American Movie Classics

Classic Movie Companion

Foreword by Andrew Sarris
A Film Preservation Message from Martin Scorsese

Edited by Robert Moses

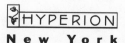HYPERION
New York

ISBN: 0-7868-8394-4

FIRST EDITION

10 9 8 7 6 5 4 3 2 1

Contributors

Senior Editor
Mary South

Contributing Writers
Alan Andres
Michael Barson
Andrea Bredau
Peter Bussian
George Callahan
Robin Dougherty
John J. Kelly
Robert Roth
Beth Rowen
Renee Scott
Carly Sommerstein
Eileen Wilkinson

Cader Books
Michael Cader
John Jusino
Marc Kehoe
Don Kennison
Andrew Goldwasser

Muze
Phil Fletcher
Robert Cavenagh
Sheila Plotnick
Kathryn Sidner
Michael Tully

Working Media
Jesse Haley
Jennifer McFarland
Alicia Potter
Kathy Whittemore

Cover and Book Design by
Charles Kreloff

Contents

Editor's Note

As Andrew Sarris remarks in his foreword, movie fans are inveterate list makers, whether it's the best new releases of the year, hunches about Oscar winners, the best Westerns of all time, or "you gotta see" recommendations for a friend. So editing the *AMC Classic Movie Companion* made a dream come true for this movie fan: the chance to create a list—a long, grand list—of Hollywood's greatest movies, and to include the kind of information about classic movies that I've always wanted to have at my fingertips.

The hard part (and the fun part) is deciding what to include and where to stop. Therefore, my guideline: the AMC Companion presents Hollywood classics from the first 50 years of the sound era, 1929 to 1979. There are special cases: I've included some silent titles that are commonly available on video and that are essential to understand the development of classic-period film. Also, British titles have been excluded (painfully, in the cases of the Emeric Pressburger–Michael Powell masterpieces, or the priceless Ealing comedies), with the following exceptions: the early Alfred Hitchcock films, which are enjoyable in their own right and that also shed light on his later work, and the James Bond films, which most viewers would expect to find here. (The eagle-eyed will notice a handful of other British titles that feature predominantly Hollywood-associated casts or directors.) While compiling the book, I came to think of the Companion as friendly recommendations from one classic-movie fan to another. Every title included has some feature that makes it worthy of viewing, whether the movie's an acknowledged screen treasure or simply features the early

work of a star or a director. You'll find beach movies and Orson Welles masterworks, Roger Corman horror quickies and sumptuous Technicolor musicals: each entry forms a piece, large or small, of the American-movie-classic mosaic.

I've been writing about film for more than 15 years, and, for a decade of that time, I've been associated with American Movie Classics as a writer, editor, and publisher. I will always be indebted to AMC for providing me the opportunity to think about, argue about, and learn about classic movies on a daily basis. There is no better place for a movie lover. This project depended on the generous support of all at AMC, particularly Kate McEnroe, Noreen O'Loughlin, Tom Barreca, Laura Masse, Marc Juris, Ellen Kroner, Lynn Weiss, Gemma Toner, Judy Krassner, and Leslie Singer.

Special thanks are due to the following: Mary South, for her unflagging support; my editor at Hyperion, David Cashion, for patience and empathy; Alan Andres, for key contributions at key points in the process; the staff at Working Media, for their generosity; all at Muze, particularly Trev Huxley, Tony Laudico, Phil Fletcher, and Robert Cavenagh, for their good humor; Cader Books, particularly Michael Cader, Charles Kreloff, and John Jusino, for their patience and understanding; Margaret Bodde at The Film Foundation, for guidance on film preservation; Holley Bishop and Kim Witherspoon at Witherspoon and Associates, for their guidance; Eric Rachlis for photographic advice; and Andrea Cannistraci, for the wise legal counsel.

As always, I relied on Noreen for inspiration and encouragement, and Caroline for smiles.

What Makes a Movie Classic?

by Andrew Sarris

Longer ago than I care to remember, my well-known passion for making lists of best movies, directors, actors, and the like provoked my esteemed polemical adversary, Pauline Kael, to ask me only semifacetiously if I were some sort of "list queen" or something. I had no immediate answer, facetious or otherwise, since the subject had never come up before as a problem in my little circle of movie buffs. But it did occur to me at the time that, to my knowledge, Ms. Kael was the only movie reviewer who had never published a ten-best list of her own. Many years after, I wrote a belated answer to her comment in the preface to someone else's book of film lists. I observed that, contrary to Ms. Kael's sly insinuation of effeminacy in the practice of list-making, lists and numbers are very much a guy thing, from childhood obsessions with passing license plates on cars to minute calculations of baseball batting averages. I have dredged up this far-from-fond memory not to renew old hostilities between warring camps of argumentative critics but, rather, to back into a discussion of the question posed in the title of this foreword to AMC's companion to American movie classics.

First, no list of best movies can ever be objective. That much I have always believed. Each of us sees a different movie on the screen, according to each of our own psyches and our different sets of personal associations with the icons and images on the screen. Stars evoke memories of parents, siblings, lovers, husbands, wives, children, and acquaintances, both pleasant and unpleasant. When my mother came to America from Greece in the '20s, she could not stand the movies of Rudolph Valentino. When asked why, she replied that he reminded her of a boy in Sparta who had been mean to her. I never got all the details, but I got the general picture.

An Affair to Remember (1957)

Andrew Sarris is most recently the author of You Ain't Heard Nothing Yet: The American Talking Film—History and Memory, 1927–1949. *He is also the film critic of* The New York Observer *and Professor of Film in the School of the Arts at Columbia University.*

The Best Years of Our Lives (1946)

Fortunately, it is still possible to salvage the talking film virtually in its entirety thanks to its residual value for the relatively new media of television, video-cassettes, laserdiscs, DVDs, and other technologies still to come—and to the valiant efforts of film preservationists, a new breed of cultural environmentalists. But they, too, have to establish a system of priorities, and that's where the film critics and historians come in.

What I did not fully realize back in the '50s when I started making my notorious lists was that I was actually in the process of preserving my most precious memories in my mind as if I could replay them by glancing at names and titles on a printed page. I was not yet arrogant enough as a revisionist film historian and a spokesman for the auteur theory in America to believe that my lists would serve as one of the many sources for establishing priorities for the preservation of American movies. Remarkably few of the movies on my lists would have seemed to qualify as "classics" in the years they first played at movie theaters. Indeed, when we look back to find Hollywood's Golden Age, we discover that people in their own time were always looking back to some previous era that put their own to shame. Similarly, the antiquarians of our own time look back from what they denounce as a Brass Age to the "good old days" when every movie was supposedly a *Citizen Kane* or a *Casablanca*.

So it is with my own biases and blind spots that I venture forth to determine the dimensions and contours of America's movie heritage, describing the special qualities that generations around the world have looked for and found in the work of successive dream-merchant colonies based mostly in a place and state of mind called Hollywood. In the beginning of the motion-picture medium, intellectuals dismissed the newfangled amusement as a circuslike curiosity, and a toy for the mindless masses. Hence, there were movies long before there were movie reviewers to apply standards of comparison. As with Aristotle and the Greek tragedians, the moviemakers created the epiphanies and the critics witnessed the glorious ascensions and needed only to describe them to their readers.

Sadly, most of our silent-film heritage has crumbled into dust in the studio vaults, and has thus vanished as completely as the missing plays of Aeschylus, Sophocles, and Euripides more than two millennia ago.

We must not despair for the movies of our own time. As always, future generations will find enough classics from our own period to hail the '90s as some kind of

Golden Age or other. The many clinkers we confront every week will either be mercifully forgotten or radically reevaluated in some sweeping new revisionist revolution. After all, the film noir so prevalent in the '90s was never taken seriously in the '40s and '50s when the serious, socially conscious film critics and historians held sway, and social significance was more highly valued than mere entertainment. Only recently, an angry letter to *The New York Observer* denounced my casual comment that Alfred Hitchcock's *Notorious* and Howard Hawks's *The Big Sleep* were better movies than William Wyler's *The Best Years of Our Lives* in 1946. That three movies released more than half a century ago could still arouse such heated controversy suggests a reason movies will never die. They are too deeply embedded in the hearts and souls of moviegoers of this century, and soon the next. I happen to be a child of the '30s, an adolescent and young man of the '40s, a burgeoning film critic of the '50s, a figure of public controversy in the '60s and '70s, an honored eminence in the '80s, a venerable mentor in the '90s, and all the time I am constantly rejuvenated by new movies and new students. With one eye on the past and one eye on the future, I have found the present infinitely renewable.

If there is a moral to these musings, it is this: We have no idea today what people will think tomorrow. Hence, total preservation should be our ideal even if it should prove impractical. As Father Flanagan insisted that there was no such thing as a bad boy, so must we say there is no such thing as a bad movie where film preservation is concerned. There are too many cross references involved, too many clues to the mystery of human life on this planet. Hence no opinion on goodness and badness can be taken as final.

The Grapes of Wrath (1940)

The secret to the cinema's immortality is its presence in real time and real space. If, as the theoreticians have argued, cinema is a language of sounds and images with a fixed vocabulary, we could stop shooting movies immediately and simply reedit the contents of our film libraries to make new movies. But that obviously would never equal what the general public considers to be "movies." As the great French film critic André Bazin once noted, movies, like the daguerreotypes and still photographs that preceded them, are less interpretations of reality such as paintings and sculpture than imprints of reality with a more intimate relationship to real time and space than the so-called fine arts. It follows that the cinema is not entirely an art, but rather a seamless fusion of life and art. No filmmaker "created" Mount Everest or Greta Garbo's cheekbones, but the cinema has endowed both of God's handiworks with the eternity and immortality of an image in ever-changing contexts.

What then is a movie classic? Any movie one thinks is a classic. If I seem evasive, it is because I have been wrong too often to claim infallibility in these matters. Of course, I would not be a critic and historian at all if I did not consider my taste superior to other people's, or, rather, if I did not have an edge on more intelligent people because they did not lie awake nights thinking about movies as I do. Contrarily, I believe also that I am not all that different from other people, and, though there are profound differences of taste among us, I can at least understand why pictures I like don't impress other people, and why pictures I dislike, do.

Some of our differences are generational, some political, and some gender-based. I happen to be a 70-year-old

Aristotelian, Greek-American, Christian-Centrist, Auteurist Male, Born in Brooklyn, Grown Up in Queens, Now Living and Working in Manhattan, but also a permanent resident of the world's movie screens. As a Christian Centrist rather than a Marxist, I believe in personal redemption more than social revolution. That is why I prefer John Ford's *The Searchers* (1956) to Ford's *The Grapes of Wrath* (1940), and Howard Hawks's *Rio Bravo* (1959) to Fred Zinnemann's *High Noon* (1952), and Alfred Hitchcock's *Vertigo* (1958) to Stanley Kramer's *The Defiant Ones* (1958), and Elia Kazan's *East of Eden* (1955) to Kazan's *Gentleman's Agreement* (1947). The Aristotelian in me prefers protagonists with a certain level of moral stature to self-pitying losers, which is why I prefer Paddy Chayefsky's *The Americanization of Emily* (1964) to Chayefsky's *Marty* (1955). This is not to say I give a free pass to the Darwinian jungle of free markets, and to the rich over the poor. Nor do I believe that the director is the sole auteur of a movie classic, or even the primary auteur, but I have found from long experience as a moviegoer that directors, more often than not, are the way to bet.

Ultimately, however, I do not expect to have it all my way in defining a movie classic, nor can the editor of this volume. Hence I am for inclusion rather than exclusion. And I do not worship the past at the expense of the present. Harold Ramis's *Groundhog Day* (1993) is as good and funny as any screwball comedy classic of the '30s; Sam Raimi's *A Simple Plan* (1998) is as tragic and moving as any American movie ever. The search goes on for American movie classics, and I hope to stay in the hunt to the next millennium and beyond.

Why Is Film Preservation Important?

by Martin Scorsese

I n the early '70s, I attended a Los Angeles screening of *The Seven Year Itch,* a film made by Billy Wilder in 1955. We were warned ahead of time that the print had faded to blue and pink. But the reality was much worse: the print had deteriorated so much that it was difficult to see the faces of the actors on the screen.

The facts about the condition of our movies are shocking. More than 50 percent of the American movies made before 1950 and 75 percent of all silent movies no longer exist. Until the '50s, films were printed on nitrate stock, which is highly flammable and disintegrates over time. Nitrate films were also routinely destroyed and recycled for their silver content.

The predominant color process used from the early '30s to the mid-'70s was Technicolor's dye-transfer (a process that separates the image into the three secondary colors: yellow, cyan, and magenta). Arguably, no better or more stable color process existed, but shooting film with it was expensive and required a heavy, cumbersome camera. In the early '50s, Kodak came out with Eastmancolor stock, which was cheaper and more sensitive (it has multiple emulsion layers on a single strip of film, and the three color separations are brought out through chemical processing). But Eastmancolor fades; in fact, all films using Eastmancolor during this period have already faded or will fade. Fortuitously, in the early '80s, Kodak created a low-fade color printing stock (LPP), which now

ensures that film prints and negatives can last for sixty to a hundred years if stored properly.

Why is it so important to save movies? The most compelling reason is that films are part of our artistic heritage—some say that film is *the* art form of the 20th century. Secondly, film is history. Movies made at a certain time, even minor ones, document ways of thinking and speaking, the behavior and the lifestyles of the people of that time. It is the most complete record we have of a particular period. And, thirdly, the older films

Martin Scorsese

All Quiet on the Western Front (1930)

provide a great reference for filmmakers, actors, and other creative artists.

As a filmmaker, when I think of a movie I don't necessarily think of its story or plot. I remember images, faces, moods, emotions, the textures created by light and shadow. The great artists of the past knew that narrative and emotion are conveyed through the detail. For example, in one of Giotto's frescoes in the Scrovegni Chapel, *The Betrayal of Christ,* the tension of the scene is captured in the movement of the cloaks, the lances, and the torches. In my movies, particularly in the period pieces I've made, I've tried to develop characters through the details of their dress, food, music. While preparing *The Age of Innocence,* for instance, I looked at images on mutoscopes from the turn of the century, and was fascinated to see how the people moved and how their clothes fit. In most movies, the costumes fit perfectly, but, in these pictures, the buttons on a jacket were a little too heavy or the vest was too tight and pulling. These details are crucial clues in narrative, and they will vanish if our film heritage is not preserved.

Cinema is only 100 years old, and yet so much of it has perished. In 1990, when I and a group of prominent directors (Woody Allen, Francis Ford Coppola, Stanley Kubrick, George Lucas, Sydney Pollack, Robert Redford, Steven Spielberg—and, in recent years, Clint Eastwood and Robert Altman have joined the board) started The Film Foundation, the movie industry was just beginning to fully appreciate the value of their libraries. Since then, we have encouraged efforts to restore and safeguard the films in the libraries, including the creation of partnerships between the studios and the archives. Many classic films have been restored through these partnerships: *All Quiet on the Western Front* (1930), *On the Waterfront* (1954), *All About Eve* (1950), *Sunrise* (1927), *My Darling Clementine* (1946), just to name a few. And AMC's annual Film Preservation Festival has raised public awareness and funds for film preservation.

Yet, there is still so much to do. With every foot of film that is lost, we lose a vital link to our culture, our past, and the present world around us.

A Film Preservation Update

The last decade has seen great strides in awareness of the need for film preservation, and the coming years promise more momentum—and the release of some intriguing, eagerly awaited restorations of classic titles.

Film preservation champions such as Martin Scorsese and The Film Foundation, American Movie Classics, and Planet Hollywood, and institutions such as the American Film Institute and the Library of Congress, have played a key role in rallying attention and much-needed financial support from the general public. And, since cable networks and video distributors have created a sharp increase in demand for movie entertainment, the movie studios themselves have focused attention on their deteriorating classic-movie archives.

The studios have brought money and a renewed sense of urgency to saving our film heritage, employing improved storage facilities and new diagnostic tools that help halt the decay of older film stocks and prevent the fading of newer stocks. Significant developments in digital processes have created advances in color negative technology and sound track restoration and remastering. The results have been illuminating and, in some cases, controversial. The 1998 release of a restored, remastered *Gone With the Wind* (1939) drew enthusiastic audiences to theaters, and sniping from some critics and preservationists who contended that the rich colors in the new negative reflected a 1954 reissue supervised by David O. Selznick rather than the muted tones of the original 1939 release. Perhaps the most interesting restoration to date was the fall 1998 rerelease of Orson Welles's

Rear Window (1954)

"The first history was written in the hope of preserving from decay the memory of what men have been. The great guerrilla war of our time is the battle between memory and forgetting. With forgetting comes the great lie, the official story, war, despair, repetition, ignorance, folly, purposelessness. Memory, as Wordsworth said, that inward eye, is the crown jewel of our evolution. Preserve it. Preserve memory. Preserve film."

Oliver Stone

Touch of Evil (1958). When Universal Pictures locked Welles out of the editing room, the director drafted a 58-page memo that detailed his intentions for the film. Forty years later, famed editor and sound mixer Walter Murch, working from the Welles memo, reconstructed a cut of the film that hews closely to Welles's vision, a fitting tribute to a film landmark that Welles claimed never to have seen after his first screening.

In 1999 the film world anticipates notable restorations of Alfred Hitchcock's *Rear Window* (1954) from the team of James Katz and Robert Harris, who supervised the revealing new look at Hitchcock's *Vertigo,* a UCLA Film and Television Archive restoration of *Joan of Arc* (1948), which was the opening-night screening at the Archive's Film Preservation Festival (a restoration supported in part by AMC's Film Preservation Festival), and a restoration of Richard Lester's *A Hard Day's Night* (1964), the Beatles movie that some say spawned music videos.

> **"We have a chance as a society to preserve a contemporary look at popular culture dating back a hundred years. No other society has had a chance to do that. For us to ignore it would be a shame. Not only for the art and the artistry of those films, but so that 400 years from now or 500 years from now, you can look back at what it was really like in 1924, or 1936, or 1947. It's important."**
>
> Ron Howard

Film Museums and Archives

Archives Supported by The Film Foundation

Academy of Motion Picture Arts and Sciences
Center for Motion Picture Study
Academy Film Archives
333 S. La Cienega Blvd.
Beverly Hills, CA 90211
(310) 247-3000

American Film Institute/National Center for Film
    and Video Preservation
John F. Kennedy Center for the Performing Arts
Washington, D.C. 20566
(202) 416-7815

George Eastman House
900 East Ave.
Rochester, NY 14607
(716) 271-3361

Library of Congress
Motion Picture, Broadcasting
    and Recorded Sound Division
Washington, D.C. 20540
(202) 707-5840

Museum of Modern Art
Department of Film
11 W. 53rd St.
New York, NY 10019
(212) 708-9602

UCLA Film and Television Archive
302 E. Melnitz Hall
University of California
405 Hilgard Ave.
Los Angeles, CA 90024
(310) 206-8013

Other Film Museums and Archives

American Museum of the Moving Image
25th Ave. at 36th St.
Astoria, NY 11106
(718) 784-4520

Carpenter Center for the Visual Arts
Harvard University
24 Quincy St.
Cambridge, MA 02138
(617) 495-4700

National Museum of Natural History/Human
    Studies Film Archives
Smithsonian Institution, Room E307
Washington, D.C. 20560
(202) 357-3349

Pacific Film Archive
University Art Museum
2625 Durant Ave.
Berkeley, CA 94720
(510) 642-1412

American Movie Classics

Classic Movie Companion

Aaron Loves Angela

(1975) Columbia
A take on the Romeo and Juliet story set in Harlem. A black man (Kevin Hooks) falls in love with a Puerto Rican woman (Cara). Against the threadbare background of the ghetto, the story is all the more poignant without the Shakespearean trappings. Early film appearance of Cara, who would go on to a singing career in *Fame* and singing the title track to *Flashdance* in the 1980s. **Cast:** Irene Cara, Kevin Hooks, Moses Gunn, Robert Hooks, Ernestine Jackson. **Credits:** Dir: Gordon Parks, Jr.; Prod: Robert J. Anderson; Story: Gerald Sanford; DP: Richard Kratina; Ed: William Anderson; Composer: José Feliciano. Color, 99 min. **VHS**

Aaron Slick from Punkin Crick

(1952) Paramount
Aaron Slick is in love with his neighbor, Josie, on the farm next door. When two big-city characters believe they've discovered oil on Josie's property, they offer to buy her out for $20,000. She accepts and leaves for the big city, much to the chagrin of the smitten Aaron. Aaron discovers, however, that the city folks are up to no good and rushes to the metropolis. **Cast:** Adele Jergens, Minerva Urecal, Martha Stewart, Fritz Feld, Veda Ann Borg, Chick Chandler, Alan Young, Dinah Shore, Robert Merrill. **Credits:** Dir: Claude Binyon; Prod: William Perlberg, George Seaton; Writer: Claude Binyon, Walter B. Hare; DP: Charles Lang; Ed: Archie Marshek; Composer: Jay Livingston, Ray Evans, Robert Emmett Dolan. Color, 95 min.

Abbott and Costello

The comedy team of Bud Abbott and Lou Costello bumbled their way through more than 36 big-screen adventures—and into the hearts of millions of fans. Abbott and Costello first teamed up in 1931 on the vaudeville stage and would complete their $10-million-grossing blockbuster, *Buck Privates,* for Universal Studios a decade later. During their illustrious careers, the two pals turned up in the strangest of locales, from Hollywood to Venus, Mexico to Transylvania, and encountered some of classic film's more supernatural denizens, including Frankenstein, the Invisible Man, Dr. Jekyll and Mr. Hyde, and the Mummy, to name a few. After a fruitful partnership in movies and on television, Abbott and Costello parted amiably in 1957. Costello appeared alone in *The 30-Foot Bride of Candy Rock* in 1959 just before his death. Abbott tried unsuccessfully to revive his career both alone and with another partner. He died in 1974.

One Night in the Tropics *(1940)*
Buck Privates *(1941)*
Hold That Ghost *(1941)*
In the Navy *(1941)*
Keep 'Em Flying *(1941)*
Who Done It? *(1942)*
Pardon My Sarong *(1942)*
Ride 'Em Cowboy *(1942)*
Rio Rita *(1942)*
Hit the Ice *(1943)*
It Ain't Hay *(1943)*
In Society *(1944)*
Lost in a Harem *(1944)*
Abbott and Costello in Hollywood *(1945)*
Here Come the Co-eds *(1945)*
The Naughty Nineties *(1945)*
Little Giant *(1946)*
The Time of Their Lives *(1946)*
Buck Privates Come Home *(1947)*
The Wistful Widow of Wagon Gap *(1947)*
Abbott and Costello Meet Frankenstein *(1948)*
Mexican Hayride *(1948)*
The Noose Hangs High *(1948)*
Abbott and Costello Meet the Killer, Boris Karloff *(1949)*
Africa Screams *(1949)*
Abbott and Costello in the Foreign Legion *(1950)*
Abbott and Costello Meet the Invisible Man *(1951)*
Comin' Round the Mountain *(1951)*
Abbott and Costello Meet Captain Kidd *(1952)*
Jack and the Beanstalk *(1952)*
Lost in Alaska *(1952)*
Abbott and Costello Go to Mars *(1953)*
Abbott and Costello Meet Dr. Jekyll and Mr. Hyde *(1953)*
Abbott and Costello Meet the Keystone Kops *(1955)*
Abbott and Costello Meet the Mummy *(1955)*
Dance with Me Henry *(1956)*

Abe Lincoln in Illinois

(1940) RKO
This screen adaptation of the Pulitzer Prize–winning play by Robert E. Sherwood depicts the life of America's 16th president. From his early days as a modest shopkeeper in Illinois to his reluctant decision to run for political office for the first time, the film delves into the personal struggles of the man the world came to know as the Great Emancipator. Massey is particularly brilliant in this role, especially in the depiction of the Lincoln-Douglas debates. **Cast:** Raymond Massey, Gene Lockhart, Ruth Gordon, Mary Howard, Dorothy Tree, Harvey Stephens, Minor Watson, Alan Baxter, Howard Da Silva. **Credits:** Dir: John Cromwell; Prod: Max Gordon; Writer: Robert E. Sherwood, Grover Jones; DP: James Wong Howe; Ed: George Hively; Composer: Roy Webb. B&W, 110 min. **VHS**

Abilene Town

(1946) United Artists
Pioneer town Abilene, Kansas, is the setting in which tensions between long-settled cattle ranchers and new homesteaders play out. Abilene sits at the tail of a livestock path that

Abraham Lincoln (1930)

stretches all the way to Texas. Its inhabitants include a dipsomaniac sheriff, a true-hearted dance-hall girl, a sweet shopkeeper, a dangerously alluring barmaid, and a two-fisted town marshal. The community-at-large is split in half between those who want this place to stay a rowdy frontier town and those who yearn to change it into a tranquil place where they can raise a family. Based on the novel *Trail Town* by Ernest Haycox. **Cast:** Randolph Scott, Ann Dvorak, Edgar Buchanan, Rhonda Fleming, Lloyd Bridges, Howard Freeman, Richard Hale, Jack Lambert, Dick Curtis, Helen Boyce. **Credits:** Dir: Edwin L. Marin; Prod: Jules Levey; Writer: Harold Shumate; DP: Archie Stout; Ed: Otho S. Lovering, Richard Heermance. B&W, 90 min. **VHS**

About Face

(1952) Warner Bros.
A comic musical about the capers of three cadets finishing their final year at Southern Military Institute, this film is a remake of *Brother Rat*. Tony, Boff, and Dave are pushed to the limits of their ingenuity as they attempt to pursue secret romances outside the con-

fines of the academy, steer the school baseball team to victory, and somehow manage to pass the class of the priggish Lieutenant Jones. Boff is actually married to his flame, a fact that becomes more difficult to hide from the Institute when she becomes pregnant with their child. **Cast:** Aileen Stanley, Jr., Eddie Bracken, Dick Wesson, Gordon MacRae, Phyllis Kirk, Aileen Stanley, Jr., Joel Grey, Larry Keating, Cliff Ferre, John Baer. **Credits:** Dir: Roy Del Ruth; Prod: William Jacobs; Writer: Peter Milne; Story: John Monks, Jr., Fred F. Finklehoffe; DP: Bert Glennon; Ed: Thomas Reilly; Prod Design: Charles H. Clarke, Lyle B. Heifsnider; Composer: Charles Tobias, Peter De Rose. Color, 93 min.

About Mrs. Leslie

(1953) Paramount
Melodrama about the early romance of a now middle-aged owner of a California rooming house. Told in flashbacks, the story follows her trail from New York City to Beverly Hills after she becomes the mistress of a man she meets in New York and pretends to be his wife. He dies and she later learns he was a rich industrialist. **Cast:**

Shirley Booth, Robert Ryan, Marjie Millar, Alex Nicol, Sam White, James Bell, Eilene Janssen, Philip Ober, Harry Morgan, Gale Page. **Credits:** Dir: Daniel Mann; Prod: Hal B. Wallis; Writer: Hal Kanter, Ketti Frings; Story: Vina Delmar; DP: Ernest Laszlo; Ed: Warren Low; Prod Design: Edith Head, John P. Fulton; Composer: Victor Young. B&W, 104 min.

Above Suspicion

(1943) MGM
On the eve of WWII, a newlywed couple (MacMurray and Crawford) about to embark on their honeymoon are suddenly given an important assignment by the British Secret Service. Despite a total lack of previous espionage experience, they accept a mission to obtain the top-secret plans for a magnetic mine. As they do their duty, the pair confronts shady characters, secret codes, assassins, complex clues, deadly traps—and Nazis. Based on the novel by Helen MacInnes. **Cast:** Joan Crawford, Fred MacMurray, Conrad Veidt, Basil Rathbone, Reginald Owen, Richard Ainley, Cecil Cunningham, Ann Shoemaker, Sara Haden, Felix Bressart. **Credits:** Dir: Richard Thorpe; Prod: Victor Saville, Leon Gordon; Writer: Keith Winter, Melville Baker, Patricia Coleman; DP: Robert Planck; Ed: George Hively; Prod Design: Randal Duell; Composer: Bronislau Kaper; Costumes: Gile Steele. B&W, 91 min. **VHS**

Abraham Lincoln

(1930) United Artists
Significant as Griffith's first talkie. Tracing the President's life from his humble birth through his political career, Griffith's sincere portrait features a standout performance by Walter Huston (father of John and grandfather of Anjelica) as Lincoln. The restored version features previously missing sequences. **Cast:** Walter Huston, Una Merkel, Edgar Dearing, Russell Simpson. **Credits:** Dir: D. W. Griffith; Writer: Stephen Vincent Benét; DP: Karl Struss; Ed: John Considine; Composer: Hugo Reisenfeld; Set Designer: William Cameron Menzies. B&W, 97 min. **VHS, LASER**

Abroad with Two Yanks

(1944) United Artists
Two WWII Marine buddies (Bendix and O'Keefe) are devoted to each other through thick and thin in the heat of battle. On furlough, however, it's every man for himself when each tries to win the heart of the same woman (Walker). Comic capers and wartime

hilarity include Marines in drag. **Cast:** William Bendix, Dennis O'Keefe, John Loder, Helen Walker. **Credits:** Dir: Allan Dwan; Prod: Edward Small; Writer: Charles Henry Blanke, John Van Druten, Lenore J. Coffee; DP: Sol Polito; Ed: Terry Morse; Prod Design: John Hughes; Composer: Franz Waxman. B&W, 80 min.

The Absent-Minded Professor

(1961) Disney
A distracted professor invents an anti-gravity goo called Flubber that makes anything it's applied to lighter-than-air, including the family flivver and the balls at the school's basketball game. MacMurray couldn't be better in patented Disney fare. Sequel is *Son of Flubber*. Academy Award Nominations: 3, including Best (Black-and-White) Cinematography. **Cast:** Fred MacMurray, Nancy Olson, Keenan Wynn, Tommy Kirk, Leon Ames, Ed Wynn, Edward Andrews. **Credits:** Dir: Robert Stevenson; Prod: Walt Disney; Writer: Bill Walsh; Story: Samuel Taylor; DP: Edward Colman; Ed: Cotton Warburton; Prod Design: Carroll Clark; Composer: George Bruns; SFX: Peter Ellenshaw, Eustace Lycett, Robert A. Mattey. B&W, 97 min. **VHS, LASER**

Across 110th Street

(1972) United Artists
The robbery of a Mafia numbers house in Harlem of $300,000 by three black men dressed as police sets off a citywide search for the perpetrators by both the Mob and the police. Quinn and Kotto give fine performances as cops with different goals in the common search. Quinn, as a cop on the take, must balance his greed and the desire for justice. **Cast:** Anthony Quinn, Yaphet Kotto, Anthony Franciosa, Paul Benjamin, Ed Bernard, Richard Ward, Norma Donaldson, Antonio Fargas, Gilbert Lewis. **Credits:** Dir: Barry Shear; Prod: Ralph Serpe, Fouad Said; Writer: Luther Davis; DP: Jack Priestly; Ed: Byron Brandt; Composer: J. J. Johnson; Art Director: Perry Watkins. Color, 144 min. **VHS**

Across the Pacific

(1942) Warner Bros.
After being given a phony dishonorable discharge, Army officer Richard Leland (Bogart) offers his services to Chiang Kai-Shek and the Chinese. On his journey through the Panama Canal, he comes across Dr. Lorenz (Greenstreet), a spy determined to blow up the Canal. It should be noted that the

characters in the movie never reach the Pacific or cross it for that matter. Huston ultimately left production literally mid-scene to join the armed forces, leaving command of the movie in the hands of young director Sherman. This second feature directed by Huston reunites most of the cast from *The Maltese Falcon* (1941). Also available in a colorized version. **Cast:** Humphrey Bogart, Keye Luke, Mary Astor, Sydney Greenstreet, Victor Sen Yung, Richard Loo. **Credits:** Dir: John Huston, Vincent Sherman; Prod: Jerry Wald, Jack Saper; Writer: Richard Macauley; DP: Arthur Edeson; Ed: Frank Magee; Composer: Adolph Deutsch; SFX: Byron Haskin; Art Director: Robert M. Haas, Hugh Reticker. B&W, 98 min. **VHS**

Across the Wide Missouri

(1951) MGM
Native American relations with white settlers in early 19th century America provide the dramatic focus here. The time is 1829 and trapper Flint Mitchell heads into the wilderness in search of valuable beaver pelts. In order to get a foothold in the hostile Blackfoot Indian territory, Mitchell marries a Blackfoot squaw, and then finds himself truly in love. Accompanied by a band of intrepid trappers, the newlyweds press deep into the untamed land despite persistent aggression from its angry native inhabitants. Spectacular Rocky Mountain photography makes this one a visual treat. **Cast:** Clark Gable, Ricardo Montalban, John Hodiak, Adolphe Menjou. **Credits:** Dir: William Wellman; Prod: Robert Sisk; Writer: Talbot Jennings; Story: Frank Cavett, Talbot Jennings; DP: William Mellor; Ed: John Dunn; Prod Design: Cedric Gibbons, James Basevi; Composer: David Raksin. Color, 101 min. **VHS**

Action in the North Atlantic

(1943) Warner Bros.
Unusual WWII adventure shines a light onto the unsung Merchant Marines who risked their lives bringing supplies to the soldiers at the front. The story begins with the Merchant Marines' tanker being torpedoed by the Nazis. The surviving men are saved after 11 days adrift at sea, and return home. But soon, the men are called back into action with a new assignment that forces them to confront the deadly seas once again. Strong ensemble acting. **Cast:** Humphrey Bogart, Raymond Massey, Alan Hale, Julie Bishop, Ruth Gordon, Sam Levene, Dane Clark. **Credits:** Dir: Lloyd Bacon; Prod: Jerry Wald; Writer: John Howard Lawson;

DP: Ted McCord; Ed: Thomas Pratt, George Amy; Composer: Adolph Deutsch; Art Director: Ted Smith. B&W, 129 min. **VHS**

An Act of Murder

(1948) Universal
March plays an unyielding judge with a dying wife who decides on suicide for himself and euthanasia for her. She is killed in his drive off a cliff but he survives and confesses to murder. O'Brien successfully defends him by establishing a mercy-killing defense. **Cast:** Fredric March, Edmond O'Brien, Florence Eldridge, Geraldine Brooks, Stanley Ridges, John McIntire, Frederic Tozere, William H. Wright, Virginia Brissac, Francis McDonald. **Credits:** Dir: Michael Gordon; Prod: Jerry Bresler; Writer: Michael Blankfort, Robert Thoeren; Story: Ernst Lothar; DP: Hal Mohr; Ed: Ralph Dawson; Composer: Daniele Amfitheatrof. B&W, 91 min.

Act of Violence

(1948) MGM
A taut, gritty drama about a WWII veteran who has miraculously—and suspiciously—survived a Nazi POW camp while the rest of his comrades, except one, have been murdered. That exception, now back in America as a physically crippled and mentally disturbed vet, embarks on a vengeful manhunt for the so-called honored hero who had actually betrayed his buddies in the camp. The "hero" wants to atone for his sins, but, in doing so, it may cost him his life. **Cast:** Van Heflin, Robert Ryan, Janet Leigh, Mary Astor, Phyllis Thaxter, Berry Kroeger, Taylor Holmes, Harry Antrim, Connie Gilchrist, Will Wright. **Credits:** Dir: Fred Zinnemann; Prod: William H. Wright; Writer: Robert L. Richards; Story: Collier Young; DP: Robert Surtees; Ed: Conrad A. Nervig; Prod Design: Cedric Gibbons; Composer: Bronislau Kaper. B&W, 82 min.

Ada

(1961) MGM
Ada, a high-class prostitute, renounces her life when she marries governor Bo Gillis. Opposed to the marriage is Gillis's scheming aide and mentor, Sylvester Marin. Marin secretly works to break up the marriage and eventually resorts to killing Gillis. The attempt fails, but leaves Gillis injured and infirmed. Ada takes over the office of her husband but her efforts are thwarted at every turn by Marin, who now wants to take the power for himself. Gillis returns at a crucial moment

to save his wife from scandal and rid the scene of the Marin. **Cast:** Susan Hayward, Dean Martin, Wilfrid Hyde-White, Ralph Meeker, Martin Balsam, Frank Maxwell, Connie Sawyer, Ford Rainey, Charles Watts, Larry Gates. **Credits:** Dir: Daniel Mann; Prod: Lawrence Weingarten; Writer: William Driskill, Arthur Sheekman; Story: Wirt Williams; DP: Joseph Ruttenberg; Ed: Ralph E. Winters; Prod Design: Edward C. Carfagno; Composer: Bronislau Kaper, Wally Fowler; Art Director: George W. Davis. Color, 109 min.

Adam Had Four Sons
(1941) Columbia
Bergman gives a warm, touching performance as a governess hired by a wealthy businessman. Though adored by the businessman's sons, she leaves for her native land after the family's economic reverses. She returns in sunnier times to encounter conflict with the oldest son's fiancée, a climbing golddigger played cunningly by Hayward. Bergman's second American film. **Cast:** Ingrid Bergman, Warner Baxter, Susan Hayward, Richard Denning, Robert Shaw, Fay Wray, Johnny Downs, June Lockhart. **Credits:** Dir: Gregory Ratoff; Prod: Robert Sherwood; Writer: William Hurlbut, Michael Blankfort; DP: Peverell Marley; Ed: Francis D. Lyon; Prod Design: Rudolph Sternad. B&W, 81 min. VHS

Adam's Rib
(1949) MGM
Tracy and Hepburn at their best as two married lawyers who take opposite sides of a front-page case. District Attorney Tracy heads the prosecution when a pistol-packing blonde goes after her girl-chasing husband and his mistress. But wife Hepburn thinks women should have the right to do exactly what men have done for years—get revenge! So it's Hepburn for the defense in a trial that proves all's fair in love, war, and court. An ahead-of-its-time script by Gordon and Kanin, combined with the matchless chemistry between Hepburn and Tracy, make this a sophisticated piece of entertainment. Later turned into a television series. A National Film Registry Outstanding Film. **Cast:** Katharine Hepburn, Spencer Tracy, Judy Holliday, Tom Ewell. **Credits:** Dir: George Cukor; Prod: Lawrence Weingarten; Writer: Ruth Gordon, Garson Kanin; DP: George J. Folsey; Ed: George Boemler; Prod Design: Cedric Gibbons; Composer: Miklos Rozsa; Costumes: Walter Plunkett; Art Direc-

tor: William Ferrari; Set Designer: Edwin B. Willis, Henry Grace. B&W, 101 min. VHS, LASER, DVD

Adventure
(1945) MGM
Gable returned from the war to this melodrama of a sailor who romances and marries a shy librarian (Garson) and then promptly returns to wandering the seas. When he returns to discover her giving birth to their child, he struggles to master his footloose ways. An uncharacteristically touching portrayal by Gable. Unpopular with critics at the time, but rewards a second look. **Cast:** Clark Gable, Greer Garson, Joan Blondell, Thomas Mitchell, Tom Tully, John Qualen, Richard Haydn. **Credits:** Dir: Victor Fleming; Prod: Sam Zimbalist; Writer: Frederick Hazlitt Brennan, Vincent Lawrence; Story: Clyde Brion Davis; DP: Joseph Ruttenberg; Ed: Frank Sullivan; Prod Design: Cedric Gibbons, Urie McCleary; Composer: Herbert Stothart; Set Designer: Edwin B. Willis. B&W, 125 min. VHS

The Adventure of Sherlock Holmes's Smarter Brother
(1978) Fox
Wilder borrows from master Mel Brooks's book in this comedy about Sherlock's less well known brother, who takes his famous relative's case overflow. Great 1970s comedy ensemble. **Cast:** Gene Wilder, Madeline Kahn, Marty Feldman, Dom De Luise. **Credits:** Dir: Gene Wilder; Prod: Richard Alan Roth; Writer: Gene Wilder; DP: Gerry Fisher; Ed: Jim Clark; Prod Design: Terry Marsh; Choreographer: Alan Johnson; Composer: John Morris; Costumes: Ruth Myers. Color, 91 min. VHS

Adventures of Don Juan
(1949) Warner Bros.
Flynn seems to be winking at his own off-screen image in the role he was born to play. As the legendary lover, he returns to Spain and takes the post of fencing instructor at the royal academy. He becomes involved in court intrigue and swordplay when he hears of a plot against his adoring Queen. The laserdisc includes the original theatrical trailer. **Academy Awards:** Best Costume Design (Color). **Cast:** Errol Flynn, Viveca Lindfors, Robert Douglas, Alan Hale. **Credits:** Dir: Vincent Sherman; Prod: Jerry Wald; Writer: George Oppenheimer, Harry Kurnitz; Story: Herbert Dalmas; DP: Elwood Bredell; Ed: Alan Crosland, Jr.; Composer: Max Steiner. B&W, 111 min. VHS, LASER

The Adventures of Huckleberry Finn
(1939) MGM
The classic film version of the beloved Mark Twain novel features Rooney in his first starring role. Considered by some to be the best of the many Huckleberry Finn movies, it was MGM's answer to the Selznick *Tom Sawyer* of the previous year. **Cast:** Mickey Rooney, Walter Connelly, William Frawley. **Credits:** Dir: Richard Thorpe; Prod: Joseph L. Mankiewicz; Writer: Hugo Butler; Story: Mark Twain; DP: John Seitz; Ed: Frank Hull; Composer: Franz Waxman. B&W, 89 min. VHS

The Adventures of Huckleberry Finn
(1960) MGM
From chicken thief to cabin boy, riverboat pilot to circus performer, Huck Finn outsmarts everyone on his way down the muddy Mississippi. This was the first color version of the Mark Twain classic. Veteran Hollywood faces, including Buster Keaton (as a lion tamer!), Sterling Holloway, Andy Devine, Judy Canova, John Carradine, and Mickey Shaughnessy provide colorful support. **Cast:** Tony Randall, Eddie Hodges, Archie Moore, Patty McCormack, Neville Brand. **Credits:** Dir: Michael Curtiz; Prod: Samuel Goldwyn; Writer: James Lee; Story: Mark Twain; DP: Ted McCord; Ed: Fredric Steinkamp; Prod Design: George W. Davis, McClure Capps; Composer: Jerome Moross; SFX: A. Arnold Gillespie. Color, 108 min. VHS

The Adventures of Marco Polo
(1938) United Artists
Cooper (!?) as the Italian explorer Marco Polo in a big-budget Hollywood fantasy adventure. Despite a host of natural obstacles, Polo and his sidekick Binguccio (Truex) arrive triumphantly in the sumptuous court of Kublai Khan (Barbier). Soon they're involved in political goings-on that threaten to undo the Khan and break up Polo's romance with lovely Asian princess Kukachin (Gurie). To battle the sinister Ahmed (Rathbone) and his usurpers, Polo enlists the aid of happy-go-lucky outlaw Kaidu (Hale) and his merry men. Their attack on the walled city is one of the great cinematic battle scenes of all time. **Cast:** Gary Cooper, Sigrid Gurie, Basil Rathbone, George Barbier, Binnie Barnes, Ernest Truex, Alan Hale, Jr., H. B. Warner, Robert Greig, Ferdinand

Gottschalk. **Credits:** Dir: Archie Mayo; Prod: Samuel Goldwyn; Writer: Robert E. Sherwood, N. A. Pogson; Ed: Fred Allen; Prod Design: Richard Day; Composer: Hugo Friedhofer. B&W, 100 min.

The Adventures of Mark Twain
(1944) Warner Bros.
The life and times of America's beloved writer and humorist. March reaches the man behind the caricature to portray the roots of Sam Clemens's storytelling art in his wanderings around still-growing America. **Cast:** Fredric March, Alexis Smith, Donald Crisp, Alan Hale, C. Aubrey Smith, John Carradine, Percy Kilbride, William Henry, Robert Barrat, Walter Hampden. **Credits:** Dir: Irving Rapper; Prod: Jesse L. Lasky; Writer: Alan LeMay, Harry Chandler, Harold Sherman; DP: Sol Polito; Ed: Ralph Dawson; Prod Design: John Hughes; Composer: Max Steiner; Set Designer: Fred M. MacLean. B&W, 130 min. **VHS**

The Adventures of Martin Eden
(1942) Columbia
Sailor Martin Eden serves on a Merchant Marine ship run by a sadistic captain. He writes of his harsh experiences in a journal, which he one day hopes to have published, exposing the cruelty and barbarity that exists in the Merchant Marines. Escaping, he sets about bringing his victimizers to justice and in the process freeing his companion Joe Dawson, who was wrongly accused of mutiny. Along the way, Eden falls in love with the impoverished Connie Dawson (Joe's sister) and rejects the wealthy Ruth Morley. **Cast:** Glenn Ford, Claire Trevor, Evelyn Keyes, Stuart Erwin, Dickie Moore, Ian MacDonald, Frank Conroy, Rafaela Ottiano, Pierre Watkin, Regina Wallace. **Credits:** Dir: Sidney Salkow; Prod: B. P. Schulberg; Writer: W. L. River; Story: Jack London; DP: Franz Planer; Ed: Al Clark. B&W, 87 min.

The Adventures of Robin Hood
(1938) Warner Bros.
Arguably Flynn's greatest role, this is the swashbuckling spectacle about the infamous outlaw and his band of merry men who "robbed from the rich and gave to the poor." Robin Hood fights for justice against the evil Sir Guy of Gisbourne, while striving to win the hand of the beautiful Maid Marian. A rollicking adventure never outdone by remakes, this epic features great

The Adventures of Robin Hood (1938)

swordplay, music, characters, and storybook. Shot in glorious Technicolor. **Academy Awards:** Best Film Editing; Best Interior Decoration (B&W); Best Original Score. **Cast:** Errol Flynn, Olivia de Havilland, Basil Rathbone, Claude Rains, Patric Knowles. **Credits:** Dir: Michael Curtiz, William Keighley; Prod: Henry Blanke; Writer: Norman Reilly Raine, Seton I. Miller; Story: Sir Walter Scott; DP: Sol Polito, Tony Gaudio; Ed: Ralph Dawson; Prod Design: Carl Jules Weyl; Composer: Erich Wolfgang Korngold; Costumes: Milo Anderson. Color, 102 min. **VHS, LASER**

The Adventures of the Wilderness Family
(1976) Pacific
An inspiring tale of a family's struggle to survive in the mountains. The Robinsons (Skip, Pat, Jenny, and Toby) flee the big city for life in the high Rockies to escape the pressures of modern city life. But Mother Nature tests them, and they must come to terms with their decision and learn to accept it, knowing that a return to the city is not the answer. (Things must go well enough, for they return a few years later in *Further Adventures of*

the Wilderness Family, Part 2.) **Cast:** Robert Logan, Susan Damante Shaw, Ham Larsen, Hollye Holmes. **Credits:** Dir: Stewart Raffill; Prod: Arthur R. Dubs; Writer: Stewart Raffill; Composer: Gene Kauer, Douglas Lackey. Color, 100 min. **VHS**

The Adventures of Tom Sawyer
(1938) United Artists
After accidentally witnessing a murder, Tom and his pals Huck and Joe run away to become pirates, swearing to never reveal their secret. But when a man is wrongfully accused of the deed, they know they've got to come forward with the truth. A mostly faithful adaptation of the Mark Twain novel. William Cameron Menzies contributes wonderful art direction. **Cast:** Walter Brennan, May Robson, Victor Jory, Tommy Kelly, Jackie Moran, Ann Gillis, Victor Kilian, Nana Bryant. **Credits:** Dir: Norman Taurog; Prod: David O. Selznick; Writer: John V. A. Weaver; Story: Mark Twain; DP: James Wong Howe, Wilfrid M. Cline; Prod Design: Lyle Wheeler; Composer: Franz Waxman, Max Steiner. Color, 93 min. **VHS, LASER**

Advise and Consent

(1962) Columbia

Preminger's political thriller examines the dark side of politics and its tragic personal repercussions for an essentially decent man. When a President nominates a controversial candidate for Secretary of State, the political dealing and infighting begins as dissident legislators are willing to stoop even to blackmail to stop his confirmation—or assure it. Preminger seemed to hit his stride lending a documentary tension to legal or political settings, and this is one of his best. Laughton's last role. **Cast:** Henry Fonda, Charles Laughton, Gene Tierney, Burgess Meredith, Peter Lawford, Walter Pidgeon, Don Murray, Lew Ayres, Franchot Tone. **Credits:** Dir: Otto Preminger; Prod: Otto Preminger; Writer: Wendell Mayes; Story: Allen Drury; DP: Sam Leavitt; Ed: Louis R. Loeffler; Prod Design: Lyle Wheeler; Composer: Jerry Fielding; Costumes: Hope Bryce; Set Designer: Eli Benneche. B&W, 139 min. VHS, LASER

Affair in Trinidad

(1952) Columbia

The *Gilda* pairing of Hayworth and Ford reunite for a steamy tropical tale. When a sexy cafe dancer's husband is murdered by an international spy, the local police ask her to snoop into the spy's affairs. But temperatures really rise when her brother-in-law arrives and they are drawn into the mystery and to each other. **Cast:** Rita Hayworth, Glenn Ford, Valerie Bettis, Torin Thatcher, Alexander Scourby. **Credits:** Dir: Vincent Sherman; Prod: Vincent Sherman; Writer: Oscar Saul, James Gunn; Story: Virginia Van Upp; DP: Joseph Walker; Ed: Viola Lawrence; Composer: George Duning; Costumes: Jean Ann Lewis; Set Designer: William Kiernan. B&W, 98 min. VHS, LASER

The Affairs of Annabel

(1938) RKO

This is the first of the Annabel series that features Lucy in late-'30s screwball mode. Ball portrays Annabel Allison, a beautiful starlet who becomes the victim of an overzealous publicity agent (Oakie) who gets her thrown in jail just to make headlines. His plans completely backfire when the show she's producing gets canceled in her absence. Followed by *Annabel Takes a Tour.* **Cast:** Lucille Ball, Jack Oakie, Ruth Donnelly, Bradley Page, Fritz Feld, Thurston Hall, James Burke. **Credits:** Dir: Benjamin Stoloff; Prod:

Lou Lusty; Writer: Paul Yawitz, Bert Granet; DP: Russell Metty; Composer: Roy Webb. B&W, 134 min. VHS, LASER

The Affairs of Cellini

(1934) Fox

A romantic comedy about the Renaissance artist Cellini. Cellini is more interested in pursuing women than his artistic pursuits. He initially flirts with his artistic model, but then succumbs to a beautiful Duchess. The duchess's husband doesn't have time to worry about Cellini romancing his wife, as he's occupied romancing Cellini's model. The artist also finds time to swashbuckle a little between romantic intrigues and painting. Academy Award Nominations: 4, including Best Actor: Frank Morgan; Best Cinematography. **Cast:** Constance Bennett, Fredric March, Frank Morgan, Fay Wray, Vince Barnett, Jessie Ralph, Louis Calhern, Jay Eaton. **Credits:** Dir: Gregory La Cava; DP: Charles Rosher, Jr.; Ed: Barbara McLean; Prod Design: Richard Day; Composer: Alfred Newman. B&W, 90 min.

The Affairs of Dobie Gillis

(1953) MGM

A boundlessly energetic musical romance, based on Max Shulman's book, which saw the creation of that archetypical girl-watcher Dobie Gillis. Sparkling tunes, freewheeling dancing, and teen comedy earned Dobie a TV series in 1959, where Dwayne Hickman took over the duties that Van introduced here. **Cast:** Debbie Reynolds, Bobby Van, Hans Conried, Lurene Tuttle, Bob Fosse, Barbara Ruick. **Credits:** Dir: Don Weis; Writer: Max Shulman; DP: William Mellor; Ed: Conrad A. Nervig; Choreographer: Alex Romero. B&W, 74 min. VHS

An Affair to Remember

(1957) Fox

In this legendary tearjerker that served as the female touchstone in *Sleepless in Seattle,* the world's most eligible bachelor (Grant) is set to marry an heiress. But unfortunately for his bride-to-be, while he's traveling alone on a luxury liner, he meets Kerr and realizes he's engaged to the wrong woman. McCarey and Grant in a sentimental mood. First made by McCarey in 1939 as *Love Affair* with Dunne and Boyer, later remade as *Love Affair* (1994) with Beatty and Bening. Academy Award Nominations: 4, including Best Song ("An Affair to Remember"). **Cast:** Cary Grant, Deborah Kerr, Cathleen Nesbitt, Neva Patterson, Richard Denning, Fortunio

Bonanova. **Credits:** Dir: Leo McCarey; Prod: Jerry Wald; Writer: Delmer Daves, Leo McCarey; Story: Mildred Cram; DP: Milton Krasner; Ed: James B. Clark; Prod Design: Lyle Wheeler, Jack Martin Smith; Composer: Hugo Friedhofer; Set Designer: Walter M. Scott, Paul S. Fox. Color, 115 min. VHS, LASER

The African Lion

(1955) Disney

Documentary featuring color footage of lions, elephants, hippos, leopards, baboons, cheetahs, giraffes, and birds of Kenya. **Credits:** Dir: James Algar; Writer: James Algar, Winston Hibler, Jack Moffitt, Ted Sears; DP: Alfred G. Milotte; Ed: James Algar; Composer: Paul Smith. Color, 75 min.

The African Queen

(1951) United Artists

The boozing, smoking, cussing captain of a tramp steamer, Charlie Allnut (Bogart), saves prim and proper Rose Sayer (Hepburn) after her brother is killed by German soldiers at the beginning of WWI in Africa. Many quarrels later, the two set sail on the *Ulonga-Bora* in order to sabotage a German ship. Based on the 1935 book by novelist C. S. Forester, the wonderful combination of Hepburn and Bogie (who won an Oscar) makes this a thoroughly enjoyable blend of comedy and adventure. Later came the book (and Clint Eastwood film) *White Hunter, Black Heart,* which chronicled Peter Viertel's experiences observing Huston throughout the making of the picture. A National Film Registry Outstanding Film. **Academy Awards:** Best Actor: Humphrey Bogart. **Cast:** Humphrey Bogart, Katharine Hepburn, Robert Morley, Theodore Bikel, Walter Gotell, Richard Marner, Peter Bull. **Credits:** Dir: John Huston; Prod: Sam Spiegel; Writer: James Agee, John Huston; Story: C. S. Forester; DP: Jack Cardiff; Ed: Ralph Kemplen; Composer: Allan Gray. Color, 105 min. VHS, LASER

African Treasure

(1952) Monogram

A typical adventure in Monogram's Bomba, the Jungle Boy series, this pits the jungle boy against two conniving diamond smugglers. The smugglers take a geologist with them in search of the blue volcanic clay that houses troves of diamonds. The district's commissioner sends Bomba to find them, but he only finds evidence that the geologist has been abandoned after serving his purpose. Bomba encounters the geologist's daughter, who is searching for her father and, summoning his mystic powers, locates the evildoers. **Cast:** Johnny Sheffield, Luez Laurette, Leonard Mudie, Arthur Space, Lane Bradford, Martin Garralaga, Lyle Talbott, Robert Whitfield, James Adamson. **Credits:** Dir: Ford Beebe; Prod: Walter Mirisch; Writer: Ford Beebe; DP: Harry Neumann; Ed: Bruce Schoengarth; Prod Design: Martin Obzina; Composer: Raoul Kraushaar; Art Director: Robert Priestly. B&W, 70 min.

Against All Flags
(1952) Universal
Flynn stars as a courageous British soldier trying to maneuver his way into a pirate fortress. When he ends up in front of a pirate tribunal, he catches the eye of stunning pirate queen O'Hara. Toward the end of Flynn's swashbuckling days, but the spirit is still willing. **Cast:** Errol Flynn, Maureen O'Hara, Anthony Quinn, Mildred Natwick. **Credits:** Dir: George Sherman; Prod: Howard Christie; Writer: Aeneas MacKenzie, Joseph Hoffman; DP: Russell Metty; Ed: Frank Gross; Prod Design: Bernard Herzbrun, Alexander Golitzen; Composer: Hans J. Salter; Costumes: Edward Stevenson; Set Designer: Russell A. Gausman, Oliver Emert. Color, 83 min. **VHS, LASER**

Agatha
(1979) Warner Bros.
An imaginative fictional speculation on the 1926 disappearance of mystery writer Agatha Christie and an American reporter's attempt to find her. Effective recreation of the time and place. **Cast:** Dustin Hoffman, Vanessa Redgrave, Helen Morse, Timothy Dalton, Timothy West, Tony Britton, Alan Badel. **Credits:** Dir: Michael Apted, Jim Clark; Prod: Jarvis Astaire, Gavrick Losey; Writer: Kathleen Tynan, Arthur Hopcraft; DP: Vittorio Storaro; Prod Design: Shirley Russell; Composer: Johnny Mandel. Color, 98 min. **VHS, LASER**

Ah, Wilderness
(1935) MGM
Eugene O'Neill's only comedy is the basis for this atmospheric story of life in small-town New England. After high school, a young man steers his way to maturity under the watchful eyes of his parents and despite his introduction to the ways of the world by Beery. Remade as *Summer Holiday* (1948), a musical starring Mickey Rooney. **Cast:** Wallace Beery, Lionel Barrymore, Aline

MacMahon, Eric Linden, Cecilia Parker, Mickey Rooney, Frank Albertson, Bonita Granville, Spring Byington, Charley Grapewin. **Credits:** Dir: Clarence Brown; Prod: Hunt Stromberg; Writer: Albert Hackett, Frances Goodrich; Story: Eugene O'Neill; DP: Clyde De Vinna; Ed: Frank Hull; Prod Design: Cedric Gibbons, William A. Horning; Composer: Herbert Stothart. B&W, 98 min. **VHS**

Air Force
(1943) Warner Bros.
The story of the crew manning a B-17 Flying Fortress in action throughout the Pacific is tailor-made for director Hawks, the undisputed master of men-under-pressure adventures. Stirring aerial battle scenes and believable dialogue lift this far above the average WWII propaganda vehicle. Academy Award Nominations: 4, including Best Original Screenplay. **Academy Awards:** Best Film Editing. **Cast:** John Garfield, John Ridgely, Gig Young, Arthur Kennedy, Charles Drake, Harry Carey, George Tobias, Stanley Ridges, Moroni Olsen, Edward Brophy. **Credits:** Dir: Howard Hawks; Prod: Hal B. Wallis; Writer: Dudley Nichols; DP: Elmer Dyer, James Wong Howe; Ed: George Amy; Composer: Franz Waxman; SFX: H. F. Koenekamp, Rex Wimpy, Roy Davidson; Art Director: John Hughes. B&W, 124 min. **VHS**

Air Mail
(1932) Universal
A drama-adventure about pilot Duke Talbot (O'Brien), a brave flyer who also happens to be a world-class show-off. He has an affair with the wife of one of his mail-service mates, and, when the betrayed husband is killed during a violent storm, Duke refuses to take his mail on to the next stage, instead choosing to elope with the newly freed wife. That job is left for Mike, the head of their station, and, along the way, the plane crashes, leaving him in what is considered to be an unlandable area. Duke leaves the lady behind and attempts the impossible. **Cast:** Pat O'Brien, Ralph Bellamy, Russell Hopton, Slim Summerville, Gloria Stuart, Lilian Bond, William Daly, Frank Albertson, Leslie Fenton, Tom Carrigan. **Credits:** Dir: John Ford; Prod: Carl Laemmle; Writer: Dale Van Every; Story: Frank Wead; DP: Karl Freund; Ed: Harry Lieb. B&W, 83 min.

Airport
(1970) Universal
One of the original "disaster" movies, this all-star nail-biter follows a series

of emergencies at a large Midwestern airport on a snowy night. The weather's bad enough, but then a passenger threatens to blow up an inbound plane. Based on Arthur Hailey's novel. Sequels include *Airport 1975, Airport '77, The Concorde—Airport '79,* and dozens of other catastrophe epics built from the same blueprint. Academy Award Nominations: 10, including Best Picture; Best (Adapted) Screenplay. **Academy Awards:** Best Supporting Actress: Helen Hayes. **Cast:** Van Heflin, Burt Lancaster, Dean Martin, George Kennedy, Helen Hayes, Jean Seberg, Maureen Stapleton, Barry Nelson, Dana Wynter, Lloyd Nolan. **Credits:** Dir: George Seaton, Henry Hathaway; Prod: Ross Hunter; Writer: George Seaton; Story: Arthur Hailey; DP: Ernest Laszlo; Ed: Stuart Gilmore; Prod Design: Alexander Golitzen, Preston Ames; Composer: Alfred Newman; Costumes: Edith Head. Color, 137 min. **VHS, LASER**

The Alamo
(1960) United Artists
The Duke directs (with the uncredited help of his friend and mentor John Ford) this flag-waving spectacular about the courageous struggle by 182 American heroes to defend a small Catholic mission to the death and eventually win Texas. The restored, widescreen edition of Wayne's epic is at original length, and includes the theatrical trailer. Academy Award Nominations: 7, including Best Picture; Best Song ("Green Leaves of Summer"). **Academy Awards:** Best Sound. **Cast:** John Wayne, Richard Widmark, Laurence Harvey, Richard Boone, Frankie Avalon. **Credits:** Dir: John Wayne; Writer: James Edward Grant; DP: William H. Clothier; Ed: Stuart Gilmore; Composer: Dimitri Tiomkin. Color, 173 min. **VHS, LASER**

Al Capone
(1959) Allied Artists
Steiger provides a fine performance in his portrayal of the famous Chicago mobster. The picture follows Capone's career from his training by a local thug, to the first exhibitions of his "talent" for violence, to his leadership of the Chicago rackets and eventual arrest on income tax charges. A latter-day revival of the classic Warner gangster movies. **Cast:** Rod Steiger, Martin Balsam, Nehemiah Persoff, Fay Spain, James Gregory, Murvyn Vye, Joe De Santis. **Credits:** Dir: Richard Wilson; Prod: John H. Burrows, Leonard J. Ackerman; Writer: Malvin Wald, Henry F. Greenberg; DP: Lucien Ballard; Ed:

Walter Hannemann; Prod Design: Hilyard Brown; Composer: David Raksin. B&W, 105 min. VHS

Alexander's Ragtime Band

(1938) Fox
A sumptuous showcase for 28 fantastic Berlin tunes. Aristocratic Power flouts family convention and takes up ragtime. He starts a band with composer Ameche and singer Faye. Over the next 30 years, two fall in love, a different two get married, one goes away to war, the band breaks up then gets back together. One of the original and still one of the best "let's put on a show" films of all time. Love, loyalty, fame, jealousy—even duty, honor, and country—all play alongside the spectacular cast in this breathtakingly appointed showbiz epic. **Academy Awards:** Best Score: Alfred Newman. **Cast:** Don Ameche, Alice Faye, Jack Haley, Jean Hersholt, Ethel Merman, Tyrone Power, Helen Westley, John Carradine, Paul Hurst, Wally Vernon. **Credits:** Dir: Henry King; Writer: Lamar Trotti, Kathryn Scola; DP: Peverell Marley; Ed: Barbara McLean; Composer: Irving Berlin, Alfred Newman; Art Director: Boris Leven, Bernard Hertzrun. B&W, 109 min. VHS

Alex in Wonderland

(1970) MGM
Mazursky wrote, directed, and performs in this semi-autobiographical film about a director who feels that fame compromises his principles so he must create a follow-up unburdened by the success his first film brought. An homage to Federico Fellini's classic tale of filmmaker's angst, *8½* with the Italian master and Jeanne Moreau appearing in cameos. **Cast:** Donald Sutherland, Ellen Burstyn, Viola Spolin, Federico Fellini, Jeanne Moreau, Paul Mazursky, Michael Lerner, Joan Delaney. **Credits:** Dir: Paul Mazursky; Prod: Larry Tucker; Writer: Paul Mazursky, Larry Tucker; DP: Laszlo Kovacs; Ed: Stuart Pappe; Prod Design: Pato Guzman; Composer: Tom O'Horgan; Set Designer: Audrey Blasdel-Goddard. Color, 109 min. VHS

Algiers

(1938) United Artists
A remake of the French film *Pepe Le Moko* in which Boyer plays Pepe, a notorious thief hiding out in the Casbah. When he falls in love with a beautiful tourist, his voluntary captivity becomes unbearable. In 1948, remade, with songs, as *Casbah.* Academy Award Nominations: 4, including Best Actor. **Cast:** Charles Boyer, Hedy Lamarr, Peter Lorre, Sigrid Gurie, Joseph Calleia, Alan Hale, Johnny Downs. **Credits:** Dir: John Cromwell; Writer: John Howard Lawson, James M. Cain; Story: Roger D'Ashelbe; DP: James Wong Howe; Ed: William H. Reynolds, Otho S. Lovering; Composer: Vincent Scotto, Mohammed Igorbouchen; Costumes: Omar Kiam, Irene; Art Director: Alexander Toluboff. B&W, 99 min. VHS

Alias Jesse James

(1959) United Artists
Hope stars as a mild-mannered life insurance agent holding Jesse James's policy, sent to the Wild West by his company to protect the outlaw from hired guns. Things get fun when James decides to collect on his own policy by setting Hope up as himself. This farcical spoof on Western flicks is loaded with star cameos. **Cast:** Bob Hope, Rhonda Fleming, Wendell Corey, Jim Davis, Gloria Talbott, James Burke. **Credits:** Dir: Norman Z. McLeod; Prod: Jack Hope; Writer: William Bowers, D. D. Beauchamp; Story: Robert St. Aubrey, Bert Lawrence; DP: Lionel Lindon; Ed: Marvin Coil, Jack Bachom; Prod Design: Hal Pereira, Roland Anderson; Costumes: Edith Head; Set Designer: Sam Comer, Bertram Granger. Color, 92 min. VHS, LASER

Alias Nick Beal

(1949) Paramount
In this modern retelling of the Faust story, an honorable judge who believes he can better serve society in a higher office makes a pact with a mysterious benefactor who is really Lucifer—alias Nick Beal—and whose identity is not revealed until the judge climbs the political ladder to become governor of his state. It is up to the governor, along with a faithful friend and his supportive wife, to outwit Lucifer and save his soul from damnation. **Cast:** Ray Milland, Audrey Totter, Thomas Mitchell, Geraldine Wall, George Macready, Henry O'Neill, Darryl Hickman, Fred Clark, Nestor Paiva, King Donovan. **Credits:** Dir: John Farrow; Prod: Andre Bohem; Writer: Jonathan Latimer; Story: Mindret Lord; DP: Lionel Linden; Ed: Eda Warren; Prod Design: Franz Bachelin; Composer: Franz Waxman. B&W, 92 min.

Ali Baba and the Forty Thieves

(1944) Universal
Ali Baba, son of the murdered Caliph, returns with his posse of forty thieves to save Baghdad, free his captured love, and reclaim the throne. This Arabian adventure is pure Technicolor escapism and the second pairing of Hall and Montez. **Cast:** Maria Montez, Jon Hall, Scotty Beckett, Turhan Bey, Kurt Katch, Andy Devine, Frank Puglia, Fortunio Bonanova, Moroni Olsen, Chris-Pin Martin. **Credits:** Dir: Arthur Lubin; Prod: Paul Malvern; Writer: Edmund L. Hartmann; DP: George Robinson, W. Howard Greene; Ed: Russell Schoengarth; Prod Design: John B. Goodman, Richard H. Riedel; Composer: Edward Ward; SFX: John Fulton; Set Designer: Russell A. Gausman, Ira Webb. Color, 87 min. VHS

Ali Baba Goes to Town

(1937) Fox
Ali Bobo, an extra working on a splashy Arabian adventure in Hollywood, falls asleep on the set and dreams he is back in ancient Arabia. There he is hired by Sultan of Baghdad to act as Chief Minister. Resolving to turn Baghdad into a peaceful, happy utopia, Ali sets about decommissioning the Sultan's army, increasing taxes on the rich, and increasing the availability of jobs. Understandably, Ali's new schemes do not wash well with all and pretty soon he has several enemies all bent on murdering him. Overcoming them with the help of a flying carpet, Ali saves the day and then wakes up to find himself back in reality. **Cast:** Eddie Cantor, Tony Martin, Roland Young, June Lang, Gypsy Rose Lee, John Carradine, Virginia Field, Alan Dinehart, Douglass Dumbrille, Maurice Cass. **Credits:** Dir: David Butler; Prod: Lawrence Schwab, Darryl F. Zanuck; Writer: C. Graham Baker, Harry Tugend, Jack Yellen, Gene Fowler, Jr.; DP: Ernest Palmer; Ed: Irene Morra; Prod Design: Bernard Herzbrun; Composer: Mack Gordon, Harry Revel, Raymond Scott, Louis Silvers. B&W, 81 min.

Alibi Ike

(1935) Warner Bros.
A lively screwball comedy. Alibi Ike is a baseball player with a talent for excuses and for inventive pitching techniques. The excuse-making threatens his romantic happiness with the sister of the wife of his team's owner, and things get even more complicated when gangsters kidnap him to keep him away from a game they've bet on. **Cast:** Joe E. Brown, Olivia de Havilland, Ruth Donnelly, Roscoe Karns, William Frawley, Eddie Shubert, Joe King, Joseph Crehan, Adrian Rosely, Paul Harvey. **Credits:** Dir: Ray Enright; Prod: Edward Chodorov; Writer: Ring

Lardner, William Wister Haines; DP: Arthur Todd; Ed: Thomas Pratt. B&W, 73 min.

Alice Adams

(1935) RKO
A small-town girl (Hepburn) attempts to climb the social ladder in a midwestern town. Hiding her reduced circumstances from her rich but unassuming beau (MacMurray), she alienates both friends and family. A mild melodrama based on the 1921 novel by Booth Tarkington. Silent version released in 1923. Academy Award Nominations: Best Picture; Best Actress. **Cast:** Katharine Hepburn, Fred MacMurray, Fred Stone, Frank Albertson, Hedda Hopper, Hattie McDaniel. **Credits:** Dir: George Stevens; Prod: Pandro S. Berman; Writer: Dorothy Yost, Mortimer Offner, Jane Murfin; Story: Booth Tarkington; DP: Robert DeGrasse; Ed: Jane Loring; Prod Design: Van Nest Polglase; Composer: Max Steiner; Costumes: Walter Plunkett. B&W, 99 min. VHS, LASER

Alice Doesn't Live Here Anymore

(1974) Warner Bros.
When a housewife is left with nothing after her husband's death, she struggles to build a new life for herself and her young son. Noteworthy as a nonviolent domestic drama from Scorsese and the basis for the long-running Linda Lavin sitcom *Alice*. Academy Award Nominations: 3, including Best Original Screenplay. **Academy Awards:** Best Actress: Ellen Burstyn. **Cast:** Ellen Burstyn, Kris Kristofferson, Harvey Keitel, Diane Ladd, Jodie Foster, Billy "Green" Bush, Vic Tayback. **Credits:** Dir: Martin Scorsese; Prod: David Susskind, Audrey Maas; Writer: Robert Getchell; DP: Kent Wakeford; Ed: Marcia Lucas; Prod Design: Toby Rafelson; Composer: Richard LaSalle. Color, 113 min. VHS, LASER

Alice in Wonderland

(1951) Disney
Based on the 1865 book by Lewis Carroll, this is the classic Disney animated version of Alice's adventures as she follows a white rabbit into a "Wonderland" of her own imagination. The usual Disney zest, and upbeat songs such as "I'm Late." Academy Award Nominations: Best Scoring of a Musical Picture. **Cast:** Sterling Holloway, Ed Wynn. **Credits:** Dir: Clyde Geronomi, Hamilton Luske, Wilfred Jackson; Prod: Walt Disney; Writer: Bill Peet, Joe Rinaldi; Story: Lewis Carroll; Composer: Oliver Wallace. Color, 75 min. VHS, LASER

All About Eve (1950)

Alice's Restaurant

(1969) United Artists
A finely wrought, and often strikingly funny, cinematic snapshot of the 1960s. After illegally dumping a load of garbage, a young man gets tangled up with both the local police and the draft board. Based on the popular Arlo Guthrie song. Academy Award Nominations: Best Director. **Cast:** Arlo Guthrie, Pat Quinn, James Broderick, Tina Chen, M. Emmet Walsh. **Credits:** Dir: Arthur Penn; Prod: Hillard Elkins, Joseph Manduke; Writer: Venable Herndon, Arthur Penn; Story: Arlo Guthrie; DP: Michael Nebbia; Ed: Dede Allen; Composer: Arlo Guthrie. Color, 111 min. VHS

Alien

(1979) Fox
While investigating an alien spacecraft ditched on a dead planet, the crew of a space freighter, including feminist heroine Weaver, picks up an uninvited passenger. This languid masterpiece of horror depicts a primal interspecies struggle for survival juxtaposed against a jungle of sci-fi hyper-technology. Followed by *Aliens,* a cathartic sequel by James Cameron, in 1986; *Alien 3* in 1992; and *Alien Resurrection* in 1997. Academy Award Nomination for Best Art Direction. **Academy Awards:** Best Visual Effects. **Cast:** Tom Skerritt, Sigourney Weaver, John Hurt, Ian Holm, Harry Dean Stanton, Veronica Cartwright, Yaphet Kotto. **Credits:** Dir: Ridley Scott; Prod: Gordon Carroll, David Giler, Walter Hill; Writer: Dan O'Bannon; Story: Ronald Shusett; DP: Derek Vanlint; Ed: Terry Rawlings, Peter Weatherly; Prod Design: Michael Seymour; Composer: Jerry Goldsmith; Costumes: John Mollo, H. R. Giger, Roger Dicken; SFX: Carlo Rambaldi, Bernard Lodge; Set Designer: Ian Whittaker. Color, 116 min. VHS, LASER

All About Eve

(1950) Fox
This brilliant, acerbic look at theater life features Davis as an aging Broadway star who takes a seemingly naive fan under her wing, only to discover the waif is scheming to take her throne. Wit and sarcasm reign supreme as the determined divas duke it out. Davis is often cited for this role, but George Sanders as the viperish columnist is oily perfection. Academy Award Nominations: 14, including two for Best Actress. Other of its multiple awards include the British Academy Best Film, and Golden Globe for Best Screenplay. A National Film Registry Outstanding Film. **Academy Awards:** Best Director; Best Supporting Actor; Best Costume

Design; Best Sound Recording; Best Screenplay; Best Picture. **Cast:** Bette Davis, Anne Baxter, George Sanders, Celeste Holm, Marilyn Monroe, Gregory Ratoff, Barbara Bates, Walter Hampden, Thelma Ritter, Hugh Marlowe. **Credits:** Dir: Joseph L. Mankiewicz; Prod: Darryl F. Zanuck; Writer: Joseph L. Mankiewicz; DP: Milton Krasner; Ed: Barbara McLean; Prod Design: Lyle Wheeler, George Davis; Composer: Alfred Newman; Costumes: Edith Head; SFX: Fred Sersen; Set Designer: Thomas Little, Walter M. Scott. B&W, 138 min. **VHS, LASER**

Allegheny Uprising
(1939) RKO
John Wayne clashes with a British military commander in order to stop the sale of guns to the Indians. Straightforward military tale with less-familiar setting of mid-1700s colonial America. **Cast:** John Wayne, Claire Trevor, George Sanders, Chill Wills, Monte Montague. **Credits:** Dir: William A. Seiter; Writer: P. J. Wolfson; Story: Neil H. Swanson; DP: Nicholas Musuraca; Ed: George Crone; Prod Design: Van Nest Polglase, Albert S. D'Agostino; Choreographer: David Robel; Composer: Anthony Collins; Costumes: Walter Plunkett; Set Designer: Darrell Silvera. B&W, 81 min. **VHS, LASER**

All Fall Down
(1962) MGM
A dissolute wanderer (Beatty) is idolized by his younger brother until he abandons the woman he's impregnated and she commits suicide. To add insult to injury, little brother had always worshiped her from afar and he now vows revenge. Written by playwright William Inge, based on the best-selling novel by James Leo Herlihy. **Cast:** Warren Beatty, Eva Marie Saint, Karl Malden, Angela Lansbury, Brandon De Wilde. **Credits:** Dir: John Frankenheimer; Prod: John Houseman; Writer: William Inge; Story: James Leo Herlihy; DP: Lionel Lindon; Ed: Fredric Steinkamp; Prod Design: George W. Davis, Preston Ames; Composer: Alex North; Costumes: Dorothy Jeakins; Set Designer: Henry Grace, George Robert Nelson. B&W, 110 min. **VHS**

All I Desire
(1953) Universal
Ten years after an illicit love affair forced a woman to abandon her husband and family, she returns to the small town hoping for a reconciliation.

But neither the town nor her children are ready to forgive. A great performance by Stanwyck in trademark Sirk material survives a happy ending tacked on by the studio over Sirk's objections. **Cast:** Barbara Stanwyck, Richard Carlson, Lyle Bettger, Maureen O'Sullivan. **Credits:** Dir: Douglas Sirk; Prod: Ross Hunter; Writer: James Gunn, Robert Blees, Gina Kaus; Story: Carol Ryrie Brink; DP: Carl Guthrie; Ed: Milton Carruth; Prod Design: Bernard Herzbrun, Alexander Golitzen; Choreographer: Kenny Williams; Composer: Joseph Gershenson; Costumes: Rosemary Odell; Set Designer: Russell A. Gausman, Julia Heron. B&W, 80 min. **VHS**

All Mine to Give
(1957) Universal
A true, moving story of a brave Scottish immigrant family and their losing battle against the rigors of the frontier wilderness. When the parents die, the children keep the family and their Wisconsin homestead together. **Cast:** Cameron Mitchell, Glynis Johns, Patty McCormack, Hope Emerson, Alan Hale, Jr. **Credits:** Dir: Allen Reisner; Prod: Sam Wiesenthal; Writer: Dale Eunson; Story: Katherine Eunson; DP: William V. Skall; Ed: Alan Crosland, Jr.; Composer: Max Steiner. Color, 102 min. **VHS**

All My Sons
(1948) Universal
A well-to-do family, headed by stern but loving airplane-parts magnate Joe Keller, grimly contends with the loss of a son in a WWII firefight. Their wounds are reopened when the lost son's former fiancée finds comfort in the arms of his surviving brother. Worse still, the fiancée's brother drives a wedge between father and son by alleging that Keller's substandard hardware contributed to the deaths of innocent flyboys—a crime for which Keller's business partner took the fall. Richly nuanced performances bring Miller's play to the big screen. **Cast:** Edward G. Robinson, Burt Lancaster, Howard Duff, Louisa Horton, Mady Christians, Arlene Francis, Henry Morgan, Elisabeth Fraser, Walter Soderling, Lloyd Gough. **Credits:** Dir: Irving Reis; Prod: Chester Erskine; Writer: Chester Erskine; Story: Arthur Miller; DP: Russell Metty; Ed: Ralph Dawson; Prod Design: Bernard Herzbrun, Hilyard Brown; Composer: Leith Stevens; Costumes: Grace Houston; SFX: David Horsley; Set Designer: Russell A. Gausman, Al Fields. B&W, 94 min. **VHS**

All Quiet on the Western Front
(1930) Universal
Based on Erich Maria Remarque's timeless antiwar novel, this moving film follows a group of German recruits during WWI as they make their personal journey from patriotism to disillusionment. Shot on an epic scale with an impressive budget of $1.25 million, the film's realism and visual art created a sensation. Author (and war veteran) Remarque was forced by the reaction to the film to relocate from his native Germany to the United States. The recently restored version includes the entire "Last Supper" sequence and removes the annoying music added to later releases. Academy Award Nominations: 4, including Best Writing. A National Film Registry Outstanding Film. **Academy Awards:** Best Director; Best Picture. **Cast:** Lew Ayres, Louis Wolheim, Russell Gleason, John Wray. **Credits:** Dir: Lewis Milestone; Prod: Carl Laemmle; Writer: Del Andrews, Lewis Milestone, George Abbott; Story: Erich Maria Remarque; DP: Karl Freund, Arthur Edeson; Ed: Edgar Adams, Milton Carruth; Prod Design: Charles D. Hall, William R. Schmidt; Composer: David Broekman; SFX: Frank H. Booth. B&W, 103 min. **VHS, LASER, DVD**

All That Heaven Allows
(1955) Universal
A wealthy suburbanite widow (Wyman) raises the eyebrows of her stodgy neighbors and the ire of her concerned children when she falls in love with a handsome, earthy—and younger!—gardener (Hudson). This is prime Sirk melodrama with his distinctive visual styling. Remade in 1974 with additional interracial themes by Rainer Werner Fassbinder as *Ali—Fear Eats the Soul.* **Cast:** Jane Wyman, Rock Hudson, Agnes Moorehead, Conrad Nagel, Virginia Grey, Gloria Talbott. **Credits:** Dir: Douglas Sirk; Prod: Ross Hunter; Writer: Peg Fenwick; Story: Edna Lee, Harry Lee; DP: Russell Metty; Ed: Frank Gross, Fred Baratta; Prod Design: Alexander Golitzen, Eric Orbom; Composer: Frank Skinner, Joseph Gershenson; Costumes: Bill Thomas; Set Designer: Russell A. Gausman, Julia Heron. Color, 89 min. **VHS**

All That Jazz
(1979) Fox
Fosse's semi-autobiographical film celebrates show business stripped of glamour or giddy illusions. The direc-

tor's energetic choreography and some exhilarating musical moments compensate for self-indulgence and an overlong finale. Academy Award Nominations: 9, including Best Picture; Best Director; Best Actor; Best Original Screenplay. **Academy Awards:** Best Film Editing; Best Costume Design; Best Art Direction—Set Decoration; Best Original Song Score and Adaptation. **Cast:** Roy Scheider, Jessica Lange, Ann Reinking, Leland Palmer, Cliff Gorman, Ben Vereen, John Lithgow. **Credits:** Dir: Bob Fosse; Prod: Robert Alan Aurthur; Writer: Robert Alan Aurthur, Bob Fosse; DP: Giuseppe Rotunno; Ed: Alan Heim; Choreographer: Bob Fosse; Composer: Ralph Burns; Costumes: Albert Wolsky; Set Designer: Philip Rosenberg. Color, 123 min. VHS, LASER

All the King's Men

(1949) Columbia
Crawford stands out in this fine drama of the rise and fall of a corrupt southern governor who promises his way to power. Once elected, his vanity and power-lust prove his downfall. Based on the 1946 novel by Robert Penn Warren, which in turn was based largely on the story of Louisiana legend Huey Long. Academy Award Nominations: 7, including Best Director; Best Screenplay. Other awards include Golden Globes for Best Director; Best Supporting Actress; Best Actor in a Drama; Best Motion Picture Drama; Most Promising Newcomer—Female. **Academy Awards:** Best Picture; Best Actor: Broderick Crawford; Best Supporting Actress: Mercedes McCambridge. **Cast:** Broderick Crawford, Mercedes McCambridge, John Ireland, John Derek, Joanne Dru. **Credits:** Dir: Robert Rossen; Prod: Robert Rossen; Writer: Robert Rossen; Story: Robert Penn Warren; DP: Burnett Guffey; Ed: Al Clark; Composer: Louis Gruenberg. B&W, 109 min. VHS, LASER

All the President's Men

(1976) Warner Bros.
A well-made thriller based on the unrelenting efforts of *Washington Post* reporters Woodward and Bernstein to uncover the Watergate scandal that ultimately ended the presidency of Richard Nixon. Robards couldn't be better as editor Ben Bradlee, and the painstaking recreations of newsroom and D.C. settings put the audience in the midst of deadline-beating tension and filled journalism schools for years after! Academy Award Nominations: 8, including Best Picture; Best Director. **Academy Awards:** Best Supporting

Actor: Jason Robards; Best Sound; Best Art Direction—Set Decoration; Best Screenplay Based on Material from Another Medium. **Cast:** Robert Redford, Dustin Hoffman, Jason Robards, John Randolph, Basil Hoffman, F. Murray Abraham. **Credits:** Dir: Alan J. Pakula; Prod: Walter Coblenz; Writer: William Goldman; Story: Carl Bernstein, Bob Woodward; DP: Gordon Willis; Ed: Robert L. Wolfe; Prod Design: George Jenkins; Composer: David Shire; Set Designer: George Gaines. Color, 139 min. VHS, LASER, DVD

All the Way Home

(1963) Paramount
A picture-perfect small-town family is shattered when Jay Follet (Preston), husband and father, is killed in a car accident. Mary Follet (Simmons) and her young son, Rufus, must now struggle to cope without their protector. Rufus, young and innocent, attempts to come to terms with the sudden disappearance of his father as well as his mother's deep depression. Comfort comes in the form of Aunt Hannah (MacMahon), who offers consolation and a little homespun advice. Mosel's adaptation of the James Agee book, *A Death in the Family.* **Cast:** Jean Simmons, Robert Preston, Pat Hingle, Aline MacMahon, Thomas Chalmers, John Cullum, Helen Carew, Ronnie Edwards, John Henry Faulk, Mary Perry. **Credits:** Dir: Alex Segal; Prod: Jack Grossberg, David Susskind; Writer: Philip Reisman, Jr.; Story: James Agee, Tad Mosel; DP: Boris Kaufman; Ed: Carl Lerner; Prod Design: Richard Sylbert; Composer: Bernard Green. B&W, 103 min.

All This and Heaven Too

(1940) Warner Bros.
A nobleman falls in love with his children's governess and then murders his wife. Unfortunately, the governess goes to jail after the royal philanderer kills himself. Great performances by Boyer as the Duke and Davis as the governess bring Rachel Field's best-selling book to life. Academy Award Nominations: 3, including Best Picture. **Cast:** Bette Davis, Charles Boyer, Barbara O'Neil, Jeffrey Lynn, June Lockhart. **Credits:** Dir: Anatole Litvak; Prod: David Lewis; Writer: Casey Robinson; Story: Rachel Field; DP: Ernest Haller; Ed: Warren Low; Prod Design: Carl Jules Weyl; Composer: Max Steiner; Costumes: Orry-Kelly. B&W, 143 min. VHS

All That Heaven Allows (1955)

All Through the Night

(1942) Warner Bros.
Bogart and Lorre spoof their screen personas in this send-up of WWII spy intrigues. Broadway big-shot and part-time gangster "Gloves" Donahue becomes a full-time amateur detective after a German friend of his is killed. Gloves's investigation lands him in a deadly web of intrigue when he discovers a Nazi spy ring is behind the murder. Fine suspense and comedy blend. **Cast:** Humphrey Bogart, Conrad Veidt, Kaaren Verne, Jane Darwell, Frank McHugh, Peter Lorre, Judith Anderson, William Demarest, Jackie Gleason, Phil Silvers. **Credits:** Dir: Vincent Sherman; Prod: Jerry Wald; Writer: Leonard Spigelgass, Edwin Gilbert; DP: Sid Hickox; Ed: Rudi Fehr; Prod Design: Max Parker; Composer: Adolph Deutsch. B&W, 107 min. VHS

Almost Angels

(1962) Disney
Perfectly fine Disney family fare about two young boys who become fast friends when chosen to be in the Vienna Boys Choir. Sumptuous Austrian settings and heavenly music. **Cast:** Peter Weck, Hans Holt, Fritz Eckhardt, Bruni Lobel, Vincent Winter. **Credits:** Dir: Steve Previn; Writer: Vernon Harris; Story: R. A. Stemmle; DP: Kurt Grigoleit. Color, 85 min. VHS

An Almost Perfect Affair

(1979) Paramount
At the Cannes film festival, a young, idealistic American filmmaker falls in love with the worldly wife of an Italian movie producer. A comedy-romance that takes a sharply observed, satirical backstage look at the movie industry. **Cast:** Keith Carradine, Monica Vitti, Raf Vallone, Christian De Sica. **Credits:** Dir: Michael Ritchie; Prod: Terry Carr; Writer: Walter Bernstein, Don Peterson; DP: Henri Decae; Ed: Richard A. Harris; Prod Design: Willy Holt; Composer: Georges Delerue; Costumes: Tanine Autre. Color, 93 min. VHS

Along Came Jones

(1945) MGM
Cooper (who was also the producer) takes a sly shot at his laconic, Western-hero image as a somewhat less-than-fearless cowboy mistaken for vicious killer Duryea. He ends up on the lam from outlaws and the law with only cranky Demarest and lovely Young to protect him. **Cast:** Gary Cooper, Loretta Young, William Demarest, Dan Duryea. **Credits:** Dir: Stuart Heisler; Prod: Gary Cooper; Writer: Nunnally

Johnson; Story: Alan LeMay; DP: Milton Krasner; Ed: Thomas L. Neff; Prod Design: Wiard Ihnen; Composer: Arthur Lange, Hugo Friedhofer, Charles Maxwell; Costumes: Walter Plunkett; Set Designer: Julia Heron. B&W, 93 min. VHS

Along the Great Divide

(1951) Warner Bros.
A cowboy yarn with all the usual elements of an innocent man facing mob justice, a powerful cattle baron willing to take the law into his own hands, and spectacular High Sierra vistas—but interesting as Douglas's first Western outing. **Cast:** Kirk Douglas, John Agar, Walter Brennan, Virginia Mayo. **Credits:** Dir: Raoul Walsh; Prod: Anthony Veiller; Writer: Walter Doniger, Lewis Meltzer; DP: Sid Hickox; Ed: Thomas Reilly; Composer: David Buttolph. B&W, 88 min. VHS

Alvarez Kelly

(1966) Columbia
A Civil War Western in which Holden plays a cattle driver at odds with Widmark, who wants him to rustle cattle for the Confederates. **Cast:** William Holden, Richard Widmark, Janice Rule, Victoria Shaw. **Credits:** Dir: Edward Dmytryk; Prod: Sol C. Siegel; Writer: Franklin Coen, Elliott Arnold; DP: Joseph MacDonald; Ed: Harold F. Kress; Composer: Johnny Green. Color, 116 min. VHS, LASER

Always Leave Them Laughing

(1949) Warner Bros.
A musical comedy that's essentially a vehicle for Uncle Miltie, who stretched his hour-long TV show into a lightly plotted feature about a struggling, pushy comedian notorious for stealing other comics' material. Embarking on the road to fame, he finds that success comes only from being original. Singing, dancing, and clowning his way through typical show-biz scenarios, the comic gets his own weekly TV show and tells his inspiring story to a young hopeful. **Cast:** Milton Berle, Iris Adrian, Jerome Cowan, Lloyd Gough, Alan Hale, Jr., Grace Hayes, Bert Lahr, Virginia Mayo, Ruth Roman, Ransom M. Sherman. **Credits:** Dir: Roy Del Ruth; Prod: Jerry Wald; Writer: Jack Rose, Melville Shavelson; Story: Richard Mealand, Max Shulman; DP: Ernest Haller; Ed: Clarence Kolster; Composer: Sammy Cahn. B&W, 115 min.

The Amazing Dobermans

(1976) Golden
Bigger-budgeted sequel to the earlier films *The Doberman Gang* and *The*

Daring Dobermans. This time, the pinschers are back, and they're even more fun than before. A federal agent taking on a powerful racketeer enlists the aid of the talented canines and their owner—the oddly cast Astaire—who is a quirky Bible-quoting ex–con man. The last film of the series, and one of Astaire's lesser known pictures; worth seeing for that alone. **Cast:** Fred Astaire, Barbara Eden, Jack Carter, James Franciscus, Parley Baer, Billy Barty. **Credits:** Dir: Byron Ross Chudnow; Prod: David Chudnow; Writer: Richard Chapman, Michael Kraike, William Goldstein; DP: Jack Adams; Ed: James Potter; Composer: Alan Silvestri. Color, 99 min. VHS

The Amazing Doctor Clitterhouse

(1938) Warner Bros.
Robinson plays Dr. Clitterhouse, a successful psychiatrist whose curiosity about the criminal psyche leads him to join a gang led by Bogart. The Doctor oversteps some legal limits and decides to retire from his new career, but the members of his gang make it difficult for the good Dr. Clitterhouse to return to normal life. **Cast:** Edgar G. Robinson, Clare Trevor, Humphrey Bogart, Allen Jenkins, Donald Crisp, Gale Page, Henry O'Neill, John Litel, Maxie Rosenbloom, Thurston Hall. **Credits:** Dir: Anatole Litvak; Prod: Robert Lord; Writer: John Huston, John Wexley; Story: Barre Lyndon; DP: Tony Gaudio; Ed: Warren Low; Prod Design: Carl Jules Weyl; Composer: Max Steiner. B&W, 87 min.

The Amazing Mrs. Holliday

(1943) Universal
French auteur Renoir began directing this pleasantly comic international production, but it was completed by the producer Manning. The lovely Durbin plays good-hearted missionary Ruth Kirke. In order to save the lives of Chinese orphans, Ruth is forced to impersonate the wife of unmarried ocean-going millionaire Commodore Holliday, who's been conveniently lost at sea. Returning to America, she brings the Chinese children to the Holliday mansion. She's too honest to keep up the lie for long but finds an understanding friend in the Commodore's grandson Tom (O'Brien). The film includes two songs by Durbin in Chinese. **Cast:** Deanna Durbin, Edmond O'Brien, Barry Fitzgerald, Arthur Treacher, Harry Davenport, Grant Mitchell, Frieda Inescort, Elisabeth Risdon, Jonathan Hale, Esther Dale. **Credits:** Dir: Bruce Manning, Jean Renoir;

Prod: Bruce Manning; Writer: Hans Jacoby; Story: Frank Ryan, Boris Inster, Leo Townsend; DP: Elwood Bredell; Ed: Ted J. Kent; Composer: Hans J. Salter, Frank Skinner. B&W, 96 min.

Ambassador Bill

(1931) Fox
Rogers plays an Oklahoma cowboy who has been appointed Ambassador to Sylvania, where he manages to impart some down-home wisdom between the weekly revolutionary skirmishes. **Cast:** Will Rogers, Ray Milland, Marguerite Churchill, Greta Nissen, Tad Alexander, Gustav Von Seyffertitz. **Credits:** Dir: Sam Taylor; Writer: Guy Bolton; Story: Vincent Sheean; DP: John Mescall; Ed: Harold Schuster. B&W, 68 min. **VHS**

The Ambassador's Daughter

(1956) United Artists
De Havilland is Joan Fisk, bored daughter of the American ambassador to France. Tired of entertaining the V.I.P. wives, she comes up with an experiment. She proposes to her father and his friends that not all soldiers are crude and untrainable in social graces, and, to prove it, accepts a date with an American G.I. (Forsythe). But as the night progresses and romance begins to blossom, she realizes that she has gotten herself into a sticky situation. Although nearing forty, de Havilland gives an inspired, believable performance as the young ingenue. **Cast:** Olivia de Havilland, John Forsythe, Myrna Loy, Adolphe Menjou, Edward Arnold, Francis Lederer, Tommy Noonan, Minor Watson. **Credits:** Dir: Norman Krasna; Prod: Norman Krasna; Writer: Norman Krasna; DP: Michel Kelber; Prod Design: Leon Barsacq; Costumes: Christian Dior. Color, 102 min. **VHS**

American Graffiti

(1973) Universal
The bittersweet innocence of pre–Kennedy assassination America is brilliantly captured in Lucas's study of a night in the lives of the Class of 1962. Cruising in their hot rods, eating at Mel's Diner, and listening to Wolfman Jack spin the latest platters draws a nostalgic pastoral with the shadow of Vietnam almost visible on the horizon. Academy Award Nominations: 5, including Best Picture; Best Director; Best (Original) Story and Screenplay. **Cast:** Richard Dreyfuss, Ron Howard, Cindy Williams, Mackenzie Phillips, Candy Clark, Harrison Ford, Paul Le Mat, Charles Martin

Smith, Suzanne Somers, Bo Hopkins, Wolfman Jack. **Credits:** Dir: George Lucas; Prod: Francis Ford Coppola, Gary Kurtz; Writer: George Lucas, Gloria Katz, Willard Huyck; DP: Jan D'Alquen, Ron Eveslage; Ed: Verna Fields, Marcia Lucas; Prod Design: Dennis Lynton Clark; Costumes: Aggie Guerard Rodgers; Set Designer: Douglas Freeman. Color, 112 min. **VHS, LASER**

American Hot Wax

(1978) Paramount
A fun look at the beginnings of rock-and-roll, focusing on pioneer rock deejay Alan Freed, who popularized the phrase "rock-and-roll." The narrative spotlights police efforts to censor the sinfully rhythmic music. The score fills the flick and includes Chuck Berry, Jerry Lee Lewis, and Screamin' Jay Hawkins. Watch for young Drescher and Leno as sidekicks, and Newman as a rising songwriter. **Cast:** Tim McIntire, Fran Drescher, Jay Leno, Laraine Newman, Jeff Altman, Moosie Drier, John Lehne, Stewart Steinberg, Jack Ellis, Richard Forbes. **Credits:** Dir: Floyd Mutrux; Prod: Fred Gallo; Writer: John Kaye, Art Linson; DP: William A. Fraker; Ed: Ronald T. Fagan, Melvin Shapiro; Prod Design: Elayne Barbara Cedar; Composer: Kenny Vance. Color, 91 min.

An American in Paris

(1951) MGM
One of the greatest of 1950s screen musicals is a happy collaboration between the grace and athleticism of Kelly and the colorful palette of Minnelli. An American G.I. lingers in Paris after the war to study painting and soon falls in love with Caron, an engaged mademoiselle, much to the chagrin of his romance-minded benefactress. Features a seventeen-minute, avant-garde ballet choreographed by Kelly to George Gershwin's unbeatable melodies. The movie's many awards include Golden Globes for Best Motion Picture and Best Musical/Comedy; and selection as a National Film Registry Outstanding Film. Academy Award Nominations: 8, including Best Director. **Academy Awards:** Best Color Cinematography; Best Scoring of a Musical; Best Picture; Best Costume Design (Color); Best Story and Screenplay; Best Art Direction—Set Decoration (Color); Honorary Award: Gene Kelly. **Cast:** Gene Kelly, Leslie Caron, Oscar Levant, Georges Guetary, Nina Foch. **Credits:** Dir: Vincente Minnelli; Prod: Arthur Freed; Writer: Alan Jay Lerner; DP: Alfred Gilks, John Alton;

Ed: Adrienne Fazan; Prod Design: Cedric Gibbons, Preston Ames; Choreographer: Gene Kelly; Composer: Johnny Green, Saul Chaplin, George Gershwin, Ira Gershwin; Costumes: Walter Plunkett, Irene Sharaff; SFX: Warren Newcombe; Set Designer: Edwin B. Willis, Keogh Gleason. Color, 115 min. **VHS, LASER**

The Americanization of Emily

(1964) MGM
A cynical American naval officer (Garner) first clashes with and then falls in love with his idealistic British driver (Andrews), a war widow. After convincing her to enjoy life, he is selected by the Navy's PR machine to become "the Unknown Sailor," the first man to die landing at Normandy on D-Day. An often brilliant script by Paddy Chayefsky elevates this one well above the average fare. **Cast:** Julie Andrews, James Garner, Melvyn Douglas, James Coburn. **Credits:** Dir: Arthur Hiller; Writer: Paddy Chayefsky; Story: William Bradford Huie; DP: Philip H. Lathrop, Christopher Challis; Ed: Tom McAdoo; Prod Design: George W. Davis; Composer: Johnny Mandel; Costumes: Bill Thomas. B&W, 117 min. **VHS, LASER**

American Madness

(1932) Columbia
Huston stars in Capra's Depression-era melodrama of a bank president who finds himself on the hot seat after making dubious loans. His loyal underlings and the grateful community to whom he made loans come to his resuce, of course. **Cast:** Walter Huston, Pat O'Brien, Kay Johnson, Constance Cummings, Gavin Gordon. **Credits:** Dir: Frank Capra; Writer: Robert Riskin; DP: Joseph Walker; Ed: Maurice Wright. B&W, 76 min. **VHS**

An American Romance

(1944) MGM
Drama follows Steve Dangos, a Czech immigrant, from his arrival on Ellis Island at the turn of the century through his old age. As a penniless new arrival, Dangos goes to work in the ore mines of Minnesota, where he meets his future wife, eventually moving to a steel mill, where he works his way up, and learns about American industry. He next becomes an auto manufacturer, and his independent values are put to the test when workers in his plant try to unionize. **Cast:** Brian Donlevy, Ann Richards, Walter Abel, John Qualen, Horace McNally. **Credits:** Dir: King

Vidor; Prod: King Vidor; Writer: Herbert Dalmas, William Ludwig, King Vidor; DP: Harold Hal Rosson; Ed: Conrad A. Nervig; Prod Design: Cedric Gibbons; Composer: Louis Gruenberg. Color, 151 min.

An American Tragedy
(1931) Warner Bros.
A young man gets a job at his uncle's factory, where he seduces an innocent coworker, getting her pregnant. Wanting to climb the social ranks, he also gets involved with a wealthy debutante with whom he falls in love. Faced with the disgrace of impregnating the factory girl and in fear of losing his rising social status, he kills the young factory girl and faces a sensational murder trial. **Cast:** Phillips Holmes, Sylvia Sidney, Frances Dee, Irving Pichel, Claire McDowell, Vivian Winston, Fredrick Burton, Albert Hart, Arnold Korff, Lucille La Verne. **Credits:** Dir: Josef von Sternberg; Prod: Josef von Sternberg; Writer: Samuel Hoffenstein, Josef von Sternberg; Story: Theodore Dreiser; DP: Lee Garmes; Art Director: Hans Dreier. B&W, 96 min.

Anastasia
(1956) Fox
A group of Russian exiles in Paris conspire to present a young woman with amnesia as Anastasia, the daughter of Czar Nicholas, so they can collect ten million pounds held in her name by the Bank of England. Bergman won her second Oscar for her winning portrayal that introduces just the right regal note of doubt about her real heritage. Remade in 1997 as Fox's first animated feature. Adapted from the play by Marcelle Maurette. **Academy Awards:** Best Actress: Ingrid Bergman. **Cast:** Ingrid Bergman, Yul Brynner, Helen Hayes, Akim Tamiroff, Martita Hunt, Felix Aylmer. **Credits:** Dir: Anatole Litvak; Prod: Buddy Adler; Writer: Arthur Laurents, Guy Bolton; Story: Marcelle Maurette; DP: Jack Hildyard; Ed: Bert Bates; Prod Design: Andre Andrejew, Bill Andrews; Composer: Alfred Newman; Costumes: Rene Hubert; Set Designer: Andrew Low. Color, 106 min. **VHS, LASER**

Anatomy of a Murder
(1959) Columbia
Director Preminger thrives in tense legal showdowns and this is perhaps his best, mostly for Stewart's cagey performance as a deceptively wily small-town lawyer. The sensationalist trial revolves around an army lieutenant who shoots a bar owner for allegedly raping his wife, an ugly crime in which no one is wholly guilty or innocent. Based on Traver's novel. Score (and onscreen appearance) by Duke Ellington. Academy Award Nominations: 7, including Best Picture; Best Director; Best Actor: James Stewart; Best (Adapted) Screenplay. **Cast:** James Stewart, George C. Scott, Murray Hamilton, Eve Arden, Lee Remick, Ben Gazzara, Orson Bean, Arthur O'Connell. **Credits:** Dir: Otto Preminger; Prod: Otto Preminger; Writer: Wendell Mayes; Story: Robert Traver; DP: Sam Leavitt; Ed: Louis Loeffler; Prod Design: Boris Leven; Composer: Duke Ellington; Set Designer: Howard Bristol. B&W, 161 min. **VHS, LASER**

Anchors Aweigh
(1945) MGM
Gangway for Sinatra and Kelly as song and dance lead the list of activities when sailors on shore leave fall in with a fatherless boy and his beautiful aunt. Includes the irresistible dance sequence with Kelly and Jerry, the cartoon mouse. Academy Award Nominations: 5, including Best Picture; Best Actor: Gene Kelly; Best Song ("I Fall in Love Too Easily"). **Academy Awards:** Best Scoring of a Musical. **Cast:** Gene Kelly, Frank Sinatra, Kathryn Grayson, Jose Iturbi, Dean Stockwell, Pamela Britton, Billy Gilbert, Henry O'Neill, James Burke. **Credits:** Dir: George Sidney; Prod: Joe Pasternak; Writer: Isobel Lennart; Story: Natalie Marcin; DP: Robert Planck, Charles Boyle; Ed: Adrienne Fazan; Prod Design: Cedric Gibbons, Randal Duell; Choreographer: Gene Kelly; Composer: George Stoll; Costumes: Irene, Kay Dean; Set Designer: Edwin B. Willis, Richard Pefferle. Color, 141 min. **VHS, LASER**

The Anderson Tapes
(1971) Columbia
After having served a ten-year prison term, an unreformed convict plans to rob an entire apartment building on the Upper East Side of Manhattan. He is backed by a gangster who organizes an assortment of characters to get in on the action, including an antiques dealer and a 40-year veteran of crime. Based on the novel by Lawrence Sanders, this fast-paced caper drama is well-constructed by Lumet, and is noticeable for its introduction of Walken in his first major role. **Cast:** Sean Connery, Dyan Cannon, Alan King, Martin Balsam, Christopher Walken. **Credits:** Dir: Sidney Lumet; Prod: Robert M. Weitman; Writer: Frank R. Pierson; Story: Lawrence Sanders; DP: Arthur J. Ornitz; Ed: Joanne Burke; Prod Design: Philip Rosenberg; Composer: Quincy Jones. Color, 99 min. **VHS, LASER**

And Justice for All
(1979) Columbia
Pacino balances a performance between comedy and bleak despair when he adds a thoroughly detestable judge accused of rape to his already miserable client list. Maybe intended as satire, maybe not. Lahti's debut film role. Academy Award Nominations: Best Actor. **Cast:** Al Pacino, Jack Warden, John Forsythe, Lee Strasberg, Christine Lahti. **Credits:** Dir: Norman Jewison; Writer: Valerie Curtin, Barry Levinson; DP: Frank Holgate; Composer: Dave Grusin. Color, 120 min. **VHS, LASER**

Androcles and the Lion
(1952) RKO
In Shaw's sparkling play set in the last days of the Roman Empire, a Christian tailor named Androcles helps a suffering lion by removing a thorn from his paw. Later, after Caesar has rounded up the Christians and sentenced them to death by the beast, the lion refuses to harm the man who has been so kind to him. **Cast:** Jean Simmons, Alan Young, Victor Mature, Robert Newton, Maurice Evans. **Credits:** Dir: Chester Erskine; Prod: Gabriel Pascal; Writer: Chester Erskine, Ken Englund; Story: George Bernard Shaw; DP: Harry Stradling; Ed: Roland Cross; Composer: Frederick Hollander; Art Director: Harry Horner. B&W, 105 min. **VHS**

The Andromeda Strain
(1971) Universal
An active satellite falls out of orbit and crash-lands in a small town. A deadly and mysterious bacteria released by the collision begins to systematically kill off the population. Scientists try to determine the basis and a cure for the deadly interloper and discover that only a small baby and the town drunk seem impervious to its spread. Anxiety rises as the researchers scramble for a cure before they too are wiped out. Based on the novel by Michael Crichton. **Cast:** James Olson, Arthur Hill, David Wayne, Kate Reid, Paula Kelly. **Credits:** Dir: Robert Wise; Prod: Robert Wise; Writer: Nelson Gidding; Story: Michael Crichton; DP: Richard H. Kline; Ed: Stuart Gilmore, Jack Holmes; Prod Design: Boris Leven; Composer: Gil Melle. Color, 130 min. **VHS, LASER, DVD**

And Then There Were None

(1945) Fox
An Agatha Christie tale told four times on film, this is still the best. Ten guests on an isolated island are murdered one by one. The only clue: a children's nursery rhyme. A black comedy-mystery with terrific performances. **Cast:** Barry Fitzgerald, Walter Huston, Judith Anderson, Louis Hayward, June Duprez, Ronald Young, Mischa Auer. **Credits:** Dir: Rene Clair; Prod: Rene Clair, Harry M. Popkin; Writer: Dudley Nichols; Story: Agatha Christie; DP: Lucien Andriot; Ed: Harvey Manger; Prod Design: Ernst Fegte. B&W, 98 min. **VHS, LASER**

Andy Hardy

After the success of *A Family Affair* (1937), which introduced the Hardy clan of Carvel, MGM's Louis B. Mayer launched the Andy Hardy series—with a few tweaks. In the 1937 film, Lionel Barrymore played flinty Judge Hardy, and Mickey Rooney, the judge's son, was only a minor player. With *You're Only Young Once* (1938), the first official series entry, Rooney became the eponymous star and Barrymore was replaced by Lewis Stone. The sentimental series perfectly captured the sensibility of the late 1930s and '40s, with Andy's red-blooded interest in girls-next-door (including Ann Rutherford as Andy's ever-patient girlfriend, Polly Benedict), and his sister, Marian (Cecilia Parker), likewise interested in boys. The siblings grew up in small-town America, under the guidance of attentive parents, Stone and the always understanding Fay Holden. Though the series may seem overly sentimental today, it remains fascinating for its insight into how America reassured itself of the values that were being fought for in WWII. It is doubly facinating because this depiction of an ideal America was created by a Russian Jewish immigrant, Mayer. The series won a special Oscar in 1942 for "its achievement in representing the American way of life." Rising stars Judy Garland, Lana Turner, Esther Williams, and Donna Reed made appearances in the films.

A Family Affair *(1937)*
You're Only Young Once *(1938)*
Judge Hardy's Children *(1938)*
Love Finds Andy Hardy *(1938)*
Out West with the Hardys *(1938)*
The Hardys Ride High *(1939)*
Andy Hardy Gets Spring Fever *(1939)*
Judge Hardy and Son *(1939)*
Andy Hardy Meets Debutante *(1940)*
Andy Hardy's Private Secretary *(1941)*
Life Begins for Andy Hardy *(1941)*

The Courtship of Andy Hardy *(1942)*
Andy Hardy's Double Life *(1942)*
Andy Hardy's Blonde Trouble *(1944)*
Love Laughs at Andy Hardy *(1946)*
Andy Hardy Comes Home *(1958)*

Andy Warhol's Dracula

(1974)
Andy Warhol's campy tribute to the Transylvanian legend is distinguished by its overt acknowledgment of the sexual metaphor of vampires. Young Dracula craves the blood of virgins in a house full of the promiscuous daughters of a country nobleman. The humor is mixed with liberal quantities of blood and sex. Caution: available in both R and unrated versions. **Cast:** Joe Dallesandro, Udo Kier, Arno Juerging, Maxine McKendry, Vittorio De Sica. **Credits:** Dir: Paul Morrissey, Antonio Margheriti; Prod: Andrew Braunsberg, Carlo Ponti, Jean-Pierre Rassam, Jean Yanne; Writer: Paul Morrissey; DP: Luigi Kuveiller; Ed: Jed Johnson, Franca Silvi; Prod Design: Enrico Job; Composer: Carlo Gizzi; SFX: Carlo Rambaldi, Roberto Arcangeli; Art Director: Gianni Giovagnoni. Color, 106 min. **VHS**

Andy Warhol's Frankenstein

(1974)
Andy Warhol's association with his filmic takes on classic horror lends an arty cachet, but these are mostly the works of director Morrissey. And they are fascinating mostly as documents of their period with media appropriation, sex, and rock-and-roll churning up traditional filmmaking. Perhaps the most violent version of the Shelley classic features shocking humor, gratuitous sex and violence, and thumb-in-the-eye attitude. Original 3-D (!) release received an X rating. **Cast:** Joe Dallesandro, Monique Van Vooren, Udo Kier. **Credits:** Dir: Paul Morrissey, Antonio Margheriti; Prod: Carlo Ponti, Andrew Braunsberg, Jean-Pierre Rassam, Jean Yanne; Writer: Tonino Guerra; DP: Luigi Kuveiller; Ed: Jed Johnson, Franca Silvi; Prod Design: Enrico Job; Composer: Carlo Gizzi; SFX: Carlo Rambaldi, Roberto Arcangeli; Art Director: Gianni Giovagnoni. Color, 95 min. **VHS**

Angel

(1937) Paramount
An intriguing combination of Dietrich with melodrama master Lubitsch promises more than is delivered here. The wife of a stuffy diplomat meets a dashing stranger (Douglas) in Paris, and their fling causes ripples in her marriage when the stranger inevitably reappears. **Cast:** Marlene Dietrich,

Herbert Marshall, Melvyn Douglas, Edward Everett Horton, Laura Hope Crews, Ernest Cossart. **Credits:** Dir: Ernst Lubitsch; Prod: Ernst Lubitsch; Writer: Samson Raphaelson, Guy Bolton, Russell Medcraft; Story: Melchior Lengyel; DP: Charles Lang; Ed: William Shea; Prod Design: Hans Dreier, Robert Usher; Composer: Frederick Hollander; Costumes: Travis Banton; SFX: Farciot Edouart; Set Designer: A. E. Freudeman. B&W, 92 min. **VHS**

Angel and the Badman

(1947) Republic
An old-fashioned Western with Wayne at his best as a gunfighter who must choose between the Quaker girl he loves and his guns, which always seem to attract the wrong kind of people. He makes a wise choice. Avoid the colorized version. **Cast:** John Wayne, Gail Russell, Bruce Cabot, Harry Carey, Tom Powers, Irene Rich. **Credits:** Dir: James Edward Grant; Prod: John Wayne; Writer: James Edward Grant; DP: Archie Stout; Ed: Harry Keller; Prod Design: Ernst Fegte; Composer: Richard Hageman. B&W, 101 min. **VHS, LASER**

Angel on My Shoulder

(1946) Fox
The writer of *Here Comes Mr. Jordan* sends a soul in the other direction as former gangster Muni gets sent by the Devil back to Earth to occupy the body of a lenient judge and increase the flow of miscreants to Hades. The ex-thug plans a little revenge on the side, though he has trouble mastering his new persona. **Cast:** Paul Muni, Claude Rains, Anne Baxter, George Cleveland, Erskine Sanford, Hardie Albright. **Credits:** Dir: Archie Mayo; Prod: David Siegel; Writer: Harry Segall, Roland Kibbee; Ed: George Arthur; Prod Design: Bernard Herzbrun; Composer: Dimitri Tiomkin; Costumes: Maria Donovan; SFX: Harry Redmond, Howard Anderson; Set Designer: Edward G. Boyle. B&W, 101 min. **VHS**

Angels Hard As They Come

(1972) New World
Jonathan Demme wrote this inventive satire of biker movies. The standard road fare culminates in a gang fight in a ghost town. Busey's debut and an early Glenn role. **Cast:** Scott Glenn, Gary Busey, Gilda Texter, James Iglehart, Charles Dierkop. **Credits:** Dir: Joe Viola; Prod: Jonathan Demme; Writer: Joe Viola, Jonathan Demme; DP: Stephen Katz; Ed: Joe Ravetz; Prod Design: Jack Fisk; Composer: Richard Hieronymous. Color, 86 min. **VHS**

Animal Crackers (1930)

Animal Crackers
(1930) Paramount
Often considered their best, this second Marx Brothers movie revolves around a stolen painting and the sprawling estate of a wealthy dowager who soon finds Chico, Zeppo, Harpo, and especially Groucho turning her life upside down. Groucho croons his famous "Hooray for Captain Spaulding" and delivers many of his most famous quips in this film based on a play by George S. Kaufman. **Cast:** Groucho Marx, Zeppo Marx, Chico Marx, Harpo Marx, Margaret Dumont, Lillian Roth, Louis Sorin, Robert Greig, Hal Thompson. **Credits:** Dir: Victor Heerman; Writer: Morrie Ryskind; Story: George S. Kaufman; DP: George J. Folsey; Composer: Bert Kalmar, Harry Ruby. B&W, 98 min. **VHS, DVD**

The Animal Kingdom
(1932) RKO
An awkward love triangle is created when a publisher (Howard) encounters a moral speed bump and engages in an affair with an open-minded artist (Harding) while married to a stodgy suburbanite (Loy). Complicating matters is the tendency of the mistress to play the role of unassuming wife while inelegant and deceptive wife acts as the mistress. Based on the successful play by Philip Barry, it was the first film shown at Radio City Music Hall. Remade as *One More Tomorrow* in 1946. **Cast:** Leslie Howard, Myrna Loy, Ann Harding, William Gargan. **Credits:** Dir: Edward H. Griffith; Prod: David O. Selznick; Writer: Horace Jackson; Story: Philip Barry; DP: Lucien Andriot; Composer: Max Steiner. B&W, 95 min. **VHS**

Anna and the King of Siam
(1946) Fox
Irene Dunne shines as the English governess who travels to Siam to instruct the King's many children. Based on a true story. Harrison's first Hollywood role; remade as a musical, *The King and I*, in 1956. Academy Award Nominations: 5, including Best Screenplay. **Academy Awards:** Best Black-and-White Cinematography; Best Black-and-White Interior Decoration. **Cast:** Irene Dunne, Rex Harrison, Linda Darnell, Lee J. Cobb, Gale Sondergaard, Mikhail Rasumny. **Credits:** Dir: John Cromwell; Prod: Louis D. Lighton; Writer: Talbot Jennings, Sally Benson; Story: Margaret Landon; DP: Arthur Miller; Prod Design: Lyle Wheeler, William S. Darling; Composer:

Angels in the Outfield
(1951) MGM
Douglas shines as Guffy McGovern, the most hard-hearted, foul-mouthed, dictatorial baseball manager in the league. His Pittsburgh Pirates are in seventh place and getting worse. Then he hears a voice telling him to "look for a miracle in the third inning." Scores of stars from baseball and Hollywood in cameo appearances join the angels who give the Pirates a lift. Remade in 1994. **Cast:** Paul Douglas, Janet Leigh, Keenan Wynn, Donna Corcoran, Spring Byington, Ellen Corby, Lewis Stone, Bruce Bennett. **Credits:** Dir: Clarence Brown; Prod: Clarence Brown; Writer: Dorothy Kingsley, George Wells; Story: Richard Conlin; DP: Paul C. Vogel; Ed: Robert J. Kern; Composer: Daniele Amfitheatrof. B&W, 102 min. **VHS**

Angels over Broadway
(1940) Columbia
Hecht brings to life the world of loners, two-bit hustlers, and has-beens that populate Times Square. Fairbanks plans to swindle a suicidal thief, but then plots with call girl Hayworth to turn his life around. Great cast in an unusually black comedy for its time. Academy Award Nomination: Best Original Screenplay. **Cast:** Douglas Fairbanks, Jr., Rita Hayworth,

Thomas Mitchell, John Qualen, George Watts, Ralph Theodore. **Credits:** Dir: Ben Hecht, Lee Garmes; Prod: Ben Hecht; Writer: Ben Hecht; DP: Lee Garmes; Ed: Gene Havlick; Prod Design: Lionel Banks; Composer: George Antheil; Costumes: Ray Howell. B&W, 80 min. **VHS, LASER**

Angels with Dirty Faces
(1938) Warner Bros.
Cagney, Bogart, and O'Brien in one of the greatest of gangster melodramas. Two boyhood pals, now a parish priest and a hardened criminal, find themselves at odds when the thug returns to his old neighborhood. O'Brien already has his hands full keeping the Dead End Kids out of trouble and now that they idolize Cagney his good works may come to nothing. Unforgettable scene of Cagney on his way to the chair. Academy Award Nominations: Best Actor: James Cagney; Best Director; Best Original Story. **Cast:** James Cagney, Pat O'Brien, Humphrey Bogart, Dead End Kids, Ann Sheridan, George Bancroft, Edward Pawley. **Credits:** Dir: Michael Curtiz; Prod: Samuel Bischoff; Writer: John Wexley, Warren Duff; Story: Roland Brown; DP: Sol Polito; Ed: Owen Marks; Prod Design: Robert M. Haas; Composer: Max Steiner. B&W, 99 min. **VHS, LASER**

Bernard Herrmann; SFX: Fred Sersen; Set Designer: Thomas Little, Frank E. Hughes. Color, 129 min. **VHS**

Anna Christie

(1930) MGM
Garbo talks! A dark O'Neill drama was Garbo's first talking picture. She plays a former prostitute who falls in love with a seaman aboard her father's barge and tries to hide her ignoble past. An alternate German version was filmed at the same time; a silent adaptation of the play was made in 1923. Academy Award Nominations: 3, including Best Director; Best Actress: Greta Garbo. **Cast:** Greta Garbo, Charles Bickford, Lee Phelps, Marie Dressler. **Credits:** Dir: Clarence Brown; Writer: Frances Marion; Story: Eugene O'Neill; DP: William Daniels; Ed: Hugh Wynn; Prod Design: Cedric Gibbons; Costumes: Adrian. B&W, 92 min. **VHS**

Anna Karenina

(1935) MGM
Could there be a better interpreter of Leo Tolstoy's ill-fated heroine—one of the most-remade film stories—than Garbo? The pains of doomed love seemed oddly suited to that stoney Nordic visage. March and Rathbone are also fine, and Garbo had plenty of preparation for the role, having starred in the silent version *(Love)* with John Gilbert. **Cast:** Greta Garbo, Fredric March, Maureen O'Sullivan, Basil Rathbone, Freddie Bartholomew, May Robson, Reginald Owen, Reginald Denny. **Credits:** Dir: Clarence Brown; Prod: David O. Selznick; Writer: Clemence Dane, Salka Viertel, S. N. Behrman; Story: Leo Tolstoy; DP: William Daniels; Ed: Robert J. Kern; Choreographer: Chester Hale, Marguerite Wallmann; Composer: Herbert Stothart. B&W, 96 min. **VHS, LASER**

Anna Lucasta

(1949) Columbia
A drama of family, greed, and revenge. When a dysfunctional Pennsylvania clan's youngest daughter is caught sinning in the barn, she's ostracized, only to be lured back when her greedy father hatches a plan to marry her to a wealthy Southern farmer. The plan backfires when the daughter genuinely falls for the farmer. **Cast:** Paulette Goddard, William Bishop, Oscar Homolka, John Ireland, Broderick Crawford, Will Geer, Gale Page, Mary Wickes, Whit Bissell, Lisa Golm. **Credits:** Dir: Irving Rapper; Prod: Phillip Yordan; Writer: Arthur Laurents; Story: Phillip Yordan; DP: Sol Polito; Ed:

Charles Nelson; Prod Design: George Brooks; Composer: Morris Stoloff. B&W, 86 min.

Anne of Green Gables

(1934) RKO
Based on Lucy Maud Montgomery's novel about a young orphan girl who steals the hearts of a lonely Canadian couple with her spirit and lively imagination. Max Steiner provides the warm musical score. Shirley assumed her character's name for her professional identity. Fans of the story will want to see the 1985 television adaptation and its 1987 sequel, *Anne of Avonlea.* **Cast:** Anne Shirley, Tom Brown, O. P. Heggie, Helen Westley, Sara Haden, Charley Grapewin. **Credits:** Dir: George Nicholls, Jr.; Prod: Kenneth MacGowan; Writer: Sam Mintz; Story: L. M. Montgomery; DP: Lucien Andriot; Ed: Arthur Schmidt; Prod Design: Van Nest Polglase, Al Herman; Composer: Max Steiner; Costumes: Walter Plunkett; SFX: Vernon Walker. B&W, 79 min. **VHS**

Anne of the Indies

(1951) Fox
A swashbuckling adventure in which Jourdan portrays Pierre Francois LaRochelle, a former pirate captain who has been caught by the British (they have also abducted his wife and ship). In order to get them back, he agrees to work as a spy against other pirates, namely the infamous Blackbeard and Captain Providence. When he happens upon their ship, he discovers, rather shockingly, that Providence is a beautiful woman. She believes his charade that he's an enemy of the British, although Blackbeard isn't quite so sure. But when she begins to fall for LaRochelle and he leads her into a trap set by the British, she escapes and kidnaps his wife for revenge. In desperation, he manages to reacquire his ship and attempts to track her down before she can sell his wife on the slave market. **Cast:** Jean Peters, Louis Jourdan, Debra Paget, Herbert Marshall, Thomas Gomez, James Robertson Justice, Francis Pierlot, Sean McClory, Holmes Herbert. **Credits:** Dir: Jacques Tourneur; Prod: George Jessel; Writer: Arthur Caesar, Philip Dunne; Story: Herbert Ravenel Sass; DP: Harry Jackson; Ed: Robert Fritch; Prod Design: Lyle Wheeler; Composer: Franz Waxman. Color, 81 min.

Anne of the Thousand Days

(1969) Universal
This lavish costume drama with rich performances to match tells of King

Henry VIII's infatuation with 18-year-old Anne Boleyn. For her hand, the king defied the Vatican, destroyed a ruling caste, and established the church of England in order to obtain a divorce from his wife. Burton is appropriately swaggering and Bujold more than worthy of her king's notice. Academy Award Nominations: 10, including Best Picture; Best Actress: Genevieve Bujold; Best Actor: Richard Burton; Best (Adapted) Screenplay. **Academy Awards:** Best Costume Design. **Cast:** Richard Burton, Genevieve Bujold, Anthony Quayle, Irene Papas, John Colicos, Michael Hordern, Katharine Blake, Peter Jeffrey, William Squire, Esmond Knight. **Credits:** Dir: Charles Jarrott; Prod: Hal B. Wallis; Writer: Bridget Boland, John Hale, Richard Sokolove; Story: Maxwell Anderson; DP: Arthur Ibbetson; Ed: Richard Marden; Prod Design: Maurice Carter; Choreographer: Mary Skeaping; Composer: Georges Delerue; Costumes: Margaret Furse; Art Director: Lionel Couch; Set Designer: Peter Howitt. Color, 146 min. **VHS**

Annie Get Your Gun

(1950) MGM
A musical adapted from the earlier stage version, this chronicles the true story of Annie Oakley Mozie, a girl from the Ozarks who became a star in Buffalo Bill's Wild West Show. The story revolves around Annie's running competition with male sharpshooter Frank Butler, a competition she must lose intentionally to win Butler's love. Borrowing from Berlin's Broadway hit, this musical includes numbers like "Doin' What Comes Naturally," "My Defenses Are Down," and the show-biz standard "There's No Business Like Show Business." **Cast:** Betty Hutton, Howard Keel, Keenan Wynn, Edward Arnold, J. Carroll Naish. **Credits:** Dir: George Sidney; Prod: Arthur Freed; Writer: Sidney Sheldon; Story: Dorothy Fields, Herbert Fields; DP: Charles Rosher, Jr. ; Ed: James E. Newman; Prod Design: Cedric Gibbons, Paul Groesse; Composer: Irving Berlin, Adolph Deutsch. Color, 107 min.

Annie Hall

(1977) United Artists
Allen cowrote, directed, and stars as a kvetchy Brooklyn comedian wistfully recalling his bygone relationship with flighty, adorable, and irrepressibly Midwestern Annie Hall. Many consider this Allen's best work, and a transition from his earlier absurdist comedies to the richer vein of thoughtful considera-

tion of relationships. In any case, the gentle narrative revolutionized the urban romantic-comedy genre, while Keaton's hip, man-tailored wardrobe set the 1977 fashion standard. The film was nominated, and won, for the Best Picture, but Allen refused to attend the ceremonies, choosing instead to play his clarinet at Michael's Pub in New York. The DVD includes trivia, production notes, and theatrical trailer. Academy Award Nominations: 5, including Best Actor. A National Film Registry Outstanding Film. **Academy Awards:** Best Director; Best Actress: Diane Keaton; Best Picture; Best Screenplay Written Directly for the Screen. **Cast:** Woody Allen, Diane Keaton, Shelley Duvall, Tony Roberts, Paul Simon, Carol Kane. **Credits:** Dir: Woody Allen; Prod: Charles H. Joffe; Writer: Woody Allen, Marshall Brickman; DP: Gordon Willis; Ed: Ralph Rosenblum, Wendy Greene Bricmont; Prod Design: Mel Bourne; Costumes: Ruth Morley, George Newman, Marilyn Putnam, Ralph Lauren, Nancy McArdle; Set Designer: Robert Drumheller. Color, 94 min. **VHS, LASER, DVD**

Annie Oakley
(1935) RKO
The story of America's most famous female sharpshooter, unforgettably performed by Stanwyck in one of her signature roles. Stevens directed this Wild West classic, which was the basis for the musical *Annie Get Your Gun,* before he helmed his Western classic, *Shane.* **Cast:** Barbara Stanwyck, Preston Foster, Melvyn Douglas, Andy Clyde, Moroni Olsen, Pert Kelton. **Credits:** Dir: George Stevens; Prod: Cliff Reid; Writer: John Sayre, John Twist; Story: Joseph Fields, Ewart Adamson; DP: J. Roy Hunt; Ed: Jack Hively; Prod Design: Van Nest Polglase, Perry Ferguson. B&W, 100 min. **VHS**

Another Language
(1933) MGM
Screen adaptation of Rose Franken's successful Broadway drama of the Hallam family, featuring several members of the original theater cast, including Hamilton. Hayes brings subtlety to the character of Stella, newly married to Victor Hallam (Montgomery). The couple returns from their honeymoon to a life dominated by Stella's new in-laws, especially the self-serving and regimented social routines of Mom Hallam. **Cast:** Helen Hayes, Robert Montgomery, Hale Closser, John Beal, Henry Travers,

Margaret Hamilton, Willard Robertson, Irene Cattell, Minor Watson, Hal K. Dawson. **Credits:** Dir: Edward H. Griffith; Prod: Walter Wanger; Writer: Herman J. Mankiewicz, Gertrude Purcell, Donald Stewart; Story: Rose Franken; Ed: Hugh Wynn; Art Director: Fredric Hope. B&W, 75 min.

Another Man, Another Chance
(1977) United Artists
The international success of *A Man and a Woman* (1966) led not only to a sequel from Lelouch twenty years later, but also this oddly languorous remake set in the waning days of the 19th century in the American West. Widow Bujold and widower Caan meet and fall in love after their spouses die. Curious. **Cast:** James Caan, Genevieve Bujold, Francis Huster, Jennifer Warren, Susan Tyrrell. **Credits:** Dir: Claude Lelouch; Prod: Alexandre Mnouchkine, Georges Dancigers; Writer: Claude Lelouch; DP: Jacques Lefrancois, Stanley Cortez; Ed: Georges Klotz, Fabien Tordjmann; Prod Design: Robert Clatworthy; Composer: Francis Lai. Color, 132 min. **VHS**

Another Part of the Forest
(1948) Universal
A darkly fascinating study of internecine greed and soul-destroying lust for power based on Lillian Hellman's second study of the Hubbard family, this time in the post–Civil War era. March is a brutal tyrant, flush with the tainted wealth of salt profiteering at the expense of the Southern cause, who torments his sons, driving O'Brien into exile. O'Brien discovers the rotten foundation of his father's wealth and proceeds to destroy him by exposing his role as a traitor. **Cast:** Fredric March, Ann Blyth, Edmond O'Brien, Dan Duryea, Florence Eldridge, John Dall, Dona Drake, Betsy Blair, Fritz Leiber, Whit Bissell. **Credits:** Dir: Michael Gordon; Prod: Jerry Bresler; Writer: Vladimir Pozner; Story: Lillian Hellman; DP: Hal Mohr; Ed: Milton Carruth; Composer: Daniele Amfitheatrof. B&W, 106 min.

Anthony Adverse
(1936) Warner Bros.
The intriguing story of a young man's globe-trotting adventures during the time of Napoleon and his struggle for personal and financial success. An excellent cast, wonderful music, and great cinematography helped make this a blockbuster of its time. Based on Hervey Allen's novel. Academy

Award Nominations: 7, including Best Picture. **Academy Awards:** Best Supporting Actress: Gale Sondergaard; Best Film Editing; Best Cinematography; Best Score. **Cast:** Fredric March, Olivia de Havilland, Gale Sondergaard, Donald Woods, Edmund Gwenn, Claude Rains, Anita Louise, Louis Hayward, Steffi Duna, Akim Tamiroff. **Credits:** Dir: Mervyn Le Roy; Prod: Henry Blanke; Writer: Sheridan Gibney; Story: Hervey Allen; DP: Tony Gaudio; Ed: Ralph Dawson; Prod Design: Anton Grot; Composer: Erich Wolfgang Korngold; Costumes: Milo Anderson. B&W, 141 min. **VHS**

Anything Can Happen
(1952) Paramount
Georgi, a kindly and honest immigrant from the Georgian area of Russia, experiences many difficulties as he tries to adapt to his adopted country. He works hard to make a place for himself in America, all the while fighting with the English language and the strange customs of an alien people. His struggles are generally successful, but only after humorous early missteps in this lighthearted family comedy. **Cast:** Jose Ferrer, Kim Hunter, Kurt Kasznar, Oscar Karlweis, Oscar Beregi, Nick Dennis, Mikhail Rasumny, Alex Danaroff, Natasha Lytess, Otto Waldis. **Credits:** Dir: George Seaton; Prod: William Perlberg; Writer: George Seaton; Story: George Papashvily, Helen Papashvily; DP: William Perlberg; Ed: Alma Macrorie; Composer: Victor Young. B&W, 107 min.

Anything Goes
(1936) Paramount
In this Cole Porter musical, good-natured Billy mistakenly thinks that a woman is being kidnapped. He follows her and her kidnappers onto an ocean liner, pretending to be a mobster in order to see her. Billy learns that Hope is actually an heiress who has run away from her family, and the two instantly fall in love. She breaks things off, however, when she thinks Billy is really a gangster. Standard nonsense in the service of those songs. **Cast:** Bing Crosby, Ethel Merman, Charlie Ruggles, Ida Lupino, Grace Bradley, Arthur Treacher, Robert McWade. **Credits:** Dir: Lewis Milestone; Prod: Benjamin Glazer; Writer: Guy Bolton, Russell Crouse, Howard Lindsay, P. G. Wodehouse; DP: Karl Struss; Ed: Eda Warren; Prod Design: Hans Dreier; Composer: Hoagy Carmichael, Frederick Hollander, Cole Porter, Leo Robin, Richard A. Whiting; Art Director: Ernst Fegte. B&W, 92 min.

Any Wednesday

(1966) Warner Bros.

Fonda plays the beautiful mistress of a high-powered industrialist, whose cozy arrangement in a company-paid "executive suite" starts to crumble one hectic afternoon when an aggressive young executive and the industrialist's wife converge on the apartment. Based on the Broadway play by Muriel Resnik. **Cast:** Jane Fonda, Jason Robards, Dean Jones, Rosemary Murphy, Ann Prentiss, King Moody. **Credits:** Dir: Robert Ellis Miller; Prod: Julius J. Epstein; Writer: Julius J. Epstein; Story: Muriel Resnik; DP: Harold Lipstein; Ed: Stefan Arnsten; Composer: George Duning; Costumes: Dorothy Jeakins. Color, 109 min. **VHS**

The Apartment

(1960) United Artists

An ambitious young insurance clerk tries to get ahead by lending his apartment key to several of the company's philandering executives for the occasional afternoon rendezvous. But when he falls in love with the building's elevator operator, he soon realizes that she's the woman his married boss has been taking to the apartment for romantic trysts. Spurred on by the exhortations of the philosophizing doctor who lives next door to him, the troubled young man eventually reexamines his priorities and decides to be true to himself and drop out of the rat race. MacMurray in an unusual turn as a scoundrel. Other awards include Golden Globes for Best Actor in a Musical or Comedy; Best Actress in a Musical or Comedy; Best Motion Picture, Comedy. A National Film Registry Outstanding Film. **Academy Awards:** Best Director; Best Film Editing; Best Picture; Best Story and Screenplay—Written Directly for the Screen; Best Art Direction—Set Decoration (B&W). **Cast:** Jack Lemmon, Shirley MacLaine, Fred MacMurray, Edie Adams, Ray Walston, Jack Kruschen, Joan Shawlee, Hope Holiday, Naomi Stevens, Joyce Jameson. **Credits:** Dir: Billy Wilder; Prod: Billy Wilder; Writer: Billy Wilder, I. A. L. Diamond; DP: Joseph La Shelle; Ed: Daniel Mandell; Composer: Adolph Deutsch. B&W, 126 min. **VHS, LASER**

Apartment for Peggy

(1948) Fox

Memorable performances from Holden, Crain, and Gwenn highlight this candid but gently comic chronicle of peacetime readjustment for the gener-

Apocalypse Now (1979)

ation that won the war. Holden is a young veteran returning to wife Crain and a different kind of struggle, making do in the close quarters of a college dorm while hoping for a bright future. **Cast:** William Holden, Jeanne Crain, Edmund Gwenn, Gene Lockhart, Griff Barnett, Randy Stuart, Marion Marshall, Pat Behrs, Henri Letondal, Houseley Stevenson. **Credits:** Dir: George Seaton; Prod: William Perlberg; Writer: George Seaton; Story: Faith Baldwin; DP: Harry Jackson; Ed: Robert Simpson; Prod Design: Thomas Little, Walter M. Scott; Composer: Lionel Newman; Art Director: Lyle Wheeler, Richard Irvine. Color, 96 min.

Apocalypse Now

(1979) Paramount

A masterful film about the moral madness of the Vietnam War, inspired by the novella *Heart of Darkness* by Joseph Conrad. A soldier is sent into the Cambodian jungle to assassinate a colonel who has become insane and now runs his own fiefdom. The grueling production and Coppola's insistence on authenticity led to vast budget overruns and physical and emotional breakdowns. Considered by many to be the best war movie of all time, incredible performances and beautifully chaotic visuals make it an absolute must-see. Available in letterbox widescreen version with a remixed

soundtrack. Also see the 1991 documentary *Hearts of Darkness: A Filmmaker's Apocalypse*. Academy Award Nominations: 8, including Best Picture; Best Director; Best (Adapted) Screenplay. **Academy Awards:** Best Cinematography; Best Sound. **Cast:** Marlon Brando, Martin Sheen, Robert Duvall, Frederic Forrest, Dennis Hopper, Scott Glenn, Harrison Ford, Laurence Fishburne, Sam Bottoms. **Credits:** Dir: Francis Ford Coppola; Prod: Francis Ford Coppola; Writer: Michael Herr, John Milius, Francis Ford Coppola; Story: Joseph Conrad; DP: Vittorio Storaro; Ed: Richard Marks; Prod Design: Dean Tavoularis; Composer: Carmine Coppola, Francis Ford Coppola; Costumes: Charles James; Art Director: Angelo Graham; Set Designer: George Robert Nelson. Color, 155 min. **VHS, LASER**

The Appaloosa

(1966) Universal.

Brando is a perpetual loner in the 1870s who decides to turn his life around and settle down as a horse breeder specializing in the colorful Appaloosas. When someone makes off with one of his prized animals, Brando gives chase and discovers a young woman attempting to escape from an overzealous and abusive lover. The two fall in love as they evade marauding bandits on their way back across the border. **Cast:** Marlon Brando, John Saxon, Anjanette Comer, Frank Silvera, Rafael Campos. **Credits:** Dir: Sidney J. Furie; Writer: James Bridges, Roland Kibbee; Story: Robert MacLeod; DP: Russell Metty; Ed: Ted J. Kent; Prod Design: Alexander Golitzen, Alfred Sweeney; Costumes: Rosemary Odell, Helen Colvig. Color, 99 min. VHS, LASER

Apple Dumpling Gang
(1975) Disney
This Disney Western has roving bachelor Bixby getting saddled with three children and a wealth of trouble when the youngsters stumble upon a huge gold nugget. They join forces with two bumbling outlaws—Knotts and Conway, of course—to fend off the greedy townspeople and are soon facing a surly gang of sharpshooters. **Cast:** Bill Bixby, Susan Clark, Don Knotts, Tim Conway, David Wayne, Slim Pickens, Harry Morgan, John McGiver, Marie Windsor, Iris Adrian. **Credits:** Dir: Norman Tokar; Prod: Bill Anderson; Writer: Don Tait; Story: Jack Bickham; DP: Frank Phillips; Ed: Ray de Leuw; Prod Design: John B. Mansbridge, Walter Tyler; Composer: Buddy Baker. Color, 100 min. VHS, LASER

Appointment in Honduras
(1953) RKO
Patriot and idealist Ford coerces a rough band of thugs and killers into helping him save a Central American country. Lots of trekking through the jungles in this adventure prove the wealthy redhead played by Sheridan is just as tough as she is rich. **Cast:** Glenn Ford, Ann Sheridan, Zachary Scott, Jack Elam, Rodolfo Acosta. **Credits:** Dir: Jacques Tourneur; Prod: Benedict E. Bogeaus; Writer: Karen DeWolf; DP: Joseph Biroc; Ed: James Leicester; Composer: Louis Forbes. Color, 79 min. VHS

Appointment with Danger
(1951) Paramount
Film noir murder mystery in which Ladd plays a detective tipped off by a nun to a killer's identity. Disguising himself as a corrupt postal worker, Ladd joins the crime syndicate responsible for his fellow agent's murder. He is constantly tested by his cronies and finally confronted by psychotic Webb in a squash court duel. When Webb attempts to put a hit on the nun, Ladd saves the day. **Cast:** Alan Ladd, Phyllis Calvert, Jan Sterling, Jack Webb, Stacy Harris, Harry Morgan, Dan Riss, Harry Antrim, Geraldine Wall, George G. Lewis. **Credits:** Dir: Lewis Allen;

Prod: Robert Fellows; Writer: Richard L. Breen, Warren Duff; Ed: LeRoy Stone; Prod Design: Hans Dreier, Albert Nozaki; Composer: Victor Young. B&W, 89 min.

The April Fools
(1969) Fox
A bored, married Wall Street stockbroker (Lemmon) finds himself falling in love with a beautiful woman (Deneuve). Little does he know that she is married as well, and to his boss at that. Undaunted by the possibility of exposure or embarrassment, he decides to give it all up and run away with her. Great cast in typical '60s sitcom. **Cast:** Jack Lemmon, Catherine Deneuve, Sally Kellerman, Charles Boyer, Harvey Korman, Myrna Loy, Jack Weston, Peter Lawford. **Credits:** Dir: Stuart Rosenberg; Prod: Gordon Carroll; Writer: Hal Dresner; DP: Michael Hugo; Ed: Robert Wyman; Prod Design: Richard Sylbert; Composer: Marvin Hamlisch. Color, 95 min. VHS

April in Paris
(1952) Warner Bros.
Dynamite Jackson is a fast-talking chorus girl who mistakenly receives an invitation to represent her country at the International Festival of Arts in Paris. On the transatlantic crossing, Dynamite meets an engaged State Department official who her shipmates decide is perfect for her. A typically sunny Doris Day musical. **Cast:** Doris Day, Ray Bolger, Claude Dauphin, Eve Miller, George Givot. **Credits:** Dir: David Butler; Prod: William Jacobs; Writer: Jack Rose, Melville Shavelson; DP: Wilfrid M. Cline; Ed: Irene Morra; Choreographer: Leroy Prinz; Composer: Sammy Cahn, Vernon Duke, E. Y. Harburg. Color, 100 min. VHS

Arabesque
(1966) Universal
Peck plays an American professor of ancient languages at Oxford University who unwittingly puts himself in danger by decoding a message in hieroglyphics. Though the plot isn't particularly deep, Peck and Loren help keep this espionage flick stylish and fast-paced. **Cast:** Gregory Peck, Sophia Loren, Alan Badel, Kieron Moore, Carl Duering. **Credits:** Dir: Stanley Donen; Prod: Stanley Donen; Writer: Julian Mitchell, Stanley Price, Peter Stone; Story: Gordon Cotler; DP: Christopher Challis; Ed: Frederick Wilson; Prod Design: Reece Pemberton; Composer: Henry Mancini. Color, 118 min. VHS

Arabian Nights
(1942) Universal
Lavish sets and costumes distinguish this story of two brothers competing for the throne of Turkey and the hand of the fiery dancing girl Scheherazade. A colorful, escapist Technicolor fantasy and the first pairing of Hall and Montez. Academy Award Nominations: 4. **Cast:** Jon Hall, Maria Montez, Sabu, Leif Erickson, Turhan Bey, Billy Gilbert, Shemp Howard, John Qualen, Thomas Gomez. **Credits:** Dir: John Rawlins; Prod: Walter Wanger; Writer: Michael Hogan; DP: Milton Krasner, William V. Skall, W. Howard Greene; Ed: Philip Cahn; Prod Design: Alexander Golitzen, Jack Otterson; Composer: Frank Skinner; Costumes: Vera West; Set Designer: Russell A. Gausman, Ira Webb. Color, 87 min. VHS

Arch of Triumph
(1948) Republic
Though unpopular in its day, this rewards a fresh viewing. Milestone, director of *All Quiet on the Western Front*, once again turned to a novel by Erich Maria Remarque for the story of a refugee doctor in pre-WWII Paris who saves the life of—and falls in love with—a despondent woman. The foreboding that enveloped Paris before the German invasion also closes in on their relationship in the last days of light before the Nazi occupation. Boyer and Bergman make a moody matched pair of brooding romantics. The special anniversary video edition includes the original film, the original theatrical trailer, and a reproduction of the original theatrical poster. **Cast:** Ingrid Bergman, Charles Boyer, Charles Laughton, Louis Calhern. **Credits:** Dir: Lewis Milestone; Prod: Lewis Milestone; Writer: Lewis Milestone, Harry Brown; Story: Erich Maria Remarque; DP: Russell Metty; Ed: Mario Castegnaro; Composer: Louis Gruenberg. B&W, 132 min. VHS

Arise, My Love
(1940) Paramount
In this Wilder-Brackett script, Colbert plays a reporter who saves a man (Milland) sentenced to death in a Spanish military prison in the aftermath of the Civil War. After he is freed, they run off to Paris but the war clouds gather. They sail for America but encounter the war once more and find themselves washed back to Europe. Academy Award Nominations: 4, including Best Cinematography; Best Score. **Academy Awards:** Best Original Story. **Cast:** Cliff Nazarro, Esther Dale, Lionel Pape, Claudette Colbert, Ray Milland, George

Zucco, Walter Abel, Frank Puglia, Dennis O'Keefe, Dick Purcell. **Credits:** Dir: Mitchell Leisen; Prod: Arthur Hornblow, Jr.; Writer: Charles Brackett, Billy Wilder; Story: Benjamin Glazer, John S. Toldy, Jaques Thery; DP: Charles Lang; Ed: Doane Harrison; Prod Design: Hans Dreier, Robert Usher; Composer: Victor Young. B&W, 113 min.

The Aristocats

(1970) Disney
Set in 1910, this Disney animated classic offers plenty of adventure, humor, and music (especially performances by Chevalier). After high-society cat Duchess (Gabor) and her three kittens inherit a fortune from their mistress, a greedy butler plots to get rid of them—and collect the cash himself. The villainous servant kidnaps the entire feline family and takes them far away from their comfortable Paris home. A bunch of animal pals come to the rescue, however, and help restore the cats to their proper place. The last film personally supervised by Walt Disney himself. **Cast:** Eva Gabor, Scatman Crothers, Phil Harris, Maurice Chevalier, Sterling Holloway, Paul Winchell, Hermione Baddeley, Roddy Maude-Roxby. **Credits:** Dir: Wolfgang Reitherman; Prod: Wolfgang Reitherman, Winston Hibler; Writer: Larry Clemmons; Ed: Tom Acosta; Prod Design: Ken Anderson; Composer: George Bruns. Color, 79 min. **VHS, LASER**

Arizona

(1940) Columbia
Arthur has the right spirit for a woman struggling to settle in the lawless frontier of 1860s Arizona. She dallies with Holden, but then gets down to business despite Indian attack and shady dealings. Academy Award Nominations: Best (Black-and-White) Interior Decoration; Best Original Score. **Cast:** William Holden, Jean Arthur, Warren William, Porter Hall, Paul Harvey, George Chandler, Byron Foulger, Regis Toomey, Edgar Buchanan. **Credits:** Dir: Wesley Ruggles; Prod: Wesley Ruggles; Writer: Claude Binyon; Story: Clarence Buddington Kelland; DP: Joseph Walker, Harry Hallenberger, Fayte Brown; Ed: Otto Meyer, William A. Lyon; Prod Design: Lionel Banks, Robert Peterson; Composer: Victor Young. Color, 121 min. **VHS**

Armored Car Robbery

(1950) RKO
Taut action film about a gang of thieves who kill a guard during an attempted armored car robbery. **Cast:**

William Talman, Charles McGraw, Adele Jergens, Steve Brodie, Douglas Fowley. **Credits:** Dir: Richard Fleischer; Prod: Herman Schlom; Writer: Earl Felton, Gerald Drayson Adams; Story: Robert Angus, Robert M. Leeds; DP: Guy Roe; Ed: Desmond Marquette; Prod Design: Albert S. D'Agostino; Set Designer: Darrell Silvera. B&W, 61 min. **VHS**

Around the World in 80 Days

(1956) United Artists
Niven is perfect as an imperturbable English gentleman who attempts to win a bet by circumnavigating the globe in 80 days. The Jules Verne story, 100 locations, 40 cameo appearances by Hollywood players, a Young score, and Perelman among the writers guarantees delightful family fare. The beginning features a prologue by esteemed journalist Edward R. Murrow and the first film to be based on a Jules Verne novel, Georges Melies's 1902 short, *A Trip to the Moon*. Shot in Mike Todd's Todd A-O widescreen process. Academy Award Nominations: 8, including Best Director. Golden Globes for Best Actor in a Musical or Comedy; Best Motion Picture; Best Drama. **Academy Awards:** Best Film Editing; Best Color Cinematography; Best Music Scoring of a Dramatic or Comedy Picture; Best Picture; Best Screenplay—Adaptation. **Cast:** David Niven, Cantinflas, Charles Boyer, Robert Newton, Shirley MacLaine, Joe E. Brown, Martine Carol, John Carradine, Charles Coburn, Ronald Colman. **Credits:** Dir: Michael Anderson; Prod: Michael Todd; Writer: S. J. Perelman, John Farrow, James Poe; Story: Jules Verne; DP: Lionel Lindon; Ed: Gene Ruggiero, Paul Weatherwax; Prod Design: James Sullivan, Ken Adams; Choreographer: Paul Godkin; Composer: Victor Young; Costumes: Miles White; SFX: Lee Zavitz; Set Designer: Ross Dowd. Color, 179 min. **VHS, LASER**

The Arrangement

(1969) Warner Bros.
Written, produced, and directed by Kazan, based on his novel. Eddie Anderson (Douglas), a successful, married advertising executive, becomes obsessed with a younger woman and carries on a torrid love affair with her. After a near-fatal car "accident," Eddie promises his faithful wife to change his ways and seek some professional help but finds it impossible to do so. Hearing from his brother that their father is ill, Eddie travels to Long Island to visit him

with his young flame in tow. His wife also follows him East as he attempts to put things right with his family. **Cast:** Kirk Douglas, Faye Dunaway, Deborah Kerr, Richard Boone, Hume Cronyn. **Credits:** Dir: Elia Kazan; Prod: Elia Kazan; Writer: Elia Kazan; DP: Robert Surtees; Ed: Stefan Arnsten; Prod Design: Malcolm Bert; Composer: David Amram. Color, 126 min. **VHS**

Arrowhead

(1953) Paramount
Heston brawls with Palance (we want to see a rematch!) when an Apache chief returns to his tribe after being schooled in the East to find his nemesis, a bitter cavalry scout, wants to continue their private war. **Cast:** Charlton Heston, Jack Palance, Brian Keith, Katy Jurado, James Burke, Milburn Stone. **Credits:** Dir: Charles Marquis Warren; Prod: Nat Holt; Writer: Charles Marquis Warren; Story: W. R. Burnett; DP: Ray Rennahan; Ed: Frank Bracht; Composer: Paul Sawtell. Color, 105 min. **VHS, LASER**

Arrowsmith

(1931) United Artists
Ford's adaptation of the novel by Sinclair Lewis presents an idealistic young medical researcher (Colman) struggling with his desire to help mankind and the temptation for personal gain. When he travels with a promising new serum to the West Indies, he inadvertently places his wife in danger and must confront his true nature. Screenwriter Howard also adapted Lewis's *Dodsworth*. Various editions in release; originally released at 110 minutes, restored version is 99 minutes. Academy Award Nominations: 4, including Best Adapted Screenplay. **Cast:** Ronald Colman, Helen Hayes, Myrna Loy, Richard Bennett, Charlotte Henry, Beulah Bondi, A. E. Anson. **Credits:** Dir: John Ford; Prod: Samuel Goldwyn; Writer: Sidney Howard; Story: Sinclair Lewis; DP: Ray June; Ed: Hugh Bennett; Prod Design: Richard Day; Composer: Alfred Newman. B&W, 100 min. **VHS**

Arsene Lupin

(1932) MGM
The first-ever screen pairing of the Brothers Barrymore, thanks to Louis B. Mayer's signing of John immediately after his contract with Warner Brothers expired. This mystery set in Paris finds John, as the glamorous crook Lupin, continually outsmarting his adversary Guerchard (Lionel), the detective on his trail. We never see an

actual crime being committed until the climax, when Lupin decides to try to steal the *Mona Lisa* from the Louvre. **Cast:** John Barrymore, Lionel Barrymore, Karen Morley, John Miljan, Tully Marshall, Henry Armetta, George W. Davis, John Davidson, James Mack, Mary Jane Irving. **Credits:** Dir: Jack Conway; Writer: Lenore J. Coffee, Bayard Veiller, Carey Wilson; Story: Francis de Croisset, Maurice Leblanc; DP: Oliver T. Marsh; Ed: Hugh Wynn; Composer: Alfred Newman. B&W, 64 min.

Arsenic and Old Lace
(1944) Warner Bros.
Beware nice old ladies offering elderberry wine! A mild-mannered drama critic discovers the shocking truth about his two elderly aunts: The seemingly harmless old ladies have the most disagreeable habit of poisoning their gentlemen callers and burying them in the cellar. One of the all-time great black comedies. **Cast:** Cary Grant, Priscilla Lane, Raymond Massey, Peter Lorre, Josephine Hull, Jean Adair, John Alexander, James Gleason, Jack Carson, Edward Everett Horton. **Credits:** Dir: Frank Capra; Prod: Frank Capra; Writer: Julius J. Epstein, Philip G. Epstein, Howard Lindsay, Russel Crouse; Story: Joseph Kesselring; DP: Sol Polito; Ed: Daniel Mandell; Prod Design: Max Parker; Composer: Max Steiner; SFX: Byron Haskin, Robert Burks. B&W, 120 min. **VHS, LASER**

Artists and Models
(1937) Paramount
Snappy musical helmed by Walsh with zippy Lupino in the lead. Mac Brewster heads an advertising agency specializing in big, splashy song-and-dance numbers. When Mac is hired to host the Annual Artists and Models Competition, one of his employees, Paula Sewell, decides to enter. She faces stiff competition from the other, better-connected models contending for the title of the Queen of the Artists and Models. Academy Award Nominations: Best Song ("Whispers in the Dark"). **Cast:** Jack Benny, Ida Lupino, Richard Arlen, Gail Patrick, Ben Blue, Judy Canova, Cecil Cunningham, Donald Meek, Hedda Hopper, Martha Raye. **Credits:** Dir: Raoul Walsh; Prod: Lewis E. Gensler; Writer: Walter DeLeon, Eve Greene, Sig Herzig, Francis Martin, Eugene Thackery, Harlan Ware; DP: Victor Milner; Ed: Ellsworth Hoagland; Prod Design: Hans Dreier; Composer: Frederick Hollander, Leo Robin; Art Director: Ernst Fegte. B&W, 90 min.

Artists and Models
(1955) Paramount
Martin and Lewis at their best as tyro comic-book artist Martin uses the feverish dreams of his daffy roommate Lewis for storylines. Turns out the comic-fueled reverie contains real government secrets, and the chase is on. Great women in support: MacLaine, Malone, Gabor, Ekberg. **Cast:** Dean Martin, Jerry Lewis, Shirley MacLaine, Dorothy Malone, Eva Gabor, Anita Ekberg, Eddie Mayehoff, George Winslow, Jack Elam. **Credits:** Dir: Frank Tashlin; Prod: Hal B. Wallis; Writer: Don McGuire, Frank Tashlin; Story: Michael Davidson, Norman Lessing; DP: Daniel Fapp; Ed: Warren Low; Choreographer: Charles O'Curran; Composer: Walter Scharf; Costumes: Edith Head. Color, 109 min. **VHS, LASER**

Artists and Models Abroad
(1938) Paramount
Leisen's take on the song-and-dance hit of the previous year. This time Benny leads a "fashion show" involving chorus girls and other Parisian performers, and romances a Texas oil millionaire's daughter. **Cast:** Jack Benny, Joan Bennett, Mary Boland, Charley Grapewin, Fritz Feld, Joyce Compton, Phyllis Kennedy, George P. Huntley, Andre Cheron, Alex Melish. **Credits:** Dir: Mitchell Leisen; Prod: Arthur Hornblow, Jr.; Writer: Ken Englund; Story: Russell Crouse, Howard Lindsay, J. P. McEvoy; DP: Ted Tetzlaff; Ed: Doane Harrison; Prod Design: Hans Dreier, Ernst Fegte; Composer: Boris Morros, Ralph Rainger, Leo Robin. B&W, 90 min.

Ask Any Girl
(1959) MGM
A young woman working at an ad agency realizes that the motivational techniques in which her firm specializes might help her snag her boss as a husband. When she enlists the expertise of her boss's older brother, they both discover that love's variables are unpredictable. **Cast:** David Niven, Shirley MacLaine, Gig Young, Rod Taylor, Jim Backus, Elisabeth Fraser, Claire Kelly. **Credits:** Dir: Charles Walters; Prod: Joe Pasternak; Writer: George Wells; Story: Winifred Wolfe; DP: Robert Bronner; Ed: John McSweeney, Jr.; Composer: Jeff Alexander; Costumes: Helen Rose. Color, 101 min. **VHS**

The Asphalt Jungle
(1950) MGM
Considered by many to be the defining film of the crime oeuvre. After many

years in prison, Doc (Jaffe), an over-the-hill criminal decides upon his release from prison to make one last go of it. His attempts to reunite the old gang and their plotting make a gripping backdrop for standout performances, including a lusty Monroe. Based on a novel by W. R. Burnett. Remade in 1958 as *Badlanders,* in 1963 as *Cairo,* and 1972 as *Cool Breeze.* **Academy Awards:** Best Director. **Cast:** Sterling Hayden, Sam Jaffe, Jean Hagen, Marilyn Monroe, Louis Calhern, James Whitmore, John McIntire, Marc Lawrence, Barry Kelley. **Credits:** Dir: John Huston; Prod: Arthur Hornblow, Jr.; Writer: Ben Maddow, John Huston; Story: W. R. Burnett; DP: Harold Rosson; Ed: George Boemler; Prod Design: Cedric Gibbons, Randal Duell; Composer: Miklos Rozsa; Set Designer: Edwin B. Willis, Jack D. Moore. B&W, 112 min. **VHS, LASER**

Assault on a Queen
(1966) Paramount
Sinatra minus the Rat Pack in another big heist. A group of adventurers plan to hold up the H.M.S. *Queen Elizabeth* using a refurbished WWII U-boat. Just for Sinatra fans. Screenplay by Rod Serling. **Cast:** Frank Sinatra, Virna Lisi, Anthony Franciosa, Richard Conte, Reginald Denny, Alf Kjellin, Errol John, Murray Matheson. **Credits:** Dir: Jack Donohue; Prod: William Goetz; Writer: Rod Serling; Story: Jack Finney; DP: William Daniels; Ed: Archie Marshek; Composer: Duke Ellington; Costumes: Edith Head. Color, 105 min. **VHS**

Assault on Precinct 13
(1976)
An early Carpenter action drama with explosive impact. A backwater L.A. police station gets lively fast when a man avenges the murder of his daughter and then takes shelter from the murderous gang in the 13th-precinct house. Purportedly an homage to Howard Hawks, but it matters little when the action starts. Carpenter also wrote the score. **Cast:** Austin Stoker, Darwin Joston, Laurie Zimmer, Martin West, Nancy Loomis, Kim Richards, Henry Brandon. **Credits:** Dir: John Carpenter; Prod: Joseph Kaufman; Writer: John Carpenter; DP: Douglas Knapp; Ed: John T. Chance; Prod Design: Tommy Lee Wallace; Composer: John Carpenter; Costumes: Louise Kyes. Color, 91 min. **VHS, LASER, DVD**

Assignment Paris
(1952) Columbia
Andrews travels to Budapest for the *Herald Tribune* to assist in an investi-

gation of a plot to overthrow the communist leadership with Tito's help. Once there, he finds a suffocating world of tension with censors, communist spies, and the constant potential for violence. He discovers photographic proof of the connection between Tito and the plotters, but is taken prisoner as a suspected spy. **Cast:** Dana Andrews, Marta Toren, George Sanders, Audrey Totter, Sandro Giglio, Don Randolph, Herbert Berghof, Ben Astar, Willis Bouchey, Earl Lee. **Credits:** Dir: Robert Parrish; Prod: Samuel Marx, Jerry Bresler; Writer: William Bowers, Paul Gallico, Pauline Gallico; DP: Burnett Guffey, Ray Cory; Ed: Charles Nelson; Composer: George Duning. B&W, 84 min.

As You Desire Me
(1932) MGM
Pirandello play yields the odd couple of Garbo and Von Stroheim as a woman with amnesia struggles to resume life with the husband she has forgotten. A curiosity worth seeing for the early Garbo performance. **Cast:** Melvyn Douglas, Greta Garbo, Erich Von Stroheim, Hedda Hopper, Rafaela Ottiano. **Credits:** Dir: George Fitzmaurice; Writer: Gene Markey; Story: Luigi Pirandello; DP: William Daniels; Ed: George Hively. B&W, 113 min. **VHS**

At Gunpoint
(1955) Republic
A timid store owner becomes the hero of a small western town when he accidently shoots and kills a bank robber. When the crook's cohorts come looking for revenge, he suddenly finds himself friendless and pulled again toward violence. **Cast:** Fred MacMurray, Dorothy Malone, Walter Brennan, Tommy Rettig, John Qualen, Skip Homeier. **Credits:** Dir: Alfred Werker; Prod: Vincent M. Fennelly; Writer: Daniel Ullman; DP: Ellsworth Fredericks; Ed: Eda Warren; Composer: Carmen Dragon. Color, 81 min. **VHS**

The Atomic City
(1952) Paramount
An acclaimed nuclear physicist (Barry) at the Los Alamos research facility is part of an elite group of scientists with knowledge of nuclear weaponry. It is his skills as a father that come into play, however, when terrorists kidnap his young son (Aaker). Hiding out in the surrounding hills, the culprits demand the plans to the H-bomb as ransom and threaten the boy's life if not delivered to their satisfaction. **Cast:** Gene Barry, Nancy Gates, Lydia Clarke, Lee Aaker, Michael J. Moore,

Milburn Stone. **Credits:** Dir: Jerry Hopper; Prod: Joseph Sistrom; Writer: Sydney Boehm; DP: Charles Lang; Ed: Archie Marshek; Composer: Leith Stevens. B&W, 85 min. **VHS**

At Sword's Point
(1952) Fox
The children of Alexandre Dumas's *Three Musketeers,* including the swashbuckling daughter of Athos, set off on adventures that rival those of their illustrious fathers. Wilde and O'Hara provide the energy in this likeable Technicolor swashbuckler. **Cast:** Cornel Wilde, Maureen O'Hara, Alan Hale, Jr., Robert Douglas, Gladys Cooper, Dan O'Herlihy, Blanche Yurka, Nancy Gates. **Credits:** Dir: Lewis Allen; Prod: Jerrold T. Brandt; Writer: Walter Ferris, Joseph Hoffman; Story: Aubrey Wisberg, Jack Pollexfen; DP: Ray Rennahan; Ed: Samuel E. Beetley, Robert Golden; Prod Design: Albert S. D'Agostino, Jack Okey; Composer: Roy Webb. Color, 81 min. **VHS, LASER**

At the Circus
(1939) MGM
The Marx Brothers save a mortgaged circus by convincing a Newport socialite to buy it for one show only. It may be past prime time for Marx films, but it's tough to beat a rousing rendition of "Lydia the Tattooed Lady." **Cast:** Chico Marx, Harpo Marx, Groucho Marx, Zeppo Marx, Margaret Dumont, Eve Arden, Nat Pendleton, Florence Rice, Kenny Baker. **Credits:** Dir: Edward Buzzell; Prod: Mervyn LeRoy; Writer: Irving Brecher; DP: Leonard Smith; Ed: William Terhune; Choreographer: Bobby Connolly; Composer: Franz Waxman, Harold Arlen, E. Y. Harburg. B&W, 87 min. **VHS, LASER**

At War with the Army
(1950) Paramount
Martin and Lewis get their first star billing in this hilarious song- and gag-filled comedy. The duo play Puccinelli and Korwin, pals who join the army and immediately get into a load of trouble on a military training base. Highlights include a sequence involving a noncooperative soda machine, Jerry Lewis performing "The Navy Gets the Gravy But the Army Gets the Beans," and the team's impersonation of the Bing Crosby–Barry Fitzgerald characters from the classic film *Going My Way.* **Cast:** Dean Martin, Jerry Lewis, Polly Bergen, Angela Greene, Mike Kellin, Jimmie Dundee. **Credits:** Dir: Hal Walker; Prod: Fred F.

Finklehoffe; Writer: Fred F. Finklehoffe; Story: James B. Allardice; DP: Stuart Thompson. B&W, 93 min. **VHS**

Auntie Mame
(1958) Warner Bros.
Sharp-witted, zippy comedy about a woman who lives life to the absolute fullest. When her orphaned 10-year-old nephew shows up on her doorstep, a new life begins for both. Mame's digs provide a cool look at what the 1950s considered bohemian hip, too. Later became the Broadway warhorse, *Mame.* Academy Award Nominations: 6, including Best Picture; Best Actress: Rosalind Russell. Other awards include Golden Globes for Best Actress in a Musical or Comedy: Rosalind Russell; Best Motion Picture; Best Comedy. **Cast:** Rosalind Russell, Forrest Tucker, Coral Browne, Fred Clark, Patric Knowles, Lee Patrick, Roger Smith, Peggy Cass, Joanna Barnes. **Credits:** Dir: Morton Da Costa; Writer: Betty Comden, Adolph Green; Story: Patrick Dennis, Jerome Lawrence, Robert E. Lee; DP: Harry Stradling; Ed: William Ziegler; Prod Design: Malcolm Bert; Composer: Bronislau Kaper; Costumes: Orry-Kelly; Set Designer: George James Hopkins. Color, 161 min. **VHS, LASER**

Autumn Leaves
(1956) Columbia
A lonely, middle-aged woman falls in love with and marries a handsome young man, only to discover the shocking, violent truth about him. Rescued by a performance from Crawford that shows vulnerability in addition to her characteristic steel. **Cast:** Joan Crawford, Cliff Robertson, Vera Miles, Lorne Greene, Ruth Donnelly, Shepperd Strudwick. **Credits:** Dir: Robert Aldrich; Prod: William Goetz; Writer: Jack Jevne, Lewis Meltzer, Robert Blees; DP: Charles Lang; Ed: Michael Luciano; Composer: Hans J. Salter. B&W, 144 min. **VHS**

Avanti!
(1972) United Artists
When a wealthy American businessman goes to Italy to claim his dead father's body, he finds himself falling in love with the daughter of his father's mistress. A late Wilder comedy that finds fun in the culture clash. Golden Globe for Best Actor: Jack Lemmon. **Cast:** Jack Lemmon, Juliet Mills, Clive Revill, Edward Andrews, Gianfranco Barra, Franco Angrisano. **Credits:** Dir: Billy Wilder; Prod: Billy Wilder; Writer: Billy Wilder, I.A.L. Diamond; Story: Samuel Taylor; DP: Luigi

The Awful Truth (1937)

Kuveiller; Ed: Ralph E. Winters; Prod Design: Ferdinando Scarfiotti; Composer: Carlo Rustichelli. Color, 144 min. **VHS**

Away All Boats

(1956) Universal
A hard-boiled U.S. Navy captain struggles to whip his men into shape before they experience the rigors of WWII combat aboard a navy transport in the Pacific. Based-on-fact story features convincing battle sequences. **Cast:** Jeff Chandler, George Nader, Julie Adams, Lex Barker, Keith Andes, Richard Boone, Frank Faylen, William Daniels. **Credits:** Dir: Joseph Pevney; Prod: Howard Christie; Writer: Ted Sherdeman; Story: Kenneth M. Dodson; DP: Clifford Stine; Ed: Ted J. Kent; Composer: Frank Skinner. B&W, 114 min. **VHS, DVD**

The Awful Truth

(1937) Columbia
In their first on-screen matchup, Grant and Dunne play a divorcing couple bent on mutual ruination. Jerry Warriner returns from a two-week Florida vacation to find his socialite wife, Lucy, has also been away. When she saunters in on the arm of the handsome Armand, Jerry looks the fool in front of society pals. But after discovering that the oranges Jerry has brought from Florida are stamped "California," Lucy realizes that her husband, too, has been up to no good. They file for divorce and begin new romances as each contrives to sabotage the other's relationship. Based on the 1922 play by Arthur Richman. Filmed previously in 1925 and 1929 and later remade as the musical *Let's Do It Again* in 1953. **Academy Awards:** Best Director. **Cast:** Cary Grant, Irene Dunne, Ralph Bellamy, Cecil Cunningham, Mary Forbes, Alex D'Arcy, Joyce Compton, Molly Lamont, Esther Dale. **Credits:** Dir: Leo McCarey; Prod: Leo McCarey; Writer: Vina Delmar; Story: Arthur Richman; DP: Joseph Walker; Ed: Al Clark; Prod Design: Stephen Goosson, Lionel Banks; Costumes: Robert Kalloch. B&W, 92 min. **VHS, LASER**

The Babe Ruth Story
(1948) Fox
An extremely sympathetic portrait of the legendary "Babe," which follows him from his troubled childhood to his last heroic day. Bendix portrays the fictional Bambino, re-creating the most memorable highlights of his life. Intermingled with actual clips of Ruth in action, adding a documentary feel to the picture. **Cast:** William Bendix, Claire Trevor, William Frawley, Charles Bickford. **Credits:** Dir: Roy Del Ruth. B&W, 107 min. **VHS**

Babes in Arms
(1939) MGM
Showbiz musical directed by Hollywood surrealist Berkeley paired Rooney and Garland for the first time as the children of former vaudevillians who team up to put on a Really Big Show to raise money for their folks. Lots of singing and dancing, with both kids doing uncanny impersonations of then-current celebrities and political figures. Includes the title song and "You Are My Lucky Star." Nominated for two Academy Awards. **Cast:** Judy Garland, Mickey Rooney, Charles Winninger, Douglas MacPhail, June Preisser, Leni Lynn. **Credits:** Dir: Busby Berkeley; Prod: Arthur Freed; Writer: Jack McGowan, Kay Van Riper; Story: Richard Rodgers, Lorenz Hart; DP: Ray June; Ed: Frank Sullivan; Prod Design: Cedric Gibbons, Merrill Pye; Choreographer: Busby Berkeley; Composer: Roger Edens, George Stoll, Lorenz Hart, Richard Rodgers; Costumes: Dolly Tree. B&W, 96 min. **VHS, LASER**

Babes in Toyland
(1934) MGM
A classic Laurel and Hardy comedy about two toy-making apprentices who live in Toyland. They're fired from their jobs after they make 100 six-feet-tall soldiers for Santa Claus instead of 600 one-foot-tall soldiers. The duo do not know how they are going to pay their room and board to Mother Peep. Mother Peep's daughter Bo is busy fending off the advances of evil Barnaby, who owns the mortgage on the Peep home. Laurel and Hardy save the day, rescuing Bo's love Tom-Tom from the land of the bogeymen, and unleashing the toy soldiers on the bogeymen who run rampant through Toyland. **Cast:** Stan Laurel, Oliver Hardy, Charlotte Henry, Felix Knight, Henry Brandon, Florence Roberts, Ferdinand Munier, William Burress, Victor Herbert. **Credits:** Dir: Gus Meins, Charles Rogers; Prod: Hal Roach; Writer: Frank Butler, Nick Grinde, Glen McDonough; DP: Francis Corby, Art Lloyd; Ed: Bert Jordan, William H. Terhune; Composer: Frank Churchill, Victor Herbert, Glen McDonough. B&W, 77 min.

Babes in Toyland
(1961) Disney
A fun-filled Disney version of Victor Herbert's engaging operetta about the world of Mother Goose. All of the classic songs are here, as well as many colorful and imaginative sets. Academy Award Nominations: 2, including Best Scoring of a Musical Picture; Best (Color) Costume Design. **Cast:** Ray Bolger, Annette Funicello, Tommy Sands. **Credits:** Dir: Jack Donohue. Color, 105 min. **VHS**

Babes on Broadway
(1941) MGM
The team from *Babes in Arms* is back with the same Berkeley-fueled formula. Mickey and Judy hit the big-time with their irrepressible act that includes spoofs of contemporary Hollywood stars and politicians. Academy Award Nomination for Best Song ("How About You?"). **Cast:** Mickey Rooney, Judy Garland, Fay Bainter, Virginia Weidler, Richard Quine, Donna Reed, Margaret O'Brien, Ray Macdonald. **Credits:** Dir: Busby Berkeley; Prod: Arthur Freed; Writer: Fred F. Finklehoffe, Elaine Ryan; DP: Lester White; Ed: Fredrick Y. Smith; Choreographer: Busby Berkeley; Composer: Burton Lane, Ralph Freed; Costumes: Robert Kalloch. B&W, 121 min. **VHS, LASER**

Baby Doll
(1956) Warner Bros.
Still controversial, this adaptation (by the playwright) of a Tennessee Williams play caused outrage upon its release. From this vantage point, Kazan's claustrophobic depiction of the sweaty competition between a dim cotton-mill owner and his business rival for the attention of the mill owner's simpering child bride is less shocking than harrowing. Academy Award Nominations: 4, including Best Actress: Carroll Baker; Best (Adapted) Screenplay. Other awards include a Golden Globe for Best Director. **Cast:** Carroll Baker, Karl Malden, Eli Wallach, Mildred Dunnock, Lonny Chapman. **Credits:** Dir: Elia Kazan; Writer: Tennessee Williams; DP: Boris Kaufman; Ed: Gene Milford; Prod Design: Richard Sylbert; Composer: Kenyon Hopkins; Costumes: Anna Hill Johnstone. B&W, 117 min. **VHS**

Baby Face
(1933) Warner Bros.
Catch this to get a glimpse of Hollywood at the height of its pre–Production Code licentiousness. Stanwyck takes the easy way from the speakeasy on the bottom floor to the penthouse executive suite of a New York office building, leaving behind a trail of discarded men in her wake. **Cast:** Barbara Stanwyck, George Brent, Donald Cook, Margaret Lindsay, Douglass Dumbrille, John Wayne, Arthur Hohl, Henry Kolker. **Credits:** Dir: Alfred E. Green; Prod: Raymond Griffith; Writer: Gene Markey, Kathryn Scola; Story: Darryl F. Zanuck; DP: James Van Trees; Ed: Howard Bretherton; Prod Design: Anton Grot; Costumes: Orry-Kelly. B&W, 72 min. **VHS**

Baby Face Harrington

(1935) MGM
A comedic gangster-movie spoof, in which a man who is already having a hard time in his job, his social life, and his marriage, is kidnapped by a bunch of thugs. News that his wife plans to divorce him almost sends him reeling over the edge before, half-unwittingly, he becomes a hero of sorts. **Cast:** Charles Butterworth, Una Merkel, Harvey Stephens, Eugene Pallette, Nat Pendleton, Ruth Selwyn, Donald Meek, Dorothy Libaire, Edward J. Nugent, Richard Carle. **Credits:** Dir: Raoul Walsh; Prod: Edgar Selwyn; Writer: William LeBaron, Edgar Selwyn, Johnson Nunnally; DP: Oliver T. Marsh; Ed: William S. Gray; Composer: Sam Wineland. B&W, 65 min.

Baby Take a Bow

(1934) Fox
Temple took a bow in her first starring vehicle as the daughter of a criminal trying to go straight. When her dad is wrongly accused of a theft, little miss pluck sets out sleuthing. **Cast:** Shirley Temple, James Dunn, Claire Trevor, Alan Dinehart, Ray Walker. **Credits:** Dir: Harry Lachman; Prod: John Stone; Writer: Philip Klein, Edward Paramore; Story: James P. Judge; DP: L. W. O'Connell. B&W, 76 min. VHS

Baby, the Rain Must Fall

(1965) Columbia
Horton Foote's screenplay from his own stage play graces this story of a man at odds with himself. A rockabilly singer on parole for a stabbing tries to settle down with his wife and daughter, but tough times and his restlessness conspire to ruin his dream of becoming a successful songwriter. Interesting chemistry between McQueen and Remick. The title song became a hit. **Cast:** Steve McQueen, Lee Remick, Paul Fix, Josephine Hutchinson, Ruth White, Charles Watts. **Credits:** Dir: Robert Mulligan; Prod: Alan J. Pakula; Writer: Horton Foote; DP: Ernest Laszlo; Ed: Aaron Stell; Prod Design: Roland Anderson; Composer: Elmer Bernstein; Set Designer: Frank A. Tuttle. B&W, 100 min. VHS, LASER

The Bachelor and the Bobby-Soxer

(1947) RKO
After love-struck teenager Temple is found in his apartment late at night, hapless painter Grant is given an unusual choice by the judge, Loy, who just happens to be the girl's sister: date the smitten high-schooler until she gets over her infatuation . . . or go to prison. The situation becomes even more complicated when the judge's initial hostility toward the philandering artist soon turns to affection. Sidney Sheldon's comic script earned him an Academy Award. **Academy Awards:** Best Original Screenplay. **Cast:** Cary Grant, Shirley Temple, Myrna Loy, Rudy Vallee, Ray Collins, Johnny Sands, Harry Davenport, Don Beddoe. **Credits:** Dir: Irving Reis; Writer: Sidney Sheldon; DP: Robert de Grasse, Nicholas Musuraca; Ed: Frederic Knudtson; Prod Design: Albert S. D'Agostino, Carroll Clark; Composer: Leigh Harline; Costumes: Edward Stevenson; SFX: Russell A. Cully; Set Designer: Darrell Silvera. B&W, 95 min. VHS, LASER

Bachelor Apartment

(1931) RKO
Rat Pack cool in the pre–Production Code days. Swinging bachelor juggles the babes (including the alluring Dunne and Murray). **Cast:** Lowell Sherman, Irene Dunne, Mae Murray, Claudia Dell, Noel Francis, Bess Flowers, Norman Kerry. **Credits:** Dir: Lowell Sherman; Prod: William LeBaron; Writer: J. Walter Ruben; Story: John Howard Lawson; DP: Leo Tover; Ed: Marie Halvey; Costumes: Max Ree. B&W, 77 min. VHS

Bachelor Bait

(1934) RKO
Erwin loses his job and starts a lonely-hearts club. He's assisted by his girl Friday who helps him make his own matrimonial choice. **Cast:** Stuart Erwin, Rochelle Hudson, Pert Kelton, Skeets Gallagher, Berton Churchill, Grady Sutton, Clarence Wilson. **Credits:** Dir: George Stevens; Writer: Glenn Tryon; Story: Edward Halperin, Victor Halperin; DP: David Abel; Ed: James Morely. B&W, 75 min. VHS

Bachelor in Paradise

(1961) MGM
Romance author Hope goes undercover in a suburban California community in order to produce a best-selling exposé on the mating habits of the natives. His plan goes awry when the housewives are (inexplicably) attracted to him. Turner's presence adds a sexy zip to the proceedings. Academy Award Nomination for Best Song ("Bachelor in Paradise"). **Cast:** Bob Hope, Lana Turner, Janis Paige, Jim Hutton, Paula Prentiss, Don Porter, Agnes Moorehead, Virginia Grey, Reta Shaw, John McGiver. **Credits:** Dir: Jack Arnold; Prod: Ted Richmond; Writer: Valentine Davies, Hal Kanter; Story: Vera Caspary; DP: Joseph Ruttenberg; Ed: Richard W. Farrell; Composer: Henry Mancini. Color, 109 min. VHS

Bachelor Mother

(1939) RKO
A young, unmarried woman stops to take a peek at a little bundle of joy abandoned on the steps of an orphanage. This innocent curiosity lands her in hot water when the home's administrators conclude that she's the baby's true mom. In no time at all, the woman is crazy about the charming infant . . . and discovering other forms of love, too. Remade with Debbie Reynolds as *Bundle of Joy* (1956). Academy Award Nomination for Best Original Story. **Cast:** Ginger Rogers, David Niven, Charles Coburn, Frank Albertson. **Credits:** Dir: Garson Kanin; Prod: B. G. DeSylva, Pandro S. Berman; Writer: Norman Krasna; Story: Felix Jackson; DP: Robert DeGrasse; Ed: Henry Berman, Robert Wise; Prod Design: Van Nest Polglase, Carroll Clark; Composer: Roy Webb; Costumes: Irene; SFX: Vernon Walker; Set Designer: Darrell Silvera. B&W, 83 min. VHS, LASER

Back at the Front

(1952) Universal
A sequel starring the comic team of Willie and Joe, this comedy takes the popular bumbles of *Up Front* to post-war Japan. After failing in a string of deceptions, aimed to secure inactive status, the boys are reassigned. Once in Japan they sir up laughs as product testers for new army gear. Left dangerously to their own devices, in their free time they get entangled in a plot to smuggle arms to North Korea. **Cast:** Richard Long, Russell Johnson, Gregg Palmer, Aram Katcher, George Ramsey, Aen-Ling Chow, Benson Fong, Tom Ewell, Harvey Lembeck, Mari Blanchard. **Credits:** Dir: George Sherman; Prod: Leonard Goldstein; Writer: Lou Breslow, Don McGuire, Oscar Brodney, Bill Mauldin; DP: Clifford Stine; Ed: Paul Weatherwax; Prod Design: Hans Dreier, Henry Bumstead; Composer: Henry Mancini, Herman Stein. B&W, 87 min.

Backdoor to Heaven

(1939) Paramount
Interesting social-problem story of a poor boy's descent into a life of crime told as his hometown schoolteacher waits for his former students to gather for a homecoming. **Cast:** Wallace Ford, Stuart Erwin, Jimmy Lydon, Aline MacMahon, William Harrigan. **Credits:**

Dir: William K. Howard; Prod: William K. Howard; Writer: John Bright, Robert Tasker; Story: William K. Howard; DP: Hal Mohr; Ed: Jack Murray. B&W, 85 min. VHS

Background to Danger
(1943) Warner Bros.
Nazis, Soviets, and American agent Raft are all after a cache of secret documents in the mysterious back alleys of WWII Turkey. A great, fast-moving spy tale handled expertly by Walsh. Based on Eric Ambler's *Uncommon Danger.* **Cast:** George Raft, Brenda Marshall, Sydney Greenstreet, Peter Lorre, Osa Massen, Kurt Katch, Turhan Bey. **Credits:** Dir: Raoul Walsh; Prod: Jerry Wald; Writer: W. R. Burnett; Story: Eric Ambler; DP: Tony Gaudio; Ed: Jack Killifer; Prod Design: Hugh Reticker; Composer: Frederick Hollander; SFX: Willard Van Enger, Warren E. Lynch; Set Designer: Casey Roberts. B&W, 81 min. VHS

Back Street
(1941) Universal
This tragic period romance jerks the tears with Sullavan as the devoted lover of the man fate refuses to give her, Walter Saxel (Boyer). After bad timing ends their first affair Boyer marries another woman overseas (O'Day), unaware that Sullivan has remained faithful. When he returns he realizes his mistake. Sullavan rejects her kind suitor (Carlson), preferring nothing at all to the wrong man. **Cast:** Charles Boyer, Margaret Sullavan, Richard Carlson, Frank McHugh, Tim Holt, Frank Jenks, Esther Dale, Samuel S. Hinds, Peggy Stewart, Nell O'Day. Academy Award Nominations: Best Score. **Credits:** Dir: Robert Stevenson; Prod: Bruce Manning; Writer: Felix Jackson, Bruce Manning; Story: Fannie Hurst; DP: William Daniels; Ed: Ted J. Kent; Prod Design: Seward Webb; Composer: Frank Skinner. B&W, 89 min.

Back Street
(1961) Universal
Probably the least involving of the three film versions of the Fannie Hurst drama about a woman who falls in love with a married man and is forced to always be the "other woman." This is the only color production, though, and, with Hayward in the lead, it's certainly eye-catching. Academy Award Nomination for Best (Color) Costume Design. **Cast:** Susan Hayward, John Gavin, Vera Miles, Virginia Grey, Charles Drake, Reginald Gardiner. **Credits:** Dir: David Miller; Prod: Ross

Hunter; Writer: Eleanore Griffin, William Ludwig; Story: Fannie Hurst; DP: Stanley Cortez; Ed: Milton Carruth; Prod Design: Alexander Golitzen; Composer: Frank Skinner; Costumes: Jean Louis. Color, 107 min. VHS

Back to Bataan
(1945) RKO
Stirring Wayne starrer with Duke an American colonel who turns Filipinos into guerrilla troops to carry on the resistance struggle after the fall of Bataan during WWII. Standard fare, but Duke's fans will enjoy it. **Cast:** John Wayne, Anthony Quinn, Beulah Bondi, Richard Loo, Fely Franquelli, Leonard Strong, Philip Ahn, Lawrence Tierney, Paul Fix. **Credits:** Dir: Edward Dmytryk; Prod: Theron Warth; Writer: Ben Barzman, Richard H. Landau; Story: Aeneas MacKenzie, William D. Gordon; DP: Nicholas Musuraca; Ed: Marston Fay; Prod Design: Albert S. D'Agostino; Composer: Roy Webb; SFX: Vernon Walker; Set Designer: Darrell Silvera. B&W, 97 min. VHS, LASER

The Bad and the Beautiful
(1952) MGM
Turner shines in a sharp portrayal of moviemaking—and climbing the Hollywood ladder. Told in flashbacks from the point of view of an actress, a writer, and a studio executive. Old Hollywood hands Minnelli and Houseman provide plenty of backstage detail. **Academy Awards:** Best Supporting Actress: Gloria Grahame; Best Screenplay; Best Black-and-White Cinematography; Best Costume Design (B&W); Best Art Direction—Set Decoration (B&W). **Cast:** Kirk Douglas, Lana Turner, Dick Powell, Gloria Grahame, Barry Sullivan, Walter Pidgeon, Gilbert Roland, Leo G. Carroll, Vanessa Brown, Paul Stewart. **Credits:** Dir: Vincente Minnelli; Prod: John Houseman; Writer: Charles Schnee; Story: George Bradshaw; DP: Robert Surtees; Ed: Conrad A. Nervig; Prod Design: Cedric Gibbons, Edward C. Carfagno; Composer: David Raskin; Costumes: Helen Rose; SFX: A. Arnold Gillespie, Warren Newcombe; Set Designer: Edwin B. Willis, Keogh Gleason. B&W, 123 min. VHS, LASER

Bad Company
(1972) Paramount
Director Benton's first feature depicts two Civil War deserters who slowly make their way west, all the time drifting deeper and deeper into a life of crime. An underestimated gem. **Cast:** Jeff Bridges, Barry Brown, Jim Davis,

John Savage, Ned Wertimer, David Huddleston. **Credits:** Dir: Robert Benton; Prod: Stanley R. Jaffe; Writer: David Newman, Robert Benton; DP: Gordon Willis; Ed: Ralph Rosenblum; Prod Design: Robert Gundlach; Composer: Harvey Schmidt; Set Designer: Audrey Blasdel-Goddard. Color, 94 min. VHS, LASER

Bad Day at Black Rock
(1955) MGM
A taut suspense story that seems to be always teetering on the edge of explosive violence. Tracy commands attention as a one-armed man who tames the ruffians who run roughshod over a weatherbeaten desert town. In the process, he uncovers the town's secrets and fulfills a promise made to the man who saved his life. A powerful, influential film. Based on Howard Breslin's novel. Academy Award Nominations: 3, including Best Director; Best Actor: Spencer Tracy; Best Screenplay. **Cast:** Spencer Tracy, Robert Ryan, Ernest Borgnine, Lee Marvin, Anne Francis, Walter Brennan, Dean Jagger, John Ericson, Russell Collins. **Credits:** Dir: John Sturges; Prod: Dore Schary; Writer: Millard Kaufman, Don McGuire; Story: Howard Briskin; DP: William C. Mellor; Ed: Newell P. Kimlin; Prod Design: Cedric Gibbons, Malcolm F. Brown; Composer: Andre Previn; Set Designer: Edwin B. Willis, Fred M. MacLean. Color, 83 min. VHS, LASER

The Badlanders
(1958) MGM
Well-realized remake of *The Asphalt Jungle,* with a western setting. Two men, the Dutchman and McBain, have just been released from the Arizona Territorial Prison. Their plan is to pull off one last heist, which will support them forever. But along comes a wandering geologist to foil their scheme by trying to steal $200,000 in gold from under their noses. As the double-crosses pile, so does the tension. Borgnine and Ladd are magnificent as the ex-cons. Based on the novel by W. R. Burnett. **Cast:** Alan Ladd, Ernest Borgnine, Katy Jurado, Claire Kelly, Kent Smith, Nehemiah Persoff, Robert Emhardt. **Credits:** Dir: Delmer Daves; Prod: Aaron Rosenberg; Writer: Richard Collins; Story: W. R. Burnett; DP: John F. Seitz. Color, 83 min. VHS

Badlands
(1973) Warner Bros.
Director Malick's debut is based on the Charles Starkweather murder spree of the 1950s. A South Dakota garbage

collector woos a high school naif away from her father—and kills him—and the two embark on a statewide killing binge. A slice of demented Americana, made all the more disturbing by Malick's understated direction and Sheen's chillingly matter-of-fact portrayal. Selected as a National Film Registry Outstanding Film. **Cast:** Martin Sheen, Sissy Spacek, Ramon Bieri, Warren Oates, Alan Vint. **Credits:** Dir: Terrence Malick; Prod: Terrence Malick; Writer: Terrence Malick; DP: Tak Fujimoto, Brian Probyn, Stevan Larner; Ed: Robert Estrin; Prod Design: Jack Fisk; Composer: George Tipton. Color, 97 min. **VHS, LASER**

Badlands of Dakota
(1941) Universal
This no-holds-barred Gold Rush Western features Calamity Jane (Farmer), General George Armstrong Custer (Richards), Wild Bill Hickok (Dix), and what appears to be most of the great Sioux Nation—all on the warpath, of course. Two rival brothers, Sheriff Jim Holliday (Stack) and outlaw Bob Holliday (Crawford), compete for the affections of the lovely Western gal Anne Grayson (Rutherford). When gold is discovered in the Black Hills history erupts around them. **Cast:** Robert Stack, Ann Rutherford, Richard Dix, Frances Farmer, Broderick Crawford, Hugh Herbert, Andy Devine, Lon Chaney, Jr., Fuzzy Knight, Addison Richards. **Credits:** Dir: Alfred E. Green; Prod: George Waggner; Writer: Gerald Geraghty, Harold Shumate; DP: Stanley Cortez; Composer: Hans J. Salter. B&W, 74 min.

The Bad Man
(1941) MGM
The story of Mexican bandit, Pancho Lopez, is told with a comic air by Wallace Beery. Lopez proves his worth by coming to the aid of future President Ronald Reagan and his grandfather, played by movie royalty, Lionel Barrymore. The two men are ranchers who are about to lose their land, having to default on their mortgage. Lopez owes the ranchers for having once saved his life. To repay the debt, he helps them attempt to save the ranch. **Cast:** Lionel Barrymore, Laraine Day, Ronald Reagan, Henry Travers, Chris-Pin Martin, Tom Conway, Chill Wills, Nydia Westman, Charles Stevens, Wallace Beery. **Credits:** Dir: Richard Thorpe; Prod: J. Walter Ruben; Writer: Wells Root; Story: Porter Emerson Browne; DP: Clyde De Vinna; Ed: Conrad A. Nervig; Prod Design: Cedric Gibbons; Composer: Franz Waxman. B&W, 70 min.

Badman's Territory
(1946) RKO
A workmanlike Western, featuring Scott as a sheriff forced to enter the lawless territory of the Dalton Boys and Jesse James. Naturally, many gunfights ensue. Stay away from the colorized version. **Cast:** Randolph Scott, Ann Richards, George "Gabby" Hayes, Ray Collins, Chief Thundercloud. **Credits:** Dir: Tim Whelan; Prod: Nat Holt; Writer: Jack Natteford, Luci Ward, Clarence Upson Young, Bess Taffel; DP: Robert DeGrasse; Ed: Philip Martin; Prod Design: Albert S. D'Agostino, Walter E. Keller; Composer: Roy Webb; Costumes: Renie; Set Designer: Darrell Silvera. B&W, 98 min. **VHS**

Bad Men of Missouri
(1941) Warner Bros.
Outlaws and the Wild West have always had a strong relationship with cinema, though this puts an oddly positive light on the Younger brothers, a criminal posse who took up with the more famous Jesse James gang. The Youngers are portrayed sympathetically, as crime becomes their way of life only after seeing their friends and family horribly murdered by carpetbaggers from the north. Though based on true characters, the truth is stretched to the extreme. **Cast:** Dennis Morgan, Wayne Morris, Arthur Kennedy, Jane Wyman, Victor Jory, Alan Baxter, Walter Catlett, Howard Da Silva, Faye Emerson, Russell Simpson. **Credits:** Dir: Ray Enright; Prod: Harlan Thompson; Writer: Charles Grayson; Story: Robert E. Kent; DP: Arthur Todd; Ed: Clarence Kolster; Composer: Howard Jackson; Costumes: Milo Anderson. B&W, 74 min.

The Bad News Bears
(1976) Paramount
An entertaining family comedy about a hopeless Little League team that scores big when it acquires a new coach. Matthau is Morris Buttermaker, a grouchy, beer-guzzling pool cleaner who takes the position for some extra cash. When he realizes that his "players" are a bunch of talentless misfits, he signs up two secret weapons: Amanda Whurlizer, the daughter of an ex-girlfriend who also happens to be an awesome pitcher, and Kelly Leak, a motorcycle-riding punk who is unarguably the best player in the area. With their new lineup in place, the Bears breeze their way into the championship game where they must battle their arch-rivals, the Yankees, in order to get revenge and win the title. **Cast:** Walter Matthau, Tatum O'Neal, Vic

Morrow, Joyce Van Patten. **Credits:** Dir: Michael Ritchie; Prod: Stanley R. Jaffe; DP: John A. Alonzo; Ed: Richard A. Harris; Prod Design: Polly Platt; Composer: Jerry Fielding; Set Designer: Cheryal Kearney. Color, 102 min. **VHS, LASER**

The Bad News Bears Go to Japan
(1978) Paramount
The delinquents of the diamond are back for the final installment of the series. Curtis is enjoyable as a talent agent who's out to exploit the kids when they travel to the Orient for the Little League World Series in Tokyo. Their opponent is a team from Japan. Their mission? Win the game and manage to return without starting World War III. **Cast:** Tony Curtis, Jackie Earle Haley, Tomisaburo Wakayama, George Wyner. **Credits:** Dir: John Berry; Prod: Michael Ritchie; Writer: Bill Lancaster; DP: Gene Polito; Ed: Richard A. Harris. Color, 102 min. **VHS, LASER**

The Bad News Bears in Breaking Training
(1977) Paramount
This is the sequel that begins with the Bears reigning supreme as the Little League champions of California. Kelly, the Bears' star player, travels with the team to the Houston Astrodome along with his estranged father, who is now the coach. They're playing a between-inning game against the local champs, the Houston Toros, for the chance to go to Japan and play the best that the east has to offer. **Cast:** William Devane, Clifton James, Jackie Earle Haley, Jimmy Baio, Chris Barnes. **Credits:** Dir: Michael Pressman; Prod: Leonard J. Goldberg; Writer: Paul Brickman; DP: Fred Koenekamp; Ed: John W. Wheeler; Composer: Craig Safan. Color, 105 min. **VHS, LASER**

The Bad Seed
(1956) Warner Bros.
A suspenseful thriller about a mother who slowly comes to the ghastly conclusion that her eight-year-old daughter is responsible for a string of brutal murders. Kelly was awarded an Oscar nomination for her strong portrayal of a woman who also discovers that the recurring nightmare she's been having is rooted in her past. Based on Maxwell Anderson's play, this picture was the inspiration for 1994's *The Good Son,* as well as the 1985 TV movie of the same name. Winner of a Golden Globe for Best Supporting Actress: Eileen Heckart. **Cast:** Nancy

Kelly, Patty McCormack, Eileen Heckart, Henry Jones, Evelyn Varden, William Hopper, Paul Fix, Jesse White. **Credits:** Dir: Mervyn Le Roy; Writer: John Lee Mahin; Story: Maxwell Anderson, William March; DP: Harold Rosson; Composer: Alex North. B&W, 129 min. **VHS, LASER**

Baker's Hawk
(1976)
A young boy's friendship with the reclusive Ives and a red-tailed hawk teaches him the importance of friendship. He also matures by helping his family fight against local extremists. This is a solid family drama with some beautiful Western scenery. **Cast:** Clint Walker, Diane Baker, Burl Ives, Lee Montgomery, Alan Young. **Credits:** Dir: Lyman Dayton; Prod: Lyman Dayton; Writer: Dan Greer, Hal Harrison; Story: Jack Bickham; DP: Bernie Abramson; Ed: Parkie Singh; Prod Design: Bill Kenney; Composer: Lex de Azevedo. Color, 98 min. **VHS, DVD**

Balalaika
(1939) MGM
A musical romance, with Eddy riding at the head of a Cossack singing regiment and falling tunefully in love with Massey. Based on the operetta by Eric Maschwitz. Academy Award Nomination for Best Sound Recording. **Cast:** Nelson Eddy, Ilona Massey, Frank Morgan, Lionel Atwill, George Tobias, Charlie Ruggles, C. Aubrey Smith, Walter Woolf King, Joyce Compton. **Credits:** Dir: Reinhold Schunzel; Prod: Lawrence Weingarten; Writer: Jacques Deval, Leon Gordon, Charles Bennett; Story: Eric Maschwitz; DP: Joseph Ruttenberg, Karl Freund; Ed: George Boemler; Prod Design: Cedric Gibbons, Eddie Imazu; Choreographer: Ernst Matray; Composer: Herbert Stothart; Costumes: Adrian; Set Designer: Edwin B. Willis. B&W, 91 min. **VHS**

Ballad of Cable Hogue
(1970) Warner Bros.
After being left to die in the desert by his unscrupulous, greedy partners, a tough prospector formulates an involved revenge scheme. A first-rate Peckinpah Western. **Cast:** Jason Robards, Stella Stevens, David Warner, Strother Martin, L. Q. Jones, Slim Pickens, Peter Whitney, R. G. Armstrong, Gene Evans. **Credits:** Dir: Sam Peckinpah; Prod: Sam Peckinpah, Phil Feldman, William D. Faralla; Writer: John Crawford, Edmund Penney; DP: Lucien Ballard; Ed: Frank Santillo, Lou Lombardo; Prod Design: Leroy Cole-

man; Composer: Jerry Goldsmith; Costumes: Robert Fletcher. Color, 122 min. **VHS, LASER**

Ball of Fire
(1941) Warner Bros.
When Cooper and his sheltered, highbrow colleagues begin work on a new encyclopedia, he enlists the aid of Stanwyck to help explain slang, unaware that she is a gangster moll being hidden by her on-the-lam boyfriend. Stanwyck's earthiness soon captivates the sheltered professor, who learns to pitch woo and fists as well as slang. Wilder and Brackett were deservedly nominated for an Academy Award for Best Original Story. Academy Award Nominations: 4, including Best Actress: Barbara Stanwyck; Best Original Story. **Cast:** Gary Cooper, Barbara Stanwyck, Oscar Homolka, Dana Andrews, Henry Travers, S. Z. Sakall, Tully Marshall, Leonid Kinskey, Richard Haydn, Aubrey Mather. **Credits:** Dir: Howard Hawks; Prod: Samuel Goldwyn; Writer: Charles Brackett, Billy Wilder, Thomas Monroe; DP: Gregg Toland; Ed: Daniel Mandell; Prod Design: Perry Ferguson; Composer: Alfred Newman; Set Designer: Howard Bristol. B&W, 116 min. **VHS, DVD**

Bambi
(1942) Disney
In Disney's legendary animated forest fable, a fawn named Bambi is born, and his mother is soon killed by a hunter. Bambi grows up befriending such memorable animal babies as the irrepressible Thumper and receiving a sometimes unkind education from Mother Nature. Eventually, he comes of age, completing the cycle of life and taking his father's place. A kids' classic that no one should miss. Academy Award Nominations: 3, including Best Song ("Love Is a Song"). Also won a Golden Globe for Special Achievements: Walt Disney. **Cast:** Peter Behn, Paula Winslowe, Bobby Stewart, Cammie King, Donnie Dunagan, Hardie Albright, John Sutherland, Sam Edwards, Sterling Holloway, Ann Gillis. **Credits:** Dir: David D. Hand; Prod: Walt Disney; Writer: Perce Pearce, Larry Morey; Story: Felix Salten; Composer: Frank Churchill, Edward Plumb. Color, 69 min. **VHS, LASER**

Bandido
(1956) United Artists
In this historical action picture toughguy soldier-of-fortune Mitchum figures the 1916 Mexican revolution could put him in the way of some serious pesos. Rebel leader Colonel Escobar (Roland)

hires him to heist an arms shipment coming by way of another American mercenary, Kennedy (Scott). It's all a matter of routine for Wilson until he gets a load of Kennedy's wife. Now he's in it for more than money. **Cast:** Robert Mitchum, Ursula Thiess, Gilbert Roland, Zachary Scott, Rodolfo Acosta, Jose Torvay, Henry Brandon, Douglas Fowley, Victor Junco, Gilbert Roland. **Credits:** Dir: Richard Fleischer; Prod: Robert Jacks; Writer: Earl Felton; DP: Ernest Laszlo; Ed: Robert Golden; Prod Design: Jack Marton Smith; Composer: Max Steiner. Color, 92 min.

Bandolero!
(1968) Fox
After being sentenced to death for their participation in a bank robbery, a pair of outlaw brothers take a beautiful woman hostage and flee across the Mexican desert. Naturally, she falls for one of them, even though her husband was killed in the bank robbery. Though the plot stretches credulity, this one's still worth watching for the odd-ball casting. **Cast:** James Stewart, Dean Martin, Raquel Welch, George Kennedy, Will Geer, Andrew Prine. **Credits:** Dir: Andrew V. McLaglen; Prod: Robert L. Jacks; Writer: James Lee Barrett; Story: Stanley L. Hough; DP: William Clothier; Ed: Folmar Blangsted; Prod Design: Alfred Sweeney, Jack Martin Smith; Composer: Jerry Goldsmith. Color, 106 min. **VHS**

The Band Wagon
(1953) MGM
Fading movie musical star Tony Hunter (Astaire), down and out in Hollywood, decides to try his luck on the Broadway stage. Unfortunately, the simple hoofer discovers that a pretentious director has control of the project, and that instead of good humor, happy songs, and a tapping chorus line, there'll be lengthy speeches, heavy drama, and lots of deep soul-searching. Even worse, Tony's expected to dance with a classical ballerina (Charisse)! The play, to no one's surprise, lays an egg. But now Tony takes charge, and he's out to prove the show must go on—his way! Some of the dazzling Astaire-Charisse dance numbers include "Triplets," "Girl Hunt," "Dancing in the Dark," and "That's Entertainment." Academy Award Nominations: 3, including Best Screenplay; Best Score. **Cast:** Fred Astaire, Cyd Charisse, Oscar Levant, Nanette Fabray, Jack Buchanan, James Mitchell. **Credits:** Dir: Vincente Minnelli; Prod: Arthur Freed; Writer: Betty Comden, Adolph Green. Color, 119 min. **VHS, LASER**

Banjo on My Knee

(1936) Fox
Riverboat musical about a man who runs away on his wedding night, thinking he has killed a man. His wife soon runs off, too, with the man her husband thinks he killed. They quickly sour on each other, and she gets a job as a dishwasher in the same town her husband is hiding in. Watchable solely for Stanwyck and McCrea. **Cast:** Barbara Stanwyck, Joel McCrea, Walter Brennan, Helen Westley. **Credits:** Dir: John Cromwell; Prod: Darryl F. Zanuck, Nunnally Johnson; Writer: Nunnally Johnson; DP: Ernest Palmer; Prod Design: Thomas Little; Composer: Harold Adamson, Arthur Lange; Art Director: Hans Peters. B&W, 95 min.

The Bank Dick

(1940) Universal
Fields, crediting himself as "Mahatma Kane Jeeves," wrote this comedy classic in which he portrays Souse (pronounced *Soo-zay*), a lush who inadvertently trips a bank robber and ends up becoming a bank detective. He takes full advantage of his new job and embezzles bank funds to finance a fly-by-night mining operation. Notable for being Fields's last major role and for what many consider to be the funniest chase sequence in cinematic history. A National Film Registry Outstanding Film. **Cast:** W. C. Fields, Cora Witherspoon, Una Merkel, Evelyn Del Rio. **Credits:** Dir: Edward Cline; Writer: W. C. Fields; DP: Milton Krasner; Ed: Arthur Hilton. B&W, 73 min. VHS, LASER

Barabbas

(1962) Columbia
This rich production (including a real solar eclipse) with an all-star cast tells the story of the murderer Barabbas, who was freed in place of Jesus. Barabbas's life and soul are forever changed as a result of the miracle he witnessed. **Cast:** Anthony Quinn, Silvana Mangano, Jack Palance, Ernest Borgnine, Katy Jurado, Harry Andrews, Vittorio Gassman, Arthur Kennedy, Valentina Cortese, Michael Gwynn. **Credits:** Dir: Richard Fleischer; Prod: Dino De Laurentiis; Writer: Christopher Fry, Nigel Balchin, Diego Fabbri, Ivo Perilli; Story: Par Lagerkvist; DP: Aldo Tonti; Ed: Raymond Poulton; Prod Design: Mario Chiari; Composer: Mario Nascimbene; Costumes: Maria DeMatteis. Color, 134 min. VHS

Barbary Coast

(1935) United Artists
Hecht and MacArthur team with Hawks for a colorful story of a music-hall performer and a saloon keeper at odds during San Francisco's bare-knuckle Gold Rush days. Academy Award Nominations: Best Cinematography. **Cast:** Walter Brennan, Miriam Hopkins, Edward G. Robinson, Joel McCrea, Frank Craven, Donald Meek. **Credits:** Dir: Howard Hawks; Prod: Samuel Goldwyn; Writer: Ben Hecht, Charles MacArthur; DP: Ray June; Ed: Edward Curtiss; Composer: Alfred Newman. B&W, 91 min. VHS, LASER

The Barefoot Contessa

(1954) United Artists
A famous film writer and director (Bogart) stands by the grave of a beautiful Hollywood star and contemplates her life in a series of flashbacks. Lovely Maria Vargas (Gardner) works as a flamenco dancer at a second-rate club when a trio of movieland bigwigs discovers her. Soon she's acquired fame, riches, and love. On the surface, it seems as if she has it all, but a dark secret in her marriage leads to jealousy, tragedy, and murder. Spicy dialogue from Mankiewicz keeps things interesting. Won a Golden Globe for Best Supporting Actor. **Academy Awards:** Best Supporting Actor: Edmond O'Brien. **Cast:** Humphrey Bogart, Ava Gardner, Edmond O'Brien, Marius Goring, Rossano Brazzi, Valentina Cortese, Elizabeth Sellars, Warren Stevens, Franco Interlenghi, Mari Aldon. **Credits:** Dir: Joseph L. Mankiewicz; Writer: Joseph L. Mankiewicz; DP: Jack Cardiff; Ed: William Hornbeck; Prod Design: Arrigo Equini; Composer: Mario Nascimbene; Costumes: Sorelle Fontana. Color, 128 min. VHS

Barefoot in the Park

(1967) Paramount
Neil Simon's comedy features Redford as a conservative young lawyer and Fonda as his spontaneous bride, roughing it in New York. This was director Gene Saks's debut. Academy Award Nominations: Best Supporting Actress: Mildred Natwick. **Cast:** Robert Redford, Jane Fonda, Charles Boyer, Mildred Natwick, Herb Edelman, Mabel Albertson, Fritz Feld. **Credits:** Dir: Gene Saks; Prod: Hal B. Wallis; Writer: Neil Simon; DP: Joseph La Shelle; Ed: William A. Lyon; Composer: Neal Hefti; Costumes: Edith Head. Color, 106 min. VHS, LASER

The Barkleys of Broadway

(1949) MGM
Astaire and Rogers, whose last joint project had been made 10 years before, come together one final time for this film. The magical pair play performers Josh and Dinah Barkley, whose act—and marriage—break up when Dinah decides to become a "serious actress." Among the unforgettable numbers are "They Can't Take That Away from Me" (which Astaire and Rogers first performed in 1937's *Shall We Dance*), "Shoes with Wings On," "Swing Trot," and "You'd Be So Hard to Replace." **Academy Awards:** Special Achievement Awards: Fred Astaire. **Cast:** Fred Astaire, Ginger Rogers, Oscar Levant, Billie Burke, Gale Robbins, Jacques Francois. **Credits:** Dir: Charles Walters; Prod: Arthur Freed; Writer: Betty Comden, Adolph Green; DP: Harry Stradling; Ed: Albert Akst; Prod Design: Cedric Gibbons, Edward C. Carfagno; Choreographer: Hermes Pan, Robert Alton; Composer: Harry Warren, Ira Gershwin; Costumes: Irene. Color, 110 min. VHS, LASER

The Barretts of Wimpole Street

(1934) MGM
A somber drama about the relationship between the poets Elizabeth Barrett and Robert Browning. The Barrett family lives in a beautiful house on Wimpole Street. But beyond the façade of their lovely home lies a tyrannical patriarch who stifles his daughter Elizabeth. The poor girl is a bed-ridden invalid who lives in solitude with her poetry and her little dog. But when she meets Browning, a handsome suitor and fellow poet, she finds the strength to make a miraculous recovery. Academy Award Nominations: Best Picture; Best Actress: Norma Shearer. **Cast:** Fredric March, Charles Laughton, Norma Shearer, Maureen O'Sullivan, Katherine Alexander, Una O'Connor, Ian Wolfe, Ralph Forbes. **Credits:** Dir: Sidney Franklin; Prod: Irving Thalberg; Writer: Ernest Vajda, Claudine West, Donald Stewart; Story: Rudolph Besier; DP: William Daniels; Ed: Margaret Booth; Prod Design: Cedric Gibbons; Costumes: Adrian. B&W, 110 min. VHS, LASER

Barry Lyndon

(1975) Warner Bros.
A breathtakingly sumptuous production based on the novel by William Thackeray. An 18th-century rogue yearns for success, but as he succeeds in his quest for riches, he finds the glittering prizes ring hollow. Kubrick's eye for detail and ear for period music combined with gorgeous natural-light cinematography. Academy Award Nominations: 7, including Best Picture; Best Director; Best (Adapted)

Screenplay. **Academy Awards:** Best Cinematography; Best Costume Design; Best Art Direction—Set Decoration; Best Original Song Score and Adaptation. **Cast:** Ryan O'Neal, Marisa Berenson, Patrick Magee, Hardy Kruger, Steven Berkoff, Gay Hamilton, Marie Kean, Murray Melvin, Andre Morell, Leonard Rossiter. **Credits:** Dir: Stanley Kubrick; Prod: Stanley Kubrick; Writer: Stanley Kubrick; Story: William Makepeace Thackeray; DP: John Alcott; Ed: Tony Lawson; Prod Design: Ken Adam; Composer: Leonard Rosenman; Set Designer: Vernon Dixon. Color, 185 min. **VHS, LASER**

Bataan
(1943) MGM
A group of doomed Americans and Filipinos hold a bridge against invading Japanese. Over-the-top flag waving made this a based-on-fact Hollywood blockbuster of the war era, despite a pretty fake-looking jungle. Avoid the colorized version. **Cast:** Robert Taylor, George Murphy, Thomas Mitchell, Lloyd Nolan, Lee Bowman, Robert Walker, Desi Arnaz, Barry Nelson, Philip Terry. **Credits:** Dir: Tay Garnett; Prod: Irving Starr; Writer: Robert Andrews; DP: Sidney Wagner; Ed: George White; Composer: Bronislau Kaper; SFX: A. Arnold Gillespie, Warren Newcombe. B&W, 114 min. **VHS**

Bathing Beauty
(1944) MGM
Esther Williams's first starring role, but this movie is notable mostly for its spectacular water-ballet finale. Lots of music, lots of watery escapades, but pretty thin laughs. **Cast:** Red Skelton, Esther Williams, Basil Rathbone, Ethel Smith, Xavier Cugat, Harry James, Keenan Wynn, Bill Goodwin. **Credits:** Dir: George Sidney; Prod: Jack Cummings; Writer: Dorothy Kingsley, Allan Boretz, Frank Waldman, Joseph Schrank; Story: Kenneth Earl, M. M. Musselman; DP: Harry Stradling; Ed: Blanche Sewell; Choreographer: John Murray Anderson; Composer: Johnny Green. Color, 101 min. **VHS, LASER**

The Battle at Apache Pass
(1952) Universal
Cochise aims to prevent Geronimo from going on the warpath in this Western. A treacherous Indian Affairs representative has stirred Geromino to action, convincing the great warrior that present treaties improperly restrain his appointed destiny. Cochise, leader of the Apaches, is concerned that Geronimo's menace will have harmful repercussions for other tribes and decides

to work with a U.S. cavalry officer to meet the threat. Bustling battles in full Technicolor splendor. **Cast:** John Lund, Jeff Chandler, Beverly Tyler, Susan Cabot, John Hudson, James Best, Regis Toomey, Richard Egan, Hugh O'Brian, Palmer Lee. **Credits:** Dir: George Sherman, Bruce Cowling; Prod: Leonard Goldstein; Writer: Gerald Drayson Adams; DP: Victor Milner; Ed: Charles Boyle; Composer: Hans J. Salter. Color, 85 min.

Battle Cry
(1955) Warner Bros.
Nonstop action in a WWII epic based on a Uris novel with an all-star cast. The heroic exploits of a Marine battalion are followed from basic training through the bloody invasion of Saipan. A newsreel and "Speedy Gonzales" cartoon are a part of the video package. Academy Award Nomination for Scoring of a Dramatic or Comedy Picture. **Cast:** Van Heflin, Aldo Ray, Mona Freeman, Nancy Olson, James Whitmore, Tab Hunter, Raymond Massey, Dorothy Malone, Anne Francis, William Campbell. **Credits:** Dir: Raoul Walsh; Prod: Raoul Walsh; Writer: Leon Uris; DP: Sid Hickox; Ed: William Ziegler; Prod Design: John Beckman; Composer: Max Steiner; Costumes: Moss Mabry; Set Designer: William Wallace. Color, 169 min. **VHS, LASER**

Battle for the Planet of the Apes
(1973) Fox
The fifth and final episode in the Planet of the Apes series. Set in the year 2670, this is the story of a superior race of apes that lives aboveground, trying to coexist peacefully with a community of conquered human mutants who reside beneath the earth. Footage from the previous installments is effective in providing background information as flashbacks in an attempt to bring the series to a logical finish. A later television series attempted to rekindle original plotlines with newer ones. **Cast:** Roddy McDowall, Claude Akins, John Huston, Paul Williams, Lew Ayres, Natalie Trundy, Severn Darden. **Credits:** Dir: J. Lee Thompson; Prod: Arthur P. Jacobs; Writer: John William Corrington, Joyce H. Corrington; Story: Paul Dehn; DP: Richard H. Kline; Ed: John C. Horger, Alan Jaggs; Composer: Leonard Rosenman. Color, 86 min. **VHS, LASER**

Battleground
(1949) MGM
The story of a U.S. Army division in the European Theater at the end of

WWII. In a last-ditch effort to turn the tide of the war, the Germans launch their famous final attack, the Battle of the Bulge. Detailed study of the drama within a fighting unit of men brought together by war. Won Golden Globes for Best Supporting Actor; Best Screenplay. **Academy Awards:** Best Black-and-White Cinematography; Best Story and Screenplay. **Cast:** Van Johnson, John Hodiak, Ricardo Montalban, George Murphy, Marshall Thompson, Denise Darcel, Richard Jaeckel, James Whitmore, James Arness, Scotty Beckett. **Credits:** Dir: William Wellman; Prod: Dore Schary; Writer: Robert Pirosh; DP: Paul C. Vogel; Ed: John Dunning; Prod Design: Cedric Gibbons, Hans Peters; Composer: Lennie Hayton; SFX: Peter Ballbusch; Set Designer: Edwin B. Willis. B&W, 118 min. **VHS, LASER**

Battle Hymn
(1957) Universal
Colonel Dean Hess, a WWII pilot, launches an air attack that inadvertently obliterates a German orphanage in the process. After the war, Hess becomes a minister and tries desperately to deal with the guilt he retains from the bombing. After the Korean War erupts, Hess learns about hundreds of Korean children left orphaned by the fighting. In an attempt to help the children and the war effort, he volunteers to fly missions and train pilots. Hoping for redemption and as an act of penance, Hess founds an orphanage for the Korean war orphans. The real Col. Dean Hess served as technical adviser for the production. The filmmakers hired actual Korean orphans, flown in to Universal Studios, to play themselves. Awarded a Golden Globe for Best Film Promoting International Understanding. **Cast:** Rock Hudson, Martha Hyer, Dan Duryea, Don DeFore, Anna Kashfi, Jock Mahoney, Carl Benton Reid, James Edwards. **Credits:** Dir: Douglas Sirk; Prod: Ross Hunter; Writer: Charles Grayson, Vincent B. Evans; DP: Russell Metty; Ed: Russell Schoengarth; Prod Design: Alexander Golitzen; Composer: Frank Skinner; Costumes: Bill Thomas; Set Designer: Oliver Emert, Russell A. Gausman. Color, 109 min. **VHS**

Battle of Midway
(1942)
A U.S. Navy–sponsored documentary about one of the most famous naval battles of WWII. Celebrated director Ford (Commander John Ford, U.S.N., Ret.) presents the battle as it happened with little comment or post-

Beach Blanket Bingo (1965)

production effects. Footage is captured from every possible vantage point, with Ford and his cameraman risking their lives. **Cast:** Donald Crisp, Henry Fonda, Jane Darwell, Charlton Heston, Robert Mitchum, Glenn Ford, Edward Albert, James Coburn, Hal Holbrook, Toshiro Mifune. **Credits:** Dir: Jack Smight; Prod: Walter Mirisch; Writer: Donald Sanford; DP: Harry Stradling; Ed: Frank J. Urioste, Robert W. Swink; Prod Design: Walter Tyler; Composer: John Williams; SFX: Jack McMasters; Set Designer: John M. Dwyer. B&W and Color, 40 min. **VHS**

Battle Zone
(1952) Allied Artists
Two U.S. Marine photographers aim to document the violent action of the Korean War while fighting for the romantic attention of the same attractive Red Cross volunteer. Their work takes place in the Yalu zone and brings them behind enemy lines more than once. The picture intersperses actual combat and camp footage of the Korean War with studio footage directed by Selander. **Cast:** John Hodiak, Linda Christian, Stephen McNally, Martin Milner, Dave Willock, Jack Larson, Richard Emory, Philip Ahn, John Fontaine, Todd Karnes. **Credits:** Dir: Lesley Selander; Prod: Walter Wanger; Writer: Steve Fisher; DP: Ernest Miller; Ed: Jack Ogilvie; Composer: Marlin Skiles. B&W, 81 min.

Beach Blanket Bingo
(1965) AIP
The fifth and arguably best known of the Avalon-Funicello surfing-beach series. Tells the story of a boy who falls in love with a beautiful girl, only to find that she is actually a mermaid. All-star ensemble cast makes for an amusing watch. Sequel is *How to Stuff a Wild Bikini.* **Cast:** Frankie Avalon, Annette Funicello, Linda Evans, Paul Lynde. **Credits:** Dir: William Asher; Prod: Samuel Z. Arkoff, James H. Nicholson; Writer: William Asher, Leo Townsend; DP: Floyd Crosby; Ed: Fred Feitshans, Eve Newman; Prod Design: Howard Campbell; Composer: Les Baxter. Color, 98 min. **VHS, LASER**

Beachhead
(1954) United Artists
War film about Marines in the Pacific who try to transport information through the jungle on the eve of a big assault. Along the way, the Marines rescue a French planter and his daughter. **Cast:** Dan Aoki, Akira Fukunaga, Tony Curtis, John Doucette, Eduard Franz, Alan Wells, Skip Homeier, Frank Lovejoy, Mary Murphy. **Credits:** Dir: Stuart Heisler; Prod: Howard W. Koch; Writer: Richard Alan Simmons. Color, 89 min.

Beach Party
(1963) AIP
An anthropologist (Cummings) and his lovely assistant travel to the wilds of Southern California's beaches to study the indigenous beach population. In their attempts to study the local population and observe customs and rituals, the two discover that the beach denizens aren't nearly so "wild" as science describes them. The first of the Avalon-Funicello beach movies to depict the social and musical scene on Southern California's beaches. It should be noted that Funicello and Avalon were not from California but Philadelphia, a town noted for neither sand nor surf. **Cast:** Robert Cummings, Dorothy Malone, Frankie Avalon, Annette Funicello, Morey Amsterdam, Vincent Price, Harvey Lembeck. **Credits:** Dir: William Asher; Prod: James H. Nicholson; Writer: Lou Rusoff; DP: Kay Norton; Ed: Homer Powell; Composer: Les Baxter; Costumes: Marjorie Corso. Color, 98 min. **VHS**

Beast from 20,000 Fathoms
(1953) Warner Bros.
A long-hibernating and ostensibly extinct rhedosaurus is roused from his eternal slumber by an atomic blast (and Harryhausen's effects). Emerging from the sea, the rhedosaurus wreaks havoc in every direction, leveling cities and amusement parks in his path. Based on Ray Bradbury's short story "The Fog Horn." **Cast:** Paul Christian, Paula Raymond, Cecil Kellaway, Donald Woods, Lee Van Cleef, Ross Elliott, Kenneth Tobey. **Credits:** Dir: Eugene Lourie; Prod: Hal E. Chester, Jack Dietz, Bernard W. Burton; Writer: Lou Morheim, Fred Freiburger; Story: Ray Bradbury; DP: Jack Russell; Composer: David Buttolph; SFX: Ray Harryhausen. B&W, 80 min. **VHS**

The Beast with Five Fingers
(1946) MGM
A partially paralyzed concert pianist continues to play with his left hand. But his sudden violent death unleashes a profound terror—his disembodied hand returns to commit a series of murders and traumatize Lorre, his secretary. No matter what Lorre tries to do to the hand (crush it, burn it, bury it), it continues to haunt the villagers. Creative camera work, as well as the interaction between Lorre and the hand, make this necessary viewing for horror historians. **Cast:** Peter Lorre, Robert Alda, Andrea King, Victor Francen, J. Carrol Naish. **Credits:** Dir: Robert Florey; Prod: William Jacobs; Writer: Curt Siodmak; DP: Wesley Anderson; Composer: Max Steiner. Color, 89 min. **VHS**

Beat the Devil

(1954) United Artists

John Huston and Truman Capote co-wrote the screenplay while working on location. A biting parody of *The Maltese Falcon* and other '40s detective movies in which Bogart often starred (and Huston often directed). The story follows a group of travelers on a steamboat who all hope to beat the others to the uranium fields of Northern Africa. While not a commercial success upon its release, the film has come to define the genre of spy movie spoofs. **Cast:** Humphrey Bogart, Jennifer Jones, Gina Lollobrigida, Peter Lorre, Robert Morley, Edward Underdown, Ivor Barnard, Bernard Lee, Marco Tulli. **Credits:** Dir: John Huston; Writer: John Huston, Truman Capote; Story: James Helvick; DP: Oswald Morris; Ed: Ralph Kemplen; Prod Design: Wilfred Shingleton; Composer: Franco Mannino. B&W, 93 min. **VHS, LASER**

Beau Brummel

(1954) MGM

Lavishly told story of George Bryan Brummel, a commoner born in the era of Napoleon who uses wit, brilliance, and sartorial flair to align himself with the future King George IV. Lush settings in authentic locations and Taylor in Regency costume make this an appealing eyeful. The 1924 silent version starred John Barrymore. **Cast:** Stewart Granger, Elizabeth Taylor, Peter Ustinov, Robert Morley, Paul Rogers, James Donald, James Hayter, Rosemary Harris, Noel Willman, Peter Bull. **Credits:** Dir: Curtis Bernhardt; Prod: Sam Zimbalist; Writer: Karl Tunberg; Story: Clyde Fitch; DP: Oswald Morris; Ed: Frank Clarke; Prod Design: Alfred Junge; Composer: Richard Addinsell; Costumes: Elizabeth Haffenden. Color, 113 min. **VHS**

Beau Geste

(1939) Paramount

An oft-remade adventure tale tells the story of three brothers who "confess" to stealing a rare gem in order to save the female culprit. The brothers in arms battle the elements and their enemies to live long enough to clear the family name. The haunting opening sequence is one of the most famous in film. Academy Award Nominations: Best Supporting Actor: Brian Donlevy; Best Interior Decoration. **Cast:** Gary Cooper, Ray Milland, Robert Preston, Susan Hayward, Brian Donlevy, J. Carrol Naish, Heather Thatcher, James Stephenson, Donald O'Connor, G. P. Huntley. **Credits:** Dir:

Beau Geste (1939)

William Wellman; Prod: William A. Wellman; Story: Robert Carson, Percival Christopher Wren; DP: Theodor Sparkuhl, Archie Stout; Ed: Thomas Scott; Prod Design: Hans Dreier, Robert Odell; Composer: Alfred Newman. B&W, 114 min. **VHS, LASER**

Beau James

(1957) Paramount

Walter Winchell himself narrates this Hollywood version of the "true story" of New York's wackiest Mayor, James J. "Jimmy" Walker (Hope). Walker's an obscure song-and-dance man who plays puppet politician for Tammany Hall gangsters. The crooks see to it he's installed in the city's most important office. As mayor, Walker spends his time chasing show-girl and movie-star Betty Compton (Miles) and avoiding the wrath of his wife Allie (Smith), while an endless assortment of crooks have their hands in the city coffers. **Cast:** Bob Hope, Vera Miles, Paul Douglas, Alexis Smith, Darren McGavin, Joe Mantell, Horace McMahon, Richard Shannon, Willis Bouchey, Sid Melton. **Credits:** Dir: Melville Shavelson; Prod: Jack Rose; Writer: Jack Rose, Melville Shavelson; Story: Gene Fowler, Jr.; DP: John F. Warren;

Ed: Floyd Knudtson; Prod Design: John B. Goodman; Composer: Joseph J. Lilley. Color, 105 min.

The Beautiful Blonde from Bashful Bend

(1949) Fox

A Sturges Western! Grable plays Freddie, a tough girl with an open mind about turning a dollar, who goes gunning for her straying boyfriend, and shoots a judge by mistake. She hides out by pretending to be a demure schoolteacher and gets involved with a mining magnate. A town dispute causes gunplay that brings Freddie to the law's attention again, inciting a shoot-out in court and another puncture to the sitting judge. Keeps getting better. **Cast:** Betty Grable, Cesar Romero, Rudy Vallee, Sterling Holloway, Olga San Juan, Hugh Herbert, El Brendel, Porter Hall, Margaret Hamilton, Esther Howard. **Credits:** Dir: Preston Sturges; Prod: Preston Sturges; Writer: Preston Sturges; Story: Earl Felton; DP: Harry Jackson; Ed: Robert Fritch; Prod Design: Lyle Wheeler, George W. Davis; Composer: Cyril Mockridge; Costumes: Rene Hubert; SFX: Fred Sersen; Set Designer: Thomas Little, Stuart A. Reiss. Color, 76 min. **VHS, LASER**

Becket

(1964) Paramount

Two of the finest actors of their generation, Burton and O'Toole, square off in this splendid production of Jean Anouilh's 1959 play. The lifelong friendship of Henry II and the Archbishop of Canterbury, Thomas Becket, is tested and ends in tragedy as Becket grows more confident and thoughtful in his position. Academy Award Nominations: 12, including Best Picture; Best Director; Best Actor: Richard Burton; Best Actor: Peter O'Toole. **Academy Awards:** Screenplay Based on Material from Another Medium. **Cast:** Richard Burton, Peter O'Toole, John Gielgud, Donald Wolfit, Martita Hunt, Pamela Brown, Sian Phillips, Paolo Stoppa. **Credits:** Dir: Peter Glenville; Prod: Hal B. Wallis; Writer: Edward Anhalt; Story: Jean Anouilh; DP: Geoffrey Unsworth; Ed: Anne V. Coates; Prod Design: Maurice Carter, John Bryan; Composer: Laurence Rosenthal; Costumes: Margaret Furse. Color, 148 min. **VHS, LASER**

Becky Sharp

(1935) RKO

The first Technicolor feature is a loose adaptation of Thackeray's *Vanity Fair*. Something of a gold digger, little orphan Becky sets her cap for Joseph Sedley, the wealthy brother of her best friend Amelia. But even the dull-witted Joseph realizes that his family would not smile upon such a union and so never proposes. Frustrated, Becky leaves the Sedley household, and, using her brains, beauty, and charm, claws her way into the upper class. Rather tough going, but worth seeing (particularly the recently restored version), a watershed movie moment. Academy Award Nomination for Best Actress: Miriam Hopkins. **Cast:** Miriam Hopkins, Frances Dee, Cedric Hardwicke, Billie Burke, Alison Skipworth, Nigel Bruce, Alan Mowbray, Colin Tapley, G. P. Huntley. **Credits:** Dir: Rouben Mamoulian; Prod: Kenneth MacGowan; Writer: Francis Edward Faragoh; Story: Langdon Mitchell, William Makepeace Thackeray; DP: Ray Rennahan; Ed: Archie Marshek; Prod Design: Robert Edmond Jones; Choreographer: Russell Lewis; Composer: Roy Webb. B&W, 83 min. VHS

The Bedford Incident
(1965) Columbia
At the peak of Cold War tensions, a U.S. naval ship discovers a Soviet submarine in the North Atlantic and proceeds to scrutinize its every move. As Captain Findlander pushes forward, relations between crew members become strained and a battle of wits ensues. Poitier plays an unfortunate reporter who went along to interview the captain, but instead gets more of a story than he'd wanted. **Cast:** Richard Widmark, Sidney Poitier, James MacArthur, Martin Balsam, Wally Cox, Donald Sutherland, Phil Brown. **Credits:** Dir: James B. Harris; Prod: James B. Harris; Writer: James Poe; DP: Gilbert Taylor; Ed: John Jympson; Composer: Gerard Schurmann. B&W, 102 min. VHS, LASER

Bedlam
(1946) RKO
An intriguing change of pace from chillmaster Lewton about an innocent girl imprisoned in a ghastly 18th-century insane asylum. Nell, an aspiring young actress, rejects the patronage of a London nobleman after learning of the aristocrat's indifference to sadistic practices at the local insane asylum. When word of Nell's accusations reach Master Sims (Karloff), the villainous director of the madhouse, the brutal "doctor" attempts to protect his own reputation by casting doubt on the young woman's sanity. Interesting because the shock depends on a more-or-less accurate depiction of authentic settings. **Cast:** Boris Karloff, Anna Lee, Richard Fraser, Ian Wolfe, Billy House, Glenn Vernon. **Credits:** Dir: Mark Robson; Prod: Val Lewton; Writer: Mark Robson, Carlos Keith; DP: Nicholas Musuraca; Ed: Lyle Boyer; Prod Design: Walter E. Keller, Albert S. D'Agostino; Composer: Roy Webb; SFX: Vernon L. Walker; Set Designer: John Sturtevant, Darrell Silvera. B&W, 79 min. VHS, LASER

Bed of Roses
(1933) RKO
This adventure-fable of redemptive love travels the Mississippi with reform-school graduates Bennett and her delightfully unsavory sidekick, Ziegfeld veteran Kelton, creating havoc as they try to steal and con their way to a life of luxury. Along the way they are rescued, literally and figuratively, by captain McCrea, who holds onboard his cotton barge the prospect of the honest love that will ultimately woo Bennett from her wayward ways and her loveless relationship with a rich New Orleans publisher. **Cast:** Constance Bennett, Joel McCrea, John Halliday, Pert Kelton, Samuel S. Hinds, Franklin Pangborn, Tom Francis. **Credits:** Dir: Gregory La Cava; Prod: Pandro S. Berman, Merian C. Cooper; Writer: Gregory La Cava, Eugene Thackery, Wanda Tuchock; DP: Charles Rosher, Jr.; Ed: Basil Wrangell; Composer: Max Steiner; Art Director: Van Nest Polglase, Charles Kirk. B&W, 70 min.

Bedtime for Bonzo
(1951) Universal
It's nature vs. nurture as Reagan steals a chimp to prove to his wouldbe father-in-law that love and a proper upbringing can improve on one's genetic inheritance. Though he provides love and understanding, the chimp unleashes no end of havoc. Perfectly good fun (though somewhat unsettling seeing the future commander in chief nursemaid to a chimp) directed by longtime *Tonight Show* producer De Cordova. **Cast:** Ronald Reagan, Diana Lynn, Walter Slezak, Jesse White, Lucille Barkley, Herbert Heyes. **Credits:** Dir: Frederick De Cordova; Prod: Michael Kraike; Writer: Val Burton, Lou Breslow; Story: Raphael Blau, Ted Berkman; DP: Carl Guthrie; Ed: Ted J. Kent; Composer: Frank Skinner. B&W, 83 min. VHS

A Bedtime Story
(1933) Paramount
Veteran tot Baby LeRoy threatens to steal the show from Chevalier as a foundling who rules the lives of his playboy foster father and his valet, the comically mournful Horton. Along the way, Chevalier has a series of amorous escapades, hires a nurse, breaks an engagement, bursts intermittently into song, falls in love with the nurse, and generally sheds his selfish, frivolous ways, in a predictably lighthearted comedy. **Cast:** Maurice Chevalier, Helen Twelvetrees, Edward Everett Horton, Adrienne Ames, Baby LeRoy, Earle Fox, Betty Lorraine, Gertrude Michael, Ernest Wood, Reginald Mason. **Credits:** Dir: Norman Taurog; Prod: Ernest Cohen; Writer: Nunnally Johnson, Waldemar Young, Benjamin Glazer; Story: Roy Horniman; DP: Charley Lang; Ed: Otto Lovering; Composer: Ralph Rainer, Leo Robin. B&W, 87 min.

Bedtime Story
(1942) Columbia
A romantic comedy that was ahead of its time. An actress (Young) wants to retire from performance, however her playwright husband (March) relentlessly begs her to star in his next play. The result is divorce. While she remarries a banker, her ex-husband never gives up hope that they will be together again. **Cast:** Fredric March, Loretta Young, Robert Benchley, Allyn Joslyn, Eve Arden, Helen Westley, Joyce Compton, Tim Ryan, Olaf Hytten, Dorothy Adams. **Credits:** Dir: Alexander Hall; Prod: B. P. Schulberg; Writer: Richard Flournoy; Story: Horace Jackson, Grant Garrett; DP: Joseph Walker; Ed: Viola Lawrence; Prod Design: Lionel Banks; Composer: Morris Stoloff. B&W, 83 min.

Beginning or the End
(1947) MGM
In an attempt to beat Paramount to the punch, MGM rushed this into production. Speed of production notwithstanding, it's a grade-A A-bomb movie. The documentary aspects of the planning, development, and deployment of the atomic warhead are well-meshed with the standard Hollywood drama. The result is an entertaining portrayal of the nuclear-age beginning. **Cast:** Brian Donlevy, Robert Walker, Jr., Tom Drake, Beverly Tyler, Audrey Totter, Hume Cronyn, Hurd Hatfield, Joseph Calleia, Godfrey Tearle. **Credits:** Dir: Norman Taurog; Prod: Samuel Marx; Writer: Frank Wead; DP: Ray June, Warren Newcombe; Ed: George Hoemier; Prod Design: Cedric Gibbons; Composer: Daniele Amfitheatrof; Art Director: Hans Peters. B&W, 112 min.

The Beguiled

(1970) Universal
A wounded Union soldier (Eastwood) is found and taken in by the residents of a decaying Southern school for girls. His presence brings to the surface the women's repressed sexual fantasies and jealousies, which he attempts to manipulate to his benefit. When he eventually seduces two of them, the women then decide to exact a strange revenge for his promiscuous actions. An oddly somnolent effort from Eastwood and Siegel, but interesting as it doesn't rely on gunplay for effect. **Cast:** Clint Eastwood, Geraldine Page, Jo Ann Harris, Elizabeth Hartman, Darleen Carr, Mae Mercer, Pamelyn Ferdin. **Credits:** Dir: Don Siegel; Writer: Albert Maltz, Irene Kamp; Story: Thomas Cullinan; DP: Bruce Surtees; Ed: Carl Pingitore; Prod Design: Ted Haworth; Composer: Lalo Schifrin; Costumes: Helen Colvig. Color, 109 min. VHS, LASER, DVD

Behold a Pale Horse

(1964) Columbia
A guerrilla leader in the Spanish Civil War continues to wage a personal campaign twenty years later until a corrupt police captain sees an opportunity to set a trap using the guerrilla's mother as bait. Prestige abounds with Peck, Quinn, Zinnemann, and a screenplay by J. P. Miller from a novel by British director Emeric Pressburger. **Cast:** Gregory Peck, Anthony Quinn, Omar Sharif, Mildred Dunnock, Raymond Pellegrin, Paolo Stoppa, Daniela Rocca, Christian Marquand. **Credits:** Dir: Fred Zinnemann; Prod: Fred Zinnemann; Writer: J. P. Miller; Story: Emeric Pressburger; DP: Jean Badal; Ed: Walter Thompson; Prod Design: Alexander Trauner; Composer: Maurice Jarre; Art Director: Auguste Capelier. B&W, 122 min. VHS

Being There

(1979) United Artists
Adapted from Kosinski's novel, this is the story of a mentally deficient gardener, who knows the outside world only through television, and his rise to political power when his idle aphorisms are interpreted as philosophical wisdom by a wealthy industrialist and, soon after, swallowed whole by the American public. Influential and provocative with a marvelously enigmatic performance by Sellers. Academy Award Nominations: 2, including Best Actor: Peter Sellers. **Academy Awards:** Best Supporting Actor: Melvyn Douglas. **Cast:** Peter Sellers, Melvyn Douglas, Shirley MacLaine,

Jack Warden, Richard Dysart, Richard Basehart. **Credits:** Dir: Hal Ashby; Prod: Andrew Braunsberg; Writer: Jerzy Kosinski; DP: Dianne Schroeder, Caleb Deschanel; Ed: Don Zimmerman; Prod Design: Michael Haller; Composer: Johnny Mandel; Art Director: James Schoppe; Set Designer: Robert Benton. Color, 130 min. VHS, LASER

Bell, Book and Candle

(1958) Columbia
Great cast in supernatural romantic comedy. When urban witch Novak casts a spell on Stewart to lure him away from a snooty former schoolmate, she finds the spell rebounding due to the intercession of a more powerful witch (Gingold). Lemmon and comic genius Kovacs add lots of laughs. Academy Award Nominations: Best Art Direction; Best Costumes. **Cast:** James Stewart, Kim Novak, Jack Lemmon, Ernie Kovacs, Hermione Gingold, Elsa Lanchester, Janice Rule. **Credits:** Dir: Richard Quine; Prod: Julian C. Blaustein; Writer: Daniel Taradash; Story: John Van Druten; DP: James Wong Howe; Ed: Charles Nelson; Prod Design: Cary Odell; Composer: George Duning. Color, 106 min. VHS, LASER

The Bellboy

(1960) Paramount
Unfortunately for the guests at the Fontainbleu Hotel, one of the bellboys is Lewis, an endearing, but accident-prone nitwit. Zany hotel hijinks abound, as the rubber-faced bellhop creates klutzy, comedic havoc. Lewis's first directorial effort, which he also produced, wrote, and, of course, starred in. Cameos by Milton Berle and Walter Winchell keep the atmosphere festive. **Cast:** Jerry Lewis, Alex Gerry, Bob Clayton, Sonny Sands, Milton Berle. **Credits:** Dir: Jerry Lewis; Prod: Jerry Lewis; Writer: Jerry Lewis; DP: Haskell Boggs; Ed: Stanley Johnson; Prod Design: Hal Pereira, Henry Bumstead; Composer: Walter Scharf. Color, 72 min. VHS, LASER

The Belle of New York

(1952) MGM
It's bustling turn-of-the-century New York City and Astaire is a playboy who falls head-over-heels in love with Vera-Ellen, a mission worker. He woos her with his charm, singing, and, of course, his dancing. Songs include: "I Wanna Be a Dancin' Man," "Let a Little Love Come In," "Baby Doll," "Seeing's Believing," "Naughty but Nice," and "Bachelor's Dinner Song." **Cast:**

Fred Astaire, Vera-Ellen, Marjorie Main, Keenan Wynn, Alice Pearce, Clinton Sundberg, Gale Robbins. **Credits:** Dir: Charles Walters; Prod: Arthur Freed; Writer: Robert O'Brien, Chester Erskine, Irving Elinson; Story: Hugh Morton; DP: Robert H. Planck; Ed: Albert Akst; Prod Design: Cedric Gibbons, Jack Martin Smith; Choreographer: Robert Alton; Composer: Johnny Mercer, Harry Warren; Costumes: Helen Rose, Gile Steele; SFX: Warren Newcombe, Irving G. Ries; Set Designer: Edwin B. Willis, Richard Pefferle. Color, 82 min. VHS

Belle of the Nineties

(1934) Paramount
Mae West's script fell victim to the censors' snips, but who can resist Mae, especially directed by McCarey? As the inevitable burlesque queen, Mae fends for herself while fending off advances in the Gay Nineties. Includes Duke Ellington and his orchestra backing West's crooning. **Cast:** Mae West, Roger Pryor, Katherine De Mille, Johnny Mack Brown, John Miljan, Duke Ellington. **Credits:** Dir: Leo McCarey; Prod: William LeBaron; Writer: Mae West; DP: Karl Struss; Ed: LeRoy Stone; Prod Design: Bernard Herzbrun, Hans Dreier; Composer: Arthur Johnston, Sam Coslow; Costumes: Travis Banton. B&W, 73 min. VHS, DVD

Belles on Their Toes

(1952) Fox
Loy reprises her role as the mother of twelve in this sequel to the hit comedy *Cheaper by the Dozen*. As before, Loy has her hands full as she manages the lives of her children, tries to go back to work, and generally does good works for the community. Things get interesting when three of her daughters find romance, and through a succession of dances, picnics, and trips to the beach she manages to solve their problems and find some romance for herself. **Cast:** Jeanne Crain, Myrna Loy, Debra Paget, Jeffrey Hunter, Edward Arnold, Hoagy Carmichael, Barbara Bates, Robert Arthur, Verna Felton, Roddy McCaskill. **Credits:** Dir: Henry Levin; Prod: Samuel G. Engel; Writer: Phoebe Ephron, Henry Ephron; DP: Arthur E. Arling; Ed: Robert Fritch; Composer: Lionel Newman, Cyril Mockridge. B&W, 89 min.

A Bell for Adano

(1945) Fox
Major Joppolo is charged with the task of reestablishing order in a small Italian village after WWII. As he helps

restore the community's civic administration, Joppolo falls in love with a local girl. He also manages to prevent the lynching of the town's former major, who had lent his support to Mussolini, and—most important—to restore the town's beloved church bell, stolen during the war. **Cast:** Gene Tierney, John Hodiak, William Bendix, Glenn Langan, Richard Conte, Stanley Prager, Harry Horgan, Monte Banks, Reed Hadley, Roy Roberts. **Credits:** Dir: Henry King; Prod: Louis D. Lighton, Lamar Trotti; Writer: Norman Raine, Lamar Trotti; Story: John Hersey; DP: Joseph LaShelle; Ed: Barbara McLean; Composer: Alfred Newman. B&W, 103 min.

The Bell Jar
(1979) Avco Embassy
A powerful drama based on the autobiographical novel by poetess Plath. The film depicts the painful mental breakdown of a dynamic, industrious woman in the '50s who works at an upscale fashion magazine. When Esther (Hassett) returns to her home in New England, her mental state continues to diminish. Somber news from every angle eventually pushes her over the edge. Manic depressives beware. **Cast:** Marilyn Hassett, Julie Harris, Barbara Barrie, Anne Bancroft. **Credits:** Dir: Larry Peerce; Writer: Marjorie Kellogg; Story: Sylvia Plath; DP: Gerald Hirschfeld; Composer: Gerald Fried; Costumes: Donald Brooks. Color, 113 min. **VHS**

Bells Are Ringing
(1960) MGM
Holliday's last screen appearance and perhaps her best, reprising her stage role in the Comden and Green musical. Holliday plays a switchboard operator at a Manhattan telephone answering service, Susanswerphone, who gets mixed up in her kooky clients' lives, acting as both muse and therapist, eventually falling in love with a client's voice. Early appearance by Stapleton, and a cameo by Holliday's husband, saxophonist Gerry Mulligan. The picture's many musical hits include "Just in Time" and "The Party's Over." Academy Award Nomination for Best Scoring of a Musical Picture. **Cast:** Dean Martin, Judy Holliday, Fred Clark, Eddie Foy, Jr., Jean Stapleton, Ruth Storey, Frank Gorshin. **Credits:** Dir: Vincente Minnelli; Prod: Arthur Freed; Writer: Betty Comden, Adolph Green; DP: Milton Krasner; Ed: Adrienne Fazan; Prod Design: George W. Davis, Preston Ames; Choreographer: Charles O'Curran; Composer: Jule

Styne, Betty Comden, Adolph Green; Costumes: Walter Plunkett. Color, 127 min. **VHS, LASER**

The Bells of St. Mary's
(1945) RKO
The sequel to *Going My Way* is a sprightly McCarey concoction again featuring the ever-likable Crosby. In this outing, Father O'Malley finds himself at cross-purposes with Bergman's Sister Superior. While helping the nuns educate and discipline the local children, and improving a little girl's unhappy family life, he also finds time to save the school from demolition by a greedy land developer. Bing sings "Adeste Fidelis," "The Bells of St. Mary's," and "O Sanctissima" with a children's choir, and sings "Aren't You Glad You're You" and "In the Land of Beginning Again" solo. Winner of the Golden Globe for Best Actress: Ingrid Bergman. Academy Award Nominations: 8, including Best Picture; Best Director; Best Actor: Bing Crosby; Best Actress: Ingrid Bergman; Best Song ("Aren't You Glad You're You"). **Academy Awards:** Best Sound. **Cast:** Bing Crosby, Ingrid Bergman, Henry Travers, William Gargan, Ruth Donnelly, Rhys Williams, Una O'Connor, Eva Novak. **Credits:** Dir: Leo McCarey; Prod: Leo McCarey; Writer: Dudley Nichols; Story: Leo McCarey; DP: George Barnes; Ed: Harry Marker; Prod Design: William Flannery; Composer: Robert Emmett Dolan; Costumes: Edith Head; Set Designer: Darrell Silvera. B&W, 126 min. **VHS, LASER, DVD**

Beloved Enemy
(1936) United Artists
A romance-adventure set against what seem to be the ever-contemporary Troubles in Ireland. Oberon makes a perfectly majestic British beauty who reveals a fiery, passionate side when she falls in love with a leader of the 1921 Irish rebellion. **Cast:** Merle Oberon, Karen Morley, Jerome Cowan, Donald Crisp, Brian Aherne, Henry Stephenson, David Niven. **Credits:** Dir: H. C. Potter; Writer: Rose Franken, William Brown Meloney, David Hart; Story: John L. Balderston; DP: Gregg Toland; Ed: Sherman Todd; Composer: Alfred Newman. B&W, 86 min. **VHS, LASER**

Bend of the River
(1952) Universal
The second of the terrific Stewart-Mann Westerns is characteristic of their pairings: adult themes played out against prairie vistas in which betrayal

and violence can erupt at any time. Formerly a vicious Missouri raider, Stewart now leads a wagon train through Indian raids and hijackings to the new boom town of Portland where he becomes embroiled in the conflict between wealthy miners and farmers. **Cast:** James Stewart, Arthur Kennedy, Julie Adams, Rock Hudson, Lori Nelson, Jay C. Flippen, Henry Morgan, Royal Dano, Stepin Fetchit. **Credits:** Dir: Anthony Mann; Writer: Borden Chase; Story: Bill Gulick; DP: Irving Glassberg; Ed: Russell Schoengarth; Prod Design: Nathan Juran, Bernard Herzbrun; Composer: Hans J. Salter; Costumes: Rosemary Odell; Set Designer: Oliver Emert, Russell A. Gausman. Color, 91 min. **VHS**

Beneath the Planet of the Apes
(1970) Fox
The second installment in the Planet of the Apes series finds an astronaut following in Heston's time-wandering footsteps to a planet ruled by highly evolved apes where he encounters a group of nuclear holocaust survivors living in Grand Central Station and worshiping the very atomic warhead that destroyed their world. Still involving, if not the breakthrough of the first outing. **Cast:** Charlton Heston, James Franciscus, Kim Hunter, Maurice Evans, Linda Harrison, Paul Richards, Victor Buono, Jeff Corey, James Gregory, Thomas Gomez. **Credits:** Dir: Ted Post; Prod: Arthur P. Jacobs; Writer: Paul Dehn, Mort Abrahams; DP: Milton Krasner; Ed: Marion Rothman; Prod Design: William Creber, Jack Martin Smith; Composer: Leonard Rosenman; Set Designer: Sven Wickman, Walter Scott. Color, 100 min. **VHS, LASER**

Beneath the 12-Mile Reef
(1953) Fox
Romance sharpens a rivalry between two families of sponge divers in the Florida Keys. Unique only for the spectacular underwater scenes in Technicolor and CinemaScope. Academy Award Nomination for Best Cinematography (Color). **Cast:** Robert Wagner, Terry Moore, Gilbert Roland, Richard Boone, Peter Graves, J. Carrol Naish, Angela Clarke, Jay Novello. **Credits:** Dir: Robert D. Webb; Prod: Robert Bassler; Writer: A. I. Bezzerides; DP: Edward Cronjager; Ed: William Reynolds; Prod Design: Lyle Wheeler; Composer: Bernard Herrmann; Costumes: Dorothy Jeakins; SFX: Ray Kellogg. Color, 102 min. **VHS, LASER, DVD**

Ben-Hur

(1959) MGM

One of the cinema's greatest epics because it's based on a compelling human story of revenge, bitterness, redemption, and forgiveness. Heston is magnificent as the Prince of Judea, Ben-Hur, who confronts the conquering Romans. His actions send him and his family into slavery—and an inspirational encounter with Jesus. The story moves from Judea to imperial Rome and back to Judea, where Heston finally meets his rival Messala in a justly famous chariot race and rescues his suffering family—after once again encountering Jesus, this time on his way to Golgotha. This was a production of unheard-of scale, exhibiting the work of literally tens of thousands of people. The 1880 novel by Lew Wallace had previously been made to great acclaim in 1927 with Ramon Navarro. The 35th Anniversary edition, which runs 282 minutes, includes a documentary narrated by Christopher Plummer on the making of the film, behind-the-scenes footage, screen tests, cast interviews, and the film's original trailer. Winner of Golden Globes for Best Director; Best Supporting Actor: Stephen Boyd; Special Achievements; Best Motion Picture, Drama. Academy Award Nominations: 12, including Best (Adapted) Screenplay. **Academy Awards:** Best Director; Best Actor: Charlton Heston; Best Supporting Actor: Hugh Griffith; Best Film Editing; Best Sound; Best Special Effects; Best Color Cinematography; Best Music Score of a Drama/Comedy; Best Picture; Best Costume Design (Color); Best Sound Effects; Best Art Direction—Set Decoration (Color). **Cast:** Charlton Heston, Jack Hawkins, Stephen Boyd, Haya Harareet, Hugh Griffith, Martha Scott, Cathy O'Donnell, Sam Jaffe, Finlay Currie, Frank Thring. **Credits:** Dir: William Wyler, Andrew Marton; Writer: Karl Tunberg; Story: Lew Wallace; DP: Robert Surtees; Ed: Ralph E. Winters, John Dunning; Prod Design: William A. Horning, Edward C. Carfagno; Composer: Miklos Rozsa; Costumes: Elizabeth Haffenden; SFX: Robert MacDonald, A. Arnold Gillespie. Color, 211 min. **VHS, LASER**

Benji

(1974)

The first screen adventure for Benji, that oh-so-lovable mutt with an iron will and a heart of gold. Benji sets out to save two kidnapped kids and finds love with a fetching female canine along the way. A kids' classic right from the start. **Cast:** Peter Breck, Deborah Walley, Edgar Buchanan,

Benji, Terry Carter, Christopher Connelly. **Credits:** Dir: Joe Camp; Prod: Joe Camp; Writer: Joe Camp; DP: Don Reddy; Ed: Leonard Smith; Prod Design: Harland Wright; Composer: Euel Box. Color, 87 min. **VHS**

The Benny Goodman Story

(1955) Universal

The music's the thing in this glossy life of Benny Goodman—and the swinging clarinet great himself supplied the sounds. The story follows Goodman from his modest upbringing in Chicago through romance and marriage to his historic concert at Carnegie Hall. Jazz buff Allen has just the right bookish kind of hep, and Harry James and Gene Krupa are among the musical cameos. **Cast:** Steve Allen, Donna Reed, Gene Krupa, Herbert Anderson. **Credits:** Dir: Valentine Davies; Prod: Aaron Rosenberg; Writer: Valentine Davies; DP: William Daniels; Ed: Russell Schoengarth; Composer: Henry Mancini. Color, 116 min. **VHS**

Berkeley Square

(1933) Fox

Grand restaging with sumptuous costumes and English cast of London's *Berkeley Square*, adapted by Balderston from his moderately successful play, loosely borrowed from Twain's *A Connecticut Yankee in King Arthur's Court*. Time travel, cultural differences, and romance are captured in Howard's superb performance as a contemporary American whose musings catapult him rearward, specifically to the London social whirl of his namesake ancestor in 1784. There, he meets the woman his forebear married, but proceeds to fall for another. Academy Award Nominations: Best Actor: Leslie Howard. **Cast:** Leslie Howard, Heather Angel, Valerie Taylor, Irene Browne, Beryl Mercer, Colin Keith-Johnston, Alan Mowbray, Lionel Barrymore, Juliette Compton, Betty Lawford. **Credits:** Dir: Frank Lloyd; Prod: Jesse Lasky, Jr.; Writer: Sonya Levien; Story: John L. Balderston; DP: Ernest Palmer; Ed: Harold Schuster; Composer: Louis De Francesco. B&W, 87 min.

Berlin Express

(1948) RKO

En route to an important conference on the future of post-WWII Germany, Dr. Bernhardt, a German diplomat, is kidnapped by die-hard Nazi operatives. A multinational team of intelligence officers cooperates to locate the missing man in Frankfurt's underworld and

bombed-out buildings. **Cast:** Robert Ryan, Merle Oberon, Paul Lukas, Charles Korvin, Robert Coote. **Credits:** Dir: Jacques Tourneur; Prod: Bert Granet; Writer: Harold Medford; Story: Curt Siodmak; DP: Lucien Ballard; Ed: Sherman Todd; Prod Design: Alfred Herman, Albert S. D'Agostino; Choreographer: Charles O'Curran; Composer: Frederick Hollander; Costumes: Orry-Kelly; Set Designer: William Stevens, Darrell Silvera. B&W, 86 min. **VHS, LASER**

Best Foot Forward

(1943) MGM

A grand MGM musical about a Hollywood star who, as part of a publicity stunt, agrees to be the guest of a young cadet at his military school prom. Probably Lucy's best film, according to Desi. The movie is based on a Broadway show and includes such big band–era hits as "Three Men on a Date," "Wish I May," "Buckle Down Winsocki," and "Two O'Clock Jump." **Cast:** Lucille Ball, June Allyson, Tommy Dix, William Gaxton, Virginia Weidler, Harry James, Gloria De Haven. **Credits:** Dir: Edward Buzzell, Charles Walters; Prod: Arthur Freed; Writer: Irving Brecher, Fred F. Finklehoffe; Story: John Cecil Holmes; DP: Leonard Smith; Ed: Blanche Sewell; Prod Design: Edward C. Carfagno, Cedric Gibbons; Composer: Hugh Martin, Ralph Blane; Costumes: Gile Steele, Irene; Set Designer: Edwin B. Willis. Color, 95 min. **VHS**

The Best Man

(1964) United Artists

An overlooked gem. Vidal adapted his own stage drama of behind-the-scenes political maneuvering during a party convention. The candidates grapple for the party's nomination, revealing their true natures as they vie for the endorsement of the ailing president. Academy Award Nomination for Best Supporting Actor: Lee Tracy. **Cast:** Henry Fonda, Cliff Robertson, Lee Tracy, Edie Adams, Margaret Leighton, Shelley Berman, Ann Sothern, Gene Raymond, Kevin McCarthy, Mahalia Jackson. **Credits:** Dir: Franklin J. Schaffner; Prod: Stuart Millar, Lawrence Turman; Writer: Gore Vidal; DP: Haskell Wexler; Ed: Robert W. Swink; Composer: Mort Lindsey; Costumes: Dorothy Jeakins. B&W, 104 min. **VHS**

The Best of Everything

(1959) Fox

Could publishing ever have been this glamorous—or heartless? Women publishing executives try to have it all in '50s New York. Crawford is tailor-made as the steely boss unnerved by her affair with a married man, and cult-fave former model Parker adds a glossy sheen. Based on Rona Jaffe's novel. **Cast:** Hope Lange, Stephen Boyd, Suzy Parker, Diane Baker, Joan Crawford, Louis Jourdan, Martha Hyer, Brian Aherne, Robert Evans. **Credits:** Dir: Jean Negulesco; Prod: Jerry Wald; Writer: Edith Sommer, Mann Rubin; Story: Rona Jaffe; DP: William Mellor; Ed: Robert Simpson; Composer: Alfred Newman; Costumes: Adele Palmer. Color, 121 min. **VHS**

Best of the Badmen
(1951) RKO
A kooky, enjoyable Western that features a group of outlaws rescuing the man sent to disband them after he's falsely arrested. Good cast and the sweetest, most talkative gang of outlaws you ever did meet. **Cast:** Robert Ryan, Claire Trevor, Robert Preston, Jack Buetel, Walter Brennan, Bruce Cabot, John Archer, Lawrence Tierney. **Credits:** Dir: William D. Russell; Prod: Herman Schlom; Writer: Robert Hardy Andrews, John Twist; DP: Edward Cronjager; Ed: Desmond Marquette; Composer: Paul Sawtell. B&W, 84 min. **VHS**

The Best Years of Our Lives
(1946) RKO
Perhaps the most memorable film about the aftermath of WWII, it unfolds with the homecoming of three veterans to the same small town. The leads all touch emotional truths: Loy seems able to express longing, joy, fear, and surprise—even with her back turned—in a particularly poignant welcome home. The movie never glosses over the reality of altered lives and the inability to communicate the experience of war on the front lines or the home front. A landmark achievement. WWII vet Russell, who lost his hands in the war, is the only person to win two Oscars for the same role, Best Supporting Actor and a special Oscar "for bringing hope and courage to his fellow veterans through his appearance." Among its many awards are a British Academy BAFTA for Best Film, Any Source; Golden Globes for Special Achievements: Harold Russell; Best Motion Picture, Drama. A National Film Registry Outstanding Film. **Academy Awards:** Best Director; Best Actor: Fredric March; Best Supporting Actor: Harold Russell; Best Film Editing; Special Achievement Awards: Harold Russell; Irving G. Thalberg Memorial

Award: Samuel Goldwyn; Best Screenplay; Best Music Score of a Drama/Comedy; Best Picture. **Cast:** Myrna Loy, Fredric March, Dana Andrews, Teresa Wright, Hoagy Carmichael, Virginia Mayo, Harold Russell, Cathy O'Donnell, Gladys George, Roman Bohnen. **Credits:** Dir: William Wyler; Prod: Samuel Goldwyn; Writer: Robert E. Sherwood; DP: Gregg Toland; Ed: Daniel Mandell; Composer: Hugo Friedhofer; Costumes: Irene Sharaff; Art Director: George Jenkins, Perry Ferguson; Set Designer: Julia Heron. B&W, 172 min. **VHS, LASER, DVD**

Betrayed
(1954) MGM
In Nazi-occupied Holland, Dutch Colonel Pieter Deventer is aligned with the British forces and searching for a traitor in his ranks. Three screen legends, Gable, Turner, and Mature, team up for this espionage thriller—Gable and Turner for the last time. **Cast:** Lana Turner, Victor Mature, Louis Calhern, Clark Gable, O. E. Hasse, Wilfrid Hyde-White, Ian Carmichael, Niall MacGinnis, Nora Swinburne. **Credits:** Dir: Gottfried Reinhardt; Prod: Gottfried Reinhardt; Writer: Ronald Millar, George Froeschel; DP: Freddie Young; Ed: Raymond Poulton, John Dunning; Prod Design: Alfred Junge; Composer: Walter Goehr; Costumes: Pierre Balmain. Color, 108 min. **VHS**

Between the Lines
(1977)
A winning and overlooked comedy about life at a Boston underground newspaper, whose staff fear it's about to be acquired by a media baron. The young cast is exceptional and were mostly unknowns at the time, though they've gone on to become household names. **Cast:** John Heard, Lindsay Crouse, Jeff Goldblum, Marilu Henner, Jill Eikenberry, Bruno Kirby, Stephen Collins, Michael J. Pollard. **Credits:** Dir: Joan Micklin Silver; Prod: Raphael Silver; Writer: Fred Barron; Story: David Helpern; DP: Kenneth Van Sickle; Ed: John Carter; Prod Design: Stuart Wurtzel; Composer: Michael Kamen; Costumes: Patrizia von Brandenstein. Color, 101 min. **VHS**

Between Two Worlds
(1944) Warner Bros.
A young couple are unable to escape the war in Europe. Despairing, they return to their apartment, and turn on the gas, determined to die. They awake on a boat bound for the Other World, and realize that they and their

fellow passengers are dead. After a lengthy journey, all are met and questioned by The Examiner, who will determine the ultimate destination of each. Initially sentenced, as suicides, to remain passengers on the purgatorial boat forever, the pair must persuade The Examiner that they deserve better. Remake of 1930's *Outward Bound*. **Cast:** Paul Henreid, Eleanor Parker, Sydney Greenstreet, John Garfield, Edmund Gwenn, George Tobias, George Coulouris, Faye Emerson. **Credits:** Dir: Edward A. Blatt; Prod: Mark Hellinger; Writer: Daniel Fuchs, Sutton Vane; DP: Carl E. Guthrie; Ed: Rudi Fehr; Prod Design: Hugh Reticker; Composer: Erich Wolfgang Korngold. B&W, 112 min.

Beware, My Lovely
(1952) RKO
A must for those fascinated by the career of Lupino. She plays a young widow held by a mentally deranged handyman. The tension of her attempts to escape build to a fierce final struggle with her captor. **Cast:** Ida Lupino, Robert Ryan, Taylor Holmes, Barbara Whiting. **Credits:** Dir: Harry Horner; Prod: Collier Young; Writer: Mel Dinelli; DP: George E. Diskant; Ed: Paul Weatherwax; Prod Design: Alfred Herman, Albert S. D'Agostino; Composer: Leith Stevens; Costumes: Michael Woulfe; Set Designer: Al Orenbach, Darrell Silvera. B&W, 77 min. **VHS, LASER**

Beyond the Forest
(1949) Warner Bros.
A small-town young woman who covets the high life enjoyed by her wealthy Chicago neighbor decides to leave her country-doctor hubby. The plot is far-fetched and Davis is not at her best in this one, though her delivery of the line "What a dump!" lives eternally. Academy Award Nomination for Best Scoring of a Dramatic or Comedy Picture. **Cast:** Bette Davis, Joseph Cotten, David Brian, Ruth Roman, Dona Drake, Regis Toomey, Minor Watson. **Credits:** Dir: King Vidor; Prod: Henry Blanke; Writer: Lenore Coffee; Story: Stuart Engstrand; DP: Robert Burks; Ed: Rudi Fehr; Composer: Max Steiner; Costumes: Edith Head. B&W, 96 min. **VHS**

Beyond the Time Barrier
(1960) AIP
A '50s jet pilot breaks through the time barrier and into World War III, circa 2024. He finds a future crowded with mutants and plagued by a deadly virus. Primitive science fiction, but amusing if you're a fan. **Cast:** Robert

Clarke, Darlene Tompkins, Arianne Arden, Vladimir Sokoloff, Stephen Bekassy. **Credits:** Dir: Edgar G. Ulmer; Prod: Robert Clarke; Writer: Arthur C. Pierce; DP: Meredith Nicholson; Ed: Jack Ruggiero; Composer: Darrell Calker; Costumes: Jack Masters. B&W, 75 min. VHS

Bhowani Junction
(1956) MGM
A young Anglo-Indian woman is forced to choose between her two races and twin allegiances when they are reflected in the men she loves. The cinematography is beautiful but the story is watered down from the more potent Masters novel. **Cast:** Ava Gardner, Stewart Granger, Bill Travers, Abraham Sofaer, Francis Matthews, Marne Maitland, Peter Illing, Freda Jackson, Edward Chapman. **Credits:** Dir: George Cukor; Prod: Pandro S. Berman; Writer: Sonya Levien, Ivan Moffat; Story: John Masters; DP: Freddie Young; Ed: George Boemler, Frank Clark; Composer: Miklos Rozsa; Costumes: Elizabeth Haffenden. B&W, 110 min. VHS, LASER

The Bigamist
(1953) Filmmakers
A salesman marries a wealthy woman (Fontaine) from a blue-blooded L.A. family and a street-smart waitress in a San Francisco Chinese restaurant. Driven to this agonizing extreme more by his big heart than lust, the bigamist strains to keep his double life a secret from the women he truly loves. Curiously nonjudgmental, particularly as it's directed by a woman, Lupino (it's also the only production in which she directed herself). **Cast:** Edmond O'Brien, Joan Fontaine, Ida Lupino, Jane Darwell, Edmund Gwenn. **Credits:** Dir: Ida Lupino; Prod: Collier Young; Writer: Collier Young; Story: Lou Schor, Larry Marcus; DP: George Diskant; Composer: Leith Stevens. B&W, 80 min. VHS

The Big Broadcast
(1932) Paramount
Comedy about a popular singer whose tardiness and other antics imperil a concert put on by a radio station. When the station owner sells out to a millionaire, the new owner uses big-name talents to put on a show. Bing Crosby, the Boswell Sisters, Cab Calloway, Kate Smith, and others appear as themselves (or performers resembling them). **Cast:** Gracie Allen, George Barbier, Connie Boswell, Martha Boswell, George Burns, Cab Calloway, Thomas Carrigan, Bing Crosby, Stuart

The Big Broadcast of 1938 (1938)

Erwin, Leila Hyams. **Credits:** Dir: Frank Tuttle; Writer: George Marion; Story: William Ford Manley; DP: George J. Folsey; Composer: Ralph Rainger, Leo Robin. B&W, 80 min.

The Big Broadcast of 1937
(1936) Paramount
Comedy featuring Burns and Allen as a husband-and-wife radio team. The station they work at is failing, and they need to put on a big show that will put them on top of the ratings and save the day (and radio station). Part of a series with the same title that featured the big radio stars of the day. **Cast:** Jack Benny, George Burns, Gracie Allen, Bobbi Burns, Martha Raye, Shirley Ross, Ray Milland, Benny Fields. **Credits:** Dir: Mitchell Leisen; Prod: Lewis E. Gensler; Writer: Edwin Gelsey, Arthur Kober, Barry Trivers; DP: Theodor Sparkuhl; Ed: Stuart Heisler; Composer: Leo Robin, Ralph Rainger. B&W, 100 min.

The Big Broadcast of 1938
(1938) Paramount
The last of the Big Broadcast vaudeville extravaganzas highlights Hope's first feature appearance—singing his signature, Oscar-winning song, "Thanks for the Memories"—and Fields fumbling through a nonsensical farce about twin brothers racing yachts to France. A horde of radio stars make their accustomed appearances. **Academy Awards:** Best Song. **Cast:** W. C. Fields, Bob Hope, Martha

Raye, Dorothy Lamour, Shirley Ross, Ben Blue, Lynne Overman, Rufe Davis, Leif Erikson, Grace Bradley. **Credits:** Dir: Mitchell Leisen; Prod: Harlan Thompson; Writer: Walter DeLeon, Francis Martin, Ken Englund, Howard Lindsay, Russel Crouse, Frederick Hazlitt; DP: Harry Fischbeck; Ed: Eda Warren, House Chandler; Prod Design: Hans Dreier; Choreographer: Leroy Prinz; Composer: Boris Morros; Costumes: Edith Head; SFX: Gordon Jennings; Art Director: Ernst Fegte. B&W, 91 min. VHS

Big Brown Eyes
(1936) Paramount
Bennett is a manicurist and Grant a detective in this comedy-mystery. Sparks fly between the two, but he is a bit wary of becoming involved with her. She ditches fingernails for sleuthing and is soon hot on the trail of a child murderer. The ensuing trial is a miscarriage of justice as the murderer uses bribery and trickery to get himself acquitted. Frustrated Grant quits and Bennett is fired. The pair next set their sights on investigating a jewel heist. **Cast:** Joan Bennett, Cary Grant, Walter Pidgeon, Isabel Jewell, Lloyd Nolan, Marjorie Gateson, Douglas Fowley. **Credits:** Dir: Raoul Walsh; Prod: Walter Wanger; Writer: James Edward Grant, Bert Hanlon, Raoul Walsh; DP: George Clemens; Ed: Robert Simpson; Composer: Boris Morros; Art Director: Alexander Toluboff. B&W, 76 min.

Big Business Girl

(1931) Warner Bros.
Loretta Young plays a career woman trying to have it all before women's lib. She works hard to save her marriage to a traveling jazz singer and advances up the corporate ladder while dodging a boss who's making advances of his own. **Cast:** Loretta Young, Ricardo Cortez, Jack Albertson, Joan Blondell, Frank Darien. **Credits:** Dir: William A. Seiter; Writer: Robert Lord; DP: Sol Polito; Ed: Peter Frisch. B&W, 75 min. **VHS**

Big City

(1937) MGM
Joe Benton (Tracy), a taxi-cab driver living in New York with his pregnant Russian wife, Anna (Rainer), is put under pressure to join local unions. When he refuses, they try to put him forcibly out of business. This proves unsuccessful, but an arson attack on one of the unions that leads to the death of several cabbies is arranged in such a way as to implicate Anna. Put on trial and found guilty, Anna is to be deported back to Russia. On the day she is to depart, Joe rushes to the mayor to convince him of Anna's innocence and overcome the corrupt union-organizers who attempt to impede him. **Cast:** Spencer Tracy, Luise Rainer, Charley Grapewin, Janet Beecher, Eddie Quillan, Victor Varconi, Oscar O'Shea, Helen Troy. **Credits:** Dir: Frank Borzage; Prod: Norman Krasna; Writer: Hugo Butler, Norman Krasna, Dore Schary; DP: Joseph Ruttenberg; Ed: Frederick Smith; Prod Design: Cedric Gibbons; Composer: Dr. William Axt. B&W, 80 min.

The Big Clock

(1948) Paramount
Crime-rag publisher Laughton tries to tag his editor (Milland) with the savage murder of the publisher's mistress when he glimpses the editor skulking out of her apartment. The twist to an otherwise familiar tale is that Laughton assigns Milland to find the killer even as the clues start pointing right at the editor himself. Based on Kenneth Fearing's novel, the film was remade in 1987 as *No Way Out*. **Cast:** Ray Milland, Charles Laughton, Maureen O'Sullivan, George Macready, Rita Johnson, Elsa Lanchester, Harold Vermilyea, James Burke, Dan Tobin, Henry Morgan. **Credits:** Dir: John Farrow; Prod: Richard Maibaum; Writer: Jonathan Latimer; DP: John Seitz; Ed: Gene Ruggiero; Prod Design: Hans Dreier; Composer: Victor Young; Costumes: Edith Head; SFX: Gordon Jennings; Art Director: Roland Anderson, Albert Nozaki; Set Designer: Sam Comer, Ross Dowd. B&W, 95 min. **VHS**

The Big Combo

(1955) Allied Artists
Shocking cruelty and explosive performances by Wilde and Conte make this a favorite of film noir cultists. The plot revolves around Wilde's determination to smash the rackets with the help of the gang boss's ex-girlfriend. As in this outing, director Lewis's deft use of low budgets made him a critical favorite. **Cast:** Cornel Wilde, Richard Conte, Jean Wallace, Brian Donlevy, Robert Middleton, Lee Van Cleef, Earl Holliman, Helen Walker, Jay Adler, John Hoyt. **Credits:** Dir: Joseph H. Lewis; Prod: Sidney Harmon; Writer: Philip Yordan; DP: John Alton; Ed: Robert S. Eisen; Prod Design: Rudi Feld; Composer: David Raskin; Costumes: Don Loper. B&W, 89 min. **VHS**

The Big Country

(1958) United Artists
Wyler's powerful Western covers a lot of territory with Peck a fish out of water as a sea captain who travels west to marry and settle, but finds himself in the middle of a bitter dispute over water rights and a jealous clash with the ranch foreman (Heston). He also discovers his fiancée isn't who he imagined and finds true romance with the local schoolmistress (Simmons). **Academy Awards:** Best Supporting Actor: Burl Ives. **Cast:** Gregory Peck, Jean Simmons, Charlton Heston, Burl Ives, Carroll Baker, Charles Bickford, Alfonso Bedoya, Chuck Connors, Jim Burk, Chuck Hayward. **Credits:** Dir: William Wyler; Prod: Gregory Peck, William Wyler; Writer: Robert Wilder, James R. Webb, Sy Bartlett, Robert Wyler; DP: Franz Planer; Ed: Robert Belcher, John Faure; Prod Design: Frank Hotaling; Composer: Jerome Moross. Color, 168 min. **VHS**

The Big Fix

(1978) Universal
A former 1960s student activist turned private detective searches for a missing Berkeley radical with whom he shared the barricades. Interesting blend of mystery yarn and '70s-cynical political setting. **Cast:** Richard Dreyfuss, Susan Anspach, Bonnie Bedelia, John Lithgow, F. Murray Abraham, Fritz Weaver, Ofelia Medina, Nicolas Coster, Michael Hershewe, Rita Karin. **Credits:** Dir: Jeremy Paul Kagan; Prod: Carl Borack, Richard Dreyfuss; Writer: Roger L. Simon; DP: Frank Stanley; Ed: Patrick Kennedy; Prod Design: Robert Boyle; Composer: Bill Conti. Color, 108 min. **VHS**

Bigger Than Life

(1956) Fox
Mason produced this dark psychodrama in which he stars as a small-town teacher who gets hooked on an experimental wonder drug. The film observes the resulting unraveling of his life. The drug causes ego inflation and soon son his relationships with his wife and his son become abusive. **Cast:** James Mason, Barbara Rush, Walter Matthau, Robert F. Simon, Christopher Olsen, Roland Winters, Rusty Lane, Rachel Stephens, Kipp Hamilton, Betty Caulfield. **Credits:** Dir: Nicholas Ray; Prod: James Mason; Writer: Cyril Hume, Richard Maibaum; Story: Gavin Lambert, James Mason, Burton Roueche, Clifford Odets; DP: Joseph MacDonald; Ed: Louis Loeffler; Composer: David Raskin. Color, 95 min.

A Big Hand for the Little Lady

(1966) Warner Bros.
Great cast elevates film based on TV version of story. A homesteader and reformed gambler passing through town learns of the annual high-stakes poker match about to take place. He recklessly throws the family fortune into the pot but soon must turn over his chair to his wife, who manages quite well to handle the cardsharps across the table. **Cast:** Henry Fonda, Joanne Woodward, Jason Robards, Charles Bickford, Burgess Meredith, Kevin McCarthy, Robert Middleton. **Credits:** Dir: Fielder Cook; Prod: Fielder Cook; Writer: Sidney Carrol; DP: Lee Garmes; Ed: George Rohr; Composer: David Raksin. Color, 95 min. **VHS**

The Big Heat

(1953) Columbia
Lang's classic film noir—and one of the darkest, most violent. When a bomb takes the life of detective Ford's wife, he determines to smash the gang responsible, enlisting the crime boss's moll (Grahame) along the way. Marvin's boiling-coffee-flinging scene still chills, mostly for the cold, serpentine menace in his eyes. **Cast:** Glenn Ford, Gloria Grahame, Jocelyn Brando, Lee Marvin, Alexander Scourby, Jeanette Nolan, Peter Whitney, Willis Bouchey, Robert Burton. **Credits:** Dir: Fritz Lang; Prod: Robert Arthur; Writer: Sydney Boehm; DP: Charles Lang; Ed: Charles Nelson; Prod Design: Robert Peterson; Composer: Daniele Amfitheatrof. B&W, 90 min. **VHS, LASER**

The Big House

(1930) MGM

Early talkie that set the stage for the countless men-behind-bars melodramas that followed. Grim depiction of the brutal conditions at an overcrowded prison that lead to a violent rebellion by angry prisoners. **Academy Awards:** Best Sound Recording; Best Screenplay. **Cast:** Wallace Beery, Robert Montgomery, Lewis Stone, Chester Morris, Karl Dane, Leila Hyams, George F. Marion, J. C. Nugent, DeWitt Jennings, Matthew Betz. **Credits:** Dir: George Hill; Prod: Irving Thalberg; Writer: Frances Marion, Joe Farnham, Martin Flavin; DP: Harold Wenstrom; Ed: Blanche Sewell; Prod Design: Cedric Gibbons. B&W, 86 min. VHS

Big Jim McLain

(1952) Warner Bros.

A no-nonsense federal agent and his war-hero partner are assigned to investigate the activities of a worldwide ring of communist terrorist spies based in Hawaii. **Cast:** John Wayne, James Arness, Nancy Olson, Veda Ann Borg, Hans Conried, Alan Napier, Gayne Whitman. **Credits:** Dir: Edward Ludwig; Prod: Robert Fellows; Writer: James Edward Grant, Richard English, Eric Taylor; DP: Archie Stout; Ed: Jack Murray; Composer: Paul Dunlap. B&W, 90 min. VHS, LASER

The Big Knife

(1955) United Artists

A dark, cynical probing of Hollywood and the studio system. When matinee idol Palance refuses to renew his studio contract, an autocratic movie mogul stoops to blackmail to force him back onto the lot. Based on an Odets play. **Cast:** Jack Palance, Ida Lupino, Shelley Winters, Rod Steiger, Wendell Corey, Everett Sloane, Jean Hagen, Ilka Chase, Wesley Addy. **Credits:** Dir: Robert Aldrich; Prod: Robert Aldrich; Writer: James Poe; Story: Clifford Odets; DP: Ernest Laszlo; Ed: Michael Luciano; Prod Design: William Glasgow; Composer: Frank de Vol. B&W, 113 min. VHS, LASER

The Big Mouth

(1967) Columbia

While he's out fishing, lamebrained Lewis encounters a scuba diver who tosses him a treasure map, which soon embroils him in a murder investigation and pursuit by criminals who want the map. Mostly for the Lewisphile, but we can take it if you can. **Cast:** Jerry Lewis, Susan Bay, Buddy Lester, Jeannine Riley, Charlie Callas,

Harold J. Stone, Del Moore, Paul Lambert, Leonard Stone, Frank de Vol. **Credits:** Dir: Jerry Lewis; Prod: Jerry Lewis; Writer: Jerry Lewis, Bill Richmond; DP: Wallace Kelley, Ernest Laszlo; Ed: Russel Wiles; Prod Design: Lyle Wheeler; Composer: Harry Betts. Color, 107 min. VHS

Big Red

(1962) Disney

The poignant Disney story of an orphan boy who is hired to care for a champion Irish setter who later saves his life. Set amid the spectacular beauty of Canada's Quebec province and based on the book by Jim Kjelgaard. **Cast:** Walter Pidgeon, Gilles Payant, Emile Genest, Janette Bertrand. **Credits:** Dir: Norman Tokar; Prod: Walt Disney, Winston Hibler; Writer: Louis Pelletier; DP: Edward Colman; Ed: Grant K. Smith; Composer: Oliver Wallace. Color, 89 min. VHS, LASER

The Big Shot

(1942) Warner Bros.

Released from prison, Duke Berne (Bogart) is pulled back into a life of crime. Joining two other hoods for a robbery, Duke backs out at the last moment at the advice of his ex-girl-friend. The robbery goes awry and Duke is framed for it. Sent to prison again, Duke escapes and kills a guard in the process. He searches for the man who ratted him out to the police, is surprised to discover who it was, and takes revenge. **Cast:** Humphrey Bogart, Irene Manning, Richard Travis, Susan Peters, Minor Watson, Stanley Ridges, Chick Chandler, Joe Downing, Howard Da Silva, Murray Alper. **Credits:** Dir: Lewis Seiler; Prod: Walter MacEwen; Writer: Abem Finkel, Daniel Fuchs, Bertram Millhauser; DP: Sid Hickox; Ed: Jack Killifer; Prod Design: John Hughes; Composer: Adolph Deutsch. B&W, 82 min.

The Big Sky

(1952) RKO

Hawks adventure with a strong performance by Douglas as a Kentucky mountaineer who embarks on a keel-boat expedition up the Missouri River in the 1830s. The perilous journey includes battles with hostile Indians and bands of outlaws—and romance with a Blackfoot princess. Pleasant frontier mythmaking based on the novel by A. B. Guthrie, the poet of America's westward expansion. Beware of colorized version. **Cast:** Kirk Douglas, Dewey Martin, Arthur Hunnicutt, Jim Davis, Elizabeth Threatt, Buddy Baer, Steven Geray, Hank Wor-

den, Henri Letondal, Booth Colman. **Credits:** Dir: Howard Hawks; Prod: Howard Hawks; Writer: Dudley Nichols; DP: Russell Harlan; Ed: Christian Nyby; Prod Design: Albert S. D'Agostino, Perry Ferguson; Composer: Dimitri Tiomkin. B&W, 122 min. VHS

The Big Sleep

(1946) Warner Bros.

Chandler's first novel introduced private detective Philip Marlowe, and *The Big Sleep* set the standard for private detective movies. Down-at-the-heels private eye Marlowe gets the assignment to clean up after the daughters of a dying millionaire, but dead people have a nasty habit of trailing in their wake. The famously tortuous story line (Hawks supposedly asked Chandler to clarify a plot point about the murder of the family chauffeur; the novelist hadn't a clue as to who did the deed) seems beside the point when Bogart and Bacall are on-screen. The final release was recut to include more of their scenes together. A must! Remade in 1978. **Cast:** Humphrey Bogart, Lauren Bacall, Dorothy Malone, John Ridgely, Louis Jean Heydt, Elisha Cook, Jr., Regis Toomey, Sonia Darrin, Bob Steele, Martha Vickers. **Credits:** Dir: Howard Hawks; Prod: Howard Hawks; Writer: William Faulkner, Jules Furthman, Leigh Brackett; DP: Sid Hickox; Ed: Christian Nyby; Prod Design: Carl Jules Weyl; Composer: Max Steiner. B&W, 114 min. VHS, LASER

The Big Sleep

(1978) United Artists

Director Winner switched the setting of Chandler's classic Marlowe mystery from 1940s Los Angeles to 1970s London, perhaps to avoid comparison with its forerunner. The 1946 Bogart-Bacall masterpiece is a tough act to follow, but this version is interesting in its own right for Mitchum's take on the fabled private eye. **Cast:** Robert Mitchum, Sarah Miles, Richard Boone, Candy Clark, James Stewart, Edward Fox, Joan Collins, John Mills, Oliver Reed, Harry Andrews. **Credits:** Dir: Michael Winner; Prod: Elliott Kastner, Michael Winner; Writer: Michael Winner; DP: Robert Paynter; Ed: Frederick Wilson; Prod Design: Harry Pottle; Composer: Jerry Fielding. Color, 101 min. VHS

The Big Steal

(1949) RKO

Early effort by action master Siegel—he would later helm Dirty Harry pictures—features terrific pairing of noir pin-ups Mitchum and Greer. A three-way chase through Mexico ensues after an army payroll is heisted. Tense, atmospheric: not for nothing is Siegel hailed by the French auteurists. **Cast:** Robert Mitchum, Jane Greer, William Bendix, Patric Knowles, Ramon Novarro, Don Alvarado, John Qualen. **Credits:** Dir: Don Siegel; Prod: Jack J. Gross; Writer: Geoffrey Homes, Gerald Drayson Adams; DP: Harry Wild; Ed: Samuel E. Beetley; Composer: Leigh Harline. B&W, 71 min. VHS

The Big Store
(1941) MGM
Groucho, Harpo, and Chico turn a big department store upside down as New York detectives trying to foil the hostile takeover of a department store and prevent a murder. Pretty late in the day for the Marxes, this was the final film in which Groucho, Harpo, and Chico appeared together—but there's still lots of fun watching the Brothers turn the emporium into their own private playground. **Cast:** Marx Brothers, Margaret Dumont, Tony Martin, Virginia Grey, Douglas Dumbrille, William Tannen, Marion Martin, Virginia O'Brien, Henry Armetta. **Credits:** Dir: Charles Riesner; Writer: Sid Kuller, Hal Fimberg, Ray Golden; DP: Charles Lawton, Jr.; Ed: Conrad A. Nervig; Composer: George Stoll. B&W, 83 min. VHS

The Big Street
(1942) RKO
Runyon's Times Square world of con men and hustlers populate the background in this tragi-comic romance, produced by Runyon himself. Unusual roles for Fonda and Ball as an innocent busboy named Little Pinks and Gloria, a glamorous nightclub singer. Hard-as-nails and dollar-wise, Gloria spurns the smitten busboy, but when an accident confines her to a wheelchair, Gloria is forced to turn to Little Pinks for help. **Cast:** Henry Fonda, Lucille Ball, Agnes Moorehead, Barton MacLane, Eugene Pallette, Sam Levene, Ray Collins, Marion Martin, William Orr, George Cleveland. **Credits:** Dir: Irving Reis; Prod: Damon Runyon; Writer: Leonard Spigelgass; DP: Russell Metty; Ed: William Hamilton; Prod Design: Albert S. D'Agostino; Composer: Roy Webb. B&W, 88 min. VHS, LASER

The Big Trail
(1930) Fox
Pioneers heading for Oregon, led by the Duke in his first starring role, endure the hardships of weather, unfriendly strangers, and internal

strife in this sophisticated early sound film. The straightforward Western tale is now overshadowed by its place in history as an early example of Fox's widescreen Grandeur process, its naturalistic sound, and prototypical Wayne performance. **Cast:** John Wayne, Marguerite Churchill, David Rollins, Tyrone Power, El Brendel, Tully Marshall, Ward Bond, Helen Parrish, Charles Stevens. **Credits:** Dir: Raoul Walsh; Prod: Raoul Walsh; Writer: Jack Peabody, Marie Boyle, Florence Postal; DP: Lucien Andriot, Arthur Edeson; Ed: Jack Dennis; Prod Design: Harold Miles; Composer: Arthur Kay. B&W, 110 min. VHS

Big Wednesday
(1978) Warner Bros.
Writer-director Milius usually dwells in a macho world of action; this brooding on the waning of youthful dreams and bravado feels awfully close to the heart. Set in the sunny surfing colony of Malibu, the first half of the film paints the joy of freedom on the waves. The second, post-Vietnam half depicts the painful road to maturity. **Cast:** Jan-Michael Vincent, William Katt, Gary Busey, Lee Purcell. **Credits:** Dir: John Milius; Prod: Buzz Feitshans; Writer: Darrell Fetty, John Milius, Dennis Aaberg; DP: Bruce Surtees, Greg MacGillivray; Ed: C. Timothy O'Meara, Robert L. Wolfe; Prod Design: Dean Mitzner; Composer: Basil Poledouris. Color, 120 min. VHS

Bikini Beach
(1964) AIP
Just about the last gasp of the classic 1960s beach movie, but features plenty of dancing, surfing, and teen romance. Before they can play in the sun, Frankie, Annette, and the gang must first deal with tough motorcycle hoods and unscrupulous land developers. **Cast:** Annette Funicello, Frankie Avalon, Keenan Wynn, Martha Hyer, Don Rickles, Harvey Lembeck, John Ashley, Boris Karloff. **Credits:** Dir: William Asher; Prod: James H. Nicholson, Samuel Z. Arkoff; Writer: William Asher, Leo Townsend, Robert Diller; DP: Floyd Crosby; Ed: Fred Feitshans; Prod Design: Daniel Haller; Composer: Les Baxter. Color, 100 min. VHS

Billie
(1965) United Artists
Patty Duke at the height of her TV cuteness stars as a natural athlete. But in the days before there was a WNBA to root for, she gets nothing but grief from beaus and parents just because she's better than the boys.

You go, girl! **Cast:** Patty Duke, Warren Berlinger, Jim Backus, Jane Greer, Billy De Wolfe, Charles Lane, Dick Sargent, Richard Deacon, Ted Bessell. **Credits:** Dir: Don Weis; Prod: Don Weis; Writer: Ronald Alexander; DP: John L. Russell, Jr.; Ed: Adrienne Fazan; Prod Design: Arthur Lonergan; Choreographer: David Winters; Composer: Dominic Frontiere. Color, 86 min. VHS, LASER

A Bill of Divorcement
(1932) RKO
Hepburn makes her screen debut as the coltish young woman who comes to know the stranger who is her father. Barrymore is quite moving as a man released from a mental institution back to the care of his wife (Burke) and daughter. **Cast:** Katharine Hepburn, John Barrymore, Billie Burke, David Manners, Paul Cavanagh, Elizabeth Patterson. **Credits:** Dir: George Cukor; Prod: David O. Selznick; Writer: Howard Estabrook, Harry Wagstaff Gribble; DP: Sid Hickox; Ed: Arthur Roberts; Composer: Max Steiner. B&W, 74 min. VHS

Bill of Divorcement
(1940) RKO
Remake of the famous melodrama tells the story of a woman about to remarry after divorcing her husband, who has been in an insane asylum for twenty years. But when the husband returns, the woman must decide between a normal life with her new love or one of duty to the man who needs her. The burden falls also on the daughter, who decides to sacrifice her own chance at love to give her mother freedom. **Cast:** Maureen O'Hara, Adolphe Menjou, Fay Bainter, Herbert Marshall, May Whitty, Patric Knowles, C. Aubrey Smith, Ernest Cossart, Kathryn Collier, Lauri Beatty. **Credits:** Dir: John Farrow; Prod: Robert Sisk; Writer: Dalton Trumbo; Story: Clemence Dane; DP: Nicholas Musuraca; Ed: Harry Marker; Prod Design: Van Nest Polglase; Composer: Roy Webb. B&W, 74 min.

Billy Budd
(1962) Allied Artists
Adapted from the last novel by Herman Melville, an allegory of good vs. evil in the story of a naive young man pressed into the service of the British Navy at the end of the 18th century. When the young sailor kills the ship's brutal master-at-arms, he's tried for murder. Overly serious, but a stunning debut for the Oscar-nominated Stamp. Academy Award Nomination for Best

Supporting Actor: Terence Stamp. **Cast:** Terence Stamp, Robert Ryan, Peter Ustinov, Melvyn Douglas, Paul Rogers, John Neville, Ronald Lewis, David McCallum, Lee Montague, John Meillon. **Credits:** Dir: Peter Ustinov; Prod: Peter Ustinov; Writer: Peter Ustinov, De Witt Bodeen, Robert Rossen; Story: Herman Melville; DP: Robert Krasker; Ed: Jack Harris; Composer: Antony Hopkins; Costumes: Anthony Mendleson. B&W, 123 min. **VHS**

Billy in the Lowlands
(1978) Theater Company of Boston
Tomaszewski's acting stands out in this independent film shot on the streets of Boston. A troubled high school dropout escapes jail and comes home when he discovers his father, now estranged, has shown up for a family funeral. Tomaszewski reforms, fulfilling his sentence and looking for a job. **Cast:** Paul Benedict, David Clennon, Ernie Lowe, David Morton, Genevieve Reale, Robert Owczarek, Henry Tomaszewski, Bronia Wheeler. **Credits:** Dir: Jan Egelson; Prod: Nick Egelson; Writer: Nick Egelson; DP: D'Arcy Marsh; Ed: Jan Egelson; Composer: Adrienne Linden. Color, 88 min.

Billy Rose's Jumbo
(1962) MGM
Doris Day stars as Kitty Wonder, the daughter of a circus owner in desperate straits. The ages-old circus tale gets lively with the songs of Rogers and Hart, and Berkeley's production numbers. Scripted by Hecht and MacArthur. Academy Award Nominations: Best (Adapted) Score. **Cast:** Doris Day, Stephen Boyd, Jimmy Durante, Martha Raye, Dean Jagger. **Credits:** Dir: Charles Walters; Prod: Joe Pasternak, Martin Melcher; Writer: Sidney Sheldon; Story: Ben Hecht, Charles MacArthur; DP: William H. Daniels; Ed: Richard W. Farrell; Prod Design: Preston Ames, George W. Davis; Choreographer: Busby Berkeley; Composer: Richard Rodgers, Lorenz Hart; Costumes: Morton Haack; SFX: J. McMillan Johnson, Robert R. Hoag, A. Arnold Gillespie; Set Designer: Hugh Hunt, Henry Grace. Color, 125 min. **VHS, LASER**

Billy the Kid
(1941) MGM
A fanciful bio of the notorious outlaw that depicts his life of crime resulting from the killing of an outlaw friend. Academy Award Nomination for Best (Color) Cinematography. **Cast:** Robert Taylor, Brian Donlevy, Ian Hunter, Mary

Howard, Gene Lockhart, Lon Chaney, Jr., Henry O'Neill, Frank Puglia, Cy Kendall, Ethel Griffies. **Credits:** Dir: David Miller; Prod: Irving Asher; Writer: Gene Fowler, Jr.; Story: Howard Emmett Rogers, Bradbury Foote; DP: Leonard Smith, William V. Skall; Ed: Robert J. Kern; Composer: David Snell. Color, 95 min. **VHS**

Billy Two Hats
(1974) MGM
A downbeat Western, though an interestingly offbeat role for Peck as a grizzled old outlaw who teams with a young half-breed for one last job. Shot in Israel. **Cast:** Gregory Peck, Desi Arnaz, Jr., Jack Warden, Sian Barbara Allen, David Huddleston. **Credits:** Dir: Ted Kotcheff, Alan Sharp; Prod: Norman Jewison, Patrick Palmer; DP: Brian West; Prod Design: Anthony Pratt; Composer: John Scott; SFX: Leslie Hillman. Color, 99 min. **VHS**

The Bingo Long Traveling All-Stars and Motor Kings
(1976) Universal
Appealing comedy about a group of black baseball players who defect from the 1930s Negro National League. As result, the talented ballplayers travel from town to town, challenging local white teams, and hiding their talents under comic shenanigans. Interesting balance of social issues and comedy. The leads are based on authentic heroes Satchel Paige and Josh Gibson. **Cast:** James Earl Jones, Richard Pryor, Billy Dee Williams, Ted Ross, Jophery Brown, Tony Burton, Rico Dawson, Sam Briston, Leon Wagner. **Credits:** Dir: John Badham; Prod: Rob Cohen; Writer: Hal Barwood, Matthew Robbins; DP: Bill Butler; Ed: David Rawlins; Prod Design: Bernard Johnson; Composer: William Goldstein. Color, 111 min. **VHS, LASER**

Birdman of Alcatraz
(1962) United Artists
A thoughtful study of the prison life of Robert Stroud, a convicted murderer who found a redemptive outlet in caring for wayward birds. Despite an unforgiving prison system favoring punishment over rehabilitation, Stroud went on to make breakthroughs in the treatment of bird diseases. Academy Award Nominations: 4, including Best Actor: Burt Lancaster. **Cast:** Burt Lancaster, Karl Malden, Thelma Ritter, Edmond O'Brien, Betty Field, Neville Brand, Hugh Marlowe, Telly Savalas, James Westerfield. **Credits:** Dir: John Frankenheimer; Prod: Stuart Millar, Guy Tros-

per; Writer: Guy Trosper; Story: Thomas E. Gaddis; DP: Burnett Guffey; Ed: Edward Mann; Composer: Elmer Bernstein. Color, 143 min. **VHS, LASER**

Bird of Paradise
(1932) RKO
A cautionary tale of romantic ecology? Exotic anyway, with McCrea beaching his yacht in the South Seas and falling in love with native looker Del Rio. When the interloper decides that he would be much happier living with his Luana in paradise than returning to his empty modern lifestyle, he upsets the girl's family . . . and maybe even the local deities. **Cast:** Dolores Del Rio, Joel McCrea, John Halliday, Lon Chaney, Jr., Skeets Gallagher, Bert Roach, Oliver Toones. **Credits:** Dir: King Vidor; Prod: David O. Selznick; Writer: Wells Root, Leonard Praskins, Wanda Tuchock; Story: Richard Walton Tully; DP: Clyde De Vinna, Edward Cronjager, Lucien Andriot; Prod Design: Carroll Clark; Choreographer: Busby Berkeley; Composer: Max Steiner. B&W, 82 min. **VHS**

The Birds
(1963) Universal
Hitchcock, the master of suspense, ventures into the realm of horror with the depiction of a world in which nature can go suddenly, terrifyingly mad. When Hedren appears in the idyllic coastal village of Bodega Bay with two lovebirds in tow, the local birds inexplicably begin to wage an all-out war on humans. Hitchcock's follow-up to *Psycho* tops even that landmark for shock value. Loosely based on a Daphne du Maurier short story. Academy Award Nominations: Best Visual Effects. **Cast:** Rod Taylor, Jessica Tandy, Tippi Hedren, Suzanne Pleshette, Veronica Cartwright, Charles McGraw, Ethel Griffies. **Credits:** Dir: Alfred Hitchcock; Prod: Alfred Hitchcock; Writer: Evan Hunter; Story: Daphne du Maurier; DP: Robert Burks; Ed: George Tomasini; Composer: Bernard Herrmann; SFX: Ub Iwerks. Color, 119 min. **VHS, LASER**

Birth of a Nation
(1915) Epoch
Griffith's enduring masterpiece tells the story of two families, one Northern and one Southern, facing the Civil War and Reconstruction periods. The Camerons, headed by "Little Colonel" Ben Cameron, and the Stonemans, headed by politician Austin Stoneman, have been friends for years, but find themselves on opposite sides of the battle lines when war comes. The Civil

War exacts a personal toll on both families, only to be followed by the equally destructive Reconstruction period. Griffith links the consequences of the war on their lives with the formation of the Ku Klux Klan, whom he credits with establishing American Romanticism, as well as Lincoln's assassination. This landmark cinematic achievement features the first use of now-standard techniques like cross-cutting and deep focus, as well as the unprecedented long shot of the Lincoln assassination and a color sequence at the end. **Cast:** Lillian Gish, Mae Marsh, Miriam Cooper, Wallace Reid, Henry B. Walthall, Erich Von Stroheim, Ralph Lewis, George Siegmann, Walter Long, Aitken Spottiswoode. **Credits:** Dir: D. W. Griffith; Prod: D. W. Griffith; Writer: D. W. Griffith, Frank Woods; DP: G. W. Bitzer; Ed: James Smith; Composer: Joseph Carl Breil, Richard Wagner. B&W, 200 min. VHS, LASER, DVD

The Birth of the Blues
(1941) Paramount
Crosby and Martin star as two jazz artists in the swinging world of 1920s New Orleans. Crosby is a clarinet player who is out to start a band called the Basin Street Hot-Shots. When Martin joins as vocalist, romance ensues. The film pays homage to jazz greats such as Duke Ellington and Louis Armstrong, and includes many musical numbers filled with cool clarinets and sizzling jam sessions such as, "Birth of the Blues," "Melancholy Baby," "St. Louis Blues," and "St. James Infirmary." **Cast:** Bing Crosby, Mary Martin, Jack Teagarden, Carolyn Lee, Eddie Anderson, Brian Donlevy. **Credits:** Dir: Victor Schertzinger; Prod: B. G. DeSylva; Writer: Harry Tugend; Story: Walter DeLeon; DP: William Mellor; Ed: Paul Weatherwax; Prod Design: Hans Dreier, Ernst Fegte; Costumes: Edith Head. B&W and Color, 76 min. VHS

The Biscuit Eater
(1940) Paramount
The heartwarming tale of a boy and his dog, a runt that has come from a famous litter of thoroughbred hunting dogs. The puppy is a gift from the owner of the plantation where his father has spent his life working. Despite the canine's mischief, the boy is determined to make a great champion of his dog. **Cast:** Tiverton Invader, Billy Lee, Cordell Hickman, Helene Millard, Richard Lane, Lester Matthews, Fred Toones, William Russell, Earl Johnson. **Credits:** Dir: Stuart

Heisler; Prod: Jack Moss; Writer: Stuart Anthony, Lillie Hayward; Story: James Street; DP: Leo Tover; Ed: Everett Douglas; Composer: Frederick Hollander. B&W, 83 min.

The Bishop's Wife
(1947) RKO
A harassed bishop's prayers are answered when an angel (played by Grant) is sent from heaven to help him raise money for a new church. A delightful holiday comedy that was remade in 1996 by Penny Marshall as *The Preacher's Wife*. Academy Award Nominations: 5, including Best Picture; Best Director. **Academy Awards:** Best Sound Recording. **Cast:** Cary Grant, David Niven, Loretta Young, Elsa Lanchester, Monty Woolley, James Gleason, Gladys Cooper, Sara Haden, Regis Toomey. **Credits:** Dir: Henry Koster; Writer: Robert E. Sherwood, Leonardo Bercovici; Story: Robert Nathan; DP: Gregg Toland; Ed: Monica Collingwood; Composer: Hugo Friedhofer. B&W, 109 min. VHS, LASER, DVD

Bite the Bullet
(1975) Columbia
Great mid-'70s cast in a grueling Denver–to–Kansas City horse race that tests the motivation and determination of a motley collection of competitors. The rivals come to respect each other as they endure one beautifully photographed hardship after another. Academy Award Nominations: 2, for Best Sound; Best Original Score. **Cast:** Gene Hackman, Candice Bergen, James Coburn, Ben Johnson, Ian Bannen, Jan-Michael Vincent, Paul Stewart. **Credits:** Dir: Richard Brooks; Prod: Richard Brooks; Writer: Richard Brooks; DP: Harry Stradling; Ed: George Granville; Prod Design: Robert Boyle; Composer: Alex North; Set Designer: Robert Signorelli. Color, 132 min. VHS, LASER

Bitter Sweet
(1940) MGM
MacDonald and Eddy vocalize through 19th-century Vienna in this second film version of Noel Coward's operetta. A must for Jeanette and Nelson fans, but tolerable also for the score and the lush Technicolor. Academy Award Nominations for Best (Color) Cinematography; Best (Color) Interior Decoration. **Cast:** Jeanette MacDonald, Nelson Eddy, George Sanders, Felix Bressart, Sig Rumann, Ian Hunter, Fay Holden, Herman Bing, Curt Bois. **Credits:** Dir: W. S. Van Dyke; Prod: Victor Saville; Writer: Lesser Samuels; DP: Oliver T.

Marsh, Allen M. Davey; Ed: Harold F. Kress; Prod Design: Cedric Gibbons, John Detlie; Choreographer: Ernst Matray; Composer: Noel Coward. B&W, 94 min. VHS

The Bitter Tea of General Yen
(1932) Columbia
Though tame by contemporary standards, Capra's tale of suggested interracial romance proved to be shocking in its day. Missionary Megan Davis (Stanwyck) travels from her staid New England home to Shanghai during China's civil unrest in the 1930s. There, she joins her fiancé, Robert Strike, but the couple is separated while trying to liberate an orphanage—and Megan falls into the hands of Chinese warlord General Yen (Asther). To their mutual surprise, Megan and General Yen develop an affinity for one another. Though he orders the massacre of hundreds during the day, Yen at night reveals a rueful, poetic side, and their affection deepens. However, the inroads made by Chinese rebels threaten to end their tentative courtship in a bloody manner that, Yen surmises, has been predetermined by his own deeds. **Cast:** Barbara Stanwyck, Nils Asther, Gavin Gordon, Toshia Mori, Richard Loo, Lucien Littlefield, Clara Blandick, Walter Connolly. **Credits:** Dir: Frank Capra; Prod: Walter Wanger; Writer: Edward Paramore; Story: Grace Zaring Stone; DP: Joseph Walker; Ed: Edward Curtiss; Composer: W. Franke Harling; Costumes: Edward Stevenson, Robert Kalloch. B&W, 87 min. VHS

Bitter Victory
(1957) Columbia
Tense WWII drama pits Jurgens against Rommel's German Afrika Korps—and one of his subordinates (Burton), who had an affair with his wife. Unusual Ray picture with international cast and production. **Cast:** Richard Burton, Curt Jurgens, Ruth Roman, Raymond Pellegrin, Sean Kelly, Anthony Bushell, Andrew Crawford, Nigel Green, Sumner Williams. **Credits:** Dir: Nicholas Ray; Prod: Paul Graetz; Writer: Gavin Lambert, Vladimir Pozner, Nicholas Ray; Story: Pauline Gallico, Rene Hardy; DP: Michel Kelber; Ed: Leonide Azar; Prod Design: Jean d'Eaubonne; Composer: Maurice Leroux. B&W, 103 min.

Black Angel
(1946) Universal
An unlikely pair of sleuths—a spurned ex-wife and a cuckolded drunk—

attempt to clear the errant husband of the murder of the drunkard's wife. As the electric chair looms larger, the wife begins to suspect her new partner of the crime. The thought begins to dawn on him, too. Terrific suspenser from a novel by Cornell Woolrich. **Cast:** Dan Duryea, June Vincent, Peter Lorre, Broderick Crawford, Constance Dowling, Wallace Ford, Hobart Cavanaugh, Fred Steele. **Credits:** Dir: Roy William Neill; Prod: Tom McKnight, Roy William Neill; Writer: Roy Chanslor; Story: Cornell Woolrich; DP: Paul Ivano; Ed: Saul A. Goodkind; Prod Design: Martin Obzina, Jack Otterson; Composer: Frank Skinner; Costumes: Vera West; Set Designer: Russell A. Gausman, E. R. Robinson. B&W, 80 min. **VHS**

The Black Arrow
(1948) Columbia
The swashbuckling hero Sir Richard Shelton returns home from the War of the Roses, only to have his uncle inform him of his father's murder. He sets out to discover the truth, guided mysteriously by a series of ominous black arrows, which lead him back to his uncle. The film climaxes with a dramatic jousting battle that will determine who lives, and who dies. Based on the Robert Louis Stevenson novel. **Cast:** Louis Hayward, Janet Blair, Edgar Buchanan, George Macready. **Credits:** Dir: Gordon Douglas; Prod: Grant Whytock; Writer: Richard Schayer, David Sheppard, Thomas Seller; DP: Charles Lawton, Jr.; Ed: Jerome Thoms. B&W, 76 min. **VHS**

Blackbeard's Ghost
(1968) Disney
Disney doings as a college track coach conjures up his ancestor, the titular pirate, to help rid himself of some pesky racketeers who have plans to turn his house into a casino. **Cast:** Peter Ustinov, Dean Jones, Suzanne Pleshette, Elsa Lanchester, Richard Deacon. **Credits:** Dir: Robert Stevenson; Prod: Bill Walsh; Writer: Bill Walsh, Don DaGradi; Story: Ben Stahl; DP: Edward Colman; Ed: Robert Stafford; Prod Design: John B. Mansbridge, Carroll Clark; Composer: Robert F. Brunner; Costumes: Bill Thomas; SFX: Robert A. Mattey, Eustace Lycett; Set Designer: Hal Gausman, Emile Kuri. Color, 108 min. **VHS**

Blackboard Jungle
(1955) MGM
Atmospheric story of a teacher's harrowing experience in the New York City school system. Navy veteran Ford is eager to start a new career as a high school teacher and his military training might come in handy. His new school is located in one of the poorest districts and is a magnet for delinquents. The new teacher's idealism fades as he struggles to make a difference to his indifferent students. Rock came to the big screen when Bill Haley's "Rock Around the Clock" bopped over the opening credits. Academy Award Nominations: 4, including Best Screenplay; Best Cinematography. **Cast:** Glenn Ford, Anne Francis, Sidney Poitier, Vic Morrow, Louis Calhern, Margaret Hayes, John Hoyt, Richard Kiley, Emile Meyer, Warner Anderson. **Credits:** Dir: Richard Brooks; Prod: Pandro S. Berman; Writer: Richard Brooks; Story: Evan Hunter; DP: Russell Harlan; Ed: Ferris Webster; Prod Design: Cedric Gibbons, Randal Duell; Composer: Charles Wolcott. B&W, 101 min. **VHS**

The Black Cat
(1934) Universal
Karloff and Lugosi together for the first time in a visually stylish film about a deadly rivalry between a friendly doctor and a sinister architect. A hapless honeymooning couple are the pawns in their game, which involves devil-worship, necrophilia, and chess. A surprisingly dark outing in the early days of Production Code enforcement. One of many similarly named films, this one has nothing to do with the Edgar Allen Poe tale that inspired the title. **Cast:** Boris Karloff, Bela Lugosi, David Manners, Jacqueline Wells, Lucille Lund, Henry Armetta, Egon Brecher. **Credits:** Dir: Edgar G. Ulmer; Prod: Carl Laemmle; Writer: Edgar G. Ulmer, Peter Ruric; DP: John Mescall; Prod Design: Charles D. Hall; Composer: Heinz Roemheld. B&W, 66 min. **VHS**

Black Friday
(1940) Universal
When a professor gets seriously hurt in a car crash with a gangster, a surgeon (Karloff) makes a risky, desperate decision: he saves his friend's life by transferring the brain of a dying gangster into the professor's body. But the surgeon's original good intentions fade when he learns that, embedded in the criminal's brain, is information regarding a hidden fortune. Determined to get the money, the doctor manipulates his patient into temporarily assuming the gangster's personality, and the criminal mind takes over, seeking revenge on a rival gangster (Lugosi). Neat mystery tale with horror overtones added by presence of monster-movie stars. **Cast:** Boris Karloff, Bela Lugosi, Stanley Ridges, Anne Nagel, Anne Gwynne, Virginia Brissac, Paul Fix. **Credits:** Dir: Arthur Lubin; Prod: Burt Kelly; Writer: Curt Siodmak, Eric Taylor; DP: Woody Bredell; Ed: Philip Cahn; Prod Design: Jack Otterson; Composer: Hans J. Salter; Costumes: Vera West; Set Designer: Russell A. Gausman. B&W, 70 min. **VHS**

Black Fury
(1935) Universal
A plainspoken coal miner earns himself a beating by the company legbreakers—and gets his friend killed—when he attempts to shine a light on the conditions down in the deep, dark holes. Muni is tough as nails in this patented Warner social-problem picture based on a true story. **Cast:** Paul Muni, Karen Morley, William Gargan, Barton MacLane, John Qualen, J. Carrol Naish, Vince Barnett, Tully Marshall, Henry O'Neill. **Credits:** Dir: Michael Curtiz; Prod: Robert Lord; Writer: Abem Finkel, Carl Erickson; Story: Harry R. Irving; DP: Byron Haskin. B&W, 95 min. **VHS**

The Black Hole
(1979) Disney
A space crew traveling the cosmos runs into a long-missing craft, manned by Dr. Hans Reinhardt. Upon meeting Reinhardt, the astronauts discover that he is not only insane, but determined to travel through a nearby "black hole," an abyss from which no one can escape. The situation darkens when Reinhardt holds the crew captive after realizing that they can help him reach his goal. Disney updated its image with sci-fi and a PG rating. **Cast:** Maximilian Schell, Anthony Perkins, Robert Forster, Joseph Bottoms, Yvette Mimieux, Ernest Borgnine, Tom McLoughlin. **Credits:** Dir: Gary Nelson; Prod: Ron Miller; Writer: Bob Barbash, Gerry Day, Richard H. Landau, Jeb Rosebrook; DP: Frank Phillips; Ed: Gregg McLaughlin; Prod Design: Peter Ellenshaw; Composer: John Barry; Costumes: Bill Thomas. Color, 97 min. **VHS, LASER**

Black Legion
(1936) Warner Bros.
After losing a promotion to a well-deserving, but foreign-born, coworker, Bogart joins a KKK-like organization, the Black Legion. His wife leaves him, and when he tells his best friend about the organization, Bogart's

coerced into killing him. **Cast:** Humphrey Bogart, Dick Foran, Erin O'Brien-Moore, Ann Sheridan, Helen Flint. **Credits:** Dir: Archie Mayo; Prod: Robert Lord; Writer: Robert Lord, William Wister Haines, Abem Finkel; DP: George Barnes; Ed: Owen Marks; Composer: Bernhard Kaun; Art Director: Robert M. Haas. B&W, 80 min.

Black Like Me

(1964)
Based on a true story and best-selling book by John Howard Griffin, a white writer colors his skin to obtain a first-hand account of racial hatred in America. Woefully, not yet a reminder of times gone by. **Cast:** Roscoe Lee Browne, James Whitmore, Sorrell Booke, Lenka Petersen. **Credits:** Dir: Carl Lerner; Writer: Gerda Lerner, Carl Lerner; Story: John Howard Griffin; DP: Henry Mueller II, Victor Lukens; Ed: Lora Hayes; Composer: Meyer Kupferman. B&W, 110 min. **VHS, LASER**

The Black Orchid

(1959) Paramount
Quinn and Loren star in this bittersweet romance. Loren helped her late husband become involved in crime, and now her son has been convicted of theft and is sent to a work program. Her life begins to take a new course when she meets and falls in love with Quinn, a simple businessman. Their children have different ideas about the budding romance. An early outing for director Ritt. **Cast:** Sophia Loren, Anthony Quinn, Ina Balin, Jimmie Baird, Mark Richman, Naomi Stevens, Frank Puglia. **Credits:** Dir: Martin Ritt; Prod: Carlo Ponti, Marcello Girosi; Writer: Joseph Stefano; DP: Robert Burks; Ed: Howard Smith; Prod Design: Hal Pereira; Composer: Alessandro Cicognini. B&W, 96 min. **VHS**

The Black Pirate

(1926) United Artists
This silent swashbuckling adventure, starring the incomparable Fairbanks, made film history as one of the first full features shot entirely in two-strip Technicolor. Here, he plays a nobleman who wants to revenge his father's murder, so he boards a pirate vessel disguised as one of the thieving, villainous rapscallions, and sets about achieving his goal. On the high seas, the athletic Fairbanks provides a rip-roaring, stunt-filled voyage—complete with a one-man takeover of a merchant ship. A National Film Registry Outstanding Film. **Cast:** Douglas Fairbanks, Donald Crisp, Billie Dove, Tempe Piggot, Sam De Grasse,

Charles Stevens, Charles Belcher, Anders Randolf. **Credits:** Dir: Albert Parker; Prod: Douglas Fairbanks; Writer: Douglas Fairbanks, Jack Cunningham; DP: Henry Sharp; Ed: William Nolan; Prod Design: Carl Oscar Borg; Composer: Mortimer Wilson. Color, 110 min. **VHS, LASER**

The Black Room

(1935) Columbia
Karloff is once again chilling and brilliant in this highly-regarded dual role. He plays twin brothers Anton and Gregor. It has been prophesied that Anton, the younger brother, will eventually murder Gregor in their castle's "Black Room." The loathed Gregor is an evil baron; Anton is revered. A murder makes the prophecy impossible to fulfill. Or does it? **Cast:** Boris Karloff, Marian Marsh, Thurston Hall, Robert Allen, Katherine DeMille, John Buckler, Henry Kolker, Colin Tapley, Torben Meyer, Egon Brecher. **Credits:** Dir: Roy William Neill; Prod: Robert North; Writer: Henry Myers; DP: Allen G. Siegler; Ed: Richard Cahoon; Costumes: Murray Mayer. B&W, 73 min. **VHS**

The Black Rose

(1950) Fox
The heroic saga of Walter of Gurnie, a rebellious Saxon nobleman chased from thirteenth-century Norman England. Walter and his partner, the expert bowman, Tristram, head for the Far East and travel to the court of Kublai Khan in the company of the Warlord Bayan. They soon realize they are merely well-kept prisoners and attempt to escape with Bayan's gift to Khan, the concubine Maryam, who has fallen in love with Walter. Welles was reportedly a pill on the set, as his attentions were diverted to developing his *Othello*. But curious to see him in a costume epic. **Cast:** Tyrone Power, Orson Welles, Cecile Aubry, Alfonso Bedoya, Robert Blake, Mary Clare, Finlay Currie, Laurence Harvey, Jack Hawkins, James Robertson Justice, Herbert Lom, Gibb McLaughlin. **Credits:** Dir: Henry Hathaway; Prod: Louis D. Lighton; Writer: Talbot Jennings; Story: Thomas B. Costain; DP: Jack Cardiff; Ed: Manuel Del Campo; Prod Design: Paul Sherrif, W. Andrews; Composer: Richard Addinsell, Muir Mathieson. Color, 120 min.

The Black Stallion

(1979) United Artists
Great family entertainment, this is a film about the adventures of a young boy and his love for a black Arabian

stallion. When the two are the only survivors of a terrible shipwreck, they form an unbreakable bond that leads them into training for a racing championship. A very solid performance by Rooney as the horse trainer helps elevate matters. Based on Walter Farley's classic novel. Academy Award Nominations for Best Supporting Actor: Mickey Rooney; Best Film Editing. **Academy Awards:** Best Sound. **Cast:** Mickey Rooney, Kelly Reno, Teri Garr, Hoyt Axton, Clarence Muse, Michael Higgins, Ed McNamara, Doghmi Larbi, John Burton, John Buchanan. **Credits:** Dir: Carroll Ballard, Francis Ford Coppola; Prod: Tom Sternberg, Fred Roos; Writer: Melissa Mathison, Jeanne Rosenberg, William D. Wittliff; DP: Caleb Deschanel; Ed: Robert Dalva; Composer: Carmine Coppola. Color, 118 min. **VHS, LASER, DVD**

Black Sunday

(1977) Paramount
Blend of suspense and disaster genres as Arab terrorists aim to commandeer the Goodyear blimp and explode it over the Super Bowl, killing 80,000 fans, including the U.S. president. Better than it sounds under Frankenheimer's management. **Cast:** Robert Shaw, Bruce Dern, Steven Keats, Marthe Keller, Fritz Weaver, Bekim Fehmiu, Michael V. Gazzo, William Daniels, Walter Gotell. **Credits:** Dir: John Frankenheimer; Prod: Robert Evans; Writer: Ernest Lehman, Kenneth Ross, Ivan Moffat; Story: Thomas Harris; DP: John A. Alonzo; Ed: Tom Rolf; Composer: John Williams. Color, 143 min. **VHS, LASER**

The Black Swan

(1942) Fox
After receiving the governorship of Jamaica, former pirate Henry Morgan—now Sir Henry Morgan—dispatches his able first mate James Waring to dispense of his former henchman, the redheaded villain, Captain Billy Leech. In the process, Waring, also a pirate turned King's loyal subject, abducts Margaret Denby, a young woman of aristocratic bearing, whom he takes along on his pursuit. But Margaret will not be trifled with, and she fights him tooth and nail up until Waring's final battle with Leech—a battle that changes the way Margaret feels about her captor. Academy Award Nominations: 3, including Best Special Effects. **Academy Awards:** Best Color Cinematography. **Cast:** Tyrone Power, Maureen O'Hara, Thomas Mitchell, George Sanders, Anthony Quinn, George Zucco, Laird

Cregar, Edward Ashley, Fortunio Bonanova, Stuart Robertson. **Credits:** Dir: Henry King; Prod: Robert Bassler; Writer: Ben Hecht, Seton I. Miller; Story: Rafael Sabatini; DP: Leon Shamroy; Ed: Barbara McLean; Prod Design: Richard Day, James Basevi; Composer: Alfred Newman. Color, 85 min. **VHS**

Black Tuesday
(1955) United Artists
Robinson conjures up his tough-guy image from younger days in this gangster film about two criminals on death row who break out together and take hostages. **Cast:** Edward G. Robinson, Jean Parker, Milburn Stone, Warren Stevens, Hal Baylor, James Bell, Peter Graves, Jack Kelly. **Credits:** Dir: Hugo Fregonese; Prod: Robert Goldstein, Leonard Goldstein; Writer: Sidney Boehm; DP: Stanley Cortez; Ed: Robert Golden, Robert Parrish; Prod Design: Hilyard Brown; Composer: Paul Dunlap; Art Director: Alfred E. Spencer. B&W, 80 min.

Blacula
(1972) AIP
Cultivated and articulate African Prince Mamuwalde is bitten by Count Dracula, and he develops the requisite insatiable hunger for blood. Two centuries later, the princely ghoul is unwittingly transported to modern-day Los Angeles where bloodthirst is a way of life. Blaxploitation and the horror genre mingle in this creature feature that inspired the sequel *Scream, Blacula, Scream.* **Cast:** William Marshall, Vonetta McGee, Denise Nicholas, Thalmus Rasulala, Charles Macaulay, Gordon Pinsent. **Credits:** Dir: William Crain; Writer: Joan Torres, Raymond Koenig; DP: John Wright Stevens; Ed: Allan Jacobs; Prod Design: Walter Scott Herndon; Composer: Gene Page. Color, 92 min. **VHS**

The Blazing Forest
(1952) Paramount
A logging boss with mysterious debts works hard to earn his check in this action-adventure. The woodcutter must push his crew and at the same time deal with the petty politics of his wife, his wayward brother, and the owner of the timberlands. When a fire endangers them all, our hero braves the flames to save his brother. **Cast:** John Payne, William Demarest, Agnes Moorehead, Richard Arlen, Susan Morrow, Roscoe Ates, Lynne Roberts, Ewing Mitchell, Walter Reed. **Credits:** Dir: Edward Ludwig; Prod: William H. Pine, William C. Thomas; Writer: Lewis

R. Foster, Winston Miller; DP: Lionel Lindon; Ed: Howard Smith; Composer: Lucien Cailliet. Color, 90 min.

Blazing Saddles
(1974) Warner Bros.
When the sheriff of a small frontier town meets a violent end, convict Bart (Little) is offered a reprieve if he is willing to take on the job. Sheriff Bart rides into town and soon realizes from the less-than-cheery welcome that the townspeople (who all seem to be named Johnson) aren't prepared for a black sheriff and that he was never meant to succeed at all. The evil LaMarr (Korman) intends to drive out the good townspeople with a hand-picked group of thugs and take over the town but the naive Bart has other plans. After a plea to the town, "You'd do it for Randolph Scott," Bart enlists every able body and the town drunk (Wilder), formerly the Waco Kid, to help save the town. A hilarious spoof of nearly every Western gag conceived, this film turns racism on its ear at every turn. Academy Award Nominations: 3, including Best Supporting Actress: Madeline Kahn. **Cast:** Cleavon Little, Gene Wilder, Madeline Kahn, Harvey Korman, Mel Brooks, Slim Pickens, Burton Gilliam, Alex Karras. **Credits:** Dir: Mel Brooks; Prod: Michael Hertzberg; Writer: Mel Brooks, Norman Steinberg, Andrew Bergman, Richard Pryor, Alan Unger; DP: Joseph Biroc; Ed: Danford B. Greene, John C. Howard; Prod Design: Peter Wooley; Choreographer: Alan Johnson; Composer: John Morris; Costumes: Vittorio Nino Novarese. Color, 93 min. **VHS, LASER, DVD**

Blessed Event
(1932) Warner Bros.
A keyhole-peeping columnist whose zest for unearthing short marriage-to-maternity spans among Broadway's notables brings him success in the tabloids. He thinks no one is exempt from his poison pen, but some sinister types intend to prove him dead wrong. Film debut for Powell. Based on a play by Manuel Seff and Forrest Wilson. **Cast:** Lee Tracy, Dick Powell, Mary Brian, Allen Jenkins, Ruth Donnelly, Emma Dunn, Walter Miller, Tom Dugan, Isabel Jewell, Ned Sparks. **Credits:** Dir: Roy Del Ruth; Writer: Howard J. Green; Story: Manuel Seff, Forrest Wilson; DP: Sol Polito; Ed: Jim Gibbons. B&W, 78 min. **VHS**

Bless the Beasts and Children
(1971) Columbia
Six troubled young misfits are forced

to attend a camp in Arizona in an effort to tame their ways. Escaping the confining camp and its counselors, they come across a herd of buffalo. Realizing that the buffalo are to be slaughtered, the boys band together and as one attempt to free the doomed animals. In the process, the boys open up to one another and reveal secrets about their difficult family lives. The music by DeVorzon and Botkin was later used by Nadia Comaneci in her gold medal–winning 1976 Olympic gymnastic routine and later became the theme song for the hit soap opera *The Young and the Restless.* **Cast:** Miles Chapin, Billy Mumy, Jesse White, Barry Robins, Ken Swofford. **Credits:** Dir: Stanley Kramer; Prod: Stanley Kramer; Writer: Mac Benoff; Story: Glendon Swarthout; DP: Michel Hugo; Composer: Barry DeVorzon, Perry Botkin. Color, 109 min. **VHS**

Blind Alley
(1939) Columbia
In this gripping criminal melodrama, a group of wanted killers, led by Morris, break into the lakeside home of an eminent psychologist, played by Bellamy, and hide out while waiting for their escape boat to pick them up. Trapped in these close quarters, Morris and Bellamy engage in a psychological struggle, with the doctor attempting to get to the core of Morris's problems in order to stop him from killing again. **Cast:** Chester Morris, Ralph Bellamy, Ann Dvorak, Joan Perry, Melville Cooper, Rose Stradner, John Eldridge, Ann Doran, Marc Lawrence, Stanley Brown. **Credits:** Dir: Charles Vidor; Prod: Fred Kohlmar; Writer: Michael Blankfort, Albert Duffy, Philip MacDonald; Story: James Warwick; DP: Lucien Ballard; Ed: Otto Meyer; Prod Design: Lionel Banks; Composer: Morris Stoloff. B&W, 68 min.

The Bliss of Mrs. Blossom
(1968) Paramount
Harriet Blossom, who's bored with her marriage, seduces Ambrose, a clumsy repairman. But Ambrose is so taken with Harriet that he moves into her attic—and refuses to leave! The idea of having a spare lover quickly grows on Harriet, and she allows him to stay. However, the lucky lady must prevent her two men from ever running into each other. Meanwhile, a couple of cops are out looking for the missing Ambrose. **Cast:** Shirley MacLaine, Richard Attenborough, James Booth, Freddie Jones, Bob Monkhouse, John Cleese, Patricia Routledge, John

Bluthal, William Rushton. **Credits:** Dir: Joseph McGrath; Prod: Josef Shaftel; Writer: Alec Coppel, Denis Norden; DP: Geoffrey Unsworth; Ed: Ralph Sheldon; Prod Design: George Lack, Bill Alexander; Composer: Riz Ortolani. Color, 93 min. VHS

Blithe Spirit
(1945) United Artists
In Lean's adaptation of Noël Coward's farce, an English mystery novelist invites a medium over for dinner in the hopes of gathering enough material for his latest book, as well as exposing her as a charlatan. As a result he's plagued by the nagging of his deceased first wife who's not too keen on wife number two. **Academy Awards:** Best Special Visual Effects. **Cast:** Rex Harrison, Constance Cummings, Margaret Rutherford, Kay Hammond, Hugh Wakefield, Joyce Carey, Jacqueline Clark. **Credits:** Dir: David Lean; Writer: Noël Coward; Story: Ronald Neame, David Lean, Anthony Havelock-Allan; DP: Ronald Neame; Ed: Jack Harris; Prod Design: C. P. Norman; Composer: Richard Addinsell. Color, 96 min. VHS, DVD

The Blob
(1958) Paramount
One of the quintessential films for lovers of those science-fiction/horror/monster/camp films of the '50s. A gigantic, gooey glob arrives from outer space and proceeds to terrorize a small town. The more it eats, the more it grows. Local teenagers, who have witnessed its obscene display of hunger, are ignored until it's too late. Can the local bad boy (McQueen, in his first leading role) save his 'burb from the sinister slime—and reform himself in the process? Great late-night viewing, but save the Jell-O for later. Remade in 1988. **Cast:** Steve McQueen, Aneta Corseaut, Earl Rowe, Olin Howlin, Stephen Chase, John Benson. **Credits:** Dir: Irvin Yeaworth, Jr.; Prod: Jack H. Harris; Writer: Theodore Simonson, Kate Phillips; DP: Thomas Spalding; Ed: Alfred Hillmann; Prod Design: William Jersey, Karl Karlson; Composer: Ralph Carmichael, Burt Bacharach, Hal David. Color, 86 min. VHS

Blockade
(1938) United Artists
Romance set against the backdrop of the Spanish Civil War, with Fonda as a courageous farmer and Carroll as a globe-trotting correspondent. **Cast:** Madeleine Carroll, Henry Fonda, Leo Carrillo, John Halliday, Vladimir

Sokolov, Robert Warwick, Reginald Denny, Peter Godfrey, Katherine De Mille, William Davidson. **Credits:** Dir: Wilhelm Dieterle; Prod: Walter Wanger; Writer: John Howard Lawson; Story: John Howard Lawson; DP: Rudolph Mate; Ed: Dorothy Spencer; Prod Design: Alexander Toluboff; Composer: Werner Janssen, Ann Ronell, Kurt Weill. B&W, 85 min.

Blonde Crazy
(1931) Warner Bros.
Cagney and Blondell make a charming pair of grifters. Bellhop Bert Harris has a little racketeering scheme in addition to his hotel duties. He uses the cash generated by this business venture to hop a ride to another town where he and his sweetheart and fellow con commit a few more scams. As they move farther west, they find it's their turn to be grifted when they meet Dapper Don Barker, a counterfeiter busy passing out bogus twenty-dollar bills. **Cast:** Joan Blondell, James Cagney, Louis Calhern, Ray Milland, Polly Walters, Nat Pendleton, Guy Kibbee, Charles Lane, Maude Eburne. **Credits:** Dir: Roy Del Ruth; Writer: Kubec Glasmon, John Bright; DP: Sid Hickox; Ed: Ralph Dawson. B&W, 81 min. VHS, LASER

Blonde Venus
(1932) Paramount
Dietrich, Marshall, and Grant star in von Sternberg's classic social drama about a young mother who enters the nightclub world to support her family. There she meets a handsome playboy. The ensuing scandal threatens her family. Characteristic von Sternberg stylistic flourishes, with the famous scene of Dietrich in the gorilla suit. **Cast:** Marlene Dietrich, Herbert Marshall, Cary Grant, Dickie Moore. **Credits:** Dir: Josef von Sternberg; Writer: Jules Furthman, S. K. Lauren; DP: Bert Glennon; Prod Design: Wiard Ihnen; Composer: Oscar Potoker; Costumes: Travis Banton. B&W, 89 min. VHS

Blondie
With the Blondie series—at 28 entries, one of the longest-running in motion-picture history—Columbia brought Chic Young's popular comic strip to life. Clever casting landed actors who actually resembled the Bumsteads of the funny pages: bleach-blonde Penny Singleton played the loopy yet endearing Blondie, and Arthur Lake portrayed the befuddled Dagwood. Unlike many series films, which saw a consistent turnover of the major players, Blondie principals

Lake and Singleton starred in all 28 installments, as did Larry Sims, who played Baby Dumpling (who later dropped the diminutive for the more mature name Alexander). Even the family pooch, Daisy, stuck around for the 12-year series. In each entry, the bumbling Dagwood found himself in some sort of misadventure, and more often than not, Blondie came to the rescue. The series was a launching pad for several up-and-comers. In *Blondie on a Budget* (1940), Rita Hayworth shows up as Dagwood's former girlfriend, and Larry Parks appears in *Blondie Plays Cupid* (1940). By the series end, the films became shopworn, falling victim to its winning formula.

Blondie *(1938)*
Blondie Meets the Boss *(1939)*
Blondie Brings Up Baby *(1939)*
Blondie Takes a Vacation *(1939)*
Blondie on a Budget *(1940)*
Blondie Has Servant Trouble *(1940)*
Blondie Plays Cupid *(1940)*
Blondie Goes Latin *(1941)*
Blondie in Society *(1941)*
Blondie Goes to College *(1942)*
Blondie's Blessed Event *(1942)*
Blondie for Victory *(1942)*
It's a Great Life *(1943)*
Footlight Glamour *(1943)*
Leave It to Blondie *(1945)*
Life with Blondie *(1946)*
Blondie's Lucky Day *(1946)*
Blondie Knows Best *(1946)*
Blondie's Big Moment *(1947)*
Blondie's Holiday *(1947)*
Blondie in the Dough *(1947)*
Blondie's Anniversary *(1947)*
Blondie's Reward *(1948)*
Blondie's Secret *(1948)*
Blondie's Big Deal *(1949)*
Blondie Hits the Jackpot *(1949)*
Blondie's Hero *(1950)*
Beware of Blondie *(1950)*

Blood Alley
(1955) Warner Bros.
Political prisoner Wilder (Wayne) is liberated by the inhabitants of a local Chinese village. The oppressed villagers are disillusioned by Communism's stranglehold and want the former Merchant Marine to sail their ship through the treacherous Formosa Straits, the infamous "Blood Alley," to Hong Kong and freedom. **Cast:** John Wayne, Lauren Bacall, Paul Fix, Joy Kim, Mike Mazurki, Berry Kroeger, Anita Ekberg. **Credits:** Dir: William Wellman; Writer: A. S. Fleischman; DP: William H. Clothier; Ed: Fred MacDowell; Prod Design: Alfred Ybarra; Composer: Roy Webb; Costumes: Gwen Wakeling. Color, 115 min. VHS, LASER

Blood and Sand

(1941) Fox

Swashbuckling Power stars in this Technicolor remake of the 1922 film that made Rudolph Valentino a household name. Juan, a poor boy from Seville, dreams of becoming a world-famous matador. He also dreams of marrying the beauteous Carmen Espinosa. Both wishes eventually come true, but at the height of his fame a sexy socialite seduces him away from his beloved wife. Power's in top form and Hayworth sizzles. **Academy Awards:** Best Color Cinematography. **Cast:** Tyrone Power, Linda Darnell, Rita Hayworth, Anthony Quinn, Nazimova, J. Carrol Naish, John Carradine, Lynn Bari, Laird Cregar, Monty Banks. **Credits:** Dir: Rouben Mamoulian; Prod: Robert T. Kane; Writer: Jo Swerling; Story: Vicente Blasco Ibanez; DP: Ernest Palmer, Ray Rennahan; Ed: Robert Bischoff; Prod Design: Richard Day, Joseph C. Wright, Thomas Little; Choreographer: Budd Boetticher, Hermes Pan; Composer: Alfred Newman; Costumes: Travis Banton. B&W, 125 min. **VHS**

Bloodbrothers

(1978) Warner Bros.

The trials and tribulations of the Italian-American De Coco family are played out in this Bronx-set story from Price. Tommy De Coco and his brother Chubby live their lives as they always have: working at their construction jobs during the day, drinking and carousing at night. Tommy's son Stony is torn between following in his father's footsteps and following his heart to work with underprivileged children. **Cast:** Richard Gere, Paul Sorvino, Tony Lo Bianco, Lelia Goldoni, Dixie King Wade. **Credits:** Dir: Robert Mulligan; Prod: Stephen Friedman; Writer: Walter Newman; Story: Richard Price; DP: Robert Surtees; Ed: Sheldon Kahn; Prod Design: Gene Callahan; Composer: Elmer Bernstein. Color, 120 min. **VHS**

Bloodhounds of Broadway

(1952) Fox

Dreaming of becoming a dancer on Broadway, Southern belle Gaynor packs up and moves north with only her pack of faithful bloodhounds to accompany her. With her beautiful voice and talented feet, she soon finds work in the Broadway world of Damon Runyon. Remade in 1989. **Cast:** Mitzi Gaynor, Marguerite Chapman, Michael O'Shea, Scott Brady, Mitzi Green, Wally Vernon, George E. Stone, Henry Slate, Edwin Max,

Richard Allen. **Credits:** Dir: Harmon Jones; Prod: George Jessel; Writer: Sy Gomberg; Story: Damon Runyon; DP: Edward Cronjager; Ed: George Gittens; Composer: Lionel Newman. Color, 90 min.

Blood on the Moon

(1948) RKO

In this adaptation of Luke Short's novel *Gunman's Choice,* a drifter finds himself caught in the middle of a battle between a rancher and a ruthless group of cattle rustlers. Jim Garry meets up with his old friend Tate Riling, who gives him a job. But when Jim realizes what Tate has in mind, he has second thoughts. Riling has been exacerbating a feud between rancher John Lufton and a group of settlers to make sure that Lufton and his family don't get grazing land for their cattle. If his scheme proves successful, Riling stands to get the Luftons' livestock at a fire-sale price. After some coaxing from John and his daughter Amy, Jim agrees to help them fight off Tate and his brutal henchmen in a thrilling climax. **Cast:** Robert Mitchum, Robert Preston, Barbara Bel Geddes, Walter Brennan. **Credits:** Dir: Robert Wise; Prod: Theron Warth; Writer: Lillie Hayward, Harold Shumate; Story: Luke Short; DP: Nicholas Musuraca; Ed: Samuel E. Beetley; Composer: Roy Webb. B&W, 88 min. **VHS**

Blood on the Sun

(1945) United Artists

Set in the 1930s, an American newspaper editor (Cagney) working in Japan discovers the insidious "Tanaka Plan" while investigating the double murder of a fellow reporter and the reporter's wife. If he is to warn the world about this Japanese plot for world domination, he must stay alive and out of the hands of the secret police with the help of Iris (Sidney), a beautiful Chinese-American spy. **Academy Awards:** Best Black-and-White Interior Decoration. **Cast:** James Cagney, Sylvia Sidney, Rosemary De Camp, Wallace Ford, Robert Armstrong, John Emery, Leonard Strong, Frank Puglia. **Credits:** Dir: Frank Lloyd; Prod: William Cagney; Writer: Lester Cole; Story: Garrett Fort; DP: Theodor Sparkuhl; Ed: Truman Wood, Walter Hannemann; Prod Design: Wiard Ihnen; Composer: Miklos Rozsa; Costumes: Robert Martien; Set Designer: Al Fields. B&W, 98 min. **VHS**

Blossoms in the Dust

(1941) MGM

The story of Edna Gladney, who after

losing her own child struggles tirelessly to bring hope, dignity, and homes to thousands of unwanted orphans. Edna enjoys a happy marriage to a loving husband and mothering her small son. The couple's little boy then dies tragically and Edna's world completely falls apart when her husband also dies suddenly. These losses, together with Edna's memory of her sister's suicide after learning that she was adopted and illegitimate, inspire Edna to help find caring parents for foundlings. **Academy Awards:** Best Color Interior Decoration. **Cast:** Greer Garson, Walter Pidgeon, Felix Bressart, Marsha Hunt, Fay Holden, Samuel S. Hinds. **Credits:** Dir: Mervyn LeRoy; Prod: Irving Asher; Writer: Anita Loos; Story: Ralph Wheelwright; DP: Karl Freund, W. Howard Greene; Ed: George Boemler; Prod Design: Cedric Gibbons, Urie McCleary; Composer: Herbert Stothart; Costumes: Gile Steele, Adrian; Set Designer: Edwin B. Willis. Color, 117 min. **VHS**

Blowing Wild

(1953) Warner Bros.

Jeff and Dutch, a pair of wildcat oil prospectors looking to get rich in Mexico, find themselves caught in a pair of explosive situations. First they get tricked into delivering a load of nitroglycerin. Then in the oil fields, Jeff (Cooper) runs into Ward (Quinn), an old friend who has become wealthy, and Ward's wife (Stanwyck), who sets her cap for Jeff. **Cast:** Barbara Stanwyck, Anthony Quinn, Gary Cooper, Ruth Roman, Ward Bond. **Credits:** Dir: Hugo Fregonese; Prod: Milton Sperling; Writer: Philip Yordan; DP: Sid Hickox; Ed: Alan Crosland, Jr.; Composer: Dimitri Tiomkin. B&W, 92 min. **VHS, LASER**

The Blue Angel

(1930) Paramount

With just one glimpse of her raw sexuality, a straitlaced professor falls into a mad passion for Lola-Lola (Dietrich), the main attraction at a smoky cabaret in Weimar Germany. Because of his obsession, he loses his position and then his dignity. This film launched Dietrich's career, and she set out for Hollywood with von Sternberg, who became her mentor (some would say her creator) even before its release, leaving behind her husband and daughter. The original English version is commonly available. Shot simultaneously in German and English, this version also contains some unexpected visual and plot variations from the German version. Features songs "Falling In

The Blue Angel (1930)

The Blue Dahlia

(1946) Paramount

When Johnny Morrison returns home at the end of the war, he expects to receive a warm welcome from his wife. Instead, he discovers that she's been unfaithful to him with the owner of the Blue Dahlia nightclub. After a heated argument, he storms out of their house. Later that night, she's murdered—and Johnny winds up the prime suspect. Joyce Harwood, the estranged wife of the club's proprietor, lends Johnny a hand and the two fall in love while tracking down the killer. This film noir classic was Chandler's first original story written directly for the screen. Academy Award Nominations: Best Screenplay. **Cast:** Alan Ladd, Veronica Lake, William Bendix, Howard Da Silva, Doris Dowling, Tom Powers, Hugh Beaumont, Howard Freeman, Don Costello, Will Wright. **Credits:** Dir: George Marshall; Prod: John Houseman; Writer: Raymond Chandler; DP: Lionel Lindon; Ed: Arthur Schmidt; Prod Design: Hans Dreier, Walter Tyler; Composer: Victor Young. B&W, 100 min. **VHS**

The Blue Gardenia

(1953) Warner Bros.

Trying to mend a broken heart, telephone operator Norah Larkin (Baxter) agrees to a date with the office stud, Harry Prebble (Burr). At his apartment later that night, Harry plies her with a drink, but Norah resists his aggressive advances, fending him off with a fireplace poker. The next morning, Harry is dead and Norah can't remember what happened. As the police investigate, newspaperman Casey Mayo takes an interest in the case. Locating Norah through appeals to her in his column, he convinces her she is a murderess. But that's before the final twist in Lang's film noir mystery. **Cast:** Anne Baxter, Raymond Burr, Richard Conte, Ann Sothern, Jeff Donnell, Nat King Cole, George Reeves. **Credits:** Dir: Fritz Lang; Prod: Alex Gottlieb; Writer: Charles Hoffman; Story: Vera Caspary; Ed: Edward Mann; Composer: Raoul Kraushaar; Art Director: Daniel Hall. B&W, 90 min.

Blue Hawaii

(1961) Paramount

Elvis stars in this return to musical comedy after several appearances in dramatic roles. Chad Gates comes home to Honolulu after a stint in the service. He shows little interest in working for his overbearing parents' pineapple plantation. Instead, Chad finds a job as a tour guide and thereby gives himself a chance to dance with,

---

Love Again" and "They Call Me Wicked Lola." Based on Heinrich Mann's novel *Professor Unrat.* **Cast:** Marlene Dietrich, Emil Jannings, Kurt Gerron, Rosa Valetti, Hans Albers. **Credits:** Dir: Josef von Sternberg; Prod: Erich Pommer; Writer: Robert Liebmann, Karl Zuckmayer, Karl Vollmoeller; Story: Heinrich Mann; DP: Gunther Rittau, Hans Schneeberger; Ed: Sam Winston; Prod Design: Otto Hunte, Emil Hasler; Composer: Frederick Hollander. B&W, 103 min. **VHS**

Bluebeard's Eighth Wife

(1938) United Artists

Mademoiselle Nicole (Colbert), the daughter of a destitute aristocrat on the French Riviera, lands a charming American millionaire (Cooper) only to find he has been married seven times previously. Determined to teach him a lesson about fidelity, Nicole is going to make sure that there will be no number nine. So begins a battle of the sexes as the wily new bride sets out to tame her Bluebeard and he tries his best to play the game his way. Cooper's a little flat-footed for the light Lubitsch touch, but a pleasant sparring partner for Colbert. **Cast:** Claudette Colbert, Gary Cooper, David Niven, Edward Everett Horton, Elizabeth Patterson, Herman Bing, Warren Hymer, Franklin Pangborn. **Credits:** Dir: Ernst Lubitsch; Prod: Ernst Lubitsch; Writer: Charles Brackett, Billy Wilder; Story: Alfred Savoir; DP: Leo Tover; Ed: William Shea; Composer: Werner Richard Heymann, Frederick Hollander. B&W, 86 min. **VHS**

Blue Collar

(1978) Universal

Three assembly-line autoworkers (two black and one white), equally angry and disenchanted at factory management and their own union, burglarize their own union's safe. Instead of finding cash as expected, they find ledgers documenting mob transactions. Their relationship is tested as they veer between blackmailing the union and testifying against it. **Cast:** Richard Pryor, Harvey Keitel, Yaphet Kotto, Ed Begley, Jr. **Credits:** Dir: Paul Schrader; Prod: Don Guest; Writer: Paul Schrader, Leonard Schrader; DP: Bobby Byrne; Ed: Tom Rolf; Composer: Jack Nitzsche, Ry Cooder. Color, 114 min. **VHS, LASER**

and sing to, a variety of Hawaii's most beautiful women. Includes musical numbers such as "Blue Hawaii," "Rock-A-Hula Baby," "Hawaiian Wedding Song," and "Island of Love," as well as the immortal "Can't Help Falling in Love." **Cast:** Elvis Presley, Angela Lansbury, Joan Blackman, Nancy Walters, Roland Winters, John Archer, Howard McNear. **Credits:** Dir: Norman Taurog; Prod: Hal B. Wallis; Writer: Hal Kanter; DP: Charles Lang; Ed: Warren Low; Composer: Joseph J. Lilley. Color, 104 min. **VHS, LASER**

The Blue Max

(1966) Fox
The "Blue Max," a coveted medal for achievement in flying, is ruthlessly sought by Peppard, a poor-boy German soldier who climbs out of the trenches and into the aristocratic air force. When he claims the title, he earns the respect of the General and the General's wife (Andress), who wants to repay him in ways that the General might not appreciate. Fantastic aerial combat sequences. **Cast:** George Peppard, James Mason, Ursula Andress, Jeremy Kemp, Karl Michael Vogler, Anton Diffring, Derren Nesbitt, Carl Schell, Peter Woodthorpe, Harry Towb. **Credits:** Dir: John Guillermin; Prod: Christian Ferry; Writer: David Pursall, Jack Seddon, Gerald Hanley; DP: Douglas Slocombe; Ed: Max Benedict; Prod Design: Fred Carter; Composer: Jerry Goldsmith. Color, 155 min. **VHS, LASER**

Blues in the Night

(1941) Warner Bros.
This adaptation of Edwin Gilbert's play examines a jazz quintet and the lifestyle of the musicians. The story takes a backseat to the strong performances, including the appearance of future directors of fame, Elia Kazan and Richard Whorf. Best remembered for its music, which includes the Academy Award–nominated title song, "Blues in the Night." **Cast:** Priscilla Lane, Betty Field, Richard Whorf, Lloyd Nolan, Jack Carson, Wallace Ford, Howard Da Silva, Elia Kazan. **Credits:** Dir: Anatole Litvak; Prod: Hal B. Wallis; Writer: Robert Rossen; Story: Edwin Gilbert; DP: Ernest Haller; Ed: Owen Marks; Prod Design: Max Parker; Composer: Heinz Roemheld. B&W, 88 min.

Blue Skies

(1946) Paramount
The owner of a nightclub (Crosby) and a dancing star (Astaire) are friends turned romantic rivals in this musical featuring the songs of Irving Berlin. A

nostalgic, loosely constructed musical that follows the years-long rivalry between two musical stars who love the same woman. Songs include "Puttin' on the Ritz," "A Couple of Song and Dance Men," "You Keep Coming Back Like a Song." **Cast:** Bing Crosby, Joan Caulfield, Fred Astaire, Billy De Wolfe, Olga San Juan, Robert Benchley, Frank Faylen, Victoria Horne, Jack Norton. **Credits:** Dir: Stuart Heisler; Prod: Sol C. Siegel; Writer: Arthur Sheekman; DP: Charles Lang, William E. Snyder; Ed: LeRoy Stone; Prod Design: Hans Dreier, Hal Pereira; Choreographer: Hermes Pan; Composer: Robert Emmett Dolan; SFX: Farciot Edouart, Paul K. Lerpae, Gordon Jennings. Color, 104 min. **VHS**

Blume in Love

(1973) Warner Bros.
Returning to Venice six years after his honeymoon there, Beverly Hills divorce lawyer Stephen Blume reminisces about the events leading to the destruction of his marriage. Even after the separation, Stephen finds that he is still in love with his former wife, who has since become involved with an out-of-work musician. Quintessential musing on marriage, '70s-style, with just the cast and director you'd expect. **Cast:** George Segal, Susan Anspach, Marsha Mason, Kris Kristofferson, Shelley Winters. **Credits:** Dir: Paul Mazursky; Prod: Paul Mazursky;

Writer: Paul Mazursky; DP: Bruce Surtees; Ed: Donn Cambern; Prod Design: Pato Guzman; Set Designer: Audrey Blasdel-Goddard. Color, 117 min. **VHS**

The Boatniks

(1970) Disney
An accident-prone Coast Guard ensign finds himself in charge of one of the busiest waterways in the United States, Newport Harbor. Endless gags on the boat docks as three bumbling thieves attempt to recover stolen jewels at the bottom of the bay while the Coast Guard tails their every clumsy move. **Cast:** Robert Morse, Stefanie Powers, Phil Silvers, Norman Fell, Mickey Shaughnessy, Wally Cox, Don Ameche, Vito Scotti, Tom Lowell, Joey Forman. **Credits:** Dir: Norman Tokar; Prod: Ron Miller; Writer: Arthur Julian; DP: William E. Snyder; Ed: Cotton Warburton; Prod Design: Hilyard Brown; Composer: Robert F. Brunner. Color, 99 min. **VHS**

Bob & Carol & Ted & Alice

(1969) Columbia
Director Mazursky depicted the changing mores of the '60s and '70s, beginning with what now looks like a quaint period piece. After married couple Carol and Bob admit, accept, and practically celebrate their extramarital affairs, their friends Ted and Alice are so shocked by their liberal standpoint that Alice must seek psychiatric treat-

The Blue Dahlia (1946)

ment. In therapy, however, Alice realizes her own illicit desires. After articulating them to her husband, Carol, and Bob, the foursome become more than just friends. It seems as remote as Henry James. **Cast:** Natalie Wood, Robert Culp, Elliott Gould, Dyan Cannon, Horst Ebersberg. **Credits:** Dir: Paul Mazursky; Prod: Larry Tucker; Writer: Paul Mazursky, Larry Tucker; DP: Charles Lang; Choreographer: Miriam Nelson; Composer: Quincy Jones; Costumes: Moss Mabry. Color, 104 min. VHS, LASER

Bobby Deerfield
(1977) Columbia
A self-absorbed champion Grand Prix driver, accustomed to facing death each time he drives, falls in love with a terminally ill Italian woman. The common ground they find brings out heretofore unknown feelings in each. Based on the Erich Maria Remarque novel *Heaven Has No Favourites*. **Cast:** Al Pacino, Marthe Keller, Anny Duperey, Walter McGinn, Romolo Valli, Jaime Sanchez. **Credits:** Dir: Sydney Pollack; Prod: Sydney Pollack; Writer: Alvin Sargent; Story: Erich Maria Remarque; DP: Henri Decae, Tony Maylam; Ed: Fredric Steinkamp; Prod Design: Stephen Grimes; Composer: Dave Grusin; Costumes: Bernie Pollack. Color, 124 min. VHS, LASER

Body and Soul
(1947) United Artists
Garfield's best role as a boxer who wins the world middleweight championship title in a fixed fight and loses his soul. The definitive ring tale. Look for onetime middleweight contender Canada Lee, who plays aging boxer Ben Chaplin. Academy Award Nominations: 3, including Best Actor: John Garfield; Best Original Screenplay. **Academy Awards:** Best Film Editing. **Cast:** John Garfield, Lilli Palmer, William Conrad, Hazel Brooks, James Burke, Anne Revere, Joseph Pevney, Canada Lee. **Credits:** Dir: Robert Rossen; Prod: Bob Roberts; Writer: Abraham Polonsky; DP: James Wong Howe; Ed: Francis D. Lyon, Robert Parrish; Prod Design: Nathan Juran; Composer: Hugo Friedhofer; Costumes: Marion Herwood Keyes; Set Designer: Edward G. Boyle. B&W, 104 min. VHS, LASER

The Body Snatcher
(1945) RKO
A 19th-century Edinburgh scientist has been relying upon a scurvy, evil grave-robber to provide him with corpses for his unlawful experiments. But when the supply of fresh cadavers

begins to dwindle and the thief begins to taunt the doctor with the knowledge that he holds the power to expose him to the authorities, murder becomes the grisly alternative. Based on the Robert Louis Stevenson story. Lewton produced this last pairing of Karloff and Lugosi. **Cast:** Boris Karloff, Bela Lugosi, Henry Daniell, Edith Atwater, Russell Wade, Rita Corday, Sharyn Moffett, Donna Lee. **Credits:** Dir: Robert Wise; Prod: Val Lewton; Writer: Philip MacDonald, Val Lewton; DP: Robert de Grasse; Ed: J. R. Whittredge; Prod Design: Albert S. D'Agostino; Composer: Roy Webb. B&W, 77 min. VHS, LASER

Boeing Boeing
(1965) Paramount
Curtis plays a newspaper correspondent based in Paris who successfully juggles living with three stewardesses. Each thinks she is his one and only until his business rival—played by a sedate Jerry Lewis—blackmails his way into the spare bedroom and all three airlines change their flight schedules. **Cast:** Tony Curtis, Jerry Lewis, Dany Saval, Christiane Schmidtmer, Suzanna Leigh, Thelma Ritter. **Credits:** Dir: John Rich; Prod: Hal B. Wallis; Writer: Edward Anhalt; Story: Marc Camoletti; DP: Lucien Ballard; Ed: Archie Marshek, Warren Low; Prod Design: Walter Tyler, Hal Pereira; Composer: Neal Hefti; Costumes: Edith Head. Color, 102 min. VHS, LASER

Bolero
(1934) Paramount
George Raft first made his mark in this drama about an obsessive dancer who rises to the top. Driven by the desire to leave the seedy places in which he performs for sophisticated Paris revues, the dancer works relentlessly to pursue his dream and gets his chance to introduce a new dance craze. His disdain for his colleagues changes when he meets Lombard. Look sharp for the rare chance to see fan-dancer Rand do her stuff. **Cast:** George Raft, Carole Lombard, William Frawley, Frances Drake, Sally Rand, Ray Milland, Gloria Shea, Gertrude Michael. **Credits:** Dir: Wesley Ruggles; Prod: Benjamin Glazer; Writer: Kubec Glasmon, Horace Jackson, Carey Wilson; Story: Ruth Ridenour; DP: Leo Tover; Ed: Hugh Bennett; Composer: Ralph Rainger. B&W, 80 min.

Bombardier
(1943) RKO
Well paced, but standard fare as young fliers learn to face the reality of

air combat. Academy Award Nominations: Best Special Effects. **Cast:** Randolph Scott, Anne Shirley, Pat O'Brien, Eddie Albert, Walter Reed, Robert Ryan, Barton MacLane. **Credits:** Dir: Richard Wallace; Prod: Robert Fellows; Writer: John Twist; Story: Martin Rackin; DP: Nicholas Musuraca; Ed: Robert Wise; Prod Design: Al Herman, Albert S. D'Agostino; Composer: Roy Webb; SFX: Douglas Travers, Vernon Walker; Set Designer: Claude Carpenter, Darrell Silvera. B&W, 99 min. VHS

Bombshell
(1933) MGM
Great performance by Harlow in this satire on the '30s Hollywood star machine. A long-suffering starlet tires of the game and quits—thoroughly frustrating her unscrupulous press agent. Based on a play by Caroline Francke and Mack Crane. **Cast:** Jean Harlow, Lee Tracy, Frank Morgan, Franchot Tone. **Credits:** Dir: Victor Fleming; Writer: Jules Furthman, John Lee Mahin; Story: Caroline Francke, Mack Crane; DP: Chester Lyons, Hal Rosson; Ed: Margaret Booth. B&W, 96 min. VHS

Bonjour Tristesse
(1958) Columbia
When young Cecile's pleasure-seeking existence is threatened by the upcoming marriage between her father and her straitlaced godmother, she devises a scheme to drive her godmother away, which takes a tragic turn. This drama, based on the sensational novel by Françoise Sagan, failed to make Seberg the star many thought she'd become. **Cast:** David Niven, Deborah Kerr, Jean Seberg, Geoffrey Horne, Mylene Demongeot, Juliette Greco, Martita Hunt, Walter Chiari, Jean Kent, Roland Culver. **Credits:** Dir: Otto Preminger; Prod: Otto Preminger; Writer: Arthur Laurents; Story: Francoise Sagan; DP: Georges Perinal; Ed: Helga Cranston; Prod Design: Roger K. Furse; Choreographer: Tutte Lemkow; Composer: Georges Auric; Costumes: Hubert de Givenchy. Color, 94 min. VHS

Bonnie and Clyde
(1967) Warner Bros.
The nuanced, ultimately bleak tale of Depression-era bank robbers Clyde Barrow and Bonnie Parker. Essentially a road film, it juxtaposes easygoing humor with stylish scenes of graphic violence. Controversial when released, it heralded the coming increase in cinematic violence, natu-

ralistic performances, and daring film style. Academy Award Nominations: 10, including Best Picture; Best Director; Best Actor: Warren Beatty; Best Actress: Faye Dunaway; Best (Original) Screenplay. **Academy Awards:** Best Supporting Actress: Estelle Parsons; Best Cinematography. **Cast:** Warren Beatty, Faye Dunaway, Estelle Parsons, Gene Hackman, Michael J. Pollard, Gene Wilder, Denver Pyle, Dub Taylor, James Stiver. **Credits:** Dir: Arthur Penn; Prod: Warren Beatty; Writer: David Newman, Robert Benton; DP: Burnett Guffey; Ed: Dede Allen; Composer: Charles Strouse; Costumes: Theadora Van Runkle. Color, 114 min. VHS, LASER, DVD

Bonzo Goes to College
(1952) Universal
This sequel to *Bedtime for Bonzo* tells the story of the brilliant ape who flees from a cruel circus owner and becomes the pet of a professor and his family. Things go well for Bonzo as he enters college and becomes a star player on the football team. When the circus owners and his flunkies show up, Bonzo must call on his new friends to save him so he can continue his smashing college career. **Cast:** Maureen O'Sullivan, Charles Drake, Edmund Gwenn, Gigi Perreau, Gene Lockhart, Irene Ryan, Frank Nelson, John Miljan, Jerry Paris, Guy Williams. **Credits:** Dir: Frederick de Cordova; Prod: Ted Richmond; Writer: Leo Lieberman; Story: Jack Henley, Raphael David Blau; DP: Ted Berkman; Ed: Ted J. Kent; Composer: Frank Skinner. B&W, 78 min.

The Boogie Man Will Get You
(1942) Columbia
Winnie Slade and Bill Leyden purchase a creepy old New England hotel from the crazed Prof. Nathaniel Billings. The hotel is already peopled by eccentrics, with the basement converted into a laboratory for Billings's experiments. When Winnie and Bill discover corpses littering their new purchase, they call in local sheriff Dr. Lorenz to investigate. Okay for Karloff fans. **Cast:** Boris Karloff, Peter Lorre, Jeff Donnell, Larry Parks, Maxie Rosenbloom, Maude Eburne, George McKay, Don Beddoe, Frank Puglia, Eddie Laughton. **Credits:** Dir: Lew Landers; Prod: Colbert Clark; Writer: Edwin Blum, Paul Gangelin; Story: Hal Fimberg, Robert B. Hunt; DP: Henry Freulich; Ed: Richard Fantl; Prod Design: Lionel Banks, Robert Peterson; Composer: Morris Stoloff. B&W, 82 min.

Boomerang!
(1947) Fox
Kazan's gangbuster film noir docudrama about an innocent man browbeaten into confessing to the murder of a minister. Andrews is the D.A. who decides to dig deeper into what seems like an open-and-shut case. Look for playwright Arthur Miller in the suspect lineup. Based on an article by Anthony Abbott in *Reader's Digest*. **Cast:** Dana Andrews, Jane Wyatt, Lee J. Cobb, Arthur Kennedy, Sam Levene, Robert Keith, Taylor Holmes, Ed Begley, Karl Malden, Cara Williams. **Credits:** Dir: Elia Kazan; Writer: Richard Murphy; DP: Norbert F. Brodine; Ed: Harmon Jones; Composer: David Buttolph. B&W, 88 min. VHS

Boom Town
(1940) MGM
Two rough-and-tumble wildcatters strike it rich in the dusty oil fields of Oklahoma. Not much of a story here but worthwhile to watch Gable and Tracy mix it up. Nominated for an Academy Award for Best (Black-and-White) Cinematography and Best Special Effects, so why bother with the colorized version? **Cast:** Clark Gable, Spencer Tracy, Claudette Colbert, Hedy Lamarr, Frank Morgan, Lionel Atwill, Chill Wills. **Credits:** Dir: Jack Conway; Prod: Sam Zimbalist; Writer: John Lee Mahin; Story: James Edward Grant; DP: Harold Rosson; Ed: Blanche Sewell; Prod Design: Cedric Gibbons, Eddie Imazu; Composer: Franz Waxman; Costumes: Gile Steele, Adrian; Set Designer: Edwin B. Willis. B&W, 120 min. VHS

Boots Malone
(1952) Columbia
Holden stars as a wiseguy jockey agent at a seedy racetrack who needs to make a fast buck. Normally he would pull a quick con or bet on a fixed race, but this time he finds a starry-eyed jockey and a second-rate horse and decides to make them into a winning combination. **Cast:** William Holden, Johnny Stewart, Stanley Clements, Basil Ruysdael, Ralph Dumke, Ed Begley, Hugh Sanders, Harry Morgan, Anna Lee, Anthony Caruso. **Credits:** Dir: William Dieterle; Prod: Milton Holmes; Writer: Milton Holmes; DP: Charles Lawton, Jr.; Ed: Al Clark; Composer: Elmer Bernstein. B&W, 103 min.

Border Incident
(1949) MGM
A hard-hitting drama that slams the corruption in supplying migrant farmworkers

to America. Shot on location in a documentary-like style, the story follows two immigration agents—one working for America, the other for Mexico—who go undercover and infiltrate a gang of smugglers dealing in human trade. The U.S. agent is discovered and brutally executed with a plow and the Mexican agent is left to fight alone. **Cast:** Ricardo Montalban, George Murphy, Howard Da Silva, James Mitchell, Arnold Moss, Alfonso Bedoya, Teresa Celli, Charles McGraw, Jose Torvay, John Ridgely. **Credits:** Dir: Anthony Mann; Prod: Nicholas Nayfack; Writer: John C. Higgins; Story: George Zuckerman; DP: John Alton; Ed: Conrad A. Nervig; Prod Design: Hans Peters; Composer: Andre Previn. B&W, 94 min.

Bordertown
(1935) Warner Bros.
An ambitious but volatile Mexican attends night school in America, becomes a lawyer, then bungles his first case so badly that he is disbarred—and embittered. He then becomes a partner in a bordertown gambling house, where his associate's wife falls in love with him. The fireworks begin, especially from Davis as the distraught would-be mistress. **Cast:** Paul Muni, Bette Davis, Margaret Lindsay, Eugene Pallette, Robert Barratt, Henry O'Neill, Hobart Cavanaugh, Gavin Gordon, William Davidson, Arthur Stone. **Credits:** Dir: Archie Mayo; Prod: Robert Lord; Writer: Robert Lord, Carroll Graham, Laird Doyle, Wallace Smith; DP: Tony Gaudio; Ed: Thomas Richards; Prod Design: Okey Jack; Composer: Leo F. Forbstein, Bernhard Kaun. B&W, 80 min.

Born Free
(1966) Columbia
The true story of Elsa the lioness, who was raised by game warden George Adamson and his wife, Joy. Based on Joy's book and one of the best family dramas of all time. **Academy Awards:** Best Song; Best Original Musical or Comedy Score. **Cast:** Virginia McKenna, Bill Travers, Geoffrey Keen, Peter Lukoye. **Credits:** Dir: James Hill; Prod: Sam Jaffe, Paul B. Radin; Writer: Gerald L. C. Copley; Story: Joy Adamson; DP: Kenneth Talbot; Ed: Don Deacon; Composer: John Barry. Color, 96 min. VHS, LASER

Born Losers
(1967) A.I.P.
The original Billy Jack film, featuring the adventures of a young half-breed who heroically attempts to save a small town from marauding bikers with his

kung fu skill. Lots of violence intended to send an anti-violence message. **Cast:** Tom Laughlin, Elizabeth James, Jeremy Slate, William Wellman, Jr., Jane Russell. **Credits:** Dir: Tom Laughlin; Writer: Tom Laughlin; DP: Gregory Sandor; Ed: John Wineld; Composer: Mike Curb. Color, 112 min. VHS, LASER

Born to Be Bad
(1950) RKO
A ruthless woman claws her way into an affair with a wealthy man while carrying on with a writer. Standard Hollywood melodrama made worthwhile by Ray, who had a unique affinity for outcasts and loners. **Cast:** Joan Fontaine, Robert Ryan, Joan Leslie, Mel Ferrer, Zachary Scott. **Credits:** Dir: Nicholas Ray; Prod: Robert Sparks; Writer: Edith Sommer, Charles Schnee, Robert Soderberg, George Oppenheimer; Story: Anne Parrish; DP: Nicholas Musuraca; Ed: Frederic Knudtson; Composer: Frederick Hollander. B&W, 94 min. VHS

Born to Dance
(1936) MGM
Yikes! Stewart sings and dances! A sailor-meets-girl story with terrific Cole Porter songs. Academy Award Nominations for Best Song ("I've Got You Under My Skin"), Best Dance Direction. **Cast:** Eleanor Powell, James Stewart, Buddy Ebsen, Una Merkel, Virginia Bruce, Frances Langford, Sid Silvers, Raymond Walburn, Reginald Gardiner. **Credits:** Dir: Roy Del Ruth; Writer: Jack McGowan, Sid Silvers; Story: B. G. DeSylva; DP: Ray June; Ed: Blanche Sewell; Prod Design: Cedric Gibbons; Choreographer: Dave Gould; Composer: Cole Porter; Costumes: Adrian. B&W, 111 min. VHS, LASER

Born to Kill
(1947) RKO
In this film noir cult favorite, Tierney marries a wealthy woman, but is irresistibly drawn to her sister. Violent and dark—and this from the director of *The Sound of Music*! **Cast:** Claire Trevor, Lawrence Tierney, Walter Slezak, Audrey Long, Philip Terry, Elisha Cook, Jr. **Credits:** Dir: Robert Wise; Writer: Eve Greene, Richard Macauley; Story: James Gunn; DP: Robert DeGrasse; Ed: Les Millbrook; Composer: Paul Sawtell. B&W, 92 min. VHS

Born Yesterday
(1950) Columbia
Holliday at her best as the unschooled girlfriend of a domineering scrap-iron tycoon who hires egghead Holden to tutor off the rough edges. Guess who

falls in love? Based on Garson Kanin's Broadway play. Remade in 1993 with Melanie Griffith. Academy Award Nominations: 5, including Best Picture; Best Director; Best Screenplay. Other awards include a Golden Globe for Best Actress in a Musical or Comedy: Judy Holliday. **Academy Awards:** Best Actress: Judy Holliday. **Cast:** Judy Holliday, William Holden, Broderick Crawford, Howard St. John. **Credits:** Dir: George Cukor; Writer: Albert Mannheimer; Story: Garson Kanin; DP: Joseph Walker; Composer: Frederick Hollander. B&W, 103 min. VHS, LASER

The Boss
(1956) United Artists
This hard-boiled social drama stars B-movie regular Payne in one of his finest roles as WWI veteran Matt Brady. Brady comes back from a ravaged Europe with nothing to lose. His brother Tim (Roberts), who runs the town's rackets, drops dead with a heart attack and Matt takes over the town. **Cast:** John Payne, William Bishop, Gloria McGhee, Doe Avedon, Roy Roberts, Rhys Williams, Robin Morse, Gil Lamb, Joe Flynn. **Credits:** Dir: Byron Haskin; Prod: John Payne, Nydia Westman; Writer: John Payne, Dalton Trumbo; DP: Hal Mohr; Ed: Ralph Dawson; Composer: Albert Glasser. B&W, 89 min.

Boston Blackie
Columbia's profitable series that featured the cool ex-con–turned–detective Boston Blackie (portrayed in the film series by Chester Morris, who began his career on Broadway at the tender age of 15 opposite Lionel Barrymore), was based on a character created in 1910 by pulp-story writer Jack Boyle. In each of the films, Blackie draws on his previous existence on the other side of the law and looks to his nefarious connections to aid in his crime solving, while Inspector Faraday (Richard Lane) relentlessly pursues the former criminal, convinced that he's on the take. Blackie, unable to count on the assistance of the suspicious men in blue, must solve the crime at hand with the aid of his sidekick, affectionately named "The Runt" (George E. Stone). After the series, Morris went back to his roots, headlining the touring companies of several Broadway plays until he died of a barbiturate overdose in 1970.

Meet Boston Blackie *(1941)*
Confessions of Boston Blackie *(1941)*

Alias Boston Blackie *(1942)*
Boston Blackie Goes Hollywood *(1942)*
After Midnight with Boston Blackie *(1943)*
The Chance of a Lifetime *(1943)*
One Mysterious Night *(1944)*
Boston Blackie Booked on Suspicion *(1945)*
Boston Blackie's Rendezvous *(1945)*
A Close Call for Boston Blackie *(1946)*
The Phantom Thief *(1946)*
Boston Blackie and the Law *(1946)*
Trapped by Boston Blackie *(1948)*
Boston Blackie's Chinese Venture *(1949)*

The Boston Strangler
(1968) Fox
The investigation of the famous murder case that haunted the citizens of Boston. Using an unusual split-screen technique, as the film follows two detectives as they track the man who raped and killed thirteen women in the early '60s. Their explorations of the crimes take them on a frightening journey into the depths of a deranged mind. Curtis gives an intense performance as the psychopath. **Cast:** Henry Fonda, Tony Curtis, George Kennedy, Sally Kellerman, Mike Kellin, Hurd Hatfield, Murray Hamilton, Jeff Corey, George Voskovec, Leora Dana. **Credits:** Dir: Richard Fleischer; Prod: Robert Fryer; Writer: Edward Anhalt; DP: Richard H. Kline; Ed: Marion Rothman; Prod Design: Jack Martin Smith, Richard Day; Composer: Lionel Newman. Color, 116 min. VHS

Bound for Glory
(1976) United Artists
A fine film biography of Woody Guthrie, the folk balladeer and poet who was the eloquent voice of America's downtrodden during the dark years of the Depression and beyond. The film lovingly evokes Guthrie's hardscrabble world and his feeling for the people. Academy Award Nominations: 6, including Best Picture; Best (Adapted) Screenplay. **Academy Awards:** Best Cinematography; Best Original Song Score and Adaptation. **Cast:** David Carradine, Ronny Cox, Melinda Dillon, Gail Strickland, John Lehne. **Credits:** Dir: Hal Ashby; Writer: Robert Getchell; Story: Woody Guthrie; DP: Haskell Wexler; Prod Design: Michael Haller; Composer: Leonard Rosenman, Woody Guthrie. Color, 149 min. VHS, LASER

The Bounty Killer
(1965)
It's the last round-up for a cast of Hollywood's greatest (and oldest!) cow-

boys—Anderson was in *The Great Train Robbery* in 1907! The story follows a loner who goes out west, is almost gunned down, and then is confronted with the decision to become a bounty hunter, an easy, well-paying job that has its obvious downsides. **Cast:** Dan Duryea, Rod Cameron, Audrey Dalton, Buster Crabbe, Fuzzy Knight, Richard Arlen, John Mack Brown, Bob Steele, Broncho Billy Anderson, Eddie Quillan, Norman Willis. **Credits:** Dir: Spencer Gordon Bennet; Prod: Alex Gordon; Writer: Ronald Alexander, Leo Gordon; DP: Frederick West; Ed: Ronald Sinclair; Prod Design: Don Ament; Composer: Ronald Stein. Color, 96 min. **VHS**

The Bowery

(1933) United Artists
Zanuck's first effort after leaving Warner Bros. is a raucous portrait of Gay Nineties New York, with personalities ranging from John L. Sullivan to Carrie Nation. It also features the return of the Wallace Beery–Jackie Cooper team from *The Champ*. Beery's saloon keeper fights for the hand of Wray with friend and rival Raft. **Cast:** Wallace Beery, George Raft, Jackie Cooper, Fay Wray, Harold Huber, Pert Kelton, George Walsh, Oscar Apfel, Fletcher Norton, John Kelly. **Credits:** Dir: Raoul Walsh; Prod: Darryl F. Zanuck, William Goetz, Raymond Griffith; Writer: Howard Estabrook, James Gleason; Story: Michael L. Simmons, Bessie Roth Solomon; Ed: Allen McNeil; Composer: Alfred Newman; Art Director: Richard Day. B&W, 92 min.

Bowery Boys

Dead End, Sidney Kingsley's caustic Broadway play about growing up in New York City's slums, had the same impact on the big screen as it did on the stage, with the young hoodlums and their shenanigans winning over sympathetic audiences. The play also inspired scores of films and four series. Lillian Hellman penned and William Wyler directed *Dead End,* the 1937 Samuel Goldwyn film that saw many of the stage's Dead End Kids, including Billy Halop, Bobby Jordan, Gabriel Dell, Huntz Hall, and Leo Gorcey, reprising their roles in the movie opposite Humphrey Bogart. Warner Bros. produced the subsequent six Dead End Kids films, with notables James Cagney (1938's *Angels with Dirty Faces*) and Bogart (1938's *Crime School*) making appearances. Universal presented the Dead End Kids and the Little Tough

Guys series in 1938 with predictable crime yarns and elements of action, comedy, and drama. More successful was Monogram Picture's East Side Kids series, featuring former Dead Enders Leo Gorcey and Bobby Jordan, Huntz Hall, and Gabriel Dell. Shot on a shoestring budget, the Monogram films added at least a note of social commentary that had been missing since the original features. Leo Gorcey was influential in retooling the series, and in 1946 he became the star of the show, with Huntz Hall his partner-in-crime(solving) in the renamed series, The Bowery Boys. Gorcey left the series in 1956, after his father, Bernard, who played the owner of the ice cream parlor–clubhouse, died. The series continued until 1958. By the end, the Boys were no longer boys—they were nearly middle-aged men.

As The Dead End Kids
Dead End *(1937)*
Crime School *(1938)*
Angels with Dirty Faces *(1938)*
They Made Me a Criminal *(1939)*
Hell's Kitchen *(1939)*
The Angels Wash Their Faces *(1939)*
On Dress Parade *(1939)*

As The Dead End Kids and The Little Tough Guys
Little Tough Guy *(1938)*
Call a Messenger *(1939)*
You're Not So Tough *(1940)*
Give Us Wings *(1940)*
Hit the Road *(1941)*
Mob Town *(1941)*
Tough as They Come *(1942)*
Mug Town *(1943)*
Keep 'Em Slugging *(1945)*

As The East Side Kids
East Side Kids *(1940)*
Boys of the City *(1940)*
That Gang of Mine *(1940)*
Pride of the Bowery *(1941)*
Flying Wild *(1941)*
Bowery Blitzkrieg *(1941)*
Spooks Run Wild *(1941)*
Mr. Wise Guy *(1942)*
Let's Get Tough *(1942)*
Smart Alecks *(1942)*
'Neath Brooklyn Bridge *(1942)*
Kid Dynamite *(1943)*
Clancy Street Boys *(1943)*
Ghosts on the Loose *(1943)*
Mr. Muggs Steps Out *(1943)*
Million Dollar Kid *(1944)*
Follow the Leader *(1944)*
Block Busters *(1944)*
Bowery Champs *(1944)*
Docks of New York *(1945)*

Mr. Muggs Rides Again *(1945)*
Come Out Fighting *(1945)*

As The Bowery Boys
Live Wires *(1946)*
In Fast Company *(1946)*
Bowery Bombshell *(1946)*
Spook Busters *(1946)*
Mr. Hex *(1946)*
Hard Boiled Mahoney *(1947)*
News Hounds *(1947)*
Bowery Buckaroos *(1947)*
Angels' Alley *(1948)*
Jinx Money *(1948)*
Smugglers' Cove *(1948)*
Trouble Makers *(1948)*
Fighting Fools *(1949)*
Hold That Baby! *(1949)*
Angels in Disguise *(1949)*
Master Minds *(1949)*
Blonde Dynamite *(1950)*
Lucky Losers *(1950)*
Triple Trouble *(1950)*
Blues Busters *(1950)*
Bowery Battalion *(1951)*
Ghost Chasers *(1951)*
Let's Go Navy *(1951)*
Crazy Over Horses *(1951)*
Hold That Line *(1952)*
Here Come the Marines *(1952)*
Feudin' Fools *(1952)*
No Holds Barred *(1952)*
Jalopy *(1953)*
Loose in London *(1953)*
Clipped Wings *(1953)*
Private Eyes *(1953)*
Paris Playboys *(1954)*
The Bowery Boys Meet the Monsters *(1954)*
Jungle Gents *(1954)*
Bowery to Bagdad *(1955)*
High Society *(1955)*
Spy Chasers *(1955)*
Jail Busters *(1955)*
Dig That Uranium *(1956)*
Crashing Las Vegas *(1956)*
Fighting Trouble *(1956)*
Hot Shots *(1956)*
Hold That Hypnotist *(1957)*
Spook Chasers *(1957)*
Looking for Danger *(1957)*
Up in Smoke *(1957)*
In the Money *(1958)*

Boxcar Bertha

(1972) AIP
Scorsese's first studio feature follows Hershey as she falls in with a gang of train robbers. Based on the book *Sister of the Road* by Boxcar Bertha Thompson. **Cast:** Barbara Hershey, David Carradine, Barry Primus, John Carradine, Bernie Casey. **Credits:** Dir: Martin Scorsese; Writer: Joyce H. Corrington, John William Corrington; DP: John M. Stephens; Composer: Thad Maxwell, Gilb Guilbeau. Color, 97 min. **VHS, LASER**

A Boy and His Dog

(1976)

A wandering survivor of an atomic holocaust depends on his telepathic dog for companionship and to lead him to food and sex. The bedraggled duo eventually discovers an underground society of survivors. A cult black comedy based on the novella by Harlan Ellison. **Cast:** Jason Robards, Don Johnson, Susanne Benton, Alvy Moore, Helen Winston, Charles McGraw. **Credits:** Dir: L. Q. Jones; Prod: Alvy Moore; Writer: L. Q. Jones; DP: John Morrill; Ed: Scott Conrad; Composer: Tim McIntire. Color, 88 min. **VHS, LASER, DVD**

Boy Meets Girl

(1938) MGM

Snappy patter enlivens this screwball parody about two Hollywood screenwriters who are running out of ideas until they decide to make their friend's baby a star. **Cast:** James Cagney, Pat O'Brien, Marie Wilson, Ralph Bellamy, Frank McHugh, Dick Foran, Penny Singleton, Ronald Reagan, James Stephenson, Bruce Lester. **Credits:** Dir: Lloyd Bacon; Writer: Bella Spewack, Samuel Spewack; DP: Sol Polito; Composer: Leo F. Forbstein. B&W, 86 min. **VHS**

Boy of the Streets

(1937) Monogram

Child star Cooper plays the ringleader of a gang of hoodlums on the Lower East Side of New York, bragging that his "big shot" dad will get him out of anything. A powerful portrait of urban decay by Hollywood maverick Rowland Brown, who was responsible for the script but yanked off directing chores. **Cast:** Marjorie Main, Jackie Cooper, Maureen O'Connor, Kathleen Burke, Robert Emmett O'Connor. **Credits:** Dir: William Nigh; Story: Roland Brown, Scott Darling; DP: Gilbert Warrenton; Ed: Russell Schoengarth. B&W, 74 min. **VHS**

The Boys from Brazil

(1978) Fox

Levin's best-selling novel is the basis for this suspenser about the propagation of a new race of Hitlers. When one of his protégés locates the elusive Nazi war criminal Dr. Josef Mengele (Peck), famed Nazi hunter Ezra Lieberman (Olivier) stumbles on Mengele's grand scheme to launch the Fourth Reich. Academy Award Nominations: 3, including Best Actor: Laurence Olivier. **Cast:** Gregory Peck, James Mason, Laurence Olivier, Lilli Palmer, Uta Hagen, Rosemary Harris, John Dehner, John Rubinstein, Anne Meara, Steven Guttenberg. **Credits:** Dir: Franklin J. Schaffner; Prod: Martin Richards, Stanley O'Toole; Writer: Heywood Gould; Story: Ira Levin; DP: Henri Decae; Ed: Robert W. Swink; Prod Design: Gil Parrondo; Composer: Jerry Goldsmith. Color, 127 min. **VHS, LASER**

The Boys in Company C

(1978) Columbia

Hard-hitting drama about a squadron of five young Marines serving in Vietnam who find their lives dramatically changed. Realism is the keynote in language and the terror of the jungle setting. **Cast:** Stan Shaw, Andrew Stevens, Michael Lembeck, James Canning, Craig Wasson, James Whitmore, Jr., Noble Willingham, Lee Ermey. **Credits:** Dir: Sidney J. Furie; Prod: Andre Morgan; Writer: Rick Natkin, Sidney J. Furie; DP: Godfrey Godar; Ed: Frank J. Urioste, Alan Pattillo, Jim Benson, Michael Berman; Prod Design: Robert Lang; Composer: Jaime Mendoza-Nava. Color, 127 min. **VHS, LASER**

The Boys in the Band

(1970) National General

Film version of Crowley's popular Broadway play. Relationships are strained and tempers tested at a birthday party thrown for a gay man by his friends. The accidental invitation and subsequent arrival of a straight friend causes everyone to rethink their roles in relationships. A breakthrough in on-screen depiction of gays. **Cast:** Frederick Combs, Leonard Frey, Cliff Gorman, Kenneth Nelson, Maud Adams, Reuben Greene, Robert La Tourneaux, Laurence Luckinbill, Keith Prentice, Peter White. **Credits:** Dir: William Friedkin; Prod: Mart Crowley; Writer: Mart Crowley; DP: Arthur J. Ornitz; Ed: Gerald Greenberg, Carl Lerner; Prod Design: John Robert Lloyd. Color, 120 min. **VHS, LASER**

Boys' Night Out

(1962) MGM

A saucy comedy about four men who flee commuter boredom by setting up a love nest in New York City with girl-toy Novak. But she's more than a pretty face—she's a sociology student observing the mating rituals of the American male. **Cast:** Kim Novak, James Garner, Tony Randall, Howard Duff, Janet Blair, Patti Page, Zsa Zsa Gabor, Howard Morris, Oscar Homolka, Jessie Royce Landis. **Credits:** Dir: Michael Gordon; Writer: Ira Wallach; DP: Arthur E. Arling; Composer: Frank de Vol. Color, 115 min. **VHS**

Boys Town

(1938) MGM

The story of Father Flanagan, who battled the courts and the community to create a home for boys that society had tossed away. Rooney plays a particularly tough challenge. Academy Award Nominations: 5, including Best Picture; Best Director; Best Screenplay. **Academy Awards:** Best Actor: Spencer Tracy; Special Achievement Award: Mickey Rooney; Best Original Story. **Cast:** Spencer Tracy, Mickey Rooney, Gene Reynolds, Henry Hull, Sidney Miller, Frankie Thomas, Bobs Watson, Tommy Noonan. **Credits:** Dir: Norman Taurog; Writer: John Meehan, Dore Schary; Story: Eleanore Griffin; DP: Sidney Wagner; Composer: Edward Ward. B&W, 96 min. **VHS, LASER**

The Boy with Green Hair

(1948) MGM

Peter Frye, a war orphan whose parents have been killed in an air raid, wakes up one morning to find his hair has turned green. He meets with suspicion and hatred, yet continues to express a belief that came to him in a vision: all wars must stop. An interesting parable with a fine performance by Stockwell as the alienated youth. **Cast:** Pat O'Brien, Robert Ryan, Barbara Hale, Dean Stockwell, Richard Lyon, Walter Catlett, Samuel S. Hinds, Regis Toomey, Charles Meredith, David Clarke. **Credits:** Dir: Joseph Losey; Prod: Stephen Ames; Writer: Ben Barzman, Alfred Lewis Levitt; DP: George Barnes; Ed: Frank Doyle; Prod Design: Albert S. D'Agostino, Ralph Berger; Composer: Leigh Harline. Color, 82 min. **VHS, LASER**

The Bravados

(1958) Fox

Peck plays an honest man who sets out to track four men he believes to be responsible for the rape and killing of his wife. The quest for revenge consumes his soul. **Cast:** Gregory Peck, Joan Collins, Henry Silva, Stephen Boyd, Albert Salmi, George Voskovec, Barry Coe, Lee Van Cleef, Herbert Rudley. **Credits:** Dir: Henry King; Prod: Herbert B. Swope; Writer: Philip Yordan; Story: Frank O'Rourke; DP: Leon Shamroy; Ed: William Mace; Prod Design: Lyle Wheeler, Mark-Lee Kirk; Composer: Lionel Newman. Color, 99 min. **VHS**

Brave Bulls

(1951) Paramount

The rise of a matador to superstardom. At the height of public attention, he loses confidence in his abilities, thinking his position is only the result of his manager's (Quinn) political ploys. He regains his prowess in time for the man-bull duel climax. Full of Mexican color and pageantry. **Cast:** Mel Ferrer, Miraslava Stern, Anthony Quinn, Eugene Iglesias, Jose Torvay, Charlita, Jose Luis Vasquez, Alfonzo Alverez, Alfredo Aguilar, Francisco Balderas. **Credits:** Dir: Robert Rossen; Prod: Robert Rossen; Writer: John Bright, Tom Lea; DP: Floyd Crosby, James Wong Howe; Ed: Henry Batista; Prod Design: Frank Tuttle. B&W, 106 min.

The Brave One

(1956) RKO

Based on an actual incident in Spain where, in 1936, a bull was pardoned and returned to his owner following a valiant performance in the ring. The film's story is transposed to Mexico, where it focuses on Leonardo, a young boy who is devoted to a pet bull he saved from a flood. When the boy's ranch-owner father dies and his stock is sold at an auction, Leonardo's favorite animal is taken away to be trained for the fights, even as Leonardo desperately tries to procure a pardon from the President. He finally succeeds but too late—the bull has already entered into the corrida to face the famous matador Fermin Rivera. Both the beast and the bullfighter show such bravery and brilliance during their face-off that the crowd votes to spare the bull's life. **Academy Awards:** Best Motion Picture Story. **Cast:** Michel Ray, Rodolpho Hoyos, Joi Lansing, Fermin Rivera, Elsa Cardenas, Carlos Navarro. **Credits:** Dir: Irving Rapper; Prod: Maurice King, Frank King; Writer: Dalton Trumbo, Harry Franklin, Merrill White; DP: Jack Cardiff; Ed: Merrill White; Composer: Victor Young. Color, 100 min. **VHS, LASER, DVD**

Breakfast at Tiffany's

(1961) Paramount

One more reason to fall in love with Audrey Hepburn is this sparkling and, at times, poignant comedy about a free-spirited young woman from the hinterlands redefining herself in New York City and her relationship with an aspiring writer. Holly Golightly partakes of all the big-city pleasures: parties, fine restaurants, and handsome,

Breakfast at Tiffany's (1961)

wealthy men who pay her way. Then she meets a new neighbor, a hopeful writer who himself lives off the generosity of a rich benefactor and soon the two begin a wistful, thorny relationship as Holly struggles to stay free. Based on a Truman Capote novella, it also features the timeless melody "Moon River" by Henry Mancini. Academy Award Nominations: 5, including Best Actress: Audrey Hepburn; Best Screenplay. **Academy Awards:** Best Song; Best Music Score of a Drama/Comedy. **Cast:** Audrey Hepburn, George Peppard, Patricia Neal, Martin Balsam, Buddy Ebsen, Mickey Rooney, John McGiver. **Credits:** Dir: Blake Edwards; Writer: George Axelrod; Story: Truman Capote; DP: Franz Planer; Ed: Howard Smith; Composer: Henry Mancini; Costumes: Edith Head. Color, 115 min. **VHS, LASER**

Breakheart Pass

(1976) United Artists

A muscular Western featuring the fisticuffs of Bronson. In 1870, the soldiers at an Army outpost in Utah are supposedly suffering from a diphtheria epidemic. A train heads toward the fort filled with soldiers, medical supplies, and Bronson, an undercover agent posing as an arrested criminal. There, he makes a stunning discovery: there is no epidemic, but there is a conspiracy between a group of

killers and a tribe of Indians. Fabled stuntman Yakima Canutt helped out, and boxer Archie Moore shows his stuff. **Cast:** Charles Bronson, Ben Johnson, Ed Lauter, Richard Crenna, Charles Durning, Jill Ireland, Archie Moore. **Credits:** Dir: Tom Gries; Prod: Jerry Gershwin; Writer: Alistair MacLean; DP: Lucien Ballard; Composer: Jerry Goldsmith. Color, 95 min. **VHS, LASER**

Breaking Away

(1979) Fox

A winning coming-of-age story with unusually well-drawn characters, social commentary, and great ensemble acting from a fresh-faced group of actors soon to be famous. The rivalry between townies and college kids sets the scene for the story of four friends figuring out their future. The star athlete, class clown, moony mascot, and a romantic dreamer in love with all things Italian pull together for a climactic bicycle race. This was the sleeper hit of 1979 and winner of the Best Picture nod from the National Society of Film Critics. Academy Award Nominations: 5, including Best Picture; Best Supporting Actress: Barbara Barrie; Best Director. **Academy Awards:** Best Screenplay. **Cast:** Dennis Christopher, Dennis Quaid, Daniel Stern, Jackie Earle Haley, Paul Dooley, Barbara Barrie, Robyn Douglass. **Credits:** Dir: Peter Yates; Prod: Peter Yates;

Breaking Away (1979)

Writer: Steve Tesich; DP: Matthew F. Leonetti; Composer: Patrick Williams. Color, 100 min. **VHS, LASER**

The Breaking Point
(1950) Warner Bros.
A remake of Warner Bros.' earlier *To Have and Have Not*, also based on Hemingway's novel of the same title, this drama follows the struggles of hapless charter captain Harry Morgan. Morgan takes on a wealthy passenger headed for Mexico. When Morgan's passenger disappears without paying, he's left unable to cover the docking fee. His financial troubles draw him into the orbit of a shifty lawyer who involves him first in a plot to smuggle Chinese and later in the transport of a bevy of crooks who nearly take his life. **Cast:** John Garfield, Patricia Neal, Phyllis Thaxter, Juano Hernandez, Wallace Ford, Edmond Ryan, Ralph Dumke, Gus Thomajan, William Campbell, Sherry Jackson. **Credits:** Dir: Michael Curtiz; Prod: Jerry Wald; Writer: Ranald MacDougall; Story: Ernest Hemingway; DP: Ted McCord; Ed: Alan Crosland; Composer: Ray Heindorf; Art Director: Edward Carrere. B&W, 97 min.

Break of Hearts
(1935) RKO
Lots of heartache and heavy drinking in this melodrama about the tortured marriage of a young composer and her conductor husband. The great conductor is a hopeless philanderer and alcoholic, and the composer reluctantly

leaves the marriage. But love conquers all, and the estranged partners find their way back into each other's arms. Pretty soupy, but Boyer and Hepburn lend class. **Cast:** Katharine Hepburn, Charles Boyer, John Beal, Jean Hersholt, Sam Hardy. **Credits:** Dir: Philip Moeller; Writer: Sarah Y. Mason, Victor Heerman, Anthony Veiller; DP: Robert DeGrasse; Composer: Max Steiner. B&W, 80 min. **VHS, LASER**

A Breath of Scandal
(1960) Paramount
An updated Molnar romance of an old-world princess romanced by an American industrialist gives Loren a chance to look stunningly beautiful. An odd outing by *Casablanca* director Curtiz. **Cast:** Sophia Loren, John Gavin, Maurice Chevalier, Isabel Jeans, Angela Lansbury. **Credits:** Dir: Michael Curtiz; Prod: Carlo Ponti; Writer: Walter Bernstein; DP: Mario Montuori; Ed: Howard Smith; Prod Design: Hal Pereira, Gene Allen. Color, 98 min. **VHS**

Brewster McCloud
(1970) MGM
In a bizarre series of murders, all of the victims of a ruthless Houston killer are found covered with bird droppings. The police soon close in on the prime suspect—a young man who lives in the Astrodome and dreams of flight. One of Altman's most offbeat, fascinating films, it includes most of the Altman stock company from *M*A*S*H*. **Cast:** Bud Cort, Sally Kellerman, Michael Murphy, Shelley

Duvall, Stacy Keach, John Schuck, William Windom, Margaret Hamilton, Rene Auberjonois. **Credits:** Dir: Robert Altman; Prod: Lou Adler; Writer: Doran William Cannon; DP: Lamar Boren, Jordan Cronenweth; Composer: Gene Page. Color, 106 min. **VHS**

Brewster's Millions
(1945) United Artists
Remade several times from silent days to the late 1980s, presumably because the story is pure escapist wish fulfillment. In this version, an ex-GI must spend a million dollars in a year's time in order to inherit an even greater fortune. **Cast:** Dennis O'Keefe, June Havoc, Helen Walker, Eddie Anderson, Gail Patrick, Mischa Auer, Joe Sawyer, Nana Bryant, John Litel, Thurston Hall. **Credits:** Dir: Allan Dwan; Writer: Sig Herzig, Charles Rogers; DP: Charles Lawton, Jr.; Composer: Hugo Friedhofer. B&W, 79 min. **VHS**

The Bride Came C.O.D.
(1941) Warner Bros.
Heiress Davis is about to elope and has hired roughneck pilot Cagney to fly her and her intended to Las Vegas for the nuptials. Joan's father, however, strenuously objects to the wedding, and offers Cagney some much-needed cash to thwart the plans. They warm up during the flight, and land in the desert—and in hot water. Odd romantic pairing of drama diva and tough guy. **Cast:** Bette Davis, James Cagney, Stuart Erwin, Eugene Pallette, Jack Carson, George Tobias, Harry Davenport, William Frawley, Edward Brophy, Chick Chandler. **Credits:** Dir: William Keighley; Prod: William Cagney; Writer: Julius J. Epstein, Philip G. Epstein; DP: Ernest Haller; Ed: Thomas Richards; Prod Design: Ted Smith; Composer: Max Steiner. B&W, 93 min. **VHS**

The Bride of Frankenstein
(1935) Universal
A sequel that surpasses the debut of the classic *Frankenstein* (and predecessor to *The House Of Frankenstein*, 1944). Having escaped the fiery castle that threatened to engulf him at the end of the 1931 horror classic, the monster is back. And he's better than ever—more civilized, more human. He's even learned to speak a few words. Henry Frankenstein, the monster's creator, tries to put his evil ways behind him. But Dr. Pretorious draws him back into the mad-scientist business by convincing Henry that he knows what the Monster really needs—a mate (Lanchester). The orig-

inal *Variety* review noted that 17 minutes were deleted from the film between the 90-minute preview print and the 73-minute release version. Consequently, some cuts of the film may run as long as 90 minutes. Frequently missing from prints of *The Bride of Frankenstein* are the murder of the burgomaster by Frankenstein's Monster and pieces of the prologue featuring Lanchester as Mary Shelley. The burgomaster sequence is often cut because of the negative light it shines on the Monster. *The Bride of Frankenstein* was remade in 1985 as *The Bride*, with Sting as Frankenstein and Jennifer Beals as the Bride. **Cast:** Boris Karloff, Elsa Lanchester, Colin Clive, Valerie Hobson, Ernest Thesiger, Dwight Frye, O. P. Heggie, Una O'Connor, E. E. Clive, Gavin Gordon. **Credits:** Dir: James Whale; Prod: Carl Laemmle; Writer: William Hurlbut, John L. Balderston; DP: John Mescall; Ed: Ted J. Kent; Prod Design: Charles D. Hall; Composer: Franz Waxman. B&W, 75 min. VHS, LASER

The Bride Wore Red
(1937) MGM
When an eccentric Italian count seeks to prove that social position is nothing more than a matter of luck, he sends chanteuse Crawford to a luxurious Swiss resort masquerading as a wealthy lady. She woos a rich bachelor away from his fiancée only to discover she is falling in love with the town's postman. **Cast:** Joan Crawford, Franchot Tone, Robert Young, Billie Burke, Reginald Owen, George Zucco, Lynne Carver, Paul Porcasi, Mary Philips, Dickie Moore. **Credits:** Dir: Dorothy Arzner; Prod: Joseph L. Mankiewicz; Writer: Bradbury Foote, Tess Slesinger; DP: George J. Folsey; Ed: Adrienne Fazan; Prod Design: Cedric Gibbons; Composer: Franz Waxman. B&W, 103 min. VHS

The Bridge at Remagen
(1969) United Artists
Based on a true account of a skirmish near the end of WWII. In an effort to commandeer an important bridge on the northern Rhine River, Allied forces do battle with retreating Germans who have every intention of destroying the bridge and cutting off the enemy route. **Cast:** George Segal, Robert Vaughn, Ben Gazzara, Bradford Dillman, E. G. Marshall, Peter Van Eyck, Anna Gael, Matt Clark, Fritz Ford, Tom Heaton. **Credits:** Dir: John Guillermin; Prod: David L. Wolper; Writer: William Roberts, Richard Yates; DP: Stanley Cortez; Ed: William

Cartwright; Prod Design: Alfred Sweeney; Composer: Elmer Bernstein. Color, 116 min. VHS

The Bridge of San Luis Rey
(1944) United Artists
Five people are killed in a freak accident when a lofty rope bridge collapses. The film details a priest's journey to discover if there was a divine reason for the bloody disaster. Set in Lima, Peru, during the 18th century. Based on the Thornton Wilder novel, and first made in 1929. **Cast:** Lynn Bari, Louis Calhern, Francis Lederer, Akim Tamiroff, Nazimova, Blanche Yurka, Donald Woods, Emma Dunn, Joan Lorring. **Credits:** Dir: Rowland V. Lee; Prod: Benedict E. Bogeaus; Writer: Howard Estabrook, Herman Weissman; Story: Thornton Wilder; DP: John W. Boyle; Ed: Harvey Manager; Composer: Dimitri Tiomkin. B&W, 89 min. VHS, LASER

The Bridge on the River Kwai
(1957) Columbia
An outstanding, psychologically complex adaptation of Pierre Boulle's 1952 novel. British POWs in Burma are forced to build a bridge to aid the war effort of their Japanese captors. British and American intelligence officers conspire to blow up the structure, but the British commander (Guinness) who supervised the bridge's construction has acquired a sense of pride in his creation and tries to foil their plans. Too late, he realizes the devastating consequences of his actions. Although credited to the director, the script was actually written by blacklisted writers Wilson and Foreman. Awards include Golden Globes for Best Director; Best Actor in a Drama: Alec Guinness; Best Motion Picture, Drama. **Academy Awards:** Best Director; Best Actor: Alec Guinness; Best Film Editing; Best Cinematography; Best Score; Best Picture; Best Screenplay Based on Material from Another Medium. **Cast:** William Holden, Alec Guinness, Jack Hawkins, Sessue Hayakawa, James Donald, Geoffrey Horne, Andre Morell, Peter Williams, Percy Herbert, Harold Goodwin. **Credits:** Dir: David Lean; Prod: Sam Spiegel; Writer: Michael Henry Wilson, Carl Foreman; DP: Jack Hildyard; Ed: Peter Taylor; Composer: Malcolm Arnold. Color, 166 min. VHS, LASER

The Bridges at Toko-Ri
(1955) Paramount
A lawyer who is a naval air reserve officer reluctantly leaves his wife and

children behind after he's called back into service. Soon, Brubaker receives his orders: to bomb five bridges that are of vital importance to the enemy. Despite his unhappiness at being back in action and his doubts about U.S. soldiers risking their lives on such a dangerous mission, Lieutenant Brubaker puts his life on the line. **Academy Awards:** Best Special Effects. **Cast:** William Holden, Grace Kelly, Fredric March, Mickey Rooney, Robert Strauss, Charles McGraw, Earl Holliman, Willis Bouchey, Keiko Awaji, Richard Shannon. **Credits:** Dir: Mark Robson; Prod: William Perlberg; Writer: Valentine Davies; Story: James A. Michener; DP: Loyal Griggs; Ed: Alma Macrorie; Prod Design: Hal Pereira, Henry Bumstead; Composer: Lyn Murray. Color, 103 min. VHS, LASER

A Bridge Too Far
(1977) United Artists
Attenborough's ambitious, all-star adaptation (by Goldman) of Cornelius Ryan's book gives an account of the Battle of Arnhem. In 1944, the Allied powers attempt to expedite the end of the war with a costly operation to capture six bridges connecting Holland to Germany. The operation ended in Allied defeat. A multitude of notables and Attenborough's mastery of the epic promise more than is ultimately delivered, but an interesting watch nonetheless. **Cast:** Dirk Bogarde, James Caan, Michael Caine, Sean Connery, Edward Fox, Elliott Gould, Gene Hackman, Laurence Olivier. **Credits:** Dir: Richard Attenborough; Prod: Joseph E. Levine, Richard Levine, Michael Stanley-Evans; Writer: William Goldman; DP: Geoffrey Unsworth; Ed: Anthony Gibbs; Composer: John Addison; Costumes: Anthony Mendleson. Color, 179 min. VHS, LASER, DVD

Brigadoon
(1954) MGM
Romance blooms for an American who stumbles upon a magical Scottish village visible for one day every hundred years. Bagpipes and brogues abound in the Technicolor Highlands, and the Lerner and Loewe score makes this one of the most underrated of the grand 1950s musicals. Awards include a Golden Globe for Best Color Cinematography. Academy Award Nominations: 3, including Best Art Direction. **Cast:** Van Johnson, Gene Kelly, Cyd Charisse, Elaine Stewart, Barry Jones, George Chakiris, Albert Shayne, Hugh Laing, Virginia Bosler, Jimmy Thompson. **Credits:** Dir: Vin-

cente Minnelli; Prod: Arthur Freed; DP: Joseph Ruttenberg; Ed: Albert Akst; Prod Design: Cedric Gibbons, Preston Ames; Composer: Alan Jay Lerner, Frederick Loewe; Costumes: Irene Sharaff. Color, 109 min. **VHS, LASER, DVD**

The Brigand
(1952) Columbia
A young dupe is recruited to pose as the king in this adventure story set in 18th-century Spain. Our hero, a young brigand, accepts his role with gusto, but gets in big trouble when he falls for the king's fiancée. The king's mistress conspires with some angry nobles to put an end to the dynasty, and only some serious swashbuckling and a good tango can save the star-crossed lovers. **Cast:** Anthony Dexter, Joey Lawrence, Gale Robbins, Anthony Quinn, Carl Benton Reid, Ron Randall, Fay Roope, Carleton Young, Ian MacDonald, Lester Matthews. **Credits:** Dir: Phil Karlson; Writer: Jesse Lasky, Jr.; Story: George Bruce; DP: W. Howard Greene; Ed: Jerome Thomas; Composer: Mario Castelnuovo-Tedasco. Color, 93 min.

Bright Eyes
(1934) Fox
Little orphan Shirley gets in the middle of a nasty custody battle. One of Temple's first and best, most famous for the song "On the Good Ship Lollipop." **Cast:** Shirley Temple, James Dunn, Jane Withers, Judith Allen. **Credits:** Dir: David Butler; Prod: Saul M. Wurtzel; Writer: William Conselman, David Butler, Edward Burke; DP: Arthur Miller; Composer: Samuel Kaylin. B&W, 90 min. **VHS**

Bright Leaf
(1950) Warner Bros.
Brant Royle and his family are driven from their Kingsmont, North Carolina, home by a tobacco baron, Major James Singleton, who wishes to keep his daughter away from the unseemly Royle. Royle vows to return to Kingsmont to wrest from Singleton his magnificent home, "Bright Leaf," and the hand of his beautiful daughter. When Royle manages to create and make himself the head of a cigarette-making syndicate that puts Singleton out of business, he finds himself in a strong position to make good his vow. **Cast:** Gary Cooper, Lauren Bacall, Patricia Neal, Jack Carson, Donald Crisp, Gladys George, Elizabeth Patterson, Jeff Corey, Taylor Holmes, Thurston Hall. **Credits:** Dir: Michael Curtiz; Prod: Henry Blanke; Writer: Ranald MacDougall;

Story: Foster Fitz-Simons; DP: Karl Freund; Ed: Owen Marks; Prod Design: Stanley Fleisher; Composer: Victor Young. B&W, 109 min.

Bright Lights
(1935) Warner Bros.
A burlesque clown and his wife are the stars of their traveling troupe. But a thrill-seeking heiress joins the company, just for adventure, and a Broadway producer's press agent convinces the society gal and the clown to take their act to the Great White Way, minus the wife. Amid many vaudevillian routines, the clown gets big-headed and falls for the heiress, then sees the error of his ways. **Cast:** Joe E. Brown, Ann Dvorak, Patricia Ellis, William Gargan, Joseph Cawthorn, Henry O'Neill, Arthur Treacher, Gordon Westcott, Joseph Crehan, Harry Ruby. **Credits:** Dir: Busby Berkeley; Prod: Michael Curtiz; Writer: Bert Kalmar, Harry Ruby, Lois Leeson, Ben Markson, Benny Rubin; DP: Sidney Hickox; Ed: Bert L'Orle; Prod Design: Anton Grot; Composer: Allie Wrubel, Bert Kalmar, Leo F. Forbstein, Allie Wrubel, Harry Ruby. B&W, 83 min.

Bright Victory
(1951) Universal
Acclaimed performance by Kennedy as a vet blinded during WWII trying to readjust to civilian life. When a lovely young nurse, Dow, helps him in his transition, he is reluctant to leave the hospital. After hometown rejection, he returns to Dow to bravely face his future without denial. Kennedy was nominated for Best Actor, but the Award went to Humphrey Bogart for *African Queen*. Watch for Rock Hudson in a small role as a corporal. **Cast:** Arthur Kennedy, Peggy Dow, Julie Adams, James L. Edwards, Will Geer, Nana Bryant, Jim Backus, Minor Watson, Joan Banks, Richard Egan. **Credits:** Dir: Mark Robson; Prod: Robert Buckner; Writer: Robert Buckner, Baynard Kendrick; DP: William H. Daniels; Ed: Russell Schoengarth; Prod Design: John P. Austin, Bernard Herzbrun; Composer: Frank Skinner. B&W, 96 min.

Bringing Up Baby
(1938) RKO
The very definition of screwball comedy, and one of the sharpest, fastest, most out-and-out hilarious movies ever made. A nonstop profusion of comic disasters, coincidences, and misunderstandings ensue when Grant, as an absentminded, straitlaced zoologist, meets Hepburn, as a flighty, accident-

prone heiress. Grant wants a donation to his museum from a wealthy widow but he seems unable to avoid the woman's niece. Soon the two are rampaging through his estate trying to find a lost dinosaur bone, searching for a missing, music-loving pet leopard named Baby, and, inevitably, falling in love. Hawks, the master of many genres, lets the whole thing run riot without ever sacrificing sense. Selected for the National Film Registry. **Cast:** Katharine Hepburn, Cary Grant, Charlie Ruggles, May Robson, Walter Catlett, Fritz Feld, Jonathan Hale, Barry Fitzgerald. **Credits:** Dir: Howard Hawks; Prod: Howard Hawks; Writer: Dudley Nichols, Hagar Wilde; DP: Russell Metty; Ed: George Hively; Prod Design: Van Nest Polglase, Perry Ferguson; Composer: Roy Webb; Costumes: Howard Greer; SFX: Vernon Walker. B&W, 102 min. **VHS, LASER**

The Brink's Job
(1978) Universal
A spirited comic crime caper based on the infamous Boston Brink's robbery that netted the amateur crooks nearly three million dollars. Based on the book *Big Stick-Up At Brinks* by Noel Behn, the movie picks up the story after the job, with less than a week to go before the statute of limitations runs out. Academy Award Nominations: Best Art Direction. **Cast:** Peter Falk, Peter Boyle, Warren Oates, Gena Rowlands, Allen Goorwitz, Paul Sorvino, Sheldon Leonard, Kevin J. O'Connor. **Credits:** Dir: William Friedkin; Prod: Ralph Serpe; Writer: Walon Green; Story: Noel Behn; DP: Norman Leigh; Ed: Bud Smith, Robert K. Lambert; Prod Design: Dean Tavoularis; Composer: Richard Rodney Bennett. Color, 103 min. **VHS**

Broadway
(1942) Universal
A famed entertainer returns to the old Paradise Club in New York where he began his career. In flashback, he recalls the club at its height, when he worked as a young hoofer, pulling in audiences with his partner, Billie. A fanciful evocation of Depression-era high times and crimes. **Cast:** George Raft, George O'Brien, Janet Blair, Broderick Crawford, Marjorie Rambeau, Anne Gwynne, S. Z. Sakall, Edward Brophy, Marie Wilson, Gus Schilling. **Credits:** Dir: William A. Seiter; Prod: Bruce Manning; Writer: John Bright, Felix Jackson; Story: George Abbott, Phillip Dunning; DP: George Barnes; Ed: Ted J. Kent; Composer: Charles Previn. B&W, 91 min.

Broadway Bill

(1934) Columbia

A sunny Capra comedy about a lover of the ponies who abandons his marriage and a job at his father-in-law's business in order to race his beloved thoroughbred Broadway Bill. He raises everyone's ire except for Loy, his unmarried sister-in-law, who believes in his dream. Capra liked the story so much he made it again in 1950 as *Riding High*. **Cast:** Myrna Loy, Warner Baxter, Margaret Hamilton, Jason Robards, Walter Connolly, Helen Vinson, Douglass Dumbrille, Raymond Walburn, Lynne Overman, Clarence Muse. **Credits:** Dir: Frank Capra; Writer: Robert Riskin; Story: Mark Hellinger; DP: Joseph A. Walker; Ed: Gene Havlick. B&W, 102 min. vhs, laser

Broadway Melody of 1936

(1935) MGM

Prime entry in series with Benny out for Taylor. Songs include "You Are My Lucky Star." Academy Award Nominations: Best Picture; Best Writing. **Academy Awards:** Best Dance Direction. **Cast:** Eleanor Powell, Jack Benny, Robert Taylor, Vilma Ebsen, Buddy Ebsen, Sid Silvers, Una Merkel, Nick Long. **Credits:** Dir: Roy Del Ruth; Prod: John Considine; Writer: Jack McGowan, Sid Silvers, Harry Conn; Story: Moss Hart; DP: Charles Rosher; Ed: Blanche Sewell; Choreographer: Albertina Rasch, Dave Gould; Composer: Arthur Freed, Nacio Herb Brown. B&W, 102 min. vhs

Broadway Melody of 1938

(1937) MGM

Something of a lull in the Broadway Melody series, but salvaged by Benchley, and a young Garland singing "Dear Mr. Gable." The plot revolves around a standard-issue struggling Broadway show, the opening of which is threatened by financial troubles. Luckily, one of the hoofers just happens to own a race horse and if it can be coaxed into winning at Saratoga, there might be enough cash to mount the production. **Cast:** Eleanor Powell, George Murphy, Judy Garland, Robert Benchley, Robert Taylor, Sophie Tucker, Buddy Ebsen, Sid Silvers, Billy Gilbert. **Credits:** Dir: Roy Del Ruth; Prod: Jack Cummings; Writer: Raymond Walburn, Jack McGowan, Sid Silvers; DP: William Daniels; Ed: Blanche Sewell; Choreographer: Dave Gould; Composer: Nacio Herb Brown, Arthur Freed. B&W, 113 min. vhs

Broadway Melody of 1940

(1940) MGM

The class of the Broadway Melody series, with the burnished talents of Astaire and Murphy, and the timeless tunes of Cole Porter. The plot, never the point of these exercises, pits two dancers in a friendly rivalry for the attentions of Powell. This was the only screen appearance together of Astaire and Powell and it makes you wish for more. **Cast:** Fred Astaire, Eleanor Powell, George Murphy, Frank Morgan, Douglas MacPhail, Florence Rice, Ian Hunter. **Credits:** Dir: Norman Taurog; Prod: Jack Cummings; Writer: Leon Gordon, George Oppenheimer; Story: Jack McGowan, Dore Schary; DP: Oliver T. Marsh, Joseph Ruttenberg; Ed: Blanche Sewell; Prod Design: Cedric Gibbons; Choreographer: Bobby Connolly; Composer: Cole Porter. B&W, 103 min. vhs, laser

Broken Arrow

(1950) Fox

Interesting depiction of diplomacy with the Indians in the frontier West focuses on the relationship between cavalry scout Stewart and Apache chief Cochise (Chandler). The scout's attempts to head off an Indian war are complicated by his love affair with an Indian woman. Winner of Golden Globe for Special Achievements. **Cast:** James Stewart, Jeff Chandler, Debra Paget, Will Geer, Basil Ruysdael, Arthur Hunnicutt, Jay Silverheels. **Credits:** Dir: Delmer Daves; Prod: Julian C. Blaustein; Writer: Michael Blankfort; Story: Elliott Arnold; DP: Ernest Palmer; Prod Design: Lyle Wheeler; Composer: Alfred Newman, Hugo Friedhofer. Color, 106 min. vhs

Broken Lance

(1954) Fox

Tracy is superb in this Western drama of an autocratic patriarch and the strife and betrayal among his sons that threatens his cattle empire. The story unfolds as one son (Wagner) returns from prison after taking responsibility for a raid led by his father. A showdown with his brother (Widmark) over the circumstances of their father's death leads to another death and the restoration of the father's legacy. Dmytryk uses widescreen to full advantage. Winner of Golden Globe for Best Film Promoting International Understanding. **Academy Awards:** Best Motion Picture Story. **Cast:** Spencer Tracy, Robert Wagner, Richard Widmark, E. G. Marshall, Jean Peters, Hugh O'Brian, Katy Jurado, Earl Holliman, Eduard Franz. **Credits:** Dir: Edward Dmytryk; Prod: Sol C. Siegel; Writer: Richard Murphy; Story: Philip Yordan; DP: Joseph MacDonald; Ed: Dorothy Spencer; Composer: Leigh Harline, Lionel Newman; Costumes: Travilla. Color, 97 min. vhs, laser

Broken Lullaby

(1932) Paramount

During WWI, a French soldier shoots a German, learning his name as he sees the dying man scribble a note to his fiancée. After the armistice, the French veteran visits the dead man's family. He endears himself to them first by putting flowers on the soldier's grave, but doesn't reveal his connection to their dead son. Soon, he and the fiancée of the dead German fall in love. **Cast:** Lionel Barrymore, George Bickel, Nancy Carroll, Louise Carter, Thomas Douglas, Emma Dunn, Phillips Holmes, Lucien Littlefield, ZaSu Pitts. **Credits:** Dir: Ernst Lubitsch; Prod: Ernst Lubitsch; Writer: Reginald Berkeley, Samson Raphaelson, Maurice Rostand, Ernest Vajada; DP: Victor Milner; Prod Design: Jan Dreier. B&W, 77 min.

Bronco Buster

(1952) Universal

In this rodeo drama, Lund plays an old roper who takes a promising young cowboy under his wing. But when the youngster gets good, he also gets full of himself, turning his back on his mentor and trying to steal his girl. That's more than the old feller can stand, so he takes it upon himself to show the kid how it's done. The film incorporates plenty of actual rodeo footage. **Cast:** John Lund, Scott Brady, Joyce Holden, Chill Wills, Don Haggerty, Dan Poore, Casey Tibbs, Bill Williams, Jerry Ambler. **Credits:** Dir: Budd Boetticher; Prod: Ted Richmond; Writer: Horace McCoy, Peter B. Kynes; Story: Lillie Hayward; DP: Clifford Stine; Ed: Edward Curtiss. B&W, 81 min.

The Brotherhood

(1968) Paramount

The elder of two brothers reluctantly guides the younger through his initiation to the mysteries of the Mob. The aging Mob boss's love and undying loyalty to his ambitious younger brother blinds him to the reality that the first hit his little brother must make is on him. **Cast:** Kirk Douglas, Alex Cord, Irene Papas, Luther Adler. **Credits:** Dir: Martin Ritt; Prod: Kirk Douglas; Writer: Lewis John Carlino; DP: Boris Kaufman; Ed: Frank Bracht; Composer: Lalo Schifrin. Color, 96 min. vhs, laser

Brother Orchid

(1940) Warner Bros.

In this offbeat gangster farce, mobster Robinson runs afoul of his former colleagues in the gang. So he cools it in a monastery, where he finds himself being reformed by the brothers. However, when he discovers his former gang preventing the monks from selling flowers, he ponders a return to his former life to settle the score. **Cast:** Edward G. Robinson, Ann Sothern, Humphrey Bogart, Ralph Bellamy, Donald Crisp, Allen Jenkins, Cecil Kellaway. **Credits:** Dir: Lloyd Bacon, Byron Haskin; Writer: Earl Baldwin; Story: Richard Connell; DP: Tony Gaudio; Ed: William Holmes; Prod Design: Max Parker; Composer: Heinz Roemheld; Costumes: Howard Shoup. B&W, 87 min. **VHS**

Brother Rat
(1938) Warner Bros.
Cadets at the Virginia Military Institute stick up for one another when one falls in love with (and secretly marries) the major's daughter. Albert reprises his stage role in his film debut. Remake in 1952 as *About Face.* Sequel: *Brother Rat and a Baby* (1940). **Cast:** Priscilla Lane, Wayne Morris, Johnnie Davis, Jane Bryan, Eddie Albert, Ronald Reagan, Jane Wyman, Henry O'Neill. **Credits:** Dir: William Keighley; Prod: Robert Lord; Writer: Richard Macaulay, Jerry Wald; Story: Fred F. Finklehoffe, John Monks, Jr.; DP: Ernest Haller; Ed: William Holmes; Prod Design: Max Parker. B&W, 89 min. **VHS**

The Brothers Karamazov
(1958) MGM
Four brothers vie for the same woman in this fine adaptation of Dostoyevsky's tale. Continually abused by their overbearing father, one takes matters into his own hands and murders the father. The horror of the father's death is further compounded by the accusation of the wrong brother as the murderer. William Shatner's screen debut. **Cast:** Yul Brynner, Claire Bloom, Lee J. Cobb, Maria Schell, William Shatner, Richard Basehart, Albert Salmi, Judith Evelyn, Harry Townes. **Credits:** Dir: Richard Brooks; Prod: Pandro S. Berman; Writer: Richard Brooks; Story: Fyodor Mikhaylovich Dostoyevsky; DP: John Alton; Ed: John Dunning; Prod Design: William A. Horning, Paul Groesse; Composer: Bronislau Kaper. Color, 147 min. **VHS**

The Buccaneer
(1958) Paramount
Swashbuckling historical adventure about the escapades of pirate Jean Lafitte—his relationship with American president Andrew Jackson during the War of 1812 and how Lafitte came to the rescue of America's fighting forces. Remake of the 1938 film by Cecil B. DeMille, who narrates the introduction. Directorial debut for actor Quinn, married at the time to Katherine DeMille, Cecil's daughter. Academy Award Nominations: Best Costumes. **Cast:** Yul Brynner, Charlton Heston, Claire Bloom, Charles Boyer, Inger Stevens, Henry Hull, E. G. Marshall, Lorne Greene, Fran Jeffries, Woody Strode. **Credits:** Dir: Anthony Quinn; Prod: Henry Wilcoxon; Writer: Jesse Lasky, Jr., Bernice Mosk; DP: Loyal Griggs; Ed: Arnie Marshek; Composer: Elmer Bernstein; Costumes: Ralph Jester, Edith Head. Color, 121 min. **VHS**

Buck and the Preacher
(1972) Columbia
Three recently freed slaves head west with the hope of starting a new life in post–Civil War America. Their progress is impeded by a sadistic racist who resents their newfound freedom. Poitier's directorial debut. **Cast:** Sidney Poitier, Ruby Dee, Harry Belafonte, Cameron Mitchell, Denny Miller, Nita Talbot, John Kelly. **Credits:** Dir: Sidney Poitier; Prod: Joel Glickman; Writer: Ernest Kinoy; Story: Drake Walker; DP: Alex Phillips; Ed: Pembroke Herring; Composer: Benny Carter; Costumes: Guy Berhille; SFX: Leon Ortega. Color, 102 min. **VHS**

Buck Benny Rides Again
(1940) Paramount
Benny (as himself) along with his usual radio colleagues (Devine, Harris, Day) find themselves on a dude ranch in Nevada. Benny tries to convince a lovely young lady that he really is a cowboy. Through a series of Western spoofs, Benny ends up having to make good on all his fictitious tales of "roughing it." "Rochester" Anderson provides much of the laughter. **Cast:** Jack Benny, Ellen Drew, Eddie Anderson, Andy Devine, Phil Harris, Virginia Dale, Lillian Cornell, Kay Linaker, Theresa Harris, Dennis Day. **Credits:** Dir: Mark Sandrich; Prod: Mark Sandrich; Writer: William Morrow, Edmund Beloin; Story: Zion Myers, Arthur Stringer; DP: Charles Lang; Ed: LeRoy Stone; Prod Design: Hans Dreier, Roland Anderson; Composer: Victor Young. B&W, 82 min.

Buckskin Frontier
(1943) United Artists
Standard Western fare about a cattle empire, threatened by an encroaching railroad, and the dirty fight to stop it. **Cast:** Richard Dix, Jane Wyatt, Lee J. Cobb, Victor Jory, Max Baer, George Reeves, Albert Dekker. **Credits:** Dir: Lesley Selander; Writer: Norman Houston, Bernard Schubert; Story: Harry Sinclair Drago. B&W, 74 min. **VHS**

The Buddy Holly Story
(1978) Columbia
A powerful biography of '50s Texas rockabilly phenomenon Buddy Holly, who took his band the Crickets to the top of the charts before a tragic airplane accident ended his life. Portrays Holly as regular, hardworking type who struggles with peers and the music industry before he makes it big with the huge hit "That'll Be the Day." Also details the final events leading up to the plane crash, en route to Minnesota in a snowstorm on February 3, 1959, which also claimed the lives of Richie Valens and the Big Bopper. **Academy Awards:** Best Original Song Score and Adaptation. **Cast:** Gary Busey, Don Stroud, Charles Martin Smith, Conrad Janis, Maria Richwine, Bill Jordan, Albert Popwell, John Goff. **Credits:** Dir: Steve Rash; Prod: Fred Bauer; Writer: Robert Gittler; DP: Stevan Larner; Ed: David Blewitt; Prod Design: Joel Schiller; Composer: Joe Renzetti. Color, 113 min. **VHS, LASER**

Buffalo Bill
(1944) Fox
Story of William F. Cody, better known as Buffalo Bill. Plenty of action as the stages of his life unfold from his early years as an Indian fighter, scout, and campaigner for Indian rights to his later years of Wild West showmanship. A good cast keeps the light fare worthwhile. **Cast:** Joel McCrea, Maureen O'Hara, Thomas Mitchell, Linda Darnell, Edgar Buchanan, Anthony Quinn, Moroni Olsen. **Credits:** Dir: William Wellman; Prod: Harry Sherman; Writer: Aeneas MacKenzie, Clemente Ripley, Cecile Kramer; Story: Frank Winch; DP: Leon Shamroy; Ed: James B. Clark; Composer: David Buttolph; SFX: Fred Sersen. Color, 90 min. **VHS**

Buffalo Bill and the Indians
(1976) United Artists
In Altman's look at Western Americana, Newman portrays Buffalo Bill as a boisterous, eccentric charlatan. Not the great director's best work but spirited and the all-star cast helps. **Cast:** Paul Newman, Geraldine Chaplin, Joel Grey, Kevin McCarthy, Burt Lancaster, Harvey Keitel, John Considine, Denver Pyle. **Credits:** Dir: Robert Altman, Richard Baskin; Prod: Robert Altman; Writer: Alan Rudolph, Robert Altman;

Story: Arthur Kopit; DP: Paul Lohmann; Ed: Dennis Hill, Peter Appleton. Color, 135 min. **VHS**

Bugsy Malone

(1976) Paramount
A real oddity; a kid's musical version of gangster films cast entirely with children. Peculiar outing highlights '70s-era Baio and Foster, so a hoot on that level. Film score by syrupmeister Paul Williams. Academy Award Nomination for Best Original Song Score. **Cast:** Jodie Foster, Scott Baio, Florrie Dugger, John Cassisi. **Credits:** Dir: Alan Parker; Prod: Alan Marshall; Writer: Alan Parker; DP: Michael Seresin, Peter Biziou; Ed: Gerry Hambling; Prod Design: Geoffrey Kirkland; Choreographer: Gillian Gregory; Composer: Paul Williams; Costumes: Monica Howe. Color, 94 min. **VHS, LASER**

Bulldog Drummond

Herman Cyril McNeile, known as "Sapper," created the adventurous Colonel Hugh "Bulldog" Drummond, a restless former British army officer who undertakes detective work to spice up his life. Though there were several silent Drummond films, the series didn't catch on until Ronald Colman appeared in 1929's *Bulldog Drummond,* in which the sleuth-for-hire saves an heiress's uncle from a crazed doctor and wins the girl's heart in the process. In Paramount's Drummond collection of the late 1930s, considered the definitive series, John Barrymore played Scotland Yard's Inspector Nielson and John Howard played the title role in seven of the crime-solving romps. The series continued until 1951, with Tim Conway, Ron Randell, and Walter Pidgeon making appearances as Drummond.

Bulldog Drummond *(1929)*
The Return of Bulldog Drummond *(1934)*
Bulldog Drummond at Bay *(1937; remade 1947)*
Bulldog Drummond Escapes *(1937)*
Bulldog Drummond Comes Back *(1937)*
Bulldog Drummond's Revenge *(1937)*
Bulldog Drummond's Peril *(1938)*
Bulldog Drummond in Africa *(1938)*
Bulldog Drummond's Secret Police *(1939)*
Bulldog Drummond's Bride *(1939)*
Arrest Bulldog Drummond *(1939)*
Bulldog Drummond Strikes Back *(1947)*
The Challenge *(1948)*
13 Lead Soldiers *(1948)*

Calling Bulldog Drummond *(1951)*
Deadlier Than the Male *(1967)*
Some Girls Do *(1969)*

Bulldog Edition

(1936) Chesterfield
Two newspapers feud it out over the number-one spot, attempting every type of intimidation and sabotage— including the employment of gangsters. Okay entry from poverty-row studio. **Cast:** Ray Walker, Evalyn Knapp, Regis Toomey, Frank Puglia, Ed LeSaint, Ruth Gillette. **Credits:** Dir: Charles Lamont; Prod: Nat Levine; Writer: Richard English, Karen DeWolf; Story: Danny Ahearn; DP: Jack Marta. B&W, 57 min. **VHS**

Bullets or Ballots

(1936) Warner Bros.
A Robinson-Bogart tough-guy yarn. A Bronx cop goes undercover so he can tip off the police to the mob's illicit activities. Bigwig businessmen and slimy politicos are in it up to their necks and they take a fall, too. Based on a true story. **Cast:** Edward G. Robinson, Joan Blondell, Barton MacLane, Humphrey Bogart, Frank McHugh, Dick Purcell, George E. Stone. **Credits:** Dir: William Keighley; Prod: Louis F. Edelman; Writer: Seton I. Miller; Story: Martin Mooney; DP: Hal Mohr; Ed: Jack Killifer; Prod Design: Carl Jules Weyl; Composer: Heinz Roemheld; SFX: Warren E. Lynch, Fred Jackman. B&W, 82 min. **VHS**

The Bullfighter and the Lady

(1951) Republic
A visiting American filmmaker vacationing in Mexico convinces the area's foremost bullfighter to give him lessons so that he may impress a beautiful local senorita. Unfortunately, the romantic interlude turns into sadness when the cocky and cavalier attitude of the amorous American toward the dangerous sport accidentally causes the death of the famous matador. Tragically, the director later spent time in Mexico, as in the story, and ironically his trip ended with the accidental death of the star bullfighter Carlos Arruza. **Cast:** Robert Stack, Gilbert Roland, Jou Page, Katy Jurado, Virginia Grey. **Credits:** Dir: Budd Boetticher; Prod: John Wayne; Writer: James Edward Grant; DP: Jack Draper; Ed: Richard Van Enger; Composer: Victor Young. B&W, 125 min. **VHS, LASER**

Bullitt

(1968) Warner Bros.
McQueen is a detective who senses that something is wrong behind his

assignment to guard a criminal witness. This edge-of-the seat thriller features one of the great car chases of cinematic history. Based on Robert L. Pike's book *Mute Witness*. Academy Award Nominations: Best Sound. **Academy Awards:** Best Film Editing. **Cast:** Steve McQueen, Robert Vaughn, Jacqueline Bisset, Don Gordon, Robert Duvall, Norman Fell, Simon Oakland. **Credits:** Dir: Peter Yates; Prod: Philip D'Antoni; Writer: Harry Kleiner, Alan R. Trustman; Story: Robert L. Pike; DP: William A. Fraker; Ed: Frank P. Keller; Prod Design: Albert Brenner; Composer: Lalo Schifrin; Costumes: Theadora Van Runkle. Color, 113 min. **VHS, LASER, DVD**

Bundle of Joy

(1956) RKO
At the height of their popularity, Fisher and Reynolds starred in this musical comedy about a salesgirl who rescues a foundling. Scandal ensues when she and her socially prominent boyfriend are mistakenly assumed to be the real parents. A remake of *Bachelor Mother.* **Cast:** Debbie Reynolds, Eddie Fisher, Adolphe Menjou, Tommy Noonan, Melville Cooper, Nita Talbot, Una Merkel, Robert H. Harris. **Credits:** Dir: Norman Taurog, Nick Castle; Prod: Edmund Grainger; Writer: Norman Krasna, Robert Carson, Arthur Sheekman; Story: Felix Jackson; DP: William E. Snyder; Ed: Harry Marker; Composer: Josef Myrow, Walter Scharf; Costumes: Howard Shoup. Color, 98 min. **VHS, LASER**

Buona Sera, Mrs. Campbell

(1968) MGM
An Italian woman has convinced three American fliers that each fathered her daughter during WWII. Their support checks have kept coming, but now it's time for the squadron's twentieth reunion and she's in a panic. **Cast:** Gina Lollobrigida, Peter Lawford, Shelley Winters, Phil Silvers, Telly Savalas, Lee Grant, Janet Margolin, Marian Moses. **Credits:** Dir: Melvin Frank; Prod: Melvin Frank; Writer: Melvin Frank, Sheldon Keller, Denis Norden; DP: Gabor Pogany; Ed: Bill Butler; Prod Design: Arrigo Equini; Composer: Riz Ortolani. Color, 113 min. **VHS, LASER**

Bureau of Missing Persons

(1933) Warner Bros.
A tough cop gets more action than he expected when transferred to the Bureau, including tangling with spitfire Davis. **Cast:** Bette Davis, Lewis Stone, Pat O'Brien, Allen Jenkins,

Ruth Donnelly, Glenda Farrell, Alan Dinehart, George Chandler, Hugh Herbert. **Credits:** Dir: Roy Del Ruth; Writer: Robert Presnell; DP: Barry McGill; Ed: James Gibbon; Prod Design: Robert M. Haas. B&W, 73 min. **VHS**

Bus Stop
(1956) Fox
Adaptation of Broadway hit by Inge ended any debate about Monroe's talent. A rancher falls for a nightclub singer while stranded at a bus stop in a blizzard. The first films for Lange and Murray, who eventually married. Academy Award Nomination for Best Actor: Don Murray. **Cast:** Marilyn Monroe, Don Murray, Arthur O'Connell, Betty Field, Eileen Heckart, Robert Bray, Hope Lange, Hans Conried, Casey Adams. **Credits:** Dir: Joshua Logan; Prod: Buddy Adler; Writer: George Axelrod; Story: William Inge; DP: Milton Krasner; Composer: Alfred Newman, Cyril Mockridge. Color, 94 min. **VHS, LASER**

Butch and Sundance: The Early Days
(1979) Fox
This prequel to the enormously successful *Butch Cassidy and the Sundance Kid* tells the story of how the infamous duo teamed up. The standard shootouts, heists, and the requisite train robbery; not up to the original standards. **Cast:** Tom Berenger, William Katt, Brian Dennehy, Jill Eikenberry, Jeff Corey, John Schuck, Michael C. Gwynne, Peter Weller. **Credits:** Dir: Richard Lester; Prod: Gabriel Katzka, Steven Bach; Writer: Allan Burns; DP: Laszlo Kovacs; Ed: George Trirogoff, Anthony Gibbs; Prod Design: Brian Eatwell, Jackson DeGovia; Composer: Patrick Williams; Costumes: William Ware Theiss. Color, 111 min. **VHS**

Butch Cassidy and the Sundance Kid
(1969) Fox
A kinder, gentler take on the outlaw myth. Based loosely on real-life Western outlaws Robert Leroy Parker and Harry Longbaugh, better known as Butch Cassidy and the Sundance Kid. Following a string of bank and train robberies in the early 1900s, the pair find themselves hotly pursued by the authorities. They escape to Bolivia with The Kid's lover, schoolteacher Etta Place, in the hopes of turning their luck around. Wistful and charming. Includes the hit "Raindrops Keep Fallin' On My Head" by Burt Bacharach and Hal David. Academy Award Nominations: 7, including Best Picture; Best Director. **Academy Awards:** Best Cinematography; Best Song; Best Story/Screenplay Written Directly for the Screen; Best Original Score. **Cast:** Paul Newman, Robert Redford, Katharine Ross, Strother Martin, Henry Jones, Jeff Corey, Cloris Leachman, Ted Cassidy, Kenneth Mars. **Credits:** Dir: George Roy Hill; Prod: John Foreman; Writer: William Goldman; DP: Conrad Hall; Ed: John Howard, Richard C. Meyer; Composer: Burt Bacharach; Costumes: Edith Head; SFX: Art Cruickshank, L. B. Abbott. Color, 112 min. **VHS, LASER**

But Not for Me
(1959) Paramount
An over-the-hill Broadway producer gets a new lease on life when he becomes the object of a much younger woman's desire. Based on the play *Accent on Life*, this comedy chronicles Gable's problems as he tries to convince financiers who think age has dampened his creative spark to put up money for his new production. Soon art is imitating life when he gives his Lolita-esque secretary the starring role in a play about a girl who falls in love with an older man. **Cast:** Clark Gable, Carroll Baker, Lilli Palmer, Barry Coe, Lee J. Cobb, Thomas Gomez. **Credits:** Dir: Walter Lang; Prod: William Perlberg, George Seaton; Writer: John Michael Hayes; Story: Samuel Raphaelson; DP: Robert Burks; Ed: Alma Macrorie; Composer: Leith Stevens. B&W, 105 min. **VHS**

Butterfield 8
(1960) MGM
Taylor's an eyeful as a sophisticated call girl wanting to go straight. The screen adaptation of O'Hara's novel grafts on a stock Hollywood ending, but the film is all Taylor's tour de force anyway. **Academy Awards:** Best Actress: Elizabeth Taylor. **Cast:** Elizabeth Taylor, Laurence Harvey, Eddie Fisher, Dina Merrill, Mildred Dunnock, Betty Field, Jeffrey Lynn, Kay Medford, Susan Oliver. **Credits:** Dir: Daniel Mann; Prod: Pandro S. Berman; Writer: Charles Schnee, John Michael Hayes; Story: John O'Hara; DP: Joseph Ruttenberg, Charles Harten; Ed: Ralph E. Winters; Prod Design: Urie McCleary, George W. Davis; Composer: Bronislau Kaper; Costumes: Helen Rose. Color, 168 min. **VHS, LASER**

Butterflies Are Free
(1972) Columbia
Film version of Leonard Gershe's Broadway play of the same name about

Bus Stop (1956)

Butch Cassidy and the Sundance Kid (1969)

a young blind man's romance with his kooky free-spirited next-door neighbor. Eileen Heckart is brilliant as his over-protective mother. **Academy Awards:** Best Supporting Actress: Eileen Heckart. **Cast:** Goldie Hawn, Edward Albert, Eileen Heckart, Mike Warren. **Credits:** Dir: Milton Katselas; Prod: M. J. Frankovich; Writer: Leonard Gershe; DP: Charles B. Lang; Ed: David Blewitt; Prod Design: Robert Clatworthy; Composer: Bob Alcivar; Costumes: Moss Mabry; Set Designer: Marvin March. Color, 110 min. VHS, LASER

Bwana Devil
(1952) United Artists
Stack plays a lion hunter in this jungle adventure. He's brought to Africa to kill off a pair of vicious man-eaters who keep eating workers during the construction of an important continental rail line. At first, he thinks it will be a walk in the park, but the lions soon change his mind. Filmed in an early 3-D process. **Cast:** Robert Stack, Barbara Britton, Nigel Bruce, Ramsey Hill, Paul McVey, Hope Miller, John

Dodsworth, Pat O'Moore, Pat Aherne, Bhogwan Singh. **Credits:** Dir: Arch Oboler; Prod: Arch Oboler; Writer: Arch Oboler; DP: Joseph Biroc, Milton Gunzburg; Ed: John Hoffman; Composer: Gordon Jenkins. Color, 79 min.

Bye Bye Birdie
(1963) Columbia
An entertaining musical about a rock-and-roll star who is drafted into the service and comes to a small town to say good-bye to an adoring fan. Top songs from what was originally a Broadway show include "Put on a Happy Face" and "A Lot of Livin' to Do." Academy Award Nominations: Best Score; Best Sound. **Cast:** Janet Leigh, Dick Van Dyke, Ann-Margret, Paul Lynde, Maureen Stapleton, Bobby Rydell, Jesse Pearson, Ed Sullivan, Robert Paige. **Credits:** Dir: George Sidney; Prod: Fred Kohlmar; Writer: Irving Brecher; DP: Joseph Biroc; Ed: Onna White; Composer: Michael Stewart, Charles Strouse, Lee Adams; Costumes: Pat Barto. Color, 112 min. VHS, LASER

By the Light of the Silvery Moon
(1953) Warner Bros.
Day and MacRae star in this musical comedy set in a small Indiana town at the end of WWI. Marjorie Winfield and her betrothed William, who has just returned from the front, have to put their matrimonial plans on hold because William wants to save some money first. But while they're waiting for the big day to arrive, they manage to get themselves into plenty of trouble. The sequel to *Moonlight Bay,* the film is based on a Booth Tarkington story. **Cast:** Doris Day, Gordon MacRae, Leon Ames, Rosemary De Camp, Mary Wickes, Billy Gray. **Credits:** Dir: David Butler; Prod: William Jacobs; Writer: Robert O'Brien, Irving Elinson; Story: Booth Tarkington; DP: Wilfrid M. Cline; Ed: Irene Morra; Choreographer: Donald Saddler; Composer: Max Steiner. Color, 100 min. VHS, LASER

Cabaret

(1972) Allied Artists

By turns amusingly tuneful and chilling, a contrast between the last, tatty gasp of romanticism and the cold dawn of the Third Reich. Minnelli gives it, if anything, too much bravura, and York seems a bit too knowing for the callow youth, but the sum is a lasting achievement. Based on the Kander-Ebb musical from John van Druten's play *I Am a Camera,* which, in turn, was based on Christopher Isherwood's novel *Goodbye to Berlin.* Academy Award Nominations: 10, including Best Picture; Best (Adapted) Screenplay. **Academy Awards:** Best Director; Best Actress: Liza Minnelli; Best Supporting Actor: Joel Grey; Best Film Editing; Best Cinematography; Best Sound; Best Art Direction—Set Decoration; Best Original Song Score and Adaptation. **Cast:** Liza Minnelli, Joel Grey, Michael York, Helmut Griem, Marisa Berenson, Fritz Wepper. **Credits:** Dir: Bob Fosse; Prod: Cy Feuer; Writer: Jay Presson Allen; Story: Christopher Isherwood; DP: Geoffrey Unsworth; Ed: David Bretherton; Prod Design: Rolf Zehetbauer; Choreographer: Bob Fosse; Composer: John Kander, Fred Ebb. Color, 150 min. **VHS, LASER, DVD**

The Cabin in the Cotton

(1932) Warner Bros.

Davis plays a vamp who toys with the feelings of a poor sharecropper's son played by Barthelmess. He works in the store owned by her father, where he finds that his employer has been systematically ripping off local farmers. **Cast:** Bette Davis, Richard Barthelmess, Dorothy Jordan, Henry B. Walthall, Tully Marshall, Berton Churchill, Hardie Albright, Clarence Muse, Edmund Breese, Dorothy Peterson. **Credits:** Dir: Michael Curtiz; Prod: Hal B. Wallis, Jack L. Warner, Darryl F. Zanuck; Writer: Paul Green; DP: Barney McGill; Ed: George Amy;

Prod Design: Esdras Hartley; Composer: Leo F. Forbstein. B&W, 79 min. **VHS**

Cabin in the Sky

(1943) MGM

Vincente Minnelli's first feature (he also directed this on Broadway) is a patronizingly simple fable from the vaunted Freed musical unit at MGM. The gloss bestows some dignity on some truly great performers. Musical highlights include Waters's singing "Happiness Is a Thing Called Joe" and the swinging Duke Ellington Orchestra. Academy Award Nominations: Best Song ("Happiness Is a Thing Called Joe"). **Cast:** Ethel Waters, Lena Horne, Louis Armstrong, Eddie Anderson, Rex Ingram, Kenneth Spencer, Ford L. Washington, John W. Sublett. **Credits:** Dir: Vincente Minnelli; Prod: Arthur Freed; Writer: Joseph Schrank; DP: Sidney Wagner; Ed: Harold F. Kress; Composer: Harold Arlen, E. Y. Harburg, Vernon Duke, John Latouche, Ted Fetter, Roger Edens; Art Director: Cedric Gibbons, Leonid Vasian. B&W, 100 min. **VHS, LASER**

Cactus Flower

(1969) Columbia

A comedy adapted from a Broadway hit about the relationship of a bachelor dentist with his nutty mistress and his rather stoic receptionist, who emerges from her shell when called upon to masquerade as his wife. **Academy Awards:** Best Supporting Actress: Goldie Hawn. **Cast:** Walter Matthau, Goldie Hawn, Ingrid Bergman, Jack Weston, Rick Lenz, Vito Scotti, Irene Hervey. **Credits:** Dir: Gene Saks; Prod: M. J. Frankovich; Writer: I. A. L. Diamond; DP: Charles Lang; Ed: Maury Winetrobe; Prod Design: Robert Clatworthy; Choreographer: Miriam Nelson; Composer: Quincy Jones. Color, 105 min. **VHS, LASER**

The Caddy

(1953) Paramount

Martin and Lewis comedy features the

boys as golfers Joe and Harvey, who team up to compete in a tournament. Harvey can't stand the tension involved in competition and becomes Joe's caddy and coach. But after a few victories, Joe's ego grows out of control, and he determines to dissolve their successful partnership. The two begin arguing and, eventually, cause hilarious chaos at a big tournament, which swiftly ends their careers as golfers and leads them to the world of entertainment instead. Features the song "That's Amore." **Cast:** Dean Martin, Jerry Lewis, Donna Reed, Fred Clark, Joseph Calleia, Barbara Bates, Clinton Sundberg, Howard Smith, Marshall Thompson, Marjorie Gateson. **Credits:** Dir: Norman Taurog; Prod: Paul Jones; Writer: Edmund L. Hartmann, Danny Arnold, Ken Englund; DP: Daniel Fapp; Ed: Warren Low; Composer: Joseph J. Lilley. B&W, 95 min. **VHS**

Caged

(1950) Warner Bros.

The class entry in women-behind-bars movies. As nineteen-year-old Parker sits in a car, waiting for her husband outside a gas station, she has no idea that she is an accomplice to a burglary in progress. When her husband is killed in the robbery attempt, she is arrested and sentenced to a term in a women's prison filled with savage inmates and brutal guards. She struggles to retain her sanity throughout cruel mistreatment, a prison pregnancy, murders, and an inmate revolt. Remade as *House of Women.* **Cast:** Eleanor Parker, Agnes Moorehead, Ellen Corby, Hope Emerson, Betty Garde, Jan Sterling, Lee Patrick, Olive Deering, Jane Darwell, Gertrude Michael. **Credits:** Dir: John Cromwell; Prod: Jerry Wald; Writer: Virginia Kellogg, Bernard C. Schoenfeld; DP: Carl E. Guthrie; Ed: Owen Marks; Prod Design: Charles H. Clarke, G. W. Bernsten; Composer: Max Steiner. B&W, 96 min.

Caged Heat

(1974) AIP

This is Demme's first picture, a women-in-prison flick that has developed a cult following for its slightly different take on the genre; that is, the women aren't simply barely dressed victims. Note the contributions of DP Tak Fujimoto and John Cale, a former member of the Velvet Underground. **Cast:** Juanita Brown, Erica Gavin, Roberta Collins, Barbara Steele, Ella Reid, Cheryl Smith, Rainbeaux Smith, Warren Miller. **Credits:** Dir: Jonathan Demme; Prod: Evelyn Purcell; Writer: Jonathan Demme; DP: Tak Fujimoto; Ed: Johanna Demetrakis, Carolyn Hicks; Composer: John Cale. Color, 84 min. VHS

Cahill—U.S. Marshal

(1973) Warner Bros.

The preachy and aged Duke's job as a U.S. Marshal is made difficult when several of his sons turn to a life of crime. For Wayne fans only. **Cast:** John Wayne, George Kennedy, Gary Grimes, Neville Brand, Marie Windsor, Royal Dano, Denver Pyle, Jackie Coogan, Clay O'Brien. **Credits:** Dir: Andrew V. McLaglen; Prod: Michael Wayne; Writer: Harry Julian Fink, Rita M. Fink; DP: Joseph Biroc; Ed: Robert Simpson; Composer: Elmer Bernstein; Art Director: Walter M. Simonds. Color, 103 min. VHS

The Caine Mutiny

(1954) Columbia

The *Caine* is a battle-scarred Navy vessel under the command of Captain Queeg (Bogart), who rules with an iron fist. But Queeg suffers from insecurity and stress, which leads to questionable judgments. The situation comes to a head during a fierce storm, in which junior officers relieve Queeg of his duties against his will in order to save the ship and the men. Queeg charges Maryk with mutiny and thus begins a dramatic court-martial. Bogart is impressive as he veers from paranoia to defiance. Based on Herman Wouk's Pulitzer Prize–winning novel of 1951. Academy Award Nominations: 7, including Best Picture; Best Actor: Humphrey Bogart; Best Supporting Actor: Tom Tully; Best Screenplay. **Cast:** Van Johnson, Humphrey Bogart, Jose Ferrer, May Wynn, Fred MacMurray, Robert Francis, Tom Tully, E. G. Marshall, Arthur Franz, Lee Marvin. **Credits:** Dir: Edward Dmytryk; Prod: Stanley Kramer; Writer: Stanley Roberts, Michael Blankfort; DP: Franz Planer;

Cabaret (1972)

Ed: William A. Lyon, Henry Batista; Prod Design: Rudolph Sternad; Composer: Max Steiner. B&W, 125 min. VHS, LASER, DVD

Calamity Jane

(1953) Warner Bros.

Day is the famous cowgirl in this musical extravaganza about the legendary female sharpshooter and her up-and-down romance with Wild Bill Hickok. Academy Award Nominations: 3, including Best Sound Recording. **Academy Awards:** Best Song. **Cast:** Doris Day, Howard Keel, Allyn Ann McLerie, Philip Carey, Dick Wesson, Paul Harvey, Chubby Johnson, Gale Robbins. **Credits:** Dir: David Butler; Prod: William Jacobs; Writer: James O'Hanlon; DP: Wilfrid M. Cline; Ed: Irene Morra; Choreographer: Jack Donohue; Composer: Ray Heindorf. Color, 101 min. VHS

California

(1946) Paramount

A Western about the American migration to California in 1848 and the quest for gold and statehood. An army deserter joins the migration to California, hoping for prosperity. He becomes entangled with a tough woman gambler, and the two team up with an equally tough miner in the war for statehood against a former slave trader whose nefarious goal is to make California his own personal territory. **Cast:** Ray Milland, Barbara Stanwyck, Barry Fitzgerald, George Coulouris, Anthony Quinn, Frank Faylen, Gavin Muir, James Burke, Eduardo Ciannelli, Albert Dekker. **Credits:** Dir: John Farrow; Prod: Seton I. Miller; Writer: Frank Butler, Theodore Strauss; Story: Boris Ingster; DP: Ray Rennahan; Ed: Eda Warren; Composer: Victor Young; Art Director: Roland Anderson, Hans Dreier. B&W, 97 min.

California Conquest

(1952) Columbia

In this pre–Civil War Western, a wealthy Spanish aristocrat teams up with a young American woman whose father has been murdered by an invading army bent on conquering California. In between swashbuckling and recruiting mercenaries, the unlikely duo falls in love. But romance must wait as they assemble their rag-tag force, then go forth to combat the bad guys, who, in a McCarthy-era twist, turn out to be the Russians. **Cast:** Cornel Wilde, Teresa Wright, Alfonso Bedoya, Lisa Ferraday, Eugene Iglesias, John Dehner, Ivan Lebedeff, Tito Renaldo, Renzo Cesana, Baynes Barron. **Credits:** Dir: Lew Landers; Prod: Sam Katzman; Writer: Robert E. Kent; DP: Ellis W. Carter; Ed: Richard Fantl; Prod Design: Paul Palmentola; Composer: Mischa Bakaleinikoff. B&W, 79 min.

California Split

(1974) Columbia

Altman's episodic look at the gambler's life. Gould plays a cool, easy-going, carefree compulsive gambler. Segal is a nervous magazine editor whose addiction has cost him his wife and is ruining his future. They meet when they are jointly mugged, and continue to gamble, at racetracks, seedy bars, and the casinos of Reno, as the hopelessness sinks in further. A loose comedy that makes its observations indirectly, in typical Altman style. **Cast:** George Segal, Elliott Gould, Ann Prentiss, Gwen Welles, Edward Walsh, Joseph Walsh, Bert Remsen, Barbara London, Barbara Ruick, Jay Fletcher. **Credits:** Dir: Robert Altman; Prod: Robert Altman, Joseph Walsh; Writer: Joseph Walsh; DP: Paul Lohmann; Ed: Lou Lombardo; Composer: Phyliss Shotwell; Art Director: Leon Ericksen. Color, 108 min.

California Suite

(1978) Columbia

Simon's *Plaza Suite* schtick set in sunnier climes, the Beverly Hills Hotel during Academy Awards weekend. The four-part storyline runs the gamut from touching introspection to outright slapstick. Academy Award Nominations: 3, including Best (Adapted) Screenplay. **Academy Awards:** Best Supporting Actress: Maggie Smith. **Cast:** Alan Alda, Michael Caine, Bill Cosby, Jane Fonda, Walter Matthau, Elaine May, Richard Pryor, Maggie Smith, Sheila Frazier. **Credits:** Dir: Herbert Ross; Prod: Ray Stark; Writer: Neil Simon; DP: David M. Walsh; Ed:

Michael A. Stevenson; Composer: Claude Bolling; Costumes: Ann Roth, Patricia Norris. Color, 103 min. **VHS, LASER**

Call Me Madam

(1953) Fox

Love is in the air in this Berlin musical about an extroverted Washington, D.C., socialite modeled on Perle Mesta, the self-proclaimed "hostess with the mostess." When she suddenly finds herself named ambassador to the tiny European hamlet of Lichtenburg, she takes her show on the road and launches a romantic coup d'état, falling in love with the Lichtenburg foreign minister, and match-making her press attaché with a genuine princess. **Cast:** Ethel Merman, George Sanders, Donald O'Connor, Vera Ellen, Billy De Wolfe, Helmut Dantine, Lilia Skala, Walter Slezak, Ludwig Stossel, Charles Dingle. **Credits:** Dir: Johnny Downs, Walter Lang; Prod: Sol C. Siegel; Writer: Arthur Sheekman; Story: Howard Lindsay, Russell Crouse; DP: Leon Shamroy; Ed: Robert Simpson; Composer: Irving Berlin, Alfred Newman; Art Director: Lyle Wheeler, John De Cuir. Color, 114 min.

Call Northside 777

(1948) Fox

In this documentary-style drama based on a true story, a reporter tries to prove that a man in prison for murder has been wrongly convicted. A great performance by Stewart as the persistent journalist. **Cast:** James Stewart, Richard Conte, Lee J. Cobb, Helen Walker, Betty Garde, Kasia Orzazewski, Howard Smith, Paul Harvey, John McIntire, Moroni Olsen. **Credits:** Dir: Henry Hathaway; Prod: Otto Lang; Writer: Jerry Cady, Jay Dratler; DP: Joseph MacDonald; Ed: J. Watson Webb; Prod Design: Lyle Wheeler, Mark-Lee Kirk; Composer: Alfred Newman. B&W, 111 min. **VHS**

The Call of the Wild

(1935) Fox

Gable plays a prospector searching for gold in Alaska in this screen adaptation of Jack London's adventure novel. Despite nay-saying townspeople, Gale is able to tame and train Buck, part dog–part wolf, to lead his sled team. Man and dog team up with rugged pal Oakie and damsel in distress Young. Adventures ensue and Buck saves the day more than once. Remade three times, but this is the real stuff. **Cast:** Clark Gable, Loretta Young, Jack Oakie, Frank Conroy, Reginald Owen. **Credits:** Dir: William Wellman; Prod:

Darryl F. Zanuck; Writer: Gene Fowler, Jr., Leonard Praskins; Story: Jack London; DP: Charles Rosher; Ed: Hanson T. Fritch; Composer: Alfred Newman. B&W, 89 min.

Camelot

(1967) Warner Bros.

The Lerner and Loewe musical about the legendary Court of King Arthur features luminous songs and an equally radiant Redgrave. The laserdisc includes restored footage and trailers. Academy Award Nominations: 5, including Best Cinematography. **Academy Awards:** Best Score; Best Costume Design; Best Art Direction—Set Decoration. **Cast:** Richard Harris, Vanessa Redgrave, David Hemmings, Franco Nero, Lionel Jeffries, Laurence Naismith, Estelle Winwood, Anthony Rogers, Pierre Olaf, Gary K. Marshall. **Credits:** Dir: Joshua Logan; Prod: Jack L. Warner; Writer: Alan Jay Lerner; DP: Richard H. Kline; Ed: Folmar Blangsted; Prod Design: Edward Carrere; Composer: Frederick Loewe; Costumes: John Truscott. Color, 180 min. **VHS, LASER, DVD**

The Cameraman

(1928) MGM

Keaton stars as a bumbling photographer who, in order to win the favor of a beautiful woman, takes a job as a newsreel cameraman. Hilarity ensues as he stumbles through a parade, a Chinese tong war, a yacht-club regatta, a crowded dressing room, and a baseball game. **Cast:** Buster Keaton, Marceline Day, Harold Goodwin, Sidney Bracey, Harry Gribbon. **Credits:** Dir: Edward Sedgwick; Writer: Richard Schayer, Lex Lipton; DP: Elgin Lesley, Reggie Manning. B&W, 70 min. **VHS**

Camille

(1936) MGM

Garbo stars as a beautiful courtesan destroyed by her love for a young French nobleman. Based on the story by Alexandre Dumas. There were three silent versions and a '70s remake, but this is definitive, for both the story and our enduring memory of Garbo. Academy Award Nominations: Best Actress: Greta Garbo. **Cast:** Greta Garbo, Robert Taylor, Lionel Barrymore, Elizabeth Allan, Henry Daniell, Lenore Ulric, Laura Hope Crews, Rex O'Malley, Jessie Ralph, E. E. Clive. **Credits:** Dir: George Cukor; Prod: Bernard Hyman; Writer: Zoe Akins, Frances Marion, James Hilton; DP: William Daniels; Ed: Margaret Booth; Composer: Herbert Stothart. B&W, 110 min. **VHS**

Can-Can

(1960) Fox

High-voltage musical talent fires this loose adaptation of the stage musical that depicts a cafe owner's introduction of the sexy title dance to the denizens of Paris. Crusading moralists and an unsympathetic legal system stand in the way of the heroine and her lawyer boyfriend and the whole damn thing stands in the way of Cole Porter's music. **Cast:** Shirley MacLaine, Frank Sinatra, Louis Jourdan, Maurice Chevalier, Juliet Prowse, Marcel Dalio, Leon Belasco, Nestor Paiva. **Credits:** Dir: Walter Lang; Prod: Jack Cummings; Writer: Dorothy Kingsley, Charles Lederer; DP: William Daniels; Ed: Robert Simpson; Prod Design: Lyle Wheeler, Jack Martin Smith; Choreographer: Hermes Pan; Composer: Cole Porter; Costumes: Irene Sharaff. Color, 131 min. **VHS, LASER**

The Candidate

(1972) Warner Bros.

An idealistic politician, son of a famous governor, is pressured into running for the U.S. Senate against the popular incumbent, with the assurance that he will lose and not have to give up his integrity or ideals. However, as the campaign deepens, he finds himself giving in and allowing himself to be manipulated as the polls slowly change and swing in his favor, and his backers decide that they want him to win after all. Ritchie's satire is made sharper by its realistic treatment of the subject. **Academy Awards:** Story/Screenplay Based on Factual Material. **Cast:** Robert Redford, Peter Boyle, Don Porter, Allen Garfield, Karen Carlson, Melvyn Douglas, Quinn Redeker. **Credits:** Dir: Michael Ritchie; Prod: Walter Coblenz; Writer: Jeremy Larner; DP: Victor J. Kemper, John Korty; Ed: Richard A. Harris, Robert Estrin; Composer: John Rubinstein; Costumes: Patricia Norris; Set Designer: Patrizia von Brandenstein. Color, 110 min. **VHS, LASER, DVD**

Candleshoe

(1977) Disney

Foster plays a streetwise L.A. kid who is planted in a mansion to help a con man bilk an elderly woman out of a fortune. Niven dons a variety of colorful disguises as the butler. **Cast:** David Niven, Jodie Foster, Helen Hayes, Leo McKern, Vivian Pickles, Veronica Quilligan, John Alderson, Ian Sharrock, Sarah Tamakuni, David Samuels. **Credits:** Dir: Norman Tokar; Prod: Ron Miller; Writer: David Swift,

Rosemary Anne Sisson; DP: Paul Beeson; Ed: Peter Boita; Composer: Ron Goodwin; Art Director: Albert Witherick. Color, 101 min. **VHS, LASER**

Cannonball

(1976) New World

Bartel (director of *Death Race 2000*) is at the helm for this high-energy action film about an illegal and lengthy marathon road race where the goal is to make it to the finish without being arrested or incinerated. Look for cameos by Martin Scorsese, Roger Corman, Joe Dante, and Sylvester Stallone. **Cast:** David Carradine, Veronica Hamel, Gerrit Graham, Bill McKinney, Judy Canova, Robert Carradine, Belinda Balaski, Carl Gottlieb, Archie Hahn. **Credits:** Dir: Paul Bartel; Prod: Samuel W. Gelfman; Writer: Paul Bartel, Donald C. Simpson; DP: Tak Fujimoto; Ed: Morton Tubor; Prod Design: Michel Levesque; Composer: David A. Axelrod. Color, 94 min. **VHS**

Canon City

(1948) Eagle Lion

Solid ensemble work and location shots highlight this documentary-style narrative of a large Colorado prison break. Minute detailing of the break's preparations are featured, as is the contrast between the mild-mannered ring leader's appearance and the dangerous reality of his plan. Rounding out the cast are the warden and some of the guards from the real Canon City prison. Initially successful, the inmates are doomed to death or capture. **Cast:** Scott Brady, Jeff Corey, Whit Bissell, Stanley Clements, Charles Russell, DeForest Kelley, Ralph Byrd, Mabel Paige, Roy Best, Alfred Linder. **Credits:** Dir: Crane Wilbur; Prod: Brian Foy, Robert T. Kane; Writer: Crane Wilbur; DP: John Alton; Ed: Louis Sackin; Composer: Irving Friedman; Art Director: Frank Durlauf. B&W, 82 min.

The Canterville Ghost

(1944) MGM

Adaptation of Oscar Wilde's famous ghost story, an American soldier encounters the supernatural when he travels to a creepy English castle. Cuffy Williams has been assigned to stay with a platoon of fellow GIs at the estate of young heiress Lady Jessica de Canterville. There, he encounters the ghost of Sir Simon de Canterville, whose father sealed him up alive in the castle 300 years earlier because of cowardice in battle. As it turns out, Cuffy is actually the spirit's descendant and therefore is the only person

who can set Simon free from his eternal suffering. **Cast:** Charles Laughton, Margaret O'Brien, William Gargan, Rags Ragland, Una O'Connor, Robert Young, Peter Lawford, Mike Mazurki. **Credits:** Dir: Jules Dassin; Writer: Edwin Blum; Story: Oscar Wilde; DP: Robert Planck. Color, 97 min. **VHS**

Can't Help Singing

(1944) Universal

When her cavalry officer fiancé heads west, the daughter (Durbin) of a Washington senator decides to follow him. She unexpectedly falls for the master of the wagon train when she learns of her fiancé's infidelity. Features an original score by Kern, including the Oscar-nominated song, "More and More." **Cast:** Deanna Durbin, David Bruce, Ray Collins, Robert Paige, Akim Tamiroff, Thomas Gomez, Leonid Kinskey, June Vincent, Andrew Tombes, Clara Blandick. **Credits:** Dir: Frank Ryan; Prod: Felix Jackson; Writer: Lewis R. Foster, Frank Ryan; DP: Woody Bredell, W. Howard Greene; Ed: Ted J. Kent; Composer: Hans J. Salter. Color, 90 min. **VHS**

Canyon Passage

(1946) Universal

A lawman retires to the Oregon Territory in hopes of a more peaceful life as a shopkeeper, but trouble follows him. Exciting plot, strong cast, and fine music make this Western a winner. **Cast:** Dana Andrews, Brian Donlevy, Susan Hayward, Patricia Roc, Ward Bond, Andy Devine, Rose Hobart, Lloyd Bridges, Stanley Ridges, Dorothy Peterson. **Credits:** Dir: Jacques Tourneur; Prod: Walter Wanger; Writer: Ernest Pascal; Story: Ernest Haycox; DP: Edward Cronjager; Ed: Milton Carruth; Prod Design: John B. Goodman, Richard H. Riedel; Composer: Frank Skinner. Color, 92 min. **VHS**

Cape Fear

(1962) Universal

Elemental good vs. evil thriller casts Mitchum as sadistic ex-con Max Cady determined to wreak revenge on the family of Sam Bowden, the good small-town lawyer who put him in jail years earlier. Stripped of legal recourse, the civilized Bowden is slowly forced to lower himself to Cady's bestial level to protect his family. Based on *The Executioners* by John D. MacDonald. Remade in 1991 by Martin Scorsese. **Cast:** Gregory Peck, Robert Mitchum, Polly Bergen, Martin Balsam, Telly Savalas, Lori Martin, Jack Kruschen, Barrie Chase, Edward Platt. **Credits:** Dir: J. Lee Thompson; Prod:

Cape Fear (1962)

Sy Bartlett; Writer: James R. Webb; Story: John D. MacDonald; DP: Sam Leavitt; Ed: George Tomasini; Prod Design: Alexander Golitzen, Robert Boyle; Composer: Bernard Herrmann; Costumes: Mary Wills. B&W, 106 min. **VHS, LASER**

Capricorn One

(1978) Warner Bros.
The government attempts to fake a mission to Mars, but when the astronauts learn that part of the scenario includes a "tragic accident" on the way home, they try to escape. Terrific aerial stunts and an all-star cast. **Cast:** Elliott Gould, James Brolin, Brenda Vaccaro, Sam Waterston, O. J. Simpson, Hal Holbrook, Telly Savalas, Karen Black, David Huddleston. **Credits:** Dir: Peter Hyams; Prod: Paul N. Lazarus III; Writer: Peter Hyams; DP: Bill Butler; Ed: James Mitchell; Composer: Jerry Goldsmith; Art Director: David Haber. Color, 124 min. **VHS, LASER, DVD**

Captain Blood

(1935) Warner Bros.
Flynn's swashbuckling film debut and the first of eight films with de Havilland. He plays a young doctor unjustly sentenced to slavery for treating rebels in one of the best swashbucklers of all time. Academy Award Nominations: Best Picture; Best Sound Recording. **Cast:** Errol Flynn, Olivia de Havilland, Basil Rathbone, Guy Kibbee, Lionel Atwill, Ross Alexander, Henry Stephenson, Forrester Harvey, Hobart Cavanaugh, Donald Meek. **Credits:** Dir: Michael Curtiz; Prod: Harry Joe Brown; Writer: Casey Robinson; DP: Hal Mohr, Ernest Haller; Ed:

George Amy; Prod Design: Anton Grot; Composer: Erich Wolfgang Korngold. B&W, 120 min. **VHS, LASER**

Captain Carey

(1950) Paramount
When Captain Webster Carey, O.S.S., sees a painting formerly hidden in his Milan hideout in the window of a New York art gallery, he thinks he has found the trail of the traitor who betrayed him and his espionage comrades during WWII. The hideout was known only to his O.S.S. partners and his Italian lover, Giulia, all killed in the war, leading him to conclude that the traitor must have smuggled the painting overseas. Traveling back to Italy, he learns that Giulia is still alive and married to a dark-looking local, and, after suspecting them both of betraying him, discovers the true identity of the culprit. **Academy Awards:** Best Song ("Mona Lisa"). **Cast:** Alan Ladd, Wanda Hendrix, Francis Lederer, Celia Lovsky, Angela Clarke, Richard Avonde, Joseph Calleia, Roland Winters, Frank Puglia, Luis Alberni. **Credits:** Dir: Mitchell Leisen; Prod: Richard Maibaum; Writer: Robert Thoeren; Story: Martha Albrand; DP: John Seitz; Ed: Alma Macrorie; Prod Design: Roland Anderson, Hans Dreier; Composer: Ray Evans, Jay Livingston, Hugo Friedhofer. B&W, 82 min.

Captain from Castille

(1947) Fox
The sweeping epic of a Spanish nobleman who seeks his fortune by enlisting with Cortez's campaign to conquer Mexico. Romantic, lavish, and highly recommended. Peters's first screen role. **Cast:** Tyrone Power, Jean Peters,

Cesar Romero, Lee J. Cobb, John Sutton, Antonio Moreno, Thomas Gomez, Alan Mowbray, Barbara Lawrence, George Zucco. **Credits:** Dir: Henry King; Prod: Lamar Trotti; Writer: Lamar Trotti; DP: Charles G. Clarke, Arthur E. Arling; Ed: Barbara McLean; Prod Design: James Basevi, Richard Day; Composer: Alfred Newman. Color, 141 min. **VHS**

Captain Horatio Hornblower

(1951) Warner Bros.
A straightforward naval adventure, based on three novels by C. S. Forester, about the heroic 19th-century British seafarer. The story sails with his ship, the *Lydia*, through battles with Spain and then France won with wit rather than might. Hornblower still finds time to romance Lady Barbara Wellesley, who roils emotional seas because she's married to his admiral. **Cast:** Gregory Peck, Virginia Mayo, Robert Beatty, Denis O'Dea, Christopher Lee, James Robertson Justice, Terence Morgan, Moultrie Kelsall, Richard Hearne, James Kenney. **Credits:** Dir: Raoul Walsh; Prod: Gerry Mitchell; Writer: Ivan Goff, Ben Roberts, Aeneas MacKenzie; Story: C. S. Forester; DP: Guy Green; Ed: Jack Harris; Composer: Robert Farnon. Color, 117 min. **VHS, LASER**

Captain January

(1936) Fox
Poor, perennially orphaned Shirley washes up from a shipwreck into the arms of a photogenically crusty lighthouse keeper who raises the little castaway with pluck and determination, qualities she'll need when the nasty truant officer tries to separate the two. Standard Temple plot, but better than average. **Cast:** Shirley Temple, Guy Kibbee, Slim Summerville, Jane Darwell, Buddy Ebsen, John Carradine, June Lang, Nella Walker, George Irving, Si Jenks. **Credits:** Dir: David Butler; Prod: Darryl F. Zanuck; Writer: Gladys Lehman, Harry Tugend; Story: Sam Hellman, Laura E. Richards; DP: John F. Seitz; Choreographer: Jack Donohue; Composer: Louis Silvers. B&W, 81 min. **VHS**

Captain Lightfoot

(1955) Universal
Action-adventure tale about swashbuckling Irish revolutionaries who vie for control of wayward rebel forces. One falls in love with the captain's lovely daughter. **Cast:** Rock Hudson, Barbara Rush, Jeff Morrow, Kathleen Ryan, Finlay Currie, Denis O'Dea, Geoffrey Toone, Milton Edwards,

Christopher Casson, Harold Goldblatt. **Credits:** Dir: Douglas Sirk; Prod: Ross Hunter; Writer: W. R. Burnett, Oscar Brodney; DP: Irving Glassberg; Ed: Frank Gross; Prod Design: Oliver Emert, Russell A. Gausman; Composer: Hans J. Salter, Joseph Gershenson; Art Director: Alexander Golitzen, Eric Orbom. Color, 91 min.

Captain Newman, M.D.
(1963) Universal
Sensitive drama in the story of a WWII doctor treating the mental scars of his soldier patients, and light comedy in his dealings with army bureaucracy, in the medical pranks that keep the hospital staff sane, and in a little romance, too. Peck manages the balancing act. Adapted from the novel by Leo Rosten, this was the last screenwriting credit for Phoebe and Henry Ephron, parents of writer-directors Nora and Delia. **Cast:** Gregory Peck, Tony Curtis, Eddie Albert, Angie Dickinson, James Gregory, Robert Duvall, Dick Sargent, Larry Storch, Bethel Leslie, Bobby Darin. **Credits:** Dir: David Miller; Prod: Robert Arthur; Writer: Richard L. Breen, Henry Ephron, Phoebe Ephron; DP: Russell Metty; Ed: Alma Macrorie; Prod Design: Alexander Golitzen, Alfred Sweeney; Composer: Frank Skinner. Color, 126 min. **VHS**

Captain Pirate
(1952) Columbia
This sequel to *Captain Blood* finds the old doctor-turned-pirate in retirement. Just when he thinks he'll never again see a cutlass or Spanish galleon, he's arrested for piracy. It seems that another cutthroat has been using his moniker to wreak havoc on the high seas. After breaking out of jail, the real Captain Blood has no choice but to gather his old gang of buccaneers and hunt down the usurper. **Cast:** Louis Hayward, Patricia Medina, John Sutton, Charles Irwin, George Givot, Rex Evans, Ted De Corsia, Malu Gatica, Sven Hugo Borg, Mario Siletti. **Credits:** Dir: Ralph Murphy; Prod: Harry Brown; Writer: Robert Libott, John Meredyth Lucas, Frank Burt; Story: Rafael Sabatini; DP: Charles Lawton, Jr.; Ed: Gene Havlick; Composer: George Duning. B&W, 85 min.

Captains Courageous
(1937) MGM
Perfect family entertainment in the classic Hollywood style. In this Kipling story, the spoiled son of a shipping magnate (Bartholomew) falls overboard from a luxury liner and is picked up by a Nantucket fishing schooner captained by the Oscar-winning Tracy. Forced to earn his keep, the boy's extended voyage and warm relationship with the captain show him what's important in life. Remade for television in 1977 and 1996. Academy Award Nominations: 4, including Best Picture; Best Screenplay. **Academy Awards:** Best Actor: Spencer Tracy. **Cast:** Spencer Tracy, Freddie Bartholomew, Lionel Barrymore, Mickey Rooney, Melvyn Douglas, Charley Grapewin, Christian Rub, John Carradine, Walter Kingsford, Leo G. Carroll. **Credits:** Dir: Victor Fleming; Prod: Louis D. Lighton; Writer: John Lee Mahin, Marc Connelly, Dale Van Every; Story: Rudyard Kipling; DP: Harold Rosson; Ed: Elmo Vernon; Prod Design: Cedric Gibbons; Composer: Franz Waxman. B&W, 116 min. **VHS, LASER**

Captains of the Clouds
(1942) Warner Bros.
Better-than-average WWII flag-waver, this time told from the point of view of the Canadians. Cagney and his daredevil flying buddies enlist in the Royal Canadian Air Force thinking that years of dangerous aerial feats have acquainted them with midair derring-do. The brash leader gets stuck with a civilian air convoy, but matures quickly when faced with a heroic decision. **Cast:** James Cagney, Dennis Morgan, Alan Hale, George Tobias, Reginald Gardiner, Brenda Marshall, Reginald Denny, Paul Cavanagh, Clem Bevans, J. M. Kerrigan. **Credits:** Dir: Michael Curtiz; Prod: William Cagney; Writer: Arthur T. Horman, Richard Macaulay, Norman Reilly Raine; DP: Sol Polito, Wilfrid M. Cline; Ed: George Amy; Prod Design: Ted Smith; Composer: Max Steiner; Costumes: Howard Shoup. Color, 113 min. **VHS**

The Captive City
(1952) Columbia
A film noir that stars John Forsythe as an idealistic newspaperman who gets a tip from a detective that the mob has moved into his home town. When our hero uncovers a gambling racket, the detective is murdered, and the police won't do anything to help. Soon the reporter is on the run from a shadowy crime lord, without a friend in the world. The film features an epilogue by an actual U.S. senator warning the public about organized crime. **Cast:** John Forsythe, Joan Camden, Harold J. Kennedy, Ray Teal, Marjorie Crosland, Victor Sutherland, Geraldine Hall, Hal K. Dawson, Martin Milner, Gladys Hurlbut. **Credits:** Dir: Robert Wise; Prod: Theron Warth; Writer: Karl Kamb, Alvin Josephy; DP: Lee Garmes; Ed: Robert Swink; Prod Design: Maurice Zuberano; Composer: Jerome Moross. B&W, 90 min.

Captive Wild Woman
(1943) RKO
Tongue-in-cheek horror as a mad scientist transforms an orangutan into a beautiful woman. She applies her innate understanding of the animal kingdom as a circus animal trainer, but her inner ape is aroused when her ardor for a fellow performer is rebuffed. Though that would seem to sum up the possibilities, this spawned 2 sequels, *Jungle Woman* (1944) and *Jungle Captive* (1945). **Cast:** John Carradine, Evelyn Ankers, Acquanetta, Milburn Stone, Lloyd Corrigan, Fay Helm, Paul Fix, Vince Barnett, Martha Vickers, William Edmunds. **Credits:** Dir: Edward Dmytryk; Prod: Ben Pivar; Writer: Griffin Jay, Henry Sucher; DP: George Robinson; Ed: Milton Carruth. B&W, 61 min. **VHS**

Carbine Williams
(1952) MGM
Stewart plays a ne'er-do-well drifter in this Western who, through a misunderstanding, finds himself in jail for killing a taxman. Once in prison, he is framed for starting a riot by his fellow inmates. As if the abuse of his fellow inmates wasn't enough, he must protect himself from the creative tortures of the evil warden. Only his indomitable will and mechanical expertise allow him to survive, and he triumphs by inventing the carbine, a new kind of rifle. **Cast:** James Stewart, Jean Hagen, Wendell Corey, Carl Benton Reid, Paul Stewart, Otto Hulett, Rhys Williams, Herbert Heyes, James Arness, Porter Hall. **Credits:** Dir: Richard Thorpe; Prod: Armand Deutsch; Writer: Arthur Cohn; DP: William Mellor; Ed: Newell P. Kimlin; Prod Design: Cedric Gibbons, Eddie Imazu; Composer: Conrad Salinger. B&W, 91 min. **VHS**

The Cardinal
(1963) Columbia
An Irish-American priest's strong commitment to social issues leads him through a labyrinth of church politics and eventually to the upper echelons of Catholic hierarchy as Cardinal. Crossing several continents, this epic traces his path and tests his faith along the way. Based on the novel by Henry Morton Robinson. **Cast:** Tom Tryon, Carol Lynley, John Saxon,

Dorothy Gish, Robert Morse, Romy Schneider, Burgess Meredith, Cecil Kellaway, John Huston, Jill Haworth. **Credits:** Dir: Otto Preminger; Prod: Otto Preminger; Writer: Robert Dozier; Story: Henry Morton Robinson; DP: Leon Shamroy; Ed: Louis Loeffler; Composer: Jerome Moross; Costumes: Donald Brooks. Color, 176 min. VHS, LASER

Career
(1959) Paramount
The standard backstage saga of a midwestern boy and his rocky road to the Broadway boards gets a treatment that carries more than the usual ring of truth. Adapted by James Lee from his off-Broadway play. Golden Globe for Best Actor in a Drama: Anthony Franciosa. **Cast:** Dean Martin, Shirley MacLaine, Anthony Franciosa, Carolyn Jones, Joan Blackman, Robert Middleton, Donna Douglas, Frank McHugh, Jerry Paris. **Credits:** Dir: Joseph Anthony; Prod: Hal B. Wallis; Writer: James Lee; DP: Joseph La Shelle; Ed: Warren Low; Prod Design: Hal Pereira; Composer: Franz Waxman. B&W, 105 min. VHS

Carefree
(1938) RKO
A comic Astaire-Rogers pairing that's more madcap than most. When stuffed-shirt Bellamy (and who can play that part better?) sends his dizzy radio-singer fiancée to a shrink to find out why she won't settle down, the dancing analyst opens her to the possibility of love and then sees his happiness heading down the aisle with the wrong man. The Irving Berlin tunes include "Change Partners." Academy Award Nominations: 3, including Best Score; Best Song ("Change Partners and Dance With Me"). **Cast:** Fred Astaire, Ginger Rogers, Ralph Bellamy, Clarence Kolb, Jack Carson, Franklin Pangborn, Walter Kingsford, Hattie McDaniel, Luella Gear, Tom Tully. **Credits:** Dir: Mark Sandrich; Prod: Pandro S. Berman; Writer: Allan Scott, Ernest Pagano; DP: Robert de Grasse; Ed: William Hamilton; Prod Design: Carroll Clark, Van Nest Polglase; Composer: William Baravalle. B&W, 83 min. VHS, LASER

The Carey Treatment
(1972) MGM
Coburn plays a pathologist, new to a Boston hospital, who attempts an investigation into a series of unexplained deaths. Each of the deaths seems to be related to abortions and recent drug burglaries. Director Edwards very publicly disavowed

responsibility for the film, feeling that MGM effectively derailed the production. Based on the novel by Michael Crichton written under the name Jeffrey Hudson. **Cast:** James Coburn, Skye Aubrey, Elizabeth Allen, Michael Blodgett, Pat Hingle, Jennifer O'Neill, Alex Dreier. **Credits:** Dir: Blake Edwards; Prod: William Belasco; Writer: Michael Crichton, Harriet Frank, Jr.; DP: Florence Stanley; Composer: Roy Budd; Art Director: Alfred Sweeney. Color, 101 min.

Caribbean
(1952) Paramount
An evil plantation lord sells Hardwicke into slavery and kidnaps his wife and daughter. Hardwicke eventually escapes and becomes a pirate bent on revenge. His wife dies, but his daughter grows up believing the evil slave trader to be her father. Our hero recruits a drifter who looks like the slaver's nephew to infiltrate his island fortress and set the stage for vengeance. **Cast:** John Payne, Arlene Dahl, Cedric Hardwicke, Francis L. Sullivan, Woody Strode, Willard Parker, Dennis Hoey, Clarence Muse, Ransay Hill, Walter Reed. **Credits:** Dir: Edward Ludwig; Prod: William H. Pine, William C. Thomas; Writer: Frank L. Moss, Edward Ludwig; DP: Lionel Lindon; Ed: Howard Smith; Composer: Lucien Calliet. B&W, 91 min.

Carmen Jones
(1954) Fox
A sizzling screen version of Bizet's *Carmen* updated for an all-black cast, including an especially sizzling Dandridge. Soldier Belafonte falls for Dandridge, a seductive factory worker. The lovers flee after the soldier kills his sergeant, but Carmen's taunting faithlessness drives her lover to a crime of passion. Hammerstein provided lyrics for Bizet's melodies, and Preminger added the snap. If you're curious what all the fuss over Dandridge is about, catch this. Golden Globe for Best Film, Musical or Comedy. **Cast:** Dorothy Dandridge, Harry Belafonte, Pearl Bailey, Roy Glenn, Diahann Carroll, Brock Peters, Joe Adams, Olga James, Sandy Lewis, Nick Stewart. **Credits:** Dir: Otto Preminger; Prod: Otto Preminger; Writer: Harry Kleiner; Story: Oscar Hammerstein; DP: Sam Leavitt; Ed: Louis R. Loeffler; Composer: Georges Bizet. Color, 108 min. VHS, LASER

Carnal Knowledge
(1971) Columbia
The bitter experiences of two middle-class, American males chronicle the

changes in America's sexual mores over the course of three decades. Nicholson, the cruel but charismatic misogynist, and Garfunkel, the bland idealist, meet as college roommates at a small New England college in the 1940s. As their friendship progresses through the '50s and '60s, their search for the ideal woman leads to failed marriages, bad relationships, and emotional emptiness. Director Nichols seems particularly adept at negotiating this kind of psychological minefield. Nicholson is fascinating to watch, but the supporting women, including Bergen and especially Ann-Margret, supply the soul. Kane's screen debut. Academy Award Nominations: Best Supporting Actress: Ann-Margret. **Cast:** Jack Nicholson, Candice Bergen, Art Garfunkel, Ann-Margret, Rita Moreno, Carol Kane, Cynthia O'Neal. **Credits:** Dir: Mike Nichols; Prod: Mike Nichols; Writer: Jules Feiffer; DP: Giuseppe Rotunno; Ed: Sam O'Steen; Prod Design: Richard Sylbert; Costumes: Anthea Sylbert. Color, 98 min. VHS, LASER

Carousel
(1956) Fox
Time (and a spectacular new Broadway staging) has been kind to the memory of this widescreen, deluxe Rodgers and Hammerstein musical. MacRae brings a blustery energy to the role of Billy Bigelow, an ill-fated carny barker. The troubled soul finally settles down with a good woman (Jones), and then gets killed during a robbery. But the angels are merciful and Bigelow returns to Earth to make good with his wife and daughter. The Broadway musical was based on a Molnar play, *Liliom*. In 1930, Frank Borzage produced a screen version starring Charles Farrell. Fritz Lang filmed a French version in 1935 (his first film after fleeing Nazi Germany), which starred Charles Boyer. **Cast:** Gordon MacRae, Shirley Jones, Cameron Mitchell, Barbara Ruick, Gene Lockhart, Robert Rounseville, Claramae Turner, Audrey Christie, Susan Luckey, John Dehner. **Credits:** Dir: Henry King; Prod: Henry Ephron; Writer: Phoebe Ephron, Henry Ephron; DP: Charles G. Clarke; Ed: William H. Reynolds; Composer: Richard Rodgers, Oscar Hammerstein; Costumes: Mary Wills. Color, 128 min. VHS, LASER

The Carpetbaggers
(1964) Paramount
This entertaining adaptation of Harold Robbins's novel of greed and sex re-

creates the early days of Hollywood. After his father dies, a ruthless young aircraft tycoon gets mixed up in numerous romantic and business shenanigans in the movie industry. Among the women he gets involved with are a flapper, who he marries and treats horribly, and a blond beauty he transforms into a sex symbol. Meanwhile, a cowboy star who's an old pal from his past attempts to reform him. **Cast:** George Peppard, Alan Ladd, Elizabeth Ashley, Robert Cummings, Carroll Baker, Martha Hyer, Lew Ayres, Martin Balsam, Ralph Taeger, Archie Moore. **Credits:** Dir: Edward Dmytryk; Prod: Joseph E. Levine; Writer: John Michael Hayes; Story: Harold Robbins; DP: Joseph MacDonald; Ed: Frank Bracht; Prod Design: Frank Caffey; Composer: Elmer Bernstein; Costumes: Edith Head; SFX: Paul K. Lerpae; Set Designer: Arthur Krams. Color, 150 min. **VHS, LASER**

Carrie
(1952) Paramount
A sterling performance by Olivier is the centerpiece of this drama based on the novel *Sister Carrie* by Theodore Dreiser. When a farm girl follows her dreams to turn-of-the-century Chicago, she enters a bleak world of grueling, poorly paid factory work. Determined to better her condition, she attaches herself to a salesman and then to a married restaurant manager, who loses everything in order to keep her. As she ascends to success in the footlights, she leaves behind the man who rescued her. Academy Award Nominations: Best Art Direction; Best Costumes. **Cast:** Jennifer Jones, Laurence Olivier, Miriam Hopkins, Eddie Albert, Mary Murphy, Basil Ruysdael, Ray Teal, Barry Kelley, William Reynolds, Harry Hayden. **Credits:** Dir: William Wyler; Prod: William Wyler; Writer: Augustus Goetz, Ruth Goodman Goetz; DP: Victor Milner; Ed: Robert W. Swink; Prod Design: Hal Pereira, Roland Anderson; Composer: David Raksin; Costumes: Edith Head. B&W, 118 min. **VHS, LASER**

Carrie
(1976) United Artists
De Palma's commercial breakout, based on a novel by Stephen King, has become something of an old-school classic in the currently resurgent, blood-soaked genre of teenage gorefests. Spacek is a shy teenager with a fiercely religious mother who struggles to come to terms with her emerging sexuality and extraordinary telekinetic powers. Taunted by her

more popular high school classmates, Carrie begins to come out of her shell when a member of the cool clique unexpectedly asks her to the senior prom. But just as she's beginning to enjoy the sudden change in her life, a cruel practical joke drives her to a monstrous act of revenge and destruction. Academy Award Nominations: Best Actress: Sissy Spacek; Best Supporting Actress: Piper Laurie. **Cast:** Sissy Spacek, John Travolta, William Katt, Nancy Allen, Piper Laurie, Amy Irving, Betty Buckley, P. J. Soles, Sydney Lassick, Stefan Gierasch. **Credits:** Dir: Brian De Palma; Prod: Paul Monash; Writer: Larry Cohen; Story: Stephen King; DP: Mario Tosi; Ed: Paul Hirsch; Prod Design: Jack Fisk, William Kenny; Composer: Pino Donaggio. Color, 98 min. **VHS, LASER, DVD**

Carson City
(1952) Warner Bros.
In this Western, Scott plays an engineer charged with building a railroad from Carson City to Virginia City. A bandit stops the work by convincing everyone in town that Scott is a crook (even his own brother). To regain his good name and win back the affection of his family and girlfriend, the engineer must defeat the bandit and finish the railroad on time. **Cast:** Randolph Scott, Lucille Norman, Don Beddoe, Raymond Massey, Richard Webb, James Millican, Larry Keating, George Cleveland, William Haade, Thurston Hall. **Credits:** Dir: Andrew De Toth; Prod: David Weisbart; Writer: Sloan Nibley, Winston Miller; DP: John W. Boyle; Ed: Robert Swanson; Composer: David Buttolph. Color, 86 min.

Car Wash
(1976) Universal
A funny day in the life of L.A. as seen through the eyes of a car-wash crew. A sampler of mid-'70s dance music provided by Rose Royce and the Pointer Sisters punctuates what there is of a plot. A sunny hit that showcased a winning cast of young black comic actors, most notably Pryor and Ajaye. **Cast:** Richard Pryor, Franklin Ajaye, George Carlin, Irwin Corey, Sully Boyar, Ivan Dixon, Antonio Fargas, Tracy Reed, Richard Brestoff, Bill Duke. **Credits:** Dir: Michael Schultz; Prod: Art Linson, Gary Stromberg; Writer: Joel Schumacher; DP: Frank Stanley; Ed: Christopher Holmes; Prod Design: Robert Clatworthy; Composer: Norman Whitfield. Color, 97 min. **VHS, DVD**

Casablanca
(1943) Warner Bros.
Perennially at the top of every all-time-greats list, and indisputably one of the landmarks of the American cinema. Bogart is an American expatriate and war profiteer in WWII Morocco, content to merely run the Café Americain until love (in the form of a luminous Bergman) returns to his life and inspires him to stand up for the French Resistance. An accidental Hollywood masterpiece, it just gets better as time goes by. The 50th anniversary release includes the documentary *You Must Remember This,* narrated by Lauren Bacall; two versions of the original theatrical trailer; a five-color booklet; original stills; original shooting script; and a numbered certificate of authenticity. National Film Registry Outstanding Film. Academy Award Nominations: 8, including Best Actor: Humphrey Bogart; Best Supporting Actor: Claude Rains; Best Cinematography. **Academy Awards:** Best Picture; Best Director; Best Screenplay. **Cast:** Humphrey Bogart, Ingrid Bergman, Claude Rains, Paul Henreid, Dooley Wilson, Conrad Veidt, Sydney Greenstreet, Peter Lorre, S. Z. Sakall, Madeline Lebeau. **Credits:** Dir: Michael Curtiz; Prod: Hal B. Wallis, Jack L. Warner; Writer: Julius J. Epstein, Howard W. Koch, Philip G. Epstein; DP: Arthur Edeson; Ed: Owen Marks; Composer: Max Steiner; Costumes: Orry-Kelly; Art Director: Carl Jules Weyl. B&W, 103 min. **VHS, LASER, DVD**

Casanova Brown
(1944) RKO
Mildly risqué comedy for its time. Cooper is set to marry his sweetheart when he discovers that his ex-wife has delivered a baby and that he's the father! But when the ex decides to put the girl up for adoption, he kidnaps the baby and prepares to raise her himself. True love, of course, is rekindled. The situation must have appealed: it was filmed twice before (1930 and 1939) as *Little Accident.* **Cast:** Gary Cooper, Teresa Wright, Frank Morgan, Anita Louise, Isobel Elsom, Patricia Collinge, Edmond Breon, Jill Esmond, Mary Treen, Halliwell Hobbes. **Credits:** Dir: Sam Wood; Prod: Nunnally Johnson; Writer: Nunnally Johnson; DP: John F. Seitz; Ed: Thomas Neff; Prod Design: Perry Ferguson; Composer: Arthur Lange. Color, 94 min. **VHS**

Casanova's Big Night
(1954) Paramount
Bob Hope in tights as a lowly tailor impersonating the renowned Latin

lover, Casanova, while wooing the royal girl of his dreams whose virtue he's meant to be testing. Plush production, but Fontaine looks baffled by the buffoonery. **Cast:** Bob Hope, Joan Fontaine, Audrey Dalton, Raymond Burr, Basil Rathbone, Vincent Price, Hugh Marlowe, John Carradine, Primo Carnera, Arnold Moss. **Credits:** Dir: Norman Z. McLeod; Prod: Paul Jones; Writer: Hal Kanter, Edmund L. Hartmann; DP: Lionel Lindon; Ed: Ellsworth Hoagland; Composer: Lyn Murray. Color, 86 min. VHS

Casbah
(1948) Universal
The third time around for this remake of *Algiers*, this time with songs by Harold Arlen. The Casbah is the eye of a romantic and criminal hurricane, the hideout of Pepe Le Moko (Martin), pursued by detective Lorre. De Carlo loves Martin, but he's after Toren. Lorre sees an opening to bag Martin and uses Toren as an unwitting dupe to lure the criminal out of hiding and into a trap at Algiers airport. **Cast:** Yvonne De Carlo, Tony Martin, Peter Lorre, Marta Toren, Hugo Haas, Thomas Gomez, Douglas Dick, Katherine Dunham, Herbert Rudley, Gene Walker. **Credits:** Dir: John Berry; Prod: Nat C. Goldstone, Eric Charell; Writer: L. Bus-Fekete, Arnold Manoff; DP: Irving Glassberg; Ed: Edward Curtiss; Choreographer: Bernard Pearce; Composer: Walter Scharf, Harold Arlen, Leo Robin; Costumes: Yvonne Wood; SFX: David Horsley. B&W, 94 min.

Cash McCall
(1959) Warner Bros.
Making money comes easy to Garner's corporate raider—but it's a lot easier when you don't fall in love with your takeover target's daughter. Pleasant comic romance that's a perfect vehicle for Garner, and Wood is typically lovely. **Cast:** James Garner, Natalie Wood, Dean Jagger, E. G. Marshall, Otto Kruger, Nina Foch, Roland Winters, Henry Jones, Edward Platt, Linda Watkins. **Credits:** Dir: Joseph Pevney; Prod: Henry Blanke; Writer: Lenore Coffee, Marion Hargrove; DP: George J. Folsey; Ed: Philip W. Anderson; Composer: Max Steiner; Costumes: Howard Shoup. Color, 116 min. VHS

Casino Royale
(1967) Columbia
This stupendous spoof on James Bond films tells of the secret agent's plans for retirement. When he relinquishes his authority to his bungling

nephew, the results are disastrous. Academy Award Nominations: Best Song ("The Look of Love"). **Cast:** Daliah Lavi, Deborah Kerr, William Holden, John Huston, Terence Cooper, George Raft, Barbara Bouchet, Charles Boyer, Woody Allen, Jean-Paul Belmondo. **Credits:** Dir: Val Guest, John Huston, Joseph McGrath, Robert Parrish, Ken Hughes; Prod: Charles K. Feldman, Jerry Bresler; Writer: Wolf Mankowitz, John Law, Michael Sayers, Billy Wilder, Val Guest, Joseph Heller, Ben Hecht, Terry Southern; Story: Ian Fleming; DP: John Wilcox, Nicolas Roeg, Jack Hildyard; Ed: Bill Lenny; Prod Design: John Howell, Lionel Couch, Ivor Beddoes; Composer: Burt Bacharach. Color, 130 min. VHS, LASER

The Cassandra Crossing
(1976) Avco Embassy
Potential train wrecks, plagues, an all-star cast, and sweeping international vistas: sounds like a disaster film. A thousand passengers traveling from Geneva to Stockholm on a luxury express train learn that there's a terrorist onboard carrying plague virus. **Cast:** Sophia Loren, Richard Harris, Burt Lancaster, Ava Gardner, O. J. Simpson, Martin Sheen, Ingrid Thulin, Lee Strasberg, John Phillip Law, Ann Turkel. **Credits:** Dir: George P. Cosmatos; Prod: Sir Lew Grade, Carlo Ponti; Writer: Tom Mankiewicz, George P. Cosmatos, Robert Katz; DP: Ennio Guarnieri; Ed: Francoise Bonnot; Prod Design: Aurelio Crugnola; Composer: Jerry Goldsmith; Costumes: Adriana Berselli; SFX: Tazio Secciaroli. Color, 132 min. VHS

William Castle
Director-producer William Castle's unabashed delight in "scaring the pants off" of his audiences made his films Saturday-afternoon classics—and guilty pleasures for generations of filmmakers (see the homage appearances in Hal Ashby's *Shampoo* and John Schlesinger's *The Day of the Locust*, both 1975). Castle's novel concept of audience participation brought an added dimension to many of his movies, such as *House on Haunted Hill* (1958), in which a glowing skeleton was propelled out over the audience (making it an irresistible target for popcorn boxes), and *The Tingler* (1959), which utilized mild electric shocks to audience members' seats at key moments in the film (faithfully reproduced for a recent Castle tribute at the Telluride Film Festival). Castle directed numerous B movies, but his most presti-

gious role was producing the classic tale of terror *Rosemary's Baby* (1968). His autobiography is *Step Right Up! I'm Gonna Scare the Pants Off America* (1976).

The Man Who Cried Wolf *(1937)*
He Stayed for Breakfast *(1940)*
The Lady in Question *(1940)*
The Chance of a Lifetime *(1943)*
The Law Rides Again *(1943)*
Klondike Kate *(1944)*
The Whistler *(1944)*
When Strangers Marry *(1944)*
She's a Soldier Too *(1944)*
The Mark of the Whistler *(1944)*
Voice of the Whistler *(1945)*
Crime Doctor's Warning *(1945)*
The Return of Rusty *(1946)*
Mysterious Intruder *(1946)*
The Crime Doctor's Man Hunt *(1946)*
Just Before Dawn *(1946)*
The Crime Doctor's Gamble *(1947)*
The Lady from Shanghai *(1948)*
The Gentleman from Nowhere *(1948)*
Texas, Brooklyn and Heaven *(1948)*
Johnny Stool Pigeon *(1949)*
Undertow *(1949)*
It's a Small World *(1950)*
The Fat Man *(1951)*
Hollywood Story *(1951)*
Cave of Outlaws *(1951)*
Conquest of Cochise *(1953)*
Slaves of Babylon *(1953)*
Serpent of the Nile *(1953)*
Fort Ti *(1953)*
Charge of the Lancers *(1953)*
Jesse James vs. the Daltons *(1954)*
Battle of Rogue River *(1954)*
Drums of Tahiti *(1954)*
The Saracen Blade *(1954)*
Masterson of Kansas *(1954)*
The Law vs. Billy the Kid *(1954)*
The Iron Glove *(1954)*
The Americano *(1955)*
New Orleans Uncensored *(1955)*
Duel on the Mississippi *(1955)*
The Gun That Won the West *(1955)*
Uranium Boom *(1956)*
The Houston Story *(1956)*
House on Haunted Hill *(1958)*
Macabre *(1958)*
The Tingler *(1959)*
13 Ghosts *(1960)*
Mr. Sardonicus *(1961)*
Homicidal *(1961)*
Zotz! *(1962)*
13 Frightened Girls *(1963)*
The Old Dark House *(1963)*
Ride the Wild Surf *(1964)*
The Night Walker *(1964)*
Strait-Jacket *(1964)*
I Saw What You Did *(1965)*
Let's Kill Uncle *(1966)*
The Spirit Is Willing *(1967)*
The Busybody *(1967)*
Project X *(1968)*

Rosemary's Baby *(1968)*
Riot *(1968)*
Shanks *(1974)*
Bug *(1975)*

Castle on the Hudson

(1940) Warner Bros.
This dark prison drama stars Garfield as a stubborn hood on his way to death row. The reform-minded warden, played by O'Brien, of course, maintains discipline inside the walls of the jail. Meredith's character instigates their failed attempt at escape. **Cast:** John Garfield, Ann Sheridan, Pat O'Brien, Burgess Meredith, Henry O'Neill, Jerome Cowan, Guinn "Big Boy" Williams, John Litel, Margot Stevenson, Willard Robertson. **Credits:** Dir: Anatole Litvak; Prod: Hal B. Wallis; Writer: Brown Holmes, Courtney Terrett, Seton I. Miller; Story: Lewis E. Lawes; DP: Arthur Edeson; Ed: Thomas Richards; Prod Design: John Hughes; Composer: Adolph Deutsch. B&W, 77 min.

The Cat and the Canary

(1939) Paramount
Comedic remake of Universal's silent film stars Hope and Goddard as potential heirs to a bayou fortune. After the will is read and the estate is left to Goddard, a number of suspicious events take place, leaving the guests unsure if the mansion is haunted or if one of the neglected heirs is trying to steal Goddard's new fortune. Hope attempts to get to the bottom of the mystery, in his typically comic manner. **Cast:** Bob Hope, Paulette Goddard, John Beal, Douglass Montgomery, Gale Sondergaard, Elizabeth Patterson, George Zucco, Nydia Westman, John Wray. **Credits:** Dir: Elliott Nugent; Prod: Arthur Hornblow, Jr.; Writer: Walter DeLeon, Lynn Starling; Story: John Willard; DP: Charles Lang; Ed: Archie Marshek; Prod Design: Hans Dreier, Robert Usher; Composer: Ernst Toch. 72 min.

The Cat and the Fiddle

(1934) MGM
MacDonald plays an American music student in Europe whose success threatens her relationship with a handsome composer played by Novarro. His troubles begin with their meeting and don't end until the premiere of his problematic stage show. The final sequence features an early experiment with three-strip Technicolor. Based on the Jerome Kern–Oscar Hammerstein musical comedy. **Cast:** Jeanette MacDonald, Ramon Novarro, Frank Morgan, Jean Hersholt, Charles

Butterworth, Vivienne Segal, Henry Armetta. **Credits:** Dir: William K. Howard; Writer: Samuel Spewack, Bella Spewack; Story: Jerome Kern, Otto A. Harbach; DP: Harold Rosson, Charles G. Clarke; Ed: Frank Hull; Composer: Herbert Stothart; Costumes: Adrian; Art Director: Alexander Toluboff; Set Designer: Edwin B. Willis. B&W, 88 min. **VHS**

Cat Ballou

(1965) Columbia
Fonda's agreeably peppery as a teacher in the Old West who wreaks vengeance on thé men who murdered her father. Marvin enlists as a drunken old gunfighter trying to retain his old glory and also portrays his twin brother, a rustler with a silver nose. A '60s-style genre spoof with enough action to keep it real. **Academy Awards:** Best Actor: Lee Marvin. **Cast:** Jane Fonda, Lee Marvin, Michael Callan, Dwayne Hickman, Nat King Cole, Stubby Kaye, Tom Nardini, John Marley, Reginald Denny, Jay C. Flippen. **Credits:** Dir: Elliot Silverstein; Prod: Harold Hecht; Writer: Frank Pierson, Walter Newman; DP: Jack Marta; Ed: Charles Nelson; Composer: Frank de Vol; Costumes: Bill Thomas. Color, 97 min. **VHS**

Catch-22

(1970) Paramount
Henry's script, based on Heller's best-selling novel, is a disturbing antiwar satire centered around a group of WWII fliers in the Mediterranean. The insanity of the goings-on mirror the insanity of war. **Cast:** Alan Arkin, Martin Balsam, Jon Voight, Orson Welles, Art Garfunkel, Richard Benjamin, Jack Gilford, Buck Henry, Bob Newhart, Anthony Perkins. **Credits:** Dir: Mike Nichols; Prod: Martin Ransohoff, John Calley; Writer: Buck Henry; Story: Joseph Heller; DP: David Watkin; Ed: Sam O'Steen; Prod Design: Richard Sylbert. Color, 121 min. **VHS, LASER**

The Catered Affair

(1956) MGM
Gore Vidal wrote this big-screen adaptation of Paddy Chayefsky's teleplay about a working-class Bronx family's struggle over the daughter's upcoming nuptials. Mother-of-the-bride Mrs. Hurley (Davis!?) wants to hold a lavish Irish wedding for her daughter that's well beyond the family's means. Even though the effort will financially ruin them, and the immediate family and prospective son-in-law are against it, she perseveres with her elaborate plans. **Cast:** Bette Davis, Ernest Borgnine, Debbie Reynolds, Barry Fitzger-

ald, Rod Taylor, Robert F. Simon, Madge Kennedy, Dorothy Stickney, Carol Veazie. **Credits:** Dir: Richard Brooks; Prod: Sam Zimbalist; Writer: Gore Vidal; Story: Paddy Chayefsky; DP: John Alton; Ed: Gene Ruggiero, Frank Santillo; Prod Design: Cedric Gibbons, Paul Groesse; Composer: Andre Previn. B&W, 95 min. **VHS**

The Cat from Outer Space

(1978) Disney
An intelligent being from another planet in the form of a cat named Jake visits earth, and enlists the aid of U.S. scientists to help rebuild his spaceship. Jake happens to be able to predict sporting-event results and attracts some military types who think they are seeking a spaceman, not a spacecat. Humorous Disney film written by cartoonist Ted Key. **Cast:** Ken Berry, Sandy Duncan, McLean Stevenson, Harry Morgan, Roddy McDowall, Jesse White, Alan Young, Hans Conried. **Credits:** Dir: Norman Tokar; Prod: Ron Miller; Writer: Ted Key; DP: Charles F. Wheeler; Ed: Cotton Warburton; Prod Design: John B. Mansbridge, Preston Ames; Composer: Lalo Schifrin; SFX: Eustace Lycett, Art Cruickshank, Danny Lee. Color, 103 min. **VHS**

Cat on a Hot Tin Roof

(1958) MGM
A blistering adaptation of Tennessee Williams's play features performances from Newman, Ives, and Taylor that have become cinematic icons (Ives's Big Daddy in acres of suit, Taylor's Maggie sprawled in her slip). A dying Southern patriarch surveys the prospects for his legacy in the hands of his sons—one a neurotic weakling and the other an alcoholic conniver—and finds them sorely lacking. Remade for television in 1984 with Jessica Lange and Tommy Lee Jones. **Cast:** Elizabeth Taylor, Paul Newman, Burl Ives, Judith Anderson, Jack Carson, Madeleine Sherwood, Larry Gates, Vaughn Taylor. **Credits:** Dir: Richard Brooks; Prod: Lawrence Weingarten; Writer: Richard Brooks, James Poe; Story: Tennessee Williams; DP: William Daniels; Ed: Ferris Webster; Prod Design: William A. Horning, Urie McCleary; Costumes: Helen Rose. Color, 109 min. **VHS, LASER, DVD**

Cat People

(1942) RKO
A young bride believes she is the victim of a curse that transforms her into a deadly panther. This is the first of several famous horror films produced

by Val Lewton. Selected for the National Film Registry. **Cast:** Simone Simon, Kent Smith, Tom Conway, Jane Randolph, Jack Holt, Alan Napier, Elizabeth Dunne, Elizabeth Russell. **Credits:** Dir: Jacques Tourneur; Prod: Val Lewton; Writer: DeWitt Bodeen; DP: Nicholas Musuraca; Ed: Mark Robson; Composer: Roy Webb. B&W, 73 min. **VHS, LASER**

The Cat's Paw
(1934) Fox
A different look for comedian Lloyd as a man who returns home after being in rural China for 20 years, having gone there as a youth with his missionary father. Upon his return he gets entangled with crooked politicians, who want to run the naive man as a bogus candidate against their own man. He wins by a landslide, however, and fearlessly goes after corruption. The crooked politicians decide to frame him, but with the help of a wise Chinese man he eludes the trap. **Cast:** Harold Lloyd, Una Merkel, George Barbier, Nat Pendleton, Grace Bradley, Alan Dinehart, Grant Mitchell, Fred Warren. **Credits:** Dir: Sam Taylor; Prod: Harold Lloyd, Jr.; Writer: Clarence Budington Kelland, Sam Taylor; DP: Walter Lundin; Ed: Bernard W. Burton; Prod Design: Harry Oliver; Composer: Alfred Newman. B&W, 101 min.

Cattle Queen of Montana
(1954) RKO
After her father is brutally murdered, a strong-willed woman struggles to keep her ranch out of the hands of greedy cattle barons and marauding Indians. Stanwyck upstages Reagan (in one of his last significant roles) but the scenery upstages both of them. **Cast:** Barbara Stanwyck, Ronald Reagan, Gene Evans, Jack Elam, Lance Fuller, Anthony Caruso, Yvette Dugay, Morris Ankrum, Chubby Johnson, Myron Healey. **Credits:** Dir: Allan Dwan; Prod: Benedict E. Bogeaus; Writer: Robert Blees, Howard Estabrook; Story: Tom Blackburn; DP: John Alton; Ed: Carlo Lodato, Jim Lekester; Prod Design: Van Nest Polglase; Composer: Louis Forbes. Color, 88 min. **LASER**

Caught
(1949) MGM
Ophuls directed this film noir about a young woman who marries a millionaire and finds wealth and security can't compensate for his abusiveness. Desperate to escape him when he's unwilling to divorce, she plots his murder. **Cast:** James Mason, Barbara Bel Geddes, Robert Ryan, Frank Fer-

guson, Curt Bois, Ruth Brady, Natalie Schafer, Art Smith, Sonia Darrin, Bernadene Hayes. **Credits:** Dir: Max Ophuls; Prod: Wolfgang Reinhardt; Writer: Arthur Laurents; DP: Lee Garmes; Ed: Robert Parrish; Prod Design: Frank Sylos; Composer: Frederick Hollander. B&W, 90 min. **VHS**

Caught in the Draft
(1941) Paramount
Bob Hope's best as a spoiled movie star who makes a play for a colonel's daughter, who is not impressed. So he sets up a phony session with an army enlistment sergeant but the bright beauty foils his game and he finds himself in a comedy of errors when Congress passes the National Draft. **Cast:** Bob Hope, Dorothy Lamour, Eddie Bracken, Lynne Overman, Clarence Kolb, Paul Hurst, Irving Bacon, Ferike Boros, Phyllis Ruth, Arthur Loft. **Credits:** Dir: David Butler; Prod: B. G. DeSylva; Writer: Harry Tugend; DP: Karl Struss; Ed: Irene Morra; Composer: Victor Young. B&W, 82 min. **VHS**

Cause for Alarm
(1951) MGM
A man recovering from illness frames his wife for his own murder when he incorrectly suspects her of having an affair. Taut pacing, fine performances, and a great plot make this a classic thriller. **Cast:** Loretta Young, Barry Sullivan, Margalo Gilmore, Carl "Alfalfa" Switzer, Bruce Cowling, Irving Bacon, Georgia Backus, Don Haggerty, Art Baker, Richard Anderson. **Credits:** Dir: Tay Garnett; Prod: Tom Lewis; Writer: Tom Lewis, Mel Dinelli; DP: Joseph Ruttenberg; Ed: James E. Newcom; Prod Design: Cedric Gibbons, Arthur Lonergan; Composer: Andre Previn. B&W, 74 min. **VHS**

Cavalcade
(1933) Fox
Fine film adaptation of Noël Coward's 1931 play traces the lives of a British family from the late 19th century through 1930. A richly nostalgic look at a family adjusting to the changes in the world as the years go by. Academy Award Nominations: 4, including Best Supporting Actress: Diana Wynyard. **Academy Awards:** Best Picture; Best Director; Best Interior Decoration (B&W). **Cast:** Diana Wynyard, Clive Brook, Herbert Mundin, Ursula Jeans, Beryl Mercer, Margaret Lindsay, Billy Bevan, Una O'Connor, Frank Lawton, Irene Browne. **Credits:** Dir: Frank Lloyd; Prod: Winfield Sheehan; Writer: Reginald Berkeley; Story: Noël Cow-

ard; DP: Ernest Palmer, William Cameron Menzies; Ed: Margaret Clancy; Composer: Louis de Francesco. B&W, 110 min. **VHS**

Ceiling Zero
(1935) Warner Bros.
Cagney plays a womanizing, devil-may-care pilot (again) who's forced to change his ways when his carelessness leads to a friend's untimely death. He makes amends with a dangerous mission. Remade in 1941 as *International Squadron.* **Cast:** James Cagney, Pat O'Brien, June Travis, Stuart Erwin, Barton MacLane, Isabel Jewell, Henry Wadsworth, Martha Tibbetts, Craig Reynolds, James Bush. **Credits:** Dir: Howard Hawks; Prod: Harry Joe Brown; Writer: Frank Wead; DP: Arthur Edeson; Ed: William Holmes; Composer: Leo F. Forbstein. B&W, 95 min. **VHS**

Centennial Summer
(1946) Fox
A Kern musical about a family with two lovely daughters living in Philadelphia in 1876. The father invents clocks but earns his living working for the railroad. The two sisters become rivals for a handsome and charming young Frenchman who arrives in Philadelphia for the Exposition of 1876. The film features the Oscar-nominated song, "All Through the Day." **Cast:** Jeanne Crain, Cornel Wilde, Linda Darnell, William Eythe, Walter Brennan, Constance Bennett, Dorothy Gish, Barbara Whiting. **Credits:** Dir: Otto Preminger; Prod: Otto Preminger; Writer: Albert E. Idell, Michael Kanin; DP: Ernest Palmer; Ed: Harry Reynolds; Composer: Oscar Hammerstein, Leo Robin, E. Y. Harburg; Art Director: Lee Fuller, Lyle Wheeler; Composer: Jerome Kern. Color, 104 min.

Central Airport
(1933) Warner Bros.
Solid performance by Barthelmess as a daredevil flier who loves a lady parachutist but refuses to marry her because of the dangers of his profession. She weds his brother instead and sparks fly, along with aerial heroics and some innovative shots. Look for one of John Wayne's early screen appearances. **Cast:** Richard Barthelmess, Sally Eilers, Tom Brown, Glenda Farrell, Harold Huber, James Murray, Grant Mitchell, Claire McDowell, Willard Robertson, Arthur Vinton. **Credits:** Dir: William Wellman, Jr.; Prod: Hal B. Wallis; Writer: Rian James, James Seymour; Story: Jack

Moffitt; DP: Sidney Hickox; Ed: James B. Morley; SFX: Franz Jackman. B&W, 75 min.

Chad Hanna
(1940) Fox
A romantic circus drama starring Fonda as a young man who runs away with the three-wagon circus. He first falls for the daring "high rider," Lamour, who is amused by his affections but eventually leaves. Fonda then falls in love with her equestrian successor, Darnell, and marries her. Filmed in Technicolor, the movie's big-top atmosphere creates a visual spectacle (the red and white rococo wagons, acrobats in pink tights and gold fringe, the blare and glare of the trombones). **Cast:** Henry Fonda, Dorothy Lamour, Linda Darnell, Guy Kibbee, Jane Darwell, John Carradine, Ted North, Roscoe Ates, Ben Carter, Frank Thomas. **Credits:** Dir: Henry King; Prod: Nunnally Johnson, Darryl F. Zanuck; Writer: Nunnally Johnson; Story: Walter D. Edmonds; DP: Ernest Palmer, Ray Rennaham; Ed: Barbara McLean; Prod Design: Richard Day; Composer: David Buttolph. Color, 86 min.

Chained
(1934) MGM
In this love triangle, Crawford can't decide if she loves Gable, whom she meets aboard a ship, or Kruger, the married businessman she's trying to forget. Pretty tame fare. **Cast:** Clark Gable, Joan Crawford, Otto Kruger, Stuart Erwin, Una O'Connor, Akim Tamiroff, Marjorie Gateson, Hooper Atchley, Phillips Smalley, Lee Phelps. **Credits:** Dir: Clarence Brown; Prod: Hunt Stromberg; Writer: John Lee Mahin; Story: Edgar Selwyn; DP: George J. Folsey; Ed: Robert J. Kern; Prod Design: Cedric Gibbons, Alexander Toluboff; Composer: Herbert Stothart. B&W, 76 min. **VHS**

The Champ
(1931) MGM
Cooper and Oscar-winner Beery star in this classic tearjerker about a young boy's love for his washed-up boxer father. Champ's fighting career has hit the skids, but he is attempting to make a comeback. However, his frequent drinking and gambling keep getting in the way. Despite Champ's failures, his son, Dink, continues to believe in him. Meanwhile, Dink's mother, Linda, has come back into their lives. Since divorcing Champ, she's remarried and now wants to gain custody of her son to raise him in a better environment. Dink and Champ reluctantly agree but,

very soon, the boy goes running back to his father—just in time to watch him face a Mexican fighter in a tough match that could be Champ's last. Remade in 1979. **Academy Awards:** Best Actor: Wallace Beery; Best Original Story. **Cast:** Wallace Beery, Jackie Cooper, Irene Rich, Roscoe Ates, Edward Brophy, Hale Hamilton. **Credits:** Dir: King Vidor; Prod: Harry Rapf; Writer: Leonard Praskins; DP: Gordon Avil. B&W, 87 min. **VHS, LASER**

The Champ
(1979) United Artists
An alcoholic ex-boxer reenters the ring in order to earn enough money to defeat his ex-wife in a custody battle for their young son. Schroder gives a touching performance as the fighter's young son. Melodramatic remake of the 1931 film. Academy Award Nomination for Best Original Score. **Cast:** Jon Voight, Faye Dunaway, Arthur Hill, Jack Warden, Rick Schroder, Strother Martin, Joan Blondell, Mary Jo Catlett, Elisha Cook, Jr. **Credits:** Dir: Franco Zeffirelli; Prod: Dyson Lovell; Writer: Walter Newman, Leonard Praskins; Story: Frances Marion; DP: Fred Koenekamp; Ed: Michael J. Sheridan; Composer: Dave Grusin; Costumes: Theoni V. Aldredge. Color, 122 min. **VHS, LASER**

Champagne for Caesar
(1950) United Artists
An unemployed genius appears on a TV quiz show and forces the jackpot to 40 million dollars. The panic-stricken sponsor then hires a femme fatale to disable the human encyclopedia in this funny spoof on the quiz-show industry. **Cast:** Ronald Colman, Celeste Holm, Vincent Price, Barbara Britton, Art Linkletter, George Fisher, Byron Foulger. **Credits:** Dir: Richard Whorf; Prod: George Moskov; Writer: Hans Jacoby, Fred Brady; DP: Paul Ivano; Ed: Hugh Bennett; Prod Design: George Van Marter; Composer: Dimitri Tiomkin. B&W, 115 min. **VHS, LASER**

Champion
(1949) United Artists
An unscrupulous boxer fights his way to the top, but eventually alienates all of the people who helped him on the way up. One of the all-time great boxing movies. Golden Globe for Best Black-and-White Cinematography. Academy Award Nominations: 6, including Best Actor: Kirk Douglas; Best Screenplay. **Academy Awards:** Best Film Editing. **Cast:** Kirk Douglas, Marilyn Maxwell, Arthur Kennedy, Ruth Roman, Paul Stewart, Lola Albright,

Luis Van Rooten, John Day, Harry Shannon. **Credits:** Dir: Mark Robson; Prod: Stanley Kramer; Writer: Carl Foreman; Story: Ring Lardner; DP: Franz Planer; Ed: Harry Gerstad; Composer: Dimitri Tiomkin. B&W, 100 min. **VHS**

Chances
(1931) First National
In this love drama, two brothers fight on the same side in WWI, and fight against each other for the affections of a beautiful woman. After this pair of soldier siblings return from R&R with eyes for the same woman, tensions rise in the trenches as both British officers, already experiencing the hell of "the war to end all wars," must now battle the passions that threaten to tear them apart. **Cast:** Douglas Fairbanks, Jr., Rose Hobart, Anthony Bushell, Holmes Herbert, Mary Forbes, Harry Allen. **Credits:** Dir: Allan Dwan; Writer: Waldemar Young; Story: A. Hamilton Gibbs; DP: Ernest Haller; Ed: Ray Curtiss; Prod Design: Esdras Hartley; Composer: David Mendoza. B&W, 72 min.

The Changeling
(1979) Associated
Well-told horror story with Scott playing the role of a widower music teacher. After the death of his wife, he moves to Seattle in hopes of starting a new life in a grand old mansion. Unfortunately, his new home turns out to be haunted by the troublesome ghost of a murdered child bent on revenge after 70 years of torment. **Cast:** George C. Scott, Melvyn Douglas, Trish Van Devere, John Colicos, Jean Marsh, Barry Morse. **Credits:** Dir: Peter Medak; Prod: Joel B. Michaels, Garth Drabinsky; Writer: William Gray, Diana Maddox; DP: John Coquillon; Ed: Lilla Ledersen; Prod Design: Reuben Freed; Composer: Rick Wilkins; SFX: Gene Grigg; Set Designer: Trevor Williams. Color, 115 min. **VHS, LASER**

Change of Habit
(1969) Universal
Presley plays a young doctor working in a free clinic who falls for Moore, one of three nuns who also work at the clinic. The Jordanaires do not appear in habits. Worth seeing once as it's Presley in his last dramatic screen role. **Cast:** Elvis Presley, Mary Tyler Moore, Barbara McNair, Jane Elliot, Ed Asner, Leora Dana, Robert Emhardt, Regis Toomey, Doro Merande, Ruth McDevitt. **Credits:** Dir: William A. Graham; Prod: Joe Connelly;

Writer: James Lee, Eric Bercovici, S. S. Schweitzer; DP: Russell Metty; Ed: Douglas Stewart; Prod Design: Alexander Golitzen; Composer: Billy Goldenberg. Color, 97 min. VHS

Chapter Two
(1979) Columbia
The film version of Simon's Broadway hit about a shy mystery writer who falls in love too soon, as he's still grieving the death of his first wife. Academy Award Nomination for Best Actress: Marsha Mason. **Cast:** James Caan, Marsha Mason, Valerie Harper, Joseph Bologna, Alan Fudge, Debra Mooney, Judy Farrell, Imogene Bliss, Isabel Cooley. **Credits:** Dir: Robert Moore; Prod: Ray Stark; Writer: Neil Simon; DP: David M. Walsh; Ed: Margaret Booth, Michael A. Stevenson; Prod Design: Peter Lansdown Smith; Composer: Marvin Hamlisch. Color, 127 min. VHS, LASER

Charade
(1963) Universal
An innocent young Parisienne widow is aided by a handsome American stranger when a cadre of hoodlums shake her down for a supposed "fortune" plundered in WWII by her late husband. Hepburn and Grant are appealing; Donen and the locations add a dash of sophistication. Based on the story "The Unsuspecting Wife" by Marc Behm and Peter Stone. Academy Award Nomination for Best Song ("Charade"). **Cast:** Audrey Hepburn, Cary Grant, Walter Matthau, James Coburn, George Kennedy, Dominique Minot, Ned Glass. **Credits:** Dir: Stanley Donen; Prod: Stanley Donen; Writer: Peter Stone; DP: Charles Lang; Ed: James P. Clark; Composer: Henry Mancini. Color, 114 min. VHS, DVD

The Charge of the Light Brigade
(1936) Warner Bros.
Loosely based on Tennyson's stirring poem, the film marks a milestone in action sequences with the tumultuous Balaklava charge. Flynn is a dashing British military man at odds with mercenary enemies. Stationed in India and later in Crimea, Flynn and cohorts vow revenge on a cruel despot who attacked their camp. Dripping with patriotism, pageantry, heroism, and thrilling action. **Academy Awards:** Best Assistant Director. **Cast:** Errol Flynn, Olivia de Havilland, Patric Knowles, David Niven, Donald Crisp, Henry Stephenson, Nigel Bruce, G. P. Huntley, Spring Byington, C. Henry Gordon. **Credits:** Dir: Michael Curtiz;

Prod: Samuel Bischoff; Writer: Michael Jacoby, Rowland Leigh; Story: Alfred Lord Tennyson; DP: Sol Polito, Fred Jackman; Ed: George Amy; Prod Design: John Hughes; Composer: Max Steiner; Costumes: Milo Anderson; SFX: H. F. Koenekamp. B&W, 117 min. VHS, LASER

Charley and the Angel
(1973) Disney
MacMurray in Disney mode as a miserly sporting goods storekeeper in the 1930s who learns from a sympathetic angel that he has only a short time to live. The news causes him to reassess his life, ease up on his family, and let their love enter his life. It aims at heartwarming. **Cast:** Fred MacMurray, Harry Morgan, Cloris Leachman, Kurt Russell, Kathleen Cody, Edward Andrews, Barbara Nichols, Vincent Van Patten, Scott Kolden, George Lindsey. **Credits:** Dir: Vincent McEveety; Prod: Bill Anderson; Writer: Roswell Rogers; Story: Will Stanton; DP: Charles F. Wheeler; Ed: Ray de Leuw, Bob Bring; Prod Design: John B. Mansbridge, Al Roelofs; Composer: Buddy Baker. Color, 94 min. VHS

Charley's Aunt
(1930) Columbia
The first talkie version of Brandon Thomas's farce (which must have been a real knee-slapper in the 23 skidoo days, as it was given multiple screen airings). Two schoolboys convince an older chum to masquerade as their aged female relation and chaperone so they can court their sweeties undisturbed. Resurfaced as the 1952 musical *Where's Charley?* **Cast:** June Collyer, Charlie Ruggles, Hugh Williams, Doris Lloyd, Halliwell Hobbes, Phillips Smalley, Wilson Benge, Flora Le Breton, Rodney McLennon. **Credits:** Dir: Al Christie; Prod: Al Christie; Writer: F. McGrew Willis; DP: Gus Peterson, Harry Zech, Leslie Rowson. B&W, 88 min. VHS

Charley's Aunt
(1941) Fox
This film, a cross-dressing farce, is performed hilariously by comedic master Benny playing Babbs, an Oxford student. When two of Benny's schoolmates need aid in wooing two young women, he comes to the rescue. Taking on the persona of a Brazilian aunt to one of the young men, he serves as chaperone for the two couples. Benny finds himself up to his wig in trouble, however, when he begins to attract the affections of a gigolo and the guardian of the two young women.

Breakneck pacing and superbly funny performances highlight this film version of Brandon Thomas's 19th-century play. **Cast:** Jack Benny, Richard Haydn, James Ellison, Laird Creeger, Edmund Gwenn, Anne Baxter, Arleen Whelan. **Credits:** Dir: Archie Mayo; Prod: William Perlberg; Writer: George Seaton; Story: Brandon Thomas; DP: Peverell Marley; Ed: Robert Bischoff; Prod Design: Nathan Juran, Richard Day, Thomas Little; Composer: Alfred Newman. B&W, 81 min.

Charley Varrick
(1973) Universal
Standard thread of small-time crook who ends up on the run with the Mob's cash is woven by director Siegel into pretty taut cloth. Baker's particularly effective. **Cast:** Walter Matthau, Joe Don Baker, Felicia Farr, John Vernon, Andy Robinson, Sheree North, Norman Fell, Benson Fong, Woodrow Parfrey, William Schallert. **Credits:** Dir: Don Siegel; Prod: Don Siegel; Writer: Dean Riesner, Howard A. Rodman; DP: Michael Butler; Ed: Frank Morriss; Prod Design: Fernando Carrere; Composer: Lalo Schifrin. Color, 111 min. VHS

Charlie Chan
Intrepid sleuth Charlie Chan (a character originally created by Earl Derr Biggers) made his first big-screen appearance in *Behind That Curtain* in 1929. Over the course of 44 movies, the Honolulu police investigator was portrayed by three non-Asian actors: Warner Oland (1931–1938), Sidney Toler (1938–1947), and Roland Winters (1947–1949). All of the films tended to follow a similar formula: one of Chan's many children, often Number One Son (portrayed by Keye Luke) and/or Number Two Son (played by Victor Sen Yung), would attempt to assist in an investigation, only to become imperiled, thus raising the stakes for Chan as he raced against the clock (sometimes in exotic locales) to solve the case at hand. The series was at its apex during Warner Oland's stint as the supersleuth, and Sidney Toler did an admirable job after Oland's death in 1937. Production values and scripts declined after the series made the move from 20th Century-Fox to Monogram in 1944, though Toler made the move, too, portraying the portly sleuth until his death in 1947.

Behind That Curtain *(1929)*
Black Camel *(1931)*
Charlie Chan in London *(1934)*

Charlie Chan in Paris *(1935)*
Charlie Chan in Egypt *(1935)*
Charlie Chan in Shanghai *(1935)*
Charlie Chan's Secret *(1936)*
Charlie Chan at the Circus *(1936)*
Charlie Chan at the Race Track *(1936)*
Charlie Chan at the Opera *(1936)*
Charlie Chan at the Olympics *(1937)*
Charlie Chan on Broadway *(1937)*
Charlie Chan at Monte Carlo *(1938)*
Charlie Chan in Honolulu *(1938)*
Charlie Chan in Reno *(1939)*
Charlie Chan at Treasure Island
  (1939)
Charlie Chan in City in Darkness
  (1939)
Charlie Chan in Panama *(1940)*
Charlie Chan's Murder Cruise *(1940)*
Charlie Chan at the Wax Museum
  (1940)
Murder over New York *(1940)*
Dead Men Tell *(1941)*
Charlie Chan in Rio *(1941)*
Castle in the Desert *(1942)*
Charlie Chan in the Secret Service
  (1944)
The Chinese Cat *(1944)*
Black Magic *(1944)*
The Jade Mask *(1945)*
The Scarlet *(1945)*
The Shanghai Cobra *(1945)*
The Red Dragon *(1945)*
Dark Alibi *(1946)*
Shadows over Chinatown *(1946)*
Dangerous Money *(1946)*
The Trap *(1947)*
The Chinese Ring *(1947)*
Docks of New Orleans *(1948)*
The Shanghai Chest *(1948)*
The Golden Eye *(1948)*
The Feathered Serpent *(1948)*
Sky Dragon *(1949)*

Charlotte's Web
(1973) Paramount
Friendly pig Wilbur makes a big splash
on the county fair circuit after Char-
lotte, the gentle spider living over his
sty, "spins" his praises in her web.
But Wilbur still has painful lessons to
learn about the ephemeral nature of
life and friendship. A charming Hanna-
Barbera musical feature based on the
best-selling novel by E. B. White.
Received the Family Award of Excel-
lence. **Cast:** Henry Gibson, Paul
Lynde, Agnes Moorehead, Debbie
Reynolds, Martha Scott, Rex Allen,
David Madden, Danny Bonaduce, Don
Messick, Herb Vigran. **Credits:** Dir:
Charles A. Nichols, Iwao Takamoto;
Prod: Joseph Barbera, William Hanna;
Writer: Earl Hamner, Jr.; Story:
E. B. White; DP: Roy Wade, Dick Blun-
dell, Dennis Weaver, Ralph Migliori;
Ed: Pat A. Foley, Larry Cowan; Prod
Design: Bob Singer, Paul Julian, Ray

Charlie Chan in City in Darkness (1939)

Aragon; Composer: Richard M. Sherman, Robert B. Sherman. Color, 94
min. **VHS, LASER**

Charly
(1968) Cinerama
Robertson delivers a heartbreaking
performance as a retarded man who
gains super-intelligence from an experimental procedure, only to experience
his newfound grasp of the world slowly
ebbing away. Bloom also fine as the
caseworker who loses her heart to her
charge. Based on Daniel Keyes's
Flowers for Algernon. Robertson had
previously appeared in the role on
television. **Academy Awards:** Best
Actor: Cliff Robertson. **Cast:** Cliff
Robertson, Claire Bloom, Lilia Skala,
Leon Janney, Dick Van Patten, Ruth
White, Barney Martin, William Dwyer,
Ed McNally, Dan Morgan. **Credits:** Dir:
Ralph Nelson; Prod: Ralph Nelson;
Writer: Stirling Silliphant; Story: Daniel
Keyes; DP: Arthur J. Ornitz; Ed: Fredric
Steinkamp; Prod Design: Charles
Rosen; Composer: Ravi Shankar.
Color, 106 min. **VHS, LASER**

Charro!
(1969) National General
A boisterous outlaw must break free
from the notorious gang he once ran
with in order to complete his reforma-
tion. Of course a must for Elvis fans,
but beware: only one song. **Cast:**
Elvis Presley, Victor French, Ina Balin,

Lynn Kellogg, James B. Sikking,
Solomon Sturges, Barbara Werle,
Paul Brinegar, Harry Landers, Tony
Young. **Credits:** Dir: Charles Marquis
Warren; Prod: Charles Marquis War-
ren; Writer: Charles Marquis Warren;
DP: Ellsworth Fredricks; Ed: Al Clark;
Prod Design: James Sullivan; Com-
poser: Hugo Montenegro. Color, 98
min. **VHS**

The Chase
(1966) Columbia
Redford escapes from prison and is
on his way to his tiny Texas hometown to see his girl (Fonda) and have
a few words with the people who sent
him to jail. Scenes of Redford's journey are interspersed with illustrations
of the sordid business of the town
that awaits him. The ineffectual sheriff (Brando) is under the thumb of the
banker (Marshall); the bank vice president (Duvall) has a shameless wife
(Dickinson) and prejudice, conspiracy,
and seedy secrets abound. Reportedly an unhappy set, but an interesting
cast at work. Based on the novel by
Foote. **Cast:** Marlon Brando, Robert
Redford, E. G. Marshall, James Fox,
Jane Fonda, Angie Dickinson, Paul
Williams, Janice Rule, Miriam Hopkins, Robert Duvall. **Credits:** Dir:
Arthur Penn; Prod: Sam Spiegel;
Writer: Lillian Hellman; Story: Horton
Foote; DP: Joseph La Shelle, Robert
Surtees; Ed: Gene Milford; Prod

Design: Richard Day; Composer: John Barry; Costumes: Donfeld; Set Designer: Frank Tuttle. Color, 135 min. VHS, LASER

The Cheap Detective
(1978) Columbia
Simon's spoof of *The Maltese Falcon* and its ilk follows private detective Lou Peckinpaugh (Falk), a man accused of killing his own partner. As Peckinpaugh follows a trail of looney characters around San Francisco, he uncovers a plot involving a dozen diamonds hidden in an egg carton. Meanwhile, he also attempts to help members of the French Resistance find safe passage to Oakland. In addition to all this lunacy, he must assist the group in the search for their missing liquor license. It was stolen by a member of the Nazi Party—which just so happens to be based in Cincinnati! Falk is hysterical in this entertaining send-up of classic cinema. **Cast:** Peter Falk, Madeline Kahn, James Coco, John Houseman, Ann-Margret, Louise Fletcher, Fernando Lamas, Eileen Brennan, Sid Caesar, Phil Silvers. **Credits:** Dir: Robert Moore; Prod: Ray Stark; Writer: Neil Simon; DP: John A. Alonzo; Ed: Sidney Levin, Michael A. Stevenson; Prod Design: Robert Luthardt; Composer: Patrick Williams; Costumes: Theoni V. Aldredge, John Anderson; Art Director: Phillip Bennett; Set Designer: Chuck Pierce. Color, 92 min. VHS

Cheaper by the Dozen
(1950) Fox
Based on the true-life story of the Gilbreths, a family of 12 raised under the firm but loving hand of Frank Bunker Gilbreth (Webb). The film chronicles the difficulties of caring for such an extensive brood, as Gilbreth and his wife navigate the family through the typical crises and events of youth: tonsillectomies (multiple, in this case), proms, school enrollment, and the like. Webb is the hero of this plotless romp, as delightfully bombastic as Loy is wise. **Cast:** Clifton Webb, Jeanne Crain, Myrna Loy, Betty Lynn, Edgar Buchanan, Barbara Bates, Mildred Natwick, Sara Allgood, Anthony Sydes, Roddy McCaskill. **Credits:** Dir: Walter Lang; Prod: Lamar Trotti; Writer: Frank B. Gilbreth, Lamar Trotti; Story: Ernestine Gilbreth Carey; DP: Leon Shamroy; Ed: J. Watson Webb; Prod Design: Leland Fuller; Composer: Cyril Mockridge, Lionel Newman. Color, 85 min.

Cheers for Miss Bishop
(1941) United Artists
And hooray for those who quietly make a difference in young lives. Perfectly pleasant portrait of the loves, triumphs, and sorrows of a midwestern teacher who served the same school for more than 50 years. **Cast:** Martha Scott, William Gargan, Edmund Gwenn, Sterling Holloway, Rosemary De Camp, Marsha Hunt, Sidney Blackmer, Mary Anderson, Dorothy Peterson, Don Douglas. **Credits:** Dir: Tay Garnett, Richard A. Rowland; Writer: Stephen Vincent Benét, Sheridan Gibney, Adelaide Heilbron; Story: Bess Streeter Aldrich; DP: Hal Mohr; Ed: William Claxton; Composer: Edward Ward. B&W, 95 min. VHS

Cheyenne
(1947) Warner Bros.
Routine Western outing for Walsh contains all the requisite characters and plot lines. A gambling man, Morgan is hired to track down a dangerous outlaw. The outlaw's wife, Wyman, in her attempt to protect her man, falls in love with Morgan. Later a TV series. **Cast:** Dennis Morgan, Jane Wyman, Janis Paige, Bruce Bennet, Alan Hale, Jr., Arthur Kennedy, John Ridgely, Barton MacLane, Tom Tyler, Bob Steele. **Credits:** Dir: Raoul Walsh; Prod: Robert Buckner; Writer: Alan LeMay, Thomas Williamson, Paul I. Wellman; DP: Sidney Hickox; Ed: Christian Nyby; Prod Design: Jack McConaghy, William McGann; Composer: Max Steiner, Leo F. Forbstein; SFX: H. F. Koenekamp; Art Director: Ted Smith. B&W, 100 min.

Cheyenne Autumn
(1964) Warner Bros.
The last Western from director Ford and a farewell to his familiar Monument Valley locations. After portraying Indians as villains in many of his classic Westerns, Ford cast them in a compassionate light in this rueful, elegiac film. The story follows the Cheyenne Indians as they flee their squalid Oklahoma reservation and return to their traditional homeland along the Yellowstone River in Wyoming. Cavalry officer Widmark gets the call to return the tribe to the reservations, but, after he sees the starvation and sickness endured by his quarry, he questions the government's decision. A cast of great stars (including a brief nod from Stewart as Wyatt Earp), and available in a restored version with additional footage. **Cast:** Richard Widmark, Carroll Baker, Karl Malden, Sal Mineo, Ricardo Montalban, James Stewart,

Edward G. Robinson, Dolores Del Rio, Gilbert Roland, Arthur Kennedy. **Credits:** Dir: John Ford; Prod: Bernard Smith; Writer: James R. Webb; DP: William Clothier; Ed: Otho S. Lovering; Prod Design: Richard Day; Composer: Alex North. Color, 158 min. VHS

The Cheyenne Social Club
(1970) National General
Kelly directed this titillation on the open range when cowboys Stewart and Fonda take over a brothel. Arriving in Cheyenne to run his brother's business, Stewart is unpleasantly surprised to discover that he's become the not so proud owner of a cathouse. His attempt to close the joint down results in a major uproar among the men of Cheyenne—and plenty of comic mishaps. Feels like a prank pulled by Hollywood icons tweaking their own images. **Cast:** Henry Fonda, James Stewart, Shirley Jones, Sue Ane Langdon, Elaine Devry, Robert Middleton, Dabbs Greer, Robert J. Wilke, Jackie Joseph. **Credits:** Dir: Gene Kelly; Prod: Gene Kelly; Writer: James Lee Barrett; DP: William Clothier; Ed: Adrienne Fazan; Prod Design: Gene Allen; Composer: Walter Scharf. Color, 103 min. VHS

A Child Is Born
(1940) Warner Bros.
A drama about the everyday life in a maternity ward. Throughout the film seven babies are born, including a set of unwanted twins, and a still-born son. The drama centers around a woman sent to the ward from prison. She is a convicted murderess who must sacrifice her own life to begin the life of her yet unborn baby daughter. Her husband is also faced with the decision between the life of their unborn child and that of his wife. This emotional tale is a remake of an earlier film titled *Life Begins*. **Cast:** Geraldine Fitzgerald, Jeffrey Lynn, Gladys George, Gale Page, Spring Byington, Johnnie Davis, Henry O'Neill, John Litel, Gloria Holden, Johnny Downs. **Credits:** Dir: Lloyd Bacon; Prod: Hal B. Wallis; Writer: Robert Rossen; Story: Mary McDougal Axelson; DP: Charles Rosher; Composer: Heinz Roemheld. B&W, 79 min.

A Child Is Waiting
(1963) United Artists
An unsympathetic, poignant drama by the always challenging Cassavetes. The setting is an institution for mentally retarded children. Lancaster is the director of the institution, a kind

yet sympathetic character. Garland is a teacher whose attentions directed toward a lonely child end up forming a stronger bond than she had anticipated, or wanted. Sobering issues are raised in Cassavetes's typical pseudo-documentary fashion, making the film resonate much more strongly than your typical Hollywood melodrama. **Cast:** Burt Lancaster, Judy Garland, Gena Rowlands, Steven Hill, Bruce Ritchey, Paul Stewart, Lawrence Tierney, Elizabeth Wilson, Barbara Pepper. **Credits:** Dir: John Cassavetes; Prod: Stanley Kramer; Writer: Abby Mann; DP: Joseph La Shelle; Ed: Gene Fowler, Jr.; Prod Design: Rudolph Sternad; Composer: Ernest Gold. B&W, 104 min. VHS, LASER

The Children of Theatre Street
(1978)
A fascinating look at one of the world's greatest schools of dance, the Kirov School in Leningrad. Renowned dancers such as Nijinsky, Karsavina, Anna Pavlova, Nureyev, Baryshnikov, and Makarova were pupils there. This documentary provides a close-up look at the regimen such dedicated young dancers must follow in order to fulfill their dream of entering the company. Narrated by Princess Grace of Monaco, a longtime dance enthusiast and supporter. Academy Award Nomination for Best Feature Documentary. **Cast:** Grace Kelly. **Credits:** Dir: Robert Dornhelm; Writer: Beth Gutcheon; DP: Karl Kofler. Color, 92 min. VHS

The Children's Hour
(1962) United Artists
Wyler remade his own screen adaptation of Hellman's play about two teachers accused of lesbianism at a private girls' school. The fomenter of the scandal is a mean-spirited and mentally unstable girl who convinces her grandmother that she and the other students have been exposed to unspeakable depravity. The younger and more emotionally vulnerable of the two teachers watches her relationship with her fiancé collapse while her alleged lover must come to terms with her own hidden desires. **Cast:** Audrey Hepburn, Shirley MacLaine, James Garner, Miriam Hopkins, Fay Bainter, Veronica Cartwright, Jered Barclay, William Mims, Hope Summers, Karen Balkin. **Credits:** Dir: William Wyler; Prod: William Wyler; Writer: John Michael Hayes; DP: Robert W. Swink; Prod Design: Fernando Carrere; Composer: Alex North. B&W, 108 min. VHS, LASER

Chilly Scenes of Winter
(1979) MGM
As bleak and gray as the title suggests, this adaptation of Ann Beattie's novel features great early performances from Heard, Hurt, and Riegert. Though the story of obsession with a lost love may strike some as adolescent, dewy-eyed romantics will relate just fine. One of the underappreciated Grahame's last roles. **Cast:** John Heard, Mary Beth Hurt, Peter Riegert, Kenneth McMillan, Gloria Grahame, Griffin Dunne, Nora Heflin, Jerry Hardin, Tarah Nutter, Mark Metcalf. **Credits:** Dir: Joan Micklin Silver; Prod: Mark Metcalf, Amy Robinson, Griffin Dunne; Writer: Joan Micklin Silver; DP: Bobby Byrne; Ed: Cynthia Scheider; Prod Design: Peter Jamison; Composer: Ken Lauber. Color, 96 min. VHS

China Gate
(1957) Fox
A Fuller war yarn set in Vietnam when conflict with the Communists was a French heartache. A multinational troop under the command of a French Foreign Legion officer sets out to seize a cache of arms with the officer's Eurasian ex-wife in tow. **Cast:** Gene Barry, Angie Dickinson, Nat King Cole, Paul Dubov, Lee Van Cleef, George Givot, Marcel Dalio, Maurice Marsac, Paul Busch. **Credits:** Dir: Samuel Fuller; Prod: Samuel Fuller; Writer: Samuel Fuller; DP: Joseph Biroc; Ed: Gene Fowler, Jr.; Composer: Victor Young, Max Steiner. B&W, 97 min. VHS

China Girl
(1943) Fox
Hathaway and Hecht team for the story of a freelance newsreel cameraman living in Mandalay during the build-up to Japan's attack on Pearl Harbor. He falls in love with a beautiful Chinese woman who was educated in the United States. In between romantic interludes, he contends with Japanese spies in search of top-secret information that will aid them in their planned invasion. **Cast:** Gene Tierney, George Montgomery, Lynn Bari, Victor McLaglen, Alan Baxter, Sig Rumann, Myron McCormick, Philip Ahn, Robert Blake, Paul Fung. **Credits:** Dir: Henry Hathaway; Prod: Ben Hecht; Writer: Ben Hecht; Story: Darryl F. Zanuck; DP: Lee Garmes; Ed: James B. Clark; Composer: Hugo Friedhofer, Alfred Newman. B&W, 95 min.

China Seas
(1935) MGM
A soggy blend of adventure, comedy, and romance on the high seas, but what a cast! Gable pilots a steamer

plying the China seas, where in one tumultuous journey he fights off pirates, foul weather, and the advances of a blond bundle of trouble known as China Doll. **Cast:** Clark Gable, Jean Harlow, Wallace Beery, Rosalind Russell, Lewis Stone, C. Aubrey Smith, Dudley Digges, Robert Benchley, William Henry, Lilian Bond. **Credits:** Dir: Tay Garnett; Prod: Albert Lewin; Writer: Jules Furthman, James Kevin McGuinness; Story: Crosbie Garstin; DP: Ray June; Ed: William LeVanway; Prod Design: Cedric Gibbons, James Havens, David Townsend; Composer: Herbert Stothart. B&W, 90 min. VHS

The China Syndrome
(1979) Columbia
In this socially-conscious thriller an ambitious female newscaster and her cameraman, an ex-'60s radical with a penchant for conspiracy theories, witness and capture on film a potentially disastrous nuclear accident. Joining forces with a concerned engineer at the plant where the near-meltdown occurred, the reporter and cameraman attempt to expose the subsequent cover-up. In a bizarre (and profitable) bit of synchronicity, the film was produced just before the March 1979 accident at the Three Mile Island nuclear power plant in Pennsylvania. **Cast:** Jane Fonda, Jack Lemmon, Michael Douglas, Scott Brady, James Hampton, Peter Donat, Wilford Brimley, Richard Herd, Daniel Valdez. **Credits:** Dir: James Bridges; Prod: Michael Douglas; Writer: Mike Gray, T. S. Cook, James Bridges; DP: James Crabe; Ed: David Rawlins; Prod Design: George Jenkins. Color, 123 min. VHS, LASER

Chinatown
(1974) Paramount
"It's just Chinatown, Jake." The opaque shrug that ends this 1970s classic embodies the film's world-weary depiction of people who are never what they seem and dark motives that dwell deep below the surface. Like the water that drives the plot, secrets in Chinatown have a way of bubbling up in the most unexpected places, as detective Jake Gittes (Nicholson) discovers when he takes on Evelyn Mulwray (Dunaway) as a client. Not so much a re-creation of the classic-era Chandler and Hammett private-eye stories as an outright celebration of the depravity they only hinted at. A stunning achievement for both Polanski and Towne. Followed by Nicholson's direction of *The Two Jakes* in 1990. Selected as a National Film Registry Outstanding Film. Academy

Award Nominations: 11, including Best Picture; Best Actor: Jack Nicholson; Best Actress: Faye Dunaway; Best Director; Best Cinematography; Best Editing; Best Score. **Academy Awards:** Best Original Screenplay. **Cast:** Jack Nicholson, Faye Dunaway, John Huston, John Hillerman, Burt Young, Perry Lopez, Diane Ladd, Darrell Zwerling, Roy Jenson, Roman Polanski. **Credits:** Dir: Roman Polanski; Prod: Robert Evans; Writer: Robert Towne; DP: John A. Alonzo; Ed: Sam O'Steen; Prod Design: Richard Sylbert; Composer: Jerry Goldsmith; Costumes: Anthea Sylbert. Color, 131 min. VHS, LASER

Chisum
(1970) Warner Bros.
A tough cattle baron fights con artists, corrupt officials—even Billy the Kid—in order to keep his ranch. Wayne's been here before, as have we. For Duke fans only. **Cast:** John Wayne, Forrest Tucker, Christopher George, Glenn Corbett, Ben Johnson, Bruce Cabot, Patric Knowles, Andrew Prine, Richard Jaeckel, Linda Day. **Credits:** Dir: Andrew V. McLaglen; Prod: Andrew J. Fenady; Writer: Andrew J. Fenady; DP: William Clothier; Ed: Robert Simpson; Prod Design: Carl Anderson; Composer: Dominic Frontiere. Color, 111 min. VHS, LASER

Chitty Chitty Bang Bang
(1968) United Artists
Van Dyke's charming as a daydreaming inventor who fixes up an old jalopy and, with the vivid imaginations of his two children and a lady friend, transforms it into a flying, floating wonder car that carries them to a magical kingdom. Inspired by an Ian Fleming idea. **Cast:** Dick Van Dyke, Sally Ann Howes, Lionel Jeffries, Benny Hill, Robert Helpmann, Gert Frobe, James Robertson Justice, Anna Quayle, Barbara Windsor. **Credits:** Dir: Ken Hughes; Prod: Albert R. Broccoli; Writer: Roald Dahl, Ken Hughes, Richard Maibaum; Story: Ian Fleming; DP: Christopher Challis; Ed: John Shirley; Composer: Irwin Kostal. Color, 145 min. VHS, LASER, DVD

A Christmas Carol
(1938) MGM
Though not quite on par with the British version starring Alistair Sim, this workmanlike adaptation is okay nonetheless. A wealthy miser learns how wonderful and fulfilling life can be with a little generosity at Christmas-time from three specters who visit him the night before Christmas. **Cast:** Reginald Owen, Gene Lockhart, Terry Kilburn, Leo G.

Carroll, Kathleen Lockhart, Barry Mackay, Lynne Carver, Lionel Braham, Ann Rutherford. **Credits:** Dir: Edwin L. Marin; Prod: Joseph L. Mankiewicz; Writer: Hugo Butler; Story: Charles Dickens; DP: Sidney Wagner; Ed: George Boemler; Prod Design: Cedric Gibbons, John Detlie; Composer: Franz Waxman. B&W, 70 min. VHS, LASER

Christmas Holiday
(1944) Universal
Durbin a bad girl? Her new husband, played by a sinister Kelly (!), turns out to have a violent temper, and to be engaged in suspicious doings with the help of his mother. Maugham story transplanted to U.S. setting. **Cast:** Deanna Durbin, Gene Kelly, Richard Whorf, Dean Harens, Gladys George, Gale Sondergaard, David Bruce. **Credits:** Dir: Robert Siodmak; Prod: Felix Jackson, Frank Shaw; Writer: Herman J. Mankiewicz; Story: W. Somerset Maugham; DP: Woody Bredell; Ed: Ted J. Kent; Prod Design: John B. Goodman, Robert Clatworthy; Composer: Hans J. Salter. B&W, 93 min.

Christmas in Connecticut
(1945) Warner Bros.
A sharp writer, who has never set foot in a kitchen, passes herself off as the consummate housewife in the column she writes for a women's magazine. When a promotional stunt plants her editor and a war veteran at her fictitious home for Christmas dinner, she has to marry her boyfriend, find a house, and prepare a spectacular meal, pronto. Life grows even more complicated when she starts to fall for the sailor. Stanwyck's perfect in this holiday confection. Remade for cable in 1992 by Arnold Schwarzenegger. **Cast:** Barbara Stanwyck, Dennis Morgan, Sydney Greenstreet, Reginald Gardiner, S. Z. Sakall, Robert Shayne, Una O'Connor, Frank Jenks, Joyce Compton. **Credits:** Dir: Peter Godfrey; Prod: Williams Jacobs; Writer: Lionel Houser, Adele Comandini; Story: Aileen Hamilton; DP: Carl E. Guthrie; Ed: Frank Magee; Prod Design: Stanley Fleischer; Composer: Frederick Hollander; Costumes: Edith Head. B&W, 103 min. VHS, LASER

Christmas in July
(1940) Paramount
Sturges's second film as director is a fast-as-lightning comedy about a store clerk who is tricked into thinking he's won $25,000 in a slogan contest. It isn't until after he's spent his "winnings" on presents for his girlfriend and everyone else who passes his way

that the clerk discovers he's been the victim of a practical joke. The Sturges stock company at its best. **Cast:** Dick Powell, Ellen Drew, Raymond Walburn, William Demarest, Ernest Truex, Al Bridge, Alexander Carr, Franklin Pangborn, Harry Hayden, Rod Cameron. **Credits:** Dir: Preston Sturges; Prod: Paul Jones; Writer: Preston Sturges; DP: Victor Milner; Ed: Ellsworth Hoagland; Composer: Sigmund Krumgold. B&W, 67 min. VHS, LASER

Christopher Strong
(1933) RKO
One of the rare films from Hollywood's classic period directed by a woman, the pioneering Dorothy Arzner, examines a woman aviator's unconventional life. The bold flier finds herself pregnant and in love with a married man, and makes a desperate decision in a world without options. Hepburn is absolutely stunning (particularly in one fireflylike evening gown) and who, after all, could better portray an independent woman in the '30s? **Cast:** Katharine Hepburn, Colin Clive, Billie Burke, Helen Chandler, Ralph Forbes, Irene Browne, Jack La Rue, Margaret Lindsay, Don Stewart. **Credits:** Dir: Dorothy Arzner; Prod: David O. Selznick, Pandro S. Berman; Writer: Zoe Akins; Story: Gilbert Frankau; DP: Bert Glennon; Ed: Arthur Roberts; Prod Design: Van Nest Polglase; Composer: Max Steiner. B&W, 77 min. VHS, LASER

Cimarron
(1931) RKO
The Best Picture of 1931 chronicles one family's experiences in the restless days of settling the American West. Adapted from Edna Ferber's sweeping novel, the story tracks the growth of an Oklahoma town and the homesteaders who came there from the 1890s through the 1920s. Remade in 1960. **Academy Awards:** Best Screenplay; Best Picture. **Cast:** Richard Dix, Irene Dunne, Estelle Taylor, Nance O'Neil, William Collier, Jr., Roscoe Ates, George E. Stone, Stanley Fields, Edna May Oliver, Robert McWade. **Credits:** Dir: Wesley Ruggles; Prod: William LeBaron; Writer: Howard Estabrook; Story: Edna Ferber; DP: Edward Cronjager; Ed: William Hamilton; Prod Design: Max Ree; Composer: Max Steiner. B&W, 130 min. VHS

Cimarron
(1960) MGM
Director Mann, a Western specialist, breathes life (along with color and

widescreen) into the lumbering Ferber novel and the dated first film version. This time Ford is the man of the Old West forging a new identity in the settling of the Oklahoma Territory. **Cast:** Glenn Ford, Maria Schell, Anne Baxter, Arthur O'Connell, Russ Tamblyn, Mercedes McCambridge, Vic Morrow, Charles McGraw, Lili Darvas, Henry Morgan. **Credits:** Dir: Anthony Mann; Prod: Edmund Grainger; Writer: Arnold Schulman; DP: Robert Surtees; Ed: John Dunning; Prod Design: George W. Davis, Addison Hehr; Composer: Franz Waxman. Color, 147 min. VHS

The Cincinnati Kid
(1965) MGM
A rising cardshark challenges a veteran player for the chance to be known as "The Man." Set in the swampy hedonism of New Orleans during the Great Depression, the card game is a gritty exploration of the manly sport of stud poker. As the men battle across the card table, the upstart realizes that someone is forcing the honest dealer to help him win. Peckinpah started the production; note the screenplay credit to Lardner and Southern. **Cast:** Steve McQueen, Ann-Margret, Edward G. Robinson, Karl Malden, Tuesday Weld, Joan Blondell, Rip Torn, Jack Weston, Cab Calloway. **Credits:** Dir: Norman Jewison; Prod: Martin Ransohoff; Writer: Ring Lardner, Terry Southern; DP: Philip H. Lathrop; Ed: Hal Ashby; Prod Design: George W. Davis, Edward C. Carfagno; Composer: Lalo Schifrin. Color, 113 min. VHS

Cinderella
(1950) Disney
The original Disney animated classic based on Charles Perrault's 17th-century fable about a poor stepdaughter transformed into a vision of beauty and sent to the royal ball by her Fairy Godmother to meet her Prince Charming and live happily ever after. Academy Award Nominations: 3, including Best Song ("Bibbidy-Bobbidi-Boo"). **Cast:** Eleanor Audley, Lucille Bliss, Verna Felton, William Phipps, Ilene Woods, James MacDonald, Rhoda Williams, Luis Van Rooten, Don Barclay, Claire DuBrey. **Credits:** Dir: Wilfred Jackson, Hamilton Luske, Clyde Geronimi; Prod: Walt Disney; Writer: Bill Peet, Ted Sears, Homer Brightman, Ken Anderson, Erdman Penner, Winston Hibler, Harry Reeves, Joe Rinaldi; Story: Charles Perrault; Ed: Donald Halliday; Composer: Oliver Wallace, Paul J. Smith. Color, 76 min. VHS, LASER

Cinderella Liberty
(1973) Fox
A good-hearted sailor begins a bittersweet romance with a prostitute who has an illegitimate black son in need of a father. When she runs away, the sailor goes AWOL to find her. Strong performances all around. **Cast:** James Caan, Marsha Mason, Kirk Calloway, Eli Wallach, Burt Young, Dabney Coleman, Allyn Ann McLerie, B. Kirby, Jr., Fred Sadoff, Allan Arbus. **Credits:** Dir: Mark Rydell; Prod: Mark Rydell; Writer: Darryl Ponicsan; DP: Vilmos Zsigmond; Ed: Donn Cambern, Patrick Kennedy; Prod Design: Leon Ericksen; Composer: John Williams. Color, 117 min. VHS

Cinderfella
(1960) Paramount
For Lewis fanatics only, a lavish remake of the Cinderella story, with Jerry as the homely servant to his Beverly Hills stepmother and stepbrother. Odd musical segments, but Count Basie joins in. **Cast:** Jerry Lewis, Ed Wynn, Anna Maria Alberghetti, Judith Anderson, Henry Silva, Robert Hutton, Count Basie. **Credits:** Dir: Jerry Lewis; Prod: Jerry Lewis; Writer: Frank Tashlin; DP: Haskell Boggs; Ed: Arthur Schmidt; Prod Design: Hal Pereira, Henry Bumstead; Composer: Walter Scharf. Color, 88 min. VHS

The Circus
(1928) United Artists
This lavish production features Chaplin directing and also doing his Little Tramp bit. This time, the hapless vagabond seeks refuge from the law among the members of a traveling circus. He soon falls in love with the beautiful equestrienne and the film audience is treated not only to a big-top spectacular, but a charming romance as well. **Cast:** Charlie Chaplin, Allan Garcia, Merna Kennedy, Harry Crocker, George Davis. **Credits:** Dir: Charlie Chaplin; Prod: Charlie Chaplin; Writer: Charlie Chaplin; DP: Rollie Totheroh, Jack Wilson, Mark Marlott. B&W, 105 min. VHS, LASER

Circus World
(1964) Paramount
Hollywood's take on the big-top life as the Duke shepherds his three-ring extravaganza through a European tour while searching for the aerialist he loved and lost—the mother of his daughter. Plenty of real circus performers and excitement balance the melodrama. **Cast:** John Wayne, Rita Hayworth, Claudia Cardinale, Richard Conte, John Smith, Lloyd Nolan, Wanda Rotha, Kay Walsh, Henri Dantes, Katharyna. **Credits:** Dir: Henry Hathaway; Prod: Samuel Bronston; Writer: Ben Hecht, Julian Halevy, James Edward Grant; Story: Philip Yordan, Nicholas Ray; DP: Jack Hildyard, Claude Renoir; Ed: Dorothy Spencer; Composer: Dimitri Tiomkin; Costumes: Renie. Color, 135 min. VHS

The Citadel
(1938) MGM
Donat stars as a devoted doctor who labors over treating Welsh miners infected with tuberculosis but ends up treating rich London patients at the risk of losing his faith in himself. The death of a close friend shakes him out of his slump and he returns to the cause of the poor. Based on the novel by A. J. Cronin. **Cast:** Robert Donat, Rosalind Russell, Rex Harrison, Ralph Richardson, Emlyn Williams, Penelope Dudley Ward, Francis L. Sullivan, Mary Clare, Cecil Parker, Nora Swinburne. **Credits:** Dir: King Vidor; Prod: Victor Saville; Writer: Ian Dalrymple, Frank Wead, Elizabeth Hill, Emlyn Williams; DP: Harry Stradling; Ed: Charles Frend; Prod Design: Lazare Meerson, Alfred Junge; Composer: Louis Levy. B&W, 114 min. VHS

Citizen Kane
(1941) RKO
Welles's greatest achievement, and a landmark of cinema history. The narrative charts the rise to power of a newspaper publisher whose wealth and power ultimately leave him alone in his castlelike refuge. Every aspect of the production marked an advance in film language: the deep-focus, deeply shadowed cinematography; the

discontinuous narrative (in a screenplay by Herman Mankiewicz); the innovative use of sound and score; the ensemble acting forged in the fires of Welles's Mercury Theater. Essential viewing. The laserdisc contains a second audio track with commentary by a noted film historian, and the 50th-anniversary release includes the restored original movie plus the 30-minute documentary *Reflections on Citizen Kane,* featuring the recollections of the actors and editors along with commentary by other filmmakers. Selected for the National Film Registry. Academy Award Nominations: 9, including Best Picture; Best Actor; Orson Welles; Best Director; Best Cinematography; Best Editing; Best Score. **Academy Awards:** Best Original Screenplay. **Cast:** Orson Welles, Joseph Cotten, Agnes Moorehead, Everett Sloane, Dorothy Comingore, Ruth Warrick, Ray Collins, Erskine Sanford, William Alland, Paul Stewart. **Credits:** Dir: Orson Welles; Prod: Orson Welles; Writer: Herman J. Mankiewicz, Orson Welles; DP: Gregg Toland; Ed: Mark Robson, Robert Wise; Prod Design: Van Nest Polglase, Perry Ferguson; Composer: Bernard Herrmann; Costumes: Edward Stevenson; SFX: Vernon L. Walker. B&W, 120 min. **VHS, LASER**

Citizens Band

(1977) Paramount
The '70s CB trend provides the backdrop for Demme's critically praised slice-of-life comedy. A two-timing truck driver who goes by the handle "Chrome Angel" has a wife and family in Portland, Oregon, and another wife and family in Dallas, Texas. Things are complicated when he has an accident in a small town and both wives are summoned to his hospital bedside. **Cast:** Paul Le Mat, Candy Clark, Ed Begley, Jr., Ann Wedgeworth, Charles Napier, Roberts Blossom, Bruce McGill, Marcia Rodd, Alix Elias. **Credits:** Dir: Jonathan Demme; Prod: Freddie Fields; Writer: Paul Brickman; DP: Jordan Cronenweth; Ed: John F. Link; Prod Design: Bill Malley; Composer: Bill Conti. Color, 98 min. **VHS**

City Across the River

(1949) Universal
A gritty urban drama focusing on youth gangs. Set in a Brooklyn slum, two members of a gang named the Amboy Dukes pick a fight with their schoolteacher and accidentally kill him. On the lam, the two friends become suspicious of each other, eventually coming to blows atop a tenement rooftop

as the police close in. **Cast:** Stephen McNally, Thelma Ritter, Luis Van Rooten, Jeff Corey, Sharon McManus, Sue England, Barbara Whiting, Richard Benedict, Anabel Shaw, Robert Osterloh. **Credits:** Dir: Maxwell Shane; Prod: Maxwell Shane; Writer: Dennis J. Cooper, Maxwell Shane; Story: Irving Shulman; DP: Maury Gertsman; Ed: Ted J. Kent; Prod Design: Bernard Herzbrun, Emrich Nicholson; Composer: Walter Scharf. B&W, 91 min.

City for Conquest

(1940) Warner Bros.
A couple who split up to pursue individual careers end up as failures. The man's attempt at becoming a boxer ends in blindness and the woman's pursuit of a dancing career is ruined due to an unsavory partner. **Cast:** James Cagney, Ann Sheridan, Frank Craven, Arthur Kennedy, Donald Crisp, Frank McHugh, George Tobias, Elia Kazan, Anthony Quinn, Jerome Cowan. **Credits:** Dir: Anatole Litvak; Prod: Anatole Litvak; Writer: John Wexley; Story: Aben Kandel; DP: Sol Polito, James Wong Howe; Ed: William Holmes; Prod Design: Robert M. Haas; Composer: Max Steiner. B&W, 101 min. **VHS**

City Lights

(1931) United Artists
A Chaplin masterpiece (and last silent film—he resisted as long as possible) about a blind girl who is restored to sight with the help and love of Chaplin's Little Tramp, who stumbles into the money for her eye surgery. A must even for those who think they don't like silent film. **Cast:** Charlie Chaplin, Virginia Cherrill, Harry Myers, Hank Mann, Florence Lee. **Credits:** Dir: Charlie Chaplin; Prod: Charlie Chaplin; Writer: Charlie Chaplin; DP: Rollie Totheroh; Composer: Alfred Newman. B&W, 87 min. **VHS, LASER**

City Streets

(1931) Paramount
Hammett's only story written expressly for the screen is also an uncharacteristic gangster drama from Mamoulian and his second feature. The daughter of a racketeer falls for The Kid, a local carnival worker. She tries to motivate her beau to join her father's rackets so that the two can live together in luxury. But after her own father turns on her, she's implicated in the crimes of her father and imprisoned. She returns from jail to find The Kid has become a gangster. Thought to be one of Al Capone's favorites. **Cast:** Guy Kibbee, Gary Cooper, Sylvia Sidney, Paul Lukas,

Wynne Gibson, Stanley Fields, William Boyd. **Credits:** Dir: Rouben Mamoulian; Prod: E. Lloyd Sheldon; Writer: Oliver H. P. Garrett, Max Marcin; Story: Dashiell Hammett; DP: Lee Garmes; Ed: Viola Lawrence, William Shea; Composer: Sidney B. Cutner. B&W, 82 min.

City That Never Sleeps

(1953) Republic
John leads the perfect double life: happily married, hardworking cop by day; wretched love slave to a chanteuse by night. When his father is murdered, he's forced to choose between his two lives in order to successfully track the killer. **Cast:** Gig Young, Mala Powers, Edward Arnold, Chill Wills, William Talman, Paula Raymond, Marie Windsor, Wally Cassell. **Credits:** Dir: John H. Auer; Prod: John H. Auer; Writer: Steve Fisher; DP: John L. Russell, Jr.; Ed: Fred Allen; Prod Design: James Sullivan; Composer: Dale Butts. B&W, 90 min. **VHS**

Civilization

(1916) Ince
This epic drama with a powerful message was the masterwork of director Thomas H. Ince, D. W. Griffith's only artistic rival in the teens. Released just before the United States' entry into WWI. Set in a make-believe kingdom called Nurma, *Civilization* makes its pacifist pleas by focusing on that mythical country's own declaration of war and its swift and catastrophic results. The horrors of battle are amply illustrated through a series of symbolic sequences and exemplary melodramatic storylines. In the end, only the intervention of Christ himself can spare further bloodshed and destruction. **Cast:** Howard Hickman, Enid Markey, Lola May, J. Barney Sherry, Raymond B. West, Reginald Barker, Herschel Mayall, George Fisher, Frank Burke. **Credits:** Dir: Thomas Ince, Raymond B. West; Prod: Thomas H. Ince; Writer: C. Gardner Sullivan; DP: Joseph H. August, Irvin Willat; Ed: LeRoy Stone; Composer: Victor Schertzinger. B&W, 102 min. **VHS**

The Clairvoyant

(1934) Fox
A fraudulent psychic (Rains at his creepiest) begins to have terrifying, authentic flashes into the future. The visions, which all seem to herald impending disasters, catch up with him and he is jailed for causing one accident that he predicted. He is saved only by his ability to tell more information about the survival of some of the

victims. Same plot was used with Edward G. Robinson in *The Night Has a Thousand Eyes* in 1948. **Cast:** Claude Rains, Fay Wray, Jane Baxter, Mary Clare, Athole Stewart, Felix Aylmer, Donald Calthrop, Jack Raine, C. Denier Warren, Ben Field. **Credits:** Dir: Maurice Elvey; Prod: Michael Balcon; Writer: Charles Bennett; DP: Glen MacWilliams; Ed: Paul Capon; Prod Design: Alfred Junge; Composer: Arthur Benjamin. B&W, 80 min. **VHS**

Clambake
(1967) United Artists
Presley stars as a millionaire playboy who decides that he doesn't need his father's money to succeed. He trades identities with a water-ski instructor in a posh Miami Beach resort, signs up for the Orange Bowl Regatta, and tries to win over a lovely young lass. But she wants to marry rich, and has no interest in the "poor" racer. So Presley sets out to make her fall for him before she finds out that he's loaded. Only for Elvis completists. **Cast:** Elvis Presley, Shelley Fabares, Will Hutchins, Bill Bixby, James Gregory, Gary Merrill, Amanda Harley, Suzie Kaye, Angelique Pettyjohn. **Credits:** Dir: Arthur Nadel; Prod: Jules Levy, Arthur Gardner, Arnold Laven; Writer: Arthur Browne, Jr.; DP: William Margulies; Ed: Tom Rolf; Prod Design: Lloyd S. Papez; Composer: Jeff Alexander. Color, 100 min. **VHS**

Clarence, the Cross-Eyed Lion
(1965) MGM
Dr. Marsh Tracy, head of an African animal-behavior center, captures an oddly placid lion whom he names Clarence. The beast's eyes, as it turns out, are crossed. When Dr. Tracy and an anthropologist are kidnapped by poachers, Clarence shows his paws, jaws, and claws work superbly. **Cast:** Betsy Drake, Cheryl Miller, Richard Haydn, Marshall Thompson, Alan Caillou, Rockne Tarkington, Maurice Marsac, Robert Doqui. **Credits:** Dir: Andrew Marton; Prod: Leonard Kaufman; Writer: Alan Caillou; Story: Marshall Thompson, Art Arthur; DP: Lamar Boren; Ed: Warren Adams; Prod Design: George W. Davis, Eddie Imazu; Composer: Al Mack. Color, 98 min. **VHS**

Clash by Night
(1952) RKO
Bruised by city life, Mae Doyle (Stanwyck) returns to the safe haven of her hometown, a small fishing community. There she finds comfort in the arms of a loving fisherman whom she marries;

but before too long Mae has thrown herself into another, more passionate affair with a bitter, angry man. She willingly abandons her husband and child to pursue this romance, only to discover that her homecoming has permanently altered her view of the world and finds she would gladly return to her husband if he can ever forgive her. Steamy potboiler based on Odets's play abetted by Lang and terrific performance by Stanwyck. **Cast:** Barbara Stanwyck, Robert Ryan, Paul Douglas, Marilyn Monroe, J. Carrol Naish, Keith Andes, Silvio Minciotti, Julius Tannen. **Credits:** Dir: Fritz Lang; Prod: Harriet Parsons; Writer: Alfred Hayes, David Dortort; Story: Clifford Odets; DP: Nicholas Musuraca; Ed: George Amy; Prod Design: Albert S. D'Agostino, Carroll Clark; Composer: Roy Webb. B&W, 105 min. **VHS, LASER**

Class of '44
(1973) Warner Bros.
Hermie, Oscy, and Benjy from *The Summer of '42* are back, and now they're living under the threat of world war as they begin their college careers. Sexual politics in the '40s. **Cast:** Gary Grimes, Jerry Houser, Oliver Conant, Sam Bottoms, William Atherton, Deborah Winters, Murray Westgate, Joe Ponazecki, Marion Waldman, Mary Long. **Credits:** Dir: Paul Bogart; Prod: Paul Bogart; Writer: Herman Raucher; DP: Andrew Laszlo; Ed: Michael A. Hoey; Prod Design: Ben Edwards; Composer: David Shire. Color, 95 min. **VHS**

Claudia
(1942) Fox
McGuire made her Hollywood debut in a role she originated on Broadway, a heartwarming domestic comedy about an innocent young bride who learns the awkward truths about marriage and life. She survives her initiation into the rites of adulthood as well as her mother's (Claire) inevitable death with her good humor sweetly intact. **Cast:** Dorothy McGuire, Robert Young, Ina Claire, Reginald Gardiner, Olga Baclanova, Jean Howard, Frank Tweddell, Elsa Janssen. **Credits:** Dir: Edmund Goulding; Prod: William Perlberg; Writer: Morrie Rysking; Story: Rose Franken; DP: Leon Shamroy; Ed: Robert Simpson; Prod Design: James Basevi, Albert Hogsett; Composer: Alfred Newman. B&W, 91 min.

Claudia and David
(1946) Fox
This sequel to *Claudia* continues the comedic story of a loving young wife.

Claudia proves herself to be an overprotective mother, and her husband worries about the faith she puts into a seer's prediction. The young wife gets jealous when a woman asks her husband for some business advice, but does not mind when a young married man flirts with her. **Cast:** Dorothy McGuire, Robert Young, Mary Astor, John Sutton, Gail Patrick, Rose Hobart, Harry Davenport, Florence Bates, Jerome Cowan. **Credits:** Dir: Walter Lang; Prod: William Perlberg; Writer: Rose Franken, William Brown Meloney; DP: Joseph Le Shelle; Ed: Robert Simpson; Composer: Cyril Mockridge. B&W, 78 min.

Cleopatra
(1934) Paramount
Grandiose, epic as only DeMille can be, and vintage early Hollywood. Colbert stars as the captivating and powerful Queen of Egypt. When Julius Caesar, the leader of the Roman Empire, succumbs to the charms of the sultry Cleopatra, he creates a scandal big enough to shake the marble pillars of Rome. The ruler pays dearly for his romance, for the outraged Roman Senate repudiates him and the fickle Cleopatra decides to protect her interests by bestowing her affections on her former lover's rival, Marc Antony. Colbert makes an elegantly imperious Queen—particularly in the milk bath! Remake of the 1917 Theda Bara vehicle. Remade in 1963 with Elizabeth Taylor and Richard Burton. **Academy Awards:** Best Cinematography. **Cast:** Claudette Colbert, Warren William, Henry Wilcoxon, Gertrude Michael, Joseph Schildkraut, Ian Keith, C. Aubrey Smith, Leonard Mudie, Irving Pichel, Arthur Hohl. **Credits:** Dir: Cecil B. DeMille; Prod: Cecil B. DeMille; Writer: Waldemar Young, Vincent Lawrence; DP: Victor Milner; Ed: Anne Bauchens; Composer: Rudolph G. Kopp. B&W, 101 min. **VHS, LASER**

Cleopatra
(1963) Fox
A long, sprawling, and epic love story depicting Cleopatra's manipulation of Caesar and Marc Antony in her ill-fated attempt to save the Egyptian Empire. Film was cut from 243 minutes to 222 at the time of its release. The most expensive film of its time, due largely to overruns caused by Taylor and Burton's tempestuous relationship on- and offscreen. Launched in the tabloids, it survived multiple starts and stops, and the near-bankruptcy of Fox, to become big box office. Acade-

Cleopatra (1963)

my Award Nominations: 9, including Best Picture; Best Actor: Rex Harrison; Best Editing. **Academy Awards:** Best Color Cinematography; Best Costume Design (Color); Best Special Visual Effects; Best Art Direction—Set Decoration (Color). **Cast:** Elizabeth Taylor, Richard Burton, Rex Harrison, Roddy McDowall, Pamela Brown, George Cole, Hume Cronyn, Cesare Danova, Kenneth Haigh, Andrew Keir. **Credits:** Dir: Joseph L. Mankiewicz; Prod: Walter Wanger; Writer: Joseph L. Mankiewicz, Ranald MacDougall, Sidney Buchman; DP: Leon Shamroy; Ed: Dorothy Spencer; Prod Design: John DeCuir; Composer: Alex North. Color, 246 min. **VHS, LASER**

The Climax
(1944) Universal
The house physician of Vienna's Royal Theater falls madly in love with their newest diva, only to murder her when success threatens to take her away. Years later, when another new star arrives with an identical voice, her young boyfriend and the doctor vie over the young soprano's fate. An unusual Technicolor creeper. **Cast:** Boris Karloff, Susanna Foster, Turhan Bey, Gale Sondergaard, Thomas Gomez, June Vincent, Jane Farrar, Scotty Beckett, George Dolenz, Ludwig Stossel. **Credits:** Dir: George Waggner; Prod: George Waggner; Writer: Curt Siodmak, Lynn Starling; DP: Hal Mohr, W. Howard Greene; Ed: Russell Schoengarth; Prod Design: John B. Goodman, Howard Golitzen; Composer: Edward Ward. Color, 86 min. **VHS**

Clive of India
(1935) United Artists
A sprawling epic centered on the English soldier-politician Robert Clive, conquering armies and facing obstacles in exotic India. The story follows him from his beginnings as an abrasive clerk with the East India Company, and sees him eventually stand trial as a betrayer of his country. Equal emphasis goes to Clive's relationship with his wife, who would like him to settle down and live safely. **Cast:** Ronald Colman, Loretta Young, Colin Clive, Francis Lister, C. Aubrey Smith, Cesar Romero, Montagu Love, Lumsden Hare, Ferdinand Munier, Gilbert Emery. **Credits:** Dir: Richard Boleslawski; Writer: W. P. Lipscomb, R. J. Minney; DP: J. Peverell Marley; Composer: Alfred Newman. B&W, 92 min.

Cloak and Dagger
(1946) Warner Bros.
An American scientist goes undercover for the O.S.S. in Lang's WWII tale of romance and espionage. Professor Alva Jesper travels through Switzerland and Italy to free a colleague who has been kidnapped by the Nazis and is being forced to construct an atomic bomb. While pursuing his spy duties, the American falls in love with the lovely Italian partisan who has been brought in to help him on his mission. **Cast:** Gary Cooper, Lilli Palmer, Robert Alda, Vladimir Sokoloff, Ludwig Stossel, J. Edward Bromberg, Helene Thimig, Marc Lawrence, Marjorie Hoshelle, Dan Seymour. **Credits:** Dir:

Fritz Lang; Prod: Milton Sperling; Writer: Albert Maltz, Ring Lardner; DP: Sol Polito; Ed: Christian Nyby; Prod Design: Max Parker; Composer: Max Steiner. B&W, 106 min. **VHS, LASER**

The Clock
(1945) MGM
All in one 48-hour leave, a soldier meets an office worker, falls in love, and marries her. The film lovingly re-creates the landmarks of New York City, especially the magnificent old Penn Station, to serve as the grand backdrop for this whirlwind courtship. Unlike many sentimental romantic tales this film is built on the small, subtle details of two people falling in love. **Cast:** Judy Garland, Robert Walker, James Gleason, Keenan Wynn, Marshall Thompson, Lucille Gleason, Ruth Brady, Chester Clute, Dick Elliott. **Credits:** Dir: Vincente Minnelli; Prod: Arthur Freed; Writer: Robert Nathan, Joseph Schrank; DP: George J. Folsey; Ed: George White; Prod Design: Cedric Gibbons, William Ferrari; Composer: George Bassman. B&W, 91 min. **VHS, LASER**

Close Encounters of the Third Kind
(1977) Columbia
Spielberg's watershed film about a man who becomes obsessed with meeting extraterrestrials after encountering a UFO on an abandoned road one night. The laserdisc features interviews with Spielberg, composer Williams, and special effects man Trumbull, as well as previously cut material. Academy Award Nominations: 8, including Best Supporting Actress: Melinda Dillon; Best Director; Best Editing; Best Score; Best Visual Effects. **Academy Awards:** Best Cinematography; Best Sound Effects Editing. **Cast:** Richard Dreyfuss, Teri Garr, Melinda Dillon, François Truffaut, Bob Balaban, Cary Guffey, Pat McNamara, Warren Kemmerling, Roberts Blossom, Lance Henriksen. **Credits:** Dir: Steven Spielberg; Prod: Michael Phillips, Julia Phillips; Writer: Steven Spielberg; DP: Vilmos Zsigmond; Ed: Michael Kahn; Prod Design: Joe Alves; Composer: John Williams; SFX: Douglas Trumbull, Roy Arbogast. Color, 277 min. **VHS, LASER**

Close to My Heart
(1951) Warner Bros.
Milland and Tierney play a sweet young couple interested in adopting a foundling that has been turned over to police headquarters. As the adoption proceeds, Tierney becomes more bonded to the baby. Milland seeks the

identity and background of the child, and the adoption agency begins to question his stability. After he discovers that the baby's father is a murderer with a date on death row he makes one final plea to the agency. **Cast:** Ray Milland, Gene Tierney, Fay Bainter, Howard St. John, Ann Morrison, Baby John Winslow, James Seay, Mary Beth Hughes. **Credits:** Dir: William Keighley; Prod: William Jacobs; Writer: William Keighley, James R. Webb; DP: Robert Burks; Ed: Clarence Kolster; Prod Design: Leo K. Kuter; Composer: Max Steiner. B&W, 90 min.

The Clown
(1952) MGM
Skelton plays a rare dramatic role as a clown whose life was shattered by alcoholism. After losing his wife to divorce and almost his son's love as well, he makes a desperate attempt to straighten out his life. **Cast:** Red Skelton, Jane Greer, Tim Considine, Loring Smith. **Credits:** Dir: Robert Z. Leonard; Prod: William Wright; Writer: Martin Rackin; DP: Paul Vogel; Ed: Gene Ruggiero; Prod Design: Cedric Gibbons, Wade Rubottom. B&W, 92 min. **VHS**

Cluny Brown
(1946) Fox
A young girl is sent away to be a maid to a wealthy, snobbish family after posing as a socially prominent young woman in order to meet a famous Czechoslovakian author. The author, who has run away from the Nazis before the outbreak of the war, stays at the family's country home. The Lubitsch touch applied to gentle social satire. **Cast:** Charles Boyer, Jennifer Jones, Peter Lawford, Helen Walker, Reginald Gardiner, Reginald Owen, C. Aubrey Smith, Richard Haydn, Margaret Bannerman. **Credits:** Dir: Ernst Lubitsch; Prod: Ernst Lubitsch; Writer: Samuel Hoffenstein, Elizabeth Reinhardt; DP: Joseph Le Shelle; Ed: Dorothy Spencer; Prod Design: Lyle Wheeler, J. Russell Spencer; Composer: Cyril Mockridge. B&W, 100 min.

Cobra Woman
(1944) Universal
Evil-twin drama. A lovely young thing is snatched on the eve of her wedding. Her fiancé follows, with a helpful native boy in tow, and discovers she has been taken to an island where her evil twin sister is tyrannical high priestess. His fiancée, it turns out, is the rightful ruler, and has been brought to take her sister's place. The struggle for control is complicated by exotic ritual, native

superstition, and the eruptions of a neighboring volcano. **Cast:** Maria Montez, Jon Hall, Lon Chaney, Jr., Edgar Barrier, Sabu. **Credits:** Dir: Robert Siodmak; Prod: George Waggner; Writer: Gene Lewis, Richard Brooks; Story: W. S. Scott Darling; DP: George Robinson, W. Howard Greene; Ed: Charles Maynard; Prod Design: Alexander Golitzen, John B. Goodman; Composer: Edward Ward. Color, 71 min.

The Cobweb
(1955) MGM
At a psychiatric care hospital, the wife of the head doctor decides the site's library is in need of new drapes. This small change sparks a conflict among the staff members that reveals covert romantic liaisons and tensions. Minnelli-directed potboiler with a great cast. **Cast:** Richard Widmark, Lauren Bacall, Gloria Grahame, Charles Boyer, Lillian Gish, John Kerr, Susan Strasberg, Oscar Levant, Tommy Rettig, Paul Stewart. **Credits:** Dir: Vincente Minnelli; Prod: John Houseman; Writer: John Paxton, William Gibson; DP: George J. Folsey; Ed: Harold F. Kress; Composer: Leonard Rosenman. Color, 125 min. **LASER**

The Cocoanuts
(1929) Paramount
The first, and widely regarded to be the zaniest, of the Marx Brothers' films. The film takes place in a Miami hotel during the land boom, and the Marxes hilariously oversee the arrival and departure of herds of comical millionaire travelers. The brothers freely reign ad-lib and riff on the Kaufman script. Florey was better known for his expressionist horror films. **Cast:** Groucho Marx, Chico Marx, Harpo Marx, Zeppo Marx, Margaret Dumont, Mary Eaton, Oscar Shaw, Kay Francis, Basil Ruysdael. **Credits:** Dir: Robert Florey, Joseph Stanley; Writer: George S. Kaufman, Morrie Ryskind; DP: George J. Folsey. B&W, 96 min. **VHS, LASER, DVD**

Coffy
(1973) AIP
Coffy is a nurse out to avenge her 11-year-old sister, who has lost her mind through the use of drugs. This film propelled leading lady Grier to Blaxploitation sex symbol stardom (and a resurgent career thanks to Quentin Tarantino and *Jackie Brown*). **Cast:** Pam Grier, Robert Doqui, Allan Arbus, Booker Bradshaw, William Elliott, Sid Haig, Barry Cahill. **Credits:** Dir: Jack Hill; Prod: Robert A. Papazian; Writer: Jack Hill; DP: Paul Lohmann; Ed:

Charles McClelland; Prod Design: Perry Ferguson; Composer: Roy Ayers. Color, 91 min. **VHS, LASER**

Cold Turkey
(1971) United Artists
Van Dyke is a minister leading his entire flock on a crusade to give up smoking for 30 days for a $25 million prize. An entire town with withdrawal symptoms is not a pretty sight but it is a funny one. **Cast:** Dick Van Dyke, Jean Stapleton, Bob Newhart, Vincent Gardenia, Pippa Scott, Tom Poston, Edward Everett Horton, Bob Elliott, Ray Goulding, Barnard Hughes. **Credits:** Dir: Norman Lear; Prod: Norman Lear; Writer: Norman Lear; DP: Charles F. Wheeler; Ed: John C. Horger; Prod Design: Arch Bacon; Composer: Randy Newman. Color, 99 min. **VHS, LASER**

Colleen
(1936) Warner Bros.
Rarely-seen musical concerning an eccentric man who buys a dress shop and then falls for the woman he puts in charge of the shop. Terrific stars from Depression-era musical comedy. **Cast:** Dick Powell, Ruby Keeler, Jack Oakie, Joan Blondell, Hugh Herbert, Louise Fazenda. **Credits:** Dir: Alfred E. Green; Writer: Herbert Hugh, Sig Herzig, Robert Lord, Peter Milne; DP: George Barns; Ed: Byron Haskin; Prod Design: Max Parker; Composer: Harry Warren. B&W, 89 min.

College Coach
(1933) Warner Bros.
A tour de force performance by O'Brien as Coach Gore highlights this sojourn into the jungle of college gridiron. The coach is a ruthless, cynical hypocrite, driven to exploit his team and win at any cost, but the film succeeds in balancing this portrayal with comic relief. Several songs, including performances by Powell (oddly anomalous in the backfield), are also included. Note early appearances of John Wayne and Ward Bond. **Cast:** Dick Powell, Ann Dvorak, Pat O'Brien, Arthur Byron, Lyle Talbot, Hugh Herbert, Guinn "Big Boy" Williams, Donald Meek, John Wayne, Ward Bond. **Credits:** Dir: William Wellman, Jr.; Prod: Robert Lord; Writer: Niven Busch, Manuel Seff; DP: Arthur Todd; Ed: Thomas Pratt; Art Director: Okey Jack. B&W, 75 min.

College Humor
(1933) Paramount
Large cast of noteworthies enlivens this lightweight musical sendup of the college movie, featuring Crosby as a

(not surprisingly) singing professor who gets the girl first and stardom later. Perhaps inevitably, there is football, with Arlen as the gridiron star supplanted romantically by Crosby and athletically by Oakie. Burns and Allen appear briefly to create mayhem at a fraternity dance. **Cast:** Bing Crosby, Jack Oakie, Richard Arlen, Mary Carlisle, Mary Kornman, George Burns, Gracie Allen, Joseph Sauers, Lona Andre, Edward J. Nugent. **Credits:** Dir: Wesley Ruggles; Writer: Claude Binyon, Frank Butler; Story: Dean Fales; DP: Leo Tover; Composer: Sam Coslow, Arthur Johnston. B&W, 68 min.

College Swing
(1938) Paramount
An incredible all-star cast that includes Burns and Allen, Hope, and a young Grable pitches in to rescue a fairly silly plot about Allen taking over a college. Based on a story by Ted Lesser, adapted by Frederick Hazlitt Brennan—and Preston Sturges took an uncredited crack at the script, too. **Cast:** Bob Hope, George Burns, Martha Raye, Edward Everett Horton, Ben Blue, Jackie Coogan, John Payne, Betty Grable, Gracie Allen. **Credits:** Dir: Raoul Walsh; Prod: Lewis E. Gensler; Writer: Walter DeLeon, Francis Martin; DP: Victor Milner; Ed: LeRoy Stone. B&W, 86 min. **VHS**

Colorado Territory
(1949) Warner Bros.
A Western set in the early days of the Wild West. Its antihero, outlaw Wes McQueen, has a long history of misdeeds and is unable to change. His love interest is an equally gutsy dance-hall girl, and together, on the run from an avenging posse, they try their best to remain alive and bullet-free. **Cast:** Joel McCrea, Virginia Mayo, Dorothy Malone, Henry Hull, John Archer, James Mitchell, Morris Ankrum, Basil Ruysdael, Frank Puglia, Ian Wolfe. **Credits:** Dir: Raoul Walsh; Prod: Anthony Veiller; Writer: Edmund H. North, John Twist; Story: W. R. Burnett; DP: Sidney Hickox; Ed: Owen Marks; Prod Design: Ted Smith; Composer: David Buttolph. B&W, 94 min.

Colossus—The Forbin Project
(1970) Universal
A U.S. Defense Department computer, named Colossus, develops a mind of its own and starts sharing classified information with its Russian counterpart, a computer called Guardian. A frighteningly believable thriller that

was ahead of its time in 1970 and, remarkably, is still timely. **Cast:** Susan Clark, Eric Braeden, Gordon Pinsent, William Schallert, Georg Stanford Brown, Willard Sage, Martin E. Brooks, Marion Ross, Leonid Rostoff, Alex Rodine. **Credits:** Dir: Joseph Sargent; Prod: Stanley Chase; Writer: James Bridges; DP: Gene Polito; Ed: Folmar Blangsted; Prod Design: John Lloyd, Alexander Golitzen; Composer: Michel Colombier. Color, 100 min. **VHS**

Coma
(1978) United Artists
Something eerie is going on at Boston Memorial—patients with minor problems are slipping into irreversible comas, and a doctor is targeted when she suspects her colleagues of foul play. A superior hospital-mystery flick based on the best-selling book by Robin Cook. **Cast:** Genevieve Bujold, Michael Douglas, Richard Widmark, Elizabeth Ashley, Rip Torn, Tom Selleck, Lois Chiles, Hari Rhodes, Gary Barton, Frank Downing. **Credits:** Dir: Michael Crichton; Prod: Martin Erlichman; Writer: Michael Crichton; DP: Victor J. Kemper, Gerald Hirschfeld; Ed: David Bretherton; Prod Design: Albert Brenner; Composer: Jerry Goldsmith. Color, 113 min. **VHS, LASER**

The Comancheros
(1961) Fox
Wayne is a Texas Ranger assigned to bring an arms-running gang to justice in this rollicking, good-humored Western. Shortly after Wayne arrests one of the criminals, matters are complicated when they wander into an area controlled by the Comancheros, a group of Anglos aiding the warring Comanche Indians. Curtiz's last film. **Cast:** John Wayne, Stuart Whitman, Lee Marvin, Ina Balin, Nehemiah Persoff, Michael Ansara, Pat Wayne, Bruce Cabot, Joan O'Brien. **Credits:** Dir: Michael Curtiz; Prod: George Sherman; Writer: James Edward Grant, Clair Huffaker; Story: Paul I. Wellman; DP: William Clothier; Ed: Louis Loeffler; Prod Design: Jack Martin Smith, Alfred Ybarra; Composer: Elmer Bernstein. Color, 108 min. **VHS, LASER**

Comanche Station
(1960) Columbia
In this exciting Boetticher-Scott Western, a loner puts aside a 10-year search for his kidnapped wife to help rescue another settler and is led into an ambush staged by a vicious outlaw. **Cast:** Randolph Scott, Nancy Gates, Claude Akins, Skip Homeier, Richard Rust, Rand Brooks, Dyke Johnson,

Foster Hood, Joe Molina. **Credits:** Dir: Budd Boetticher; Prod: Harry Joe Brown, Budd Boetticher, Randolph Scott; Writer: Burt Kennedy; DP: Charles Lawton, Jr.; Ed: Edwin Bryant. Color, 73 min. **VHS**

Come and Get It
(1936) Goldwyn
Those curious about the actress depicted in the biopic *Frances* (1982) will want to watch her in this, her best and biggest role playing both a mother and daughter. Arnold portrays a timber baron who sacrifices family for success. Based on an Edna Ferber novel. Academy Award Nominations: 2, including Best Film Editing. **Academy Awards:** Best Supporting Actor: Walter Brennan. **Cast:** Edward Arnold, Joel McCrea, Frances Farmer, Walter Brennan, Andrea Leeds, Mady Christians, Mary Nash, Clem Bevans, Edwin Maxwell, Frank Shields. **Credits:** Dir: Howard Hawks, William Wyler; Prod: Samuel Goldwyn; Writer: Jules Furthman, Jane Murfin; DP: Gregg Toland, Rudolph Mate; Ed: Edward Curtiss; Prod Design: Richard Day; Composer: Alfred Newman. B&W, 99 min. **VHS, LASER**

Come Back, Little Sheba
(1952) Paramount
An attractive boarder stirs the barely hidden seeds of contempt between a tired, disappointed housewife and her husband, a washed-up alcoholic doctor. Great performances bring William Inge's 1950 play to life on the big screen. Golden Globe for Best Actress in a Drama: Shirley Booth. Academy Award Nominations: 3, including Best Supporting Actress: Terry Moore; Best Film Editing. **Academy Awards:** Best Actress: Shirley Booth. **Cast:** Burt Lancaster, Shirley Booth, Terry Moore, Richard Jaeckel, Philip Ober, Lisa Golm, Walter Kelley. **Credits:** Dir: Daniel Mann; Prod: Hal B. Wallis; Writer: Ketti Frings; DP: James Wong Howe; Ed: Warren Low; Composer: Franz Waxman. B&W, 99 min. **VHS, LASER**

Come Blow Your Horn
(1963) Paramount
Sinatra's a young bachelor-about-town who has it all: wall-to-wall girls, a kid brother who wants to be just like him, and a disapproving father. Frank looks a little long in the tooth for the ring-a-ding stuff. Producer-director team later made a bigger mark on TV. Based on Neil Simon's first Broadway hit. Academy Award Nominations: Best (Color) Art Direction—Set Decoration. **Cast:** Frank Sinatra, Lee J. Cobb, Tony Bill, Molly

Picon, Barbara Rush, Jill St. John, Dan Blocker, Carole Wells, Phyllis McGuire, Herbie Faye. **Credits:** Dir: Bud Yorkin; Prod: Bud Yorkin, Norman Lear; Writer: Norman Lear; DP: William Daniels; Ed: Frank P. Keller; Prod Design: Hal Pereira, Roland Anderson; Composer: Nelson Riddle. Color, 115 min. **VHS**

The Comedians
(1967) MGM
Another of the Taylor-Burton sagas that seems to run as long as one of their marriages. Political drama adapted by Greene from his novel about an odd assortment of characters living and coping in 1960s Haiti under the regime of dictator "Papa Doc" Duvalier and his infamous secret police, the Ton Ton Macoute. **Cast:** Elizabeth Taylor, Richard Burton, Alec Guinness, Peter Ustinov, Paul Ford, Lillian Gish, Raymond St. Jacques, Zakes Mokae, Gloria Foster, Georg Stanford Brown. **Credits:** Dir: Peter Glenville; Prod: Peter Glenville; Writer: Graham Greene; DP: Henri Decae; Ed: Francoise Javet; Prod Design: Francois de Lamothe; Composer: Laurence Rosenthal. Color, 148 min. **VHS**

Come Fill the Cup
(1951) Warner Bros.
In one of his most brilliant film performances, Cagney plays an alcoholic reporter who loses his girlfriend and his job to the bottle. After going on a bender, he is found collapsed in a street gutter and is put in a drunk tank, where he is forced to go through a painful withdrawal. He joins an AA-like group and moves in with a friend played by Gleason. Recovered, he again retains his job, advancing to editorial duties. His boss, Massey, asks him to wet-nurse his nephew played by Young (who, in real life, died of alcohol addiction). By mistake, Young causes the death of Gleason because of former Mob connections. Not of the caliber of *The Lost Weekend* but Cagney's portrayal of drunkenness is unparalleled. (Cagney was never a tippler but his dad was an alcoholic.) In one sequence Gleason places an unopened bottle of liquor in his cabinet to remind Cagney that just one drink will return him to the dregs again. His portrayal of wanting something he can't have leaves your mouth watering. Academy Award Nomination for Best Supporting Actor: Gig Young. **Cast:** James Cagney, Phyllis Thaxter, Raymond Massey, James Gleason, Selena Royle, Larry Keating, Gig Young, Sheldon Leonard, Charlita, John Kellogg. **Credits:** Dir: John H.

Auer; Prod: Henry Blanke; Writer: Ivan Goff, Ben Roberts, Harlan Ware; DP: Robert Burks; Ed: Alan Crosland; Prod Design: Leo K. Kuter; Composer: Ray Heindorf. B&W, 113 min.

Come Live with Me
(1941) MGM
An appealing love story with an appealing cast including Lamarr and Stewart. Lamarr, a refugee facing deportation, is having an affair with a wealthy married publisher. She arranges to marry a poor writer, Stewart, so that she may remain in America, agreeing to pay him for his troubles. Stewart, of course, then falls for Lamarr. The business-romance triangle is completed when Stewart sells his novel to Lamarr's other man, the publisher. **Cast:** Barton MacLaine, Edward Ashley, Ann Codee, King Baggot, James Stewart, Hedy Lamarr, Ian Hunter, Verree Teasdale, Donald Meek. **Credits:** Dir: Clarence Brown; Prod: Clarence Brown; Writer: Patterson McNutt; Story: Virginia Van Upp; DP: George Folsey, Jr.; Ed: Frank E. Hull; Prod Design: Randal Duell, Cedric Gibbons, Edwin B. Willis; Composer: Herbert Stothart. B&W, 86 min.

Comes a Horseman
(1978) United Artists
A Western drama with many beautiful panoramic scenes tells the story of rivalry between ranch owners (Robards and Fonda) in the 1940s. Academy Award Nomination for Best Supporting Actor: Richard Farnsworth. **Cast:** Jane Fonda, James Caan, Jason Robards, George Grizzard, Basil Hoffman, Richard Farnsworth, Jim Davis, Mark Harmon, Macon McCalman. **Credits:** Dir: Alan J. Pakula; Prod: Gene Kirkwood, Dan Paulson; Writer: Dennis Lynton Clark; DP: Gordon Willis; Ed: Marion Rothman; Prod Design: George Jenkins; Composer: Michael Small. Color, 118 min. **VHS**

Come September
(1961) Universal
Hudson plays an amorous American tycoon with a villa on the Italian Riviera who arrives unexpectedly to find his butler using it as a hotel. Darin married costar Dee. **Cast:** Rock Hudson, Gina Lollobrigida, Sandra Dee, Bobby Darin, Joel Grey, Walter Slezak, Rosanna Rory, Ronald Howard, Brenda De Banzie. **Credits:** Dir: Robert Mulligan; Prod: Robert Arthur; Writer: Stanley Shapiro, Maurice Richlin; DP: William Daniels; Ed: Russell Schoengarth; Prod Design: Ernest B. Wehmeyer; Composer: Hans J. Salter. Color, 114 min. **VHS**

Come to the Stable
(1949) Fox
A pair of French nuns fulfill their promise to God by moving to New England to found a children's hospital. A pleasingly warm movie based on a story by Clare Boothe Luce. Academy Award Nominations: 7, including Best Actress: Loretta Young; Best Supporting Actress: Celeste Holm. **Cast:** Loretta Young, Celeste Holm, Hugh Marlowe, Elsa Lanchester, Regis Toomey, Mike Mazurki, Thomas Gomez, Dorothy Patrick, Basil Ruysdael, Dooley Wilson. **Credits:** Dir: Henry Koster; Prod: Samuel G. Engel; Writer: Oscar Millard, Sally Benson; DP: Joseph La Shelle; Ed: William H. Reynolds; Prod Design: Lyle Wheeler, Joseph C. Wright; Composer: Cyril J. Mockridge. B&W, 95 min. **VHS**

The Comic
(1969) Columbia
A popular silent-picture comedian has difficulty in making the transition to talkies. Unable to cope with the advances of the industry, he sinks into despair. Van Dyke narrates this sharp recreation of silent-era Hollywood from his coffin! **Cast:** Dick Van Dyke, Mickey Rooney, Michele Lee, Cornel Wilde, Nina Wayne, Pert Kelton, Steve Allen, Ed Peck, Jeannine Riley. **Credits:** Dir: Carl Reiner; Prod: Carl Reiner, Aaron Ruben; Writer: Carl Reiner, Aaron Ruben; DP: Wallace Kelley; Ed: Adrienne Fazan; Prod Design: Walter M. Simonds; Composer: Jack Elliott. Color, 96 min. **VHS, LASER**

Coming Home
(1978) United Artists
A critically acclaimed film about the lingering wounds inflicted by the Vietnam War, this powerful drama examines the growing relationship between an officer's wife, who volunteers to help disabled vets, and a bitter paraplegic under her care. Impassioned advocacy filmmaking. Academy Award Nominations: 8, including Best Picture; Best Director. **Academy Awards:** Best Actor: Jon Voight; Best Actress: Jane Fonda; Best Screenplay Written Directly for the Screen. **Cast:** Jane Fonda, Jon Voight, Bruce Dern, Robert Carradine, Penelope Milford, Robert Ginty, Charles Cyphers, Mary Jackson, Tresa Hughes, Kenneth Augustine. **Credits:** Dir: Hal Ashby; Prod: Jerome Hellman; Writer: Waldo Salt, Robert C. Jones; DP: Haskell Wexler; Ed: Don Zimmerman; Prod Design: Michael Haller. Color, 127 min. **VHS, LASER**

Command Decision

(1948) MGM

The agonizing decision: whether to send men on WWII missions from which they won't return. Fascinating study of Gable's struggle between doing what is right and what looks good to the public. **Cast:** Clark Gable, Walter Pidgeon, Van Johnson, Brian Donlevy, Charles Bickford, John Hodiak, Edward Arnold, Marshall Thompson, Richard Quine, Cameron Mitchell. **Credits:** Dir: Sam Wood; Prod: Sidney Franklin; Writer: William R. Laidlaw, George Froeschel; DP: Harold Rosson; Ed: Harold F. Kress; Prod Design: Cedric Gibbons, Urie McLeary; Composer: Miklos Rozsa. Color, 113 min. **VHS, LASER**

The Company She Keeps

(1950) RKO

When a beautiful convict is released from prison she promptly falls in love with her female parole officer's intended. The parole officer must decide whether to have her put back in jail or to allow the romance to continue. When the former inmate involves herself rather innocently in new legal trouble, the question is brought to a head. Great showdown between noir babes Scott and Greer. **Cast:** Lizabeth Scott, Jane Greer, Dennis O'Keefe, Fay Baker, John Hoyt, James Bell, Don Beddoe, Bert Freed, Irene Tedrow, Marjorie Wood. **Credits:** Dir: John Cromwell; Prod: John Houseman; Writer: Ketti Frings; DP: Nicholas Musuraca; Ed: Robert Swink; Composer: Leigh Harline. B&W, 82 min.

Compulsion

(1959) Fox

A tough dramatization of the famous Leopold and Loeb murder case in which two college students kidnapped and killed a boy purely for kicks. Welles plays the defense attorney who knows the truth and hopes only to forestall the death sentence. An adaptation of reporter Meyer Levin's novel. **Cast:** Orson Welles, Diane Varsi, Dean Stockwell, Bradford Dillman, E. G. Marshall, Martin Milner, Richard Anderson, Robert Simon, Edward Binns, Robert Burton. **Credits:** Dir: Richard Fleischer; Prod: Richard D. Zanuck; Writer: Richard Murphy; Story: Meyer Levin; DP: William Mellor; Ed: William H. Reynolds; Composer: Lionel Newman; Costumes: Charles LeMaire. B&W, 105 min. **VHS**

The Computer Wore Tennis Shoes

(1969) Disney

After a strange encounter with the new college computer, a half-wit student is transformed into a genius. The only problem is that he has learned more than is good for him. **Cast:** Kurt Russell, Cesar Romero, Joe Flynn, Alan Hewitt, William Schallert, Richard Bakalyan, Michael McGreevey, Jon Provost. **Credits:** Dir: Robert Butler; Prod: Bill Anderson; Writer: Joseph L. McEveety; DP: Frank Phillips; Ed: Cotton Warburton; Prod Design: John B. Mansbridge; Composer: Robert F. Brunner. Color, 87 min. **VHS**

Comrade X

(1940) MGM

Comedy, intrigue, and suspense are combined in this *Ninotchka*-inspired satire. Gable is an American correspondent in Moscow who is blackmailed into marrying a die-hard communist played by Lamarr. Academy Award Nomination for Best Original Story. **Cast:** Clark Gable, Hedy Lamarr, Sig Rumann, Oscar Homolka, Felix Bressart, Eve Arden, Vladimir Sokoloff, Edgar Barrier, John Picorri, Mikhail Rasumny. **Credits:** Dir: King Vidor; Prod: Gottfried Reinhardt; Writer: Ben Hecht, Charles Lederer; Story: Walter Reisch; DP: Joseph Ruttenberg; Ed: Harold F. Kress; Prod Design: Cedric Gibbons; Composer: Bronislau Kaper. B&W, 90 min. **VHS**

Coney Island

(1943) Fox

This lush period musical set in turn-of-the-century New York stars Grable as an ambitious showgirl caught between club owner Romero and smooth-talking Montgomery, who starts managing Grable's career and wants more than just her name in the lights. As the rivals bicker, Grable lights up the boardwalk. Songs include "Pretty Baby," "Live from Louisville," "Oh Susanna," "Deep River," and "Cuddle Up a Little Closer." **Cast:** Betty Grable, George Montgomery, Cesar Romero, Charles Winninger, Phil Silvers, Matt Briggs, Paul Hurst, Frank Orth. **Credits:** Dir: Walter Lang; Prod: William Perlberg; Writer: George Seaton; DP: Ernest Palmer; Ed: Robert Simpson; Prod Design: Richard Day, Joseph C. White; Composer: Alfred Newman, Ralph Rainger, Leo Robin. Color, 96 min.

Confession

(1937) Warner Bros.

A cabaret singer is put on trial for the murder of a philandering concert pianist. Before the jury, she recounts how, as a young woman, an encounter with him was responsible for her separation from her husband and baby girl. **Cast:** Kay Francis, Ian Hunter, Basil Rathbone, Jane Bryan, Donald Crisp, Mary Maguire, Dorothy Peterson, Laura Hope Crews, Robert Barratt, Ben Welden. **Credits:** Dir: Joe May; Prod: Henry Blanke; Writer: Julius J. Epstein, Margaret P. Levino, Hans Rameau; DP: Sidney Hickox; Ed: James Gibbon; Prod Design: Anton Grot; Composer: Peter Kreunder. B&W, 86 min.

Confessions of a Nazi Spy

(1939) Warner Bros.

Using the style of a wartime propaganda film, this pseudo-documentary is based on evidence presented by former G-men during the 1938 spy trials that resulted in the conviction of four persons. The film presents the belief that German leaders used German-American rallies and other tactics to unravel democracy. Along with the staged action, the film uses newsreel shots of Hitler and a commentator's voice-over to add to its authenticity. **Cast:** Edward G. Robinson, Francis Lederer, George Sanders, Paul Lukas, Henry O'Neill, Lya Lys, Grace Stafford, James Stephenson, Sig Rumann. **Credits:** Dir: Anatole Litvak; Prod: Robert Lord; Writer: John Wexley, Milton Krims; Story: Leon G. Turrou; DP: Sol Polito; Ed: Owen Marks; Composer: Max Steiner. B&W, 110 min.

Confidential Agent

(1946) Warner Bros.

A famous concert pianist in '30s Spain travels to London to purchase a consignment of coal for the Loyalist struggle and prevent the Nazis from getting their hands on it. There he meets the beautiful Bacall and falls in love with her. **Cast:** Charles Boyer, Lauren Bacall, Katina Paxinou, Peter Lorre, George Coulouris, Wanda Hendrix, John Warburton, Dan Seymour, George Zucco, Ian Wolfe. **Credits:** Dir: Herman Shumlin; Prod: Robert Buckner; Story: Graham Greene; DP: James Wong Howe; Ed: George Amy; Prod Design: Leo K. Kuter; Composer: Franz Waxman. B&W, 118 min.

Conflict

(1945) Warner Bros.

Bogart plays a man who plots his wife's murder when she won't divorce him so that he can marry her younger sister. But with her body missing, her perfume in the air, a glimpse of her on the street, he starts to wonder if she's really dead after all. A psychological thriller. **Cast:** Humphrey Bogart, Alexis Smith, Sydney Greenstreet,

Tom Doherty on Pre-Code Hollywood

For four years—from March 31, 1930, when the Motion Picture Producers and Distributors of America formally pledged to abide by the Production Code, until July 2, 1934, when the MPPDA empowered the Production Code Administration to enforce it—studio compliance with motion-picture censorship was a verbal agreement that as producer Sam Goldwyn might have said, wasn't worth the paper it was written on. That four-year interval marks a fascinating and anomalous passage in American motion-picture history: the so-called pre-Code era, when censorship was lax and Hollywood made the most of it. More unbridled, salacious, subversive, and just plain bizarre than what came afterward, the films of pre-Code Hollywood look like golden-age Hollywood cinema, but the moral terrain is so off-kilter that they seem imported from a parallel universe. In a sense, pre-Code Hollywood *is* from another universe. It lays bare what Hollywood under the Production Code did its best to cover up and push off screen: sexual liaisons unsanctified by the laws of God or man; marriage ridiculed and redefined; ethnic lines crossed and racial barriers ignored; economic injustice exposed and political corruption assumed; vice unpunished and virtue unrewarded—in sum, pretty much the raw stuff of American culture, unvarnished and unveiled. Listed below, however, are some personal favorites from the more obscure pre-Code archives:

Warner Bros.' *Skyscraper Souls* **(1932)** and *Employee's Entrance* **(1932)** are two low-rent versions of MGM's *Grand Hotel* **(1932)**, workplace melodramas where the girls trade on their looks to move up the economic ladder. Both also star the electrifying Warren William, pre-Code Hollywood's cad of choice.

Red Headed Woman **(1932)** and *Baby Face* **(1933)** were probably the most scandalous of the pre-Code "bad girl" films. In the former, platinum-blonde Jean Harlow proves men prefer her in any hair color. In the latter, Barbara Stanwyck makes a vertical ascent in business via horizontal means. Each actress is deliciously mercenary as she cuts a swath through the hapless male population.

Massacre **(1934)** is an oddball "social consciousness" film featuring Richard Barthelmess as a Native American who trades heartthrob status at a Wild West show to go on the warpath against the evil Indian agents back at his reservation. Weird but highly intriguing, though, as *Variety* wisecracked: "When surrounded by other big chiefs who are Indians on the up and up, Barthelmess doesn't look like an Indian any more than Jimmy Durante looks like a Chinaman."

Night Nurse **(1931)** stars Barbara Stanwyck as a spunky nurse who foils a sinister plot by evil chauffeur Clark Gable to kill the rich children under her care. The drunken and irresponsible mother of the kids has the best line: "I'm a dipsomaniac and I like it!"

This Day and Age **(1933)** is Cecil B. DeMille's deranged foray into social consciousness in which mobs of teenage vigilantes dangle gangster Charles Bickford over a pit of rats. It has to be seen to be believed.

Goona-Goona **(1932)** and *Virgins of Bali* **(1932)** are sexy expeditionary films enlivened by purely educational anthropology lessons featuring topless native girls. Both very popular in their day, for obvious reasons. *Goona-Goona* is the better docudrama, but *Virgins of Bali* is more fun just because it is so shamelessly voyeuristic.

Wild Boys of the Road **(1933)** and *Heroes for Sale* **(1933)** are two searing social-consciousness films directed by William Wellman, Warner Bros.' job-of-work genius. Each includes an uplifting New Deal ending that does nothing to soothe the raw nerves exposed in these wrenching journeys through Great Depression America.

Freaks **(1932)** is at once warmly humanist and starkly terrifying. Tod Browning's one-of-a-kind film presents a cracked-mirror world where the strong and beautiful are ignoble and cruel, the deformed and repulsive honorable and kind.

Island of Lost Souls **(1932)** showcases pre-Code horror at its most perverse. A bestial lumpenproletariat revolts against its tyrannical creator-ruler, played by a sadomasochistic Charles Laughton. "Are we not men?" chant the men-beasts.

The Story of Temple Drake **(1933)** is a sordid version of William Faulkner's *Sanctuary*, featuring Miriam Hopkins as a flirty Southern belle who teases the polite young men of the town, works them into a lather, and then leaves them hot and bothered—until the gangster Trigger (Jack LaRue) enters her life.

Call Her Savage **(1932)** is a misfired comeback attempt by actress Clara Bow, the sexy "It" girl of the 1920s. As extravagantly profligate as Bow's private life, it checks off a litany of Production Code violations: marital infidelity, interracial marital infidelity, sadomasochistic whipping, erotic frolicking with a Great Dane, prurient exposure of female flesh, kept women, femme-on-femme cat fights, a demented husband who tries to rape his wife, prostitution, gigolos, and a pair of mincing homosexual waiters. Required pre-Code viewing.

Tom Doherty is the author of *Pre-Code Hollywood: Immorality and Insurrection in American Cinema, 1930–1934.*

Rose Hobart, Charles Drake, Grant Mitchell, Patrick O'Moore, Ann Shoemaker, Frank Wilcox, James Flavin. **Credits:** Dir: Curtis Bernhardt; Prod: William Jacobs; Writer: Arthur T. Horman, Dwight Taylor; Story: Robert Siodmak; DP: Merritt Gerstad; Ed: David Weisbart; Prod Design: Ted Smith; Composer: Frederick Hollander. B&W, 109 min. **VHS**

A Connecticut Yankee
(1931) Fox
One of the many adaptations of Twain's novel. A Connecticut radio salesman, struck unconscious by a falling suit of armor, awakens in England in the year 528. What follows is a series of situations where the misplaced Yank uses his modern knowledge and homespun wisdom to impress the court. Rogers is charming in the lead role. **Cast:** Will Rogers, Myrna Loy, William Farnum, Frank Albertson, Maureen O'Sullivan, Brandon Hurst, Mitchell Harris. **Credits:** Dir: David Butler; Writer: William Conselman, Owen Davis; Story: Mark Twain; DP: Ernest Palmer; Ed: Irene Morra; Prod Design: William S. Darling. B&W, 96 min. **VHS**

A Connecticut Yankee in King Arthur's Court
(1949) Paramount
The musical version of the oft-made Twain novel. Bing plays a blacksmith who is knocked out and wakes up in the days of King Arthur. He is proclaimed a wizard and experiences many knightly adventures. Songs crooned include "Busy Doing Nothing" and "Once and For Always." **Cast:** Bing Crosby, Rhonda Fleming, William Bendix, Cedric Hardwicke, Murvyn Vye, Virginia Field, Henry Wilcoxon, Richard Webb, Joseph Vitale. **Credits:** Dir: Tay Garnett; Prod: Robert Fellows; Writer: Edmund Beloin; Story: Mark Twain; DP: Ray Rennahan; Ed: Archie Marshek; Prod Design: Hans Dreier, Roland Anderson; Composer: Victor Young. Color, 108 min. **VHS**

The Connection
(1961) Allen, Clarke
The Living Theatre's production of the play by Jack Gelber. Independent filmmaker Clarke, who also made dance and abstract films, here delves into the world of a drug dealer and his heroin-addicted clients as they await his "connection." At the same time, a documentary filmmaker records everything that happens in the room, including an impromptu jazz session by some of the junkies. But when Cowboy arrives, pan-

demonium erupts when one person virtually overdoses. Intense early independent film. **Cast:** William Redfield, Warren Finnerty, Garry Goodrow, James Anderson, Carl Lee, Roscoe Lee Browne. **Credits:** Dir: Shirley Clarke; Prod: Lewis Allen, Shirley Clarke; Writer: Jack Gelber; DP: Arthur J. Ornitz; Ed: Shirley Clarke; Composer: Freddie Redd. Color, 105 min. **VHS**

The Conquerors
(1932) RKO
Family saga about Easterners who strike out for Fort Allen, Nebraska, in 1870. They start a family, fight outlaws, and protect their town. Later, they start the town's first bank, which stays in business until the financial panic of 1892. Tragedy strikes when a train hits the buggy their son is riding in. Years later, a grandson brings honor to the family through his heroic deeds in WWI. **Cast:** Wally Albright, Donald Cook, Richard Dix, Ann Harding, Julie Haydon, Harry Holman, Guy Kibbee, Marilyn Knowlden, Edna May Oliver, Walter Walker. **Credits:** Dir: William Wellman, Jr.; Prod: David O. Selznick; Writer: Robert Lord; Story: Howard Estabrook; DP: Edward Cronajer; Ed: William Hamilton; Prod Design: Carroll Clark; Composer: Max Steiner. B&W, 86 min.

Conquest
(1937) MGM
This lavish epic centers on the romance between Napoleon Bonaparte and the Polish Countess Marie Walewska. An expensive flop despite good performances. Academy Award Nominations: Best Actor: Charles Boyer; Best Interior Decoration. **Cast:** Greta Garbo, Charles Boyer, Leif Erickson, Reginald Owen, Alan Marshal, Henry Stephenson, Dame May Whitty, C. Henry Gordon, Maria Ouspenskaya, Claude Gillingwater. **Credits:** Dir: Clarence Brown; Prod: Bernard Hyman; Writer: Samuel Hoffenstein, Salka Viertel, S. N. Behrman; DP: Karl Freund; Ed: Tom Held; Prod Design: Cedric Gibbons; Composer: Herbert Stothart. B&W, 115 min. **VHS**

Conquest of the Planet of the Apes
(1972) Fox
An intelligent ape from the far future leads an army of monkey servants in a revolt against their human masters. The fourth film in the Planet of the Apes series and the reduced budgets are starting to show. **Cast:** Roddy McDowall, Ricardo Montalban, Don Murray, Natalie Trundy, Hari Rhodes,

Severn Darden, Lou Wagner, John Randolph, David Chow. **Credits:** Dir: J. Lee Thompson; Prod: Arthur P. Jacobs; Writer: Paul Dehn; Story: Pierre Boulle; DP: Bruce Surtees; Ed: Marjorie Fowler, Alan Jaggs; Prod Design: Philip M. Jefferies; Composer: Tom Scott. Color, 88 min. **VHS, LASER**

Conrack
(1974) Fox
A creative teacher in an impoverished school district in South Carolina comes into conflict with the school superintendent because of his unusual commonsense teaching methods. Based on Pat Conroy's book *The Water Is Wide*. **Cast:** Jon Voight, Hume Cronyn, Paul Winfield, Madge Sinclair, Tina Andrews, Antonio Fargas, Ruth Attaway, James O'Reare. **Credits:** Dir: Martin Ritt; Prod: Martin Ritt, Harriet Frank, Jr.; Writer: Irving Ravetch, Harriet Frank, Jr.; Story: Pat Conroy; DP: John A. Alonzo; Ed: Frank Bracht; Prod Design: Walter Scott Herndon; Composer: John Williams. Color, 111 min. **VHS**

Consolation Marriage
(1931) RKO
A man and a woman marry after they're both jilted by their respective mates, but years later must decide what to do when the former lovers return. **Cast:** Irene Dunne, Myrna Loy, Pat O'Brien, Matt Moore, Lester Vail. **Credits:** Dir: Paul Sloane; Prod: William LeBaron; Writer: Humphrey Pearson; DP: J. Roy Hunt; Ed: Archie Marshek; Composer: Max Steiner; Art Director: Max Ree. B&W, 82 min. **VHS**

The Conspirators
(1944) Warner Bros.
Spy drama following a resistance fighter known as The Flying Dutchman, who flees Holland for Lisbon, where he is sheltered by the underground. There he meets and falls in love with a woman who is married to a German official sympathetic to the cause of the resistance. When an underground agent is killed on a secret mission back in Holland, suspicion initially falls on the Dutchman, who must then hatch a plot to expose the real traitor and defeat the Nazi spies who surround him. **Cast:** Hedy Lamarr, Paul Henreid, Sydney Greenstreet, Peter Lorre, Victor Francen. **Credits:** Dir: Jean Negulesco; Prod: Jack Chertok; Writer: Vladimir Posner, Leo Rosten, Jack Moffitt; Story: Frederic Prokosch; DP: Arthur Edeson; Ed: Rudi Fehr; Prod Design: Anton Grot; Composer: Max Steiner. B&W, 100 min.

The Constant Nymph

(1943) Warner Bros.
Romantic melodrama of a young composer living in Switzerland with his mentor and the man's four young daughters, one of whom is secretly in love with the dashing composer. When the mentor dies, a wealthy uncle comes to take the girls to England. With him is his daughter, whom the composer marries after a whirlwind courtship. Back in England, however, he's suffocated by his new life of money and prestige, and his music suffers. When his mentor's daughter comes to him after fleeing her repressive boarding school, he realizes, a bit too late, that she is his true love, and the real inspiration for his art. Under her influence, he composes again, but tragedy strikes during the triumphant performance of his new work. **Cast:** Charles Boyer, Joan Fontaine, Alexis Smith, Charles Coburn, Brenda Marshall, May Whitty, Peter Lorre, Basil Dean. **Credits:** Dir: Edmund Goulding; Prod: Henry Blanke; Writer: Kathryn Scola; Story: Margaret Kennedy; DP: Tony Gaudio; Ed: David Weisbert; Prod Design: Carl Jules Weyl; Composer: Erich Wolfgang Korngold. B&W, 112 min.

The Conversation

(1974) Paramount
Coppola's haunting film focuses on a detached surveillance expert who finds himself becoming a victim of the same modern technology he uses to destroy others. It begins with a seemingly routine job trailing an unfaithful wife and her lover. But the case involves him in a murderous intrigue in which he may have played an unwitting role. A masterpiece of paranoia and personal responsibility. Won the Palme d'Or at Cannes. **Cast:** Gene Hackman, John Cazale, Allen Garfield, Cindy Williams, Frederic Forrest, Harrison Ford, Teri Garr, Robert Duvall, Michael Higgins, Elizabeth MacRae. **Credits:** Dir: Francis Ford Coppola; Prod: Francis Ford Coppola; Writer: Francis Ford Coppola; DP: Bill Butler; Ed: Walter Murch, Richard Chew; Prod Design: Dean Tavoularis; Composer: David Shire. Color, 113 min. **VHS, LASER**

Convoy

(1978) United Artists
A mile-long convoy of protesting truckers speeds along the Arizona highway toward the Mexican border. Peckinpah builds tense action to an incredible climax featuring one of the most elaborate crash scenes ever filmed. **Cast:** Kris Kristofferson, Ali MacGraw, Ernest Borgnine, Burt Young, Madge Sinclair, Franklin Ajaye, Brian Davies, Seymour Cassel, Cassie Yates, Walter Kelley. **Credits:** Dir: Sam Peckinpah; Prod: Robert M. Sherman; Writer: B. W. L. Norton; DP: Harry Stradling; Ed: Graeme Clifford, John Wright, Garth Craven; Prod Design: Fernando Carrere; Composer: Chip Davis. Color, 106 min. **VHS**

Coogan's Bluff

(1968) Universal
Another great Siegel-Eastwood pairing. Eastwood plays an Arizona sheriff who escorts his extradited prisoner to New York City. When the convict escapes, a wild and dangerous chase through New York ensues. Source of the TV series, *McCloud.* **Cast:** Clint Eastwood, Lee J. Cobb, Susan Clark, Don Stroud, Tisha Sterling, Betty Field, Tom Tully, James Edwards, David Doyle. **Credits:** Dir: Don Siegel; Prod: Don Siegel; Writer: Herman Miller, Dean Riesner, Howard A. Rodman; DP: Bud Thackery; Ed: Sam E. Waxman; Prod Design: Alexander Golitzen, Robert C. MacKichan; Composer: Lalo Schifrin. Color, 100 min. **VHS, LASER**

Cooley High

(1975) AIP
In this black *American Graffiti,* two high school boys get into trouble with the law after innocently taking a joy ride with the neighborhood pals who stole the vehicle. Great late-period Motown soundtrack. **Cast:** Glynn Turman, Lawrence Hilton-Jacobs, Garrett Morris, Cynthia Davis, Corin Rogers, Maurice Leon Havis. **Credits:** Dir: Michael Schultz; Prod: Steve Krantz; Writer: Eric Monte; DP: Paul Von Brack; Ed: Christopher Holmes; Prod Design: William Fosser; Composer: Freddie Perren. Color, 107 min. **VHS, LASER**

Cool Hand Luke

(1967) Warner Bros.
"What we have here is a failure to communicate." Newman wakes up on a Southern chain gang after a destructive drunken spree. Stuck in a stink hole of a prison, he refuses to give up his dignity or humor to abusive authorities. Academy Award Nominations: 4, including Best Actor: Paul Newman; Best (Adapted) Screenplay; Best Original Music Score. **Academy Awards:** Best Supporting Actor: George Kennedy. **Cast:** Paul Newman, George Kennedy, Jo Van Fleet, J. D. Cannon, Strother Martin, Lou Antonio, Robert Drivas, Clifton James, Morgan Woodward, Luke Askew. **Credits:** Dir: Stuart Rosenberg; Prod: Gordon Carroll; Writer: Donn Pearce, Frank R. Pierson; DP: Conrad Hall; Ed: Sam O'Steen; Prod Design: Cary Odell; Composer: Lalo Schifrin. Color, 127 min. **VHS, LASER, DVD**

The Cool World

(1963) Cinema 5
Another bleakly cool Clarke docudrama, this time following a young black man through the streets of Harlem. After hearing a Black Muslim make an empowering speech claiming black supremacy and a disdain for white people, Duke (Clanton) tries to assert his authority with a street gang. Very cool jazz soundtrack. **Cast:** Gloria Foster, Hampton Clanton, Carl Lee. **Credits:** Dir: Shirley Clarke; Prod: Frederick Wiseman; Writer: Shirley Clarke; DP: Baird Bryant; Ed: Shirley Clarke; Composer: Dizzy Gillespie, Yuseff Lateef, Mal Waldron. B&W, 107 min. **VHS**

Copacabana

(1947) United Artists
Groucho plays an agent who books the same nightclub singer at the Copacabana under two different names—the Brazilian Bombshell and Mademoiselle Fifi. Always fun to see Groucho and Carmen, but otherwise . . . **Cast:** Groucho Marx, Carmen Miranda, Andy Russell, Steve Cochran, Gloria Jean, Ralph Sanford. **Credits:** Dir: Alfred E. Green; Prod: Sam Coslow; Writer: Laszlo Vadnay, Allan Boretz, Howard Harris; DP: Bert Glennon; Composer: Edward Ward. B&W, 92 min. **VHS, LASER**

Cops and Robbers

(1973) United Artists
Two New York cops who plan a 10-million-dollar heist learn that even the perfect crime can turn into the perfect mess. A strong comic caper with an equal measure of fast-moving action. **Cast:** Cliff Gorman, Joseph Bologna, Dick Ward, Shepperd Strudwick, John P. Ryan, Ellen Holly, Dolph Sweet, Joe Spinell. **Credits:** Dir: Aram Avakian; Prod: Elliott Kastner; Writer: Donald E. Westlake; DP: David Quaid; Ed: Barry Malkin; Prod Design: Gene Rudolf; Composer: Michel Legrand. Color, 89 min. **VHS**

Roger Corman

Roger Corman is, without a doubt, one of the most prolific filmmakers in Hollywood. Best known for his contribution to America's stockpile of B movies (who could forget 1957's *The Saga of the Viking Women and Their*

Voyage to the Waters of the Great Sea Serpent?), Corman began his career in Hollywood as an errand boy at Twentieth Century-Fox. After graduate work at Oxford, he worked his way up to producer-director. Oftentimes working with meager budgets in the neighborhood of $50,000, Corman managed to churn out an astounding volume of guilty pleasures, and some visually rich, financially successful features. His films also launched the careers of future luminaries such as Francis Ford Coppola, Martin Scorsese, Peter Bogdanovich, and Jack Nicholson. Though he proved himself the master of all genres, Corman won devoted fans with his series based on the short stories of Edgar Allen Poe, all of which starred Vincent Price. These particular films were adored by horror fans because of the singularly creepy mood that they evoked. The subject of a feature documentary entitled *Roger Corman: Hollywood's Wild Angel* (1978), Corman has also written an autobiography, *How I Made a Hundred Movies in Hollywood and Never Lost a Dime* (1990).

The Fast and the Furious *(1954)*
The Monster from the Ocean Floor *(1954)*
Highway Dragnet *(1954)*
Swamp Women *(1955)*
Apache Woman *(1955)*
Five Guns West *(1955)*
The Day the World Ended *(1956)*
It Conquered the World *(1956)*
The Gunslinger *(1956)*
The Oklahoma Woman *(1956)*
Naked Paradise *(1957)*
Rock All Night *(1957)*
Teenage Doll *(1957)*
Sorority Girl *(1957)*
Attack of the Crab Monsters *(1957)*
Carnival Rock *(1957)*
The Undead *(1957)*
Not of This Earth *(1957)*
Gunslinger *(1957)*
The Saga of the Viking Women and Their Voyage to the Waters of the Great Sea Serpent *(1957)*
Night of the Blood Beast *(1958)*
Teenage Caveman *(1958)*
Stakeout on Dope Street *(1958)*
She-Gods of Shark Reef *(1958)*
I, Monster *(1958)*
The Brain Eaters *(1958)*
Machine Gun Kelly *(1958)*
War of the Satellites *(1958)*
Attack of the Giant Leeches *(1958)*
A Bucket of Blood *(1959)*
High School Big Shot *(1959)*
T-Bird Gang *(1959)*
The Wasp Woman *(1959)*
The Little Shop of Horrors *(1960)*

The Last Woman on Earth *(1960)*
Atlas *(1960)*
House of Usher *(1960)*
Ski Troop Attack *(1960)*
The Wild Ride *(1960)*
Battle of Blood Island *(1960)*
Pit and the Pendulum *(1961)*
The Creature from the Haunted Sea *(1961)*
Tales of Terror *(1961)*
The Intruder *(1961)*
The Premature Burial *(1962)*
Tower of London *(1962)*
Battle Beyond the Sun *(1963)*
The Haunted Palace *(1963)*
The Raven *(1963)*
X—The Man with the X-Ray Eyes *(1963)*
The Terror *(1963)*
Dementia 13 *(1963)*
The Young Racers *(1963)*
The Tomb of Ligeia *(1964)*
The Masque of the Red Death *(1964)*
The Secret Invasion *(1964)*
Beach Ball *(1965)*
Voyage to the Planet of Prehistoric Women *(1966)*
Planet of Blood *(1966)*
The Wild Angels *(1966)*
The St. Valentine's Day Massacre *(1967)*
Devil's Angels *(1967)*
The Trip *(1967)*
The Wild Racers *(1968)*
Targets *(1968)*
Target: Harry *(1968)*
Bloody Mama *(1970)*
Beast of the Yellow Night *(1970)*
The Dunwich Horror *(1970)*

Cornered

(1945) RKO
After his release from prison camp, Powell travels the world in pursuit of the Nazi who killed his French wife and child during WWII. Story by Hecht. The colorized version can be skipped. **Cast:** Dick Powell, Walter Slezak, Micheline Cheirel, Nina Vale, Morris Carnovsky. **Credits:** Dir: Edward Dmytryk; Writer: John Paxton; Story: John Wexley, Ben Hecht; DP: Harry Wild; Ed: Joseph Noriega; Prod Design: Albert S. D'Agostino, Carroll Clark; Composer: Roy Webb. B&W, 102 min. **VHS, LASER**

The Corn Is Green

(1945) Warner Bros.
A spinster teacher lives to educate the poor children of a Wales mining village. She discovers that one of her students has promise, maybe even a shot at Oxford, and they both begin to come out of their shells. Academy Award Nominations: Best Supporting Actor: John Dall; Best Supporting Actress:

Joan Lorring. **Cast:** Bette Davis, Nigel Bruce, John Dall, Joan Lorring, Rhys Williams, Rosalind Ivan, Mildred Dunnock, Gwyneth Hughes. **Credits:** Dir: Irving Rapper; Prod: Jack Chertok; Writer: Casey Robinson, Frank Cavett; DP: Sol Polito; Ed: Frederick Richards; Prod Design: Carl Jules Weyl; Composer: Max Steiner. B&W, 115 min. **VHS**

Coroner Creek

(1948) Columbia
Vengeance-seeking Scott tracks down the man responsible for causing his fiancée's suicide in a stagecoach raid, and dukes it out spectacularly with Tucker. Solid action Western with top-notch Scott. **Cast:** Randolph Scott, Marguerite Chapman, George Macready, Sally Eilers, Edgar Buchanan, Barbara Reed, Wallace Ford, Forrest Tucker, William Bishop, Douglas Fowley. **Credits:** Dir: Ray Enright; Prod: Harry Joe Brown; Writer: Kenneth Gamet; Story: Luke Short; DP: Fred Jackman; Ed: Harvey Manger; Composer: Rudolph Schrager. Color, 90 min. **VHS**

The Corsican Brothers

(1941) United Artists
Dumas, endless source of costume-epic plots, supplied the story of Siamese twins, sons of a Corsican nobleman, who are separated and hidden just as the entire family is wiped out by a robber baron. Twenty years later the two young men meet. One grew up in Paris, the other sheltered by a family retainer in Corsica. The brothers have a telepathic link and feel each other's emotions. They once again separate, but this time to confuse and wreak vengeance on the villain responsible for the demise of their kin. Great dual role for Fairbanks. Academy Award Nominations: Best Score. **Cast:** Douglas Fairbanks, Jr., Ruth Warrick, Akim Tamiroff, H. B. Warner, J. Carrol Naish, John Emery, Henry Wilcoxon, Gloria Holden, Walter Kingsford, Nana Bryant. **Credits:** Dir: Gregory Ratoff; Prod: Edward Small; Writer: George Bruce; DP: Harry Stradling; Ed: Grant Whytock, William Claxton; Composer: Dimitri Tiomkin. B&W, 111 min. **VHS, DVD**

Corvette K-225

(1943) Universal
A war film about one of the corvettes that protected Allied supply ships from U-boats. A Canadian returns home after losing a ship to German fire. While waiting for his new command, he meets and woos a woman who lost an older brother at sea and is reluc-

tant to get involved with a naval officer. The captain compounds the situation by taking her younger brother, Paul, with him when he heads to sea in his new boat. There the corvette is beset by storms, shelled by Nazi airplanes, and surrounded by sneaky U-boats. Shot, in part, onboard Atlantic corvettes in combat. An early Mitchum appearance. **Cast:** Randolph Scott, James Brown, Ella Raines, Noah Beery, Jr., Barry Fitzgerald, Andy Devine, Fuzzy Knight, Richard Lane, Robert Mitchum. **Credits:** Dir: Richard Rosson; Prod: Howard Hawks; Writer: John Rhodes Sturdy; DP: Tony Gaudio, Harry Perry; Ed: Edward Curtiss; Prod Design: Robert Boyle; Composer: John B. Goodman. B&W, 98 min.

Cotton Comes to Harlem
(1970) MGM
Two black cops in Harlem suspect a preacher's back-to-Africa campaign is a swindle in this crime comedy based on the book by Chester Himes. **Cast:** Godfrey Cambridge, Raymond St. Jacques, Calvin Lockhart, Judy Pace, Redd Foxx, Emily Yancy, Cleavon Little. **Credits:** Dir: Ossie Davis; Writer: Ossie Davis, Arnold Perl; Story: Chester Himes; DP: Gerald Hirschfeld; Ed: John Carter, Robert Q. Lovett; Prod Design: Manny Gerard; Composer: Galt MacDermot; Costumes: Anna Hill Johnstone; SFX: Sol Stern; Set Designer: Robert Drumheller. Color, 97 min. **VHS**

Counsellor at Law
(1933) Universal
A riveting drama featuring a fine performance from The Great Profile, sure-footed direction and pacing from Wyler, who adds to the intensity by confining most of the action to the arena of the law office, and fine ensemble support work. Barrymore plays a successful lawyer of Jewish ancestry, and a complex man, at the center of a professional and personal maelstrom that includes a bewildering array of clients, a cheating wife, and a loving secretary. **Cast:** John Barrymore, Bebe Daniels, Doris Kenyon, Onslow Stevens, Isabel Jewell, Melvyn Douglas, Thelma Todd, Marvin Kline, Conroy Washburn, John Qualen. **Credits:** Dir: William Wyler; Prod: Carl Laemmle, Jr.; Writer: Elmer Rice; DP: Norbert F. Brodine; Ed: Daniel Mandell; Art Director: Charles D. Hall. B&W, 80 min.

Countdown
(1968) Warner Bros.
Early, less well known Altman offering depicts the drama and adventure of

man's first lunar landing (though it hadn't yet happened). Recut by the studio and disavowed by the director, but interesting for Altman fans. Based on a novel by WWII pilot Hank Searls. **Cast:** James Caan, Joanna Moore, Robert Duvall, Charles Aidman, Barbara Baxley, Steve Ihnat. **Credits:** Dir: Robert Altman; Prod: William Conrad; Writer: Loring Mandel; Story: Hank Searls; DP: William W. Spencer; Ed: Gene Milford; Composer: Leonard Rosenman. Color, 102 min. **VHS**

The Counterfeit Traitor
(1962) Paramount
Based on a shocking true story, this film tells of the true adventures of Eric Erickson, a naturalized Swede born in America, who poses as a Nazi sympathizer while actually spying for Allied forces. When a fellow spy, with whom he has fallen in love, is discovered and murdered in front of his eyes, he must control his anger in order to stay out of the Gestapo clutches. Holden is riveting in this suspenseful thriller. **Cast:** William Holden, Lilli Palmer, Hugh Griffith, Erica Beer, Werner Peters, Phil Brown, Eva Dahlbeck, Ulf Palme, Carl Raddatz, Ernst Schroder. **Credits:** Dir: George Seaton; Prod: William Perlberg; Writer: George Seaton; DP: Jean Bourgoin; Ed: Hans Ebel, Alma Macrorie; Composer: Alfred Newman. Color, 140 min. **VHS, LASER**

A Countess from Hong Kong
(1967) United Artists
Leaving Hong Kong after a stopover, an American diplomat discovers a stowaway in his stateroom: the Countess Natascha Alexandra, whose family had fled from Russia. Fearful of losing his job, he tries to keep his new

roomie hidden while they try unsuccessfully to keep from falling in love. This was director Chaplin's final film. **Cast:** Marlon Brando, Patrick Cargill, Charlie Chaplin, Geraldine Chaplin, Sydney Chaplin, Tippi Hedren, Sophia Loren, Margaret Rutherford, John Paul, Bill Nagy. **Credits:** Dir: Charlie Chaplin; Prod: Jerome Epstein, Charlie Chaplin; Writer: Charlie Chaplin; DP: Arthur Ibbetson; Ed: Gordon Hales; Prod Design: Don Ashton; Composer: Charlie Chaplin. Color, 108 min. **VHS**

The Count of Monte Cristo
(1934) United Artists
A classic swashbuckler based on the 1844 novel by Dumas. It tells the story of Edmond Dantes, a sailor who was unjustly imprisoned but escapes to look for the culprits who framed him. Donat's performance put him in the running for *Captain Blood* and *The Adventures of Robin Hood*, which he lost to the then-unknown Errol Flynn. **Cast:** Robert Donat, Louis Calhern, Sidney Blackmer, Irene Harvey, Elissa Landi, Raymond Walburn, O. P. Heggie, William Farnum, Georgia Caine. **Credits:** Dir: Rowland V. Lee; Prod: Edward Small; Writer: Philip Dunne, Dan Totheroh, Rowland V. Lee; DP: Peverell Marley; Ed: Grant Whytock; Composer: Alfred Newman. B&W, 119 min. **VHS**

The Country Girl
(1954) Paramount
A deeply moving story about a has-been actor struggling to make a comeback. Frank Elgin, a broken-down entertainer, has long taken refuge in booze. But now he's given one last chance to make a comeback and save his relationship with his long-suffering

Gene Autry's Cowboy Code

1. A cowboy never takes unfair advantage—even of an enemy.

2. A cowboy never betrays a trust.

3. A cowboy always tells the truth.

4. A cowboy is kind to small children, old folks, and animals.

5. A cowboy is free from racial and religious prejudice.

6. A cowboy is helpful, and when anyone is in trouble, he lends a hand.

7. A cowboy is a good worker.

8. A cowboy is clean about his person, and in thought, word, and deed.

9. A cowboy respects womanhood, his parents, and the laws of his country.

10. A cowboy is a patriot.

wife. Based on the play by Clifford Odets. Remade in 1982 with Dick Van Dyke and Faye Dunaway. Golden Globe for Best Actress in a Drama: Grace Kelly. **Academy Awards:** Best Actress: Grace Kelly; Best Screenplay. **Cast:** Bing Crosby, Grace Kelly, William Holden, Anthony Ross, Gene Reynolds, Jacqueline Fontaine, Eddie Ryder, Robert Kent. **Credits:** Dir: George Seaton; Prod: William Perlberg, George Seaton; Writer: George Seaton; DP: John F. Warren; Ed: Ellsworth Hoagland; Prod Design: Hal Pereira, Roland Anderson; Composer: Victor Young. B&W, 104 min. VHS

The Court Jester
(1956) Paramount
A 12th-century court jester in England becomes involved with a desperate band of outlaws who are attempting to overthrow the king. A delightful comedy that features a particularly fine cast. **Cast:** Danny Kaye, Glynis Johns, Basil Rathbone, Angela Lansbury, Cecil Parker, Mildred Natwick, Robert Middleton, Michael Pate, Herbert Rudley. **Credits:** Dir: Melvin Frank, Norman Panama; Prod: Norman Panama, Melvin Frank; Writer: Norman Panama, Melvin Frank; DP: Ray June; Ed: Tom McAdoo; Prod Design: Hal Pereira, Roland Anderson; Composer: Vic Schoen. Color, 101 min. VHS, LASER

The Court-Martial of Billy Mitchell
(1955) Warner Bros.
A courtroom drama from master of legal fireworks Preminger based on the true story of an American general court-martialed for accusing the military of negligence. In the wake of WWI, General Billy Mitchell considered the military's failure to build the Air Force as akin to treason. In the trial that followed, he predicted a situation not unlike the bombing of Pearl Harbor that occurred two decades later. **Cast:** Gary Cooper, Charles Bickford, Ralph Bellamy, Rod Steiger, Elizabeth Montgomery, Darren McGavin, Fred Clark, James Daly, Jack Lord, Peter Graves. **Credits:** Dir: Otto Preminger; Prod: Milton Sperling; Writer: Milton Sperling, Emmett Lavery; DP: Sam Leavitt; Ed: Folmar Blangsted; Prod Design: Malcolm Bert; Composer: Dimitri Tiomkin. Color, 100 min. VHS

The Courtship of Eddie's Father
(1963) MGM
Director Ron Howard began his career as an actor in such wholesome fare as this. After his grief subsides, wid-

ower Ford begins to date again, with his opinionated 6-year-old, Howard, helping out. This spawned the '60s TV series. **Cast:** Glenn Ford, Ron Howard, Shirley Jones, Stella Stevens, Dina Merrill, Roberta Sherwood, Jerry Van Dyke. **Credits:** Dir: Vincente Minnelli; Prod: Joe Pasternak; Writer: John Gay; DP: Milton Krasner; Ed: Adrienne Fazan; Prod Design: George W. Davis; Composer: George Stoll. Color, 117 min. VHS

The Covered Wagon
(1923) Paramount
A silent forerunner of Western epics, this film follows two wagon caravans as they depart from the newly crowned Kansas City and begin their journey westward, determined to settle in Oregon. Along the way, the pioneers must combat Indians and the elements (first desert heat, then mountain snow). Adding even more drama is a love triangle that develops between a pretty woman and two male travelers. History has obviously lessened the emotional impact of the film, but beautiful photography makes it a visual treat. **Cast:** J. Warren Kerrigan, Lois Wilson, Alan Hale, Ernest Torrence, Tully Marshall, Ethel Wales, Guy Oliver. **Credits:** Dir: James Cruze; Writer: Jack Cunningham, Emerson Hough; DP: Karl Brown; Ed: Dorothy Arzner; Composer: Hugo Riesenfeld. B&W, 83 min. VHS, LASER

Cover Girl
(1944) Columbia
This Jerome Kern and Ira Gershwin musical traces a chorus girl's rise to stardom as a cover girl. Very funny with great dancing by Kelly and lots of good music. Academy Award Nominations: 5. **Academy Awards:** Best Scoring of a Musical. **Cast:** Rita Hayworth, Gene Kelly, Phil Silvers, Eve Arden, Lee Bowman, Jinx Falkenberg, Otto Kruger, Edward Brophy. **Credits:** Dir: Charles Vidor; Prod: Arthur Schwartz; Writer: Virginia Van Upp, Marion Parsonnet, Paul Gangelin; Story: Erwin Gelsey; DP: Rudolph Mate, Allen M. Davey; Ed: Viola Lawrence; Prod Design: Lionel Banks, Cary Odell; Choreographer: Stanley Donen, Val Raset, Seymour Felix, Gene Kelly; Composer: Carmen Dragon; Costumes: Travis Banton, Gwen Wakeling, Muriel King, Kenneth Hopkins; Set Designer: Fay Babcock. Color, 107 min. VHS, LASER

Cowboy
(1958) Columbia
Excellent Western in which Lemmon plays hotel clerk turned cattle driver

Frank Harris. Great detail, picturesque southwestern locations, and lots and lots of cows give this one an intelligent, authentic flavor. **Cast:** Glenn Ford, Jack Lemmon, Anna Kashfi, Brian Donlevy, Dick York, Richard Jaeckel, King Donovan. **Credits:** Dir: Delmer Daves; Prod: Julian C. Blaustein; Writer: Edmund H. North; Story: Frank Harris; DP: Charles Lawton, Jr.; Ed: Al Clark, William A. Lyon; Prod Design: Cary Odell; Composer: George Duning; Set Designer: William Kiernan. Color, 92 min. VHS

The Cowboy and the Lady
(1938) United Artists
In this entertaining romantic comedy, a rodeo rider falls in love with a woman he believes is a maid, but who is actually the daughter of a wealthy presidential candidate. Without letting him know her true identity, she elopes with him aboard a ship. Much humorous confusion transpires. **Academy Awards:** Best Sound Recording. **Cast:** Gary Cooper, Merle Oberon, Patsy Kelly, Walter Brennan, Fuzzy Knight, Harry Davenport, Henry Kolker, Emma Dunn, Walter Walker, Mabel Todd. **Credits:** Dir: H. C. Potter; Prod: Samuel Goldwyn; Writer: S. N. Behrman, Sonya Levien; DP: Gregg Toland; Ed: Sherman Todd; Prod Design: Richard Day, James Basevi; Composer: Alfred Newman. B&W, 91 min. VHS

The Cowboys
(1972) Warner Bros.
After being deserted by his hands, a veteran rancher hires a classroomful of young boys to drive his cattle to market protected by an over-the-hill shootist, Wayne. The length of the trip and the 400 cattle make for an impromptu classroom on the range, complete with a group of savage outlaws. Wayne actually expires in this one, and the boys have to fend for themselves against the rustlers. **Cast:** John Wayne, Roscoe Lee Browne, Slim Pickens, Colleen Dewhurst, Bruce Dern, Lonny Chapman, Charles Tyner, A Martinez. **Credits:** Dir: Mark Rydell; Prod: Mark Rydell; Writer: Irving Ravetch, Harriet Frank, Jr., William Dale Jennings; DP: Robert Surtees; Ed: Robert W. Swink, Neil Travis; Prod Design: Philip M. Jefferies; Composer: John Williams. Color, 135 min. VHS, LASER

Crack in the Mirror
(1960) Fox
A scheming wife and her lover plan and carry out the murder of the

woman's construction-worker husband. Accused of the crime they face a jury, are found guilty, and are sent to prison. Meanwhile the man who defends them is likewise having an affair with a married woman and plots the murder of the woman's successful attorney husband, who also happens to be his mentor. Unlike the case he has defended, however, his own crimes go unpunished. **Cast:** Orson Welles, Juliette Greco, Bradford Dillman, Alexander Knox, Eugene Deckers, William Lucas, Catherine Lacey, Austin Willis, Cec Linder, Eugene Deckers. **Credits:** Dir: Richard Fleischer; Prod: Darryl F. Zanuck; Writer: Darryl F. Zanuck; Story: Marcel Haedrick; DP: William C. Mellor; Ed: Craig McKay; Prod Design: Jean d'Eaubonne; Composer: Maurice Jarre. B&W, 97 min.

Crack-Up
(1936) Fox
Expert test pilot Ace Martin is hounded by a mysterious spy ring seeking secret plans to an experimental plane. Eluding them, Martin escapes with the plans in another experimental plane alongside the plane's designer, Fleming, copilot, Randall, and Gimpy, the airplane's eccentric mascot. When the plane crash-lands in the ocean, however, Gimpy reveals himself to be the spy-ring's leader and demands that Martin hand over the plans. Neat spy yarn. **Cast:** Peter Lorre, Brian Donlevy, Gloria Roy, Ralph Morgan, Thomas Beck, Kay Linaker, Lester Matthews, Earl Foxe, J. Carrol Naish, Helen Wood. **Credits:** Dir: Malcolm St. Clair; Prod: Samuel G. Engel; Writer: John F. Goodrich, Charles Kenyon, Sam Mintz; Ed: Fred Allen; Prod Design: Duncan Cramer; Composer: Harry Akst, Sidney Clare, Samuel Kaylin; Art Director: Lewis H. Creber. B&W, 71 min.

Crack-Up
(1946) RKO
Film noir about an art critic who blacks out and must reconstruct the missing hours in order to prove an art forgery conspiracy. A taut thriller that's become a minor classic of suspense. **Cast:** Pat O'Brien, Claire Trevor, Herbert Marshall, Wallace Ford, Ray Collins. **Credits:** Dir: Irving Reis; Writer: John Paxton, Raymond Spencer; Story: Fredric Brown; DP: Robert de Grasse; Ed: Frederic Knudtson; Prod Design: Albert S. D'Agostino, Jack Okey; Composer: Leigh Harline; Costumes: Renie; Set Designer: Darrell Silvera. B&W, 93 min. **VHS**

Craig's Wife
(1936) Columbia
Russell's big break is a powerful drama about a married woman whose unrelenting greed and ambition eventually cause her own downfall. Based on a Pulitzer Prize–winning play by George Kelly. Remade as *Harriet Craig*. **Cast:** Rosalind Russell, John Boles, Dorothy Wilson, Jane Darwell, Billie Burke, Alma Kruger, Thomas Mitchell, Elisabeth Risdon, Raymond Walburn. **Credits:** Dir: Dorothy Arzner; Writer: Mary McCall, George Kelly; DP: Lucien Ballard. B&W, 78 min. **VHS**

Crash Dive
(1943) Fox
This romantic adventure, set during WWII, features two Navy men vying for the love of the same woman. While heading to Washington, Lieutenant Ward Stewart meets teacher Jean Hewlitt, quickly falls for her, and eventually succeeds in gaining her affection. However, Lieutenant Stewart soon discovers that his new girlfriend is already engaged to his commanding officer. Further complications develop when both officers get assigned to the same submarine and must set off together on a dangerous mission to destroy a Nazi base. **Academy Awards:** Best Special Effects; Best Sound Effects. **Cast:** Tyrone Power, Anne Baxter, Dana Andrews, James Gleason, Dame May Whitty, Henry Morgan, Frank Conroy, Minor Watson. **Credits:** Dir: Archie Mayo; Prod: Milton Sperling; Writer: Jo Swerling; Story: W. R. Burnett; DP: Leon Shamroy; Ed: Walter Thompson; Prod Design: Richard Day, Wiard Ihnen; Composer: David Buttolph; Costumes: Earl Luick; SFX: Fred Sersen; Set Designer: Thomas Little, Paul S. Fox. Color, 105 min. **VHS**

Crazy Mama
(1975) New World
Demme's B-movie masterpiece follows three generations of female outlaws as they journey back to their hometown to repossess the family farm that was lost during the Depression. On the way they pick up a number of odd men, each with a criminal bent. **Cast:** Ann Sothern, Cloris Leachman, Linda Purl, Stuart Whitman, Jim Backus, Donald Most, Sally Kirkland, Bryan Englund, Merie Earle, Clint Kimbrough. **Credits:** Dir: Jonathan Demme; Prod: Julie Corman; Writer: Robert Thom; DP: Bruce Logan; Ed: Allan Holzman, Lewis Teague; Prod Design: Peter Jamison. Color, 81 min. **VHS**

Creature from the Black Lagoon
(1954) Universal
A group of scientists discover a terrifying prehistoric monster they dub "Gill-man" with an appetite for beautiful women in an Amazonian lagoon, where it has existed undisturbed since the Devonian Period. The creature begins to attack the humans after they invade their quiet habitat, but falls prey to the charms of the female research assistant whom he tries to spirit off to his underwater hideaway. A sci-fi/horror classic, originally shown in 3-D. The film spawned two sequels: *Revenge of the Creature* and *The Creature Walks Among Us*. **Cast:** Richard Carlson, Julie Adams, Richard Denning, Antonio Moreno, Nestor Paiva, Whit Bissell, Ben Chapman, Syd Mason, Ricou Browning. **Credits:** Dir: Jack Arnold; Prod: William Alland; Writer: Harry Essex, Arthur Ross; Story: Maurice Zimm; DP: William E. Snyder, Charles S. Welbourne; Ed: Ted J. Kent; Prod Design: Hilyard Brown, Bernard Herzbrun; Composer: Herman Stein, Hans J. Salter, Milton Rosen, Henry Mancini, Robert Emmett Dolan. B&W, 80 min. **VHS, LASER**

Crime and Punishment
(1935) Columbia
Von Sternberg's take on Dostoyevsky with Lorre in the lead. Roderick Raskolnikov believes he can commit the perfect crime and murders an old man. His conscience soon begins to destroy him, however, and the detective in charge of the case is determined to wring a confession out of him. **Cast:** Edward Arnold, Peter Lorre, Marian Marsh, Tala Birell, Elisabeth Risdon, Robert Allen. **Credits:** Dir: Josef von Sternberg; Prod: B. P. Schulberg; Writer: S. K. Lauren, Joseph Anthony; DP: Lucien Ballard; Ed: Richard Cahoon; Composer: Louis Silvers. B&W, 88 min. **VHS, LASER**

Crime Doctor
Based on Max Mancin's radio show, Columbia's short, snappy film series had criminal–turned–criminal psychologist Dr. Ordway, played by Warner Baxter, solving perplexing mysteries. The first entry, *Crime Doctor* (1943), sets the stage, with the former mob kingpin taking a nasty blow to the head, which leaves him with amnesia. Unable to recall anything about his past, he reinvents himself as a crime-solving psychiatrist. His past catches up with him, and he's arrested, though his reputation helps him get off with a suspended sentence. Look

for Lloyd Bridges and Reginald Denny in *Crime Doctor's Strangest Case* (1943) and George Zucco in *Shadows in the Night* (1944). William Castle directed three of the entries: *Crime Doctor's Warning* (1945); *Crime Doctor's Man Hunt* (1946); and *Crime Doctor's Gamble* (1947).

Crime Doctor (1943)
Crime Doctor's Strangest Case
    (1943)
Shadows in the Night *(1944)*
Crime Doctor's Courage *(1945)*
Crime Doctor's Warning *(1945)*
Crime Doctor's Man Hunt *(1946)*
Just Before Dawn *(1946)*
The Millerson Case *(1947)*
Crime Doctor's Gamble *(1947)*
Crime Doctor's Diary *(1949)*

Crime of Passion

(1957) United Artists
Stanwyck plays an antiheroine for the '50s as ace columnist Kathy Ferguson. Kathy is chic, smart, and famous, but she makes a big mistake: she falls in love with an L.A. detective. Putting all of her energies into helping her unambitious husband become an inspector, Kathy even offers her body to Inspector Pope, her husband's boss. When he rejects her, she loses control. **Cast:** Barbara Stanwyck, Sterling Hayden, Raymond Burr, Fay Wray, Virginia Grey, Royal Dano. **Credits:** Dir: Gerd Oswald; Prod: Herman Cohen; Writer: Jo Eisinger; DP: Joseph La Shelle; Ed: Marjorie Fowler; Prod Design: Leslie Thomas; Composer: Paul Dunlap; Costumes: Grace Houston; Set Designer: Morrie Hoffman. Color, 84 min. **VHS**

Crime School

(1938) Warner Bros.
Reform-school drama stars Bogart as the warden who tries to actually change these boys' lives for the better. An unlikely role for Bogart but very fitting casting for the pack of delinquents. The rough pack of rowdies give the warden quite a workout. He manages to "reform" a few. The film is quite reminiscent of an old Cagney film, *The Mayor of Hell*. **Cast:** Humphrey Bogart, Sue Warren, Bobby Jordan, Huntz Hall, Leo Gorcey, Bernard Punsley, Gabriel Dell, George Offerman, Weldon Heyburn. **Credits:** Dir: Lewis Seiler; Prod: Bryan Foy; Writer: Vincent Sherman, Crane Wilbur; Story: Crane Wilbur; DP: Arthur Todd; Ed: Terry O. Morse; Prod Design: Charles Novi; Composer: Hugo Friedhofer, George Parrish, Max Steiner. B&W, 86 min.

The Criminal Code

(1931) Columbia
A young man, unjustly jailed for killing another man in self-defense, finds himself in for a hard time when the district attorney who successfully convicted and jailed him turns up as the new warden. Remade as *Penitentiary* in 1938 and as *Convicted* in 1950. **Cast:** Walter Huston, Phillips Holmes, Constance Cummings, Boris Karloff, Mary Doran, DeWitt Jennings, Otto Hoffman, John Sheehan. **Credits:** Dir: Howard Hawks; Prod: Harry Cohn; Writer: Fred Niblo, Seton I. Miller; DP: James Wong Howe; Ed: Edward Curtiss. B&W, 98 min. **VHS**

The Crimson Pirate

(1952) Warner Bros.
A tongue-in-cheek adventure spoof, set in the late 18th century, of swashbuckling pirates. Lancaster is the captain who takes over royal ships on the high seas by having his crew feign death by scurvy. Lancaster is joined by his circus buddy Cravat in spirited stunts. **Cast:** Burt Lancaster, Eva Bartok, Nick Cravat, Torin Thatcher, James Hayter, Leslie Bradley, Margot Grahame, Noel Purcell, Frederick Leister, Eliot Makeham. **Credits:** Dir: Robert Siodmak; Prod: Harold Hecht; Writer: Roland Kibbee; DP: Otto Heller; Ed: Jack Harris; Prod Design: Paul Sheriff; Composer: William Alwyn, Dimitri Tiomkin. Color, 104 min. **VHS, LASER**

Cripple Creek

(1952) Columbia
A Western about a pair of undercover agents chasing a smuggling gang. During the lawless hysteria of the Gold Rush, the agents join the band of smugglers in order to incriminate them. It is dangerous work, and they are often on the verge of being discovered. After they assist with a shipment of gold being sent overseas, they have enough proof to arrest the criminals. **Cast:** George Montgomery, Karin Booth, Jerome Courtland, William Bishop, Richard Egan, Don Porter, John Dehner, Roy Roberts. **Credits:** Dir: Ray Nazarro; Prod: Edward Small; Writer: Richard Schayer; DP: William V. Skall; Ed: Richard Fantl; Composer: Mischa Bakaleinikoff. Color, 78 min.

Criss Cross

(1948) Universal
A hardworking, honest armored-truck driver has a fatal passion for his ex-wife, a gold digger now married to a notorious gangster. When their tryst is discovered by her husband, they con-

vince the hoodlum that they only met to get his help in robbing an upcoming payroll shipment and now the honest Joe must plan a real robbery or die. Film debut for Tony Curtis. **Cast:** Burt Lancaster, Yvonne De Carlo, Dan Duryea, Stephen McNally, Richard Long, Tom Pedi, Alan Napier. **Credits:** Dir: Robert Siodmak; Prod: Michael Kraike; Writer: Daniel Fuchs; Story: Don Tracy; DP: Franz Planer; Ed: Ted J. Kent; Prod Design: Bernard Herzbrun, Boris Leven; Composer: Miklos Rozsa; Costumes: Yvonne Wood; SFX: David Horsley; Set Designer: Russell A. Gausman, Oliver Emert. B&W, 98 min. **VHS, LASER**

Crossfire

(1947) RKO
A rare Hollywood indictment of anti-Semitism and bigotry. Four soldiers on leave spend a drunken evening with a girl and her Jewish boyfriend, whom they meet in a nightclub. When the guys argue with the boyfriend, Ryan kills him with his bare hands. In an effort to throw the detectives off his path, he kills one of his friends. Then, another soldier agrees to work with the police and sets up Ryan. Based on the novel *The Brick Foxhole* by Richard Brooks. Academy Award Nominations: Best Picture; Best Supporting Actor: Robert Ryan; Best Supporting Actress: Gloria Grahame; Best Director; Best Screenplay. **Cast:** Robert Young, Robert Mitchum, Robert Ryan, Gloria Grahame, Paul Kelly, Sam Levene, Jacqueline White, Steve Brodie. **Credits:** Dir: Edward Dmytryk; Prod: Adrian Scott; Writer: John Paxton; Story: Richard Brooks; DP: J. Roy Hunt; Ed: Harry Gerstad; Prod Design: Albert S. D'Agostino, Alfred Herman; Composer: Roy Webb; SFX: Russell A. Cully; Set Designer: Darrell Silvera, John Sturtevant. B&W, 86 min. **VHS**

Cross of Iron

(1977) Avco Embassy
A strong antiwar message film, set during WWII and told from the German perspective. A German Army sergeant doggedly struggles to keep his platoon intact while surviving the horrors of the Russian front in 1943. **Cast:** James Coburn, Maximilian Schell, Senta Berger, James Mason, David Warner, Klaus Lowitsch, Walter Kelley. **Credits:** Dir: Sam Peckinpah; Prod: Wolf C. Hartwig; Writer: James Hamilton, Julius J. Epstein; Story: Willi Heinrich; DP: John Coquillon; Ed: Michael Ellis, Tony Lawson; Composer: Ernest Gold; SFX: Richard Richtsfeld. Color, 132 min. **VHS**

The Cross of Lorraine

(1943) MGM

Drama about a group of soldiers who surrender to the Germans when France falls. The group is taken to a concentration camp, where they are tormented by sadistic Nazi guards. After a priest is shot while conducting mass for the prisoners, a French soldier attacks the Nazi sergeant responsible, and is cruelly rewarded with torture. As he is recovering in the infirmary, his comrade Paul helps him to escape, and the two make their way to a small German town. When the Nazis arrive to get recruits, Paul steps forward to confront them. **Cast:** Jean-Pierre Aumont, Gene Kelly, Cedric Hardwicke, Richard Whorf, Joseph Calleia, Peter Lorre, Hume Cronyn. **Credits:** Dir: Tay Garnett; Prod: Edwin H. Knopf; Writer: Robert Hardy Andrews, Alexandre Esway, Michael Kanin, Ring Lardner; Story: Robert Aisner, Lilo Damert, Hans Habe; DP: Sidney Wagner; Ed: Dan Milner; Prod Design: Daniel B. Cathcart, Cedric Gibbons; Composer: Bronislau Kaper, Eric Zeisl. B&W, 89 min.

Crossroads

(1942) MGM

French diplomat David Talbot marries the beautiful Lucienne, but shortly afterward finds himself being blackmailed by crooks who insist he once murdered a man. The problem is that Talbot believes he is suffering from amnesia and has cause to think that he did indeed commit the murder he is accused of. A supposed ex-flame, Michelle Allaine, corroborates the blackmailer's claims, as does a photo of Talbot and Michelle out on the town together. **Cast:** William Powell, Hedy Lamarr, Claire Trevor, Basil Rathbone, Margaret Wycherly, Felix Bressart, Sig Rumann, H. B. Warner, Philip Merivale, Vladimir Sokoloff. **Credits:** Dir: Jack Conway; Prod: Edwin H. Knopf; Writer: Guy Trosper; Story: John H. Kafka, Howard Emmett Rogers; DP: Joseph Ruttenberg; Ed: George Boemler; Prod Design: Cedric Gibbons; Composer: Bronislau Kaper. B&W, 84 min.

The Crowd Roars

(1932) Warner Bros.

A race car driver becomes jealous of his younger brother, an up-and-coming racer who marries the older brother's onetime sweetheart. In a race to settle the rivalry—one of the film's several high-energy racing sequences—the older sibling causes a crash that kills another driver. Later, he regains his hero status. **Cast:** William Arnold,

Criss Cross (1948)

Joan Blondell, James Cagney, Ann Dvorak, Ralph Hepburn, Eric Lindon, Guy Kibbee, Frank McHugh, Leo Nomis, Regis Toomey. **Credits:** Dir: Howard Hawks; Writer: John Bright, Niven Busch, Kubec Glasmon, Howard Hawks, Seton I. Miller; DP: Sidney Hickcox; Ed: Thomas Pratt; Prod Design: Jack Okey; Composer: Leo F. Forbstein. B&W, 84 min.

The Crusades

(1935) Paramount

An epic depiction of the Third Crusade, where a united force of countries embark on a mission to wrest Jerusalem from the hands of Saladin and his infidels. King Richard the Lion-Hearted leads the French, German, and English armies against the haughty Saladin. Hoping to gather more supplies, Richard offhandedly agrees to marry the daughter of a French ruler in an exchange for betrothal. By letting a proxy take part rather than in person, Richard scorns the woman who upon meeting he realizes is beautiful. Love conquers all when the two are finally joined, even as conquering armies enter Jerusalem. **Cast:** Loretta Young, Henry Wilcoxon, Ian Keith, C. Aubrey Smith, Joseph Schildkraut, Alan Hale, Katherine DeMille. **Credits:** Dir: Cecil B. DeMille; Prod: Cecil B. DeMille; Writer: Harold Lamb, Waldemar Young, Dudley Nichols; DP: Victor Milner; Ed: Anne Bauchens; Composer: Rudolph G. Kopp. Color, 126 min. **VHS**

Cry Danger

(1951) RKO

Parrish's debut as a director, following a long career as an actor and an editor. An innocent man just released from prison searches for the people who framed him and for the stashed $100,000 bankroll. Along the way he meets the wife of a fellow con still on the inside, who was framed for the same crime. Back-stabbing and deception surround him as he works to clear his name and stay alive. **Cast:** Dick Powell, Rhonda Fleming, William Conrad, Regis Toomey, Jay Adler. **Credits:** Dir: Robert Parrish, Richard Erdman; Prod: Sam Wiesenthal, W. R. Frank; Writer: William Bowers; Story: Jerry Cady; DP: Joseph Biroc; Ed: Bernard W. Burton; Prod Design: Richard Day; Composer: Emil Newman, Paul Dunlap. B&W, 80 min. **VHS**

Cry Havoc
(1943) MGM
A war movie about 9 women thrown together as volunteers in a Bataan field hospital. The majority of the action takes place in a bomb shelter, where the women (one a waitress, one a southern belle, one a former burlesque queen, etc. . . .) share their feelings about war, men, and life in general. A courageous Army nurse keeps them in line while they wait for the inevitable arrival of the Japanese troops. **Cast:** Margaret Sullavan, Ann Sothern, Joan Blondell, Fay Bainter, Marsha Hunt, Ella Raines, Frances Gifford, Diana Lewis, Heather Angel, Dorothy Morris. **Credits:** Dir: Richard Thorpe; Prod: Edwin H. Knopf; Writer: Paul Osborn; Story: Allen R. Kenward; DP: Karl Freund; Ed: Ralph E. Winters; Prod Design: Cedric Gibbons, Stephen Goosson; Composer: Daniele Amfitheatrof. B&W, 96 min.

Cry Terror
(1958) MGM
Fast-paced film filled with bombs, murders, kidnappings, the F.B.I., shootings, drug addicts, and psychopaths. An extortionist convinces an electronics expert to build a bomb. The bomb is planted on an airplane, but the authorities are warned in time. The next time, however, there will be no warning, and the extortionist holds the electronics expert, his wife, and their young daughter hostage. **Cast:** James Mason, Rod Steiger, Inger Stevens, Angie Dickinson, Jack Klugman, Carleton Young, Jack Kruschen, Neville Brand, Kenneth Tobey, Barney Phillips. **Credits:** Dir: Andrew L. Stone; Prod: Virginia Lively Stone, Andrew L. Stone; Writer: Andrew L. Stone; DP: Walter Strenge; Ed: Virginia Lively Stone; Composer: Howard Jackson. B&W, 96 min.

Cry Wolf
(1947) Warner Bros.
After Sandra Marshall's secret wedding, her young husband suddenly dies mysteriously. Without disclosing her identity to his family, Sandra

attends the wake to take stock of her spouse's relatives. The young widow is disturbed by what she sees, and becomes convinced that her husband's uncle, Mark Caldwell, has somehow contributed to the young man's demise. Sandra gradually learns more, realizing that Mark could not have committed a murder. However, not all is right with the Caldwell family and she means to discover what it is. Film debut for actress Brooks. **Cast:** Errol Flynn, Barbara Stanwyck, Geraldine Brooks, Richard Basehart, Helene Thimig. **Credits:** Dir: Peter Godfrey; Prod: Henry Blanke; Writer: Catherine Turney; Story: Marjorie Carleton; DP: Carl Guthrie; Ed: Folmar Blangsted; Prod Design: Carl Jules Weyl; Composer: Franz Waxman; Costumes: Travilla, Edith Head; SFX: William McGann, Robert Burks. B&W, 83 min. **VHS**

Cuba
(1979) United Artists
Satire about Cuban dictatorships and revolutions. A cynical British mercenary is dispatched to Havana by the Batista government in an attempt to end Castro's reign. Along the way he meets a variety of similarly cynical types as well as an old girlfriend. As the government falls down around them, each realizes a different set of values toward the conflict. **Cast:** Sean Connery, Brooke Adams, Jack Weston, Hector Elizondo, Denholm Elliott, Chris Sarandon, Lonette McKee, Martin Balsam. **Credits:** Dir: Richard Lester; Prod: Arlene Sellers, Alex Winitsky; Writer: Charles Wood; DP: David Watkin; Ed: John Victor Smith; Prod Design: Gil Parrondo; Composer: Patrick Williams; Costumes: Shirely Russell. Color, 121 min. **VHS**

Curly Top
(1935) Fox
Remake of the 1919 Mary Pickford production *Daddy Long Legs*. Shirley is the destitute little orphan girl who lives in an orphanage and plays cupid for her beautiful sister. They are discovered by a bachelor millionaire who whisks them off to his Park Avenue abode and promptly falls in love with the older sister. Never one to abandon her roots, Temple returns to the orphanage for some rousing song-and-dance routines with her friends. Features the hit songs "Curly Top," "When I Grow Up," and "Animal Crackers in My Soup." Remade again in 1955 with Fred Astaire and Leslie Caron. **Cast:** Shirley Temple, John Boles, Arthur Treacher, Jane Darwell,

Rochelle Hudson, Esther Dale, Etienne Girardot. **Credits:** Dir: Irving Cummings; Prod: Winfield Sheehan; Writer: Patterson McNutt, Arthur Beckhard; Story: Jean Webster; DP: John Seitz; Choreographer: Jack Donohue; Composer: Ray Henderson, Ted Koehler, Edward Heyman, Irving Caesar. B&W, 75 min. **VHS**

Curse of the Cat People
(1944) Universal
A child (Carter) explores her late mother's life and discovers her maternal bloodline is cursed. In her dreams, she visits her mother (Simon, the star of the earlier film titled *Cat People*) and learns her people become panthers when their blood is aroused. This sequel delves into childhood fantasy rather than suspense and horror. **Cast:** Simone Simon, Kent Smith, Jane Randolph, Elizabeth Russell, Ann Carter, Eve March, Julia Dean, Erford Gage, Sir Lancelot, Joel Davis. **Credits:** Dir: Robert Wise, Gunther von Fritsch; Prod: Val Lewton; Writer: De Witt Bodeen; DP: Nicholas Musuraca; Ed: J. R. Whittredge. B&W, 73 min. **VHS, LASER**

Cyrano de Bergerac
(1950) United Artists
Ferrer stars as the poetry-spouting soldier with the oversized nose in this faithful adaptation of Edmond Rostand's romantic tragedy. Using the handsome but inarticulate Christian as a conduit for his feelings, the ugly but eloquent Cyrano pours his heart out to the lovely Roxanne. And she, wooed by the beauty of the words, falls in love with Christian, not realizing that it is Cyrano whose voice has aroused her passion. Golden Globes for Best Black-and-White Cinematography; Best Actor in a Drama: Jose Ferrer. **Academy Awards:** Best Actor: Jose Ferrer. **Cast:** Jose Ferrer, Mala Powers, William Prince, Morris Carnovsky, Elena Verdugo, Ralph Clanton, Virginia Farmer, Edgar Barrier, Albert Cavens, Arthur Blake. **Credits:** Dir: Michael Gordon; Prod: Stanley Kramer; Writer: Carl Foreman; DP: Franz Planer; Ed: Harry Gerstad; Composer: Dimitri Tiomkin. B&W, 112 min. **VHS, LASER**

Daddy Long Legs
(1955) Fox
Globe-trotting playboy Astaire spies a young woman living in an orphanage, and on impulse decides to anonymously sponsor her college education. The mystery of her benefactor's identity fuels romantic speculation in the girl, and her letters fuel romantic speculation in Astaire. Caron may not be Astaire's greatest partner, but she's adorable and the score's pleasant. Academy Award Nominations: 3, including Best Score; Best Song ("Something's Gotta Give"). **Cast:** Fred Astaire, Leslie Caron, Thelma Ritter, Fred Clark, Terry Moore, Larry Keating, Charlotte Austin, Kathryn Givney, Kelly Brown, Sara Shane. **Credits:** Dir: Jean Negulesco; Prod: Samuel G. Engel; Writer: Phoebe Ephron, Henry Ephron; DP: Leon Shamroy; Ed: William Reynolds; Choreographer: Roland Petit, David Robel, Fred Astaire; Composer: Alfred Newman, Alex North. Color, 126 min. **VHS, LASER**

Daddy's Gone A-Hunting
(1969) Warner Bros.
A young woman eagerly awaits the birth of her first child—until her psychotic ex shows up demanding atonement for the life of their aborted child: a life for a life. Creepy psychological thriller. **Cast:** Carol White, Paul Burke, Scott Hylands, Rachel Ames, Mala Powers, Barry Cahill, Matilda Calnan, Andrea King, Gene Lyons, Ron Masak. **Credits:** Dir: Mark Robson; Prod: Mark Robson; Writer: Larry Cohen, Lorenzo Semple, Jr.; DP: Ernest Laszlo; Ed: Dorothy Spencer; Composer: John Williams; Costumes: Travilla; Art Director: James Sullivan; Set Designer: Charles S. Thompson. Color, 108 min. **VHS**

Daisy Kenyon
(1947) Fox
Typical love triangle with atypically strong cast and Preminger's touch for tension. Crawford has been carrying on a love affair with a married man, Andrews, who has no intention of leaving his wife. She meets Fonda, who has returned home from the war and intends to return to his simple life in Massachusetts. Crawford marries him, leaving her lover behind. When Andrews finally divorces his wife, he arrives at the cottage of the newlyweds to win back his mistress. The two men put the decision to Crawford, who must now choose between the wealthy former lover and the poor WWII veteran who has won her heart. **Cast:** Joan Crawford, Henry Fonda, Dana Andrews, Ruth Warrick, Martha Stewart, Peggy Ann Garner, Connie Marshall, Nicholas Joy. **Credits:** Dir: Otto Preminger; Prod: Otto Preminger; Writer: David Hertz, Elizabeth Janeway; DP: Leon Shamroy; Ed: Lewis Loeffler; Prod Design: Lyle Wheeler, Thomas Little; Composer: Alfred Newman; SFX: Fred Sersen; Art Director: George W. Davis. B&W, 99 min.

Daisy Miller
(1974) Paramount
Better than the critics of the time said. Bogdanovich's version of the Henry James story clearly was an attempt to give Shepherd, his muse at the time, a more serious profile. But she may have been just right for the role. Daisy, a rich American, takes the grand tour of Europe to mingle with others of her class and hope that breeding rubs off. But Daisy's youthful high spirits and American frankness clash with Continental etiquette. **Cast:** Cybill Shepherd, Eileen Brennan, Cloris Leachman, Barry Brown, Mildred Natwick, Duilio Del Prete, James McMurtry, Nicholas Jones, George Morfogen, Jean Pascal Bongard. **Credits:** Dir: Peter Bogdanovich; Prod: Peter Bogdanovich; Writer: Frederic Raphael; DP: Alberto Spagnoli; Ed: Verna Fields; Prod Design: Ferdi-nando Scarfiotti; Costumes: John Furness; Set Designer: Gianni Silvestri. Color, 93 min. **VHS**

Dallas
(1950) Warner Bros.
When former Confederate guerrilla Cooper comes to Dallas under the guise of a U.S. marshal, he finds the frontier town much to his liking. There is plenty of room to ride and beautiful Roman, with whom he falls in love. Unfortunately, the town is run by the nefarious Marlow brothers. When Hollister learns that they were responsible for the burning of his family's home during the war and that they now plan to drive Robles's father off of his extensive lands, he takes aim for the Marlow siblings. **Cast:** Gary Cooper, Ruth Roman, Steve Cochran, Raymond Massey, Barbara Payton, Leif Erickson, Antonio Moreno, Jerome Cowan, Reed Hadley, Gil Donaldson. **Credits:** Dir: Stuart Heisler; Prod: Anthony Veiller; Writer: John Twist; DP: Ernest Haller; Ed: Clarence Kolster; Prod Design: Douglas Bacon, George James Hopkins; Composer: Max Steiner. Color, 94 min.

Dames
(1934) Warner Bros.
Perhaps the ne plus ultra of Berkeley choreography, this backstage musical features dancing ironing boards and puzzle pieces among its surreal delights. Blondell, Keeler, and Powell sing, dance, and chew up the scenery in a hoary plot about a rich bluenose's attempts to close down a Broadway show. Never mind; just keep your eyes on those chorus lines in numbers such as "Girl at the Ironing Board" and "I Only Have Eyes for You." **Cast:** Dick Powell, Joan Blondell, Ruby Keeler, ZaSu Pitts, Hugh Herbert, Guy Kibbee, Arthur Vinton, Sammy Fain, Phil Regan, Arthur Aylesworth. **Credits:** Dir: Ray Enright; Prod: Robert Lord; Writer: Delmer Daves; DP: Sid

"She is the emerald shower which succeeds the initial explosion of a skyrocket."

New York Times film critic Bosley Crowther on 19-year-old Maureen O'Hara

Hickox; Ed: Harold McLernon; Prod Design: Robert M. Haas; Choreographer: Busby Berkeley; Costumes: Orry-Kelly; Art Director: Willy Pogany. B&W, 95 min. **VHS, LASER**

Damien: Omen II
(1978) Fox
The Omen series drew surprisingly great casts, perhaps because the emphasis was as much on suspense as gore. In this follow-up to *The Omen* (1976), the demon child is visited upon relatives Holden and Grant. Not as shocking, as we know what to expect, but still hair-raising. **Cast:** William Holden, Lee Grant, Lew Ayres, Jonathan Scott-Taylor, Sylvia Sidney, Robert Foxworth, Nicholas Pryor, Lance Henriksen, Lucas Donat, Allan Arbus. **Credits:** Dir: Don Taylor, Mike Hodges; Prod: Harvey Bernhard; Writer: Stanley Mann; DP: Bill Butler; Ed: Robert Brown; Prod Design: Philip M. Jefferies, Fred Harpman; Composer: Jerry Goldsmith. Color, 110 min. **VHS, LASER**

The Damned Don't Cry
(1950) Warner Bros.
Traces the transformation of a poor laborer's wife to the haughty, elegant mistress of a crime boss. Crawford, in a typically hard-boiled role, leaves her husband and squalid surroundings behind intent on finding a better life. In the big city, she proffers love to a talented accountant who, with Crawford's prodding, becomes allied with a mobster. Crawford quickly leaves her man for the powerful gang boss but ends up back where she began, wounded and wiser. **Cast:** Joan Crawford, David Brian, Steve Cochran, Kent Smith, Hugh Sanders, Selena Royle, Jacqueline De Wit, Morris Ankrum, Sara Perry, Richard Egan. **Credits:** Dir: Vincent Sherman; Prod: Jerry Wald; Writer: Harold Medford, Jerome Weidman; Story: Gertrude Walker; DP: Ted McCord; Ed: Rudi Fehr; Prod Design: Robert M. Haas, William L. Kuehl; Composer: Danielle Amfitheatrof. B&W, 103 min.

Damn Yankees
(1958) Warner Bros.
The ever-dim prospects of the Washington Senators suddenly improve when the team's most avid fan strikes a bargain with the devil to make him the club's newest slugger. A vivacious, buoyant adaptation of the Broadway hit directed by musical mavens Donen and Abbott, Mr. Broadway himself. Their seductive mambo made stars out of choreographer Bob Fosse and the brilliant Verdon, who played Lola, a seductive siren in the service of Satan. Songs include "Whatever Lola Wants" and "(You Got to Have) Heart." **Cast:** Gwen Verdon, Ray Walston, Tab Hunter, Russ Brown, Shannon Bolin, Nathaniel Frey; Jimmie Komack, Rae Allen, Robert Shafer, Jean Stapleton. **Credits:** Dir: George Abbott, Stanley Donen; Writer: George Abbott; DP: Harold Lipstein; Ed: Frank Bracht; Prod Design: William Eckart, Jean Eckart; Composer: Jerry Ross, Richard Adler; Costumes: William Eckart, Jean Eckart; Art Director: Stanley Fleischer. Color, 110 min. **VHS, LASER**

A Damsel in Distress
(1937) RKO
A carefree American dancer taking London by storm has less success with an aristocratic lady and her stiff-upper-lip family. The Wodehouse story suits Astaire to a T, and Burns and Allen add plenty of comic relief as Astaire's annoying agent and his agent's wife. Gershwin songs include "Foggy Day in London Town," "Nice Work If You Can Get It," and "Stiff Upper Lip." Prime Astaire. Academy Award Nominations: Best Art Direction. **Academy Awards:** Best Dance Direction. **Cast:** Fred Astaire, George Burns, Gracie Allen, Joan Fontaine, Reginald Gardiner, Ray Noble, Constance Collier, Montagu Love, Harry Watson, Jan Duggan. **Credits:** Dir: George Stevens; Prod: Pandro S. Berman; Writer: Ernest Pagano; Story: P. G. Wodehouse; DP: Joseph H. August; Ed: Henry Berman; Choreographer: Hermes Pan, Fred Astaire; SFX:

Dance, Fools, Dance
(1931) MGM
An interesting early appearance by Gable as a bootlegger tangled up with spoiled rich girl turned reporter Crawford. Depression-era potboiler enlivened with pre-Code violence and naughty glimpses of Crawford in her undies. **Cast:** Joan Crawford, Clark Gable, Cliff Edwards, Earl Foxe, Lester Vail, Natalie Moorhead, Joan Marsh. **Credits:** Dir: Harry Beaumont, Claude Autant-Lara; Writer: Richard Schayer, Aurania Rouverol; DP: Charles Rosher; Ed: George Hively; Prod Design: Cedric Gibbons. B&W, 81 min. **VHS**

Dance, Girl, Dance
(1940) RKO
O'Hara as a lovely, young aspiring ballerina who falls into a livelier life in burlesque as a result of her competition with Bubbles (Ball), a firecracker burlesque dancer. Her efforts to redeem herself and direction by pioneer female director Arzner make this a favorite among feminists. In any case, interesting for the early O'Hara and Ball roles. **Cast:** Maureen O'Hara, Lucille Ball, Louis Hayward, Virginia Field, Ralph Bellamy, Maria Ouspenskaya, Mary Carlisle, Katharine Alexander, Edward Brophy, Walter Abel. **Credits:** Dir: Dorothy Arzner, Robert Wise; Prod: Erich Pommer; Writer: Tess Slesinger, Frank Davis; DP: Russell Metty; Choreographer: Ernst Matray; Composer: Edward Ward, Chester Forrest; Art Director: Van Nest Polglase. B&W, 89 min. **VHS, LASER**

Dancing Lady
(1933) MGM
Crawford and Gable star in the story of a young burlesque dancer seeking stardom on Broadway while being romanced by two boyfriends. Mostly noted as the screen debuts of Astaire and Eddy (it even features a hilarious early appearance by The Three Stooges!). Includes songs by Burton Lane and Rodgers and Hart—one even sung by Clark! **Cast:** Joan Crawford, Clark Gable, Fred Astaire, Franchot Tone, Nelson Eddy, The Three Stooges, May Robson, Michael Robson, Winnie Lightner. **Credits:** Dir: Robert Z. Leonard; Prod: David O. Selznick; Writer: Allen Rivkin, P. J. Wolfson; DP: Oliver T. Marsh; Ed: Margaret Booth; Prod Design: Cedric Gib-

bons; Choreographer: Sammy Lee, Leroy Prinz; Composer: Louis Silvers. B&W, 94 min. VHS

The Dancing Pirate
(1936) RKO
Rodgers and Hart songs in a musical comedy about a dance instructor kidnapped by pirates who finds romance south of the border. Early Technicolor experiment, not much else. **Cast:** Frank Morgan, Charles Collins, Steffi Duna, Luis Alberni, Victor Varconi, Jack La Rue. **Credits:** Dir: Lloyd Corrigan; Prod: John Speaks; Writer: Francis Edward Faragoh, Ray Harris; DP: William V. Skall; Ed: Archie Marshek; Prod Design: Robert Jones; Composer: Richard Rodgers; Art Director: Wiard Ihnen. B&W, 84 min. VHS

Danger—Love at Work
(1937) Fox
Preminger's debut as director follows a dedicated young lawyer from New York City who's sent to a small town to negotiate the sale of a family home. The family invites him to have dinner and to spend the night, promising they will sign all necessary documents in due time. Reluctantly, the attorney agrees to humor the eccentric hosts. As excuses and incidents delay the signing of the document, he leaves with the family's love-struck daughter eagerly in tow. The family follows to New York. **Cast:** Ann Sothern, Jack Haley, Edward Everett Horton, John Carradine, Walter Catlett, Bennie Bartlett, Maurice Cass, Alan Dinehart, Etienne Girardot, E. E. Clive. **Credits:** Dir: Otto Preminger; Prod: Harold Wilson; Writer: Ben Markson; Story: James Edward Grant; DP: Virgil Miller; Ed: Jack Murray; Prod Design: Duncan Cramer; Composer: David Buttolph. B&W, 81 min.

Dangerous
(1935) Warner Bros.
Tempestuous former Broadway star Davis, now an alcoholic, gets another chance when an admiring architect falls in love with her and breaks off his engagement to the wealthy socialite who adores him. He even bankrolls her comeback, but Davis harbors a secret that could put an end to their plans. Davis's first Oscar-winning role. **Academy Awards:** Best Actress: Bette Davis. **Cast:** Bette Davis, Franchot Tone, Margaret Lindsay, Dick Foran, Alison Skipworth, John Eldredge, Pierre Watkin, Walter Walker, George Irving, William B. Davidson. **Credits:** Dir: Alfred E. Green; Prod: Harry J. Brown; Writer: Laird Doyle; DP: Ernest Haller; Ed:

Thomas Richards; Composer: Bernhard Kaun; Art Director: Hugh Reticker. B&W, 78 min. VHS, LASER

Dangerous Corner
(1934) RKO
Neat drama based on Priestley play with a trick ending about a theft of government bonds that results in the mysterious suicide of the chief suspect. Those who knew him best get together for a long dinner that turns into a truth-telling session in which illicit loves and forbidden passions surface. **Cast:** Melvyn Douglas, Conrad Nagel, Virginia Bruce, Erin O'Brien-Moore, Betty Furness, Henry Wadsworth, Doris Lloyd, Ian Keith. **Credits:** Dir: Phil Rosen; Prod: Arthur Sibcom; Writer: Anne Morrison Chapin, J. B. Priestley, Madeleine Ruthven; DP: Roy Hunt; Ed: Archie Marshek; Prod Design: Van Nest Polglase. B&W, 65 min.

Dangerous Holiday
(1937) Republic
A young violin prodigy hits the road when practicing all day means he can't roughhouse like a typical boy. His disappearance has alarms ringing. Fine family picture featuring Hopper in pre-Hollywood-columnist days. **Cast:** Hedda Hopper, Jack La Rue, Guinn "Big Boy" Williams, Franklin Pangborn, Ronald Sinclair, Jed Prouty, Lynne Roberts, William Bakewell, Fern Emmett. **Credits:** Dir: Nicholas Barrows; Prod: William Berke; Writer: Nicholas Barrows, William DeWolf; DP: William Nobles; Ed: Roy V. Livingston; Composer: Alberto Colombo. B&W, 54 min. VHS

Dangerous When Wet
(1953) MGM
Aquatic star Williams in a bubbly musical about a healthy farm family that goes to Europe so their daughter can swim the English Channel. They hope to win money for the family farm, but they bring in a bigger prize when their lovely daughter charms a French champagne producer. Williams gets to share the pool with cartoon stars Tom and Jerry, and met her future husband in costar Lamas. **Cast:** Esther Williams, Fernando Lamas, Jack Carson, Charlotte Greenwood, Denise Darcel, William Demarest, Donna Corcoran, Barbara Whiting, Bunny Waters, Henri Letondal. **Credits:** Dir: Charles Walters; Prod: George Wells; Writer: Dorothy Kingsley; DP: Harold Rosson; Ed: John McSweeney, Jr.; Choreographer: Billy Daniel, Charles Walters; Composer: Arthur Schwartz. Color, 96 min. VHS, LASER

Darby O'Gill and the Little People
(1959) Disney
A man with the Irish gift of gab finds himself face-to-face with the magical little people in an underestimated Disney classic. One of the old storyteller's tall tales comes true when he captures the King of the Leprechauns, who must grant him three wishes. They all backfire in amusing, and sometimes frightening, ways. Great special effects and scenery. **Cast:** Albert Sharpe, Janet Munro, Sean Connery, Kieron Moore, Jimmy O'Dea, Estelle Winwood, Walter Fitzgerald, Denis O'Dea, J. G. Devlin, Jack MacGowran. **Credits:** Dir: Robert Stevenson; Prod: Walt Disney; Writer: Lawrence Edward Watkin; DP: Winton C. Hoch; Ed: Stanley Johnson; Prod Design: Carroll Clark; Composer: Oliver Wallace. Color, 93 min. VHS

Darby's Rangers
(1957) Warner Bros.
Interesting combination of old pro Wellman and Garner in his first starring role. He portrays the leader of an elite commando brigade that faced the Axis powers in North Africa and Italy. Garner spends an equal amount of time preparing his troops and sorting out their amours. **Cast:** James Garner, Jack Warden, Peter Brown, Stuart Whitman, David Janssen, Edd Byrnes, Etchika Choureau, Torin Thatcher, Venetia Stevenson, Joan Elan. **Credits:** Dir: William Wellman, Max Steiner; Prod: Martin Rackin; Writer: Guy Trosper; DP: William Clothier; Ed: Owen Marks; Costumes: Marjorie Best; Art Director: William Campbell. B&W, 122 min. VHS

The Dark Angel
(1935) United Artists
Three friends in this sentimental romance—Alan, Kitty, and Gerald—grow up in the English countryside, the boys vying gently for the affections of Kitty. Just before war separates them, Kitty commits herself to Alan, who is then believed killed. Kitty and Gerald draw closer, but just as they prepare to marry they discover that Alan still lives. They seek him out and realize he has been blinded, and was hiding himself because he does not want to be a burdensome husband to Kitty. Standard three-corner romance weepy with more than the usual star appeal. **Cast:** Fredric March, Merle Oberon, Herbert Marshall, Janet Beecher, John Halliday, Henrietta Crosman, Frieda Inescort, Claude Allister, George P. Breakston, Fay

Chaldecott. **Credits:** Dir: Sidney Franklin; Prod: Samuel Goldwyn; Writer: Guy Bolton, Lillian Hellman; DP: Gregg Toland; Composer: Alfred Newman; Art Director: Richard Day. B&W, 105 min.

The Dark at the Top of the Stairs
(1960) Warner Bros.
Family trials and tribulations in '20s Oklahoma. Preston gives a poignant portrayal of a husband who chooses the warmth of another woman over his cold wife and familial duties. His daughter falls in love with a Jewish boy who commits suicide due to anti-Semitic pressure. Meanwhile, young Sonny must come to terms with the evil he imagines to exist in the dark at the top of the stairs. **Cast:** Robert Preston, Dorothy McGuire, Eve Arden, Angela Lansbury, Shirley Knight, Lee Kinsolving, Frank Overton, Robert Eyer, Penny Parker, Ken Lynch. **Credits:** Dir: Delbert Mann; Prod: Michael Garrison; Writer: Harriet Frank, Jr., Irving Ravetch; Story: William Inge; DP: Harry Stradling; Ed: Folmar Blangsted; Prod Design: Leo K. Kuter; Composer: Max Steiner. Color, 124 min.

Dark City
(1950) Paramount
Brooding noir begins after an unlucky patsy commits suicide when he is cleaned out in a rigged poker game, and four con men are hunted down by the mark's brother. As his colleagues are murdered one by one, the leader of the ring travels to Los Angeles to investigate the mysterious killer. While the revenge killer stalks the ringleader, a cop is also on his trail. Heston's big-screen debut. **Cast:** Charlton Heston, Lizabeth Scott, Viveca Lindfors, Dean Jagger, Don Defore, Jack Webb, Ed Begley, Jr., Harry Morgan, Walter Sande, Mark Keuning. **Credits:** Dir: William Dieterle; Prod: Hal B. Wallis; Writer: Larry Marcus, John Meredyth Lucas, Ketti Frings; DP: Victor Milner; Ed: Warren Low; Composer: Franz Waxman; Art Director: Franz Bachelin, Hans Dreier. B&W, 82 min.

The Dark Command
(1940) Republic
A Civil War tale based on the exploits of the notorious outlaw Quantrill. Wayne plays a U.S. marshal out to stop the cutthroat raider and his band. Based on the novel by W. R. Burnett. **Cast:** John Wayne, Claire Trevor, Walter Pidgeon, Roy Rogers, George "Gabby" Hayes, Porter Hall, Marjorie Main. **Credits:** Dir: Raoul Walsh; Prod:

Sol C. Siegel; Writer: Grover Jones, Lionel Houser, F. Hugh Herbert, Jan Fortune; Story: W. R. Burnett; DP: Jack Marta; Ed: Murray Seldeen, William Morgan; Composer: Victor Young; Art Director: John Victor MacKay. B&W, 94 min. **VHS**

The Dark Corner
(1946) Fox
Twisty, riveting film noir about a private detective, formerly framed by his partner, who finds himself framed again—this time for his partner's murder. Ball plays his trusty secretary, who aids him in tracking down the real killer. **Cast:** Mark Stevens, Lucille Ball, Clifton Webb, William Bendix, Cathy Downs, Kurt Kreuger, Reed Hadley, Constance Collier. **Credits:** Dir: Henry Hathaway; Prod: Fred Kohlmar; Writer: Jay Dratler, Bernard C. Schoenfeld; Story: Leo Rosten; DP: Joseph MacDonald; Ed: J. Watson Webb; Prod Design: James Basevi; Composer: Cyril J. Mockridge; Costumes: Kay Nelson; SFX: Fred Sersen; Art Director: Leland Fuller; Set Designer: Thomas Little, Paul S. Fox. B&W, 99 min. **VHS**

The Dark Mirror
(1946) Universal
De Havilland plays two roles in this entertaining psychological drama. A sister and her disturbed twin are implicated in a Hollywood murder and a police detective must figure out which one's the killer. **Cast:** Olivia de Havilland, Lew Ayres, Thomas Mitchell, Richard Long, Garry Owen. **Credits:** Dir: Robert Siodmak; Writer: Nunnally Johnson; Story: Vladimir Pozner; DP: Milton Krasner; Ed: Ernest Nims; Prod Design: Duncan Cramer; Composer: Dimitri Tiomkin; Costumes: Irene Sharaff; SFX: Paul K. Lerpae, Devereaux Jennings; Set Designer: Hugh Hunt. B&W, 85 min. **VHS**

Dark Passage
(1947) Warner Bros.
Bogart and Bacall headline a wild tale of an escapee from a San Quentin murder sentence who has his face surgically altered to allow him the freedom to find his wife's real killer. Now a man without a past, he meets a sultry stranger willing to put him up until his face heals and they can solve the mystery. **Cast:** Humphrey Bogart, Lauren Bacall, Agnes Moorehead, Bruce Bennett, Tom D'Andrea, Clifton Young, Douglas Kennedy, Rory Mallinson, Houseley Stevenson, Bob Farber. **Credits:** Dir: Delmer Daves; Prod: Jerry Wald; Writer: Delmer

Daves; DP: Sid Hickox; Prod Design: Charles H. Clarke; Composer: Franz Waxman. B&W, 107 min. **VHS, LASER**

The Dark Past
(1949) Columbia
A psychopathic killer opens the wrong door when he takes a cool-headed psychiatrist and his family hostage. They engage in a mental duel for survival that becomes a compelling "battle of the psyches." An overlooked thriller with an unforgettable climax. **Cast:** William Holden, Lee J. Cobb, Nina Foch, Adele Jergens, Stephen Dunne. **Credits:** Dir: Rudolph Mate; Prod: Buddy Adler; Writer: Philip MacDonald, Michael Blankfort, Malvin Wald; Story: Oscar Saul, James Warwick; DP: Joseph Walker; Ed: Viola Lawrence; Prod Design: Cary Odell; Composer: George Duning; Costumes: Jean Louis; Set Designer: Frank Tuttle. B&W, 75 min. **VHS**

Dark Star
(1974)
Sci-fi cinema geniuses, the early years! Carpenter's directorial debut, aided and abetted by future *Alien* writer O'Bannon. A knowing satire of sci-fi flicks as three astronauts pursue their mission to seek and destroy unstable planets that are hazardous to space colonies. Their onboard computer and weapons systems have different ideas. **Cast:** Brian Narelle, Dan O'Bannon, Dre Pahich, Carl Kuniholm, Joe Sanders. **Credits:** Dir: John Carpenter; Prod: John Carpenter; Writer: John Carpenter; DP: Douglas Knapp; Ed: Dan O'Bannon; Composer: John Carpenter. Color, 91 min. **VHS, LASER**

Dark Victory
(1939) Warner Bros.
In one of the roles most identified with Davis, she shows her quicksilver ability to change emotional tempo from flighty high-handedness to despair to brave resignation. As a beautiful, effervescent social butterfly she leads a carefree life until she learns she has a fatal brain tumor. Given a respite by the healing hands of her handsome young doctor, she falls in love with both him and life itself. Beware of colorized version. **Cast:** Bette Davis, George Brent, Humphrey Bogart, Geraldine Fitzgerald, Ronald Reagan, Henry Travers, Cora Witherspoon, Virginia Brissac, Dorothy Peterson, Charles Richman. **Credits:** Dir: Edmund Goulding; Prod: David Lewis; Writer: Casey Robinson; DP: Ernest Haller; Ed: William Holmes; Prod

Design: Robert M. Haas; Composer: Max Steiner. B&W, 106 min. **VHS, LASER, DVD**

Darling, How Could You?

(1951) Paramount

Minor Leisen outing with Fontaine and Lund starring as parents who return home to reacquaint themselves with their three children after spending five years helping to dig the Panama Canal. Watch for Burke (Glenda in *The Wizard of Oz*) in a cameo as Rosie. Based on James M. Barrie's stage play, *Alice Sit-by-the-Fire*. **Cast:** Joan Fontaine, John Lund, Mona Freeman, Peter Hanson, David Stollery, Virginia Farmer, Angela Clarke, Lowell Gilmore, Robert Barratt, Gertrude Michael. **Credits:** Dir: Mitchell Leisen; Prod: Harry Tugend; Writer: Lesser Samuels, Dodie Smith, James M. Barrie; DP: Daniel Fapp; Ed: Alma Macrorie; Prod Design: Roland Anderson, Hal Periera; Composer: Frederick Hollander. B&W, 96 min.

A Date with Judy

(1948) MGM

Interesting early postwar musical that combines the musicomedy warhorses of the '40s with the rising Hollywood stars of the '50s, including the lovely Taylor. Choreography by Donen distinguishes plot of teenage doings before a big dance. Includes the songs "It's a Most Unusual Day" and "Cuanto La Gusta" (with Miranda!). **Cast:** Jane Powell, Wallace Beery, Elizabeth Taylor, Carmen Miranda, Xavier Cugat, Robert Stack, Selena Royle, Scotty Beckett, Leon Ames, George Cleveland. **Credits:** Dir: Richard Thorpe, Harold F. Kress; Prod: Joe Pasternak; Writer: Dorothy Cooper, Dorothy Kingsley; DP: Robert Surtees; Prod Design: Cedric Gibbons; Choreographer: Stanley Donen. Color, 114 min. **VHS, LASER**

Daughters Courageous

(1939) Warner Bros.

A successful entry in the *Four Daughters* franchise, again directed by Curtiz with most of the same cast, this warm follow-up is based on the return of the daughters' father, Rains, who left his wife and family 20 years earlier only to return just as his ex-wife has decided to remarry. The drama involves whether or not Rains will be accepted again by the family he abandoned, and how his presence will affect the balance that all in the family have worked so hard to achieve. **Cast:** John Garfield, Claude Rains, Jeffrey Lynn, Fay Bainter, Donald Crisp, May Robson, Frank McHugh, Dick Foran,

George Humbert, Berton Churchill. **Credits:** Dir: Michael Curtiz; Prod: Henry Blanke; Writer: Julius J. Epstein, Philip G. Epstein; Story: Dorothy Bennett, Irving White; DP: James Wong Howe; Ed: Ralph Dawson, W. Donn Hayes; Prod Design: John Hughes; Composer: Max Steiner. B&W, 107 min.

David and Bathsheba

(1951) Fox

A better-than-average biblical tale with an all-too-modern moral. King David's infatuation with Bathsheba, the wife of one of his soldiers, nearly causes the destruction of his kingdom when he brings the wrath of God upon his land. Peck has just the right mix of gravity and matinee-idol appeal. **Cast:** Gregory Peck, Susan Hayward, Raymond Massey, James Robertson Justice, Kieron Moore, Jayne Meadows, John Sutton, Dennis Hoey, Francis X. Bushman, Jr., George Zucco. **Credits:** Dir: Henry King; Prod: Darryl F. Zanuck; Writer: Philip Dunne; DP: Leon Shamroy; Ed: Barbara McLean; Prod Design: Lyle Wheeler, George W. Davis; Composer: Alfred Newman. Color, 116 min. **VHS, LASER**

David and Lisa

(1962) Continental

Renowned independent feature from the '60s. Dullea and Margolin meet in a mental institution—he locked inside his anxieties, she a fragile, whimsical compulsive—and fall in love. Heartbreakingly poignant with artistically low-budget flourishes. Remade for television in 1998. Academy Award Nominations: Best Screenplay; Best Director. **Cast:** Keir Dullea, Janet Margolin, Howard Da Silva, Clifton James, Neva Patterson, Richard McMurray. **Credits:** Dir: Frank Perry; Prod: Paul M. Heller; Writer: Eleanor Perry, Theodore Isaac Rubin; DP: Leonard Hirschfield; Ed: Irving Oshman; Composer: Mark Lawrence. B&W, 94 min. **VHS, LASER**

David Copperfield

(1935) MGM

The definitive Hollywood version of Dickens's 1850 tale of a young boy despised by his stepfather who overcomes early years of poverty. No film can ever come close to conveying the detail and depth of a Dickens novel, but, perhaps more than any other, Cukor's version captures the spirit of his words. Bartholomew is endearing and the deep cast of characters in support includes a priceless turn by Fields as Micawber. **Cast:** Freddie Bartholomew, W. C. Fields, Maureen

O'Sullivan, Edna May Oliver, Lionel Barrymore, Madge Evans, Lewis Stone, Frank Lawton, Elizabeth Allan, Roland Young. **Credits:** Dir: George Cukor; Prod: David O. Selznick; Writer: Howard Estabrook, Hugh Walpole; Story: Charles Dickens; DP: Oliver T. Marsh; Ed: Robert J. Kern; Prod Design: Cedric Gibbons; Composer: Herbert Stothart. B&W, 131 min. **VHS, LASER**

David Holzman's Diary

(1968) Paradigm

A legendary independent film satire in the form of a cinema verité diary movie. As the young filmmaker records more of his life, he understands it less. Made for only $2,500, it met with approval on the festival circuit. Director McBride went on to direct *The Big Easy* and *The Wrong Man,* among others. Selected for the National Film Registry. **Cast:** L. M. Kit Carson, Eileen Dietz, Louise Levine, Lorenzo Mans. **Credits:** Dir: Jim McBride; Prod: Jim McBride; Writer: Jim McBride; DP: Michael Wadleigh. B&W, 74 min. **VHS**

Dawn of the Dead

(1978) United

Romero's tongue-in-cheek sequel to *Night of the Living Dead* is so grotesque that it achieves a kind of comic bliss. In the modern cathedral of materialism, a shopping mall, flesh-eating zombies browse for more victims. Four horrified survivors fend off the gruesome shoppers as the mall fills with the once-living. The director's cut features 11 minutes of ultra-gory footage not included in the theatrical release, and includes a bonus tape with the domestic and international theatrical trailers. **Cast:** David Emge, Ken Foree, Scott Reiniger, Tom Savini, Gaylen Ross, David Crawford, George A. Romero, The Zombies. **Credits:** Dir: George A. Romero; Prod: Richard P. Rubinstein; Writer: George Romero; DP: Michael Gornick; Prod Design: Barbara Lifsher, Josie Caruso. Color, 131 min. **VHS, LASER**

The Dawn Patrol

(1938) Warner Bros.

The harrowing tale of WWI British fighter pilots whose jobs are to keep the German planes behind enemy lines. An engaging drama about the stresses and friendships of wartime, with fine performances by an all-star cast. Remake of Howard Hawks's 1930 version. **Cast:** Errol Flynn, David Niven, Basil Rathbone, Donald Crisp, Melville Cooper, Barry Fitzgerald, Carl Esmond.

Credits: Dir: Edmund Goulding; Prod: Seton I. Miller; Writer: Dan Totheroh; Story: John Monk Saunders; DP: Tony Gaudio; Ed: Ralph Dawson; Composer: Max Steiner; SFX: Edwin A. DuPar; Art Director: John Hughes. B&W, 108 min. VHS

A Day at the Races
(1937) MGM
This Marx Brothers outing turns the boys loose in a sanatorium. Groucho moves up in life from ministering to horses at the track to minding the hypochondriacal ills of patients such as Dumont. One of their best! **Cast:** Groucho, Harpo, and Chico Marx, Maureen O'Sullivan, Allan Jones, Sig Rumann, Margaret Dumont, Douglas Dumbrille, Esther Muir. **Credits:** Dir: Sam Wood; Prod: Max Siegel; Writer: Robert Pirosh, Bob Seaton; Story: George Oppenheimer; DP: Joseph Ruttenberg; Ed: Frank Hull; Choreographer: Dave Gould; Composer: Bronislau Kaper, Walter Jurmann, Gus Kahn. B&W, 111 min. VHS, LASER

A Day of Fury
(1956) Universal
This winning Western depicts loner Robertson struggling to maintain his rugged individuality against the civilized encroachments of modernity. After saving the town marshal's life, Robertson goes to the the lawman's wedding party and has a little too much fun. He blows up the local saloon, imports a host of showgirls, and puts a couple of bullets in a man who may or may not have been gunning for him. The town's in an uproar, having outgrown such frontier behavior long ago. But when an outlaw shows up, they're glad Robertson's around. **Cast:** Dale Robertson, Mara Corday, Jock Mahoney, Carl Benton Reid, Jan Merlin, John Dehner, Dee Carroll, Sheila Terry, James Bell, Dani Crayne. **Credits:** Dir: Harmon Jones; Prod: Robert Arthur; Writer: James Edmiston, Oscar Brodney; Story: James Edmiston; DP: Ellis W. Carter; Ed: Sherman Todd; Prod Design: Robert F. Boyle, Alexander Golitzen; Composer: Henry Mancini. Color, 78 min.

The Day of the Dolphin
(1973) Avco Embassy
Scientist Scott and his wife train his dolphins to speak but find they have been kidnapped and that the military has other plans for them, including assassination. Henry wrote the script and performed the dolphin voices (no doubt providing more grist for his satiric mill). **Cast:** George C. Scott, Trish Van Devere, Paul Sorvino, Fritz Weaver, Jon Korkes, Edward Herrmann, Leslie Charleson, John David Carson, Victoria Racimo, John Dehner. **Credits:** Dir: Mike Nichols; Prod: Robert E. Relyea; Writer: Buck Henry; Story: Robert Merle; DP: William A. Fraker; Ed: Sam O'Steen; Prod Design: Richard Sylbert; Composer: Georges Delerue. Color, 104 min. VHS, LASER

The Day of the Jackal
(1973) Universal
This suspense thriller about a daring plot to murder Charles De Gaulle is based on Forsyth's best-seller. The movie's deliberate, suspenseful pace is tied to the careful, intricate planning of the man code-named "the Jackal" as he prepares for the hit. Watered down and remade in 1997 as *The Jackal*. Academy Award Nominations: Best Editing. **Cast:** Edward Fox, Alan Badel, Terrence Alexander, Cyril Cusack, Michel Auclair, Tony Britton, Maurice Denham, Vernon Dobtcheff, Jacques Francois, Olga Georges-Picot. **Credits:** Dir: Fred Zinnemann; Prod: John Woolf, David Deutsch, Julien Derode; Writer: Kenneth Ross; Story: Frederick Forsyth; DP: Jean Tournier; Ed: Ralph Kemplen; Prod Design: Willy Holt, Ernest Archer; Composer: Georges Delerue. Color, 143 min. VHS, LASER, DVD

The Day of the Locust
(1975) Paramount
An absorbing look at the desperate characters who populated Hollywood in the 1930s, based on West's satirical novel. A young artist encounters a dismal world of broken people, shattered dreams, and phony healers pandering to the lost where he had hoped to find glamour. All collide at a disastrous Hollywood premiere. Academy Award Nominations: Best Supporting Actor: Burgess Meredith; Best Cinematography. **Cast:** Donald Sutherland, Karen Black, Burgess Meredith, William Atherton, Geraldine Page, Richard A. Dysart, Bo Hopkins, Lelia Goldoni, Pepe Serna, Billy Barty. **Credits:** Dir: John Schlesinger; Prod: Jerome Hellman; Writer: Waldo Salt; Story: Nathanael West; DP: Conrad Hall; Ed: Jim Clark; Prod Design: Richard MacDonald; Composer: John Barry. Color, 144 min. VHS, LASER

The Day of the Triffids
(1963) Allied Artists
A meteor shower disrupts the earth's ecosystem, blinds all who observed it, and awakens meat-eating plants. As the hungry foliage grow ever faster, a sighted sailor and an alcoholic scientist help save humanity from becoming plant food. Script originally credited to Philip Yordan, who acted as a blacklist-era "front" for Michael Gordon. **Cast:** Howard Keel, Nicole Maurey, Kieron Moore, Janette Scott, Alexander Knox, Mervyn Johns, Janina Faye, Alison Leggatt, Ewan Roberts. **Credits:** Dir: Steve Sekely; Prod: George Pitcher; Writer: Philip Yordan; Story: John Wyndham; DP: Ted Moore; Ed: Spencer Reeve; Prod Design: Cedric Dawe; Composer: Ron Goodwin. Color, 95 min. VHS, LASER

Days of Heaven
(1978) Paramount
Malick's lyrical screen poem about life in America at the turn of the century. When a Chicago steel-mill worker (Gere) is fired after a fight with his supervisor, he hops a train for the Great Plains with his girlfriend (Adams) and his younger sister (Manz). The trio join itinerant workers following the farming seasons, and find a place with a quiet, lonely landowner. As the year passes and the harvest nears, a fateful love triangle develops with fiery consequences. The spare dialogue and strong performances match Almendros's moody compositions in this elegy for the pre-modern prairie. Academy Award Nominations: 4, including Best Score. **Academy Awards:** Best Cinematography. **Cast:** Richard Gere, Brooke Adams, Sam Shepard, Linda Manz, Bob Wilke, Stuart Margolin, Timothy Scott, Jackie Shultis. **Credits:** Dir: Terrence Malick; Prod: Bert Schneider, Harold Schneider; Writer: Terrence Malick; DP: Nestor Almendros; Ed: Billy Weber; Prod Design: Jack Fisk; Composer: Ennio Morricone. Color, 95 min. VHS, LASER

Days of Wine and Roses
(1962) Warner Bros.
Biting drama about a young couple's struggle with alcoholism. Edwards gives Lemmon plenty of room—the production is more naturalistic than the original teleplay—and he makes the best of it. Excellent score by Mancini, and the title song became a hit. The *Playhouse 90* teleplay was directed by John Frankenheimer and starred Cliff Robertson and Piper Laurie; fascinating, and also available on video. Academy Award Nominations: 5, including Best Actor: Jack Lemmon; Best Actress: Lee Remick. **Academy Awards:** Best Song. **Cast:** Jack Lemmon, Lee Remick, Jack Albertson, Jack Klugman, Charles Bickford, Alan

Hewitt, Maxine Stuart, Tom Palmer, Debbie Megowan, Katherine Squire. **Credits:** Dir: Blake Edwards; Prod: Martin Manulis; Writer: J. P. Miller; DP: Philip H. Lathrop; Ed: Patrick McCormack; Prod Design: Joseph C. Wright; Composer: Henry Mancini. B&W, 138 min. VHS

The Day the Earth Stood Still
(1951) Fox
Though it lacks digital-era special effects (and the hero's giant robot companion looks as menacing as an industrial Maytag), this may be one of the greatest science-fiction films of all time. Soberly, almost solemnly, it depicts the arrival of an alien dignitary who has come to earth to deliver a message: stop warring among yourselves or you will be destroyed. Bidden to Washington, the world's leaders squabble until the alien ambassador loses patience and slips into the world to learn why humans can't hear the truth. Herrmann wrote the haunting score. Golden Globe for Best Film Promoting International Understanding. **Cast:** Michael Rennie, Patricia Neal, Hugh Marlowe, Sam Jaffe, Billy Gray, Frances Bavier, Lock Martin, Drew Pearson, Frank Conroy, Edith Evanson. **Credits:** Dir: Robert Wise; Prod: Julian C. Blaustein; Writer: Edmund H. North; DP: Leo Tover; Ed: William H. Reynolds; Prod Design: Lyle Wheeler, Addison Hehr; Composer: Bernard Herrmann. B&W, 92 min. VHS, LASER

Day-Time Wife
(1939) Fox
Power stars in this romantic comedy as the husband who loves his wife, Darnell, but still takes his secretary out for the occasional night on the town. Darnell suspects his playful nature and gets a job in the office of one of her husband's associates, where she can track her husband on the sly. She ultimately follows her husband and his associate to a restaurant where they plan to dine with their respective secretaries, a funny climax to this comedic game of cat-and-spouse. **Cast:** Tyrone Power, Linda Darnell, Warren William, Binnie Barnes, Wendy Barrie, Joan Davis, Joan Valerie, Leonid Kinskey, Mildred Glover, Renie Riano. **Credits:** Dir: Gregory Ratoff; Prod: Darryl F. Zanuck; Writer: Art Arthur, Robert Harari; Story: Rex Taylor; DP: Peverell Marley; Ed: Francis Lyons; Prod Design: Richard Day, Joseph C. Wright; Composer: Cyril Mockridge. B&W and Color, 71 min.

D-Day, the Sixth of June
(1956) Fox
Hollywood looks back once again at the undeniably compelling story of D-Day, this time through the device of two officers, an American and a Brit, facing the coming battle and recalling their love for the same woman. Solid battle sequences, but the atypical plot is the hook. **Cast:** Robert Taylor, Dana Wynter, Richard Todd, Edmond O'Brien, John Williams, Jerry Paris, Robert Gist, Richard Stapley, Ross Elliott, Alex Finlayson. **Credits:** Dir: Henry Koster; Prod: Charles Brackett; Writer: Ivan Moffat, Harry Brown; DP: Lee Garmes; Ed: William Mace; Prod Design: Lyle Wheeler; Composer: Lyn Murray; Costumes: Charles LeMaire; SFX: Ray Kellogg; Art Director: Lewis Creber. Color, 106 min. VHS

Dead End
(1937) United Artists
Prototypical social-problem drama about a Manhattan slum in the 1930s. Hellman's engaging script, based on Sidney Kingsley's hit play, finds the neighborhood's residents struggling to get by, some choosing hard work, some taking the easier route of crime. When gangster Bogart starts to hang around his old haunts, he becomes an unwelcome influence on the street kids. Those kids became known as the Dead End Kids and, later, the Bowery Boys. Academy Award Nominations: 4, including Best Picture; Best Supporting Actress: Claire Trevor; Best Cinematography. **Cast:** Humphrey Bogart, Sylvia Sidney, Joel McCrea, Wendy Barrie, Claire Trevor, Allen Jenkins, Dead End Kids, Marjorie Main, James Burke, Ward Bond. **Credits:** Dir: William Wyler; Prod: Samuel Goldwyn; Writer: Lillian Hellman; DP: Gregg Toland; Ed: Daniel Mandell; Prod Design: Richard Day; Composer: Alfred Newman. B&W, 92 min. VHS, LASER

Dead Heat on a Merry-Go-Round
(1966) Columbia
Conman Coburn spends his time in prison figuring out how to win release and get to work on his next big job. Once on the outside, he plans to rob the bank at L.A. International Airport. But does he land the loot he intended? Ford makes his 1-line debut as a hotel employee. **Cast:** James Coburn, Camilla Sparv, Aldo Ray, Nina Wayne, Robert Webber, Todd Armstrong, Marian Moses, Severn Darden, James Westerfield, Harrison Ford. **Credits:** Dir: Bernard Girard; Prod: Carter

DeHaven; Writer: Bernard Girard, Lionel Lindon; Ed: William A. Lyon; Composer: Stu Phillips; Art Director: Walter M. Simonds. Color, 107 min. VHS

Deadline
(1952) Fox
Drama stars Bogart as an honorable editor of a respected newspaper. He is in danger of losing the paper to the late owner's greedy daughters, who in turn will sell it to the paper's competition. At the same time, he's caught up in trying to expose a Mob boss. He and his dedicated reporters uncover the crime syndicate and are close to pinning a murder on the boss until the witness is killed. **Cast:** Humphrey Bogart, Ethel Barrymore, Kim Hunter, Ed Begley, Jr., Warren Stevens, Paul Stewart, Martin Gabel, Joe Desantis, Joyce MacKenzie, Audrey Christie. **Credits:** Dir: Richard Brooks; Prod: Sol C. Siegel; Writer: Richard Brooks; DP: Milton Krasner; Ed: William B. Murphy; Prod Design: Lyle Wheeler; Composer: Sol Kaplan, Cyril Mockridge. B&W, 87 min.

Deadline at Dawn
(1946) RKO
Group Theater guru Clurman's only outing as a screen director is an atmospheric murder mystery about a naive sailor framed for a woman's death. Hayward mixes in as an aspiring actress who believes the sailor's story. Based on an Odets script from a Woolrich novel. **Cast:** Paul Lukas, Susan Hayward, Lola Lane, Bob Williams, Osa Massen, Joseph Calleia, Jerome Cowan, Marvin Miller, Roman Bohnen, Steven Geray. **Credits:** Dir: Harold Clurman; Prod: Adrian Scott; Writer: Clifford Odets; Story: Cornell Woolrich; DP: Nicholas Musuraca; Ed: Roland Gross; Prod Design: Albert S. D'Agostino, Jack Okey; Composer: Hanns Eisler. B&W, 91 min. VHS

The Deadly Affair
(1967) Columbia
Lumet directs a decidedly un-007-like spy thriller. In this adaptation of John le Carré's *Call for the Dead*, Mason plays a dyspeptic, underpaid counterespionage agent. When a routine check of a foreign service officer turns up a dead body, Mason, against orders from headquarters, quits his post to investigate this fishy "suicide" at a high personal and professional cost. **Cast:** Michael Bryant, James Mason, Maximilian Schell, Charles Kay, Harriet Andersson, Margaret

Lacey, Harry Andrews, Simone Signoret, David Warner. **Credits:** Dir: Sidney Lumet; Prod: Sidney Lumet; Writer: Paul Dehn; Story: John le Carré; DP: Frederick Young; Ed: Thelma Connell; Prod Design: John Howell; Composer: Quincy Jones. Color, 107 min.

The Deadly Companions
(1961) Pathé
Peckinpah's first feature follows a funeral procession through hostile Apache territory as it's led by the man who accidentally killed the boy in the coffin. The soldier who made the promise of protection to the boy's mother hopes to settle more than one score at the end of the journey. **Cast:** Maureen O'Hara, Brian Keith, Chill Wills, Steve Cochran, Strother Martin, Will Wright. **Credits:** Dir: Sam Peckinpah; Prod: Charles B. FitzSimons; Writer: A. S. Fleischman; DP: William H. Clothier; Ed: Stanley Rabjohn; Composer: Marlin Skiles. Color, 90 min. **VHS, LASER**

Dead Reckoning
(1947) Columbia
A made-for-Bogart role as a WWII veteran who becomes an amateur sleuth when his buddy goes missing on the way to Washington. His investigation takes him to his friend's hometown in the South where he discovers a murder and more than he wanted to know about his pal. **Cast:** Humphrey Bogart, Lizabeth Scott, Morris Carnovsky, William Prince, Charles Cane, Marvin Miller, Wallace Ford, James Bell, George Chandler, William Forrest. **Credits:** Dir: John Cromwell; Prod: Sidney Biddell; Writer: Oliver H. P. Garrett, Steve Fisher, Allen Rivkin; DP: Leo Tover; Ed: Gene Havlick; Composer: Marlin Skiles. B&W, 100 min. **VHS, LASER**

Dead Ringer
(1964) Warner Bros.
A Davis-fest as the screen diva plays twin sisters at odds over a man stolen from the meeker sister by the devious sister. Directed by Davis's *Now, Voyager* costar (and *Casablanca* star) Henreid. **Cast:** Bette Davis, Karl Malden, Peter Lawford, Jean Hagen, George Macready, Estelle Winwood, George Chandler, Cyril Delevanti, Paul Henreid. **Credits:** Dir: Paul Henreid; Prod: William H. Wright; Writer: Albert Beich, Oscar Millard; DP: Ernest Haller; Ed: Folmar Blangsted; Composer: Andre Previn; Art Director: Perry Ferguson. B&W, 116 min. **VHS, LASER**

Dear Brigitte
(1965) Fox
A 10-year-old math whiz, with a knack for picking the horses and a crush on Brigitte Bardot, beats all the odds and ends up meeting his beloved Brigitte. Stewart in his 1960s befuddled family-man persona. Okay for kids (but you'll have to explain who Bardot is). **Cast:** James Stewart, Billy Mumy, Fabian, Glynis Johns, Ed Wynn, Brigitte Bardot, Cindy Carol, John Williams, Jack Kruschen, Alice Pearce. **Credits:** Dir: Henry Koster; Prod: Henry Koster; Writer: Hal Kanter; DP: Lucien Ballard; Ed: Marjorie Fowler; Prod Design: Jack Martin Smith, Malcolm F. Brown; Composer: George Duning. Color, 100 min. **VHS**

Death of a Gunfighter
(1969) Universal
Off-beat Western tale of an ex-gunslinger sheriff who doesn't match the up-to-date image the town wants to project to Eastern investors. And there's only one way to fire an ex-gunslinger. Directed by Totten and Siegel, this was the first screen credit for Alan Smithee, the pseudonym of choice for unhappy directors. **Cast:** Richard Widmark, Lena Horne, John Saxon, Carroll O'Connor, David Opatoshu, Kent Smith, Jacqueline Scott, Morgan Woodward, Larry Gates, Dub Taylor. **Credits:** Dir: Robert Totten, Don Siegel; Prod: Richard E. Lyons; DP: Andrew Jackson; Ed: Robert F. Shugrue; Prod Design: Alexander Golitzen; Composer: Oliver Nelson. Color, 100 min. **VHS**

Death on the Nile
(1978) Paramount
A deluxe version of Agatha Christie's favorite mystery story, published in 1937, and a thematic follow-up to her *Murder on the Orient Express*. Set aboard a steamship cruising down the Nile, an extremely unpopular heiress is murdered and everyone on the ship is suspect. The passengers include the eminent detective Hercule Poirot (Ustinov), who cuts short his vacation in order to solve the mystery. The cast features the cream of '70s Hollywood and even includes classic-era stars Davis and Niven. **Academy Awards:** Best Costume Design. **Cast:** Peter Ustinov, Jane Birkin, Lois Chiles, Bette Davis, Mia Farrow, Olivia Hussey, Jon Finch, George Kennedy, Angela Lansbury, David Niven. **Credits:** Dir: John Guillermin; Prod: John Brabourne, Richard Goodwin; Writer: Anthony Shaffer; Story: Agatha Christie; DP: Jack Cardiff; Ed: Malcolm Cooke; Prod

Design: Peter Murton; Composer: Nino Rota; Costumes: Anthony Powell. Color, 135 min. **VHS, LASER**

Death Race 2000
(1975) New World
More delightfully sick humor from Bartel (*Eating Raoul*). In a boorish future, the government sponsors a popular, but bloody, cross-country race in which points are scored by mowing down pedestrians—bonus points for the elderly! Five teams, each comprised of a male and female, compete using cars equipped with deadly weapons. Frankenstein, the mysterious returning champion, has become America's hero, but this time he has a passenger from the underground resistance. A legendary cult film. **Cast:** David Carradine, Sylvester Stallone, Mary Woronov, Roberta Collins, Louisa Moritz. **Credits:** Dir: Paul Bartel; Prod: Roger Corman; Writer: Robert Thom, Charles B. Griffith; Story: Ib Melchior; DP: Tak Fujimoto; Ed: Tina Hirsch; Composer: Paul Chihara; SFX: Richard MacLean. Color, 103 min. **VHS, DVD**

Death Takes a Holiday
(1934) Paramount
In this fanciful allegory, Death, bored with his somber job, visits Earth in the guise of a handsome prince. While all living creatures enjoy a mysterious respite from death, the Reaper falls in love with a beautiful Italian, then agonizes over revealing his true identity. Remade for TV in 1971 and again as *Meet Joe Black* (with Brad Pitt as Death) in 1998. **Cast:** Fredric March, Evelyn Venable, Guy Standing, Katherine Alexander, Gail Patrick, Helen Westley, Kathleen Howard, Henry Travers, Kent Taylor. **Credits:** Dir: Mitchell Leisen; Prod: E. Lloyd Sheldon; Writer: Maxwell Anderson, Gladys Lehman, Walter Ferris; Story: Alberto Casella; DP: Charles Lang; Prod Design: Hans Dreier, Ernst Fegte. Color, 79 min. **VHS**

Death Wish
(1974) Paramount
After his wife has been murdered and his daughter raped by a trio of ruthless muggers, a mild-mannered businessman becomes judge, jury, and executioner when he hunts down the criminals himself. The first and best of a long series that became gratuitously violent and plot-thin. **Cast:** Charles Bronson, Vincent Gardenia, William Redfield, Hope Lange, Steven Keats, Stuart Margolin, Stephen Elliott, Kathleen Tolan, Jack Wallace, Fred Scollay. **Credits:** Dir: Michael Winner; Prod:

Hal Landers, Bobby Roberts, Michael Winner; Writer: Wendell Mayes; DP: Arthur J. Ornitz; Ed: Bernard Gribble; Prod Design: Robert Gundlach; Composer: Herbie Hancock. Color, 93 min. VHS, LASER

Deception
(1946) Warner Bros.
Davis and Rains shine in a romantic melodrama set in the world of concert music. Davis is a pianist torn between her wealthy, jealous patron and her cellist husband. Could have been too weepy, but stops just short. **Cast:** Bette Davis, Claude Rains, Paul Henreid, John Abbott, Benson Fong. **Credits:** Dir: Irving Rapper; Prod: Henry Blanke; Writer: John Collier, Joseph Than; Story: Louis Verneuil; DP: Ernest Haller; Ed: Alan Crosland, Jr.; Prod Design: Anton Grot; Composer: Erich Wolfgang Korngold; Costumes: Bernard Newman; Set Designer: George James Hopkins. Color, 113 min. VHS

Decision Before Dawn
(1952) Fox
A WWII spy thriller in which a young German soldier becomes a spy for the United States. While being held prisoner, a young medic overhears a fellow German prisoner criticizing Hitler and the Nazis. When the prisoner is later found murdered, the medic soon agrees to work for the Allies in hopes of ending the war that is destroying his country. He is dropped behind enemy lines, with orders to find a panzer division that supposedly wants to stop fighting, where he faces many perils, including a German spy. **Cast:** Richard Basehart, Gary Merrill, Oskar Werner, Hildegard Knef, Dominique Blanchar, Oberst von Ecker, Wilfried Seyferth, Hans-Christian Blech, Helen Thimig, Robert Freytag. **Credits:** Dir: Anatole Litvak; Prod: Anatole Litvak, Frank McCarthy; Writer: George Howe, Peter Viertel; DP: Frank Planer; Ed: Dorothy Spencer; Prod Design: Ludwig Reiber; Composer: Franz Waxman. B&W, 119 min.

The Deep
(1977) Columbia
While diving in the Bahamas, a vacationing couple discover pieces of gold, and assume that they've stumbled upon a legendary lost treasure. But as they return for more, they cross paths with divers intent on a more dangerous treasure. Posters of Bisset underwater in a T-shirt adorned many a dorm wall. Based on the novel by Peter Benchley. **Cast:** Robert Shaw,

Jacqueline Bisset, Nick Nolte, Louis Gossett, Jr., Eli Wallach. **Credits:** Dir: Peter Yates; Prod: Peter Guber; Writer: Peter Benchley, Tracy Keenan Wynn; DP: Christopher Challis; Ed: Robert Wolfe, David Berlatsky; Composer: John Barry; Prod Design: Tony Masters. Color, 127 min. VHS, LASER

Deep in My Heart
(1954) MGM
Donen stage-manages a musical biography about the life and career of Hungarian composer Sigmund Romberg that features everyone on the MGM lot, and includes a sleekly elegant Cyd Charisse turn. **Cast:** Jose Ferrer, Merle Oberon, Helen Traubel, Doe Avedon, Tamara Toumanova, Paul Stewart, Jim Backus, Walter Pidgeon, Paul Henreid, Ann Miller. **Credits:** Dir: Stanley Donen; Writer: Leonard Spigelgass; Story: Elliott Arnold; DP: George Folsey, Jr.; Ed: Adrienne Fazan; Prod Design: Cedric Gibbons; Choreographer: Eugene Loring; Composer: Sigmund Romberg; SFX: Warren Newcombe; Art Director: Edward C. Carfagno. Color, 133 min. VHS, LASER

The Deep Six
(1958) Warner Bros.
A Quaker naval officer is called to active duty in WWII. He struggles to balance his beliefs with the need to serve, and is offered the chance to prove himself and redeem himself in the eyes of his mates with a dangerous mission. **Cast:** Alan Ladd, William Bendix, James Whitmore, Dianne Foster, Efrem Zimbalist, Jr., Keenan Wynn, Joey Bishop, Jeanette Nolan, Ross Bagdasarian, Walter Reed. **Credits:** Dir: Rudolph Mate; Prod: Martin Rackin; Writer: John Twist, Harry Brown; DP: John F. Seitz; Ed: Roland Gross; Prod Design: Leo K. Kuter; Composer: David Buttolph; Costumes: Howard Shoup. Color, 110 min. VHS

Deep Valley
(1947) Warner Bros.
A young farm girl, Lupino, finds the love and comfort that is missing from her family in the arms of an escaped convict (Clark) she shelters. Their love blossoms in the family barn, until he is discovered by a sheriff's posse intent on returning him to the chain gang. A more stylish than usual tearjerker with a somber resolution. Shot entirely on location in Big Sur and Big Bear, California. **Cast:** Ida Lupino, Dane Clark, Wayne Morris, Fay Bainter, Henry Hull, Willard Robertson, Rory Mallinson, Jack Mower. **Credits:** Dir: Jean Negulesco; Prod: Henry Blanke;

Writer: Stephen Morehouse Avery, Salka Vieretel; Story: Dan Totheroh; DP: Ted McCord; Ed: Owen Marks; Prod Design: Max Parker; Composer: Max Steiner; Art Director: Frank Durlauf. B&W, 103 min.

The Deer Hunter
(1978) Universal
Cimino's ambitious, wrenching epic about the effect of the Vietnam War on three boyhood friends from a Pennsylvania steel town. The story follows three sons of immigrants, blue-collar workers who believe in the American dream and accept America's involvement in the war. But once in Vietnam, their ideas about honor and what it means to be a man—expressed in their homefront ritual of an annual deer-hunting expedition—get blown away in the face of war's bloody mayhem. A rewarding, if grueling, experience that reaches for emotional truths rather than political postures. Also won Golden Globe and DGA awards for Cimino. Selected for the National Film Registry. Academy Award Nominations: 9, including Best Actor: Robert De Niro; Best Supporting Actress: Meryl Streep; Best Screenplay. **Academy Awards:** Best Picture; Best Director; Best Supporting Actor: Christopher Walken; Best Film Editing; Best Sound. **Cast:** Robert De Niro, Meryl Streep, Christopher Walken, John Savage, John Cazale, George Dzundza, Chuck Aspegren, Shirley Stoler, Rutanya Alda. **Credits:** Dir: Michael Cimino; Prod: Barry Spikings, Michael Deeley, Michael Cimino, John Peverall; Writer: Deric Washburn; DP: Vilmos Zsigmond; Ed: Peter Zinner; Prod Design: Ron Hobbs, Kim Swados; Composer: Stanley Myers. Color, 183 min. VHS, LASER, DVD

The Defiant Ones
(1958) MGM
Two escaped convicts—one black (Poitier), one white (Curtis), and both shackled in the same pair of handcuffs—battle the elements and each other as they travel Southern back roads eluding the ever-approaching posse. Though the device of binding two racial antagonists together for survival may be rather obvious, the performances make the result compelling. Watch for Chaney, Jr., along the way. Golden Globe for Best Motion Picture, Drama. **Academy Awards:** Best Black-and-White Cinematography; Story/Screenplay Written Directly for the Screen. **Cast:** Tony Curtis, Sidney Poitier, Theodore Bikel, Charles McGraw, King Donovan, Cara Williams, Kevin Coughlin, Lon Chaney, Jr.,

Claude Akins. **Credits:** Dir: Stanley Kramer; Prod: Stanley Kramer; Writer: Nathan E. Douglas, Harold Jacob Smith; DP: Sam Leavitt; Ed: Frederic Knudtson; Prod Design: Rudolph Sternad; Composer: Ernest Gold. B&W, 97 min. **VHS, LASER**

The Delicate Delinquent

(1957) Paramount
Wanting to prove a point, good-hearted cop McGavin enrolls bumbling delinquent Lewis in the police academy, where he distinguishes himself with ineptitude and heart. One of the most successful Lewis movies, and his first outing without Dino. **Cast:** Jerry Lewis, Martha Hyer, Darren McGavin, Horace McMahon, Robert Ivers, Richard Bakalyan, Mary Webster, Milton Frome. **Credits:** Dir: Don McGuire; Prod: Jerry Lewis; Writer: Don McGuire; DP: Haskell Boggs; Ed: Howard Smith; Prod Design: Hal Pereira, Earl Hedrick; Composer: Buddy Bregman. B&W, 101 min. **VHS, LASER**

Deliverance

(1972) Warner Bros.
Based on Dickey's novel (and he wrote the screenplay), this harrowing film tells the story of an ill-fated canoe trip in deep backwoods America, where the people are as scary as the country is beautiful. Film debut of Beatty and Cox and Reynolds's best film. The scene that sets the stage for the horror to follow spawned the hit song "Dueling Banjos." Academy Award Nominations: Best Picture; Best Director; Best Editing. **Cast:** Burt Reynolds, Jon Voight, Ned Beatty, Ronny Cox, Ed O'Neill, James Dickey. **Credits:** Dir: John Boorman; Prod: John Boorman; Writer: James Dickey; DP: Vilmos Zsigmond, Tom Priestley; Prod Design: Fred Harpman; Composer: Eric Weissberg; Costumes: Bucky Rous; SFX: Marcel Vercoutere. Color, 109 min. **VHS, LASER**

Demetrius and the Gladiators

(1954) Fox
Emperor Caligula has two things on his mind: gladiatorial displays and gaining possession of the robe that fell from Jesus on the cross and is now in the hands of Demetrius. The sequel to *The Robe.* **Cast:** Victor Mature, Jay Jackson, Susan Hayward, Debra Paget, Anne Bancroft, Michael Rennie, Jay Robinson, Barry Jones, William Marshall, Richard Egan. **Credits:** Dir: Delmer Daves; Prod: Frank Ross; Writer: Philip Dunne; DP: Milton

Krasner; Ed: Dorothy Spencer, Robert Fritch; Prod Design: Lyle Wheeler; Choreographer: Stephen Papick; Composer: Franz Waxman, Alfred Newman; Costumes: Charles LeMaire; SFX: Ray Kellogg; Art Director: George W. Davis. Color, 101 min. **VHS, LASER**

Demon Seed

(1977) MGM
A brilliant scientist of the future creates a computer with almost limitless intelligence. The super-machine gets out of hand, however, when it decides that it wants to produce offspring and stalks the scientist's wife. **Cast:** Julie Christie, Fritz Weaver, Gerrit Graham, Berry Kroeger, Lisa Lu. **Credits:** Dir: Donald Cammell; Prod: Herb Jaffe; Writer: Robert Jaffe, Roger O. Hirson; Story: Dean R. Koontz; DP: Bill Butler; Ed: Frank Mazzola; Prod Design: Edward C. Carfagno; Composer: Jerry Fielding; Costumes: Joie Hutchinson, Bucky Ross, Sandy Cole; SFX: Tom Fisher. Color, 97 min. **VHS, LASER**

The Desert Fox

(1951) Fox
Mason is utterly convincing as Nazi Field Marshal Rommel (a role that became something of a specialty: see *The Desert Rats*), who gained notoriety for his successful North African campaigns. The big-budget actioner portrays not only his victories and ultimate defeat but also his personal doubts and conflicts with his superiors back in Berlin. **Cast:** James Mason, Jessica Tandy, Luther Adler, Leo G. Carroll, Cedric Hardwicke, Everett Sloane, George Macready, Richard Boone, Eduard Franz, Desmond Young. **Credits:** Dir: Henry Hathaway; Prod: Nunnally Johnson; Writer: Nunnally Johnson; DP: Norbert F. Brodine; Ed: James B. Clark; Prod Design: Lyle Wheeler, Maurice Ransford; Composer: Daniele Amfitheatrof. B&W, 88 min. **VHS, LASER**

The Desert Rats

(1953) Fox
British commando captain Burton takes charge of a hopelessly outnumbered but stubbornly defiant Australian division in their heroic stand against Field Marshal Rommel in North Africa. Their new leader wastes no time in alienating his men, but the Australians prove themselves both plucky and amusing. Another sweeping evocation of the North Africa campaign (an undeniably photogenic setting), with Mason's Rommel once again lurking over the next dune. **Cast:** Richard

Burton, James Mason, Robert Newton, Chips Rafferty, Torin Thatcher, Robert Douglas, Charles Tingwell, Charles Davis, Ben Wright, James Lilburn. **Credits:** Dir: Robert Wise; Prod: Robert L. Jacks; Writer: Richard Murphy; DP: Lucien Ballard; Ed: Barbara McLean; Prod Design: Lyle Wheeler, Addison Hehr; Composer: Leigh Harline. B&W, 88 min. **VHS**

Design for Living

(1933) Paramount
The Hays Code forced the team of Lubitsch and Hecht to rework the script of Coward's original play, which Hecht proceeded to do with a thoroughness that left only the shell of a ménage à trois, with Hopkins, in the employ of advertising executive Horton, serving as the romantic and artistic muse for best friends playwright March and artist Cooper. Attempts at keeping it all platonic succumb to the simmering, competitive passions of March and Cooper and the inability of the muse to make up her mind. **Cast:** Fredric March, Gary Cooper, Miriam Hopkins, Edward Everett Horton, Franklin Pangborn, Isabel Jewell, Harry Dunkminson, Helena Phillips, James Donlin, Vernon Steele. **Credits:** Dir: Ernst Lubitsch; Prod: Ernst Lubitsch; Writer: Ben Hecht; Story: Noël Coward; DP: Victor Milner; Ed: Frances Marsh; Costumes: Travis Banton; Art Director: Hans Dreier. B&W, 90 min.

Designing Woman

(1957) MGM
Stylish domestic romp with Peck a guy's-guy sports reporter who marries an elegant dress designer, Bacall. The odd-couple comedy begins when they try to blend their homes and friends, and soon suspect they have nothing at all in common. **Academy Awards:** Best Story/Screenplay. **Cast:** Gregory Peck, Lauren Bacall, Dolores Gray, Sam Levene, Mickey Shaughnessy, Chuck Connors, Tom Helmore, Jesse White, Jack Cole. **Credits:** Dir: Vincente Minnelli; Prod: Dore Schary; Writer: George Wells; DP: John Alton; Composer: Andre Previn. Color, 118 min. **VHS, LASER**

Desire

(1936) Paramount
A crafty, alluring jewel thief (Dietrich) steals a priceless pearl necklace and hides it in the coat pocket of a man who then becomes an unwitting smuggler (Cooper). In order to retrieve the gems, she feigns romantic feelings, which leads, of course, to real love. Second outing for successful pairing

from *Morocco* (1930). **Cast:** Marlene Dietrich, Gary Cooper, John Halladay, William Frawley, Ernest Cossart, Akim Tamiroff, Alan Mowbray, Zeffie Tilbury. **Credits:** Dir: Frank Borzage; Prod: Ernst Lubitsch; Writer: Edwin Justus Mayer, Waldemar Young, Samuel Hoffenstein; Story: R. A. Stemmle; DP: Charles Lang, Victor Milner; Ed: William Shea; Prod Design: Hans Dreier; Composer: Frederick Hollander; Costumes: Travis Banton; Art Director: Robert Usher. B&W, 96 min. **VHS**

Desiree
(1954) Fox
Historical fiction about Napoleon's love affair with a 17-year-old who proves distracting to his empire building. More battles in the boudoir than on the battlefield. Academy Award Nominations: Best (Color) Art Direction—Set Direction; Best (Color) Costume Design. **Cast:** Marlon Brando, Jean Simmons, Michael Rennie, Merle Oberon, Cameron Mitchell, Elizabeth Sellars, Charlotte Austin, Cathleen Nesbitt, Isobel Elsom. **Credits:** Dir: Henry Koster; Prod: Julian C. Blaustein; Writer: Daniel Taradash; Story: Annemarie Selinko; DP: Milton Krasner; Ed: William Reynolds; Prod Design: Lyle Wheeler; Choreographer: Stephen Papich; Composer: Alex North; Art Director: Leland Fuller. Color, 110 min. **VHS, LASER**

Desire Me
(1947) MGM
Before being released, this remake of the German film *Homecoming* (1928) endured a recasting of the leads, directoral switches, and an 18-month stint on the shelves of MGM's vault. The final product is somewhat understandably choppy. Garson stars as a woman who has unknowingly betrayed her husband, Mitchum, whom she thought had died in WWII with Hart, the man her husband had helped escape from a POW camp. Mitchum returns to reclaim his wife, resulting in a deadly confrontation between the two men. Cukor shot most of this though he asked for his name to be removed from the credits. **Cast:** Robert Mitchum, Greer Garson, Richard Hart, George Zucco, Morris Ankrum, Cecil Humphreys, David Hoffman, Florence Bates, Max Willenz. **Credits:** Dir: George Cukor; Prod: Arthur Hornblow, Jr.; Writer: Marguerite Roberts, Zoe Atkins, Frank Leonhard; DP: Joseph Ruttenberg; Ed: Joseph Dervin; Prod Design: Cedric Gibbons; Composer: Herbert Stothart; Art Director: Urie McCleary. B&W, 91 min.

Desk Set (1957)

Desire Under the Elms
(1958) Paramount
A young man succumbs to his passion for his father's beautiful new bride in the film version of O'Neill's play. Loren's Hollywood debut finds her a fish out of water in 19th-century New England. Academy Award Nomination for Best (Black-and-White) Cinematography. **Cast:** Sophia Loren, Anthony Perkins, Burl Ives, Frank Overton, Eugene O'Neill, Anne Seymour. **Credits:** Dir: Delbert Mann; Writer: Irwin Shaw; Story: Eugene O'Neill; DP: Daniel Fapp; Composer: Elmer Bernstein. B&W, 115 min. **VHS, LASER** 110

Desk Set
(1957) Fox
Hired to computerize a TV network's operations, an efficiency expert (Tracy) clashes with the head of the research department (Hepburn), even as he falls slowly, surely in love with her. Classic Hepburn and Tracy banter and twinkle in the eye. Adapted from the William Marchant play by Henry and Phoebe Ephron. **Cast:** Spencer Tracy, Katharine Hepburn, Joan Blondell, Gig Young, Dina Merrill, Neva Patterson. **Credits:** Dir: Walter Lang; Prod: Henry Ephron; Writer: Henry Ephron, Phoebe Ephron; Story: William Marchant; DP: Leon Shamroy; Ed: Robert Simpson; Prod Design: Lyle Wheeler; Composer: Cyril Mockridge; Costumes: Charles LeMaire; SFX: Ray Kellogg; Set Designer: Walter M. Scott, Paul S. Fox. Color, 103 min. **VHS, LASER**

The Desperadoes
(1943) Columbia
A better-than-average Scott Western gets a lift from old hand Vidor. Ford's an outlaw trying to go straight after visiting his old friend Scott, now a lawman, and falling in love with a local gal. When the town's bank is robbed, the townspeople know who to suspect. The outlaw and the lawman ride together to bring the real bandits to justice. **Cast:** Randolph Scott, Glenn Ford, Claire Trevor, Evelyn Keyes, Edgar Buchanan, Raymond Walburn, Guinn "Big Boy" Williams, Porter Hall, Joan Woodbury, Bernard Nedell. **Credits:** Dir: Charles Vidor; Prod: Harry Joe Brown; Writer: Robert Carson; DP: George Meehan, Allen M. Davey; Ed: Gene Havlick; Prod Design: Lionel Banks; Composer: Morris Stoloff. Color, 85 min. **VHS**

Desperate
(1947) RKO
Director Mann (also the director of the great *T-Men*, 1947) in film noir mode. A trucker who stumbles on a crime is forced to flee with his wife when he is victimized by racketeers and tailed by

the cops. **Cast:** Steve Brodie, Audrey Long, Raymond Burr, Douglas Fowley, William Challee, Jason Robards, Sr., Ilka Gruning. **Credits:** Dir: Anthony Mann; Prod: Michael Kraike; Writer: Harry Essex, Martin Rackin; Story: Anthony Mann; DP: George E. Diskant; Ed: Marston Fay; Composer: Paul Sawtell; SFX: Russell A. Cully; Art Director: Albert S. D'Agostino, Walter E. Keller; Set Designer: Darrell Silvera. B&W, 73 min. **VHS**

Desperate Characters
(1971) Paramount
A story of a childless, middle-aged couple whose crumbling marriage and daily struggle with the stresses of city life have them trapped in a hell they're too depleted to leave. Strong performance by MacLaine. **Cast:** Shirley MacLaine, Kenneth Mars, Sada Thompson, Jack Somack, Rose Gregorio, Carol Kane, Gerald S. O'Loughlin. **Credits:** Dir: Frank D. Gilroy; Prod: Frank D. Gilroy; Writer: Frank D. Gilroy; Story: Paula Fox; DP: Urs Furrer; Ed: Robert Q. Lovett; Composer: Lee Konitz, Jim Hall, Ron Carter; Art Director: Edgar Lansbury; Set Designer: Herbert F. Mulligan. Color, 88 min. **VHS, LASER**

The Desperate Hours
(1955) Paramount
Escaped convicts hold a family hostage in this classic nail-biter adapted from the novel and Broadway play by Joseph Hayes, which were inspired by an actual case. The intruders' brutish behavior brings out Dad's courageous side. Remade in 1990. **Cast:** Humphrey Bogart, Fredric March, Arthur Kennedy, Martha Scott, Gig Young, Dewey Martin, Mary Murphy, Robert Middleton, Richard Eyer. **Credits:** Dir: William Wyler; Prod: William Wyler; Writer: Joseph Hayes; DP: Lee Garmes; Ed: Robert W. Swink; Prod Design: Hal Pereira, Joseph MacMillan Johnson; Composer: Gail Kubik. B&W, 112 min. **VHS, LASER**

Desperate Journey
(1942) Warner Bros.
Five Allied airmen, including Flynn and Reagan, shot down over the eastern front, fight their way back to England. Typical of morale-boosting genre, but interesting now for the curious starring duo. Academy Award Nomination for Best Special Effects. **Cast:** Errol Flynn, Raymond Massey, Ronald Reagan, Alan Hale, Arthur Kennedy, Nancy Coleman, Sig Rumann, Patrick O'Moore, Ronald Sinclair, Albert Basserman. **Credits:** Dir: Raoul

Walsh; Writer: Arthur T. Horman; DP: Bert Glennon; Ed: Rudi Fehr; Composer: Max Steiner; Costumes: Milo Anderson; SFX: Edwin A. DuPar; Art Director: Carl Jules Weyl. B&W, 119 min. **VHS**

Desperate Search
(1952) MGM
Adventure story follows the struggle of a young brother and sister to survive after their airplane crashes. They persevere through bitterly cold weather, and stay one step ahead of a cougar that is tracking them as their father, mother, and the father's wife desperately search. **Cast:** Howard Keel, Jane Greer, Patricia Medina, Keenan Wynn, Robert Burton, Lee Aaker, Linda Lowell, Michael Dugan, Elaine Stewart, Jonathan Cott. **Credits:** Dir: Joseph H. Lewis; Prod: Matthew Rapf; Writer: Walter Doniger, Arthur Mayse; DP: Harold Lipstein; Ed: Joseph Dervin; Composer: Rudolph G. Kopp; Art Director: Cedric Gibbons, Eddie Imazu. B&W, 71 min.

Destination Moon
(1950) Eagle-Lion
A privately-funded lunar expedition goes awry when the crew lacks sufficient fuel for the return trip. Based on Heinlein's *Rocketship Galileo*. George Pal created the special effects. Academy Award Nominations: 2, including Best (Color) Art Direction—Set Direction. **Academy Awards:** Best Special Effects. **Cast:** Warner Anderson, John Archer, Tom Powers, Dick Wesson. **Credits:** Dir: Irving Pichel; Prod: George Pal; Writer: Rip Van Ronkel, James O'Hanlon; Story: Robert A. Heinlein; DP: Lionel Lindon; Composer: Leith Stevens. Color, 91 min. **VHS, LASER**

Destination Tokyo
(1943) Warner Bros.
Men-under-fire drama under the sea lifted by the high-calibre cast. The crew of a U.S. submarine sent into Japanese waters learns to work together while cruising into danger. Academy Award Nomination for Best Original Story. **Cast:** Cary Grant, John Garfield, Alan Hale, John Ridgely, Dane Clark, Warner Anderson, William Prince, John Forsythe, Robert Hutton, Tom Tully. **Credits:** Dir: Delmer Daves; Prod: Jerry Wald; Writer: Albert Maltz, Delmer Daves; Story: Steve Fisher; DP: Bert Glennon; Ed: Christian Nyby; Composer: Franz Waxman; SFX: Lawrence Butler, Willard Van Enger; Art Director: Leo K. Kuter; Set Designer: Walter Tilford. B&W, 136 min. **VHS**

Destroyer
(1943) Columbia
Wartime men-under-fire drama on the seas follows a young officer showing up his superior (Robinson) onboard a WWII destroyer. In the end, experience wins the day. **Cast:** Edward G. Robinson, Glenn Ford, Leo Gorcey, Edgar Buchanan, Marguerite Chapman, Regis Toomey, Edward Brophy. **Credits:** Dir: William A. Seiter; Prod: Louis F. Edelman; Writer: Frank Wead, Lewis Meltzer, Borden Chase; DP: Franz Planer; Ed: Gene Havlick; Composer: Anthony Collins; Art Director: Lionel Banks. B&W, 97 min. **VHS**

Destry Rides Again
(1939) Universal
This Western satire features a laconic Stewart as a lawman with an aversion to guns who comes to clean up a hopelessly lawless town. Dietrich's dance-hall girl, Frenchy, sings "See What the Boys in the Back Room Will Have" between cat fights. One of the great barroom brawl choreographies of all time as she hurls everything within reach at a grinning Stewart. Great fun. Selected for the national Film Registry. **Cast:** Marlene Dietrich, James Stewart, Brian Donlevy, Charles Winninger, Mischa Auer, Irene Harvey, Una Merkel, Allen Jenkins, Warren Hymer, Samuel S. Hinds. **Credits:** Dir: George Marshall; Prod: Joe Pasternak; Writer: Felix Jackson, Henry Myers, Gertrude Purcell; Story: Max Brand; DP: Hal Mohr; Ed: Milton Carruth; Prod Design: Jack Otterson; Composer: Frank Skinner, Frederick Hollander, Frank Loesser; Costumes: Vera West. B&W, 94 min. **VHS, LASER**

Detective Story
(1951) Paramount
An embittered cop (Douglas) and his mercurial temper affect life in a New York City police precinct. His wife, Parker, suffers from neglect and his sympathetic boss tries to counsel him. Explosive drama takes place almost entirely in the claustrophobic confines of the precinct house. Based on Kingsley's Broadway play, this seminal cop drama was a prototype for everything from *Hill Street Blues* to *NYPD Blue*. Academy Award Nominations: 4, including Best Director; Best Actress: Eleanor Parker; Best Screenplay. Grant won the Best Actress award at Cannes for her screen debut. **Cast:** Kirk Douglas, Eleanor Parker, Lee Grant, Horace McMahon, William Bendix, Craig Hill, Joseph Wiseman, Gladys George, Frank Faylen, Warner Anderson. **Credits:** Dir: William Wyler; Prod: William

Wyler; Writer: Philip Yordan, Robert Wyler; Story: Sidney Kingsley; DP: Lee Garmes; Ed: Robert W. Swink; Costumes: Edith Head; Art Director: Hal Pereira, Earl Hedrick; Set Designer: Emile Kuri. B&W, 103 min. VHS

The Devil and Daniel Webster

(1941) RKO

An 1840s New Hampshire farmer who sold his soul to the Devil decides that the price he paid was too high, and sends for silver-tongued lawyer Webster to plead his case. An all-around treat, based on Benét's short story. Herrmann's evocative score won an Oscar. The restored version includes footage missing from the truncated television versions, but still clocks in a few minutes short of the original running time. **Academy Awards:** Best Music Score of a Drama/Comedy. **Cast:** Walter Huston, Edward Arnold, Anne Shirley, James Craig, Simone Simon, Jane Darwell, Gene Lockhart, John Qualen, H. B. Warner. **Credits:** Dir: William Dieterle; Prod: William Dieterle; Writer: Dan Totheroh; Story: Stephen Vincent Benét; DP: Joseph H. August; Ed: Robert Wise; Prod Design: Van Nest Polglase; Composer: Bernard Herrmann. B&W, 109 min. VHS, LASER

The Devil and Miss Jones

(1941) RKO

The Bill Gates of his day (Coburn) discovers an effigy of himself hanging outside a department store he didn't even know he owned. Curious, he ventures inside and becomes a clerk in order to investigate further. Naturally, the view from street level brings a new perspective and romance. A witty script given a big lift from Arthur and Coburn. **Cast:** Jean Arthur, Robert Cummings, Charles Coburn, Spring Byington, S. Z. Sakall, William Demarest, Walter Kingsford, Montagu Love, Richard Carle, Charles Waldron. **Credits:** Dir: Sam Wood, Norman Krasna; Prod: Frank Ross; Writer: Norman Krasna; DP: Harry Stradling; Ed: Sherman Todd; Prod Design: William Cameron Menzies; Composer: Roy Webb. B&W, 92 min. VHS

The Devil at 4 O'Clock

(1961) Columbia

When a volcano erupts near a children's hospital in the South Pacific, three convicts and a priest must rescue the patients and staff. A forerunner of the volcano-disaster pics of 1997 (and no more successful), but with a solid-gold cast. **Cast:** Spencer Tracy, Frank Sinatra, Gregoire Aslan, Jean-Pierre

Aumont, Kerwin Mathews, Alexander Scourby, Barbara Luna, Cathy Lewis, Bernie Hamilton, Martin Brandt. **Credits:** Dir: Mervyn Le Roy; Prod: Fred Kohlmar; Writer: Liam O'Brien; Story: Max Catto; DP: Joseph Biroc; Ed: Charles Nelson; Prod Design: John Beckman; Composer: George Duning. Color, 127 min. VHS, LASER

The Devil Commands

(1941) Columbia

Horror movie hall-of-famer Karloff does his mad scientist routine this time as Dr. Julian Blair, who obsessively attempts to communicate with his dead wife by using robot suits, kidnapped people, and plenty of Frankenstein-like electricity effects. Dmytryk and Karloff do their best to infuse the film with life. **Cast:** Boris Karloff, Amanda Duff, Shirley Warde, Richard Fiske, Anne Revere, Ralph Penny, Dorothy Adams, Walter Baldwin, Kenneth MacDonald. **Credits:** Dir: Edward Dmytryk; Prod: Wallace MacDonald; Writer: Milton Gunzburg, Robert D. Andrews; Story: William Sloane; DP: Allen G. Siegler; Ed: Al Clark; Prod Design: Lionel Banks; Composer: Morris Stoloff. B&W, 65 min.

The Devil Doll

(1936) MGM

An escaped convict uses the shrinking serum of his fellow prisoner on Devil's Island, a mad scientist, to create miniature people. He then sends out the little henchmen in the form of innocent dolls to settle some old scores. A creepy revelation from horror master Browning that features a script by von Stroheim. **Cast:** Lionel Barrymore, Maureen O'Sullivan, Frank Lawton, Robert Greig, Lucy Beaumont, Henry B. Walthall, Pedro De Cordoba, Rafaela Ottiano, Erich von Stroheim. **Credits:** Dir: Tod Browning; Prod: Edward J. Mannix; Writer: Garret Fort, Guy Endore, Tod Browning; DP: Leonard Smith; Ed: Fredrick Y. Smith; Prod Design: Cedric Gibbons; Composer: Franz Waxman. B&W, 80 min. VHS

The Devil Is a Woman

(1935) Paramount

Dietrich plays Concha Perez, a Spanish courtesan so beautiful and scheming that she ruthlessly ensnares even the respectable Don Pasqual. His downfall is told in flashbacks as he warns a young friend away from the same fate. But, smitten, the friend ignores the advice, and Concha runs off with him, only to eventually confirm Don Pasqual's warning. Von Sternberg and Dietrich enliven an otherwise weary

melodrama. **Cast:** Marlene Dietrich, Cesar Romero, Lionel Atwill, Alison Skipworth, Don Alvarado, Morgan Wallace, Tempe Pigott, Jill Dennett, Lawrence Grant, Edward Everett Horton. **Credits:** Dir: Josef von Sternberg; Prod: Adolph Zukor; Writer: John Dos Passos, Sam Winston; Story: Pierre Louys; DP: Lucien Ballard, Josef von Sternberg; Ed: Sam Winston; Composer: Ralph Rainger, Andrea Setaro, Nicolai Rimsky-Korsakoff, Leo Robin; Art Director: Hans Drier, Josef von Sternberg. B&W, 76 min.

The Devil's Brigade

(1968) United Artists

Standard WWII fantasyland fare as Holden grabs a thankless detail: create a fit commando troop from a gaggle of down-and-dirty Canadian and American misfits. Big-budget, big-screen treatment and curious assortment of stars doesn't add up to much, but choosing the Italian Alps as a theater of war is refreshing. **Cast:** William Holden, Cliff Robertson, Vince Edwards, Michael Rennie, Dana Andrews, Carroll O'Connor, Gretchen Wyler, Andrew Prine, Claude Akins, Richard Jaeckel. **Credits:** Dir: Andrew V. McLaglen; Prod: David L. Wolper; Writer: William Roberts; DP: William Clothier; Ed: William Cartwright; Composer: Alex North; Art Director: Alfred Sweeney. Color, 130 min. VHS

Devil's Doorway

(1950) Paramount

Former Sergeant Lance Poole, a full-blooded Shoshone Indian and winner of a Congressional Medal of Honor for service at Gettysburg, comes home to Wyoming and finds himself in the middle of a dispute between homesteading sheepherders and Shoshone, who are being driven from their traditional lands. The sheepherders are innocent of malice, but have settled the Shoshone land at the suggestion of an Indian-hating lawyer. Poole foolishly hopes that he is in a position to gain some legal justice for his tribe, but is eventually left with no choice but to lead them into battle against the white settlers. **Cast:** Robert Taylor, Louis Calhern, Paula Raymond, Marshall Thompson, James Mitchell, Edgar Buchanan, Rhys Williams, Spring Byington, James Millican, Bruce Cowling. **Credits:** Dir: Anthony Mann; Prod: Nicholas Nayfack; Writer: Guy Trosper; DP: John Alton; Ed: Conrad A. Nervig; Prod Design: Cedric Gibbons; Composer: Danielle Amfitheatrof; Art Director: Leonid Vasian. B&W, 84 min.

Devotion

(1931) Warner Bros.
A film biography of English novelists Charlotte Brontë (*Jane Eyre*) and her sister Emily Brontë (*Wuthering Heights*), focusing on their lives before they became writers—including the love triangle that entangled them. **Cast:** Leslie Howard, Ann Harding, Robert Williams, O. P. Heggie, Louise Closser Hale, Dudley Digges. **Credits:** Dir: Robert Milton; Writer: Horace Jackson, Graham John; Story: Pamela Wynne. B&W, 81 min. **VHS**

Dial M for Murder

(1954) Warner Bros.
Hitchcock's intriguing cinematic adaptation of Frederick Knott's play about a woman who slowly comes to realize that her husband is trying to murder her for her money. She foils an intruder with a sharp pair of scissors in a scene even more electrifying in the original 3-D. **Cast:** Ray Milland, Grace Kelly, Robert Cummings, John Williams, Anthony Dawson. **Credits:** Dir: Alfred Hitchcock; Prod: Alfred Hitchcock; Writer: Frederick Knott; DP: Robert Burks; Ed: Rudi Fehr; Composer: Dimitri Tiomkin. Color, 109 min. **VHS, LASER**

Diamond Head

(1962) Columbia
An oppressive agricultural tycoon alienates his entire family when he forbids his baby sister to marry a Hawaiian. **Cast:** Charlton Heston, Yvette Mimieux, George Chakiris, James Darren, France Nuyen, Aline MacMahon, Elizabeth Allen. **Credits:** Dir: Guy Green; Prod: Jerry Bresler; Writer: Marguerite Roberts; Story: Peter Gilman; DP: Sam Leavitt; Ed: William A. Lyon; Prod Design: Malcolm F. Brown; Composer: John Williams; Costumes: Pat Barto; Set Designer: William Kiernan. Color, 107 min. **VHS, LASER**

Diamond Jim

(1935) Universal
Biography of railroad tycoon James Brady traces the protagonist from his childhood in the slums through his first job as baggage handler to his later life as an oversized, extravagant adult. He first falls in love with a woman from his hometown, then when she rejects him, he has an affair with actress Lillian Russell. Sturges had a hand in the screenplay. **Cast:** Edward Arnold, Jean Arthur, Binnie Barnes, Eric Blore, Helen Brown, William Demarest, Bill Houlahan, Cesar Romero, George Sidney. **Credits:** Dir:

A. Edward Sutherland; Prod: Edmund Grainger; Writer: Nydia Westman, Henry Clork, Doris Malloy, Preston Sturges; DP: George Robinson; Ed: Daniel Mandell. B&W, 93 min.

Diamonds Are Forever

(1971) United Artists
Connery is back in the seventh Bond film and the first to utilize American locations. Bond follows diamond smugglers to Las Vegas where a Howard Hughes–like millionaire appears to be using them in a deadly space weapon. Academy Award Nomination for Best Sound. **Cast:** Sean Connery, Jill St. John, Lana Wood, Charles Gray, Bruce Glover, Jimmy Dean, Bruce Cabot, Bernard Lee, Lois Maxwell. **Credits:** Dir: Guy Hamilton; Prod: Harry Saltzman, Albert R. Broccoli; Writer: Richard Maibaum, Tom Mankiewicz; Story: Ian Fleming; DP: Ted Moore; Ed: Bert Bates; Prod Design: Ken Adam, Bill Kenney; Composer: John Barry; Costumes: Elsa Fennell, Donfeld; SFX: Leslie Hillman, Albert J. Whitlock, Wally Veevers; Set Designer: Peter Lamont, John Austin. Color, 120 min. **VHS, LASER**

Diary of a Chambermaid

(1946) United Artists
One of French master Renoir's Hollywood outings. An outspoken maid in a household full of eccentrics has her eye on the wealthy master of the house, but is pursued by a fellow servant. Meredith wrote the script and produced. Remade in 1964. **Cast:** Paulette Goddard, Hurd Hatfield, Francis Lederer, Burgess Meredith, Irene Ryan, Reginald Owen, Judith Anderson, Florence Bates, Almira Sessions. **Credits:** Dir: Jean Renoir; Prod: Burgess Meredith; Writer: Burgess Meredith; Story: Octave Mirbeau; DP: Lucien Andriot; Ed: James Smith; Prod Design: Eugene Lourie; Composer: Michel Michelet; SFX: Lee Zavitz. B&W, 86 min. **VHS**

Diary of a Mad Housewife

(1970) Universal
As an act of both boredom and vengeance, a frustrated young housewife takes a lover but finds it doesn't fix her problems. Based on the novel by Sue Kaufman. Academy Award Nomination for Best Actress: Carrie Snodgress. **Cast:** Richard Benjamin, Frank Langella, Carrie Snodgress, Lorraine Cullen, Frannie Michel. **Credits:** Dir: Frank Perry; Prod: Frank Perry; Writer: Eleanor Perry; Story: Sue Kaufman; DP: Gerald Hirschfeld; Ed: Sidney Katz; Prod Design: Peter

Dohanos; Costumes: Ruth Morley; Set Designer: Robert Drumheller. Color, 100 min. **VHS**

The Diary of Anne Frank

(1959) Fox
Pulitzer Prize–winning play is translated to film in this gripping account of WWII Jewish refugees hiding in occupied Amsterdam. Frank's celebrated diary of the harrowing experience reveals her flourishing spirit in one of the darkest of our times. Highly successful new production of the play on Broadway in 1997–98. Golden Globe for Best Film Promoting International Understanding. Academy Award Nominations: 8, including Best Picture; Best Supporting Actor: Ed Wynn; Best Director; Best Score. **Academy Awards:** Best Supporting Actress: Shelley Winters; Best Black-and-White Cinematography; Best Art Direction—Set Decoration (B&W). **Cast:** Millie Perkins, Joseph Schildkraut, Shelley Winters, Richard Beymer, Gusti Huber, Lou Jacobi, Diane Baker, Douglas Spencer, Dody Heath, Ed Wynn. **Credits:** Dir: George Stevens, Jack Cardiff; Prod: George Stevens; Writer: Frances Goodrich, Albert Hackett; DP: William Mellor; Ed: Robert W. Swink, William Mace, David Bretherton; Composer: Alfred Newman. B&W, 151 min. **VHS, LASER**

Dillinger

(1945) Monogram
A fine production (one of several Hollywood versions of this brutal life story), which follows the feared gangster from street hood to the top of the FBI's "Most Wanted List," and, finally, to his violent death in a police ambush. Academy Award Nomination for Best Original Screenplay. **Cast:** Lawrence Tierney, Edmund Lowe, Anne Jeffreys, Elisha Cook, Jr., Eduardo Ciannelli. **Credits:** Dir: Max Nosseck; Prod: Maurice King; Writer: Philip Yordan, Leon Charles; DP: Jackson Rose; Ed: Otho S. Lovering, Edward Mann; Composer: Dimitri Tiomkin; SFX: Robert Clark. B&W, 89 min. **VHS**

Dillinger

(1973) AIP
The first feature film from man's-man director Milius is a violent, hard-hitting account of Public Enemy No.1, John Dillinger. The last half of his criminal career is dramatically retold until his notorious finale outside the Biograph Theatre. Check out the cast: Oates, Johnson, and Stanton in one film! **Cast:** Warren Oates, Ben Johnson, Cloris Leachman, Harry Dean Stanton,

Richard Dreyfuss, Michelle Phillips. **Credits:** Dir: John Milius; Prod: Buzz Feitshans; Writer: John Milius; DP: Jules Brenner; Ed: Fred Feitshans; Prod Design: Trevor Williams; Composer: Barry Devorzon; Costumes: Barbara Siebert; SFX: A. D. Flowers, Clifford P. Wenger; Set Designer: Chuck Pierce. Color, 106 min. VHS, LASER

Dimples
(1936) Fox
Shirley Temple's grandfather is a charming oldster with a bad case of "sticky fingers." When Grandpa is caught thieving from a wealthy lady, Shirley takes the blame and her honesty unexpectedly leads to a career in showbiz. **Cast:** Shirley Temple, Frank Morgan, Stepin Fetchit, Robert Kent, Helen Westley, Astrid Allwyn, Delma Byron, Benton Churchill. **Credits:** Dir: William A. Seiter; Prod: Darryl F. Zanuck; Writer: Arthur Sheekman, Nat Perrin; Story: Nunnally Johnson; DP: Bert Glennon; Ed: Herbert Levy; Choreographer: Bill Robinson; Art Director: William S. Darling; Set Designer: Thomas Little. B&W, 78 min. VHS

Dinner at Eight
(1933) MGM
Three of Hollywood's greatest scriptwriters and most of the stars on the MGM backlot combine for a glamorous, giddy comedy of Depression-era manners. A Park Avenue snob performs a series of brilliant manipulations in order to bring about a dinner party for an English peer. Based on the play by Ferber and Kaufman. **Cast:** Marie Dressler, John Barrymore, Jean Harlow, Wallace Beery, Lionel Barrymore, Lee Tracy, Edmund Lowe, Billie Burke, Madge Evans, Jean Hersholt. **Credits:** Dir: George Cukor; Prod: David O. Selznick; Writer: Frances Marion, Herman J. Mankiewicz, Donald Ogden Stewart; Story: George S. Kaufman, Edna Ferber; DP: William Daniels; Ed: Ben Lewis; Prod Design: Cedric Gibbons; Costumes: Adrian; Set Designer: Hobe Erwin, Fred Hope. B&W, 113 min. VHS, LASER

Dirigible
(1931) Columbia
Early Capra follows two navy pilots commanding separate airships as they race to the South Pole. The two men also compete for the love of the same woman. When one dirigible crashes in the icy plain of Antarctica, one man must choose between staying home with the woman and risking his life to save his rival. **Cast:** Hobart Bosworth, Ralph Graves, Jack Holt, Roscoe Karns, Fay Wray. **Credits:** Dir: Frank Capra; Prod: Harry Cohn; Writer: Dorothy Howell, Jo Swerling; Story: Frank Wead; DP: Elmer Dyer, Joe Wilbur; Ed: Maurice Wright. B&W, 100 min.

The Dirty Dozen
(1967) MGM
An all-star cast leads this classic WWII action drama about 12 condemned American military prisoners pressed into service as a crack commando team. The incarcerated soldiers, most of whom are facing death sentences for a variety of violent crimes, are given a chance to redeem themselves if they attempt an extremely risky guerrilla raid in Nazi-occupied France just before D-Day. Three sequels made for TV. **Academy Awards:** Best Sound Effects Editing. **Cast:** Lee Marvin, Ernest Borgnine, Jim Brown, John Cassavetes, Robert Ryan, Charles Bronson, Donald Sutherland, George Kennedy, Trini Lopez. **Credits:** Dir: Robert Aldrich, Nunnally Johnson; Prod: Kenneth Hyman; Writer: Lukas Heller; DP: Edward Scaife; Ed: Michael Luciano; Composer: Frank DeVol. Color, 151 min. VHS, LASER, DVD

Dirty Harry
(1971) Warner Bros.
Eastwood and director Siegel in the defining moment for both. Harry Callahan, a San Francisco detective, hunts down a psychopathic serial killer. His muscular brand of justice pits Harry against his superiors in the department as well as the killer. A modern archetype that wedded the counterculture antihero to a reactionary response to crime. Four sequels followed. **Cast:** Clint Eastwood, Harry Guardino, Reni Santoni, John Vernon, John Larch, Andrew Robinson, John Mitchum. **Credits:** Dir: Don Siegel; Prod: Don Siegel; Writer: Harry Julian Fink, Rita M. Fink; DP: Bruce Surtees; Ed: Carl Pingitore; Prod Design: Dale Hennesy; Composer: Lalo Schifrin; Costumes: Glenn T. Wright; Set Designer: Robert DeVestel. Color, 102 min. VHS, LASER, DVD

Dirty Mary Crazy Larry
(1974) Fox
Fast action results when race-driver Fonda and mechanic Roarke smash every car in sight while escaping with their loot and a babe from a supermarket robbery. **Cast:** Peter Fonda, Susan George, Adam Roarke, Vic Morrow, Eugene Daniels, Roddy McDowall, Kenneth Tobey. **Credits:** Dir: John Hough; Prod: Norman T. Herman; Writer: Leigh Chapman, Antonio Santean; Story: Richard Unekis; DP: Michael D. Margulies; Ed: Christopher Holmes; Composer: Jimmie Haskell. Color, 91 min. VHS

Dishonored
(1931) Paramount
Dietrich and von Sternberg in a brooding version of the Mata Hari story. In WWI Vienna, the widow of an Austrian soldier is approached to pass on sensitive information. She turns the man in instead but is then thanked by being forced to infiltrate the home of a high-ranking traitor by becoming his mistress. **Cast:** Marlene Dietrich, Warner Oland, Lew Cody, Victor McLaglen, Gustav Von Seyffertitz, Barry Norton, Wilfred Lucas, Davison Clark. **Credits:** Dir: Josef von Sternberg; Writer: Danny Rubin; Story: Josef von Sternberg; DP: Lee Garmes; Prod Design: Hans Dreier; Composer: Karl Hajos, Josef von Sternberg; Costumes: Travis Banton. B&W, 91 min. VHS

The Disorderly Orderly
(1964) Paramount
The master of comedic chaos turned loose in a hospital—so much for managed care! Not more than you would expect, but one of Jerry's best. **Cast:** Jerry Lewis, Glenda Farrell, Susan Oliver, Everett Sloane, Karen Sharpe, Kathleen Freeman, Del Moore, Alice Pearce, Jack E. Leonard, Barbara Nichols. **Credits:** Dir: Frank Tashlin; Prod: Paul Jones; Writer: Frank Tashlin; DP: Wallace Kelley; Ed: John Woodcock, Russel Wiles; Composer: Joseph J. Lilley; Costumes: Edith Head; Art Director: Hal Pereira. Color, 90 min. VHS

Distant Drums
(1951) Warner Bros.
A small but daring group of men led by Cooper venture into the Florida Everglades to battle the hostile Seminole Indians during their rebellion of 1840. **Cast:** Gary Cooper, Mari Aldon, Richard Webb, Robert Barratt, Ray Teal, Arthur Hunnicutt. **Credits:** Dir: Raoul Walsh; Prod: Milton Sperling; Writer: Niven Busch, Martin Rackin; DP: Sid Hickox; Ed: Folmar Blangsted; Composer: Max Steiner; Costumes: Marjorie Best; Art Director: Douglas Bacon; Set Designer: William Wallace. Color, 101 min. VHS, LASER

Dive Bomber
(1941) Warner Bros.
Exciting action movie about a military flight surgeon obsessed with finding

the cure for pilot "blackout" was released right before Pearl Harbor. Uncharacteristically sincere Flynn performance. Academy Award Nomination for Best (Color) Cinematography. **Cast:** Errol Flynn, Ralph Bellamy, Fred MacMurray, Alexis Smith, Robert Armstrong, Regis Toomey, Craig Stevens, Allen Jenkins, Herbert Anderson, Moroni Olsen. **Credits:** Dir: Michael Curtiz; Writer: Frank Wead, Robert Buckner; DP: Bert Glennon, Winton C. Hoch; Ed: George Amy; Prod Design: Robert M. Haas; Composer: Max Steiner; SFX: Byron Haskin, Rex Wimpy. Color, 130 min. **VHS**

Divorce American Style
(1967) Columbia
In a black comedy about the debilitating process of divorce, an average American ex-couple realize that after matchmaking hell, alimony-avoiding schemes, and commiserating with fellow divorcées, married life doesn't seem so bad. Producer and director Yorkin and Lear went on to TV greatness. **Cast:** Dick Van Dyke, Debbie Reynolds, Jason Robards, Jean Simmons, Van Johnson, Joe Flynn, Shelley Berman, Lee Grant, Tom Bosley, Eileen Brennan. **Credits:** Dir: Bud Yorkin; Prod: Norman Lear; Writer: Norman Lear; Story: Robert Kaufman; DP: Conrad Hall; Ed: Ferris Webster; Prod Design: Edward Stephenson; Composer: Dave Grusin. Color, 103 min. **VHS**

The Divorcee
(1930) MGM
After several blissful years of marriage, Shearer catches her husband in a compromising position and forces him to confess his infidelities. Her solution to the problem is to match him tryst for tryst. Early talkie with pre-Code va-va-va-voom. Based on *Ex-Wife*, the controversial novel by Ursula Parrott. **Academy Awards:** Best Actress: Norma Shearer. **Cast:** Norma Shearer, Robert Montgomery, Conrad Nagel, Chester Morris, Florence Eldridge, Robert Elliott, Mary Doran, Tyler Brooke, Zelda Sears, Helene Millard. **Credits:** Dir: Robert Z. Leonard; Prod: Robert Z. Leonard; Writer: Nick Grinde, Zelda Sears, John Meehan; DP: Norbert F. Brodine; Ed: Hugh Wynn, Truman Wood; Prod Design: Cedric Gibbons; Costumes: Adrian. B&W, 95 min. **VHS**

Dixie
(1943) Paramount
A musical loosely based on the life of songwriter ("Dixie") and blackface minstrel Daniel Decatur Emmet. Newly

arrived in New Orleans, small-town Kentucky boy Emmet falls in love with Millie and decides to break things off with hometown sweetheart Jean so he can marry her. When he returns to Kentucky, he discovers Jean has polio and, in sympathy, marries her instead. Emmet grinds out a living in the music halls but can't seem to get the big break. When the two return to New Orleans, they run into Millie again, and the stricken Jean, feeling she stands in the way of his happiness, tries to leave. A backstage fire during a performance resolves the romantic dilemma and the creative crisis at once. Average backstage bio, but with unusual setting. **Cast:** Bing Crosby, Dorothy Lamour, Marjorie Reynolds, Billy DeWolfe, Eddie Foy, Jr., Lynne Overman, Tom Herbert, Olin Howin, Raymond Walburn, Robert Warwick. **Credits:** Dir: A. Edward Sutherland; Prod: Paul Jones; Writer: Claude Binyon, Karl Tunberg, Darrell Ware; Story: William Rankin; DP: William Mellor; Ed: William Shea; Prod Design: William Flannery; Composer: Johnny Burke, James Van Heusen, Dan Emmet. Color, 89 min.

D.O.A.
(1950) United Artists
This famous film noir murder mystery features an inventive twist: the victim as "detective," desperately trying to solve his own murder. A real-estate salesman on vacation in San Francisco gets a dose of slow-acting, lethal poison in a misdirected murder attempt. He then begins a desperate search for the individual responsible for his impending demise. Irresistible plot given remakes in 1969 as *Color Me Dead*, and in 1988 starring Meg Ryan and Dennis Quaid. **Cast:** Edmond O'Brien, Luther Adler, Pamela Britton, Neville Brand, Beverly Garland, Lynne Baggett, William Ching, Henry Hart, Laurette Luez, Jess Kirkpatrick. **Credits:** Dir: Rudolph Mate; Prod: Leo C. Popkin; Writer: Russell Rouse, Clarence Greene; DP: Ernest Laszlo; Ed: Arthur H. Nadel; Composer: Dimitri Tiomkin; Costumes: Maria Donovan; Art Director: Duncan Cramer; Set Designer: Al Orenbach. B&W, 85 min. **VHS**

The Docks of New York
(1928) Paramount
Von Sternberg's first Hollywood production is one of the greatest achievements of the silent cinema. As he wanders the smoky dives along New York's decaying waterfront at night, a dockworker saves a despairing woman

from suicide and his life is dramatically changed. The zenith of silent-era cinematography (by Rossen) that, matched with a haunting score, created the thick atmosphere of impending doom. **Cast:** George Bancroft, Betty Compson, Olga Baclanova, Mitchell Lewis. **Credits:** Dir: Josef von Sternberg; DP: Harold Rossen. B&W, 80 min. **VHS**

Doctor Bull
(1933) Fox
Ford and Rogers come to Connecticut, with Rogers as a professionally awkward but personally upright country doctor who weathers small-town gossip, petty politicking, and an epidemic, while scandalizing the community by socializing with a widow and foiling his detractors with honesty and a ready wit. **Cast:** Will Rogers, Marion Nixon, Vera Allen, Howard Lally, Berton Churchill, Louise Dresser, Andy Devine, Rochelle Hudson, Ralph Morgan, Tempe Pigott. **Credits:** Dir: John Ford; Writer: Paul Green, Jane Storm; Story: James Gould Cozzens; DP: George Schneiderman; Composer: Samuel Kaylin; Costumes: Rita Kaufman; Art Director: William S. Darling. B&W, 75 min.

Doctor Dolittle
(1967) Fox
A musical about an English doctor who becomes disillusioned with human beings and drifts off to commune with the birds and the beasts. Based on Hugh Lofting's stories from the '20s. Okay for family time. Academy Award Nominations: 9, including Best Picture; Best Original Music Score. **Academy Awards:** Best Song; Best Special Visual Effects. **Cast:** Rex Harrison, Samantha Eggar, Anthony Newley, Peter Bull, William Dix, Richard Attenborough. **Credits:** Dir: Richard Fleischer; Prod: Arthur P. Jacobs; Writer: Leslie Bricusse; Story: Hugh Lofting; DP: Robert Surtees; Ed: Samuel E. Beetley, Marjorie Fowler; Prod Design: Mario Chiari; Choreographer: Herbert Ross; Costumes: Ray Aghayan; SFX: L. B. Abbott, Art Cruickshank, Howard Lydecker, Emil Kosa; Art Director: Jack Martin Smith, Ed Graves; Set Designer: Walter M. Scott, Stuart A. Reiss. Color, 152 min. **VHS**

The Doctor Takes a Wife
(1940) Columbia
Zippy screwball outing for Milland and Young, not a duo that first comes to mind for madcap hijinks. An independent, career-minded woman writer who detests dominating males and a hard-

working medical-college instructor get caught up in a publicity mix-up. Despite their differences, the two are forced to pretend to be married. **Cast:** Loretta Young, Ray Milland, Reginald Gardiner, Gail Patrick, Edmund Gwenn, Frank Sully, Georges Metaxa, Charles Halton, Chester Clute. **Credits:** Dir: Alexander Hall; Prod: William Perlberg; Writer: George Seaton, Ken Englund; DP: Sid Hickox; Ed: Viola Lawrence; Composer: Frederick Hollander. B&W, 89 min. **VHS**

Doctor X
(1932) Warner Bros.
When the moon is full, murder stalks the streets of New York in this early talking chiller about a mad scientist with no arms conducting grisly flesh regeneration experiments. Interesting for its use of lighting, sets, and an early two-strip Technicolor process. **Cast:** Lionel Atwill, Fay Wray, Lee Tracy, Preston Foster, George Rosener, Mae Busch, Arthur Edmond Carewe, John Wray. **Credits:** Dir: Michael Curtiz; Prod: Hal Wallis; Writer: Earl Baldwin, Robert Tasker; DP: Ray Rennahan; Ed: George Amy; Prod Design: Anton Grot; Composer: Leo F. Forbstein. Color, 80 min. **VHS, LASER**

Doctor Zhivago
(1965) MGM
The ultimate in mid-'60s, big-budget Hollywood filmmaking, with casts of thousands, exotic locations, strikingly beautiful stars, and the sheen that only money can buy. Based on the Pulitzer Prize–winning novel by Boris Pasternak, about a Russian surgeon and poet, married to one woman yet in love with another, who becomes a victim of the Russian Revolution. The 30th Anniversary edition includes a documentary on the making of the film and is remastered. Academy Award Nominations: 10, including Best Picture; Best Director; Best Film Editing. **Academy Awards:** Best Color Cinematography; Best Costume Design (Color); Best Screenplay Based on Material from Another Medium; Best Original Music Score; Best Art Direction—Set Decoration (Color). **Cast:** Omar Sharif, Julie Christie, Geraldine Chaplin, Alec Guinness, Tom Courtenay, Siobhan McKenna, Ralph Richardson, Rod Steiger, Rita Tushingham, Adrienne Corri. **Credits:** Dir: David Lean; Prod: Carlo Ponti; Writer: Robert Bolt; Story: Boris Pasternak; DP: Freddie Young; Ed: Norman Savage; Prod Design: John Box; Composer: Maurice Jarre; Costumes: Phyllis

Dalton; SFX: Eddie Fowlie; Art Director: Terence Marsh; Set Designer: Dario Simoni. Color, 200 min. **VHS, LASER, DVD**

Dodge City
(1939) Warner Bros.
Cowpoke Flynn takes on the job of sheriff in the legendary Wild West town of Dodge City to rid his townfolk of a murderous gang. He also wins the hand of frequent costar de Havilland. Deep in supporting costars. **Cast:** Errol Flynn, Olivia de Havilland, Bruce Cabot, Ward Bond, Alan Hale, Ann Sheridan, Frank McHugh, John Litel, Victor Jory, Henry Travers. **Credits:** Dir: Michael Curtiz; Prod: Robert Lord; Writer: Robert Buckner; DP: Ray Rennahan, Sol Polito; Ed: George Amy; Composer: Max Steiner; Costumes: Milo Anderson; SFX: Byron Haskin, Rex Wimpy; Art Director: Ted Smith. Color, 105 min. **VHS, LASER**

Dodsworth
(1936) Goldwyn
A retired auto manufacturer travels to Europe with his vain, shallow wife. When she leaves him for a European baron, he is disconsolate until he meets a pretty young widow. A superb film adaptation of the Lewis novel handled well by Wyler and a big cast of Hollywood's best. Payne's screen debut. Academy Award Nominations: 7, including Best Picture; Best Director; Best Actor: Walter Huston; Best Screenplay. **Academy Awards:** Best Interior Decoration (B&W). **Cast:** Walter Huston, Ruth Chatterton, Paul Lucas, Mary Astor, David Niven, John Payne, Spring Byington, Gregory Gaye, Maria Ouspenskaya, Odette Myrtil. **Credits:** Dir: William Wyler; Prod: Samuel Goldwyn; Writer: Sidney Howard; Story: Sinclair Lewis; DP: Rudolph Mate; Ed: Daniel Mandell; Composer: Alfred Newman; Costumes: Omar Kiam; SFX: Ray Binger; Art Director: Richard Day. B&W, 101 min. **VHS, LASER**

Dog Day Afternoon
(1975) Warner Bros.
When a nervous thief (Pacino) holds up a Brooklyn bank, he inadvertently draws a city-sized crowd. All he wanted was money for his lover's sex change operation. Considered by many to be Pacino's finest early performance, it also underlines the tragedy of Cazale's early death. An "only in New York" true story told by quintessential New York director Lumet. Academy Award Nominations: 6, including Best Picture; Best Actor: Al Pacino; Best Director.

Academy Awards: Best Original Screenplay. **Cast:** Al Pacino, John Cazale, Charles Durning, James Broderick, Chris Sarandon, Carol Kane. **Credits:** Dir: Sidney Lumet; Prod: Martin Bregman, Martin Elfand; Writer: Frank Pierson; DP: Victor J. Kemper; Ed: Dede Allen; Prod Design: Charles Bailey; Costumes: Anna Hill Johnstone; Art Director: Douglas Higgins; Set Designer: Robert Drumheller. Color, 130 min. **VHS, LASER, DVD**

Dollars
(1972) Columbia
A security specialist installs a sophisticated alarm system in a bank he and his ditzy girlfriend plan to rob. This comic caper was filmed on location in Germany. **Cast:** Warren Beatty, Goldie Hawn, Scott Brady, Gert Frobe, Robert Webber, Arthur Brauss. **Credits:** Dir: Richard Brooks; Prod: M. J. Frankovich; Writer: Richard Brooks; DP: Petrus Schloemp; Composer: Quincy Jones. Color, 119 min. **VHS, LASER**

Doll Face
(1946) Fox
Pleasant musical features the time-worn tale of a burlesque queen who schemes to make it big on Broadway. Includes an early crooning hit from Como, if that's your thing. **Cast:** Vivian Blaine, Dennis O'Keefe, Perry Como, Carmen Miranda, Reed Hadley, Martha Stewart, George E. Stone, Donald McBride, Michael Dunne, Edgar Norton. **Credits:** Dir: Lewis Seiler; Prod: Bryan Foy; Writer: Leonard Praskins, Harold Buchman; DP: Joseph La Shelle; Ed: Norman Colbert; Prod Design: Lyle Wheeler, Boris Leven; Composer: Emil Newman, Charles Henderson. B&W, 80 min. **VHS**

The Dolly Sisters
(1945) Fox
Pinup favorite Grable and Haver star in this comedic bio of Jenny and Rosie Dolly, a Hungarian sister act who took Europe by storm in the early 1900s. The story focuses on the romance between singer-songwriter Harry Fox and the beautiful Jenny Dolly. Includes the song "I Can't Begin to Tell You," among the other creaky musical standards that were nostalgic 50 years ago. Standard Fox-Grable musical, and that's pretty okay. **Cast:** Betty Grable, John Payne, June Haver, Reginald Gardiner, Frank Latimore, S. Z. Sakall, Gene Sheldon, Sig Rumann, Trudy Marshall. **Credits:** Dir: Irving Cummings; Prod: George Jessel; Writer: John Larkin, Marian Spitzer; DP: Ernest Palmer; Ed: Barbara McLean;

Double Indemnity (1944)

Prod Design: Lyle Wheeler, Leland Fuller; Composer: Alfred Newman, Charles Henderson, Gene Rose, James V. Monaco, Mack Gordon. Color, 114 min. **VHS**

Donovan's Brain
(1953) United Artists
A scientist preserves the brain of a dead multimillionaire, but it starts to exercise control over him. Based on a novel by Curt Siodmak, the story was inexplicably made three times. **Cast:** Lew Ayres, Gene Evans, Nancy Davis, Steve Brodie, Lisa Howard, Tom Powers, Michael Colgan, Kyle James, Stapleton Kent, Peter Adams. **Credits:** Dir: Felix Feist; Prod: Tom Gries; Writer: Felix Feist; Story: Curt Siodmak; DP: Joseph Biroc; Ed: Herbert L. Strock; Prod Design: Boris Leven; Composer: Eddie Dunstedter. B&W, 85 min. **VHS, LASER**

Donovan's Reef
(1963) Paramount
A snooty Boston girl arrives on a tiny South Pacific isle in search of her missing father and encounters two old salty dogs. The mismatched trio creates an abundance of lighthearted fun in this last Ford-Wayne pairing. **Cast:** John Wayne, Lee Marvin, Elizabeth Allen, Jack Warden, Dorothy Lamour, Cesar Romero, Mike Mazurki, Marcel Dalio, Jacqueline Malouf. **Credits:** Dir: John Ford; Prod: John Ford; Writer: Frank S. Nugent, James Edward Grant; DP: William Clothier; Ed: Otho S. Lovering; Prod Design: Hal Pereira, Eddie Imazu; Composer: Cyril J. Mockridge. Color, 109 min. **VHS**

Don't Give Up the Ship
(1959) Paramount
Lewis portrays a former sailor accused of stealing a battleship on his wedding night. Brought before a military council, Lewis tells of his exploits onboard the ship, and it eventually transpires that the ship was sunk while acting as a target for shooting practice. He has to prove his innocence to return to his newly wedded (and as yet unbedded) wife. **Cast:** Jerry Lewis, Claude Akins, Hugh Sanders, Dina Merrill, Diana Spencer, Mickey Shaughnessy, Mabel Albertson, Robert Middleton, Gale Gordon, Richard Shannon. **Credits:** Dir: Norman Taurog; Prod: Hal B. Wallis; Writer: Ellis Kadison, Herbert Baker, Edmund Beloin, Henry Garson; DP: Haskell B. Boggs; Ed: Warren Low, Walter Tyler; Composer: Walter Scharf. B&W, 89 min.

Don't Look Back
(1967)
The rock-and-roll doc that launched a thousand imitations. Pennebaker's loose shooting style and focused interviewing illuminates Dylan's celebrated 1965 tour of England and features appearances by Joan Baez and Dylan's manager Albert Grossman. Includes one-of-a-kind performances of "The Times, They Are a Changin'," "It's All Over Now, Baby Blue," and "Subterranean Homesick Blues." Pennebaker also shot the unreleased tour doc meant for ABC television and shelved after Dylan edited it. **Cast:** Bob Dylan, Joan Baez, Albert Grossman. **Credits:** Dir: D. A. Pennebaker. B&W, 95 min. **VHS, LASER**

Don't Raise the Bridge, Lower the River
(1968) Columbia
An American in England schemes to get rich quick by renting out his English wife's ancestral manor as a discotheque. Just funny enough to keep watching. **Cast:** Jerry Lewis, Terry-Thomas, Jacqueline Pearce, Bernard Cribbins, Patricia Routledge, Nicholas Parsons, Michael Bates, Colin Gordon, John Bluthal. **Credits:** Dir: Jerry Paris; Prod: Walter Shenson; Writer: Max Wilk; DP: Otto Heller; Ed: Bill Lenny; Prod Design: John Howell; Composer: David Whitaker. Color, 99 min. **VHS**

Double Dynamite
(1951) RKO
An innocent bank teller (Sinatra), preparing to be married, hits it big at the racetrack but lands in a mess when his winnings are taken in a bank robbery. Farce distinguished only by its oddball cast. **Cast:** Frank Sinatra, Jane Russell, Groucho Marx, Don McGuire, Howard Freeman, Harry Hayden, Nestor Paiva, Joe Devlin, Frank Orth. **Credits:** Dir: Irving Cummings; Prod: Irving Cummings; Writer: Melville Shavelson, Harry Crane; DP: Robert de Grasse; Ed: Harry Marker; Prod Design: Albert S. D'Agostino, Feild M. Gray; Composer: Leigh Harline. B&W, 80 min. **VHS**

Double Indemnity
(1944) Paramount
Perhaps the most famous film noir of all. An insurance salesman (MacMurray) looking for a bigger score than the next whole-life policy and a scheming

blond viper with bangs, shades, and an intriguing anklet persuade her husband to sign a policy that pays double for accidental death—an accident they plan to make happen. MacMurray's past tense voice-over adds a rueful, bitterly world-weary tone. The electrifying script was written by Wilder and Chandler, based on the novel by James M. Cain. Academy Award Nominations: 7, including Best Picture; Best Director; Best Adapted Screenplay. **Cast:** Fred MacMurray, Barbara Stanwyck, Edward G. Robinson, Porter Hall, Tom Powers, Jean Heather, Byron Barr, Richard Gaines, Fortunio Bonanova. **Credits:** Dir: Billy Wilder; Prod: Joseph Sistrom; Writer: Raymond Chandler, Billy Wilder; Story: James M. Cain; DP: John Seitz; Ed: Doane Harrison; Prod Design: Hans Dreier, Hal Pereira; Composer: Miklos Rozsa, Cesar Franck. B&W, 107 min. **VHS, LASER, DVD**

A Double Life
(1947) Universal
In what many considered (at the time of its release) the role of Colman's career, the matinee idol gets to play both a veteran stage actor and perform great scenes from Othello. Colman falls victim to the actors' malady of mixing roles with reality, a particularly dangerous affliction when playing the jealous Moor and also when playing opposite one's wife. This is a sharp, lovingly observed look at the acting life presented by a team that knows whereof it speaks: writers Kanin and Gordon and director Cukor. **Cast:** Ronald Colman, Signe Hasso, Edmond O'Brien, Shelley Winters, Ray Collins, Philip Loeb, Millard Mitchell, Joe Sawyer, Whit Bissell, Ruth Gordon. **Credits:** Dir: George Cukor; Prod: Michael Kanin; Writer: Garson Kanin, Ruth Gordon; DP: Milton Krasner; Ed: Robert Parrish; Prod Design: Harry Horner; Composer: Miklos Rozsa; Art Director: Bernard Herzbrun. B&W, 103 min. **VHS**

The Double McGuffin
(1979)
Kura, the beautiful prime minister of a Middle Eastern country, and her daughter are due to make an appearance at an ordinary American school. An assassination plot is quickly discovered by three smart kids who can't get the police to listen, so they take matters into their own hands. **Cast:** Ernest Borgnine, George Kennedy, Elke Sommer, Vincent Spano, Lisa Whelchel, Ed "Too Tall" Jones, Lyle Alzado, Rod Browning, Orson Welles.

Credits: Dir: Joe Camp; Prod: Joe Camp; Writer: Joe Camp; DP: Don Reddy; Ed: Leon Seith; Prod Design: Harland Wright; Composer: Euel Box. Color, 101 min. **VHS**

Double Trouble
(1967) MGM
While performing in Europe, a surprisingly mod Elvis falls for a young heiress who is being chased by both gangsters and the police. Nine top songs are featured, including "Could I Fall in Love" and "It Won't Be Long." Elvis tries to get hip: watch for the far-out yoga scene. **Cast:** Elvis Presley, Annette Day, John Williams, Yvonne Romain, Chips Rafferty, Norman Rossington, Michael Murphy, Leon Askin, John Alderson, Stanley Adams. **Credits:** Dir: Norman Taurog; Prod: Judd Bernard, Irwin Winkler; Writer: Jo Heims; DP: Daniel Fapp; Ed: John McSweeney, Jr.; Prod Design: George W. Davis, Merrill Pye; Composer: Jeff Alexander. Color, 91 min. **VHS**

Double Wedding
(1937) MGM
Romantic screwball comedy about opposites—in this case a nose-to-the-grindstone Loy and layabout bohemian-type Powell—attracting. The seventh pairing of Powell and Loy. Based on *Great Love* by Ferenc Molnar. **Cast:** Myrna Loy, William Powell, Florence Rice, Edgar Kennedy, Sidney Toler, Mary Gordon, John Beal, Jessie Ralph, Katherine Alexander, Donald Meek. **Credits:** Dir: Richard Thorpe; Prod: Joseph L. Mankiewicz; Writer: Waldo Salt, Jo Swerling; DP: William Daniels; Ed: Frank Sullivan; Prod Design: Cedric Gibbons; Composer: Edward Ward. B&W, 87 min. **VHS**

Doubting Thomas
(1935) Fox
A man has misgivings about his wife's amateur theatrical career but can't dissuade her. This remake of a George Kelly play called *The Torch Bearers* was Rogers's last and in theaters when his plane crashed. Rogers and Burke make an appealing double bill. **Cast:** Will Rogers, Frank Albertson, Frances Grant, Billie Burke, Alison Skipworth, Sterling Holloway, Andrew Tombes, Gail Patrick, John Qualen, Johnny Arthur. **Credits:** Dir: David Butler; Prod: B. G. DeSylva; Writer: William Conselman, Bartlett Cormack; DP: Joseph A. Valentine; Prod Design: Jack Otterson; Composer: Arthur Lange. B&W, 78 min. **VHS**

Doughboys
(1930) MGM
A wealthy man accidentally enlists as a WWI army recruit and ineptly wades through basic training. Keaton's second talkie. **Cast:** Buster Keaton, Sally Eilers, Cliff Edwards, Edward Brophy, Victor Potel, Frank Mayo. **Credits:** Dir: Edward Sedgwick; Prod: Lawrence Weingarten; Writer: Al Boasberg, Richard Schayer, Sidney Lazarus; DP: Leonard Smith; Ed: William Le Vanway; Prod Design: Cedric Gibbons; Composer: Howard Johnson, Edward Sedgwick, Joseph Meyer. B&W, 80 min. **VHS**

Down Argentine Way
(1940) Fox
Patented Fox musical notable as Miranda's first American film appearance. An American socialite on vacation in Argentina falls in love with a wealthy racehorse owner. Carmen and her band give Hollywood's Pan-American drive for new markets in wartime a big boost. Academy Award Nominations: 3, including Best (Color) Cinematography; Best Song ("Down Argentine Way"). **Cast:** Betty Grable, Don Ameche, Carmen Miranda, Charlotte Greenwood, J. Carrol Naish, Henry Stephenson, Leonid Kinskey, Nicholas Brothers, Chris-Pin Martin, Gregory Gaye. **Credits:** Dir: Irving Cummings; Prod: Harry Joe Brown; Writer: Darrell Ware, Karl Tunberg; DP: Leon Shamroy, Ray Rennahan; Ed: Barbara McLean; Prod Design: Joseph C. Wright, Richard Day; Composer: Emil Newman. Color, 92 min. **VHS, LASER**

Downhill Racer
(1969) Paramount
Dazzling ski scenes are the best part of this sports drama about an undisciplined young skier on the U.S. Olympic Team. Novelist Salter's study of a restless soul on the run from his own emptiness. **Cast:** Robert Redford, Gene Hackman, Camilla Sparv, Dabney Coleman, Joe Jay Jalbert, Timothy Kirk, Karl Michael Vogler, James McMullan, Christian Doermer, Kathleen Crowley. **Credits:** Dir: Michael Ritchie; Prod: Richard Gregson; Writer: James Salter; DP: Brian Probyn; Ed: Nick Archer; Prod Design: Ian Whittaker; Composer: Kenyon Hopkins. Color, 102 min. **VHS, LASER**

Down to the Sea in Ships
(1949) Fox
Set back in the days when whales were hunted for oil, this actioner takes place almost entirely aboard a whaling

ship in the North Atlantic, and the story's principal characters are the ship's old captain (played with much sympathy by Barrymore), his young grandson (Dean Stockwell), and their first mate. On their voyage northward, the whale hunt turns dangerous as the ship encounters dense fog and an impending impact with an iceberg. **Cast:** Cecil Kellaway, Gene Lockhart, Berry Kroeger, John McIntire, Harry Morgan, Harry Davenport, Paul Harvey, Richard Widmark, Lionel Barrymore. **Credits:** Dir: Henry Hathaway; Prod: Louis D. Lighton; Writer: John Lee Mahin; Story: Sy Bartlett; DP: Joseph MacDonald; Ed: Dorothy Spencer; Prod Design: Ben Hayne; Composer: Alfred Newman. B&W, 120 min.

Dracula

(1931) Universal
The most famous screen version of Bram Stoker's celebrated tale launched Lugosi's career in the role he seemed destined to play. Browning had the right macabre sensibility and Freund's images are moody and shadowy. You know the lines by heart, but have you ever really looked at the scene in which Lugosi stands at the top of a sweeping staircase, haloed by spiderwebs, and intones, "I am . . . Dracula"? There was a Spanish-language version filmed at the same time that, with the exception of Lugosi's embodiment of the count, is considered superior. Try to give it a watch. **Cast:** Bela Lugosi, David Manners, Helen Chandler, Dwight Frye, Edward Van Sloan. **Credits:** Dir: Tod Browning; Prod: Carl Laemmle; Writer: Garret Fort; Story: Hamilton Deane, John L. Balderston, Bram Stoker; DP: Karl Freund; Ed: Milton Carruth, Maurice Pivar; Composer: Peter Ilich Tchaikovsky, Richard Wagner; Art Director: Charles D. Hall. B&W, 75 min. VHS, LASER

Dracula

(1979) Universal
Langella's acclaimed Broadway characterization as the famous count is effectively repeated on the silver screen, though the script falls flat when it strays from the original story. Made its romantic leading man a cinema sex symbol. **Cast:** Frank Langella, Laurence Olivier, Kate Nelligan, Donald Pleasence, Trevor Eve. **Credits:** Dir: John Badham; Prod: Walter Mirisch; Writer: W. D. Richter; Story: Hamilton Deane, John L. Balderston, Bram Stoker; DP: Gilbert Taylor; Ed: John Bloom; Prod Design: Peter Murton; Composer: John Williams;

Costumes: Julie Harris; SFX: Roy Arbogast; Art Director: Brian Ackland-Snow. Color, 109 min. VHS, LASER, DVD

Dracula's Daughter

(1936) Universal
The sequel to the 1931 *Dracula* finds his daughter, the beautiful and apparently bisexual countess Marya Zaleska, haunting London. Unfortunately, she's got Dad's appetite. Creepy fun. **Cast:** Gloria Holden, Otto Kruger, Marguerite Churchill, Irving Pichel, Edward Van Sloan, Nan Grey, Hedda Hopper, Gilbert Emery, Claud Allister, E. E. Clive. **Credits:** Dir: Lambert Hillyer; Story: Garret Fort, John L. Balderston, Bram Stoker; DP: George Robinson; Ed: Milton Carruth; Composer: Heinz Roemheld; SFX: John Fulton; Art Director: Albert S. D'Agostino. B&W, 71 min. VHS

Dragnet

(1954) Warner Bros.
A full-length feature film based on the popular police series of the 1950s. Watch it for its memorable evocation of its pre–Miranda Warning times. **Cast:** Jack Webb, Ben Alexander, Richard Boone, Ann Robinson, Stacy Harris, Virginia Gregg, Vic Perrin. **Credits:** Dir: Jack Webb; Writer: Richard Breen; DP: Edward Colman; Ed: Robert M. Leeds; Composer: Walter Schumann. Color, 88 min. VHS

Dragon Seed

(1944) MGM
A heroic young Chinese woman leads her fellow villagers in an uprising against Japanese invaders. Good intentions. Based on Pearl S. Buck's 1942 novel. Academy Award Nominations: 2, Best Supporting Actress: Aline MacMahon, Best (Black-and-White) Cinematography. **Cast:** Katharine Hepburn, Walter Huston, Turhan Bey, Agnes Moorehead, Aline MacMahon, Akim Tamiroff, Hurd Hatfield, Frances Rafferty, Henry Travers, Robert Lewis. **Credits:** Dir: Harold S. Bucquet, Jack Conway; Prod: Pandro S. Berman; Writer: Marguerite Roberts, Jane Murfin; Story: Pearl S. Buck; DP: Sidney Wagner; Ed: Harold F. Kress; Prod Design: Cedric Gibbons, Lyle Wheeler; Composer: Herbert Stothart; Costumes: Irene, Valles; SFX: Warren Newcombe; Set Designer: Edwin B. Willis, Hugh Hunt. B&W, 149 min. VHS

Dragonwyck

(1946) Fox
Mankiewicz's directorial debut is a Gothic mystery set in a prototypical gloomy mansion. Price resents his wife because she has only given him a daughter and no son. Her lovely

cousin comes to help take care of the wife and the daughter, and Price falls in love with her. He murders his wife and then proposes to the unsuspecting girl. She accepts, and a son is soon born and quickly dies. The local doctor discovers the truth about Price just as he is about to kill again. **Cast:** Gene Tierney, Walter Huston, Vincent Price, Glenn Langan, Anne Revere, Spring Byington, Connie Marshall, Harry Morgan, Vivienne Osborne, Jessica Tandy. **Credits:** Dir: Joseph L. Mankiewicz; Prod: Darryl F. Zanuck; Writer: Joseph L. Mankiewicz, Anya Seton; DP: Arthur Miller; Ed: Dorothy Spencer; Composer: Alfred Newman; Art Director: J. Russell Spencer, Lyle Wheeler. B&W, 103 min.

Dr. Broadway

(1942) Paramount
Dr. Timothy Kane is a doctor working Times Square in the heart of New York's theater world. Unwittingly, Kane befriends a murderer who asks him to deliver $100,000 to his daughter. Kane agrees, but shortly afterward, his newfound friend is killed by the mob and Kane is accused of the murder. In between treating Broadway crazies, Kane must prove his innocence to the police and find the responsible gangsters. Director Mann's debut feature. **Cast:** Macdonald Carey, Jean Phillips, J. Carrol Naish, Eduardo Ciannelli, Richard Lane, Joan Woodbury, Warren Hymer, Frank Bruno, Sid Melton, William Haade. **Credits:** Dir: Anthony Mann; Prod: Sol C. Siegel; Writer: Art Arthur; DP: Theodor Sparkuhl; Ed: Arthur Schmidt; Prod Design: Hans Dreier, A. Earl Hedrick. B&W, 68 min.

Dr. Cyclops

(1940) Paramount
A mad scientist shrinks a team of explorers in this Technicolor fantasy known for its groundbreaking special effects. Academy Award Nomination for Best Special Effects. **Cast:** Albert Dekker, Thomas Coley, Janice Logan, Victor Kilian, Charles Halton, Frank Yaconelli, Paul Fix, Frank Reicher. **Credits:** Dir: Ernest B. Schoedsack; Prod: Dale Van Every; Writer: Tom Kilpatrick; DP: Henry Sharp, Winton C. Hoch; Ed: Ellsworth Hoagland; Prod Design: A. E. Freudeman; Composer: Ernst Toch, Gerard Carbonara, Albert Hay Malotte. Color, 76 min. VHS, LASER

Dream Girl

(1947) Paramount
Hutton's a rich girl whose mother and sister just don't understand her

dreamy ways. Hutton is up to the episodic role, whether subjected to her mean sister's maudlin musings or pivoting adroitly from opera understudy who gets her moment in the limelight to an emotionally broken harlot who chooses a saloon to take her own life. **Cast:** Betty Hutton, Macdonald Carey, Patric Knowles, Virginia Field, Walter Abel, Peggy Wood, Carolyn Butler, Lowell Gilmore, Zamah Cunningham, Frank Puglia. **Credits:** Dir: Mitchell Leisen; Prod: P. J. Wolfson; Writer: Arthur Sheekman; Story: Elmer Rice; DP: Daniel L. Fapp; Ed: Alma Macrorie; Composer: Victor Young; Costumes: Edith Head; SFX: Gordon Jennings; Art Director: Hans Dreier, John Meehan. B&W, 85 min.

Dreaming Out Loud
(1940) RKO
Popular radio characters Lum and Abner pull off a number of capers to bring progress to the town of Pine Ridge in their big-screen debut. **Cast:** Phil Harris, Lum and Abner, Frank Craven, Clara Blandick, Frances Langford, Chester Lauck, Norris Goff. **Credits:** Dir: Harold Young; Writer: Howard J. Green, Barry Trivers, Robert D. Andrews; DP: Phillip Tannura; Ed: Otto Ludwig; Composer: Lud Gluskin; Art Director: Bernard Herzbrun. B&W, 89 min. **VHS**

A Dream of Kings
(1969) National General
A marvelous performance by Quinn as a Greek immigrant in Chicago who grasps for a second chance at love with a younger woman (Stevens) and scrambles to raise enough money to take his ailing son home to Greece. Stevens's performance demonstrates what a loss her suicide was; this was her last screen appearance. **Cast:** Anthony Quinn, Irene Papas, Inger Stevens, Sam Levene, Val Avery, Peter Mamakos, Alan Reed, H. B. Haggerty, Alberto Morin. **Credits:** Dir: Daniel Mann; Prod: Jules Schermer; Writer: Harry Mark Petrakis, Ian McLellan Hunter; DP: Richard H. Kline; Ed: Ray Daniels, Walter Hannemann; Prod Design: Boris Leven; Composer: Alex North. Color, 111 min. **VHS**

Dr. Ehrlich's Magic Bullet
(1940) Warner Bros.
Biographical drama about a dedicated doctor whose research helped develop a cure for syphilis. Dr. Ehrlich's work puts him in conflict with the staff at the late-19th-century hospital in which he works. **Cast:** Edward G. Robinson, Ruth Gordon, Otto Kruger, Donald

Crisp, Maria Ouspenskaya, Montagu Love, Sig Rumann, Donald Meek, Henry O'Neill, Albert Bassermann. **Credits:** Dir: William Dieterle; Prod: Hal B. Wallis; Writer: John Huston, Heinz Herald, Norman Burnside; Story: Norman Burnside; DP: James Wong Howe; Ed: Warren Low; Prod Design: Carl Jules Weyl; Composer: Max Steiner. B&W, 103 min.

The Driver
(1978) Fox
O'Neal stars as The Driver, a conniving, talented getaway driver who's continually on the run from a detective obsessed with capturing him. Told from the getaway driver's point of view. Early effort from action maven Hill. **Cast:** Ryan O'Neal, Bruce Dern, Isabelle Adjani, Ronee Blakley, Matt Clark, Felice Orlandi, Joseph Walsh, Rudy Ramos, Frank Bruno. **Credits:** Dir: Walter Hill; Prod: Lawrence Gordon; Writer: Walter Hill; DP: Philip H. Lathrop; Ed: Tina Hirsch, Robert K. Lambert; Prod Design: Harry Horner; Composer: Michael Small. Color, 131 min. **VHS**

Dr. Jekyll and Mr. Hyde
(1932) Paramount
Robert Louis Stevenson's spine-chilling tale of a doctor who becomes tormented by his success in separating man's good and evil natures was filmed several times. With spooky gaslit scenes of London and an excellent cast, this is still the most cinematically satisfying version. Seventeen minutes of previously censored material are now included. Academy Award Nominations: 3, including Best Adapted Screenplay. **Academy Awards:** Best Actor: Fredric March. **Cast:** Fredric March, Miriam Hopkins, Rose Hobart, Holmes Herbert, Halliwell Hobbes, Arnold Lucy, Tempe Pigott, Eric Wilton, Percy Heath. **Credits:** Dir: Rouben Mamoulian; Prod: Rouben Mamoulian; Writer: Samuel Hoffenstein; Story: Robert Louis Stevenson; DP: Karl Struss; Ed: William Shea; Prod Design: Hans Dreier. B&W, 98 min. **VHS, LASER**

Dr. Jekyll and Mr. Hyde
(1941) MGM
This version of Robert Louis Stevenson's tale about a scientist who develops a potion that separates man's good and evil natures accentuates the emotional characteristics of the Hyde figure, rather than the terror angle. Don't bother with the colorized version. Academy Award Nominations: 3. **Cast:** Spencer Tracy, Lana Turner,

Ingrid Bergman, Donald Crisp, Ian Hunter, Barton MacLane, C. Aubrey Smith, Sara Allgood, Frederic Worlock. **Credits:** Dir: Victor Fleming, Peter Godfrey, Harold F. Kress; Prod: Victor Fleming; Writer: John Lee Mahin; Story: Robert Louis Stevenson; DP: Joseph Ruttenberg; Composer: Franz Waxman. B&W, 114 min. **VHS, LASER**

Dr. Kildare
ER without the gore. The Dr. Kildare ensemble films, based on Max Brand's characters, followed Lew Ayres (after Joel McCrea portrayed Kildare in the opener, *Internes Can't Take Money*), the young do-gooder doctor of the title, and Lionel Barrymore, his irascible yet nurturing superior, Dr. Gillespie, as they tended to the infirm, often with state-of-art techniques. In addition to dealing with the doctors' personal dramas, each installment had a web of subplots, with a broad supporting cast to provide plenty of melodrama as well as comic relief. The secondary players included soon-to-be-a-star Laraine Day as Kildare's sweetheart; Walter Kingsford as Blair General Hospital's chief; Nat Pendleton as an ambulance driver; and Nell Craig as Nurse Parker. Van Johnson, Lana Turner, Ava Gardner, Robert Young, and Red Skelton also made appearances. When MGM dropped WWII-conscientious-objector Ayres from the cast after *Dr. Kildare's Victory* (1942), Barrymore took over as leading man. Philip Dorn and James Craig each played Kildare, but these later entries lacked the depth of the earlier films.

Internes Can't Take Money *(1937)*
Young Dr. Kildare *(1938)*
Calling Dr. Kildare *(1939)*
The Secret of Dr. Kildare *(1939)*
Dr. Kildare Goes Home *(1940)*
Dr. Kildare's Crisis *(1940)*
Dr. Kildare's Strange Case *(1940)*
The People vs. Dr. Kildare *(1941)*
Dr. Kildare's Wedding Day *(1941)*
Dr. Kildare's Victory *(1942)*
Calling Dr. Gillespie *(1942)*
Dr. Gillespie's New Assistant *(1942)*
Dr. Gillespie's Criminal Case *(1943)*
Three Men in White *(1944)*
Between Two Women *(1944)*
Dark Delusion *(1947)*

Dr. No
(1962) United Artists
In his investigation of strange occurrences in Jamaica, Bond uncovers a sinister plot by master criminal Dr. No. The first of the James Bond films and, with the exception of *License to Kill*,

the most serious portrayal of Bond. **Cast:** Sean Connery, Ursula Andress, Jack Lord, Joseph Wiseman, John Kitzmiller, Bernard Lee, Lois Maxwell, Zena Marshall, Eunice Gayson, Anthony Dawson. **Credits:** Dir: Terence Young; Prod: Harry Saltzman, Albert R. Broccoli; Writer: Richard Maibaum, Johanna Harwood, Berkeley Mather; Story: Ian Fleming; DP: Ted Moore; Ed: Peter Hunt; Prod Design: Ken Adam; Composer: John Barry, Monty Norman. Color, 111 min. **VHS, LASER, DVD**

The Drowning Pool

(1975) Warner Bros.
Sophisticated private eye Lew Harper returns, this time coming to the rescue of old flame Iris Devereaux. Iris is being victimized by an anonymous blackmailer who's threatening to reveal her infidelities to her husband. Sequel to *Harper* (1966). **Cast:** Paul Newman, Joanne Woodward, Anthony Franciosa, Melanie Griffith, Linda Haynes, Coral Browne, Murray Hamilton, Gail Strickland, Richard Jaeckel. **Credits:** Dir: Stuart Rosenberg; Prod: Lawrence Turman; Writer: Tracy Keenan Wynn, Lorenzo Semple, Jr., Walter Hill; DP: Gordon Willis; Ed: John C. Howard; Prod Design: Paul Sylbert; Composer: Michael Small, Charles Fox. Color, 109 min. **VHS**

Dr. Rhythm

(1938) Paramount
Musical comedy based on a short story by O. Henry, "The Badge of Policeman O'Roon." Veterinary surgeon Crosby disguises himself on a whim as a policeman. As a cop, the innocent singing doctor takes his first assignment, as bodyguard to experienced showgirl Carlisle, directly to heart and, hopefully, the chapel. Songs include "This Is My Night to Dream," "On the Sentimental Side," "Doctor Rhythm," and "P.S. 43." **Cast:** Bing Crosby, Mary Carlisle, Beatrice Lillie, Andy Devine, Rufe Davis, Laura Hope Crews, Fred Keating, John Hamilton, Sterling Holloway, Henry Wadsworth. **Credits:** Dir: Frank Tuttle; Prod: Emanuel Cohen; Writer: Don Ethelradge, Richard Connell, Jo Swerling, O. Henry; DP: Floyd Crosby; Ed: Alex Troffey; Composer: Johnny Burke. B&W, 80 min.

Dr. Socrates

(1935) Warner Bros.
At gunpoint, a small-town doctor unwillingly treats a bank robber and soon becomes doctor of choice for a gang of criminals. He protects an outcast townswoman that he's falling for,

rescuing her from the gang by telling the criminals she has a contagious disease. Later, as the gangsters prepare for attack, he gives them a sleep-inducing drug. **Cast:** Robert Barratt, Raymond Brown, Ann Dvorak, Olin Howlin, Marc Lawrence, Helen Lowell, Barton MacLane, Paul Muni, Grace Stafford. **Credits:** Dir: Wilhelm Dieterle; Prod: Robert Lord; Writer: W. R. Burnett, Robert Lord, Mary C. McCall; DP: Anton Grot; Composer: Leo F. Forbstein. B&W, 74 min.

Dr. Strangelove or: How I Learned to Stop Worrying and Love the Bomb

(1964) Columbia
When a psychotic U.S. general launches a preemptive strike against "the Commies," the American president (Sellers, in one of three roles) must deal with gung-ho military brass, bureaucratic bumbling, a drunken Soviet premier, and a twisted German rocket scientist. Horribly funny. Based on the novel *Red Alert* by Peter George. Selected for the National Film Registry. Academy Award Nominations: 4, including Best Picture; Best Director; Best Actor: Peter Sellers; Best (Adapted) Screenplay. **Cast:** Peter Sellers, George C. Scott, Sterling Hayden, Slim Pickens, Peter Bull, Keenan Wynn, James Earl Jones, Tracy Reed, Jack Creley. **Credits:** Dir: Stanley Kubrick; Prod: Stanley Kubrick; Writer: Terry Southern, Stanley Kubrick, Peter George; DP: Gilbert Taylor; Ed: Anthony Harvey; Prod Design: Ken Adam; Composer: Laurie Johnson. B&W, 93 min. **VHS, LASER, DVD**

Dr. Syn, Alias the Scarecrow

(1962) Disney
Pastor of his flock by day, and courageous defender of the hard-pressed farmers and villagers by night, Dr. Syn dons scarecrow disguise to fight the oppression of King George III. **Cast:** Patrick McGoohan, George Cole, Tony Britton, Kay Walsh, Geoffrey Keen, Patrick Wymark, Alan Dobie, Eric Pohlmann. **Credits:** Dir: James Neilson; Prod: Walt Disney, Bill Anderson; Writer: Robert Westerby; Story: Russell Thorndike, William Buchanan; DP: Paul Beeson; Composer: Gerard Schurmann. Color, 129 min. **VHS**

Drum Beat

(1954) Warner Bros.
Ladd plays an Indian fighter who is sent to negotiate peace with a warring Indian tribe. His mission is ambushed by a renegade chief. Based on a real

incident. **Cast:** Alan Ladd, Charles Bronson, Audrey Dalton, Marisa Pavan, Robert Keith, Rodolfo Acosta, Warner Anderson, Elisha Cook, Jr., Anthony Caruso, Richard Gaines. **Credits:** Dir: Delmer Daves; Writer: Delmer Daves; DP: Peverell Marley; Ed: Clarence Kolster; Composer: Victor Young; SFX: H. F. Koenekamp; Art Director: Leo K. Kuter; Set Designer: William L. Kuehl. Color, 111 min. **VHS**

Drums Along the Mohawk

(1939) Fox
Fonda and Colbert star as newlyweds whose simple life in the Mohawk Valley is savagely disrupted by Indian raids. Colbert is terrific as the city girl adjusting to life on the frontier. Ford's only film set in colonial America. Academy Award Nominations: 2, Best Cinematography; Best Supporting Actress: Edna May Oliver. **Cast:** Henry Fonda, Claudette Colbert, John Carradine, Edna May Oliver, Eddie Collins, Dorris Bowdon, Jessie Ralph, Arthur Shields, Robert Lowery, Roger Imhof. **Credits:** Dir: John Ford; Prod: Raymond Griffith; Writer: Lamar Trotti, Sonya Levien; Story: Walter D. Edmonds; DP: Bert Glennon, Ray Rennahan; Ed: Robert Simpson; Prod Design: Mark-Lee Kirk; Composer: Alfred Newman; Costumes: Gwen Wakeling; Art Director: Richard Day; Set Designer: Thomas Little. Color, 104 min. **VHS, LASER**

DuBarry Was a Lady

(1943) MGM
Two talented redheads cavort through the court of King Louis XV in one of MGM's lightest and frothiest musical concoctions. Adapted from a Cole Porter Broadway show but missing most of its best songs, it's still a treat to see Tommy Dorsey and His Orchestra in powdered wigs. **Cast:** Red Skelton, Lucille Ball, Gene Kelly, Zero Mostel, Virginia O'Brien. **Credits:** Dir: Roy Del Ruth; Prod: Arthur Freed; Writer: Irving Brecher, Nancy Hamilton, Wilkie Mahoney, Albert Mannheimer, Jack McGowan, Mary McCall; Story: B. G. DeSylva, Herbert Fields; DP: Karl Freund; Ed: Blanche Sewell; Prod Design: Cedric Gibbons; Choreographer: Charles Walters; Composer: Cole Porter, Tommy Dorsey; Costumes: Irene, Howard Shoup, Gile Steele; Set Designer: Edwin B. Willis, Henry Grace. Color, 112 min. **VHS**

Duck Soup

(1933) Paramount
One of the Marx Brothers' funniest, loaded with zany antics and a famous battle scene, which has been copied

by many. Groucho plays the incompetent king of Fredonia who wages war on a neighboring country. **Cast:** Harpo Marx, Zeppo Marx, Chico Marx, Groucho Marx, Margaret Dumont, Louis Calhern, Raquel Torres, Edgar Kennedy. **Credits:** Dir: Leo McCarey; Writer: Bert Kalmar, Harry Ruby, Arthur Sheekman, Nat Perrin; DP: Henry Sharp; Prod Design: Hans Dreier; Composer: Bert Kalmar, Harry Ruby; Art Director: Wiard Ihnen. B&W, 72 min. **VHS, LASER, DVD**

Duel at Diablo
(1966) United Artists
Violent Western about racism, in which a loner, an outcast bride, her bitter husband, and a proud Cavalry officer are forced to put their differences aside in order to fight for their lives against Apache warriors. **Cast:** James Garner, Sidney Poitier, Dennis Weaver, Bibi Andersson, Bill Travers, William Redfield, John Hoyt, John Crawford, John Hubbard. **Credits:** Dir: Ralph Nelson; Prod: Fred Engel, Ralph Nelson; Writer: Marvin H. Albert, Michel Grilikhes; DP: Charles F. Wheeler; Ed: Fredric Steinkamp; Composer: Neal Hefti; Costumes: Yvonne Wood; SFX: Roscoe Cline, Lawrence A. Hampton; Art Director: Alfred Ybarra; Set Designer: Victor A. Gangelin. Color, 130 min. **VHS**

Duel in the Sun
(1946) Fox
In Selznick's *amour fou* of a Western, two brothers become bitter rivals after a beautiful half-Indian woman comes to live on their sprawling ranch. Overheated potboiler set in the West, played out in lurid Technicolor. Academy Award Nominations: 2, Best Actress: Jennifer Jones; Best Supporting Actress: Lillian Gish. **Cast:** Gregory Peck, Lionel Barrymore, Joseph Cotten, Jennifer Jones, Lillian Gish, Walter Huston, Charles Bickford, Herbert Marshall, Joan Tetzel, Harry Carey. **Credits:** Dir: King Vidor, B. Reeves Eason, Otto Brower; Prod: David O. Selznick; Writer: Oliver H. P. Garrett, David O. Selznick; Story: Niven Busch; DP: Lee Garmes, Harold Rosson, Ray Rennahan, Charles Boyle, Allen M. Davey; Ed: Hal C. Kern, William Ziegler, John Faure, Charles Freeman; Prod Design: J. McMillan Johnson; Choreographer: Tilly Losch; Composer: Dimitri Tiomkin; Costumes: Walter Plunkett; SFX: Clarence Slifer, Jack Cosgrove; Art Director: James Basevi; Set Designer: Emile Kuri. Color, 138 min. **VHS, LASER**

Duel in the Sun (1946)

The Duke Is Tops
(1938)
Presaging her successes in *Cabin in the Sky* and *Stormy Weather,* a young Horne makes her feature-film debut in this all-black production as a singing sensation whose manager— in an unusual plot twist for the era— sacrifices his ambition for her sake. **Cast:** Lena Horne, Ralph Cooper, Lawrence Criner, Neva Peoples, Rubberneck Holmes, Edward Thompson, Monte Hawley, Vernon McCalla, Johnny Taylor, Guernsey Morrow. **Credits:** Dir: William Nolte; Prod: Harry M. Popkin; Writer: Phil Dunham; DP: Robert Cline; Choreographer: Lew Crawson; Composer: Basin Street Boys, The Cats and the Fiddle. B&W, 80 min. **VHS**

Dumbo
(1941) Disney
In this classic animated Disney film, a baby circus elephant is cruelly mocked until he realizes that his enormous ears are a blessing in disguise: he can fly. Soon, Dumbo becomes the greatest show on earth. Academy Award Nomination for Best Song ("Baby Mine"). **Academy Awards:** Best Scoring of a Musical. **Cast:** Edward Brophy, Herman Bing, Verna Felton, Sterling Holloway, Cliff Edwards. **Credits:** Dir: Ben Sharp-steen; Prod: Walt Disney; Writer: Joe Grant, Dick Huemer; Story: Helen Aberson, Harold Pearl. Color, 64 min. **VHS, LASER**

Dust Be My Destiny
(1939) Warner Bros.
In this Warner prison melodrama, Garfield plays a hardened tough who has just served a prison sentence for a crime he didn't commit. After he's picked up as a vagabond, he's sent to a country workfarm. There he falls in love with Lane, and the couple decides to run off and get married— after a fight with Lane's father. They later discover that Lane's father has died and Garfield is wanted for the murder. **Cast:** John Garfield, Priscilla Lane, Alan Hale, Frank McHugh, Billy Halop, Bobby Jordan, Charley Grapewin, Henry Armetta, Stanley Ridges, John Litel. **Credits:** Dir: Lewis Seiler; Prod: Louis F. Edelman; Writer: Robert Rossen; Story: Jerome Odlum; DP: James Wong Howe; Ed: Warren Low; Prod Design: Hugh Reticker; Composer: Max Steiner. B&W and Color, 88 min.

Each Dawn I Die

(1939) Warner Bros.
A reporter, framed and sent to prison for a crime he didn't commit, befriends a mobster in the pen. Half of the story is completely implausible but Cagney's performance is superb. **Cast:** James Cagney, George Raft, George Bancroft, Jane Bryan, Maxie Rosenbloom, Stanley Ridges, Alan Baxter, Victor Jory, Willard Robertson, Paul Hurst. **Credits:** Dir: William Keighley, David Lewis; Writer: Norman Reilly Raine, Warren Duff; DP: Arthur Edeson; Ed: Thomas Richards; Prod Design: Max Parker; Composer: Max Steiner. B&W, 92 min. **VHS**

The Eagle and the Hawk

(1933) Paramount
Three Americans (March, Grant, and Oakie) go blustering off to volunteer for duty in the Royal Air Force in WWI. The reality of war sobers March quickly, but Grant's ill-advised derring-do results in tragedy. The romantic subplot involves dishy Lombard. A remarkably fresh antiwar film reportedly actually helmed by Mitchell Leisen. **Cast:** Fredric March, Cary Grant, Jack Oakie, Carole Lombard, Sir Guy Standing, Adrienne D'Ambricourt, Forrester Harvey. **Credits:** Dir: Stuart Walker; Writer: Seton I. Miller, Bogart Rogers; Story: John Monk Saunders; DP: Harry Fischbeck. B&W, 73 min. **VHS**

The Eagle Has Landed

(1977) Columbia
Fast-moving WWII drama based on a best-selling novel by Jack Higgins places Nazi officer Duvall at the head of a squad of German commandos whose mission is to kidnap Winston Churchill. Their object: deliver Churchill to Adolf Hitler so the two leaders can hammer out a peace plan. An additional twist comes from the addition of the Irish Troubles to the plot in the form of Irish nationalist guerrilla Sutherland. **Cast:** Michael Caine, Donald Sutherland, Robert Duvall, Jenny Agutter, Donald Pleasence, Anthony Quayle, Jean Marsh, Sven-Bertil Taube, John Standing, Judy Geeson. **Credits:** Dir: John Sturges; Writer: Tom Mankiewicz; Story: Jack Higgins; DP: Anthony Richmond, Peter Allwork; Ed: Irene Lamb, Anne V. Coates; Prod Design: Peter Murton; Composer: Lalo Schifrin; Costumes: Yvonne Blake; SFX: Roy Whybrow; Art Director: Charles Bishop; Set Designer: Peter James. Color, 134 min. **VHS**

Earth vs. the Flying Saucers

(1956) Columbia
A young space scientist and his wife are working on a secret missile project, but every time their rockets are launched, they are intercepted and destroyed by the more advanced technology of mysterious flying saucers hovering near the earth. Almost too good to be a B movie, with Harryhausen's special effects. **Cast:** Hugh Marlowe, Joan Taylor, Donald Curtis, Morris Ankrum, Thomas Brown Henry, Grandon Rhodes, Larry Blake, Harry Lauter, Charles Evans. **Credits:** Dir: Fred F. Sears, Fred Jackman; Prod: Charles H. Schneer; Writer: George Worthing Yates; Ed: Danny B. Landres; SFX: Ray Harryhausen. B&W, 83 min. **VHS, LASER**

Earthworm Tractors

(1936) Warner Bros.
A hilarious comedy with Brown's trademark blustery, broad comedy in which a tractor salesman will go to any length to make a sale. Built around the character "Alexander Botts," who first appeared in the *Saturday Evening Post*. **Cast:** Joe E. Brown, Guy Kibbee, Dick Foran, Gene Lockhart, June Travis, Carol Hughes, Olin Howlin, Joseph Crehan, Sarah Edwards, Charles C. Wilson. **Credits:** Dir: Ray Enright; Prod: Samuel Bischoff; Writer: Richard Macaulay, Joe Traub, Hugh Cummings; DP: Arthur Todd; Ed: Doug Gould. B&W, 69 min. **VHS**

Easter Parade

(1948) MGM
An Irving Berlin spectacular in which Astaire plays the part of a dance man whose partner abandons the act. Fortunately, his new partner turns out to be Garland. This is the only picture in which the two superstars worked together. **Academy Awards:** Best Scoring of a Musical. **Cast:** Judy Garland, Fred Astaire, Peter Lawford, Ann Miller, Jules Munshin, Clinton Sundberg, Jeni Le Gon, Richard Beavers, Richard Simmons, Jimmie Bates. **Credits:** Dir: Charles Walters; Prod: Arthur Freed; Writer: Frances Goodrich, Albert Hackett, Sidney Sheldon, Guy Bolton; DP: Harry Stradling; Ed: Albert Akst; Prod Design: Cedric Gibbons; Composer: Johnny Green; Art Director: Jack Martin Smith. Color, 109 min. **VHS, LASER**

East of Eden

(1955) Warner Bros.
The strong screen adaptation of John Steinbeck's 1952 novel features the debut of Dean. Like Cain with Abel, a black sheep competes with his brother for his father's love—with tragic results. Dean immediately fixed himself in cinema history as the brooding son who feels his mother's absence as a searing wound. Golden Globe for Best Motion Picture, Drama. Academy Award Nominations: 4, including Best Actor: James Dean; Best Director; Best Screenplay. **Academy Awards:** Best Supporting Actress: Jo Van Fleet. **Cast:** James Dean, Julie Harris, Raymond Massey, Jo Van Fleet, Richard Davalos, Burl Ives, Albert Dekker, Lois Smith, Harold B. Gordon, Timothy Carey. **Credits:** Dir: Elia Kazan; Prod: Elia Kazan; Writer: Paul Osborn; DP: Ted McCord; Ed: Owen Marks; Prod

Design: James Basevi; Composer: Leonard Rosenman; Costumes: Anna Hill Johnstone; Art Director: Malcolm Bert; Set Designer: George James Hopkins. Color, 240 min. VHS, LASER

East Side, West Side

(1949) MGM
A gracious society matron desperately wants to save her marriage, but the ex-mistress is back in town and ready to fight for the man she desires in this drama based on the novel by Marcia Davenport. **Cast:** Barbara Stanwyck, James Mason, Ava Gardner, Van Heflin, Cyd Charisse, Gale Sondergaard, William Frawley, Nancy Davis. **Credits:** Dir: Mervyn Le Roy; Prod: Voldemar Vetluguin; Writer: Isobel Lennart; DP: Charles Rosher; Ed: Harold F. Kress; Prod Design: Cedric Gibbons; Composer: Miklos Rozsa. B&W, 110 min. VHS

Easy Come, Easy Go

(1967) Paramount
Presley is a frogman on an underwater adventure to look for buried treasure. Even the music doesn't keep this one afloat for long. Songs include the title number, "The Love Machine," and "I'll Take Love." **Cast:** Elvis Presley, Dodie Marshall, Pat Priest, Elsa Lanchester, Frank McHugh, Skip Ward, Elaine Beckett, Shari Nims, Sandy Kenyon. **Credits:** Dir: John Rich; Prod: Hal B. Wallis; Writer: Allan Weiss, Anthony Lawrence; DP: William Margulies; Ed: Archie Marshek; Composer: Joseph J. Lilley; Art Director: Hal Pereira. Color, 95 min. VHS

Easy Living

(1949) RKO
An aging football star struggles to cope with a fading career and a grasping wife in this gridiron melodrama based on an Irwin Shaw story. Interesting portrait of a man who knows his best days are behind him, with one of Mature's better performances. **Cast:** Victor Mature, Lucille Ball, Lizabeth Scott, Sonny Tufts, Lloyd Nolan, Paul Stewart, Jack Paar, Jeff Donnell, Art Baker, Gordon Jones. **Credits:** Dir: Jacques Tourneur; Prod: Robert Sparks; Writer: Charles Schnee; DP: Harry Wild; Ed: Frederic Knudtson; Composer: Roy Webb; Art Director: Albert S. D'Agostino, Alfred Herman. B&W, 77 min. VHS, LASER

Easy Rider

(1969) Columbia
Two motorcyclists embark on a coast-to-coast odyssey in search of real America, encountering the many faces of its big cities and small towns, a hip-pie commune, drugs, and sex in a New Orleans bawdy house. This often-imitated road movie defined a generation and has a memorable soundtrack. Written by the leads and Southern, the subject of later dispute. Academy Award Nominations: Best Supporting Actor: Jack Nicholson; Best (Original) Story and Screenplay. **Cast:** Peter Fonda, Dennis Hopper, Jack Nicholson, Karen Black, Phil Spector, Warren Finnerty, Luke Askew, Sabrina Scharf, Robert Walker, Jr.. **Credits:** Dir: Dennis Hopper; Prod: Peter Fonda; Writer: Peter Fonda, Dennis Hopper, Terry Southern; DP: Laszlo Kovacs; Ed: Donn Cambern. Color, 94 min. VHS, LASER

Easy to Love

(1953) MGM
The resident water queen of Cypress Gardens, Florida, swims, dives, and water-skis her way through a series of romantic entanglements, accompanied by the music of Cole Porter and choreography by Busby Berkeley. **Cast:** Esther Williams, Van Johnson, Tony Martin, John Bromfield, Carroll Baker, Edna Skinner, Eddie Oliver, Benny Rubin. **Credits:** Dir: Charles Walters, King Donovan; Prod: Joe Pasternak; Writer: Laslo Vadney, William Roberts; DP: Ray June; Ed: Gene Ruggiero; Prod Design: Cedric Gibbons. Color, 97 min. VHS

Edge of Darkness

(1943) Warner Bros.
A Norwegian fisherman (Flynn) leads his village's resistance against Nazi invaders in this stirring war drama directed by Milestone. The camerawork is magnificent and Rossen's script moves the action briskly to its inspiring conclusion. **Cast:** Errol Flynn, Ann Sheridan, Walter Huston, Ruth Gordon, Nancy Coleman, Helmut Dantine, Judith Anderson, John Beal, Roman Bohnen. **Credits:** Dir: Lewis Milestone; Prod: Henry Blanke; Writer: Robert Rossen; DP: Sid Hickox; Ed: David Weisbart; Prod Design: Robert M. Haas; Composer: Franz Waxman. B&W, 120 min. VHS

Edge of the City

(1957) MGM
Cassavetes and Poitier shine in this riveting exploration of race and the working class on New York City's docks. Cassavetes plays a drifter let out of the army but on the run for the murder of his brother, which he didn't commit. With nowhere else to go he arrives at New York's docks, and falls under the wing of a black worker (Poitier). They clash with the corrupt union Mob boss. Ritt's first feature. Aurthur developed the script from his own teleplay. **Cast:** John Cassavetes, Sidney Poitier, Jack Warden, Kathleen Maguire, Ruby Dee, Robert F. Simon, Ruth White, William A. Lee, Val Avery, John Kellogg. **Credits:** Dir: Martin Ritt; Prod: David Susskind; Writer: Robert Alan Aurthur; DP: Joseph Brun; Ed: Sidney Meyers; Prod Design: Richard Sylbert; Composer: Leonard Rosenman. B&W, 85 min.

Edison, the Man

(1940) MGM
Tracy portrays Thomas Edison in this sentimental version of the genius's life, and follow-up to *Young Tom Edison*. Middling, but sincere. Academy Award Nomination for Best Original Story. **Cast:** Spencer Tracy, Rita Johnson, Lynne Overman, Charles Coburn, Gene Lockhart, Henry Travers, Felix Bressart, Frank Faylen, Byron Foulger. **Credits:** Dir: Clarence Brown, Peter Godfrey; Prod: John Considine; Writer: Talbot Jennings, Bradbury Foote; DP: Harold Rosson; Ed: Fredrick Y. Smith; Prod Design: Cedric Gibbons; Composer: Herbert Stothart. B&W, 108 min. VHS

Edward, My Son

(1949) MGM
A drama that traces both the rise of a modest, hardworking family man and the decline of his marriage and morals. A happily married man and doting father soon increases his fortune, has an affair with his secretary, and eventually receives a knighthood under false pretenses. His wife, meanwhile, turns into a drunken, bitter person understood only by the family doctor (who has a crush on her). Experimental narrative with characters addressing the camera and the title character referred to in the third person and never seen. Academy Award Nominations: Best Actress: Deborah Kerr. **Cast:** Spencer Tracy, Deborah Kerr, Ian Hunter, Leueen McGrath, Mervyn Johns, Felix Aylmer, Julian d'Albie, Walter Fitzgerald, Colin Gordon, Ernest Jay. **Credits:** Dir: George Cukor; Prod: Edwin H. Knopf; Writer: Donald O. Stewart; Story: Noel Langley, Robert Morley; DP: Freddie Young; Ed: Raymond Poulton; Prod Design: Alfred Junge; Composer: John Wooldridge. B&W, 112 min.

The Egg and I

(1947) Universal
Green Acres '40s style! Colbert hits just the right note of exasperation in

this lighthearted comedy about a society girl whose new husband (MacMurray) convinces her to move out to the canebrake and start a chicken farm. The finishing-school graduate struggles with the hardships of rural living—and keeps an eye out for the seductive neighbor down the road. Features the first film appearance of Ma and Pa Kettle. **Cast:** Claudette Colbert, Fred MacMurray, Marjorie Main, Percy Kilbride, Louise Allbritton, Richard Long, Billy House, Ida Moore, Donald MacBride. **Credits:** Dir: Chester Erskine; Prod: Chester Erskine; Writer: Chester Erskine, Fred F. Finklehoffe; Story: Betty MacDonald; DP: Milton Krasner; Ed: Russell Schoengarth; Prod Design: Bernard Herzbrun; Composer: Frank Skinner. B&W, 108 min. VHS, LASER

El Dorado (1967)

The Eiger Sanction

(1975) Universal
A James Bond–like movie about a retired former hit-man (Eastwood) who becomes involved with his old profession. The climax includes exciting action in the Swiss Alps during which Eastwood must carry out another assassination. Based on the novel by Trevanian. **Cast:** Clint Eastwood, George Kennedy, Jack Cassidy, Thayer David, Vonetta McGee, Heidi Bruhl. **Credits:** Dir: Clint Eastwood; Writer: Hal Dresner, Warren B. Murphy, Rod Whitaker; DP: Frank Stanley, Peter Pilafian, Peter White, Jeff Schoolfield, John Cleare; Ed: Ferris Webster; Prod Design: George C. Webb; Composer: John Williams; Costumes: Charles Waldo; Art Director: Aurelio Crugnola. Color, 128 min. VHS, LASER

El Cid

(1961) Allied Artists
This costume adventure follows the legendary exploits of the 11th-century Spanish knight-errant (Heston) as he battles the Moorish invaders while wooing back his wife (Loren) with his faith and bravery. This marks director Mann's brief excursion into widescreen historical epics after he distinguished himself with his Westerns. (He would begin work on *Spartacus* only to be replaced by Stanley Kubrick, then later follow these with *The Fall of the Roman Empire*.) Restored under the supervision of Martin Scorsese, who also knows something about the intersection of spiritual inspiration and muscular action. Academy Award Nominations: 3: Best Art Direction, Best Score, Best Song. **Cast:** Charlton Heston, Sophia Loren, Raf Vallone, Genevieve Page, Herbert Lom. **Credits:** Dir: Anthony Mann; Prod: Samuel Bronston, Anthony Mann; Writer: Philip Yordan, Fredric Frank; DP: Robert Krasker; Ed: Robert Lawrence; Prod Design: Venierio Colasanti, John Moore; Composer: Miklos Rosza. Color, 182 min. VHS

El Dorado

(1967) Paramount
An embattled sheriff (Mitchum) must first win his struggle with the bottle before he can hope to oust a band of desperate, greedy cattlemen. Wayne comes to the rescue. Funny turn by Caan. Many similarities to Hawks's earlier Western *Rio Bravo*. **Cast:** John Wayne, Robert Mitchum, James Caan, Michele Carey, Charlene Holt, Arthur Hunnicutt, R. G. Armstrong, Edward Asner, Paul Fix, Christopher George. **Credits:** Dir: Howard Hawks; Prod: Howard Hawks; Writer: Leigh Brackett; Story: Harry Brown; DP: Harold Rosson; Ed: John Woodcock; Composer: Nelson Riddle; Costumes: Edith Head; Art Director: Carl Anderson. Color, 126 min. VHS, LASER

Electra Glide in Blue

(1973) MGM
Blake's Arizona motorcycle cop compensates for his stature with his giant Harley of the title and his brains. Reactionary response to perception of society gone to hell. Lots of stylish violence and great action sequences shot in Monument Valley. **Cast:** Robert Blake, Billy "Green" Bush, Elisha Cook, Jr., Mitchell Ryan, Jeannine Riley, Royal Dano, Peter Cetera, Lee Loughnane. **Credits:** Dir: James William Guercio; Prod: James William Guercio; Writer: Robert Boris, Michael

Butler; DP: Conrad Hall; Ed: Jim Benson, Jerry Greenberg, John F. Link. Color, 114 min. **VHS, LASER**

The Electric Horseman
(1979) Columbia
A fading, alcoholic ex–world champion rodeo cowboy (Redford) rides away from a Las Vegas casino atop a multimillion-dollar racehorse, and a relentless broadcast journalist (Fonda) is determined to discover why. The story gives an environmentalist twist to the better-than-average chase and romance plot. **Cast:** Robert Redford, Jane Fonda, Valerie Perrine, Willie Nelson, Basil Hoffman, Wilford Brimley, Allan Arbus, John Saxon, James B. Sikking. **Credits:** Dir: Sydney Pollack; Prod: Ray Stark; Writer: Robert Garland; Story: Paul Gaer, Shelly Burton; DP: Owen Roizman; Ed: Sheldon Kahn; Prod Design: Stephen Grimes; Composer: Dave Grusin; Costumes: Bernie Pollack; SFX: Augie Lohman; Set Designer: Mary Swanson. Color, 120 min. **VHS, LASER, DVD**

Elephant Boy
(1937) United Artists
The engaging story of a young Indian boy who discovers the location of the fabled elephant burial ground. This film marked Sabu's debut performance and is now available in remastered stereo. **Cast:** Sabu, W. E. Holloway, Allan Jeayes, Robert Flaherty, Walter Hudd, Bruce Gordon. **Credits:** Dir: Robert Flaherty; Prod: Zoltan Korda; Writer: John Collier; DP: Osmond H. Borradaile; Ed: William Hornbeck. B&W, 91 min. **VHS**

Elephant Walk
(1954) Paramount
A new bride on a Ceylon tea plantation must cope with her strange new environment, as well as her domineering husband. The elephants' charge marks the high point. Vivien Leigh was replaced in the lead by Taylor. **Cast:** Elizabeth Taylor, Dana Andrews, Peter Finch, Abraham Sofaer, Abner Biberman, Rosalind Ivan, Barry Bernard, Philip Tonge, Edward Ashley. **Credits:** Dir: William Dieterle; Prod: Irving Asher; Writer: John Lee Mahin; DP: Loyal Griggs; Ed: George Tomasini; Prod Design: Joseph MacMillan Johnson; Choreographer: Ram Gopal; Composer: Franz Waxman; Art Director: Hal Pereira. Color, 103 min. **VHS**

Elmer Gantry
(1960) United Artists
Fine adaptation of Sinclair Lewis's 1927 novel about a charismatic ex–football player who becomes an evangelist, plagiarizing speeches to promote himself above all else as he successfully exploits the folks of America's Corn Belt during the '20s. Academy Award Nominations: 5, including Best Picture. Other awards include a Golden Globe for Best Actor in a Drama: Burt Lancaster. **Academy Awards:** Best Actor: Burt Lancaster; Best Supporting Actress: Shirley Jones; Best Screenplay Based on Material from Another Medium. **Cast:** Burt Lancaster, Jean Simmons, Dean Jagger, Arthur Kennedy, Shirley Jones, Patti Page, Edward Andrews, John McIntire. **Credits:** Dir: Richard Brooks; Prod: Bernard Smith; Writer: Richard Brooks; Story: Sinclair Lewis; DP: John Alton; Ed: Marjorie Fowler; Composer: Andre Previn; Costumes: Dorothy Jeakins; Art Director: Edward Carrere. Color, 147 min. **VHS, LASER**

Elmer the Great
(1933) Warner Bros.
This adaptation of the Cohan-Lardner play was made for the manic gifts of comic Brown. There is mugging aplenty as witless Elmer with his magical gift for timely home runs stumbles through brawls, gambling joints, cheating Yankee pitchers, police stations, and, finally, romance. Brown's experience as a professional baseball player adds realism to his performance on the diamond. A remake of *Fast Company* (1929), starring Jack Oakie. **Cast:** Joe E. Brown, Patricia Ellis, Frank McHugh, Claire Dodd, Preston Foster, Russell Hopton, Sterling Holloway, Emma Dunn, Charles C. Wilson, Jessie Ralph. **Credits:** Dir: Mervyn LeRoy; Prod: Raymond Griffith; Writer: Tom J. Geraghty; Story: George M. Cohan, Ring Lardner; DP: Arthur Todd; Ed: Thomas Pratt; Composer: Leo F. Forbstein; Costumes: Orry-Kelly; Art Director: Robert M. Haas. B&W, 64 min.

Emil and the Detectives
(1964) Disney
Shot in Germany, this Disney remake of a 1931 film is about a 10-year-old boy who is robbed by a mysterious pickpocket while on his way to visit his grandmother. With the help of a group of enterprising young boys, Emil and his newfound friends track down the thief. **Cast:** Walter Slezak, Bryan Russell, Roger Mobley, Heinz Schubert. **Credits:** Dir: Peter Tewksbury; Prod: Walt Disney; Writer: A. J. Carothers; Story: Erich Kastner; Ed: Thomas Stanford, Cotton Warburton. Color, 92 min. **VHS**

Emma
(1932) MGM
A housekeeper (Dressler) marries her widowed employer of 20 years. His youngest son loves her but she wins the scorn of his three grown children. When her husband dies, Emma learns he has left her all his money. His older children trump up charges of manslaughter. She is acquitted but soon heartbroken when she learns horrible news about the youngest boy. Written for Dressler by her longtime friend, Hollywood great Marion. Academy Award Nominations: Best Actress: Marie Dressler. **Cast:** Leila Bennett, Katherine Crawford, Richard Cromwell, Marie Dressler, Dale Fuller, Jean Hersholt, Barbara Kent, Myrna Loy, George Meeker, Purnell Pratt. **Credits:** Dir: Clarence Brown; Writer: Leonard Praskins, Zelda Sears; Story: Frances Marion; DP: Oliver T. Marsh; Ed: William Levanway; Prod Design: Cedric Gibbons. B&W, 70 min.

The Emperor Jones
(1933) United Artists
Accomplished actor, singer, athlete, and scholar Robeson debuts in this adaptation of the O'Neill play. Haughty and volatile, a Pullman porter's fiery disposition loses him his job and lands him in jail. While on the chain gang, he kills a white guard and escapes, retreating to Haiti, where he overthrows the monarch and crowns himself Emperor Jones. According to historian Donald Bogle, Washington had to wear heavy makeup and darken her fair complexion as producers were concerned white audiences would think Robeson was playing a romantic lead opposite a white actress. Screenwriter Heyward also wrote *Porgy*, on which *Porgy and Bess* was based. The Home Vision video release includes the Academy Award–winning documentary *Paul Robeson: Tribute to an Artist.* **Cast:** Paul Robeson, Dudley Digges, Frank Wilson, Fredi Washington, Ruby Elzy, Brandon Evans, Rex Ingram, Jackie Mayble, Blueboy O'Connor, Gordon Taylor. **Credits:** Dir: Dudley Murphy; Prod: Gifford Cochran, John Krimsky; Writer: DuBose Heyward; Story: Eugene O'Neill; DP: Ernest Haller; Ed: Grant Whytock; Composer: Rosamond Johnson, Frank Tours. B&W, 101 min. **VHS**

The Emperor's Candlesticks
(1937) MGM
Baron Stephen Wolensky and Countess Olga Mironova are rival spies working in pre-WWI Europe. When an antique pair of candlesticks—each

containing documents hidden there by Wolensky and Mironova—are stolen, both spies are hot on their trail, tracking enemy spies through Czarist Russia and Venice. En route, sufficient time is spent in hostile entanglements that Wolensky and Mironova fall madly in love. When the documents are finally retrieved they are no longer on the opposite sides of the fence. A chance to see the intriguing Rainer at work. **Cast:** William Powell, Louise Rainer, Robert Young, Maureen O'Sullivan, Frank Morgan, Henry Stephenson, Bernadine Hayes, Donald Kirke, Douglass Dumbrille. **Credits:** Dir: George Fitzmaurice; Prod: John Considine; Writer: Harold Goldman, Monckton Hoffe; Story: Baroness Emmuska Orczy; DP: Harold Rosson; Ed: Conrad A. Nervig; Prod Design: Cedric Gibbons; Composer: C. Bakaleinikoff, Clifford Vaughan, Franz Waxman. B&W, 89 min.

The Emperor Waltz
(1948) Paramount
Crosby plays a phonograph salesman plying his wares—romantic and musical—in the Viennese court of Franz Joseph. He sees an opportunity to show his stuff to the royal household by wooing a countess (Fontaine in her accustomed regal mode); love prevails over commerce. Curiously workmanlike script from normally hard-boiled types Wilder and Brackett. **Cast:** Bing Crosby, Joan Fontaine, Roland Culver, Richard Haydn, Lucile Watson, Sig Rumann, Julia Dean, Harold Vermilyea. **Credits:** Dir: Billy Wilder; Prod: Charles Brackett; Writer: Charles Brackett, Billy Wilder; DP: George Barnes; Ed: Doane Harrison; Prod Design: Hans Dreier, Franz Bachelin; Choreographer: Billy Daniels; Composer: Victor Young, Johnny Burke, Jimmy Van Heusen; Costumes: Edith Head, Gile Steele; SFX: Gordon Jennings; Set Designer: Sam Comer, Paul Huldschinsky. B&W, 106 min. **VHS**

Employees' Entrance
(1933) Warner Bros.
A penniless young woman is forced to take a job with a reptilian executive who is in charge of a large department store. When she falls in love with his apprentice, their jobs are threatened. A racy pre-Code potboiler. **Cast:** Warren William, Loretta Young, Wallace Ford, Alice White, Allen Jenkins, Marjorie Gateson. **Credits:** Dir: Roy Del Ruth; Writer: Robert Presnell; Story: David Boehm; DP: Barney McGill; Prod Design: Robert M. Haas. B&W, 75 min. **VHS**

Enchanted April
(1935) RKO
Character study about British women who, bored and rejected by their husbands and finding themselves feeling the doldrums of middle age, take rooms in an Italian villa for a prolonged vacation. Here they entertain visiting husbands and others, who help them regain their optimistic perspective. Remade to great acclaim by British director Mike Newell in 1991. **Cast:** Katherine Alexander, Jane Baxter, Ralph Forbes, Ann Harding, Charles Judels, Frank Morgan, Jessie Ralph, Rafaela Ottiano, Reginald Owen. **Credits:** Dir: Harry Beaumont; Prod: Kenneth MacGowan; Writer: Kane Campbell, Ray Harris, Samuel Hoffenstein, Elizabeth Von Arnim; DP: Edward Cronjager; Ed: George Hively; Composer: Max Steiner. B&W, 66 min.

The Enchanted Cottage
(1944) RKO
The legendary height of Hollywood melodramatic fantasy. On the eve of his wedding, a handsome, wealthy man is called to active duty. The young flier returns disfigured and embittered after a plane crash. His fiancée deserts him, and he hides in the cottage that would have been their honeymoon love nest. A plain, painfully shy woman also hiding from the world's cruelty lingers by the seaside cottage. The unwanted loners befriend each other and agree to marry as no one else will have them. Their love transforms them: he is restored to his former self and she becomes lovely in the enchanted space their love has created. A gusher. **Cast:** Dorothy McGuire, Robert Young, Herbert Marshall, Mildred Natwick, Spring Byington, Richard Gaines, Hillary Brooke. **Credits:** Dir: John Cromwell; Prod: Harriet Parsons; Writer: De Witt Bodeen, Herman J. Mankiewicz; Story: Sir Arthur Wing Pinero; DP: Ted Tetzlaff; Ed: Joseph Noriega; Prod Design: Carroll Clark; Composer: Roy Webb; Costumes: Edward Stevenson; SFX: Vernon L. Walker; Art Director: Albert S. D'Agostino; Set Designer: Darrell Silvera, Harley Miller. B&W, 92 min. **VHS, LASER**

The Enchanted Forest
(1945)
A kindly old hermit who has lived in the California redwood forest for so long that he can commune with the birds and animals saves an infant after a train crash. He raises the child in the forest until the day comes when he reunites the boy with his mother

and at the same time saves his beloved sylvan glade. An overlooked family gem from a minor studio. **Cast:** Edmund Lowe, Brenda Joyce, Harry Davenport, William Severn, John Litel. **Credits:** Dir: Lew Landers; Writer: Robert Johnson, Louis Brock, John Lebar; DP: Marcel Le Picard; Ed: Roy V. Livingston; Prod Design: F. Paul Sylos; Composer: Albert Hay Malotte. Color, 78 min. **VHS**

The End
(1978) United Artists
Slapstick black comedy about a man (Reynolds) who finds that he hasn't much longer to live, and his bungled his attempts at suicide. He gets an assist from a crazed DeLuise. Reynolds directed a winning cast. **Cast:** Burt Reynolds, Sally Field, Joanne Woodward, Dom DeLuise, Strother Martin, David Steinberg, Norman Fell, Myrna Loy, Pat O'Brien, Kristy McNichol. **Credits:** Dir: Burt Reynolds; Writer: Jerry Belson; DP: Bobby Byrne; Ed: Donn Cambern; Prod Design: Jan Scott; Composer: Paul Williams; Costumes: Norman Salling; SFX: Clifford P. Wenger, Carol Wenger. Color, 100 min. **VHS, LASER**

The Endless Summer
(1966)
Longtime surfing chronicler Brown documents the ultimate surfer safari for what most dudes consider the never-bested granddaddy of all surfing movies. Two California surfers who are among the best in the world travel the globe in search of the perfect wave. The balance of their personalities and Brown's laconic observations make this enjoyable even for the landlocked. Followed in 1994 by *Endless Summer II* with a new generation of surfers. **Credits:** Dir: Bruce Brown; Prod: Bruce Brown; Writer: Bruce Brown. Color, 90 min. **VHS, LASER**

End of the Road
(1970) Allied Artists
Unorthodox treatment from a psychiatrist pushes an unstable young college professor right to the edge. He loses his already-shaky hold on reality after embarking on an affair with another professor's wife. Adapted from a John Barth novel, this was originally released with an X rating. **Cast:** James Earl Jones, Stacy Keach, Harris Yulin, Dorothy Tristan. **Credits:** Dir: Avram Avakian; Prod: Terry Southern, Stephen F. Kesten; Writer: Dennis McGuire, Terry Southern, Avram Avakian; Story: John Barth; DP: Gordon Willis; Ed: Robert Q. Lovett, Barry

Malkin; Prod Design: Jack Wright; Composer: Teo Macero. Color, 110 min. **VHS**

The Enemy Below
(1957) Fox
It's Mitchum vs. Jurgens as the commanders of an American destroyer and a German U-boat play a deadly game of cat and mouse. Noted for its underwater effects. Directed by musical comedy star Powell, who became a producer/director for feature films and for Four Star Television. **Academy Awards:** Best Special Effects. **Cast:** Robert Mitchum, Curt Jurgens, Theodore Bikel, Doug McClure, David Hedison. **Credits:** Dir: Dick Powell; Prod: Dick Powell; Writer: Wendell Mayes; Story: D. A. Rayner; DP: Harold Rosson; Ed: Stuart Gilmore; Prod Design: Lyle Wheeler; Composer: Leigh Harline; SFX: L. B. Abbott; Art Director: Albert Hogsett. Color, 98 min. **VHS, LASER**

The Enforcer
(1950) Warner Bros.
Told in a series of flashbacks, this tense, moody film noir drama concerns the attempts of district attorney Bogart to crack a ring of hired killers. Just as victory is at hand, the key witness dies and the DA, after four years on the case, must start again from square one. Painstakingly retracing the murderers' gruesome steps, the dedicated DA searches for the necessary evidence with which to convict the gang leader. Based on the Murder, Inc. trials. **Cast:** Humphrey Bogart, Zero Mostel, Patricia Joiner, Everett Sloane, Ted De Corsia, Roy Roberts, King Donovan. **Credits:** Dir: Bretaigne Windust; Prod: Milton Sperling; Writer: Martin Rackin; DP: Robert Burks; Ed: Fred Allen; Prod Design: Charles H. Clarke; Composer: David Buttolph; Set Designer: William L. Kuehl. B&W, 87 min. **VHS, LASER**

The Enforcer
(1976) Warner Bros.
In this third installment of the Dirty Harry series, Detective Callahan wages war on a terrorist group and his by-the-books superiors. His partner for this mission is a determined female officer who refuses to be bullied by male-chauvinist cops. Callahan and partner save the mayor, Dirty Harry–style. Followed by *Sudden Impact*. **Cast:** Clint Eastwood, Tyne Daly, Harry Guardino, Bradford Dillman, John Mitchum, Albert Popwell, John Crawford, DeVeren Bookwlater. **Credits:** Dir: James Fargo; Prod:

Robert Daley; Writer: Stirling Silliphant, Dean Riesner; Composer: Jerry Fielding. Color, 97 min. **VHS, LASER**

Ensign Pulver
(1964) Warner Bros.
In this sequel to *Mr. Roberts*, the crew of the U.S.S. *Reluctant* find themselves docked beside an island that boasts a barrack full of attractive nurses. Not as good as its predecessor but it's fun to spot the many future stars in the cast. **Cast:** Robert Walker, Burl Ives, Walter Matthau, Jack Nicholson, James Coco, James Farentino, Timothy Sands, Millie Perkins, Kay Medford, Larry Hagman. **Credits:** Dir: Joshua Logan; Prod: Joshua Logan; Writer: Joshua Logan, Thomas Heggen; DP: Charles Lawton, Jr.; Ed: William Reynolds; Composer: George Duning; Costumes: Dorothy Jeakins; Art Director: Leo K. Kuter. Color, 105 min. **VHS**

Enter Laughing
(1967) Columbia
A loosely autobiographical account of Reiner's early professional life in which an aspiring Bronx funnyman struggles to get his acting career off the ground. Adapted from the successful Broadway show and not quite as winning on the big screen, but a treat for Reiner fans as he wrote, directed, and produced. **Cast:** Reni Santoni, Jose Ferrer, Elaine May, Shelley Winters, Jack Gilford, Janet Margolin, David Opatoshu, Michael J. Pollard, Rob Reiner. **Credits:** Dir: Carl Reiner; Prod: Carl Reiner, Joseph Stein; Writer: Carl Reiner, Joseph Stein; DP: Joseph Biroc; Ed: Charles Nelson; Composer: Quincy Jones. Color, 112 min. **VHS**

Enter the Dragon
(1973) Warner Bros.
A trend-setting martial arts film with masterful kung fu action by the leg-

The Enforcer (1950)

endary Lee. The opium-smuggling plot is secondary to amazing and violent action scenes. The 25th anniversary edition features additional footage, an interview with Lee's widow, Linda Lee Caldwell, and *Bruce Lee: In His Own Words*, a behind-the-scenes documentary. **Cast:** Bruce Lee, John Saxon, Jim Kelly, Ahna Capri, Bob Wall, Shih Kien. **Credits:** Dir: Robert Clouse; Writer: Michael Allin; DP: Gilbert Hubbs; Composer: Lalo Schifrin. Color, 103 min. **VHS, LASER, DVD**

Equus
(1977) MGM
A powerful drama about a psychiatrist's struggle to understand one of his patients—a stable boy who, for some seemingly inexplicable reason, blinded six horses. Burton gives a performance of depth and maturity. Adapted from the more successful play by Shaffer. Academy Award Nominations: 3, including Best Actor: Richard Burton; Best (Adapted) Screenplay. **Cast:** Richard Burton, Peter Firth, Joan Plowright, Colin Blakely, Jenny Agutter, Harry Andrews, Eileen Atkins, Kate Reid. **Credits:** Dir: Sidney Lumet; Writer: Peter Shaffer; DP: Oswald Morris; Prod Design: Tony Walton; Composer: Richard Rodney Bennett. Color, 145 min. **VHS, LASER**

Eraserhead
(1976) Libra
A surreal, existentialist nightmare on celluloid in which a quivering couple produce a hideous, mutant baby in a ghastly urban environment. Originally Lynch's film-school project, this cult favorite was his feature-film debut. **Cast:** Charlotte Stewart, Jeanne Bates, John Nance, Joseph Allen, Judith Roberts. **Credits:** Dir: David Lynch; Writer: David Lynch; DP: David Elmes, Herbert Cardwell. B&W, 90 min. **VHS, LASER**

The Errand Boy
(1961) Paramount
The bustling activity at a movie studio gives Lewis plenty of opportunity to raise havoc in this spoof of Hollywood mores and manners. Jerry runs into (literally, most of the time) the cast of *Bonanza* and lots of familiar faces from Hollywood's golden past. **Cast:** Jerry Lewis, Brian Donlevy, Howard McNear, Iris Adrian, Sig Rumann, Isobel Elsom, Fritz Feld. **Credits:** Dir: Jerry Lewis; Writer: Jerry Lewis; DP: Wallace Kelley; Ed: Stanley Johnson; Choreographer: Nick Castle; Costumes: Edith Head; Art Director: Hal

Pereira, Arthur Lonergan; Set Designer: Sam Comer. B&W, 95 min. **VHS, LASER**

Escape
(1940) MGM
The story of a young American man who arrives in prewar Germany in search of his actress mother. His inquiries are met with mysterious evasion. He then discovers that his mother has been sent to a concentration camp and will soon be executed. He enlists the aid of an American-born countess, who turns against her German lover, a general, in order to help the boy sneak his mother to safety. A doctor in the concentration camp also proves to be a helpful accomplice in getting the mother across the border. **Cast:** Norma Shearer, Robert Taylor, Conrad Veidt, , Felix Bressart, Albert Basserman, Philip Dorn, Bonita Granville, Edgar Barrier, Blanche Yurka. **Credits:** Dir: Mervyn LeRoy; Prod: Mervyn LeRoy; Writer: Marguerite Roberts, Arch Obeler; Story: Ethel Vance; DP: Robert Planck; Ed: George Boemler; Prod Design: Urie McCleary; Composer: Eugene Zador, C. Bakaleinikoff, Franz Waxman. B&W, 104 min.

Escape
(1948) Fox
Former RAF squadron leader Harrison has the misfortune to survive air battles of WWII only to accidentally kill a policeman while defending a prostitute. Unjustly convicted and imprisoned, Harrison quickly finds life behind bars to be intolerable and escapes. He finds shelter first with Cummins, then in a church. He is too noble a man to allow the minister to lie to shield him for very long and he decides to give himself up, with the prospect of a reunion with Cummins upon release. Galsworthy story had a previous outing in 1930. **Cast:** Rex Harrison, Peggy Cummins, William Hartnell, Betty Ann Davies, Norman Wooland, Jill Esmond, Frederick Piper, Cyril Cusack, Marjorie Rhodes, John Slater. **Credits:** Dir: Joseph L. Mankiewicz; Prod: William Perlberg; Writer: Philip Dunne; Story: John Galsworthy; DP: Freddie Young; Ed: Alan Jaggs, K. Heely-Ray; Composer: William Alwyn; Art Director: Alex Vetchinsky. B&W, 79 min.

Escape from Alcatraz
(1979) Paramount
Another Siegel/Eastwood action-suspenser is the true story of how three men broke out of a maximum security prison that was thought to be inescapable. The carefully plotted

story is made all the more exciting because the men were never heard from again and no one ever duplicated their feat. Danny Glover's debut. **Cast:** Clint Eastwood, Patrick McGoohan, Roberts Blossom, Fred Ward, Jack Thibeau, Larry Hankin. **Credits:** Dir: Don Siegel; Prod: Don Siegel; Writer: Richard Tuggle; Story: J. Campbell Bruce; DP: Bruce Surtees; Ed: Ferris Webster; Prod Design: Allen Smith; Set Designer: Edward R. McDonald. Color, 112 min. **VHS, LASER**

Escape from Fort Bravo
(1953) MGM
This Civil War–era Western bristles with action as it's Union vs. Confederacy and settlers vs. Indians and every man for himself. Holden plays a tough Union cavalry officer at odds with both a band of restless Confederate prisoners and deadly Mescalero Indians. **Cast:** William Holden, Eleanor Parker, John Forsythe, Polly Bergen, William Demarest. **Credits:** Dir: John Sturges; Prod: Nicholas Nayfack; Writer: Frank Fenton; Story: Michael Pate; DP: Robert Surtees; Ed: George Boemler; Prod Design: Cedric Gibbons; Composer: Jeff Alexander; Costumes: Helen Rose; SFX: Warren Newcombe; Art Director: Malcolm F. Brown; Set Designer: Edwin B. Willis, Ralph S. Hurst. Color, 98 min. **VHS**

Escape from the Planet of the Apes
(1971) Fox
This third installment in the Planet of the Apes series finds Cornelius and Zira in modern-day Los Angeles. They have traveled back in time but soon find that they have enemies in the past as well as the present. This is thought by many to be the best of the sequels as it nicely blends humor with the sci-fi fantasy. The trip to the present was the result of limited budgets: ape suits cost money! **Cast:** Roddy McDowall, Kim Hunter, Ricardo Montalban, Sal Mineo, Eric Braeden, Bradford Dillman, Natalie Trundy, William Windom. **Credits:** Dir: Don Taylor; Prod: Arthur P. Jacobs; Writer: Paul Dehn; DP: Joseph Biroc; Ed: Marion Rothman; Prod Design: William Creber; Composer: Jerry Goldsmith; SFX: John Chambers, Howard Anderson; Art Director: Jack Martin Smith; Set Designer: Walter M. Scott, Stuart A. Reiss. Color, 98 min. **VHS, LASER**

Escape to Burma
(1955) RKO
Set in the lush jungles near Rangoon, this adventure follows a man on the

run for a crime he didn't commit. While evading the authorities, he finds more than refuge on a plantation owned by a beautiful, strong-willed woman. **Cast:** Barbara Stanwyck, Robert Ryan, David Farrar, Murvyn Vye, Reginald Denny. **Credits:** Dir: Allan Dwan; Prod: Benedict E. Bogeaus; Writer: Talbot Jennings, Herbert Donavan; DP: John Alton; Ed: James Leicester; Composer: Louis Forbes; Costumes: Gwen Wakeling; SFX: Lee Zavitz; Art Director: Van Nest Polglase; Set Designer: Fay Babcock. Color, 86 min. **VHS**

Escape to Glory
(1940) Columbia
This WWII-era programmer takes place on a British ship bound for the west at the outbreak of the war. The freighter's passengers include a college professor and his wife, a crooked district attorney, a German doctor, a gunman hiding out, and a soldier of fortune. The drama escalates as the temporarily disabled ship must hide from a Nazi submarine. As doom approaches, the passengers' true natures come to the fore. **Cast:** Pat O'Brien, Constance Bennett, John Halliday, Melville Cooper, Alan Baxter, Edgar Buchanan, Marjorie Gateson, Francis Pierlot, Jesse Busley, Stanley Logan. **Credits:** Dir: John Brahm; Prod: Samuel Bishoff; Writer: P. J. Wolfson; Story: Sidney Biddell, Fredric M. Frank; DP: Franz Planer; Ed: Al Clark; Composer: M. W. Stoloff. B&W, 74 min.

Escape to Witch Mountain
(1975) Disney
Two psychic orphans head for Witch Mountain to escape the evil plans of Milland and find their real identities. Pleasant Disney adventure was followed by *Return from Witch Mountain*. **Cast:** Eddie Albert, Ray Milland, Donald Pleasence, Kim Richards, Ike Eisenmann, Walter Barnes, Reta Shaw, Denver Pyle. **Credits:** Dir: John Hough; Writer: Robert Malcolm Young; Story: Alexander Key; DP: Frank Phillips; Ed: Robert Stafford; Prod Design: John B. Mansbridge; Composer: Johnny Mandel; Costumes: Chuck Keehne, Emily Sundby; SFX: Art Cruickshank, Danny Lee; Art Director: Al Roelofs; Set Designer: Hal Gausman. Color, 97 min. **VHS, LASER**

Eternally Yours
(1939) United Artists
Young plays the wife of Niven the Magician, whose career may make his marriage disappear. Clever banter. Academy Award Nomination for Best

Original Score. **Cast:** David Niven, Loretta Young, Hugh Herbert, C. Aubrey Smith, Eve Arden, ZaSu Pitts, Broderick Crawford, Billie Burke, Raymond Walburn, Virginia Field. **Credits:** Dir: Tay Garnett; Prod: Walter Wanger; Writer: Gene Towne, Graham Baker, John Meehan; DP: Merritt Gerstad, Ray Binger; Ed: Dorothy Spencer; Prod Design: Alexander Golitzen; Composer: Werner Janssen. B&W, 95 min. **VHS**

Evelyn Prentice
(1934) MGM
Powell and Loy, who made such an enticingly lighthearted couple in *The Thin Man*, reunite for this considerably darker noirish courtroom melodrama. This pairing finds them in the middle of cheating, blackmailing, and murder. Russell's screen debut has her in the role of "the other woman." **Cast:** William Powell, Myrna Loy, Una Merkel, Rosalind Russell, Isabel Jewell, Harvey Stephens, Cora Sue Collins, Edward Brophy, Henry Wadsworth. **Credits:** Dir: William K. Howard; Prod: John Considine; Writer: Lenore Coffee; Story: W. E. Woodward; DP: Charles G. Clarke; Ed: Frank Hull; Prod Design: Cedric Gibbons, A. Arnold Gillespie; Costumes: Dolly Tree; Art Director: Edwin B. Willis. B&W, 78 min. **VHS**

Everybody Does It
(1949) Fox
A screwball comedy set in the usually stuffy opera world. The story revolves around a rough-edged wrecking contractor and his young Park Avenue wife, who desperately wants to become a concert singer despite a lack of talent. A successful diva discovers that it's the contractor who has a wonderful baritone and she convinces him to take to the stage himself. An unlikely subject for a Cain story. Made earlier as *Wife, Husband, Friend* (1939). **Cast:** Paul Douglas, Linda Darnell, Celeste Holm, Charles Coburn, Millard Mitchell, Lucile Watson, John Hoyt, George Tobias, Leon Belasco, Tito Vuolo. **Credits:** Dir: Edmund Goulding; Prod: Nunnally Johnson; Writer: Nunnally Johnson; Story: James M. Cain; DP: Joseph La Shelle; Ed: Robert Fritch; Prod Design: Richard Irvine, Lyle Wheeler; Composer: Alfred Newman. B&W, 98 min.

Everybody Sing
(1938) MGM
A quirky theatrical family and their equally eccentric hired help populate this less well known MGM musical. Dad's a frustrated playwright, Mom's

an emotionally unstable actress, and the kids sing, so they put on a show. It's not even as good as it sounds unless you have an obsession with Garland. **Cast:** Judy Garland, Fanny Brice, Billie Burke, Allan Jones, Reginald Owen, Reginald Gardiner, Lynne Carver, Monty Woolley, Henry Armetta. **Credits:** Dir: Edwin L. Marin; Prod: Harry Rapf; Writer: Florence Ryerson, Edgar Allan Woolf, James Gruen; DP: Joseph Ruttenberg; Ed: William S. Gray. B&W, 91 min. **VHS**

Every Day's a Holiday
(1937) Paramount
West plays Peaches O'Day, a Gay '90s con artist who can sell anything, including the Brooklyn Bridge. She returns to New York from banishment in disguise to exact her revenge on the police commissioner. As usual West's script slides a few past the censor's snips. Her last picture for Paramount. Academy Award Nomination for Best Interior Decoration. **Cast:** Mae West, Edmund Lowe, Charles Butterworth, Charles Winninger, Walter Catlett, Lloyd Nolan, Herman Bing, Chester Conklin, Louis Armstrong, Roger Imhof. **Credits:** Dir: A. Edward Sutherland; Prod: Emanuel Cohen; Writer: Mae West; DP: Karl Struss; Ed: Ray Curtiss; Choreographer: Leroy Prinz; Costumes: Basia Bassett; Art Director: Wiard Ihnen. B&W, 79 min. **VHS**

Every Girl Should Be Married
(1948) RKO
A breezy comedy about a shopgirl determined to marry a dashing bachelor doctor, with Tone waiting in the wings. In real life, Drake and Grant were married shortly after this movie. **Cast:** Cary Grant, Franchot Tone, Diana Lynn, Betsy Drake, Alan Mowbray, Elisabeth Risdon, Richard Gaines. **Credits:** Dir: Don Hartman; Prod: Don Hartman; Writer: Don Hartman, Stephen Morehouse Avery; Story: Eleanor Harris; DP: George E. Diskant; Ed: Harry Marker; Prod Design: Carroll Clark; Composer: Leigh Harline; Costumes: Irene Sharaff; SFX: Russell A. Cully; Art Director: Albert S. D'Agostino; Set Designer: Darrell Silvera, William Stevens. B&W, 84 min. **VHS, LASER**

Everything Happens at Night
(1939) Fox
Skating legend Henie sports her way into the hearts of two newspapermen covering a political story in Switzerland. Henie navigates the emotional

peaks and valleys as well as the ski slopes and ice rinks. **Cast:** Sonja Henie, Ray Milland, Robert Cummings, Alan Dinehart, Fritz Feld, Jody Gilbert, Victor Varconi, Maurice Moscovich, Leonid Kinskey. **Credits:** Dir: Irving Cummings; Prod: Harry Joe Brown; Writer: Art Arthur, Robert Herari; DP: Edward Cronjager; Ed: Walter Thompson; Choreographer: Nick Castle. B&W, 77 min. **vhs**

Everything You Always Wanted to Know About Sex, but Were Afraid to Ask
(1972) United Artists
Seven humorous sketches depict the human sex drive and the absurd behavior it causes. The sketches include scenes in which an average middle-aged Jewish man sneaks upstairs to try on a dinner hostess's dresses; Wilder falls gradually in love with a sheep; and Allen's girlfriend can only reach satisfaction by having sex in public places. A satire of '70s sexual mores with not much to do with the book by Dr. David Reuben except for its title. **Cast:** Woody Allen, John Carradine, Lou Jacobi, Louise Lasser, Anthony Quayle, Tony Randall, Lynn Redgrave, Burt Reynolds, Gene Wilder. **Credits:** Dir: Woody Allen; Prod: Charles H. Joffe; Writer: Woody Allen; DP: David M. Walsh; Ed: James Heckert, Eric Albertson; Prod Design: Dale Hennesy; Composer: Mundell Lowe; Set Designer: Marvin March. Color, 88 min. **vhs, laser**

Exclusive
(1937) Paramount
The publisher of *The Mountain City World* juggles the blossoming affair between his ace reporter and his determined daughter (Farmer) and corrupt local political leaders. Complications ensure when his daughter joins the gutter-press rival, hot on the same story. **Cast:** Fred MacMurray, Frances Farmer, Charlie Ruggles, Lloyd Nolan, Fay Holden, Ralph Morgan, Edward H. Robins, Willard Robertson, Horace McMahon. **Credits:** Dir: Alexander Hall; Prod: Benjamin Glazer; Writer: Rian James, Sidney Salkow; Story: Jack Moffitt; DP: Geoffrey Erb, Geoffrey Erb, William Mellor; Ed: Paul Weatherwax. B&W, 85 min.

Executive Suite
(1954) MGM
After the sudden death of its president, a giant furniture company's seven board members battle for control. Sophisticated soap with a jaundiced view of the corporate rat race. The

basis for a later TV series. **Academy Award Nominations:** 4, including Best Supporting Actress: Nina Foch; Best Cinematography **Cast:** William Holden, June Allyson, Barbara Stanwyck, Fredric March, Walter Pidgeon, Shelley Winters, Paul Douglas, Louis Calhern, Dean Jagger, Nina Foch. **Credits:** Dir: Robert Wise; Writer: Ernest Lehman; Story: Cameron Hawley; DP: George J. Folsey; Ed: Ralph E. Winters; Prod Design: Cedric Gibbons; Costumes: Helen Rose; SFX: A. Arnold Gillespie; Art Director: Edward C. Carfagno; Set Designer: Edwin B. Willis, Emile Kuri. B&W, 105 min. **vhs**

The Exile
(1947) Universal
The story of Charles II benefits from Fairbanks's love of all things British. Charles has left England for Holland to escape Oliver Cromwell and the Puritans. While there he is held safely at the estate of a beautiful countess. The American debut of director Ophuls. **Cast:** Milton Owen, Douglas Fairbanks, Jr., Maria Montez, Paula Croset, Henry Daniell, Nigel Bruce, Robert Coote, Otto Waldis, Mort Shuman, Eldon Gorst. **Credits:** Dir: Max Ophuls; Prod: Douglas Fairbanks, Jr.; Writer: Douglas Fairbanks, Jr., Cosmo Hamilton; DP: Franz Planer; Ed: Ted J. Kent; Prod Design: Bernard Herzbrun, Howard Bay; Composer: Frank Skinner; SFX: David Horsley; Art Director: Hilyard Brown. B&W, 95 min.

Ex-Lady
(1933) Warner Bros.
An independent artist has no problem "living in sin" with her boyfriend. But when he starts pressuring her to marry him, their problems begin. A remake of Barbara Stanwyck's 1931 movie *Illicit*. **Cast:** Bette Davis, Gene Raymond, Frank McHugh, Claire Dodd, Ferdinand Gottschalk, Monroe Owsley. **Credits:** Dir: Robert Florey; Writer: David Boehm; Story: Edith Fitzgerald, Robert Riskin; DP: Tony Gaudio; Ed: Harold McLernon; Costumes: Orry-Kelly; Art Director: Jack Okey. B&W, 67 min. **vhs**

The Ex-Mrs. Bradford
(1936) RKO
When the innocent Dr. Bradford finds himself implicated in a string of murders, his meddling ex-wife uses the opportunity to reenter his life. The squabbling pair must now join forces to solve the crimes and clear the good doctor's name. Great fun with Powell and Arthur making a likable team. **Cast:** William Powell, Jean Arthur,

James Gleason, Eric Blore, Robert Armstrong, Lila Lee, Grant Mitchell, Ralph Morgan. **Credits:** Dir: Stephen Roberts; Prod: Edward Kaufman; Writer: Anthony Veiller; Story: James Edward Grant; DP: J. Roy Hunt; Ed: Arthur Roberts; Prod Design: Van Nest Polglase; Composer: Roy Webb; Costumes: Bernard Newman; Art Director: Perry Ferguson; Set Designer: Darrell Silvera. B&W, 80 min. **vhs, laser**

Exodus
(1960) United Artists
Based on Leon Uris's novel, *Exodus* is the epic saga of the founding of Israel in the days following WWII. Newman stars as an Israeli resistance fighter involved in the effort to bring a group of 600 European Jews from British-blockaded Cyprus into newly partitioned Palestine, right before the United Nations is to vote on making it a Jewish homeland. Golden Globe for Best Supporting Actor: Sal Mineo. **Academy Awards:** Best Music Score of a Drama/Comedy. **Cast:** Paul Newman, Eva Marie Saint, Lee J. Cobb, Sal Mineo, Ralph Richardson, John Derek, Hugh Griffith, Gregory Ratoff, Felix Aylmer, David Opatoshu. **Credits:** Dir: Otto Preminger; Prod: Otto Preminger; Writer: Dalton Trumbo; Story: Leon Uris; DP: Sam Leavitt; Ed: Louis Loeffler; Composer: Ernest Gold; Costumes: Joe King, Rudi Gernreich, Hope Bryce, Margo Slater, May Walding; SFX: Winston Ryder; Art Director: Richard Day, William E. Hutchinson; Set Designer: Dario Simoni. Color, 218 min. **vhs, laser**

The Exorcist
(1973) Warner Bros.
The movie you can't stand to watch and yet can't turn away from. A horrifying, riveting film based on William Peter Blatty's best-seller (he also wrote the screenplay). In the ultimate transformation plot, a 12-year-old girl (Blair) becomes possessed by the devil. Soon, the once sweet child is transformed into a murderous, vomit-spewing, bed-twirling hellhound. A dedicated but naive priest attempts to exorcise Satan from Blair's body—and in the process is forced to confront personal demons of his own. The theatrical release led to outrage, fainting, nausea—and huge box office receipts. The result was two cash-in sequels, the second directed by Blatty. The 25th anniversary video release includes a documentary on the making of the film, an introduction by director Friedkin, and a commemorative 52-page book, *The Exorcist: The*

Making of a Classic Motion Picture.
Academy Award Nominations: 10, including Best Picture; Best Actress: Ellen Burstyn; Best Supporting Actor: Jason Robards; Best Supporting Actress: Linda Blair; Best Director; Best Cinematography; Best Editing. **Academy Awards:** Best Screenplay Based on Material from Another Medium. **Cast:** Ellen Burstyn, Max von Sydow, Lee J. Cobb, Kitty Winn, Jack MacGowran, Jason Miller, Linda Blair. **Credits:** Dir: William Friedkin; Writer: William Peter Blatty; DP: Owen Roizman, Billy Williams; Ed: Norman Gay, Jordan Leondopoulos, Evan Lottman, Bud Smith; Prod Design: Bill Malley; Composer: Jack Nitzsche; Songs: Mike Oldfield; Set Designer: Jerry Wunderlich. Color, 120 min. **VHS, LASER, DVD**

Exorcist 2—The Heretic
(1977) Warner Bros.
This sequel to the 1973 groundbreaking box office hit finds Blair under psychiatric treatment, still recovering from the effects of personally hosting evil. Burton's a priest who thinks it's not over yet. The special effects are good but the story is so weak that Boorman recut the film the day after it premiered—the home video features the original version, though. **Cast:** Richard Burton, Linda Blair, Louise Fletcher, James Earl Jones, Max von Sydow, Kitty Winn, Paul Henreid, Ned Beatty. **Credits:** Dir: John Boorman; Prod: Richard Lederer, John Boorman; Writer: William Goodhart; DP: William A. Fraker; Ed: Tom Priestley; Prod Design: Richard MacDonald; Composer: Ennio Morricone; Costumes: Robert De Mora; SFX: Albert J. Whit-

lock, Chuck Gaspar, Jeff Jarvis, Jim Blount, Roy Kelly, Wayne Edgar; Art Director: Jack Collins; Set Designer: John Austin. Color, 118 min. **VHS**

Experiment in Terror
(1962) Columbia
A psychopathic extortionist kidnaps a bank teller's younger sister and uses her to force the teller to embezzle money. Excellent performances by a good cast, a wonderful Mancini score, great shots of San Francisco, and a tight, realistic story all contribute to making this suspenseful thriller well worth it. **Cast:** Lee Remick, Stefanie Powers, Ross Martin, Glenn Ford. **Credits:** Dir: Blake Edwards; Prod: Blake Edwards; Writer: Gordon Gordon, Mildred Gordon; DP: Philip H. Lathrop; Composer: Henry Mancini. B&W, 123 min. **VHS, LASER**

Experiment Perilous
(1944) RKO
A famous psychiatrist (Brent) becomes involved with a beautiful new patient (Lamarr) who happens to be married to a very rich and jealous man (Lukas). She fears her husband and when Brent comes to spirit her away, the angry husband lashes out with deadly consequences. **Cast:** Hedy Lamarr, George Brent, Paul Lukas, Albert Dekker. **Credits:** Dir: Jacques Tourneur; Prod: Warren Duff; Writer: Warren Duff; Story: Margaret Wycherly; DP: Tony Gaudio; Ed: Ralph Dawson; Composer: Roy Webb; Costumes: Leah Rhodes, Edward Stevenson; SFX: Vernon Walker; Art Director: Albert S. D'Agostino, Jack Okey; Set Designer: Darrell Silvera, Claude Carpenter. B&W, 92 min. **VHS**

Eyes in the Night
(1942) MGM
An early Zinnemann outing follows a blind detective who is hired by an old friend to investigate a murder. The victim was an actor who had been seeing the friend's stepdaughter, but in the past had been her lover. On the case, the detective uncovers a ring of Nazi spies searching for a secret formula. **Cast:** Edward Arnold, Ann Harding, Donna Reed, Katherine Emery, Stephen McNally, Allen Jenkins, Stanley Ridges, Reginald Denny, Rosemary De Camp, John Emery. **Credits:** Dir: Fred Zinnemann; Prod: Jack Chertok; Writer: Howard Emmett Rogers, Guy Trosper; Story: Baynard Kendrick; DP: Charles Lawton, Jr., Robert Planck; Ed: Ralph E. Winters; Prod Design: Cedric Gibbons, Stan Rogers; Composer: Lennie Hayton. B&W, 80 min.

Eyes of Laura Mars
(1978) Columbia
Dunaway plays a fashion photographer who starts to "see" murders through her camera lens and gradually realizes she's being stalked by a killer. Jones is the detective trying to figure the who and why. Carpenter cowrote this fairly suspenseful thriller with a couple of tricky twists. Barbra Streisand sings the title song. **Cast:** Faye Dunaway, Tommy Lee Jones, Brad Dourif, Raul Julia, Rene Auberjonois, Frank Adonis, Darlanne Fluegel, Rose Gregorio, Bill Boggs. **Credits:** Dir: Irvin Kershner; Prod: Jon Peters; Writer: John Carpenter, David Zelag Goodman; DP: Victor J. Kemper; Ed: Michael Kahn; Prod Design: Gene Callahan; Composer: Artie Kane. Color, 104 min. **VHS, LASER**

The Fabulous Dorseys
(1947) United Artists
Big-band greats Tommy and Jimmy (along with fellow bandleader Whiteman and a full stage of top-drawer musicians) star in their own biopic. You could watch this with your eyes closed and not miss anything, but the sounds are so hep it's worth the time. The numbers include "At Sundown," "Green Eyes," "Runnin' Wild," and many more. **Cast:** Tommy and Jimmy Dorsey, Janet Blair, Paul Whiteman, William Lundigan. **Credits:** Dir: Alfred E. Green; Prod: John W. Rogers; Writer: Richard English, Art Arthur, Curtis Kenyon; DP: James Van Trees; Ed: George Arthur; Choreographer: Charles Baron; Composer: Leo Shuken; SFX: Alfred Schmid. B&W, 91 min. **VHS, LASER**

The Face Behind the Mask
(1941) Columbia
This haunting, starkly-lit minimalist film follows the suffering of Hungarian refugee Lorre as he struggles through a miserable existence in an alienating, cruel urban America. His face melted in a fire, Szaby wears a frightening expressionistic mask as he makes an attempt to raise the money necessary for plastic surgery. He gets mixed up with a criminally dangerous crew and when the blind girl he loves, Keyes, is blown to bits, Lorre learns it is possible to lose more than your face. Florey was one of the greatest exponents of German Expressionist film working in Hollywood. **Cast:** Peter Lorre, Evelyn Keyes, Don Beddoe, George E. Stone, John Tyrell, Stanley Brown, Alan Seymour, James Seay, Warren Ashe, Charles C. Wilson. **Credits:** Dir: Robert Florey; Prod: Wallace MacDonald; Writer: Paul Jarrico; DP: Franz Planer; Ed: Charles Nelson; Prod Design: Lionel Banks; Composer: Morris Stoloff. B&W, 69 min.

A Face in the Crowd
(1957) Warner Bros.
A savagely funny look at the way sudden notoriety and power corrupt. A small-town windbag (Griffith in his film debut) becomes an overnight success when the TV show created for him by network and advertising execs hits the top of the ratings. But behind the scenes he turns out to be a vindictive monster, and the reporter who brought him out of the woods determines to expose him. Based on the short story "The Arkansas Traveler" by Schulberg, who also wrote the script. **Cast:** Andy Griffith, Lee Remick, Walter Matthau, Patricia Neal, Anthony Franciosa, Percy Waram, Rod Brasfield, Paul McGrath, Kay Medford. **Credits:** Dir: Elia Kazan; Prod: Elia Kazan; Writer: Budd Schulberg; DP: Harry Stradling, Gayne Rescher; Composer: Tom Glazer. B&W, 126 min. **VHS**

Faces
(1968) Continental
Regarded as the first American independent film to cross over to mainstream audiences, this stark tale of infidelity follows a couple who abandon their marriage after 14 years. As each turns to another for companionship they realize life on the outside isn't what they expected. Cassavetes's famed improvisational technique is particularly well suited to the heightened emotions in relationship drama such as this. Academy Award nominations for Best Supporting Actress: Lynn Carlin; Best Supporting Actor: Seymour Cassel; Best Original Screenplay. **Cast:** John Marley, Gena Rowlands, Lynn Carlin, Seymour Cassel, Fred Draper, Val Avery, Dorothy Gulliver. **Credits:** Dir: John Cassavetes; Prod: Maurice McEndree; Writer: John Cassavetes; DP: Al Ruban; Ed: John Cassavetes, Maurice McEndree, Al Ruban; Composer: Jack Ackerman. B&W, 129 min. **VHS**

The Facts of Life
(1960) United Artists
Comedy giants Ball and Hope heat things up as two romantically connected souls whose respective spouses don't appreciate their indiscreet dalliances. A surprisingly cosmopolitan comedy about love and romance and their meaning within and without marriage. **Cast:** Bob Hope, Lucille Ball, Ruth Hussey, Don Defore, Louis Nye, Philip Ober. **Credits:** Dir: Melvin Frank; Writer: Norman Panama, Melvin Frank; DP: Charles Lang; Prod Design: Joseph MacMillan Johnson; Composer: Leigh Harline; Art Director: Kenneth Reid. Color, 103 min. **VHS, LASER**

Fail-Safe
(1964) Columbia
A gripping Cold War drama about a computer malfunction that sends American bombers to destroy Moscow. The U.S. president is then forced to make a decision in order to prevent an all-out nuclear exchange. Based on the novel by Eugene Burdick and Harvey Wheeler, this features an excellent debut performance by Larry Hagman. **Cast:** Dan O'Herlihy, Walter Matthau, Henry Fonda, Fritz Weaver, Larry Hagman, Frank Overton, Edward Binns, Russell Collins, William Hansen, Russell Hardie. **Credits:** Dir: Sidney Lumet; Prod: Max E. Youngstein; Writer: Walter Bernstein; DP: Gerald Hirschfeld; Ed: Ralph Rosenblum; Prod Design: Albert Brenner. B&W, 113 min. **VHS, LASER**

The Falcon
The well-crafted series had striking similarities to The Saint entries, with an urbane, playboy detective taking on cases involving everything from murder to international intrigue, with more than a few starlets thrown into the mix. The similarities were not a coincidence. In fact, George Sanders left The Saint to play Gay Lawrence, a.k.a. The Falcon,

in RKO's newly launched series that was as much comedy as it was mystery. Sanders stuck around for the first four installments, leaving after *The Falcon's Brother* (1942). In the film, The Falcon looks to his brother, played by Tom Conway, Sanders's real-life brother, to help him thwart the assassination of a Latin diplomat. When The Falcon dies in the process, his brother vows to take over his brother's work and does so in the remaining nine films of the series. *The Falcon Takes Over* was based on Raymond Chandler's *Farewell, My Lovely*, later remade as *Murder, My Sweet* (1944).

The Gay Falcon *(1941)*
A Date with the Falcon *(1941)*
The Falcon Takes Over *(1942)*
The Falcon's Brother *(1942)*
The Falcon Strikes Back *(1943)*
The Falcon and the Co-eds *(1943)*
The Falcon in Danger *(1943)*
The Falcon in Hollywood *(1944)*
The Falcon in Mexico *(1944)*
The Falcon Out West *(1944)*
The Falcon in San Francisco *(1945)*
The Falcon's Alibi *(1946)*
The Falcon's Adventure *(1946)*

Fallen Angel
(1945) Fox
Eric Stanton is waylaid in Walton after having been thrown off a bus (heading to San Francisco) because he cannot afford the fare. There he meets up with the wealthy June Mills, who falls for him immediately. Stanton, however, has fallen for a sultry waitress, Stella, who urges him to marry June for her money and then divorce her. Stanton agrees, but when Stella is suddenly and mysteriously murdered, he becomes the prime suspect. While trying to prove his innocence and locate the real killer, Stanton comes to rely on June and eventually falls in love with her. An early Preminger with uncharacteristic roles for Faye and Darnell. **Cast:** Alice Faye, Dana Andrews, Linda Darnell, Charles Bickford, Anne Revere, Bruce Cabot, John Carradine, Percy Kilbride, Olin Howlin, Mira McKinney. **Credits:** Dir: Otto Prem-inger; Prod: Otto Preminger; Writer: Harry Kleiner; Story: Marty Holland; DP: Joseph LaShelle; Ed: Harry Reynolds; Prod Design: Lyle Wheeler, Leland Fuller; Composer: David Raksin. B&W, 98 min.

The Fallen Sparrow
(1943) RKO
Tormented by his experiences as a prisoner during the Spanish Civil War, Garfield returns home to a snare set

for him by Slezak's ring of Nazis and a trio of beautiful women. Good performance from Garfield as the man with a secret he won't give up no matter what torture Slezak deals out. **Cast:** John Garfield, Maureen O'Hara, Walter Slezak, Patricia Morison, Martha O'Driscoll, Bruce Edwards, John Banner, John Miljan. **Credits:** Dir: Richard Wallace; Prod: Robert Fellows; Writer: Warren Duff; Story: Dorothy B. Hughes; DP: Nicholas Musuraca; Ed: Robert Wise; Prod Design: Van Nest Polglase, Mark-Lee Kirk; Composer: Roy Webb; SFX: Vernon L. Walker; Art Director: Albert S. D'Agostino. B&W, 94 min. **VHS, LASER**

The Fall of the Roman Empire
(1964) Paramount
The success of Mann's wide-screen epic *El Cid* (1961) led to this even grander undertaking, one of Hollywood's periodic infatuations with the decadence of Imperial Rome. After murdering his father, Emperor Marcus Aurelius Commodus drifts into a life of wanton depravity as the Gothic hordes gather at the Empire's borders. A Hollywood spectacular in the grand tradition, but Mann manages to elicit some terrific performances among the mob scenes. According to the trailer, the

film contains "Not just three or four, but ALL of the known emotions!" Academy Award Nominations: Best Score. **Cast:** Stephen Boyd, Alec Guinness, Christopher Plummer, James Mason, Sophia Loren, Omar Sharif, Mel Ferrer, John Ireland, Anthony Quayle, Eric Porter. **Credits:** Dir: Anthony Mann; Prod: Samuel Bronston; Writer: Ben Barzman, Basilio Franchina; DP: Robert Krasker; Ed: Robert Lawrence; Prod Design: Veniero Colasanti, John Moore; Composer: Dimitri Tiomkin; Costumes: Gloria Mussetta; SFX: Alex Weldon. Color, 187 min. **VHS**

False Faces
(1932) World Wide
A charming quack insinuates his way into the new field of plastic surgery to prey on the vanity of wealthy women. When his butchery catches up to him, and the legion of disfigured women finally succeed in bringing him to court, he is utterly without remorse. A surprise ending caps this dark and strange drama that weaves sick humor, sexual subtext, and even romance into a unique film for its time. **Cast:** Lila Lee, Joyce Compton, Lowell Sherman, Peggy Shannon, Berton Churchill, David Landau. **Credits:** Dir: Lowell Sherman; Prod: Lowell Sher-

Faces (1968)

man; Writer: Kubec Glasmon, Llewellyn Hughes; DP: Ray Binger, Ted McCord; Ed: Rose Loewinger. B&W, 80 min. **VHS**

The Family Jewels

(1965) Paramount
Lewis a control freak? As producer, director, writer, and performer of seven different roles in this patented comedy, Jerry does it all. A little orphan is about to inherit $30 million, and she must choose which of her six zany uncles (played by guess who) will be her guardian. **Cast:** Jerry Lewis, Donna Butterworth, Sebastian Cabot, Robert Strauss, Milton Frome. **Credits:** Dir: Jerry Lewis; Prod: Jerry Lewis; Writer: Jerry Lewis, Bill Richmond; DP: Wallace Kelley; Ed: Arthur Schmidt, John Woodcock; Prod Design: Hal Pereira; Composer: Pete King; Costumes: Edith Head; SFX: Paul K. Lerpae; Art Director: Jack Poplin; Set Designer: Sam Comer, Robert R. Benton. Color, 100 min. **VHS**

Family Plot

(1976) Universal
A cab driver and a phony psychic team up to find a missing heir in order to claim a $10,000 reward. This is Hitch's last and he's relying on our knowledge of his greatness to smooth over the rough spots, but always interesting to see the work of a master. **Cast:** Bruce Dern, Barbara Harris, William Devane, Karen Black, Ed Lauter, William Prince, Marge Redmond, Cathleen Nesbitt. **Credits:** Dir: Alfred Hitchcock; Prod: Alfred Hitchcock; Writer: Ernest Lehman; DP: Leonard J. South; Ed: J. Terry Williams; Prod Design: Henry Bumstead; Composer: John Williams. Color, 121 min. **VHS, LASER**

The Fan

(1949) Fox
Based on Oscar Wilde's story "Lady Windermere's Fan," this is a society drama set in Victorian England, and it tells the tale of a young and attractive mother who hovers around her marriageable daughter and tries to persuade her not to repeat her own mistake of eloping. Carroll's last film. **Cast:** Jeanne Crain, Madeleine Carroll, George Sanders, Richard Greene, Martita Hunt, John Sutton, Hugh Dempster, Richard Ney, Virginia McDowall, Hugh Murray. **Credits:** Dir: Otto Preminger; Prod: Otto Preminger; Writer: Walter Reisch, Dorothy Parker, Ross Evans; Story: Oscar Wilde; DP: Joseph La Shelle; Ed: Louis Loeffler; Prod Design: Lyle Wheeler, Leland Fuller. B&W, 79 min.

Fancy Pants

(1950) Paramount
Bob Hope successfully takes the Laughton role as butler from *Ruggles of Red Gap* (1935). A nouveau riche American family aspires to class by hiring Hope as their British butler. Unfortunately, Hope is neither a butler nor British; he's actually an out of work American actor. Fun performances by Hope and Ball, and the incomparable Blore. **Cast:** Bob Hope, Lucille Ball, Bruce Cabot, Jack Kirkwood, Lea Penman, Eric Blore, John Alexander, Norma Varden, Joseph Vitale, Hugh French. **Credits:** Dir: George Marshall; Prod: Robert L. Welch; Writer: Edmund L. Hartmann, Robert O'Brien; DP: Charles B. Lang; Ed: Archie Marshek; Prod Design: Hans Dreier, Earl Hedrick; Composer: Nathan Van Cleave. Color, 92 min. **VHS, LASER**

Fanny

(1961) Warner Bros.
Marcel Pagnol's trilogy about the girlfriend of a sailor who finds herself pregnant after he returns to sea. She enters into a marriage of convenience with an older man that matures into real love and real family. Their life together is threatened when the sailor returns from the sea. This version is lovingly photographed, beautifully scored, and a touching melodrama; great to see older stars from Hollywood's past in the leads. **Cast:** Leslie Caron, Horst Buchholz, Maurice Chevalier, Charles Boyer, Georgette Anys, Salvatore Baccaloni, Lionel Jeffries, Raymond Bussieres, Victor Francen. **Credits:** Dir: Joshua Logan; Prod: Joshua Logan; Writer: Julius J. Epstein, Joshua Logan, Marcel Pagnol; DP: Jack Cardiff; Ed: William H. Reynolds; Composer: Harold J. Rome, Morris Stoloff, Harry Sukman. Color, 148 min. **VHS**

Fantasia

(1940) Disney
The movie many consider Disney's greatest animation achievement is a series of eight animated fantasies set to classical music conducted by Leopold Stokowski. Swirling, surrealistic, colorful, it's long been considered a classic (particularly among generations of substance-enhanced audiences). Look for Mickey Mouse in the famous "Sorcerer's Apprentice" segment. **Academy Awards:** Special Achievement Award: Leopold Stokowski. **Cast:** Mickey Mouse, Deems Taylor, Leopold Stokowski. **Credits:** Dir: Samuel Armstrong, James Algar, Bill Roberts,

Paul Satterfield, Hamilton Luske, Jim Handley, Ford Beebe, Walt Disney, Norman Ferguson, Wilfred Jackson; Prod: Walt Disney; Writer: Elmer Plummer, Otto Englander, Webb Smith, Erdman Penner, Joseph Sabo, Joe Grant, Dick Huemer. Color, 120 min. **VHS, LASER**

Fantastic Voyage

(1966) Fox
A life-threatening blood clot is battled by a crew of medical scientists who are shrunk to microscopic size and injected into the body to destroy the clot. Great premise from the Isaac Asimov novel, and the special effects do it justice. **Academy Awards:** Best Art Direction—Set Decoration (Color). **Cast:** Stephen Boyd, Raquel Welch, Edmond O'Brien, Donald Pleasence, Arthur Kennedy, Arthur O'Connell, William Redfield, Jean Del Val, Barry Coe. **Credits:** Dir: Richard Fleischer; Prod: Saul David; Writer: Harry Kleiner, David Duncan; DP: Ernest Laszlo; Ed: William B. Murphy; Prod Design: Jack Martin Smith, Dale Hennessy; Composer: Leonard Rosenman. Color, 100 min. **VHS, LASER**

The Far Country

(1955) Universal
One of the best Mann-Stewart Westerns of the '50s, with a refreshing Yukon setting. Stewart drives cattle north on an arduous trek to Alaska. When he reaches his destination, his payoff for his trouble is double-cross and violence. **Cast:** James Stewart, Ruth Roman, Corinne Calvet, Walter Brennan, John McIntire, Jay C. Flippen, Harry Morgan, Steve Brodie, Royal Dano. **Credits:** Dir: Anthony Mann; Prod: Aaron Rosenberg; Writer: Borden Chase; DP: William Daniels; Ed: Russell Schoengarth; Prod Design: Bernard Herzbrun, Alexander Golitzen; Composer: Joseph Gershenson. Color, 115 min. **VHS**

Farewell, My Lovely

(1975) Avco Embassy
Another detective story by Raymond Chandler set in the 1940s has Philip Marlowe on two cases, searching for a thug's girl and a jade necklace at the same time. What Marlowe doesn't realize is that the two seemingly unrelated cases are actually one and the same. Third remake of the story after *The Falcon Takes Over* (1942) and *Murder, My Sweet* (1944). Although the original sequel, *The Big Sleep* (1946), was set in Los Angeles, the 1977 remake (again with Mitchum) was set in London. **Cast:** Robert

Mitchum, Charlotte Rampling, Sylvia Miles, Jack O'Halloran, John Ireland, Anthony Zerbe, Kate Murtagh, Harry Dean Stanton, John O'Leary. **Credits:** Dir: Dick Richards; Prod: George Pappas, Jerry Bruckheimer; Writer: David Zelag Goodman; Story: Raymond Chandler; DP: John A. Alonzo; Ed: Walter Thompson, Joel Cox; Prod Design: Dean Tavoularis; Composer: David Shire. Color, 98 min. VHS

A Farewell to Arms
(1932) Paramount
The original, highly acclaimed adaptation of Ernest Hemingway's 1929 novel about the poignant, ill-fated wartime romance between an American paramedic and an English nurse in WWI. A remake followed in 1957. A quality treatment with the cream of Hollywood in the leads. Academy Award Nominations: Best Picture; Best Art Direction. **Academy Awards:** Best Cinematography; Best Sound **Cast:** Helen Hayes, Gary Cooper, Adolphe Menjou, Mary Philips, Jack La Rue, Blanche Frederici, Henry Armetta, George Humbert, Fred Mala-testa, Mary Forbes. **Credits:** Dir: Frank Borzage; Writer: Benjamin Glazer; Story: Ernest Hemingway; DP: Charles Lang; Ed: Otho S. Lovering; Prod Design: Hans Dreier; Composer: Ralph Rainger, John Leipold, Bernhard Kaun, Paul Marquardt; Art Director: Roland Anderson. B&W, 83 min. VHS, LASER

A Farewell to Arms
(1957) Fox
The third film version of Ernest Hemingway's novel succumbs to the incessant meddling of producer Selznick, who crafted the film as a vehicle for his wife Jones. She plays the young nurse (though she was 38) who falls tragically in love with an ambulance driver (Hudson) in WWI. Director John Huston began production but left, fed up with Selznick, and was replaced by Vidor. Italian director De Sica is intriguing as Major Rinaldi. Mostly of interest in comparison to the 1932 version. Academy Award Nomination for Best Supporting Actor: Vittorio De Sica. **Cast:** Rock Hudson, Jennifer Jones, Vittorio De Sica, Alberto Sordi, Mercedes McCambridge, Oscar Homolka, Elaine Strich. **Credits:** Dir: Charles Vidor; Prod: David O. Selznick; Writer: Ben Hecht; Story: Ernest Hemingway; DP: Oswald Morris, Piero Potralupi; Ed: Gerard Wilson, John Foley; Prod Design: Mario Garbuglia. Color, 152 min.

The Far Country (1955)

The Farmer's Daughter
(1947) RKO
Young moves from maid of the house to Member of the House in this delightful comedy. Swedish housekeeper for Congressman Cotten sees how the political game's played and decides she can improve it as the Reform candidate. One of Young's signature roles. Later a TV series starring Inger Stevens. Academy Award Nominations: Best Supporting Actor: Charles Bickford. **Academy Awards:** Best Actress: Loretta Young. **Cast:** Loretta Young, Joseph Cotten, Ethel Barrymore, Charles Bickford, Rose Hobart, Rhys Williams, Harry Davenport, Tom Powers. **Credits:** Dir: H. C. Potter; Prod: Dore Schary; Writer: Allen Rivkin, Laura Kerr; Story: Juhni Tervataa; DP: Milton Krasner; Ed: Harry Marker; Composer: Leigh Harline. B&W, 97 min. VHS

The Farmer Takes a Wife
(1935) Fox
Small-town comedy set in boats and on the shores by the Erie Canal in the 1850s. Colorful characters banter about life on the water and the possible threat of seeing it all end when the railroad is up and running. A would-be farmer wins a boat in a lottery and falls in love with a woman who doesn't want to marry a farmer. He hopes she'll eventually change her mind. Henry Fonda's film debut. **Cast:** Charles Bickford, Andy Devine, Henry Fonda, Janet Gaynor, Margaret Hamilton, Roger Imhof, Sig Rumann, Slim Summerville, Jane Withers. **Credits:** Dir: Victor Fleming; Prod: Nydia Westman; Writer: Edwin Burke, Marc Connelly, Walter D. Edmonds, Frank B. Elser; DP: John Seitz; Ed: Harold Schuster; Composer: Arthur Lange, Oscar Bradley. B&W, 94 min.

Fashions of 1934
(1934) First National
Choreographed by Busby Berkeley, this musical comedy follows a fashion designer (Powell) with a reputation for stealing other people's ideas. All of his spies are well known in Paris, so he takes his two assistants (one with a mini-camera in a cane) to France to steal ideas themselves. Along the way, they meet a feather vendor pushing his wares and a

struggling songwriter. The designer also runs into his ex-fiancée, who is now posing as a Russian noblewoman. **Cast:** William Powell, Bette Davis, Frank McHugh, Verree Teasdale, Reginald Owen, Hobart Cavanaugh, Henry O'Neill, Phillip Reed. **Credits:** Dir: Wilhelm Dieterle; Prod: Henry Blanke; Writer: Harry Collins, Warren Duff, Carol Erickson, Herbert Hugh, Gene Markey, Kathryn Scola; DP: William Rees; Ed: Jack Killifer; Composer: Sammy Fain, Irving Kahal; Art Director: Jack Okey, Willy Pogany. B&W, 80 min. **VHS**

Fast and Loose

(1939) MGM
Montgomery and Russell take over the roles as married rare-book dealers who were meant to compete on Nick and Nora territory in three MGM programmers, of which this is the second. This sequel to *Fast Company* (1938) deals with the disappearance of rare books from the library of a tycoon. An insurance company hires Montgomery to work as an amateur detective and track down the missing editions. Three murders sufficiently muddle the investigation, as does the assistance of Russell. An interesting and less well known Hollywood series. **Cast:** Robert Montgomery, Rosalind Russell, Reginald Owen, Ralph Morgan, Etienne Girardot, Alan Dinehart, Joann Sayers, Joan Marsh, Tom Collins, Sidney Blackmer. **Credits:** Dir: Edwin L. Marin; Prod: Frederick Stephani; Writer: Harry Kurnitz; DP: George Folsey, Jr.; Ed: Elmo Vernon; Prod Design: Cedric Gibbons; Composer: Douglas Shearer. B&W, and Color, 78 min.

Fast Break

(1979) Columbia
Seventies TV icon Kaplan makes his feature debut as a New York delicatessen worker who talks his way into a position as head basketball coach at a Nevada college. He accepts the job on the condition that he can bring his streetwise New York City players with him. The players are standouts on the court but lost in the classroom, which leads to trouble. **Cast:** Gabe Kaplan, Harold Sylvester, Mike Warren, Reb Brown, Bert Remsen, Randee Heller, Laurence Fishburne, Mavis Washington. **Credits:** Dir: Jack Smight; Prod: Stephen Friedman; Writer: Sandor Stern; DP: Charles Correll; Ed: Frank J. Urioste; Prod Design: Norm Baron, John Barry; Composer: David Shire, James DiPasquale. Color, 107 min. **VHS**

Fastest Gun Alive

(1956) MGM
Ford plays a storekeeper who keeps to himself, but shootists keep remembering his prowess with the six-guns. Slow, almost somber Western with a difference. Don't bother with the colorized version. **Cast:** Glenn Ford, Jeanne Crain, Broderick Crawford, Russ Tamblyn, Allyn Joslyn, Leif Erickson, John Dehner, Noah Beery , J. M. Kerrigan, Rhys Williams. **Credits:** Dir: Russell Rouse; Prod: Clarence Greene; Writer: Frank D. Gilroy, Russell Rouse; DP: George J. Folsey; Ed: Ferris Webster, Harry Knapp; Prod Design: Cedric Gibbons, Merrill Pye; Composer: Andre Previn. B&W, 92 min. **VHS**

Fat City

(1972) Columbia
Late-period Huston entry is a ring tale that follows a punch-drunk, washed-up pugilist and his unpromising young protégé. Tyrrell scores as the fighter's washed-up gal pal. **Cast:** Stacy Keach, Jeff Bridges, Candy Clark, Susan Tyrrell, Nicholas Colasanto, Art Aragon. **Credits:** Dir: John Huston; Prod: Ray Stark; Writer: Leonard Gardner; DP: Conrad Hall; Ed: Margaret Booth; Prod Design: Richard Sylbert; Composer: Marvin Hamlisch. Color, 100 min. **VHS**

Father Goose

(1964) Universal
An Australian beach bum with a strong penchant for drinking finds himself "drafted" by a naval commander to man a strategic observation post in the South Pacific during WWII. When a French schoolteacher and her seven female pupils move in with him, a comical battle of the sexes ensues. The 30th anniversary release includes the original trailer, a reproduction of two original lobby cards, and is digitally remastered from the original film negative. Academy Award Nominations: 3, including Best Film Editing. **Academy Awards:** Best Story/Screenplay Written Directly for the Screen. **Cast:** Cary Grant, Leslie Caron, Trevor Howard, Jack Good, Verina Greenlaw, Pip Sparke. **Credits:** Dir: Ralph Nelson; Prod: Robert Arthur; Writer: Frank Tarloff, Peter Stone; Story: S. H. Barnett; DP: Charles B. Lang; Ed: Ted J. Kent; Prod Design: Alexander Golitzen, Henry Bumstead; Composer: Cy Coleman. Color, 118 min. **VHS**

Father of the Bride

(1950) MGM
The comic trials and tribulations that beset a family, mostly the father, prior to their daughter's wedding day. Taylor

and Tracy give wonderful performances and it's so effortlessly charming, it's easy to understand why this was remade in 1991. The colorized version doesn't add much. Academy Award Nominations: Best Picture; Best Actor: Spencer Tracy; Best Screenplay. **Cast:** Spencer Tracy, Joan Bennett, Elizabeth Taylor, Billie Burke, Don Taylor, Moroni Olsen, Leo G. Carroll, Taylor Holmes, Melville Cooper, Paul Harvey. **Credits:** Dir: Vincente Minnelli; Prod: Pandro S. Berman; Writer: Frances Goodrich, Albert Hackett; DP: John Alton; Ed: Ferris Webster; Prod Design: Cedric Gibbons, Leonid Vasian; Composer: Adolph Deutsch. B&W, 106 min. **VHS, LASER**

Father's Little Dividend

(1951) MGM
This sequel to the hugely popular *Father of the Bride* reunited the entire cast for another charming turn. Although Tracy's hoping for some peace and quiet now that Taylor's been married off, he soon learns he's in for more chaos as an expectant grandfather. Equally fun as the original, and, of course, this premise was repeated in *Father of the Bride Part II* (1995). **Cast:** Spencer Tracy, Joan Bennett, Elizabeth Taylor, Don Taylor, Bill Burke, Billie Burke, Moroni Olsen, Richard Rober, Marietta Canty, Russ Tamblyn. **Credits:** Dir: Vincente Minnelli; Prod: Pandro S. Berman; Writer: Frances Goodrich, Albert Hackett; DP: John Alton; Ed: Ferris Webster; Prod Design: Cedric Gibbons, Leonid Vasian; Composer: Albert Sendrey. B&W, 88 min. **VHS**

Father Was a Fullback

(1949) Fox
A light family comedy about a hapless college football coach who's got trouble at home and on the field. His daughters have reached that worrisome age and the alumni association is badgering him for some wins. One young man might be the answer to all his problems. **Cast:** Fred MacMurray, Maureen O'Hara, Betty Lynn, Rudy Vallee, Thelma Ritter, Natalie Wood, Jim Backus, Richard Tyler. **Credits:** Dir: John M. Stahl; Prod: Fred Kohlmar; Writer: Aleen Leslie, Casey Robinson, Mary Loos, Richard Sale; DP: Lloyd Ahern; Ed: J. Watson Webb; Prod Design: Lyle Wheeler, Chester Gore; Composer: Cyril Mockridge. B&W, 84 min. **VHS**

The FBI Story

(1959) Warner Bros.
The career of straight-arrow FBI agent Stewart from the Prohibition-era found-

ing of the bureau to the Cold War as he struggles between loyalty to his family and dedication to his career. Interesting to see the story told from the street-level point of view of an ordinary agent with actual cases, and to get behind the scenes and into the labs and document files of the bureau's Washington, D.C., headquarters. It was made with the cooperation of the agency, so it's not just the facts, ma'am. **Cast:** James Stewart, Vera Miles, Murray Hamilton, Nick Adams, Diane Jergens, Larry Pennell. **Credits:** Dir: Mervyn LeRoy; Prod: Mervyn LeRoy; Writer: Richard Breen, John Twist; Story: Don Whitehead; DP: Joseph Biroc; Ed: Philip W. Anderson; Prod Design: John Beckman; Composer: Max Steiner; Costumes: Adele Palmer; Set Designer: Ralph S. Hurst. Color, 149 min. **VHS, LASER**

Fear in the Night

(1947) Paramount
A film noir–ish shocker in which De Forrest Kelley dreams he murders someone and wakes up to find it may not have been a dream. Twisty plot has him enlisting a cop pal (Paul Kelly) to track down his dream-crimes. The secret lies in a mirrored room in a creepy mansion. Based on the story "Nightmare" by Cornell Woolrich and produced under that title in 1956. **Cast:** De Forest Kelley, Paul Kelly, Ann Doran, Jeff York, Charles Victor, Janet Warren, Michael Harvey, Kay Scott, Robert Emmett Keane. **Credits:** Dir: Maxwell Shane; Prod: William H. Pine, William C. Thomas; Writer: Maxwell Shane; DP: Jack Greenhalgh; Ed: Howard Smith; Prod Design: F. Paul Sylos; Composer: Rudolph Schrager. B&W, **VHS**

Fear Strikes Out

(1957) Paramount
One of the most memorable sports film sagas (remember the scene of Perkins scaling the wall into the stands?) is the story of courageous Red Sox outfielder Jimmy Piersall, who played 17 seasons in the majors, with a lifetime batting average of .272, while battling mental illness. Perkins's trademark intensity brings the ballplayer's nightmare to life and Malden is perfect as his overbearing father. **Cast:** Anthony Perkins, Karl Malden, Norma Moore, Adam Williams, Peter Votrian, Perry Wilson, Dennis McMullen, Gail Land. **Credits:** Dir: Robert Mulligan; Prod: Alan J. Pakula; Writer: Ted Berkman, Raphael Blau; DP: Haskell Boggs; Ed: Aaron Stell; Composer: Elmer Bernstein. B&W 100 min. **VHS, LASER**

Female

(1933) Warner Bros.
A comic feminist movie that's way ahead of its time. A wealthy president of a motorcar company—Chatterton, by the way—who is married to her job and takes her pleasure where she may among her male underlings (harassment!) finally meets her match (in real-life husband, Brent). Bemusing to think that the humor here comes from the very idea of a strong-willed female executive. Full of wildly extravagant period detail. From a story by Donald Henderson Clark. **Cast:** Ruth Chatterton, George Brent, Ferdinand Gottschalk, Philip Faversham, Ruth Donnelly, Lois Wilson, Gavin Gordon, Johnny Mack Brown, Douglas Dumbrille. **Credits:** Dir: Michael Curtiz; Writer: Gene Markey, Kathryn Scola, William A. Wellman; DP: Sid Hickox; Ed: Jack Killifer; Prod Design: Jack Okey; Composer: Leo F. Forbstein. B&W, 60 min. **VHS**

Female Trouble

(1975) New Line
A weird, campy romp through modern society's outer fringe, this early flick from Baltimore's Bard lightheartedly zeros in on feminine foibles and hazards. The Waters ensemble, including the divine Divine, at their most flamboyant. **Cast:** Divine, David Lochary, Edith Massey, Mink Stole, Mary Vivian Pearce, Cookie Mueller, Susan Walsh. **Credits:** Dir: John Waters; Prod: John Waters; Writer: John Waters; DP: John Waters; Ed: Charles Roggero. Color, 95 min. **VHS**

The Feminine Touch

(1941) MGM
This madcap comedy has professor Ameche turning to his pen when he loses his job for actually trying to teach a member of the football team. Luckily, his witty wife Russell lands a job in New York working for big-shot literary lion Heflin. In no time, Heflin fancies Russell and his colleague, the gorgeous, elegant Francis, isn't at all turned off by Ameche. As misunderstandings and flirtations fly, the poor professor's simply trying to finish his magnum opus on jealousy. **Cast:** Rosalind Russell, Don Ameche, Kay Francis, Van Heflin, Donald Meek, Gordon Jones, Henry Daniell, Sidney Blackmer, Grant Mitchell, David Clyde. **Credits:** Dir: W. S. Van Dyke; Prod: Joseph L. Mankiewicz; Writer: Edmund L. Hartmann, Ogden Nash, George Oppenheimer; DP: Ray June; Ed: Albert Akst; Prod Design: Cedric Gibbons, Paul Groesse; Composer: Franz Waxman. B&W, 97 min.

F for Fake

(1973)
Welles's fascination with magic and sleight of hand extends to this doc on confidence artists who work in, shall we say, a grander scale. It includes examinations of art forger Elmyr de Hory, Howard Hughes pseudo-biographer Clifford Irving, and, finally, Welles himself, from his *War of the Worlds* radio broadcast to the accusation that he stole a writer's credit on *Citizen Kane*. This was one of Welles's last films, and though it defies easy categorization, no Welles fan should miss it. **Cast:** Orson Welles, Joseph Cotten, Paul Stewart, Laurence Harvey, Oja Kodar. **Credits:** Dir: Orson Welles; Prod: Dominique Antoine, Francois Reichenbach; Writer: Orson Welles, Oja Palinkas; DP: Gary Graver, Christian Odasso; Ed: Marie-Sophie Dubus, Dominique Engerer; Composer: Michel Legrand. Color, 98 min. **VHS**

Fiddler on the Roof

(1971) United Artists
Ukrainian milkman Tevye clings desperately to the old Jewish traditions while all around him the world changes, day by day. His three daughters marry men he considers more and more unacceptable, and the ruling Russian government's anti-Semitism threatens to drive him from his home. Based on the enormously successful Broadway show with great performances and unforgettable songs. Academy Award Nominations: 8, including Best Picture; Best Director; Best Actor: Topol. **Academy Awards:** Best Cinematography; Best Sound; Best Original Song Score and Adaptation. **Cast:** Topol, Molly Picon, Leonard Frey, Paul Michael Glaser, Norma Crane, Theodore Bikel, Paul Mann, Rosalind Harris, Michele Marsh. **Credits:** Dir: Norman Jewison; Prod: Norman Jewison; Writer: Joseph Stein; Story: Sholem Aleichem; DP: Oswald Morris; Ed: Antony Gibbs, Robert Lawrence; Prod Design: Michael Stringer; Composer: John Williams. Color, 181 min. **VHS, LASER, DVD**

The Fifth Musketeer

(1979) Columbia
A fine, lavish remake of the Alexandre Dumas story *The Man in the Iron Mask*. Louis XIV of France and his twin brother, Philippe, are both adroitly played by Beau Bridges. Every generation seems to renew their love affair with the derring-do of Dumas; witness the most recent adaptation with Leonardo DiCaprio and John

Malkovich. **Cast:** Beau Bridges, Ursula Andress, Sylvia Kristel, Jose Ferrer, Lloyd Bridges, Rex Harrison, Olivia de Havilland. **Credits:** Dir: Ken Annakin; Prod: Ted Richmond; Writer: David Ambrose; DP: Jack Cardiff; Prod Design: Theo Harisch; Composer: Riz Ortolani. Color, 104 min. **VHS**

The Fighter
(1952) United Artists
Conte, a young Mexican who lost his family and his girlfriend in a raid by Mexican dictator Diaz's soldiers, falls in with a group of revolutionaries across the border in El Paso. Led by Cobb, the group is plotting to overthrow the regime. All they need is money, so Conte turns pugilist and boxes a top contender for a large purse. In the process, Conte wins not only the money but the heart of another patriot, Brown. Adapted from Jack London's story "The Mexican." **Cast:** Richard Conte, Vanessa Brown, Lee J. Cobb, Frank Silvera, Martin Garralaga, Rodolpho Hoyos, Roberta Haynes, Hugh Sanders, Claire Carleton, Argentina Brunetti. **Credits:** Dir: Hernert Kline; Prod: Alex Gottlieb; Writer: Aben Kandel, Jack London; DP: James Wong Howe; Ed: Edward Mann; Composer: Vicente Gomez. B&W, 78 min.

Fighter Squadron
(1948) Warner Bros.
A taut film that addresses the inexorable human arithmetic of the air war against the Nazis. O'Brien is the leader of a fighter squadron who must face the ugly realties of a savage battle of attrition against an implacable foe. The psychological studies of fear, stress, and the problems of command are deftly balanced with graphic aerial-combat footage. Also notable for the first screen appearance of Rock Hudson. **Cast:** Edmond O'Brien, Robert Stack, John Rodney, Tom D'Andrea, Henry Hull, James Holden, Walter Reed, Shepperd Strudwick, Arthur Space, Jack Larson. **Credits:** Dir: Raoul Walsh; Prod: Seton I. Miller; Writer: Seton I. Miller, Martin Rankin; DP: Sidney Hickox, Wilfred Cline; Ed:

Christian Nyby; Composer: Max Steiner, Ray Heindorf; Art Director: Ted Smith. Color, 96 min.

Fighting Caravans
(1931) Paramount
Early Cooper role distinguishes one of the first big-budget Westerns, based on a Zane Grey novel. Cooper convinces a fellow traveler on a westbound caravan to pose as his wife to help disguise him, then saves the caravan from an Indian attack. And falls in love, of course. **Cast:** Gary Cooper, Lili Damita, Ernest Torrence, Eugene Pallette, Fred Kohler, Tully Marshall, Roy Stewart. **Credits:** Dir: Otto Brewer, David Burton; Writer: Edward Paramore, Keene Thompson, Agnes Brand Leahy; Story: Zane Grey; DP: Lee Garmes, Henry Gerrard; Ed: William Shea; Prod Design: Robert Odell; Composer: John Leipold, Oscar Potoker, Karl Hajos, Sigmund Krumgold, Emil Bierman, Max Bergunker, Emil Hilb, Herman Hand, A. Cousminer. B&W, 91 min. **VHS**

Fighting Father Dunne
(1948) RKO
A sentimental Hollywood tearjerker based on a true story, which will remind all of *Boys Town* (1938). A tough parish priest befriends a group of newsboys from poor or broken homes in St. Louis at the turn of the century. **Cast:** Pat O'Brien, Darryl Hickman, Charles Kemper, Una O'Connor, Arthur Shields, Harry Shannon, Joe Sawyer, Anna Q. Nilsson. **Credits:** Dir: Ted Tetzlaff; Prod: Phil L. Ryan; Writer: Frank Davis, Martin Rackin; DP: George E. Diskant; Ed: Frederic Knudtson; Prod Design: Albert S. D'Agostino, Walter E. Keller; Composer: Roy Webb. B&W, 93 min. **VHS**

The Fighting Kentuckian
(1949) Republic
Wayne's in action on the frontier of the early 1800s as a Kentucky soldier who pauses on his way home from the Battle of New Orleans to battle land-claim jumpers and woo the daughter of a French general. Standard stuff with nonstandard part for Hardy. **Cast:**

John Wayne, Oliver Hardy, Marie Windsor, Vera Ralston, Philip Dorn, Mae Marsh, John Howard, Hugo Haas, Grant Withers. **Credits:** Dir: George Waggner; Prod: John Wayne; Writer: George Waggner; DP: Lee Garmes; Ed: Richard L. Van Enger; Prod Design: James Sullivan; Composer: George Antheil. B&W, 102 min. **VHS**

The Fighting O'Flynn
(1948) Universal
A swashbuckling adventure vehicle for Fairbanks, Jr. (written and produced by Douglas as well), this is an actioner centered on "The O'Flynn," a mercenary soldier on his way home to an Irish castle willed to him by an uncle. On the way, he rescues a young lass besieged by stagecoach bandits. The woman delivers an important message to her father, Viceroy of Ireland, warning him of an impending attack by Napoleon, who eyes Britain via Ireland. It's up to The O'Flynn to smash a French spy ring and boot Napoleon's vandals from both his castle and his homeland. **Cast:** Douglas Fairbanks, Jr., Helena Carter, Patricia Medina, Richard Greene, Arthur Shields, J. M. Kerrigan, Ludwig Donath, Lumsden Hare, Otto Waldis, Henry Brandon. **Credits:** Dir: Arthur Pierson; Prod: Douglas Fairbanks, Jr.; Writer: Douglas Fairbanks, Jr., Robert Thoeren; Story: Justin Huntly McCarthy; DP: Arthur Edeson; Ed: Russell Schoengarth; Prod Design: Bernard Herzbrun; Composer: Frank Skinner. B&W, 94 min.

The Fighting Prince of Donegal
(1966) Disney
Disney action-adventure entry set in 16th-century Ireland pits Red Hugh of Donegal against the invading English. High-quality production makes this a rousing family swashbuckler. **Cast:** Peter McEnery, Susan Hampshire, Tom Adams, Gordon Jackson, Andrew Keir, Richard Leech, Norman Wooland, Maurice Roeves, Donal McCann, Peter Jeffrey. **Credits:** Dir: Michael O'Herlihy; Writer: Robert Westerby; Story: Robert Reilly; DP: Arthur Ibbetson; Ed: Peter Boita; Prod Design: Maurice Carter; Composer: George Bruns. Color, 110 min. **VHS**

Fighting Seabees
(1944) Republic
The story of how the Navy's Seabees, a construction-worker fighting unit, were formed. Wayne stars as the foreman of a work battalion close to enemy lines and Hayward's reporter–love interest. More action than the story of a

"If Bess and I had a son, we'd want him to be just like Jimmy Stewart."

President Harry S. Truman

construction unit would imply. The anniversary release includes a reproduction of an original lobby card and two black-and-white, behind-the-scenes photos, and is digitally remastered from the original film negative. Academy Award Nomination for Best Scoring of a Dramatic or Comedy Picture. **Cast:** John Wayne, Susan Hayward, Dennis O'Keefe, Paul Fix, William Frawley, Duncan Renaldo, Addison Richards, Leonid Kinskey, J. M. Kerrigan, Grant Withers. **Credits:** Dir: Edward Ludwig; Prod: Albert J. Cohen; Writer: Borden Chase, Aeneas MacKenzie; DP: William Bradford; Ed: Richard L. Van Enger; Composer: Walter Scharf, Roy Webb. B&W, 100 min. VHS

The Fighting 69th
(1940) Warner Bros.
A made-for-Cagney part as a cocky Brooklyn kid who likes nothing better than a fight. He gets all he can handle as a member of "The Fighting 69th," the celebrated Irish-American unit that goes "over there" and into the trenches of WWI. His bravado melts as the Kaiser's guns rain death onto the Allied positions. A fine blend of fighting action, humor, and real emotion. Avoid the colorized version. **Cast:** James Cagney, Pat O'Brien, George Brent, Jeffrey Lynn, Frank McHugh, Dennis Morgan, Alan Hale, William Lundigan, Dick Foran, Guinn Williams. **Credits:** Dir: William Keighley; Writer: Norman Reilly Raine, Fred Niblo, Dean Franklin; DP: Tony Gaudio; Ed: Owen Marks; Composer: Adolph Deutsch; SFX: Byron Haskin, Rex Wimpy; Art Director: Ted Smith. B&W, 90 min. VHS

The Fighting Sullivans
(1944) Fox
This emotionally gripping depiction of the Sullivan boys of Waterloo, Iowa, is the wartime forerunner of the story told in *Saving Private Ryan* (1998). Amid all the tales of personal tragedy in WWII, this one stands out. The five inseparable brothers enlisted together after Pearl Harbor and were all assigned to a battleship that ended up at Guadalcanal—where all five brothers died in action. A moving tribute to those who gave their lives in the last world war. **Cast:** Thomas Mitchell, Anne Baxter, Selena Royle, Ward Bond, Bobby Driscoll, Addison Richards, Trudy Marshall, John Campbell, James Cardwell, John Alvin. **Credits:** Dir: Lloyd Bacon; Prod: Sam Jaffe; Writer: Mary McCall; DP: Lucien Andriot; Composer: Alfred Newman. B&W, 113 min. VHS

The File on Thelma Jordan
(1949) Paramount
A noir-ish courtroom drama in which an assistant D.A., after a fight with his wife, meets and falls for a femme fatale with a rich aunt. When the aunt is found murdered, the D.A. must prosecute his lover, who is charged with the crime, but he deliberately loses the case by secretly helping the defense. When the femme fatale reveals it was all a plot there are tragic consequences. Is there anyone who could play these roles better than Stanwyck? **Cast:** Barbara Stanwyck, Wendell Corey, Paul Kelly, Joan Tetzel, Stanley Ridges, Richard Rober, Minor Watson, Barry Kelley, Laura Elliot, Barry Ruysdael. **Credits:** Dir: Robert Siodmak; Prod: Hal B. Wallis; Writer: Ketti Fringes; Story: Marty Holland; DP: George Barnes; Ed: Warren Low; Prod Design: Hans Dreier, A. Earl Hedrick; Composer: Victor Young. B&W, 100 min.

A Fine Madness
(1966) Warner Bros.
Sixties vintage madman-against-a-mad-society comedy with Connery appealing as a rowdy, rebellious poet with a chip on his shoulder and an eye for the ladies. His creative block, hyperactive libido, and belligerent binges threaten to bring about his undoing when a cadre of know-it-all psychiatrists prescribes a lobotomy. Based on the novel by Baker. **Cast:** Sean Connery, Joanne Woodward, Jean Seberg, Colleen Dewhurst, Patrick O'Neal, Clive Revill, Werner Peters, John Fiedler, Kay Medford, Jackie Coogan. **Credits:** Dir: Irvin Kershner; Prod: Jerome Hellman; Writer: Elliot Baker; DP: Ted McCord; Ed: William Ziegler; Composer: John Addison. Color, 104 min. VHS

Fingers
(1978)
Keitel is forced to work as a debt collector for his mobster father even though he dreams of becoming a concert pianist. When he is drawn to a prostitute, the tension between his two worlds becomes unbearable. A disturbing and memorable debut from director and screenwriter Tobak. **Cast:** Harvey Keitel, Tisa Farrow, Jim Brown, Tanya Roberts, Danny Aiello, Marian Seldes, Carole Francis, Georgette Muir, Dominic Chianese. **Credits:** Dir: James Toback; Prod: George Barrie; Writer: James Toback; DP: Michael Chapman; Ed: Robert Lawrence; Prod Design: Gene Rudolf. Color, 91 min. VHS

Finian's Rainbow
(1968) Warner Bros.
Could there have been a worse year than 1968, with its riots, assassinations, and war, to release a whimsical musical starring a nostalgic star from yesteryear? Don't be put off by its somewhat obvious appeal for equality; this is too long overlooked. Finian manages to steal a pot of gold from an unlucky leprechaun and spirit it back to the Deep South. Burying it for safety, and in the hopes that it will multiply, the gold becomes the target of the leprechaun Og. An interesting outing for director Coppola, who seems to possess a sentimental streak; Astaire's last full-length musical role. Academy Award Nominations: Best Score; Best Sound. **Cast:** Fred Astaire, Petula Clark, Tommy Steele, Don Francks, Keenan Wynn, Barbara Hancock, Al Freeman, Jr., Ronald Colby, Dolph Sweet. **Credits:** Dir: Francis Ford Coppola; Prod: Joseph Landon; Writer: E. Y. Harburg, Fred Saidy; DP: Philip H. Lathrop; Ed: Melvin Shapiro; Prod Design: Hilyard Brown; Choreographer: Hermes Pan. Color, 142 min. VHS, LASER

Finnegans Wake
(1965) Grove Press
An ambitious independent attempt to cast James Joyce's inscrutable masterpiece into filmic terms, an impossible task by its very definition. While the novel is highly allusive and engages in literate word-play, this film sticks to the plot, in so far as that can be agreed upon: In the course of one night, Finnegan dreams his own death and the behavior of the mourners of his wake. In his dream, his actions, and those of his family, are cast in mythic historical, biblical terms. Revealed as a representative for Everyman, Finnegan wakes with expanded self-awareness. **Cast:** Martin Kelley, Peter Haskell, Jane Reilly, Page Johnson, Robert Lord, John V. Kelleher, Ray Flanagan, Maura Pryor, Jo Jo Slavin. **Credits:** Dir: Mary Ellen Bute; Prod: Mary Ellen Bute; Writer: Mary Ellen Bute, Ted Nemeth, Jr., Romana Javitz; Story: James Joyce, Mary Manning; DP: Ted Nemeth; Ed: Mary Ellen Bute, Yoshio Kishi, Paul Ronder, Thelma Schoonmaker, Catherine Pichonnier; Composer: Elliot Kaplin. B&W, 92 min.

Firecreek
(1968) Warner Bros.
A villainous gang of outlaws, led by vicious gunfighter Fonda, has the residents of Firecreek living in fear. Although rancher Stewart considers

Five Easy Pieces (1970)

himself a man of peace, he agrees to become the town's sheriff and put an end to the bad guys' campaign of terror once and for all. A dark, menacing Western with an unbeatable starring duo. **Cast:** James Stewart, Henry Fonda, Inger Stevens, Gary Lockwood, Dean Jagger, Ed Begley, Jack Elam, Barbara Luna, Jay C. Flippen, James Best. **Credits:** Dir: Vincent McEveety; Prod: Philip Leacock; Writer: Calvin Clements; DP: William Clothier; Ed: William Ziegler; Composer: Alfred Newman; Costumes: Yvonne Wood; Art Director: Howard Hollander; Set Designer: William L. Kuehl. Color, 104 min. **VHS**

First Lady
(1937) Warner Bros.
Lady Chase-Wayne, daughter of the former president of the United States and wife of the secretary of state, is in no way content with her current status. Eager to become First Lady, she sets about grooming her husband for the Oval Office while pulling strings to get him elected. The only problem is that Irene Hibberd, the wife of a conniving judge, is after the very same thing. Colliding missions bring both women together in a catfight for the position of First Lady. Arch script by Kaufman based on his play. **Cast:** Kay Francis, Anita Louise, Verree Teasdale, Preston Foster, Walter Connolly, Harry Davenport, Louise Fazenda, Victor Jory, Marjorie Gateson, Marjorie Rambeau. **Credits:** Dir: Stanley Logan; Prod: Harry Joe Brown; Writer: George S. Kaufman; Story: Katharine Dayton; DP: Sid Hickox; Prod Design: Max Parker; Composer: Max Steiner. B&W, 82 min.

The First Legion
(1951) United Artists
A thoughtful drama directed by Sirk about a Jesuit priest who investigates a seeming miracle in his community.

Notable for the quietly powerful performance by Boyer. **Cast:** Charles Boyer, Barbara Rush, William Demarest, Leo G. Carroll, Lyle Bettger, Walter Hampden, George Zucco, Taylor Holmes, Wesley Addy, H. B. Warner. **Credits:** Dir: Douglas Sirk; Prod: Douglas Sirk; Writer: Emmett Lavery; DP: Robert de Grasse; Ed: Francis D. Lyon; Composer: Hans Sommer. B&W, 86 min. **VHS**

First Love
(1939) Universal
Durbin grows up (and puckers up, with Stack). This light Cinderella-ish comedy focuses on the travails of adopted daughter Durbin as she competes with her wealthy family's spoiled biological daughter for a handsome beau on the eve of their debutante ball. Featuring a host of musical numbers. **Cast:** Deanna Durbin, Robert Stack, Eugene Pallette, Helen Parrish, Lewis Howard, Leatrice Joy. **Credits:** Dir: Henry Koster; Writer: Bruce Manning, Lionel Houser; DP: Joseph A. Valentine; Ed: Bernard W. Burton; Prod Design: Jack Otterson; Composer: Frank Skinner; Art Director: Martin Obzina. B&W, 85 min. **VHS**

The First Time
(1952) Columbia
The "first time" in this innocent comedy refers to the trials, tribulations, and triumphs of the childrearing. Cummings and Hale play new parents who find out the hard way that raising a child costs a lot more than they ever expected—financially and emotionally. **Cast:** Robert Cummings, Barbara Hale, Bill Goodwin, Jeff Donnell, Carl Benton Reid, Mona Barrie, Kathleen Comegys, Paul Harvey, Cora Witherspoon, Bea Benadaret. **Credits:** Dir: Frank Tashlin; Prod: Harold Hecht; Writer: Hugh Butler; Story: Jean Rouverol, Frank Tashlin, Dane Lussier; DP: Ernest Laszlo; Ed: Viola Lawrence; Composer: Frederick Hollander. B&W, 89 min.

A Fistful of Dollars
(1964) United Artists
The first in the Leone "Dollars" trilogy. This exemplary spaghetti Western is about a nameless drifter who plays two feuding families off each other to his own benefit. As members of each family are planted in the ground, the gold in his pocket gets heavier and heavier. This violent remake of Kurosawa's *Yojimbo* made Eastwood a star, and set the standard for revisionist Westerns. **Cast:** Clint Eastwood, Gian Maria Volonte, Marianne Koch,

Mario Brega. **Credits:** Dir: Sergio Leone; Prod: Giorgio Papi; Writer: Sergio Leone, Duccio Tessari, G. Schock, Victor A. Catena; DP: Massimo Dallamano; Ed: Roberto Cinquini; Composer: Ennio Morricone. Color, 102 min. VHS, LASER

Fitzwilly
(1967) United Artists
A well-meaning butler enlists the aid of his fellow servants in a series of capers to maintain an illusion of prosperity for their elderly employer—even though she's flat broke. Based on Tyler's novel, *A Garden of Cucumbers*, this marks the film debut of Sam Waterston and Feldon. **Cast:** Dick Van Dyke, Barbara Feldon, Edith Evans, John McGiver, Harry Townes, John Fiedler, Norman Fell, Cecil Kellaway, Stephen Strimpell, Anne Seymour. **Credits:** Dir: Delbert Mann; Prod: Walter Mirisch; Writer: Isobel Lennart; Story: Poyntz Tyler; DP: Joseph Biroc; Ed: Ralph E. Winters; Prod Design: Robert Boyle; Composer: John Williams. Color, 102 min. VHS

Five Against the House
(1955) Columbia
In this high-rolling casino caper Al Mercer (Madison) works out the perfect robbery as a gag. His buddy Brick (Keith) gets the crazy idea the heist is for real and before they know it five college boys are up against a Reno house. The beautiful Kay Greylek (Novak) only entices the foolish kids into a tighter squeeze. **Cast:** Guy Madison, Kim Novak, Brian Keith, Alvy Moore, Kerwin Mathews, William Conrad, George Brand, Jean Willes, John Zaremba, Mark Hanna. **Credits:** Dir: Phil Karlson; Prod: Helen Ainsworth; Writer: John Barnwell, William Bowers, Stirling Silliphant; Story: Jack Finney; DP: Lester White; Ed: Jerome Thoms; Prod Design: Robert Peterson; Composer: George Duning. B&W, 84 min.

Five Easy Pieces
(1970) Columbia
The black sheep of a well-to-do family abandons a promising career as a classical pianist to work on an oil rig, but when he returns home to his father's deathbed, he meets a sophisticated woman and falls in love . . . too late. A moody, reflective performance by Nicholson, and, of course, the famous chicken-salad sandwich scene. Academy Award Nominations: Best Picture; Best Actor: Jack Nicholson; Best Supporting Actress: Karen Black; Best Screenplay. **Cast:** Jack

Nicholson, Karen Black, Susan Anspach, Sally Struthers, Billy "Green" Bush, Fannie Flagg, Marlena MacGuire, Richard Stahl, Lois Smith, Helena Kallianiotes. **Credits:** Dir: Bob Rafelson; Prod: Richard Wechsler; Writer: Bob Rafelson, Adrien Joyce; DP: Laszlo Kovacs; Ed: Gerald S. Shepard, Christopher Holmes; Costumes: Bucky Rous. Color, 98 min. VHS, LASER

Five Fingers
(1952) Fox
Mankiewicz directs this intriguing WWII story of a valet to the British ambassador to Turkey who uses his position to gain access to intelligence documents, which he sells to German agents. Mason is perfect as the suave, shifty traitor and the cinematography enhances the tension of the final pursuit of Mason by both British authorities and German cutthroats. Golden Globe for Best Screenplay. **Cast:** James Mason, Danielle Darrieux, Michael Rennie, Walter Hampden, Richard Loo, Oscar Karlweis, Herbert Berghof, John Wengraf, Michael Pate. **Credits:** Dir: Joseph L. Mankiewicz; Prod: Otto Lang; Writer: Michael Henry Wilson; Story: L. C. Moyzisch; DP: Norbert F. Brodine; Ed: James B. Clark; Prod Design: Lyle Wheeler; Composer: Bernard Herrmann; SFX: Fred Sersen; Art Director: George W. Davis. B&W, 108 min. VHS

Five Graves to Cairo
(1943) Paramount
The Sahara heats up as Allied spies try to outwit "Desert Fox" Rommel in this political thriller ably helmed by Wilder. Tone takes refuge in an oasis hotel run by Tamiroff just after the Afrika Korps rumbles through. He assumes a dead hotel waiter's identity, who also happens to have been a spy for Rommel. The intelligent Wilder-Brackett screenplay keeps things bouncing along with intense suspense and a dash of humor. Academy Award Nominations: 3, including Best Cinematography. **Cast:** Franchot Tone, Anne Baxter, Akim Tamiroff, Erich von Stroheim, Peter Van Eyck, Fortunio Bonanova, Miles Mander. **Credits:** Dir: Billy Wilder; Prod: Charles Brackett; Writer: Charles Brackett, Billy Wilder; Story: Lajos Biro; DP: John Seitz; Ed: Doane Harrison; Prod Design: Hans Dreier; Composer: Miklos Rozsa; Costumes: Edith Head; Art Director: Ernst Fegte; Set Designer: Bertram Granger. B&W, 97 min. VHS

The Five Pennies
(1959) Paramount
The musical biopic of jazz great Red Nichols features a healthy dose of melodrama along with the melodies. As the famed Dixieland cornetist, he runs into opposition to his sound, but breaks through to success. He marries a warm, patient woman (Bel Geddes) and even finds time to raise a family. Then tragedy strikes when their daughter contracts polio. The jazzman puts down his horn to stand by her. Among the musical cameos is a hot turn by Armstrong in a duet with Kaye. **Cast:** Danny Kaye, Tuesday Weld, Louis Armstrong, Bob Crosby, Bobby Troup, Ray Anthony, Shelly Manne, Barbara Bel Geddes, Harry Guardino, Susan Gordon. **Credits:** Dir: Melville Shavelson; Prod: Jack Rose; Writer: Melville Shavelson, Jack Rose; DP: Daniel Fapp; Ed: Frank P. Keller; Prod Design: Hal Pereira, Tambi Larsen; Composer: Leith Stevens. Color, 117 min. VHS, LASER

Five Star Final
(1931) Warner Bros.
When the editor of the *New York Gazette* attempts to increase readership of his paper, he assigns his ace muckraker to dig up the dirt on an unsolved murder that has baffled the local police for more than 20 years. The reporter cracks the case only to discover the guilty party in this crime of passion is now a well-to-do housewife and mother. When her story is published, the result is tragic, as she cannot bear to remember her acts from years past. Fascinating early talkie potboiler with muscular Robinson and different role for Karloff. **Cast:** Edward G. Robinson, H. B. Warner, Boris Karloff, Marian Marsh, Anthony Bushell, Frances Starr, Ona Munson. **Credits:** Dir: Mervyn LeRoy; Prod: Hal B. Wallis; Writer: Robert Lord, Byron Morgan; Story: Louis Weitzenkorn; DP: Sol Polito; Ed: Frank Ware; Composer: Leo F. Forbstein; Art Director: Jack Okey. B&W, 89 min.

Five Weeks in a Balloon
(1962) Fox
A group of daring adventurers set out in a unicorn-shaped balloon on a trip across the African continent. During their perilous travels they battle everything from sandstorms to Sultans. Based on a novel by Verne. **Cast:** Fabian, Cedric Hardwicke, Red Buttons, Barbara Eden, Peter Lorre, Richard Haydn, Barbara Luna, Billy Gilbert, Herbert Marshall, Reginald Owen. **Credits:** Dir: Irwin Allen; Prod:

Irwin Allen; Writer: Irwin Allen, Charles Bennett, Albert Gail; Story: Jules Verne; DP: Winton C. Hoch; Ed: George Boemler; Prod Design: Jack Martin Smith; Composer: Paul Sawtell; Art Director: Alfred Ybarra. Color, 101 min. **VHS**

The Fixer
(1968) MGM
In prerevolutionary Russia, Yakov Bok (Bates), a "fixer," or handyman, moves to Kiev from the *shtetl* and is unjustly accused of the ritual murder of a gentile boy. Bok is innocent of this atrocious crime, but he is guilty of being a Jew. He's tortured, deprived of any outside contact, legal help, or a glimmer of hope for three long years, and becomes a cause célèbre outside Russia. When the czar declares a general amnesty, Bok is pardoned, but demands a trial to prove his innocence. Bogarde comes to his defense. From the Bernard Malamud novel. **Cast:** Alan Bates, Dirk Bogarde, Georgia Brown, Hugh Griffith, Ian Holm, Jack Gilford, Elizabeth Hartman, David Warner, Carol White, Murray Melvin. **Credits:** Dir: John Frankenheimer; Prod: Edward Lewis; Writer: Dalton Trumbo; Story: Bernard Malamud; DP: Marcel Grignon; Ed: Henry Berman; Prod Design: Bela Zeichan; Composer: Maurice Jarre. Color, 132 min. **VHS**

The Flame and the Arrow
(1950) Warner Bros.
Lancaster returns to his circus-acrobat roots (with his vaudeville partner Cravat in tow) as Dardo the Arrow, the leader of a fearless band of rebels in medieval Italy. Mostly interesting for early Lancaster appearance and his obvious joy in doing his own acrobatic stunts. **Cast:** Burt Lancaster, Virginia Mayo, Aline MacMahon, Nick Cravat, Robert Douglas, Frank Allenby, Lynne Baggett, Gordon Gebert, Norman Lloyd, Victor Kilian. **Credits:** Dir: Jacques Tourneur; Prod: Harold Hecht, Frank Ross; Writer: Waldo Salt; DP: Ernest Haller; Ed: Alan Crosland, Jr.; Prod Design: Edward Carrere; Composer: Max Steiner. Color, 88 min. **VHS, LASER**

Flame of Araby
(1951) Universal
Threatened with a forced marriage to a prince from Barbarossa, a Tunisian princess arranges for her Bedouin paramour to challenge her betrothed to a horse race. If he wins, he gets her hand; if she wins, she gets her freedom. Now she needs a horse.

O'Hara's lovely and that's the story here. **Cast:** Maureen O'Hara, Jeff Chandler, Maxwell Reed, Susan Cabot, Lon Chaney, Jr., Richard Egan, Buddy Baer. **Credits:** Dir: Charles Lamont; Writer: Gerald Drayson Adams; DP: Russell Metty; Ed: Ted J. Kent; Art Director: Bernard Herzbrun. Color, 77 min. **VHS**

The Flame of New Orleans
(1941) Universal
Dietrich lights up New Orleans as European adventuress Claire Ledoux in this madcap romance. Sultry and elegant Mme. Ledoux shows up on the Mississippi and makes herself flagrantly available. Millionaire Young is drawn to the flame and it looks like the rugged seaman Cabot doesn't stand a chance. But when Auer shows up from Europe claiming that Mme. Ledoux isn't the lady she pretends to be, she pulls off a series of intricate stunts to place the blame on her fictional cousin. Giraud can't help being confused. Meanwhile Captain Latour is waiting patiently, very patiently. French director Clair's first Hollywood picture. Academy Award Nominations: Best Art Direction. **Cast:** Marlene Dietrich, Bruce Cabot, Roland Young, Mischa Auer, Andy Devine, Frank Jenks, Eddie Quillan, Laura Hope Crews, Franklin Pangborn, Theresa Harris. **Credits:** Dir: Rene Clair; Prod: Joe Pasternak; Writer: Rene Clair, Norman Krasna; DP: Rudolph Mate; Ed: Frank Gross; Prod Design: Jack Otterson; Composer: Charles Previn, Frank Skinner. B&W, 80 min.

Flame of the Barbary Coast
(1945) Republic
A cowboy competes with a gambling tycoon on the Barbary Coast for the hand of a beautiful dance-hall queen. The 1906 San Francisco earthquake shakes up the plot and provides the climax. **Cast:** John Wayne, Ann Dvorak, Joseph Schildkraut, Virginia Grey. **Credits:** Dir: Joseph Kane; Prod: Joseph Kane; Writer: Borden Chase; Story: Prescott Chaplin; DP: Robert DeGrasse; Ed: Richard L. Van Enger; Composer: Dale Butts; SFX: Howard Lydecker, Theodore Lydecker; Art Director: Gano Chittenden. B&W, 92 min. **VHS**

Flamingo Road
(1949) Warner Bros.
Life in a small southern town heats up when a sexy dancer (Crawford) gets stranded by a traveling carnival. She wins the hearts of two men and gets a taste of local politics when she

butts heads with a corrupt sheriff. Apparently Crawford only accepted the role after Jack Warner ordered rewrites and spruced up the production. Squalid and steamy. **Cast:** Joan Crawford, Zachary Scott, Sydney Greenstreet, David Brian, Gertrude Michael, Gladys George, Virginia Huston, Fred Clark. **Credits:** Dir: Michael Curtiz; Prod: Jerry Wald; Writer: Robert Wilder, Edmund H. North; Story: Sally Wilder; DP: Ted McCord; Ed: Folmar Blangsted; Composer: Max Steiner; Costumes: Travilla; Art Director: Leo K. Kuter; Set Designer: Howard Winterbottom. B&W, 94 min. **VHS, LASER**

Flat Top
(1952) Allied Artists
A steel-nerved skipper (Hayden) trains Navy carrier pilots during WWII while battling the kind commander of another group new to the carrier. His hard-won lessons come in handy when the flyboys hit air combat. The actual newsreel footage adds realism to the picture. **Cast:** Sterling Hayden, Richard Carlson, Keith Larson, Bill Phipps, John Bromfield, Walter Coy, Dave Willock, Phyllis Coates, Todd Karns, William Schallert. **Credits:** Dir: Lesley Selander; Prod: Walter Mirisch; Writer: Steve Fisher; DP: Harry Neumann; Ed: William Austin; Prod Design: Dave Milton; Composer: Marlin Skiles. Color, 85 min. **VHS, LASER**

The Fleet's In
(1942) Paramount
The Countess of Swingland (Lamour) is a cold, aloof singer in a wartime nightclub who entertains soldiers on leave. When Casey Kirby (Bracken), a mild-mannered sailor—who, oddly enough, has a reputation as a womanizer—arrives on the scene, the irreproachable Countess has her own reputation put to the test. To win a bet, Casey attempts to seduce the singer and melt her icy veneer. It proves to be an even more difficult task than he imagined. Hutton debuts in a star turn, and music is provided by the Jimmy Dorsey Orchestra. **Cast:** Dorothy Lamour, William Holden, Eddie Bracken, Betty Hutton, Cass Daley, Gil Lamb, Leif Erickson, Betty Rhodes, Jack Norton. **Credits:** Dir: Victor Schertzinger; Prod: Paul Jones; Writer: Walter DeLeon, Sid Silvers; Story: Kenyon Nicholson, J. Walter Ruben, Brice Monte, Charles Robinson; DP: William Mellor; Ed: Paul Weatherwax; Prod Design: Hans Dreier, Ernst Fegte; Composer: Johnny Mercer, Victor Schertzinger. B&W, 93 min.

Flesh

(1932) MGM

A German waiter and sometime wrestler (Beery) falls in love with an American dancer (Morley) and marries her. She has a child, he becomes the German wrestling champion, and together they travel to the U.S., where the wife's old partner resurfaces and becomes the fighter's manager. The wrestler's wife leaves him for the manager, who beats her. Learning of this brutality, the wrestler strangles the manager but doesn't know if he's dead. The fighter is arrested for murder after winning a big championship. Curious melodrama from Ford. **Cast:** Vince Barnett, Wallace Beery, Herman Bing, Edward Brophy, Ricardo Cortez, Karen Morley, Jean Hersholt, Greta Meyer, John Miljan. **Credits:** Dir: John Ford; Writer: Moss Hart, Leonard Praskins, Edgar Allan Woolf; Story: Edmund Goulding; DP: Arthur Edelson; Ed: William S. Gray. B&W, 95 min.

Flesh and Fantasy

(1943) Universal

The film presents three individual supernatural tales linked by two men discussing their dreams. The first vignette is set in New Orleans at Mardi Gras. Field, frustrated by her looks, is given a beauty mask from a mysterious man. The man assures her it will change her life. She accepts the mask, and is then able to win the favor of a young student, Cummings. In the second tale, a psychic (Mitchell) predicts that Robinson will commit a murder in the future. Robinson, now obsessed with the prediction, tries to take fate into his own hands. The third story tells of a circus performer who meets a woman he has seen before in his dreams. **Cast:** Robert Benchley, David Hoffman, Betty Field, Robert Cummings, Thomas Mitchell, Edgar G. Robinson, Charles Boyer, Barbara Stanwyck. **Credits:** Dir: Julien Duvivier; Prod: Julien Duvivier, Charles Boyer; Writer: Ernest Pascal, Samuel Hoffenstein, Ellis St. Joseph, Lasio Vadnay, Oscar Wilde; DP: Stanley Cortez, Paul Ivano; Ed: Arthur Hilton; Prod Design: Robert Boyle, John B. Goodman, Russell A. Gausman, Richard Reidel, E. R. Robinson; Composer: Alexandre Tansman, Charles Previn. B&W, 93 min.

Flesh and Fury

(1952) Universal

Curtis is a deaf and mute boxer fighting his way to a shot at the title, but he finds himself vulnerable to Sterling, a self-serving blonde who sees an easy mark in the handicapped athlete.

Enter hard-boiled reporter Freeman, who falls for Curtis and steps in to protect him, getting him an operation to restore his hearing. Curtis loses it again, along with the title, in the big fight, but he gains true love, and permanent hearing to boot, when he dumps Sterling for Freeman. **Cast:** Tony Curtis, Jan Sterling, Mona Freeman, Wallace Ford, Connie Gilchrist, Katherine Locke, Joe Gray, Ron Hargrave, Harry Guardino, Harry Shannon. **Credits:** Dir: Joseph Pevney; Prod: Leonard Goldstein; Writer: William Alland; Story: Bernard Gordon; DP: Irving Glassberg; Ed: Virgil Vogel; Prod Design: Bernard Herzbrun; Composer: Hans J. Salter; Art Director: Emrich Nicholson. B&W, 82 min.

Flesh and the Devil

(1927) MGM

A seductive temptress drives a wedge between two old friends, a division that leads to death and banishment. Garbo's finest (and she's truly gorgeous). The offscreen sparks between Garbo and Gilbert are apparent. **Cast:** Greta Garbo, John Gilbert, Lars Hanson, Barbara Kent. **Credits:** Dir: Clarence Brown; Writer: Benjamin Glazer; DP: William Daniels; Ed: Lloyd Nosler; Prod Design: Cedric Gibbons, Frederick Hope. B&W, 113 min. **VHS**

Flight from Destiny

(1941) Warner Bros.

A strange adventure follows Mitchell after he learns of his imminent death. With only three months to live, the professor seeks some way to give his life meaning. When he sees the potential happiness of his favorite students Fitzgerald and Lynn threatened by vindictive shrew Maris, the professor finds his unlikely destiny in helping dispel a murder charge. **Cast:** Geraldine Fitzgerald, Thomas Mitchell, Jeffrey Lynn, James Stephenson, Mona Maris, Jonathan Hale, David Bruce, Thurston Hall, Mary Gordon, John Eldredge. **Credits:** Dir: Vincent Sherman; Prod: Edmund Grainger; Writer: Anthony Berkeley, Barry Trivers; DP: James Van Trees; Ed: Thomas Richards; Prod Design: Esdras Hartley; Composer: Heinz Roemheld. B&W, 73 min.

The Flight of the Phoenix

(1965) Fox

A small cargo-passenger plane carrying oil workers and military personnel crashes, stranding a group of survivors in the Sahara Desert. The conscientious pilot struggles with his

doubts as a fanatical German model-aircraft designer attempts to build, out of the wreckage, a single-engine plane that will lift them out of the desert before the heat and sand take their toll. Intriguing cast and taut story line. Based on Trevor's novel. **Cast:** James Stewart, Richard Attenborough, Peter Finch, Hardy Kruger, Ernest Borgnine, George Kennedy, Ian Bannen, Dan Duryea, Ronald Fraser, Christian Marquand. **Credits:** Dir: Robert Aldrich; Prod: Robert Aldrich; Writer: Lukas Heller; Story: Elleston Trevor; DP: Joseph Biroc; Ed: Michael Luciano; Prod Design: William Glasgow; Composer: Frank DeVol. Color, 147 min. **VHS, LASER**

The Flim-Flam Man

(1967) Fox

Winning, rare lighthearted role for Scott as a scam artist working the back roads down South. He takes on a young army deserter (Sarrazin) as an apprentice. Much to Scott's disappointment, Sarrazin starts to stray toward the straight and narrow. **Cast:** George C. Scott, Michael Sarrazin, Jack Albertson, Slim Pickens, Sue Lyon, Harry Morgan, Alice Ghostley, Albert Salmi, Strother Martin, George Mitchell. **Credits:** Dir: Irvin Kershner; Prod: Lawrence Turman; Writer: William Rose; DP: Charles B. Lang; Ed: Robert W. Swink; Prod Design: Jack Martin Smith, Robert Smith, Lewis Creber; Composer: Jerry Goldsmith. Color, 115 min. **VHS**

Flipper

(1963) MGM

The son of a Florida fisherman nurses an injured dolphin. Their relationship develops into true friendship as the animal returns to health. But when the father orders that the dolphin be returned to his natural habitat, the boy is disappointed. Flipper returns, however, to save the day at a drastic moment, sealing the bond that the son always knew was there. **Cast:** Chuck Connors, Luke Halpin, Flipper, Kathleen Maguire, Connie Scott. **Credits:** Dir: James B. Clark; Prod: Ivan Tors; Writer: Arthur Weiss; Story: Ricou Browning, Jack Cowden; DP: Lamar Boren, Joseph Brun; Ed: Warren Adams; Composer: Henry Vars. Color, 91 min. **VHS**

Flower Drum Song

(1961) Universal

This film version of the Rodgers and Hammerstein Broadway smash tells the story of a traditional young Chinese woman (Umeki) who travels to

scientist wants to reverse the process, but first he must catch that fly. Hilarious as well as horrific, this spawned two sequels in the '50s (*Return of the Fly* and *Curse of the Fly*) before starting another cycle in the '80s, beginning with David Cronenberg's elegant updating (*The Fly*, 1986). **Cast:** Vincent Price, Herbert Marshall, David Hedison, Patricia Owens, Kathleen Freeman, Betty Lou Gerson, Charles Herbert, Eugene Borden, Torben Meyer, Harry Carter. **Credits:** Dir: Kurt Neumann; Prod: Kurt Neumann; Writer: James Clavell; DP: Karl Struss; Ed: Merrill White; Composer: Paul Sawtell. Color, 94 min. **VHS, LASER**

Flying Down to Rio
(1933) RKO
This is the first of the Astaire-Rogers musicals, about an American bandleader who romances a pretty South American socialite on two continents. The highlights are a production number on the wings of a moving airplane, and, of course, the chemistry between the two stars, of which we were soon to see much, much more. **Cast:** Fred Astaire, Ginger Rogers, Dolores Del Rio, Gene Raymond, Blanche Frederici, Walter Walker, Eric Blore, Franklin Pangborn. Academy Award Nominations: Best Song ("The Carioca"). **Credits:** Dir: Thornton Freeland; Prod: Louis Brock; Writer: Cyril Hume, Erwin Gelsey, H. W. Hanemann; Story: Anne Caldwell, Louis Brock; DP: J. Roy Hunt; Ed: Jack Kitchin; Prod Design: Carroll Clark; Choreographer: Hermes Pan, Dave Gould; Composer: Vincent Youmans; Costumes: Walter Plunkett; SFX: Vernon L. Walker; Art Director: Van Nest Polglase. B&W, 89 min. **VHS**

Flying Leathernecks
(1951) RKO
Action-packed war film utilizing actual battle footage to create a tense drama. Two U.S. Marine fighter pilots try to fight their own personal battles while still banding together to fight the war. Wayne delivers his standard performance as the flying officer whose determination is hated by his men as well as the enemy. **Cast:** John Wayne, Robert Ryan, Don Taylor, Janis Carter, William Harrigan, Jay C. Flippen, James Bell. **Credits:** Dir: Nicholas Ray; Prod: Edmund Grainger; Writer: James Edward Grant; Story: Kenneth Gamet; DP: William E. Snyder; Ed: Sherman Todd; Composer: Roy Webb; Art Director: Albert S. D'Agostino, James Sullivan. Color, 102 min. **VHS, LASER**

The Fly (1958)

San Francisco from Hong Kong to fulfill an arranged marriage. The problem is that her prospective husband, an up-to-date, Westernized Chinese-American nightclub owner (Shigeta), has other plans, including his romance with singer Kwan. Not completely successful in its translation to the screen, it remains, nonetheless, an appealing presentation of a seldom-seen setting. Academy Award Nominations: 5, including Best Cinematography; Best Score. **Cast:** Nancy Kwan, Jack Soo, James Shigeta, Miyoshi Umeki, Juanita Hall, Victor Sen Yung. **Credits:** Dir: Henry Koster; Prod: Ross Hunter; Writer: Joseph Fields; Story: C. Y. Lee; DP: Russell Metty; Ed: Mil-

ton Carruth; Prod Design: Alexander Golitzen, Joseph C. Wright; Choreographer: Hermes Pan; Composer: Richard Rodgers, Oscar Hammerstein; Costumes: Irene Sharaff. Color, 133 min. **VHS, LASER**

The Fly
(1958) Fox
The classic science fiction–horror film about a scientist's (Price) two "teleport" machines, one of which dissolves atoms, while the other reconstructs them. When Price unwittingly shares the machine with a common housefly, he turns into a hideous hybrid of man and insect—and begins to literally bug out. The

Flying Tigers

(1942) Republic
Wayne is the leader of a squadron of American pilots-for-hire in WWII China. The men are desperately outnumbered by the Japanese, and also deal with difficulties within their own ranks. Excellent air-combat scenes, some taut military-court drama, and even a little romance between Wayne and a lovely British nurse. **Cast:** John Wayne, Anna Lee, John Carroll, Paul Kelly, Mae Clarke. **Credits:** Dir: David Miller; Prod: Edmund Grainger; Writer: Kenneth Gamet, Barry Trivers; DP: Jack Marta; Ed: Ernest Nims; Composer: Victor Young; SFX: Howard Lydecker; Art Director: Russell Kimball. B&W, 101 min. **VHS, LASER**

FM

(1978) Universal
The groovy deejays at L.A.'s hippest radio station rail against the revenue-hungry corporation that pulls all the strings. Company bigwigs want to load up the airwaves with snazzy rock-and-roll commercials for the army, but the jocks bristle at the new "improvements" and eventually go on strike to regain control. A crowd of supporters gathers outside as the radio personalities commandeer the station in order to spread their positive, carefree message to the public. Great Mull performance (in his screen debut), major contemporary music star power in cameos and performances (REO Speedwagon, anybody?), and a sizzling sound track. **Cast:** Michael Brandon, Eileen Brennan, Alex Karras, Cleavon Little, Martin Mull, Cassie Yates, Linda Ronstadt, Jimmy Buffet. **Credits:** Dir: John A. Alonzo; Prod: Rand Holston; Writer: Ezra Sacks; DP: David Myers; Ed: Jeff Gourson; Prod Design: Lawrence G. Paull. Color, 105 min. **VHS, LASER**

Fog over Frisco

(1934) Warner Bros.
A sweet young socialite reads a newspaper story reporting that her stepsister has been keeping company with gangsters at a nightclub. Upset, the girl seeks the reporter out and scolds him for the piece. He takes her to the nightclub, where she sees the truth for herself. The stepsister is using her fiancé to sell stolen securities acquired from crooks. She gives the concerned young girl an envelope that will expose the crooks if anything happens to her. The stepsister is soon kidnapped by her cohorts, who believe her too dangerous. Early Davis role as the flighty socialite. **Cast:** Bette Davis, Donald Woods, Margaret Lindsay, Lyle Talbot, Hugh Herbert, Arthur Byron,

Robert Barrat, Irving Pichel, Douglass Dumbrille. **Credits:** Dir: William Dieterle; Prod: Robert Lord; Writer: George Dyer, Robert N. Lee, Eugene Solow; DP: Tony Gaudio; Ed: Harold McLernon; Prod Design: Jack Okey; Composer: Leo F. Forbstein. B&W, 68 min.

Folies Bergère

(1935) Fox
Musical comedy about a Baron who needs to be two places at the same time. A Paris cabaret star, who greatly resembles him, is hired to impersonate the Baron. The actor falls in love with the Baroness, while the Baron finds himself attracted to the actor's girlfriend. The Baron eventually realizes that his wife is in love with the man impersonating him. Oberon's American debut. **Cast:** Walter Byron, Maurice Chevalier, Ferdinand Gottschalk, Robert Greig, Lumsden Hare, Halliwell Hobbes, Merle Oberon, Ann Sothern, Eric Blore, Ferdinand Munier. **Credits:** Dir: Roy Del Ruth; Prod: William Goetz, Raymond Griffith, Darryl F. Zanuck; Writer: Hans Adler, Hal Long, Rudolph Lothar, Bess Meredyth; DP: J. Peverell Marley; Ed: Allen McNeil, Sherman Todd, William S. Darling; Composer: Jak Meskill, Jack Stern, Burton Lane, Harold Adamson. B&W, 83 min.

Follow Me, Boys!

(1966) Disney
Fred MacMurray charms in this sweet story of a good-natured chap who looks for, finds, and settles in a small country town. He courts and marries a beautiful girl (Miles) and wins over the youth population, eventually becoming scoutmaster, with his easygoing nature and musical talents. **Cast:** Fred MacMurray, Vera Miles, Lillian Gish, Charlie Ruggles, Elliot Reid, Kurt Russell, Luana Patten, Ken Murray. **Credits:** Dir: Norman Tokar; Prod: Walt Disney, Winston Hibler; Writer: Louis Pelletier; Story: MacKinlay Kantor; DP: Clifford Stine; Ed: Robert Stafford; Prod Design: Carroll Clark; Composer: George Bruns; Costumes: Bill Thomas; SFX: Eustace Lycett; Art Director: Marvin Aubrey Davis; Set Designer: Emile Kuri, Frank McKelvy. Color, 120 min. **VHS**

Follow Me Quietly

(1949) RKO
Unique film noir in which a psychotic killer, known as the Judge, ends the lives of those he deems unworthy. Police use information from witnesses to create a life-size mannequin of their quarry, which they keep in the sta-

tion, setting the stage for a daring switcheroo. Great performance by Lundigan as the obsessed detective. **Cast:** William Lundigan, Dorothy Patrick, Jeff Corey, Nestor Paiva, Charles D. Brown, Paul Guilfoyle, Edwin Max. **Credits:** Dir: Richard Fleischer; Prod: Herman Schlom; Writer: Lillie Hayward; Story: Anthony Mann, Francis Rosenwald; DP: Robert de Grasse; Ed: Elmo Williams; Composer: Leonid Raab; Art Director: Albert S. D'Agostino, Walter E. Keller; Set Designer: Darrell Silvera, James Altweis. B&W, 59 min. **VHS**

Follow That Dream

(1962) United Artists
Elvis stars as an innocent Georgia country boy whose ragtag family moves to the Florida coast to set up a homestead. A nosy social worker and a meddlesome land commissioner try to prevent the family's settling in. Elvis's songs include "What a Wonderful Life," "Angel," and the title tune. **Cast:** Elvis Presley, Arthur O'Connell, Anne Helm, Joanna Moore, Jack Kruschen. **Credits:** Dir: Gordon Douglas; Prod: David Weisbart; Writer: Charles Lederer; DP: Leo Tover; Ed: William B. Murphy; Composer: Hans J. Salter; Art Director: Malcolm Bert. Color, 111 min. **VHS, LASER**

Follow the Fleet

(1936) RKO
When he is rejected by his lady love, a song-and-dance man enlists in the navy. The estranged couple later meet again and join forces to solve the romantic difficulties of another star-crossed pair. An Astaire-Rogers musical featuring some of Irving Berlin's best songs, including "Let's Face the Music and Dance," "Let Yourself Go," "We Saw the Sea." Typical but delightful. **Cast:** Fred Astaire, Ginger Rogers, Randolph Scott, Harriet Hilliard, Astrid Allwyn, Harry Beresford, Russell Hicks, Lucille Ball, Betty Grable, Tony Martin. **Credits:** Dir: Mark Sandrich; Prod: Pandro S. Berman; Writer: Dwight Taylor, Allan Scott; Story: Hubert Osborne; DP: David Abel; Ed: Henry Berman; Prod Design: Carroll Clark; Choreographer: Hermes Pan, Fred Astaire; Composer: Irving Berlin; Costumes: Bernard Newman; SFX: Vernon L. Walker; Art Director: Van Nest Polglase; Set Designer: Darrell Silvera. B&W, 110 min. **VHS, LASER**

Follow the Sun

(1951) Fox
A bio-drama of the true story of golf pro Ben Hogan, whose comeback

after a devastating car accident was as inspirational as it was remarkable. Growing up a poor child in Texas, Hogan learns the game of golf as a caddy and eventually overcomes stereotypes and barriers to join the pro tour. Based on a magazine article by Brennan. **Cast:** Glenn Ford, Anne Baxter, Dennis O'Keefe, June Havoc, Larry Keating, Roland Winters, Nana Bryant. **Credits:** Dir: Sidney Lanfield; Prod: Samuel G. Engel; Writer: Frederick Hazlitt Brennan; DP: Leo Tover; Ed: Barbara McLean; Prod Design: Lyle Wheeler; Composer: Cyril J. Mockridge; Art Director: Rich Irvine. B&W, 94 min. **VHS**

Foolish Wives

(1922) Universal
Erich von Stroheim's psychologically penetrating and visually gorgeous study of "innocent Americans" abroad, and their inability to understand the long-standing rules of behavior followed by their sophisticated European counterparts. An American diplomat and his wife journey to Monte Carlo, where he proceeds to bury himself in work. His wife, bored and upset with her husband's inattentiveness, and longing to experience the Continental nightlife, gradually succumbs to the flirtations of an elegant and charming "count"—who, in actuality, is merely a Russian military officer out to seduce her. As events come tumbling to a disastrous conclusion, the woman learns a valuable lesson about the meaning of true nobility and the difference between appearance and reality. **Cast:** Erich von Stroheim, Cesare Gravina, Maud George, Mae Busch, Harrison Ford. **Credits:** Dir: Erich von Stroheim; Writer: Erich von Stroheim, Marian Ainslee; DP: William Daniels. B&W, 117 min. **VHS, LASER**

A Fool There Was

(1915) Fox
The vehicle for Bara's initiation into the cult of vamp movies. Based on Rudyard Kipling's "The Vampire," the film details the story of a just and moral man who falls from grace at the insidious hands of the unrepentant vamp. Notorious title cards and the indelible image of Bara mark this as a landmark piece of cinema: "Kiss me, my fool!" **Cast:** Theda Bara, Edward Jose, Runa Hodges, Clifford Bruce, Frank Powell, Creighton Hale, Mabel Frenyear, May Allison, Victor Benoit, Minna Gale. **Credits:** Dir: Frank Powell; Prod: William Fox; Writer: Frank Powell, Roy L. McCardell; Story: Rudyard Kipling. B&W, 86 min. **VHS**

Footlight Parade

(1933) Warner Bros.
A stage producer discovers that talking pictures have killed the demand for musical shows, so he rechannels his talents into creating live musical numbers for movie theaters to present between features. His fledgling business is threatened by unscrupulous business partners, conniving gold diggers, and spying competitors. Featured hits include "By a Waterfall," "Shanghai Lil," and "Honeymoon Hotel." **Cast:** Ruby Keeler, Joan Blondell, Dick Powell, James Cagney, Guy Kibbee, Ruth Donnelly, Claire Dodd, Hugh Herbert, Frank McHugh, Herman Bing. **Credits:** Dir: Lloyd Bacon; Prod: Robert Lord; Writer: Manuel Seff, James Seymour; DP: George Barnes; Ed: George Amy; Prod Design: Anton Grot; Choreographer: Busby Berkeley; Composer: Harry Warren, Al Dubin, Sammy Fain, Irving Kahal; Costumes: Milo Anderson; Art Director: Jack Okey. B&W, 105 min. **VHS, LASER**

Footlight Serenade

(1942) Fox
A champion heavyweight fighter takes a role in a Broadway show and makes a play for one of the dancers who, for career reasons, does not want it known she is married. Her husband is also an actor in the show and finds it increasingly difficult to watch the lady-killer champ going after his wife. **Cast:** Betty Grable, Victor Mature, John Payne, Jane Wyman, James Gleason, Phil Silvers, June Lang, Mantan Moreland, Cobina Wright. **Credits:** Dir: Gregory Ratoff; Prod: William LeBaron; Writer: Robert Ellis, Helen Logan, Lynn Starling; Story: Kenneth Earl, Fidel LaBarba; DP: Lee Garmes; Ed: Robert Simpson; Prod Design: Richard Day; Choreographer: Hermes Pan; Composer: Ralph Rainger, Leo Robin; Art Director: Roger Hemen. B&W, 81 min. **VHS**

Footsteps in the Dark

(1941) Warner Bros.
In an atypically nonhistorical role, Flynn plays investment consultant Francis Warren leading a double life as a suspense crime author. Playing detective at night to gather information for his stories, Warren works unbeknownst to his sleeping wife. He becomes implicated in an actual murder, and must do his own investigating to save his marriage and life. **Cast:** Errol Flynn, Brenda Marshall, Ralph Bellamy, Alan Hale, Lee Patrick, Allen Jenkins, Lucile Watson, William

Frawley, Roscoe Karns, Grant Mitchell. **Credits:** Dir: Lloyd Bacon; Prod: Robert Lord; Writer: Lester Cole, John Wexley; Story: Ladislaus Fodor, Bernard Merivale, Jeffrey Dell; DP: Ernest Haller; Ed: Owen Marks; Prod Design: Max Parker; Choreographer: Robert Vreeland; Composer: Frederick Hollander; Costumes: Howard Shoup; SFX: Rex Wimpy. B&W, 96 min. **VHS**

For a Few Dollars More

(1965) United Artists
Second of Leone and Eastwood's "Dollar" trilogy. The Man with No Name (Eastwood) teams up with a gunslinger (Van Cleef) in order to extract reward money from Volonte, a vicious bandit. There is little doubt as to Eastwood's financial intentions, but Van Cleef seems to be driven by something a bit deeper. A series of flashbacks (which would become a Leone signature device) provides the background for Van Cleef's anger and desire for revenge after Volonte raped and murdered his younger sister. Morricone's score and Leone's trademark long, lingering shots have entered movie iconography. **Cast:** Clint Eastwood, Lee Van Cleef, Gian Maria Volonte, Klaus Kinski, Rosemarie Dexter, Mario Brega, Aldo Sambrell, Luigi Pistilli. **Credits:** Dir: Sergio Leone; Prod: Alberto Grimaldi; Writer: Luciano Vincenzoni, Sergio Leone; DP: Massimo Dallamano; Composer: Ennio Morricone. Color, 131 min. **VHS, LASER, DVD**

Forbidden

(1932) Columbia
A married district attorney meets a single woman when he accidentally wanders into her cabin on a cruise ship. The two visit Havana together, and when they return to New York she is pregnant. The D.A., when his wife is out of town, takes the woman in and she poses as the baby's nurse. When the wife returns, she and the D.A. adopt the baby. Years later, the single woman becomes a reporter and works for an editor, trying to unseat the D.A. To protect the father of her child, the woman marries the editor, an act which ultimately doesn't resolve her dilemma. **Cast:** Ralph Bellamy, Thomas Jefferson, Adolphe Menjou, Dorothy Peterson, Barbara Stanwyck, Myrna Fresholt, Charlotte Henry. **Credits:** Dir: Frank Capra; Prod: Harry Cohn; Writer: Frank Capra, Jo Swerling; DP: Joseph Walker; Ed: Maurice Wright; Composer: Irving Bibo, Pete Fylling. B&W, 87 min.

Forbidden Planet

(1956) MGM

Shakespeare's *The Tempest* is transformed in this landmark science-fiction film with groundbreaking special effects. Spacemen travel to a planet ruled by expatriate Pidgeon, who has built a kingdom with his daughter and obedient robot Robby. There the good doctor is plagued by his mad quest for knowledge through his "brain booster" machine, and by Freudian "monsters from the id," as his daughter discovers other men and learns to kiss. **Cast:** Walter Pidgeon, Anne Francis, Leslie Nielsen, Warren Stevens, Earl Holliman, Jack Kelly, Richard Anderson, George Wallace, James Drury, Harry Harvey, Jr.. **Credits:** Dir: Fred M. Wilcox; Prod: Nicholas Nayfack; Writer: Cyril Hume; Story: Irving Block, Allen Adler; DP: George J. Folsey; Ed: George Folsey, Jr., Ferris Webster; Prod Design: Cedric Gibbons, Arthur Lonergan; Composer: Bebe Barron, Louis Barron; SFX: A. Arnold Gillespie, Warren Newcombe, Irving Reis, Joshua Meador. Color, 98 min. **VHS, LASER, DVD**

Force of Evil

(1949) MGM

A lawyer gets caught in a three-way squeeze between his racketeer boss, his racketeer brother, and the anti-crime tactics of a new prosecutor who would like to jail the entire lot. Based on the novel *Tucker's People* by Ira Wolfert. Directorial debut for the blacklisted Polonsky. A National Film Registry Outstanding Film. **Cast:** John Garfield, Beatrice Pearson, Thomas Gomez, Marie Windsor, Howland Chamberlin, Roy Roberts, Paul McVey, Tim Ryan. **Credits:** Dir: Abraham Polonsky; Prod: Bob Roberts; Writer: Abraham Polonsky, Ira Wolfert; Story: Ira Wolfert; DP: George Barnes; Ed: Walter Thompson, Arthur Seidel; Prod Design: Richard Day; Composer: David Raksin. B&W, 82 min. **VHS, LASER**

A Foreign Affair

(1948) Paramount

Wilder's tongue-in-cheek look at de-Nazification has Arthur and Dietrich in fine form as opposite ends of a Lund taffy pull. The postwar Berlin setting casts Arthur as a congresswoman monitoring the fraternization between Germans and Americans, while Dietrich stakes out familiar territory as the steamy chanteuse, this time with Nazi-infested past. She manages to ensnare Lund while singing numbers like "The Ruins of Berlin," but Arthur, who counters by cooing "Iowa Corn Song," is wise to her and seems to have fallen for Lund herself. **Cast:** Jean Arthur, Marlene Dietrich, John Lund, Millard Mitchell, Bill Murphy, Stanley Prager, Peter Von Zerbeck, Raymond Bond, Boyd Davis, Robert Malcolm. Academy Award Nominations: Best Screenplay; Best Cinematography. **Credits:** Dir: Billy Wilder; Prod: Charles Brackett; Writer: Robert Harari, Charles Brackett, Billy Wilder, Richard Breen; DP: Charles Lang; Ed: Doane Harrison; Composer: Frederick Hollander; Art Director: Hans Dreier, Walter Tyler. B&W, 116 min.

Foreign Correspondent

(1940) United Artists

Classic Hitchcock. It is 1939 and Johnny Jones, a naive police reporter, is sent by his even more naive boss to cover a "crime" story that's unfolding in Europe: the potential outbreak of a second world war. Unprepared for the dangerous political landscape he's entering, Johnny manages to land smack in the middle of a spy ring that is masquerading as a peace organization. **Cast:** Joel McCrea, Laraine Day, Herbert Marshall, George Sanders, Albert Basserman, Edmund Gwenn, Eduardo Ciannelli, Robert Benchley, Harry Davenport, Martin Kosleck. **Credits:** Dir: Alfred Hitchcock; Prod: Walter Wanger; Writer: Charles Bennett, Joan Harrison, James Hilton, Robert Benchley; DP: Rudolph Mate; Ed: Otho S. Lovering, Dorothy Spencer; Prod Design: Alexander Golitzen; Composer: Alfred Newman. B&W, 120 min. **VHS, LASER**

The Forest Rangers

(1942) Paramount

Tough-guy forest ranger Don Stuart (MacMurray) is investigating a rash of fires in his jurisdiction when he falls for Celia Huston (Goddard), an uppity rich girl from town. The more rugged Tana "Butch" Mason (Hayward) thinks she's better suited for Don and tries to convince him to try her out for size. When both women are caught by a vicious fire, Don hitches a ride from pilot Frank Hatfield (Toomey), only to discover he's the arsonist. Don, Celia, and "Butch" have to put out this real fire before they can address the flames in their hearts. **Cast:** Fred MacMurray, Paulette Goddard, Susan Hayward, Lynne Overman, Albert Dekker, Eugene Pallette, Regis Toomey, Rod Cameron, Clem Bevans, James Brown. **Credits:** Dir: George Marshall; Prod: Robert Sisk; Writer: Harold Shumate; Story: Thelma Strabel; DP: Charles Lang, William V. Skall; Ed: Paul Weatherwax; Prod Design: Hans Dreier, A. Earl Hedrick; Composer: Victor Young. Color, 87 min.

Forever Amber

(1947) Fox

The post-WWII screen scorcher based on Kathleen Winsor's novel, a progenitor of the modern romance novel. The big-budget bodice buster caused gossip and censorship in its day. The story follows a stunningly beautiful peasant girl as she sleeps her way into the British aristocracy. Academy Award Nominations: Best Score. **Cast:** Cornel Wilde, Linda Darnell, Anne Revere, Richard Greene, George Sanders, Jessica Tandy, Glenn Langan, Richard Haydn, Robert Coote, John Russell. **Credits:** Dir: Otto Preminger, Philip Dunne; Prod: William Perlberg; Writer: Ring Lardner, Jerry Cady; Story: Kathleen Winsor; DP: Leon Shamroy; Ed: Louis Loeffler; Prod Design: Lyle Wheeler; Composer: David Raksin. Color, 140 min. **VHS**

Forever and a Day

(1943) RKO

In this entertaining film featuring an all-star cast, the history of a London mansion and its many occupants from 1804 through WWII is told in epic fashion. The film demonstrates how a house—and, by extension, England itself—is able to survive despite war and other outside threats. **Cast:** Ray Milland, Merle Oberon, Ida Lupino, Charles Laughton, Claude Rains, Anna Neagle, Buster Keaton, Herbert Marshall, Kent Smith, Robert Cummings. **Credits:** Dir: Rene Clair, Edmund Goulding, Frank Lloyd, Victor Saville, Robert Stevenson, Herbert Wilcox, Cedric Hardwicke; Prod: Rene Clair, Edmund Goulding, Cedric Hardwicke, Frank Lloyd, Victor Saville, Robert Stevenson, Herbert Wilcox; Writer: Charles Bennett, C. S. Forester, Lawrence Hazard, Michael Hogan, W. P. Lipscomb, Alice Duer Miller, John Van Druten, Alan Campbell, Peter Godfrey, Sig Herzig, Christopher Isherwood, Gene Lockhart, R. C. Sherriff, Claudine West, Norman Corwin, James Hilton, Emmett Lavery, Frederick Lonsdale, Donald Ogden Stewart, Keith Winter; DP: Robert de Grasse, Lee Garmes, Russell Metty, Nicholas Musuraca; Ed: Elmo Williams, George Crone; Prod Design: Albert S. D'Agostino, L. P. Williams, Al Freeman, Jr.; Composer: Anthony Collins. B&W, 106 min. **VHS**

Forever Female

(1953) Paramount

Charming farce about glamorous backstage Broadway with Rogers as an actress past her prime and Holden as a novice playwright. Holden has just finished his first play, which catches the attention of leading actress Rogers and her ex-husband (Douglas), a theater producer. Things get romantically dicey when Holden ages a character so he can cast Rogers. **Cast:** Ginger Rogers, William Holden, Paul Douglas, Pat Crowley, James Gleason, Marjorie Rambeau, Alan Reeves, George Reeves, Maidie Norman, King Donovan. **Credits:** Dir: Irving Rapper; Prod: Pat Duggan; Writer: Julius J. Epstein, Philip G. Epstein; DP: Harry Stradling; Ed: Archie Marshek, Doane Harrison; Prod Design: Hal Pereira, Joseph MacMillan; Composer: Victor Young. Color, 93 min. **VHS, LASER**

Forgotten Women

(1932) Monogram

A rising newspaperman has flings with two different women. Ditching one for the other, he realizes that the woman scorned has taken up with a gangster. In trying to bring the gangsters to justice, he must decide whether to pursue his career or re-ignite his forgotten relationship. **Cast:** Marion Shilling, Rex Bell, Beryl Mercer, Virginia Lee Corbin, Carmelita Geraghty, Edna Murphy, Edward Earle, Eddie Kane. **Credits:** Dir: Richard Thorpe; Writer: Adele S. Buffington; Story: Wellyn Totman; DP: Archie Stout, Charles Van Enger; Ed: W. Donn Hayes. Color, 62 min. **VHS**

For Me and My Gal

(1942) MGM

Kelly made his film debut in this boy-woos-girl classic. An ambitious song-and-dance man and a pretty singer with dreams of hitting the big time team up to work the vaudeville circuit. Their professional relationship gradually becomes romantic, but both suffer a series of setbacks and disappointments. As they finally seem poised on the verge of success, WWI breaks out and threatens to tear them apart forever. **Cast:** Judy Garland, Gene Kelly, George Murphy, Keenan Wynn, Marta Eggerth, Ben Blue, Richard Quine, Stephen McNally. **Credits:** Dir: Busby Berkeley; Prod: Arthur Freed; Writer: Richard Sherman, Fred F. Finklehoffe, Sid Silvers, Jack McGowan, Irving Brecher; Story: Howard Emmett Rogers; DP: William Daniels; Ed: Ben Lewis; Prod Design: Cedric Gibbons, Gabriel Scognamillo; Composer: George Stoll, Roger Edens. B&W, 104 min. **VHS, LASER**

For Pete's Sake

(1977) Columbia

Streisand stars as a Brooklyn housewife in this comedy set in the '30s. Her husband is a down-on-his-luck cabbie who happens upon an investment tip for pork belly futures. With no money of their own, the couple borrow from a loan shark and spend the rest of the movie trying to keep their heads above water and out of the Mob's noose. **Cast:** Barbra Streisand, Michael Sarrazin, Estelle Parsons, Molly Picon, William Redfield, Louis Zorich, Richard Ward, Heywood Hale Broun, Joseph Maher. **Credits:** Dir: Peter Yates; Prod: Martin Erlichman, Stanley Shapiro; Writer: Stanley Shapiro, Maurice Richlin; DP: Laszlo Kovacs; Ed: Frank P. Keller; Prod Design: Gene Callahan; Composer: Artie Butler. Color, 90 min. **VHS**

Forsaking All Others

(1934) MGM

Jilted by one suitor and consoled by another, Crawford demonstrates a sly sense of humor and a confused heart. This rollicking comedy, chock-full of MGM stars, revolves around a daffy romantic quadrangle. Jeff has quietly been in love with Mary for 20 years. Mary, who's unaware of Jeff's affections, plans to marry Dill. But Dill leaves Mary at the altar when he falls for a cunning temptress named Connie. Originally a stage play starring Tallulah Bankhead. **Cast:** Joan Crawford, Clark Gable, Robert Montgomery, Billie Burke, Charles Butterworth, Frances Drake, Rosalind Russell, Arthur Treacher. **Credits:** Dir: W. S. Van Dyke; Prod: Bernard Hyman; Writer: Joseph L. Mankiewicz; DP: Gregg Toland, George J. Folsey; Ed: Tom Held; Prod Design: Cedric Gibbons; Composer: William Axt. B&W, 84 min. **VHS**

Fort Apache

(1948) RKO

The first of Ford's acclaimed Cavalry trilogy. After a distinguished military career in the Civil War, a rigid, by-the-book colonel (Fonda) is assigned to the remote western cavalry post of Fort Apache. Viewing his assignment as a demotion, Fonda resists the advice of his more experienced men, including Wayne. Fonda's ignorance of the territory and Indian ways leads to a tragic blunder, despite Wayne's impassioned pleas for his men's safety. A superbly constructed portrait of life on the frontier and the army routine that secured the territory for settlement. **Cast:** Henry Fonda, John Wayne, Ward Bond, Shirley Temple, John Agar, Pedro Armendariz, Irene Rich, George O'Brien, Victor McLaglen, Anna Lee. **Credits:** Dir: John Ford; Prod: John Ford, Merian C. Cooper; Writer: Frank S. Nugent; DP: Archie Stout; Ed: Jack Murray; Prod. Design: James Basevi; Composer: Richard Hageman. B&W, 127 min. **VHS, LASER**

For the Love of Benji

(1977)

A sequel to the successful *Benji*, featuring the thoroughly lovable mop of a dog. This adventure takes Benji on a vacation to Greece, where the pooch becomes involved with foreign dog-snatchers. Dependable family fare. **Cast:** Patsy Garrett, Cynthia Smith, Allen Fiuzat, Ed Nelson, Benji, Peter Bowles. **Credits:** Dir: Joe Camp; Prod: Ben Vaughn; Writer: Joe Camp; DP: Don Reddy; Ed: Leon Seith; Prod Design: Harland Wright; Composer: Euel Box. Color, 90 min. **VHS**

For the Love of Mary

(1948) Universal

A perky switchboard operator for the White House makes not one but three love connections, and her attempts to keep each Romeo on the line leads to a lot of crossed wires. Contains an alternate ending not included in the theatrical release. **Cast:** Deanna Durbin, Edmond O'Brien, Harry Davenport, Don Taylor, Jeffrey Lynn, Ray Collins, Hugo Haas, Griff Barnett, Katherine Alexander, James Todd. **Credits:** Dir: Frederick De Cordova; Prod: Robert Arthur; Writer: Oscar Brodney; DP: William Daniels; Ed: Ted J. Kent; Composer: Frank Skinner. B&W, 99 min. **VHS**

The Fortune

(1975) Columbia

Nichols directs odd comedy pairing of Nicholson and Beatty in a minor Roaring Twenties comedy. As rival hucksters who vie for the attention—and the bank book—of a dizzy heiress, the stars are just okay, but worth catching for lesser-known work of the talents involved. **Cast:** Stockard Channing, Warren Beatty, Jack Nicholson, Florence Stanley, Richard B. Shull, John Fiedler, Scatman Crothers, Dub Taylor, Ian Wolfe, Rose Michtom. **Credits:** Dir: Mike Nichols; Prod: Mike Nichols, Don Devlin; Writer: Adrien Joyce; DP: John A. Alonzo; Ed: Stu Linder; Prod Design: Richard Sylbert; Composer: David Shire. Color, 88 min. **VHS**

The Fortune Cookie

(1966) United Artists

A TV cameraman (Lemmon) hatches an insurance-fraud scheme with his brother-in-law (Matthau), a larcenous lawyer, when he's injured while working a football game. While wrestling with his conscience, the cameraman must also wrestle with the difficulties of masquerading as a wheelchair-bound invalid and with his greedy ex-wife, who returns to the fold in anticipation of a large settlement. Typically cynical Wilder comedy with the unbeatable team of Lemmon and Matthau in good form. **Academy Awards:** Best Supporting Actor: Walter Matthau. **Cast:** Jack Lemmon, Walter Matthau, Judi West, Ron Rich, Cliff Osmond, Lurene Tuttle, Les Tremayne, Marge Redmond, Noam Pitlik, Ann Shoemaker. **Credits:** Dir: Billy Wilder; Prod: Billy Wilder; Writer: Billy Wilder, I. A. L. Diamond; DP: Joseph La Shelle; Ed: Daniel Mandell; Prod Design: Robert Luthardt; Composer: Andre Previn. Color, 125 min. **VHS, LASER**

Forty Little Mothers

(1940) MGM

While temporarily unemployed, a teacher of philosophy, ancient history, and romantic languages finds an abandoned baby in a waiting room. He gets caught while stealing a bottle of milk to feed the hungry baby. The judge in the police court happens to be an old college friend. The judge helps his old chum out and recommends him for the professorship in a young ladies' seminary. Unable to abandon the baby again, he brings the child along and hence the title of the film; the little baby boy becomes an honorary part of the school curriculum. **Cast:** Eddie Cantor, Judith Anderson, Ralph Morgan, Rita Johnson, Bonita Granville, Diana Lewis, Nydia Westman, Margaret Early, Martha O'Driscoll, Charlotte Munier. **Credits:** Dir: Busby Berkeley; Prod: Harry Rapf; Writer: Dorothy Yost, Ernest Pagano; Story: Jean Guitton; DP: Charles Lawton, Jr.; Ed: Ben Lewis. B&W, 88 min.

For Whom the Bell Tolls

(1943) Paramount

Based on Ernest Hemingway's 1940 novel, this screen adaptation sensitively explores the tragic and passionate relationship between American mercenary Cooper and Maria (Bergman), a Spanish orphan who is a resistance fighter during the Spanish Civil War. Their love is intensified as Cooper, a munitions expert, risks his life to help a band of Loyalist guerril-

For Whom the Bell Tolls (1943)

las destroy an enemy bridge. Romance, wartime drama, and striking photography make this among the most worthy Hemingway adaptations. Golden Globes for Best Supporting Actor: Akim Tamiroff; Best Supporting Actress: Katina Paxinou. Academy Award Nominations: 9, including Best Picture; Best Actor: Gary Cooper; Best Actress: Ingrid Bergman; Best Supporting Actor: Akim Tamiroff; Best Cinematography; Best Editing. **Academy Awards:** Best Supporting Actress: Katina Paxinou. **Cast:** Gary Cooper, Ingrid Bergman, Akim Tamiroff, Artur De Cordova, Joseph Calleia, Katina Paxinou, Vladimir Sokoloff, Mikhail Rasumny, Victor Varconi, Alexander Granach. **Credits:** Dir: Sam Wood; Prod: Sam Wood; Writer: Dudley Nichols; Story: Ernest Hemingway; DP: Ray Rennahan; Ed: Sherman Todd, John F. Link; Prod Design: William Cameron Menzies; Composer: Victor Young. Color, 166 min. **VHS, LASER**

Foul Play

(1978) Paramount

Sweet, unassuming librarian Gloria Mundy stumbles upon a plot to kill the Pope, who will be visiting soon. When Gloria realizes she's been marked for murder, she goes to detective Tony Carlson for help. Together the twosome set out to unravel the wacky but heinous murder plot. Along the way they encounter a deadly midget, a shadowy albino, a wild and kinky swinger (with an unbelievable bedroom), vanishing cadavers, and much more, culminating in a wild car chase through the steep streets of San Francisco. And as they make their way through all the lunacy, Gloria and Tony might just be falling in love, too. Chase and Hawn are the reasons to watch this Hitchcockian update. **Cast:** Goldie Hawn, Chevy Chase, Burgess Meredith, Rachel Roberts, Dudley Moore, Eugene Roche, Marilyn Sokol, Brian Dennehy, Marc Lawrence, Chuck McCann. **Credits:** Dir: Colin Higgins; Prod: Thomas L. Miller; Writer: Colin Higgins; DP: David M. Walsh; Ed: Pembroke Herring; Prod Design: Alfred Sweeney; Composer: Charles Fox. Color, 118 min. VHS, LASER

The Fountainhead
(1949) Warner Bros.
A cinema monolith based on Rand's 1943 monolithic tome about an idealistic architectural genius (Cooper) who battles with his corporate sponsors over the designs for a housing project. When Cooper learns that the plans were changed over his objections, he destroys the finished building and is forced to defend his unyielding position in court. Cooper looks the part but this is as cold as marble. **Cast:** Gary Cooper, Patricia Neal, Raymond Massey, Kent Smith, Robert Douglas, Henry Hull, Ray Collins, Moroni Olsen, Jerome Cowan, Paul Harvey. **Credits:** Dir: King Vidor; Prod: Henry Blanke; Writer: Ayn Rand; DP: Robert Burks; Ed: David Weisbart; Prod Design: Edward Carrere; Composer: Max Steiner. B&W, 114 min. VHS, LASER

Four Daughters
(1938) Warner Bros.
A touching drama about a musical family with four lovely girls. The quiet existence of their Connecticut household is shattered by a parade of men who enter the family's life. One of these characters is the melancholy Mickey Borden—a morose piano player whose arrival causes emotional havoc for one of the daughters and for the other man who loves her, too. A wonderfully acted film that inspired two sequels, as well as a remake. **Cast:** Claude Rains, Rosemary Lane, Lola Lane, Priscilla Lane, Gale Page, John Garfield, Jeffrey Lynn, Frank McHugh, May Robson, Dick Foran. **Credits:** Dir: Michael Curtiz; Prod: Henry Blanke; Writer: Julius J. Epstein, Lenore Coffee; DP: Ernest Haller; Ed: Ralph Dawson; Prod Design: John Hughes; Composer: Max Steiner. B&W, 90 min. VHS

Four Faces West
(1948) United Artists
Ross McEwen robs a bank in the town of Santa Maria in order to help his father save his ranch. Not being a dishonest person at heart, he leaves an IOU, which he sincerely intends to honor. Coincidentally, famed U.S. Marshal Pat Garrett is in Santa Maria at the same time and takes up the chase. Ross manages to elude him until a final showdown where Garrett finally catches up with him on a range where he had stopped to help nurse a family of Mexicans dying of diphtheria. Well made all around. **Cast:** Joel McCrea, Frances Dee, Charles Bickford, Joseph Calleia, William Conrad, Martin Garralaga, John Parrish. **Credits:** Dir: Alfred E. Green; Prod: Harry Sherman; Writer: Graham Baker, Teddi Sherman, William Brent, Milarde Brent; DP: Russell Harlan; Ed: Edward Mann; Composer: Paul Sawtell. B&W, 89 min. VHS

The Four Feathers
(1939) United Artists
When a man's friends and lover think he's a coward, he heads for the distant war in Egypt to redeem himself. An adventure classic with a stunning cast. Academy Award Nomination for Best Color Cinematography. **Cast:** Ralph Richardson, John Clements, C. Aubrey Smith, June Duprez, Allan Jeayes, Jack Allen, Donald Gray, Henry Oscar, John Laurie, Frederick Culley. **Credits:** Dir: Alexander Korda; Prod: Alexander Korda; Writer: R. C. Sherriff, Lajos Biro, Arthur Wimperis; Story: A. E. W. Mason; DP: Georges Perinal, Osmond H. Borradaile, Jack Cardiff; Ed: William Hornbeck, Henry Cornelius; Prod Design: Vincent Korda; Composer: Miklos Rozsa. Color, 130 min. VHS, LASER

The Four Horsemen of the Apocalypse
(1961) MGM
Set in occupied France during WWII, the tale revolves around a French family whose members swear opposite political allegiances. **Cast:** Glenn Ford, Ingrid Thulin, Lee J. Cobb, Yvette Mimieux, Charles Boyer, Paul Henreid, Paul Lukas. **Credits:** Dir: Vincente Minnelli; Prod: Julian C. Blaustein; Writer: Robert Ardrey, John Gay; DP: Milton Krasner; Ed: Adrienne Fazan, Ben Lewis; Prod Design: George W. Davis, Urie McCleary, Elliot Scott; Composer: Andre Previn. Color, 154 min. VHS

Four Hours to Kill
(1935) Paramount
Melodrama set in the lobby of a midtown Manhattan theater. Characters—an expectant father, an escaped convict, the detective handcuffed to the convict, a rich woman and her lover, a hat-check boy and the usherette who is blackmailing him—all come and go as their stories intertwine. **Cast:** Richard Barthelmess, Roscoe Karns, Lois Kent, Joe Morrison, Helen Mack, Gertrude Michael, Ray Milland, Bruce Mitchell, Henry Travers, Dorothy Tree. **Credits:** Dir: Mitchell Leisen; Prod: Arthur Hornblow, Jr.; Writer: Norman Krasna; DP: Theodor Sparkuhl; Ed: John Harrison; Composer: Ralph Rainger, Leo Robin. B&W, 71 min.

Four Jacks and a Jill
(1942) RKO
Four musicians search for a new singer when the gangster boyfriend of their current one disallows her to continue playing in the band. Their new recruit (Shirley) is an innocent type who has drawn the attentions of a cab driver who claims to be a king. A remake of both *That Girl from Paris* and *Street Girl.* **Cast:** Ray Bolger, Anne Shirley, June Havoc, Desi Arnaz, Jack Durant, Eddie Foy, Jr., Fritz Feld, Henry Daniell. **Credits:** Dir: Jack Hively; Prod: John Twist; Writer: John Twist; DP: Russell Metty; Ed: George Hively. B&W, 68 min. VHS

Four Jills in a Jeep
(1944) Fox
Francis, Landis, Raye, and Mayfair reenact their own true-life experiences entertaining the troops overseas during WWII, making for musical patriotism—and a little romance added for poetic license. Jimmy Dorsey and his orchestra are on hand to back up the ladies. **Cast:** Kay Francis, Carole Landis, Martha Raye, Mitzi Mayfair, Phil Silvers, Dick Haymes, Jimmy Dorsey, John Harvey, Alice Faye, Betty Grable. **Credits:** Dir: William A. Seiter; Prod: Irving Starr; Writer: Robert Ellis, Helen Logan, Snag Werris; Story: Froma Sand, Fred Niblo; DP: Peverell Marley; Ed: Ray Curtiss; Prod Design: James Basevi, Albert Hogsett; Composer: Emil Newman, Charles Henderson. Color, 89 min. VHS

Four Men and a Prayer
(1938) Fox
Ford follows the four Leigh brothers (Greene, Sanders, Niven, and Henry) as they circle the globe in effort to clear their name and solve the murder of their beloved father, disgraced military hero Colonel Loring Leigh (Smith). The far-ranging settings and wide spectrum of characters encountered, from London to South America to Egypt to the United States, leave room enough for romance between Young

and Greene. **Cast:** Loretta Young, Richard Greene, George Sanders, David Niven, C. Aubrey Smith, J. Edward Bromberg, William Henry, John Carradine, Alan Hale, Reginald Denny. **Credits:** Dir: John Ford; Prod: Darryl F. Zannuck, Kenneth MacGowan; Writer: Walter Ferris, Sonya Levien, Richard Sherman, William Faulkner, David Garth; DP: Ernest Palmer; Ed: Louis Loeffler; Prod Design: Bernard Herzbrun, Rudolph Sternad; Composer: Louis Silvers. B&W, 85 min.

Four Mothers

(1941) Warner Bros.
This sequel to *Four Daughters* and *Four Wives* follows the Lemp sisters (played by the Lane sisters) into adulthood. Husbands and babies abound, but when their father, Adam (Rains), has the entire town investing in the real estate deal proposed by Thea's husband Ben (McHugh), things suddenly look grim. The market collapses and the Lemp family is responsible for the economic ruin of their community. Luckily, the other husbands are a strong, self-reliant crew and with a little hard work (another baby, too) they're able to set everything right. **Cast:** Eddie Albert, Dick Foran, Gale Lane, Lola Lane, Priscilla Lane, Rosemary Lane, Vera Lewis, Jeffrey Lynn, Frank McHugh, Gale Page. **Credits:** Dir: William Keighley; Writer: Stephen Morehouse Avery; Story: Fannie Hurst; DP: Charles Rosher; Ed: Ralph Dawson. B&W, 85 min.

The Four Musketeers

(1975) Fox
Chapter two of Lester's winking, rollicking takes on Dumas's famous swordsmen, produced at the same time as his *Three Musketeers* with the same leads. Great swordplay (executed by the stars; York claims each was injured during shooting) and two great female stars in Dunaway and Welch. **Cast:** Oliver Reed, Raquel Welch, Richard Chamberlain, Frank Finlay, Faye Dunaway, Michael York, Charlton Heston, Christopher Lee, Jean-Pierre Cassel, Sybil Danning. **Credits:** Dir: Richard Lester; Prod: Alexander Salkind, Ilya Salkind; Writer: George MacDonald Fraser; Story: Alexandre Dumas; DP: David Watkin; Ed: John Victor Smith; Prod Design: Brian Eatwell; Composer: Lalo Schifrin. Color, 160 min. VHS, DVD

The Four Poster

(1952) Columbia
Staged as a series of seven bedroom vignettes, this drama of a married couple's ups and downs is adapted from the stage play of the same name. With the master bedroom's great four-poster bed as the visual and symbolic center of this self-consciously theatrical production, Harrison and Palmer feel their way with humor and pathos through the formative events of their union—childrearing, infidelities, and the losing of a son in WWI. Interspersed with the drama are animated shorts, which offer a quirky commentary on this human comedy. **Cast:** Rex Harrison, Lilli Palmer. **Credits:** Dir: Irving Reis; Prod: Stanley Kramer; Writer: Allan Scott; Story: Jane De Hertog; DP: Hal Mohr; Ed: Henry Batista; Prod Design: Rudolph Sternad; Composer: Dimitri Tiomkin. B&W, 103 min.

Four's a Crowd

(1938) Warner Bros.
Flynn plays against type in this screwball comedy, playing handsome PR wizard Robert Kensington Lanford. Lanford's out to make his name by giving greedy robber baron John Dillingwell (Connolly) the public relations makeover of all time. All it will take is the help of newspaperman Patterson Buckley (Knowles) and dame reporter Jean Cristy (Russell). When Dillingwell's beautiful daughter Lorri (de Havilland) gets mixed up in the plot, the flirting flies fast and furious. Lanford and Buckley hope to get the girls and the old man wants his image. **Cast:** Errol Flynn, Olivia de Havilland, Rosalind Russell, Patric Knowles, Walter Connolly, Melville Cooper, Franklin Pangborn, Herman Bing, Joseph Crehan, Dennie Moore. **Credits:** Dir: Michael Curtiz; Prod: Hal B. Wallis; Writer: Sig Herzig, Casey Robinson, Wallace Sullivan; DP: Ernest Haller; Ed: Clarence Kolster; Prod Design: Max Parker; Composer: Leo F. Forbstein. B&W, 92 min.

Fourteen Hours

(1951) Fox
Filmed in semidocumentary style, this is a tense drama about a troubled young man (Basehart) who threatens to throw himself off of the ledge of a New York skyscraper. The action centers around a cop (Douglas) who attempts to talk him out of it. Basehart wants nothing to do with smothering mother Moorehead or girlfriend Bel Geddes. Many vignettes are presented of New York characters whose lives are changed by the spectacle. In her first film, Kelly plays a wife who decides not to sign a divorce agreement as she watches from a law office. Watch for Ossie Davis as a cabby. The story is based on the real-life suicide of John Warde, who jumped 17 floors from the Hotel Gotham on July 26, 1938, after attempts by cops to dissuade him. **Cast:** Paul Douglas, Richard Basehart, Barbara Bel Geddes, Debra Paget, Agnes Moorehead, Robert Keith, Howard Da Silva, Jeffrey Hunter, Martin Gabel, Grace Kelly. **Credits:** Dir: Henry Hathaway; Prod: Sol Siegel; Writer: John Paxton, Joel Sayre; DP: Joseph MacDonald; Ed: Dorothy Spencer; Prod Design: Leland Fuller, Lyle Wheeler; Composer: Alfred Newman. B&W, 92 min.

Four Wives

(1939) Warner Bros.
In this uplifting sequel to *Four Daughters*, one of the sisters, Ann Lemp, played by Priscilla Lane, finds another husband, while the other sisters all discover motherhood. The drama hinges on Lane's discovering—on the day of her new engagement—that she is to be the mother of her former husband's child. The story unfolds in a tender, yet believable manner that moves toward a happy ending. **Cast:** Claude Rains, Jeffrey Lynn, John Garfield, Eddie Albert, Frank McHugh, May Robson, Gale Page, Dick Foran, Henry O'Neill, Vera Lewis. **Credits:** Dir: Michael Curtiz; Prod: Hal B. Wallis; Writer: Julius J. Epstein, Philip G. Epstein, Maurice Hanline; DP: Sol Polito; Ed: Ralph Dawson; Composer: Max Steiner. B&W, 110 min.

The Foxes of Harrow

(1947) Fox
A gambler wins a large New Orleans estate in a card game. He meets a society woman and marries her, but the marriage dissolves when the woman confronts the gambler's past. The gambler leaves, their son is killed, and the woman runs the estate. Her husband returns before a bad crop nearly ruins the place and the couple bond anew. Academy Award Nominations: Best Art Direction. **Cast:** Vanessa Brown, Joseph Crehan, William B. Davis, Rex Harrison, Richard Haydn, Gene Lockhart, Celia Lovsky, Victor McLaglen, Patricia Medina, Maureen O'Hara. **Credits:** Dir: John M. Stahl; Prod: William A. Bacher; Writer: Wanda Tuchock; Story: Frank Yerby; DP: Joseph LaShelle; Ed: James B. Clark; Prod Design: Paul S. Fox, Thomas Little; Composer: David Buttolph, Alfred Newman; Art Director: Maurice Ransford, Lyle Wheeler. B&W, 117 min.

F.P.1

(1932) Fox
This is the English-language edition of *F.P.1 Doesn't Answer*, which was filmed simultaneously in German with a German cast and in English with a different cast. Colossal Floating Platform 1 is a mid-Atlantic airport refueling station that's being sabotaged and, a pilot's determined to stop it in this early sci-fi thriller. Peter Lorre had the Veidt role in the German version. **Cast:** Conrad Veidt, Jill Esmond, Leslie Fenton, George Merritt, Donald Calthrop. **Credits:** Dir: Karl Hartl; Prod: Erich Pommer; Writer: Curt Siodmak, Walter Reisch, Robert Stevenson, Peter Macfarlane; DP: Gunther Rittau, Konstantin Tochet; Prod Design: Erich Kettelhut; Composer: Allan Gray. B&W, 74 min. **VHS**

Francis (The Talking Mule)

The notion of a film series based on a talking beast of burden may on its face seem preposterous, but the Francis (The Talking Mule) series showed America gamely trying to laugh at its recent wartime experience. It certainly wasn't lost on the ex-serviceman audience that the army mule shared a voice with the general (Chill Wills) in *Francis Joins the WACs* (1954). The acerbic Francis teamed up with West Point cadet G.I. Peter Sterling (Donald O'Connor) in the first film of the series, *Francis* (1949), to crack a Nazi spy ring. Sterling, formerly thought to be quite mad by his fellow cadets (due to his insistence that Francis did indeed posses the gift of gab) becomes a hero, and Francis gets . . . an extra bag of oats. O'Connor and director Arthur Lubin (who later directed TV's *Mr. Ed!*) left the series before the last installment (1956's *Francis in the Haunted House*), but you'll recognize Francis's new pal in that film as young Mickey Rooney.

Francis *(1949)*
Francis Goes to the Races *(1951)*
Francis Goes to West Point *(1952)*
Francis Covers the Big Town *(1953)*
Francis Joins the WACs *(1954)*
Francis in the Navy *(1955)*
Francis in the Haunted House *(1956)*

Frankenstein

(1931) Universal
The monster that mocked the sanctity of God's creation and brought ruin to his mad-scientist master firmly established a fertile movie genre and saved a studio in the bargain. Though the definitive monster movie, it succeeds purely because of the glimmer of humanity that Karloff allows us to see through the stitching and bolts, and the pathos of a barely human consciousness trapped in a hideous body. The versions available since the late '80s have restored the famously brutal sequence of the monster's encounter with a little girl at a lake shore. The laserdisc offers trailers, photos, and study sequences. Those interested in the career of the movie's director will want to search for *Gods and Monsters* (1998), an impeccably played portrait of Whale. Followed by *Bride of Frankenstein*, possibly an even better movie if not the equal in historical importance. **Cast:** Boris Karloff, Colin Clive, Mae Clarke, John Boles, Dwight Frye, Edward Van Sloan, Frederick Kerr, Lionel Belmore, Michael Mark, Marilyn Harris. **Credits:** Dir: James Whale; Prod: Carl Laemmle; Writer: Garrett Fort, Francis Edward Faragoh, John L. Balderston, Robert Florey; Story: Mary Shelley, Peggy Webling; DP: Arthur Edeson; Ed: Maurice Pivar, Clarence Kolster; Prod Design: Charles D. Hall; Composer: David Broekman. B&W, 71 min. **VHS, LASER**

Frankenstein Meets the Wolfman

(1942) Universal
It's Lugosi's turn to play the monster in this fourth installment of Universal's monster skein. On a moonlit night, grave robbers unwittingly unearth the tomb of the Wolfman, who then begins a desperate search for a cure for his "condition." The search eventually leads him to a climactic confrontation with, of all creatures, Frankenstein's monster. Sequel to *Ghost of Frankenstein* and *The Wolf Man*; later followed by *House of Frankenstein*. **Cast:** Lon Chaney, Jr., Bela Lugosi, Patric Knowles, Lionel Atwill, Maria Ouspenskaya, Ilona Massey, Dennis Hoey, Don Barclay, Rex Evans, Dwight Frye. **Credits:** Dir: Roy William Neill; Prod: George Waggner; Writer: Curt Siodmak; DP: George Robinson; Ed: Edward Curtiss; Prod Design: John B. Goodman; Composer: Hans J. Salter. B&W, 73 min. **VHS, LASER**

Frankie and Johnny

(1936) Republic
The first version of the ill-fated love story of Frankie and Johnny, this musical features Morgan singing "Frankie and Johnny" to the accompaniment of the Victor Young Orchestra. **Cast:** Helen Morgan, Chester Morris, Florence Reed, Walter Kingsford, William Harrigan, John Larkin, Cora Witherspoon, Lilyan Tashman. **Credits:** Dir: Chester Erskine, John H. Auer; Prod: William Saal; Writer: Moss Hart, Lou Goldberg; Story: Jack Kirkland; DP: Joseph Ruttenberg; Composer: Victor Young. B&W, 67 min. **VHS**

Frankie and Johnny

(1966) United Artists
Elvis pairs with Douglas of TV's *The Beverly Hillbillies* for a romantic musical set on a riverboat. Presley plays a riverboat gambler down on his luck and out of a girlfriend when he becomes involved with a redhead, a Gypsy, and a roulette wheel. Features some uncharacteristic Elvis songs such as "When the Saints Go Marchin' In" and "Down by the Riverside." **Cast:** Elvis Presley, Donna Douglas, Harry Morgan, Sue Ane Langdon, Nancy Kovack, Audrey Christie, Jerome Cowan, Robert Strauss, Anthony Eisley. **Credits:** Dir: Frederick De Cordova; Prod: Edward Small; Writer: Alex Gottlieb; Story: Nat Perrin; DP: Jacques Marquette; Ed: Grant Whytock; Prod Design: Walter M. Simonds; Composer: Fred Karger. Color, 88 min. **VHS**

Freaks

(1932) MGM
Browning's cult classic about the close-knit world of carnival performers and sideshow "freaks" has oddly touching moments along with the shock value. One of the midgets in the show falls for a beautiful acrobat, and is overjoyed when she agrees to marry him. But her apparent affection is merely a cover for her sinister plans, which lead to a horrifying conclusion. Not for everyone's tastes, but there are scenes of immense power that stand up strongly to modern "shock" pictures. It's even selected as a National Film Registry Outstanding Film. **Cast:** Wallace Ford, Olga Baclanova, Leila Hyams, Roscoe Ates, Henry Victor, Daisy Earles, Harry Earles, Rose Dione, Daisy and Violet Hilton. **Credits:** Dir: Tod Browning; Prod: Tod Browning; Writer: Willis Goldbeck, Leon Gordon, Edgar Allan Woolf, Al Boasberg; DP: Merritt Gerstad; Ed: Basil Wrangell. B&W, 66 min. **VHS, LASER**

Freaky Friday

(1977) Disney
It could only happen on Friday the 13th. While simultaneously desiring that they could change places, a mother and daughter experience a strange miracle—their wish is granted. The result of their realized fantasy is a great amount of magical fun in this live-action Disney comedy.

Cast: Barbara Harris, Jodie Foster, John Astin, Dick Van Patten, Kaye Ballard, Ruth Buzzi, Patsy Kelly, Sorrell Booke, Marie Windsor. **Dir:** Gary Nelson; Writer: Mary Rodgers; Ed: Cotton Warburton; Prod Design: John B. Mansbridge; Composer: Johnny Mandel; Costumes: Chuck Keehne, Evelyn Kennedy; SFX: Eustace Lycett, Danny Lee, Art Cruickshank; Art Director: Jack Senter; Set Designer: Robert R. Benton. Color, 98 min. VHS, LASER

Free and Easy
(1930) MGM
A grease monkey–"talent manager" takes a young beauty-contest winner and her frightening mother from Kansas to Hollywood. They manage to get on the MGM lot, where they disrupt sets, wreak scenes, bedevil directors, and ultimately gain some unexpected notices of their own. Interesting Keaton vehicle with glimpses of the real Hollywood during the early talkie period. **Cast:** Buster Keaton, Anita Page, Robert Montgomery, Edgar Dearing, Lionel Barrymore, Dorothy Sebastian, Trixie Friganza. **Credits:** Dir: Edward Sedgwick; Writer: Richard Schayer, Al Boasberg, Paul Dickey; DP: Leonard Smith; Ed: William LeVanway, George Todd. B&W, 92 min. VHS

A Free Soul
(1931) MGM
Barrymore shines as an alcoholic lawyer who successfully defends dashing gangster Gable on a murder charge only to find that his headstrong daughter has fallen in love with his client. He makes her a deal: he'll stop drinking if she'll stop seeing Ace. She agrees to the arrangement, but begins to see the criminal again after her father goes back to the bottle—though she later comes to see the mobster's less-than-dashing side. Remade as *The Girl Who Has Everything* (1953). Based on a book by Adela Rogers St. John. **Academy Awards:** Best Actor: Lionel Barrymore. **Cast:** Norma Shearer, Lionel Barrymore, Clark Gable, Leslie Howard, James Gleason, Lucy Beaumont, Claire Whitney, Frank Sheridan, E. Alyn Warren, George Irving. **Credits:** Dir: Clarence Brown; Writer: John Meehan; Ed: Hugh Wynn; Composer: William Axt. B&W, 91 min. VHS

The French Connection
(1971) Fox
This account of one of the largest U.S. drug busts at the time, loosely based on a true story and Robin Moore's book, features one of the most famous chase scenes in film history, as cars careen below the elevated train tracks dodging city traffic. The chase begins when a pair of hard-boiled New York City narcotics detectives uncover an elaborate heroin-smuggling ring headed by a French crime boss. Hackman makes a lasting impression as tough-guy cop Popeye Doyle. Wunderkind Friedkin made his commercial breakthrough and won an Oscar for Best Director. The sequel, *French Connection II* (1975), directed by John Frankenheimer, is okay, too. Academy Award Nominations: 8, including Best Supporting Actor: Roy Scheider; Best Cinematography. **Academy Awards:** Best Director; Best Actor: Gene Hackman; Best Film Editing; Best Picture; Best Screenplay Based on Material from Another Medium. **Cast:** Gene Hackman, Fernando Rey, Roy Scheider, Tony Lo Bianco, Bill Hickman, Marcel Bozzufi, Frederic de Pasquale, Ann Rebbot, Harold Gary, Sonny Grosso. **Credits:** Dir: William Friedkin, Philip D'Antoni; Writer: Ernest Tidyman; DP: Owen Roizman; Ed: Jerry Greenberg; Prod Design: Ben Kazaskow; Composer: Don Ellis. Color, 102 min. VHS, LASER

French Connection II
(1975) Fox
New York City police detective Popeye Doyle travels to France in pursuit of the heroin kingpin whom he failed to capture in the first French Connection movie. After he is captured by dealers, Doyle is forced to become an addict himself. Hackman, once again, delivers a riveting performance. **Cast:** Gene Hackman, Fernando Rey, Bernard Fresson, Cathleen Nesbitt. **Credits:** Dir: John Frankenheimer, Robert L. Rosen; Writer: Alexander Jacobs, Robert Dillon, Laurie Dillon; DP: Claude Renoir; Ed: Tom Rolf; Prod Design: Jacques Saulnier, Georges Glon; Composer: Don Ellis; Costumes: Jacques Fonteray; SFX: Logan Frazee; Art Director: Gerard Viard. Color, 119 min. VHS, LASER

Frenchman's Creek
(1944) Paramount
A Daphne du Maurier novel brought to glorious, colorful life by Leisen features a lovely aristocrat fleeing a wimpy husband and his sinister pals—straight into the arms of a pirate. This proto-bodice-ripper set in 17th-century England offers astounding sets, costumes, and score, satisfying romantic melodrama, and swash-buckling action. **Academy Awards:** Best Art Direction. **Cast:** Joan Fontaine, Arturo De Cordova, Basil Rathbone, Nigel Bruce, Cecil Kellaway, Ralph Forbes, Billy Daniels, Moyna MacGill, Mary Field, Charles Coleman. **Credits:** Dir: Mitchell Leisen; Prod: B.G. DeSylva; Writer: Talbot Jennings; Story: Daphne du Maurier; DP: George Barnes; Ed: Alma Macrorie; Prod Design: Hans Dreier; Composer: Victor Young; Costumes: Raoul Pene Du Bois; SFX: Gordon Jennings; Art Director: Ernst Fegte; Set Designer: Sam Comer. Color, 112 min. VHS

French Quarter
(1977) Crown
Down in New Orleans where the jazz is hot and the magic is deadly, a beautiful woman takes a trip back in time to a world of decadence and voodoo. Not seen often, but interesting and worthwhile. **Cast:** Lance Le Gault, Alisha Fontaine, Bruce Davison, Virginia Mayo, Lindsay Bloom, Anne Michelle. **Credits:** Dir: Dennis Kane; Prod: Dennis Kane; Writer: Barney Cohen, Dennis Kane; DP: Jerry Kalogeratos; Ed: George T. Norris, Ed Fricke; Choreographer: Donnis Hunnicutt; Composer: Dick Hyman; Costumes: Ellen Mirojnick. Color, 101 min. VHS

Frenzy
(1972) Universal
Hitchcock goes mod with this blackly comic story about a sex criminal— the "Necktie Killer"—plaguing post-Carnaby London. Naturally, an innocent man who is suspected by police as the murderer must fight to nab the real perpetrator and clear his name. Although it didn't do well at the box office, this marked a striking return to form for the famed director, following a series of lackluster pictures. **Cast:** Jon Finch, Alec McCowen, Barry Foster, Anna Massey, Barbara Leigh-Hunt, Vivien Merchant, Billie Whitelaw. **Credits:** Dir: Alfred Hitchcock; Prod: Alfred Hitchcock; Writer: Anthony Shaffer; Story: Arthur LaBern; DP: Gilbert Taylor; Ed: John Jympson; Prod Design: Syd Cain; Composer: Ron Goodwin; Set Designer: Simon Wakefield. Color, 116 min. VHS, LASER

Freud
(1962) Universal
Vienna doctor Sigmund Freud takes an extended leave from his position at the Vienna General Hospital to pursue his studies in hypnotherapy. His work in this area unites him with Dr. Joseph Breuer. Together they begin to analyze Cecily Koertner and Carl Von

Schlossen. Cecily is a sexually repressed woman suffering from acute cases of hysteria and father fixation. Von Schlossen, who attempted to murder his father, suffers from repressed desire to sexually consummate his relationship with his mother. Both cases offer the young Freud a starting point from which develop his later, groundbreaking theories of sexuality and human psychology. **Cast:** Montgomery Clift, Susannah York, Susan Kohner, Eileen Herlie, Fernand Ledoux, David McCallum, Rosalie Crutchley, David Kossoff, Joseph Furst, Larry Parks. **Credits:** Dir: John Huston; Prod: Wolfgang Reinhardt; Writer: Charles Kaufman, Wolfgang Reinhardt, Jean-Paul Sartre; DP: Douglas Slocombe; Ed: Ralph Kemplen; Prod Design: Stephen B. Grimes; Composer: Jerry Goldsmith. B&W, 139 min.

Friendly Persuasion
(1956) Allied Artists
The tranquil existence of a family of Quakers living in Indiana during the time of the Civil War is shattered when one of the sons decides to enlist in the army. His decision raises difficult questions about courage and faith, and the evil of violence. While the patriarch of the clan competes with a friend to be the first to church on Sundays, his son is torn between his faith in nonviolence and his desire to prove his bravery in battle. Written without credit by blacklisted writer Michael Wilson. **Cast:** Gary Cooper, Anthony Perkins, Dorothy McGuire, Marjorie Main, Mark Richman, Richard Eyer, Robert Middleton, Walter Catlett. **Credits:** Dir: William Wyler; Prod: William Wyler; Writer: Michael Wilson; Story: Jessamyn West; DP: Ellsworth Fredericks; Ed: Robert W. Swink, Edward A. Biery, Robert Belcher; Prod Design: Ted Haworth; Composer: Dimitri Tiomkin; Costumes: Dorothy Jeakins; Set Designer: Joseph Kish. Color, 138 min. **VHS, LASER**

Frisco Jenny
(1933) Warner Bros.
Chatterton portrays the daughter of a San Francisco saloonkeeper orphaned during the 1906 earthquake. The story traverses her giving birth to an illegitimate son, who is then adopted by a wealthy family, follows her emergence as a financially successful bordello proprietress and underworld power, and her demise as she kills a crony who would have murdered her son. **Cast:** Ruth Chatterton, Donald Cook, James Murray, Louis Calhern, Frank McGlynn, J. Pat O'Malley,

Robert Warwick, Harold Huber, Helen Jerome Eddy, Hallam Cooley. **Credits:** Dir: William Wellman; Prod: Raymond Griffith; Writer: Robert Lord, Wilson Mizner; Story: John Larkin, Lillie Hayward, Gerald Beaumont; DP: Sid Hickox; Ed: James B. Morley; Costumes: Orry-Kelly; Art Director: Robert M. Haas. B&W, 70 min.

The Frisco Kid
(1979) Warner Bros.
Mild comedy as a sweetly innocent Polish rabbi travels through 1850s America, and forms an uneasy alliance with an inept outlaw bank robber on his way to his new congregation and wife in San Francisco. **Cast:** Gene Wilder, Harrison Ford, Ramon Bieri, Penny Peyser, Leo Fuchs, Val Bisoglio, George Dicenzo, William Smith, Jack Somack. **Credits:** Dir: Robert Aldrich; Prod: Mace Neufeld; Writer: Michael Elias, Frank Shaw; DP: Robert B. Hauser; Ed: Maury Winetrobe, Irving C. Rosenblum; Prod Design: Terence Marsh, Josan F. Russo; Composer: Frank DeVol. Color, 119 min. **VHS**

From Here to Eternity
(1953) Columbia
Landmark example of Hollywood melodrama at its finest. An all-star cast brought what was considered an unfilmable novel to the screen with skill and grace. The story portrays the loves, hopes, and dreams of those in a close-knit army barracks in Hawaii shortly before the attack on Pearl Harbor. Clift plays a former boxer who refuses to fight after blinding a friend in the ring and is sent to the remote outpost as punishment for his insubordination. Reed plays spectacularly against type as a bar girl who comforts Clift. Lancaster and Kerr have their illicit sprawl in the surf, and Sinatra makes a remarkable movie-career rebound. A big story with performances to match. Based on the novel by James Jones. Golden Globes for Best Director; Best Supporting Actor: Frank Sinatra. Academy Award Nominations: 13, including Best Actor: Montgomery Clift; Best Actor: Burt Lancaster; Best Actress: Deborah Kerr; Best Score. **Academy Awards:** Best Director; Best Supporting Actor: Frank Sinatra; Best Supporting Actress: Donna Reed; Best Film Editing; Best Sound Recording; Best Black-and-White Cinematography; Best Picture. **Cast:** Burt Lancaster, Montgomery Clift, Deborah Kerr, Donna Reed, Frank Sinatra, Ernest Borgnine, Philip Ober, Jack Warden, Mickey Shaughnessy. **Credits:** Dir: Fred Zinnemann; Prod: Buddy Adler;

Writer: Daniel Taradash; DP: Burnett Guffey; Ed: William A. Lyon; Composer: George Duning; Costumes: Jean Louis; Art Director: Cary Odell; Set Designer: Frank Tuttle. B&W, 118 min. **VHS, LASER**

From the Terrace
(1960) Fox
The melodramatic story of one man's single-minded pursuit of the American Dream—and his eventual rejection of that world, once he's gained his final victory. Newman is Alfred Eaton, a man married to old money and on his way up the corporate ladder in a successful Wall Street firm. But Eaton's dissatisfaction with the values that once ruled his life and his illicit love affair with a like-minded young woman turn his world upside down at the moment of his greatest reward. **Cast:** Paul Newman, Joanne Woodward, Myrna Loy, Ina Balin, Leon Ames, Barbara Eden, George Grizzard, Elizabeth Allen, Patrick O'Neal, Felix Aylmer. **Credits:** Dir: Mark Robson; Prod: Mark Robson; Writer: Ernest Lehman; Story: John O'Hara; DP: Leo Tover; Ed: Dorothy Spencer; Prod Design: Lyle Wheeler; Composer: Elmer Bernstein; Costumes: Travilla; SFX: James B. Gordon, L. B. Abbott; Set Designer: Walter M. Scott, Paul S. Fox. Color, 144 min. **VHS, LASER**

From This Day Forward
(1946) RKO
A dramatic story of a marriage told through a flashback. A couple meet and fall in love in the Bronx tenements. They marry, but he soon loses his job. The wife must support both of them on her meager salary as a bookstore clerk. The husband does find a job but is subsequently drafted for the war. The flashback ends at the employment office, where it looks as if he will get a good job. **Cast:** Joan Fontaine, Bobby Driscoll, Mary Treen, Mark Stevens, Harry Morgan, Wally Brown, Rosemary DeCamp, Queenie Smith. **Credits:** Dir: John Berry; Prod: William Pereira, Alfred Herman; Writer: Thomas Bell, Hugo Butler, Garson Kanin, Charles Schnee, Edith Sommer; DP: George Barnes; Ed: Frank Doyle; Composer: Leigh Harline; Art Director: Albert S. D'Agostino. B&W, 95 min.

The Front
(1976) Columbia
A dark comedy set in the Hollywood blacklist days of the '50s. Allen couldn't be better as a bookie, desperately in need of cash to cover his losses, who agrees to do a favor for

his old schoolfriend Alfred, a blacklisted screenwriter who wants Allen to "sign" his screenplays so they can be produced. What starts out as a favor becomes a career when Allen's pool of writers and screenplays becomes larger. The director, writer, and some of the performers were themselves blacklisted. Academy Award Nominations: Best Screenplay. **Cast:** Woody Allen, Zero Mostel, Herschel Bernardi, Michael Murphy, Andrea Marcovicci, Lloyd Gough, Remak Ramsay. **Credits:** Dir: Martin Ritt; Prod: Martin Ritt; Writer: Walter Bernstein; DP: Michael Chapman; Ed: Sidney Levin; Prod Design: Charles Bailey; Composer: Dave Grusin. Color, 94 min. **VHS, LASER**

Frontier Marshal
(1939) Fox
Using equal parts dramatic action, gunplay, and romantic tension, this melodramatic Western tells the story of the infamous Wyatt Earp and his arrival in Tombstone, Arizona. Earp, played by reliably photogenic Scott, arrives in Tombstone and takes over as marshal. After a brush with outlaw Romero, Wyatt sets out to avenge his loss and bring law and order to Tombstone. **Cast:** Randolph Scott, Nancy Kelly, Cesar Romero, Binnie Barnes, John Carradine, Edward Norris, Eddie Foy, Jr., Ward Bond, Lon Chaney, Jr., Chris-Pin Martin. **Credits:** Dir: Allan Dwan; Prod: Sol M. Wurtzel; Writer: Sam Hellman, Stuart N. Lake; DP: Charles G. Clarke; Ed: Red Allen. B&W, 72 min.

The Front Page
(1931) United Artists
The first screen version of the successful Hecht-MacArthur play. In 1920s Chicago, ace reporter Hildy Johnson is rescued from the brink of retirement by his fast-talking editor, who needs Hildy to cover "one last" story: the politically charged execution of a cop-killing radical. Interesting contrast to the remake, *His Girl Friday* (1940), particularly in the handling of the familiar roles by Menjou and O'Brien, and, in some ways, as enjoyable. Academy Award Nominations: Best Picture; Best Actor: Adolphe Menjou; Best Director. **Cast:** Adolphe Menjou, Pat O'Brien, Mary Brian, Mae Clarke, Edward Everett Horton, Walter Catlett, George E. Stone, Slim Summerville, Matt Moore, Frank McHugh. **Credits:** Dir: Lewis Milestone; Prod: Howard Hughes; Writer: Bartlett Cormack, Ben Hecht, Charles Lederer; Story: Ben Hecht, Charles MacArthur; DP: Glen MacWilliams, Hal Mohr, Tony

Gaudio; Ed: Duncan Mansfield; Prod Design: Richard Day. B&W, 101 min. **VHS**

The Front Page
(1974) Universal
The crack comedy team of Wilder, Lemmon, and Matthau take on the film and stage warhorse. A ruthless managing editor of a Chicago newspaper angrily learns his ace reporter plans to leave the paper to get married. While he trains a replacement, all hell breaks loose and a convicted killer escapes from right under the nose of the bumbling sheriff and gives the reporter an irresistible exclusive interview. **Cast:** Jack Lemmon, Walter Matthau, Vincent Gardenia, Susan Sarandon, Allen Garfield, David Wayne, Charles Durning, Austin Pendleton, Carol Burnett, Herb Edelman. **Credits:** Dir: Billy Wilder; Prod: Paul Monash; Writer: Billy Wilder, I. A. L. Diamond; Story: Ben Hecht, Charles MacArthur; DP: Jordan Cronenweth; Ed: Ralph E. Winters; Prod Design: Henry Bumstead; Composer: Billy May. Color, 105 min. **VHS, LASER**

Front Page Woman
(1935) Warner Bros.
Romantic comedy about two rival newspaper reporters who were once romantically involved. (The relationship suffers because the man thinks women shouldn't be reporters.) When a high-profile murder occurs, she gets the scoop. He challenges her to find the murderer. As the murder trial of one suspect ends, he plots a way to discover the verdict before it is announced and tells her the opposite of what it is. She falls for the con, prints the incorrect verdict, and gets fired. Still, she thinks the wrong man was sentenced. Eventually, she gets a confession from the real killer and gains the opportunity to win back her job. **Cast:** Joseph Crehan, Dorothy Dare, Bette Davis, George Brent, Roscoe Karns, June Martel, J. Carrol Naish, Winifred Shaw, Walter Walker, Gordon Westcott. **Credits:** Dir: Michael Curtiz; Prod: Samuel Bishoff; Writer: Roy Chanslor, Laird Doyle, Lillie Hayward, Richard Macaulay; DP: Tony Gaudio; Ed: Terry Morse; Prod Design: John Hughes; Composer: Leo F. Forbstein. B&W, 81 min.

The Fugitive
(1947) RKO
Fonda gives one of his greatest performances as a Catholic priest who finds himself pursued by the military when his Latin American country outlaws religion. His faith and loyalty

compel him to remain with the peasants he ministers to even as the new government forces him to become a fugitive. Ford considered it one of his best works, and the critics of the time compared it favorably to *The Informer*, but it undeservedly receives far less notice today. Based on Greene's novel *The Power and the Glory*. **Cast:** Henry Fonda, Dolores Del Rio, Pedro Armendariz, J. Carrol Naish, Leo Carrillo, Ward Bond, Robert Armstrong, John Qualen. **Credits:** Dir: John Ford; Prod: John Ford, Merian C. Cooper; Writer: Dudley Nichols; Story: Graham Greene; DP: Gabriel Figueroa; Ed: Jack Murray; Prod Design: Alfred Ybarra; Composer: Richard Hageman. B&W, 99 min. **VHS, LASER**

The Fugitive Kind
(1959) United Artists
This film adaptation of Williams's play *Orpheus Descending* follows wanderer Brando to a sleepy southern town, where his brooding sexual magnetism ignites the passions of three of the town's women—with tragic consequences. Uneven results, but the chance to watch some of the screen's finest actors in Brando, Magnani, Woodward, and Stapleton. **Cast:** Marlon Brando, Anna Magnani, Joanne Woodward, Maureen Stapleton, Victor Jory, R. G. Armstrong, Emory Richardson, Madame Spivy, Sally Gracie, Lucille Benson. **Credits:** Dir: Sidney Lumet; Prod: Martin Jurow, Richard Shepherd; Writer: Meade Roberts, Tennessee Williams; DP: Boris Kaufman; Ed: Carl Lerner; Prod Design: Richard Sylbert; Composer: Kenyon Hopkins. B&W, 135 min. **VHS**

Full of Life
(1956) Columbia
This charming domestic comedy puts nonbelieving Emily Rocco (Holliday) in the household of her very Catholic in-laws. Emily's husband Nick (Conte) is a starving writer, forced to depend on his father's assistance. When pregnant Emily falls through a hole in the floor, Papa decides to build the couple a new fireplace. Mama (Minciotti) won't be satisfied until the couple says their vows all over again in front of the altar, this time. Holliday sparkles with beauty and a bad temper. **Cast:** Judy Holliday, Richard Conte, Salvatore Baccaloni, Esther Minciotti, Silvio Minciotti. **Credits:** Dir: Richard Quine; Prod: Fred Kohlmar; Writer: John Fante; DP: Charles Lawton; Ed: Charles Nelson; Prod Design: William Flannery; Composer: George Duning. B&W, 91 min.

Funny Face (1957)

Funny Face
(1957) Paramount
A photographer and a fashion editor, looking for a fresh face to grace the pages of their magazine, discover an alluring, intellectual bohemian in a Greenwich Village bookstore. But both the charming gamine and the cynical photographer are in for the surprise—and the romance—of their lives as they discover that they've jumped to some wrong conclusions about themselves and others . . . and that Paris in the springtime is delightful indeed. This Gershwin musical was to be produced by MGM but was given to Paramount so that Hepburn could star. Academy Award Nominations: 4, including Best Screenplay, Best Cinematography. **Cast:** Fred Astaire, Audrey Hepburn, Kay Thompson, Suzy Parker, Michel Auclair, Robert Flemyng. **Credits:** Dir: Stanley Donen; Prod: Roger Edens; Writer: Leonard Gershe; DP: Ray June; Ed: Frank Bracht; Prod Design: George W. Davis; Choreographer: Fred Astaire, Eugene Loring; Composer: George Gershwin, Ira Gershwin, Roger Edens, Leonard Gershe; Costumes: Edith Head, Hubert de Givenchy; SFX: John Fulton; Art Director: Hal Pereira; Set Designer: Sam Comer, Ray Moyer. Color, 103 min. **VHS**

Funny Girl
(1968) Columbia
Film debut for Streisand in a reprisal of her Broadway role as Ziegfeld star Fanny Brice in this highly fictionalized musical biopic. Brice, a poor Jewish girl from the Lower East Side, rose to fame and won audiences' hearts everywhere with her comic antics and powerful singing. Unfortunately, she had far less success in her personal life, and the film focuses on her doomed romance with her first husband, gambler Nicky Arnstein. Academy Award Nominations: 8, including Best Picture; Best Supporting Actress: Kay Medford; Best Cinematography; Best Editing. **Academy Awards:** Best Actress: Barbra Streisand. **Cast:** Barbra Streisand, Omar Sharif, Kay Medford, Anne Francis, Walter Pidgeon, Mae Questel, Gerald Mohr, Frank Faylen. **Credits:** Dir: William Wyler; Prod: Ray Stark; Writer: Isobel Lennart; DP: Harry Stradling; Ed: Maury Winetrobe, William Sands; Prod Design: Gene Callahan; Choreographer: Herbert Ross; Composer: Jule Styne, Robert Merrill; Costumes: Irene Sharaff; Art Director: Robert Luthardt; Set Designer: William Kiernan. Color, 169 min. **VHS, LASER**

Funeral in Berlin
(1966) Paramount
Second in the series of Harry Palmer spy thrillers by Len Deighton, the first being *The Ipcress File* and the third, *Billion Dollar Brain*. An intriguing spy film about an agent who is sent to Berlin to assist a possible Russian defector. More twists and turns than a Sherlock Holmes novel. **Cast:** Michael Caine, Oscar Homolka, Eva Renzi, Paul Hubschmid, Hugh Burden, Guy Doleman, Rachel Gurney. **Credits:** Dir: Guy Hamilton; Prod: Charles Kasher; Writer: Evan Jones; Story: Len Deighton; DP: Otto Heller; Ed: John Bloom; Prod Design: Ken Adam; Composer: Konrad Elfers. Color, 102 min. **VHS, LASER**

Fun in Acapulco
(1963) Paramount
Presley has his hands full as a would-be cliff diver and former aerialist attempting to simultaneously cure his acrophobia and win the hand of an aloof displaced royal (Andress). Add to the mix a pint-sized impresario hoping to break our hero as a lounge act, the inevitable swarthy romantic rival, and a sultry lady bullfighter, and you'll see why "You Can't Say No in Acapulco." Distinguished by a particularly peppy production number, "Bossa Nova Baby." **Cast:** Elvis Presley, Ursula Andress, Paul Lukas, Elsa Cardenas, Larry Domasin. **Credits:** Dir: Richard Thorpe; Prod: Hal B. Wallis; Writer: Allan Weiss; DP: Daniel Fapp; Ed: Stanley Johnson; Prod Design: Hal Pereira; Choreographer: Charles O'Curran; Composer: Joseph J. Lilley; Costumes: Edith Head; SFX: Paul K. Lerpae; Art Director: Walter Tyler; Set Designer: Sam Comer, Robert R. Benton. Color, 97 min. **VHS**

Funny Lady
(1975) Columbia
The story of vaudeville entertainer-comedian Fanny Brice after her separation from playboy millionaire Nick Arnstein, and her subsequent professional and personal relationship with Broadway producer, songwriter, and entrepreneur Billy Rose. The sequel to William Wyler's Oscar-winning *Funny Girl* (1968). Academy Award Nominations: 5, including Best Cinematography; Best Score; Best Song ("How Lucky Can You Get?"). **Cast:** Barbra Streisand, James Caan, Omar Sharif, Roddy McDowall, Ben Vereen, Carole Wells. **Credits:** Dir: Herbert Ross; Prod: Ray Stark; Writer: Arnold Schulman, Jay Allen; DP: James Wong Howe; Ed: Marion Rothman; Prod Design: George Jenkins; Choreographer: Betty Walberg; Costumes: Ray Aghayan, Bob Mackie, Shirlee Strahm; SFX: Albert J. Whitlock; Set Designer: Audrey Blasdel-Goddard. Color, 137 min. **VHS**

A Funny Thing Happened on the Way to the Forum
(1966) MGM
Based on the Broadway musical comedy, this farce set in Ancient Rome follows slave and scam-artist Pseudolus (Mostel, in a signature role) as he attempts to win his freedom by brokering the sale of a virgin. Sondheim's score adds to the appeal. Recently renewed its popularity on the stage with Nathan Lane in the lead. **Academy Awards:** Best Scoring of a Musical. **Cast:** Zero Mostel, Phil Silvers, Jack Gilford, Buster Keaton, Michael Crawford, Michael Hordern, Patricia Jessel, Myrna White. **Credits:** Dir: Richard Lester; Prod: Melvin Frank; Writer: Michael Pertwee; DP: Nicolas Roeg; Ed: John Victor Smith; Prod Design: Tony Walton; Composer: Stephen Sondheim. Color, 100 min. **VHS, LASER**

Fun with Dick and Jane
(1977) Columbia
Before there were Yuppies, there were . . . Yuppies—they just didn't go by that name. Dick and Jane, an upscale Los Angeles couple, face a severe drop in their standard of living when Dick loses his high-paying executive position. Desperate, the white-collar pair turn to blue-collar crime to solve their cash-flow problems. **Cast:** George Segal, Jane Fonda, Ed McMahon, Dick Gautier, Allan Miller. **Credits:** Dir: Ted Kotcheff; Prod: Peter Bart, Max Palevsky; Writer: David Giler, Jerry Belson, Mordecai Richler; Story: Gerald Gaiser; DP: Fred Koenekamp; Ed: Danford B. Greene; Prod Design: James Hulsey; Composer: Ernest Gold, Lamont Dozier, Gene Page; Costumes: Donfeld, Lambert Marks, Margo Baxley; Set Designer: Jack Stevens. Color, 104 min. **VHS**

The Furies
(1950) Paramount
From a hard man comes a hard daughter in Mann's Western. T. C. Jeffords's determination built his huge New Mexico cattle ranch and his spirit has been passed down to Vance Jeffords. Father and daughter clash over T.C.'s choice of a new bride, but engage in open war when the senior Jeffords hangs a man that Vance loves, Juan Herrera, leader of a group of squatters living on ranch land. With the help of another flame, the gambler Rip Darrow, Vance aims to drive her father from his estate, "The Furies," and expose him to the elements and justice of the plains. **Cast:** Barbara Stanwyck, Walter Huston, Wendell Corey, Judith Anderson, Gilbert Roland, Thomas Gomez, Blanche Yurka, John Bromfield, Wallace Ford, Beulah Bondi. **Credits:** Dir: Anthony Mann; Prod: Hal B. Wallis; Writer: Charles Schnee; Story: Niven Busch; DP: Victor Milner; Ed: Archie Marshek; Prod Design: Hans Dreier, Henry Bumstead; Composer: Franz Waxman. B&W, 109 min.

Fury
(1936) MGM
Joe Wilson, an ethical young man, is forced to confront his own mortality and morality after he is wrongly accused and jailed for kidnapping. A lynch mob burns down the jail, and believes he died in the inferno. He survives to exact revenge on the vigilantes. **Cast:** Spencer Tracy, Sylvia Sidney, Walter Abel, Bruce Cabot, Edward Ellis, Walter Brennan, Frank Albertson. **Credits:** Dir: Fritz Lang; Prod: Joseph L. Mankiewicz; Writer: Bartlett Cormack, Fritz Lang; Story: Norman Krasna; DP: Joseph Ruttenberg; Ed: Frank Sullivan; Prod Design: Cedric Gibbons, William A. Horning; Composer: Franz Waxman; Costumes: Dolly Tree; Art Director: Edwin B. Willis. B&W, 96 min. **VHS**

The Fury
(1978) Fox
Another De Palma tale of young people with psychokinetic powers, but this goes for suspense rather than the gorefest of *Carrie*. Douglas plays a father, head of a psychic research lab, who attempts to protect his psychically gifted son from government use in secret mind-control experiments. **Cast:** Kirk Douglas, John Cassavetes, Carrie Snodgrass, Charles Durning, Amy Irving, Andrew Stevens, Fiona Lewis, Carol Rossen. **Credits:** Dir: Brian De Palma; Prod: Frank Yablans; Writer: John Farris; DP: Richard H. Kline; Ed: Paul Hirsch; Prod Design: Bill Malley; Composer: John Williams. Color, 118 min. **VHS**

Futureworld
(1976) AIP
Sequel to *Westworld*, where the robots have rebuilt the theme park. Not content with capitalism, the robots, led by Hill, are now bent on complete global domination. When powerful leaders are invited to the park, they uncover a sinister cloning plan. **Cast:** Peter Fonda, Blythe Danner, Arthur Hill, Yul Brynner, Stuart Margolin, John P. Ryan, Jim Antonio. **Credits:** Dir: Richard T. Heffron; Prod: James Aubrey; Writer: Mayo Simon, George Schenck; DP: Sol Polito, Howard Schwartz; Ed: James Mitchell; Prod Design: Trevor Williams; Composer: Fred Karlin; SFX: Gene Grigg, Brent Sellstrom; Set Designer: Marvin March, Dennis Peeples. Color, 104 min. **VHS**

Gabriel over the White House

(1933) MGM
A startling Hollywood answer to the perception of chaos overrunning the Depression-plagued country. After being elected president as the candidate of organized crime and corrupt interests, Huston has a Damascus-road moment when visited by an angel who advises a change of heart. When he turns with a vengeance on the crooked elements who got him elected, they fight back by alleging that he's lost his mind. The film feels almost like a prayer for deliverance, and is truly remarkable. **Cast:** Walter Huston, Karen Morley, Franchot Tone, Dickie Moore, C. Henry Gordon, Samuel S. Hinds, Jean Parker, David Landau, William Pawley. **Credits:** Dir: Gregory La Cava; Prod: Walter Wanger; Writer: Carey Wilson, Bertram Bloch; DP: Bert Glennon; Ed: Basil Wrangell; Prod Design: Cedric Gibbons; Composer: William Axt. B&W, 87 min. **VHS**

The Gallant Hours

(1960) United Artists
This docudrama traces the days before the World War II battle of Guadalcanal, in which Admiral William F. Halsey, commander of the South Pacific forces, makes courageous and crucial decisions that start to turn the tide against the Japanese. More a biography than a war picture, this film focuses on leadership in war and is not for those who crave battle-scene action. **Cast:** James Cagney, Dennis Weaver, Ward Costello, Richard Jaeckel, Carl Benton Reid, Robert Montgomery. **Credits:** Dir: Robert Montgomery; Prod: Robert Montgomery; Writer: Frank D. Gilroy, Beirne Lay; DP: Joseph MacDonald; Ed: Fredrick Y. Smith; Art Director: Wiard Ihnen; Set Designer: Frank McKelvy. B&W, 116 min. **VHS**

Gal Young 'Un

(1979)
Based on an award-winning story by Marjorie Kinnan Rawlings about Mattie Siles, a widow recently married to a whiskey distiller. Her new husband spends all her money on the still and then spurns her for a younger woman. Set in the backwoods of Florida during the Prohibition era. Director Nunez's debut and a Sundance Grand Jury Prize winner in 1981. **Cast:** Dana Preu, David Peck, J. Smith-Cameron, Gene Densmore, Timothe McCormack, Casey Donovan, Jennie Stringfellow, Mike Garlington, Marshal New, Bruce Cornwell. **Credits:** Dir: Victor Nunez; Prod: Victor Nunez; Writer: Victor Nunez; DP: Victor Nunez; Ed: Victor Nunez. Color, 105 min. **VHS**

Gambit

(1966) Universal
Caine, a bumbling but debonair English cat burglar, and MacLaine, a beautiful Eurasian dancer, team up to steal a priceless statue—which bears an uncanny resemblance to MacLaine—from the impregnable mansion of a billionaire recluse. Caine's Hollywood debut. **Cast:** Shirley MacLaine, Michael Caine, Herbert Lom, Arnold Moss, Roger C. Carmel, John Abbott, Richard Angarola, Maurice Marsac. **Credits:** Dir: Ronald Neame; Prod: Leo L. Fuchs; Writer: Alvin Sargent, Jack Davies; DP: Clifford Stine; Ed: Alma Macrorie; Prod Design: Alexander Golitzen, George C. Webb; Composer: Maurice Jarre. Color, 109 min. **VHS**

The Gambler

(1974) Paramount
A distinguished NYU literature professor from a wealthy family is also a compulsive gambler, in debt for $44,000 he lost in Las Vegas. When he can't stop, his life ends up in the hands of the Mob. This worthy portrayal of an addicted personality

was well written by Toback. **Cast:** James Caan, Paul Sorvino, Lauren Hutton, Burt Young, Morris Carnovsky, Jacqueline Brookes. **Credits:** Dir: Karel Reisz; Prod: Robert Chartoff, Irwin Winkler; Writer: James Toback; DP: Victor J. Kemper; Ed: Roger Spottiswoode; Prod Design: Philip Rosenberg; Composer: Gustav Mahler; Costumes: Albert Wolsky; Set Designer: Edward Stewart. Color, 111 min. **VHS**

Gambling Lady

(1934) Warner Bros.
A drama starring Stanwyck as a gambler with honor. The daughter of a gambler who killed himself after he went bankrupt, she meets and marries a wealthy man (McCrea). When doubts are cast on her real motives, Stanwyck almost loses the man she loves. The marriage is saved when he realizes she loves him more than gambling. **Cast:** Barbara Stanwyck, Joel McCrea, Pat O'Brien, Claire Dodd, C. Aubrey Smith, Phillip Reed, Robert Barratt, Robert Elliott, Ferdinand Gottshalk, Arthur Vinton. **Credits:** Dir: Archie Mayo; Writer: Ralph Block, Doris Malloy; DP: George Barnes; Ed: Harold McLernon; Prod Design: Anton Grot. B&W, 66 min.

Gangs, Inc.

(1941) Producers
When a woman is imprisoned for a hit-and-run accident that was really committed by an irresponsible playboy, she sets her mind on murderous revenge. A better-than-average low-budget thriller that features an early role for Ladd. **Cast:** Alan Ladd, Joan Woodbury, Lash La Rue, George Pembroke, Harry Depp, Gavin Gordon. **Credits:** Dir: Phil Rosen; Prod: Frank King, Maurice King; Writer: Martin Mooney; DP: Arthur Martinelli. B&W, 72 min. **VHS**

Gangster Story

(1960)
A gangland tale with an emphasis on the personal relations rather than the gunplay. Matthau's girlfriend keeps the heat on to leave the Mob behind. Matthau directed himself in this dryly satirical noir. **Cast:** Walter Matthau, Carol Grace, Bruce McFarlan, Garrett Wallberge. **Credits:** Dir: Walter Matthau; Prod: Jonathan Daniels; Writer: Paul Purcell; Composer: Leonard Barr, Donald Bloomberg. B&W, 65 min. **VHS**

The Garden of Allah

(1936) United Artists
A society girl (Dietrich), mourning the death of her father, travels to the Sahara Desert. There she finds romance with a monk who has recently abandoned the monastic life but remains torn between religious devotion and worldly desire, particularly desire for the exceptionally alluring Marlene (she was photographed so beautifully the cameramen won special Oscars). Lots of moonlit desert scenery in early Technicolor. Academy Award Nominations: Best Score. **Cast:** Marlene Dietrich, Charles Boyer, Tilly Losch, Basil Rathbone, C. Aubrey Smith, Joseph Schildkraut, John Carradine, Alan Marshal, Lucile Watson, Henry Brandon. **Credits:** Dir: Richard Boleslawski; Prod: David O. Selznick; Writer: W. P. Lipscomb, Lynn Riggs; DP: Harold Rosson, W. Howard Greene; Ed: Hal C. Kern, Anson Stevenson; Prod Design: Lansing C. Holden; Composer: Max Steiner. Color, 85 min. **VHS, LASER**

Garden of the Moon

(1938) Warner Bros.
This happy-go-lucky Berkeley musical focuses on the relationship between O'Brien, owner of the nightclub Garden of the Moon; his bandleader, Payne; and their ongoing competition with each other. But when dame singer Lindsay lights up the place, they're suddenly playing for keeps. Songs include "The Girl of Whirling Dervish," "The Lady on the Two Cent Stamp," "Confidentially," and "Garden of the Moon." **Cast:** Pat O'Brien, Margaret Lindsay, John Payne, Johnnie Davis, Jimmie Fidler, Melville Cooper, Isabel Jeans, Mabel Todd, Penny Singleton, Dick Purcell. **Credits:** Dir: Busby Berkeley; Prod: Louis F. Edelman; Writer: Jerry Wald, Richard Macaulay, H. Bedford Jones, Barton Browne; DP: Tony Gaudio; Ed: George Amy; Composer: Leo F. Forbstein, Harry Warren, Al Dubin. B&W, 94 min.

Gaslight

(1944) MGM
Cukor captures the smoky, smoggy feel of Victorian London for this atmospheric mystery. The husband of innocent new bride Bergman may have a dark past, and he may be trying to drive her insane to get his hands on her family's jewels. Lansbury's film debut. Golden Globe for Best Actress: Ingrid Bergman. Academy Award Nominations: 7, including Best Picture; Best Actor: Charles Boyer; Best Supporting Actress: Angela Lansbury; Best Screenplay; Best Cinematography. **Academy Awards:** Best Actress: Ingrid Bergman; Best Interior Decoration (B&W). **Cast:** Charles Boyer, Ingrid Bergman, Joseph Cotten, Angela Lansbury, Dame May Whitty, Barbara Everest, Edmund Breon, Halliwell Hobbes. **Credits:** Dir: George Cukor; Prod: Arthur Hornblow, Jr.; Writer: John Van Druten, Walter Reisch, John L. Balderston; DP: Joseph Ruttenberg; Ed: Ralph E. Winters; Prod Design: Cedric Gibbons, William Ferrari; Composer: Bronislau Kaper. B&W, 114 min. **VHS, LASER**

Gates of Heaven

(1978)
Independent doc maker Morris (*Thin Blue Line*, *Fast Cheap and Out of Control*) interviews pet cemetery proprietors, pet owners, and embalmers, as they talk candidly about their feelings for the dear departed and their work dealing with the bereaved. A typically off-center look at American obsessions. **Cast:** Cal Harberts, Phil Harberts, Scottie Harberts, Lucille Billingsley, Zella Graham. **Credits:** Dir: Errol Morris; DP: Ned Burgess; Ed: Errol Morris; Composer: Dan Harberts. Color, 90 min. **VHS**

The Gauntlet

(1977) Warner Bros.
An alcoholic, rather dim-witted police detective is sent to Las Vegas to extradite a prostitute with Mob connections. The routine assignment grows more complicated when the pair is pursued by vengeful gangsters and corrupt cops intent on preventing her testimony. Watch this for Eastwood's performance and an action-packed plot. **Cast:** Clint Eastwood, Sondra Locke, Pat Hingle, William Prince. **Credits:** Dir: Clint Eastwood; Prod: Robert Daley; Writer: Michael Butler, Dennis Shryack; DP: Rexford Metz; Ed: Ferris Webster, Joel Cox; Composer: Jerry Fielding; Costumes: Glenn T. Wright; SFX: Chuck Gaspar; Art Director: Allen Smith. Color, 111 min. **VHS, LASER**

The Gay Deception

(1935) Fox
A romantic comedy about a prince who masquerades as a bellhop at the Waldorf Plaza Hotel. Confusion and romance ensue when he meets a stenographer pretending to be rich after wining $5,000 in a lottery. An early Wyler effort. **Cast:** Luis Alberni, Frances Dee, Benita Hume, Francis Lederer, Alan Mowbray, Lennox Pawle, Adele St. Mauer, Lionel Stander, Akim Tamiroff. **Credits:** Dir: William Wyler; Prod: Jesse L. Lasky; Writer: Stephen Avery, Don Hartman, Arthur Richman; DP: Joseph A. Valentine; Ed: Robert Simpson; Composer: Louis De Francesco. B&W, 75 min.

The Gay Divorcee

(1934) RKO
A lively adaptation of the stage musical, which featured Astaire and his sister, Adele, and the first film in which Astaire and Rogers actually received star billing. While vacationing at an English seaside resort, a soon-to-be-divorced woman mistakes a lovestruck song-and-dance man for her paid corespondent. As usual, the plot's not important when you see these two and hear classics like Cole Porter's "Night and Day." Academy Award Nominations: 5, including Best Picture; Best Score. **Academy Awards:** Best Song ("The Continental"). **Cast:** Fred Astaire, Ginger Rogers, Alice Brady, Edward Everett Horton, Erik Rhodes, Betty Grable, Eric Blore, Lillian Miles. **Credits:** Dir: Mark Sandrich; Prod: Pandro S. Berman; Writer: George Marion, Dorothy Yost, Edward Kaufman; Story: Dwight Taylor; DP: David Abel; Ed: William Hamilton; Prod Design: Carroll Clark; Choreographer: Fred Astaire, Hermes Pan; Composer: Cole Porter, Max Steiner; Costumes: Walter Plunkett; SFX: Vernon L. Walker; Art Director: Van Nest Polglase. B&W, 107 min. **VHS, LASER**

Gay Purr-Ee

(1962) Warner Bros.
The story follows Mewsette, a French country cat, who spurns the romantic overtures of her country bumpkin boyfriend in favor of seeking out the high life and *l'amour* in the big city. The guileless feline immediately falls into the paws of some unscrupulous cat snatchers. Garland and Goulet provide the voices and song stylings. Written by the peerless Jones and featuring songs by Arlen and Harburg. **Cast:** Judy Garland, Robert Goulet, Red Buttons, Hermione Gingold, Mel Blanc, Paul Frees, Morey Amsterdam. **Credits:** Dir:

> ## "The only person who has the right attitude about boxing in the movies for me was Buster Keaton."
>
> Martin Scorsese, director of *Raging Bull* (1980)

Abe Levitow; Prod: Henry G. Saperstein; Writer: Chuck Jones, Ralph Wright, Dorothy Jones; DP: Roy Hutchcroft, Jack Stevens, Dan T. Miller, Duane Keegan; Ed: Sam Horta, Ted Baker, Earl Bennett; Composer: Harold Arlen, E. Y. Harburg. Color, 85 min. **VHS, LASER**

The Gazebo
(1959) MGM
A TV writer is being blackmailed by someone who has old nude photos of his Broadway star wife. He decides to kill the blackmailer and bury him under the backyard gazebo without realizing he's left just enough clues to get everyone involved in his case. Reynolds sings "Something Called Love" in this offbeat comedy-mystery. Academy Award Nominations: Best (Black-and-White) Costume Design. **Cast:** Glenn Ford, Debbie Reynolds, Carl Reiner, Doro Merande, John McGiver, Mabel Albertson, Martin Landau. **Credits:** Dir: George Marshall; Prod: Lawrence Weingarten; Writer: George Wells, Alec Coppel; DP: Paul C. Vogel; Ed: Adrienne Fazan; Prod Design: Paul Groesse; Composer: Jeff Alexander; Costumes: Helen Rose; Art Director: George W. Davis. B&W, 100 min. **VHS**

The Geisha Boy
(1958) Paramount
Pleshette's film debut in this Lewis comedy about a clumsy magician who signs up for a USO tour of Japan and Korea. He befriends a shy Japanese boy and falls in love with his mother. Lewis fans will enjoy the sight gags and the well-known appearance by the Los Angeles Dodgers. **Cast:** Jerry Lewis, Suzanne Pleshette, Marie McDonald, Sessue Hayakawa, Nobu McCarthy, Barton MacLane. **Credits:** Dir: Frank Tashlin; Prod: Jerry Lewis; Writer: Frank Tashlin; DP: Haskell Boggs; Ed: Alma Macrorie; Prod Design: Tambi Larsen; Composer: Walter Scharf; Costumes: Edith Head; Art Director: Hal Pereira; Set Designer: Sam Comer, Robert R. Benton. Color, 98 min. **VHS**

The Gene Krupa Story
(1960) Columbia
A fairly clichéd story of the musical genius who transformed the sound of jazz percussion. A young Mineo convincingly portrays the drummer's great career, which was temporarily derailed by drug addiction, though he "sticksynchs" along to the Krupa sound track. **Cast:** Sal Mineo, James Darren, Susan Kohner, Susan Oliver, Yvonne Craig, Lawrence Dobkin, Celia Lovsky, Red Nichols, Shelly Manne, Buddy Lester. **Credits:** Dir: Don Weis; Prod: Philip A. Waxman; Writer: Orin Jannings; DP: Charles Lawton, Jr.; Composer: Leith Stevens. B&W, 101 min. **VHS, LASER**

The General
(1927) United Artists
Keaton's greatest achievement grew out of an authentic episode of American history—the theft of a strategically important locomotive during the Civil War. Keaton takes the train, belching smoke, on a single-handed wild ride, shielding his beloved while fending off Union soldiers. The chase sequence culminates in Keaton's grandest stunt as the train crashes into the river. This silent gem was selected by the Library of Congress for the National Film Registry. **Cast:** Buster Keaton, Marion Mack, Charles Smith, Frank Barnes, Joe Keaton. **Credits:** Dir: Buster Keaton, Clyde Bruckman. Prod: Joseph Schenck; Writer: Al Boasberg, Charles Smith; DP: J. Devereaux Jennings, Bert Haines; Ed: Sherman Kell; Prod Design: Fred Gabourie. B&W, 107 min (running times vary by supplier). **VHS, LASER**

The General Died at Dawn
(1936) Paramount
Cooper finds intrigue in the East and romance with Carroll. In China during the '20s, a soldier of fortune tries to deliver arms money to peasants who are battling a ruthless warlord, but he is waylaid by a beautiful spy. Milestone (*All Quiet on the Western Front*) directed Odets's first screenplay.

Cast: Gary Cooper, Madeleine Carroll, William Frawley, Akim Tamiroff, Dudley Digges, Porter Hall, J. M. Kerrigan, Philip Ahn, Lee Tung Foo, Leonid Kinskey. **Credits:** Dir: Lewis Milestone; Prod: William LeBaron; Writer: Clifford Odets; DP: Victor Milner; Ed: Eda Warren; Prod Design: Hans Dreier, Ernst Fegte; Composer: Werner Janssen. B&W, 97 min. **VHS**

Gentle Giant
(1967) Paramount
A young boy living in Florida befriends an orphaned black bear cub and raises him until he gains his adult size and must be returned to the wild. The basis for the *Gentle Ben* TV series. **Cast:** Dennis Weaver, Vera Miles, Ralph Meeker, Clint Howard, Huntz Hall. **Credits:** Dir: James Neilson; Prod: Ivan Tors; Writer: Edward Lasko, Andy White; Story: Walt Morey; DP: Howard Winner; Ed: Warren Adams, Peter Colbert; Prod Design: Bruce Bushman; Composer: Samuel Matlovsky. Color, 93 min. **VHS**

Gentleman Jim
(1942) Warner Bros.
A high-spirited biopic that depicts the life of dashing heavyweight champ Jim Corbett (Flynn). Set in turn-of-the-century San Francisco, the story brings to life the colorful world of 19th-century fisticuffs and climaxes in the legendary championship match between Corbett and John L. Sullivan (Bond). Flynn adds just the right note of swagger to what was one of his favorite roles. **Cast:** Errol Flynn, Alexis Smith, Jack Carson, Ward Bond, Alan Hale, Jr., John Loder, William Frawley, Rhys Williams, Arthur Shields. **Credits:** Dir: Raoul Walsh; Prod: Robert Buckner; Writer: Vincent Lawrence, Horace McCoy; DP: Sid Hickox; Ed: Jack Killifer; Prod Design: Ted Smith; Composer: Heinz Roemheld. B&W, 104 min. **VHS**

Gentleman's Agreement
(1947) Fox
The best of the few Hollywood treatments of anti-Semitism. Peck gives the right gravity to his role of a magazine reporter who comes to understand in a personal way the barriers imposed by prejudice when, to add depth to his magazine feature, he takes on a Jewish identity. Hart wrote the script, based on the novel by Laura Z. Hobson. Academy Award Nominations: 8, including Best Actor: Gregory Peck; Best Actress: Dorothy McGuire; Best Supporting Actress: Anne Revere; Best Screenplay. **Academy Awards:** Best Picture; Best Sup-

porting Actress: Celeste Holm; Best Director. **Cast:** Gregory Peck, Dorothy McGuire, John Garfield, Celeste Holm, Anne Revere, June Havoc, Albert Dekker, Jane Wyatt, Dean Stockwell, Sam Jaffe. **Credits:** Dir: Elia Kazan; Prod: Darryl F. Zanuck; Writer: Moss Hart; DP: Arthur Miller; Ed: Harmon Jones; Prod Design: Lyle Wheeler, Mark-Lee Kirk; Composer: Alfred Newman. B&W, 118 min. **VHS, LASER**

Gentlemen Prefer Blondes
(1953) Fox
Fifties screen sirens Monroe and Russell in made-to-order roles. A pair of gold-digging showgirls from the cane-brake—a sassy, street-smart brunette and a sexy, naive blonde—pursue potential husbands on an ocean cruise. Glossy, big-budget Hawks adaptation of the Broadway hit based on an Anita Loos story. Jule Styne's songs include "Diamonds Are a Girl's Best Friend." **Cast:** Marilyn Monroe, Jane Russell, Charles Coburn, Elliott Reid, Tommy Noonan, Norma Varden, George Winslow, Marcel Dalio, Taylor Holmes. **Credits:** Dir: Howard Hawks; Prod: Sol C. Siegel; Writer: Charles Lederer; DP: Harry Wild; Ed: Hugh S. Fowler; Prod Design: Lyle Wheeler, Joseph C. Wright; Composer: Lionel Newman. Color, 92 min. **VHS, LASER**

George Washington Slept Here
(1942) Warner Bros.
Hilarious Kaufman-and-Hart cautionary tale about the dangers of moving to the country. Benny gets the opportunity for many double takes, as his comfortable city life moves north to a rambling wreck in Connecticut. The new country squire tries to rein in his wife (Sheridan) while holding the workmen and neighbors at bay. Prime Benny performance of a terrific script. **Cast:** Jack Benny, Ann Sheridan, Charles Coburn, Hattie McDaniel, Percy Kilbride, Franklin Pangborn, William Tracy, Lee Patrick, John Emery, Charles Dingle. **Credits:** Dir: William Keighley; Prod: Jerry Wald; Writer: Everett Freeman; DP: Ernest Haller; Ed: Ralph Dawson; Prod Design: Max Parker, Mark-Lee Kirk; Composer: Adolph Deutsch. Color, 91 min. **VHS**

George White's Scandals
(1934) Fox
A standard backstage musical based on the popular Broadway extravaganzas known as *George White's Scandals*. Small-town music-hall gal Faye catches the eye of the famous impresario and heads to the big city, where

success on the boards isn't all it's cracked up to be. Eleanor Powell's debut. The first of a series of tried-and-true backstage musicals with the same name; see the original and you've seen 'em all. **Cast:** Rudy Vallee, Jimmy Durante, Alice Faye, Adrienne Ames, Gregory Ratoff, Cliff Edwards, Dixie Dunbar, Thomas Jackson. **Credits:** Dir: Thornton Freeland, Harry Lachman, George White; Prod: George White; Writer: Jack Yellen; DP: Lee Garmes, George Schneiderman; Ed: Paul Weatherwax; Composer: Irving Caesar, Ray Henderson, Jack Yellen. B&W, 83 min.

George White's Scandals
(1945) RKO
A run-of-the-mill backstage musical based on the *George White's Scandals* stage extravaganzas that wowed Broadway for years. Produced by White himself, and best during the musical numbers that were the high-point of the *Scandals* and of the series of films based on the shows. See this one for Davis. **Cast:** Joan Davis, Jack Haley, Philip Terry, Ethel Smith, Margaret Hamilton, Glenn Tryon, Jane Greer, Fritz Feld, Rufe Davis, Martha Holliday. **Credits:** Dir: Felix Feist; Prod: George White; Writer: Howard Snyder, Parke Levy, Howard J. Green, Hugh Wedlock, Jr.; DP: Robert de Grasse; Ed: Joseph Noriega; Prod Design: Albert S. D'Agostino, Ralph Berger; Composer: Leigh Harline. B&W, 95 min. **VHS**

The Getaway
(1972) National General
McQueen and MacGraw star as husband-and-wife bank robbers. Mac-Graw's early prison release plan ignites McQueen's violent jealousy, which is heightened when he realizes they're being set up after fulfilling a promise to pull off one more robbery. Peckinpah keeps this one fast and furious, and the sparks between the stars offscreen make it onto the screen as well. Remade in a less compelling version in 1994 with Alec Baldwin and Kim Basinger, also an off-screen couple. Future action-director Hill based his screenplay on a Jim Thompson novel. Features music by Quincy Jones. **Cast:** Steve McQueen, Ali MacGraw, Ben Johnson, Bo Hopkins, Sally Struthers, Al Lettieri, Slim Pickens. **Credits:** Dir: Sam Peckinpah; Prod: David Foster, Mitchell Brower; Writer: Walter Hill; Story: Jim Thompson; DP: Lucien Ballard; Ed: Robert L. Wolfe; Prod Design: Angelo Graham; Composer: Quincy Jones; SFX: Bud

Hulburd; Art Director: Ted Haworth; Set Designer: Gene Nelson. Color, 123 min. **VHS, DVD**

Get Christie Love!
(1974)
That '70s blaxploitation show! An undercover police detective (Graves, who was the black woman in a bikini on *Laugh-In*) sheds her double-knit togs along with her identity to break a drug ring. Later became a TV series. **Cast:** Teresa Graves, Harry Guardino, Louise Sorel, Paul Stevens, Andy Romano, Debbie Dozier. **Credits:** Dir: William A. Graham. Color, 100 min. **VHS**

Getting Gertie's Garter
(1945) United Artists
A retired scientist, now happily married, had romanced the woman who plans to marry his best friend. He had given the woman a sexy garter, which she insists on wearing should her impending marriage fail and they ever want to renew their romance. The scientist determines to retrieve the incriminating evidence of his premarriage romance. Gertie's garter is finally got but not before much humorous embarrassment. **Cast:** Dennis O'Keefe, Marie MacDonald, Barry Sullivan, Binnie Barnes, Sheila Ryan, J. Carrol Naish, Jerome Cowan, Vera Marshe, Don Beddoe, Frank Fenton. **Credits:** Dir: Allan Dwan; Prod: Edward Small; Writer: Karen DeWolf, Allan Dwan; Story: Avery Hopwood, Wilson Collison; DP: Charles Lawton, Jr.; Ed: Walter Hannemann, Truman K. Wood; Prod Design: Joseph Sternad; Composer: Louis Forbes. B&W, 72 min.

Getting Straight
(1970) Columbia
A kind of *Man in the Gray Flannel Suit* for the counterculture generation. Gould makes a strong impression as a returning Vietnam vet who goes back to college in the heady days of campus unrest. He's turned off by stodgy academia and too soon back from the real world of war to commit to the political radicals. A violent student riot leads Gould to realize he's neither part of the Revolution nor the Establishment. **Cast:** Elliott Gould, Candice Bergen, Jeff Corey, Max Julien, Cecil Kellaway, Robert F. Lyons, Jeannie Berlin, John Rubinstein, Brenda Sykes, Harrison Ford. **Credits:** Dir: Richard Rush; Prod: Richard Rush; Writer: Robert Kaufman; DP: Laszlo Kovacs; Ed: Maury Winetrobe; Prod Design: Sydney Litwack; Composer: Ronald Stein. Color, 124 min. **VHS**

The Ghost and Mrs. Muir (1947)

Get to Know Your Rabbit

(1972) Warner Bros.

Early De Palma effort finds humor in Smothers's abandoning career to become a tap-dancing magician. Rough but has its moments, with interesting cast. **Cast:** Tom Smothers, Katharine Ross, John Astin, Orson Welles, Suzanne Zenor, Allen Garfield, Hope Summers, Charles Lane, Samantha Jones, M. Emmet Walsh. **Credits:** Dir: Brian De Palma; Prod: Steven Bernhardt; Writer: Jordon Crittenden; DP: John A. Alonzo; Ed: Frank J. Urioste, Peter Colbert; Prod Design: Bill Malley; Composer: Jack Elliott, Allyn Ferguson. Color, 92 min. **VHS**

The Ghost and Mrs. Muir

(1947) Fox

The lovingly made romantic fantasy of a lonely widow (the radiant Tierney) who refuses to be scared by the ghost of a salty sea captain in her cottage. When her debts mount, he helps her write a successful novel about his life, and, ultimately, she is forced to choose between her love for this endearing denizen of the spirit world or for a flesh-and-blood romance. Based on the R. A. Dick novel. Academy Award Nominations: Best (B&W) Cinematography. **Cast:** Gene Tierney, Rex Harrison, George Sanders, Edna Best, Vanessa Brown, Anna Lee, Robert Coote, Natalie Wood, Isobel Elsom. **Credits:** Dir: Joseph L. Mankiewicz; Prod: Fred Kohlmar; Writer: Philip Dunne; Story: R. A. Dick; DP: Charles B. Lang; Ed: Dorothy Spencer; Prod Design: Richard Day; Composer: Bernard Herr-mann; Costumes: Oleg Cassini; SFX: Fred Sersen; Art Director: George W. Davis; Set Designer: Thomas Little, Stuart A. Reiss. B&W, 104 min. **VHS, LASER**

Ghost Breakers

(1940) Paramount

Bob Hope and Paulette Goddard seemed to bring out the best in each other in their comedy thrillers, and this is the best of the lot. Goddard inherits a creepy Cuban castle. Meanwhile, thinking that he's killed a man, Hope hides away in a steam trunk that, unbeknownst to him, is bound for Cuba. They team up to face down death threats and ghouls. **Cast:** Bob Hope, Paulette Goddard, Richard Carlson, Paul Lukas, Anthony Quinn, Willie Best, Lloyd Corrigan, Noble Johnson, Pedro De Cordoba, Virginia Brissac. **Credits:** Dir: George Marshall; Prod: Arthur Hornblow, Jr.; Writer: Walter DeLeon; DP: Charles B. Lang; Ed: Ellsworth Hoagland; Prod Design: Hans Dreier, Robert Usher; Composer: Ernst Toch. B&W, 85 min. **VHS, LASER**

The Ghost Goes West

(1936) United Artists

Clair's first English film is an odd charmer about a matchmaking ghost played by Donat. When an American woman inherits a Scottish castle and decides to move it lock, stock, and barrel to Florida, a 200-year-old ghost goes along for the ride. The descendant of the cranky specter also comes along as caretaker to pursue his romance with the new owner's daughter. Written by Sherwood. Now available in a digitally remastered version that includes the original trailer. **Cast:** Robert Donat, Jean Parker, Eugene Pallette, Elsa Lanchester, Ralph Bunker, Patricia Hilliard, Everly Gregg, Morton Selten. **Credits:** Dir: Rene Clair; Prod: Alexander Korda; Writer: Robert E. Sherwood, Rene Clair, Eric Keown; DP: Harold Rosson, Harold Rosson; Ed: Henry Cornelius; Prod Design: Vincent Korda; Composer: Mischa Spoliansky; Costumes: Rene Hubert, John Armstrong; SFX: Ned Mann. B&W, 86 min. **VHS**

The Ghost of Frankenstein

(1942) Universal

Lugosi's back as Ygor in this fourth of Universal's Frankenstein flicks. This time, Dr. Frankenstein (the orginal mad scientist's second son) thinks his monster could be cured if he only had a normal brain, so with the help of Ygor, they try it again, from the top. **Cast:** Ralph Bellamy, Bela Lugosi, Lon Chaney, Jr., Cedric Hardwicke, Lionel Atwill, Evelyn Ankers. **Credits:** Dir: Erle C. Kenton; Prod: George Waggner; Writer: W. Scott Darling; Story: Eric Taylor; DP: Milton Krasner, Elwood Bredell; Ed: Ted J. Kent; Prod Design: Jack Otterson; Composer: Charles Previn; SFX: John Fulton. B&W, 68 min. **VHS**

The Ghost Ship

(1943) RKO

Creepy Lewton-produced drama with silent star Dix playing a sadistic ship's captain. The plot takes a mutinous turn when a crew member finally subdues the captain. The dark mood is carried throughout by an omniscient deaf-mute's narration. *The Ghost Ship* was removed from distribution for bearing a striking resemblance to a play of a similar name. **Cast:** Richard Dix, Dewey Robinson, Skelton Knaggs, Alec Craig, Russell Wade, Edith Barrett, Edmond Glover, Lawrence Tierney. **Credits:** Dir: Mark Robson; Prod: Val Lewton; Writer: Donald Henderson Clarke, Leo Mittler; DP: Nicholas Musuraca; Ed: John Lockert; Prod Design: Albert S. D'Agostino, Walter E. Keller, Claude Carpenter; Composer: Roy Webb, C. Bakaleinikoff; Art Director: Darrel Silvera. B&W, 69 min. **VHS, LASER**

Giant

(1956) Warner Bros.
This fabled family saga follows the lives and loves of a wealthy Texan rancher and a cowpoke who strikes it rich in the Texas oil fields. Rich with the period's greatest actors, including not only Dean's last performance and Taylor and Hudson in top form, but also support from McCambridge, Hopper, Baker, and Mineo. Dean's performance as a prosperous former ranch hand with an attachment to his former boss's wife (Taylor) has become legendary. The 40th-anniversary enhanced version includes a restored sound track and color as well as 60 minutes of archival footage, a special introduction from the director, and the original theatrical trailer. The deluxe boxed set includes *George Stevens: A Filmmaker's Journey*, a full-length documentary about the acclaimed director. The Limited Collector's Edition includes a 72-page book. Academy Award Nominations: 10, including Best Picture; Best Actor: Rock Hudson; Best Actor: James Dean; Best Adapted Screenplay. **Academy Awards:** Best Director. **Cast:** Rock Hudson, James Dean, Elizabeth Taylor, Mercedes McCambridge, Chill Wills, Sal Mineo, Jane Withers, Carroll Baker, Dennis Hopper, Rod Taylor. **Credits:** Dir: George Stevens; Prod: George Stevens, Henry Ginsberg; Writer: Fred Guiol, Ivan Moffat; Story: Edna Ferber; DP: William Mellor; Ed: William Hornbeck, Fred Bohanan, Philip W. Anderson; Prod Design: Boris Leven; Composer: Dimitri Tiomkin. Color, 202 min. **VHS, LASER**

G.I. Blues

(1960) Paramount
Presley put his recent army service to good use in this better-than-average outing. While stationed in Germany, rock-and-rolling Sergeant Presley bets his army buddy band mates he can make time with beautiful but standoffish dancer Prowse. Songs include "Blue Suede Shoes," "Shopping Around," and "Pocketful of Rainbows." **Cast:** Elvis Presley, Juliet Prowse, Robert Ivers, Leticia Roman, Arch Johnson, Sigrid Maier, The Jordanaires. **Credits:** Dir: Norman Taurog; Prod: Hal B. Wallis; Writer: Edmund Beloin, Henry Garson; DP: Loyal Griggs; Ed: Warren Low; Prod Design: Hal Pereira, Walter Tyler; Composer: Joseph J. Lilley. Color, 104 min. **VHS**

Gidget

(1959) Columbia
The first and best of the Gidget movies, which spawned equally popular television series (two of them!). The pert 'n' perky Dee, a California tomboy, spends the summer in Malibu learning how to surf—and learning about love from a cool surfer and a beach bum. Novelist Fredrick Kohner based the character on his daughter. **Cast:** Sandra Dee, James Darren, Cliff Robertson, Arthur O'Connell, Joby Baker, Tom Laughlin, Robert Ellis, Mary LaRoche. **Credits:** Dir: Paul Wendkos; Prod: Lewis J. Rachmil; Writer: Gabrielle Upton; DP: Burnett Guffey; Ed: William A. Lyon; Composer: George Duning. Color, 95 min. **VHS, LASER**

Gidget Goes Hawaiian

(1961) Columbia
The pert California girl (Walley takes over from Dee) and her family take Hawaii by storm. With her rad surfing technique and perky good looks, Gidget attracts lots of boys—causing problems with her boyfriend. Meanwhile, a jealous rival spreads a vicious rumor. **Cast:** Deborah Walley, James Darren, Michael Callan, Carl Reiner, Peggy Cass, Eddie Foy, Jr., Jeff Donnell, Vicki Trickett, Joby Baker. **Credits:** Dir: Paul Wendkos; Prod: Jerry Bresler; Writer: Ruth Brookes Flippen; DP: Robert Bronner; Ed: William A. Lyon; Prod Design: Walter Holscher; Composer: George Duning. Color, 102 min. **VHS**

Gidget Goes to Rome

(1963) Columbia
On vacation with two girlfriends, her boyfriend Moondoggie, and his pal Clay, Gidget takes in the Eternal City with her dad's wartime pal, Paolo Cellini. Gidget doesn't realize that her dad has asked his friend to keep an eye on her while she's there. But he didn't plan on Gidget falling for Paolo. Moondoggie's back again, but Carol takes the Gidget baton from Walley. **Cast:** Cindy Carol, James Darren, Peter Brooks, Cesare Danova, Jessie Royce Landis, Joby Baker. **Credits:** Dir: Paul Wendkos; Prod: Jerry Bresler; Writer: Ruth Brookes Flippen, Katherine Eunson, Dale Eunson; DP: Enzo Barboni, Robert Bronner; Ed: William A. Lyon; Prod Design: Tony Sarzi Braga, Robert Peterson; Composer: John Williams. Color, 104 min. **VHS**

Gigi

(1958) MGM
Set in Paris at the turn of the century, this delightful Lerner-and-Loewe musi-
cal, based on a story by Colette, follows a precocious French girl as she is groomed into a would-be courtesan and blossoms into a stunning woman. The story provides plenty of opportunity for Minnelli and MGM to pull out all the stops in its first musical production shot on location. Paris and Caron never looked lovelier, and Jourdan and Chevalier are so French, no? Songs include "Gigi," "Thank Heaven for Little Girls," and "Ah, Yes, I Remember It Well." Academy Award Nominations: 9. Golden Globes for Best Director; Best Supporting Actress: Hermione Gingold; Best Motion Picture: Musical/Comedy. **Academy Awards:** Best Director; Best Film Editing; Best Song; Best Color Cinematography; Best Scoring of a Musical; Best Picture; Best Screenplay Based on Material from Another Source; Best Art Direction—Set Decoration (B&W or Color); Best Costume Design (B&W or Color). **Cast:** Leslie Caron, Louis Jourdan, Maurice Chevalier, Jacques Bergerac, Hermione Gingold, Isabel Jeans, Eva Gabor, John Abbott, Monique Van Vooren. **Credits:** Dir: Vincente Minnelli; Prod: Arthur Freed; DP: Joseph Ruttenberg, Ray June; Ed: Adrienne Fazan; Composer: Alan Jay Lerner, Frederick Loewe; Costumes: Cecil Beaton. Color, 119 min. **VHS, LASER**

Gigot

(1962) Fox
Gleason is disarming as a simple mute working at a pension in Paris. One day he encounters and befriends a young prostitute, Colette, and her daughter, Nicole. Colette and Nicole have hit upon hard times and Gigot offers to take them in. He forms a friendship with Nicole, but it only makes the local townsfolk suspicious. Gigot is branded a child molester and is pursued by an angry mob. He falls into the Seine and is believed dead. Afterward, when Gigot's innocence is established, the townsfolk are overcome with remorse and design an elaborate funeral. **Cast:** Jackie Gleason, Katherine Kath, Gabrielle Dorziat, Jean Lefevre, Jacques Marin, Albert Remy, Yvonne Constant, Germaine Delbat, Albert Dinan, Diane Gardner. **Credits:** Dir: Gene Kelly; Prod: Kenneth Hyman; Writer: John Patrick; DP: Jean Bourgoin; Ed: Roger Dwyre; Prod Design: Auguste Capelier; Composer: Jackie Gleason, Michel Magne. Color, 104 min.

Gilda

(1946) Columbia
This is the film that gave the world the indelible image of Hayworth in that

tight gown, lovingly removing that long glove as she sings "Put the Blame on Mame." That's enough to justify a viewing, but the film has more, including a bewitched, bothered, etc. performance by Ford. An intricate noir in which Hayworth, as the titular femme fatale, is placed by her mobster club-owner husband in the care of Ford, a small-time hood who also happens to be her ex-lover. **Cast:** Rita Hayworth, Glenn Ford, Joseph Calleia, George Macready, Steve Geray, Joe Sawyer, Gerald Mohr, Ludwig Donath, Don Douglas, Lionel Royce. **Credits:** Dir: Charles Vidor; Prod: Virginia Van Upp; Writer: Marion Parsonnet; DP: Rudolph Mate; Ed: Charles Nelson; Prod Design: Stephen Goosson, Van Nest Polglase; Composer: Hugo Friedhofer. B&W, 110 min. **VHS, LASER**

The Gilded Lily
(1935) Paramount
One of several MacMurray-Colbert pairings, this romantic comedy about a friendship between a newspaper reporter and a stenograper made Fred a star. Colbert meets a man in the subway without realizing he's a British lord. After learning the man's true identity, the stenographer think she's been tricked and rejects him. Her reporter friend MacMurray dubs her the "No Girl," and she becomes a minor celebrity. Thinking that the lord may still love her, she tracks him down. She has to choose heart over head when she finds him. **Cast:** Luis Alberni, Claudette Colbert, Eddie Craven, Forrester Harvey, Claude King, Fred MacMurray, Donald Meek, Ray Milland, C. Aubrey Smith. **Credits:** Dir: Wesley Ruggles; Prod: Albert Lewis; Writer: Melville Baker, Claude Binvon; Jack Kirkland; DP: Victor Milner; Ed: Otto Lovering; Composer: Arthur Johnston, Sam Coslow. B&W, 85 min.

Gimme Shelter
(1970)
The Maysles brothers unwittingly captured the end of the '60s as they documented the Rolling Stones' tragic 1970 free concert at Altamont, California. The backstage world of touring superstars and the logistics that go into planning an event that was to be attended by 300,000 people pales as the Hell's Angels stomp an audience member to death while Jagger helplessly shrieks "Sympathy for the Devil." Terrifying and electrifying filmmaking. **Cast:** Jefferson Airplane, Ike Turner, Tina Turner, The Rolling Stones, Marty Balin, Melvin Belli, Paul

Kantner, Grace Slick. **Credits:** DP: George Lucas, Albert Maysles, David Maysles; Ed: Joanne Burke, Ellen Giffard, Kent McKinney; Color, 91 min. **VHS, LASER**

Ginger in the Morning
(1973) National
A young hitchhiker overcomes her suspicions and becomes romantically attached to a middle-aged businessman when he picks her up. Spacek's first starring role. **Cast:** Sissy Spacek, Monte Markham, Susan Oliver, Mark Miller, Slim Pickens, David Doyle. **Credits:** Dir: Gordon Wiles. Color, 90 min. **VHS**

A Girl, a Guy and a Gob
(1941) RKO
Ball finds herself caught up in a comic love triangle and unable to choose between her men. B-picture, but always enjoyable to watch the young Lucy. **Cast:** George Murphy, Lucille Ball, Edmond O'Brien, Henry Travers, Franklin Pangborn, George Cleveland, Marguerite Churchill, Lloyd Corrigan, Mady Correll, Frank Mc-Glynn. **Credits:** Dir: Richard Wallace; Prod: Harold Lloyd; Writer: Frank Ryan, Bert Granet; DP: Russell Metty; Ed: George Crone; Composer: Roy Webb. B&W, 91 min. **VHS**

The Girl Can't Help It
(1956) Fox
In Mansfield's first starring role, she portrays the outrageously voluptuous but tone-deaf girlfriend of a retired racketeer. He hires a talent agent to transform her into a movie star and they fall in love. High-voltage, candy-colored camp by comic maven Tashlin, which features some great early rock-and-roll performances from The Platters, Little Richard, and Fats Domino. **Cast:** Jayne Mansfield, Edmond O'Brien, Tom Ewell, Julie London, Henry Jones, John Emery, Ray Anthony, Little Richard, Fats Domino. **Credits:** Dir: Frank Tashlin; Prod: Frank Tashlin; Writer: Frank Tashlin, Herbert Baker; DP: Leon Shamroy; Ed: James B. Clark; Prod Design: Lyle Wheeler; Costumes: Charles LeMaire; Art Director: Leland Fuller. Color, 99 min. **VHS, LASER**

Girl Crazy
(1943) MGM
A wealthy Manhattanite, fed up with his son's romantic escapades, ships the budding playboy to a men-only southwestern university. There, the would-be Romeo falls for the pretty but uninterested dean's granddaughter and saves the school from finan-

cial ruin. This eighth pairing of Rooney and Garland includes many classic Gershwin songs, such as "I Got Rhythm," "Fascinating Rhythm," and "Embraceable You." **Cast:** Mickey Rooney, Judy Garland, Guy Kibbee, Gil Stratton, Rags Ragland, June Allyson, Nancy Walker, Tommy Dorsey, Robert E. Strickland, Frances Rafferty. **Credits:** Dir: Norman Taurog; Prod: Arthur Freed; Writer: Fred F. Finklehoffe, Dorothy Kingsley, Sid Silvers, William Ludwig; DP: William Daniels, Robert Planck; Ed: Albert Akst; Prod Design: Cedric Gibbons; Composer: George Gershwin, Ira Gershwin. B&W, 100 min. **VHS, LASER**

Girlfriends
(1978) Warner Bros.
Believable relationship story of a young woman who is trying to make it on her own, juggling work, romance, and friendship, and has to accept the marriage of her best friend. Nice performance by Mayron. **Cast:** Melanie Mayron, Anita Skinner, Eli Wallach, Christopher Guest, Bob Balaban, Amy Wright, Viveca Lindfors, Mike Kellin, Jean De Baer, Kenneth McMillan. **Credits:** Dir: Claudia Weill; Prod: Claudia Weill, Jan Saunders; Writer: Vicki Polon; DP: Fred Murphy; Ed: Suzanne Pettit; Prod Design: Patrizia von Brandenstein; Composer: Michael Small. Color, 88 min. **VHS**

The Girl from Mexico
(1939) RKO
Energetic slapstick comedy about an obscure Mexican singer, Velez, who is brought from her homeland to New York to star on an American radio program. Woods, the advertising executive who discovers Velez, falls in love with her along the way, but the film is at its best when Lupe kicks up her heels. Errol also stands out as Lupe's comedic sidekick. This first appearance by Velez led to her *Mexican Spitfire* series. **Cast:** Lupe Velez, Donald Woods, Leon Errol, Linda Hayes, Donald MacBride, Edward Raquello, Elisabeth Risdon, Ward Bond. **Credits:** Dir: Leslie Goodwins; Prod: Leslie Goodwins; Writer: Lionel Houser; DP: Jack MacKenzie; Ed: Desmond Marquette; Prod Design: Van Nest Polglase; Composer: Roy Webb. B&W, 71 min.

The Girl from Missouri
(1934) MGM
The cowriters of *Gentlemen Prefer Blondes* also penned this delightful comedy. Would-be gold digger Harlow wants to land playboy millionaire Tone, who in turn sees her as just another

possible conquest. Lots of laughs, especially from the sharp-tongued Kelly, who plays Harlow's pal. **Cast:** Jean Harlow, Lionel Barrymore, Franchot Tone, Lewis Stone, Patsy Kelly, Alan Mowbray. **Credits:** Dir: Jack Conway; Prod: Bernard Hyman; Writer: Anita Loos, John Emerson; DP: Ray June; Ed: Tom Held; Composer: William Axt. B&W, 72 min. **VHS**

The Girl from Petrovka
(1974) Universal
Hawn stars as a feisty Russian ballerina who falls in love with Holbrook, a visiting U.S. correspondent. In order for their relationship to survive, they must overcome the obstacles that the secret police throw their way. An interesting Cold War artifact and not a bad bittersweet-comedy, either. **Cast:** Goldie Hawn, Hal Holbrook, Anthony Hopkins, Gregoire Aslan, Anton Dolin, Bruno Wintzell, Zoran Andric, Hanna Hertelendy, Maria Sokolov, Zitto Kazann. **Credits:** Dir: Robert Ellis Miller; Prod: Richard D. Zanuck, David Brown; Writer: Chris Bryant, Allan Scott; Story: George Feifer; DP: Vilmos Zsigmond; Ed: John F. Burnett; Composer: Henry Mancini; Costumes: Deirdre Clancy. Color, 103 min. **VHS**

The Girl from 10th Avenue
(1935) Warner Bros.
In an early starring role, Davis plays Miriam, the "girl" of the title. In a drunken haze, she marries a Park Avenue man who, also drunk, had been trying to drown his sorrows of losing to another man the society queen he really loved. Under Miriam's influence, however, he straightens himself out in many regards, and she humbly agrees to free him from the mishap marriage—until his old flame tries to rekindle their romance. **Cast:** Bette Davis, Ian Hunter, Colin Clive, Alison Skipworth, John Eldredge, Katherine Alexander, Helen Jerome Eddy, Gordon Elliot, Adrian Rosely, Andre Cheron. **Credits:** Dir: Alfred E. Green; Prod: Harry Blanke, Robert Lord; Writer: Hubert Henry Davies, Charles Kenyon; DP: James Van Trees; Ed: Owen Marks; Composer: Leo F. Forbstein; Art Director: John Hughes. B&W, 69 min.

Girl Happy
(1965) MGM
Elvis and the Jordanaires hit the beaches of sunny Fort Lauderdale to "babysit" the beautiful, brainy daughter of their nightclub-owner boss in exchange for a booking. Naturally, a springtime romance blossoms

between the King and his ward. One of the better Elvis comedies, enlivened by the presence of Presley's favorite costar, the talented Fabares, and by his only screen appearance in drag. **Cast:** Elvis Presley, Shelley Fabares, Mary Ann Mobley, Harold J. Stone, Gary Crosby, Nita Talbot, Joby Baker, Fabrizio Mioni, Jackie Coogan. **Credits:** Dir: Boris Sagal; Prod: Joe Pasternak; Writer: Harvey Bullock, R. S. Allen; DP: Philip H. Lathrop; Ed: Rita Roland; Prod Design: George W. Davis, Addison Hehr; Composer: George Stoll. Color, 96 min. **VHS**

The Girl in White
(1952) MGM
Based on *Bowery to Bellevue*, the autobiography of Dr. Emily Dunning Barringer, the film relates in a semi-documentary style a female doctor's struggle to gain respect from her peers and the freedom to pursue a meaningful career in the male-dominated profession. Following her rise from medical school to a post at New York's Bellevue Hospital and marriage to a colleague, the film is a non-confrontational, '50s-era examination of the life of a feminist pioneer. **Cast:** June Allyson, Arthur Kennedy, Gary Merrill, Mildred Dunnock, Jesse White, Marilyn Erskine, Guy Anderson, Gar Moore, Don Keefer, Ann Tyrrell. **Credits:** Dir: John Sturges; Prod: Armand Deutch; Writer: Emily Dunning Barringer; Story: Philip Stevenson, Allen Vincent, Irma von Cube; DP: Paul C. Vogel; Ed: Ferris Webster; Prod Design: Cedric Gibbons; Composer: David Raksin; Art Director: Leonid Vasian. B&W, 92 min.

The Girl Most Likely
(1957) RKO
Leisen directs this old-fashioned musical with a second-tier cast about a young woman (Powell) who sets out to marry a rich man and attracts three potential suitors. Standout feature is the choreography by Broadway legend Gower Champion. Remake of *Tom, Dick and Harry* (1941). Songs include "The Girl Most Likely," "I Don't Know What I Want," and "Crazy Horse." **Cast:** Cliff Robertson, Jane Powell, Kaye Ballard, Keith Andes, Tommy Noonan, Una Merkel, Kelly Brown, Judy Nugent, Frank Cady. **Credits:** Dir: Mitchell Leisen; Prod: Stanley Rubin; Writer: Devery Freeman; DP: Robert Planck; Ed: Harry Marker, Dean Harrison; Prod Design: Albert S. D'Agostino, George W. Davis; Composer: Nelson Riddle, Ralph Blane, Hugh Martin. Color, 98 min. **VHS, LASER**

The Girl of the Golden West
(1938) MGM
An Eddy-MacDonald musical about a good girl who falls for an outlaw and saves him from lynching by playing poker with the handsome but lonely sheriff, the stakes being her hand in marriage. Not the best MacDonald and Eddy, but worthwhile for fans. Puccini used the same play for the basis of his opera of the same name. **Cast:** Jeanette MacDonald, Nelson Eddy, Walter Pidgeon, Buddy Ebsen, Leo Carrillo, Olin Howlin. **Credits:** Dir: Robert Z. Leonard; Prod: William Anthony McGuire; Writer: Isabel Dawn, Boyce DeGaw, David Belasco; DP: Oliver T. Marsh; Ed: W. Donn Hayes; Prod Design: Cedric Gibbons; Choreographer: Albertina Rasch; Composer: Herbert Stothart, Sigmund Romberg, Gus Kahn; Costumes: Adrian; Set Designer: Edwin B. Willis. B&W, 121 min. **VHS**

Girl Rush
(1944) RKO
The zany stars of San Francisco vaudeville show *The Frisco Follies* head out in search of gold. While panning for gold, they restage their act in the little town of Red Creek, despite the efforts to foil their performance by a wicked gambler (Mitchum, in an early screen appearance). **Cast:** Alan Carney, Wally Brown, Frances Langford, Paul Hurst, Vera Vague, Robert Mitchum, Sarah Padden, Cy Kendall, John Merton, Patti Brill. **Credits:** Dir: Gordon Douglas; Prod: John H. Auer; Writer: Robert E. Kent; DP: Nicholas Musuraca; Ed: Duncan Mansfield; Prod Design: Albert S. D'Agostino, Walter E. Keller; Composer: Gene Rose. B&W, 65 min. **VHS**

Girls About Town
(1931) Paramount
Francis and Tashman live large on the kindness of wealthy men, including McCrea. When McCrea proposes to Francis, she reveals that she's already married. Early Cukor with pre-Code sensationalism. **Cast:** Louise Beavers, Alan Dinehart, Kay Francis, Joel McCrea, Eugene Pallette, Lilyan Tashman, Lucile Gleason. **Credits:** Dir: George Cukor; Writer: Raymond Griffith, Brian Marlow; Story: Zoe Akins; DP: Ernest Haller; Costumes: Travis Banton. B&W, 82 min.

Girls! Girls! Girls!
(1962) Paramount
Better than the title would suggest and also featuring a genuine hit, "Return to Sender." Elvis moonlights

singing in a club in order to get his dad out of hock. A rich girl slumming by the shore may prove to be his answer. Hits include "I Don't Want To," "Because of Love," and "Song of the Shrimp." **Cast:** Elvis Presley, Stella Stevens. **Credits:** Dir: Norman Taurog; Writer: Edward Anhalt; DP: Loyal Griggs. Color, 106 min. **VHS**

Give a Girl a Break
(1953) MGM
Broadway's greatest dancers and choreographers—Marge and Gower Champion, Bob Fosse, and the movie world's dance master, Stanley Donen—combine for a backstage tale that's more knowing than most. Three young performers up for the lead in a Broadway show think they've got it wired when they form romantic attachments to the men with the show. Two songs in the picture are the only (and only moderately successful) collaboration between lyricist Ira Gershwin and composer Lane. **Cast:** Marge Champion, Gower Champion, Debbie Reynolds, Kurt Kasznar, Larry Keating, Bob Fosse, Richard Anderson, William Ching, Lurene Tuttle, Donna Martell. **Credits:** Dir: Stanley Donen; Prod: Jack Cummings; Writer: Albert Hackett, Frances Goodrich; DP: William Mellor; Ed: Adrienne Fazan; Prod Design: Cedric Gibbons, Paul Groesse; Choreographer: Stanley Donen, Gower Champion; Composer: Burton Lane, Ira Gershwin. Color, 82 min. **VHS**

Give Me a Sailor
(1938) Paramount
In this sailors-on-leave romantic screwball comedy, Hope and Raye agree to help each other get the girl and guy of their dreams, respectively. Two sisters—one beautiful, the other homely—meet two swabbies on shore leave. Grable (the pretty one) sings, and Hope and Raye mug. Good fun. **Cast:** Bob Hope, Martha Raye, Betty Grable, Jack Whiting, Clarence Kolb, J. C. Nugent, Nana Bryant, Emerson Treacy, Bonnie Jean Churchill. **Credits:** Dir: Elliott Nugent; Prod: Jeff Lazarus; Writer: Doris Anderson, Frank Butler; DP: Victor Milner; Ed: William Shea; Prod Design: Hans Dreier; Composer: Boris Morros, Leo Robin, Ralph Rainger. B&W, 78 min. **VHS**

The Glass Bottom Boat
(1966) MGM
All-American Doris Day is mistaken for a Communist spy in this slapstick romantic comedy. When her secretly smitten boss at the aerospace lab

asks her to write his biography as a ploy to spend time with her, suspicious heads turn—especially since her dog is named Vladimir! Day croons "Que Sera, Sera," and the Man from U.N.C.L.E. shows up to lend a hand. **Cast:** Doris Day, Rod Taylor, Arthur Godfrey, Paul Lynde, Eric Fleming, Alice Pearce, Ellen Corby, John McGiver, Edward Andrews, Dick Martin. **Credits:** Dir: Frank Tashlin; Prod: Martin Melcher; Writer: Everett Freeman; DP: Leon Shamroy; Ed: John McSweeney, Jr.; Prod Design: George W. Davis; Composer: Frank DeVol; Costumes: Ray Aghayan; SFX: J. McMillan Johnson; Art Director: Edward C. Carfagno; Set Designer: Henry Grace, Hugh Hunt. Color, 110 min. **VHS, LASER**

The Glass Key
(1935) Paramount
In this murder mystery–melodrama adapted from a Hammett novel, a popular but none-too-honest politician decides to clean up his act, aligning himself with a senator. But when he closes down the gambling operation of an underworld gangster, the gangster spreads the rumor that the politician is responsible for the mysterious death of the senator's son. Further complicating the whodunnit scenario is the politician's daughter, who was in love with the murder victim. **Cast:** George Raft, Claire Dodd, Edward Arnold, Rosalind Keith, Ray Milland, Robert Gleckler, Guinn Williams, Tammany Young, Harry Tyler, Charles Richman. **Credits:** Dir: Frank Tuttle; Prod: E. Lloyd Sheldon; Writer: Dashiell Hammett, Kubec Glasmon, Kathryn Scola, Harry Ruskin; DP: Henry Sharp; Ed: Hugh Bennett. B&W, 77 min.

The Glass Key
(1942) Paramount
A classic murder mystery, based on the Hammett novel and said to be the inspiration for Kurosawa's *Yojimbo.* When a corrupt politician is accused of murder, his assistant hunts the real killer, avoiding amorous advances from his boss's fiancée and attacks from gangsters along the way. Ladd and Lake make this a better version than the 1935 film of the same name. **Cast:** Brian Donlevy, Veronica Lake, Alan Ladd, William Bendix, Bonita Granville, Richard Denning, Joseph Calleia, Moroni Olsen. **Credits:** Dir: Stuart Heisler; Prod: Fred Kohlmar; Writer: Jonathan Latimer; Story: Dashiell Hammett; DP: Theodor Sparkuhl; Ed: Archie Marshek; Prod

Design: Hans Dreier; Composer: Victor Young; Art Director: Haldane Douglas. B&W, 85 min. **VHS, LASER**

The Glass Menagerie
(1950) Warner Bros.
Tennessee Williams's stage drama has proved irresistible to actors and moviemakers, seemingly remade once a generation. This adaptation sticks closely to the original text but injects some lighter notes. Laura, a retiring girl with a clubbed foot, shuts herself away with her menagerie of glass figurines. Her brother, Tom, the story's narrator, earns the family's wages at a warehouse. They share a faded St. Louis tenement with their nagging mother, who harasses Laura to socialize and Tom to find a better job and a man for his sister. Compare to the Paul Newman–directed version of 1987. **Cast:** Jane Wyman, Kirk Douglas, Gertrude Lawrence, Arthur Kennedy, Ralph Sanford, Ann Tyrrell, John Compton, Gertrude Graner, Sarah Edwards, Louise Lorrimer. **Credits:** Dir: Irving Rapper; Prod: Jerry Wald, Charles K. Feldman; Writer: Tennessee Williams, Peter Berneis; DP: Robert Burks; Ed: David Weisbart; Composer: Max Steiner; Art Director: Robert M. Haas. B&W, 106 min.

The Glass Slipper
(1955) MGM
In this musical version of Cinderella, the stepdaughter (Caron) is a beautiful, gifted tomboy, her fairy godmother is a loony old kleptomaniac who shoplifts a gown, and the prince has been schooled at the best universities, cafés, and boudoirs. The Paris Ballet has some beautiful dance sequences in this winningly oddball fairy tale. **Cast:** Leslie Caron, Michael Wilding, Keenan Wynn, Estelle Winwood, Elsa Lanchester, Amanda Blake, Barry Jones. **Credits:** Dir: Charles Walters; Prod: Edwin H. Knopf; Writer: Helen Deutsch; DP: Arthur E. Arling; Ed: Ferris Webster; Prod Design: Cedric Gibbons; Choreographer: Roland Petit; Composer: Bronislau Kaper; Costumes: Helen Rose, Walter Plunkett; Art Director: Daniel B. Cathcart. Color, 95 min. **VHS**

The Glass Web
(1953) Universal
When a real murder is committed on the set of the popular, reality-based TV program *Crime of the Week,* the show's writers and performers aren't just suspects, they're investigators too. The murdered actress had carried

on a series of affairs and was blackmailing some of her conquests, so plenty of people wanted her out of the way. As the heinous crime is worked into the script for next week's broadcast, however, the real killer slips up, accidentally writing a crucial clue into the script. With the cameras rolling, police nab their man during the performance. Neat mystery with early TV setting. **Cast:** Edgar G. Robinson, John Forsythe, Marcia Henderson, Kathleen Hughes, Richard Denning, Hugh Sanders, Jean Willes, Harry Tyler. **Credits:** Dir: Jack Arnold; Prod: Albert J. Cohen; Writer: Robert Blees, Leonard Lee; Story: Max Erlich; DP: Maury Gertsman; Ed: Ted J. Kent; Composer: Joseph Gershenson, Herman Stein; Art Director: Bernard Herzbrun. B&W, 81 min.

Glen and Randa
(1971)
Independent filmmaker McBride (*David Holzman's Diary*) follows a hedonistic, innocent young couple as they roam the post-apocalyptic world in search of a fabled, unspoiled city of dreams. Caution: Originally rated X. **Cast:** Steven Curry, Shelley Plimpton, Woodrow Chambliss, Garry Goodrow. **Credits:** Dir: Jim McBride; Prod: Sidney Glazier; Writer: Lorenzo Mans, Jim McBride, Rudy Wurlitzer; DP: Alan Raymond; Ed: Jack Baran, Mike Levine. Color, 94 min. **VHS, LASER**

The Glenn Miller Story
(1953) Universal
Stewart gives a warm performance as the legendary bandleader who met an untimely end in a WWII airplane crash. Though much of Miller's story has been glossed over here, the great big-band music is really what it's all about. Includes performances of "Little Brown Jug," "Moonlight Serenade," "Pennsylvania 6-5000," "In the Mood," and many more. Interesting Mann-Stewart picture that takes place away from the Wild West. Academy Award Nominations: 3, including Best Story and Screenplay; Best Scoring of a Musical Picture. **Academy Awards:** Best Sound Recording. **Cast:** James Stewart, June Allyson, Harry Morgan, Charles Drake, Frances Langford, Louis Armstrong, Gene Krupa. **Credits:** Dir: Anthony Mann; Prod: Aaron Rosenberg; Writer: Valentine Davies, Oscar Brodney; DP: William Daniels; Ed: Russell Schoengarth; Choreographer: Kenny Williams; Composer: Joseph Gershenson. Color, 116 min. **VHS, LASER**

Glen or Glenda
(1953) Paramount
An Ed Wood curiosity about transvestism and sex changes. Exploitative in its time and filled with sinister characters and spooky settings, the film is a major hoot for today's viewers. Lugosi plays a ghoulish narrator-puppetmaster who threatens to "Pull the string!" of helpless mortals. **Cast:** Bela Lugosi, Lyle Talbot, Daniel Davis, Dolores Fuller, Timothy Farrell, Tommy Haynes, Conrad Brooks. **Credits:** Dir: Edward D. Wood, Jr.; Prod: George Weiss; Writer: Edward D. Wood, Jr.; DP: William C. Thompson; Ed: Bud Schelling. B&W, 79 min. **VHS**

Glory Alley
(1952) MGM
A New Orleans boxer skips town the night before a big prizefight. He's branded a coward, so he joins the army and wins the Congressional Medal of Honor in Korea. He returns a hero in name, but the father of his dancer girlfriend, Caron, will not consent to their marriage. Haunted by his past, he begins training for the fight that will win back his honor. Includes a blistering burlesque-house performance by Louis Armstrong and Caron. **Cast:** Ralph Meeker, Leslie Caron, Kurt Kasznar, Gilbert Roland, John McIntire, Louis Armstrong, Jack Teagarden, Dan Seymour, Larry Gates, Pat Goldin. **Credits:** Dir: Raoul Walsh; Prod: Nicholas Nayfack; Writer: Arthur Cohn; DP: William Daniels; Ed: Gene Ruggeiro; Composer: George E. Stoll; Art Director: Malcolm Brown, Cedric Gibbons. B&W, 79 min.

G Men
(1935) Warner Bros.
One of the best of the Hollywood F.B.I. stories finds Cagney fighting for the good guys after being raised with the Mob. When a vicious mobster rubs out attorney Cagney's friend (a federal agent, or "G-Man"), he trades in the law for a lawman's badge. He makes good use of his background in his search for the killers. A thriller and a top Cagney performance. **Cast:** James Cagney, Margaret Lindsay, Ann Dvorak, Robert Armstrong, Barton MacLane, Lloyd Nolan, William Harrigan, Edward Pawley, Russell Hopton, Noel Madison. **Credits:** Dir: William Keighley; Prod: Louis F. Edelman; Writer: Seton I. Miller; DP: Sol Polito; Ed: Jack Killifer; Prod Design: John Hughes. B&W, 86 min. **VHS**

The Gnome-Mobile
(1967) Disney
A winning live-action children's film from the Disney studio, this effort

stars former *Mary Poppins* kids Garber and Dotrice. On a drive through the country with their timber-tycoon grandfather (Brennan), the children discover a gnome who fears he may be the last of his enchanted race. They agree to help the wood sprite find his friends, who, they discover at last, live in the heart of the California redwood forest. In the end, Grandfather has a change of heart and deeds a plot of forest to the gnomes in this ecology-minded tall tale. **Cast:** Walter Brennan, Matthew Garber, Karen Dotrice, Richard Deacon, Tom Lowell, Sean McClory, Ed Wynn, Jerome Cowan, Charles Lane, Carol Kane. **Credits:** Dir: Robert Stevenson; Prod: Walt Disney; Writer: Ellis Kadison; Story: Upton Sinclair; DP: Edward Coleman; Ed: Norman Palmer; Prod Design: Carol Clarke, William H. Tuntke; Composer: Buddy Baker. Color, 83 min.

The Goddess
(1957) Columbia
Said to be loosely based by writer Paddy Chayefsky on the story of Marilyn Monroe, the film focuses on a woman with radiant, sexual charisma and a driving ambition to become a star. Though she does whatever it takes to get there, she finds that fame and fortune do not end her loneliness and discontent. Academy Award Nominations: Best (Original) Story and Screenplay. **Cast:** Patty Duke, Kim Stanley, Lloyd Bridges, Steven Hill, Betty Lou Holland. **Credits:** Dir: John Cromwell; Prod: Milton Perlman; Writer: Paddy Chayefsky; DP: Arthur J. Ornitz; Ed: Carl Lerner; Prod Design: Ted Haworth; Composer: Virgil Thompson; Costumes: Frank Thompson. B&W, 105 min. **VHS, LASER**

The Godfather
(1972) Paramount
One of the great movies of all time, which spawned an equally successful sequel and a third chapter as well. This atmospheric epic follows the fortunes of the Corleones, a powerful Mafia family with its own separate code of honor, justice, law, and loyalty. Flawless performances from an all-star cast, a dramatic narrative full of authentic detail taken from Puzo's blockbuster novel, unforgettable music, and groundbreaking cinematography combine to make this a film that rewards multiple screenings. The entire Corleone saga is available in one video release, *The Godfather 1902–1959: The Complete Epic*. Its many awards include the Directors

The Godfather Part II (1974)

ered a landmark of '70s filmmaking, the film garnered multiple honors, including Director's Guild Best Director; National Society of Film Critics, Best Director, Best Cinematography; Writer's Guild, Best Screenplay. Selected for the National Film Registry. Academy Award Nominations: 11, including Best Actor: Al Pacino; 3 nominations for Best Supporting Actor: Robert De Niro, Michael V. Gazzo, Lee Strasberg; and Best Supporting Actress: Talia Shire. **Academy Awards:** Best Picture; Best Director; Best (Adapted) Screenplay; Best Supporting Actor: Robert De Niro; Best Score. **Cast:** Al Pacino, Robert De Niro, Robert Duvall, Talia Shire, Diane Keaton, Lee Strasberg, John Cazale, Michael V. Gazzo, Troy Donahue. **Credits:** Dir: Francis Ford Coppola; Writer: Francis Ford Coppola, Mario Puzo; DP: Gordon Willis; Ed: Peter Zinner, Barry Malkin, Richard Marks; Prod Design: Dean Tavoularis; Composer: Nino Rota; Costumes: Theadora Van Runkle; SFX: A. D. Flowers, Joe Lombardi; Art Director: Angelo Graham; Set Designer: George Robert Nelson. Color, 200 min. **VHS, LASER**

God Is My Co-Pilot
(1945) Warner Bros.
True story of Robert Scott, ace fighter pilot and WWII hero. From his early dreams of one day becoming an airplane pilot, through his West Point training, and, later still, as a mail pilot flying a cargo of mail through a blinding storm, we wait for his shining moment. He gets his chance when Japan bombs Pearl Harbor, and Scott is sent to fight the Japanese over China with General Claire Chennault's "Flying Tigers." **Cast:** Dennis Morgan, Dane Clark, Raymond Massey, Alan Hale, Andrea King, John Ridgely, Stanley Ridges, Craig Stevens, Warren Douglas, Mark Stevens. **Credits:** Dir: Robert Florey; Prod: Robert Buckner; Writer: Abem Finkel, Peter Milne, William Faulkner; Story: Robert Scott; DP: Sidney Hickox; Ed: Folmar Blangsted; Prod Design: Stanley Fleischer, John Hughes; Composer: Franz Waxman. B&W, 90 min.

God's Little Acre
(1958) United Artists
The lives of Georgia farmers aren't as pastoral as they might seem, at least as shown in this fine drama directed by Mann. The movie follows the lives of several Georgia farmers, including one who thinks there may be treasure buried on his property. Yordan wrote the script from the novel by Caldwell.

Guild Best Supporting Actor: Robert Duvall and Outstanding Directorial Achievement; Golden Globes for Best Actor: Marlon Brando; Best Director; Best Score; Best Screenplay; National Society of Film Critics Best Actor: Al Pacino; Writers Guild Best Screenplay. Selected for the National Film Registry. Academy Award Nominations: 10, including Best Director; 3 nominations for Best Supporting Actor (Caan, Duvall, Pacino). **Academy Awards:** Best Actor: Marlon Brando; Best Picture; Best Screenplay Based on Material from Another Medium. **Cast:** Marlon Brando, Al Pacino, James Caan, Robert Duvall, Talia Shire, Diane Keaton, Sterling Hayden, John Cazale, Richard Castellano, John Marley. **Credits:** Dir: Francis Ford Coppola; Writer: Francis Ford Coppola; Story: Mario Puzo; DP: Gordon Willis; Ed: Peter Zinner; Prod De-

sign: Dean Tavoularis; Composer: Nino Rota; Costumes: Anna Hill Johnstone; SFX: A. D. Flowers, Joe Lombardi, Dick Smith, Sass Bedig; Set Designer: Philip Smith. Color, 175 min. **VHS, LASER**

The Godfather Part II
(1974) Paramount
One of the few sequels in film history that surpasses the original, this outstanding film compares the young Vito Corleone, an immigrant finding power in crime, to his son Michael, who moves the family affairs into the modern world. An operatic family saga that has an inexorable sense of dread and fate that comes from the sins of the father's being paid for by the sons. Puzo and Coppola endow the parallel stories with vibrant historical detail and the real sense of seeing the inner workings of a secret world. Consid-

Cast: Robert Ryan, Aldo Ray, Tina Louise, Jack Lord, Buddy Hackett, Vic Morrow, Rex Ingram, Helen Westcott, Lance Fuller, Michael Landon. **Credits:** Dir: Anthony Mann; Prod: Sidney Harmon; Writer: Philip Yordan; Story: Erskine Caldwell; DP: Ernest Haller; Ed: Richard C. Meyer; Composer: Elmer Bernstein. B&W, 118 min. **VHS**

Go for Broke!

(1951) MGM
The 442nd Regiment, comprised of Nisei—loyal Americans of Japanese ancestry—exhibits heroism beyond the call of duty, overcoming the Nazis as well as the prejudice of white Americans who cannot accept "Japs" on their side. Johnson plays one of those bigots. Academy Award Nomination for Best Story and Screenplay. **Cast:** Van Johnson, Warner Anderson, Gianna Canale, Lane Nakano, Don Haggerty, George Miki, Akira Fukunaga, Ken K. Okamoto, Henry Oyasato, Harry Hamada. **Credits:** Dir: Robert Pirosh; Prod: Dore Schary; Writer: Robert Pirosh; DP: Paul C. Vogel; Ed: James E. Newcom; Prod Design: Cedric Gibbons, Eddie Imazu; Composer: Alberto Colombo. B&W, 92 min. **VHS**

Going Hollywood

(1933) MGM
William Randolph Hearst's Cosmopolitan Pictures was set up to make Davies, the magnate's muse, a major star. While she never attained the heights Hearst had in mind, she was an affable, appealing comedian (and often had great material provided by Hearst's money and friends such as Frances Marion). This is prime Davies, and Crosby's first MGM outing. Davies is an unassuming French teacher in love with radio singer Crosby. When he follows his star to Hollywood, so does she, where she encounters a rival for his affections on the set of his big breakthrough film. Davies quickly dispatches the starlet and finds herself in the lights. **Cast:** Marion Davies, Bing Crosby, Fifi D'Orsay, Stuart Erwin, Ned Sparks, Patsy Kelly, Bobby Watson, Lennie Hayton, Clara Blandick, Sterling Holloway. **Credits:** Dir: Raoul Walsh; Prod: Walter Wanger; Writer: Donald Stewart; DP: George Folsey, Jr.; Ed: Frank Sullivan; Art Director: Merrill Pye. B&W, 78 min. **VHS**

Going in Style

(1979) Warner Bros.
Terrific cast of coots—Burns, Strasberg, and Carney—pull a daring bank heist out of sheer boredom. The difficulties begin when they actually pull

off the caper and are faced with a new career. Funny script and three Hollywood legends. **Cast:** George Burns, Art Carney, Lee Strasberg, Charles Hallahan, Pamela Payton-Wright, Marty Keegan, Brian Neville, Constantine Hartofolis. **Credits:** Dir: Martin Brest; Prod: Tony Bill, Fred T. Gallo; Writer: Martin Brest; DP: Billy Williams; Ed: Robert W. Swink, C. Timothy O'Meara; Composer: Michael Small. Color, 99 min. **VHS**

Going My Way

(1944) Paramount
Lovable McCarey picture is a sentimental favorite. Dynamic young priest Bing adds sparkle to a parish, overseen by crusty old priest (Fitzgerald), that could sure use some. Crosby single-handedly wins over the local toughs by organizing a football team and bolsters the parish's coffers with a little ditty he sells. The whole thing just sings, particularly "Would You Like to Swing on a Star?" Golden Globes for Best Director; Best Supporting Actor: Barry Fitzgerald; Best Motion Picture, Drama. Academy Award Nominations: 10, including Best Actor: Barry Fitzgerald (the last actor to be nominated for two Academy Awards for the same role); Best Cinematography (B&W); Best Film Editing. **Academy Awards:** Best Director; Best Actor: Bing Crosby; Best Supporting Actor: Barry Fitzgerald; Best Song; Best Original Story; Best Screenplay; Best Picture. **Cast:** Bing Crosby, Barry Fitzgerald, Frank McHugh, James Brown, June Lockhart, Rise Stevens, William Frawley, Jean Heather, Porter Hall. **Credits:** Dir: Leo McCarey; Prod: Leo McCarey; Writer: Frank Butler, Frank Cavett; DP: Lionel Lindon; Ed: LeRoy Stone; Prod Design: Hans Dreier; Composer: Robert Emmett Dolan; Art Director: William Flannery. B&W, 126 min. **VHS**

Goin' South

(1978) Paramount
Nicholson's second directorial effort (and the screen debuts of Steenburgen and Belushi) is this humorous Western. Nicholson nearly has his neck in a noose before he finds a loophole that lets him avoid the gallows by slipping a wedding ring on a lonely spinster. Belushi's a hoot and Almendros contributed the striking color. **Cast:** Jack Nicholson, Mary Steenburgen, Danny De Vito, John Belushi, Christopher Lloyd, Veronica Cartwright, Richard Bradford, Jeff Morris, Tracey Walter, Ed Begley, Jr. **Credits:** Dir: Jack

Nicholson; Prod: Harry Gittes, Harold Schneider; Writer: John Herman Shaner, Al Ramrus, Charles Shyer, Alan Mandel; DP: Nestor Almendros; Ed: Richard Chew, John Fitzgerald; Prod Design: Toby Rafelson; Composer: Van Dyke Parks, Perry Jr. Botkin. Color, 109 min. **VHS**

Goin' to Town

(1935) Paramount
Mae's in the money in this one, after she inherits a gushing oil field. With cash in her kitty, she trys to add a touch of class to snare the heart of an engineer. West's in great form. **Cast:** Mae West, Monroe Owsley, Paul Cavanagh, Ivan Lebedeff, Marjorie Gateson, Fred Kohler, Tito Coral, Grant Withers, Luis Alberni. **Credits:** Dir: Alexander Hall; Prod: William LeBaron; Writer: Mae West; DP: Karl Struss; Ed: LeRoy Stone; Prod Design: Hans Dreier, Robert Usher; Composer: Sammy Fain. B&W, 71 min. **VHS**

Go into Your Dance

(1935) Warner Bros.
Stage crooner Jolson's fondness for Mexican sprees has caused his producers to force him out of showbiz. Luckily his adoring and clever sister, Molly (Farrell), doesn't give up on him. She sets him up with an ambitious and beautiful dancer (Keeler, Jolson's off-screen wife), and the two light up Chicago. Al returns to Broadway to make a splash with his own new nightclub but gets mixed up with a gangster (MacLane) and a nightclub owner (Morgan). Songs include "I'm a Latin from Manhattan," "About a Quarter to Nine," and "Cielito Lindo." **Cast:** Al Jolson, Ruby Keeler, Glenda Farrell, Barton MacLane, Patsy Kelly, Akim Tamiroff, Helen Morgan, Sharon Lynn, Benny Rubin, Phil Regan. **Credits:** Dir: Archie Mayo, Robert Florey, Michael Curtiz; Writer: Earl Baldwin; Story: Bradford Ropes; DP: Tony Gaudio; Ed: Harold McLernon; Composer: Al Dubin, Harry Warren; Art Director: John Hughes. B&W, 89 min.

Go, Johnny, Go!

(1958) Hal Roach
A rock-fueled jet back to the days when rock was new. A rock music promoter (Freed himself, rock-'n'-roll's first impresario) goes in search of a mystery contestant who won his star-making talent contest. The new teen idol, Johnny Melody, is surrounded with rare performances by rock's founding fathers, including Chuck Berry, Eddie Cochran, Ritchie Valens (his only screen appearance), Jackie

Wilson, The Cadillacs, and many others. **Cast:** Alan Freed, Jimmy Clanton, Chuck Berry, Sandy Stewart, Herb Vigran, Frank Wilcox, Barbara Woodell, Milton Frome. **Credits:** Dir: Paul Landres; Prod: Alan Freed; Writer: Gary Alexander; DP: Ed Fitzgerald; Ed: Walter Hannemann; Prod Design: McClure Capps; Composer: Leon Klatzkin. B&W, 75 min. VHS, LASER

Gold Diggers of 1933

(1933) Warner Bros.
It's Busby Berkeley time! The plot involves the usual nonsense about an upper-crust songwriter and his show-girl fiancée who stage an elaborate musical production, much to the consternation of his proper society family. Blondell's brassy fun, and watch for a young Rogers dancing to "We're in the Money." Another highlight: the dark, moody, and politically fascinating "Remember My Forgotten Man" number. Followed by two sequels. Academy Award Nomination for Best Sound Recording. **Cast:** Joan Blondell, Dick Powell, Ruby Keeler, Warren William, Aline MacMahon, Guy Kibbee, Ned Sparks, Ginger Rogers, Bobby Agnew, Sterling Holloway. **Credits:** Dir: Mervyn LeRoy; Prod: Robert Lord; Writer: Erwin Gelsey, James Seymour, David Boehm, Ben Markson; DP: Sol Polito; Ed: George Amy; Prod Design: Anton Grot; Costumes: Orry-Kelly. B&W, 98 min. VHS, LASER

Gold Diggers of 1935

(1935) Warner Bros.
Berkeley himself directed as well as choreographed the second Gold Diggers musical. What there is of a plot involves a young medical student escorting a beautiful debutante to a charity ball. A show must be put on! Love, comedy, singing, and dancing naturally follow. Includes "Lullaby of Broadway." **Cast:** Dick Powell, Adolphe Menjou, Gloria Stuart, Alice Brady, Hugh Herbert, Glenda Farrell, Frank McHugh, Joseph Cawthorn, Grant Mitchell, Dorothy Dare. **Credits:** Dir: Busby Berkeley; Prod: Robert Lord; Writer: Manuel Seff, Peter Milne; DP: George Barnes; Ed: George Amy; Prod Design: Anton Grot; Composer: Al Dubin, Harry Warren. B&W, 96 min. VHS

Gold Diggers of 1937

(1936) Warner Bros.
A musical that proves even insurance salesmen can be fun song-and-dance guys. This late entry in the Gold Diggers series presents an insurance salesman who falls in love with an

ex–chorus girl. The couple joins the girl's friend in a scheme to get $1 million in insurance money from a Broadway producer when he dies. The producer is a hypochondriac, however, and it eventually becomes clear that the only way for the four to make money is if they put on a show the producer has had in the works. **Cast:** Dick Powell, Joan Blondell, Glenda Farrell, Victor Moore. **Credits:** Dir: Lloyd Bacon; Prod: Hal B. Wallis; Writer: Warren Duff; Story: George Haight, Richard Maibaum, Michael Wallace; DP: Arthur Edeson; Ed: Thomas Richards; Composer: Al Dubin, E. Y. Harburg. B&W, 101 min.

The Golden Arrow

(1936) Warner Bros.
A comedy in which cafeteria worker Davis is hired by a cosmetics company to pose as an heiress and company spokeswoman. Trying to rid herself of pesky fortune hunters, she and a newspaper reporter get married out of convenience. He will have enough money to support himself while he writes a novel, and she won't have to worry about men after her for her supposed riches. The reporter sours on the deal, but truly falls in love with Davis when a rival heiress exposes her as a fraud. **Cast:** Bette Davis, George Brent, Eugene Pallette, Dick Foran, Carol Hughes. **Credits:** Dir: Alfred E. Green; Prod: Sam Bischoff; Writer: Michael Arlen, Charles Kenyon, Giorgio Prosperi; DP: Arthur Edeson; Ed: Thomas Pratt; Prod Design: Anton Grot; Composer: Franke Harling, Heinz Roemheld. B&W, 60 min.

Golden Boy

(1939) Columbia
In his debut performance, Holden scores as a violin prodigy who makes some extra dough on the side as a prizefighter. Not likely, but the performances make it work, particularly Stanwyck's as a corrupting influence. Tragic consequences result when she lures the golden boy from practicing his scales. Based on Clifford Odets's 1937 play. Academy Award Nomination for Best Original Score. **Cast:** William Holden, Barbara Stanwyck, Lee J. Cobb, Adolphe Menjou, Joseph Calleia, Sam Levene, Edward Brophy, Don Beddoe, Frank Jenks, Charles Halton. **Credits:** Dir: Rouben Mamoulian, Karl Freund; Prod: William Perlberg; Writer: Lewis Meltzer, Daniel Taradash, Sarah Y. Mason, Victor Heerman; DP: Nicholas Musuraca; Ed: Otto Meyer; Composer: Victor Young; Art Director: Lionel Banks. B&W, 99 min. VHS, LASER

Golden Earrings

(1947) Paramount
Dietrich and Milland don't strike many sparks, but Marlene's alluringly exotic. A former British spy (Milland) receives a set of gold earrings in the mail and recalls his wartime journey across Germany disguised as a Gypsy and accompanied by a beautiful Gypsy woman. During the trip, he gathers damaging information against the Nazis as he falls in love with the woman who hides him. **Cast:** Marlene Dietrich, Ray Milland, Quentin Reynolds, Murvyn Vye, Reinhold Schunzel, Bruce Lester, Dennis Hoey, Ivan Triesault, Hermine Sterler, Frank Butler. **Credits:** Dir: Mitchell Leisen, Abraham Polonsky; Prod: Harry Saltzman, Albert R. Broccoli; Writer: Harry Tugend, Helen Deutsch; Story: Richard Maibaum; DP: Daniel Fapp, Ted Moore; Ed: Alma Macrorie, Peter Hunt; Prod Design: Hans Dreier, John Meehan, Ken Adam, Peter Murton; Composer: Victor Young. B&W, 95 min. VHS

The Golden Hawk

(1952) Columbia
It's high fun on the high seas in this swashbuckling adventure comedy. Fleming plays a tough and sexy lady pirate who's being held captive by the governor. Hayden, the pirate "Golden Hawk," is her liberator, who unlocks some secrets about both their pasts, namely that Fleming is really a fallen society dame who's turned privateer to recover her stolen plantation fortune. **Cast:** Rhonda Fleming, Sterling Hayden, Helena Carter, John Sutton, Paul Cavanagh, Michael Ansara, Raymond Hatton, Alex Montoya, Poppy A. del Vando, Albert Pollet. **Credits:** Dir: Sidney Salkow; Prod: Sam Katzman; Writer: Robert E. Kent; Story: Frank Yerby; DP: William V. Skall; Ed: Edwin Bryant; Prod Design: Paul Palmentola; Composer: Mischa Bakaleinikoff. Color, 83 min.

Goldfinger

(1964) United Artists
In the third James Bond adventure, the dangerously suave spy's objective is to terminate criminal capitalist Auric Goldfinger (and his assistants Pussy Galore and Oddjob) and foil his plan to contaminate Fort Knox's gold with atomic radiation, a strategy that would dramatically increase the value of Goldfinger's own hoard. With the help of the usual bevy of beautiful women and ingenious gadgets, 007 spoils Goldfinger's fun. Based on Ian Fleming's 1959 novel. The laser release

includes interviews, trailers, photos, and more. **Academy Awards:** Best Sound Effects. **Cast:** Sean Connery, Gert Frobe, Honor Blackman, Shirley Eaton, Harold "Oddjob" Sakata. **Credits:** Dir: Guy Hamilton; Prod: Harry Saltzman, Albert Broccoli; Writer: Richard Maibaum, Paul Dehn; DP: Ted Moore; Ed: Peter Hunt; Composer: John Barry; Prod Design: Ken Adam. Color, 112 min. VHS, LASER, DVD

The Gold Rush
(1925) United Artists
This Chaplin classic finds Charlie in the Klondike searching for gold. Maintains a careful balance of masterful slapstick, romantic tenderness, and wry social satire. Also contains the celebrated "dancing dinner rolls" gag. Rerelease in 1942 featured sound narration. **Cast:** Charles Chaplin, Georgina Hale, Mack Swain. **Credits:** Dir: Charles Chaplin; Prod: Charles Chaplin; Writer: Charles Chaplin; DP: Roland Totheroh; Prod Design: Charles Hall. B&W, 80 min. VHS, LASER

The Goldwyn Follies
(1938) United Artists
This elaborate musical extravaganza centers around a Hollywood producer who hires an ordinary person to preview his movies before the public sees them. There are about a gazillion star cameos, a Hecht script, and lots of tunes by George and Ira Gershwin, but the proceedings are still pretty silly. Fans of the Ritz Brothers take note. Academy Award Nominations: Best Score; Best Interior Decoration. **Cast:** Edgar Bergen, Ritz Brothers, Adolphe Menjou, Helen Jepson, Vera Zorina, Kenny Baker, Andrea Leeds, Phil Baker, Bobby Clark, Jerome Cowan. **Credits:** Dir: George Marshall; Prod: Samuel Goldwyn; Writer: Ben Hecht; DP: Gregg Toland; Ed: Sherman Todd; Choreographer: George Balanchine; Costumes: Omar Kiam; Art Director: Richard Day. Color, 115 min. VHS, DVD

Gone Are the Days
(1963) Hammer
Having ordained himself a minister, Purlie Victorious returns with his wife, Lutievelle, to his hometown in Georgia. There he attempts to buy up an old barn owned by miser Captain Cotchipee in an attempt to build a church. The captain refuses to sell his barn, gleeful at the opportunity to quench Purlie's dreams. Purlie is determined, however, and enlists the aid of the captain's son Charlie. Charlie wrangles the barn for Purlie and it is soon converted into a church. Alda's debut. **Cast:** Ruby Dee, Ossie Davis, Sorrell Booke, Godfrey Cambridge, Hilda Haynes, Alan Alda, Beah Richards, Charles Welch, Ralph Roberts. **Credits:** Dir: Nicholas Webster; Prod: Nicholas Webster; Writer: Ossie Davis; DP: Boris Kaufman; Ed: Ralph Rosenblum; Prod Design: Kim Swados; Composer: Henry Cowen, Milton Okun. B&W, 97 min.

Gone With the Wind
(1939) MGM
One of the great cinematic achievements, technically as well as in enduring appeal, this is a movie that keeps finding an audience with every successive generation (it was restored—somewhat controversially—and re-released theatrically in 1998). The story and characters are familiar to even the most casual moviegoer: an indomitable southern belle (Leigh) loves and loses and loves again a slyly dashing war profiteer as she struggles to protect her family and beloved plantation, Tara, from the ravages of the Civil War. Based on Margaret Mitchell's 1936 novel, which at the time of the film's release, had surpassed 1.5 million copies sold. Selznick paid $50,000 for rights to the book and brought in a number of screenwriters in addition to Sidney Howard to help him shape the material. Among them were Edwin Justin Mayer, John Van Druten, Ben Hecht, F. Scott Fitzgerald, and Jo Swerling. For the part of Scarlett O'Hara, Selznick conducted a national talent search that has in itself become Hollywood legend and the basis of a movie. Scores of famous actresses tested for the part, including Bette Davis, Katharine Hepburn, Miriam Hopkins, Joan Crawford, Margaret Sullivan, Barbara Stanwyck, Paulette Goddard,

---

Raymond Benson's Favorite James Bond Movies

1. *From Russia with Love* **(1963)** because it captures the essence of Ian Fleming's novel(s) better than any other entry in the series. It has the best ensemble cast (Sean Connery at his best, Robert Shaw, Lotte Lenya, and my favorite Bond girl, Daniela Bianchi), and it is a serious, topical spy thriller from the Cold War era.

2. *Dr. No* **(1962)** because it is the first in the series, with a well-told story and good characterizations. Sean Connery's cool-as-hell first appearance as 007 in the casino, uttering the famous line, "Bond . . . James Bond," is *classic* cinema.

3. *Goldfinger* **(1964)** because it is the blueprint for the rest of the series. Humor became a more important element, but it is still handled darkly, with tongue in cheek, and it has the right mixture of glitz, action, sex, and gadgetry.

4. *On Her Majesty's Secret Service* **(1969)** because it is the one film that is the closest to Ian Fleming's original novel. And, despite George Lazenby in his one-shot as Bond (in a vastly underrated performance), it is a fond favorite among hard-core Bond fans.

5. Tie: *Thunderball* **(1965)** because it represents the bigness that the series became and is the high point of the "spy boom" of the '60s, and because of the groundbreaking underwater photography and Oscar-winning visual effects that set new standards for action-adventure films. *License to Kill* **(1989)**: A controversial choice (even among die-hard Bond fans), it's listed here because Timothy Dalton's intensely ruthless performance as Bond is the closest and most accurate portrayal of Ian Fleming's literary character ever presented on-screen. It is lean, mean, tough, and violent—the only film in the series that realistically presents the truly dangerous world Bond inhabits.

Raymond Benson is the official author of the James Bond adventures, chosen by the Ian Fleming estate.

Lana Turner, Jean Arthur, Mae West, Tallulah Bankhead, and Lucille Ball. In all, 32 actresses did screen tests for the film. Leigh was given the part on Christmas Day, 1938. Ronald Colman, Errol Flynn, and Gary Cooper were considered for the part of Rhett Butler, but the character was written with Clark Gable in mind. George Cukor was the film's original director, and Fleming was Cukor's successor. When Fleming fell sick, Sam Wood took over, but only for a short time. In addition to its nine Oscars, *GWTW* also won special Academy recognition for production designer Menzies's outstanding contribution to the use of color. *GWTW* was shot in three-strip Technicolor. At the time, there were only seven Technicolor cameras in existence, all of which were used for the production. McDaniel's Best Supporting Actress award was the first given to an African American. Chosen for the National Film Registry. Academy Award Nominations: 13, including Best Actor: Clark Gable; Best Supporting Actress: Olivia de Havilland; Best Score. **Academy Awards:** Best Actress: Vivien Leigh; Best Color Cinematography; Best Director; Best Film Editing; Best Interior Decoration; Best Screenplay; Best Supporting Actress: Hattie McDaniel; Best Picture. **Cast:** Clark Gable, Vivien Leigh, Leslie Howard, Olivia de Havilland, Hattie McDaniel, Thomas Mitchell, Barbara O'Neil, Evelyn Keyes, Ann Rutherford, George Reeves. **Credits:** Dir: Victor Fleming; Prod: David O. Selznick; Writer: Sidney Howard; Story: Margaret Mitchell; DP: Ernest Haller, Lee Garmes, Ray Rennahan; Ed: Hal C. Kern, James E. Newcom; Prod Design: William Cameron Menzies; Composer: Adolph Deutsch, Max Steiner, Hugo Friedhofer, Heinz Roemheld; Costumes: Walter Plunkett. Color, 233 min. **VHS, LASER, DVD**

Goodbye, Again
(1961) United Artists
Sophisticated meller set in Paris and starring a luminous, lovely Bergman. A 40-ish interior decorator's despair over her wealthy lover's (Montand) unfaithful ways drives her into the arms of a younger man, the son of a client. **Cast:** Ingrid Bergman, Anthony Perkins, Yves Montand, Jessie Royce Landis, Diahann Carroll, Jackie Lane, Pierre Dux, Jean Clarke, Ralph Taeger. **Credits:** Dir: Anatole Litvak; Prod: Anatole Litvak; Writer: Samuel Taylor; DP: Armand Thirard; Ed: Bert Bates; Prod Design: Alexander Trauner; Composer: Georges Auric. B&W, 120 min. **VHS**

Goodbye, Columbus
(1969) Paramount
Philip Roth's biting satire of middle-class Jewish life brought to the screen. Benjamin stars in his film debut as an innocent, bookish type from the Bronx thrown into the maelstrom of MacGraw's (her film debut) well-to-do Westchester family as they plan their wedding. Sharply observed comedy of class and manners. Academy Award Nominations: Best (Adapted) Screenplay. **Cast:** Richard Benjamin, Jack Klugman, Ali MacGraw, Nan Martin, Michael Meyers, Lori Shelle, Royce Wallace, Sylvie Straus. **Credits:** Dir: Larry Peerce, Ralph Rosenblum; Prod: Stanley R. Jaffe; Writer: Arnold Schulman; DP: Gerald Hirschfeld; Composer: Charles Fox; Art Director: Manny Gerard. Color, 105 min. **VHS**

The Goodbye Girl
(1977) Warner Bros.
This intimate Simon comedy launched Dreyfuss's career. A divorcée (Mason) and her daughter are forced to share their apartment with an actor (Dreyfuss), and their reluctantly shared struggle to survive in New York leads unexpectedly to love. Later made into a Broadway musical. Academy Award Nominations: 5, including Best Picture; Best Actress: Marsha Mason; Best (Original) Screenplay. **Academy Awards:** Best Actor: Richard Dreyfuss. **Cast:** Richard Dreyfuss, Marsha Mason, Quinn Cummings, Paul Benedict, Barbara Rhoades. **Credits:** Dir: Herbert Ross; Prod: Ray Stark; Writer: Neil Simon; DP: David M. Walsh; Ed: John F. Burnett; Prod Design: Albert Brenner; Composer: Dave Grusin; Costumes: Ann Roth; SFX: Al Griswold; Set Designer: Jerry Wunderlich. Color, 110 min. **VHS, LASER**

Goodbye, Mr. Chips
(1939) MGM
The touching story of a shy Latin professor at an English boys' school who finds happiness and fulfillment with an outgoing, vivacious woman. But after her tragic death, he dedicates his life to his charges. Garson was nominated for an Oscar in her film debut, and Donat won for his best-remembered role. Based on the novel by James Hilton. Academy Award Nominations: 7, including Best Picture; Best Director; Best Actress: Greer Garson; Best Actor: Robert Donat; Best Adapted Screenplay. **Academy Awards:** Best Actor: Robert Donat. **Cast:** Robert Donat, Greer Garson, John Mills, Terry Kilburn, Paul Hen-

reid, Judith Furse, Lyn Harding, Milton Rosmer, Frederick Leister. **Credits:** Dir: Sam Wood, Sidney Franklin; Prod: Victor Saville; Writer: R. C. Sherriff, Claudine West, Eric Maschwitz; DP: Freddie Young; Ed: Charles Frend; Composer: John Williams, Richard Addinsell. B&W, 114 min. **VHS, LASER**

Goodbye, Mr. Chips
(1969) MGM
Musical remake of the 1939 film about a proper British schoolmaster (O'Toole) who falls in love with a music-hall girl (pop star Petula Clark in a rare film role). O'Toole seems right for the character but struggles with the musical aspects of the performance. Director Ross's debut. Based on James Hilton's 1934 novel. Academy Award Nominations: Best Actor: Peter O'Toole; Best Score of a Musical Picture. **Cast:** Peter O'Toole, Petula Clark, Michael Redgrave, George Baker, Sian Phillips, Michael Bryant, Jack Hedley, Alison Leggatt, Clinton Greyn, Barbara Couper. **Credits:** Dir: Herbert Ross; Prod: Arthur P. Jacobs; Story: Terence Rattigan; DP: Oswald Morris; Ed: Ralph Kemplen; Prod Design: Ken Adam; Composer: John Williams; Art Director: Maurice Fowler. Color, 156 min. **VHS, LASER**

Goodbye, My Fancy
(1951) Warner Bros.
Crawford stars as an ambitious congresswoman who returns to finish her degree at the school from which she was expelled 20 years earlier for having an affair with a professor. Sparks reunite as soon as Young, now the school president, lays eyes on Crawford again. A triangle develops when a photographer-reporter vies to break up the romance. Watch for Corby (Grandma Walton) and Arden in small roles. **Cast:** Joan Crawford, Robert Young, Frank Lovejoy, Eve Arden, John Alvin, Mary Carver, Lucius Cook, Ellen Corby, Morgan Farley, Virginia Gibson, Creighton Hale, Fred Howard. **Credits:** Dir: Vincent Sherman; Prod: Henry Blanke; Writer: Ivan Goff, Fay Kanin, Ben Roberts; DP: Ted McCord; Ed: Rudi Fehr; Prod Design: Stanley Fleischer; Composer: Ray Heindorf. B&W, 107 min.

Goodbye, My Lady
(1956) Warner Bros.
Wellman directed this poignant tale of a young boy (De Wilde), an elderly man (Brennan), and the dog that brings joy to their lives. Fine family viewing. **Cast:** Walter Brennan, Phil Harris, Brandon De Wilde, Sidney

Poitier, William Hopper, Louise Beavers. **Credits:** Dir: William Wellman; Writer: A. S. Fleischman; DP: William Clothier; Ed: Fred MacDowell; Composer: Laurindo Almeida, George Field. B&W, 95 min. **VHS, LASER**

Good Day for a Hanging
(1958) Columbia
A marshal who solves the murder of a town's sheriff becomes an enemy of the people when a lawyer turns the townsfolk against him. However, the bandit's attorney manages to convince most of the townspeople that the jailed man is really not to blame for the crime. Before long, even the new marshal's daughter, who once was romantically involved with the defendant, turns against her father. Even when the culprit is found guilty there's no support in town for his death sentence. A Western drama with an interestingly different twist. **Cast:** Fred MacMurray, Maggie Hayes, Robert Vaughn, Joan Blackman, James Drury, Denver Pyle, Wendell Holmes, Edmon Ryan. **Credits:** Dir: Nathan Juran; Prod: Charles H. Schneer; Writer: Daniel Ullman; DP: Henry Freulich; Ed: Jerome Thoms; Art Director: Robert Peterson. Color, 85 min. **VHS**

The Good Earth
(1937) MGM
Excellent, painstaking adaptation of Pearl S. Buck's 1931 tome about a Chinese peasant family whose rise to wealth nearly destroys them, save for the saintly O-Lan. The special effects and the cinematography are wonderful, and Rainer won the second of her consecutive Oscars for Best Actress. This was Thalberg's last production and is dedicated to his memory. Academy Award Nominations: 5, including Best Picture; Best Director. **Academy Awards:** Best Actress: Luise Rainer; Best Cinematography. **Cast:** Paul Muni, Luise Rainer, Walter Connolly, Keye Luke, Tillie Losch, Charley Grapewin, Jessie Ralph, Harold Huber. **Credits:** Dir: Sidney Franklin; Prod: Irving Thalberg; Writer: Talbot Jennings, Tess Slesinger, Frances Marion, Claudine West; Story: Pearl S. Buck; DP: Karl Freund; Ed: Basil Wrangell; Prod Design: Cedric Gibbons; Composer: Herbert Stothart; Costumes: Dolly Tree; Set Designer: Edwin B. Willis. B&W, 138 min. **VHS**

The Good Fairy
(1935) Universal
In this goofy comedy, small-on-sense-big-on-dreams Sullavan forsakes her Hungarian asylum for show-biz: she finds a job as usherette in a movie theater. Her plot is to secretly support the needy Dr. Sporum (Marshall) by passing on gifts laid out for her by the millionaire Konrad (Morgan), whose intentions, apparently, are the worst possible. Misunderstandings abound, until her friend, the gigantic waiter Detlaff (Owen), intervenes, not quite saving the day. Future director Sturges wrote the script from a Molnar play. Remade in 1947 with Deanna Durbin as *I'll Be Yours*. **Cast:** Margaret Sullavan, Herbert Marshall, Frank Morgan, Reginald Owen, Eric Blore, Beulah Bondi, Alan Hale, Cesar Romero, Luis Alberni. **Credits:** Dir: William Wyler; Prod: Carl Laemmle; Writer: Preston Sturges, Ferenc Molnar; DP: Norbert F. Brodine; Ed: Daniel Mandell; Prod Design: Charles D. Hall; Composer: Heinz Roemheld. B&W, 98 min.

Good Girls Go to Paris
(1939) Columbia
Wacky romantic comedy with spunky Blondell, a waitress who confides to one of her professors that her greatest ambition is to marry into money and see the world. Her scheme quickly gets out of control, however, as she becomes the recipient of four simultaneous proposals, gets accused of both blackmail and being a hit-and-run driver, and is accused of being a home wrecker. **Cast:** Melvyn Douglas, Joan Blondell, Walter Connolly, Alan Curtis, John Bennett Perry, Isabel Jeans, Stanley Brown, Alex D'Arcy, Henry Hunter, Clarence Kolb. **Credits:** Dir: Alexander Hall; Prod: William Perlberg; Writer: Gladys Lehman; Story: William Joyce Cowen, Lenore J. Coffee; DP: Henry Freulich; Ed: Al Clark; Composer: Morris Stoloff. B&W, 75 min.

The Good Guys and the Bad Guys
(1969) Warner Bros.
A comedy-Western that uses the tough-guy personas of the stars to examine what happens when bad guys get too old to be bad. Mitchum plays an aging sheriff tracking down his longtime nemesis Kennedy, who has nowhere to turn when his gang gives the old gunslinger an unwelcome early retirement. **Cast:** Robert Mitchum, George Kennedy, David Carradine, John Carradine, Tina Louise, Martin Balsam, Douglas Fowley, Lois Nettleton, John Davis Chandler, Marie Windsor. **Credits:** Dir: Burt Kennedy; Prod: Ronald Cohen, Dennis Shryack; Writer: Ronald M. Cohen, Dennis Shryack; DP: Harry Stradling; Ed: Otho S. Lovering; Prod Design: Stan Jolley; Composer: William Lava; Costumes: Yvonne Wood; Art Director: Ralph S. Hurst. Color, 90 min. **VHS**

Good Morning, Miss Dove
(1955) Fox
This heartwarming picture gives a long, loving look at the life of a New England schoolteacher (Jones) whose life has been devoted to her students. As she nears death, the film presents flashbacks showing the profound effect her interest, wisdom, and kindness played in the lives of her students. Tough, quiet Connors owes Miss Dove for helping him keep out of jail. The playwright (Paris) would never have had the necessary confidence without her. Even her doctor (Stack) who just might be able to save her life owes his practice to Miss Dove. **Cast:** Jennifer Jones, Kipp Hamilton, Robert Douglas, Peggy Knudsen, Marshall Thompson, Chuck Connors, Robert Stack, Jerry Paris, Mary Wickes, Richard Deacon. **Credits:** Dir: Henry Koster; Prod: Samuel G. Engel; Writer: Eleanore Griffin, Frances Gray Patton; DP: Leon Shamroy; Ed: William Reynolds; Prod Design: Mark-Lee Kirk; Composer: Leigh Harline. Color, 120 min.

Good Neighbor Sam
(1964) Columbia
A delightful Lemmon performance in the story of an advertising executive who good-naturedly agrees to pose as the husband of his attractive neighbor (Schneider) so that she can inherit a fortune. When his biggest client also falls for the ruse, the bogus couple find themselves the centerpiece of a new campaign. **Cast:** Jack Lemmon, Romy Schneider, Dorothy Provine, Edward G. Robinson, Mike Connors, Anne Seymour, Charles Lane, Louis Nye, Edward Andrews, Robert Q. Lewis. **Credits:** Dir: David Swift; Prod: David Swift; Writer: James Fritzell, Everett Greenbaum; DP: Burnett Guffey; Ed: Charles Nelson; Prod Design: Dale Hennesy; Composer: Frank DeVol. Color, 131 min. **VHS**

Good News
(1947) MGM
Lawford tries on his dancing shoes in a Comden-Green refurbishing of a vintage '20s musical. College football star Lawford recruits brainy Allyson to tutor him in French and finds unexpected romance, but a vampy coed is just itching to get in the way. Includes nostalgic numbers such as "The Best

Things in Life Are Free" and "Varsity Drag." Academy Award Nominations: Best Song ("Pass That Peace Pipe"). **Cast:** June Allyson, Peter Lawford, Joan McCracken, Patricia Marshall, Ray McDonald, Mel Torme, Robert Strickland, Donald MacBride, Tom Dugan, Adolph Green. **Credits:** Dir: Charles Walters; Prod: Arthur Freed; Writer: Betty Comden; DP: Charles Schoenbaum; Ed: Albert Akst; Prod Design: Cedric Gibbons; Art Director: Edward C. Carfagno. Color, 95 min. **VHS, LASER**

The Good, the Bad and the Ugly

(1966) United Artists
The culmination of Leone's renowned Dollars series that includes *A Fistful of Dollars* (1964) and *For a Few Dollars More* (1965). Set during the Civil War, this wagonload of grit carries three desperadoes whose squinting eyes are fixed on a Confederate treasure. While dodging authorities, they keep busy stabbing each other firmly in the back. A typical Leone picture with brooding vistas, leisurely pacing, operatic violence, and a haunting score from Morricone. **Cast:** Clint Eastwood, Eli Wallach, Lee Van Cleef, Mario Brega, Aldo Giuffre, Chelo Alonso, Luigi Pistilli, Rada Rassimov, Enzo Petito, Claudio Scarchilli. **Credits:** Dir: Sergio Leone; Prod: Alberto Grimaldi; Writer: Sergio Leone; Story: Luciano Vincenzoni; DP: Tonino Delli Colli; Ed: Nino Baragli, Eugenio Alabiso; Composer: Ennio Morricone; Art Director: Carlo Simi. Color, 161 min. **VHS, LASER, DVD**

The Gorgeous Hussy

(1936) MGM
In this tale of political drama and romantic scandals, Crawford plays Andrew Jackson's mistress, who has both romantic and political aspirations, and winds up embarrassing everyone around her. A great cast, beautiful costumes, and rich setting can't save this somewhat tedious period piece. Academy Award Nominations: 2. **Cast:** Joan Crawford, Lionel Barrymore, Robert Taylor, Franchot Tone, Melvyn Douglas, James Stewart, Louis Calhern, Alison Skipworth, Beulah Bondi, Melville Cooper. **Credits:** Dir: Clarence Brown; Prod: Joseph L. Mankiewicz; Writer: Stephen Morehouse Avery, Ainsworth Morgan; Story: Samuel Hopkins Adams; DP: George J. Folsey; Ed: Blanche Sewell; Prod Design: Cedric Gibbons; Choreographer: Val Raset; Composer: Herbert Stothart; Costumes: Adrian. B&W, 103 min. **VHS**

Gorilla at Large

(1954) Fox
Thriller filmed in 3-D and set in an amusement park whose main attraction is a live gorilla act. When three murders occur, a law student who works part-time in a gorilla suit is accused, and so is the husband of the trapeze artist. The true murderer gets carried off by the real gorilla, who scales a roller coaster before he is shot. Hilarious and actually not a bad mystery. **Cast:** Cameron Mitchell, Anne Bancroft, Lee J. Cobb, Raymond Burr, Charlotte Austin, Peter Whitney, Lee Marvin, Warren Stevens, John Kellogg, Charles Tannen. **Credits:** Dir: Harmon Jones; Prod: Robert Jacks; Writer: Leonard Praskins, Barney Slater; DP: Lloyd Ahern; Ed: George Gittens, Paul Weatherwax; Composer: Lionel Newman; Art Director: Addison Hehr, Lyle Wheeler. Color, 84 min.

Go Tell the Spartans

(1978) Avco Embassy
A less-well-known Vietnam War picture with an interesting point of view, formed while memories of the war were still fresh. Lancaster plays a tough U.S. military adviser in 1964 assigned to the abandoned French outpost of Muc Wa, where he must assemble a platoon out of inexperienced American soldiers and hardened Vietnamese mercenaries. As he witnesses the conditions firsthand, his doubts about U.S. involvement grow. **Cast:** Burt Lancaster, Craig Wasson, Jonathan Goldsmith, Marc Singer, Joe Unger, Dennis Howard, David Clennon, Evan Kim, John Megna, Hilly Hicks. **Credits:** Dir: Ted Post; Prod: Allan F. Bodoh, Mitchell Cannold; Writer: Wendell Mayes; DP: Harry Stradling; Ed: Millie Moore; Prod Design: Jack Senter; Composer: Dick Halligan. Color, 114 min. **VHS, LASER**

Go West

(1940) MGM
The way the West wasn't won. The Marx Brothers mess with manifest destiny when they head to the Wild West with the railroad. Late for the Brothers and it shows, but there's always a laugh or two. **Cast:** Marx Brothers, John Carroll, Diana Lewis, Robert Barratt, Walter Woolf King, Mitchell Lewis, Tully Marshall. **Credits:** Dir: Edward Buzzell; Prod: Jack Cummings; Writer: Irving Brecher; DP: Leonard Smith; Ed: Blanche Sewell; Prod Design: Cedric Gibbons; Composer: Bronislau Kaper, Roger Edens. B&W, 82 min. **VHS**

Go West Young Man

(1936) Paramount
The celebrated Mae West, this time a brassy Hollywood sexpot accustomed to getting her way, gets stranded in a small town during a publicity tour for her latest movie. Scott helps her pass the time, when she can stay out of the clutches of her oily publicist. Because her studio contract stipulates that she remain "available," Mae never finds Mr. Right. It doesn't stop her from looking. **Cast:** Mae West, Warren William, Randolph Scott, Elizabeth Patterson, Lyle Talbot, Isabel Jewell, Margaret Perry, Alice Brady, Etienne Girardot, Maynard Holmes. **Credits:** Dir: Henry Hathaway; Prod: Emanuel Cohen; Writer: Mae West; DP: Karl Struss; Ed: Ray Curtiss; Composer: George Stoll. B&W, 80 min. **VHS**

The Graduate

(1967) Avco Embassy
A satirical coming-of-age comedy that became an emotional touchstone for an entire generation. In the late '60s, a confused college graduate is pulled in myriad directions by family, friends, and associates just days after receiving his diploma. Seduced by an older friend of the family, the young man carries on an affair with the married woman even as he chases his heart's desire with her engaged daughter. This established Nichols as a major director and was Hoffman's first major role. Its impact on popular culture is immeasurable: "Plastics" will live on eternally as depressing but solid career advice, and older women will never eye younger men without fear of becoming a "Mrs. Robinson." Henry cowrote the influential screenplay based on the novel by Webb. The special 25th-anniversary video edition includes the original film plus *The Graduate at 25,* a short documentary on the making of the film, and a new cut of "Mrs. Robinson" performed by the Lemonheads. The laserdisc version includes an audio essay analyzing the film, several screen tests, candid photos and wardrobe stills, and a feature depicting the evolution of the screenplay. Its many honors include the Cannes prize for Best New Actor: Dustin Hoffman. Academy Award Nominations: 7, including Best Picture; Best Actor: Dustin Hoffman; Best Actress: Anne Bancroft; Best Supporting Actress: Katharine Ross; Best (Adapted) Screenplay. **Academy Awards:** Best Director. **Cast:** Anne Bancroft, Dustin Hoffman, Katharine Ross, Murray Hamilton, William Daniels, Elizabeth Wilson, Brian Avery, Walter Brooke, Norman Fell, Elisabeth Fraser. **Credits:**

Dir: Mike Nichols; Prod: Lawrence Turman; Writer: Calder Willingham, Buck Henry; Story: Charles Webb; DP: Robert Surtees; Ed: Sam O'Steen; Prod Design: Richard Sylbert; Composer: Dave Grusin, Simon and Garfunkel; Costumes: Patricia Zipprodt; Set Designer: George Robert Nelson. Color, 106 min. VHS, LASER

Grand Hotel
(1932) MGM
The Best Picture of 1932 established the episodic narrative device of following the diverse stories of various characters who drift through a location. It was to be repeated onboard ships, trains, and planes, in apartment buildings, resorts, anywhere the camera could observe comings and goings and the drama inherent in everyday life. Garbo stands out in an outstanding crowd of the screen's great faces as a world-weary ballerina pining for her jewel-thief lover (John Barrymore). Other stories found in a Berlin hotel where "people come, people go, nothing ever happens" revolve around Lionel Barrymore's imminent death, Crawford's social climber, and Beery's business traveler. One of the greats. Reworked for a less-successful Broadway musical. **Academy Awards:** Best Picture. **Cast:** Greta Garbo, John Barrymore, Wallace Beery, Joan Crawford, Lionel Barrymore, Jean Hersholt, Robert McWade, Purnell Pratt, Ferdinand Gottschalk, Rafaela Ottiano. **Credits:** Dir: Edmund Goulding; Writer: William A. Drake; Ed: Blanche Sewell; Prod Design: Cedric Gibbons. B&W, 114 min. VHS, LASER

Grand Prix
(1966) MGM
Frankenheimer once again pushes the stylistic envelope with this high-speed, realistic drama about Grand Prix auto racing complete with up-to-the-minute '60s techniques of panoramic widescreen, split-screen, and cameras mounted on the cars. Garner stars as a race-car driver competing for the world championship in a series of races that takes him from Monte Carlo to Mexico City. **Academy Awards:** Best Film Editing; Best Sound. **Cast:** James Garner, Eva Marie Saint, Yves Montand, Toshiro Mifune, Brian Bedford, Jessica Walter, Antonio Sabato, Adolfo Celi, Claude Dauphin, Enzo Fiermonte. **Credits:** Dir: John Frankenheimer; Prod: Edward Lewis; Writer: Robert Alan Aurthur, William Hanley; DP: Lionel Lindon; Ed: Fredric Steinkamp; Prod Design:

Richard Sylbert; Composer: Maurice Jarre; SFX: Milt Rice. Color, 178 min. VHS, LASER

Grand Theft Auto
(1977) New World
Howard made his directorial debut and wrote the script for this car-chase collage. A rich heiress elopes to Las Vegas with her boyfriend in a stolen Rolls-Royce, prompting her father to offer a reward for her return. The promise of the reward motivates a cross-country chase and spectacular crashes. **Cast:** Ron Howard, Nancy Morgan, Marion Ross, Peter Isacksen, Barry Cahill, Hoke Howell, Lew Brown, Rance Howard. **Credits:** Dir: Ron Howard; Prod: Jon Davison; Writer: Ron Howard, Rance Howard; DP: Gary Graver; Ed: Joe Dante; Composer: Peter Ivers; Art Director: Keith Michaels. Color, 84 min. VHS

The Grapes of Wrath
(1940) Fox
Ford directs what many consider to be Fonda's greatest role. Based on Steinbeck's Pulitzer Prize–winning 1939 novel, the story follows an Oklahoma family's escape from the Dustbowl to join the migration to California's fruit harvest. Fonda shines as Tom Joad, a poor farmer who refuses to be beaten down by misfortune and oppression, and Darwell is moving as the loving backbone of the Joad family. An unusually compassionate and socially conscious film, it's like a series of Dorothea Lange photos from the Depression, full of suffering and dignity. Selected as a National Film Registry Outstanding Film. Academy Award Nominations: 7, including Best Picture; Best Actor: Henry Fonda; Best Screenplay. **Academy Awards:** Best Director; Best Supporting Actress: Jane Darwell. **Cast:** Henry Fonda, Jane Darwell, John Carradine, Doris Bowden, Charley Grapewin, Russell Simpson, O. Z. Whitehead, John Qualen, Eddie Quillan, Zeffie Tilbury. **Credits:** Dir: John Ford; Prod: Nunnally Johnson; Writer: Nunnally Johnson; Story: John Steinbeck; DP: Gregg Toland; Ed: Robert Simpson; Prod Design: Mark-Lee Kirk; Costumes: Gwen Wakeling; Art Director: Richard Day; Set Designer: Thomas Little. B&W, 129 min. VHS, LASER

Gray Lady Down
(1978) Universal
The tense story of the nuclear submarine *Neptune*, which is rammed by a Norwegian freighter, plummeting 1,400 feet before coming to rest on a crum-

bling sea-shelf. Using his untested two-man sub, a diving expert embarks upon a daring rescue attempt. Late-'70s vintage disaster flick with better-than-average performances. **Cast:** Charlton Heston, David Carradine, Stacy Keach, Ned Beatty, Stephen McHattie, Ronny Cox, Dorian Harewood, Rosemary Forsyth, Hilly Hicks, Charles Cioffi. **Credits:** Dir: David Greene; Prod: Walter Mirisch; Writer: Howard Sackler, James Whittaker; DP: Stevan Larner; Ed: Robert W. Swink; Prod Design: William Tuntke; Composer: Jerry Fielding. Color, 111 min. VHS

Grease
(1978) Paramount
The zippy smash-hit translation to the screen from the Broadway musical tribute to the fabulous '50s. As a new school year begins, wholesome Australian exchange student Sandy (pop star Olivia Newton-John) and ducktailed, leather-jacket-clad Danny (John Travolta) parlay their summertime romance into an on-and-off attraction that may or may not cross clique lines. Sandy seriously cramps Danny's style, so he dumps her. In response, Sandy begins dating a wholesome athlete, but, as a hedge, she also joins the gum-chewin', tough-talkin' clique known as the Pink Ladies. The popular sound track includes "You're the One That I Want," "Hopelessly Devoted to You," "Summer Nights," and the title tune. Academy Award Nomination for Best Song ("Hopelessly Devoted to You"). **Cast:** John Travolta, Olivia Newton-John, Stockard Channing, Jeff Conaway, Eve Arden, Barry Pearl, Michael Tucci, Kelly Ward, Didi Conn, Jamie Donnelly. **Credits:** Dir: Randal Kleiser; Prod: Robert Stigwood, Allan Carr; Writer: Bronte Woodard, Allan Carr; DP: Bill Butler; Ed: John F. Burnett; Prod Design: Philip M. Jeffries; Choreographer: Patricia Birch; Composer: John Farrar, Bill Oakes, Louis St. Louis; Costumes: Albert Wolsky. Color, 110 min. VHS, LASER

Greaser's Palace
(1972)
Robert Downey, Sr. (*Putney Swope*), directed this parody of the life of Christ, set in a small western town. A bizarre drifter reveals his spiritual destiny and wanders the town performing healing "miracles." Downey, Jr., age seven, makes an appearance as an injured child. **Cast:** Albert Henderson, Allan Arbus, Luana Anders, George Morgan. **Credits:** Dir: Robert Downey; Prod: Cyma Rubin; Writer: Robert Downey; DP: Peter Powell; Ed: Bud

Smith; Composer: Jack Nitzsche; Set Designer: David Forman. Color, 91 min. **VHS**

The Great American Broadcast
(1941) Fox
This whirlwind musical comedy also depicts the early days of radio. Two war buddies, Payne and Oakie, come back from the Great War and with little to lose embark on careers in the newest business around: radio. Some hard work and good ideas have them rising to the top of the industry when a romance between Payne's girl Faye and his buddy threatens to spoil everything. While the two men smolder, Faye becomes a singing sensation. Lots of cameos and songs from radio stars of the era. **Cast:** Alice Faye, Jack Oakie, John Payne, Cesar Romero, James Newill, Mary Beth Hughes, Eula Morgan, William Pawley, Lucien Littlefield, Edward Conrad. **Credits:** Dir: Archie Mayo; Prod: Darryl F. Zanuck; Writer: Edwin Blum, Robert Ellis, Don Ettlinger; DP: J. Peverell Marley, Leon Shamroy; Ed: Robert Simpson; Prod Design: Richard Hogsett; Composer: Alfred Newman. B&W, 90 min.

The Great Caruso
(1951) MGM
This satisfying fictionalized biography explores the life and loves of the great tenor from Naples who became the toast of the Metropolitan Opera in New York City but died just as he reached his peak. Lanza is magnificent in the role, and the score is an opera lover's dream, with 27 musical numbers, including arias from *La Boheme, I Pagliacci,* and *Rigoletto.* **Academy Awards:** Best Sound Recording. **Cast:** Mario Lanza, Ann Blyth, Jarmila Novotna, Dorothy Kirsten, Carl Benton Reid, Eduard Franz, Ludwig Donath. **Credits:** Dir: Richard Thorpe; Prod: Joe Pasternak; Writer: Sonya Levien, William Ludwig; DP: Joseph Ruttenberg; Ed: Gene Ruggiero; Choreographer: Peter Herman Adler; Composer: Johnny Green; Costumes: Helen Rose, Gile Steele; SFX: Peter Ballbusch, Warren Newcombe; Art Director: Gabriel Scognamillo; Set Designer: Jack D. Moore, Edwin B. Willis. Color, 109 min. **VHS, LASER**

Great Day in the Morning
(1956) RKO
Just prior to the outbreak of the Civil War, northern and southern partisans begin violently drawing sides while also joining in the Gold Rush fever.

Okay Western directed by Tourneur. **Cast:** Virginia Mayo, Robert Stack, Ruth Roman, Alex Nicol, Raymond Burr, Regis Toomey. **Credits:** Dir: Jacques Tourneur; Prod: Edmund Grainger; Writer: Lesser Samuels; Story: Robert Hardy Andrews; DP: William E. Snyder; Ed: Harry Marker; Prod Design: Albert S. D'Agostino; Composer: Leith Stevens; Costumes: Gwen Wakeling; Art Director: Jack Okey. Color, 92 min. **VHS**

The Great Dictator
(1940) United Artists
Chaplin has a dual role in this film, his first with full dialogue: a sweet-natured Jewish barber and a murderous Hitler-type dictator. The film had huge satirical impact and made Chaplin a detested enemy of the Reich. Particularly delectable comic scenes are Hynkel's balletic "pas de deux" with a globe, and a cream-cake fight between Hynkel and Napoloni, the dictator of Bacteria (Oakie). **Cast:** Charlie Chaplin, Paulette Goddard, Jack Oakie, Reginald Gardiner, Henry Daniell, Billy Gilbert, Maurice Moscovich, Emma Dunn, Grace Hayle, Carter DeHaven. **Credits:** Dir: Charles Chaplin; Prod: Charles Chaplin; Writer: Charles Chaplin; DP: Roland Totheroh, Karl Struss; Ed: Willard Nico; Composer: Meredith Willson; Art Director: J. Russell Spencer. B&W, 128 min. **VHS, LASER**

The Great Escape
(1963) United Artists
An all-star cast comprises the American, British, and Canadian prisoners in a German P.O.W. camp as they join in a single mass break for freedom to distract the Nazi war effort. This epic film, filled with three-dimensional characters, great attention to detail, and arch humor, was based on a true story from the book by Paul Brickhill. Academy Award Nominations: Best Editing. **Cast:** Steve McQueen, James Garner, James Coburn, Richard Attenborough, James Donald, Charles Bronson, Donald Pleasence, David McCallum, Gordon Jackson, John Leyton. **Credits:** Dir: John Sturges; Prod: John Sturges; Writer: W. R. Burnett, James Clavell; DP: Daniel Fapp; Ed: Ferris Webster; Prod Design: Fernando Carrere; Composer: Elmer Bernstein. Color, 172 min. **VHS, LASER, DVD**

The Greatest
(1977) Columbia
Ali portrays himself in this film autobiography. The docudrama follows Ali's career from gold medal victories at

the Olympic Games to the heavyweight championship of the world. **Cast:** Muhammad Ali, Ernest Borgnine, Robert Duvall, James Earl Jones, Lloyd Haynes, John Marley, David Huddleston, Ben Johnson, Dina Merrill, Roger E. Mosley. **Credits:** Dir: Tom Gries; Prod: John Marshall; Writer: Ring Lardner; Story: Muhammad Ali; DP: Harry Stradling; Ed: Byron Brandt; Prod Design: Robert Smith; Composer: Michael Masser; Costumes: Eric Seelig, Sandra Stewart; SFX: Candy Flanagin; Set Designer: Solomon Brewer. Color, 101 min. **VHS**

The Greatest Show on Earth
(1952) Paramount
A dazzling, only-by-DeMille spectacle focusing on life with a traveling three-ring circus. Stewart appears in an unfamiliar guise as a clown hiding from his past (as a doctor!), and there is romance and adventure under this big top, too. Look for many guest appearances. DeMille went all out recreating the color and pageantry of the circus, even traveling with Barnum and Bailey to learn the rhythms of big-top life. Golden Globes for Best Director; Best Color Cinematography; Best Motion Picture, Drama. Academy Award Nominations: 5, including Best Director; Best Editing. **Academy Awards:** Best Picture; Best Motion Picture Story. **Cast:** Betty Hutton, Charlton Heston, Dorothy Lamour, James Stewart, Gloria Grahame, Cornel Wilde, Lyle Bettger, Henry Wilcoxon, Lawrence Tierney, John Kellogg. **Credits:** Dir: Cecil B. DeMille; Prod: Cecil B. DeMille; Writer: Fredric M. Frank, Barre Lyndon; Story: Frank Cavett; DP: George Barnes, Peverell Marley, Wallace Kelley; Ed: Anne Bauchens; Prod Design: Hal Pereira; Choreographer: Richard Barstow; Composer: Victor Young; Costumes: Miles White, Edith Head, Dorothy Jeakins; SFX: Gordon Jennings, Paul K. Lerpae, Devereaux Jennings; Art Director: Walter Tyler; Set Designer: Sam Comer, Ray Moyer. Color, 149 min. **VHS, LASER**

The Greatest Story Ever Told
(1965) United Artists
Hollywood's big-screen rendering of the life of Christ. Von Sydow stars as the Son of God, but biblical strongman Heston steals the show as the impassioned John the Baptist. Look for cameos and breathtaking photography. Academy Award Nominations: 5, including Best Cinematography; Best Score. **Cast:** Max Von Sydow, Charlton Heston, Sidney Poitier, Claude Rains. **Credits:** Dir:

George Stevens; Prod: George Stevens; Writer: George Stevens, James Lee Barret; DP: William Mellor, Loyal Griggs; Ed: Harold Kress, Argyle Nelson, Frank O'Neill; Prod Design: Richard Day, William Creber, David Hall; Composer: Alfred Newman. Color, 199 min. VHS, LASER

Great Expectations
(1934) United Artists
One of several Hollywood versions of the Dickens novel (the latest being the 1997 reworking of the plot line), this one is overshadowed in performance and direction by the 1946 David Lean adaptation. Orphan Pip prospers in the Victorian social elite under the financial auspices of an anonymous provider. Watchable as contrast to what would follow. **Cast:** Henry Hull, Phillips Holmes, Jane Wyatt, Florence Reed, Alan Hale, Francis L. Sullivan, Walter Brennan, Rafaela Ottiano. **Credits:** Dir: Stuart Walker; Prod: Ronald Neame; Writer: Gladys Unger; Story: Charles Dickens; DP: George Robinson; Ed: Edward Curtiss; Prod Design: Albert S. D'Agostino; Composer: Edward Ward. B&W, 102 min. VHS

Great Expectations
(1946) Universal
The definitive version of the Dickens classic about an orphaned British boy befriended by a mysterious benefactor who enables him to become a gentleman of means. In the gloom of a country graveyard, a young boy encounters an escaped convict, a chance meeting that years later leads the boy to mysterious adventure, wealth, and joy. Lean's achievement is in setting once-in-a-lifetime performances in a vibrant narrative that maintains rich detail but never bogs down. Considered by many to be among the greatest films ever made. Selected as a National Board of Review 10 Best Films of the Year. Academy Award Nominations: 5, including Best Picture; Best Director; Best Screenplay. **Academy Awards:** Best Black-and-White Cinematography; Best Art Direction—Set Decoration (B&W). **Cast:** John Mills, Alec Guinness, Valerie Hobson, Jean Simmons, Bernard Miles, Francis L. Sullivan, Martita Hunt, Finlay Currie, Anthony Wager, Ivor Barnard. **Credits:** Dir: David Lean; Prod: Ronald Neame; Writer: David Lean, Ronald Neame, Anthony Havelock-Allan, Kay Walsh; Story: Charles Dickens; DP: Guy Green; Ed: Jack Harris; Prod Design: John Bryan; Composer: Walter Goehr; Costumes: Sophia Harris; Art Director: Wilfred Shingleton. B&W, 118 min. VHS

Great Expectations (1946)

The Great Flamarion
(1946) Republic
A woman-hating sideshow performer refuses to let down his guard after being hurt many years before. When his lovely assistant starts to fall for him, he stages an accident that kills her husband and leaves her available. When she runs off with another performer, the Great Flamarion gets burned yet again. Based on the story "Big Shot" by Vicki Baum. **Cast:** Dan Duryea, Erich von Stroheim, Mary Beth Hughes, Stephen Barclay, Lester Allen, Esther Howard, Michael Mark, John Hamilton. **Credits:** Dir: Anthony Mann; Prod: W. Lee Wilder; Writer: Heinz Herald, Anne Wigton, Richard Weil; DP: James S. Brown, Jr.; Ed: John F. Link; Prod Design: F. Paul Sylos; Composer: Alexander Laszlo. B&W, 80 min. VHS

The Great Gambini
(1937) Paramount
The Great Gambini is a suave, sophisticated clairvoyant whose nightclub shows are the talk of the town. Unknown to the public, however, is Gambini's other profession: murder. But when the police begin snooping around the clairvoyant while investigating a series of mysterious deaths, Gambini offers to help them in their search. Giving phony predictions as to who will be the murderer's next victim, Gambini leads Detectives Buckie and Kirby in circles. It all comes to an end, however, when Gambini unwittingly implicates himself. A promotional stunt involved a pause at the end to let audiences try their hand at guessing the murderer's identity. **Cast:** Akim Tamiroff, Edward Brophy, William Demarest, John Trent, Marian Marsh, Genevieve Tobin, Reginald Denny, Lya Lys, Alan Birmingham, Toland Drew. **Credits:** Dir: Charles Vidor; Prod: B. P. Schulberg; Writer: Frederick J. Jackson, Frank Partos, Howard Young; DP: Leon Shamroy; Ed: Robert Bischoff; Composer: Boris Morror. B&W, 70 min.

The Great Garrick
(1937) Warner Bros.
Real-life 19th-century British actor David Garrick makes a disparaging remark aimed at French actors on the eve of visiting the Comedie Française in Paris. In retaliation, the company at the Comedie Française decide to embarrass the Great Garrick and send him back to Britain shamed and ridiculed. Taking over the Adam and Eve Inn where Garrick is scheduled to stay, they put on an elaborate show designed to scare Garrick out of his wits. The great actor becomes suspicious and foils their plans, winning the heart of the Countess Germaine—the only guest at the Inn who is not involved in the actors' machinations in the process. **Cast:** Brian Aherne, Olivia de Havilland, Edward Everett

Horton, Melville Cooper, Lionel Atwill, Luis Alberni, Lana Turner, Marie Wilson, Linda Perry, Fritz Leiber. **Credits:** Dir: James Whale; Prod: Mervyn LeRoy; Writer: Ernest Vajda; DP: Ernest Haller; Ed: Warren Low; Prod Design: Anton Grot; Composer: Adolph Deutsch. B&W, 91 min.

The Great Gatsby
(1949) Paramount
The second screen adaptation (after the silent 1926 version) of Fitzgerald's story features a fine performance by Ladd in the Nick Carraway role. A searching young man observes the Jazz Age society of Long Island as go-between for an upwardly mobile gangster and a frivolous woman trying to rekindle a romantic spark. The novel's mixture of envy and repulsion seems to resist big-screen treatment. **Cast:** Alan Ladd, Betty Field, Macdonald Carey, Ruth Hussey, Barry Sullivan, Howard Da Silva, Shelley Winters, Henry Hull, Ed Begley, Elisha Cook, Jr. **Credits:** Dir: Elliott Nugent; Prod: Richard Maibaum; Writer: Cyril Hume, Richard Maibaum; Story: F. Scott Fitzgerald; Ed: Ellsworth Hoagland; Prod Design: Hans Dreier; Composer: Robert Emmett Dolan; Costumes: Edith Head. B&W, 92 min. **VHS**

The Great Gatsby
(1974) Paramount
Adapted for the screen by Coppola from Fitzgerald's 1925 masterpiece about a handsome and enigmatic millionaire. Though he has always been in love with the same woman, now that he can afford her, she's married to a boorish philanderer. A richly successful evocation of the Jazz Age, but the performers wear the period detail like a heavy winter coat on an Indian summer day. **Academy Awards:** Best Costume Design; Best Original Song Score and Adaptation. **Cast:** Robert Redford, Mia Farrow, Bruce Dern, Karen Black, Sam Waterston, Scott Wilson, Lois Chiles. **Credits:** Dir: Jack Clayton; Prod: David Merrick; Writer: Francis Ford Coppola; Story: F. Scott Fitzgerald; DP: Douglas Slocombe; Ed: Tom Priestley; Prod Design: John Box; Choreographer: Tony Stevens; Composer: Nelson Riddle; Costumes: Theoni V. Aldredge; Art Director: Gene Rudolf. Color, 146 min. **VHS, LASER**

The Great Gildersleeve
RKO's successful radio series about pompous Springfield water commissioner Throckmorton P. Gildersleeve made the jump to the big screen in 1943's *The Great Gildersleeve*. Slen-

der radio actor Harold Peory went through an arduous weight-gain regimen in order to reprise his role as the corpulent commissioner for the film. As in the radio series, Gildersleeve had to navigate the topsy-turvy political climate of Springfield while trying to evade the marriage schemes of amorous spinster Mary Field (Amelia Hooker). Gildersleeve's guardianship of his niece (Nancy Gates) and nephew (Freddie Mercer) served to keep the commissioner's stubborn pride in check. Peory went on to star in a new series called Honest Harold, but the project was unsuccessful and he appeared in few films after his career had reached its zenith in the Gildersleeve series.

The Great Gildersleeve *(1943)*
Gildersleeve's Bad Day *(1943)*
Gildersleeve on Broadway *(1943)*
Gildersleeve's Ghost *(1944)*

The Great Impostor
(1961) Universal
The true story of Ferdinand Waldo Demara, Jr., one of the world's great frauds. In the '50s, Demara (Curtis) conned many by successfully impersonating a professor, a surgeon, a monk, a schoolteacher, and a prison warden—always with the FBI chasing his still-warm trail. Despite the incredible story, the movie is pretty humdrum. **Cast:** Tony Curtis, Edmond O'Brien, Arthur O'Connell, Raymond Massey, Karl Malden, Gary Merrill, Joan Blackman, Robert Middleton, Frank Gorshin. **Credits:** Dir: Robert Mulligan; Prod: Robert Arthur; Writer: Liam O'Brien; Story: Robert Crichton; DP: Robert Burks; Ed: Frederic Knudtson; Prod Design: Alexander Golitzen; Composer: Henry Mancini; Set Designer: Julia Heron. B&W, 112 min. **VHS**

The Great Lie
(1941) Warner Bros.
A thoroughly entertaining drama with Astor and Davis battling it out as catty rivals for the love of a pilot. When he's presumed dead in a crash, the pregnant ex-wife and the new widow must come to terms with their unconventional triangle. Astor's short haircut started a fashion craze. Awarded National Board of Review Best Supporting Actress: Mary Astor. **Academy Awards:** Best Supporting Actress: Mary Astor. **Cast:** Bette Davis, Mary Astor, George Brent, Hattie McDaniel, Lucile Watson, Grant Mitchell, Jerome Cowan. **Credits:** Dir: Edmund Goulding; Prod: Henry Blanke; Writer: Lenore Coffee; Story: Polan Blanks;

DP: Tony Gaudio; Ed: Ralph Dawson; Composer: Max Steiner; Costumes: Orry-Kelly; SFX: Byron Haskin, Robert Burks; Art Director: Carl Jules Weyl. B&W, 107 min. **VHS**

The Great Locomotive Chase
(1956) Disney
A colorful Walt Disney production based on the true story of Andrews' Raiders, who captured a Confederate railroad train during the Civil War and were then pursued by another Confederate locomotive. Buster Keaton featured the same story in his classic silent *The General* (1927). **Cast:** Fess Parker, Jeffrey Hunter, Jeff York, John Lupton, Kenneth Tobey. **Credits:** Dir: Francis D. Lyon; Prod: Lawrence Edward Watkin; Writer: Lawrence Edward Watkin; DP: Charles Boyle; Ed: Ellsworth Hoagland; Prod Design: Carroll Clark; Composer: Paul J. Smith; Costumes: Chuck Keehne; Set Designer: Emile Kuri. Color, 87 min. **VHS**

The Great Lover
(1949) Paramount
A classic comedy results when reporter Hope reluctantly agrees to chaperone a bunch of schoolboys on an ocean liner that's also carrying a cardshark, a duchess, and a murderer. If you're a Hope fan, this has to be near the top of your list. **Cast:** Bob Hope, Rhonda Fleming, Roland Young, Roland Culver, George Reeves, Jim Backus. **Credits:** Dir: Alexander Hall; Prod: Edmund Beloin; Writer: Edmund Beloin, Melville Shavelson, Jack Rose; DP: Charles Lang; Ed: Ellsworth Hoagland; Prod Design: Hans Dreier; Costumes: Edith Head; SFX: Gordon Jennings, Farciot Edouart; Art Director: Earl Hedrick; Set Designer: Sam Comer, Ross Dowd. B&W, 80 min. **VHS**

The Great Man
(1956) Universal
Ferrer cowrote, directed, and stars in this hard-hitting drama exposing the world behind the cameras of a television network. Ferrer plays an idealistic reporter who's hired by his network's president (Jagger) to put together a memorial report celebrating the life of a deceased reporter, the title's "Great Man." Ferrer uncovers evidence of the Great Man's greed, immorality, and perverse desire to lie to the public. He wants to go straight with his report on air but Carleton says no way, leaving him with the most important choice of his life. No-holds-barred examination of ethics in broadcasting. **Cast:** Jose Ferrer, Dean Jagger, Keenan Wynn,

Julie London, Joanne Gilbert, Ed Wynn, Jim Backus, Russ Morgan, Edward C. Platt, Robert Foulk. **Credits:** Dir: Jose Ferrer; Prod: Aaron Rosenberg; Writer: Al Morgan, Jose Ferrer; DP: Harold Lipstein; Ed: Sherman Todd, Joseph Albrecht; Prod Design: Eric Orbom, Richard H. Riedel; Composer: Herman Stein. B&W, 92 min.

The Great Man's Lady
(1942) Paramount
The 109-year-old wife of the founder of Hoyt City recounts her long life with her husband for a young biographer. Told in flashbacks, Stanwyck plays herself from age 16 to 109 and demonstrates the old adage that behind every great man (in this case two men, McCrea and Donlevy, who battle for Stanwyck's attention) is a great woman. Based on the story "The Human Side" by Vina Delmar. **Cast:** Barbara Stanwyck, Joel McCrea, Brian Donlevy, K. T. Stevens, Thurston Hall, Lloyd Corrigan. **Credits:** Dir: William Wellman; Prod: William Wellman; Writer: W. L. Rivers, Seena Owen; Story: Vina Delmar; DP: William Mellor; Ed: Thomas Scott; Prod Design: Hans Dreier; Composer: Victor Young; Costumes: Edith Head; SFX: Gordon Jennings; Art Director: Earl Hedrick. B&W, 91 min. **VHS**

The Great Man Votes
(1938) RKO
Barrymore is wonderful as a widowed former professor who has taken to the bottle. Just as he risks losing his children in a custody battle, he feels a newfound sense of importance and responsibility when his ballot becomes the tie-breaker in the local election. A marvelously funny movie with Kanin's lightly satirical touch. **Cast:** John Barrymore, Peter Holden, Virginia Weidler, Donald MacBride, William Demarest. **Credits:** Dir: Garson Kanin; Prod: Cliff Reid; Writer: John Twist; DP: Russell Metty; Ed: Jack Hively; Composer: Roy Webb; Art Director: Van Nest Polglase. B&W, 72 min. **VHS**

The Great McGinty
(1940) Paramount
Sturges's directorial debut tells the story of a corrupt politician who comes to power using every dirty trick in the book. Naturally, when he cleans up his act, he's run out of office. Sturges's cast of comic characters (who would soon be recognized as his fabled stock company) and his Oscar-winning dialogue make this a must for Sturges fans. **Academy Awards:** Best Original Screenplay. **Cast:** Brian Donlevy, Muriel Angelus, Akim Tamiroff, Allyn Joslyn, Louis Jean Heydt, Arthur Hoyt. **Credits:** Dir: Preston Sturges; Prod: Paul Jones; Writer: Preston Sturges; DP: William Mellor; Ed: Hugh Bennett; Prod Design: Hans Dreier; Composer: Frederick Hollander; Costumes: Edith Head; Art Director: Earl Hedrick. B&W, 82 min. **VHS, LASER**

The Great Moment
(1944) Paramount
An unusual film from Sturges, this biography of the dentist who pioneered the use of ether in dental procedures employs flashbacks that veer back and forth from comedy to drama. Still, Sturges fans will want to see it—and to remember that this film was taken away from Sturges and re-edited. Always fun to see the Sturges company at work, though. **Cast:** Joel McCrea, Betty Field, Harry Carey, William Demarest, Franklin Pangborn, Porter Hall, Grady Sutton. **Credits:** Dir: Preston Sturges; Prod: Preston Sturges; Writer: Preston Sturges; Story: Rene Fulop-Miller; DP: Victor Milner; Ed: Stuart Gilmore; Prod Design: Hans Dreier; Composer: Victor Young; Art Director: Ernst Fegte. B&W, 87 min. **VHS**

The Great Northfield Minnesota Raid
(1972) Universal
Based on the true story of the last, failed bank robbery by the James and Younger brothers, this film is notable for showing the unraveling heist from the outlaws' side. Duvall and Robertson give meaningful peformances as the doomed duo. **Cast:** Cliff Robertson, Robert Duvall, Luke Askew, R. G. Armstrong, Elisha Cook, Jr. **Credits:** Dir: Philip Kaufman; Prod: Jennings Lang; Writer: Philip Kaufman; DP: Bruce Surtees; Ed: Douglas Stewart; Prod Design: Alexander Golitzen; Composer: Dave Grusin; Costumes: Helen Colvig; Art Director: George C. Webb; Set Designer: Hal Gausman. Color, 91 min. **VHS**

The Great Race
(1965) Warner Bros.
An Edwards period comedy about a transcontinental auto race with a raft of memorable characters. Along their way, they encounter a polar bear, get into saloon brawls, challenge each other to duels, and have a colossal pie fight—which involved more than 2,000 pies! This is a sporadically successful effort that makes you wish they'd drive a little bit faster. **Acad-emy Awards:** Best Sound Effects. **Cast:** Jack Lemmon, Tony Curtis, Natalie Wood, Peter Falk, Keenan Wynn, Blake Edwards, Arthur O'Connell, Vivian Vance, Dorothy Provine, Larry Storch. **Credits:** Dir: Blake Edwards; Prod: Martin Jurow; Writer: Arthur Ross; Story: Arthur Ross, Blake Edwards; DP: Russell Harlan; Ed: Ralph E. Winters; Prod Design: Fernando Carrere; Choreographer: Hermes Pan; Composer: Henry Mancini; Costumes: Edith Head; Set Designer: George James Hopkins. Color, 160 min. **VHS, LASER**

The Great Santini
(1979) Orion
Duvall gives a rich, emotional performance as a Marine fighter pilot who funnels his frustrated desire to fight into creating a tip-top battalion out of his own emotionally battered family. His adolescent son suffers the most from the colonel's inability to express love through anything but discipline. This critically acclaimed movie has become a touchstone for dysfunctional families and is based on the Pat Conroy novel. Academy Award Nominations: Best Actor: Robert Duvall; Best Supporting Actor: Michael O'Keefe. **Cast:** Robert Duvall, Michael O'Keefe, Blythe Danner, David Keith, Stan Shaw, Lisa Jane Persky, Julie Anne Haddock. **Credits:** Dir: Lewis John Carlino; Prod: Charles Pratt; Writer: Lewis John Carlino; Story: Pat Conroy; DP: Ralph Woolsey; Prod Design: Jack Poplin; Composer: Elmer Bernstein. Color, 116 min. **VHS**

The Great Train Robbery
(1903) Edison
This picture, directed and scripted by Edwin S. Porter, introduced the first cinematic cowboy star, Bronco Billy Anderson. Anderson plays several roles in this action-packed depiction of outlaws ambushing a steam train. A breakthrough achievement in motion picture history, remarkable for being the first film narrative and the first of a genre (the first film Western), as well as its technical advancements, including its use of close-ups and Porter's camera movements (what we now refer to as "panning"). Mandatory viewing for the cinephile. **Cast:** Bronco Billy Anderson, Billy Whiskers, Marie Murray, George Barnes, Morgan Jones, Tom London, A. C. Abadie, Walter Cameron, Frank Hanaway. **Credits:** Dir: Edwin S. Porter; Prod: Hans A. Spanuth; Writer: Edwin S. Porter; DP: Edwin S. Porter, Blair Smith. B&W, 42 min. **VHS**

The Great Waldo Pepper

(1975) Universal
Another excellent period adventure film from director George Roy Hill in which Redford plays a stunt pilot who travels from town to town dazzling midwesterners with his aerobatic talents. Notable for its reuniting of the team from *Butch Cassidy* and *The Sting*, its script by Goldman, and some great flying footage. **Cast:** Robert Redford, Bo Svenson, Susan Sarandon, Margot Kidder, Bo Brundin, Geoffrey Lewis. **Credits:** Dir: George Roy Hill; Prod: George Roy Hill; Writer: William Goldman; DP: Robert Surtees; Ed: Peter Berkos, William Reynolds; Prod Design: Henry Bumstead; Composer: Henry Mancini; Costumes: Edith Head; Set Designer: James Payne. Color, 107 min. **VHS, LASER, DVD**

The Great Waltz

(1938) MGM
A film biography of composer Johann Strauss, which is also a fine romantic musical comedy. The alluring Rainer is the apex of a romantic triangle that serves as a backdrop for the stirring score. Far more compelling than the 1972 version. **Academy Awards:** Best Cinematography. **Cast:** Luise Rainer, Fernand Gravet, Miliza Korjus, Hugh Herbert, Lionel Atwill, Curt Bois, Herman Bing. **Credits:** Dir: Julien Duvivier, Josef von Sternberg; Prod: Bernard Hyman; Writer: Samuel Hoffenstein, Walter Reisch; Story: Gottfried Reinhardt; DP: Joseph Ruttenberg; Ed: Tom Held; Prod Design: Cedric Gibbons; Choreographer: Albertina Rasch; Composer: Dimitri Tiomkin. B&W, 102 min. **VHS, LASER**

The Great White Hope

(1970) Fox
The first black heavyweight boxing champion of the world is a man who bows before no man, in the ring or out. After winning the title, the boxer enrages the racists in boxing and law enforcement with his relationship with a white woman and his outspoken ways. A plan is schemed to bring about his downfall. Adapted for the screen by Sackler, from his stage play. Alexander's film debut. **Cast:** James Earl Jones, Jane Alexander, Chester Morris, Hal Holbrook, Moses Gunn, Lou Gilbert, Joel Fluellen, Robert Webber. **Credits:** Dir: Martin Ritt; Prod: Lawrence Turman; Writer: Howard Sackler; Story: Howard Sackler; DP: Burnett Guffey; Ed: William H. Reynolds; Prod Design: John DeCuir; Choreographer: Donald McKayle; Costumes: Irene Sharaff; Art Director: Jack Martin Smith; Set Designer: Walter M. Scott, Raphael Bretton. Color, 103 min. **VHS**

The Great Ziegfeld

(1936) MGM
The Best Picture of 1936 still sets a high standard for grand musicals. The larger-than-life career of stage genius Florenz Ziegfeld (Powell, in a winning performance) is aptly celebrated in this marvelous musical biography. The colorful story and all-star cast are bolstered by a catalog of nostalgic hit songs, including "If You Knew Susie," "Shine On, Harvest Moon," and "A Pretty Girl Is Like a Melody." Rainer was chosen as the New York Film Critics Circle Best Actress. Academy Award Nominations: 6, including Best Director; Best Screenplay. **Academy Awards:** Best Actress: Luise Rainer; Best Dance Direction; Best Picture. **Cast:** William Powell, Myrna Loy, Fanny Brice, Luise Rainer, Frank Morgan, Ray Bolger, Virginia Bruce, Reginald Owen, Dennis Morgan, Nat Pendleton. **Credits:** Dir: Robert Z. Leonard; Prod: Hunt Stromberg; Writer: William Anthony McGuire; DP: Ray June, Oliver T. Marsh, Karl Freund, Merritt Gerstad, George J. Folsey; Ed: William S. Gray; Prod Design: Cedric Gibbons, Eddie Imazu, Edwin B. Willis; Choreographer: Seymour Felix; Composer: Arthur Lange; Costumes: Adrian. B&W, 176 min. **VHS, LASER**

Greed

(1924) MGM
A silent-era monument, and intended by its director to achieve monumental length: eight hours. Even with studio-enforced cuts, von Stroheim's story (from the Frank Norris novel *McTeague*) remains powerful. A dentist loses everything because of his wife's (Pitts) fixation on money. He becomes a fugitive maddened by lust for money, and kills his captor, only to find himself handcuffed to a corpse and the gold he desires out of his reach. The video release includes a prologue hosted by film historian Kevin Brownlow explaining the controversy around cuts made to the film and the music score. **Cast:** ZaSu Pitts, Gibson Gowland, Jean Hersholt, Chester Conklin. **Credits:** Dir: Erich von Stroheim; Prod: Erich von Stroheim, Samuel Goldwyn; Writer: Erich von Stroheim, June Mathis; Story: Frank Norris; DP: William Daniels, Ben Reynolds, Ernest Schoedsack; Ed: Frank Hull, Joseph Farnham; Prod Design: Richard Day, Erich von Stroheim. B&W, 133 min. **VHS, LASER**

The Green Berets

(1968) Warner Bros.
One of the first American films specifically about the Vietnam War was also one of the most hawkish, offering a pro-intervention perspective at the height of the conflict. A gung-ho colonel battles the vicious Viet Cong while protecting innocent civilians, befriending an orphaned boy, and reforming a liberal newspaperman's misguided political views. A lowpoint for the Duke, and watchable mostly as a time capsule. **Cast:** John Wayne, Aldo Ray, Raymond St. Jacques, David Janssen, Jim Hutton, Bruce Cabot, Patrick Wayne, Luke Askew. **Credits:** Dir: John Wayne, Ray Kellogg; Prod: Michael Wayne; Writer: James Lee Barret; DP: Winton Hoch; Ed: Otho Lovering; Composer: Miklos Rozsa. Color, 142 min. **VHS, LASER, DVD**

Green Dolphin Street

(1947) MGM
An exotic setting for a standard '40s romantic drama. After deserting from the British Navy and settling in New Zealand, a young sailor sends for his lady love but gets her also-smitten sister as well. The journey includes exciting depictions of tidal waves and earthquakes. Academy Award Nominations: 4, including Best B&W Cinematography; Best Film Editing; Best Sound. **Academy Awards:** Best Sound Effects; Best Special Visual Effects. **Cast:** Lana Turner, Van Heflin, Donna Reed, Richard Hart, Edmund Gwenn. **Credits:** Dir: Victor Saville; Prod: Carey Wilson; Writer: Samson Raphaelson; Story: Elizabeth Goudge; DP: George J. Folsey; Ed: George White; Prod Design: Cedric Gibbons; Composer: Bronislau Kaper; Costumes: Walter Plunkett, Valles; SFX: Warren Newcombe, A. Arnold Gillespie; Art Director: Malcolm F. Brown; Set Designer: Edwin B. Willis. B&W, 141 min. **VHS, LASER**

Greenwich Village

(1944) Fox
Musical about a young classical composer who comes to 1922 Greenwich Villiage in search of a career. Once arrived, he meets up with the inhabitants of a speakeasy, falling in love with its featured performer, Bonnie. While our hero hopes his concerto will make it to Carnegie Hall, the speakeasy owner has other plans, and the two adapt the refrain for a popular musical, which is a huge success. **Cast:** Carmen Miranda, Don Ameche, William Bendix, Vivian Blaine, Felix Bressart, Tony Demarco, Betty Com-

den, Adolph Green, Sally Demarco. **Credits:** Dir: Walter Lang; Prod: William LeBaron; Writer: Earl Baldwin, Walter Bullock, Michael Fessier, Ernest Pagano; Story: Frederick Hazlitt Bresman; DP: Leon Shamroy, Harry Jackson; Ed: Robert Simpson; Composer: Emil Newman, Charles Henderson, Nacio Herb Brown. Color, 82 min.

The Green Years
(1946) MGM
A coming-of-age story based on a popular novel. A poor Irish orphan is taken in by his Scottish grandparents and develops a bond with his grandfather, an amiable man who likes to drink. As he grows older, the boy falls in love for the first time and experiences other expected growing pains. When he becomes a young man he wants to go to college but feels guilty because the money for tuition would come from his grandfather's life insurance. **Cast:** Charles Coburn, Tom Drake, Dean Stockwell, Beverly Tyler, Hume Cronyn, Gladys Cooper, Selena Royle, Jessica Tandy. **Credits:** Dir: Victor Saville; Prod: Leon Gordon; Writer: Robert Ardrey, A. J. Cronin, Sonya Levien; DP: George Folsey, Jr.; Ed: Robert J. Kern; Composer: Herbert Stothart; Art Director: Cedric Gibbons, Hans Peters. B&W, 127 min.

Greetings
(1968) Sigma III
An early De Palma satire featuring De Niro and his efforts to help his best friend fail an army physical. The '60s time capsule also features a fascination with the JFK assassination and voyeuristic moviemaking. Originally received an X rating. **Cast:** Robert De Niro, Jonathan Warden, Gerrit Graham, Allen Garfield, Megan McCormick. **Credits:** Dir: Brian De Palma; Prod: Charles Hirsch; Writer: Brian De Palma, Charles Hirsch; DP: Robert Florey; Ed: Brian De Palma. Color, 88 min. **VHS, LASER**

Grey Gardens
(1975) Portrait Films
A truly weird and fascinating documentary study of Edith Bouvier Beale and her daughter, Edie, who live in an unkempt, weed-strangled old home in East Hampton, Long Island, surrounded by faded memories and kitty droppings. They are, antithetically, the aunt and cousin of Jackie Kennedy Onassis and Lee Radizwill. One scene, reminiscent of *Whatever Happened to Baby Jane,* has Miss Edie turbaning her nearly bald head in dish towels and recalling her social life that once was and her never-realized showbiz dreams. Mummy Edith sits atop her cat-filled bed gaily singing "Tea for Two." Produced by the Maysles brothers, this cinema verité still arouses controversy. **Credits:** Prod: Albert Maysles, David Maysles; DP: Albert Maysles, David Maysles; Ed: Susan Fromke, Ellen Hovde, Muffie Meyer. Color, 95 min.

The Grissom Gang
(1971) Cinerama
This typically violent but also darkly funny movie is a slight change of pace for Aldrich. A young heiress is kidnapped by a freakish family and things go terribly awry once love makes its unlikely appearance. Based on the film *No Orchids for Miss Blandish.* **Cast:** Kim Darby, Scott Wilson, Connie Stevens, Tony Musante, Irene Dailey. **Credits:** Dir: Robert Aldrich; Prod: Robert Aldrich; Writer: Leon Griffiths; DP: Joseph Biroc; Ed: Michael Luciano; Composer: Gerald Fried. Color, 128 min. **VHS**

The Groom Wore Spurs
(1951) Universal
In this light comedy, Rogers plays an attorney who marries then divorces a rugged cowboy. When he gets into trouble with the law, she feels compelled to defend him. Naturally, he turns out to be not so tough after all. **Cast:** Ginger Rogers, Jack Carson, Joan Davis. **Credits:** Dir: Richard Whorf; Prod: Howard Welsch; Writer: Robert Carson, Robert Libott; Frank Burt; DP: Peverell Marley; Ed: Otto Ludwig. B&W, 81 min. **VHS**

The Group
(1966) United Artists
A group of women who attend a Vassar-esque college during the Great Depression grow to realize the pact they made to remain friends may be more difficult than they thought. Bergen, Hackett, and Holbrook made their film debuts in this provocative drama based on the Mary McCarthy novel. **Cast:** Candice Bergen, Joan Hackett, Elizabeth Hartman, Hal Holbrook, Shirley Knight. **Credits:** Dir: Sidney Lumet; Prod: Sidney Buchman; Writer: Sidney Buchman; DP: Boris Kaufman; Ed: Ralph Rosenbloom; Composer: Charles Gross. Color, 152 min. **VHS**

Guadalcanal Diary
(1943) Fox
Wartime account of the Marine invasion of the Solomon Islands during WWII. Clearly intended to bolster home-front morale, but the better-than-average cast of tough guys and the proximity of the release to the events themselves give the action an added urgency. **Cast:** Preston Foster, Lloyd Nolan, Richard Conte, William Bendix, Anthony Quinn, Richard Jaeckel, Roy Roberts, Minor Watson, Ralph Byrd, Lionel Stander. **Credits:** Dir: Lewis Seiler; Prod: Bryan Foy; Writer: Lamar Trotti, Jerry Cady; Story: Richard Tregaskis; DP: Charles G. Clarke; Ed: Fred Allen; Prod Design: James Basevi; Composer: David Buttolph; SFX: Fred Sersen; Art Director: Leland Fuller. B&W, 93 min. **VHS, LASER**

The Guardsman
(1931) MGM
Testing his wife's loyalty and his own acting talent, a husband disguises himself and seduces his own wife. Based on the Broadway show in which Lunt and Fontanne also starred, this was the only film appearance for the lauded stage duo. Academy Award nominations: Best Actor: Alfred Lunt; Best Actress: Lynn Fontanne. **Cast:** Alfred Lunt, Lynn Fontanne, Roland Young, ZaSu Pitts, Maude Eburne, Herman Bing. **Credits:** Dir: Sidney Franklin; Prod: Irving Thalberg, Albert Lewin; Writer: Ernest Vadja, Claudine West; DP: Norbert Brodine; Ed: Conrad Nervig. B&W, 83 min. **VHS**

Guess Who's Coming to Dinner
(1967) Columbia
A liberal white couple (Hepburn and Tracy, in Tracy's last appearance) put their platitudes to the test. They always taught their daughter (Houghton, Hepburn's niece) that all people are created equal, regardless of race or religion . . . until she unexpectedly brings home a black doctor (Poitier) and announces that they're engaged. Mostly interesting for a look at '60s attitudes toward race and the performances of Tracy and Hepburn. Academy Award Nominations: 10, including Best Picture; Best Director; Best Actor: Spencer Tracy. **Academy Awards:** Best Actress: Katharine Hepburn; Best Story/Screenplay Written Directly for the Screen. **Cast:** Katharine Hepburn, Spencer Tracy, Katharine Houghton, Sidney Poitier, Isabel Sanford, Cecil Kellaway, Roy Glenn, Beah Richards, Virginia Christine. **Credits:** Dir: Stanley Kramer; Prod: Stanley Kramer; Writer: William Rose; DP: Sam Leavitt; Ed: Robert C. Jones; Prod Design: Robert Clatworthy; Costumes: Jean Louis, Joe King; SFX: Geza Gaspar. Color, 112 min. **VHS, LASER**

Guest in the House

(1944) United Artists

Baxter once again proves to be a wolf in sheep's clothing as a manipulative young woman who moves in with the family of her betrothed (Bellamy, for once not the jilted suitor), who also happens to be her psychiatrist. She gradually turns the house full of happy, loving people against one another, and they are powerless to stop her. Academy Award Nomination for Best Scoring of a Dramatic or Comedy Picture. **Cast:** Anne Baxter, Ralph Bellamy, Marie McDonald, Margaret Hamilton, Ruth Warrick, Aline MacMahon, Scott McKay, Jerome Cowan, Percy Kilbride. **Credits:** Dir: John Brahm; Prod: Hunt Stromberg; Writer: Ketti Frings; Story: Hagar Wilde, Dale Eunson; DP: Lee Garmes; Ed: James E. Newcom, Walter Hannemann; Prod Design: Nicolai Remisoff; Composer: Werner Janssen. B&W, 121 min. **VHS**

Guest Wife

(1945) United Artists

A journalist (Ameche) is long overdue for a vacation, but he's got to convince his family-man boss that he needs the time to be with his wife. There's only one problem: he isn't married. A pal (Foran) comes to the rescue, suggesting his wife (Colbert) pose as the journalist's wife. Old-reliable mistaken-identity plot, but the pairing of Ameche and Colbert is a winner. Academy Award Nomination for Best Scoring of a Dramatic or Comedy Picture. **Cast:** Don Ameche, Claudette Colbert, Dick Foran, Charles Dingle, Grant Mitchell. **Credits:** Dir: Sam Wood; Prod: Jack Skirball; Writer: Bruce Manning, John Klorer; DP: Joseph A. Valentine; Ed: William Morgan; Art Director: Lionel Banks; Set Designer: George Sawley. B&W, 88 min. **VHS**

A Guide for the Married Man

(1967) Fox

Kelly's light-footed tour guide to the psyche of the suburban male, circa mid-'60s. Veteran skirt chaser Matthau gives his buddy Morse a thorough grounding in the rules of the extramarital affair. Plenty of cameos in this sophisticated sex comedy. **Cast:** Walter Matthau, Robert Morse, Jack Benny, Lucille Ball, Polly Bergen, Joey Bishop, Sid Caesar, Art Carney, Wally Cox, Inger Stevens. **Credits:** Dir: Gene Kelly; Prod: Frank McCarthy; Writer: Frank Tarloff; DP: Joseph MacDonald; Ed: Dorothy Spencer; Prod Design: Jack Martin Smith, William Glasgow; Composer: Johnny Williams. Color, 91 min. **VHS**

The Guilt of Janet Ames

(1947) Columbia

Years after her husband is killed in WWII from throwing himself on a live grenade, a woman (Russell) visits the five men in his unit that he saved. When she's injured in an accident and suffers psychosomatic paralysis, one of her husband's comrades (Douglas) treats her for hysteria. Under hypnosis, she's able to come to terms with her husband's death. **Cast:** Betsy Blair, Sid Caesar, Charles Cane, Melvyn Douglas, Nina Foch, Bruce Harper, Frank Orth, Rosalind Russell, Arthur Space, Harry Von Zell. **Credits:** Dir: Henry Levin; Writer: Devery Freeman, Louella MacFarlane, Allen Rivkin; Story: Lenore J. Coffee; DP: Joseph Walker; Ed: Charles Nelson; Prod Design: George Montgomery, Frank Tuttle; Composer: George Duning, Morris Stoloff, Allan Roberts, Doris Fisher; Art Director: Stephen Goosson, Walter Holscher. B&W, 81 min.

Guilty Hands

(1931) MGM

When the former district attorney (Barrymore) finds out that the local millionaire playboy (Mowbray) is looking to marry his impressionable daughter, the lawyer takes matters into his own hands. Barrymore openly threatens to murder the Casanova if he continues to court his daughter. A twisty little suspenser with surprises and great performances. **Cast:** Kay Francis, Madge Evans, William Bakewell, C. Aubrey Smith, Polly Moran, Alan Mowbray, Forrester Harvey, Charles Crokett, Henry A. Barrows, Lionel Barrymore. **Credits:** Dir: W. S. Van Dyke; Writer: Bayard Veiller; DP: Merritt Gerstad; Ed: Anne Bauchens; Composer: Douglas Shearer; Costumes: Rene Hubert. B&W, 71 min.

Gulliver's Travels

(1939) Paramount

Dave and Max Fleischer's feature-length, color, animated version of Jonathan Swift's classic of 1726 about a British sailor's adventures in Lilliput, an island inhabited by tiny people. Academy Award Nominations: 2, Best Original Score; Best Song: "Faithful Forever." **Cast:** Jessica Dragonette, Lanny Ross, Pinto Colvig, Jack Mercer, Sam Parker. **Credits:** Dir: Dave Fleischer; Prod: Max Fleischer; DP: Charles Schettler; Composer: Ralph Rainger, Leo Robin. Color, 80 min. **VHS, LASER**

The Gumball Rally

(1976) Warner Bros.

A group of wacky characters compete in an illegal auto race known as the Gumball Rally. It starts in New York and finishes in Long Beach, California: that's the sum and total of the rules. This is the road-race comedy that all the others imitate, and it's based on a real event. **Cast:** Michael Sarrazin, Tim McIntire, Gary Busey, Raul Julia, John Durren, Susan Flannery, Steven Keats, Joanne Nail, Nicholas Pryor, J. Pat O'Malley. **Credits:** Dir: Chuck Bail; Prod: Chuck Bail; Writer: Leon Capetanos; DP: Richard Glouner. Color, 107 min. **VHS, LASER**

Gun Crazy

(1949) United Artists

The forerunner of *Bonnie and Clyde* (1968) has become a cult favorite. It inspired a remake in 1992 by former music-video director Tamra Davis and an homage in Jim McBride's version of *Breathless* (1983). A wild young couple with a love of guns (she was a trick shooter in a Wild West show) and a knack for violence go on a spree. The camera work has a jar-ring immediacy, and the leads have a contemporary-feeling, snarling attitude. **Cast:** Peggy Cummins, John Dall, Berry Kroeger, Morris Carnovsky, Harry Lewis, Anabel Shaw, Russ Tamblyn. **Credits:** Dir: Joseph H. Lewis; Prod: Maurice King; Writer: MacKinlay Kantor, Millard Kaufman, Dalton Trumbo; Story: MacKinlay Kantor; DP: Russell Harlan; Ed: Harry Gerstad; Prod Design: Gordon Wiles; Composer: Victor Young; Costumes: Norma; Set Designer: Raymond Boltz. B&W, 87 min. **VHS**

Gunfight at the O.K. Corral

(1957) Paramount

Straightforward account of the events leading up to the famous Tombstone gunfight, involving lawman Wyatt Earp and gunman Doc Holliday as they battled the Clanton gang. Oft-made but not with this distinction or with the two-fisted combination of Douglas and Lancaster. Well worth seeing. Note the Leon Uris screenplay and early Dennis Hopper appearance. Academy Award Nominations: Best Film Editing; Best Sound. **Cast:** Burt Lancaster, Kirk Douglas, Rhonda Fleming, Jo Van Fleet, John Ireland, Frank Faylen, Kenneth Tobey, Earl Holliman, Lyle Bettger, Ted De Corsia. **Credits:** Dir: John Sturges; Prod: Hal B. Wallis; Writer: Leon Uris; DP: Charles B. Lang; Ed: Warren Low; Prod Design: Hal Pereira, Walter Tyler; Composer: Dimitri Tiomkin. Color, 122 min. **VHS, LASER**

The Gunfighter

(1950) Fox

A famed gunfighter seeking peace and quiet visits his estranged wife and their small son. The sheriff, who is an old friend, warns the gunfighter that his presence is upsetting the town and it would be best if he moves on. But before he can, challengers seeking to make their own reputations come after him for a gunfight. Academy Award Nominations: Best Motion Picture Story. **Cast:** Gregory Peck, Helen Westcott, Millard Mitchell, Jean Parker, Karl Malden. **Credits:** Dir: Henry King; Prod: Nunnally Johnson; Writer: William Bowers, William Sellers, Nunnally Johnson, Andre De Toth; DP: Arthur Miller; Ed: Barbara McLean; Composer: Alfred Newman; Prod Design: Lyle Wheeler, Richard Irvine. B&W, 85 min. **VHS, LASER**

Gun Fury

(1953) Columbia

A Civil War vet takes off in hot pursuit after an outlaw gang who ambushed a stagecoach and kidnapped his bride-to-be. Typical Walsh Western, originally shown in 3-D. **Cast:** Rock Hudson, Donna Reed, Philip Carey, Roberta Haynes, Lee Marvin, Neville Brand. **Credits:** Dir: Raoul Walsh; Prod: Louis Rachmil; Writer: Irving Wallace, Roy Huggins; DP: Lester White; Ed: James H. Sweeney, Jerome Thoms; Art Director: Ross Bellah. Color, 83 min. **VHS, LASER**

Gunga Din

(1939) RKO

The prototypical Hollywood action adventure–buddy film is loosely based on the poem by Rudyard Kipling and adapted by MacArthur-Hecht (basing character relationships from their hit play *The Front Page*) and William Faulkner, who goes uncredited. Three soldier-comrades (Grant, Fairbanks, and McLaglen) help suppress a native uprising in 19th-century India with the help of their intrepid waterboy, Gunga Din. Archivally restored to 117 minutes (from 96), it is also available in a less impressive colorized version. Academy Award Nominations: Best (B&W) Cinematography. **Cast:** Cary Grant, Douglas Fairbanks, Jr., Victor McLaglen, Sam Jaffe, Eduardo Ciannelli, Joan Fontaine, Montagu Love, Robert Coote, Cecil Kellaway, Abner Biberman. **Credits:** Dir: George Stevens; Prod: George Stevens; Writer: Fred Guiol; Story: Rudyard Kipling; DP: Joseph H. August; Ed: Henry Berman, John Lockert; Prod Design: Van Nest Polglase, Perry Ferguson; Composer: Alfred Newman. B&W, 117 min. **VHS, LASER**

Gunman's Walk

(1958) Columbia

In this CinemaScope Western, a retired gunslinger-turned-rancher (Heflin) struggles to raise his two sons on the frontier. One son, Ed, has a penchant for violence and wants to outshoot his dad while the other falls in love with a half-breed Sioux woman whose brother was killed by Ed. When Ed grows more and more uncontrollable his father must make a desperate decision. **Cast:** Van Heflin, Tab Hunter, Kathryn Grant, James Darren, Mickey Shaughnessy, Robert F. Simon, Edward Platt, Ray Teal, Paul Birch. **Credits:** Dir: Phil Karlson; Prod: Fred Kohlmar; Writer: Frank S. Nugent; DP: Charles Lawton, Jr.; Ed: Jerome Thoms; Prod Design: Robert Peterson; Composer: George Duning. Color, 95 min. **VHS**

The Guns of August

(1964)

A documentary about WWI, based on the Pulitzer Prize–winning book by Tuchman, which examines the years between 1910 and 1918. Interesting use of rare footage, photographs, and documents make this is a must for history buffs. **Credits:** Dir: Nathan Kroll; Story: Barbara Tuchman. B&W, 100 min. **VHS, LASER**

The Guns of Fort Petticoat

(1957) Columbia

A solid Western, with Murphy as a moralistic army officer who refuses to take part in an unauthorized raid on an Indian tribe. But when the Indians strike back, it falls to Murphy to hold the fort. His best defense is to train a group of women to fend off the foes. **Cast:** Audie Murphy, Kathryn Grant, Hope Emerson, Jeff Donnell. **Credits:** Dir: George Marshall; Prod: Harry Joe Brown; Writer: Walter Doniger; DP: Ray Rennahan; Ed: Al Clark. Color, 81 min. **VHS**

The Guns of Navarone

(1961) Columbia

Fine war movie with an all-star cast and a gripping plot based on the Alistair MacLean novel. A commando team is sent to a Greek Island to destroy the giant Nazi guns that are controlling a strategic channel in the Aegean Sea. This was a groundbreaker in the Special Effects department. Golden Globes for Best Original Score; Best Motion Picture, Drama. Academy Award Nominations: 7, including Best Picture; Best Director; Best (Adapted) Screenplay. **Academy Awards:** Best Film; Best Special Effects; Best Sound Effects. **Cast:** Gregory Peck, David Niven, Anthony Quinn, Stanley Baker, Anthony Quayle, Gia Scala. **Credits:** Dir: J. Lee Thompson; Writer: Carl Foreman; DP: Oswald Morris; Ed: Alan Osbiston; Composer: Dimitri Tiomkin; Prod Design: Geoffrey Drake. Color, 157 min. **VHS, LASER**

Guns of the Magnificent Seven

(1969) United Artists

In this third remake of Kurosawa's *The Seven Samurai,* the "seven" gunslingers free Mexican political prisoners, train them as warriors, and fight alongside them in an attack upon a Mexican fortress in an attempt to free a revolutionary leader. Filmed in Panavision with an Elmer Bernstein score, the film offers nothing new but is highly entertaining. It spawned a sequel, *The Magnificent Seven Ride.* **Cast:** George Kennedy, James Whitmore, Monte Markham, Joe Don Baker, Bernie Casey, Scott Thomas, Reni Santoni, Michael Ansara, Fernando Rey, Frank Silvera. **Credits:** Dir: Paul Wendkos; Prod: Vincent M. Fennelly; Writer: Herman Hoffman; DP: Antonio Macasoli; Ed: Walter Hannemann; Prod Design: Jose Marie Tapiador; Composer: Elmer Bernstein. Color, 106 min. **VHS**

Gus

(1976) Disney

Wholesome family fun in this Disney comedy about an inept, last-place football team, the California Atoms, which is turned around with the help of their new star player . . . a football-kicking mule! The villainous competition then attempts the kidnapping of Gus, leading to slapstick results. **Cast:** Edward Asner, Don Knotts, Gary Grimes, Tim Conway, Dick Van Patten, Harold Gould, Liberty Williams, Bob Crane, Tom Bosley, Ronnie Schell. **Credits:** Dir: Vincent McEveety; Prod: Ron Miller; Writer: Arthur Alsberg, Don Nelson; DP: Frank Phillips; Ed: Robert Stafford; Prod Design: John B. Mansbridge, Al Roelofs; Composer: Robert F. Brunner. Color, 96 min. **VHS**

A Guy Named Joe

(1943) MGM

Reassuring WWII-era fantasy about a flier who visits Earth to guide a younger pilot through the hazards of battle. He also lends a hand through the minefields of the heart when he steers the young pilot toward his grieving girlfriend. Steven Spielberg mined the story line for his *Always* (1989). **Cast:** Spencer Tracy, Irene Dunne, Van

Guys and Dolls (1955)

Johnson, Ward Bond, James Gleason, Lionel Barrymore, Barry Nelson, Don Defore, Henry O'Neill. **Credits:** Dir: Victor Fleming; Prod: Everett Riskin; Writer: Dalton Trumbo; DP: George J. Folsey, Karl Freund; Ed: Frank Sullivan; Prod Design: Cedric Gibbons, Lyle Wheeler; Composer: Herbert Stothart. B&W, 121 min. **VHS**

Guys and Dolls
(1955) Fox
Brando's bold musical debut based on the Damon Runyon comedy—adapted by director Mankiewicz—about gamblers and a Salvation Army lass. Sky Masterson (Brando), veteran gambler, takes a bet from Sinatra that he can win the heart of a "soldier" in the Salvation Army. The Loesser tunes include "Luck Be a Lady," and Blaine, Kaye, Pully, and Silver reprise their Broadway roles. Golden Globes for Best Actress in a Musical or Comedy: Jean Simmons; Best Motion Picture, Musical/Comedy. Academy Award Nominations: Best Cinematography; Best Art Direction; Best Costumes; Best Scoring of a Musical. **Cast:** Marlon Brando, Frank Sinatra, Jean Simmons, Vivian Blaine, Robert Keith, Stubby Kaye, B. S. Pully, Sheldon Leonard, George E. Stone, Johnny Silver. **Credits:** Dir: Joseph L. Mankiewicz; Prod: Samuel Goldwyn; Writer: Joseph L. Mankiewicz; Story: Damon Runyon; DP: Harry Stradling; Ed: Daniel Mandell; Prod Design: Oliver Smith; Choreographer: Michael Kidd; Composer: Frank Loesser. Color, 150 min. **VHS, LASER**

Gypsy
(1962) Warner Bros.
A colorful adaptation of the Broadway play about the early life of the queen of burlesque, Gypsy Rose Lee. After years of putting her own ambitions on hold to raise a family, Mama Rose (Russell) attempts to make her young daughters—the pretty and talented June and the uncoordinated tomboy Louise—vaudeville stars. June became June Havoc, and Louise became Gypsy Rose. Remade in 1993 for TV with Bette Midler. Songs performed include "Everything's Coming Up Roses," "Let Me Entertain You," and "Small World." Academy Award Nominations: Best (Color) Cinematography; Best (Adapted) Score; Best (Color) Costume Design. **Cast:** Rosalind Russell, Natalie Wood, Karl Malden, Paul Wallace, Betty Bruce, Harvey Korman, Parley Baer, Ann Jillian, Harry Shannon, Morgan Brittany. **Credits:** Dir: Mervyn LeRoy; Prod: Mervyn LeRoy; Writer: Leonard Spigelgass; DP: Harry Stradling; Ed: Philip W. Anderson; Prod Design: John Beckman; Choreographer: Robert Tucker; Composer: Jule Styne, Stephen Sondheim. Color, 143 min. **VHS**

Hail the Conquering Hero

(1944) Paramount

Another comic gem from writer-director-producer Sturges. At the start of WWII, Bracken eagerly enlists in the service only to be soon discharged for his chronic hay fever. His hometown lays out the red carpet when he's mistakenly credited with bravery at Guadalcanal. The Sturges gang's all here, with particularly hilarious showings by Demarest and Pangborn. Academy Award Nomination for Best Original Screenplay. **Cast:** Eddie Bracken, Ella Raines, William Demarest, Franklin Pangborn, Raymond Walburn, Elizabeth Patterson, Georgia Caine, Alan Bridge, Freddie Steele, Jimmy Conlin. **Credits:** Dir: Preston Sturges; Prod: Preston Sturges; Writer: Preston Sturges; Ed: Stuart Gilmore; Prod Design: Hans Dreier; Composer: Werner Richard Heymann. B&W, 101 min. **VHS**

Hair

(1979) MGM

The Age of Aquarius is captured for all time in Forman's version of the hit '60s Broadway musical by Rado and MacDermot. A clean-cut midwestern kid (Savage) comes to New York and joins up with a nomadic tribe of hippies in Central Park. Notable for its hit songs, such as "Let the Sun Shine In," its choreography by Twyla Tharp, a cameo by the late Nicholas Ray (as a general), and for jump-starting the careers of Williams and D'Angelo. A time capsule from groovier days, but the story and characters hold up. Nell Carter, Ellen Foley, Melba Moore, and others appear and sing on the sound track. **Cast:** Treat Williams, John Savage, Beverly D'Angelo, Annie Golden, Dorsey Wright. **Credits:** Dir: Milos Forman; Prod: Lester Persky, Michael Butler; Writer: Michael Weller; DP: Miroslav Ondricek, Richard Kratina; Ed: Lynzee Klingman; Prod Design: Stuart Wurtzel; Choreographer: Twyla Tharp; Composer: Gerome Ragni,

James Rado, Galt MacDermot; Costumes: Ann Roth; SFX: Al Griswold. Color, 121 min. **VHS, LASER**

The Hairy Ape

(1944) United Artists

Bendix plays a hulking, beastial ship stoker who falls for Hayward, a haughty socialite, during an ocean voyage. Based on the Eugene O'Neill play, this film production lost something on-screen, though the casting of Hayward as a siren and brutal Bendix holds fascinating possibilities. **Cast:** William Bendix, Susan Hayward, John Loder, Dorothy Comingore, Roman Bohnen, Alan Napier, Tom Fadden, Charles Cane. **Credits:** Dir: Alfred Santell; Prod: Jules Levey; Writer: Robert D. Andrews, Decla Dunning; Story: Eugene O'Neill; DP: Lucien Andriot; Ed: William Ziegler; Prod Design: James Sullivan; Composer: Michel Michelet, Edward Paul. B&W, 94 min. **VHS**

The Half-Naked Truth

(1932) RKO

Comedy based on stories about legendary New York publicist Harry Reichenbach, a one-time carnival worker whose most famous real-life exploits (duplicated in the film) included putting a live lion inside a piano box and lifting it into a downtown hotel suite. He uses this stunt to get publicity for a woman whom he dubs Princess Exotica (Velez). She is involved with a theatrical producer,

whom the press agent embarrasses with photographs of his liaisons. Early Velez with pre-Code sauciness, and typically hilarious performances by Pallette and Morgan. **Cast:** Shirley Chambers, Mary Mason, James Donlon, Robert McKenzie, Charles Dow Clark, Eugene Pallette, Lee Tracy, Lupe Velez, Frank Morgan, Franklin Pangborn. **Credits:** Dir: Gregory LaCava; Prod: David O. Selznick; Writer: Bartlett McCormack, Corey Ford, Gregory LaCava; Story: David Freedman, Ben Markson, Harry Reichenbach, H. N. Swanson; DP: Bert Glennon; Ed: Charles Kimball; Composer: Max Steiner. B&W, 75 min.

Hallelujah

(1929) MGM

This first Hollywood picture to feature an all-black cast is worth a viewing for more than that historical and racial distinction. Vidor pioneered not only impressive advances in film technique, but also an expansive, humanist vision of the drama in everyday life (*The Crowd* in 1928, or 1931's *Street Scene*, for example). This melodramatic musical depicts the life of black southern sharecroppers while following the life of one farmworker who becomes a preacher and falls prey to his more earthbound desires. Academy Award Nomination for Best Director. **Cast:** Daniel L. Haynes, Nina Mae McKinney, William Fountaine, Everett McGarrity, Victoria Spivey. **Credits:** Dir:

> **"I did all my directing when I wrote the screenplay. It was probably harder for a regular director. He probably had to read the script the night before shooting started."**
>
> Preston Sturges

King Vidor; Prod: King Vidor; Writer: Wanda Tuchock, Ransom Rideout; DP: Gordon Avil; Ed: Hugh Wynn, Anson Stevenson; Composer: Irving Berlin. B&W, 90 min. **VHS**

Hallelujah, I'm a Bum
(1933) United Artists
Jolson sings Rodgers and Hart in this offbeat Depression-era tale about a hobo who tries to upgrade his station in life in order to romance the woman of his dreams. Cowritten by Hecht, it features rhyming dialogue between songs (!), and a rare Rodgers and Hart cameo as photographers. Songs include "You Are Too Beautiful," which was written expressly for the movie. Beware of edited versions entitled *Hallelujah, I'm a Tramp*; *The Heart of New York*; *Happy Go Lucky*; and *Lazy Bones*. **Cast:** Al Jolson, Madge Evans, Frank Morgan, Chester Conklin, Harry Langdon. **Credits:** Dir: Lewis Milestone; Prod: Lewis Milestone; Writer: S. N. Behrman, Ben Hecht; DP: Lucien Andriot; Composer: Richard Rodgers, Lorenz Hart; Art Director: Richard Day. B&W, 83 min. **VHS**

The Hallelujah Trail
(1965) United Artists
Comedy Western with Mitchum a cavalry officer assigned to protect a wagon train loaded with whiskey on its way to Denver miners. A bitterly cold winter's on the way and if temperance leader Remick has anything to say about it, it'll be a dry one, too. Based on the novel by Bill Gulick. **Cast:** Burt Lancaster, Lee Remick, Jim Hutton, Brian Keith, Martin Landau, Donald Pleasence, Pamela Tiffin, James Burke, John Anderson, Tom Stern. **Credits:** Dir: John Sturges; Prod: John Sturges; Writer: John Gay; DP: Robert Surtees; Ed: Ferris Webster; Prod Design: Cary Odell; Composer: Elmer Bernstein. Color, 167 min. **VHS, LASER**

Halloween
(1978) Compass
The film that ushered in the modern age of horror (and introduced as well the referential humor of second-generation hits such as *Scream*) stands well above its many sequels and clones because Carpenter's taut screenplay and direction make it truly scary without drenching the audience in gore. Curtis, in her debut role, plays a baby-sitter who must protect herself from the deadly Michael Myers, a mental institution escapee who killed his sister on Halloween 15 years earlier. Called "the most successful independent motion picture of all time,"

this low-budget film also started the career of writer-turned-producer Debra Hill. **Cast:** Donald Pleasence, Jamie Lee Curtis, P. J. Soles, Nancy Loomis, Charles Cyphers, Kyle Richards, Arthur Malet, David Kyle, Nick Castle. **Credits:** Dir: John Carpenter; Prod: Debra Hill; Writer: John Carpenter, Debra Hill; DP: Dean Cundey; Ed: Tommy Lee Wallace, Charles Bornstein; Prod Design: Tommy Lee Wallace; Composer: John Carpenter; Set Designer: Craig Stearns. Color, 92 min. **VHS, LASER, DVD**

Halls of Montezuma
(1950) Fox
A big, loud, and grim WWII action flick in which a troop of U.S. Marines in the Pacific theater embarks on a scouting mission to capture a strategic Japanese rocket base. Notable for the great performances by Malden, Palance, Widmark, and Webb, and for the very young Wagner. This late-period Milestone seems far removed from his earlier, antiwar masterpiece, *All Quiet on the Western Front* (1930). **Cast:** Richard Widmark, Jack Palance, Robert Wagner, Jack Webb, Karl Malden, Reginald Gardiner, Philip Ahn, Richard Hylton, Richard Boone, Skip Homeier. **Credits:** Dir: Lewis Milestone; Prod: Robert Bassler; Writer: Michael Blankfort; DP: Winton C. Hoch, Harry Jackson; Ed: William Reynolds; Composer: Sol Kaplan; Costumes: Charles LeMaire; SFX: Fred Sersen; Art Director: Albert Hogsett; Set Designer: Bruce MacDonald. Color, 113 min. **VHS**

Hamlet
(1948) GFD
Critically acclaimed and beloved by the Academy, Olivier stars in and directs Shakespeare's masterpiece about a disconsolate prince seeking revenge for the secret murder of his father by his uncle. Though the Rosencrantz and Guildenstern scenes were cut, the authentic setting (shot in Elsinore, Denmark) helped it earn seven Academy Award nominations and four Oscars. The film's many other awards include a British Academy award for Best Film, Any Source and a Golden Globe for Best Actor: Laurence Olivier. **Academy Awards:** Best Actor: Laurence Olivier; Best Picture; Best Costume Design; Best Art Direction—Set Decoration. **Cast:** Laurence Olivier, Jean Simmons, Eileen Herlie, Basil Sydney, Felix Aylmer, Norman Wooland, Terence Morgan, Peter Cushing, Stanley Holloway, Sterling Holloway. **Credits:** Dir: Laurence

Olivier; Prod: Laurence Olivier; Writer: Alan Dent; Story: William Shakespeare; DP: Desmond Dickinson; Ed: Helga Cranston; Prod Design: Roger K. Furse; Composer: William Walton; SFX: Paul Sheriff; Art Director: Carmen Dillon. Color, 153 min. **VHS, LASER**

Hands Across the Table
(1935) Paramount
A classic screwball romantic comedy with Lombard as a gold-digging manicurist working in the barber shop of a swanky hotel who meets a former millionaire playboy (MacMurray), who is himself about to marry for money. Bellamy, predating his role in *His Girl Friday*, plays the heroine's patient suitor. The ghoulish will want the opportunity to catch Prevost, whose grisly, untimely demise was the subject of a '70s Nick Lowe ditty. **Cast:** Carole Lombard, Fred MacMurray, Ralph Bellamy, William Demarest, Astrid Allwyn, Ruth Donnelly, Marie Prevost, Edward Gargan. **Credits:** Dir: Mitchell Leisen; Prod: E. Lloyd Sheldon; Writer: Michel Krasna, Herbert Fields; Story: Vina Delmar; DP: Ted Tetzlaff; Ed: William Shea; Composer: Sam Coslow, Frederick Hollander; Costumes: Travis Banton. B&W, 80 min. **VHS**

Hang 'Em High
(1968) United Artists
The first spaghetti Western made in America (sans Leone) and Eastwood's first star vehicle made outside Europe. Eastwood's innocent cowboy miraculously survives his own hanging (though he has to hide a nasty scar under his bandanna) by vigilantes and then treks across the frontier to bring his would-be hangmen to justice. Highly entertaining, with leathery performances from Johnson and Begley, and support from Bruce Dern, Dennis Hopper, and cowboy veteran Bob Steele as a dungeon prisoner. **Cast:** Clint Eastwood, Inger Stevens, Ed Begley, Pat Hingle, Arlene Golonka, James MacArthur, Ben Johnson, L. Q. Jones. **Credits:** Dir: Ted Post; Prod: Leonard Freeman; Writer: Leonard Freeman, Mel Goldberg; DP: Leonard J. South, Richard H. Kline; Ed: Gene Fowler; Composer: Dominic Frontiere; Costumes: George Murray; SFX: George Swartz; Art Director: John B. Goodman; Set Designer: Arthur Krams. Color, 115 min. **VHS, LASER, DVD**

The Hanging Tree
(1959) Warner Bros.
One of Cooper's last roles and one of his least-heralded but most effective.

Cooper portrays a secretive frontier doctor with a mysterious past. When a blind girl who's the lone survivor of a stagecoach robbery is placed under his care, a jealous cowboy stirs up trouble. Fine performances from all in this thinking-man's Western. Scott's screen debut. **Cast:** Gary Cooper, Karl Malden, George C. Scott, Maria Schell, Ben Piazza, Karl Swenson, Virginia Gregg, John Dierkes, King Donovan, Guy Wilkerson. **Credits:** Dir: Delmer Daves; Prod: Martin Jurow, Richard Shepherd; Writer: Wendell Mayes, Halstead Welles; DP: Ted McCord; Ed: Owen Marks; Composer: Max Steiner. Color, 108 min. **VHS**

Hangmen Also Die!

(1942) United Artists
Bertolt Brecht wrote the story and Fritz Lang directs this grim WWII noir thriller, which makes a vehement wartime commentary on Nazi terror and betrayal. Donlevy plays a gunman hiding out with the Resistance in Prague after the 1942 assassination of Hitler henchman Reinhard Heydrich. Academy award Nominations: Best Score; Best Sound. **Cast:** Brian Donlevy, Anna Lee, Walter Brennan, Gene Lockhart, Dennis O'Keefe, Alexander Granach, Margaret Wycherly, Nana Bryant, Jonathan Hale, Lionel Stander. **Credits:** Dir: Fritz Lang; Prod: Fritz Lang; Writer: John Wexley; Story: Bertolt Brecht, Fritz Lang; DP: James Wong Howe; Composer: Hanns Eisler. Color, 134 min. **VHS**

Hangover Square

(1945) Fox
The director and star of Jack the Ripper tale *The Lodger* (1944) present another suspenseful mystery movie. George Harvey Bone (Cregar), a talented composer, has one tragic flaw—whenever he hears a loud, discordant noise he is immediately incited to murderous impulses and wanders the streets of turn-of-the-century London looking for someone on whom to vent his aggression. When the composer's romantic interest becomes a victim, Scotland Yard is called in to investigate. Notable score by Herrmann. **Cast:** Laird Cregar, Linda Darnell, George Sanders, Glenn Langan, Faye Marlowe, Alan Napier, Frederic Worlock, J. W. Austin, Leyland Hodgson, Clifford Brooke. **Credits:** Dir: John Brahm; Prod: Robert Bassler; Writer: Barre Lyndon; Story: Patrick Hamilton; DP: Joseph LaShelle; Ed: Harry Reynolds; Prod Design: Lyle Wheeler, Maurice Ransford; Composer: Bernard Herrmann. B&W, 77 min.

Hanover Street

(1979) Columbia
Notable as one of Ford's first starring roles post–*Star Wars*. Ford plays a WWII American bomber pilot who falls in love with a married British nurse and then is sent on a risky mission behind enemy lines, where he ends up working with his lover's husband. **Cast:** Harrison Ford, Lesley-Anne Down, Christopher Plummer, Alec McCowen, Richard Masur, Michael Sacks, Max Wall. **Credits:** Dir: Peter Hyams; Prod: Paul Lazarus; Writer: Peter Hyams; DP: David Watkin; Ed: James Mitchell; Prod Design: Philip Harrison; Composer: John Barry; Costumes: Joan Bridge; SFX: Martin Gutteridge; Art Director: Malcolm Middleton. Color, 110 min. **VHS**

Hans Christian Andersen

(1952) RKO
Kaye doing what he does best in this colorful musical written by Hart with songs by Loesser: portraying an endearing character and singing family favorites, including "Thumbelina," "Inchworm," and "Ugly Duckling." Kaye's Andersen woos a glamorous Copenhagen actress while amusing the Danish kids. Top-notch family viewing. Academy Award nominations: 6, including Best Song ("Thumbelina"). **Cast:** Danny Kaye, Farley Granger, Zizi Jeanmaire, Philip Tonge, Roland Petit, Erik Bruhn. **Credits:** Dir: Charles Vidor; Prod: Samuel Goldwyn; Writer: Moss Hart; Story: Myles Connolly; DP: Harry Stradling; Ed: Daniel Mandell; Choreographer: Roland Petit; Composer: Frank Loesser; Costumes: Mary Wills, Antoni Clave, Barbara Karinska; Art Director: Richard Day; Set Designer: Howard Bristol. Color, 112 min. **VHS, LASER**

The Happiest Millionaire

(1967) Disney
Wouldn't we all be happy in Disney's land? A delightful Disney musical adapted from a stage play about the comic misadventures of an immigrant butler who takes a job with an eccentric millionaire family. Among other things, they keep pet alligators in the conservatory, and operate a Bible-and-boxing school in the stables. Based on the book *My Philadelphia Father* by Kyle Crichton. **Cast:** Fred MacMurray, Tommy Steele, Greer Garson, Geraldine Page, John Davidson, Gladys Cooper, Lesley Ann Warren, Hermione Baddeley, Paul Petersen, Eddie Hodges. **Credits:** Dir: Norman Tokar; Prod: Walt Disney, Bill Anderson; Writer: A. J. Carothers; DP: Edward

Colman; Ed: Cotton Warburton; Prod Design: Carroll Clark, John B. Mansbridge; Composer: Richard M. Sherman, Robert B. Sherman, Jack Elliott. Color, 144 min. **VHS**

Happy Birthday, Wanda June

(1971) Columbia
Kurt Vonnegut's own adaptation of his play. Steiger plays a big-game hunter who returns from the jungles of the Amazon after being written off as dead eight years before and finds that his values have been rendered equally moribund. His previously batty wife (York) has since become quite the intellectual and is preparing to remarry. Hickey is outstanding as the oddball Looseleaf. Fine evocation of the Vonnegut upside-down world. **Cast:** Rod Steiger, Susannah York, Don Murray, Steven Paul, William Hickey, George Grizzard, Pamelyn Ferdin. **Credits:** Dir: Mark Robson; Prod: Lester Goldsmith; Writer: Kurt Vonnegut, Jr.; DP: Fred J. Koenekamp; Ed: Dorothy Spencer; Prod Design: Boris Leven. Color, 105 min.

Happy Landing

(1938) Fox
Typical Henie outdoor romance finds the ice queen of Hollywood (no, not Joan Crawford) torn between the affections of all-American Ameche and robust Romeo Romero when Ameche's plane ditches near Henie's Norwegian home. **Cast:** Sonja Henie, Don Ameche, Cesar Romero, Ethel Merman, Jean Hersholt, Billy Gilbert, Wally Vernon, El Brendel. **Credits:** Dir: Roy Del Ruth; Prod: David Hempstead; Writer: Milton Sperling, Boris Ingster; DP: John Mescall; Ed: Louis Loeffler; Choreographer: Harry Losee. B&W, 102 min. **VHS**

The Happy Time

(1952) Columbia
Driscoll is an innocent 12-year-old who grows into maturity as he discovers love and the fairer sex at his family's ancestral home in Ottawa. Born to a family of free-spirited French Canadians, Driscoll navigates the shoals of first love, eventually discarding his infatuation with the curvy new maid (a former showgirl) in favor of the girl next door. **Cast:** Charles Boyer, Louis Jourdan, Marsha Hunt, Kurt Kraznar, Linda Christian, Bobby Driscoll, Jeanette Nolan, Richard Erdman, Jack Raine. **Credits:** Dir: Richaard Fleisher; Prod: Stanley Kramer; Writer: Earl Felton; DP: Charles Lawton, Jr.; Ed: William A. Lyon; Composer: Dimitri Tiomkin; Art Director: Carl Anderson. B&W, 94 min.

The Happy Years
(1950) MGM
When John Humperdink Stover disappoints his respectable family by getting expelled from school for the second time in his young life, he is shipped off to Lawrenceville, a prestigious New Jersey preparatory academy. This family comedy, based on the popular magazine series "The Lawrenceville School Stories" by Owen Johnson, traces Stover's development from a stubborn delinquent to a young man of character. Stover grows through his experience on the football field, where he learns to accept a former rival as a teammate and friend, and in the classroom, where he is given the opportunity to cheat on a Latin test he is ill prepared for. **Cast:** Darryl Hickman, Scotty Beckett, Leon Ames, Margalo Gilmore, Leo G. Carroll, Donn Gift, Peter Thompson, Jerry Mickelsen, Alan Dinehart, David Bair. **Credits:** Dir: William Wellman; Prod: Carey Wilson; Writer: Harry Ruskin, Owen Johnson; DP: Paul C. Vogel; Ed: John Dunning; Composer: Leigh Harline, Alfred Newman; Art Director: Cedric Gibbons, Daniel B. Cathcart. Color, 109 min.

Hardcore
(1979) Columbia
This early feature from writer-director Schrader features what may be Scott's best performance. The daughter of a midwestern businessman (Hubley) disappears on a trip to Los Angeles sponsored by their Calvinist church. Shattered when she turns up in a porno movie, the grieving father descends into the sordid realm of the hard-core sex industry determined to retrieve her. In the process of his search, Scott befriends a sympathetic prostitute and the two discover they have more in common than they would have imagined. Schrader's own strict upbringing gives his story depth in its portrayal of a man whose moral compass is suddenly in question. **Cast:** George C. Scott, Peter Boyle, Ed Begley, Season Hubley, Dick Sargent, Leonard Gaines. **Credits:** Dir: Paul Schrader; Prod: Buzz Feitshans; Writer: Paul Schrader; DP: Michael Chapman; Ed: Tom Rolf; Prod Design: Paul Sylbert; Composer: Jack Nitzsche; Art Director: Edwin O'Donovan; Set Designer: Bruce Weintraub. Color, 111 min. VHS, LASER

The Harder They Come
(1973) New World
Reggae music serves as both sound track and plot element in this cross between a crime yarn and backstage musical. Reggae star Cliff portrays a poor Jamaican youth who looks to better himself through success in the recording industry but finds corruption everywhere he turns. He turns to crime just as his career ignites. The best-selling sound track features songs such as "You Can Get It If You Really Want It," "Many Rivers to Cross," "The Harder They Come," and "Sitting in Limbo." **Cast:** Jimmy Cliff, Janet Barkley, Carl Bradshaw, Toots and the Maytals, Ras Daniel Hartman, Basil Keane. **Credits:** Dir: Perry Henzell; Prod: Perry Henzell; Writer: Perry Henzell, Trevor Rhone; DP: Peter Jessop, David McDonald, Frank St. Juste; Ed: Seicland Anderson, John Victor Smith, Richard White; Prod Design: Sally Henzell; Composer: Jimmy Cliff. Color, 104 min. VHS, LASER

The Harder They Fall
(1956) Columbia
A stinging sucker punch of a ring yarn that features Bogart's last role. An unemployed sportswriter (Bogart) finds a simple fighter for corrupt boxing manager Steiger to promote. He plays both sides, though, as he uses his access to boxing corruption to write an exposé on the racket. Bogart died soon after filming. From Schulberg's novel. Academy Award Nomination: Best Cinematography; **Cast:** Humphrey Bogart, Rod Steiger, Jan Sterling, Mike Lane, Max Baer, Edward Andrews, Harold J. Stone, Carlos Montalban, Nehemiah Persoff, Felice Orlandi. **Credits:** Dir: Mark Robson; Prod: Philip Yordan; Writer: Philip Yordan, Budd Schulberg; DP: Burnett Guffey; Ed: Jerome Thoms; Prod Design: William Flannery; Composer: Hugo Friedhofer, Lionel Newman. B&W, 109 min. VHS

Hard, Fast and Beautiful
(1951) RKO
A selfish mother's (Trevor) ambition pushes her daughter to the top of the pro tennis world. Manipulated into giving up her sweetheart, the girl (Forrest) finally sees that her mother and promoter (Young) are using her for their own greedy interests, and she gives up her career to return to her true love. Lupino directs and appears in a cameo. Based on John R. Tunis's novel *Mother of a Champion*. **Cast:** Clare Trevor, Sally Forrest, Carleton Young, Robert Clarke, Kenneth Patterson, Marcella Cisney, Joseph Kearns, George Fisher, Arthur Little, Bert Whitley. **Credits:** Dir: Ida Lupino; Prod: Collier Young, Norman A. Cook; Writer: Martha Wilkerson; Story: John R. Tunis; DP: Archie Stout; Ed: George C. Shrader, William Ziegler; Composer: Roy Webb. B&W, 78 min.

Hard Times
(1975) Columbia
Action film writer-director Hill's first feature is a hard-hitting story with rich period detail about a bareknuckle streetfighter (Bronson) who drifts into Depression-era New Orleans and hooks up with a small-time gambler. The gambler takes over the boxer's career, arranging illegal fights and involving him in a scheme to fleece some gangsters. Hill's eye for atmosphere is combined with Bronson's best tough-guy role. **Cast:** Charles Bronson, James Coburn, Jill Ireland, Margaret Blye, Strother Martin. **Credits:** Dir: Walter Hill; Prod: Lawrence Gordon; Writer: Bryan Gindorff, Bruce Henstell, Walter Hill; DP: Philip H. Lathrop; Ed: Roger Spottiswoode; Prod Design: Trevor Williams; Composer: Barry Devorzon; Set Designer: Dennis Peeples. Color, 97 min. VHS, LASER

Hard to Get
(1938) Warner Bros.
This musical screwball comedy pits poor but talented architect Powell against spoiled little rich girl de Havilland. He humiliates the hopeless de Havilland at his filling station, not knowing that she's the daughter of an eccentric millionaire (Winninger) who wants to hire him to design a hotel chain. Okay variation on a tried-and-true theme. Songs include "There's a Sunny Side to Every Situation" and "You Must Have Been a Beautiful Baby." **Cast:** Dick Powell, Olivia de Havilland, Charles Winninger, Allen Jenkins, Bonita Granville, Melville Cooper, Granville Bates, Thurston Hall, Penny Singleton, Nella Walker. **Credits:** Dir: Ray Enright; Prod: Hal B. Wallis; Writer: Jerry Wald, Maurice Leo, Richard Macauley; DP: Charles Rosher; Ed: Thomas Richards; Prod Design: Anton Grot; Composer: Johnny Mercer, Harry Warren. B&W, 80 min.

The Hard Way
(1942) Warner Bros.
Small-town housewife Lupino is stuck in nowheresville and she's not going to let the same thing happen to her lovely little sister, Leslie. Keeping her away from potential ruin at the hands of men, Helen forces Katherine into a rigorous showbiz career. Katherine has success onstage but her sister's obsession with every aspect of her career threatens to destroy her life. To

reach her final success, she must cast away her clinging sister. Hard-hearted melodrama, and no one's better than Lupino at that. Songs include "Was I Blue?" "Goodnight My Darling," and "I Love to Dance." **Cast:** Ida Lupino, Joan Leslie, Dennis Morgan, Jack Carson, Gladys George, Faye Emerson, Paul Cavanagh, Roman Bohnen, Julie Bishop. **Credits:** Dir: Vincent Sherman; Prod: Jerry Wald; Writer: Daniel Fuchs, Peter Viertel; Story: Jerry Wald; DP: James Wong Howe; Ed: Thomas Pratt; Composer: Heinz Roemheld, M. K. Jerome, Max Scholl; Costumes: Orry-Kelly. B&W, 108 min. **VHS, LASER**

Harem Girl

(1952) Columbia
An exotic Hollywood Araby is the setting for this comedy, which has Davis, a harem girl, trying to foil a murder plot afoot in the palace. Intent on seizing the kingdom's oil supply, an evil sheikh, Randolph, schemes to kill the princess, Castle. Davis does all that she can to save her mistress. **Cast:** Joan Davis, Peggie Castle, Arthur Blake, Paul Marion, Don Randolph, Henry Brandon, Minerva Urecal, Peter Mamakos, John Dehner, Peter Brocco. **Credits:** Dir: Edward Bernds; Prod: Wallace MacDonald; Writer: Edward Bernds, Elwood Ullman; DP: Lester White; Ed: Richard Fantl; Composer: Mischa Bakaleinikoff; Art Director: Paul Palmentola. B&W, 70 min.

Harlan County, USA

(1976)
An Academy Award–winning documentary about the strike by Kentucky mine workers against the Eastover Mining Company. Film traces the effects of the strike and union organizing efforts on 180 coal-mining families. This acclaimed documentary was selected in 1990 for permanent preservation by the National Film Registry. **Academy Awards:** Best Documentary Feature. **Credits:** Dir: Barbara Kopple; Prod: Barbara Kopple; DP: Phil Parmet, Hart Perry; Ed: Nancy Baker, Mirra Bank, Lora Hays, Mary Lampson; Composer: Merle Travis. Color, 103 min. **VHS**

Harlow

(1965) Paramount
A lurid biopic of the tragic, glamorous movie queen, Jean Harlow. This focuses on Harlow's various relationships, including those with her mother and stepfather, agent Arthur Landau, and husband, studio executive Paul Bern, who committed suicide. Baker

manages to at least look a little like Harlow, and Lansbury adds some needed class. Not to be confused with film of the same title released the same year (what was the fascination with platinum blondes in '65?). **Cast:** Carroll Baker, Martin Balsam, Red Buttons, Mike Connors, Angela Lansbury, Peter Lawford, Michael Dante, Raf Vallone, Leslie Nielsen, Mary Murphy. **Credits:** Dir: Gordon Douglas; Prod: Joseph E. Levine; Writer: John Michael Hayes; DP: Joseph Ruttenberg; Composer: Neal Hefti. Color, 125 min. **VHS**

Harold and Maude

(1971) Paramount
A whimsical black comedy that became a cult and campus favorite, tapping into an inexplicable early-'70s zeitgeist. Harold is a rich 20-year-old obsessed with slashed wrists, self-inflicted gunshots, personal vivisection, drowning, hanging, and being burned alive—just to annoy his mother. Maude is a poor 80-year-old optimist who has a peerless affinity for all things living. Together, they attend strangers' wakes and find in each other a most unlikely romantic partner. This was originally writer Colin Higgins's UCLA thesis. Features a score by Cat Stevens. **Cast:** Ruth Gordon, Bud Cort, Vivian Pickles, Cyril Cusack. **Credits:** Dir: Hal Ashby; Prod: Charles B. Mulvehill, Colin Higgins; Writer: Colin Higgins; DP: John A. Alonzo; Ed: William Sawyer, Edward A. Warschilka; Prod Design: Michael Haller; Composer: Cat Stevens; Costumes: William Ware Theiss; SFX: A. D. Flowers. Color, 91 min. **VHS, LASER**

Harper

(1966) Warner Bros.
Private-eye mystery based on MacDonald's Lew Archer novels. When a millionaire businessman turns up missing, his estranged, invalid wife (Bacall) hires a private detective (Newman) to find him. The P.I. quickly discovers that the victim has been kidnapped by some of those nearest and dearest to him, and uncovers a tangled web of smuggling, greed, drugs, and petty family jealousies. Note script by Goldman. Followed by *The Drowning Pool* (1975). **Cast:** Paul Newman, Lauren Bacall, Julie Harris, Shelley Winters, Arthur Hill, Janet Leigh, Pamela Tiffin, Robert Wagner, Robert Webber, Strother Martin. **Credits:** Dir: Jack Smight; Writer: William Goldman; Story: Ross MacDonald; DP: Conrad Hall; Composer: Johnny Mandel. Color, 121 min. **VHS, LASER**

The Harrad Experiment

(1973) Cinerama
A sensuous screen production of the best-seller by Robert Rimmer—and, from this distance, an almost touchingly innocent look back at bygone sexual mores. Two relationships are intimately explored in an experimental coed college that encourages sexual freedom. Costars Hedren and Johnson were romantically involved during filming; years later Johnson married Hedren's daughter Melanie Griffith (who appears as an extra). **Cast:** Laurie Walters, Don Johnson, Tippi Hedren, James Whitmore, Victoria Thompson, Bruno Kirby, Robert Middleton. **Credits:** Dir: Ted Post; Prod: Dennis F. Stevens; Writer: Ted Cassedy, Michael Werner; DP: Richard H. Kline; Ed: Bill Brame; Composer: Artie Butler. Color, 95 min. **VHS**

Harriet Craig

(1950) Columbia
Crawford, in a dream role, plays shrewish, perfectionist Harriet Craig, who is so obsessively house-proud that she drives everyone around her crazy. She can't resist trying to run people's lives, and almost destroys her cousin's romance. Then Mrs. Craig interferes in her husband's career—until she goes too far. In the end, she's left alone with her true love: her spotlessly clean home. Though the premise sounds like campy fun (and indeed it has been satirized onstage), that stony Crawford visage makes Harriet a little too real. Remake of 1936's *Craig's Wife*. **Cast:** Joan Crawford, Wendell Corey, Lucile Watson, Ellen Corby, Allyn Joslyn, William Bishop, K. T. Stevens, Raymond Greenleaf. **Credits:** Dir: Vincent Sherman; Prod: William Dozier; Writer: Anne Froelick, James Gunn; Story: George Kelly; DP: Joseph Walker; Prod Design: Walter Holscher; Composer: George Duning; Costumes: Sheila O'Brien. B&W, 94 min. **VHS**

Harry and Tonto

(1974) Fox
An offbeat comedy-drama with a great central performance by Carney. A 72-year-old widower takes off on a cross-country odyssey with his cat, Tonto, after he's evicted from his Manhattan apartment building. Along the way, he visits his grown children as well as his first love. Among the gallery of other memorable characters he meets on the road are a young female hitchhiker, a hooker, and a down-on-his-luck Indian chief. Golden

Globe for Best Actor: Art Carney. Academy Award Nominations: Best Original Screenplay. **Academy Awards:** Best Actor: Art Carney. **Cast:** Art Carney, Ellen Burstyn, Larry Hagman, Chief Dan George, Geraldine Fitzgerald, Arthur Hunnicutt, Herbert Berghof. **Credits:** Dir: Paul Mazursky; Prod: Paul Mazursky; Writer: Paul Mazursky, Josh Greenfeld; DP: Michael Butler; Ed: Richard Halsey; Prod Design: Ted Haworth; Composer: Bill Conti; Costumes: Albert Wolsky; Set Designer: John Godfrey. Color, 115 min. **VHS**

Harum Scarum
(1965) MGM
One of the stranger plots for an Elvis flick. The King plays a matinee idol on a visit to the desert kingdoms of the Middle East. His uneventful goodwill tour takes a turn for the weird when a team of assassins try to force him to exterminate their king. But Elvis has already captured the heart of the king's daughter (Mobley). Songs include "My Desert Serenade," "Shake That Tambourine," and "So Close Yet So Far (From Paradise)." **Cast:** Elvis Presley, Mary Ann Mobley,

Fran Jeffries, Michael Ansara, Jay Novello, Theodore Marcuse, Billy Barty. **Credits:** Dir: Gene Nelson; Prod: Sam Katzman; Writer: Gerald Drayson Adams; DP: Fred Jackman; Ed: Ben Lewis; Choreographer: Earl Barton; Composer: Fred Karger; Costumes: Margo Weintz; Art Director: George W. Davis; Set Designer: Henry Grace. Color, 95 min. **VHS, LASER**

Harvey
(1950) Universal
Elwood is a good-natured, slightly sloshed man whose faithful companion is a 6-feet-3½-inches-tall rabbit that only he can see. When his sister Veta (Hull) tries to have him committed, she's taken in instead. It's up to Elwood and Harvey to straighten out the mess. Stewart in his best amiable, bumbling mode. Based on Mary Chase's Pulitzer Prize–winning play. Golden Globe for Best Supporting Actress: Josephine Hull. Academy Award Nominations: 2, including Best Actor: James Stewart. **Academy Awards:** Best Supporting Actress: Josephine Hull. **Cast:** James Stewart, Josephine Hull, Charles Drake, Cecil Kellaway, Jesse White, Victoria Horne, Wallace Ford, Peggy Dow, Nana Bryant. **Credits:** Dir: Henry Koster; Prod: John Beck; Writer: Oscar Brodney, Mary Chase; Story: Mary Chase; DP: William Daniels; Ed: Ralph Dawson; Composer: Frank Skinner; Art Director: Nathan Juran. B&W, 104 min. **VHS, LASER**

The Harvey Girls
(1946) MGM
A chain of railroad station restaurants bring the frontier a touch of civilization along with a hot meal in this nostalgic musical comedy from the legendary MGM Freed unit. There's high-wattage star power (Garland, Foster, Charisse, Bolger, Lansbury) expended on a negligible tale of an eastern gal who heads west to work in one of the elegant restaurants. The Mercer-Warren score includes the Award-winning "On the Atchison, Topeka and Santa Fe," "The Wild, Wild West," "It's a Great Big World," and many others. Academy Award Nominations: 2, including Best Scoring of a Musical Picture. **Academy Awards:** Best Song. **Cast:** Judy Garland, Ray Bolger, John Hodiak, Angela Lansbury, Cyd Charisse, Preston Foster, Virginia O'Brien, Marjorie Main, Chill Wills, Kenny Baker. **Credits:** Dir: George Sidney; Prod: Arthur Freed; Writer: Edmund Beloin, Nathaniel Curtis, Harry Crane, James O'Hanlon, Sam-

Harvey (1950)

son Raphaelson; Ed: George J. Folsey, Albert Akst; Prod Design: Cedric Gibbons, William Ferrari; Composer: Lennie Hayton, Johnny Mercer, Harry Warren. Color, 102 min. VHS, LASER

Has Anybody Seen My Gal?
(1952) Universal
Sirk directs the story of an aging millionaire (Coburn) who wants to leave his fortune to the family of a woman who once spurned his proposal to marry. After anonymously donating the first $100,000, he poses as a border in the house to see if they're worthy of the rest. While dad sells the drugstore and mom takes to social climbing with vengeance, the younger generation shows they're made of stronger stuff when Laurie refuses to dump her true love, soda jerk Hudson. Dean has an early, small role. **Cast:** Piper Laurie, Rock Hudson, Gigi Perreau, Charles Coburn, Lynn Bari, Larry Gates, William Reynolds, Paul Harvey, Frank Ferguson, James Dean. **Credits:** Dir: Douglas Sirk; Prod: Ted Richmond; Writer: Joseph Hoffman; Story: Eleanor H. Porter; DP: Clifford Stine; Ed: Russell Schoengarth; Prod Design: Hilyard Brown, Bernard Herzbrun; Composer: Joseph Gershenson. Color, 88 min.

Hatari!
(1962) Paramount
Wayne leads the way in an exciting action adventure about big-game hunters in Africa. The wildlife photography is top-notch and there's just enough of a story to bridge the action sequences. Interesting to watch how the hunters safely capture their prey for sale to zoos. Academy Award Nomination for Best (Color) Cinematography. **Cast:** John Wayne, Elsa Martinelli, Red Buttons, Hardy Kruger. **Credits:** Dir: Howard Hawks; Prod: Howard Hawks; Writer: Leigh Brackett; Story: Harry Kurnitz; DP: Russell Harlan; Ed: Stuart Gilmore; Composer: Henry Mancini; Costumes: Edith Head; SFX: John Fulton; Art Director: Hal Pereira; Set Designer: Sam Comer. Color, 158 min. VHS, LASER

The Hatchet Man
(1932) First National
In this early Wellman, Robinson plays a hatchet man, or Chinese gangster, in San Francisco's Chinatown, assigned by Tong leaders to kill his best friend. He has already agreed to look after the friend's daughter, and marries her. The hatchet man is then ordered to kill her bodyguard but feels bound by duty to his old friend and

sends the pair out of the country instead. When he learns she is selling drugs in China, he goes after her and her lover. **Cast:** Edward G. Robinson, Loretta Young, Edmund Breese, Dudley Digges, Leslie Fenton, Blanche Frederici, Ralph Ince, Noel Madison, Tully Marshall, J. Carrol Naish. **Credits:** Dir: William Wellman; Writer: J. Grubb Alexander, David Belasco; Story: Achmed Abdullah; DP: Sidney Hickox; Ed: Owen Marks. B&W, 74 min.

The Haunting
(1963) MGM
A paranormal investigator invites two women with psychic powers to help him examine Hill House, a sinister family estate haunted by the angry souls from its troubled past. Tamblyn plays the cocksure heir to the house who will learn to respect its wrath. Based on Shirley Jackson's lyrical novel *The Haunting of Hill House*. A remake is in the offing. **Cast:** Julie Harris, Claire Bloom, Russ Tamblyn, Richard Johnson, Lois Maxwell, Valentine Dyall, Fay Compton, Rosalie Crutchley, Ronald Adam. **Credits:** Dir: Robert Wise; Prod: Robert Wise; Writer: Nelson Gidding; Story: Shirley Jackson; DP: David Boulton; Ed: Ernest Walter; Prod Design: Elliot Scott; Composer: Humphrey Searle. B&W, 112 min. VHS, LASER

Having a Wild Weekend
(1965) Warner Bros.
Boorman directed this me-too feature about Merseybeat also-rans the Dave Clark Five. Life as movie stuntmen grows wearisome for Dave and the lads, so they escape, with a beautiful model in tow, to a tropical island to get away from it all. But they soon discover that their paradise has plenty of surprises. The songs are the point, and they include the hit "Catch Us If You Can," "I Can't Stand It," and the title tune. **Cast:** Dave Clark Five, Barbara Ferris, David Lodge, Robin Bailey, David De Keyser, Yootha Joyce, Robert Lang, Clive Swift, Ronald Lacey, Hugh Walters. **Credits:** Dir: John Boorman; Prod: David Deutsch; Writer: Peter Nichols; DP: Manny Wynn; Ed: Gordon Pilkington; Prod Design: Tony Woollard; Costumes: Sally Jacobs. Color, 91 min. VHS

Having Wonderful Crime
(1945) RKO
Fun, fast-moving comedy-mystery that teams honeymooners Murphy and Landis with their criminal attorney friend O'Brien to solve the disappearance of a magician. **Cast:** Pat O'Brien, George Murphy, Carole Landis. **Cred-**

its: Dir: A. Edward Sutherland; Prod: Robert Fellows; Writer: Howard J. Green, Parke Levy; DP: Frank Redman; Ed: Gene Milford; Composer: Leigh Harline; SFX: Vernon L. Walker; Art Director: Albert S. D'Agostino; Set Designer: Darrell Silvera. B&W, 70 min. VHS, LASER

Hawaii
(1966) United Artists
An epic film adapted from Michener's historical novel that depicts the tropical islands in the early part of the 19th century. A Protestant missionary from New England ministers to the native Hawaiians with the help of his devoted wife. He is tested through the years by natural disasters, the clash between European and native cultures, and the visits of a seafaring rival for his wife's affections. Academy Award Nominations: 7, including Best (Color) Cinematography. **Cast:** Max von Sydow, Julie Andrews, Richard Harris, Gene Hackman, Carroll O'Connor, Torin Thatcher, Jocelyn Lagarde. **Credits:** Dir: George Roy Hill; Prod: Walter Mirisch; Writer: Dalton Trumbo, Daniel Taradash; Story: James A. Michener; DP: Russell Harlan; Prod Design: Cary Odell; Composer: Elmer Bernstein; Costumes: Dorothy Jeakins; SFX: Linwood Dunn; Set Designer: Edward G. Boyle. Color, 188 min. VHS, LASER

Head
(1968) Columbia
It's a trip, man! The Monkees parlayed their television success to the big screen. But they didn't settle for a bigger-budget version of the sitcom. Instead, they created a mind-blowing excursion, courtesy of writer and director Nicholson and Rafelson. There's no story and none of their hit songs is here, can you dig it? But the psychedelic excursion includes "Porpoise Song," "Daddy's Song," and "Circle Sky." **Cast:** The Monkees, Victor Mature, Frank Zappa, Annette Funicello, Carol Doda, Teri Garr, Sonny Liston, Peter Tork, Davy Jones, Mickey Dolenz. **Credits:** Dir: Bob Rafelson; Prod: Bob Rafelson; Writer: Bob Rafelson, Jack Nicholson; DP: Michel Hugo; Ed: Mike Pozen; Choreographer: Toni Basil; Composer: Ken Thorne; SFX: Chuck Gaspar; Set Designer: Ned Parsons. Color, 99 min. VHS, DVD

Heartbeat
(1946) RKO
Guttersnipe Rogers graduates from Rathbone's school for pickpockets only to get her hand stuck in heartthrob

Aumont's hip pocket. They fall immediately in love. Remake of French farce *Battement de Coeur* (1939) doesn't translate that well and is something of a stretch for Rogers (she plays an 18-year-old). **Cast:** Ginger Rogers, Jean-Pierre Aumont, Adolphe Menjou, Basil Rathbone, Melville Cooper, Mikhail Rasumny, Mona Maris, Henry Stephenson. **Credits:** Dir: Sam Wood; Prod: Robert Hakim, Raymond Hakim; Writer: Morrie Ryskind, Roland Leigh; Story: Hans Wilhelm, Max Kolpe, Michel Duran; DP: Joseph A. Valentine; Ed: Roland Gross; Prod Design: Lionel Banks; Composer: Paul Misraki. B&W, 102 min. vhs

The Heartbreak Kid
(1972) Fox
In this bitter Simon-scripted comedy, Grodin decides on his honeymoon that he absolutely can't stand his irritatingly idiosyncratic wife and becomes obsessed with a ravishing, but frosty, WASP coed (the inevitable Shepherd). Well directed by May and adapted by Simon from a Bruce Jay Friedman story. **Cast:** Cybill Shepherd, Charles Grodin, Eddie Albert, Jeannie Berlin, Audra Lindley, William Prince, Art Metrano, Marilyn Putnam. **Credits:** Dir: Elaine May; Prod: Edgar J. Scherick; Writer: Neil Simon; DP: Owen Roizman; Ed: John Carter; Composer: Garry Sherman. Color, 106 min. vhs, laser

The Heart Is a Lonely Hunter
(1968) Warner Bros.
Locke and Keach both made their film debuts in this fine cinematic adaptation of McCullers's heart-wrenching story. A deaf-mute man living in a small town in Alabama befriends a lonely adolescent girl. Arkin is superb and Howe's photography is first-rate. Academy Award Nominations: Best Actor: Alan Arkin; Best Supporting Actress: Sondra Locke. **Cast:** Alan Arkin, Sondra Locke, Cicely Tyson, Stacy Keach, Laurinda Barrett, Chuck McCann, Biff McGuire, Percy Rodriguez. **Credits:** Dir: Robert Ellis Miller; Prod: Thomas C. Ryan, Marc Merson; Writer: Thomas C. Ryan, Carson McCullers; DP: James Wong Howe; Ed: John F. Burnett; Prod Design: Leroy Deane; Composer: Dave Grusin. Color, 125 min. vhs

Heartland
(1979) Filmhaus
The quiet dignity of life on the prairie in the early part of this century has powerful performances from Torn and Ferrell. Ferrell portrays a widow who survives by becoming the taciturn Torn's

housekeeper. The hardships and pleasures are treated simply, with great attention to detail and emotional nuance. Based on the frontier diaries of Elinore Randall Stewart. **Cast:** Rip Torn, Conchata Ferrell, Barry Primus, Lilia Skala. **Credits:** Dir: Richard Pearce; Prod: Michael Hausman, Beth Ferris; Writer: Beth Ferris; Story: Elinore Randall Stewart; DP: Fred Murphy; Ed: Bill Yahraus; Composer: Charles Gross; Costumes: Hilary Rosenfeld; Art Director: Carl Copeland. Color, 95 min. vhs

Hearts and Minds
(1974) Warner Bros.
This Academy Award–winning documentary is a sweeping survey of the United States' cataclysmic involvement in Vietnam and the cost of the war at home and abroad. The filmmaker combines interviews with American politicians and army officers, Vietnamese peasants, war veterans, and antiwar activists with newsreel footage, excerpts from Hollywood war movies, and material he shot himself in Vietnam to create an indelible visual essay against war. **Academy Awards:** Best Documentary Feature. **Cast:** Clark Clifford, George Coker, Daniel Ellsberg, J. W. Fulbright, Brian Holden, Lyndon Johnson, Robby Muller, Richard Milhous Nixon, George S. Patton. **Credits:** Dir: Peter Davis; Ed: Lynzee Klingman. Color, 115 min. vhs, laser

Hearts Divided
(1936) Warner Bros.
Dramatic true story of the romance between Napoleon Bonaparte's younger brother, Jerome (Powell), and an American girl from Maryland (Davies). Jerome is on a goodwill tour of the United States when he meets Betsy Patterson at a horse track. At first she rebuffs him, but the pair quickly fall in love. Both families oppose the romance, hers because they think he is only a French tutor and his because Napoleon wants him to marry European royalty. **Cast:** Marion Davies, Dick Powell, Claude Rains, Charlie Ruggles, Edward Everett Horton. **Credits:** Dir: Frank Borzage; Prod: Harry Brown; Writer: Doyle Laird, Casey Robinson, Johnson Rida Young; DP: George Folsey, Jr.; Ed: William Holmes; Prod Design: Robert M. Haas; Composer: Al Dubin, Harry Warren. B&W, 70 min.

Hearts of the West
(1975) United Artists
A movielover's movie starring Bridges as a young man who moves to Holly-

wood in the '30s with hopes of becoming a writer of Western pulp novels. Instead he finds himself in front of the camera in cowboy films. Loosely based on the unlikely cowboy stars, such as Tom Mix, who literally rode onto sets as cowpokes and rode off as stars. **Cast:** Jeff Bridges, Andy Griffith, Alan Arkin, Blythe Danner, Donald Pleasence, Richard B. Shull, Herb Edelman, Tony Bill. **Credits:** Dir: Howard Zieff; Prod: Tony Bill; Writer: Rob Thompson; DP: Mario Tosi; Composer: Ken Lauber. Color, 103 min. vhs, laser

The Heat's On
(1943) Columbia
Screen siren West took a 27-year break after this. Though she did write her own dialogue, she had almost no control over the rest of this uneven musical production. She plays an actress in a Broadway flop whose producer uses scandal to pump up the ticket sales, and launches a new venture with hypocritical Legion of Purity members. Mildly amusing satire on Mae's own troubles with the Legion of Decency and studio censors. **Cast:** Mae West, Victor Moore, William Gaxton, Lester Allen, Almira Sessions, Hazel Scott, Alan Dinehart, Lloyd Bridges, Xavier Cugat, Mary Roche. **Credits:** Dir: Gregory Ratoff; Prod: Gregory Ratoff; Writer: Fitzroy Davis, George S. George, Fred Schiller; DP: Franz Planer; Ed: Otto Meyer; Prod Design: Nicolai Remisoff; Composer: John Leipold. B&W, 79 min. vhs

Heaven Can Wait
(1943) Fox
A sharp romantic comedy with the Lubitsch touch. When a dearly departed former playboy (Ameche) goes to Hell, he must convince the ruler of the realm of darkness that he has come to the right place. He recounts his life story, including his unfaithfulness to his beautiful wife (Tierney), but as his life flashes in front of his eyes, he and the Devil find he was a terribly good father, a horribly loyal husband, and a hideously kindhearted soul. Academy Award Nominations: Best Color Cinematography; Best Picture; Best Director. **Cast:** Gene Tierney, Don Ameche, Laird Cregar, Charles Coburn, Marjorie Main, Louis Calhern, Signe Hasso, Eugene Pallette, Allyn Joslyn, Spring Byington. **Credits:** Dir: Ernst Lubitsch; Prod: Ernst Lubitsch; Writer: Samson Raphaelson; Story: Lazlo Bus-Fekete; DP: Edward Cronjager; Ed: Dorothy Spencer; Prod Design: James Basevi;

Composer: Alfred Newman; Costumes: Rene Hubert; Set Designer: Thomas Little. Color, 112 min. **VHS, LASER**

Heaven Can Wait

(1978) Paramount

When L.A. Rams quarterback Joe Pendleton (Beatty) is plucked from Earth too soon by an overzealous angel, he is sent back to Earth in another, older body. He struggles to regain his old spot in the lineup while straightening out his host's tangled affairs. The story by May and Beatty is based not on the 1943 movie of the same name, but on 1941's *Here Comes Mr. Jordan*. Academy Award Nominations: 9, including Best Picture; Best Actor: Warren Beatty; Best Director; Best Adapted Screenplay. **Academy Awards:** Best Art Direction—Set Decoration. **Cast:** Warren Beatty, Julie Christie, James Mason, Jack Warden, Dyan Cannon, Charles Grodin, Vincent Gardenia, Joseph Maher, Hamilton Camp, Arthur Malet. **Credits:** Dir: Buck Henry; Prod: Warren Beatty, Howard W. Koch, Charles McGuire; Writer: Elaine May, Warren Beatty; Story: Harry Segall; DP: William A. Fraker; Ed: Robert C. Jones, Don Zimmerman; Prod Design: Paul Sylbert, Edwin O'Donovan; Composer: Dave Grusin; Costumes: Richard Bruno, Theadora Van Runkle; SFX: Robert MacDonald. Color, 100 min. **VHS, LASER**

Heaven Knows, Mr. Allison

(1957) Fox

While hiding from a Japanese military offensive on a desolate Pacific island, a Marine sergeant (Mitchum) and his only fellow survivor, an Irish Roman Catholic novitiate on a humanitarian mission (Kerr), search for food, engage in philosophical sparring, avoid sexual tension, and struggle to survive. Huston again pairs a hardened hero with an indomitable woman (think *African Queen*) and lets the sparks fly. Academy Award Nominations: Best Adapted Screenplay; Best Actress: Deborah Kerr. **Cast:** Deborah Kerr, Robert Mitchum. **Credits:** Dir: John Huston; Prod: Buddy Adler; Writer: John Huston, John Lee Mahin; Story: Charles Shaw; DP: Oswald Morris; Ed: Russell Lloyd; Composer: Georges Auric; Costumes: Elizabeth Haffenden; Art Director: Stephen Grimes. Color, 107 min. **VHS**

Heidi

(1937) Fox

Spyri's much-loved children's novel combined with Hollywood's most popular child star, Temple. When the

The Heiress (1949)

newly orphaned Heidi first comes to live with her grandfather, she finds him cold and distant. But it isn't long before the sunny child manages to warm his heart and change his disposition. But their happiness is threatened by a mean governess. Primal drama for the wee ones. **Cast:** Shirley Temple, Helen Westley, Arthur Treacher, Jean Hersholt, Pauline Moore, Thomas Beck, Mary Nash, Sidney Blackmer, Mady Christians, Sig Rumann. **Credits:** Dir: Allan Dwan; Prod: Raymond Griffith; Writer: Walter Ferris, Julien Josephson; Story: Johanna Spyri; DP: Arthur C. Miller; Ed: Allen McNeil; Prod Design: Hans Peters. B&W, 88 min. **VHS, LASER**

The Heiress

(1949) Paramount

A superb cinematic version of Henry James's novel *Washington Square*. After discovering that his bride-to-be (de Havilland) is going to be disinherited by her brutally overbearing father (Richardson), a handsome young fortune hunter (Clift) jilts her on the night of their elopement. Years later, when the woman's fortune is secured, the man returns and again asks for her hand, but his erstwhile sweetheart exacts her revenge. Copland's score is magnificent. Golden Globe for Best Actress: Olivia de Havilland. Academy Award Nominations: 8, including Best Picture; Best Director. **Academy Awards:** Best Actress: Olivia de Havil-

land; Best Black-and-White Cinematography; Best Music Score of a Drama/Comedy; Best Costume Design (B&W); Best Art Direction—Set Decoration (B&W). **Cast:** Olivia de Havilland, Montgomery Clift, Ralph Richardson, Miriam Hopkins, Vanessa Brown, Mona Freeman, Ray Collins. **Credits:** Dir: William Wyler; Prod: William Wyler; Writer: Ruth Goodman Goetz, Augustus Goetz; DP: Leo Tover; Ed: William Hornbeck; Prod Design: John Meehan, Harry Horner; Composer: Aaron Copland. Color, 115 min. **VHS, LASER**

Heller in Pink Tights

(1960) Paramount

Something of a disappointment as the promise of a Cukor Western is, well, interesting. The director is at least on familiar backstage turf in the story of a Wild West theatrical troupe that stays one step ahead of Indians and the bill collectors as it travels the frontier. Curious casting and swell production make this watchable. Based on a L'Amour story. **Cast:** Sophia Loren, Anthony Quinn, Margaret O'Brien, Steve Forrest, Edmund Lowe, Eileen Heckart, Ramon Novarro. **Credits:** Dir: George Cukor; Prod: Carlo Ponti, Marcello Girosi; Writer: Dudley Nichols, Walter Bernstein; Story: Louis L'Amour; DP: Harold Lipstein; Ed: Howard Smith; Prod Design: Hal Pereira; Choreographer: Val Raset; Composer: Daniele

Amfitheatrof; Costumes: Edith Head; Art Director: Gene Allen. Color, 101 min. VHS

Hellfighters

(1968) Universal
In one of Wayne's less spectacular later dramas from 1968, he plays real-life character Red Adair, owner of a Texas company that puts out oil-well fires. Ross, fresh from earning an Academy Award nomination for *The Graduate* in '67, plays his feisty daughter. Available in letterbox. **Cast:** John Wayne, Katharine Ross, Jim Hutton, Vera Miles, Jay C. Flippen, Bruce Cabot, Barbara Stuart. **Credits:** Dir: Andrew V. McLaglen; Prod: Robert Arthur; Writer: Clair Huffaker; DP: William Clothier; Ed: Folmar Blangsted; Prod Design: Alexander Golitzen; Composer: John McCarthy, Leonard Rosenman; Costumes: Edith Head; SFX: Fred Knoth. Color, 121 min. VHS, LASER

Hellgate

(1952) Lippert
Hayden is wrongly accused of fighting with a covert guerrilla group during the Civil War and is sent to New Mexico's Hellgate Prison. The warden nurses a grudge against the guerrillas—his family was killed in one of their raids—and he treats Hayden severely. After managing to escape the cruelty of Hellgate, he is recaptured, but he eventually gains a full pardon after helping to halt the spread of an epidemic in the prison. **Cast:** Sterling Hayden, Joan Leslie, James Arness, Ward Bond, Marshall Bradford, Peter Coe, Richard Paxton, John Pichard, Patricia Coleman, Robert J. Wilke. **Credits:** Dir: Charles Marquis Warren; Prod: John C. Champion; Writer: Charles Marquis Warren; DP: Ernest Miller; Ed: Elmo Williams; Composer: Paul Dunlap. B&W, 79 min.

Hell in the Pacific

(1968) Cinerama
Two soldiers, one American and the other Japanese, find themselves stranded on a deserted isle during WWII. Their deeply embedded prejudices and the antagonisms created by war get a cathartic release as the pair cooperate to escape the remote rock. The explosive team of director Boorman and star Marvin (they also paired in *Point Blank*) broke through to wider attention with this fascinating allegory. **Cast:** Lee Marvin, Toshiro Mifune. **Credits:** Dir: John Boorman; Prod: Reuben Bercovitch; Writer: Alexander Jacobs, Eric Bercovici; Story: Reuben Bercovitch; DP: Conrad Hall; Ed:

Thomas Stanford; Prod Design: Anthony Pratt; Composer: Lalo Schifrin. Color, 103 min. VHS, LASER

Hell Is for Heroes

(1962) Paramount
The two-fisted action team of director Siegel and star McQueen (they later paired in *Bullitt*, 1968) take on the WWII foxhole drama. A group of American G.I.s try to defend a key battle line against enemy fire, but to do so they must convince the Nazis that they are a large Allied task force. Fierce fighting, bravery under fire, even comic relief from Newhart. **Cast:** Steve McQueen, Bobby Darin, Fess Parker, Nick Adams, Bob Newhart, James Coburn, Harry Guardino. **Credits:** Dir: Don Siegel; Prod: Henry Blanke; Writer: Robert Pirosh, Richard Carr; DP: Harold Lipstein; Ed: Howard Smith; Composer: Leonard Rosenman; Costumes: Wally Harton; SFX: Dick Webb; Art Director: Hal Pereira; Set Designer: Sam Comer. B&W, 90 min. VHS, LASER

Hello, Dolly!

(1969) Fox
Streisand directed by Kelly with a popular Herman score—this film is one of the last big, splashy Hollywood musicals. Playing widow Dolly Levi, a matchmaker, Streisand finally finds herself a match. Bumptious egos clashed during filming, but the musical set pieces survive. Based on Thornton Wilder's successful Broadway play *The Matchmaker*, the film earned 7 Academy Award Nominations, including Best Picture. **Academy Awards:** Best Sound; Best Scoring of a Musical; Best Art Direction—Set Decoration. **Cast:** Barbra Streisand, Walter Matthau, Michael Crawford, Louis Armstrong, Marianne McAndrew, E. J. Peaker, Tommy Tune, David Hurst. **Credits:** Dir: Gene Kelly; Writer: Ernest Lehman; Story: Thornton Wilder; DP: Harry Stradling; Ed: William H. Reynolds; Prod Design: John DeCuir; Choreographer: Michael Kidd; Composer: Jerry Herman; Costumes: Irene Sharaff; SFX: L. B. Abbott; Art Director: Jack Martin Smith; Set Designer: Walter M. Scott. Color, 146 min. VHS, LASER

Hello, Frisco, Hello

(1943) Fox
Patented Faye–Fox musical set in San Francisco's Barbary Coast at the turn of the century. The romantic musical features a love triangle in which Faye is a singer hired by saloon owner Payne. She develops a crush on him

but he's interested in a society girl. Faye becomes an international star and Payne pines. Songs include "San Francisco," "Strike Up the Band," "Has Anybody Here Seen Kelly?" and "Ragtime Country Joe." Academy Award Nominations: Best Color Cinematography; Best Song ("You'll Never Know"). **Academy Awards:** Best Song. **Cast:** Alice Faye, John Payne, Jack Oakie, Lynn Bari, Ward Bond, June Havoc, George Barbier, Laird Cregar, Aubrey Mather, Frank Orth. **Credits:** Dir: H. Bruce Humberstone; Prod: Milton Sperling; Writer: Robert Ellis, Helen Logan, Richard Macauley; DP: Charles G. Clarke, Allen M. Davey; Ed: Barbara McLean; Prod Design: James Basevi, Thomas Little; Choreographer: Val Raset, Hermes Pan; Costumes: Helen Rose; SFX: Fred Sersen; Art Director: Boris Leven. Color, 99 min. VHS

Hell's Angels

(1930) United Artists
Mogul Howard Hughes's legendary aviation epic about WWI pilots launched Harlow's career with the sensational line, "Would you be shocked if I slipped into something more comfortable?" Three years and three directors in the making (Whale finally stepped in after Hughes fired directors Howard Hawks and Luther Reed), the film's dazzling dogfights earned it an Academy Award Nomination for Best Cinematography. A two-color Technicolor party scene (the only color footage of Harlow) and tinted night scenes were restored in 1989. **Cast:** Ben Lyon, James Hall, Jean Harlow, John Darrow, Lucien Prival, Roy Wilson. **Credits:** Dir: Howard Hughes, James Whale; Prod: Howard Hughes; Writer: Harry Behn, Howard Estabrook; Story: Neil Marshall, Joseph Moncure March; DP: Tony Gaudio, Harry Perry, E. Burton Steene; Prod Design: Carroll Clark; Composer: Hugo Riesenfeld. B&W, 129 min. VHS

The Hellstrom Chronicle

(1971) Columbia
This remarkable quasi-documentary on insects features amazing microphotography, which lends support to the film's theory that insects will one day rule the earth. Uneven but a big award winner at the time, which enjoyed a cult following, especially among the stoned. The forerunner of 1997's international festival hit, *Microcosmos*. **Academy Awards:** Best Documentary Feature. **Cast:** Conlan Carter, Lawrence Pressman. **Credits:** Dir: Walon Green; Prod: David L. Wolper; Composer: Lalo Schifrin. Color, 90 min. VHS

Hell to Eternity

(1960) Paramount
Based on the true story of WWII hero Guy Gabaldon, a Marine who was raised by a Japanese-American family. He daringly went behind enemy lines and convinced 2,000 Japanese soldiers to surrender. Packed with action, the film features Janssen before he found wider fame as TV's "Fugitive." **Cast:** Jeffrey Hunter, David Janssen, Vic Damone, Patricia Owens, Richard Eyer, Sessue Hayakawa. **Credits:** Dir: Phil Karlson; Prod: Irving H. Levin; Writer: Ted Sherdeman, Walter Robert Schmidt; Story: Gil Doud; DP: Burnett Guffey; Ed: George White; Composer: Leith Stevens. B&W, 132 min. VHS

Hell Town

(1937) Paramount
Called Wayne's best B-movie (after his many outings at Monogram), this buddy tale based on Zane Grey's novel is about a cowboy who tracks down a cattle rustler and the grateful rancher who then saves him from a cardshark. **Cast:** John Wayne, Marsha Hunt, Johnny Mack Brown, Monte Blue, Syd Saylor, Earl Devine, Alan Ladd, John Patterson, Nick Lukats, Lucien Littlefield. **Credits:** Dir: Charles Barton; Prod: William T. Lackey, William LeBaron; Writer: Stuart Anthony, Robert Yost; DP: Devereaux Jennings; Ed: John F. Link; Prod Design: Hans Dreier, Robert Odell; Composer: Boris Morros. B&W, 51 min. VHS

Hellzapoppin'

(1941) Universal
This loony vaudeville variety comedy takes a famous stage-destroying antiplay to the silver screen. Olsen and Johnson, as themselves, don't appreciate being in a movie. It's hard enough to get the girl and all that, but with those lights and cameras and the director always yelling through a bullhorn? Who is this Count Pepi (Auer) and why is he chasing Raye around the set? Sight gags, terrible jokes, pointless sexiness abound. **Cast:** Ole Olsen, Chic Johnson, Robert Paige, Jane Frazee, Lewis Howard, Martha Raye, Clarence Kolb, Nella Walker, Mischa Auer, Richard Lane. **Credits:** Dir: H. C. Potter; Prod: Jules Levy; Writer: Warren Wilson, Nat Perrin; Story: Nat Perrin; DP: Elwood Bredell; Ed: Milton Carruth; Composer: Gene de Paul. B&W, 84 min.

Henry Aldrich

Before there was *Dumb and Dumber,* there was Henry Aldrich, a bumbling high school student from middle America, whose haplessness landed him in hot water with family and friends, though he found vindication by the end of each film. The first entry of the Paramount series, *What a Life* (1939), scripted by Billy Wilder and Charles Brackett, was based on the 1938 Broadway play and subsequent radio series. Jackie Cooper played the title role in the first two installments, before Jimmy Lydon and a new supporting cast took over for the remaining nine entries (produced in just four years!). Along with top-notch supporting players such as John Litel, who played Henry's strict father, and Charles Smith as Henry's wily sidekick, established character actors such as Frances Gifford (*Henry Aldrich Gets Glamour,* 1943); Francis Pierlot (*Henry Aldrich, Editor,* 1942); and Fritz Feld (*Henry Aldrich Swings It,* 1943) made appearances in the films. The Henry Aldrich series is sly, breezy fun.

What a Life *(1939)*
Life with Henry *(1941)*
Henry Aldrich for President *(1941)*
Henry and Dizzy *(1942)*
Henry Aldrich, Editor *(1942)*
Henry Aldrich Gets Glamour *(1943)*
Henry Aldrich Swings It *(1943)*
Henry Aldrich Haunts a House *(1943)*
Henry Aldrich, Boy Scout *(1944)*
Henry Aldrich Plays Cupid *(1944)*
Henry Aldrich's Little Secret *(1944)*

Henry V

(1945) United Artists
The young English King Harry overcomes his youthful reputation and miraculous odds to defeat the French at Agincourt. Olivier's production of Shakespeare's 1599 play is full of pomp and pageantry, retaining more of the flavor of a stage production than the comparatively realistic treatment given the play by Kenneth Branagh in 1989. Academy Award Nominations: 4, including Best Picture; Best Actor: Laurence Olivier. **Academy Awards:** Special Achievement Awards: Laurence Olivier. **Cast:** Laurence Olivier, Robert Newton, Leslie Banks, Renee Asherton, Esmond Knight, Leo Genn, Felix Aylmer, Ralph Truman, Harcourt Williams, Ernest Thesiger. **Credits:** Dir: Laurence Olivier; Prod: Laurence Olivier; Writer: Laurence Olivier, Alan Dent; Story: William Shakespeare; DP: Robert Krasker; Ed: Reginald Beck; Composer: William Walton; Costumes: Roger K. Furse; Art Director: Paul Sheriff. Color, 138 min. VHS

Herbie Rides Again

(1974) Disney
Family fare from Disney, this sequel to *The Love Bug* has the extraordinarily personable and powerful Volkswagen "Bug" help elderly Hayes save her property from an evil real estate tycoon who wants to erect a giant skyscraper. Herbie rode onward into two more sequels in '77 and '80 (and then into television!). **Cast:** Helen Hayes, Stefanie Powers, John McIntire, Ken Berry, Keenan Wynn, Huntz Hall. **Credits:** Dir: Robert Stevenson; Prod: Bill Walsh; DP: Frank Phillips; Ed: Cotton Warburton; Prod Design: John B. Mansbridge; Composer: George Burns; Costumes: Chuck Keehne; SFX: Art Cruickshank; Set Designer: Hal Gausman. Color, 88 min. VHS

Here Comes Mr. Jordan

(1941) Columbia
A beguiling fantasy comedy that accompanies a restless spirit from Earth to Heaven and back again. Montgomery has a happy-go-lucky charm as professional boxer Joe Pendleton. When the fighter's plane crashes after a bout, his spirit is removed—too early—from his body by the inexperienced heavenly messenger (Horton, in one of his best roles). A new body must be found. First, Joe occupies the body of a millionaire about to be murdered in his tub, and later a heavyweight boxer who runs afoul of the Mob. Throughout his celestial journeys, he finds his way to the winsome Keyes and his manager, Gleason. Followed by the 1947 sequel *Down to Earth* and the inspiration for 1978's *Heaven Can Wait.* The laserdisc features a second audio track with commentary by Montgomery's daughter, Elizabeth Montgomery, who discusses the film, her father, and her own career. Academy Award Nominations: 7, including Best Picture; Best Director; Best Actor: Robert Montgomery. **Academy Awards:** Best Original Story; Best Screenplay. **Cast:** Robert Montgomery, Claude Rains, Evelyn Keyes, Rita Johnson, Edward Everett Horton, James Gleason, John Emery, Donald MacBride, Don Costello, Halliwell Hobbes. **Credits:** Dir: Alexander Hall; Writer: Sidney Buchman, Seton I. Miller; Story: Harry Segall; DP: Joseph Walker; Ed: Viola Lawrence; Prod Design: Lionel Banks; Composer: Frederick Hollander; Costumes: Edith Head. B&W, 94 min. VHS, LASER

Here Comes the Groom

(1951) Paramount
A Capra musical! Crosby croons in this romantic comedy about a newspaper

reporter who wants to adopt two war orphans. In order to do so, though, he must have a wife, and, unfortunately, his former fiancée (a stunning Wyman) is about to wed a dashing millionaire (Tone). The reporter must win her back in five days, with whatever it takes: songs, cute kids, even a little help from the F.B.I. Academy Award Nominations: Best Motion Picture Story; Best Song. **Academy Awards:** Best Song. **Cast:** Bing Crosby, Jane Wyman, Franchot Tone, Alexis Smith, James Barton, Anna Maria Alberghetti, James Burke, Beverly Washburn, Connie Gilchrist, Walter Catlett. **Credits:** Dir: Frank Capra; Prod: Frank Capra; Writer: Virginia Van Upp, Liam O'Brien, Myles Connolly; DP: George Barnes; Ed: Ellsworth Hoagland; Composer: Joseph J. Lilley; Art Director: Hal Pereira. B&W, 114 min. VHS, LASER

Here Come the Girls
(1953) Paramount
Hope plays an incompetent chorus boy who gets his big break—but he's being used as the bait to catch a killer by filling in for the leading man. Not one of Bob's brightest, but Clooney fans will enjoy seeing her at age 25. **Cast:** Bob Hope, Arlene Dahl, Rosemary Clooney, Tony Martin, Fred Clark, Robert Strauss, Millard Mitchell, William Demarest. **Credits:** Dir: Claude Binyon; Prod: Paul Jones; Writer: Edmund L. Hartmann, Hal Kanter; DP: Lionel Lindon; Ed: Arthur Schmidt; Prod Design: Hal Pereira; Choreographer: Nick Castle; Art Director: Roland Anderson. Color, 100 min. VHS, LASER

Here Come the Waves
(1944) Paramount
In this snappy Crosby musical comedy, he plays a popular Sinatra-like crooner doing Navy WAVE shows who meets identical twins (both played by Hutton). He falls hard but can't tell one from the other—and one twin hates him. Arlen-Mercer score includes "That Old Black Magic" and Academy Award–nominated "Accentuate the Positive." **Cast:** Bing Crosby, Betty Hutton, Sonny Tufts, Ann Doran, Gwen Crawford, Noel Neill, Catherine Craig, Marjorie Henshaw. **Credits:** Dir: Mark Sandrich; Prod: Mark Sandrich; Writer: Allan Scott, Ken Englund, Zion Myers; DP: Charles Lang; Ed: Ellsworth Hoagland; Prod Design: Hans Dreier; Composer: Robert Emmett Dolan, Harold Arlen, Johnny Mercer; SFX: Gordon Jennings, Paul K. Lerpae; Art Director: Roland Anderson; Set Designer: Ray Moyer. B&W, 99 min. VHS

Heritage of the Desert
(1932) Paramount
The first of the Hathaway-Scott Westerns is also Randy's first screen appearance. He plays a young desert rancher who comes to the aid of an orphan girl and tries to stop claim-jumpers from stealing his land. Based on a novel by Zane Grey. **Cast:** Randolph Scott, J. Farrell MacDonald, Guinn "Big Boy" Williams, Sally Blane, David Landau, Gordon Westcott, Vince Barnett, Susan Fleming, Charles Stevens, Fred Burns. **Credits:** Dir: Henry Hathaway; Prod: Harold Hurley; Writer: Harold Shumate, Frank Partos; DP: Archie Stout. B&W, 63 min. VHS

Her Jungle Love
(1938) Paramount
Classic B-movie jungle adventure has pilot Denning crashing on an uncharted island where he discovers, among the flora and fauna, the sexpot queen of the jungle, Lamour. Two rescuers, Overman and Milland, find themselves enchanted as well—but the dastardly, sinister villain of the jungle, Naish, has other plans for the visitors. **Cast:** Richard Denning, Dorothy Lamour, Lynne Overman, Ray Milland, J. Carrol Naish, Sonny Chorre, Edward Earle, Jonathan Hale, Archie Twitchell, Virginia Vale. **Credits:** Dir: George Archainbaud; Prod: George M. Arthur; Writer: Lillie Hayward, Joseph Moncure March, Eddie Welch; Story: Gerald Geraghty, Curt Siodmak; DP: Ray Rennahan; Ed: Hugh Bennett; Prod Design: Nathalie Kalmis, Hans Dreier, A. Earl Hedrick; Composer: Gregory Stone. Color, 81 min.

A Hero Ain't Nothin' But a Sandwich
(1978) New World
A moving drama about an intelligent but alienated black ghetto youth who battles with drugs, and tries to keep his family together in spite of it. **Cast:** Cicely Tyson, Paul Winfield, Larry B. Scott, Helen Martin, Glynn Turman, David Groh. **Credits:** Dir: Ralph Nelson; Prod: Robert B. Radnitz; Writer: Alice Childress; DP: Frank Stanley; Ed: Fred Chulack; Prod Design: Walter Scott Herndon; Costumes: Nedra Watt; Set Designer: Cheryal Kearney. Color, 107 min. VHS, LASER

Heroes
(1977) Universal
Winkler stretches from his starring TV role as the Fonz to play a Vietnam vet who escapes from a mental hospital to meet a war buddy (Ford, in a pre-

stardom appearance) with plans to start a worm farm. Along the way he meets charming oddball Field and they join destinies. A typical road film with winning performances and a dash of social commentary, too. **Cast:** Henry Winkler, Sally Field, Harrison Ford, Val Avery, Olivia Cole, Hector Elias, Dennis Burkley, Tony Burton, Michael Cavanaugh, Helen Craig. **Credits:** Dir: Jeremy Paul Kagan; Prod: David Foster, Lawrence Turman; Writer: Jim Carabatsos; DP: Frank Stanley; Ed: Patrick Kennedy; Composer: Jack Nitzsche, Richard Hazard. Color, 97 min. VHS

Heroes for Sale
(1933) Warner Bros.
A fascinating social-problem story about a wounded ex-doughboy who comes home addicted to the needle. He befriends a crackpot anarchist, who makes them both millionaires when he creates a washing machine. Odd mixture of familiar Warner social-problem film and wishful, Depression-era romantic fantasy. Early Young role. **Cast:** Richard Barthelmess, Loretta Young, Aline MacMahon, Grant Mitchell, Douglass Dumbrille, Ward Bond, Robert Barratt, Charley Grapewin. **Credits:** Dir: William Wellman, Howard Bretherton; Writer: Robert Lord, Wilson Mizner; DP: James Van Trees; Art Director: Jack Okey. B&W, 73 min. VHS

Hester Street
(1975)
A Jewish immigrant woman from eastern Europe (Kane) travels to New York's Lower East Side in 1896 to join her husband. The husband, Jake, has rapidly assimilated, wanting desperately to shed any trace of what he views as provincial, ethnic, and old-country. His wife, Gitl, frightened and unused to American ways, finds solace and security in the ways of the old country, divorces Jake and marries his scholarly friend. Jake, in turn, marries his Americanized girlfriend, who runs a dance hall. Directorial debut for Kane. An adaptation of a story by Abraham Cahan. Academy Award Nominations: Best Actress: Carol Kane. **Cast:** Carol Kane, Mel Howard, Dorrie Kavanaugh, Steven Keats, Doris Roberts, Stephen Strimpell, Lauren Frost, Paul Freedman, Zvee Scooler. **Credits:** Dir: Joan Micklin Silver; Prod: Raphael Silver; Writer: Joan Micklin Silver; DP: Kenneth Van Sickle; Ed: Katherine Wenning; Composer: William Bolcom. B&W, 89 min. VHS

He Walked by Night

(1948) Eagle-Lion

A burglar becomes a cold-blooded cop killer and is hunted down on the streets of Los Angeles. The men in blue manage to track their suspect down into the bowels of the city—the labyrinth sewer system. Noir veteran Anthony Mann, though uncredited, co-directed the film. Well done and supposedly an inspiration for Jack Webb's *Dragnet* TV series. **Cast:** Richard Basehart, Scott Brady, Jack Webb, Roy Roberts, Whit Bissell. **Credits:** Dir: Alfred Werker; Prod: Robert Kane; Writer: John C. Higgins, Crane Wilbur; DP: John Alton; Prod Design: Edward L. Ilou; Composer: Leonid Raab; SFX: George J. Teague. B&W, 78 min. **VHS**

Hide-Out

(1934) MGM

A New York City crook (Montgomery) wounded during a shoot-out with the police eludes his pursuers and makes his way to an upstate farm, where he collapses and tells the farmer he was shot by crooks. While he recuperates, the crook spends time with a farmgirl (O'Sullivan makes a fetching farmer's daughter) who teaches him rural feats such as tossing hay onto a wagon and how to milk a cow. The law finally catches up with him, and he must tell the girl he now loves the truth. Remade as *I'll Wait for You* (1941). **Cast:** Robert Montgomery, Maureen O'Sullivan, Elizabeth Patterson, Whitford Kane, Mickey Rooney, Muriel Evans, Edward Brophy, Edward Arnold, C. Henry Gordon. **Credits:** Dir: W. S. Van Dyke; Prod: Hunt Stromberg; Writer: Frances Goodrich, Mauri Grashin, Albert Hackett; DP: Ray June, Sidney Wagner; Ed: Basil Wrangell; Composer: Dr. William Axt; Art Director: Cedric Gibbons. B&W, 80 min. **VHS**

The High and the Mighty

(1954) Warner Bros.

As a washed-up pilot, Wayne steers a plane full of vacationers on a trip from Honolulu to San Francisco. A long list of famous faces play travelers, who include a couple headed for a divorce, a mail-order bride, a would-be murderer of another passenger, and a theater producer. Soon after takeoff, Wayne senses something is not right with the plane. The beleaguered pilot then faces the choice between landing in the water or trying to make it to San Francisco. Wayne produced this tense prototype of disaster flicks like *Airport* and its sequels and only took the lead when his intended star, Spencer Tracy, dropped out. Academy Award Nomina-

tions: 6, including Best Supporting Actress: Jan Sterling; Best Supporting Actress: Claire Trevor; Best Director; Best Editing. **Academy Awards:** Best Score. **Cast:** John Wayne, Claire Trevor, Lorraine Day, Robert Stack, Jan Sterling, Phil Harris, Robert Newton, David Brian, Paul Kelly, Sidney Blackmer. **Credits:** Dir: William Wellman, Jr.; Prod: Robert Fellows, John Wayne; Story: Ernest K. Gann; DP: Archie Stout, William Clothier; Ed: Ralph Dawson; Composer: Dimitri Tiomkin; Costumes: Gwen Wakeling; Art Director: Alfred Ybarra. Color, 147 min.

High Anxiety

(1977) Fox

Brooks stars, directs, writes, and produces this comic send-up of Hitchcock's best-known and most-loved thrillers, including parodies of famous scenes from *Psycho, Vertigo, Spellbound,* and *The Birds*. Brooks plays Dr. Richard Thorndyke, who takes a job at the Institute for the Very, Very Nervous only to find himself ensnared in a spiraling eddy of deception, conspiracies, and naughty nurses. Brooks hits consistently in one of his most popular comedies. **Cast:** Mel Brooks, Madeline Kahn, Cloris Leachman, Harvey Korman, Dick Van Patten, Ron Carey, Howard Morris, Jack Riley, Charlie Callas. **Credits:** Dir: Mel Brooks; Prod: Mel Brooks; Writer: Mel Brooks, Ron Clark, Rudy DeLuca, Barry Levinson; DP: Paul Lohmann; Ed: John C. Howard; Composer: John Morris. Color, 94 min. **VHS, LASER**

Higher and Higher

(1943) RKO

Sinatra's first big starring role is in a musical comedy about a bankrupt businessman (Errol) who schemes with his household staff to come up with some cash. They choose to hoodwink the boy-next-door (Sinatra), who happens to be filthy rich, into marrying a maid who's posing as the businessman's daughter. The plan is scuttled when con man Borge happens on to the scene, imitating a wealthy aristocrat. Okay musical, but mostly notable for young Frank. Academy Award Nominations: 2, including Best Song ("I Couldn't Sleep a Wink Last Night"). **Cast:** Frank Sinatra, Leon Errol, Michele Morgan, Jack Haley, Victor Borge, Mary Wickes, Elisabeth Risdon, Barbara Hale, Mel Torme, Paul Hartman. **Credits:** Dir: Tim Whelan; Prod: Tim Whelan; Writer: Jay Dratler, Ralph Spence, William Bowers, Howard Harris; DP: Robert de Grasse; Ed: Gene

Milford; Composer: Roy Webb; Art Director: Albert S. D'Agostino, Jack Okey. B&W, 90 min. **VHS, LASER**

High Noon

(1952) United Artists

Cooper is Hollywood's perfect hero, the very embodiment of integrity and grace in this greatest of Westerns. As a newly married town marshal, he must balance an innate sense of justice and duty with loyalty to his beautiful new—and pacifist—bride when he is left by an ungrateful town to face a gang of deadly outlaws alone. As we watch spellbound, film time is real time as the showdown grows ever closer. This masterpiece is frequently interpreted as a parable about artists left to "stand alone" and face persecution during the HUAC Hollywood blacklisting. (However, Howard Hawks allegedly devised *Rio Bravo* as an answer to this film's "wimpiness." Also, John Wayne once declared *High Noon* un-American. He was apparently offended by the ending of the film, which shows Sheriff Kane removing his badge and tossing it in the dirt.) The deluxe 40th anniversary video edition was digitally remastered and includes *The Making of High Noon*, a behind-the-scenes documentary narrated by Leonard Maltin, a hardbound book, *The Complete Films of Gary Cooper*, a limited edition collector's reproduction of four original lobby cards and poster, and an individually-numbered gift box. The laserdisc includes an audio essay, a photo essay of stills and storyboards, and the original theatrical trailer. A made-for-TV sequel, *High Noon Part II: Return of Will Kane*, aired in 1980. The film's many honors include Golden Globes for Best Supporting Actress: Katy Jurado; Best Black-and-White Cinematography; Best Original Score; Best Actor in a Drama: Gary Cooper. Selected as a National Film Registry Outstanding Film. Academy Award Nominations: 7, including Best Picture; Best Director; Best Screenplay. **Academy Awards:** Best Actor: Gary Cooper; Best Film Editing; Best Song; Best Music Score of a Drama/Comedy. **Cast:** Gary Cooper, Grace Kelly, Thomas Mitchell, Lloyd Bridges, Katy Jurado, Otto Kruger, Lon Chaney, Jr., Harry Morgan, Ian MacDonald, Eve McVeagh. **Credits:** Dir: Fred Zinnemann; Prod: Stanley Kramer, Elmo Williams; Writer: Carl Foreman; DP: Floyd Crosby; Ed: Harry Gerstad; Prod Design: Rudolph Sternad; Composer: Dimitri Tiomkin. B&W, 111 min. **VHS, LASER, DVD**

High Plains Drifter

(1973) Universal
Eastwood's second time in the director's chair is a bleak morality play about a man who protects a frontier town from outlaws, more out of contempt for the outlaws than love for the cowardly townspeople. Violent, operatic in the best spaghetti-Western style. The laserdisc features letterbox format and trailers. **Cast:** Clint Eastwood, Verna Bloom, Marianna Hill, Billy Curtis, Mitchell Ryan, Jack Ging, Stefan Gierasch, Ted Hartley, Geoffrey Lewis, Scott Walker. **Credits:** Dir: Clint Eastwood; Prod: Robert Daley; Writer: Ernest Tidyman; DP: Bruce Surtees; Ed: Ferris Webster; Prod Design: Henry Bumstead; Composer: Dee Barton. Color, 106 min. VHS, LASER, DVD

High Pressure

(1932) Warner Bros.
This early talkie, a get-rich-quick pipe dream for the Depression-era audience, sports the eminently watchable Powell as a big-thinking grifter whose dummy company raises capital from stockholders by promising an alchemy that will turn garbage into synthetic rubber. The twist is that the scientist who supposedly holds the secret formula is nuts, but not to worry, as investors from a real rubber company are right around the corner, and Powell has a chance to stay in the money and out of jail. **Cast:** William Powell, Evelyn Brent, George Sidney, Frank McHugh, Guy Kibbee, Evalyn Knapp, Ben Alexander, Harry Beresford, John Wray, Charles Judels. **Credits:** Dir: Mervyn LeRoy; Writer: Aben Kandel, Joseph Jackson; Story: S. J. Peters; DP: Robert Kurrle; Ed: Ralph Dawson; Composer: Leo F. Forbstein. B&W, 72 min.

High School Confidential!

(1958) MGM
Teen-pic exploitation classic that purports to depict the hard-hitting reality of high school drug abuse. Following a Jerry Lee Lewis performance of the title song on the back of a flatbed truck, mysterious new kid in town Tamblyn quickly ingratiates himself into the biggest pot ring in school while hiding the truth—he's a narc! On the home front, he must ward off the amorous advances of his curvaceous "aunt" (Van Doren), while wooing one of his lovely teachers. Check out appearances by Michael Landon, and famous names Charles Chaplin, Jr., and William Wellman, Jr. **Cast:** Russ Tamblyn, Mamie Van Doren, Diane Jergens, Jan Sterling, John Drew Barry-

more, Jerry Lee Lewis, Ray Anthony, Jackie Coogan, Charles Chaplin, Burt Douglas. **Credits:** Dir: Jack Arnold; Prod: Albert Zugsmith; Writer: Lewis Meltzer, Robert Blees; DP: Harold J. Marzorati; Ed: Ben Lewis; Prod Design: William A. Horning. B&W, 85 min. VHS, LASER

High Sierra

(1941) Warner Bros.
A seminal gangster film that focused attention on Bogart and writer Huston. Bogart plays a violent criminal just released from prison who knows he's got just one more job in him. An aging gang boss wants Bogart to lead a jewel heist at a resort. When he sees the inexperienced men he'll be leading (and fends off the attentions of Lupino, the girlfriend of one of the thugs), Bogart suspects there will be trouble, and there is when a cop is killed during the robbery. A manhunt drives Bogart to the highest peak in the High Sierras where he awaits death at the hands of the police. A gripping portrait of a desperate outlaw and a breakthrough for its creators. **Cast:** Humphrey Bogart, Ida Lupino, Alan Curtis, Arthur Kennedy, Joan Leslie, Henry Hull, Barton MacLane, Henry Travers, Elisabeth Risdon, Cornel Wilde. **Credits:** Dir: Raoul Walsh; Prod: Mark Hellinger; Writer: John Huston; Story: W. R. Burnett; DP: Tony Gaudio; Ed: Jack Killifer; Composer: Adolph Deutsch, Leo F. Forbstein. B&W, 100 min. VHS, LASER

High Society

(1955) MGM
Porter adds the tunes and Sinatra the ring-a-ding to this swinging musical remake of *The Philadelphia Story*. A prim socialite (Kelly in her last role before becoming Her Serene Highness) finds herself in the middle of a comic mess when her ex-husband (Crosby) and an amorous reporter (Sinatra) come to cover the preparations for her upcoming wedding. Adding to the tension is her skirt-chasing father, who's also returned home for the ceremony. The resulting confusion—and several potent drinks—melts the ice princess's frosty exterior. It isn't long before she sees through her society-climbing fiancé, and warms up again to her crooning jazz musician ex-husband. Rare chance to see rivals Crosby and Sinatra together. Includes such hit numbers as "True Love," "You're Sensational," and "Did You Evah." Academy Award Nominations: 3, including Best Motion Picture Story. **Cast:** Bing Crosby, Frank

Sinatra, Grace Kelly, Louis Armstrong, Celeste Holm, John Lund, Louis Calhern, Sidney Blackmer, Margalo Gillmore, Gordon Richards. **Credits:** Dir: Charles Walters; Prod: Sol C. Siegel; Writer: John Patrick; DP: Paul C. Vogel; Ed: Ralph E. Winters; Prod Design: Cedric Gibbons, Hans Peters; Choreographer: Charles Walters; Composer: Cole Porter, Johnny Green, Saul Chaplin. Color, 107 min. VHS, LASER

High, Wide, and Handsome

(1937) Paramount
A Mamoulian musical of the roughneck days in the Pennsylvania oil fields. Scott's a tough oil prospector who strikes it rich in the booming town of Titusville, Pennsylvania. In an attempt to push them off their claim, evil railway baron Hale refuses to ship their oil to the refinery. Scott organizes the other prospectors to build a pipeline that will carry the oil to the refinery without the help of the railway. Scott finds unlikely help in La-mour, a sideshow performer who drafts several circus elephants to aid in the construction of the pipeline. **Cast:** Irene Dunne, Randolph Scott, Alan Hale, Dorothy Lamour, Akim Tamiroff, Raymond Walburn, Charles Bickford, Ben Blue, Elizabeth Patterson, Lucien Littlefield, Helen Lowell. **Credits:** Dir: Rouben Mamoulian; Prod: Arthur Hornblow, Jr.; Writer: Oscar Hammerstein, George O'Neil; DP: Victor Milner, Theodor Sparkuhl; Ed: Archie Marshek; Prod Design: Hans Dreier; Composer: Jerome Kern; Art Director: John Goodman. B&W, 112 min.

The Hill

(1965) MGM
The cruel conditions of a British military stockade in Africa during WWII are symbolized by The Hill, a mound of rock and sand created by the prisoners. Connery plays an officer sent to the stockade for disobeying an order that would have meant sure death, and his reshaping is the film's centerpiece. Fine performances by all. **Cast:** Sean Connery, Harry Andrews, Ian Hendry, Michael Redgrave, Ian Bannen, Alfred Lynch, Ossie Davis, Roy Kinnear, Jack Watson. **Credits:** Dir: Sidney Lumet; Prod: Kenneth Hyman; Writer: Ray Rigby, R. S. Allen; DP: Oswald Morris; Ed: Thelma Connell; Prod Design: Herbert Smith. B&W, 123 min. VHS

Hills of Home

(1948) MGM
One of the better entries in the Lassie series finds the loyal collie roaming

the Scottish highlands, but with a fear of water. She overcomes her fear to save the local doctor who has been training her from a roaring river. Early Leigh role. **Cast:** Edmund Gwenn, Donald Crisp, Tom Drake, Janet Leigh, Lassie, Rhys Williams, Reginald Owen, Edmund Breon, Alan Napier, Hugh Green. **Credits:** Dir: Fred M. Wilcox; Prod: Robert Sisk; Writer: William Ludwig; DP: Charles Schoenbaum; Ed: Ralph E. Winters; Prod Design: Cedric Gibbons; Composer: Herbert Stothart, Albert Sendrey, Robert Franklyn. Color, 98 min. VHS

Hi, Nellie!
(1934) Warner Bros.
A newspaper's proud managing editor is judged to have missed a big angle on a story, and is demoted to authoring the paper's advice column to the heartsick. Furious at first, he eventually warms to the task and does a glowing job. But in order to win back his old position, he also embarks on a quest to reveal the cause behind an unsolved embezzlement case. **Cast:** Paul Muni, Glenda Farrell, Douglass Dumbrille, Robert Barrat, Ned Sparks, Hobart Cavanaugh, Pat Wing, Edward Ellis, Berton Churchill, Sidney Miller. **Credits:** Dir: Mervyn LeRoy; Prod: Robert Presnell, Sr.; Writer: Roy Chanslor, Abem Finkel, Sidney Sutherland; DP: Sol Polito; Ed: William Holmes; Art Director: Robert M. Haas. B&W, 75 min.

The Hired Hand
(1971) Universal
Peter Fonda directs this offbeat Western. Two drifting cowboys (Fonda and Oates) go back to the farm and the wife (Bloom) Fonda deserted seven years earlier. The warmth of hearth and home reinvigorates the dormant marriage. Brilliant camerawork by Zsigmond. **Cast:** Peter Fonda, Warren Oates, Verna Bloom, Robert Pratt, Severn Darden, Ted Markland. **Credits:** Dir: Peter Fonda; Prod: William Hayward; Writer: Alan Sharp; DP: Vilmos Zsigmond; Ed: Frank Mazzola; Prod Design: Lawrence G. Paull; Composer: Bruce Langhorne. Color, 93 min. VHS

Hired Wife
(1940) Universal
Russell plays a secretary who falls in love with her skirt-chasing boss. She marries him not as a "matter of the heart" but to save him from legal action being taken against the company. Hoping their honeymoon would be a time for peace and quiet (and

hopefully love), instead she spends her time observing the beautiful bombshell who tries to "influence" her husband away. It is up to her to end his "chasing days" by convincing him of what a gem he's already got. **Cast:** Rosalind Russell, Brian Aherne, Virginia Bruce, Robert Benchley, John Carroll, Hobart Cavanaugh, Richard Lane, William Davidson, Leonard Carey, Selmer Jackson. **Credits:** Dir: William A. Seiter; Prod: William A. Seiter; Writer: Richard Connell, Gladys Lehman; Story: George Beck; DP: Milton Krasner; Ed: Milton Carruth; Prod Design: Jack Otterson; Composer: Frank Skinner. B&W, 93 min.

His Brother's Wife
(1936) MGM
A melodrama about a woman (Stanwyck) in love with an epidemiologist (Taylor) who leaves her behind in order to cure a disease in the tropics. Before he leaves he asks his brother for help with gambling debts, and his brother agrees to help him on the condition that he end his relationship with the woman. She is devastated when he leaves, and seeks revenge by marrying his brother. The doctor eventually returns from the tropics to find his brother miserable and the woman still in love with him. **Cast:** Barbara Stanwyck, Robert Taylor, Jean Hersholt, John Eldredge, John Calleia. **Credits:** Dir: W. S. Van Dyke; Prod: Lawrence Weingarten; Writer: George Auerback, Leon Gordon, John Meehan; DP: Oliver T. Marsh; Ed: Conrad A. Nervig; Prod Design: Cedric Gibbons; Composer: Franz Waxman; Art Director: Harry McAfee. B&W, 91 min.

His Double Life
(1933) Paramount
A favorite story of the silent era gets its first talkie treatment. When a valet dies and is buried under his master's name, the boss, a famous artist, assumes his identity and lives it up as the dead valet. Adapted from Arnold Bennett's play *Buried Alive*; remade in 1943 as *Holy Matrimony*. **Cast:** Roland Young, Lillian Gish, Lucy Beaumont, Montagu Love, Lumsden Hare, Charles Richman, Gerald Oliver Smith, Philip Tonge, Ben Jackson. **Credits:** Dir: Arthur Hopkins; Writer: Arthur Hopkins, Clara S. Beranger; DP: Arthur Edeson; Ed: Arthur Ellis. B&W, 67 min. VHS

His Girl Friday
(1940) Columbia
Arguably one of the funniest screen comedies, but indisputably the fastest.

How the leads managed to get their lines out at the pace Hawks set is a marvel. This witty adaptation of the Hecht and MacArthur stage hit *The Front Page* (also the basis of the 1931 film) gives the ace reporter role to Russell, who takes it and runs. The action begins when Russell informs Grant, her suave managing editor and new ex-husband, that she's leaving the paper and planning to remarry. Grant, a handsome, hard-boiled type, wouldn't dare show his true feelings for Hildy, but he gets his way through the only true love of his ex's life: a breaking, front-page headline story. Her intended, Bellamy, stands by with hat in hand, his accustomed Hollywood role. Remade again in 1974, and, as *Switching Channels,* in 1988 set in a TV news environment. Selected as a National Film Registry Outstanding Film. **Cast:** Cary Grant, Rosalind Russell, Ralph Bellamy, Gene Lockhart, Helen Mack, Porter Hall, Ernest Truex, Cliff Edwards, Clarence Kolb, Roscoe Karns. **Credits:** Dir: Howard Hawks; Prod: Howard Hawks; Writer: Charles Lederer; Story: Ben Hecht, Charles MacArthur; DP: Joseph Walker; Ed: Gene Havlick; Composer: Morris Stoloff; Art Director: Lionel Banks. B&W, 95 min. VHS, LASER

His Kind of Woman
(1951) RKO
Cult favorite with explosive pairing of Mitchum and Russell, one of the screen's more combustible duos. Gambler Mitchum goes to Mexico on an ill-defined mission that should net him 50 grand. It may also cost him his life as he's being set up by mobster Burr, who wants to reenter the country with his face and identity transformed into Mitchum's. Mitchum gets an assist from good-time girl Russell and hammy actor Price. **Cast:** Robert Mitchum, Jane Russell, Vincent Price, Tim Holt, Charles McGraw, Marjorie Reynolds, Raymond Burr, Leslye Banning, Jim Backus, Philip Van Zandt. **Credits:** Dir: John Farrow, Stanley Fleischer; Prod: Robert Sparks; Writer: Gerald Drayson Adams, Frank Fenton, Jack E. Leonard; DP: Harry Wild; Ed: Frederic Knudtson, Eda Warren; Prod Design: Albert S. D'Agostino; Composer: Leigh Harline. B&W, 120 min.

His Majesty O'Keefe
(1953) Warner Bros.
Lancaster plays a daring 19th-century American sea captain whose mutinous crew dumps him unceremoniously into the ocean. The trusty mariner manages to stay alive and lands on a Polynesian

island where he makes the best of his predicament by embarking on a career as a coconut oil trader. The island's natives view the buccaneer as a kind of god, so he "goes native" himself, taking a local woman as his wife. In order to make his fortune, however, O'Keefe must first battle hostile tribal chiefs who want to keep control of their island's wealth and incursions by other traders. This was the first movie ever shot in the Fiji islands. **Cast:** Burt Lancaster, Joan Rice, Benson Fong, Philip Ahn, Grant Taylor, Andre Morell, Abraham Sofaer, Archie Savage, Charles Horvath. **Credits:** Dir: Byron Haskin; Prod: Harold Hecht; Writer: Borden Chase, James Hill; DP: Otto Heller. Color, 92 min. **VHS, LASER**

History Is Made at Night
(1937) United Artists
A romance, murder mystery, and disaster movie rolled into one, this is a valentine to the indestructibility of love. Fleeing from her jealous husband (Clive), Arthur finds true passion in the arms of a Parisian waiter, Boyer. But to be together the lovers must overcome seemingly insurmountable obstacles—including a frame-up for murder and a shipwreck at sea. **Cast:** Charles Boyer, Jean Arthur, Colin Clive, Leo Carrillo, Ivan Lebedeff, George Meeker, Lucien Prival, Georges Renavent, George Davis. **Credits:** Dir: Frank Borzage; Prod: Walter Wanger; Writer: Gene Towne, Graham Baker; DP: Gregg Toland; Ed: Margaret Clancy. B&W, 98 min. **VHS, LASER**

The Hitch-Hiker
(1952) RKO
Lupino's acclaimed film noir thriller in which two vacationing men (O'Brien and Lovejoy) are held captive by a hitchhiking psychopath with one eye that never closes (Talman). Though years of more intense violence and suspense make this seem tame in comparison, this was way ahead of its time. Considered among Lupino's best work, this film was the progenitor of many films that would follow in its tire treads. **Cast:** Frank Lovejoy, William Talman, Edmond O'Brien, Clark Howat, Jose Torvay, Sam Hayes, Wendell Niles, Jean Del Val, Natividad Vacio, Rodney Bell. **Credits:** Dir: Ida Lupino; Prod: Collier Young; Writer: Ida Lupino, Collier Young, Robert L. Joseph; DP: Nicholas Musuraca; Ed: Douglas Stewart; Prod Design: Albert S. D'Agostino, Walter E. Keller; Composer: Leith Stevens. B&W, 71 min. **VHS**

Hitler's Children
(1943) RKO
Grim portrayal of youths caught in the horror of the Nazi regime meant to excite home-front passions. When Holt, an enthusiastic student at a German school for Hitler Youth, meets Granville, a student at the American school next door, they fall in love despite her misgivings about his fascism. When the war breaks out, Granville's caught in the brutality of Nazi Germany face-to-face. **Cast:** Bonita Granville, Tim Holt, Otto Kruger, Kent Smith, Edward A. Golden, H. B. Warner, Lloyd Corrigan, Erford Gage, Hans Conreid, Nancy Gates. **Credits:** Dir: Edward Dmytryk; Prod: Edward A. Golden; Writer: Emmett Lavery; DP: Russell Metty; Ed: Joseph Noriega; Composer: Roy Webb; Art Director: Albert S. D'Agostino. B&W, 83 min. **VHS**

Hitler's Madman
(1943) MGM
Sirk draws upon his experiences in Nazi Germany in WWII for his first American film. Carradine stars as the Nazi in charge of a Czech town. In a revolt against his oppression, the Czech resistance successfully assassinates him. The brief celebration of this triumph is quickly silenced as Himmler and his troops sweep through the town. **Cast:** John Carradine, Howard Freeman, Alan Curtis, Patricia Morison, Ralph Morgan, Ludwig Stossel, Edgar Kennedy, Jimmy Conlin, Jorja Rollins, Ava Gardner. **Credits:** Dir: Douglas Sirk; Prod: Seymour Nebenzal; Writer: Peretz Hirshbein, Melvin Levy, Doris Malloy; Story: Emil Ludwig, Albrecht Joseph, Bart Lytton; DP: Jack Greenhaigh, Eugene Schuftan; Ed: Dan Milner; Prod Design: Fred Preble; Composer: Karl Hajos; Art Director: Edward Willens. B&W, 84 min.

H. M. Pulham, Esq.
(1941) MGM
True love isn't enough to break the bonds of social class in this portrait of a man too good for his own good. Harry Pulham (Young), the wealthy son of Bostonians, shocks everyone when he takes up with lively Iowan copywriter, Lamarr. Mr. Pulham, Sr., unfortunately, cannot stomach the prospect of his new daughter-in-law-to-be, and Harry is bullied into letting his beauty go. He marries a Bostonian bore, though Lamarr hasn't given up. **Cast:** Hedy Lamarr, Robert Young, Ruth Hussey, Charles Coburn, Van Heflin, Fay Holden, Bonita Granville, Douglas

Wood, Charles Halton, Leif Erickson. **Credits:** Dir: King Vidor; Prod: King Vidor; Writer: Elizabeth Hill, King Vidor; Story: John P. Marquand; DP: Ray June; Ed: Harold F. Kress; Prod Design: Cedric Gibbons, Malcolm Brown; Composer: Bronislau Kaper. B&W, 120 min.

Hold Back the Dawn
(1941) Paramount
In a backstage glimpse at director Leisen at work, a hard-luck romantic plot is told by Boyer to director Leisen for the 500 bucks he needs to help his girl, de Havilland. Boyer relays his plight as a hopeless refugee from a war-ravaged Europe holed up in a Mexican border town. Trouble-making Goddard tells him that U.S. citizenship can be had by marrying an American. Luckily for Boyer, the innocent, trusting de Havilland is in town leading a school trip. She falls deeply for Boyer and she touches his heart as well. But then Goddard turns up and spills the beans. **Cast:** Charles Boyer, Olivia de Havilland, Paulette Goddard, Victor Francen, Walter Abel, Curt Bois, Rosemary De Camp, Eric Feldary, Nestor Paiva, Eva Puig. **Credits:** Dir: Mitchell Leisen; Prod: Arthur Hornblow; Writer: Charles Brackett, Billy Wilder; Story: Ketti Frings; DP: Leo Tover; Ed: Doane Harrison; Prod Design: Hans Dreier, Robert Usher; Composer: Victor Young. B&W, 115 min.

Hold Your Man
(1933) MGM
A sharp Loos script for unbeatable combo of Gable and Harlow. She's Ruby, one tough cookie. He's Eddie. Even his smile is crooked. Together, they set out to clip the world. When a scam goes sour, Ruby ends up in reform school. She's in trouble, and he's not around—or so she thinks. Entertaining, well-produced mix of crime-flick spoof and drama. **Cast:** Jean Harlow, Clark Gable, Stuart Erwin, Elizabeth Patterson, Blanche Friderici, Dorothy Burgess, Muriel Kirkland, Garry Owen, Paul Hurst, Theresa Harris. **Credits:** Dir: Sam Wood; Prod: Sam Wood; Writer: Anita Loos, Howard Emmett Rogers; DP: Harold Rosson; Prod Design: Cedric Gibbons; Art Director: Merrill Pye. B&W, 88 min. **VHS**

A Hole in the Head
(1959) United Artists
A Capra musical that the Chairman of the Board keeps bouncy. Frank's a small-time hotel owner with delusions of grandeur forced to face the music of adult responsibilities (voiced by his

disapproving brother, Robinson) in order to keep his adoring young son. Nonetheless, he hangs on to the far-fetched dreams. Sinatra songs include the Oscar-winning "High Hopes" and "All My Tomorrows." **Academy Awards:** Best Song. **Cast:** Frank Sinatra, Edward G. Robinson, Eleanor Parker, Carolyn Jones, Thelma Ritter, Eddie Hodges, Keenan Wynn, Joi Lansing, Jimmie Komack. **Credits:** Dir: Frank Capra; Prod: Frank Capra; Writer: Arnold Schulman; DP: William Daniels; Ed: William Hornbeck; Prod Design: Eddie Imazu; Composer: Nelson Riddle. Color, 121 min. VHS, LASER

Holiday
(1938) Columbia
Hepburn and Grant shine in this gentle Cukor screwball comedy about a wrong marriage halted and the right one joyously celebrated. Grant's a free spirit who thinks he's just met the girl of his dreams. But he soon discovers that his lovely new bride-to-be comes from a blueblood Park Avenue family. He meets his true match in his intended's unconventional sister, Hepburn, who wants something different than the life her family has mapped out. Based on the play by Phillip Barry, the author of *The Philadelphia Story,* which would become a triumph for the some of the same crew two years later. **Cast:** Cary Grant, Katharine Hepburn, Doris Nolan, Lew Ayres, Edward Everett Horton, Henry Kolker, Binnie Barnes, Jean Dixon, Henry Daniell, Charles Trowbridge. **Credits:** Dir: George Cukor; Prod: Everett Riskin; Writer: Donald Ogden Stewart, Sidney Buchman; DP: Franz Planer; Ed: Otto Meyer, Al Clark; Composer: Sidney Cutner; Art Director: Stephen Goosson, Lionel Banks. B&W, 93 min. VHS, LASER

Holiday Affair
(1949) RKO
This Christmas story centers on a widowed mother who is about to marry an old friend. The mother, eager to give her boy a very merry Christmas, allows a charming sales clerk to buy her son a toy train set, much to her fiancé's chagrin. The triangle is in place. Steve, the clerk, understands that to win her heart, he must first win over her son. Based on the story by John D. Weaver. Remade for television in 1996. **Cast:** Robert Mitchum, Janet Leigh, Wendell Corey, Gordon Gebert, Griff Barnett, Henry O'Neill, Henry Morgan, Helen Hayes Brown, James Griffith, Frances Morris. **Credits:** Dir: Don Hartman; Prod: Don Hartman; Writer: Isobel Lennart; Story: John D.

Weaver; DP: Milton Krasner; Ed: Harry Marker; Composer: Roy Webb. B&W, 87 min. VHS, LASER

Holiday for Sinners
(1952) MGM
Set against the festive backdrop of Mardi Gras, this is the story of a young doctor debating whether he should leave the violent New Orleans neighborhood where he grew up. Young, who inherited his father's practice, questions whether it's worth staying to care for his poor patients. His love for Rule, and his boyhood friendships with Wynn, a former boxer, and Anderson, a priest, make it hard for him to let go. **Cast:** Gig Young, Keenan Wynn, Janice Rule, William Campbell, Richard Anderson, Michael Chekhov, Sandro Giglio, Edith Barrett, Porter Hall, Ralph Dumke. **Credits:** Dir: Gerald Mayer; Prod: John Houseman; Writer: A.I. Bezzerides; Story: Hamilton Basso; DP: Paul C. Vogel; Ed: Frederick Smith; Composer: Alberto Colombo; Art Director: Cedric Gibbons, Arthur Longersan. B&W, 72 min.

Holiday in Mexico
(1946) MGM
Mexico is an unforgettable adventure for a U.S. ambassador (Pidgeon) and his precocious teenage daughter (Powell). Determined to run her father's personal life, she's disappointed when he falls for a beautiful singer. She in turn develops a crush on an older pianist (Iturbi). Engaging performances, many musical numbers performed by Cugat and his orchestra, such as "Italian Street Song" from Powell, and Iturbi's performance of Chopin highlight this musical postcard. **Cast:** Walter Pidgeon, Ilona Massey, Roddy McDowall, Jose Iturbi, Xavier Cugat, Jane Powell, Hugo Haas, Mikhail Rasumny, Helene Stanley, William F. Phillips. **Credits:** Dir: George Sidney; Prod: Joe Pasternak; Writer: Isobel Lennart; DP: Harry Stradling; Ed: Adrienne Fazan; Prod Design: Cedric Gibbons; Choreographer: Stanley Donen; Composer: George Stoll; Art Director: Jack Martin Smith. Color, 127 min. VHS

Holiday Inn
(1942) Paramount
Two retiring showmen (Astaire and Crosby) start a New England country inn with the unique and, one would think, self-defeating idea of being open only on national holidays; however, in this delightful fluff-fest, they achieve instantaneous success. Conflicts arise when they fall for the same

woman, and sparks fly as fast as their feet in a variety of inventive, holiday-themed song-and-dance productions. Perhaps the best film ever inspired by a song. Berlin's Yuletide chestnut "White Christmas" was introduced in this film in a cozy scene of Bing crooning by the trimmed tree. Remade in 1954 with Crosby and Danny Kaye as *White Christmas.* Other songs include "Happy Holidays," "Be Careful It's My Heart," "Let's Start the New Year Right," and "Let's Say It With Firecrackers." Academy Award Nominations: Best Story; Best Score. **Academy Awards:** Best Song ("White Christmas"). **Cast:** Bing Crosby, Fred Astaire, Marjorie Reynolds, Walter Abel, Louise Beavers, Virginia Dale. **Credits:** Dir: Mark Sandrich; Prod: Mark Sandrich; Writer: Claude Binyon, Elmer Rice; DP: David Abel; Ed: Ellsworth Hoagland; Choreographer: Danny Dare; Composer: Irving Berlin; Costumes: Edith Head. B&W, 101 min. VHS

Hollow Triumph
(1948) Eagle-Lion
Film noir drama in which a sophisticated con man, who has just stolen from the Mob, is forced to impersonate a psychiatrist who looks just like him, even cutting himself on the cheek to duplicate a similar scar on the doctor. When he takes matters even further, he's forced to pay the debts of his double. **Cast:** Joan Bennett, Jack Webb, Paul Heinreid, Eduard Franz, Leslie Brooks, John Qualen, Mabel Paige, Herbert Rudley, Paul E. Burns, Charles Trowbridge. **Credits:** Dir: Steve Sekely; Prod: Paul Henreid; Writer: Daniel Fuchs; DP: John Alton; Ed: Fred Allen; Prod Design: Edward L. Ilou, Frank Durlauf; Composer: Sol Kaplan. B&W, 83 min. VHS

Hollywood Boulevard
(1936) Paramount
A backstage Hollywood drama about a faded actor, Halliday, whose desperation forces him to write a tell-all serialized memoir for a sleazy magazine publisher. His family is mortified when the first installment of the serial appears in print. Blakeford begs the publisher not to print the rest of the series, but the publisher refuses. The two argue and the publisher shoots and kills Blakeford. Blakeford's daughter is considered the prime suspect, but her resourceful fiancé comes to her rescue and clears her name. The film features a number of cameo appearances by silent-film stars, and is directed by Expressionist master Florey. **Cast:** John Halliday, Marsha

Hunt, Robert Cummings, C. Henry Gordon, Frieda Inescort, Francis X. Bushman. **Credits:** Dir: Robert Florey; Prod: A. M. Botsford; Writer: Faith Thomas, Marguerite Robert; DP: George Clemens; Ed: Harvey Johnson, William Shea; Prod Design: Hans Dreier; Composer: Gregory Stone; Art Director: A. Earl Hedrick. B&W, 75 min.

Hollywood Canteen
(1944) Warner Bros.
A musical set in the USO nightclub where the biggest names in show business entertained the troops during WWII. The story revolves around a young G.I. (Hutton) who has a crush on one of the female performers—and is lucky enough to win a night out on the town with her when he's named the Canteen's millionth visitor. Watch for many guest stars, including Crawford, Ida Lupino, Barbara Stanwyck, Peter Lorre, Sydney Greenstreet, Benny, and Roy Rogers. Plenty of the era's greatest hits, too. Acadamy Award Nominations: 3. **Cast:** Bette Davis, John Garfield, Joan Leslie, Robert Hutton, Dane Clark, Janis Paige, Jack Benny, Joe E. Brown, Eddie Cantor, Joan Crawford. **Credits:** Dir: Delmer Daves; Prod: Alex Gottlieb; Writer: Delmer Daves; DP: Bert Glennon; Ed: Christian Nyby; Prod Design: Leo K. Kuter; Composer: Ray Heindorf. B&W, 124 min. **VHS, LASER**

Hollywood Cavalcade
(1939) Fox
In the motion picture industry's first large-scale attempt to dramatize its own history, this follows the story of a young director's (Ameche) rise, fall, and subsequent resurfacing in Hollywood. This "movie about the movies" provides a means for numerous stars to re-create the roles that originally made them famous. Members of Mack Sennett's original troupe, including the Keystone Kops, along with Mack himself, appear in the film, as do Keaton and Al Jolson, who re-creates a sequence from *The Jazz Singer*. **Cast:** Alice Faye, Don Ameche, J. Edward Bromberg, Alan Curtis, Stuart Erwin, Jed Prouty, Donald Meek, George Givot, Chick Chandler, Buster Keaton. **Credits:** Dir: Irving Cummings; Prod: Darryl F. Zanuck; Writer: Ernest Pascal, Hilary Lynn, Brown Holmes; DP: Allen M. Davey; Composer: David Raksin. B&W, 100 min.

Hollywood Hotel
(1937) Warner Bros.
This energetic Berkeley musical tells the story of a saxophonist (Powell)

sent to the West Coast after winning a 10-week contract. He is relieved of his duties when he leaves with the star's double (Lola Lane, Rosemary's sister) instead of the star (Rosemary Lane). He's hired back only after filling in as a voice double for the male lead in the show. Benny Goodman and his Orchestra perform no less than eight musical numbers (with encores), including "Sing Sing Sing," and the production numbers include the famous Mercer and Whiting anthem, "Hooray for Hollywood." **Cast:** Dick Powell, Rosemary Lane, Lola Lane, Hugh Herbert, Ted Healy, Glenda Farrell, Johnnie Davis, Alan Mowbray, Mabel Todd, Frances Langford. **Credits:** Dir: Busby Berkeley; Writer: Richard Macauley; DP: George Barnes, Charles Rosher; Ed: George Amy; Prod Design: Busby Berkeley; Composer: Johnny Mercer, Richard A. Whiting. B&W, 109 min.

Hollywood or Bust
(1956) Paramount
The last screen pairing of Martin and Lewis tells the story of a nebbish movie fanatic and a debauched crooner who share first prize in a local contest. The award is a sleek, new convertible—so the two use the prize to set off for Hollywood. As Lewis, his suave friend, and a sloppy Great Dane make their way across the country, they warble a few waggish ditties and get tangled up in comic hijinks. In the end, of course, Dean-o gets the girl and Jerry gets . . . the dog! **Cast:** Jerry Lewis, Dean Martin, Anita Ekberg, Pat Crowley, Maxie Rosenbloom, Willard Waterman, Michael Ross. **Credits:** Dir: Frank Tashlin; Prod: Hal B. Wallis; Writer: Erna Lazarus; DP: Daniel Fapp; Ed: Howard Smith; Composer: Walter Scharf. Color, 95 min. **VHS**

Holy Matrimony
(1943) Fox
A reclusive artist, played by Woolley, has been living and painting on an island in the Pacific for two decades. When he is summoned back to England to be knighted, he reluctantly returns with his valet. On the journey, his valet dies, and the artist swaps identities with the dead butler. In his assumed life, he finds that he must marry a woman to whom the real valet has professed to love. Everything is turned upside down, though, when the first wife of the valet shows up with their three children to reclaim the husband she hasn't seen in 20 years. Classy remake of *His Double Life*

(1933), with great character actors Pangborn and Blore in the background. **Cast:** Monty Woolley, Gracie Fields, Laird Cregar, Una O'Connor, Alan Mowbray, Melville Cooper, Franklin Pangborn, Ethel Griffies, Eric Blore, Montagu Love. **Credits:** Dir: John M. Stahl; Prod: Nunnally Johnson; Writer: Nunnally Johnson; Story: Arnold Bennett; DP: Lucien Ballard; Ed: James B. Clark; Prod Design: James Basevi, Thomas Little; Composer: Emil Newman, Cyril Mockridge; SFX: Paul Sersen; Art Director: Russell Spencer. B&W 87 min.

Hombre
(1967) Fox
In this Western with a message, Newman gives a sharp performance as a white man raised by Native Americans. As he joins a stagecoach filled with hostile, bigoted whites journeying through the Old West, Newman is forced to confront his own anti-white bias to save the lives of his traveling companions. Adapted from a Leonard story. **Cast:** Paul Newman, Fredric March, Richard Boone, Diane Cilento, Martin Balsam, Barbara Rush, Cameron Mitchell, Peter Lazer. **Credits:** Dir: Martin Ritt; Prod: Martin Ritt, Irving Ravetch; Writer: Irving Ravetch, Harriet Farnk, Jr.; Story: Elmore Leonard; DP: James Wong Howe; Ed: Frank Bracht; Prod Design: Jack Martin Smith, Robert Smith; Composer: David Rose. Color, 111 min. **VHS, LASER**

Home Before Dark
(1958) Warner Bros.
A college professor drives his wife (Simmons) to insanity with his chilly indifference. Upon his wife's return from a mental hospital, the husband insists that they sleep apart as he cavorts about town with her stepsister, who now lives in Simmons's home. A gentle member of the college faculty is also boarding in the home and proves to be a source of enticing comfort for the still-fragile wife. **Cast:** Jean Simmons, Dan O'Herlihy, Rhonda Fleming, Efrem Zimbalist, Jr., Mabel Albertson, Stephen Dunne, Joanna Barnes, Kathryn Card, Marjorie Bennett, Joan Weldon. **Credits:** Dir: Mervyn LeRoy; Prod: Mervyn LeRoy; Writer: Eileen Bassing, Robert Bassing; DP: Joseph Biroc; Ed: Philip W. Anderson; Composer: Ray Heindorf. B&W, 137 min.

Homecoming
(1948) MGM
Told in flashback, this wartime romantic melodrama depicts the repercus-

sions of an extramarital affair on the front lines. Gable enlists as an army surgeon, leaving behind a wife (Baxter) and home. He finds comfort in the arms of Turner, a battlefield nurse. They survive and love as the bombs fly. A postwar potboiler with a better-than-average cast. Based on Sidney Kingsley's story "The Homecoming of Ulysses." **Cast:** Clark Gable, Lana Turner, Anne Baxter, John Hodiak, Ray Collins, Cameron Mitchell, Gladys Cooper, Marshall Thompson, Art Baker, Lurene Tuttle. **Credits:** Dir: Mervyn LeRoy; Prod: Sidney Franklin; Writer: Paul Osborn, Jan Lustig; DP: Harold Rosson; Ed: John Dunning; Prod Design: Cedric Gibbons, Randal Duell; Composer: Bronislau Kaper. B&W, 113 min. **VHS**

Home from the Hill
(1960) MGM
Minnelli directs a southern melodrama about a father's (Mitchum) relationship with his two sons (Hamilton and Peppard), one of whom is the illegitimate result of an affair with a local woman. Damaged by his mother's scorn and his father's callousness, Hamilton carries on his father's legacy by mistreating his own girlfriend. His impoverished half-brother Peppard grew up in the shadow of his spoiled brother. Peppard comes to terms with his brother, his absent father, and the life that was denied him. Superb performances by all. **Cast:** Robert Mitchum, Eleanor Parker, George Peppard, George Hamilton, Luana Patten, Everett Sloane, Constance Ford, Ray Teal, Anne Seymour. **Credits:** Dir: Vincente Minnelli; Prod: Edmund Grainger; Writer: Frank Harriet; DP: Milton Krasner; Ed: Harold F. Kress; Prod Design: George W. Davis, Preston Ames; Composer: Bronislau Kaper, Charles Wolcott. Color, 150 min. **VHS, LASER**

Home of the Brave
(1949) United Artists
A young black G.I. (Edwards) suffers a nervous breakdown, induced by his wartime experience on a reconnaissance mission in which he suffers at the hands of the enemy and his fellow soldiers, and by a lifetime of racial discrimination. Crippled by rage, he develops psychosomatic paralysis. But if he can overcome his anger and frustration, he might just walk again. A strong cry for racial justice that's still relevant. **Cast:** Lloyd Bridges, Frank Lovejoy, James Edwards, Steve Brodie, Jeff Corey, Douglas Dick, Cliff Clark. **Credits:** Dir: Mark Robson;

Prod: Stanley Kramer; Writer: Carl Foreman; Story: Arthur Laurents; DP: Robert de Grasse; Ed: Harry Gerstad; Prod Design: Rudolph Sternad; Composer: Dimitri Tiomkin. B&W, 86 min. **VHS, LASER**

Hondo
(1953) Warner Bros.
This sparkling Western has Wayne as a half-Indian cavalry scout who, with his feral dog companion, finds a young woman and her son living on an isolated ranch in unfriendly Apache country. A poetic and exciting script, outstanding performances, and breathtaking scenery make this an indisputable classic. Based on the L'Amour story "The Gift of Cochise." Page's debut. Produced in 3-D. **Cast:** John Wayne, Geraldine Page, Ward Bond, Michael Pate, James Arness, Rodolfo Acosta, Leo Gordon, Lee Aaker, Paul Fix, Tom Irish. **Credits:** Dir: John Farrow; Prod: Robert Fellows, John Wayne; Writer: James Edward Grant; Story: Louis L'Amour; DP: Robert Burks, Archie Stout; Ed: Ralph Dawson; Prod Design: Alfred Ybarra; Composer: Hugo Friedhofer, Alfred Newman. Color, 84 min. **VHS**

Honeymoon in Bali
(1939) Paramount
A spunky comedy-drama in which Carroll plays a successful career woman who decides that love is something that must be sacrificed in order to maintain her career. Her stance softens, however, after meeting the man from Bali (MacMurray). Tamiroff, as the advice-giving window washer, stands out in a supporting role. **Cast:** Fred MacMurray, Madeleine Carroll, Allan Jones, Akim Tamiroff, Helen Broderick, Osa Massen, Carolyn Lee, Astrid Allwyn, Georgia Caine, William Davidson. **Credits:** Dir: Edward H. Griffith; Prod: Jeff Lazarus; Writer: Katharine Brush, Virginia Van Upp, Grace Sartwell Mason; DP: Ted Tetzlaff; Ed: Eda Warren. B&W, 95 min. **VHS**

The Honeymoon Killers
(1970) Cinerama
In this stark film based on the '40s Lonely Hearts murders, a handsome gigolo (LoBianco) cons lonely women out of money with the promise of marriage, and his lover, an obese nurse (Stoler), takes murderous revenge on the vulnerable women. Initially scheduled for direction by Scorsese, this film has developed a cult following for its powerful depiction of deadly loneliness. **Cast:** Tony LoBianco, Shirley

Stoler, Mary Jane Higby, Doris Roberts, Kip McArdle, Barbara Cason, Marilyn Chris, Dortha Duckworth. **Credits:** Dir: Leonard Kastle; Prod: Warren Steibel; Writer: Leonard Kastle; DP: Oliver Wood; Ed: Stanley Warnow, Richard Brophy; Composer: Gustav Mahler. B&W, 103 min. **VHS, LASER**

The Honey Pot
(1967) United Artists
Writer-director Mankiewicz updates Molière's *Volpone*, with Harrison as the sly guy who pretends to be dying in order to test the love of his former mistresses. But greed for an inheritance emerges as their primary feeling when they gather at his bedside. An amusing black comedy and whodunit. **Cast:** Rex Harrison, Maggie Smith, Susan Hayward, Cliff Robertson, Capucine, Edie Adams, Adolfo Celi, Herschel Bernardi, Cy Grant, Frank Latimore. **Credits:** Dir: Joseph L. Mankiewicz; Prod: Charles K. Feldman, Joseph L. Mankiewicz; Writer: Joseph L. Mankiewicz; DP: Gianni Di Venanzo; Ed: David Bretherton; Prod Design: John DeCuir; Composer: John Addison. Color, 131 min. **VHS**

Honky Tonk
(1941) MGM
Tired of being run out of respectable burgs, gambler Gable decides to get wise and take over a town of his own, Yellow Creek, Nevada. Once there, he marries the daughter of the local justice of the peace and expands his illicit activities, until love turns him to the straight and narrow. This was the first pairing of Gable and Turner, but the obvious chemistry between the two leads ensured that it wouldn't be the last. **Cast:** Clark Gable, Lana Turner, Frank Morgan, Claire Trevor, Marjorie Main, Albert Dekker, Chill Wills, Henry O'Neill, Betty Blythe, John Maxwell. **Credits:** Dir: Jack Conway; Prod: Pandro S. Berman; Writer: Marguerite Roberts, John Sanford; DP: Harold Rosson; Ed: Blanche Sewell; Prod Design: Cedric Gibbons, Eddie Imazu; Composer: Franz Waxman. B&W, 106 min. **VHS**

Honolulu
(1939) MGM
A cinema heartthrob finds trouble in paradise when he trades places with his double, a Hawaiian plantation owner (both roles played by Young). He's arrested, thrown in jail, and forced to marry his look-alike's sweetheart, all the while falling in love with a girl of his own. Young is fun to watch

in the lead roles, the musical numbers keep matters light and festive, and Burns and Allen (in their last film pairing) crack jokes. **Cast:** Eleanor Powell, Robert Young, George Burns, Gracie Allen, Rita Johnson, Willie Fung, Ruth Hussey, Sig Rumann, Clarence Kolb, Eddie Anderson. **Credits:** Dir: Edward Buzzell; Prod: Jack Cummings; Writer: Herbert Fields, Frank Partos; DP: Ray June; Choreographer: Bobby Connolly; Composer: Franz Waxman. B&W, 84 min. **VHS**

Hoodlum Empire
(1952) Republic
It's a deadly play for power when a Mafia chieftain's top gun goes straight after a stint in combat, and threatens to testify against the big boss and his nationwide network of crime. The picture, which was shot in a semi-documentary style, was inspired by the Kefauver investigations of 1950–51. **Cast:** Brian Donlevy, Claire Trevor, Forrest Tucker, Luther Adler, Vera Ralston, John Russell, Gene Lockhart, Grant Withers, Taylor Holmes, Roy Barcroft. **Credits:** Dir: Joseph Kane; Prod: Herbert J. Yates; Writer: Bruce Manning, Bob Considine; DP: Reggie Lanning; Ed: Richard L. Van Enger; Prod Design: Frank Arrigo; Composer: Nathan Scott; Costumes: Adele Palmer. B&W, 98 min. **VHS**

The Hoodlum Priest
(1961) United Artists
Murray stars in this true story (as well as coproducing and cowriting) of Rev. Charles Dismas Clark, a Jesuit priest who dedicated his life to working with former convicts in St. Louis. Dullea, in his first screen appearance, has trouble making the adjustment to life outside the big house. **Cast:** Don Murray, Larry Gates, Keir Dullea, Logan Ramsey, Cindi Wood. **Credits:** Dir: Irvin Kershner; Prod: Walter Wood, Don Murray; Writer: Joseph Landon, Don Murray; DP: Haskell Wexler; Ed: Maurice Wright; Prod Design: Jack Poplin; Composer: Richard Markowitz. B&W, 101 min. **VHS**

The Hook
(1963) MGM
A striking morality play set on the last day of the Korean War. After U.S. forces fish a downed North Korean pilot out of the drink, the commanding officer, a snarling Douglas, orders his men, Walker and Adams, to kill him, which they refuse to do. Word reaches them of the armistice, and when they try to release the prisoner, Magalona, he's accidentally killed in a scuffle.

Cast: Kirk Douglas, Robert Walker, Jr., Nick Adams, Enrique Magalona, Nehemiah Persoff, Mark Miller, John Bleifer. **Credits:** Dir: George Seaton; Prod: William Perlberg; Writer: Henry Denker; Story: Vahe Katcha; DP: Joseph Ruttenberg; Ed: Robert J. Kern; Prod Design: George W. Davis, Hans Peters; Composer: Larry Adler. B&W, 98 min.

Hooper
(1978) Warner Bros.
Behind the scenes in Hollywood, stuntmen compete with one another for the title "best in town." A young upstart (Vincent) challenges aging stuntman Reynolds for the crown, forcing him to deliver one more dangerous stunt that could either kill him or make him a living legend. The team from *Smokey and the Bandit* provides flashes of humor, and the action scenes are energetically photographed. **Cast:** Burt Reynolds, Sally Field, Brian Keith, Jan-Michael Vincent, Robert Klein, John Marley, James Best, Adam West, Terry Bradshaw. **Credits:** Dir: Hal Needham; Prod: Hank Moonjean; Writer: Bill Kerby, Thomas Rickman; DP: Bobby Byrne; Ed: Donn Cambern; Composer: Bill Justis; Costumes: Norman Salling. Color, 100 min. **VHS, LASER**

Hooray for Love
(1935) RKO
Raymond plays a big-time musical producer on the down-and-out who falls for talented showgirl Sothern. By manipulating her aging father (Hall) into a profitable marriage with an old heiress (Kane), who's not, thankfully, as dour as she looks, the couple raise the cash necessary to salvage Raymond's career and catapult Sothern to musical stardom. There's enough story to string together a series of classic performances by the likes of Fats Waller, Bill "Bojangles" Robinson, Maria Gambarelli, and Sothern herself. Hot numbers include "Hooray for Love," "Palsie Walsie," "I'm Living in a Great Big Way," and "Got a Snap in My Fingers." **Cast:** Ann Sothern, Gene Raymond, Bill Robinson, Maria Gambarelli, Thurston Hall, Pert Kelton, Georgia Kane, Lionel Stander, Etienne Girardot, Fats Waller. **Credits:** Dir: Walter Lang; Prod: Felix Young; Writer: Lawrence Hazard, Marc Lachmann; Story: Ray Harris; DP: Lucien N. Andriot; Ed: George Crone; Prod Design: Van Nest Polglase, Perry Ferguson; Composer: Dorothy Fields, Jimmy McHugh. B&W, 72 min.

Hoosier Schoolboy
(1937) Monogram
Set against the background of a 1936 strike by midwestern milk farmers, this picture concerns a troubled young man (Rooney) who must battle his neighbors and classmates as they taunt and mock his drunken father. When his father gets his act together and begins driving a milk truck, tragedy eventually strikes, leaving the boy an orphan. As the school tries to expel him for his disruptive behavior, a new teacher (Nagel) understands his troubled situation and defends him. This was Rooney's first starring role, and he gives a mature, powerful performance. **Cast:** Mickey Rooney, Anne Nagel, Frank Shields, Edward Pawley, William Gould. **Credits:** Dir: William Nigh; Prod: Ken Goldsmith; Writer: Robert Johnson; DP: Paul Ivano. B&W, 63 min. **VHS**

Horizons West
(1952) Universal
Ryan and Hudson play half brothers who survive the Civil War but find that in peacetime their paths diverge. Hudson moves west, settles down, and becomes a rancher. The unscrupulous Ryan, however, embarks on a one-man campaign of violence and intimidation to take control of the territory. After killing rival overlord Burr and commanding the affections of his widow, Adams, Ryan's destiny leads him to a showdown with Hudson. A sprawling tale directed by Boetticher with a powerhouse cast. **Cast:** Robert Ryan, Julie Adams, Rock Hudson, John McIntire, Judith Braun, Raymond Burr, James Arness, Frances Bavier, Dennis Weaver, Tom Powers. **Credits:** Dir: Budd Boetticher; Prod: Albert J. Cohen; Writer: Louis Stevenson; DP: Charles Boyle; Ed: Ted J. Kent; Prod Design: Robert Clatworthy, Bernard Herzbrun; Composer: Joseph Gershenson. B&W, 81 min.

The Horn Blows at Midnight
(1945) Warner Bros.
Benny plays a big-band trumpeter who falls asleep and dreams he is an archangel, sent to destroy Earth because persecution and hatred are out of control. A lighthearted fantasy with the unlikely subject of the Apocalypse. Quite enjoyable, for the premise and for Benny's performance. **Cast:** Jack Benny, Alexis Smith, Guy Kibbee, Reginald Gardiner, Robert Blake, James Burke, Dolores Moran, Allyn Joslyn, Franklin Pangborn, John Alexander. **Credits:** Dir: Raoul Walsh; Prod: Mark Hellinger; Writer: Sam Hell-

Horse Feathers (1932)

man, James V. Kern; DP: Sid Hickox; Ed: Irene Morra; Prod Design: Hugh Reticker; Composer: Franz Waxman, Leo F. Forbstein. B&W, and Color, 78 min. **VHS**

Horse Feathers

(1932) Paramount
The Marx Brothers parody college life in this gag-filled, fast-paced comedy. The fast-talking new president of Huxley College needs to scrounge up some top-flight ringers for his football team, but ends up with a bootlegger and a mute dogcatcher instead. More laughs than most Marx comedies (and that's saying something), in a script cowritten by humorist Perelman. **Cast:** Groucho, Harpo, Chico, and Zeppo Marx, Thelma Todd, David Landau, Robert Greig, Florine McKinney, Nat Pendleton, Reginald Barlow. **Credits:** Dir: Norman Z. McLeod; Prod: Herman J. Mankiewicz; Writer: Bert Kalmar, Harry Ruby, S. J. Perelman, William B. Johnstone; DP: Ray June; Composer: Bert Kalmar, Harry Ruby. B&W, 68 min. **VHS, LASER, DVD**

Horse in the Gray Flannel Suit

(1968) Disney
Disney family comedy that finds harried New York ad executive (Jones) in trouble at home as well as the office. His daughter is a gifted equestrian who wants to own her own horse, but not on dad's meager budget. His boss orders Jones to invent an ad campaign for a new product, a stomach

pill called "Aspercel." When he decides that the best thing to do is to buy a horse for his daughter and name it "Aspercel," the results aren't an immediate success. **Cast:** Dean Jones, Ellen Janov, Diane Baker, Pamela Franklin, Fred Clark, Kurt Russell, Morey Amsterdam, Lloyd Bochner, Lurene Tuttle, Alan Hewitt. **Credits:** Dir: Norman Tokar; Prod: Winston Hibler; Writer: Louis Pelletier; Story: Eric Hatch; DP: William E. Snyder; Ed: Robert Stafford; Prod Design: Carroll Clark, John B. Mansbridge; Composer: George Bruns. Color, 114 min. **VHS**

The Horsemen

(1971) Columbia
A young man (Sharif) is forced to play in a violent Bozkeshi tournament, and loses his leg trying to please his father. Trumbo's script is an odd mixture of action, adventure, and drama but the Afghan and Spanish scenery (photographed by Claude Renoir) and performances by Sharif and Palance make this worth seeing. **Cast:** Omar Sharif, Jack Palance, Leigh Taylor-Young, Peter Jeffrey, Eric Pohlmann, David De Keyser, George Murcell, Vernon Dobtcheff. **Credits:** Dir: John Frankenheimer; Prod: Edward Lewis; Writer: Dalton Trumbo; Story: Joseph Kessel; DP: Claude Renoir, Vladimir Ivanoff, Andre Domage; Ed: Harold F. Kress; Prod Design: Pierre-Louis Thevenet; Composer: Georges Delerue. Color, 109 min. **VHS**

The Horse Soldiers

(1959) United Artists
Union colonel Wayne leads a daring commando raid 300 miles into Confederate territory in an attempt to destroy a railway hub. Along the way, he butts heads with Holden, a doctor with misgivings about the mission. Ford's only Civil War movie. **Cast:** John Wayne, William Holden, Constance Towers, Hoot Gibson, Althea Gibson, Anna Lee, Russell Simpson, Carleton Young, Basil Ruysdael. **Credits:** Dir: John Ford; Prod: John Lee Mahin, Martin Rackin; Writer: John Lee Mahin, Martin Rackin; Story: Harold Sinclair; DP: William Clothier; Ed: Jack Murray; Prod Design: Frank Hotaling; Composer: David Buttolph. Color, 119 min. **VHS, LASER**

The Hospital

(1971) United Artists
This black comedy features an alcoholic doctor-turned-administrator who tries to manage an overburdened and chaotic hospital, with fatal results. The script by Chayefsky is dead-on in this satire on modern bureaucracies and the plight of a rational man in an irrational environment. Sadly, this cult favorite still rings true in our HMO age. Selected as a National Film Registry Outstanding Film. Academy Award Nominations: 2, including Best Actor: George C. Scott. **Academy Awards:** Best Story/Screenplay Based on Factual Material. **Cast:** George C. Scott, Diana Rigg, Barnard Hughes, Nancy Marchand, Stockard Channing, Roberts Blossom, Robert Walden, Richard Dysart, Lenny Baker, Frances Sternhagen. **Credits:** Dir: Arthur Hiller; Prod: Howard Gottfried; Writer: Paddy Chayefsky; DP: Victor J. Kemper; Ed: Eric Albertson; Prod Design: Gene Rudolf; Composer: Morris Surdin. Color, 103 min. **VHS, LASER**

Houdini

(1953) Paramount
Biopic of the great magician spanning the years from age 21 to his death, with fascinating re-creations of his most famous stunts. The movie chronicles his early career as an illusionist in New York City, his quick courtship and marriage to wife Bess, and his subsequent trip to Europe, where his escape artistry brought him fame. Upon his return to the U.S., Houdini began performing death-defying acts across the country, and soon became a household name. However, he was unable to dodge fate—or death—forever: on Halloween night, 1926, he succumbed while attempting to

escape from a water tank. Hollywood-isms aside, this is still an entertaining and revealing motion picture. **Cast:** Tony Curtis, Janet Leigh, Torin Thatcher, Ian Wolfe, Sig Rumann, Angela Clarke, Stefan Schnabel, Michael Pate, Connie Gilchrist. **Credits:** Dir: George Marshall; Prod: George Pal; Writer: Philip Yordan; Story: Harold Kellock; DP: Ernest Laszlo; Ed: George Tomasini; Prod Design: Hal Pereira, Albert Nozaki; Composer: Roy Webb; Costumes: Edith Head. Color, 107 min. VHS

Hour of Thirteen
(1952) MGM
Rat-packer Lawford plays a mercurial jewel thief in this remake of the 1934 film, *The Mystery of Mr. X.* Aided by accomplices Gordon and Dwyer, Lawford pulls off the heist of a prized emerald at a high-society soiree. At the same time, a cop killer murders another bobby and it's Lawford who draws the heat from Scotland Yard. With the assistance of the Chief Inspector's daughter, Addams, Lawford sets a trap for the killer. **Cast:** Peter Lawford, Dawn Addams, Roland Culver, Derek Bond, Leslie Dwyer, Michael Hordern, Colin Gordon, Heather Thatcher, Jack McNaughton, Campbell Cotts. **Credits:** Dir: Harold French; Prod: Hayes Goetz; Writer: Leon Gordon; Story: Philip MacDonald, Howard Emmett Rogers; DP: Guy Green; Ed: Raymond Poulton, Robert Watts; Prod Design: Alfred Junge; Composer: John Addison. B&W, 79 min.

Houseboat
(1958) Paramount
When Grant's estranged wife dies in a sudden accident, he's left alone to raise their three children. They haven't seen hide nor hair of their father in ages, and they aren't about to let him play the perfect parent now. In steps Loren, a lovely lady who's willing to do anything to escape her strict father. She goes to work for Grant as a live-in nanny, and, predictably, they all become one big, happy family. The casting of Grant and Loren promises more than the situation delivers. Academy Award Nominations: 2, including Best Screenplay. **Cast:** Cary Grant, Sophia Loren, Martha Hyer, Harry Guardino, Eduardo Ciannelli. **Credits:** Dir: Melville Shavelson; Prod: Jack Rose; Writer: Jack Rose, Melville Shavelson; DP: Ray June; Ed: Frank Bracht; Prod Design: Hal Pereira; Composer: George Duning; Costumes: Edith Head; SFX: John Fulton; Art

Director: John B. Goodman; Set Designer: Sam Comer. Color, 110 min. VHS

House by the River
(1950) Republic
Evil has a way of coming back to haunt its practitioners in Lang's disturbing drama. Hayward plays a married writer living on the banks of a dark river who accidentally kills his young maid during a rebuffed attempt to romance her. He first tries to dispose of the body in the river, but when the corpse washes ashore, he decides to pin the crime on his crippled brother (Bowman). When the writer's wife (Wyatt) discovers his crime, she joins the accused brother in exposing her husband. Twisted psychological intrigue. **Cast:** Louis Hayward, Lee Bowman, Jane Wyatt, Dorothy Patrick, Ann Shoemaker, Jody Gilbert, Peter Brocco, Howland Chamberlin, Margaret Seddon, Sarah Padden. **Credits:** Dir: Fritz Lang; Prod: Howard Welsch; Writer: Mel Dinelli, A. P. Herbert; DP: Edward Cronjager; Ed: Arthur Hilton; Prod Design: Bert Leven; Composer: George Antheil. B&W, 88 min.

House Calls
(1978) Universal
A hilarious comedy about a newly widowed surgeon (Matthau) who tries to make up for 31 years of fidelity by seeing as many women as possible. Then he becomes enamored of a prickly nurse (Jackson) who doesn't take to the idea of just playing house. Carney is especially fine as the not-too-with-it head of surgery at the hospital. **Cast:** Walter Matthau, Glenda Jackson, Art Carney, Richard Benjamin, Candice Azzara, Thayer David, Dick O'Neill, Anthony Holland, Sandra Kerns, Brad Dexter. **Credits:** Dir: Howard Zieff; Prod: Alex Winitsky, Arlene Sellers; Writer: Max Shulman, Julius J. Epstein, Alan Mandel, Charles Shyer; DP: David M. Walsh; Ed: Edward A. Warschilka; Prod Design: Henry Bumstead; Composer: Henry Mancini. Color, 98 min. VHS, LASER

House of Dracula
(1945) Universal
Another horror feast featuring the Wolfman (Chaney, Jr.), Dracula (Carradine), and the Frankenstein monster (Strange), with a female hunchbacked assistant thrown in. They have all come to Dr. Edelman (Stevens) seeking cures for their monstrous conditions, but the angry villagers, torches

ready, don't appreciate the good doctor's clientele. Sequel to *House of Frankenstein*, and the Universal monster spree is starting to wear thin. **Cast:** Lon Chaney, Jr., John Carradine, Martha O'Driscoll, Onslow Stevens, Glenn Strange, Lionel Atwill, Jane Adams, Ludwig Stossel. **Credits:** Dir: Erle C. Kenton; Prod: Paul Malvern; Writer: Edward T. Lowe; DP: George Robinson, John Fulton; Ed: Russell Schoengarth; Prod Design: John B. Goodman, Martin Obzina; Composer: Edgar Fairchild. B&W, 67 min. VHS

House of Frankenstein
(1944) Universal
After being found guilty of performing bizarre experiments on dead bodies, Dr. Gustav Niemann (Karloff this time) escapes from the asylum and, along with his hunchbacked assistant, resurrects Dracula (Carradine, his first time wearing fangs), the Wolfman (Chaney, Jr.), and the Frankenstein monster (Strange) in order to exact revenge on all those who wronged him. This was the studio's first attempt at a horror "all star" picture, bringing all their monstrous creations together for maximum box-office effect. The result is great Saturday afternoon fun. **Cast:** Boris Karloff, Lon Chaney, Jr., John Carradine, Elena Verdugo, Anne Gwynne, Lionel Atwill, Peter Coe, George Zucco, Glenn Strange, J. Carrol Naish. **Credits:** Dir: Erle C. Kenton; Prod: Paul Malvern; Writer: Edward T. Lowe; Story: Curt Siodmak; DP: George Robinson; Ed: Philip Cahn; Prod Design: John B. Goodman, Martin Obzina; Composer: Hans J. Salter. B&W, 71 min. VHS

The House of Rothschild
(1934) Fox
The story of two generations of the Rothschild family as it becomes a formidable financial power and major financer of the war against Napoleon. Mayer Rothschild and, later, his five sons (one of them played by Arliss, who also plays Mayer), prove they can withstand both hard times and anti-Semitism. Handsomely mounted, with an early use of color in the final sequence. Academy Award Nominations: Best Picture. **Cast:** George Arliss, Boris Karloff, Loretta Young, Robert Young, C. Aubrey Smith, Arthur Byron, Helen Westley, Reginald Owen, Florence Arliss, Alan Mowbray. **Credits:** Dir: Alfred Werker; Prod: Darryl F. Zanuck, William Goetz, Raymond Griffith; Writer: George Humbert Westley, Nunnally Johnson; DP: J. Peverell Marley; Ed:

Barbara McLean, Allen McNeil; Prod
Design: Richard Day; Composer:
Alfred Newman. B&W, 94 min.

House of Strangers
(1949) Fox
A ruthless banker (Robinson) uses his
four sons in any way necessary to
build his empire. When the favorite
goes to prison for his father's sins,
the other three take over and drive the
older man to his death. The fourth
brother swears an oath of vengeance
to be exacted upon his release.
Unusually tough domestic drama from
Mankiewicz. **Cast:** Edward G. Robin-
son, Richard Conte, Susan Hayward,
Luther Adler, Paul Valentine, Efrem
Zimbalist, Jr., Debra Paget, Hope
Emerson, Esther Minciotti, Diana
Douglas. **Credits:** Dir: Joseph L. Man-
kiewicz; Prod: Sol C. Siegel; Writer:
Philip Yordan; Story: Jerome Weidman;
DP: Milton Krasner; Ed: Harmon
Jones; Prod Design: Lyle Wheeler,
George W. Davis; Composer: Daniele
Amfitheatrof. B&W, 101 min. VHS

House of Wax
(1953) Warner Bros.
The masterpiece of 3-D, this remains
a drive-in favorite and marks Price's
entrance into the macabre roles that
would fill the second half of his long
career. After a talented wax sculptor's
hyperrealistic creations are destroyed
by fire, the madman transforms fresh
corpses into lifelike works of art.
Watch for Bronson as the sculptor's
mute assistant. **Cast:** Vincent Price,
Frank Lovejoy, Phyllis Kirk, Carolyn
Jones, Charles Bronson, Paul Picerni,
Roy Roberts, Angela Clarke, Paul
Cavanagh, Dabbs Greer. **Credits:** Dir:
Andre De Toth; Prod: Bryan Foy;
Writer: Crane Wilbur; DP: Bert Glen-
non, Peverell Marley; Ed: Rudi Fehr;
Prod Design: Stanley Fleischer; Com-
poser: David Buttolph. Color, 88 min.
VHS, LASER

House on Haunted Hill
(1958) Allied Artists
The wealthy, eccentric owner of a
haunted house offers a group of
strangers a fortune if they spend one
entire night in his ghost-infested domi-
cile. While doing so, they are terror-
ized by decapitated human heads,
crashing chandeliers, and enormous
vats of lye in what appears to be an
elaborate ruse to kill the homeowner's
wife, the latest in a long line who
seem to meet bad ends. *Saturday the
14th* (1981) sends up this Price
spooker. **Cast:** Vincent Price, Carol
Ohmart, Alan Marshal, Richard Long,

House on Haunted Hill (1958)

Carolyn Craig, Elisha Cook, Julie
Mitchum, Leona Anderson, Howard
Hoffman. **Credits:** Dir: William Castle;
Prod: William Castle; Writer: Robb
White; DP: Carl E. Guthrie; Ed: Roy V.
Livingston; Composer: Von Dexter;
SFX: Herman E. Townsley. B&W, 75
min. VHS, LASER

The House on 92nd Street
(1945) Fox
A groundbreaking film for its docudrama feel, this depicts counterespionage efforts against Nazi spies in
New York, and was produced with the
cooperation of the F.B.I. using actual
locations. The story's based on an
incident in which Nazi agents
attempted to steal atom bomb secrets
and adds newsreel footage for atmo-
sphere and authenticity. **Academy
Awards:** Best Original Story. **Cast:**
William Eythe, Lloyd Nolan, Signe
Hasso, Gene Lockhart, Leo G. Carroll,
Lydia St. Clair, Harry Bellaver, Reed
Hadley, William Post, Jr. **Credits:** Dir:
Henry Hathaway; Prod: Louis de
Rochemont; Writer: Barre Lyndon,
Charles G. Booth, John Monks, Jr.;
Story: Charles G. Booth; DP: Norbert
F. Brodine; Ed: Harmon Jones; Prod
Design: Lyle Wheeler, Lewis Creber;
Composer: David Buttolph, Emil New-
man. B&W, 89 min. VHS

The Howards of Virginia
(1940) Columbia
A grand historical epic about a Virginia
couple (Grant and Scott) from differing
backgrounds during the Revolutionary

War. Their families' growing involvement in the conflict force them to
choose between their feelings for one
another and their differing political
beliefs. Quite interesting if you're fascinated by all things Colonial, but otherwise pretty standard. Academy
Award Nominations: 2, including Best
Score. **Cast:** Cary Grant, Martha
Scott, Cedric Hardwicke, Alan Marshal, Richard Carlson, Paul Kelly, Irving Bacon, Elisabeth Risdon, Anne
Revere, Tom Drake. **Credits:** Dir: Frank
Lloyd; Prod: Frank Lloyd; Writer: Sidney Buchman; DP: Bert Glennon; Ed:
Paul Weatherwax; Prod Design: John
B. Goodman; Composer: Richard
Hageman. B&W, 117 min. VHS

How Green Was My Valley
(1941) Fox
Ford's vivid recounting of a childhood
spent in the lush hills of Wales. A
Welsh coal-mining family experiences
labor unrest and personal tragedy as
their traditional way of life collides
with the 20th century. Beautifully
realized and deeply felt portrayal of
the sustaining power of home and
family. And O'Hara was never lovelier.
The Oscars have solidified its place in
history as one of the top tearjerkers
of all time. Adapted from Richard
Llewellyn's best-selling novel. Academy Award Nominations: 10, including
Best Supporting Actress: Sara Allgood; Best Screenplay. **Academy
Awards:** Best Director; Best Supporting Actor: Donald Crisp; Best Black-
and-White Cinematography; Best

Black-and-White Interior Decoration; Best Picture. **Cast:** Walter Pidgeon, Maureen O'Hara, Donald Crisp, Anna Lee, Roddy McDowall, John Loder, Sara Allgood, Barry Fitzgerald, Patric Knowles, Rhys Williams. **Credits:** Dir: John Ford; Prod: Darryl F. Zanuck; Writer: Philip Dunne, Richard Llewellyn; DP: Arthur Miller; Ed: James B. Clark; Prod Design: Nathan Juran, Thomas Little; Composer: Alfred Newman; Costumes: Gwen Wakeling; Art Director: Richard Day. B&W, 118 min. **VHS, LASER**

How the West Was Won
(1962) MGM
Epic, episodic tale of the development of the American West from the 1830s through the Civil War to the end of the century, as seen through the eyes of the pioneer Prescott family. As the Prescotts struggle with danger and loss, and newfound love, the vast canvas of U.S. manifest destiny unfolds around them. The breadth of the material required the contributions of the three greatest Western directors, Ford, Hathaway, and Marshall. With top-notch production values and a "who's who" of Hollywood stars, it was projected theatrically in the three-screen Cinerama process. The letterbox version on the laserdisc approximates the sweep of the gigantic Cinerama screen. Academy Award Nominations: 8, including Best Picture; Best Cinematography; Best Score.

Academy Awards: Best Film Editing; Best Sound; Best Story/Screenplay Written Directly for the Screen. **Cast:** Robert Preston, Henry Fonda, Debbie Reynolds, James Stewart, Carroll Baker, Lee J. Cobb, Carolyn Jones, Karl Malden, Gregory Peck, George Peppard. **Credits:** Dir: John Ford, Henry Hathaway, George Marshall; Prod: Bernard Smith; Writer: James R. Webb; DP: Joseph La Shelle, Charles B. Lang, William Daniels, Milton Krasner, Harold Wellman; Ed: Harold F. Kress; Prod Design: George W. Davis, William Ferrari, Addison Hehr; Composer: Alfred Newman, Ken Darby. Color, 166 min. **VHS, LASER, DVD**

How to Commit Marriage
(1969) Cinerama
Above-average Hope fare about a one-time model couple who, after 19 years of apparent bliss, have decided to call it quits. The only trouble is that no one remembered to call their daughter. The fun begins when she arrives home with plans to marry Gleason's son, a wacky musician. The groovy humor seems antique, but there's an ironic chuckle or two. **Cast:** Bob Hope, Jackie Gleason, Jane Wyman, Maureen Arthur, Tim Matheson, Leslie Nielsen, Tina Louise, Irwin Corey, Paul Stewart, Joanna Cameron. **Credits:** Dir: Norman Panama; Prod: Bill Lawrence; Writer: Ben Starr, Michael Kanin; DP: Charles B. Lang; Composer: Joseph J. Lilley. Color, 98 min. **VHS**

How to Marry a Millionaire
(1953) Fox
Monroe, Bacall, and Grable conspire to nab a millionaire husband. They pool their resources and rent an expensive penthouse in an attempt to lure in their likely prey. Powell tries to slip the noose. The glamorous trio bring Johnson's hysterical script (based on *The Greeks Had a Word for Them*, 1932) to life. Academy Award Nominations: Best Costumes. **Cast:** Marilyn Monroe, Betty Grable, Lauren Bacall, William Powell, Cameron Mitchell, David Wayne, Rory Calhoun, Alex D'Arcy, Fred Clark, George Dunn. **Credits:** Dir: Jean Negulesco; Prod: Nunnally Johnson; Writer: Nunnally Johnson; DP: Joseph MacDonald; Ed: Louis Loeffler; Prod Design: Lyle Wheeler, Leland Fuller; Composer: Alfred Newman, Cyril J. Mockridge. Color, 96 min. **VHS, LASER**

How to Murder Your Wife
(1965) United Artists
Cartoonist Lemmon, a confirmed bachelor, attends a party one evening and is bewitched by a blond Italian knockout (Lisi) who pops out of a cake. He marries her on the spot. Though his new wife is a happy homemaker, Lemmon has no stomach for domestic bliss. Known for acting out his hero's scenarios before putting ink to page, he stages her murder and sketches a cartoon based on the scheme. When his wife sees the funny pages, she is frightened and vanishes. Mission accomplished. Not so fast, however, as the police appear and now want to ask him a few questions about his wife's whereabouts. **Cast:** Jack Lemmon, Virna Lisi, Terry-Thomas, Eddie Mayehoff, Sidney Blackmer, Claire Trevor, Max Showalter, Jack Albertson, Alan Hewitt, Mary Wickes. **Credits:** Dir: Richard Quine; Prod: George Axelrod; Writer: George Axelrod; DP: Harry Stradling; Ed: David Wages; Prod Design: Richard Sylbert; Composer: Neal Hefti. Color, 119 min. **VHS, LASER**

How to Steal a Million
(1966) Fox
A million-dollar art museum heist is the chewy center of this chocolate truffle as the dashing O'Toole and precious Hepburn pair off in an aristocratic romantic comedy. The daughter of a Parisian art collector (Hepburn), in truth a forger, unwittingly solicits the aid of a man she believes to be a thief (O'Toole) to steal a famous "Cellini Venus" statue—sculpted by her grandfather—from a museum. But

How to Marry a Millionaire (1953)

in actuality, the "thief" is a private detective specializing in exposing forgeries. The chemistry of the two leads makes this well worth the watch. **Cast:** Audrey Hepburn, Peter O'Toole, Hugh Griffith, Charles Boyer, Eli Wallach, Fernand Gravet, Marcel Dalio, Jacques Marin. **Credits:** Dir: William Wyler; Prod: Fred Kohlmar; Writer: Harry Kurnitz; DP: Charles B. Lang; Ed: Robert W. Swink; Prod Design: Alexander Trauner; Composer: Johnny Williams. Color, 127 min. **VHS**

How to Succeed in Business Without Really Trying

(1967) United Artists
Using his wits—and a dog-eared paperback—to guide him, a window washer takes a stab at success in the corporate world. In short order, he goes from the mail room to the sales office to the boardroom as a top executive at Vallee's Worldwide Wicket Co. But he discovers that making it in business isn't all it's cracked up to be, as he finds himself dodging vengeful superiors, back-stabbing underlings, and a buxom secretary. Energetic update of the successful Broadway play. **Cast:** Robert Morse, Michele Lee, Rudy Vallee, Anthony Teague, Maureen Arthur, Sammy Smith, Murray Matheson, John Myhers. **Credits:** Dir: David Swift; Prod: David Swift; Writer: David Swift; DP: Burnett Guffey; Ed: Ralph E. Winters, Allan Jacobs; Prod Design: Robert Boyle; Composer: Nelson Riddle. Color, 121 min. **VHS, LASER**

Huckleberry Finn

(1931) Paramount
Riverfront waif Huckleberry Finn fails at school, competes with friend Tom Sawyer for Becky Thatcher's affections, and—in order to flee his drunken father—takes off down the river with Tom on a small raft. On the water, the two meet a pair of gamblers recently thrown off a steamboat who tell the boys they are a king and duke. In Huckleberry's absence, his father is accused of killing him and Huckleberry rushes back to save him. Meanwhile, Aunt Polly becomes a candidate for the custody of Huck. Early talkie follow-up to *Tom Sawyer* of previous year. **Cast:** Jackie Coogan, Junior Durkin, Mitzi Green, Jackie Searl, Eugene Pallette, Clarence Muse, Clara Blandwick, Jane Darwell, Oscar Apfel, Warner Richmond. **Credits:** Dir: Norman Taurog; Writer: Grover Jones, William Stevens McNutt; Story: Mark Twain. B&W, 79 min.

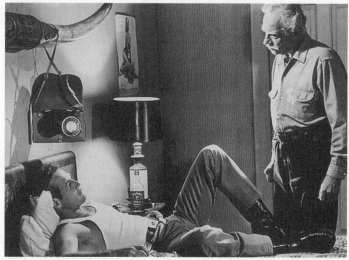

Hud (1963)

The Hucksters

(1947) MGM
Kerr made her American debut in this drama about the advertising business. The story pits Gable, an ex-G.I. who returned from the war with ideals, against the ranks of yes-men vying for the approval of a sadistic soap tycoon (Greenstreet). Kerr and Gardner vie for his attention when he's not busy fighting the agency wars. **Cast:** Clark Gable, Deborah Kerr, Sydney Greenstreet, Adolphe Menjou, Ava Gardner, Keenan Wynn, Edward Arnold, Aubrey Mather, Richard Gaines, Frank Albertson. **Credits:** Dir: Jack Conway; Prod: Arthur Hornblow, Jr.; Writer: Luther Davis, Edward Chodorov, George Wells; Story: Frederic Wakeman; DP: Harold Rosson; Ed: Frank Sullivan; Prod Design: Cedric Gibbons, Urie McCleary; Composer: Lennie Hayton. B&W, 116 min. **VHS, LASER**

Hud

(1963) Paramount
A career-defining role for Newman as Hud Bannon, a worthless heel whose womanizing, drinking, and arrogance constantly pit him against his father, Homer (Douglas). Widening the rift between the two is an incident that occurred 15 years ago, which resulted in the death of Hud's brother, Norman. The discord between father and son erupts when Homer desperately needs his son's help. Hud makes a bad situation even worse by romantically pursuing family housekeeper Neal. Hated by everyone—maybe even himself—Hud is clearly on a downward spiral, heading for a

life of even more loneliness and pain. Based on Larry McMurtry's novel *Horseman, Pass By*. Stark, haunting cinematography by Howe. Academy Award Nominations: 7, including Best Actor: Paul Newman; Best Director; Best Screenplay. **Academy Awards:** Best Actress: Patricia Neal; Best Supporting Actor: Melvyn Douglas; Best Black-and-White Cinematography. **Cast:** Paul Newman, Patricia Neal, Melvyn Douglas, Brandon De Wilde, John Ashley, Whit Bissell, Crahan Denton, Val Avery, Sheldon Allman. **Credits:** Dir: Martin Ritt; Prod: Martin Ritt, Irving Ravetch; Writer: Irving Ravetch, Harriet Farnk, Jr.; Story: Larry McMurtry; DP: James Wong Howe; Ed: Frank Bracht; Prod Design: Hal Pereira, Tambi Larsen; Composer: Elmer Bernstein. B&W, 112 min. **VHS, LASER**

Hudson's Bay

(1940) Fox
An adventure story about the formation of the Hudson Bay trading company. Muni plays Pierre Radisson who, along with his mountainous friend Cregar, sets off into Canada to gather furs in hopes of starting a trading company. When the French governor tries to grab their furs, they set off for England and get the help of King Charles for the backing of their business. Again they head off to Hudson's Bay to gather up more furs, bringing along with them an English troublemaker who ends up selling brandy to the Indians. Expensively mounted historical adventure in a setting that feels remote in more than

geography. **Cast:** Paul Muni, Gene Tierney, Laird Cregar, John Sutton, Virginia Field, Nigel Bruce, Vincent Price, Morton Lowry, Robert Greig, Chief Thundercloud. **Credits:** Dir: Irving Pichel; Prod: Kenneth MacGowan; Writer: Lamar Trotti; DP: J. Peverell Marley; Ed: Robert Simpson; Prod Design: Richard Day, Wiard Ihnen; Composer: Alfred Newman. B&W, 95 min.

The Human Comedy
(1943) MGM
Small-town life during WWII illuminated by Saroyan's story and Rooney's performance. The sentimental story depicts a telegram delivery boy (Rooney) whose messages almost always spell disaster. The lad learns about life from his widowed mother and philosophical old boss. One of Rooney's best roles. Stay away from the colorized version. Academy Award Nominations: 5, including Best Picture; Best Director; Best Actor: Mickey Rooney. **Academy Awards:** Best Original Story. **Cast:** Mickey Rooney, Frank Morgan, Fay Bainter, James Craig, Robert Mitchum, Donna Reed, Marsha Hunt, Jackie Jenkins, Ray Collins, Van Johnson. **Credits:** Dir: Clarence Brown; Prod: Clarence Brown; Writer: Howard Estabrook; Story: William Saroyan; DP: Harry Stradling; Ed: Conrad A. Nervig; Prod Design: Cedric Gibbons; Choreographer: Ernst Matray; Composer: Herbert Stothart. B&W, 118 min. **VHS, LASER**

Humoresque
(1946) Warner Bros.
With the encouragment of his mother, a poor but talented violinist (Garfield) rises in the music world. But he also receives a more physical form of assistance from a wealthy, married patron of the arts with amorous intentions (Crawford). Their involvement has tragic repercussions for both of them. High-class melodrama scripted by Odets. Academy Award Nominations: Best Score. **Cast:** Joan Crawford, John Garfield, Oscar Levant, Craig Stevens, J. Carrol Naish, Joan Chandler, Tom D'Andrea, Ruth Nelson, Peggy Knudsen, Paul Cavanagh. **Credits:** Dir: Jean Negulesco; Prod: Jerry Wald; Writer: Clifford Odets, Zachary Gold; Story: Fannie Hurst; DP: Ernest Haller; Ed: Rudi Fehr; Prod Design: Hugh Reticker; Composer: Franz Waxman. B&W, 126 min. **VHS, LASER**

The Hunchback of Notre Dame
(1923) Universal
The first screen version of Hugo's 1831 novel is a silent masterpiece. Chaney's finest moment as he plays the deformed bell-ringer who is smitten by a beautiful dancing girl (Miller) persecuted by the wicked Bishop of Notre Dame. **Cast:** Lon Chaney, Patsy Ruth Miller, Ernest Torrence, Tully Marshall. **Credits:** Dir: Wallace Worsley; Writer: Edward Lowe, Perley Poore Sheehan; DP: Robert Newhard, Tony Komman. B&W, 137 min. **VHS, LASER**

The Hunchback of Notre Dame
(1939) RKO
The second and best version of Hugo's tale of the benevolent but hideous bell-ringer of Notre Dame, Quasimodo, who rescues a beautiful Gypsy girl (O'Hara) from the clutches of a sadistic bishop. Laughton evokes both pity and fear in one of his greatest performances. The Hollywood debut for O'Hara and O'Brien. Remade for TV in 1982, and as an odd Disney animated feature in 1996. Academy Award Nominations: 2. **Cast:** Charles Laughton, Maureen O'Hara, Edmond O'Brien, Cedric Hardwicke, Thomas Mitchell, Harry Davenport, Walter Hampden, Alan Marshal, George Zucco, Katherine Alexander. **Credits:** Dir: William Dieterle; Prod: Pandro S. Berman; Writer: Sonya Levien, Bruno Frank; Story: Victor Hugo; DP: Joseph H. August; Ed: William Hamilton, Robert Wise; Prod Design: Van Nest Polglase; Composer: Alfred Newman. B&W, 117 min. **VHS, LASER**

The Hurricane
(1937) United Artists
A Ford tropical fantasy and a wonderful adventure story set on an idyllic island, where a young couple (Lamour and Hall) and their clash with the local governor (Massey) are made insignificant by the impending natural disaster of the title. Newman wrote the lush film score, and the special effects are still pretty impressive. Unfortunately remade in 1979. Academy Award Nominations: Best Supporting Actor: Thomas Mitchell; Best Score. **Academy Award:** Best Sound. **Cast:** Dorothy Lamour, Jon Hall, Raymond Massey, Mary Astor, C. Aubrey Smith, Thomas Mitchell, John Carradine, Jerome Cowan. **Credits:** Dir: John Ford, Stuart Heisler; Prod: Samuel Goldwyn; Writer: Dudley Nichols, Oliver H. P. Garrett; DP: Bert Glennon; Ed: Lloyd Nosler; Prod Design: Richard Day, Alexander Golitzen; Composer: Alfred Newman. B&W, 103 min. **VHS, LASER**

Hurricane Smith
(1952) Paramount
This swashbuckling romantic comedy is set on the high seas, in blazing Technicolor. Ireland plays a pirate stranded on a desert island. He and his accomplices capture a passing slave ship to take it to Australia, where they meet scientist De Carlo. Before the hero and heroine are united, the pair navigate their way through treachery, swordfights, mutinies, a lashing at the masthead,

The Hustler (1962)

and a hunt for buried treasure. **Cast:** Yvonne De Carlo, John Ireland, James Craig, Forrest Tucker, Lyle Bettger, Richard Arlen, Mike Kellin, Murray Matheson, Henry Brandon, Emile Meyer. **Credits:** Dir: Claude Hopper; Prod: Nat Holt; Writer: Frank Gruber; Story: Gordon Ray Young; DP: Ray Rennahan; Ed: Frank Bracht; Composer: Paul Sawtell; Art Director: Hal Pereira, Walter Tyler. Color, 90 min.

Hush...Hush, Sweet Charlotte

(1965) Fox

Two Hollywood grande dames rejuvenate their careers in a chilling story of a reclusive spinster (de Havilland) haunted by memories of her murdered fiancé (Cotten). When the state decides to tear down her mansion, she calls on her cousin (Davis) for help, but ends up fighting for her sanity instead. As the 37 years of nightmares continue to haunt her, she discovers the truth of what really happened. Originally intended as a follow-up to *Whatever Happened to Baby Jane?* (1962), the celebrity death match between Davis and Crawford, this actually benefits from de Havilland's more restrained performance. **Cast:** Bette Davis, Olivia de Havilland, Joseph Cotten, Agnes Moorehead, Mary Astor, Bruce Dern, Victor Buono, Cecil Kellaway, William Campbell, Wesley Addy. **Credits:** Dir: Robert Aldrich; Prod: Robert Aldrich; Writer: Henry Farrell, Lukas Heller; DP: Joseph Biroc; Ed: Michael Luciano; Prod Design: William Glasgow; Composer: Frank DeVol. Color, 133 min. **VHS**

Hush . . . Hush, Sweet Charlotte (1965)

The Hustler

(1962) Fox

An arrogant and amoral hustler haunts poolrooms skinning suckers waiting to get a crack at bringing down Minnesota Fats. When he starts to have real feelings for a woman, he's faced with a dilemma. To pick up Fast Eddie's story years later, see *The Color of Money* (1987), an excellent sequel for which Newman won the Best Actor Oscar. Academy Award Nominations: 9, including Best Picture; Best Director; Best Actor: Paul Newman; Best Adapted Screenplay. **Academy Awards:** Best Black-and-White Cinematography; Best Art Direction—Set Decoration (B&W). **Cast:** Paul Newman, Jackie Gleason, Piper Laurie, George C. Scott, Myron McCormick, Murray Hamilton, Michael Constantine, Stefan Gierasch, Jake LaMotta. **Credits:** Dir: Robert Rossen; Prod: Robert Rossen; Writer: Sidney Carroll, Robert Rossen; Story: Walter S. Tevis; DP: Eugen Schufftan; Ed: Dede Allen; Prod Design: Harry Horner; Composer: Kenyon Hopkins. B&W, 134 min. **VHS, LASER**

I Am a Fugitive from a Chain Gang

(1932) Warner Bros.
Groundbreaking docudrama with hard-hitting performance by Muni as a victim of a legal injustice. When WWI vet Muni tramps the country, he finds a place on a Georgia chain gang after befriending a stick-up man. After escaping, he becomes hardened by life on the run. Based on Robert E. Burns's autobiographical story, this is a still-powerful portrait of the little guy battling injustice, and an insight into Depression-era America. Selected for the National Film Registry. Academy Award Nominations: 3, Best Picture; Best Actor: Paul Muni; Best Sound. **Cast:** Paul Muni, Glenda Farrell, Helen Vinson, Preston Foster, Allen Jenkins, Berton Churchill, Edward Ellis, Edward J. Macnamara, John Wray, Hale Hamilton. **Credits:** Dir: Mervyn LeRoy; Prod: Hal B. Wallis; Writer: Howard J. Green, Brown Holmes, Sheridan Gibney; Story: Robert E. Burns; DP: Sol Polito; Ed: William Holmes; Prod Design: Jack Okey. B&W, 93 min. **VHS, LASER**

I Am the Law

(1938) Columbia
Robinson is just as tough when he walks on the right side of the law as a dynamic law professor who's drafted by civic leaders to act as special prosecutor and put an end to the city's gangster activity. When all his witnesses turn up dead, the professor uses his students for help and eventually points the finger at the civic leader for being involved with the rackets all along. Not exactly a surprising movie but plenty entertaining. **Cast:** Edward G. Robinson, Otto Kruger, John Beal, Wendy Barrie, Marc Lawrence, Barbara O'Neil, Arthur Loft, Douglas Wood, Robert Middlemass, Ivan Miller. **Credits:** Dir: Alexander Hall; Prod: Everett Riskin; Writer: Jo Swerling; DP: Henry Freulich; Ed: Viola

Lawrence; Prod Design: Stephen Goosson, Lionel Banks; Costumes: Robert Kalloch. B&W, 83 min. **VHS, LASER**

I Can Get It for You Wholesale

(1951) Fox
This adaptation of the rag-trade novel by Weidman later became the basis for a Broadway musical that introduced young Barbra Streisand to the world singing "Mrs. Marmelstein." Hayward plays a young runway model with aspirations to become owner of her own fashion company. She starts her own firm, but nearly drops her new partnership when Sanders sweeps her off her feet and promises to make her a world-famous fashion designer. **Cast:** Susan Hayward, Dan Dailey, George Sanders, Sam Jaffe, Randy Stuart, Marvin Kaplan, Harry Von Zell, Barbara Whiting, Vicki Cummings, Ross Elliot. **Credits:** Dir: Michael Gordon; Prod: Sol Siegel; Writer: Vera Caspary, Abraham Polonsky; Story: Jerome Weidman; DP: Milton Krasner; Ed: Robert Simpson; Prod Design: John De Cuir, Lyle Wheeler; Composer: Sol Kaplan. B&W, 90 min.

Iceland

(1942) Fox
The setting provides a lift to the standard Henie romantic musical. Icelandic girl Henie falls for a Marine (Payne) stationed on the island while singing and flashing her skates. She pledges to marry Payne so that her little sister can make her own marriage plans. Now she has to convince Payne. The songs help: "There Will Never Be Another You," Lover's Knot," "You Can't Say No to a Soldier," and more. **Cast:** Sonja Henie, John Payne, Jack Oakie, Felix Bressart, Osa Massen, Joan Merrill, Fritz Feld, Sterling Holloway, Adeline de Walt Reynolds, Ludwig Stossel. **Credits:** Dir: H. Bruce Humberstone; Prod: William LeBaron; Writer: Helen Logan; DP: Arthur Miller;

Ed: James B. Clark; Prod Design: Richard Day; Composer: Emil Newman. B&W, 80 min. **VHS**

The Iceman Cometh

(1973) American Film Theatre
Based on O'Neill's play set in 1912. The defeated, apathetic patrons of Harry Hope's Bar live through their memories. Enter Hickey, a hardware salesman, who stops by once a year to check in. As he points out each person's problems, he makes them confront their demons, assuring them that only through self-reflection can they become alive again. When they realize that he destroyed his demons by killing his own wife, the barflies return safely to their dreams and memories. At four hours, this is a challenging work, but the performances, Frankenheimer's unobtrusive direction, and O'Neill's words make it a worthwile investment. **Cast:** Lee Marvin, Fredric March, Robert Ryan, Jeff Bridges, Bradford Dillman, Sorrell Booke, Hildy Brooks, Nancy Juno Dawson, Evans Evans, Martin Green. **Credits:** Dir: John Frankenheimer; Prod: Ely Landau; Writer: Eugene O'Neill, Thomas Quinn Curtiss; DP: Ralph Woolsey; Ed: Harold F. Kress; Prod Design: Jack Marton Smith. Color, 239 min.

Ice Palace

(1960) Warner Bros.
The rambunctious history of the founding of the 49th state in an adaptation of the Ferber novel. Burton and Ryan go adventuring in the great white north as friends and become lifelong rivals as the developing frontier offers them opportunities. Okay historical drama, interesting mostly for the stars. **Cast:** Richard Burton, Robert Ryan, Martha Hyer, Carolyn Jones, Jim Backus, Ray Danton, Diane McBain, Karl Swenson, Shirley Knight. **Credits:** Dir: Vincent Sherman; Prod: Henry Blanke; Writer: Harry Kleiner; Story:

Edna Ferber; DP: Joseph Biroc; Ed: William Ziegler; Composer: Max Steiner; Costumes: Howard Shoup. Color, 144 min. **VHS**

Ice Station Zebra
(1968) MGM
A Cold War nail-biter from the pen of Alastair MacLean. Nuclear submarine commander Hudson cruises toward the polar ice cap, and, unwittingly, toward an international incident involving a Soviet satellite and a trap laid by British agent McGoohan. A big-budget, handsomely made espionage thriller. Academy Award Nominations: Best Cinematography; Best Special Visual Effects. **Cast:** Rock Hudson, Jim Brown, Ernest Borgnine, Tony Bill, Patrick McGoohan, Lloyd Nolan, Gerald S. O'Loughlin, Alf Kjellin, Ted Hartley, Ron Masak. **Credits:** Dir: John Sturges; Prod: Martin Ransohoff, John Calley; Writer: Douglas Heyes; DP: Daniel Fapp; Ed: Ferris Webster; Prod Design: George W. Davis, Addison Hehr; Composer: Michel Legrand. Color, 150 min. **VHS, LASER**

I Confess
(1953) Warner Bros.
A minor Hitchcock crime drama with an interesting moral dilemma at its center. Clift plays a young priest who hears the confession of a murderer who killed a blackmailer, a man who knew of Clift's youthful affair with Baxter. When the murderer ends up dead, Clift is accused of the crime, and torn between his vows of silence and the need to clear himself. Based on the play by Anthelme. **Cast:** Montgomery Clift, Anne Baxter, Karl Malden, Brian Aherne, Dolly Haas, O. E. Hasse, Roger Dann, Charles Andre, Judson Pratt. **Credits:** Dir: Alfred Hitchcock; Prod: Alfred Hitchcock; Writer: George Tabori, William Archibald; Story: Paul Anthelme; DP: Robert Burks; Ed: Rudi Fehr; Prod Design: Edward S. Haworth, George James Hopkins; Composer: Dimitri Tiomkin. B&W, 95 min. **VHS, LASER**

I Cover the Waterfront
(1933) United Artists
Lyon plays a reporter hot on the story of a fisherman suspected of smuggling Chinese immigrants into the country on his boat—wrapped in shark skins! He starts romancing the fisherman's daughter (Colbert) for the obvious journalistic reasons but you can guess what happens eventually. Hard-hitting crime drama with newsroom angle. **Cast:** Claudette Colbert, Ben Lyon, Ernest Torrence, Hobart

Cavanaugh, Maurice Black, Harry Beresford, Purnell Pratt, George Humbert. **Credits:** Dir: James Cruze; Prod: Edward Small; Writer: Wells Root, Jack Jevne; Story: Max Miller; DP: Ray June; Ed: Grant Whytock; Composer: Alfred Newman. B&W, 74 min. **VHS**

I'd Climb the Highest Mountain
(1951) Fox
A warm tale of life in rural Georgia, filmed on location and beloved by Southerners. Lundigan plays a pastor who tends a flock in the Georgia hill country. When he brings his new, city-raised wife (Hayward) to his hometown, she must overcome the local suspicions and her own misgivings to become part of the community. **Cast:** Susan Hayward, William Lundigan, Rory Calhoun, Barbara Bates, Gene Lockhart, Lynn Bari, Ruth Donnelly, Alexander Knox, Kathleen Lockhart. **Credits:** Dir: Henry King; Prod: Lamar Trotti; Writer: Lamar Trotti; DP: Edward Cronjager; Ed: Barbara McLean; Prod Design: Lyle Wheeler, Maurice Ransford; Composer: Sol Kaplan. Color, 88 min. **VHS**

Idiot's Delight
(1939) MGM
Musical comedy plays eerily as WWII hovers just on the horizon. *Grand Hotel*-like plot finds a munitions profiteer (Arnold) and his phony Russian countess companion (Shearer, in a Garboesque role) thrown together with a hoofer (Gable)—her ex-boyfriend—in an Italian hotel. This features the legendary sequence of Gable attempting a song-and-dance routine to "Puttin' On the Ritz." The antiwar message from Sherwood's Pulitzer-winning play peeks through now and again. **Cast:** Clark Gable, Norma Shearer, Edward Arnold, Charles Coburn, Burgess Meredith, Joseph Schildkraut, Laura Hope Crews, Skeets Gallagher, Pat Paterson, Fritz Feld. **Credits:** Dir: Clarence Brown; Prod: Hunt Stromberg; Writer: Robert E. Sherwood; DP: William Daniels; Ed: Robert J. Kern; Prod Design: Cedric Gibbons, Wade B. Rubottom; Composer: Herbert Stothart. B&W, 107 min. **VHS, LASER**

I Dream Too Much
(1935) RKO
Opera star Pons plays a singer whose dreams of stardom come true when she falls in love with Fonda, a young composer. Unfortunately, after he pushes her to success, their love affair is marred by jealousy. Pons was

cast in response to Columbia's successful launching of opera singer Grace Moore's screen career. Early role for Ball as a tourist. Academy Award Nomination for Best Sound Recording. **Cast:** Lily Pons, Henry Fonda, Eric Blore, Osgood Perkins, Lucille Ball, Lucien Littlefield, Esther Dale, Mischa Auer, Paul Porcasi. **Credits:** Dir: John Cromwell; Prod: Pandro S. Berman; Writer: James Gow, Edmund H. North; DP: David Abel; Ed: William Morgan; Prod Design: Van Nest Polglase; Composer: Jerome Kern, Dorothy Fields. B&W, 97 min. **VHS**

If I Had A Million
(1932) Paramount
This episodic fantasy studies the personal effects of capricious fortune. An ailing wealthy man gives a million dollars each to strangers randomly chosen from the phone book rather than watch grasping relatives wait for him to die. The results are portrayed by luminaries such as Lubitsch, Taurog, Laughton, and W. C. Fields. Downtrodden employees, streetwalkers, golden-agers, and sick-of-it-all drivers deliver triumphant raspberries to their oppressors, a forger literally can't give it away, a condemned man still dies, and a Marine thinks it an April Fool's prank. Perfect example of Depression-era wish-fulfillment genre. **Cast:** Gary Cooper, W. C. Fields, Gertrude Norman, George Raft, Ernest Truex, Wynne Gibson, Emma Tansey, Charles Laughton, William V. Mong, Jack Oakie, Margaret Seddon. **Credits:** Dir: Ernst Lubitsch, Norman Taurog, Stephen Roberts, Norman Z. McLeod, James Cruze, William A. Seiter, H. Bruce Humberstone, Lothar Mendes; Prod: Louis D. Lighton; Writer: Claude Binyon, Whitney Bolton, Malcolm Stuart Boyland, John Bright, Sidney Buchanan, Lester Cole, Isabel Dawn, Boyce DeGaw, Walter DeLeon, Oliver H. P. Garrett, Harvey Gates, Grover Jones, Ernst Lubitsch, Lawton Mackall, Joseph L. Mankiewicz, William Slavens McNutt, Seton I. Miller, Robert Sparks, Toffany Thayer. B&W, 88 min.

If It's Tuesday, This Must Be Belgium
(1969) MGM
Nine countries in 18 days and we see them all in this jet-paced comedy. Familiar '60s TV faces (including Pleshette, Ingels, Fell) stumble through Europe on the package tour encountering cultural differences and famous personalities wherever they disembark. Dated enough to be kind

of campy fun. **Cast:** Suzanne Pleshette, Ian McShane, Mildred Natwick, Murray Hamilton, Sandy Baron, Michael Constantine, Norman Fell, Peggy Cass, Joan Collins, Marty Ingels. **Credits:** Dir: Mel Stuart; Prod: Stan Margulies; Writer: David Shaw; DP: Vilis Lapenieks, Fritz Roland; Ed: David Saxon; Prod Design: Marc Frederix; Composer: Walter Scharf. Color, 141 min. VHS, LASER

If I Were Free
(1933) RKO
Dunne and Brook are in fine form in this quality domestic melodrama as despairing lovers ensnared in bad marriages. He is a lawyer whose drinking and career are stumbling blocks to their happiness, as well as his wife's refusal to grant a divorce and the specter of the lingering, potentially fatal effects of his old war wound. Dunne's husband returns after a long absence to heighten the tension. **Cast:** Irene Dunne, Clive Brook, Nils Asther, Henry Stephenson, Vivian Tobin, Tempe Pigott, Lorraine MacLean, Laura Hope Crews, Halliwell Hobbs. **Credits:** Dir: Elliott Nugent; Prod: Merian C. Cooper, Kenneth MacGowan; Writer: Dwight Taylor; Story: John Van Druten; DP: Edward Cronjager; Ed: Arthur Roberts; Composer: Max Steiner; Art Director: Charles Kirk, Van Nest Polglase. B&W, 65 min.

If I Were King
(1938) Paramount
The great writer-director Preston Sturges called the screenplay of this classic period piece one of his greatest accomplishments. The lavishly produced epic sets real-life rogue and poet François Villon (Colman) on a fictional adventure in the court of Louis XI (Rathbone) of France. After killing a government official in a fair, if drunken, fight, Villon is hauled before the King. The hard-drinking man of letters proves a match for the king's wicked wit and he ends up saving his head and gains the hand of the beautiful lady-in-waiting Katherine de Vaucelles (Dee). **Cast:** Ronald Colman, Basil Rathbone, Frances Dee, Ellen Drew, C. V. France, Henry Wilcoxon, Heather Thatcher, Stanley Ridges, Bruce Lester, Alma Lloyd. **Credits:** Dir: Frank Lloyd; Prod: Frank Lloyd, Louise Smith; Writer: Preston Sturges, Justin Huntly McCarthy; DP: Theodor Sparkuhl; Ed: Hugh Bennett; Prod Design: Hans Dreier, John Goodman; Composer: Richard Hageman. B&W, 100 min.

I. F. Stone's Weekly
(1973)
A documentary portrait of Isadore Feinstein Stone, the maverick publisher intent on exposing the ignorance and hypocrisy of American government officials. He established his own weekly newsletter in 1952, which he finally abandoned in 1971 in order to write for the *New York Review of Books*. The footage includes selected speeches as well as personal interviews, giving the viewer insight into the mind of one of America's last muckrakers. **Cast:** I. F. Stone, Tom Wicker. **Credits:** Dir: Jerry Bruck, Jr.; Prod: Jerry Bruck, Jr.; DP: Jerry Bruck, Jr.; Ed: Jerry Bruck, Jr. B&W, 62 min.

If You Could Only Cook
(1935) Columbia
In this screwball comedy version of a gangster picture, Arthur, a lovely poor girl with a heart of gold, enlists the aid of not-so-nerdy automobile inventor, Marshall, to infiltrate a mobster's estate. Disguising themselves as servants, the sleuthing partners fall in love and zany events follow. Even gangster boss Carrillo gets a happy ending. **Cast:** Herbert Marshall, Jean Arthur, Leo Carrillo, Lionel Stander, Anthony Edwards, Frieda Inescort, Gene Morgan, Ralf Harolde, Matt McHugh, Richard Powell. **Credits:** Dir: William A. Seiter; Prod: Everett Riskin; Writer: Howard J. Green, Gertrude Purcell, Hugh Herbert; DP: John Stumar; Ed: Gene Havlick; Prod Design: Stephen Goosson. B&W, 70 min.

If You Knew Susie
(1948) RKO
Every down-on-his-luck hoofer's dream comes true for Cantor and Davis. Aging vaudevillians find a will—signed by George Washington (we're in fantasyland here, folks)—that makes the team heirs to an immense fortune. Lots of music-hall vintage song and dance, anyway, including the title song, "We're Living the Life We Love," "My Brooklyn Love Song," "My How the Time Goes By," and more. **Cast:** Eddie Cantor, Joan Davis, Allyn Joslyn, Charles Dingle, Phil Brown, Bobby Driscoll, Sheldon Leonard, Joe Sawyer, Douglas Fowley. **Credits:** Dir: Gordon Douglas; Prod: Eddie Cantor; Writer: Oscar Brodney, Warren Wilson, Bud Pearson, Lester A. White; DP: Frank Redman; Ed: Philip Martin; Prod Design: Albert S. D'Agostino, Ralph Berger; Composer: Edgar Fairchild. B&W, 90 min. VHS

I Live My Life
(1935) MGM
Another patented Crawford performance as a bored, wealthy socialite who falls in love with a dedicated archaeologist. Already engaged, she must choose between wedded bliss with the poor scholar she now loves or the comfortable life of cocktail parties, shopping, and butlers she would have with her rich, socially correct fiancé. A stylish but lightweight effort. Note Mankiewicz among the scribes. **Cast:** Joan Crawford, Brian Aherne, Frank Morgan, Aline MacMahon, Eric Blore, Jessie Ralph, Arthur Treacher, Hedda Hopper, Etienne Girardot, Edward Brophy. **Credits:** Dir: W. S. Van Dyke; Prod: Bernard Hyman; Writer: Joseph L. Mankiewicz, Gottfried Reinhardt, Ethel Borden; DP: George J. Folsey; Ed: Tom Held; Prod Design: Cedric Gibbons; Composer: Dimitri Tiomkin; Costumes: Adrian. B&W, 97 min. VHS

I'll Cry Tomorrow
(1955) MGM
Another of Hayward's signature portrayals of a suffering woman who finds reserves of pride and strength. This biopic of actress Lillian Roth based on her memoir follows her roller-coaster life and career through bad marriages and battles with the bottle. Hayward won the Best Actress award at Cannes. Songs include: "When the Red, Red Robin Comes Bob, Bob Bobbin' Along," "Happiness Is a Thing Called Joe," and "Sing You Sinners." Academy Award Nominations: 4, including Best Actress: Susan Hayward. **Cast:** Susan Hayward, Richard Conte, Jo Van Fleet, Eddie Albert, Don Taylor, Ray Danton, Margo, Virginia Gregg, Don "Red" Barry. **Credits:** Dir: Daniel Mann; Prod: Lawrence Weingarten; Writer: Helen Deutsch, Jay Richard Kennedy; DP: Arthur E. Arling; Ed: Harold F. Kress; Prod Design: Cedric Gibbons, Malcolm F. Brown; Composer: Alex North. B&W, 120 min. VHS, LASER

Illicit
(1931) Warner Bros.
Early talkie and early role for Stanwyck. A romantic adventuress fears that marriage to Rennie will cramp her style, which, of course, it does. Each finds solace in others' arms. Fans of screen divas will want to compare Bette Davis in the same role in *Ex-Lady* (1933). **Cast:** Barbara Stanwyck, James Rennie, Ricardo Cortez, Joan Blondell, Charles Butterworth, Natalie Moorhead, Claude Gillingwater. **Cred-**

its: Dir: Archie Mayo; Writer: Harvey Thew; DP: Robert Kurrle. B&W, 81 min. **VHS**

The Illustrated Man
(1969) Warner Bros.
Steiger plays a man tattooed from head to toe in this sci-fi fantasy based on a collection of stories by Bradbury. The "illustrated man" searches for the woman who painted him (Bloom). During his trek, the drifter meets a young man, who envisions three futuristic science-fiction tales, each based on a different tattoo: "The Long Rain," "The Veldt," and "The Last Night of the World." **Cast:** Rod Steiger, Claire Bloom, Robert Drivas, Jason Evers, Don Dubbins, Tim Weldon, Christie Matchett. **Credits:** Dir: Jack Smight; Prod: Howard B. Kreitsek, Ted Mann; Writer: Howard B. Kreitsek; Story: Ray Bradbury; DP: Philip H. Lathrop; Composer: Jerry Goldsmith. Color, 103 min. **VHS**

I Love Melvin
(1953) MGM
A perky musical comedy with O'Connor as a guy Friday at *Look* magazine who poses as their famous photographer in order to impress Reynolds, an aspiring screen queen who desperately wants to be on the cover. Songs include "A Lady Loves," "I Wanna Wander," "Life Has Its Funny Ups and Downs," and "Where Did You Learn to Dance?" **Cast:** Donald O'Connor, Debbie Reynolds, Una Merkel, Allyn Joslyn, Jim Backus, Richard Anderson, Noreen Corcoran, Les Tremayne, Barbara Ruick, Robert Taylor. **Credits:** Dir: Don Weis; Prod: George Wells; Writer: George Wells, Ruth Brookes Flippen; Story: Laszlo Vadnay; DP: Harold Rosson; Ed: Adrienne Fazan; Prod Design: Cedric Gibbons, Jack Martin Smith, Eddie Imazu; Composer: Skip Martin, George Stoll. Color, 76 min. **VHS**

I Love You Again
(1940) MGM
Powell and Loy take a break from Thin Man pairings to work their screwball magic in this delightful comedy about a fuddy-duddy, small-town businessman who's about to be divorced by his fed-up wife when a head injury cures his previously unsuspected amnesia. Though Powell recalls that he's a big-city con man with a dynamic personality, he still loves Loy, and has to figure out which life to choose. Lots of laughs from both the situation and the witty dialogue. **Cast:** William Powell, Myrna Loy, Frank McHugh, Edmund Lowe, Donald Douglas, Nella Walker,

Pierre Watkin, Morgan Wallace, Charles Arnt, Harlan Briggs. **Credits:** Dir: W. S. Van Dyke; Prod: Lawrence Weingarten; Writer: Charles Lederer, George Oppenheimer, Harry Kurnitz; DP: Oliver T. Marsh; Ed: Gene Ruggiero; Prod Design: Cedric Gibbons, Daniel B. Cathcart; Composer: Franz Waxman. B&W, 99 min. **VHS**

I Love You, Alice B. Toklas
(1968) Warner Bros.
Sellers had a unique gift for multiple-personality roles, and this is one of his best as a buttoned-down, uptight lawyer who flips out and joins the hippie generation. Script by Mazursky, the Bard of the middle-age meltdown. **Cast:** Peter Sellers, Jo Van Fleet, Leigh Taylor-Young, Joyce Van Patten, David Arkin, Herb Edelman, Grady Sutton, Salem Ludwig, Louis Gottlieb. **Credits:** Dir: Hy Averback; Prod: Charles H. Maguire; Writer: Paul Mazursky, Larry Tucker; DP: Philip H. Lathrop; Ed: Robert C. Jones; Prod Design: Pato Guzman; Composer: Elmer Bernstein. Color, 93 min. **VHS, LASER**

Images
(1972) Columbia
An early Altman psycho-thriller in which York plays a mad housewife who writes children's books. She imagines she has gotten a phone call warning her about her husband's extramarital fling. When she and her husband visit their vacation cottage, she imagines that her dead lover and an artist friend have appeared. She shoots the lover only to find she has shattered her husband's camera, and knifes the artist, discovering he is actually there, but all she has murdered are her images. Filmed in Dublin and Loch Bray, Ireland, the film's vivid imagery, filmed by Zsigmond, is the high point. **Cast:** Susannah York, Rene Auberjonois, Marcel Bozzulfi, Hugh Millais, Cathryn Harrison. **Credits:** Dir: Robert Altman; Prod: Tommy Thompson; Writer: Robert Altman; Story: Susannah York; DP: Vilmos Zsigmond; Ed: Graeme Clifford; Prod Design: Leon Erickson; Composer: John Williams. Color, 101 min.

I Married a Monster from Outer Space
(1958) Paramount
Basically a reworking of *Invasion of the Body Snatchers*, this cult favorite can hold its own in the '50s paranoia hall of fame. Aliens come to earth disguised as humans to pump up the population on their home planet by procreating here on Earth. An unsus-

pecting Earthling (Talbott) marries one of the intergalactic beings and gradually catches on. **Cast:** Tom Tryon, Gloria Talbott, Ken Lynch, Maxie Rosenbloom, Robert Ivers, Valerie Allen, John Eldredge, Alan Dexter, Chuck Wassil, Ty Hungerford. **Credits:** Dir: Gene Fowler, Jr.; Prod: Gene Fowler, Jr.; Writer: Louis Vittes; DP: Haskell Boggs; Ed: George Tomasini; Prod Design: Hal Pereira, Henry Bumstead; SFX: John Fulton. B&W, 78 min. **VHS, LASER**

I Married an Angel
(1942) MGM
MacDonald and Eddy's last film together is an adaptation of a Rodgers and Hart musical about a playboy who is seduced by his dream that he's married an angel. Comes off as rather odd, but the title song and "Spring is Here" are highlights. **Cast:** Jeanette MacDonald, Nelson Eddy, Edward Everett Horton, Binnie Barnes, Reginald Owen, Douglass Dumbrille, Mona Maris, Janis Carter, Inez Cooper. **Credits:** Dir: W. S. Van Dyke; Prod: Hunt Stromberg; Writer: Anita Loos; DP: Ray June; Ed: Conrad A. Nervig; Prod Design: Cedric Gibbons, John Detlie; Composer: Richard Rodgers. B&W, 84 min. **VHS**

I Married a Witch
(1942) United Artists
A delightful comedy based on an unfinished novel by Thorne Smith, the author of *Topper*. Smith once again turns to the supernatural for comedy: A witch (Lake) and her sorcerer father who were burned at the stake several centuries ago return to the present to haunt the descendant of the man who condemned them (March). Romance ensues. One of French director Clair's few Hollywood pictures after he escaped the war. Academy Award Nomination for Best Scoring of a Dramatic or Comedic Picture. **Cast:** Fredric March, Veronica Lake, Susan Hayward, Robert Benchley, Cecil Kellaway, Elizabeth Patterson, Robert Warwick, Eily Malyon, Nora Cecil, Emory Parnell. **Credits:** Dir: Rene Clair; Prod: Preston Sturges; Writer: Robert Pirosh, Dalton Trumbo, Marc Connelly; DP: Ted Tetzlaff; Ed: Eda Warren; Prod Design: Hans Dreier, Ernst Fegte; Composer: Roy Webb. B&W, 82 min. **VHS, LASER**

I Met Him in Paris
(1937) Paramount
This romantic comedy centers around a hardworking young lady (Colbert) who has been saving for years to take her

dream trip to Paris. While in Paris, she meets a gentleman (Douglas) who falls for her and invites her to go along with him to Switzerland. Enter a playwright (Young) who also loves her. Skeptical of the other man, he decides to accompany her to Switzerland as a "chaperone." Then, of course, there is the young man she has at home. Her dream trip becomes a shopping trip for the right man. **Cast:** Claudette Colbert, Melvyn Douglas, Robert Young, Lee Bowman, Mona Barrie, George Davis, Fritz Feld, Rudolph Amendt, Alexander Cross, Louis LaBey. **Credits:** Dir: Wesley Ruggles; Prod: Adolph Zukor, Wesley Ruggles; Writer: Claude Binyon, Helen Meinardi; DP: Leo Tover; Ed: Otho Lovering; Composer: Boris Morros; Art Director: Hans Dreier, Ernst Fegte. B&W, 86 min.

I Met My Love Again
(1938) United Artists
This sentimental love story begins in a small Vermont town where two youngsters—brash, lively Bennett and serious, quiet Fonda—enjoy a fledgling romance. All is ruined when Bennett falls hopelessly for the irresistibly cosmopolitan Marshal and elopes with him to Paris. Ten years later, after her husband has drunk himself to death, Bennett brings her child back to

Vermont, where she discovers that Fonda, now a professor, hasn't married. **Cast:** Joan Bennett, Henry Fonda, Louise Platt, Alan Marshal, May Whitty, Alan Baxter, Dorothy Stickney, Tim Holt, Florence Lake, Elise Cavanna. **Credits:** Dir: Joshua Logan, Arthur Ripley; Prod: Walter Wanger; Writer: David Hertz, Allene Corliss; DP: Hal Mohr; Ed: Otho Lovering, Edward Mann; Prod Design: Alexander Toluboff; Composer: Heinz Roemheld. B&W, 77 min. **VHS**

Imitation of Life
(1934) Universal
The first adaptation of Hurst's famous melodrama of two hardworking women and their daughters. Widowed Colbert strives to provide for her daughter, translating a pancake recipe into a chain of restaurants. Her success in the business world, however, drives her away from her daughter. Beavers's daughter, meanwhile, discovers she can pass for white. Academy Award Nominations: Best Picture, Best Sound. **Cast:** Claudette Colbert, Louise Beavers, Warren William, Rochelle Hudson, Ned Sparks, Henry Armetta. **Credits:** Dir: John Stahl; Prod: Carl Laemmle; Writer: William Hurlbut; Story: Fannie Hurst; DP: Merritt Gerstad; Ed: Philip Cahn. B&W, 109 min.

Imitation of Life
(1959) Universal
Sirk's beautifully composed remake of the 1934 Colbert melodrama. If anything, Turner makes a more icily perfect star for the story of a driven actress whose passion for the stage drains her of time and affection for her daughter (Dee), who grows up mostly in the company of her warm maid (Moore) and the maid's daughter (Kohner). Both mothers come into conflict with their daughters: Turner and Dee compete for the attention of Gavin, and Moore finds that Kohner has been passing as white. No one else in Hollywood handled this kind of material as well as Sirk. Golden Globe for Best Supporting Actress: Susan Kohner. Academy Award Nomination for Best Supporting Actress: Susan Kohner. **Academy Awards:** Best Supporting Actress: Juanita Moore. **Cast:** Lana Turner, John Gavin, Sandra Dee, Dan O'Herlihy, Susan Kohner, Robert Alda, Juanita Moore, Mahalia Jackson. **Credits:** Dir: Douglas Sirk; Prod: Ross Hunter; Writer: Eleanore Griffin, Allan Scott; Story: Fannie Hurst; DP: Russell Metty; Ed: Milton Carruth; Prod Design: Alexander Golitzen, Richard H. Riedel; Composer: Frank Skinner, Joseph Gershenson. Color, 124 min. **VHS**

I'm No Angel
(1933) Universal
One of two riotous pairings of Grant and West, with Mae scoring most of the points as a circus performer who spends most of her offstage time fleecing her would-be suitors. Slippery ladies' man Grant's a more difficult catch, and the spurned West throws the whole thing into a madcap courtroom scene. Plenty of opportunity for sly double entendres as West must confront her many dalliances. **Cast:** Mae West, Cary Grant, Kent Taylor, Edward Arnold, Gregory Ratoff, Gertrude Michael, Ralf Harolde, Russell Hopton, Dorothy Peterson, William B. Davidson. **Credits:** Dir: Wesley Ruggles; Prod: William LeBaron; Writer: Mae West, Harlan Thompson; DP: Leo Tover; Ed: Otho S. Lovering; Prod Design: Hans Dreier, Bernard Herzbrun; Composer: Gladys Dubois, Harvey Brooks. B&W, 88 min. **VHS, DVD**

Impact
(1949) United Artists
Twisty crime melodrama builds real tension from standard plot of an unfaithful wife (Raines) plotting with her lover to do in the woman's wealthy husband. Neat little movie with less-often-seen cast (look for turns by

I'm No Angel (1933)

Sheilah Graham and Mae Marsh). An unusual outing for director Lubin, who more often handled costume epics or comedies (e.g., the Francis the Talking Mule series). **Cast:** Brian Donlevy, Ella Raines, Charles Coburn, Helen Walker. **Credits:** Dir: Arthur Lubin; Prod: Harry M. Popkin; Writer: Dorothy Davenport; DP: Ernest Laszlo. B&W, 111 min. VHS

The Impossible Years
(1968) MGM
Domestic comedy with Niven as a respected psychiatrist teaching at a local college. Despite having written numerous books on dealing and coping with teenage children, he finds himself unable to follow his own advice in handling his own teenage children. Based on the hit Broadway play by Bob Fisher and Arthur Marx, it features (in a bit of casting irony) TV dad Nelson in a supporting role. **Cast:** David Niven, Lola Albright, Chad Everett, Ozzie Nelson, Cristina Ferrare, Ned Wertimer, Jeff Cooper, John Harding, Michael McGreevey, Don Beddoe. **Credits:** Dir: Michael Gordon; Prod: Lawrence Weingarten; Writer: George Wells; DP: William Daniels; Ed: James E. Newcom; Composer: Don Costa; Art Director: George W. Davis, Preston Ames. Color, 92 min. VHS

In a Lonely Place
(1950) Columbia
A stinging, no-holds-barred performance from Bogart highlights this taut, noirish tale of paranoia. An unstable, temperamental screenwriter throws out a desperate emotional lifeline to starlet Grahame. She grabs on for a dangerous ride; when he's suspected of murder, she confirms his alibi and then begins to wonder if one day she might be next. The down-at-the-heels underside to Hollywood glamour sets the tone of last-chance lives being led at the margins. One of director Ray's greatest, and a marvelous role for the underappreciated Grahame, then Ray's wife. **Cast:** Humphrey Bogart, Gloria Grahame, Frank Lovejoy, Robert Warwick, Carl Benton Reid, Art Smith, Jeff Donnell, Martha Stewart, Morris Ankrum. **Credits:** Dir: Nicholas Ray; Prod: Robert Lord; Writer: Andrew Solt; DP: Burnett Guffey; Ed: Viola Lawrence; Prod Design: Robert Peterson; Composer: George Antheil. B&W, 93 min. VHS

In Caliente
(1935) Warner Bros.
This Latin-flavored song-and-dance picture is set in Agua Caliente and stars Del Rio as sexy Mexican dancer Rita

In a Lonely Place (1950)

Gomez. Without meaning to, Rita ignites a burning passion in a wise-cracking American critic, O'Brien, who's panned her act. Mucho dancing, crooning, and courting ensue, lit up by Busby Berkeley's production numbers. Songs include "To Call You My Own," "In Caliente," "Muchacha," and "The Lady in Red." **Cast:** Dolores Del Rio, Pat O'Brien, Leo Carillo, Glenda Farell, Edward Everett Horton, Phil Regan, Winifred Shaw, Dorothy Dare, Harry Holman. **Credits:** Dir: Lloyd Bacon; Prod: Edward Chodorov; Writer: Edward Chodorov, Julius J. Epstein, Jerry Wald, Ralph Block, Warren Duff; DP: Sol Polito; Ed: James Gibbon; Composer: Leo F. Forbstein, Mort Dixon, Allie Wrubel, Al Dubin, Harry Warren; Art Director: Robert M. Haas. B&W, 74 min.

Incendiary Blonde
(1945) Paramount
The real-life story of famed Jazz Age hostess Texas Guinan (Hutton) begins with young Texas struggling to make ends meet with her mother and father. Winning a rodeo championship, Texas begins a lucrative career, which leads to Broadway and national renown. Despite now being married, she gets involved with gangster Bill Kilgannon and ends up having to flee from him to Hollywood, where she embarks on a career in silent films. Later, during Prohibition, Texas returns to the East Coast where she becomes the famed "Queen of the Nightclubs." Fanciful history with plenty of period music and a colorful central character. **Cast:**

Betty Hutton, Arturo De Cordova, Charlie Ruggles, Albert Dekker, Barry Fitzgerald, Mary Phillips, Bill Goodwin, Eduardo Ciannelli, Maurice Rocco. **Credits:** Dir: George Marshall; Prod: Joseph Sistrom; Writer: Claude Binyon, Frank Butler; DP: Ray Rennehan; Ed: Archie Marshek; Prod Design: Hans Dreier, William Flannery; Composer: Robert Emmett Dolan. Color, 113 min.

The Incident
(1967) Fox
Sheen made his film debut in this gritty urban drama, which caused some controversy upon its release. Sheen and Musante terrorize a group of passengers aboard a New York City subway train late at night. The victims are more concerned with their own problems than helping each other and pray that they won't be next. Also featuring the debut of Donna Mills. **Cast:** Martin Sheen, Tony Musante, Thelma Ritter, Beau Bridges, Brock Peters, Ruby Dee, Jack Gilford, Ed McMahon, Diana Van Der Vlis, Mike Kellin. **Credits:** Dir: Larry Peerce; Prod: Monroe Sachson, Edward Meadow; Writer: Nicholas Baehr; DP: Gerald Hirschfeld; Ed: Armond Lebowitz; Prod Design: Manny Gerard; Composer: Terry Knight, Charles Fox. B&W, 107 min. VHS, LASER

In Cold Blood
(1967) Columbia
A stark, haunting re-creation of a brutally senseless killing that is as groundbreaking in film as the based-

on-fact narrative constructed by Truman Capote was in the literary world. Blake and Wilson are two wanderers who plan a robbery and merciless execution of an innocent farm family. The movie depicts their crime, their capture, and their state of mind as they await their final judgment. Hall's cinematography is at once harsh and darkly brooding; the scene in which rain on a window drains in reflection down Blake's face as he waits on death row is poetic and unsparing. Remade for TV in 1996. Academy Award Nominations: 3, including Best Director; Best (Adapted) Screenplay. **Cast:** Robert Blake, Scott Wilson, John Forsythe, Paul Stewart, Gerald S. O'Loughlin, Jeff Corey, James Flavin, Charles McGraw, John Gallaudet. **Credits:** Dir: Richard Brooks; Prod: Richard Brooks; Writer: Richard Brooks; Story: Truman Capote; DP: Conrad Hall; Ed: Peter Zinner; Prod Design: Robert Boyle; Composer: Quincy Jones. B&W, 134 min. **VHS, LASER**

The Incredible Journey
(1963) Disney
A classic Disney animal feature. Shortly after a Canadian businessman leaves on his annual hunting trip, his three pets—a Labrador retriever, a bull terrier, and a Siamese cat—trek 250 miles across Canada's forbidding wilderness to find him. Based on the book by Sheila Burnford, it was successfully remade in 1993 as *Homeward Bound: The Incredible Journey,* with the voices of Michael J. Fox, Sally Field, and Don Ameche. **Cast:** Emil Genest, John Drainie, Tommy Tweed, Sandra Scott, Syme Jago, Marion Finlayson, Robert Christie, Beth Lockerbie, Jan Rubes. **Credits:** Dir: Fletcher Markle; Prod: Walt Disney, James Algar; Writer: James Algar; DP: Kenneth Peach; Ed: Norman Palmer; Prod Design: Carroll Clark; Composer: Oliver Wallace. Color, 80 min. **VHS**

The Incredible Mr. Limpet
(1964) Warner Bros.
A family-friendly deep-sea adventure with a whimsical premise. A bespectacled bookkeeper (Knotts) loves his pet fish so much that he longs to be one. The simple life of Henry the fish, however, proves more exciting than he imagined as he falls in aquatic love and helps the U.S. Navy defeat the Nazis during WWII. Based on a novel by Theodore Pratt. **Cast:** Don Knotts, Jack Weston, Elizabeth MacRae, Andrew Duggan, Carole Cook, Larry Keating, Charles Meredith, Oscar

Beregi, Paul Frees. **Credits:** Dir: Arthur Lubin; Prod: Jack Rose; Writer: Jack Rose, Jameson Brewer, Joe DiMona; DP: Harold E. Stine. Color, 102 min. **VHS, LASER**

The Incredible Shrinking Man
(1957) Universal
When an ordinary businessman encounters a mysterious radioactive mist during a boating trip, his life takes a bizarre and frightening twist. Soon he finds he is shrinking, and within weeks he's just two inches tall; suddenly, familiar people, animals, and objects are monumentally different. This sci-fi classic boasts both an intelligent story (including the questioning finale as the brave hero faces infinity) and outstanding special effects (including a battle with a spider, armed only with a straight pin), and set a new benchmark for the genre. Scripter Matheson—a sci-fi master who also wrote scripts for *Twilight Zone* along with many noted novels and original screenplays—adapted his own novel for his first screenplay. **Cast:** Grant Williams, Randy Stuart, April Kent, Raymond Bailey, Paul Langton, William Schallert, Frank Scannell, Helene Marshall, Diana Darrin. **Credits:** Dir: Jack Arnold, Albert Zugsmith; Writer: Richard Matheson; DP: Ellis W. Carter; Ed: Al Joseph; Prod Design: Alexander Golitzen; Composer: Fred Carling, Elliot Lawrence; Art Director: Robert Clatworthy. B&W, 81 min. **VHS, LASER**

The Indian Fighter
(1955) United Artists
This grand CinemaScope Western stars Douglas as a scout leading a wagon train across dangerous Dakota Sioux territory in 1870. He tries to make peace with a Sioux leader but a secret Indian gold mine and romance with the chief's beautiful daughter (Martinelli) defeat his good intentions. Note that Hecht wrote the script. **Cast:** Kirk Douglas, Walter Matthau, Elsa Martinelli, Walter Abel, Lon Chaney, Jr., Diana Douglas. **Credits:** Dir: Andre De Toth; Prod: William Schorr; Writer: Ben Hecht; DP: Wilfrid M. Cline; Ed: Richard Cahoon; Art Director: Wiard Ihnen. Color, 88 min. **VHS**

Indian Uprising
(1951) Columbia
This cavalry picture places Montgomery, as the captain of the troops, in the middle of a dispute between white settlers and distrustful Indians. When greedy speculators plot to get their hands on the reservation's rich

gold deposits, Geronimo and his tribe declare war. **Cast:** Joe Sawyer, Robert Dover, Eddy Waller, Cliff Kennedy, George Montgomery, Audrey Long, Carl Benton Reid, Eugene Iglesias, John Baer. **Credits:** Dir: Ray Nazarro; Prod: Bernard Small; Story: Richard Schayer; DP: Ellis W. Carter; Ed: Richard Fantl; Composer: Rose DiMaggio; Art Director: Walter Holscher. Color, 75 min.

Indiscreet
(1931) United Artists
An early talkie romantic comedy directed by McCarey featuring Swanson's arching eyebrows feigning emotion, sterling examples of Deco styling, and two songs sung by Gloria. The plot involves fashion designer Swanson concealing her past romantic adventures as she attempts to keep her ex, Lyon, away from her sister. **Cast:** Gloria Swanson, Ben Lyon, Barbara Kent, Arthur Lake, Monroe Owsley, Maude Eburne, Henry Kolker, Nella Walker. **Credits:** Dir: Leo McCarey; Prod: Lew Brown, B. G. DeSylva, Ray Henderson, Joseph M. Schenck; Writer: B. G. DeSylva, Lew Brown, Ray Henderson; DP: Ray June, Gregg Toland; Ed: Hal C. Kern. B&W, 92 min. **VHS**

Indiscreet
(1958) Warner Bros.
Lilting romantic comedy with a sure-fire cast. Grant plays a dashing diplomat who can't get his flirtation with a famous actress, Bergman, out of his head. Though he maintains a fictional wife as protection from entanglement, the truth will out. Donen has a light touch for this kind of winking romance and the combination of Grant and Bergman in anything guarantees a pleasant watch. The special anniversary video edition includes the original theatrical trailer and a reproduction of the original theatrical poster. Remade as a TV movie in 1988. **Cast:** Cary Grant, Ingrid Bergman, Phyllis Calvert, Cecil Parker, David Kossoff, Megs Jenkins, Oliver Johnston, Michael Anthony. **Credits:** Dir: Stanley Donen; Prod: Stanley Donen; Writer: Norman Krasna; DP: Freddie Young; Ed: Jack Harris; Composer: Richard Rodney Bennett, Ken Jones; Art Director: Don Ashton. Color, 102 min. **VHS**

Indiscretion of an American Wife
(1953) Columbia
Rare Hollywood outing for Italian director De Sica (*The Bicycle Thief, Shoeshine*). Emotions rise, fade, shift, and turn for two illicit lovers as married

American Jones meets her lover, Clift, for the last time. The romantic turmoil plays against the rushing crowds of Rome's central railway station and we wonder about the dramas that pass by unnoticed every day in the streets. Edited heavily for the U.S. release; De Sica's 87-minute cut has been restored under the Italian title, *Terminal Station*. Academy Award Nomination for Best (Black-and-White) Costume Design. **Cast:** Jennifer Jones, Montgomery Clift, Richard Beymer, Gino Cervi, Paolo Stoppa, Clelia Matania, Maria Pia Casilio, Nando Bruno, Enrico Viarisio, Giuseppe Forelli. **Credits:** Dir: Vittorio De Sica; Prod: Vittorio De Sica; Writer: Cesare Zavattini, Luigi Chiarini, Giorgio Prosperi, Truman Capote; DP: G. R. Aldo; Ed: Eraldo da Roma, Jean Barker; Prod Design: Virgilio Marchi; Composer: Franco Ferrara. B&W, 63 min. VHS

I Never Promised You a Rose Garden
(1977) New World
An excellent, though at times disturbing, account of a teenager's struggle with schizophrenia, focusing on the intense relationship between the patient (Quinlan) and her psychiatrist (Andersson). An emotionally powerful adaptation of the autobiographical best-seller by Joanne Greenberg. Academy Award Nomination for Best (Adapted) Screenplay. **Cast:** Bibi Andersson, Kathleen Quinlan, Sylvia Sidney, Martine Bartlett, Signe Hasso, Ben Piazza, Lorraine Gary, Reni Santoni, Susan Tyrrell, Darlene Craviotto. **Credits:** Dir: Anthony Page; Prod: Terence F. Deane, Michael Hausman, Daniel H. Blatt; Writer: Lewis John Carlino, Gavin Lambert; DP: Bruce Logan; Ed: Garth Craven; Prod Design: Toby Rafelson; Composer: Paul Chihara. Color, 90 min. VHS

I Never Sang for My Father
(1970) Columbia
A fine cinematic version of Anderson's semiautobiographical stage play about a middle-aged widower, played by Hackman, who is still trying to win the approval of his distant father (Douglas). The family's old patterns emerge when Hackman's forced to choose between moving away to marry the woman he loves or staying to care for his parent. His mother and sister add their own pressures. Thoughtful drama that strikes home with emotional honesty. Academy Award Nominations: Best Actor: Melvyn Douglas; Best Supporting Actor: Gene Hackman; Best Adapted Screenplay. **Cast:** Melvyn

Douglas, Gene Hackman, Estelle Parsons, Dorothy Stickney, Elizabeth Hubbard, Lovelady Powell, Daniel Keyes, Conrad Bain. **Credits:** Dir: Gilbert Cates; Prod: Gilbert Cates; Writer: Robert Anderson; DP: Morris Hartzband, George Stoetzel; Ed: Angelo Ross; Prod Design: Hank Aldrich; Composer: Barry Mann, Al Gorgoni. Color, 90 min. VHS, LASER

The Informer
(1935) RKO
A hard-hitting Academy Award–winning drama directed by Ford. Set during the 1922 Irish Sinn Fein Rebellion, the film follows the downward spiral of a hard-drinking Dubliner (McLaglen) who informs on a fellow IRA fighter for 20 pounds that he hopes will give him passage to America. After his friend dies in custody, he drinks the reward money away and the IRA exacts its revenge. Based on a novel by Liam O'Flaherty. Academy Award Nominations: 6, including Best Picture. **Academy Awards:** Best Director; Best Actor: Victor McLaglen; Best Score; Best Screenplay. **Cast:** Victor McLaglen, Preston Foster, Margot Grahame, Wallace Ford. **Credits:** Dir: John Ford; Prod: Cliff Reid; Writer: Dudley Nichols; DP: Joseph August; Ed: George Hively; Prod Design: Van Nest Polglase, Charles Kirk; Composer: Max Steiner. B&W, 91 min. VHS, LASER

In Harm's Way
(1965) Paramount
Sprawling, messy recreation of the early days of the war in the Pacific, but the cast reads like roll call in the Hollywood Hall of Fame. The starry troop is led by hard-guy Wayne as a naval commander who has to crank up the war machine. Heaven for fans of the Duke and WWII action. Academy Award Nomination for Best (Black-and-White) Cinematography. **Cast:** John Wayne, Kirk Douglas, Henry Fonda, Patricia Neal, Carroll O'Connor, Tom Tryon, Paula Prentiss, Brandon De Wilde, Stanley Holloway, Burgess Meredith. **Credits:** Dir: Otto Preminger; Prod: Otto Preminger; Writer: Wendell Mayes; Story: James Bassett; DP: Loyal Griggs; Ed: George Tomasini, Hugh S. Fowler; Prod Design: Lyle Wheeler; Composer: Jerry Goldsmith. B&W, 165 min. VHS, LASER

Inherit the Wind
(1960) United Artists
Two of the best actors of their generation take the lead in this evergreen American drama. Generations of high school drama clubs have not dimmed

the power in the story based on the 1925 Scopes Monkey Trial that pitted the greatest lawyers and orators of the day, William Jennings Bryan and Clarence Darrow, against each other in the trial of a Tennessee biology teacher who taught the theory of evolution. Tracy (as Darrow) and March (as Bryan) give eloquent readings and are supported by a cast deep in great performers. A definitive courtroom drama, and a still-relevant piece of American history. Based on the play by Jerome Lawrence and Robert E. Lee, and remade for TV in 1988. Academy Award Nominations: 4, including Best Actor: Spencer Tracy; Best (Adapted) Screenplay. **Cast:** Spencer Tracy, Fredric March, Gene Kelly, Florence Eldridge, Dick York, Donna Anderson, Harry Morgan, Elliot Reid. **Credits:** Dir: Stanley Kramer; Prod: Stanley Kramer; Writer: Nathan E. Douglas, Harold Jacob Smith; DP: Ernest Laszlo; Ed: Frederic L. Knudtson; Prod Design: Rudolph Sternad; Composer: Ernest Gold. B&W, 128 min. VHS, LASER

The In-Laws
(1979) Warner Bros.
Falk plays a wily C.I.A. agent (or so he says) who meets his son's father-in-law-to-be, Arkin, a respected New York City dentist, just days before their children are to wed. Falk leads a mildly neurotic Arkin into a wild plot against a South American dictator-counterfeiter. Directed nimbly by Hiller, it is based on an early-career script by Bergman. Good mix of domestic comedy with action-adventure. **Cast:** Peter Falk, Alan Arkin, Ed Begley, Jr., Michael Lembeck, Nancy Dussault, Richard Libertini, Penny Peyser, Paul L. Smith, Carmine Caridi, Sammy Smith. **Credits:** Dir: Arthur Hiller; Prod: Arthur Hiller, William Sackheim; Writer: Andrew Bergman; DP: David M. Walsh; Ed: Robert W. Swink; Composer: John Morris. Color, 103 min. VHS, LASER

In Like Flint
(1967) Fox
The sequel to *Our Man Flint* (1966) continues the exploits of superspy Coburn. This installment finds the debonair man of the world facing a conspiracy of comely women with designs on world domination by brainwashing women through their hair dryers. Coburn's just the man for the job in these spy-genre satires that have as much sly appeal as some of the Bond pictures they spoof. **Cast:** James Coburn, Lee J. Cobb, Andrew

Duggan, Jean Hale, Yvonne Craig, Anna Lee, Hanna Landy, Totty Ames. **Credits:** Dir: Gordon Douglas; Prod: Saul David; Writer: Hal Fimberg; DP: William Daniels; Ed: Hugh S. Fowler; Composer: Jerry Goldsmith; Art Director: Jack Martin Smith, Dale Hennesy. Color, 114 min. VHS, LASER

In Name Only
(1939) RKO
A terrific pairing of Lombard and Grant in an absorbing domestic melodrama. The run-of-the-mill situation of a soulful, wealthy Grant stuck with ice-cube-in-a-gown Francis and his attempts to free himself to pursue the simple pleasures with Lombard gets a big lift from the innate appeal of the leads. **Cast:** Cary Grant, Carole Lombard, Kay Francis, Charles Coburn, Helen Vinson, Katharine Alexander, Jonathan Hale, Maurice Moscovich. **Credits:** Dir: John Cromwell; Prod: George Haight; Writer: Richard Sherman; DP: J. Roy Hunt; Ed: William Hamilton; Composer: Roy Webb; Art Director: Van Nest Polglase, Perry Ferguson. B&W, 102 min. VHS, LASER

The Inner Circle
(1946) Rebublic
When a gossip-mongering radio reporter is murdered, a private eye who's been framed for murder by his secretary must clear his name before time runs out. **Cast:** Adele Mara, Warren Douglas, Ricardo Cortez, Virginia Christine, Ken Niles, Will Wright, Dorothy Adams, Edward Gargan, Fred Graham, Eddie Parker. **Credits:** Dir: Philip Ford; Prod: William J. O'Sullivan; Writer: Dorrell McGowan, Stuart McGowan; DP: Reggie Lanning; Ed: Tony Martinelli; Prod Design: Fred A. Ritter; Composer: Mort Glickman. B&W, VHS

The Inn of the Sixth Happiness
(1958) Fox
Well-done, true-life drama based on the life of an English servant girl, Gladys Aylward (Bergman), who became a missionary and led a group of children on a perilous evacuation through war-ravaged 1930s China. Based on *The Small Woman* by Alan Burgess. Shot in CinemaScope and featuring Robert Donat's final performance. Golden Globe for Best Film Promoting International Understanding. Academy Award Nomination for Best Director. **Cast:** Ingrid Bergman, Curt Jurgens, Robert Donat, Ronald Squire, Noel Hood, Joan Young, Moultrie Kelsall, Edith Sharpe, Richard

Wattis. **Credits:** Dir: Mark Robson; Prod: Buddy Adler; Writer: Isobel Lennart; DP: Freddie Young; Ed: Ernest Walter; Composer: Malcolm Arnold; Art Director: Geoffrey Drake. Color, 158 min. VHS

In Old California
(1942) Republic
Wayne Western portrays the travails of a mild-mannered pharmacist (Duke?!) who migrates west and right into a heap of trouble with the local crime kingpin. It doesn't take long for Wayne to get riled. **Cast:** John Wayne, Albert Dekker, Binnie Barnes, Helen Parrish, Edgar Kennedy, Patsy Kelly, Dick Purcell, Harry Shannon, Charles Halton. **Credits:** Dir: William McGann; Prod: Robert North; Writer: Gertrude Purcell, Frances Hyland; Story: J. Robert Bren, Gladys Atwater; DP: Jack Marta; Ed: Murray Seldeen, Howard O'Neill; Composer: David Buttolph; Art Director: Russell Kimball. B&W, 90 min. VHS

In Old Santa Fe
(1934) Mascot
Autry's first film is a roundup of '30s-era cowboy stars, including Maynard, Hayes, and Burnette. Maynard finds himself framed for murder, while Gene and Smiley prove they can sing as well as they ride. Great nostalgic fun, and notable for early performances by Saturday matinee idols. **Cast:** Ken Maynard, George "Gabby" Hayes, H. B. Warner, Kenneth Thompson, Gene Autry, Smiley Burnette, Wheeler Oakman, Evalyn Knapp. **Credits:** Dir: David Howard; Prod: Nat Levine; Writer: Colbert Clark, James Gruen; DP: Ernest Miller, William Nobles; Ed: Thomas Scott. B&W, 64 min. VHS

Inside Daisy Clover
(1965) Warner Bros.
The time-honored tale of an actress clawing her way to the top of Hollywood's heap in the '30s gets a grim '60s point of view and better-than-it-deserves performances. Wood goes from guttersnipe to glamour queen, first under the sponsorship of studio head Plummer, then as the wife of matinee idol Redford. She discovers, as she must, that the price for big-screen glory is too high. Academy Award Nominations: 3, including Best Supporting Actress: Ruth Gordon. **Cast:** Natalie Wood, Robert Redford, Christopher Plummer, Roddy McDowall, Ruth Gordon, Bard Katharine, Betty Harford, John Hale. **Credits:** Dir: Robert Mulligan; Prod: Alan J. Pakula; Writer: Gavin Lambert; DP: Charles B. Lang; Ed: Aaron Stell;

Prod Design: Robert Clatworthy; Composer: Andre Previn. Color, 129 min. VHS, LASER

Inspector Clouseau
(1968) United Artists
Middle-period Clouseau entry between the first two hilarious films directed by Blake Edwards (*A Shot in the Dark*, *The Pink Panther*) and the later films with Edwards back at the helm. Here Arkin takes the Peter Sellers role as the bumbling French detective, and Yorkin directs. Most of the interest is seeing a talent as large as Arkin's taking on a role so closely associated with comic genius Sellers. **Cast:** Alan Arkin, Frank Finlay, Barry Foster, Patrick Cargill, Beryl Reid, Clive Francis, Delia Boccardo, John Bindon. **Credits:** Dir: Bud Yorkin; Prod: Lewis J. Rachmil; Writer: Tom Waldman, Frank Waldman; DP: Arthur Ibbetson; Ed: John Victor Smith; Prod Design: Michael Stringer; Composer: Ken Thorne. Color, 98 min. VHS

The Inspector General
(1949) Warner Bros.
Classic Kaye performance as a quack medicine man with a traveling carnival who is mistakenly identified as the feared Inspector General when he visits an Eastern European village. Plenty of opportunity for patented Kaye befuddlement when he's invited to the Russian Imperial court. Based on the story by Russian dramatist Nikolay Gogol. Songs include "The Gypsy Drinking Song," "The Medicine Show," "The Inspector General," "Happy Times," and "Onward Onward." Golden Globe for Best Score. **Cast:** Danny Kaye, Walter Slezak, Elsa Lanchester, John Carradine, Barbara Bates, Gene Lockhart, Alan Hale, Walter Catlett, Rys Williams. **Credits:** Dir: Henry Koster; Prod: Jerry Wald; Writer: Philip Rapp, Harry Kurnitz; DP: Elwood Bredell; Ed: Rudi Fehr; Prod Design: Robert M. Haas; Composer: Johnny Green. Color, 103 min. VHS

Inspiration
(1931) MGM
One of the several Garbo vehicles Brown directed in the early talkie era. Standard fare about a courtesan whose past indiscretions cause her to shun the love of her life (Montgomery) to avoid tainting him with her scarlet reputation. Interesting mostly to see two of MGM's workhorses on familiar territory. **Cast:** Greta Garbo, Robert Montgomery, Lewis Stone, Marjorie Rambeau, Beryl Mercer, Oscar Apfel, John Miljan, Edwin Maxwell. **Credits:** Dir: Clarence Brown;

Prod: Clarence Brown; Writer: Gene Markey; DP: William Daniels; Ed: Conrad A. Nervig. B&W, 77 min. **VHS**

Interiors
(1978) United Artists
The success of *Annie Hall* must have given Allen the confidence to take his work in a radically different direction. This amounts to an homage to the psychological dramas of Ingmar Bergman, with a similarly bleak view of the emotional repercussions of personal decisions on relationships and a frosty cold visual style. The daughters of Marshall react with bewilderment and anger when he leaves their mother for another woman. Fine performances by Keaton, Hurt, Page, and Stapleton in extraordinarily difficult material. Fascinating, especially for Allen fans. Academy Award Nominations: 5, including Best Director; Best (Original) Screenplay; Best Actress: Geraldine Page. **Cast:** Diane Keaton, Geraldine Page, E. G. Marshall, Maureen Stapleton, Kristin Griffith, Mary Beth Hurt, Sam Waterston, Richard Jordan. **Credits:** Dir: Woody Allen; Prod: Charles H. Joffe; Writer: Woody Allen; DP: Gordon Willis; Ed: Ralph Rosenblum; Prod Design: Mel Bourne. Color, 99 min. **VHS, LASER**

Intermezzo
(1939) United Artists
Bergman made her Hollywood debut in a role she had played three years earlier in Sweden. She is absolutely luminous as the concert pianist who diverts violin virtuoso Howard from his wife and children. After a whirlwind tour together, Howard finds the pull of family too much, leaving Bergman alone with her music. The classic romantic melodrama with a classical-music setting. Jascha Heifetz dubbed Howard's violin parts. Academy Award Nominations: Best Black-and-White Cinematography, Best Score. **Cast:** Ingrid Bergman, Leslie Howard, Edna Best, Cecil Kellaway, John Halliday, Enid Bennett, Ann E. Todd, Scott Douglas. **Credits:** Dir: Gregory Ratoff; Prod: David O. Selznick; Writer: George O'Neil; DP: Gregg Toland; Ed: Hal C. Kern, Francis D. Lyon; Art Director: Lyle Wheeler. B&W, 91 min. **VHS, LASER**

International House
(1933) Paramount
Legendary surreal comedy with hilarious lineup of vaudeville performers, including Fields, Burns and Allen, Vallee, and Lugosi (!). An early television device draws an assortment of oddballs and characters to a Shanghai

hotel for a demonstration and bidding for the rights to manufacture (an interesting situation demonstrating that early television devices appeared as far back as the '20s, when it was considered a logical extension of the radio craze; the devices, available in kit form, picked up broadcasts that were barely visible pantomime performances). Baby Rose Marie and Cab Calloway (singing the naughty "Reefer Man") appear on the TV device. **Cast:** W. C. Fields, Peggy Hopkins Joyce, Rudy Vallee, Stuart Erwin, George Burns, Gracie Allen, Sara Maritza, Bela Lugosi. **Credits:** Dir: A. Edward Sutherland; Writer: Francis Martin, Walter DeLeon; DP: Ernest Haller. B&W, 72 min. **VHS, LASER**

Internes Can't Take Money
(1937) Paramount
The first film to introduce the Dr. Kildare character from the Max Brand books; it later became a movie series featuring Lew Ayers as the young doctor and Lionel Barrymore as his irascible mentor, Dr. Gillespie. This stands on its own, however, with McCrea saving the life of a gangster in order to help Stanwyck, a bank robber's widow, find her daughter. **Cast:** Barbara Stanwyck, Joel McCrea, Lloyd Nolan, Stanley Ridges, Lee Bowman, Irving Bacon, Gaylord Pendleton, Barry Macollum. **Credits:** Dir: Alfred Santell; Prod: Benjamin Glazer; Writer: Rian James, Theodore Reeves; DP: Theodor Sparkuhl; Ed: Doane Harrison; Composer: Boris Morros; Art Director: Hans Dreier, Roland Anderson. B&W, 79 min. **VHS**

Interrupted Melody
(1955) MGM
Another film bio featuring a performer struck down at her height only to show pluck and determination in resuming a career (it seemed to be a mid-'50s obsession). Parker is fine (in what could have been a Susan Hayward role) as Australian opera star Marjorie Lawrence, who contracts polio and then battles to regain her place on the Metropolitan Opera stage. Well done and much-honored. Academy Award Nominations: 3, including Best Actress: Eleanor Parker. **Academy Awards:** Best Story and Screenplay. **Cast:** Eleanor Parker, Glenn Ford, Roger Moore, Cecil Kellaway, Ann Codee, Stephen Bekassy, Peter Leeds, Walter Baldwin. **Credits:** Dir: Curtis Bernhardt; Prod: Jack Cummings, John Dunning; Writer: William Ludwig, Sonya Levien; DP: Joseph Ruttenberg, Paul C. Vogel; Prod Design:

Cedric Gibbons; Composer: Adolph Deutsch; Art Director: Daniel B. Cathcart. Color, 106 min. **VHS**

In the Good Old Summertime
(1949) MGM
Garland and Johnson bicker constantly as they work in a music store (giving us a chance to hear lots of nostalgic tunes), but are blissfully unaware that they are sweethearts as pen pals. Doesn't have the reputation of the other Garland MGM musicals, but lots of winning songs, including "Meet Me Tonight in Dreamland," "Put Your Arms Around Me Honey," "Wait Till the Sun Shines, Nellie," and "Merry Christmas." Little Liza's in the last scene. **Cast:** Judy Garland, Van Johnson, Buster Keaton, S. Z. Sakall, Spring Byington, Clinton Sundberg, Lillian Bronson, Marcia Van Dyke. **Credits:** Dir: Robert Z. Leonard; Prod: Joe Pasternak; Writer: Samson Raphaelson, Frances Goodrich, Ivan Tors, Albert Hackett; DP: Harry Stradling. Color, 104 min. **VHS, LASER**

In the Heat of the Night
(1967) United Artists
Two powerful actors in a bitter showdown take this murder mystery to a higher level. Backwoods southern sheriff Steiger, in an Academy Award–winning role, doesn't appreciate the assistance offered by black, big-city detective Poitier. The uneasy pair reluctantly join forces to solve the strange murder of a wealthy industrialist. The element of racial tension gives Silliphant's screenplay a dimension and depth most detective tales can't match. Poitier returned as Tibbs in *They Call Me Mr. Tibbs!* (1970) and *The Organization* (1971). The characters appeared again in a TV series. Academy Award Nominations: 7, including Best Director. **Academy Awards:** Best Picture; Best Actor: Rod Steiger; Best Film Editing; Best Sound; Irving G. Thalberg Memorial Award: Walter Mirisch; Best Screenplay Based on Material from Another Medium. **Cast:** Sidney Poitier, Rod Steiger, Warren Oates, Lee Grant, Quentin Dean, James Patterson, William Schallert, Scott Wilson. **Credits:** Dir: Norman Jewison; Prod: Walter Mirisch; Writer: Stirling Silliphant; DP: Haskell Wexler; Ed: Hal Ashby; Composer: Quincy Jones; Art Director: Paul Groesse. Color, 111 min. **VHS, LASER**

In This Our Life
(1942) Warner Bros.
Sisters Davis and de Havilland struggle over the affections of Morgan.

Davis wins the contest but her conniving costs her in the end. Huston and the flashing temperaments of the female leads give this domestic melodrama (an unusual genre for Huston) an uncharacteristic bite. Watch for background appearances by the cast of Huston's recently completed *The Maltese Falcon* in a barroom scene. Based on a novel by Ellen Glasgow. **Cast:** Bette Davis, Olivia de Havilland, George Brent, Charles Coburn, Hattie McDaniel, Dennis Morgan, Frank Craven, Billie Burke. **Credits:** Dir: John Huston; Prod: David Lewis; Writer: Howard Koch, John Huston; DP: Ernest Haller; Ed: William Holmes; Composer: Max Steiner; Art Director: Robert M. Haas. B&W, 101 min. **VHS**

Intolerance

(1916)
Griffith's mammoth achievement, spanning several centuries and cultures. The silent film presents four stories linked solely by a single common thread: intolerance. Three of the stories are based on historical fact: medieval France during the reign of Charles IX; the birth and crucifixion of Christ; and the fall of Babylon. The fourth tale is a "modern" story of greed, cruelty, and betrayal. *Intolerance* had its New York premiere on September 5, 1916; it was released two years after *The Birth of a Nation*, and it is widely regarded as Griffith's protest and self-defense against the charges of racism leveled at him for *Birth*'s glorification of the Ku Klux Klan. Composer Carl Davis created a new score for a recent release. Selected for the National Film Registry. **Cast:** Lillian Gish, Robert Harron, Mae Marsh, Constance Talmadge, Elmo Lincoln, Eugene Pallette. **Credits:** Dir: D. W. Griffith; Prod: D. W. Griffith; Writer: D. W. Griffith, Tod Browning; DP: G. W. Bitzer, Karl Brown; Ed: James Smith, D. W. Griffith, Rose Smith; Prod Design: D. W. Griffith; Composer: Joseph Carl Breil, D. W. Griffith. B&W, 208 min. **VHS, LASER, DVD**

Intruder in the Dust

(1949) MGM
When a black man (Hernandez) is accused of murder in a small southern town, the ugly drumbeat of the lynch mob begins to be heard. Gripping story of racial hatred adapted from a William Faulkner novel (and filmed near Oxford, Mississippi) presents a detailed portrait of a community torn apart by its animosities as well as the fear instilled by the reign

of mob terror. **Cast:** David Brian, Claude Jarman, Jr., Juano Hernandez, Porter Hall, Elizabeth Patterson, Charles Kemper, Will Geer, David Clarke. **Credits:** Dir: Clarence Brown; Prod: Clarence Brown; Writer: Ben Maddow; DP: Robert Surtees; Ed: Robert J. Kern; Prod Design: Cedric Gibbons; Composer: Adolph Deutsch. B&W, 87 min. **VHS**

Invaders from Mars

(1953) Fox
The classic invasion-of-the-little-green-men movie from Hollywood stylist Menzies. A boy can't get anyone, including his parents, to listen when he claims to have seen a flying saucer land nearby. Of course, everyone he meets has already succumbed to the invasion. Remade in 1986 by Tobe Hooper. **Cast:** Arthur Franz, Helena Carter, Jimmy Hunt, Leif Erickson, Morris Ankrum, Hillary Brooke, Max Wagner, Milburn Stone. **Credits:** Dir: William Cameron Menzies; Prod: Edward L. Alperson; Writer: Richard Blake, John Tucker Battle, William Cameron Menzies; DP: John F. Seitz; Ed: Arthur Roberts; Prod Design: William Cameron Menzies; Composer: Raoul Kraushaar. Color, 78 min. **VHS, LASER, DVD**

Invasion of the Body Snatchers

(1956) Allied Artists
This is the height of paranoid science-fiction terror made at the height of McCarthy-era paranoia. A small-town doctor (McCarthy) becomes the last man with a conscience when pods from outer space begin to reproduce inside their human hosts, draining all humanity from them. When he gleans the truth, a race begins to get the word out before it's too late. Long seen as a parable about individuality and the danger of conformity and group-think. Breathless, suspenseful, and the best of its kind. Remade successfully in 1978. The laser release includes a wide-screen version, commentary, including an interview with director Siegel, and trailers. Based on the serialized story in *Collier's* magazine by Jack Finney. Selected as a National Film Registry Outstanding Film. **Cast:** Kevin McCarthy, Dana Wynter, Carolyn Jones, Larry Gates, Virginia Christine, Ralph Dumke, Jean Willes, King Donovan. **Credits:** Dir: Don Siegel; Prod: Walter Wanger; Writer: Geoffrey Homes; DP: Ellsworth Fredricks; Ed: Robert S. Eisen; Prod Design: Joseph Kish; Composer: Carmen Dragon. B&W, 80 min. **VHS, LASER, DVD**

Invasion of the Body Snatchers

(1978) United Artists
Built on the outlines of the earlier terror masterpiece, this updated version has surprises of its own. The story moves from a small desert town to the city of San Francisco, where the dense population makes for even higher stakes for humanity. Sutherland takes over the McCarthy role as a man who can trust no one as he tries to rein in the spreading menace. The director and star of the original show up here as well. **Cast:** Donald Sutherland, Brooke Adams, Veronica Cartwright, Jeff Goldblum, Leonard Nimoy, Art Hindle, Lelia Goldoni, Don Siegel. **Credits:** Dir: Philip Kaufman; Prod: Robert H. Solo; Writer: W. D. Richter; DP: Michael Chapman; Ed: Douglas Stewart; Prod Design: Charles Rosen; Composer: Denny Zeitlin. Color, 117 min. **VHS, LASER, DVD**

The Invisible Man

(1933) Universal
In this classic Universal horror film based on the H. G. Wells novella, Rains (in his debut, a role that monster master Boris Karloff turned down) plays a mad scientist whose formula for invisibility wreaks havoc on his mind, and he begins to lust for power. Directed by one of Hollywood's most distinctive stylists, Whale (*Frankenstein*), it costars Stuart long before her Academy Award–nominated role in *Titanic*. **Cast:** Claude Rains, Gloria Stuart, William Harrigan, Una O'Connor, Henry Travers, Forrester Harvey, Holmes Herbert, E. E. Clive, Dudley Digges, Harry Stubbs. **Credits:** Dir: James Whale; Prod: Carl Laemmle, Jr.; Writer: Philip Wylie, R. C. Sherriff; DP: Arthur Edeson; Composer: W. Franke Harling; Art Director: Charles D. Hall. B&W, 72 min. **VHS, LASER**

The Invisible Man Returns

(1940) Universal
Made seven years after the original, this tongue-in-cheek sequel stars Price as the invisible man's brother who uses the same formula to clear himself of a murder charge. Thought to be Price's first journey into the macabre on-screen. Academy Award Nomination for Best Special Effects. **Cast:** Cedric Hardwicke, Vincent Price, John Sutton, Nan Grey, Cecil Kellaway, Alan Napier, Forrester Harvey, Frances Robinson, Ivan Simpson, Edward Fielding. **Credits:** Dir: Joe May; Prod: Ken Goldsmith; Writer: Lester Cole, Cecil Belfrage, Curt Siodmak; DP: Milton

Krasner; Ed: Frank Gross; Composer: Frank Skinner, H. J. Salter. B&W, 82 min. VHS

The Invisible Ray

(1936) Universal
Karloff and Lugosi duke it out in this sci-fi thriller. Karloff's mad scientist becomes radioactive from a meteorite and develops the uncanny ability to deliver death with the mere touch of his hand. Lugosi's hero must stop the murdering monster. Though not one of the best Karloff-Lugosi pairings, the great special effects—see a man burst into flames!—compensate for the script's failings. **Cast:** Boris Karloff, Bela Lugosi, Frances Drake, Frank Lawton, Beulah Bondi, Nydia Westman, Georges Renavent, Frank Reicher, Paul Weigel. **Credits:** Dir: Lambert Hillyer; Prod: Edmund Grainger; Writer: John Colton. B&W, 90 min. VHS, LASER

Invisible Stripes

(1940) Warner Bros.
The "invisible stripes" are the regulation attire of the Big House and they dog a man even after he tries to go clean. Raft and Bogie are fresh out of the pen, but Bogie is not interested in the straight and narrow. Raft tries but his past catches up with him, and to help his brother (played by a young Holden) set up a nest egg, Raft briefly rejoins Bogart, then goes straight again. Holden ends up implicated in their activities and jailed, and Raft must clear him by going after Bogie himself. **Cast:** George Raft, Jane Bryan, William Holden, Humphrey Bogart, Flora Robson, Paul Kelly, Lee Patrick, Henry O'Neill, Frankie Thomas, Moroni Olsen. **Credits:** Dir: Lloyd Bacon; Prod: Louis F. Edelman; Writer: Warren Duff, Lewis E. Lawes, Jonathan Finn; DP: Ernest Haller; Ed: James Gibbon; Prod Design: Max Parker; Composer: Heinz Roemheld. B&W, 82 min.

The Invisible Woman

(1940) Universal
An entertaining sci-fi comedy starring Barrymore as a likably odd professor who manages to render a beautiful model invisible, thus gaining the attention of his rich playboy backer (Howard) and a greedy gangster (Homolka). Great cast of top character actors in support. Based on a story by Joe May and Curt Siodmak, who wrote *The Invisible Man Returns* the same year (1940). Academy Award Nomination for Best Special Effects. **Cast:** John Barrymore, Virginia Bruce, John

Howard, Charlie Ruggles, Oscar Homolka, Edward Brophy, Donald MacBride, Margaret Hamilton, Shemp Howard. **Credits:** Dir: A. Edward Sutherland; Prod: Burt Kelly; Writer: Robert Lees, Frederic I. Rinaldo, Gertrude Purcell; DP: Elwood Bredell; Ed: Frank Gross; Prod Design: Jack Otterson. B&W, 83 min. VHS

Invitation

(1952) MGM
McGuire plays a young wife who has everything—a handsome doctor husband and a dream house, as well as a deep-pocketed father, Calhern. But she's racked by mysterious chest pains. Through a series of flashbacks, we learn that she has a terminal heart condition and that her father paid her husband to marry her. After she confronts her husband, Johnson, he admits the plot but says he has learned to love her truly. This sooths McGuire as she prepares for the operation that may save her life. **Cast:** Van Johnson, Dorothy McGuire, Ruth Roman, Louis Calhern, Ray Collins, Michael Chekov, Lisa Golm, Diane Cassidy, Stapleton Kent, Barbara Ruick. **Credits:** Dir: Gottfried Reinhardt; Prod: Lawrence Weingarten; Writer: Paul Osborn; Story: Jerome Weidman; DP: Ray June; Ed: George Boemler; Prod Design: Cedric Gibbons; Composer: Cyril Mockridge; Art Director: Urie McCleary. B&W, 84 min.

Invitation to the Dance

(1956) MGM
Kelly's filmic valentine to the dance features three stories told entirely in music and dance, the most interesting of which is Kelly's second teaming with Hanna-Barbera animated characters (after the Tom and Jerry sequence in *Anchors Aweigh*). The score includes works by Rimsky-Korsakov, Previn, and Ibert. Winner of a Golden Bear at the Berlin Film Festival. **Cast:** Gene Kelly, Igor Youskevitch, Claire Sombert, Carol Haney, David Kasday, David Paltenghi, Claude Bessy, Diana Adams. **Credits:** Dir: Gene Kelly; Prod: Arthur Freed; Writer: Gene Kelly; DP: Freddie Young, Joseph Ruttenberg; Ed: Raymond Poulton, Adrienne Fazan, Robert Watts; Prod Design: Cedric Gibbons, Randal Duell; Composer: Jacques Ibert, Andre Previn, Roger Edens, Nikolai Andreevich; Art Director: Alfred Junge. Color, 93 min. VHS

I Remember Mama

(1948) RKO
A touching drama about a Norwegian immigrant family's struggle to survive

in early-20th-century San Francisco is lovingly brought to life in rich and rewarding detail. As the pillar of strength, the always dignified Dunne is perfectly cast as Mama. Superb supporting performances animate the story, which is based on the play by John Van Druten, who based his work on the memoirs of Kathryn Forbes. This nostalgic treat later became the TV series, *Mama*. Golden Globe for Best Supporting Actress: Ellen Corby. Academy Award Nominations: 5, including Best Actress: Irene Dunne. **Cast:** Irene Dunne, Barbara Bel Geddes, Oscar Homolka, Philip Dorn, Edgar Bergen, Ellen Corby, Florence Bates, Cedric Hardwicke, Barbara O'Neil, Rudy Vallee. **Credits:** Dir: George Stevens; Prod: Harriet Parsons; Writer: De Witt Bodeen; DP: Nicholas Musuraca; Ed: Robert W. Swink, Tholen Gladden; Prod Design: Albert S. D'Agostino, Carroll Clark; Composer: Roy Webb. B&W, 134 min. VHS, LASER

Irma La Douce

(1963) United Artists
Wilder took away the music from the Broadway production, but left the heart. It's all MacLaine's show as the happy-go-lucky hooker who snares gendarme Lemmon's heart when he cleans out a red-light district bordello. Adult comedy with Wilder's bawdy sensibility. Academy Award Nominations: 3, including Best Actress: Shirley MacLaine. **Academy Awards:** Best Music Score, Adaptation or Treatment. **Cast:** Shirley MacLaine, Jack Lemmon, Lou Jacobi, Herschel Bernardi, Bruce Yarnell, Hope Holiday, Joan Shawlee, Grace Lee Whitney, Tura Satana, Harriette Young. **Credits:** Dir: Billy Wilder; Prod: Billy Wilder; Writer: Billy Wilder, I. A. L. Diamond; DP: Joseph La Shelle; Ed: Daniel Mandell; Prod Design: Alexander Trauner; Composer: Andre Previn; Costumes: Orry-Kelly. Color, 147 min. VHS, LASER

The Iron Curtain

(1948) Fox
This slice of Cold War wish-fulfillment puts the squeeze on Andrews as a would-be Soviet defector whose knowledge of the Russian spy network puts his life in danger and threatens to escalate into an international incident. Andrews's wife Tierney stiffens his resolve. The score includes work by Shostakovich and Prokofiev. **Cast:** Dana Andrews, Gene Tierney, June Havoc, Barry Kroeger, Edna Best, Stefan Schnabel, Nicholas

Joy, Eduard Franz, Frederic Tozere, Noel Cravat. **Credits:** Dir: William Wellman; Prod: Sol Siegel; Writer: Milton Krims, Igor Gouzenko; DP: Charles Clark; Ed: Louis Loeffler; Composer: Dmitry Shostakovich, Sergey Prokofiev, Aram Khachaturian, Nicholas Miaskovsky, Alfred Newman; Art Director: Lyle Wheeler, Mark-Lee Kirk. B&W, 87 min.

The Iron Major
(1943) RKO
Made as a wartime morale booster, this sentimental biopic stars O'Brien as Frank Cavanaugh, the disabled WWI hero who became an inspirational football coach. Costars Warrick as Cavenaugh's wife, who wrote his story. **Cast:** Pat O'Brien, Robert Ryan, Ruth Warrick, Leon Ames, Russell Wade, Bruce Edwards, Richard Martin, Robert Bice, Virginia Brissac, Bud Geary. **Credits:** Dir: Ray Enright; Prod: Robert Fellows; Writer: Aben Kandel, Warren Duff; DP: Robert de Grasse; Ed: Robert Wise, Philip Martin; Prod Design: Carroll Clark; Composer: Roy Webb; Art Director: Albert S. D'Agostino. B&W, 85 min. **VHS**

The Iron Mistress
(1952) Warner Bros.
A lush, well-financed vehicle for Ladd's first effort with Warner, this is a loose account of the life of Jim Bowie before he achieved fame at the Alamo. Ladd's Bowie is a backwoods kid introduced to New Orleans society by painter John James Audubon. After falling in love with the gorgeous but fickle society dame, Mayo, he builds up a fortune gambling and speculating, as well as a reputation by wielding his specifically forged knife. Unsuccessful with his suit for Mayo, Ladd gives up society and heads out to Texas. **Cast:** Alan Ladd, Virginia Mayo, Joseph Calleia, Phyllis Kirk, Alf Kjellin, Douglas Dick, Nedrick Young, George Voskovec, Richard Carlyle, Robert Emhardt. **Credits:** Dir: Gordon Douglas; Prod: Henry Blanke; Writer: James E. Webb; Story: Paul I. Wellman; DP: John Seitz; Ed: Alan Crosland; Prod Design: John Beckman; Composer: Max Steiner. Color, 110 min.

Isadora
(1968) Universal
Extravagantly talented, beautiful, and artistically audacious, Isadora Duncan was a tabloid sensation before there were such things. Redgrave's portrayal of the '20s dancer became an icon of the flower-power generation searching for antiestablishment

forebears. Duncan's life provides plenty of material, with affairs, groundbreaking and bluenose-twitting performances, and even a live-fast, die-young last act. Redgrave won many acting awards, including the Oscar, National Film Critics, and Cannes prizes. The director restored 22 minutes to the rerelease. **Academy Awards:** Best Actress: Vanessa Redgrave. **Cast:** Vanessa Redgrave, James Fox, Jason Robards, Ivan Tchenko, John Fraser, Bessie Love, Cynthia Harris, Tony Vogel. **Credits:** Dir: Karel Reisz; Prod: Robert Hakim, Raymond Hakim; Writer: Melvyn Bragg, Clive Exton, Margaret Drabble; DP: Larry Pizer; Ed: Tom Priestley; Composer: Maurice Jarre; Art Director: Michael Seymour. Color, 168 min. **VHS**

The Island of Dr. Moreau
(1977) AIP
Lancaster gives a memorable performance as the demented Doctor Moreau, who performs bizarre genetic experiments on animals—turning them into man-beasts known as humanimals. His experiments continue uninterrupted until a mariner named Braddock shipwrecks on Moreau's island. Shocked by the immoral nature of Moreau's work, Braddock tries to stop the Doctor but finds that he has an army of humanimals to reckon with first. Based on H. G. Wells's 1896 novel and a remake of the 1933 horror classic, *Island of Lost Souls*—and much more enjoyable than the most recent, 1996 version starring Marlon Brando. **Cast:** Burt Lancaster, Michael York, Barbara Carrera, Nigel Davenport, Richard Basehart, Nick Cravat, Bob Ozman, Fumio Demura, Gary Baxley, John Gillespie. **Credits:** Dir: Don Taylor; Prod: Skip Steloff, John Temple-Smith, Samuel Z. Arkoff; Writer: John Herman Shaner, Al Ramrus; DP: Gerry Fisher; Ed: Marion Rothman; Prod Design: Philip M. Jefferies; Composer: Laurence Rosenthal. Color, 104 min. **VHS**

Island of Lost Souls
(1933) Universal
One of the most horrifying of horror movies is based on H. G. Wells's *The Island of Dr. Moreau*. Exiled to a tropical island far from shore, a mad scientist (Laughton) tampers with the evolutionary process to produce creatures that are half-man, half-jungle creature. A shipwreck survivor (Arlen) gives the doctor an opportunity for some further exploration by mating the man with his

panther-woman. The premise of a mad doctor performing sadistic experiments on humans and animals may be even more hideous in light of the real-life events that would come just a few years later. Remade twice as *The Island of Dr. Moreau* (1977 and 1996). Also the source of Devo's cry "Are we not men?" **Cast:** Charles Laughton, Bela Lugosi, Richard Arlen, Stanley Fields, Kathleen Burke, Leila Hyams, Arthur Hohl, Bob Kortman. **Credits:** Dir: Erle C. Kenton; Writer: Philip Wylie, Waldemar Young; DP: Karl Struss. B&W, 71 min. **VHS**

Islands in the Stream
(1977) Paramount
Scott makes a suitable Ernest Hemingway stand-in in one of the better adaptations of Papa's novels. An American painter and sculptor lives in splendid isolation on the island of Bimini until his solitary existence is threatened by the arrival of his three sons and their expectations for reconciliation, and the increasing tension building toward WWII. Academy Award Nomination for Best Cinematography. **Cast:** George C. Scott, David Hemmings, Claire Bloom, Susan Tyrrell, Gilbert Roland, Richard Evans, Hart Bochner, Brad Savage. **Credits:** Dir: Franklin J. Schaffner; Prod: Peter Bart, Max Palevsky; Writer: Denne Bart Petitclerc; Story: Ernest Hemingway; DP: Fred Koenekamp; Ed: Robert W. Swink; Prod Design: William Greber; Composer: Jerry Goldsmith. Color, 110 min. **VHS, LASER**

Is Paris Burning?
(1966) Paramount
Coppola and Vidal wrote the script for this international production that depicts the Nazi withdrawal from France and their threat to set fire to the City of Lights. The pseudodocumentary style adds immediacy and impact and the huge list of famous faces make for fun star-spotting. From the best-seller by Larry Collins and Dominique Lapierre. Academy Award Nominations: 2, including Best (Black-and-White) Cinematography. **Cast:** Jean-Paul Belmondo, Charles Boyer, Leslie Caron, Jean-Pierre Cassel, Claude Dauphin, Alain Delon, Kirk Douglas, Glenn Ford, Gert Frobe, Daniel Gelin. **Credits:** Dir: Rene Clement; Prod: Paul Graetz; Writer: Gore Vidal, Francis Ford Coppola, Jean Aurenche, Pierre Bost, Claude Brule, Marcel Moussy, Beate von Molo; DP: Marcel Grignon; Ed: Robert Lawrence; Composer: Maurice Jarre; Art Director: Willy Holt. Color, 173 min. **VHS, LASER**

It Came from Beneath the Sea

(1955) Columbia
A giant octopus rises from beneath the Pacific Ocean and makes its way toward San Francisco to satisfy its immense appetite for humans. Typical mid-'50s creature feature with the distinction of having effects by the inimitable Harryhausen. **Cast:** Kenneth Tobey, Faith Domergue, Donald Curtis, Ian Keith, Harry Lauter, Eddie Fisher. **Credits:** Dir: Robert Gordon; Prod: Charles H. Schneer; Writer: George Worthing Yates, Hal Smith; DP: Henry Freulich; Ed: Jerome Thoms; Composer: Mischa Bakaleinikoff; SFX: Ray Harryhausen, Jack Erickson. B&W, 80 min. **VHS, LASER**

It Came from Outer Space

(1953) Universal
This screen adaptation of Bradbury's own story, "The Meteor," predates *Invasion of the Body Snatchers* (1956) with a similar creepy theme. When a spaceship crashes in the Arizona desert, the crew assumes the identities of local townspeople as they try to make repairs on their craft. Filmed in 3-D. Remade for TV in 1996. **Cast:** Richard Carlson, Barbara Rush, Charles Drake, Russell Johnson, Kathleen Hughes, Joe Sawyer, Dave Willock, Alan Dexter. **Credits:** Dir: Jack Arnold; Prod: William Alland; Writer: Harry Essex; Story: Ray Bradbury; DP: Clifford Stine; Composer: Herman Stein, Joseph Gershenson. B&W, 81 min. **VHS**

It Could Happen to You

(1937) Republic
A politically charged story about a man who dabbles in crime, with disastrous results, to gain the capital he needs to purchase a school where immigrants are prepared for American citizenship. The school's European teacher dreams of a fascist America. Based on a story by West and Samuel Ornitz, who was one of the Hollywood Ten blacklisted during the McCarthy era. **Cast:** Alan Baxter, Andrea Leeds, Owen Davis, Jr., Walter Kingsford, Al Shean, Christian Rub, Elsa Janssen, Stanley King. **Credits:** Dir: Phil Rosen; Prod: Leonard Fields; Writer: Nathanael West; DP: Jack A. Marta; Ed: Murray Seldeen, Ernest Nims; Composer: Alberto Colombo. B&W, 65 min. **VHS**

It Grows on Trees

(1952) Universal
A light comedy with Dunne, in the last role of her career, as a housewife who discovers that money does indeed grow on trees—specifically, five- and ten-dollar bills on two trees in her own backyard. Her husband, Jagger, is doubtful, until the Treasury department grudgingly admits the cash is legal tender. Dunne amuses herself on shopping sprees until she discovers that the bills, unlike leaves, crumble to dust. **Cast:** Dean Jagger, Joan Evans, Richard Crenna, Les Treymayne, Dee Pollock, Sandy Descher, Irene Dunne, Forrest Lewis, Edith Meiser, Frank Ferguson. **Credits:** Dir: Arthur Lubin; Prod: Leonard Goldstein; Writer: Leonard Praskins, Barney Slater; DP: Maury Gertsman; Ed: Milton Carruth; Prod Design: Alexander Golitzen, Bernard Herzbrun; Composer: Frank Skinner. B&W, 84 min.

It Had to Be You

(1947) Columbia
Whimsical comedy about a rich woman (Rogers) who is about to marry for the fourth time but who always changes her mind. Meanwhile, she meets the man (Wilde)—who appears to be a Native American—she's been in love with from afar all her life, who turns out to be a New York City fireman. **Cast:** Billy Bevan, Spring Byington, Ginger Rogers, Ron Randell, Charles Evans, Thurston Hall, Harry Morgan, Frank Orth, Cornel Wilde, Percy Waram. **Credits:** Dir: Don Hartman, Rudolph Mate; Prod: Don Hartman; Writer: Melvin Frank, Norman Panama; Story: Allen Boretz; DP: Vincent J. Farrar, Rudolph Mate; Ed: Gene Havlick; Prod Design: Wilbur Menefee, William Kiernan; Composer: Heinz Roemheld, Morris Stoloff; Costumes: Jean Louise; Art Director: Stephen Goosson, Rudolph Sternad. B&W, 98 min.

It Happened at the World's Fair

(1963) MGM
Better than most Elvis pictures mostly due to its vibrant setting and bouncy songs. An adorable little Chinese girl plays tour guide and Cupid as she leads Presley and O'Brien through the Seattle World's Fair. A young Kurt Russell made his screen debut. Songs include "Take Me to the Fair," "I'm Falling in Love Tonight," "Cotton Candy Land," and "A World of Our Own." **Cast:** Elvis Presley, Gary Lockwood, Ginny Tiu, Joan O'Brien, Edith Atwater, Guy Raymond, Dorothy Green, Yvonne Craig. **Credits:** Dir: Norman Taurog; Prod: Ted Richmond; Writer: Simon Rose, Seaman Jacobs; DP: Joseph Ruttenberg; Composer: Leith Stevens. Color, 105 min. **VHS**

It Happened in Brooklyn

(1947) MGM
The Chairman of the Board and The Schnozzola make unlikely bunkmates (and share a duet, "The Song's Gotta Have Heart") in this easygoing show-biz musical. Ex-sailor Sinatra finds a place to stay with janitor Durante as he and his pals try to hit the big time in the big town. **Cast:** Frank Sinatra, Kathryn Grayson, Jimmy Durante, Peter Lawford, Gloria Grahame, Aubrey Mather, Tamara Shayne, William Haade. **Credits:** Dir: Richard Whorf; Writer: Isobel Lennart; DP: Robert Planck; Ed: Blanche Sewell; Prod Design: Cedric Gibbons; Composer: Johnny Green; Art Director: Leonid Vasian. B&W, 104 min. **VHS, LASER**

It Happened One Night

(1934) Columbia
Capra built an enduring romantic comedy from the standard madcap runaway heiress routine with wit, crackling performances, and expert pacing. Heiress Colbert ignites a nationwide, tabloid-fueled chase when she abandons her wealthy lifestyle to seek simpler joys. She shares a seat on a bus and trades barbs with reporter Gable, who thinks he knows just where to find real life. Their road trip becomes a mutual education and a movie delight, with images that have passed into the American culture, such as sleeping in a haystack, the hitchhiking scene, and sharing a tourist bungalow separated only by Gable's jury-rigged walls of Jericho. It was recognized as a masterpiece upon release (winning all five major Oscars, the first to do so) and remains so today. Remade twice as the musicals *Eve Knew Her Apples* (1945) and *You Can't Run Away from It* (1956). Selected for the National Film Registry Outstanding Film. **Academy Awards:** Best Picture; Best Director; Best Actor: Clark Gable; Best Actress: Claudette Colbert; Best Adaptation. **Cast:** Clark Gable, Claudette Colbert, Walter Connolly, Alan Hale, Roscoe Karns, Ward Bond, Henry Wadsworth, Claire McDowell. **Credits:** Dir: Frank Capra; Writer: Robert Riskin; DP: Joseph Walker; Ed: Gene Havlick; Composer: Louis Silvers; Art Director: Stephen Goosson. B&W, 105 min. **VHS, LASER**

It Happened Tomorrow

(1944) United Artists
Powell is a young reporter at the turn of the century who, thanks to his friendship with a deceased librarian, gets the newspaper a day early, allowing him to anticipate newsworthy

events before they happen. Forewarned, Powell shows up for the big bank robbery and wins at the races with his spiritualist girlfriend. On the third day, however, he reads his own obituary, and, despite all his efforts, circumstances conspire to bring him to the hotel lobby where he is supposed to die. Fascinating fantasy, and the premise for the TV series *Early Edition*. **Cast:** Dick Powell, Linda Darnell, Jack Oakie, Edgar Kennedy, John Philliber. **Credits:** Dir: Rene Clair; Prod: Arnold Pressburger; Writer: Dudley Nichols, Rene Clair, Helene Fraenkel; Story: Lord Dunsany, Hugh Wedlock, Howard Snyder, Lewis R. Foster; DP: Archie Stout; Ed: Fred Pressburger; Prod Design: Ern Metzner; Composer: Robert Stolz. B&W, 85 min.

It Happens Every Spring

(1949) Fox
Great fun, especially for baseball fans. Bookish chemistry professor Milland discovers a wood-repelling compound while working on a bug repellent. Being a baseball fan, he sees the possibilities of applying the substance to baseballs. The result is a rapid-fire rise in the majors, pitching perfect games under an assumed name to raise money for marriage to Peters. Her family assumes that his disappearance has to do with shady dealings. Funny physical comedy (his catcher ends up with the stuff on his hairbrush) and understated Milland make this enjoyable family fare. Academy Award Nomination for Best Motion Picture Story. **Cast:** Ray Milland, Jean Peters, Paul Douglas, Ed Begley, Ray Collins, Ted De Corsia, Jessie Royce Landis, William R. Murphy, Alan Hale. **Credits:** Dir: Lloyd Bacon; Prod: William Perlberg; Writer: Valentine Davies; DP: Joseph MacDonald; Ed: Bruce B. Pierce; Composer: Leigh Harline; Art Director: Lyle Wheeler, J. Russell Spencer. B&W, 87 min. **VHS**

It Happens Every Thursday

(1953) Universal
Fed up with the daily grind of his beat at a big-city newspaper, reporter Bob MacAvoy and his pregnant wife head to California, where they take over operations of a small, weekly paper. They struggle to keep the paper afloat financially, all the while trying to be accepted as part of the local community. To win over the locals, and increase his paper's circulation, MacAvoy turns to hatching a spectacular publicity stunt. **Cast:** Edgar Buchanan, John Forsythe, Frank McHugh, Dennis Weaver, Loretta Young, Jimmy Conlin,

Jane Darwell. **Credits:** Dir: Joseph Pevney; Prod: Leonard Goldstein, Anton Leader; Writer: Dane Lussier, Leonard Praskins, Barney Slater; Story: Jane McIlvaine; DP: Russell Metty; Ed: Frank Gross; Composer: Henry Mancini, Joseph Gershenson; Art Director: Robert Clatworthy, Bernard Herzbrun. B&W, 80 min.

It's a Date

(1940) Universal
Deanna sings her way through an awkward adolescence of competing with her mother for work and romance. Francis first loses a Broadway role to Durbin and her magnificent voice, and then finds her beau, Pidgeon, wooing Durbin as well. Remarkably good-humored given the circumstances, with tuneful songs and a refreshing Hawaiian setting. Remade with Jane Powell as *Nancy Goes to Rio*. Songs include "Ave Maria," "Love Is All," "Musetta's Waltz," and "Rhythm of the Islands." **Cast:** Deanna Durbin, Walter Pidgeon, Kay Francis, Eugene Pallette, Lewis Howard, S. Z. Sakall, Samuel S. Hinds, Cecilia Loftus. **Credits:** Dir: William A. Seiter; Prod: Joe Pasternak; Story: Norman Krasna; DP: Joseph A. Valentine; Ed: Bernard W. Burton; Composer: Charles Previn. B&W, 105 min. **VHS**

It's a Gift

(1934) Paramount
Considered one of Fields's greatest, though this earlier outing may be less well known than titles such as *The Bank Dick* (1940) or *My Little Chickadee* (1940). Fields plays Harold Bissonette (pronounced by his wife "Bisson-ay"), a grocer who picks up and moves west with ambitions to make his mark in the orange groves. He, of course, meets with frustrations at every turn. A reworking of the Fields silent, *It's the Old Army Game* (1926), itself an extended Ziegfeld Follies sketch costarring Louise Brooks. **Cast:** W. C. Fields, Baby LeRoy, Kathleen Howard, Tommy Bupp, Jean Rouverol, Tammany Young, Morgan Wallace, Charles Sellon, Julian Madison. **Credits:** Dir: Norman Z. McLeod; Prod: William LeBaron; Writer: Jack Cunningham; Story: W. C. Fields; DP: Henry Sharp; Art Director: Hans Dreier, John B. Goodman. B&W, 73 min. **VHS, LASER**

It's a Great Feeling

(1949) Warner Bros.
And what could be a better title for a Doris Day movie? An early Day role in which she gets to wander wide-eyed

through a Hollywood backlot encountering all the Warner greats. Waitress and aspiring actress Day gets her shot at the silver screen when everyone else in Hollywood refuses to work with obnoxious star Carson. After he drives her away, the production execs hear Day singing in the dailies and make Carson track her down to her hometown in cow country. **Cast:** Dennis Morgan, Doris Day, Jack Carson, Bill Goodwin, Irving Bacon, Claire Carleton, Jacqueline De Wit, Wilfred Lucas, Harlan Warde. **Credits:** Dir: David Butler; Prod: Alex Gottlieb; Writer: Jack Rose; Story: Melville Shavelson; DP: Wilfrid M. Cline; Ed: Irene Morra; Composer: Ray Heindorf; Art Director: Stanley Fleischer. Color, 85 min. **VHS, LASER**

It's Always Fair Weather

(1955) MGM
The unbeatable musical-comedy team of Kelly and Donen (*Singin' in the Rain*, 1952) direct this less well known Comden and Green musical about life's changing seasons. Kelly, Dailey, and Kidd meet up 10 years after their WWII discharge to reminisce over old times and hard times, and find that they hardly know—or like— one another anymore. Charisse adds leggy elegance to "Baby, You Knock Me Out." Academy Award Nomination for Best Scoring of a Musical Picture. **Cast:** Gene Kelly, Cyd Charisse, Dan Dailey, Dolores Gray, Michael Kidd, David Burns, Jay C. Flippen, Richard Simmons. **Credits:** Dir: Stanley Donen, Gene Kelly; Prod: Arthur Freed; Writer: Betty Comden, Adolph Green; DP: Robert Bronner; Ed: Adrienne Fazan; Composer: Andre Previn; Art Director: Cedric Gibbons, Arthur Lonergan. Color, 102 min. **VHS, LASER**

It's a Mad, Mad, Mad, Mad World

(1963) United Artists
They emptied the comedy hall of fame to make this frantic epic. It's like a wide-screen, big-budget disaster movie —only played for laughs—in which half the fun is pointing to famous faces. Tracy is the relatively calm center of a whirlwind as a detective keeping an eye on a herd of citizens out to uncover a stash of stolen bank loot. He has his hands full following Berle, Caesar, Rooney, Winters, Durante, Adams, et al. and on and on. At more than three hours in the restored version, this gets a little wearing. Academy Award Nominations: 6, including Best Cinematogra-

phy, Best Editing. **Academy Awards:** Best Sound Effects. **Cast:** Spencer Tracy, Milton Berle, Sid Caesar, Buddy Hackett, Edie Adams, Ethel Merman, Jonathan Winters, Jimmy Durante, Mickey Rooney, Dick Shawn. **Credits:** Dir: Stanley Kramer; Prod: Stanley Kramer; Writer: William Rose, Tania Rose; DP: Ernest Laszlo; Ed: Frederic Knudtson, Robert C. Jones, Gene Fowler, Jr.; Prod Design: Rudolph Sternad; Composer: Ernest Gold; Art Director: Gordon Gurnell. Color, 155 min./192 min. VHS, LASER

It's a Wonderful Life
(1946) RKO
Now the essential Hollywood Christmas movie classic, Capra's fable of finding sustenance in the humdrum of everyday life is a surprisingly dark vision for such a holiday icon. After all, this is a portrait of a man, played with great feeling and emotion by Stewart, driven to despair by potential financial ruin and the loss of his youthful dreams. It also features one of the angriest romantic clinches in all of movie history, as Stewart sees his future in Reed's eyes and knows it doesn't include the foreign adventures that have kept him going day to day in his broken-down savings and loan. But all this loss and compromise is balanced by genuine warmth and joy, as Stewart lassoes the moon for Reed, when she welcomes him to their improvised honeymoon suite, when, finally, all is put right by the community Stewart selflessly served—and by an angel named Clarence. More complex than most holiday fare, and maybe that's why it remains in our hearts. The restored video includes a digitally transferred print with trailer; the laserdisc includes commentary by Jeanine Basinger, stills, and production notes. The special 45th-anniversary video edition includes the documentary featurette, *The Making of It's a Wonderful Life*; the deluxe collector's set includes a digitally remastered edition duplicated from the original film negative, the "making of" featurette, lobby cards, a compact disc, production photos, original poster reproduction, the *It's a Wonderful Life Book*, and a letter from the director's son. The DVD contains the behind-the-scenes featurette and an interview with director Capra. Avoid the colorized version. Academy Award Nominations: Best Picture; Best Director; Best Actor: James Stewart; Best Editing; Best Sound. **Cast:** James Stewart, Donna Reed, Lionel

It's a Wonderful Life (1946)

Barrymore, Thomas Mitchell, Henry Travers, Beulah Bondi, Frank Faylen, Ward Bond, Gloria Grahame, H. B. Warner. **Credits:** Dir: Frank Capra; Prod: Frank Capra; Writer: Jo Swerling, Frank Capra, Frances Goodrich, Albert Hackett; Story: Philip Van Doren Stern; DP: Joseph Walker, Joseph Biroc; Ed: William Hornbeck; Composer: Dimitri Tiomkin; Costumes: Edward Stevenson; Art Director: Jack Okey. B&W, 132 min. VHS, LASER, DVD

It's a Wonderful World
(1939) MGM
It's also a wonderful screwball comedy with a strong cast, script, and direction, from what many regard as the greatest year Hollywood ever had. Stewart is a novice private dick who is assigned to trail a loose cannon of a

millionaire. Instead he finds both of them headed for a slew of picaresque misadventures, beginning with arrest and transportation to the Big House for murder. Stewart escapes and abducts poet Colbert, forcing her to help him as he assumes an absurd gallery of disguises. Along the way Colbert falls for him and together they exonerate Stewart and the millionaire. Note the script by Hecht from a story by him and Mankiewicz. **Cast:** Claudette Colbert, James Stewart, Guy Kibbee, Nat Pendleton, Frances Drake, Edgar Kennedy, Ernest Truex, Richard Carle, Cecilia Callejo, Sidney Blackmer. **Credits:** Dir: W. S. Van Dyke; Prod: Frank Davis; Writer: Ben Hecht; Story: Ben Hecht, Herman J. Mankiewicz; DP: Oliver T. Marsh; Ed: Harold Kress; Art Director: Cedric Gibbons. B&W, 86 min.

It Should Happen to You

(1954) Columbia
One of the best of the tragically few Holliday comedies, and one of her best performances. As aspiring actress Gladys Glover, Holliday puts her own name in lights by plastering it on a New York billboard. Cukor directs Kanin's script with characteristic light touch. Lemmon's screen debut. Academy Award Nomination for Best (Black-and-White) Costume Design. **Cast:** Judy Holliday, Jack Lemmon, Peter Lawford, Michael O'Shea, Connie Gilchrist, Vaughn Taylor, Heywood Hale Broun, Rex Evans. **Credits:** Dir: George Cukor; Prod: Fred Kohlmar; Writer: Garson Kanin; DP: Charles Lang; Ed: Charles Nelson; Composer: Frederick Hollander; Art Director: John Meehan. B&W, 88 min. **VHS, LASER**

It's in the Bag

(1945) United Artists
Radio star Allen made only a handful of movies, and this is the best. The plot—a threadbare nobleman searches for a fortune—is merely an excuse to put Allen in sketches with cohorts Benchley, Benny, Ameche, and Vallee. **Cast:** Fred Allen, Don Ameche, Jack Benny, William Bendix, Binnie Barnes, Robert Benchley, Rudy Vallee, Victor Moore, John Carradine, Jerry Colonna. **Credits:** Dir: Richard Wallace; Prod: Jack H. Skirball; Writer: Jay Dratler, Lewis R. Foster, Fred Allen; Story: Alma Reville; DP: Russell Metty; Ed: William Morgan; Composer: Werner Richard Heymann. B&W, 87 min. **VHS**

It's Love I'm After

(1937) Warner Bros.
In this romantic comedy, Howard plays an ego-inflated actor whose fiancée-costar, Davis, becomes jealous after he befriends eyelash-batting de Havilland. Pretty leads, witty script, and Blore in support make this entertaining. **Cast:** Leslie Howard, Bette Davis, Olivia de Havilland, Eric Blore, George Barbier, Bonita Granville, Spring Byington, Georgia Caine, Veda Ann Borg, Patric Knowles. **Credits:** Dir: Archie Mayo; Prod: Hal B. Wallis; Writer: Casey Robinson, Maurice Hanline; DP: James Van Trees; Ed: Owen Marks; Prod Design: Carl Jules Weyl; Composer: Heinz Roemheld. B&W, 90 min.

It's Only Money

(1962) Paramount
Better-than-usual Lewis entry, with Jerry a TV repairman who wants to be a private investigator. When he sees O'Brien on television inquiring about the whereabouts of her long-lost nephew—who is shortly to become heir to a fortune—Lewis decides to seek him out, but the clues all point to him! Instead of being a detective, Lewis becomes a target for several murder attempts by O'Brien's greedy attorney, who wants the fortune for himself. **Cast:** Jerry Lewis, Joan O'Brien, Zachary Scott, Jack Weston, Jesse White, Mae Questal, Pat Dahl, Barbara Pepper, Francine York, Michael Ross. **Credits:** Dir: Frank Tashlin; Prod: Paul Jones; Writer: John Murray; DP: W. Wallace Kelley; Ed: Arthur Schmidt; Composer: Walter Scharf. B&W, 84 min.

It Started in Naples

(1960) Paramount
American lawyer Gable ventures to Italy to finalize his brother's estate and discovers his nephew living with vivacious stripper Loren. He immediately begins a custody battle but may end up losing custody of his heart. Mostly interesting for the romantic combination of leads: Gable is nearly at the end of his career; Loren still has plenty of oomph. Academy Award Nomination for Best (Color) Art Direction—Set Decoration. **Cast:** Clark Gable, Sophia Loren, Vittorio De Sica, Marietto, Paolo Carlini, Claudio Ermelli, Giovanni Filidoro. **Credits:** Dir: Melville Shavelson; Prod: Jack Rose; Writer: Melville Shavelson, Jack Rose; Story: Suso Cecchi D'Amico; DP: Robert Surtees; Ed: Frank Bracht; Composer: Alessandro Cicognini, Carlo Savina. Color, 100 min. **VHS**

It Started with a Kiss

(1959) MGM
Whimsical comedy of whirlwind romance as Reynolds gives up her gold-digging plans to impulsively marry Air Force officer Ford. When he's transferred to Spain, they have to adjust to their new home and each other as Reynolds decides whether she made the right decision. Pleasant enough. **Cast:** Glenn Ford, Debbie Reynolds, Eva Gabor, Fred Clark, Edgar Buchanan, Harry Morgan, Robert Warwick. **Credits:** Dir: George Marshall; Prod: Aaron Rosenberg; Writer: Charles Lederer; DP: Robert Bronner; Ed: John McSweeney; Composer: Jeff Alexander; Art Director: Hans Peters, Urie McCleary. Color, 104 min. **VHS**

It Started with Eve

(1941) Universal
Sparkling romantic musical comedy with a grown-up Durbin. As wealthy Laughton languishes on his deathbed, he makes a gasping request to see the girl his son (Cummings) is about to marry. As she's not close at hand, Cummings grabs hat-check girl Durbin, who charms the old guy right back from the abyss. Now Cummings needs a plan, and Durbin is rather charming, after all. Remade as *I'd Rather Be Rich.* **Cast:** Deanna Durbin, Charles Laughton, Robert Cummings, Guy Kibbee, Margaret Tallichet, Catharine Doucet, Walter Catlett, Charles Coleman, Clara Blandick. **Credits:** Dir: Henry Koster; Writer: Norman Krasna; Story: Leo Townsend; DP: Rudolph Mate; Ed: Bernard W. Burton; Composer: H. J. Salter, Charles Previn; Art Director: Jack Otterson. B&W, 92 min. **VHS**

It! The Terror from Beyond Space

(1958) United Artists
The prototype for the *Alien* movies can be found in this late-'50s monster-from-outer-space-flick. A spaceship makes an expedition to Mars to retrieve the sole survivor of the first manned exploration. He's believed to have murdered his spacemates, but the real killer, a Martian native, has already gotten aboard and begins to eliminate the astronauts one by one. **Cast:** Marshall Thompson, Shawn Smith, Kim Spalding, Ann Doran, Paul Langton, Robert Bice, Richard Benedict, Ray Corrigan, Dabbs Greer, Richard Hervey. **Credits:** Dir: Edward L. Cahn; Prod: Robert E. Kent; Writer: Jerome Bixby; DP: Kenneth Peach; Ed: Grant Whytock; Composer: Paul Sawtell, Bert Shefter; Art Director: William Glasgow. B&W, 70 min. **VHS**

Ivanhoe

(1952) MGM
Attractive cast and location atmospherics make this the definitive screen version of Sir Walter Scott's knights-and-damsels epic. A chiseled Taylor fights for the return of Richard the Lionhearted, who was captured on his return journey from the Crusades. He captures the attention of two incomparably beautiful damsels in distress, Taylor and Fontaine, as he keeps them from the clutches of evil Prince John (Sanders). Remade for TV in 1982 with Anthony Andrews and James Mason. Academy Award Nominations: 3, including Best Picture. **Cast:** Robert Taylor, Elizabeth Taylor, Joan Fontaine, George Sanders, Emlyn Williams, Robert Douglas, Finlay Currie, Felix Aylmer. **Credits:** Dir: Richard

Thorpe; Prod: Pandro S. Berman; Writer: Noel Langley; Story: Sir Walter Scott; DP: Freddie Young; Ed: Frank Clarke; Composer: Miklos Rozsa; Art Director: Alfred Junge. Color, 107 min. **VHS, LASER**

I've Always Loved You
(1946) Republic
Classical-music lovers will want to catch this romantic melodrama set in the world of an orchestra and featuring a lush sound track that includes works by Beethoven, Tchaikovsky, Chopin, Liszt, Rachmaninoff, Wagner, and more performed by piano virtuoso Arthur Rubinstein. This very definition of the "quality picture" presents a romantic showdown between a tempestuous conductor and a willful concert pianist. Available in a restored version that reveals vibrant Technicolor and pristine sound. **Cast:** Philip Dorn, Catherine McLeod, William Carter, Maria Ouspenskaya, Felix Bressart, Fritz Feld, Elizabeth Patterson, Vanessa Brown, Lewis Howard, Adele Mara. **Credits:** Dir: Frank Borzage; Prod: Frank Borzage; Writer: Borden Chase; DP: Tony Gaudio; Ed: Richard L. Van Enger; Prod Design: Ernst Fegte; Composer: Sergey Rachmaninoff, Frederic Chopin, Ludwig van Beethoven, Felix Mendelssohn, Richard Wagner, J. S. Bach. Color, 117 min. **VHS, LASER**

Ivy
(1947) Universal
Melodrama set in early-20th-century England. A woman named Ivy (Fontaine) poisons her husband and sets up her lover, who is a doctor, as the murderer. Meanwhile, she pursues a third man. When the doctor is convicted and condemned to death, Ivy's crime is uncovered. Middling production but with a classy cast. **Cast:** Joan Fontaine, Patric Knowles, Herbert Marshall, Richard Ney, Cedric Hardwicke, Lucile Watson, Sara Allgood, Henry Stephenson, Rosalind Ivan, Lillian Fontaine. **Credits:** Dir: Sam Wood; Prod: William Cameron Menzies; Writer: Charles C. Bennett; Story: Marie Belloc-Lowndes; DP: Russell Metty; Ed: Ralph Dawson; Prod Design: Russell A. Gausman, T. F. Offenbecker; Composer: Daniele Amfitheatrof, Hoagy Carmichael; Art Director: Richard H. Riedel. B&W, 98 min.

I Wake Up Screaming
(1941) Fox
An entertaining mystery about a beautiful young actress (Landis) who is believed by brutal detective Cregar to

have been murdered by the promoter who was working to make her a star (Mature). Grable plays the victim's sister, who takes a shine to the suspect, in her first nonmusical performance. Keep watching for a clever plot twist at the end. Remade in 1953 as *Vicki*. **Cast:** Betty Grable, Carole Landis, Victor Mature, Laird Cregar, William Gargan, Alan Mowbray, Allyn Joslyn, Elisha Cook, Chick Chandler, Morris Ankrum. **Credits:** Dir: H. Bruce Humberstone; Prod: Milton Sperling; Writer: Dwight Taylor; Story: Steve Fisher; DP: Edward Cronjager; Ed: Robert Simpson; Prod Design: Richard Day, Nathan Juran; Composer: Cyril J. Mockridge. B&W, 82 min. **VHS**

I Walked with a Zombie
(1943) RKO
A creepy Tourneur-Lewton production about a nurse (Dee) who is hired to treat the catatonic matriarch of a Caribbean family. When the nurse explores local healing techniques, she finds dark legends, strange creatures, and eerie voodoo rituals. A better-than-average spooky story (vaguely related to *Jane Eyre*) and an intense atmosphere make this one to watch with someone else. **Cast:** James Ellison, Frances Dee, Tom Conway, Edith Barrett, James Bell, Sir Lancelot, Christine Gordon, Theresa Harris, Jeni Le Gon. **Credits:** Dir: Jacques Tourneur; Prod: Val Lewton; Writer: Curt Siodmak, Ardell Wray; DP: J. Roy Hunt; Ed: Mark Robson; Prod Design: Albert S. D'Agostino, Walter E. Keller; Composer: Roy Webb. B&W, 69 min. **VHS, LASER**

I Wanna Hold Your Hand
(1978) Warner Bros.
Spielberg protégé Zemeckis's (*Back to the Future*, *Forrest Gump*) first feature is a sweetly comic re-creation of the Beatles' invasion of New York. Teenage friends (including Allen) try any subterfuge necessary to score tickets for the Fab Four's appearance on *The Ed Sullivan Show*. A charmer of special interest for Beatles and pop music fans as the sound track includes 17 Beatles songs. **Cast:** Nancy Allen, Bobby Di Cicco, Marc McClure, Theresa Saldana, Susan Kendall Newman, Wendie Jo Sperber, Eddie Deezen, Christian Juttner, Will Jordan. **Credits:** Dir: Robert Zemeckis; Prod: Tamara Asseyev, Alex Rose; Writer: Robert Zemeckis, Bob Gale; DP: Donald M. Morgan; Ed: Frank Morriss; Prod Design: Peter Jamison; Composer: The Beatles. Color, 104 min. **VHS, LASER**

I Want a Divorce
(1940) Paramount
Real-life husband and wife Blondell and Powell star in this marital comedy. Snappy young Blondell weds successful lawyer Powell, and all is well until Powell takes on several divorce cases. Getting emotionally involved in her husband's work, Blondell takes a look at her own marriage. **Cast:** Joan Blondell, Dick Powell, Gloria Dickson, Frank Fay, Jessie Ralph, Harry Davenport, Conrad Nagel, Mickey Kuhn, Dorothy Burgess, Sidney Blackmer. **Credits:** Dir: Ralph Murphy; Prod: George M. Arthur; Writer: Frank Butler; Story: Adela Rogers St. John; DP: Ted Tetzlaff; Ed: LeRoy Stone; Prod Design: Hans Dreier, Ernst Fegte; Composer: Victor Young. B&W, 75 min.

I Wanted Wings
(1941) Paramount
Constance Kern changed her name to Veronica Lake for this, her feature film debut. An unabashed piece of WWII propaganda, it follows three hot-shot pilots, Milland, Holden, and Morris, as they earn their wings under the impeccably straight Donlevy. Holden's a New York City rich kid with curvaceous photographer Moore documenting his progress, and Milland's a handsome workingman who makes the trampy Lake feel warm all over. The plot's machinations are secondary to the expert aerial photography and special effects. **Academy Awards:** Best Special Effects. **Cast:** Ray Milland, William Holden, Wayne Morris, Brian Donlevy, Constance Moore, Veronica Lake, Harry Davenport, Phil Brown, Edward Fielding, Willard Robertson. **Credits:** Dir: Mitchell Leisen; Prod: Arthur Hornblow, Jr.; Writer: Sig Herzig, Richard Maibaum, Beirne Lay; Story: Eleanore Griffin, Frank Wead, Beirne Lay; DP: Leo Tover; Ed: Hugh Bennett; Prod Design: Hans Dreier; Composer: Victor Young. B&W, 131 min.

I Want to Live!
(1958) United Artists
Hayward's most impressive performance as a tough gal wrongly accused of murder and her attempts to avoid the gas chamber. When an elderly lady is murdered, a prostitute named Barbara Graham takes the fall. Hayward's defiance and then pathos as the case becomes a clear miscarriage of justice earned her the Best Actress Oscar. An important statement about capital punishment. Hayward won a Golden Globe for Best Actress in a Drama. Academy Award Nominations: 6, including Best Director; Best (Adapted)

I Was a Male War Bride (1949)

Screenplay. **Academy Awards:** Best Actress: Susan Hayward. **Cast:** Susan Hayward, Simon Oakland, Theodore Bikel, Virginia Vincent, Wesley Lau, Philip Coolidge, Lou Krugman, James Philbrook, Bartlett Robinson, Gage Clarke. **Credits:** Dir: Robert Wise; Prod: Walter Wanger; Writer: Nelson Gidding, Don Mankiewicz; DP: Lionel Lindon; Ed: William Hornbeck; Prod Design: Ted Haworth; Composer: Johnny Mandel. B&W, 123 min. **VHS, LASER**

I Want You
(1951) RKO
The Korean War comes to small-town America in a fascinating portrayal of the country's attitudes toward another foreign conflict just as the wounds of WWII have begun to heal. A WWII vet (Andrews) struggles with his wife's

objections and his own misgivings about reenlisting, and two young men receive conflicting messages from their fathers about the meaning of duty and service. Historically and dramatically interesting. Script by novelist Irwin Shaw. **Cast:** Dana Andrews, Dorothy McGuire, Farley Granger, Peggy Dow, Robert Keith, Mildred Dunnock, Martin Milner, Ray Collins, Jim Backus. **Credits:** Dir: Mark Robson; Prod: Samuel Goldwyn; Writer: Irwin Shaw; DP: Harry Stradling; Ed: Daniel Mandell; Prod Design: Richard Day; Composer: Leigh Harline; Costumes: Mary Wills. B&W, 102 min. **VHS**

I Was a Male War Bride
(1949) Fox
Hawks finds timeless comedy in the confusion of postwar Europe, and provides one of Grant's funniest moments

(in a cross-dressing sequence that rivals *Bringing Up Baby*'s dressing-gown scene). French officer Grant meets his true love in WAC Sheridan, and they make their plans for a home in the U.S. The only hitch? Bureaucratic logic dictates that war brides may be shipped back to the States—but where does that leave Grant? **Cast:** Cary Grant, Ann Sheridan, Marion Marshall, Randy Stuart, John Whitney, Kenneth Tobey, Joe Haworth, Gene Garrick, Ruben Wendorf. **Credits:** Dir: Howard Hawks; Prod: Sol C. Siegel; Writer: Charles Lederer, Leonard Spigelgass, Hagar Wilde; Story: Henri Rochard; DP: Norbert F. Brodine, Osmond H. Borradaile; Ed: James B. Clark; Prod Design: Lyle Wheeler, Albert Hogsett; Composer: Cyril J. Mockridge. B&W, 105 min. **VHS**

The Jackie Robinson Story
(1950) Eagle-Lion Films
In this biopic of major league base-ball's first black player, Robinson stars as himself in a straightforward account of his dramatic life from ath-letic excellence at UCLA and in the Negro League to his momentous meeting with Branch Rickey of the no-less-legendary Brooklyn Dodgers and his major league career. Considering that this was filmed well before the civil rights era, it deals with the racial issues plainly and is notable as social history as well as being a ter-rific baseball movie. A TV movie called *The Court Martial of Jackie Robinson* was made four decades later. **Cast:** Jackie Robinson, Ruby Dee, Minor Watson, Louise Beavers, Richard Lane, Harry Shannon, Ben Lessy, Joel Fluellen. **Credits:** Dir: Alfred E. Green; Prod: Mort Briskin; Writer: Lawrence Taylor, Arthur Mann. B&W, 81 min. **VHS**

Jacques Brel Is Alive and Well and Living in Paris
(1973) American Film Theater
A cinema adaptation of the off-Broadway cabaret hit conceived by Eric Blau and Mort Shuman and fea-turing the lyrics and music of Belgian writer Jacques Brel, which played 1,800 performances at N.Y.C.'s famed Village Gate. The 26-song revue begins with the principals, including a lady shopper, a Marine, and a taxi driver, who run to a theater to get out of a downpour. There, each character finds himself onstage and each song unfolds as its own fantasy. In this poignant look at Brel's bitter-sweet view of life, Brel himself sings his most well known ballad, "Ne Me Quittes Pas." **Cast:** Elly Stone, Joe Masiell, Jacques Brel. **Credits:** Dir: Denis Heroux; Prod: Claude Heroux; DP: Rene Verzier; Ed: Yves Langlois; Prod Design: Jean Andre; Composer: Jacques Brel. Color, 93 min.

Jailhouse Rock
(1957) MGM
Considered by many to be Presley's best film because of its eerie narra-tive prescience, noirish setting, and quality songs (note the poolside per-formance of "You're So Square"). In any case, a must for those who need convincing of Presley's revolutionary sexual magnetism. After learning to play guitar and sing during a stint in the Big House for manslaughter, a punk kid (Presley) becomes a rock star with a little help from a beautiful agent (Tyler). He progresses from wide-eyed gratitude to surly petulance. The justly famous title-song sequence, with sliding down the fire pole and dancing with a chair, was choreo-graphed by the King himself. Other songs include "Treat Me Nice," "Baby, I Don't Care," and "I Wanna Be Free." **Cast:** Elvis Presley, Judy Tyler, Vaughn Taylor, Dean Jones, Mickey Shaugh-nessy, Jennifer Holden, Anne Neyland, Hugh Sanders. **Credits:** Dir: Richard Thorpe; Prod: Pandro S. Berman; Story: Guy Trosper; DP: Robert Bron-ner; Ed: Ralph E. Winters; Composer: Jeff Alexander; Art Director: William A. Horning, Randall Duell. B&W, 98 min. **VHS, LASER, DVD**

Jamaica Inn
(1939) Paramount
The last British Hitchcock, and the first of his adaptations of a Daphne du Maurier novel (he achieved an immedi-ate Hollywood success with *Rebecca* the following year). A vicious band of highwaymen, led by nobleman Laughton, create havoc on the 19th-century Cornwall moors. A young woman (O'Hara) who visits her aunt discovers she's residing in a haven for the criminals. Careful, literal filmmak-ing, but interesting to see the master ready to spread his wings and truly fly. An early role for the stunningly beauti-ful O'Hara; she and Laughton teamed again the same year for the indelible

Hunchback of Notre Dame. **Cast:** Charles Laughton, Maureen O'Hara, Robert Newton, Leslie Banks, Herbert Lomas, Mervyn Jones, Emlyn Williams, Edwin Greenwood. **Credits:** Dir: Alfred Hitchcock; Prod: Erich Pom-mer, Charles Laughton; Writer: Sidney Gilliat, Joan Harrison, J. B. Priestley; Story: Alma Reville; DP: Harry Stradling, Bernard Knowles; Ed: Robert Hamer; Composer: Eric Fenby. B&W, 98 min. **VHS, LASER**

Jane Eyre
(1934) Monogram
A curiosity notable for being the first talking version of Brontë's novel about an orphaned governess who moves to a mysterious mansion and falls in love with its brooding owner. Also interest-ing as a bid by poverty row–studio Monogram to move up in class. **Cast:** Virginia Bruce, Colin Clive, Beryl Mer-cer, Jameson Thomas, Aileen Pringle, David Torrence, Lionel Belmore, Joan Standing, Edith Fellows, John Rodgers. **Credits:** Dir: Christy Cabanne; Prod: Ben Verschleiser; Writer: Adele Co-mandini; Story: Charlotte Brontë; DP: Robert H. Planck; Ed: Carl Pierson. B&W, 67 min. **VHS**

Jane Eyre
(1944) Fox
The most satisfying version of Charlotte Brontë's oft-filmed novel, with moody atmosphere and Welles's glow-ering mystery (some say director Stevenson benefited from—or suffered through—Welles's presence on the set). Fontaine is convincing as the orphan girl who becomes a governess, experiences the light of love with her employer, and then sees her future cru-elly snatched away by Mr. Rochester's dark secret. An early role for Taylor. **Cast:** Joan Fontaine, Orson Welles, Margaret O'Brien, Elizabeth Taylor, Hillary Brooke, Peggy Ann Garner, Henry Daniell, Sara Allgood, Agnes Moorehead, John Sutton. **Credits:** Dir:

Robert Stevenson; Prod: William Goetz; Writer: Aldous Huxley, Robert Stevenson, John Houseman; Story: Charlotte Brontë; DP: George Barnes; Ed: Walter Thompson; Composer: Bernard Herrmann; Art Director: James Basevi, Wiard Ihnen. B&W, 96 min. VHS, LASER

Janie

(1944) Warner Bros.
Wartime comedy about the effects on small-town life of an army camp. Although her newspaperman father has written editorials opposing it, Janie (Reynolds) is delighted when an army post is established near her small town. Determined to land herself a soldier boyfriend, she meets and falls for a young private (Hutton), and invites him over for an intimate evening when her parents are scheduled to be away from home. Her regular high school sweetie, seeing his opportunity to intervene, counters by inviting half of the base along, too. All this makes for a giant bash, at which both Janie's parents and the M.P.s are inevitable arrivals. **Cast:** Joyce Reynolds, Robert Hutton, Edward Arnold, Ann Harding, Robert Benchley, Alan Hale. **Credits:** Dir: Michael Curtiz; Prod: Alex Gottlieb; Writer: Agnes Christine Johnson, Charles Hoffman; Story: Josephine Bentham, Herschel V. Williams, Jr.; DP: Carl E. Guthrie; Ed: Owen Marks; Prod Design: Robert Hass; Composer: Heinz Roemheld, Franz Waxman. B&W, 102 min.

Janis

(1974)
One of the few documentary looks at the life of blues-rock singer Janis Joplin, and one of the more colorful—and tragic—of rock's greatest period. It traces Janis from childhood in blue-collar Texas, through her performances with Big Brother and the Holding Co. at the height of the Haight-Ashbury psychedelic scene, to superstardom after Woodstock. Contains 14 songs, including "Piece of My Heart," "Me and Bobby McGee," "Tell Mama," and "Ball and Chain." Filmed with the cooperation of her family, so it doesn't get as real as it might have, but a rare glimpse at a meteoric talent. **Cast:** Janis Joplin. **Credits:** Dir: Howard Alk; Writer: Howard Alk, Seaton Findlay; DP: James Desmond, Michael Wadleigh; Composer: Janis Joplin. Color, 96 min. VHS

Japanese War Bride

(1952) Fox
Anti-Japanese sentiment, festering since WWII, causes friction between neighbors and family when a returning Korean War veteran brings home a new Japanese wife. One of the last of Hollywood legend Vidor's directing career; interesting to see the lion in winter handling B-movie sensationalism and budget. **Cast:** Shirley Yamaguchi, Don Taylor, Cameron Mitchell, Marie Windsor, James Bell, Louise Lorimer, Philip Ahn, Sybil Merritt, Lane Nakano, Kathleen Mulqueen. **Credits:** Dir: King Vidor; Prod: Joseph Bernhard, Anson Bond; Writer: Catherine Turney; DP: Lionel Lindon; Ed: Terry Morse; Prod Design: Daniel Hall; Composer: Emil Newman, Arthur Lange. B&W, 91 min. VHS

Jason and the Argonauts

(1963) Columbia
Greek mythology comes to life in this exciting film adaptation of the story of Jason's quest for the Golden Fleece. Harryhausen's special effects in this picture are legendary, especially a sword fight between three live actors and seven skeletons. Loosely based on the *Argonautica* of Apollonius of Rhodes (c. 250 B.C.). The laserdisc features an interview with Harryhausen. A wonderful film to watch with the kids. **Cast:** Todd Armstrong, Gary Raymond, Nancy Kovack, Honor Blackman, Douglas Robinson, John Crawford, Nigel Green, Andrew Faulds. **Credits:** Dir: Don Chaffey; Prod: Charles H. Schneer; Writer: Beverly Cross; Ed: Maurice Rootes; Prod Design: Geoffrey Drake, Herbert Smith; Composer: Bernard Herrmann; SFX: Ray Harryhausen. Color, 104 min. VHS, LASER, DVD

Jaws

(1975) Universal
The box-office smash that created the event-movie mentality in Hollywood and to which all theme-park-ride movies get compared—and it still makes you think twice before a trip to the beach. A seaside community (it was filmed on Martha's Vineyard, Massachusetts) succumbs to terror, and writes off a tourist season, when a Great White shark seems to target the town's beaches for a hunting ground. Local sheriff Scheider joins with a bespectacled academic (Dreyfuss) and a salty-dog fisherman (Shaw) in an Ahab-like hunt for the monster. A young Spielberg (all of 27!) stage-manages the bounding main action, and a recalcitrant mechanical shark named Bruce, to produce a modern classic of archetypal terror. Williams's score can still evoke shivers. Based on the best-selling book by Benchley. Followed by three sequels. The laserdisc includes an original, two-hour "making of" documentary featuring interviews with the cast and crew, behind-the-scenes footage, outtakes, and more. Academy Award Nominations: 4, including Best Picture. **Academy Awards:** Best Film Editing; Best Sound; Best Original Score. **Cast:** Roy Scheider, Richard Dreyfuss, Robert Shaw, Lorraine Gary, Murray Hamilton, Peter Benchley, Carl Gottlieb, Jay Mello, Lee Fierro, Jeffrey Kramer. **Credits:** Dir: Steven Spielberg; Prod: Richard D. Zanuck, David Brown; Writer: Peter Benchley, Carl Gottlieb, Howard Sackler; Story: Peter Benchley; DP: Bill Butler; Ed: Verna Fields; Prod Design: Joe Alves; Composer: John Williams; Set Designer: John M. Dwyer. Color, 124 min. VHS, LASER

Jaws 2

(1978) Universal
An almost inevitably disappointing sequel, given the absences of Dreyfuss, Shaw, and Spielberg. But notable for the even more elaborate shark-terror scenes. Amity police chief Scheider discovers that there's more than one fish in the sea—the Great White shark he destroyed has a hungry mate that comes to the all-you-can-eat buffet at the seaside resort, and the sheriff must stop him before he dines and dashes. Don't bother with the next two *Jaws* sequels, though. **Cast:** Roy Scheider, Lorraine Gary, Murray Hamilton, Joseph Mascolo, Jeffrey Kramer, Collin Wilcox, Ann Dusenberry, Mark Gruner, Barry Coe, Susan French. **Credits:** Dir: Jeannot Szwarc; Prod: Richard D. Zanuck, David Brown; Writer: Carl Gottlieb, Michael Butler; DP: Michael Butler; Ed: Neil Travis, Steve Potter, Arthur Schmidt, Freeman Davies, Michael Elias, Robert Hernandez, Sherrie Sanet Jacobson, Joe Alves; Composer: John Williams; Costumes: Bill Jobe; Set Designer: Phil Abramson. Color, 117 min. VHS, LASER

The Jazz Singer

(1927) Warner Bros.
A cinema landmark, this is the film most identified with the coming of sound. Though sound schemes had been envisioned at the dawn of motion pictures (even sound-on-film techniques similar to modern methods), *The Jazz Singer* made the commercial potential of sound apparent. The major studios had resisted disrupting the profitable silent-film production engine that had only recently been standardized, and making the huge investment required retrofitting studios and theaters for sound. Sam

Warner must be credited with taking a chance on a sound-on-disk system developed by their Vitaphone subsidiary; he died just before the thronged premiere that proved his prescience. The first Vitaphone feature film depicts the dilemma of a cantor's son who garners show business success over his father's objections. With the line, "You ain't heard nuthin' yet!," movie history changed forever. Note that *The Jazz Singer* is mostly silent, with just some Jolson ad-libbed asides in addition to the synch-sound (more or less) musical segments. The first all-talking feature was *Lights of New York*, a squalid little potboiler that featured dialogue in 22 scenes. Songs include "Mammy," "Toot, Toot, Tootsie," "Blue Skies," and more. Academy Award Nominations: 2, including Best Adapted Writing. **Academy Awards:** Special Award for technical achievement. **Cast:** Al Jolson, May McAvoy, Eugenie Besserer, Warner Oland, Myrna Loy, William Demarest. **Credits:** Dir: Alan Crosland; Writer: Jack Jarmouth; Story: Samson Raphaelson; Ed: Harold McCord; Cinematographer: Hal Mohr. B&W, 90 min. **VHS**

The Jazz Singer

(1953) Warner Bros.
Thomas takes the Jolson role in a straightforward rendition of the by-now familiar tale of the cantor's son who chooses show biz over filial duty. Not as compelling without the historical context, but interesting for Curtiz's direction, Thomas's feeling for the role, and the appearance of Lee. Academy Award Nomination for Best Scoring of a Musical. **Cast:** Danny Thomas, Peggy Lee, Eduard Franz, Allyn Joslyn, Mildred Dunnock, Tom Tully, Alex Gerry. **Credits:** Dir: Michael Curtiz; Prod: Louis F. Edelman; Writer: Frank Davis, Leonard Stern. Color, 107 min. **VHS**

Jennie Gerhardt

(1933) Paramount
Sidney again shines in a Dreiser tragedy adapted for the screen (she also appeared in *An American Tragedy*, 1931). This time around, she leaves home to find betrayal at the hands of powerful benefactor Senator Brander, superbly played by Arnold. When he's killed in an accident, he leaves her with a daughter, forcing her to return home in shame. She is driven to the household staff of the wealthy Kane family, and finds both unrequited love with Lester Kane and the death of her daughter. **Cast:** Sylvia Sidney, Donald Cook, Mary Astor, Edward Arnold, H.

B. Warner, Theodore von Eltz, Dorothy Libaire, Greta Meyer, Dave O'Brien. **Credits:** Dir: Marion Gering; Prod: B. P. Schulberg; Writer: S. K. Lauren, Joseph Moncure March, Frank Partos; Story: Theodore Dreiser; DP: Leon Shamroy. B&W, 85 min.

Jeremiah Johnson

(1972) Warner Bros.
Redford stars as the title character, a man who flees civilization for the wilderness in the mid-1800s. Despite a constant struggle to survive challenges from nature and the local Indians, he becomes one with his surroundings. This is a beautifully photographed and atmospheric film that no nature buff, or Redford fan, will want to miss. Man's-man film writer-director Milius must have contributed the notion of the spiritual peace found in the battle with nature. **Cast:** Robert Redford, Will Geer, Stefan Gierasch, Josh Albee, Allyn Ann McLerie, Charles Tyner, Delle Bolton, Joaquin Martinez, Paul Benedict, Matt Clark. **Credits:** Dir: Sydney Pollack; Prod: Joe Wizan; Writer: John Milius, Edward Anhalt; DP: Duke Callaghan; Ed: Thomas Stanford; Prod Design: Ted Haworth; Set Designer: Raymond Molyneaux. Color, 116 min. **VHS, LASER, DVD**

Jericho

(1937) General Films
A rare chance to see Robeson, this time as a corporal in a black unit of the U.S. expeditionary forces stationed in France during WWI. He's court-martialed and sentenced to die after accidentally killing his brutal sergeant in a fight. He escapes and lives among a North African tribe. A curiosity that showcases the powerful appeal (and powerful voice) of Robeson. Songs include "My Way," "Golden River," "Deep Desert," "Silent Night," and "Shortnin' Bread." **Cast:** Paul Robeson, Henry Wilcoxon, Wallace Ford, John Laurie, James Carew. **Credits:** Dir: Thornton Freeland; Prod: Walter Futter; Writer: Robert N. Lee, Frances Marion, Peter Ruric, George Barraud; DP: John W. Boyle; Ed: Edward B. Jarvis; Composer: Michael Carr, Jimmy Kennedy; Art Director: Edward Carrick. B&W, 77 min. **VHS**

The Jerk

(1979) Universal
Martin fans will love him in his first starring role. He narrates and stars, telling us the story of his absurd life from his birth ("I was born a poor black child") to his happy middle years

as a successful inventor of a device meant to eliminate annoying eyeglass nose-slide, and up to the down-on-his-luck present. This is absolutely silly comedy based on Martin's rubbery-faced persona developed on TV's *Saturday Night Live*; directed by Reiner, who knows a thing or two about TV comedy himself. **Cast:** Steve Martin, Bernadette Peters, Catlin Adams, Mabel King, M. Emmet Walsh, Dick Anthony Williams, Dick O'Neill, Maurice Evans, Pepe Serna, Carl Gottlieb. **Credits:** Dir: Carl Reiner; Prod: David V. Picker, William E. McEuen; Writer: Steve Martin, Carl Gottlieb, Michael Elias; Story: Carl Gottlieb, Steve Martin; DP: Victor J. Kemper; Ed: Bud Molin; Prod Design: Jack T. Collis; Composer: Jack Elliott; Costumes: Theadora Van Runkle. Color, 104 min. **VHS, LASER, DVD**

Jesse James

(1939) Fox
Power and Fonda bring the James brothers legend to the big screen in fine style. This rich production paints a dubious historical portrait of Jesse as driven to crime by the destruction of his family's farm at the hands of the railroad, but the talent involved makes it easy to overlook the inaccuracy and view the movie as pure Hollywood drama. Fonda appeared again as Frank James in *Return of Frank James* (1940), directed by Fritz Lang. **Cast:** Tyrone Power, Henry Fonda, Randolph Scott, Nancy Kelly, Henry Hull, John Carradine, Jane Darwell, Donald Meek, Slim Summerville, J. Edward Bromberg. **Credits:** Dir: Henry King; Prod: Nunnally Johnson; Writer: Nunnally Johnson; DP: W. Howard Greene, George Barnes; Ed: Barbara McLean; Art Director: William S. Darling. Color, 106 min. **VHS, LASER**

Jesus Christ Superstar

(1973) Universal
The film version of the Webber and Rice smash record and the Broadway musical sensation about the last week of Christ's life. At the time, its pairing of rock music with a sacred subject was thought to be bordering on the sacrilegious but who could resist those songs? This film version presents the story as told by young people in Israel, opening up the stage to natural vistas of the Holy Land. The stage production has shown remarkable longevity, being revived periodically in road shows and on Broadway. Songs include the title song, "I Don't Know How to Love Him," "Everything's Alright," "What's the Buzz," and more.

"I keep your face and figure in my mind as I write."

John Steinbeck in a letter to Henry Fonda

Academy Award Nomination for Best Song Score. **Cast:** Ted Neeley, Carl Anderson, Yvonne Elliman, Barry Dennen, Bob Bingham, Larry Marshall, Josh Mostel, Kurt Yaghjian, Philip Toubus. **Credits:** Dir: Norman Jewison; Prod: Robert Stigwood; Writer: Norman Jewison, Melvyn Bragg; DP: Douglas Slocombe; Ed: Anthony Gibbs; Prod Design: Richard MacDonald; Composer: Tim Rice, Andrew Lloyd Webber. Color, 108 min. **VHS, LASER**

Jet Pilot
(1957) Universal
A flier's dream with right-stuff guy Chuck Yeager doing the stunt flying. The tense Cold War plot has American Air Force colonel Wayne falling in love with defected Russian pilot Leigh. His suspicions take them back into the heart of the evil empire. The aerial sequences are the highlight. Producer Hughes once again takes to the skies on film, aiming at the fascination and box-office success he found with *Hell's Angels* (1930) a generation before. The last von Sternberg film released, though it was shot in 1950 before *Macao* (1952) and *Anatahan* (1953). **Cast:** John Wayne, Janet Leigh, Jay C. Flippen, Paul Fix, Richard Rober, Roland Winters, Hans Conried, Ivan Triesault, John Bishop, Joyce Compton. **Credits:** Dir: Josef von Sternberg; Prod: Howard Hughes; Writer: Jules Furthman; DP: Winton C. Hoch; Ed: Harry Marker, James Wilkinson, Michael R. McAdam; Prod Design: Albert S. D'Agostino, Feild M. Gray; Composer: Bronislau Kaper. Color, 113 min. **VHS, LASER**

Jewel Robbery
(1932) Warner Bros.
Powell just can't help being captivating, so he might as well put it to good use, for instance, by relieving a beautiful (but-pining-from-ennui) banker's wife (Francis) of all those heavy jewels while he romances her. Powell sailing through high society turns this into something special. **Cast:** William Powell, Kay Francis, Hardie Albright, André Luquet, Henry Kolker, Spencer Charters, Alan Mowbray, Helen Vinson,

Lawrence Grant. **Credits:** Dir: William Dieterle; Writer: Edwin Gelsey, Laszlo Fodor, William Keighley; DP: Robert Kurrle; Art Director: Robert M. Haas. B&W, 63 min.

Jezebel
(1938) Warner Bros.
The role perhaps most closely associated with Davis is an utter triumph. As a coquettish belle in the Civil War South, Davis taunts and teases the men who desire her (Fonda and Brent) until her options vanish and she's faced with life alone. She realizes her shallowness and the depth of her potential loss when Fonda becomes ill. Wyler and Davis were famous combatants, but the director was able to elicit her best work (here and in *The Little Foxes*, 1941). He was noted for endless takes and for mise-en-scène, allowing scenes to develop in one shot rather than by intercutting close-ups and reaction shots. This required discipline and concentration from actors. The results, as in this, were worth the effort. Academy Award Nominations: 5, including Best Picture; Best Cinematography. **Academy Awards:** Best Actress: Bette Davis; Best Supporting Actress: Fay Bainter. **Cast:** Bette Davis, Henry Fonda, George Brent, Margaret Lindsay, Donald Crisp, Fay Bainter, Richard Cromwell, Henry O'Neill, John Litel, Gordon Oliver. **Credits:** Dir: William Wyler; Prod: Henry Blanke; Writer: Abem Finkel, John Huston, Robert Buckner; Story: Clements Ripley; DP: Ernest Haller; Ed: Warren Low; Composer: Max Steiner; Art Director: Robert M. Haas. B&W, 105 min. **VHS, LASER, DVD**

Jimi Hendrix
(1973)
This absorbing documentary about one of rock's greatest innovators, guitarist Jimi Hendrix, features both interviews with contemporaries such as Clapton and band mates Mitchell and Cox, and rare performances from his club dates in London to sequences from the Monterey Pop, Woodstock, and Isle of Wight music festivals. A

must for rock fans and those who want a rare insight into one of the most fertile talents in rock. **Cast:** Jimi Hendrix, Eric Clapton, Mick Jagger, Little Richard, Pete Townshend. **Credits:** Dir: Joe Boyd, Gary Weis, John Head; Prod: Joe Boyd, John Head, Gary Weis; Ed: Peter Colbert. Color, 102 min. **VHS**

Jim Thorpe—All American
(1951) Warner Bros.
Athletic Lancaster plays a cool Native American before Native American was cool. Curtiz directs the biopic of the multifaceted athlete who was stripped of his Olympic medals when he decided to play major league baseball. Not more than expected, but a winner for sports fans. **Cast:** Burt Lancaster, Charles Bickford, Steve Cochran, Phyllis Thaxter, Dick Wesson, Alfonso Mejia, Nestor Paiva, Jim Moss, Billy Gray, Edwin Max. **Credits:** Dir: Michael Curtiz; Prod: Everett Freeman; Writer: Douglas Morrow, Frank Davis, Everett Freeman; DP: Ernest Haller; Ed: Folmar Blangsted; Composer: Max Steiner. B&W, 107 min. **VHS, LASER**

Joan of Arc
(1948) RKO
A radiant Bergman makes an apt choice for director Fleming's (*Wizard of Oz*, 1939, and *Gone With the Wind*, 1939) sincere depiction of Joan of Arc, the young peasant girl who united France and was martyred for her beliefs. Based on Anderson's 1946 play, *Joan of Lorraine*. Note: a restored version due in 1999 adds footage cut after initial release. Academy Award Nominations: 7, including Best Actress: Ingrid Bergman and Best Supporting Actor: Jose Ferrer. **Academy Awards:** Best Color Cinematography; Best Costume Design (Color). **Cast:** Ingrid Bergman, Jose Ferrer, Francis L. Sullivan, J. Carrol Naish, Ward Bond, Shepperd Strudwick, Gene Lockhart, Leif Erikson, Cecil Kellaway, Selena Royle. **Credits:** Dir: Victor Fleming, Andrew Solt; Prod: Walter Wanger; Writer: Maxwell Anderson; DP: Joseph A. Valentine; Ed: Frank Sullivan; Composer: Hugo Friedhofer. Color, 100 min. **VHS, LASER**

Joe
(1970) Cannon
A business executive and a hard-hat bigot team up to find the executive's runaway daughter and form a partnership that explodes into violence and then mutual suspicion. Their search becomes a journey through the counterculture, a world foreign and repugnant to them both. The Hippie vs.

Redneck theme places us firmly in 1970, but Boyle shines as the flag-waver. Sarandon steps onto the celluloid scene for the first time. Academy Award Nomination for Best (Original) Screenplay. **Cast:** Peter Boyle, Dennis Patrick, Susan Sarandon, Audrey Caire, K. Callan, Tim Lewis, Estelle Omens, Marlene Warfield, Patrick O'Neal. **Credits:** Dir: John G. Avildsen; Prod: David Gil; Writer: Norman Wexler; DP: John G. Avildsen; Ed: George T. Norris. Color, 107 min. **VHS, LASER**

Joe and Ethel Turp Call on the President
(1939) MGM
An entertaining comedy that is also a democratic fantasy. Originating with Runyon, it chronicles events surrounding a postal worker suspended for tampering with the mail, albeit with a noble motive: to protect his sweetheart from bad news. Apparently eager to overlook a federal crime, the Flatbush neighborhood mobilizes around his cause, and worlds collide when the Turps actually succeed in arguing their case in the Oval Office before granite-faced president Stone. **Cast:** Ann Sothern, Lewis Stone, Walter Brennan, William Gargan, Marsha Hunt, Tom Neal, James Bush, Don Costello, Muriel Hutchinson, Jack Norton. **Credits:** Dir: Robert B. Sinclair; Prod: Edgar Selwyn; Writer: Damon Runyon, Melville Baker; DP: Leonard Smith; Ed: Gene Ruggiero. B&W, 70 min.

Joe Kidd
(1972) Universal
Eastwood and Duvall clash in a Western set in territorial New Mexico. Eastwood is hired by wealthy Duvall to fight off some Mexicans in a land dispute, but then falls in love with one, complicating matters. When he discovers his own spread has been destroyed, he reverses his allegiance. Note writing credit for novelist Leonard. **Cast:** Clint Eastwood, Robert Duvall, John Saxon, Don Stroud, Stella Garcia, James Wainwright, Paul Koslo, Gregory Walcott, Dick Van Patten, John Carter. **Credits:** Dir: John Sturges; Prod: Sidney Beckerman; Story: Elmore Leonard; DP: Bruce Surtees; Ed: Ferris Webster; Composer: Lalo Schifrin; Art Director: Alexander Golitzen. Color, 88 min. **VHS, LASER, DVD**

The Joe Louis Story
(1953) United Artists
The story of the heavyweight champion of the world who was both a hero in the ring, becoming a national symbol

of pride after knocking out Nazi Germany's Max Schmeling, and a potent instrument of racial equality. Though this didn't have much of a budget and is in many ways a fairly straightforward biopic, it does have a couple of strengths: Wallace, who plays the champ, was a boxer and newsreel clips lend an air of authenticity. An early role for Davis. **Cast:** Coley Wallace, Paul Stewart, James Edwards, Ossie Davis, Dots Johnson, John Marley, Tiger Joe Marsh. **Credits:** Dir: Robert Gordon; Prod: Stirling Silliphant; Writer: Robert Sylvester; Composer: George Bassman. B&W, 88 min. **VHS**

Joe Palooka
(1934) United Artists
Fight movie has Durante singing his famous "Inka-Dinka-Doo." Fast, funny, well-directed comedy about a fight promoter (Durante) and his main man (Erwin). Erwin fights James Cagney's little brother, William. **Cast:** Jimmy Durante, Lupe Velez, Marjorie Rambeau, Stuart Erwin, Robert Armstrong, Mary Carlisle, William Cagney, Thelma Todd. **Credits:** Dir: Benjamin Stoloff; Prod: Edward Small; Writer: Jack Jevne, Arthur Kober, Gertrude Purcell, Murray Roth, Ham Fisher, Ben Ryan; DP: Arthur Edeson; Ed: Grant Whytock; Composer: Constantin Bakaleinikoff; Art Director: Albert S. D'Agostino. B&W, 86 min. **VHS**

Johnny Angel
(1945) RKO
Raft takes a turn at the tough-guy gangster picture as a merchant marine sailor who comes home from the war and searches for his father's murderer. As he uncovers the mystery, he busts up the local mob. Two-fisted fun. **Cast:** George Raft, Claire Trevor, Hoagy Carmichael, Signe Hasso, Lowell Gilmore, Marvin Miller, Margaret Wycherly, J. Farrell MacDonald, Mack Gray, Jason Robards, Sr. **Credits:** Dir: Edwin L. Marin; Prod: William L. Pereira; Writer: Steve Fisher, Frank Gruber; Story: Charles G. Booth; DP: Harry Wild; Ed: Les Millbrook; Composer: Leigh Harline; Art Director: Albert S. D'Agostino, Jack Okey. B&W, 80 min. **VHS, LASER**

Johnny Apollo
(1940) Fox
Power impresses as a college student who slips into a life of crime in order to bail out his wealthy father (Arnold), who gets caught manipulating his books. Life on the wrong side of the law has its benefits, including gal pal

Lamour, but he winds up sharing a cell block with Dad. Director Hathaway was noted for his action pictures, and here he roughs up Power's pretty-boy image. **Cast:** Tyrone Power, Dorothy Lamour, Edward Arnold, Lloyd Nolan, Lionel Atwill, Charley Grapewin, Emmett Vogan, Harry Tyler, Stanley Andrews. **Credits:** Dir: Henry Hathaway; Prod: Darryl F. Zanuck; Writer: Philip Dunne, Rowland Brown; Story: Samuel G. Engel; DP: Arthur Miller; Ed: Robert Bischoff; Composer: Frank Loesser, Alfred Newman, Lionel Newman, Mack Gordon; Art Director: Richard Day, Wiard Ihnen. B&W, 94 min. **VHS**

Johnny Belinda
(1948) Warner Bros.
A patient, compassionate doctor (Ayres) in a rural community teaches a deaf-mute girl (Wyman) to communicate. After the young lady is brutally raped by a local villager, the bucolic populace suspects the doctor of being the father of the child she later delivers. Just as Wyman's life is looking up the father of the child comes to claim it. Better-than-average melodrama much admired at the time. Director Negulesco was competent with both sweeping romantic drama and tough-minded noirs. This may be his shining moment, but he and this film receive less notice now. Golden Globes for Best Actress in a Drama: Jane Wyman and Best Motion Picture, Drama. Academy Award Nominations: 12, including Best Picture; Best Director; Best Actor: Lew Ayres; Best Supporting Actor: Charles Bickford; Best Supporting Actress: Agnes Moorehead; Best Cinematography; Best Screenplay. **Academy Awards:** Best Actress: Jane Wyman. **Cast:** Jane Wyman, Lew Ayres, Charles Bickford, Jan Sterling, Rosalind Ivan, Dan Seymour, Mabel Paige, Ida Moore, Alan Napier, Monte Blue. **Credits:** Dir: Jean Negulesco; Prod: Jerry Wald; Writer: Irmgard Von Cube, Allen Vincent; Story: Elmer Harris; DP: T. D. McCord; Ed: David Weisbart; Composer: Max Steiner; Art Director: Robert M. Haas. B&W, 103 min. **VHS**

Johnny Come Lately
(1943) United Artists
An ex-newspaperman is saved from a vagrancy rap by the elderly editor of a failing paper. The two band together to expose political corruption through the written word, disregarding threats from a rival newspaperman. Academy Award Nomination for Best Scoring of a Dramatic or Comedy Picture. **Cast:**

James Cagney, Grace George, Hattie McDaniel, Marjorie Main, Marjorie Lord, Edward McNamara. **Credits:** Dir: William K. Howard; Prod: William Cagney; Writer: John Van Druten. B&W, 97 min. **VHS, LASER**

Johnny Eager

(1942) MGM
Unusual MGM entry into the crime melodrama racket benefits from the high-budget treatment and attractive stars. Johnny, a cagey racketeer looking to tighten his grip on local gambling operations, gets involved with a vulnerable society girl—and the daughter of the local D.A.—who becomes a tool for his criminal schemes. **Academy Awards:** Best Supporting Actor: Van Heflin. **Cast:** Robert Taylor, Lana Turner, Edward Arnold, Van Heflin, Robert Sterling, Patricia Dane, Glenda Farrell. **Credits:** Dir: Mervyn LeRoy; Prod: John W. Considine, Jr.; DP: Harold Rossen; Ed: Albert Akst; Prod Design: Cedric Gibbons, Stan Rogers; Composer: Bronislau Kaper; Writer: James Edward Grant, John Lee Mahin. B&W, 107 min. **VHS**

Johnny Got His Gun

(1971) Cinemation
A moving drama that realistically depicts the horrifying results of war, this stirring antiwar film is based on Trumbo's novel (he also directed) about an armless, legless, deaf, mute, and blind WWI bomb victim who lies in a dim, depressing hospital ward reflecting on his life and what might have been. Released at the height of the antiwar movement, its relevance to current events could not be ignored. Winner of Cannes Film Festival Grand Jury Prize. **Cast:** Timothy Bottoms, Kathy Fields, Marsha Hunt, Jason Robards, Donald Sutherland, Diane Varsi, Don Barry, Peter Brocco, Ken Clarke, Eric Christmas. **Credits:** Dir: Dalton Trumbo; Prod: Bruce Campbell; Writer: Dalton Trumbo; DP: Jules Brenner; Ed: William P. Dornisch; Prod Design: Harold Michelson; Composer: Jerry Fielding. Color, 111 min. **VHS, LASER**

Johnny Guitar

(1954) Republic
Women wear the pants (and guns) in one of the oddest, and most rewarding, Westerns ever brought to the screen. Iconoclast Ray corralled his quarreling costars, Crawford and McCambridge, long enough to get them brawling on-screen. McCambridge wants saloon owner Crawford to take her bar trade

elsewhere or face a lynching. Crawford's determined to stay, and when mysterious guitar-playing Brady (Lawrence Tierney's younger brother) gets involved, the six-shooters come out—in the hands of the ladies. **Cast:** Joan Crawford, Sterling Hayden, Ernest Borgnine, Scott Brady, Ben Cooper, Ward Bond, John Carradine, Mercedes McCambridge. **Credits:** Dir: Nicholas Ray; Prod: Herbert J. Yates; Writer: Philip Yordan; DP: Harry Stradling; Ed: Richard L. Van Enger. Color, 110 min. **VHS, LASER**

Johnny Tremain

(1957) Disney
This Disney classic follows the life of young Johnny Tremain (Stalmaster) during the American Revolution. Young Tremain is apprenticed to a Boston silversmith until he burns his hand in an accident. Career prospects over, Johnny falls in with revolutionaries after an Englishman (Cabot) accuses him of a theft he didn't commit. Noted silversmith Paul Revere (Sande) himself helps Johnny discover his revolutionary destiny. The film climaxes with the Boston Tea Party and the Battle of Lexington. A must for patriotic young-uns. **Cast:** Hal Stalmaster, Luana Patten, Jeff York, Sebastian Cabot, Richard Beymer, Rusty Lane, Walter Sande, Whit Bissell, Walter Coy, Will Wright. **Credits:** Dir: Robert Stevenson; Prod: Peter Ellenshaw; Writer: Thomas W. Blackburn; Story: Esther Forbes; DP: Charles P. Boyle; Ed: Stanley E. Johnson; Prod Design: Caroll Clark; Composer: George Bruns. Color, 80 min.

The Joker Is Wild

(1957) Paramount
This historical look at Chicago in the wild '20s stars Sinatra as real-life nightclub crooner-comedian Joe E. Lewis. When Lewis says no to some gangsters and gets his throat cut, his singing days are done. Bitter and brooding, Lewis starts telling nasty jokes and falls into a career as a comedian on the low-brow circuit. He quickly draws the attentions of two dames, the classy Letty Page (Crain) and the not-so-classy dancer Martha Stewart (Gaynor). Meanwhile, Lewis drinks himself to some place where nothing much bothers him. **Cast:** Frank Sinatra, Mitzi Gaynor, Jeanne Crain, Eddie Albert, Beverly Garland, Jackie Coogan, Barry Kelley, Ted De Corsia, Leonard Graves, Valerie Allen. **Credits:** Dir: Charles Vidor; Prod: Samuel J. Briskin; Writer: Oscar Saul;

Story: Arthur Cohn; DP: Daniel L. Fapp; Ed: Everett Douglas; Prod Design: Roland Anderson; Composer: Walter Scharf, James Van Heusen, Sammy Cahn. B&W, 126 min.

The Jolson Story

(1946) Columbia
One of the top musical bios of all time is about a performer who was at a historical crossroads of movie and entertainment history. Parks gives a dynamic performance (and Jolson himself dubbed the songs) as the cantor's son who rose from a humble background to become first a vaudeville performer and then a world-famous Broadway and film star. Parks became an overnight success and followed with the sequel, *Jolson Sings Again* (1949). His career came to an abrupt end when he admitted membership in the Communist Party to the House Un-American Activities Committee. Songs include "April Showers," "By the Light of the Silvery Moon," "Rock-A-Bye Your Baby with a Dixie Melody," "My Mammy," "Swanee," and many more nostalgic favorites. **Academy Awards:** Best Sound Recording; Best Scoring of a Musical. **Cast:** Larry Parks, Evelyn Keyes, William Demarest, Bill Goodwin, Ludwig Donath, Tamara Shayne, John Alexander. **Credits:** Dir: Alfred E. Green; Prod: Sidney Skolsky; Writer: Stephen Longstreet, Harry Chandlee; Composer: Morris Stoloff. Color, 129 min. **VHS, LASER**

The Journey

(1959) MGM
A group of travelers, attempting to escape to Austria, are detained at the Hungarian border by Russian soldiers during the ill-fated revolution of 1956. One of the group, Lady Diana Ashmore (Kerr), becomes enamored with mysterious Paul Kedes (Robards), as Diana catches the eye of Major Surov (Brynner), the Russian commander. In love with Kedes and desperate to help him escape, Diana offers herself up to Surov for his life. Surov is taken aback by her willingness to sacrifice herself and allows her and Kedes to go free. As they cross the border, Surov is killed by a resistance fighter. Debuts for Robards and Howard. **Cast:** Deborah Kerr, Yul Brynner, Jason Robards, Robert Morley, E. G. Marshall, Anne Jackson, Ron Howard, Flip Mark, Kurt Kasznar, David Kossoff. **Credits:** Dir: Anatole Litvak; Prod: Anatole Litvak, Carl Szokoll; Writer: George Tabori; DP: Jack Hildyard; Ed: Dorothy Spencer; Composer:

Georges Auric, Michel Michelet; Art Director: Isabella Schlichting, Werner Schlichting. Color, 125 min.

Journey for Margaret
(1942) MGM
A WWII tearjerker about a couple (Young and Day) stationed in London who lose their unborn infant and are robbed of their chance of ever becoming parents when she is injured during an air raid. Day heads back to the States but Young carries on as a war reporter, eventually befriending and trying to adopt two British orphans to take home to his wife. Based on the book by J. L. White. O'Brien's screen debut. **Cast:** Laraine Day, Fay Bainter, Robert Young, Margaret O'Brien, William Severn, Nigel Bruce, G. P. Huntley, Doris Lloyd, Jill Esmond. **Credits:** Dir: W.S. Van Dyke; Prod: B. P. Fineman; Writer: David Hertz, William Ludwig; DP: Ray June; Ed: George White; Prod Design: Cedric Gibbons, Wade B. Rubottom; Composer: Franz Waxman; Costumes: Robert Kalloch. B&W, 81 min. **VHS**

Journey into Fear
(1942) RKO
Started by Welles, this spy thriller follows Cotten as an American munitions expert who goes on an arms smuggling mission to Istanbul and becomes a target for Nazi agents. Welles and Cotten wrote this adaptation of the Eric Ambler novel. Remade in 1972 by Daniel Mann. **Cast:** Joseph Cotten, Dolores Del Rio, Agnes Moorehead, Ruth Warrick, Jack Durant, Everett Sloane, Eustace Wyatt, Frank Readick, Edgar Barrier. **Credits:** Dir: Norman Foster; Prod: Orson Welles; Writer: Orson Welles, Joseph Cotten; Ed: Mark Robson; Prod Design: Mark-Lee Kirk; Composer: Roy Webb; Art Director: Albert S. D'Agostino. B&W, 69 min. **VHS, LASER**

Journey to the Center of the Earth
(1959) Fox
A scientist (Mason) and a student (Boone) go on an old-fashioned exploration adventure to find the center of the earth and happen upon the lost underwater city of Atlantis. Mason makes an inspiring expedition leader. Note the Herrmann score. Based on Verne's 1864 novel. Academy Award Nominations: 3. **Cast:** Pat Boone, James Mason, Arlene Dahl, Diane Baker, Thayer David, Peter Ronson, Robert Adler. **Credits:** Dir: Henry Levin, Stuart Gilmore; Prod: Charles Brackett; Writer: Charles Brackett,

Johnny Guitar (1954)

Walter Reisch; Story: Jules Verne; DP: Leo Tover; Ed: Jack W. Holmes; Composer: Bernard Herrmann. Color, 130 min. **VHS, LASER**

Joy of Living
(1938) RKO
A wonderful lighthearted romantic musical comedy featuring dashing yachting-type Fairbanks and oh-so-proper chanteuse Dunne in tailor-made roles. When opposites attract, Fairbanks encourages Dunne to loosen up and plenty of opportunities for song, dance, and farce arise. Look for Ball in an early role. Kern-Fields songs include "You Couldn't Be Cuter" and "Just Let Me Look at You." **Cast:** Irene Dunne, Douglas Fairbanks, Jr., Alice Brady, Guy Kibbee, Jean Dixon, Eric Blore, Lucille Ball, Warren Hymer, Billy Gilbert. **Credits:** Dir: Tay Garnett; Prod: Felix Young; Writer: Gene Towne, Graham Baker, Allan Scott; DP: Joseph Walker; Ed: Jack Hively; Composer: Jerome Kern, Dorothy Fields; Art Director: Van Nest Polglase. B&W, 100 min. **VHS, LASER**

Juarez
(1939) Warner Bros.
Muni portrayed so many historical personages he must have felt as if he was in a Warner Bros. time machine. This big-budget biopic is the inspiring story of Benitez Pablo Juarez, a peasant rebel leader who overthrew the Mexican government and became president. Muni and Garfield give strong performances and Rains is magnificent as Napoleon III. A well-done biography with the cream of the Warner backlot in attendance. Academy Award Nominations: 2, including Best Supporting Actor: Brian Aherne. **Cast:** Paul Muni, John Garfield, Brian Aherne, Bette Davis, Gale Sondergaard, Donald Crisp, Gilbert Roland, Claude Rains, Joseph Calleia, Henry O'Neill. **Credits:** Dir: William Dieterle; Prod: Henry Blanke; Writer: John Huston, Wolfgang Reinhardt, Aeneas MacKenzie; DP: Tony Gaudio; Ed: Warren Low; Composer: Erich Wolfgang Korngold; Art Director: Anton F. Grot. B&W, 132 min. **VHS**

Jubal

(1956) Columbia
A Western take on *Othello* in which rancher Borgnine seeks advice on pleasing a wife from cowhand Ford. Steiger stirs things up by implying that Ford may be practicing those very tips on Borgnine's wife. An unusually adult approach to horse opera. **Cast:** Glenn Ford, Ernest Borgnine, Rod Steiger, Valerie French, Felicia Farr, Charles Bronson, Noah Beery, Jr. **Credits:** Dir: Delmer Daves; Prod: William Fadiman; Writer: Russell Hughes, Delmer Daves; DP: Charles Lawton, Jr.; Ed: Al Clark; Composer: David Raskin; Art Director: Carl Anderson. Color, 101 min. **VHS, LASER**

Judge Priest

(1934) Fox
Rogers is perfect as a small-town judge who metes out justice with a serving of common sense. A less-acclaimed Ford—its view of small-town America seems badly dated—but full of sharply observed detail and rich characterizations. Worth a look for Ford fans. This was based on the stories by Irvin S. Cobb and later remade by Ford as *The Sun Shines Bright* (1953). **Cast:** Will Rogers, Anita Louise, Tom Brown, Hattie McDaniel, Stepin Fetchit, Henry B. Walthall, Rochelle Hudson, David Landau. **Credits:** Dir: John Ford; Prod: Saul M. Wurtzel; Writer: Dudley Nichols, Lamar Trotti; DP: George Schneiderman; Composer: Cyril J. Mockridge. B&W, 90 min. **VHS**

Judgment at Nuremberg

(1961) United Artists
This rare drama of ideas is one of the most thought-provoking of Hollywood's many considerations of WWII, and one of the most acclaimed. American jurist Tracy presides as Chief Justice over the Nuremberg tribunal that judges responsibility for war crimes. He balances the emotional testimony of Holocaust victims with the defense of individuals having no personal responsibility for institutional madness (Schell is magnificent as the German defense counsel) as well as the political pressures brought to bear outside his courtroom. A stellar cast working at the top of their form for Kramer, who earlier showed his ability with courtroom drama as director of *Inherit the Wind* (1960). Based on a *Playhouse 90* broadcast. Golden Globes for Best Director; Best Actor in a Drama: Richard Widmark. Academy Award Nominations: 11, including Best Picture; Best Director; Best Actor: Spencer Tracy. **Academy**

Awards: Best Actor: Maximilian Schell; Best Screenplay. **Cast:** Spencer Tracy, Burt Lancaster, Marlene Dietrich, Maximilian Schell, Montgomery Clift, Richard Widmark, William Shatner, Edward Binns. **Credits:** Dir: Stanley Kramer; Prod: Stanley Kramer; Writer: Abby Mann; DP: Ernest Laszlo; Ed: Frederic Knudtson; Prod Design: Rudolph Sternad; Composer: Ernest Gold. B&W, 188 min. **VHS, LASER**

Judith of Bethulia

(1913) Biograph
Griffith's retelling of the biblical tale of a woman who saves her city from Assyrian invasion by seducing and killing the opposition's leader. The last picture that Griffith directed for Biograph, before making cinema history in 1915 with *The Birth of a Nation*. **Cast:** Lillian Gish, Dorothy Gish, Blanche Sweet, Mae Marsh, Henry B. Walthall, Lionel Barrymore, Robert Harron, Kate Bruce, Harry Carey, Sr., J. Jiquel Lanoe. **Credits:** Dir: D. W. Griffith; Prod: D. W. Griffith; Writer: D. W. Griffith, Frank Woods; DP: Billy Bitzer; Ed: James Smith. B&W, 108 min. **VHS**

Juke Girl

(1942) Warner Bros.
In this agrarian murder mystery, Reagan, if you can believe it, plays a drifter and left-wing labor organizer. His friendship with Whorf is threatened when the two wind up on different sides in a labor dispute at the Florida tomato plant where they both work, and in a romantic tussle for Sheridan. When a farmer gets murdered, Reagan gets framed. **Cast:** Ronald Reagan, Ann Sheridan, Richard Whorf, George Tobias, Gene Lockhart, Alan Hale, Betty Brewer, Howard Da Silva, Donald MacBride, Willard Robertson, Faye Emerson. **Credits:** Dir: Curtis Bernhardt; Prod: Hal B. Wallis; Writer: A. I. Bezzerides, Kenneth Gamet; Story: Theodore Pratt; DP: Bert Glennon; Ed: Warren Low; Prod Design: Robert M. Haas; Composer: Adolph Deutsch, M. K. Jerome, Max Scholl. B&W, 90 min.

Julia

(1977) Fox
The film adaptation of *Pentimento*, in which author Lillian Hellman (Fonda) recounts how she came to be involved in the resistance during WWII for the sake of her passionate and irrepressible childhood friend, Julia (Redgrave). Both leads are outstanding, and Robards, as Hellman's companion, mystery writer Dashiell Hammett, provides colorful support. This was

Streep's big-screen debut. Note the evocative Delerue score. One of the most honored films of the late '70s, it won multiple BAFTA awards, and Golden Globes for Best Actress: Jane Fonda; Best Supporting Actress: Vanessa Redgrave. Academy Award Nominations: 11, including Best Picture; Best Director; Best Actress; Best Cinematography; Best Supporting Actor; Best Original Score. **Academy Awards:** Best Supporting Actor: Jason Robards; Best Supporting Actress: Vanessa Redgrave. Best Screenplay Based on Material from Another Medium. **Cast:** Jane Fonda, Vanessa Redgrave, Jason Robards, Maximilian Schell, Hal Holbrook, Rosemary Murphy, Meryl Streep. **Credits:** Dir: Fred Zinnemann; Prod: Richard Roth; Writer: Alvin Sargent; DP: Douglas Slocombe; Ed: Walter Murch, Marcel Durham; Prod Design: Willy Holt, Gene Callahan, Carmen Dillon; Composer: Georges Delerue; Set Designer: Tessa Davies. Color, 118 min. **VHS, LASER**

Julia Misbehaves

(1948) MGM
A slapstick comedy about a showgirl (Garson, in an unusual role for the ordinarily dignified actress) returning to the very proper husband (Pidgeon, of course) and refined daughter (Taylor) she abandoned 18 years earlier to be at her daughter's wedding in the south of France. The trip from England to the French chateau provides plenty of opportunity for mishaps, including inviting a circus troupe along for the party. Based on Margery Sharp's novel, *The Nutmeg Tree*. **Cast:** Elizabeth Taylor, Greer Garson, Walter Pidgeon, Peter Lawford, Cesar Romero, Mary Boland, Nigel Bruce, Reginald Owen, Arthur Wimperis. **Credits:** Dir: Jack Conway; Prod: Everett Riskin, John Dunning; Writer: William Ludwig, Harry Ruskin, Gina Kaus, Monckton Hoffe; DP: Joseph Ruttenberg; Prod Design: Cedric Gibbons; Composer: Adolph Deutsch; Art Director: Daniel B. Cathcart. Color, 99 min. **VHS**

Julius Caesar

(1953) MGM
Astonishing display of acting talent brings immediacy and power to a fine screen adaptation of the Shakespeare play that portrays the political infighting in Julius Caesar's Roman Empire. Producer Houseman was a veteran of the stage and Mankiewicz one of the most literate of Hollywood writer-directors. The first production from Mankiewicz's own company attracted universal acclaim. Academy Award

Nominations: 5, including Best Picture; Best Actor: Marlon Brando. **Academy Awards:** Best Art Direction—Set Decoration (B&W). **Cast:** John Gielgud, Marlon Brando, James Mason, Greer Garson, Deborah Kerr, George Macready, Louis Calhern, Edmond O'Brien, Michael Pate. **Credits:** Dir: Joseph L. Mankiewicz; Prod: John Houseman; Writer: Joseph L. Mankiewicz; DP: Joseph Ruttenberg; Ed: John Dunning; Prod Design: Cedric Gibbons; Composer: Miklos Rozsa; Art Director: Edward C. Carfagno. B&W, 121 min. **VHS**

Jumping Jacks
(1952) Paramount
Martin and Lewis hit the silks instead of the nightclub stage when they volunteer to entertain the troops overseas and wind up diving out of a plane. The duo's second attack on the military life, following *At War with the Army* (1950). **Cast:** Dean Martin, Jerry Lewis, Mona Freeman, Robert Strauss, Don Defore, Ray Teal, Danny Arnold, Richard Erdman. **Credits:** Dir: Norman Taurog; Prod: Hal B. Wallis; Writer: Robert Lees, Frederic I. Rinaldo, Herbert Baker, James B. Allardice; DP: Daniel Fapp; Ed: Stanley Johnson; Prod Design: Hal Pereira. B&W, 96 min. **VHS, LASER**

June Bride
(1948) Warner Bros.
Breezy comedy with Davis in a rare light-romantic role. Montgomery and Davis are a correspondent and editor of a woman's magazine who were once sweethearts and rivals for bylines. They end up on an assignment to do a seasonal feature on June brides. The romance of white lace and promises melts even the normally hard-boiled Davis and cures Montgomery of his reporter's cynicism. Debbie Reynolds makes her feature bow. **Cast:** Bette Davis, Robert Montgomery, Fay Bainter, Tom Tully, Barbara Bates, Jerome Cowan, Mary Wickes, James Burke. **Credits:** Dir: Bretaigne Windust; Prod: Henry Blanke; Writer: Ranald MacDougall; DP: Ted McCord; Ed: Owen Marks; Prod Design: Anton Grot; Composer: David Buttolph. B&W, 97 min. **VHS**

The Jungle Book
(1942) United Artists
Quality Korda treatment for the timeless 1894 Rudyard Kipling tale of the boy raised by wolves in India. Sabu (made a star by Korda's *The Elephant Boy*, 1937) stars as Mowgli. Academy Award Nominations: 4, including Best (Black-and-White) Cinematography.

Cast: Sabu, Joseph Calleia, John Qualen, Frank Puglia, Rosemary De Camp. **Credits:** Dir: Zoltan Korda; Prod: Alexander Korda; Writer: Laurence Stallings; Story: Rudyard Kipling; SFX: Lawrence Butler. Color, 109 min. **VHS, LASER**

The Jungle Book
(1967) Disney
The 17th animated feature produced by Disney studios and the last film supervised by Walt Disney himself, this endearing feature is based on Rudyard Kipling's story about a boy named Mowgli raised by wolves in the wilderness of India. During his delightfully scary adventures with a series of wild creatures, Mowgli learns he must leave the jungle and be what nature intended him to be—a man. Delightful jazz-inspired songs, including "Trust In Me," "I Wanna Be Like You," and "Bare Necessities," make this a Disney classic. The 30th Anniversary Limited Edition includes a featurette entitled *The Making of The Jungle Book* and a songbook featuring lyrics from the sound track. **Cast:** Sebastian Cabot, Phil Harris, Louis Prima, George Sanders. **Credits:** Dir: Wolfgang Reitherman; Prod: Walt Disney; Writer: Larry Clemmons, Ralph Wright, Ken Anderson; Story: Rudyard Kipling. Color, 100 min. **VHS, LASER**

The Jungle Princess
(1936) Paramount
Lamour's first outing in her sarong is an adventure story about a young woman raised alone in the jungle. A young man (Milland) is hunting when he is attacked by a tiger. Ulah (Lamour), the mistress of the tiger, appears and nurses Milland back to health and he teaches her English in return. When he is well he heads back to his camp, where his fiancée waits for him. Lamour, who has fallen in love with him, follows. An exotic setting for the usual triangle, but Dotty looks great in that sarong! **Cast:** Dorothy Lamour, Ray Milland, Akim Tamiroff, Lynne Overman, Molly Lamont, Hugh Buckler. **Credits:** Dir: Wilhelm Thiele; Prod: E. Lloyd Sheldon; Writer: Gerald Geraghty, Cyril Hume, Gouverneur Morris, Max Marcin; DP: Harry Fischbeck; Ed: Ellsworth Hoagland; Composer: Frederick Hollander, Leo Robin. B&W, 82 min.

Junior Bonner
(1972) Cinerama
A fading competitor on the rodeo circuit, McQueen reaches for inner strength to make one last, face-saving

showing in the hometown he left behind. Along with his dignity, he restores the bonds broken with his family (Preston and Lupino) many years before. Peckinpah knows these people and gives them a rough grace, aided by the camerawork of Ballard. **Cast:** Steve McQueen, Robert Preston, Ida Lupino, Ben Johnson, Joe Don Baker, Barbara Leigh, Mary Murphy, Bill McKinney. **Credits:** Dir: Sam Peckinpah; Prod: Joe Wizan; Writer: Jeb Rosebrook; DP: Lucien Ballard; Composer: Jerry Fielding. Color, 110 min. **VHS**

Juno and the Paycock
(1930) Wardour
Early British Hitchcock film is interesting as it shows the director at work on a stage adaptation. O'Casey's tragic play about a poor family during the Irish uprising who receive word that they are due an inheritance gets a surprisingly straight reading, but essential viewing for the Hitchcock cult. Fitzgerald's screen debut. **Cast:** Sara Allgood, Edward Chapman, Barry Fitzgerald, John Longden, John Laurie, Donald Calthrop, Kathleen O'Regan, Maire O'Neill, Dave Morris, Fred Schwartz. **Credits:** Dir: Alfred Hitchcock; Prod: John Maxwell; Writer: Alfred Hitchcock, Alma Reville; Story: Sean O'Casey; DP: Jack Cox; Ed: Emile DeRuelle; Art Director: Norman Arnold. B&W, 99 min. **VHS**

Just Across the Street
(1952) Universal
An innocuous romantic comedy that casts Lund as a successful, if gullible, plumber and Sheridan as the secretary who falls for him. He mistakenly believes poor Sheridan is the daughter of a banker, and she does nothing to discourage him, allowing him to drop her off at "home" in front of an expensive suburban estate. Soon the charade involves the home's middle-aged owners and the expected mistaken identity hilarity ensues before all is set straight. **Cast:** Ann Sheridan, John Lund, Robert Keith, Cecil Kellaway, Alan Mowbray, Natalie Schafer, George Eldredge, Burt Mustin, Billie Bird. **Credits:** Dir: Joseph Pevney; Prod: Leonard Goldstein; Writer: Joel Malone, Roswell Rogers; DP: Maury Gertsman; Ed: Virgil Vogel; Composer: Joseph Gershenson; Art Director: Bernard Herzbrun, Emrich Nicholson. B&W, 78 min.

Just Around the Corner
(1938) Fox
There were breaks in the clouds of the Depression in 1938 and prosperity

must have seemed just around the corner once again. There could be no more hope-filled movie than this. Little miss sunshine Temple convinces a stingy millionaire to come across with jobs, just in time to save her janitor father from despair. Shirley's fourth outing with "Bojangles" Robinson. Songs include "Just Around the Corner," "I'll Be Lucky With You," "I Love to Walk in the Rain," and "Brass Buttons and Epaulets." **Cast:** Shirley Temple, Joan Davis, Bill Robinson, Bert Lahr, Charles Farrell, Franklin Pangborn, Amanda Duff, Cora Witherspoon, Claude Gillingwater. **Credits:** Dir: Irving Cummings; Prod: David Hempstead; Writer: Ethel Hill, J. P. McEvoy. B&W, 71 min. VHS

Just for You
(1952) Paramount
Crooner Crosby climbs the rungs of stage success and leaves his kids behind. Wyman takes charge of family life and brings Bing back to the fold. Pleasant enough, if unremarkable, and Wyman fits comfortably in the maternal role. Note early appearance by Wood, and grande dame Barrymore. Based on Stephen Vincent Benét's novel, *Famous*. Songs include "Zing a Little Zong," "He's Crazy for Me," "Just for You," and "On the 10:10." Academy Award Nomination for Best Song ("Zing a Little Zong"). **Cast:** Bing Crosby, Jane Wyman, Ethel Barrymore, Bob Arthur, Natalie Wood, Cora Witherspoon, Ben Lessy, Art Smith, Regis Toomey, Willis Bouchey.

Credits: Dir: Elliott Nugent; Prod: Pat Duggan; Writer: Robert Carson; DP: George Barnes; Ed: Doane Harrison; Composer: Harry Warren; Art Director: Hal Pereira. Color, 104 min. VHS

Justine
(1969) Fox
Cukor's valiant attempt to tame Durrell's dense, colorful *Alexandria Quartet*. An international cast do their best to imbue this with the simmering sexuality and alluring mystery of the novels, but the result suffers from the confusion many experienced with the books. Aimee is properly sultry in the role of a Middle Eastern prostitute married to one of Egypt's wealthiest bankers in pre-WWII Alexandria. With her husband's consent, she continues to enflame other men and is also deeply involved in a plot to arm Palestinian Jews about to revolt against English rule. **Cast:** Anouk Aimee, Michael York, Dirk Bogarde, Robert Forster, Jack Albertson, Cliff Gorman, Anna Karina, Philippe Noiret, John Vernon, George Baker. **Credits:** Dir: George Cukor; Prod: Pandro S. Berman; Writer: Lawrence B. Marcus; Story: Lawrence Durrell; DP: Leon Shamroy; Ed: Rita Roland; Composer: Jerry Goldsmith; Costumes: Irene Sharaff. Color, 116 min. VHS

Just This Once
(1952) MGM
Lawford plays a free-spending playboy in this romantic comedy. Leigh plays the young attorney who is improbably

retained as his guardian and fiscal watchdog. In order to control his extravagance, Leigh puts him on a slim weekly allowance and moves in with him. The mismatched pair cutesy-talk themselves into love, and after Leigh drops her fiancé, they rush headlong into marriage. **Cast:** Janet Leigh, Peter Lawford, Lewis Stone, Richard Anderson, Douglas Fowley, Hanley Stafford, Henry Slate, Jerry Hausner, Benny Rubin, Charles Watts. **Credits:** Dir: Don Weis; Prod: Henry Berman; Writer: Sidney Sheldon; Story: Max Trell; DP: Ray June; Ed: Frederick Smith; Art Director: James Basevi, Cedric Gibbons. B&W, 90 min.

J. W. Coop
(1972) Columbia
Robertson scored a hat trick as writer, director, and actor and shines in all departments. He plays a drifter who's struggling to set his life straight by becoming the greatest rodeo rider on the circuit after 10 years in prison. An effective debut as director for Robertson, whose career got snagged when he started the ball rolling in the Columbia-David Begelman scandal. **Cast:** Cliff Robertson, Geraldine Page, Cristina Ferrare, R. G. Armstrong, John Crawford, Paul Harper, Richard Kennedy, Bruce Kirby. **Credits:** Dir: Cliff Robertson; Prod: Cliff Robertson; Writer: Cliff Robertson, Bud Shrake, Gary Cartwright; DP: Frank Stanley, Adam Holender, Fred Waugh, Ross Lowell; Ed: Alex Beaton; Composer: Don Randi, Louie Shelton. Color, 112 min. VHS

Kangaroo
(1952) Fox
Two con men want to swindle an elderly Australian cattle rancher out of his money. They convince the rancher and his beautiful daughter (an always beautiful O'Hara) that the younger man is actually the rancher's long lost son. In an effort to gain his favor, they assist the rancher and daughter in a cattle drive to bring the thirsty cattle to water. They battle stampedes, brush fires, and other life-threatening challenges until the law catches up with the two con men. **Cast:** Maureen O'Hara, Peter Lawford, Finlay Currie, Richard Boone, Chips Rafferty, Charles Tingwell, Letty Craydon, Guy Doleman, Ron Whelan. **Credits:** Dir: Lewis Milestone; Prod: Robert Bassler; Writer: Harry Kleiner; Story: Martin Berkeley; DP: Charles G. Clarke; Ed: Nick DeMaggio; Prod Design: Jack-Lee Kirk, Lyle Wheeler; Composer: Sol Kaplan. Color, 84 min.

Kansas City Confidential
(1952) United Artists
A hard-hitting film noir about an ex-con (Payne) sent up the river for an armored car heist he didn't commit. When he's released, he devotes himself to nailing the corrupt ex-cop who set him up, chasing him all the way to Central America. Sure to please fans of the genre. **Cast:** John Payne, Coleen Gray, Preston Foster, Dona Drake, Jack Elam, Neville Brand, Lee Van Cleef, Carleton Young. **Credits:** Dir: Phil Karlson; Prod: Edward Small; Writer: George Bruce, Harry Essex; DP: George E. Diskant. B&W, 98 min. **VHS**

Keeper of the Flame
(1942) MGM
An interesting look at public images and private lives. Tracy is a reporter assigned to write a piece about a recently deceased, beloved American patriot. Hepburn is the widow who continues to protect the public from

the secret life behind the facade. The reporter's story gets complicated when he falls for the widow. Tracy and Hepburn in the able hands of Cukor, with a script by writer Stewart (*The Philadelphia Story,* 1940) based on the story by A. I. R. Wylie. **Cast:** Spencer Tracy, Katharine Hepburn, Richard Whorf, Margaret Wycherly, Forrest Tucker, Frank Craven, Percy Kilbride, Stephen McNally. **Credits:** Dir: George Cukor; Prod: Victor Saville; Writer: Donald Ogden Stewart; DP: William Daniels. B&W, 101 min. **VHS**

Kelly's Heroes
(1970) MGM
The late '60s invade WWII! An anti-establishment version of the tried-and-true WWII adventure movie as the laid-back members of a misfit gang plan an unusual, and unusually dangerous, expedition to steal a cache of gold hidden behind enemy lines. The action scenes are enthusiastic and the attitude is hipper than most. Eastwood and Savalas seem to wink at their hard-guy images, and Sutherland does his half-stoned *M*A*S*H* bit. **Cast:** Clint Eastwood, Telly Savalas, Don Rickles, Donald Sutherland, Carroll O'Connor, Gavin MacLeod, Hal Buckley, Stuart Margolin. **Credits:** Dir: Brian G. Hutton; Prod: Gabriel Katzka; Writer: Troy Kennedy Martin; Composer: Lalo Schifrin. Color, 150 min. **VHS, LASER**

The Kentuckian
(1955) United Artists
Lancaster stars in and directs this CinemaScope Western. A rugged frontiersman and his son travel to 1820s Texas in search of a place where they can begin a new life. Matthau made his film debut as a whip-wielding brute in this solid Western. Based on the novel *The Gabriel Horn* by Felix Holt. **Cast:** Burt Lancaster, Diana Lynn, Walter Matthau, John McIntire, Dianne Foster, Una Merkel, John Carradine.

Credits: Dir: Burt Lancaster; Prod: Harold Hecht; DP: Ernest Laszlo; Composer: Bernard Herrmann. Color, 104 min. **VHS**

Kentucky
(1938) Fox
This bluegrass, horse-racing romance has the love between two young Kentuckians, Young and Greene, hampered by the smoldering feud that has separated their southern families for generations. Though Greene despises this legacy, Young's pride breaks them up and the family conflict is only resolved in the great Kentucky Derby, with each family's horse running neck and neck. Young's bitter, unforgiving uncle (Brennan), dies before he sees his horse win. With his death, the lovers have a chance to bring the feud to an end. Prime Young melodrama. **Academy Awards:** Best Supporting Actor: Walter Brennan. **Cast:** Loretta Young, Richard Greene, Walter Brennan, Douglass Dumbrille, Karen Morley, Moroni Olsen, Russell Hicks, Willard Robertson, Charles Waldron, George Reed. **Credits:** Dir: David Butler; Prod: Gene Markey; Writer: Lamar Trotti, John Tainor Foote; Story: John Tainor Foote; DP: Ernest Palmer, Ray Rennahan; Ed: Irene Morra; Prod Design: Bernard Herzbrun; Composer: Louis Silvers. Color, 95 min.

Kentucky Fried Movie
(1977) United Film
The title for this satiric look at commercials, television, and movies comes from the Kentucky Fried Theatre, a Madison, Wisconsin, theater troupe that was the launching pad for Abrahams and the Zucker brothers. They became better known as the auteurs behind *Airplane!* (1980), but this earlier work features plenty of their patented sight gags. Also gave director Landis his first big shot in an outing with a comedic sensibility not far removed from his breakthrough the

next year with *National Lampoon's Animal House*. **Cast:** Bill Bixby, Jerry Zucker, Evan Kim, George Lazenby, Henry Gibson, Tony Dow, Donald Sutherland. **Credits:** Dir: John Landis; Prod: Robert K. Weiss; Writer: David Zucker, Jerry Zucker, Jim Abrahams; DP: Stephen Katz; Ed: George Folsey, Jr.; Costumes: Deborah Nadoolman. Color, 90 min. **VHS**

Kept Husbands
(1931) RKO
After an employee bravely saves the lives of other workers in an industrial accident, the boss invites him to the big house on the hill for dinner. Although romance blooms between the employee and the boss's daughter, they find that their varying pedigrees cause plenty of relationship problems. Dated situation, but the romantic dilemma is well played. **Cast:** Joel McCrea, Dorothy Mackaill, Robert McWade, Florence Roberts, Clara Kimball Young, Mary Carr. **Credits:** Dir: Lloyd Bacon; Prod: Louis Sarecky; Writer: Alfred Jackson, Forrest Halsey; DP: Jack Mackenzie. B&W, 95 min. **VHS**

The Key
(1934) Warner Bros.
This romantic military melodrama, set in Ireland during the revolution of 1920, embraces both a love triangle and sweeping skirmish scenes. Captain Andrew Kerr of the British Intelligence (Clive) introduces his wife (Best) to a friend, Captain Tennant of the British Army (Powell), never suspecting that the two were once in love. Distraught at finding them together later, Kerr goes on a drinking expedition and is abducted by the Irish. Tennant then has to redeem himself by attempting to set things right. Terrific cast, supported by colorful character actors such as Treacher and Crisp. **Cast:** William Powell, Edna Best, Colin Clive, Hobart Cavanaugh, Halliwell Hobbes, Henry O'Neill, Phil Regan, Donald Crisp, J. M. Kerrigan, Arthur Treacher. **Credits:** Dir: Michael Curtiz; Prod: Robert Sr. Presnell; Writer: R. Gore Brown, J. L. Hardy, Laird Doyle; DP: Ernest Haller; Ed: William Clemens. B&W, 82 min.

Key Largo
(1948) Warner Bros.
A notorious gangster (Robinson, in a trademarked performance) holds the residents of a Florida Keys hotel hostage during a hurricane. Bogart looks like the only hope for a way out, but he's had enough violence, until

Bacall is threatened. Huston directed this adaptation of the Maxwell Anderson play. Bogart and Bacall are still on a roll, and it's a prime period for all involved. **Academy Awards:** Best Supporting Actress: Claire Trevor. **Cast:** Humphrey Bogart, Edward G. Robinson, Lauren Bacall, Claire Trevor, Lionel Barrymore, Thomas Gomez, John Rodney. **Credits:** Dir: John Huston; Prod: Jerry Wald; Writer: Richard Brooks, John Huston; DP: Karl Freund; Composer: Max Steiner. B&W, 102 min. **VHS, LASER**

The Keys of the Kingdom
(1944) Fox
An early role for a perfectly cast Peck earned him an Oscar nomination. Peck portrays a Scottish missionary doing God's work in a China beset by war and poverty. Also features McDowall as the missionary's boyhood self. Based on the novel by A. J. Cronin. **Academy Award Nominations:** 3, including Best Actor: Gregory Peck. **Cast:** Gregory Peck, Vincent Price, Thomas Mitchell, Rose Stradner, Roddy McDowall, Edmund Gwenn, Cedric Hardwicke, Peggy Ann Garner. **Credits:** Dir: John M. Stahl; Prod: Joseph L. Mankiewicz; Writer: Joseph L. Mankiewicz, Nunnally Johnson; DP: Arthur Miller; Prod Design: James Basevi; Composer: Alfred Newman. B&W, 137 min. **VHS**

Key to the City
(1950) MGM
A light comedy-romance about a couple of small-town mayors who meet at a big convention in San Francisco. Their Honors Gable (a former longshoreman) and Young (a prim and proper Harvard graduate) toss the barbed remarks after being arrested in a nightclub brawl, but meanwhile they're falling in love. **Cast:** Clark Gable, Loretta Young, Frank Morgan, Marilyn Maxwell, Raymond Burr, James Gleason, Lewis Stone, Raymond Walburn. **Credits:** Dir: George Sidney; Prod: Z. Wayne Griffin; Writer: Robert Riley Crutcher; DP: Harold Rosson. B&W, 101 min. **VHS**

The Kid
(1921) First National
Chaplin's first feature is a touching comedy about a woman who abandons her child with the intention of committing suicide. Chaplin's Little Tramp finds the kid (Coogan, in the role that made him an overnight sensation) and takes him under his wing. When the woman, Purviance, becomes an opera star five years later, she spends her

extra time doing charity work for youngsters who live in the slums, hoping that she will find her son. Eventually, the truth comes out and the authorities take the baby away from Chaplin. He steals the child back, but is soon discovered and separated once again from him. A reunion at the mother's mansion resolves things happily, yet the earlier somber tone prevails, making this sweet and heartwarming story resonate. **Cast:** Charlie Chaplin, Jackie Coogan, Chuck Reisner, Edna Purviance. **Credits:** Dir: Charlie Chaplin; Prod: Charlie Chaplin; Writer: Charlie Chaplin; DP: Rollie Totheroh, Jack Wilson; Prod Design: Charles D. Hall. B&W, 85 min. **VHS**

The Kid from Brooklyn
(1946) RKO
In the late '40s, Kaye was just hitting his stride, as his third starring feature amply demonstrates. The musical comedy remake of the Harold Lloyd silent, *The Milky Way*, stars Kaye again as an everyman plunged into fantastic circumstances (a year before his finest role in *The Secret Life of Walter Mitty*), a musically inclined milkman who accidentally becomes a prizefighter by knocking out the champ in a street fight. Note the camerawork by Toland. The video release includes a digitally remastered stereo mix and the original trailer. Songs include "Sunflower Song," "You're the Cause of It All," "I Love an Old-Fashioned Song," and "Josie." **Cast:** Danny Kaye, Virginia Mayo, Eve Arden, Steve Cochran, Walter Abel, Lionel Stander, Fay Bainter. **Credits:** Dir: Norman Z. McLeod; Prod: Samuel Goldwyn; Writer: Don Hartman, Melville Shavelson; DP: Gregg Toland; Ed: Daniel Mandell; Composer: Carmen Dragon; Art Director: Perry Ferguson. Color, 114 min. **VHS, LASER**

The Kid from Spain
(1932) United Artists
Cantor stars in this early screwball musical with choreography by Berkeley. College kid Cantor witnesses a bank robbery and then flees to his friend Young's place in Mexico. There he's mistaken for a bullfighter and must enter the ring. Fine example of director McCarey's early work as the director of choice for the major comedians of the time, including Cantor, the Marx Brothers, Mae West, W. C. Fields, and Harold Lloyd. Look quick to see Betty Grable and Paulette Goddard in a Berkeley-fueled chorus line. Songs include "Look What You've Done," "In the Moonlight," and "What

a Perfect Combination." **Cast:** Eddie Cantor, Lyda Roberti, Robert Young, Ruth Hall, John Miljan, Stanley Fields. **Credits:** Dir: Leo McCarey; Prod: Samuel Goldwyn; Writer: William Anthony McGuire, Bert Kalmar, Harry Ruby; DP: Gregg Toland; Choreographer: Busby Berkeley. B&W, 96 min. **VHS**

Kid Galahad

(1937) Warner Bros.
Said to be one of the greatest pictures of the fight game ever made, it certainly features a powerhouse cast— Robinson, Davis, Bogart—and capable direction from Curtiz (*Casablanca*, 1942). Hard-bitten fight promoter Robinson discovers that bellhop Morris can punch, and makes him a heavyweight contender. Along the way, his gal pal Davis loses her heart to the innocent boxer, and Robinson loses control of his shot at the big time. Remade as *The Wagons Roll at Night* in 1941 with a circus setting (and Bogart again), and as an Elvis vehicle in 1962. **Cast:** Edward G. Robinson, Bette Davis, Humphrey Bo-gart, Wayne Morris, Jane Bryan, Harry Carey, Veda Ann Borg. **Credits:** Dir: Michael Curtiz; Prod: Samuel Bischoff; Writer: Seton I. Miller; DP: Tony Gaudio; Composer: Max Steiner. B&W, 101 min. **VHS**

Kid Galahad

(1962) United Artists
Elvis struts his stuff as a boxing novice who winds up punching his way to fame. In between winning championships and bouts of wishing he could go back to his quiet life as a garage mechanic and start a family, the King does sing. If you love Elvis, you'll love this. If you love boxing, stick with the 1937 version. Songs include "I Got Lucky," "Home Is Where the Heart Is," and "Riding the Rainbow." **Cast:** Elvis Presley, Lola Albright, Charles Bronson, Gig Young, Michael Dante, Ned Glass, Robert Emhardt, David Lewis. **Credits:** Dir: Phil Karlson; Prod: David Weisbart; Writer: William Fayman; DP: Burnett Guffey. Color, 97 min. **VHS, LASER**

Kid Glove Killer

(1942) MGM
This hard-boiled murder mystery was Heflin's first role and the great director Zinnemann's first stint in the director's chair. Heflin plays a relentless police pathologist on the trail of the mayor's slayer. He comes smack up against star lawyer Litel and his attention to detail just might cost him his life. Look for an early Gardner bit part as a carhop. **Cast:** Van Heflin, Marsha Hunt, Lee Bowman, Samuel S. Hinds, Cliff Clarke, Eddie Quillan, John Litel, Catherine Lewis, Nella Walker, Ava Gardner. **Credits:** Dir: Fred Zinnemann; Prod: Jack Chertok; Writer: John C. Higgins, Allen Rivkin; DP: Paul C. Vogel; Ed: Ralph E. Winters; Prod Design: Edwin B. Willis; Composer: David Snell. B&W, 74 min.

Kid Millions

(1934) United Artists
Nostalgic musical comedy with a line-up of vaudeville greats, including Cantor, Merman, Murphy, and the dancing Nicholas Brothers. The negligible story line concerns a poor Brooklyn boy who must travel to Egypt to collect his 77-million-dollar inheritance. The ice cream fantasy finale features early Technicolor, and Lucille Ball can be glimpsed as a Goldwyn Girl. **Cast:** Eddie Cantor, Ethel Merman, Ann Sothern, George Murphy, Berton Churchill, Warren Hymer, Paul Harvey. **Credits:** Dir: Roy Del Ruth; Prod: Samuel Goldwyn; Writer: Arthur Sheekman, Nat Perrin, Nunnally Johnson; DP: Ray June. B&W, 90 min. **VHS, LASER**

Kidnapped

(1960) Disney
Classic Disney version of Stevenson's 1886 novel about a boy (MacArthur) who's sold into slavery by his evil uncle, and his quest for his rightful inheritance. Filmed in England with a vivid setting of the historical time period. Screen debut for O'Toole. **Cast:** Peter Finch, James MacArthur, Bernard Lee, Peter O'Toole, John Laurie, Niall MacGinnis. **Credits:** Dir: Robert Stevenson; Prod: Walt Disney; Writer: Robert Louis Stevenson; Story: Robert Louis Stevenson; DP: Paul Beeson. Color, 95 min. **VHS, LASER**

The Killer Inside Me

(1976) Warner Bros.
Thompson's great pulp novel is adapted for this Western, starring Keach as a deputy sheriff of a small, midwestern town whose cheerful demeanor disguises a walking time bomb of hidden evil ready to explode into a psychotic rage. Director Kennedy is a Western specialist who got his start writing scripts for action master Budd Boetticher and directing episodes of TV's *Combat*. **Cast:** Stacy Keach, Susan Tyrrell, Tisha Sterling, Keenan Wynn, John Carradine, John Dehner. **Credits:** Dir: Burt Kennedy; Prod: Michael W. Leighton; Writer: Edward Mann; Story: Jim Thompson. Color, 99 min. **VHS, DVD**

Killer McCoy

(1947) MGM
A young song-and-dance man (Rooney) befriends a boxer who talks him into becoming a fighter as well. He deserts the dance act he's put together with his alcoholic father and ends up in a championship bout with his friend. The ex-dancer kills his boxer friend in the ring, and his life unravels. The daughter of his unsavory fight promoter (Blyth) falls in love with him and he leaves boxing behind. A remake of *The Crowd Roars* (1938) with Robert Taylor and Edward Arnold. **Cast:** Mickey Rooney, James Bell, Ann Blyth, Brian Donlevy, James Dunn, Gloria Holden, Sam Levene, Walter Sande, Tom Tully. **Credits:** Dir: Roy Rowland; Prod: Sam Zimbalist; Writer: Frederick Hazlitt Brennan; Story: George Bruce, George Oppenheimer; DP: Joseph Ruttenberg; Ed: Ralph E. Winters; Composer: David Snell, Stanley Donen; Art Director: Cedric Gibbons. B&W, 104 min.

The Killers

(1946) Universal
An insurance investigator (O'Brien) digs up crime, betrayal, and a glamorous woman (Gardner in best femme fatale mode) behind an ex-fighter's (and current gas-station attendant's) death. Classic noir from Siodmak, a master of the genre, scripted by Veiller with an uncredited assist from Huston, based on a story by Ernest Hemingway. Lancaster made a sizzling film debut in the role of Swede, the murdered boxer. Rozsa's main theme was later borrowed for the opening sequence of TV's *Dragnet*. Academy Award Nominations: 4, including Best Director and Best Screenplay. **Cast:** Burt Lancaster, Ava Gardner, Edmond O'Brien, Albert Dekker, Sam Levene, Vince Barnett, Virginia Christine, Jack Lambert, Charles D. Brown, Donald MacBride. **Credits:** Dir: Robert Siodmak; Prod: Mark Hellinger; Writer: John Huston, Anthony Veiller; DP: Elwood Bredell; Ed: Arthur Hilton; Composer: Miklos Rozsa; Costumes: Vera West. B&W, 105 min. **VHS**

The Killers

(1964) Universal
Siegel directed this late-period noir loosely based on the Ernest Hemingway short story. Two hit men, hoping they'll figure out a way to make a million-dollar score, investigate the life of the teacher they've just killed. Reagan's final movie casts him as a villain. Composer Williams provided the score. Originally shot for TV but deemed "too violent" and given a theatrical release.

The King and I (1956)

wife, child, and a couple claiming to be Elcott's relations. Herries comes to the terrible realization that she has fallen under the power of a ring of con artists and is forced to watch as Elcott and his partners systematically sell off her valuable possessions. Her only chance at survival is to escape her own home. Made once before, in 1936, with Basil Rathbone. Academy Award Nomination for Best Costumes. **Cast:** Ethel Barrymore, Maurice Evans, Angela Lansbury, Keenan Wynn, Betsy Blair, John Williams, Doris Lloyd, Henri Letondal, Moyna MacGill. **Credits:** Dir: John Sturges; Prod: Armand Deutch; Writer: Jerry Davis, Edward Chodorov, Charles C. Bennett, Hugh Walpole; DP: Joseph Ruttenberg; Ed: Ferris Webster; Prod Design: Cedric Gibbons, William Ferrari. B&W, 77 min.

King and Four Queens
(1956) United Artists
Gable plays an outlaw on the lam who hides out in a ghost town whose only other occupants are a mother and her three daughters. When he learns that they're searching for $100,000 in gold stolen from a stagecoach by one of their husbands, he turns on the toothy charm, trying to seduce each of them into giving up their secrets. Directed by Walsh toward the end of his career, but still turning out man's-man adventures. **Cast:** Clark Gable, Eleanor Parker, Jo Van Fleet, Jean Willes, Barbara Nichols, Sara Shane, Jay C. Flippen, Roy Roberts. **Credits:** Dir: Raoul Walsh; Prod: David Hempstead; Writer: Margaret Fitts, Richard Alan Simmons; DP: Lucien Ballard; Ed: Louis R. Loeffler, David Brotherton; Composer: Alex North; Art Director: Wiard Ihnen. Color, 87 min. **VHS**

The King and I
(1956) Fox
Excellent Rodgers and Hammerstein musical with delightful songs, a heartwarming plot, and romantic, exotic settings and costumes. Kerr is a widowed teacher with her hands full bringing the King's brood up to date on the modern world—and with Brynner, in his iconic role as the tough-on-the-outside King of Siam. A remake of the nonmusical *Anna and the King of Siam* (1946), based on Margaret Landon's life story. Marni Nixon, often heard on Hollywood sound tracks (she was also used for *West Side Story* and *My Fair Lady*), doubles for Kerr on the sound track. Songs include "Getting to Know You," "Hello Young Lovers," "A Puzzlement," "Something

Cast: Lee Marvin, Angie Dickinson, Ronald Reagan, John Cassavetes, Claude Akins, Norman Fell, Virginia Christine. **Credits:** Dir: Don Siegel; Writer: Don Siegel, Gene L. Coon; Ed: Richard Belding; Composer: John Williams. Color, 95 min. **VHS**

Killer's Kiss
(1955) United Artists
Kubrick's second feature film tells the story of a struggling New York boxer who gets in trouble with gangsters when he protects a nightclub dancer. Kubrick raised the money for this film from friends and family. It's rough and wanders a bit but fans will find it an interesting early display of Kubrick's talent as he handles nearly every production chore. **Cast:** Frank Silvera, Jamie Smith, Irene Kane, Ruth Sobotka, Felice Orlandi, Ralph Roberts, Jerry Jarret, Mike Dana. **Credits:** Dir: Stanley Kubrick; Prod: Stanley Kubrick, Morris Bousel; Writer: Stanley Kubrick, Howard Sackler; DP: Stanley Kubrick; Ed: Stanley Kubrick; Composer: Gerald Fried. B&W, 67 min. **VHS**

The Killing
(1956) United Artists
Kubrick's perfect noir jump-started his career. Hayden stars as the ringleader in a racetrack heist that goes terribly wrong. Featuring Cook as the sympathetic fall guy, a nihilistic final image often copied, and a tight script, which

Kubrick adapted from the novel *Clean Break* by Lionel White. **Cast:** Sterling Hayden, Elisha Cook, Jr., Timothy Carey, Coleen Gray, Vince Edwards, Jay C. Flippen, Marie Windsor. **Credits:** Dir: Stanley Kubrick; Prod: James B. Harris; Writer: Stanley Kubrick; DP: Lucien Ballard. B&W, 83 min. **VHS, LASER**

Kim
(1950) MGM
Hollywood's version of Kipling's 1901 tale about a boy's adventures in India in the 1890s with a horse trader and a secret agent, who introduces him to the dangerous game of espionage. Remade for TV in 1984 with Peter O'Toole in the Flynn role. **Cast:** Errol Flynn, Dean Stockwell, Paul Lukas, Thomas Gomez, Cecil Kellaway, Arnold Moss, Reginald Owen, Laurette Luez. **Credits:** Dir: Victor Saville; Prod: Leon Gordon; Writer: Leon Gordon, Helen Deutsch, Richard Schayer; Story: Rudyard Kipling; DP: William V. Skall; Ed: George Boemler; Prod Design: Cedric Gibbons, Hans Peters; Composer: Andre Previn. Color, 113 min. **VHS**

Kind Lady
(1951) MGM
Henry Elcott (Evans), a young artist, convinces the elderly Mary Herries (Barrymore), a wealthy patron of the arts, to take him into her home. Suddenly, new guests begin to appear in the Herries' home as Elcott prevails upon the trusting widow to shelter his

Wonderful," and many others. Golden Globes for Best Film, Musical or Comedy; Best Actress in a Musical or Comedy: Deborah Kerr. Academy Award Nominations: 9, including Best Picture; Best Director; Best Actress: Deborah Kerr. **Academy Awards:** Best Sound Recording; Best Scoring of a Musical; Best Costume Design (Color); Best Art Direction—Set Decoration (Color). **Cast:** Deborah Kerr, Yul Brynner, Rita Moreno, Martin Benson, Terry Saunders, Rex Thompson, Carlos Rivas, Patrick Adiarte. **Credits:** Dir: Walter Lang; Prod: Charles Brackett; Writer: Ernest Lehman; DP: Leon Shamroy; Songs: Richard Rodgers, Oscar Hammerstein; Composer: Alfred Newman, Ken Darby; Costumes: Irene Sharaff. Color, 133 min. **VHS, LASER**

King and the Chorus Girl
(1937) Warner Bros.
A romantic comedy about an expatriate king (Gravet) on the search for new thrills. He ends up at the Folies Bergere, where a chorus girl in the can-can ensemble (Blondell) catches his eye. A farcical chase ensues between the two and the young lady ends up with a broken heart. When the king learns of the lady's possible departure back to Brooklyn (because of her distraught condition) he decides to mend her heart in a rare majestic moment. Written by Groucho! **Cast:** Fernand Gravet, Joan Blondell, Edward Everett Horton, Alan Mowbray, Jane Wyman, Mary Nash, Luis Alberni, Armand Kaliz, Ben Welden, Lionel Pape. **Credits:** Dir: Mervyn LeRoy; Prod: Mervyn LeRoy; Writer: Norman Krasna, Groucho Marx; Composer: Werner R. Heymann, Ted Koehler. B&W, 94 min.

King Creole
(1958) Paramount
Elvis is surprisingly good when he gets capable direction, in this case Curtiz. This noirish version of Harold Robbins's *A Stone for Danny Fisher* features Elvis as a busboy who becomes a star when he's forced to sing in a mobster's (Matthau) New Orleans club. Though he's gone straight, his youthful ties to organized crime threaten to end his career. Songs include "Hard-Headed Woman," "King Creole," and "Trouble." **Cast:** Elvis Presley, Walter Matthau, Carolyn Jones, Dean Jagger, Dolores Hart, Liliane Montevecchi, Paul Stewart, Vic Morrow. **Credits:** Dir: Michael Curtiz; Prod: Hal B. Wallis; Writer: Herbert Baker, Michael V. Gazzo; DP: Russell Harlan; Ed: Warren Low; Prod Design:

Joseph MacMillan Johnson; Composer: Walter Scharf; Art Director: Hal Pereira. B&W, 115 min. **VHS, LASER**

A King in New York
(1957) Archway
Chaplin made this bitter story of a deposed European king who observes the American scene, bewildered, in England, and it was widely viewed at the time as an attack on the country that made him an international superstar. Chaplin had a knack for annoying American Babbits, going all the way back to his marriages to teenage actresses in the teens and '20s. But it was his pacifist movie *Monsieur Verdoux* (1947) and his early, outspoken calls to open a Russian front in WWII that aroused the attention of the House Un-American Activities Committee. Though he wired the committee that he had never belonged to any political party, he was informed while aboard a ship sailing for London that he would not be readmitted to the U.S. without testifying as to his moral fitness. He remained exiled in Switzerland until returning in 1972 to accept a special Academy Award for his contribution to movie history. *A King in New York* was finally released in the U.S. in 1973. **Cast:** Charlie Chaplin, Dawn Addams, Oliver Johnston, Maxine Audley, Phil Brown, Alan Gifford, Shani Wallis, Michael Chaplin, Harry Green, Sid James. **Credits:** Dir: Charlie Chaplin; Prod: Charlie Chaplin; Writer: Charlie Chaplin; DP: Georges Perinal; Ed: John Seabourne; Composer: Charlie Chaplin. B&W, 105 min. **VHS**

King Kong
(1933) RKO
A masterpiece of movie exotica and one of the top moneymakers of the '30s. Fortune hunters travel to Skull Island in search of the fabled giant

ape "King Kong." Enticing him with the lovely Wray, they capture Kong and bring him back to New York to become a sideshow attraction. The rampaging ape escapes and ransacks the city searching for Wray, ending his quest swatting biplanes as he dangles from the Empire State Building in one of the most famous images in movie history. Directors Cooper and Schoedsack met as fliers in WWI Poland. They specialized in exotic documentaries and then adventure films with far-flung locations. Cooper later became a producer for David O. Selznick, and then produced John Ford masterpieces such as *Fort Apache* (1948) and *The Quiet Man* (1952), and one of the biggest hits of the '50s, *This Is Cinerama* (1952). Followed by *Son of Kong* (1934), a 1976 remake, and the related monkeyshines of *Mighty Joe Young* (1949). The special edition video includes archival footage, such as the scene in which Kong peels Wray like a banana and the excised giant spider scene. The laserdisc includes a second audio track with historical commentary from film historian Ronald Haver. Selected for the National Film Registry. **Cast:** Fay Wray, Bruce Cabot, Robert Armstrong, Frank Reicher, Sam Hardy, Noble Johnson, James Flavin, Victor Wong. **Credits:** Dir: Merian C. Cooper, Ernest B. Schoedsack; Prod: Merian C. Cooper, Ernest B. Shoedsack; Writer: Ruth Rose, James Creelman; DP: Vernon Walker, Eddie Linden, J. O. Taylor; Ed: Ted Cheesman; Prod Design: Carroll Clark; Composer: Max Steiner; Art Director: Al Herman, Van Nest Polglase. B&W, 105 min. **VHS, LASER**

King Kong
(1976) Paramount
Lange makes her screen debut as the giant ape's object of affection in this

---

Professor Harold Bloom Rates Shakespeare Movies

My first two choices are the Akira Kurosawa films *Ran* (1985), which is his splendid version of *King Lear*, and *Throne of Blood* (1957), a much earlier adaptation of *Macbeth*. Then I would select Larry Olivier's *Richard III* (1955), but most decidedly not his *Hamlet* (1948). For that matter, the Kenneth Branagh *Henry V* (1989) is to be avoided at all costs, as are all of Orson Welles's dreadful versions of the Bard [*Macbeth* (1948), *Chimes at Midnight* (1966), *Othello* (1951)].

Professor Harold Bloom is the author of *Shakespeare: Reinventing the Human.*

variation on the 1933 classic. The central element of unrequited love between big beast and the beauty is still here, but this time Kong is dragged from his island to the Big Apple by oil-company executives. He does some serious damage to an excellent re-creation of New York and is altogether more lifelike in this update. Academy Award Nominations: 2, including Best Cinematography; Best Sound. **Academy Awards:** Best Visual Effects. **Cast:** Jeff Bridges, Charles Grodin, Jessica Lange, John Randolph, Rene Auberjonois, Julius Harris, Jack O'Halloran, Dennis Fimple. **Credits:** Dir: John Guillermin; Prod: Dino De Laurentiis; Writer: Lorenzo Semple, Jr.; DP: Richard H. Kline; Ed: Ralph E. Winters; Prod Design: Mario Chiari, Dale Hennesy; Composer: John Barry. Color, 135 min. **VHS, LASER**

King of Alcatraz

(1938) Paramount
This fine adventure at sea begins as a lighthearted romance in which two hotshot radio operators, Nolan and Preston, are put onboard the same ship with lovely nurse Patrick. Before the situation is resolved, the boat is boarded by a gang of vicious criminals, headed by Alcatraz escapee Naish. A routine crime tale directed by Florey. **Cast:** Lloyd Nolan, Gail Patrick, Harry Carey, Robert Preston, Anthony Quinn, J. Carrol Naish, Dennis Morgan, Porter Hall, Richard Denning, Tom Tyler, Konstantin Shayne. **Credits:** Dir: Robert Florey; Prod: William Thomas; Writer: Irving Reis; DP: Harry Fischbeck; Ed: Eda Warren; Prod Design: A. Earl Hedrick; Composer: Boris Morros. B&W, 56 min.

King of Kings

(1961) MGM
Director Ray, who led what might charitably be described as a colorful life, would seem at first to be an odd choice for a big-budget, wide-screen epic depiction of the life of Christ. But remember also that Ray gave us our most indelible images of the soulful outsider; here we have a Jesus who is a rebel with the highest possible cause. The emphasis is on the spiritual, the healing moments, Jesus' contact with the people who would become his followers, not a trivial accomplishment in an undertaking on this scale. Orson Welles narrates, and the cast includes actors' actors such as Torn, McKenna, and Lindfors. **Cast:** Jeffrey Hunter, Siobhan McKenna, Robert Ryan, Hurd Hatfield, Viveca

Lindfors, Harry Guardino, Rip Torn, Ron Randell. **Credits:** Dir: Nicholas Ray; Prod: Samuel Bronston; Writer: Philip Yordan; DP: Franz Planer, Milton Krasner, Manuel Berenguer; Ed: Harold F. Kress, Renee Lichtig; Composer: Miklos Rozsa. Color, 230 min. **VHS, LASER**

The King of Marvin Gardens

(1972) Columbia
Nicholson reteamed with director Rafelson (*Head*, 1968; *Five Easy Pieces*, 1970) for this character study of a radio DJ who returns to Atlantic City to try to convince his dreamer brother (Dern) to forget a dangerous fast-money scheme but ends up involved. Featuring Burstyn in a fine performance as Dern's fading-beauty girlfriend and beautiful cinematography by Kovacs. **Cast:** Jack Nicholson, Ellen Burstyn, Bruce Dern, Julia Anne Robinson, Scatman Crothers. **Credits:** Dir: Bob Rafelson; Prod: Bob Rafelson; Writer: Jacob Brackman; DP: Laszlo Kovacs. Color, 104 min. **VHS**

King of the Gypsies

(1978) Paramount
Intriguing glimpse into the life of Gypsies with a terrific cast. Roberts is the grandson of Gypsy King Hayden. Though Roberts has tried to distance himself from his heritage, his grandfather bestows his title on him, enraging his jealous father. Roberts's screen debut. Note the camerawork of Nykvist, Ingmar Bergman's cinematographer, and the score by jazz violinist Grappelli and Grisman. **Cast:** Sterling Hayden, Shelley Winters, Susan Sarandon, Judd Hirsch, Eric Roberts, Brooke Shields, Annette O'Toole, Annie Potts. **Credits:** Dir: Frank Pierson; Prod: Federico De Laurentiis; Writer: Frank R. Pierson; DP: Sven Nykvist; Ed: Paul Hirsch; Prod Design: Gene Callahan; Composer: Stephane Grappelli and David Grisman. Color, 112 min. **VHS, LASER**

King of the Underworld

(1939) Warner Bros.
Bogie in a fable on the dangers of vice. Francis and her husband are both prominent surgeons who have everything and proceed to lose it when his penchant for gambling drives him into the clutches of underworld boss Bogart, who uses him to minister to his gang. Bogie kills her husband, but Francis tracks him down in a small town where she sets up shop and seizes the opportunity to get her revenge. Same plot as Muni-starrer *Dr. Socrates* (1935) with a gender

twist. **Cast:** Humphrey Bogart, Kay Francis, James Stephenson, John Eldredge, Jesse Busley, Arthur Aylesworth, Raymond Brown, Harland Tucker, Ralph Remley, Murray Alper. **Credits:** Dir: Lewis Seiler; Writer: W. R. Burnett, Vincent Sherman, George Bricker; DP: Sidney Hickox; Ed: Frank Dewar; Composer: Leo F. Forbstein; Art Director: Charles Novi. B&W, 69 min.

King Rat

(1965) Columbia
Well-played ensemble drama set in a Japanese prisoner-of-war camp in WWII. Segal, the monarch of the title, runs the camp's black-market trade and is able to set himself up in more comfortable fashion than his fellow prisoners, a polyglot of captives from England, Australia, and the U.S. From James Clavell's novel. Academy Award Nominations: 2, including Best (Black-and-White) Cinematography. **Cast:** George Segal, Tom Courtenay, Patrick O'Neal, James Fox, Todd Armstrong, Joseph Turkel, William Fawcett, Denholm Elliott. **Credits:** Dir: Bryan Forbes; Prod: James Woolf; Writer: Bryan Forbes; DP: Burnett Guffey; Ed: Walter Thompson; Composer: John Barry; Art Director: Robert Smith. B&W, 133 min. **VHS**

Kings Go Forth

(1958) United Artists
A romantic triangle that plays the race card to tip the balance. Two soldiers (Sinatra and Curtis) in WWII France understandably fall for the same girl, Wood. When she tells Sinatra one of her parents is black, he maintains it doesn't matter. Wood still refuses him, her heart set on Curtis, who has no real feelings for her. A standard potboiler with an unusual setting and dressed up as a social-problem film. **Cast:** Frank Sinatra, Tony Curtis, Natalie Wood, Leora Dana, Karl Swenson, Ann Codee, Eddie Ryder, Red Norvo. **Credits:** Dir: Delmer Daves; Prod: Frank Ross, Richard Lee Ross; Writer: Merle Miller; DP: Daniel L. Fapp; Ed: William B. Murphy; Composer: Elmer Bernstein; Art Director: Fernando Carrere. Color, 110 min. **VHS**

King Solomon's Mines

(1937) Gaumont
A most authentic treatment for the oft-made Haggard African adventure novel. This British version is interesting mostly for the performance by Robeson as King Umbopa, considered by most critics to be his best on film. Explorer Allan Quartermain (Hard-

wicke) crosses the Sahara into remote Africa in search of the legendary diamond mines. Shot on location. **Cast:** Cedric Hardwicke, Paul Robeson, Roland Young, Anna Lee, John Loder, Robert Adams, Frederick Leister, Sidney Fairbrother. **Credits:** Dir: Robert Stevenson; Prod: Geoffrey Barkas; Writer: Michael Hogan, A. R. Rawlinson, Roland Pertwee, Ralph Spence, Charles Bennett; Story: H. Rider Haggard; DP: Glen MacWilliams, Cyril Knowles; Ed: Michael Gordon; Prod Design: Alfred Junge; Composer: Mischa Spoliansky. B&W and Color, 81 min. **VHS**

King Solomon's Mines

(1950) MGM
A color update of the Haggard adventure that focuses on the relationship between Kerr and big white hunter Granger. Nothing new to add to the story, but the production is solid. The footage from Africa ended up in several African adventures. Academy Award Nominations: 3, including Best Picture. **Academy Awards:** Best (Color) Cinematography; Best Film Editing. **Cast:** Andrew Marton, Deborah Kerr, Stewart Granger, Richard Carlson, Hugo Haas, Lowell Gilmore, John Banner. **Credits:** Dir: Compton Bennett; Prod: Sam Zimbalist; Writer: Helen Deutsch; Story: H. Rider Haggard; DP: Robert Surtees; Ed: Ralph E. Winters, Conrad A. Nervig; Prod Design: Cedric Gibbons; Art Director: Conrad A. Nervig. Color, 103 min. **VHS**

Kings Row

(1942) Warner Bros.
The highest expression of the soap-opera device of tearing the facade from small-town life to discover the seething pit of rivalries, petty jealousies, and squalid affairs that lie beneath. In pre-WWI mid-America, two young men (Reagan and Cummings) grow tangled roots in a small town touched by madness and murder. Considered to be Reagan's best performance (not including Commander in Chief). **Cast:** Ann Sheridan, Robert Cummings, Ronald Reagan, Betty Field, Charles Coburn, Claude Rains, Judith Anderson, Maria Ouspenskaya. **Credits:** Dir: Sam Wood; Prod: David Lewis; Writer: Casey Robinson; DP: James Wong Howe; Ed: Ralph Dawson; Composer: Erich Wolfgang Korngold; Art Director: Carl Jules Weyl. B&W, 127 min. **VHS**

The King Steps Out

(1936) Columbia
A von Sternberg musical that tells the romantic story of Elizabeth of Austria.

Emperor Franz Josef is smitten with a young princess who does not reciprocate his feelings. The unhappy princess is to marry the Emperor until her sister comes to her aid. Posing as a dressmaker, the sister wins the love of the Emperor for herself and becomes his bride. **Cast:** Grace Moore, Franchot Tone, Walter Connolly, Raymond Walburn, Victor Jory, Elisabeth Risdon, Nana Bryant, Frieda Inescort. **Credits:** Dir: Josef von Sternberg; Prod: William Perlberg; Writer: Sidney Buchman; Story: Ernst Decsey, Gustav Holm, Hubert Marischka; DP: Lucien Ballard; Ed: Viola Lawrence; Prod Design: Stephen Goosson; Composer: Fritz Kreisler. Color, 85 min.

The King's Thief

(1955) MGM
Debonair Niven stars as a duke involved in a nefarious plot to steal the crown jewels from England's King Charles II. Look for a young, pre-Bond Moore. **Cast:** David Niven, Roger Moore, Ann Blyth, George Sanders, Edmund Purdom, John Dehner. **Credits:** Dir: Robert Z. Leonard; Prod: Edwin H. Knopf; Writer: Christopher Knopf; DP: Robert Planck; Composer: Miklos Rozsa. Color, 78 min. **VHS**

Kismet

(1955) MGM
The big-budget Minnelli musical version of the Broadway hit. The hoary Arabian Nights tale has beggar-poet Keel conniving his way into the Wazir's harem so that he can woo Blyth. Score adapted from Borodin; show-stopping songs include "Baubles, Bangles and Beads," "Bagdad," "The Olive Tree," and "Sands of Time." The laserdisc release is letterboxed and includes trailers. Also see the 1944 nonmusical version with Ronald Colman winning Marlene Dietrich's heart. **Cast:** Howard Keel, Ann Blyth, Dolores Gray, Monty Woolley, Vic Damone, Sebastian Cabot, Jay C. Flippen, Mike Mazurki. **Credits:** Dir: Vincente Minnelli; Prod: Arthur Freed; Writer: Charles Lederer, Luther Davis; DP: Joseph Ruttenberg; Ed: Adrienne Fazan; Prod Design: Cedric Gibbons; Composer: Andre Previn, Jeff Alexander; Art Director: Preston Ames. Color, 114 min. **VHS, LASER**

A Kiss Before Dying

(1956) United Artists
In this dark crime picture, young Wagner seduces the innocent Woodward with an eye on her family's great wealth. When he impregnates her, their

chances for the family's approval go out the window. Enraged, Wagner murders Woodward, making sure it looks like suicide. When her sister, Leith, starts poking around, Wagner tries to turn the charm on one more time. Remade with Matt Dillon in 1991. **Cast:** Robert Wagner, Jeffrey Hunter, Joanne Woodward, George Macready, Howard Petrie, Bill Walker, Mollie McCart, Marlene Felton, Virginia Leith, Mary Astor. **Credits:** Dir: Gerd Oswald; Prod: Robert Jacks; Writer: Lawrence Roman, Ira Levin; DP: Lucien Ballard; Ed: George A. Gittens; Prod Design: Addison Hehr; Composer: Lionel Newman. Color, 94 min.

The Kiss Before the Mirror

(1933) Universal
A murder-suspense-courtroom drama set in Vienna, with Morgan as a trial attorney defending a jealous husband accused of killing his faithless wife. The attorney begins to see some ominous parallels between the behavior of his client's victim and his own wife, and he contemplates a similar solution. Solid direction from Whale (he shot this on his sets from *Frankenstein!*), and cinematography by Freund, of *Metropolis* fame. Whale made this once again in 1938 as *Wives Under Suspicion*. **Cast:** Nancy Carroll, Frank Morgan, Gloria Stuart, Jean Dixon, Donald Cook, Charley Grapewin, Walter Pidgeon, Reginald Mason, Paul Lukas. **Credits:** Dir: James Whale; Prod: Carl Laemmle; Writer: Laszlo Fodor, William Anthony McGuire; DP: Karl Freund; Ed: Ted J. Kent; Composer: Franke Harling; Art Director: Charles D. Hall. B&W, 67 min.

Kisses for My President

(1964) Warner Bros.
The comic premise here may be outmoded soon: MacMurray has to come to terms with his new role as first husband when wife Bergen is elected president. MacMurray, America's father figure of the '60s, handles his ceremonial chores with good humor, of course. Mild humor that will soon seem as curiously remote as silent newsreels. Academy Award Nomination for Best (Black-and-White) Costume Design. **Cast:** Polly Bergen, Fred MacMurray, Arlene Dahl, Edward Andrews, Eli Wallach, Donald May, Anna Capri, Bill Walker. **Credits:** Dir: Curtis Bernhardt; Prod: Curtis Bernhardt; Writer: Claude Binyon, Robert G. Kane; DP: Robert Surtees; Ed: Sam O'Steen; Composer: Bronislau Kaper; Art Director: Herman A. Blumenthal. B&W, 113 min. **VHS, LASER**

Kiss Me Deadly (1955)

Kissin' Cousins
(1964) MGM
Elvis times two as the King pulls a Patty Duke and becomes identical cousins, one a hillbilly singer and the other an Air Force officer on the lookout for a new missile site. Singing, including "Barefoot Ballad," seals the deal. Not prime Presley. **Cast:** Elvis Presley, Arthur O'Connell, Glenda Farrell, Pamela Austin, Yvonne Craig, Donald Woods, Tommy Farrell, Beverly Powers. **Credits:** Dir: Gene Nelson; Prod: Sam Katzman; Writer: Gerald Drayson Adams, Gene Nelson; DP: Ellis W. Carter. Color, 97 min. **VHS**

Kiss Me Deadly
(1955) United Artists
Triumphant '50s-vintage tough-guy film, pulp-detective-novel style. Mickey Spillane's brutal private eye Mike Hammer (Meeker) follows the trail of a murdered dame right into the heart of nuclear-age paranoia. Angry, stylish filmmaking that combines sci-fi and noir into one violent explosion. Aldrich's early masterpiece planted seeds that blossomed in such French New Wave classics as *Breathless* (1961). The restored video version contains the original theatrical ending, which was thought lost and possibly censored before it was discovered in the director's print in the UCLA film vaults. **Cast:** Ralph Meeker, Albert Dekker, Paul Stewart, Cloris Leachman, Maxine Cooper, Gaby Rodgers, Jack Elam, Strother Martin, Jack Lambert. **Credits:** Dir: Robert Aldrich; Prod: Robert Aldrich; Writer: A. I.

Bezzerides; DP: Ernest Laszlo; Ed: Michael Luciano; Composer: Frank DeVol; Art Director: William Glasgow. B&W, 106 min. **VHS, LASER**

Kiss Me Kate
(1953) MGM
Porter's brilliant musical retelling of Shakespeare's *The Taming of the Shrew* presents married performers Keel and Grayson taking their onstage roles offstage and vice versa. Watch for Fosse's big number. Produced in 3-D! Songs include "From This Moment On," "Wunderbar," "So In Love," "Where Is the Life That Late I Led?" and many more. Academy Award Nomination for Best Scoring of a Musical Picture. **Cast:** Kathryn Grayson, Howard Keel, Ann Miller, Bobby Van, Keenan Wynn, James Whitmore, Kurt Kasznar, Bob Fosse. **Credits:** Dir: George Sidney; Prod: Jack Cummings; Writer: Dorothy Kingsley; DP: Charles Rosher; Ed: Ralph E. Winters; Prod Design: Cedric Gibbons, Urie McCleary; Composer: Cole Porter. Color, 111 min. **VHS, LASER**

Kiss Me, Stupid
(1964) Lopert
Dino doesn't stretch much as a night-club singer stuck in small-town Nevada. A failed local songwriter (Walston) wants to sell some tunes but keep the lecherous singer's hands off his beautiful wife (Novak), so he convinces a local bimbo to pose as his spouse. Wilder's love of twitting bluenoses reached its apex with this sex comedy that was condemned by

churches and critics alike. Thirty-five years later, it's time to take another look. **Cast:** Dean Martin, Ray Walston, Kim Novak, Felicia Farr, Cliff Osmond, Barbara Pepper, Doro Merande, Henry Gibson, John Fiedler, Mel Blanc. **Credits:** Dir: Billy Wilder; Prod: Billy Wilder; Writer: Billy Wilder, I. A. L. Diamond; DP: Joseph La Shelle; Ed: Daniel Mandell; Prod Design: Alexander Trauner; Composer: Andre Previn. B&W, 126 min. **VHS, LASER**

Kiss of Death
(1947) Fox
There's nowhere for paroled thief Mature to turn when he rats on a gang in this famously gritty New York noir scripted by Hecht and Lederer. Widmark makes one of the screen's great debuts as the psychopathic killer on Mature's trail (the scene of him pushing a wheelchair-bound old lady down the stairs remains shocking despite all that has followed). Golden Globe for Most Promising Newcomer, Male: Richard Widmark. Academy Award Nominations: Best Supporting Actor: Richard Widmark; Best Original Story. **Cast:** Victor Mature, Richard Widmark, Brian Donlevy, Coleen Gray, Karl Malden, Taylor Holmes, Howard Smith, Anthony Ross. **Credits:** Dir: Henry Hathaway; Prod: Fred Kohlmar; Writer: Ben Hecht, Charles Lederer; DP: Norbert F. Brodine; Ed: J. Watson Webb; Prod Design: Lyle Wheeler, Leland Fuller; Composer: David Buttolph. B&W, 99 min. **VHS**

Kiss the Blood Off My Hands
(1948) Universal
Lancaster stars as a combat veteran and ex-POW with post-traumatic symptoms. The results are fisticuffs, and prison, the lash, and some homicide thrown in for good measure. Burt takes it on the lam at Fontaine's suggestion after being seen at one killing, but ends up in jail after beating a cop. The black-marketeering witness to the killing surfaces repeatedly to harass and threaten Lancaster and Fontaine, but his attempts to coerce Lancaster into participating in crime end with Fontaine taking action against him, and Lancaster taking the rap. **Cast:** Joan Fontaine, Burt Lancaster, Robert Newton, Jay Novello, Colin Keith-Johnston, Reginald Sheffield. **Credits:** Dir: Norman Foster; Prod: Harold Hecht, Richard Vernon; Writer: Gerald Butler, Leonardo Bercovici, Walter Bernstein; DP: Russell Metty; Ed: Milton Carruth; Composer: Miklos Rozsa; Art Director: Bernard Herzbrun, Nathan Juran. B&W, 79 min.

Kiss the Boys Goodbye

(1941) Paramount
This backstage musical stars sparkling Martin as a southern belle who can belt out a tune. When the lil' ole nobody auditions for the lead role in a Broadway musical show, the producers, Ameche and Levant, are charmed into giving the new girl the part. But after no time Martin's fired for unprofessionalism. As soon as she's gone, Ameche realizes he has more than professional interest in the spunky singer, and he's off on the chase. **Cast:** Mary Martin, Don Ameche, Oscar Levant, Virginia Dale, Barbara Jo Allen, Raymond Walburn, Elizabeth Patterson, Jerome Cowan, Connee Boswell, Eddie Anderson. **Credits:** Dir: Victor Schertzinger; Prod: William LeBaron; Writer: Dwight Taylor, Harry Tugend; Story: Clare Booth; DP: Ted Tetzlaff; Ed: Paul Weatherwax; Composer: Victor Young. B&W, 85 min.

Kiss Tomorrow Goodbye

(1950) Warner Bros.
Cagney's on familiar turf in the story of a ruthless mobster's rise and fall, but the action is more violently explosive than in the '30s Warner gangster films Cagney made famous. Note the depth of character actors in support: Bond, MacLane, Adler, Neville Brand. **Cast:** James Cagney, Barbara Payton, Luther Adler, Ward Bond, Helena Carter, Barton MacLane, Steve Brodie, Rhys Williams. **Credits:** Dir: Gordon Douglas; Prod: William Cagney; Writer: Harry Brown; DP: Peverell Marley; Ed: Walter Hannemann, Truman Wood; Prod Design: Wiard Ihnen; Composer: Carmen Dragon. B&W, 102 min. **VHS, LASER**

Kit Carson

(1940) United Artists
Hall gets the chance to shine away from the Maria Montez exotica in this straightforward depiction of the frontier scout leading a wagon train west. Cavalry officer Andrews comes to the rescue when Indians attack but becomes a rival for Bari. Look for future Lone Ranger Moore. **Cast:** Jon Hall, Dana Andrews, Lynn Bari, Harold Huber, Ward Bond, Renie Riano, Clayton Moore, Raymond Hatton. **Credits:** Dir: George B. Seitz; Prod: Edward Small; Writer: George Bruce; DP: John Mescall, Robert Pittack; Ed: Fred Feitshans, William Claxton; Composer: Edward Ward; Art Director: John DuCasse Schulze. Color, 101 min. **VHS**

Kitty

(1945) Paramount
A signature role for Goddard as an impoverished, beautiful young Cockney girl in 18th-century England. She is spotted by artist Thomas Gainsborough and has her portrait painted. The painting catches the eye of Sir Hugh Marcy, a nobleman who takes her in and decides to turn her into a lady. This he does successfully and Kitty has a marriage arranged for her to an aging ironmonger. Her husband dies shortly afterward and Kitty moves on, marrying another man while pregnant from her first husband. When her second husband also dies, Kitty finally manages to find love with the one who has loved her all the while. A rich costume romance with Leisen's customary good taste. Academy Award Nomination for Best Art Direction. **Cast:** Paulette Goddard, Ray Milland, Patric Knowles, Reginald Owen, Cecil Kellaway, Constance Collier, Dennis Hoey, Sara Allgood, Eric Blore, Gordon Richards. **Credits:** Dir: Mitchell Leisen; Prod: Mitchell Leisen; Writer: Karl Tunberg, Darrell Ware; Story: Rosamond Marshall; DP: Daniel L. Fapp; Ed: Alma Macrorie; Prod Design: Hans Dreier, Raoul Pene Du Bois, Walter Tyler; Composer: Victor Young. B&W, 103 min.

Kitty Foyle

(1940) Paramount
Rogers turned her career in a new direction (and won an Oscar) when she stepped out of her dancing shoes and into the starring role in this romantic melodrama. As an average working-girl secretary, Rogers faces compromising her self-image and relationships with her friends and coworkers when she falls in love with a married man. Based on the popular novel by Christopher Morley. Academy Award Nominations: 5, including Best Picture; Best Director; Best Screenplay. **Academy Awards:** Best Actress: Ginger Rogers. **Cast:** Ginger Rogers, Dennis Morgan, Eduardo Ciannelli, James Craig, Ernest Cossart, Gladys Cooper, Odette Myrtil, Mary Treen. **Credits:** Dir: Sam Wood; Prod: David Hempstead; Writer: Dalton Trumbo, Donald Ogden Stewart; DP: Robert de Grasse; Ed: Henry Berman; Composer: Roy Webb; Art Director: Van Nest Polglase, Mark-Lee Kirk. B&W, 108 min. **VHS, LASER**

Klondike Annie

(1936) Paramount
One of West's best, with direction by Walsh and a leading man who can take what she dishes out in rugged McLaglen. When Mae defends her honor by killing her assailant, she hides out on a steamship heading for the Yukon. McLaglen lends a hand and loses his heart, and the two concoct a phony mission to save souls. The sight of West retailing the Gospels is funny enough, but then the situation gets funnier as she starts to get serious. **Cast:** Mae West, Helen Jerome Eddy, Victor McLaglen, Philip Reed, Harold Huber, Conway Tearle, Lucille Gleason, Esther Howard. **Credits:** Dir: Raoul Walsh; Prod: William LeBaron; Writer: Mae West; DP: George Clemens; Ed: Stuart Heisler; Art Director: Hans Dreier, Bernard Herzbrun. B&W, 77 min. **VHS, DVD**

Klute

(1971) Warner Bros.
This could have been no better than an episode of TV's *McCloud*, with a small-town sheriff (Sutherland) loose in the big city on a missing-persons case. But Fonda invests her role as the prostitute who needs Sutherland's help and who may hold the key to his investigation with such understanding, ambivalence, and longing that she becomes the centerpiece of the picture. A fine performance justly awarded an Oscar. Fonda also won a Golden Globe for Best Actress and the National Society of Film Critics Best Actress prize. Academy Award Nominations: 2, including Best (Original) Story and Screenplay. **Academy Awards:** Best Actress: Jane Fonda. **Cast:** Jane Fonda, Donald Sutherland, Roy Scheider, Rita Gam, Charles Cioffi, Nathan George, Dorothy Tristan, Jean Stapleton. **Credits:** Dir: Alan J. Pakula; Prod: Alan J. Pakula, David Lang; Writer: Andy K. Lewis, David P. Lewis; DP: Gordon Willis; Ed: Carl Lerner; Composer: Michael Small; Art Director: George Jenkins. Color, 114 min. **VHS, LASER**

Knock on Wood

(1954) Paramount
Kaye's in top form in this comic thriller about a ventriloquist with a dummy that talks at inappropriate times. Unbeknownst to him, the dummy is used as a hiding place for plans for a new secret weapon. Two different political groups search for the dummy and get caught up in the outrageous situations, such as dancing in a ballet as Kaye tries to avoid the gangsters. Along the way, he falls in love with a psychiatrist. Academy Award Nomination for Best Screenplay. **Cast:** Danny Kaye, Mai Zetterling, Torin Thatcher, David Burns, Leon

Askin, Abner Biberman, Gavin Gordon, Otto Waldis, Steven Geray, Diana Adams. **Credits:** Dir: Melvin Frank, Norman Panama; Prod: Melvin Frank, Norman Panama; Writer: Norman Panama, Melvin Frank; DP: Daniel Fapp; Ed: Alma Macrorie; Choreographer: Michael Kidd; Composer: Sylvia Fine, Victor Young; Art Director: Hal Pereira. Color, 103 min.

Knute Rockne—All American
(1940) Warner Bros.
Famous biopic of Notre Dame football coach has probably been more referenced than seen because of its performance by Reagan as gridiron star George Gipp and the so-quotable line, "Tell the boys to win just one for the Gipper." But O'Brien gives it the necessary fire and brimstone and this is one of Reagan's signature roles as the dying player, so sports fans in particular should try to catch it. Selected for the National Film Registry. **Cast:** Pat O'Brien, Gale Page, Ronald Reagan, Donald Crisp, Albert Basserman, John Litel, Henry O'Neill, John Qualen. **Credits:** Dir: Lloyd Bacon; Prod: Robert Fellows; Writer: Robert Buckner; DP: Tony Gaudio; Ed: Ralph Dawson; Composer: Ray Heindorf; Art Director: Robert M. Haas. B&W, 98 min. **VHS**

Kongo
(1932) MGM
Huston performed in the stage version in the 1920s and Tod Browning directed a silent version of the same story as *West of Zanzibar,* starring Lon Chaney, in 1928. That's quite a pedigree in the world of the bizarre, and with a dash of Joseph Conrad, we descend to the metaphorical no-man's-land of the Congo. Huston etches a graphic portrait of a crippled white trader who ruthlessly controls a native tribe, though his violent thirst for revenge leads to a gruesome comeuppance. **Cast:** Walter Huston, Lupe Velez, Conrad Nagel, Virginia Bruce, C. Henry Gordon, Mitchell Lewis, Forrester Harvey. **Credits:** D ir: William Joyce Cowen; Writer: Leon Gordon; DP: Harold Rosson; Ed: Conrad A. Nervig; Art Director: Cedric Gibbons. B&W, 86 min.

Kon-Tiki
(1951)
Beloved by boomer-generation boys, this adventurous documentary has fueled plenty of oceangoing adventure daydreams. Anthropologist Heyerdahl proves his theory of ancient ocean migrations by lashing together a raft and sailing it from Peru to Tahiti. Share the memory with this generation of daydreamers. **Academy Awards:** Best Documentary. **Cast:** Thor Heyerdahl. **Credits:** Dir: Ben Grauer, Thor Heyerdahl; Prod: Olle Nordemar. Color, 73 min. **VHS**

Kotch
(1971) Cinerama
Lemmon debuts as director with familiar sidekick Matthau in the lead and support from wife Farr. The tailor-made role for Matthau finds the children of an elderly grump trying to encourage him to slow down and retire. He wants none of it. Terrific script from Paxton. Academy Award Nominations: 4, including Best Actor: Walter Matthau; Best Song ("Life Is What You Make It"). **Cast:** Walter Matthau, Deborah Winters, Felicia Farr, Charles Aidman, Ellen Geer, Darrell Larson, Paul Picerni, Lucy Saroyan. **Credits:** Dir: Jack Lemmon; Prod: Richard Carter; Writer: John Paxton; DP: Richard H. Kline; Ed: Ralph E. Winters; Composer: Marvin Hamlisch; Art Director: Jack Poplin. Color, 114 min. **VHS**

Krakatoa, East of Java
(1969) Cinerama
An international cast goes in search of sunken treasure and encounters an erupting volcano. Much nonsensical business leads up to genuinely stirring action sequences. Based on an actual massive eruption in the 1800s, which devastated the island of Java and killed thousands. Boomer-age audiences will probably remember the promotional campaign more than the film itself, but probably spent a Saturday afternoon watching this at some point. The lengths of various editions vary wildly. **Cast:** Maximilian Schell, Sal Mineo, Diane Baker, Brian Keith, Barbara Werle, John Leyton, Rossano

Brazzi, J. D. Cannon. **Credits:** Dir: Bernard L. Kowalski; Prod: Lester A. Sansom, William R. Forman; Writer: Bernard Gordon, Clifford Newton Gould; DP: Manuel Berenguer; Ed: Maurice Rootes, Warren Low, Walter Hannemann; Composer: Frank DeVol; Art Director: Eugene Lourie. Color, 128 min. **VHS**

Kramer vs. Kramer
(1979) Columbia
This is the film that captured all the searching and heartbreak that marked the mid-'70s revolution in marriage roles as it captivated audiences. Hoffman's advertising executive sacrifices family time for his career until wife Streep announces that she's abandoning her husband and child to find fulfillment on her own terms. Henry reveals himself to be a marvelous actor at a tender age as he registers shock and bewilderment, and, finally, trust that everything will work out. Just as he makes an accommodation to his new situation, Henry becomes the spoils of a custody war. There are scenes of real humor (Hoffman preparing breakfast in a kitchen with which he is painfully unfamiliar) to balance the heartbreak. Justly awarded virtually every honor possible, including Golden Globes for Best Actor: Dustin Hoffman; Best Drama; Best Supporting Actress: Meryl Streep; and Best Screenplay. Benton deserves particular mention for his script adapted from Avery Corman's novel, and his sensitive direction that kept the explosive emotions in balance. Academy Award Nominations: 8. **Academy Awards:** Best Picture; Best Director; Best Actor: Dustin Hoffman; Best Supporting Actress: Meryl Streep; Best Screenplay Based on Material from Another Medium. **Cast:** Dustin Hoffman, Justin Henry, Meryl Streep, Jane Alexander, Howard Duff, George Coe, JoBeth Williams, Bill Moor. **Credits:** Dir: Robert Benton; Prod: Stanley R. Jaffe; Writer: Robert Benton; DP: Nestor Almendros; Ed: Jerry Greenberg; Prod Design: Paul Sylbert; Composer: Henry Purcell, Antonio Vivaldi. Color, 105 min. **VHS, LASER**

Ladies in Retirement

(1941) Columbia
This creepy, hair-raising drama features Lupino as the housekeeper and personal maid to rich, has-been actress Elsom. When Lupino's two strange sisters move into the dark mansion, the lady of the house objects. Fearing what might happen to the weird sisters on the outside, Lupino strangles her mistress. Soon after, Hayward, a curious young relative, shows up at the door asking questions. **Cast:** Ida Lupino, Louis Hayward, Evelyn Keyes, Elsa Lancaster, Edith Barrett, Isobel Elsom, Emma Dunn, Clyde Cook, Queenie Leonard. **Credits:** Dir: Charles Vidor; Prod: Lester Cowan; Writer: Garrett Fort, Reginald Denham; Story: Reginald Denham, Edward Percy; DP: George Barnes; Ed: Al Clark; Prod Design: Lionel Banks; Composer: Morris Stoloff, Ernst Toch. B&W, 91 min.

The Ladies' Man

(1961) Paramount
Nice setup for Jerry as the nutty handyman in an all-girl boardinghouse. Lots of opportunity for doors slamming and general mayhem. One of Lewis's better efforts. Cameos from Raft as, inevitably, a gangster, and Harry James. **Cast:** Jerry Lewis, Helen Traubel, Kathleen Freeman, George Raft, Marty Ingels, Buddy Lester, Gloria Jean, Jack LaLanne, Pat Stanley. **Credits:** Dir: Jerry Lewis; Prod: Jerry Lewis; Writer: Jerry Lewis, Bill Richmond; DP: Wallace Kelley; Ed: Stanley Johnson; Composer: Walter Scharf; Art Director: Hal Pereira, Ross Bellah. Color, 106 min. **VHS, LASER**

Ladies of Leisure

(1930) Columbia
In one of her first roles, Stanwyck plays a gold digger who decides to change her ways and find true love. On her way back from a yachting party she runs into a ladies' man and artist (Graves) who asks her to pose for a portrait he wants to paint. Although the painter comes from money, Stanwyck curbs the wisecracks long enough to fall in love with him. Enter the artist's wealthy parents. Routine early talkie potboiler with the attraction of a fiery young Stanwyck. **Cast:** Barbara Stanwyck, Ralph Graves, Lowell Sherman, Marie Prevost, George Fawcett, Juliette Compton, Johnnie Walker. **Credits:** Dir: Frank Capra; Prod: Harry Cohn; Writer: Jo Swerling; Story: Milton Herbert Gropper; DP: Joseph Walker; Ed: Maurice Wright; Composer: Constantine Bakaleinikoff; Art Director: Harrison Wiley. B&W, 98 min. **VHS**

Ladies They Talk About

(1933) Warner Bros.
Stanwyck gives a knockout performance as a jailbird in this tough-talking, pre-Code prison drama. Stanwyck, a gun moll, gets sent to the female ward at San Quentin after her gang of bank robbers is caught. Based on the play *Women in Prison*, cowritten by Dorothy Mackaye, an actress who found herself behind bars when her husband was killed by another actor. **Cast:** William Keighley, Barbara Stanwyck, Lyle Talbot, Dorothy Burgess, Maude Eburne, Preston Foster, Lillian Roth, Harold Huber. **Credits:** Dir: Howard Bretherton; Prod: Raymond Griffith; Writer: Sidney Sutherland, Brown Holmes, William McGrath; DP: John F. Seitz; Ed: Basil Wrangell; Prod Design: Esdras Hartley. B&W, 70 min. **VHS**

Lady and the Tramp

(1955) Disney
Disney's animated classic is a romantic adventure about two dogs from the opposite sides of the kennel. Lady, a pedigreed cocker spaniel who's run away from home, meets Tramp, a wild mutt who comes to her defense, and they fall in love. Featuring the voice and music of Peggy Lee, this was Disney's first CinemaScope cartoon, requiring animators to draw some scenes twice, once in CinemaScope and once in the regular aspect ratio. Based on Ward Greene's short story "Happy Dan, the Whistling Dog." Songs include "He's a Tramp" and "Peace on Earth." **Cast:** Peggy Lee, Barbara Luddy, Larry Roberts, Bill Thompson, Bill Baucon, Stan Freberg, Verna Felton, Alan Reed. **Credits:** Dir: Hamilton Luske, Clyde Geronimi, Wilfred Jackson; Prod: Walt Disney; Writer: Erdman Penner, Joe Rinaldi, Ralph Wright, Don DaGradi; Ed: Donald Halliday; Composer: Oliver Wallace. Color, 77 min. **VHS, LASER**

Lady Be Good

(1941) MGM
A musical feast based on a Gershwin backstage musical, updated to feature the songs of Oscar Hammerstein, the Gershwins, Jerome Kern, and George Bassman, this comedy follows the life of a married couple who write beautiful music together when they're not hating each other. Starring Young and Sothern (with routines by comedian Skelton and dancer Powell), and based on the 1924 Gershwin Broadway hit, it features the songs "Lady Be Good," "You'll Never Know," and Kern's Oscar-winning "The Last Time I Saw Paris." **Academy Awards:** Best Song. **Cast:** Ann Sothern, Robert Young, Eleanor Powell, Red Skelton, Lionel Barrymore, John Carroll, Virginia O'Brien, Dan Dailey, Jimmy Dorsey. **Credits:** Dir: Norman Z. McLeod; Prod: Arthur Freed; Writer: Jack McGowan, Kay Van Riper, Ralph Spence, Herman Wouk, Vincente Minnelli, John McClain, Arnold Auerbach, Robert MacGunigle; DP: George J. Folsey, Oliver T. Marsh; Ed: Fredrick Y. Smith; Prod Design: Cedric Gibbons, John Detlie; Composer: George E. Stoll. B&W, 111 min. **VHS**

Ladybug, Ladybug

(1963) United Artists
Made on a shoestring budget and based on a true incident that occurred during the Cuban Missile Crisis of 1962, this film tells the story of what happens after an air-raid warning alarm accidentally goes off at an elementary school. Twelve-year-old Playten invites some of her friends into her family's air-raid shelter, and, after telling one girl that there is no room for her, the girl runs off to hide and suffocates in a junked refrigerator. Interesting early independent feature from the writer-director team that produced *David and Lisa* in 1962. **Cast:** Jane Connell, William Daniels, James Frawley, Richard Hamilton, Kathryn Hays, Jane Hoffman, Nancy Marchand, Alice Playten. **Credits:** Dir: Frank Perry; Prod: Frank Perry; Writer: Eleanor Perry; Art Director: Albert Brenner. B&W, 81 min.

Lady by Choice

(1934) Columbia
Lombard stars in this highly entertaining, Depression-era comedy as a burlesque dancer who, after getting arrested for a public performance, "adopts" a homeless woman as her mother on the advice of her press agent. "Mother" transforms her into a lady, complete with wealthy suitor Pryor waiting in the wings. Co-starring Robson as the "mother," reprising her role from the 1933 prequel, Capra's *Lady for a Day*. **Cast:** Carole Lombard, May Robson, Roger Pryor, Walter Connolly, Arthur Hohl, Raymond Walburn, James Burke, Henry Kolker. **Credits:** Dir: David Burton; Prod: Robert North; Writer: Jo Swerling; DP: Ted Tetzlaff; Ed: Viola Lawrence. B&W, 78 min. VHS

The Lady Eve

(1941) Paramount
This is perhaps the perfect movie comedy, with a runaway heiress—or, in this case, heir—double identities, barbed wit, inspired pratfalls, and the Sturges collection of supporting characters. One could ask for no more. Beer scion Fonda would rather spend his time chasing snakes up exotic rivers than running the family business, until he becomes fascinated with con girl Stanwyck and her crooked pop, Coburn, on an ocean liner. Of course, she falls for Fonda and then loses him when he learns of her occupation. She gets another chance in the guise of visiting royalty and charms everyone at a reception in her honor, including Fonda's tycoon father Pallette. Our favorite line: after Fonda has most of the formal dinner

and drinks spilled on his tux and, finally, on his out-of-season dinner jacket, Pallette intones, "Why don't you put on a bathing suit!" Well, you have to see it. Selected for the National Film Registry. Academy Award Nomination for Best Original Story. **Cast:** Barbara Stanwyck, Henry Fonda, Charles Coburn, Eugene Pallette, William Demarest, Eric Blore, Melville Cooper, Martha O'Driscoll. **Credits:** Dir: Preston Sturges; Prod: Paul Jones; Story: Preston Sturges; DP: Victor Milner; Ed: Stuart Gilmore; Composer: Sigmund Krumgold; Art Director: Hans Dreier, Ernst Fegte. B&W, 97 min. VHS, LASER

Lady for a Day

(1933) Columbia
Capra directs this heartfelt adapation of Damon Runyon's story "Madame La Gimp," in which a softhearted gangster (William) organizes his entire gang of thugs to help transform an elderly apple vendor (Robson) into a perfect society lady. Reportedly one of Capra's favorites among his own films, he remade it in 1961 with Bette Davis. Academy Award Nominations: Best Picture; Best Director; Best Actress: May Robson; Best Adapted Screenplay. **Cast:** Warren William, May Robson, Guy Kibbee, Glenda Farrell, Walter Connolly, Nat Pendleton, Ned Sparks, Jean Parker. **Credits:** Dir: Frank Capra; Writer: Robert Riskin; DP: Joseph Walker; Ed: Gene Havlick; Composer: Constantin Bakaleinikoff; Art Director: Stephen Goosson. B&W, 96 min. VHS, LASER

Lady for a Night

(1942) Republic
Blondell stars in this drama about the wealthy female owner of a casino riverboat who tries to break into high society by blackmailing a southern aristocrat (Wayne) into marrying her and ends up facing a murder charge when she dodges a dose of poison meant for her. **Cast:** John Wayne, Joan Blondell, Ray Middleton, Philip Merivale, Blanche Yurka, Edith Barrett, Leonid Kinskey, Dorothy Burgess. **Credits:** Dir: Leigh Jason; Prod: Albert J. Cohen; Writer: Boyce DeGaw, Isabel Dawn; Story: Garrett Fort; DP: Norbert F. Brodine; Ed: Murray Seldeen, Ernest Nims; Composer: David Buttolph; Art Director: John Victor MacKay. B&W, 88 min. VHS

The Lady from Shanghai

(1948) Columbia
Welles constructs a series of brilliant set pieces that don't quite add up to a

movie, but the result is fascinating nonetheless. Beautiful viper Hayworth weaves a snare for Welles as an Irish sailor who she hires to work on her crippled husband's yacht for a Pacific ocean cruise, a cruise from which she doesn't intend the husband to return. A showdown in the San Francisco Playland's hall of mirrors culminates in a shower of glass and a justly renowned piece of movie history. Hayworth, Mrs. Welles during the production, filed for divorce when the shooting stopped, and the film's lack of box-office success hampered Welles's career for years. **Cast:** Orson Welles, Rita Hayworth, Everett Sloane, Glenn Anders, Ted De Corsia, Erskine Sanford, Gus Schilling, Harry Shannon. **Credits:** Dir: Orson Welles; Prod: Orson Welles; Story: Orson Welles; DP: Charles Lawton, Jr.; Ed: Viola Lawrence; Composer: Heinz Roemheld; Art Director: Stephen Goosson, Sturges Carne. B&W, 87 min. VHS, LASER

The Lady Gambles

(1949) Universal
A drama about a married woman (Stanwyck) with a dangerous passion for Las Vegas and a terrible gambling habit. Abandoning her hubby, the gambler teams up with a professional but she eventually destroys their relationship with her excessive behavior, and in the end she gets set straight by her supportive spouse and a shrink. A social-problem melodrama with a powerful performance by Stanwyck. Watch for an early appearance by Tony Curtis. **Cast:** Barbara Stanwyck, Robert Preston, Stephen McNally, Edith Barrett, John Hoyt, Elliott Sullivan, John Harmon, Philip Van Zandt, Leif Erickson, Curt Conway. **Credits:** Dir: Michael Gordon; Prod: Kraike Michael; Writer: Roy Huggins, Halsted Welles; Story: Lewis Meltzner, Oscar Saul; DP: Russell Metty; Ed: Milton Carruth; Prod Design: Alexander Golitzen; Composer: Frank Skinner. B&W, 99 min.

Lady Godiva

(1955) Universal
The statuesque O'Hara takes on the title role as the legendary 11th-century Saxon maid who rides naked through Canterbury to prove the loyalty of the Saxons to King Edward. A rote costumer notable entirely for O'Hara's presence. Eastwood appears in an early bit role. **Cast:** Maureen O'Hara, George Nader, Victor McLaglen, Torin Thatcher, Robert Warwick, Alex Harford, Clint Eastwood, Eduard Franz. **Credits:** Dir: Arthur Lubin; Prod: Robert Arthur; Writer: Oscar Brodney,

Harry Ruskin; DP: Carl Guthrie; Ed: Paul Weatherwax; Prod Design: Alexander Golitzen; Composer: Joseph Gershenson; Art Director: Robert Boyle. Color, 89 min. **VHS**

Lady in a Cage

(1963) Paramount

This brutal shocker has a simple setup—a wealthy widow (de Havilland) is trapped by a power outage in a stalled elevator in her home—but a remorseless tension. A gang of thugs who respond to her cries for help terrify the woman seemingly just for kicks. Caan has a believable menace in his first featured role. A small-scale masterpiece of urban horror, with striking camerawork by Garmes.
Cast: Olivia de Havilland, James Caan, Jennifer Billingsley, Rafael Campos, William Swan, Jeff Corey, Ann Sothern, Charles Seel. **Credits:** Dir: Walter Grauman; Prod: Luther Davis; Writer: Luther Davis; DP: Lee Garmes; Ed: Leon Barsha; Composer: Paul Glass; Art Director: Hal Pereira. B&W, 95 min. **VHS**

Lady in the Dark

(1944) Paramount

Rogers has an intriguing role as a successful magazine editor-in-chief who is troubled by seemingly inexplicable symptoms, and unwillingly seeks the services of a psychoanalyst. She explores a series of dreams, presented in delirious Technicolor, and the analysis takes her progressively further back into her unhappy childhood. In the meantime, Rogers is beset by romantic troubles, losing interest in a recent divorcé and a hunky movie star, and doing battle with her handsome but stubborn coworker. Unsurprisingly, the lessons she learns in analysis resolve psychological distress and her romantic quandary at once. A curious Hollywood treatment of the then-voguish interest in Freudian analysis. Based on a Broadway musical. Academy Award Nominations: 3, including Best Cinematography; Best Score. **Cast:** Ginger Rogers, Ray Milland, Jon Hall, Warner Baxter, Barry Sullivan, Mischa Auer. **Credits:** Dir: Mitchell Leisen; Prod: Richard Blumenthal; Writer: Frances Goodrich, Albert Hackett; Story: Moss Hart; DP: Ray Rennahan; Ed: Alma Macrorie; Composer: Kurt Weill, Ira Gershwin, Johnny Burke, James Van Heusen. Color, 100 min.

Lady in the Iron Mask

(1952) Fox

The classic Three Musketeers story with a gender switch. The twin sister of the reigning princess has been imprisoned in a dungeon by an evil duke. There is a kidnapping plot to switch the sisters so the imprisoned one will marry the snooty prince of Spain. The Three Musketeers learn of the plot and free the now-imprisoned princess. Instead of returning her to the throne, however, they leave her sister in charge and the four set off for the States. **Cast:** Louis Hayward, Patricia Medina, Alan Hale, Judd Holdren, Steve Brodie, John Sutton, Hal Gerard, Lester Matthews. **Credits:** Dir: Ralph Murphy; Prod: Eugene Frenke, Walter Wanger; Writer: Jack Pollexfen; DP: Ernest Laszlo; Ed: Merrill White; Prod Design: Martin Obzina; Composer: Dimitri Tiomkin. Color, 78 min.

Lady in the Lake

(1946) MGM

Noir fans debate this noble experiment, but it makes for fascinating viewing, particularly for fans of the hard-boiled private-eye genre. Montgomery directs (after earning high marks for taking over John Ford's seat in *They Were Expendable*, 1945, after Ford was injured) a Chandler-Marlowe yarn about a missing-wife case. The innovation is Montgomery's attempt to provide the narrative with the same first-person bite as the book by giving the camera Marlowe's point of view in one of the first uses of the handheld camera. The detective is seen only twice, once in the prologue and once as he passes in front of the mirror—too bad, as Montgomery makes a convincingly smooth Marlowe. An interest-ing twist, but Montgomery didn't direct again for 16 years, turning his attention to producing for television. **Cast:** Robert Montgomery, Audrey Totter, Lloyd Nolan, Tom Tully, Leon Ames, Jayne Meadows, Morris Ankrum, Lila Leeds, William Frawley. **Credits:** Dir: Robert Montgomery; Prod: George Haight; Writer: Steve Fisher, Raymond Chandler; DP: Paul C. Vogel; Ed: Gene Ruggiero; Prod Design: Cedric Gibbons; Composer: David Snell; Art Director: Preston Ames. B&W, 104 min. **VHS**

The Lady Is Willing

(1942) Columbia

Have a hard time imagining Dietrich as a devoted mother? Audiences in the '40s must have drawn the same conclusion, and that's the root of the humor here. Dietrich is a theater diva who finds an abandoned child and whimsically decides she wants to be a mother. But she can't adopt until she has a husband. Pediatrician MacMurray conveniently provides the child-rearing knowledge, and wins a place in Dietrich's heart as well. Basically the *Bachelor Mother* routine, but the mix of Marlene and America's Dad is too good to pass up. **Cast:** Marlene Dietrich, Fred MacMurray, Aline MacMahon, Arline Judge, Stanley Ridges, Roger Clark, Marietta Canty, Ruth Ford. **Credits:** Dir: Mitchell Leisen; Prod: Mitchell Leisen; Story: James Edward Grant; DP: Ted Tetzlaff; Ed: Eda Warren; Composer: W. Franke Harling; Art Director: Rudolph Sternad, Lionel Banks. B&W, 91 min. **VHS**

Robert B. Parker Picks Five Favorite Private-Eye Movies

1. *The Lady in the Lake* **(1946)** because of that fascinating camera work. And Robert Montgomery is OK as Marlowe.

2. *The Maltese Falcon* **(1941)** because it's so faithful to Hammett's great novel about Sam Spade."

3. *Murder, My Sweet* [a.k.a. *Farewell, My Lovely*] **(1944)** because Dick Powell made such a great Marlowe, completely reinventing his screen image.

4. *Marlowe* **(1969)** because James Garner looked great in the part even though he didn't have the inner toughness that you expect Marlowe to have.

5. Any of the Chester Morris Boston Blackie programmers. And if I weren't being loyal to Boston, I'd throw in the Tom Conway Falcon series, too.

Robert B. Parker is the author of the Spenser private-eye series.

Lady Killer

(1933) Warner Bros.
In a pre-Code premonition of our own time when mere notoriety is enough to launch a Hollywood career, Cagney reprises his tough-guy bit (with an assist from his *Public Enemy* costar Clarke doing her gum-cracking moll bit) as a movie-theater usher who rises in the Mob and ascends to greater heights on the silver screen. While hiding out in Hollywood, Cagney gets discovered, but also by his former gang associates, who see the opportunity for blackmail. A sly satire of Hollywood and the gangster genre. **Cast:** James Cagney, Mae Clarke, Leslie Fenton, Margaret Lindsay, Henry O'Neill, Raymond Hatton, George Chandler, Willard Robertson. **Credits:** Dir: Roy Del Ruth; Prod: Henry Blanke; Writer: Ben Markson, Lillie Hayward; DP: Tony Gaudio; Ed: George Amy; Prod Design: Robert M. Haas. B&W, 77 min. **VHS**

Lady of Burlesque

(1943) United Artists
For her delightful mystery novel, *The G-String Murders,* Gypsy Rose Lee used her burlesque background to fashion a mystery tale with an alluring setting, the world of striptease artists. Stanwyck stars in this screen adaptation as an undercover detective searching for the killer who strangles strippers with their own G-strings. Real burlesque queens and vaudeville settings give this crime tale a pungently original kick. Academy Award Nomination for Best Scoring of a Dramatic or Comedy Picture. **Cast:** Barbara Stanwyck, Michael O'Shea, J. Edward Bromberg, Iris Adrian, Charles Dingle, Marion Martin, Pinky Lee, Frank Conroy. **Credits:** Dir: William Wellman; Prod: Hunt Stromberg; Writer: James Gunn; DP: Robert de Grasse; Ed: James E. Newcomb; Composer: Arthur Lange; Art Director: Bernard Herzbrun. B&W, 92 min. **VHS**

Lady on a Train

(1945) Universal
A winning Durbin vehicle that combines mystery and comedy with a little singing, of course. As a rich girl on her way to New York for the Christmas holidays, Deanna's just sure she saw a murder as her train passes. Not being able to convince anyone of her story, she locates a handsome mystery writer (Bruce) for inspiration and sets out sleuthing. The trail leads to an eccentric family and a surprise ending. Great supporting cast including Bellamy, Horton, Duryea, Frawley. From a Leslie Charteris story. **Cast:** Deanna Durbin, Ralph Bellamy, Dan Duryea, Willian Frawley, Edward Everett Horton, George Couloris, David Bruce, Patricia Morison, Maria Palmer. **Credits:** Dir: Charles David; Prod: Felix Jackson; Writer: Edmund Beloin, Robert O'Brien; DP: Elwood Bredell; Ed: Ted J. Kent; Prod Design: Robert Clatworthy; Composer: Miklos Rozsa; Art Director: John B. Goodman. B&W, 95 min. **VHS**

Lady Sings the Blues

(1972) Paramount
The story of blues singer Billie Holiday makes an impressive vehicle for Ross's screen debut. The rise and fall of a showbiz star is well-trodden ground in Hollywood, but the less well known setting, the timeless music as interpreted by pop stylist Ross, and her compelling, knowing performance as the blues artist haunted by racism and drug addiction lifts the story out of the expected. Pryor shines in support. Academy Award Nominations: 5, including Best Actress: Diana Ross; Best (Original) Screenplay; Best Song Score. **Cast:** Diana Ross, Billy Dee Williams, Richard Pryor, James Callahan, Paul Hampton, Sid Melton, Virginia Capers, Scatman Crothers. **Credits:** Dir: Sidney J. Furie; Prod: Jay Weston, James S. White; Writer: Terence McCloy, Chris Clark, Suzanne De Passe; DP: John A. Alonzo; Ed: Argyle Nelson; Prod Design: Carl Anderson; Composer: Michel Legrand. Color, 144 min. **VHS, LASER**

A Lady Takes a Chance

(1943) RKO
The oddball comedy pairing of Wayne and Arthur makes this standard romance about a city girl with her cap set on a rodeo star who wants only to wander the range just intriguing enough to merit a viewing. Note the story from Kanin. **Cast:** John Wayne, Jean Arthur, Phil Silvers, Charles Winninger, Mary Field, Don Costello, Grady Sutton, Grant Withers, John Philliber. **Credits:** Dir: William A. Seiter; Prod: Frank Ross; Writer: Robert Ardrey; Story: Garson Kanin; DP: Frank Redman; Ed: Theron Warth; Composer: Roy Webb; Art Director: Albert S. D'Agostino, Alfred Herman. B&W, 86 min. **VHS**

The Lady Vanishes

(1938) MGM
The high point of Hitchcock's British films is a beguiling mystery story. A group of English travelers on a train across Europe includes a sweet old woman (Whitty) . . . for a while. Lockwood and Redgrave get pulled into a web of intrigue when, after Lockwood gets beaned on the head, the lady disappears, leaving only her name written in frost on the window. When they set out to find her, Lockwood's memory and sanity are questioned, particularly by a scheming Lukas. The Hitchcock touches, the sly wit, the unsuspecting hero plunged into a baffling situation, are already apparent. The special edition video includes a documentary on Hitchcock's famous cameo appearances. Remade in 1979 with Elliott Gould and Cybill Shepherd. **Cast:** Michael Redgrave, Paul Lukas, Margaret Lockwood, May Whitty, Cecil Parker, Linden Travers, Mary Clare, Naunton Wayne, Basil Radford, Googie Withers. **Credits:** Dir: Alfred Hitchcock; Prod: Edward Black; Writer: Alma Reville, Sidney Gilliat; Story: Frank Launder; DP: Jack Cox; Ed: Alfred Roome, R. E. Dearing; Composer: Louis Levy. B&W, 99 min. **VHS, LASER, DVD**

The Lady Wants Mink

(1953) Republic
How far will an ordinary housewife go to enjoy the finer things in life? If owning a mink coat of her own is financially out of the question, then hardworking Arden will have to grow one of her own. Raising minks in their city apartment, however, soon leads to eviction and the loss of her husband's job. The couple settles in the countryside with their fur-bearing animals, and later decides city life no longer suits them. **Cast:** Eve Arden, William Demarest, Ruth Hussey, Gene Lockhart, Dennis O'Keefe, Tommy Rettig, Hope Emerson. **Credits:** Dir: William A. Seiter; Prod: William A. Seiter; Writer: Richard Simmons, Lou Schor; DP: Reggie Lanning; Ed: Fred Allen; Composer: Stanley Wilson. Color, 92 min.

Lafayette Escadrille

(1958) Warner Bros.
Wellman builds on his own experience with the famous flying aces in WWI to create this action-packed war drama. When American fliers volunteer to aid the Allies in the skies over France, they encounter danger and romance. Hunter's suitable and Wellman's son portrays a character that must be similar to his dad. Watch for an early Eastwood appearance. **Cast:** Tab Hunter, Clint Eastwood, Tom Laughlin, William Wellman, Jr., David Janssen, Jody McCrea, Marcel Dalio, Will Hutchins, Paul Fix. **Credits:** Dir: William Wellman; Prod: William A. Wellman; Writer: A. S. Fleischman; DP: William H. Clothier;

Ed: Owen Marks; Composer: Leonard Rosenman; Art Director: John Beckman. B&W, 93 min. **VHS**

Lancer Spy

(1937) Fox
This solo directorial debut by Ratoff presents the story of British naval officer Michael Bruce (Sanders), who, at the behest of His Majesty, must pose as a German officer who's been taken prisoner and whom he resembles closely. Placed in Germany, singer Del Rio is recruited by secret police captain Lorre to confirm his suspicions. When she falls for Sanders, she's forced to choose between her man and her country. This made Sanders a hot property, and Ratoff, a colorful émigré who had studied at the Moscow Art Theater, would soon go on to direct Ingrid Bergman in her Hollywood debut, *Intermezzo* (1939). **Cast:** George Sanders, Dolores Del Rio, Peter Lorre, Virginia Field, Sig Rumann, Joseph Schildkraut, Maurice Mosocovich, Lionel Atwill, Luther Adler, Fritz Feld. **Credits:** Dir: Gregory Ratoff; Prod: Samuel G. Engel, Darryl F. Zanuck; Writer: Philip Dunne, Marthe McKenna; Ed: Louis Loeffler; Prod Design: Albert Hogsett; Composer: Arthur Lange. B&W, 84 min.

The Landlord

(1970) United Artists
Director Ashby's first film follows the story of a rich kid (Bridges) who buys a run-down tenement in Brooklyn to rehab it into a palatial home for himself. His plans run headlong into the lives of the current tenants and, after overcoming racial differences, the new landlord eventually becomes part of the building's community. Sweet-tempered comedy that's fully of its era. Based on the novel by Kristin Hunter. **Cast:** Beau Bridges, Lee Grant, Diana Sands, Pearl Bailey, Susan Anspach, Robert Klein, Trish Van Devere, Louis Gossett, Jr. **Credits:** Dir: Hal Ashby; Prod: Norman Jewison; Story: Bill Gunn; DP: Gordon Willis; Ed: Edward A. Warschilka, William Sawyer; Prod Design: Robert Boyle; Composer: Al Kooper. Color, 110 min. **VHS**

Larceny, Inc.

(1942) Warner Bros.
This hilarious screwball gangster picture (penned in part by humorist Perelman) has ex-con Pressure Maxwell (Robinson) teaming up with jail buddies Jug Martin (Crawford) and Weepy Davis (Brophy) to purchase a luggage store conveniently located across the

street from a bank. All they have to do is dig a tunnel across the street from the basement, but with all the well-wishing good-neighbor types who constantly step in to wish Pressure luck with the store, and with his annoyingly reliable niece Denny Costello (Wyman), there's never enough time to do wrong! When jealous violent convict Leo Dexter (Quinn) escapes from prison and decides to get in on the action, the whole thing, literally, blows up in Pressure's face. **Cast:** Edward G. Robinson, Jane Wyman, Broderick Crawford, Jack Carson, Anthony Quinn, Edward Brophy, Harry Davenport, John Qualen, Barbara Jo Allen, Grant Mitchell. **Credits:** Dir: Lloyd Bacon; Prod: Hal B. Wallis, Jack Saper, Jerry Wald; Writer: Everett Freeman, Edwin Gilbert; Story: Laura Perelman, S. J. Perelman; DP: Tony Gaudio; Ed: Ralph Dawson; Prod Design: John Hughes; Composer: Adolph Deutsch. B&W, 95 min.

Lassie Come Home

(1943) MGM
This is the first and best of the famous family series about a devoted collie dog. A wonderful cast, including young McDowall and Taylor, portray the story of a poor boy whose family is forced to sell his beloved dog. Though taken far away, Lassie overcomes every obstacle to be reunited with her family. Taylor's second screen appearance and her first for MGM, the studio that made her a star. Selected as a National Film Registry Outstanding Film. Academy Award Nomination for Best (Color) Cinematography. **Cast:** Roddy McDowall, Donald Crisp, Elsa Lanchester, Elizabeth Taylor, Dame May Whitty, Edmund Gwenn, Nigel Bruce, J. Pat O'Malley. **Credits:** Dir: Fred M. Wilcox; Prod: Samuel Marx; Writer: Hugo Butler; Story: Eric Knight; DP: Leonard Smith; Ed: Ben Lewis; Prod Design: Cedric Gibbons, Paul Groesse; Composer: Daniele Amfitheatrof. Color, 88 min. **VHS, LASER**

The Last American Hero

(1973) Fox
A backwoods moonshine runner (Bridges) becomes a famous speed-demon on the stock-car circuit in this biopic of motorsports legend Junior Johnson. Great supporting cast includes Busey, Fitzgerald, Beatty, and Lund. Amiable little-guy-against-the-system story based on a magazine profile by Tom Wolfe. **Cast:** Jeff Bridges, Art Lund, Gary Busey, Geraldine Fitzgerald, Ned Beatty, Valerie Perrine, Ed Lauter, Gregory Walcott.

Credits: Dir: Lamont Johnson; Prod: William Roberts, John Cutts; Story: William Roberts; DP: George Silano. Color, 100 min. **VHS**

The Last Angry Man

(1959) Columbia
Muni's bravura last role as a dedicated doctor whose devotion to his Brooklyn community attracts the interest of his nephew, a TV producer with whom the crusty old family practitioner clashes. Muni was Warner's class act, the choice for seemingly every prestigious historical biopic. Interesting mostly for being his valedictory. Academy Award Nominations: 2, Best Actor: Paul Muni; Best Art Direction—Set Decoration (B&W). **Cast:** Paul Muni, Joby Baker, Cicely Tyson, Billy Dee Williams, Claudia McNeil, Godfrey Cambridge, Betsy Palmer, Luther Adler, David Wayne. **Credits:** Dir: Daniel Mann; Prod: Fred Kohlmar; Writer: Gerald Green; Story: Richard Murphy; DP: James Wong Howe; Ed: Charles Nelson; Composer: George Duning; Art Director: Carl Anderson. B&W, 100 min. **VHS**

The Last Command

(1955) Republic
The story of American hero Jim Bowie (Hayden) culminates in the battle for the Alamo. Bowie was a Mexican citizen living in Texas when the struggle for the republic began in earnest. Hayden initially urges his neighbors Borgnine and Carlson to be cautious, but sides with them when the fighting begins. Most watchable during the realistically portrayed battle for the Alamo. Originally a John Wayne vehicle, studio head Herbert Yates balked at the movie's price tag. Wayne returned to the setting for his own directorial debut, *The Alamo* (1960). **Cast:** Sterling Hayden, Richard Carlson, Ernest Borgnine, Anna Maria Alberghetti, Arthur Hunnicutt, A. Carrol Naish, Ben Cooper, John Russell. **Credits:** Dir: Frank Lloyd; Prod: Frank Lloyd; Story: Warren Duff; DP: Jack Marta; Ed: Tony Martinelli; Composer: Max Steiner; Art Director: Frank Arrigo. Color, 110 min. **VHS**

The Last Days of Pompeii

(1934) RKO
A Christians vs. Romans spectacle produced by the makers of *King Kong* (!), Schoedsack and Cooper. Foster stars as a blacksmith who turns to the gladiators' arena after the tragic death of his wife and child. He becomes a star of the arena and parlays his renown into a fortune, and, in

remorse, adopts the child of one of his victims. He raises the child in Judea, where he befriends Pontius Pilate (Rathbone), makes a fortune with vicious raids, and, after "the great prophet" heals his son, witnesses Jesus' death after refusing to help him. Foster and son return to Pompeii where they live in splendor, though the young man falls for a Christian slave. When Vesuvius erupts, Foster turns at last to the good and saves fleeing Christians, earning a blessing from a vision of Christ. An attempt at De Mille–like grandeur, with the special effects and Rathbone having the most impact. **Cast:** Preston Foster, Basil Rathbone, Dorothy Wilson, Alan Hale, John Wood, Lóuis Calhern, David Holt, Wyrley Birch. **Credits:** Dir: Ernest B. Schoedsack; Prod: Merian C. Cooper; Writer: Ruth Rose; Story: Boris Ingster; DP: J. Roy Hunt, Eddie Linden; Ed: Archie Marshek; Composer: Roy Webb. B&W, 93 min. **VHS**

The Last Detail
(1974) Columbia
One of Nicholson's least-mannered performances is a gritty story of the last days of freedom for a misguided young sailor. Nicholson and Young are two Navy lifers put on a detail transporting Quaid to a brig for stealing a pittance from a base charity box. The sailor's guilelessness wears away the two wardens' crusty shell and they begin to warm to their charge. Determined to show Quaid one last good time and part of the world before he enters prison, the trio go on a spree that ends in a pitiful attempted escape from a brothel. Based on a novel by Darryl Ponicsan (whose *Cinderella Liberty* was also made into a movie in 1974), screenwriter Towne (*Chinatown*, 1974) and director Ashby paint a desolate picture of lives lived from one shore leave to the next. Look for an early cameo by Gilda Radner. Academy Award Nominations: 3, including Best Actor: Jack Nicholson; Best Supporting Actor: Randy Quaid; Best (Adapted) Screenplay. **Cast:** Jack Nicholson, Otis Young, Randy Quaid, Michael Moriarty, Nancy Allen, Carol Kane, Luana Anders, Kathleen Miller. **Credits:** Dir: Hal Ashby; Prod: Gerald Ayres; Writer: Robert Towne; DP: Michael Chapman; Ed: Robert C. Jones; Prod Design: Michael Haller; Composer: Johnny Mandel. Color, 105 min. **VHS, LASER**

Last Embrace
(1979) United Artists
Director Demme's ode to Hitchcock has C.I.A. agent Scheider on the run

after seeing his wife killed in an ambush. Thinking he's marked for death, the agent tries to beat the assassin to the punch. Precise plotting builds to a tense climax by Niagara Falls. Effective Rozsa score. **Cast:** Roy Scheider, Janet Margolin, Christopher Walken, John Glover, Sam Levene, Charles Napier, Jacqueline Brookes, David Margulies. **Credits:** Dir: Jonathan Demme; Prod: Michael Taylor, Dan Wigutow; Writer: David Shaber; DP: Tak Fujimoto; Ed: Barry Malkin; Composer: Miklos Rozsa; Art Director: James Taylor. Color, 98 min. **VHS**

The Last Flight
(1931) Warner Bros.
German director Dieterle's Hollywood debut is an emotional drama that follows four Americans living in Europe in the '20s. The three survivors of the horrors of WWI and their gal companion suffer from the aimlessness and emotional trauma that earned the period between the wars the nickname "the Lost Generation." Tragedy ensues when the group heads to Spain. Dieterle's first film, in 1923, featured a 21-year-old Dietrich. **Cast:** Richard Barthelmess, David Manners, Johnny Mack Brown, Helen Chandler, Elliott Nugent, Walter Byron. **Credits:** Dir: Wilhelm Dieterle; Writer: John Monk Saunders; DP: Sidney Hickox; Ed: Alexander Hall; Prod Design: Earl Luick; Composer: Leo F. Forbstein; Art Director: Jack Okey. B&W, 80 min.

The Last Gangster
(1937) MGM
A crook of Slavic background (Robinson) returns to his native land to find a wife and bring her back to the U.S. Just about the time his son is to be born, he gets arrested for tax evasion and is sent to prison for 10 years. While in the slammer, his wife learns of his misdeeds and deserts him. With a new name and a new town, she meets a journalist who marries her and treats her son as his own. When the crook finally gets out of prison after brooding on his son that he's never seen, he searches for his runaway family. Better-than-average gangster flick with a story by Wellman. **Cast:** Edward G. Robinson, James Stewart, Rose Stradner, Lionel Stander, John Carradine, Sidney Blackmer, Edward Brophy, Alan Baxter, Grant Mitchell. **Credits:** Dir: Edward Ludwig; Prod: J. J. Cohen; Writer: John Lee Mahin, Robert Carson, William Wellman; DP: William Daniels; Ed: Ben Lewis; Prod Design: Daniel B. Cath-

cart; Composer: Edward Ward; Art Director: Cedric Gibbons, Edwin B. Willis. B&W, 81 min.

The Last Gentleman
(1934) Fox
An eccentric, opinionated Massachusetts millionaire (Arliss) approaches his final days determined to bequeath his fortune in exactly the way he pleases, and makes sure with his filmed final testament. **Cast:** George Arliss, Edna May Oliver, Janet Beecher, Charlotte Henry, Ralph Morgan, Edward Ellis, Frank Albertson, Rafaela Ottiano, Donald Meek, Joseph Cawthorn. **Credits:** Dir: Sidney Lanfield; Prod: William Goetz, Joseph Schenck, Raymond Griffith, Darryl F. Zanuck; Writer: Katharine Clugeton, Leonard Praskins; DP: Barney McGill; Ed: Maurice Wright; Prod Design: Richard Day; Composer: Alfred Newman. B&W, 78 min.

The Last Hurrah
(1958) Columbia
Edwin O'Connor's colorful novel of the Boston political scene comes to life in this adaptation by Ford. Tracy revels in his role as an old-time Irish-American pol, the longtime mayor of Boston, who runs afoul of the gentry (in the form of newspaper publisher Carradine and banker Rathbone) and his idealistic nephew (Hunter), a reporter for Carradine's paper who rejects his uncle's rough-and-tumble backroom politicking but respects and admires his devotion to the city's working people. The story culminates in Tracy's last, losing campaign for office. **Cast:** Spencer Tracy, John Carradine, Basil Rathbone, Jeffrey Hunter, Dianne Foster, Pat O'Brien, Donald Crisp, James Gleason. **Credits:** Dir: John Ford; Prod: John Ford; Writer: Frank S. Nugent; DP: Charles Lawton, Jr.; Ed: Jack Murray; Art Director: Robert Peterson. B&W, 121 min. **VHS, LASER**

The Last Mile
(1932) World Wide
An unrelenting, hard-hearted glimpse at life on Death Row told through the eyes of an innocent man sentenced to die (Phillips). While waiting on Death Row as his family and friends work for his release, Phillips comes to know the hard cases who surround him, including Killer Mears (Foster). Foster gets a chance to make a break for it by killing a particularly sadistic guard, and leads a desperate prison rebellion that ends in a final, fatal shootout with the guards. Inspired by a spate of prison rebellions in 1929, the prologue

features an actual prison warden. The only directorial effort by Bischoff, who later produced hard-boiled fare such as *San Quentin* (1937), *Angels With Dirty Faces* (1938), and *The Roaring Twenties* (1939). Spencer Tracy played the Killer Mears role on Broadway, and Clark Gable took the part in Los Angeles. **Cast:** Preston Foster, Howard Phillips, Noel Madison, George E. Stone, Alan Roscoe, Paul Fix, Al Hill, Daniel L. Haynes. **Credits:** Dir: Sam Bischoff; Prod: E. W. Hammons; Writer: Seton I. Miller; DP: Arthur Edeson; Ed: Rose Loewinger, Martin Cohn; Composer: Val Burton. B&W, 70 min. **VHS**

The Last Movie
(1971) Universal
Hoping to cash in on the success of *Easy Rider*, Universal gave Hopper $1 million to make a movie. He returned after a sojourn in Peru with a six-hour cut, which he then labored for a year to make theatrical-release length. The result is fascinating mostly for the lengthy list of Hopper's pals that either worked on or appeared in his opus. The story revolves around a stuntman (Hopper) left behind after a movie crew (led by director Sam Fuller) pulls out of a small village in Peru. He becomes involved in the life of the community, searches for gold, and even finds himself a local deity. Tough going for all but the most devoted cineastes, but intriguing to see the result of a major studio trying deperately to keep up with the youth culture. **Cast:** Dennis Hopper, Peter Fonda, Kris Kristofferson, Michelle Phillips, Dean Stockwell, Sylvia Miles, Julie Adams, Russ Tamblyn, Rod Cameron. **Credits:** Dir: Dennis Hopper; Prod: Paul Lewis; Story: Stewart Stern; DP: Laszlo Kovacs; Ed: Dennis Hopper, David Berlatsky, Antranig Mahakian; Composer: Kris Kristofferson, Severn Darden, John Buck Wilkin, Chabuca Granda; Art Director: Leon Ericksen. Color, 108 min. **VHS**

The Last of Mrs. Cheyney
(1937) MGM
Crawford and Powell team up to fleece the bluebloods in this crime-caper comedy. Crawford, aided by Powell posing as her butler, makes a hit on the debutante circuit as she trolls for jewels to heist. Montgomery makes a dashing mark until all are revealed and Crawford has to resort to blackmail to make an exit. Remake of the 1929 early talkie starring Norma Shearer, and remade again in 1951 as *The Law and the Lady*. After Boleslawski died during production,

Fitzmaurice took over his duties. **Cast:** Joan Crawford, William Powell, Robert Montgomery, Frank Morgan, Jessie Ralph, Nigel Bruce, Benita Hume, Melville Cooper. **Credits:** Dir: Richard Boleslawski, George Fitzmaurice; Prod: Lawrence Weingarten; Writer: Leon Gordon, Samson Raphaelson; Story: Monckton Hoffe; DP: George J. Folsey; Ed: Frank Sullivan; Composer: William Axt; Art Director: Cedric Gibbons. B&W, 99 min. **VHS**

The Last of Sheila
(1973) Warner Bros.
This is a real curiosity and a terrific whodunit with an intricate, witty script by composer-lyricist Sondheim and actor Perkins. An assortment of Hollywood types repair to producer Coburn's yacht harbored in the south of France one year after his wife was struck and killed by a hit-and-run driver. Coburn has plans to snare the killer with an elaborate game, a game that has unintended consequences. **Cast:** Richard Benjamin, Dyan Cannon, James Coburn, Joan Hackett, James Mason, Ian McShane, Raquel Welch, Yvonne Romain. **Credits:** Dir: Herbert Ross; Prod: Herbert Ross; Writer: Stephen Sondheim, Anthony Perkins; DP: Gerry Turpin; Ed: Edward Warschilka; Composer: Billy Goldenberg; Prod Design: Ken Adam. Color, 119 min. **VHS**

Last of the Comanches
(1952) Columbia
A Western about a sergeant who takes his weary soldiers on a 100-mile mission. The situation couldn't seem worse when they begin to run out of food and water, then they meet a group of Indians suffering the same fate. Fearing attack and exhausted by the trek, the soldiers seek shelter in an abandoned mission. As the Indians prepare to strike, another cavalry group arrives to save the day. **Cast:** George Mathews, Hugh Sanders, Ric Roman, Chubby Johnson, Martin Milner, Milton Parsons, Jack Woody, Broderick Crawford, Barbara Hale, Johnny Stewart. **Credits:** Dir: Andre De Toth; Prod: Buddy Adler; Writer: Kenneth Gamet; DP: Ray Cory, Charles Lawton, Jr.; Ed: Al Clark; Prod Design: Ross Bellah; Composer: Charles Duning. Color, 85 min.

The Last of the Mohicans
(1936) United Artists
James Fenimore Cooper's adventure set in the days of the French and Indian Wars has been a Hollywood perennial, having been filmed as far

back as 1911 and continuing through the terrifically realistic 1992 version starring Daniel Day-Lewis. Though there have been other notable adaptations, including a silent 1922 feature starring Wallace Beery and a 1932 serial with Harry Carey, this is classic Hollywood's definitive version. Scott makes a muscular Hawkeye, the white man raised by Indians who finds himself with divided loyalties when the tribes take sides in the settlers' conflict, and along the way he draws the amorous attention of the colonel's daughter he's escorting through Indian territory. Academy Award Nomination for Best Assistant Director: Clem Beauchamp. **Cast:** Randolph Scott, Binnie Barnes, Heather Angel, Hugh Buckler, Henry Wilcoxon, Bruce Cabot, Robert Barrat, Phillip Reed. **Credits:** Dir: George B. Seitz; Prod: Edward Small, Harry M. Goetz; Writer: Philip Dunne, John L. Balderston, Paul Perez; Story: Daniel Moore; DP: Robert H. Planck; Ed: Jack Dennis, Harry Marker; Composer: Roy Webb; Art Director: John DuCasse Schulze. B&W, 91 min. **VHS**

The Last Outlaw
(1936) RKO
Little-seen Western with a satirical edge from a story penned by John Ford, who had made a silent version in 1919. Interesting plot has old-timer Carey, lost in the changing world after being locked away behind bars for 25 years. When a gang of thieves takes his daughter hostage, he straps on the six-shooters one more time. **Cast:** Harry Carey, Hoot Gibson, Tom Tyler, Henry B. Walthall, Frank M. Thomas, Russell Hopton, Frank Jenks, Maxine Jennings, Margaret Callahan. **Credits:** Dir: Christy Cabanne; Prod: Robert Sisk; Writer: John Twist, Jack Townley, E. Murray Campbell; DP: Jack Mackenzie; Ed: George Hively. B&W, 72 min. **VHS**

The Last Outpost
(1935) Paramount
This romantic adventure allies two handsome English soldiers with Armenians battling tribes of Kurds and the savage wilds of southwest Asia. After an injury escaping the Kurds, Grant falls deeply in love with his nurse (Michael), who turns out to be the estranged wife of the other, Rains. Rains is killed beside his friend in battle with the Turks and Grant enjoys happily-ever-after with the blushing widow. **Cast:** Cary Grant, Claude Rains, Gertrude Michael, Kathleen Burke, Colin Tapley, Georges

The Last Picture Show (1971)

Ravenant, Akim Tamiroff, Billy Bevan. **Credits:** Dir: Charles Barton, Louis Gasnier; Prod: E. Lloyd Sheldon; Writer: Charles Brackett, Philip Mac-Donald, Frank Partos, F. Britten Austin; DP: Theodor Sparkhul; Ed: Jack Dennis; Prod Design: Hans Dreier, A. Earl Hedrick. B&W, 72 min.

The Last Picture Show

(1971) Columbia
With only his second feature, director Bogdanovich earned a place in movie history alongside his mentors John Ford and Orson Welles. As spare and haunting as the Texas plains in which it is set, this was a breakthrough for many of the previously little-known stars as well as Bogdanovich. The story, based on Larry McMurtry's novel, follows two friends (Bottoms and Bridges), high school football heroes in a dusty, Texas backwater in the '50s. Their future in the dying town

(the local throwback to cowboy glory, Johnson, dies and the local café and theater, the centers of life in the town, are right behind him) starts to constrict like a noose around their necks. Through desperate, lonely affairs, brawls, and attempts at escape, both struggle to find a way out. Outstanding performances by all, but especially Leachman, Burstyn, Johnson, and Shepherd. The laserdisc special edition includes a new cut from Bogdanovich with seven minutes of additional footage, audio commentary by the director, interviews with the cast, original screen tests, original theatrical trailer, location-scouting footage, and excerpts from the original screenplay and from the *Texasville* screenplay. Followed by the sequel, *Texasville*, in 1990. Academy Award Nominations: 8, including Best Picture; Best Director; Best Screenplay. **Academy Awards:** Best Supporting Actor: Ben Johnson;

Best Supporting Actress: Cloris Leach-man. **Cast:** Jeff Bridges, Cybill Shep-herd, Cloris Leachman, Ben Johnson, Timothy Bottoms, Ellen Burstyn, Eileen Brennan, Randy Quaid, Sam Bottoms. **Credits:** Dir: Peter Bogdanovich; Prod: Stephen Friedman; Writer: Peter Bog-danovich; Story: Larry McMurtry; DP: Robert Surtees; Ed: Donn Cambern; Prod Design: Polly Platt. B&W 118 min. VHS, LASER

The Last Remake of Beau Geste

(1977) Universal
Mel Brooks stock company player Feldman takes his turn in the director's seat for a Brooks-inspired parody of Foreign Legion movies. The plot, based on the 1939 version starring Cooper (who even makes an appearance here via film clip), is recognizable, if played for laughs by a deep cast of '70s stars. Feldman and York play twins who escape to the Foreign Legion. More fun if you know the original. **Cast:** Marty Feldman, Ann-Margret, Michael York, Peter Ustinov, James Earl Jones, Henry Polic II, Trevor Howard, Ed McMahon. **Credits:** Dir: Marty Feldman; Prod: William S. Gilmore; Writer: Marty Feld-man; Story: Chris J. Allen; DP: Gerry Fisher; Ed: Jim Clark, Arthur Schmidt; Prod Design: Brian Eatwell; Composer: John Morris; Art Director: Leslie Dilley. Color, 85 min. VHS

Last Summer

(1969) Allied Artists
A wonderfully acted film from Hunter's novel about the experiences of teenagers initiated into the rites of friendship, sex, and love while spend-ing the summer on Fire Island. When a dare goes too far, the youths are bound together for life by a terrible secret. Academy Award Nomination for Best Supporting Actress: Catherine Burns. From the writer-director team of Eleanor and Frank Perry. Note that this originally carried an X rating. **Cast:** Barbara Hershey, Richard Thomas, Bruce Davison, Catherine Burns, Ralph Waite, Conrad Bain. **Credits:** Dir: Frank Perry; Prod: Sidney Beckerman, Alfred W. Crown; Writer: Eleanor Perry; Story: Evan Hunter; DP: Gerald Hirschfeld; Ed: Sidney Katz; Prod Design: Phillip Goldfarb; Com-poser: John Simon; Costumes: Theoni V. Aldredge; Art Director: Peter Dohanos. Color, 97 min. VHS

The Last Time I Saw Paris

(1954) MGM
An MGM-glossy version of F. Scott Fitzgerald's melodrama that's a per-

fect vehicle for a young Taylor. Just after WWII, would-be writer Johnson soaks in the literary expatriate scene in Paris. He meets and falls in love with wealthy Taylor despite the disapproval of Taylor's sister, Reed. As he attempts to finish his first novel, Johnson turns more often to the bottle than the typewriter, alienating Taylor and neglecting their child. When he locks his wife out of their apartment in a rainstorm, she dies of pneumonia and their daughter is taken by Reed. Johnson reforms, begins a successful career, and goes back to Paris to reclaim his memories and his child. **Cast:** Elizabeth Taylor, Van Johnson, Eva Gabor, Walter Pidgeon, Donna Reed, Roger Moore, Kurt Kasznar, George Dolenz. **Credits:** Dir: Richard Brooks; Prod: Jack Cummings; Writer: Richard Brooks, Julius J. Epstein; DP: Joseph Ruttenberg; Ed: John Dunning; Composer: Conrad Salinger; Art Director: Cedric Gibbons, Randall Duell. Color, 116 min. VHS, LASER

Last Train from Gun Hill
(1959) Paramount
A dark, brooding Western that transplants a revenge fantasy more typical of noir to the Wild West. Douglas plays a U.S. Marshal who traces the man who raped and killed his wife to Gun Hill only to discover he is the son of a good friend (Quinn) who will stop at nothing to prevent the marshal from bringing his boy to justice. **Cast:** Kirk Douglas, Anthony Quinn, Carolyn Jones, Earl Holliman, Brad Dexter, Brian Hutton, Bing Russell, Val Avery. **Credits:** Dir: John Sturges; Prod: Hal B. Wallis; Writer: James Poe; DP: Charles B. Lang; Ed: Warren Low; Composer: Dimitri Tiomkin; Art Director: Walter Tyler, Hal Pereira. Color, 94 min. VHS

The Last Train from Madrid
(1937) Paramount
Fleeing the heat of the Spanish Civil War, an impressive cast mingles during the last few hours before a train is to bring them to the safety of Valencia. The limited number of passes available to board the train builds the suspense as the various vignettes unfold. One of the first films to deal with the resistance to Spanish fascism in the '30s. Inserted newsreel footage shows the actual bombardment of Madrid. **Cast:** Dorothy Lamour, Lew Ayres, Gilbert Roland, Karen Morely, Lionel Atwill, Helen Mack, Robert Cummings, Olympe Bradna, Anthony Quinn, Lee Bowman. **Credits:** Dir: James Hogan; Prod: George K. Arthur, Hugh Bennett; Writer: Louis Stevens, Robert Wyler,

Elsie Fox, Paul Hervey Fox; DP: Harry Fischbeck; Ed: Everett Douglas; Composer: Boris Morros. B&W, 85 min.

The Last Tycoon
(1977) Paramount
This has everything going for it: an unfinished story by F. Scott Fitzgerald; a terrific lineup of international stars, including De Niro, Mitchum, Moreau, Curtis, Milland, and Nicholson; script by renowned playwright Pinter; and direction from Kazan. But the backstage Hollywood story (loosely based on the career of prototypical producer Irving Thalberg) never rises above the level of expensive potboiler. Fascinating for the movie fan who wants a glimpse of early Hollywood and stars working harder than they should. Academy Award Nomination for Best Art Direction—Set Decoration. **Cast:** Robert De Niro, Jack Nicholson, Robert Mitchum, Jeanne Moreau, Tony Curtis, Ingrid Boulting, Theresa Russell, Ray Milland. **Credits:** Dir: Elia Kazan; Prod: Sam Spiegel; Story: Harold Pinter; DP: Victor J. Kemper; Ed: Richard Marks; Prod Design: Gene Callahan; Composer: Maurice Jarre; Art Director: Jack Collins. Color, 125 min. VHS, LASER

The Last Voyage
(1960) MGM
Though most writers point to *The Poseidon Adventure* (1972) as the starting point of the disaster-movie genre, this tense thriller marks an earlier prototype. Though it doesn't have the cast of a thousand stars of its '70s offspring, it does feature fine performances from Malone and Stack as a couple looking forward to a romantic ocean cruise—until the liner starts smoking and then sinking. Sanders and O'Brien try to take command as Stack searches frantically for his wife. The realistic effects were aided by the use of a real ocean liner, the *Ile de France*, on its way to the scrap yard. Academy Award Nomination for Best Special Effects. **Cast:** Robert Stack, George Sanders, Dorothy Malone, Edmond O'Brien, Woody Strode, Jack Kruschen, Richard Norris, Andrew Hughes. **Credits:** Dir: Andrew L. Stone; Prod: Andrew L. Stone, Virginia Lively Stone; Writer: Andrew L. Stone; DP: Hal Mohr; Ed: Virginia Stone; Composer: Rudolph Schrager. Color, 87 min. VHS

The Last Wagon
(1956) Fox
This violent, action-packed epic Western has outlaw Comanche Todd (Wid-

mark) on the run for murdering the crooks who killed his family. When a sheriff captures him, he hooks the convict up with a passing wagon train—literally. What's that over the hill: Apaches! In the fight that follows, the great wagon train is decimated and the innocents massacred. But Todd's alive and he helps the other survivors, a bunch of kids, make it out of Indian country in the last wagon. **Cast:** Richard Widmark, Felicia Farr, Susan Kohner, Tommy Rettig, Stephanie Griffin, Ray Stricklyn, Nick Adams, Carl Benton Reid, Richard Kennedy, George Mathews. **Credits:** Dir: Delmer Daves; Prod: William B. Hanks; Writer: Delmer Daves, James Edward Grant; DP: Wilfred Cline; Ed: Hugh Fowler; Prod Design: Lyle Wheeler; Composer: Lionel Newman. Color, 98 min.

The Last Waltz
(1976) MGM
By 1976, The Band had been present throughout rock's first golden age, as the backup band for rock-n-roll wandering minstrel (and wildman) Ronnie Hawkins, then with Dylan as he made a literally electrifying break with his folkie past, and, finally, stepping into the spotlight to make the connection between rock's rural roots and its mass-culture present. In the face of the second-generation upheavals of punk and dance music, The Band made the most graceful exit possible, a farewell concert filmed with respect, admiration, and insight by Scorsese. Guests from throughout their career— Dylan, Neil Young, Joni Mitchell, Eric Clapton—stop by to perform and comment on The Band's influence. An essential for anyone even marginally interested in rock. **Cast:** The Band, Bob Dylan, Ringo Starr, Muddy Waters, Neil Young. **Credits:** Dir: Martin Scorsese; Prod: Robbie Robertson; DP: Michael Watkins, Vilmos Zsigmond; Prod Design: Boris Leven. Color, 117 min. VHS, LASER

The Late George Apley
(1947) Fox
Mankiewicz directs a not particularly faithful adaptation of the Marquand novel of the same name. A Boston Brahmin (Colman) finds his dreams of perfect family life ruined when his son falls in love with a woman from another city and his daughter dates a Yale man. He tries to put an end to his son's romance, but is persuaded by his future daughter-in-law to give the couple his blessing, and his heart also softens one more time so

that his daughter also marries the man she loves. **Cast:** Ronald Colman, Vanessa Brown, Richard Haydn, Charles Russell, Richard Ney, Percy Waram, Mildred Natwick, Edna Best, Nydia Westman. **Credits:** Dir: Joseph L. Mankiewicz; Prod: Fred Kohlmar; Writer: Philip Dunne; Story: George S. Kaufman, John P. Marquand; DP: Joseph LaShelle; Ed: James B. Clark; Prod Design: Edwin B. Willis, Paul S. Fox; Composer: Cyril Mockridge, Alfred Newman; Costumes: Rene Hubert; Art Director: James Basevi, J. Russell Spencer. B&W, 93 min.

The Late Show
(1976) Warner Bros.
Altman (he produced) protégé Benton's second film is a subtle, character-driven private-eye movie with touching performances by Carney and Tomlin. In a classic setup (think *Maltese Falcon*), aging private eye Carney tries to solve his partner's murder (he had been on a missing-cat case) and finds himself embroiled in the life of his client, Tomlin. True to the form, they form a warm bond. The difference here is in Carney's portrayal of a hard-boiled type with a soft center who knows his last days are on the horizon. Benton's wise script won an Oscar nomination. Academy Award Nomination for Best (Original) Screenplay. **Cast:** Art Carney, Lily Tomlin, Bill Macy, Eugene Roche, Joanna Cassidy,

Laura (1944)

John Considine, Ruth Nelson, Howard Duff. **Credits:** Dir: Robert Benton; Prod: Robert Altman; Writer: Robert Benton; DP: Charles Rosher; Ed: Lou Lombardo, Peter Appleton; Composer: Ken Wannberg. Color, 94 min.
VHS, LASER

Laughing Sinners
(1931) MGM
The romantic chemistry of Crawford and Gable—who were teaming up behind the scenes, too—lights up this romantic melodrama. Crawford's a debutante who's saved from a suicide attempt by Salvation Army worker Gable after being dumped by boyfriend Hamilton. Based on the play *Torch Song* by Nicholson. **Cast:** Joan Crawford, Clark Gable, Neil Hamilton, Johnny Mack Brown, Marjorie Rambeau, Guy Kibbee, Roscoe Karns, Cliff Edwards. **Credits:** Dir: Harry Beaumont; Writer: Bess Meredyth, Martin Flavin, Edith Fitzgerald; Story: Kenyon Nicholson; DP: Charles Rosher; Ed: George Hively; Prod Design: Cedric Gibbons; Costumes: Adrian. B&W, 72 min. **VHS**

Laura
(1944) Fox
A classic noirish mystery with a consummate ensemble of actors. Andrews adroitly plays the detective who delves into the murder of the stunningly beautiful Laura (Tierney, in her signature role), with whom it

seems everyone, including the detective himself, is understandable in love. But Webb steals the show as Laura's creepily elegant mentor, society columnist Waldo Lydecker. Based on the novel by Caspary. Preminger took over the direction of this compelling mystery classic, which was originally in the hands of Rouben Mamoulian. The restored video includes previously excised footage. Academy Award Nominations: 4, including Best Director. **Academy Awards:** Best Black-and-White Cinematography. **Cast:** Gene Tierney, Dana Andrews, Clifton Webb, Vincent Price, Judith Anderson, James Flavin, Clyde Fillmore, Ralph Dunn, Grant Mitchell, Kathleen Howard. **Credits:** Dir: Otto Preminger; Prod: Otto Preminger; Writer: Jay Dratler, Elizabeth Reinhardt, Samuel Hoffenstein, Ring Lardner, Jerry Cady; Story: Vera Caspary; DP: Joseph La Shelle; Ed: Louis Loeffler; Prod Design: Thomas Little, Paul S. Fox; Composer: David Raksin; Costumes: Bonnie Cashin; SFX: Fred Sersen. B&W, 88 min. **VHS, LASER**

Laurel and Hardy
Reportedly, Leo McCarey put Stan Laurel and Oliver Hardy together at the Hal Roach Studios in 1926. For that alone he should be in every movie-lover's heart. Laurel and Hardy may be the perfect screen-comedy team. A study in opposites, slim Stan and hefty Hardy often played to their extreme physical differences with great physical comedy skills. But their genius lay in the step-by-step dissolution of order and common sense as they burrow deeper into an everyday dilemma such as piano moving or ice delivery. Although the duo shared screen time in several silent films, it wasn't until 1927's *The Second Hundred Years* that they were actually billed as a team. Twenty-seven features and dozens of shorts followed. Wanting more creative freedom, the duo eventually left Roach's studio in 1940, moving on to 20th Century-Fox and MGM. Ironically, the eight films produced in this period (1940–1945) withered under the respective studios' heavy-handedness. In 1947 Laurel and Hardy went on the road, performing to sold-out crowds in Europe and the British Isles. They returned to a resurgence of popularity in the States, thanks in part to television's frequent airing of their films, though preparations for a movie comeback ended with Hardy's 1957 stroke. Laurel continued to write, out of the public eye, until his death in 1965.

Laurel and Hardy Silent Films

Lucky Dog *(1918)*
45 Minutes From Hollywood *(1926)*
Duck Soup *(1927)*
Slipping Wives *(1927)*
Love 'Em and Weep *(1927)*
Why Girls Love Sailors *(1927)*
With Love and Hisses *(1927)*
Sugar Daddies *(1927)*
Sailors, Beware! *(1927)*
The Second Hundred Years *(1927)*
Call of the Cuckoos *(1927)*
Hats Off *(1927)*
Do Detectives Think? *(1927)*
Putting Pants on Philip *(1927)*
The Battle of the Century *(1927)*
Leave 'Em Laughing *(1928)*
Flying Elephants *(1928)*
The Finishing Touch *(1928)*
From Soup to Nuts *(1928)*
You're Darn Tootin' *(1928)*
Their Purple Moment *(1928)*
Should Married Men Go Home?
 (1928)
Early to Bed *(1928)*
Two Tars *(1928)*
Habeas Corpus *(1928)*
We Faw Down *(1928)*
Liberty *(1929)*
Wrong Again *(1929)*
That's My Wife *(1929)*
Big Business *(1929)*
Double Whoopee*(1929)*
Bacon Grabbers *(1929)*
Angora Love *(1929)*

Laurel and Hardy Sound Films

Unaccustomed As We Are *(1929)*
Berth Marks *(1929)*
Perfect Day *(1929)*
They Go Boom *(1929)*
The Hoose-Gow *(1929)*
Night Owls *(1930)*
Blotto *(1930)*
Brats *(1930)*
Below Zero *(1930)*
The Rogue Song *(1930)*
Hog Wild *(1930)*
The Laurel and Hardy Murder Case
 (1930)
Another Fine Mess *(1930)*
Be Big *(1931)*
Chickens Come Home *(1931)*
The Stolen Jools (cameo) *(1931)*
Laughing Gravy *(1931)*
Our Wife *(1931)*
Pardon Us *(1931)*
Come Clean *(1931)*
One Good Turn *(1931)*
Beau Hunks *(1931)*
Helpmates *(1932)*
Any Old Port *(1932)*
The Music Box *(1932)*
The Chimp *(1932)*
County Hospital *(1932)*
Scram! *(1932)*
Pack Up Your Troubles *(1932)*

Their First Mistake *(1932)*
Towed in a Hole *(1932)*
Twice Two *(1933)*
Me and My Pal *(1933)*
The Devil's Brother/
Fra Diavolo *(1933)*
The Midnight Patrol *(1933)*
Busy Bodies *(1933)*
Wild Poses (cameo) *(1933)*
Dirty Work *(1933)*
Sons of the Desert *(1933)*
Oliver the Eighth *(1934)*
Going Bye Bye! *(1934)*
Them Thar Hills *(1934)*
Babes in Toyland *(1934)*
The Live Ghost *(1934)*
Tit For Tat *(1935)*
The Fixer Uppers *(1935)*
Thicker Than Water *(1935)*
Bonnie Scotland *(1935)*
The Bohemian Girl *(1936)*
Our Relations *(1936)*
Way Out West *(1937)*
Swiss Miss *(1938)*
Block-Heads *(1938)*
The Flying Deuces *(1939)*
A Chump At Oxford *(1940)*
Saps At Sea *(1940)*
Great Guns *(1941)*
A-Haunting We Will Go *(1942)*
The Tree in a Test Tube *(1943)*
Air Raid Wardens *(1943)*
The Big Noise *(1944)*
The Bullfighters *(1945)*
Nothing But Trouble *(1945)*
Robinson Crusoeland *(1950)*

The Law and Jake Wade

(1958) MGM
An ungrateful Widmark kidnaps former partner-in-crime Taylor after the bank robber turned marshal saves him from a hanging. The lucky bandit forces Taylor to reveal where he had hidden the take from an earlier robbery, Taylor's last, up in the High Sierras. A panoramic color Western with a slam-bang finale. **Cast:** Patricia Owens, Robert Taylor, Richard Widmark, Robert Middleton, Henry Silva, DeForest Kelley, Burt Douglas, Eddie Firestone. **Credits:** Dir: John Sturges; Prod: William B. Hawks; Writer: William Bowers; Story: Marvin H. Albert; DP: Robert Surtees; Ed: Ferris Webster; Art Director: Daniel B. Cathcart. Color, 87 min. **VHS**

"I do not welcome advice from actors,
they are here to act."

Director Otto Preminger

Law and Order

(1932) Universal
A melancholy study of the close relationship between violence and justice in the old West, notable for its collaboration between the Hustons, scriptwriter John and leading man Walter, as the righteous sheriff who would clean up the corruption and lawlessness in Tombstone. Unfortunately for Huston and Tombstone, the price of peace and justice is dear, as he must resort to frequent gunplay to vanquish the enemy in the dusty streets. **Cast:** Walter Huston, Russell Simpson, Russell Hopton, Andy Devine, Walter Brennan, Ralph Ince, Harry Woods, Richard Alexander. **Credits:** Dir: Edward L. Cahn; Writer: John Huston; Story: W. R. Burnett; Ed: Milton Carruth. B&W, 70 min.

The Lawless

(1950) Paramount
A fight at a northern California dance hall breaks out along racial lines, inflaming existing tensions between Mexican "fruit tramps," employed to harvest the town's fruit and vegetables, and the local whites. A Mexican youth must flee for his life after striking a cop in the brawl as the whites organize themselves into violent mobs to hunt for the fugitive. A sympathetic white newspaperman places himself at the center of their fury by attempting to defend the fleeing youth. As both sides turn to violence, townspeople in the middle on the racial issue are forced to choose sides. An early Losey effort. **Cast:** Macdonald Carey, Gail Russell, Johnny Sands, Lee Patrick, John Hoyt, Paul Rodriguez, Maurice Jara, Walter Reed, Guy Anderson, Argentina Brunetti. **Credits:** Dir: Joseph Losey; Prod: Nicholas Nayfack; Writer: Geoffrey Homes; DP: Roy Hunt; Ed: Howard Smith; Prod Design: Lewis H. Creber, Al Kegerris; Composer: David Chudnow. B&W, 83 min.

The Lawless Breed

(1953) Universal
Hudson's first starring role is portraying savage killer John Wesley Hardin in this Walsh Western. Though the real

Hardin was something of a madman, here he's given the standard excuses for his life of crime, a romance with the always-lovely Adams, and a son whom he cares enough about to steer away from following in his footsteps. **Cast:** Rock Hudson, Julie Adams, Mary Castle, John McIntire, Hugh O'Brian, Dennis Weaver, Forrest Lewis, Michael Ansara, Lee Van Cleef, Glenn Strange. **Credits:** Dir: Raoul Walsh; Prod: William Alland; Story: Bernard Gordon; DP: Irving Glassberg; Ed: Frank Gross; Composer: Joseph Gershenson; Art Director: Bernard Herzbrun, Richard H. Riedel. Color, 83 min. **VHS**

Lawman
(1971) United Artists
A thought-provoking Western about a relentless lawman determined to chase down six cowhands involved in an accidental death, without regard to what's moral or popular. Even when the entire town turns against him, he persists in delivering them to "justice." A moody and violent picture with fine performances from Lancaster as the marshal and Ryan as the spineless local sheriff who lives in the safety of the past. **Cast:** Burt Lancaster, Robert Ryan, Lee J. Cobb, Robert Duvall, Sheree North, Albert Salmi, Joseph Wiseman, J. D. Cannon, Richard Jordan, John McGiver. **Credits:** Dir: Michael Winner; Prod: Michael Winner; Writer: Gerald Wilson; DP: Robert Paynter; Ed: Frederick Wilson; Composer: Jerry Fielding; Art Director: Herbert Westbrook. Color, 97 min. **VHS**

Lawrence of Arabia
(1962) Columbia
Here is one of the great Hollywood epics of all time and O'Toole's first major screen appearance, which established him as an international star overnight. He gives a superb performance as T. E. Lawrence, a British military observer who, in rejecting British tradition and adapting Arab attire, became a figure of enduring mystique while helping to unite the warring Arab factions into a guerrilla front against the Turks. The restored video includes 35 minutes of previously missing footage. The 30th anniversary special edition features the original theatrical trailer and a 32-page companion booklet, plus a film short on the making of the film including interviews and behind the scenes footage. The laserdisc edition features a collection of production photos, *Wind, Sand and Star*, a featurette doc-

umenting production, footage from the 1962 New York premiere, and silent newsreel production footage. Lean's masterpiece justly swept the '62 Academy Awards. Its many other honors include the British Academy BAFTA: Best Film; Best Actor; Best Screenplay; Best British Film. Golden Globes for Best Director; Best Supporting Actor: Omar Sharif; Best Color Cinematography; Best Male Newcomer: Omar Sharif; Best Motion Picture, Drama. Directors Guild DGA award for Outstanding Directorial Achievement. Selected as a National Film Registry Outstanding Film. Academy Award Nominations: 10, including Best Actor: Peter O'Toole; Best Supporting Actor: Omar Sharif; Best (Adapted) Screenplay. **Academy Awards:** Best Picture; Best Director; Best Cinematography; Best Editing; Best Score; Best Art Direction; Best Sound. **Cast:** Peter O'Toole, Alec Guinness, Anthony Quinn, Jack Hawkins, Omar Sharif, Jose Ferrer, Claude Rains, Anthony Quayle, Arthur Kennedy, I. S. Johar. **Credits:** Dir: David Lean; Prod: Robert A. Harris, Sam Spiegel, David Lean; Writer: Robert Bolt, Michael Wilson; Story: T. E. Lawrence; DP: Freddie Young; Ed: Anne V. Coates; Prod Design: John Box; Composer: Maurice Jarre; Costumes: Phyllis Dalton. Color, 216 min. **VHS, LASER**

Lawyer Man
(1932) Warner Bros.
This requires a certain suspension of disbelief as it presents a character played by Powell as not being the epitome of suave. Powell carries the film as a young attorney who seizes opportunities to further his career and place in society, as he surrenders his ethics. Spotted as a rising star by a venerable, successful attorney, he proceeds to traffic on this boost by making a name on his own as a defender of criminals. Along the way he is acquitted of blackmail and hires Blondell as a snappy secretary. **Cast:** William Powell, Joan Blondell, Helen Vinson, Alan Dinehart, Allen Jenkins, David Landau, Claire Dodd, Sheila Terry, Kenneth Thomson, Jack LaRue. **Credits:** Dir: William Dieterle; Prod: Hal B. Wallis; Writer: Ryan James, James Seymour; DP: Robert Kurrle; Ed: Thomas Pratt. B&W, 68 min.

Leadbelly
(1976) Paramount
This well-made biopic about the legendary African-American folk musician Huddie Ledbetter opens with his last

stay in prison and utilizes flashbacks to tell the story. Mosley portrays him as winning, giving, and stubborn at the same time. A dozen-plus songs are woven throughout as performed by Hitide Harris. **Cast:** Roger E. Mosley, Paul Benjamin, Vivian Bonnell, James E. Brodhead, Art Evans, John Henry Faulk, Albert Hall, Dana Manno, Alan Manson, Madge Sinclair. **Credits:** Dir: Gordon Parks; Prod: Marc Merson; Writer: Ernest Kinoy; DP: Bruce Surtees; Ed: Moe (III) Howard; Prod Design: Robert Boyle; Composer: Fred Karlin. Color, 126 min.

The Learning Tree
(1969) Warner Bros.
Former *Life* magazine photographer Parks wrote the screenplay (based on his semiautobiographical novel), produced, directed, and even wrote the music for this portrait of growing up black in '20s Kansas City. Along the way, Johnson faces the usual trials of growing up—first love, brushes with crime and death, temptations and choices—always making his way through racial obstacles with the strong moral teaching of his mother, that every event in life is a branch on "the learning tree." A nuanced, thoughtful message film with an absorbing narrative, too. After this first effort, Parks went on to direct the Shaft series of black action films. Selected as a National Film Registry Outstanding Film. **Cast:** Kyle Johnson, Alex Clarke, Estelle Evans, Dana Elcar, Jimmy Rushing, Mira Waters, Joel Fluellen, Malcolm Atterbury. **Credits:** Dir: Gordon Parks; Prod: Gordon Parks; Writer: Gordon Parks; DP: Burnett Guffey; Ed: George R. Rohrs; Composer: Gordon Parks, Tom McIntosh; Art Director: Ed Engoron. Color, 107 min. **VHS**

Leave Her to Heaven
(1945) Fox
Tierney positively eats the camera in this darkly beautiful Technicolor portrait of a pathologically possessive wife who will do whatever she has to to keep her husband all to herself, even from beyond the grave. Worth watching just for Tierney's scary, neurotic beauty. Adapted from the novel by Ben Ames. Academy Award Nominations: 2, including Best Actress: Gene Tierney. **Academy Awards:** Best Color Cinematography. **Cast:** Gene Tierney, Cornel Wilde, Jeanne Crain, Vincent Price, Mary Philips, Ray Collins, Darryl Hickman, Gene Lockhart. **Credits:** Dir: John M. Stahl; Prod: William A. Bacher; Writer: Jo

Swerling; DP: Leon Shamroy; Ed: James B. Clark; Prod Design: Lyle Wheeler, Maurice Ransford; Composer: Alfred Newman. Color, 111 min. VHS

The Left-Handed Gun
(1958) Warner Bros.
Penn's first theatrically released feature builds an intriguing portrait of Billy the Kid, seeing him as a damaged youth whose devotion to a murdered rancher who was his father figure sets him on his murderous rampage. Newman attempts to find the psychological basis for the Kid's spree, giving an edgy, irritable reading. This was based on *The Death of Billy the Kid*, a teleplay written by Vidal (and directed for TV by Penn). **Cast:** Paul Newman, Lita Milan, John Dehner, Hurd Hatfield, James Congdon, James Best, John Dierkes, Wally Brown. **Credits:** Dir: Arthur Penn; Prod: Fred Coe; Writer: Leslie Stevens; Story: Gore Vidal; DP: Peverell Marley; Ed: Folmar Blangsted; Composer: Alexander Courage; Art Director: Art Loell. B&W, 102 min. VHS

The Left Hand of God
(1955) Fox
One of Bogart's last roles is an exotic military adventure tale set in post–WWII China. After pilot Bogart crashes in a remote mountain village, he throws in with a warlord improbably played by Cobb. After a killing of a priest, Bogart flees, knowing he'll be blamed. He takes refuge in a mission where he poses as a priest, and warms to the lovely Tierney, a missionary nurse. But his past reappears when Cobb threatens to destroy the village if he doesn't come back to lead his forces. **Cast:** Humphrey Bogart, Gene Tierney, Lee J. Cobb, Agnes Moorehead, E. G. Marshall, Jean Porter, Carl Benton Reid, Victor Sen Yung, Philip Ahn, Benson Fong. **Credits:** Dir: Edward Dmytryk; Writer: Alfred Hayes; Story: William E. Barrett; DP: Franz Planer; Ed: Dorothy Spencer; Prod Design: Lyle Wheeler, Maurice Ransford; Composer: Victor Young. Color, 87 min. VHS

Le Mans
(1971) National General
McQueen did his own stunt driving in this film about a man who chases his own demons as he chases the checkered flag of the 24-hour Le Mans race. Despite a mighty thin plot, the exciting racetrack footage keeps this worthwhile as a realistic peek into the world of Grand Prix auto racing. Many consider this the best racing film ever.

Cast: Steve McQueen, Siegfried Rauch, Ronald Leigh-Hunt, Elga Andersen, Luc Merenda, Angelo Infanti, Carlo Cecchi, Hale Hamilton. **Credits:** Dir: Lee H. Katzin; Prod: Jack N. Reddish; Writer: Harry Kleiner; DP: Robert B. Hauser, Rene Guissart; Ed: Donald W. Ernst, John Woodcock; Composer: Michel Legrand; Art Director: Nikita Knatz. Color, 108 min. VHS, LASER

The Lemon Drop Kid
(1951) Paramount
This second filming of Runyon's story of a bookie on the lam from a gangster provides Hope with one of his best settings and he runs with it. Hope lets gang boss Nolan in on a sure thing, which finishes out of the money, and has to do some fast talking and fast walking to keep one step ahead of him. The 1934 version starring Lee Tracy also had Frawley in the cast. This introduced the Yuletide chestnut, "Silver Bells." **Cast:** Bob Hope, Marilyn Maxwell, Lloyd Nolan, Jane Darwell, Andrea King, Fred Clark, Jay C. Flippen, William Frawley, Harry Bellaver, Sid Melton. **Credits:** Dir: Sidney Lanfield, Frank Tashlin; Prod: Robert L. Welch; Writer: Edmund L. Hartmann, Robert O'Brien; Story: Edmund Beloin, Damon Runyon; DP: Daniel L. Fapp; Ed: Archie Marshek; Composer: Jay Livingston, Ray Evans; Art Director: Hal Pereira, Franz Bachelin. B&W, 91 min. VHS, LASER

Lenny
(1974) United Artists
The life of nightclub comic Lenny Bruce doesn't make entertainment for the whole family, but it is an absorbing portrait of a brilliantly misguided missile. Bruce, who pioneered the comedic trend of foul-mouthed, scathingly political humor, is well-played by Hoffman, and Perrine convinces as his wife, stripper Honey Harlowe. Bruce would have been pleased by the controversy that surrounded this biopic adapted from the Broadway play by Barry. Academy Award Nominations: 6, including Best Picture; Best Director; Best Actor: Dustin Hoffman; Best Actress: Valerie Perrine; Best (Adapted) Screenplay. **Cast:** Dustin Hoffman, Valerie Perrine, Jan Miner, Stanley Beck, Gary Morton, Rashel Novikoff, Guy Rennie, Mark Harris. **Credits:** Dir: Bob Fosse; Prod: Marvin Worth; Writer: Julian Barry; DP: Bruce Surtees; Ed: Alan Heim; Prod Design: Joel Schiller. Color, 112 min. VHS, LASER

The Leopard Man
(1943) RKO
The thriller producer-director team of Lewton and Tourneur (*Cat People*, 1942) created another suspenseful shocker with this tale of a killer on the loose. A public-relations stunt turns macabre when a leopard escapes and kills a young girl. When similar killings horrify the New Mexico town, the blame is put on the wild animal. But the PR man (O'Keefe) investigates and comes to a very different conclusion. Based on a Woolrich novel. **Cast:** Dennis O'Keefe, Margo, Jean Brooks, Isabel Jewell, James Bell, Margaret Landry, Abner Biberman, Richard Martin, Tula Parma, Ben Bard. **Credits:** Dir: Jacques Tourneur; Prod: Val Lewton; Writer: Ardell Wray, Edward Dein; Story: Cornell Woolrich; DP: Robert de Grasse; Composer: Roy Webb; Art Director: Albert S. D'Agostino, Walter E. Keller. B&W, 66 min. VHS, LASER

Lepke
(1975) Warner Bros.
An excellent gangster film that follows the life of Louis Buchalter from the reformatory to C.E.O. of Murder, Inc. to the electric chair in 1944. Curtis makes a believable mobster despite his boyish good looks. Berle makes a rare, albeit short, appearance in a dramatic role as Lepke's father-in-law. **Cast:** Tony Curtis, Anjanette Comer, Michael Callan, Warren Berlinger, Gianni Russo, Vic Tayback, Mary Wilcox, Milton Berle. **Credits:** Dir: Menahem Golan; Prod: Menahem Golan; Writer: Wesley Lau, Tamar Simon Hoffs; DP: Andrew Davis; Ed: Dov Hoenig, Aaron Stell; Prod Design: Jackson DeGovia; Composer: Kenneth Wannberg. Color, 110 min. VHS

Les Girls
(1957) MGM
This charming Cukor musical revolves around three showgirls who feel betrayed when one of them writes a memoir about their days in a French cabaret act. In flashbacks, each of them recounts a relationship with the leader of the troupe, Kelly. Porter's score (his last written for the screen) is just too, too and includes "Les Girls," "Flower Song," and "You're Just Too, Too." Adapted from Vera Caspary's novel. Golden Globes for Best Actress in a Musical or Comedy: Kay Kendall; Best Motion Picture, Musical/Comedy. Academy Award Nominations: 3. **Academy Awards:** Best Costume Design. **Cast:** Gene Kelly, Mitzi Gaynor, Kay Kendall, Taina

Elg, Jacques Bergerac, Leslie Phillips, Henry Daniell, Patrick MacNee. **Credits:** Dir: George Cukor; Prod: Sol C. Siegel; Writer: John Patrick; DP: Robert Surtees; Ed: Ferris Webster; Prod Design: William A. Horning, Gene Allen; Composer: Cole Porter. Color, 115 min. **VHS, LASER**

Les Miserables
(1935) United Artists
This is the first of, to date, six versions of Victor Hugo's famous story about moral thievery and immoral justice. March steals bread, March repents and becomes a respectable public figure, Laughton pursues him with a frightening vengeance. The cinematography by Toland is beautiful, the pacing is perfect, and the details are wonderful. And the story must be great; there were two big-budget versions made in the last three years. Academy Award Nominations: 4, including Best Picture. **Cast:** Fredric March, Charles Laughton, Cedric Hardwicke, Frances Drake, Rochelle Hudson, Marilyn Knowlden, John Beal, Jessie Ralph. **Credits:** Dir: Richard Boleslawski; Prod: Darryl F. Zanuck; Writer: W. P. Lipscomb; DP: Gregg Toland; Ed: Barbara McLean; Composer: Alfred Newman. B&W, 104 min. **VHS, LASER**

Let Freedom Ring
(1939) MGM
Nelson Eddy proves that he can use his fists as well as his voice as a lawyer who returns to his hometown to fight corruption and the encroachment of the railroad led by scheming tycoon Arnold. Sentimental where it means to be stirring, but Hecht's fine scriptwriting saves the day. **Cast:** Nelson Eddy, Virginia Bruce, Victor McLaglen, Lionel Barrymore, Edward Arnold, Guy Kibbee, Raymond Walburn, Charles Butterworth. **Credits:** Dir: Jack Conway; Prod: Harry Rapf; Writer: Ben Hecht; DP: Sidney Wagner; Ed: Fredrick Y. Smith; Prod Design: Cedric Gibbons, Daniel B. Cathcart; Composer: Arthur Lange. B&W, 100 min. **VHS**

Let's Dance
(1950) Paramount
With the help of her USO-show dance partner (Astaire), a war widow (Hutton) fights a legal battle and gains custody of her child. Not one of Astaire's better-known films, but lots of fun just the same. Fabulous dancing from Astaire and Hutton (with choreography from longtime Astaire collaborator Hermes Pan), including the celebrated "Piano Dance" routine, and a lovely

score from Loesser, including "Tunnel of Love," "Can't Stop Talking," and "Why Fight the Feeling?" **Cast:** Fred Astaire, Betty Hutton, Roland Young, Ruth Warrick, Lucile Watson, Gregory Moffett, Barton MacLane, Shepperd Strudwick. **Credits:** Dir: Norman Z. McLeod; Prod: Robert Fellows; Writer: Allan Scott, Dane Lussier; DP: George Barnes; Ed: Ellsworth Hoagland; Prod Design: Hans Dreier, Roland Anderson; Composer: Frank Loesser, Robert Emmett. Color, 112 min. **VHS, LASER**

Let's Do It Again
(1953) Columbia
Musical comedy about a woman (Wyman) married to a philanderer (Milland) who decides to get back at her husband by having an affair. She isn't serious but the husband asks for a divorce. Apart, each continues to try to make the other jealous, until they decide to remarry. A remake of *The Awful Truth* (1937) with songs. **Cast:** Jane Wyman, Ray Milland, Aldo Ray, Leon Ames, Valerie Bettis, Tom Helmore, Karin Booth, Mary Treen, Kathryn Givney, Herbert Heyes. **Credits:** Dir: Alexander Hall; Prod: Oscar Saul; Writer: Mary Loos, Richard Sale; DP: Charles Lawton, Jr.; Ed: Charles Nelson; Composer: George Duning, Morris Stoloff. Color, 95 min.

Let's Do It Again
(1975) Warner Bros.
Cosby and Poitier play working-class guys in Atlanta who really want to raise some money for their lodge. They decide to hypnotize Walker into believing he's a boxer, then set up a fight to separate big-time gamblers from their greenbacks. This comic caper was the sequel to *Uptown Saturday Night* (1974). **Cast:** Sidney Poitier, Bill Cosby, Jimmie Walker, Calvin Lockhart, John Amos, Denise Nicholas, Lee Chamberlin, Mel Stewart. **Credits:** Dir: Sidney Poitier; Prod: Melville Tucker; Writer: Richard Wesley; DP: Donald M. Morgan; Ed: Pembroke Herring; Prod Design: Alfred Sweeney; Composer: Curtis Mayfield. Color, 113 min. **VHS**

Let's Make Love
(1960) Fox
A millionaire (Montand) is out to squelch a show that makes fun of him until he meets cast member Monroe. To get closer to her, he decides to join the cast and hires Milton Berle, Gene Kelly, and Bing Crosby (as themselves) to teach him the performing arts. Monroe and Montand were carrying on a frank dalliance during produc-

tion. A delightful Cukor backstage musical with many memorable songs, including "My Heart Belongs to Daddy" and "You With the Crazy Eyes." Academy Award Nomination for Best Scoring of a Musical Picture. **Cast:** Marilyn Monroe, Yves Montand, Tony Randall, Frankie Vaughan, Wilfrid Hyde-White, David Burns, Michael David, Mara Lynn. **Credits:** Dir: George Cukor; Prod: Jerry Wald; Writer: Norman Krasna, Hal Kanter; DP: Daniel Fapp; Ed: David Bretherton; Prod Design: Lyle Wheeler; Composer: Lionel Newman; Art Director: Gene Allen. Color, 118 min. **VHS**

Let's Scare Jessica to Death
(1971) Paramount
Jessica (Lampert) goes home with her husband (Heyman) to recuperate after a nervous breakdown—but drownings, corpses, ghosts, séances, and even an old woman who turns out to be a vampire make her question her recovery. **Cast:** Zohra Lampert, Barton Heyman, Kevin J. O'Connor, Gretchen Corbett, Alan Manson, Mariclare Costello. **Credits:** Dir: John Hancock; Prod: Charles Moss; Writer: Norman Jonas, Ralph Rose; DP: Bob Baldwin; Ed: Murray Solomon, Joe Ryan; Costumes: Mariette Pinchart. Color, 89 min. **VHS**

The Letter
(1940) Warner Bros.
Another stellar performance by Davis in a Wyler film after their 1938 success with *Jezebel*. It's almost possible to see the cold, calculating machinery in Davis's mind as she plays the wife of a Malayan rubber-plantation owner who kills her lover and then claims that he attacked her. Her husband (Marshall) defends her until the victim's wife comes forward with a letter Davis had written to her husband—and a blackmail demand. The Maugham story had been filmed once before in 1929 (and was remade again in 1947 as *The Unfaithful* with Ann Sheridan, and again for TV) and Davis reportedly based her performance on the star of that silent version, Jeanne Eagels. The unfortunate Eagels was a heroin addict and a brilliant, raw actress; she died soon after her appearance in *The Letter*. Academy Award Nominations: 7, including Best Picture; Best Director; Best Actress: Bette Davis. **Cast:** Bette Davis, Herbert Marshall, James Stephenson, Gale Sondergaard, Bruce Lester, Cecil Kellaway, Victor Sen Yung, Doris Lloyd, Willie Fung, Tetsu Komai. **Credits:** Dir: William Wyler; Prod: Robert Lord; Writer: Howard Koch;

Story: W. Somerset Maugham; DP: Tony Gaudio; Ed: George Amy; Composer: Max Steiner; Art Director: Carl Jules Weyl. B&W, 96 min. VHS, LASER

Letter from an Unknown Woman

(1948) Universal

A lush, haunting romance from German director Ophuls, and his most successful Hollywood film, about a woman (Fontaine) who maintains her love for a concert pianist (Jourdan) so self-absorbed that he fails to recognize her from one long-ago rendezvous to the next—though, unknown to him, she gave birth to their child. Produced by Fontaine's own production company. The 45th anniversary edition has been digitally remastered and also includes a reproduction of an original theatrical lobby card and the theatrical trailer. **Cast:** Joan Fontaine, Louis Jourdan, Marcel Journet, Mady Christians, Art Smith, Carol Yorke, Howard Freeman, Erskine Sanford. **Credits:** Dir: Max Ophuls; Prod: John Houseman; Writer: Howard Koch; DP: Franz Planer; Ed: Ted J. Kent; Prod Design: Alexander Golitzen; Composer: Daniele Amfitheatrof. B&W, 87 min. VHS, LASER

Letter of Introduction

(1938) Universal

A struggling actress (Leeds) seeks the advice of an older, famous actor (Menjou). A warm friendship grows between them and when it's revealed that he is her father, she decides not to damage his ego by making that knowledge public. It's the relationship between Menjou and Leeds that keeps this family drama with a backstage setting alive. **Cast:** Adolphe Menjou, Andrea Leeds, Edgar Bergen, Eve Arden, Mortimer Snerd, Charlie McCarthy, George Murphy, Rita Johnson. **Credits:** Dir: John M. Stahl; Prod: John M. Stahl; Writer: Sheridan Gibney, Leonard Spigelgass; DP: Karl Freund; Ed: Ted J. Kent. B&W, 104 min. VHS

A Letter to Three Wives

(1949) Fox

A letter is received by three women from a mutual "friend" (voiced by the unseen Holm) informing them she has run off with one of their husbands. Each woman reflects, through flashbacks, on her marriage. A neat twist on a soapy formula. Multiple award-winner, including Directors Guild DGA award for Outstanding Directorial Achievement. Academy Award Nominations: 3, including Best Picture. **Academy Awards:** Best Director; Best Screenplay. **Cast:** Jeanne Crain, Linda Darnell, Ann Sothern, Kirk Douglas, Paul Douglas, Thelma Ritter, Celeste Holm, Barbara Lawrence. **Credits:** Dir: Joseph L. Mankiewicz; Prod: Sol C. Siegel; Writer: Joseph L. Mankiewicz; Story: Vera Caspary; DP: Arthur Miller; Ed: J. Watson Webb; Composer: Alfred Newman; Art Director: Lyle Wheeler, J. Russell Spencer. B&W, 103 min. VHS, LASER

Let the Good Times Roll

(1973) Columbia

A documentary that recaptures the birth of the rock-n-roll era in the '50s, featuring performances by early rock's biggest names. Footage is drawn from two 1972 concerts (Long Island's Nassau Coliseum and Detroit's Cobo Hall), as well as a Fats Domino performance at Las Vegas's Flamingo Hotel. Intercut with 33 songs are backstage interviews with the artists, as well as film excerpts and stills from the '50s. Highlights include Bo Diddley and Chuck Berry teaming up for "Johnny B. Goode," and Little Richard, who performs three of his classics. **Cast:** Chuck Berry, Little Richard, Fats Domino, Chubby Checker, Bo Diddley, The Five Satins, The Coasters, Bill Haley, Danny and the Juniors, The Shirelles. **Credits:** Dir: Robert Abel, Sidney Levin; Prod: Gerald I. Isenberg; DP: Robert Thomas; Ed: Hyman Kaufman, Bud Friedgen, Yeu Bun-Yee; Composer: James E. Webb, Jr., Joe Tully. Color, 98 min.

Let There Be Light

(1945)

To explore the psychological rehabilitation of soldiers returning from WWII battlefields, Director Huston took a crew of Signal Corps cameramen to Mason General Hospital in Long Island, New York. This is a film on the subject of war's impact on the human spirit and a tribute to the raw courage of the men themselves. **Cast:** Walter Huston. **Credits:** Dir: John Huston; Writer: Charles Kaufman; DP: Stanley Cortez, John Doran, Lloyd Fromm, Joseph Jackman, George Smith; Composer: Dimitri Tiomkin. B&W, 60 min. VHS

Let Us Live

(1939) Columbia

The wrong men are arrested and sentenced to die for a crime, but the staunch fiancée of one works tirelessly to persuade the police to have a closer look at the case. Fonda is one of the condemned men, O'Sullivan plays the fiancée, and Bellamy is the lieutenant who reopens the case. Based on a 1934 Lynn, Massachusetts, theater robbery case. **Cast:** Maureen O'Sullivan, Henry Fonda, Ralph Bellamy, Alan Baxter, Stanley Ridges, Henry Kolker, Peter Lynn, George Douglas, Philip Trent, Martin Spellman. **Credits:** Dir: John Brahm; Prod: William Perlberg; Writer: Joseph F. Dineen, Anthony Veiller, Allen Rivkin; DP: Lucien Ballard; Ed: Al Clark; Composer: Karol Rathaus, Morris Stoloff; Art Director: Lionel Banks. B&W, 66 min.

Libeled Lady

(1936) MGM

Fast-paced, classic Hollywood comedy with Tracy as a newspaper editor who employs his fiancée Harlow and his former employee Powell to dig up the dirt on heiress Loy. Of course, nothing goes as planned and the complications are wonderfully entertaining. All four stars are marvelous in this movie that was remade as a musical a decade later called *Easy to Wed*. Academy Award Nomination for Best Picture. **Cast:** Jean Harlow, William Powell, Myrna Loy, Spencer Tracy, Walter Connolly, Charley Grapewin, Cora Witherspoon, Charles Trowbridge. **Credits:** Dir: Jack Conway; Prod: Lawrence Weingarten; Writer: Maurine Watkins, Howard Emmett Rogers, George Oppenheimer; DP: Norbert F. Brodine; Ed: Fredrick Y. Smith; Prod Design: Cedric Gibbons, William A. Horning; Composer: William Axt. B&W, 99 min. VHS, LASER

The Liberation of L. B. Jones

(1970) Columbia

A turbulent domestic situation leads to murder and vengeance in Wyler's last film. Black undertaker Browne wants to divorce his wife (Falana, in her debut) after her affair with a white policeman (Zerbe). The cop and his partner trump up charges against Browne, and his futile escape leads only to killings. A fairly routine revenge drama with the racial angle adding the only interest. **Cast:** Lola Falana, Roscoe Lee Browne, Anthony Zerbe, Lee J. Cobb, Lee Majors, Barbara Hershey, Yaphet Kotto, Arch Johnson, Chill Wills, Zara Cully. **Credits:** Dir: William Wyler; Prod: Ronald Lubin; Writer: Stirling Silliphant, Jesse Hill Ford; DP: Robert Surtees; Ed: Robert W. Swink, Carl Kress; Prod Design: Kenneth Reid; Composer: Elmer Bernstein. Color, 102 min. VHS

The Life and Times of Judge Roy Bean

(1972) National General

Huston takes a crack at the revisionist Western that reexamined the national mythology during the Vietnam era, following *Butch Cassidy and the Sundance Kid* (1969) and *McCabe and Mrs. Miller* (1971). Newman plays the infamous hanging Judge Bean (an anti-hero if there ever was one) with a pungent swagger. After killing half the town of Vinageroon, Texas, Newman sets himself up as a judge, renames the town Langtry in honor of actress Lily, and proceeds to make himself and the town rich by preying on the honest and dishonest who pass his way. Wild, surrealist Western from the pen of a young Milius. Watch for appearances by Gardner as Lily Langtry and Huston as Grizzly Adams. Academy Award Nomination for Best Song ("Marmalade, Molasses and Honey"). **Cast:** Paul Newman, Ava Gardner, Victoria Principal, Anthony Perkins, Howard Morton, John Huston, Stacy Keach, Roddy McDowall, Ned Beatty, Anthony Zerbe. **Credits:** Dir: John Huston; Prod: John Foreman; Writer: John Milius; DP: Richard Moore; Ed: Hugh S. Fowler; Composer: Maurice Jarre; Art Director: Tambi Larsen. Color, 124 min. **VHS, LASER**

Life Begins
(1932) Warner Bros.
A maternity ward is the hub for a web of stories juxtaposing birth and death, innocence and guilt. Farrell portrays a hard-bitten nightclub singer who croons "Frankie and Johnny" to her twins, and Young plays a convicted murderer facing a difficult birth. In giving life to her child, this woman who has taken life now will give her own, leaving her husband to come to terms with her loss as well as his new child. **Cast:** Loretta Young, Eric Linden, Aline MacMahon, Glenda Farrell, Dorothy Peterson, Vivienne Osborne, Frank McHugh, Gilbert Roland, Hale Hamilton, Herbert Mundin. **Credits:** Dir: James Flood, Elliott Nugent; Prod: Raymond Griffith; Writer: Earl Baldwin; DP: James Van Trees; Ed: George Marks. B&W, 71 min.

Life Begins at Eight-Thirty
(1942) Fox
Aging stage star Woolley has a drinking problem that threatens to sink his career and his relationship with his saintly, crippled daughter, Lupino. As he deteriorates, reduced to playing a drunken Santa in department stores, his lively wit becomes increasingly deranged and vicious. It will take the threat of losing his daughter for good to her suitor Wilde to force the great actor to piece himself back together, redeem himself in his daughter's eyes, and, as King Lear, give the performance of his life. **Cast:** Monty Woolley, Ida Lupino, Cornel Wilde, Sara Allgood, Melville Cooper, J. Edward Bromberg, William Demarest. **Credits:** Dir: Irving Pichel; Prod: Nunnally Johnson; Writer: Nunnally Johnson; Story: Emlyn Williams; DP: Edward Cronjager; Ed: Fred Allen; Prod Design: Richard Day, Boris Leven; Composer: Alfred Newman. B&W, 85 min.

Life Begins at Forty
(1935) Fox
This often humorous, populist look at the relationship between graft and small-town politics stars Rogers as a dogged reporter helping out a good kid, Cromwell, who's been imprisoned for a bank heist he didn't commit. Typically wry commentary from Rogers accompanies the plot. **Cast:** Will Rogers, Richard Cromwell, Rochelle Hudson, Thomas Beck, George Barbier, Slim Summerville, Jane Darwell, Sterling Holloway. **Credits:** Dir: George Marshall; Prod: Sol M. Wurtzel; Writer: Dudley Nichols, Lamar Trotti, Robert Quillen, William Counselman, Walter B. Pitkin; DP: Harry Jackson; Ed: Alex Troffey; Prod Design: Duncan Cramer, Albert Hogsett. B&W, 85 min.

Lifeboat
(1944) Fox
A Hitchcock wartime thriller based on a story by Steinbeck (who made a first attempt at the script; Ben Hecht did some polishing to Swerling's script). An escape from a torpedoed ship becomes a desperate struggle for survival after the occupants of a lifeboat take in the captain of the U-boat that preyed upon their ship. The setting made for a difficult production (Bankhead contracted pneumonia) and required three differently configured boats. It also presented a dilemma for the famous Hitchcock cameo: watch the newspaper ads! Academy Award Nominations: 3, including Best Director; Best Original Story. **Cast:** Tallulah Bankhead, William Bendix, Walter Slezak, Mary Anderson, Henry Hill, John Hodiak, Heather Angel, Hume Cronyn, Canada Lee. **Credits:** Dir: Alfred Hitchcock; Prod: Kenneth MacGowan; Writer: Jo Swerling; Story: John Steinbeck; DP: Glen MacWilliams; Ed: Dorothy Spencer; Prod Design: James Basevi, Maurice Ransford; Composer: Hugo Friedhofer. B&W, 96 min. **VHS, LASER**

The Life of Emile Zola
(1937) Warner Bros.
Another successful Muni biopic as the French man of letters who risked his career and freedom to stand up for an unfairly accused man. Muni stars as the French novelist Zola, who rose from scandal to national treasure, and who threw his reputation and rhetorical skill behind Alfred Dreyfus, who had been wrongly accused of treason and sent to Devil's Island. Dieterle had previously directed Muni in the historical dramas *The Story of Louis Pasteur* (1936) and *Juarez* (1939). Academy Award Nominations: 10, including Best Director; Best Actor: Paul Muni; Best Supporting Actor; Best Original Story. **Academy Awards:** Best Supporting Actor: Joseph Schildkraut; Best Screenplay; Best Picture. **Cast:** Paul Muni, Joseph Schildkraut, Gale Sondergaard, Gloria Holden, Donald Crisp, Erin O'Brien-Moore, John Litel, Henry O'Neill, Morris Carnovsky, Louis Calhern. **Credits:** Dir: William Dieterle; Prod: Henry Blanke; Writer: Norman Reilly Raine, Heinz Herald, Geza Herczeg; DP: Tony Gaudio; Ed: Warren Low; Prod Design: Anton Grot; Composer: Max Steiner. B&W, 116 min. **VHS**

A Life of Her Own
(1950) MGM
A well-handled soaper from Cukor about a beautiful girl from the Midwest (Turner) who comes to New York to be a top model and succeeds. She's taken under the wing of old hand Dvorak, and, once on top of the modeling heap, looks for love. When she falls for a married man, her bed of roses turns out to have thorns. **Cast:** Lana Turner, Ray Milland, Tom Ewell, Louis Calhern, Ann Dvorak, Margaret Phillips, Jean Hagen, Barry Sullivan, Phyllis Kirk. **Credits:** Dir: George Cukor; Prod: Voldemar Vetluguin; Writer: Isobel Lennart; DP: George J. Folsey; Ed: George White; Composer: Bronislau Kaper, Johnny Green; Art Director: Cedric Gibbons, Arthur Lonergan. B&W, 108 min. **VHS**

The Life of Jimmy Dolan
(1933) Warner Bros.
The prototype for *They Made Me a Criminal* (1939) places the distinctly unmarred features of Douglas Fairbanks, Jr., in harm's way as an orphan-turned-prizefighter whose judgment is clouded by alcohol, and whose fists become lethal weapons to an indiscreet reporter. Fairbanks takes it on the lam, but is double-crossed by his manager, who steals his girl, money, and watch. A car accident burns the manager beyond recognition, but the watch misidentifies him as the fugitive pugilist. Fairbanks, assuming a new identity, returns to

the ring to try to save a home for crippled children. Watch for Rooney and Wayne. **Cast:** Douglas Fairbanks, Jr., Loretta Young, Fifi D'Orsay, Aline MacMahon, Guy Kibbee, Lyle Talbot, Harold Huber, Mickey Rooney, John Wayne. **Credits:** Dir: Archie Mayo; Prod: Hal B. Wallis; DP: Arthur Edeson; Composer: Leo F. Forbstein; Costumes: Orry-Kelly. B&W, 85 min.

The Life of Riley
(1949) Universal
In a clear-cut argument for "the good old days," conscience gets in the way of career advancement for Bendix in a role that jumped from successful radio show to successful film to successful TV series. He dreams of more from his job than a life punching rivets into planes, but never imagined that his daughter could get it for him in a dynastic marriage to the boss's son. Bendix displays a nobility far greater than his appearance when he breaks up the wedding and returns his daughter to her true love. **Cast:** William Bendix, Rosemary DeCamp, James Gleason, Beulah Bondi, Meg Randall, Richard Long, Lanny Rees, Mark Daniels, Ted De Corsia, Bill Goodwin. **Credits:** Dir: Irving Brecher; Prod: Irving Brecher; Writer: Irving Brecher; DP: William Daniels; Ed: Milton Carruth; Prod Design: Bernard Herzbrun, John De Cuir; Composer: Frank Skinner. B&W, 87 min.

Life with Father
(1947) Warner Bros.
A family favorite adapted from a Broadway show inspired by Clarence O'Day, Jr.'s memoir of his childhood in turn-of-the-century New York City. The family, including three carrot-topped brothers and a wise mother (Dunne, in one of her specialties), revolves around the stern, but eccentric and loving father (Powell). Based on Howard Lindsay and Russell Crouse's Broadway play. Academy Award Nominations: 4, including Best Actor: William Powell. **Cast:** William Powell, Irene Dunne, Elizabeth Taylor, ZaSu Pitts, Martin Milner, Edmund Gwenn, James Lydon, Emma Dunn. **Credits:** Dir: Michael Curtiz; Prod: Robert Buckner; Writer: Donald Ogden Stewart; DP: Peverell Marley, William V. Skall; Ed: George Amy; Prod Design: Robert M. Haas; Composer: Max Steiner. Color, 130 min. **VHS**

The Light in the Forest
(1958) Disney
A wonderful Disney drama for young folks about a young white man raised by Indians who finds difficulty adjusting to his old home. Parker oversees MacArthur's return to his white family after a peace treaty with the Indians is signed. Lynley, in her first role, initially despises and then comes to love MacArthur and helps him make the adjustment. **Cast:** Carol Lynley, James MacArthur, Fess Parker, Wendell Corey, Joanne Dru, Jessica Tandy, Joseph Calleia, John McIntire, Rafael Campos, Frank Ferguson, Marian Seldes. **Credits:** Dir: Herschel Daugherty; Prod: Walt Disney; Writer: Lawrence Edward Watkin; Story: Conrad Richter; DP: Ellsworth Fredericks; Ed: Stanley Johnson. Color, 92 min. **VHS**

The Light That Failed
(1939) Paramount
Superb retelling with fine cast of Kipling's work set against the panorama of British imperial ambition in the Sudan. Colman brings greatness to the role of the war correspondent-artist slowly losing his sight to a war wound. He creates a sensation with his portrait of courtesan Lupino (in the portrayal that made her a star), who falls in love with him but proves unable to surmount class distinctions. Rather than accepting his blindness, Colman opts for the noble gesture, seeking death in battle against the fuzzy-wuzzies. The third film try in 25 years for this Kipling story. **Cast:** Muriel Angelus, Ida Lupino, Dudley Digges, Ernest Cossart, Ferike Boros, Pedro De Cordoba, Colin Tapley, Fay Helm, Ronald Colman, Walter Huston. **Credits:** Dir: William Wellman; Prod: William Wellman; Writer: Robert Carson; Story: Rudyard Kipling; DP: Theodor Sparkuhl; Ed: Thomas Scott; Composer: Victor Young; Art Director: Hans Dreier. B&W, 97 min.

Lili
(1953) MGM
A warm, poignant musical fable about a teenage French orphan girl (Caron) who joins a carnival, moons over a magician (Aumont), and winds up in love with a bitter, wounded puppeteer (Ferrer). Caron sings the lyrical hit song "Hi-Lili, Hi-Lo." A delightful romance from Paul Gallico's story and the Broadway musical, *Carnival*. Golden Globe for Best Screenplay. Academy Award Nominations: 6, including Best Actress: Leslie Caron; Best Screenplay. **Academy Awards:** Best Music Score of a Drama/Comedy. **Cast:** Leslie Caron, Mel Ferrer, Jean-Pierre Aumont, Zsa Zsa Gabor, Kurt Kasznar, Amanda Blake, Alex Gerry, Ralph Dumke. **Credits:** Dir:

Charles Walters; Prod: Edwin H. Knopf; Writer: Helen Deutsch; DP: Robert Planck; Ed: Ferris Webster; Prod Design: Cedric Gibbons, Paul Groesse; Composer: Bronislau Kaper. Color, 81 min. **VHS**

Lilies of the Field
(1963) United Artists
Poitier won a well-deserved Oscar, a first for an African-American, for his performance as a pragmatic U.S. Army vet who agrees to build a chapel for and teach English to five East German nuns. A subtly powerful small movie that won hearts. Academy Award Nominations: 5, including Best Picture; Best (Adapted) Screenplay. **Academy Awards:** Best Actor: Sidney Poitier. **Cast:** Sidney Poitier, Lilia Skala, Lisa Mann, Isa Crino, Stanley Adams, Ralph Nelson. **Credits:** Dir: Ralph Nelson; Prod: Ralph Nelson; Writer: James Poe; Story: William E. Barrett; DP: Ernest Haller; Ed: John McCafferty; Composer: Jerry Goldsmith. B&W, 94 min. **VHS**

Lilith
(1964) Columbia
Director Rossen's (*All the King's Men*, 1949; *The Hustler*, 1961) final film, a portrait of a troubled mind, may have reflected the writer-director's own feelings of being divided against himself. An inactive member of the Communist Party in the '40s, Rossen first refused to name for the House Un-American Activities Committee his associates in Hollywood; at a later special session he did, a tormenting decision. He withdrew from sight, coming back in the early '60s with *The Hustler* and this turbulent, stark story of a young psychiatrist (Beatty) who falls for a schizophrenic patient (Seberg). Rossen died before its release. **Cast:** Warren Beatty, Jean Seberg, Kim Hunter, Peter Fonda, Gene Hackman, Jessica Walter, James Patterson, Robert Reilly. **Credits:** Dir: Robert Rossen; Prod: Robert Rossen; Writer: Robert Rossen; Story: J. R. Salamanca; DP: Eugen Schufftan; Ed: Aram Avakian; Prod Design: Richard Sylbert; Composer: Kenyon Hopkins. B&W, 114 min. **VHS**

Limelight
(1951) United Artists
A winsome fable of music-hall performer Chaplin regaining his love of life after turning a young ballerina (a radiant, 19-year-old Bloom) from suicide. Chaplin and Keaton's only screen appearance together comes in a nostalgic vaudeville skit. Chaplin

also wrote the lovely score, for which he earned an Oscar (in 1971!). Chaplin's daughter Geraldine makes her screen debut. **Academy Awards:** Best Original Dramatic Score. **Cast:** Charlie Chaplin, Claire Bloom, Sydney Chaplin, Geraldine Chaplin, Nigel Bruce, Buster Keaton, Andre Eglevsky, Melissa Hayden, Norman Lloyd. **Credits:** Dir: Charlie Chaplin; Prod: Charlie Chaplin; Writer: Charlie Chaplin; DP: Karl Struss; Ed: Joe Inge; Art Director: Eugene Laurie; Composer: Charlie Chaplin. B&W, 137 min. **VHS, LASER**

The Lion in Winter
(1968) Avco Embassy
O'Toole's second appearance as Henry II (he first played the role in *Becket*, 1964) is a magnificent portrait of a man facing the passage of his time on Earth and a monarch ambivalently yielding the reins of power. Hepburn won an Oscar—she shared it with Streisand for *Funny Girl*—for her portrayal of Henry's wife, Eleanor of Aquitaine, as a flinty advocate for her agenda in the succession struggle between their three sons. Hopkins and Dalton make their film debuts. Adapted by Goldman from his play. The 25th anniversary video release includes a digitally remastered edition packaged in a distinctive, book-style box with behind-the-scenes stories and exclusive photos of the making of the film. Academy Award Nominations: 7, including Best Picture; Best Director; Best Actor: Peter O'Toole. **Academy Awards:** Best Actress: Katharine Hepburn; Best Screenplay Based on Material from Another Medium; Best Original Score. **Cast:** Peter O'Toole, Katharine Hepburn, Jane Merrow, Timothy Dalton, Anthony Hopkins, John Castle, Nigel Stock, Nigel Terry. **Credits:** Dir: Anthony Harvey; Prod: Martin H. Poll; Writer: James Goldman; DP: Douglas Slocombe; Ed: John Bloom; Prod Design: Peter Murton, Gilbert Margerie; Composer: John Barry; Set Designer: Peter James. Color, 135 min. **VHS, LASER**

A Lion Is in the Streets
(1953) Warner Bros.
A spunky street con man in Louisiana puts his pitching skills to good use on the campaign trail when he decides to become a politician. Cagney's the one to watch in this Walsh fable loosely based on the mythology of Huey Long. **Cast:** James Cagney, Barbara Hale, Anne Francis, Warner Anderson, John McIntire, Jeanne Cagney, Lon Chaney, Jr., Frank McHugh. **Credits:** Dir: Raoul Walsh; Prod: William Cagney; Story: Luther Davis; DP: Harry Stradling; Ed: George Amy; Prod Design: Wiard Ihnen; Composer: Franz Waxman. Color, 88 min. **VHS, LASER**

Listen, Darling
(1938) MGM
Garland and Bartholomew play matchmakers for their widowed mother (Astor) in Garland's first starring role. Pidgeon fits the bill nicely, and Judy gets to sing "Zing! Went the Strings of My Heart," "Nobody's Baby," "Ten Pins in the Sky," and "On the Bumpy Road to Love." **Cast:** Judy Garland, Freddie Bartholomew, Mary Astor, Walter Pidgeon, Alan Hale, Scotty Beckett. **Credits:** Dir: Edwin L. Marin; Prod: Jack Cummings; Writer: Elaine Ryan, Anne Morrison Chapin; DP: Charles Lawton, Jr.; Ed: Blanche Sewell; Prod Design: Cedric Gibbons. B&W, 75 min. **VHS**

The List of Adrian Messenger
(1963) Universal
A retired army officer (Scott) receives a list from a friend who later dies in a plane crash. When Scott pursues information about the men on the list, he uncovers a brilliantly devious traitor who informed on his comrades in a Japanese prison camp in Burma, and who is eliminating those who know about it. Complex, intriguing mystery directed by Huston. Cameos by Mitchum, Sinatra, Lancaster, Douglas, and Huston. Adapted from the novel by Philip MacDonald. **Cast:** Kirk Douglas, George C. Scott, Dana Wynter, Robert Mitchum, Burt Lancaster, Tony Curtis, Frank Sinatra, Clive Brook, Herbert Marshall, Gladys Cooper. **Credits:** Dir: John Huston; Prod: Edward Lewis; Writer: Anthony Veiller; Story: Philip MacDonald; DP: Joseph MacDonald; Ed: Terry O. Morse, Hugh S. Fowler; Composer: Jerry Goldsmith; Art Director: Alexander Golitzen, Stephen Grimes, George C. Webb. B&W, 98 min. **VHS**

Little Big Man
(1970) National General
The memories of a 121-year-old survivor of Little Big Horn form the story line of this showcase for Hoffman's acting skill. As Jack Crabbe, Hoffman ages from a young man in the Wild West who is something of an innocent bystander to history in his various incarnations as a gunfighter, medicine-show huckster, adopted Indian, and intimate of Wild Bill Hickok and Custer. Hoffman gets colorful support from players such as Dunaway, Chief Dan George, Hickey, and Balsam. From Thomas Berger's novel. Academy Award Nomination for Best Supporting Actor: Chief Dan George. **Cast:** Dustin Hoffman, Martin Balsam, Faye Dunaway, Richard Mulligan, Chief Dan George, Jeff Corey, William Hickey, Aimee Eccles, Kelly Jean Peters. **Credits:** Dir: Arthur Penn; Prod: Stuart Millar; Writer: Calder Willingham; DP: Harry Stradling; Ed: Dede Allen; Prod Design: Dean Tavoularis; SFX: Dick Smith; Art Director: Angelo Graham. Color, 149 min. **VHS, LASER**

Little Boy Lost
(1953) Paramount
Drama about a war correspondent (Crosby) trying to find his young son, who was lost in the war. In France, he finds an eight-year-old in an orphanage he thinks may be his own and then discovers that the kid is pretending to be his at the behest of the orphanage's Mother Superior, who wants him to find a good home. **Cast:** Bing Crosby, Claude Dauphin, Gabrielle Dorziat, Nicole Maurey, Michael Moore, Peter Baldwin. **Credits:** Dir: George Seaton; Prod: William Perlberg; Writer: George Seaton; DP: George Barnes; Composer: Johnny Burke, James Van Heusen, Victor Young; Art Director: Henry Bumstead. B&W, 95 min.

Little Caesar
(1930) Warner Bros.
This role made Robinson a star and set the standard for the innumerable Warner gangster pics that followed. The familiar story (based loosely on the career of Al Capone) follows the rise of Rico Bandello from street tough to emperor of gangland—and his equally rapid fall from power. Robinson's two-fisted performance and trademark delivery, *see*, erased memories of his 15-year career on Broadway and made it hard for Hollywood to see him as anything but a ruthless mobster for years. We see this as an interesting film genre forerunner, but in its own time it had the impact of a tabloid headline. Academy Award Nomination for Best Adapted Writing. **Cast:** Edward G. Robinson, Douglas Fairbanks, Jr., Stanley Fields, Glenda Farrell, Thomas Jackson. **Credits:** Dir: Mervyn LeRoy; Prod: Hal B. Wallis; Writer: W. R. Burnett, Robert N. Lee, Darryl F. Zanuck, Francis Edward Faragoh; DP: Tony Gaudio; Ed: Ray Curtiss; Prod Design: Anton Grot. B&W, 81 min. **VHS**

The Little Colonel

(1935) Fox

Little Shirley generally manages to bring sunshine to every situation, and here she even brings harmony to the hard feelings left over from the Civil War. Barrymore can't stand the thought of his daughter (Venable) being married to a damn Yankee (Lodge), and it rankles to have to take them in when times get hard. Temple wins him over in her own benign version of Reconstruction. This features the famous step dance with Bill Robinson and it helps offset the otherwise patronizing tone. **Cast:** Shirley Temple, Bill Robinson, Lionel Barrymore, Evelyn Venable, John Lodge, Sidney Blackmer, Stephan Chase. **Credits:** Dir: David Butler; Prod: B. G. DeSylva; Writer: William Conselman; Story: Annie Fellows Johnston; DP: Arthur C. Miller, William V. Skall; Composer: Arthur Lange, Cyril Mockridge; Art Director: William S. Darling. B&W, 80 min. **VHS, LASER**

The Little Foxes

(1941) RKO

The third of Davis's portrayals of icy women for director Wyler (the others were *Jezebel*, 1938, and *The Letter*, 1940), and perhaps the finest, though she never thought so herself and clashed constantly with the director on the set. Davis manipulates, blackmails, and finally needles her husband (Marshall) to an early grave in one of the boldest portrayals of avarice ever put on-screen. When her brothers come to her needing money for an exploitative business scheme, she sends for Marshall, who's recuperating from a heart attack. The would-be mill owners realize they'll never see the money from their principled brother-in-law and resort to stealing bonds from him. Davis seizes the opportunity to blackmail her brothers, and when her husband foils her scheme, she ignores his cries for help as he suffers another attack. Scripted by Hellman from her play (though with help from Dorothy Parker, among others), and with justly renowned camerawork by Toland, who also shot *Citizen Kane* (1941). Here, Toland employs the same deep-focus techniques that made *Kane* a cinema breakthrough. Hellman's prequel is *Another Part of the Forest* (1948). Academy Award Nominations: 9, including Best Picture; Best Director; Best Actress: Bette Davis; Best Screenplay. **Cast:** Bette Davis, Herbert Marshall, Dan Duryea, Teresa Wright, Richard Carlson, Patricia Collinge, Charles Dingle,

The Little Foxes (1941)

Carl Benton Reid, Russell Hicks. **Credits:** Dir: William Wyler; Prod: Samuel Goldwyn; Writer: Lillian Hellman, Arthur Kober, Dorothy Parker, Alan Campbell; DP: Gregg Toland; Ed: Daniel Mandell; Composer: Meredith Willson; Art Director: Stephen Goosson; Set Designer: Howard Bristol. B&W, 116 min. **VHS, LASER, DVD**

Little Fugitive

(1953)

When a seven-year-old Brooklyn boy's older brother tricks him into thinking the tyke has killed him, the youngster takes what money he can find and hightails it to Coney Island. While his brother searches for him, the runaway Gene Autry fan encounters adventures among the summer throngs. A pioneering independent film from writer-producer-director Engel, it won the Silver Lion Award at the 1953 Venice Film Festival. Selected for the National Film Registry in 1997. Academy Award Nomination for Best Motion Picture Story. **Cast:** Richie Andrusco, Ricky Brewster, Will Lee. **Credits:** Dir: Morris Engel, Ruth Orkin, Ray Ashley; Prod: Morris Engel, Ray Ashley; Writer: Morris Engel, Ray Ashley, Ruth Orkin; Composer: Eddy Manson. B&W, 80 min. **VHS**

The Little Girl Who Lives Down the Lane

(1976) AIP

There's something odd about young Foster. No one has seen her father for some time now and Foster seems to take care of all the household affairs.

The self-sufficient teenager has plenty of chores to do, including keeping snooping neighbors away from her basement. Sheen gets more than he bargains for when he tries to upset the perfect, adult-free world Foster creates with Jacoby. A chilling tale with plenty of surprises. **Cast:** Jodie Foster, Martin Sheen, Alexis Smith, Scott Jacoby, Mort Shuman. **Credits:** Dir: Nicolas Gessner; Prod: Zev Braun; Writer: Richard S. Lochte, Laird Koenig; DP: Rene Verzier; Ed: Yves Langlois; Prod Design: Robert Prevost; Composer: Christian Gaubert. Color, 94 min. **VHS, LASER**

Little Lord Fauntleroy

(1936) United Artists

A crusty, old British nobleman (Smith) and a lonely, orphaned New York lad (Bartholomew) each find the warmth and attachment they need when the poor boy is discovered to be the heir to a British peerage. Rags-to-riches tales had an obvious appeal in the Depression era, but the winning performances and well-loved story make this terrific family fare for today as well. Remade for TV here and in Britain. Based on Burnett's 1886 story. **Cast:** C. Aubrey Smith, Freddie Bartholomew, Mickey Rooney, Dolores Costello, Guy Kibbee, Henry Stephenson, Eric Alden, Jackie Searl, Reginald Barlow, Ivan Simpson, E. E. Clive. **Credits:** Dir: John Cromwell; Prod: David O. Selznick; Writer: Hugh Walpole; Story: Frances Hodgson Burnett; DP: Charles Rosher; Ed: Hal C. Kern; Composer: Max Steiner. B&W, 105 min. **VHS**

Little Man, What Now?

(1934) Universal
A German couple, and eventually their infant son (the "Little Man" of the title), struggle to retain employment and make ends meet during difficult times when they move from their little village to the wide-open big city of Berlin. The love between the husband and wife endures trials and poverty. A rare glimpse at the hardships of Weimar Germany directed by Borzage, one of the great practitioners of the sentimental Hollywood romance. **Cast:** Douglass Montgomery, Alan Hale, Catharine Doucet, Fred Kohler, Mae Marsh, De Witt Jennings, Alan Mowbray, Mort Shuman, Hedda Hopper, Sarah Padden. **Credits:** Dir: Frank Borzage; Prod: Carl Laemmle; Writer: Hans Fallada, William Anthony McGuire; DP: Norbert F. Brodine; Ed: Milton Carruth; Art Director: Charles D. Hall. B&W, 95 min.

The Little Minister

(1934) RKO
The first talkie version of Barrie's novel (it was a play, a radio drama, and there were two silent-film versions) was also an early outing for a spirited Hepburn. Proper young minister Beal meets free-spirit Hepburn, whom he believes to be a Gypsy, when she covertly aids the local weavers in their battle with the manufacturers. After they fall in love, he learns she is really the ward of the local earl. Pleasant enough costumer with Hepburn's youthful fire. **Cast:** Katharine Hepburn, Donald Crisp, John Beal, Andy Clyde, Beryl Mercer, Bill Watson, Dorothy Stickney, Mary Gordon, Frank Conroy, Barlowe Borland. **Credits:** Dir: Richard Wallace; Prod: Pandro S. Berman; Writer: Jane Murfin, Sarah Y. Mason, Victor Heerman, Mortimer Offner, Jack Wagner; Story: J. M. Barrie; DP: Henry Gerrard; Ed: William Hamilton; Composer: Max Steiner. B&W, 110 min. **VHS, LASER**

Little Miss Broadway

(1938) Fox
Shirley brings sunshine to the fading denizens of a residential hotel populated by ex–show people, including song-and-dance man Durante. Manager Oliver despises her colorful clientele, but her nephew Murphy cozies up to the old codgers. Trademark Temple tunes include "Be Optimistic," "If All the World Were Paper," "Swing Me an Old-Fashioned Song," "I'll Build a Broadway for You," and "We Should Be Together." **Cast:** Shirley Temple, Jimmy Durante, George Murphy, Phyllis Brooks, Edna May Oliver. **Credits:**

Dir: Irving Cummings; Prod: Darryl F. Zanuck; Writer: Harry Tugend, Jack Yellen; DP: Arthur Miller; Ed: Walter Thompson. B&W, 70 min. **VHS**

Little Miss Marker

(1934) Paramount
The Runyon tale of bookie Sorrowful Jones is a Hollywood favorite (there are at least four versions), but this is the best of the lot. Menjou couldn't be better as Jones, who receives Temple as the collateral on a debt. Little Miss Sunshine warms up the wisecrackers and racetrack rogues who populate Runyon's world. Remakes include *Sorrowful Jones* (1949) and *Forty Pounds of Trouble* (1962). **Cast:** Shirley Temple, Adolphe Menjou, Dorothy Dell, Charles Bickford, Lynne Overman, Garry Owen, Willie Best. **Credits:** Dir: Alexander Hall; Prod: B. P. Schulberg; Writer: William R. Lipman, Sam Hellman, Gladys Lehman; DP: Alfred Gilks; Ed: William Shea. B&W, 79 min. **VHS**

Little Murders

(1971) Fox
The Newquists are a typical American family, living in a terror-ridden neighborhood in an explosive city. They have already lost a son to a street sniper and, tired of being victims, take up guns and become snipers in their own right and fight back. A grim view of New York in the black comedy of an ambivalent romance. Feiffer adapted his own bleakly humorous play, directed by actor Arkin. **Cast:** Elliott Gould, Donald Sutherland, Vincent Gardenia, Alan Arkin, Lou Jacobi, Marcia Rodd, Jon Korkes, Elizabeth Wilson. **Credits:** Dir: Alan Arkin; Prod: Jack Brodsky, Elliott Gould; Writer: Jules Feiffer; DP: Gordon Willis; Ed: Howard Kuperman; Prod Design: Gene Rudolf; Composer: Fred Kaz; Set Designer: Philip Smith. Color, 107 min. **VHS**

Little Nellie Kelly

(1940) MGM
Grim premise for an otherwise light-hearted Garland musical. Garland plays both an Irish immigrant who dies in childbirth, and also her daughter, who negotiates between her Irish cop husband (Murphy) and her father (Winninger) while trying to make it on Broadway. Wear green while watching this one. Songs include "Nellie Is a Darling," "It's a Great Day for the Irish," "Danny Boy," and "Singing in the Rain." **Cast:** Judy Garland, George Murphy, Charles Winninger, Douglas McPhail, Arthur Shields, Forrester Harvey. **Credits:** Dir: Norman Taurog;

Prod: Arthur Freed; Writer: Jack McGowan; DP: Ray June; Ed: Fredrick Y. Smith; Prod Design: Cedric Gibbons; Composer: Roger Edens; Set Designer: Edwin B. Willis. B&W, 100 min. **VHS**

A Little Night Music

(1978) New World
An international adaptation of Sondheim's most hummable musical, which was itself based on Ingmar Bergman's film *Smiles of a Summer Night*. A group of old friends meet at a country house and renew old romances, wounds, and friendships. Directed by Prince, who had handled the Broadway chores as well. The magnificent songs include the familiar "Send in the Clowns," "Every Day a Little Death," and "You Must Meet My Wife." **Academy Awards:** Best Original Song Score and Adaptation. **Cast:** Elizabeth Taylor, Diana Rigg, Len Cariou, Lesley-Anne Down, Hermione Gingold, Christopher Guard, Chloe Franks, Jonathan Tunick, Laurence Guittard, Heinz Maracek. **Credits:** Dir: Harold Prince; Prod: Elliott Kastner; Story: Hugh Wheeler; DP: Arthur Ibbetson; Ed: John Jympson; Prod Design: Laci von Ronay; Composer: Stephen Sondheim; Art Director: Thomas Riccabona, Herta Pischinger. Color, 124 min. **VHS, LASER**

The Little Prince

(1974) Paramount
Donen directs a deep roster of musical veterans in a film adaptation of the timeless fable by Saint-Exupery. Lerner and Loewe songs and Fosse choreography are high points; the whimsical tale suffers somewhat in the translation. Academy Award Nominations: Best Song ("Little Prince"); Best Original Song Score. **Cast:** Richard Kiley, Bob Fosse, Steven Warner, Gene Wilder, Donna McKechnie, Joss Ackland, Clive Revill, Victor Spinetti, Graham Crowden. **Credits:** Dir: Stanley Donen; Prod: Stanley Donen; Writer: Alan J. Lerner; Story: Antoine De Saint-Exupery; DP: Christopher Challis; Ed: Peter Boita; Composer: Frederick Loewe. Color, 88 min. **VHS**

The Little Princess

(1939) Fox
One of Temple's most memorable films, and her first Technicolor production. After escaping from a miserable boarding school, little Shirley rides to the rescue of her wounded pop (Hunter) as he languishes in a Boer War field hospital. She charms his memory back and all is well. Standard Temple plot with more action than

most. **Cast:** Shirley Temple, Richard Greene, Ian Hunter, Cesar Romero, Arthur Treacher, Mary Nash, Sybil Jason, Miles Mander, Marcia Mae Jones, Beryl Mercer. **Credits:** Dir: Walter Lang; Prod: Gene Markey; Writer: Ethel Hill, Walter Ferris; Story: Frances Hodgson Burnett; DP: Arthur Miller, William V. Skall; Ed: Louis R. Loeffler; Composer: Walter Bullock, Samuel Pokrass. Color, 94 min. VHS, LASER, DVD

A Little Romance
(1979) Orion
An American girl (Lane) in Paris as her mother (Kellerman) chases a movie director meets a charming French boy (Bernard) who is a dedicated movie fan and has an equally high IQ. The two teens fall in love and pursue a romantic odyssey when charming petty thief Olivier passes on a legend about the enduring love of those who kiss under Venice's Bridge of Sighs. Utterly delightful. Academy Award Nominations: Best (Adapted) Screenplay; Best Original Score. **Academy Awards:** Best Original Score. **Cast:** Laurence Olivier, Thelonius Bernard, Diane Lane, Arthur Hill, Sally Kellerman, Broderick Crawford, David Dukes, Andrew Duncan. **Credits:** Dir: George Roy Hill; Prod: Robert L. Crawford, Yves Rousset-Rouard; Story: Allan Burns; DP: Pierre-William Glenn; Ed: William H. Reynolds; Prod Design: Henry Bumstead; Composer: Georges Delerue; Art Director: Francois de Lamothe. Color, 105 min. VHS

Little Shop of Horrors
(1960) AIP
Corman's most famous horror parody (mostly for being shot in record time) has spawned a musical and a 1986 screen version of the musical starring Rick Moranis. The story, such as it is, introduces a mild-mannered florist's helper, who turns a houseplant into a ravenous, talking ("Feed me! Feed me!"), man-eating monster, Audrey, Jr. Nicholson appears in an equally famous scene as a dental patient who can take as much pain as the dentist can dish out. Good, silly fun. **Cast:** Dick Miller, Jack Nicholson, Jackie Joseph, Jonathan Haze, Mel Welles. **Credits:** Dir: Roger Corman; Prod: Roger Corman; Writer: Charles B. Griffith; DP: Arch Dalzell; Ed: Marshal Neilan; Composer: Fred Katz. B&W, 73 min. VHS, LASER

The Littlest Horse Thieves
(1976) Disney
In turn-of-the-century England, three young folks rescue the horses who work in the mines from their cruel hardships. They succeed in hiding the horses, but the little herd may end up in the slaughterhouse unless their stepfather convinces the miners to come to their rescue. Beautifully filmed on location in England. **Cast:** Peter Barkworth, Maurice Colbourne, Susan Tebbs, Alistair Sim, Geraldine McEwan, Chloe Franks, Prunella Scales. **Credits:** Dir: Charles Jarrott; Prod: Ron Miller; Writer: Rosemary Anne Sisson; DP: Paul Beeson; Ed: Richard Marden. Color, 104 min. VHS

The Littlest Outlaw
(1954) Disney
An unusual Disney drama that reaches for the impact of docudrama. A Mexican boy takes pity on a horse that's being trained through torture and which is ordered killed when it throws the daughter of the local general. He rides away with the steed and their bond grows as they face dangers such as the pursuing general and a turn around the bullring. Well done adventure for older kids. **Cast:** Pedro Armendariz, Joseph Calleia, Rodolfo Acosta, Andres Velasquez, Pedro Vargas. **Credits:** Dir: Roberto Gavaldon; Prod: Larry Lansburgh; Writer: Bill Walsh; Story: Larry Lansburgh; DP: Alex Phillips; Ed: Carlos Savage; Composer: William Lava. Color, 73 min. VHS

The Littlest Rebel
(1935) Fox
Little Shirley comes to the rescue of a parent once again, this time Boles as a rebel officer trying to sneak through Union lines to visit his sick wife. When her pop's about to be executed, little miss sunshine drops by the White House for a chat with Honest Abe, thus sparing Dad and the president. Dancing with Robinson ("Polly Wolly Doodle") is again the highlight. **Cast:** Shirley Temple, John Boles, Bill Robinson, Jack Holt, Karen Morley, Willie Best, Frank McGlynn. **Credits:** Dir: David Butler; Prod: B. G. DeSylva; Writer: Edwin Burke, Harry Tugend; Story: Edward Peple; DP: John F. Seitz; Ed: Irene Morra; Art Director: William S. Darling; Set Designer: Thomas Little. B&W, 73 min. VHS

Little Women
(1933) RKO
Could there be a better Jo than Hepburn, the flashing pride, the determined set of jaw, the coltish energy? Director Cukor sets Hepburn at the center of a wonderful cast that includes Oliver, Bennett, Byington, and lets her light up the screen. This is the cream of the many adaptations (it was also produced in 1949, 1978, and 1994) of Alcott's beloved novel of teenage girls finding their way to adulthood during the Civil War that has taken the men from their lives. Marvelously entertaining family fare. Academy Award Nominations: 3, including Best Picture; Best Director. **Academy Awards:** Best Adapted Screenplay. **Cast:** Katharine Hepburn, Joan Bennett, Frances Dee, Jean Parker, Edna May Oliver, Paul Lukas, Henry Stephenson, Douglass Montgomery, John Lodge, Spring Byington. **Credits:** Dir: George Cukor; Prod: Kenneth MacGowan; Writer: Victor Heerman, Sarah Y. Mason; Story: Louisa May Alcott; DP: Henry Gerrard; Ed: Jack Kitchin; Composer: Max Steiner; Costumes: Maryann Plunkett; SFX: Harry Redmond. B&W, 116 min. VHS, LASER

Little Women
(1949) MGM
Postwar version of Alcott's story of four New England sisters at the time of the Civil War adds Technicolor and Taylor, and worth watching as a comparison to the incomparable 1933 version. Academy Award Nominations: Best (Color) Cinematography; Best Art Direction—Set Decoration (Color). **Academy Awards:** Best Art Direction—Set Decoration (Color). **Cast:** June Allyson, Peter Lawford, Margaret O'Brien, Elizabeth Taylor, Janet Leigh, Rossano Brazzi, Mary Astor. **Credits:** Dir: Mervyn LeRoy; Prod: Mervyn LeRoy; Writer: Andrew Solt; Story: Louisa May Alcott; DP: Robert Planck; Ed: Ralph E. Winters; Prod Design: Cedric Gibbons; Composer: Adolph Deutsch; Art Director: Paul Groesse. Color, 122 min. VHS

Live a Little, Love a Little
(1968) MGM
Elvis is a busy boy on the job front and juggling girls. Presley sheds his wholesome on-screen image and goes mod as a jet-setting, turtlenecked playboy photographer whose swingin' lifestyle is derailed by a flaky, domineering vixen with designs on his bachelorhood. Vallee tries to stay hip. Songs include "A Little Less Conversation," "Edge of Reality," and "Wonderful World." **Cast:** Elvis Presley, Rudy Vallee, Michele Carey, Dick Sargent, Don Porter, Sterling Holloway, Celeste Yarnall, Eddie Hodges. **Credits:** Dir: Norman Taurog; Prod: Douglas Laurence; Writer: Michael A. Hoey; DP: Fred Koenekamp; Ed: John McSweeney, Jr.; Composer: Billy

Strange; Art Director: George W. Davis, Preston Ames; Set Designer: Henry Grace. Color, 90 min. **VHS, LASER**

Live and Let Die
(1973) United Artists
The first Bond incarnation by Moore seems to pump up the volume and chase scenes to distract from the lack of Sean Connery. Bond's opponent: Dr. Kananga, a black criminal mastermind who combines drugs and voodoo into a potent weapon for world domination. The title song was a hit for Paul McCartney and Wings. Academy Award Nomination for Best Song ("Live and Let Die"). **Cast:** Roger Moore, Jane Seymour, Yaphet Kotto, Clifton James, Julius Harris, Geoffrey Holder, David Hedison, Gloria Hendry. **Credits:** Dir: Guy Hamilton; Prod: Albert R. Broccoli, Harry Saltzman; Writer: Tom Mankiewicz; DP: Ted Moore; Ed: Bert Bates, Raymond Poulton, John Shirley; Prod Design: Syd Cain; Composer: George Martin; Art Director: Syd Cain. Color, 121 min. **VHS, LASER**

The Lives of a Bengal Lancer
(1935) Paramount
One of the greatest of Hollywood adventure stories and a breakthrough for both Cooper and director Hathaway, who became known for his attention to detail and use of authentic locations. Hathaway himself shot some of the exotic northwestern India locations for this heart-quickening tale of three soldiers in the famous British regiment. Cooper is the old hand who reins in gung-ho Tone and takes Cromwell, the bitter son of the commander, under his wing. Much derring-do, including a climactic battle that finds the trio fighting from inside the enemy's mountain fortress as the Lancers lay siege from the outside. Academy Award Nominations: 8, including Best Picture; Best Director; Best Screenplay. **Academy Awards:** Best Assistant Director. **Cast:** Gary Cooper, Franchot Tone, Richard Cromwell, Guy Standing, C. Aubrey Smith, Monte Blue, Kathleen Burke, Colin Tapley, Jameson Thomas, Rollo Lloyd. **Credits:** Dir: Henry Hathaway; Prod: Louis D. Lighton; Writer: Waldemar Young, John L. Balderston, Achmed Abdullah, Grover Jones, William Slavens McNutt; Story: Major Francis Yeats-Brown; DP: Charles B. Lang, Ernest B. Schoedsack; Ed: Ellsworth Hoagland; Composer: Milan Roder; Art Director: Hans Dreier, Roland Anderson. B&W, 110 min. **VHS, LASER**

Living in a Big Way
(1947) MGM
A musical based on an emotional consequence of wartime works when Kelly dances. Kelly stars as an ex-G.I. who has to get to know his hurriedly romanced wartime bride (McDonald) and her overbearing father (Winninger) and family. Minor-league but worthwhile for Kelly enthusiasts. **Cast:** Spring Byington, Gene Kelly, Marie McDonald, Phyllis Thaxter, Charles Winninger, Clinton Sundberg. **Credits:** Dir: Gregory La Cava; Prod: Pandro S. Berman; Writer: Gregory La Cava, Irving Ravetch; DP: Harold Rosson; Ed: Ferris Webster; Prod Design: Cedric Gibbons; Choreographer: Gene Kelly; Art Director: William Ferrari. B&W, 104 min. **VHS**

Living It Up
(1954) Paramount
Martin and Lewis step into the *Nothing Sacred* (1937) scenario as Lewis, who believes he has but a few months to live, accepts an offer of a last fling by newspaper reporter Leigh. Better-than-average outing for the boys, mostly for the pedigree of the material. Songs include "How Do You Speak to an Angel," "Champagne and Wedding Cake," and "Money Burns a Hole in My Pocket." **Cast:** Dean Martin, Jerry Lewis, Janet Leigh, Edward Arnold, Fred Clark, Sheree North, Sam White, Richard Loo, Raymond Greenleaf. **Credits:** Dir: Norman Taurog; Prod: Paul Jones; Writer: Jack Rose, Melville Shavelson; Story: Ben Hecht, Jule Styne; DP: Daniel Fapp; Ed: Archie Marshek; Choreographer: Nick Castle; Composer: Walter Scharf; Art Director: Albert Nozaki, Hal Pereira. Color, 94 min.

Local Boy Makes Good
(1931) Warner Bros.
Early talkie romantic comedy showcase for Brown, as a quiet, well-mannered florist whose infatuation for the lovely Lee occupies his daydreams. Brown writes Lee a love letter, which he never intends to mail, and it contains a few embellishments regarding his athletic prowess at the local university. But when John's friend mails the letter, Julia's interests are piqued and our young hero must rise to the occasion, becoming the track star he described. **Cast:** Joe E. Brown, Dorothy Lee, Ruth Hall, Edward Woods, Edward J. Nugent. **Credits:** Dir: Mervyn LeRoy; Prod: Robert Lord; Writer: Robert Lord; Story: Elliott Nugent; DP: Sol Polito; Ed: Jack Killifer; Composer: Leo F. Forbstein; Art Director: Jack Okey. B&W, 67 min.

The Lodger
(1944) Fox
Jack the Ripper haunts the London of 1889 in this superior remake of Alfred Hitchcock's 1926 silent. When a middle-aged couple and their actress daughter (Oberon) take in a lodger (Cregar), he refuses to join them at meals, leaves the house at night with a little black bag, and, when at home, locks himself in his room performing unspecified experiments. His suspicious behavior piques the interest of Oberon's boyfriend (Sanders), a Scotland Yarder on the trail of the Ripper. The policeman's growing suspicions turn to action just in time to protect Oberon from the lodger's unwholesome attentions. Cregar made something of a specialty of these creepy roles, though his obsession with becoming a matinee idol led to his death from a starvation diet just after this was released. **Cast:** Laird Cregar, George Sanders, Merle Oberon, Cedric Hardwicke, Sara Allgood. **Credits:** Dir: John Brahm; Prod: Robert Bassler; Writer: Barre Lyndon; Story: Marie Belloc Lowndes; DP: Lucien Ballard; Ed: J. Watson Webb, Jr.; Prod Design: James Basevi, John Ewing; Composer: Hugo Friedhofer. B&W, 84 min.

Logan's Run
(1976) United Artists
In 2274, life is an unending pursuit of pleasure. The catch is that life ends at the age of 30. York plays a policeman nearing the statutory limit who refuses to go gracefully. A handsome cast including Fawcett and Agutter, and an intriguing sci-fi premise based on the novel by William Nolan and George Clayton. Academy Award Nominations: 2, including Best Cinematography. **Academy Awards:** Best Visual Effects. **Cast:** Michael York, Jenny Agutter, Peter Ustinov, Richard Jordan, Farrah Fawcett, Roscoe Lee Browne. **Credits:** Dir: Michael Anderson; Prod: Saul David; Writer: David Zelag Goodman; DP: Ernest Laszlo; Ed: Bob Wyman; Prod Design: Dale Hennesy; Composer: Jerry Goldsmith. Color, 126 min. **VHS, LASER, DVD**

Lolita
(1962) MGM
The novel that remains an unquenchable controversy as adapted for the screen by its author, Nabokov. While the novel, though once banned, is accepted in most quarters as a masterpiece, this film version by Kubrick is hotly debated. A professor (Mason) who takes rooms in a widow's home conceives a distracting obsession with

her teenage daughter, eventually marrying the grasping mother (Winters) in order to remain close to Lolita (Lyon). The triangle results in murder and humiliation. Lyon seems a bit too knowing as the object of obsession, and Sellers's Quilty seems to have dropped in on his way to Mars, but the overall effect is as absorbing and repellent as a slow-motion car crash. The 1998 remake by Adrian Lyne starring Jeremy Irons renewed the controversy with an even closer reading of the novel and its resultant inability to find a U.S. release until the Showtime cable network stepped forward. Academy Award Nomination for Best (Adapted) Screenplay. **Cast:** James Mason, Shelley Winters, Peter Sellers, Sue Lyon, Jerry Stovin, Gary Cockrell, Diana Decker. **Credits:** Dir: Stanley Kubrick; Prod: James B. Harris; Writer: Vladimir Nabokov; DP: Oswald Morris; Ed: Anthony Harvey; Composer: Nelson Riddle; Art Director: Bill Andrews; Set Designer: Andrew Low, Peter James. B&W, 152 min. VHS, LASER

Lonely Are the Brave
(1962) Universal
An elegy for the passing of the West's cult of the resourceful individual who bucks the constraints of fences and boundaries. Douglas embodies the spirit perfectly in this modern-day Western as a cowboy who makes a break from jail and leads his pursuers on a chase by horseback. He's no match for the police and their cars, radios, and other modern means of pursuit. Trumbo wrote the script based on the novel *The Brave Cowboy* by Edward Abbey. **Cast:** Kirk Douglas, Walter Matthau, George Kennedy, Carroll O'Connor, Gena Rowlands, William Schallert, Karl Swenson. **Credits:** Dir: David Miller; Prod: Edward Lewis; Writer: Dalton Trumbo; DP: Philip H. Lathrop; Ed: Leon Barsha, Edward Mann; Composer: Jerry Goldsmith; Art Director: Alexander Golitzen, Robert Smith. B&W, 107 min. VHS, LASER

Lonelyhearts
(1958) United Artists
Adaptation of a story from the author of *The Day of the Locust* finds aspiring reporter Clift working his way up from the bottom of the newspaper heap as the paper's "agony aunt" columnist, Miss Lonelyhearts. His boredom turns to an almost sick fascination with the problems of his readers, and his involvement in their lives causes more harm than good. Great cast, including Stapleton's debut as a pitifully lonely letter-writer. Academy Award Nomina-

tion for Best Supporting Actress: Maureen Stapleton. **Cast:** Montgomery Clift, Myrna Loy, Robert Ryan, Dolores Hart, Maureen Stapleton, Frank Maxwell, Jackie Coogan, Mike Kellin, Frank Overton. **Credits:** Dir: Vincent J. Donehue, William Reilly; Prod: Dore Schary; Story: Nathanael West; DP: John Alton; Ed: Aaron Stell, John Faure; Composer: Conrad Salinger; Art Director: Serge Krizman; Set Designer: Darrell Silvera. B&W, 104 min. VHS

The Lonely Man
(1957) Paramount
An attempt to recast the 1941 Wayne starrer *Shepherd of the Hills*, with the attention now on the relationship between the gunfighter father and his resentful son. Palance comes back to the family ranch after 17 years to retire his well-used six-shooter and reclaim the love of his son, Perkins, who harbors a smoldering hatred for the father who deserted him. Palance also has to face retribution from Van Cleef and Brand for taking Brand's woman. More emotional depth than the average oater. **Cast:** Jack Palance, Anthony Perkins, Neville Brand, Robert Middleton, Elaine Aiken, Lee Van Cleef, Claude Akins, Elisha Cook, Denver Pyle. **Credits:** Dir: Henry Levin; Prod: Pat Duggan; Writer: Harry Essex, Rob Smith; DP: Lionel Lindon; Ed: William B. Murphy; Art Director: Hal Pereira, Roland Anderson. B&W, 87 min. VHS

Lone Star
(1952) MGM
The brawling history of Texas as told by Hollywood. Cattle rancher Gable takes an assignment from Andrew Jackson (Barrymore) to prevent Texas from becoming a republic. Crawford, as Texas founding father Sam Houston, battles Gable over territory—and romance with Gardner. Okay Western with interesting, if fanciful, premise, and appealing leads. **Cast:** Clark Gable, Ava Gardner, Lionel Barrymore, Beulah Bondi, Broderick Crawford, Ed Begley, James Burke. **Credits:** Dir: Vincent Sherman; Prod: Z. Wayne Griffin; Writer: Howard Estabrook; DP: Harold Rosson; Ed: Ferris Webster; Prod Design: Cedric Gibbons, Hans Peters; Composer: David Buttolph. B&W, 94 min. VHS

Lone Wolf
The Lone Wolf character, created by mystery writer Louis Joseph Vance, had been in celluloid for years, first featured in silent films and early talkies, before Columbia revived the series in 1935 with the rerelease of

the 1926 film *The Lone Wolf Returns*. Melvyn Douglas played Michael Lanyard, aka the Lone Wolf, the gallant former jewel thief who often returned to his previous profession to solve a mystery. Douglas only stuck around for the first entry in the stylish, long-running series. Francis Lederer took over in *The Lone Wolf in Paris* (1938). Warren William signed on for the lead in *The Lone Wolf Spy Hunt* (1939), beginning a nine-film run as the title character (and which features the best cast of the series, including Ida Lupino and Rita Hayworth). In this version of the series, the Lone Wolf often enlisted his trusty valet, Jamison (masterfully played by Eric Blore), who proved to have sticky yet nimble fingers himself. The series lasted until 1949, with Gerald Mohr playing the title role in three of the last four entries.

The Lone Wolf Returns *(1935)*
The Lone Wolf in Paris *(1938)*
The Lone Wolf Spy Hunt *(1939)*
The Lone Wolf Strikes *(1940)*
The Lone Wolf Meets a Lady *(1940)*
The Lone Wolf Takes a Chance *(1941)*
The Lone Wolf Keeps a Date *(1941)*
Secrets of the Lone Wolf *(1941)*
Counter-Espionage *(1942)*
One Dangerous Night *(1943)*
Passport to Suez *(1943)*
The Notorious Lone Wolf *(1946)*
The Lone Wolf in London *(1947)*
The Lone Wolf in Mexico *(1947)*
The Lone Wolf and His Lady *(1949)*

Long Day's Journey into Night
(1962) Embassy
The definitive film version of Eugene O'Neill's bleak drama of a family torn by secrets, vices, and guilt. Lumet's obvious skill with actors (a child actor himself, he directed for the off-Broadway stage and for live television) produces powerhouse performances from Hepburn as the mother who takes drugs to numb her abandonment, Richardson as her preening actor husband, Robards as the alcoholic son, and Stockwell as the son wasting away from TB. Harrowing drama presented by experienced talent. The 30th anniversary video release is digitally remastered and includes the original theatrical trailer. Academy Award Nomination for Best Actress: Katharine Hepburn. **Cast:** Katharine Hepburn, Jason Robards, Ralph Richardson, Dean Stockwell, Jeanne Barr. **Credits:** Dir: Sidney Lumet; Prod: Ely Landau, Jack J. Dreyfus; Writer: Eugene O'Neill; DP: Boris Kauf-

man; Ed: Ralph Rosenblum; Prod Design: Richard Sylbert; Composer: Andre Previn; Art Director: Richard Sylbert. B&W, 170 min. **VHS, LASER**

The Longest Day

(1962) Fox
Before *Saving Private Ryan* (1998), this was Hollywood's definitive statement on the D-Day assault, and the difference is revealing. Where Steven Spielberg opts for a grueling, first-person, infantryman's slog up the beach, Zanuck marshaled every resource and every star at hand to provide an omniscient general's-eye view of the unfolding battles from both sides of the front lines. Which is not to say that there aren't personal battles and moments of terror and bravery (Buttons dangling by his parachute from a church steeple, for example) amid the massive armies on the move. This ambitious undertaking by studio head Zanuck (this was a personal obsession and he supervised the production) was the most expensive black-and-white movie of the time at $10 million, and it shows in the dedication to detail as well as the stars in the field. Golden Globe for Best Black-and-White Cinematography. Academy Award Nominations: 5, including Best Picture; Best Editing. **Academy Awards:** Best Special Effects; Best Black-and-White Cinematography; Best Sound Effects. **Cast:** John Wayne, Robert Mitchum, Henry Fonda, Richard Burton, Sean Connery, Paul Anka, Robert Wagner, Red Buttons. **Credits:** Dir: Ken Annakin, Andrew Marton, Bernhard Wicki, Gerd Oswald; Prod: Darryl Zanuck; Writer: Cornelius Ryan, Romain Gary, James Jones, David Pursall, Jack Seddon; Story: Cornelius Ryan; DP: Jean Bourgoin, Henri Persin, Walter Wottitz, Guy Tabary; Ed: Samuel E. Beetley; Prod Design: Ted Haworth; Composer:

Maurice Jarre; Art Director: Leon Barsacq, Vincent Korda. B&W, 183 min. **VHS, LASER**

The Longest Yard

(1974) Paramount
Capable action film from Aldrich pits the prisoners against the guards in a no-holds-barred game of football. Former pro ballplayer Reynolds steals his girl's car and ends up in the pen under the thumb of Albert. He puts together a team to take on Albert's ringers (football fans will have fun spotting the pros, including Joe Kapp, Nitschke, and Ernie Wheelwright). Academy Award Nomination for Best Editing. **Cast:** Burt Reynolds, Eddie Albert, Dino Washington, Ray Nitschke, Sonny Sixkiller, Michael Conrad, James Hampton, Harry Caesar, John Steadman. **Credits:** Dir: Robert Aldrich, Tracy Keenan Wynn; Prod: Albert S. Ruddy; Story: Albert S. Ruddy; DP: Joseph Biroc; Ed: Michael Luciano, Allan Jacobs, George Hively; Prod Design: James D. Vance; Composer: Frank DeVol. Color, 123 min. **VHS, LASER**

The Long Goodbye

(1973) United Artists
A Philip Marlowe for the antiestablishment era, as Gould shuffles amiably through Altman's take on the private-eye genre. Gould ferries a friend (former baseball ne'er-do-well Bouton) to Tijuana before learning that he is wanted for the murder of his wife. Gould's investigation turns up eccentric psychologists, affairs, and theft. From Chandler's next-to-last novel, though Altman's version may render it unrecognizable to those who only know the book. Director Rydell (*On Golden Pond*, 1981) appears as a vicious mobster whose henchman is Schwarzenegger in his second film appearance. Screenwriter Brackett had cowritten *The Big Sleep* (1946).

Cast: Elliott Gould, Nina Van Pallandt, Sterling Hayden, Henry Gibson, Mark Rydell, Jim Bouton, David Arkin, Warren Berlinger, Arnold Schwarzenegger. **Credits:** Dir: Robert Altman; Prod: Jerry Bick; Writer: Leigh Brackett; Story: Raymond Chandler; DP: Vilmos Zsigmond; Ed: Lou Lombardo; Composer: John Williams. Color, 113 min. **VHS, LASER**

The Long Gray Line

(1955) Columbia
A respectful biography of a West Point institution, the assistant athletic director who was a father figure for generations of cadets. As he looks back at his life from his retirement day, Power delivers a powerful performance as an Irish immigrant who, with the guidance of Bond and the love of O'Hara, settles into a life devoted to the boys who become soldiers and men at West Point. Ford invests his picture with real feeling for the institution and the code of honor that feeds its sense of pride and duty. **Cast:** Tyrone Power, Maureen O'Hara, Robert Francis, Ward Bond, Donald Crisp, Betsy Palmer, Philip Carey, William Leslie, Patrick Wayne. **Credits:** Dir: John Ford; Prod: Robert Arthur; Writer: Edward Hope; Story: Marty Maher; DP: Charles Lawton, Jr.; Ed: William A. Lyon; Composer: Morris Stoloff; Art Director: Robert Peterson. Color, 138 min. **VHS**

The Long Hot Summer

(1958) Fox
This sultry drama based on Faulkner's novel *The Hamlet* and two of his stories is given a steamy reading by a terrific ensemble. Newman strikes sparks with Woodward (they were married the same year), as small-town big daddy Welles compares Newman's virile toughness with his dissolute son, Franciosa, and decides he would make a fine match for old-maid daughter, Woodward. Franciosa takes desperate measures as he sees his patrimony slipping away. An early effort for Ritt, who directed Newman again in *Hud* (1963) and *Hombre* (1968). **Cast:** Paul Newman, Joanne Woodward, Anthony Franciosa, Orson Welles, Lee Remick, Angela Lansbury, Richard Anderson, Sarah Marshall, George Dunn. **Credits:** Dir: Martin Ritt; Prod: Jerry Wald; Writer: Irving Ravetch, Harriet Frank, Jr.; Story: William Faulkner; DP: Joseph La Shelle; Ed: Louis R. Loeffler; Prod Design: Lyle Wheeler, Maurice Ransford; Composer: Alex North. Color, 117 min. **VHS, LASER**

The Long, Long Trailer

(1954) MGM
Lucy and Desi hit the highway in a trailer that looks to be a mile long in a lighthearted domestic comedy written by Hackett and Goodrich and directed by Minnelli. **Cast:** Lucille Ball, Desi Arnaz, Marjorie Main, Keenan Wynn, Gladys Hurlbut, Moroni Olsen, Bert Freed, Madge Blake. **Credits:** Dir: Vincente Minnelli; Prod: Pandro S. Berman; Writer: Albert Hackett, Frances Goodrich; Story: Clinton Twiss; DP: Robert Surtees; Ed: Ferris Webster; Prod Design: Cedric Gibbons, Edward C. Carfagno; Composer: Adolph Deutsch. Color, 97 min. VHS

The Long Night

(1947) RKO
Fonda's first role upon his return from WWII service is a grim portrayal of a life spun out of control. The movie opens with Fonda preparing to battle police after accidentally killing traveling magician Price in a fight precipitated by his taunts about seducing Fonda's wife, Bel Geddes. Fonda recalls his small-town past, his romance with his wife and her dreams of escape, and the events that led to his predicament as he prepares for a desperate final shoot-out. **Cast:** Henry Fonda, Howard Freeman, Barbara Bel Geddes, Ann Dvorak, Vincent Price, Elisha Cook, Jr., David Clarke, Moroni Olsen. **Credits:** Dir: Anatole Litvak; Prod: Robert Hakim, Raymond Hakim, Anatole Litvak; Writer: John Wexley; DP: Sol Polito; Ed: Robert Swank; Prod Design: Eugene Lourie; Composer: Dimitri Tiomkin. B&W, 101 min.

The Long Voyage Home

(1940) United Artists
Four one-acts by O'Neill add up to a gripping account of men thrown together by war facing danger from the enemy under the waves and from the raging sea itself. Wayne portrays a young Swede gaining his sea legs and just trying to make it home so he can settle on a farm of his own. He's taken in hand by the Ford stock company—Mitchell, Fitzgerald, Bond—and together they weather a fatal storm, suspicions of treason, a strafing by enemy planes, and the equally hazardous shore leave. One of Ford's finest, and that's saying plenty; O'Neill reportedly considered it the best adaptation of his work. Note the photography by Toland. Academy Award Nominations: 6, including Best Picture; Best Screenplay. **Cast:** John Wayne, Thomas Mitchell, Ward Bond, Ian Hunter, Barry Fitzgerald, John Qualen, Mildred Natwick, Wilfred Lawson. **Credits:** Dir: John Ford; Prod: Walter Wanger; Writer: Dudley Nichols; Story: Eugene O'Neill; DP: Gregg Toland; Ed: Sherman Todd; Prod Design: James Basevi; Composer: Richard Hageman. B&W, 106 min. VHS

Looking for Mr. Goodbar

(1977) Paramount
A period piece from a not-too-distant period that might as well be the Middle Ages. The portrayal of casual sex and copious drugs in the mid-'70s New York singles scene effectively evokes the numbing frivolity of the time, but drains it of the hope and exhilaration of old attitudes being destroyed that also characterized the era. Interesting particularly for Keaton fans, as she plays the lonely schoolteacher whose one-night stands and accelerating drug use end in violence and degradation. Caution: strong sexual scenes and violence. Academy Award Nominations: Best Supporting Actress: Tuesday Weld; Best Cinematography. **Cast:** Diane Keaton, Tuesday Weld, Richard Gere, Richard Kiley, William Atherton, Alan Feinstein, Tom Berenger, Priscilla Pointer. **Credits:** Dir: Richard Brooks; Prod: Freddie Fields; Writer: Richard Brooks; DP: William A. Fraker; Ed: George Grenville; Composer: Artie Kane; Costumes: Jodie Tillen; Art Director: Edward C. Carfagno; Set Designer: Ruby Levitt. Color, 136 min. VHS

Lord Jim

(1965) Columbia
In this faithful adaptation of Conrad's 1900 novel, O'Toole plays a ship's officer in the 19th-century British merchant marines who is disgraced by abandoning his ship in a lashing storm, an act of cowardice that will always hang over him. Dismissed from

The Longest Yard (1974)

his post, he sets out to recover his self-respect in the Far East by taking a dangerous shipment of dynamite for Lukas to a rebellious tribe. A capable cast and wonderful location production. **Cast:** Peter O'Toole, James Mason, Curt Jurgens, Eli Wallach, Paul Lukas, Daliah Lavi, Jack Hawkins, Tatsu Saito. **Credits:** Dir: Richard Brooks; Prod: Richard Brooks; Writer: Richard Brooks; Story: Joseph Conrad; DP: Freddie Young; Ed: Alan Osbiston; Prod Design: Geoffrey Drake; Composer: Bronislau Kaper; Art Director: Ernest Archer. Color, 154 min. **VHS**

Lord Love a Duck
(1966) United Artists
A Southern California high school student with super-intelligence (McDowall) woos a stuck-up coed (Weld) by making all her dreams come true. The result is suicide, murder, and unhappy marriage. Based on Al Hine's novel lampooning youth culture. Director Axelrod wrote *Will Success Spoil Rock Hunter* (1957) and *The Seven-Year Itch* (1957). **Cast:** Roddy McDowall, Tuesday Weld, Lola Albright, Martin West, Ruth Gordon, Harvey Korman, Martin Gabel. **Credits:** Dir: George Axelrod; Prod: George Axelrod; Writer: George Axelrod; DP: Daniel Fapp; Ed: William A. Lyon; Composer: Neal Hefti; Art Director: Malcolm F. Brown. B&W, 105 min. **VHS**

The Lord of the Rings
(1978) United Artists
Animator Bakshi was most noted for his X-rated cartoons such as *Fritz the Cat*. Here he takes on the beloved Tolkien trilogy with a combination of live-action and animation. A fellowship of 9 sets out to destroy an evil ring of power and are beset upon by the Dark Lord of Mordor and his evil servants. Primarily of interest for fans of the books. **Credits:** Dir: Ralph Bakshi; Prod: Saul Zaentz; Writer: Chris Conkling, Peter Beagle; Story: J. R. R. Tolkien; Composer: Leonard Rosenman. Color, 133 min. **VHS**

The Lords of Flatbush
(1974) Columbia
The first featured role for Stallone leads the list of young actors in this cast who later made a mark in Hollywood: King, Winkler, Blakely, Assante, Sharkey. A tough gang with soul roams the streets of Brooklyn in the '50s getting into mild trouble with authority and their girls. A likably nostalgic look back. **Cast:** Sylvester Stallone, Henry Winkler, Perry King, Susan Blakely, Paul Jabara, Barbara Reed,

Armand Assante, Ray Sharkey, Joseph Stern, Dolph Sweet, Antonia Rey. **Credits:** Dir: Martin Davidson, Stephen Verona; Prod: Stephen Verona; Writer: Stephen F. Verona, Martin Davidson, Sylvester Stallone; DP: Joseph Mangine, Ed Lachman; Ed: Stan Siegel, Muffie Meyer; Composer: Joe Brooks, Paul Jabara, J. D. Nicholas; Art Director: Glenda Miller. Color, 88 min. **VHS, LASER**

The Lost Command
(1966) Columbia
A colorful military adventure set in the less-familiar terrain of the French-Algerian conflict of the late '50s. A hard-headed officer (Quinn), determined to become a hero at any cost, leads his defeated French army out of Indochina, to learn he's been relieved of command. Given another chance he launches a bloody battle against an Arab terrorist. Quinn takes charge of a motley unit in order to help quell the North African uprising and win the hand of a wealthy expatriate (Morgan). Good support from an international cast, including Segal, Delon, and Cardinale. **Cast:** Anthony Quinn, Michele Morgan, George Segal, Claudia Cardinale, Alain Delon, Maurice Ronet, Gregoire Aslan, Jean Servais, Jacques Marin. **Credits:** Dir: Mark Robson; Prod: Mark Robson; Writer: Nelson Gidding; Story: Jean Larteguy; DP: Robert Surtees; Ed: Dorothy Spencer; Composer: Franz Waxman; Art Director: John Stoll. Color, 129 min. **VHS**

Lost Horizon
(1937) Columbia
Capra's version of James Hilton's book is as timeless as the inhabitants of his carefully created Shangri-La—and one of his most unusual films. Known for his depictions of the plucky heart of the little people, here Capra takes on a grand vision of a place beyond the reach of war, financial panic, and governments. British diplomat Colman rescues refugees from the revolution in China, and herds them into a plane that heads not for the West but to the top of the world, Tibet. When they crash-land, the party is met with guides and warm clothes for their trip to a beautiful valley of peace and calm where time has virtually stopped. Colman has been selected to take over for the head lama, and, seemingly, for romance with an ethereally beautiful Wyatt. When his buddy (Howard) convinces him to leave, Colman struggles back to England where he is haunted by his

reveries of the idyllic valley and Wyatt. He mounts a dangerous expedition to return. The restored video version has 20 minutes of previously excised footage. Thrilling, fantastic entertainment. Academy Award Nominations: 7, including Best Picture; Best Supporting Actor: H. B. Warner; Best Score. **Academy Awards:** Best Film Editing; Best Interior Decoration (B&W). **Cast:** Ronald Colman, Jane Wyatt, John Howard, Margo, Thomas Mitchell, Edward Everett Horton, Sam Jaffe, Isabel Jewell. **Credits:** Dir: Frank Capra; Prod: Frank Capra; Writer: Robert Riskin; DP: Joseph Walker; Ed: Gene Havlick, Gene Milford; Composer: Dimitri Tiomkin, Max Steiner; Art Director: Stephen Goosson. B&W, 134 min. **VHS, LASER**

The Lost Moment
(1947) Universal
An odd, dark drama based on James's *The Aspern Papers*. Publisher Cummings ventures to Venice in order to review a cache of letters left by a poet who mysteriously vanished. He encounters a 105-year-old woman (Moorehead), who was the recipient of the letters, and her beautiful niece, Hayward. Hayward suffers from delusions that she is her aunt and that Cummings is the missing poet. When the letters are stolen, secrets are revealed. **Cast:** Robert Cummings, Susan Hayward, Eduardo Ciannelli, Agnes Moorehead, Joan Lorring, Minerva Urecal, William Edmunds. **Credits:** Dir: Martin Gabel; Writer: Leonardo Bercovici; Story: Henry James; DP: Hal Mohr; Prod Design: Alexander Golitzen; Composer: Daniele Amfitheatrof. B&W, 90 min. **VHS**

The Lost Weekend
(1945) Paramount
This portrait of alcohol's deadly grip is perhaps the greatest of the social-problem films, and a rewarding, harrowing movie experience. Milland gives the performance of a lifetime as a writer who encounters the depths of his soul on a weekend alone in New York. When his brother (Terry) goes on vacation, leaving Milland alone to write, the bottles come out before the typewriter. Before the weekend is over, Milland will have lost his money, his freedom, and his grip on reality as he descends into the alcoholic abyss. Justly praised upon its first, limited release, the movie was almost scrapped when the alcoholic beverage industry offered millions for the negative, and studio executives questioned

its commercial potential. Milland explored the darkest corners of society researching the role, spending the night in New York's Bellevue Hospital (the setting for some of the most disturbing sequences) on the alcoholic ward. Based on Charles Jackson's 1944 novel. Its multiple honors include the Cannes festival award for Best Actor: Ray Milland, and the Palme d'Or; Golden Globes for Best Director; Best Actor: Ray Milland; Best Motion Picture, Drama. Academy Award Nominations: 7, including Best Editing; Best Cinematography. **Academy Awards:** Best Picture; Best Director; Best Actor: Ray Milland; Best Screenplay. **Cast:** Ray Milland, Jane Wyman, Philip Terry, Howard Da Silva, Doris Dowling, Frank Faylen, Mary Young, Anita Bolster. **Credits:** Dir: Billy Wilder; Writer: Charles Brackett; DP: John Seitz; Ed: Doane Harrison; Prod Design: Hans Dreier; Composer: Miklos Rozsa; SFX: Gordon Jennings. B&W, 101 min. **VHS, LASER**

The Lost World
(1925) First National
The original, silent version of the story of the dinosaur-inhabited land time forgot, featuring wonderful early stop-motion animation by O'Brien. Based on a work by Sir Arthur Conan Doyle. **Cast:** Bessie Love, Wallace Beery, Lewis Stone, Lloyd Hughes. **Credits:** Dir: Harry Hoyt, William Dowling; Writer: Marion Dowling; DP: Arthur Edeson; Ed: George McGuire; SFX: Willis O'Brien. B&W, 72 min. **VHS, DVD**

Louisa
(1950) Universal
Hal Norton (Reagan), a suburban family man, has no idea how much trouble he has on his hands when his mother, Louisa (Byington), comes to live with him. When an elderly local grocer (Gwenn) falls in love with Louisa and is soon contested romantically by Hal's powerful bachelor boss (Coburn), family comedy ensues. Hal has to readjust his assumption that his mother is too old for love, as Louisa unexpectedly becomes the most amorously active member of his household. **Cast:** Ronald Reagan, Charles Coburn, Ruth Hussey, Edmund Gwenn, Spring Byington, Piper Laurie, Scotty Beckett, Bruce Gilchrist, Willard Waterman, Marjorie Crossland. **Credits:** Dir: Mitchell Leisen; Prod: Jerry Wald; Writer: Virginia Kellogg, Bernard C. Schoenfeld; DP: Carl E. Guthrie; Ed: Owen Marks; Prod Design: Charles H. Clarke, G. W. Bernsten; Composer: Max Steiner. B&W, 82 min.

The Lost Weekend (1945)

The Louisiana Story
(1948)
Renowned documentary maker Robert Flaherty's last film depicts the oil industry's effect on the bayou country of Louisiana. A Cajun boy living in the marshlands of Petit Anse Bayou observes the growing industrialization of his state as he watches the offshore oil platforms rise and the drillers at work. Composer and critic Virgil Thomson supplies the score. Equally hearty as explorer and filmmaker, Flaherty first brought back silent footage from the far north (*Nanook of the North,* 1922) and the lush exotica of *Moana* (1926), and with F. W. Murnau, *Tabu* (1933). This was produced for Standard Oil. Selected as a National Film Registry Outstanding Film. Academy Award Nomination for Best Motion Picture Story. **Cast:** Joseph Boudreaux, Lionel Le Blanc, E. Bienvenu, Frank Hardy, C. P. Guedry. **Credits:** Dir: Robert Flaherty; Prod: Robert Flaherty; Writer: Robert Flaherty, Frances H. Flaherty; DP: Richard Leacock; Ed: Helen van Dongen; Composer: Virgil Thomson. B&W, 79 min. **VHS**

Love Affair
(1932) Columbia
Bogie does an aerial turn as an aviator and mechanic waiting for his ship to come in. But he's also a gifted inventor with a hot new motor for a brainchild. He gives flying lessons to a beautiful heiress (Mackaill) and, as the sparks fly, she agrees to back him. When she loses her fortune, Bogie saves her from suicide. **Cast:** Dorothy Mackaill, Humphrey Bogart, Bradley Page, Hale Hamilton, Jack Kennedy, Astrid Allwyn. **Credits:** Dir: Thornton Freeland; Writer: Jo Swerling, Dorothy Howell; DP: Ted Tetzlaff; Ed: Jack Dennis. B&W, 87 min.

Love Affair
(1939) RKO
Director McCarey's first version of the all-time great sudser that he later remade as *An Affair to Remember* (1957) with Cary Grant and Deborah Kerr. Boyer and Dunne are the shipboard lovers who vow to meet again in six months to test their love. An enduring romance classic that was made again in 1994 by Warren Beatty with Annette Bening. Academy Award

Love Affair (1939)

Nominations: 6, including Best Picture; Best Actress: Irene Dunne; Best Original Story. **Cast:** Irene Dunne, Charles Boyer, Maria Ouspenskaya, Lee Bowman, Astrid Allwyn, Maurice Moscovich. **Credits:** Dir: Leo McCarey; Prod: Leo McCarey; Writer: Delmer Daves, Donald Ogden Stewart; Story: Mildred Cram, Leo McCarey; DP: Rudolph Mate; Ed: Edward Dmytryk, George Hively; Composer: Roy Webb; Art Director: Van Nest Polglase, Al Herman. B&W, 87 min. **VHS**

Love and Death
(1975) United Artists
Allen spoofs melodramatic Russian literature in this comedy about Boris, a timid Russian soldier in the Napoleonic wars condemned to death for plotting to assassinate Napoleon, whose life flashes, very slowly, before his eyes. Quite funny, especially if you know Russian novels or movies, though it works on its own, too. Music by Prokofiev. **Cast:** Woody Allen, Diane Keaton, Alfred Lutter, Harold Gould, George Birt, Tony Jay. **Credits:** Dir: Woody Allen; Prod: Charles H. Joffe; Writer: Woody Allen; DP: Ghislain Cloquet; Ed: Ron Kalish, Ralph Rosenblum; Art Director: Willy Holt; Set Designer: Claude Reytinas; Composer: Sergey Prokofiev. Color, 85 min. **VHS, LASER**

Love at First Bite
(1979) AIP
In this vampire-movie spoof, Hamilton plays the blood-sucking Count, whose gloomy home is confiscated so that the Romanian government can train gymnasts there. He creeps through New York discos and preys upon St. James,

whose psychiatrist boyfriend (Benjamin) is determined to bring her back from the undead. This revived Hamilton's formerly pallid career. **Cast:** George Hamilton, Susan St. James, Arte Johnson, Richard Benjamin, Dick Shawn, Isabel Sanford, Barry Gordon. **Credits:** Dir: Stan Dragoti; Prod: Joel Freeman; Writer: Robert Kaufman; Ed: Alan Jacobs, Mort Fallick; Prod Design: Serge Krizman; Composer: Charles Bernstein. Color, 96 min. **VHS**

The Loved One
(1965) MGM
One of novelist Evelyn Waugh's most vicious satires, set among the last resting places for people and animals in Hollywood. Morse comes to Hollywood to visit his uncle (Gielgud), a movie art director who hangs himself when he loses his job. Morse is then in the hands of Morley and twin funeral directors (one for humans, one for animals), both played by the sur-really funny Winters. A wickedly wry look at death and Hollywood. Script by Southern and Isherwood. **Cast:** Robert Morse, Robert Morley, Rod Steiger, Jonathan Winters, John Gielgud, Paul Williams, Dana Andrews, Milton Berle, James Coburn. **Credits:** Dir: Tony Richardson; Prod: John Calley; Writer: Terry Southern, Christopher Isherwood; DP: Haskell Wexler; Ed: Anthony Gibbs; Composer: John Addison; SFX: Geza Gaspar; Art Director: Sydney Litwack. B&W, 122 min. **VHS, LASER**

Love Happy
(1949) United Artists
The Marx Brothers' last film together features Groucho as Sam Grunion,

private eye, who takes on the case in which he must find the missing Romanoff diamonds. The jewels are hidden in a sardine tin, which somehow makes its fishy way to the backstage of a theatrical troupe Harpo supports. Famous for a Marilyn Monroe bit. **Cast:** Groucho, Harpo, and Chico Marx, Ilona Massey, Vera Ellen, Raymond Burr, Marion Hutton, Bruce Gordon. **Credits:** Dir: David Miller; Prod: Lester Cowan; Writer: Frank Tashlin, Mac Benoff; DP: William Mellor; Ed: Basil Wrangell, Al Joseph; Art Director: Gabriel Scognamillo. B&W, 91 min. **VHS, LASER**

Love in the Afternoon
(1957) Allied Artists
This romantic comedy written and directed by Wilder makes marvelous use of its Parisian settings, though the sight of 56-year-old Cooper romantically crossing swords with gamine Hepburn strains credulity. Hepburn saves Cooper from the spying of her father, private detective Chevalier, earning her his amorous attention. When Chevalier listens to Cooper's musings about his situation, he offers his services to track her down, then discovers it is his daughter he's tailing. **Cast:** Gary Cooper, Audrey Hepburn, Maurice Chevalier, John McGiver. **Credits:** Dir: Billy Wilder; Prod: Billy Wilder; Writer: Billy Wilder, I. A. L. Diamond; Ed: Leonide Azar; Prod Design: Alexander Trauner; Composer: Franz Waxman. B&W, 130 min. **VHS, LASER**

Love Is a Many Splendored Thing
(1955) Fox
This romantic melodrama set in Hong Kong during the Korean War features the photogenic pairing of Holden as a married American war correspondent and Jones as a beautiful Eurasian doctor. Their affair meets prejudice, frustration, and, ultimately, tragedy when Holden returns to the front. Famous for its swelling title song. Based on the novel by Han Suyin. Golden Globe for Best Film Promoting International Understanding. Academy Award Nominations: 8, including Best Picture; Best Actress: Jennifer Jones. **Academy Awards:** Best Song; Best Music Score of a Drama/Comedy; Best Costume Design (Color). **Cast:** Jennifer Jones, William Holden, Isobel Elsom, Richard Loo, Torin Hatcher. **Credits:** Dir: Henry King; Prod: Buddy Adler; Writer: John Patrick; DP: Leon Shamroy; Ed: William H. Reynolds; Prod Design: Lyle Wheeler; Com-

poser: Alfred Newman; Art Director: George W. Davis. Color, 102 min. **VHS, LASER**

Love Is Better Than Ever
(1952) MGM
This frothy comedy-romance features Taylor as a small-town dance instructor who falls for Parks, a talent agent she meets at a New York City convention. She's determined to win this carefree man-about-town but he's not interested in giving up his fun and freedom. The film's release was delayed when Parks was blacklisted by the HUAC. **Cast:** Elizabeth Taylor, Larry Parks, Josephine Hutchinson, Tom Tully, Ann Doran, Elinor Donahue, Kathleen Freeman. **Credits:** Dir: Stanley Donen; Prod: William H. Wright; Writer: Ruth Brookes Flippen; DP: Harold Rosson; Ed: George Boemler; Prod Design: Cedric Gibbons, Gabriel Scognamillo; Composer: Lennie Hayton. Color, 81 min. **VHS**

Love Is on the Air
(1937) Warner Bros.
Reagan's film debut finds him a brash radio announcer whose popular show uncovers the dirt on local politics. His cautious boss has trouble with the sponsors and demotes Reagan to the kids' show, but in the end Reagan (who began his career as a radio announcer) has the last word. **Cast:** Ronald Reagan, June Travis, Eddie Acuff, Ben Weldon, Robert Barrat, Addison Richards, Raymond Hatton, Dick Jones, Willard Parker, Spec O'Donnell. **Credits:** Dir: Nick Grinde; Prod: Brian Foy; Writer: Morton Grant, Roy Chanslor; DP: James Van Trees. B&W, 61 min.

Love Letters
(1945) Paramount
In this sparkling, *Cyrano*-like tale, Jones marries a soldier (Sully) after his friend (Cotten) writes her beautiful letters. When her husband dies at the hand of her stepmother after he attacks her, Jones is stricken with amnesia. Cotten comes to investigate his friend's murder, and the author of the letters finds his love rekindled. Novelist Rand adapted the screenplay from Chris Massie's novel, *Pity My Simplicity*. Academy Award Nominations: 4, including Best Actress: Jennifer Jones. **Cast:** Jennifer Jones, Joseph Cotten, Robert Sully, Ann Richards, Gladys Cooper, Anita Louise, Reginald Denny, Cecil Kellaway. **Credits:** Dir: William Dieterle; Prod: Hal B. Wallis; Writer: Ayn Rand; DP: Lee Garmes; Composer: Victor Young; Art Director: Hans Dreier, Roland Anderson. B&W, 102 min. **VHS**

Lovely to Look At
(1952) MGM
Broadway veterans Grayson, Keel, and Skelton raise money for a show of their own by taking over the Parisian dress shop owned by Skelton's deceased aunt. They lift sales by turning it into a musical parade with the help of the Champions. Great songs by Kern and choreography by Hermes Pan. A remake of *Roberta* (1935). **Cast:** Kathryn Grayson, Red Skelton, Howard Keel, Ann Miller, Marge Champion, Gower Champion, Zsa Zsa Gabor, Kurt Kasznar. **Credits:** Dir: Mervyn LeRoy; Prod: Jack Cummings; Writer: George Wells, Harry Ruby, Andrew Solt; DP: George J. Folsey; Ed: John McSweeney, Jr.; Prod Design: Cedric Gibbons; Composer: Jerome Kern; Art Director: Gabriel Scognamillo. Color, 105 min. **VHS, LASER**

Love Me or Leave Me
(1955) MGM
Day's finest performance in a role that lets her be bold, bad, and sexy, and that allows her plenty of room to sing the great tunes from the '20s. Day plays Jazz Age nightclub singer Ruth Etting, who balances the romantic aspirations of Chicago gangster Cagney and her true love, pianist Mitchell. Academy Award Nominations: 6, including Best Actor: James Cagney; Best Screenplay; Best Song ("I'll Never Stop Loving You"). **Academy Awards:** Best Motion Picture Story. **Cast:** James Cagney, Doris Day, Cameron Mitchell, Robert Keith, Tom Tully, Harry Bellaver, Richard Gaines, Peter Leeds. **Credits:** Dir: Charles Vidor; Prod: Joe Pasternak; Writer: Daniel Fuchs, Isobel Lennart, Arthur E. Arling; Ed: Ralph E. Winters; Prod Design: Cedric Gibbons, Urie McCleary; Composer: Percy Faith. Color, 150 min. **VHS, LASER**

Love Me Tender
(1956) Fox
Presley's first film centers on a family torn apart by Civil War politics and by two brothers' love for the same woman. Aside from his debut, the King's crooning is really the highlight of this period drama as he sings "Love Me Tender," "Poor Boy," "Let Me," and others. **Cast:** Elvis Presley, Debra Paget, Richard Egan, Robert Middleton, William Campbell, Neville Brand, Mildred Dunnock, Bruce Bennett. **Credits:** Dir: Robert D. Webb; Prod: David Weisbart; Writer: Robert Buckner; Story: Maurice Geraghty; DP: Leo Tover; Ed: Hugh S. Fowler; Prod Design: Maurice Ransford, Lyle

Wheeler; Composer: Vera Matson, Lionel Newman, Elvis Presley. Color, 89 min. **VHS**

Love Me Tonight
(1932) Paramount
A remarkable step forward for film musicals, this is one of the most carefully imagined screen musicals in film history. The Rodgers and Hart songs are deployed with imagination and flair, woven into the narrative in a manner that seems utterly natural, passed like a musical baton from character to character. The light-as-meringue story revolves around tailor Chevalier, whose generosity to a profligate aristocrat (Ruggles) enables him to pursue his love for MacDonald's aloof princess. A treasure. **Cast:** Maurice Chevalier, Jeanette MacDonald, Charles Ruggles, Charles Butterworth, Myrna Loy, C. Aubrey Smith, Elizabeth Patterson, Joseph Cawthorn. **Credits:** Dir: Rouben Mamoulian; Writer: Samuel Hoffenstein, Waldemar Young, George Marion; DP: Victor Milner; Ed: William Shea; Composer: Richard Rodgers, Lorenz Hart; Prod Design: Hans Dreier; Costumes: Edith Head, Travis Banton. B&W, 104 min.

Love on the Run
(1936) MGM
International correspondents Gable and Tone compete for stories and for the attention of heiress on the run Crawford. The three cross paths when Crawford asks for help getting out of her upcoming wedding and they steal a plane belonging to aeronaut and spy, Owen. A chase across Europe— and romance—ensues. **Cast:** Joan Crawford, Clark Gable, Franchot Tone, William Demarest, Reginald Owen, Mona Barrie, Ivan Lebedeff, Charles Judels. **Credits:** Dir: W. S. Van Dyke; Prod: Joseph L. Mankiewicz; Writer: John Lee Mahin, Manuel Seff, Gladys Hurlbut; DP: Oliver T. Marsh; Ed: Frank Sullivan; Prod Design: Cedric Gibbons; Composer: Franz Waxman. B&W, 80 min. **VHS**

Lover Come Back
(1962) Universal
Frantic comedy pairing of Day and Hudson as rival advertising executives. After battling each other over clients, Hudson woos Day impersonating the head of a company that makes a mysterious product called "Vip," which he insists will rival Coca-Cola. Day throws herself at him to get the account, only to discover that Hudson made up the product to support a bogus campaign he created to help

him with Adams. Vip, though, has remarkable properties that break down the romantic barriers. Academy Award Nomination for Best (Original) Story and Screenplay. **Cast:** Doris Day, Rock Hudson, Tony Randall, Edie Adams, Jack Oakie, Jack Kruschen, Ann B. Davis, Joe Flynn. **Credits:** Dir: Delbert Mann; Prod: Stanley Shapiro, Martin Melcher; Writer: Stanley Shapiro, Paul Henning; DP: Arthur E. Arling; Ed: Marjorie Fowler; Prod Design: Alexander Golitzen, Robert Clatworthy; Composer: Frank DeVol. B&W, 107 min. **VHS**

Lovers and Other Strangers
(1970) Cinerama
A romantic rondo that centers on a young couple (Bedelia and Brandon) who decide to marry after secretly living together for 18 months. They discover their parents have remarkable romantic secrets of their own, the bride's sister's marriage is failing, and a blind date with one of the ushers leads to disaster. Keaton and Castellano in their first major roles. Academy Award Nominations: 3, including Best Supporting Actor: Richard Castellano; Best (Adapted) Screenplay. **Academy Awards:** Best Song. **Cast:** Gig Young, Beatrice Arthur, Bonnie Bedelia, Michael Brandon, Anne Jackson, Richard Castellano, Harry Guardino, Diane Keaton, Cloris Leachman. **Credits:** Dir: Cy Howard; Prod: David Susskind; Writer: Renee Taylor, Joseph Bologna, David Zelag Goodman; DP: Andrew Laszlo; Ed: David Bretherton, Sidney Katz; Prod Design: Ben Edwards; Composer: Fred Karlin. Color, 106 min. **VHS**

Love Story
(1970) Paramount
The millionth screen soaper depicting a poor girl surmounting all obstacles to land her rich beau only to have the glittering prize snatched from her grasp, in this case by a fatal illness. But this telling for the psychobabble era deserves a look for its attractive leads (MacGraw and O'Neal) and the antiestablishment disdain with which the Radcliffe coed played by MacGraw lures O'Neal's preppy Harvard man. Only in the '60s would being rich, handsome, educated, and athletic mean having to say you're sorry. Followed by *Oliver's Story* in 1978, in which O'Neal pines until equally wealthy Candice Bergen steps into his life, thus ushering in the '80s era. Academy Award Nominations: 7, including Best Picture; Best Director; Best Actor: Ryan O'Neal; Best Actress: Ali MacGraw; Best (Adapted) Screenplay. **Academy Awards:** Best Original

Score. **Cast:** Ryan O'Neal, Ali MacGraw, Ray Milland, John Marley, Russell Nype, Sydney Walker, Robert Modica, Walker Daniels. **Credits:** Dir: Arthur Hiller; Prod: Howard G. Minsky; Writer: Erich Segal; Ed: Robert C. Jones; Composer: Francis Lai; Art Director: Robert Gundlach. Color, 100 min. **VHS**

Love That Brute
(1950) Fox
There is only one problem with Chicago gangster "Big Ed" Hanley's (Douglas) plan to hire Ruth Manning (Peters), a woman he has fallen for, as a governess. He doesn't have any children. The solution, in this romantic comedy, is to go out and "hire" a son, but Harry, a lippy street youth, turns out to be more than Hanley can handle. When Manning pieces together the ruse and leaves his home, "Big Ed" decides it is time to make peace with his top rival (Romero), go straight, and reveal his soft side. **Cast:** Paul Douglas, Jean Peters, Cesar Romero, Keenan Wynn, Joan Davis, Arthur Treacher, Peter Edward Price, Jay C. Flippen, Barry Kelley, Leon Belasco. **Credits:** Dir: Alexander Hall; Prod: Fred Kohlmar; Writer: Karl Tunberg; DP: Lloyd Ahern II; Ed: Nick DeMaggio; Composer: Cyril Mockridge, Lionel Newman; Art Director: Lyle Wheeler, Richard Irvine. B&W, 85 min.

Love Thy Neighbor
(1940) Paramount
This comedic farce centers around the long-running radio "feud" between Mr. Allen and Mr. Benny. The tale begins when Allen, on his way to greet his niece (Martin) who is returning from a cruise, bumps into Benny and unpleasant words are exchanged. It turns out Benny is producing a musical in which Allen's niece ends up getting a job in order to help mend the "feud." The two fall in love. Mostly interesting as a translation of a radio program to the big screen. **Cast:** Jack Benny, Fred Allen, Mary Martin, Barbara Jo Allen, Eddie Anderson, Virginia Dale, Theresa Harris, Richard Denning, Jack Carson, Barnett Parker. **Credits:** Dir: Mark Sandrich; Prod: Mark Sandrich; Writer: Edmund Beloin, William Morrow, Ernest Pagano; DP: Ted Tetzlaff; Ed: LeRoy Stone; Composer: Johnny Burke, Cole Porter, James Van Heusen. B&W, 82 min.

Love with the Proper Stranger
(1963) Paramount
A tough and tender love story about a footloose jazz musician (McQueen)

and the Macy's salesgirl (Wood) who is carrying his child. Though they decide to end the pregnancy, and Wood's parents push her to marry the local grocer, she and McQueen make a last-minute decision to give love a chance. Academy Award Nominations: 4, including Best Actress: Natalie Wood; Best (Original) Story and Screenplay. **Cast:** Natalie Wood, Steve McQueen, Edie Adams, Herschel Bernardi, Tom Bosley, Harvey Lembeck, Penny Santon, Virginia Vincent. **Credits:** Dir: Robert Mulligan; Prod: Alan J. Pakula; Writer: Arnold Schulman; DP: Milton Krasner; Ed: Aaron Stell; Composer: Elmer Bernstein; Art Director: Hal Pereira, Roland Anderson. B&W, 102 min. **VHS, LASER**

Loving You
(1957) Paramount
Elvis plays a Hollywood version of himself in his second big-screen outing. Small-town truck driver Elvis stops at a rally long enough to sing and impress Scott, a PR agent. As she helps build his career, Elvis's attention wanders from her to the girl singer in the band (Hart). Not bad, and includes Elvis hits "Teddy Bear" and "Got a Lot of Livin' to Do." **Cast:** Elvis Presley, Wendell Corey, Lizabeth Scott, Dolores Hart, James Gleason, Paul Smith, Jana Lund, Ralph Dumke. **Credits:** Dir: Hal Kanter; Prod: Hal B. Wallis; Writer: Hal Kanter, Herbert Baker; DP: Charles B. Lang; Ed: Howard Smith; Composer: Walter Scharf; Art Director: Hal Pereira, Albert Nozaki. Color, 102 min. **VHS, LASER**

Lt. Robin Crusoe, U.S.N.
(1966) Disney
Daniel Defoe's story takes a Disney turn when Van Dyke, a U.S. Navy pilot, crash-lands on a South Sea island. The other inhabitants are a space chimp whose capsule landed on the island and the alluring Kwan, whose dad, a tribal chieftain, makes trouble. Disney comedy with a spirited Van Dyke performance. The story is credited to Retlaw Yensid (spell it backwards!). **Cast:** Dick Van Dyke, Nancy Kwan, Akim Tamiroff, Arthur Malet, Tyler McVey, John Dennis, Nancy Hsueh, Ian Dury. **Credits:** Dir: Byron Paul; Prod: Bill Walsh, Ron Miller; Writer: Bill Walsh, Don DaGradi; DP: William E. Snyder; Ed: Cotton Warburton; Prod Design: Carroll Clark, Carl Anderson; Composer: Robert F. Brunner. Color, 113 min. **VHS**

Lullaby of Broadway

(1950) Warner Bros.

Day gets the chance to sing a basketful of nostalgic songs as an aspiring actress who comes to New York City and discovers that her mother isn't who she thought she was. In addition to the title number, the songs include "Zing! Went the Strings of My Heart" and "You're Getting to Be a Habit With Me." **Cast:** Doris Day, Gene Nelson, Gladys George, S. Z. Sakall, Billy de Wolfe, Florence Bates, Anne Triola, Hanley Stafford. **Credits:** Dir: David Butler; Prod: William Jacobs; Writer: Earl Baldwin; DP: Wilfrid M. Cline; Ed: Irene Morra; Art Director: Douglas Bacon. Color, 93 min. **VHS**

Lured

(1947) United Artists

An early Hollywood outing for Sirk and an interesting non-comedy role for Ball. The mystery begins with a young taxi dancer in London (Ball) whose friend is murdered by a madman who leaves notes for the police written in poetry. After turning up false leads (including an appearance by Karloff), Ball agrees to act as a lure for the police and answers a newspaper ad taken out by the murderer. Her boyfriend, Sanders, is a nightclub owner who has a partner, Hardwicke, who begins to behave rather oddly. A tight, no-nonsense thriller. **Cast:** George Sanders, Lucille Ball, Charles Coburn, Boris Karloff, Alan Mowbray, Cedric Hardwicke, George Zucco, Joseph Calleia, Alan Napier. **Credits:** Dir: Douglas Sirk; Prod: James Nasser; Writer: Leo Rosten; DP: William Daniels; Ed: John Foley, James E. Newcom; Composer: Michel Michelet; Art Director: Nicolai Remisoff. B&W, 102 min.

Lust for Life

(1956) MGM

Exhaustive research for the role earned Douglas an Academy Award nomination for his searing portrayal of Vincent van Gogh in Minnelli's biographical film of the famously talented and tormented painter. Based on the novel by Irving Stone and featuring many original van Gogh paintings from private collections, this also earned an Academy Award for Best Supporting Actor for Quinn as Paul Gauguin. Golden Globe for Best Actor in a Drama: Kirk Douglas. Academy Award Nominations: 4, including Best Actor: Kirk Douglas; Best (Adapted) Screenplay. **Academy Awards:** Best Supporting Actor: Anthony Quinn. **Cast:** Kirk Douglas, Anthony Quinn, James Donald, Pamela Brown, Everett Sloane, Niall MacGinnis, Noel Purcell, Henry Daniell. **Credits:** Dir: Vincente Minnelli; Prod: John Houseman; Writer: Norman Corwin; DP: Freddie Young, Russell Harlan; Ed: Adrienne Fazan; Prod Design: Cedric Gibbons, Hans Peters, Preston Ames; Composer: Miklos Rozsa. Color, 123 min. **VHS, LASER**

The Lusty Men

(1952) RKO

The competition for a woman and for a man's place in the world drives this beautifully photographed cowboy melodrama set in the world of professional rodeos. Director Ray elicts one of Mitchum's best performances as a top rodeo rider facing retirement after being gored by a bull. He limps back to his family ranch in Oklahoma where he encounters Kennedy and Hayward and their desire to buy the place. Kennedy recognizes the former rodeo star and asks him for training to compete in the local events Kennedy has entered. Mitchum and Hayward strike sparks and Kennedy rises in the rodeo rankings, setting up a final showdown in the dusty ring. Footage from actual rodeos and a script from real cowboy Dortort add to the authentic atmosphere. **Cast:** Robert Mitchum, Susan Hayward, Arthur Kennedy, Arthur Hunnicutt, Frank Faylen, Walter Coy, Carole Nugent, Lorna Thayer. **Credits:** Dir: Nicholas Ray; Prod: Jerry Wald; Writer: Horace McCoy, David Dortort; DP: Lee Garmes; Ed: Ralph Dawson; Composer: Roy Webb; Art Director: Albert S. D'Agostino. B&W, 113 min. **VHS, LASER**

Lydia Bailey

(1952) Fox

A historical drama set during Napoleon's 1802 attempted takeover of Haiti, this tells the story of an American lawyer, Robertson, who arrives in Haiti and must reach a beautiful local aristrocrat (Francis) to settle an estate. He recruits one of the Haitian rebels to lead him to this French sympathizer. The lawyer and rebel arrive in time to save the young woman, her wealthy fiancé, and the fiancé's son from French soldiers. In the end, the woman leaves her preference for the French and her fiancé behind, choosing the American lawyer instead. **Cast:** Dale Robertson, Anne Francis, William Marshall, Charles Korvin, Adeline de Walt Reynolds, Luis Van Rooten, Gladys Holland, Roy Glenn, Will Wright. **Credits:** Dir: Jean Negulesco; Prod: Jules Schermer; Writer: Michael Blankfort, Philip Dunne; DP: Harry Jackson; Ed: Dorothy Spencer; Prod Design: Lyle Wheeler, J. Russell Spencer; Composer: Hugo Friedhofer. Color, 89 min.

M

M

(1951) Columbia
Losey's remake of Fritz Lang's German classic brings the story to Los Angeles. An obsessive man, whose compulsions play out in the murder of little girls, raises the fears of an entire community. The police, under heavy pressure from the populace, set out to find the killer, while the underworld, under pressure from police raids resulting from the investigation, organize their own search for the man. When the underworld catches him first, it is the murderer's turn to feel terror, as this frightened, unstable man is put through an informal trial to determine his fate. **Cast:** David Wayne, Howard Da Silva, Martin Gabel, Luther Adler, Steve Brodie, Glenn Anders, Norman Lloyd, Walter Burke, Raymond Burr, Karen Morley. **Credits:** Dir: Joseph Losey; Prod: Seymour Nebenzal; Writer: Norman Raine, Leo Katcher, Waldo Salt; DP: Ernest Laszlo; Ed: Edward Mann; Prod Design: Martin Obzina; Composer: Michel Michelet. B&W, 88 min.

Ma and Pa Kettle

Loveable country bumpkins Ma and Pa Kettle were never the critics' darlings, but they entertained many and their low-budget films were highly profitable. The hillbilly couple made their first appearance as peripheral characters in *The Egg and I* (1947), starring Fred MacMurray and Claudette Colbert, the story of an urban couple forced to move to the country. Audiences were so taken by the yokels that Ma and Pa (and their very large brood of children) earned their very own series. Most of the humor in this Universal series centers on the good-hearted couple's encounters with new-fangled technology. In the first film of the series, Ma and Pa Kettle (1949), Pa wins a contest by writing a new slogan for a local tobacco. The prize is a totally automated home of the future

and the Kettles hilariously try to figure out all the "whatsamagiggys and whoosits" built in to their deluxe new habitation. Main came to the series after a rather prolific career. After co-starring on Broadway early on with W. C. Fields, she was featured in more than 100 films for MGM, many on the arm of Wallace Beery, before creating the character of Ma. Main died in 1975. Kilbride began his career in regional stock theater companies and as a character actor in Hollywood before bringing the character of Pa to the screen. He exited the series in 1955 and made no more movies. Kilbride died in 1964

Ma and Pa Kettle *(1949)*
Ma and Pa Kettle Go to Town *(1950)*
Ma and Pa Kettle Back on The Farm *(1951)*
Ma and Pa Kettle at the Fair *(1952)*
Ma and Pa Kettle on Vacation *(1953)*
Ma and Pa Kettle at Home *(1954)*
Ma and Pa Kettle at Waikiki *(1955)*
The Kettles in the Ozarks *(1956)*
The Kettles on Old Macdonald's Farm *(1957)*

Macao

(1952) RKO
"Adventure! . . . Intrigue! . . . In the mysterious Orient!" Mitchum and Russell star in a story about an ex-G.I. on the lam, a sassy singer, and a New York detective (Bendix) chasing the head of a gambling ring. Russell is hired to sing in a nightclub owned by mobster Dexter, much to the consternation of Grahame, playing (once again) the gangster's moll. Meanwhile Mitchum is mistaken for the cop and things turn nasty. Von Sternberg's atmospheric touches are in evidence, especially in a waterfront chase through fishing nets, however Nicholas Ray shot additional scenes after troublesome preview screenings, and von Sternberg eventually disowned the film. **Cast:** Robert

Mitchum, Jane Russell, William Bendix, Gloria Grahame, Thomas Gomez, Brad Dexter, Edward Ashley, Philip Ahn. **Credits:** Dir: Josef Von Sternberg, Nicholas Ray; Prod: Alex Gottlieb; Writer: Bernard C. Schoenfeld, Stanley Rubin; DP: Harry Wild; Ed: Samuel E. Beetley, Robert Golden; Prod Design: Ralph Berger; Composer: Anthony Collins; Art Director: Albert S. D'Agostino. B&W, 80 min. **VHS, LASER**

MacArthur

(1979) Universal
What began as an attempt to repeat the success of *Patton* (1970) resulted in an admiring Hollywood biopic, greatly enhanced by a spirited and introspective performance by Peck as the flamboyant, controversial, and brilliant general. Framed by his West Point farewell speech ("Old soldiers never die . . . they just fade away . . . "), flashbacks capture his career, including recreations of the famous landing in the Philippines and the Japanese surrender on the battleship *Missouri*, as well as the ultimate showdown with Harry Truman (Flanders) that led to his dismissal. **Cast:** Gregory Peck, Ed Flanders, Dan O'Herlihy, Sandy Kenyon, Ivan Bonar, Ward Costello, Nicolas Coster, Marj Dusay. **Credits:** Dir: Joseph Sargent; Prod: Frank McCarthy; Writer: Hal Barwood, Matthew Robbins; DP: Mario Tosi; Ed: George Jay Nicholson; Composer: Jerry Goldsmith; Art Director: John Lloyd. Color, 130 min. **VHS, LASER**

Macbeth

(1948) Republic
Welles's first screen adaptation of Shakespeare was shot on a Republic studios Western soundstage in three days. Even though it looks like a '20s German expressionist film shot on a rubber-boulder-covered *Star Trek* planet, this low-budget film has a lot going for it. While not totally successful, it is never dull. Welles himself

described this as "a violent charcoal sketch of a great play," and he added characters—in particular, Napier's Holy Father—to emphasize the paganism of the three witches vs. Christianity. Look for the Mercury Theater regulars: William Alland and Erskine Sanford. Originally cut to 89 minutes for theatrical release, the film has been restored to Welles's intended 105 minutes. Nominated for an award in the 1948 Venice Film Festival. **Cast:** Orson Welles, Jeanette Nolan, Dan O'Herlihy, Roddy McDowall, Edgar Barrier, Alan Napier, Erskine Sanford, Peggy Webber, John Dierkes, Robert Coote. **Credits:** Dir: Orson Welles; Prod: Orson Welles; Writer: Orson Welles; Story: William Shakespeare; DP: John L. Russell, Jr., William Bradford; Ed: Louis Lindsay; Prod Design: Fred A. Ritter; Composer: Jacques Ibert; Costumes: Orson Welles, Fred A. Ritter, Adele Palmer; SFX: Howard Lydecker, Theodore Lydecker. B&W, 112 min. **VHS, LASER**

Mackenna's Gold

(1969) Columbia
One of the last of the traditional Westerns, with Peck as Sheriff Mackenna, the only person who knows the location of a legendary canyon of gold coveted by a Mexican bandit (Sharif), countless prospectors, and Apaches. The Apaches want the gold to fight the white men, despite a decree from their elders, while Sharif is only looking for an easy ticket to Paris. Well-populated with wonderful actors in small roles (Cobb, Robinson, Massey, Meredith, and Newmar as an Apache maiden). Produced by longtime Hollywood soundtrack composer Tiomkin. **Cast:** Gregory Peck, Omar Sharif, Keenan Wynn, Telly Savalas, Julie Newmar, Lee J. Cobb, Camilla Sparv, Raymond Massey, Burgess Meredith, Anthony Quayle, Edward G. Robinson. **Credits:** Dir: J. Lee Thompson; Prod: Carl Foreman, Dimitri Tiomkin; Writer: Carl Foreman; DP: Joseph MacDonald; Ed: Bill Lenny; Prod Design: Geoffrey Drake; Composer: Quincy Jones. Color, 128 min. **VHS, LASER**

The Mackintosh Man

(1973) Warner Bros.
An international spy thriller set in England and Ireland directed by Huston (and penned by future director Hill) with Newman as an Australian assassin hired by British intelligence to expose reactionary politician Mason. Sanda is the romantic interest added for the international film market. Yet what should have been a *North By*

Macbeth (1948)

Northwest–style thriller seldom engages and even Huston admitted this was one of his least favorite films. Based on Bagley's novel *The Freedom Trap*. **Cast:** Paul Newman, James Mason, Dominique Sanda, Harry Andrews, Ian Bannen, Michael Hordern, Nigel Patrick, Peter Vaughan, Roland Culver, Percy Herbert. **Credits:** Dir: John Huston; Prod: John Foreman; Writer: Walter Hill; Story: Desmond Bagley; DP: Oswald Morris; Ed: Russell Lloyd; Prod Design: Terence Marsh, Alan Tomkins; Composer: Maurice Jarre. Color, 100 min. **VHS**

The Macomber Affair

(1947) United Artists
A wholly satisfying adaptation of the Ernest Hemingway story about a rich man (Preston) who hires a professional game hunter (Peck) as a guide in Africa. The man's wife (Bennett) pursues the hunter with romantic intentions. She shoots her husband as he is charged by a buffalo and is tried for his murder. **Cast:** Gregory Peck, Joan Bennett, Robert Preston, Reginald Denny, Jean Gillie, Carl Harbord, Earl E. Smith, Francis Worlock, Vernon Downing. **Credits:** Dir: Zoltan Korda; Prod: Benedict Bogeaus, Arthur M. Landau, Casey Robinson; Writer: Seymour Bennett, Frank Arnold, Casey

Robinson; Story: Ernest Hemingway; DP: Karl Struss, O. H. Borradaile, John Wilcox; Ed: George Feld, Jack Wheeler, James Smith; Prod Design: Ern Metzner, Fred Widdowson; Composer: Miklos Rozsa. B&W, 89 min.

Mad About Music

(1938) Universal
A popular Durbin vehicle in which she plays a film star's daughter who gets shipped off to a posh Swiss boarding school. Prohibited from revealing her true parentage, she concocts the story of a fantasy father, an explorer and big-game hunter. When her bluff is endangered, Durbin enlists the help of a kind vacationing composer (Marshall) to masquerade as the great man. Remade in 1956 as *Toy Tiger* with Jeff Chandler in the role of the fantasy father. **Cast:** Deanna Durbin, Herbert Marshall, Arthur Treacher, Gail Patrick, Marcia Mae Jones, Jackie Moran, William Frawley, Helen Parrish. **Credits:** Dir: Norman Taurog; Prod: Joe Pasternak; Writer: Bruce Manning, Felix Jackson; DP: Joseph A. Valentine; Ed: Philip Cahn. B&W, 92 min. **VHS**

Madame Bovary

(1949) MGM
Gustave Flaubert's classic tale of a bourgeois wife who sacrifices every-

thing for love is often considered a highlight of director Minnelli's career. Jones is the unhappy Emma, married to doctor Heflin, with a young Jourdan as her lover. Framing the narrative is Flaubert's morals trial, with Mason in the role of the author. A spectacular ball sequence with a score by Rozsa is one of the highlights. Three other theatrical versions have been made, by Albert Ray (as *Unholy Love*, 1932), Jean Renoir (1934), and Claude Chabrol (1991). Academy Award Nomination for Best (Black-and-White) Art Direction—Set Decoration. **Cast:** Van Heflin, Jennifer Jones, James Mason, Louis Jourdan, Gene Lockhart, Frank Allenby, Gladys Cooper, John Abbott. **Credits:** Dir: Vincente Minnelli; Prod: Pandro S. Berman; Writer: Robert Ardrey; DP: Robert Planck; Ed: Ferris Webster; Prod Design: Cedric Gibbons; Composer: Miklos Rozsa; Art Director: Jack Martin Smith. B&W, 115 min. VHS, LASER

Madame Curie
(1943) MGM
Garson and Pidgeon return a year after the triumph of *Mrs. Miniver* in this biopic about the famous husband-and-wife team who discovered radium. Though the love story between the shy Pierre (Pidgeon) and the Polish student Marie (Garson) gets center stage, this is an unusually intelligent look at the scientific quest that produced one of the century's major triumphs, but ended in tragedy. Dignified and moving. Academy Award Nominations: 7, including Best Picture; Best Actor: Walter Pidgeon; Best Actress: Greer Garson. **Cast:** Greer Garson, Walter Pidgeon, Henry Travers, Albert Basserman, Robert Walker, C. Aubrey Smith, Victor Francen, Reginald Owen. **Credits:** Dir: Mervyn LeRoy; Prod: Sidney Franklin; Writer: Paul Osborn, Paul H. Rameau; DP: Joseph Ruttenberg; Ed: Harold F. Kress; Prod Design: Cedric Gibbons, Paul Groesse; Composer: Herbert Stothart. B&W, 113 min. VHS, LASER

Madame X
(1937) MGM
Alexandre Bisson's 1909 tearjerker play had already reached the screen three times by 1929; eight years later it was time for another go-round. The story of a woman blackmailed and then wrongly accused of murder, who finds herself defended by a son unaware of his parentage, was produced to highlight the talents of Gladys George. Her judgmental husband is played by Warren William;

Beal, her son Raymond. Beal's defense to the court is both moving and delivered with conviction. **Cast:** Gladys George, John Beal, Warren William, Reginald Owen, William Henry, Henry Daniell, Phillip Reed, Ruth Hussey. **Credits:** Dir: Sam Wood; Prod: James Kevin McGuinness; Writer: John Meehan; DP: John F. Seitz; Ed: Frank Hull; Prod Design: Cedric Gibbons; Composer: David Snell. B&W, 96 min. VHS

Madame X
(1966) Universal
This time it's Turner who portrays the wronged woman in a color version of the oft-filmed Alexandre Bisson soap opera. Forsythe plays her distant political husband, Montalban her lover, and Dullea her public-defender son. An attempt by Universal's Hunter to recapture the old stars and old stories of Hollywood's golden age, this was a flop, which caused one critic to quip: "She's not Madame X, she's Brand X; she's not an actress, she's a commodity." **Cast:** Lana Turner, John Forsythe, Ricardo Montalban, Burgess Meredith, Constance Bennett, Keir Dullea, John Van Dreelan, Virginia Grey. **Credits:** Dir: David Lowell Rich; Prod: Ross Hunter; Writer: Jean Holloway; DP: Russell Metty; Ed: Milton Carruth; Prod Design: Alexander Golitzen; Composer: Frank Skinner; Art Director: George C. Webb. Color, 100 min. VHS

Made for Each Other
(1939) Fox
A romantic drama with a light touch, thanks mostly to Lombard's winning ways. Young attorney Stewart has high hopes for a partnership, but sees them dashed when he marries Lombard instead of the boss's daughter, Weston. His attempts to win over the senior partner (Coburn) are fruitless until he desperately needs help to get medicine for his child on a snowy New Year's Eve. **Cast:** James Stewart, Carole Lombard, Charles Coburn, Ward Bond, Lucile Watson, Ruth Weston, Harry Davenport, Donald Briggs, Eddie Quillan. **Credits:** Dir: John Cromwell; Prod: David O. Selznick; Writer: Jo Swerling, Frank Ryan; DP: Leon Shamroy; Ed: James E. Newcomb, Hal C. Kern; Prod Design: Lyle Wheeler; Composer: Louis Forbes. B&W, 107 min. VHS

Mademoiselle Fifi
(1943) RKO
The first feature by director Wise, who had moved up from editor on *Citizen*

Kane (1941) and *The Magnificent Ambersons* (1942), is a low-budget adaptation of two Guy de Maupassant short stories that take place in the 19th century, but were clearly intended to allude to the world war raging when this film was produced. A stagecoach journey during the Franco-Prussian war brings a laundress, a Prussian officer, and other passengers to a defining moment where courage is tested and loyalties are questioned. **Cast:** Simone Simon, John Emery, Kurt Kreuger, Alan Napier, Helen Freeman, Jason Robards, Sr., Norma Varden, Fay Helm. **Credits:** Dir: Robert Wise; Prod: Val Lewton; Writer: Peter Ruric, Josef Mischel; DP: Harry Wild; Ed: J.R. Whittredge; Composer: Werner Richard Heymann; Art Director: Albert S. D'Agostino, Walter E. Keller. B&W, 69 min. VHS

Madigan
(1968) Universal
Director Siegel's big-city cop drama seems a run-through for his 1972 hit *Dirty Harry*, with Widmark as the cynical, hard-nosed cop chasing after a psycho killer (Ihnat). Widmark is supported by a wonderful cast, including Guardino as his partner, Stevens as his wife, Fonda as a conflicted police commissioner, and Whitmore as Widmark's longtime friend dealing with a corruption investigation. One of Siegel's most accomplished and finely crafted features, which later spawned a short-lived TV show in which Widmark reprised his role. **Cast:** Richard Widmark, Henry Fonda, Inger Stevens, Harry Guardino, James Whitmore, Susan Clark, Michael Dunn, Steve Ihnat. **Credits:** Dir: Don Siegel; Prod: Frank P. Rosenberg; Writer: Howard A. Rodman, Abraham Polonsky, Harry Kleiner; DP: Russell Metty; Ed: Milton Shifman; Prod Design: Alexander Golitzen; Composer: Don Costa; Art Director: George C. Webb. Color, 101 min. VHS

Mad Love
(1935) MGM
The most famous version of Maurice Renard's famous horror story, "The Hands of Orlac." Here Lorre, in his American screen debut, plays a surgeon who operates on the hands of a noted pianist. Atmospherically directed by the noted Czech cinematographer Freund (*Metropolis*, 1926; *The Mummy*, 1932). Critic Pauline Kael speculates that Lorre's cue-ball makeup was the inspiration for Orson Welles's aged Charles Fos-

ter Kane. **Cast:** Peter Lorre, Frances Drake, Colin Clive, Isabel Jewell, Ted Healy, Sara Haden, Edward Brophy, Keye Luke. **Credits:** Dir: Karl Freund; Prod: John Considine; Writer: Guy Endore, P. J. Wolfson, John L. Balderston; DP: Chester Lyons, Gregg Toland; Ed: Hugh Wynn; Composer: Dimitri Tiomkin. B&W, 83 min. **VHS**

The Madwoman of Chaillot
(1969) Warner Bros.
Katharine Hepburn plays the deluded Parisian Countess Aurelia, who retains her placid illusions while the world spins out of control around her, in what was intended as an allusion to modern social decline. Giradoux's play features an all-star, international cast in this filmed stage adaptation produced by Landau and directed by the deft Forbes, who took over after John Huston was fired. **Cast:** Katharine Hepburn, Charles Boyer, Claude Dauphin, Edith Evans, John Gavin, Paul Henreid, Richard Chamberlain, Yul Brynner, Danny Kaye, Oscar Homolka. **Credits:** Dir: Bryan Forbes; Prod: Ely Landau; Writer: Edward Anhalt; Story: Jean Giradoux; DP: Claude Renoir, Burnett Guffey; Ed: Roger Dwyer; Prod Design: Ray Simm; Composer: Michael J. Lewis. Color, 132 min. **VHS, LASER**

Magic Town
(1947) RKO
A prescient Capra-like comedy in which Stewart plays a pollster who discovers Grandview, the perfectly average American town. Once the secret is out, and the town becomes aware of its stature, all goes awry. A wonderful premise with a script written by frequent Capra screenwriter Riskin and wry direction by Wellman. **Cast:** James Stewart, Jane Wyman, Regis Toomey, Kent Smith, Ned Sparks, Ann Doran, Donald Meek, Ann Shoemaker. **Credits:** Dir: William Wellman; Prod: Robert Riskin; Writer: Robert Riskin; DP: Joseph Biroc; Ed: Sherman Todd, Richard Wray; Composer: Roy Webb; Art Director: Lionel Banks. B&W, 103 min. **VHS**

The Magnificent Ambersons
(1942) RKO
Both one of the supreme works of the American cinema and one of its most notorious "ruined" films, Welles's follow-up to *Citizen Kane* (1941) keeps him behind the camera, though his presence is felt in every frame. Tarkington's novel about a turn-of-the-century family's conflicts is transformed by Welles into a eulogy for a slower,

simpler, and decent past, and this is a more personal film for Welles than his stunning debut the year before. Now missing close to 30 minutes and containing a saccharine "happy ending" shot by another crew while Welles was filming in South America, this version of *Ambersons* is the only one that survives. The Welles regulars are all here (Cotten, Moorehead, Collins), aided by Cortez's astounding cinematography and Herrmann's fitting score. The laserdisc contains interviews and original storyboards. Academy Award nominations: Best Picture; Best Supporting Actress: Agnes Moorehead; Best Art Direction—Set Decoration; Best Cinematography. **Cast:** Joseph Cotten, Anne Baxter, Tim Holt, Agnes Moorehead, Dolores Costello, Ray Collins, Erskine Sanford, Richard Bennett, J. Louis Johnson, Donald Dillaway. **Credits:** Dir: Orson Welles, Freddie Fleck, Robert Wise; Prod: Orson Welles; Writer: Orson Welles; Story: Booth Tarkington; DP: Stanley Cortez, Russell Metty, Harry Wild; Ed: Robert Wise, Jack Moss, Mark Robson; Prod Design: Mark-Lee Kirk; Composer: Bernard Herrmann, Roy Webb; Costumes: Edward Stevenson; SFX: Vernon L. Walker. B&W, 88 min. **VHS, LASER**

Magnificent Brute
(1936) Universal
A romantic triangle about two men fighting for the love of a woman set in the roughhouse world of steel mills. Big Steve (McLaglen) is a good man who takes up a collection for the widow of one of his mill helpers. He gives it to Barnes for safekeeping. Unfortunately greedy, she's easily persuaded by the hero's rival (Hall) to give it to him so that he can gamble with it. He pockets the money and tells Barnes that he lost it. The two are on their way out of town when kindhearted boardinghouse owner Dixon stops them. **Cast:** Binnie Barnes, William Hall, Henry Armetta, Victor McLaglen, Jean Dixon. **Credits:** Dir: John G. Blystone; Prod: Edmund Grainger, Charles Rogers; Writer: Lewis R. Foster, Bertram Millhauser, Owen Francis; DP: Merritt Gerstad; Ed: Ted J. Kent; Composer: Arthur Lange; Art Director: Albert S. D'Agostino, Jack Otterson. B&W, 77 min.

Magnificent Doll
(1946) Universal
A richly appointed historical drama based on the life of Dolley Madison. After Dolley (Rogers) loses her first husband, she and her mother open up a boardinghouse in Washington, D.C.

James Madison (Meredith) and Aaron Burr (Niven) vie for her attention, and Dolley has a brief affair with the evil Burr before she falls in love with Madison and marries him. Dolley is chiefly responsible for her husband's presidency, pushing him to run after he becomes Secretary of State under Thomas Jefferson. **Cast:** Ginger Rogers, David Niven, Burgess Meredith, Horace McNally, Peggy Wood, Robert Barrat, Grandon Rhodes. **Credits:** Dir: Frank Borzage; Prod: Bruce Manning, Jack H. Skirball; Writer: Irving Stone; DP: Joseph A. Valentine; Ed: Ted J. Kent; Prod Design: Alexander Golitzen; Composer: Hans J. Salter. B&W, 93 min.

The Magnificent Matador
(1955) Fox
Director Boetticher was apparently as enthralled by bullfighting as by CinemaScope, both of which are in ample evidence in this melodrama about Mexico's greatest matador (Quinn) facing middle age and training his illegitimate son to take his place. Much ado about macho pride; the scenes in the bullring are the highlight. **Cast:** Anthony Quinn, Maureen O'Hara, Manuel Rojas, Richard Denning, Thomas Gomez, Lola Albright, William Ching, Anthony Caruso. **Credits:** Dir: Budd Boetticher; Prod: Edward L. Alperson; Writer: Charles Lang; DP: Lucien Ballard; Ed: Richard Cahoon; Composer: Raoul Kraushaar, Edward L. Alperson. Color, 94 min. **VHS**

Magnificent Obsession
(1935) Universal
This is a melodrama that weaves a rich patchwork of guilt, desire, crime, and punishment. Robert Merrick's (Taylor) drinking has caused the death of a better man. Trying to make amends he accidentally blinds the beautiful widow Helen Hudson (Dunne). Obsessed with his guilt and his love for Helen, Merrick disappears and returns transformed into a Nobel-winning physician capable of curing the blindness he's caused. Remade in 1954 by Douglas Sirk. **Cast:** Irene Dunne, Robert Taylor, Charles Butterworth, Betty Furness, Sara Haden, Ralph Morgan, Henry Armetta, Gilbert Emery, Arthur Treacher, Beryl Mercer. **Credits:** Dir: John M. Stahl; Prod: E. M. Asher, John M. Stahl; Writer: Sarah Y. Mason, Victor Heerman, George O'Neill, Lloyd C. Douglas; DP: John J. Mescall; Ed: Milton Carruth; Composer: Franz Waxman; Art Director: Charles D. Hall. B&W, 112 min.

Magnificent Obsession (1954)

Magnificent Obsession
(1954) Universal
This is the second adaptation of novelist Lloyd C. Douglas's (*The Robe*) best-selling melodrama about a doctor's spiritual redemption when he chooses to abandon his youthful indiscretions to devote his life to restoring the eyesight of a woman he accidentally blinded. After minor roles in programmers and forgettable Westerns, Hudson here found his first popular starring role, opposite Wyman (both of whom appeared together again in Sirk's *All That Heaven Allows* a year later). Glossy and meticulously crafted, Sirk's version of the soaper has built a cult following. Previously filmed with Robert Taylor and Irene Dunne in 1935. Academy Award Nomination for Best Actress: Jane Wyman. **Cast:** Jane Wyman, Rock Hudson, Barbara Rush, Otto Kruger, Agnes Moorehead, Gregg Palmer, Sara Shane, Paul Cavanagh. **Credits:** Dir: Douglas Sirk; Prod: Ross Hunter; Writer: Robert Blees, Wells Root; DP: Russell Metty; Ed: Milton Carruth; Composer: Frank Skinner; Art Director: Bernard Herzbrun, Emrich Nicholson. Color, 108 min. **VHS**

The Magnificent Seven
(1960) United Artists
Among the most celebrated Westerns, this remake of Japanese director Akira Kurosawa's *Seven Samurai* chronicles the saga of 7 gunfighters hired to protect a small Mexican village from a group of marauding bandits. As much a star as the familiar faces (Brynner, McQueen, Wallach, Bronson, Coburn, Vaughn) is Bernstein's score, perhaps the most quoted piece of Western film music in history (and famous later for its use in TV cigarette commercials). Although he had labored in countless B pictures, this role was McQueen's breakthrough, appearing for the first time above the title. A television show and three sequels followed: *Return of the Magnificent Seven*, *Guns of the Magnificent Seven*, and *The Magnificent Seven Ride*. Parodied in *Three Amigos*. Academy Award Nomination for Best Scoring of a Dramatic or Comedy Picture. **Cast:** Yul Brynner, Eli Wallach, Steve McQueen, Horst Buchholz, James Coburn, Robert Vaughn, Charles Bronson, Brad Dexter, Vladimir Sokoloff, Rosenda Monteros. **Credits:** Dir: John Sturges; Prod: John Sturges, Lou Morheim; Writer: William Roberts, Walter Newman, Walter Bernstein; Story: Akira Kurosawa; DP: Charles Lang; Ed: Ferris Webster; Prod Design: Edward Fitzgerald; Composer: Elmer Bernstein; SFX: Milt Rice. Color, 138 min. **VHS, LASER, DVD**

The Magnificent Yankee
(1950) MGM
This life of jurist Oliver Wendell Holmes, based on the popular play by Lavery, is a showcase for the fine acting of Calhern, in the title role, and Harding, playing his devoted wife. Very little time is spent in the courtroom, with the drama largely confined to the domestic matters of this loving couple and a celebration of Holmes's 80th birthday. Academy Award Nominations: 2, including Best Actor: Louis Calhern. **Cast:** Louis Calhern, Ann Harding, Eduard Franz, James Lydon, Philip Ober, Ian Wolfe, Edith Evanson, Richard Anderson, Herbert Anderson. **Credits:** Dir: John Sturges; Prod: Armand S. Deutsch; Writer: Emmett Lavery; DP: Joseph Ruttenberg; Ed: Ferris Webster; Prod Design: Cedric Gibbons; Composer: David Raksin; Art Director: Arthur Lonergan. Color, 80 min. **VHS**

Magnum Force
(1973) Warner Bros.
After the success of 1971's *Dirty Harry*, it was inevitable the San Francisco cop who writes his own rules would return with his .44 Magnum. In an intriguing variation on the premise of the first film, here Harry Callahan (Eastwood) takes on a secret cabal of vigilante cops under the command of police captain Holbrook. The story, penned by soon-to-be directors Milius (*Big Wednesday*, 1978) and Cimino (*The Deer Hunter*, 1978), offers plenty of action and even a few comic asides. The ambiguity of Holbrook's character stems partially from having starred as a Kennedy-like liberal politician in a highly acclaimed 1970s TV series, *The Senator*. Sequel: *The Enforcer* (1976). **Cast:** Clint Eastwood, Hal Holbrook, David Soul, Robert Urich, Mitchell Ryan, Felton Perry, Tim Matheson, Kip Niven. **Credits:** Dir: Ted Post; Prod: Robert Daley; Writer: John Milius, Michael Cimino; DP: Frank Stanley; Ed: Ferris Webster; Composer: Lalo Schifrin; Art Director: Jack Collis. Color, 124 min. **VHS, LASER**

Maid of Salem

(1937) Paramount
This drama is set during the 1692 witch trials in Salem. Colbert plays the voice of reason in a town filled with suspicion. Granville stirs up the village, and when it is discovered that Colbert has been meeting with the outsider MacMurray, she is in danger of being branded a witch. **Cast:** Claudette Colbert, Fred MacMurray, Harvey Stephens, Gale Sondergaard, Louise Dresser, Edward Ellis, Virginia Weidler, E. E. Clive, Bonita Granville, Bennie Bartlett. **Credits:** Dir: Frank Lloyd; Prod: Frank Lloyd; Writer: Walter Ferris, Durward Grimstead, Bradley King; DP: Leo Tover; Ed: Hugh Bennett; Prod Design: Hans Dreier; Composer: Victor Young; Art Director: Bernard Herzbrun. B&W, 86 min.

The Main Event

(1979) Warner Bros.
A star vehicle for Streisand and O'Neal, teamed together in the hope of recapturing the success of 1972's *What's Up, Doc?* Streisand is a perfume magnate whose luck has turned sour, O'Neal a former boxer who has been coerced back into the ring. Yet another attempt to breathe life into the screwball-comedy genre, but the results are hardly a knockout. This was one of Streisand's projects co-produced with former hairdresser Peters. **Cast:** Barbra Streisand, Ryan O'Neal, Patti D'Arbanville, Paul Sand, Richard Lawson, James Gregory, Whitman Mayo, Richard Altman, Seth Banks. **Credits:** Dir: Howard Zieff; Prod: Jon Peters, Barbra Streisand; Writer: Gail Parent, Andrew Smith; DP: Mario Tosi; Ed: Edward A. Warschilka; Prod Design: Charles Rosen. Color, 109 min. **VHS, LASER**

Main Street to Broadway

(1953) MGM
Writer Raphaelson's (*The Shop Around The Corner, Heaven Can Wait*) inside story of the struggle for success in showbiz, featuring two obscure leads and plenty of Broadway cameos, including Lilli Palmer, Helen Hayes, Henry Fonda, Mary Martin, and Louis Calhern. The story charts a playwright's opening on Broadway, yet the main attraction remains the walk-ons. **Cast:** Lionel Barrymore, Tom Morton, Mary Murphy, Agnes Moorehead, Rosemary DeCamp, Tallulah Bankhead, Shirley Booth, Cornel Wilde, Rex Harrison. **Credits:** Dir: Tay Garnett; Prod: Lester Cowan; Writer: Samson Raphaelson; DP: James Wong Howe; Ed: Gene Fowler, Jr.; Composer: Ann Ronell; Art Director: Perry Ferguson. B&W, 102 min. **VHS**

Maisie

A tough girl with a good heart, Maisie (a character created by novelist Wilson Collison), played with great pizzazz by Ann Sothern, made her way through a series that tested her sass and endurance, as well as reflected new roles for women as America went to war. Most of the plots revolved around Maisie's ability to straighten out the lives of those individuals she encounters: clearing a foreman (Robert Young) of a false murder charge in *Maisie* (1939) and preventing a young couple's divorce in *Maisie Goes to Reno* (1944). Despite surprisingly poor production quality for an MGM project and rather banal scripts, Sothern's vitality managed to carry the films. Ava Gardner appears in *Maisie Goes to Reno* and Maureen O'Sullivan helps out in *Maisie Was a Lady* (1941).

Maisie *(1939)*
Congo Maisie *(1940)*
Gold Rush Maisie *(1940)*
Maisie Was a Lady *(1941)*
Ringside Maisie *(1941)*
Maisie Gets Her Man *(1942)*
Swing Shift Maisie *(1943)*
Maisie Goes to Reno *(1944)*
Up Goes Maisie *(1946)*
Undercover Maisie *(1947)*

The Major and the Minor

(1942) Paramount
After writing some of the wittiest scripts of the 1930s, Wilder was finally given the opportunity by Paramount to direct this comedy about a destitute New York career woman (Rogers) who decides to return to Iowa at reduced train fare by masquerading as a 12-year-old. On her journey, she meets the dignified, proper Milland, the commander of a military school, who takes it upon himself to see to her welfare. The predictable misunderstandings ensue as Rogers falls in love with Milland while the cadets start making passes at the new visitor. Very popular when released, it's interesting to view now in light of its *Lolita*-like subtext, of which Wilder was certainly more than aware. An adaptation of Fannie Kilbourne's short story "Sunny Goes Home." **Cast:** Ginger Rogers, Ray Milland, Rita Johnson, Robert Benchley, Diana Lynn, Edward Fielding, Frankie Thomas. **Credits:** Dir: Billy Wilder; Prod: Arthur Hornblow, Jr.; Writer: Billy Wilder, Charles Brackett; DP: Leo Tover; Ed: Doane Harrison; Composer: Robert Emmett Dolan; Costumes: Edith Head. B&W, 101 min. **VHS**

Major Dundee

(1965) Columbia
Peckinpah's second feature was taken from his control and recut, yet still contains action sequences and the sweep of the Western landscape that bear his mark. Heston plays Dundee, a conflicted Union cavalry officer commanding an assortment of renegades on a rescue mission to save three children kidnapped by Apaches. Dundee clashes with the charismatic Capt. Benjamin Tyreen (Harris), the commander of Confederate prisoners mustered into service. The story suffers from occasional incoherence (Peckinpah intended to shoot an additional hour of footage), but remains a fascinating epic. Look for some of the Peckinpah stock company: L. Q. Jones, Oates, and Johnson. **Cast:** Charlton Heston, Richard Harris, Jim Hutton, James Coburn, Senta Berger, Brock Peters, Warren Oates, Slim Pickens, Ben Johnson. **Credits:** Dir: Sam Peckinpah; Prod: Jerry Bresler; Writer: Harry Julian Fink, Oscar Saul, Sam Peckinpah; DP: Sam Leavitt; Ed: William A. Lyon, Don Starling, Howard Kunin; Composer: Daniele Amfitheatrof; Art Director: Alfred Ybarra. Color, 124 min. **VHS, LASER**

A Majority of One

(1961) Warner Bros.
Guinness playing a Japanese widower courted by Russell as a Jewish Brooklyn widow? Based on a Broadway hit and popular in its time, this talky LeRoy comedy is very much a film of its time. Russell is often endearing and entertaining, yet Guinness, who has played everything from Victorian matrons to Jedi knights, seems more comfortable in a Saville Row suit than a kimono. Based on the play by Spigelgass. Russell won her fourth Golden Globe award for Best Actress for this performance, and the film won for Best Film Promoting International Understanding and Best Motion Picture, Comedy. Academy Award Nomination for Best (Color) Cinematography. **Cast:** Alec Guinness, Rosalind Russell, Ray Danton, Madlyn Rhue, Mae Questel, Gary Vinson, Sharon Hugueny, Frank Wilcox. **Credits:** Dir: Mervyn LeRoy; Prod: Mervyn LeRoy; Writer: Leonard Spigelgass; DP: Harry Stradling; Ed: Philip W. Anderson; Art Director: John Beckman. Color, 153 min. **VHS**

Make Haste to Live

(1954) Republic

McGuire plays a New Mexico newspaper owner who has been secretly living under an assumed name while her mobster husband serves time for murder: hers! After 18 years, McGuire has raised a daughter and lives in peace—until her vengeful husband comes looking for her. **Cast:** Dorothy McGuire, Stephen McNally, Mary Murphy, Edgar Buchanan, Carolyn Jones, John Howard, Eddy Waller, Ron Hagerthy, Pepe Hern. **Credits:** Dir: William A. Seiter; Prod: William A. Seiter; Writer: Warren Duff; DP: John L. Russell, Jr.; Ed: Fred Allen; Composer: Elmer Bernstein. B&W, 90 min. **VHS**

Make Mine Music

(1946) Disney

An animated film comprised of 10 separate sequences. Considered a pop version of *Fantasia* at the time, the film features the story of "Casey at the Bat" and "Peter and the Wolf" along with original bits about a whale whose greatest wish is to sing at the Metropolitan Opera, feuding mountain people, and Benny Goodman and His Orchestra. **Cast:** Nelson Eddy, Dinah Shore, Jerry Colonna, Andy Russell, David Lichine, Sterling Holloway, Tania Riabouchinskaya. **Credits:** Dir: Robert Cormack, Clyde Geronimi, Jack Kinney, Hamilton Luske, Joshua Meador; Prod: Joe Grant; Writer: Walt Disney, James Bodrero, Homer Brightman, Erdman Penner, Dick Huemer, Dick Kinney, John Walbridge, Tom Oreb, Dick Shaw, Eric Gurney, Sylvia Holland, Dick Kelsey, Jesse Marsh, Roy Williams, Cap Palmer, Erwin Graham; Prod Design: Mary Blair; Composer: Eliot Daniel, Ray Gilbert, Allie Wrubel, Allan Cameron, Richard Wagner; Art Director: Elmer Plummer, John Hench. Color, 74 min.

Make Way For Tomorrow

(1937) Paramount

This is one of the most exquisitely sad motion pictures ever made, by one of the screen's greatest directors of madcap humor, McCarey. Ma and Pa Cooper (Moore and Bondi) can't make their payments to the bank and their house is repossessed. Left with no alternative, they seek help from their children. With neither the space nor the time, their children cannot accommodate them and so the couple are forced to separate after years of living together. She is to go to a retirement home for women, he is to travel south as his health requires a warmer cli-

mate. Ma and Pa say farewell to each other at the same train station from which they had embarked on their honeymoon. McCarey had a pronounced sentimental streak (he also directed *Going My Way*, and made the story that became *An Affair to Remember* twice) and here it finds its greatest expression, with fine interpretations by the entire cast. Not a big hit in the weary latter days of the Depression, it may have more relevance today. **Cast:** Victor Moore, Beulah Bondi, Fay Bainter, Thomas Mitchel, Porter Hall, Barbara Read, Maurice Moscovich, Elisabeth Risdon, Minna Gombell, Ray Mayer. **Credits:** Dir: Leo McCarey; Prod: Leo McCarey, Adolph Zukor; Writer: Vina Delmar, Josephine Lawrence; Story: Henry Leary, Noah Leary; DP: William Mellor; Ed: LeRoy Stone; Prod Design: Hans Dreier; Composer: Victor Young, George Antheil. B&W, 92 min.

The Male Animal

(1942) Warner Bros.

New Yorker magazine writer Thurber's popular battle-of-the-sexes stage drama (cowritten by director Nugent) with classic performances from Fonda as a clueless, distracted college professor, de Havilland as his neglected wife, and Carson as the homecoming football hero who comes between them. Remade as a musical, *She's Working Her Way Through College* (1952); with Ronald Reagan in the role of the professor. **Cast:** Henry Fonda, Olivia de Havilland, Joan Leslie, Jack Carson, Eugene Pallette, Herbert Anderson, Hattie McDaniel, Don Defore. **Credits:** Dir: Elliott Nugent; Prod: Wolfgang Reinhardt; Writer: Julius J. Epstein, Philip G. Epstein, Stephen Morehouse Avery; Story: James Thurber, Elliott Nugent; DP: Arthur Edeson; Ed: Thomas Richards; Composer: Heinz Roemheld. B&W, 101 min. **VHS**

The Maltese Falcon

(1941) Warner Bros.

One of the most popular crime films of all time has Bogart playing Hammett's private detective Sam Spade as he sleuths the backyard of San Francisco in search of an elusive black bird statuette and crosses wits with Astor's treacherous Brigid O'Shaughnessy and fat man Kaspar Gutman (Greenstreet). Memorable supporting performances by Lorre and Cook, Jr., playing two of the quirkiest villains of the '40s, only add to the unsettling atmosphere of this cynical parable of greed and deceit. After a brief career

as screenwriter, this was Huston's directorial debut, and launched a career that spanned nearly half a century. Based on the Hammett novel that was previously filmed in 1931 as *Dangerous Female*, in 1936 as *Satan Met a Lady* starring Bette Davis, and poorly redone in 1975 as *The Black Bird*. Selected as a National Film Registry Outstanding Film. Academy Award Nominations: Best Picture; Best Supporting Actor: Sydney Greenstreet; Best Screenplay. **Cast:** Humphrey Bogart, Mary Astor, Peter Lorre, Sydney Greenstreet, Gladys George, Ward Bond, Elisha Cook, Jr., Walter Huston, Barton MacLane, Lee Patrick. **Credits:** Dir: John Huston; Prod: Henry Blanke; Writer: John Huston; Story: Dashiell Hammett; DP: Arthur Edeson; Ed: Thomas Richards; Prod Design: Robert M. Haas; Composer: Adolph Deutsch; Costumes: Orry-Kelly. B&W, 101 min. **VHS, LASER**

Mambo

(1954) Paramount

An international star vehicle for Italian sensation Mangano (*Bitter Rice*, *Anna*), this was shot on location in Venice. She plays a salesclerk embroiled in romances with a gambler and sickly aristocrat and who suddenly becomes a popular mambo dancer. Mangano, a former model and later wife of Dino de Laurentiis, never achieved the American popularity of her contemporaries Gina Lollobrigida or Sophia Loren, but later in her career made a number of notable films in Italy. **Cast:** Silvana Mangano, Michael Rennie, Vittorio Gassman, Shelley Winters, Katherine Dunham, Eduardo Ciannelli, Mary Clare, Julie Robinson, Walter Zappolini. **Credits:** Dir: Robert Rossen; Prod: Dino de Laurentiis, Carlo Ponti; Writer: Guido Piovene, Ivo Perilli, Ennio De Concini, Robert Rossen; DP: Harold Rosson; Ed: Adriana Novelli; Prod Design: Andre Andrejew; Composer: Nino Rota, Angelo Francesco Lavagnino, Bernardo Noriega. B&W, 94 min. **VHS**

Mame

(1974) Warner Bros.

The Broadway musical adaptation of Patrick Denis's *Auntie Mame,* the story of an eccentric, wealthy woman who teaches her nephew how to live life to the fullest, comes to the screen starring Ball in her final screen appearance (Ball, 64 when this was made, plays a woman 20 years younger). The novel, play, and earlier Rosalind Russell film of this story of an irrepressible, extroverted, and outrageous rich Bohemian in 1920s New

York has had a lasting cult following, but this final incarnation met with little enthusiasm and did nothing to bolster the flagging Hollywood musical. Theadora van Runkle's costumes are one of the film's charms. Featured songs include "Mame," "If He Walked Into My Life," and "We Need a Little Christmas." **Cast:** Lucille Ball, Beatrice Arthur, Robert Preston, Jane Connell, Ned Wertimer, Bruce Davison, Joyce Van Patten, Don Porter. **Credits:** Dir: Gene Saks; Prod: Robert Fryer, James Cresson; Writer: Paul Zindel; DP: Philip H. Lathrop; Ed: Maury Winetrobe; Composer: Ralph Burns; Art Director: Harold Michelson. Color, 132 min. **VHS, LASER**

A Man Alone
(1955) Republic
Notable as actor Milland's directorial debut, he plays a gunslinger suspected of murder hiding out from an angry mob in a small town. Befriended by the daughter of a corrupt sheriff (Murphy), Milland tries to clear his name while dealing with heavies Burr and Van Cleef. Bond is notable as the sheriff who has a change of heart. Milland went on to direct five more features. **Cast:** Ray Milland, Raymond Burr, Mary Murphy, Ward Bond, Arthur Space, Lee Van Cleef, Alan Hale, Douglas Spencer, Thomas Brown Henry, Grandon Rhodes. **Credits:** Dir: Ray Milland; Prod: Mort Briskin, Herbert J. Yates; Writer: John Tucker Battle; DP: Lionel Lindon; Ed: Richard L. Van Enger; Composer: Victor Young; Art Director: Walter E. Keller. Color, 96 min. **VHS**

The Man Behind the Gun
(1952) Warner Bros.
This Western is about a cavalry officer (Scott) who goes undercover to foil plans for California to secede from the Union. He arrives in Los Angeles to complete his mission and soon falls in love with a charming schoolteacher (Wymore) and exposes the power-mad senator Roberts. **Cast:** Randolph Scott, Patrice Wymore, Dick Wesson, Philip Carey, Lina Romay, Roy Roberts, Morris Ankrum, Katharine Warren, Alan Hale, Douglas Fowley. **Credits:** Dir: Felix E. Feist; Prod: Robert Sisk; Writer: Robert Buckner, John Twist; DP: Bert Glennon; Ed: Owen Marks; Composer: David Buttolph. Color, 82 min.

A Man Betrayed
(1941) Republic
A small-town lawyer (Wayne) goes to the big city to investigate the murder of a friend, a young basketball player. During the course of his investigation

the lawyer ends up exposing a corrupt political ring and numerous underworld associates, and falls in love with the corrupt politician's daughter (Dee). **Cast:** John Wayne, Frances Dee, Edward Ellis, Ward Bond, Wallace Ford, Harold Huber, Alexander Granach, Barnett Parker, Ed Stanley, Harry Hayden. **Credits:** Dir: John H. Auer; Prod: Armand Schaefer; Writer: Isabel Dawn, Tom Kilpatrick; Story: Jack Moffitt; DP: Jack A. Marta, Ernest Miller; Ed: Charles Craft; Prod Design: John MacKay; Composer: Cy Feuer. B&W, 82 min.

A Man Called Horse
(1970) National General
Primarily remembered for its graphic depiction of the Sioux Sun Vow ceremony, this gritty clash-of-cultures story stars Harris as an English nobleman captured, tortured, and eventually adopted by the Sioux. An odd mix of primitive romanticism and racial clichés, this, along with *Little Big Man* and *Soldier Blue* (both also released in 1970), was an attempt to authentically present Native American history at the twilight of the traditional Hollywood Western. A sequel, *The Return of a Man Called Horse*, followed in 1976. **Cast:** Richard Harris, Judith Anderson, Manu Tupou, Jean Gascon, Corinna Tsopei, Dub Taylor, William Jordan, James Gammon. **Credits:** Dir: Elliot Silverstein; Prod: Sandy Howard; Writer: Jack DeWitt; Story: Dorothy M. Johnson; DP: Robert Hauser; Ed: Philip W. Anderson, Gene Fowler, Jr.; Prod Design: Dennis Lynton Clark; Composer: Leonard Rosenman, Lloyd One Star. Color, 115 min. **VHS**

A Man Called Peter
(1955) Fox
Produced during the decade of countless biblical sagas, this biopic of U.S. Senate chaplain Peter Marshall (Todd) is one of the few truly moving religious films created in Hollywood. Based on a popular book by his widow, Catherine, this chronicles Marshall's career from humble beginnings in Scotland to his struggles with tuberculosis. Unusual for its approach to religion in a contemporary world: a highlight is Todd's Pearl Harbor sermon to Naval Academy midshipmen. The fine cinematography by Lipstein earned an Academy Award Nomination. Academy Award Nomination for Best (Black-and-White) Cinematography. **Cast:** Richard Todd, Jean Peters, Marjorie Rambeau, Jill Esmond, Les Tremayne, Robert Burton, Gladys Hurlbut, Billy Chapin. **Credits:** Dir: Henry Koster; Prod:

Samuel G. Engel; Writer: Eleanore Griffin; Story: Catherine Marshall; DP: Harold Lipstein; Ed: Robert Simpson; Prod Design: Lyle Wheeler, Maurice Ransford; Composer: Alfred Newman. Color, 119 min. **VHS**

The Manchurian Candidate
(1962) United Artists
Among the most lauded political thrillers of all time, this film was amazingly prescient in light of the recent attraction of conspiracy theories. Korean War hero Harvey is a brainwashed human time bomb engineered to further a hidden Communist takeover, with Sinatra the one man who stands in his way. A mix of black-comic political satire (Gregory, in his finest performance as a Joe McCarthy–like demagogue) and an energetic, violent, and disturbing exercise in suspense, the film has resonance like few others of its time. Perhaps the finest work by Frankenheimer, featuring an outstanding cast (Lansbury, in the role of her career as Harvey's scheming mother) and one of the saddest scores of all time by Amram. Not to be missed. Based on Richard Condon's harrowing novel. The laserdisc collector's edition is digitally remastered and includes the original theatrical trailer. Golden Globe for Best Supporting Actress: Angela Lansbury, and selected as a National Film Registry Outstanding Film. Academy Award Nominations: Best Film Editing; Best Supporting Actress: Angela Lansbury. **Cast:** Frank Sinatra, Laurence Harvey, Angela Lansbury, Janet Leigh, James Gregory, Henry Silva, Leslie Parrish, John McGivern. **Credits:** Dir: John Frankenheimer; Prod: George Axelrod; Writer: George Axelrod; DP: Lionel Lindon; Ed: Ferris Webster; Prod Design: Richard Sylbert; Composer: David Amram; SFX: Paul Pollard. B&W, 136 min. **VHS, LASER, DVD**

The Man from Laramie
(1955) Columbia
In the last of the justly renowned Mann-Stewart Westerns, Stewart plays a vengeance-driven cowboy trying to uncover the reasons behind his brother's death. He discovers a tragic feud between rival ranchers in New Mexico and runs afoul of the sadistic son of a dying patriarch (Crisp). Mann's Westerns are moral parables about family, land, greed, and revenge. The other Mann-Stewart collaborations were *Winchester '73* (1950), *Bend of the River* (1952), *The Naked Spur* (1953), and *The Far Coun-*

try (1955). **Cast:** James Stewart, Arthur Kennedy, Donald Crisp, Cathy O'Donnell, Alex Nicol, Aline MacMahon, Wallace Ford, Jack Elam, John War Eagle, Frank Cordell. **Credits:** Dir: Anthony Mann; Prod: William Goetz; Writer: Philip Yordan, Frank Burt; Story: Thomas T. Flynn; DP: Charles B. Lang; Ed: William A. Lyon; Composer: George Duning; Art Director: Cary Odell. Color, 104 min. **VHS**

The Man from the Alamo

(1953) Universal
Ford plays the sole survivor of the Alamo massacre, branded a coward after he escapes from the Alamo to warn others in this Boetticher Western. As in most other Boetticher pictures, it's the action sequences that sing, particularly an attack on a wagon train by Jory's marauding gang dressed as Mexican soldiers. Cinematography by veteran cameraman Metty (*Touch of Evil*) deserves special note. **Cast:** Glenn Ford, Julie Adams, Hugh O'Brian, Chill Wills, Victor Jory, Jeanne Cooper, Neville Brand, Edward Norris, Guy Williams. **Credits:** Dir: Budd Boetticher; Prod: Aaron Rosenberg; Writer: Steve Fisher, D. D. Beauchamp; Story: Niven Busch, Oliver Crawford; DP: Russell Metty; Ed: Virgil Vogel; Composer: Frank Skinner; Art Director: Alexander Golitzen. Color, 80 min. **VHS**

Man from Yesterday

(1932) Paramount
Nurse Colbert marries Brook's captain and conceives a child with him just before he returns to the WWI front. He is gassed, left for dead, and taken prisoner. A buddy mistakenly reports his demise to Colbert, who has since begun to assist doctor Boyer, but refused to become involved with him pending news of her husband. Doctor and nurse fall in love, but Brook returns, and fails to successfully re-enter what was once his life. **Cast:** Charles Boyer, Clive Brook, Claudette Colbert, Andy Devine, Alan Mowbray, Ronnie Cosbey, Emil Chautard, George W. Davis, Reginald Pasch, Christian Rub. **Credits:** Dir: Berthold Viertel; Writer: Neil Blackwell, Roland G. Edwards; Story: Oliver H. P. Garrett; DP: Karl Struss. B&W, 68 min.

Manhattan

(1979) United Artists
Among Allen's most praised films, it is probably the most beloved of all valentines to New York City. A skillfully constructed and beautifully shot slice-of-life portrait of a neurotic writer (Allen,

naturally) and his circle, for which happiness with everyday life seems an elusive impossibility. Both comic and introspective and set to the familiar strains of Gershwin, the film features many familiar faces from the Allen ensemble in some of their finest work. An early role for Streep as Allen's ex-wife. Academy Award Nominations: Best Supporting Actress: Mariel Hemingway; Best (Original) Screenplay. **Cast:** Woody Allen, Diane Keaton, Mariel Hemingway, Meryl Streep, Michael Murphy, Anne Byrne, Karen Ludwig, Michael O'Donoghue. **Credits:** Dir: Woody Allen; Prod: Charles H. Joffe; Writer: Woody Allen, Marshall Brickman; DP: Gordon Willis; Ed: Susan E. Morse; Prod Design: Mel Bourne; Composer: George Gershwin. B&W, 96 min. **VHS, LASER**

Manhattan Merry-Go-Round

(1937) Republic
One of those '30s musical-variety films in which celebrities of all types appear in cameo performance numbers barely held together by a purely incidental script. Sentimental racketeer Carrillo's gangsters muscle into the recording business, and Autry, Calloway, big-band star Ted Lewis, and even Joe DiMaggio get in the act. Featuring such nostalgic melodies as "Mamma I Wanna Make Rhythm" and "It's Round-up Time in Reno." Based on a hit radio show that ran from 1932 to 1949. Academy Award Nomination for Best Interior Decoration. **Cast:** Phil Regan, Ann Dvorak, Leo Carrillo, James Gleason, Kay Thompson, Cab Calloway, Joe DiMaggio, Gene Autry. **Credits:** Dir: Charles Riesner; Prod: Harry Sauber; Writer: Harry Sauber; DP: Jack Marta; Ed: Murray Seldeen, Ernest Nims; Composer: Alberto Colombo. B&W, 89 min. **VHS**

Man Hunt

(1941) Fox
This taut Lang spy thriller follows Captain Alan Thorndike (Pidgeon) on a hunting expedition in the Austrian Alps. By accident, he stumbles on the mountain hideaway of none other than Adolf Hitler himself. One bullet is all it would take, and Thorndike's about to save the world a whole lot of trouble when he's captured by the Gestapo. Beaten, tossed out for dead, Captain Thorndike survives and makes his way to England, where he gets mixed up in the seamy underworld, killing the mysterious Imposter (Carradine) in self defense and briefly romancing lovely Bennett. At the end, Captain Thorndike parachutes back into the

European mainland with his hunting rifle looking for a second chance. **Cast:** Walter Pidgeon, Joan Bennett, Ludwig Stossel, Heather Thatcher, John Carradine, Roger Imhof, Egon Brecher, Carl Ekberg, Lucien Prival, Fredrik Vogeding, Eily Malyon, Herbert Evans. **Credits:** Dir: Fritz Lang; Prod: Kenneth MacGowan; Writer: Dudley Nichols; DP: Arthur C. Miller; Ed: Allen McNeil; Prod Design: Richard Day, Wiard Ihnen; Composer: Alfred Newman. B&W, 105 min.

The Man I Love

(1946) Warner Bros.
Walsh soaper about a torch singer (Lupino) visiting her family romanced by a nightclub pianist (Alda). Notable as the inspiration for Martin Scorsese's *New York, New York* (1977). The closest Walsh came to making a film noir featuring one of his favorite actresses, Lupino. **Cast:** Ida Lupino, Robert Alda, Bruce Bennett, Andrea King, Dolores Moran, Martha Vickers, Alan Hale, Craig Stevens, William Edmunds, Thomas Quinn. **Credits:** Dir: Raoul Walsh; Prod: Arnold Albert; Writer: Catherine Turney, Jo Pagano; Story: Maritta M. Wolff; DP: Sidney Hickox; Ed: Owen Marks; Composer: Max Steiner; Art Director: Stanley Fleischer. B&W, 96 min. **VHS**

The Man I Married

(1940) Fox
A WWII drama about an American woman married to a German-American. When she and their small son return to the fatherland for a visit, she meets an American journalist who aids her in seeing more clearly the regimentation and frightful mass meetings of the Nazi Party. Her husband ends up slipping into the spell of the German fanaticism but she manages to flee Germany with her son and returns to America. A fascinating glimpse at the period's anti-Nazi propaganda. **Cast:** Joan Bennett, Francis Lederer, Lloyd Nolan, Anna Sten, Otto Kruger, Maria Ouspenskaya, Ludwig Stossel, Johnny Russell, Lionel Royce, Fredrik Vogeding. **Credits:** Dir: Irving Pichel; Prod: Darryl F. Zanuck; Writer: Oliver H. P. Garrett; Story: Oscar Schisgall; DP: J. Peverell Marley; Ed: Robert Simpson; Prod Design: Richard Day, Hans Peters; Composer: David Buttolph. B&W, 77 min.

Man in the Gray Flannel Suit

(1956) Fox
One of Peck's best films, it applies his natural sincerity to balance the lead character's confusion and guilt.

Office and money pressures, home life, and secrets from the wartime past weigh on decent, but fallible, Peck, who must choose between an accelerating career and his suburban home life and wife (Jones). His first success presents a fork in the road leading to either a 9-to-5 life that lets him watch his children grow or a hard-charging career that leads to loneliness at the top. Outstanding are March as the troubled public-relations tycoon and the music by Herrmann, who took a breather from Hitchcock thrillers and fantasy epics. **Cast:** Jennifer Jones, Fredric March, Lee J. Cobb, Gregory Peck, Keenan Wynn, Marisa Pavan, Ann Harding, Gene Lockhart, Gigi Perreau, Arthur O'Connell. **Credits:** Dir: Nunnally Johnson; Prod: Darryl F. Zanuck; Writer: Nunnally Johnson; Story: Sloan Wilson; DP: Charles G. Clarke; Ed: Dorothy Spencer; Prod Design: Charles H. Clarke, Lyle Wheeler; Composer: Bernard Herrmann; Costumes: Charles LeMaire; Art Director: Jack Martin Smith. Color, 153 min. **VHS, LASER**

The Man in the Iron Mask
(1939) United Artists
This famous Dumas costume adventure is about a twin brother of Louis XV kept hidden away in a prison and forced to wear an iron mask to hide his identity. This second of five versions was directed by Whale (*Frankenstein*) and features Hayward in the dual roles of Louis and his brother, and William as swordsman D'Artagnan. First made with Douglas Fairbanks in 1929 as *The Iron Mask*, with later versions made in 1976, 1978 (*The Fifth Musketeer*), and 1998. Academy Award Nomination for Best Original Score. **Cast:** Louis Hayward, Joan Bennett, Joseph Schildkraut, Warren William, Alan Hale, Miles Mander, Bert Roach, Walter Kingsford, Marion Martin, Montagu Love, Doris Kenyon. **Credits:** Dir: James Whale; Prod: Edward Small; Writer: George Bruce; Story: Alexandre Dumas; DP: Robert H. Planck; Ed: Grant Whytock; Composer: Lucien Moraweck. B&W, 119 min. **VHS**

The Man in the Shadow
(1957) Universal
An honest sheriff (Chandler) stands up to a wealthy, despotic rancher (the magnificently sinister Welles) when one of the rancher's laborers is brutally murdered on the job. A minor, low-budget Western notable as the film that briefly brought Welles to Universal and led to his opportunity to

direct *Touch of Evil* shortly thereafter. Script by classic *Star Trek* writer Coon and directed by Arnold (*It Came from Outer Space*, 1953). **Cast:** Jeff Chandler, Orson Welles, Colleen Miller, James Gleason, Ben Alexander, Barbara Lawrence, John Larch, Royal Dano, Paul Fix, Leo Gordon. **Credits:** Dir: Jack Arnold; Prod: Albert Zugsmith; Writer: Gene L. Coon; DP: Arthur E. Arling; Ed: Edward Curtiss; Composer: Joseph Gershenson; Costumes: Bill Thomas. B&W, 80 min. **VHS**

Mannequin
(1937) MGM
Crawford and Tracy appear here in their only film together. She's a Lower East Side factory girl married to a small-time hood, he's a lonely, wealthy shipping magnate. Tracy wins her over, only to have the ex return for his share of the pie. A typical Crawford soaper produced with all the famed MGM glamour. Ironically, the year this film was made theater exhibitors were taking out full-page ads declaring Crawford "box office poison." Academy Award Nomination for Best Song ("Always and Always"). **Cast:** Joan Crawford, Spencer Tracy, Alan Curtis, Ralph Morgan, Leo Gorcey, Elisabeth Risdon, Mary Philips, Oscar O'Shea. **Credits:** Dir: Frank Borzage; Prod: Joseph L. Mankiewicz; Writer: Lawrence Hazard; DP: George J. Folsey; Ed: Fredrick Y. Smith; Prod Design: Cedric Gibbons, Paul Groesse; Composer: Edward Ward. B&W, 95 min. **VHS**

Man of Aran
(1934)
A near-plotless, epic film poem about men and the sea, this is shot on the rugged rocky islands off the west coast of Ireland. Director Flaherty, the most influential American documentary filmmaker of his generation, used native talent and fudged with reality (the islands had electricity and the seafarers hadn't fished for basking sharks for 60 years by the time the film was made) to create one of the most admired and memorable films of the 1930s. One of the very few commercially distributed documentaries of the era. **Cast:** Colman "Tiger" King, Maggie Dirrane, Michael Dillane, Pat Mullin, Patch "Red Beard" Ruadh, Patcheen Faherty. **Credits:** Dir: Robert Flaherty; Writer: Robert J. Flaherty; DP: Robert J. Flaherty; Ed: John Goldman; Composer: John Greenwood. B&W, 77 min. **VHS**

Man of a Thousand Faces
(1957) Universal
Cagney excels in this life of Lon Chaney, Sr., silent star of *Phantom of the Opera* and *The Hunchback of Notre Dame*. Strong on characterization and family background—Chaney achieved his sympathetic depiction of "outsiders" by calling upon his upbringing by two deaf-mute parents—the film triumphs, re-creating the world of vaudeville and early silent-film productions in the 1920s. Greer and Malone are strong as Chaney's two wives and Bud Westmore was respon-

The Man in the Iron Mask (1939)

sible for the memorable makeup. Academy Award Nomination for Best (Original) Story and Screenplay. **Cast:** James Cagney, Dorothy Malone, Jane Greer, Marjorie Rambeau, Jim Backus, Roger Smith, Robert Evans, Celia Lovsky. **Credits:** Dir: Joseph Pevney; Prod: Robert Arthur; Writer: Ivan Goff; DP: Russell Metty; Ed: Ted J. Kent; Prod Design: Alexander Golitzen; Composer: Frank Skinner; Art Director: Eric Orbom. B&W, 122 min. **VHS, LASER, DVD**

Man of La Mancha
(1972) United Artists
Leigh and Joe Darion's long-running Broadway musical retelling of Don Quixote, the knight who still believes in chivalry and adventure in a world that has left him behind, came to the screen with two surprising leads never noted for their singing talent. O'Toole (with Simon Gilbert as his invisible singing voice) plays both the novelist Miguel de Cervantes and Quixote, while Loren doubles as Dulcinea and Aldonza (yes, she does her own singing). Ironically, Cervantes's greatest creation was intended as literary satire and an object of ridicule, while La Mancha's Quixote is a heroic madman following "the impossible dream." Coco is the always loyal Sancho Panza. Academy Award Nomination for Best Song Score. **Cast:** Peter O'Toole, Sophia Loren, James Coco, Harry Andrews, John Castle, Brian Blessed, Ian Richardson, Julie Gregg. **Credits:** Dir: Arthur Hiller; Prod: Arthur Hiller; Writer: Dale Wasserman; DP: Giuseppe Rotunno; Ed: Robert C. Jones, Folmar Blangsted; Composer: Mitch Leigh; Art Director: Luciano Damiani. Color, 130 min. **VHS, LASER**

Man of the West
(1958) United Artists
Mann, who created a number of stylish yet often neglected Westerns during the 1950s, directs Cooper as a reformed gunslinger whose past catches up with him when he is robbed of a town's treasury and later captured along with two others (O'Connell and London) by Cooper's former gang, headed by Cobb. As tension builds, including a forced striptease by London, Cooper realizes he must resort to the violence he has forsworn. A tragedy about the changing West set against an epic landscape, this was Mann's final Western and one of his best. **Cast:** Gary Cooper, Julie London, Lee J. Cobb, Arthur O'Connell, Jack Lord, John Dehner, Royal Dano, Bob Wilke. **Credits:** Dir: Anthony Mann; Prod: Walter Mirisch;

Writer: Reginald Rose; DP: Ernest Haller; Ed: Richard Heermance; Composer: Leigh Harline; Art Director: Hilyard Brown. Color, 100 min. **VHS**

Man of the World
(1931) Paramount
Expatriate in Paris Michael Trevor (Powell) is many things: a sometime scandal-rag publisher, playboy, and con artist. The ever-suave Powell makes his living by preying on unsuspecting American women vacationing in Paris—until he falls in love with Mary Kendall (Lombard), a debutante previously in his sights. When he decides to go straight to win Lombard, his mistress (Gibson) blackmails him back onto the crooked path. An early Powell vehicle that shows off his rakish charm. **Cast:** George Chandler, Wynne Gibson, Guy Kibbee, Carole Lombard, William Powell, Lawrence Gray, Tom Costello, Andre Cheron, Tom Ricketts, Maude Truax. **Credits:** Dir: Richard Wallace, John B. Goodman; Writer: Herman J. Mankiewicz; DP: Victor Milner. B&W, 71 min.

Man on a String
(1960) Columbia
A successful film producer by day, Boris Mitrov (Borgnine) moonlights as a spy for the Russians. Mitrov, however, works not out of love of country, but for the safe release of his father held in a Russian prison. When the F.B.I. is made aware of Mitrov's activities, he offers to help the U.S. government put an end to the spy syndicate. Sent on a whirlwind adventure through Cold War Europe, and stopping along the way in Moscow and Berlin, Mitrov safely returns to the U.S. with invaluable information. **Cast:** Ernest Borgnine, Kerwin Mathews, Glenn Corbett, Alexander Scourby, Colleen Dewhurst, Vladimir Sokoloff, Friedrich Joloff, Richard Kendrick, Ed Prentiss. **Credits:** Dir: Andre De Toth; Prod: Louis de Rochemont; Writer: John H. Kafka, Virginia Shaler, Boris Morros; DP: Charles Lawton, Jr., Pierre Poincarde, Gayne Rescher, Albert Benitz; Ed: Al Clark; Prod Design: Carl Anderson; Composer: George Duning. B&W, 92 min.

Man on the Eiffel Tower
(1949) RKO
The only film directed by Meredith is a suspense melodrama adapted from the Georges Simenon novel, *A Battle of Nerves*. French police inspector Maigret (Laughton) tries to trap a wily murder suspect (Tone). Authentic Parisian locations, outstanding performances, and Cortez's cinematography

make this independent production worth seeking out. **Cast:** Charles Laughton, Franchot Tone, Burgess Meredith, Robert Hutton, Jean Wallace, Patricia Roc, George Thorpe, William Phipps. **Credits:** Dir: Burgess Meredith; Prod: Irving Allen; Writer: Harry Brown; DP: Stanley Cortez; Ed: Louis Sackin; Composer: Michel Michelet; Art Director: Rene Renoux. Color, 97 min. **VHS**

Man on the Flying Trapeze
(1935) Paramount
This W. C. Fields classic follows the high-wire stumblings of the unlucky sap Ambrose Wolfinger as he bumbles through two harrowing days at the mercy of his wife, daughter, in-laws, boss, coworkers, stairway, local police department, several burglars, some professional wrestlers, large quantities of alcohol, Hookalakah Mishabob, a luxury convertible, and one suddenly drenching downpour. A hilarious middle-class nightmare that is one of Fields's greatest achievements. **Cast:** W. C. Fields, Mary Brian, Kathleen Howard, Vera Lewis, Grady Sutton, Oscar Apfel, Lucien Littlefield, Walter Brennan, Harry Ekezian. **Credits:** Dir: Clyde Bruckman; Prod: William LeBaron; Writer: Jack Cunningham, Ray Harris, Bobby Vernon, W. C. Fields, Sam Hardy; DP: Alfred Gilks; Ed: Richard C. Currier. B&W, 65 min.

Manpower
(1942) Warner Bros.
This amounts to a romantic-triangle melodrama, but in a tough-guy setting directed by action expert Walsh. Two workers (Robinson and Raft) on the high-power lines battle the elements, the dangers of their job—and each other after they meet fading bar singer Dietrich. Dietrich marries Robinson though she's in love with Raft, which she makes clear when Raft is injured and comes to live with the newlyweds. The result is a terrific fight that ends in tragedy. The set was nearly as dangerous as the action depicted: the story calls for Raft to slug Dietrich; he missed and knocked her down a flight of steps, breaking her ankle. The feud between Robinson and Raft on-screen carried on for years offscreen as well. **Cast:** Edward G. Robinson, Marlene Dietrich, George Raft, Alan Hale, Frank McHugh, Eve Arden, Barton MacLane, Ward Bond, Walter Catlett, Joyce Compton. **Credits:** Dir: Raoul Walsh; Prod: Mark Hellinger; Writer: Richard Macaulay, Jerry Wald; DP: Ernest Haller; Ed: Ralph Dawson; Prod Design: Max Parker; Composer: Adolph Deutsch. B&W, 105 min.

A Man's Castle

(1933) Columbia

A pre-Code, Depression-era story with surprisingly adult themes from master of melodrama Borzage. Tracy, like millions of Americans, is down on his luck and living in a Hooverville-style shack. When he sees the plight of Young, who doesn't even have a place to lay her head, he takes her in and they soon begin a relationship. However, Tracy's head is turned by a dancer (Farrell) who offers a trip down Easy Street. But Tracy discovers Young is pregnant, and to do the honorable thing, he tries to rob a factory payroll safe. **Cast:** Spencer Tracy, Loretta Young, Glenda Farrell, Walter Connolly, Arthur Hohl, Marjorie Rambeau, Dickie Moore, Harvey Clark, Henry Roquemore, Hector V. Samo. **Credits:** Dir: Frank Borzage; Writer: Jo Swerling; Story: Lawrence Hazard; DP: Joseph H. August; Ed: Viola Lawrence; Composer: Franke Harling, Constantine Bakaleinikoff. B&W, 70 min.

Man's Favorite Sport?

(1963) Universal

The man in question is Hudson, a fishing equipment salesman for Abercrombie & Fitch whose knowledge of flycasting is limited to demonstrations in department-store showrooms. The sport in question is actually the pursuit of women, and the woman in question is Prentiss, playing another version of Hawks's sassy, confident heroines. This was Hawks's return to screwball comedy, after such notable outings as *Bringing Up Baby* (1938), *Ball of Fire* (1941), and *His Girl Friday* (1940). **Cast:** Rock Hudson, Paula Prentiss, Maria Perschy, Charlene Holt, John McGiver, Roscoe Karns, Forrest Lewis, Regis Toomey. **Credits:** Dir: Howard Hawks; Prod: Howard Hawks; Writer: John Fenton Murray, Steve McNeil; DP: Russell Harlan; Ed: Stuart Gilmore; Prod Design: Alexander Golitzen; Composer: Henry Mancini; Art Director: Tambi Larsen. Color, 121 min. **VHS**

The Man They Could Not Hang

(1939) Columbia

Karloff stars as a scientist who invents a mechanical heart, then is wrongly accused of a killing and hung. His student uses the experimental device to restore him to life and he comes back to seek vengeance. First in a series of movies in which Karloff played hanged men who return with a chip on their shoulder. **Cast:** Boris Karloff, Lorna Gray, Robert Wilcox,

Roger Pryor, Don Beddoe, Ann Doran, Dick Curtis, Byron Foulger. **Credits:** Dir: Nick Grinde; Prod: Wallace MacDonald; Writer: Karl Brown; Story: Leslie T. White; DP: Benjamin H. Kline; Ed: William A. Lyon. B&W, 72 min. **VHS**

The Man Who Knew Too Much

(1934) Gaumont

Hitchcock's first go at this tale of a kidnapping by a cabal of political terrorists planning to assassinate a head of state at a posh Albert Hall concert. Banks and Best play the parents with Pilbeam (later to star for Hitch in *Young and Innocent*, 1937) as their abducted daughter. The grotesque assassin is played by Lorre in his En-glish-language film debut. A fine atmospheric thriller with memorable set pieces. Remade by Hitch in Hollywood, with James Stewart and Doris Day, in 1956. **Cast:** Leslie Banks, Edna Best, Peter Lorre, Nova Pilbeam, Hugh Wakefield, Pierre Fresnay, George Curzon, Henry Oscar, Emlyn Williams. **Credits:** Dir: Alfred Hitchcock; Prod: Michael Balcon; Writer: A. R. Rawlinson, Charles Bennett, D. B. Wyndham-Lewis, Edwin Greenwood; DP: Curt Courant; Ed: Hugh Stewart; Composer: Arthur Benjamin; Art Director: Alfred Junge. B&W, 84 min. **VHS, LASER**

The Man Who Knew Too Much

(1956) Paramount

Twenty-two years after his earlier version of this story of a family's accidental involvement in a political assassination plot, Hitchcock cast Stewart and Day in the leads as an American doctor and his retired-singer wife. Shot in color and on location, this entertaining thriller moves swiftly to its justly famous climax at a concert of Arthur Benjamin's *Storm Clouds* cantata at London's Albert Hall. It is fascinating to compare the two film versions, which are sometimes identical in shot composition and action. For the most part, the second version is the superior production, blessed with a fine cast and a superb score by Herrmann (who makes his only film cameo as the concert conductor). **Academy Awards:** Best Song ("Que Sera, Sera"). **Cast:** James Stewart, Doris Day, Brenda De Banzie, Bernard Miles, Daniel Gelin, Christopher Olsen, Reggie Nalder, Richard Wattis, Noel Willman. **Credits:** Dir: Alfred Hitchcock; Prod: Alfred Hitchcock; Writer: John Michael Hayes, Angus MacPhail; Story: Charles Bennett, D. B. Wyndham-Lewis; DP: Richard

Mueller; Ed: Luigi Tomasini, George Tomasini; Composer: Bernard Herrmann; Art Director: Hal Pereira, Henry Bumstead. Color, 120 min. **VHS, LASER**

The Man Who Loved Cat Dancing

(1973) MGM

One of the last classic-style Hollywood Westerns has Reynolds in his first big role as a train robber on the run for murdering the man who raped his Indian wife (the Cat Dancing of the title), and Miles on the run from her husband (Hamilton). The most interesting star is the dramatic cinematography. Miles's husband, playwright Robert Bolt, is rumored to have had a hand in the screenplay. **Cast:** Burt Reynolds, Sarah Miles, George Hamilton, Jack Warden, Lee J. Cobb, Bo Hopkins, Robert Donner, Larry Littlebird, Nancy Malone. **Credits:** Dir: Richard C. Sarafian; Prod: Martin H. Poll, Eleanor Perry; Writer: Eleanor Perry; DP: Harry Stradling; Ed: Tom Rolf; Prod Design: Edward C. Carfagno; Composer: John Williams. Color, 127 min. **VHS**

The Man Who Shot Liberty Valance

(1962) Paramount

In director Ford's swan song for the conventional frontier Western, he answers the Death Valley panorama of his classical frontier films with the demise of the archetypal gunfighter-hero, with Wayne and Stewart representing wilderness vs. civilization. Stewart plays Ransom Stoddard, a law-school graduate from the East who tries to bring peace to the burgeoning town of Shinbone, which suffers under the tyranny of Valance (Marvin). After a series of run-ins and a hopeless attempt by Tom Doniphon (Wayne), a gritty Western hero, to teach him to shoot, Stoddard agrees to a showdown with Valance, but the real shooter—and savior—of Shinbone is his friendly rival, Doniphon. As peace comes to Shinbone, Stoddard wins an election and the hand of Doniphon's girl (Miles), while Doniphon never tells the townspeople the truth about the killing. A wonderfully realized film, which is both an elegy to a dying way of life and a wise commentary on the fragility of modern society. A keystone in Ford's career. Gene Pitney's title song was a million-seller. **Cast:** James Stewart, John Wayne, Lee Marvin, Vera Miles, Dutton Peabody, Andy Devine, Ken Murray, John Carradine, Jeanette Nolan, John Qualen. **Credits:** Dir: John Ford;

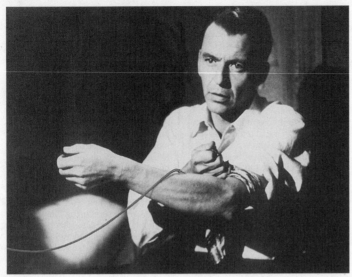

The Man with the Golden Arm (1955)

Prod: Willis Goldbeck; Writer: Willis Goldbeck, James Warner Bellah; Story: Dorothy Johnson; DP: William Clothier; Ed: Otto Lovering; Composer: Cyril Mockridge, Alfred Newman; Costumes: Edith Head; Art Director: Hal Pereira, Eddie Imazu. B&W, 122 min. **VHS, LASER**

The Man Who Would Be King

(1975) Allied Artists
Connery and Caine in Huston's grand adventure based on a Kipling novel about two army rogues who arrive in 1880s India and are treated as deities in Kaifiristan. Beautifully told, this is part comedy, part boys' heroic yarn, framed by scenes of Plummer as Kipling. After a string of disappointing small films in the 1960s and early 1970s, Huston proved he could still work the old magic. Academy Award Nominations: 4, including Best (Adapted) Screenplay. **Cast:** Sean Connery, Michael Caine, Christopher Plummer, Saeed Jaffrey, Jack May, Doghmi Larbi, Shakira Caine, Paul Antrim. **Credits:** Dir: John Huston; Prod: John Foreman; Writer: John Huston, Gladys Hill; Story: Rudyard Kipling; DP: Oswald Morris; Ed: Russell Lloyd; Prod Design: Alexander Trauner; Composer: Maurice Jarre; Art Director: Tony Inglis. Color, 129 min. **VHS, LASER, DVD**

The Man with Nine Lives

(1940) Columbia
In this science-fiction tale, Karloff plays Dr. Kravaal, a scientist who discovers a revolutionary treatment for cancer. His method is to put the patient to sleep with a strong drug, then put him in an ice chamber and slowly reduce the body temperature to below freezing, which will then kill any cancerous growth. The doctor is accused by the district attorney, and a coroner, for wanting to use a "wealthy patient" as a guinea pig. His idea is brushed off but when he accidentally locks himself and some unwilling subjects in the ice chamber for 10 years, his theory holds up quite well. **Cast:** Boris Karloff, Roger Pryor, Byron Foulger, Stanley Brown, Joann Sayers, John Dilson, Ernie Adams, Lee Willard, Ivan Miller. **Credits:** Dir: Nick Grinde; Prod: Irving Briskin, Wallace MacDonald; Writer: Karl Brown; Story: Harold Shumate; DP: Benjamin H. Kline; Ed: Al Clark; Prod Design: Lionel Banks. B&W, 73 min.

Man Without a Star

(1955) Universal
The conflict between ranchers and cattle owners is center stage in this intelligent Western skillfully directed by veteran Vidor, his last Western. Conflicted as well is likable cowboy Douglas, enlisted by a ruthless and manipulative cattle baroness, Crain, to further her intent of increasing the size of her herds despite a lack of grazing area. Douglas initiates young Campbell into the ways of the cowboy, and reveals in his scars his aversion to dividing the western prairies with barbed wire. A strong supporting cast, featuring Trevor in the familiar role of the madam with a heart of gold and Boone as the menacing gunfighter, all raise the quality of this familiar story. Remade as *A Man Called Gannon* with Tony Franciosa in 1969. **Cast:** Kirk Douglas, Jeanne Crain, Claire Trevor, Richard Boone, William Campbell, Mara Corday, Jay C. Flippen, George Wallace. **Credits:** Dir: King Vidor; Prod: Aaron Rosenberg; Writer: Borden Chase, D. D. Beauchamp; DP: Russell Metty; Ed: Virgil Vogel; Prod Design: Alexander Golitzen; Composer: Joseph Gershenson; Art Director: Richard H. Reidel. Color, 89 min. **VHS**

The Man with the Golden Arm

(1955) United Artists
Preminger's adaptation of Algren's novel about drummer Frankie Machine's (Sinatra) battle with narcotics was daring when released, and still remains powerful. The film stays confined to a few locales, concentrating on Frankie's torments of addiction and withdrawal. Parker plays the dependent wife, Novak the neighbor downstairs. Important to the look and feel of the film are Saul Bass's title designs and Elmer Bernstein's justly celebrated jazz score. Academy Award Nominations: 3, including Best Actor: Frank Sinatra. **Cast:** Frank Sinatra, Eleanor Parker, Kim Novak, Darren McGavin, Robert Strauss, Arnold Stang, George Mathews, John Conte. **Credits:** Dir: Otto Preminger; Prod: Otto Preminger; Writer: Walter Newman; Story: Nelson Algren; DP: Sam Leavitt; Ed: Louis R. Loeffler; Composer: Elmer Bernstein. B&W, 120 min. **VHS**

The Man with the Golden Gun

(1974) United Artists
Moore's second time to don the dinner jacket as James Bond (the 10th film in the series). In this outing, the superagent is assigned the task of recovering a valuable piece of technical equipment capable of harnessing the sun's energy. The arch-villain (Lee) is Scaramagna, an international hit man who uses a trademark golden gun on his victims and who has set up a base in the Far East. **Cast:** Roger Moore, Christopher Lee, Britt Ekland, Maud Adams, Soon-Teck Oh, Richard Loo, Marc Lawrence, Bernard Lee. **Credits:** Dir: Guy Hamilton; Prod: Albert R. Broccoli; Story: Richard Maibaum; DP: Ted Moore; Ed: John Shirley; Composer: John Barry; SFX: John Stears; Art Director: Peter Lamont. Color, 125 min. **VHS, LASER**

Many Happy Returns

(1934) Paramount

A vehicle for the comedy team of Burns and Allen, this romp begins in New York, where Allen's character wreaks havoc on her father's property. Her father becomes convinced that the best way to get her off his hands is to have her marry Burns, and pay him by the mile to take her away. Plenty of music from Guy Lombardo. **Cast:** Gracie Allen, George Burns, Joan Marsh, George Barbier, Franklin Pangborn, Ray Milland, Egon Brecher, Stanley Fields, John Kelly, William Demarest. **Credits:** Dir: Norman Z. McLeod; Writer: J. P. McEvoy, Claude Binyon, Keene Thompson, Ray Harris; Story: Lady Mary Cameron; DP: Henry Sharp; Ed: Richard Currier. B&W, 62 min.

Mara Maru

(1952) Warner Bros.

A late-period Flynn adventure that still shows some swashbuckling spirit. Flynn's salvage diver is hired by a scheming Burr to retrieve an ancient cross from the waters off Manila's shores. Once he retrieves the treasure, the chase is on. The diver races to return the cross to the small church from which it was stolen at the beginning of WWII, with Burr close on his tail. **Cast:** Errol Flynn, Ruth Roman, Raymond Burr, Paul Picerni, Richard Webb, Dan Seymour, Georges Renavent, Robert Cabal, Henry Marco, Nestor Paiva. **Credits:** Dir: Gordon Douglas; Prod: David Weisbart; Writer: Phillip Yordan, Sidney Harmon, Hollister Noble, N. Richard Nash; DP: Robert Burks; Ed: Robert Swanson; Prod Design: Stanley Fleischer; Composer: Max Steiner. B&W, 98 min.

Marathon Man

(1976) Paramount

Goldman wrote both the novel and screenplay to this thriller with Olivier as a vicious Nazi war criminal on the loose in New York. Unwittingly, graduate student Hoffman (the marathon runner of the title) finds himself embroiled in a convoluted plot involving stolen diamonds, his mysterious brother (Scheider), U.S. intelligence agents, and perhaps the most famous dental scene in film history. Directed by Schlesinger (*Midnight Cowboy*, 1969). Academy Award Nomination for Best Supporting Actor: Laurence Olivier. **Cast:** Dustin Hoffman, Laurence Olivier, Marthe Keller, Roy Scheider, William Devane, Fritz Weaver, Richard Bright, Marc Lawrence. **Credits:** Dir: John Schlesinger; Prod: Robert Evans, Sidney Beckerman; Writer: William

Goldman; DP: Conrad Hall; Ed: Jim Clark; Prod Design: Richard MacDonald; Composer: Michael Small. Color, 125 min. **VHS**

Margie

(1946) Fox

A charming trip down memory lane to Jazz Age high school romance, this movie begins with Crain telling her teenage daughter what the '20s were like, when she was a pretty flapper who put rouge on her knees. She has a boyfriend, but nevertheless harbors a big crush on the handsome, young French teacher at her school (Langan). The teenage girl listens with a smile on her face, as the French teacher is her father. Includes a long list of the popular tunes of the day. **Cast:** Jeanne Crain, Glenn Langan, Lynn Bari, Alan Young, Barbara Lawrence, Conrad Janis, Esther Dale, Hobart Cavanaugh, Ann Todd, Hattie McDaniel. **Credits:** Dir: Henry King; Prod: Walter Morosco; Writer: F. Hugh Herbert; Story: Richard Bransten, Ruth McKenney; DP: Charles G. Clarke; Ed: Barbara McLean; Composer: Alfred Newman; Art Director: James Basevi, Russell Spencer, Lyle Wheeler. B&W, 94 min.

Marie Antoinette

(1938) MGM

A long, lavish biopic chronicling the life of the French queen (Shearer) who wanted only a simple life on a farm, but was finally consumed by the French Revolution. Central to the film's story, adapted from the best-selling biography by Stefan Zweig, are the intrigues at Versailles and the scandal of the diamond necklace. Power, on loan from Fox (in exchange for Spencer Tracy's appearance in *Stanley and Livingstone*), plays Marie's Swedish lover Ferson and Morley is excellent as weak Louis XVI. A big-budget showcase for Shearer's return after a two-year absence while she grieved the loss of husband and MGM production chief Irving Thalberg. While Sidney Franklin spent years preparing to direct the film, studio boss Mayer forced him to stand back and allow no-nonsense Van Dyke to take over. Academy Award Nominations: 4, including Best Actress: Norma Shearer. **Cast:** Norma Shearer, Tyrone Power, John Barrymore, Robert Morley, Gladys George, Anita Louise, Joseph Schildkraut, Henry Stephenson. **Credits:** Dir: W. S. Van Dyke, Julien Duvivier; Prod: Hunt Stromberg; Writer: Claudine West, Donald Ogden Stewart, Ernest Vajda, F. Scott Fitzger-

ald; DP: William Daniels; Ed: Robert J. Kern; Prod Design: Cedric Gibbons, William A. Horning; Composer: Herbert Stothart. B&W, 160 min. **VHS, LASER**

Marjoe

(1972) Cinema 5

This Oscar-winning documentary about sham evangelist Marjoe Gortner was meant as an exposé of religious fundamentalism, but was as much a launch pad for the brief acting career of the charismatic Gortner (*Earthquake*, 1974; *Star Crash*, 1978). Marjoe (the name is a contraction of Mary and Joseph) is a master manipulator of his flock, the film's makers, and the film audience. Viewed from the perspective of 30 years later (after Jim Bakker and Jimmy Swaggart), the film lacks its original bite; however it is seldom boring and offers a revealing snapshot of America. **Academy Awards:** Best Documentary Feature. **Cast:** Marjoe Gortner. **Credits:** Dir: Sarah Kernochan, Howard Smith; Prod: Sarah Kernochan, Howard Smith; DP: Ed Lynch, David Myers, Richard Pearce, Thomas Reichman, Kenneth Van Sickle, Mike Shea; Ed: Larry Silk. Color, 88 min. **VHS**

Marjorie Morningstar

(1958) Warner Bros.

This Wood vehicle was based on a Wouk best-seller about the coming-of-age of an upper-middle-class Jewish Hunter College student who disavows her Orthodox heritage (changing her name from Morgenstern to Morningstar). Along the way she kindles a summer romance with a singer-dancer (Kelly), and dives into the world of Manhattan's bohemia before landing in the reality of '50s suburbia. Wynn is outstanding as her uncle and Milner plays her loyal boyfriend. A fascinating look at '50s Hollywood's idea of a woman's quest to find herself. The 35th-anniversary video edition is digitally remastered and includes the film's original theatrical trailer. Academy Award Nomination for Best Song ("A Very Precious Love"). **Cast:** Gene Kelly, Natalie Wood, Claire Trevor, Ed Wynn, Everett Sloane, Martin Milner, Carolyn Jones, George Tobias, Martin Balsam, Jesse White. **Credits:** Dir: Irving Rapper; Prod: Milton Sperling; Writer: Everett Freeman; Story: Herman Wouk; DP: Harry Stradling; Ed: Folmar Blangsted; Choreographer: Jack Baker; Composer: Max Steiner; Costumes: Howard Shoup; Art Director: Malcolm Bert. Color, 125 min. **VHS**

Marked Woman

(1937) Warner Bros.
In 1936 Davis, distressed about her career and the poor quality of scripts she was offered, refused Warners' next assignment and sailed to Europe to make films in England and France. A lawsuit followed and the studio brought her back and cast her in this criminal melodrama, which proved to be a career turning point. Bogart plays a crusading district attorney after a Lucky Luciano–like mobster (Ciannelli) who uses hostess Davis as a key witness in his investigation. Warners stalwarts Bogart and Davis both deliver strong performances, and eventually appeared in 8 films together. **Cast:** Bette Davis, Humphrey Bogart, Eduardo Ciannelli, Lola Lane, Jane Bryan, Isabel Jewell, Allen Jenkins, Mayo Methot. **Credits:** Dir: Lloyd Bacon; Prod: Louis F. Edelman; Writer: Robert Rossen, Abem Finkel, Seton I. Miller; DP: George Barnes; Ed: Jack Killifer; Prod Design: Max Parker; Composer: Bernhard Kaun, Heinz Roemheld. B&W, 97 min. **VHS, LASER**

Mark of the Vampire

(1935) MGM
Lugosi clad in familiar evening dress and cape plays the leader of a troupe of actors responsible for mysterious vampire-like murders in this remake of the Lon Chaney silent classic, *London After Midnight* (1927), also directed by Browning. Atwill is the police inspector and Barrymore a vampire expert and hypnotist leading the investigation. Noted for its atmospheric cinematography by veteran cameraman Howe. **Cast:** Lionel Barrymore, Bela Lugosi, Elizabeth Allan, Lionel Atwill, Holmes Herbert, Jean Hersholt, Donald Meek, Ivan Simpson. **Credits:** Dir: Tod Browning; Prod: Edward J. Mannix; Writer: Guy Endore, Bernard Schubert; DP: James Wong Howe; Ed: Ben Lewis; Prod Design: Cedric Gibbons, Harry Oliver. B&W, 61 min. **VHS**

The Mark of Zorro

(1920) United Artists
This is Fairbanks's first costume swashbuckler and the prototype for many classic adventures. Don Diego Vega, a carefree young nobleman in California, fills with horror as the rich landowners mistreat their workers. Finally, the outraged Vega devises a scheme to right the wrongs he sees: during the day he poses as a cowardly fop but at night he battles evil as the masked avenger, Zorro. The great-grandfather of the subsequent Zorro films and serials (including the 1940 version starring Tyrone Power and the 1998 version starring Antonio Banderas) as well as the TV series of the late '50s. **Cast:** Douglas Fairbanks, Noah Beery, Marguerite De La Motte, Claire McDowell, Robert McKim, Charles Mailes, Walt Whitman, Snitz Edwards. **Credits:** Dir: Fred Niblo; Prod: Douglas Fairbanks; Writer: Douglas Fairbanks; Story: Johnston McCulley; DP: Harry Thorpe, William McGann; Prod Design: Edward Langley. B&W, 91 min. **VHS, LASER**

Marlowe

(1969) MGM
Garner's turn to play Raymond Chandler's famed detective, here engaged by a woman from Kansas searching for her brother. One of the odder adaptations (based on the novel *The Little Sister*), which abandons atmospheric '40s noir for sunny late-'60s southern California, and portrays Marlowe as a bewildered man-in-a-maze, not unlike Garner's later Jim Rockford. An outstanding supporting cast includes O'Connor as a slow cop, Moreno in a memorable striptease, and Lee in a tiny role in which he uses his martial arts talents to redesign Marlowe's office. Among the many other stars who have played Philip Marlowe are Humphrey Bogart, Robert Montgomery, Elliott Gould, Dick Powell, Robert Mitchum, George Montgomery, and James Caan. **Cast:** James Garner, Gayle Hunnicutt, Carroll O'Connor, Rita Moreno, Sharon Farrell, William Daniels, Jackie Coogan, Bruce Lee. **Credits:** Dir: Paul Bogart; Prod: Gabriel Katzka, Sidney Beckerman; Writer: Stirling Silliphant; DP: William Daniels; Ed: Gene Ruggiero; Composer: Peter Matz; Art Director: George W. Davis, Addison Hehr. Color, 95 min. **VHS**

Marnie

(1964) Universal
When first released this was generally considered one of Hitchcock's lesser efforts, yet it has grown in critical estimation over the years. Hitchcock discovery Hedren (*The Birds*, 1963) plays a repressed kleptomaniac with a hidden past and Connery the insurance investigator whose obsessions with her dark secrets are nearly as troubled. Hitchcock returns to the theme of
sexual obsession seven years after *Vertigo*, and while not of the same caliber as his 1957 masterpiece, this is a psychologically intriguing film that remains in the mind. Featuring a young Dern in an important small role, and one of Herrmann's finest scores. **Cast:** Tippi Hedren, Sean Connery, Diane Baker, Bruce Dern, Martin Gabel, Louise Latham, Bob Sweeney, Milton Selzer. **Credits:** Dir: Alfred Hitchcock; Prod: Alfred Hitchcock; Writer: Jay Presson Allen; DP: Robert Burks; Ed: George Tomasini; Prod Design: Robert Boyle; Composer: Bernard Herrmann. Color, 130 min. **VHS, LASER**

The Marrying Kind

(1952) Columbia
Young, urban newlyweds Holliday and Ray run into the inevitable emotional tremors in this Gordon and Kanin–penned slice-of-life drama. As they testify at their divorce hearing, the film flashes back to their meeting in a park, wedding, children: the countless joys and tragedies of married life. This was Ray's film debut, while Holliday strengthened her dramatic credentials following her Oscar for *Born Yesterday* (1950), also directed by Cukor from a script by Gordon and Kanin. Also interesting for some now-nostalgic footage of Manhattan in the early '50s. **Cast:** Judy Holliday, Aldo Ray, Madge Kennedy, Sheila Bond, John Alexander, Rex Williams, Phyllis Povah, Peggy Cass, Mickey Shaughnessy, Griff Barnett. **Credits:** Dir: George Cukor; Prod: Bert Granet; Writer: Ruth Gordon, Garson Kanin; DP: Joseph Walker; Ed: Charles Nelson; Composer: Hugo Friedhofer; Art Director: John Meehan. B&W, 92 min. **VHS**

Marty

(1955) United Artists
This icon of the '50s was first seen as Paddy Chayefsky's teleplay for Goodyear Playhouse two years earlier. Borgnine, in an Oscar-winning performance, plays a lonely Bronx butcher who discovers that, even though he doesn't look like Tyrone Power, he can still find love. Produced at the time when Hollywood was fighting television with wide-screen formats and stereophonic sound, *Marty*'s naturalistic dialogue and modest humanistic story were revolutionary in their own quiet way. Awarded the Golden Globe for Best Actor in a Drama: Ernest Borgnine, and selected as a National Film Registry Outstanding Film. Academy Award Nominations: 8, including Best Supporting Actor: Joe Mantell; Best Supporting Actress: Betsy Blair. **Academy Awards:** Best Picture; Best Director; Best Actor: Ernest Borgnine; Best Screenplay. **Cast:** Ernest Borgnine, Betsy Blair, Joe De Santis, Joe Mantell, Esther Minciotti, Karen

Steele, Jerry Paris, Frank Sutton, Walter Kelley, Robin Morse. **Credits:** Dir: Delbert Mann; Prod: Harold Hecht; Writer: Paddy Chayefsky; Story: Paddy Chayefsky; DP: Joseph LaShelle; Ed: Alan Crosland, Jr.; Prod Design: Edward S. Haworth, Walter Simonds, Robert Priestley; Composer: Roy Webb; Costumes: Norma. B&W, 91 min. VHS, LASER

Mary Burns, Fugitive
(1935) Paramount
Innocent Mary Burns (Sidney) falls for Baxter not knowing that he's a mobster and a killer. Mary's naivete makes her the perfect victim of a set-up and she's imprisoned for a murder she didn't commit. When she escapes from jail, Douglas hides her until she can clear her name. Routine material given better than it deserves by an appealing cast, most notably the sloe-eyed Sidney and Baxter, a Group Theater actor in his screen debut. **Cast:** Sylvia Sidney, Helene Chadwick, Alan Baxter, Melvyn Douglas, Brian Donlevy, Esther Dale, Wallace Ford, Daniel L. Haynes, Frances Gregg, Grace Hayle, Pert Kelton. **Credits:** Dir: William K. Howard; Prod: Walter Wanger; Writer: C. Graham Baker, Gene Towne, Louis Stevens; DP: Leon Shamroy; Ed: Peter Fritsch; Costumes: Helen Taylor. B&W, 84 min.

Mary of Scotland
(1936) RKO
Hepburn plays Mary Stuart, the Queen of Scotland who refuses to renounce her claim to the throne of England, supported by March as Bothwell, her adviser and lover. One of director Ford's few costume dramas (based on a play by Maxwell Anderson), this concentrates on a complicated intrigue and deceit rather than on the romantic melodrama. While the story is familiar and has been told a number of times, Ford's direction, shadowy cinematography, and impressive art direction all make this memorable. Hepburn, by the way, is descended from the Bothwell family. Mary was later played by Vanessa Redgrave and Kathy Burke, among others. **Cast:** Katharine Hepburn, Fredric March, John Carradine, Florence Eldridge, Douglas Walton, Robert Barrat, Gavin Muir, Ian Keith. **Credits:** Dir: John Ford; Prod: Pandro S. Berman; Writer: Dudley Nichols; DP: Joseph H. August; Ed: Jane Loring; Prod Design: Carroll Clark; Composer: Max Steiner; Art Director: Van Nest Polglase. B&W, 123 min. VHS, LASER

Mary Poppins
(1964) Disney
After triumphs on Broadway and the London stage (and the disappointment of not being cast in the film adaptation of *My Fair Lady*), Andrews made her screen debut in this magical, musical Disney version of Travers's children's classic about a flying governess who takes over the house of a turn-of-the-century London banker and wins the hearts of his two children. Andrews's fresh appeal is in ample evidence here, and she was embraced by audiences around the world for this and for *The Sound of Music,* made the following year. A lanky Van Dyke, in the standout screen role of his career, plays Bert, the chimney sweep, and sings and dances the popular "Chim-Chim-Cheree" and "Supercalifragilistic-expialidocious." The limited-release deluxe collector's set features the remastered original film, the original theatrical trailer, footage of the world premiere at Grauman's Chinese Theatre, and a commemorative book, *The Music of Mary Poppins.* Academy Award Nominations: 13, including Best Picture; Best Director; Best (Adapted) Screenplay. **Academy Awards:** Best Actress: Julie Andrews; Best Film Editing; Best Song ("Chim-Chim-Cheree"); Best Music Score; Best Special Visual Effects. **Cast:** Julie Andrews, Dick Van Dyke, David Tomlinson, Glynis Johns, Hermione Baddeley, Karen Dotrice, Matthew Garber, Reta Shaw, Elsa Lanchester, Arthur Treacher. **Credits:** Dir: Robert Stevenson; Prod: Walt Disney, Bill Walsh; Writer: Bill Walsh, Don DaGradi; Story: P. L. Travers; DP: Edward Colman; Ed: Cotton Warburton; Prod Design: Carroll Clark, William H. Tuntke; Choreographer: Marc Breaux, Dee Dee Wood; Composer: Irwin Kostal, Richard M. Sherman, Robert B. Sherman; Costumes: Tony Walton; SFX: Peter Ellenshaw, Eustace Lycett, Robert A. Mattey. Color, 155 min. VHS, LASER, DVD

M*A*S*H
(1970) Fox
A Korean War black comedy produced at the height of the Vietnam War, this was director Altman's breakthrough feature, and, with *Easy Rider*, one of the films that ushered in the New Hollywood of the 1970s. Grittier and more cynical than the later popular TV series, *M*A*S*H* (Mobile Army Surgical Hospital) made immediate stars of Sutherland and Gould as the cool surgeons Hawkeye and Trapper John. If irony is born from the horrors of war, its enemy is protocol and rigidity, here personified by Kellerman and Duvall as Hot Lips Houlihan and Frank Burns. The irreverent mix of football, wisecracks, martini highballs, and shower voyeurism are desperate measures to deal with the spurting blood and waste of lives that frame the film. Remember this was made only two years after John Wayne's *The Green Berets.* Golden Globe for Best Film, Musical or Comedy. Academy Award Nominations: 5, including Best Picture; Best Director. **Academy Awards:** Best Screenplay Based on Material from Another Medium. **Cast:** Elliott Gould, Donald Sutherland, Sally Kellerman, Tom Skerritt, Robert Duvall, Jo Ann Pflug, Rene Auberjonois, Roger Bowen. **Credits:** Dir: Robert Altman; Prod: Ingo Preminger; Writer: Ring Lardner; DP: Harold E. Stine; Ed: Danford B. Greene; Composer: Johnny Mandel; Art Director: Jack Martin Smith, Arthur Lonergan. Color, 116 min. VHS, LASER

Mask of Dimitrios
(1944) Warner Bros.
In an intriguing, exotic noir spy tale, Lorre is a mystery writer vacationing in Istanbul who becomes fascinated by the life of Dimitrios, a violent master criminal (Scott) who had been mixed up with the Bulgarian patriotic front. With his steps dogged by Greenstreet, a former associate of Dimitrios, the writer tracks the story of the enigmatic criminal whose body had washed up on the Turkish coast. After Greenstreet comes clean about his interest in the case, Lorre gets an up-close look at his subject when it turns out Dimitrios is not quite as dead as everyone thought. **Cast:** Sydney Greenstreet, Zachary Scott, Faye Emerson, Peter Lorre, Victor Francen. **Credits:** Dir: Jean Negulesco; Prod: Henry Blanke; Writer: Frank Gruber; Story: Eric Ambler; DP: Arthur Edeson; Ed: Frederick Richards; Prod Design: Ted Smith; Composer: Adolph Deutsch. B&W, 95 min.

The Mask of Fu Manchu
(1932) MGM
Karloff takes over the role of Sax Rohmer's deadly master criminal from Warner Oland in this melodrama made the same year as *The Mummy* and *The Old Dark House.* Fu Manchu searches for and finds the scimitar of Genghis Khan that will give him power over the white man. Contemporary audiences may find the film politically incorrect, but it's great, campy fun and engrossing in its own way. Karloff in long fingernails isn't the only one to

watch: Loy appears as Fu Manchu's sadistic sex-starved daughter, torturing men and turning them into love slaves—the last of a long parade of "Oriental" roles for Loy. **Cast:** Boris Karloff, Lewis Stone, Karen Morley, Myrna Loy, Charles Starrett, Jean Hersholt, Lawrence Grant, David Torrence. **Credits:** Dir: Charles Brabin; Prod: Irving Thalberg; Writer: Irene Kuhn, Edgar Allan Woolf, John Willard; Story: Sax Rohmer; DP: Tony Gaudio; Ed: Ben Lewis; Prod Design: Cedric Gibbons. B&W, 67 min. **VHS**

The Master of Ballantrae
(1952) Warner Bros.
An aging Flynn stars in the last of his great costume adventures. This swashbuckling adventure, adapted from Robert Louis Stevenson, is considered Flynn's best film since *The Sea Hawk* 13 years earlier. Scottish, English, and Sicilian locations add greatly to this colorful tale of piracy and intrigue aimed at restoring the Stuarts to the British throne. Remade as a TV film in 1984 with Michael York in the Flynn role. **Cast:** Errol Flynn, Roger Livesey, Anthony Steel, Yvonne Furneaux, Felix Aylmer, Mervyn Johns, Charles Goldner. **Credits:** Dir: William Keighley; Writer: Herb Meadow; DP: Jack Cardiff; Ed: Jack Harris; Composer: William Alwyn; Art Director: Ralph Brinton. Color, 89 min.
VHS, LASER

Master of the World
(1961) AIP
In a low-budget Jules Verne thriller, Price is the megalomaniac mad scientist, Robur, trying to blackmail the governments of the world to outlaw war. Playing like "20,000 Leagues in the Air," Price cruises the sky in a clipper ship with rotor blades instead of sails. Bronson, who memorably appeared with Price in *House of Wax*, here plays the heroic lead, a government agent intent on destroying the airship. **Cast:** Vincent Price, Charles Bronson, Mary Webster, Henry Hull, David Frankham, Richard Harrison, Vito Scotti, Wally Campo. **Credits:** Dir: William Witney; Prod: James H. Nicholson; Writer: Richard Matheson; DP: Gilbert Warrenton, Kay Norton; Ed: Anthony Carras; Prod Design: Daniel Haller; Composer: Les Baxter. Color, 95 min. **VHS**

The Master Race
(1944) RKO
WWII-era Nazi espionage melodrama has Coulouris as a German officer attempting to undermine the post–D-Day liberation forces. Engaging WWII propaganda to warn against the belief the war had been won. From the producers of *Hitler's Children* (1943). **Cast:** George Coulouris, Stanley Ridges, Osa Massen, Lloyd Bridges, Carl Esmond, Nancy Gates, Morris Carnovsky, Helen Beverly. **Credits:** Dir: Herbert J. Biberman; Prod: Robert S. Golden; Writer: Herbert J. Biberman; DP: Russell Metty; Ed: Ernie Leadlay; Composer: Roy Webb; Costumes: Renie; Art Director: Albert S. D'Agostino. B&W, 96 min. **VHS**

Mata Hari
(1932) MGM
Garbo is the ultimate femme fatale in a sober, involved melodrama and star vehicle for her and Novarro. As the notorious seducer, Garbo wins secrets for the Germans from her French officer lovers. Garbo could never take herself seriously playing a vamp, though she has the opportunity here to re-create Mata Hari's seductive dances that lure her victims. Reportedly Garbo was more interested in playing Joan of Arc than Mata Hari; one wonders what von Sternberg and Dietrich might have made of this material (they made *Dishonored*, with Dietrich as a spy, the same year). **Cast:** Greta Garbo, Ramon Novarro, Lionel Barrymore, Lewis Stone, Karen Morely, Alec B. Francis, Edmund Breese, Helen Jerome Eddy, Frank Reicher. **Credits:** Dir: George Fitzmaurice; Prod: Irving Thalberg; Writer: Benjamin Glazer, Leo Birinski, Doris Anderson, Gilbert Emery; DP: William Daniels; Ed: Frank Sullivan. B&W, 90 min. **VHS**

The Matchmaker
(1958) Paramount
Thornton Wilder's play (which later evolved into the musical *Hello, Dolly!*) is about a turn-of-the-century New York matchmaker (Booth) and her attempts to find a wife for a widowed millionaire (Paul Ford). Strong performances from the younger supporting cast: Perkins as a naive, endearing hayseed, Morse as his pal, and, especially, 22-year-old MacLaine as a lovelorn milliner. Occasional stage asides to the audience add an ironic distance to the nostalgia. **Cast:** Shirley Booth, Anthony Perkins, Shirley MacLaine, Paul Ford, Robert Morse, Wallace Ford, Perry Wilson, Russell Collins, Rex Evans. **Credits:** Dir: Joseph Anthony; Prod: Don Hartman; Writer: John Michael Hayes; DP: Charles B. Lang; Ed: Howard Smith; Composer: Adolph Deutsch; Art Director: Hal Pereira. B&W, 110 min. **VHS, LASER**

The Mating Game
(1959) MGM
A '50s comedy of the sexes with Randall as a traveling IRS investigator looking into the finances of a family farm and Reynolds as the proverbial farmer's daughter he falls for, supported by the ubiquitous supporting faces of the period: Douglas and Clark. The leads are a refreshing reminder of an era and sensibility now long gone. An Americanization of Bates's popular British comic novel, *The Darling Buds of May*, a U.K. *Tobacco Road*, which came to TV briefly in the '90s. **Cast:** Debbie Reynolds, Tony Randall, Paul Douglas, Fred Clark, Una Merkel, Philip Ober, Charles Lane, Trevor Bardette. **Credits:** Dir: George Marshall; Prod: Philip Barry; Writer: William Roberts; Story: H. E. Bates; DP: Robert Bronner; Ed: John McSweeney, Jr.; Prod Design: William A. Horning; Composer: Jeff Alexander; Costumes: Helen Rose; Art Director: Malcolm F. Brown. Color, 96 min. **VHS**

The Mating Season
(1951) Paramount
Just when former factory worker Lund thinks he's left his humble beginnings behind by marrying wealthy and fashionable Tierney, his mother (Ritter) comes to the family mansion as they're throwing their first ball. Her son reluctantly agrees to her wish to blend in as household help. Ritter's decency, good sense, and wit, however, win over her daughter-in-law and fill her son with pride. Great production by Leisen of a Brackett script, and a terrific performance by Ritter, the perennial Oscar nominee who stole *All About Eve* from a cast of notable scene-stealers. Academy Award Nomination: Best Supporting Actress: Thelma Ritter. **Cast:** Larry Keating, James Lorimer, Gene Tierney, Cora Witherspoon, Malcolm Keen, Gladys Hurlbut, Ellen Corby, Billie Bird, Mary Young, Thelma Ritter, John Lund. **Credits:** Dir: Mitchell Leisen; Prod: Charles Brackett; Writer: Charles Brackett, Walter Reisch, Richard Breen; DP: Charley Lang; Ed: Frank Bracht; Prod Design: Hal Pereira, Roland Anderson; Composer: Joseph J. Lilley. B&W, 101 min.

The Maverick Queen
(1956) Republic
Stanwyck in iron-willed Western-woman mode here oversees a saloon and runs a cattle-rustling ring on the side. Familiar '50s Western faces Sullivan, playing a Pinkerton detective,

and Brady, as the nasty Sundance Kid, complete the triangle. This relatively big-budget Republic feature (based on the writing of Zane Grey) shares some slight relation to the better-known *Butch Cassidy and the Sundance Kid* (1969). The first film shot in Republic's wide-screen process, Naturama. **Cast:** Barbara Stanwyck, Barry Sullivan, Mary Murphy, Scott Brady, Wallace Ford, Howard Petrie, Jim Davis, Emile Meyer. **Credits:** Dir: Joseph Kane; Prod: Herbert J. Yates; Writer: Kenneth Gamet; DP: Jack Marta; Ed: Richard L. Van Enger; Composer: Victor Young; Art Director: Walter E. Keller. Color, 92 min. VHS

Maytime
(1937) MGM
The past proves itself a truly foreign country when viewing this once popular, now neglected Eddy-MacDonald vehicle. Here is a prime example of popular Depression-era entertainment, considered by aficionados as the pinnacle of the duo's career together, whose appeal is completely lost on contemporary audiences. He plays a poor singer, she a married opera star who meet in Paris and must deal with Barrymore as the jealous husband. Filled with musical numbers including "Mammy's L'il Baby Loves Shortnin' Bread," "Will You Remember, Sweetheart?" and an uncalled for adaptation of Tchaikovsky's Fifth Symphony with modern lyrics. Academy Award Nominations: Best Sound Recording; Best Score. **Cast:** Jeanette MacDonald, Nelson Eddy, John Barrymore, Herman Bing, Tom Brown, Lynne Carver, Rafaela Ottiano, Charles Judels. **Credits:** Dir: Robert Z. Leonard; Prod: Hunt Stromberg; Writer: Noel Langley; DP: Oliver T. Marsh; Ed: Conrad A. Nervig; Prod Design: Cedric Gibbons; Composer: Herbert Stothart; Art Director: Fred Hope. B&W, 132 min. VHS, LASER

McCabe and Mrs. Miller
(1971) Warner Bros.
This bleak Western set in a Pacific Northwest mining camp was Altman's first major film following his breakthrough success with *M*A*S*H*. McCabe (Beatty) is a sardonic gambler who partners in business with local madame Mrs. Miller (Christie, in a wonderful performance). Their business runs afoul of the local mining company's enforcers, ending in an atypical snowstorm showdown just as the church bell gets lifted to the steeple. This looked and sounded unlike any other American film of the period, a

blend of the romantic cinematography by Zsigmond, gritty, dimly lit sets, brutal realism, and a subdued, multi-layered sound track. Academy Award Nomination for Best Actress: Julie Christie. **Cast:** Warren Beatty, Julie Christie, Rene Auberjonois, Keith Carradine, John Schuck, Bert Remsen, William Devane, Corey Fischer. **Credits:** Dir: Robert Altman; Prod: David Foster, Mitchell Brower; Writer: Robert Altman, Brian McKay; DP: Vilmos Zsigmond; Ed: Lou Lombardo; Prod Design: Leon Ericksen; Composer: Leonard Cohen. Color, 121 min. VHS

The McConnell Story
(1955) Warner Bros.
Captain Joseph McConnell (Ladd) was America's first air ace of the Korean War, and, in typical military biopic fashion, this film chronicles his story in the air and on the ground with the support from understanding yet worried wife, Allyson (playing nearly the same role as in *Strategic Air Command*, made the same year). The entire reason to watch is the flying sequences, which include experimental vehicles and air-to-air combat. **Cast:** Alan Ladd, June Allyson, James Whitmore, Frank Faylen, Robert Ellis, Willis Bouchey, Sarah Selby, Gregory Walcott. **Credits:** Dir: Gordon Douglas; Prod: Henry Blanke; Writer: Ted Sherdeman; DP: John F. Seitz; Ed: Owen Marks; Composer: Max Steiner; Art Director: John Beckman. Color, 107 min. VHS, LASER

The McKenzie Break
(1970) United Artists
British-American production about another "Great Escape" during WWII. German U-boat POWs attempt a break from a Scottish prison castle. Keith is the hard-drinking intelligence agent assigned to preventing any escapes, Griem his intelligent adversary. Blessed with a literate script and fine performances from the dueling leads, directed by TV-movie veteran Johnson. **Cast:** Brian Keith, Helmut Griem, Ian Hendry, Jack Watson, Patrick O'Connell, Horst Janson, Alexander Allerson, Tom Kempinski, Eric Allan, John Abineri. **Credits:** Dir: Lamont Johnson; Prod: Jules Levy; Writer: William Norton; DP: Michael Reed; Ed: Tom Rolf; Composer: Riz Ortolani. Color, 106 min. VHS

McLintock!
(1963) United Artists
Wealthy cattle baron Wayne settles into a cozy existence with cook De

Carlo and her kids (played by Wayne's brood) until his estranged wife O'Hara returns from the East after a two-year separation. She vows to divorce him and the two of them turn the entire town upside down with a hilarious romantic showdown featuring the notorious "spanking" scene. **Cast:** John Wayne, Maureen O'Hara, Patrick Wayne, Stefanie Powers, Edgar Buchanan, Jerry Van Dyke, Yvonne De Carlo, Jack Kruschen. **Credits:** Dir: Andrew V. McLaglen; Prod: Michael Wayne; Writer: James Edward Grant; DP: William Clothier; Ed: Otho S. Lovering; Composer: Frank DeVol; Art Director: Hal Pereira, Eddie Imazu. Color, 140 min. VHS, DVD

Me and the Colonel
(1958) Columbia
An anti-Semitic Polish colonel (Jurgens) and a Jewish refugee (Kaye) team up to seek passage out of France on the eve of the Nazis' strike. Along the way, life, love, and war bring the two men to a better understanding of each other. Based on *Jacobowsky and the Colonel* by Franz Werfel. **Cast:** Danny Kaye, Curt Jurgens, Nicole Maurey, Françoise Rosay, Akim Tamiroff, Martita Hunt, Alexander Scourby, Liliane Montevecchi. **Credits:** Dir: Peter Glenville; Prod: Sally Shuter; Writer: S. N. Behrman, George Froeschel; DP: Burnett Guffey; Ed: William A. Lyon, Charles Nelson; Prod Design: Walter Holscher; Composer: George Duning; Art Director: Georges Wakhevitch. B&W, 110 min. VHS

Meanest Man in the World
(1943) Fox
A classic Benny comedy. Benny is a perfectly friendly lawyer, convinced by his valet Anderson that he will do much better in his profession if he turns meaner. True enough, the nastier he becomes the more money he makes. His pinnacle of meanness is achieved when he is photographed literally stealing candy from a baby. His girlfriend, Lane, doesn't like the change. **Cast:** Jack Benny, Priscilla Lane, Eddie Anderson, Edmund Gwenn, Matt Briggs, Anne Revere, Margaret Seddon, Helene Reynolds, Don Douglas. **Credits:** Dir: Sidney Lanfield; Prod: William Perlberg; Writer: George Seaton, Allan House; Story: Austin MacHugh, George M. Cohan; DP: J. Peverell Marley; Ed: Robert Bischoff; Prod Design: Richard Day, Thomas Little; Composer: Emil Newman, Cyril Mockridge; Art Director: Albert Hogsett. B&W, 57 min.

Mean Streets

(1973) Warner Bros.
This is Scorsese's breakout feature, and arguably his most heartfelt film, with career-making performances by Keitel and De Niro. A group of friends in New York's Little Italy hang out, get in scrapes, and struggle with what comes next. Keitel is the conflicted nephew of a local Mob boss in Little Italy, struggling with his Catholic faith, his desire to go straight and own a restaurant, and the life promised by the Mob; De Niro is a frighteningly unstable hood, a human stick of dynamite capable of igniting at whim. A triumph, with dazzling scenes in which dialogue veers from the hilarious to the chilling, supported by spectacular editing and sound, this film established Scorsese as a master filmmaker and became one of the most influential films of the '70s. Remember, never call anyone a "mook." Selected for the National Film Registry. **Cast:** Robert De Niro, Harvey Keitel, David Proval, Amy Robinson, Richard Romanus, Cesare Danova, Victor Argo, George Memmoli. **Credits:** Dir: Martin Scorsese; Prod: Jonathan Taplin; Writer: Martin Scorsese, Mardik Martin; DP: Kent Wakeford; Ed: Sidney Levin. Color, 112 min. **VHS, LASER, DVD**

A Medal for Benny

(1945) Paramount
A WWII satire (based on a story by Steinbeck) on the nature of heroism and public image. When Benny, a local troublemaker, earns a posthumous Congressional Medal of Honor, all who once knew (and disliked) him laud him as a hero. His father, Naish, refuses to cash in and his onetime girlfriend, Lamour, finds love with De Cordova, who goes off to war in an effort to live up to the image of his predecessor. Academy Award Nominations: Best Supporting Actor: J. Carroll Naish; Best Original Screenplay. **Cast:** Dorothy Lamour, Arturo De Cordova, J. Carrol Naish, Mikhail Rasumny, Fernando Alvarado, Charles Dingle, Frank McHugh, Rosita Moreno, Grant Mitchell, Douglass Dumbrille. **Credits:** Dir: Irving Pichel; Prod: Paul Jones; Writer: Frank Butler, Jack Wagner, John Steinbeck; DP: Lionel Linden; Ed: Arthur Schmidt; Prod Design: Hans Dreier, Hal Pereira; Composer: Victor Young. B&W, 77 min.

Medium Cool

(1969) Paramount
Cinematographer Wexler's groundbreaking, compelling indy feature about a dispassionate news cameraman influenced a generation of American filmmakers. Shot on location in Chicago during the notorious Democratic convention of 1968, *Medium Cool* is also a time capsule of the late '60s, with hippies, war protests, and actual scenes of revolutionary turmoil. The police response to the protesters gets uncomfortably close to the filmmakers. In one scene, you hear a cameraman shout, "Look out, Haskell, it's real!" just before Wexler is struck by a tear-gas canister and drops his camera. Forster (whose career revived in 1998's *Foxy Brown*) is the cameraman who experiences the action on the street as he helps look for the son of a woman from Kentucky in whom he takes an interest. Bonerz (later a regular on *The Bob Newhart Show*) plays his soundman. The film remains a moving, intelligent exploration of the responsibility of the artist to society. **Cast:** Robert Forster, Verna Bloom, Marianna Hill, Peter Bonerz, Harold Blankenship, Peter Boyle, Felton Perry, Robert Paige. **Credits:** Dir: Haskell Wexler; Prod: Jerry Wexler, Haskell Wexler, Tully Friedman; Writer: Haskell Wexler; DP: Haskell Wexler; Ed: Verna Fields; Composer: Michael Bloomfield; Art Director: Leon Ericksen. Color, 111 min. **VHS, LASER**

Meet Danny Wilson

(1951) Universal
Sinatra is a saloon singer who becomes snarled in the dealings of gangster Burr. Despite the melodrama, this is likable entertainment, with a vibrant performance by Winters as the singer distracting both Sinatra and his pianist sidekick. Memorable numbers include: "All of Me," "That Old Black Magic," and "A Good Man Is Hard to Find." **Cast:** Frank Sinatra, Shelley Winters, Raymond Burr, Alex Nicol, Tommy Farrell, Vaughn Taylor, Donald MacBride, Carl Sklover. **Credits:** Dir: Joseph Pevney; Prod: Leonard Goldstein; Writer: Don McGuire; DP: Maury Gertsman; Ed: Virgil Vogel; Composer: Joseph Gershenson; Art Director: Bernard Herzbrun, Nathan Juran. B&W, 88 min. **VHS**

Meet John Doe

(1941) Warner Bros.
With *Mr. Smith Goes to Washington* (1939) and *Mr. Deeds Goes to Town* (1936), this is Capra's third Depression-era parable illustrating the decency of the common man triumphing over cynicism, big-money influence, and power. A suicidal down-and-outer, "John Doe" (Cooper), is manipulated by an ambitious politician (Arnold) and a newspaper writer (Stanwyck) to appeal to the masses, only to discover too late the nature of the deception. Capra and frequent collaborator Riskin's ode to populism once again makes its points with well-drawn characters, wonderful performances, and a number of powerful scenes, including a giant rally in the rain where Cooper is denounced as a fraud. Academy Award Nomination for Best Original Story. **Cast:** Gary Cooper, Barbara Stanwyck, Edward Arnold, Walter Brennan, James Gleason, Spring Byington, Gene Lockhart, Rod La Rocque, Irving Bacon. **Credits:** Dir: Frank Capra; Prod: Frank Capra; Writer: Robert Riskin; DP: George Barnes; Ed: Daniel Mandell; Composer: Dimitri Tiomkin. B&W, 135 min. **VHS**

Meet Me in Las Vegas

(1956) MGM
It's not the story but the dance numbers that make this Dailey-Charisse CinemaScope romantic comedy about a gambler who only wins when he holds the hand of his lady luck. The highlight is a ballet based on the folk legend "Frankie and Johnny" (with lyrics by Sammy Cahn and sung by Sammy Davis, Jr.). Look for guest appearances by Horne singing "If You Can Dream" and Laine, then at the height of his career, singing "Hell Hath No Fury," cameos by Frank Sinatra and Debbie Reynolds, as well as a young George Chakiris (*West Side Story*) among the dancers. Academy Award Nomination for Best Scoring of a Musical Picture. **Cast:** Dan Dailey, Cyd Charisse, Agnes Moorehead, Lili Darvas, Jim Backus, Jerry Colonna, Paul Henreid, Lena Horne, Frankie Laine, Mitsuko Sawamura. **Credits:** Dir: Roy Rowland; Prod: Joe Pasternak; Writer: Isobel Lennart; DP: Robert Bronner; Ed: Albert Akst; Prod Design: Cedric Gibbons, Urie McCleary; SFX: Warren Newcombe; Set Designer: Edwin B. Willis. Color, 103 min. **VHS, LASER**

Meet Me in St. Louis

(1944) MGM
On nearly every list of the best Hollywood musicals of all time, Minnelli's slice of Americana set during the 1904 World's Fair was unusual for its failure to employ a "backstage" plot device to set up the songs. More important, it served to reestablish Garland's career and established Minnelli (Garland's future husband) as a major American filmmaker. The story

of the well-to-do Alonzo Smith (Ames) and his family is a nostalgic portrait of an idealized happy American household, where the biggest worries concern the romantic futures of daughters Garland and Bremer and a possible move to New York. With songs like "The Boy Next Door," "Have Yourself a Merry Christmas," and the famous "Trolley Song," this soon became MGM's second most successful film, bested only by GWTW. Selected as a National Film Registry Outstanding Film. Academy Award Nominations: 4, including Best Screenplay; Best Song ("The Trolley Song"). **Cast:** Judy Garland, Mary Astor, Tom Drake, Margaret O'Brien, Harry Davenport, Lucille Bremer, June Lockhart, Marjorie Main, Leon Ames. **Credits:** Dir: Vincente Minnelli; Prod: Arthur Freed; Writer: Irving Brecher, Fred F. Finklehoffe; DP: George J. Folsey; Ed: Albert Akst; Prod Design: Cedric Gibbons; Set Designer: Edwin B. Willis. Color, 113 min. VHS, LASER

The Member of the Wedding
(1953) Columbia
A reverent if stagebound adaptation of Carson McCullers's novel and play, with notable screen debuts by Harris and de Wilde. Harris plays 12-year-old Frankie, the central figure who imagines herself part of her big brother's wedding party and who runs away from home only to confront her own blossoming maturity. Harris (who was 26 when the film was shot), along with de Wilde, Waters, Hansen, and Bolden, all repeat their Broadway roles. Golden Globe for Special Achievement: Brandon de Wilde. Academy Award Nomination: Best Actress: Julie Harris. **Cast:** Ethel Waters, Julie Harris, Brandon de Wilde, Arthur Franz, Nancy Gates, James Edwards, Dickie Moore, June Hedin, Ann Carter, Harry Bolden, William Hansen. **Credits:** Dir: Fred Zinnemann; Prod: Stanley Kramer; Writer: Edna Anhalt, Edward Anhalt; DP: Hal Mohr; Ed: Harry Gerstad, William Lyon; Composer: Alex North. B&W, 91 min. VHS

The Memphis Belle
(1944)
Director William Wyler's Technicolor documentary short about a B-17 Flying Fortress on dangerous missions over Germany is one of the landmark war documentaries of its era, made for the War Activities Commission. Its images were recycled into scores of later combat films. This served as the inspiration for the 1990 dramatic film of the same name. Color, 43 min. VHS, LASER

The Men
(1950) United Artists
In his film debut, Brando plays a sullen wheelchair-bound paraplegic war veteran who learns to deal with his self-pity and adjust to life. Brando's performance was a departure from Hollywood acting of the period and he prepared for the role by living in a ward with veterans. Despite good reviews and much press about Hollywood's latest antistar, the film did little business and it took Brando's next film, A Streetcar Named Desire (1951), to make him a screen sensation. Academy Award Nomination for Best Story and Screenplay. **Cast:** Marlon Brando, Teresa Wright, Everett Sloane, Jack Webb, Richard Erdman, Virginia Farmer, Dorothy Tree, Howard St. John, John Miller. **Credits:** Dir: Fred Zinnemann; Prod: Stanley Kramer; Writer: Carl Foreman; DP: Robert de Grasse; Ed: Harry Gerstad; Prod Design: Rudolph Sternad; Composer: Dimitri Tiomkin. B&W, 85 min. VHS

Men in War
(1957) United Artists
The '50s saw an endless number of isolated platoon films; it's a wonder all those lost soldiers didn't finally collide with each other. Here the Korean War platoon is led by Ryan, aided by ubiquitous Ray. We see few clichés or heroics as one by one the men confront the usual travails and misery in a bleak portrayal of the futility of combat. Morrow (soon to command his own platoon on TV's Combat), Marlowe, Pine, and Persoff are among the familiar dogfaces. A departure for director Mann, though known for his acute understanding of the psychological tension of men under stress. **Cast:** Robert Ryan, Aldo Ray, Robert Keith, Vic Morrow, Scott Marlowe, Philip Pine, Nehemiah Persoff, James Edwards. **Credits:** Dir: Anthony Mann; Prod: Sidney Harmon; Writer: Philip Yordan; DP: Ernest Haller; Ed: Richard C. Meyer. B&W, 105 min. VHS

Men in White
(1934) MGM
An early dramatic role for Gable as a dedicated young doctor who must choose between the lively lifestyle urged on him by his society fiancée (Loy) and the demanding career of service he craves. Meanwhile, he attracts the attention and affection of a nurse who understands his motivations better than his wife-to-be. The two have a brief affair, with dire consequences for the nurse. **Cast:** Clark Gable, Myrna Loy, Jean Hersholt, Elizabeth Allan,

C. Henry Gordon. **Credits:** Dir: Richard Boleslawski; Prod: Monta Bell; Writer: Sidney Kingsley, Waldemar Young; DP: George Folsey, Jr.; Ed: Frank Sullivan; Composer: Dr. William Axt; Art Director: Cedric Gibbons, Merrill Pye. B&W, 80 min.

Men of America
(1932) RKO
Boyd was soon to rise to fame and fortune as Hopalong Cassidy, but first he had to pay his dues by taking on gangsters after moving to a western town. It seems residents suspect the newcomer as an accomplice to the recent crime wave, but he shows his true-blue colors by forming an alliance with the owner of the general store and successfully battling the bad guys. Director Ince was the brother of Thomas Ince, the father of the modern role of producer. Ralph Ince was also a prolific actor and director in the silent era, appearing in 500 films and directing 150 by the time the sound era dawned. **Cast:** William Boyd, Dorothy Wilson, Charles Sale, Ralph Ince, Henry Armetta, Eugene Strong, Ernie Adams, Theresa Maxwell Conover, Alphonz Ethier, Fatty Layman. **Credits:** Dir: Ralph Ince; Prod: Pandro S. Berman; Writer: Jack Jungmeyer, Samuel Ornitz; Story: Henry McCarty, Humphrey Pearson; DP: J. Roy Hunt; Ed: Edward Schroeder. B&W, 57 min.

Men of Boys Town
(1941) MGM
Tracy reprising his Oscar-winning role of Father Flanagan costars with Rooney in this routine sequel to the successful and beloved Boys Town (1938). In dire need of money to finance new facilities at Boys Town, Father Flanagan comes to the aid of a young man convicted of murder. **Cast:** Spencer Tracy, Mickey Rooney, Lee J. Cobb, Darryl Hickman, Henry O'Neill, Mary Nash. **Credits:** Dir: Norman Taurog; Prod: John Considine; Writer: James Kevin McGuinness; DP: Harold Rosson; Ed: Fredrick Y. Smith; Prod Design: Cedric Gibbons; Composer: Herbert Stothart. B&W, 106 min. VHS

Men of the Fighting Lady
(1954) MGM
The Fighting Lady is the aircraft-carrier setting of this Korean War naval aviation drama. The plot is fairly routine, with the usual mix of brash young pilots and stock combat footage, the stories linked by Calhern's narrative, here playing writer James A. Michener. Rozsa provided the stirring score, which proves particularly effective in a

scene where blinded pilot Martin is talked down to the flight deck by Johnson. This film was so beloved by President Ronald Reagan that he reportedly incorporated lines from Pidgeon's role into speeches about real events. **Cast:** Van Johnson, Walter Pidgeon, Louis Calhern, Dewey Martin, Keenan Wynn, Frank Lovejoy, Robert Horton, Bert Freed. **Credits:** Dir: Andrew Marton; Prod: Henry Berman; Writer: Art Cohn; DP: George J. Folsey; Ed: Gene Ruggiero; Prod Design: Cedric Gibbons; Composer: Miklos Rozsa; Set Designer: Edwin B. Willis. Color, 81 min. **VHS**

Men with Wings
(1938) Paramount
An aerial romance (the best kind for former WWI pilot Wellman, who also directed *Wings* in 1929) takes to the skies to resolve the romantic tensions among a triangle of childhood friends who share a passion for airplanes. Campbell and her husband MacMurray see longtime friend Milland as their number-one colleague and pal. But Milland has been harboring romantic feelings for Campbell since they were kids and, if she can accept it, his love for her will lighten the tragedy of her husband's death in the skies of China. The plot takes a backseat to the remarkable aerial sequences, featuring extraordinary stunt pilot Paul Mantz directing the mid-air photography. **Cast:** Fred MacMurray, Ray Milland, Walter Abel, Andy Devine, Louise Campbell, Kitty Kelly, Donald O'Connor, George Chandler, Porter Hall, Russell Hicks. **Credits:** Dir: William Wellman; Prod: William Wellman; Writer: Robert Carson; DP: W. Howard Greene, Paul Mantz; Ed: Thomas Scott. Color, 105 min.

The Mephisto Waltz
(1971) Fox
In this complicated occult thriller, a journalist's young wife (Bisset) is concerned with the changes she sees in her husband (Alda) after a rare interview with a famous, terminally ill pianist. She should be, as a group of Satan worshipers led by the pianist (Jurgens) is taking possession of them. TV producer and director Martin and Wendkos's attempt to capture the success of *Rosemary's Baby*, with creepy asides about a devil child, blood transfusions, and a dog with a human head. Based on a novel by Fred Mustard Stewart. **Cast:** Alan Alda, Curt Jurgens, Jacqueline Bisset, Barbara Parkins, Bradford Dillman, William Windom, Kathleen Widdoes,

Pamelyn Ferdin, Curt Lowens. **Credits:** Dir: Paul Wendkos; Prod: Quinn Martin; Writer: Ben Maddow; DP: William W. Spencer; Composer: Jerry Goldsmith; SFX: Howard Anderson; Art Director: Richard Haman. Color, 109 min. **VHS**

Merrill's Marauders
(1962) Warner Bros.
Fuller, never known for subtle understatement, directed this brutal, relentless WWII film set in the jungles of Burma. Chandler, in his final screen appearance, plays the famed Brigadier General Frank Merrill, and gives a moving portrayal of the man who commanded a volunteer unit to march 500 miles through swamps and forests to stem the Japanese onslaught. Supported by faces familiar from countless other war films (Akins, Hutchins, and Hardin). Fuller was a master of wide-screen composition and this color CinemaScope feature is among the finest displays of his genius. Not your typical WWII combat saga. **Cast:** Jeff Chandler, Ty Hardin, Claude Akins, Peter Brown, Andrew Duggan, Will Hutchins. **Credits:** Dir: Samuel Fuller; Prod: Milton Sperling; Writer: Samuel Fuller, Milton Sperling; DP: William H. Clothier; Ed: Folmar Blangsted. Color, 99 min. **VHS, LASER**

Merrily We Live
(1938) MGM
A delightful, less well known screwball comedy. Cynical writer Aherne unwittingly infiltrates a loony house of philanthropists. Mrs. Emily Kilbourne (Burke) runs a household that, due to her charitable nature, is as much hobo jungle as happy home. When he joins the menage, Aherne falls head over heels in love with Bennett, the eldest daughter. Academy Award Nominations: 5, including Best Supporting Actress: Billie Burke. **Cast:** Constance Bennett, Brian Aherne, Billie Burke, Alan Mowbray, Pat Kelly, Ann Dvorak, Tom Brown, Marjorie Rambeau, Phillip Reed, Clarence Kolb. **Credits:** Dir: Norman Z. McLeod; Prod: Hal Roach, Milton Bren; Writer: Jack Jevne, Eddie Moran; DP: Norbert F. Brodine; Ed: William H. Terhune; Prod Design: Charles D. Hall; Composer: Phil Craig, Arthur Quenzer. B&W, 90 min.

The Merry Widow
(1934) MGM
This is the very definition of the much-heralded "Lubitsch touch," that flair for light humor that gave a lilt to costume romances such as this. Chevalier plays the dashing prince

who is the last chance for a tiny municipality when the wealthy widow (MacDonald) who supports the economy decamps for the bright lights of Paris. A magnificent production of the popular (and often-filmed) 1905 Lehar operetta, it includes new lyrics by Lorenz Hart and fine supporting performances by Horton and Merkel. **Academy Awards:** Best Interior Decoration (B&W). **Cast:** Jeanette MacDonald, Maurice Chevalier, Una Merkel, Edward Everett Horton, George Barbier, Minna Gombell, Sterling Holloway, Henry Armetta, Donald Meek, Ruth Channing. **Credits:** Dir: Ernst Lubitsch; Prod: Irving Thalberg; Writer: Samson Raphaelson; DP: Oliver T. Marsh; Ed: Frances Marsh; Prod Design: Cedric Gibbons; Choreographer: Albertina Rasch; Composer: Franz Lehar. B&W, 99 min. **VHS, LASER**

The Merry Widow
(1952) MGM
This is the third screen version of the Lehar operetta, this time in Technicolor with Turner and Lamas in the leads. An attempt by MGM to remake Turner as a musical star (Enzio Pinza costarred with her in *Mr. Imperium* of 1951), but the film was a notorious failure. The trappings are fine as is Lamas, and Turner, with dubbed singing voice, wears her gowns with style. Academy Award Nominations: 2, including Best (Color) Costume Design. **Cast:** Lana Turner, Fernando Lamas, Una Merkel, Richard Haydn, Thomas Gomez, John Abbott, Marcel Dalio, King Donovan, Robert Coote. **Credits:** Dir: Curtis Bernhardt; Prod: Joe Pasternak; Writer: Sonya Levien; DP: Robert Surtees; Ed: Conrad A. Nervig; Prod Design: Cedric Gibbons; Choreographer: Jack Cole; Composer: Franz Lehar. Color, 105 min. **VHS**

Message to Love: The Isle of Wight Festival
(1970)
An eye-opening, no-holds-barred documentary of 1970's legendary five-day Isle of Wight rock-and-roll festival, featuring the final stage performances of Jimi Hendrix and The Doors with Jim Morrison. Other highlights include The Who's "Young Man's Blues" and "Naked Eyes," along with footage of Free, Taste, Tiny Tim, John Sebastian, Donovan, Ten Years After, The Moody Blues, Kris Kristofferson, Joni Mitchell, Miles Davis, Leonard Cohen, ELP, Joan Baez, and Jethro Tull. **Credits:** Dir: Murray Lerner; Prod: Rocky Oldham, Avril MacRory, Malcolm Gerrie; Writer: Murray Lerner; DP: Jack

Hazan, Nic Knowland, Norman Langley, Charles Stewart, Mike Whittaker, Andy Carchrae, Richard Stanley; Ed: Howard Alk, Greg Sheldon, Stanley Warnow, Einar Westerlund. Color, 137 min. **VHS, DVD**

Mexican Spitfire

RKO knew it had scored a winner with the farcical comedy *The Girl from Mexico* (1939), which had the saucy, charismatic Lupe Velez playing Carmelita, a tempestuous Mexican entertainer recruited to New York by Donald Wood's uptight ad executive, Dennis. Carmelita and Dennis fall in love and marry, though Carmelita finds she has more in common with Dennis's loopy uncle Matt, played by Leon Errol. In subsequent entries, attention shifts to the rapport between Velez and Errol, whose Ziegfeld-style comic talent is put to good use, especially when he assumed a second role, that of Matt's boss, uppity British businessman Lord Epping. This is a one-note series, but Lupe hit the perfect Pan-American note for wartime sales to Latin America. Velez is a somewhat tragic figure in Hollywood history, moving from fiery leading roles in late-silent and early-talkie classics such as *Lady of the Pavement* (1929) for D. W. Griffith and *The Squaw Man* (1931) for Cecil B. DeMille to the stereotypical Spitfire series. Her private life matched her tempestuous on-screen persona. After public affairs —and equally public humiliations—with Gary Cooper among others and a rocky marriage to Johnny Weismuller, Velez committed suicide in 1944.

The Girl from Mexico *(1939)*
Mexican Spitfire *(1939)*
Mexican Spitfire Out West *(1940)*
Mexican Spitfire's Baby *(1941)*
Mexican Spitfire at Sea *(1942)*
Mexican Spitfire Sees a Ghost *(1942)*
Mexican Spitfire's Elephant *(1942)*
Mexican Spitfire's Blessed Event
    (1943)

Oscar Micheaux

A prolific and controversial African-American independent filmmaker of the '20s and '30s, Micheaux was best known for his tenacity in producing his own work. When negotiations with the Lincoln Film Company (one of the first African-American studios) to produce the film version of Micheaux's novel, *The Homesteaders*, broke down in 1918, Micheaux simply pulled up stakes and moved to

Chicago, taking over the abandoned Selig Studio and making the film himself. Many more followed, but Micheaux was continually plagued by lack of funding and as a result, his films tend to be of a rather poor technical quality. Scenes had to be shot in a single take, often in poor lighting. Micheaux's movies were not always well received by African-American audiences, who tended to be turned off by the director-producer's rather bourgeois, ambivalent treatment of the race issue (particularly in *The Exile*, 1931). Micheaux's attempts to emulate Hollywood genres and to promote African-American stars were for the most part unsuccessful. Most of Micheaux's actors were amateurs with the exception of Paul Robeson, who starred in *Body and Soul* (1924).

Within Our Gates *(1924)*
Birthright *(1924)*
Body and Soul *(1925)*
A Daughter of the Congo *(1930)*
Easy Street *(1930)*
Veiled Aristocrats *(1932)*
Ten Minutes to Live *(1932)*
Girl from Chicago *(1932)*
Ten Minutes to Kill *(1933)*
Harlem After Midnight *(1934)*
Murder in Harlem *(1935)*
Temptation *(1936)*
Underworld *(1937)*
God's Stepchildren *(1937)*
Thirty Years Later *(1938)*
Swing! *(1938)*
Lying Lips *(1939)*
The Betrayal *(1948)*

Midnight

(1939) Paramount
Colbert is featured in one of her best roles in an early script by the masters of wit and sophistication, Wilder and Brackett. Produced the same year as the team's much better known *Ninotchka*, this society comedy finds showgirl Colbert in Paris courted by a poor Hungarian cabdriver (Ameche) and a multimillionaire (Barrymore) who needs her participation in a scheme to win back his wife (Astor). The deceptions multiply and the dialogue's memorable in a film some critics have described as the coincidental bookend to Jean Renoir's enduring classic *Rules of the Game*, made the same year. Considered by many to be the best film directed by Leisen. **Cast:** Claudette Colbert, Don Ameche, John Barrymore, Francis Lederer, Mary Astor, Hedda Hopper, Rex O'Malley. **Credits:** Dir: Mitchell Leisen; Prod: Arthur Hornblow, Jr.;

Writer: Charles Brackett, Billy Wilder; DP: Charles Lang; Ed: Doane Harrison; Composer: Frederick Hollander; Art Director: Hans Dreier, Robert Usher. B&W, 94 min. **VHS**

Midnight Cowboy

(1969) United Artists
One of the finest American films of the '60s, this flew in the face of the Hollywood establishment and helped advance the trend toward difficult subject matter, naturalistic acting, and location shooting. Rated X when first released, this bitter story follows the slow-witted hustler Joe Buck (Voight) and his desperate friendship with the sickly Ratso Rizzo (Hoffman), two drifters lost in the canyons and crowds of New York. Its bleak, cynical view of modern America as a collection of lonely abusers and dispirited victims is often depressing, yet is balanced by a sardonic wit often as cruel as the actions portrayed on the screen. Very much a period piece of the early Nixon era and an America in political and artistic conflict. Standout performances by the two leads, who swiftly became among the most important stars of the next decade. The deluxe, remastered video edition features a behind-the-scenes documentary, the original and rerelease trailers, and a newly mixed sound track. Golden Globe for Best Male Newcomer: Jon Voight, the Directors Guild DGA for Outstanding Directorial Achievement, and selected as a National Film Registry Outstanding Film. Academy Award Nominations: 7, including Best Actor: Dustin Hoffman and Jon Voight. **Academy Awards:** Best Picture; Best Director; Best Screenplay Based on Material from Another Medium. **Cast:** Dustin Hoffman, Jon Voight, Sylvia Miles, Brenda Vaccaro, John McGiver, Ruth White, Barnard Hughes, Bob Balaban, Viva, Paul Morrissey. **Credits:** Dir: John Schlesinger; Prod: Jerome Hellman; Writer: Waldo Salt; Story: James Leo Herlihy; DP: Adam Holender; Ed: Hugh A. Robertson; Prod Design: John Robert Lloyd; Composer: John Barry; SFX: Dick Smith. Color, 113 min. **VHS, LASER, DVD**

Midnight Lace

(1960) Universal
A Ross Hunter thriller in which Day returns to London yet fails to re-create the energy and suspense of Hitchcock's *The Man Who Knew Too Much*, which featured Day (and London) four years earlier. Day is the American wife of a British tycoon (Harrison) threat-

> **"Joan Crawford is doubtless the best example of the flapper, the girl you see at smart nightclubs, gowned to the apex of sophistication, toying with iced glasses with a remote, faintly bitter expression, dancing deliciously, laughing a great deal with wide, hurt eyes."**
>
> F. Scott Fitzgerald

ened by menacing telephone calls and near-fatal accidents. Everyone becomes a potential murderer, including her debonair husband, an adoring next-door neighbor, and a construction foreman working nearby. A fine supporting cast can't save a fairly routine script. Academy Award Nomination for Best Costumes. **Cast:** Doris Day, Rex Harrison, John Gavin, Myrna Loy, Roddy McDowall, Herbert Marshall, Natasha Parry, John Williams, Hermione Baddeley. **Credits:** Dir: David Miller; Prod: Ross Hunter; Martin Melcher; Writer: Ivan Goff; DP: Russell Metty; Ed: Russell Schoengarth, Leon Barsha; Prod Design: Alexander Golitzen; Composer: Frank Skinner; Art Director: Robert Clatworthy. Color, 108 min. **VHS**

Midnight Mary
(1933) MGM
Less than masterful meeting of two masters, director Wellman (*The Public Enemy*, 1931) and writer Loos (*Gentlemen Prefer Blondes*, 1953), flashes back over the life of a woman on trial for murder, Young, who gives a memorable performance cast against type. The chronicle of how Young turned bad follows her from 10-year-old orphan to adult companion of the gangster she will later jeopardize to save her new love. Notable early performance by Devine. **Cast:** Loretta Young, Ricardo Cortez, Franchot Tone, Andy Devine, Harold Huber, Warren Hymer, Una Merkel, Frank Conroy, Ivan Simpson, Sandy Roth. **Credits:** Dir: William Wellman; Prod: Lucien Hubbard; Writer: Gene Markey, Kathryn Scola; Story: Anita Loos; DP: James Van Trees; Ed: William S. Gray; Composer: William Axt. B&W, 71 min.

A Midsummer Night's Dream
(1935) Warner Bros.
German experimental theater director Reinhardt's only sound feature is now most often remembered for casting an energetic Cagney as Bottom and 15-year-old Rooney in the role of Puck. Hollywood's first major talking attempt at Shakespeare, it also featured the film debut of de Havilland as Hermia, Jory as Oberon, and Brown as Flute. Replacement cinematographer Mohr was awarded an Oscar for his lush images, the only time a write-in candidate has won. Mendelssohn's music was adapted by Erich Wolfgang Korngold, and some sophisticated ballet sequences created by Bronislawa Nijinska were later re-choreographed as if they were Busby Berkeley production numbers. Academy Award Nominations: 3, including Best Picture. **Academy Awards:** Best Cinematography; Best Film Editing. **Cast:** James Cagney, Mickey Rooney, Olivia de Havilland, Dick Powell, Gary Cooper, Joe E. Brown, Jean Muir, Hugh Herbert, Ian Hunter, Victor Jory. **Credits:** Dir: Max Reinhardt; Prod: Max Reinhardt; Writer: Charles Kenyon, Mary McCall; Story: William Shakespeare; DP: Hal Mohr; Ed: Ralph Dawson; Prod Design: Anton Grot; Composer: Felix Mendelssohn. B&W, 150 min. **VHS, LASER**

Midway
(1976) Universal
One of the last megabudgeted WWII battle films has a large cast of familiar faces, character actors, and stars in decline, who join forces with radio-controlled models, stock footage, and explosions to re-create this saga of the massive air and sea battle of June 1942. Fonda plays Fleet Commander Chester W. Nimitz and Mifune his Japanese counterpart Admiral Yamamoto (with voice dubbed by the ubiquitous Paul Frees). Meanwhile there is a subplot involving Captain Garth (Heston) and his son's intent to marry a Hawaiian woman of Japanese descent. Long and loud, but quieter now than when first released: original theatrical showings used Universal's "Sensurround" process, which utilized low-frequency speakers in theaters to shake the floors and walls. **Cast:** Charlton Heston, Henry Fonda, Glenn Ford, Robert Mitchum, Edward Albert, Hal Holbrook, James Coburn, Robert Wagner, Toshiro Mifune. **Credits:** Dir: Jack Smight; Prod: Walter Mirisch; DP: Harry Stradling; Ed: Robert W. Swink, Frank J. Urioste; Composer: John Williams; SFX: Jack McMasters; Art Director: Walter Tyler; Set Designer: John M. Dwyer. Color, 132 min. **VHS, LASER, DVD**

Mighty Joe Young
(1949) RKO
The first semi-remake of the King Kong story features special effects by O'Brien and a very young Harryhausen (later responsible for *The Seventh Voyage of Sinbad*, *Earth vs. the Flying Saucers*, among many others). This time Moore has the female lead and the music is by Webb, reminding us of the important part played by Fay Wray and Max Steiner in the original *Kong*. The tone is lighter as well and Joe eventually triumphs, making this a slight entertainment without the dark, tragic notes of the earlier film. Remade in 1998. The laserdisc contains a historical overview. **Academy Awards:** Best Special Effects. **Cast:** Terry Moore, Ben Johnson, Robert Armstrong, Douglas Fowley, Paul Guilfoyle, Nestor Paiva, Regis Toomey. **Credits:** Dir: Ernest B. Schoedsack; Prod: John Ford, Merian C. Cooper; Writer: Ruth Rose; DP: J. Roy Hunt; Ed: Ted Cheesman; SFX: Ray Harryhausen, Willis H. O'Brien, Harold E. Stine, Bert Willis, Linwood Dunn, Pete Peterson; Composer: Roy Webb. B&W, 94 min. **VHS, LASER**

Mikey and Nicky
(1976) Paramount
One of the quintessential New York theater films of the period, the third feature by former comic May (*The Heartbreak Kid*, 1972) is the story of two thugs and longtime friends (Cassavetes and Falk) on the run from a hired assassin (Beatty) . . . or perhaps he is really only after one of them. Choppy and experimental, the film is a

wonderful set piece for both leads as the true nature of their friendship and character is revealed. Storied New York acting coach Meisner plays the gang lord who fingers Cassavetes. **Cast:** John Cassavetes, Peter Falk, Ned Beatty, Joyce Van Patten, Sanford Meisner, Carol Grace, William Hickey. **Credits:** Dir: Elaine May; Prod: Michael Hausman; Writer: Elaine May; DP: Victor J. Kemper; Ed: John Carter, Sheldon Kahn; Prod Design: Paul Sylbert; Composer: Johann Strauss II; Set Designer: John Austin. Color, 106 min. **VHS**

Mildred Pierce
(1945) Warner Bros.
Crawford is at her finest in her Oscar-winning role as James M. Cain's sacrificing mother who rises from waitress to restaurant-chain owner only to find her undoing in a mean-spirited, ungrateful daughter, Blyth. A first-class soap directed with deft aplomb by Warner A-teamer Curtiz (*Casablanca*, 1942). The title role, which revived Crawford's career, was reportedly first offered to Bette Davis and Barbara Stanwyck before producer Wald was approached by Crawford. Academy Award Nominations: 6, including Best Picture; Best (Adapted) Screenplay; Best Supporting Actress: Eve Arden and Ann Blyth. **Academy Awards:** Best Actress: Joan Crawford. **Cast:** Joan Crawford, Ann Blyth, Jack Carson, Zachary Scott, Eve Arden, Bruce Bennett, George Tobias, Lee Patrick, Moroni Olsen, Barbara Brown. **Credits:** Dir: Michael Curtiz; Prod: Jerry Wald; Writer: Ranald MacDougall; Ed: David Weisbart; Prod Design: Anton Grot; Composer: Max Steiner. B&W, 120 min. **VHS, LASER**

Milhouse—A White Comedy
(1971)
A year prior to the Watergate break-in, this black-comic compilation of newsclips from Richard Nixon's career confirmed what many of his detractors had said for a long time: his entire political life had been a parade of deception and grandstanding. Here are the famous "pumpkin papers," the notorious "Checkers Speech," and his 1962 promise to withdraw from politics so the press "won't have Dick Nixon to kick around anymore." De Antonio, who previously had compiled the McCarthy documentary *Point of Order*, edits and manipulates the material for the most devastating effect. **Credits:** Dir: Emile De Antonio; DP: Ed Emshwiller, Mike Gray; Ed: Mary Lampson. B&W, 90 min. **VHS**

The Milkman
(1950) Universal
Durante stars in this comedy about a milkman and his hapless young protégé. When Roger Bradley (O'Connor) comes back from WWII, he asks his father, a milk magnate, for a delivery job at his dairy. Roger Bradley, Sr., believes the cure for his boy, who seems to have picked up a permanent case of nerves during the war, is leisure, and refuses his son's request. The elder Bradley's dairy is better off for this refusal, for when Roger gets a job at a rival dairy through his friend Breezy Albright (Durante), his missteps derail his older partner's smooth path to retirement. **Cast:** Donald O'Connor, Jimmy Durante, Joyce Holden, William Conrad, Piper Laurie, Henry O'Neill, Paul Harvey, Jess Barker, Elisabeth Risdon, Frank Nelson. **Credits:** Dir: Charles Barton; Prod: Ted Richmond; Writer: Albert Beich, James O'Hanlon, Leonard Stern; Story: Martin Ragaway; DP: Clifford Stine; Ed: Russell Schoengarth; Prod Design: Bernard Herzbrun, Robert Boyle; Composer: Milton Rosen. B&W, 87 min.

The Milky Way
(1936) Paramount
Lloyd's first major talkie is about a timid milkman pressured into the ring by a fight promoter (Menjou) after he mistakenly knocks out the middleweight champion. Lloyd made only six sound films, and this is the only one that approaches the invention and flair of his justly celebrated silents. Remade 10 years later as *The Kid from Brooklyn* with Danny Kaye, again directed by McCarey. **Cast:** Harold Lloyd, Adolphe Menjou, Dorothy Wilson, Helen Mack, William Gargan, George Barbier, Lionel Stander, Charles Lane, Marjorie Gateson. **Credits:** Dir: Leo McCarey; Prod: E. Lloyd Sheldon; Writer: Grover Jones; DP: Alfred Gilks; Ed: LeRoy Stone; Prod Design: Hans Dreier. B&W, 89 min. **VHS, LASER**

A Millionaire for Christy
(1951) Fox
In this fast and furious screwball comedy, Christy Sloane (Parker), secretary for a legal firm, is hoping for romance when she travels to California to inform MacMurray of an unexpected large inheritance. The problem is that he's about to be married and the best man (Carlson), secretly in love with the intended, disappears to stall the wedding. Parker and MacMurray search for him and fall in love during a series of madcap adventures on the road. **Cast:**

Fred MacMurray, Eleanor Parker, Richard Carlson, Kay Buckley, Una Merkel, Raymond Greenleaf, Nestor Paiva, Douglass Dumbrille, Chris-Pin Martin, Ralph Hodges. **Credits:** Dir: George Marshall; Prod: Bert Friedlob; Writer: Ken Englund, Robert Harari; DP: Harry Stradling; Ed: Daniel Mandell; Prod Design: Boris Leven; Composer: Victor Young. B&W, 91 min.

Million Dollar Legs
(1932) Paramount
With Fields, Oakie, and Turpin in leading roles, it's safe to assume that the proceedings will be dangerously nutty. Fields has assumed the presidency of the republic of Klopstokia through the usual means: by besting his opponent in an arm-pulling contest. However, inspired silliness is not the best way to ensure a country's financial stability, and there is dissension within the cabinet at the empty treasury. Fortunately, Klopstokians are blessed with preternatural speed, and Olympic games provide a sure means of raising revenue. **Cast:** Jack Oakie, W. C. Fields, Andy Clyde, Susan Fleming, Lyda Roberti, Ben Turpin, Hugh Herbert, George Barbier, Dickie Moore, Billy Gilbert. **Credits:** Dir: Edward Cline; Writer: Nicholas Barrows, Ben Hecht, Henry Myers; Story: Joseph L. Mankiewicz; DP: Arthur Todd. B&W, 82 min.

Million Dollar Legs
(1939) Paramount
A proving ground for future luminaries, with an appropriate title: Grable is featured long before she acquired that famous sobriquet, but in this movie the legs are attached to a horse. Specifically, it's the horse on which Hartley will bet the money collected from his college crew team in order to finance new boats without asking his rich father. Watch for a single line from a young William Holden, and Crabbe, back from Buck Rogers's intergalactic sojourns to coach the team. **Cast:** Betty Grable, John Hartley, Donald O'Connor, Jackie Coogan, Buster Crabbe, Peter Lind Hayes, Dorothea Kent, Richard Denning, Philip Warren, Edward Arnold. **Credits:** Dir: Nick Grinde, Edward Dmytryk; Prod: William C. Thomas; Writer: Richard English; Story: Lewis R. Foster; DP: Harry Fischbeck; Ed: Stuart Gilmore. B&W, 59 min.

Min and Bill
(1930) MGM
Matronly silent-film star Dressler, in an Academy Award–winning perfor-

mance, is here teamed with Beery playing a couple of colorful waterfront characters trying to retain custody of Dressler's daughter. Moving and sentimental, though saddled by the limitations of early sound technology. Dressler's late career is most often recalled wedded to fog-shrouded docks in films like this, *Anna Christie* (1930), and *Tugboat Annie* (1933, also costarring Beery). Written for Dressler by her friend Marion. **Academy Awards:** Best Actress: Marie Dressler. **Cast:** Marie Dressler, Wallace Beery, Dorothy Jordan, Marjorie Rambeau, Frank McGlynn, Donald Dillaway, DeWitt Jennings, Russell Hopton. **Credits:** Dir: George Hill; Writer: Frances Marion; Prod Design: Cedric Gibbons; Costumes: Rene Hubert. B&W, 70 min. **VHS**

Ministry of Fear
(1944) Paramount
This Lang noir-spy thriller follows a man (Milland) recently released from a British insane asylum who accidentally wins a cake with a secret message at a carnival run by a Nazi espionage organization. Milland excels as the innocent man in the wrong place dealing with a world crazier than the asylum he just left. Lang's direction creates constant suspense, the sets and cinematography are suitably atmospheric, the plot quirky and engaging,

and the performances of high caliber. Based on a Greene novel of the same name. **Cast:** Ray Milland, Marjorie Reynolds, Carl Esmond, Hillary Brooke, Dan Duryea, Alan Napier, Erskine Sanford, Percy Waram. **Credits:** Dir: Fritz Lang; Prod: Seton I. Miller; Writer: Seton I. Miller; Story: Graham Greene; DP: Henry Sharp; Ed: Archie Marshek; Composer: Miklos Rozsa, Victor Young; Costumes: Edith Head. B&W, 85 min. **VHS**

The Miniver Story
(1950) MGM
After *Mrs. Miniver* captured six 1943 Oscars, including Best Film, Actress, and Director, it was inevitable that Hollywood would pair Garson and Pidgeon once again and reunite the family for a postwar follow-up. While actual British locations replace MGM soundstages and despite a subplot concentrating on the next generation, this is particularly melodramatic, with Garson courageously showing her resolve against a fatal illness. **Cast:** Greer Garson, Walter Pidgeon, John Hodiak, Leo Genn, Cathy O'Donnell, Henry Wilcoxon, Reginald Owen, Peter Finch. **Credits:** Dir: H. C. Potter; Prod: Sidney Franklin; Writer: Ronald Millar; DP: Joseph Ruttenberg; Ed: Harold F. Kress; Composer: Herbert Stothart; Art Director: Alfred Junge. B&W, 104 min. **VHS**

The Miracle of Morgan's Creek
(1944) Paramount
While this celebrated screwball comedy may not rise to the sophisticated heights of his previous masterpieces *The Lady Eve* (1941) and *The Palm Beach Story* (1942), Sturges's familiar blend of fast dialogue and zany slapstick is still apparent. Hutton finds herself pregnant after a night with a soldier she thinks was named "Ratsky-Watsky or something like that" and needs to find a husband, a position that falls to milquetoast bank clerk Bracken. What follows is a chaotic assault on everything sacred in WWII America: motherhood, the military, and family values. Academy Award Nomination for Best Original Screenplay. **Cast:** Eddie Bracken, Betty Hutton, William Demarest, Diana Lynn. **Credits:** Dir: Preston Sturges; Prod: Preston Sturges; Writer: Preston Sturges; DP: Joh Seitz; Ed: Stuart Gilmore; Composer: Leo Shuken, Charles Bradshaw; Prod Design: Hans Dreier, Ernest Fegte. B&W, 98 min. **VHS, LASER**

Miracle of Our Lady of Fatima
(1952) Warner Bros.
A sober recounting of the apparition of the Virgin Mary seen by three rural Portuguese children in 1917 is an odd footnote in Hollywood history. This anti-Communist McCarthy-era religious epic was reportedly Jack Warner's penance for having produced the pro-Stalinist *Mission to Moscow* nine years earlier. A better script than might be expected considering the circumstances. Academy Award Nomination for Best Scoring of a Dramatic or Comedy Picture. **Cast:** Gilbert Roland, Susan Whitney, Sherry Jackson, Sammy Ogg, Angela Clark, Frank Silvera, Jay Novello, Richard Hale, Carol Dee. **Credits:** Dir: John Brahm; Prod: Bryan Foy; Writer: Crane Wilbur, James O'Hanlon; DP: Edwin A. DuPar; Ed: Thomas Reilly; Composer: Max Steiner; Art Director: Edward Carrere. Color, 102 min. **VHS**

Miracle on 34th Street
(1947) Fox
After *It's a Wonderful Life* (1946), this is the ultimate Hollywood Christmas movie, featuring Gwenn as the real Kris Kringle playing a department-store Santa who teaches the true meaning of Christmas to a doubting 9-year-old Wood, O'Hara's daughter. A sentimental slice of Americana that still brings a smile. Ritter's screen

Ministry of Fear (1944)

debut. Remade in 1973 and 1994. The 50th-anniversary edition includes remastered footage and a promotional short. Golden Globes for Best Supporting Actor: Edmund Gwenn; Best Screenplay. Academy Award Nominations: 4, including Best Picture. **Academy Awards:** Best Supporting Actor: Edmund Gwenn; Best Original Story; Best Screenplay. **Cast:** Maureen O'Hara, John Payne, Edmund Gwenn, Thelma Ritter, Gene Lockhart, Natalie Wood, William Frawley. **Credits:** Dir: George Seaton; Prod: William Perlberg; Writer: George Seaton; Story: Valentine Davies; DP: Charles H. Clarke, Lloyd Ahern II; Ed: Robert Simpson; Composer: Cyril Mockridge; SFX: Fred Sersen. B&W, 97 min. VHS, LASER

The Miracle Woman
(1931) Columbia
This early Capra satire, with the director's favorite, Stanwyck, as an evangelical minister turned confidence trickster, was reportedly inspired by the life of Aimee Semple Macpherson. Following her minister father's death, which she ascribes to his ouster from the pulpit by church elders, a young woman falls under the control of a con man who convinces her to take her rage and passion on the road as an evangelist. As her newfound career blossoms—complete with staged "healings" and overblown spectacle— a blind war veteran falls in love with her, threatening her handler's meal ticket. A big-budget, daring film for its time, based on a play, *Bless You Sister,* which was cowritten by frequent Capra screenwriter Robert Riskin. **Cast:** Barbara Stanwyck, David Manners, Beryl Mercer, Russell Hopton, Sam Hardy, Charles Middleton, Eddie Boland, Aileen Carlyle, Al Stewart. **Credits:** Dir: Frank Capra; Prod: Harry Cohn; Writer: Jo Swerling, Dorothy Howell; DP: Joseph Walker; Ed: Maurice Wright; Prod Design: Max Parker. B&W, 90 min. VHS

The Miracle Worker
(1962) United Artists
The remarkable story of deaf and blind Helen Keller (Duke) and her relationship with her teacher, Annie Sullivan (Bancroft), won Oscars for both leads (at the time Duke, 16, was the youngest recipient of a Best Supporting Actress award). Penn re-creates his Broadway success presenting a great story and an enduring tale of the triumph of the spirit with his two stage leads. This was the second film for Penn (*Bonnie and Clyde,* 1967), who cut his teeth directing early TV dra-

mas, and was produced by TV-drama legend Coe. Academy Award Nominations: 5, including Best Director; Best (Adapted) Screenplay. **Academy Awards:** Best Actress: Anne Bancroft; Best Supporting Actress: Patty Duke. **Cast:** Anne Bancroft, Patty Duke, Victor Jory, Inga Swenson, Andrew Prine, Beah Richards. **Credits:** Dir: Arthur Penn; Prod: Fred Coe; Writer: William Gibson; Ed: Aram Avakian; Composer: Laurence Rosenthal; Art Director: George Jenkins. B&W, 107 min. VHS

Mirage
(1965) Universal
An ambitious attempt to make a Hitchcock-like thriller. Peck appears to lose his memory while trying to rescue a man who falls from a building during a power blackout. As the familiar people and places of his life vanish or turn against him, Peck turns for help from detective Matthau. Shot on location in New York City, with innovative direction from Dmytryk. Often entertaining, but don't expect the plot to be explained. **Cast:** Gregory Peck, Diane Baker, Walter Matthau, Kevin McCarthy, George Kennedy, Walter Abel, Leif Erikson, Jack Weston. **Credits:** Dir: Edward Dmytryk; Prod: Harry Keller; Writer: Peter Stone; DP: Joseph MacDonald; Ed: Ted J. Kent; Composer: Quincy Jones; Art Director: Alexander Golitzen, Frank Arrigo; Set Designer: John McCarthy, John Austin. B&W, 108 min. VHS

The Misfits
(1961) United Artists
Principally remembered as Monroe's and Gable's last movie, this Huston film written by Miller (for his then-wife Monroe) about a newly divorced young dancer and a solitary, aging cowboy in Nevada is an ambitious attempt to explore the death of the Old West and the essential loneliness of modern America. Huston departs from traditional Hollywood filmmaking of the period, using mobile camera platforms in the famous mustang roundup scenes, and Gable endows his role with dignity and strength. Notoriously plagued with on-set contretemps, the final result has aged well. **Cast:** Clark Gable, Marilyn Monroe, James Barton, Montgomery Clift, Eli Wallach, Thelma Ritter, Estelle Winwood, Kevin McCarthy, Denise Shaw, Philip Mitchell. **Credits:** Dir: John Huston; Prod: Frank E. Taylor; Writer: Arthur Miller; DP: Russell Metty; Ed: George Tomasini; Composer: Alex North; Art Director: Stephen Grimes. B&W, 124 min. VHS, LASER

Miss Annie Rooney
(1942) United Artists
A late Temple feature, best remembered for showing her first screen kiss (Moore has the honor), this remake of an ancient Mary Pickford favorite about a poor girl smitten with the son of a moneybags was met with apathy by wartime audiences, and signaled the end of her long string of popular features. Two years later she would play her first adult role in *Since You Went Away.* **Cast:** Shirley Temple, William Gargan, Guy Kibbee, Dickie Moore, Peggy Ryan, Jonathan Hale, Gloria Holden, Mary Field, George Lloyd. **Credits:** Dir: Edwin L. Marin; Prod: Edward Small; Writer: George Bruce; DP: Lester White; Ed: Fred Feitshans; Choreographer: Nick Castle; Costumes: Royer; Art Director: John DuCasse Schulze. B&W, 86 min. VHS

The Missing Juror
(1944) Columbia
Six members of a jury who convicted a man of murder and sent him to the electric chair have been murdered. The police are baffled and can find neither clues nor a motive, as the only person who could possibly have held a grudge is now dead. Enter Joe Keats (Bannon), a newspaper reporter who investigates the matter and discovers that the convicted man is anything but dead—and he's bent on revenge. Taut mystery from Boetticher. **Cast:** Jim Bannon, Janis Carter, George Macready, Jean Stevens, Joseph Crehan, Carole Mathews, Cliff Clark, Edmund Cobb, Mike Mazurki, George Lloyd. **Credits:** Dir: Budd Boetticher; Prod: Wallace MacDonald; Writer: Charles O'Neal; DP: L. William O'Connell; Ed: Paul Borofsky; Prod Design: George Brooks; Composer: Mischa Bakaleinikoff. B&W, 66 min.

Mission to Moscow
(1943) Warner Bros.
Based on the memoir of Ambassador Joseph E. Davies, this borders on being a well-produced Soviet propaganda film. Davies (Huston), the U.S. Ambassador to Moscow from 1936 through 1938, used his memoir to allay the American fears of Communism and show how the Soviets were an important friend and ally in the battle against the Nazis. Scenes from Soviet life are historically interesting, if homogenized. This film (oddly, produced while Warner was headed by staunch anti-Communist Jack Warner), and those involved in making

it, were noted by the HUAC. **Cast:** Walter Huston, Ann Harding, Oscar Homolka, George Tobias, Gene Lockhart, Frieda Inescort, Eleanor Parker, Dudley Field Malone, Richard Travis, Helmut Dantine. **Credits:** Dir: Michael Curtiz; Prod: Robert Buckner; Writer: Howard W. Koch, Jr.; Story: Joseph E. Davies; DP: Bert Glennon; Ed: Owen Marks; Composer: Leo F. Forbstein; Art Director: Carl Jules Weyl. B&W, 123 min.

Mississippi

(1935) Paramount
In this fast-moving, screwball comedy on a riverboat, northerner Crosby wants to marry the southern belle Patrick. He's rejected when he refuses to fight a duel with her southern suitor, but her younger sister, Bennett, takes a shine to him as he signs on for a crooning gig on a riverboat captained by none other than Fields. Onboard, Bing accidentally kills a man in a fight. Fields has him dubbed the "singing killer" and it takes much persuasion to convince sweet Bennett her lover isn't a ruthless killer. **Cast:** Bing Crosby, W. C. Fields, Joan Bennett, Gail Patrick, Queenie Smith, Claude Gillingwater, John Milian, Fred Kohler, Edward Pawley, Theresa Maxwell Conover. **Credits:** Dir: A. Edward Sutherland; Prod: Arthur Hornblow, Jr.; Writer: Claude Binyon, Jack Cunningham, Herbert Fields, Francis Martin, Booth Tarkington; DP: Charles Lang, Jr.; Ed: Chandler House; Prod Design: Hans Dreier; Composer: Lorenz Hart, Richard Rodgers; Art Director: Bernard Herzbrun. B&W, 73 min.

The Missouri Breaks

(1976) United Artists
Penn's famously odd Western written by veteran novelist McGuane stars Brando as an eccentric bounty hunter and Nicholson as a rustler who just wants to settle down. The scenes of Brando outfitted in dress and bonnet or lying in a bubble bath, and Nicholson's exaggerated performance, confounded critics and viewers at the time of its release. Over time, the film has gained champions. One of the very last major-studio Westerns. **Cast:** Marlon Brando, Jack Nicholson, Kathleen Lloyd, Randy Quaid, Frederic Forrest, Harry Dean Stanton, John McLiam, John Ryan, Sam Gilman. **Credits:** Dir: Arthur Penn; Prod: Elliott Kastner; Writer: Thomas McGuane; DP: Michael Butler; Ed: Jerry Greenberg; Composer: John Williams. Color, 126 min. **VHS, LASER**

Miss Sadie Thompson

(1954) Columbia
Somerset Maugham's story, previously filmed in 1928 with Gloria Swanson and later, in 1932, as *Rain* with Joan Crawford and Walter Huston, here returns as a musical with Hayworth playing the notorious tramp of the South Seas. Shot in Hawaii in glorious Technicolor and 3-D (!), this film has authentic, lush locales and a pulsating, jazzy score. This time Ferrer plays the Huston role of Alfred Davidson, no longer a missionary but the traveling chairman of the mission's board, intent on keeping the islands free of sin. Ray makes one of his frequent '50s appearances in military uniform as Marine Sergeant O'Hara. Academy Award Nomination for Best Song ("Sadie Thompson's Song [Blue Pacific Blues]"). **Cast:** Rita Hayworth, Jose Ferrer, Aldo Ray, Charles Bronson, Diosa Costello, Harry Bellaver, Wilton Graff, Peggy Converse, Rudy Bond, Frances Morris. **Credits:** Dir: Curtis Bernhardt; Prod: Jerry Wald; Writer: Harry Kleiner; DP: Charles Lawton, Jr.; Ed: Viola Lawrence; Prod Design: Carl Anderson; Composer: George Duning. Color, 91 min. **VHS, LASER**

Mister 880

(1950) Fox
This warm romance features a fine comedic performance for Gwenn as a cheerful counterfeiter who cranks out one-dollar bills mostly for the love of printing on his beloved press, nicknamed "Cousin Henry." Lancaster, a Treasury agent, is assigned the case, and he tracks one of those dollar bills to Gwenn's attractive neighbor (McGuire), who he romances, and eventually to the counterfeiter himself, forcing a decision about whether to prosecute the kindly old man. Academy Award Nomination for Best Supporting Actor: Edmund Gwenn. **Cast:** Burt Lancaster, Dorothy McGuire, Edmund Gwenn, Millard Mitchell, Minor Watson, Howard St. John, Hugh Sanders, James Millican, Howland Chamberlin, Larry Keating. **Credits:** Dir: Edmund Goulding; Prod: Julian Blaustein; Writer: Robert Riskin; Story: St. Clair McKelway; DP: Joseph La-Shelle; Ed: Robert Fritch; Prod Design: Lyle Wheeler, George W. Davis; Composer: Lionel Newman. B&W, 90 min.

Mister Roberts

(1955) Warner Bros.
One of the great WWII comedies, this tale of day-to-day life on the cargo ship *Reluctant* satirizes the boredom, pettiness, cruelty, and illogic of the mili-

tary. Fonda re-creates his acclaimed Broadway role of the decent Lieutenant Roberts who, while enduring a crew of half-wits and a nasty captain with an inferiority complex (Cagney), fears the Pacific naval war will be over before he ever sees anything more explosive than a fire extinguisher of home-brewed "jungle juice." Director Ford includes a number of his stock company, such as Curtis and Bond. Followed by *Ensign Pulver* in 1964. Academy Award Nominations: 2, including Best Picture. **Academy Awards:** Best Supporting Actor: Jack Lemmon. **Cast:** Henry Fonda, Jack Lemmon, James Cagney, Betsy Palmer, Ward Bond, Philip Carey, Nick Adams, Harry Carey, Jr., Ken Curtis, Frank Aletter. **Credits:** Dir: John Ford, Mervyn LeRoy; Prod: Leland Hayward; Writer: Joshua Logan, Frank S. Nugent; DP: Winton C. Hoch; Ed: Jack Murray; Composer: Franz Waxman; Costumes: Moss Mabry; Art Director: Art Loell; Set Designer: William L. Kuehl. Color, 123 min. **VHS, DVD**

Mister Scoutmaster

(1953) Fox
Comedy about a TV star (Webb, in a patented role of the crisp professional with no time for warm, fuzzy feelings) who becomes a scoutmaster in order to understand the kids who watch his show. He takes the troop camping and ends up adopting one orphaned boy. **Cast:** Clifton Webb, Frances Dee, Edmund Gwenn, Jimmy Hawkins, Orley Lindgren, Jim Moss, Sammy Ogg, Skip Torgerson, George "Foghorn" Winslow. **Credits:** Dir: Henry Levin; Prod: Leonard Goldstein; Writer: Leonard Praskins, Barney Slater; Story: Rice E. Cochran; DP: Joseph La Shelle; Ed: William B. Murphy; Composer: Cyril Mockridge, Lionel Newman; Costumes: Renie; Art Director: Lyle Wheeler, Albert Hogsett. B&W, 87 min.

Misty

(1961) Fox
An admirable adaptation of Marguerite Henry's children's classic *Misty of Chincoteague* about two children (David Ladd, son of Alan Ladd, and Smith) and the wild pony they come to love. O'Connell and Seymour play the adults who help the children win the pony at the annual auction. The main attractions are the attractive Virginia coastal island locations and the scenes of wild horses running in the ocean waves. **Cast:** David Ladd, Pam Smith, Arthur O'Connell, Anne Seymour. **Credits:** Dir: James B. Clark; Prod: Robert B. Radnitz; Writer: Ted

Sherdeman; DP: Leo Tover, Lee Garmes; Ed: Fredrick Y. Smith; Composer: Paul Sawtell, Bert Shefter; Art Director: Duncan Cramer; Set Designer: Walter M. Scott, Stuart A. Reiss. Color, 93 min. **VHS, LASER**

Moana
(1926)
A poetic silent doumentary by the master of early documentary film, Flaherty. Filmed on one of the Samoan islands, this captures the pristine beauty of life in the South Seas. **Credits:** Dir: Robert Flaherty. B&W, 76 min. **VHS**

Moby Dick
(1930) Warner Bros.
First sound version of the Melville classic about a sea captain obsessed with hunting down and killing the white whale that destroyed his leg. Here, Ahab (Barrymore, in a role he first played in the silent *The Sea Beast*, 1926) competes with his stepbrother (Hughes) for the love of a woman named Faith (Bennett). Hughes pushes Ahab off the ship's deck and into the mouth of the whale, and the captain loses a leg (after it's gruesomely cauterized onboard). Faith deserts Ahab when she learns he has a peg leg, and he becomes obsessed with wreaking vengeance on the whale. **Cast:** John Barrymore, Joan Bennett, Lloyd Hughes, Nobel Johnson, Nigel De Brulier, Walter Long, May Boley, Tom O'Brien, Virginia Sale, Will Walling. **Credits:** Dir: Lloyd Bacon; Writer: J. Grubb Alexander; Story: Herman Melville; DP: Robert Kurrle. B&W, 75 min.

Moby Dick
(1956) Warner Bros.
After making a number of fine films based on good, yet hardly classic novels, Huston decided to tackle "the big one," Herman Melville's monumental classic of one man's obsession with a great white whale. Huston chose fantasy writer Bradbury to adapt the story and cast Peck as the maniacal Captain Ahab, leaving ashore most of the ruminations about man's quarrel with God to concentrate on the action and adventure. The results are better than might have been expected, despite a performance by Peck as stiff as his whalebone peg leg. The film looks terrific (Huston shot the film in an experimental color process to simulate the look of 19th-century wood engravings), with good performances by Basehart as Ishmael, Welles in a cameo as Father Mapple, and Austrian count Ledebur as a sympathetic

Queequeg, the harpooner from the South Seas. The excellent music is by English symphonic composer Stainton, his only film score, and considered the major composition of his career. **Cast:** Gregory Peck, Richard Basehart, Orson Welles, Leo Genn, Harry Andrews, Bernard Miles, Mervyn Johns, Noel Purcell, Frederick Ledebur, James Robertson Justice. **Credits:** Dir: John Huston; Prod: John Huston; Writer: John Huston, Ray Bradbury; DP: Oswald Morris; Ed: Russell Lloyd; Prod Design: Stephen B. Grimes; Composer: Philip Stainton; Art Director: Ralph Brinton, Stephen Grimes. Color, 116 min. **VHS, LASER**

The Model and the Marriage Broker
(1951) Fox
Character-actor great Ritter stars as a marriage broker who makes model Crain her personal business. When she learns that young and winning Crain is romantically attached to a married man, she decides to set her up with X-ray technician Brady. This comedy relies heavily on humorous portrayals of the marriage service's customers, but turns sweet as Ritter wages her unyielding campaign to unite the young couple. She's surprised to discover there is something in it for her. Academy Award Nomination: Best Costume Design. **Cast:** Jeanne Crain, Scott Brady, Thelma Ritter, Zero Mostel, Michael O'Shea, Helen Ford, Frank Fontaine, Dennie Moore, John Alexander, Jay C. Flippen. **Credits:** Dir: George Cukor; Writer: Charles Brackett, Walter Reisch, Richard Breen; DP: Milton Krasner; Ed: Robert Simpson; Prod Design: Lyle Wheeler, Don DeCuir; Composer: Cyril Mockridge, Lionel Newman. B&W, 103 min.

Modern Times
(1936) United Artists
In Chaplin's classic comedy, machine-age dehumanization remains as biting in the era of downsizing and the Internet as it was when first released. As an assembly-line worker who becomes too enthusiastically engaged in his work, Chaplin launches into a series of set pieces commenting on the frustrations of the modern world. His first film after the success of *City Lights* (1931), and last silent, is very much a one-man show, with Chaplin directing, writing, producing, scoring, and starring along with then-wife Goddard. A National Film Registry Outstanding Film. **Cast:** Charlie Chaplin, Paulette Goddard, Henry Bergman, Chester

Conklin, Tiny Sandford, Hank Mann, Stanley Blystone, Allan Garcia. **Credits:** Dir: Charlie Chaplin; Prod: Charles Chaplin; Writer: Charles Chaplin; DP: Rollie Totheroh, Ira Morgan; Composer: Charles Chaplin, Alfred Newman; Art Director: Charles D. Hall, J. Russell Spencer. B&W, 89 min. **VHS, LASER**

Mogambo
(1953) MGM
Gable, Kelly, and Gardner go on an African safari where they look glamorous enough to have just wandered by for cocktails. Gable plays the magnetic macho great white hunter, and Gardner the woman hunting the hunter while trying to distract the wandering eyes of the cool, married Kelly. A more sensual remake of *Red Dust*, in which Gable costarred with Jean Harlow 21 years earlier, aided by the assured direction of Ford and a dazzling cast. Golden Globe for Best Supporting Actress: Grace Kelly. Academy Award Nominations: Best Actress: Ava Gardner; Best Supporting Actress: Grace Kelly. **Cast:** Clark Gable, Ava Gardner, Grace Kelly, Donald Sinden, Philip Stainton, Eric Pohlmann, Laurence Naismith, Denis O'Dea. **Credits:** Dir: John Ford; Prod: Sam Zimbalist; Story: John Lee Mahin; DP: Robert Surtees, Freddie Young; Ed: Frank Clarke; Art Director: Alfred Junge. Color, 116 min. **VHS, LASER**

Molly and Me
(1945) Fox
A Hollywood vehicle for British actress and singer Fields paired again with her costar from *Holy Matrimony* (1943), Woolley. Here she plays a maid who helps out a group of out-of-work actors by hiring them to be the domestic staff for stuffy aristocrat Woolley (in a story supposedly based on an incident that happened to silent screen star Marie Dressler). Woolley is her difficult employer and McDowall his son. This was Fields's penultimate film, and she sings several songs, including "Christopher Robin" and "Bring Back My Bonnie to Me." **Cast:** Gracie Fields, Monty Woolley, Roddy McDowall, Reginald Gardiner, Natalie Schafer, Edith Barrett, Aminta Dyne, Queenie Leonard, Clifford Brooke. **Credits:** Dir: Lewis Seiler; Prod: Robert Bassler; Writer: Leonard Praskins, Roger Burford; Story: Frances Marion; DP: Charles G. Clarke; Ed: John McCafferty; Composer: Cyril J. Mockridge, Emil Newman; Art Director: Lyle Wheeler, Albert Hogsett. B&W, 76 min. **VHS**

The Molly Maguires

(1970) Paramount

Hollywood has presented few stories of the American labor movement. This film about a Pennsylvania coal-mine uprising by Irish laborers is the rare exception. Connery plays the leader of the miners' revolt, and Harris an infiltrator hired by management. A better-than-average script that presents an ambivalent portrait of both men, and fine cinematography by veteran Howe, greatly aid this Ritt (*Norma Rae*, 1979) production. Academy Award Nomination for Best Art Direction. **Cast:** Sean Connery, Richard Harris, Samantha Eggar, Frank Finlay, Anthony Zerbe, Bethel Leslie, Arthur Lundquist, Anthony Costello, Philip Bourneuf, Brendan Dillon, Jr. **Credits:** Dir: Martin Ritt; Prod: Martin Ritt; Writer: Walter Bernstein; DP: James Wong Howe; Ed: Frank Bracht; Prod Design: Tambi Larsen; Composer: Henry Mancini. Color, 123 min. **VHS, LASER**

Monkey Business

(1931) Paramount

One of the earlier Marx Brothers features, it was the first written for the screen (based on a story by humorist Perelman, among others). This takes place onboard an ocean liner, with the brothers running all over the ship to keep from being thrown in the brig as stowaways. Along the way the Marxes get involved in a gang feud, a Punch and Judy show, and there are the usual musical numbers by Chico and Harpo. **Cast:** Groucho, Harpo, Chico, and Zeppo Marx, Thelma Todd, Ruth Hall, Harry Woods, Tom Kennedy, Ben Taggart, Otto Fries. **Credits:** Dir: Norman Z. McLeod; Writer: Arthur Sheekman, William B. Johnstone, S. J. Perelman; DP: Arthur Todd. B&W, 77 min. **VHS, LASER, DVD**

Monkey Business

(1952) Fox

This Hawks screwball comedy has no relation to the Marx Brothers classic of 1931. Here Grant is a chemist in quest of a youth elixir, actually concocted by a marauding monkey let lose in the lab. An assault on American manners and decorum, in which Grant and his wife (Rogers) accidentally revert back to unrestrained pre-teenagers. Monroe has an early role as a dumb secretary. One of Hawks's best comedies, up there with *His Girl Friday* (1940) and *Bringing Up Baby* (1938). Screenplay by Hecht. **Cast:** Cary Grant, Ginger Rogers, Marilyn Monroe, Charles Coburn, Hugh Marlowe, Henri Letondal, Robert Corn-thwaite, Larry Keating. **Credits:** Dir: Howard Hawks; Prod: Sol C. Siegel; Writer: Ben Hecht, Charles Lederer; Story: I. A. L. Diamond; DP: Milton Krasner; Ed: William B. Murphy; Composer: Leigh Harline, Lionel Newman; Art Director: Lyle Wheeler, George Patrick. B&W, 97 min. **VHS, LASER**

Monsieur Beaucaire

(1946) Paramount

A Hope swashbuckler comedy made at the height of his popularity. Based on a Booth Tarkington novel that had a previous film version starring Rudolph Valentino, Hope plays a court barber at the time of Louis XV who, rather than face execution, is sent on a deadly espionage mission masquerading as the ambassador to Spain. **Cast:** Bob Hope, Joan Caulfield, Patric Knowles, Reginald Owen, Cecil Kellaway, Marjorie Reynolds, Joseph Schildkraut, Constance Collier. **Credits:** Dir: George Marshall; Prod: Paul Jones; Writer: Melvin Frank; Story: Norman Panama; DP: Lionel Lindon; Ed: Arthur Schmidt; Composer: Robert Emmett Dolan; Art Director: Hans Dreier, Earl Hedrick. B&W, 93 min. **VHS**

Monsieur Verdoux

(1947) United Artists

Chaplin's notorious film about Landru, the Parisian bank clerk who murdered a string of wealthy widows, is a mixture of a straight thriller and black comedy, with an unsettling tone that originally kept away postwar audiences and alienated Chaplin fans. Nevertheless, there is much to recommend this amusing critique of a modern society that values money more than human lives. Big-mouthed comedienne Raye has her finest role as the widow who proves Verdoux's ultimate challenge. Ahead of its time when produced, the film has since moved from cult status to classic and is now widely hailed as one of Chaplin's essential works. Academy Award Nomination for Best Original Screenplay. **Cast:** Charlie Chaplin, Martha Raye, Isobel Elsom, Marilyn Nash, Mady Correll, Robert Lewis, Marjorie Bennett, Irving Bacon. **Credits:** Dir: Charlie Chaplin; Prod: Charlie Chaplin; Story: Charlie Chaplin; DP: Curt Courant, Rollie Totheroh, Wallace Chewing; Ed: Willard Nico; Composer: Charlie Chaplin; Art Director: John Beckman. B&W, 123 min. **VHS, LASER**

Montana Belle

(1952) RKO

Russell overshadows the entire male cast playing outlaw Belle Starr in this Dwan Western. Starr leaves the Dalton gang and strikes out on her own, robbing banks with Tucker and Lambert and seducing Brent for his fortune. Howard Hughes held Russell's contract, and the film was unreleased for years due to Hughes's desire to wait until Russell was established as a star. **Cast:** Jane Russell, George Brent, Scott Brady, Andy Devine, Forrest Tucker, Jack Lambert, John Litel, Ray Teal. **Credits:** Dir: Allan Dwan; Prod: Howard Welsch; Writer: Horace McCoy; Story: Norman S. Hall; DP: Jack A. Marta; Ed: Arthur Roberts; Composer: Nathan Scott; Art Director: Frank Arrigo. B&W, 81 min. **VHS**

Monte Carlo

(1930) Paramount

This is the landmark early sound musical comedy in which Lubitsch proved talking and singing stars didn't need to hover near microphones hidden in flower vases. The story follows a countess (MacDonald) who deserts her fiancé and hops a train to Monte Carlo. She then tries to win back her lost fortune by gambling, and at the casino she meets a count (Buchanan), who becomes smitten with her. He masquerades as her hairdresser and chauffeur, and also serenades her nightly without revealing his identity. She learns his true identity when she goes to the opera and sees him sitting in an adjacent box. **Cast:** Jeanette MacDonald, John Roche, ZaSu Pitts, Claude Allister, Jack Buchanan, Albert Conti, Helen Garden, Lionel Belmore, Tyler Brooks. **Credits:** Dir: Ernst Lubitsch; Prod: Adolph Zukor; Writer: Ernst Vadja, Vincent Lawrence, Evelyn Sutherland; Story: Hans Mueller, Booth Tarkington; DP: Victor Milner; Ed: Merrill White; Prod Design: Hans Dreier; Composer: Franke Harling, Richard A. Whiting, Leo Robin. B&W, 90 min.

Monterey Pop: The Film

(1967)

Pennebaker's cinematic scrapbook of the epic Monterey Pop festival, which was a turning point for rock. Featuring The Who, the Mamas and the Papas, Jimi Hendrix, Big Brother and the Holding Company, and many more. This version includes 9 minutes of never-before-seen footage. **Cast:** Jimi Hendrix, Big Brother and the Holding Company, the Mamas and the Papas, Canned Heat, Jefferson Airplane, The Animals, The Who, Otis Redding, Ravi Shankar. **Credits:** Dir: D. A. Pennebaker; Prod: Lou Adler. Color, 98 min. **VHS**

Chuck Maland Picks Political Films

***Gabriel over the White House* (1933).** The strange tale of a newly elected president who, after having a vision following a car accident, assumes dictatorial powers to solve the country's problems. The movie's hysteria hints at the social anxieties in the darkest years of the Depression.

***Mr. Smith Goes to Washington* (1939).** A prototypical Frank Capra story of a young senator (Jimmy Stewart) struggling to maintain his political idealism in the face of corrupt politics, led by Boss Jim Taylor (Edward Arnold) and Senator Joseph Paine (Claude Raines).

***The Great McGinty* (1940).** Preston Sturges's howling and thinly veiled satire on Chicago politics, featuring a bum (Brian Donlevy) who rises to the governor's mansion, getting his start by voting 37 times in the same election. Contains usual Sturges cast of supporting characters.

***The Great Dictator* (1940).** The Little Tramp takes on Hitler: Chaplin's first talking film aims its social satire and invective at Adenoid Hynkel, the Phooey of Tomania. Wonderful performance by Chaplin in two roles: the dictator and a gentle, humanistic Jewish barber.

***All the King's Men* (1949).** Robert Rossen's adaptation of Robert Penn Warren's Pulitzer Prize–winning novel. Fueled by Broderick Crawford's performance as Willie Stark, this won the 1949 Oscars for Best Picture and Best Actor.

***The Last Hurrah* (1958).** John Ford's affectionate look at old-style city politics, from a novel loosely based on the life of Boston mayor James Curley. Great cast led by Spencer Tracy as Mayor Frank Skeffington, who fails in his bid to win a fifth term as mayor, losing to an inferior candidate who uses television to his advantage.

***The Manchurian Candidate* (1962).** Stylistically audacious, this strange, paranoid, John Frankenheimer Cold War thriller follows a brainwashed Korean War hero (Lawrence Harvey) and his cold, ambitious mother (Angela Lansbury), who wants to get her Joseph McCarthy–like husband elected to the presidency as another war vet (Frank Sinatra) tries to unravel the mystery.

***Dr. Strangelove or: How I Learned to Stop Worrying and Love the Bomb* (1964).** Stanley Kubrick's brilliant Cold War black comedy about the zaniness of nuclear proliferation and the threat of accidental nuclear war. Great satiric performances by Peter Sellers (in three roles); Sterling Hayden as Jack D. Ripper; Slim Pickens as Major Kong; and George C. Scott as Buck Turgidson.

***The Candidate* (1972).** Michael Ritchie film about the pressures on a young social-activist lawyer (Robert Redford) running for the U.S. Senate. The candidate comes to lament how much he must compromise if he hopes to get elected in a television-dominated age.

***All the President's Men* (1976).** Alan Pakula's adaption of the Bernstein-Woodward book on Watergate and the fall of Richard Nixon; in the film, the investigative journalists (Dustin Hoffman and Robert Redford) become the story's crusading protagonists.

***Wag the Dog* (1997).** This hard-edged, disturbingly hilarious satire shows how politics and the media intertwine in contemporary America, as a presidential adviser (Robert De Niro) hires a Hollywood producer (Dustin Hoffman) to invent a war that will distract the public from a sexual scandal involving the president.

Chuck Maland is a Lindsay Young Professor of Film Studies and American Studies at the University of Tennessee. He is the author of *Chaplin and American Culture* and is working on a cultural history of American movies, titled *American Dreams, American Nightmares*.

Monte Walsh
(1970) National General
Marvin and Palance give outstanding performances as anachronistic cowboys in this end-of-the-West Western. Romantic and sad, this elegy to a passing time and way of life slowly chronicles the daily routine of the two men as their ranch closes, they contemplate marriage, and their skills are now valued only for Wild West Show entertainment. French star Moreau plays Marvin's tubercular mistress. Cinematographer Fraker's (*Bullitt*, 1968) first feature as director; based on a novel by veteran Western novelist Jack Schaefer (*Shane*). **Cast:** Lee Marvin, Jack Palance, Jeanne Moreau, Mitchell Ryan, Jim Davis, Michael Conrad, Tom Heaton, G. D. Spradlin. **Credits:** Dir: William A. Fraker; Prod: Hal Landers, Bobby Roberts; Writer: Lukas Heller; Story: David Z. Goodman; DP: David M. Walsh; Ed: Robert L. Wolfe, Ray Daniels, Richard Brockway, Gene Fowler, Jr.; Prod Design: Albert Brenner; Composer: John Barry; Art Director: Ward Preston. Color, 100 min. **VHS**

The Moon and Sixpence
(1942) United Artists
Maugham's famous novel about a Paul Gauguin–like painter (Sanders) who quits his job as a stockbroker, abandons family and civilization, and moves to a South Seas island gets a reverent and literary treatment. Despite an encompassing narration

by Marshall playing Maugham, this is Sanders's film and his transformation from cad to introspective artist is both convincing and moving. Filmed in black and white, with Gauguin's paintings in color at the conclusion. Academy Award Nomination for Best Scoring of a Dramatic or Comedy Picture. **Cast:** George Sanders, Herbert Marshall, Doris Dudley, Eric Blore, Elena Verdugo, Florence Bates, Albert Basserman, Molly Lamont. **Credits:** Dir: Albert Lewin; Prod: David Loew; Writer: Albert Lewin; Story: W. Somerset Maugham; DP: John F. Seitz; Ed: Richard L. Van Enger; Prod Design: Gordon Willis; Composer: Dimitri Tiomkin. B&W, 89 min. VHS

Moonfleet

(1955) MGM
This swashbuckler about 18th-century English smugglers and an inherited diamond was an unusual departure for director Lang. A splashy Technicolor costume epic with an outstanding cast including Granger, Sanders, and the plummy voiced Greenwood, and Lang's assured direction,makes for this an enjoyable exercise in style and panache. **Cast:** Stewart Granger, Jon Whiteley, George Sanders, Viveca Lindfors, Joan Greenwood, Ian Wolfe, Liliane Montevecchi, Melville Cooper. **Credits:** Dir: Fritz Lang; Prod: John Houseman, Jud Kinberg; Writer: Jan Lustig, Margaret Fitts; DP: Robert Planck; Ed: Albert Akst; Prod Design: Cedric Gibbons, Hans Peters; Composer: Miklos Rozsa, Vicente Gomez. Color, 89 min. LASER

The Moon Is Blue

(1953) United Artists
Preminger tried to break barriers and generate publicity with this once-notorious Broadway play, which caused outrage when first released. What was the fuss? The film concerns the seduction of a virgin and the audience actually hears the words "virgin," "mistress," and "pregnant" in spoken dialogue. Actually it is a fairly routine farce about a bachelor (Holden), a young woman (McNamara), his apartment, and misunderstandings resulting from her changing a dress due to a wine stain. Niven revived his faltering screen career by playing Holden's fiancée's lecherous father. McNamara was nominated for an Oscar and made only three other films before committing suicide in 1978. Golden Globe for Best Actor in a Musical or Comedy: David Niven. Academy Award Nominations: Best Actress: Maggie McNamara; Best Editing; Best Song. **Cast:** William Holden, David Niven, Maggie Mc Namara, Tom Tully, Dawn Addams, Fortunio Bonanova, Gregory Ratoff, Hardy Kruger, Johanna Matz. **Credits:** Dir: Otto Preminger; Prod: Otto Preminger; Writer: F. Hugh Herbert; DP: Ernest Laszlo; Ed: Ronald Sinclair; Composer: Herschel Burke Gilbert; Art Director: Nicolai Remisoff. B&W, 100 min. VHS, LASER

The Moon Is Down

(1943) Fox
Grim but engrossing film adaptation of the best-selling John Steinbeck novel and play that traces the effects of Nazi occupation on a Norwegian town. The German commandant believes that cooperation is the key to the village's survival and tries to subdue his men's cruelty. The town forms a resistance movement and the Nazis round up the town officials for a public hanging. Revenge ultimately comes, but at a high cost. **Cast:** Cedric Hardwicke, Henry Travers, Doris Bowdon, Margaret Wycherly, Lee J. Cobb, Peter Van Eyck, Henry Rowland. **Credits:** Dir: Irving Pichel; Prod: Nunnally Johnson; Writer: Nunnally Johnson; Story: John Steinbeck; DP: Arthur Miller; Ed: Louis Loeffler; Prod Design: James Basevi; Composer:Alfred Newman. B&W, 90 min.

Moon over Miami

(1941) Fox
This Grable musical was produced at the height of her popularity. Texas gold diggers Grable and Landis head to Miami with their aunt (Greenwood) in search of eligible bachelors by pretending to be a millionairess and her servant. They target the once-wealthy Ameche and Cummings, but all ends as expected. Haley and Greenwood add welcome support in this blazing Technicolor musical, along with some memorable dancing by the Condos Brothers and songs such as "You Started Something." A musical remake of *Three Blind Mice* (1938), and later made again as *Three Little Girls in Blue* (1946). **Cast:** Betty Grable, Carole Landis, Charlotte Greenwood, Don Ameche, Robert Cummings, Jack Haley, Robert Greig, Minor Watson. **Credits:** Dir: Walter Lang; Prod: Harry Joe Brown; Writer: Vincent Lawrence, Brown Holmes, George Seaton, Lynn Starling; DP: Peverell Marley, Leon Shamroy, Allen M. Davey; Ed: Walter Thompson; Composer: Alfred Newman; Art Director: Richard Day, Wiard Ihnen. Color, 91 min. VHS

Moon Pilot

(1962) Disney
This Disney feature produced the year of John Glenn's orbital mission centers around a NASA astronaut (Tryon) selected for a solitary moon mission (by a space monkey!) visited by a sexy alien (Saval). Keith plays the blustering military general. An unusually sharp Disney comedy. Director Neilson was a stalwart Disney features director for the next decade. **Cast:** Tom Tryon, Brian Keith, Edmond O'Brien, Tommy Kirk, Dany Saval, Bob Sweeney, Kent Smith, Bert Remsen. **Credits:** Dir: James Neilson; Prod: Bill Anderson; Writer: Maurice Tombragel; DP: William E. Snyder; Ed: Cotton Warburton; Prod Design: Carroll Clark; Composer: Paul J. Smith; Art Director: Marvin Aubrey Davis. Color, 98 min. VHS

Moonraker

(1979) United Artists
The 12th James Bond feature and the fourth go-round for Moore, this time finds him fighting villain Drax (Lonsdale) on a space station, a setting that required a huge budget. Kiel (Jaws), who appeared in *The Spy Who Loved Me*, returns, as do Lee as M (his final appearance) and the invaluable Barry, who once again composed the score. Gadgets, girls, and the usual single entendres. Academy Award Nomination for Best Visual Effects. **Cast:** Roger Moore, Lois Chiles, Richard Kiel, Michael Lonsdale, Corinne Clery, Bernard Lee, Geoffrey Keen, Desmond Llewelyn. **Credits:** Dir: Lewis Gilbert; Prod: Albert R. Broccoli; Writer: Christopher Wood; DP: Jean Tournier; Ed: John Glen; Composer: John Barry; Art Director: Max Douy, Charles Bishop. Color, 128 min. VHS, LASER, DVD

Moonrise

(1948) Republic
An unusual and neglected film noir about a young man (Clark) with a haunted family history who kills one of his tormentors and escapes into the swampy wilderness of the deep South only to find redemption and release from his guilt. One of the last films by director Borzage, better known for romantic features. This was originally intended as a William Wellman film starring James Stewart or John Garfield. Academy Award Nomination for Best Sound Recording. **Cast:** Dane Clark, Gail Russell, Ethel Barrymore, Allyn Joslyn, Lloyd Bridges, Harry Morgan, Phil Brown, Rex Ingram. **Credits:** Dir: Frank Borzage; Prod: Charles F. Haas; Writer: Charles Haas; DP: John

L. Russell, Jr.; Ed: Harry Keller; Prod Design: Lionel Banks; Composer: William Lava. B&W, 90 min. **VHS, LASER**

The Moon's Our Home
(1936) Paramount
This underrated screwball comedy stars real-life married and divorced husband and wife Fonda and Sullavan. She is heiress Sara Brown, an actress who appears on-screen as Cherry Chester; he is the adventurous best-selling travel writer John Smith, who uses the pen name Anthony Amberton. After they fall in love with their public personas, they find their private selves a bad match. Dorothy Parker (uncredited) is reported to have contributed greatly to the dialogue. **Cast:** Margaret Sullavan, Henry Fonda, Charles Butterworth, Beulah Bondi, Henrietta Crosman, Lucien Littlefield, Walter Brennan, Brandon Hurst, Spencer Charters, Margaret Hamilton. **Credits:** Dir: William A. Seiter; Prod: Walter Wanger; Writer: Isabel Dawn; DP: Joseph A. Valentine; Ed: Dorothy Spencer; Composer: Boris Morros; Art Director: Alexander Tolaboff. B&W, 83 min. **VHS**

The Moon-Spinners
(1964) Disney
Disney dramatic feature from Gothic novelist Mary Stewart places Mills and Greenwood in Crete. Spectacular location photography frames a standard young-adult suspense tale of jewel thieves and assorted villains, headed by Wallach. Mills gets her first screen romance, silent screen star Negri has a small role as a fence, and contemporary viewers get a look at Crete before the package-tour boom of recent years. **Cast:** Hayley Mills, Peter McEnery, Eli Wallach, Pola Negri, Joan Greenwood, Irene Papas, Sheila Hancock, Michael Davis, John Le Mesurier. **Credits:** Dir: James Neilson; Prod: Bill Anderson; Writer: Michael Dyne; DP: Paul Beeson; Ed: Gordon Stone, Elmo Veron; Composer: Edward Kane. Color, 118 min. **VHS, LASER**

Moontide
(1942) Fox
This hard-luck tale features French film star Gabin in his Hollywood debut as the happy-go-lucky sailor Bobo, who can't penetrate his hangover to remember if he committed last night's murder. His mate Tiny (Mitchell) assures him he did, and Tiny promises he won't tell if he can get a little help from Bobo on some shady business. Bobo falls for waitress Anna (Lupino) and she discovers that it's

Tiny who's guilty after all. The fight that follows sends one of the sailors into the ocean. Lang was replaced by Mayo after four shooting days. Note the contributions of gifted writers O'Hara and Johnson. Academy Award Nomination: Best Cinematography. **Cast:** Jean Gabin, Ida Lupino, Thomas Mitchell, Claude Rains, Jerome Cowan, Helene Reynolds, Ralph Byrd, William Halligan, Victor Sen Yung, Chester Gan. **Credits:** Dir: Fritz Lang, Archie Mayo; Prod: Mark Hellinger; Writer: John O'Hara, Nunnally Johnson; Story: Willard Robinson; DP: Lucien Ballard, Charles G. Clarke; Ed: William Reynolds; Prod Design: James Basevi, Richard Day; Composer: David Buttolph, Cyril Mockridge. B&W, 94 min.

The More the Merrier
(1943) Columbia
Stevens's wartime romantic comedy finds millionaire Coburn, Army Air Force sergeant McCrea, and Arthur sharing a cramped Washington apartment during the wartime housing shortage. Coburn is wonderful as the matchmaking Mr. Dingle, and was awarded an Oscar. Garson Kanin (uncredited) has claimed responsibility for the entire screenplay. Remade less successfully as *Walk Don't Run* (1966) with Cary Grant. Academy Award Nominations: 6, including Best Picture; Best Director; Best Actress: Jean Arthur; Best Original Story; Best Screenplay. **Academy Awards:** Best Supporting Actor: Charles Coburn. **Cast:** Jean Arthur, Joel McCrea, Charles Coburn, Richard Gaines, Bruce Bennett, Frank Sully, Clyde Fillmore, Stanley Clements, Donald Douglas, Ann Savage. **Credits:** Dir: George Stevens; Prod: George Stevens; Writer: Robert Russell; DP: Ted Tetzlaff; Ed: Otto Meyer; Composer: Leigh Harline; Art Director: Lionel Banks. B&W, 104 min. **VHS, LASER**

Morning Glory
(1933) RKO
Hepburn's third film and first Oscar-winning performance is an adaptation of a Zoe Atkins play about a very determined woman from New England trying to succeed on the New York stage. Along the way she has to deal with a triangle involving Menjou and Fairbanks. Remade by Sidney Lumet in 1958 as *Stage Struck* with Susan Strasberg. **Academy Awards:** Best Actress: Katharine Hepburn. **Cast:** Katharine Hepburn, Adolphe Menjou, Douglas Fairbanks, Jr., C. Aubrey Smith, Mary Duncan, Don Alvarado,

Richard Carle, Tyler Brooke. **Credits:** Dir: Lowell Sherman; Prod: Pandro S. Berman; Story: Howard J. Green; DP: Bert Glennon; Ed: William Hamilton; Composer: Max Steiner; Art Director: Van Nest Polglase, Charles Kirk. B&W, 75 min. **VHS, LASER**

Morocco
(1930) Paramount
This is the American screen debut of Dietrich, directed by her Svengali, von Sternberg, who made her a world sensation earlier the same year in *The Blue Angel*. The story concerns a cabaret singer who must choose between Foreign Legionnaire Cooper and moneybags Menjou, but it is really Dietrich and von Sternberg's picture. Dietrich dresses in top hat and tails and sings three numbers, including "What Am I Bid?" Academy Award Nominations: 4, including Best Director; Best Actress: Marlene Dietrich. **Cast:** Gary Cooper, Marlene Dietrich, Adolphe Menjou, Francis McDonald, Juliette Compton, Albert Conti, Eve Southern, Michael Visaroff. **Credits:** Dir: Josef von Sternberg; Prod: Hector Turnbull; Writer: Jules Furthman; Story: Benno Vigny; DP: Lee Garmes, Lucien Ballard; Ed: Sam Winston; Prod Design: Hans Dreier; Composer: Karl Hajos. B&W, 92 min. **VHS, LASER**

The Mortal Storm
(1940) MGM
Phyllis Bottome's prewar best-seller about a family's attempts to escape from Nazi Germany was made into a strong antifascist statement that resulted in the banning of all MGM films in Germany. The story is solid Hollywood melodrama, with Sullavan rejecting Stewart in favor of a fascist youth and later changing her mind when her professor father is removed from his position for his outspoken beliefs. **Cast:** Margaret Sullavan, James Stewart, Robert Young, Frank Morgan, Robert Stack, Bonita Granville, Irene Rich, Maria Ouspenskaya. **Credits:** Dir: Frank Borzage; Prod: Sidney Franklin, Victor Saville; Writer: Claudine West, Anderson Ellis, George Froeschel; Story: Phyllis Bottome; DP: William Daniels; Ed: Elmo Veron; Prod Design: Cedric Gibbons, Wade B. Rubottom; Composer: Edward Kane, Eugene Zador. B&W, 100 min. **VHS**

The Most Dangerous Game
(1932) RKO
Popular adventure yarn about a man and a woman (McCrea and Wray) stalked like wild animals by the

demented millionaire hunter Count Zaroff (Banks) on his remote jungle island. Despite countless remakes and variations of this story in TV series, this original film still has a perverse edge. Schoedsack and Cooper produced *King Kong* a few months later. Note the score by Steiner. **Cast:** Leslie Banks, Joel McCrea, Fay Wray, Robert Armstrong, Noble Johnson, Hale Hamilton, Steve Clemente. **Credits:** Dir: Irving Pichel, Ernest B. Shoedsack; Prod: Merian C. Cooper, Ernest B. Schoedsack; Writer: James Creelman; Story: Richard Connell; DP: Henry Gerrard; Ed: Archie Marshek; Composer: Max Steiner. B&W, 63 min. **VHS**

Mother Carey's Chickens
(1938) RKO
This heartwarming melodrama follows a strong-willed widow, Nancy Carey (Bainter), as she struggles for the future of her beautiful daughters Nancy (Shirley) and Kitty (Keeler) and her beloved son Peter (Dunagan). Good humor and folksy grit help Mother Carey keep poverty and the wrong fellows for her daughters at bay. **Cast:** Anne Shirley, Ruby Keeler, James Ellison, Fay Bainter, Walter Brennan, Donnie Dunagan, Frank Albertson, Alma Kruger, Jackie Moran, Margaret Hamilton. **Credits:** Dir: Rowland V. Lee; Prod: Pandro S. Berman; Writer: S. K. Lauren, Gertrude Purcell, Rachel Crothers, Kate Douglas Wiggin; DP: J. Roy Hunt; Ed: George Hively; Composer: Frank Tours. B&W, 82 min.

Mother Is a Freshman
(1949) Fox
A Technicolor comedy about a poor young widow (Young) who becomes eligible for a "family scholarship" to the college her daughter (Lynn) is attending. All the girls on campus have a crush on a certain literature professor (Johnson), but it is "mother" who eventually charms him with her intelligence and beauty, much to her daughter's dismay. **Cast:** Loretta Young, Van Johnson, Rudy Vallee, Betty Lynn, Barbara Lawrence, Robert Arthur, Griff Barnett, Kathleen Hughes, Eddie Dunn, Claire Mead, Henri Letondal. **Credits:** Dir: Lloyd Bacon; Prod: Walter Morosco; Writer: Mary Loos, Richard Sale; Story: Raphael Blau; DP: Arthur E. Arling; Ed: William Reynolds; Prod Design: Maurice Ransford; Composer: Alfred Newman. Color, 81 min.

Mother Wore Tights
(1947) Fox
Musical comedy about a woman who quits the vaudeville circuit to raise two daughters. She returns to work when her girls are grown, but almost fatally embarrasses one of them by performing in a theater near the daughter's school. The girl's schoolchums show up, however, and are impressed. **Cast:** Betty Grable, Dan Dailey, Mona Freeman, Connie Marshall, Vanessa Brown, Robert Arthur, Sara Allgood, William Frawley, Ruth Nelson, Anabel Shaw. **Credits:** Dir: Walter Lang; Prod: Lamar Trotti; Writer: Lamar Trotti; Story: Miriam Young; DP: Harry Jackson; Ed: J. Watson Webb, Jr.; Composer: Josef Myrow, Alfred Newman, Charles Henderson; Art Director: Richard Day, Joseph C. Wright. Color, 107 min.

Moulin Rouge
(1952) United Artists
Ferrer stars as post-Impressionist painter Henri Toulouse-Lautrec in Huston's ambitious chronicle of the painter's Parisian life and the Belle Epoque nightspots and bawdy houses he frequented. Ferrer excels as the physically challenged Lautrec (his legs were stunted after a childhood accident), while Huston and cinematographer Morris make an admirable attempt to capture Lautrec's palette and compositions on the Technicolor screen. Academy Award Nominations: 7, including Best Picture; Best Director; Best Actor: Jose Ferrer. **Academy Awards:** Best Costume Design (Color); Best Art Direction—Set Decoration (Color). **Cast:** Jose Ferrer, Zsa Zsa Gabor, Suzanne Flon, Eric Pohlmann, Colette Marchand, Katherine Kath, Mary Clare, Harold Kasket. **Credits:** Dir: John Huston; Prod: John Huston; Writer: Anthony Veiller; Story: John Huston; DP: Oswald Morris; Ed: Ralph Kemplen; Composer: Georges Auric; Art Director: Paul Sheriff. Color, 123 min. **VHS, LASER**

Mourning Becomes Electra
(1947) RKO
This condensation of O'Neill's melancholy dramatic trilogy (*The Homecoming, The Hunted, The Haunted*) set in Civil War–era New England was reduced from the stage length of six hours to a screen time of three. As the war ends, a father (Massey) returns home to find his wife (Paxinou) is having an affair with a sea captain (Genn). Their daughter (Russell), who dotes on her father, hates her mother for her infidelity. The mother murders the father, then the daughter and her brother (Redgrave) murder the sea captain, driving Paxinou to kill herself. Just as grim as it sounds, and stagebound to boot, but a fascinating look at extremely high-caliber actors working on extremely difficult material. Acadmey Award Nominations: Best Actor: Michael Redgrave; Best Actress: Rosalind Russell. **Cast:** Rosalind Russell, Michael Redgrave; Raymond Massey, Katina Paxinou, Leo Genn, Kirk Douglas, Nancy Coleman, Henry Hull, Sara Allgood, Thurston Hall. **Credits:** Dir: Dudley Nichols; Prod: Edward Donahue, Dudley Nichols; Writer: Dudley Nichols, Eugene O'Neill; DP: George Barnes; Ed: Roland Gross, Chandler House; Prod Design: William Flannery; Composer: Richard Hageman, Constantine Bakaleinikoff; Art Director: Albert S. D'Agostino. B&W, 173 min.

The Mouthpiece
(1932) Warner Bros.
William is sharp as an assistant D.A., embittered after sending an innocent man to the chair. Turning to the bottle, he makes a Faustian pact, twisting a flair for sensational courtroom performances into equally spectacular financial success in the defense of mobsters and embezzlers. Salvation comes in the person of girl-next-door stenographer Fox. She spurns William's love, but he dies nobly in the defense of her guiltless boyfriend against the Mob. Loosely based on the life of New York lawyer William J. Fallon. Remade as *The Man Who Talked Too Much* (1940) and *Illegal* (1955). **Cast:** Warren William, Sidney Fox, Aline MacMahon, John Wray, William Janney, Polly Walters, Ralph Ince, Mae Madison, Noel Francis, Morgan Wallace. **Credits:** Dir: James Flood, Elliott Nugent; Writer: Earl Baldwin, Frank Collins, Jr., Joseph Jackson; Ed: George Amy; Costumes: Earl Luick; Art Director: Esdras Hartley. B&W, 90 min.

Movie Crazy
(1932) Paramount
This looney Lloyd talkie follows our bespectacled hero as he bumbles his starstruck way from Kansas to Hollywood, and as he brings mayhem to a movie set. Accidentally donning a magician's coat for a formal party at the big film producer's house, Lloyd unwittingly unleashes a menagerie and creates a showcase for superb comic timing. Happily the big producer has glimpsed the raw comic genius behind the rube, and fame and fortune await. **Cast:** Harold Lloyd, Constance Cummings, Kenneth Thomp-

son, Sidney Jarvis, Louise Closser Hale, Robert McWade. **Credits:** Dir: Clyde Bruckman, Gaylord Lloyd; Prod: Harold Lloyd; Writer: Vincent Lawrence; Story: Agnes Christine Johnson, John Grey, Felix Adler; DP: Walter Lundin; Ed: Bernard W. Burton. B&W, 81 min.

Mr. and Mrs. North
(1941) MGM
This madcap murder mystery features Allen as Pamela North in a rare appearance without George Burns. Pamela and her husband Gerald (Post) return to their ordinary home after a weekend away; when they open the closet door, out falls a dead body. The Norths aren't exactly intimidated by the corpse; they're quite willing to believe that one of their oddball friends is responsible, it's just a matter of figuring out which one. It will take many silly questions and even some moments of danger for the two to get their man. **Cast:** Gracie Allen, William Post, Jr., Paul Kelly, Rose Hobart, Virginia Grey, Tom Conway, Porter Hall, Millard Mitchell, Lucien Littlefield, Inez Cooper. **Credits:** Dir: Robert B. Sinclair; Prod: Irving Asher; Writer: S. K. Lauren; Story: Francis Lockridge, Richard Lockridge, Owen Davis, Jr.; DP: Harry Stradling; Ed: Ralph E. Winters; Prod Design: Cedric Gibbons. B&W, 68 min.

Mr. and Mrs. Smith
(1941) RKO
Hitchcock's only comedy without suspense elements is a battle-of-the-sexes screwball with Lombard and Montgomery. A happily bantering married couple discover that a legal loophole has nullified their wedding; Montgomery's wry refusal to hold a quick ceremony infuriates Lombard and leaves the door open for other possibilities. Lombard and Hitchcock were great pals, and this is the production on which Lombard tweaked Hitchcock's statement about actors being cattle by corralling on the set three calves with the stars' names hung on them. This was Lombard's penultimate film, followed by Ernst Lubitsch's *To Be or Not to Be* (1942), before her untimely death. **Cast:** Carole Lombard, Robert Montgomery, Gene Raymond, Jack Carson, Philip Merivale, Betty Compson, Lucile Watson, William Tracy. **Credits:** Dir: Alfred Hitchcock; Prod: Harry E. Edington; Writer: Norman Krasna; DP: Harry Stradling; Ed: William Hamilton; Composer: Edward Ward, Roy Webb; Art Director: Van Nest Polglase, L. P. Williams. B&W, 95 min. **VHS, LASER**

Mr. Arkadin
(1955) Talbot
A Welles thriller, and one of his few films based on his own original material. Filmed on a low budget in Europe (and looking like it), this is another Welles portrait of a mysterious, rich, and powerful man. Here Welles plays a reclusive billionaire who fakes a case of amnesia, then hires the man who has been seeing his daughter to investigate his own past. Weak leads and some plot holes will disappoint some, but Welles's audacity, imagination, and literate dialogue more than compensate for its shortcomings. Arkadin's daughter is played by Mori, an Italian countess who became Welles's third wife. Welles tried out the concept as a radio drama first. The original European version, released in English and Spanish seven years before the eventual 1962 U.S. release, was entitled *Confidential Report.* **Cast:** Orson Welles, Michael Redgrave, Patricia Medina, Akim Tamiroff, Mischa Auer, Robert Arden, Katina Paxinou, Jack Watling, Paola Mori. **Credits:** Dir: Orson Welles; Writer: Orson Welles; Story: Orson Welles; DP: Jean Bourgoin; Ed: Renzo Lucidi; Composer: Paul Misraki; Art Director: Orson Welles. B&W, 99 min. **VHS, LASER**

Mr. Blandings Builds His Dream House
(1948) RKO
A lively satire of the postwar American housing boom when optimism was epidemic and prosperity seemed a realistic dream for any working stiff. City resident Blandings (Grant) endures the trials and tribulations of architects, contractors, neighbors, and his suspicions about his wife (Loy) and lawyer (Douglas) as a first-time country homeowner. **Cast:** Cary Grant, Myrna Loy, Melvyn Douglas, Reginald Denny, Sharyn Moffett, Connie Marshall, Louise Beavers, Harry Shannon, Ian Wolfe. **Credits:** Dir: H. C. Potter; Prod: Norman Panama, Melvin Frank; Writer: Norman Panama, Melvin Frank; Story: Eric Hodgins; DP: James Wong Howe; Ed: Harry Marker; Prod Design: Albert S. D'Agostino, Carroll Clark; Composer: Leigh Harline. B&W, 93 min. **VHS, LASER**

Mr. Deeds Goes to Town
(1936) Columbia
Capra's populist favorite is about a Vermont hayseed (Cooper) who inherits a fortune and his encounters with the cynical, heartless metropolis. Small-town "pixilated" poet and guile-

less good guy Longfellow Deeds inherits $20 million, and, when he wants to use it to help the needy, various unsavory types try to get him declared insane. As might be expected, Cooper embodies the simple virtues and wins over hardened newspaper reporter Arthur. Capra favorite Riskin wrote the screenplay and Capra won his second Oscar for the direction. Both leads worked for Capra again in *Meet John Doe* (Cooper) and *Mr. Smith Goes to Washington* (Arthur). Based on "Opera Hat," a *Saturday Evening Post* story by Clarence Budington Kelland. Academy Award Nominations: 5, including Best Picture; Best Actor: Gary Cooper; Best Screenplay. **Academy Awards:** Best Director. **Cast:** Gary Cooper, Jean Arthur, George Bancroft, Lionel Stander, Douglass Dumbrille, Raymond Walburn, H. B. Warner, Warren Hymer, Margaret Matzenauer. **Credits:** Dir: Frank Capra; Prod: Frank Capra, Jr.; Story: Robert Riskin; DP: Joseph Walker; Ed: Gene Havlick; Composer: Howard Jackson; Art Director: Stephen Goosson. B&W, 115 min. **VHS, LASER**

Mr. Hobbs Takes a Vacation
(1962) Fox
Stewart and O'Hara as the typical American husband and wife encounter comedic travails and family problems while attempting to vacation at an old crumbling house on the Pacific seaside. This comedy captures Hollywood's idea of the American family, which may seem refreshingly innocent to contemporary eyes. Stewart and O'Hara are winning as always. **Cast:** James Stewart, Maureen O'Hara, Fabian, John Saxon, Laurie Peters, John McGiver, Reginald Gardiner, Lili Gentle, Marie Wilson, Valerie Varda. **Credits:** Dir: Henry Koster; Prod: Jerry Wald; Writer: Nunnally Johnson; DP: William Mellor; Ed: Marjorie Fowler; Composer: Henry Mancini; Costumes: Don Feld; Art Director: Jack Martin Smith, Malcolm F. Brown. Color, 116 min. **VHS**

Mr. Lucky
(1943) RKO
Apolitical wartime gambler Grant tries to move his gaming ship to Cuba and avoid the draft by assuming the name and identity of a dying man who was classified 4-F. Finding he can't ignore Day or his conscience, he ends up working for the war effort. Better than to be expected due to Grant's charismatic performance. Later an inspiration for the early TV series of the same name. The story was developed by Holmes, the onetime tennis pro at

the Beverly Hills Tennis Club. **Cast:** Cary Grant, Laraine Day, Charles Bickford, Gladys Cooper, Alan Carney, Henry Stephenson, Paul Stewart, Kay Johnson, Erford Gage. **Credits:** Dir: H. C. Potter; Prod: David Hempstead; Writer: Milton Holmes, Adrian Scott; DP: George Barnes; Ed: Theron Warth; Prod Design: William Cameron Menzies; Composer: Roy Webb. B&W, 99 min. **VHS, LASER**

Mr. Music
(1950) Paramount
Crosby, playing a songwriter who would rather spend his time on the golf course than write tunes (a plotline apparently suggested by Bing's own attitudes), is coaxed into work by a college student (Olson). Agreeable fluff with Jimmy Van Heusen and Johnny Burke tunes, including "Life Is So Peculiar" sung by Crosby and Lee. A remake of *Accent on Youth* (1935), later the inspiration for *But Not for Me* (1959) with Clark Gable. Note dance pros Gower and Marge Champion and Groucho in the cast. **Cast:** Bing Crosby, Nancy Olson, Charles Coburn, Ruth Hussey, Marge Champion, Gower Champion, Peggy Lee, Groucho Marx. **Credits:** Dir: Richard Haydn; Prod: Robert L. Welch; Story: Arthur Sheekman; DP: George Barnes; Ed: Doane Harrison, Everett Douglas; Composer: Troy Sanders; Art Director: Hans Dreier, Earl Hedrick. B&W, 113 min. **VHS, LASER**

Mr. Peabody and the Mermaid
(1948) Universal
Midlife crisis for Powell as an unassuming gentleman who falls for a mermaid (Blyth) while fishing in the Caribbean. He takes her home and puts her in his pond. Unfortunately, his wife (Hervey) doesn't share his nautical tastes. Powell, professional as always, rises above the material. An early American independent production distributed by Universal. The 45th-anniversary video includes a digitally remastered edition from the original film negative, a reproduction of the original theatrical poster, and the original theatrical trailer. **Cast:** William Powell, Ann Blyth, Irene Hervey, Andrea King, Clinton Sundberg, Art Smith, Hugh French, Lumsden Hare. **Credits:** Dir: Irving Pichel; Prod: Nunnally Johnson; Writer: Nunnally Johnson; DP: Russell Metty, David Horsley; Ed: Marjorie Fowler; Composer: Robert Emmett Dolan; Art Director: Bernard Herzbrun, Boris Leven. B&W, 89 min. **VHS**

Mr. Robinson Crusoe
(1932) United Artists
A showcase for the aging, yet still agile Fairbanks, whose acrobatics are on display as a wealthy aristocrat who bets he can live alone on a desert island for a year without any support. All goes well until he discovers his "Saturday": a woman (Alba). Notable for its early score by Hollywood legend Newman. **Cast:** Douglas Fairbanks, William Farnum, Maria Alba, Earle Browne. **Credits:** Dir: A. Edward Sutherland; Prod: Douglas Fairbanks; Writer: Tom Geraghty; DP: Max Dupont; Ed: Robert J. Kern; Composer: Alfred Newman. B&W, 76 min. **VHS, LASER**

Mr. Skeffington
(1944) Warner Bros.
This popular Warner melodrama has Davis as a society beauty who marries to prevent her brother from being arrested for embezzlement. She never forgives Rains, her banker husband, and they divorce. When their daughter flees her and she contracts a withering case of diphtheria, Davis learns that Rains has survived a concentration camp and is blind and poor. The onetime beauty returns to the onetime rich man. A strong script and two star performances, which garnered Academy Award nominations. Davis and Rains starred opposite each other four times in seven years (1939–1946). This was their third film together, the others being *Juarez* (1939); *Now, Voyager* (1942); and *Deception* (1946). Academy Award Nominations: Best Actress: Bette Davis; Best Supporting Actor: Claude Rains. **Cast:** Bette Davis, Claude Rains, Richard Waring, Walter Abel, George Coulouris, Robert Shayne, John Alexander, Jerome Cowan, Margorie Riordan. **Credits:** Dir: Vincent Sherman; Prod: Julius J. Epstein, Philip G. Epstein; Writer: Julius J. Epstein, Philip G. Epstein; DP: Ernest Haller; Ed: Ralph Dawson; Prod Design: Robert M. Haas; Composer: Franz Waxman. B&W, 147 min. **VHS, LASER**

Mr. Skitch
(1933) Fox
A studio-bound vehicle for Rogers, whose genuine personality shines through the production's limitations. In what is nearly *The Grapes of Wrath* retold as a Depression-era comedy, Rogers plays the head of a poor Missouri family heading west on the road to California and better opportunities. One of Rogers's last films before his death in a plane crash two years later.

Cast: Will Rogers, ZaSu Pitts, Rochelle Hudson, Florence Desmond, Harry Green, Charles Starrett, Eugene Pallette. **Credits:** Dir: James Cruze; Prod: James Cruze; Writer: Ralph Spence, Sonya Levien; Story: Anne Cameron; DP: John Seitz; Composer: Louis de Francesco; Art Director: William S. Darling. B&W, 70 min. **VHS**

Mrs. Miniver
(1942) MGM
Garson in her Oscar-winning portrayal personified the British resolve against Nazi aggression. An immensely popular piece of wartime propaganda, Wyler's film follows Mrs. Miniver, her husband (Pidgeon), their children, and their small English town as the war comes closer to their lives. The family endures the departure of the father for the beaches at Dunkirk, the discovery of a wounded Nazi pilot, the death of the daughter-in-law in an air raid, and the entry of the son into the Royal Air Force. The scenes culminate in a morale-boosting final speech that President Franklin Roosevelt ordered printed and air-dropped over war-torn Europe. The romance of her eldest son coincides with the first bombs and the destruction of the village church, yet through all the strife upper lips remain stiff and even the smallest traditions are maintained. Adapted from the novel by Jan Struther. Academy Award Nominations: 12, including Best Actor: Walter Pidgeon. **Academy Awards:** Best Picture; Best Director; Best Actress: Greer Garson; Best Supporting Actress: Teresa Wright; Best Screenplay; Best Black-and-White Cinematography. **Cast:** Greer Garson, Walter Pidgeon, May Whitty, Teresa Wright, Reginald Owen, Henry Travers, Miles Mander, Henry Wilcoxon, Richard Ney, Rhys Williams. **Credits:** Dir: William Wyler; Prod: Sidney Franklin; Writer: Arthur Wimperis, George Froeschel, James Hilton, Claudine West; Story: Jan Struther; DP: Joseph Ruttenberg; Ed: Harold F. Kress; Prod Design: Cedric Gibbons, Urie McCleary; Composer: Herbert Stothart; Costumes: Robert Calloch. B&W, 134 min. **VHS, LASER**

Mr. Smith Goes to Washington
(1939) Columbia
Capra's enduring favorite has Stewart as the idealistic, yet naive, politician sent to Washington as junior senator who runs afoul of the political corruption in his state. Capra favorite Arthur plays his cynical secretary and Rains

the powerful senior senator who expects Smith to be nothing more than a rubber stamp. As with the best of Capra's films, the sentiment and moralizing are kept in check by wonderful acting and genuine emotion. Based on Lewis R. Foster's novel *The Gentleman from Montana*. Selected as a National Film Registry Outstanding Film. Academy Award Nominations: 11, including Best Picture; Best Director; Best Actor: James Stewart; Best Supporting Actor: Harry Carey. **Academy Awards:** Best Original Story. **Cast:** Jean Arthur, James Stewart, Claude Rains, Edward Arnold, Thomas Mitchell, Beulah Bondi, Guy Kibbee, H. B. Warner, Harry Carey, Astrid Allwyn. **Credits:** Dir: Frank Capra; Prod: Frank Capra; Writer: Sidney Buchman; Story: Lewis R. Foster; DP: Joseph Walker; Ed: Gene Havlick, Al Clark; Composer: Dimitri Tiomkin; Costumes: Robert Kalloch; Art Director: Lionel Banks. B&W, 130 min. **VHS, LASER**

Mrs. Parkington

(1944) MGM
Garson and Pidgeon are together again in this lavish melodrama about a miner who becomes a millionaire and his ambitious wife. A vehicle designed for Garson and Pidgeon, attempting to repeat the success of *Mrs. Miniver*. Garson and Pidgeon appeared together in nine features between 1941 and 1953; this was the fifth. Golden Globe for Best Supporting Actress: Agnes Moorehead. Academy Award Nominations: Best Actress: Greer Garson; Best Supporting Actress: Agnes Moorehead. **Cast:** Greer Garson, Walter Pidgeon, Edward Arnold, Gladys Cooper, Agnes Moorehead, Peter Lawford, Dan Duryea, Lee Patrick. **Credits:** Dir: Tay Garnett; Prod: Leon Gordon; Writer: Robert Thoeren, Polly James; Story: Louis Bromfield; DP: Joseph Ruttenberg; Ed: George Boemler; Prod Design: Cedric Gibbons; Composer: Bronislau Kaper; Art Director: Randall Duell. B&W, 124 min. **VHS**

Mrs. Wiggs of the Cabbage Patch

(1934) Paramount
Fields and Pitts give memorable performances in this oft-filmed melodrama about a family facing eviction, and a late-in-life romance in the poverty-stricken Cabbage Patch. This popular 1901 novel was made a number of times: 1914, 1919, and again in 1942. **Cast:** Pauline Lord, ZaSu Pitts, W. C. Fields, Kent Taylor,

Charles Middleton, Donald Meek, Jimmy Butler, George Breakston, Edith Fellows, Virginia Weidler. **Credits:** Dir: Norman Taurog; Prod: Douglas MacLean; Writer: William Slavens McNutt, Jane Storm; DP: Charles B. Lang; Ed: Anne Bauchens; Art Director: Hans Dreier, Robert Odell. B&W, 80 min. **VHS**

Mrs. Wiggs of the Cabbage Patch

(1942) Paramount
Good-hearted old lady Elvira Wiggs (Bainter) has five unruly children to raise without her husband, who hasn't been seen in years. In the impoverished neighborhood called "The Cabbage Patch," her hands are especially full: her eccentric old neighbor Mr. Marcus Throckmorton is hearing wedding bells, her one boy is sick in the hospital, her other children are up for adoption, and men are hounding her daughters. This was a trademarked role for Bainter as another in a long line of suffering matrons. **Cast:** Carolyn Lee, Hugh Herbert, Vera Vague, Betty Brewer, Harry Shawn, Carl "Alfalfa" Switzer, Moroni Olsen, Janet Beecher, Fay Bainter. **Credits:** Dir: Ralph Murphy; Prod: Ralph Murphy, Sol C. Siegel; Writer: Doris Anderson; Story: Anne Crawford Flexner, Alice Hegan Rice; DP: Leo Tover; Ed: Anne Bauchens; Prod Design: Hans Dreier; Composer: Victor Young. B&W, 80 min.

Mr. Winkle Goes to War

(1944) Columbia
Robinson is Mr. Winkle, a henpecked husband who is mistakenly drafted during WWII and finds it's the best thing that ever happened to him. Once in the service, he demonstrates a courage and competence that shocks everyone who knows him. He returns to a hero's welcome and to try to repair his marriage. Script by future blacklist victim Salt. **Cast:** Edward G. Robinson, Ruth Warrick, Richard Lane, Robert Armstrong, Richard Gaines, Walter Baldwin, Art Smith, Ann Shoemaker, Paul Stanton, George Tyne. **Credits:** Dir: Alfred E. Green; Prod: Jack Moss; Writer: Waldo Salt, George Corey, Louis Solomon; Story: Theodore Pratt; DP: Joseph Walker; Ed: Richard Fantl; Prod Design: Lionel Banks, Rudolph Sternad; Composer: Carmen Dragon, Paul Sawtell. B&W, 80 min. **VHS**

The Mummy

(1932) Universal
An icon of American cinema horror features Karloff following his perfor-

mance as the Frankenstein Monster in the starring role as the cursed Im-Ho-Tep. When archaeologist Van Sloan opens the crypt containing the mummified remains of a disgraced Egyptian prince, he steps into a moody mystery of ancient curses and slowly revivifying remains. The makeup, by master Jack Pierce, is unforgettable (and took eight hours to apply!). This was Freund's first American film as director following his notable career as cameraman for Fritz Lang (*Metropolis*, 1926) and F. W. Murnau (*The Last Laugh*, 1924). The laserdisc includes the original theatrical trailer, plus a special selection of stills from the movie. **Cast:** Boris Karloff, Zita Johann, David Manners, Bramwell Fletcher, Arthur Byron, Edward Van Sloan, Leonard Mudie, Kathleen Byron, Eddie Kane, Henry Victor. **Credits:** Dir: Karl Freund; Prod: Carl Laemmle, Jr.; Writer: John L. Balderston; DP: Charles Stumar; Ed: Milton Carruth; Art Director: Willy Pogany. B&W, 72 min. **VHS, LASER**

The Mummy's Hand

(1940) Universal
This is a remake of *The Mummy* with Western actor Tyler taking over the role made famous by Karloff. The mummy in question is Kharis (Im-Ho-Tep having met a dusty demise earlier), who is revived and immediately sets out to kill off more archaeologists. Effective horror (with some nice touches, like the dragging paralyzed leg) preceded by some labored comedy. Kharis proved so popular there were three sequels: *The Mummy's Tomb* (1942), *The Mummy's Ghost* (1944), and *The Mummy's Curse* (1944). **Cast:** Dick Foran, Cecil Kellaway, George Zucco, Eduardo Ciannelli, Charles Trowbridge, Tom Tyler, Sig Arno. **Credits:** Dir: Christy Cabanne; Prod: Ben Pivar; Writer: Griffin Jay; DP: Elwood Bredell; Ed: Philip Cahn. B&W, 70 min. **VHS**

The Muppet Movie

(1979) Associated
The first big-screen spin-off from the popular TV variety show has Kermit and Miss Piggy and company setting off for Hollywood. Along the way there are plenty of bad puns and sly allusions to old movies. Cameos by many stars slightly past their prime, from Berle to Orson Welles. Academy Award Nominations: Best Original Song ("The Rainbow Connection"); Best Original Song Score. **Cast:** Edgar Bergen, Milton Berle, Mel Brooks, Steve Martin, The Muppets, Elliott Gould, Carol

Kane, Madeline Kahn. **Credits:** Dir: James Frawley; Prod: Jim Henson; Writer: Jerry Juhl; DP: Isidore Mankofsky; Ed: Christopher Greenbury; Composer: Paul Williams; Art Director: Les Gobruegge. Color, 95 min. VHS

Murder

(1930) British International
An early, British Hitchcock talkie has Marshall playing a noted actor who, after sitting on a jury that has sentenced a woman to death, has second thoughts and tries to solve the murder. An interesting exercise in a whodunit with many of the familiar Hitchcock touches: rapid montage, a literate, witty script, interior dialogue, and outré sexuality. **Cast:** Herbert Marshall, Nora Baring, Phyllis Constam, Edward Chapman, Donald Calthrop, Esme Percy, Claire Greet. **Credits:** Dir: Alfred Hitchcock; Prod: John Maxwell; Writer: Alma Reville, Walter Mycroft, Alfred Hitchcock; Story: Clemence Dane, Helen Simpson; DP: Jack Cox; Ed: Emile De Ruelle, Rene Harrison; Composer: John Reynders. B&W, 105 min. VHS

Murder at the Vanities

(1934) Paramount
This Hollywood musical murder mystery takes place backstage at Earl Carroll's famed revue. Now remembered for a scene that depicts a singer killed while performing a ditty entitled "Sweet Marijuana." The mystery takes second stage to the variety acts that follow, including many song-and-dance numbers and the "Cocktails for Two" production number. Duke Ellington appears briefly. **Cast:** Carl Brisson, Victor McLaglen, Jack Oakie, Kitty Carlisle, Dorothy Stickney, Gertrude Michael, Jessie Ralph, Charles Middleton, Gail Patrick, Donald Meek. **Credits:** Dir: Mitchell Leisen; Prod: E. Lloyd Sheldon; Writer: Carey Wilson, Sam Hellman, Joseph Gollomb; Story: Earl Carroll, Rufus King; DP: Leo Tover; Ed: William Shea; Composer: Arthur Johnston. B&W, 91 min. VHS

Murder, He Says

(1945) Paramount
MacMurray was fresh off the set of *Double Indemnity* when he played this slapstick variation of that role in a black comedy about an insurance-company pollster (MacMurray) who finds himself trapped in a house with a family of murderous, feuding hillbillies. An odd mixture of *Ma and Pa Kettle* and *Cold Comfort Farm*. Main tweaks her most famous role with a twisted version of Ma Kettle. Unusually ghoulish for a Hollywood comedy of its time,

but plenty of fun. **Cast:** Fred MacMurray, Helen Walker, Marjorie Main, Porter Hall, Peter Whitney, Barbara Pepper, James Flavin, Jean Heather, Mabel Paige, Walter Baldwin. **Credits:** Dir: George Marshall; Prod: E. D. Leshin; Writer: Lou Breslow; Story: Jack Moffitt; DP: Theodor Sparkuhl; Ed: LeRoy Stone; Composer: Robert Emmett Dolan. Color, 91 min. VHS

The Murder Man

(1935) MGM
This grim hard-boiled melodrama has eccentric tough-guy crime-beat reporter Steve Grey (Tracy) out for revenge. Despite attentions and aid from the drama reporter Mary Shannon (Bruce), Grey winds up in more trouble than he solves. Grifter Henry Mander (Stephens) kills Grey's father and causes his wife's suicide. Grey solves the crime, then kills Mander's right-hand man and frames Mander for the job. Triumphant, Grey visits Mander in prison to taunt him, but is overcome suddenly by his good angels. He confesses his crime and accepts his fate. The film features Jimmy Stewart's first role as scoop reporter Shorty. **Cast:** Spencer Tracy, Virginia Bruce, Lionel Atwill, Harvey Stephens, Robert Barrat, James Stewart, William Collier, Sr., Bob Watson, William Demarest, John Sheehan. **Credits:** Dir: Tim Whelan; Prod: Harry Rapf; Writer: John C. Higgins, Guy Bolton, Tim Whelan; DP: Lester White; Ed: James E. Newcom; Prod Design: Cedric Gibbons; Composer: William Axt. B&W, 70 min.

Murder, My Sweet

(1944) RKO
The earliest screen depiction of famed detective Philip Marlowe is an adaptation of Raymond Chandler's *Farewell, My Lovely*. Former '30s song-and-dance man Powell was an unlikely candidate to play the ultimate cynical dick with the code of honor but he does it quite successfully (some contend he was the best screen Marlowe). The plot concerns a quest for the missing girlfriend of bruiser Moose Malloy (Mazurki). Director Dmytryk skillfully captures Marlowe's psychological disorientation as he moves from millionaire mansions to the seedy urban underbelly with a muted expressionism. The original title, "Farewell, My Lovely," was changed so that Powell's fans wouldn't mistake the film for a musical comedy, his career staple; the 1975 remake with Robert Mitchum retains the original title. **Cast:** Dick Powell, Claire Trevor, Anne Shirley,

Mike Mazurki, Miles Mander, Douglas Walton, Ralf Harolde, Esther Howard, Shimen Ruskin. **Credits:** Dir: Edward Dmytryk; Prod: Adrian Scott; Writer: John Paxton; Story: Raymond Chandler; DP: Harry Wild; Ed: Joseph Noriega; Prod Design: Albert S. D'Agostino, Carroll Clark; Composer: Roy Webb; SFX: Vernon L. Walker. B&W, 95 min. VHS, LASER

Murder on the Orient Express

(1974) Paramount
The first and best of the all-star adaptations of Christie's Hercule Poirot mysteries set in the art deco 1930s. Belgian detective Poirot (Finney) finds himself involved in a murder investigation onboard the luxurious Orient Express, and there are plenty of suspects. A stylish bit of entertainment with a wonderful cast and a lilting score by Bennett. Followed by *Death on the Nile* (1978) and *Evil Under the Sun* (1982) with Peter Ustinov behind Poirot's waxed mustache. Academy Award Nominations: 6, including Best Actor: Albert Finney; Best (Adapted) Screenplay. **Academy Awards:** Best Supporting Actress: Ingrid Bergman. **Cast:** Lauren Bacall, Ingrid Bergman, Martin Balsam, Jacqueline Bisset, Jean-Pierre Cassel, John Gielgud, Wendy Hiller, Anthony Perkins, Richard Widmark, Michael York. **Credits:** Dir: Sidney Lumet; Prod: John Brabourne, Richard Goodwin; Writer: Paul Dehn; Story: Agatha Christie; DP: Geoffrey Unsworth; Ed: Anne V. Coates; Prod Design: Tony Walton; Composer: Richard Rodney Bennett; Art Director: Jack Stephens. Color, 131 min. VHS, LASER

Murders in the Rue Morgue

(1932) Universal
Lugosi stars in the second go-round for Poe's classic tale about Parisian murders carried out by a great ape. Heavily influenced by German expressionist silent films of the previous decade, Lugosi's Dr. Mirakle, a fairground hypnotist, is closer to Dr.Caligari than to a Poe creation. An unforgettable exercise in horror from the golden age of American fright classics. Certainly the only movie in which future *What's My Line* panelist Francis is tortured, bled to death on a rack, and then dumped in the river. **Cast:** Bela Lugosi, Sidney Fox, Leon Ames, Brandon Hurst, Arlene Francis, Bert Roach, Noble Johnson, Herman Bing. **Credits:** Dir: Robert Florey; Story: Edgar Allan Poe. B&W, 75 min. VHS

Murders in the Zoo

(1933) Paramount
This neglected horror classic portrays a jealous zoo curator (Atwill) who imaginatively dispatches his wife's real and imagined suitors within the confines of the zoo. The majority of the story concerns disposing of bodies; one is fed to the lions, another is left to die in the snake cage. Ruggles struggles as the zoo press agent trying to calm public fears. **Cast:** Lionel Atwill, Charlie Ruggles, Randolph Scott, Gail Patrick, Kathleen Burke, Harry Beresford, John Lodge. **Credits:** Dir: Edward Sutherland; Writer: Philip Wylie, Seton I. Miller; DP: Ernest Haller. B&W, 62 min. VHS

Murph the Surf

(1975) AIP
TV actor Conrad (*The Wild Wild West*) stars as the infamous cat burglar who stole the Star of India sapphire in a daring heist in the 1960s. Stroud plays his beefy partner. A low-budget American International feature with a good heist scene and speedboat race, supported by a cast of '70s TV actors, and directed by small-screen veteran Chomsky (*Roots, Star Trek*). **Cast:** Robert Conrad, Don Stroud, Donna Mills, Robyn Millan, Luther Adler, Paul Stewart, Morgan Paull, Ben Frank, Burt Young, Pepper Martin. **Credits:** Dir: Marvin J. Chomsky; Prod: Chuck Courtney, J. Skeet Wilson; Writer: Arthur Kean; DP: Michel Hugo; Ed: Howard Smith; Prod Design: James D. Vance; Composer: Philip Lambro. Color, 101 min. VHS

Muscle Beach Party

(1964) AIP
The second in the string of beach-party films of the mid-'60s with the official wholesome couple of the suntan lotion and hairspray set: Avalon and Funicello. A fascinating look at '60s pop culture promoting the California dream of surf, sand, and ideal physiques. Hackett, Rickles, and Amsterdam supply some labored comic relief. Notable for appearances by Stevie Wonder, surf guitarist Dick Dale, and Peter Lorre (his last screen role). **Cast:** Frankie Avalon, Annette Funicello, Buddy Hackett, Don Rickles, Morey Amsterdam, Stevie Wonder, Dan Haggerty, Larry B. Scott. **Credits:** Dir: William Asher; Prod: James H. Nicholson, Robert Dillon; Writer: Robert Dillon; Story: William Asher; DP: Harold Wellman; Ed: Eve Newman; Composer: Les Baxter; Art Director: Lucius Croxton; Set Designer: Harry Reif. Color, 96 min. VHS, LASER

Music in the Air

(1934) Fox
Swanson plays the operetta prima donna, and Boles her lyric-writing love, in this backstage musical set in Germany. They quarrel, then decide to get even with each other by pairing ºoff with a visiting country girl and her schoolmaster sweetheart. The prima donna plays on the schoolmaster's affections, the lyricist offers to make a star of the country girl, and comedy ensues, set to the music of Kern and Hammerstein. **Cast:** Gloria Swanson, John Boles, Douglass Montgomery, June Lang, Al Shean, Reginald Owen, Joseph Cawthorn, Hobart Bosworth, Sara Haden, Marjorie Main. **Credits:** Dir: Joe May; Prod: Erich Pommer; Writer: Oscar Hammerstein, Jerome Kern, Robert Liebmann, Billy Wilder, Howard Young; DP: Ernest Palmer; Composer: Jerome Kern, Franz Waxman. B&W, 85 min.

The Music Man

(1962) Warner Bros.
Perennially popular Meredith Willson musical stars Preston as Professor Harold Hill, con man and traveling salesman, who arrives in River City, Iowa, and convinces the citizens to form a boys' band, which he plans to lead (and to which he will sell instruments). A mixture of small-town nostalgia, Americana, and infectious music, the film shines with a wonderful cast circling around Preston, in a role he will own for eternity. Among the most popular songs are: "Trouble," "Till There Was You," "Gary, Indiana," and "76 Trombones." Lost to *Lawrence of Arabia* for the Academy Award for Best Picture, but winner of the Golden Globe for Best Motion Picture, Musical. Academy Award Nominations: 6, including Best Picture; Best Art Direction; Best Costume Design. **Academy Awards:** Best Music Score, Adaptation or Treatment. **Cast:** Robert Preston, Buddy Hackett, Hermione Gingold, Paul Ford, Pert Kelton, Shirley Jones, Timmy Everett, Ron Howard. **Credits:** Dir: Morton Da Costa; Prod: Morton Da Costa; Writer: Marion Hargrove; DP: Robert Burks; Ed: William Ziegler; Prod Design: Paul Groesse; Choreographer: Onna White; Composer: Meredith Willson. Color, 152 min. VHS, LASER

Mutiny on the Bounty

(1935) MGM
The first, and arguably the best, telling of the famous 18th-century naval story, with Gable and Laughton facing off on the H.M.S. *Bounty* in the remote South Seas. Gable, in a role he undertook reluctantly, assuming he would look silly in breeches, is fittingly noble and heroic, Laughton a sneering portrait of cruel, arrogant authority. English conscripts sailing on a mission to Tahiti buckle under to cruel Captain William Bligh (Laughton). The captain's grotesque abuses of power, including a brutal flogging that results in the death of the sick, old ship's doctor, finally inspire a mutiny on the return voyage, conducted under the leadership of fair-minded officer Fletcher Christian (Gable). Two years in production and grossly over budget, the film was a huge international success, establishing Gable as one of the leading men of the 1930s. Academy Award Nominations: 8, including 3 Best Actors (Gable, Laughton, and Tone); Best Director; Best Screenplay; Best Editing; Best Score. **Academy Awards:** Best Picture. **Cast:** Charles Laughton, Clark Gable, Dudley Digges, Donald Crisp, Franchot Tone, Herbert Mundin, Eddie Quillan, Henry Stephenson, Spring Byington, Mamo Clark. **Credits:** Dir: Frank Lloyd; Prod: Irving Thalberg; Writer: Talbot Jennings, Jules Furthman, Carey Wilson; Story: Charles Nordhoff, James Norman Hall; DP: Arthur Edeson; Ed: Margaret Booth; Prod Design: Cedric Gibbons, Arnold Gillespie; Composer: Herbert Stothart. B&W, 135 min. VHS, LASER

Mutiny on the Bounty

(1962) MGM
The second Hollywood version of the most famous British naval mutiny, with Brando as Fletcher Christian and Howard as Captain Bligh. While in production, this long, big-budget epic garnered nearly as much press as Fox's *Cleopatra* (1963). With the passing years the film's merits (Howard's performance, magnificent cinematography, and score by Kaper) dim when compared to the 1935 original. Remade again in 1984 with Mel Gibson and Anthony Hopkins. Academy Award Nominations: 7, including Best Picture. **Cast:** Marlon Brando, Trevor Howard, Richard Harris, Hugh Griffith, Richard Haydn, Tim Seely, Percy Herbert, Gordon Jackson, Noel Purcell, Duncan Lamont. **Credits:** Dir: Lewis Milestone; Prod: Aaron Rosenberg; Writer: Charles Lederer; Story: Charles Nordhoff, James Norman Hall; DP: Robert Surtees; Ed: John McSweeney, Jr.; Prod Design: Joseph MacMillan Johnson; Composer: Bronislau Kaper; Art Director: George Davis. Color, 185 min. VHS, LASER

My Blue Heaven

(1950) Fox

Two television personalities, Molly and Jack Moran (Grable and Dailey), have their dreams of a family shattered when a car accident causes Molly to lose the baby she is carrying. Learning that Molly is now unable to conceive, they turn to the adoption agencies. The unexpected ensues in this musical, as they attempt to convince a mistrusting agency that television personalities can reliably parent. They are overjoyed when they successfully adopt, crushed when the baby is taken back, thrilled when they receive a new child, and stunned when the first child is returned to them. The greatest surprise, however, is yet to come. **Cast:** Betty Grable, Dan Dailey, David Wayne, Jane Wyatt, Mitzi Gaynor, Una Merkel, Don Hicks, Louise Beavers, Laura Pierpont. **Credits:** Dir: Henry Koster; Prod: Sol C. Siegel; Writer: Lamar Trotti, Claude Binyon; Story: S. K. Lauren; DP: Arthur E. Arling; Ed: James B. Clark; Prod Design: Lyle Wheeler, Joseph C. Wright; Composer: Harold Arlen, Alfred Newman. Color, 96 min.

My Cousin Rachel

(1952) Fox

Burton, in his Hollywood debut, plays a wealthy young man in 19th-century England who receives letters from his cousin (and best friend) that seem to imply that the man's wife (de Havilland) is poisoning him. The cousin dies, and his attractive widow soon comes for a visit. Burton initially mistrusts her, but he soons falls in love with her, giving her everything he owns. His suspicions revive, with catastrophic consequences when her lawyer (Dolenz) arrives at the estate, and he coaxes Burton to try some of de Havilland's tea. His anger and suspicions lead to a death that leaves many questions unanswered. De Havilland returned to the screen after a three-year absence to take the role of the murderously attractive widow. **Cast:** Olivia de Havilland, Richard Burton, George Dolenz, Audrey Dalton, Ronald Squire. **Credits:** Dir: Henry Koster; Prod: Earl Johnson; Writer: Daphne du Maurier, Nunnally Johnson; DP: Joseph La Shelle; Ed: Louis Loeffler; Prod Design: John De Cuir, Lyle Wheeler; Composer: Franz Waxman. B&W, 98 min.

My Darling Clementine

(1946) Fox

Fonda plays Wyatt Earp in Ford's celebrated telling of the gunfight at the OK Corral. Mature is a solid Doc Holliday, the cultured Bostonian turned gunfighter. Ford includes long, nostalgic passages that with loving detail evoke daily life in the West, as much the theme of the film as Fonda's quest for his brother's killers and the inevitable showdown at the conclusion. One of Ford's best. **Cast:** Henry Fonda, Linda Darnell, Victor Mature, Walter Brennan, Cathy Downs, Tim Holt, Ward Bond, Alan Mowbray, John Ireland, Roy Roberts. **Credits:** Dir: John Ford; Prod: Samuel G. Engel; Writer: Winston Miller, Samuel G. Engel; Story: Sam Hellman, Stuart N. Lake; Ed: Dorothy Spencer; Prod Design: James Basevi, Lyle Wheeler; Composer: Cyril Mockridge, David Buttolph; Costumes: Rene Hubert. B&W, 97 min.
VHS, LASER

My Fair Lady

(1964) Warner Bros.

Lerner and Loewe's Broadway success comes to the screen with a ravishing Hepburn in the title role made famous onstage by Julie Andrews and Harrison repeating the character of Dr. Henry Higgins. The now-familiar story of the Cockney market girl who conquers society as well as her mentor's heart is beautifully realized by Cukor, assisted by sets and costumes designed by famed photographer Cecil Beaton (the Ascot Races sequence is a virtual runway fashion show of Beaton's glamorous handiwork), and the invisible Marni Nixon as Hepburn's singing voice. Memorable songs include: "I've Grown Accustomed to Her Face," "The Rain in Spain Stays Mainly in the Plain," "I Could Have Danced All Night," and "You Did It!" among many others. This quintessential film musical was based on Shaw's 1913 play, *Pygmalion*. The 30th-anniversary video includes a fully restored print, the original theatrical trailer, promotional film, and CBS news footage of the star-studded premiere. Golden Globes for Best Director; Best Actor in a Musical or Comedy: Rex Harrison; Best Film, Musical or Comedy. Academy Award Nominations: 12, including Best (Adapted) Screenplay. **Academy Awards:** Best Picture; Best Director; Best Actor: Rex Harrison; Best Sound; Best Color Cinematography; Best Costume Design (Color); Best Music Score, Adaptation or Treatment; Best Art Direction—Set Decoration (Color). **Cast:** Audrey Hepburn, Rex Harrison, Wilfrid Hyde-White, Stanley Holloway, Jeremy Brett, Theodore Bikel, Gladys Cooper, Henry Daniell, Isobel Elsom, Mona Washbourne. **Credits:** Dir: George Cukor; Prod: Jack Warner; Story: Frederick Loewe, George Bernard Shaw; DP: Harry Stradling; Ed: William Ziegler; Choreographer: Hermes Pan; Composer: Alan Jay Lerner, Frederick Loewe; Costumes: Cecil Beaton; Art Director: Gene Allen; Set Designer: George James Hopkins. Color, 171 min. **VHS, LASER, DVD**

My Favorite Blonde

(1942) Paramount

A wartime spy comedy with Carroll enlisting vaudevillian Hope and his trained penguin in a coast-to-coast espionage mission that gets progressively more absurd. Hitchcock's *The 39 Steps* (1935), the progenitor of nearly all spy chase films, which also starred Carroll, appears to have served as the inspiration for this popular romp. Crosby makes a very brief appearance in a memorable scene. **Cast:** Bob Hope, Madeleine Carroll, Gale Sondergaard, George Zucco, Bing Crosby, Lionel Royce, Walter Kingsford, Victor Varconi, Otto Reichow, Charles Cane. **Credits:** Dir: Sidney Lanfield; Prod: Paul Jones; Writer: Don Hartman, Frank Butler; Story: Melvin Frank, Norman Panama; DP: William Mellor; Ed: William O'Shea; Composer: David Buttolph. B&W, 78 min. **VHS**

My Favorite Brunette

(1947) Paramount

Another vehicle for Hope and Lamour: he plays a baby photographer, she is a baroness looking for a missing husband. Along the way there are run-ins with a horde of international criminals led by Lorre, a quest for a hidden map, and two classic cameo appearances. One of 15 films Hope made with Lamour. **Cast:** Bob Hope, Dorothy Lamour, Peter Lorre, Lon Chaney, Jr., John Hoyt, Charles Dingle, Reginald Denny, Frank Puglia, Ann Doran, Willard Robertson. **Credits:** Dir: Elliott Nugent; Prod: Danny Dare; Writer: Edmund Beloin, Jack Rose; DP: Lionel Lindon; Ed: Ellsworth Hoagland; Composer: Robert Emmett Dolan. B&W, 87 min. **VHS, LASER**

My Favorite Spy

(1951) Paramount

This Hope vehicle stars the comedian as both international spy Eric Augustine and Peanuts White, a bumbling comic, in a parody of murky spy tales. When Augustine is kidnapped, the government sends look-alike White overseas in his place to pick up a valuable strip of microfilm. White meets his contact but finds himself in danger from a criminal ring seeking the microfilm. He romances the spy's girl, Lily (Lamarr), but when she turns out to be part of the ring, only the comic's charm can save him. **Cast:** Bob Hope, Hedy Lamarr, Francis L. Sullivan, Arnold Moss, Tonio Selwart, Stephan Chase, John Archer, Morris Ankrum, Marc Lawrence, Iris Adrian. **Credits:** Dir: Norman Z. McLeod; Prod: Paul Jones; Writer: Edmund Hartman, Jack Sher, Hal Kanter, Edmund Beloin, Lou Breslow; DP: Victor Milner; Ed: Frank Bracht; Prod Design: Hal Pereira; Composer: Victor Young. B&W, 93 min.

My Favorite Wife
(1940) RKO
In this marital screwball comedy, newly married Grant discovers his first wife (Dunne) wasn't lost seven years earlier in a South Seas typhoon as was presumed. Grant, Dunne, and producer McCarey try to repeat the success of *The Awful Truth* (1937). The pace is fast and the situations absurd, but the cast keeps everything humming delightfully. Later remade as *Move Over, Darling* (1963) with Doris Day and James Garner (which began life as the unfinished Marilyn Monroe vehicle *Something's Got to Give*). Academy Award Nominations: 3, including Best Original Story. **Cast:** Cary Grant, Irene Dunne, Gail Patrick, Randolph Scott, Ann Shoemaker, Scotty Beckett, Donald MacBride, Granville Bates, Leon Belasco. **Credits:** Dir: Garson Kanin; Prod: Leo McCarey; Writer: Samuel Spewack, Bella Spewack; Story: Leo McCarey; DP: Rudolph Maté; Ed: Robert Wise; Composer: Roy Webb. B&W, 88 min. **VHS, LASER**

My Forbidden Past
(1951) RKO
The only pairing of Mitchum and Gardner is this turn-of-the-century tale of a vengeful New Orleans femme fatale who inherits money and determines to break up the marriage of the man she loves. Gardner looks wonderful in the dresses of the period; Mitchum looks more comfortable in a trench coat. **Cast:** Robert Mitchum, Ava Gardner, Melvyn Douglas, Janis Carter, Gordon Oliver, Basil Ruysdael, Clarence Muse, Walter Kingsford, Will Wright. **Credits:** Dir: Robert Stevenson; Prod: Robert Sparks, Polan Banks, Malcom Gerrie, Avril MacRory; Writer: Marion Parsonnet, Leopold Atlas; Story: Polan Banks; DP: Harry Wild, Andy Carchrae; Ed: George Shrader; Composer: Fred-

erick Hollander; Art Director: Albert S. D'Agostino, Alfred Herman. B&W, 81 min. **VHS**

My Friend Flicka
(1943) Fox
Family favorite about a boy (McDowall) and his wild pony and its effect on his family. Fine performances by McDowall, Foster, and Johnson and spectacular color cinematography lift this from average fare. Followed by *Thunderhead, Son of Flicka* (1945). **Cast:** Roddy McDowall, Preston Foster, Rita Johnson, Jeff Corey, James Bell, Jimmie Aubrey, Arthur Loft. **Credits:** Dir: Harold Schuster; Prod: Ralph Dietrich; Writer: Lillie Hayward, Francis Edward Faragoh; DP: Dewey Wrigley; Ed: Robert Fritch; Prod Design: Richard Day, Chester Gore; Composer: Alfred Newman. Color, 89 min. **VHS**

My Gal Sal
(1942) Fox
This period-piece musical comedy traces the career of 1890s songwriter Paul Dreiser (Mature), brother to the novelist Theodore Dreiser, as he leaves Indiana for Broadway. In New York City, Paul encounters the dazzling show-stopper Sally Elliott (Hayworth). The two don't exactly hit it off, but their bumbling romance—with the help of Paul's tune "My Gal Sal"—hits the big time. Songs include "I's Your Honey If You Wants Me Liza Jane," "Mr. Volunteer," "On the Big White Way," and "The Convict and the Bird." **Cast:** Rita Hayworth, Victor Mature, John Sutton, Carole Landis, James Gleason, Phil Silvers, Walter Catlett, Mona Maris, Frank Orth, Stanley Andrews. **Credits:** Dir: Irving Cummings; Prod: Robert Bassler; Writer: Seton I. Miller, Karl Tunberg, Darrell Ware; Story: Theodore Dreiser; DP: Ernest Palmer; Ed: Robert Simpson; Prod Design: Richard Day, Joseph C. Wright; Composer: Ralph Rainger. Color, 102 min.

My Geisha
(1962) Paramount
A madcap story about an American film actress (MacLaine) who masquerades as a geisha to win the part of Madame Butterfly in her film-director husband's (Montand) production. MacLaine and the Japanese locations make this watchable, however the sitcom situation deteriorates into an embarrassing commentary on the role of women in the early '60s. Robinson is a welcome addition as the producer. Academy Award Nomination for Best (Color) Costume Design. **Cast:**

Shirley MacLaine, Yves Montand, Edward G. Robinson, Robert Cummings, Yoko Tani, Tatsu Saito, Alex Gerry. **Credits:** Dir: Jack Cardiff; Prod: Steve Parker; Writer: Norman Krasna; DP: Shunichiro Nakao; Ed: Archie Marshek; Composer: Franz Waxman; Art Director: Hal Pereira, Arthur Lonergan. Color, 120 min. **VHS, LASER**

My Life with Caroline
(1941) RKO
This loony comedy features Colman as Anthony Mason, a publishing baron more dedicated to his work than to Caroline (Lee), his pretty young wife. Caroline goes on a love spree to get her husband back, suddenly assembling what seems to Anthony a smorgasbord of lovers. There's the long-ago romance with South American millionaire Paco Del Valle (Roland) and her current beau, sculptor Paul Martindale (Gardiner)—both a lot younger than he is. Out of the office for the first time in years, Anthony finds himself back on the trail of his errant wife under the hot sun of Palm Beach. A departure for the normally somber Milestone. **Cast:** Ronald Colman, Anna Lee, Charles Winninger, Reginald Gardiner, Gilbert Roland, Katherine Leslie, Hugh O'Connell, Murray Alper, Caroline Moses, Matt Moore. **Credits:** Dir: Lewis Milestone; Prod: Lewis Milestone; Writer: Arnold Belgard, John Van Druten; Story: Georges Berr, Louis Verneuil; DP: Victor Milner; Ed: Henry Berman; Prod Design: Nicolai Remisoff; Composer: Werner R. Heymann. B&W, 81 min.

My Little Chickadee
(1940) Universal
The immortal pairing of West and Fields way out West, respectively playing a woman of dubious reputation and a shady gambler, has hilarious moments. It's terrific fun to see these two movie icons together in a film they reportedly cowrote, although most sounds like West's handiwork. Fields has a memorable poker scene and even ends up in bed with a goat ("Darling, did you change your perfume?") as West pursues a romance with a dashing masked man. **Cast:** Mae West, W. C. Fields, Joseph Calleia, Dick Foran, Margaret Hamilton, George Moran, Si Jenks, Gene Austin, Fuzzy Knight. **Credits:** Dir: Edward Cline; Prod: Lester Cowan; Writer: Mae West, W. C. Fields; DP: Joe Valentine; Ed: Edward Curtiss; Composer: Frank Skinner; Art Director: Jack Otterson. B&W, 91 min. **VHS, LASER**

My Lucky Star

(1938) Fox

The fourth vehicle for Norwegian skating star Sonja Henie, who turned professional after the 1936 Olympics. Here she plays—surprise—an iceskater discovered by department store heir Romero hoping to impress his dad by having her perform in his showroom. The highlight is Henie's "Alice in Wonderland" ice ballet. Gypsy Rose Lee and Ebsen appear in small supporting roles. **Cast:** Sonja Henie, Richard Greene, Cesar Romero, Buddy Ebsen, Arthur Treacher, George Barbier, Gypsy Rose Lee, Billy Gilbert, Paul Hurst, Cully Richards. **Credits:** Dir: Roy Del Ruth; Prod: Harry Joe Brown; Writer: Harry Tugend, Jack Yellen; Story: Karl Tunberg, Don Ettlinger; DP: John Mescall; Ed: Allen McNeil. B&W, 90 min. **VHS**

My Man and I

(1952) MGM

A proud Mexican (Montalban) treasures his new U.S. citizenship. He takes a job working for a man (Corey) who hates Mexicans and has to rebuff the advances of the man's lonely wife (Trevor). When the boss tries to cheat the man out of his wages, there is a fight. The husband and wife lie to the police and accuse the Mexican of attacking them, and he's thrown in jail, but his friends save the day by coercing the couple into retracting their statement. **Cast:** Shelley Winters, Ricardo Montalban, Wendell Corey, Claire Trevor, Jose Torvay, Jack Elam, Pascual Garcia Pena, George Chandler, Juan Torena. **Credits:** Dir: William Wellman; Prod: Stephen Ames; Writer: John Fante; DP: William Mellor; Ed: John Dunning; Prod Design: James Baseui; Art Director: Cedric Gibbons. B&W, 99 min.

My Man Godfrey

(1936) Universal

One of the all-time great screwball comedies of the '30s features winning performances by Lombard as a flighty heiress and Powell as the bum she finds in a scavenger hunt and later hires as a butler. A bitterly satiric view of the idle rich and the nobility of the common man made in the darkest days of the Depression, with Pallette as the nutty father and Auer playing an artist who does monkey imitations. Powell and Lombard were husband and wife from 1931 to 1933. Remade in 1957. Academy Award Nominations: 7, including Best Director; Best Actor: William Powell; Best Actress: Carole Lombard; Best Screenplay.

Cast: William Powell, Carole Lombard, Mischa Auer, Eugene Pallette, Alice Brady, Jean Dixon, Pat Flaherty, Jean Rogers. **Credits:** Dir: Gregory La Cava; Prod: Gregory La Cava; Writer: Morrie Ryskind, Eric Hatch, Gregory La Cava; DP: Ted Tetzlaff; Ed: Ted J. Kent; Composer: Charles Previn; Art Director: Charles D. Hall. B&W, 95 min. **VHS**

My Man Godfrey

(1957) Universal

A remake of the 1936 favorite, featuring Allyson and Niven. Niven holds his own as the "forgotten man" who reminds the wealthy about some basic realities of life, but Allyson lacks the comic flair and the mischievous intelligence of Lombard's original performance. This was Allyson's next-to-last film, departing the large screen two years later for her own TV show. **Cast:** June Allyson, David Niven, Martha Hyer, Eva Gabor, Jeff Donnell, Jessie Royce Landis, Robert Keith, Jay Robinson. **Credits:** Dir: Henry Koster; Prod: Ross Hunter; Writer: Everett Freeman, Peter Berneis, William Bowers; DP: William Daniels; Ed: Milton Carruth; Composer: Frank Skinner; Art Director: Alexander Golitzen, Richard H. Riedel. Color, 93 min. **VHS**

My Reputation

(1946) Warner Bros.

A soapy melodrama, though hugely successful, this stars Stanwyck as a widow facing life alone caring for her two sons by herself. She rebuffs the advances of married men who are looking for a mistress or just a good time. When her friends convince her to join them on a vacation, she meets a handsome bachelor (Brent). An attraction develops, but he makes it clear that he will never marry. While nothing untoward happened with the bachelor, gossip spreads and her own sons turn against her for insulting their father's memory. She realizes she must choose between a boring suitor and the man she loves. **Cast:** Barbara Stanwyck, George Brent, Warner Anderson, Lucile Watson, John Ridgely, Eve Arden, Esther Dale, Jerome Cowan, Leona Maricle, Scotty Beckett. **Credits:** Dir: Curtis Bernhardt; Prod: Henry Blanke; Writer: Catherine Turney; Story: Clare Jaynes; DP: James Wong Howe; Ed: David Weisbart; Composer: Max Steiner; Art Director: Anton Grot. B&W, 94 min.

My Side of the Mountain

(1969) Paramount

Good outdoorsy, family entertainment

about a 13-year-old boy (Eccles) who decides to go it alone in the Canadian mountains. Bikel plays a mountain folksinger who acts as savior when the winter snows threaten. Spectacular nature cinematography. **Cast:** Teddy Eccles, Theodore Bikel, Tudi Wiggins, Frank Perry, Tom Harvey, Paul Herbert, Maxie Rosenbloom. **Credits:** Dir: James B. Clark; Prod: Robert B. Radnitz; Writer: Ted Sherdeman, Jane Klove, Joanna Crawford; Story: Jean George; DP: Denys Coop, Peter Thornton; Ed: Alastair McIntyre; Composer: Wilfred Josephs; Art Director: George Lack. Color, 100 min. **VHS**

My Sister Eileen

(1942) Columbia

This charming urban comedy has two sisters from the Ohio sticks arriving in New York City's Greenwich Village, eager to make a go of it. With romance budding up for the younger, Eileen (Blair), and a possible writing career for the elder, Ruth (Russell), the country girls encounter a variety of busy city-folk and downtown oddballs. They even receive a surprise visit to their basement apartment from the subway-tunneling Three Stooges. Academy Award Nomination: Best Actress: Rosalind Russell. **Cast:** Rosalind Russell, Brian Aherne, Janet Blair, George Tobias, Allyn Joslyn, Elizabeth Patterson, Grant Mitchell, Richard Quine, June Havoc, Donald MacBride. **Credits:** Dir: Alexander Hall; Prod: Max Gordon; Writer: Jerome Chodorov, Joseph Fields; Story: Ruth McKenney; DP: Joseph Walker; Ed: Viola Lawrence; Prod Design: Lionel Banks. B&W, 96 min.

My Sister Eileen

(1955) Columbia

Musical-comedy remake of the 1942 Rosalind Russell film about two Ohio girls (Leigh and Garrett) who take a bite of The Big Apple by setting themselves up in a Greenwich Village apartment. Lemmon, who won an Oscar for his breakthrough role in *Mister Roberts* the same year, plays Garrett's suitor, and Fosse performs in and choreographed a number of the dances. Originally based on a play by Joseph Fields and Jerome Chodorov, inspired by *New Yorker* stories by Ruth McKenney. **Cast:** Betty Garrett, Janet Leigh, Jack Lemmon, Kurt Kasznar, Dick York, Bob Fosse, Horace McMahon, Hal March, Queenie Smith. **Credits:** Dir: Richard Quine; Prod: Fred Kohlmar; Writer: Blake Edwards, Richard Quine; DP: Charles Lawton,

Jr.; Ed: Charles Nelson; Prod Design: Walter Holscher; Composer: George Duning; Set Designer: William Kiernan. Color, 108 min. **VHS**

My Six Convicts
(1952) Columbia
Based on the best-seller about a psychologist who comes to work in a prison, this is an uncommon story of prison life filled with genuine humor and drama. Six convicts make up the psychologist's staff: a safecracker, an embezzler, a psychopathic killer, an alcoholic taking the rap for a girl, a sensitive romantic, and a guy sentenced for an unarmed holdup. As the doubting warden looks on, the psychologist works to develop a system for rehabilitating the incarcerated men, and the convicts grow to trust and admire him. **Cast:** Millard Mitchell, Gilbert Roland, John Beal, Marshall Thompson, Alf Kjellin, Harry Morgan, Jay Adler, Regis Toomey, Fay Roope, Carleton Young. **Credits:** Dir: Hugo Fregonese; Prod: Stanley Kramer; Writer: Michael Blankfort, Donald Powell Wilson; DP: Guy Roe; Ed: Gene Havlick; Composer: Dimitri Tiomkin. B&W, 104 min.

My Son John
(1952) Paramount
Straight-faced propaganda for the McCarthy era, this is one of the most inexplicable episodes in film history, with talents such as Hayes and McCarey involved. Hayes is a mother of three sons, two on their way to Korea and the third (Walker) a pseudo-intellectual fellow traveler. Her eyes slowly open and her son finally renounces his Party spying, just in time to take a bullet from the Reds, expiring on the steps of the Lincoln Memorial. Absolutely loony scenes of patriotic paranoia (Jagger clouting his son with the Bible) make for a fascinating watch. Academy Award Nomination for Best Original Screenplay.

Cast: Helen Hayes, Robert Walker, Van Heflin, Dean Jagger, Minor Watson, Frank McHugh, Irene Winston, James Young, Richard Jaeckel, Todd Karns. **Credits:** Dir: Leo McCarey; Prod: Leo McCarey; Writer: Myles Connolly, Leo McCarey; Story: John Lee Mahin; DP: Harry Stradling; Ed: Marvin Coil; Composer: Robert Emmett Dolan. B&W, 121 min.

The Mystery of Edwin Drood
(1935) Universal
Rains stars in an ambitious attempt to complete Charles Dickens's final unfinished thriller about a repellent opium-addicted choirmaster (Rains) and his desire for his nephew's fiancée (Angel). Drood, the nephew (Manners), is dispatched by Rains and an innocent man is charged. Unsuccessfully remade in 1992. **Cast:** Claude Rains, Douglass Montgomery, Heather Angel, Valerie Hobson, David Manners, Zeffie Tillbury, Francis L. Sullivan, Ethel Griffies, E. E. Clive. **Credits:** Dir: Stuart Walker; Prod: Edmund Grainger; Writer: John L. Balderston; DP: George Robinson; Ed: Edward Curtiss; Composer: Edward Ward; Art Director: Albert S. D'Agostino. B&W, 85 min. **VHS**

The Mystery of Mr. X
(1934) MGM
In foggy London a mystery unfolds as Scotland Yard tries to determine who is killing policemen. A jewel thief (Montgomery) finds himself in the unfortunate position of possessing a diamond believed to be stolen by the murderer; he's also in love with the Scotland Yard Commissioner's daughter. In order to save himself, he must solve the mystery. **Cast:** Robert Montgomery, Elizabeth Allan, Lewis Stone, Ralph Forbes, Henry Stephenson, Forrester Harvey, Ivan Simpson, Leonard Mudie, Alec B. Francis, Charles Irwin. **Credits:** Dir: Edgar Selwyn; Prod: Lawrence Weingarten; Writer: Philip

MacDonald, Howard Emmett Rogers; DP: Oliver T. Marsh; Ed: Hugh Wynn; Prod Design: Merill Pye. B&W, 85 min.

The Mystery of the Wax Museum
(1933) Warner Bros.
Here is the familiar story of the disfigured sculptor (Atwill) who hides his murder victims as waxwork displays. The locale is contemporary New York City, and the story is structured as a whodunit with a few labored comedy scenes. Notable as one of the first films released in an early two-color Technicolor process. More successfully remade as the better-known *House of Wax*, with Vincent Price (1953), set in turn-of-the-century Baltimore. **Cast:** Lionel Atwill, Fay Wray, Glenda Farrell, Frank McHugh, Gavin Gordon, Edwin Maxwell, Holmes Herbert, Arthur Edmond Carewe, Allen Vincent. **Credits:** Dir: Michael Curtiz; Prod: Henry Blanke; Writer: Carl Erickson; DP: Ray Rennahan; Ed: George Amy; Art Director: Anton F. Grot. Color, 77 min. **VHS**

My Wife's Best Friend
(1952) Fox
While flying to Honolulu to celebrate their eighth wedding anniversary, a couple experiences turbulence of the sort that prompts "I may never see you again" confessions. The woman apologizes for not being a good wife and the husband confesses to almost having an affair with her best friend three years prior. Not surprisingly, the plane lands safely and the movie takes off as the wife adopts many different means of torturing the husband who said more than he should. **Cast:** Anne Baxter, Macdonald Carey, Cecil Kellaway, Casey Adams, Katherine McLeod, Leif Erickson, Frances Bavier, Mary Sullivan, Martin Milner, Billie Bird. **Credits:** Dir: Richard Sale; Prod: Robert Bassler; Writer: Isobel Lennart, John Harding Briard; DP: Leo Tover; Ed: Robert Simpson; Composer: Leigh Harline. B&W, 87 min.

The Naked and the Dead

(1958) Warner Bros.
Walsh's bleak adaptation of Norman
Mailer's blockbuster follows the
descent of a platoon of American sol-
diers into the hell of a Japanese-held
Pacific island. Death and the chronic
indifference of the high command are
their constant companions as the
grinding, violent attrition comes to its
inexorable conclusion. A strong cast,
with Massey, Robertson, and Ray, and
a fine score by Herrmann. **Cast:** Cliff
Robertson, Raymond Massey, Aldo
Ray, Joey Bishop, Lili St. Cyr, William
Campbell, Barbara Nichols, Richard
Jaeckel. **Credits:** Dir: Raoul Walsh;
Prod: Paul Gregory; Writer: Denis
Sanders, Terry Sanders; DP: Joseph
La Shelle; Composer: Bernard Herrmann. Color, 131 min. **VHS**

The Naked City

(1948) Universal
This fine film adroitly uses a police
murder investigation as the vehicle for
a cinematic meditation on the grim
realities of city life. The story is a
based-on-fact account of a young
woman who is brutally murdered on
the streets of New York City and the
subsequent manhunt for her killer.
Producer Hellinger was also responsible for the Bogart-Cagney film *The
Roaring Twenties* (1939) and drew
once more on his experiences as a
tabloid reporter to infuse this film with
raw energy and deft pacing. Fitzgerald
is the cop, Duff is the killer, and the
renowned Daniels is responsible for
the starkly beautiful cinematography.
Academy Award Nominations: 3,
including Best Motion Picture Story.
Academy Awards: Best Film Editing;
Best Black-and-White Cinematography.
Cast: Barry Fitzgerald, Howard Duff,
Dorothy Hart, Don Taylor, Ted De Cor-
sia, House Jameson, Tom Pedi, Enid
Markey. **Credits:** Dir: Jules Dassin;
Prod: Mark Hellinger; Writer: Albert
Maltz, Malvin Wald; DP: William

Daniels; Ed: Paul Weatherwax; Prod
Design: John DeCuir; Composer: Miklos Rozsa, Frank Skinner. B&W, 96
min. **VHS**

The Naked Edge

(1961) United Artists
Cooper, Kerr, Marlon Brando's production company, and a taut murder mystery should have added up to more.
Unfortunately, Cooper was dying of
cancer in real life and is visibly weak-
ened. England is the backdrop for a
case in which Cooper's testimony puts
a coworker in jail for robbery and murder. Cooper subsequently finds himself rich, to the suspicious bewilderment of his wife, Kerr. Blackmail, then
the attempted murder of Kerr, follow
as Cooper seeks to expose the real
culprit. **Cast:** Gary Cooper, Deborah
Kerr, Eric Portman, Diane Cilento,
Hermione Gingold, Michael Wilding,
Peter Cushing, Ronald Howard. **Credits:** Dir: Michael Anderson; Prod: Walter Seltzer, George Glass; Writer:
Joseph Stefano; DP: Erwin Hillier; Ed:
Gordon Pilkington; Prod Design: Carmen Dillon; Composer: William Alwyn.
Color, 97 min. **VHS**

The Naked Jungle

(1954) Paramount
Years ahead of the curve for movies
with insects as the central characters,
this Technicolor adventure was based
on Carl Stephenson's story "Leiningen
Versus the Ants." Heston is the tough-
as-nails plantation owner who rejects
mail-order bride Parker until she supports his will to resist the elemental
destructive power of a city-sized
swarm of ants. Great special effects
(this was produced by Pal). And it's
amusing to see Heston swathed in
grease sprinting to blow up the dam.
Cast: Eleanor Parker, Charlton Heston, Abraham Sofaer, William Conrad,
Romo Vincent, Douglas Fowley, John
Dierkes, Leonard Strong. **Credits:** Dir:
Byron Haskin; Prod: George Pal;

Writer: Philip Yordan, Ranald Mac-
Dougall; DP: Ernest Laszlo; Ed: Everett
Douglas; Composer: Daniele Amfithe-
atrof. Color, 95 min. **VHS, LASER**

The Naked Kiss

(1964) Allied Artists
In this harsh, misanthropic drama by
Fuller, a prostitute (Towers) finally
sickens of her life's degradations,
kills her pimp, and heads for the
canebrake to start again. She works
with crippled children and draws the
attention of local rich man Dante.
They're about to tie the knot when
Towers discovers him about to molest
one of the children she cares for. She
kills again in rage and heads back to
a world where the insanity is less
cloaked. Shockingly effective noir
melodrama. **Cast:** Constance Towers,
Anthony Eisley, Virginia Grey, Betty
Bronson, Michael Dante, Patsy Kelly,
Linda Francis, Barbara Perry. **Credits:**
Dir: Samuel Fuller; Prod: Samuel
Fuller; Writer: Samuel Fuller; DP:
Stanley Cortez; Ed: Jerome Thoms;
Composer: Paul Dunlap; Art Director:
Eugene Lourie. B&W, 90 min. **VHS,
LASER, DVD**

The Naked Prey

(1965) Paramount
Wilde produced and directed this fast-
paced and harrowing tale of white
arrogance leading to the capture and
graphically depicted torture of members of an African safari by tribesmen.
After his charges are roasted,
butchered, and snake-bitten, guide
Wilde is given the chance to outrun an
elite tribal cadre of lion-killers. During
production, Wilde was bitten by a
lizard, a manager was fanged by a
cobra, crew members were hospital-
ized after being attacked by bees,
Wilde contracted a dangerous fever,
and his home was robbed. Ouch.
Beautiful cinematography in this realistic and almost dialogue-free film.
Academy Award Nomination for Best

(Original) Story and Screenplay. **Cast:** Cornel Wilde, Ken Gampu, Gert Van Den Bergh, Patrick Mynhardt, John Marcus, Bella Randels, Jose Sithole, Richard Mashiya, Eric Sabela. **Credits:** Dir: Cornel Wilde; Prod: Cornel Wilde; Writer: Clint Johnston, Don Peters; DP: H. A. R. Thomson; Ed: Roger Cherrill. Color, 94 min. **VHS, LASER**

The Naked Spur
(1953) MGM
Mann continued his quest to reinvent the Western with this superb outing that boasts an Oscar-nominated screenplay. Adventure, striking location shots, and sharply etched psychological studies are woven seamlessly as disillusioned Civil War veteran Stewart becomes a bounty hunter after losing his land. He's after Ryan, who's running with Leigh, while Stewart picks up Meeker and Mitchell. They catch Ryan, who sows dissension and selfishness. When the smoke clears, only two are left standing. Academy Award Nomination for Best Story and Screenplay. **Cast:** James Stewart, Robert Ryan, Janet Leigh, Ralph Meeker, Millard Mitchell. **Credits:** Dir: Anthony Mann; Prod: William Wright; Writer: Sam Rolfe, Harold Jack Bloom; DP: William Mellor; Ed: George White; Prod Design: Cedric Gibbons, Malcolm Brown; Composer: Bronislau Kaper. Color, 93 min. **VHS**

Namu, the Killer Whale
(1966) United Artists
Inspired by the life of a killer whale of the same name, which was studied at the Seattle Public Aquarium in the '60s. Lansing is a marine biologist who captures a killer whale and hopes to keep it for research purposes. But whales feed on the same salmon the local fishermen depend on for their livelihood. They would rather see Namu destroyed than understood. Tensions mount between the local element and the scientific interests. **Cast:** Robert Lansing, John Anderson, Lee Meriwether, Richard Erdman, Robin Mattson, Michael Sheard, Joe Higgins, Mike Shea. **Credits:** Dir: Laslo Benedek; Prod: Laslo Benedek; Writer: Arthur Weiss; DP: Lamar Boren; Ed: Warren Adams; Composer: Samuel Matlovsky; Art Director: Eddie Imazu. Color, 89 min. **VHS**

Nana
(1934) United Artists
Zola's famous courtesan (Sten) here ascends to the heights of Parisian music-hall fame when coached by an egotistical manger. Her celebrated beauty causes men to fall at her feet, including the Grand Duke played by Grant and two brothers played by Atwill and Holmes. She extricates herself from the predicament with a dramatic exit. Meant to introduce Russian actress Sten to the world; she became known as "Goldwyn's Folly." Directed by pioneer woman director Arzner. **Cast:** Anna Sten, Lionel Atwill, Phillips Holmes, Richard Bennett, Muriel Kirkland, Reginald Owen, Helen Freeman, Lawrence Grant, Jessie Ralph, Ferdinand Gottschalk. **Credits:** Dir: Dorothy Arzner; Prod: Samuel Goldwyn; Writer: Emile Zola, Willard Mack, Harry Wagstaff Gribble; DP: Gregg Toland; Ed: Frank Lawrence; Composer: Lorenz Hart, Alfred Newman; Art Director: Richard Day. B&W, 87 min.

Nancy Drew
Carolyn Keene penned more than 100 Nancy Drew mysteries, beginning in 1930, though only one of them, *Nancy Drew and the Hidden Staircase* (1939), was specifically adapted for the big screen. (The other three films in the series were based upon Keene's characters.) Nevertheless, the short-lived series was well received, with snappily paced films and a well-cast Bonita Granville making Nancy plucky, smart, and unflappable. In each of the four films, Frankie Thomas, Jr., played Nancy's boyfriend and fellow gumshoe, and John Litel played her lawyer father who always, to no avail, urged Nancy to keep her nose out of the murder and mayhem.

Nancy Drew, Detective (1938)
Nancy Drew—Reporter (1939)
Nancy Drew—Troubleshooter (1939)
Nancy Drew and the Hidden Staircase (1939)

Nanook of the North
(1922)
One of the landmarks of documentary film, this remains a fascinating view of a vanishing culture. Flaherty, having ventured to the Hudson Bay twice before (and having brought a camera in 1913), went again with backing from a fur company. He returned with a majestic portrait of man's battle with the elements. The video release features an original score recorded by the Tashi Ensemble under the direction of Peter Serkin. Selected as a National Film Registry Outstanding Film. **Credits:** Dir: Robert Flaherty. B&W, 69 min. **VHS**

The Narrow Corner
(1933) Warner Bros.
In this adaptation of a Maugham story, Fairbanks, Jr., plays a man who commits a murder in Australia, then flees to open seas. When his ship puts in at a remote island, he meets an eccentric British family and falls in love with the daughter (Ellis). She's engaged (to poor benighted Bellamy, of course), and their blossoming affair

Nanook of the North (1922)

leads to suicide, which again points the finger at Fairbanks. Remade as *Isle of Fury* (1936) with Humphrey Bogart. **Cast:** Douglas Fairbanks, Jr., Patricia Ellis, Dudley Digges, Ralph Bellamy, Arthur Hohl, Henry Kolker, Willie Fung, Reginald Owen, William V. Mong, Josef Swickard. **Credits:** Dir: Alfred E. Green; Prod: Hal B. Wallis; Writer: Robert Presnell Sr.,; Story: W. Somerset Maugham; DP: Tony Gaudio; Ed: Bert Levy. B&W, 71 min.

Nashville
(1975) Paramount
Altman's bold masterpiece is a marvel of film structure, following 24 characters throughout the course of one weekend in Nashville, Tennessee, without losing track of their motivations or story lines. Both a major music festival and a political rally for a shadowy candidate are on the weekend's agenda. For some, like nervous rodeo sweetheart Blakley, it means a comeback; for folkie lothario Carradine, more women to bed; for waitressing wannabe Welles, the scene is a shot at stardom; for Chaplin, the BBC telejournalist, it's a curious microcosm of American society. Standouts also include Gibson as a country superstar and Tomlin as the unhappy wife of promoter Beatty. Features a superb sound track with songs written by the actors. Assistant director Alan Rudolph went on to his own idiosyncratic career as director. Selected for the National Film Registry. Academy Award Nominations: 6, including Best Picture; Best Director; Best (Adapted) Screenplay; Best Supporting Actress: Ronee Blakley; Best Supporting Actress: Lily Tomlin. **Academy Awards:** Best Song ("I'm Easy"). **Cast:** Henry Gibson, Lily Tomlin, Ronee Blakley, Keith Carradine, Geraldine Chaplin, Gwen Welles, Ned Beatty, Barbara Harris, Karen Black, Dave Peel. **Credits:** Dir: Robert Altman; Prod: Robert Altman; Writer: Joan Tewkesbury; DP: Paul Lohmann; Ed: Sidney Levin, Dennis Hill; Composer: Richard Baskin. Color, 159 min. **VHS, LASER**

National Velvet
(1944) MGM
Here is the poignant story of Velvet Brown (a 12-year-old Taylor), a young working-class girl who wins a horse in a raffle and, with the help of a skittish, gun-shy ex-jockey (Rooney), trains it to enter the prestigious Grand National race. When their jockey pulls out, Velvet disguises herself as a boy and rides to victory in a thrilling race sequence. This uplifting adaptation of

Bagnold's novel features stunning photography of coastal England. Academy Award Nominations: 5, including Best Director; Best (Color) Cinematography. **Academy Awards:** Best Supporting Actress: Anne Revere; Best Film Editing. **Cast:** Elizabeth Taylor, Mickey Rooney, Donald Crisp, Anne Revere, Angela Lansbury, Jackie Jenkins, Arthur Treacher, Reginald Owen, Terry Kilburn, Norma Varden. **Credits:** Dir: Clarence Brown; Prod: Pandro S. Berman; Writer: Theodore Reeves, Helen Deutsch; Story: Enid Bagnold; DP: Leonard Smith; Ed: Robert J. Kern; Prod Design: Cedric Gibbons, Urie McCleary; Composer: Herbert Stothart; Costumes: Irene; SFX: Warren Newcombe. Color, 125 min. **VHS, LASER, DVD**

Naughty Marietta
(1935) MGM
This is the film debut of the movie operetta team of Eddy and MacDonald. A French mademoiselle is scheduled to be married to a Spaniard against her will. Instead, she swaps destinies with her maid, who is soon to board ship for New Orleans. When pirates attack the ship and carry off the lovelies, scouts led by Eddy come to the rescue. MacDonald gives him the once-over, but he's off in a flash. Later, he repents his error and searches for his true love in New Orleans. Featuring over a thousand extras and elaborate sets, this box-office smash tickled the fancy of the times. Hard to figure now. Academy Award Nominations: 2, including Best Picture. **Academy Awards:** Best Sound Recording. **Cast:** Jeanette MacDonald, Nelson Eddy, Frank Morgan, Elsa Lanchester, Douglas Dumbrille, Joseph Cawthorn, Cecilia Parker, Walter Kingsford. **Credits:** Dir: W. S. Van Dyke; Prod: Hunt Stromberg; Writer: John Lee Mahin, Frances Goodrich, Albert Hackett; Story: Victor Herbert, Rida Johnson Young; DP: William Daniels; Ed: Blanche Sewell; Prod Design: Cedric Gibbons. B&W, 106 min. **VHS, LASER**

Navy Blue and Gold
(1937) MGM
Stewart is the center on Navy's football team. When false rumors spread about his late father, Stewart stands up in class to offer the truth. He gets suspended for his insubordination, and the team leaves for the season's big game against Army without him. He is pardoned just in time to join his teammates for the play that wins the game. **Cast:** Robert Young, James Stewart, Florence Rice, Billie Burke,

Lionel Barrymore, Tom Brown, Samuel S. Hinds, Paul Kelly. **Credits:** Dir: Sam Wood; Prod: Sam Zimbalist; Writer: George Bruce; DP: John Seitz; Ed: Robert J. Kern; Prod Design: Cedric Gibbons, Urie McCleary; Composer: Edward Ward; Set Designer: Edwin B. Willis. B&W, 94 min. **VHS**

Navy Blues
(1941) Warner Bros.
This screwball musical at sea has two wise-guy sailors, Oakie and Haley, trying to trick farm-boy Anderson into winning the marksmanship contest for their ship. Since his stint in the navy is up before the contest day, the two persuade him to sign up again with the lovely Sheridan, who ends up melting for the big lug. Meanwhile, Oakie's old lady Raye shows up fighting mad. Songs include "In Waikiki," "You're a Natural," "Navy Blues," and "When Are We Going to Land Abroad?" **Cast:** Ann Sheridan, Jack Oakie, Martha Raye, Jack Haley, Herbert Anderson, Jack Carson, William Orr, Jackie Gleason, John Ridgely, Howard Da Silva. **Credits:** Dir: Lloyd Bacon; Prod: Jack Saper; Writer: Richard Macaulay, Sam Perrin, Jerry Wald; Story: Arthur T. Horman; DP: Tony Gaudio, James Wong Howe, Sol Polito; Ed: Rudi Fehr; Prod Design: Robert M. Haas; Composer: Leo F. Forbstein, Johnny Mercer, Arthur Schwartz. B&W, 109 min.

Nazi Agent
(1942) MGM
This Dassin WWII propaganda picture has Veidt playing German-born twins. One, a vicious Nazi, extorts the aid of the other, a democratic, upstanding American citizen, in an espionage plot. But the good brother kills his evil twin and takes his place in the Third Reich. **Cast:** Conrad Veidt, Anne Ayars, Frank Reicher, Dorothy Tree, Ivan Simpson, William Tannen, Martin Kosleck, Marc Lawrence, Sidney Blackmer, Moroni Olsen. **Credits:** Dir: Jules Dassin; Prod: Irving Asher; Writer: Paul Gangelin, John Meehan; Story: Lothar Mended; DP: Harry Stradling; Ed: Frank E. Hull; Composer: Lennie Hayton. B&W, 83 min.

Neptune's Daughter
(1949) MGM
A bathing-suit designer (Williams, of course) fights off wolfish Montalban, while her sister (Garrett) sets her sights on masseur Skelton, who she believes to be fabulously wealthy. Mostly an excuse for singing, dancing, and aquatic sports. **Academy Awards:** Best Song ("Baby, It's Cold Outside").

Cast: Esther Williams, Red Skelton, Keenan Wynn, Ricardo Montalban, Betty Garrett, Mel Blanc, Frank Mitchell, Matt Moore, Richard Simmons. Credits: Dir: Edward Buzzell; Prod: Jack Cummings; Writer: Dorothy Kingsley, Raymond Singer; DP: Charles Rosher; Ed: Irving Warburton; Prod Design: Cedric Gibbons; Art Director: Edward C. Carfagno. Color, 94 min. VHS, LASER

Network

(1976) United Artists
Chayefsky prophetically, scathingly satirizes the lurid depths to which TV will sink for ratings (though he must be in writers' heaven chuckling about the current craze for true-crime, surveillance-camera specials). A ruthless network executive (Dunaway) realizes a news anchorman (Finch), driven crazy by the plunge in standards and full of righteous indignation, is worth more to her crazy than sane (his cri de coeur, "I'm mad as hell, and I'm not going to take it anymore," makes a brilliant on-air promo). News veteran Holden is the weary voice of sanity as he watches the business (and the woman) he loves sink deeper into the morass. TV veteran Chayefsky is a master of portraying the madness of institutions (see *Hospital*, 1971), and here his script is prevented from slipping into mere parody by Lumet and the cast. Finch died soon after the production. Academy Award Nominations: 10, including Best Picture; Best Director; Best Actor: William Holden. Academy Awards: Best Actor: Peter Finch; Best Actress: Faye Dunaway; Best Supporting Actress: Beatrice Straight; Best Screenplay Written Directly for the Screen. Cast: Faye Dunaway, William Holden, Peter Finch, Robert Duvall, Wesley Addy, Ned Beatty, Beatrice Straight, Arthur Burghardt, Bill Burrows, Jordan Charney. Credits: Dir: Sidney Lumet; Prod: Howard Gottfried; Writer: Paddy Chayefsky; DP: Owen Roizman; Ed: Alan Heim; Composer: Elliot Lawrence. Color, 122 min. VHS, LASER, DVD

Nevada Smith

(1966) Paramount
In this prequel to *The Carpetbaggers*, also by beach-novel auteur Robbins, McQueen is the future cowboy star who searches for his parents' killer with the help of sharpshooter Keith. Believed to be based on '30s cowboy-movie star Ken Maynard. Featuring edge-of-your-seat action scenes and spectacular footage of northern California. Cast: Steve McQueen, Karl

Malden, Brian Keith, Suzanne Pleshette, Arthur Kennedy, Howard Da Silva, Martin Landau, Paul Fix, Gene Evans. Credits: Dir: Henry Hathaway; Prod: Henry Hathaway; Writer: John Michael Hayes; Story: Harold Robbins; DP: Lucien Ballard; Ed: Frank Bracht; Composer: Alfred Newman; Art Director: Hal Pereira, Tambi Larsen, Al Roelofs. Color, 139 min. VHS, LASER

Never Fear

(1950) Eagle-Lion
This well-made melodrama was Lupino's first film as director. Forrest and Brasselle, partners in both romance and dance, see a promising career and a happy marriage before them as they celebrate a successful premiere on the Los Angeles nightclub circuit. Then Forrest is tragically stricken with polio, wrecking their plans, and despite Brasselle's unwavering affections, the couple breaks apart under the stress of Forrest's ailment. The stricken dancer turns inward, but finds the strength to rehabilitate herself and her relationship. Cast: Sally Forrest, Keefe Brasselle, Hugh O'Brian, Eve Miller, Larry Dobkin, Rita Lupino, Herbert Butterfield, Red Dawson, Stanley Waxman, Jerry Housner. Credits: Dir: Ida Lupino; Prod: Collier Young; Writer: Ida Lupino, Collier Young; DP: Archie Stout; Ed: William Ziegler, Harvey Manger; Composer: John Franco, William Earley. B&W, 81 min.

Never Give a Sucker an Even Break

(1941) Universal
Fields's best days were behind him and he knew it, so he let go with a vicious satire of the movie business for his last starring role. Fields essentially plays himself (he's billed as The Great Man; he even inserts a scene in which kids make fun of his last release, *The Bank Dick*) as he goes about trying to get his film made. Hilarious and pointed. Cast: W. C. Fields, Margaret Dumont, Gloria Jean, Leon Errol, Anne Nagel, Franklin Pangborn, Mona Barrie, Susan Miller, Charley Lang, Nell O'Day. Credits: Dir: Edward Cline; Writer: John T. Neville, Prescott Chaplin; Story: W. C. Fields; DP: Charles Van Engler; Ed: Arthur Hilton; Composer: Frank Skinner. B&W, 71 min. VHS, LASER

Never Let Me Go

(1953) MGM
Gable and Haydn unite in postwar Moscow to fight the communist forces that prevent their respective Russian

wives from leaving the country with them. The battling husbands buy a boat and arrange a rendezvous somewhere in the Baltic. Gable proves his love for Tierney, a comely ballerina, by single-handedly besting the Reds and snatching her right from the theater. But wouldn't you if you were married to Tierney? Cast: Clark Gable, Gene Tierney, Bernard Miles, Richard Haydn, Kenneth More, Belita, Theodore Bikel, Anton Dolin. Credits: Dir: Delmer Daves; Prod: Clarence Brown; Writer: Ronald Millar, George Froeschel; Story: Roger Bax; DP: Robert Krasker; Ed: Frank Clarke; Composer: Hans May. B&W, 94 min. VHS

Never on Sunday

(1960) United Artists
Writer-director Dassin also costars as Homer, an American in Piraeus. He loves everything Greek, including the local prostitute (played by his wife, Mercouri), who is proud of her career choice. She works hard throughout the week but reserves Sunday for watching Greek plays. He tries to change her ways, but in the end it's Homer who sees her profession in a new light. Golden Globe for Special Achievement. Academy Award Nominations: 5, including Best Director; Best Actress: Melina Mercouri. Academy Awards: Best Song ("Never On Sunday"). Cast: Melina Mercouri, Jules Dassin, Tito Vandis, George Foundas, Despo Diamantidou, Dimitris Papamichael, Mitsos Liguisos, Dimos Starenios, Alexis Salomos. Credits: Dir: Jules Dassin; Prod: Jules Dassin; Writer: Jules Dassin; DP: Jacques Natteau; Ed: Roger Dwyer; Composer: Manos Hadjidakis; Costumes: Denny Vachlioti. B&W, 94 min. VHS

Never Say Die

(1939) Paramount
A confusion of his test results with those of a dog convinces neurotic rich man Hope that he is about to die. He falls in love with Texas oil heiress Raye, who loves poor Devine. Hope comes up with a simple plan that will make everyone happy: marry Raye, die, and leave her all his money and the freedom to follow her heart with Devine. They marry and honeymoon, with Devine along for the ride. Just when the plan seems to be falling into place, Hope realizes the mistake. Cast: Bob Hope, Martha Raye, Andy Devine, Alan Mowbray, Gale Sondergaard, Sig Rumann, Ernest Cossart, Paul Harvey, Frances Arms, Ivan Simpson. Credits: Dir: Elliott Nugent; Prod: Paul Jones; Writer: Don Hartman,

Frank Butler, Preston Sturges; Story: William Post, Jr.; DP: Leo Tover; Ed: James Smith; Composer: Boris Morros; Art Director: Hans Dreier, Ernst Fegte. B&W, 80 min.

Never So Few
(1959) MGM
Action director Sturges (*The Magnificent Seven*, 1960) presents the story of 600 U.S. guerrilla fighters who take on 40,000 Japanese troops in WWII Burma. Sinatra leads a successful mission, but when his troops are attacked by a Chinese warlord, he follows the trail into China and discovers double-dealing. He attacks despite orders not to and faces a court-martial. This is vintage Sinatra and gave a significant boost to McQueen and Bronson. **Cast:** Frank Sinatra, Gina Lollobrigida, Peter Lawford, Steve McQueen, Charles Bronson, Dean Jones, Philip Ahn, John Hoyt. **Credits:** Dir: John Sturges; Prod: Edmund Grainger; Writer: Millard Kaufman; Story: Tom T. Chamales; DP: William Daniels; Ed: Ferris Webster; Prod Design: Hans Peters, Addison Hehr; Composer: Hugo Friedhofer. Color, 125 min. VHS

Never Steal Anything Small
(1958) Universal
In his last musical, Cagney stars as a not-so-honest union official who stops at nothing to win an election—and the wife of an attorney (Jones) against whom he trumps up charges. You don't see many singing and dancing stevedore-union bosses these days. **Cast:** James Cagney, Shirley Jones, Cara Williams, Roger Smith, Royal Dano, Anthony Caruso, Virginia Vincent, Bob Wilke. **Credits:** Dir: Charles Lederer; Prod: Aaron Rosenberg; Writer: Charles Lederer; Story: Maxwell Anderson; DP: Harold Lipstein; Ed: Russell Schoengarth; Composer: Allie Wrubel; Art Director: Alexander Golitzen, Robert Clatworthy. Color, 94 min. VHS

The New Centurions
(1972) Columbia
The gritty realism of ex-cop Joseph Wambaugh's crime saga makes gripping viewing. The story teams rookie cop and law student Keach with veteran Scott and his "ends justifying the means" police work. The stresses of front-line policing cause emotional wreckage: Keach's marriage to Alexander dissolves, Keach is seriously wounded, and Scott retires, only to commit suicide. Keach finds a new love, but tragedy awaits. Watch for soon-to-be television stars Estrada,

James, and Sanford. **Cast:** George C. Scott, Stacy Keach, Jane Alexander, Rosalind Cash, Isabel Sanford, Scott Wilson, Erik Estrada, Clifton James. **Credits:** Dir: Richard Fleischer; Prod: Irwin Winkler, Robert Chartoff; Writer: Stirling Silliphant; DP: Ralph Woolsey; Ed: Robert C. Jones; Prod Design: Boris Leven; Composer: Quincy Jones. Color, 103 min. VHS, LASER

A New Kind of Love
(1963) Paramount
Newsman Newman meets up with Woodward (twice) in the City of Lights in this gossamer romantic comedy. Woodward barely rates a second glance from Newman as a department-store spy in Paris to copy designs, but when she dons a wig and becomes an exotic, erotic call girl, Newman's profile of her hits the front page as she steals his heart. The fashion setting is sumptuous as are the designs by Dior, Saint-Laurent, Lanvin, and Cardin, and studio stalwart Head, who won an Oscar nomination. Academy Award Nominations: 2, including Best (Adapted) Score; Best (Color) Costume Design. **Cast:** Paul Newman, Joanne Woodward, Maurice Chevalier, Thelma Ritter, Eva Gabor, George Tobias, Marvin Kaplan, Robert Clary. **Credits:** Dir: Melville Shavelson; Prod: Melville Shavelson; Writer: Melville Shavelson; DP: Daniel Fapp; Ed: Frank Bracht; Composer: Leith Stevens, Erroll Garner; Art Director: Hal Pereira, Arthur Lonergan; Costumes: Edith Head. Color, 110 min. VHS

The New Moon
(1940) MGM
MacDonald and Eddy hit the high seas heading for New Orleans (in what amounts to a second run around the block for *Naughty Marietta*). She's a noblewoman on her way to claim a plantation, he's a nobleman disguised as a servant on the lam from the king. Guess who falls in love? Songs include: "One Kiss," "Lover Come Back to Me," and more. **Cast:** Jeanette MacDonald, Nelson Eddy, Mary Boland, George Zucco, H. B. Warner, Grant Mitchell, Stanley Fields, Claude King. **Credits:** Dir: Robert Z. Leonard; Prod: Robert Z. Leonard; Writer: Jacques Deval, Robert Arthur; DP: William Daniels; Ed: Harold F. Kress; Prod Design: Cedric Gibbons; Composer: Sigmund Romberg; Art Director: Eddie Imazu. B&W, 106 min. VHS, LASER

New Orleans
(1947) United Artists
The history of jazz in New Orleans gets a glossy, romanticized treatment

in a film mostly notable for the only feature-length performance by Holiday and multiple numbers by Armstrong. The forgettable story involves a rich woman who falls in love with a man running a gambling operation and with the jazz music that he plays in his club. Flashbacks recount how the gambler tried to popularize jazz. **Cast:** John Alexander, Louis Armstrong, Charles Beale, Red Callendat, Arturo De Cordova, Richard Hageman, Billie Holiday, Woody Herman, Dorothy Patrick, Irene Rich. **Credits:** Dir: Arthur Lubin; Prod: Jules Levey; Writer: Herbert J. Biberman, Dick Irving Hyland, Elliot Paul; DP: Lucien N. Andriot; Ed: Bernard W. Burton; Composer: Nathaniel Finston; Art Director: Rudi Feld. B&W, 89 min.

New York, New York
(1977) United Artists
Scorsese's take on the backstage nightclub musical has all the genre conventions but with uncompromising, unsparing work from director and cast. The story follows hard-headed sax player De Niro and singer Minnelli as they meet, hook up on the road, become lovers, spouses, and parents, and then drift apart and nearly back together again as their careers diverge. Threaded through the story is the story of the decline of the big bands and the rise of pop and small-combo jazz. The nightclub world is beautifully rendered as are the musical set pieces (the restored video has footage from a performance center-piece that was cut from the initial release). This deserves a bigger audience. The special edition video release includes the shooting script illustrated with the director's notes, trailers, interviews, director's commentary, and deleted footage including a different, more upbeat ending. **Cast:** Liza Minnelli, Robert De Niro, Lionel Stander, Georgie Auld, Mary Kay Place, George Memmoli, Barry Primus, Dick Miller, Diahnne Abbott. **Credits:** Dir: Martin Scorsese; Prod: Irwin Winkler, Robert Chartoff; Writer: Earl Mac Rauch, Mardik Martin; DP: Laszlo Kovacs; Ed: Irving Lerner, Marcia Lucas, Bert Lovitt, David Ramirez, Tom Rolf; Prod Design: Boris Leven; Composer: Ralph Burns. Color, 165 min. VHS, LASER

New York Town
(1941) Paramount
Down on his luck, but determined to make it big, MacMurray shares a run-down apartment with art professor Tamiroff. When his path crosses that

of Martin, a beautiful young innocent alone in the Big Apple, he takes her in and offers to help her get settled—with a rich man. Running through a list of eligible bachelors, MacMurray finally gets Martin hooked up with wealthy Preston, only to discover that he is now in love with her himself. Routine, but among the infrequent screen roles for Martin. **Cast:** Fred MacMurray, Mary Martin, Akim Tamiroff, Robert Preston, Lynne Overman, Eric Blore, Fuzzy Knight, Cecil Kellaway, Edward McNamara. **Credits:** Dir: Charles Vidor; Prod: Anthony Veiller; Writer: Lewis Meltzer, Preston Sturges, Jo Swerling; DP: Charles Edgar Schoenbaum; Ed: Doane Harrison; Prod Design: Hans Dreier, William Pereira; Composer: Leo Shuken. B&W, 94 min.

The Next Man
(1976) Allied Artists
Connery is vaguely Bondian in this spy thriller enlivened by great shots of locales ranging from New York to Bavaria and Morocco, not to mention the lovely Sharpe. Connery plays an Arab diplomat attempting to broker a peace settlement with Israel, and Sharpe is the sexy assassin hired by Arab extremists to kill him. While this is all too familiar, not every assassin looks like Sharpe and not every diplomat is Connery, and they reach their own very amicable settlement. **Cast:** Sean Connery, Cornelia Sharpe, Albert Paulsen, Adolfo Celi, Charles Cioffi, Salem Ludwig, Tom Klunis, Michael Storm. **Credits:** Dir: Richard C. Sarafian; Prod: Martin Bregman; Writer: Morton Fine, Alan R. Trustman, David S. Wolf, Richard C. Sarafian; DP: Michael Chapman; Ed: Aram Avakian, Robert Q. Lovett; Prod Design: Gene Callahan; Composer: Michael Kamen. Color, 108 min. **VHS**

Next Time We Love
(1936) Universal
This sudsy melodrama features an unusually glum Stewart and an uncredited script by Sturges. Stewart and Sullavan are a married couple who often find their personal ambition stronger than their love. He is a writer who travels to Rome on assignment; she is an actress with dreams of Broadway. While in Rome, he finds out she is pregnant and races home to be with his wife, getting fired in the process. After a short time starting all over again, the discontented Stewart goes back to work in Rome. His best friend Milland lends a hand to Sullavan's acting ambitions and finally

Niagara (1953)

reveals that he is in love with the actress. He asks for her hand in marriage, and the wife goes to the husband to sort things out. He confesses he is dying of a terminal illness, and she tearfully commits to be by his side until the end. **Cast:** Margaret Sullavan, James Stewart, Ray Milland, Grant Mitchell, Anna Demetrio, Robert McWade, Florence Robert, Christian Rub, Hattie McDaniel. **Credits:** Dir: Edward H. Griffith; Prod: Paul Kohner; Writer: Melville Baker, Preston Sturges; Story: Ursula Parrott; DP: Joseph A. Valentine; Ed: Ted J. Kent; Prod Design: Charles D. Hall; Composer: Franz Waxman. B&W, 87 min.

The Next Voice You Hear
(1950) MGM
An oddity that plays better than it sounds, this message picture asks what would happen if God decides to make Himself known to the world through a series of radio broadcasts.

The focus is on "every couple" Whitmore and Davis (the future Mrs. Reagan), and the suddenly altered dynamic of their happy world. Wellman's masterful hand guided this picture to completion in three weeks and $200,000 under budget. **Cast:** James Whitmore, Nancy Davis, Lillian Bronson, Jeff Corey, Gary Gray, Art Smith, Tom D'Andrea, George Chandler. **Credits:** Dir: William Wellman; Prod: Dore Schary; Writer: Charles Schnee; DP: William Mellor; Ed: John Dunning; Prod Design: Cedric Gibbons; Composer: David Raksin; Art Director: Eddie Imazu. B&W, 85 min. **VHS**

Niagara
(1953) Fox
In a Niagara Falls honeymoon motel, the voluptuous, seductive Monroe plots to murder her older husband, the decidedly creepy Cotten. A newlywed couple (Peters and Adams) observe the comings and goings, his fits, her infidelities, and finally begin to suspect

the murder plot when a death occurs, but not to the expected party. This was the film (her 18th) that launched Monroe into Hollywood superstardom. **Cast:** Marilyn Monroe, Joseph Cotten, Jean Peters, Casey Adams, Richard Allan, Don Wilson, Max Showalter, Denis O'Dea, Lurene Tuttle, Russell Collins. **Credits:** Dir: Henry Hathaway; Prod: Charles Brackett; Writer: Charles Brackett; DP: Joseph MacDonald; Ed: Barbara McLean; Prod Design: Lyle Wheeler; Composer: Sol Kaplan. Color, 89 min. VHS, LASER

Nice Girl?
(1941) Universal
Durbin plays a young woman with a crush on an older professor (Tone) visiting her family's suburban home. She schemes to spend time alone with him in an attempt to leave her "nice girl" image behind, but he manages to fend off the girl's romantic advances. When he is unable to keep rumors about the pair from spreading, he returns to set the record straight. Includes the songs "Love at Last" and "Perhaps." The video release includes an alternate ending. **Cast:** Deanna Durbin, Franchot Tone, Robert Stack, Walter Brennan, Robert Benchley, Helen Broderick, Ann Gillis, Anne Gwynne. **Credits:** Dir: William A. Seiter; Prod: Joe Pasternak; Writer: Richard Connell; DP: Joseph A. Valentine; Ed: Bernard W. Burton; Composer: Charles Previn; Art Director: Jack Otterson. B&W, 99 min. VHS

Nick Carter
Detective Nick Carter sprung to life in the 1880s and appeared in hundreds of short stories, pulp-magazine stories, and novels before his big-screen career began in the silents. He never made much of an impact on audiences until MGM cast Walter Pidgeon in 1939's *Nick Carter—Master Detective* as the suave sleuth. The series only lasted for three well-made, fast-paced installments, enough time for the amateur gumshoe to get mixed up with espionage, sabotage, and Nazi spies. Donald Meek's oddball Bartholomew, the Bee-Man, whom Carter reluctantly used as an assistant, often upstaged Pidgeon.

Nick Carter—Master Detective *(1939)*
Phantom Raiders *(1940)*
Sky Murder *(1940)*

Nickelodeon
(1976) Columbia
A gift to film fans from director Bogdanovich recalls the early days of motion pictures. Ryan O'Neal plays a lawyer who accidentally begins a career as a director, Reynolds is a roustabout turned leading man, and Tatum O'Neal portrays an industrious country girl who rents equipment to film companies. Watch for Ritter in one of his earliest roles, as a cameraman who teaches direction to Tatum O'Neal. **Cast:** Ryan O'Neal, Burt Reynolds, Tatum O'Neal, Brian Keith, Stella Stevens, John Ritter, Frank Marshall. **Credits:** Dir: Peter Bogdanovich; Prod: Irwin Winkler, Robert Chartoff; Writer: Richard Hazard, W. D. Richter; DP: Laszlo Kovacs; Ed: William C. Carruth; Prod Design: Richard Berger; Composer: Richard Hazard. Color, 121 min.

Night After Night
(1932) Paramount
In Raft's first leading role and West's first talkie, Raft is a creep with more cash than class. Looking to break into the upper crust, he opens a nightclub on the very spot where downtrodden Cummings's family mansion once stood. Raft arranges a quiet dinner for the two at his club, which is crashed by (among several others) Raft's old flame, West, who steals the show. **Cast:** Mae West, George Raft, Constance Cummings, Wynne Gibson, Alison Skipworth, Roscoe Karns, Louis Calhern, Bradley Page. **Credits:** Dir: Archie Mayo; Prod: William LeBaron; Writer: Vincent Lawrence; DP: Ernest Haller. B&W, 73 min. VHS

Night and Day
(1946) Warner Bros.
Grant portrays Cole Porter in this biopic about the composer's life from his early days at Yale and in WWI through his successful music career on the stage and the screen. Highlighted by Martin's performance of "My Heart Belongs to Daddy." Academy Award Nominations: Best Scoring of a Musical. **Cast:** Cary Grant, Alexis Smith, Monty Woolley, Ginny Simms, Jane Wyman, Mary Martin, Eve Arden, Victor Francen, Alan Hale. **Credits:** Dir: Michael Curtiz; Prod: Arthur Schwartz; Writer: Michael Hoffman; DP: Peverell Marley; Ed: David Weisbart; Choreographer: Leroy Prinz; Composer: Max Steiner; Art Director: John Hughes. Color, 128 min. VHS

Night and the City
(1950) Fox
This film–noir landmark uncompromisingly depicts the tawdry ambitions and inevitable bad ends of the lowlife hustlers who populate the underworld. Widmark is outstanding as a hustler working for London nightclub owner Sullivan, who has big ideas of his own. Using everyone he knows, including his true love Tierney and his mistress (and boss's wife) Withers, he puts together his big play, a wrestling match that ends in death and with him on the run from gangster Lom. **Cast:** Richard Widmark, Gene Tierney, Herbert Lom, Francis L. Sullivan, Hugh Marlowe, Googie Withers, Stanislaus Zbyszko, Mike Mazurki, Charles Farrell. **Credits:** Dir: Jules Dassin; Prod: Samuel G. Engel; Writer: Jo Eisinger; Story: Gerald Kersh; DP: Mutz Greenbaum; Ed: Sidney Stone, Nick DeMaggio; Composer: Franz Waxman; Art Director: C. P. Norman. Color, 104 min. VHS

A Night at the Opera
(1935) MGM
Probably the finest hour in the Marx Brothers' stellar career, this was their first film for MGM and their first without Zeppo. It was assembled after Irving Thalberg's dictate that the show go on the road before it went in front of the cameras. The result was a polished, blissful union of critical and commercial smash. It features the seminal Marx Brothers juxtapositions of high society and absurdly crooked con men, in this case Groucho trying to waylay the fortune of perennial nemesis Dumont by persuading her to invest in an opera company. The stowaways in the jammed stateroom scene is one of the greatest bits of comedy ever put on film. **Cast:** Groucho Marx, Harpo Marx, Chico Marx, Kitty Carlisle, Allan Jones, Sig Rumann, Walter Woolf King, Margaret Dumont, Edward Keane, Gino Corrado, Claude Payton, Samuel Marx. **Credits:** Dir: Sam Wood; Prod: Irving Thalberg; Writer: George S. Kaufman, Morrie Ryskind, Al Boasberg, Bert Kalmar, Harry Ruby, James Kevin McGuinness; DP: Merritt Gerstad; Ed: William Le Vanway; Prod Design: Cedric Gibbons; Composer: Herbert Stothart; Art Director: Ben Carre. B&W, 92 min. VHS, LASER

Night Club Scandal
(1937) Paramount
Barrymore plays a cunning doctor who suspects that his wife is having an affair. He murders her and arranges the scene to implicate his wife's lover, Naish. While the police ignore his protests, dedicated reporter Overman comes to suspect a setup and embarks on his own investigation. Remake of early talkie *Guilty as Hell* (1932). **Cast:** John Barrymore, Lynne

Overman, Louise Campbell, Charles Bickford, Harvey Stevens, J. Carrol Naish, Evelyn Brent, Elizabeth Patterson, Cecil Cunningham, Barlowe Borland. **Credits:** Dir: Ralph Murphy; Writer: Lillian Hayward; Story: Daniel N. Rubin; DP: Leo Tover; Ed: Archie Marshek; Prod Design: A. Earl Hedrick; Composer: Boris Morros. B&W, 70 min.

Night Has a Thousand Eyes
(1948) Paramount
In this film noir with a bizarre supernatural twist, Robinson is a psychic whose visions haunt him with lurid images of suicide and tragedy. The frequency and accuracy of his second sight makes him a suspect when a friend dies in a plane crash. Robinson's horrible visions free him from jail, prove his innocence, and then bring about his own demise. Based on a story by Woolrich. **Cast:** Edward G. Robinson, Gail Russell, John Lund, Virginia Bruce, William Demarest, Richard Webb, Jerome Cowan, Onslow Stevenson, John Alexander, Roman Bohnan. **Credits:** Dir: John Farrow; Prod: Andre Bohem; Writer: Cornell Woolrich, Barre Lyndon, Jonathan Latimer; DP: John Seitz; Ed: Eda Warren; Composer: Victor Young; Art Director: Hans Dreier, Franz Bachelin. B&W, 80 min.

A Night in Casablanca
(1946) United Artists
It's not *A Night at the Opera*, but as James Agee said, "the worst thing they might ever make would be better worth seeing than most other things I can think of." Groucho is the new manager of the Casablanca Hotel. Several previous managers have been bumped off by a sadistic Nazi, who also happens to be Harpo's employer. Harpo's gags were orchestrated by Tashlin, director of *The Girl Can't Help It* (1956) and *Will Success Spoil Rock Hunter?* (1957). **Cast:** Groucho Marx, Harpo Marx, Chico Marx, Lisette Verea, Charles Drake, Lois Collier, Sig Rumann, Dan Seymour, Lewis L. Russell. **Credits:** Dir: Archie Mayo; Prod: David Loew; Writer: Joseph Fields, Roland Kibbee, Frank Tashlin; DP: James Van Trees; Ed: Gregg C. Pallas; Composer: Werner Janssen. B&W, 85 min. **VHS**

Night into Morning
(1951) MGM
Milland is a college professor who loses his family in a sudden violent accident while he's teaching. Unable to come to grips with his tragedy, he begins a slow spiral downward lubricated by a mixture of drink and depression. With the help of friends Hodiak and Davis (Mrs. Reagan), he climbs back from the precipice. **Cast:** Dawn Addams, Ray Milland, John Hodiak, Nancy Davis, Lewis Stone, Jean Hagen, Rosemary DeCamp, Jonathan Cott, Gordon Gebert, Katharine Warren. **Credits:** Dir: Fletcher Markle; Prod: Edwin H. Knopf; Writer: Karl Tunberg, Leonard Spigelgass; DP: George Folsey, Jr.; Ed: George White, Robert Watts; Composer: Carmen Dragon; Art Director: Cedric Gibbons, James Basevi. B&W, 86 min.

Nightmare Alley
(1947) Fox
Here is a truly horrific story of degradation and greed, with a most unusual role for dashing leading-man type Power. He plays a carnival barker who becomes part of a mind-reading act with veterans Blondell and Keith. Power learns that the carnival's alcoholic geek—the guy who bites heads off of live chickens—once had a spectacular mind-reading act. After seducing both Blondell and a young sideshow assistant (Gray), Power marries Gray, moves to Chicago, and starts up a nightclub act in which he reads fortunes. He begins to con rich people, at one point convincing his wife to pretend to be the ghost of a rich man's wife, a pitiful scene that makes Gray break down and reveal the hoax. Broken, outcast, Power hits the bottle and winds up back at the carny—as the geek. **Cast:** Tyrone Power, Joan Blondell, Coleen Gray, Helen Walker, Taylor Holmes, Mike Mazurki, Ian Keith, Julia Dean, James Flavin, Roy Roberts. **Credits:** Dir: Edmund Goulding; Prod: George Jessel; Writer: Jules Furthman; Story: William Lindsay Gresham; DP: Lee Garmes; Ed: Barbara McLean; Composer: Cyril Mockridge, Lionel Newman; Art Director: J. Russell Spencer, Lyle Wheeler. B&W, 111 min.

Night Moves
(1975) Warner Bros.
Hackman is a private eye in trouble in this updated film noir directed by Penn. He earns his living from petty divorce actions and runaway-children complaints and finds that when he gets his first big case, he really doesn't know what to do. Hired by Ward, an actress, to track down her runaway daughter (the debut for 17-year-old

Nightmare Alley (1947)

Griffith), the trail leads him to the Florida Keys, and back again when the young girl is killed in a movie stunt. An unusual take on the private-eye genre with a detective who's always a step behind. **Cast:** Gene Hackman, Susan Clark, Jennifer Warren, Janet Ward, Melanie Griffith, Edward Binns, Kenneth Mars, James Woods, Anthony Costello, John Crawford. **Credits:** Dir: Arthur Penn; Prod: Robert M. Sherman; Writer: Alan Sharp; DP: Bruce Surtees; Ed: Dede Allen; Prod Design: George Jenkins; Composer: Michael Small. Color, 100 min. **VHS**

Night Must Fall
(1937) MGM
This fantastic thriller is adapted from Emlyn Williams's play. Montgomery is terrifying as the creepy visitor toting a heavy hatbox. When he suddenly shows up at Whitty's cottage, Russell begins to suspect he's connected with the disappearance of a female guest from a nearby inn. But she's the only one, as his charm seems to prevent anyone from seeing the truth. But when Whitty turns up dead, Russell knows who to look for—and what's in the hatbox. Academy Award Nominations: Best Actor: Robert Montgomery; Best Supporting Actress: Dame May Whitty. **Cast:** Robert Montgomery, Rosalind Russell, Dame May Whitty, Alan Marshal, Merle Tottenham, Kathleen Harrison, Matthew Boulton, Eily Malyon, E. E. Clive. **Credits:** Dir: Richard Thorpe; Prod: Hunt Stromberg; Writer: John Van Druten; DP: Ray June; Ed: Robert J. Kern; Prod Design: Cedric Gibbons; Composer: Edward Ward. B&W, 105 min. **VHS**

Night Nurse
(1931) Warner Bros.
A rich woman's two children are the sole beneficiaries of a family fortune, so she and Gable, her greedy chauffeur boyfriend, plan to starve the kids and spend the fortune. Stanwyck is a nurse in the house who gets wind of their murderous intentions, and then finds her own life at risk when Blondell encourages her to go to the police. Just to show he's serious, Gable gives her a pop on the kisser. Stanwyck comes back with an armed bootlegger (Lyon) in tow. Pre-Code potboiler with plenty of peeps at Stanwyck and Blondell, and Gable taking a turn at the Warner Bros. gangster routine. **Cast:** Barbara Stanwyck, Joan Blondell, Clark Gable, Ben Lyon, Charles Winninger, Eddie Nugent, Blanche Frederici, Allan "Rocky" Lane. **Credits:** Dir: William Wellman; Writer:

Oliver H. P. Garrett; DP: Barney McGill; Ed: E. M. McDermott; Prod Design: Max Parker; Costumes: Earl Luick. B&W, 73 min. **VHS**

The Night of the Hunter
(1955) United Artists
In this eerie meditation on good and evil, a murderous "preacher" with the elemental forces of "love" and "hate" tattooed on each hand relentlessly hunts two small children across the Depression-era Bible Belt to get at their dead father's stolen fortune. He marries then kills their mother (Winters), and the children flee on a nighttime river odyssey to the protection of Gish. In the only directorial effort by Laughton (from a screenplay by Agee), Mitchum turns in the performance of his career, with Gish as costar and camerawork by Cortez, of *The Magnificent Ambersons* (1942). A dreamlike parable laced with stunningly orchestrated symbolism. Despite current critical acclaim, it was a box-office flop and was nominated for no Academy Awards. Selected for the National Film Registry. **Cast:** Robert Mitchum, Shelley Winters, Lillian Gish, Peter Graves, Evelyn Varden, Gloria Castillo, Don Beddoe, Billy Chapin, James Gleason, Sally Jane Bruce. **Credits:** Dir: Charles Laughton; Prod: Paul Gregory; Writer: James Agee; Story: Davis Grubb; DP: Stanley Cortez; Ed: Robert Golden; Composer: Walter Schumann; Costumes: Jerry Bros. B&W, 94 min. **VHS, LASER**

The Night of the Iguana
(1964) MGM
Huston's adaptation of the Tennessee Williams play is a sometimes confounding, sometimes penetrating film. A defrocked, dissolute Burton squires teachers around Mexico while getting into hot water over a romantic dalliance with a much younger Lyon (in her first role after *Lolita*). Gardner crackles as the hotel owner who tries to keep him from being torn in two by heaven and earth, but he meets poor, wandering artist Kerr and begins a romantic triangle with her and Gardner. The tour leaves, followed by Kerr, and moral exhaustion or inertia holds Burton and Gardner together at the hotel. Academy Award Nominations: 4, including Best Supporting Actress: Grayson Hall; Best Cinematography. **Academy Awards:** Best Costume Design (B&W). **Cast:** Richard Burton, Deborah Kerr, Ava Gardner, Sue Lyon, Grayson Hall, James Ward, Cyril Delevanti, Emilio Fernandez, Mary Boylan, Gladys Hill. **Credits:** Dir: John Huston;

Prod: Ray Stark; Writer: Anthony Veiller, John Huston; DP: Gabriel Figueroa; Ed: Ralph Kemplen; Composer: Benjamin Frankel; Art Director: Stephen Grimes. B&W, 125 min. **VHS**

Night of the Living Dead
(1968) Continental
In this grisly benchmark of American horror film, the dead return and terrorize the living. A group of strangers seek refuge in an abandoned house by locking themselves inside. The living dead slowly penetrate the fortress, killing friends and relatives in search of a good meal. Followed by a sequel (so hilariously graphic it briefly earned an X-rating) entitled *Dawn of the Dead* (1978) and remade in 1990. **Cast:** Judith O'Dea, Russell Streiner, Duane Jones, Keith Wayne, Karl Hardman. **Credits:** Dir: George A. Romero; Prod: Russell W. Streiner, Karl Hardman; Writer: John A. Russo; Story: George Romero; DP: George Romero; Ed: George Romero; Prod Design: Vincent Survinski. B&W, 96 min. **VHS, LASER, DVD**

Night Passage
(1957) Universal
Two brothers (Stewart and Murphy) run on opposite sides of the law. Murphy's a gunslinging train robber and Stewart's been enlisted to get the payroll to the end of the line. The rotten brother's gang holds the train up and Stewart has to track him down. This was meant to be a Mann-Stewart Western, but the director didn't like the looks of the script. **Cast:** James Stewart, Audie Murphy, Dan Duryea, Dianne Foster, Elaine Stewart, Brandon De Wilde, Jay C. Flippen, Herbert Anderson, Robert J. Wilke. **Credits:** Dir: James Nielson; Prod: Aaron Rosenberg; Writer: Borden Chase, Norman Fox; DP: William Daniels; Ed: Sherman Todd; Composer: Dimitri Tiomkin. Color, 90 min.

The Night They Raided Minsky's
(1968) United Artists
TV legend Lear produced and cowrote the screenplay for this comedic story of the birth of striptease. Robards wants to thumb his nose at decency groups by hyping dancer Ekland as a stripper—when all she actually intends to do is an interpretive dance of the Bible (!). The best-laid plans go awry as Ekland's Amish father appears and rips her dress trying to drag her away just as the cops burst in. Rudy Vallee is the singing narrator. An early effort by a young Friedkin.

Cast: Jason Robards, Britt Ekland, Norman Wisdom, Forrest Tucker, Harry Andrews, Joseph Wiseman, Denholm Elliott, Jack Burns, Bert Lahr, Elliott Gould. **Credits:** Dir: William Friedkin; Prod: Norman Lear; Writer: Arnold Schulman, Norman Lear, Sidney Michaels; DP: Andrew Laszlo; Ed: Ralph Rosenblum; Composer: Charles Strouse; Art Director: John Lloyd. Color, 100 min. VHS

Night Tide
(1961) AIP
This creepy tale of obsession has Hopper as a sailor on leave who falls for an orphan girl working as a mermaid in a California sideshow. She believes she is descended from sea creatures who must kill on the full moon. **Cast:** Dennis Hopper, Linda Lawson, Luana Anders, Gavin Muir, Marjorie Eaton, Tom Dillon, Bruno Ve Sota. **Credits:** Dir: Curtis Harrington; Prod: Aram Kantarian; Writer: Curtis Harrington; DP: Vilis Lapenieks; Ed: Jodie Copelan; Prod Design: Paul Mathison; Choreographer: Benjamin Zemach; Composer: David Raksin. B&W, 87 min. VHS, LASER

A Night to Remember
(1943) Columbia
Aherne does a turn reminiscent of TV's *Murder, She Wrote* as a whodunit author whose wife, ably played by Young, convinces him that a change of scene will help him switch genres and finish that romance novel he's been working on. But life doggedly imitates art as their backyard becomes the center of a murder investigation, and Aherne follows the impulse to solve the crime himself. **Cast:** Loretta Young, Brian Aherne, Sidney Toler, Gale Sondergaard, Jeff Donnell, William Wright, Donald MacBride, Lee Patrick. **Credits:** Dir: Richard Wallace; Prod: Samuel Bischoff; Writer: Richard Flournoy, Jack Henley; DP: Joseph Walker; Ed: Charles Nelson; Composer: Werner Richard Heymann; Art Director: Lionel Banks. B&W, 91 min. VHS

The Night Walker
(1964) Universal
Bloch was the author of *Psycho* and producer-director Castle was notorious for sensationalized effects, but the film failed to live up to its promise. Stanwyck is married to Rorke, a blind genius who is jealous of her dreams of another lover. Rorke's killed in an accident, and Stanwyck is propelled by her dreams into an eerie world of paranoia and murderous duplicity, where Taylor, who offed Rorke, and private eye Bochner are both trying to kill her. Stanwyck and Taylor were husband and wife at the time. **Cast:** Barbara Stanwyck, Robert Taylor, Lloyd Bochner, Hayden Rorke, Judi Meredith, Rochelle Hudson, Marjorie Bennett, Jess Barker. **Credits:** Dir: William Castle; Prod: William Castle; Writer: Robert Bloch; DP: Harold E. Stine; Ed: Edwin Bryant; Prod Design: Alexander Golitzen; Composer: Vic Mizzy; Art Director: Julia Heron. B&W, 86 min. VHS

Night Without Sleep
(1952) Fox
Waking from a hangover with the feeling he has done something awful, volatile composer Merrill tries to remember the details of the night before. He quarreled with his wife (Vincent) as she prepared to leave town. He quarreled with his mistress (Neff). He also met a friend, lovely actress Darnell, at a party. After phoning both the actress and his mistress and finding them in one piece, he makes his way upstairs and suddenly recalls what happened. He murdered his wife: Doh! **Cast:** Linda Darnell, Gary Merrill, Hildegarde Neff, Joyce MacKenzie, June Vincent, Don Randolph, Hugh Beaumont, Louise Lorimer, William Forrest, Steven Geray. **Credits:** Dir: Roy Ward Baker; Prod: Robert Bassler; Writer: Frank Partos, Elick Moll; DP: Lucien Ballard; Ed: Nick DeMaggio; Composer: Cyril Mockridge. B&W, 77 min.

Night World
(1932) Universal
This taut little early-talkie thriller features three early roles for actors who had just completed career-defining roles: Karloff in *Frankenstein,* Raft in *Scar-Face,* and Ayres in *All Quiet on the Western Front*—and with Berkeley's choreography! Among the denizens of Karloff's nightclub are a wealthy young drunk (Ayres) with family problems (i.e., his mother callously murdered his father), Clarke as a dancer who would love him away from the clutches of gangster Raft, and Karloff's own wife (Revier), who is in love with a producer. **Cast:** Lew Ayres, Mae Clarke, Boris Karloff, George Raft, Dorothy Revier, Russell Hopton, Bert Roach, Dorothy Peterson, Hedda Hopper, Paisley Noon. **Credits:** Dir: Hobart Henley; Prod: Carl Laemmle; Writer: Richard Schayer; Story: P. J. Wolfson, Allen Rivkin; DP: Merritt Gerstad; Ed: Maurice Pivar; Choreographer: Busby Berkeley; Composer: Alfred Newman. B&W, 60 min.

Nikki—Wild Dog of the North
(1961) Disney
In this engrossing blend of nature film and family adventure a pair of animal pals, a wild dog and a bear cub, fight for survival in the Canadian wilderness when the pup gets separated from his master. **Cast:** Jean Coutu, Emile Genest, Uriel Luft, Don Haldane. **Credits:** Dir: Jack Couffer; Prod: Walt Disney; Writer: Winston Hibler; DP: Lloyd Beebe; Ed: Grant K. Smith; Composer: Oliver Wallace. Color, 73 min. VHS

Ninotchka
(1939) MGM
"Garbo Laughs!" The cool beauty's first comedy was a triumph and she never looked more beautiful or performed so gracefully. When the Soviet Union sends a committee to Paris to exchange royal jewels for tractors, former Russian Grand Duchess Claire dispatches her lover and a former count (Douglas) to liberate her diamonds. He successfully corrupts the comrades and the Soviets send in a secret weapon, the utterly humorless, businesslike Garbo. Douglas goes to work showing her the delights of capitalist life and of love, and, though he loses the battle for the jewels, wins her heart. Directed with a light touch by Lubitsch from a sparkling script by Wilder and Brackett. Remade as *Comrade X* (1940) with Clark Gable and Hedy Lamarr, and *Iron Petticoat* (1956) with Katharine Hepburn and Bob Hope. Selected for the National Film Registry. Academy Award Nominations: 4, including Best Picture; Best Actress: Greta Garbo; Best Original Story. **Cast:** Greta Garbo, Melvyn Douglas, Bela Lugosi, Ina Claire, Sig Rumann, Felix Bressart, Alexander Granach, Gregory Gaye, Dorothy Adams. **Credits:** Dir: Ernst Lubitsch; Prod: Ernst Lubitsch; Writer: Charles Brackett, Billy Wilder, Walter Reisch; DP: William Daniels; Ed: Gene Ruggiero; Prod Design: Cedric Gibbons; Composer: Werner Richard Heymann. B&W, 155 min. VHS, LASER

Nob Hill
(1945) Fox
In turn-of-the-century San Francisco, Raft runs a Gold Coast saloon and has a relationship with his singer, Blaine. When Garner, a young Irish girl, arrives on the scene in search of

> "[Hitchcock] said, 'I don't want you going back to sink-to-sink movies. You do movies where you wash the dishes looking drab in an apron. The audience wants to see their leading ladies dressed up.' He saw me as others didn't."
>
> Eva Marie Saint on Alfred Hitchcock

her dead uncle, Raft looks after her and she introduces him to Bennett, a society gal from Nob Hill. While the romance has its ups and downs, Garner does her best to keep her newly adopted parents together. Standard fare done well with plenty of nostalgic music, including "I Don't Care Who Knows It," "San Francisco," and "Chinatown, My Chinatown." **Cast:** George Raft, Joan Bennett, Vivian Blaine, Peggy Ann Garner, Alan Reed, B. S. Pully, Emil Coleman, Edgar Barrier, George Anderson, Don Costello. **Credits:** Dir: Henry Hathaway; Prod: Andre Daven; Writer: Norman Raine, Wanda Tuchock; DP: Edward Cronjager; Ed: Harmon Jones; Prod Design: Lyle Wheeler, J. Russell Spencer; Composer: David Buttolph. B&W, 95 min.

Nobody Lives Forever
(1946) Warner Bros.
This early Negulesco film noir ranges the country from New York to California. Garfield, an ex-gambler with Mob ties, returns home from the war to find that his girlfriend has taken all of his money and left town with another man. He collects interest from his gambling cronies and leaves for California. When he encounters his former crime boss, he gets embroiled in a plot to swindle a young widow (Fitzgerald). Garfield falls in love with her instead, and saves his new love from his former partners. **Cast:** John Garfield, Geraldine Fitzgerald, Walter Brennan, Faye Emerson, George Coulouris, George Tobias, Robert Shayne, Richard Gaines, James Flavin, Ralph Peters. **Credits:** Dir: Jean Negulesco; Prod: Robert Buckner; Writer: W. R. Burnett; DP: Arthur Edeson; Ed: Rudi Fehr; Prod Design: Hugh Reticker; Composer: Adolph Deutsch, Jerome Morros. B&W, 100 min.

Nocturne
(1946) RKO
Frequent Hitchcock writer Harrison produced this tight little noir with Raft a detective that won't let the death of a composer go. When the department rules the death a suicide, Raft continues his investigation even after the police force suspends him. He targets Bari, one of the composer's many mistresses, and then falls for her. She leads him to the real killer, who reveals himself with a musical clue. **Cast:** George Raft, Lynn Bari, Virginia Huston, Joseph Pevney, Myrna Dell, Edward Ashley, Walter Sande, Mabel Paige, Queenie Smith, Mack Gray. **Credits:** Dir: Edwin L. Marin; Prod: Joan Harrison; Writer: Jonathan Latimer; DP: Harry Wild; Ed: Elmo Williams; Prod Design: Robert Boyle; Composer: Leigh Harline; Art Director: Albert S. D'Agostino, Robert Boyle. B&W, 88 min. **VHS**

No Down Payment
(1957) Fox
Ritt's second feature depicts the lives led by wage slaves who live from paycheck to paycheck in the faceless suburbs created by the postwar housing boom. Though the houses look the same, the lives within are twisted with economic woes, marriages on the rocks, alcoholism, even rape and murder. **Cast:** Joanne Woodward, Sheree North, Tony Randall, Jeffrey Hunter, Cameron Mitchell, Patricia Owens, Barbara Rush, Pat Hingle, Robert Harris. **Credits:** Dir: Martin Ritt; Prod: Jerry Wald; Writer: Philip Yordan, John McPartland; DP: Joseph La Shelle; Ed: Louis Loeffler; Composer: Leigh Harline. B&W, 105 min.

No Highway in the Sky
(1951) Fox
Stewart plays an eccentric scientist who theorizes that Britain's new Rein-deer airplanes will disintegrate after 1440 hours in the air. Finding himself aboard one of the planes as it is reaching the stress point, he manages to convince an actress onboard (Dietrich) of their danger. Based on Shute's novel. **Cast:** James Stewart, Marlene Dietrich, Glynis Johns, Jack Hawkins, Janette Scott. **Credits:** Dir: Henry Koster; Prod: Louis D. Lighton; Writer: R. C. Sherriff, Oscar Millard, Alec Coppel; Story: Nevil Shute; DP: Georges Perinal; Ed: Manuel Del Campo; Costumes: Christian Dior; Art Director: C. P. Norman. B&W, 98 min. **VHS**

No Man of Her Own
(1933) Paramount
This romantic comedy pairs the future Mr. and Mrs. Gable for the first time on-screen. When gambler Gable hides out in a small town, he marries the sweet local librarian (Lombard) as cover, then falls for her. When his past catches up to him, he comes clean to protect Lombard and she continues to adore him. The chemistry between the stars was real and clearly visible. **Cast:** Clark Gable, Carole Lombard, Dorothy Mackaill, Grant Mitchell, George Barbier, Elizabeth Patterson, J. Farrell MacDonald, Tommy Conlon, Walter Walker, Paul Ellis. **Credits:** Dir: Wesley Ruggles; Prod: Albert E. Lewis; Writer: Maurine Watkins, Milton H. Gropper; DP: Leo Tover; Costumes: Travis Banton. B&W, 81 min. **VHS, LASER**

No Name on the Bullet
(1959) Universal
The townfolk of a tranquil hamlet out West get a shock when notorious hired gun Murphy blows into town. They assume he's there for a killing, but they anxiously try to discover who the intended victim is. Tense Western with unexpected final showdown. **Cast:** Audie Murphy, Charles Drake, Joan Evans, Virginia Grey, Warren Stevens, R. G. Armstrong, Karl Swenson, Charles Watts, Whit Bissell. **Credits:** Dir: Jack Arnold; Prod: Jack Arnold, Howard Christie; Writer: Gene L. Coon; DP: Harold Lipstein; Ed: Frank Gross; Composer: Herman Stein. Color, 77 min. **VHS**

None but the Brave
(1965) Warner Bros.
A battle of wits and weapons ensues and unlikely alliances are forged when a crashed planeload of U.S. Marines and a Japanese army platoon are all stranded on a tiny South Pacific island during WWII. Notable only as Sinatra's

producing and directing debut. **Cast:** Frank Sinatra, Clint Walker, Tommy Sands, Brad Dexter, Tony Bill, Sammy Jackson, Tatsuya Mihashi, Takeshi Kato. **Credits:** Dir: Frank Sinatra; Prod: Frank Sinatra; Writer: John Twist, Katsuya Suzaki; DP: Harold Lipstein; Ed: Sam O'Steen; Composer: Johnny Williams; SFX: Eiji Tsuburaya; Set Designer: George James Hopkins. Color, 106 min. **VHS, LASER**

None but the Lonely Heart
(1944) RKO
Odets wrote and directed this unsparing melodrama that depicts the bond of love and devotion in the face of hopeless poverty. Grant is a carefree ne'er-do-well in London's slums, barely on speaking terms with his mother, Barrymore, who runs a secondhand furniture shop. When he learns that she is soon to die, he becomes a devoted son, working in the shop and caring for her. They develop a real bond, and, in order to see that her son is taken care of, Barrymore starts getting involved with some of Grant's former criminal companions. Academy Award Nominations: 4, including Best Actor: Cary Grant. **Academy Awards:** Best Supporting Actress: Ethel Barrymore. **Cast:** Cary Grant, Ethel Barrymore, Barry Fitzgerald, Jane Wyatt, June Duprez, George CouEdouris, Dan Duryea, Konstantin Shayne, Morton Lowry, Helene Thimig. **Credits:** Dir: Clifford Odets; Prod: David Hempstead; Writer: Clifford Odets; DP: George Barnes; Ed: Roland Gross; Prod Design: Mordecai Gorelik; Composer: Hanns Eisler; Art Director: Albert S. D'Agostino, Jack Okey. B&W, 113 min. **VHS, LASER**

None Shall Escape
(1944) Columbia
Crippled during WWI, Knox returns to his village embittered and angry. Taking up his old job as teacher, Knox tries to live his life as he did before the war but things have changed irrevocably. Seduced by the ideologies of the growing Nazi Party, he grows more and more hate-filled, losing his fiancée in the process. When accused of sexually assaulting a young girl, he is forced to leave his own town, but vows revenge and returns years later as a high-ranking Nazi official to carry it out. **Cast:** Marsha Hunt, Alexander Knox, Henry Travers, Eric Rolf, Richard Crane, Dorothy Morris, Richard Hale, Ruth Nelson, Kurt Kreuger, Shirley Mills. **Credits:** Dir: Andre De Toth; Prod: Sam Bischoff; Writer: Lester

Cole; Story: Alfred Neumann, Joseph Than; DP: Lee Garmes; Ed: Charles Nelson; Prod Design: Lionel Banks; Composer: Ernst Toch. B&W, 85 min.

Norma Rae
(1979) Fox
This updated social-problem film by Ritt, a master of the genre, has a sterling script by Ravetch and Frank. Field won an Oscar for her portrayal of a cotton-mill worker who matures as she shoulders the burden of waking up her fellow workers to the need for a union. Bridges, as her jealous new husband, and Leibman, as the union organizer, are fine in support. Golden Globe for Best Actress (Drama): Sally Field. Academy Award Nominations: 4, including Best Picture; Best (Adapted) Screenplay. **Academy Awards:** Best Actress: Sally Field; Best Song. **Cast:** Sally Field, Ron Leibman, Beau Bridges, Pat Hingle, Barbara Baxley, Gail Strickland, Morgan Paull, John Calvin, Booth Colman, Bob Minor. **Credits:** Dir: Martin Ritt; Prod: Tamara Asseyev, Alex Rose; Writer: Irving Ravetch, Harriet Frank, Jr., Jr.; DP: John A. Alonzo; Prod Design: Walter Scott Herndon; Composer: David Shire; Art Director: Tracy Bousman; Set Designer: Gregory Garrison. Color, 117 min. **VHS, LASER**

No Room for the Groom
(1952) Fox
In a rare Sirk comedy, a newlywed couple tries in vain to be together in a house filled with relatives. Curtis, a G.I., elopes with the object of his affection (Laurie) and is shipped to Korea soon after the nuptials. Upon his return, his home is loaded with relatives who have no idea he is now a married man. The antics revolve around breaking the news of the wedding, a mother-in-law who wants to fix her daughter up with another man, and a couple who simply cannot find room to be alone. **Cast:** Tony Curtis, Piper Laurie, Don Defore, Spring Byington, Lillian Bronson, Paul McVey, Stephan Chase, Lee Aeker, Jack Kelly, Frank Sully. **Credits:** Dir: Douglas Sirk; Prod: Ted Richmond; Writer: Joseph Hoffman, Darwin L. Teilher; DP: Clifford Stine; Ed: Russell Schoengarth; Composer: Frank Skinner. B&W, 82 min.

North Avenue Irregulars
(1979) Disney
This lively Disney comedy is about six churchgoing ladies who team up with a new pastor (Herrmann) to fight crime when Kelly loses their church

funds to a bookie. **Cast:** Edward Herrmann, Barbara Harris, Karen Valentine, Susan Clark, Michael Constantine, Cloris Leachman, Patsy Kelly, Douglas Fowley. **Credits:** Dir: Bruce Bilson; Prod: Ron Miller, Tom Leetch; Writer: Don Tait; DP: Leonard J. South; Ed: Gordon D. Brenner; Prod Design: John B. Mansbridge; Composer: Robert F. Brunner; Art Director: Jack Collis. Color, 99 min. **VHS**

North by Northwest
(1959) MGM
This is one of Hitchcock's greatest, with suspense, action, and comedy in one non-stop motion picture. In one of his patented ordinary-man-in-exceptional-circumstances plots, advertising executive Grant gets kidnapped from a business engagement and winds up in a baffling, twisting battle with enemy agents and on the run from both police and the agents. This technically superb film yielded some of Hitchcock's best-known images: the crop duster bearing down on Grant in a remote cornfield, Grant and Saint dangling from Mt. Rushmore, Saint's frank seduction of Grant on a train. Essential viewing. The laserdisc includes an audio commentary by Frank Danielle, dean of USC Film School, with special screenplay analysis. Academy Award Nominations: 3, including Best (Original) Screenplay. **Cast:** Cary Grant, Eva Marie Saint, James Mason, Leo G. Carroll, Jessie Royce Landis, Philip Ober, Josephine Hutchinson, Martin Landau. **Credits:** Dir: Alfred Hitchcock; Prod: Alfred Hitchcock; Writer: Ernest Lehman; DP: Robert Burks; Ed: George Tomasini; Prod Design: William A. Horning; Composer: Bernard Herrmann; Art Director: Merrill Pye. Color, 136 min. **VHS, LASER**

North Dallas Forty
(1979) Paramount
This screen adaptation of former Dallas wide receiver Gent's best-selling novel about a team's relationship with a troublesome player (Nolte) is one of the greatest gridiron movies ever made. Though he begins to see the game for what it is and knows that he can't play the off-the-field games, Nolte longs for the Sunday action. Winning debut for Davis. **Cast:** Nick Nolte, Charles Durning, Bo Svenson, Mac Davis, John Matuszak, Dabney Coleman, Steve Forrest, Brian Dennehy, Dayle Haddon. **Credits:** Dir: Ted Kotcheff; Prod: Frank Yablans; Writer: Frank Yablans, Ted Kotcheff, Peter Gent; DP: Paul Lohmann; Ed: Jay

Kamen; Prod Design: Alfred Sweeney; Composer: John Scott. Color, 119 min. **VHS, LASER**

Northern Lights

(1979) Cine Manifest
Based on the real-life diaries of Ray Sorenson, this is a tale of Swedish immigrant farmers in 1915 North Dakota struggling to save their farms, families, and way of life from the elements and the powers that control both commerce and government. **Cast:** Joe Spano, Robert Behling, Susan Lynch, Henry Martinson, Marianna Astrom-De Fina, Ray Ness, Helen Ness, Thorbjorn Rue. **Credits:** Dir: John Hanson, Rob Nilsson; Prod: John Hanson, Rob Nilsson; Writer: John Hanson, Rob Nilsson; DP: Judy Irola; Ed: John Hanson, Rob Nilsson. Color, 96 min. **VHS**

Northern Pursuit

(1943) Warner Bros.
Dashing Flynn stars as a Canadian Mountie with German parents who poses as a traitor in an attempt to infiltrate a Nazi spy ring. Filmed on location in Canada by Walsh. **Cast:** Errol Flynn, Julie Bishop, Helmut Dantine, John Ridgely, Gene Lockhart, Tom Tully, Bernard Nedell, Warren Douglas, Monte Blue. **Credits:** Dir: Raoul Walsh; Prod: Jack Chertok; Writer: Frank Gruber, Alvah Bessie; DP: Sid Hickox; Ed: Jack Killifer; Composer: Adolph Deutsch; Art Director: Leo K. Kuter. B&W, 94 min. **VHS**

The North Star

(1943) RKO
President Franklin Roosevelt initiated this project with a personal plea to depict the gallant Soviet defense against the Nazis. His son James was president of Goldwyn Studios and Hellman developed a screenplay, ultimately directed by Milestone and shot by Howe, with a very impressive cast, including the debut of Granger. The story focused on the tenacious defense of a village near Kiev by a group of citizen-partisans against barbarous Nazis. However, Hellman's work was altered and the movie condemned by the Hearst organization as Bolshevist. The film was then savaged by HUAC in the 1950s, mangled, and rereleased in 1957 as *Armored Command* with every use of the word "comrade" carefully deleted. Academy Award Nominations: 6, including Best Original Screenplay. **Cast:** Anne Baxter, Dana Andrews, Walter Huston, Ann Harding, Erich von Stroheim, Farley Granger, Jane Withers, Eric Roberts. **Credits:** Dir: Lewis Milestone; Prod: William Cameron Menzies; Writer: Lillian Hellman; DP: James Wong Howe; Ed: Daniel Mandell; Prod Design: McClure Capps; Composer: Aaron Copland; Art Director: Perry Ferguson. B&W, 154 min. **VHS**

North to Alaska

(1960) Fox
Hathaway and Wayne seem to have a rollicking good time winking at their rough-and-tough Western images with this uproarious comedy Western. Having struck it rich in the gold fields of Alaska, Wayne heads to Seattle for supplies and to pick up his partner, Granger's fiancée. Discovering her married already, he heads to a brothel to select a substitute (Capucine).

Along the way, they fall in love, which sets off a battle royal upon their return to Nome. **Cast:** John Wayne, Stewart Granger, Ernie Kovacs, Fabian, Capucine, Mickey Shaughnessy, Karl Swenson, Joe Sawyer, Kathleen Freeman. **Credits:** Dir: Henry Hathaway; Prod: Henry Hathaway; Writer: John Lee Mahin, Martin Rackin, Claude Binyon; DP: Leon Shamroy; Ed: Dorothy Spencer; Choreographer: Josephine Earle; Composer: Lionel Newman; Art Director: Duncan Cramer, Jack Martin Smith. Color, 120 min. **VHS, LASER**

Northwest Mounted Police

(1940) Paramount
History according to DeMille and his first excursion into Technicolor. This carefully manicured action-adventure takes place in the deep forests and expansive mountains of the Canadian Northwest (really a pine forest built by DeMille on the Paramount backlot). The Canadian Riel Rebellion, an uprising by half-breed rebels and Indians, rages in the background as Texas Ranger Cooper comes looking for murderer Bancroft. He moves in with the red-coated Mounted Police and attracts the attention of both Mountie Foster's girl Carroll and the half-breed temptress Goddard. Academy Award Nominations: 5, including Best Cinematography. **Academy Awards:** Best Editing. **Cast:** Gary Cooper, Madeleine Carroll, Paulette Goddard, Preston Foster, Robert Preston, George Bancroft, Lynne Overman, Akim Tamiroff, Walter Hampden, Lon Chaney, Jr. **Credits:** Dir: Cecil B. DeMille; Prod: Cecil B. DeMille; Writer: Jesse Lasky, Jr., Alan LeMay, C. Gardner Sullivan; Story: R. C. Fetherstonhaugh; DP: W. Howard Greene, Victor Milner; Ed: Anne Bauchens; Prod Design: Roland Anderson, Hans Dreier; Composer: Victor Young. Color, 125 min.

Northwest Passage

(1940) MGM
In 1759, real-life pioneer Major Robert Rogers (Tracy) and his band of Rangers set out to blaze a trail from the colonies to the Pacific Ocean. Cartoonist Young turns into a mapmaker and learns the ways of the frontier when he signs on with Tracy's troops and their battle with French-backed Indians. A masterwork from director Vidor based on the novel by Kenneth Roberts. Academy Award Nomination for Best (Color) Cinematography. **Cast:** Spencer Tracy, Robert Young, Walter Brennan, Ruth Hussey, Nat Pendleton,

Capra's Reel War

War pictures are a staple of the Hollywood film diet, of course. But perhaps the most important American war pictures weren't made in Hollywood at all; they were made by Maj. Frank Capra in Washington for the Defense Department during World War II. Capra's "Why We Fight" series is hailed as one of his greatest achievements, yet Capra was initially reluctant to take the job. At Capra's first meeting with Gen. George C. Marshall, the Chief of Staff told him that he wanted to make a series of films that would explain to the troops why and for which principles they were fighting. The director protested, "General Marshall, it's only fair to tell you that I've never made a documentary film. In fact, I've never even been near anybody that made one." "Capra," the General interrupted, "I have never been Chief of Staff before. Thousands of young Americans have never had their legs shot off before. Boys are commanding ships today who a year ago had never seen the ocean before." "I'm sorry, sir," the chastened director replied, "I'll make the best damned documentary films ever made."

Robert Barrat, Lumsden Hare, Donald MacBride. **Credits:** Dir: King Vidor; Prod: Hunt Stromberg; Writer: Laurence Stallings, Talbot Jennings; DP: Sidney Wagner, William V. Skall; Ed: Conrad A. Nervig; Prod Design: Cedric Gibbons; Composer: Herbert Stothart. Color, 127 min. vhs

No Sad Songs for Me
(1950) Columbia
A real weeper, this follows the story of a young mother (Sullavan) who learns that she has cancer and only six months to live. Sullavan decides to hide her condition from her husband (Quine), choosing to enjoy her last months as much as possible. Already pregnant, she prepares to bring another child into the world while she contemplates leaving her husband and daughter (Wood) behind. And in a final show of nobility, she encourages Lindfors, recipient of her husband's occasional flirting attention, to remain to comfort him after she is gone. **Cast:** Margaret Sullavan, Richard Quine, Jeanette Nolan, Dorothy Tree, Raymond Greenleaf, Wendell Corey, Viveca Lindfors, Natalie Wood, John McIntire, Ann Doran. **Credits:** Dir: Rudolph Maté; Prod: Buddy Adler; Writer: Ruth Southard, Howard W. "Hawk" Koch, Jr.; DP: Joseph Walker; Ed: William A. Lyon; Composer: George Duning; Art Director: Cary O'Dell. B&W, 89 min.

Not as a Stranger
(1955) United Artists
Mitchum and Sinatra as callow young interns (!) star in this weeper. Mitchum needs money to stay in med school, so he marries wealthy nurse de Havilland. They move to a small town where he becomes insufferable and takes up with wealthy patient Grahame. He gets his comeuppance when he fails to save Bickford on the operating table. Academy Award Nomination for Best Sound Recording. **Cast:** Olivia de Havilland, Robert Mitchum, Frank Sinatra, Charles Bickford, Gloria Grahame, Broderick Crawford, Lee Marvin, Lon Chaney, Harry Morgan, Virginia Christine. **Credits:** Dir: Stanley Kramer; Prod: Stanley Kramer; Writer: Edna Anhalt, Edward Anhalt; DP: Franz Planer; Ed: Frederic Knudtson; Prod Design: Rudolph Sternad; Composer: George Antheil. Color, 136 min. vhs

Nothing but a Man
(1964) Cinema 5
An African-American railroad worker in the '60s South endeavors to make a life for himself despite adversities.

The story follows Dixon as he meets a preacher's daughter (Lincoln) and moves with her to Birmingham, where he faces racism and frustration. He eventually reunites with his illegitimate son and with Lincoln. A powerful, independently made film. *Nothing but a Man* was a crowd favorite at the 1964 New York Film Festival. Selected as a National Film Registry Outstanding Film. **Cast:** Ivan Dixon, Abbey Lincoln, Gloria Foster, Yaphet Kotto, Julius Harris, Martin Priest, Leonard Parker, Stanley Greene, Helen Lounck. **Credits:** Dir: Michael Roemer; Prod: Robert Young, Michael Roemer, Robert Rubin; Writer: Michael Roemer; DP: Robert Young; Ed: Luke Bennett. B&W, 92 min. vhs, laser

Nothing but the Truth
(1941) Paramount
Hope plays a mild-mannered stockbroker who has a problem with the truth—he never seems able to speak it. A compulsive liar, he enters a wager that he can tell the truth, and nothing but the truth, for 24 hours straight. As the stakes get higher and higher, Hope's fiancée Goddard ups the bets by placing $10,000 on his ability to be truthful. Remade with Jim Carrey as *Liar Liar* in 1996. **Cast:** Bob Hope, Paulette Goddard, Edward Arnold, Leif Erickson, Helen Vinson, Willie Best, Glenn Anders, Grant Mitchell, Catharine Doucet, Rose Hobart. **Credits:** Dir: Elliott Nugent; Prod: Arthur Hornblow, Jr.; Writer: Ken Englund, Don Hartman; Story: James Montgomery, Frederic S. Isham; DP: Charles Lang; Ed: Alma Macrorie; Prod Design: Hans Dreier, Robert Usher; Composer: Andrea Setaro. B&W, 90 min.

Nothing Sacred
(1937) United Artists
This is one of the great screwball comedies and a clever satire on all-too-relevant tabloid frenzy. Screenwriter Hecht borrowed from his experience as a Chicago newspaperman to create the March character, a tabloid reporter not afraid to create a little news if none comes his way. His editor (Connolly) busts him to the obits when he discovers one such ruse. March finds a way back to the front page with the story of Hazel Flagg (Lombard, in her best-loved role), a Vermont girl whose rural doctor makes a grim diagnosis of radioactive poisoning. Though the doctor changes his mind, March smells a story and Lombard's fate grips New York. March gets her to go along by promising to show her the big city, which he does in grand style. When

the ruse wears thin, the two, now in love, make a splendid getaway. Great fun throughout and not a moment wasted. Remade in 1954 as *Living It Up* with Martin and Lewis. The DVD edition includes Gable and Lombard home movies and short subjects. **Cast:** Carole Lombard, Fredric March, Walter Connolly, Charles Winninger, Sig Rumann, Frank Fay, Maxie Rosenbloom, Margaret Hamilton. **Credits:** Dir: William Wellman; Prod: David O. Selznick; Writer: Ben Hecht; DP: W. Howard Greene; Ed: Hal C. Kern; Prod Design: Lyle Wheeler; Composer: Oscar Levant. Color, 100 min. vhs, laser, dvd

No Time for Comedy
(1940) Warner Bros.
Stewart is an unassuming young playwright who travels to New York for some last revisions to his successful play, where he falls in love and marries the leading actress (Russell). After a string of four successful comedies, he becomes the toast of the town and a snobby sophisticate. His wife's rival convinces him he is wasting his time on "light material" and should take on more serious drama. But after the failure of Stewart's "serious play," the playwright realizes his true callings—in both genre and in love. Pleasant enough and with winning performances by Stewart and Russell. **Cast:** James Stewart, Rosalind Russell, Charlie Ruggles, Genevieve Tobin, Louise Beavers, Allyn Joslyn, Clarence Kolb, Robert Greig, J. M. Kerrigan, Lawrence Grosmith. **Credits:** Dir: William Keighley; Prod: Hal B. Wallis, Jack Warner; Writer: Julius J. Epstein, Philip G. Epstein; Story: S. N. Behrman; DP: Ernest Haller; Ed: Owen Marks; Composer: Heinz Roemheld. B&W, 98 min.

No Time for Flowers
(1952) RKO
Cold War claptrap (made with government cooperation) about the secretary (Lindfors) to a Czech communist official who tempts her with American comforts such as gowns and champagne to determine her party loyalty. They fall in love and flee Czechoslovakia for the American zone of Austria. **Cast:** Viveca Lindfors, Paul Christian, Ludwig Stossel, Adrienne Gessner, Peter Preses, Manfred Inger, Peter Czeyke, Frederick Berger, Oscar Wegostrek, Helmut Janatsch. **Credits:** Dir: Don Siegel; Prod: Mort Briskin; Writer: Lasio Vadnay, Hans Wilheim; DP: Toni Braun; Ed: Arthur Nadel; Composer: Herschel Burke Gilbert. B&W, 83 min.

No Time for Love

(1943) Paramount
This Leisen-directed comedy of manners stars Paramount's winning comedy team of Colbert and MacMurray. Colbert's a New York City photographer with an assignment to photograph men digging a tunnel under the Hudson River. There she meets MacMurray, a burly laborer dripping sweaty blue-collar appeal. When her photographs of this Superman slugging a coworker are published, he's suspended, and the guilt-stricken Colbert offers him a job as her assistant. Colbert learns to love the hunk and is jealous of his flirtation with model Havoc. She comes to the rescue of his career as an engineer when her photographs help demonstrate his tunneling device. Academy Award Nomination: Best Art Direction. **Cast:** Claudette Colbert, Fred MacMurray, Ilka Chase, Richard Haydn, Paul McGrath, June Havoc, Marjorie Gateson. **Credits:** Dir: Mitchell Leisen; Prod: Mitchell Leisen, Fred Kohlmar; Writer: Claude Binyon, Warren Duff; Story: Robert Lees, Frederic I. Rinaldo; DP: Charles Lang; Ed: Alma Macrorie; Prod Design: Hans Dreier, Robert Usher; Composer: Victor Young. B&W, 83 min.

Notorious

(1946) RKO
In one of the most stylish works by the master of suspense, American agent Grant gets the assignment to watch international playgirl Bergman, whose father is a Nazi sympathizer. He soon realizes she abhors his beliefs and they begin to work in tandem, an assignment that means she must marry Nazi agent Rains in Rio despite their mutual attraction. When Rains becomes suspicious of Bergman, he begins slowly poisoning her, and Grant comes to the rescue. The intricate plot revolves around Rains's hoard of uranium, a top-secret material at the time, and a plot point that earned writer Hecht and Hitch an F.B.I. tail during production. This also features one of Hitchcock's greatest shots, the descending crane shot from the top of a grand staircase to the key to Rains's wine cellar held tight in Bergman's hand. The laserdisc edition includes audio commentary and production background, with a theatrical trailer, telecast clips, deleted scenes from the script with stills, and the Lux Radio Theatre Broadcast. Academy Award Nominations: Best Original Screenplay; Best Supporting Actor:

Claude Rains. **Cast:** Cary Grant, Ingrid Bergman, Claude Rains, Louis Calhern, Reinhold Schunzel, Moroni Olsen, Ivan Triesault, Alexis Minotis, Wally Brown. **Credits:** Dir: Alfred Hitchcock; Prod: Alfred Hitchcock; Writer: Ben Hecht; DP: Ted Tetzlaff; Ed: Theron Warth; Composer: Roy Webb; Art Director: Albert S. D'Agostino. B&W, 103 min. **VHS, LASER**

Now and Forever

(1934) Paramount
The combination of Lombard, Cooper, and Temple is promising in a woolly tale about a con man who considers taking $75,000 for the custody rights to the daughter he hasn't seen since she was an infant. But when he meets Temple, he decides to take her with him and his conning girlfriend (Lombard) and try to go straight. **Cast:** Gary Cooper, Carole Lombard, Shirley Temple, Guy Standing, Charlotte Granville, Gilbert Emery, Henry Kolker, Tetsu Komai, Jameson Thomas, Harry Stubbs. **Credits:** Dir: Henry Hathaway; Prod: Louis D. Lighton; Writer: Vincent Lawrence, Sylvia Thalberg; DP: Harry Fischbeck; Ed: Ellsworth Hoagland; Prod Design: Hans Dreier. B&W, 82 min. **VHS**

No Way Out

(1950) Fox
When a young black doctor (Poitier) fails to save a gangster's brother suffering from gunshot wounds, the bigoted mobster (Widmark) orchestrates race riots as his means of revenge. When Widmark is injured, Poitier has to choose between his feelings and his Hippocratic oath. A provocative social-problem melodrama from Mankiewicz, featuring the debut film performances of Poitier, Dee, and Davis. Academy Award Nomination: Best Story and Screenplay. **Cast:** Richard Widmark, Linda Darnell, Stephen McNally, Sidney Poitier, Ruby Dee, Ossie Davis, Bill Walker, Mildred Joanne Smith, Harry Bellaver. **Credits:** Dir: Joseph L. Mankiewicz; Prod: Darryl F. Zanuck; Writer: Joseph L. Mankiewicz, Lesser Samuels; DP: Milton Krasner; Ed: Barbara McLean; Prod Design: Lyle Wheeler; Composer: Alfred Newman; Costumes: Travilla; Art Director: George W. Davis. B&W, 106 min. **VHS**

No Way to Treat a Lady

(1968) Paramount
A master of disguise (Steiger) stalks the streets of New York, strangling his female victims while phoning clues into the detective on the case (Segal)

to keep the chase interesting. Now he wants to up the ante once more—his next target is the detective's girlfriend! A black comedy based on the novel by William Goldman. **Cast:** Rod Steiger, Lee Remick, George Segal, Eileen Heckart, Murray Hamilton, Michael Dunn, Barbara Baxley, Doris Roberts, David Doyle. **Credits:** Dir: Jack Smight; Prod: Sol C. Siegel; Writer: John Gay; DP: Jack Priestley; Ed: Archie Marshek; Composer: Stanley Myers; Art Director: Hal Pereira, George Jen-kins; Set Designer: George Jenkins. Color, 108 min. **VHS**

Now, Voyager

(1942) Warner Bros.
"Now, Voyager, sail forth to seek and find." Rains is a psychiatrist who quotes this line from Walt Whitman to inspire the repressed Davis. Soon, the shy, sheltered spinster is brought out of her shell and falls in love with handsome, suave Henreid, though she knows he will never leave his wife. Through years of trials, their love endures and she becomes a surrogate mother to Henreid's daughter (Wilson). The quintessential Hollywood tear-jerker, with a lush Steiner score. Academy Award Nominations: 3, including Best Actress: Bette Davis; Best Supporting Actress: Gladys Cooper. **Academy Awards:** Best Music Score of a Drama/Comedy. **Cast:** Bette Davis, Paul Henreid, Claude Rains, Gladys Cooper, Janis Wilson, Bonita Granville, Ilka Chase, John Loder, Lee Patrick, James Rennie. **Credits:** Dir: Irving Rapper; Prod: Hal B. Wallis; Writer: Casey Robinson; DP: Sol Polito; Ed: Warren Low; Composer: Max Steiner; Art Director: Robert M. Haas. B&W, 118 min. **VHS, LASER**

Number 17

(1932)
This early British Hitchcock humorous mystery about a gang of jewel thieves in the London train yards is mostly of interest to see the work of the young master. **Cast:** Leon M. Lion, Anne Grey, John Stuart, Donald Calthrop, Barry Jones, Garry Marsh, Ann Casson, Henry Caine, Herbert Langley. **Credits:** Dir: Alfred Hitchcock; Prod: John Maxwell; Writer: Alfred Hitchcock, Alma Reville; DP: Jack Cox; Ed: A. C. Hammond; Art Director: Wilfred Arnold. B&W, 66 min. **VHS, DVD**

The Nun's Story

(1959) Warner Bros.
Hepburn is magnificent as the daughter of a Belgian colonial doctor who

enters a nursing order in the Congo, in a warm, engrossing film about the religious life, with thought-provoking questions about the limits of faith in the face of injustice. After providing a rare glimpse at the life inside the cloister under the stern hand of Evans, the story follows Hepburn as she's reassigned to Holland just as the Nazis invade. When she looks into the face of evil, she has to make a choice between her vows and the service she can perform in the resistance. Moving and provocative. Academy Award Nominations: 8, including Best Picture; Best Director; Best Actress: Audrey Hepburn; Best (Adapted) Screenplay. **Cast:** Audrey Hepburn, Peter Finch, Edith Evans, Peggy Ashcroft, Dean Jagger, Mildred Dunnock, Beatrice Straight, Colleen Dewhurst. **Credits:** Dir: Fred Zinnemann; Prod: Henry Blanke; Writer: Robert Anderson; DP: Franz Planer; Ed: Walter Thompson; Prod Design: Alexander Trauner; Composer: Franz Waxman. Color, 151 min. **VHS**

Nurse Edith Cavell
(1939) RKO
Neagle portrays the brave nurse who shuttles refugees and political prisoners out of Belgium via an underground railroad in WWI and was executed for her work. Ironically, released just as WWII was beginning to rage. A remake of Wilcox's 1928 silent. Academy Award Nomination for Best Original Score. **Cast:** Anna Neagle, Edna May Oliver, George Sanders, ZaSu Pitts, May Robson, H. B. Warner, Sophie Stewart, Mary Howard, Robert Coote, Martin Kosleck. **Credits:** Dir: Herbert Wilcox; Prod: Herbert Wilcox; Writer: Michael Hogan; DP: Freddie Young; Ed: Elmo Williams; Composer: Anthony Collins; Art Director: L. P. Williams. B&W, 108 min. **VHS**

The Nutty Professor
(1963) Paramount
It's Jerry Lewis and Mr. Hyde as he assumes the roles of star (in a dual role), coproducer, director, and coscriptwriter developing his own idea. In what is probably his most famous film, Lewis plays an irretrievably nerdy professor whose love for student Stevens drives the creation of a suave potion that turns him into his lounge lizard alter ego. Remade with great success by Eddie Murphy in 1996. **Cast:** Jerry Lewis, Stella Stevens, Henry Gibson, Del Moore, Kathleen Freeman, Skip Ward, Norman Alden, Howard Morris. **Credits:** Dir: Jerry Lewis; Prod: Jerry Lewis, Ernest D. Glucksman; Writer: Jerry Lewis, Bill Richmond; DP: Wallace Kelley; Ed: John Woodcock; Composer: Walter Scharf; Art Director: Hal Pereira, Walter Tyler. Color, 108 min. **VHS, LASER**

Objective, Burma!
(1945) Warner Bros.
Flynn gives one of his most heroic performances as the leader of a paratroop squad in WWII Burma. After a successful mission to dismantle a Japanese radar station, the soldiers must split up and trek 150 miles through hostile jungle. The hardships of the jungle pale in comparison to the withering attacks of the Japanese. Stirring wartime propaganda from Walsh and a story by writer Bessie, later a member of the Hollywood 10. Academy Award Nominations: 3, including Best Original Story. **Cast:** Errol Flynn, William Prince, James Brown, George Tobias, Henry Hull, Warner Anderson, John Alvin, Mark Stevens. **Credits:** Dir: Raoul Walsh; Prod: Jerry Wald; Writer: Ranald MacDougall, Lester Cole; Story: Alvah Bessie; DP: James Wong Howe; Ed: George Amy; Composer: Franz Waxman; Art Director: Ted Smith. B&W, 142 min. **VHS**

Obsession
(1976) Columbia
Director De Palma tips his cap to Hitchcock's *Vertigo* (1958) in this thriller starring Robertson as a man possessed by the image of his wife, who was presumed dead after a kidnapping. When he sees her double (a dual role for Bujold) 16 years later, he becomes obsessed with finding out her identity. Score by Hitchcock favorite Herrmann, who received a posthumous Oscar nomination. Academy Award Nomination: Best Score. **Cast:** Cliff Robertson, Genevieve Bujold, Wanda Blackman, John Lithgow, Sylvia Kuumba Williams, Pat McNamara, Stocker Fontelieu, Don Hood. **Credits:** Dir: Brian De Palma; Prod: George Litto, Harry N. Blum; Story: Brian De Palma, Paul Schrader; DP: Vilmos Zsigmond; Ed: Paul Hirsch; Composer: Bernard Herrmann. Color, 98 min. **VHS, LASER**

An Occurrence at Owl Creek Bridge
(1962)
This Academy Award–winning short subject, based on a story by Ambrose Bierce, is a devastating film revealing the final moments of a man about to be hung for sabotage. Available on video as a double feature with *The Red Balloon*. **Cast:** Roger Jacquet, Anne Cornaly. **Credits:** Dir: Robert Enrico. B&W, 29 min. **VHS**

Oceans 11
(1960) Warner Bros.
Sinatra, Martin, Davis, Lawford, and the rest of the Rat Pack do that Ring-a-Ding-Ding thing in their neon stomping ground—Las Vegas. The Pack plays a group of ex-soldiers who plan to knock off the strip's biggest casinos on New Year's Eve. Most interesting as social anthropology of a lost culture circa early '60s. **Cast:** Frank Sinatra, Dean Martin, Sammy Davis, Jr., Peter Lawford, Angie Dickinson, Richard Conte, Cesar Romero, Patrice Wymore. **Credits:** Dir: Lewis Milestone; Prod: Lewis Milestone; Writer: Harry Brown, Charles Lederer; DP: William Daniels; Ed: Philip W. Anderson; Composer: Nelson Riddle; Art Director: Nicolai Remisoff. Color, 127 min. **VHS, LASER**

The Odd Couple
(1968) Paramount
Simon's justifiably famous pair was based on the real experiences of his scriptwriting brother living with two bachelors in Hollywood. Lemmon replaced Art Carney from the stage smash in the role of Matthau's new roommate, and the other principals brought finely tuned ensemble work to the film, infusing depth to the characterizations of sloppy, curmudgeonly Madison and his poker-buddy circle. Lemmon brought a shrill neurosis to fussy Felix that is the perfect foil. Watch for cameos by a host of late-'60s baseball greats, ranging

from Roberto Clemente and Maury Wills to Bud Harrelson. The basis for the long-running TV series starring Tony Randall and Jack Klugman. Academy Award Nominations: Best (Adapted) Screenplay; Best Film Editing. **Cast:** Jack Lemmon, Walter Matthau, John Fiedler, Herb Edelman, David Sheiner, Monica Evans, Carole Shelley, Iris Adrian. **Credits:** Dir: Gene Saks; Prod: Howard W. Koch; Writer: Neil Simon; DP: Robert B. Hauser; Ed: Frank Bracht; Composer: Neal Hefti; Art Director: Hal Pereira, Walter Tyler. Color, 106 min. **VHS, LASER**

Odds Against Tomorrow
(1959) United Artists
In what is considered one of the last great film noirs from the classic period of the '40s and '50s, Belafonte is a drug-addicted nightclub singer who teams with a remorseless killer and a crooked cop to make some money the old-fashioned way: steal it. But first they have to overcome not only the obstacles of the job but also their racial prejudices. **Cast:** Harry Belafonte, Robert Ryan, Shelley Winters, Ed Begley, Gloria Grahame, Richard Bright, Lew Gallo, Fred Scollay. **Credits:** Dir: Robert Wise; Prod: Robert Wise; Writer: John O. Killens, Nelson Gidding; DP: Joseph Brun; Ed: Dede Allen; Composer: John Lewis; Art Director: Leo Kerz. B&W, 120 min. **VHS**

The Odessa File
(1974) Columbia
The follow-up to the successful *The Day of the Jackal* (1973), this is also a taut, sophisticated, and subtly shaded international espionage film. Voight gives a superior performance as the son of a German soldier who infiltrates the network of Nazi sympathizers code-named Odessa in the early '60s. He searches for SS monster Schell after being trained to infiltrate Odessa by Israeli experts and

goaded by the haunting diary of a survivor. Based on the novel by Frederick Forsythe. **Cast:** Jon Voight, Maximilian Schell, Derek Jacobi, Maria Schell, Mary Tamm, Peter Jeffrey, Klaus Lowitsch, Kurt Meisel. **Credits:** Dir: Ronald Neame; Prod: John Woolf; Writer: George Markstein, Kenneth Ross; DP: Oswald Morris; Ed: Ralph Kemplen; Prod Design: Rolf Zehetbauer; Composer: Andrew Lloyd Webber. Color, 130 min. **VHS, LASER**

Of Human Bondage
(1934) RKO
Considered to be the best of the three film versions of Maugham's 1915 novel about a crippled doctor's passion for a waitress and the destructive romance that follows. Howard plays the sensitive artist turned doctor, and Davis his shrewish waitress lover. Davis's Best Actress Oscar the following year for *Dangerous* was widely acknowledged as a compensation for not winning an Oscar for this role, which made her a star. **Cast:** Leslie Howard, Bette Davis, Kay Johnson, Frances Dee, Alan Hale, Reginald Owen, Reginald Denny, Reginald Sheffield. **Credits:** Dir: John Cromwell; Prod: Pandro S. Berman; Writer: Lester Cohen; Story: W. Somerset Maugham; DP: Henry Gerrard; Ed: William Morgan; Prod Design: Carroll Clark; Composer: Max Steiner; Art Director: Van Nest Polglase. B&W, 84 min. **VHS, LASER**

Of Human Hearts
(1938) MGM
Bondi is magnificent, stoic, and proud in this melodrama set in pre–Civil War Ohio. Stewart, the resentful son of a stern preacher, becomes a doctor through his mother's sacrifice. But after he moves East and enters the war, he ignores his family. Bondi fears that he has been killed and writes to President Lincoln (Carradine) asking if he knows of her son's whereabouts. The president sternly presses a reconciliation between Stewart and his dying mother. Academy Award Nominations: Best Supporting Actress: Beulah Bondi. **Cast:** Walter Huston, James Stewart, Gene Reynolds, Beulah Bondi, Guy Kibbee, Charles Coburn, John Carradine, Ann Rutherford. **Credits:** Dir: Clarence Brown; Prod: John Considine; Writer: Bradbury Foote; DP: Clyde De Vinna; Ed: Frank Hull; Prod Design: Cedric Gibbons; Composer: Herbert Stothart; Art Director: Harry Oliver, Edwin B. Willis. B&W, 100 min. **VHS**

Of Mice and Men
(1939) United Artists
In this adaptation of Steinback's dark, richly textured masterpiece, the uncertainties of the Depression-era world resonate in the story of two drifters who cling to the dream of their own ranch. Meredith plays the self-appointed guardian of the innocent, slow, but potentially dangerous Chaney, Jr., who gives perhaps his finest performance. Their comforting fantasy of a better life is shattered by the ugly realities of the ranch where they find work: a tormenting ranch owner (Steele), the cruel foreman, and his promiscuous wife (Field). Academy Award Nominations: 3, including Best Picture. **Cast:** Burgess Meredith, Lon Chaney, Jr., Betty Field, Charles Bickford, Roman Bohnen, Bob Steele, Noah Beery, Oscar O'Shea, Granville Bates, Leigh Whipper, Leona Roberts. **Credits:** Dir: Lewis Milestone; Prod: Lewis Milestone, Frank Ross; Writer: Eugene Solow; Story: John Steinbeck; DP: Norbert F. Brodine; Ed: Bert Jordan; Composer: Aaron Copland; SFX: Roy Seawright; Art Director: Nicolai Remisoff. B&W, 107 min.

Oh Dad, Poor Dad, Mamma's Hung You in the Closet and I'm Feelin' So Sad
(1967) Paramount
Offbeat black comedy with Russell as Mme. Rosepettle, the domineering mom who leads her dead husband (stuffed and in a casket), their bizarre 25-year-old "baby," and his oversexed nanny on a vacation in the Caribbean. Weird fun, based on Arthur L. Kopit's stage play. **Cast:** Jonathan Winters, Rosalind Russell, Robert Morse, Barbara Harris, Hugh Griffith, Lionel Jeffries, Cyril Delevanti, Hiram Sherman. **Credits:** Dir: Richard Quine, Alexander Mackendrick; Prod: Ray Stark, Stanley Rubin; Writer: Pat McCormick, Herbert Baker, Ian Bernard; DP: Geoffrey Unsworth; Ed: Warren Low, David Wages; Composer: Neal Hefti; Art Director: Philip M. Jefferies. Color, 86 min. **VHS**

O. Henry's Full House
(1952) Fox
This quintet of classic O. Henry short stories is well cast and lavishly produced by some of the period's best directors. One piece follows a vagrant's (Laughton) unsuccessful attempts (including harassing Monroe) to get arrested and spend the cold winter months in a warm jail cell. Adaptations of "The Ransom of Red Chief," in which kidnappers Allen and Levant have their hands full with a bratty captive, and "The Gift of the Magi," with poor newlyweds Granger and Crain offering sacrificial gifts, are also standouts. **Cast:** Charles Laughton, Marilyn Monroe, David Wayne, Dale Robertson, Fred Allen, Oscar Levant, Jeanne Crain, Farley Granger, Richard Widmark, Joyce MacKenzie, Richard Rober, Anne Baxter, Jean Peters, John Steinbeck (narrator). **Credits:** Dir: Henry Koster, Henry Hathaway, Jean Negulesco, Howard Hawks, Henry King; Prod: Andre Hakim; Writer: Richard Breen, Ivan Goff, Ben Roberts, Nunnally Johnson, Walter Bullock, Lamar Trotti; DP: Joseph MacDonald, Lloyd Ahern, Lucien Ballard, Milton Krasner; Ed: Nick DeMaggio, Barbara McLean, William B. Murphy; Composer: Alfred Newman. B&W, 116 min.

Oh, God
(1977) Warner Bros.
Denver plays an assistant grocery-store manager who is summoned by God (Burns, of course, in the role that brought him back) to spread the gospel. Denver's wife (Teri Garr) as well as everyone else think he has gone off the deep end. Burns was so adored as The Man Upstairs that two sequels followed. Directed and written by TV mavens Reiner (*The Dick Van Dyke Show*) and Gelbart (*M*A*S*H*). Academy Award Nominations: Best (Adapted) Screenplay. **Cast:** George Burns, John Denver, Teri Garr, Paul Sorvino, Ralph Bellamy, Dinah Shore, Barry Sullivan, Donald Pleasence. **Credits:** Dir: Carl Reiner; Prod: Jerry Weintraub; Writer: Larry Gelbart; DP: Victor J. Kemper; Ed: Bud Molin; Composer: Jack Elliott; Art Director: Jack Senter. Color, 104 min. **VHS, LASER**

Oil for the Lamps of China
(1935) Warner Bros.
In this melodramatic indictment of a worker's dedication to his job, O'Brien, the Atlantis Oil Co.'s man in China, gives more than his all to his job: he allows the death of his firstborn child, fires his best friend, nearly loses his wife (Hutchinson), and takes a bullet from the communists instead of giving over $15,000 in company funds. When he's finally on his feet again, his company offers him a demotion. A last-minute happy ending doesn't change the film's message of corporate brutality. **Cast:** Pat O'Brien, Josephine Hutchinson, Jean Muir, Lyle Talbott, Arthur S. Byron, John Eldredge, Donald Crisp, Willie Fung, Tetsu Komai, Henry O'Neill. **Credits:** Dir: Mervyn LeRoy; Prod: Robert Lord; Writer: Laird

Doyle, Alice Tisdale Hobart; DP: Tony Gaudio; Ed: William Clemens; Prod Design: Robert M. Haas; Composer: Leo F. Forbstein. B&W, 105 min.

Okinawa
(1952) Columbia
The WWII story of a Navy destroyer crew and their life at sea as told in their dialogue about home, family, and strategy. Actual sea and air war footage is threaded throughout the film and easily becomes the real standout. **Cast:** Pat O'Brien, Cameron Mitchell, Richard Denning, Rhys Williams, James Dobson, Richard Benedict, Buddy Robles, Donal Gibson, George Cooper, Alan Dreeben. **Credits:** Dir: Leigh Jason; Prod: Wallace MacDonald; Writer: Jameson Brewer, Arthur Ross; Story: Leonard Stern; DP: Henry Freulich; Ed: Jerome Thomas; Composer: Herschel Burke Gilbert. B&W, 67 min.

Oklahoma!
(1955) Fox
In this beloved Rodgers and Hammerstein musical (their first brought to the screen), an adorable 19-year-old Jones, in her screen debut, must choose a suitor to accompany her to a social, the riotous cowboy (MacRae) or the brooding farm hand (Steiger). From this simple scenario develops humor, fighting, dancing (including a breakthrough dream sequence choreographed by Agnes De Mille), and singing. The entire production was filmed twice, with one take for the new Todd A-O format and one for the regular CinemaScope aspect ratio. There is now a laserdisc version of the Todd A-O takes, which some consider vastly superior. Includes the enduring songs "People Will Say We're in Love," "Oh, What a Beautiful Mornin'," "Oklahoma!" and many more. Academy Award Nominations: 4, including Best Cinematography; Best Editing. **Academy Awards:** Best Sound Recording; Best Scoring of a Musical. **Cast:** Gordon MacRae, Shirley Jones, Rod Steiger, Gloria Grahame, Gene Nelson, Charlotte Greenwood, Eddie Albert, James Whitmore. **Credits:** Dir: Fred Zinnemann; Prod: Arthur Hornblow, Jr.; Writer: Sonya Levien, William Ludwig; DP: Robert Surtees; Ed: Gene Ruggiero; Prod Design: Oliver Smith; Choreographer: Agnes De Mille; Composer: Richard Rodgers, Oscar Hammerstein. Color, 146 min. **VHS, LASER**

The Oklahoma Kid
(1939) Warner Bros.
Worth seeing, if only to watch Bogie and Cagney sporting Western duds, and Cagney singing a lullaby while playing a guitar. Set during the Oklahoma land rush, it pits Bogie as the crooked gambling hall–saloon owner against Sothern's efforts to clean up Tulsa. What Bogie doesn't realize is that one of Sothern's sons happens to be Cagney, the notorious Oklahoma Kid. When Bogie's machinations kill Sothern, Cagney's bent on revenge. **Cast:** James Cagney, Humphrey Bogart, Rosemary Lane, Donald Crisp, Harvey Stephens, Hugh Sothern, Charles Middleton, Ward Bond. **Credits:** Dir: Lloyd Bacon; Prod: Samuel Bischoff; Writer: Warren Duff, Robert Buckner, Edward Paramore; DP: James Wong Howe; Ed: Owen Marks; Prod Design: Esdras Hartley; Composer: Max Steiner. B&W, 85 min. **VHS**

The Old Dark House
(1932) Universal
Karloff is a horribly disfigured butler in a Welsh mansion that serves as refuge for two stranded couples in this Gothic horror classic. Among the other denizens of the house are the 102-year-old father, a pyromaniac son, a Bible-thumping daughter, and an atheistic eldest son. Based on J. B. Priestley's novel *Benighted*. **Cast:** Boris Karloff, Melvyn Douglas, Charles Laughton, Gloria Stuart, Lilian Bond, Ernest Thesiger, Raymond Massey, Eva Moore. **Credits:** Dir: James Whale; Prod: Carl Laemmle, Jr.; Writer: Benn W. Levy, R. C. Sherriff; DP: Arthur Edeson; Ed: Clarence Kolster; Art Director: Charles D. Hall. B&W, 72 min. **VHS, LASER**

The Old-Fashioned Way
(1934) Paramount
Here is a showcase for Fields, who plays the head of a traveling troupe of

Oklahoma! (1955)

actors and tries to keep his charges ahead of the bill collectors and sheriffs. Fields gets to display all of his comedic and vaudeville talents, including a hilarious juggling routine. **Cast:** W. C. Fields, Joe Morrison, Judith Allen, Jan Duggan, Nora Cecil, Baby LeRoy, Jack Mulhall, Joe Millis, Samuel Ethridge, Emma Ray. **Credits:** Dir: William Beaudine; Prod: William LeBaron; Writer: W. C. Fields, Jack Cunningham, Garnett Weston; DP: Ben F. Reynolds; Composer: Harry Revel. B&W, 74 min.

The Old Maid
(1939) Warner Bros.
Adapted from a Pulitzer Prize–winning play that in turn was derived from a 1924 Edith Wharton novel, this film features a tour de force performance from Davis. Set during and just after the Civil War, it begins with Davis picking up the pieces with Brent after Hopkins leaves him, then Davis bearing his child just before he is killed at Vicksburg. Davis migrates to Philadelphia to set up an orphanage where her child can disappear in the crowd. She loses a second love, and gives the child to Hopkins for adoption to provide her with a family name, never revealing her dark past. **Cast:** Bette Davis, Miriam Hopkins, George Brent, Jane Bryan, Donald Crisp, Louise Fazenda, James Stephenson, Jerome Cowan. **Credits:** Dir: Edmund Goulding; Prod: Henry Blanke; Writer: Casey Robinson; DP: Tony Gaudio; Ed: George Amy; Prod Design: Robert M. Haas; Composer: Max Steiner. B&W, 96 min. **VHS**

The Old Man and the Sea
(1958) Warner Bros.
Hemingway personally approved the adaptation of his work for the screen and the selection of Tracy as the star. He also participated in one of the fishing excursions attempting to shoot the landing of a giant marlin. Nevertheless, problems dogged the picture, which eventually cost $6 million and sundered what had been a close relationship between Tracy and Hemingway. Tracy rose to the occasion anyway. The richly metaphorical tale of the old salt's heroic struggle with nature and his rising to meet his destiny would finally be filmed in the Warner Brothers tank—with stock footage borrowed from Disney. The video release includes a short documentary featuring footage of Hemingway himself fishing for marlin. Academy Award Nominations: 3, including Best Actor: Spencer Tracy; Best Cine-

The Old Dark House (1932)

matography. **Academy Awards:** Best Original Dramatic Score. **Cast:** Spencer Tracy, Harry Bellaver, Felipe Pazos, Don Diamond, Don Blackman, Mauritz Hugo, J. Ray, Tony Rosario. **Credits:** Dir: John Sturges; Prod: Leland Hayward; Writer: Peter Viertel; Story: Ernest Hemingway; DP: James Wong Howe, Floyd Crosby, Lamar Boren, Tom Tutwiler; Ed: Arthur Schmidt; Composer: Dimitri Tiomkin; Art Director: Art Loell, Edward Carrere. Color, 95 min. **VHS, LASER**

Old Yeller
(1957) Disney
A heartfelt Disney story of a poor 1860s Texas family and the yellow dog who befriends them. When father Parker heads off on a three-month cattle drive, Kirk is in charge of his little brother (Corcoran). Old Yeller follows Corcoran home, and Kirk wants nothing to do with the stray. But Old Yeller quickly proves himself a loyal friend to the lonely little boy and the two become inseparable pals—until rabies forces a fateful decision. This Disney film was one of the top grossing movies of 1957, and convinced the studio to branch out from animation and produce more live-action movies. **Cast:** Dorothy McGuire, Fess Parker, Tommy Kirk, Kevin Corcoran, Jeff York, Chuck Connors, Beverly Washburn, Spike. **Credits:** Dir: Robert Stevenson; Prod: Walt Disney; Writer: Fred Gipson, William Tunberg; DP: Charles Boyle; Ed: Stanley Johnson; Prod Design: Carroll Clark; Composer: Oliver Wallace. Color, 84 min. **VHS, LASER**

Oliver!
(1968) Columbia
This is a delightful musical version of Dickens's tale of a young orphan who is introduced to a life of petty crime, adapted from the stage musical by Bart. Songs include "Boy for Sale" and "You've Got to Pick a Pocket or Two." Won a slew of Academy Awards, including a special choreography award for White. Academy Award Nominations: 11, including Best Actor: Ron Moody; Best (Adapted) Screenplay. **Academy Awards:** Best Picture; Best Director; Best Sound; Best Scoring of a Musical; Best Art Direction—Set Decoration. **Cast:** Mark Lester, Jack Wild, Ron Moody, Oliver Reed, Shani Wallis, Harry Secombe, Hugh Griffith, Hugh O'Conor, Peggy Mount, Leonard Rossiter. **Credits:** Dir: Carol Reed; Prod: John Woolf; Writer: Vernon Harris; Story: Lionel Bart, Charles Dickens; DP: Oswald Morris; Ed: Ralph Kemplen; Prod Design: John Box; Choreographer: Onna White; Composer: Lionel Bart; Costumes: Phyllis Dalton; SFX: Allan Bryce. Color, 153 min. **VHS, LASER, DVD**

Oliver Twist
(1933) Monogram
This first film version of the 1839 Dickens classic set in the downtrodden classes of 19th-century England was produced by Poverty Row studio Monogram, and though it can't hold a candle to the British adaptations that follow, it's interesting to see for comparison. Orphaned Oliver spends his childhood in the workhouse being

treated harshly at the hands of the parish authorities until he runs away to London. There he meets Fagin, an old criminal who controls a gang of young thieves and who introduces Oliver to a life of crime. **Cast:** Dickie Moore, Irving Pichel, William Boyd, Doris Lloyd, Barbara Kent, Alec B. Francis, George K. Arthur, Clyde Cook. **Credits:** Dir: William J. Cowan; Prod: I. E. Chadwick; Writer: Elizabeth Meehan; Story: Charles Dickens; DP: J. Roy Hunt; Ed: Carl Pierson. B&W, 77 min. **VHS**

Olsen and Johnson

The wacky humor and slapstick shtick of vaudeville duo Ole Olsen and Chic Johnson rarely got old on the big screen, despite the fact that many of the plots of their films were contrived to showcase their "nut" humor and to parade big-name specialty acts across the screen. The King Cole Trio shows up, dressed as cooks, in *See My Lawyer* (1945), and Count Basie and *Sherlock Holmes*'s Basil Rathbone and Nigel Bruce turn up in *Crazy House* (1943). The comedy team is best remembered for the raucous *Hellzapoppin'*, the 1941 film adaptation of their anything-goes Broadway hit that combined musical comedy, sight gags, audience-participation bits, and more than a few dirty jokes.

Oh! Sailor! Behave! *(1930)*
Country Gentlemen *(1936)*
Cinema Circus *(1937)*
All Over Town *(1937)*
Hellzapoppin' *(1941)*
Crazy House *(1943)*
Ghost Catchers *(1944)*
See My Lawyer *(1945)*

O'Malley of the Mounted

(1933) Fox
A lawless gang preys on towns along the U.S.-Canadian border. O'Brien is the Mountie who goes undercover to break them up. Based on a story by silent cowboy star William S. Hart. **Cast:** George O'Brien, Irene Ware, Stanley Fields, James Bush, Victor Potel, Reginald Barlow, Dick Cramer, Tom London. **Credits:** Dir: David Howard; Prod: Sol Lesser; Writer: Dan Jarrett, Frank Clark; DP: Frank B. Good; Ed: Arthur Hilton. B&W, 59 min. **VHS**

The Omega Man

(1971) Warner Bros.
The last survivor of germ warfare hides from nocturnal mutants in a fortified mansion, gathering supplies by day from a deserted L.A. whose streets are strewn with the post-

apocalyptic flotsam of the super-funky '70s. Orson Welles apparently recommended Richard Matheson's *I Am Legend* to Heston, who then backed the production. Made before as *The Last Man on Earth* (1964) with Vincent Price—and watch for a remake by director Ridley Scott to star Arnold Schwarzenegger. **Cast:** Charlton Heston, Anthony Zerbe, Rosalind Cash, Paul Koslo, Lincoln Kilpatrick, Eric Laneuville, John Dierkes, Monika Henreid. **Credits:** Dir: Boris Sagal; Prod: Walter Seltzer; Writer: John William Corrington, Joyce H. Corrington; DP: Russell Metty; Ed: William Ziegler. Color, 98 min. **VHS**

The Omen

(1976) Fox
This film doesn't shy away from graphic violence in an occasionally arresting examination of the ultimate evil penetrating the otherwise comfortable existence of a diplomat, Peck, and his wife, Remick. After grieving the loss of a stillborn child, Peck and Remick adopt a child, Damien, who is actually, um, the Antichrist. Damien leaves the film littered with corpses after unsuccessful attempts to eliminate him end with his being adopted by the president of the United States (!). The unique climax paved the way for the two popular sequels, *Damien—Omen II* (1978) and *Final Conflict* (1981). A fourth was intended, but as interest in the franchise declined, the project was scrapped. Academy Award Nominations: 2, including Best Original Song ("Ave Satani"). **Academy Awards:** Best Original Score. **Cast:** Gregory Peck, Lee Remick, David Warner, Billie Whitelaw, Leo McKern, Patrick Troughton, Martin Benson, Harvey Stevens, Holly Palance, Nicholas Campbell. **Credits:** Dir: Richard Donner; Prod: Harvey Bernhard; Writer: David Seltzer; DP: Gilbert Taylor; Ed: Stuart Baird; Prod Design: Carmen Dillon; Composer: Jerry Goldsmith; SFX: John Richardson. Color, 111 min. **VHS, LASER**

On a Clear Day You Can See Forever

(1970) Paramount
In an attempt to curb her smoking habit, Streisand heads to a hypnotist (Montand). But beneath the smoke, it seems she has ESP, and soon she's reliving a past life in 19th-century En-gland. The good doctor finds her past self enticing. Wonderful songs by Lerner and Lane, direction from Minnelli, as well as appearances by

Nicholson and Newhart. **Cast:** Barbra Streisand, Yves Montand, Bob Newhart, Jack Nicholson, Larry Blyden, Simon Oakland, John Richardson, Pamela Brown. **Credits:** Dir: Vincente Minnelli; Prod: Howard W. Koch; Writer: Alan Jay Lerner; DP: Harry Stradling; Ed: David Bretherton; Prod Design: John DeCuir; Composer: Burton Lane. Color, 129 min. **VHS, LASER**

On Any Sunday

(1971)
This classic motorcycle documentary conveys the danger and thrill of the high-speed chase, the rugged freedom of off-roading, and the true spirit of motorcycling. The video also features a tribute to McQueen, who was an avid cyclist. **Cast:** Steve McQueen, Mert Lawwill, Malcolm Smith. **Credits:** Dir: Bruce Brown; Prod: Bruce Brown. Color, 96 min. **VHS**

On Borrowed Time

(1939) MGM
Crusty old Barrymore struggles to raise his grandson alone until he receives a familiar visitor: death, in the form of Hardwicke. Barrymore engages the Reaper in a debate and forces him up an apple tree, thereby holding his own demise at bay until he arrives at a solution for his grandson's care. An unusual metaphysical allegory based on a play by Paul Osborne. **Cast:** Lionel Barrymore, Cedric Hardwicke, Beulah Bondi, Una Merkel, Ian Wolfe, Philip Terry, Bobs Watson, Nat Pendleton. **Credits:** Dir: Harold S. Bucquet; Prod: Sidney Franklin; Writer: Alice Duer Miller, Frank O'Neill, Claudine West; DP: Joseph Ruttenberg; Ed: George Boemler. B&W, 99 min. **VHS**

Once in a Lifetime

(1932) Universal
A broadly brushed version of the Kaufman and Hart send-up of Hollywood has a trio of vaudevillians traveling from New York to make a fast buck by selling diction lessons to actors in the new talking pictures. They find improbable success after an insult to a producer is interpreted as genius, and produce a work of art from a script rescued from the garbage. Oakie infuses a caricatured role with real personality, and watch for the screen debut of Ladd. **Cast:** Jack Oakie, Sidney Fox, Aline MacMahon, Russell Hopton, ZaSu Pitts, Louise Fazenda, Gregory Ratoff, Onslow Stevens, Robert McWade, Alan Ladd. **Credits:** Dir: Russell Mack; Prod: Carl Laemmle; Writer: Seton I. Miller; Story:

Moss Hart, George S. Kaufman; DP: George Robinson; Ed: Robert Carlisle. B&W, 90 min.

Once Upon a Time
(1944) Columbia
A backstage fairy tale with producer Grant facing the imminent closure of his theater. A chance encounter with young Donaldson introduces his dancing caterpillar. Grant is soon back in top form hosting a series of shows featuring the caterpillar that make him the toast of the town. His shameless exploitation of the boy comes to an end when the caterpillar can't be found—until a musical butterfly suddenly appears. **Cast:** Cary Grant, Janet Blair, James Gleason, Ted Donaldson, William Demarest, Howard Freeman, Art Baker, John Abbott, Ian Wolfe, Jack Lee. **Credits:** Dir: Alexander Hall; Prod: Louis F. Edelman; Writer: Lewis Meltzer, Oscar Saul, Irving Fineman; Story: Norman Corwin, Lucille Fletcher; DP: Franz Planer; Ed: Gene Havlick; Prod Design: Lionel Banks, Edward C. Jewell; Composer: Frederick Hollander. B&W, 89 min.

Once Upon a Time in the West
(1969) Paramount
Leone's greatest achievement is a blood-drenched elegy for the mythic Western gunfighter. From its opening sequence, as three gunmen await the arrival of killer Bronson, the anticipation of sudden violence builds into a full-scale war that leaves none of the combatants standing except the mysterious Bronson. Much of the shock is in Leone's casting of movie icon Fonda as one of the most callous killers ever seen on-screen. Literally operatic in its linking musical themes to character, Morricone's influential score (written before production started) sets the pace and supports the action. A must-see. Filmmakers Dario Argento and Bernardo Bertolucci contributed to the screenplay. **Cast:** Henry Fonda, Jason Robards, Charles Bronson, Claudia Cardinale, Jack Elam, Frank Wolff, Gabriele Ferzetti, Keenan Wynn. **Credits:** Dir: Sergio Leone; Prod: Fulvio Morsella; Writer: Sergio Leone, Sergio Donati; DP: Tonino Delli Colli; Ed: Nino Baragli; Composer: Ennio Morricone; Art Director: Carlo Simi. Color, 165 min. VHS, LASER

On Dangerous Ground
(1951) RKO
Ryan is a big-city detective whose strong-arm tactics get him pushed out to the country to investigate a killing.

There, he encounters the father (Bond) of the murdered girl, a man equally full of hate, and falls for the murderer's blind sister (Lupino), who offers him a softer vision of humanity. Bond is bent on avenging his daughter's death. The investigation comes to a bad end despite Ryan's best effort, and he reaches out for a different life with Lupino. Another dark tale from Ray of an uncompromising outsider. **Cast:** Robert Ryan, Ida Lupino, Ward Bond, Ed Begley, Charles Kemper, Anthony Ross, Ian Wolfe, Gus Schilling. **Credits:** Dir: Nicholas Ray; Prod: John Houseman; Writer: A. I. Bezzerides, Nicholas Ray; DP: George E. Diskant; Ed: Roland Gross; Prod Design: Ralph Berger; Composer: Bernard Herrmann; Art Director: Albert S. D'Agostino. B&W, 82 min. VHS, LASER

One and Only Genuine, Original Family Band
(1968) Disney
This Disney tale tells the story of a musical family from 1880s Dakota territory who try to make it to the Democratic Convention in swanky St. Louis. The convention was famous for selecting Grover Cleveland, who loses the election to Benjamin Harrison though he won the popular vote. Songs include "Drummin' Drummin' Drummin'" and "The Happiest Girl Alive." Goldie Hawn makes her big-screen debut in a bit as "The Giggly Girl." **Cast:** Walter Brennan, Buddy Ebsen, Lesley Ann Warren, John Davidson, Janet Blair, Wally Cox, Kurt Russell, Richard Deacon. **Credits:** Dir: Michael O'Herlihy; Prod: Bill Anderson; Writer: Lowell S. Hawley; DP: Frank Phillips; Ed: Cotton Warburton; Prod Design: Carroll Clark; Composer: Richard M. Sherman, Robert B. Sherman; Art Director: Herman A. Blumenthal. Color, 110 min. VHS, LASER

One Big Affair
(1952) United Artists
An American schoolteacher (Keyes), on a sight-seeing tour of Mexico with colleagues, is accidentally left in a small town. She meets and hits it off with an American lawyer (O'Keefe) who is more than happy to offer her assistance. The other schoolteachers, meanwhile, report their missing friend to the authorities. The couple, having grown fond of each other, do not wish to be found. The two take off for Acapulco with the help of warmhearted locals, all the while attempting to avoid interference from the police and the concerned group of teachers.

Cast: Evelyn Keyes, Dennis O'Keefe, Mary Anderson, Connie Gilchrist, Thurston Hall, Gus Schilling, Jose Torvay, Carles Musqued, Andrew Velazquez. **Credits:** Dir: Peter Godfrey; Prod: Benedic Bocceaus; Writer: Leo Townsend, George Bricker; Story: Francis Swan; DP: Jose Ortiz Ramos; Ed: George Crome; Composer: L. Breton Hernandez. B&W, 80 min.

One-Eyed Jacks
(1961) Paramount
After Brando took over direction of this film from Stanley Kubrick, he proceeded to shoot more than one million feet of film in the course of six months. It also cost $6 million, three times its original budget. What emerged was quintessential Brando: brooding, introspective, often difficult to fathom but fascinating. Elements of the Billy the Kid story were grafted onto a dark fable of double crossing and subsequent revenge. Brando and Malden rob a bank, but Malden takes the money and leaves Brando in the lurch, goes straight, and becomes the sheriff of Monterey. Brando, living for revenge, arrives in town years later with a new gang. Academy Award Nominations: Best (Color) Cinematography. **Cast:** Marlon Brando, Karl Malden, Katy Jurado, Ben Johnson, Pina Pellicer, Slim Pickens, Sam Gilman, Larry Duran. **Credits:** Dir: Marlon Brando; Prod: Frank P. Rosenberg; Writer: Guy Trosper, Calder Willingham; DP: Charles Lang; Ed: Archie Marshek; Prod Design: Joseph MacMillan Johnson; Composer: Hugo Friedhofer; Art Director: Hal Pereira. Color, 141 min. VHS, LASER, DVD

One Flew over the Cuckoo's Nest
(1975) United Artists
The antiheroic struggle of a flamboyant personality against a bureaucratic institution makes a perfect vehicle for Nicholson. In one of his signature roles as McMurphy, Nicholson escapes a prison work farm by feigning insanity. When he arrives at the institution, he discovers the inmates to be no more nutty than the average joe, and sets about organizing their resistance to their nemesis, Nurse Ratched (Fletcher). This powerful, and powerfully funny, film is based on Kesey's novel. The debuts of Lloyd and Dourif, and the breakthrough for DeVito. Selected as a National Film Registry Outstanding Film. Academy Award Nominations: 9, including Best Supporting Actor: Brad Dourif. **Academy Awards:** Best Picture; Best Direc-

tor; Best Actor: Jack Nicholson; Best Actress: Louise Fletcher; Best Screenplay Adapted from Other Material. **Cast:** Jack Nicholson, Louise Fletcher, William Redfield, Danny DeVito, Christopher Lloyd, Scatman Crothers, Will Sampson, Brad Dourif, Michael Berryman, Peter Brocco. **Credits:** Dir: Milos Forman; Prod: Michael Douglas, Saul Zaentz; Writer: Bo Goldman, Lawrence Hauben; Story: Ken Kesey; DP: Bill Butler, Haskell Wexler, William A. Fraker; Ed: Richard Chew, Sheldon Kahn, Lynzee Klingman; Prod Design: Paul Sylbert; Composer: Jack Nitzsche; Costumes: Aggie Guerard Rodgers. Color, 133 min. **VHS, LASER, DVD**

One Foot in Heaven
(1941) Warner Bros.
This is a moving story of a Methodist minister (March) who travels from assignment to assignment building the faith of the communities he finds. After training to be a doctor, he decides to quit his studies and offer up his life to God, setting out with his wife (Scott). So begins a life on the road, landing in communities in need of uplift and then setting off again once their mission is done. Academy Award Nomination: Best Picture. **Cast:** Fredric March, Martha Scott, Beulah Bondi, Gene Lockhart, Elisabeth Fraser, Harry Davenport, Laura Hope Crews, Grant Mitchell, Moroni Olsen, Frankie Thomas. **Credits:** Dir: Irving Rapper; Prod: Robert Lord; Writer: Casey Robinson; Story: Hartzell Spence; DP: Charles Rosher; Ed: Warren Low; Composer: Max Steiner. B&W, 108 min.

One Hour with You
(1932) Paramount
Lubitsch improves on his 1924 silent *The Marriage Circle* with this Chevalier vehicle interspersed with song and punctuated with humorous asides to the audience. Chevalier is an amorous Parisian doctor happily married to MacDonald, though beset by the advances of his wife's best friend (Tobin). When her husband's suspicions are aroused, he hires a detective and discovers his wife's appointment with Chevalier. The doctor tells his wife about the situation and she decides to have an affair with Ruggles, after which they agree never to stray again. Academy Award Nomination: Best Picture. **Cast:** Maurice Chevalier, Jeanette MacDonald, Genevieve Tobin, Charlie Ruggles, Roland Young, George Barbier, Josephine Dunn, Richard Carle, Charles Judels, Barbara Leonard.

Credits: Dir: George Cukor, Ernst Lubitsch; Prod: Ernst Lubitsch; Writer: Samson Raphaelson, Lothar Schmidt; DP: Victor Milner; Composer: Oscar Straus, Richard A. Whiting, Leo Robin. B&W, 80 min.

One in a Million
(1936) Fox
In her smash debut movie, Olympic skating champion Henie plays a Swiss gold medalist who hooks up with Menjou's traveling vaudeville troupe. Ameche tries to keep her away from the sharpies until she makes a dazzling appearance at Madison Square Garden. Not much of a stretch for Henie in the role, but she shows a winning grace and healthy appeal. She went on to be a solid box-office performer and retired early and wealthy after making some shrewd investments. **Cast:** Sonja Henie, Adolphe Menjou, Don Ameche, Ned Sparks, Jean Hersholt, Ritz Brothers, Arline Judge, Borrah Minevich. **Credits:** Dir: Sidney Lanfield; Prod: Raymond Griffith; Writer: Leonard Praskins, Mark Kelly; DP: Edward Cronjager; Ed: Robert Simpson. B&W, 95 min. **VHS**

One Man's Way
(1964) United Artists
Post–*Bus Stop* Murray is cast as Norman Vincent Peale, one of the pioneers for that all-too-familiar figure of the modern media landscape: the broadcasting preacher. While the author of *The Power of Positive Thinking* was not possessed of the fire and brimstone obvious in his TV progeny, his New Testament–style gospel of love and turning the other cheek was controversial in its own way. This film makes a serious attempt to deal with the complexities of the man and his faith, and Murray and the supporting cast deliver strong performances. **Cast:** Don Murray, Diana Hyland, Veronica Cartwright, Ian Wolfe, Virginia Christine, Carol Ohmart, William Windom, Liam Sullivan. **Credits:** Dir: Denis Sanders; Prod: Frank Ross; Writer: Eleanore Griffin, John W. Bloch; DP: Ernest Laszlo; Ed: Philip W. Anderson; Composer: Richard Markowitz; Art Director: Edward C. Jewell. Color, 105 min. **VHS**

One Million B.C.
(1940) United Artists
A look at prehistoric sociology as Mature, an outcast from the warrior Klang people, finds a home with the peace-loving Shell people along with pretty Neanderthal Landis. The romance lifts eyebrows in the tribe,

but the warring clans join together at the end for survival. D. W. Griffith was hired to direct, but his contribution is uncertain. Remade by Hammer Studios in 1967 with Ray Harryhausen effects and Racquel Welch in a bikini. Academy Award Nominations: Best Original Score; Best Special Effects. **Cast:** Victor Mature, Carole Landis, Lon Chaney, Jr., Mamo Clark, Conrad Nagel, John Hubbard, Robert Kent, Inez Palange. **Credits:** Dir: Hal Roach, D. W. Griffith; Prod: Hal Roach; Writer: Mickell Novak, George Baker, Joseph Frickert, Grover Jones; DP: Norbert F. Brodine; Ed: Ray Snyder; Composer: Werner Richard Heymann; Art Director: Charles D. Hall. B&W, 80 min. **VHS**

One Minute to Zero
(1952) RKO
Democracy is saved as Mitchum tackles the Communist hordes while keeping his heart safe for Blyth. It's a standard Korean War picture, but Mitchum was an actor capable of a riveting performance in any role, and his approach seems utterly natural in a war film. If you feel that life is not complete without hearing Mitchum sing, he does a duet with Blyth on the Japanese smash "Tell Me Golden Moon." **Cast:** Robert Mitchum, Ann Blyth, William Talman, Richard Egan, Charles McGraw, Margaret Sheridan, Eduard Franz, Robert Gist. **Credits:** Dir: Tay Garnett; Prod: Edmund Grainger; Writer: Milton Krims, William Wister Haines; DP: William E. Snyder; Ed: Sherman Todd, Robert Belcher; Composer: Victor Young; Art Director: Albert S. D'Agostino, Jack Okey. B&W, 105 min. **VHS**

One More River
(1934) Universal
Superb melodrama about an abused wife (Wynyard) who leaves her husband (Clive) and forms a platonic relationship with a younger man (Lawton). When Clive has his wife followed by a detective, he learns of the relationship and uses it to press a divorce suit. A quiet, somber look at the course of love from director Whale with some of Britain's greatest actors (including a role for Mrs. Campbell). **Cast:** Frank Lawton, Mrs. Patrick Campbell, Jane Wyatt, Colin Clive, Reginald Denny, C. Aubrey Smith, Henry Stephenson, Lionel Atwill, Alan Mowbray, Diana Wynyard. **Credits:** Dir: James Whale; Prod: Carl Laemmle, James Whale; Writer: R. C. Sherriff, John Galsworthy; DP: John J. Mescall; Ed: Ted J. Kent; Composer: Franke Harling; Art Director: Charles D. Hall. B&W, 90 min.

One Night of Love

(1934) Columbia

This is a delightful musical about an aspiring opera singer and her relationship with her demanding vocal coach. An amorous reiteration of the maxim that there is no such thing as overnight success and that stardom is often won on the field of broken dreams. Moore's operatic aspirations are shattered initially so she migrates to Europe, where she is discovered. Unfortunately she falls for her impresario and torpedoes herself with a spasm of jealousy. Happily, her talent finally carries her to fame—and the film to a happy ending. Academy Award Nominations: 6, including Best Picture; Best Director; Best Actress: Grace Moore. **Academy Awards:** Best Sound Recording; Best Score. **Cast:** Grace Moore, Tullio Carminati, Lyle Talbot, Mona Barrie, Jessie Ralph, Luis Alberni, Andreas De Segurola, Nydia Westman. **Credits:** Dir: Victor Schertzinger; Prod: Sara Risher; Writer: S. K. Lauren, James Gow, Edmund H. North; DP: Joseph Walker; Ed: Gene Milford; Composer: Louis Silvers; Art Director: Stephen Goosson. B&W, 80 min. **VHS, LASER**

One on One

(1976) Warner Bros.

Hollywood bequeathed a rich legacy in the college athletics genre, with a shotgun-spread of approaches embracing Harold Lloyd's gemlike spoofing to Reagan's Gipper and even The Three Stooges. Benson, as co-scriptwriting auteur, attempts a serious study of motivation and pain in the jungle of college basketball. Neither a vaguely sadistic coach, who employs his goons to deliver elbow after elbow to our hero's delicate features, nor a lustful secretary, nor the disdain of his snotty tutor (who grows to love him) deter Benson from taking it strong to the hoop. **Cast:** Robby Benson, Annette O'Toole, G. D. Spradlin, Gail Strickland, Melanie Griffith, Lamont Johnson, James G. Richardson, Hector Morales, Cory Faucher. **Credits:** Dir: Lamont Johnson; Prod: Martin Hornstein; Writer: Robby Benson, Jerry Segal; DP: Donald M. Morgan; Ed: Robbe Roberts; Composer: Charles Fox; Art Director: Sherman Loudermilk. Color, 105 min. **VHS**

One Potato, Two Potato

(1964) Fox

A heartbreakingly honest independent production, this film explores the deep strains of racism uncovered in an Ohio town by an interracial marriage. Barrie plays a single mother whose husband (Mulligan) abandons her to work in South America. She takes a job and falls in love with Hamilton, a black coworker. They marry and return to his parents' farm in Ohio. When Mulligan returns, he fights for custody of his child. Academy Award Nomination: Best Original Screenplay. **Cast:** Barbara Barrie, Bernie Hamilton, Richard Mulligan, Harry Bellaver, Mart Mericka, Robert Earl Jones, Vinnette Carroll, Faith Burwell, Anthony Spinelli, Jack Stamberger. **Credits:** Dir: Larry Peerce; Prod: Sam Weston; Writer: Raphael Hayes; Story: Orville Hampton; DP: Andrew Laszlo; Ed: Robert Fritch; Composer: Gerald Fried. B&W, 92 min.

One Rainy Afternoon

(1936) United Artists

With a pinch of Continental charm, European leading man Lederer accidentally smooches Lupino in a dark theater. His troubles are just beginning, for Lupino is not a woman to be kissed lightly. She has him arrested, but he soon becomes famous and she sees his attributes in a much more appealing light. **Cast:** Francis Lederer, Ida Lupino, Hugh Herbert, Roland Young, Erik Rhodes, Joseph Cawthorn, Donald Meek, Georgia Caine. **Credits:** Dir: Rowland V. Lee; Prod: Jesse L. Lasky; Writer: Stephen Morehouse Avery; DP: Peverell Marley; Ed: Margaret Clancy; Composer: Alfred Newman; Art Director: Richard Day. B&W, 79 min. **VHS**

One Sunday Afternoon

(1948) Warner Bros.

This is the third try at the Hagan musical about a turn-of-the-century singing dentist (Morgan), lost love, and the pleasant surprise of finding true love on the rebound. Lots of nostalgic songs enliven this otherwise erratic Walsh effort, including the immortal "In My Merry Oldsmobile." Reworking of the reworked *Strawberry Blonde* (1941), also directed by Walsh. **Cast:** Dennis Morgan, Janis Paige, Don Defore, Dorothy Malone, Ben Blue, Oscar O'Shea, Alan Hale, Jr., George Neise, Jim Nolan, Douglas Kennedy. **Credits:** Dir: Raoul Walsh; Prod: Jerry Wald; Writer: Robert L. Richards; Story: James Hagan; DP: Sidney Hickox, Wilfred Cline; Ed: Christian Nyby; Composer: Ralph Blaine; Costumes: Leah Rhodes; Art Director: Anton Grot, Fred M. McLean. Color, 90 min.

One Third of a Nation

(1939) Paramount

A Depression-era melodrama with a WPA pedigree, this also features future director Lumet in his sole appearance on the other side of the camera playing a crippled New York City slum child who just happens to have Sidney for an older sister. They eke out a depressing existence until Erickson inherits their building and falls for Sidney. A strong depiction of the plight of the urban poor, with gritty cinematography. Title stems from FDR's famous speech, wherein he saw one third of a nation "ill-housed, ill-clad, ill-fed." **Cast:** Sylvia Sidney, Leif Erikson, Myron McCormick, Hiram Sherman, Sidney Lumet, Percy Waram, Iris Adrian, Charles Dingle. **Credits:** Dir: Dudley Murphy; Prod: Dudley Murphy; Writer: Oliver H. P. Garrett, Dudley Murphy; DP: William J. Miller, Edward Hyland; Ed: Duncan Mansfield; Composer: Nathaniel Shilkret. B&W, 79 min. **VHS**

One Touch of Venus

(1948) Universal

Nash, Weill, and Perelman sound like a dream writing team for a musical comedy and Gardner as Venus could probably make a pagan out of anyone. Walker plays the obscure department-store window dresser who animates a statue of Venus with a kiss, bringing love to the store while she lingers. Unfortunately, the adaptation doesn't completely cash in on its assets, the visual presentation of goddess Gardner excepted. The 45th anniversary edition has been digitally remastered from the original film negative, and includes a reproduction of an original theatrical lobby card and the original theatrical trailer. **Cast:** Ava Gardner, Robert Walker, Eve Arden, Dick Haymes, Olga San Juan, Tom Conway, James Flavin, Sara Allgood. **Credits:** Dir: William A. Seiter; Prod: Lester Cowen; Writer: Harry Kurnitz, Frank Tashlin; Story: S. J. Perelman, Ogden Nash, Kurt Weill; DP: Franz Planer; Ed: Otto Ludwig; Composer: Ann Ronell, Kurt Weill, Ann Ronell, Ogden Nash; Art Director: Bernard Herzbrun, Emrich Nicholson. B&W, 82 min. **VHS**

One, Two, Three

(1961) United Artists

Yet another great Wilder effort (he also wrote the blistering screenplay with longtime collaborator Diamond), this time a sprinting comedy of clashing ideologies subverted by love. Cagney's last film finds him as a fast-talking, hard-driving head of the

German branch of Coca-Cola. Worlds collide as he volunteers to baby-sit Tiffin, the teenage daughter of a Coke executive from the home office. He loses her, then finds her in love with East German communist beatnik, Buchholtz. Cagney frames him to get him away from Tiffin, then discovers that he and Tiffin are not just married, but expecting. Cagney rescues the kid, but then loses his job to the reformed communist. Notable score by Previn. Academy Award Nominations: Best (Black-and-White) Cinematography. **Cast:** James Cagney, Horst Buchholz, Arlene Francis, Pamela Tiffin, Lilo Pulver, Howard St. John, Leon Askin, Peter Capell. **Credits:** Dir: Billy Wilder; Prod: Billy Wilder; Writer: Billy Wilder, I. A. L. Diamond; DP: Daniel Fapp; Ed: Daniel Mandell; Prod Design: Alexander Trauner; Composer: Andre Previn. B&W, 110 min. **VHS, LASER**

One Way Passage
(1932) Warner Bros.
This seagoing melodrama of doomed lovers features Powell in a typically fine performance as a convict headed for the electric chair, and Francis as a dying woman. Comic relief is provided by the able supporting troika of shady MacMahon, posing as The Countess, and drunken thief McHugh, both of whom distract the dim-witted cop, Hymer. Director Garnett wrote the story for what some call his best film from Lord's concept, but was dissuaded from taking screen credit by producer Wallis. It won Lord an Oscar. **Academy Award:** Best Original Screenplay. **Cast:** Kay Francis, Warren Hymer, Aline MacMahon, Fredrick Burton, Douglas Gerrard, Herbert Mundin, Roscoe Karns, Wilson Mizner, Stanley Fields, William Powell, Frank McHugh. **Credits:** Dir: Tay Garnett; Prod: Robert Lord, Hal B. Wallis; Writer: Tay Garnett, Joseph Jackson, Wilson Mizner; Story: Robert Lord; DP: Robert Kurrle; Ed: Ralph Dawson; Composer: Franke Harling; Art Director: Anton Grot. B&W, 69 min.

On Her Majesty's Secret Service
(1969) United Artists
When Sean Connery refused to play Agent 007 again, Australian model Lazenby was brought in to play Bond. Rigg is the requisite love interest (Bond's only wife), and Savalas is Ernst Stavro Blofeld, the master criminal intent on destroying the world's agricultural economy. A credible performance from Lazenby. **Cast:** George Lazenby, Diana Rigg, Telly Savalas, Gabriele Ferzetti, Ilse Steppat, Bernard Horsfall, George Baker, Bernard Lee. **Credits:** Dir: Peter H. Hunt; Prod: Albert R. Broccoli, Harry Saltzman; Writer: Richard Maibaum, Simon Raven; DP: Michael Reed, Roy Ford, John Jordan, Willy Bogner, Ken Higgins, Egil Woxholt, Alex Barbey; Ed: John Glen; Prod Design: Syd Cain; Composer: John Barry. Color, 142 min. **VHS, LASER**

Onionhead
(1958) Warner Bros.
Griffith isn't getting much out of his college experience, but WWII offers a way out: join the Coast Guard and see the world. Unfortunately, most of the world that he sees is the galley of the boat, and he gets all the action he can handle from his boss, the ever-curmudgeonly Matthau. As if having Matthau for a taskmaster wasn't bad enough, Matthau's fiancée seems to be irresistibly attracted to Griffith. It's a very long way from Mayberry for all concerned. **Cast:** Andy Griffith, Felicia Farr, Walter Matthau, Erin O'Brien, Joe Mantell, Ray Danton, James Gregory, Joey Bishop, Claude Akins. **Credits:** Dir: Norman Taurog; Prod: Jules Schermer; Writer: Nelson Gidding; DP: Harold Rosson; Ed: William Ziegler; Composer: David Buttolph; Art Director: Leo K. Kuter. B&W, 111 min. **VHS**

Only Angels Have Wings
(1939) Columbia
A sparkling cast, well directed, highlights a film that represented the comeback of Barthelmess, a major leading man of the silent era. Grant plays the flinty director of a trans-Andes air courier operation. He is the eye of a hurricane of women who want him, Barthelmess, who may be responsible for the death of Mitchell's brother, and the nearly blind Mitchell himself, who dies on a dangerous mission while trying to spare Grant the risk. When the storm clears we glimpse a humanized Grant with Arthur on his arm. Academy Award Nominations: Best (Black-and-White) Cinematography; Best Visual Effects. **Cast:** Cary Grant, Rita Hayworth, Richard Barthelmess, Jean Arthur, Thomas Mitchell, Allyn Joslyn, Sig Rumann, Victor Kilian. **Credits:** Dir: Howard Hawks; Prod: Howard Hawks; Writer: William Rankin, Eleanore Griffin, Jules Furthman; DP: Joseph Walker, Elmer Dyer; Ed: Viola Lawrence; Composer: Dimitri Tiomkin, Manuel Maciste, Morris Stoloff; Art Director: Lionel Banks. B&W, 121 min. **VHS**

Only the Valiant
(1950) Warner Bros.
Peck plays a martinet captain who assembles a hand-picked force to literally head the Apaches off at the pass. But it seems that all the men hate Peck and one of them is about to lose his girl to him. The captain's response is to order his rival to certain death. Only by risking his own neck to fulfill the mission does Peck redeem himself in the eyes of his men. **Cast:** Gregory Peck, Gig Young, Lon Chaney, Barbara Payton, Ward Bond, Neville Brand, Jeff Corey, Warner Anderson. **Credits:** Dir: Gordon Douglas; Prod: William Cagney; Writer: Edmund H. North, Harry Brown; DP: Lionel Lindon; Ed: Walter Hannemann; Prod Design: Wiard Ihnen; Composer: Franz Waxman. B&W, 105 min. **VHS, LASER**

Only Yesterday
(1933) Universal
This is that rare romantic weeper that sympathetically portrays both an unwed mother and the unknowing father. Sullavan and Boles meet just as he's about to ship off for the Great War and they enjoy a pleasant night of love. When she becomes pregnant, she heads to New York and her aunt (Burke) and cares for her child by starting a thriving business. After the war, she finds Boles, but he fails to recognize her and marries another. A decade later, they meet again and once more enjoy each other's company, but for Boles, it's no more than a passing fancy. But as the Great Crash pushes Boles toward suicide, he makes a startling discovery, though not in time to be reunited with Sullavan. Debut for Sullavan, and it made her an instant sensation. **Cast:** Margaret Sullavan, John Boles, Billie Burke, Reginald Denny, Jimmy Butler, Edna May Oliver, Benita Hume, George Meeker, June Clyde, Marie Prevost. **Credits:** Dir: John M. Stahl; Writer: William Hurlbut, George O'Neil, Arthur Richman; Story: Fred Allen; DP: Gerstad Merrit; Ed: Milton Carruth; Prod Design: Charles D. Hall; Composer: Max Steiner. B&W, 105 min.

On Our Merry Way
(1948) United Artists
An omnibus picture, each chapter here depicts how having a baby changes a life. Old pals Fonda and Stewart get together for the first time, in a story segment written by John O'Hara and directed by both John Huston and George Stevens. Interesting mostly for the talent involved. **Cast:** Burgess Meredith, Paulette

Goddard, Fred MacMurray, James Stewart, Dorothy Lamour, Hugh Herbert, William Demarest, Henry Fonda. **Credits:** Dir: King Vidor; Prod: Benedict Bogeaus; Writer: Lawrence Stallings, Lou Breslow; DP: John Seitz, Ernest Laszlo; Ed: James Smith; Composer: Heinz Romheld; Art Director: Ernest Fegte, Duncan Cramer. B&W, 107 min.

On the Avenue
(1937) Fox
Socialite Carroll becomes enraged, accusing a Broadway producer (Powell) of parodying her in a revue. She turns out to be mistaken, and love arises, but her rival (Faye) has other plans. Lively, funny musical featuring the Berlin songs "The Girl on the Police Gazette," "This Year's Kisses," "Let's Go Slumming," and "I've Got My Love to Keep Me Warm." **Cast:** Dick Powell, Madeleine Carroll, Alice Faye, Ritz Brothers, George Barbier, Cora Witherspoon, Alan Mowbray, Walter Catlett. **Credits:** Dir: Roy Del Ruth; Prod: Gene Markey; Writer: William Conselman, Gene Markey; DP: Lucien Andriot; Ed: Allen McNeil; Prod Design: Mark-Lee Kirk; Composer: Irving Berlin; Art Director: William S. Darling. B&W, 89 min. **VHS**

On the Beach
(1959) United Artists
After the entire Northern Hemisphere is destroyed by a nuclear war, a group of survivors in Australia prepare for their own inevitable demise. As a deadly cloud of radiation creeps toward the continent, some survivors cling to hopes that life as they know it has continued somewhere, hopes that are fed by the discovery of a mysterious, erratic radio signal emanating from San Diego. Others, such as Astaire's sardonic, race-car driving physicist and Gardner's world-weary, tippling party girl, throw their energies into squeezing the last drops from their lives. A grim, unflinching clarion call for sanity that evolves at a deliberate, suspenseful pace. Based on the novel by Shute. Golden Globe for Best Original Score. Academy Award Nominations: Best Editing; Best Score. **Cast:** Gregory Peck, Ava Gardner, Fred Astaire, Anthony Perkins, Donna Anderson, John Tate, Lola Brooks, John Meillon, Lou Vernon, Guy Doleman. **Credits:** Dir: Stanley Kramer; Prod: Stanley Kramer; Writer: John Paxton, Jim Barrett; Story: Nevil Shute; DP: Giuseppe Rotunno, Daniel Fapp; Ed: Frederic Knudtson; Prod Design: Rudolph Sternad; Composer:

Ernest Gold; Costumes: The Fontana Sisters; SFX: Lee Zavitz. B&W, 135 min. **VHS**

On the Double
(1961) Paramount
Double-identity comedy with Kaye as an American solider stationed in England who is the spitting image of England's commanding officer. He takes an assignment from the British government to pose as the General, a decoy to confuse Nazi spies. His guise goes over too well and soon Kaye finds himself a prisoner of the Nazis and en route to Germany. He escapes by using his gift of mimicry. Includes songs by Kaye's wife Sylvia Fine. **Cast:** Danny Kaye, Dana Wynter, Wilfrid Hyde-White, Margaret Rutherford, Diana Dors, Allan Cuthbertson, Jesse White, Gregory Walcott, Terrence DeMarney. **Credits:** Dir: Danny Kaye; Prod: Jack Rose; Writer: Jack Rose, Melville Shavelson; DP: Harry Stradling, Geoffrey Unsworth; Ed: Frank Bracht; Composer: Leith Stevens; Art Director: Hal Pereira, Arthur Lonergan. Color, 92 min.

On the Riviera
(1951) Fox
Kaye stars in a dual role as the famous pilot, Henri Duran, and the American entertainer, Jack Martin. When Duran meets his double, Martin, he hatches a scheme for Martin to take his place at a party, freeing him to attend to a business matter in London without alarming his rival. Martin enjoys the company of Duran's beautiful wife (Tierney), who is ignorant of the switch, but is pushed to the limits of his ingenuity when he encounters a number of Duran's "other" women at the party as well as the rival. Academy Award Nominations: 2, including Best Score. **Cast:** Danny Kaye, Gene Tierney, Corinne Calvet, Marcel Dalio, Jean Murat, Henri Letondal, Clinton Sundberg, Sig Rumann, Joyce MacKenzie, Monique Chantal. **Credits:** Dir: Walter Lang; Prod: Sol Siegel; Writer: Valentine Davies, Phoebe Ephron, Henry Ephron, Rudolph Lothar, Hans Adler; DP: Leon Shamroy; Ed: J. Watson Webb; Composer: Alfred Newman; Art Director: Lyle Wheeler, Leland Fuller. Color, 90 min.

On the Town
(1949) MGM
Bernstein's (with Comden and Green) great musical comedy gets the full Technicolor treatment with fine singing and dancing. Three sailors (Kelly, Munshin, and Sinatra) with 24 hours of shore leave seek excitement and

romance in New York City, an excitement conjured especially in the famous "New York, New York" number. They team with Garrett, Miller, and Vera-Ellen, and they are off gallivanting around N.Y.C. Doubly directed by Kelly and Donen (their first directorial pairing), this fast-moving musical is not only contagious fun, but also a splendid look at New York City ("a helluva town") in the 1940s. **Academy Awards:** Best Scoring of a Musical. **Cast:** Gene Kelly, Frank Sinatra, Vera-Ellen, Ann Miller, Betty Garrett, Jules Munshin, Florence Bates, Alice Pearce. **Credits:** Dir: Stanley Donen, Gene Kelly; Prod: Arthur Freed; Writer: Adolph Green, Betty Comden; DP: Harold Rosson; Ed: Ralph E. Winters; Prod Design: Cedric Gibbons; Choreographer: Stanley Donen; Composer: Leonard Bernstein, Roger Edens, Saul Chaplin, Conrad Salinger; Art Director: Jack Martin Smith. Color, 98 min. **VHS, LASER**

On the Waterfront
(1954) Columbia
One of the most powerful film dramas of all time springs from the lives of hard men who work the docks and their resistance to the brass-knuckle politics of the waterfront unions. Union corruption wasn't a popular fim subject, and neither were director Kazan and writer Schulberg after testifying to the HUAC. But the product of their collaboration forged a powerful impression on generations of moviegoers. Brando gives a remarkable, intuitive, physical performance as a washed-up boxer turned errand boy for the corrupt union boss. But when he contributes to a killing and falls in love with the victim's sister (Saint), he begins to see the consequences of the union grip on the waterfront. Under the wing of crusading priest Malden, Brando begins to challenge the mob, eventually becoming a bloody symbol of resistance. Stirring, important filmmaking. Golden Globes for Best Director; Best Black-and-White Cinematography; Best Actor in a Drama: Marlon Brando; Best Motion Picture, Drama. Selected as a National Film Registry Outstanding Film. Academy Award Nominations: 12. **Academy Awards:** Best Picture; Best Director; Best Actor: Marlon Brando; Best Supporting Actress: Eva Marie Saint; Best Film Editing; Best Black-and-White Cinematography; Best Story and Screenplay; Best Art Direction—Set Decoration (B&W). **Cast:** Marlon Brando, Lee J. Cobb, Rod Steiger, Eva Marie Saint, Karl

Malden, Leif Erickson, John Hamilton, Nehemiah Persoff, James Westerfield, Rudy Bond. **Credits:** Dir: Elia Kazan; Prod: Sam Spiegel; Writer: Budd Schulberg; DP: Boris Kaufman; Ed: Gene Milford; Composer: Leonard Bernstein; Costumes: Anna Hill Johnstone; Art Director: Richard Day. B&W 108 min. **VHS, LASER**

On Your Toes
(1939) Warner Bros.
This remains a slight adaptation of the Broadway smash despite the participation of Rodgers and Hart, Ballanchine, and Howe. Albert is a composer who aspires to something more fulfilling than vaudeville. The wagon to his star could be a Russian dance troupe with whom his former sweetheart (Zorina, Ballanchine's wife at the time) dances. Watch for a very young O'Connor and Ballanchine's choreography of "Slaughter on Tenth Avenue." **Cast:** Vera Zorina, Eddie Albert, Alan Hale, Frank McHugh, James Gleason, Leonid Kinskey, Gloria Dickson, Queenie Smith, Donald O'Connor, Erik Rhodes. **Credits:** Dir: Ray Enright; Prod: Robert Lord; Writer: Jerry Wald, Richard Macaulay, Sig Herzig, Lawrence Riley; Story: Richard Rodgers, Lorenz Hart, George Abbott; DP: James Wong Howe, Sol Polito; Ed: Clarence Kolster; Choreographer: George Ballanchine; Composer: Lorenz Hart. B&W, 93 min.

Opening Night
(1977) Faces
A typically gritty Cassavetes work, this pivots on the psychodramas attendant on the frenetic preparations for a Broadway production. The action is compressed to the few days just before the show and follows star Rowlands on her collision course with a breakdown. Neuroses and self-examination are at the heart of the somewhat claustrophobic matter, but it is enlivened by Cassavetes's way with a solid cast. **Cast:** Gena Rowlands, John Cassavetes, Peter Falk, Ben Gazzara, Paul Stewart, Zohra Lampert, Joan Blondell, Laura Johnson. **Credits:** Dir: John Cassavetes; Prod: Al Ruban; Writer: John Cassavetes; DP: Al Ruban; Ed: Tom Cornwell; Composer: Bo Harwood; Art Director: Bryan Ryman. Color, 144 min. **VHS, LASER, DVD**

Operation Crossbow
(1965) MGM
An international cast is featured in an international production that depicts a WWII Allied espionage effort to trace the whereabouts of the V-1 rocket,

Nazi Germany's newest weapon, and act as pathfinders for the bombing mission that will eliminate the launching sites. The covert operation, with captures and evil interrogations, blown covers and silent killing, boasts a more than adequate share of tension. **Cast:** George Peppard, Sophia Loren, Trevor Howard, Tom Courtenay, Anthony Quayle, John Mills, Sylvia Syms, Richard Todd, Lilli Palmer. **Credits:** Dir: Michael Anderson, Carlo Ponti; Writer: Derry Quinn, Emeric Pressburger, Richard Imrie; DP: Erwin Hillier; Ed: Ernest Walter; Composer: Ron Goodwin; Art Director: Elliot Scott. Color, 116 min. **VHS, LASER**

Operation Pacific
(1951) Warner Bros.
The Duke portrays a submariner haunted by the specter of drowned captain Bond, who gave Wayne the order that would kill him. He's also plagued by his less-than-manly role in ending his marriage to nurse Neal after the death of their son. The course of the film draws them inexorably together again, but not without the obstacle of Captain Bond's son, who also loves Neal and now hates Wayne for doing his duty. A complex character for a Wayne action film. **Cast:** John Wayne, Patricia Neal, Ward Bond, Scott Forbes, Philip Carey, Paul Picerni, William Campbell, Kathryn Givney. **Credits:** Dir: George Waggner; Prod: Louis F. Edelman; Writer: George Waggner; DP: Bert Glennon; Ed: Alan Crosland, Jr.; Composer: Max Steiner; Art Director: Leo K. Kuter. B&W, 110 min. **VHS, LASER**

Operation Petticoat
(1959) Universal
Edwards is responsible for the deft pacing, and the long string of successful comic setups is courtesy of screenwriters Shapiro and Richlin, who wrote *Pillow Talk* (1959). The plot is almost incidental, but concerns the WWII exploits of a sub captained by Grant, and the often unmilitary results of his evacuating beautiful nurses. The sub ends up pink and Grant and Curtis, in superb comic turns, both end up married to nurses. The 35th anniversary video includes the original theatrical trailer, a reproduction of the original theatrical poster, and is digitally remastered from the original film negative. Academy Award Nomination: Best Screenplay. **Cast:** Cary Grant, Tony Curtis, Gene Evans, Dina Merrill, Arthur O'Connell, Gavin MacLeod, Marion Ross, Dick Sargent. **Credits:** Dir: Blake Edwards; Prod: Robert

Arthur; Writer: Stanley Shapiro, Maurice Richlin; Story: Paul King, Joseph Stone; DP: Russell Harlan, Clifford Stine; Ed: Ted J. Kent, Frank Gross; Prod Design: Alexander Golitzen; Composer: David Rose; Art Director: Robert Smith. Color, 122 min. **VHS, LASER**

Operation Secret
(1952) Warner Bros.
This unusual WWII espionage tale makes brilliant use of actual Nazi footage to tell the story of an American French Foreign Legionnaire (Wilde) working for the resistance who goes behind enemy lines to inspect bomb damage and comes away with a cache of films. When his plane goes down he's presumed dead. His exploits are told in flashback after the war from the proceedings of his trial for the murder of a former comrade. Based on the exploits of a real agent. **Cast:** Cornel Wilde, Karl Malden, Steve Cochran, Phyllis Thaxter, Paul Picerni, Lester Matthews, Dan O'Herlihy, Wilton Graff, Dan Riss, Jay Novello. **Credits:** Dir: Lewis Seiler; Prod: Henry Blanke; Writer: James R. Webb, Harold Medford, John Twist; Story: Alvin Joseph; DP: Ted McCord; Ed: Clarence Kolster; Composer: Roy Webb. B&W, 107 min.

The Opposite Sex
(1956) MGM
An irreproachable pedigree was one of this film's hallmarks. It was a Broadway smash for Clare Booth Luce in 1936 as *The Women*, as was the 1939 film of the same title with Norma Shearer, Rosalind Russell, Joan Fontaine, and Paulette Goddard. Another hallmark was bankable, eclectic star power in the by-now familiar story of plain-Jane Allyson losing her man to sexy Collins until she adopts the ways of the jungle to win him back. **Cast:** June Allyson, Joan Collins, Joan Blondell, Ann Miller, Agnes Moorehead, Dolores Gray, Ann Sheridan, Jeff Richards. **Credits:** Dir: David Miller; Prod: Joe Pasternak; Writer: Fay Kanin, Michael Kanin; DP: Robert Bronner; Ed: John McSweeney; Prod Design: Cedric Gibbons; Composer: Nicholas Brodszky; Art Director: Daniel B. Cathcart. Color, 117 min. **VHS, LASER**

Orchestra Wives
(1942) Fox
In spite of their widely publicized and microscopically examined breakup, The Beatles didn't invent the concept of a band on the rocks due to troublesome romances. A swingin' story of

tension on the road, replete with a jealous young wife (Rutherford), a flirty singer with the hots for Rutherford's husband (Bari), and a chorus of sensible, veteran road wives. And, of course, Glenn Miller's band, in Miller's last screen appearance before his plane disappeared over the English Channel. Watch for a young jazz aficionado soon to be known as "The Great One" (Gleason) as the bass player. Contains the songs "I've Got a Gal in Kalamazoo," "At Last," and "Serenade in Blue." Academy Award Nominations: Best Song ("I've Got a Gal in Kalamazoo"). **Cast:** George Montgomery, Glenn Miller, Carole Landis, Cesar Romero, Ann Rutherford, Virginia Gilmore, Mary Beth Hughes, Lynn Bari, Jackie Gleason, Nicholas Brothers, Harry Morgan. **Credits:** Dir: Archie Mayo; Prod: William LeBaron; Writer: Karl Tunberg, Darrell Ware; DP: Lucien Ballard; Ed: Robert Bischoff; Prod Design: Joseph C. Wright; Composer: Alfred Newman; Art Director: Richard Day. B&W, 98 min. **VHS**

The Organization
(1971) United Artists
Poitier reprises his *In the Heat of the Night* character for a third time. In this outing, Tibbs goes outside proper police channels to infiltrate a murderous drug operation and comes into conflict with his superiors. He is suspended from the force, but cracks the ring. **Cast:** Sidney Poitier, Barbara McNair, Raul Julia, Sheree North, Gerald S. O'Loughlin, Fred Beir, Allen Garfield, Bernie Hamilton. **Credits:** Dir: Don Medford; Prod: Walter Mirisch; Writer: James R. Webb; DP: Joseph Biroc; Ed: Ferris Webster; Composer: Gil Melle; Art Director: George Chan. Color, 107 min. **VHS**

O.S.S.
(1946) Paramount
Ladd, Fitzgerald, and other elite American troops parachute into WWII France to destroy a German supply route. Paramount employed 30 former O.S.S. (Office of Strategic Services, forerunner of the C.I.A.) agents as technical directors to add realism. **Cast:** Alan Ladd, Geraldine Fitzgerald, Patric Knowles, John Hoyt, Richard Benedict, Harold Vermilyea, Don Beddoe, Onslow Stevens. **Credits:** Dir: Irving Pichel; Prod: Richard Maibaum; Writer: Richard Maibaum; DP: Lionel Lindon; Ed: William Shea; Prod Design: Hans Dreier; Composer: Daniele Amfitheatrof, Heinz Roemheld; Art Director: Haldane Douglas. B&W, 108 min. **VHS**

The Other
(1972) Fox
Tryon adapted his own novel into this chilling tale of a bad seed in rural New England. It seems that not all is well in the town, what with grave robbing, children impaled while at play, and such. At the same time, grandmother Hagen begins to interpret the mysterious aura of evil emanating from one of her twin grandsons, even as the other appears to be normal. **Cast:** Uta Hagen, Diana Muldaur, John Ritter, Chris Udvarnoky, Martin Udvarnoky, Victor French, Norma Connolly, Lou Frizzell. **Credits:** Dir: Robert Mulligan; Prod: Robert Mulligan; Writer: Tom Tryon; DP: Robert Surtees; Ed: Folmar Blangsted. Color, 108 min. **VHS**

Other Men's Women
(1931) Warner Bros.
This early Wellman love triangle features prestardom parts for Cagney and Blondell. Tensions rise when a railroad conductor and his wife let a fireman come into their home and into their lives. The jealous engineer is quick to observe the leering eyes of both his wife and the fireman. The result is a fight that renders the train engineer blind. **Cast:** Mary Astor, James Cagney, Regis Toomey, Grant Withers, Fred Kohler, Walter Long, Joan Blondell. **Credits:** Dir: William Wellman; Writer: William K. Wells; Story: Maude Fulton; DP: Barney McGill; Ed: Edward McDermott; Composer: Louis Silvers, Leo F. Forbstein; Costumes: Earl Luick. B&W, 70 min.

The Other Side of Midnight
(1977) Fox
This strangely dark film of love and vengeance, from the torrid Sidney Sheldon novel, stars Beck as the WWII flier who jilts French *fille* Pisier. She gets her revenge by becoming a famous actress who marries a Greek millionaire, while he fails in business and in marriage with Sarandon. Pisier hires Beck as her pilot, they reunite, and plot to kill Sarandon, but she is swept out to sea before they do. The plotting lovers face the consequences for her killing, even as Sarandon reappears at a convent. Academy Award Nominations: Best Costume Design. **Cast:** Noelle Page, John Beck, Marie-France Pisier, Susan Sarandon, Raf Vallone, Clu Gulager, Christian Marquand, Michael Lerner. **Credits:** Dir: Charles Jarrott; Prod: Frank Yablans; Writer: Herman Raucher, Daniel Taradash; DP: Fred Koenekamp; Ed: Donn Cambern,

Harold F. Kress; Prod Design: John DeCuir; Composer: Michel Legrand. Color, 165 min. **VHS**

The Other Side of the Mountain
(1975) Universal
This is the inspirational autobiography of Olympic skier Jill Kinmont, whose career ended in a paralyzing accident. The movie chronicles her trials in coming to terms with her loss, redoubled by the breakup of her engagement with a fiancé unable to bear the weight of her disability. Enter Bridges, with whom she falls in love and begins a new life as a teacher, only to renew her acquaintance with tragedy again. Academy Award Nominations: Best Song ("Richard's Window"). **Cast:** Marilyn Hassett, Beau Bridges, Dabney Coleman, Belinda J. Montgomery, Nan Martin, William Bryant, Hampton Fancher, William Roerick. **Credits:** Dir: Larry Peerce; Prod: Edward S. Feldman; Writer: David Seltzer; DP: David M. Walsh; Ed: Eve Newman; Composer: Charles Fox. Color, 102 min. **VHS**

Our Betters
(1933) RKO
In this adaptation of a Maugham comedy, down-to-earth Bennett, a hardware heiress, marries a stiff-upper-lip British lord, and proceeds to turn society decorum upside down. An early effort by Cukor, who had been a Broadway director and dialogue coach (most notably for Lewis Milestone's *All Quiet on the Western Front*, 1930). After being relieved from the helm of Paramount's *One Hour with You* (1932), he followed Selznick to RKO for this. Bennett and Roland soon became Mr. and Mrs. **Cast:** Constance Bennett, Gilbert Roland, Charles Starrett, Anita Louise, Grant Mitchell, Hugh Sinclair, Alan Mowbray, Minor Watson, Violet Kemble-Cooper, Tyrell Davis. **Credits:** Dir: George Cukor; Prod: David O. Selznick; Writer: Harry Wagstaff Gribble, Jane Murfin, W. Somerset Maugham; DP: Charles Rosher; Ed: Jack Kitchin; Prod Design: Hobe Erwin; Composer: Max Steiner; Art Director: Van Nest Polglase. B&W, 83 min.

Our Daily Bread
(1934) United Artists
Vidor portrays the nobility of the common man in the face of titanic hardship in a film whose gestures toward group action as a solution to problems smacked of socialism to studio heads. With a slashed budget, he forged ahead with an elemental story

of hardship, temptation, conscience, and survival. Morley and Keene set up what is essentially a commune to help their farm survive, but Keene runs off with one of the women, only to stumble on a water source in the midst of a drought and return to save the farm. **Cast:** Karen Morley, Tom Keene, John Qualen, Barbara Pepper, Addison Richards, Billy Engle, Henry Hall, Lynton Brent. **Credits:** Dir: King Vidor; Prod: King Vidor; Writer: King Vidor, Elizabeth Hill, Joseph L. Mankiewicz; DP: Robert Planck; Ed: Lloyd Nosler; Composer: Alfred Newman. B&W, 80 min. **VHS, LASER**

Our Gang (The Little Rascals)

Legend has it that the idea for the Our Gang series came to producer Hal Roach as he watched some small children fight over a piece of wood. Roach, who detested the "professional children" who were common in the films of the day, decided to create young characters who behaved like real children rather than as pint-sized adults. Spanky (George "Spanky" McFarland); Alfalfa (Carl Switzer); Buckwheat (Bill "Buckwheat" Thomas); Darla (Darla Hood); and the indomitable spotted pooch, Petie, were born. These were just a few of the better-known actors that made up the Our Gang ensemble, many of whom went on to successful film and television careers (Jackie Cooper and Robert Blake perhaps the most notable). The cast rotated frequently due to the simple fact that members literally outgrew their roles. The shorts—often screened together— were enormously popular and found an even wider audience when television began airing them. The list below indicates some commonly available video packages of the Our Gang shorts.

The Return of Our Gang (1925)
Our Gang (1926)
Little Rascals, Vol. 1 (1929)
Little Rascals, Vol. 2 (1930)
Little Rascals: Pups Is Pups / Three Smart Boys (1930)
The Best of the Little Rascals (1931)
Little Rascals: Readin' and Writin'/ Mail and Female (1931)
Little Rascals: Bear Facts / Hook and Ladder (1932)
Little Rascals: Spanky / Feed 'em and Weep (1932)
Little Rascals: Choo Choo / Fishy Tales (1932)
Little Rascals: Mush and Milk / Three Men in a Tub (1933)

Little Rascals: Fish Hooky / Spooky Hooky (1933)
General Spanky / Our Gang Shorts (1936)
Little Rascals: Pay As You Exit / Kid from Borneo (1936)
Little Rascals: Bored of Education / Arbor Day (1936)
Little Rascals: Roamin' Holiday / Free Eats (1937)
Little Rascals: Rushin' Ballet / Lucky Corner (1937)
Little Rascals on Parade (1937)
Our Gang Comedies (1940)
Who Killed Doc Robbin? (1948)

Our Hearts Were Growing Up

(1946) Paramount
Two young women get into various antics by attending a Princeton University football weekend, and then by braving exciting Greenwich Village for the Christmas holiday. Along the way they cross paths with a good-natured bootlegger who helps them reconcile with their boyfriends. A sequel to Our Hearts Were Young and Gay (1944). **Cast:** Gail Russell, Diana Lynn, Brian Donlevy, Bill Edwards, William Demarest, Billy De Wolfe, Sharon Douglas, Mary Hatcher, James Brown. **Credits:** Dir: William Russell; Prod: Danny Dare; Writer: Melvin Frank, Norman Panama; Story: Frank Waldman; DP: Stuart Thompson; Ed: Doane Harrison; Composer: Victor Young; Art Director: Haldene Douglas, Hans Dreier. B&W, 83 min.

Our Little Girl

(1935) Fox
Temple's cute dimples should not obscure significant realities: She was a superstar, a guaranteed box-office knockout, and was formidably talented. She could shoulder the burden for a formulaic, feel-good plot and still make it enjoyable. She does so here, as the irrepressible bundle of precociousness who jump-starts her parents' stalled marriage by running away. **Cast:** Shirley Temple, Rosemary Ames, Joel McCrea, Lyle Talbot, Erin O'Brien-Moore, Poodles Hanneford, Margaret Armstrong, Leonard Carey. **Credits:** Dir: John S. Robertson; Prod: Edward Butcher; Writer: Stephen Morehouse Avery, Allen Rivkin, Jack Yellen; DP: John F. Seitz. B&W, 65 min. **VHS**

Our Man Flint

(1966) Fox
Coburn is appropriately wry in his first starring role as an International Man of Mystery saving the world through judicious use of ludicrously lethal gad-

gets and adroit maneuvering through bevys of blondes and armed guards. Somewhere in the range between James Bond and Austin Powers, you might say. And it's very '60s. Seems that peace and love are not on the agenda of GALAXY, however, and Coburn must go undercover to stop their plot to manipulate world weather. **Cast:** James Coburn, Lee J. Cobb, Gila Golan, Edward Mulhare, Benson Fong, Rhys Williams, Russ Conway, Ena Hartman. **Credits:** Dir: Daniel Mann; Prod: Saul David; Writer: Hal Fimberg, Ben Starr; DP: Daniel Fapp; Ed: William H. Reynolds; Composer: Jerry Goldsmith; Art Director: Jack Martin Smith, Ed Graves. Color, 107 min. **VHS, LASER**

Our Town

(1940) United Artists
Wilder's Pulitzer Prize–winning play is treated with sensitivity and given nuanced, innovative direction. It also boasts consistently strong performances and a shimmering score by Copland. Wilder's famous work is an episodic study of small-town New England life, emphasizing the maturation, courtship, and loss experienced by Holden and Scott, told in three sequences depicting the decades before WWI. Academy Award Nominations: 5, including Best Picture; Best Actress: Martha Scott. **Cast:** William Holden, Martha Scott, Thomas Mitchell, Frank Craven, Beulah Bondi, Fay Bainter, Guy Kibbee, Stuart Erwin. **Credits:** Dir: Sam Wood; Prod: Sol Lesser; Writer: Thornton Wilder, Frank Craven, Harry Chandlee; DP: Bert Glennon; Ed: Sherman Todd; Prod Design: William Cameron Menzies, Harry Horner; Composer: Aaron Copland. B&W, 90 min. **VHS**

Our Vines Have Tender Grapes

(1945) MGM
A narrative scripted by the deft hand of HUAC victim Trumbo, this is a charming paean to the virtues of community and small-town America. Released just as WWII was ending, it also represents a reassuring assessment of the values Americans fought to preserve. Robinson and O'Brien are tender as the widower father and daughter, sharing lessons ranging from life and death to Christian charity. Gifford plays the new, sophisticated schoolteacher who learns that there is more to real community than worldly trappings. **Cast:** Edward G. Robinson, Margaret O'Brien, James Craig, Frances Gifford, Agnes Moore-

head, Morris Carnovsky, Jackie Jenkins, Sara Haden. **Credits:** Dir: Roy Rowland; Prod: Robert Sisk; Writer: Dalton Trumbo; DP: Robert Surtees; Ed: Ralph E. Winters; Prod Design: Cedric Gibbons; Composer: Bronislau Kaper; Art Director: Edward C. Carfagno. B&W, 106 min. **VHS**

The Outcasts of Poker Flat
(1952) Fox
After a robbery, the thief (Mitchell) drops the cash with his wife on his way out of town. Enraged with this lawless act, the townspeople run the wife (Baxter), a gambler (Robertson), and two ladies of ill repute out of town. With a blizzard approaching, the group holes up in a mountain cabin and an attraction develops between the wife and the gambler. Then the thieving husband shows up at the cabin and holds all inside captive. After two hostages are killed, Robertson takes his shot with Mitchell. **Cast:** Anne Baxter, Dale Robertson, Miriam Hopkins, Cameron Mitchell, Craig Hill, Barbara Bates, Billy Lynn, Dick Rich, Tom Greenway. **Credits:** Dir: Joseph M. Newman; Prod: Julian Blaustein; Writer: Edmund H. North; Story: Bret Harte; DP: Joseph La Shelle; Ed: William Reynolds; Composer: Hugo Friedhofer. B&W, 80 min.

The Outlaw
(1943) RKO
An odd amalgam of sublime potential and fascinatingly silly result, this is now remembered mostly for one of the most famous ballyhoo campaigns ever executed for a movie. Huston and Mitchell were capable of delivering memorable performances, Toland was Orson Welles's preferred cinematographer, and Hawks a more than competent director. Unfortunately, they were no match for mogul Hughes's obsession with busty new starlet Russell and a pulpy, virtually fact-free story line having something to do with Billy the Kid. Release was delayed for years as Hughes plastered the countryside with posters featuring a sultry Russell as he built a story of censorship and licentiousness that successfully reeled in the suckers. **Cast:** Jane Russell, Walter Huston, Jack Beutel, Thomas Mitchell, Joe Sawyer, Frank Darien, Pat West, Carl Stockdale. **Credits:** Dir: Howard Hawks, Howard Hughes, Otho Loverling; Prod: Howard Hughes; Writer: Jules Furthman; DP: Gregg Toland; Ed: Otho S. Lovering, Wallace Grissell; Composer: Victor Young; Art Director: Perry Ferguson. B&W, 117 min. **VHS, LASER**

Outlaw Blues
(1977) Warner Bros.
Fonda is no Merle Haggard, but then Haggard was never nominated for an Oscar. Fonda is a country singer with a past. Released from prison, he is hunting for Callahan, another singer, who purloined one of his tunes. Unfortunately for Fonda, he catches up with him and Callahan somehow ends up dead. Fonda takes it on the lam with Callahan's girl, played with zest by St. James, and she turns out to be a marketing genius who makes him famous. **Cast:** Peter Fonda, Susan St. James, James Callahan, John Crawford, Michael Lerner, Matt Clark, Jeffrey Friedman, James N. Harrell. **Credits:** Dir: Richard T. Heffron; Prod: Steve Tisch; Writer: B. W. L. Norton; DP: Jules Brenner; Ed: Danford B. Greene, Scott Conrad; Composer: Charles Bernstein; Art Director: Jack Marty. Color, 101 min. **VHS**

The Outlaw Josey Wales
(1976) Warner Bros.
One of the last major studio Westerns (until Eastwood's *Unforgiven*, 1992), this is also a testament to Eastwood's feeling for the genre. True to form, Eastwood's Josey Wales becomes a man alone in the violence of a divided Missouri during the Civil War, driven to murderous revenge by the killing of his family and pillaging of his farm. Here, though, the avenging loner begins to show a human face again after years of war and killing when he rescues an Indian friend (George) and a farm family from raiders. An interesting evolution from Eastwood's man-without-a-name character that promised even more fully imagined Western characters to come. Academy Award Nominations: Best Original Score. **Cast:** Clint Eastwood, Chief Dan George, Sondra Locke, Bill Mc-Kinney, John Vernon, Paula Trueman, Sam Bottoms, Woodrow Parfrey. **Credits:** Dir: Clint Eastwood; Prod: Robert Daley; Writer: Philip Kaufman, Sonia Chernus; DP: Bruce Surtees; Ed: Ferris Webster; Prod Design: Tambi Larsen; Composer: Jerry Fielding. Color, 136 min. **VHS, LASER**

Out of the Fog
(1941) Warner Bros.
Garfield, a Brooklyn hood, puts the pressure on two Brooklyn fishermen (Mitchell and Qualen) for a slice of their profits. Handing over their savings, and all possibilities of buying a new boat, the bitter fishermen plot the thug's death. Complications arise as Mitchell's daughter, Lupino, falls in love with Garfield. The murder attempt is botched, but the sea claims the rightful victim. Based on an Irwin Shaw play. **Cast:** John Garfield, Thomas Mitchell, Eddie Albert, John Qualen, George Tobias, Aline MacMahon, Robert Homans, Bernard Gorcey, Leo Gorcey, Ida Lupino. **Credits:** Dir: Anatole Litvak; Prod: Hal B. Wallis, Henry Blanke; Writer: Richard Macaulay, Robert Rossen, Jerry Wald; Story: Irwin Shaw; DP: James Wong Howe; Ed: Warren Low; Prod Design: Carl Jules Weyl; Composer: Leo F. Forbstein. B&W, 93 min.

Out of the Past
(1947) RKO
Mitchum's past catches up with him in this web of deceit and double and triple crossings. Greer first manipulates underworld gambling czar Douglas then fixes her crosshairs on Mitchum, sent by Douglas to find her. The pair is then set upon by Mitchum's former investigative partner. All of them end up, in noir fashion, dead. A seminal film noir. Pulp novelist James M. Cain did uncredited script work. **Cast:** Robert Mitchum, Kirk Douglas, Jane Greer, Rhonda Fleming, Richard Webb, Steve Brodie, Virginia Huston, Paul Valentine. **Credits:** Dir: Jacques Tourneur; Prod: Warren Duff; Writer: Geoffrey Homes; DP: Nicholas Musuraca; Ed: Samuel E. Beetley; Composer: Roy Webb; Art Director: Albert S. D'Agostino, Jack Okey. B&W, 97 min. **VHS, LASER**

The Out-of-Towners

(1970) Paramount

When a middle-aged Ohio couple travels to New York for the husband's job interview, husband Lemmon is tossed like a neurotic hot potato from airport to mugger to hijacker with improbable but hilarious frequency until he is little more than a frayed, raw nerve. Dennis is his hysterical, then numb, wife in this Simon comedy of terrors. **Cast:** Jack Lemmon, Sandy Dennis, Anne Meara, Sandy Baron, Robert Nichols, Ann Prentiss, Ron Carey, Philip Bruns. **Credits:** Dir: Arthur Hiller; Prod: Paul Nathan; Writer: Neil Simon; DP: Andrew Laszlo; Ed: Fred Chulack; Composer: Quincy Jones; Art Director: Charles Bailey, Walter Tyler. Color, 98 min. **VHS, LASER**

The Outsider

(1961) Universal

Curtis plays a Pima Indian who becomes a national hero when he helps raise the American flag on Iwo Jima. He meets Franciscus at boot camp, and the two become friends and go off to WWII. After the battle on Iwo Jima, Curtis witnesses his friend's death, and though he's welcomed home as a hero, he suffers from survivor's guilt and begins to drink heavily. He returns to the Marines, then back to the reservation after the war, never fitting in. The one-time hero ends his battle with the bottle alone at the top of a mountain. **Cast:** Tony Curtis, James Franciscus, Gregory Walcott, Bruce Bennett, Vivian Nathan, Edmund Hashim, Paul Comi, Stanley Adams, Wayne Heffley, Ralph Moody. **Credits:** Dir: Delbert Mann; Prod: Sy Bartlett; Writer: William Bradford Huie; DP: Joseph LaShelle; Ed: Marjorie Fowler; Prod Design: Ted Haworth; Composer: Leonard Rosenman. B&W, 105 min.

Outward Bound

(1930) Warner Bros.

In this eerie allegorical fantasy, two young people in love find themselves the only living passengers on a strange vessel destined for nowhere. From The Examiner, we learn that their dog had shattered a window in their flat, foiling their suicide attempt. The first Hollywood role for Howard. **Cast:** Leslie Howard, Douglas Fairbanks, Jr., Beryl Mercer, Dudley Digges, Helen Chandler, Alec B. Francis, Montagu Love, Lyonel Watts, Alison Skipworth, Walter Kingsford. **Credits:** Dir: Robert Milton; Writer: J. Grubb Alexander; Story: Sutton Vane; DP: Hal Mohr; Ed: Ralph Dawson; Composer: Louis Silvers. B&W, 84 min.

Over the Edge

(1979) Warner Bros.

Dillon's screen debut turns out to be an intriguing, realistic assessment of suburban adolescents, driven by the banality and tedium of their world to seek escape, inevitably through drugs and violence. When a misunderstanding causes the death of a mischievous, but harmless, teenager, the kids rebel, inciting a riot that the parents and authorities are unable to control. Though not an unqualified success, the film does convey an authentic feel for teen angst. Music by punk rock legends The Ramones, and Cheap Trick. Breakthroughs for Dillon, Spano, and director Kaplan (*Heart Like a Wheel*, 1983). **Cast:** Michael Kramer, Pamela Ludwig, Matt Dillon, Vincent Spano, Tom Ferguson, Harry Northrup, Andy Romano, Ellen Geer. **Credits:** Dir: Jonathan Kaplan; Prod: George Litto; Writer: Tim Hunter, Charles Haas; DP: Andrew Davis; Ed: Robert Barrere; Prod Design: James William Newport; Composer: Sol Kaplan. Color, 95 min. **VHS**

Over 21

(1945) Columbia

Dunne is a famous writer married to Knox, a hotshot editor who works for a big-time newspaper. When the middle-aged Knox decides to enlist in the army, Dunne must adjust to life alone. Knox comes to terms with his age as younger, fitter recruits show him up in training. Through the efforts of Dunne and Knox's publisher, Coburn, Knox gets his old life and job back. An adaptation of a Gordon play based on her own wartime experiences. **Cast:** Irene Dunne, Alexander Knox, Charles Coburn, Jeff Donnell, Loren Tindall, Lee Patrick, Phil Brown, Cora Witherspoon, Charles Evans, Pierre Watkin. **Credits:** Dir: Charles Vidor; Prod: Sidney Buchman; Writer: Sidney Buchman; Story: Ruth Gordon; DP: Rudolph Maté; Ed: Otto Meyer; Prod Design: Stephen Goosson, Rudolph Sternad; Composer: Marlin Skiles. B&W, 102 min.

The Owl and the Pussycat

(1970) Columbia

Buck Henry scripted this boisterous adaptation of a Broadway play by Bill Manhoff, an intermittently hilarious Streisand-Segal vehicle. She's the call-girl sex kitten who spies the tiger lurking beneath the nerd and is bent on unveiling it. By the finish, bookish Segal has been evicted from his apartment, smoked pot, bathed with her, and fallen for her, in spite of her being a prostitute and having a best friend played by soon-to-be porn star Marilyn Chambers. Streisand's first nonsinging role. **Cast:** Barbra Streisand, George Segal, Robert Klein, Allen Garfield, Roz Kelly, Jack Manning, Grace Carney, Kim Chan. **Credits:** Dir: Herbert Ross; Prod: Ray Stark; Writer: Buck Henry; DP: Harry Stradling, Andrew Laszlo; Ed: Margaret Booth, John F. Burnett; Prod Design: Philip Rosenberg; Composer: Dick Halligan; Art Director: Robert Wightman. Color, 96 min. **VHS, LASER**

The Ox-Bow Incident

(1943) Fox

Wellman kept his eyes on the prize to make this great Western, promising two more films to Darryl Zanuck, sidestepping a producer who wanted to shoehorn Mae West into the cast (!), and eventually buying the rights to the book himself. His dogged perseverance paid off with one of the most quietly powerful Western stories ever committed to film. Fonda and Morgan stop at a saloon and get mixed up in a posse when word comes that a rancher has been murdered. A deputy (Conroy) organizes a lynch mob, and finds a suspicious trio of outsiders, including wanted criminal Quinn. The mob gives the men time to write letters, recaptures Quinn after an attempted escape, and then strings up the strangers despite Fonda's pleas for justice. When the posse gets back to town they learn of the enormity of their actions. Academy Award Nomination: Best Picture. **Cast:** Henry Fonda, Jane Darwell, Anthony Quinn, Dana Andrews, Harry Morgan, William Eythe, Harry Davenport, Frank Conroy. **Credits:** Dir: William Wellman; Prod: Lamar Trotti; Writer: Lamar Trotti; Story: Walter Van Tilburg Clark; DP: Arthur Miller; Ed: Allen McNeil; Prod Design: James Basevi; Composer: Cyril J. Mockridge; Art Director: Richard Day. B&W, 75 min. **VHS, LASER**

The Painted Desert

(1932) Pathe-American
This is Gable's first featured role and his first talkie. A boy found in the desert by Farnum and MacDonald grows up to be Boyd. When he returns from college, he gets involved with his father in a long-standing feud, romances Twelvetrees, and tangles with Twelvetrees's other beau, Gable. **Cast:** William Boyd, Helen Twelvetrees, Clark Gable, William Farnum, J. Farrell MacDonald, Edward Hearn, Charles Sellon, Edmund Breese. **Credits:** Dir: Howard Higgin; Prod: E. B. Derr; Writer: Howard Higgin, Tom Buckingham; DP: Edward Snyder, Ed: Clarence Kolster. B&W, 83 min. **VHS**

The Painted Veil

(1934) MGM
A magnificent Garbo illuminates this Maugham story set in China. When doctor Marshall ventures to China to combat cholera, neglected Garbo finds herself entangled with politician Brent. She rallies to Marshall's side when he needs her most, nursing epidemic victims and her wounded husband. Remade as *The Seventh Sin* (1957) with Eleanor Parker. **Cast:** Greta Garbo, Herbert Marshall, George Brent, Warner Oland, Jean Hersholt, Beulah Bondi, Katharine Alexander, Cecilia Parker. **Credits:** Dir: Richard Boleslawski; Prod: Hunt Stromberg; Writer: John Meehan, Salka Viertel, Edith Fitzgerald; Story: W. Somerset Maugham; DP: William H. Daniels; Ed: Hugh Wynn; Prod Design: Cedric Gibbons; Composer: Herbert Stothart. B&W, 86 min. **VHS**

Paint Your Wagon

(1969) Paramount
This is a truly bizarre excursion to the Wild West, with unlikely song-and-dance men Eastwood and Marvin. The playful Western comedy follows Eastwood and Marvin as they stake a place in the California Gold Rush by establishing a mining boomtown. They import a wagonload of prostitutes and Marvin buys a wife, Seberg, but both men share her affections. The Lerner and Loewe score (with additions from Andre Previn) includes Eastwood singing "I Talk to the Trees" and "I Still See Elisa," the growly Marvin attempting "Hand Me Down That Can of Beans," and Presnell (fortunately) singing "They Call the Wind Maria." Has to be seen to be believed. Academy Award Nomination for Best Score of a Musical Picture. **Cast:** Clint Eastwood, Lee Marvin, Jean Seberg, Ray Walston, Harve Presnell, Tom Ligon, Alan Dexter, William O'Connell, Benny Baker, Alan Baxter. **Credits:** Dir: Joshua Logan, Tom Shaw; Prod: Alan J. Lerner; Writer: Alan J. Lerner, Paddy Chayefsky; DP: William A. Fraker; Ed: Robert C. Jones; Prod Design: John Truscott; Composer: Frederick Loewe; Art Director: Carl Braunger. Color, 164 min. **VHS, LASER**

Pajama Game

(1957) Warner Bros.
Mr. Broadway, Abbott, teams with the master of film musicals, Donen, to produce and direct one of the great musicals of the '50s. Workers in a pajama factory demand a pay raise, but their negotiator (Day) spoils the arbitration by falling for the shop supervisor. Notable choreography by Bob Fosse and songs that include the title song, "Steam Heat," "There Once Was a Man," and many more. **Cast:** Doris Day, John Raitt, Carol Haney, Reta Shaw, Eddie Foy, Jr., Barbara Nichols, Ralph Dunn, Ralph Volkie. **Credits:** Dir: George Abbott, Stanley Donen; Prod: George Abbott, Stanley Donen; Writer: George Abbott, Richard Bissell; DP: Harry Stradling; Ed: William Ziegler; Art Director: Malcolm Bert. Color, 101 min. **VHS, LASER**

The Paleface

(1948) Paramount
This hilarious send-up of gunslinging oaters has Hope's mail-order dentist encountering famed outlaw Calamity Jane, played by a sly, luscious Russell. Hoping for a reprieve from the law, wisecracking Jane marries the nervous, shy dentist and gets him involved in her operation, and Hope manages to make the inadvertent transition to bad, brave gunslinger. A sequel, *Son of Paleface,* followed four years later, and remade as *The Shakiest Gun in the West* in 1968 with Don Knotts. **Academy Awards:** Best Song ("Buttons and Bows"). **Cast:** Bob Hope, Jane Russell, Robert Armstrong, Iris Adrian, Bobby Watson, Jackie Searle, Joseph Vitale, Charles Trowbridge, Clem Bevans. **Credits:** Dir: Norman Z. McLeod; Prod: Robert L. Welch; Writer: Edmund L. Hartmann, Frank Tashlin, Jack Rose; DP: Ray Rennahan; Ed: Ellsworth Hoagland; Composer: Victor Young; Art Director: Hans Dreier, Earl Hedrick. Color, 91 min. **VHS, LASER**

Pal Joey

(1957) Columbia
One of Sinatra's best musical performances is this production of the racy Broadway hit based on stories by John O'Hara. A brash singer (Sinatra) lands in San Francisco determined to make it big, but scores his biggest hits with a wealthy widow (Hayworth) and a chorus-line cutie (Novak). He's faced with a dilemma when Hayworth offers to open a club with his name on it, but only if Novak hits the road. Sinatra makes the right choice while singing classic Rodgers and Hart tunes such as "Bewitched, Bothered and Bewildered" and "I Could Write a Book." Golden Globe for Best Actor in a Musical or Comedy: Frank Sinatra. Academy Award Nominations: 4, including Best Film Editing; Best Art Direction. **Cast:** Frank Sinatra, Rita Hayworth, Kim Novak, Barbara Nichols, Bobby Sherwood, Hank Henry, Elizabeth Patterson, Robin Morse. **Credits:** Dir: George Sidney; Prod: Fred Kohlmar; Writer: Dorothy Kingsley; DP: Harold

Lipstein; Ed: Viola Lawrence, Jerome Thoms; Prod Design: Walter Holscher; Composer: Nelson Riddle. Color, 111 min. **VHS, LASER**

The Palm Beach Story
(1942) Paramount
One of the high points in Sturges's career is this screwball comedy starring Colbert and McCrea as a husband and wife whose scheme to finance his inventions leads to a wild excursion to Palm Beach. In a plan that McCrea finds a little too sophisticated, Colbert plans to divorce him and find a rich husband whose money will bankroll his airport design. Into their lives steps the half-deaf "wienie king" (Dudley)—one of Sturges's most eccentric characters in a filmography loaded with them—as well as billionaire Vallee, his carefree sister Astor and her incomprehensible companion (Arno), and a train full of tipsy hunters led by Demarest. The dialogue's snappy, the situations teeter on the edge of insanity, and the whole is a delight. **Cast:** Claudette Colbert, Joel McCrea, Mary Astor, Rudy Vallee, William Demarest, Sig Arno, Robert Dudley, Robert Warwick, Torben Meyer, Victor Potel. **Credits:** Dir: Preston Sturges; Prod: Paul Jones; Writer: Preston Sturges; DP: Victor Milner; Ed: Stuart Gilmore; Composer: Victor Young; Art Director: Hans Dreier, Ernst Fegte. B&W, 88 min. **VHS, LASER**

The Palm Beach Story (1942)

Palm Springs Weekend
(1963) Warner Bros.
This beach-party movie transported to the California desert has a dark undertone shading the shenanigans. A college basketball team and hundreds of fun-seeking kids descend on the desert resort for a wild Easter-week fling. Troy and the police chief's daughter (Powers) find each other, but trouble drives a T-Bird with Conrad at the wheel. **Cast:** Troy Donahue, Connie Stevens, Ty Hardin, Stefanie Powers, Robert Conrad, Jerry Van Dyke, Andrew Duggan, Jack Weston. **Credits:** Dir: Norman Taurog; Prod: Michael A. Hoey; Writer: Earl Hamner, Jr.; DP: Harold Lipstein; Ed: Folmar Blangsted; Composer: Frank Perkins; Art Director: Leroy Deane. Color, 101 min. **VHS, LASER**

Palmy Days
(1931) United Artists
Notable for Berkeley's signature kaleidoscopic choreography, in this follow-up to *Whoopee!* (1930) Cantor plays the stooge when he gets involved with a phony psychic. He winds up at a bakery with purloined cash in a loaf of bread and a romance with athletic Greenwood. Betty Grable appears with the Goldwyn Girls as one of the aproned bakery girls. A typically energetic Cantor role, and with an early appearance by Raft. **Cast:** Eddie Cantor, Charlotte Greenwood, Charles

Middleton, George Raft, Walter Catlett, Spencer Charters, Barbara Weeks, Harry Woods. **Credits:** Dir: Edward Sutherland; Prod: Samuel Goldwyn; Writer: Morrie Ryskind, Keene Thompson, Eddie Cantor, David Freedman; DP: Gregg Toland; Ed: Sherman Todd; Choreographer: Busby Berkeley; Composer: Alfred Newman; Art Director: Richard Day. B&W, 77 min. **VHS**

Palooka
(1934) United Artists
The comic strip comes to life as Durante plays Knobby Walsh, a flashy boxing promoter, and Erwin the goofy young boxer who might have a future in the ring. Cagney's look-alike younger brother plays his opponent in the ring. Snappy dialogue and a lot of laughs, and the Schnozz gets to sing "Inka-Dinka-Doo." **Cast:** Jimmy Durante, Stuart Erwin, Lupe Velez, Marjorie Rambeau, Robert Armstrong, Louise Beavers, William Cagney, Mary Carlisle. **Credits:** Dir: Benjamin Stoloff; Prod: Edward Small; Writer: Ben Ryan, Murray Roth, Gertrude Purcell, Jack Jevne, Arthur Kober; DP: Arthur Edeson. B&W, 86 min. **VHS**

Panama Hattie
(1942) MGM
This quickie version of a Broadway hit from MGM's vaunted Freed unit features one great song after another (from Porter, "Yip" Harburg, and other luminaries of the day) and not much plot. Sothern runs a speakeasy for American G.I.s in Panama where spies and Nazis run rampant. Horne's second film appearance. **Cast:** Ann Sothern, Red Skelton, Rags Ragland, Ben Blue, Marsha Hunt, Virginia O'Brien, Alan Mowbray, Lena Horne, Dan Dailey, Carl Esmond. **Credits:** Dir: Norman Z. McLeod; Prod: Arthur Freed; Writer: Jack McGowan, Wilkie Mahoney; DP: George J. Folsey; Ed: Blanche Sewell; Prod Design: Cedric Gibbons; Composer: Cole Porter. B&W, 81 min. **VHS**

Pan-Americana
(1945) RKO
Long is a writer working for *Western World* magazine, a slick publication that sends her in search of glamorous stories. While traveling through South America with handsome photographer Terry, Long plans a rendezvous with her workaholic fiancé Cramer, who lives in Rio. Along the way, however, Long falls in love with Terry between colorful south-of-the-border musical interludes. Prime example of Hollywood's wartime Pan-American market-

ing, and a must for fans of Latin music. **Cast:** Philip Terry, Eve Arden, Robert Benchley, Audrey Long, Marc Cramer, Jane Greer, Valerie Hall, Lita Baron, Ernest Truex. **Credits:** Dir: John H. Auer; Prod: John H. Auer; Writer: Lawrence Kimble; DP: Frank Redman; Ed: Harry Marker; Prod Design: Albert S. D'Agostino; Composer: Constantin Baka-leinikoff. B&W, 84 min.

Panic in the Streets
(1950) Fox
A dead man on the waterfront is found to have had the black plague, igniting a desperate search for a man who doesn't want to be found, the murderer. A brilliant situation for a taut, suspenseful police drama with an unusual detective, the doctor played with steely resolve by Widmark. Kazan depicts the seedy waterfront of New Orleans with care and Palance makes a sinister rat. **Academy Awards:** Best Motion Picture Story. **Cast:** Richard Widmark, Paul Douglas, Barbara Bel Geddes, Jack Palance, Zero Mostel, Dan Riss, Alexis Minotis, Tommy Cook. **Credits:** Dir: Elia Kazan; Prod: Sol C. Siegel; Writer: Richard Murphy, Daniel Fuchs; DP: Joseph MacDonald; Ed: Harmon Jones; Prod Design: Lyle Wheeler, Maurice Ransford; Composer: Alfred Newman. B&W, 96 min. **VHS**

Panic in Year Zero
(1962) AIP
A family heads for its usual vacation spot only to pause when a nuclear attack leaves Los Angeles in chaos and ignites panic throughout the city. They pick up some supplies and hole up in a cave, fending off lunatic hoodlums. Milland directs with more seriousness than the sensational material probably deserves, but he gives this real tension. **Cast:** Ray Milland, Frankie Avalon, Jean Hagen, Mary Mitchell, Joan Freeman, Richard Garland, Richard Bakalyan, Willis Bouchey, Neil Nephew, Rex Holman. **Credits:** Dir: Ray Milland; Prod: Lou Rusoff, Arnold Houghland; Writer: John Morton, Jay Simms; DP: Gilbert Warrenton; Ed: William Austin, Anthony Carras; Composer: Les Baxter; Art Director: Daniel Haller. B&W, 92 min. **VHS**

Papa's Delicate Condition
(1963) Paramount
Gleason is the inebriated Papa whose shenanigans keep his family on their toes. Based on silent screen star Corinne Griffith's autobiographical account of growing up at the turn of the century in Texas. The Oscar for Best Song went to it: "Call Me Irre-

Paper Moon (1973)

sponsible" (by James Van Heusen and Sammy Cahn). "Bill Bailey Won't You Please Come Home" debuted here, too. **Academy Awards:** Best Song. **Cast:** Jackie Gleason, Glynis Johns, Charlie Ruggles, Laurel Goodwin, Ned Glass, Murray Hamilton, Charles Lane, Benny Baker, Linda Bruhl, Elisha Cook, Jr.. **Credits:** Dir: George Marshall; Prod: Jack Rose; Writer: Jack Rose; DP: Loyal Griggs; Ed: Frank P. Keller; Composer: Joseph J. Lilley; Art Director: Hal Pereira, Arthur Lonergan. Color, 98 min. **VHS, LASER**

The Paper Chase
(1973) Fox
Houseman's portrayal of a wise, tough Harvard Law professor won him an Academy Award and the film became the basis for the very successful television series of the same name. First-year Harvard Law School student Bottoms struggles with the intense pressures of the Ivy League and falls in love (unwittingly) with the

legendary professor's divorced daughter. Based on the novel by Osborn, Academy Award Nominations: 3, including Best (Adapted) Screenplay. **Academy Awards:** Best Supporting Actor: John Houseman. **Cast:** Timothy Bottoms, Lindsay Wagner, John Houseman, Graham Beckel, Craig Richard Nelson, James Naughton, Regina Baff. **Credits:** Dir: James Bridges, Robert C. Thompson; Prod: Robert C. Thompson, Rodrick Paul; Writer: James Bridges; Story: John Jay Osborn, Jr.; DP: Gordon Willis; Ed: Walter Thompson; Composer: John Williams; Art Director: George Jenkins. Color, 111 min. **VHS, LASER**

Paper Moon
(1973) Paramount
Bogdanovich brilliantly re-creates the Depression-era road movie with two appealing leads: Tatum O'Neal, in her debut, a tough-talking orphan who hitches a ride from her mom's funeral with con artist Ryan O'Neal. They work

the Great Plains with a variety of scams as they grow closer together. Funny and touching, with winning performances. Academy Award Nominations: 4, including Best Screenplay. **Academy Awards:** Best Supporting Actress: Tatum O'Neal. **Cast:** Ryan O'Neal, Tatum O'Neal, Madeline Kahn, John Hillerman, James N. Harrell, Noble Willingham, Burton Gilliam, Randy Quaid, P. J. Johnson, Jessie Lee Fulton. **Credits:** Dir: Peter Bogdanovich; Prod: Peter Bogdanovich; Writer: Alvin Sargent; DP: Laszlo Kovacs; Ed: Verna Fields; Prod Design: Polly Platt. B&W, 114 min. VHS, LASER

Papillon
(1973) Allied Artists
In this richly detailed action-adventure, McQueen plays a famous '30s French criminal sent to the Devil's Island penal colony from which no one had ever escaped. On the way he meets Hoffman, a stock swindler, and they set about preparing to escape. Determined to flee, they succeed, are recaptured, then escape again. Gritty scenes of prison life and great performances. Academy Award Nomination for Best Original Dramatic Score. **Cast:** Steve McQueen, Dustin Hoffman, Victor Jory, Anthony Zerbe, Don Gordon, Robert Deman, Woodrow Parfrey, Billy Mumy. **Credits:** Dir: Franklin J. Schaffner; Prod: Robert Dorfmann, Franklin J. Schaffner; Writer: Dalton Trumbo, Lorenzo Semple, Jr.; Story: Henri Charrière; DP: Fred J. Koenekamp; Ed: Robert W. Swink; Prod Design: Tony Masters; Composer: Jerry Goldsmith; Art Director: Jack Maxsted. Color, 150 min. VHS

The Paradine Case
(1947) Fox
This is the last of the films Hitchcock directed under producer Selznick, who cowrote the script. A happily married English barrister (Peck) falls in love with a beautiful client (Valli) accused of murdering her husband. Peck learns of Valli's affair with her stableman (Jourdan) and calls him to the stand. The result is a stunning reversal and death. An unhappy collaboration between Hitch and Selznick resulting in a second-rank Hitchcock. In pure Selznick style, nearly a third of the film's budget went to re-creating the original courtroom on the set. Valli and Jourdan's American film debuts. Academy Award Nomination for Best Supporting Actress: Ethel Barrymore. **Cast:** Gregory Peck, Ann Todd, Charles Laughton, Ethel Barrymore, Louis Jourdan, Alida Valli, Leo G. Carroll,

Joan Tetzel. **Credits:** Dir: Alfred Hitchcock; Prod: David O. Selznick; Writer: Alma Reville, James Bridie, Robert Hichens, David O. Selznick; DP: Lee Garmes; Ed: Hal C. Kern, John Faure; Prod Design: J. McMillan Johnson; Composer: Franz Waxman. B&W, 125 min. VHS, LASER

The Parallax View
(1974) Paramount
This taut political thriller features a terrific performance by Beatty as a reporter nosing around for a story when witnesses to a political assassination start turning up dead. He tracks the source of the killings to the shadowy Parallax Corporation and puts himself in danger as another senator is in harm's way. **Cast:** Warren Beatty, Paula Prentiss, Hume Cronyn, William Daniels, Kelly Thordsen, Earl Hindman, Chuck Waters, Jim Davis. **Credits:** Dir: Alan J. Pakula; Prod: Alan J. Pakula; Writer: David Giler, Lorenzo Semple, Jr.; Story: Loren Singer; DP: Gordon Willis; Ed: John W. Wheeler; Composer: Michael Small; Art Director: George Jenkins. Color, 102 min. VHS

Pardners
(1956) Paramount
In this Martin and Lewis remake of *Rhythm on the Range* (1936), Lewis plays a Manhattan millionaire who becomes sheriff of a small Western town and helps ranch-hand Martin get rid of the bad guys. Made after Martin and Lewis broke up their nightclub act. **Cast:** Dean Martin, Jerry Lewis, Lori Nelson, Jeff Morrow, Jackie Loughery, John Baragrey, Agnes Moorehead, Milton Frome, Lon Chaney, Jr. **Credits:** Dir: Norman Taurog; Prod: Paul Jones; Writer: Sidney Sheldon; Story: Jerry Davis; DP: Daniel Fapp; Ed: Archie Marshek; Composer: Frank DeVol; Art Director: Hal Pereira, Roland Anderson. Color, 88 min. VHS

Pardon My Past
(1945) Columbia
Leaving the army behind them, MacMurray and Demarest decide to invest their savings in a mink farm. Heading to a small Wisconsin town, they meet with a cool welcome as MacMurray is mistaken for a local playboy who is in debt to half the town, particularly Tamiroff and his thugs. MacMurray gets caught up in the devious machinations of his alter-ego's family, not to mention his double's wife, who is anything but happy with her husband's philandering. An old wheeze but MacMurray in a double role adds interest. **Cast:** Fred MacMurray, Akim Tamiroff,

William Demarest, Rita Johnson, Harry Davenport, Douglass Dumbrille, Karolyn Grimes, Dewey Robinson, Tom Moffatt, Marguerite Chapman. **Credits:** Dir: Leslie Fenton; Prod: Leslie Fenton; Writer: Leslie Fenton, Karl Kamb; Story: Patterson McNutt, Harlan Ware; DP: Russell Metty; Ed: Otto Lovering, Richard Herrmance; Prod Design: Bernard Herzbrun; Composer: Dimitri Tiomkin. B&W, 89 min.

The Parent Trap
(1961) Disney
The ultimate, reassuring fantasy of children of divorced parents made a much-loved family film. Mills plays twins separated years before when their parents (Keith and O'Hara) separate. When Keith moves to remarry, together they hatch an ingenious plot to reunite their family. Remade in 1998. Academy Award Nominations: 2, including Best Film Editing. **Cast:** Hayley Mills, Maureen O'Hara, Brian Keith, Charlie Ruggles, Una Merkel, Leo G. Carroll, Joanna Barnes, Cathleen Nesbitt, Crahan Denton. **Credits:** Dir: David Swift; Prod: George Golitzen; Writer: David Swift; Story: Erich Kastner; DP: Lucien Ballard; Ed: Philip W. Anderson; Composer: Paul J. Smith. Color, 129 min. VHS, LASER

Paris Blues
(1961) United Artists
Jazz fans take note: cool sounds by great artists here. Newman studies classical music but hangs out with buddy Poitier playing jazz in a cabaret, until tourists Woodward and Carroll make the scene. Carroll helps Poitier overcome his distaste for America's racial hatred and head back home, and Woodward nearly entices Newman away from his studies. A well-intentioned melodrama with Ritt's near-documentary style, but the real treat here is the music, with Ellington and Armstrong leading the way. Academy Award Nomination for Best Scoring of a Musical Picture. **Cast:** Paul Newman, Joanne Woodward, Diahann Carroll, Sidney Poitier, Louis Armstrong, Serge Reggiani, Barbara Laage, Marie Versini, Andre Luguet. **Credits:** Dir: Martin Ritt; Prod: Sam Shaw; Writer: Jack Sher, Irene Kamp, Walter Bernstein, Lulla Adler; DP: Christian Matras; Ed: Roger Dwyre; Composer: Duke Ellington; Art Director: Alexander Trauner. B&W, 98 min. VHS

Paris Calling
(1941) Universal
Bergner, a wealthy Parisian socialite, joins the French underground resis-

tance when the Nazis invade. Her lover Rathbone, also a member of the underground, becomes an informer for the Nazis and betrays the movement. Meanwhile, disgusted by Rathbone's betrayal, she falls in love with an American fighter pilot, Scott. Routine WWII programmer. **Cast:** Elisabeth Bergner, Randolph Scott, Basil Rathbone, Gale Sondergaard, Lee J. Cobb, Charles Arnt, Eduardo Ciannelli, Elisabeth Risdon, Georges Renavent, William Edmunds. **Credits:** Dir: Edwin L. Marin; Prod: Benjamin Glazer; Writer: Charles Kaufman; Story: John S. Toldy; DP: Milton Krasner; Ed: Edward Curtiss; Prod Design: Jack Otterson; Composer: Richard Hageman. B&W, 95 min.

Paris Holiday
(1958) United Artists
Sturges makes a rare screen appearance in this affable farce. Hope arrives in Paris to pick up a new screenplay by a successful writer, but it's not so easy, as Ekberg wants it too. He flees French gangsters and a mental institution. **Cast:** Bob Hope, Fernandel, Anita Ekberg, Martha Hyer, Andre Morell, Jean Murat, Yves Brainville, Alan Gifford, Preston Sturges. **Credits:** Dir: Gerd Oswald; Prod: Bob Hope; Writer: Edmund Beloin, Dean Riesner; DP: Roger Hubert; Ed: Ellsworth Hoagland; Prod Design: Georges Wakhevitch; Composer: Joseph J. Lilley. Color, 100 min. VHS

Paris When It Sizzles
(1964) Paramount
The romantic pairing from *Sabrina* (1954) reunites for a quirky comedy shot on location in Paris. Holden is trying desperately to finish a screenplay and hires Hepburn as his secretary. She is understandably irresistible and the two fall in love as they act out the possible scenarios. An all-star cast, including Dietrich and Sinatra, show up for a party. This was a painful experience for Holden, who had fallen in love with Hepburn on the *Sabrina* set and still carried a brightly burning torch. The hopelessness of his attraction fueled drinking binges and a wrecked Ferrari during shooting. The result seems forlorn rather than sparkling. **Cast:** William Holden, Audrey Hepburn, Noel Coward, Gregoire Aslan, Raymond Bussieres, Tony Curtis, Fred Astaire, Frank Sinatra, Christian Duvallex, Marlene Dietrich. **Credits:** Dir: Richard Quine; Prod: Richard Quine, George Axelrod; Writer: George Axelrod; DP: Charles

Lang; Ed: Archie Marshek; Composer: Nelson Riddle; Art Director: Jean D'Eaubonne. Color, 110 min. VHS

Park Row
(1952) United Artists
Tough-guy director Fuller maps the origins of the contemporary American press. The story follows the efforts of an idealistic newspaper editor (Evans) who joins forces with an equally optimistic printer to start their own paper, *The Globe.* A circulation war ensues with the attractive and feisty owner of his rival publication, *The Star.* Realizing they both support freedom of the press, the two end the duel in favor of romance. An early effort from a director better known for slam-bang action. **Cast:** Gene Evans, Mary Welch, Bela Kovacs, Herbert Heyes, Tina Rome, George O'Hanlon, Jr., J. M. Kerrigan, Forrest Taylor, Don Orlando, Neyle Morrow. **Credits:** Dir: Samuel Fuller; Prod: Samuel Fuller; Writer: Samuel Fuller; DP: Jack Russell; Ed: Phillip Cahn; Composer: Paul Dunlap; Prod Design: Theobold Holsopple. B&W, 83 min.

Parlor, Bedroom and Bath
(1931) MGM
Keaton's first sound film finds him coming to the romantic rescue of Edwards by wooing his sister, Christy. But his teacher in love, Greenwood, starts to have eyes for her pupil and the deal's off. Filmed at Keaton's mansion in Beverly Hills. **Cast:** Buster Keaton, Charlotte Greenwood, Reginald Denny, Cliff Edwards, Dorothy Christy, Joan Peers, Sally Eilers, Natalie Moorhead, Edward Brophy. **Credits:** Dir: Edward Sedgwick; Prod: Edward Sedgwick; Writer: Richard Schayer, Robert E. Hopkins; DP: Leonard Smith; Ed: William LeVanway. B&W, 80 min. VHS

The Party
(1968) United Artists
The *Pink Panther* team of director Edwards and Sellers reunite for the story of a bumbling Indian actor in Hollywood to star in a remake of *Gunga Din.* After knocking down most of the set, Sellers starts to work on the home of a producer. Sight gags make up for what little plot exists. **Cast:** Peter Sellers, Claudine Longet, Marge Champion, Denny Miller, Gavin MacLeod, Buddy Lester, Carol Wayne, Allan Jung. **Credits:** Dir: Blake Edwards; Prod: Blake Edwards; Writer: Blake Edwards, Tom Waldman, Frank Waldman; DP: Lucien Ballard; Ed: Ralph E. Winters; Prod Design: Fernando Carrere; Composer: Henry Mancini. Color, 99 min. VHS, LASER

Party Girl
(1958) MGM
Ray's brooding style lifts a steamy potboiler above its material. Taylor is a crippled attorney representing Chicago mobster Cobb's gunmen until he falls hard for a nightclub dancer (Charisse) who convinces him to call it quits and find another line of work. He bitterly reveals that he's married to a woman who rejects him because of his affliction. Charisse sticks by him through a restorative operation, and they prepare for a new life until he takes one last case. In his final encounter with the gangster, he is wounded, arrested by the cops, and forced to testify against the gang, but the Mob's got Charisse as a hostage to keep him quiet. Another Ray portrait of a bitter loner who makes one last grab for life. **Cast:** Robert Taylor, Cyd Charisse, Lee J. Cobb, John Ireland, Kent Smith, Claire Kelly, Corey Allen, Lewis Charles, Kem Dibbs. **Credits:** Dir: Nicholas Ray; Prod: Joe Pasternak; Writer: George Wells; Story: Leo Katcher; DP: Robert Bronner; Ed: John McSweeney, Jr.; Prod Design: William A. Horning, Randal Duell; Composer: Jeff Alexander. Color, 100 min. VHS, LASER

Party Wire
(1935) Columbia
A comedy perhaps made incomprehensible by advancing technology. When his estranged father dies, young Jory returns to his small town to take over the family dairy business. Though all the eligible (and some not-so-eligible) women swoon over the romantic stranger, Jory only has eyes for small-town beauty Arthur. The anonymous gossips who pick up tidbits on the party line (ask your grandparents) almost spoil what should be a storybook romance with their prattling. Always worth watching Arthur, here in a less well known role. **Cast:** Jean Arthur, Victor Jory, Helen Lowell, Robert Allen, Charley Grapewin, Clara Blandick, Geneva Mitchell, Maude Eburne, Matt McHugh, Oscar Apfel. **Credits:** Dir: Erle C. Kenton; Writer: Ethel Hill, John Howard Lawson, Vera Caspary, Bruce Manning; DP: Allen G. Siegler; Ed: Viola Lawrence; Prod Design: Stephen Goosson. B&W, 70 min.

Passage to Marseilles
(1944) Warner Bros.
Curtiz rounds up the male leads from *Casablanca* for another gripping, atmospheric wartime tale. The story centers on Bogart, a bombardier on a Free France bomber who drops let-

ters to his wife and son trapped in occupied France. Through flashbacks we see the story of his prewar romance, resistance to fascism, his arrest, and eventual escape from a penal colony. Though Bogie never makes it back alive, Rains ensures his last letter will be delivered. Stirring and action-packed. **Cast:** Humphrey Bogart, Michele Morgan, Claude Rains, Philip Dorn, Peter Lorre, Sydney Greenstreet, George Tobias, Victor Francen. **Credits:** Dir: Michael Curtiz; Prod: Hal B. Wallis; Writer: Casey Robinson, John C. Moffitt; Story: Charles Robinoff, James Norman Hall; DP: James Wong Howe; Ed: Owen Marks; Composer: Max Steiner; Art Director: Carl Jules Weyl. B&W, 110 min. **VHS**

The Passionate Plumber
(1932) MGM
One of the few Keaton talkies, mostly of interest for the pairing with Durante. The story has to do with Keaton fending off a Spanish nobleman's advances on his girl. **Cast:** Buster Keaton, Jimmy Durante, Irene Purcell, Polly Moran, Gilbert Roland, Mona Maris, Maude Eburne, Henry Armetta, Paul Porcasi, Jean del Val. **Credits:** Dir: Edgar Sedgwick; Writer: Nydia Westman, Ralph Spence, Jacques Deval, Laurence E. Johnson; DP: Norbert F. Brodine; Ed: William S. Gray. B&W, 73 min.

Pat and Mike
(1952) MGM
Cukor directs the seventh pairing of Hepburn and Tracy and, in one of their best outings, the sparring has an athletic setting to match the verbal gymnastics. Tracy plays a sports promoter who discovers a natural in Hepburn's small-college phys ed instructor. He keeps the gamblers at bay and she deals with her boring administrator beau as she warms to Tracy. Hepburn was indeed a natural athlete and she gets to show off in the company of some noted athletes. Bronson makes an early appearance (as a criminal) and Connors (then a ballplayer) makes his debut. Academy Award Nominations: Best Original Screenplay. **Cast:** Katharine Hepburn, Spencer Tracy, Jim Backus, Charles Bronson, Chuck Connors, Aldo Ray, William Ching, Sammy White. **Credits:** Dir: George Cukor; Prod: Lawrence Weingarten; Writer: Ruth Gordon, Garson Kanin; DP: William Daniels; Ed: George Boemler; Prod Design: Cedric Gibbons; Composer: David Raksin. B&W, 96 min. **VHS**

A Patch of Blue
(1965) MGM
Exquisite performances by Winters, Poitier, and Hartman, who debuted as a young blind woman who falls in love with a black man. Winters is unforgettable as the tortured mother who blinded her daughter and then seems determined to rob her of life itself. Hartman's frail beauty was seen only occasionally on-screen through the '80s, and she died in 1987, a presumed suicide. Academy Award Nominations: 5, including Best Actress: Elizabeth Hartman. **Academy Award:** Best Supporting Actress: Shelley Winters. **Cast:** Sidney Poitier, Elizabeth Hartman, Shelley Winters, Wallace Ford, Ivan Dixon, John Qualen, Elisabeth Fraser, Kelly Flynn. **Credits:** Dir: Guy Green; Prod: Pandro S. Berman; Writer: Guy Green; Story: Elizabeth Kata; DP: Robert Burks; Ed: Rita Roland; Prod Design: George W. Davis, Urie McCleary; Composer: Jerry Goldsmith. Color, 106 min. **VHS**

Pat Garrett and Billy the Kid
(1973) MGM
Aging gunfighter Garrett (Coburn) sees the handwriting on the wall and opts to pin on a badge, which leads him to a confrontation with his old friend, the notorious Billy the Kid (Kristofferson). Hard-bitten, beautifully photographed Western that replaces the usual gunplay bravado with ambivalence and guilt. A wonderful supporting cast includes old hands such as Pickens and Wills and intriguingly cast newcomers such as Dylan and Rita Coolidge (Kristofferson's wife at the time). Dylan's sound track includes "Knockin' on Heaven's Door," signaling his return to the pop charts. Peckinpah saw what he considered one of his best works disastrously reedited by the studio; his cut is once again available. **Cast:** Kris Kristofferson, James Coburn, Bob Dylan, Katy Jurado, Jason Robards, Jr., Richard Jaeckel, Slim Pickens, Chill Wills. **Credits:** Dir: Sam Peckinpah; Prod: Gordon Carroll; Writer: Rudy Wurlitzer; DP: John Coquillon; Ed: Roger Spottiswoode; Prod Design: Ted Haworth; Composer: Bob Dylan. Color, 122 min. **VHS, LASER**

The Pathfinder
(1952) Columbia
Based on Cooper's tale of a British scout (Montgomery) sent to spy on a French fortress. An interpreter accompanies him and discovers French schemes to dominate the Great Lakes regions. The two are unmasked, and

the British army arrives in the nick of time to deliver the couple from death. Okay historical adventure. **Cast:** George Montgomery, Helena Carter, Jay Silverheels, Walter Kingsford, Rodd Redwing, Stephen Bekassy, Elena Verdugo, Bruce Lester. **Credits:** Dir: Sidney Salkow; Prod: Sam Katzman; Writer: Robert E. Kent; Story: James Fenimore Cooper; DP: Henry Freulich; Ed: Sidney Salkow, Jerome Thoms. Color, 78 min.

Paths of Glory
(1957) United Artists
This is a cinema landmark and the most moving indictment of war's brutality since *All Quiet on the Western Front* (1930). Kubrick's restless camera moves through WWI trenches as Douglas commands a French company waiting for the whistle that sends them over the top and into the teeth of enemy machine-gun fire. Douglas makes a plea to the heartless commanders (Macready and Menjou) to relieve his weary men, but callous disregard for human life coupled with ambition wins the day. When one company refuses to sacrifice themselves, a court-martial ensues, with Douglas pleading the cases of the condemned men. Kubrick revisited the horror of war with *Full Metal Jacket* 30 years later. Selected for the National Film Registry. **Cast:** Kirk Douglas, Ralph Meeker, Adolphe Menjou, George Macready, Wayne Morris, Richard Anderson, Joseph Turkel, Timothy Carey. **Credits:** Dir: Stanley Kubrick; Prod: James B. Harris; Writer: Stanley Kubrick, Calder Willingham; Story: Jim Thompson; DP: George Krause; Ed: Eva Kroll; Composer: Gerald Fried; Art Director: Ludwig Reiber. B&W, 86 min. **VHS, LASER**

The Patsy
(1964) Paramount
Lorre's last film (he died just after shooting was completed) was this minor Lewis vehicle. Shark producers who've just lost their star comedian to the Grim Reaper select an inept bellhop to make over into a comedy king. Many Hollywood cameos, including a Jerry appearance on the *Ed Sullivan Show*. **Cast:** Jerry Lewis, Ina Balin, Everett Sloane, Keenan Wynn, Peter Lorre, John Carradine, Hans Conried, Del Moore. **Credits:** Dir: Jerry Lewis; Prod: Ernest D. Glucksman; Writer: Jerry Lewis, Bill Richmond; DP: Wallace Kelley; Ed: John Woodcock; Composer: David Raksin; Art Director: Hal Pereira, Cary Odell. Color, 106 min. **VHS, LASER**

Patterns

(1955) United Artists

A sleeper, with roots in mid-'50s TV drama. Future *Twilight Zone* auteur Rod Serling wrote (from his *Kraft Playhouse* script) and TV veteran Cook directed this story of corporate greed, which stands up well today. Sloane is a ruthless and greedy chariman of the board who aims to crush the humanists in his midst. Begley is a kindhearted older man who is manipulated into a confrontation with Heflin, a young, ambitious executive. A tense, realistic view of life swimming with sharks in corporate America. **Cast:** Ed Begley, Richard Kiley, Elizabeth Montgomery, Van Heflin, Everett Sloane, Beatrice Straight, Elizabeth Wilson, Sally Gracie. **Credits:** Dir: Fielder Cook; Prod: Michael Myerberg; Writer: Rod Serling; DP: Boris Kaufman; Ed: David Kummins, Carl Lerner; Prod Design: Richard Sylbert. B&W, 84 min. **VHS**

Patton

(1970) Fox

This three-dimensional bio of WWII general George S. Patton, who wrote poetry, fired pistols at strafing fighter planes, and loved America and the military with a fierce zeal, traces his personal rivalry with Rommel, his problematic treatment of his own men, and his nearly runaway contempt for diplomacy. The film triumphs with Scott's fully inhabited portrait of a complex, larger-than-life figure. The special edition video includes a behind-the-scenes feature, production stills, and audio commentary on the production. Academy Award Nominations: 10, including Best Cinematography; Best Score. **Academy Awards:** Best Picture; Best Director; Best Actor: George C. Scott; Best Film Editing; Best Sound; Best Story/Screenplay; Best Art Direction—Set Decoration. **Cast:** George C. Scott, Karl Malden, Stephen Young, Michael Strong, Michael Bates, Edward Binns, Lawrence Dobkin, John Doucette. **Credits:** Dir: Franklin J. Schaffner; Prod: Frank McCarthy, Frank Caffey; Writer: Francis Ford Coppola, Edmund H. North; Story: Omar N. Bradley; DP: Fred Koenekamp; Ed: Hugh S. Fowler; Prod Design: Urie McCleary; Composer: Jerry Goldsmith; Art Director: Gil Parrondo. Color, 172 min. **VHS, LASER**

Paula

(1952) Columbia

A hit-and-run driver renders a young orphan boy (Rettig) mute. A young married couple, unable to have children, are prevailed upon to take the child into their home. The wife (Young) begins the difficult task of teaching the youngster to speak again, and in the course of her interaction reveals she is the individual unwittingly responsible for the accident. The angry youth works diligently to speak again so that he can denounce her. The search for the driver gets uncomfortably close to the young woman, but in the end she is spared and wins the boy's affection. **Cast:** Loretta Young, Kent Smith, Alexander Knox, Tommy Rettig, Otto Hulett, William H. Wright, Raymond Greenleaf, William Veder. **Credits:** Dir: Rudolph Maté; Prod: Buddy Adler; Writer: James Poe, Jerry Sackhelm, Larry Marcus; DP: Viola Lawrence; Composer: George Dunning. B&W, 80 min.

The Pawnbroker

(1965) AIP

Lumet pushed hard on societal and filmmaking conventions to produce this unsparing portrait of a man robbed of his humanity by unspeakable cruelty. Steiger's portrayal of a Harlem pawnbroker haunted by the rape and killing of his wife and sons in the Nazi death camps is a lasting achievement. Steiger makes a claustrophobic world for himself in the confines of the shop, almost daring the customers and thieves who come in the door to find a glimmer of emotion in him. Feelings intrude, manifested as nearly subliminal flashes of the past created by editor Rosenblum. The 30th-anniversary edition includes a reproduction of the original theatrical poster in German, the original theatrical trailer, and is digitally remastered from the original film negative. Academy Award Nominations: Best Actor: Rod Steiger. **Cast:** Rod Steiger, Geraldine Fitzgerald, Brock Peters, Jaime Sanchez, Thelma Oliver, Marketta Kimbrell, Baruch Lumet, Linda Geiser. **Credits:** Dir: Sidney Lumet; Prod: Roger Lewis, Philip Langner; Writer: David Friedkin, Morton Fine; Story: Edward Lewis Wallant; DP: Boris Kaufman; Ed: Ralph Rosenblum; Composer: Quincy Jones; Art Director: Richard Sylbert. B&W, 116 min. **VHS, LASER**

Payday

(1972) Cinerama

Torn stars in this powerful little drama as a country-music star on the downside of the music-business roller coaster as he tours the small-town circuit trying to make his way back to the top in Nashville. An unflinching look at show business day-to-day, the seedy hotels, the boredom, the haggard groupies. Fine performances in a little-seen gem. **Cast:** Rip Torn, Ahna Capri, Cliff Emmich, Elayne Heilveil, Michael C. Gwynne, Jeff Morris, Henry O. Arnold, Michael Edwards. **Credits:** Dir: Daryl Duke; Prod: Don Carpenter, Martin Fink; Writer: Don Carpenter; DP: Richard C. Glouner; Ed: Richard Halsey. Color, 98 min. **VHS**

Payment Deferred

(1932) MGM

Laughton honed his portrayal of middle-class murderer Marble onstage, so it is not surprising that this understated film captures his finely etched portrait of a man driven to murder by debt. Laughton kills his visiting nephew for ready investment capital, then buries him in the garden behind the house. He proceeds to make a fortune, but is yoked into killing both by his terror of leaving the scene where he buried the evidence and the specter of his guilt. In a twist on an-eye-for-an-eye, Laughton is falsely accused of another crime and must face the consequences. **Cast:** Charles Laughton, Ray Milland, Maureen O'Sullivan, Neil Hamilton, Halliwell Hobbes, Dorothy Peterson, William Stack, Verree Teasdale. **Credits:** Dir: Lothar Mendes; Writer: Ernest Vajda, Claudine West; Story: Jeffrey Dell, C. S. Forester; DP: Merritt Gerstad; Ed: Frank Sullivan. B&W, 81 min.

Payment on Demand

(1951) RKO

Davis stars as a woman scorned who finds herself facing the prospect of a lonely life. Davis is shocked when her wealthy husband of 20 years, Sullivan, asks for a divorce. Sullivan has tired of his wife's relentless pursuit of social ascendancy, and begun dating a teacher. Davis wins an enormous settlement, leaves for a cruise, and begins an onboard affair, but reconsiders her actions after visiting another wealthy divorcée living the "high life" of an aging gigolo magnet. Realizing her responsibility in driving her husband away, she heads home to attempt reconciliation. Soapy, but franker than most treatments of the subject. **Cast:** Bette Davis, Barry Sullivan, Frances Dee, Kent Taylor, Peggie Castle, Betty Lynn, Richard Anderson, Brett King, Otto Kruger, Jane Cowl. **Credits:** Dir: Curtis Bernhardt; Prod: Jack H. Skirball, Bruce Manning; Writer: Bruce Manning, Curtis Bernhardt; DP: Leo Tover; Ed: Harry

Marker; Prod Design: Albert S. D'Agostino, Carroll Clark; Composer: Victor Young. B&W, 90 min.

Peck's Bad Boy
(1934) Fox
A boy and his mother move in and try to drive apart Cooper and the man who adopted him. A fine family drama, and a remake of a 1921 silent film based on stories by George Wilbur Peck. **Cast:** Jackie Cooper, Thomas Meighan, Jackie Searl, Dorothy Peterson, O. P. Heggie, Charles Evans, Harvey Clark, Lloyd Ingraham. **Credits:** Dir: Edward F. Cline; Prod: Sol Lesser; Writer: Bernard Schubert, Marguerite Roberts; Story: George W. Peck; DP: Frank B. Good; Ed: W. Donn Hayes. B&W, 68 min. **VHS**

Peg o' My Heart
(1933) MGM
Irish lass (Davies) must leave her beloved village and father to live among the aristocrats in England if she is to receive two million pounds. She doesn't last long among the monied set. Written as a vehicle for the bright charms of Davies by her friend Frances Marion. **Cast:** Marion Davies, Onslow Stevens, John Farrell MacDonald, Juliette Compton, Irene Browne, Tyrell Davis, Alan Mowbray, Doris Lloyd, Robert Greig, Nora Cecil. **Credits:** Dir: Robert Z. Leonard; Writer: Frank R. Adams, Frances Marion; Story: J. Hartley Manners; DP: George Barnes; Ed: Margaret Booth; Composer: Herbert Stothart. B&W, 89 min.

Penny Serenade
(1941) Columbia
One of the saddest tales put in front of the camera is played by consummate actors Dunne and Grant, who had a lighthearted hit with *The Awful Truth* (1937). Dunne and Grant are about to part, having endured the tragedy of losing a child by miscarriage and then, after struggling to adopt, raising a beloved daughter who also dies. Just when they (and the audience) are about to succumb to grief, a small ray of light appears. Academy Award Nomination for Best Actor: Cary Grant. **Cast:** Cary Grant, Irene Dunne, Edgar Buchanan, Beulah Bondi, Ann Doran, Wallis Clark, Walter Soderling, Edmund Elton. **Credits:** Dir: George Stevens; Prod: George Stevens; Writer: Morrie Ryskind; Story: Martha Cheavens; DP: Joseph Walker; Ed: Otto Meyer; Composer: W. Franke Harling; Art Director: Lionel Banks. B&W, 125 min. **VHS, LASER**

Penrod
Based on the popular novel by Booth Tarkington, the Penrod series featured the exploits of the freckle-faced all-American boy Penrod Schofield (portrayed alternately by Billy Mauch and Ben Alexander). Growing up in small-town middle America, Penrod managed to get into plenty of trouble . . . and to catch a few bad guys along the way. Cast in rather stereotypical strokes, the inhabitants of Penrod's Indiana hometown provided the fodder for his adventures. The schoolmarm (Martha Mattox), the town drunk (Vic Potel), the wimp, and the toady were all there, providing audiences of the period with Hollywood's version of wholesome midwestern charm. *Penrod and Sam* was so popular that three different versions of Tarkington's novel of the same name were brought to the big screen.

Penrod *(1922)*
Penrod and Sam *(1923)*
Penrod and Sam *(1931)*
Penrod and Sam *(1937)*
Penrod and His Twin Brother *(1938)*
Penrod's Double Trouble *(1938)*

Penthouse
(1933) MGM
In this crime comedy, Baxter plays a white-shoe lawyer who dabbles in defending gangsters and in the process gets drawn into crime-solving. He's joined in his sleuthing by Loy as his Mob client's moll. The director and writing team joined with Loy to create the *Thin Man* series the next year. **Cast:** Warner Baxter, Myrna Loy, Charles Butterworth, Mae Clarke, Phillips Holmes, Martha Sleeper, Nat Pendleton, Georgie Stone, C. Henry Gordon, Robert Emmet O'Connor. **Credits:** Dir: W. S. Van Dyke; Prod: Hunt Stromberg; Writer: Frances Goodrich, Albert Hackett; Story: Arthur Somers Roche; DP: Lucien N. Andriot, Harold Rossen; Ed: Robert J. Kern. B&W, 90 min.

People Will Talk
(1935) Paramount
This charming domestic comedy reunites Ruggles and Boland as parents tricking their beloved daughter, Hyams, into forgiving her husband, Jagger, for flirting with sexy Stevens at their first anniversary party. But as the parents begin their mock argument, it suddenly turns real and Hyams, newly educated on forgiveness, must employ similar methods to bring them back together. **Cast:** Leila Hyams, Charlie Ruggles, Mary Boland,

Ruthelma Stevens, Stanley Andrews, Edward Brophy, Hans Steinke, Dean Jagger. **Credits:** Dir: Alfred Santell; Prod: Douglas Maclean; Writer: Sophie Kerr, Herbert Fields, F. Hugh Herbert; DP: Alfred Gilks; Ed: Richard Currier. B&W, 67 min.

People Will Talk
(1951) Fox
The *New York Times* called Mankiewicz's unusual drama a "significant milestone in the moral emancipation of American film." A surgeon (Grant) has to defend himself against the medical establishment when he proclaims the unorthodox view that the mind can heal the body. Not only does he keep company with some oddball characters (Slezak and Currie), but he falls in love with one of his students, a young, single woman—who is pregnant. Much talk, but interesting subject matter and finely calibrated performances. **Cast:** Cary Grant, Jeanne Crain, Walter Slezak, Hume Cronyn, Finlay Currie, Sidney Blackmer, Basil Ruysdael, Katherine Locke. **Credits:** Dir: Joseph L. Mankiewicz; Prod: Darryl F. Zanuck; Writer: Joseph L. Mankiewicz; DP: Milton Krasner; Ed: Barbara McLean; Prod Design: Lyle Wheeler; Composer: Johannes Brahms, Richard Wagner; Art Director: George W. Davis. B&W, 110 min. **VHS**

A Perfect Couple
(1979) Fox
This Altman film pairs a meek middle-aged Dooley with Heflin, who plays a rock singer in a group headed by Neeley (who appeared in *Jesus Christ Superstar*). In addition to this seeming mismatch, both deal badly with authority. The couple attempts to shrug off their oppressive situations and find peace with each other. **Cast:** Paul Dooley, Marta Heflin, Tito Vandis, Belita Moreno, Henry Gibson, Dimitra Arliss, Allan Nicholls, Anne Ryerson, Ted Neeley, Heather MacRea. **Credits:** Dir: Robert Altman; Prod: Robert Altman; Writer: Robert Altman, Allan Nicholls; DP: Edmond L. Koons; Ed: Tony Lombardo; Prod Design: Leon Erickson; Composer: Allan Nicholls. Color, 110 min.

The Perfect Furlough
(1958) Universal
Psychologist Leigh comes up with the morale-boosting idea of creating custom-design furloughs for 300 soldiers. Playboy Curtis dreams up a trip to Paris with a starlet. Leigh

comes along and winds up with the soldier boy. Curtis and Leigh were married at the time. **Cast:** Tony Curtis, Keenan Wynn, Linda Cristal, Janet Leigh, Elaine Stritch, Marcel Dalio, King Donovan, Troy Donohue. **Credits:** Dir: Blake Edwards; Prod: Robert Arthur; Writer: Stanley Shapiro; DP: Philip H. Lathrop; Ed: Milton Carruth; Composer: Frank Skinner; Art Director: Alexander Golitzen. B&W, 94 min. **VHS**

The Perfect Marriage
(1946) Paramount
After 10 years of marriage, a happy couple (Niven and Young) decides to call it quits after a simple misunderstanding that happens on their anniversary. Their daughter comes to the rescue. Good performances, sharp dialogue, and elegant evening clothes enhance a simple plot. The romantic pairing of Niven and Young would reappear to more acclaim the next year in *The Bishop's Wife.* **Cast:** David Niven, Loretta Young, Eddie Albert, Virginia Field, Rita Johnson, ZaSu Pitts, Charlie Ruggles, Jerome Cowan. **Credits:** Dir: Lewis Allen; Prod: Hal B. Wallis; Writer: Leonard Spigelgass; Story: Samson Raphaelson; DP: Russell Metty; Ed: Ellsworth Hoagland; Composer: Frederick Hollander; Art Director: Lionel Banks. B&W, 88 min. **VHS**

The Perfect Specimen
(1937) Warner Bros.
Flynn, in his only comic turn, plays a sheltered millionaire living a life of ease in his secluded mansion, awaiting the day when he will take over the family business. Hoping to nab an exclusive story, a woman reporter (the bustling Blondell) penetrates the mansion and returns with the heir to the outside world. Though the police believe he's been kidnapped, he relishes his time spent among the unwashed masses with the journalist. A curiosity (comedy wasn't Curtiz's forte, either) but good fun. **Cast:** Errol Flynn, Joan Blondell, Hugh Herbert, Edward Everett Horton, Dick Foran, Beverly Roberts, May Robson, Allen Jenkins, Hugh O'Connell, James Burke. **Credits:** Dir: Michael Curtiz; Prod: Harry Joe Brown, Hal B. Wallis; Writer: Fritz Falkenstein, Brewster Morse, Norman Raine, Lawrence Riley; Story: Samuel Hopkins Adams; DP: Jack A. Marta, Charles Rosher; Ed: Terrell O. Morse; Prod Design: Robert Hass; Composer: Heinz Roemheld. B&W, 97 min.

The Perils of Pauline
(1947) Paramount
Here is a delightful musical-comedy look at the silent-movie days in Hollywood in a glossy biopic of silent cliff-hanger star Pearl White. Plenty of cameos from the days when they had faces, highlighted by the songs of Frank Loesser, including Hutton's hit, "Poppa Don't Preach to Me." Academy Award Nomination for Best Song ("I Wish I Didn't Love You So"). **Cast:** Betty Hutton, John Lund, Constance Collier, William Demarest, Frank Faylen, William Farnum, Paul Panzer, Snub Pollard, Creighton Hale. **Credits:** Dir: George Marshall; Prod: Sol C. Siegel; Writer: P. J. Wolfson, Frank Butler; DP: Ray Rennahan; Ed: Arthur Schmidt; Composer: Robert Emmett Dolan; Art Director: Hans Dreier, Roland Anderson. Color, 96 min. **VHS**

Period of Adjustment
(1962) MGM
Director Hill's first film was this Williams comedy (!) about the inevitable adjustments newlyweds make. The story follows two couples, one a newly married couple, played by Hutton and Fonda, working out their own intimacy issues when they visit Franciosa and Nettleton and figure they have it pretty good. A witty and unusually warm comedy for Williams and fine performances by the entire cast. Academy Award Nomination for Best Art Direction. **Cast:** Jane Fonda, Jim Hutton, Lois Nettleton, John McGiver, Jack Albertson, Anthony Franciosa, Mabel Albertson. **Credits:** Dir: George Roy Hill; Prod: Lawrence Weingarten; Writer: Isobel Lennart; Story: Tennessee Williams; DP: Paul C. Vogel; Ed: Fredric Steinkamp; Prod Design: George W. Davis, Edward C. Carfagno; Composer: Lyn Murray. Color, 112 min. **VHS**

Pete Kelly's Blues
(1955) Warner Bros.
Future TV star Webb produced, directed, and stars in this hard-edged depiction of the jazz scene in 1920s Kansas City (predating Robert Altman's *Kansas City* by a generation). Legendary vocalists Fitzgerald and Lee are jazz singers in the rough and tumble world of a speakeasy. Trouble breaks out when racketeers (led by O'Brien) try to muscle in on the music business and lean too hard on a club musician, Webb. A shoot-out ensues when the gangsters go to murderous extremes. Joe Venuti, Matty Matlock, Dick Cathcart, and Eddie Miller are just some of the great musicians

backing the vocalists in renditions of "Hard Hearted Hannah," "Sing a Rainbow," and "He Needs Me." **Cast:** Jack Webb, Edmond O'Brien, Peggy Lee, Janet Leigh, Lee Marvin, Jayne Mansfield, Andy Devine, Ella Fitzgerald. **Credits:** Dir: Jack Webb; Prod: Jack Webb; Writer: Richard Breen; DP: Harold Rosson; Ed: Robert M. Leeds; Prod Design: Feild M. Gray; Composer: Ray Heindorf, Sammy Cahn, Arthur Hamilton. Color, 95 min. **VHS, LASER**

Pete 'n' Tillie
(1972) Universal
This impressive slice-of-life drama has two appealing characters, played by comedy stars Matthau and Burnett. Two misfits meet at a party and begin a life together that holds joy and fulfillment, and tragedy and loss. When their doted-upon son dies of leukemia, the marriage suffers until a final reconciliation in the face of a return to loneliness. Academy Award Nominations: Best Adapted Screenplay; Best Supporting Actress: Geraldine Page. **Cast:** Walter Matthau, Carol Burnett, Geraldine Page, Rene Auberjonois, Barry Nelson, Henry Jones, Kent Smith, Philip Bourneuf. **Credits:** Dir: Martin Ritt; Prod: Julius J. Epstein; Writer: Julius J. Epstein; DP: John A. Alonzo; Ed: Frank Bracht; Composer: John Williams; Art Director: George C. Webb. Color, 100 min. **VHS**

Peter Ibbetson
(1935) Paramount
In this surreal, metaphysical romance, sweethearts separated as children are mystically reunited after death. Peter Ibbetson (Cooper) is a Parisian architect with a commission to design stables on Duke Towers's (Halliday) property. In the lovely Duchess Mary (Harding), Ibbetson discovers the long-lost childhood friend with whom he played in the garden he is redesigning. His attentions to her are quickly misjudged by the jealous Duke. In the scuffle that follows, Ibbetson accidentally kills the Duke and is given life in prison. Here he is treated to a series of surreal visions of Mary and a promise of eternal happiness, which, after the lovers die many years later, we actually get to see. A favorite of the European Surrealists. **Cast:** Gary Cooper, Ann Harding, John Halliday, Ida Lupino, Douglass Dumbrille, Virginia Weidler, Dickie Moore, Doris Lloyd. **Credits:** Dir: Henry Hathaway; Prod: Louis D. Lighton; Writer: Vincent Lawrence, Edwin Justus Mayer, John Meehan, Waldemar Young, John Nathaniel Raphael, George L. du Mau-

rier, Constance Collier; DP: Charles Lang; Ed: Stuart Heisler; Prod Design: Hans Dreier; Composer: Ernst Toch; Art Director: Robert Usher. B&W, 88 min.

The Petrified Forest
(1936) Warner Bros.
In the role that made him a star (and typecast him for years as a gangster), Bogart reprises his stage appearance as murdering thug Duke Mantee. Howard, who had won the role for Bogart, plays a drifting intellectual who places himself in Bogart's path to help yearning poet Davis when Bogart and his band of hoodlums hold the patrons of an Arizona desert diner hostage. Based on Sherwood's play. **Cast:** Humphrey Bogart, Leslie Howard, Bette Davis, Dick Foran, Joe Sawyer, Porter Hall, Charley Grapewin, Paul Harvey, Eddie Acuff. **Credits:** Dir: Archie Mayo; Prod: Henry Blanke; Writer: Charles Kenyon, Delmer Daves; Story: Robert E. Sherwood; DP: Sol Polito; Ed: Owen Marks; Composer: Bernhard Kaun; Art Director: John Hughes. B&W, 90 min. **VHS**

Petulia
(1968) Warner Bros.
Scott finds it difficult to adjust to the swinging singles scene in '60s San Francisco when he runs into troubled free spirit Christie. She fascinates the committed doctor, and he pursues his fascination though she returns to her abusive husband, Chamberlain. A mod time capsule with sharp social commentary directed by hip filmmaker Lester (*A Hard Day's Night*, 1964), and shot by future director Roeg. Watch for glimpses of The Grateful Dead and Big Brother and the Holding Company. **Cast:** Julie Christie, George C. Scott, Richard Chamberlain, Arthur Hill, Shirley Knight, Joseph Cotten, Pippa Scott, Kathleen Widdoes. **Credits:** Dir: Richard Lester; Prod: Raymond Wagner; Writer: Larry Marcus, Barbara Turner; DP: Nicolas Roeg; Ed: Anthony Gibbs; Prod Design: Dean Tavoularis; Composer: John Barry. Color, 105 min. **VHS**

Peyton Place
(1957) Fox
Based on the scandalous and biggest best-selling book of its time, this glossy adaptation set the standard for movie soap and spawned a sequel and a long-running prime-time TV series. Lust, deception, scandal, and murder lurk beneath the surface of a picture-perfect New England town, where personal dramas and intrigues are hidden from view by deceptively quaint clap-

board and shuttered houses. A murder trial brings writer Varsi back to her small town, spurring revelations and reconciliations. Academy Award Nominations: 9, including Best Picture; Best Director; Best Actress: Lana Turner; Best (Adapted) Screenplay. **Cast:** Lana Turner, Hope Lange, Russ Tamblyn, Arthur Kennedy, Diane Varsi, Lee Philips, Lloyd Nolan, Terry Moore. **Credits:** Dir: Mark Robson; Prod: Jerry Wald; Writer: John Michael Hayes; Story: Grace Metalious; DP: William Mellor; Ed: David Bretherton; Prod Design: Lyle Wheeler; Composer: Franz Waxman; Art Director: Jack Martin Smith. Color, 162 min. **VHS, LASER**

Phantom Lady
(1944) Universal
This film is an expressionist cruise through the neon-lit New York nightlife, with a murder lurking in the background. Siodmak directs this stylish thriller in which Curtis heads to a bar after a tiff with his wife and spends the evening with a mysterious woman (Helm). When he arrives home, he finds his wife dead, strangled by his necktie, and he is accused of the crime. The babe who is his alibi cannot be found; nobody even remembers her. Only his loyal secretary (Raines) believes in his innocence and sets out to solve the crime. Based on the novel by Woolrich. **Cast:** Franchot Tone, Ella Raines, Alan Curtis, Fay Helm, Elisha Cook, Jr., Andrew Tombes, Regis Toomey, Joseph Crehan, Doris Lloyd, Virginia Brissac. **Credits:** Dir: Robert Siodmak; Prod: Joan Harrison; Writer: Bernard C. Schoenfeld; Story: Cornell Woolrich; DP: Elwood Bredell; Ed: Arthur Hilton; Prod Design: Robert Clatworthy; Composer: Hans J. Salter; Costumes: Vera West, Kenneth Hopkins; Art Director: John B. Goodman. B&W, 87 min. **VHS**

Phantom of Santa Fe
(1936)
Notable as the earliest color Western, this was originally shot in 1931. When a priceless treasure is stolen, the townsfolk suspect a mysterious, Zorro-like figure known as "The Phantom of Santa Fe." Kerry was a silent Western star. **Cast:** Norman Kerry, Nena Quartaro, Carmelita Geraghty, Frank Mayo, Jack Mower, Tom O'Brien. **Credits:** Dir: Jacques Jaccard; Writer: Charles F. Royal. B&W, 75 min. **VHS**

The Phantom of the Opera
(1925) Universal
This is the high point of silent horror films and one of Chaney's most

famous performances, which fixed the character and story in history and led to several remakes and the long-running Broadway musical. Hideously disfigured composer catches the eye of a young singer (Philbin) at the Paris Opera. He makes her a star through coaching and intimidation of the Opera's star, then wants her as his own. The scene in which Philbin can't resist temptation and lifts the Phantom's mask still sends shivers. **Cast:** Lon Chaney, Mary Philbin, Norman Kerry, Snitz Edwards, Gibson Gowland. **Credits:** Dir: Rupert Julian; Story: Gaston Leroux; DP: Virgil Miller, Charles Van Enger, Milton Bridenbecker; Art Director: Charles D. Hall. B&W, 79 min. **VHS, LASER, DVD**

The Phantom of the Opera
(1943) Universal
The first sound version of the classic backstage thriller is more of a costume romance than a horror film. Rains draws a sympathetic rendering of the phantom who obsesses over a young soprano (Foster). Here he is a meek violinist who worships Foster from afar and devotes his life to her career. Academy Award Nominations: 4. **Academy Awards:** Best Color Cinematography; Best Color Interior Decoration. **Cast:** Nelson Eddy, Susanna Foster, Claude Rains, Edgar Barrier, Hume Cronyn, Jane Farrar, J. Edward Bromberg, Fritz Feld, Frank Puglia, Steven Geray. **Credits:** Dir: Arthur Lubin; Prod: George Waggner; Writer: Eric Taylor, Hans Jacoby, Samuel Hoffenstein; Story: Gaston Leroux; DP: Hal Mohr, W. Howard Greene; Ed: Russell Schoengarth; Composer: Edward Ward, George Wagner; Art Director: John B. Goodman, Alexander Golitzen. Color, 93 min. **VHS, LASER**

Phantom of the Paradise
(1974) Fox
De Palma's rock musical is about a talented young composer (Finley) whose music is stolen and whose life is destroyed by a ruthless record tycoon named Swan (Williams), who's sold his soul in exchange for eternal youth. The ruined composer becomes the phantom, haunting Swan's Rock Palace, the "Paradise." One of De Palma's best, and most overlooked, films, with set designs by prestardom Sissy Spacek and her husband Fisk, and a voice-over by Rod Serling. Academy Award Nomination for Best Original Song Score. **Cast:** Paul Williams, William Finley, Jessica Harper, George Memmoli, Gerrit

Graham, Archie Hahn, Gene Gross, Ken Carpenter. **Credits:** Dir: Brian De Palma; Prod: Edward R. Pressman; Writer: Brian De Palma; DP: Larry Pizer; Ed: Paul Hirsch; Prod Design: Jack Fisk; Composer: Paul Williams, George Tipton. Color, 92 min. **VHS, LASER**

The Phantom Tollbooth
(1969) MGM
Animator Jones's first feature is a delight. A bored young boy (Patrick) quells a war between numbers and letters when he drives his toy car through a mysterious tollbooth into a world of puns and adventure. Accompanied by a watchdog named Tock and the crusty but lovable Humbug, he visits Alphabet City, passes through the doldrums, stops at a point of view, meets a giant-midget-fat man-thin man, and ultimately sets off on a quest to save the princesses Rhyme and Reason. **Cast:** Mel Blanc, Daws Butler, Hans Conreid, June Foray, Butch Patrick, Candy Candido, Patti Gilbert, Shepard Menken, Cliff Norton, Larry Thor. **Credits:** Dir: Chuck Jones, Abe Levitow, David Monahan; Prod: Chuck Jones, Abe Levitow, Les Goldman; Writer: Chuck Jones, Sam Rosen; Story: Norton Juster; DP: Lester Shorr; Ed: Jim Faris; Prod Design: Maurice Noble; Composer: Dean Elliott. Color, 90 min. **VHS, LASER**

The Phenix City Story
(1955) Allied Artists
Here is the high point in the career of critical and cult favorite Karlson. This taut, hard-boiled exposé of the event that almost destroyed the town of Phenix City, Alabama, and earned it the tag "America's Wickedest City" was produced as the trial for the events it depicts was in progress. The sensational story begins after a prologue of testimony from actual participants. Idealistic lawyer Kiley goes on a personal crusade to clean up a town overrun with sleazy nightclubs, prostitution, blackmail, and extortion when his district attorney father (McIntire) is killed by goons working for boss Andrews. With the help of some vigilante citizens and the National Guard, Kiley triumphs. Karlson went to extremes of authenticity, even having McIntire wear clothes worn by the murder victim. **Cast:** John McIntire, Richard Kiley, Kathryn Grant, Edward Andrews, Lenka Peterson, Biff McGuire, Truman Smith, Jean Carson, Kathy Marlowe, John Larch. **Credits:** Dir: Phil Karlson; Prod: Sam Bischoff, David Diamond; Writer: Daniel Main-

waring; DP: Harry Neumann; Ed: George White; Prod Design: Stanley Fleischer. B&W, 100 min.

The Philadelphia Story
(1940) MGM
Hepburn shines (the Stewart character describes her character as being "lit from within") as Tracy Lord, the role that probably continues to define our vision of her. And she took a strong hand in the production, bankrolling the play, in which she also starred, and hand-picking the director, screenwriter, and stars. This perennial favorite, a film version of Barry's smart play, depicts the topsy-turvy events around the impending wedding of a wealthy society girl who's torn between her millionaire fiancé (Howard), and a cynical, voice-of-the-people reporter (Stewart) turned loose among the Main Line set. Remade in musical form in 1956 as *High Society* with Bing Crosby, Frank Sinatra, and Grace Kelly. Selected for the National Film Registry. Academy Award Nominations: 6, including Best Picture; Best Director; Best Actress: Katharine Hepburn. **Academy Awards:** Best Actor: James Stewart; Best Screenplay. **Cast:** Cary Grant, Katharine Hepburn, James Stewart, Ruth Hussey, John Howard, Roland Young, John Halliday, Virginia Weidler, Henry Daniell. **Credits:** Dir: George Cukor; Prod: Joseph L. Mankiewicz; Writer: Donald Ogden Stewart; Story: Philip Barry; DP: Joseph Ruttenberg; Ed: Frank Sullivan; Composer: Franz Waxman; Costumes: Adrian. B&W, 112 min. **VHS, LASER, DVD**

Philo Vance
Though several actors took turns playing the title role, William Powell is best remembered as S. S. Van Dine's refined, sophisticated sleuth, starring in the first three Paramount whodunits (1929's *Canary Murder Case*; 1929's *The Greene Murder Case*; and 1930's *Bishop Murder Case*). Each entry had the plucky gumshoe facing puzzling, often outrageous murders. Powell returned in 1933's *The Kennel Murder Case*. Arguably the best of the series, it boasted direction by Michael Curtiz (*Casablanca*); it was remade, less effectively, by Warners in 1940 as *Calling Philo Vance*. The body count was often high in the Philo Vance films; in *The Greene Murder Case*, no fewer than 10 corpses pile up. Warners, Paramount, and MGM all made Vance titles. While the clever storylines were engaging, sluggish pacing and B-level budgets often tested audi-

ence patience. *Calling Philo Vance* with James Stephenson was the last entry by a major studio. In 1947 low-budget producer PRC revived the series to surprisingly good effect.

Canary Murder Case (1929)
The Greene Murder Case (1929)
Bishop Murder Case (1930)
Benson Murder Case (1930)
The Kennel Murder Case (1933)
The Dragon Murder Case (1934)
Casino Murder Case (1935)
The Garden Murder Case (1936)
Night of Mystery (1937)
The Gracie Allen Murder Case (1939)
Calling Philo Vance (1940)
Philo Vance Returns (1947)
Philo Vance's Gambit (1947)
Philo Vance's Secret Mission (1947)

Phone Call from a Stranger
(1952) Fox
This haunting melodrama wraps several story lines in a neat narrative device. Recently separated Merrill becomes confidant to a number of passengers flying to Los Angeles: an ex-stripper returning forlornly to L.A. after losing a role, a salesman (Wynn) who brags about his stunning wife, a doctor (Rennie) facing a difficult revelation. When the plane crashes, leaving him the lone survivor, Merrill makes it his mission to visit the families of those whose lives he touched en route, righting wrongs and discovering an inspirational story when he visits Davis, the salesman's wife. **Cast:** Bette Davis, Shelley Winters, Gary Merrill, Keenan Wynn, Evelyn Varden, Michael Rennie, Warren Stevens, Beatrice Straight. **Credits:** Dir: Jean Negulesco; Prod: Nunnally Johnson; Writer: Nunnally Johnson; DP: Milton Krasner; Ed: Hugh S. Fowler; Prod Design: Lyle Wheeler; Composer: Franz Waxman; Art Director: J. Russell Spencer. B&W, 96 min. **VHS**

Pickup on South Street
(1953) Fox
This hysterical McCarthy-era noir is about a skid-row pickpocket (Widmark) who dips into the wrong pocketbook and winds up with top-secret microfilm, which was being unwittingly couriered by Peters for her communist boyfriend (Kiley). The contraband hot potato puts him on the run from communist spies and federal agents. A critical favorite by slam-bang director Fuller. **Cast:** Richard Widmark, Jean Peters, Thelma Ritter, Richard Kiley, Murvyn Vye, Willis Bouchey, Milburn Stone, Jerry O'Sullivan, Harry Carter. **Credits:** Dir: Samuel Fuller; Prod:

Picnic (1956)

Jules Schermer; Writer: Samuel Fuller; Story: Dwight Taylor; DP: Joseph Mac-Donald; Ed: Nick DeMaggio; Prod Design: Lyle Wheeler, George Patrick; Composer: Leigh Harline. B&W, 81 min. **VHS**

Picnic

(1956) Columbia
This screen adaptation of William Inge's play about a drifter, played by Holden, who visits an old pal (Robertson) in a small Kansas town and steals the heart of his girlfriend, Novak, as well as the interest of every other woman in town, including Strasberg and Russell, focused on the dark passions hidden in small-town America and signaled Hollywood's turn toward the more naturalistic material of the era's playwrights. Their steamy scenes also made sex symbols of Holden (at age 37) and Novak, in her first major role. Top-notch technical credits, including stunning cinematography from Howe, complement fine directing and performances, including Robertson in his first big part. Golden Globe for Best Director. Academy Award Nominations: 6, including Best Picture; Best Director. **Academy Awards:** Best (Color) Art Direction—Set Decoration; Best Film Editing. **Cast:** Susan Strasberg, William Holden, Kim Novak, Rosalind Russell, Cliff Robertson, Betty Field, Arthur O'Connell, Verna Felton. **Credits:** Dir: Joshua Logan; Prod: Fred Kohlmar; Writer: Daniel Taradash; Story: William Inge; DP: James Wong Howe; Ed: Charles Nelson, William A. Lyon; Composer: George Duning; Art Director: William Flannery. Color, 113 min. **VHS, LASER**

The Picture of Dorian Gray

(1945) MGM
This adaptation of the novel by Wilde is about a vain young man (Hatfield) who makes a pact with the devil to retain his youth. As a portrait in the attic changes with the years to reflect his true age and his evil nature, Dorian Gray retains his outward youth and beauty. The stark black-and-white cinematography is wonderfully affecting, particularly when the portrait pops out in lurid Technicolor. Golden Globe for Best Supporting Actress: Angela Lansbury. Academy Award Nominations: 3, including Best Supporting Actress: Angela Lansbury. **Academy Awards:** Best Black-and-White Cinematography. **Cast:** Hurd Hatfield, Angela Lansbury, Sibyl Vane, George Sanders, Donna Reed, Peter Lawford, Richard Fraser, Douglas Walton, Renee Carson, Lillian Bond. **Credits:** Dir: Albert Lewin; Prod: Pandro S. Berman; Writer: Albert Lewin; Story: Oscar Wilde; DP: Harry Stradling; Ed: Ferris Webster; Prod Design: Cedric Gibbons, Hans Peters; Composer: Herbert Stothart. B&W, 110 min. **VHS, LASER**

A Piece of the Action

(1977) Warner Bros.
Poitier directed this third outing with his partner from *Uptown Saturday Night* (1974), Cosby. The story finds the black con artists getting arm-twisted by Jones into doing some good for the kids in their ghetto neighborhood and end up getting something out of it for themselves. The combination of crime, comedy, and a little preaching at the end make it a feel-good film. **Cast:** Sidney Poitier, Bill Cosby, James Earl Jones, Denise Nicholas, Hope Clarke, Tracy Reed, Titos Vandis, Frances Foster. **Credits:** Dir: Sidney Poitier; Prod: Melville Tucker; Writer: Charles Blackwell; Story: Timothy March; DP: Donald M. Morgan; Ed: Pembroke Herring; Prod Design: Alfred Sweeney; Composer: Curtis Mayfield. Color, 135 min. **VHS**

The Pied Piper

(1942) Fox
After losing his only son in the opening days of the war, the last thing the grieving Woolley wants to have interrupt his French fishing vacation are more children. Yet as the Germans plow through Belgium, two English children, McDowall and Baxter, are put in his hands. Wooley's task of getting them to the English Channel before the war catches up snowballs and he is leading a small troop of kids when he encounters a German major played by Preminger. Prime WWII morale-booster. Academy Award Nominations: 3, including Best Picture; Best Actor: Monty Woolley. **Cast:** Monty Woolley, Roddy McDowall, Anne Baxter, Otto Preminger, J. Carrol Naish, Lester Matthews, Jill Esmond, Ferike Boros, Peggy Ann Garner, Merrill Rodin. **Credits:** Dir: Irving Pichel; Prod: Nunnally Johnson; Writer: Nunnally Johnson; Story: Nevil Shute; DP: Edward Cronjager; Ed: Allen McNeil; Prod Design: Richard Day; Composer: Alfred Newman. B&W, 86 min.

Pilgrimage

(1933) Fox
In this most unusual melodrama by director Ford, he keeps the sentiment in check as he unfolds a truly touching story. A possessive mother (theater diva Crosman) sends her son to war to separate him from his girlfriend (Nixon), unaware that she is pregnant. After he is killed, she travels to France with other Gold Star Mothers and meets a young couple, seemingly doomed to follow in the steps of her lost child. By sharing experiences with other bereaved mothers, she finds it in herself to help the lovers and reconcile with Nixon and her grandson. **Cast:** Henrietta Crosman, Heather Angel, Norman Foster, Marion Nixon, Maurice Murphy, Lucille LaVerne, Charley Grapewin, Hedda Hopper, Robert Warwick, Betty Blythe. **Credits:** Dir: John Ford; Writer: Barry Connors, Philip Klein; Story: I. A. R. Wylie; DP: George Schneiderman; Ed: Louis Loeffler; Prod Design: William S. Darling; Composer: Samuel Kayline, R. H. Bassett. B&W, 95 min.

Pillow Talk

(1959) Universal
The first film pairing of Hudson and Day as romantic leads, this sparkling comedy may be the unintended grandmother of phone sex. Day shares a party line with Hudson, a playboy songwriter whose lines with women she's forced to hear on the line. He assumes she's a nagging old scold, but gets a pleasant surprise when she shows up with beau Randall. He dons a silly disguise as a guileless Texan to woo her. A prime example of '50s screen comedy. Academy Award Nominations: 5, including Best Actress: Doris Day. **Academy Awards:** Best Story/Screenplay. **Cast:** Rock Hudson, Doris Day, Tony Randall, Thelma Ritter, Nick Adams, Julia Meade, Allen Jenkins, Marcel Dalio. **Credits:** Dir: Michael Gordon; Prod: Ross Hunter, Martin Melcher; Writer: Stanley Shapiro, Maurice Richlin; DP: Arthur E. Arling; Ed: Milton Carruth; Prod Design: Alexander Golitzen, Richard H. Riedel; Composer: Frank DeVol. Color, 102 min. **VHS, LASER**

Pink Flamingos

(1973)
Writer-director Waters found an immediate niche as an on-campus favorite with this crude—but funny—film. His muse, Divine, a heavyweight transvestite, has entered the World's Filthiest Person Competition and is determined to win the title. Win it she does and just how is now famous. Waters has toned down a bit since this early success, which now has a huge cult audience, but beware, this was originally billed as the most disgusting film of all time. The 25th-anniversary edition includes the original theatrical trailer and running audio commentary by Waters. **Cast:** Divine, Edith Massey, Mink Stole, David Lochary, John Waters, Mary Vivian Pearce, Danny Mills, Cookie Mueller. **Credits:** Dir: John Waters; Prod: John Waters; Writer: John Waters; DP: John Waters; Ed: John Waters. Color, 108 min. **VHS, LASER**

The Pink Jungle

(1968) Universal
This offbeat, low-budget '60s adventure-comedy has Garner playing a fashion photographer on location in South America with fashion model Renzi. Romance and adventure ensue once they get caught up in a race to find a lost diamond mine. The film is based on the novel *Snake Water* by Alan Williams. **Cast:** James Garner, Eva Renzi, George Kennedy, Nigel Green, Michael Ansara, George Rose,

Fabrizio Mioni, Vincent Beck, Val Avery, Robert Carricart. **Credits:** Dir: Delbert Mann; Prod: Stan Margulies; Writer: Charles Williams; Story: Alan A. Williams; DP: Russell Metty; Ed: William B. Murphy; Composer: Ernie Freeman; Costumes: Edith Head; Art Director: Alexander Golitzen, Alfred Ybarra. Color, 94 min. **VHS**

The Pink Panther

(1964) United Artists
Sellers introduces Inspector Clouseau in this first of the Pink Panther series, which had five sequels. Sellers became inextricably associated with the bungling French policeman who dogs the steps of a suave jewel thief called The Phantom (Niven). Edwards and Sellers seemed to bring out the best in each other, and this madcap cop comedy set the tone for their frequent collaborations. Academy Award Nominations: Best (Original) Score. **Cast:** Peter Sellers, David Niven, Capucine, Robert Wagner, Claudia Cardinale, Brenda De Banzie, Fran Jeffries, Colin Gordon, Martin Miller. **Credits:** Dir: Blake Edwards; Prod: Martin Jurow; Writer: Blake Edwards, Maurice Richlin; DP: Philip H. Lathrop; Ed: Ralph E. Winters, Marshall M. Borden; Composer: Henry Mancini; Art Director: Fernando Carrere. Color, 118 min. **VHS, LASER**

The Pink Panther Strikes Again

(1976) United Artists
The fifth installment in the Pink Panther series quickly followed the successful *The Return of the Pink Panther* (1974). Inspector Clouseau (again played by Sellers) investigates his former boss, who has had a nervous breakdown and is intent on destroying the world (and, in particular, Clouseau) with a deadly ray gun. Mostly watchable for Sellers's mania. Academy Award Nomination for Best Song, "Come to Me." **Cast:** Peter Sellers, David Niven, Robert Wagner, Claudia Cardinale, Phil Brown, Burt Kwouk, Paul Maxwell, Dudley Sutton. **Credits:** Dir: Blake Edwards; Prod: Blake Edwards; Writer: Blake Edwards, Frank Waldman; DP: Harry Waxman; Ed: Alan Jones; Prod Design: Peter Mullins; Composer: Henry Mancini; Art Director: John Siddall. Color, 110 min. **VHS, LASER**

Pinky

(1949) Fox
Fox head Zanuck tackles the sensitive subject of interracial romance and society's intolerance. A southern

black girl (Crain) who is able to pass for white while working as a nurse in New England attracts the affections of a white doctor (Lundigan). She rejects his sincere attention and returns to her hometown and works for wealthy matron Barrymore, from whom she inherits a large estate. Barrymore's family contests the bequest, and the hearing reveals their racial bias. John Ford started shooting but was replaced by a director with more political commitment. Academy Award Nominations: Best Actress: Jeanne Crain; Best Supporting Actress: Ethel Barrymore; Best Supporting Actress: Ethel Waters. **Cast:** Jeanne Crain, Ethel Barrymore, Ethel Waters, William Lundigan, Basil Ruysdael, Kenny Washington, Nina Mae McKinney, Griff Barnett. **Credits:** Dir: Elia Kazan; Prod: Darryl F. Zanuck; Writer: Dudley Nichols, Philip Dunne; DP: Joseph MacDonald; Ed: Harmon Jones; Prod Design: Lyle Wheeler; Composer: Alfred Newman. B&W, 102 min. **VHS**

Pinocchio

(1940) Disney
Walt Disney's beautiful animated feature (his second) is rich with complex and sympathetic characters, a fascinating story, and dazzling animation artistry. A brilliant piece of filmmaking, based on a story by Collodi about a puppet who is brought to life by a fairy but wants more than anything to become a real boy. Classic children's entertainment, which engages audiences at all levels. The collector's edition includes photos of the animators, early concept drawings and scene paintings, original theatrical trailers, publicity materials, an exclusive commemorative lithograph and booklet, plus a newly remastered compact disc of the film's original sound track. Selected as a National Film Registry Outstanding Film. **Academy Awards:** Best Original Score; Best Song ("When You Wish Upon a Star"). **Cast:** Dick Jones, Christian Rub, Cliff Edwards, Evelyn Venable, Walter Catlett, Frankie Darro, Charles Judels, Don Brodie. **Credits:** Dir: Ben Sharpsteen, Hamilton Luske; Prod: Walt Disney; Writer: Ted Sears, Otto Englander, Webb Smith; Story: C. Collodi; Composer: Paul Smith; Art Director: Charles Philippi. Color, 88 min. **VHS, LASER**

Pin Up Girl

(1944) Fox
This is a patriotic vehicle for poster-girl Grable, but which unfortunately has

nothing to do with the famous photo. Here she plays a mousy secretary who visits a U.S.O. canteen and falls in love with a Navy hero. She pretends to be a Broadway star so she can be near him and a U.S.O. performance leads her, overnight, to actual stardom. Mostly an excuse for much song and dance, including "Once Too Often" (with dancing by choreographer Pan) and "Yankee Doodle Dandy" as sung by Raye. **Cast:** Betty Grable, John Harvey, Martha Raye, Joe E. Brown, Eugene Pallette, Dorothea Kent, Dave Willock, Robert E. Homans. **Credits:** Dir: H. Bruce Humberstone; Prod: William LeBaron; Writer: Robert Ellis; DP: Ernest Palmer; Ed: Robert Simpson; Prod Design: James Basevi; Choreographer: Hermes Pan; Composer: Emil Newman. Color, 83 min. **VHS, LASER**

Piranha
(1978) New World
Independent filmmaker Sayles (who also made a name for himself as a Hollywood script doctor) wrote this *Jaws* parody about a scientist who develops a man-eating species of fish as a weapon for the Americans in the Vietnam War. The fish have found their way to rich resort waters and are eating up vacationers in Texas. Well written for the genre, and the first solo outing for director Dante (*Gremlins,* 1984). Film buffs will enjoy the inside jokes. **Cast:** Bradford Dillman, Heather Menzies, Kevin McCarthy, Keenan Wynn, Dick Miller, Barbara Steele, Belinda Balaski, Melody Thomas. **Credits:** Dir: Joe Dante; Prod: Jon Davison; Writer: John Sayles; DP: Jamie Anderson; Ed: Mark Goldblatt; Prod Design: Bill Milling; Composer: Pino Donaggio. Color, 90 min. **VHS**

The Pirate
(1948) MGM
Kelly and Garland with a Porter score, set in the West Indies, and with great costumes and dancing, shining in the grand Minnelli-MGM style. Kelly plays a street musician who poses as an infamous Caribbean pirate so he can woo Garland, who has spurned him. Academy Award Nomination for Best Scoring of a Musical Picture. **Cast:** Judy Garland, Gene Kelly, Gladys Cooper, Reginald Owen, George Zucco, Lester Allen, Cully Richards. **Credits:** Dir: Vincente Minnelli; Prod: Arthur Freed; Writer: Albert Hackett, Frances Goodrich, Joseph Than, Anita Loos, Wilkie Mahoney; Story: S. N. Behrman; DP: Harry Stradling; Ed: Blanche Sewell; Prod Design: Cedric

Gibbons; Composer: Cole Porter; Art Director: Jack Martin Smith. Color, 102 min. **VHS, LASER**

Pitfall
(1948) United Artists
In this biting film noir, Powell is an insurance investigator with a ho-hum suburban life and perfect wife (Wyatt) whose life goes awry when he looks for diversion with an investigation of stolen goods. A chillingly amoral tale of adultery, thievery, and corruption with a cold-blooded performance by Burr. **Cast:** Dick Powell, Lizabeth Scott, Jane Wyatt, Raymond Burr, John Litel, Byron Barr, Jimmy Hunt, Ann Doran, Selmer Jackson, Margaret Wells. **Credits:** Dir: Andre De Toth; Prod: Samuel Bischoff; Writer: Karl Kamb; Story: Jay Dratler; DP: Harry Wild; Ed: Walter Thompson; Composer: Louis Forbes; Art Director: Arthur Lonergan. B&W, 88 min. **VHS, LASER**

Pittsburgh
(1942) Universal
Wayne and Scott are coal miners when Dietrich returns to her old neighborhood, inspiring them to improve their lot in life. Both are attracted to Dietrich's vitality and beauty, but as Wayne prospers with his own mill, she's spurned by Wayne for a lady of high social standing (Allbritton). When Wayne clashes with his workers, his business fails and he loses his wife. A reteaming of the trio from *The Spoilers* (1942). **Cast:** Marlene Dietrich, John Wayne, Randolph Scott, Thomas Gomez, Frank Craven, Louise Allbritton, Shemp Howard, Ludwig Stossel, Samuel S. Hinds, Paul Fix. **Credits:** Dir: Lewis Seiler; Prod: Charles K. Feldman; Writer: Kenneth Gamet, Tom Reed; DP: Robert de Grasse; Ed: Paul Landres; Composer: Frank Skinner, H. J. Salter; Art Director: John B. Goodman. B&W, 92 min. **VHS**

A Place in the Sun
(1951) Paramount
A landmark, blockbuster melodrama about class striving and the loss of a man's moral bearings. This remake of the 1930 von Sternberg film based on the Dreiser novel *An American Tragedy* updates the setting to a '50s resort town in upstate New York. A beautiful, rich girl (Taylor) gives a handsome young laborer (Clift) entree to her world of privilege through a powerful, overwhelming passion. Just as he sees himself leaving behind a lifetime of wage slavery, his plain, needy former girlfriend (Winters) reveals that she's pregnant. Wracked with guilt

and longing, he takes her for a last ride on the lake. When she accidentally drowns, he is tried for murder. A national sensation, with performances that etched Taylor and Clift, who began a lifelong friendship, in the public mind; even the party dress Taylor wears became a best-seller. Golden Globe for Best Motion Picture, Drama. Academy Award Nominations: 9, including Best Picture; Best Actor: Montgomery Clift. **Academy Awards:** Best Director; Best Film Editing; Best Screenplay; Best Black-and-White Cinematography; Best Music Score of a Drama/Comedy; Best Costume Design (B&W). **Cast:** Montgomery Clift, Elizabeth Taylor, Shelley Winters, Raymond Burr, Herbert Heyes, Shepperd Strudwick, Frieda Inescort, Kathryn Givney, Walter Sande. **Credits:** Dir: George Stevens; Prod: George Stevens; Writer: Michael Wilson, Harry Brown; Story: Theodore Dreiser, Patrick Kearney; DP: William Mellor; Ed: William Hornbeck; Composer: Franz Waxman; Art Director: Hans Dreier, Walter Tyler. B&W, 122 min. **VHS, LASER**

The Plainsman
(1937) Paramount
DeMille's extravagant way with history is here applied to the oft-filmed tale of Wild Bill Hickok and Calamity Jane. The two (Cooper and Arthur, fresh from their success in *Mr. Deeds Goes to Town*) get mixed up with Buffalo Bill and a sneak who's selling guns to the Indians. Arthur tries to come to the rescue and gets herself and Cooper captured. The source of the famous Hollywood story about Quinn answering a casting call for real Indians (and DeMille did stock the cast with authentic native Americans and performing a Cheyenne war dance with gibberish. He got the part, and won the hand of the director's daughter. **Cast:** Gary Cooper, Jean Arthur, Charles Bickford, Anthony Quinn, James Ellison, Victor Varconi, Granville Bates, Purnell Pratt. **Credits:** Dir: Cecil B. DeMille; Prod: Cecil B. DeMille; Writer: Waldemar Young, Harold Lamb, Lynn Riggs, Jeanie Macpherson; Story: Frank J. Wilstach, Courtney Riley Cooper, Grover Jones; DP: Victor Milner, George Robinson; Ed: Anne Bauchens; Prod Design: Hans Dreier; Composer: George Antheil; Art Director: Roland Anderson. B&W, 115 min. **VHS, LASER**

Planet of the Apes
(1967) Fox
Astronauts on a deep-space expedition land on an Earth-like planet only

to find evolution gone awry: apes rule and treat humans like animals. Heston makes contact with two sympathetic scientists (MacDowall and Hunter) and forces them to face their origins. He also gets a lesson in man's fate in the final sequence when he comes upon a half-submerged Statue of Liberty. Smart sci-fi with social commentary and wry humor, based on the novel by Pierre Boulle with a screenplay cowritten by Rod Serling. Four sequels and two television series followed. Academy Award Nominations: Best Score; Best Costume Design. **Academy Awards:** Honorary Award to John Chambers for special achievement in makeup effects. **Cast:** Charlton Heston, Roddy McDowall, Kim Hunter, Maurice Evans, James Whitmore, James Daly, Linda Harrison, Robert Gunner, Lou Wagner, Woodrow Parfrey. **Credits:** Dir: Franklin J. Schaffner; Prod: Arthur P. Jacobs; Writer: Michael Wilson; Story: Pierre Boulle; DP: Leon Shamroy; Ed: Hugh S. Fowler; Composer: Jerry Goldsmith; Art Director: Jack Martin Smith. Color, 112 min. VHS, LASER

Plan 9 from Outer Space
(1959) Distributors
Wood, the inspiration for Tim Burton's 1994 tongue-in-cheek biopic *Ed Wood*, produced what has been hailed as the worst film ever made. Aliens from outer space want to rule the earth and decide to use corpses to help them to their evil end. If they dig up the dead, they can turn them against the living. Special effects include flying saucers that look like paper plates. Lugosi died two days into shooting and was replaced by a chiropractor who hid his face behind a cape. An unintentionally hilarious film and a favorite of film cultists. **Cast:** Bela Lugosi, Lyle Talbot, Tor Johnson, Vampira, Paul Marco. **Credits:** Dir: Edward D. Wood, Jr.; Prod: Edward Wood, Jr.; Writer: Edward Wood, Jr.; DP: William Thompson; Ed: Edward Wood, Jr.; Composer: Gordon Zahler. B&W, 79 min. VHS, LASER

Platinum Blonde
(1931) Columbia
Capra love triangle with a hard-boiled newspaper setting. Reporter Williams gets a cache of love letters that figure in a tawdry affair, but holds them so he can make time with Harlow. Meanwhile, fellow reporter Young watches with her own romantic interest. **Cast:** Jean Harlow, Loretta Young, Robert Williams, Louise Closser Hale, Donald Dillaway, Reginald Owen, Walter Catlett, Edmund Breese, Halliwell Hobbes, Claud Allister. **Credits:** Dir: Frank Capra; Prod: Harry Cohn; Writer: Jo Swerling, Dorothy Howell; DP: Joseph Walker; Ed: Gene Milford. B&W, 89 min. VHS

Play It Again, Sam
(1972) Paramount
Consummate film buff Allen created the ultimate film buff's fantasy, the merging of real life and the big screen. Allen takes the lead in this adaptation of his play, which also features other members of the Broadway cast, as a movie fan whose passivity messes up his relationships with women—until his hero, Bogart, starts dispensing advice. Interesting to see someone else (Ross) directing Allen material, and a hoot for film fans. **Cast:** Woody Allen, Diane Keaton, Susan Anspach, Tony Roberts, Jerry Lacy, Jennifer Salt, Viva, Joy Bang, Mari Fletcher, Diana Davila. **Credits:** Dir: Herbert Ross; Prod: Arthur P. Jacobs; Writer: Woody Allen; DP: Owen Roizman; Ed: Marion Rothman; Prod Design: Ed Wittstein; Composer: Billy Goldenberg. Color, 87 min. VHS, LASER

Play Misty for Me
(1971) Universal
Eastwood's first venture into directing is a well-made, gripping thriller. A late-night disc jockey (Eastwood), on the rebound from a breakup, gets a nightly call to play the title song. When he is seduced into meeting the woman caller (Walter), he becomes the object of her obsession. She eventually reveals herself to be deeply disturbed and is placed in a sanitarium. Eastwood thinks his troubles are over until he gets a haunting request once more. Eastwood gives a nod to his mentor, director Siegel, with a cameo as a barkeep. Features the Roberta Flack song, "The First Time Ever I Saw Your Face." **Cast:** Clint Eastwood, Jessica Walter, Donna Mills, John Larch, Jack Ging, Irene Hervey, James McEachin, Clarice Taylor, Don Siegel. **Credits:** Dir: Clint Eastwood; Prod: Robert Daley; Writer: Jo Heims, Dean Riesner; DP: Bruce Surtees; Ed: Carl Pingitore; Composer: Dee Barton; Art Director: Alexander Golitzen. Color, 103 min. VHS, LASER

Plaza Suite
(1971) Paramount
Matthau stars as three different characters in a successful adaptation of a Broadway hit by Simon (the fourth episode in the stage version became *The Out-of-Towners*, 1970). The three vignettes all take place in the same hotel room in New York City. In the first, a couple celebrates their wedding anniversary with a trip to the hotel. As the wife sentimentalizes, the husband plans to meet his mistress. In another, a producer puts the make on an old flame (Harris). In the third, a father tries to coax his anxious, about to be married, daughter out of the bathroom. **Cast:** Walter Matthau, Maureen Stapleton, Barbara Harris, Lee Grant, Louise Sorel, Tom Carey, Jose Ocasion, Dan Ferrone, Jenny Sullivan. **Credits:** Dir: Arthur Hiller; Prod: Howard W. Koch; Writer: Neil Simon; Story: Neil Simon; DP: Jack A. Marta; Ed: Frank Bracht; Composer: Maurice Jarre; Art Director: Arthur Lonergan. Color, 115 min. VHS, LASER

Please Don't Eat the Daisies
(1960) MGM
Based on the book by Jean Kerr, Day and Niven star as city sophisticates (he's a drama critic) who decide to move to the country with the dog and the kids, and are hilariously traumatized by the experience. An amusing family comedy, supported by the fine comic performances of Paige, Kelly, and Byington. The film was the basis for a successful television series. **Cast:** David Niven, Doris Day, Janis Paige, Spring Byington, Richard Haydn, Patsy Kelly, Jack Weston, John Harding, Margaret Lindsay, Charles Herbert. **Credits:** Dir: Charles Walters; Prod: Joe Pasternak; Writer: Isobel Lennart; Story: Jean Kerr; DP: Robert Bronner; Ed: John McSweeney; Composer: David Rose; Art Director: George W. Davis. Color, 111 min. VHS, LASER

The Pleasure of His Company
(1961) Paramount
Astaire is a carefree playboy who returns to San Francisco after 15 years to visit his ex-wife Palmer and daughter Reynolds. Reynolds is about to be married to Hunter, a local rancher. Astaire insinuates his way into the wedding preparations and the lives of the household, much to Merrill's, Palmer's wealthy husband, aggravation. Reynolds becomes besotted with her father's Continental suavity and decides to spend the next few years with him instead of getting married. When Astaire realizes the mess he is making of both the family and their wedding preparations, he bids farewell to his daughter and wishes her the best. Lilting dialogue

and the assured presence of Astaire make this slight romantic comedy special. **Cast:** Fred Astaire, Debbie Reynolds, Gary Merrill, Lillie Palmer, Tab Hunter, Charlie Ruggles, Harold Fong, Elvia Allman, Edith Head. **Credits:** Dir: George Seaton; Prod: William Perlberg; Writer: Sam Taylor, Cornelia Otis Skinner; DP: Robert Burks; Ed: Alma Macrorie; Prod Design: Hal Pereira, Tambi Larsem; Composer: Alfred Newman. Color, 115 min.

The Plough and the Stars
(1936) RKO
A stormy relationship with RKO makes this minor-league Ford, but interesting to see his treatment of a subject he also dealt with in *The Informer*. This historical drama based on O'Casey's play about the 1916 Easter rebellion in Ireland features Stanwyck who owns a boardinghouse with her husband (Foster), a member of the Irish Citizen Army. She convinces him to resign from the group, but he rejoins once he learns he has been promoted to commander. The studio brought in another director to reshoot romantic interludes and Ford threatened to have his name removed from the credits. **Cast:** Barbara Stanwyck, Preston Foster, Barry Fitzgerald, Denis O'Dea, F. J. McCormick, Arthur Shields, Una O'Connor. **Credits:** Dir: John Ford; Prod: Cliff Reid, Robert Sisk; Writer: Dudley Nichols; Story: Sean O'Casey; DP: Joseph H. August; Ed: George Hively; Prod Design: Darrel Silvera; Composer: Roy Webb; Art Director: Van Nest Polglase. B&W, 72 min.

Plymouth Adventure
(1952) MGM
The Mayflower saga serves as background for a romantic, historical adventure. Gruff Tracy shepherds the pilgrims across the tossing sea, and tries to start a romantic adventure with future governor William Bradford's wife (Tierney). She resists, and he gains respect for the colonists, but not in time to save her from drowning in a violent storm. **Academy Award:** Best Visual Effects. **Cast:** Spencer Tracy, Gene Tierney, Van Johnson, Leo Genn, Dawn Addams, Lloyd Bridges, Barry Jones, John Dehner, Tommy Ivo, Lowell Gilmore. **Credits:** Dir: Clarence Brown; Prod: Dore Schary; Writer: Ernst Gabler, Helen Deutsch; DP: William Daniels; Ed: Robert J. Kern; Composer: Miklos Rozsa; Art Director: Cedric Gibbons, Urie McCleary. Color, 105 min.

Pocketful of Miracles
(1961) Columbia
Capra's star-studded, sentimental final film is a remake of his 1934 *Lady for a Day* and both are based on the hoary Damon Runyon tale. An aging apple-seller (Davis) passes herself off as a woman of wealth in order to help her daughter marry into a well-to-do family. Assisting her in the comic charade is a motley group of small-time gangsters led by a disarming Falk. Ann-Margret made her film debut. Academy Award Nominations: 3, including Best Supporting Actor: Peter Falk; Best Song ("Pocketful of Miracles"). Golden Globe for Best Actor in a Musical or Comedy: Glenn Ford. **Cast:** Bette Davis, Glenn Ford, Hope Lange, Arthur O'Connell, Peter Falk, Jack Elam, Ann-Margret, Thomas Mitchell, Edward Everett Horton, Mickey Shaughnessy. **Credits:** Dir: Frank Capra; Prod: Frank Capra; Writer: Hal Kanter, Harry Tugend; Story: Damon Runyon; DP: Robert Bronner; Ed: Frank P. Keller; Prod Design: Hal Pereira; Choreographer: Nick Castle; Composer: Walter Scharf. Color, 138 min. **VHS, LASER**

Pocket Money
(1972) National General
In a modern Western written by cult director Malick (*Badlands*, 1974, and *The Thin Red Line*, 1998), Newman and Marvin star as a couple of slow-witted cowpokes who try to improve their luck by getting into business with a slick cattle rancher. On a trip to Mexico, they meet an old pal with a few schemes still left up his sleeve. Kovacs's cinematography of the Western landscape is memorable. The first offering from the production consortium of '70s stars known as First Artists. **Cast:** Paul Newman, Lee Marvin, Hector Elizondo, Christine Belford, Wayne Rogers, Strother Martin, Kelly Jean Peters, Fred Graham, Gregory Sierra. **Credits:** Dir: Stuart Rosenberg; Prod: John Foreman; Writer: Terrence Malick; DP: Laszlo Kovacs; Ed: Bob Wyman; Composer: Alex North; Art Director: Tambi Larsen. Color, 100 min. **VHS**

Point Blank
(1967) MGM
Boorman directed this taut, bloody thriller, borrowing techniques from the French New Wave. Marvin stars as a husband left for dead by his wife and her gangster boyfriend, but he returns to get what he deserves from the double-crossers, with the help of Dickinson. Now considered one of the most stylish films of the late '60s, it marked a fruitful collaboration between Boorman and Marvin. Adapted from *The Hunter* by Donald E. Westlake (writing as Richard Stark). **Cast:** Lee Marvin, Angie Dickinson, Carroll O'Connor, Keenan Wynn, Lloyd Bochner, Michael Strong, John Vernon, Sharon Acker, James B. Sikking. **Credits:** Dir: John Boorman; Prod: Judd Bernard; Writer: Alexander Jacobs; Story: Donald E. Westlake; DP: Philip H. Lathrop; Ed: Henry Berman; Composer: Johnny Mandel; Art Director: George W. Davis. Color, 89 min. **VHS, LASER**

Pollyanna
(1960) Disney
A Disney remake of the 1921 Mary Pickford original, based on the Eleanor Porter story, this is a heartwarming tale of a young girl (Mills) who brings goodwill and happiness to the residents of a New England town. The entire cast is first-rate. Mills won a special Oscar for "the most outstanding juvenile performance." **Academy Awards:** Honorary Award: Hayley Mills. **Cast:** Hayley Mills, Richard Egan, Jane Wyman, Karl Malden, Adolphe Menjou, Nancy Olson, Donald Crisp, Agnes Moorehead, Kevin Corcoran, James Drury. **Credits:** Dir: David Swift; Prod: Walt Disney; Writer: David Swift; Story: Eleanor Porter; DP: Russell Harlan; Ed: Frank Gross; Prod Design: Carroll Clark; Composer: Paul J. Smith. Color, 134 min. **VHS, LASER**

Pony Express
(1953) Paramount
Buffalo Bill Cody and Wild Bill Hickok (Heston and Tucker) are commissioned to establish Pony Express stations along a route to Sacramento. The local stagecoach company wants to keep the profitable government mail contract and attempts to sabotage their efforts. **Cast:** Charlton Heston, Forrest Tucker, Rhonda Fleming, Jan Sterling, Michael Moore, Porter Hall, Richard Shannon, Henry Brandon, Stuart Randall, Lewis Martin. **Credits:** Dir: Jerry Hopper; Prod: Nat Holt; Writer: Charles Marquis Warren; DP: Ray Rennahan; Ed: Eda Warren; Prod Design: Hal Pereira; Composer: Paul Sawtell. Color, 101 min. **VHS**

Pony Soldier
(1952) Fox
As a Canadian Mountie, Power tries to avert an Indian war as he escorts the Cree Indians back to Canada after they illegally entered the United States to hunt buffalo. Based on a

true story. **Cast:** Tyrone Power, Cameron Mitchell, Robert Horton, Thomas Gomez, Penny Edwards, Earl Holliman, Adeline de Walt Reynolds. **Credits:** Dir: Joseph M. Newman; Prod: Samuel G. Engel; Writer: John C. Higgins; DP: Harry Jackson; Ed: John McCafferty; Prod Design: Lyle Wheeler; Composer: Alex North. Color, 81 min. **VHS**

The Poor Little Rich Girl
(1936) Fox
One of Temple's best has her as a motherless rich girl who runs away from her father and lands in the home, and stage act, of a husband-and-wife team of entertainers. She makes them stars as she performs the tunes "I Love a Military Man," "Oh, My Goodness," and "When I'm with You." **Cast:** Shirley Temple, Alice Faye, Frank Haley, Gloria Stuart, Michael Whalen, Sara Haden, Jane Darwell, Arthur Hoyt. **Credits:** Dir: Irving Cummings; Prod: Raymond Griffith; Writer: Sam Hellman, Gladys Lehman, Harry Tugend; Story: Ralph Spence; DP: John Seitz; Ed: Jack Murray; Prod Design: Rudolph Sternad; Art Director: William S. Darling. B&W, 72 min. **VHS, LASER**

Poppy
(1936) Paramount
This is a Fields comedy in which a carnival medicine-show con man and his adopted daughter move to a small town and run a scam. The carny learns that a wealthy estate is about to be claimed by the long-lost daughter of the owners. He convinces his daughter to pose as the heiress, but the ruse is soon discovered. Featured are some of Fields's best-loved routines ("never give a sucker an even break"), and based on his silent film *Sally of the Sawdust* (1925) that was directed by D. W. Griffith. **Cast:** W. C. Fields, Rochelle Hudson, Richard Cromwell, Lynne Overman, Catharine Doucet, Granville Bates. **Credits:** Dir: A. Edward Sutherland; Prod: William LeBaron; Writer: Dorothy Donnelly, Waldemar Young, Virginia Van Upp; DP: William Mellor; Ed: Stuart Heisler; Prod Design: Hans Dreier, Bernard Herzbrun; Composer: Ralph Rainger, Leo Robin. B&W, 75 min.

Pork Chop Hill
(1959) United Artists
Milestone's third antiwar masterpiece features a cast of young stars-to-be, with Peck in the lead, as soldiers fighting one of the last, futile battles of the Korean War. Peck is a soldier ordered to send his men up the title hill under withering fire from the communists as the politicians negotiating the end of the "police action" continue to talk. Impressive directing and performances in this gripping story set in the less-depicted Korean conflict. **Cast:** Gregory Peck, Harry Guardino, Rip Torn, George Peppard, James Edwards, Bob Steele, Woody Strode, Norman Fell, Robert Blake, Biff Elliot. **Credits:** Dir: Lewis Milestone; Prod: Sy Bartlett; Writer: James R. Webb; DP: Sam Leavitt; Ed: George Boemler; Composer: Leonard Rosenman; Art Director: Nicolai Remisoff. B&W, 98 min. **VHS, LASER**

Port of Seven Seas
(1938) MGM
This screen version of French writer Pagnol's romantic novel *Fanny* stars O'Sullivan as Madelon, lover of the young sailor Marius (Beal). When the sea calls her beau away, Madelon discovers she is pregnant. Panisse (Morgan), longtime friend of her father Caesar (Beery), marries Madelon to save her reputation. When Marius returns he must decide whether to destroy Madelon's new marriage or to give her up for the sake of his child's future. A curious attempt to graft Continental sensibility onto a Hollywood production, with a script by Sturges and direction by Whale. **Cast:** Maureen O'Sullivan, John Beal, Wallace Beery, Frank Morgan, Etienne Girardot, Cora Witherspoon, E. Alyn Warren, Jessie Ralph. **Credits:** Dir: James Whale; Prod: Carl Laemmle, Henry Henigson; Writer: Preston Sturges, Ernest Vajda; Story: Marcel Pagnol; DP: Karl Freund; Ed: Frederick Smith; Prod Design: Cedric Gibbons; Composer: Franz Waxman. B&W, 81 min.

Portrait of Jennie
(1948) Goldwyn
A penniless artist (Cotten) meets a strange girl (Jones) who seems to be of another time and place. As she appears to him as the seasons and years pass, he finally paints her at the height of her beauty and the painting marks his artistic breakthrough. He falls in love with the girl and tracks her to a New England boarding school where she had died in a terrible storm. A haunting tale of a mystical affair. Academy Award Nominations: 2. **Academy Awards:** Best Special Visual Effects. **Cast:** Jennifer Jones, Joseph Cotten, Ethel Barrymore, Lillian Gish, Cecil Kellaway, David Wayne, Albert Sharpe, Florence Bates, Henry Hull. **Credits:** Dir: William Dieterle; Prod: David O. Selznick; Writer: Paul Osborn; Story: Robert Nathan; DP: Joseph H. August; Ed: William Morgan; Prod Design: J. McMillan Johnson; Composer: Bernard Herrmann, Dimitri Tiomkin. B&W, 86 min. **VHS, LASER**

The Poseidon Adventure
(1972) Fox
The granddaddy of disaster flicks. When an earthquake sends a tidal wave over a luxury liner on New Year's Eve, the top-heavy vessel capsizes. Ten survivors journey through the ship to escape; worthwhile simply to see Winters squeezing through air shafts, and the toppling Christmas tree. It spawned a terrible sequel, *Beyond the Poseidon Adventure*, along with countless imitators. Academy Award Nominations: 8, including Best Actress: Shelley Winters. **Academy Awards:** Best Song ("There's Got to Be a Morning After"). **Cast:** Gene Hackman, Ernest Borgnine, Carol Lynley, Red Buttons, Shelley Winters, Jack Albertson, Stella Stevens, Roddy McDowall, Pamela Sue Martin, Arthur O'Connell. **Credits:** Dir: Ronald Neame; Prod: Irwin Allen; Writer: Stirling Silliphant, Wendell Mayes; Story: Paul Gallico; DP: Harold E. Stine; Ed: Harold F. Kress; Prod Design: William J. Creber; Composer: John Williams. Color, 117 min. **VHS, LASER, DVD**

Posse
(1975) Paramount
Douglas directs and portrays a U.S. marshal with political ambitions. But when he vows to put a bandit behind bars, the electorate takes the side of the outlaw. An interesting study of outright lawlessness and hidden corruption. Beautifully photographed by Koenekamp. **Cast:** Kirk Douglas, Bruce Dern, Bo Hopkins, James Stacy, Luke Askew, David Canary, Alfonso Arau, Kate Woodville, Mark Roberts, Beth Brickell. **Credits:** Dir: Kirk Douglas; Prod: Kirk Douglas; Writer: William Roberts; DP: Fred Koenekamp; Ed: John W. Wheeler; Prod Design: Lyle Wheeler; Composer: Maurice Jarre. Color, 94 min. **VHS, LASER**

Possessed
(1931) MGM
Crawford stars in a fascinating, juicy pre-Code potboiler. A lower-class working girl (Crawford) thinks she's hit the jackpot when she becomes a Park Avenue lawyer's mistress. Gable has political ambitions but wants his cake and to eat it, too. A routine melodrama with the benefit of fireworks from

Gable and Crawford. **Cast:** Joan Crawford, Clark Gable, Wallace Ford, Skeets Gallagher, John Miljan, Frank Conroy, Marjorie White, Clara Blandick. **Credits:** Dir: Clarence Brown; Prod: Clarence Brown; Writer: Lenore Coffee; DP: Oliver T. Marsh; Ed: William LeVanway; Prod Design: Cedric Gibbons; Costumes: Adrian. B&W, 78 min. **VHS**

Possessed
(1947) Warner Bros.
An emotionally unstable woman (Crawford) is torn between two men. Her obsession compels her to marry the one she doesn't love (Massey), and to kill the man she does (Heflin). Brooks made her charming film debut. Academy Award Nomination for Best Actress: Joan Crawford. **Cast:** Joan Crawford, Van Heflin, Raymond Massey, Geraldine Brooks, Stanley Ridges, Moroni Olsen, John Ridgely, Nana Bryant, Erskine Sanford, Peter Miles. **Credits:** Dir: Curtis Bernhardt; Prod: Jerry Wald; Writer: Silvia Richards; DP: Joseph A. Valentine; Ed: Rudi Fehr; Prod Design: Anton F. Grot; Composer: Franz Waxman. B&W, 110 min. **VHS, LASER**

The Postman Always Rings Twice
(1946) MGM
The first and the sexiest of the three films made of James M.Cain's novel (he also wrote *Double Indemnity*). The chemistry between a drifter (Garfield) and a waitress (Turner) at a roadside cafe waiting for a chance to escape her suffocating life and husband is so explosive that it leads to killing the woman's husband. The pair get off when charged with murder, but their lawyer (Cronyn) gets the goods on them for a blackmail scheme. In a twist of fate, each of the murderers gets their comeuppance in an unexpected way. The story and direction make the murder seem almost inevitable. MGM tried for more than a decade to get a script that would pass the Breen office censors. In the meantime, Italian director Luchino Visconti made a version entitled *Ossessione* in 1942. Remade with more blatant sexuality in 1980 with Jack Nicholson and Jessica Lange. **Cast:** Lana Turner, John Garfield, Cecil Kallaway, Hume Cronyn, Leon Ames, Audrey Totter, Alan Reed, Jeff York. **Credits:** Dir: Tay Garnett; Prod: Carey Wilson; Writer: Harry Ruskin, Niven Busch; DP: Sidney Wagner; Ed: George White; Prod Design: Cedric Gibbons; Composer: George Bassman; Art Director: Randall Duell. B&W, 113 min. **VHS, LASER**

The Power and the Glory
(1933) Fox
A cinema breakthrough, this film was hailed at the time for its unconventional structure (dubbed "narratage" and often seen as the basis for the structure of *Citizen Kane*) and the debuts of Tracy in a leading role and Sturges as writer. A corrupt tycoon rises from a poor young idealist to an uncaring robber baron. His faithful wife helps him to build his empire, then suffers from his selfishness as his power grows. It was renowned as much for Sturges's deal with studio head Lasky for a percentage of its gross as for its structure. **Cast:** Spencer Tracy, Colleen Moore, Ralph Morgan, Helen Vinson, Philip Trent, Henry Kolker, Sarah Padden, Billy O'Brien, Cullen Johnson, J. Farrell MacDonald. **Credits:** Dir: William K. Howard; Prod: Jesse L. Lasky; Writer: Preston Sturges; DP: James Wong Howe; Ed: Paul Weatherwax; Prod Design: Max Parker; Composer: Louis De Francesco, J. S. Zamecnik, Peter Brunelli. B&W, 76 min.

Presenting Lily Mars
(1943) MGM
A sprightly musical with a young Garland in the lead. From a Booth Tarkington novel, the story follows a girl from a small town who badgers a producer to take her to New York City. Her dreams come true when she is selected for the lead in a new show. Tommy Dorsey and Bob Crosby provide the music and Judy sings "Every Little Movement Has a Meaning of Its Own." **Cast:** Judy Garland, Van Heflin, Fay Bainter, Richard Carlson, Spring Byington, Marta Eggerth, Connie Gilchrist, Leonid Kinskey. **Credits:** Dir: Norman Taurog; Prod: Joe Pasternak; Writer: Richard Connell; Story: Booth Tarkington; DP: Joseph Ruttenberg; Ed: Albert Akst; Prod Design: Cedric Gibbons; Choreographer: Ernst Matray. B&W, 105 min. **VHS, LASER**

The President's Analyst
(1967) Paramount
A brilliant political satire about a shrink (Coburn) who is appointed in secret to treat the President, who appears to have a galloping paranoia. When the shrink quits this high-pressure job, he finds himself pursued by intelligence agents from every side of the Cold War and wonders about not only the President's sanity but his own. **Cast:** James Coburn, Godfrey Cambridge, Severn Darden, Pat Harrington, Jr., Joan Delaney, Barry Maguire, Eduard Franz, Walter Burke. **Credits:** Dir: Theodore J.

Flicker; Prod: Stanley Rubin; Writer: Theodore J. Flicker; DP: William A. Fraker; Ed: Stuart Pappe; Prod Design: Pato Guzman; Composer: Lalo Schifrin; Art Director: Hal Pereira, Al Roelofs. Color, 100 min. **VHS, LASER**

The President's Lady
(1953) Fox
Lush, romanticized biopic of President Andrew Jackson (Heston) and his wife Rachel Donelson Robards (Hayward), who bond when Jackson escorts Robards, then married to another man, on a dangerous riverboat trip from Nashville to Natchez, Miss. They fall in love and decide to marry once her first marriage is annulled. Some question the legitimacy of their marriage since it took place before her divorce was final, and they marry again. Jackson wins his party's nomination and runs for president and wins, but the new First Lady dies before the couple moves into the White House. Academy Award Nominations: Best Art Direction; Best Costume Design. **Cast:** Susan Hayward, Charlton Heston, John McIntire, Fay Bainter, Carl Betz, Gladys Hurlbut, Whitfield Connor, Charles Dingle. **Credits:** Dir: Henry Levin; Prod: Sol C. Siegel; Writer: John Patrick; Story: Ruth Attaway; DP: Leo Tover; Ed: William B. Murphy; Prod Design: Charles Le Maire, Renie; Composer: Alfred Newman; Art Director: Leland Fuller, Lyle Wheeler. B&W, 96 min.

The President's Mystery
(1936) Republic
The only movie based on an idea conceived by President Franklin Delano Roosevelt (or any other president!), it was developed as an article for *Liberty* magazine before it became a screenplay written by West, who used his experience to later write the blistering satire *The Day of the Locust*. A Depression-era lawyer whose practice helps greedy capitalists exploit working people gives up his wife and his practice in disgust. He tries to reinvent himself, and falls in love with another woman (Furness). **Cast:** Sidney Blackmer, Betty Furness, Henry Wilcoxon, Evelyn Brent, Barnett Parker, Wade Boteler, John Wray, Guy Usher. **Credits:** Dir: Phil Rosen; Prod: Nat Levine; Writer: Lester Cole, Nathanael West; DP: Ernest Miller; Ed: Murray Seldeen, Robert Simpson. B&W, 80 min. **VHS**

Pressure Point
(1962) United Artists
This is an intelligent though sometimes convoluted drama based on a

true story adapted from *The Fifty-Minute Hour,* a memoir by Dr. Robert M. Lindner. A prison psychiatrist (Poitier) has trouble treating a racist patient (Darin), who is also an active member of the American Nazi Party. The two clash after Poitier frees Darin's mind and he prepares to be paroled. Darin and Poitier make a strong pairing. **Cast:** Sidney Poitier, Peter Falk, Carl Benton Reid, Mary Munday, Barry Gordon, Howard Caine, Bobby Darin, James Anderson. **Credits:** Dir: Hubert Cornfield; Prod: Stanley Kramer; Writer: Hubert Cornfield; Story: Robert M. Lindner; DP: Ernest Haller; Ed: Frederic L. Knudtson; Prod Design: Rudolph Sternad; Composer: Ernest Gold. Color, 88 min. **VHS**

Pretty Baby
(1978) Paramount
French director Malle's first American film marked the celebrated debut of 12-year-old Shields as a brothel child who gets involved with, then marries, an older photographer (Carradine as real-life photographer E. J.Bellocq) in 1910 New Orleans. Sarandon is Shields's prostitute mother. Nykvist's photography makes a compelling evocation of old New Orleans, and what could have been merely tawdry becomes an interesting look at a bygone way of life. Academy Award Nomination for Best Score. **Cast:** Keith Carradine, Brooke Shields, Susan Sarandon, Frances Faye, Antonio Fargas, Gerrit Graham, Mae Mercer, Diana Scarwid. **Credits:** Dir: Louis Malle; Prod: Louis Malle; Writer: Polly Platt; Story: Louis Malle, Polly Platt; DP: Sven Nykvist; Ed: Suzanne Baron; Prod Design: Trevor Williams; Composer: Jerry Wexler. Color, 109 min. **VHS, LASER**

Pretty Maids All in a Row
(1971) MGM
Director Vadim came to Hollywood with this mordant black comedy starring Hudson as a high school counselor who takes female students to bed and later murders them. Hudson shows Carson the ropes. Written and produced by Roddenberry, known for TV's *Star Trek.* **Cast:** Rock Hudson, Angie Dickinson, John David Carson, Telly Savalas, Roddy McDowall, Keenan Wynn, James Doohan, Barbara Leigh, Aimee Eccles. **Credits:** Dir: Roger Vadim; Prod: Gene Roddenberry; Writer: Gene Roddenberry; DP: Charles Rosher; Ed: Bill Brame; Prod Design: George W. Davis; Composer: Lalo Schifrin. Color, 92 min. **VHS**

Pride and Prejudice
(1940) MGM
Jane Austen's classic comedy of manners is vividly adapted with a charming cast. Five sisters in 19th-century England are all concerned with finding a husband. The most opinionated of the lot (Garson) rejects a man who has been chosen for her (Olivier) because she finds him full of pride. She changes her mind and wins him when she acknowledges her own pride is hindering her happiness. Huxley was among the writers of the screenplay. **Academy Awards:** Best Black-and-White Interior Decoration. **Cast:** Greer Garson, Laurence Olivier, Edna May Oliver, Edmund Gwenn, Maureen O'Sullivan, Mary Boland, Ann Rutherford, Frieda Inescort. **Credits:** Dir: Robert Z. Leonard; Prod: Hunt Stromberg; Writer: Aldous Huxley; DP: Karl Freund; Ed: Robert J. Kern; Prod Design: Cedric Gibbons; Composer: Herbert Stothart. B&W, 118 min. **VHS, LASER**

The Pride and the Passion
(1957) United Artists
International superstars enhance a lavish epic of Spain's 1810 effort to rebuff Napoleon Bonaparte. An intrepid band of resistance fighters must first haul a six-ton cannon across the wide expanse of Spain's mountains. During their perilous journey, a dramatic love triangle emerges between a dashing resistance fighter (Sinatra), his sultry mistress (Loren), and a British navy captain (Grant) recruited for the cause. **Cast:** Cary Grant, Frank Sinatra, Sophia Loren, Theodore Bikel, John Wengraf, Jay Novello, Jose Nieto. **Credits:** Dir: Stanley Kramer; Prod: Stanley Kramer; Writer: Edna Anhalt, Edward Anhalt; Story: C. S. Forester; DP: Franz Planer; Ed: Frederic Knudtson, Ellsworth Hoagland; Prod Design: Rudolph Sternad; Composer: George Antheil, Ernest Gold. Color, 132 min. **VHS**

The Pride of St. Louis
(1952) Fox
In this biopic of Dizzy Dean (Dailey), a baseball star turns to sports commentary after an injury takes him permanently out of the game. After a bout with self-pity and the bottle, with the help of his devoted wife, Dru, he makes a new life. In an early appearance, Chet Huntley of NBC News fame can be seen as a sports broadcaster. Academy Award Nomination for Best Motion Picture Story. **Cast:** Dan Dailey, Joanne Dru, Richard Hylton, Richard Crenna, Hugh Sanders, James Brown, Kenny Williams, Stuart Randall. **Credits:** Dir: Harmon Jones;

Prod: Jules Schermer; Writer: Herman J. Mankiewicz, Guy Trosper; DP: Leo Tover; Ed: Robert Simpson; Prod Design: Lyle Wheeler; Composer: Arthur Lange; Art Director: Addison Hehr. B&W, 93 min. **VHS**

Pride of the Marines
(1945) Warner Bros.
This gripping depiction of the aftermath of WWII shows that some of the most courageous moments of war come in facing its consequences. Garfield, in one of his favorite roles, plays Al Schmid, a real-life war hero. He marries Parker on the eve of Japan's invasion of Pearl Harbor and finds himself on his way to Guadalcanal. He heroically defends himself and his troops from the Japanese (killing 200 or more in the process, in some of the most savage war scenes ever filmed). He's blinded in the battle and returns home to a Navy Cross and a difficult, bitter rehabilitation. With the help and patience of his wife, he begins the long, difficult journey toward readjusting to life. Academy Award Nomination for Best Original Screenplay. **Cast:** Warren Douglass, John Garfield, Eleanor Parker, Dane Clark, John Ridgely, Rosemary DeCamp, Ann Doran, Ann Todd, Tom D'Andrea, Don McGuire. **Credits:** Dir: Delmer Daves; Prod: Jerry Wald; Writer: Albert Maltz, Marvin Borowsky, Delmer Daves; Story: Herbert Butterfield; DP: J. Peverell Marley; Ed: Owen Marks; Prod Design: Leo K. Kuter; Composer: Franz Waxman. B&W, 119 min.

The Pride of the Yankees
(1942) RKO
This is one of the greatest of sports films and a much-lauded portrait of courage. Cooper plays Lou Gehrig, the first baseman for the fabled Yanks of the golden age of baseball, who suffered from a crippling and incurable disease that came to bear his name. The film's final scene of his farewell address at Yankee Stadium is a moving valedictory to a storied career. Academy Award Nominations: 11, including Best Picture; Best Actor: Gary Cooper; Best Actress: Teresa Wright; Best Original Story. **Academy Awards:** Best Film Editing. **Cast:** Gary Cooper, Teresa Wright, Babe Ruth, Walter Brennan, Ludwig Stossel, Bill Dickey, Ernie Adams. **Credits:** Dir: Sam Wood; Prod: Samuel Goldwyn; Writer: Jo Swerling, Herman J. Mankiewicz; Story: Paul Gallico; DP: Rudolph Maté; Ed: Daniel Mandell; Prod Design:

William Cameron Menzies, Perry Ferguson, McClure Capps; Composer: Leigh Harline. B&W, 128 min. **VHS**

The Prime of Miss Jean Brodie
(1969) Fox
An inspirational, controversial teacher (Smith) at an exclusive girls' school in Scotland in the '30s finds her unorthodox methods—and romantic idealization of the Italian fascists—place her career in jeopardy. Her romantic entanglements and competition with one of her students also complicate her life. Based on Jay Presson Allen's play (which starred Vanessa Redgrave) of Muriel Spark's novel. Academy Award Nominations: 2, including Best Song ("Jean"). **Academy Awards:** Best Actress: Maggie Smith. **Cast:** Maggie Smith, Robert Stephens, Pamela Franklin, Gordon Jackson, Celia Johnson, Jane Carr, Rona Anderson, Ann Way. **Credits:** Dir: Ronald Neame; Prod: Robert Fryer; Writer: Jay Presson Allen; DP: Ted Moore; Ed: Norman Savage; Prod Design: John Howell; Composer: Rod McKuen. Color, 116 min. **VHS**

The Primrose Path
(1940) RKO
This gritty romantic melodrama features Rogers as the daughter of an aging prostitute (Rambeau) who lures a hamburger-stand owner (McCrea) into marriage. Once he learns about her family, the marriage is off and Rogers is faced with following in her mother's footsteps. Rambeau was a noted beauty in the silent-film days but by this time played mostly aging harlots. Academy Award Nomination for Best Supporting Actress: Marjorie Rambeau. **Cast:** Ginger Rogers, Joel McCrea, Marjorie Rambeau, Miles Mander, Henry Travers, Joan Carroll, Vivienne Osborne, Gene Morgan. **Credits:** Dir: Gregory La Cava; Prod: Gregory La Cava; Writer: Allan Scott, Gregory La Cava; Story: Robert Buckner, Walter Hart; DP: Joseph H. August; Ed: William Hamilton; Prod Design: Van Nest Polglase, Carroll Clark; Composer: Werner Richard Heymann. B&W, 93 min. **VHS**

The Prince and the Pauper
(1937) Warner Bros.
This is the first and best of the three films made based on Twain's classic story of the young Prince Edward VI of En-gland and his look-alike orphan friend, who trade places. Flynn appears in the second half as the hero who rescues the boys from trou-

ble. Score by Korngold. **Cast:** Errol Flynn, Billy Mauch, Bobby Mauch, Claude Rains, Alan Hale, Elspeth Dudgeon, Helen Valkis. **Credits:** Dir: William Keighley; Prod: Robert Lord; Writer: Laird Doyle; Story: Mark Twain, Catherine Cushing; DP: Sol Polito; Ed: Ralph Dawson; Composer: Erich Wolfgang Korngold; Art Director: Robert M. Haas. B&W, 119 min. **VHS, LASER**

The Prince and the Showgirl
(1957) Warner Bros.
In London for the 1911 Coronation of George V, an American chorus girl (Monroe) meets the Prince of Carpathia (Olivier). The differences in class and upbringing make for an intriguing sexual tension and a winning romantic comedy. Monroe financed the production and Olivier directed in what would be a surprisingly fruitful collaboration between a great light comedienne and the world's most renowned actor. **Cast:** Marilyn Monroe, Laurence Olivier, Sybil Thorndike, Jeremy Spenser, Esmond Knight, Paul Hardwicke, Rosamund Greenwood, Maxine Audley. **Credits:** Dir: Laurence Olivier; Prod: Laurence Olivier; Writer: Terence Rattigan; DP: Jack Cardiff; Ed: Jack Harris; Composer: Richard Addinsell. Color, 117 min. **VHS, LASER**

Prince of Foxes
(1949) Fox
Welles playing Cesare Borgia (in order to finance his own films) offers reason enough to see this, but Power also shines as the henchman of the treacherous Renaissance despot, who uses Power's considerable charms to avoid taking fortresses by storm. Welles soon discovers that his devilish ruses come up short compared to the wiles of Cupid as Power manages to seduce his way into the duke's fortress, but finds himself in love with the daughter. Academy Award Nominations: Best Cinematography; Best Costume Design. **Cast:** Orson Welles, Wanda Hendrix, Marina Berti, Katina Paxinou, Felix Aylmer, Leslie Bradley, Joop van Hulzen, James Carney, Tyrone Power, Everett Sloane. **Credits:** Dir: Henry King; Prod: Sol C. Siegel; Writer: Milton Krims; Story: Samuel Shellabarger; DP: Leon Shamroy; Ed: Barbara McLean; Prod Design: Lyle Wheeler, Mark-Lee Kirk; Composer: Alfred Newman. B&W, 107 min.

The Princess and the Pirate
(1944) RKO
Hope stars as a 17th-century entertainer who falls for a princess (Mayo), whom he'd saved from pirates. Great

costumes, great sight gags (including a walk-on from rival Bing Crosby), great pirates, particularly Brennan. Academy Award Nominations: 2, including Best Scoring of a Dramatic or Comedy Picture. **Cast:** Bob Hope, Walter Slezak, Walter Brennan, Virginia Mayo, Marc Lawrence, Hugo Haas, Maude Eburne, Brandon Hurst, Tom Tyler. **Credits:** Dir: David Butler; Prod: Don Hartman; Writer: Don Hartman, Melville Shavelson, Everett Freeman, Allan Boretz, Curtis Kenyon; Story: Sy Bartlett; DP: Victor Milner, William E. Snyder; Ed: Daniel Mandell; Composer: David Rose; Art Director: Ernst Fegte. Color, 94 min. **VHS, LASER, DVD**

The Princess Comes Across
(1936) Paramount
In this fizzy cocktail of comedy and murder, Lombard plays a Brooklyn actress trying to improve her chances of success by posing as a Swedish princess on a transatlantic voyage who wants a movie career. The ship's bandleader (MacMurray) falls for her, but an old boyfriend spots her, and threatens to expose her. When he's murdered, suspicion falls on Lombard and MacMurray. **Cast:** Carole Lombard, Alison Skipworth, Fred Mac-Murray, Douglass Dumbrille, William Frawley, Porter Hall, George Barbier, Lumsden Hare, Sig Rumann, Mischa Auer. **Credits:** Dir: William K. Howard; Prod: Arthur Hornblow, Jr.; Writer: Walter DeLeon, Francis Martin, Frank Butler, Don Hartman; Story: Phillip MacDonald, Louis Lucien Rogger; DP: Ted Tetzlaff; Ed: Paul Weatherwax; Prod Design: Hans Dreier, Ernst Fegte. B&W, 77 min. **VHS**

Princess O'Rourke
(1943) Warner Bros.
When his plane is forced to return to the ground, pilot Cummings takes charge of a pretty passenger (de Havilland) who has taken sleeping pills for the trip, and can't be revived. He brings her back to his apartment, she recovers, and the two are soon smitten, becoming engaged almost immediately. Much to Cummings's surprise, his anonymous houseguest-fiancée turns out to be a princess in the U.S. looking for a husband. Though a pilot isn't what father Coburn had in mind, he approves and plans for a wedding at the White House. But Cummings objects when he will have to renounce his U.S. citizenship to marry the girl he loves. Made with the participation of First Film Fan FDR and his Scottie dog Fala, who both appear. **Cast:** Olivia de Havilland, Robert Cummings,

Charles Coburn, Jack Carson, Jane Wyman. **Credits:** Dir: Norman Krasna; Prod: Hal B. Wallis; Writer: Norman Krasna; DP: Ernest Haller; Ed: Warren Low; Prod Design: Max Parker. B&W, 93 min.

The Prisoner of Second Avenue
(1975) Warner Bros.
An adaptation by Simon of his Broadway hit. An ad executive (Lemmon) loses confidence in himself and the future when he's handed his pink slip. In addition he and wife Bancroft suffer New York indignities including apartment break-ins. Occasionally funny, but with plenty of dark moments. Stallone and F. Murray Abraham have early small roles. **Cast:** Jack Lemmon, Anne Bancroft, M. Emmet Walsh, Gene Saks, Sylvester Stallone, Stack Pierce, Ivor Francis. **Credits:** Dir: Melvin Frank; Prod: Melvin Frank; Writer: Neil Simon; DP: Philip H. Lathrop; Ed: Bob Wyman; Composer: Marvin Hamlisch; Art Director: Preston Ames. Color, 105 min. **VHS, LASER**

Prisoner of Shark Island
(1936) Fox
Here is Ford's dramatization of the true story of Dr. Samuel Mudd (Baxter), the doctor who fixed fugitive John Wilkes Booth's ankle and was subsequently charged with conspiracy to murder President Lincoln. He is taken away from his loving wife (Stuart) and family and sentenced to life at Fort Jefferson Prison on Shark Island. Dr. Mudd soon is recognized by prisoners as an honorable man and a gentleman by the prison guards. A yellow fever epidemic breaks out among the prisoners and guards and Dr. Mudd risks his own life to save the victims. His heroic deed is recognized and his case is reopened. **Cast:** Warner Baxter, Gloria Stuart, Claude Gillingwater, Arthur Byron, O. P. Heggie, Henry Carey, Sr., Francis Ford. **Credits:** Dir: John Ford; Prod: Darryl F. Zanuck; Writer: Nunnally Johnson; DP: Bert Glennon; Ed: Jack Murray; Prod Design: William S. Darling, Thomas Little. B&W, 95 min.

The Prisoner of Zenda
(1937) United Artists
The definitive adaptation (others were made in 1914, 1922, 1952, and 1979) of the Anthony Hope novel. The swashbuckling adventure tells the story of a commoner (Colman) thrust into the royal household when he is called on to impersonate a look-alike king who has been kidnapped by a band of rebels. There he falls in love with a regal beauty (Carroll). Academy Award Nominations: Best Interior Decoration; Best Score. **Cast:** Ronald Colman, Madeleine Carroll, Mary Astor, Douglas Fairbanks, Jr., Raymond Massey, David Niven, Eleanor Wesselhoeft, Byron Foulger. **Credits:** Dir: John Cromwell; Prod: David O. Selznick; Writer: John L. Balderston, Wells Root, Donald Ogden Stewart; Story: Anthony Hope, Edward Rose; DP: James Wong Howe; Ed: Hal C. Kern, James E. Newcomb; Prod Design: Lyle Wheeler; Composer: Alfred Newman. B&W, 102 min. **VHS**

The Prisoner of Zenda
(1952) MGM
Remake of the 1937 film about a commoner (Granger) who fills in for the king in his coronation ceremony because the king has been kidnapped by revolutionaries. Stone, cast as an elderly cardinal, starred in the 1922 version. **Cast:** Stewart Granger, Deborah Kerr, Jane Greer, Louis Calhern, James Mason, Lewis Stone, Robert Douglas, Robert Coote. **Credits:** Dir: Richard Thorpe; Prod: Pandro S. Berman; Writer: John L. Balderston, Noel Langley; Story: Anthony Hope; DP: Joseph Ruttenberg; Ed: George Boemler; Prod Design: Cedric Gibbons, Hans Peters; Composer: Alfred Newman. Color, 100 min. **VHS**

The Private Affairs of Bel Ami
(1947) United Artists
A juicy adaptation of de Maupassant's novel, *Bel Ami*, performed by an excellent cast. Set in Paris in the 1880s, it is a chronicle of a young cad (Sanders) who makes his way by charming women out of money and influence and throwing them away when he gets what he wants. But he misses out on a true love with Lansbury. **Cast:** George Sanders, Angela Lansbury, Ann Dvorak, Frances Dee, Albert Basserman, Warren William, John Carradine, Leonard Mudie. **Credits:** Dir: Albert Lewin; Prod: David Loew; Writer: Albert Lewin; Story: Guy de Maupassant; DP: Russell Metty; Ed: Al Joseph; Composer: Darius Milhaud. B&W, 119 min. **VHS**

Private Hell 36
(1954) Filmmakers
This low-budget, independent film noir was co-written and coproduced by Lupino, and directed by action auteur Siegel. Cochran and Duff pursue stolen money from New York to Los Angeles, where nightclub chanteuse Lupino puts them on the trail of the thieves. When one of the bad guys dies in a chase, Cochran and Duff get their hands on some of the loot. But their new wealth leads to a deadly struggle—with their consciences and each other. **Cast:** Howard Duff, Ida Lupino, Dorothy Malone, Steve Cochran, Dean Jagger, Jerry Hausner, Dabbs Greer, King Donovan. **Credits:** Dir: Don Siegel; Prod: Collier Young, Ida Lupino; Writer: Collier Young, Ida Lupino; DP: Burnett Guffey; Ed: Stanford Tischler; Composer: Leith Stevens; Art Director: Walter E. Keller. B&W, 81 min. **VHS, LASER**

The Private Life of Sherlock Holmes
(1970) United Artists
This is a great Wilder film that deserves more attention. An acerbic look at the romantic and melancholic interior life of Sherlock Holmes, here a bored, cocaine-addicted sleuth. The story line manages to involve a Russian ballerina, the Loch Ness Monster, six missing midgets, and Queen Victoria. Stephens portrays Holmes's complexity with a great sympathy. **Cast:** Robert Stephens, Colin Blakely, Genevieve Page, Irene Handl, Stanley Holloway, Christopher Lee, Clive Revill, Peter Madden. **Credits:** Dir: Billy Wilder; Prod: Billy Wilder; Writer: Billy Wilder, I. A. L. Diamond; Story: Sir Arthur Conan Doyle; DP: Christopher Challis; Ed: Ernest Walter; Prod Design: Alexander Trauner; Composer: Miklos Rozsa; Art Director: Tony Inglis. Color, 125 min. **VHS**

Private Lives
(1931) MGM
An adaptation of Coward's comedy about a bickering couple who find they can't live with or without each other. Montgomery and Shearer have split long ago and are married to others (Denny and Merkel). The two couples meet at a French resort, and the old magic is rekindled between Montgomery and Shearer. Sharp, witty, and immortal. **Cast:** Norma Shearer, Robert Montgomery, Una Merkel, Reginald Denny, Jean Hersholt, George Davis. **Credits:** Dir: Sidney Franklin; Prod: Sidney Franklin; Writer: Hans Kraly, Richard Schayer, Claudine West; Story: Noel Coward; DP: Ray Binger; Ed: Conrad A. Nervig; Prod Design: Cedric Gibbons; Costumes: Adrian. B&W, 84 min. **VHS, LASER**

The Private Lives of Elizabeth and Essex

(1939) Warner Bros.

Curtiz directs an all-star cast in a lavish historical epic that featured as many fireworks on the set between Davis and Flynn as appeared onscreen. Davis makes an imperious Elizabeth who is both drawn to and suspicious of the dashing Essex (Flynn), who returns in triumph from Spain. Academy Award Nominations: 5. **Cast:** Errol Flynn, Bette Davis, Olivia de Havilland, Donald Crisp, Vincent Price, Henry Stephenson, Henry Daniell, Nanette Fabray, Ralph Forbes. **Credits:** Dir: Michael Curtiz; Prod: Robert Lord; Writer: Norman Reilly Raine, Aeneas MacKenzie; Story: Maxwell Anderson; DP: Sol Polito, W. Howard Greene; Ed: Owen Marks; Prod Design: Anton Grot; Composer: Erich Wolfgang Korngold. Color, 106 min. **VHS**

The Private War of Major Bensen

(1955) Universal

A hard-nosed, maverick Army major (Heston) loses his assignment after going public with some less than acceptable views. Disgraced, he takes a job as an ROTC instructor at a school run by nuns, ultimately winning the respect of his young charges—and romance with the camp doctor, to boot. This film served as the basis for the 1996 Damon Wayans comedy *Major Payne*. **Cast:** Charlton Heston, Julie Adams, William Demarest, Tim Considine, Sal Mineo, Nana Bryant, Mary Field, Tim Hovey, Don Haggerty. **Credits:** Dir: Jerry Hopper; Prod: Howard Pine; Writer: William Roberts, Richard Alan Simmons; Story: Joe Connelly, Bob Mosher; DP: Harold Lipstein; Ed: Ted J. Kent; Art Director: Alexander Golitzen, Robert Boyle. Color, 104 min. **VHS**

The Prize

(1963) MGM

When a group of honorees arrive in Stockholm for the Nobel Prize ceremony, the American winner for fiction (Newman) confesses he suspects the German physicist is an impostor. Before long, he finds himself involved with communist agents, a murder, and a near-drowning . . . his own. Script by Lehman (*Rear Window*, 1954). **Cast:** Paul Newman, Edward G. Robinson, Elke Sommer, Diane Baker, Micheline Presle, Leo G. Carroll, Don Dubbins, Lester Matthews. **Credits:** Dir: Mark Robson; Prod: Pandro S. Berman; Writer: Ernest Lehman; Story: Irving Wallace; DP: William Daniels; Ed: Adrienne Fazan; Prod Design: George W. Davis, Urie McCleary; Composer: Jerry Goldsmith. Color, 136 min. **VHS**

The Producers

(1968) Avco Embassy

Brooks's received an Oscar for writing this backstage farce, his first feature. Mostel gives a hysterical performance as a Broadway producer who cons old ladies into financing dismal plays he needs to have flop to make his accounting work. Wilder is the mealy-mouthed accountant he hires to cover his financing. The two scheme to get rich by producing a sure-thing flop called *Springtime for Hitler*. Academy Award Nominations: 2, including Best Supporting Actor: Gene Wilder. **Academy Awards:** Best Story/Screenplay Written Directly for the Screen. **Cast:** Zero Mostel, Gene Wilder, Dick Shawn, Kenneth Mars, Estelle Winwood, Christopher Hewett, Andreas Voutsinas, Renee Taylor. **Credits:** Dir: Mel Brooks; Prod: Sidney Glazier; Writer: Mel Brooks; DP: Joe Coffey; Ed: Ralph Rosenblum; Prod Design: Charles Rosen; Composer: John Morris. Color, 88 min. **VHS, LASER**

The Professionals

(1966) Columbia

Brooks was Oscar-nominated in both writing and direction for this tightly spun action thriller set in the last days of the West. Bellamy is a wealthy Western cattleman who hires four veteran mercenaries (Lancaster, Ryan, Marvin, and Strode) with special talents to recover his wife (a luscious Cardinale) from greedy Mexican kidnapper Palance. Full of suspense and beautifully photographed by the great Hall, who also was nominated for an Oscar. Based on the novel by O'Rourke. Academy Award Nominations: Best Director; Best (Adapted) · Screenplay; Best (Black-and-White) Cinematography. **Cast:** Burt Lancaster, Robert Ryan, Lee Marvin, Claudia Cardinale, Jack Palance, Ralph Bellamy, Woody Strode, Joe De Santis, Rafael Bertrand. **Credits:** Dir: Richard Brooks; Prod: Richard Brooks; Writer: Richard Brooks; Story: Frank O'Rourke; DP: Conrad Hall; Ed: Peter Zinner; Prod Design: Ted Haworth; Composer: Maurice Jarre. Color, 117 min. **VHS, LASER**

Professor Beware

(1938) Paramount

This madcap comedy stars Lloyd as an absentminded archaeology professor. His generosity to a needy gangster gets him in trouble with the law, and he goes AWOL from the Egyptian expedition he's meant to be heading to find a lost tablet. Two bums (Walburn and Stander) and a young beauty (Welch) help the bumbling genius save the day. **Cast:** Harold Lloyd, Phyllis Welch, Raymond Walburn, Lionel Stander, William Frawley, Thurston Hall, Cora Witherspoon, Sterling Holloway, Mary Lou Lender, Montagu Love. **Credits:** Dir: Elliott Nugent; Prod: Harold Lloyd, Adolph Zukor;

The Producers (1968)

Writer: Clyde Bruckman, Jack Cunningham, Delmer Daves, Francis M. Cockrell, Marion B. Cockrell, Crampton Davis; DP: Archie Stout; Ed: W. Duncan Mansfield; Prod Design: Albert S. D'Agostino. B&W, 95 min.

Promise Her Anything
(1966) Paramount
A struggling single mom (Caron) sets her sights on marrying her boss, a child psychologist (Cummings) who hates children. She asks her cute neighbor, a would-be filmmaker who makes a living producing soft-core films (Beatty), to hide the baby from Cummings while she seduces the psychologist. But the blue filmmaker has had his eye on Caron and uses the baby to win her affection. **Cast:** Warren Beatty, Leslie Caron, Lionel Stander, Keenan Wynn, Hermione Gingold, Robert Cummings, Cathleen Nesbitt, Michael Bradley, Asa Maynor. **Credits:** Dir: Arthur Hiller; Prod: Ray Stark; Writer: William Peter Blatty; Story: William Peter Blatty, Arne Sultan, Marvin Worth; DP: Douglas Slocombe; Ed: John Shirley; Prod Design: Wilfred Shingleton; Choreographer: Lionel Blair; Composer: Lyn Murray. Color, 98 min. **VHS**

The Proud Rebel
(1958) Buena Vista
After seeing his home destroyed in the Civil War, a young boy (David Ladd) goes mute. He and his father, a stubborn southern widower (Alan Ladd), travel the breadth of the Great Plains searching for a cure. When they get into a scrape, rancher de Havilland takes them in and finds a way to communicate with the boy. Curtiz directed what might have been an overly sentimental tale in other hands and with lesser actors. **Cast:** Alan Ladd, Olivia de Havilland, Dean Jagger, Harry Dean Stanton, David Ladd, Cecil Kellaway, James Westerfield, Henry Hull. **Credits:** Dir: Michael Curtiz; Prod: Samuel Goldwyn; Writer: Joseph Petracca, Lillie Hayward; DP: Ted McCord; Ed: Aaron Stell; Prod Design: McClure Capps; Composer: Jerome Moross, Emil Newman. Color, 103 min. **VHS, LASER**

The Prowler
(1951) United Artists
Losey directs this sinister little noir about a cop lured into homicide by lust and greed. Detective Heflin is summoned to an opulent Los Angeles home by a woman's (Keyes) prowler complaint. She's young, attractive, and frequently left alone at night by her older husband, an overnight radio personality. Heflin seduces her and learns of an insurance policy on her husband, a policy that might fund his dream of owning a Las Vegas motel. After becoming a prowler himself, Heflin murders the husband and makes it look like self-defense. More trouble arises when Keyes reveals her pregnancy, a condition her husband couldn't have left her in. **Cast:** Van Heflin, Evelyn Keyes, John Maxwell, Emerson Treacy, Wheaton Chambers, Madge O. Blake, Sherry Hall, Robert Osterloh, Katherine Warren, Louise Lorimer. **Credits:** Dir: Joseph Losey; Prod: Sam Spiegel; Writer: Hugo Butler, Robert Thoeren, Hans Wilhelm; DP: Arthur Miller; Ed: Paul Weatherwax; Composer: Lyn Murray, Irving Friedman; Art Director: Boris Leven, Jacques Mapes. B&W, 92 min.

Psycho
(1960) Paramount
Hitchcock's mesmerizing thriller broke the rules of filmmaking with its cunning, psychologically based plot, and changed the perception of Hollywood horror films forever. On a relatively small budget, Hitchcock carefully constructs a maze that leads to an inevitable, gruesome conclusion, a conclusion that the audience has seen coming and dreads. From the first shot, a magnificent crane shot whose camera perches on a hotel window from which we can observe an adulterous affair between Marion Crane (Leigh) and Gavin, the audience is complicit in the action, voyeurs who can't look away. After impulsively stealing a bundle of cash, Leigh heads for the highway. When she wearies and is advised to find a room, she turns into the Bates Motel, where she first encounters the nervously birdlike proprietor, Norman Bates (Perkins). Perkins's sly, almost charming performance as the haunted momma's boy builds a near-sympathy that is quickly erased by the famous shower scene, the most graphic depiction of a murder seen on film to that time. Through careful shooting and editing, the intensity of the act is multiplied in the minds of the audience until the last traces of blood swirl down the drain. As Crane's sister, Miles, and detective Balsam uncover her fate, one more shock remains. A blueprint for cinema terror, which has been followed, discussed, and now remade almost shot for shot by Gus Van Sant in 1998 (he also followed Hitchcock's promotional blueprint, not allowing critics to prescreen the film). Hitchcock had the last laugh on Paramount when they insisted that he finance much of the budget; *Psycho* was an international sensation that made him a wealthy man. Herrmann's chilling score, one of his finest, remains ever recognizable. Followed by three sequels and the 1998 remake. Though the film was nominated for Oscars for Best Director, Cinematography, Supporting Actress, and Art Direction, it received none, though it won a Golden Globe for Best Supporting Actress: Janet Leigh. Selected for the National Film Registry. Academy Award Nominations: 4, including Best Director; Best Supporting Actress. The collector's edition DVD includes a "making of" featurette, cast and crew interviews, and other material. **Cast:** Anthony Perkins, Janet Leigh, Martin Balsam, Vera Miles, John Gavin, John McIntire, Simon Oakland, Vaughn Taylor, Frank Albertson, Lurene Tuttle. **Credits:** Dir: Alfred Hitchcock; Prod: Alfred Hitchcock; Writer: Joseph Stefano; Story: Robert Bloch; DP: John L. Russell, Jr.; Ed: George Tomasini; Prod Design: Robert Clatworthy, Joseph Hurley; Composer: Bernard Herrmann; Costumes: Helen Colvig; SFX: Clarence Champagne. B&W, 109 min. **VHS, LASER, DVD**

> ## "I haven't seen a movie of mine in twenty years. There are too many other things in life. I'm not the least interested in my movies, old or new. It's like watching a ghost, and I'm not interested in seeing my ghost."
>
> Jack Palance

> **"Contrary to what a lot of people say, he did have respect for actors. He would always say to me, 'I'm sure you can get it, old girl.'"**
>
> Janet Leigh on Alfred Hitchcock

Psycho (1960)

PT 109
(1963) Warner Bros.
The WWII heroics of a man who would be president, John F. Kennedy, are drawn from JFK's experience as a naval lieutenant commanding a PT boat in the South Pacific. This screen bio centers on the evacuation of Marines from a Pacific island and their escape when a Japanese war ship shatters the small boat. Robertson makes a suitably upright young commander, and the action scenes are well rendered. **Cast:** Cliff Robertson, Robert Culp, Ty Hardin, James Gregory, Grant Williams, Lew Gallo, Errol John, Michael Pate. **Credits:** Dir: Leslie Martinson; Prod: Bryan Foy; Writer: Richard L. Breen; DP: Robert Surtees; Ed: Folmar Blangsted; Composer: William Lava; Art Director: Leo K. Kuter. Color, 163 min. **VHS, LASER**

The Public Enemy
(1931) Warner Bros.
This is Wellman's brutal pre-Code depiction of young Chicago hoodlums in the '20s. His last-minute casting of Cagney as the lead mobster launched his career as the movies' gangster king and typecast him for years. Two Irish boys (Cagney and Woods) grow up hard on the South Side, taking part in small-time heists until they kill a cop. With Prohibition comes the opportunity for more money and they become bootleggers, splurging on booze and women, including floozies Blondell, Clarke, and Harlow. When Cagney tires of Clarke, their argument leads to the infamous grapefruit scene in which a surprised Clarke gets half a grapefruit in the kisser. The hoodlums come to a bad end, of course, but not before a truly shocking amount of gunplay. This and *Little Caesar* (1930) are the twin pillars of the gangster genre. Academy Award Nominations: Best Writing (Original Story). **Cast:** James Cagney, Jean Harlow, Eddie Woods, Beryl Mercer, Joan Blondell, Donald Cook, Mae Clarke, Leslie Fenton. **Credits:** Dir: William Wellman; Prod: Darryl F. Zanuck; Writer: Kubec Glasmon; DP: Devereaux Jennings; Ed: Ed McCormick; Prod Design: Max Parker; Composer: David Mendoza. B&W, 84 min. **VHS, LASER**

Pulp
(1972) United Artists
This is a cult favorite of film fans for its many inside references to gangster and private-eye pictures. Caine's an ex–funeral director who now hacks out popular detective pulp-fiction novels. He sees easy money when he agrees

to ghost-write the memoirs of an ailing, onetime Hollywood star (Rooney) who has retired to the Mediterranean. Caine enjoys the work as the star had been a good friend to gangsters in the '30s and his story is a colorful one. But when Rooney is assassinated, Caine finishes the tale by following a blackmail conspiracy. Great support from Stander and Scott. **Cast:** Michael Caine, Mickey Rooney, Lionel Stander, Lizabeth Scott, Nadia Cassini, Al Lettieri, Dennis Price, Leopoldo Trieste. **Credits:** Dir: Mike Hodges; Prod: Michael Klinger; Writer: Michael Klinger; DP: Ousama Rawi; Ed: John Glen; Composer: George Martin; Art Director: Darrell Lass. Color, 95 min. **VHS**

Pumping Iron
(1977) Cinema 5
Here is the documentary that brought Schwarzenegger to the attention of Hollywood. The film is a fascinating examination of the world of men's bodybuilding and follows the behind-the-scenes work that goes into preparing for the Mr. Olympia competition. **Cast:** Arnold Schwarzenegger, Lou Ferrigno, Franco Columbu, Mike Katz, Ken Waller. **Credits:** Dir: George Butler, Robert Fiore; Writer: George Butler; Story: Charles Gaines; Composer: Michael Small. Color, 87 min. **VHS, LASER**

The Purchase Price
(1932) Warner Bros.
This early Wellman potboiler stars Brent as a North Dakota farmer who sends for a mail-order bride and ends up with snappy Stanwyck, a nightclub singer who's been around the block more than a few times. Not love at first sight, their commitment is tested when financial misfortune falls, a neighbor thinks some monetary help in exchange for the farmer's wife is a fair deal, and Stanwyck's old bootlegging beau shows up. **Cast:** Barbara Stanwyck, George Brent, Lyle Talbot, Hardie Albright, David Landau, Leila Bennett, Matt McHugh, Clarence Wilson. **Credits:** Dir: William A. Wellman; Writer: Robert Lord; DP: Sid Hickox; Ed: William Holmes; Art Director: Jack Okey. B&W, 68 min. **VHS**

The Purple Heart
(1944) Fox
Zanuck produced and co-wrote this harrowing WWII film about two captured Air Force bomber crews, their trial, and eventual execution. This somber tale was directed by Milestone (*All Quiet on the Western Front*, 1930), and he handles the torture and propaganda elements with care. **Cast:** Richard Conte, Tala Birell, Dana Andrews, Farley Granger, Sam Levene, Nestor Paiva, Benson Fong, Richard Loo. **Credits:** Dir: Lewis Milestone; Prod: Darryl F. Zanuck; Writer: Jerry Cady; Story: Darryl F. Zanuck; DP: Arthur Miller; Ed: Douglas Biggs; Prod Design: James Basevi; Composer: Alfred Newman; Art Director: Lewis Creber. B&W, 99 min. **VHS**

Pursued
(1947) Warner Bros.
In a dark Western that is as much family melodrama as action picture, Mitchum flees from a mob as we see in flashback the events that led to the pursuit. The central mystery of who he is and why he is being followed is kept until the fiery conclusion. Wright is fine in support—first as Mitchum's enemy, then his wife. **Cast:** Robert Mitchum, Teresa Wright, Judith Anderson, Dean Jagger, Alan Hale, Harry Carey, Jr., John Rodney, Clifton Young. **Credits:** Dir: Raoul Walsh; Prod: Milton Sperling; Writer: Niven Busch; DP: James Wong Howe; Ed: Christian Nyby; Composer: Max Steiner; Art Director: Ted Smith. B&W, 105 min. **VHS**

Putney Swope
(1969) Cinema 5
Downey directed this pioneering indy-film satire on black power at the height of white fear of the Black Panthers and other revolutionary groups. A token black at an advertising agency (Johnson) is inadvertently elected Chairman of the Board. He seizes the opportunity to revolutionize the company and renames it Truth and Soul, Inc., hiring an all-black staff, jettisoning the capitalist-tool clients, and enduring assassination attempts. Blistering parody of advertising and the counterculture. **Cast:** Arnold Johnson, Laura Greene, Allen Garfield, Stan Gottlieb, Bert Lawrence, Pepi Hermine, George Morgan, Allan Arbus. **Credits:** Dir: Robert Downey; Prod: Ron Sullivan; Writer: Robert Downey; DP: Gerald Cotts; Ed: Bud Smith; Composer: Charley Cuva; Art Director: Gary Weist. B&W, and Color, 88 min. **VHS**

Quality Street
(1937) RKO
Hepburn's sterling performance elevates this adaptation of James M. Barrie's lighthearted turn-of-the-century play. In 1790s London, Hepburn attracts the affection of physician Tone before he does his duty in the protracted Napoleonic wars. By the time he returns many years later, Tone no longer recognizes the faithful Hepburn, who has settled into life as a spinster teacher. She masquerades as her 16-year-old niece in order to attract Tone's attention once again. An old chestnut at its time of release, this was produced as a silent in 1927 with Marion Davies. Academy Award Nomination for Best Score. **Cast:** Katharine Hepburn, Franchot Tone, Fay Bainter, Eric Blore, Cora Witherspoon, Estelle Winwood, Florence Lake, Roland Varno. **Credits:** Dir: George Stevens; Prod: Pandro S. Berman; Writer: Mortimer Offner, Allan Scott; DP: Robert de Grasse; Ed: Henry Berman; Composer: Roy Webb; Art Director: Hobe Erwin. B&W, 84 min. **VHS, LASER**

Queen Bee
(1955) Columbia
Here's another trademark, hard-as-nails performance from Crawford as a southern grande dame whose insidious scheming dominates her household. She drives her husband (Sullivan) to drink, and she breaks up her sister-in-law's (Palmer) impending marriage to the estate's caretaker (Ireland), with whom Crawford had a longtime affair, driving Palmer to suicide. After Sullivan finds Marlow sympathetic, Ireland arranges Crawford's death to stop her meddling. Academy Award Nominations: Best Cinematography; Best Costume Design. **Cast:** Joan Crawford, Barry Sullivan, Betsy Palmer, Fay Wray, John Ireland, Tim Hovey, Lucy Marlow, William Leslie. **Credits:** Dir: Ranald

MacDougall; Prod: Jerry Wald; Writer: Ranald MacDougall; DP: Charles Lang; Ed: Viola Lawrence; Composer: George Duning; Art Director: Ross Bellah; Costumes: Jean Louis. B&W, 94 min. **VHS**

Queen Christina
(1933) MGM
The finest Garbo performance illuminates a passionate love story in which the enigmatic actress was paired once more with her leading man (and lover) from the silent era, Gilbert. The controversial, 17th-century Swedish queen, wise and beloved by her subjects, brings peace to her country while avoiding politically inspired marriages. While out riding, she meets a dashing stranger (Gilbert), who is the Spanish ambassador to Sweden. To test his character, Garbo disguises herself as a young man. Satisfied with Gilbert's worthiness, she reveals her status and he reveals that he has traveled to Sweden to ask for her hand—for his king. The lovers continue to meet and Garbo announces her abdication to follow her heart to Spain, but a jealous courtier (Keith) destroys their dreams. Garbo couldn't be more lovely or effective, a performance that many credit to her pairing, after many years, with Gilbert. MGM had abandoned Gilbert in the sound era, but Garbo exercised her right of cast approval to keep Gilbert in the production (though Olivier had rehearsed in the role). **Cast:** Greta Garbo, John Gilbert, Ian Keith, Lewis Stone, C. Aubrey Smith, Reginald Owen, Georges Renavent, Gustav Von Seyffertitz. **Credits:** Dir: Rouben Mamoulian; Prod: Walter Wanger; Writer: H. M. Harwood, Salka Viertel, S. N. Behrman; DP: William Daniels; Ed: Blanche Sewell; Composer: Herbert Stothart; Art Director: Alexander Toluboff. B&W, 101 min. **VHS, LASER**

Queen of Outer Space
(1958) Allied Artists
This campy, sci-fi hoot follows a crew of Earthling rocketeers who crash on Venus and discover that beautiful women rule the planet named for the goddess of love. Mission leader Fleming woos a delightfully outrageous Gabor, though they run afoul of Mitchell, the bitter queen who harbors a deep hatred of men. Whether the humor is intentional or not, it's still hilarious. And famed screenwriter Hecht created the story! **Cast:** Zsa Zsa Gabor, Eric Fleming, Laurie Mitchell, Paul Birch, Barbara Darrow, Dave Willock, Lisa Davis, Mary Ford. **Credits:** Dir: Edward Bernds; Prod: Ben Schwalb; Writer: Charles Beaumont; Story: Ben Hecht; DP: William Whitley; Ed: William Austin; Prod Design: Dave Milton; Composer: Marlin Skiles. Color, 80 min. **VHS**

Quicksand
(1950) United Artists
This brisk, hard-nosed crime drama depicts a simple man who sinks deeper into criminality when he falls for the wrong girl. Rooney, a garage mechanic, dips into the till for 20 bucks so he can score with Cagney (Jimmy's sister). When the auditor comes early, Rooney scrambles for the money, starting the dominoes falling toward a shoot-out with the cops. Lorre depicts a shady carnival operator; this was meant to be the start of a multi-picture collaboration between Rooney and Lorre, surely one of the oddest-couple business partnerships in Hollywood. This was the only result of the deal. **Cast:** Mickey Rooney, Peter Lorre, Jeanne Cagney, Barbara Bates, Taylor Holmes, Art Smith, Wally Cassell, John Gallaudet. **Credits:** Dir: Irving Pichel; Prod: Mort Briskin; Writer: Robert Smith; DP: Lionel Lindon; Ed: Walter Thompson; Composer: Louis Gruenberg, Emil Newman; Art Director: Boris Leven. B&W, 79 min. **VHS**

The Quiet Man

(1952) Republic

One of Ford's greatest and most loved films is at once a rollicking, robust comedy, a passionate love story, and a misty-eyed ode to Ford's Irish homeland. Wayne, a boxer returned to his birthplace in the small village of Innisfree, stumbles on the local customs and the resentment and suspicions of the townspeople, particularly a despised bully played by McLaglen. He also loses his heart to McLaglen's beautiful sister (O'Hara, who was never lovelier). Their rivalry comes to an explosive, hilarious climax when O'Hara refuses to consider herself married until Wayne receives her dowry from McLaglen. The secretive American finally unleashses his fists and earns his wife's love and respect. Ford's brother Francis, a silent-era actor and director, appears in a funny cameo as an old man who refuses to expire until he witnesses the battle royal. This is a rewarding look directly into Ford's heart. Academy Award Nominations: 7, including Best Picture; Best Supporting Actor: Victor McLaglen; Best Screenplay. **Academy Awards:** Best Director; Best Cinematography. **Cast:** John Wayne, Maureen O'Hara, Barry Fitzgerald, Ward Bond, Victor McLaglen, Mildred Natwick, Francis Ford, Arthur Shields. **Credits:** Dir: John Ford; Prod: Merian C. Cooper, John Ford, Michel Killanin; Writer: Frank S. Nugent, Richard Llewellyn; Story: Maurice Walsh; DP: Winton C. Hoch, Archie Stout; Ed: Jack Murray; Composer: Victor Young; Art Director: Frank Hotaling. Color, 153 min. **VHS, LASER**

Quintet

(1979) Fox

This bizarre Altman concoction is interesting mostly for fans of the director and star, and those curious to see an ambitious misfire. Newman and his wife, Fossey, wander a postnuclear landscape in the grip of a new Ice Age, where they get caught up in a deadly game called Quintet. Violent, rambling, and fascinating in its setting and the challenges it offers the cast. **Cast:** Paul Newman, Bibi Andersson,

The Quiet Man (1952)

Fernando Rey, Vittorio Gassman, David Langton, Brigitte Fossey, Nina Van Pallandt, Monique Mercure. **Credits:** Dir: Robert Altman; Prod: Robert Altman; Writer: Frank Barhydt, Robert Altman, Patricia Resnick; DP: Jean Boffety; Ed: Dennis Hill; Prod Design: Leon Ericksen, Wolf Kroeger; Composer: Tom Pierson. Color, 118 min. **VHS**

Quo Vadis

(1951) MGM

This colossal MGM blockbuster launched dozens of biblical epics but remains one of the most successful. Ustinov steals the show with a leering, unhinged performance as Nero, the Roman emperor who burned his capital to clear the way for his new city and blamed the conflagration on Christians. Taylor shines as a Roman general who returns to the Eternal City after a victorious campaign. Attracted by Christian captive Kerr, he takes her as a slave, but can't convince her to become his lover. They draw closer when he follows her to a secret Christian service. Together they face Nero's wrath, and their torment inspires a revolt. The big-budget re-creation of the ancient world was based on an often-filmed story, the first adaptation going back to the early days of cinema, and including a famous 12-reel silent, Italian version that toured the world in 1912. An updating of the story was intended for director John Huston, but this more traditional version went before the cameras instead. Successful as eye-popping spectacle, and fascinating for its central performances. Golden Globes for Best Supporting Actor: Peter Ustinov; Best Color Cinematography. Academy Award Nominations: 8, including Best Picture; Best Supporting Actor: Peter Ustinov; Best Supporting Actor: Leo Genn. **Cast:** Robert Taylor, Deborah Kerr, Peter Ustinov, Leo Genn, Patricia Laffan, Finlay Currie, Abraham Sofaer, Marina Berti. **Credits:** Dir: Mervyn LeRoy; Prod: Sam Zimbalist; Writer: John Lee Mahin; DP: Robert Surtees; Ed: Ralph E. Winters; Prod Design: Cedric Gibbons; Composer: Miklos Rozsa. Color, 171 min. **VHS, LASER**

Rachel and the Stranger

(1948) RKO

Not quite a musical, not quite a romance, not quite a historical adventure, but wholly entertaining. A widower in the frontier Northwest, Holden decides his son (Gray) needs looking after, so he buys (then marries) housekeeper Young, but dwells in the past. A wandering scout (Mitchum) pays a visit, and seeing Young's neglect, courts her (even pulling out a guitar and singing a few tunes). Holden becomes jealous, and both men nearly lose her, until they draw together during an Indian attack. **Cast:** Loretta Young, William Holden, Robert Mitchum, Gary Gray, Tom Tully, Sara Haden, Frank Ferguson, Walter Baldwin, Joe Conlan. **Credits:** Dir: Norman Foster; Prod: Richard Berger; Writer: Waldo Salt; DP: Maury Gertsman; Ed: Lee Milbrook; Composer: Roy Webb; Art Director: Walter E. Keller, Jack Okey, Albert S. D'Agostino; Costumes: Edith Head. B&W, 93 min. **VHS, LASER**

Rachel, Rachel

(1968) Warner Bros.

Newman's debut as director is the sensitive story of a lonely woman who reaches for a last chance at love and leaves her bland, comfortable life behind. Woodward gives a thoughtful, openhearted performance as a New England schoolteacher who realizes how circumscribed her emotional life has been when she gets swept up in a church revival meeting, and when her best friend (Parsons) presses her to begin a different type of relationship. Woodward turns to an old friend (Olson) to experience physical love and gets her heart broken. The process prods her to move forward with her life. Neither Newman nor his cast makes a false step. Academy Award Nominations: 4, including Best Picture; Best Actress: Joanne Woodward; Best Supporting Actress: Estelle Parsons; Best (Adapted) Screenplay.

Cast: Joanne Woodward, Estelle Parsons, James Olson, Geraldine Fitzgerald, Kate Harrington, Donald Moffat, Terry Kiser, Bernard Barrow, Frank Corsaro. **Credits:** Dir: Paul Newman; Prod: Paul L. Newman; Story: Stewart Stern; DP: Gayne Rescher; Ed: Dede Allen; Composer: Jerome Moross, Erik Satie, Robert Schumann; Art Director: Robert Gundlach. Color, 102 min. **VHS**

The Rack

(1956) MGM

This dark courtroom drama was based on a Rod Serling teleplay, and proved to be (along with *Somebody Up There Likes Me,* 1956) young Newman's breakthrough role. Newman plays an officer accused of collaborating with enemy interrogators during the Korean War. As his defenders attempt to show that his mental state exposed him to tortures as extreme as the medieval rack, Newman's buttoned-up father (Pidgeon), an army colonel, must come to terms with his own role in his son's collapse. **Cast:** Paul Newman, Wendell Corey, Walter Pidgeon, Edmond O'Brien, Anne Francis, Lee Marvin, Cloris Leachman, Robert Burton, Robert F. Simon, Trevor Bardette. **Credits:** Dir: Arnold Laven; Prod: Arthur M. Loew; Writer: Stewart Stern, Rod Serling; DP: Paul C. Vogel; Ed: Harold F. Kress, Marshall Neilan; Prod Design: Cedric Gibbons, Merill Pye; Composer: Adolph Deutsch. B&W, 100 min.

The Racket

(1951) RKO

Mitchum stays on the right side of the law as a tough cop who faces down a brutal gangster and the corruption in city hall. Gangster Ryan runs the underground from his nightclub, and controls the police commissioner and mayor. Mitchum busts the mobster with the help of nightclub singer Scott. Well made, and topical at the time as the televised Kefauver police corruption hearings gripped the nation. **Cast:**

Robert Mitchum, Robert Ryan, William Conrad, Lizabeth Scott, Ray Collins, Robert Hutton, Virginia Huston, Walter Sande. **Credits:** Dir: John Cromwell; Prod: Edmund Grainger; Writer: William Haines, W. R. Burnett; DP: George E. Diskant; Ed: Sherman Todd; Composer: Paul Sawtell, Roy Webb; Art Director: Albert S. D'Agostino, Jack Okey. B&W, 90 min. **VHS**

Racket Busters

(1938) Warner Bros.

This classic hard-boiled Warner gangster drama is based on court records of a trucking racket in New York City. Bogart dominates the trucking business, demanding protection money. Brent and his partner Jenkins refuse to give in until Bogart's brutality makes them buckle. But new D.A. Abel makes use of Brent's bitterness to score a direct hit on the rackets. **Cast:** Humphrey Bogart, George Brent, Gloria Dickson, Allen Jenkins, Walter Abel, Henry O'Neill, Penny Singleton, Antony Averill, Oscar O'Shea, Elliott Sullivan. **Credits:** Dir: Lloyd Bacon; Prod: Samuel Bischoffs; Writer: Leonardo Bercovici, Robert Rossen; DP: Arthur Edeson; Ed: James Gibbon; Composer: Adolph Deutsch. B&W, 71 min.

Raffles

(1930) United Artists

This is the first sound version of the popular story of an amateur thief, and Goldwyn's last production released in both sound and silent versions. Colman makes an appealing rogue as a professional cricket player who occupies his time as an amateur safecracker. When invited by comely Francis to a weekend at a royal retreat, Colman sets his eye on a fabulous necklace to help a destitute friend. He manages to elude Scotland Yard inspector Torrence, and slip away with paramour Francis. Originally filmed in 1917 with John Barrymore, followed by two more remakes, in 1925 and in

1940. Academy Award Nomination for Best Sound. **Cast:** Ronald Colman, Kay Francis, Bramwell Fletcher, Frances Dade, Alison Skipworth, David Torrence, Frederick Kerr, Wilson Benge. **Credits:** Dir: Harry D'Arrast, George Fitzmaurice; Prod: Samuel Goldwyn; Writer: Sidney Howard; Story: E. W. Hornung; DP: George Barnes, Gregg Toland; Ed: Stuart Heisler; Art Director: William Cameron Menzies, Park French. B&W, 72 min. VHS

Raffles
(1940) United Artists
Niven takes the Colman role as an adventurous British cricket star and amateur thief who baffles the best of Scotland Yard. In this version, Niven decides to give up crime when he falls in love with de Havilland. He returns a purloined necklace and arouses the suspicion of inspector Digges. The nimble Niven slips the trap, saves the day for a desperate friend, and makes off with his leading lady. A well-produced updating with a charming performance by Niven. **Cast:** David Niven, Olivia de Havilland, May Whitty, Dudley Digges, Douglas Walton, Lionel Pape, E. E. Clive, Peter Godfrey, Margaret Seddon, Gilbert Emery. **Credits:** Dir: Sam Wood; Prod: Samuel Goldwyn; Writer: John Van Druten; Story: E. W. Hornung; DP: Gregg Toland; Ed: Sherman Todd; Prod Design: James Basevi; Composer: Victor Young. B&W, 72 min.

The Rage of Paris
(1938) Universal
In this sophisticated comedy French actress Darrieux made her Hollywood debut. A French model who comes to New York looking for work, she answers a call for a nude model but ends up disrobing in the wrong office for a bemused Fairbanks. Thinking he's being set up for a blackmail plot, Fairbanks gives her the boot, but she turns up again when her "managers," Auer and Broderick, take aim at Hayward. Also the debut of Mary Martin. **Cast:** Mischa Auer, Danielle Darrieux, Douglas Fairbanks, Jr., Louis Hayward, Helen Broderick, Charles Coleman, Samuel S. Hinds, Nella Walker. **Credits:** Dir: Henry Koster; Prod: B. G. DeSylva; Writer: Bruce Manning, Felix Jackson; DP: Joseph A. Valentine; Ed: Bernard W. Burton; Art Director: Jack Otterson. B&W, 78 min. VHS

Raging Bull
(1980) United Artists
This is the only entry from the '80s in this volume, simply because it would be impossible to leave out what many consider to be the finest Hollywood film of its time. The rise and fall of middleweight champion Jake LaMotta hurtles inexorably toward tragedy, the violence and hubris of its protagonist ending in lonely dissolution. De Niro famously altered his physique to play the boxer from lean contender to bloated has-been, but his emotional preparation must have been similarly excruciating. De Niro blunders through his life paying little heed to the consequences of abandoning his wife for Moriarty and then torturing her with jealous fury, and succumbing to the temptations of the Mob introduced by his sycophantic brother, Pesci. Chap-

Raging Bull (1980)

man's photography, with subjective camera, explosions of flashbulbs, and slow-motion sprays of sweat, has been as acclaimed as De Niro's performance. A masterwork and an enduring movie classic. Selected for the National Film Registry. Golden Globe for Best Actor: Robert De Niro. Academy Award Nominations: 8, including Best Picture; Best Supporting Actor: Joe Pesci; Best Supporting Actress: Cathy Moriarty; Best Director; Best Cinematography; Best Sound. **Academy Awards:** Best Actor: Robert De Niro; Best Editing. **Cast:** Robert De Niro, Joe Pesci, Cathy Moriarty, Frank Vincent, Nicholas Colasanto, Theresa Saldana, Frank Adonis, Mario Gallo, Frank Topham. **Credits:** Dir: Martin Scorsese; Prod: Irwin Winkler, Robert Chartoff; Writer: Paul Schrader, Mardik Martin; Story: Jake LaMotta; DP: Michael Chapman; Ed: Thelma Schoonmaker; Prod Design: Gene Rudolph. B&W (with color sequence), 129 min. VHS, LASER, DVD

Railroaded
(1947) Eagle-Lion
In Mann's elegantly directed noir, Ireland stuns as a perverse killer who eliminates the investigators of a cop-killer. When a policeman is killed in a gangland shoot-out during a botched robbery, the cops put the heat on one of the captured robbers. The thug implicates his innocent friend (Kelly), and when Kelly's sister and a decent cop (Beaumont) try to find the real killer, they earn a bullet for their trouble. **Cast:** John Ireland, Sheila Ryan, Hugh Beaumont, Jane Randolph, Charles D. Brown, Keefe Brasselle, Roy Gordon, Ed Kelly, Clancy Cooper, Peggy Converse. **Credits:** Dir: Anthony

---

John Hassan Picks
10 Classics for Sports Fans

1. **Raging Bull** *(1980)*

2. **The Longest Yard** *(1974)*

3. **Caddyshack** *(1980)*

4. **Hoosiers** *(1986)*

5. **Champion** *(1949)*

6. **Slap Shot** *(1977)*

7. **North Dallas Forty** *(1979)*

8. **Field of Dreams** *(1989)*

9. **Requiem for a Heavyweight** *(1962)*

10. **Rocky** *(1976)*

John Hassan is a senior editor at *ESPN: The Magazine.*

Mann; Prod: Charles Riesner, Benjamin Stoloff; Writer: John C. Higgins; Story: Gertrude Walker; DP: Guy Roe; Ed: Louis Sackin; Composer: Alvin Levin; Costumes: Frances Ehren. B&W, 74 min. **VHS, LASER**

Rain

(1932) United Artists
Crawford gives a fascinating performance in the Sadie Thompson role that was a landmark challenge for actresses after the compelling interpretations delivered by Gloria Swanson and Jeanne Eagels in silent days, and Huston provides the definitive reading of the obsessed missionary role. When a tramp steamer deposits trampy Crawford on Pago Pago, the sex-starved men of the island, particularly simple Gargan, take immediate notice. She also catches the attention of a fire-and-brimstone missionary (Huston) for whom she becomes an extra-credit project. As his ministry begins to crack her cynicism, her wiles defeat his faith, and he becomes drawn inexorably toward sin and suicidal guilt. Meanwhile, the incessant rain beats an oppressive drumbeat. Milestone provides an appropriately steamy setting for Somerset Maugham's famous story. **Cast:** Joan Crawford, Walter Huston, Guy Kibbee, William Gargan, Beulah Bondi, Walter Catlett, Matt Moore, Kendall Lee, Ben Hendricks, Jr., Fred Howard. **Credits:** Dir: Lewis Milestone; Prod: Joseph M. Schenck; Writer: Maxwell Anderson; DP: Oliver T. Marsh; Ed: Duncan Mansfield; Art Director: Richard Day. B&W, 93 min. **VHS**

Rainbow 'Round My Shoulder

(1952) Columbia
This Edwards-Quine collaboration is a wheezy tale of a determined young girl (Austin) trying to get a break in Hollywood. Her reward is an appearance in a new Frankie Laine movie. Interesting mainly for the inside look at the bustling Columbia studio, and several songs from Laine and Daniels. **Cast:** Frankie Laine, Billy Daniels, Charlotte Austin, Arthur Franz, Ida Moore, Lloyd Corrigan, Barbara Whiting, Ross Ford, Arthur Space, Frank Wilcox. **Credits:** Dir: Richard Quine; Prod: Jonie Taps; Writer: Blake Edwards, Jane Alexander, Richard Quine; DP: Ellis W. Carter; Ed: Richard Fantl; Composer: George Duning. Color, 78 min.

The Rainmaker

(1956) Paramount
A sweltering southwestern burg gets a new lease on life when flimflam man Lancaster breezes into town. Claiming

he can start the rains falling, he boards with Prud'homme while working his magic. He also works magic in the life of Hepburn, a fading flower whom Lancaster fills with a breath of spring, giving her the confidence to prod her sometime suitor Corey. Stage director Anthony brings his Broadway success (which began life as a TV play) to the screen. Golden Globe for Best Supporting Actor: Earl Holliman. Academy Award Nominations: Best Actress: Katharine Hepburn; Best Score. **Cast:** Burt Lancaster, Katharine Hepburn, Wendell Corey, Lloyd Bridges, Earl Holliman, Cameron Prud'homme, Wallace Ford, Yvonne Lime. **Credits:** Dir: Joseph Anthony; Prod: Hal B. Wallis; Writer: N. Richard Nash; DP: Charles B. Lang; Ed: Warren Low; Composer: Alex North; Art Director: Hal Pereira, Walter Tyler. Color, 121 min. **VHS, LASER**

Rain or Shine

(1930) Columbia
This is an early Capra outing based on the Broadway comedy starring Cook. Peers inherits a circus that's about to go under. Cook portrays the manager who pitches in by putting on a one-man juggling and tightrope-walking show. Of historical interest only. **Cast:** Joe Cook, Louise Fazenda, Joan Peers, William Collier, Jr., Tom Howard, Dave Chasen, Alan Roscoe, Adolph Milar, Clarence Muse. **Credits:** Dir: Frank Capra; Prod: Harry Cohn; Writer: Dorothy Howell, Jo Swerling; Story: James Gleason; DP: Joseph Walker; Ed: Maurice Wright; Composer: Jack Yellen, Milton Anger, Jack Dougherty. B&W, 90 min.

The Rain People

(1969) Warner Bros.
This brooding, feminist road movie indicated that director and writer Coppola had moved from promising-prodigy status to a mature filmmaker with a personal vision. A Long Island housewife (Knight) takes to the road when she discovers that she's pregnant. Looking for experience outside her small world, a sign of what her future holds, or just time to think, Knight first picks up Caan, a brain-damaged young drifter, and then crosses policeman Duvall when he stops her for speeding. Difficult, but rewarding. **Cast:** James Caan, Shirley Knight, Robert Duvall, Tom Aldredge, Marya Zimmet, Andrew Duncan, Sally Gracie, Robert Modica, Alan Manson. **Credits:** Dir: Francis Ford Coppola; Prod: Bart Patton, Ronald Colby; Writer: Francis Ford Coppola; DP:

Wilmer Butler; Ed: Blackie Malkin; Composer: Ronald Stein; Art Director: Leon Ericksen. Color, 102 min. **VHS**

The Rains Came

(1939) Fox
This exotic romantic melodrama follows a bored, sensation-hungry aristocrat (Loy) who changes her life when she falls in love with a committed Indian doctor (Power). Loy follows her husband to India, where she sheds her careless past to work side by side with Power helping the poor of Ranchipur after a flood causes a malaria outbreak. Their love comes to a tragic end as she succumbs to the disease. Remade as *The Rains of Ranchipur* (1955) with Lana Turner and Richard Burton. Academy Award Nominations: 5, including Best Editing; Best Score. **Academy Awards:** Best Visual Effects. **Cast:** Myrna Loy, Tyrone Power, George Brent, Brenda Joyce, Nigel Bruce, Jane Darwell, Marjorie Rambeau, Henry Travers, H. B. Warner. **Credits:** Dir: Clarence Brown; Prod: Harry Joe Brown; Writer: Philip Dunne, Julien Josephson; DP: Arthur Miller; Ed: Barbara McLean; Composer: Alfred Newman; Art Director: William S. Darling; SFX: E. H. Hansen, Fred Sersen. B&W, 104 min. **VHS**

Raintree County

(1957) MGM
This Civil War potboiler was meant to rival *Gone With the Wind*, but wallows in the histrionics of its stars (both on- and offscreen). Southern belle Taylor raises the temperature of a small Indiana town, seducing Clift away from faithful Saint, and tricking him into marriage. Their union is as sundered as the Union by the Civil War, with Clift away fighting for the North while Taylor flees with their son to the South. She succumbs to family madness and Clift searches frantically for his son. Clift made a spectacle of himself on location, and Taylor was preoccupied with her new affair with Mike Todd. But interesting to watch the two friends in the leads, their first pairing since *A Place in the Sun* (1951). Academy Award Nominations: 4, including Best Actress: Elizabeth Taylor; Best Score. **Cast:** Montgomery Clift, Elizabeth Taylor, Eva Marie Saint, Lee Marvin, Nigel Patrick, Rod Taylor, Agnes Moorehead, Walter Abel. **Credits:** Dir: Edward Dmytryk; Prod: David Lewis; Writer: Millard Kaufman; DP: Robert Surtees; Ed: John Dunning; Composer: Johnny Green; Art Director: William A. Horning, Urie McCleary. Color, 178 min. **VHS, LASER**

A Raisin in the Sun

(1961) Columbia

Lorraine Hansberry adapts her Broadway success, and most of that production's cast make the transition to the screen in this penetrating drama about a working-class black family living in a tiny Chicago tenement. When matriarch McNeil receives a settlement on her late husband's insurance, a struggle breaks out in the family. McNeil wants to buy a home away from their dangerous neighborhood and fund her daughter's (Sands) medical-school education. Her son, Poitier, wants to buy into a liquor store and build his own business. Poitier makes an ill-advised deal, and jeopardizes the family's way out of the ghetto. **Cast:** Sidney Poitier, Claudia McNeil, Louis Gossett, Jr., Ruby Dee, Diana Sands, Ivan Dixon, Steve Perry, Joel Fluellen. **Credits:** Dir: Daniel Petrie; Prod: David Susskind, Philip Rose; Writer: Lorraine Hansberry; DP: Charles Lawton, Jr.; Ed: William A. Lyon, Paul Weatherwax; Composer: Laurence Rosenthal; Art Director: Carl Anderson. B&W, 128 min. **VHS**

Rancho Deluxe

(1975) United Artists

Bridges and Waterston play modern-day cattle rustlers in this comedy adventure from a screenplay by novelist Thomas McGuane. After petty thieves Bridges and Waterston unsuccessfully try to reform, they make plans for one big score. When one of their gang gets involved with private detective Pickens's daughter, the scheme unravels. Wryly humorous and carefully observed. **Cast:** Jeff Bridges, Sam Waterston, Elizabeth Ashley, Charlene Dallas, Clifton James, Slim Pickens, Harry Dean Stanton, Richard Bright, Patti D'Arbanville. **Credits:** Dir: Frank Perry; Prod: Elliott Kastner; Writer: Thomas McGuane; DP: William A. Fraker; Ed: Sidney Katz; Composer: Jimmy Buffett; Art Director: Michael Haller. Color, 93 min. **VHS**

Rancho Notorious

(1952) RKO

In Lang's intensely emotional version of a Western, Dietrich plays the mistress of a ranch used as a hiding place by notorious outlaws. Her nest is exposed when Kennedy tracks his fiancée's murderers to Dietrich's Chuck-a-Luck ranch, named for a legendary game of chance. Kennedy plays the characteristic Lang hero whose basic goodness gets twisted by a thirst for revenge. **Cast:** Marlene Dietrich, Arthur Kennedy, Mel Ferrer,

Lloyd Gough, Gloria Henry, William Frawley, Lisa Ferraday, Jack Elam, John Raven. **Credits:** Dir: Fritz Lang; Prod: Howard Welsch; Writer: Daniel Taradash; DP: Hal Mohr; Ed: Otto Ludwig; Prod Design: Wiard Ihnen; Composer: Emil Newman. Color, 89 min. **VHS, LASER**

Random Harvest

(1942) MGM

In the hands of any other cast and crew, the implausibility of this plot would torpedo the whole production. But LeRoy and his leads, Colman and Garson, make this a touching romantic melodrama that transcends the story. Industrial scion Colman emerges from the WWI trenches mute and amnesiac. When he wanders from his ward into a small town, showgirl Garson takes him in, soothes his injuries, and nurtures his writing ability. While away from Garson and their son, an injury jars his memory, though he loses the years spent with Garson. Back at work in the family factories, Colman hires Garson as an assistant without recognizing her. While revisiting the small town with Garson, his memories return and the couple is fully reunited. Academy Award Nominations: 7, including Best Picture; Best Director; Best Actor: Ronald Colman; Best Supporting Actress: Susan Peters; Best Screenplay. **Cast:** Greer Garson, Ronald Colman, Philip Dorn, Susan Peters, Reginald Owen, Edmund Gwenn, Henry Travers, Margaret Wycherly. **Credits:** Dir: Mervyn LeRoy; Prod: Sidney Franklin; Writer: Claudine West, George Froeschel, Arthur Wimperis; Story: James Hilton; DP: Joseph Ruttenberg; Ed: Harold F. Kress; Composer: Herbert Stothart; Art Director: Cedric Gibbons, Randall Duell. B&W, 128 min. **VHS**

Randy Rides Alone

(1934) Monogram

After Wayne enters a saloon filled with murdered patrons, he finds himself accused of being the killer. In a brave attempt to prove his innocence, he sets a trap for the real criminals and comes up against a hunchback known as "Matt the Mute." One of Wayne's best early oaters, and he even heaves out with a song. **Cast:** John Wayne, George "Gabby" Hayes, Alberta Vaughan, Earl Dwire, Yakima Canutt, Tex Palmer, Tex Phelps, Artie Ortego, Herman Hack. **Credits:** Dir: Henry Frazer; Prod: Paul Malvern; Writer: Lindsley Parsons; DP: Archie Stout; Ed: Carl Pierson; Composer: Abe Meyer. B&W, 60 min. **VHS**

The Rare Breed

(1966) Universal

Widowed O'Hara enlists cowpoke Stewart in her quixotic attempt to breed a longhorn bull with her prize English Hereford. Keith initially backs the concept, but begins to doubt. After escorting O'Hara and her cow, Stewart becomes a believer and, after the bull dies, searches the prairie for a half-Hereford calf. Well made, with convincing performances. **Cast:** James Stewart, Maureen O'Hara, Brian Keith, Juliet Mills, Don Galloway, David Brian, Jack Elam, Ben Johnson, Harry Carey, Jr. **Credits:** Dir: Andrew V. McLaglen; Prod: William Alland; Writer: Ric Hardman; DP: William H. Clothier; Ed: Russell Schoengarth; Composer: John Williams; Art Director: Alexander Golitzen, Alfred Ybarra. Color, 97 min. **VHS**

Rasputin and the Empress

(1932) MGM

Here is a landmark historical drama written by MacArthur and featuring the only on-screen appearance of the three reigning members of acting's royal family, the Barrymores. Lionel Barrymore portrays the mad monk whose corruption distracted the Romanov rulers as their empire collapsed around them. John Barrymore, a royal relative, comes to court to warn the emperor (Morgan) and empress (Ethel Barrymore) of the restlessness among the peasants. The family, though, is preoccupied with the condition of their hemophiliac son, whose bleeding could be stopped only by Rasputin. John Barrymore finally manages to dispatch the monk, though it leads to his disgrace and comes too late. A fascinating look at the famous family and a great chance to watch Ethel Barrymore work. Academy Award Nomination for Best Original Screenplay. **Cast:** John Barrymore, Ethel Barrymore, Lionel Barrymore, Ralph Morgan, Diana Wynyard, Tad Alexander, C. Henry Gordon, Edward Arnold, Jean Parker. **Credits:** Dir: Richard Boleslawski; Prod: Bernard Hyman; Writer: Charles MacArthur; DP: William Daniels; Ed: Tom Held; Composer: Herbert Stothart; Art Director: Cedric Gibbons, Alexander Toluboff. B&W, 123 min. **VHS, LASER**

The Raven

(1935) Universal

This is the second teaming of Lugosi and Karloff (following *The Black Cat*, 1934), with Lugosi a mad surgeon who collects gruesome paraphernalia associated with macabre Poe stories. When he's spurned by a judge's

The Raven (1935)

daughter (Ware), Lugosi invites her, her fiancé, and her father to a dinner at which he means to get revenge. Lugosi intends to unleash Karloff, a horrible criminal with a twisted visage that Lugosi created, but Karloff has his own revenge in mind. Available on a double-bill video with *The Black Cat*. **Cast:** Boris Karloff, Bela Lugosi, Irene Ware, Lester Matthews, Samuel S. Hinds, Ian Wolfe, Spencer Charters, Maidel Turner, Arthur Hoyt. **Credits:** Dir: Lew Landers; Prod: David Diamond, Carl Laemmle; Writer: David Boehm, Jim Tully; DP: Charles Stumar; Ed: Albert Akst; Composer: W. Franke Harling, Heinz Roemheld, Clifford Vaughan; Art Director: Albert S. D'Agostino. B&W, 62 min. **VHS**

Raw Deal
(1948) Eagle-Lion
This masterful, relentless noir is directed by Mann and shot by the great Alton. O'Keefe was framed by his shady associates and sent up for a hard stretch in prison. He escapes

with the help of his girlfriend (Trevor) and sets out for revenge. When he takes his social worker (Hunt) hostage, she starts to enjoy the electricity of being so close to crime and becomes fully enmeshed in the underworld when she saves O'Keefe by killing a thug (Ireland). The growing attraction between O'Keefe and Hunt annoys Trevor, but, before the situation comes to a head, O'Keefe has a final showdown with firebug Burr. **Cast:** Dennis O'Keefe, Claire Trevor, Marsha Hunt, Raymond Burr, John Ireland, Richard Fraser, Whit Bissell, Cliff Clark, Curt Conway, Chili Williams. **Credits:** Dir: Anthony Mann; Prod: Edward Small; Writer: Leopold Atlas, John C. Higgins; DP: John Alton; Ed: Al DeGaetano; Composer: Paul Sawtell. B&W, 79 min. **VHS**

The Razor's Edge
(1946) Fox
W. Somerset Maugham's acclaimed 1944 novel gets a respectful, well-appointed treatment. After serving in

WWI, Power returns to his Chicago home to find his life and his fiancée (Tierney) superficial, so he sets out first to Paris and then the Far East to find the meaning of existence. An encounter with a guru gives him a mission of service, a mission he gets to follow when he runs into old friend Baxter in Paris, now a widow grieving the tragic loss of her husband and family, and consoling herself with drink. Power decides to rehabilitate Baxter, but Tierney's jealous scheming leads to her death and Power's departure, once again on a journey to find himself. Though Baxter got an Oscar for a heartrending performance, Power shines brightest, investing what could have been a soupy role with dignity and real passion for enlightenment. Perhaps his recent experiences as a Marine in WWII gave him personal insight into the character. Remade in 1984 with Bill Murray. Golden Globes for Best Supporting Actor: Clifton Webb; Best Supporting Actress: Anne Baxter. Academy Award Nominations: 4, including Best Picture; Best Supporting Actor: Clifton Webb; Best (Black-and-White) Interior Decoration. **Academy Awards:** Best Supporting Actress: Anne Baxter. **Cast:** Tyrone Power, Gene Tierney, Anne Baxter, Clifton Webb, Herbert Marshall, Lucile Watson, Elsa Lanchester, Fritz Kortner. **Credits:** Dir: Edmund Goulding; Prod: Darryl F. Zanuck; Writer: Lamar Trotti; Story: Somerset Maugham; DP: Arthur Miller; Ed: J. Watson Webb; Composer: Alfred Newman; Art Director: Richard Day, Nathan Juran. B&W, 144 min. **VHS, LASER**

Reaching for the Moon
(1931) United Artists
This light romance between Fairbanks, a financier who has weathered the stock-market crash, and aviatrix Daniels has plenty of twists and turns. The opening shot is remarkable, as the camera swoops over an intricate Art Deco miniature of a fantastic city designed by Menzies. Notable also for an early appearance by Crosby. **Cast:** Douglas Fairbanks, Bebe Daniels, Edward Everett Horton, Bing Crosby, Jack Mulhall, Claude Allister, Walter Walker, Helen Jerome Eddy, June MacCloy. **Credits:** Dir: Edmund Goulding; Writer: Edmund Goulding, Elsie Janis; DP: Ray June, Robert Planck; Ed: Lloyd Nosler, Hal C. Kern; Prod Design: William Cameron Menzies; Composer: Irving Berlin. B&W, 90 min. **VHS**

The Real Glory

(1939) United Artists
In a stirring wartime adventure directed by action master Hathaway, Cooper is an army medic in the Philippines after the Spanish-American War. An uprising by Moro tribesmen leads to the evacuation of all but a small army outpost manned by Filipinos and led by a small contingent of American officers. The Moros seem impervious to the soldiers' bullets, so Cooper disobeys orders to spy on their rituals. The tribesmen draw the soldiers out by damming their water supply, then attack the fort. **Cast:** Gary Cooper, Reginald Owen, David Niven, Andrea Leeds, Kay Johnson, Broderick Crawford, Vladimir Sokoloff, Henry Kolker. **Credits:** Dir: Henry Hathaway; Prod: Samuel Goldwyn; Writer: Jo Swerling, Robert Presnell; Story: Charles L. Clifford; DP: Rudolph Maté; Ed: Daniel Mandell; Prod Design: James Basevi. B&W, 96 min. **VHS**

Real Life

(1979) Paramount
Brooks's brilliant, savage satire of a culture so media-saturated that nothing seems real unless it's on TV predates by 20 years recent explorations of the theme such as *The Truman Show* (1998) or *Ed TV* (1999). Brooks plays a desperate documentary producer who decimates a family when he turns his probing cameras on their daily life for one year. His film loses steam when nothing much happens, so Brooks starts a little action to save the project. Clearly based on the concept of the PBS series of the '70s, *An American Family*. Produced by Spheeris, who would unleash her own documentary havoc with *The Decline of Western Civilization* (1981). **Cast:** Albert Brooks, Charles Grodin, Frances Lee McCain, J. A. Preston, Matthew Tobin, James L. Brooks, Adam Grant, David Spielberg. **Credits:** Dir: Albert Brooks; Prod: Penelope Spheeris; Writer: Albert Brooks, Monica Johnson, Harry Shearer; DP: Eric Saarinen; Ed: David Finfer; Composer: Mort Lindsey; Art Director: Linda Spheeris, Linda Marder. Color, 99 min. **VHS**

Reap the Wild Wind

(1942) Paramount
In a DeMille potboiler at sea, 19th-century ship captain Wayne fights for his reputation with shipping company investigator Milland, for his ship with salvage pirates Massey and Preston, and for his life with a giant red octopus. Salvage-company owner Goddard nurses Wayne back to health after a shipwreck, though she loses him to the sea creature. Academy Award Nominations: 2, including Best Cinematography. **Academy Awards:** Best Special Effects. **Cast:** John Wayne, Susan Hayward, Ray Milland, Paulette Goddard, Raymond Massey, Robert Preston, Lynne Overman, Charles Bickford. **Credits:** Dir: Cecil B. DeMille; Prod: Cecil B. DeMille; Writer: Alan LeMay, Charles Bennett, Jeanie Macpherson, Jesse Lasky, Jr.; Story: Thelma Strabel; DP: Victor Milner, William V. Skall; Ed: Anne Bauchens; Composer: Victor Young; Art Director: Hans Dreier, Roland Anderson; SFX: Farciot Eduoart, Gordon Jennings, William Pereira, Louis Mesenkop. Color, 124 min. **VHS**

Rear Window

(1954) Paramount
This thoroughly enjoyable mystery classic from Hitchcock pokes amiably at the inherent voyeurism of the movie audience. Restless magazine photographer Stewart bides his time while confined to a wheelchair with observing the behavior of his neighbors from the vantage point of his rear window. His only other distractions during the day are visits from his model girlfriend Kelly and nurse Ritter. After waking in the night, Stewart is convinced he sees salesman Burr disposing of evidence that would indicate a hideous murder, with his nagging wife the obvious victim. But when Stewart's story doesn't wash with a policeman pal, he sends Kelly into the apartment to search for more clues. As Stewart watches helplessly, Burr returns to his apartment. Now aware of Stewart's snooping, Burr attacks the wheelchair-bound voyeur. Witty and beautifully produced (Hitchcock constructed the largest set of its time at Paramount—31 full-scale apartments), this is an enduring popular and critical favorite. A restored version of this Hitchcock masterpiece (by the team that accomplished wonders with *Vertigo*) is due to be released in the fall of 1999. Selected for the National Film Registry. Academy Award Nominations: Best Director; Best Screenplay; Best Cinematography; Best Sound. **Cast:** James Stewart, Grace Kelly, Wendell Corey, Thelma Ritter, Raymond Burr, Judith Evelyn, Sara Berner, Frank Cady, Georgine Darcy. **Credits:** Dir: Alfred Hitchcock; Prod: Alfred Hitchcock; Writer: John Michael Hayes; Story: Cornell Woolrich; DP: Robert Burks; Ed: George Tomasini; Prod Design: Hal Pereira, Joseph MacMillan Johnson; Composer: Franz Waxman; Costumes: Edith Head. Color, 112 min. **VHS, LASER, DVD**

Rebecca

(1940) United Artists
Hitchcock's American debut was a smashing success, and an intriguing change of pace after his British murder mysteries. Here, Hitchcock takes a subtler, psychologically-based approach to the 1938 novel by Daphne du Maurier, more akin to William Wyler's brooding *Wuthering Heights*

Rebecca (1940)

(1939) than to the crime genre. Olivier meets shy, retiring Fontaine on vacation and soon marries her. When they settle at Olivier's estate, Fontaine discovers that Olivier's deceased first wife still rules the household through the servants (particularly a creepy housekeeper played by Anderson) and a looming portrait. Though Fontaine hears nothing but adulation for the dead woman, her true character is revealed when the remains of her boat wash to shore, making clear that the craft was intentionally sunk. Olivier then tells Fontaine of the torment his first wife made of his life, setting free his conscience as the housekeeper consumes the first wife's memory in the flames of the burning estate. The laserdisc edition includes screen tests by Vivien Leigh, Anne Baxter, Loretta Young, and Fontaine for the lead; coverage of the 1940 Oscar ceremonies; trailers, radio broadcasts, production stills, and a second audio track that contains comment derived from interviews with Hitchcock. Academy Award Nominations: 11, including Best Director; Best Actor: Laurence Olivier; Best Actress: Joan Fontaine; Best Supporting Actress: Judith Anderson; Best Adapted Screenplay; Best Editing; Best Score. **Academy Awards:** Best Picture; Best Black-and-White Cinematography. **Cast:** Joan Fontaine, Laurence Olivier, George Sanders, Judith Anderson, Nigel Bruce, C. Aubrey Smith, Reginald Denny, Gladys Cooper. **Credits:** Dir: Alfred Hitchcock; Prod: David O. Selznick; Writer: Robert E. Sherwood, Joan Harrison; Story: Daphne du Maurier; DP: George Barnes; Ed: James E. Newcom, Hal C. Kern; Composer: Franz Waxman; Art Director: Lyle Wheeler. B&W, 130 min. **VHS, LASER**

Rebecca of Sunnybrook Farm
(1917) Artcraft
This silent version of the Kate Douglas Wiggin children's book stars Pickford as the spunky young girl. Pickford comes from a large, loving, but poor family. In hopes of providing her with a better future, her parents send her to live with a stern aunt (Cromwell). Although Pickford's fun-loving antics vex her prickly aunt, the plucky girl ultimately triumphs, wedding the wealthiest man in town (O'Brien). **Cast:** Mary Pickford, Helen Jerome Eddy, Eugene O'Brien, Josephine Cromwell, Mayme Kelso, Marjorie Daw, ZaSu Pitts. **Credits:** Dir: Marshall Neilan; Writer: Frances Marion; DP: Walter Stradling; Composer: Gaylord Carter. B&W, 71 min. **VHS, LASER**

Rebecca of Sunnybrook Farm
(1938) Fox
Temple plays a talented little girl who becomes a sensational radio star. Standard Temple fare with a medley of her greatest hits ("On the Good Ship Lollipop," "When I'm with You," and "Animal Crackers") and a dance with Robinson to "Parade of the Wooden Soldiers." Available on laserdisc with *The Little Colonel*. **Cast:** Shirley Temple, Jack Haley, Randolph Scott, Bill Robinson. **Credits:** Dir: Allan Dwan; Prod: Raymond Griffith; Writer: Karl Tunberg, Karl Ettlinger; Story: Kate Douglas Wiggin; DP: Arthur Miller; Ed: Allen McNeil. B&W, 81 min. **VHS**

The Rebel Set
(1959) Allied Artists
Cool, man. A '50s crime caper with Beat-era overtones. Coffeehouse-owner Palmer plans an armored-car heist and enlists his beatnik friends. They succeed, but face a showdown with the cops. **Cast:** Gregg Palmer, Edward Platt, Don Sullivan, Ned Glass, Stanford Jolley, Robert Shayne. **Credits:** Dir: Gene Fowler, Jr.; Prod: Earle Lyon; Writer: Louis Vittes, Bernard Girard; DP: Karl Struss; Ed: William Austin; Prod Design: Dave Milton; Composer: Paul Dunlap. B&W, 73 min. **VHS**

Rebel Without a Cause
(1955) Warner Bros.
What could have been merely a teen-exploitation flick became, in the hands of director Ray (perhaps the greatest screen interpreter of alienated outsiders), a timeless study of maturity formed in rebellion and tragedy. Dean's brooding, troubled character (along with Brando's character in *The Wild One*, 1954) also set the stage for the countless teen pictures to follow as the restless youth of the mid-'50s defined teen culture. Dean and his family settle in Los Angeles, the latest in a series of moves driven by Dean's delinquency. Confused by his father's (Backus) surrender to his domineering mother (Doran), Dean tries to establish himself with fisticuffs and daredevil stunts. When he meets Wood and Mineo at the police station, his pursuit of Wood leads to a deadly hot-rod showdown and a tragic run from the police. In the face of pursuit by the authorities, and with no effective adults to turn to, the three form an imitation family of their own until Backus finally finds the courage to reach out to his son. Ray dignifies the story with his characteristically careful compositions and by drawing electrify-

ing performances from his cast. Selected for the National Film Registry. Academy Award Nominations: Best Supporting Actor: Sal Mineo; Best Supporting Actress: Natalie Wood; Best Motion Picture Story. **Cast:** James Dean, Natalie Wood, Sal Mineo, Jim Backus, Ann Doran, Dennis Hopper, Nick Adams, Jack Simmons, Marietta Canty. **Credits:** Dir: Nicholas Ray; Prod: David Weisbart; Writer: Stewart Stern; DP: Ernest Haller; Ed: William Ziegler; Prod Design: William Wallace; Composer: Leonard Rosenman. Color, 140 min. **VHS, LASER**

Reckless
(1935) MGM
Selznick's misguided attempt to turn Harlow into a song-and-dance star is fascinating for her game effort and also for the pairing with Powell. Harlow's marriage to wealthy Tone is on the rocks, so she turns to her agent, Powell. Tone commits suicide, and Harlow is suspected of murder. Loyal Powell puts on a show that answers every suspicion, winning her heart for good. In a macabre sidelight, Harlow's husband, studio executive Paul Bern, did commit suicide, and Harlow and Powell did become an item a year after this was released. **Cast:** Jean Harlow, William Powell, Franchot Tone, May Robson, Ted Healy, Nat Pendleton, Rosalind Russell, Henry Stephenson, Leon Waycoff, Mickey Rooney. **Credits:** Dir: Victor Fleming; Prod: David O. Selznick; Writer: P. J. Wolfson; DP: George J. Folsey; Ed: Margaret Booth; Prod Design: Cedric Gibbons; Choreographer: Carl Randall; Composer: Victor Baravalle. B&W, 97 min. **VHS**

The Red Badge of Courage
(1951) MGM
This is a spare, devastating version by Huston of the 1895 Stephen Crane classic that depicts a young soldier's experiences in the Civil War. War hero Murphy portrays a young recruit in the Union Army who matures into manhood as he first flees the horrors of the battlefield and then leads the charge after seeing his friends die. Reportedly a favorite of Huston's, he nevertheless left the cutting of his picture to the studio to be on the set of *The African Queen* (1951). **Cast:** Audie Murphy, Bill Mauldin, Arthur Hunnicutt, John Dierkes, Royal Dano, Douglas Dick, Andy Devine, Robert Easton, Smith Ballew, Glenn Strange. **Credits:** Dir: John Huston; Prod: Gottfried Reinhardt; Writer: John Huston,

Michael Barson Picks the Greatest Teen Movies of All Time

1. Rebel Without a Cause *(1955).* James Dean achieved supernova stardom on the basis of his performance here as Jim, the troubled transplant to a status-conscious L.A. high school. Unfortunately, he was dead at the time, having cracked up his Porsche less than two months before the film's release. But you already knew that. We also like Natalie Wood as the object of Dean's desire, but Sal Mineo is way too much as the anguished Plato.

2. Fast Times at Ridgemont High *(1982).* Amy Heckerling directs the apotheosis of '80s teen culture, brilliantly embodied by Sean Penn's Spicoli and his contest of wills with Ray Walston's pitiless—but ultimately overmatched—teacher. Judge Reinhold, Phoebe Cates, and Jennifer Jason Leigh are nearly as great. Pizza, anyone?

3. Girl's Town *(1959);* **High School Confidential** *(1958);* **Untamed Youth** *(1957);* **Running Wild** *(1955).* Mamie, Mamie, Mamie Van Doren—"the girl built like a platinum powerhouse," and that ain't lyin'—ended up in more girls' reformatories than Ma Barker. Well, Marilyn was way past making teen flicks by the mid-fifties, so that left it to the capable Mamie, ponytail and all. Extra points for her half-decent warbling on the sound tracks of the above. And more points for her excellent sneer.

4. American Graffiti *(1973).* Set in the Southern California of 1962, this sleeper—directed by the pre–*Star Wars* George Lucas—went on to become one of the most profitable films of all time. Richard Dreyfuss is a bit hard to buy as a teen, but Ron Howard, Cindy Williams, and Candy Clark are beyond perfect, and Paul Le Mat elevates the mythic figure of the brooding drag racer to near-tragic proportions. And, oh, that sound track!

5. Clueless *(1995).* Has there ever been a more winning star-making performance than that submitted by Alicia Silverstone in this frothy updating of—can it be?—Jane Austen's *Emma*? We especially dug how Alicia's crush on a patently gay guy was handled, and Dan Hedaya makes one of the great dads in all of Teen Pic history. Deserves repeated viewings, as do all of the above nominees.

Teen Pic Honorable Mentions

Youth Runs Wild *(1944).* Featuring Bonita Granville and adapted from the *Look* magazine article about delinquency, "Are These Our Children?"

City Across the River *(1949).* The so-so film version of Irving Shulman's seminal novel, *The Amboy Dukes*, with a young Tony Curtis—he was born ten years too soon!

Rock, Rock, Rock *(1956).* Thanks to perky Tuesday Weld and primo musical performances by Frankie Lymon and the Teenagers, and Chuck Berry—plus Alan Freed, Rock's Pied Piper.

Dino *(1957).* Sal Mineo at his best, struggling to connect with true love despite problems at home and school.

The Lords of Flatbush *(1974).* Sly Stallone before he became Sly Stallone does nicely as a tough greaser roped into an early marriage, and we like Perry King nearly as much. Henry Winkler was so good here he was cast as The Fonz on *Happy Days*, thus ruining a truly promising career.

The Wanderers *(1979).* Ken Wahl and Karen Allen are right-on embodiments of Richard Price's young Bronx lovers trying to escape peer pressure, but Phil Kaufman lays on the mythic overtones a little more heavily than we needed.

Over the Edge *(1979).* Scary stuff from director Jonathan Kaplan, with troubled teens Matt Dillon and Michael Kramer trying to overcome anomie in their planned community somewhere in the desert of the southwest. No sweet sound track here to take away the sting.

Valley Girl *(1982).* Nick Cage before he was Nick Cage is irresistibly sweet as he tries to win the girl of his dreams.

Sixteen Candles *(1984).* Molly Ringwald is winning, Anthony Michael Hall is cute, and John Cusack is funny, while director-producer John Hughes holds back his impulse toward bathos for the first and, alas, last time. Or didn't you see *The Breakfast Club* and *St. Elmo's Fire*?

Michael Barson is most recently the coauthor (with Steve Heller) of *Teenage Confidential!*.

Albert Band; Story: Stephen Crane; DP: Harold Rosson; Ed: Ben Lewis; Prod Design: Cedric Gibbons, Hans Peters; Composer: Bronislaw Kaper. B&W, 70 min. VHS

Red Ball Express
(1952) Universal
This is a slam-bang Boetticher WWII tale about the officer (Chandler) assigned to provide fuel to General Patton's tank divisions as they made their way toward Paris, outrunning their supply lines in Nazi-held territory. In addition to the Nazis, Chandler contends with racism in the ranks directed toward Poitier. **Cast:** Jeff Chandler, Alex Nicol, Sidney Poitier, Charles Drake, Judith Braun, Jacqueline Duval, Jack Kelly. **Credits:** Dir: Budd Boetticher; Prod: Aaron Rosenberg; Writer: John Michael Hayes; DP: Maury Gertsman; Ed: Edward Curtiss; Art Director: Bernard Herzbrun. B&W, 84 min. VHS

Red Dust
(1932) MGM
The second pairing of Gable and Harlow is a steamy potboiler set on an equally steamy Indochina rubber plantation. Plantation foreman Gable first woos wisecracking prostitute Harlow when she arrives by ship, then takes up with the wife of an engineer (Astor) after he puts Harlow on a steamer. When Harlow returns and wants Gable back, Astor flies into a murderously jealous rage. Tragedy struck the set when Harlow's husband, studio executive Paul Bern, committed suicide during production. MGM considered a substitute, but the public demanded to see Harlow on-screen. Remade as *Mogambo,* again with Gable, in 1953. **Cast:** Clark Gable, Jean Harlow, Mary Astor, Donald Crisp, Gene Raymond, Tully Marshall, Willie Fung, Forrester Harvey. **Credits:** Dir: Victor Fleming; Prod: Victor Fleming; Writer: John Lee Mahin; Story: Wilson Collison; DP: Harold Rosson; Ed: Blanche Sewell; Prod Design: Cedric Gibbons. B&W, 83 min. VHS

Red Garters
(1954) Paramount
In a stylized musical satire of Westerns, Mitchell comes to Limbo County to avenge the death of his brother. As he searches for the culprit, he gets ensnared in a romantic triangle with saloon singer Clooney and lawyer Carson. The highlights include Clooney singing the title song and "Man and Woman." Academy Award Nomination for Best (Color) Art Direction—Set Decoration. **Cast:** Rosemary Clooney, Jack Carson, Guy Mitchell, Pat Crowley, Gene Barry, Cass Daley, Frank Faylen, Buddy Ebsen. **Credits:** Dir: George Marshall; Prod: Pat Duggan; Writer: Michael Fessier; DP: Arthur E. Arling; Ed: Arthur Schmidt; Art Director: Hal Pereira, Roland Anderson. Color, 91 min. VHS

Red-Headed Woman
(1932) MGM
In this pre-Code comedy that made a star of Harlow, a saucy redhead vamps her boss (Morris) away from his wife and then cats around town with wealthy Stephenson and her chauffeur (Boyer). When Morris objects, she pulls a gun and he retreats back to his calmer previous life. Harlow turns up later, now the mistress of a titled gentleman. Snappy lines from Loos delivered with Harlow's lovable trampiness. **Cast:** Jean Harlow, Chester Morris, Una Merkel, Lewis Stone, May Robson, Leila Hyams, Charles Boyer, Henry Stephenson, Harvey Clark. **Credits:** Dir: Jack Conway; Prod: Paul Bern; Writer: Anita Loos; Story: Katherine Brush; DP: Harold Rosson; Ed: Blanche Sewell; Prod Design: Cedric Gibbons. B&W, 81 min. VHS

The Redhead from Wyoming
(1953) Universal
This straightforward oater has O'Hara the feisty proprietress of a saloon who gets framed for a murder when she crosses Bishop's plans to start a range war. Sheriff Nicol helps her clear her name. **Cast:** Maureen O'Hara, Alex Nicol, William Bishop, Robert Strauss, Alexander Scourby, Palmer Lee, Jack Kelly, Jeannie Cooper, Dennis Weaver, Stacy Harris. **Credits:** Dir: Lee Sholem; Prod: Leonard Goldstein; Writer: Polly James, Herb Meadow; DP: Winton C. Hoch; Ed: Milton Carruth; Art Director: Bernard Herzbrun, Hilyard Brown. Color, 81 min. VHS

Red, Hot and Blue
(1949) Paramount
Blond knockout Hutton, who is dating the director of her Broadway show (Mature), finds herself in a pickle when the show's producer (a gangster) gets murdered while she's visiting his apartment. Mature wants to know why she was there and the gangsters want to know what she knows. Mostly an excuse for the Loesser songs and Hutton's rambunctious performance. **Cast:** Betty Hutton, Victor Mature, William Demarest, June Havoc, Jane Nigh, Frank Loesser, William Talman, Art Smith. **Credits:** Dir: John Farrow; Prod: Robert Fellows; Writer: John Farrow, Hagar Wilde; Story: Charles Lederer; DP: Daniel L. Fapp; Ed: Eda Warren; Prod Design: Hans Dreier, Franz Bachelin, Sam Comer; Composer: Joseph J. Lilley. B&W, 84 min.

The Red House
(1947) United Artists
This suspenseful thriller has Robinson a crippled farmer who harbors a deep secret and forbids anyone to go near a red house hidden in the woods. His ward (Roberts) and farmhand (McCallister) snoop until they uncover the house and its mysterious past. **Cast:** Edward G. Robinson, Judith Anderson, Lon McCallister, Rory Calhoun, Allene Roberts, Julie London, Ona Munson, Harry Shannon. **Credits:** Dir: Delmer Daves; Prod: Sol Lesser; Writer: Delmer Daves; DP: Bert Glennon; Ed: Merrill White; Prod Design: McClure Capps; Composer: Miklos Rozsa. B&W, 100 min. VHS

Red Line 7000
(1965) Paramount
Late in his career, Hawks directed what amounts to a romantic potboiler set in the world of international auto racing. Racers die, dashing new drivers emerge, and beautiful women lose their hearts against their better judgment. Watchable for fans of the sport, it includes some terrific racing footage. **Cast:** James Caan, Laura Devon, Gail Hire, Charlene Holt, John Crawford, Marianna Hill, James Ward, Norman Alden. **Credits:** Dir: Howard Hawks; Prod: Howard Hawks; Writer: George Kirgo; DP: Milton Krasner, Haskell Boggs; Ed: Stuart Gilmore, Bill Brame; Composer: Nelson Riddle; Art Director: Hal Pereira, Arthur Lonergan. Color, 110 min. VHS

Red Planet Mars
(1952) United Artists
This bizarre sci-fi head-scratcher has to be seen to be believed. A scientist develops equipment that receives transmissions from Mars. The news sets off pandemonium and a religious revolution that overthrows the Soviet government. Though an ex-Nazi claims to have created the device to bring down world governments, further transmissions claim that God is in fact the ruler of Mars. **Cast:** Peter Graves, Andrea King, Marvin Miller, Herbert Berghof, House Peters, Orley Lindgren, Bayard Veiller, Walter Sande. **Credits:** Dir: Harry Horner; Prod:

Anthony Veiller, Donald Hyde; Writer: Anthony Veiller, John L. Balderston; DP: Joseph Biroc; Ed: Francis D. Lyon; Prod Design: Charles D. Hall; Composer: M. A. Merrick, David Chudnow. B&W, 87 min. **VHS**

The Red Pony

(1949) Republic
This is great family entertainment, with a distinguished pedigree: written by John Steinbeck, directed by Lewis Milestone, and featuring one of the few scores written directly for the screen by Aaron Copland. A young boy's admiration for a ranch hand (Mitchum) causes friction with his city-bred father (Strudwick) and mother (Loy). When the boy's adored pony gets loose and falls ill, he blames Mitchum. His father comes home and helps his son through the crisis, and Mitchum gives the boy a new pony when his mare has a foal. Remade for TV in 1972 with Henry Fonda. The 45th anniversary video edition is digitally remastered from the original negative, and includes the original theatrical trailer and lobby-card reproductions. **Cast:** Myrna Loy, Robert Mitchum, Shepperd Strudwick, Louis Calhern, Peter Miles, Margaret Hamilton, Beau Bridges, Tom Sheridan, George Tyne. **Credits:** Dir: Lewis Milestone; Prod: Lewis Milestone; Writer: John Steinbeck; DP: Tony Gaudio; Ed: Harry Keller; Composer: Aaron Copland; Art Director: Victor Greene. Color, 89 min. **VHS, LASER**

Red River

(1948) United Artists
With Hawks's first Western he showed his mastery of the genre, producing an enduring classic that features one of Wayne's finest performances. Wayne splits from an ill-fated wagon train heading west, and steers toward Texas with his friend Brennan and a young Indian-attack survivor who grows up to be Clift. Wayne establishes the biggest spread in Texas, and runs it with the ruthlessness he showed in seizing the land. When he drives thousands of cattle north to Missouri, Wayne ignores the advice of his hands about the new Chisholm Trail, and runs the drive with an iron fist that leads to killings and mutiny. Clift finally establishes his own claim to the ranch's heritage by defying Wayne and heading to Kansas despite Wayne's threat to kill him. After a climactic brawl, Wayne acknowledges Clift's claim and the men are reconciled. A big, muscular drama with Clift's quiet steel making a nice contrast to

Red River (1948)

Wayne's grit, and Brennan's comic turn adding a lighter note. The director's restored version contains eight minutes of previously excised footage. Academy Award Nominations: Best Screenplay; Best Editing. **Cast:** John Wayne, Montgomery Clift, Walter Brennan, Joanne Dru, Coleen Gray, John Ireland, Noah Beery, Harry Carey. **Credits:** Dir: Howard Hawks; Prod: Howard Hawks; Writer: Borden Chase, Charles Schnee; DP: Russell Harlan; Ed: Christian Nyby; Composer: Dimitri Tiomkin; Art Director: John Datu Arensman. B&W, 125/133 min. **VHS, LASER, DVD**

Red Skies of Montana

(1952) Fox
The red skies are forest fires roaring in glorious Technicolor and Widmark is a seasoned campaigner, parachuting into the inferno. He loses a squad to a fire and emerges from the flames with amnesia and an accusation of cowardice from the son (Hunter) of a man who was lost in the blaze. Widmark redeems himself after training new recruits, including Hunter, to battle forest fires. **Cast:** Richard Widmark, Constance Smith, Jeffrey Hunter, Richard Boone, Warren Stevens, James Griffith, Joe Sawyer, Gregory Wolcott, Richard Crenna, Bob Nichols. **Credits:** Dir: Joseph M. Newman; Prod: Samuel G. Engel; Writer: Arthur Cohn; Story: Harry Kleiner; DP: Charles G. Clarke; Ed: William Reynolds; Composer: Lionel Newman; Art Director: Lyle Wheeler, Chester Gore. Color, 89 min.

Reflections in a Golden Eye

(1967) Warner Bros.
This Huston misfire was supposed to exploit the box-office dynamite of a Brando-Taylor pairing. But with Brando a repressed homosexual army camp commandant and Taylor a braying, spiteful tramp, there's not much chance of chemistry. Add a salacious plot that plays like bargain-basement Tennessee Williams, and audience indifference is guaranteed. A curiosity suitable only for hard-core Huston completists, or fans of Brando and Taylor. **Cast:** Elizabeth Taylor, Marlon Brando, Brian Keith, Julie Harris, Gordon Mitchell, Zorro David, Irvin Dugan, Douglas Stark, Al Mulock. **Credits:** Dir: John Huston; Prod: Ray Stark; Writer: Chapman Mortimer, Gladys Hill; Story: Carson McCullers; DP: Aldo Tonti; Ed: Russell Lloyd; Prod Design: Stephen Grimes; Composer: Toshiro Mayuzumi. Color, 109 min. **VHS**

The Reivers

(1969) National General
This turn-of-the-century adventure tale with nostalgic good humor was written by William Faulkner. The arrival of Geer's new Winton automobile in a Mississippi town sets off a boisterous trip to Memphis when Geer's son (Vogel), chauffeur (McQueen), and a black relation (Crosse) borrow the car. While McQueen looks up an old acquaintance (Farrell) in a bordello and Vogel learns a little street wisdom, Crosse trades the car for a racehorse.

Academy Award Nominations: Best Supporting Actor: Rupert Crosse; Best Score. **Cast:** Steve McQueen, Sharon Farrell, Will Geer, Michael Constantine, Rupert Crosse, Mitch Vogel, Lonny Chapman, Clifton James. **Credits:** Dir: Mark Rydell; Prod: Irving Ravetch; Writer: Irving Ravetch, Harriet Frank, Jr.; Story: William Faulkner; DP: Richard Moore; Ed: Thomas Stanford; Composer: John Williams; SFX: Paul Pollard; Art Director: Charles Bailey, Joel Schiller. Color, 107 min. **VHS**

The Reluctant Debutante
(1958) MGM
Minnelli directs a delightful romantic comedy with Harrison and Kendall presenting his daughter from a previous marriage (Dee) at a London society ball. Though they hope for a well-born British husband to materialize, Dee's more interested in hepcat American musician Saxon. Everybody's happy when Saxon receives a large inheritance. Kendall and Harrison were also married offscreen at the time. **Cast:** Rex Harrison, Kay Kendall, John Saxon, Sandra Dee, Angela Lansbury, Peter Myers, Diane Clare, Sheila Raynor. **Credits:** Dir: Vincente Minnelli; Prod: Pandro S. Berman; Writer: William Douglas Home; DP: Joseph Ruttenberg; Ed: Adrienne Fazan; Composer: Eddie Warner; Art Director: Jean D'Eaubonne; Set Designer: Robert Christides. Color, 94 min. **VHS, LASER**

The Remarkable Andrew
(1942) Paramount
This unusual fantasy from screenwriter Trumbo unfolds when meek accountant and secretary of the local Andrew Jackson historical society Andrew Long (Holden) is falsely accused of embezzlement. Poor Holden's put in prison for a crime he didn't commit, but there he's visited by a spectral procession of great Americans, including Andrew Jackson, George Washington, Ben Franklin, and Thomas Jefferson. The hallowed and spirited spirits argue among themselves and marvel at moden wonders as they engineer Holden's jailbreak, the clearing of his good name, and his happy reunion with his fiancée (Drew). **Cast:** Brian Donlevy, William Holden, Ellen Drew, Montagu Love, Gilbert Emery, Brandon Hurst, George Watts, Rod Cameron, Jimmy Conlin, Richard Webb. **Credits:** Dir: Stuart Heiser; Prod: Richard Blumenthal; Writer: Dalton Trumbo; DP: Theodor Sparkuhl; Ed: Archie Marshek; Prod Design: Hans Dreier, A. Earl Hedrick; Composer: Victor Young. B&W, 81 min.

Remember Last Night?
(1935) Universal
In this comic murder mystery, hard-drinking, wisecracking socialites Cummings and Young cooperate with good-humored detective Arnold as he investigates a series of killings in their wild set. Unfortunately, their constant inebriation requires the use of a German hypnotist (von Seyffertitz) who, of course, gets his as he gets closer to the truth. An unusually light-hearted romp through serial murders with director Whale's characteristic off-hand elegance. **Cast:** Edward Arnold, Constance Cummings, Robert Armstrong, Reginald Denny, Robert Young, Sally Eilers, Monroe Owsley, Arthur Treacher, Gustav von Seyffertitz. **Credits:** Dir: James Whale; Prod: Carl Laemmle; Writer: Lois Kent, Louise Henry, Doris Malloy, Dan Totheroh, Adam Hobhouse; DP: Joseph A. Valentine; Ed: Ted J. Kent; Prod Design: Charles D. Hall; Composer: Franz Waxman. B&W, 81 min.

Remember My Name
(1978) Columbia
Director Rudolph, previously Robert Altman's assistant director and a remarkable film stylist in his own right, refers to this film as "A Contemporary Blues Fable." Perkins plays a construction worker happily remarried to Berenson whose marriage and his wife's life are threatened when Chaplin, his ex-wife, gets out of jail. Chaplin gets a job in a nearby five-and-dime store owned by Goldblum, and terrorizes Perkins and Berenson in a sad, misguided attempt to win Perkins back. A complex mystery drama accentuated by Alberta Hunter's bluesy voice on the sound track. **Cast:** Geraldine Chaplin, Anthony Perkins, Moses Gunn, Berry Berenson, Jeff Goldblum, Tim Thomerson, Alfre Woodard, Marilyn Coleman, Jeffrey Perry, Alan Autry. **Credits:** Dir: Alan Rudolph; Prod: Robert Altman; Writer: Alan Rudolph; DP: Tak Fujimoto; Ed: William A. Sawyer, Tom Walls; Composer: Alberta Hunter. Color, 94 min.

Remember the Day
(1941) Fox
Colbert, an elderly schoolteacher, prepares to meet a former pupil, Strudwick, now a candidate for president. She recalls the politician as a boy, his schoolboy crush, and his jealousy when he discovered that she was secretly married to a fellow schoolteacher. Colbert's reminiscences turn to her relationship with the teacher, his enlistment in the Canadian forces

during WWI, and his death in the trenches. Colbert remembers the comfort she took in her students, especially young Strudwick. A heart-warmer with a winning performance from Colbert. **Cast:** Claudette Colbert, John Payne, Shepperd Strudwick, Ann Todd, Douglas Croft, Jane Seymour, Anne Revere, Frieda Inescort, Harry Hayden, Francis Pierlot. **Credits:** Dir: Henry King; Prod: William Perlberg; Writer: Frank Davis, Allan Scott, Tess Slesinger, Henry King; Story: Philo Higley; DP: George Barnes; Ed: Barbara McLean; Prod Design: Richard Day; Composer: Alfred Newman. B&W, 86 min.

Remember the Night
(1940) Paramount
Leisen directs a Sturges script and the result is a terrific combination of witty romance and heartwarming comedy. Stanwyck's a shoplifter who gets caught with a diamond necklace just before the Christmas hoildays. When D.A. MacMurray discovers she's from his home state of Indiana, he gets her released to his custody for the holiday. When her own mother doesn't want her around, MacMurray takes her to his home where she revels in the warmth and family affection. As the unlikely duo fall in love, Stanwyck decides to plead guilty and hope for the best. **Cast:** Barbara Stanwyck, Fred MacMurray, Beulah Bondi, Elizabeth Patterson, Sterling Holloway, Charles Waldron, Virginia Brissac, Spencer Charters, Paul Guilfoyle, Willard Robertson. **Credits:** Dir: Mitchell Leisen; Prod: Mitchell Leisen; Writer: Preston Sturges; DP: Ted Tetzlaff; Ed: Doane Harrison; Prod Design: Hans Dreier, Roland Anderson; Composer: Frederick Hollander; Costumes: Edith Head. B&W, 94 min. **VHS**

Requiem for a Heavyweight
(1962) Columbia
This is the big-screen adaptation of Rod Serling's landmark live-TV drama about an aging boxer (Quinn) facing life outside the ring. As Mountain Rivera, Quinn takes a beating from Ali, after which the ring doctor advises him to quit or chance blindness. He lasted too long against Ali, though, for his friend and manager Gleason to collect on his bet against him and Gleason presses him to fight or come up with the money. Quinn searches for a new job with the help of employment counselor Harris, but Gleason undermines his efforts. When Gleason becomes desperate, Quinn accepts the indignity of the professional

wrestling ring. The TV version introduced Jack Palance and won 5 Emmy Awards: Best New Program Series; Best Single Program; Best Single Performance (Palance); Best Direction; Best Teleplay (Serling). **Cast:** Anthony Quinn, Jackie Gleason, Mickey Rooney, Julie Harris, Muhammad Ali (screen credit as Cassius Clay), Stanley Adams, Madame Spivy, Herbie Faye, Jack Dempsey. **Credits:** Dir: Ralph Nelson; Prod: David Susskind; Writer: Rod Serling; DP: Arthur J. Ornitz; Ed: Carl Lerner; Prod Design: Burr Smidt; Composer: Laurence Rosenthal. B&W, 100 min. **VHS**

The Rescuers
(1977) Disney
An urgent note in a bottle from a kidnapped orphan girl leads two adventuresome mice (voiced by Newhart and Gabor) on a "wild albatross chase" to Devil's Bayou and a madcap encounter with the villainous Madame Medusa. A hit, and among the best of Disney's '70s efforts. Academy Award Nomination for Best Song ("Someone's Waiting for You"). **Cast:** Eva Gabor, Bob Newhart, Geraldine Page, Joe Flynn, Jeanette Nolan, Pat Buttram, Jim Jordan, John McIntire, Bernard Fox. **Credits:** Dir: Wolfgang Reitherman, John Lounsbury, Art Stevens; Prod: Wolfgang Reitherman; Writer: Ken Anderson, Vance Gerry, Larry Clemmons, Dave Michener, Burny Mattinson, Frank Thomas, Ted Berman; Story: Margery Sharp; Ed: Jim Koford, James Melton; Composer: Artie Butler; Art Director: Don Griffith. Color, 77 min. **VHS**

The Return of Frank James
(1940) Fox
German director Lang was a bold choice for the sequel to Fox's popular *Jesse James* (1939), but the result is a classic of the genre. Lang's first color film, and his first Western, stars Fonda as the notorious outlaw Jesse James's brother Frank, who has returned to his farm after Jesse's killing by the Ford brothers. When he hears that the Fords have been pardoned, Fonda sets out with Cooper to administer a little justice of his own. Tierney makes her debut as a reporter who gets the story from the legend himself. **Cast:** Henry Fonda, Jackie Cooper, Gene Tierney, John Carradine, J. Edward Bromberg, Donald Meek, Eddie Collins, George Barbier, Ernest Whitman. **Credits:** Dir: Fritz Lang; Prod: Kenneth MacGowan; Writer: Sam Hellman; DP: George Barnes, William V. Skall; Ed: Walter Thompson;

Composer: David Buttolph; Art Director: Richard Day, Wiard Ihnen. Color, 92 min. **VHS, LASER**

Return of the Bad Men
(1948) RKO
The sequel to *Badman's Territory* (1946) features the same fanciful premise, as Ryan assembles a gang of criminal superstars, including the Youngers, the Daltons, Billy the Kid, the Arkansas Kid, and Wild Bill Doolin, to rampage through the Oklahoma Territory. Scott stands between the gang and anarchy with support from sidekick Hayes and reformed lady gunslinger Jeffreys. This features all the Western clichés, but given such an enthusiastic reading it's hard to resist. **Cast:** Randolph Scott, Robert Ryan, Anne Jeffreys, George "Gabby" Hayes, Jacqueline White, Jason Robards, Tom Keene, Robert Bray. **Credits:** Dir: Ray Enright; Prod: Nat Holt; Writer: Jack Natteford; DP: J. Roy Hunt; Ed: Samuel E. Beetley; Composer: Paul Sawtell; Art Director: Albert S. D'Agostino. B&W, 90 min. **VHS**

The Return of the Pink Panther
(1974) United Artists
After Alan Arkin took over the title role in *Inspector Clouseau* (1968) under Bud Yorkin's direction, Sellers returns to star in the comedy series that he made famous in a sequel written and directed by series originator Edwards. The bumbling inspector dashs around Europe on the trail of a retired jewel thief (Plummer) who is suspected in a rash of robberies. The innocent thief is as anxious to solve the crime as Sellers. A return to form for the series. **Cast:** Peter Sellers, Christopher Plummer, Catherine Schell, Herbert Lom, Peter Arne, Burt Kwouk, Andre Maranne, Gregoire Aslan, Peter Jeffrey. **Credits:** Dir: Blake Edwards; Prod: Blake Edwards; Writer: Frank Waldman, Blake Edwards; DP: Geoffrey Unsworth; Ed: Tom Priestley; Composer: Henry Mancini; Art Director: Peter Mullins. Color, 113 min. **VHS, LASER**

Return of the Texan
(1952) Fox
When Robertson's wife dies, the Texas native flees the city with his father (Brennan) and sons, and heads back to the family ranch. The men build up the neglected ranch under the suspicious eye of wealthy rancher Boone. Robertson finds a new love interest in Dru as the family adjusts to their new surroundings. A fine family

drama. **Cast:** Dale Robertson, Joanne Dru, Walter Brennan, Richard Boone, Tom Tully, Robert Horton, Helen Westcott, Lonnie Thomas, Dennis Ross, Robert Adler. **Credits:** Dir: Howard Bretherton; Prod: Sam Bischoff; Writer: Dudley Nichols; Story: Fred Gipson; DP: Lucien Ballard; Ed: Louis Loeffler; Composer: Lionel Newman; Art Director: Lyle Wheeler, Albert Hoysett. B&W, 88 min.

Return to Peyton Place
(1961) Fox
The sequel to the popular potboiler that became a long-running soap opera mirrors author Grace Metalious's own experiences after her roman à clef was published. In this outing, young author Lynley faces cold shoulders in her hometown after her book, which reveals the petty gossip and backbiting that infest a small New England town, is published. Worse, her father (Sterling) loses his job. Meanwhile, not much has changed, as a meddling mother (Astor) interferes in her son's happy marriage, rape victim Weld struggles with intimacy with her boyfriend, and even Lynley must make a decision about her own adulterous affair. **Cast:** Carol Lynley, Tuesday Weld, Jeff Chandler, Eleanor Parker, Mary Astor, Robert Sterling, Brett Halsey, Luciana Paluzzi, Gunnar Hellstrom, Bob Crane. **Credits:** Dir: Jose Ferrer; Prod: Jerry Wald; Writer: Ronald Alexander; DP: Charles G. Clarke; Ed: David Bretherton; Composer: Franz Waxman; Art Director: Jack Martin Smith. Color, 123 min. **VHS**

Reunion in France
(1942) MGM
Crawford meets Wayne in a story set in a rather glamorous Nazi-occupied Paris. Wealthy Parisienne Crawford lives in splendor and prepares to marry her industrial-designer boyfriend Dorn. Their idyll gets interrupted by the Nazi invasion, and Crawford begins to suspect Dorn is a collaborator. Disillusioned and forced into a cramped apartment, Crawford's patriotism surfaces. She gets to exercise her new commitment when she shelters downed RAF flier Wayne, and the two begin to fall in love. When she turns in desperation to her old flame, she discovers he's actually an important member of the Resistance. **Cast:** John Wayne, Joan Crawford, Philip Dorn, Reginald Owen, Albert Basserman, John Carradine, Anne Ayars, J. Edward Bromberg. **Credits:** Dir: Jules Dassin; Prod: Joseph L.

Mankiewicz; Writer: Jan Lustig, Marvin Borowsky; DP: Robert Planck; Ed: Elmo Veron; Prod Design: Cedric Gibbons; Composer: Franz Waxman. B&W, 100 min. **VHS**

Revenge of the Pink Panther
(1978) United Artists
By the fifth installment, the Pink Panther series gets a little winded, but there are laughs to be found anytime Sellers is in the cast. This time out, the bumbling inspector travels the world to track down the narcotics ring that tried to assassinate him. Sellers's supposed death allows him to pursue his quarry to Hong Kong incognito. **Cast:** Peter Sellers, Herbert Lom, Dyan Cannon, Robert Webber, Burt Kwouk, Paul Stewart, Robert Loggia, Graham Stark. **Credits:** Dir: Blake Edwards; Prod: Blake Edwards; Writer: Frank Waldman; DP: Ernest Day; Ed: Alan Jones; Prod Design: Peter Mullins; Composer: Henry Mancini. Color, 100 min. **VHS, LASER**

Rhapsody
(1954) MGM
A soapy romance with a classical music backdrop, and a stunningly beautiful Taylor in the lead. Taylor plays the muse first for a devoted violinist (Gassman) and then a pianist (Ericson), whom she marries when she can't distract Gassman from his scales. When she tries to win back Gassman's affections, he rejects her and then wants her back again after she's proved her devotion to her pianist husband. Ericson's parts are played by maestro Claudio Arrau. **Cast:** Elizabeth Taylor, Vittorio Gassman, John Ericson, Louis Calhern, Michael Chekhov, Barbara Bates, Richard Hageman, Richard Lupino. **Credits:** Dir: Charles Vidor; Prod: Lawrence Weingarten; Writer: Fay Kanin, Michael Kanin, Ruth Goetz, Augustus Goetz; DP: Robert Planck; Ed: John Dunning; Prod Design: Cedric Gibbons; Composer: Bronislau Kaper, Pyotr Tchaikovsky, Sergey Rachmaninoff, Franz Liszt. Color, 115 min. **VHS**

Rhapsody in Blue
(1945) Warner Bros.
This is the life of George Gershwin presented in a glossy Hollywood version whose main attribute is the subject's immortal music. The Gershwin brothers rise from the Lower East Side of New York to international acclaim with all the standard stumbles and triumphs. Levant outshines the rest of the cast, including young Alda in his

second screen appearance. Academy Award Nominations: Best Sound Recording; Best Scoring of a Musical Picture. **Cast:** Robert Alda, Joan Leslie, Alexis Smith, Oscar Levant, Charles Coburn, Julie Bishop, Albert Basserman, Morris Carnovsky, Herbert Rudley, Rosemary De Camp. **Credits:** Dir: Irving Rapper; Prod: Jesse L. Lasky; Writer: Howard Koch, Elliot Paul; DP: Sol Polito; Ed: Folmar Blangsted; Composer: George Gershwin; Art Director: John Hughes. B&W, 142 min. **VHS, LASER**

Rhubarb
(1951) Paramount
In a whimsical farce based on H. Allen Smith's popular comic novel, Lockhart, an eccentric millionaire, adopts Rhubarb, a snarling alley cat who impresses the tycoon with his spirit and pluck. He names Rhubarb the primary beneficiary of his will, making the cat a multimillionaire and owner of his Brooklyn baseball club upon his death. With Rhubarb as mascot, the team starts winning, so when gamblers betting against Brooklyn catnap the tom, Milland, the cat's caretaker and the team press agent, mobilizes the fans. **Cast:** Ray Milland, Jan Sterling, Gene Lockhart, Taylor Holmes, Elsie Holmes, William Frawley, Willard Waterman, Henry Slate, Jim Hayward, Anthony Redecki. **Credits:** Dir: Arthur Lubin; Prod: William Perlberg, George Seaton; Writer: Dorothy Davenport, Francis M. Cockrell, H. Allen Smith; DP: Lionel Lindon; Ed: Alma Macrorie; Prod Design: Hal Pereira; Composer: Van Cleave; Art Director: Henry Bumstead. B&W, 95 min.

Rhythm on the Range
(1936) Paramount
Bing plays a singing cowboy who corrals a society dame (Farmer) fleeing a bad marriage on his way back to his ranch from a rodeo at Madison Square Garden. His buddy Burns romances Raye. When Farmer gets kidnapped, the crooner and his sidekick save the day. The songs in Bing's first of only two Westerns include "I'm an Old Cowhand," "Empty Saddles," and "If You Can't Sing It, You'll Have to Swing It." Raye's screen debut. **Cast:** Bing Crosby, Frances Farmer, Martha Raye, Bob Burns, Samuel S. Hinds, Lucille Gleason, Warren Hymer, George E. Stone. **Credits:** Dir: Norman Taurog; Prod: Benjamin Glazer; Writer: John C. Moffitt; DP: Karl Struss; Ed: Ellsworth Hoagland; Prod Design: Hans Dreier; Composer: Boris Morros. B&W, 88 min. **VHS**

Rhythm on the River
(1940) Paramount
Paramount followed Crosby's success with *Rhythm on the Range* with this backstage musical romance about two songwriters (Crosby and Martin) who meet when hired to assist famous songwriter Rathbone. Rathbone's blocked and needs tunes for a new Broadway show, but Crosby and Martin decide to go it alone. They become a hit when Rathbone uses a love song they wrote for each other. The songs include "Only Forever," "When the Moon Rises over Madison Square," "Rhythm on the River," and "Ain't It a Shame About Mame." Billy Wilder had a hand in the story. Academy Award Nomination: Best Song ("Only Forever"). **Cast:** Bing Crosby, Mary Martin, Basil Rathbone, Oscar Levant, William Frawley, Oscar Shaw, Charley Grapewin, Jeanne Cagney. **Credits:** Dir: Victor Schertzinger; Prod: William LeBaron; Writer: Dwight Taylor; DP: Ted Tetzlaff; Ed: Hugh Bennett; Prod Design: Hans Dreier; Composer: Victor Young. B&W, 94 min. **VHS**

Richest Girl in the World
(1934) RKO
In a witty romantic comedy with Hopkins a millionairess who wants assurance that a man will marry her for her personal allure and not her money, the rich girl switches roles with her secretary (Wray) and becomes smitten with McCrea. Academy Award Nomination: Best Original Screenplay. **Cast:** Miriam Hopkins, Joel McCrea, Fay Wray, Henry Stephenson, Reginald Denny, George Meeker, Wade Boteler, Fred Howard, Herbert Bunston, Burr McIntosh. **Credits:** Dir: William A. Seiter; Prod: Pandro S. Berman; Writer: Norman Krasna; DP: Nicholas Musuraca; Ed: George Crone; Composer: Max Steiner. B&W, 76 min.

Rich Kids
(1979) United Artists
A 12-year-old girl (Alvarado) gets advice from a brainy friend (Levy) as her parents (Lithgow and Walker) drift toward divorce. A thoughtful, provocative look at divorce from the kid's point of view. Robert Altman executive produced. **Cast:** John Lithgow, Kathryn Walker, Trini Alvarado, Jeremy Levy, Terry Kiser, David Selby, Roberta Maxwell, Paul Dooley. **Credits:** Dir: Robert M. Young; Prod: George W. George, Michael Hausman; Writer: Judith Ross; DP: Ralf D. Bode; Ed: Edward Beyer; Composer: Craig Doerge; Art Director: David Mitchell. Color, 101 min. **VHS**

Ride in the Whirlwind

(1967) Favorite

This is an oddball low-budget Western, but interesting as it's written, produced, and stars Nicholson and directed by cult favorite Hellman. Nicholson and two fellow cowboys get mixed up in crime when they stop at Stanton's cabin to rest. When a posse shows up, they make a run for it, but Nicholson ends up killing a man and becoming the outlaw he was mistaken for at the outset. Shot in six weeks concurrent with Hellman's *The Shooting.* Roger Corman executive produced both. **Cast:** Jack Nicholson, Cameron Mitchell, Millie Perkins, Harry Dean Stanton, Katherine Squire, George Mitchell, Brandon Carroll, Rupert Crosse. **Credits:** Dir: Monte Hellman; Prod: Monte Hellman, Jack Nicholson; Writer: Jack Nicholson; DP: Gregory Sandor; Ed: Monte Hellman; Composer: Robert Drasnin. Color, 83 min. **VHS, LASER**

Riders of Destiny

(1933) Monogram

In his first Western for Monogram, Wayne plays a Secret Service agent sent on a mission to help ranchers whose water supply is threatened by a gang of crooks. He's a singing agent, mind you, but when he and legendary stuntman Canutt tangle, he cuts out the musical foolishness. Writer and director Bradbury was cowboy star Bob Steele's father. **Cast:** John Wayne, Cecilia Parker, George "Gabby" Hayes, Forrest Taylor, Earl Dwire, Al St. John, Heinie Conklin, Lafe McKee, Yakima Canutt. **Credits:** Dir: Robert N. Bradbury; Prod: Paul Malvern; Writer: Robert N. Bradbury; DP: Archie Stout; Ed: Carl Pierson. B&W, 55 min. **VHS**

Ride the Pink Horse

(1947) Universal

Actor and occasional director Montgomery presents a film noir written by Hecht and Lederer, and produced by Hitchcock collaborator Harrison. Montgomery stars as a blackmailer who goes to a New Mexico resort in search of a crime boss (Clark). The FBI agent tailing him wants the evidence Montgomery's going to use against Clark, but he's intent on his scheme even after being beaten by Clark's goons. Montgomery gets revenge, and the agent kills the gangster in a shoot-out in which the blackmailer nearly loses his life, too. Montgomery also directed *The Lady in the Lake* (1946). Academy Award Nomination: Best Supporting Actor: Thomas Gomez. **Cast:** Robert Montgomery, Thomas Gomez, Andrea King, Fred Clark, Rita Conde, Iris Flores, Wanda Hendrix, Grandon Rhodes, Tito Renaldo, Richard Gaines. **Credits:** Dir: Robert Montgomery; Prod: Joan Harrison; Writer: Ben Hecht, Charles Lederer; Story: Dorothy B. Hughes; DP: Russell Metty; Ed: Ralph Dawson; Composer: Frank Skinner; Art Director: Robert Boyle, Bernard Herzbrun. B&W, 101 min.

Ride the Wild Surf

(1964) Columbia

Here's a classic surfing flick with California boys Fabian, Hunter, and Brown taking their boards to Hawaii for the monster winter swells. They face the locals and 40-foot waves while romancing Eden, Fabares, and Hart. Excellent surf rock from Jan and Dean on the sound track. **Cast:** Fabian, Tab Hunter, Barbara Eden, Anthony Hayes, Shelley Fabares, Jim Mitchum, Peter Brown, Susan Hart. **Credits:** Dir: Don Taylor; Prod: Jo Napoleon, Art Napoleon; Writer: Art Napoleon, Jo Napoleon; DP: Joseph Biroc; Ed: Eda Warren, Howard Smith. Color, 101 min. **VHS**

Riding High

(1950) Paramount

Capra's remake of his own *Broadway Bill* (1934) finds Crosby maintaining his allegiance to his horse, despite jealous interference from fiancée Gray. Crosby lets Gray walk out, but the horse comes through with flying colors. Demarest and Hardy have funny bits. Crosby sings "Sunshine Cake," "We've Got a Sure Thing," and "The Horse Told Me." **Cast:** Bing Crosby, Oliver Hardy, Coleen Gray, Charles Bickford, William Demarest, Frances Gifford, Raymond Walburn, James Gleason. **Credits:** Dir: Frank Capra; Prod: Frank Capra; Writer: Robert Riskin, Melville Shavelson; DP: George Barnes; Ed: William Hornbeck; Prod Design: Hans Dreier; Composer: Victor Young. B&W, 112 min. **VHS, LASER**

Riffraff

(1935) MGM

Harlow and Tracy star in this rough-and-tumble romance between a gutsy cannery gal and a two-fisted fisherman. When Tracy's agitation for a strike gets him kicked out of the fishermen's union, he hits the skids. Harlow gets money for him by stealing and gets sent to jail, where she gives birth to their child. Tracy gets his position back by foiling a sabotage attempt and waits for his wife's release. Note the collaboration between the top women writers of the day, Marion and Loos. **Cast:** Jean Harlow, Spencer Tracy, Una Merkel, Joseph Calleia, Victor Kilian, Mickey Rooney, J. Farrell MacDonald, Roger Imhof. **Credits:** Dir: J. Walter Ruben; Prod: Irving Thalberg; Writer: Frances Marion, Anita Loos, H. W. Haneman; DP: Ray June; Ed: Frank Sullivan; Prod Design: Cedric Gibbons; Composer: Edward Ward. B&W, 94 min. **VHS**

Riffraff

(1947) RKO

Tetzlaff, the DP for Hitchcock's *Notorious* (1946) and *The Enchanted Cottage* (1945), steps to the director's chair for this action adventure about O'Brien's attempt to find a map that will foil a takeover of Panamanian oil fields by Slezak. **Cast:** Pat O'Brien, Anne Jeffreys, Walter Slezak, Jason Robards, Percy Kilbride, Jerome Cowan, George Givot, Julian Rivero. **Credits:** Dir: Ted Tetzlaff; Prod: Nat Holt; Writer: Martin Rackin; DP: George E. Diskant; Ed: Philip Martin; Composer: Roy Webb; Art Director: Albert S. D'Agostino. B&W, 80 min. **VHS, LASER**

Right Cross

(1950) MGM

Montalban stars as a Mexican-American boxer who fears that prejudice will harm his career and damage his relationship with his trainer (Barrymore) and his girlfriend (Allyson), Barrymore's daughter. To show he can provide for Allyson, Montalban takes on a series of questionable bouts, and then damages his main asset, his right hand, in a fight with a sportswriter (Powell). After losing his title, Montalban regains Allyson's affections. Look for an early bit part by Monroe. **Cast:** June Allyson, Dick Powell, Ricardo Montalban, Lionel Barrymore, Teresa Celli, Barry Kelly, Marilyn Monroe. **Credits:** Dir: John Sturges; Prod: Armand Deutsch; Writer: Charles Schnee; DP: Norbert Brodine; Ed: James Newcom; Prod Design: Cedric Gibbons, James Scognamillo; Composer: David Raksin. B&W, 90 min.

The Ring

(1952) United Artists

A Mexican-American (Rios) from the streets of L.A. takes to the boxing ring after prejudice bars him from a decent job outside the fight game. Though his family objects, he's determined to succeed in order to provide for his girlfriend (Moreno). When he takes a beating in a championship bout, Rios faces the battle on the other side of the ropes. **Cast:** Rita Moreno, Lalo Rios, Jack Elam, Gerald Mohr, Art Aragon, Pepe Hern, Peter Brocco, Martin Garralaga. **Credits:** Dir: Kurt Neumann; Prod: Maurice King, Herman King, Frank King; Writer: Irving Shulman; DP: Russell Harlan; Ed: Bruce Pierce. B&W, 92 min. VHS

Rings on Her Fingers
(1942) Fox
In this wisecracking romantic comedy, con artists (Cregar and Byington) enlist the aid of first-time crook Tierney to divest a heap of cash from a handy sucker. When a simple-seeming accountant (Fonda) shows up with his hard-earned savings in search of the yacht he's been dreaming of his whole life, Tierney's sent to entice him away from his money. But Fonda's not the simpleton he seems and Tierney's not the crook she might be; their new romance survives the con artists dangling a real millionaire under Tierney's nose. **Cast:** Henry Fonda, Gene Tierney, Laird Cregar, John Shepherd, Spring Byington, Frank Orth, Henry Stephenson, Marjorie Gateson, George Lessey, Iris Adrian. **Credits:** Dir: Rouben Mamoulian; Prod: Milton Sperling; Writer: Ken Englund; Story: Robert Pirosh, Joseph Schrank; DP: George Barnes; Ed: Barbara McLean; Prod Design: Richard Day, Albert Hogsett; Composer: Cyril Mockridge, Alfred Newman. B&W, 86 min.

Rio Bravo
(1959) Warner Bros.
Reportedly director Hawks and star Wayne were so put off by *High Noon* (1952) and the Cooper character's requests for help from the townspeople that they filmed this rough-and-tumble Western in rebuttal. It is, in any case, a terrific story, and features themes and characters that Hawks used again in *El Dorado* (1967) and *Rio Lobo* (1970). No-nonsense Texas bordertown sheriff Wayne arrests the bullying cattle baron (Akins) who dominates the town for murder, though he knows Akins's men will come after their boss. Wayne gets little help from Martin, his deputy, who's become a hopeless drunk, and Brennan, an old man who's little more than a mascot. When wagon-train boss Bond shows up with a gunslinging Nelson in tow, Wayne first resists Nelson's help. But when Akins's men shoot Bond, Nelson joins the fray. Martin straightens up, Nelson proves his mettle, and the Duke and Brennan flush out the bad guys with an explosive climactic gunfight. Wayne even gets the girl, saloon

singer Dickinson. **Cast:** John Wayne, Dean Martin, Angie Dickinson, Ricky Nelson, Walter Brennan, Ward Bond, John Russell, Claude Akins. **Credits:** Dir: Howard Hawks; Prod: Howard Hawks; Writer: Jules Furthman, Leigh Brackett; DP: Russell Harlan; Ed: Folmar Blangsted; Composer: Dimitri Tiomkin; Art Director: Leo K. Kuter. Color, 141 min. VHS, LASER

Rio Conchos
(1964) Fox
A U.S. cavalry captain (Whitman) arrests Boone with a stolen rifle, and turns him into an ally against O'Brien, a Confederate sympathizer who's determined to reignite the Civil War by giving the stolen weapons to the Apaches. Brown's first screen appearance. **Cast:** Richard Boone, Stuart Whitman, Edmond O'Brien, Anthony Franciosa, Jim Brown, Wende Wagner, Warner Anderson, Rodolfo Acosta. **Credits:** Dir: Gordon Douglas; Prod: David Weisbart; Writer: Joseph Landon, Clair Huffaker; DP: Joseph MacDonald; Ed: Joseph Silver; Composer: Jerry Goldsmith; Art Director: William J. Creber. Color, 107 min. VHS

Rio Grande
(1950) Republic
The third entry in Ford's "Cavalry Trilogy" finds Wayne the commander of a Western fort. When his son (Jarman) gets assigned to his command, Wayne's estranged wife (O'Hara) follows. After 15 years' separation, caused by Wayne's refusal to disobey orders that he burn down O'Hara's family's plantation, Wayne courts his wife again as he tries to instill his feeling for the military in his son. After a wagon train leading women and children to safety is attacked by Indians, Jarman proves his courage and ability to his father. A stirring portrait by Ford of the men who made the southwest safe, and the sense of duty that kept them at their hard, hazardous profession. This was Wayne and O'Hara's first pairing and they were clearly meant for each other, making five films together. The 45th anniversary video edition includes a special program, "The Making of Rio Grande," hosted by Leonard Maltin. **Cast:** John Wayne, Maureen O'Hara, Ben Johnson, Chill Wills, Claude Jarman, Harry Carey, Jr., J. Carrol Naish, Victor McLaglen. **Credits:** Dir: John Ford; Prod: John Ford, Merian C. Cooper; Writer: James Kevin McGuinness; DP: Bert Glennon; Ed: Jack Murray; Prod Design: Frank Hotaling; Composer: Victor Young. B&W, 105 min. VHS, LASER, DVD

Rio Lobo
(1970) National General
Hawks's final outing doesn't stand comparison to his best, but it boasts an easygoing performance by Wayne. After the Civil War, former Union officer Wayne hooks up with two ex-Confederates to track a stolen shipment of gold. Their search leads to a town under the thumb of a rotten lawman. Wayne and company demonstrate how to liberate the town. Look for studio executive Lansing in her screen-ingenue days. **Cast:** John Wayne, Jennifer O'Neill, Jorge Rivero, Jack Elam, Victor French, Susana Dosamantes, Christopher Mitchum, Mike Henry, Sherry Lansing. **Credits:** Dir: Howard Hawks; Prod: Howard Hawks; Writer: Burton Wohl, Leigh Brackett; DP: William H. Clothier; Ed: John Woodcock; Composer: Jerry Goldsmith; Art Director: Robert Smith. Color, 114 min. VHS, LASER

Riot in Cell Block 11
(1954) Allied Artists
Siegel's hard-hitting entry in the prison-movie genre was shot on location in Folsom Prison, and it succeeds with a documentary-like feel in building suspense and action without sentimentalizing the prisoners or turning the authorities into stereotypes. Brand leads a revolt in his cell block when he can longer abide the conditions and the treatment by the guards. He accomplishes the first stage of the uprising with the fists of Gordon, but his accomplice is a pathological criminal who has no interest in Brand's agenda. The prison riot spreads to other cell blocks as Brand tries to negotiate with a sympathetic warden (Meyer) and keep Gordon under control. Producer Wanger had done time in a California work farm when he fired at his wife's agent for disrupting his home. **Cast:** Neville Brand, Leo Gordon, Emile Meyer, Frank Faylen, Paul Frees, Don Keefer, Alvy Moore, Dabbs Greer. **Credits:** Dir: Don Siegel; Prod: Walter Wanger; Writer: Richard Collins; DP: Russell Harlan; Ed: Bruce B. Pierce; Prod Design: Robert Priestley; Composer: Herschel Burke Gilbert. B&W, 80 min. VHS

Riptide
(1934) MGM
Shearer portrays an American romantic adventuress who snares an English lord (Marshall). Their marriage is threatened when an old boyfriend (Montgomery) turns up at a society event while Marshall is in the States on business. Montgomery's amorous

misadventure leads to a separation until Shearer and Marshall renew their vows. A rare chance to see English stage diva Mrs. Patrick Campbell. **Cast:** Norma Shearer, Robert Montgomery, Herbert Marshall, Mrs. Patrick Campbell, Skeets Gallagher, Ralph Forbes, Lilyan Tashman, Helen Jerome Eddy, Art Jarrett. **Credits:** Dir: Edmund Goulding; Prod: Irving Thalberg; Writer: Edmund Goulding; DP: Ray June; Ed: Margaret Booth; Prod Design: Edwin B. Willis; Art Director: Alexander Toluboff. B&W, 90 min. **VHS**

The Rise and Fall of Legs Diamond
(1960) Warner Bros.
Boetticher takes a turn at the crime genre with this study of brutal gangster Legs Diamond (Danton). Danton makes his way from petty thief to bodyguard for the head of a mob to control of the bootlegging rackets in New York. Along the way, he kills his associates, lets his brother (Oates) die alone and poor, and ignores his wife (Steele) until she leaves him. Finally alone in the world, the old-style gangster is eliminated by the new Italian syndicate. Academy Award Nomination for Best (Black-and-White) Costume Design. **Cast:** Ray Danton, Karen Steele, Elaine Stewart, Jesse White, Simon Oakland, Robert Lowery, Warren Oates, Sid Melton. **Credits:** Dir: Budd Boetticher; Prod: Milton Sperling; Writer: Joseph Landon; DP: Lucien Ballard; Ed: Folmar Blangsted; Composer: Leonard Rosenman; Art Director: Jack Poplin. B&W, 101 min. **VHS, LASER**

The Ritz Brothers
The Ritz Brothers were actually the Brooklyn- and New Jersey–raised Joachim brothers—Al, Jimmy, and Harry. The fourth brother, George, served as their agent. The popular vaudeville song-and-dance men made their big-screen debut in the two-reel comedy *Hotel Anchovy* (1934) and made their feature debut in *Sing, Baby, Sing* (1936). Their popularity earned them a starring vehicle for their zany antics, *Life Begins in College* (1937), and a lucrative deal with 20th Century-Fox. But the brothers' egos soured their relationship with Fox, and soon after their best outing—*The Three Musketeers* (1939), a surprisingly faithful adaptation of Alexander Dumas's novel in which Don Ameche played D'Artagnan—Fox terminated the association. Universal signed the team and produced a series of low-budget, campy musicals

with thin plots contrived solely to showcase the Ritzes' shtick. The Andrews Sisters made their big-screen debut in *Argentine Nights* (1940). The Ritz Brothers continued to entertain in nightclubs and on early television variety shows; their act ended with Al's death in 1965. Watch for brother Harry in *Silent Movie* (1976).

Sing, Baby, Sing *(1936)*
One in a Million *(1936)*
Life Begins in College *(1937)*
You Can't Have Everything *(1937)*
On the Avenue *(1937)*
The Goldwyn Follies *(1938)*
Straight, Place and Show *(1938)*
Kentucky Moonshine *(1938)*
Pack Up Your Troubles *(1939)*
The Three Musketeers *(1939)*
The Gorilla *(1939)*
Argentine Nights *(1940)*
Behind the Eight Ball *(1942)*
Never a Dull Moment *(1943)*
Hi'ya, Chum *(1943)*

River of No Return
(1954) Fox
This rousing Western, and Preminger's only outing in the genre, pairs an amiable Monroe and Mitchum. On his way back to his farm in the Canadian Rockies after serving a prison term for a killing, Mitchum gathers up his son (Rettig) and takes note of the saloon singer (Monroe) who had befriended the boy. When he later saves Monroe and her gambler boyfriend (Calhoun), he gets a gun butt in the head for his bravery but also the admiration of Monroe. After facing off with Calhoun once more, Mitchum claims Monroe for good. Well-done and good fun. **Cast:** Robert Mitchum, Marilyn Monroe, Rory Calhoun, Tommy Rettig, Murvyn Vye, Douglas Spencer, Don Beddoe, Edmund Cobb. **Credits:** Dir: Otto Preminger; Prod: Stanley Rubin; Writer: Frank Fenton; DP: Joseph La Shelle; Ed: Louis Loeffler; Prod Design: Lyle Wheeler; Choreographer: Jack Cole; Composer: Cyril J. Mockridge. Color, 91 min. **VHS, LASER**

The River's Edge
(1957) Fox
Milland steals a million dollars and beats it for the Mexican border. Knowing he needs a way to evade the border crossings, he coerces Quinn, his former girlfriend's (Paget) husband and a rugged outdoorsman, to guide him over the rough terrain. When Milland kills an old prospector, Quinn and Paget realize what a desperate situation they're in and struggle to free themselves. One of cinema veteran

Dwan's final films. **Cast:** Ray Milland, Anthony Quinn, Debra Paget, Chubby Johnson, Harry Carey, Jr., Byron Foulger, Tom McKee, Frank Gerstle. **Credits:** Dir: Allan Dwan; Prod: Benedic Burgeaus; Writer: Harold Jacob Smith, James Leicester; DP: Harold Lipstein; Ed: James Leicester; Composer: Louis Forbes, Bobby Troup. Color, 87 min.

The Road Back
(1937) Universal
Director Whale reportedly created a searing sequel to the antiwar classic *All Quiet on the Western Front* (1930), but the studio at the last minute decided to tone down the antiwar sentiments in an unsuccessful attempt to have a ban on the film lifted by Nazi Germany. What remains follows the surviving characters from the platoon in *All Quiet* as they attempt to adjust to life in defeated Germany. Summerville manages to calm a mob bent on looting a shop owned by his town's mayor (earning the hand of the mayor's daughter), and Murphy kills the war profiteer who's been dallying with his wife. The ending reveals another generation of young boys playing at war as they goose-step across the schoolyard. An intriguing cinematic might-have-been. **Cast:** Andy Devine, Barbara Read, Louise Fazenda, Noah Beery, Maurice Murphy, Lionel Atwill, Larry J. Blake, John Emery, Richard Cromwell, John King, Slim Summerville. **Credits:** Dir: James Whale; Prod: Edmund Grainger; Writer: R. C. Sherriff; DP: John J. Mescall; Ed: Ted J. Kent; Prod Design: Charles D. Hall; Composer: Dimitri Tiomkin. B&W, 97 min.

Road House
(1948) Fox
This famously perverse film noir stars Lupino as the singer who comes between two friends, roadhouse owner Widmark and his manager, Wilde. Lupino takes a shine to Wilde, but Widmark becomes obsessed with her. When Wilde finally gives in to Lupino (to Holm's distress), Widmark stages a robbery that implicates Wilde and has him released into his custody where he can tempt Wilde with Lupino and to make a run for his freedom. Wilde makes a break for it, and Widmark hunts him down, but Lupino takes aim at Widmark. **Cast:** Ida Lupino, Cornel Wilde, Celeste Holm, Richard Widmark, O. Z. Whitehead, Robert Karnes, Edward Chodorov, Ian MacDonald. **Credits:** Dir: Jean Negulesco; Prod: Edward Chodorov; Writer:

Edward Chodorov; Story: Margaret Gruen, Oscar Saul; DP: Joseph La Shelle; Ed: James B. Clark; Prod Design: Lyle Wheeler; Composer: Cyril J. Mockridge. B&W, 95 min. VHS

Road Show

(1941) United Artists
Menjou has been put in a mental institution against his will, so he and eccentric millionaire Hubbard take off and hook up with a broken-down carnival run by Landis. Note the writing credit for silent comedian Langdon. **Cast:** Adolphe Menjou, Carole Landis, John Hubbard, Patsy Kelly, Charles Butterworth, George E. Stone, Polly Ann Young, Edward Norris, Marjorie Woodworth. **Credits:** Dir: Hal Roach; Prod: Hal Roach; Writer: Arnold Belgard, Harry Langdon, Mickell Novak; DP: Norbert F. Brodine; Ed: Bert Jordan; Composer: George Stoll; Art Director: Charles D. Hall. B&W, 87 min. VHS

Road to Bali

(1952) Paramount
The sixth "Road" movie, and the only one in color, finds Hope and Crosby on the run from some angry fathers in Australia. They hook up with a sea captain who transports them to Bali, where they encounter the lovely Lamour in her sarong. Lots of cameos (including Humphrey Bogart and Dean Martin and Jerry Lewis) as the boys sing, clown, and fight off wild natives, jungle creatures, and Russell. **Cast:** Bob Hope, Bing Crosby, Dorothy Lamour, Murvyn Vye, Jane Russell, Peter Coe, Ralph Moody, Leon Askin. **Credits:** Dir: Hal Walker; Prod: Harry Tugend; Writer: Frank Butler; DP: George Barnes; Ed: Archie Marshek; Prod Design: Hal Pereira; Composer: Joseph J. Lilley. Color, 91 min. VHS

Road to Glory

(1936) Fox
Hawks and author William Faulkner constructed this WWI drama from a celebrated French WWI film, *Wooden Crosses*. French commander Baxter struggles with the horrors of war and the loss of his fellow soldiers, coping with the help of a steady ration of liquor. His situation worsens when Barrymore, his father and the oldest enlisted man in the army, enters his regiment, and when junior officer March becomes a rival for the attention of nurse Lang. **Cast:** Fredric March, Warner Baxter, Lionel Barrymore, June Lang, Gregory Ratoff, Victor Kilian. **Credits:** Dir: Howard Hawks; Prod: Darryl F. Zanuck; Writer: William Faulkner, Joel Sayre; DP: Gregg

Toland; Ed: Edward Curtiss; Prod Design: Thomas Little; Composer: Louis Silvers. B&W, 103 min.

The Road to Hong Kong

(1962) United Artists
The last of the "Road" movies has an updated, space-age plot. Aging vaudevillians Hope and Crosby give up the road for a confidence scam, do-it-yourself spaceships. While being chased by the cops, Hope loses his memory after a bump on the head (diagnosed by Peter Sellers). That leads to a monastery, a spy intrigue with Collins, hiding out with Lamour in Hong Kong, a trip to the moon and back, and a final space shot to a remote planet (where they encounter a Rat Pack beachhead established by Frank Sinatra and Dean Martin). As this was filmed in England, the usual cameos get augmented by British character actors. **Cast:** Bob Hope, Bing Crosby, Joan Collins, Dorothy Lamour, Robert Morley, Walter Gotell, Felix Aylmer, Peter Madden. **Credits:** Dir: Norman Panama; Prod: Melvin Frank; Writer: Norman Panama, Melvin Frank; DP: Jack Hildyard; Ed: Alan Osbiston, John Smith; Prod Design: Roger K. Furse; Composer: Robert Farnon; Art Director: Syd Cain. B&W, 92 min. VHS, LASER

Road to Morocco

(1942) Paramount
Third time's a charm for the "Road" series. The third entry is classic film comedy at its best, and the best of the series. Hope and Crosby aim at Arabian Nights fantasies, and the set pieces send up every cliché in the form. Shipwreck survivors Hope and Crosby hitch a ride on a wisecracking passing camel and head for Morocco where Bing sells Bob into slavery. It turns out to be love slavery as Crosby finds Hope in the lap of luxury, and Lamour's lap, as he awaits a royal marriage. Sheik Quinn has another idea. Wonderful fun with a snappy script, the usual asides, and cameos. Academy Award Nominations: Best Original Screenplay; Best Sound. **Cast:** Bing Crosby, Bob Hope, Dorothy Lamour, Vladimir Sokoloff, Dona Drake, Monte Blue, Yvonne De Carlo, Anthony Quinn, Jerry Colonna. **Credits:** Dir: David Butler; Prod: Paul Jones; Writer: Frank Butler; DP: William Mellor; Ed: Irene Morra; Prod Design: Hans Dreier; Composer: Victor Young. B&W, 83 min. VHS, DVD

Road to Rio

(1947) Paramount
The fifth in the "Road" series finds Hope and Crosby stowing away on a

southbound steamship after setting fire to the carnival in which they were working. Onboard, they notice Lamour, who is alternately inviting and indifferent. They discover that she's been hypnotized by her aunt into marrying a man she doesn't love. The boys find work in Rio with a trio, and crash Lamour's wedding just in time. Hope gets the girl in this one, with a little hocus-pocus of his own. Fewer set pieces, more plot, same riotous comedy. One of the best in the series. Academy Award Nomination for Best Scoring of a Musical Picture. **Cast:** Bob Hope, Bing Crosby, Dorothy Lamour, Gale Sondergaard, Frank Faylen, Joseph Vitale, Frank Puglia, Nestor Paiva. **Credits:** Dir: Norman Z. McLeod; Prod: Daniel Dare; Writer: Edmund Beloin, Jack Rose; DP: Ernest Laszlo; Ed: Ellsworth Hoagland; Prod Design: Hans Dreier, Earl Hedrick; Choreographer: Billy Daniel, Bernard Pearce; Composer: Robert Emmett Dolan. B&W, 100 min. VHS

Road to Singapore

(1940) Paramount
The first of the "Road" movies was a surprise success for Paramount, and started a seven-film series. Though the series picked up steam as it went along, this entry introduces the familiar characters. Crosby's the scion of Coburn's industrial empire, but the idle playboy doesn't want any part of desk duty, so he rounds up pal Hope for a journey to the other side of the planet. In Singapore, they rescue Lamour from a dangerous whip act (starring Quinn) and make her their housekeeper. As both fall in love with her, Lamour refuses to choose. **Cast:** Bing Crosby, Bob Hope, Dorothy Lamour, Charles Coburn, Judith Barrett, Anthony Quinn, Jerry Colonna, Johnny Arthur. **Credits:** Dir: Victor Schertzinger; Prod: Harlan Thompson; Writer: Don Hartman, Frank Butler; DP: William Mellor; Ed: Paul Weatherwax; Prod Design: Hans Dreier, Frank Odell; Composer: Victor Young. B&W, 84 min. VHS

Road to Utopia

(1946) Paramount
The fourth "Road" movie, and one of the most gag-filled, opens with old married couple Hope and Lamour comfortable in their mansion reminiscing about their past in the Yukon gold country. Vaudevillians Hope and Crosby escaped San Francisco on a steamer heading north, impersonating vicious killers and with a stolen mine deed in their pockets. Lamour, the daughter of the rightful owner and a

dance-hall singer, woos both to get her hands on the deed. Hope gets the girl, but their child looks like Bing! Humorist Robert Benchley narrates. Academy Award Nomination for Best Original Screenplay. **Cast:** Bob Hope, Bing Crosby, Dorothy Lamour, Hillary Brooke, Douglas Dumbrille, Jack LaRue, Robert Barrat, Nestor Paiva. **Credits:** Dir: Hal Walker; Prod: Paul Jones; Writer: Norman Panama, Melvin Frank; DP: Lionel Lindon; Ed: Stuart Gilmore; Prod Design: Hans Dreier; Composer: Leigh Harline; Art Director: Hans Dreier, Roland Anderson. B&W, 90 min. VHS, LASER, DVD

Road to Zanzibar
(1941) Paramount
The second "Road" movie takes on jungle epics with Hope and Crosby playing con men on the run after selling a worthless diamond mine. As they head toward Zanzibar, the boys run into Lamour and Merkel, who convince them to help rescue Lamour's brother. But Hope and Crosby discover they've been conned, and, worse, end up in a cannibal tribe's stewpot. **Cast:** Bing Crosby, Bob Hope, Dorothy Lamour, Una Merkel, Eric Blore, Iris Adrian, Lionel Royce, Buck Woods. **Credits:** Dir: Victor Schertzinger; Prod: Paul Jones; Writer: Frank Butler, Don Hartman; DP: Ted Tetzlaff; Ed: Alma Macrorie; Prod Design: Hans Dreier; Composer: Victor Young; Art Director: Robert Usher. B&W, 92 min. VHS

The Roaring Twenties
(1939) Warner Bros.
The summation of the Warner tough-guy gangster movies of the '30s depicts the entire Prohibition era in the rise and fall of three WWI doughboys. Cagney tries to return to the taxi business he loves, but gets involved in bootlegging. Bogart, an icy killer, first becomes a Cagney lieutenant, then ascends to the top of the rackets as Cagney becomes a down-and-outer. The third buddy (Lynn) first makes a mark as Cagney's attorney, then becomes a crusading D.A. When Lynn turns his investigators on Bogart, Cagney comes to the aid of the woman he still loves (Lane), though she's married to Lynn, and asks Bogart to spare Lynn's life. At the end of the climactic confrontation, both gangsters, the kingpin and the one "who used to be a big shot," die violent deaths. Walsh punctuates the decade with a brisk, brilliant look back at a lawless time that created the mythology of the gangster. **Cast:** James Cagney, Humphrey Bogart, Jeffrey

Lynn, Priscilla Lane, Frank McHugh, Paul Kelly, Elisabeth Risdon, Edward Keane, Joe Sawyer. **Credits:** Dir: Raoul Walsh, Anatole Litvak; Prod: Samuel Bischoff; Writer: Jerry Wald, Richard Macaulay, Robert Rossen; Story: Mark Hellinger; DP: Ernest Haller; Ed: Jack Killifer; Prod Design: Max Parker; Composer: Heinz Roemheld, Ray Heindorf. B&W, 106 min. VHS, LASER

The Robe
(1953) Fox
This is the biblical epic that introduced the world to CinemaScope and made Burton a star. As a Roman tribune who helps to crucify Christ, and who later converts to the new religion, Burton gives a marvelous performance. Christian influences enter Burton's life from both his Greek servant Mature, who witnesses the wonders worked by Christ's robe, and his wife (Simmons), and the callous soldier gains dignity and courage as he faces the wrath of emperor Caligula (Robinson). Golden Globe for Best Motion Picture, Drama. Academy Award Nominations: 5, including Best Picture; Best Actor: Richard Burton; Best Cinematography. **Academy Awards:** Best Costume Design (Color); Best Art Direction—Set Decoration (Color). **Cast:** Richard Burton, Jean Simmons, Victor Mature, Michael Rennie, Jay Robinson, Dean Jagger, Torin Thatcher, Richard Boone, Jeff Morrow, Ernest Thesiger. **Credits:** Dir: Henry Koster; Prod: Frank Ross; Writer: Philip Dunne; Story: Lloyd C. Douglas; DP: Leon Shamroy; Ed: Barbara McLean; Prod Design: Lyle Wheeler; Composer: Alfred Newman; Art Director: George Davis. Color, 135 min. VHS, LASER

Roberta
(1935) RKO
This overlooked Fred and Ginger gem adapted from the Broadway hit by Jerome Kern and Otto Harbach includes some of Kern's greatest songs, including "Smoke Gets in Your Eyes" and "Lovely to Look At." Astaire and Scott travel to Paris with their band, where they meet former Russian princess Dunne, now a famous fashion designer, and Astaire's old flame, Rogers, who's posing as a Polish countess. Lucille Ball has a bit in a fashion show sequence. Academy Award Nomination: Best Song ("Lovely to Look At"). **Cast:** Ginger Rogers, Fred Astaire, Irene Dunne, Randolph Scott, Helen Westley, Victor Varconi, Claire Dodd, Luis Alberni. **Credits:** Dir: William A.

Seiter; Prod: Pandro S. Berman; Writer: Jane Murfin, Sam Mintz, Allan Scott, Glenn Tryon; DP: Edward Cronjager; Ed: William Hamilton; Prod Design: Carroll Clark; Composer: Jerome Kern; Art Director: Van Nest Polglase. B&W, 106 min. VHS, LASER

Robin and the Seven Hoods
(1964) Warner Bros.
The Rat Pack assembles in Prohibition-era Chicago with Sinatra and Falk taking over Robinson's territory when the old mobster gets rubbed out. Martin hooks up with Sinatra's gang for a battle with Falk, and Rush, Robinson's daughter, gives Sinatra money to find her father's killers. Sinatra gives the money to Davis, who gives it to Crosby, who runs an orphanage. The publicity makes Sinatra the Robin Hood of Chicago. Everyone has a ring-a-ding time and the in-jokes fly. Douglas became Sinatra's choice director because his brisk shooting never held up the party. Academy Award Nominations: Best Song ("My Kind of Town"); Best Score. **Cast:** Frank Sinatra, Dean Martin, Bing Crosby, Sammy Davis, Jr., Peter Falk, Barbara Rush, Edward G. Robinson, Victor Buono. **Credits:** Dir: Gordon Douglas; Prod: Frank Sinatra; Writer: David R. Schwartz; DP: William Daniels; Ed: Sam O'Steen; Composer: Nelson Riddle; Art Director: Leroy Deane. Color, 123 min. VHS

Robin Hood
(1922) United Artists
This is the archetypal Fairbanks swashbuckler with the producer–silent idol building a magnificent castle set and then filling it with the grandest derring-do on-screen. As the Earl of Huntington, Fairbanks joins King Richard (Beery) on a crusade, but returns as Robin Hood when Prince John (De Grasse) threatens to usurp the throne. Terrific action and a dashing spirit make this a silent-era must-see. **Cast:** Douglas Fairbanks, Wallace Beery, Enid Bennett, Alan Hale, Sam De Grasse. **Credits:** Dir: Allan Dwan; Prod: Douglas Fairbanks; Writer: Lotta Woods; DP: Arthur Edeson; Ed: William Nolan; Prod Design: Wilfred Buckland, Irvin Martin; Costumes: Mitchell Leisen. B&W, 110 min. VHS

The Robin Hood of El Dorado
(1936) MGM
A peaceful farmer's wife is murdered by a band of desperadoes after the farmer (Baxter) refuses to abandon his land. The farmer, consumed by hate, becomes the leader of an outlaw gang. A moderately interesting Wellman

Western. **Cast:** Warner Baxter, Ann Loring, Bruce Cabot, Margo, J. Carrol Naish, Soledad Jiminez, Carlos De Valdez. **Credits:** Dir: William Wellman; Prod: John Considine; Writer: Walter Barnes, Joseph Calleia, Melvin Levy, William Wellman; DP: Chester A. Lyons; Ed: Robert J. Kern; Composer: Herbert Stothart; Costumes: Dolly Tree; Art Director: Gabriel Scognamillo, David Townsend. B&W, 84 min.

Rock-a-Bye Baby
(1958) Paramount
A Hollywood actress (Maxwell) due to star in a biblical epic delivers triplets following a one-day marriage to a Mexican bullfighter. Worried about her image, she leaves the babies on the doorstep of the goofy TV repairman (Lewis) who once loved her. Jerry marries Maxwell's sister (Stevens), and she delivers quints. Tashlin based his story on Preston Sturges's screenplay for *The Miracle of Morgan's Creek*. One of Lewis's better efforts. **Cast:** Jerry Lewis, Marilyn Maxwell, Connie Stevens, Salvatore Baccaloni, Reginald Gardiner, Hans Conried, Ida Moore, Gary Lewis, Judy Franklin, Isobel Elsom. **Credits:** Dir: Frank Tashlin; Prod: Jerry Lewis; Writer: Frank Tashlin; DP: Haskell B. Boggs; Ed: Alma Macrorie; Composer: Walter Scharf, Sammy Cahn, Harry Warren. Color, 95 min.

Rock, Rock, Rock
(1956) Distributors
Here is one of the better early rock-n-roll movies, featuring the era's best musical talent and Weld's screen debut. Weld raises money with a show that features terrific performances from Chuck Berry, La Vern Baker, and Frankie Lymon and the Teenagers (who sing the classic "I'm Not a Juvenile Delinquent"). **Cast:** Tuesday Weld, Chuck Berry, Alan Freed, Fats Domino, Frankie Lymon, Fran Manfred, Jack Collins, David Winters. **Credits:** Dir: Will Price; Prod: Milton Subotsky, Max Rosenberg; Writer: Milton Subotsky; DP: Morris Hartzband; Ed: Blandine Hafela. B&W, 78 min. **VHS**

Rocky
(1976) United Artists
This is the plucky crowd-pleaser that took courage and determination on Stallone's part to produce. While trying to make it as a screenwriter, the unknown Stallone created his famous character after watching the Ali-Wepner bout, and clearly drawing parallels with his own underdog status. He insisted on playing the lead, though offered much-needed cash to sell the script; he made the right choice, as Stallone's character and the movie became international sensations, touching the plucky underdog in every audience. Washed-up canvas-back Stallone gets the chance of a lifetime when cocky champion Weathers lets an unknown take a shot at his title. With his trainer Meredith and shy girlfriend Shire supporting him, Stallone hits the pavement to train for his moment of glory. Golden Globe for Best Motion Picture, Drama. Academy Award Nominations: 10, including Best Actor: Sylvester Stallone; Best Actress: Talia Shire; Best Supporting Actor: Burgess Meredith; Best Supporting Actor: Burt Young; Best (Original) Screenplay. **Academy Awards:** Best Picture; Best Director; Best Film Editing. **Cast:** Sylvester Stallone, Talia Shire, Burt Young, Burgess Meredith, Carl Weathers, Thayer David, Joe Spinell, Aldo Silvani, Frank Stallone, Joe Frazier. **Credits:** Dir: John Avildsen; Prod: Irwin Winkler, Robert Chartoff; Writer: Sylvester Stallone; DP: James Crabe; Ed: Richard Halsey, Scott Conrad; Prod Design: William Cassidy; Composer: Bill Conti; Costumes: Robert Cambel, Joanne Hutchinson. Color, 125 min. **VHS, LASER, DVD**

Rocky 2
(1979) United Artists
Stallone writes and directs himself in the sequel to the *Rocky* phenomenon. Stallone, now married to Shire and expecting a family, finds life outside the ring worrisome. He's been told that boxing risks his sight, but Shire goes into a coma while delivering their child. Stallone gets another shot at Weathers and proves his first showing was no fluke. Not up to the first, but still entertaining, with touching moments and great fight sequences. **Cast:** Sylvester Stallone, Talia Shire, Carl Weathers, Burgess Meredith, Burt Young, Tony Burton, Joe Spinell, Leonard Gaines. **Credits:** Dir: Sylvester Stallone; Prod: Irwin Winkler, Robert Chartoff; Writer: Sylvester Stallone; DP: Bill Butler; Ed: Danford B. Greene, Stanford C. Allen, Janice Hampton, James Symons; Composer: Bill Conti; Art Director: Richard Berger. Color, 120 min. **VHS, LASER, DVD**

The Rocky Horror Picture Show
(1975) Fox
This is the movie that started the midnight-screening madness in which audience members dress as their favorite characters and perform and sing-along with the action on-screen. A flat tire on a rainy night brings Bostwick and Sarandon to Dr. Frank N. Furter's castle on the night he is to unveil his latest creation—Rocky Horror, the ultimate, voraciously sexual being—to an audience of interplanetary transsexuals. Curry gives the good doctor a crazed good humor as the proceedings become increasingly decadent. The video release includes a prologue highlighting the *Rocky Horror* midnight-movie phenomenon and concludes with a new music video of "Time Warp." **Cast:** Barry Bostwick, Susan Sarandon, Tim Curry, Charles Gray, Richard O'Brien, Nell Campbell, Patricia Quinn, Meat Loaf, Jeremy Newson. **Credits:** Dir: Jim Sharman; Prod: Michael White, John Goldstone; Writer: Jim Sharman, Richard O'Brien; DP: Peter Suschitzky; Ed: Graeme Clifford; Prod Design: Brian Thomson; Composer: Richard O'Brien. Color, 106 min. **VHS, LASER**

Rogue Cop
(1954) MGM
A cop on the take (Taylor) from Mob boss Raft has a younger brother (Forrest), a rookie on the force, who won't look the other way after witnessing a Mob hit. Neither Taylor nor a bribe can convince the younger man to be silent, so Raft permanently silences him. Taylor then takes his revenge, though he knows he'll do time. An okay film noir. Academy Award Nomination: Best Cinematography. **Cast:** Robert Taylor, Janet Leigh, George Raft, Steve Forrest, Anne Francis, Robert F. Simon, Anthony Ross, Alan Hale, Jr., Peter Brocco, Robert Ellenstein. **Credits:** Dir: Roy Rowland; Prod: Nicholas Nayfack; Writer: Andre Bohem, William P. McGivern; DP: John Seitz; Ed: James E. Newcom; Composer: Jeff Alexander; Art Director: Cedric Gibbons, Hans Peters. B&W, 92 min.

Romance
(1930) MGM
An older clergyman uses his own sad story to convince his grandson not to marry an actress. As a young man (Gordon), the curate was seduced by a glamorous, older opera star (Garbo). She reveals that she is the kept woman of wealthy Stone, and when she goes to announce her leaving to Stone, Gordon sees her and assumes she's been unfaithful. Gordon then pleads for her to make love, and Garbo rejects him, knowing that he has no higher motivation than any other man. Pretty soupy, but Garbo

fascinates as usual. Academy Award Nominations: Best Director; Best Actress: Greta Garbo. **Cast:** Greta Garbo, Lewis Stone, Gavin Gordon, Elliott Nugent, Florence Lake, Clara Blandick, Henry Armetta, Mathilde Comont, Countess De Liguoro. **Credits:** Dir: Clarence Brown; Writer: Edwin Justus Mayer, Bess Meredyth, Edward Sheldon; DP: William H. Daniels; Ed: Leslie Wilder, Hugh Wynn; Prod Design: Cedric Gibbons; Costumes: Adrian. B&W, 78 min. **VHS**

Romance on the High Seas

(1948) Warner Bros.
Doris Day stars in her first feature role as a struggling nightclub singer who agrees to take a cruise posing as a wealthy socialite (Paige) who would rather stay home to spy on her husband (Defore). Her scheme is foiled when the private detective (Carson) hired to spy on the vacationing wife falls in love with the imposter. Day's role was intended for Judy Garland, who was replaced with Betty Hutton, who got pregnant, leaving the field open for Day, who was the singer in Les Brown's band. Academy Award Nominations: Best Song ("Romance on the High Seas"); Best Scoring of a Musical Picture. **Cast:** Jack Carson, Janis Paige, Don Defore, Doris Day, Oscar Levant, S. Z. Sakall, Fortunio Bonanova, Eric Blore, Franklin Pangborn. **Credits:** Dir: Michael Curtiz; Prod: Alex Gottlieb; Writer: Julius J. Epstein, Philip G. Epstein, I. A. L. Diamond; DP: Elwood Bredell; Ed: Rudi Fehr; Prod Design: Anton Grot. Color, 99 min. **VHS**

Roman Holiday

(1953) Paramount
Hepburn steps lightly into the starring spotlight with this whimsical romance. As a rebellious young princess who longs to see the world beyond her velvet prison, Hepburn steals away from her entourage and links up with reporter Peck, who's been trying to get a glimpse of the beautiful royal. The two fall in love as they evade the prying eyes of other reporters and Hepburn's guardians. The Oscar-winning story from then-blacklisted Trumbo was fronted by McLellan Hunter; Trumbo was awarded a posthumous Oscar in 1993. Golden Globe Award for Best Actress: Audrey Hepburn. Academy Award Nominations: 10, including Best Picture; Best Director; Best Screenplay. **Academy Awards:** Best Actress: Audrey Hepburn; Best Motion Picture Story; Best Costume Design (B&W). **Cast:** Gregory Peck, Audrey Hepburn, Eddie Albert,

Roman Holiday (1953)

Tullio Carminati, Hartley Power, Harcourt Williams, Margaret Rawlings, Paolo Carlini. **Credits:** Dir: William Wyler; Prod: William Wyler; Writer: Dalton Trumbo, Ian McLellan Hunter, John Dighton; DP: Franz Planer, Henri Alekan; Ed: Robert W. Swink; Composer: Georges Auric; Art Director: Hal Pereira, Walter Tyler; Costumes: Edith Head. B&W, 118 min. **VHS, LASER**

Romanoff and Juliet

(1961) Universal
Peter Ustinov's play comes to the screen with its auteur performing every task but sweeping up the stage. Ustinov rules Concordia, a small European country inconsequential in every way. But when Ustinov abstains from a UN vote, the fate of the world hangs in the balance. Both Russia and the U.S. pursue Ustinov with bags of aid money, but he maintains his neutrality. Instead of choosing sides, he orchestrates a budding romance between the Russian ambassador's son (Gavin) and the U.S. ambassador's daughter (Dee). **Cast:** Peter Ustinov, Sandra Dee, John Gavin, Akim Tamiroff, Alix Talton, Rik Von Nutter, John Phillips,

Peter Jones, Tamara Shayne, Suzanne Cloutier. **Credits:** Dir: Peter Ustinov; Prod: Peter Ustinov; Writer: Peter Ustinov; DP: Robert Krasker; Ed: Renzo Lucidi; Prod Design: Alexander Trauner; Composer: Mario Nascimbene. Color, 103 min.

Roman Scandals

(1933) United Artists
In this Cantor smash-hit comedy, the slapstick star plays a delivery boy in West Rome, Oklahoma, who dreams himself back to ancient Rome, where he becomes the chief food-taster for emperor Arnold. Look closely for Ball in the Goldwyn Girl lineup wearing a long blond wig and a smile. **Cast:** Eddie Cantor, Lucille Ball, Marjorie Main, Edward Arnold, Ruth Etting, Gloria Stuart, David Manners, Verree Teasdale. **Credits:** Dir: Frank Tuttle; Prod: Samuel Goldwyn; Writer: William Anthony McGuire, George Oppenheimer, Arthur Sheekman, Nat Perrin; DP: Gregg Toland; Ed: Stuart Heisler; Composer: Alfred Newman; Art Director: Richard Day; Choreography: Busby Berkeley. B&W, 92 min. **VHS, LASER**

The Roman Spring of Mrs. Stone

(1961) Warner Bros.
In her next-to-last role, Leigh plays an aging actress who travels to Rome. Lonely and confused after her husband dies en route, Leigh ends up consulting Lenya, a pimp who supplies her with Beatty, her latest sensation. Leigh becomes entranced with the young man, though Lenya breaks up the unprofitable arrangement by introducing him to St. John. Despondent, Leigh throws herself at a shadowy stranger. Based on Tennessee Williams's only novel. Academy Award Nomination for Best Supporting Actress: Lotte Lenya. **Cast:** Vivien Leigh, Warren Beatty, Lotte Lenya, Jill St. John, Jeremy Spencer, Josephine Brown, Peter Dyneley, Carl Jaffe. **Credits:** Dir: Jose Quintero; Prod: Louis de Rochemont; Writer: Gavin Lambert, Jan Read; Story: Tennessee Williams; DP: Harry Waxman; Ed: Ralph Kamplen; Prod Design: Roger K. Furse; Composer: Richard Addinsell. Color, 104 min. **VHS**

Rome Adventure

(1962) Warner Bros.
Pleshette, a spinstery New England schoolteacher, heads for the Eternal City in search of romance. She gets more than she could have dreamed with a handsome student (Donahue), a dashing older man (Brazzi)—and competition from a glamorous woman of the world (Dickinson). **Cast:** Suzanne Pleshette, Troy Donahue, Angie Dickinson, Rossano Brazzi, Constance Ford, Al Hirt, Chad Everett, Hampton Fancher. **Credits:** Dir: Delmer Daves; Prod: Delmer Daves; Writer: Delmer Daves; DP: Charles Lawton, Jr.; Ed: William Ziegler; Composer: Max Steiner; Art Director: Leo K. Kuter. Color, 119 min. **VHS, LASER**

Romeo and Juliet

(1936) MGM
MGM production chief Thalberg lavished his personal attention on this reverent treatment of Shakespeare's classic love story as his wife, Shearer, was cast in the lead. Shearer and Howard make an earnest pair, but the fizz in the production comes from Barrymore's delightful Mercutio. Interesting as a comparison of the classic acting style of the '30s with the more naturalistic treatment of the 1968 British-Italian version directed by Franco Zeffirelli. Academy Award Nominations: 4, including Best Picture; Best Actress: Norma Shearer; Best Supporting Actor: Basil Rathbone. **Cast:** Norma Shearer, Leslie Howard, John Barrymore, Edna May Oliver, Basil Rathbone, C. Aubrey Smith, Andy Devine, Reginald Denny, Ralph Forbes. **Credits:** Dir: George Cukor; Prod: Irving Thalberg; Writer: Talbot Jennings; DP: William Daniels; Ed: Margaret Booth; Prod Design: Cedric Gibbons; Composer: Herbert Stothart. B&W, 126 min. **VHS, LASER**

Room for One More

(1952) Warner Bros.
Offscreen mates Grant and Drake add familial warmth to a heart-tugging story of a family that always has room for one more child in need. Based on the true story of a New Jersey family that took in troubled kids, the film handles the implications for the marriage and for the emotionally scarred children lightly, but its deft blend of comedy and drama is uplifting. **Cast:** Cary Grant, Betsy Drake, Lurene Tuttle, Randy Stuart, John Ridgely, Irving Bacon, Mary Treen, Hayden Rorke, Iris Mann, George Winslow. **Credits:** Dir: Norman Taurog; Prod: Henry Blanke; Writer: Jack Rose; Story: Anna Perrott Rose, Melville Shavelson; DP: Robert Burks; Ed: Alan Crosland; Composer: Max Steiner; Art Director: Douglas Bacon. B&W, 98 min.

Room Service

(1938) RKO
A successful stage farce gets a less-successful treatment in this production, but the Marx Brothers add their patented mania. The Marxes are holed up in a hotel room waiting for financing to come through for the show. In the meantime, virtually everyone associated with the show, including the writer (Albertson) who shows up wide-eyed to see how his work's progressing, occupies the room. Miller comes in to introduce a new act and falls for Albertson, and Ball announces a new angel, and just in time as hotel executive MacBride is about to evict the whole crew. Remade as *Step Lively* (1944) with Frank Sinatra. **Cast:** Lucille Ball, Groucho Marx, Chico Marx, Harpo Marx, Ann Miller, Frank Albertson, Donald MacBride, Philip Loeb, Philip Wood, Alexander Asro. **Credits:** Dir: William A. Seiter; Prod: Pandro S. Berman; Writer: Morrie Ryskind; DP: J. Roy Hunt; Ed: George Crone; Composer: Roy Webb; Art Director: Van Nest Polglase, Al Herman. B&W, 79 min. **VHS**

Rooster Cogburn

(1975) Universal
This less-than-stellar sequel to *True Grit* is watchable mainly for the clash between movie titans Hepburn and Wayne. Wayne's character from *True Grit*, Rooster Cogburn, has a chance to redeem his sheriff's star if he can get back a shipment of nitroglycerin stolen by outlaws. Hepburn's Scripture-quoting schoolmarm joins in to see the men who killed her father brought to justice. **Cast:** John Wayne, Katharine Hepburn, Anthony Zerbe, Strother Martin, Richard Jordan, John McIntire, Richard Romancito, Warren Vanders. **Credits:** Dir: Stuart Millar; Prod: Hal B. Wallis; Writer: Martin Julien; DP: Harry Stradling; Ed: Robert W. Swink; Composer: Laurence Rosenthal; Art Director: Preston Ames. Color, 108 min. **VHS, LASER, DVD**

Rope

(1948) Warner Bros.
This is one of the most famous technical achievements in movie history, a Hitchcock mystery that seems to unfold in a single, continuous shot (though there are two brief reverse-angle shots). The story of a thrill killing (based on the 1924 Leopold and Loeb murder) takes place as two pseudo-intellectuals (Granger and Dall) murder a friend and then host a dinner party. The guests include the victim's father (Hardwicke), his fiancée (Chandler), and Stewart, a professor whose lectures on Nietzsche inspired their deed. Dall toys with the guests, daring them to uncover the secret of the body that he's hidden in the chest from which they serve dinner. To his chagrin, Stewart begins to understand Dall's taunts. The technical challenge appealed to Hitchcock's formidable production-planning skills. The set consisted of wild walls that could move out of the camera's path, and the set dressing had to move silently as well. As night falls, the light had to change both on the set and on the carefully rendered Manhattan skyline that serves as a backdrop. Hitchcock organized a massive army of technicians and crew, and the resulting film (which Hitchcock referred to as a "stunt") consists of eight apparently seamless 10-minute takes. **Cast:** James Stewart, John Dall, Farley Granger, Cedric Hardwicke, Constance Collier, Joan Chandler, Edith Evanson, Douglas Dick. **Credits:** Dir: Alfred Hitchcock; Prod: Sidney Bernstein, Alfred Hitchcock; Writer: Arthur Laurents, Hume Cronyn, Ben Hecht; DP: Joseph A. Valentine, William V. Skall; Ed: William Ziegler; Composer: David Buttolph; Art Director: Perry Ferguson; Costumes: Adrian. Color, 81 min. **VHS, LASER**

Rope of Sand

(1949) Paramount

Thievery, murder, love, and intrigue fill this *Casablanca*-esque film set in South Africa's diamond-mining country. *Casablanca* alumni Henreid, Rains, and Lorre join Lancaster in a search for stolen diamonds. Lancaster had helped a now-deceased diamond thief to escape. Now, being the only man who knows where they are hidden, he withstands torture and blackmail at the hands of the mining company's chief of security (Henreid). Lancaster agrees to turn over the diamonds to save the life of a woman (Calvet) first enlisted to betray him but who subsequently has fallen in love with him. Engaging suspense and a great cast. **Cast:** Burt Lancaster, Paul Henreid, Claude Rains, Peter Lorre, Corinne Calvet, Sam Jaffe, John Bromfield, Mike Mazurki, Kenny Washington. **Credits:** Dir: William Dieterle; Prod: Hal B. Wallis; Writer: Walter Doniger, John Paxton; DP: Charles Lang; Ed: Warren Low; Prod Design: Hans Dreier, Franz Bachelin; Composer: Franz Waxman. B&W, 104 min.

Rosalie

(1937) MGM

This ponderous, lavishly produced musical romance should have been lighthearted, but is still interesting to see what profligate spending could buy in Depression-era Hollywood. West Point football hero Eddy falls in love with a Vassar student (Powell) who also happens to be the princess of a tiny Balkan nation. When he flies his own plane to her principality, he discovers the nation in chaos and the princess gives him a cold shoulder. Mainly an excuse for an entire portfolio of Cole Porter songs, including the title song, "In the Still of the Night," "I've Got a Strange New Rhythm in My Heart," and "Who Knows?" The producers threw out the Broadway show's score by Sigmund Romberg and George Gershwin! **Cast:** Eleanor Powell, Nelson Eddy, Frank Morgan, Ray Bolger, Ilona Massey, Edna May Oliver, Billy Gilbert, Reginald Owen. **Credits:** Dir: W. S. Van Dyke; Prod: William Anthony McGuire; Writer: William Anthony McGuire; DP: Oliver T. Marsh; Ed: Blanche Sewell; Prod Design: Cedric Gibbons; Composer: Cole Porter, Herbert Stothart. B&W, 125 min. **VHS**

Roseland

(1977) Cinema Shares

This quickie, low-budget memory drama from Merchant and Ivory shows flashes of their adroit way with actors and story. The trilogy set in New York City's Roseland Ballroom depicts the lives of three regulars on the dance floor: Wright and Jacobi relive their glory days at the famed ballroom; gigolo Walken shows tenderness toward a dying woman (Copeland); and Skala portrays a poor woman who works hard all week to find a few hours of magic at the ballroom. **Cast:** Teresa Wright, Lou Jacobi, Geraldine Chaplin, Helen Gallagher, Joan Copeland, Christopher Walken, Conrad Janis, Lilia Skala. **Credits:** Dir: James Ivory; Prod: Ismail Merchant; Writer: Ruth Prawer Jhabvala; DP: Ernest Vincze; Ed: Humphrey Dixon, Richard Schmiechen; Composer: Michael Gibson. Color, 103 min. **VHS**

Rose Marie

(1936) MGM

This is the most famous of the MacDonald-Eddy movie operettas (and the one most lampooned, with its keynote song, "Indian Love Call," providing irresistible material for comedians). Opera star MacDonald tours Canada and makes an appeal for the release of her ne'er-do-well brother (Stewart) from prison. But before the appeal can go through, Stewart escapes and kills a Mountie. MacDonald trails after him, enlists an Indian guide to bring her into the deep forest, and attracts the attention of a Mountie (Eddy) who's tracking her brother. When MacDonald's left alone in the woods, Eddy comes to the rescue and love blooms. The famous Friml-Stothart score includes the title song, "The Mounties," "Indian Love Call," and "Just for You." The stage production was brought to the screen first in 1928 as *Rose-Marie* with Joan Crawford. **Cast:** Nelson Eddy, Jeanette MacDonald, James Stewart, Reginald Owen, Robert Greig, Jimmy Conlin, Lucien Littlefield, Alan Mowbray. **Credits:** Dir: W. S. Van Dyke; Prod: Hunt Stromberg; Writer: Frances Goodrich, Albert Hackett, Alice Duer Miller; DP: William Daniels; Ed: Blanche Sewell; Prod Design: Cedric Gibbons, Joseph C. Wright; Composer: Rudolf Friml, Herbert Stothart; Art Director: Edwin B. Willis. B&W, 112 min. **VHS, LASER**

Rose Marie

(1954) MGM

This is a similar setting but a different story for the Friml-Stothart operetta. Here, Blyth is a native of the beautiful Canadian Rockies in love with a mean-tempered trapper (Lamas) on the run from Mountie Keel. Mostly notable as the first color CinemaScope musical and for being one of Berkeley's last pictures as choreographer. **Cast:** Ann Blyth, Howard Keel, Fernando Lamas, Bert Lahr, Marjorie Main, Joan Taylor, Ray Collins, James Logan. **Credits:** Dir: Mervyn LeRoy; Prod: Mervyn LeRoy; Writer: Ronald Millar, George Froeschel; DP: Paul C. Vogel; Ed: Harold F. Kress; Prod Design: Cedric Gibbons; Composer: Rudolf Friml, Herbert Stothart; Art Director: Merrill Pye; Choreography: Busby Berkeley. Color, 115 min. **VHS, LASER**

Rosemary's Baby

(1968) Paramount

This terrifying film redefines and updates Gothic horror for the modern (and more explicit) age. Cassavetes

Rosemary's Baby (1968)

and Farrow move into a huge, creepy—and suspiciously affordable—apartment. They're taken under the wing of elderly neighbors Blackmer and Gordon, and good things start to happen in Cassavetes's marginal acting career. When the couple decides to have a child, Gordon takes over Farrow's care, and a strange dream that Farrow has of mating with a hideous beast begins to seem possible. Farrow's suspicions are treated as paranoid delusions, until they take shape in the form of her baby, the spawn of Satan. Polanski creates a truly frightening world from Ira Levin's sensational novel in which no one is who they seem and the dreaded underworld exists side by side with everyday life. Golden Globe Award for Best Supporting Actress: Ruth Gordon. Academy Award Nominations: 2, including Best (Adapted) Screenplay. **Academy Awards:** Best Supporting Actress: Ruth Gordon. **Cast:** Mia Farrow, John Cassavetes, Ruth Gordon, Ralph Bellamy, Sidney Blackmer, Maurice Evans, Victoria Vetri, Patsy Kelly. **Credits:** Dir: Roman Polanski; Prod: William Castle; Writer: Roman Polanski; Story: Ira Levin; DP: William A. Fraker; Ed: Sam O'Steen, Bob Wyman; Composer: Krzysztof Komeda; Art Director: Joel Schiller. Color, 136 min. **VHS, LASER**

Rose of Washington Square
(1939) Fox
In a sprightly Fox musical, Faye is a Ziegfeld starlet who stands by her thieving husband, Power. The story comes close to being a biopic of vaudeville comedienne Fanny Brice; Brice sued. But mostly this is a chance to see Jolson at the end of his career having a ball reprising his signature numbers, including "My Mammy," "California, Here I Come," and "Rock-a-Bye Your Daddy with a Dixie Melody." Faye sings "My Man" and "I'm Just Wild About Harry." **Cast:** Alice Faye, Tyrone Power, Al Jolson, William Frawley, Horace McMahon, Moroni Olsen, Joyce Compton, Hobart Cavanaugh. **Credits:** Dir: Gregory Ratoff; Prod: Nunnally Johnson; Writer: Nunnally Johnson; DP: Karl Freund; Ed: Louis Loeffler; Prod Design: Rudolph Sternad; Art Director: Richard Day. B&W, 86 min. **VHS**

The Rose Tattoo
(1955) Paramount
Magnani's Hollywood debut caused a sensation for her earthy, natural portrayal of a working-class widow. Magnani holds dear the memory of her banana-boat-worker husband, but

when Lancaster, also a banana hauler with a rose tattooed on his chest, comes around, she's torn between her memories and her desires. Her teenage daughter (Pavan) also faces the temptations of the flesh with sailor Cooper. Tennessee Williams wrote the part specifically for Magnani and she revels in the role. Golden Globes for Best Actress in a Drama: Anna Magnani; Best Supporting Actress: Marisa Pavan. Academy Award Nominations: 8, including Best Picture; Best Supporting Actress: Marisa Pavan. **Academy Awards:** Best Actress: Anna Magnani; Best Black-and-White Cinematography; Best Art Direction—Set Decoration (B&W). **Cast:** Anna Magnani, Burt Lancaster, Marisa Pavan, Ben Cooper, Virginia Grey, Jo Van Fleet, Sandro Giglio. **Credits:** Dir: Daniel Mann; Prod: Hal B. Wallis; Writer: Hal Kanter, Tennessee Williams; DP: James Wong Howe; Ed: Warren Low; Prod Design: Hal Pereira, Tambi Larsen; Composer: Alex North. B&W, 117 min. **VHS, LASER**

The Rounders
(1965) MGM
This is an underrated, contemporary comic Western with Fonda and Ford as a couple of middle-aged cowpokes scratching together a living breaking horses while they dream of a big score. They almost get their chance when they accept a mean, unbreakable horse as payment from rancher Wills. When they enter the steed in a local rodeo, Fonda and Ford make a pile betting on the horse, but when it tears down the stable, it's back to the ranch and dreams of desert isles "where there ain't no grass, and there ain't no horses." **Cast:** Glenn Ford, Henry Fonda, Sue Ane Langdon, Hope Holiday, Chill Wills, Edgar Buchanan, Kathleen Freeman, Joan Freeman. **Credits:** Dir: Burt Kennedy; Prod: Richard E. Lyons; Writer: Burt Kennedy; DP: Paul C. Vogel; Ed: John McSweeney, Jr.; Prod Design: George W. Davis; Composer: Jeff Alexander. Color, 85 min. **VHS**

Roustabout
(1964) Paramount
In one of the best Elvis outings, the proceedings are dignified by Stanwyck's participation as the operator of a carnival. After hitting the road following a fight in a coffeehouse, Elvis becomes a handyman at Stanwyck's show, and romances Freeman. His fists fly again when he attracts the attention of a sleazy rival. Welch makes her screen debut in a bit part

as a college girl. Includes the songs "Hard Knocks," "One Track Heart," "It's a Wonderful World," and "Big Love, Big Heartache." **Cast:** Elvis Presley, Barbara Stanwyck, Raquel Welch, Joan Freeman, Leif Erickson, Sue Ane Langdon, Pat Buttram, Joan Staley. **Credits:** Dir: John Rich; Prod: Hal B. Wallis; Writer: Anthony Lawrence, Allan Weiss; DP: Lucien Ballard; Ed: Warren Low; Composer: Joseph J. Lilley; Art Director: Hal Pereira, Walter Tyler. Color, 101 min. **VHS**

Roxie Hart
(1942) Fox
Rogers delivers the laughs—and the legs—in this high-spirited adaptation of the stage production that was the basis for the Bob Fosse musical *Chicago* and a 1927 silent. Rogers plays the title character, a publicity-seeking dance-hall girl in the Roaring '20s who gladly takes the rap for a murder her husband (Chandler) commits in order to boost her career. Defense attorney Menjou sways the jury with Ginger's gams and gum-snapping sex appeal. Action master Wellman makes this fly. **Cast:** Ginger Rogers, Adolphe Menjou, George Montgomery, Nigel Bruce, Phil Silvers, George Chandler, William Frawley, Lynne Overman. **Credits:** Dir: William Wellman; Prod: Nunnally Johnson; Writer: Nunnally Johnson; DP: Leon Shamroy; Ed: James B. Clark; Composer: Alfred Newman; Art Director: Richard Day, Wiard Ihnen. Color, 75 min. **VHS**

The Royal Family of Broadway
(1930) Paramount
This ultimate in backstage comedy is directed by Cukor, an experienced theater director who demonstrates real affection for his characters and setting. The wicked parody of the Barrymores finds March coming home after a sojourn in Hollywood. His arrival causes an uproar outside the home and inside, as the family matriarch Crosman views his movie career as beneath the family. She also worries that the family legacy is fading as her daughter (Claire) retires from the stage to marry and the next generation proves unwilling to carry on. Crosman hits the boards once again, which threatens her health but re-inspires her children. Academy Award Nomination for Best Actor: Fredric March. **Cast:** Ina Claire, Fredric March, Mary Brian, Henrietta Crosman, Arnold Korff, Frank Conroy, Charles Starrett, Royal C. Stout, Mur-

ray Alper, Elsie Edmond. **Credits:** Dir: George Cukor, Cyril Gardner; Writer: Herman J. Mankiewicz, Gertrude Powell; Story: Edna Ferber, George S. Kaufman; DP: George Folsey, Jr.; Ed: Edward Dmytryk. B&W, 82 min.

A Royal Scandal
(1945) Fox
Lubitsch was meant to direct this, but contented himself with watching over Preminger's shoulder when he became ill. His light touch is evident in this romantic depiction of the notorious czarina, Catherine the Great. Portrayed by an imperious Bankhead, Catherine welcomes a soldier (Eythe) who warns her of an overthrow plot in the ranks. The czarina becomes attached to the handsome young officer and he quickly rises to the rank of general. But when he falls in love with a sweet lady-in-waiting (Baxter), Catherine sends the girl away. Heartbroken, the new general nevertheless does his duty and successfully defends the czarina, and is rewarded with the return of his true love. **Cast:** Tallulah Bankhead, Charles Coburn, Anne Baxter, William Eythe, Vincent Price, Mischa Auer, Sig Ruman, Vladimir Sokoloff, Grady Sutton. **Credits:** Dir: Otto Preminger; Prod: Ernst Lubitsch; Writer: Bruno Frank, Edwin Justus Mayer; DP: Arthur Miller; Ed: Dorothy Spencer; Composer: Alfred Newman; Art Director: Mark-Lee Kirk, Lyle Wheeler. B&W, 94 min.

Royal Wedding
(1951) MGM
Some of Astaire's most elaborate dance sequences appear in this musical romance, including his run around the walls and ceiling, and his pas de deux with a hat rack. He and Powell play a brother-sister dance team in Britain who get involved with two locals, Churchill and Lawford. Powell makes a fine partner for Astaire in Donen's solo directing debut. The Lerner and Lane songs include "Too Late Now," "You're All the World to Me," "The Happiest Day in My Life," and "What a Lovely Day for a Wedding." Academy Award Nomination for Best Song ("Too Late Now"). **Cast:** Fred Astaire, Jane Powell, Keenan Wynn, Peter Lawford, Sarah Churchill, Albert Sharpe, Henri Letondal, James

Finlayson. **Credits:** Dir: Stanley Donen; Prod: Arthur Freed; Writer: Alan Jay Lerner; DP: Robert Planck; Ed: Albert Akst; Prod Design: Cedric Gibbons, Jack Martin Smith; Composer: Alan Jay Lerner, Burton Lane. Color, 100 min. VHS, LASER, DVD

Ruggles of Red Gap
(1935) Paramount
Director McCarey, responsible for so many cinema classics, presents one of the best—and funniest—screen comedies. Laughton makes an unlikely comedian, but he is winning and adept as the perfect English valet who journeys to the Wild West when his employer (Young) loses him in a card game to an American rancher (Ruggles). Once in the land of the free, Laughton frees himself of the class restrictions he once took for granted, finding happiness with Pitts and opening a restaurant. This features Laughton's surprisingly affecting reading of the Gettysburg Address—while slightly sloshed. Academy Award Nomination: Best Picture. **Cast:** Charles Laughton, Mary Boland, Charlie Ruggles, ZaSu Pitts, Roland Young, Leila Hyams, Maude Eburne, Lucien Littlefield. **Credits:** Dir: Leo McCarey; Prod: Arthur Hornblow, Jr.; Writer: Walter DeLeon, Harlan Thompson, Humphrey Pearson; DP: Alfred Gilks; Ed: Edward Dmytryk; Prod Design: Hans Dreier; Composer: Ralph Rainger, Sam Coslow; Art Director: Robert Odell. B&W, 90 min. VHS, LASER

Run of the Arrow
(1956) Universal
This fascinating, graphically violent Fuller Western stars Steiger as a Confederate soldier who finally comes to grips with the end of the war. Steiger fires the last bullet of the war, and flees to the West after the South's loss. There his bitterness drives him to live outside the Union by becoming a Sioux warrior (his initiation is known as the "run of the arrow") and taking an Indian bride. When the cavalry establishes a fort nearby, Steiger is torn between the Union and his new tribe when he sees the Indians savagely attack the soldiers. **Cast:** Rod Steiger, Brian Keith, Charles Bronson, Jay C. Flippen, Sarita Montiel, Ralph Meeker, Olive Carey, Frank De Kova.

Credits: Dir: Samuel Fuller; Prod: Samuel Fuller; Writer: Samuel Fuller; DP: Joseph Biroc; Ed: Gene Fowler, Jr.; Composer: Victor Young; Art Director: Albert S. D'Agostino, Jack Okey. Color, 85 min. VHS, LASER

Run Silent, Run Deep
(1958) United Artists
Gable and Lancaster butt heads as a WWII submarine commander and his executive officer. Gable survived the sinking of his submarine by a Japanese destroyer. The crew on his new assignment don't trust Gable, and Lancaster openly questions his judgment. Gable, meanwhile, plots to get his revenge on the Japanese ship despite orders to avoid it. **Cast:** Clark Gable, Burt Lancaster, Brad Dexter, Jack Warden, Don Rickles, Nick Cravat, Mary LaRoche, Rudy Bond. **Credits:** Dir: Robert Wise; Prod: Harold Hecht; Writer: John Gay; Ed: George Boemler; Composer: Franz Waxman; Art Director: Edward Carrere. B&W, 93 min. VHS

The Russians Are Coming, the Russians Are Coming
(1966) United Artists
This is a terrific comedy and satire of Cold War tensions. When Russian sub commander Bikel maneuvers his craft onto a sandbar near the New England coastline, he sends Arkin and a small squad to find a motorboat to pull them off. They beach near Manhattan TV writer Reiner's summer house, and soon the entire resort town is either fascinated or up in arms about their foreign visitors. Romances bloom and tensions rise, but the sub crew and townspeople pull together to save a child. Arkin's screen debut. Based on the novel *The Off-Islanders* by Nathaniel Benchley, father of *Jaws* author Peter Benchley. Academy Award Nominations: 4, including Best Picture; Best Actor: Alan Arkin; Best Adapted Screenplay. **Cast:** Carl Reiner, Eva Marie Saint, Alan Arkin, Brian Keith, Jonathan Winters, Theodore Bikel, Paul Ford, Tessie O'Shea. **Credits:** Dir: Norman Jewison; Prod: Norman Jewison; Writer: William Rose; DP: Joseph Biroc; Ed: Hal Ashby, J. Terry Williams; Prod Design: Robert Boyle; Composer: Johnny Mandel. Color, 126 min. VHS

Sabotage

(1936) Gaumont
One of Hitchcock's most successful British mysteries is also one of the most controversial. A terrorist bomber (Homolka) uses a movie theater to mask his activities. As undercover Scotland Yard agent Loder starts to move in, the bomber's wife (Sidney) becomes suspicious and Homolka gives her little brother a dangerous package. When the bomb explodes on a bus, Sidney takes her revenge and the terrorists destroy the theater to cover up their deeds. Hitchcock almost got a punch in the nose and received general condemnation for killing a child and innocents on-screen. The director based many of the settings on remembered places from his childhood. Based on Joseph Conrad's *Secret Agent.* **Cast:** Oscar Homolka, Sylvia Sidney, John Loder, Desmond Tester, Matthew Boulton, Austin Trevor, Torin Thatcher, Aubrey Mather. **Credits:** Dir: Alfred Hitchcock; Prod: Michael Balcon, Ivor Montagu; Writer: Charles Bennett, Ian Hay, Alma Reville, Helen Simpson, E. V. H. Emmett; DP: Bernard Knowles; Ed: Charles Frend; Composer: Louis Levy. B&W, 93 min. **VHS, LASER**

Saboteur

(1942) Universal
Hitchcock's briskly paced wartime thriller was made famous by the unforgettable climax that has the film's villain dangling from the torch of the Statue of Liberty. An aircraft worker (Cummings) becomes a fugitive when he's falsely accused of sabotaging the factory where he works. On a cross-country chase to clear his name, he remains a step ahead of the police and a step behind the real culprit, who's part of a ring of Nazi spies. A fascinating, twisty tale penned by Parker, Harrison, and Viertel, with the action set in some of America's most recognizable locations, including Radio City Music Hall, Boulder Dam, and, of course, the Statue of Liberty. **Cast:** Robert Cummings, Priscilla Lane, Otto Kruger, Norman Lloyd, Alan Baxter, Clem Bevans, Alma Kruger, Vaughan Glaser. **Credits:** Dir: Alfred Hitchcock; Prod: Frank Lloyd, Jack H. Skirball; Writer: Peter Viertel, Joan Harrison, Dorothy Parker; DP: Joseph A. Valentine; Ed: Otto Ludwig; Prod Design: Jack Otterson; Composer: Charles Previn, Frank Skinner. B&W, 108 min. **VHS, LASER**

Sabrina

(1954) Paramount
This classic romance showcases Hepburn's grace and natural beauty. Hepburn, a chauffeur's daughter who lives over a mansion's garage, returns home from a French cooking school as a charming sophisticate. She had been sent away after losing her heart to her father's employer's playboy son (Holden). Upon Hepburn's homecoming, her new appearance and polish knock Holden off his feet. But Holden's brother, Bogart, a nose-to-the-grindstone businessman, has plans for Holden to marry a rival's daughter (Hyer) in a practical, if not romantic, merger. Bogart advises Hepburn to watch her heart, but then finds himself enchanted. Wilder's astringent dialogue and a sly performance from Bogart lift this above the suds. Remade in 1995 by Sydney Pollack with Harrison Ford in the Bogart role. Golden Globe for Best Screenplay. Academy Award Nominations: 5, including Best Director; Best Screenplay. **Academy Awards:** Best Costume Design (B&W). **Cast:** Humphrey Bogart, Audrey Hepburn, William Holden, Martha Hyer, John Williams, Walter Hampden, Joan Vohs, Marcel Dalio. **Credits:** Dir: Billy Wilder; Prod: Billy Wilder; Writer: Billy Wilder, Samuel Taylor, Ernest Lehman; DP: Charles B. Lang; Ed: Arthur Schmidt; Composer: Frederick Hollander; Art Director: Hal Pereira, Walter Tyler; Costumes: Edith Head. B&W, 113 min. **VHS, LASER**

Saddle the Wind

(1958) MGM
A former gunslinger (Taylor) settles down in a quiet town of farmers and cattle ranchers. But unstable younger brother Cassavetes shows up with a gun and a dance-hall girl (London). After killing a man who had earlier threatened his brother, he uses his newfound sense of power to harass some squatters. When Taylor tries to put an end to the violence, Cassavetes uses the gun on himself. Serling wrote this unusual, psychologically gripping Western, an equally unusual setting for Cassavetes. **Cast:** Robert Taylor, Julie London, John Cassavetes, Donald Crisp, Charles McGraw, Royal Dano, Richard Erdman, Douglas Spencer, Ray Teal. **Credits:** Dir: Robert Parrish; Prod: Armand Deutsch; Writer: Rod Serling; Story: Thomas Thompson; DP: George Folsey, Jr.; Ed: John McSweeney; Composer: Elmer Bernstein. Color, 84 min.

Sadie McKee

(1934) MGM
Crawford plays the perennial small-town girl in the heartless big city in this early talkie potboiler. As a maid in the home of Tone's parents, Crawford takes an early shine to the rich boy. But convinced she really loves troubled Raymond, she follows him to New York where she discovers him shacked up with a floozy (Ralston). Alone in the big city, she finds a job in a nightclub and a loveless marriage with a surprisingly sympathetic Arnold. But when she meets Tone again, the sparks turn to flame. The leads make this worth watching, particularly favorite character actor Arnold. This introduced the chestnut "All I Do Is Dream of You." **Cast:** Joan Crawford, Franchot Tone, Gene Raymond,

Edward Arnold, Esther Ralston, Leo G. Carroll, Akim Tamiroff, Gene Austin. **Credits:** Dir: Clarence Brown; Prod: Lawrence Weingarten; Writer: John Meehan; DP: Oliver T. Marsh; Ed: Hugh Wynn. B&W, 93 min. VHS

Sadie Thompson

(1928) United Artists
A San Francisco prostitute (Swanson) arrives in Pago Pago to hide her immoral past. She marries a sailor (Walsh), but a religious zealot (Barrymore) threatens to expose her. When Barrymore becomes obsessed with Swanson, he seduces her and his guilt drives him to suicide. A steamy, damp treatment for this oft-filmed, erotically-charged classic. Academy Award Nominations: 2, including Best Actress: Gloria Swanson. **Cast:** Gloria Swanson, Lionel Barrymore, Raoul Walsh, Charles Lane, Blanche Federici, Florence Midgely. **Credits:** Dir: Raoul Walsh; Prod: Gloria Swanson; Writer: Raoul Walsh; Story: W. Somerset Maugham; DP: Oliver Marsh, George Barnes, Robert Kurrle; Ed: C. Gradner Sullivan; Prod Design: William Cameron Menzies. B&W, 97 min. VHS, LASER

Safe at Home!

(1962) Columbia
In a dream come true for Yankees fans, Roger Maris, Mickey Mantle, Whitey Ford, and manager Ralph Houk make appearances in this feel-good kids' flick. When Little Leaguer and big-league storyteller Russell moves to Florida from New York, he tries to convince his teammates that he's tight with the dynamic duo of Mantle and Maris. When his friends call his bluff, Russell tracks down the players, who teach him the virtues of telling the truth, and invite Russell's team to spring training. **Cast:** Bryan Russell, Mickey Mantle, Roger Maris, William Frawley, Patricia Barry, Don Collier, Charles Martin, Whitey Ford, Tom Naud. **Credits:** Dir: Walter Doniger; Prod: Tom Naud; Writer: Robert Dillon; DP: Irving Lippman; Ed: Frank Keller. B&W, 84 min. VHS

Safety Last

(1923) Hal Roach
Lloyd's brightest moment is this film that features one of the most famous images from the silent era—Lloyd dangling from a clock over downtown Los Angeles. Lloyd moves to the big city to make enough money to marry his beloved (Davis), but only lands a salesclerk position. When Lloyd pretends to be a big shot, Davis's mother

Sabrina (1954)

sends her after her beau. Lloyd needs cash to keep up appearances, so he hatches a publicity stunt that involves his acrobat friend climbing the outside of the store. When his friend gets collared for an earlier stunt, Lloyd performs the daring climb himself. Selected for the National Film Registry. **Cast:** Harold Lloyd, Mildred Davis, Bill Strother, Noah Young, Westcott Clarke, Mickey Daniels. **Credits:** Dir: Sam Taylor, Fred Newmeyer; Prod: Hal Roach; Writer: Hal Roach, Tim Whelan, Sam Taylor; DP: Walter Lundin; Ed: Fred Guiol; Prod Design: Fred Guiol. B&W, 78 min. VHS

Sagebrush Trail

(1933) Monogram
Wayne appears at the dawn of his career in his second Western for Monogram. Accused of a murder he didn't commit, Wayne escapes from jail and sets out for the West to find the real killer. He hooks up with gunslinger Chandler, not realizing Chandler's the culprit. Watch for master stuntman Canutt. **Cast:** John Wayne, Nancy Shubert, Lane Chandler, Yakima Canutt, Hal Taliaferro, Art Mix, Robert E. Burns, Henry Hall. **Credits:** Dir: Armand Schaefer; Prod: Paul Malvern; Writer: Lindsley Parsons; DP: Archie Stout. B&W, 58 min. VHS, LASER

Sahara

(1943) Columbia
In a premier WWII adventure set under the relentless, blistering Saharan sun, Bogart mans a crippled tank retreating

into the Libyan desert. As they search desperately for water, the tank squad picks up various stragglers from defeated Allied units. The growing band fights off air attacks and then vies with a Nazi battalion for a nearly dry well at a desert ghost town. There, Bogart spurs the defeated, parched men into making a stand against the overwhelming numbers of Germans. Never predictable, the script from future Hollywood Ten member Lawson fills the screen with action and memorable characters. Academy Award Nominations: 3, including Best Supporting Actor: J. Carrol Naish; Best (Black-and-White) Cinematography. **Cast:** Humphrey Bogart, Bruce Bennett, Dan Duryea, Lloyd Bridges, Rex Ingram, J. Carrol Naish, Louis Mercier, Patrick O'Moore. **Credits:** Dir: Zoltan Korda; Prod: Harry Joe Brown; Writer: John Howard Lawson, Zoltan Korda, James O'Hanlon; DP: Rudolph Maté; Ed: Charles Nelson; Composer: Miklos Rozsa; Art Director: Lionel Banks, Eugene Lourie. B&W, 97 min. VHS, LASER

Sailor Beware

(1951) Paramount
Martin and Lewis star as new naval recruits. Martin, of course, sings and looks exasperated as Lewis gets into undersea trouble when the duo are assigned to a submarine. Supposedly based on *The Fleet's In* (1942) but that worthy wartime musical is mostly obscured by the frenzy. **Cast:** Dean Martin, Dick Stabile, Donald MacBride,

Louis Jean Heydt, Mike Mahoney, Jerry Lewis, Corinne Calvet, Marion Marshall, Robert Strauss, Leif Erickson. **Credits:** Dir: Hal Walker; Prod: Hal B. Wallis; Writer: Martin Rackin, Elwood Ullman, Kenyon Nicholson; DP: Daniel L. Fapp; Ed: Warren Low; Prod Design: Hal Pereira, Henry Bumstead; Composer: Joseph J. Lilley. B&W, 108 min.

Sailor's Luck
(1933) Fox
In this comedy, Dunn plays a seaman who falls for Eilers but can't marry her because of his contract with the service. When duty calls and he sets sail, he tries to keep in contact and mistakenly believes that she's seeing a gangster. He calls in his shipmates to help get her back, resulting in an all-out brawl between the men in white and the Mob. Notable only as an early talkie from Walsh. **Cast:** James Dunn, Sally Eilers, Sammy Cohen, Frank Moran, Victor Jory, Esther Muir, Will Stanton, Armand Wright, Jerry Mandy, Lucien Littlefield. **Credits:** Dir: Raoul Walsh; Writer: Marguerite Roberts, Charlotte Miller, Bert Hanlon, Ben Ryan; Story: Roberts Miller; DP: Arthur Miller; Ed: Jack Murray. B&W, 78 min.

The Saint
The popularity of the first Saint film, *The Saint in New York* (1938), inspired a series, though it proved only a modest success for RKO. Odd, because the character had been and remains enduringly intriguing in radio, TV, and film right up to today. RKO's problem seemed to be in casting. The high turnover of actors portraying novelist Leslie Charteris's suave Simon Templar resulted in an uneven group of films. Louis Hayward, George Sanders—who starred in five of the nine installments—and Hugh Sinclair each took turns playing the globetrotting, debonair criminal-turned-detective who had a taste for fine wine and a nose for adventurous crime-solving capers. Sanders left the series after 1941's *The Saint in Palm Springs* to star in another series, The Falcon, which was nearly indistinguishable from The Saint. The British television series, imported to the U.S. in the '60s, found more success, with Roger Moore as Templar, warming up for his future role as James Bond. The series returned to television in the '70s and '80s, and a new feature film, *The Saint*, starring Val Kilmer as Templar, debuted in 1997.

The Saint in New York *(1938)*
The Saint Strikes Back *(1939)*

The Saint in London *(1939)*
The Saint's Double Trouble *(1940)*
The Saint Takes Over *(1940)*
The Saint in Palm Springs *(1941)*
The Saint's Vacation *(1941)*
The Saint Meets the Tiger *(1943)*
The Saint's Girl Friday *(1954)*

Saint Jack
(1979) New World
In a fine performance by Gazzara, an American pimp in Singapore seeks protection from the local mob by signing up with an American mobster played by Bogdanovich. Gazzara's forced into photographing a senator with a young male prostitute for blackmail and begins to question his life. Director Bogdanovich once again hooks up with Corman, who had produced his screenwriting debut, *The Wild Angels* (1966). Explicit sexual situations. **Cast:** Ben Gazzara, Denholm Elliott, James Villiers, Peter Bogdonovich, David Lazenby, Joss Ackland, Rodney Bewes, Mark Kingston, Lisa Lu. **Credits:** Dir: Peter Bogdanovich; Prod: Roger Corman; Writer: Peter Bogdanovich, Howard Sackler, Paul Theroux; DP: Robby Muller; Ed: William Carruth; Art Director: David Ng. Color, 112 min. **VHS**

Sally and Saint Anne
(1952) Universal
When Hollywood set out to make a heartwarming comedy about an Irish family, certain ingredients would surely appear in the stew: the local priest, the amusingly idiosyncratic older relative (often a tippler), fisticuffs, and a wonderfully superstitious brand of Catholicism. Those time-tested elements flavor this sweetly charming domestic comedy. Blyth prays to St. Anne to use her influence for a successful outcome of her brother's boxing, her battle to save the family home, and her love life. Gwenn shines as her hypochondriacal grandfather. **Cast:** Ann Blyth, Edmund Gwenn, John McIntire, Palmer Lee, Gregg Palmer, Hugh O'Brian, Jack Kelly, Frances Bevier, Otto Hulett, Kathleen Hughes. **Credits:** Dir: Rudolph Maté; Prod: Leonard Goldstein; Writer: James O'Hanlon, Herb Meadow; DP: Irving Glassberg; Ed: Edward Curtiss; Composer: Frank Skinner; Art Director: Bernard Herzbrun, Hilyard Brown. B&W, 90 min.

Salome
(1953) Columbia
This biblical potboiler amounts to little more than an excuse to have Hollywood's most erotic classic star, Hayworth, perform an ecstatic strip tease—but wickedly entertaining performances by Laughton as King Herod and Anderson as his queen make the buildup watchable. Somehow Salome has become a reluctant participant in Herod's torture of John the Baptist (Badel) as she tries to stay out of her stepfather Herod's clutches and pitch woo with recent convert Granger. Silly, but colorful. **Cast:** Rita Hayworth, Charles Laughton, Stewart Granger, Judith Anderson, Cedric Hardwicke, Basil Sydney, Alan Badel, Rex Reason. **Credits:** Dir: William Dieterle; Prod: Buddy Adler; Writer: Harry Kleiner; DP: Charles B. Lang; Ed: Viola Lawrence; Composer: George Duning, Daniele Amfitheatrof; Art Director: John Meehan. Color, 103 min. **VHS**

Salt of the Earth
(1953)
This is a historically important film made outside the Hollywood system by blacklisted producer Jarrico and director Biberman, backed by the International Union of Mine, Mill and Smelt Workers and using actual mine workers (the head of the miners' local, Chacon, has the lead). The film was produced clandestinely after Screen Actors Guild president Walter Pidgeon alerted HUAC, and RKO owner Howard Hughes managed to stop the filmmakers' access to processing and distribution. Local New Mexico thugs also broke up sets and set fire to the union headquarters. The controversy flared over a story of Hispanic mine workers demanding better living and working conditions, and the realistic depiction of their harsh lives. When the strike leader's wife (Revueltas) rallies the miners' wives to the picket lines for their jailed husbands, the men begin to recognize the importance of the women's contributions to their lives and to their strike. Geer (also a blacklist victim) is one of the only professional actors in the film; the other, Revueltas, was blacklisted in her native Mexico and never worked again. Finally available on video after being suppressed for 30 years. Selected for the National Film Registry. **Cast:** Juan Chacon, Will Geer, Rosaura Revueltas, Mervin Williams, Charles Coleman. **Credits:** Dir: Herbert J. Biberman; Prod: Paul Jarrico, Adolfo Barela; Writer: Michael Wilson, Michael Biberman; DP: Leonard Stark, Stanley Meredith; Ed: Ed Spiegel, Joan Laird; Prod Design: Sonja Dahl Biberman, Adolfo Barela; Composer: Sol Kaplan. B&W, 94 min. **VHS, LASER, DVD**

Salty O'Rourke

(1945) Paramount

In a sprightly Ladd vehicle directed by Walsh, racetrack hound Ladd and his friend (Demarest) scheme to pay back a gambling debt before there are dire consequences. They find a fast horse but it's rideable only by a banned jockey (Clements). They finagle him into the race by using his underage brother's ID, but that means he has to go back to jockey school. There he takes a liking to his teacher (Russell), but so does Ladd. Academy Award Nomination for Best Original Screenplay. **Cast:** Alan Ladd, Gail Russell, Stanley Clements, William Demarest, Spring Byington, Bruce Cabot, Marjorie Woodworth. **Credits:** Dir: Raoul Walsh; Prod: E. D. Leshin; Writer: Milton Holmes; DP: Theodor Sparkuhl; Ed: William Shea; Composer: Robert Emmett Dolan; Art Director: Hans Dreier, Haldene Douglas. B&W, 97 min.

Same Time, Next Year

(1978) Universal

Mulligan's tender film, based on Bernard Slade's long-running play, observes the sea changes not only in his characters but also in America as a couple (Alda and Burstyn) carry on an affair for 26 years. After an ecstatic first tryst at a resort in the '50s, the young marrieds decide to stay in their own marriages, but rekindle their romance once a year at the resort. Academy Award Nominations: 4, including Best Actress: Ellen Burstyn; Best Adapted Screenplay. **Cast:** Ellen Burstyn, Alan Alda, Ivan Bonar, Bernie Kuby, Cosmo Sardo, David Northcutt, William Cantrell. **Credits:** Dir: Robert Mulligan; Prod: Walter Mirisch, Morton Gottlieb; Writer: Bernard Slade; DP: Robert Surtees; Ed: Sheldon Kahn; Prod Design: Henry Bumstead; Composer: Marvin Hamlisch. Color, 119 min. **VHS, LASER**

Samson and Delilah

(1949) Paramount

This is DeMille's grandest biblical epic and that's saying something. At a cost of $3 million, DeMille created a Technicolor version of the Old Testament world of the Danite shepherd who slays his Philistine captors with the jaw of an ass, but who succumbs to the wiles of a woman. As the hunky hero, Mature is in top form, his chiseled face straining as he fells his enemies but its fleshiness also hinting at his weakness. Lamarr also struts and poses to great effect, but the main attraction here is the spectacle itself, from Samson's shows of strength, his battles with the Philistines, and his climactic destruction of the temple. Academy Award Nominations: 5, including Best Cinematography. **Academy Awards:** Best Costume Design (Color); Best Art Direction—Set Decoration (Color). **Cast:** Hedy Lamarr, Victor Mature, Angela Lansbury, George Sanders, Henry Wilcoxon, Olive Deering, Fay Holden, Julia Faye. **Credits:** Dir: Cecil B. DeMille; Prod: Cecil B. DeMille; Writer: Vladimir Jabotinsky, Harold Lamb, Jesse Lasky, Jr., Fredric M. Frank; DP: Dewey Wrigley, George Barnes; Ed: Anne Bauchens; Prod Design: Hans Dreier; Composer: Victor Young; Art Director: Walter Tyler. Color, 128 min. **VHS, LASER**

San Antonio

(1945) Warner Bros.

This Technicolor Western features Flynn as a cattleman who uncovers the rustling operation being operated from the saloon owned by Kelly. Smith sings in the saloon, and Flynn thinks she might be in on the scheme, but that doesn't prevent him from romancing her. Pleasant enough, with action, romance, and a few songs thrown in. Academy Award Nominations: Best Song; Best (Color) Interior Decoration. **Cast:** Errol Flynn, Alexis Smith, S. Z. Sakall, Victor Francen, Florence Bates, John Litel, Paul Kelly, John Alvin. **Credits:** Dir: David Butler; Prod: Robert Buckner; Writer: Alan LeMay, W. R. Burnett; DP: Bert Glennon; Ed: Irene Morra; Composer: Max Steiner; Art Director: Ted Smith. Color, 111 min. **VHS**

The Sand Pebbles

(1966) Fox

Big-budget action drama based on an actual incident in which the Japanese sunk an American gunboat when they invaded China. Primarily remembered for McQueen's fine performance as a machinist's mate who angers his fellow Americans by releasing the coolies that did the crew's chores, and for the screen debut of 20-year-old Bergen. Notable performances from Crenna as the inexperienced lieutenant in command, and Attenborough as a sailor who falls in love with a Chinese prostitute. This was Wise's first film after the worldwide success of *The Sound of Music*. Academy Award Nominations: 8, including Best Picture; Best Actor: Steve McQueen; Best Supporting Actor: Mako; Best Cinematography; Best Editing. **Cast:** Steve McQueen, Mako, Richard Crenna, Candice Bergen, Richard Attenborough, Marayat Andriane, Larry Gates, Charles Robinson, Simon Oakland. **Credits:** Dir: Robert Wise; Prod: Robert Wise; Writer: Robert Anderson; DP: Joseph MacDonald; Ed: William H. Reynolds; Prod Design: Boris Leven; Composer: Jerry Goldsmith. Color, 182 min. **VHS, LASER**

The Sandpiper

(1965) MGM

The fourth Burton-Taylor vehicle (following *Cleopatra*, *The VIPs*, and *Night of the Iguana*) is a steamy love triangle drama formed by an Episcopal minister (Burton), his wife (Saint), and a bohemian painter (Taylor). Free-loving Taylor, outfitted in grimy sweatshirt and black tights, plays Hollywood's idea of the Beat Generation. She catches the eye of Burton when her son (played by Morgan Mason, son of James Mason) gets sent to his boarding school. Written by Trumbo and directed by Minnelli, this mostly serves to remind us of the intense screen chemistry of Burton and Taylor and the endless fascination they hold for audiences. **Academy Awards:** Best Song ("The Shadow of Your Smile"). **Cast:** Elizabeth Taylor, Richard Burton, Eva Marie Saint, Charles Bronson, Robert Webber, James Edwards, Torin Thatcher, Tom Drake. **Credits:** Dir: Vincente Minnelli; Prod: Martin Ransohoff; Writer: Dalton Trumbo, Michael Wilson; DP: Milton Krasner; Ed: David Bretherton; Composer: Johnny Mandel; Art Director: George W. Davis. Color, 117 min. **VHS**

Sands of Iwo Jima

(1949) Republic

This is an outstanding WWII action movie with real drama and believable performances substituting for hollow flag-waving. Lifelong Marine Wayne drills his men relentlessly, knowing that training will be their salvation in the bloody Pacific battles ahead. Agar, the son of a Marine hero, particularly resents his tough treatment of the recruits. Tested on Tarawa, his men see Wayne's steel when he lets his friend Brown scream through the night without responding so he doesn't give their position away. After a leave in Hawaii that reveals the men's human side, they're sent to the devastation of Iwo Jima. The special anniversary edition includes *The Making of Sands of Iwo Jima* hosted by Leonard Maltin, a reproduction of an original theatrical poster and a lobby card, and the original theatrical trailer. Academy Award Nominations: 4, including Best Actor: John Wayne; Best Original Screenplay. **Cast:** John

Wayne, Adele Mara, Forrest Tucker, John Agar, Richard Jaeckel, Wally Cassell, James Brown, Richard Webb. **Credits:** Dir: Allan Dwan; Prod: Edmund Grainger; Writer: Harry Brown, James Edward Grant; DP: Reggie Lanning; Ed: Richard L. Van Enger; Composer: Victor Young; Art Director: James Sullivan. B&W, 110 min. **VHS, LASER, DVD**

San Francisco
(1936) MGM
One of the all-time greats of the classic era, this rousing period drama opens in the early days of the fateful year 1906. Barbary Coast music-hall owner Gable looks over a new singing prospect, MacDonald, and then meets up with pal Tracy, a priest, for a brisk workout in the ring. As Gable molds MacDonald's style to fit his rambunctious clientele, he sees she's a quality lady, also not overlooked by his rival, Holt, the impresario of the opera house. The rivalry for MacDonald's attention and the controversy over Gable's bawdy entertainment comes to a sharp conclusion when the earth splits open (in some of the most ingenious effects of the day) in the Great Earthquake of 1906. Academy Award Nominations: 5, including Best Picture; Best Director; Best Actor: Spencer Tracy; Best Original Story. **Academy Awards:** Best Sound Recording. **Cast:** Clark Gable, Jeanette MacDonald, Spencer Tracy, Jack Holt, Jessie Ralph, Ted Healy, Shirley Ross, Al Shean. **Credits:** Dir: W. S. Van Dyke; Prod: John Emerson, Bernard Hyman; Writer: Anita Loos, Erich Von Stroheim; DP: Oliver T. Marsh; Ed: Tom Held; Prod Design: Cedric Gibbons; Composer: Edward Ward; SFX: A. Arnold Gillespie. B&W, 117 min. **VHS, LASER**

The San Francisco Story
(1952) Warner Bros.
In an action drama set in Gold Rush days, when fortunes were made overnight and power relied on brutal frontier methods, former miner McCrea backs up his newspaper editor friend Stevens in a campaign to rid San Francisco of corrupt political boss Blackmer. De Carlo is the politician's girlfriend who switches her allegiance to McCrea. **Cast:** Joel McCrea, Yvonne De Carlo, Sidney Blackmer, Richard Erdman, Florence Bates, Onslow Stevens, John Raven, O. Z. Whitehead, Ralph Dumke, Robert Foulk. **Credits:** Dir: Robert Parrish; Prod: Howard Welsch; Writer: Richard Sum-

mers, D. D. Beauchamp; DP: John Seitz; Ed: Otto Ludwig; Prod Design: George Jenkins; Composer: Emil Newman, Paul Dunlap, Joseph Gershenson; Costumes: Yvonne Wood; Art Director: Bernard Herzbrun, Robert Clatworthy. B&W, 80 min.

San Quentin
(1937) Warner Bros.
This is a realistic depiction of life behind bars shot on location in one of the most famous prisons in the world. O'Brien comes to San Quentin to reform the hard-bitten treatment of prisoners by MacLane, who stirs up trouble. He meets nightclub singer Sheridan, whose brother Bogart is a troublemaker locked up in the prison. O'Brien starts to favor Bogart and the con makes a break for it, running to his sister's apartment where he encounters O'Brien. The hardened con reforms too late. One of O'Brien's ex-con pals counseled Bacon on authentic action and dialogue. **Cast:** Pat O'Brien, Humphrey Bogart, Ann Sheridan, Barton MacLane, Joe Sawyer, Veda Ann Borg. **Credits:** Dir: Lloyd Bacon; Prod: Samuel Bischoff; Writer: Peter Milne, Humphrey Cobb; DP: Sidney Hickox; Ed: William Holmes; Composer: Heinz Roemhold, David Raksin; Art Director: Esdras Hartley. B&W, 70 min.

San Quentin
(1946) RKO
Men-behind-bars action-adventure depicts the founding of an organization, The Inmates Welfare League, to prepare the jailed men for the outside. When a member escapes and goes on a rampage, a former inmate member (Tierney) helps capture the escapee to ensure the survival of the group. Raymond Burr's film debut. **Cast:** Lawrence Tierney, Marian Carr, Barton MacLane, Carol Forman, Tom Keene, Joe Devlin, James Robbins, Harry Shannon, Lee Bonnell, Robert Clarke. **Credits:** Dir: Gordon Douglas; Prod: Martin Mooney; Writer: Lawrence Kimble, Arthur Ross, Howard Green; DP: Frank Redman; Ed: Marvin Celli; Composer: Paul Sawtell; Art Director: Albert D'Agostino. B&W, 66 min.

Santa Fe
(1951) Columbia
In an okay Western, Scott plays a former Confederate soldier resolved to live peacefully in the reunited nation working for the Santa Fe railroad. His brothers refuse to accept defeat and throw in with a gang led by Roberts. When they decide to hold up the

Santa Fe line, the brothers square off. **Cast:** Randolph Scott, Janis Carter, Jerome Courtland, Peter Thompson, John Archer, Warner Anderson, Roy Roberts, Jock Mahoney. **Credits:** Dir: Irving Pichel; Prod: Harry Joe Brown; Writer: Kenneth Gamet; DP: Charles Lawton, Jr.; Ed: Gene Havlick; Prod Design: Walter Holscher. Color, 87 min. **VHS**

Santa Fe Trail
(1940) Warner Bros.
Curtiz directs Flynn as J. E. B. Stuart, one of the Confederacy's greatest generals. This follows Stuart from his entrance at West Point (where he is one of an illustrious class that led both sides of the Civil War), his friendship with Custer (Reagan), and rivalry with Heflin, who gets tossed out for abolitionist agitating. The rivals meet again when Flynn is assigned to the Kansas regiment sent to quell the abolitionist uprising led by John Brown (Massey). **Cast:** Ronald Reagan, Errol Flynn, Olivia de Havilland, Van Heflin, Raymond Massey, Alan Hale, Guinn "Big Boy" Williams, Henry O'Neill. **Credits:** Dir: Michael Curtiz; Prod: Robert Fellows; Writer: Robert Buckner; DP: Sol Polito; Ed: George Amy; Composer: Max Steiner; Art Director: John Hughes. B&W, 110 min. **VHS**

Saratoga
(1937) MGM
Harlow's last film features one of her best performances. Raised among the Saratoga horse farms, Harlow's been sheltered from the racetrack by her father (Hale). But after her father loses his farm to gambler Gable and dies of a heart attack, she and her fiancé, wealthy stockbroker Pidgeon (who also owes Gable money), work out a scheme to get the money back. Meanwhile, Gable wants more of Pidgeon's money, and Harlow, too. Harlow collapsed before shooting was complete, and a double was used for some of her scenes. After a personally disastrous few years, Harlow succumbed to uremic poisoning after her mother, a devotee of faith healing, was slow to seek medical attention. **Cast:** Jean Harlow, Clark Gable, Lionel Barrymore, Frank Morgan, Walter Pidgeon, Una Merkel, Cliff Edwards, George Zucco, Margaret Hamilton, Jonathan Hale, Hattie McDaniel. **Credits:** Dir: Jack Conway; Prod: Bernard Hyman; Writer: Anita Loos, Robert E. Hopkins; DP: Ray June; Ed: Elmo Veron; Prod Design: Cedric Gibbons; Composer: Edward Ward; Art Director: John Detlie. B&W, 92 min. **VHS**

Saratoga Trunk

(1946) Warner Bros.

Cooper and Bergman reunite after their success in *For Whom the Bell Tolls* (1943). This costume drama based on an Edna Ferber novel finds Bergman a Creole belle returning to New Orleans from Paris in 1875. She's determined to find a rich husband and wreak havoc on her father's despised family, though the first man she lays eyes on is Texas gambler Cooper. She follows him to the ritzy watering hole of Saratoga Springs where she pretends to be a wealthy French mademoiselle. Bergman snares financier Warburton, but the arrangements fall apart when she sees Cooper, the man she truly loves, in danger. Elegantly produced if something of a yawner. Academy Award Nomination for Best Supporting Actress: Flora Robson. **Cast:** Gary Cooper, Ingrid Bergman, Flora Robson, Jerry Austin, John Warburton, Florence Bates. **Credits:** Dir: Sam Wood; Prod: Hal Wallis; Writer: Casey Robinson; DP: Ernest Haller; Ed: Ralph Dawson; Composer: Max Steiner. B&W, 135 min. **VHS**

Satan Met a Lady

(1936) Warner Bros.

The second screen version of Dashiell Hammett's *Maltese Falcon* is of interest mostly for Davis in the lead and for comparison to Huston's later classic version. This outing adds humor and changes the names, but to no good effect. Her refusal at first to take this assignment began one of Davis's legendary battles with Jack Warner. **Cast:** Bette Davis, Warren William, Alison Skipworth, Arthur Treacher, Winifred Shaw, Marie Wilson, Porter Hall, Maynard Holmes. **Credits:** Dir: William Dieterle; Prod: Henry Blanke; Writer: Brown Holmes; DP: Arthur Edeson; Ed: Max Parker; Prod Design: Max Parker. B&W, 75 min. **VHS**

Saturday Night Fever

(1977) Paramount

Not much more than a teen potboiler revolving around a Brooklyn disco, this nevertheless became a pop-culture phenomenon not only at the box office but with its double-album sound track that sold tens of millions of copies. From the opening sequence of Travolta's impeccably shod feet stepping confidently down the Brooklyn streets, a '70s icon was born. The plot follows paint-store clerk Travolta as he comes alive every Saturday night at the disco, where he rules the floor. His horizons start to expand when he

teams for a dance contest with Gorney, an ambitious secretary who has her sights set on Manhattan, and a friend dies. Credit Travolta's easy sexiness in the dance sequences, the sound track (including the Bee Gees songs written for the movie) that blasted from every radio for months, and the exquisite timing of the release that caught the national mood of hedonism and restlessness for making this a perfect time capsule. A sequel, *Staying Alive*, appeared in 1983. Academy Award Nomination for Best Actor: John Travolta. **Cast:** John Travolta, Karen Lynn Gorney, Donna Pescow, Barry Miller, Bruce Ornstein, Julie Bovasso, Sam Coppola, Denny Dillon. **Credits:** Dir: John Badham; Prod: Robert Stigwood; Writer: Norman Wexler; DP: Ralf D. Bode; Ed: David Rawlins; Prod Design: Charles Bailey; Composer: Barry Gibb, Robin Gibb, Maurice Gibb, David Shire. Color, 118 min. **VHS**

Saturday's Children

(1940) Warner Bros.

This is a story about two young New Yorkers who fall in love and face the challenge of making it work when money's tight. Shirley plays a hardworking office girl and Garfield plays the dreamy inventor she sets her sights on. Shirley's sister (Patrick) plots their marriage before Garfield can slip off to the Philippines while their father (Rains) schemes to get the young lovers some cash. **Cast:** John Garfield, Anne Shirley, Claude Rains, Lee Patrick, George Tobias, Roscoe Karns, Dennie Moore, Elisabeth Risdon, Berton Churchill, John Ridgely. **Credits:** Dir: Vincent Sherman; Prod: Henry Blanke, Hal B. Wallis; Writer: Julius J. Epstein, Philip G. Epstein; Story: Maxwell Anderson; DP: James Wong Howe; Ed: Owen Marks; Prod Design: Hugh Reticker; Composer: Adolph Deutsch. B&W, 101 min.

The Savage

(1952) Paramount

Heston stars as a white man raised by the Sioux whose loyalty to his adopted tribe is questioned when white soldiers and settlers move into the area. He demonstrates his allegiance by agreeing to lead the cavalry into an ambush after his Indian lover is killed. But when he finds himself unwilling to incite further bloodshed, he is ostracized by the tribe. He leaves his Indian home with a warning of more bloodshed to come. **Cast:** Ted De Corsia, Ian MacDonald, Milburn Stone, Angela

Clarke, Charlton Heston, Susan Morrow, Peter Hanson, Joan Taylor, Richard Rober, Don Porter. **Credits:** Dir: George Marshall; Prod: George Marshall; Writer: Sidney Boehm; DP: John Seitz; Ed: Arthur Schmidt; Art Director: Hal Pereira, William Flannery. B&W, 95 min.

Savage Sam

(1963) Disney

In this sequel to *Old Yeller*, the famous dog's offspring saves his masters from a group of Apache Indians. The intrepid canine must brave wolves and wildcats before accomplishing his task. Not up to the usual Disney standards, but okay for kids if everything else is rented. **Cast:** Brian Keith, Tommy Kirk, Kevin Corcoran, Dewey Martin, Jeff York, Royal Dano, Marta Kristen, Rafael Campos. **Credits:** Dir: Norman Tokar; Prod: Bill Anderson; Writer: Fred Gipson, William Tunberg; DP: Edward Colman; Ed: Grant K. Smith; Prod Design: Carroll Clark; Composer: Oliver Wallace; Art Director: Marvin Aubrey Davis. Color, 103 min. **VHS**

Save the Tiger

(1973) Paramount

Lemmon performs magnificently in a bleak story that depicts an outwardly successful man questioning the value of the material prosperity he's desperately trying to maintain. Lemmon and Gilford run an apparel company and are in deep financial straits. In the course of two days, Lemmon considers torching his warehouse for the insurance settlement, his main client suffers a heart attack in a tryst Lemmon arranged, he dabbles with free love but makes no contact with a free-spirit hitchhiker, and breaks down at the premiere of his company's new line. Thoughtful and full of wonderful actors in well-written roles. Academy Award Nominations: 3, including Best (Original) Story and Screenplay. **Academy Awards:** Best Actor: Jack Lemmon. **Cast:** Jack Lemmon, Jack Gilford, Patricia Smith, Laurie Heineman, Norman Burton, Thayer David, William Hansen, Harvey Jason. **Credits:** Dir: John G. Avildsen; Prod: Steve Shagan; Writer: Steve Shagan; DP: James Crabe; Ed: David Bretherton; Composer: Marvin Hamlisch; Art Director: Jack Collis. Color, 100 min. **VHS, LASER**

Sayonara

(1957) Warner Bros.

In an insightful, tragic romantic drama, prejudice takes its toll on American servicemen and their Japanese lovers, but can't stop true love. During the Korean War, Brando is given a plum assignment to Japan, against his wishes, courtesy of his future father-in-law. There he experiences the base rules against fraternization and meets Buttons, who has fallen in love with a Japanese woman and intends to marry her. Brando earns the wrath of his fiancée (Owens) and her family when he stands up with his friend at his wedding, and then becomes entranced himself with a member of a famous Japanese dance troupe. The two become lovers despite the objections of both the Americans and the Japanese. When the base commander orders servicemen with Japanese wives home without their spouses, Buttons and Brando are arrested, and Buttons's relationship comes to a tragic end. Brando and Logan clashed offscreen but each produced some of his best work for the screen. Golden Globe for Best Supporting Actor: Red Buttons. Academy Award Nominations: 10, including Best Picture; Best Director; Best Actor: Marlon Brando; Best (Adapted) Screenplay. **Academy Awards:** Best Supporting Actor: Red Buttons; Best Supporting Actress: Miyoshi Umeki; Best Sound; Best Art Direction—Set Decoration. **Cast:** Marlon Brando, James Garner, Ricardo Montalban, Red Buttons, Miyoshi Umeki, Patricia Owens, Martha Scott, Miiko Taka. **Credits:** Dir: Joshua Logan; Prod: William Goetz; Writer: Paul Osborn; DP: Ellsworth Fredricks; Ed: Arthur Schmidt; Prod Design: Ted Haworth; Composer: Franz Waxman. Color, 148 min. VHS, LASER

Scandalous John
(1971) Disney
This touching Disney comedy is about an impoverished rancher (Keith) who believes in the code of the Old West, and his attempt to save his land from a developer. With the developer's son and Keith's daughter, Keith goes on one last cattle drive, herding only a lonely steer. **Cast:** Brian Keith, Alfonso Arau, Michele Carey, Rick Lenz, Harry Morgan, Simon Oakland, Bill Williams, Christopher Dark. **Credits:** Dir: Robert Butler; Prod: Bill Walsh; Writer: Bill Walsh, Don DaGradi; DP: Frank Phillips; Ed: Cotton Warburton; Prod Design: John B. Mansbridge. Color, 113 min. VHS

Scandal Sheet
(1952) Columbia
This excellent noir full of savagely ironic twists is directed by Karlson from a novel, *The Dark Page,* by

Samuel Fuller. Crawford takes over a venerable, but ailing, New York daily and resuscitates it as a scandal sheet with outrageous publicity stunts. Crawford cultivates a successor in Derek, but Derek's girlfriend (Reed) is appalled by the paper's new direction. At a paper-sponsored Lonely Hearts Ball, Crawford sees the wife he left penniless (DeCamp), who tries to blackmail him. After Crawford murders the woman, Derek emulates his boss by going after the big story. He winds up with a very different front-page exclusive than he intended. A gripping story well told. **Cast:** John Derek, Donna Reed, Broderick Crawford, Rosemary DeCamp, Henry O'Neil, Harry Morgan, James Millican, Griff Barnett, Jonathan Hale, Pierre Watkin. **Credits:** Dir: Phil Karlson; Prod: Edward Small; Writer: Ted Sherdeman, Eugene Ling, James Poe; DP: Burnett Guffey; Ed: Jerome Thoms; Composer: George Duning, Morris Stoloff; Art Director: Robert Peterson. B&W, 82 min.

Scaramouche
(1952) MGM
In this expensively-mounted, robust adaptation of Raphael Sabatini's 1921 novel, Granger wanders revolutionary France seeking his real father and avenging the death of his friend at the hands of the marquis, a deadly swordsman (Ferrer). He also falls in love with both aristocratic Leigh and Parker, an actress in the theater company he joins to hide and learn the art of swordplay. Once equipped with fencing skills, he pursues the marquis in a climactic swordfight that is one of the most colorful fencing matches ever put on film. **Cast:** Stewart Granger, Eleanor Parker, Janet Leigh, Mel Ferrer, Henry Wilcoxon, Nina Foch, Richard Anderson, Robert Coote. **Credits:** Dir: George Sidney; Prod: Carey Wilson; Writer: Ronald Millar, George Froeschel; DP: Charles Rosher; Ed: James E. Newcom; Prod Design: Cedric Gibbons, Hans Peters; Composer: Victor Young. Color, 118 min. VHS, LASER

Scarecrow
(1973) Warner Bros.
Ex-con Hackman hooks up with itinerant sailor Pacino for a road movie that explores the growing friendship between the two men. Hackman trades his plans for his own business to care for his new pal after Pacino breaks down. A sensitive drama, it won a Golden Palm Award at Cannes. **Cast:** Gene Hackman, Al Pacino,

Dorothy Tristan, Eileen Brennan, Ann Wedgeworth, Richard Lynch, Penny Allen, Rutanya Alda. **Credits:** Dir: Jerry Schatzberg; Prod: Robert Sherman; Writer: Garry Michael White; DP: Vilmos Zsigmond; Ed: Evan Lottman; Prod Design: Albert Brenner; Composer: Fred Myrow. Color, 112 min. VHS, LASER

Scared Stiff
(1953) Paramount
In a better-than-average Martin and Lewis, the boys flee the Mob onto an island owned by heiress Scott, and Jerry does a great Carmen Miranda imitation. Scott's island home turns out to be a haunted (mostly by gangsters) castle that holds a load of gold. Based on the Hope vehicle *The Ghost Breakers* (1940). **Cast:** Jerry Lewis, Dean Martin, Lizabeth Scott, Carmen Miranda, Dorothy Malone, George Dolenz, William Ching, Jack Lambert. **Credits:** Dir: George Marshall; Prod: Hal B. Wallis; Writer: Herbert Baker, Walter DeLeon, Ed Simmons, Norman Lear; DP: Ernest Laszlo; Ed: Warren Low; Prod Design: Franz Bachelin; Composer: Leith Stevens; Art Director: Hal Pereira. B&W, 109 min. VHS, LASER

Scar-Face
(1932) United Artists
The explosion of gangster films in the first years of the Depression reached a violent, incendiary crescendo with this classic from Hawks. Also known as "The Shame of a Nation," this follows the rise of a power-mad, ruthless killer (Muni) as he murders his way to the top of the Chicago gangs. Writer Hecht drew on his Chicago newspaper experience and Hawks received plenty of advice from real mobsters to create what was clearly a portrait of Al Capone, Johnny Torrio, and Bugs Moran and the killing sprees that enraged and fascinated the public. From the first scene, it's clear that Muni is a remorseless murderer, stupidly arrogant, rather than the rakish outlaws that Hollywood was in the process of mythologizing. He first kills on order from his boss, Perkins, but soon goads Perkins into rubbing out his boss, Vejar. Muni soon turns the gun on Perkins and takes over his operation and his moll, Morley. Throughout, Muni and his friend Raft have a running battle with North Side gang boss Karloff, a duel that culminates in a slaughter modeled after the St. Valentine's Day Massacre. When Muni discovers that Raft has been living with Dvo-

rak, Muni's sister, with whom he has a near-incestuous attachment, he kills his only friend and then faces, sniveling, the guns of the cops. Hawks pushes the action as fast as the bullets fly, using innovative camera moves and insisting on realism, with live machine-gun fire used to decimate sets and multiple car crashes. The result was a box-office smash (it was also popular with its subjects; Capone himself owned a print) and both Muni and Raft became instant stars, but it also created a tangle with the censors. Hughes released both Hawks's cut, which depicts Muni's ignominious death in a gutter, and a version that has Muni tried and sentenced to death. The laserdisc contains both the original ending and the Motion Picture Producers' Association ending. Remade with Al Pacino in 1983. Selected as a National Film Registry Outstanding Film. **Cast:** Paul Muni, Ann Dvorak, George Raft, Boris Karloff, Karen Morley, Osgood Perkins, Harry Vejar, Vince Barnett, C. Henry Gordon. **Credits:** Dir: Howard Hawks; Prod: Howard Hughes; Writer: W. R. Burnett, Ben Hecht, Seton I. Miller, John Lee Mahin, Fred Pasley; Story: Armitage Trail; DP: Lee Garmes, L. W. O'Connell; Ed: Edward Curtiss; Prod Design: Harry Olivier; Composer: Adolph Tandler, Gus Arnheim. B&W, 93 min. **VHS, LASER**

Scar-Face (1932)

The Scarlet Empress

(1934) Paramount
Von Sternberg created a landmark of the early sound era with this intricately detailed biopic of Catherine the Great of Russia, embodied by his great discovery, Dietrich. Taken from her Prussian family as a teenager and wed to the lunatic Peter (Jaffe in a remarkable portrayal of madness), Dietrich survives palace intrigue and multiple affairs to emerge as the ruler of Russia. Von Sternberg lavishes his command of film style on his muse, and Dietrich emerges from a believable adolescence to an imperious beauty with a commanding hauteur. **Cast:** Marlene Dietrich, John Lodge, Sam Jaffe, C. Aubrey Smith, Louise Dresser, Olive Tell, Gavin Gordon, Jameson Thomas, Maria Sieber. **Credits:** Dir: Josef von Sternberg; Writer: Manuel Komroff; DP: Bert Glennon; Ed: Josef von Sternberg; Composer: Felix Mendelssohn, Richard Wagner, Josef von Sternberg, Pyotr Ilich Tchaikovsky; Art Director: Hans Dreier, Peter Ballbusch, Richard Kollorsz; Costumes: Travis Banton. B&W, 105 min. **VHS**

Scarlet Street

(1945) Universal
This bleak Lang noir depicts the downward spiral of a meek store clerk (Robinson) whom fate marks as a patsy. Robinson, who spends his free time painting, defends Bennett from a mugging and becomes fascinated with her, telling her he's a famous artist. Bennett and her petty criminal boyfriend Duryea set Robinson up for a score, with Bennett leading him on until they can relieve him of the cash his passion has forced him to embezzle. When Robinson catches the two in a clinch, he kills Bennett and frames Duryea for the murder. Now homeless and jobless, Robinson wanders the streets, his only satisfaction coming from the surge of electricity being sent toward Duryea's chair. Grim, but fascinating. **Cast:** Edward G. Robinson, Joan Bennett, Dan Duryea, Margaret Lindsay, Rosalind Ivan, Jess Barker, Arthur Loft, Samuel S. Hinds. **Credits:** Dir: Fritz Lang; Prod: Fritz Lang; Writer: Dudley Nichols; DP: Milton Krasner; Ed: Arthur Hilton; Composer: H. J. Salter; Art Director: Alexander Golitzen, John B. Goodman. B&W, 105 min. **VHS**

The Scoundrel

(1935) Paramount
This curiosity from Hecht and MacArthur must count as one of America's earliest art films. With beautifully written dialogue, Hecht and MacArthur create an acid portrait of a louse (Coward, in his first starring role). Callous, eager to destroy the virtue of any innocent who crosses his experienced path, he crushes the romance of good-hearted Haydon, and then meets his match in Williams. When Coward perishes in a plane crash, he gets a chance to return to see if he can find anyone who regrets his passing. **Academy Awards:** Best Original Story. **Cast:** Noel Coward, Julie Haydon, Hope Williams, Helen Strickland, Lionel Stander, Everly Gregg, Dawn O'Day, Frank Conlon, Ernest Cossart, Harry Davenport. **Credits:** Dir: Ben Hecht, Charles MacArthur; Prod: Ben Hecht, Charles MacArthur; Writer: Charles McGraw, Ben Hecht, Charles MacArthur; DP: Lee Garmes; Ed: Arthur Ellis; Prod Design: Walter E. Keller; Composer: George Antheil. B&W, 75 min.

The Sea Chase

(1955) Warner Bros.
In perhaps the most unusual casting of Wayne's career, he plays an anti-Nazi German freighter captain at the beginning of WWII attempting to sail his ship from Australia to the North Sea rather than risk internment. Both Allied and German ships follow in pursuit, while Wayne battles storms, sharks, and romances. **Cast:** John Wayne, Lana Turner, Tab Hunter, James Arness, Lyle Bettger, David Farrar, Dick Davalos, John Qualen. **Credits:** Dir: John Farrow; Prod: John Farrow; Writer: James Warner Bellah; DP: William Clothier; Ed: William Ziegler; Prod Design: Franz Bachelin; Composer: Roy Webb. Color, 117 min. **VHS, LASER**

The Sea Gypsies

(1978) Warner Bros.

Logan and his kids are joined by a magazine writer and a stowaway for a seagoing expedition. The adventurers' around-the-world cruise comes to an end when they are shipwrecked on an Aleutian Island. Faced with dangerous animals and the onset of the brutal Alaskan winter, they decide to construct an escape craft. Family adventure. **Cast:** Robert Logan, Mikki Jamison-Olsen, Heather Rattray, Cjon Damitri Patterson, Shannon Saylor. **Credits:** Dir: Stewart Raffill; Prod: Joseph C. Raffill; Writer: Stewart Raffill; DP: Thomas McHugh; Ed: R. Hansel Brown, Art Stafford; Composer: Fred Steiner. Color, 102 min. **VHS**

The Sea Hawk

(1940) Warner Bros.

This spirited swashbuckler cemented Flynn's dashing image he'd created with *Captain Blood* (also directed by Curtiz) with his derring-do as Capt. Geoffrey Thorpe, an English buccaneer battling the Spanish at the behest of Elizabeth I (Robson). There was no expense spared for the battles at sea and some of the most spirited sword-play ever seen on film. Flynn did his own stunts, driven to the edge of disaster by a slave-driving Curtiz. A rousing score by Korngold. Koch's first screenplay was based on a classic adventure novel by Rafael Sabatini, author of *Scaramouche*. Academy Award Nominations: 4, including Best Score; Best Sound. **Cast:** Errol Flynn, Flora Robson,, Brenda Marshall, Henry Daniell, Claude Rains, Donald Crisp, Alan Hale, Una O'Connor. **Credits:** Dir: Michael Curtiz; Prod: Henry Blanke; Writer: Howard Koch; DP: Sol Polito; Ed: George Amy; Prod Design: Anton Grot; Composer: Erich Wolfgang Korngold. B&W, 128 min. **VHS, LASER**

The Sea of Grass

(1947) MGM

Tracy and Hepburn star in director Kazan's second film, an adaptation of Conrad Richter's generational saga about homesteaders in conflict with ranchers. Stubborn cattle baron Tracy loses the sympathy of wife Hepburn after he turns to violence to rid himself of homesteaders. Fleeing to the city, she meets a Denver attorney (Douglas) who had defended the homesteaders' rights and he eventually fathers her child. Hepburn returns home, but years later, the boy, plagued by his illegitimacy, grows up to become an outlaw (Walker). In retrospect, this seems the least typical film in the careers of Tracy and Hepburn, as well as that of Kazan. **Cast:** Katharine Hepburn, Spencer Tracy, Melvyn Douglas, Phyllis Thaxter, Robert Walker, Edgar Buchanan, Harry Carey, Ruth Nelson. **Credits:** Dir: Elia Kazan; Prod: Pandro S. Berman; Writer: Marguerite Roberts; DP: Harry Stradling; Ed: Robert J. Kern; Prod Design: Cedric Gibbons; Composer: Herbert Stothart. B&W, 133 min. **VHS**

The Search

(1948) MGM

Audiences around the world saw Clift first in this moving story of displaced European war orphans shot on location in the ruins of Europe. (He had previously made *Red River* for Howard Hawks, released a few months after this.) Clift, playing an American G.I. caring for a young survivor of a concentration camp (Jandl), joins Corey in an attempt to maneuver through the postwar bureaucracy and reunite the boy with his family's survivors. Golden Globes for Best Screenplay; Special Achievement: Ivan Jandl. Academy Award Nominations: 4, including Best Director; Best Actor: Montgomery Clift; Best Screenplay. **Academy Awards:** Best Motion Picture Story; Special Achievement Award: Ivan Jandl. **Cast:** Montgomery Clift, Ivan Jandl, Aline MacMahon, Jarmila Novotna, Wendell Corey, William Penn Adair Rogers, Mary Patton, E. G. Morrison. **Credits:** Dir: Fred Zinnemann; Prod: Lazar Wechsler; Writer: Richard Schweizer, David Wechsler, Paul Jarrico; DP: Emil Berna; Ed: Hermann Haller; Composer: Robert Blum. B&W, 105 min. **VHS**

The Searchers

(1956) Warner Bros.

Arguably the finest Western in the Ford and Wayne canon, this appears perennially on every list of the greatest American films of all time. After Comanches kill his brother's family and kidnap their daughters, bitter Confederate veteran Wayne sets forth on a hate-ridden quest to find his nieces (Scott and Wood) and save them from the "savages." He reluctantly brings along young Hunter, the adopted son of a family also killed by Indians. Their quest leads them hundreds of miles over seven agonizing years of dead ends and double crosses. As it becomes clear that Wood has accepted her life among the Comanches, Wayne resolves not to rescue her but to save her from disgrace by killing her, a resolve that comes to a heart-stopping, emotional climax. Ford's story of moral ambiguity lives in Wayne's dense, richly layered characterization of a man whose brutal tendencies, hardened by his experiences of war and the frontier, balance with a tender, forlorn longing for home and family, expressed in his words to the frightened girl as he holds her life in his hands: "Let's go home, Debbie." The character dramatically upends Wayne's heroic archetype; it's rumored that after shooting the film, Ford, who had directed Wayne many times before, exclaimed, "I didn't know he could act!" Highly influential to a generation of filmmakers. Selected as a National Film Registry Outstanding Film. **Cast:** John Wayne, Jeffrey Hunter, Vera Miles, Ward Bond, Natalie Wood, Pippa Scott, John Qualen, Olive Carey, Henry Brandon. **Credits:** Dir: John Ford; Prod: Merian C. Cooper, C. V. Whitney; Writer: Frank S. Nugent; Story: Alan LeMay; DP: Winton C. Hoch; Ed: Jack Murray; Composer: Max Steiner; Art Director: Frank Hotaling, James Basevi. Color, 144 min. **VHS, LASER, DVD**

The Searching Wind

(1946) Paramount

This antiwar melodrama might have been better received if not released just as peace settled on the world. An American diplomat in Italy (Young) wavers in the face of fascism as he longs for fiery reporter Sidney, with whom he has had a long-running affair. His father (Digges), an influential newspaper publisher, becomes impatient with Young's policy, and the diplomat's son (Dick) loses a leg in the war and makes an impassioned case to end all wars. **Cast:** Robert Young, Sylvia Sidney, Ann Richards, Douglas Dick, Dudley Digges, Albert Bassermann, Dan Seymour, Marietta Canty, Charles D. Brown, Don Castle. **Credits:** Dir: William Dieterle; Prod: Hal B. Wallis; Writer: Lillian Hellman; DP: Lee Garmes; Ed: Warren Low; Composer: Victor Young; Art Director: Franz Bachelin, Hans Dreier. B&W, 108 min.

The Sea Wolf

(1941) Warner Bros.

This is the finest version of the often-filmed Jack London novel, with Robinson as the vicious Wolf Larsen, captain of the sinister ship the *Ghost*. Garfield plays the sailor running away from his past, while Knox and Lupino play a writer and an escapee of a reformatory rescued after a collision at sea. A moody exercise, with the fog-enshrouded world of the ship comprising the film's entire universe. Notable direction by Curtiz and a fine score by Korngold. Most recently remade in 1993 as a cable-TV film with Charles Bronson and Christopher Reeve. Academy Award Nomination for Best Special Effects. **Cast:** Edward G. Robinson, John Garfield, Ida Lupino, Alexander Knox, Gene Lockhart, Barry Fitzgerald, Stanley Ridges, Francis McDonald. **Credits:** Dir: Michael Curtiz; Prod: Henry Blanke; Writer: Robert Rossen; DP: Sol Polito; Ed: George Amy; Prod Design: Anton Grot; Composer: Erich Wolfgang Korngold; SFX: Byron Haskin, Nathan Levinson. B&W, 90 min. VHS

Second Chance
(1953) RKO
Mitchum and Darnell each try to make a new beginning south of the border. He's a prizefighter disturbed by his killing of an opponent and Darnell's a mobster's girlfriend on the run from a commission that wants her to testify. They fall in love but hit man Palance is determined to find Darnell before the commission does. The terrific climax, with a disabled cable car dangling high above an abyss as the cables snap one by one, makes great use of the original 3-D format. **Cast:** Robert Mitchum, Linda Darnell, Jack Palance, Reginald Sheffield, Rodolfo Hoyos, Roy Roberts, Maurice Jara, Judy Walsh. **Credits:** Dir: Rudolph Maté; Prod: Sam Wiesenthal; Writer: Oscar Millard, Sydney Boehm; DP: William E. Snyder; Ed: Robert Ford; Composer: Roy Webb; Art Director: Carroll Clark, Albert S. D'Agostino. Color, 82 min. LASER

Second Chorus
(1940) Paramount
In an Astaire curiosity, he and Meredith bide their time in college as each vies for a place in Artie Shaw's show. A delicious Goddard manages both and they compete for a place in her heart as well. Offscreen, Meredith took the prize and married Goddard a few years after this production. Academy Award Nominations: Best Song ("Love of My Life"); Best Score. **Cast:** Fred Astaire, Paulette Goddard, Burgess Meredith, Artie Shaw, Charles Butterworth, Frank Melton, Jimmy Conlin, Adia Kuznetzoff. **Credits:** Dir: Frank Cavett; Prod: Boris Morros, Robert Stillman; Writer: Elaine Ryan, Ian McLellan Hunter, Johnny Mercer; DP: Theodor Sparkuhl; Ed: Jack Dennis; Choreography: Hermes Pan. B&W, 90 min. VHS, LASER

Second Fiddle
(1939) Fox
In this Irving Berlin musical the leads Power and Henie don't sing! Other-

wise it is a perfectly enjoyable minor musical with skating champion Henie up for a big role in Hollywood. Studio PR man Power convinces her aunt (Oliver) to let the skater make the trip to Tinseltown, and then creates a PR stunt romance between Henie and her costar, Vallee. Innocent Henie gets her heart broken, but Power wants to be her leading man and creates a romantic scenario for himself. Academy Award Nomination for Best Song ("I Poured My Heart into a Song"). **Cast:** Edna May Oliver, Tyrone Power, Lyle Talbot, Rudy Vallee, Sonja Henie, Mary Healy, Alan Dinehart, Minna Gombell. **Credits:** Dir: Sidney Lanfield; Prod: Gene Markey; Writer: Harry Tugend; Story: George Bradshaw; DP: Leon Shamroy; Ed: Robert Simpson; Composer: Irving Berlin; Art Director: Richard Day. B&W, 87 min. VHS

Second Honeymoon
(1937) Fox
Young's second husband (Talbot) makes a dull, conservative comparison with the excitement and energy she felt with first husband Power, which she's reminded of when they meet again in Florida. When Talbot has sudden business back home, he leaves Young with Power, who promptly woos his ex. After confusion over a gabby young gold digger (Weaver), Young begins a second honeymoon with Power. **Cast:** Tyrone Power, Loretta Young, Stuart Erwin, Lyle Talbot, J. Edward Bromberg, Paul Hurst, Jayne Regan, Hal K. Dawson, Claire Trevor, Marjorie Weaver. **Credits:** Dir: Walter Lang; Prod: Darryl F. Zanuck, Raymond Griffith; Writer: Kathryn Scola, Darrell Ware, Philip Wylie; DP: Ernest Palmer; Ed: Walter Thompson; Prod Design: Bernard Herzbrun; Composer: David Buttolph; Art Director: David Hall. B&W, 79 min.

Seconds
(1966) Paramount
This cult classic is now available on video in its original, unexpurgated version. Randolph gets the chance, for a fee, to escape his humdrum, workaday world and aging wife when offered the chance to become a "second," with a surgically altered face and a new name, home, and occupation. After a trip under the knife, Randolph becomes Hudson, a painter in the bohemian capital of Venice, California. But Hudson's uneasy with his new life and finds his way back home, where he discovers he can have his old identity back—if he can find a replacement. Some consider this Hudson's

best work on-screen. Academy Award Nomination for Best Cinematography. **Cast:** Rock Hudson, John Randolph, Salome Jens, Will Geer, Richard Anderson, Murray Hamilton, Karl Swenson. **Credits:** Dir: John Frankenheimer, Frances Reid; Prod: Edward Lewis; Writer: Lewis John Carlino; DP: James Wong Howe; Ed: Ferris Webster; Prod Design: Ted Haworth; Composer: Jerry Goldsmith. B&W, 107 min. VHS

Secret Agent
(1936) Gaumont
In the middle entry of Hitchcock's British spy trilogy following *The 39 Steps* (1935), Gielgud and Carroll pose as man and wife to pursue a secret agent in Switzerland. Paid assassin Lorre comes along to finish the job. The heroes first kill the wrong man, and then discover their quarry is a talkative American (Young) who has attached himself to Carroll. Interesting portrayals by Gielgud as an agent with empathy and Lorre as a cold-blooded killer. **Cast:** Robert Young, Madeleine Carroll, Peter Lorre, John Gielgud, Percy Marmont, Lilli Palmer, Charles Carson, Andreas Malandrinos, Florence Kahn. **Credits:** Dir: Alfred Hitchcock; Prod: Michael Balcon, Ivor Montagu; Writer: Charles Bennett, Ian Hay, Jesse Lasky, Jr., Alma Reville; Story: W. Somerset Maugham; DP: Bernard Knowles; Ed: Charles Frend; Composer: Louis Levy; Costumes: Joe Strassner. B&W, 93 min. VHS, LASER

The Secret Beyond the Door
(1948) Universal
This moody drama from Lang is about a wealthy heiress (Bennett) who marries Redgrave, the mysterious publisher of an architectural journal, in a romantic whirlwind and later comes to believe that he's a demented killer. Reportedly, Lang had Rozsa record his score in reverse and then played it back normally on the sound track to add a creepy effect to the music. **Cast:** Joan Bennett, Michael Redgrave, Anne Revere, Barbara O'Neil, Natalie Schafer, Paul Cavanagh, Anabel Shaw, James Seay. **Credits:** Dir: Fritz Lang; Prod: Fritz Lang; Writer: Silvia Richards; Story: Rufus King; DP: Stanley Cortez; Ed: Arthur Hilton; Prod Design: Max Parker; Composer: Miklos Rozsa. B&W, 99 min. VHS

The Secret Bride
(1935) Warner Bros.
This early Stanwyck vehicle is both love story and political whodunit. To avoid publicity, state attorney general

William marries the governor's daughter (Stanwyck) in a secret, out-of-state ceremony. The happy couple returns home to discover that her father (Byron) has been implicated in a graft case. An investigator gets murdered, and it's up to Stanwyck and William to solve the crime and clear her father's name. Until then, their marriage must remain a secret. **Cast:** Barbara Stanwyck, Warren William, Glenda Farrell, Grant Mitchell, Arthur Byron, Henry O'Neill, Douglass Dumbrille, Arthur Aylesworth, Willard Robertson, William Davidson. **Credits:** Dir: William Dieterle; Prod: Henry Blanke; Writer: Tom Buckingham, F. Hugh Herbert, Mary C. McCall; Story: Leonard Ide; DP: Ernest Haller; Ed: Owen Marks; Prod Design: Anton Grot; Composer: Leo F. Forbstein. B&W, 64 min.

The Secret Garden
(1949) MGM
Here is a touching children's classic from Frances Hodgson Burnett's novel about a sickly rich boy Colin (Stockwell) who lives with his somber father (Marshall) and his cousin, an orphan girl who comes to stay with them (O'Brien). After the death of Marshall's wife, he forbids entrance to her favorite garden. But O'Brien discovers the key, and begins to resurrect the lush greenery with the help of a neighbor boy. When they bring Stockwell to their colorful world (the scenes in the garden are in Technicolor), it brings the boy back to life. A noble adaptation of a story rich in metaphor and notable for its depiction of a troubled male world remade by a headstrong female outsider. Remade for TV in 1987, and then by Agnieszka Holland in 1993. **Cast:** Margaret O'Brien, Dean Stockwell, Herbert Marshall, Gladys Cooper, Elsa Lanchester, Reginald Owen, Aubrey Mather, George Zucco. **Credits:** Dir: Fred M. Wilcox; Prod: Clarence Brown; Writer: Robert Ardrey; DP: Ray June; Ed: Robert J. Kern; Prod Design: Cedric Gibbons, Urie McCleary; Composer: Bronislau Kaper. B&W and Color, 92 min. **VHS**

The Secret Heart
(1946) MGM
Colbert's stepdaughter, Allyson, refuses to accept the fact of her father's suicide and her behavior becomes alarming enough to ask a psychiatrist to intervene. He insists that Allyson visit the site of her father's death, but the plan backfires when she tries to kill herself. An unusual psychological melodrama.

Cast: Claudette Colbert, Walter Pidgeon, June Allyson, Lionel Barrymore, Robert Sterling, Marshall Thompson, Elizabeth Patterson, Richard Derr, Patricia Medina, Eily Malyon. **Credits:** Dir: Robert Z. Leonard; Prod: Edwin H. Knopf; Writer: Anne Morrison Chapin, Whitfield Cook; Story: William Brown Meloney, Rose Franken; DP: George Folsey, Jr.; Ed: Adrienne Fazan; Prod Design: Edwin B. Willis, Henry W. Grace; Composer: Bronislau Kaper; Art Director: Edward C. Carfagno, Cedric Gibbons. B&W, 97 min.

The Secret Life of Walter Mitty
(1947) RKO
The high point of Kaye's career comes as James Thurber's daydreaming everyman who escapes the mundane world by losing himself in adventurous, heroic fantasies. A proofreader for a pulp fiction magazine, Kaye's dreams of adventure include Western shoot-outs, seafaring derring-do, and aerial dogfights. His fantasies also include sexy Mayo, and she becomes a dream come true when she asks Kaye for help with some jewel thieves. Thurber's story didn't need the additional "real life" subplot, which tends to blur the ironic division between reality and Mitty's fantasy world, and Thurber hated the movie. But audiences loved it and continue to love it still. **Cast:** Danny Kaye, Virginia Mayo, Boris Karloff, Fay Bainter, Ann Rutherford, Thurston Hall, Konstantin Shayne, Florence Bates. **Credits:** Dir: Norman Z. McLeod; Prod: Samuel Goldwyn; Writer: Ken Englund, Everett Freeman; DP: Lee Garmes; Ed: Monica Collingwood; Composer: David Raksin; Art Director: George Jenkins, Perry Ferguson. Color, 110 min. **VHS, LASER, DVD**

The Secret of Santa Vittoria
(1969) United Artists
Following his signature role as Zorba, Quinn appeared in a series of films in which he reprised his personification of the human life force. Here he plays the drunken mayor of a small northern Italian hill town who, upon hearing that a retreating force of German soldiers is about to enter the village, rallies the citizens to hide their most precious treasure, millions of bottles of vintage wine. Based on the bestselling comic novel by Robert Crichton, which reportedly originated as a local legend, Kramer's film delivers the familiar character of the lovable Italian peasant who outwits the cold, methodical German. Academy Award

Nominations: Best Editing; Best Score. **Cast:** Anthony Quinn, Anna Magnani, Virna Lisi, Hardy Kruger, Sergio Franchi, Renato Rascel, Giancarlo Giannini, Eduardo Ciannelli, Leopoldo Trieste, Quinto Parmeggiani. **Credits:** Dir: Stanley Kramer; Prod: Stanley Kramer; Writer: William Rose, Ben Maddow; DP: Giuseppe Rotunno; Ed: William A. Lyon; Prod Design: Robert Clatworthy; Composer: Ernest Gold. Color, 139 min. **VHS**

The Secret Six
(1931) MGM
This slam-bang gangster movie more typical of Warner than MGM features early appearances by Harlow and Gable, the first of their five films together. Despite the sinister name, The Secret Six is a group of businessmen out to end the bootlegging and murder of a mob run by Beery and drunken lawyer Stone. After Beery bumps off their partner, Bellamy, two newspapermen (Gable and Brown) dig into the gang's activities, and Beery hires Harlow to watch the reporters. She switches sides after her boss kills Brown, and gets saved from Beery's kidnappers by Gable. Marion supposedly based the Beery character on Al Capone (a frequent model for vicious thugs). A pre-Code crime flick often banned for excessive violence. **Cast:** Wallace Beery, Ralph Bellamy, Johnny Mack Brown, Clark Gable, Jean Harlow, John Miljan, Marjorie Rambeau, Lewis Stone, Tom London. **Credits:** Dir: George W. Hill; Writer: Frances Marion; DP: Harold Wenstrom; Ed: Blanche Sewell; Composer: Douglas Shearer; Costumes: Rene Hubert; Art Director: Cedric Gibbons. B&W, 83 min.

The Secret War of Harry Frigg
(1968) Universal
Newman stars in a rare comedy outing as a rebel WWII private who gets promoted to general and assigned to rescue a group of Allied generals from an Italian villa. They're reluctant to go, however, and so's Newman once he meets Koscina. When the Germans take over, the mission gets complicated. **Cast:** Paul Newman, Sylva Koscina, Andrew Duggan, Tom Bosley, John Williams, Charles Gray, Vito Scotti, Jacques Roux. **Credits:** Dir: Jack Smight; Prod: Hal E. Chester; Writer: Peter Stone; DP: Russell Metty; Ed: Terry Williams; Prod Design: Alexander Golitzen; Composer: Carlo Rustichelli. Color, 123 min. **VHS**

The Seduction of Joe Tynan

(1979) Universal

After his popular starring role in TV's *M*A*S*H*, Alda briefly became Hollywood's idea of the new sensitive man, in touch with his feelings and unthreatened by independent women. In this attempt to explore the realities of American politics as well as the changing role of the American man, Alda, who wrote the screenplay, created a role for himself as a liberal senator with a wife and two kids who becomes transformed by political power and involved in an extramarital affair with a young lobbyist (Streep in one of her early starring performances). Harris and Douglas are notable in the respective roles of Alda's wife and his political mentor. Made long before the names Donna Rice, Gennifer Flowers, and Monica Lewinsky were in the national lexicon, this is a look at late-'70s American politics and masculinity. **Cast:** Alan Alda, Meryl Streep, Barbara Harris, Rip Torn, Melvyn Douglas, Charles Kimbrough, Carrie Nye, Michael Higgins. **Credits:** Dir: Jerry Schatzberg; Prod: Martin Bregman; Writer: Alan Alda; DP: Adam Holender; Ed: Evan Lottman; Prod Design: David Chapman; Composer: Bill Conti. Color, 107 min. **VHS, LASER**

See Here, Private Hargrove

(1944) MGM

Walker plays a young reporter, and the bane of his editor's existence, who joins the army and promptly becomes his boot camp C.O.'s worst nightmare. Fumbling orders, breaking military equipment, and tripping up and knocking over high-ranking officials leave him almost permanently on K.P. duty. Aided and abetted by his friend Wynn, Walker manages to keep himself alive and (just about) keep romance blooming with his gal back home, Reed. This memoir of army life by Marion Hargrove was endearing enough that a sequel, *What's Next, Corporal Hargrove?*, appeared the next year. Tay Garnett directed a new ending after an unsuccessful preview. **Cast:** Robert Walker, Donna Reed, Robert Benchley, Keenan Wynn, Bob Crosby, Ray Collins, Chill Wills, Martha Linden, Grant Mitchell, George Offerman. **Credits:** Dir: Wesley Ruggles; Prod: George Haight; Writer: Harry Kurnitz; DP: Charles Lawton; Ed: Frank E. Hull; Prod Design: Cedric Gibbons; Composer: David Snell. B&W, 101 min.

Semi-Tough

(1977) United Artists

In a satire of both professional football and the self-help movements of the '70s, teammates Kristofferson and Reynolds are buddies and rivals for the hand of Clayburgh, daughter of their team's owner (Preston). Kristofferson's new devotion to Convy's cult makes him an early favorite until Reynolds pokes a hole in his plans. Lots of pro players in cameos. A spin-off TV series fumbled its way to early cancellation. **Cast:** Burt Reynolds, Kris Kristofferson, Jill Clayburgh, Robert Preston, Bert Convy, Lotte Lenya, Richard Masur, Carl Weathers, Brian Dennehy, Roger E. Mosley. **Credits:** Dir: Michael Ritchie; Prod: David Merrick; Writer: Walter Bernstein; DP: Charles Rosher; Ed: Richard A. Harris; Prod Design: Walter Scott Herndon; Composer: Jerry Fielding. Color, 108 min. **VHS, LASER**

The Senator Was Indiscreet

(1948) Universal

Algonquin Round Table wit and Pulitzer Prize–winning playwright Kaufman's only film as director is a political satire about a dim-witted U.S. Senator(Powell) who loses a diary containing intimate dirt on all his opponents. When Powell runs for president on a hilarious platform, his PR man Hayes finds his boss's intimate writings with dirt on all his colleagues. When he turns it over to his reporter girlfriend (Raines), the politicos head for the hills. An amusing and often startlingly prescient script by MacArthur. Powell won the best actor award from the New York Film Critics. **Cast:** William Powell, Ella Raines, Peter Lind Hayes, Hans Conried, Charles D. Brown, Allen Jenkins, Ray Collins, Arleen Whelan, Francis Pierlot, Cynthia Corley. **Credits:** Dir: George S. Kaufman; Prod: Nunnally Johnson; Writer: Charles MacArthur; DP: William Mellor; Ed: Sherman A. Rose; Composer: Daniele Amfitheatrof; Art Director: Bernard Herzbrun, Boris Leven. B&W, 81 min. **VHS**

Send Me No Flowers

(1964) Universal

In the last of the Hudson-Day romantic comedies, Hudson plays a hypochondriac under the false impression that he's dying. When he tries to fix up his soon-to-be-widowed wife (Day) with a successor, including her old beau Walker, Day thinks Hudson's feeling guilty over an extramarital affair. Not their best moment, but pleasant enough. **Cast:** Rock Hudson, Doris Day, Tony Randall, Clint Walker, Paul Lynde, Hal March, Edward Andrews, Patricia Barry. **Credits:** Dir: Norman Jewison; Prod: Harry Keller; Writer: Julius J. Epstein; DP: Daniel Fapp; Ed: Terry Williams; Prod Design: Alexander Golitzen; Composer: Frank DeVol. Color, 100 min. **VHS**

Sensations of 1945

(1944) United Artists

Old-fashioned showman Pallette is willing to go to any length to attract customers to his shows. O'Keefe, Pallette's son and the junior member of the company, prefers advertising to the humbug of his senior. Exasperated with his son, Pallette turns over the reins to dancer Powell who adds even more flamboyance, eventually landing her in jail. Romance ensues when O'Keefe bails her out. Basically a primer on old-time vaudeville with a variety of acts, including W. C. Fields's last screen appearance. Academy Award Nomination for Best Score. **Cast:** Eleanor Powell, Dennis O'Keefe, C. Aubrey Smith, Eugene Pallette, Mimi Forsythe, Lyle Talbot, Hubert Castle, Richard Hageman, Marie Blake, Stanley Andrews. **Credits:** Dir: Andrew L. Stone; Prod: Andrew L. Stone; Writer: Dorothy Bennett, Andrew L. Stone; Story: Frederick J. Jackson; DP: J. Peverell Marley, John J. Mescall; Ed: James Smith; Prod Design: Charles Odds; Composer: Mahlon Merrick, Alfred Sherman, Harry Tobias. B&W, 86 min.

September Affair

(1950) Paramount

When married man Cotten and classical pianist Fontaine miss their plane after engine trouble gives them a few hours sight-seeing in Naples, they also miss the plane crash that kills everyone on their flight. Listed as passengers, the two are given a chance at a new life together, but when Cotten's wife shows up, their Italian idyll crashes too. This revived the hit "September Song." Golden Globe for Best Original Score. **Cast:** Joseph Cotten, Joan Fontaine, Francoise Rosay, Jessica Tandy, Robert Arthur, James Lydon, Fortunio Bonanova, Grazia Narciso. **Credits:** Dir: William Dieterle; Prod: Hal B. Wallis; Writer: Robert Thoeren; DP: Charles B. Lang; Ed: Warren Low; Prod Design: Hans Dreier; Composer: Victor Young. B&W, 105 min. **VHS**

September 30, 1955

(1977) Universal

This is a little-seen sleeper about the effect actor James Dean's death has on a group of teenage friends. Thomas and Blount organize a mystical ceremony leading to drinking and a run from the police that has tragic consequences. An unusually sincere look at the feelings teens invest in idols on their way to adulthood. Quaid made his film debut in this provocative drama. **Cast:** Richard Thomas, Susan Tyrrell, Deborah Benson, Lisa Blount, Tom Hulce, Dennis Quaid, Mary Kai Clark, Dennis Christopher, Collin Wilcox. **Credits:** Dir: James Bridges; Prod: Jerry Weintraub, Jack Larson; Writer: James Bridges; DP: Gordon Willis; Ed: Jeff Gourson; Composer: Leonard Rosenman. Color, 107 min. VHS, LASER

Sergeant Madden
(1939) MGM
Von Sternberg's crime melodrama hints at Greek tragedy. Beery plays the archetypal Irish cop, with unbounded respect for the law. His son, Curtis, becomes a cop but alienates his colleagues with his ambition. When he shoots a suspect in a theft, he's set up for a prison stint. After his release, Curtis goes on a crime spree, one that puts him face-to-face with his father's retribution. **Cast:** Wallace Beery, Tom Brown, Alan Curtis, Lorraine Day, Fay Holden, Marc Lawrence, Marion Martin, David Gorcey, Donald Haines, Ben Welden. **Credits:** Dir: Josef von Sternberg; Prod: J. Walter Ruben; Writer: Wells Root; Story: William Ullman; DP: John Seitz; Ed: Conrad A. Nervig; Composer: Dr. William Axt; Art Director: Randal Duell, Cedric Gibbons. B&W, 82 min.

Sergeant York
(1941) Warner Bros.
This is one of the greatest of war sagas because it is the true story of a simple man who accomplishes extraordinary feats through quiet determination and faith. Cooper deservedly won acclaim for his portrayal of the WWI hero (York himself insisted that Cooper take the role if his story was filmed) from rural east Tennessee. At first hot-headed, with fast fists and no direction, Cooper first changes his life with hard work meant to earn land for a farm that will win him the hand of Leslie. He then takes a devout turn after divine intervention prevents him from murdering his rival for Leslie's affections. Reluctantly enlisted in WWI after denied conscientious objector status, Cooper performs heroic feats motivated by his desire to stop a German machine-gun nest from killing. Upon his return, Cooper is greeted with parades, Leslie's love, and a farm of his own presented by the people of Tennessee, bounty Cooper ascribes to God's grace. A compelling story, expertly directed by Hawks, of

inner strength from inspired purpose first seen in York's personal struggles and then his actions on behalf of his comrades. Academy Award Nominations: 11, including Best Picture; Best Director; Best Original Screenplay. **Academy Awards:** Best Actor: Gary Cooper; Best Film Editing. **Cast:** Gary Cooper, Walter Brennan, George Tobias, Noah Beery, Joan Leslie, June Lockhart, Dickie Moore, Clem Bevans, Howard Da Silva. **Credits:** Dir: Howard Hawks; Prod: Jesse L. Lasky; Writer: Abem Finkel, Harry Chandlee; DP: Sol Polito; Ed: William Holmes; Composer: Max Steiner; Art Director: John Hughes. B&W, 134 min. VHS, LASER

Serpico
(1973) Paramount
Among Pacino's finest performances is this story of real-life New York detective Frank Serpico, whose insistence on staying clear of police corruption led to real reforms. A detective who refuses to take his share of the protection money that washes through every precinct to which he's assigned, Pacino first reports to his police department bosses and, when nothing happens, to the newspapers. His one-man integrity campaign earns him personal turmoil, a bullet in the face, and then public notoriety after his testimony to the Knapp Commission. (The real Frank Serpico was forced to move all the way to Italy because his life was in such danger.) Terrific script from the great Salt. Academy Award Nominations: Best Actor: Al Pacino; Best (Adapted) Screenplay. **Cast:** Al Pacino, John Randolph, Jack Kehoe, Biff McGuire, Barbara Eda-Young, Tony Roberts, Cornelia Sharpe, John Medici. **Credits:** Dir: Sidney Lumet; Prod: Martin Bregman; Writer: Waldo Salt; DP: Arthur J. Ornitz; Ed: Dede Allen; Prod Design: Charles Bailey; Composer: Mikis Theodorakis. Color, 129 min. VHS, LASER

The Set-Up
(1949) RKO
This was unsurpassed as a dark, emotionally stirring portrait of boxing until release of Martin Scorsese's *Raging Bull* (1980). The film's story unfolds in real time as Ryan, an over-the-hill fighter, prepares for his bout at the end of the night's card. His long-suffering wife (Totter) pleads for him to quit and tells him she won't watch this fight. His manager, meanwhile, takes a payoff from a mobster meant to ensure that Ryan tanks in the second round. After he climbs into the ring and sees Totter's seat empty, Ryan reaches down for a determina-

tion to win, even after his trainer finally tells him of the setup. Ryan ultimately wins, but at a high cost. Compact storytelling with a feeling for the ring and the men, good and bad, who live their lives in the boxing arena. The story originated as a narrative poem by Joseph Moncure March. Noted photographer Weegee has a small cameo as the Timekeeper. **Cast:** Robert Ryan, Audrey Totter, Alan Baxter, George Tobias, Wallace Ford, Percy Helton, Hal Baylor, Darryl Hickman. **Credits:** Dir: Robert Wise; Prod: Richard Goldstone; Writer: Art Cohn; DP: Milton Krasner; Ed: Roland Gross; Art Director: Albert S. D'Agostino, Jack Okey. B&W, 72 min. VHS, LASER

Seven Brides for Seven Brothers
(1954) MGM
One of the highlights of the '50s musical, this is a rollicking romance with rousing songs and spirited dancing. Keel and six brothers run a ranch in Oregon in the mid-1800s, a lonely life and one noticeably lacking in female companionship. So Keel ventures to town where he convinces Powell to accompany him to the ranch without clueing her in to the six unwashed brothers also sharing the house. After Powell mops up the household, the brothers yearn for a little companionship themselves and run off with six girls from town. An avalanche conveniently strands the mob on the ranch for the winter, after which a mass marriage seals the deal. Academy Award Nominations: 5, including Best Picture; Best Screenplay; Best (Color) Cinematography. **Academy Awards:** Best Scoring of a Musical. **Cast:** Howard Keel, Jane Powell, Jeff Richards, Russ Tamblyn, Howard Petrie, Virginia Gibson, Ian Wolfe, Marc Platt. **Credits:** Dir: Stanley Donen; Prod: Jack Cummings; Writer: Albert Hackett; DP: George J. Folsey; Ed: Ralph E. Winters; Prod Design: Cedric Gibbons; Composer: Adolph Deutsch. Color, 104 min. VHS, LASER

Seven Days in May
(1964) Paramount
This is a tense political thriller that depicts a military coup in 1974. After the signing of a nuclear treaty, chairman of the joint chiefs Lancaster plans to replace the commander in chief (March) and recruits the heads of each service. Military attaché Douglas notices suspicious activity around a secret base and warns the president that he suspects a coup.

Frankenheimer (who also directed another exercise in political paranoia, *The Manchurian Candidate*) keeps the plot threads written by Serling tightly woven. Houseman's first on-screen appearance after an illustrious career in theater and as a producer. Academy Award Nominations: Best Supporting Actor: Edmond O'Brien; Best ArtDirection. **Cast:** Burt Lancaster, Kirk Douglas, Fredric March, Ava Gardner, Edmond O'Brien, Martin Balsam, George Macready, Whit Bissell, John Houseman. **Credits:** Dir: John Frankenheimer; Prod: Edward Lewis; Writer: Rod Serling; DP: Ellsworth Fredricks; Ed: Ferris Webster; Composer: Jerry Goldsmith; Art Director: Cary Odell. B&W, 118 min. **VHS, LASER**

Seven Days' Leave
(1942) RKO
This wartime musical comedy features plenty of big names from radio days. Mature (who joined up for real after finishing his role) plays an army private who has a week to earn himself an inheritance of one hundred thousand dollars if he can get a wealthy heiress (Ball) to marry him. Problem is, this wealthy beauty has already promised to marry somebody else. Fans of Freddy Martin's and Les Brown's bands should catch this one. **Cast:** Lucille Ball, Victor Mature, Harold Peary, Ginny Simms, Peter Lind Hayes, Arnold Stang, Ralph Edwards, Walter Reed. **Credits:** Dir: Tim Whelan; Prod: Tim Whelan; Writer: William Bowers; DP: Robert de Grasse; Ed: Robert Wise; Art Director: Albert S. D'Agostino. B&W, 87 min. **VHS**

7 Faces of Dr. Lao
(1963) MGM
One of director Pal's masterpieces of imagination this time is set in the Wild West as Randall's circus comes to the town of Abalone and deals with a land-grabbing gang while helping crusading newspaperman Ericson woo Eden. Pal's puppet creations, including a seven-headed sea monster, mop up the bad guys. Makeup genius William Tuttle won the Academy's special award; he won a special commendation again for *Planet of the Apes* (1968). **Academy Awards:** Special Award for Best Visual Effects. **Cast:** Tony Randall, Barbara Eden, Arthur O'Connell, John Ericson, Noah Beery, Minerva Urecal, Frank Kreig. **Credits:** Dir: George Pal; Prod: George Pal; Writer: Charles Beaumont, Ben Hecht; Story: Charles G. Finney; DP: Robert Bronner; Ed:

George Tomasini; Composer: Leigh Harline; Art Director: George W. Davis. Color, 101 min. **VHS, LASER**

Seven Keys to Baldpate
(1947) RKO
This is a mystery comedy (and the fifth screen version of the story) about a writer (Terry) trying to finish a book in 24 hours. To get peace and quiet, he holes up in the Baldpate Inn, where he makes a wager with the owner, who then tries to keep him from making his deadline. Meanwhile, jewel thieves show up fresh from a big job, providing more distraction. The 1935 version features Gene Raymond as the writer, with the inimitable Eric Blore as the detective on the robbery case. **Cast:** Philip Terry, Jacqueline White, Eduardo Cianelli, Margaret Lindsay, Arthur Shields, Jimmy Conlin, Tony Barrett, Richard Powers, Jason Robards. **Credits:** Dir: Lew Landers; Prod: Herman Schlom; Writer: George M. Cohan, Lee Loeb; Story: Earl Derr Biggers; DP: Jack MacKenzie; Ed: J. R. Whittredge; Prod Design: Lucius O. Croxton, Albert S. D'Agostino; Composer: Paul Sawtell, C. Bakaleinikoff. B&W, 68 min.

The Seven Little Foys
(1955) Paramount
In a valentine to vaudeville days, Hope plays Eddie Foy, the real-life patriarch of The Singing and Dancing Foys. Though he always worked alone, without their mother to care for them, Hope has to work the kids into the act. Hope is comfortable in the scenes that play onstage, however, following the death of Mrs. Foy (Vitale), this biopic veers toward a ragtime dysfunctional-family soaper. In a cameo appearance, Cagney reprises his famous role as George M. Cohan, as he and Hope do a fantastic dance routine to "Yankee Doodle Dandy." Academy Award Nomination for Best Story and Screenplay. **Cast:** Bob Hope, Milly Vitale, Billy Gray, George Tobias, James Cagney, Angela Clarke, Herbert Heyes, Richard Shannon. **Credits:** Dir: Melville Shavelson; Prod: Jack Rose; Writer: Melville Shavelson; DP: John F. Warren; Ed: Ellsworth Hoagland; Art Director: Hal Pereira, John B. Goodman. Color, 95 min. **VHS**

Seven Men from Now
(1956) Warner Bros.
This tense Western drama from Boetticher (the first to team Scott with Boetticher and writer Kennedy) features Scott as a grim ex-lawman on the warpath to revenge his wife's murder

at a courier station holdup. Seven men did the deed. Scott's got help from tough guy Reed and his wife, Russell, and untrustworthy gunman Marvin, who's out to clean up on the bounty and Reed's money after the battle. Marvin's performance as the turncoat is a standout. **Cast:** Randolph Scott, Gail Russell, Lee Marvin, Walter Reed, John Larch, Don "Red" Barry. **Credits:** Dir: Budd Boetticher; Prod: Andrew V. McLaglen, Robert E. Morrison, John Wayne; Writer: Burt Kennedy; DP: William Clothier; Ed: Everett Sutherland; Prod Design: A. Leslie Thomas; Composer: Henry Vars. Color, 78 min.

The Seven-Per-Cent Solution
(1976) Universal
Nicholas Meyer's best-seller pairs the world's greatest detective—Sherlock Holmes (Williamson)—with the world's leading investigator of the human mind—Sigmund Freud (Arkin)—in a tale of two entwined mysteries. In the first, Dr. Watson (Duvall) engages Dr. Freud to delve into Holmes's troubled past and the origin of the detective's cocaine addiction (the formula alluded to in the film's title). In the second, Freud and Holmes investigate the kidnapping of a former patient (Redgrave). A clever film with an outstanding cast including Olivier as a very different Professor Moriarty. A breakthrough for author Meyer, who became a feature-film director (*Time After Time*, 1979; *Star Trek II: The Wrath of Khan*, 1982). Academy Award Nominations: Best (Adapted) Screenplay; Best Costume Design. **Cast:** Alan Arkin, Nicol Williamson, Laurence Olivier, Robert Duvall, Vanessa Redgrave, Joel Grey, Samantha Eggar, Jeremy Kemp. **Credits:** Dir: Herbert Ross; Prod: Herbert Ross; Writer: Nicholas Meyer; DP: Oswald Morris; Ed: Chris Barnes; Prod Design: Peter Lamont; Composer: John Addison. Color, 113 min. **VHS, LASER, DVD**

Seven Sinners
(1940) Universal
Dietrich plays the tramp of the South Seas, moving from island to island when trouble follows. After once more being deported with pals Crawford and Auer, Dietrich performs aboard a ship carrying troublesome old flame Dekker, and draws the attention of by-the-book navy man Wayne. With her siren song at the Seven Sinners Cafe, Dietrich nearly lures Wayne from his home on the bounding main, but Crawford sets her straight. Great fun with two screen icons. This production was also the source of the famous story about Diet-

rich and director Garnett passing Wayne in the Universal commissary whereupon Dietrich breathily exhaled, "Daddy, buy me that!" **Cast:** Marlene Dietrich, John Wayne, Albert Dekker, Broderick Crawford, Mischa Auer, Billy Gilbert, Oscar Homolka, Anna Lee. **Credits:** Dir: Tay Garnett; Prod: Joe Pasternak; Writer: John Meehan; DP: Rudolph Maté; Ed: Ted J. Kent; Prod Design: Jack Otterson; Composer: Frank Skinner. B&W, 87 min. VHS

Seventeen
(1940) Paramount
Cooper plays an adolescent in the throes of first love with Field, a dazzling young lady who incites him to taste the nightlife and grow up faster than his parents prefer, and distracting him from his schoolbooks. Harmless fun for Cooper fans. **Cast:** Jackie Cooper, Betty Field, Otto Kruger, Ann Shoemaker, Norma Nelson, Betty Moran, Thomas Ross, Peter Lind Hayes, Donald Haines, Buddy Pepper. **Credits:** Dir: Louis King; Prod: Stuart Walker; Writer: Agnes Christine Johnston, Stuart Palmer; Story: Booth Tarkington, Stuart Walker, Hugh Stanislaus Stange, Stanford Mears; DP: Victor Milner; Ed: Arthur Schmidt; Prod Design: Hans Dreier, Franz Bachelin. B&W, 78 min.

The Seventh Cross
(1944) MGM
This is a wartime melodrama and a strong anti-Nazi statement from Austrian-born director Zinnemann. Seven escapees from a concentration camp have seven crosses nailed to trees awaiting their capture. Six are used for crucifixions; only embittered Tracy, who gradually learns to trust his fellow man again, makes his way to Holland. An effective, atmospheric thriller with great performances from Tracy, Cronyn, and Tandy (in her screen debut). Academy Award Nomination for Best Supporting Actor: Hume Cronyn. **Cast:** Spencer Tracy, Signe Hasso, Hume Cronyn, Agnes Moorehead, Jessica Tandy, George Macready, Kaaren Verne, George Zucco, Felix Bressart. **Credits:** Dir: Fred Zinnemann; Prod: Pandro S. Berman; Writer: Helen Deutsch; DP: Karl Freund; Ed: Thomas Richards; Prod Design: Cedric Gibbons; Composer: Roy Webb; Art Director: Leonid Vasian. B&W, 112 min. VHS

Seven Thieves
(1960) Fox
Robinson plays a more lighthearted criminal type than his famous Warner gangsters. Here, he's an aging scientist who wants one more thrill before he goes, in this case, executing the perfect crime. To accomplish his planned casino heist, Robinson rounds up a crew of ex-con Steiger, glamour-girl Collins and her friend Wallach, safecracker Dante, inside-man Scourby, and getaway driver Kroeger. The script is refreshingly upbeat with an ironic twist. Adapted from the Max Catto novel *Lions at the Kill*. Academy Award Nomination for Best (Black-and-White) Costume Design. **Cast:** Edward G. Robinson, Rod Steiger, Joan Collins, Eli Wallach, Michael Dante, Alexander Scourby, Berry Kroeger, Sebastian Cabot. **Credits:** Dir: Henry Hathaway; Prod: Sydney Boehm; Writer: Sydney Boehm; DP: Sam Leavitt; Ed: Dorothy Spencer; Prod Design: Lyle Wheeler; Composer: Dominic Frontiere. B&W, 102 min. VHS

The Seventh Victim
(1943) RKO
Horror master Lewton produced this creepy thriller about a naive young woman (Hunter, in her film debut) who learns from the nuns at her convent school that her sister (Brooks) has disappeared. She joins Brooks's husband (Beaumont) in a search that yields a shocking discovery: her sister has given her soul to a secret cult of Satan worshipers. She encounters a world obsessed with death and despair, finally making the acquaintance of a consumptive prostitute (Russell) in a bleak rooming house. This was veteran director Robson's first film. **Cast:** Tom Conway, Kim Hunter, Jean Brooks, Hugh Beaumont, Erford Gage, Isabel Jewell, Evelyn Brent, Eve March, Elizabeth Russell. **Credits:** Dir: Mark Robson; Prod: Val Lewton; Writer: DeWitt Bodeen, Charles O'Neal; DP: Nicholas Musuraca; Ed: John Lockert; Composer: Roy Webb; Art Director: Albert S. D'Agostino, Walter E. Keller. B&W, 71 min. VHS, LASER

The Seventh Voyage of Sinbad
(1958) Columbia
This special-effects fantasy features the work of the legendary Harryhausen in a story he had cherished for years and his first color production. When Sinbad (Mathews) and his intended (Grant) sail toward Baghdad, they're waylaid by a sorcerer who refuses to give up a magic lantern to the Cyclops who owns it. When he miniaturizes the princess, Mathews has to return to the Cyclops's island for the egg of a roc. This includes the famous sequence with Sinbad sword-fighting with a skeleton. Composer Herrmann provides the suspenseful score. **Cast:** Kerwin Mathews, Kathryn Grant, Richard Eyer, Torin Thatcher, Alec Mango, Danny Green, Harold Kasket, Alfred Brown. **Credits:** Dir: Nathan Juran; Prod: Charles H. Schneer; Writer: Ken Kolb; DP: Wilkie Cooper; Ed: Edwin Bryant, Jerome Thoms; Composer: Bernard Herrmann; SFX: Ray Harryhausen. Color, 94 min. VHS, LASER

The Seven-Ups
(1973) Fox
Scheider, who played a supporting role to Gene Hackman in *The French Connection* (1971), takes the lead as a tough-guy undercover New York cop on the trail of hardened criminals eligible for more than seven years hard time. Directed by the producer of *The French Connection*, the action again relies on a highly choreographed and artfully edited urban car chase. **Cast:** Roy Scheider, Tony Lo Bianco, Bill Hickman, Richard Lynch, Victor Arnold, Jerry Leon, Ken Kercheval, David Wilson. **Credits:** Dir: Philip D'Antoni; Prod: Philip D'Antoni; Writer: Albert Ruben, Alexander Jacobs; DP: Urs Furrer; Ed: Jerry Greenberg, Stephen A. Rotter, John C. Horger; Prod Design: Ed Wittstein; Composer: Don Ellis. Color, 109 min. VHS

The Seven Year Itch
(1955) Fox
One of Monroe's funniest, finest performances came in Wilder's classic comedy. Happily married Manhattanite Ewell reverts to bachelor fantasies when his wife (Keyes) and child leave for a summer vacation. His dreams come true when he meets his new neighbor, Monroe. While in the film Ewell remains torn between his fantasies and guilt, the play upon which the film was based reached the same happy ending though Ewell succeeds in bedding his neighbor, something Hollywood would never have allowed during the '50s. The origin of perhaps the decade's most lasting icon: Monroe radiating her smile while that famous white summer dress billows above a subway grating. Golden Globe for Best Actor in a Musical or Comedy: Tom Ewell. **Cast:** Marilyn Monroe, Tom Ewell, Sonny Tufts, Evelyn Keyes, Robert Strauss, Oscar Homolka, Marguerite Chapman, Victor Moore. **Credits:** Dir: Billy Wilder; Prod: Charles K. Feldman, Billy Wilder; Writer: Billy Wilder, George Axelrod; Story: George Axelrod; DP: Milton Krasner; Ed: Hugh S. Fowler; Prod Design: Lyle Wheeler;

Composer: Alfred Newman; Art Director: George W. Davis. Color, 105 min. VHS, LASER

Sex and the Single Girl
(1964) Warner Bros.
This slapstick sex comedy has absolutely nothing to do with *Cosmopolitan* magazine publisher Helen Gurley Brown's book, but does boast a script by Joseph Heller, the author of *Catch-22*. Curtis gets an assignment to expose the director of "The International Institute of Advanced Marital and Pre-Marital Studies" (Wood) as a virgin. Featuring Fonda and Bacall, Curtis's battling neighbors, who get mixed up in the scheme when the reporter uses Fonda's name as an alias. This seemed sophisticated then. **Cast:** Natalie Wood, Tony Curtis, Lauren Bacall, Henry Fonda, Mel Ferrer, Fran Jeffries, Leslie Parrish, Edward Everett Horton, Larry Storch. **Credits:** Dir: Richard Quine; Prod: William T. Orr; Writer: Joseph Heller; DP: Charles Lang; Composer: Neal Hefti; Art Director: Cary O'Dell. Color, 110 min. VHS, LASER

Shack Out on 101
(1955) Allied Artists
Deep in the heart of the Cold War, this cult film follows the heroic efforts of a waitress (Moore) who uncovers communist scheming inside a diner while slinging hash. While fending off the advances of scientist Lovejoy, Moore overhears his dealings with foreign agent Marvin. **Cast:** Lee Marvin, Frank Lovejoy, Terry Moore, Keenan Wynn, Whit Bissell, Jess Barker, Donald Murphy. **Credits:** Dir: Edward Dein; Prod: William F. Broidy, Mort Millman; Writer: Edward Dein, Mildred Dein; DP: Floyd Crosby; Composer: Paul Dunlap; Art Director: Lou Croyton. B&W, 80 min. VHS

Shadow of a Doubt
(1943) Universal
In this enthralling story (and Hitchcock's personal favorite), an average small town receives a visit from the Merry Widow murderer. Cotten gives an intense, quiet performance as Wright's Uncle Charlie, whose visit she and her family eagerly anticipate. Fresh from his latest killing, Cotten charms his sister's family, especially Wright, who feels she and her worldly uncle have a special bond. But as his dark torment starts to surface, Wright is endangered when Cotten realizes she sees through him. A terrific script from Wilder perfectly establishes the small-town atmosphere (a particularly winning touch is the running dialogue

between Travers and Cronyn, two mystery buffs who enliven their humdrum lives with a debate on techniques for the perfect murder), and the shadow cast by the presence of pure evil. Academy Award Nomination for Best Original Story. **Cast:** Joseph Cotten, Teresa Wright, Macdonald Carey, Wallace Ford, Hume Cronyn, Patricia Collinge, Henry Travers, Clarence Muse. **Credits:** Dir: Alfred Hitchcock; Prod: Jack H. Skirball; Writer: Thornton Wilder; DP: Joseph A. Valentine; Ed: Milton Carruth; Composer: Dimitri Tiomkin; Art Director: John B. Goodman. B&W, 108 min. VHS, LASER

The Shadow of the Eagle
(1932) Mascot
Prior to reaching the pinnacle of Hollywood stardom, Wayne spent many years on Saturday matinee screens in adventure serials and B Westerns. *The Shadow of the Eagle*, a Poverty Row 12-part serial, stars a young Wayne as a WWI air ace suspected of being a skywriting extortionist called "The Eagle." **Cast:** John Wayne, Dorothy Gulliver, Walter Miller, Kenneth Harlan, Yakima Canutt, Pat O'Malley, Little Billy, Edward Hearn. **Credits:** Dir: Ford Beebe; Prod: Nat Levine; Writer: Ford Beebe, Colbert Clark, Wyndham Gittens; DP: Benjamin H. Kline, Victor Scheurich; Ed: Ray Snyder; Composer: Lee Zahler. B&W, 240 min. VHS

Shadows
(1960) Lion International
Cassavetes's first feature exhibits the improvisation and jumpy, nervous energy that would remain his hallmarks. Hurd, a bitter black jazz musician, hangs out with his friends and gigs in dives when he can to support his brother (Carruthers). Meanwhile, their light-skinned sister Goldoni makes the art scene and attracts a white man (Ray) who leaves her once he meets her family. Great music (by jazz bassist Mingus) and a cameo by Cassavetes, who shows up briefly in front of a seedy movie theater on 42nd Street. After winning the Critics' Award at Cannes and gaining international acclaim, this became a surprise art-house hit in the U.S. An early look at a priceless talent and at the bohemian, Beat scene of the late '50s. Selected for the National Film Registry. **Cast:** Ben Carruthers, Lelia Goldoni, Hugh Hurd, Anthony Ray, Rupert Cross, David Jones, Jack Ackerman, Tom Allen, Dennis Sallas, David Pokitillow. **Credits:** Dir: John Cassavetes; Prod: Maurice McEndree;

DP: Erich Kollmar; Ed: Maurice McEndree; Composer: Charlie Mingus. B&W, 87 min. VHS, LASER, DVD

Shaft
(1971) MGM
One of the emblematic films of the early '70s features Roundtree as a private detective hired to find the kidnapped daughter of a king of the streets. His search leads him through the crime- and drug-infested mean streets as he infiltrates the Mob with the help of black militant St. John. The second feature by black photographer Parks. Based on the novel by Ernest Tidyman. Followed by *Shaft's Big Score* (1972) and *Shaft in Africa* (1973). Academy Award Nominations: 2, including Best Original Dramatic Score. **Academy Awards:** Best Song ("Theme from Shaft"). **Cast:** Richard Roundtree, Moses Gunn, Charles Cioffi, Antonio Fargas, Christopher St. John, Gwenn Mitchell, Lawrence Pressman, Victor Arnold. **Credits:** Dir: Gordon Parks; Prod: Joel Freeman; Writer: John D. F. Black, Ernest Tidyman; DP: Urs Furrer; Ed: Hugh A. Robertson; Composer: Isaac Hayes; Art Director: Emanuel Gerard. Color, 98 min. VHS, LASER

The Shaggy D.A.
(1976) Disney
In a sequel of sorts to *The Shaggy Dog* (made 17 years later) Jones plays the adult Wilby Daniels, a lawyer running for district attorney who finds the ring that transformed Tommy Kirk into a sheepdog back in 1959. Pleshette plays his long-suffering wife and his rival for office is Wynn. **Cast:** Dean Jones, Tim Conway, Suzanne Pleshette, Keenan Wynn, Jo Anne Worley, Dick Van Patten, Vic Tayback, John Myhers. **Credits:** Dir: Robert Stevenson; Prod: Bill Anderson; Writer: Don Tait; DP: Frank Phillips; Ed: Bob Bring, Norman Palmer; Prod Design: John B. Mansbridge; Composer: Buddy Baker; Art Director: Perry Ferguson. Color, 91 min. VHS, LASER

The Shaggy Dog
(1959) Disney
This early Disney live-action comedy features studio stalwart Kirk as the teenage son of MacMurray who transforms into an English sheepdog when a magic ring falls into his pants cuff. To break the spell he must perform acts of heroism, something he gets plenty of opportunity to do when he discovers a cabal of Soviet spies living next door. Loosely based on Felix Salten's *The Hound of Florence*.

Remade as a TV film in 1994. **Cast:** Fred MacMurray, Jean Hagen, Tommy Kirk, Annette Funicello, Tim Considine, Kevin Corcoran, Cecil Kellaway, Alexander Scourby. **Credits:** Dir: Charles Barton; Prod: Walt Disney, Bill Walsh; Writer: Bill Walsh, Lillie Hayward; DP: Edward Colman; Ed: James D. Ballas; Prod Design: Carroll Clark; Composer: Paul J. Smith. B&W, 104 min. **VHS, LASER**

Shall We Dance
(1937) RKO
Astaire and Rogers pair for the seventh time as dancers (he a Russian ballet dancer, she a Broadway musical star) who feign marriage as a publicity angle and then fall head over heels. Terrific Gershwin score, including the famous duet "Let's Call the Whole Thing Off," the title-song finale, and the wistful melody of "They Can't Take That Away From Me." Typically high-gloss production and haute-Deco trappings make this a high point of the classic-era musical. Academy Award Nomination for Best Song ("They Can't Take That Away From Me"). **Cast:** Fred Astaire, Ginger Rogers, Eric Blore, Edward Everett Horton, Ann Shoemaker, Jerome Cowan, Harriet Hoctor, Ben Alexander. **Credits:** Dir: Mark Sandrich; Prod: Pandro S. Berman; Writer: Allan Scott, Ernest Pagano, P. J. Wolfson; DP: David Abel; Ed: William Hamilton; Composer: George Gershwin; Art Director: Van Nest Polglase, Carroll Clark; Choreographer: Hermes Pan, Harry Losee. B&W, 116 min. **VHS**

Shampoo
(1975) Columbia
This biting satire portrays the moral sea-change from the boundary-breaking free love of the '60s into the shallow hunt for self-gratification in the '70s. On Election Day in 1968, as Nixon becomes president, Beatty, a hairstylist to the rich and neurotic of Beverly Hills, untangles the messy strands of his affairs as he runs from one unhappy client-lover to the next and tries to stake a claim in the world by raising the money to open his own salon. He ends a bleak round of parties and bedrooms alone. Fisher makes her film debut as Grant's daughter, who shares Beatty's attentions. Academy Award Nominations: 4, including Best Original Screenplay; Best Supporting Actor: Jack Warden. **Academy Awards:** Best Supporting Actress: Lee Grant. **Cast:** Warren Beatty, Lee Grant, Jack Warden, Julie Christie, Goldie Hawn, Carrie Fisher, Howard Hesseman, Tony Bill. **Credits:** Dir: Hal Ashby; Prod: Warren

Beatty; Writer: Robert Towne; DP: Laszlo Kovacs; Ed: Robert C. Jones; Composer: Paul Simon; Art Director: Stewart Campbell. Color, 112 min. **VHS, LASER**

Shane
(1953) Paramount
Considered one of the greatest Westerns, this is Ladd's finest role. Like *High Noon*, with which it shares some similarity, *Shane* proposes that the stain of killing can't be washed away, even if the death comes in a righteous cause. Ladd gets involved in a nasty skirmish between ranchers and farmers when he rides up to Heflin's farmhouse looking for water. From the first, he impresses young De Wilde with his instinctual quick draw and then earns Heflin's trust when he backs down bullying Meyer. Ladd seems to be putting down roots as he fights for the farmers. But after a final showdown with steely-eyed Palance, he rides away from the farm he's made secure, knowing that his mere presence will bring more death. A landmark Western, beautifully directed and photographed. Selected for the National Film Registry. Academy Award Nominations: 6, including Best Picture; Best Director; Best Screenplay; Best Supporting Actor: Jack Palance; Best Supporting Actor: Brandon de Wilde. **Academy Awards:** Best Color Cinematography. **Cast:** Van Heflin, Alan Ladd, Jean Arthur, Brandon De Wilde, Jack Palance, Ben Johnson, Edgar Buchanan, Emile Meyer, Elisha Cook, Jr., John Dierkes. **Credits:** Dir: George Stevens; Prod: George Stevens; Writer: A. B. Guthrie; Story: Jack Schaefer; DP: Loyal Griggs; Ed: William Hornbeck; Prod Design: Hal Pereira; Composer: Victor Young. Color, 118 min. **VHS, LASER**

Shanghai Express
(1932) Paramount
Von Sternberg's exotic adventure has glamorous courtesan Dietrich encountering ex-lover Brook aboard a Chinese train destined for trouble. Rebellion surrounds the journey with danger, and the train carries the rebel chieftain (Oland) disguised as a businessman. When he orders the train stopped at a rebel stronghold, Oland forces Dietrich to become his lover in order to save Brook. But Wong takes revenge for an earlier attack by Oland. Academy Award Nominations: 3, including Best Picture; Best Director. **Academy Awards:** Best Cinematography. **Cast:** Marlene Dietrich, Anna May Wong, Warner Oland, Clive Brook, Eugene

Pallette, Louise Closser Hale, Gustav Von Seyffertitz, Emile Chautard. **Credits:** Dir: Josef von Sternberg; Writer: Jules Furthman; DP: Lee Garmes; Prod Design: Hans Dreier; Composer: W. Franke Harling. B&W, 82 min. **VHS**

The Shanghai Gesture
(1941) United Artists
After the cycle of seven celebrated features with Dietrich that ended with *The Devil Is a Woman*, von Sternberg's directorial career never again gained those heights. The closest he came to his earlier glory was this melodrama of depravity and blackmail featuring Tierney as a half-caste who becomes a pawn in a war to shut down Munson's notorious gambling den. Despite the strong arm of the Hays Office, the film supplies a campy atmospheric maze of disturbing depravity. An ailing von Sternberg directed much of the film lying on a cot and didn't make another film until *Jet Pilot* in 1950. Academy Award Nominations: Best Interior Decoration and Best Score. **Cast:** Victor Mature, Gene Tierney, Ona Munson, Walter Huston, Phyllis Brooks, Albert Basserman, Maria Ouspenskaya, Eric Blore. **Credits:** Dir: Josef von Sternberg; Prod: Arnold Pressburger; Writer: Josef von Sternberg, Karl Vollmoeller, Geza Herczeg, Jules Furthman; DP: Paul Ivano; Ed: Sam Winston; Composer: Richard Hageman; Art Director: Boris Leven. B&W, 106 min. **VHS, LASER**

She
(1935) RKO
Created by the producer of *King Kong*, this fantasy adventure follows an expedition seeking the Flame of Eternal Life, a fire that burns so brightly it conserves rather than destroys. When captured by Mongol natives after an avalanche, Scott gets an introduction to She-Who-Must-Be-Obeyed. She (Gahagan) bathed in the Flame and is now immortal, and long ago had killed Scott's explorer father when he spurned her advances. Now she wants Scott. This was Gahagan's only screen appearance. After marrying Melvyn Douglas, she earned fame running as a liberal for Congress and losing her Senate campaign against Richard Nixon. Steiner provides an outstanding score. **Cast:** Randolph Scott, Helen Gahagan, Helen Mack, Nigel Bruce, Gustav Von Seyffertitz, Samuel S. Hinds, Noble Johnson, Lumsden Hare. **Credits:** Dir: Irving Pichel, Lansing C. Holden; Prod: Merian C. Cooper; Writer: Ruth Rose, Dudley Nichols; Story: H.Ryder Haggard;

DP: J. Roy Hunt; Composer: Max Steiner; Art Director: Van Nest Polglase, Al Herman. B&W, 95 min. VHS

Sheba Baby
(1974) AIP
This blaxploitation flick stars Grier, who made a comeback in 1997's *Jackie Brown*. Grier plays a private detective hired to find out who's trying to ruin her rich father and his loan company. Meant to capitalize on the sexy star's success in *Coffy* (1973) and *Foxy Brown* (1974). **Cast:** Pam Grier, Austin Stoker, Dick Merrifield, Rudy Challenger, Charles Kissinger, Christopher Joy, Maurice Downes, Ernest Cooley. **Credits:** Dir: William Girdler; Prod: David Sheldon; Writer: William Girdler; DP: William Asman; Ed: Jack Davies; Prod Design: J. Patrick, III Kelly; Composer: Monk Higgins. Color, 90 min. VHS

She Couldn't Say No
(1954) RKO
In an attempt to repay citizens of her home town for their kindness in her childhood, an oil-rich woman (Simmons) showers the townsfolk with money only to see her actions disrupt their lives in ways she never imagined. When she decides to stop her well-intentioned meddling and leave, local doctor Mitchum convinces her to marry him. A mild comedy that was a contract obligation for Simmons. **Cast:** Jean Simmons, Robert Mitchum, Arthur Hunnicutt, Wallace Ford, Edgar Buchanan. **Credits:** Dir: Lloyd Bacon; Prod: Robert Sparks; Writer: D. D. Beauchamp, William Bowers, Richard Flournoy; DP: Harry Wild; Ed: George Amy; Composer: Roy Webb. B&W, 89 min. VHS

She Couldn't Take It
(1935) Columbia
This madcap gangster comedy places millionaire Connolly in a jail cell where he gets a respite from his free-spending family. In prison, he meets Raft, a bootlegger who's used his time to educate himself in the prison library. Impressed with his industriousness, Connolly names Raft his executor and then promptly drops dead. Raft runs headlong into the millionaire's nasty widow (Burke) and daffy daughter (Bennett), who gets Raft in hot water, and romance, when she fakes her own kidnapping. Future director Oscar Rudolph, father of independent filmmaker Alan, plays a newsboy. **Cast:** Walter Connolly, Joan Bennett, James Blakeley, Billie Burke, Stanley Andrews, Frank Conroy, May-

nard Holmes, George Raft. **Credits:** Dir: Tay Garnett; Prod: B. P. Schulberg; Writer: Oliver H. P. Garrett, Gene Towne; DP: Leon Shamroy; Prod Design: Stephen Goosson. B&W, 77 min.

She Done Him Wrong
(1933) Universal
This is the movie that made West a star and features one of her most famous performances. West plays Diamond Lil, who runs a saloon on the Bowery for Beery. She takes a shine to young missionary Grant, who reveals himself to be an undercover cop investigating the crime spree Beery runs out of the saloon when he claims West's heart. Based on her stage play *Diamond Lil*, this includes the bawdy numbers "Frankie and Johnny," "I Like a Guy What Takes His Time," and "Easy Rider." Academy Award Nomination for Best Picture. **Cast:** Mae West, Cary Grant, Owen Moore, Noah Beery, Gilbert Roland, David Landau, Rafaela Ottiano, Dewey Robinson. **Credits:** Dir: Lowell Sherman; Prod: William LeBaron; Writer: Mae West; DP: Charles Lang; Ed: Alex Hall; Choreographer: Harold Hecht; Art Director: Robert Usher. B&W, 65 min. VHS, LASER

The Sheik
(1921) Paramount
The silent classic that created the silver-screen legend of Valentino is a routine melodrama that wouldn't be remembered today if not for the sensation caused by its male star. Despite her countrymen's warning against traveling into the desert alone, Lady Diana (Ayres) rides out onto the sandy plain with only one guide to protect her. Miles into the desert, she's captured by Sheik Ahmed Ben Hassan (Valentino). Bewitched by her beauty, the Sheik keeps the British aristocrat locked away in a love nest hoping to make her his concubine. Ayres protects her virtue, but is then captured by an evil sheik (Long). When Valentino rides to her rescue, Ayres realizes her captor's not the uncivilized brute she mistook him for. **Cast:** Rudolph Valentino, Agnes Ayres, Adolphe Menjou, Walter Long, Lucien Littlefield, George Waggner, Patsy Ruth Miller, Frank Butler. **Credits:** Dir: George Melford; Prod: George Melford; Writer: Monte M. Katterjohn; DP: William Marshall. B&W, 79 min. VHS

She Loves Me Not
(1934) Paramount
In an early Crosby outing, a Philadelphia cabaret dancer (Hopkins) wit-

nesses a murder and flees to Princeton where she disguises herself as a male student so that she can hide in the room of two Good Samaritan Princeton students (Crosby and Nugent). She escapes the gangsters, but a movie producer hears of a girl being hidden in a Princeton dorm room, ruining Crosby's romance with the dean's daughter. **Cast:** Bing Crosby, Miriam Hopkins, Kitty Carlisle, Edward J. Nugent, Lynne Overman, Henry Stephenson, Warren Hymer, Judith Allen, George Barbier, Henry Kolker. **Credits:** Dir: Elliott Nugent; Prod: Benjamin Glazer; Writer: Benjamin Glazer; Story: Edward Hope, Howard Lindsay; DP: Charles Lang; Ed: Hugh Bennett; Composer: Ralph Rainger, Harry Revel, Leo Robin. B&W, 83 min.

Shenandoah
(1965) Universal
A nuanced performance by Stewart depicts the pain of loss, a steely determination to survive, and the futility of revenge. The Civil War intrudes on widower Stewart's Virginia farm where he raised six sons and a daughter though he has sworn neutrality. When one son (Alford) is captured, and son-in-law McClure gets called up, Stewart takes his remaining sons on a search for their brother, leaving pregnant Ross and her husband (Wayne) behind. When he returns to find them murdered, a desolate Stewart retreats back to his faith and tries to reconstruct his simple life. Ross makes her film debut as Stewart's daughter. Academy Award Nomination for Best Sound. **Cast:** James Stewart, Doug McClure, Glenn Corbett, Patrick Wayne, Katharine Ross, Phillip Alford, Rosemary Forsyth, Charles Robinson. **Credits:** Dir: Andrew V. McLaglen; Prod: Robert Arthur; Writer: James Lee Barrett; DP: William Clothier; Ed: Otho S. Lovering; Prod Design: Alexander Golitzen; Composer: Frank Skinner. Color, 107 min. VHS, LASER

The Shepherd of the Hills
(1941) Paramount
Wayne is featured in a less conventional role as a bitter Ozark moonshiner whose love for Field is only matched by his hatred for his father (Carey), who abandoned his family and caused the death of his mother. When Carey comes back to the mountains, known only as The Shepherd for the good that he does in the community, Wayne befriends him until he discovers that Carey is his long-lost father. A powerful performance by Wayne that

drew attention to his acting skills outside his accustomed action pictures. Hathaway's Technicolor film was adapted from a sentimental novel by Harold Bell Wright, previously filmed in 1919 and 1928. **Cast:** John Wayne, Betty Field, Harry Carey, Sr., Beulah Bondi, James Barton, Samuel S. Hinds, Marjorie Main, Ward Bond. **Credits:** Dir: Henry Hathaway; Prod: Jack Moss; Writer: Grover Jones, Stuart Anthony; DP: Charles B. Lang, W. Howard Greene; Ed: Ellsworth Hoagland; Prod Design: Hans Dreier; Composer: Gerard Carbonara; Art Director: Roland Anderson. Color, 98 min. **VHS**

Sherlock Holmes

While there have been several British Sherlock Holmes series, only one has been produced on these shores. In 1939 Basil Rathbone and Nigel Bruce made their debuts as Sir Arthur Conan Doyle's master sleuth Holmes and his sidekick, Dr. Watson, in 20th Century-Fox's *The Hound of the Baskervilles*. Fox also produced *The Adventures of Sherlock Holmes* in 1939. The pairing proved to be the best of all Holmes-Watson teams, with deft filmmaking enhancing their appeal. Though both were critically and commercially successful, three years passed before another entry appeared, *Sherlock Holmes and The Voice of Terror,* this time for Universal. Rathbone and Bruce resumed their roles, though the films jumped ahead in time about a half century to the WWII years and often featured Holmes battling the Nazis. The most memorable entries featured Holmes going head-to-head with archnemesis Professor Moriarty, variously portrayed by George Zucco, Lionel Atwill, and Henry Daniell. Later installments lacked the stylized dialogue and moody cinematography of the early entries and were heavy on wartime propaganda. Nevertheless, the on-screen chemistry between Rathbone's intrepid sleuth and Bruce's blundering Watson consistently entertained.

The Hound of the Baskervilles *(1939)*
The Adventures of Sherlock Holmes *(1939)*
Sherlock Holmes and the Voice of Terror *(1942)*
Sherlock Holmes and the Secret Weapon *(1942)*
Sherlock Holmes in Washington *(1943)*
Sherlock Holmes Faces Death *(1943)*
Sherlock Holmes and the Spider Woman *(1944)*

The Scarlet Claw *(1944)*
The Pearl of Death *(1944)*
The House of Fear *(1945)*
The Woman in Green *(1945)*
Pursuit to Algiers *(1946)*
Dressed to Kill *(1946)*
Terror by Night *(1946)*

She's Working Her Way Through College

(1952) Warner Bros.
Ex–burlesque gal Mayo goes to college and disrupts the life of married and somewhat bookish professor Reagan. He's used to directing staid versions of the classics for the student theater, but Mayo has something more lively in mind. When her past is exposed by the jealous girlfriend of a would-be suitor, the college president demands her expulsion and Reagan jumps to Mayo's defense. His motives get questioned when an old beau of his wife (Thaxter) shows up. Based on a play cowritten by Thurber, with songs including the title number, "I'll Be Loving You," "The Stuff That Dreams Are Made Of," and "Am I In Love?" **Cast:** Virginia Mayo, Ronald Reagan, Gene Nelson, Don Defore, Phyllis Thaxter, Patrice Wymore, Roland Winters, Raymond Greenleaf, Norman Batrold, Armanda Randolph. **Credits:** Dir: H. Bruce Humberstone; Prod: Williams Jacobs; Writer: Peter Milne; Story: James Thurber, Elliott Nugent; DP: Wilfred Cline; Ed: Clarence Kolster; Choreographer: Leroy Prinz; Composer: Sammy Cahn, Vernon Duke, Al Dubin, Harry Warren, Ray Heindorf; Art Director: Charles H. Clarke. Color, 101 min.

She Wore a Yellow Ribbon

(1949) RKO
The second of director Ford's Cavalry Trilogy (preceded by *Fort Apache,* followed by *Rio Grande*) depicts the passing of an era in the settlement of the West as one generation hands over its claim to the future to the next generation. Cavalry officer Wayne draws a frustrating assignment of shepherding women to a stagecoach as storm clouds build with the local Indians. Ready to go once more into the fray, Wayne gets reminded that his retirement is now effective and that the young, inexperienced lieutenants (Agar and Carey) have to earn their stripes under fire. An affecting performance from Wayne with Ford's usual empathy for the human stories that comprise our history. **Academy Awards:** Best Color Cinematography. **Cast:** John Wayne, Joanne Dru, Ben Johnson, John Agar, Harry Carey, Jr.,

Victor McLaglen, Mildred Natwick, George O'Brien. **Credits:** Dir: John Ford; Prod: John Ford; Writer: Frank S. Nugent; DP: Winton C. Hoch; Ed: Jack Murray; Prod Design: James Basevi; Composer: Richard Hageman. Color, 103 min. **VHS, LASER**

She Wouldn't Say Yes

(1945) Columbia
In a romantic comedy, psychiatrist Russell searches for a test subject to prove her theory about the healthy effects of reining in the emotions. She chooses cartoonist Bowman, whose character, Nixie, is an id run rampant. After the philosophical sparring, love wins out. This gets a lift from the ever-lovable Russell. **Cast:** Rosalind Russell, Lee Bowman, Adele Jergens, Charles Winninger, Harry Davenport, Sara Haden, Percy Kilbride, Lewis Russell. **Credits:** Dir: Alexander Hall; Prod: Virginia Van Upp; Writer: Virginia Van Upp, Hans Jacoby, Sarett Tobias; DP: Joseph Walker; Composer: Marlin Skiles; Art Director: Stephen Goosson, Van Nest Polglase. B&W, 87 min.

The Shining Hour

(1938) MGM
Crawford stars in a familiar melodrama about a nightclub singer who marries wealthy Douglas and goes to live on the family estate. Tensions arise as sister-in-law Bainter takes an instant dislike to her and brother-in-law Young finds her irresistible. Coscripted by poet Ogden Nash. **Cast:** Joan Crawford, Margaret Sullavan, Robert Young, Melvyn Douglas, Fay Bainter, Allyn Joslyn, Hattie McDaniel, Frank Albertson. **Credits:** Dir: Frank Borzage; Prod: Joseph L. Mankiewicz; Writer: Jane Murfin, Ogden Nash; DP: George J. Folsey; Ed: Frank Hull; Prod Design: Cedric Gibbons, Paul Groesse; Composer: Franz Waxman. B&W, 80 min. **VHS**

Ship Ahoy

(1942) MGM
A leggy dancer on a cruise ship (Powell) makes her way to Puerto Rico in the company of hack writer Skelton, the Dorsey Band, and a singer named Sinatra. Ignore the silly spy plot and watch Sinatra sing "Last Call for Love," "On Moonlight Bay," and "Poor You." **Cast:** Eleanor Powell, Frank Sinatra, Red Skelton, Virginia O'Brien, Bert Lahr, Tommy Dorsey, William Post, Jr., John Emery, Bernard Nedell, Moroni Olsen. **Credits:** Dir: Edward Buzzell; Prod: Jack Cummings; Writer: Harry Clork, Harry Kurnitz, Irving Brecher; DP: Leonard Smith, Robert Planck; Ed: Blanche

Sewell; Prod Design: Cedric Gibbons; Choreographer: Bobby Connolly; Composer: Axel Stordahl, Leo Arnaud, George Bassman, George Stoll, Sy Oliver, Basil Adlam, Henry Russell; Costumes: Robert Kalloch; Art Director: Harry McAfee; Set Designer: Edwin B. Willis. B&W, 95 min. **VHS**

Ship of Fools
(1965) Columbia
A microcosm of the world and the human experience unfolds aboard an ocean liner bound for Europe in the '30s. A compelling, episodic treatment of the 1962 novel by Katherine Anne Porter that depicts wealthy German passengers who espouse Nazi ideas from the captain's table while a Jew and a dwarf are made to sit elsewhere, a drunken baseball player reveling in the past (Marvin), a divorcée who cruelly toys with men (Leigh, in her last film role), Segal and Ashley as a passionate young couple, and Werner and Signoret, who fall in love though she must face political charges in Spain. Academy Award Nominations: 8, including Best Picture; Best Actor: Oskar Werner; Best Actress: Simone Signoret; Best (Adapted) Screenplay. **Academy Awards:** Best Black-and-White Cinematography; Best Art Direction—Set Decoration (B&W). **Cast:** Vivien Leigh, Simone Signoret, Oskar Werner, Heinz Ruehmann, Jose Ferrer, Lee Marvin, George Segal, Elizabeth Ashley, Jose Greco, Heinz Ruhmann. **Credits:** Dir: Stanley Kramer; Prod: Stanley Kramer; Writer: Abby Mann; DP: Ernest Laszlo; Ed: Robert C. Jones; Prod Design: Robert Clatworthy; Costumes: Bill Thomas, Jean Louis; SFX: Albert J. Whitlock, Farciot Edouart, John Burke; Set Designer: Joseph Kish. B&W, 149 min. **VHS**

Shock Corridor
(1963) Allied Artists
What could have been merely a cheap exploitation picture becomes a shockingly bizarre crime thriller in the hands of Fuller. Breck badgers his editor with his plan to win a Pulitzer: contrive a way into a mental institution with a sick tale of incest and assault in order to solve a recent murder. But once inside, the reporter starts to lose his grip, imagining lurid scenarios with his stripper girlfriend, suffering an attack by nymphomaniacs, and undergoing shock treatments. He manages to uncover the truth behind the killings, but the sordid tale further unhinges his mind, leading to catatonia—and a Pulitzer. An infamously brutal chapter in Fuller's career. **Cast:** Peter Breck,

Constance Towers, Gene Evans, Hari Rhodes, James Best, Larry Tucker, Philip Ahn, John Matthews, Frank Gerstle, Paul Dubov. **Credits:** Dir: Samuel Fuller; Prod: Samuel Fuller; Writer: Samuel Fuller; DP: Stanley Cortez, Samuel Fuller; Ed: Jerome Thoms; Prod Design: Eugene Lourie; Choreographer: Jon Gregory; Composer: Paul Dunlap; SFX: Charles Duncan, Lynn Dunn; Set Designer: Charles S. Thompson. B&W and Color, 101 min. **VHS, LASER, DVD**

The Shocking Miss Pilgrim
(1947) Fox
In late-19th-century Boston, Grable raises a ruckus in Beantown by agitating for women's rights. Somehow, Haymes overcomes his horror at her behavior and they fall in love to dancing choreographed by Pan and music by the Gershwins. Mostly ho-hum but curious to see Grable in long skirts! **Cast:** Betty Grable, Dick Haymes, Anne Revere, Allyn Joslyn, Gene Lockhart, Elizabeth Patterson, Elizabeth Risdon, Arthur Shields, Charles Kemper, Roy Roberts. **Credits:** Dir: George Seaton; Prod: William Perlberg; Writer: Ernest Maas, Frederick Maas; Story: George Seaton; DP: Leon Shamroy; Ed: Robert Simpson; Choreographer: Hermes Pan; Composer: Alfred Newman, Charles Henderson, George Gershwin, Ira Gershwin; Art Director: James Basevi, Boris Leven. Color, 87 min.

Shockproof
(1949) Columbia
Sirk directs a film noir coauthored by future action director Fuller. The tale of ill-fated lovers follows paroled murderer Knight and her affair with her parole officer, Wilde. Wilde risks his budding political career by marrying an ex-con, but their troubles begin in earnest when Knight's old lover appears on the scene. **Cast:** Cornel Wilde, Patricia Knight, John Baragray, Esther Minciotti, Howard St. John, Russell Collins, Charley Bates, Gilbert Barnett, Frank Jaquet. **Credits:** Dir: Douglas Sirk; Prod: S. Sylvan Simon, Helen Deutsch; Writer: Helen Deutsch, Samuel Fuller; DP: Charles Lawton; Ed: Gene Havlik; Prod Design: Carl Anderson; Composer: George Duning. B&W, 79 min.

The Shoes of the Fisherman
(1968) MGM
This is an overlong, big-budget version of the Morris West novel about a Russian priest (Quinn) released from a Siberian labor camp who's eventually elected Pope. In the process, he

is forced to confront global Cold War politics and world famine. Though he was placed in Rome for political reasons by the Russian premier (Olivier), Quinn soon espouses his own radical solutions to help the needy of the world, including selling the Church's treasures to feed the starving. Notable mostly for the high-wattage acting talent on-screen. Academy Award Nominations: Best Art Direction—Set Decoration; Best Original Score. **Cast:** Anthony Quinn, Leo McKern, Laurence Olivier, John Gielgud, Oskar Werner, David Janssen, Vittorio De Sica, Barbara Jefford. **Credits:** Dir: Michael Anderson; Prod: George Englund; Writer: John Patrick, James Kennaway; DP: Erwin Hillier; Ed: Ernest Walter; Composer: Alex North; Art Director: George W. Davis, Edward C. Carfagno. Color, 164 min. **VHS, LASER**

The Shooting
(1967) AIP
A low-budget Western from cult favorite Hellman features a performance from a young, prestardom Nicholson (who also coproduced). Perkins (best remembered for her role as Anne Frank a decade earlier) engages bounty hunter Oates to avenge the death of her husband and child, while mystery gunman Nicholson trails them. Often described as an existential Western, the film features a fragmented narrative that culminates in a surprise ending, and barren Utah vistas suitable for a Samuel Beckett drama. Shot simultaneously with Hellman's *Ride the Whirlwind*, which also featured Nicholson and Perkins. Writer Joyce later scripted *Five Easy Pieces* (1970). **Cast:** Jack Nicholson, Will Hutchins, Warren Oates, Millie Perkins, Charles Eastman. **Credits:** Dir: Monte Hellman; Prod: Monte Hellman, Jack Nicholson; Writer: Adrien Joyce; DP: Gregory Sandor; Ed: Monte Hellman. Color, 83 min. **VHS, LASER**

The Shootist
(1976) Paramount
Wayne's last film is an elegy for both the Western and its main star, who died from cancer three years after it was released. Ironically, Wayne plays a legendary gunfighter (after clips from Wayne films that establish his prowess and renown) who is informed by doctor Stewart that he has cancer. Wayne realizes that as the world around him changes, he needs to confront his own legacy and give his death meaning. This, in turn, leads him to a relationship with his landlady Bacall's son, Howard, which forms the heart of the picture. Wayne moves

through the role with a dignified awareness of his own myth that invests his character with a wry wit and a knowledge that he must pass as surely as the West that he once dominated. One of Wayne's finest films, directed with economy and finesse by master craftsman Siegel. Academy Award Nomination for Best Art Direction—Set Decoration. **Cast:** John Wayne, Lauren Bacall, Ron Howard, James Stewart, Bill McKinney, Richard Boone, John Carradine, Scatman Crothers, Richard Lenz, Harry Morgan. **Credits:** Dir: Don Siegel; Prod: M. J. Frankovich, William Self; Writer: Miles Hood Swarthout, Scott Hale; DP: Bruce Surtees; Ed: Douglas Stewart; Prod Design: Robert Boyle; Composer: Elmer Bernstein. Color, 100 min. **VHS, LASER**

The Shop Around the Corner
(1940) MGM
One of Lubitsch's most beloved romantic comedies is about two feuding employees (Stewart and Sullavan) in Morgan's Budapest store who, unbeknownst to each other, are actually carrying on an amorous pen pal correspondence. On the night the correspondents finally agree to meet, each expecting a proposal, Morgan fires Stewart and makes Sullavan stay late. But through circumstance and one more letter, the scales finally drop from the eyes of the epistolary lovers. Truly a sweet tale with winning performances by Stewart and Sullavan. Remade in 1949 as a musical, *In the Good Old Summertime* (with Judy Garland and Van Johnson), a Broadway play, *She Loves Me*, and most recently via e-mail as *You've Got Mail* (1998), with Tom Hanks and Meg Ryan. **Cast:** James Stewart, Margaret Sullavan, Frank Morgan, Sara Haden, Joseph Schildkraut, Felix Bressart, William Tracy, Inez Courtney. **Credits:** Dir: Ernst Lubitsch; Prod: Ernst Lubitsch; Writer: Samson Raphaelson; DP: William Daniels; Ed: Gene Ruggiero; Prod Design: Cedric Gibbons, Wade B. Rubottom; Composer: Werner Richard Heymann. B&W, 100 min. **VHS, LASER**

The Shopworn Angel
(1938) MGM
First a hit in 1929 with Gary Cooper, this outing pairs Stewart and Sullavan as a naive Texas doughboy and a streetwise New York chorine. Just before he is to ship overseas to the trenches of WWI, Sullavan nearly mows Stewart down with her car and winds up showing him the town, much

to the consternation of her boyfriend, socialite Pidgeon. Before he ships out, Sullavan makes her ill-fated doughboy's dreams come true by marrying him in a whirlwind ceremony. First screenplay by renowned screenwriter Salt. **Cast:** Margaret Sullavan, James Stewart, Walter Pidgeon, Hattie McDaniel, Sam Levene, Nat Pendleton, Alan Curtis, Charley Grapewin. **Credits:** Dir: H. C. Potter; Prod: Joseph L. Mankiewicz; Writer: Waldo Salt; DP: Joseph Ruttenberg; Ed: W. Donn Hayes; Prod Design: Cedric Gibbons, Joseph C. Wright; Composer: Edward Ward. B&W, 81 min. **VHS**

Short Eyes
(1977) Paramount
A brutal prison drama told with disturbing realism. When a child molester (Davison) goes behind bars, he's threatened, tortured, and eventually executed by his fellow inmates who despise child molesters. Shot on location at the now closed New York City Men's House of Detention, also known as the Tombs. Based on the script and the Joe Papp stage production by Pinero, an ex-con himself. **Cast:** Bruce Davison, Jose Perez, Nathan George, Donald Blakely, Shawn Elliott, Freddy Fender. **Credits:** Dir: Robert M. Young; Prod: Lewis Harris; Writer: Miguel Pinero; DP: Peter Sova; Ed: Edward Beyer; Composer: Curtis Mayfield; Costumes: Paul Martino. Color, 100 min. **VHS**

A Shot in the Dark
(1964) United Artists
The second installment in the Inspector Clouseau series established Sellers's bumbling detective as one of classic film's most hilarious slapstick characters. In this madcap comedy–murder mystery, Clouseau is determined to prove the beautiful maid in a French estate (Sommer) has been framed for the murder of her lover, though every clue points directly to her. The high points include a chase through a nudist camp and the explosive finale. Probably the best in the series. Note the coauthor: Blatty, who would later pen *The Exorcist*. **Cast:** Peter Sellers, Elke Sommer, George Sanders, Herbert Lom, Tracy Reed, Graham Stark, Andre Maranne, Douglas Wilmer. **Credits:** Dir: Blake Edwards; Prod: Blake Edwards; Writer: Blake Edwards, William Peter Blatty; DP: Christopher Challis; Ed: Bert Bates; Prod Design: Michael Stringer; Composer: Henry Mancini. Color, 103 min. **VHS, LASER**

Show Boat
(1936) Universal
This is the second of three film versions of the Kern-Hammerstein musical based on the Edna Ferber novel, and is justly renowned for the performances by Robeson (including his powerful rendition of "Old Man River") and Morgan as Julie, the mulatto girl, and her signature song, "Bill." Directed by Whale, whose credentials as the expressionist director of *Frankenstein* would seem an odd entrée to this assignment, but he carries the day with style and a lively pace. Filmed originally in 1929 and for a third time in 1951. The laserdisc includes an audio essay, historical shorts and photos, and clips from both the 1929 version and the stage production. Selected for the National Film Registry. **Cast:** Irene Dunne, Allan Jones, Helen Morgan, Paul Robeson, Charles Winninger, Hattie McDaniel, Sammy White, Arthur Hohl, Charles Middleton, Francis X. Mahoney. **Credits:** Dir: James Whale; Prod: Carl Laemmle, Jr.; Writer: Oscar Hammerstein; DP: John Mescall; Ed: Ted J. Kent, Bernard W. Burton; Prod Design: Charles D. Hall; Choreographer: Leroy Prinz; Composer: Jerome Kern, Oscar Hammerstein; Costumes: Vera West, Doris Zinkeisen; SFX: John Fulton. B&W, 115 min. **VHS, LASER**

Show Boat
(1951) MGM
MGM's Freed musical unit went all out to render America's most venerable musical in vivid Technicolor, spending more than $2.3 million overall and $100,000 alone on the 171-foot paddle-wheeler, the *Cotton Blossom*. A reluctant Gardner earned raves for her performance as Julie, the half-black star of the showboat's troupe, though her voice was dubbed. Not as historically interesting as the 1936 version, but all the standards—"Bill," "Can't Help Loving That Man," and "Old Man River"—get a rousing treatment and the production values shine. The laserdisc includes historical shorts, the original trailer, and commentary. Academy Award Nominations: Best (Color) Cinematography; Best Scoring of a Musical Picture. **Cast:** Kathryn Grayson, Ava Gardner, Howard Keel, Joe E. Brown, Gower Champion, Robert Sterling, Agnes Moorehead, Adele Jergens, Leif Erickson. **Credits:** Dir: George Sidney; Prod: Arthur Freed; Writer: John Lee Mahin, George Wells, Jack McGowan; DP: Charles Rosher; Ed: John Dunning; Prod Design: Cedric Gibbons, Jack Martin Smith; Choreog-

rapher: Robert Alton; Composer: Jerome Kern, Oscar Hammerstein; Costumes: Walter Plunkett, Alfred E. Spencer; SFX: Peter Ballbusch; Set Designer: Edwin B. Willis. Color, 107 min. VHS, LASER, DVD

A Shriek in the Night
(1933) Allied
This mystery thriller reunites the creators and stars (Rogers and Talbot) from *The Thirteenth Guest* (1932). This time Rogers and Talbot play competing reporters who team up to solve a string of murders by a killer who leaves behind a menacing calling card. Don't look too closely at the film's poster: it gives away the ending! **Cast:** Ginger Rogers, Lyle Talbot, Louise Beavers, Arthur Hoyt, Frances Hyland, Lillian Harmer, Purnell Pratt, Harvey Clark, Maurice Black. **Credits:** Dir: Albert Ray; Prod: M. H. Hoffman; Writer: Frances Hyland; Story: Kurt Kempler; DP: Harry Neumann; Ed: L. R. Brown; Composer: Abe Meyer; Art Director: Gene Hornbostel. B&W, 66 min. VHS

Side Street
(1950) MGM
This Mann noir follows a regular guy with money worries who tumbles from temptation to a panicked escape through New York's seamy underworld. Granger has hopes and dreams for himself and his wife O'Donnell that he can't reach with his mailman's salary. When he spots an envelope full of cash on his route, the easy pickings lead to a blackmail plot, a run from gangsters and the police, and a bullet. An early use of location shooting on New York's streets. **Cast:** Farley Granger, Cathy O'Donnell, James Craig, Paul Kelly, Jean Hagan, Paul Harvey, Edmond Ryan, Charles McGraw, Edwin Max, Adele Jergens. **Credits:** Dir: Anthony Mann; Prod: Sam Zimbalist; Writer: Sidney Boehm; DP: Joseph Ruttenberg; Ed: Conrad A. Nervig; Prod Design: Cedric Gibbons; Composer: Lennie Hayton. B&W, 83 min.

Sidewalks of New York
(1931) MGM
Here's silent-comic genius Keaton's first talkie feature. As a hapless New York millionaire landlord, Keaton falls for an inner-city gal, Page. Some funny moments as Keaton tries to win over Page by stopping her brother from joining a tough street gang. Unfortunately, as this demonstrates, Keaton's work never returned to the height of his silent classics. White went on to a semi-glorious career directing the Three Stooges. **Cast:** Buster Keaton,

Zion Myers, Anita Page, Cliff Edwards, Frank Rowan, Norman Phillips, Oscar Apfel, Syd Saylor, Clark Marshall. **Credits:** Dir: Jules White, Zion Myers; Prod: Lawrence Weingarten; Writer: George Landy, Paul Gerard Smith, Eric Hatch; DP: Leonard Smith; Ed: Charles Hochberg. B&W, 74 min. VHS

The Sign of the Cross
(1932) Paramount
DeMille's version of Nero's Rome allowed him to depict vice, naked women, homosexuality, lesbians, and cannibalism—all in the name of moral instruction. Laughton plays Nero in a campy performance reportedly based on Mussolini, while Colbert, as Poppea, bathes in real asses' milk (which apparently turned to hideously foul-smelling cheese under the lights) and makes eyes at the captain of the guard, March. March, though, only desires the pure Landi, a Christian convert. When she's led into the arena after Nero blames his conflagration on the Christians, March nobly joins his true love in her sacrifice. In typical DeMille fashion, the film's press kit boasted of a cast of more than 4,000 and a menagerie gathered from 12 zoos. **Cast:** Elissa Landi, Claudette Colbert, Charles Laughton, Fredric March, Ian Keith, Vivian Tobin, Harry Beresford, Ferdinand Gottschalk. **Credits:** Dir: Cecil B. DeMille; Prod: Cecil B. DeMille; Writer: Waldemar Young, Sidney Buchman; DP: Karl Struss; Ed: Anne Bauchens; Composer: Rudolph G. Kopp. B&W, 125 min. VHS

The Sign of the Ram
(1948) Columbia
This is a macabre footnote in film history and a truly odd movie. Peters had a promising career as a screen ingenue until a hunting accident left her spine damaged and made her dependent on a wheelchair. This was her comeback, playing a wicked stepmother confined to a wheelchair. After breaking up one stepson's love affair and harassing the other stepson's fiancée until she attempts suicide, Peters wheels her chair over a cliff. Weird. **Cast:** Susan Peters, Alexander Knox, Phyllis Thaxter, Peggy Ann Garner, Ron Randell, May Whitty, Allene Roberts, Ross Ford, Diana Douglas, Margaret Tracey. **Credits:** Dir: John Sturges; Prod: Irving Cummings; Writer: Charles C. Bennett; Story: Margaret Ferguson; DP: Burnett Guffey; Ed: Aaron Stell; Composer: Morris Stoloff; Art Director: Stephen Goosson. B&W, 88 min.

Silent Running
(1971) Universal
This sci-fi fantasy that deserves more acclaim was penned by the writers of *The Deer Hunter* (1978) and directed by the special effects master who worked on *2001* (1968) and *Close Encounters of the Third Kind* (1977). In a grim not-so-distant future, Earth is so polluted by a nuclear disaster that plants can no longer survive. Giant greenhouses in orbit around Saturn carry samples of Earth's dying forests, waiting for the day when Earth can be replanted. When the government decides they're too expensive to maintain, one committed crew member (Dern) takes Earth's future in his own hands. Classical music fans will want to note the score by parodist "P.D.Q. Bach" Schickele. **Cast:** Bruce Dern, Cliff Potts, Ron Rifkin, Jesse Vint, Steve Brown. **Credits:** Dir: Douglas Trumbull; Prod: Michael Gruskoff; Writer: Michael Cimino, Deric Washburn, Steven Bochco; DP: Charles F. Wheeler; Ed: Aaron Stell; Composer: Peter Schickele. Color, 90 min. VHS, LASER, DVD

Silk Stockings
(1957) MGM
This MGM Freed unit musical update of *Ninotchka* adds debonair songs by Porter to the familiar story of a Soviet cadre entranced by romance and the west. When Astaire ventures to Paris to produce a movie, he asks a famed Soviet composer for a score. This brings the disapproving trio of Lorre, Munshin, and Buloff from Russia to retrieve the maestro before he defects. Once exposed to the temptations of the west, however, they're happy to go along until the party sends the sternest comrade of all, Charisse. After a brisk tour of factories and the sewers, the beautiful apparatchik softens under the spell of boutiques and nightspots before she ushers her charges back to Russia. When the trio returns to Paris, Astaire wins Charisse over for good. This includes songs written for the stage adaptation (by George S. Kaufman) as well as new songs for the movie. They include "Too Bad," "Fated to Be Mated," "All of You," and the title number. **Cast:** Fred Astaire, Cyd Charisse, Janis Paige, Peter Lorre, Jules Munshin, Barrie Chase, Joseph Buloff, George Tobias, Belita. **Credits:** Dir: Rouben Mamoulian; Prod: Arthur Freed; Writer: Leonard Gershe, Harry Kurnitz, Leonard Spigelgass; DP: Robert Bronner; Ed: Harold F. Kress; Prod Design: William A. Horning, Randal Duell; Choreographer: Hermes

Pan, Eugene Loring; Composer: Cole Porter; Costumes: Helen Rose; Set Designer: Edwin B. Willis, Hugh Hunt. Color, 117 min. **VHS, LASER**

The Silver Chalice
(1954) Warner Bros.
This is perhaps the oddest biblical epic produced during Hollywood's "swords and sandals" heyday. A profoundly out-of-place Yale Drama School actor named Paul Newman made his Hollywood debut in this notorious multimillion-dollar disaster about the slave who fashioned the cup from which Christ drank at the Last Supper. (Newman himself later described his performance as "very, very bad" in "the worst motion picture filmed during the '50s.") Yet this film, with its strange minimalist sets and bizarre costumes, occasionally feels more like a science-fiction allegory than a biblical epic, and it has its cult fans, reportedly including Martin Scorsese. Palance, fresh from his menacing role in *Shane* (1953), is equally memorable as the revolutionary sorcerer, and Waxman's Oscar-nominated score is a secondary highlight. Academy Award Nominations: Best (Color) Cinematography; Best Score. **Cast:** Paul Newman, Virginia Mayo, Pier Angeli, Jack Palance, Lorne Greene, Natalie Wood, Alexander Scourby, Joseph Wiseman. **Credits:** Dir: Victor Saville; Prod: Victor Saville; Writer: Lesser Samuels; Story: Thomas B. Costain; DP: William V. Skall; Ed: George White; Composer: Franz Waxman; Art Director: Boris Leven. Color, 144 min. **VHS**

The Silver Cord
(1933) RKO
Crews chews the scenery in a plum role as a grasping mother. Scientist Dunne managed to spirit new husband McCrea overseas to get him away from Mom. But when they return for a visit, Crews puts on quite a show, including a feigned heart condition. Younger son Linden doesn't manage to escape the gravitational pull and loses Dee. **Cast:** Irene Dunne, Joel McCrea, Frances Dee, Eric Linden, Laura Hope Crews, Helen Cromwell, Gustav Von Seyffertitz, Reginald Pasch, Perry Ivins. **Credits:** Dir: John Cromwell; Prod: Pandro S. Berman; Writer: Jane Murfin; DP: Charles Rosher; Ed: George Nichols; Prod Design: Van Nest Polglase; Composer: Max Steiner. B&W, 74 min.

Sinbad the Sailor
(1947) RKO
The younger Fairbanks picks up the swashbuckling mantle in this Arabian Nights adventure. When Sinbad's ship is nearly sold out from under him while on the trail of lost treasure, the sailor catches the eye of beautiful princess O'Hara. When a wicked prince (Quinn) threatens Sinbad, fellow sailor Slezak comes to the rescue, or does he? Fine family entertainment. **Cast:** Douglas Fairbanks, Jr., Maureen O'Hara, Anthony Quinn, Walter Slezak, George Tobias, Jane Greer, Mike Mazurki, Sheldon Leonard. **Credits:** Dir: Richard Wallace; Prod: Stephen Ames; Writer: John Twist; Story: George Worthing Yates; DP: George Barnes; Ed: Sherman Todd, Frank Doyle; Prod Design: Albert S. D'Agostino, Carroll Clark; Composer: Roy Webb. Color, 117 min. **VHS, LASER**

Since You Went Away
(1944) United Artists
This touching WWII picture focuses on the home front and the war's impact on the lives of average Americans. Colbert keeps her household and two daughters (Jones and Temple) together as they face day-to-day life without the man of the family. The family deals with economic pressures (they take on boarder Woolley) and romances (Jones's relationship with soldier Walker, her real-life husband at the time). Based on Wilder's letters to her overseas husband, adapted by producer Selznick. Academy Award Nominations: 9, including Best Picture; Best Actress: Claudette Colbert; Best Supporting Actor: Monty Woolley; Best Supporting Actress: Jennifer Jones; Best Cinematography; Best Editing. **Academy Awards:** Best Music Score of a Drama/Comedy. **Cast:** Claudette Colbert, Jennifer Jones, Joseph Cotten, Shirley Temple, Lionel Barrymore, Hattie McDaniel, Robert Walker, Monty Wooley, Agnes Moorehead, Guy Madison. **Credits:** Dir: John Cromwell; Prod: David O. Selznick; Writer: David O. Selznick; Story: Margaret Buell Wilder; DP: Stanley Cortez, Lee Garmes, Jack Cosgrove; Ed: Hal C. Kern, James E. Newcomb, Don DiFaure, Arthur Fellows, Wayland M. Hendrys; Prod Design: William L. Pereira; Composer: Max Steiner, Louis Forbes. B&W, 180 min. **VHS, LASER**

Sing, Baby, Sing
(1936) Fox
This early role for Faye is a story of a drunk Shakespearean actor (Menjou) who catches Faye's nightclub act and falls into a booze-induced infatuation. Her agent (Ratoff) thinks this is her big break, and tries to line up a joint radio appearance. The actor's cousin (Love) shoves Menjou on a train bound for L.A. to shield him from the manager and singer, who leap on a train in hot pursuit. The Ritz Brothers make their debut. Academy Award Nomination for Best Song. **Cast:** Alice Faye, Adolphe Menjou, Gregory Ratoff, Patsy Kelly, Montagu Love. **Credits:** Dir: Sidney Lanfield; Prod: Darryl F. Zanuck; Writer: Milton Sperling, Harry Tugend, Jack Yellen; DP: Peverell Marley; Ed: Barbara McLean; Composer: Louis Alter, Walter Bullock, Sidney D. Mitchell, Lewis Pollack, Louis Silvers, Richard A. Whiting, Jack Yellen. B&W, 90 min.

Singin' in the Rain
(1952) MGM
Perhaps the finest screen musical of all time is a particular treat for classic-movie fans as it portrays the frantic period when Hollywood's pictures learned to talk. But this is no dry history lesson: it moves with a nimble grace through flashbacks and a romantic storyline while featuring a selection of the best Freed-Brown numbers from MGM's musicals of the preceding two decades. The silver-screen characters from the late '20s include matinee-idol Kelly and his silent diva leading lady Hagen, whose voice ensures that she won't make the transition to sound, and fresh-faced Reynolds as an aspiring actress and singer who wins Kelly's heart with her voice and good nature. The justly famous numbers include Charisse's slinky "Broadway Ballet" and, of course, Kelly's exuberant stomp through the title song. Other musical numbers include: "You Were Meant for Me," "Make 'Em Laugh," "You Are My Lucky Star," and "All I Do Is Dream of You." Golden Globe for Best Actor in a Musical or Comedy: Gene Kelly. Selected for the National Film Registry. Academy Award Nominations: Best Supporting Actress: Jean Hagen; Best Scoring of a Musical Picture. **Cast:** Gene Kelly, Debbie Reynolds, Donald O'Connor, Cyd Charisse, Rita Moreno, Jean Hagen, Millard Mitchell, Douglas Fowley, King Donovan, Kathleen Freeman. **Credits:** Dir: Stanley Donen, Gene Kelly; Prod: Arthur Freed; Writer: Betty Comden, Adolph Green; DP: Harold Rosson; Ed: Adrienne Fazan; Prod Design: Cedric Gibbons, Randal Duell; Choreographer: Stanley Donen; Composer: Arthur Freed, Nacio Herb Brown; Costumes: Walter Plunkett. Color, 119 min. **VHS, LASER, DVD**

Sing You Sinners

(1938) Paramount
Crosby stars as a likable dreamer who avoids work at all costs. When he sets out to make his fortune in Los Angeles, he's followed by his brothers (steady, dependable Mac-Murray and teenaged O'Connor) and their mother. They find Crosby playing the horses and investing his money in a broken-down nag of his own. After besting some gangsters, Crosby promises his mother to spend more time in the family singing act. Songs include "I've Got a Pocketful of Dreams," "Laugh and Call It Love," and "Small Fry." **Cast:** Bing Crosby, Fred MacMurray, Donald O'Connor, Elizabeth Patterson, Ellen Drew. **Credits:** Dir: Wesley Ruggles; Prod: Wesley Ruggles; Writer: Claude Binyon; DP: Karl Struss; Ed: Alma Macrorie; Art Director: Hans Drier, Ernst Fegte. B&W, 88 min.

Sinner's Holiday

(1930) Warner Bros.
Cagney's film debut already sets his early image as a tough guy. La Verne runs a penny arcade with her daughter Knapp while son Cagney works for sideshow boss and bootlegger Hymer. When Hymer accuses Cagney of embezzling their illegal gains, Cagney shoots him and flees to his mother's side. La Verne tries to plant the gun on Knapp's suitor Withers, but Knapp blows the whistle on her brother. **Cast:** Grant Withers, Evalyn Knapp, James Cagney, Lucille La Verne, Noel Madison, Joan Blondell, Otto Hoffman, Warren Hymer, Ray Gallagher, Hank Mann. **Credits:** Dir: John G. Adolfi; Writer: George Rosener, Harvey F. Thew; Story: Marie Baumer; DP: Ira Morgan; Ed: James Gibbon; Composer: Leo F. Forbstein. B&W, 60 min.

Sinners in Paradise

(1938) Universal
This melodramatic adventure is set in motion when a plane carrying a load of corrupt, troubled individuals crashes on a mysterious jungle island. The survivors must cope with the native wildlife and a violent ex-con. Notable only as a nonhorror feature directed by Whale. **Cast:** John Boles, Bruce Cabot, Dwight Frye, Madge Evans, Marion Martin, Gene Lockhart, Nana Bryant, Milburn Stone. **Credits:** Dir: James Whale; Prod: Ken Goldsmith; Writer: Lester Cole, Louis Stevens; DP: George Robinson; Ed: Maurice Wright; Art Director: Jack Otterson. B&W, 64 min. **VHS**

The Sin of Harold Diddlebock

(1947) United Artists/RKO
An uneven comedy from Sturges (and silent great Lloyd's last feature), yet it contains some of the funniest scenes in movies. In the first scenes, Lloyd's football-star character from *The Freshman* (1925) is revealed to have descended from gridiron exploits to a long, dull career as a clerk with a wistful, unrequited longing for a fellow employee. When he's summarily fired after 20 years, Lloyd goes on a hilarious bender that fizzes over into comic madness when he guzzles a concoction that the bartender names The Diddlebock in his honor. It causes him to bray like a mule and boosts his gumption so that he ends up owner of a down-at-the-heels circus and dangling out of a building. After Sturges and Lloyd battled on the set, this was released to lukewarm reception. Producer Hughes sliced nine minutes out and rereleased it as *Mad Wednesday* in 1950. **Cast:** Harold Lloyd, Frances Ramsden, Jimmy Conlin, Rudy Vallee, Edgar Kennedy, Raymond Walburn, Arline Judge, Franklin Pangborn, Lionel Stander, Margaret Hamilton. **Credits:** Dir: Preston Sturges; Prod: Howard Hughes, Preston Sturges; Writer: Preston Sturges; DP: Robert Pittack; Ed: Thomas Neff, Stuart Gilmore; Composer: Werner Richard Heymann, Harry Rosenthal; Art Director: Robert Usher. B&W, 102 min. **VHS**

The Sin of Madelon Claudet

(1931) MGM
Hayes made her first sound film and won a Best Actress Oscar in this soaper written by husband MacArthur that was filmed no fewer than eight times from 1915 to 1981. An innocent French country girl is seduced by an artist (Hamilton), living joyously with him until he leaves to marry another woman. Her next affair ends with Stone arrested for a jewel heist and a suicide from shame. Hayes eventually resorts to walking the streets to support her illegitimate child (Young), a child who grows up to become a dedicated doctor. Depression-era audiences loved melodramas of motherly sacrifice such as this tale of Madame X, and because of Hayes's performance this remains one of the best. **Academy Awards:** Best Actress: Helen Hayes. **Cast:** Helen Hayes, Lewis Stone, Neil Hamilton, Robert Young, Cliff Edwards, Jean Hersholt, Marie Prevost, Karen Morley. **Credits:** Dir: Edgar Selwyn; Writer: Charles MacArthur; DP: Oliver Marsh; Ed: Tom Held; Prod Design: Cedric Gibbons. B&W, 76 min. **VHS**

Sin Town

(1942) Universal
This quickly paced Western shoot-'em-up stars Crawford and Bennett as drifting grifters who arrive at a new boomtown in 1910 and start getting ready to count the suckers' cash. After saving Bond from the hangman, they gain ownership of the local saloon, but feisty newspaperwoman Gwynne doesn't much like what she sees. When she winds up apparently dead, Crawford and Bennett just might lose their lives too. **Cast:** Broderick Crawford, Constance Bennett, Anne Gwynne, Patric Knowles, Andy Devine, Leo Carrillo, Ward Bond, Arthur Aylesworth, Ralf Harolde, Charles Wagenheim, Billy Wayne. **Credits:** Dir: Ray Enright; Prod: George Waggner; Writer: Richard Brooks, Scott Darling, Gerald Geraghty; DP: George Robinson; Ed: Edward Curtiss; Prod Design: Jack Otterson; Composer: Hans J. Salter. B&W, 73 min.

Sirocco

(1951) Columbia
Bogart stars as a gunrunner stuck between the French and the rebels led by Stevens in war-torn '20s Syria. When he falls in love with Toren, the girlfriend of the French intelligence chief (Cobb), he becomes a go-between as the French try to work out a peace settlement. His reward will be two passes to Cairo for Toren and him, if he survives. Atmospheric action drama. **Cast:** Humphrey Bogart, Zero Mostel, Lee J. Cobb, Everett Sloane,

Onslow Stevens, Marta Toren, Gerald Mohr, Nick Dennis, Ludwig Donath, Vincent Renno, Leo Penn. **Credits:** Dir: Curtis Bernhardt; Prod: Robert Lord; Writer: A. I. Bezzerides, Hans Jacoby; Story: Joseph Kessel; DP: Burnett Guffey; Ed: Viola Lawrence; Composer: George Antheil; Art Director: Robert Peterson. B&W, 111 min. VHS, LASER

Sister Kenny
(1946) RKO
Russell gives a moving performance as Elizabeth Kenny, the dedicated nurse who pioneered her own method of treatment for infantile paralysis. Knox plays the doctor who gives her encouragement and champions her rehabilitation method to the medical community. Kenny came to the U.S. in 1940 and set up a facility in Minnesota. Golden Globe for Best Actress: Rosalind Russell. Academy Award Nomination for Best Actress: Rosalind Russell. **Cast:** Rosalind Russell, Dean Jagger, Alexander Knox, Beulah Bondi, Charles Dingle, John Litel, Fay Helm. **Credits:** Dir: Dudley Nichols; Prod: Dudley Nichols; Writer: Dudley Nichols, Alexander Knox, Mary McCarthy, Milton Gunzburg; Story: Elizabeth Kenny, Martha Ostenso; DP: George Barnes; Ed: Roland Gross; Composer: Alexandre Tansman; Art Director: Albert S. D'Agostino, William Flannery. B&W, 116 min. VHS

The Sisters
(1938) Warner Bros.
A soapy Warner melodrama set at the turn of the century follows the romantic fortunes of three sisters from Montana (Davis, Louise, and Bryan) and their husbands, who they meet at the 1904 inaugural ball. Two sisters have their ups and downs, but Davis marries Flynn, an arrogant newspaperman in San Francisco, who drinks, chases other women, and eventually runs off in shame to Singapore. In her grief, Davis suffers a miscarriage and then has to deal with the 1906 earthquake. Flynn returns eventually after Davis has found a new life with Hunter. **Cast:** Bette Davis, Errol Flynn, Anita Louise, Ian Hunter, Donald Crisp, Beulah Bondi, Jane Bryan, Lee Patrick. **Credits:** Dir: Anatole Litvak; Prod: David Lewis; Writer: Milton Krims; Story: Myron Brinig; DP: Tony Gaudio; Ed: Warren Low; Composer: Max Steiner, Leo F. Forbstein; Art Director: Carl Jules Weyl. B&W, 99 min. VHS

Sisters
(1973) AIP
This delightfully horrific murder mystery is the first of director De Palma's

homages to themes explored by Hitchcock. Reporter Salt spies a murder next door, and is mystified when the police find no evidence of a crime. She tracks her suspect, Kidder, to a mental institution where she discovers that Kidder is one of a pair of separated Siamese twins. Clever storytelling and a score by Hitchcock's favorite composer, Herrmann. **Cast:** Margot Kidder, Jennifer Salt, Charles Durning, Barnard Hughes, Bill Finley, Lisle Wilson, Dolph Sweet. **Credits:** Dir: Brian De Palma; Prod: Edward R. Pressman; Writer: Brian De Palma, Louisa Rose; DP: Gregory Sandor; Ed: Paul Hirsch; Composer: Bernard Herrmann; Art Director: Gary Weist. Color, 92 min. VHS

Sitting Pretty
(1948) Paramount
In a career-defining role for Webb, his brilliantly acerbic portrayal of Lynn Belvedere also spawned two Mr. Belvedere sequels and a TV series. O'Hara and Young play harried suburban parents of three little barbarians who make short work of a phone book full of baby-sitters. Webb guarantees that his method of child-rearing will civilize the behavioral nightmare and his interactions with the children produce results and truly memorable comedy. However, all is not as it seems, as Webb is actually doing research for an unflattering best-seller describing the community of Hummingbird Hill. Followed by *Mr. Belvedere Goes to College* (1949) and *Mr. Belvedere Rings the Bell* (1951). Academy Award Nomination for Best Actor: Clifton Webb. **Cast:** Robert Young, Maureen O'Hara, Clifton Webb, Richard Haydn, Louise Allbritton, Randy Stuart, Larry Olsen, Johnny Russell, Betty Lynn, Willard Robertson. **Credits:** Dir: Walter Lang; Prod: Samuel G. Engel; Writer: Hugh Herbert; Story: Gwen Davenport; DP: Norbert F. Brodine; Ed: Harmon Jones; Composer: Alfred Newman; Art Director: Lyle Wheeler, Leland Fuller. B&W, 85 min.

Six of a Kind
(1934) Paramount
McCarey directs a roster of comedians in this hilarious road comedy. Ruggles and Boland want to save money on the travel for their second honeymoon and advertise for a couple to share expenses. They wind up with Burns and Allen and an enormous Great Dane. Their trip gets further complicated when a crooked colleague at Ruggles's bank puts $50,000 in

embezzled funds in Ruggles's suitcase. The cops put out an all-points bulletin, which introduces Fields as a pool-playing sheriff, one of his best routines. **Cast:** George Burns, Gracie Allen, Charlie Ruggles, Mary Boland, W. C. Fields, Alison Skipworth, Bradley Page, Grace Bradley. **Credits:** Dir: Leo McCarey; Writer: Walter DeLeon, Harry Ruskin; Story: Douglas MacLean; DP: Henry Sharp; Ed: LeRoy Stone; Composer: Ralph Rainger; Art Director: Hans Dreier, Robert Odell. B&W, 63 min. VHS

The Skin Game
(1931) British International
One of Hitchcock's earliest sound features is based on a play by John Galsworthy (*The Forsythe Saga*) about two rival neighbors, a nouveau riche industrialist (Gwenn), and a member of the old gentry (France). An atypical British Hitchcock feature of interest mainly for Hitchcock scholars, who will note his experiments with subjective dolly shots and whip-panning in the courtroom scenes. **Cast:** Edmund Gwenn, Jill Esmond, John Longden, C. V. France, Phyllis Konstam, Helen Hayes, Frank Lawton, Edward Chapman. **Credits:** Dir: Alfred Hitchcock; Prod: John Maxwell; Writer: Alfred Hitchcock, Alma Reville; Story: John Galsworthy; DP: Jack Cox. B&W, 85 min. VHS

Skippy
(1931) Paramount
This wonderful children's adventure follows two boys, one rich and the other poor, and their dogs. Nine-year-old Cooper and his friend Coogan have to raise three bucks fast when Coogan's dog is nabbed by the dog-catcher. They put on a show, sell lemonade, and try to break into Cooper's piggy bank before they learn that Coogan's dog has died. Cooper tries to ease the pain by trading for a new dog to give to Coogan, but really comes through when he convinces his dad not to tear down Coogan's neighborhood. Academy Award Nominations: 4, including Best Picture; Best Actor: Jackie Cooper; Best Adapted Screenplay. **Academy Awards:** Best Director. **Cast:** Enid Bennett, Robert Coogan, Jackie Cooper, Mitzi Green, Donald Haines, Willard Robertson, Jackie Searl. **Credits:** Dir: Norman Taurog; Prod: Louis D. Lighton; Writer: Joseph L. Mankiewicz, Percy Crosby, Norman Z. McLeod, Don Marquis, Sam Mintz; DP: Karl Struss. 85 min.

Skylark

(1941) Paramount

In a witty romantic comedy, Colbert is the dissatisfied wife of ad exec Milland, whose interests lie more with his work than his marriage. Colbert heads to Reno to start divorce proceedings, and hooks up with wealthy playboy Aherne on a cruise. Though he falls madly in love with Colbert, she's trying to figure out how to get back with Milland. Academy Award Nomination for Best Sound. **Cast:** Claudette Colbert, Ray Milland, Brian Aherne, Binnie Barnes, Walter Abel, Grant Mitchell, Mona Barrie, Ernest Cossart, James Rennie, Fritz Feld. **Credits:** Dir: Mark Sandrich; Prod: Mark Sandrich; Writer: Zion Myers, Allan Scott; Story: Samson Raphaelson; DP: Charles Lang; Ed: LeRoy Stone; Prod Design: Hans Dreier, Roland Anderson; Composer: Victor Young. B&W, 92 min.

Skyscraper Souls

(1932) MGM

In this famously hot-stuff, pre-Code potboiler, William plays a ruthless financial wizard who owns a 100-story monument to his ego. Inside the building, romantic and financial shenanigans lead to heartbreak and death. Risqué enough to still raise eyebrows. **Cast:** Warren William, Maureen O'Sullivan, Gregory Ratoff, Anita Page, Verree Teasdale, Norman Foster, Hedda Hopper, George Barbier. **Credits:** Dir: Edgar Selwyn; Writer: C. Gardner Sullivan, Elmer Harris; Story: Faith Baldwin; DP: William Daniels; Ed: Tom Held; Prod Design: Cedric Gibbons. B&W, 99 min. **VHS**

The Sky's the Limit

(1943) RKO

In 1939, RKO studio heads chose to foster the dramatic career of Ginger Rogers at the expense of Fred Astaire, whom theater owners had pronounced box-office poison. After films at MGM and Paramount, including the successful *Holiday Inn* (1942), RKO was happy to welcome him back for this Harold Arlen wartime musical. Astaire plays one of Col. Chenault's Flying Tiger pilots in New York for a hero's welcome who decides to see the town incognito. A news photographer (Leslie) catches his eye, but she mistakenly assumes he's a shirker. Astaire brings her around with song and dance. Algonquin Round Table humorist Benchley is also on hand, presenting his classic routine, "Treasurer's Report." Songs include "One for My Baby and One for the Road"

and "My Shining Hour." Academy Award Nominations: Best Scoring of a Musical Picture; Best Song ("My Shining Hour"). **Cast:** Fred Astaire, Joan Leslie, Robert Ryan, Robert Benchley, Elizabeth Patterson, Marjorie Gateson, Richard Davies, Clarence Kolb. **Credits:** Dir: Edward H. Griffith; Prod: David Hempstead; Writer: Frank Fenton, Lynn Root; DP: Russell Metty; Ed: Roland Gross; Composer: Leigh Harline; Art Director: Albert S. D'Agostino, Carroll Clark. B&W, 89 min. **VHS**

Slap Shot

(1977) Universal

Great performance by Newman as the coach of a minor-league hockey team whose owner plans to sell as the steel mill that supplies fans is on its last legs. Newman spurs his team to victory with dirty play, raising a conflict with clean-cut, college-boy player Ontkean. The team makes it to a climactic brawl of a championship game. Notoriously foul language. **Cast:** Paul Newman, Strother Martin, Jennifer Warren, Michael Ontkean, Lindsay Crouse, Jerry Houser, Andrew Duncan, Steve Carlson, Allan Nicholls. **Credits:** Dir: George Roy Hill; Prod: Robert J. Wunsch, Stephen Friedman; Writer: Nancy Dowd; DP: Victor J. Kemper; Ed: Dede Allen; Composer: Elmer Bernstein; Art Director: Henry Bumstead. Color, 123 min. **VHS, LASER**

Slattery's Hurricane

(1949) Fox

As Widmark flies a dangerous assignment for the Weather Service, an assignment he took to atone for trying to steal his pal's wife, flashbacks tell how he arrived at his critical moment. A heroic WWII navy pilot, Widmark takes a job flying planes for a candy company with a sideline of shipping dope for the Mafia and gets involved with a junkie, Lake. Widmark then discovers that an old navy pal, Russell, is married to an old flame of his (Darnell), and the flame stills burns. Darnell helps him to reform and Widmark volunteers to take Russell's place on the dangerous mission. Lake's last major appearance. **Cast:** Richard Widmark, Linda Darnell, Veronica Lake, Johnny Russell, Walter Kingsford, Stanley Waxman, Gary Merrill, Raymond Greenleaf. **Credits:** Dir: Andre De Toth; Prod: William Perlberg; Writer: Herman Wouk, Richard Murphy; DP: Charles G. Clarke; Prod Design: Lyle Wheeler; Composer: Lionel Newman; SFX: Ray Kellog; Art Director: Albert Hogsett. B&W, 83 min.

Slaughterhouse-Five

(1972) Universal

Director Hill took on a daunting assignment with Kurt Vonnegut's surreal novel. The story of Billy Pilgrim (Sacks) jumps through time and space, following the bewildered everyman as he comes "unstuck in time" from his WWII service in Europe where he was a prisoner in Dresden at the time of the firebombing, to the suburban sprawl of the '60s, to his captivity with porn star Perrine in a human zoo on the planet Trafalmadore. A challenging, entertaining experience. **Cast:** Michael Sacks, Ron Leibman, Valerie Perrine, Perry King, Eugene Roche, Sharon Gans, Roberts Blossom, Sorrell Booke, Kevin Conway, Gary Waynesmith. **Credits:** Dir: George Roy Hill; Prod: Paul Monash; Writer: Stephen Geller; Story: Kurt Vonnegut; DP: Miroslav Ondricek; Ed: Dede Allen; Prod Design: Henry Bumstead; Composer: Glenn Gould; SFX: John Chambers. Color, 104 min. **VHS, LASER, DVD**

Slaughter on Tenth Avenue

(1957) Universal

Egan plays a young, inexperienced assistant district attorney who battles the mob that runs the waterfront. When longshoreman Shaughnessy gets shot, Egan goes undercover to break the dock workers' code of silence with the support of Shaughnessy's wife, Sterling, and his own wife, Adams. With his last words, the longshoreman lets go of the secrets that convict gangster Matthau and his toughs. Based on a real case. The theme music is from Rodgers's ballet for *On Your Toes*. **Cast:** Richard Egan, Jan Sterling, Dan Duryea, Julie Adams, Charles Matthau, Sam Levene, Mickey Shaughnessy, Harry Bellaver, Nick Dennis. **Credits:** Dir: Arnold Laven; Prod: Albert Zugsmith; Writer: Lawrence Roman, William J. Keating, Richard Carter; DP: Fred Jackman; Ed: Russell Schoengarth; Composer: Richard Rodgers. B&W, 103 min.

Slave Ship

(1937) Fox

Baxter, captain of the *Albatross*, a slave ship crewed by a ruthless band of cutthroats, meets and falls in love with a beautiful young woman, Allan. Vowing to reform, he makes known his intentions to sell the boat and free the ship's slaves. Mutiny ensues. Rooney provides laughs; Faulkner contributed to the script. **Cast:** Warner Baxter, Wallace Beery, Elizabeth Allan, Mickey Rooney, George Sanders, Jane Darwell,

Joseph Schildkraut, Miles Mander, Arthur Hohl, Scott Douglas. **Credits:** Dir: Tay Garnett; Prod: Darryl F. Zanuck, Nunnally Johnson; Writer: Sam Hellman, Gladys Lehman, William Faulkner, Lamar Trotti; Story: George King; DP: Ernest Palmer; Ed: Lloyd Nosler; Prod Design: Hans Peters; Composer: Alfred Newman. B&W, 92 min.

Sleeper
(1973) United Artists
A 20th-century health-food-store owner wakes up to a future in which science has proven deep-fried foods and chocolate to be healthy, machines stimulate orgasms, and the world is dominated by a disembodied nose. In Allen's brilliant sci-fi parody, his neurotic character joins the underground resistance and brings wealthy housewife Keaton with him. Futuristic hilarity ensues. **Cast:** Woody Allen, Diane Keaton, Mary Gregory, John Beck, Marya Small, Bartlett Robinson, Peter Hobbs, Brian Avery. **Dir:** Dir: Woody Allen; Prod: Jack Grossberg; Writer: Marshall Brickman; DP: David M. Walsh; Ed: Ralph Rosenblum; Prod Design: Dale Hennesy; Composer: Woody Allen; Art Director: Dianne Wager. Color, 88 min. VHS, LASER

Sleeping Beauty
(1959) Disney
This is the most expensive animated film of its time and a landmark achievement for Disney, and it has grown more popular over time. The still-beloved story depicts a beautiful princess born in a faraway kingdom destined by a witch's terrible curse to fall into a deep sleep, and she can be awakened only by true love's first kiss. This family classic makes wondrous use of Tchaikovsky's same-titled ballet score. The limited, collector's edition video includes a bonus program entitled *Once Upon a Dream: The Making of Sleeping Beauty*, plus a behind-the-scenes booklet. In addition, the collector's edition widescreen version features the original theatrical trailer and bonus footage. Academy Award Nominations: Best Scoring of a Musical Picture. **Cast:** Mary Costa, Eleanor Audley, Barbara Luddy, Taylor Holmes, Bill Shirley, Barbara Jo Allen. **Credits:** Dir: Clyde Geronimi; Writer: Erdman Penner; Ed: Roy M. Brewer, Jr., Donald Halliday; Prod Design: Don DaGradi, Ken Anderson. Color, 91 min. VHS, LASER

Sleep, My Love
(1948) United Artists
In a complex psychological thriller and murder mystery from director Sirk,

Ameche attempts to drive wealthy wife Colbert to suicide, leaving Ameche and his lover with her estate. This hall of mirrors, complete with dummy psychiatrist, seems to be working according to plan until Colbert bumps into Cummings, who falls for her. It doesn't take him long to unravel Ameche's plot, and just in time. **Cast:** Claudette Colbert, Robert Cummings, Don Ameche, Rita Johnson, George Coulouris, Hazel Brooks, Anne Triola, Queenie Smith, Keye Luke, Fred Nurney. **Credits:** Dir: Douglas Sirk; Prod: Ralph Cohn, Charles Rogers; Writer: St. Clair McKelway; Story: Leo Rosten, Cyril Endfield, Decla Dunning; DP: Joseph A. Valentine; Ed: Lynn Harrison; Art Director: William Ferrari. B&W, 97 min.

The Slender Thread
(1965) Paramount
This interesting drama is set in Seattle with Poitier as a telephone volunteer on a suicide prevention hotline trying to keep Bancroft, a housewife who has taken an overdose, on the line so that a rescue crew can trace the call before it is too late. The tense situation, expanded with a few flashbacks detailing Bancroft's past, marked Pollack's first film following his work in TV drama. Written by veteran TV dramatist Silliphant, based on a real incident detailed in a magazine article by Alexander. Academy Award Nominations: Best (Black-and-White) Art Direction—Set Decoration; Best (Black-and-White) Costume Design. **Cast:** Sidney Poitier, Anne Bancroft, Telly Savalas, Steven Hill, Edward Asner, Dabney Coleman, John Benson, Paul Newlan. **Credits:** Dir: Sydney Pollack; Prod: Stephen Alexander; Writer: Stirling Silliphant; Story: Shana Alexander; DP: Loyal Griggs; Ed: Thomas Stanford; Composer: Quincy Jones; Art Director: Hal Pereira, Jack Poplin. B&W, 98 min. VHS

Sleuth
(1972) Fox
A sparkling succession of surprises pop up in a puzzle-box of a movie that keeps twisting at every turn. Caine visits mystery writer Olivier where he's informed that Olivier knows about his affair with his wife. When he suggests that Caine fake a jewel heist to support his lover, the games begin. The advantage shifts between the rivals, with elaborate disguises, fake deaths, blank guns, and, finally, deadly revenge. Based on Shaffer's play. Academy Award Nominations: 4, including Best Actor: Lau-

rence Olivier; Best Actor: Michael Caine; Best Director. **Cast:** Laurence Olivier, Michael Caine, Alec Cawthorne, Ted Martin. **Credits:** Dir: Joseph L. Mankiewicz, John Matthews; Prod: Morton Gottlieb; Writer: Anthony Shaffer; DP: Oswald Morris; Ed: Richard Marden; Prod Design: Ken Adam; Composer: John Addison; Art Director: Peter Lamont. Color, 139 min. VHS, LASER

A Slight Case of Murder
(1938) Warner Bros.
This is a hilarious send-up by Robinson of his tough-guy gangster movies. As a beer tycoon who could only have thrived during Prohibition, Robinson decides to settle down on his country estate after the 21st Amendment passes. But first he discovers the corpses of rival gangsters scattered around the grounds, and then his future son-in-law decides to become a cop. Good fun with characters from a Damon Runyon play. **Cast:** Edward G. Robinson, Allen Jenkins, Jane Bryan, Ruth Donnelly, Willard Parker, John Litel, Edward Brophy, Harold Huber, Willard Parker, Paul Harvey. **Credits:** Dir: Lloyd Bacon; Prod: Sam Bischoff; Writer: Earl Baldwin, Joseph Schrank, Howard Lindsay, Damon Runyon; DP: Sid Hickox; Ed: James Gibbon; Composer: M. K. Jerome, Jack Scholl. B&W, 85 min.

Slightly French
(1949) Columbia
This reworking of 1934's *Let's Fall in Love* features the Harold Arlen–Ted Koehler title song, and Sirk's bemused look at directorial ego. Ameche gets fired from a picture after reducing the star to shambles, but finds the right vehicle to realize his ambitions in Lamour, who exchanges her Brooklyn "dese" and "dose" for the elegance of French and, incidentally, wins Ameche's heart. An uncharacteristically lighthearted outing from Sirk. **Cast:** Dorothy Lamour, Don Ameche, Janis Carter, Willard Parker, Adele Jergens, Jeanne Manet, Frank Ferguson, Myron Healey, Leonard Carey, Earl Hodgins. **Credits:** Dir: Douglas Sirk; Prod: Irving Starr; Writer: Karen DeWolf; Story: Herbert Fields; DP: Charles Lawton; Ed: Al Clark; Composer: George Duning, Morris Stoloff; Costumes: Jean Louis; Art Director: Carl Anderson. B&W, 81 min.

Slightly Scarlet
(1955) RKO
A wide-screen, Technicolor noir! Mob underling Payne gets the assignment to dig up the dirt on a reform candi-

date for mayor. He sniffs around the politician's secretary (Fleming) and discovers an ex-con sister (Dahl). But when Payne falls for Fleming, he switches sides, ratting on his boss (De Corsia) and taking over the gang. Payne's conflicted by his love for Fleming and confronts the Mob boss one final time. An interesting, less well known noir from Dwan. Based on a James M. Cain novel, *Love's Lovely Counterfeit*. **Cast:** Rhonda Fleming, John Payne, Arlene Dahl, Kent Taylor, Ted De Corsia, Lance Fuller, Frank Gerstle, Buddy Baer. **Credits:** Dir: Allan Dwan; Prod: Benedict Bogeaus; Writer: Robert Blees; DP: John Alton; Ed: James Leicester; Prod Design: Van Nest Polglase; Composer: Louis Forbes. Color, 99 min. **VHS**

Slim

(1937) Warner Bros.

Fonda plays a young farmhand anxious to leave his rural life behind, and he sees the chance when he meets high-power lineman O'Brien. O'Brien trains Fonda in their dangerous occupation and introduces him to the hard-drinking lifestyle of the linemen. He also introduces him to his girlfriend (Lindsay) and sparks start to fly off the job as well. The two stay pals, however, and bravely face a power outage in a raging storm. The plot would make its reappearance in *Manpower* (1941). **Cast:** Craig Reynolds, John Litel, Jane Wyman, Pat O'Brien, Henry Fonda, Stuart Erwin, Margaret Lindsay, J. Farrell MacDonald, Dick Purcell, Joe Sawyer. **Credits:** Dir: Ray Enright; Prod: Hal B. Wallis, Sam Bischoff; Writer: William Haines; DP: Sidney Hickox; Ed: Owen Marks; Prod Design: Ted Smith; Composer: Max Steiner. B&W, 80 min.

Smart Money

(1931) Warner Bros.

This bristling crime melodrama was the only on-screen pairing of Warner's two top tough guys, Robinson and Cagney. Robinson had become a star with the release of *Little Caesar* and Cagney was making *The Public Enemy* at the same time as this. Robinson plays a small-town barber who knows his way around the card table. When he beats crooked gambler Karloff, his friends stake him to a big score. But once in the city, Robinson loses the money in a setup that relies on his attraction to Francis. He and Cagney come to the city looking for revenge, and they get it, but once more Robinson takes a fall because of a dame, Knapp this time. Academy Award Nom-

ination for Best Original Screenplay. **Cast:** James Cagney, Edward G. Robinson, Boris Karloff, Polly Walters, Ralf Harolde, Margaret Livingston, Maurice Black, Noel Francis, Evalyn Knapp. **Credits:** Dir: Alfred E. Green; Writer: John Bright, Kubec Glasmon, Lucien Hubbard; DP: Robert Kurrle; Ed: Jack Killifer; Composer: Leo F. Forbstein. B&W, 90 min.

Smash-Up, the Story of a Woman

(1947) Universal

Here is Hayward's first major role, and what a performance. Hayward's a nightclub singer who abandons her successful career to get married and have a family. After helping singer and songwriter husband Bowman to the top, she finds herself alone in their home as he pursues the limelight. Hayward takes comfort in the bottle, eventually driving her husband away and losing custody of their daughter. When she makes a desperate grab for the child, it leads to a disastrous fire and the first steps to recovery. Dorothy Parker wrote the story. Academy Award Nominations: Best Actress: Susan Hayward; Best Original Story. **Cast:** Susan Hayward, Eddie Albert, Lee Bowman, Marsha Hunt, Carl Esmond, Carleton Young, Charles D. Brown, Robert Shayne. **Credits:** Dir: Stuart Heisler; Prod: Walter Wanger; Writer: John Howard Lawson, Lionel Wiggam; DP: Stanley Cortez; Ed: Milton Carruth; Prod Design: Alexander Golitzen; Composer: Daniele Amfitheatrof. B&W, 106 min. **VHS**

Smile

(1975) United Artists

This hilarious satire on the emptiness of middle America is considered by many to be one of the most underrated comedies of the '70s. Ritchie sets his story in the midst of a real beauty contest being held in Santa Rosa, California. As the young beauties (including a young Griffith) compete for the "Young American Miss" title, various stories unfold. Mobile-home dealer Dern catches his son peddling nude photos of the contestants, Kidd sees his choreographic career descend to the depths, and contest judge Feldon turns away from husband Pryor. As in Robert Altman's *Nashville*, also produced in 1975, the many fragmented story lines (and the actual beauty contest) lend a near-documentary feeling. **Cast:** Bruce Dern, Barbara Feldon, Melanie Griffith, Annette O'Toole, Michael Kidd, Geoffrey Lewis, Nicholas Pryor, Colleen

Camp. **Credits:** Dir: Michael Ritchie; Prod: Michael Ritchie; Writer: Jerry Belson; DP: Conrad Hall; Ed: Richard A. Harris; Composer: Leroy Holmes, Charles Chaplin, Daniel Osborn. Color, 113 min. **VHS, LASER**

Smilin' Through

(1932) MGM

The first sound version of this romantic melodrama features the queen of MGM, Shearer, in a dual role as murdered bride and vivacious niece. Howard plays the bereft bridegroom whose marriage to Shearer and his happiness are destroyed when an insanely jealous rival (March) murders his bride with a misplaced shot. After years of bitter loneliness, Shearer, Howard's niece, brightens his life. The clouds gather once again when his niece meets the killer's son (March again), and Howard forbids them to see each other. The ghost of the murdered bride urges Howard to let the lovers be together. Director Franklin also directed the original, silent version in 1922. Academy Award Nomination for Best Picture. **Cast:** Norma Shearer, Fredric March, Leslie Howard, Ralph Forbes, O. P. Heggie, Beryl Mercer, Cora Sue Collins, Forrester Harvey. **Credits:** Dir: Sidney Franklin; Writer: Ernest Vajda, Claudine West, Donald Ogden Stewart, James Fagan; DP: Lee Garmes; Ed: Margaret Booth; Prod Design: Cedric Gibbons; Costumes: Adrian. B&W, 100 min. **VHS**

Smilin' Through

(1941) MGM

The third screen version of this romantic melodrama features MacDonald and her real-life husband Raymond in dual roles, and it adds music to the tragedy. MacDonald's guardian (Aherne) forbids her to see dashing American Raymond before he ships off to WWI. The reason? Raymond's father, a jilted suitor, had killed Aherne's intended (also MacDonald) on their wedding day. Raymond returns wounded and the murder victim from the past comes back to urge MacDonald to his side. MacDonald sings "Smilin' Through" and the tender "A Little Love, A Little Kiss." **Cast:** Jeanette MacDonald, Gene Raymond, Brian Aherne, Ian Hunter, Patrick O'Moore, Frances Robinson, Frances Carson, Wyndham Standing. **Credits:** Dir: Frank Borzage; Prod: Victor Saville; Writer: Donald Ogden Stewart, John L. Balderston; DP: Leonard Smith; Ed: Frank Sullivan; Prod Design: Cedric Gibbons; Composer: Herbert Stothart. Color, 100 min. **VHS**

Smith!

(1969) Disney
Ford stars in the Disney version of the plight of the Native American. Young Indian Ramirez hides from a murder rap on Ford's ranch. Though Ford's pal George turns in his fellow Indian, Ford steps forward to defend the boy. A gentle portrayal of a difficult social problem. **Cast:** Glenn Ford, Nancy Olson, Dean Jagger, Keenan Wynn, Warren Oates, Chief Dan George, Frank Ramirez, John Randolph. **Credits:** Dir: Michael O'Herlihy; Prod: Bill Anderson; Writer: Louis Pelletier; DP: Robert Moreno; Ed: Robert Stafford; Prod Design: John B. Mansbridge; Composer: Robert F. Brunner. Color, 101 min. **VHS**

The Snake Pit

(1948) Fox
This is one of the best examples of the classic social-problem film and one of the first mainstream films to deal sympathetically with mental illness. In an award-winning performance, de Havilland portrays with insight and dignity a woman institutionalized in a crowded state hospital due to a breakdown following depression. The snake pit of the title is the hospital's room of horrors, an open ward in which the hopeless cases are confined. Popular in its day and still disturbing, but the film presents some dated therapies that may surprise contemporary audiences. Academy Award Nominations: 6, including Best Picture; Best Director; Best Actress: Olivia de Havilland; Best Screenplay. **Academy Awards:** Best Sound. **Cast:** Olivia de Havilland, Mark Stevens, Leo Genn, Celeste Holm, Glenn Langan, Helen Craig, Leif Erickson, Beulah Bondi, Lee Patrick, Isabel Jewell. **Credits:** Dir: Anatole Litvak; Prod: Anatole Litvak, Robert Bassler; Writer: Frank Partos, Millen Brand; Story: Mary Jane Ward; Ed: Dorothy Spencer; Prod Design: Lyle Wheeler, Joseph C. Wright; Composer: Alfred Newman; Costumes: Bonnie Cashin; Set Designer: Thomas Little, Ernest Lansing. B&W, 108 min. **VHS, LASER**

The Sniper

(1952) Columbia
This marks blacklist victim Dmytryk's return to directing from political exile in England and a jail term in the U.S. This is also a superbly modulated, frank attempt to grapple with society's reaction to homicidal mental illness. Franz plays the title character, a man who lives the terror of recognizing his own mental instability and urge toward violence, while the world ignores his pleas for help. He gets the attention he desperately needs when he begins shooting women with whom he has had contact. Cop Menjou is the first to realize the shootings are a cry for help. Dmytryk echoes Franz's mental state in his dark, noirish imagery. **Cast:** Adolphe Menjou, Arthur Franz, Gerald Mohr, Marie Windsor, Frank Faylen, Richard Kiley, Mabel Paige, Marlo Dwyer, Geraldin Carr, Jay Novello. **Credits:** Dir: Edward Dmytryk; Prod: Stanley Kramer; Writer: Harry Brown; Story: Edna Anhalt, Edward Anhalt; DP: Burnett Guffey; Ed: Harry Gerstad, Aaron Stell; Prod Design: Rudolph Sternad; Composer: Morris Stoloff; Art Director: Walter Holscher. B&W, 87 min.

The Snows of Kilimanjaro

(1952) Fox
In one of the best Ernest Hemingway adaptations, Peck is a hunter and writer, revisiting his life as he lies close to death from a hunting accident on the African veldt. In flashbacks, Peck recalls life in Paris during the '20s, his burning passion for and failed marriage to Gardner, and his days fighting alongside the Loyalists during the Spanish Civil War. Throughout his wandering, Peck has searched for the meaning that would invest his work and his life with purpose. Meanwhile, Hayward, his safari companion, nurses him through the night, a devotion that Peck comes to see as the meaning for which he's been searching. The original short story gets freighted with extra baggage, but Peck brings the right soulfulness and Gardner the combustible beauty to make for a rewarding movie. This also features a wistful score by Herrmann, including his famous "Memory Waltz." Academy Award Nominations: 2, including Best (Color) Cinematography. **Cast:** Gregory Peck, Ava Gardner, Susan Hayward, Leo G. Carroll, Hildegarde Neff, Torin Thatcher, Helene Stanley, Marcel Dalio, Richard Allan, Leonard Carey. **Credits:** Dir: Henry King; Prod: Darryl F. Zanuck; Writer: Casey Robinson; DP: Leon Shamroy; Ed: Barbara McLean; Prod Design: Lyle Wheeler, John DeCuir; Composer: Bernard Herrmann; Costumes: Charles LeMaire; SFX: Ray Kellogg; Set Designer: Thomas Little, Paul S. Fox. Color, 117 min. **VHS**

Snow White and the Seven Dwarfs

(1937) Disney
Disney's first full-length animated masterpiece is perhaps the "fairest of them all" in the history of animation. Walt Disney took a big risk making this adaptation of the Brothers Grimm fairy tale (it took two years and cost $1.5 million). While many scoffed at the idea, Disney had the last laugh as generations have been delighted by this tale of pure and simple love. Because a jealous queen wants her dead, Snow White flees into the forest where she's taken in by seven little diamond-mine workers. A poisonous apple sent by the queen puts her soundly to sleep until her Prince Charming rouses her with a kiss. The animators modeled their work on live actors (Margary Belcher as Snow White, Louis Hightower as the Prince, and La Verne as the evil Queen). Great music and spectacular images make classic family entertainment. And who can't sing along with "Heigh Ho," "Whistle While You Work," and "Someday My Prince Will Come." Selected for the National Film Registry. Academy Award Nomination for Best Score. **Academy Awards:** Special Award for "Significant Screen Innovation." **Cast:** Adriana Caselotti, Harry Stockwell, Lucille La Verne, Moroni Olsen, Billy Gilbert, Pinto Colvig, Otis Harlan, James MacDonald. **Credits:** Dir: David D. Hand, Perce Pearce, Larry Morey, William Cottrell, Wilfred Jackson, Ben Sharpsteen; Prod: Walt Disney; Writer: Ted Sears, Otto Englander, Earl Hurd, Dorothy Anne Blank, Dick Richards, Merrill De Maris, Webb Smith, Richard Creedon; Composer: Frank Churchill, Leigh Harline, Paul J. Smith, Larry Morey. Color, 84 min. **VHS, LASER**

Soak the Rich

(1936) Paramount
In a Hecht-MacArthur comedy with a political angle, a young heiress (Taylor) returns from Europe to attend the college her father owns. She promptly falls in love with the leader of the college radicals (Howard), and joins his campaign to prevent her father from firing a professor whose book, *Soak the Rich*, advocates the overthrow by taxes of her class. Romance eventually cools the political passions. **Cast:** Walter Connolly, Mary Taylor, John Howard, Alice D. G. Miller, Ilka Chase, Edwin Phillips, Lionel Stander. **Credits:** Dir: Ben Hecht, Charles MacArthur; Prod: Ben Hecht, Charles MacArthur; Writer: Ben Hecht, Charles MacArthur; DP: Leon Shamroy, Charles Hansen; Ed: Leo Zockling. B&W, 86 min.

So Big

(1953) Warner Bros.

In the often-produced melodrama based on Edna Ferber's novel, Wyman stars as a woman from a wealthy midwestern that founders on hard times. She takes a job as a teacher in rural Illinois and marries a farmer, Hayden. Disappointed when their son (Forrest) goes into business rather than the arts, she becomes a surrogate mother to a boy who does want to become an artist. Then Forrest meets artist Olson in Paris and she encourages him to pursue his love of architecture. Made three times previously, once in 1932 with Barbara Stanwyck. **Cast:** Jane Wyman, Sterling Hayden, Nancy Olson, Steve Forrest, Elisabeth Fraser, Martha Hyer, Walter Coy, Richard Beymer, Tommy Rettig, Roland Winters. **Credits:** Dir: Robert Wise; Prod: Henry Blanke; Writer: John Twist; DP: Ellsworth Fredericks; Ed: Thomas Reilly; Prod Design: Milo Anderson, Howard Shoup; Composer: Max Steiner; Art Director: John Beckman. B&W, 101 min.

So Dear to My Heart

(1958) Disney

This heartwarming Disney production lovingly re-creates, with a mix of live-action and animation, the simpler life of America at the turn of the century and the pure heart of a young boy. Driscoll raises his little black lamb and, with the encouragement of Ives, hopes to enter it in the state fair. He works hard to raise the money to make the trip, but his lamb gets lost in a storm. Driscoll asks God to help him find the lamb and he'll love the animal without aspiring to bring it to the fair. But his grandmother Bondi has already made a bargain with the Lord, and Driscoll and his lamb enter the fair's judging. Lovely family entertainment with a flock of great songs. Academy Award Nomination for Best Song ("Lavender Blue [Dilly Dilly]"). **Cast:** Burl Ives, Beulah Bondi, Bobby Driscoll, Luana Patten, Harry Carey, Walter Soderling, John Beal, Raymond Bond. **Credits:** Dir: Harold Schuster; Prod: Walt Disney, Perce Pearce; Writer: John Tucker Battle, Maurice Rapf, Ted Sears; DP: Winton C. Hoch; Ed: Thomas Scott, Lloyd Richardson; Composer: Paul J. Smith; Art Director: John Ewing. Color, 82 min. VHS

So Ends Our Night

(1941) United Artists

This features striking performances by March, as a German who leaves his wife and home to flee Hitler's society, and Sullavan and Ford as a Jewish couple also on the run. March returns to visit his dying wife despite the SS agents on his tail, and Ford and Sullavan make it to the temporary safety of Paris. A trademark evil-Nazi role for Von Stroheim in an adaptation of Erich Maria Remarque's novel *Flotsam*. Academy Award Nomination for Best Scoring of a Dramatic Picture. **Cast:** Fredric March, Erich Von Stroheim, Margaret Sullavan, Glenn Ford, Frances Dee, Anna Sten, Leonid Kinskey, Joseph Cawthorn. **Credits:** Dir: John Cromwell; Prod: David Loew, Albert Lewin; Writer: Talbot Jennings; DP: William Daniels; Ed: William H. Reynolds; Prod Design: Jack Otterson. B&W, 117 min. VHS

Soldier in the Rain

(1963) Allied Artists

Gleason and McQueen make an odd pairing for a buddy movie, but this service comedy with dramatic moments features a terrific performance by Gleason. A career enlisted man, Gleason turns a deaf ear to fellow sergeant McQueen's dreams of riches outside the service: all his needs are provided as he waits to retire on a desert isle. The dreams expire after he saves McQueen from a beating by MPs. Director Edwards cowrote this adaptation of a William Goldman novel. **Cast:** Steve McQueen, Jackie Gleason, Tuesday Weld, Tony Bill, Tom Poston, Ed Nelson, Adam West, Chris Noel, Lew Gallo. **Credits:** Dir: Ralph Nelson; Prod: Martin Jurow; Writer: Maurice Richlin, Blake Edwards; Story: William Goldman; DP: Philip H. Lathrop; Ed: Ralph E. Winters; Composer: Henry Mancini; Art Director: Phil Barber, James Payne. B&W, 88 min. VHS

Soldier of Fortune

(1955) Fox

Hayward searches for her missing photographer husband in Hong Kong, and signs up gunrunner Gable to help out. Gable, policeman Rennie, and Hayward take a dangerous journey into Communist China to smuggle out the photographer. A standard adventure, but the leads and the crackling action directed by Dmytryk make an entertaining package. All of Hayward's scenes were shot in the studio as her divorce didn't allow her to take her children on location. **Cast:** Clark Gable, Susan Hayward, Michael Rennie, Gene Barry, Alex D'Arcy, Tom Tully, Anna Sten, Russell Collins. **Credits:** Dir: Edward Dmytryk; Prod: Buddy Adler; Writer: Ernest K. Gann; DP: Leo Tover; Ed: Dorothy Spencer; Prod Design: Lyle Wheeler; Composer: Hugo Friedhofer; Art Director: Jack Martin Smith. Color, 96 min. VHS

Soldiers Three

(1951) MGM

Three British comrades-in-arms (Granger, Newton, and Cusack) in 1890s India annoy their commanding officer (Pidgeon) with their drinking and brawling, despite his best efforts to break up the threesome. Granger deserts to join his pals on a routine mission and they come under attack from Indian rebels. Pidgeon comes to the rescue, kills the leader of the rebels, and earns a promotion. Granger gets busted back to private where he can carouse with his buddies again. A period military comedy based on Kipling short stories by the producer of *Gunga Din* (1939). **Cast:** Stewart Granger, Walter Pidgeon, David Niven, Robert Newton, Cyril Cusack, Greta Gynt, Frank Allenby, Robert Coote, Dan O'Herlihy, Michael Ansara. **Credits:** Dir: Tay Garnett; Prod: Pandro S. Berman; Writer: Marguerite Roberts, Tom Reed, Malcolm Stuart Boylan; Story: Rudyard Kipling; DP: William Mellor; Ed: Robert J. Kern; Prod Design: Cedric Gibbons, Malcolm Brown; Composer: Adolph Deutsch. B&W, 87 min.

The Solid Gold Cadillac

(1956) Columbia

This is George S. Kaufman and Howard Teichmann's Broadway satire of American corporate corruption defeated by a plucky small shareholder played by Holliday. When Holliday, who owns 10 shares of stock in a huge corporation, makes waves at an annual board meeting, former chief executive Douglas takes note of the new management's sharp practices and organizes all the small shareholders for a proxy battle. Sharp comedy with a famous role for Holliday. Academy Award Nominations: 2, including Best Art Direction. **Academy Awards:** Best Costume Design (B&W). **Cast:** Judy Holliday, Paul Douglas, Fred Clark, John Williams, Arthur O'Connell, Hiram Sherman, Neva Patterson, Ray Collins, Richard Deacon. **Credits:** Dir: Richard Quine; Prod: Fred Kohlmar; Writer: Abe Burrows; DP: Charles Lang; Ed: Charles Nelson; Composer: Cyril Mockridge; Costumes: Jean Louis; Art Director: Ross Bellah; Set Designer: William Kiernan. B&W, 99 min. VHS

"I have discussed this with my doctor and my psychiatrist and they tell me I'm too old and too rich to go through this again."

Billy Wilder, after directing Marilyn Monroe in *Some Like It Hot* (1959)

Solomon and Sheba

(1959) United Artists
Director Vidor's swan song also has the unfortunate renown as the scene of Tyrone Power's death. When he suffered a heart attack after completion of most of the principal filming, Vidor reshot his scenes with Brynner. The Queen of Sheba (Lollobrigida) seduces Solomon (Brynner) to distract him after his military victories strike fear into the Egyptian king (Farrar). After striving with his brother (Sanders), building the Temple in Jerusalem, and then seeing it destroyed, Solomon is reunited with his newly reformed Sheba. This colorful, wide-screen biblical epic strains for DeMille seriousness but only manages to equal the master for salaciousness in its orgy sequences. **Cast:** Yul Brynner, Gina Lollobrigida, George Sanders, Marisa Pavan, John Crawford, Laurence Naismith, Jose Nieto, Alejandro Rey, David Farrar. **Credits:** Dir: King Vidor; Prod: Ted Richmond; Writer: Anthony Veiller, George Bruce, Paul Dudley; DP: Freddie Young; Ed: John Ludwig; Composer: Mario Nascimbene; Art Director: Richard Day, Alfred Sweeney. Color, 142 min. VHS, LASER

Somebody Loves Me

(1952) Paramount
An appealing biopic of vaudevillian Blossom Seeley starring musical comedy star Hutton. Hutton leaves the vaudeville halls of San Francisco for the Broadway stage. There she meets Meeker, as the love of Seeley's life, vaudevillian Benny Fields. Though he hooks his star to Hutton's career, Meeker doesn't attain his dreams until Hutton retires to focus attention on his career. Elaborate costumes, grand production, and many musical contributions, including the title Gershwin tune, "Rose Room," and "I Can't Tell You Why I Love You." **Cast:** Betty Hutton, Ralph Meeker, Robert Keith, Adele Jergens, Billie Bird, Henry Slate, Sid Tomack, Ludwig Stossel, Sydney Mason. **Credits:** Dir: Irving Brecher; Prod: William Perlberg, George Sea-

ton; Writer: Irving Brecher; DP: George Barnes; Ed: Frank Bracht; Composer: Emil Newman; Art Director: Hal Pereira, Earl Hedrick. Color, 97 min.

Somebody Up There Likes Me

(1956) MGM
This biopic of middleweight boxing champ Rocky Graziano scores big, and made a young Newman a star with his third screen appearance. After hanging out in the streets with Mineo and earning a stretch in a reformatory, when Newman ends up doing hard time in Leavenworth, the prison's gym instructor sees potential and straps a pair of gloves on his hands. Started on the way to self-respect, Newman finds even greater reason to clean up his act when he meets and falls in love with Angeli. Months of research and talks with Graziano give Newman's performance a realistically gritty edge in a well-crafted story. Look quickly for the film debut of McQueen. Academy Award Nominations: 3, including Best Editing. **Academy Awards:** Best Black-and-White Cinematography; Best Art Direction—Set Decoration (B&W). **Cast:** Paul Newman, Sal Mineo, Pier Angeli, Robert Loggia, Steve McQueen, Michael Dante, Everett Sloane, Eileen Heckart. **Credits:** Dir: Robert Wise; Prod: Charles Schnee; Writer: Ernest Lehman; DP: Joseph Ruttenberg; Ed: Albert Akst; Prod Design: Cedric Gibbons; Composer: Bronislau Kaper; Art Director: Malcolm F. Brown. B&W, 113 min. VHS

Some Came Running

(1958) MGM
Sinatra teams with his Rat Pack buddy Martin for the first time as a struggling writer who finds you can never go home again. Floozy MacLaine and Sinatra come back to his midwestern small town, much to the displeasure of Sinatra's businessman brother Kennedy and his frosty wife, Dana, and hook up with town drunk Martin. Sinatra also intrigues local English

teacher Hyer, though she resists his questionable charms. Minnelli condensed Jones's enormous novel to focus on Sinatra's romantic dilemmas. As might be expected, there's a nice rapport between Sinatra, Martin, and MacLaine. Academy Award Nominations: 5, including Best Actress: Shirley MacLaine; Best Supporting Actress: Martha Hyer; Best Supporting Actor: Arthur Kennedy; Best Song ("To Love and Be Loved"). **Cast:** Frank Sinatra, Dean Martin, Shirley MacLaine, Martha Hyer, Arthur Kennedy, Nancy Gates, Leora Dana, Betty Lou Keim. **Credits:** Dir: Vincente Minnelli; Prod: Sol C. Siegel; Writer: John Patrick, Arthur Sheekman; Story: James Jones; DP: William Daniels; Ed: Adrienne Fazan; Prod Design: William A. Horning, Urie McCleary; Composer: Elmer Bernstein. Color, 137 min. VHS, LASER

Some Like It Hot

(1959) United Artists
Wilder's comedy masterpiece spoofs Warner gangster movies and, with Wilder's characteristic biting wit, many in the cast seem to be winking at their on-screen personas. Lemmon and Curtis, two unemployed musicians in the Roaring '20s, flee Chicago after they witness a gangland massacre. They take refuge in an all-woman band, dressing as women and taking the train with them to Florida. With one look at the band's lead singer, Monroe (she walks like "Jell-O on springs," Lemmon sighs), Curtis is in love but trapped in drag. Learning that she's after money, Curtis doffs his dress for Cary Grant trappings to woo her. Meanwhile, Lemmon has attracted the attention of bona fide millionaire Brown, and he's tempted to marry the persistent suitor after receiving a diamond bracelet. After witnessing another rubout, Lemmon and Curtis go on the lam again, this time with their sweethearts in tow. What about the gender problem between Lemmon and Brown? "Nobody's perfect," exclaims Brown. An unqualified success, and considered by many to be among the funniest films ever made. Monroe was said to be a nightmare during production, arriving late and forgetting lines, and Curtis compared kissing her to "kissing Hitler." Monroe's absences, though, forced Wilder and Diamond to concoct the film's famous "Nobody's perfect" last line as a way of shooting around her. Songs by Monroe include "I Wanna Be Loved By You" and "I'm Through With Love." Golden Globes for Best Actor in

a Musical or Comedy: Jack Lemmon; Best Actress in a Musical or Comedy: Marilyn Monroe; Best Motion Picture, Comedy. Selected as a National Film Registry Outstanding Film. Academy Award Nominations: 6, including Best Director; Best Actor: Jack Lemmon; Best Screenplay. **Academy Awards:** Best Costume Design (B&W). **Cast:** Marilyn Monroe, Tony Curtis, Jack Lemmon, George Raft, Pat O'Brien, Joe E. Brown, Nehemiah Persoff, Joan Shawlee, Billy Gray, George E. Stone. **Credits:** Dir: Billy Wilder; Prod: Billy Wilder; Writer: I. A. L. Diamond, Billy Wilder; DP: Charles Lang; Ed: Arthur Schmidt; Prod Design: Ted Haworth; Composer: Adolph Deutsch; Costumes: Orry-Kelly, Milt Rice. B&W, 122 min. **VHS, LASER**

Something for the Birds
(1952) Fox
Conservationist Neal fights to save the habitat of the California condor and to do it she works her way into the affections of Mature, a representative of the oil company that wants the land for their own purposes. True love wins over the oil man to the politically correct side. Gwenn adds a comic touch as the social impostor who becomes Neal's guide to the Washington labyrinth. Note the script contribution of frequent Wilder collaborator Diamond. **Cast:** Victor Mature, Patricia Neal, Edmund Gwenn, Larry Keating, Gladys Hurlbut, Hugh Sanders, Christian Rub, Wilton Graff, Archer MacDonald, Richard Garrick. **Credits:** Dir: Robert Wise; Prod: Samuel G. Engel; Writer: I. A. L. Diamond, Boris Ingster, Alvin Josephy, Joseph Petracca; DP: Joseph LaShelle; Ed: Hugh Fowler; Composer: Lionel Newman; Art Director: Lyle Wheeler, George Patrick. B&W, 81 min.

Something in the Wind
(1947) Universal
Durbin stars as a deejay who becomes romantically involved with Dall, a radio rival, after he kidnaps her. Dall thinks Durbin's a gold digger who's preying on his wealthy Uncle Chester (Winninger). O'Connor dances to the defense of the singing deejay. Songs include the title tune, "You Wanna Keep Your Baby Lookin Right," and "Happy Go Lucky and Free." **Cast:** Deanna Durbin, Donald O'Connor, John Dall, Charles Winninger, Helena Carter, Margaret Wycherly, Jan Peerce, Jean Adair. **Credits:** Dir: Irving Pichel; Prod: Joseph Sistrom; Writer: Harry Kurnitz, William Bowers; DP: Milton Krasner; Ed: Otto Ludwig; Composer: Johnny Green. B&W, 89 min. **VHS**

Something of Value
(1957) MGM
In a brilliant performance, Poitier is a man trapped between his feelings for a boyhood friend and his loyalty to his own people. Poitier and Hudson grow up together in Kenya, and Hudson, though he wants to harvest the riches of the land, realizes that the whites must work with the local people. After a series of violent raids, the lines between the friends are drawn when Poitier joins the Mau Mau rebellion. Based on the book by Robert Ruark. **Cast:** Rock Hudson, Sidney Poitier, Wendy Hiller, Dana Wynter, Juano Hernandez, William Marshall, Robert Beatty, Walter Fitzgerald. **Credits:** Dir: Richard Brooks; Prod: Pandro S. Berman; Writer: Richard Brooks; DP: Russell Harlan; Ed: Ferris Webster; Prod Design: William A. Horning; Composer: Miklos Rozsa; Art Director: Edward C. Carfagno. B&W, 113 min. **VHS**

Something to Live For
(1952) Paramount
Milland reprises his *Lost Weekend* problems with the bottle as a married man who gets involved with actress Fontaine as she struggles with her own drinking problem. Their mutual support soon leads to something more. Wright, Milland's wife, sticks by him and the illicit lovers realize that dealing with their affair will help them deal with their addiction. **Cast:** Joan Fontaine, Ray Milland, Teresa Wright, Richard Derr, Douglas Dick, Herbert Heyes, Harry Bellaver, Paul Valentine, Frank Orth, Bob Cornthwaite. **Credits:** Dir: George Stevens; Prod: George Stevens; Writer: Dwight Taylor; DP: George Barnes; Ed: William Hornbeck; Composer: Victor Young; Art Director: Hal Pereira, Walter Tyler. B&W, 89 min.

Something to Sing About
(1937) Grand National
Cagney gets to show off his hoofer's background as a bandleader looking for a big break in Hollywood. After beating the streets, he retreats to a cozy marriage with his former singer (Daw), but after the happy couple return from their honeymoon, the studios dangle a movie contract—if he remains single. Academy Award Nomination for Best Score. **Cast:** James Cagney, Evelyn Daw, William Frawley, Mona Barrie, Gene Lockhart, Candy Candido, Cully Richards, William B. Davidson. **Credits:** Dir: Victor Schertzinger; Prod: Zion Myers; Writer: Austin Parker; DP: John Stumar; Ed: Gene Milford; Composer:

Constantin Bakaleinikoff; Art Director: Robert Lee, Paul Murphy. B&W, 94 min. **VHS**

Sometimes a Great Notion
(1971) Universal
Newman's second directorial outing presents Ken Kesey's brawling family drama of lumbermen in the Northwest. Fonda's the patriarch of a timber business in Oregon that includes his sons, Newman and Jaeckel. The old man puts his business and his family's lives in danger when he refuses to honor a strike by other logging companies. After threats and the destruction of their trucks, the family, now including half-brother Sarrazin, make a desperate decision to float their logs downriver. The family is further sundered when Newman's wife Remick gets involved with Sarrazin. A stirring drama that deserves another viewing. Academy Award Nominations: Best Supporting Actor: Richard Jaeckel; Best Song ("All His Children"). **Cast:** Paul Newman, Henry Fonda, Lee Remick, Michael Sarrazin, Richard Jaeckel, Linda Lawson, Cliff Potts, Sam Gilman. **Credits:** Dir: Paul Newman; Prod: John Foreman; Writer: John Gay; Story: Ken Kesey; DP: Richard Moore; Ed: Bob Wyman; Composer: Henry Mancini; Art Director: Philip M. Jefferies. Color, 115 min. **VHS, LASER**

Somewhere I'll Find You
(1942) MGM
Gable and Turner star in a WWII romantic melodrama as newspaper correspondents whose attraction takes a temporary backseat to the war. Gable and his brother Sterling come home from Europe on orders from their editor who ignores their predictions of imminent war. Once back in New York, they run into Turner, another correspondent, who's involved with Sterling despite her flirtation with Gable. She's assigned to cover the war in Indochina, and Gable and his brother follow soon after. There, her smuggling of orphans melts Gable's heart as Sterling enlists for active duty. Gable forced himself to complete this project despite the tragic death of his wife, Carole Lombard, just three days into production. **Cast:** Lana Turner, Clark Gable, Robert Sterling, Reginald Owen, Lee Patrick, Rags Ragland, Van Johnson, Patricia Dane. **Credits:** Dir: Wesley Ruggles; Prod: Pandro S. Berman; Writer: Marguerite Roberts, Walter Reisch; DP: Harold Rosson; Ed: Frank Hull; Prod Design: Cedric Gibbons; Composer: Bronislau Kaper; Art Director: Malcolm F. Brown. B&W, 117 min. **VHS**

Somewhere in the Night

(1946) Fox

A Marine with amnesia (Hodiak) gets involved in the criminal underworld when he tracks down his identity. Clues at his home lead him to a nightclub and a singer (Guild), and a beating from mobsters. He soon realizes that the man he's chasing is himself and that he was once a partner with the criminals. After locating a briefcase full of cash, Hodiak faces a showdown with his former partners. Whip-snap direction from Mankiewicz; note the script credit for acting guru Strasberg. **Cast:** John Hodiak, Nancy Guild, Richard Conte, Lloyd Nolan, Josephine Hutchinson, Fritz Kortner, Sheldon Leonard, Lou Nova, Margo Woode, Johnny Russell. **Credits:** Dir: Joseph L. Mankiewicz; Prod: Anderson Lawler; Writer: Howard Dimsdale, Joseph L. Mankiewicz, Lee Strasberg; Story: Marvin Borowsky; DP: Norbert F. Brodine; Ed: James Clarke; Composer: David Buttolph, Emil Newman; Art Director: James Basevi, Maurice Ransford. B&W, 100 min.

A Song Is Born

(1948) RKO

Director Hawks puts his own *Ball of Fire* (1941) to music, with the help of guest stars Benny Goodman, Louis Armstrong, Lionel Hampton, and Tommy Dorsey. While researching the history of jazz for a collaborative project, a group of tweedy professors led by Kaye gets a lively lesson from a sultry nightclub singer (Mayo) on the lam from both her gangster boyfriend and the district attorney. As spirited as its predecessor, this boasts charismatic performances, especially from the above-mentioned big-band guests and other musical stars such as Mel Powell, Buck and Bubbles, and Charlie Barnet. **Cast:** Danny Kaye, Virginia Mayo, Hugh Herbert, Steve Cochran, Felix Bressart, Tommy Dorsey, Louis Armstrong, Benny Goodman. **Credits:** Dir: Howard Hawks; Prod: Samuel Goldwyn; Writer: Harry Tugend; DP: Gregg Toland; Ed: Daniel Mandell; Prod Design: George Jenkins; Composer: Emil Newman. Color, 113 min. **VHS**

The Song of Bernadette

(1943) Fox

This is a reverent depiction of the young 19th-century French peasant girl (Jones, in her first featured performance) who beheld a vision of the Virgin Mary at Lourdes. The film follows her story from ridicule by the townspeople, including a wicked Price who wants to have the girl committed to an asylum, to the discovery of the healing springs in the famed grotto, her acceptance in a convent, and eventual canonization. A restrained adaptation of Werfel's novel that benefits from Jones's open-faced expression of piety and purity. Golden Globes for Best Actress: Jennifer Jones; Best Motion Picture, Drama. Academy Award Nominations: 12, including Best Picture; Best Screenplay; Best Supporting Actor: Charles Bickford; Best Supporting Actress: Gladys Cooper; Best Supporting Actress: Anne Revere; Best Director. **Academy Awards:** Best Actress: Jennifer Jones; Best Black-and-White Cinematography; Best Black-and-White Interior Decoration; Best Music Score of a Drama/Comedy. **Cast:** Charles Bickford, Lee J. Cobb, Jennifer Jones, William Eythe, Vincent Price, Gladys Cooper, Anne Revere, Blanche Yurka, Mary Anderson, Edith Barrett. **Credits:** Dir: Henry King; Prod: William Perlberg; Writer: George Seaton; Story: Franz Werfel; DP: Arthur Miller; Ed: Barbara McLean; Prod Design: James Basevi, William S. Darling; Composer: Alfred Newman; Costumes: Rene Hubert; SFX: Fred Sersen; Set Designer: Thomas Little, Frank E. Hughes. B&W, 156 min. **VHS, LASER**

Song of Love

(1947) MGM

Hepburn lifts this too-precious biopic of Clara and Robert Schumann. Hepburn gives up her career as a pianist to marry composer Henreid. After they raise seven children, Henreid goes mad from his exertions teaching and composing. One of his former students, Brahms (Walker), now a famous composer, offers to marry Hepburn, but she chooses instead to return to her career and devote herself to interpreting her husband's work. The lush score boasts piano playing by Arthur Rubinstein. **Cast:** Katharine Hepburn, Paul Henreid, Robert Walker, Henry Daniell, Leo G. Carroll, Gigi Perreau, Tala Birell, Henry Stephenson, Else Janssen. **Credits:** Dir: Clarence Brown; Prod: Clarence Brown; Writer: Ivan Tors, Irmgarde Von Cube, Allen Vincent, Robert Ardrey; DP: Harry Stradling; Ed: Robert J. Kern; Prod Design: Cedric Gibbons; Composer: Johannes Brahms, Franz Liszt, Robert Schumann. B&W, 121 min. **VHS**

The Song of Songs

(1933) Paramount

Mamoulian takes Josef von Sternberg's reins for Dietrich's first Hollywood feature without her mentor. The romantic melodrama finds Dietrich in the familiar role of a woman who risks scandal for the sake of love. A poor girl working in her aunt's bookstore, Dietrich's beauty catches the eye of a sculptor (Aherne) who becomes her lover as she poses for a nude statue. Art collector Atwill, a local baron, sees the statue and lusts after the model, convincing Aherne that the relationship distracts him from his art. After marrying a forlorn Dietrich, Atwill attempts to mold her into a society matron, but Dietrich's heart belongs to Aherne even through a scandal that drives her into the decadent world of Berlin's nightclubs. **Cast:** Marlene Dietrich, Brian Aherne, Lionel Atwill, Alison Skipworth, Hardie Albright, Morgan Wallace, Wilson Benge, Hans Schumm, Eric Wilton, Richard Bennett. **Credits:** Dir: Rouben Mamoulian; Prod: Rouben Mamoulian; Writer: Leo Birinski, Samuel Hoffenstein; Story: Hermann Sudermann, Edward Sheldon; DP: Victor Milner; Prod Design: Hans Dreier; Composer: Nathaniel Finston, Karl Hajos. B&W, 90 min.

Song of the Islands

(1942) Fox

An Irish planter (Mitchell) gets involved in a feud with a cattle baron (Barbier) over a stretch of Hawaiian beach, setting up a Romeo and Juliet tale that unfolds in a tropical paradise. The cattle man's son (Mature) returns from the States and falls in love with the planter's daughter (Grable), to the strenuous objection of the feuding parents. Plenty of Technicolor singing and dancing, including "O'Brien Has Gone Hawaiian," "Sing Me a Song of the Islands," and "What's Buzzin', Cousin?" **Cast:** Betty Grable, Thomas Mitchell, George Barbier, Victor Mature, Jack Oakie, Billy Gilbert, Hal K. Dawson, Alex Pollard. **Credits:** Dir: Walter Lang; Prod: William LeBaron; Writer: Joseph Schrank, Robert Pirosh, Robert Ellis, Helen Logan; DP: Ernest Palmer; Ed: Robert Simpson; Composer: Ralph Freed, Mack Gordon, Leleiohaku, Alfred Newman, Johnny Noble, Harry Owens, Al Stillman, R. Alex Anderson; Costumes: Gwen Wakeling; Art Director: Richard Day. Color, 75 min. **VHS, LASER**

Song of the South

(1946) Disney

Disney brings the Uncle Remus tales to life, earning big box office but also condemnation by African-American organizations that protested the stereotypes and rosy view of the South's Reconstruction days. A boy (Disney perennial Driscoll) whose father leaves the family goes to his grandmother's home with his mother, but runs away. Along the way, he meets a former slave, Uncle Remus (Baskett), who tells him stories about Brer Rabbit, Brer Fox, and Brer Bear, as he gently convinces Driscoll to stay at home. The blend of animation and live action is remarkable, due largely to Baskett's ability to interact with the animated creatures, a performance that earned him an honorary Oscar. Academy Award Nominations: 2, including Best Score. **Academy Awards:** Best Song ("Zip a Dee Doo Dah"); Honorary Award to James Baskett. **Cast:** Ruth Warrick, Bobby Driscoll, James Baskett, Luana Patten, Lucile Watson, Hattie McDaniel, Erik Rolf, Glenn Leedy, George Nokes, Gene Holland. **Credits:** Dir: Harve Foster, Wilfred Jackson; Prod: Walt Disney, Perce Pearce; Writer: Morton Grant, Joel Chandler Harris, Bill Peet, Maurcie Rapf, Dalton Raymond, George Stallings, Ralph Wright; DP: Gregg Toland; Ed: William Morgan; Composer: Daniele Amfitheatrof, Foster Carling, Eliot Daniel, Ray Gilbert, Robert MacGimsey, Paul J. Smith, Charles Wolcott, Allie Wrubel; Art Director: Perry Ferguson. B&W, 94 min.

A Song to Remember
(1945) Columbia
A portrait of a famous romance is featured in this biopic that plays fast and loose with the story of the most beloved composer of the Romantic era, Frederic Chopin (Wilde). After fleeing Poland with his teacher (Muni) for refusing to play for the Czarist governor, Chopin settles in Paris, becomes a fashionable composer, runs away to Majorca with writer George Sand (Oberon). Muni attempts to coax the prodigy back to touring, and Oberon encourages him to stay with her and write. Wilde's patriotism wins out and he returns to the stage to raise money for Polish revolutionaries. First-rate music (Jose Iturbi played Wilde's parts, and his version of the "Polonaise" actually hit the charts) and Wilde and Oberon make a dashingly romantic pairing, so who cares if the story doesn't match the history books? Academy Award Nominations: 6, including Best Actor: Cornel Wilde; Best Original Story; Best Cinematography. **Cast:** Cornel Wilde, Paul Muni, Merle Oberon, Nina Foch, George Coulouris, Howard Freeman, Stephen Bekassy, George Macready. **Credits:** Dir: Charles Vidor; Prod: Louis F. Edelman; Writer: Sidney

Buchman; DP: Tony Gaudio; Ed: Charles Nelson; Prod Design: Lionel Banks; Composer: Miklos Rozsa. Color, 113 min. **VHS, LASER**

Song Without End
(1960) Columbia
Here is the romantic story of Hungarian pianist Franz Liszt (Bogarde), the troubled virtuoso whose scandalous affair with a married countess (Capucine) led to his work as a composer and his eventual seclusion in the Church. On a concert tour, he meets Capucine and she encourages him to focus on his composing rather than his piano playing. When they fall in love, she requests an annulment of her marriage. When the annulment gets rescinded, the princess refuses to live out of wedlock and Bogarde takes holy orders. Begun by Vidor but, upon his death during production, Cukor finished the film. Golden Globe for Best Motion Picture, Musical. **Academy Awards:** Best Scoring of a Musical. **Cast:** Dirk Bogarde, Capucine, Genevieve Page, Patricia Morison, Ivan Desny, Martita Hunt, Lou Jacobi. **Credits:** Dir: George Cukor, Charles Vidor; Prod: William Goetz; Writer: Oscar Millard; DP: James Wong Howe; Ed: William A. Lyon; Prod Design: Walter Holscher; Composer: Franz Liszt. Color, 141 min. **VHS, LASER**

Son of Dracula
(1943) Universal
Lon Chaney, Jr., portrays the king of the night, Count Alucard, who travels to New Orleans to claim a local black-arts aficionado (Allbritton) as his bride, much to her former boyfriend's distress. Terrific effects and the unusual setting make this one of the most atmospheric of the second generation of Universal horror movies. **Cast:** Lon Chaney, Jr., Louise Allbritton, Robert Paige, Frank Craven, Evelyn Ankers, J. Edward Bromberg, Samuel S. Hinds, Adeline de Walt Reynolds. **Credits:** Dir: Robert Siodmak; Prod: Ford Beebe; Writer: Eric Taylor; DP: George Robinson; Ed: Saul A. Goodkind; Composer: H. J. Salter; Art Director: John B. Goodman, Martin Obzina. B&W, 80 min. **VHS, LASER**

Son of Flubber
(1963) Disney
In a real gas of a sequel to Disney's huge hit, *The Absent Minded Professor* (1961), MacMurray discovers the new ways to use his Flubber as he untangles all the business possibilities. Kirk uses his professor's inven-

tion to rule the college football league. Pleasant family fun. **Cast:** Fred MacMurray, Nancy Olson, Keenan Wynn, Tommy Kirk, Charlie Ruggles, Elliott Reid, Joanna Moore, Leon Ames. **Credits:** Dir: Robert Stevenson; Prod: Bill Walsh, Ron Miller; Writer: Bill Walsh, Don DaGradi; DP: Edward Colman; Ed: Cotton Warburton; Prod Design: Carroll Clark, William H. Tuntke; Composer: George Bruns. B&W, 106 min. **VHS, LASER**

Son of Frankenstein
(1939) Universal
Universal's second sequel to the 1931 classic features Karloff's last appearance as the monster. Baron von Frankenstein's son, Rathbone, returns from America to tidy up the family's affairs, an arrival greeted with suspicion by the townspeople who have a right to be wary of a new generation of Frankensteins. Rathbone pledges to police officer Atwill, one of the monster's victims, that he will never resume his father's experiments. But when he meets a grossly deformed Lugosi (his neck was broken when he was hung by the townspeople for obtaining bodies for the old Baron), he learns that his father's creation is still very much alive. Lugosi's creation of the shepherd Ygor is fascinating; he reappears in *The Ghost of Frankenstein* (1942). This led the resurgence of Universal's monsters into a second generation of box-office success. **Cast:** Bela Lugosi, Basil Rathbone, Boris Karloff, Lionel Atwill, Josephine Hutchinson, Donnie Dunagan, Emma Dunn, Edgar Norton. **Credits:** Dir: Rowland V. Lee; Prod: Rowland V. Lee; Writer: Willis Cooper; DP: George Robinson; Ed: Ted J. Kent; Prod Design: Jack Otterson; Composer: Frank Skinner. B&W, 99 min. **VHS, LASER**

Son of Fury
(1942) Fox
Power stars as the 18th-century heir to an English estate who grows up under the thumb of a greedy uncle (Sanders) who makes off with his fortune. Power flees to a desert isle where he meets luscious native Tierney, and grows a fortune pearl-diving with his friend Carradine, but revenge is always on his mind. An expensively mounted costume adventure. Remade in 1953 as *The Treasure of the Golden Condor*. **Cast:** Tyrone Power, Gene Tierney, George Sanders, Frances Farmer, Roddy McDowall, Kay Johnson, John Carradine, Elsa Lanchester. **Credits:** Dir: John Cromwell; Prod: William Perlberg; Writer: Philip Dunne;

DP: Arthur Miller; Ed: Walter Thompson; Prod Design: James Basevi; Composer: Alfred Newman; Art Director: Richard Day. B&W, 98 min. VHS

Son of Kong
(1933) RKO
The Kong team created a sequel that presents a kinder, gentler member of the Kong clan. When Armstrong and Reicher flee the New York lawyers who expect reparations for King Kong's rampage, they return to Skull Island in search of treasure. There they find the relatively diminutive, white-maned son of Kong who protects the adventurers from the prehistoric creatures that inhabit the island. Wonderful special effects again by Willis O'Brien and his team in this humorous adventure. **Cast:** Robert Armstrong, Helen Mack, Victor Wong, John Marston, Frank Reicher, Ed Brady, Lee Kohlmar, Clarence Wilson. **Credits:** Dir: Ernest B. Schoedsack; Prod: Archie Marshek; Writer: Ruth Rose; DP: Eddie Linden, Vernon Walker, J. O. Taylor; Ed: Ted Cheesman; Composer: Max Steiner; Art Director: Van Nest Polglase, Al Herman. B&W, 70 min. VHS

Son of Lassie
(1945) MGM
Lassie's son Laddie goes to war when he stows away on master Lawford's bomber. When they're shot down over Germany, Laddie goes to fetch help several times, but as he hasn't read the papers, he always brings back the darn Nazis. Children will enjoy this and adults will be curious to see sometime Rat Packer Lawford. **Cast:** Peter Lawford, Donald Crisp, June Lockhart, Nigel Bruce, William Severn, Leon Ames, Fay Helm, Donald Curtis, Nils Asther, Terry Moore. **Credits:** Dir: S. Sylvan Simon; Prod: Samuel Marx; Writer: Jeanne Bartlett; Ed: Ben Lewis; Prod Design: Cedric Gibbons; Composer: Herbert Stothart. Color, 100 min. VHS

Son of Paleface
(1952) Paramount
Onetime cartoonist Tashlin gets his first director's credit with this sequel to Hope's comedic masterpiece. Hope plays the son of his character in *The Paleface*, an Ivy Leaguer headed west to claim the inheritance left by his frontier dentist dad. He and Rogers run down a crook who's been holding up gold shipments. Hope once again joins saloon-singer Russell as they send up every Western cliché in the classic Hollywood book. Plenty of songs, including a reprise of "Buttons

and Bows" and "Am I In Love." Academy Award Nomination for Best Song ("Am I In Love"). **Cast:** Bob Hope, Jane Russell, Roy Rogers, Iron Eyes Cody, Bill Williams, Lloyd Corrigan, Paul E. Burns, Douglas Dumbrille. **Credits:** Dir: Frank Tashlin; Prod: Robert L. Welch; Writer: Frank Tashlin; DP: Harry Wild; Ed: Eda Warren; Composer: Lyn Murray; Art Director: Hal Pereira. Color, 95 min. VHS, LASER

The Sons of Katie Elder
(1965) Paramount
Wayne, nearing the end of his fifth decade and having beaten his first bout with cancer, continued to make at least a film a year (often more than one), many of them Westerns, this being among the most popular of the period. He plays the eldest Elder son, John, a Texas gunslinger reunited at his mother's funeral with brothers Martin, a gambler, Holliman, and college boy Anderson. The brothers begin investigating the death of their father despite being warned off by the local sheriff, and when they discover that Gregory and his son Hopper were the only witnesses, trouble starts. Bernstein contributed another of his signature Western scores. **Cast:** John Wayne, Dean Martin, Martha Hyer, Earl Holliman, Michael Anderson, Jeremy Slate, James Gregory, Paul Fix, George Kennedy, Dennis Hopper. **Credits:** Dir: Henry Hathaway; Prod: Hal B. Wallis; Writer: William H. Wright, Allan Weiss, Harry Essex; DP: Lucien Ballard; Ed: Warren Low; Prod Design: Hal Pereira, Walter Tyler; Composer: Elmer Bernstein; Costumes: Edith Head; Set Designer: Sam Comer, Ray Moyer. Color, 122 min. VHS, LASER

So Proudly We Hail
(1943) Paramount
Paramount's reigning divas, Colbert, Lake, and Goddard, appear in unglamorous roles as three nurses who survive the most brutal Pacific-theater battles of WWII. Director Sandrich accentuates the danger and hard conditions as he depicts the courage and the daily routines of women who worked at the front. This novel approach made a big impact on the homefront audiences used to seeing glossy renditions of wartime romance. This also displayed Lake's new, short hairdo, ordered by the war department to prevent female war workers from catching their long, Lake-like tresses in factory machinery. Academy Award Nominations: 4, including Best Supporting Actress: Paulette Goddard; Best Original Screenplay; Best Cine-

matography. **Cast:** Claudette Colbert, Paulette Goddard, Veronica Lake, George Reeves, Barbara Britton, Walter Abel, Sonny Tufts, Mary Servoss. **Credits:** Dir: Mark Sandrich; Prod: Mark Sandrich; Writer: Allan Scott; DP: Charles Lang; Ed: Ellsworth Hoagland; Prod Design: Hans Dreier; Composer: Miklos Rozsa; Art Director: Earl Hedrick. B&W, 126 min. VHS

So Red the Rose
(1935) Paramount
Sullavan plays a Scarlett-like southern belle, the daughter of a wealthy plantation owner. As her family suffers through the Civil War, she falls for her cousin (Scott), a conscientious objector who's been forced onto the front lines of the fight. Sullavan must play Penelope to her absent love for the duration of the war, while the picturesque, sheltering world of her youth collapses around her. **Cast:** Margaret Sullavan, Walter Connolly, Janet Beecher, Harry Ellerbe, Robert Cummings, Charles Starrett, Johnny Downs, Daniel L. Haynes, Randolph Scott, Elizabeth Patterson. **Credits:** Dir: King Vidor; Prod: Douglas MacLean; Writer: Maxwell Anderson, Edwin Justus Mayer, Laurence Stillings; DP: Victor Milner; Ed: Eda Warren; Prod Design: Hans Dreier; Composer: Franke Harling; Art Director: Ernst Fegte. B&W, 82 min.

Sorrowful Jones
(1949) Paramount
The critical estimation of Hope's acting rose after this remake of *Little Miss Marker* (1934). Hope makes a colorfully Runyonesque character as a gambler who receives a six-year-old girl (an appealing Saunders) as a marker for a bet. The father never returns, leaving Hope and Saunders to search for him among the denizens of Runyon's world, including a run-in with a sympathetic chorine, Ball. **Cast:** Bob Hope, Lucille Ball, Bruce Cabot, William Demarest, Mary Jane Saunders, Thomas Gomez, Tom Pedi, Paul Lees, Houseley Stevenson. **Credits:** Dir: Sidney Lanfield; Prod: Robert L. Welch; Writer: Melville Shavelson, Edmund Hartman, Jack Rose; DP: Daniel Fapp; Ed: Arthur Schmidt; Prod Design: Hans Dreier; Composer: Robert Emmett Dolan. B&W, 88 min. VHS, LASER

Sorry, Wrong Number
(1948) Paramount
Director Litvak and writer Fletcher turn her 22-minute radio play (one of the most famous radio dramas, it featured a wonderful performance by Agnes

Moorehead) into a gripping, feature-length murder mystery. Wealthy Stanwyck stays tethered to her bedroom by neuroses and fear, making contact with the world only through her telephone. While on the phone trying to locate husband Lancaster, she overhears a woman's murder being plotted and comes to believe she's the target. Lancaster, who has indeed started a plot in motion, listens helplessly as his scheme bears evil fruit. Stanwyck gives a remarkable performance, balancing the helplessness of the victim with a spiky unpleasantness. Academy Award Nomination for Best Actress: Barbara Stanwyck. **Cast:** Barbara Stanwyck, William Conrad, Burt Lancaster, Wendell Corey, Ed Begley, Ann Richards, Harold Vermilyea, Leif Erickson. **Credits:** Dir: Anatole Litvak; Prod: Hal B. Wallis; Writer: Lucille Fletcher; DP: Sol Polito; Ed: Warren Low; Prod Design: Hans Dreier, Earl Hedrick; Composer: Franz Waxman. B&W, 89 min. **VHS**

So This Is New York

(1948) United Artists
This breezy comedy set in the New York of the Roaring Twenties follows the misadventures of a visiting country hick (Morgan), his wife, and his marriageable sister-in-law. After making their way through the bewildering urban jungle, the trio find themselves in the middle of a big swindle at the horse races. Morgan brings his simple-country-cousin routine from the radio to the screen, and the Dead End Kids lead the mayhem. **Cast:** Harry Morgan, Rudy Vallee, Bill Goodwin, Herbert Hugh, Leo Gorcey, Virginia Grey, Dona Drake, Frank Orth, Jerome Cowan, Dave Willock. **Credits:** Dir: Richard Fleischer; Prod: Stanley Kramer; Writer: Herbert Baker, Carl Foreman, Ring Lardner; DP: Jack Russell; Ed: Walter Thompson; Prod Design: Eloise Jennson; Composer: Dimitri Tiomkin. B&W, 79 min.

Souls at Sea

(1937) Paramount
Based on the true story of the William Brown murders, this combination of seafaring adventure and courtroom drama tells the story of a ship's first mate, Nuggin Taylor (Cooper), who is tried and convicted for mass murder at sea before evidence arrives that the Queen of England enlisted him to sabotage the slave trade. After first being tried for mutiny after he and Raft set free a slaver's cargo, British agents recruit the firebrand for a mission to disrupt the slave trade to the

U.S. Raft dies nobly in this one rather than in a hail of police bullets. Academy Award Nominations: Best Score; Best Art Direction. **Cast:** Gary Cooper, George Raft, Frances Dee, Henry Wilcoxon, Harry Carey, Olympe Bradna, Robert Cummings, George Zucco, Porter Hall, Joseph Schildkraut. **Credits:** Dir: Henry Hathaway; Prod: Henry Hathaway; Writer: Grover Jones, Dale Van Every, Richard Talmadge; DP: Charles Lang; Ed: Ellsworth Hoagland; Prod Design: Hans Dreier, Roland Anderson; Composer: W. Franke Harling, Milan Roeder, Bernhard Kaun. B&W, 93 min. **VHS**

Soul to Soul

(1971)
A soulful concert video that brings together the top names in '60s R&B. The concert honoring Ghanian independence features performances by Wilson Pickett, Santana, the Staple Singers, Ike and Tina Turner, Eddie Harris, and Roberta Flack. Filmed in Ghana with traditional African music and local footage included, the film expertly depicts the high point of American sweet soul music. **Credits:** Dir: Denis Sanders. Color, 95 min. **VHS**

Sounder

(1972) Fox
In this much-loved family classic, a warm black family in Depression-era rural Louisiana struggles to survive by sharecropping and hunting. After a night of hunting turns up nothing to eat, the father (Winfield) steals a ham for his family (Tyson, Kevin and Eric Hooks, and Jarrell), and is subsequently imprisoned. Kevin Hooks hits the road with the family dog, Sounder, to find his beloved father. When he gets lost on the way home, Hooks strays into a school for black kids that boosts confidence and learning. After his father comes home injured, Hooks gets an invitation to the school, and has a dilemma: stay to help his family or take advantage of a once-in-a-lifetime opportunity to better his life. Look for an engaging performance by singer Taj Mahal in his acting debut. Followed by a TV movie sequel in 1976. Academy Award Nominations: 4, including Best Picture; Best Actor: Paul Winfield; Best Actress: Cicely Tyson; Best (Adapted) Screenplay. **Cast:** Cicely Tyson, Paul Winfield, Carmen Mathews, Kevin Hooks, Taj Mahal, Janet MacLachlan, James Best, Yvonne Jarrell. **Credits:** Dir: Martin Ritt; Prod: Robert B. Radnitz; Writer: Lonne Elder, III; DP: John A. Alonzo; Ed: Sidney Levin; Prod

Design: Walter Scott Herndon; Composer: Taj Mahal; Costumes: Nedra Watt. Color, 105 min. **VHS, LASER**

Sound Off

(1952) Columbia
An early screenplay by future director Edwards finds Rooney uncomfortably inducted into the army. He's an entertainer who has been around the block once or twice and wakes up to find himself drafted, but lands on his feet entertaining the troops after a series of close encounters with rigid army regulations. **Cast:** George Duning, Mickey Rooney, Anne James, Helen Ford, John Archer, Gordon Jones, Wally Cassell, Arthur Space, Patrick Williams, Marshall Reed. **Credits:** Dir: Richard Quine; Prod: Jonie Taps; Writer: Richard Quine, Blake Edwards; Ed: Charles Nelson; Choreographer: Leroy Prinz; Composer: Bob Russell, Freddy Karger, Paul Mertz, Charles Stoloff, Lester Lee, Mickey Rooney; Art Director: Carl Anderson. Color, 83 min.

The Sound of Music

(1965) Fox
This box-office champ of the '60s (ousting previous champ, 1939's *Gone With the Wind*, and retaining the title until *The Godfather* in 1972), and the most successful musical of all time, brought families into theaters for repeat viewings. The trilling voice and wholesome appeal of Andrews and the music of Rodgers and Hammerstein are highlights of the romantic musical that follows a convent novitiate who becomes caretaker for a widowed Austrian captain's brood of seven children. Her good nature brings smiles to the children and eventually wins the heart of the stern Plummer. Guided by her musical talent, the whole bunch forms the Von Trapp Family Singers. They take the show on the road when Nazis threaten their idyllic life. The story greatly benefits from the charm of Andrews, who had just won an Oscar for *Mary Poppins*. Much as he had done with *West Side Story* (1961), director Wise opened the visual possibilities of the musical with location shooting among Alpine vistas. Songs include: "Climb Every Mountain," "Something Good," "How Do You Solve a Problem Like Maria?" "Sixteen, Going on Seventeen," "My Favorite Things," "Edelweiss." Academy Award Nominations: 10, including Best Actress: Julie Andrews. **Academy Awards:** Best Picture; Best Director; Best Film Editing; Best Sound; Best Costume Design (Color); Best Score. **Cast:** Julie Andrews, Christopher

Plummer, Richard Haydn, Peggy Wood, Eleanor Parker, Heather Menzies, Nicholas Hammond, Angela Cartwright, Ben Wright, Norma Varden. **Credits:** Dir: Robert Wise; Prod: Robert Wise, Boris Leven; Writer: Ernest Lehman; DP: Ted McCord; Ed: William H. Reynolds; Choreographer: Dee Dee Wood; Composer: Richard Rodgers, Irwin Kostal; Costumes: Dorothy Jeakins; SFX: L. B. Abbott, Emil Kosa; Set Designer: Walter M. Scott. Color, 175 min. **VHS, LASER**

The Southerner
(1945) United Artists
Famed French director Renoir fled Europe and arrived in Hollywood in early 1941, where he made 5 films. He described this as his "least unsatisfactory," and as a film in which every character is a hero in their struggle to build a life on the land. The near-documentary story follows a family of sharecroppers led by Scott as they carve out their own farm from an unpromising piece of land. In the course of one year, they establish their crops, deal with illness and despair, and battle nature, eventually securing their tenuous foothold in the earth. Renoir wrote the script in English, with some assistance with dialect from Johnson and uncredited story help from Faulkner. Set designer Lourie worked on Renoir's greatest films, *Grand Illusion* and *Rules of the Game.* When released the film was a financial failure and was viewed by many southerners as an insulting portrayal of their region; boycotts and pickets followed its exhibition. It was, however, a critical success and won the International Award at the Venice Film Festival. Based on a story by George Sessions Perry, "Hold Autumn in Your Hand." Academy Award Nominations: 3, including Best Director; Best Score. **Cast:** Zachary Scott, Betty Fields, Beulah Bondi, J. Carrol Naish, Norman Lloyd, Jack Norworth, Nestor Paiva, Estelle Taylor, Dorothy Granger, Noreen Nash. **Credits:** Dir: Jean Renoir; Writer: Jean Renoir, Hugo Butler, William Faulkner, Nunnally Johnson; DP: Lucien Andriot; Ed: Greg Tallas; Composer: Werner Janssen; Set Designer: Eugene Lourie. B&W, 98 min. **VHS**

A Southern Yankee
(1948) MGM
This is a great role for Skelton (with most of his best bits written by an uncredited Buster Keaton) as a lovable bellboy who becomes a secret agent for the Union after a notorious

Southern spy is captured. He goes behind Confederate lines seeking information and finds romance with belle Dahl. **Cast:** Red Skelton, Brian Donlevy, Arlene Dahl, George Coulouris, Lloyd Gough, John Ireland, Charles Dingle, Joyce Compton. **Credits:** Dir: Edward Sedgwick; Prod: Paul Jones; Writer: Harry Tugend; DP: Ray June; Ed: Ben Lewis; Prod Design: Cedric Gibbons; Composer: David Snell. B&W, 91 min. **VHS**

South Pacific
(1958) Fox
The Rodgers and Hammerstein songs from this musical classic rank with the best of their prodigious careers. This film adaptation of the unprecedented Broadway smash, directed by its stage director, Logan, may not have the boisterous energy found on recordings of the renowned stage production starring Mary Martin, but it substitutes lush Hawaiian locations and sumptuous photography. The story builds two love affairs, one between a midwestern nurse (Gaynor) and an older planter (Brazzi) with children and an ambivalence to the war that encroaches on his paradise, and one between a native girl (Nuyen) and a young American sailor (Kerr). Songs include "Some Enchanted Evening," "I'm in Love with a Wonderful Guy," and "Bali H'ai." Academy Award Nominations: 3, including Best Cinematography. **Academy Awards:** Best Sound. **Cast:** Mitzi Gaynor, Rossano Brazzi, John Kerr, Ray Walston, Juanita Hall, France Nuyen, Tom Laughlin, Russ Brown. **Credits:** Dir: Joshua Logan; Prod: Buddy Adler; Writer: Paul Osborn; DP: Leon Shamroy; Ed: Robert Simpson; Prod Design: Lyle Wheeler; Color, 170 min. **VHS, LASER**

Soylent Green
(1973) MGM
In a controversial sci-fi fantasy, cop Heston pursues a murder in the murky environment of 21st-century New York City. Overpopulation has forced consumption of wafers presumably processed from vegetable matter by the giant Soylent company. As the clues lead to Soylent executive Cotten and his bodyguard Connors, Heston's roommate Robinson, an aging researcher, elects to take the government's offer to die. As Robinson heads for the conveyor belt, Heston discovers the real composition of Soylent Green. Chosen the best science-fiction film of the year. Robinson's last movie. **Cast:** Charlton Heston, Leigh Taylor-Young, Chuck Connors, Joseph

Cotten, Edward G. Robinson, Dick Van Patten, Stephen Young, Paula Kelly, Brock Peters. **Credits:** Dir: Richard Fleischer; Prod: Walter Seltzer; Writer: Stanley R. Greenberg; DP: Richard H. Kline; Ed: Samuel E. Beetley; Composer: Fred Myrow; Art Director: Edward C. Carfagno. Color, 100 min. **VHS, LASER**

The Spanish Main
(1945) RKO
This rousing Technicolor pirate adventure has Henreid as a Dutch naval captain who turns pirate after nearly being hung by Spanish governor Slezak. Henreid and his men get their revenge by stealing Slezak's fiancée, O'Hara, and though Henreid's men fear reprisals, love blooms between the pirate and the lady. Note the score by Bertolt Brecht collaborator Eisler. Academy Award Nomination for Best (Color) Cinematography. **Cast:** Maureen O'Hara, Paul Henreid, Walter Slezak, Binnie Barnes, John Emery, Barton MacLane, Fritz Leiber, Nancy Gates. **Credits:** Dir: Frank Borzage; Prod: Stephen Ames; Writer: George Worthing Yates, Herman Mankiewicz; DP: George Barnes; Ed: Ralph Dawson; Prod Design: Carroll Clark; Composer: Hanns Eisler; Art Director: Albert S. D'Agostino. Color, 100 min. **LASER**

Spartacus
(1960) Universal
Director Kubrick marshals the proverbial cast of thousands in an early example of his celebrated concern for authenticity. The result is one of the finest movie depictions of the ancient Roman world. Douglas gives a muscular, emotional performance as a slave brought to the Roman gladiator school by its master, Ustinov. There he befriends and then bests Strode in an unwanted contest to the death staged for the pleasure of senator Olivier. When guards taunt Douglas with the news that Olivier has taken away Simmons, the slave girl with whom he's in love, Douglas leads a slave rebellion that shakes the foundations of the empire. Though the epic struggle ends with Douglas's crucifixion, Simmons lifts up to him his free son before he dies. Director Anthony Mann was replaced with Kubrick by executive producer Douglas after the first scenes. Trumbo's compelling script was his first after being blacklisted. The film's stunning music score was composed by Alex North. Golden Globe for Best Motion Picture, Drama. Academy Award Nominations: 6, including Best Editing; Best Score. **Academy**

Awards: Best Supporting Actor: Peter Ustinov; Best Color Cinematography; Best Costume Design (Color); Best Art Direction—Set Decoration (Color). **Cast:** Kirk Douglas, Laurence Olivier, Jean Simmons, Charles Laughton, Peter Ustinov, Tony Curtis, John Gavin, Nina Foch, Woody Strode. **Credits:** Dir: Stanley Kubrick; Prod: Edward Lewis; Writer: Dalton Trumbo; Story: Howard Fast; DP: Russell Metty, Clifford Stine; Ed: Robert Lawrence, Robert Schulte, Fred Chulack; Prod Design: Alexander Golitzen; Composer: Alex North.Color, 196 min. **VHS, LASER, DVD**

Spawn of the North

(1938) Paramount
Alaskan salmon fishermen Fonda and Raft find themselves in a face-off when Raft joins a Russian salmon-poaching gang. The plot simply transports the standard Western fare to the chilly waters of Alaska, but Hathaway's keen eye makes this easy sailing. Winner of a Special Academy Award for outstanding achievements in special effects and photography. **Cast:** Henry Fonda, George Raft, Dorothy Lamour, Akim Tamiroff, John Barrymore, Lynne Overman, Fuzzy Knight, Louise Platt. **Credits:** Dir: Henry Hathaway; Prod: Albert Lewin; Writer: Jules Furthman, Talbot Jennings; DP: Charles Lang; Ed: Ellsworth Hoagland; Prod Design: Hans Dreier; Composer: Dimitri Tiomkin. B&W, 110 min. **VHS**

Speak Easily

(1932) MGM
Here's another of Keaton's less than stellar sound-era efforts, but it's always worth a look at the great stone face. Butler Durante gives his boring boss, professor Keaton, a boost when he concocts a phony inheritance. Keaton sets out to make whoopee and finds a struggling theater troupe. Their show's a stinker until the prof accidentally hits the stage. **Cast:** Buster Keaton, Jimmy Durante, Ruth Selwyn, Thelma Todd, Hedda Hopper, Sidney Toler, William Pawley, Lawrence Grant. **Credits:** Dir: Edward Sedgwick; Writer: Ralph Spence, Laurence Johnson; DP: Harold Wenstrom. B&W, 82 min. **VHS**

Specter of the Rose

(1946) Republic
When renowned screenwriter Hecht produced and directed his own films, the results were always entertaining, if idiosyncratic. This is surely one of the most unusual psychological mysteries on film. Famous ballet star

Kirov had previously knifed his costar wife in an hallucination caused by his role in the ballet *Spectre de la Rose*. Thinking he's cured, his new young costar (Essen) marries him, but soon the knife comes out when the music plays. **Cast:** Judith Anderson, Michael Chekhov, Ivan Kirov, Viola Essen, Lionel Stander, Charles Marshall, Billy Gray, Ferike Boros. **Credits:** Dir: Ben Hecht; Prod: Ben Hecht; Writer: Ben Hecht; DP: Lee Garmes; Choreographer: Tamara Geva; Composer: George Antheil. B&W, 90 min. **VHS**

Speed

(1936) MGM
This includes exciting racing action with Stewart as the creator of a new high-performance carburetor. He finds an ally and a love interest in his company president's niece (Barrie), who works in the publicity department. She introduces him to her engineering friend (Heyburn), and a romantic rivalry soon develops. After a crash endangers the life of their test driver (Healy), it's back to the drawing board before the Indianapolis 500. **Cast:** James Stewart, Wendy Barrie, Una Merkel, Weldon Heyburn, Ted Healy, Ralph Morgan. **Credits:** Dir: Edwin L. Marin; Prod: Lucien Hubbard; Writer: Michael Fessier; DP: Lester White; Ed: Harry Poppe; Prod Design: Cedric Gibbons. B&W, 70 min.

Speedway

(1968) MGM
The King once again plays a stock-car driver and good ol' boy, a milieu he must have enjoyed. Just as Elvis discovers that manager Bixby has squandered his winnings, IRS agent Sinatra shows up. Notable mostly for the pairing of Presley and Sinatra, this is getting late in the day for Elvis movies. The songs include "Let Yourself Go," "Mine," "Going Home," and the title tune. **Cast:** Elvis Presley, Nancy Sinatra, Bill Bixby, Gale Gordon, William Schallert, Victoria Paige Meyerink, Ross Hagen, Carl Ballantine. **Credits:** Dir: Norman Taurog; Prod: Douglas Laurence; Writer: Phillip Shuken; DP: Joseph Ruttenberg; Ed: Richard W. Farrell; Composer: Jeff Alexander; Art Director: George W. Davis. Color, 95 min. **VHS, LASER**

Spellbound

(1945) United Artists
Hitchcock's psychological mystery makes engrossing use of the contemporary fascination with Freudian analysis. It stars Bergman as a coolly intellectual analyst who grows to suspect that the new director of the institute

(Peck) is not who he claims to be. As a bond of love grows between the two, Bergman is torn between her rational fear that Peck may be the murderer of the director they were expecting, and her heart telling her that he's an innocent man suffering an emotional trauma. As her love opens mental doors for Peck, the experience brings warmth to Bergman's character. The typical mystery-story chase sequence is here a search for clues in Peck's psyche. The production began with producer Selznick's interest in analysis. It features famous set pieces depicting Peck's mental state, including a dream sequence designed by surrealist artist Salvador Dalí. The sequence (Dalí created material for 22 minutes, nearly all of it cut) was directed by an uncredited William Cameron Menzies. Academy Award Nominations: 6, including Best Picture; Best Director. **Academy Awards:** Best Music Score of a Drama/Comedy. **Cast:** Ingrid Bergman, Gregory Peck, Leo G. Carroll, Michael Chekhov, Rhonda Fleming, John Emery, Norman Lloyd, Steven Geray. **Credits:** Dir: Alfred Hitchcock; Prod: David O. Selznick; Writer: Ben Hecht; DP: George Barnes; Ed: William Ziegler; Prod Design: James Basevi; Composer: Miklos Rozsa. B&W, 111 min. **VHS, LASER**

Spencer's Mountain

(1963) Warner Bros.
The Earl Hamner, Jr., novel that also served as inspiration for the long-running TV series *The Waltons* gets a lustier treatment here. Fonda plays the patriarch of a clan that shares a mountain household with nine kids and Fonda's parents. He's an earthy, God-fearing type who's an honest man, but who doesn't want religion's restrictions on his drinking, cussing, or his good-old-fashioned (and understandable) lust for his wife, O'Hara. When eldest son MacArthur graduates from high school with an eye toward college, Fonda is faced with giving up his dream of larger quarters or accepting help in the form of a religious scholarship. MacArthur's scenes with local girl Farmer show the apple hasn't fallen far from the tree. **Cast:** Henry Fonda, Maureen O'Hara, James MacArthur, Donald Crisp, Wally Cox, Mimsy Farmer, Veronica Cartwright, Victor French, Virginia Gregg. **Credits:** Dir: Delmer Daves; Prod: Delmer Daves; Writer: Delmer Daves; DP: Charles Lawton, Jr.; Ed: David Wages; Prod Design: Carl Anderson; Composer: Max Steiner. Color, 118 min. **VHS**

The Sphinx

(1933) Monogram

This is a Poverty Row thriller about a deaf-mute millionaire (Atwill) accused of murders he couldn't possibly have committed. A reporter (Newton) remains suspicious. His girlfriend (Terry), the paper's society editor, is charmed by the philanthropist until she discovers the shocking secret: the real murderer, a deaf-mute twin brother! Remade again by Monogram in 1941 as *The Phantom Killer*. **Cast:** Sheila Terry, Theodore Newton, Lionel Atwill, George "Gabby" Hayes, Wilfred Lucas, Hooper Atchley, Lillian Leighton, Paul Fix, Lucien Prival, Robert Ellis. **Credits:** Dir: Phil Rosen, Wilfred Lucas; Prod: Trem Carr; Writer: Albert DeMond; DP: Gilbert Warrenton. B&W, 63 min. **VHS**

Spinout

(1966) MGM

Race driver Elvis rock and rolls, too. That's a potent combination guaranteed to drive girls crazy, and it keeps him hopping between rich magazine editor Fabares and his drummer, Walley. He gets the first two married off, but then needs a drummer, so he's in the romantic soup again with Marshall. The whole thing's pretty soupy, but it's better than his 1968 flick, *Speedway*. Songs include "Beach Shack," "Adam and Evil," and "Smorgasbord." **Cast:** Elvis Presley, Shelley Fabares, Carl Betz, Will Hutchins, Cecil Kellaway, Una Merkel, Deborah Walley, Dodie Marshall. **Credits:** Dir: Norman Taurog; Prod: Joe Pasternak; Writer: Theodore J. Flicker, George Kirgo; DP: Daniel Fapp; Ed: Rita Roland; Composer: George E. Stoll; Art Director: George W. Davis. Color, 95 min. **VHS, LASER**

The Spiral Staircase

(1946) RKO

This is the ultimate Gothic horror film, complete with a spooky, dark house, a mysterious old invalid, a young woman in distress, and an insane killer hiding in the enveloping shadows. McGuire plays a mute caretaker engaged to attend to a wealthy widowed matron (Barrymore) in a large mansion at the turn of the century. The young woman is a delight, and she draws the attention of several suitors, including the local doctor (Smith), who tells her that her trauma-induced condition may be reversible; the widow's stepson (Brent), a bookish professor; and the widow's wild-child son, Oliver. A serial killer with a fetish for eliminating handicapped women is on the loose, and

McGuire has a suspicion she may be next. Her fears turn out to be justified as the killer has been observing her from inside the house itself. A stylish thriller directed by Siodmak, made the same year as his noir classic, *The Killers*. Remade in Britain in 1976. Academy Award Nomination for Best Supporting Actress: Ethel Barrymore. **Cast:** Dorothy McGuire, George Brent, Ethel Barrymore, Kent Smith, Rhonda Fleming, Gordon Oliver, Elsa Lanchester, James Bell, Charles Wagenheim, Ellen Corby. **Credits:** Dir: Robert Siodmak; Prod: Dore Schary; Writer: Mel Dinelli; DP: Nicholas Musuraca; Ed: Harry Marker, Harry Gerstad; Composer: Roy Webb; Art Director: Albert S. D'Agostino. B&W, 83 min. **VHS, LASER**

The Spirit of St. Louis

(1957) Warner Bros.

This straightforward biopic with Stewart playing aviator Charles Lindbergh may be the least typical film of director Wilder's career. Concentrating on his famous 1927 solo flight across the Atlantic, the film presents in flashbacks moments from Lindbergh's early career as a barnstormer and mail pilot. Stewart, who at 49 was playing a man half that age, is genuine and engaging in what is essentially a one-person film. Contemporary audiences found this curiously unappealing and it became a notorious money-loser; it has grown in estimation over the years, perhaps along with Wilder's renown. Notable for an outstanding score by Waxman. Academy Award Nomination for Best Special Effects. **Cast:** James Stewart, Patricia Smith, Murray Hamilton, Marc Connelly, Sheila Bond, Robert Cornthwaite, Arthur Space, Harlan Warde, Dabbs Greer, Paul Birch. **Credits:** Dir: Billy Wilder; Prod: Leland Hayward; Writer: Wendell Mayes, Charles Lederer; DP: Robert Burks, Peverell Marley; Ed: Arthur Schmidt; Composer: Franz Waxman; SFX: H. F. Koenekamp; Art Director: Art Loell; Set Designer: William L. Kuehl. Color, 138 min. **VHS, LASER**

Splendor

(1935) United Artists

This standard movie melodrama has poor girl Hopkins marrying rich kid McCrea, much to his family's dismay. In order to bolster their fading fortunes, the family pushes Hopkins into an affair with a wealthy financier (Cavanagh). Niven's first featured role. **Cast:** Miriam Hopkins, David Niven, Joel McCrea, Paul Cavanagh, Helen Westley, Billie Burke, Katherine Alexander, Ivan Simpson. **Credits:** Dir:

Elliott Nugent; Prod: Samuel Goldwyn; Writer: Rachel Crothers; DP: Gregg Toland; Ed: Margaret Clancy; Composer: Alfred Newman; Art Director: Richard Day. B&W, 77 min. **VHS**

Splendor in the Grass

(1961) Warner Bros.

This tale of repressed sexuality leading to emotional turmoil marked the screen debut of Beatty, in a role Inge wrote for the young actor after he starred in his play *A Loss of Roses* on Broadway. Beatty portrays a rich midwestern boy in the '20s whose passion for a gorgeous, simmering Wood remains unconsummated as a result of their parents' dominance. Disasters befall both, and neither finds again the romantic love that they found with each other in the golden days of youth. This was also Dennis's debut. Academy Award Nominations: 2, including Best Actress: Natalie Wood. **Academy Awards:** Best Original Story/Screenplay. **Cast:** Natalie Wood, Warren Beatty, Audrey Christie, Pat Hingle, Barbara Loden, Zohra Lampert, Fred Stewart, Gary Lockwood, Sandy Dennis. **Credits:** Dir: Elia Kazan; Prod: Elia Kazan; Writer: William Inge; DP: Boris Kaufman; Ed: Gene Milford; Prod Design: Richard Sylbert; Composer: David Amram. Color, 124 min. **VHS**

The Spoilers

(1942) Universal

Dietrich, Wayne, and Scott star in the fourth version of Rex Beach's popular Western about Alaskan Gold Rush prospectors. The ownership of Wayne and Carey's mine is questioned by crooked gold commissioner Scott, who's in cahoots with the presiding judge. So the two prospectors plot to steal back their own assets from the bank. Saloon girl Dietrich helps Wayne at a key moment, winning him away from scheming Lindsay. The highlight is the brutal, bare-knuckle brawl between Wayne and Scott. A year later all three stars re-created their triangle in Universal's *Pittsburgh*. Yukon poet Robert W. Service ("The Shooting of Dan McGrew") appears in an unusual cameo. The story was rendered in 1914, 1923, for the first time with sound and Gary Cooper in 1930, and again, this time in color, in 1955. Academy Award Nomination for Best (Black-and-White) Interior Decoration. **Cast:** John Wayne, Randolph Scott, Marlene Dietrich, Margaret Lindsay, Harry Carey, Richard Barthelmess, George Cleveland, Samuel S. Hinds. **Credits:** Dir: Ray Enright; Prod: Frank Lloyd; Writer: Lawrence Hazard, Tom

Reed; DP: Milton Krasner; Ed: Clarence Kolster; Prod Design: Jack Otterson, John Goodman; Composer: H. J. Salter. B&W, 104 min. **VHS, LASER**

Springfield Rifle

(1952) Warner Bros.
Cooper follows his appearance in the most extraordinary Western of movie history, *High Noon*, with this, one of the most ordinary. Union soldier Cooper gets himself ejected from the army in order to infiltrate a pack of Confederate raiders. At the inevitable gunfight climax, Cooper pulls out the experimental rifle of the title. Fine for Cooper fans. **Cast:** Gary Cooper, Lon Chaney, Phyllis Thaxter, David Brian, Paul Kelly, Philip Carey, Guinn "Big Boy" Williams, James Millican, Martin Milner. **Credits:** Dir: Andre De Toth; Prod: Louis F. Edelman; Writer: Charles Marquis Warren, Frank Davis; DP: Edwin A. DuPar; Ed: Robert L. Swanson; Prod Design: John Beckman; Composer: Max Steiner. Color, 93 min. **VHS**

Spring Parade

(1940) Universal
This delightful Durbin musical comedy takes place in springtime Vienna. A whimsical baker employs Durbin to work in his shop. She's a cheery young thing who likes to sing and dance, and flirt with the army drummer (Cummings) who frequents the shop. Cummings wants to compose despite army regulations, so Durbin forwards one of his waltzes to the Emperor and earns them both a command performance. An innocent musical fantasy. Academy Award Nominations: 4, including Best Cinematography; Best Score. **Cast:** Deanna Durbin, Robert Cummings, Mischa Auer, Henry Stephenson, S. Z. Sakall, Walter Catlett, Anne Gwyne, Allyn Joslyn, Peggy Moran. **Credits:** Dir: Henry Koster; Prod: Joe Pasternak; Writer: Felix Jackson, Bruce Manning; Story: Ernst Marischka; DP: Joseph A. Valentine; Ed: Bernard W. Burton; Prod Design: Richard H. Riedel; Composer: Charles Previn, Gus Kahn, Robert Stoltz. B&W, 89 min.

Springtime in the Rockies

(1942) Fox
The epitome of the Fox Technicolor musical takes full advantage of the vivacious Fox musical queen, Grable, and added comic relief with Miranda. Grable and Payne make a song-and-dance team and an on-again, off-again romantic duo. When Grable makes Payne jealous with suave new dance

partner Romero, Payne woos secretary Miranda. The Canadian Rockies make a picturesque backdrop, and Harry James and his orchestra add the big-band swing. Grable married James the following year. **Cast:** Betty Grable, John Payne, Carmen Miranda, Cesar Romero, Charlotte Greenwood, Edward Everett Horton, Frank Orth, Harry Hayden. **Credits:** Dir: Irving Cummings; Prod: William LeBaron; Writer: Walter Bullock, Ken Englund, Jacques Tery; DP: Ernest Palmer; Ed: Robert Simpson; Prod Design: Richard Day, Joseph Wright; Composer: Alfred Newman. Color, 91 min. **VHS**

The Spy Who Loved Me

(1977) United Artists
Thi is Moore's third go-round as James Bond, and the 11th film in the series. Russian spy Bach joins Moore to defeat underwater criminal Stromberg (Jurgens), whose evil scheme involves destroying the world from his submarines so that he can rule from below. To dispatch 007, he sends seven-foot, steel-fanged Jaws (Kiel). Carly Simon had a hit with the theme song, "Nobody Does It Better." Editor Glen became a Bond director himself. Academy Award Nominations: 3, including Best Song. **Cast:** Roger Moore, Barbara Bach, Curt Jurgens, Richard Kiel, Caroline Munro, Walter Gotell, Geoffrey Keen, Bernard Lee. **Credits:** Dir: Lewis Gilbert; Prod: Albert R. Broc-

coli; Writer: Christopher Wood, Richard Maibaum; DP: Lamar Boren, Claude Renoir; Ed: John Glen; Prod Design: Ken Adam; Composer: Marvin Hamlisch. Color, 125 min. **VHS, LASER, DVD**

The Squaw Man

(1931) MGM
In 1914, Cecil B. DeMille made his directorial debut with the original film version of *The Squaw Man*. The production, one of the early features filmed in Hollywood, literally endangered DeMille's life as he suffered burns from misfiring explosions and was shot at by agents from the Motion Picture Patent Trust. The result was a great success. This remake, DeMille's third time around with the story, is less successful. The plot once again follows a young English nobleman (Baxter) who abandons his title when he escapes to the American frontier after pleading guilty to a crime he did not commit to protect the woman he loved (Boardman). But once on the American plains, the dashing soldier marries a beautiful Indian woman (Velez) only to find himself torn between two worlds when his former lover arrives in America. Upon the release of his first version, DeMille threatened to remake the story every 10 years. Fortunately, his experience with this production cooled his enthusiasm. **Cast:** Warner Baxter, Charles Bickford, Eleanor Boardman, Chris-Pin Martin, Raymond

Springtime in the Rockies (1942)

Hatton, De Witt Jennings, John Farrell MacDonald, Dickie Moore, Lupe Velez, Roland Young. **Credits:** Dir: Cecil B. DeMille; Prod: Cecil B. DeMille; Writer: Lucien Hubbard, Elsie Janis, Edwin Milton Royle; DP: Harold Hal Rosson; Ed: Anne Bauchens; Prod Design: Mitchell Leisen; Composer: Herbert Stothart. B&W, 106 min.

Stagecoach
(1939) United Artists
This film is the greatest Western entry in Hollywood's *annus mirabilis* of 1939, and Ford's prototype for the Western genre he dignified. This also marked Wayne's commercial breakthrough and a new level of maturity in his performances. A motley crowd—a loose woman, a gambler, a banker with a mysterious satchel, an expectant young bride, a whiskey salesman, and a drunk doctor—set out from a dusty New Mexico town with Devine at the reins and Bancroft riding shotgun and with eye out for the escaped outlaw, the Ringo Kid (Wayne). They pick up Wayne soon enough, and alliances and suspicions are forged in the tension of anticipating an Indian attack. The first of many Westerns filmed in the forbidding majesty of Monument Valley. Academy Award Nominations: 7, including Best Picture; Best Director; Best Cinematography; Best Editing. **Academy Awards:** Best Supporting Actor: Thomas Mitchell; Best Score. **Cast:** John Wayne, Claire Trevor, John Carradine, Thomas Mitchell, Donald Meek, Andy Devine, George Bancroft, Tim Holt. **Credits:** Dir: John Ford; Prod: Walter Wanger; Writer: Dudley Nichols; Story: Ernest Haycox; DP: Bert Glennon; Ed: Dorothy Spencer, Walter Reynolds; Composer: Richard Hageman, Frank Harling, Louis Gruenberg, Leo Shuken, John Leipold; Art Director: Alexander Toluboff. B&W, 99 min. **VHS, LASER, DVD**

Stage Door
(1937) RKO
A boardinghouse for aspiring actresses is the setting for one of the greatest of backstage dramas. When heiress Hepburn moves in with tough-cookie Rogers, sparks fly. The women compete for Broadway parts and men, including producer Menjou. When Menjou gets an offer from Hepburn's father (Hinds) to back his latest show, Hepburn gets the lead, causing jealousy and despair. The cast is deep in great supporting actors (Ball, Miller, Arden, Franklin Pangborn) and the lines roll off the women's sharp

tongues with spiteful elegance. That's remarkable due to the number of hands on the script; George S. Kaufman commented acidly that the production should have been called *Screen Door*. Academy Award Nominations: Best Picture; Best Director; Best Screenplay; Best Supporting Actress: Andrea Leeds. **Cast:** Katharine Hepburn, Ginger Rogers, Lucille Ball, Ann Miller, Eve Arden, Andrea Leeds, Adolphe Menjou, Pierre Watkin, Samuel Hinds. **Credits:** Dir: Gregory La Cava; Prod: Pandro S. Berman; Writer: Morrie Ryskind, Anthony Veiller, Gregory La Cava; DP: Robert de Grasse; Ed: William Hamilton; Prod Design: Van Nest Polglase, Carroll Clark. B&W, 92 min. **VHS, LASER**

Stage Door Canteen
(1943) United Artists
Dozens of the biggest Hollywood stars make appearances in this wartime musical parade with the Benny Goodman, Guy Lombardo, Count Basie, and Freddy Martin bands adding the swing. The ignorable story follows three soldiers who meet three girls before going overseas. But don't miss the chance to get a rare look at stage great Katherine Cornell, Lunt and Fontanne, Harpo Marx, and everyone else in Hollywood and on Broadway. The profits went to the American Theater Wing to support the Stage Door Canteens that offered good times to hundreds of thousands of enlisted men during WWII. Academy Award Nominations: 2, including Best Song ("We Mustn't Say Good Bye"). **Cast:** Lon McCallister, Cheryl Walker, William Terry, Katharine Hepburn, Helen Hayes, Edgar Bergen, Harpo Marx, Judith Anderson, Tallulah Bankhead, Ed Wynn. **Credits:** Dir: Frank Borzage; Prod: Sol Lesser; Writer: Delmer Daves; DP: Harry Wild; Ed: Hal C. Kern; Prod Design: Harry Horner, Hans Peters; Composer: Freddie Rich. B&W, 147 min. **VHS, LASER**

Stage Fright
(1950) Warner Bros.
This later British production from Hitchcock features an outstanding cast. Acting student Wyman's ex-boyfriend (Todd) comes to her with a dilemma: his mistress, nightclub chanteuse Dietrich, came to him spattered with blood and with the news that her husband has been murdered. The police, naturally, suspect Todd, and Wyman's the only one he can turn to. Not Hitchcock's best, but entertaining enough. **Cast:** Jane Wyman, Marlene Dietrich, Michael Wilding,

Richard Todd, Sybil Thorndike, Alastair Sim, Kay Walsh, Miles Malleson, Joyce Grenfell. **Credits:** Dir: Alfred Hitchcock; Prod: Alfred Hitchcock; Writer: Whitfield Cook, Alma Reville, James Bridie, Ranald MacDougall; DP: Wilkie Cooper; Ed: E. B. Jarvis; Composer: Leighton Lucas. B&W, 110 min. **VHS, LASER**

Stage Struck
(1958) RKO
This aged backstage tale won Katharine Hepburn acclaim when she appeared in *Morning Glory* 25 years earlier. In this updating, aspiring young actress Strasberg climbs the ladder of theatrical success with the encouragement and romantic entanglement of producer Fonda, playwright Plummer, and aging Broadway star Marshall. She reaches the top when she steps into a part meant for Greenwood. Strasberg's and Plummer's screen debuts and Lumet's second directorial outing. **Cast:** Henry Fonda, Susan Strasberg, Christopher Plummer, Joan Greenwood, Herbert Marshall, Pat Harrington, Frank Campanella, Sally Gracie. **Credits:** Dir: Sidney Lumet; Prod: Stuart Millar; Writer: Ruth Goetz, Augustus Goetz; DP: Franz Planer, Morris Hartzband; Ed: Stuart Gilmore; Composer: Alex North; Art Director: Kim Swados. Color, 95 min. **VHS, LASER**

Stalag 17
(1953) Paramount
One of the greatest of the postwar WWII movies isn't a flag-waving storm-the-beaches epic or a homefront melodrama, but this POW-camp adventure with a black-comic edge. Wilder's biting, cynical dialogue looks presciently forward to the antihero war movies that would follow in the late'60s and the '70s. In a camp run with an iron fist by sadistic commandant Preminger, G.I.s keep themselves sane by planning escapes and pulling pranks on the guards. Keeping his mates at arm's length, Holden rejects the patriotic motivations of his comrades and engages in black-market trade with his captors and the women's compound. When a spy infiltrates the ranks, Holden's the obvious suspect. But after a beating, Holden uncovers the culprit and volunteers—for his own commercial reasons—for a heroic assignment. One of Wilder's greatest scripts (and he shot it nearly word-for-word), given a terrific reading from Holden and a deep cast of supporting actors. Academy Award Nominations: 3, including Best Director; Best Sup-

porting Actor: Robert Strauss. **Academy Awards:** Best Actor: William Holden. **Cast:** William Holden, Don Taylor, Otto Preminger, Neville Brand, Peter Graves, Robert Strauss, Harvey Lembeck, Sig Rumann. **Credits:** Dir: Billy Wilder; Prod: Billy Wilder; Writer: Billy Wilder, Edwin Blum; DP: Ernest Laszlo; Ed: Doane Harrison, George Tomasini; Composer: Franz Waxman; Art Director: Hal Pereira, Franz Bachelin. B&W, 120 min. **VHS, LASER**

Stamboul Quest
(1934) MGM
Loy steps out in her first solo starring performance as a German spy in WWI. Spymaster Atwill sends her to Constantinople to stem a leak from a military attaché. Her mission is threatened by the medical student who loves her (Brent) and tags after her to Turkey without a clue as to her real occupation. Atwill, fearing the mission will be compromised, tells Loy that Brent has been shot, sending her into a mental crisis from guilt. The lovers are reunited and Loy leaves her dangerous game. **Cast:** Myrna Loy, George Brent, Lionel Atwill, C. Henry Gordon, Rudolph Amendt, Mischa Auer, Douglass Dumbrille, Hooper Atchley, Leo G. Carroll, Walter Brennan. **Credits:** Dir: Sam Wood; Prod: Bernard H. Hyman; Writer: Herman J. Mankiewicz; Story: Leo Birinski; DP: James Wong Howe; Ed: Hugh Wynn; Prod Design: Cedric Gibbons, Stan Rogers. B&W, 88 min.

Stand-In
(1937) United Artists
This is an unusual comedy role for Bogart in a fish-out-of-water satire set in Hollywood, with Howard a financial genius sent to evaluate the credit worthiness of Colossal Studios. The studio is under pressure from a competitor, and director Mowbray and woeful producer Bogart aren't up to saving it until stand-in Blondell rallies the little people who really do the work on the backlot. Great fun for movie fans to see what contemporaries thought of classic Hollywood. **Cast:** Leslie Howard, Humphrey Bogart, Joan Blondell, Alan Mowbray, Jack Carson, Tully Marshall, J. C. Nugent, William V. Mong. **Credits:** Dir: Tay Garnett; Prod: Walter Wanger; Writer: Gene Towne, Graham Baker; Story: Clarence Buddington Kelland; DP: Charles G. Clarke; Ed: Otho S. Lovering, Dorothy Spencer; Prod Design: Alexander Toluboff, Wade B. Rubottom; Composer: Heinz Roemheld. B&W, 93 min. **VHS**

Stand Up and Fight
(1939) MGM
An aptly-titled picture, as standing up and fighting comprises most of Taylor and Beery's action. When the dust from the brawling occasionally settles, antebellum Maryland emerges, with Taylor as a down-on-his-luck plantation owner who tries to force the slave-trading stagecoach line that Beery works for out of business. Their personal vendettas are buried when Beery kills the local slave trader who has been using him, and Taylor withholds damaging evidence. It just so happens that Beery's boss at the stage line (Rice) is pretty enough for Taylor to fall for, too. **Cast:** Robert Taylor, Wallace Beery, Florence Rice, Helen Broderick, Charles Bickford, Barton MacLane, Charley Grapewin, John Qualen, Clinton Rosemond, Jonathan Hale. **Credits:** Dir: W. S. Van Dyke; Prod: Mervyn LeRoy; Writer: James M. Cain, Forbes Parkhill, Jane Murfin; Story: Harvey Ferguson; DP: Leonard Smith; Ed: Frank Sullivan; Composer: Dr. William Axt; Art Director: Cedric Gibbons. B&W, 105 min.

Stanley and Livingstone
(1939) Fox
This adventure-filled biopic depicts the journey to Africa of journalist Henry Stanley (Tracy), and his quest to determine the fate of the Scottish missionary Dr. Livingstone (Hardwicke). After enduring unspeakable hardships and disease, Tracy encounters Hardwicke and emerges from Africa with a new perspective on life. A fine performance from Tracy. Filmed on location in Kenya, Uganda, and Tanzania. **Cast:** Spencer Tracy, Cedric Hardwicke, Nancy Kelly, Walter Brennan, Richard Greene, Charles Coburn, Henry Hull, Henry Travers. **Credits:** Dir: Henry King; Prod: Kenneth MacGowan; Writer: Philip Dunne, Julien Josephson; DP: George Barnes, Otto Brower; Ed: Barbara McLean; Composer: Alan Bennett, David Buttolph, Louis Silvers, R. H. Bassett, Cyril J. Mockridge, Rudolph Schrager; Art Director: William S. Darling, Geoff Dudley. B&W, 101 min. **VHS**

The Star
(1952) Fox
Davis gives a remarkable performance in a bitter examination of fickle Hollywood celebrity. Once a bright light on the silver screen, Davis now scratches for roles that never come, and she's reduced to selling her property. Now that she's broke, friends and family who depended on her earnings fade

away, and her hope of being reunited with daughter Wood gets dashed. One-time costar Hayden, now a marina owner, offers her love and a life away from the brutal battle to stay in movies. Academy Award Nomination for Best Actress: Bette Davis. **Cast:** Bette Davis, Sterling Hayden, Natalie Wood, Warner Anderson, Minor Watson, June Travis, Kay Riehl, Barbara Woodell. **Credits:** Dir: Stuart Heisler; Prod: Bert Friedlob; Writer: Katherine Albert; DP: Ernest Laszlo; Ed: Otto Ludwig; Composer: Victor Young; Art Director: Boris Leven. B&W, 91 min. **VHS**

Star!
(1968) Fox
This musical biopic of Gertrude Lawrence became a famous flop upon release (the studio edited out nearly an hour and rereleased it, to no avail), but over the years it has gained partisans who appreciate the sumptuous production values employed by experienced musical director Wise, the winning score, and a bustling choreography by Kidd. It follows British stage star Lawrence (Andrews) from the WWI years through her ascent to the stage with her friend Noel Coward (Massey). Her theatrical destiny leads to a break-up with her first husband (Crenna) and alienation from her daughter (Agutter). Academy Award Nominations: 7, including Best Song ("Star!"); Best Score of a Musical Picture. **Cast:** Julie Andrews, Richard Crenna, Daniel Massey, Michael Craig, Robert Reed, Jenny Agutter, Bruce Forsyth, Beryl Reid, John Collin. **Credits:** Dir: Robert Wise; Prod: Saul Chaplin; Writer: William Fairchild; DP: Ernest Laszlo; Ed: William H. Reynolds; Prod Design: Boris Leven; Choreography: Michael Kidd; Composer: Lennie Hayton. Color, 172 min. **VHS**

A Star Is Born
(1937) United Artists
The archetypal Hollywood tragedy, this depicts the star-crossed romance of two silver-screen stars, one just starting to shine, the other falling to earth. March plays an aging matinee idol whose battle with the bottle has made him a risk to studio executive Menjou and a constant problem for PR man Stander. At a party, March offhandedly offers to make Gaynor, a young hopeful waiting for her big break, a movie star. After their first screen appearance together, March's offer is fulfilled, and Gaynor becomes adored as he becomes unemployable, falling first to a sanitarium, then to jail, and, finally, to suicidal despair. The mar-

velous, fully imagined characters borrow aspects of the lives of classic-era stars such as John Gilbert, John Barrymore, and Wallace Reid. The script was worked by many hands, but the biting dialogue bears the stamp of famed wit Dorothy Parker. This fascinates film fans for its insider's look at the making of a star and life at the '30s-era studios. It also inspired two remakes, in 1954 and 1976. Academy Award Nominations: 6, including Best Picture; Best Actor: Fredric March; Best Actress: Janet Gaynor; Best Director; Best Screenplay. **Academy Awards:** Best Original Story, and a special award honoring the film's color photography. **Cast:** Fredric March, Janet Gaynor, Adolphe Menjou, May Robson, Andy Devine, Lionel Stander, Owen Moore, Elizabeth Jenns. **Credits:** Dir: William Wellman; Prod: David O. Selznick; Writer: Dorothy Parker, Alan Campbell, William Wellman, Robert Carson; DP: W. Howard Greene; Ed: James E. Newcom; Prod Design: Lyle Wheeler; Composer: Max Steiner. Color, 112 min. **VHS, LASER, DVD**

A Star Is Born
(1954) Warner Bros.
A close remake of the fabled 1937 Hollywood tragedy (with aspects of Cukor's own 1932 *What Price Hollywood?*) is elevated by Garland's finest, most-esteemed performance. The feeling of impending doom is intensified for today's audience by our knowledge of Garland's own experience and career. The story follows the original, with singer Garland getting her big break by giving screen star Mason a hand onstage. The more emotional performances characteristic of the '50s make this version somewhat overwrought, with Mason's degradation more shocking than Fredric March's decline. Drastic cuts made by the studio after its initial release were restored in the early '80s, and nearly 30 minutes of additional footage are available on the laserdisc. The Harold Arlen–Ira Gershwin score introduced the Garland versions of "The Man That Got Away," "Somewhere There's a Someone," "Melancholy Baby," and "Born in a Trunk." Golden Globe for Best Actor in a Musical or Comedy: James Mason; Best Actress in a Musical or Comedy: Judy Garland. Academy Award Nominations: 6, including Best Actor: James Mason; Best Actress: Judy Garland; Best Score; Best Song ("The Man That Got Away"). **Cast:** Judy Garland, James Mason, Jack Carson, Charles Bickford, Tommy Noonan, Lucy Mar-

low, Amanda Blake, Irving Bacon. **Credits:** Dir: George Cukor; Prod: Sidney Luft; Writer: Moss Hart; DP: Sam Leavitt; Ed: Folmar Blangsted; Prod Design: Gene Allen; Composer: Harold Arlen. Color, 154 min. **VHS, LASER, DVD**

A Star Is Born
(1976) Warner Bros.
This is the least satisfying and most recent adaptation of the classic backstage tragedy. Streisand's performance as a singer plucked from obscurity by skidding rock star Kristofferson will delight her fans. The sound track became a major hit. Academy Award Nominations: 4, including Best Cinematography; Best Song Score. **Academy Awards:** Best Song ("Evergreen"). **Cast:** Barbra Streisand, Kris Kristofferson, Gary Busey, Paul Mazursky, Oliver Clark, Sally Kirkland, Joanne Linville. **Credits:** Dir: Frank Pierson; Prod: Jon Peters; Writer: John Gregory Dunne, Joan Didion, Frank Pierson; DP: Robert Surtees; Ed: Peter Zinner; Prod Design: Polly Platt; Choreographer: David Winters; Composer: Paul Williams, Barbra Streisand. Color, 140 min. **VHS, LASER**

Stars and Stripes Forever
(1952) Fox
In an entertaining biopic of the "March King," John Philip Sousa, Webb portrays the composer's engaging idiosyncracies, and the Gay '90s milieu is colorfully rendered. The story follows Webb from his Marine Corps days to the worldwide tours with his own band. **Cast:** Clifton Webb, Robert Wagner, Ruth Hussey, Debra Paget, Finlay Currie, Roy Roberts, Thomas Brown Henry, Lester Matthews. **Credits:** Dir: Henry Koster; Prod: Lamar Trotti; Writer: Lamar Trotti, Ernest Vajda; Story: John Philip Sousa; DP: Charles G. Clarke; Ed: James B. Clark; Prod Design: Lyle Wheeler, Joseph C. Wright. Color, 89 min. **VHS**

Stars in My Crown
(1950) MGM
Director Tourneur constructs one year in the life of a small, 19th-century southern town, with persuasive preacher McCrea helping the residents deal with an epidemic, economic hard times, and dissension sowed by nightriding KKK thugs. Look for Arness and Blake, who would later costar in TV's *Gunsmoke*. **Cast:** Joel McCrea, Ellen Drew, Dean Stockwell, Alan Hale, Lewis Stone, Ed Begley, Amanda Blake, James Arness. **Credits:** Dir: Jacques Tourneur; Prod: William H. Wright; Writer: Margaret Fitts; Story:

Joe David Brown; DP: Charles Schoenbaum; Ed: Gene Ruggiero; Prod Design: Gene Ruggiero, Cedric Gibbons; Composer: Adolph Deutsch. B&W, 89 min. **VHS**

Star Spangled Rhythm
(1942) Paramount
Paramount opens the famous front gates and gives classic-movie fans a cinematic time machine back to wartime days. Most anyone associated with the studio at the time (actors and directors both) shows up in this charming story of a soldier (Bracken) coming home to visit his father (Moore), once a cowboy star and now the studio gatekeeper. Moore and switchboard operator Hutton have convinced Bracken that Pop runs the place, and the studio personnel love him enough to keep up the façade. A rare chance to get a glimpse at studio life of the classic era. Academy Award Nominations: Best Score; Best Song ("That Old Black Magic"). **Cast:** Eddie Bracken, Victor Moore, Bing Crosby, Betty Hutton, Bob Hope, Fred MacMurray, Franchot Tone, Vera Zarina, Ray Milland, Mary Martin, Dick Powell, Alan Ladd. **Credits:** Dir: George Marshall; Prod: Joseph Sistrom; Writer: Harry Tugend, George S. Kaufman, Arthur Ross, Fred Saidy, Norman Panama, Melvin Frank; DP: Leo Tover, Theodor Sparkuhl; Ed: Paul Weatherwax; Composer: Robert Emmett Dolan; Art Director: Hans Dreier, Ernst Fegte. B&W, 100 min. **VHS**

Starting Over
(1979) Paramount
Reynolds gives the best performance of his career (until his recent renaissance) as a bewildered man whose wife (Bergen) leaves him for a dubious singing career. He stumbles into a tentative relationship with Clayburgh. Previously seen only in macho roles, Reynolds here manages to show with real insight the hurt, off-balance soul of the wounded male. Academy Award Nominations: Best Actress: Jill Clayburgh; Best Supporting Actress: Candice Bergen. **Cast:** Burt Reynolds, Jill Clayburgh, Candice Bergen, Charles Durning, Frances Sternhagen, Austin Pendleton, Mary Kay Place, Macintyre Dixon, Jay O. Sanders, Charles Kimbrough. **Credits:** Dir: Alan J. Pakula; Prod: Alan J. Pakula, James L. Brooks; Writer: James Brooks; Story: Dan Wakefield; DP: Sven Nykvist; Ed: Marion Rothman; Prod Design: George Jenkins; Composer: Marvin Hamlisch. Color, 106 min. **VHS, LASER**

Start the Revolution Without Me

(1970) Warner Bros.
This charming farce satirizes the great costume adventures of classic Hollywood. Sutherland and Wilder play two sets of mismatched twins, one raised into dueling hellions by aristocratic parents, the other simple peasants who join the Revolution. The possibilities for confusion multiply as the comedy builds to a hilarious costume ball. **Cast:** Gene Wilder, Donald Sutherland, Billie Whitelaw, Hugh Griffith, Jack MacGowran, Victor Spinetti, Orson Welles, Ewa Aulin. **Credits:** Dir: Bud Yorkin; Prod: Bud Yorkin; Writer: Fred Freeman, Larry Cohen; DP: Jean Tournier; Ed: Ferris Webster; Composer: John Addison; Art Director: Francois de Lamothe. Color, 98 min. **VHS**

Star Wars

(1977) Fox
This is our first look at Lucas's remarkable, fully-imagined future in which the fighters for good, relying on the force of righteous belief, battle the overwhelming power of an evil empire. If that sounds simplistic, it is only simple in the way that mythology makes for sharply drawn, dynamic drama. We enter in the middle of a nine-film cycle, when a captured princess (Fisher) on the empire's Death Star sends a last-ditch plea embedded in her comic duo of robots, R2D2 and C3PO, to former Jedi knight Obi Wan Kenobi (Guinness) to come to her defense. The robots are sold for scrap on a desert planet to a farmer and his nephew (Hamill), who discovers their message. This leads to a fateful encounter with Guinness through which he learns of his heroic patrimony and his future role. Hamill and the robots link up with intergalactic mercenary Ford and his skeptical Wookie to rescue the princess. The astonishing effects created demand for high-tech spectacle and lifted Hollywood's use of technology to a higher level, yet they never outshone the dialogue and the characterizations of the actors. Through ubiquitous merchandising (another *Star Wars* innovation), sequels, and rerelease of the original in special video editions and theatrically, *Star Wars* has become accepted as our modern mythology. Selected for the National Film Registry. Golden Globe for Best Score. Academy Award Nominations: 10, including Best Picture; Best Director; Best (Original) Screenplay. **Academy Awards:** Best Film Editing; Best Sound; Best Costume Design; Best Art Direction—Set Decoration; Best Sound Effects; Best Visual Effects; Best Original Score. **Cast:** Carrie Fisher, Mark Hamill, Harrison Ford, Alec Guinness, Anthony Daniels, Peter Cushing, Kenny Baker, Peter Mayhew, David Prowse, James Earl Jones. **Credits:** Dir: George Lucas; Prod: Gary Kurtz; Writer: George Lucas; DP: Gilbert Taylor; Ed: Paul Hirsch, Marcia Lucas, Richard Chew; Prod Design: John Barry, Norman Reynolds, Leslie Dilley; Composer: John Williams; Costumes: John Mollo, Ron Beck; SFX: Rick Baker, John Dykstra. Color, 121 min. **VHS, LASER**

State Fair

(1933) Fox
This quaint, loving story set at the Iowa State Fair springs from Hollywood's deep feeling for its version of rural America, and audiences returned the affection. This drew the blueprint for the two musical versions that followed. Homespun philosopher Rogers plays a farmer who has a chance for a blue ribbon with his prize hog, Blue Bell; his wife, Dresser, has high hopes for her mincemeat recipe; son Foster takes an adolescent shine to worldly trapeze artist Eilers; and daughter Gaynor wins the heart of a newsman with a roving eye, Ayres. The plot may be as simple as the desires of the characters, but the picture never condescends, making this a warmhearted portrait of another time and place. Academy Award Nominations: Best Picture; Best Adapted Screenplay. **Cast:** Will Rogers, Janet Gaynor, Lew Ayres, Sally Eilers, Norman Foster, Louise Dresser, Frank Craven, Victor Jory, Franklin Melton, John Sheehan. **Credits:** Dir: Henry King; Prod: Winfield R. Sheehan; Writer: Paul Green, Sonya Levien; Story: Phil Strong; DP: Hal Mohr; Ed: Robert Bischoff; Composer: Louis De Francesco; Art Director: Duncan Cramer. B&W, 96 min.

State Fair

(1945) Fox
The Rodgers and Hammerstein songs lift this remake of the 1933 original. This hews close to the original story about an Iowa farm family's journey to the state fair: Winninger has high hopes for his prize hog, Bainter spikes her mincemeat, Haymes woos singer Blaine (and gets to keep her in this version), and Crain attracts a newsman lothario (Andrews). Rodgers and Hammerstein seemed to become the chroniclers of America's rural heritage after the successes of *Oklahoma!*, *Carousel*, and this. Their songs are memorable and heartfelt: "It Might As Well Be Spring," "It's a Grand Night for Singing," and "Our State Fair" are standouts. Academy Award Nominations: Best Score; Best Song. **Academy Awards:** Best Song ("It Might As Well Be Spring"). **Cast:** Jeanne Crain, Dana Andrews, Dick Haymes, Vivian Blaine, Charles Winninger, Fay Bainter, Donald Meek, Frank McHugh, Phil Brown. **Credits:** Dir: Walter Lang; Prod: William Perlberg; Writer: Oscar Hammerstein, Sonya Levien, Paul Green; DP: Leon Shamroy; Ed: J. Watson Webb; Prod Design: Lyle Wheeler; Art Director: Lewis Creber. Color, 100 min. **VHS, LASER**

State Fair

(1962) Fox
The bloom's off the third version of this movie chestnut as it updates the story of a rural family's experiences at the state fair to modern Texas, while retaining the Rodgers and Hammerstein songs. Here, Ewell and Faye play the parents, with Boone hoping for success on the car-racing dirt track and with showgirl Ann-Margret, and Tiffin getting the eye from TV star Darin. The sentiments inherent in the story and songs make for an uneasy fit with the '60s setting, but Ann-Margret supplies a spark. **Cast:** Pat Boone, Bobby Darin, Ann-Margret, Pamela Tiffin, Tom Ewell, Alice Faye, Wally Cox, David Brandon. **Credits:** Dir: Jose Ferrer; Prod: Charles Brackett; Writer: Richard Breen, Oscar Hammerstein, Sonya Levien, Paul Green; DP: William Mellor; Ed: David Bretherton; Composer: Alfred Newman; Art Director: Jack Martin Smith, Walter M. Simonds. Color, 118 min. **VHS**

State of the Union

(1948) MGM
Hepburn and Tracy are ably guided by Capra in a fascinating political drama that becomes a warm romance. Aircraft manufacturer Tracy takes a run at the presidency, but finds his campaign hindered by what we would call the "character issue." He's been separated from wife Hepburn for years, and dallies with newspaper publisher Lansbury. Tracy convinces Hepburn to stand with him during the campaign and the romantic feelings return. But their new affection is threatened by Tracy's willingness to sacrifice his ideals for political expediency. Based on a Pulitzer Prize–winning play by Howard Lindsay and Russel Crouse. **Cast:** Katharine Hepburn, Spencer

Tracy, Angela Lansbury, Van Johnson, Adolphe Menjou, Lewis Stone, Howard Smith, Maidel Turner. **Credits:** Dir: Frank Capra; Prod: Frank Capra; Writer: Anthony Veiller, Myles Connolly; DP: George J. Folsey; Ed: William Hornbeck; Prod Design: Cedric Gibbons, Urie McCleary; Composer: Victor Young. B&W, 124 min. **VHS, LASER**

State's Attorney
(1931) RKO
Barrymore plays a D.A. who rose from reform school to law school. After first representing crime boss Boyd, he turns over a new leaf and wins Twelvetrees's affections. But his new position as D.A. leads to a run-in with his old boss. **Cast:** John Barrymore, Helen Twelvetrees, William Boyd, Ralph Ince, Frederick Burton, Leon Ames, Lee Phelps. **Credits:** Dir: George Archainbaud; Prod: James Kevin McGuinness; Writer: Gene Fowler, Rowland Brown; DP: Leo Tover; Ed: Charles L. Kimball, William Hamilton; Prod Design: Carroll Clark. B&W, 81 min. **VHS**

Station West
(1948) RKO
Powell goes after noir-babe Greer as he tracks the murderers of a gold shipment's guards. Greer runs a gambling house, and Powell takes a job as a bouncer in order to get close to the gang. An entertaining Western mystery based on a story by Luke Short. **Cast:** Dick Powell, Jane Greer, Tom Powers, Raymond Burr, Regis Toomey, Olin Howlin, Michael Steele, Dan White. **Credits:** Dir: Sidney Lanfield; Prod: Robert Sparks; Writer: Frank Fenton, Winston Miller; Story: Luke Short; DP: Harry Wild; Ed: Frederic Knudtson; Prod Design: Albert S. D'Agostino, Feild M. Gray; Composer: Heinz Roemheld. B&W, 79 min. **VHS**

Stay Hungry
(1976) United Artists
Rafelson (director of *Five Easy Pieces*, 1970) revisits the clash between rich and poor in the U.S. Wealthy Bridges pursues a real-estate development that stumbles on the refusal by a bodybuilding-gym owner to move his business. When he comes to know the owner and his patrons, Bridges gets involved with the gym rats who call it home, including Schwarzenegger, in his first movie role, who's training to be Mr. Universe. Bridges also falls for Field, a girl who's never been part of his country-club set. **Cast:** Jeff Bridges, Sally Field, Arnold Schwarzenegger, R. G. Armstrong, Robert

Englund, Helena Kallianiotes, Roger E. Mosley, Woodrow Parfrey. **Credits:** Dir: Bob Rafelson; Prod: Harold Schneider; Writer: Bob Rafelson, Charles Gaines; DP: Victor J. Kemper; Ed: John F. Link; Composer: Bruce Langehorne, Byron Berline; Art Director: Toby Rafelson. Color, 102 min. **VHS**

The Steel Helmet
(1951) Lippert
In what might be considered the spiritual antecedent of Steven Spielberg's *Saving Private Ryan* (1998) or Terrence Malick's *The Thin Red Line*, Fuller's first war movie depicts men engaged in a struggle to survive the confusion and terror of war. Fuller produced this savage depiction of the Korean War in just 10 days, and only six months after the start of that conflict, but it remains a timeless statement. WWII veteran Evans survives his unit's slaughter, and, accompanied by a Korean boy who helped him escape sniper fire, joins up with a unit of untested new recruits. They withstand a withering assault and eventually seize a Buddhist temple and the North Korean officer defending it. But there is no sense of pride, heroism, or patriotism. In the confusion of war, connection means risk and death are random. This resonated with audiences familiar with the real costs of WWII and was a surprise hit when released, marking Fuller's Hollywood breakthrough. **Cast:** Gene Evans, James Edwards, Harold Fong, Robert Hutton, Richard Loo, Steve Brodie, Sid Melton, Lynn Stalmaster. **Credits:** Dir: Samuel Fuller; Prod: Samuel Fuller; Writer: Samuel Fuller; DP: Ernest Miller; Ed: Philip Cahn; Composer: Paul Dunlap; Art Director: Theobold Holsopple. B&W, 84 min. **VHS**

The Steel Trap
(1952) Fox
In a suspenseful comedy about an essentially decent man, Cotten succumbs to a million-dollar temptation at the bank where he works. His dream of riches stumbles when he takes wife Wright and family along for the getaway. When the usual family circus causes them to miss the plane to Brazil, Cotten's conscience reasserts itself, he tells Wright about his misadventure, and he has the money safely back in the bank for Monday's opening. **Cast:** Joseph Cotten, Teresa Wright, Eddie Marr, Aline Towne, Bill Hudson, Beny Burt, Joey Ray, Sam Flint, Charlie Collins, Kurt Martell. **Credits:** Dir: Andrew Stone; Writer:

Andrew Stone; DP: Ernest Laszlo; Ed: Otto Ludwig; Composer: Dimitri Tiomkin, Stan Jones, Mort Shuman. B&W, 85 min.

Stella Dallas
(1937) United Artists
One of the most famous Hollywood soaps, this was first a best-selling novel, a play, a silent film, and a radio serial that ran for 18 years. Stanwyck's performance as the devoted mother gives depth and humanity to an overly familiar story, and she considered it her best work in a career of notable performances. Stanwyck, a good-hearted girl from the hard side of a mill town, meets and marries down-on-his-luck heir Boles and they have a daughter. When Boles gets the chance to return to his privileged life in New York, Stanwyck worries that she won't fit in and stays behind with the girl. She returns to the hard-living crowd she used to know and comes to realize that she's holding back her now-grown daughter (Shirley). She strikes a soul-rending bargain with Boles's new, society-bred wife that allows Shirley to marry into a wealthy family. The last scene is a legendary tearjerker. Academy Award Nominations: Best Actress: Barbara Stanwyck; Best Supporting Actress: Anne Shirley. **Cast:** Barbara Stanwyck, Anne Shirley, John Boles, Barbara O'Neil, Alan Hale, Marjorie Main, Edmund Elton, George Walcott. **Credits:** Dir: King Vidor; Prod: Samuel Goldwyn; Writer: Sarah Y. Mason, Victor Heerman; Story: Olive Higgins Prouty, Harry Wagstaff Gribble, Gertrude Purcell; DP: Rudolph Maté; Ed: Sherman Todd; Composer: Alfred Newman; Art Director: Richard Day. B&W, 110 min. **VHS, LASER**

The Stepford Wives
(1975) Columbia
Like the phrase "Catch-22," the title of this early feminist-era thriller about a secret conspiracy of husbands who replace their wives with vapid, subservient robots has entered the national lexicon. Ross and Prentiss play two newcomers to a Connecticut community where they notice that the wives all seem a little too content with their lives. When they get curious about a men's club run by O'Neal, they start to unravel the mystery of what's happened to the Stepford wives. The novel by Ira Levin was adapted by renowned scripter Goldman. Followed by the made-for-television sequel *Revenge of the Stepford Wives*. **Cast:** Katharine Ross, Paula Prentiss, Peter Masterson, Nanette Newman,

Tina Louise, Carol Rossen, Patrick O'Neal, William Prince, Mary Stuart Masterson, Dee Wallace. **Credits:** Dir: Bryan Forbes; Prod: Edgar J. Scherick; Writer: William Goldman; DP: Owen Roizman; Ed: Timothy Gee; Prod Design: Gene Callahan; Composer: Michael Small. Color, 115 min. **VHS, DVD**

Step Lively
(1944) RKO
Sinatra makes it to the top of the credits in this musical version of the Broadway chestnut *Room Service* (also the basis of the 1938 Marx Brothers film). When Sinatra follows up on the script and money he sent to producer Murphy, he discovers the impresario rehearsing another show in his hotel room, a show paid for with Sinatra's money. Pallette offers backing from a mystery Broadway angel if his protégée Jeffreys gets the lead. Meanwhile, the bills are mounting and hotel boss Menjou wants his money. Sinatra sings Sammy Cahn and Jule Styne songs, including "As Long as There's Music," "Come Out, Come Out," and "Where Does Love Begin." Academy Award Nomination for Best (Black-and-White) Art Direction. **Cast:** Frank Sinatra, George Murphy, Adolphe Menjou, Gloria De Haven, Anne Jeffreys, Walter Slezak, Eugene Pallette, Wally Brown, Grant Mitchell. **Credits:** Dir: Tim Whelan; Prod: Robert Fellows; Writer: Warren Duff, Peter Milne; Story: John Murray, Allan Boretz; DP: Robert de Grasse; Ed: Gene Milford; Prod Design: Albert S. D'Agostino, Carroll Clark. B&W, 88 min. **VHS, LASER**

Step Lively, Jeeves!
(1937) Fox
Treacher makes an ideal Jeeves, P. G. Wodehouse's oh-so-English gentleman's gentleman. In Fox's second attempt to import the Jeeves stories to Hollywood, the butler gets hilariously mixed up with a bunch of American gangsters when he believes he's the long-lost heir to the gold of Sir Francis Drake. The ruse is part of a complicated plot by two gangsters to relieve Mob boss Harrington of a large amount of loot. **Cast:** Arthur Treacher, Patricia Ellis, Robert Kent, Alan Dinehart, George Givot, Helen Flint, John Harrington, George Cooper, Arthur Housman, Max Wagner. **Credits:** Dir: Eugene Ford; Prod: John Stone; Writer: Frank Fenton, Lynn Root, Frances Hyland; Story: P. G. Wodehouse; DP: Daniel B. Clark; Ed: Fred Hamilton; Composer: Samuel Kaylin. B&W, 69 min.

The Sterile Cuckoo
(1969) Paramount
After producing a number of notable films in the '60s (*To Kill a Mockingbird*; *Up the Down Staircase*), Pakula stepped behind the camera to direct his first feature, and it's a remarkable debut. The story follows a lonely misfit, Pookie Adams (Minnelli, in her second film role), as she meets shy, bookish Burton on the bus to their respective colleges. Minnelli never knew her mother and was shunted from camp to boarding school by her father, so she clings to the emotional attachment that she and Burton find. Though she thrusts herself awkwardly into Burton's life, their love affair is tender and bittersweet as we know it must come to an end. Minnelli overshadows the rest of the players with her now-familiar mixture of brassy vamping and nervy, naked vulnerability. A coming-of-age picture unmarred by phony nostalgia or sentiment. Academy Award Nominations: Best Actress: Liza Minnelli; Best Song ("Come Saturday Morning"). **Cast:** Liza Minnelli, Wendell Burton, Tim McIntire, Elizabeth Harrower, Austin Green, Sandy Faison, Fred Lerner. **Credits:** Dir: Alan Pakula; Prod: Alan Pakula; Writer: Alvin Sargent; DP: Milton Krasner; Ed: Sam O'Steen, John W. Wheeler; Composer: Fred Karlin; Art Director: Roland Anderson. Color, 107 min. **VHS**

The Sting
(1973) Universal
Redford, Newman, and director Hill return four years after their success with *Butch Cassidy and the Sundance Kid* to create the most popular of all the buddy movies spawned by their earlier success. The '20s-era comedy-adventure revolves around an elaborate con set up to avenge the murder of Redford's pal, a small-time grifter, by a Chicago mobster (Shaw). Redford seeks out the king of the con, Newman, and finds him living in squalor. After Redford gets Newman on his feet, the old pro and the willing apprentice set up a gambling con game that unfolds like a Chinese puzzle box. Great family entertainment. Hamlisch's score based on Scott Joplin tunes created a brief revival of ragtime music. Academy Award Nominations: 10, including Best Actor: Robert Redford; Best Cinematography. **Academy Awards:** Best Picture; Best Director; Best Film Editing; Best Costume Design; Best Art Direction—Set Decoration; Best Original Song Score and Adaptation; Best

Story/Screenplay. **Cast:** Paul Newman, Robert Redford, Robert Shaw, Eileen Brennan, Charles Durning, Ray Walston, Harold Gould, Dana Elcar, Jack Kehoe, Dimitra Arliss. **Credits:** Dir: George Roy Hill; Prod: Julia Phillips, Michael Phillips, Tony Bill; Writer: David S. Ward; DP: Robert Surtees; Composer: Marvin Hamlisch; Costumes: Edith Head. Color, 129 min. **VHS, LASER, DVD**

St. Louis Blues
(1939) Paramount
Lamour seems to wink at her public image as she packs her sarong and runs away from a New York manager who exploits her to a Missouri riverboat where Nolan puts her in his new show. Nolan's competitor (Frawley) tries to stop the successful show by revealing that Lamour walked out on a contract. This is mostly an excuse to stage W. C. Handy's title masterpiece and the many other songs. For more deeply felt performances of the music, see the 1958 film with the same title. **Cast:** Dorothy Lamour, Lloyd Nolan, William Frawley, Jerome Cowan, Mary Parker, Cliff Nazarro, Joseph Crehan, Florence Dudley, Tito Guizar, Virginia Howell. **Credits:** Dir: Raoul Walsh; Prod: Jeff Lazarus; Writer: John C. Moffitt, Malcolm Stuart Boylan, Frederick Hazlitt Brennan, Virginia Van Upp; Story: William Rankin, Eleanore Griffin; DP: Theodor Sparkuhl; Ed: William Shea; Choreographer: Leroy Prinz; Composer: Frank Loesser; Art Director: Hans Dreier. B&W, 92 min.

St. Louis Blues
(1958) Paramount
The reigning kings and queens of jazz and pop appear in a fictionalized biopic of blues pioneer W. C. Handy. The film presents Handy's life as a kind of black version of *The Jazz Singer*, with Handy (Cole) getting heat from his minister father for playing the devil's music. Future '60s rock star Billy Preston plays young Handy. The point, though, is the performances of classic blues such as the title song, "Beale St. Blues," "Hesitating Blues," and "Careless Love." **Cast:** Nat King Cole, Eartha Kitt, Pearl Bailey, Cab Calloway, Ella Fitzgerald, Mahalia Jackson, Ruby Dee. **Credits:** Dir: Alan Reisner; Prod: Robert Smith; Writer: Robert Smith, Ted Sherdeman; DP: Haskell Boggs; Ed: Eda Warren; Composer: W. C. Handy; Art Director: Hal Pereira, Roland Anderson. B&W, 93 min.

A Stolen Life

(1946) Warner Bros.
In this soapy romantic melodrama, Davis plays identical twins, one a shy artist, the other a predatory man-trap. On a vacation to Martha's Vineyard, both set their sights on engineer Ford. The bad girl wins, of course, though the good twin gets another chance some years later when her sister drowns in a boating accident and everyone assumes that the survivor was Ford's wife. But when she assumes her sister's identity, what Davis learns about her sister makes her flee the marriage. Ford lets her back in his heart, suspecting all along that he ended up with the right twin. This remake of a 1939 film was Davis's only outing as producer. Academy Award Nomination for Best Special Effects. **Cast:** Bette Davis, Glenn Ford, Dane Clark, Walter Brennan, Charlie Ruggles, Bruce Bennett, Peggy Knudsen, Esther Dale. **Credits:** Dir: Curtis Bernhardt; Prod: Bette Davis; Writer: Catherine Turney; DP: Sol Polito; Ed: Rudi Fehr; Prod Design: Robert M. Haas; Composer: Max Steiner; SFX: William McGann; Nathan Levinson. B&W, 114 min. **VHS**

The Stooge

(1951) Paramount
In a plot that comes uncomfortably close to their real story, Martin plays a going-nowhere vaudeville accordion player who teams with madcap comedian Lewis. The act takes off, but Martin wants to reestablish his own career. He does, with disastrous results. Martin's wife (Bergen) convinces him that two heads are funnier than one. **Cast:** Dean Martin, Jerry Lewis, Polly Bergen, Eddie Mayehoff, Marion Marshall. **Credits:** Dir: Norman Taurog; Prod: Hal Wallis; Writer: Fred Finklehoff, Elwood Ullmann, Martin Rackin; DP: Daniel Fapp; Ed: Warren Low; Prod Design: Hal Pereira, Franz Bachelin. B&W, 100 min. **VHS**

The Stork Club

(1945) Paramount
This is a minor Hutton musical comedy in which she plays a hat-check girl at the Stork Club who lucks into a fortune by saving from drowning a millionaire masquerading as a bum (Fitzgerald). When Fitzgerald puts her in the lap of luxury, her new lifestyle sparks the jealousy of her G.I. boyfriend (Defore). Rumored to have been partly financed by the New York nightspot as a lavish advertisement. Songs include "Doctor, Lawyer, Indian Chief." **Cast:** Betty Hutton, Barry Fitzgerald, Don Defore, Robert Benchley, Bill Goodwin, Andy Russell, Noel Neill, Mae Busch. **Credits:** Dir: Hal Walker; Prod: B. G. DeSylva; Writer: B. G. DeSylva, Jack McGowan; DP: Charles Lang, Farciot Edouart; Ed: Gladys Carley; Art Director: Hans Dreier, Earl Hedrick. B&W, 99 min. **VHS**

Storm Warning

(1951) Warner Bros.
This taut drama features Day's first nonsinging role. New York model Rogers visits her sister (Day) in a small town, and witnesses the Klan murder of an investigative reporter. She is shocked when she finds that one of the faces she saw under the hoods belongs to her sister's husband (Cochran). Her pregnant sister begs her to keep silent for the sake of her child and she agrees, but later feels pressure from a D.A. (Reagan) trying to find a witness so he can break the Klan secrecy. Rogers keeps her word to her sister, but after Cochran threatens her and Day at a victory celebration, Rogers decides to testify. The Klan kidnaps Rogers, but Day comes to her rescue. **Cast:** Ginger Rogers, Ronald Reagan, Doris Day, Steve

Cochran, Hugh Sanders, Lloyd Gough, Raymond Greenleaf, Ned Glass, Paul E. Burns, Walter Baldwin. **Credits:** Dir: Stuart Heisler; Prod: Jerry Wald; Writer: Daniel Fuchs, Richard Brooks; DP: Carl E. Guthrie; Ed: Clarence Kolster; Prod Design: Leo K. Kuter, G. W. Bernsten; Composer: Daniele Amfitheatrof. B&W, 93 min.

Stormy Weather

(1943) Fox
This musical is significant for the many standout performances by the greatest black musical stars of the day. Robinson ruminates on his career in show business and his on-again, off-again relationship with his wife (Horne). The backstage story provides many musical set pieces, including Horne giving her smoky rendition of the title song, Fats Waller singing "Ain't Misbehavin'," a duet by the leads on "I Can't Give You Anything but Love, Baby," Cab Calloway's "Rhythm Cocktail" and "Geechy Joe," and the Nicholas Brothers dancing to "Jumpin' Jive." A treasure. **Cast:** Lena Horne, Bill Robinson, Cab Calloway, Dooley Wilson, Fats Waller, Eddie Anderson, Johnny Lee, Ernest Whitman. **Credits:** Dir: Andrew L. Stone; Prod: William LeBaron; Writer: Frederick Jackson, Ted Koehler, Jerry Horwin; DP: Leon Shamroy; Ed: James B. Clark; Prod Design: James Basevi, Joseph C. Wright. Choreographer: Katherine Dunham. B&W, 88 min. **VHS, LASER**

The Story of Alexander Graham Bell

(1939) Fox
Ameche became forever associated with his role in this straightforward biopic of the inventor of the telephone. The movie recounts the story of the Scottish immigrant who comes to America to work with the deaf, including Young, his future wife and the comely daughter of rich Coburn. While continuing his work with the deaf, Ameche gets backing from his father-in-law to perfect a device that would transmit voices over Western Union's telegraph lines. Fonda plays his assistant, Watson. Look for appearances by all four Young sisters. **Cast:** Don Ameche, Loretta Young, Henry Fonda, Charles Coburn, Gene Lockhart, Spring Byington, Polly Ann Young, Jonathan Hale. **Credits:** Dir: Irving Cummings; Prod: Kenneth MacGowan; Writer: Lamar Trotti; Story: Ray Harris; DP: Leon Shamroy; Ed: Walter Thompson. B&W, 97 min. **VHS**

Stormy Weather (1943)

The Story of Dr. Wassell

(1944) Paramount
DeMille added his characteristic taste for the spectacular to the true story of an Arkansas doctor (Cooper) who risks his life to evacuate wounded American sailors from Java. First a missionary doctor, then a navy medic, Cooper disregards orders and takes badly wounded men aboard a train and fights his way to one of the last ships to breach the Japanese blockade. The film was DeMille's war benefit, with the real doctor's fee and the profits going to the Naval Relief Fund. Novelist Hilton, who adapted the story for the screen, also turned the story into a book. Academy Award Nomination for Best Visual Effects. **Cast:** Gary Cooper, Laraine Day, Signe Hasso, Dennis O'Keefe, Carol Thurston, Carl Esmond, Stanley Ridges, Richard Loo. **Credits:** Dir: Cecil B. DeMille; Prod: Cecil B. DeMille; Writer: Alan LeMay, Charles Bennett, James Hilton; DP: William E. Snyder, Victor Milner; Ed: Anne Bauchens; Composer: Victor Young; Art Director: Hans Dreier, Roland Anderson; SFX: Farciot Edouart, Gordon Jennings, George Dutton. Color, 137 min. **VHS**

The Story of G.I. Joe

(1945) United Artists
Mitchum's big break came in Wellman's harrowing biopic of WWII correspondent Ernie Pyle. Pyle (Meredith) follows an exhausted platoon as they fight their way from town to town in Italy. The platoon's captain (Mitchum) becomes the focus of his men's lives

and of the film. Privately, he anguishes over having to send his men into mortal danger and writes letters to the mothers of all the soldiers who have died under his command. Pyle records the emotional breakdowns and physical courage of the common foot soldier, a point of view that endeared him to the soldiers and his readers. Pyle saw only a rough cut of this fine war drama before he was killed in a Pacific battle. Academy Award Nominations: Best Supporting Actor: Robert Mitchum; Best Original Screenplay. **Cast:** Burgess Meredith, Robert Mitchum, Wally Cassell, Jimmy Lloyd, Jack Reilly, William Murphy, Fred Steele. **Credits:** Dir: William Wellman; Prod: Lester Cowan; Writer: Leopold Atlas, Guy Endore, Philip Stevenson; DP: Russell Metty; Ed: Albrecht Joseph, Otho Lovering; Prod Design: David Hall, James Sullivan; Composer: Louise Applebaum, Ann Ronell. B&W, 109 min.

The Story of Louis Pasteur

(1936) Warner Bros.
Muni shines in another of his famed film biography performances, this time winning an Oscar in the role of the famed French scientist who discovered a cure for anthrax and rabies. The '30s saw countless reverent biopics, typically celebrating a visionary scientist, following their humble beginnings, visionary theories, and public ridicule to eventual triumph. This is among the best known and is blessed with a better than average screenplay, which also garnered an

Academy Award. Ironically, Warner didn't have faith in the production, and, to cut corners, a Busby Berkeley nightclub set was redressed as the French Academy of Sciences. Only critical and popular esteem lifted the picture from its original release on the second spot of a double bill. Academy Award Nominations: 3, including Best Picture. **Academy Awards:** Best Actor: Paul Muni; Best Screenplay. **Cast:** Paul Muni, Josephine Hutchinson, Anita Louise, Donald Woods, Porter Hall, Akim Tamiroff, Walter Kingsford, Halliwell Hobbes. **Credits:** Dir: William Dieterle; Prod: Henry Blanke; Writer: Sheridan Gibney, Pierre Collings; DP: Tony Gaudio; Ed: Ralph Dawson; Prod Design: Robert M. Haas. B&W, 85 min. **VHS**

The Story of Robin Hood
(1952) Disney
This wonderful Disney retelling of the classic tale about Robin Hood (Todd), his true love Maid Marian (Rice), his band of Merrie Men, and their fight to preserve the throne for King Richard and shield the people from the oppressive reign of the evil Prince John and the Sheriff of Nottingham. This lavish version was produced in England with a British cast, including Justice as Little John and Finch as the evil Sheriff. For baby boomers growing up in the '50s and '60s unaware of Errol Flynn, Todd (and, later, TV's Richard Greene) was Robin Hood. This was the first of three British Disney productions, the other two being *The Sword and the Rose* and *Rob Roy, the Highland Rogue*. **Cast:** Richard Todd, Joan Rice, Peter Finch, James Hayter, James Robertson Justice, Martita Hunt, Hubert Gregg. **Credits:** Dir: Ken Annakin; Prod: Perce Pearce; Writer: Lawrence Edward Watkin; DP: Guy Green; Ed: Gordon Pilkington; Prod Design: Carmen Dillon; Composer: Clifton Parker; Art Director: Arthur Lawson. Color, 84 min. **VHS, LASER**

The Story of Ruth
(1960) Fox
This is one of the last of the widescreen biblical epics of the Eisenhower era, written by veteran radio dramatist Corwin. Ruth (Eden, in her one starring role) is an ex–pagan priestess accused of idolatry after marrying Judean Tryon. The hirsute Whitman plays her protector, Boaz. Despite the massive success of *Ben-Hur* a year earlier, audiences for biblical epics turned their attention elsewhere, and *Barabbas*, *Sodom and Gomorrah*, and *The Greatest Story Ever Told* were

among the final productions in the decade-long vogue for the genre. Years later, the son of composer Waxman turned his father's film score into a dramatic narrative for symphony orchestra. **Cast:** Elana Eden, Stuart Whitman, Tom Tryon, Peggy Wood, Viveca Lindfors, Jeff Morrow, Elana Eden, Thayer David, Les Tremayne. **Credits:** Dir: Henry Koster; Prod: Samuel G. Engel; Writer: Norman Corwin; DP: Arthur E. Arling; Ed: Jack W. Holmes; Prod Design: Lyle Wheeler; Composer: Franz Waxman; Art Director: Franz Bachelin. Color, 132 min. **VHS**

The Story of Three Loves
(1953) MGM
Here is a triptych of romantic stories that take place on an ocean liner. "The Jealous Lover" is about a choreographer who reminisces, in flashbacks, about his most famous ballet, starring a ballerina with a heart disease. "Mademoiselle" is about a governess whose young charge meets a witch. A spell changes the boy into a grown-up who falls in love with the nanny. "Equilibrium" is about a trapeze artist who falls in love with a retired circus performer. **Cast:** Zsa Zsa Gabor, Farley Granger, James Mason, Agnes Moorehead, Moira Shearer, Ricky Nelson, Richard Anderson, Ethel Barrymore, Leslie Caron, Kirk Douglas. **Credits:** Dir: Vincente Minnelli, Gottfried Reinhardt; Prod: Sidney Franklin; Writer: John Collier, George Froeschel, Jan Lustig; Story: Arnold Phillips, Ladislao Vajda, Jacques Maret; DP: Charles Rosher; Ed: Ralph E. Winters; Prod Design: E. Preston Ames, Edward C. Carfagno, Cedric Gibbons, Preston Ames, Gabriel Scognamillo. Color, 122 min.

The Story of Vernon and Irene Castle
(1939) RKO
The last of the RKO Astaire-Rogers musicals tells the story of the early-20th-century dancing duo who were among the most famous people of their day. The story follows the meeting of the doctor's daughter and the vaudeville star, their rise from vaudeville to ballroom dancing, and Astaire's service as a WWI flier. Word of Astaire's on-screen demise may have deterred audiences looking for light escapist entertainment and, despite the depiction of a final duet in the hereafter, the film was a box-office failure. Irene Castle served as a consultant and supervised the dance sequences. Among the dozens of

musical numbers are "Only When You're in My Arms," "The Missouri Waltz," "By the Light of the Silvery Moon," "Waiting for the Robert E. Lee," "Too Much Mustard," and "A Beautiful Doll." **Cast:** Fred Astaire, Ginger Rogers, Edna May Oliver, Walter Brennan, Lew Fields, Etienne Girardot, Janet Beecher, Sonny Lamont. **Credits:** Dir: H. C. Potter; Prod: George Haight, Pandro S. Berman; Writer: Richard Sherman, Oscar Hammerstein, Dorothy Yost; Story: Irene Castle; DP: Robert de Grasse; Ed: William Hamilton; Art Director: Van Nest Polglase, Perry Ferguson. B&W, 93 min. **VHS, LASER**

The Story of Will Rogers
(1952) Warner Bros.
Here is an above-average biopic of the rope-twirling icon, whose laconic, hayseed delivery was just a sheath for his rapier wit. Curtiz directs Rogers's son in the role, which lends an effortless authenticity to the mannerisms and delivery. Even though we know the outcome, the cumulative effect of witnessing Rogers's humble Okie origins, domineering political father, his Ziegfeld vaudeville years, film superstardom, and untimely death is moving. **Cast:** Will Rogers, Jr., Jane Wyman, Carl Benton Reid, Eve Miller, James Gleason, Slim Pickens, Noah Beery, Mary Wickes, Steve Brodie, Pinky Tomlin. **Credits:** Dir: Michael Curtiz; Prod: Robert Arthur; Writer: Frank Davis, Stanley Roberts, John C. Moffit; Story: Betty Blake Rogers; DP: Wilfred Cline; Ed: Folmar Blangsted; Composer: Victor Young; Art Director: Edward Carrere. Color, 84 min.

The Story on Page One
(1959) Fox
This marks renowned playwright Odets's second attempt at movie directing, and it's a curiosity notable mostly for those curious about Odets and an older, wiser, but still gorgeous Hayworth. Adulterous wife Hayworth and her lover (Young) are accused of murdering her husband, Ryder. In flashback, Ryder abuses Hayworth, who seeks comfort with Young. Walking in on an embrace, Ryder pulls a gun and clumsily kills himself with it. Down-at-the-heels mouthpiece Franciosa defends the illicit lovers in court. **Cast:** Rita Hayworth, Anthony Franciosa, Gig Young, Mildred Dunnock, Hugh Griffith, Sanford Meisner, Robert Burton, Alfred Ryder, Katherine Squire, Raymond Greenleaf. **Credits:** Dir: Clifford Odets; Prod: Jerry Wald; Writer: Clifford Odets; DP: James

Wong Howe; Ed: Hugh Fowler; Prod Design: Howard Richmond; Composer: Elmer Bernstein. B&W, 123 min.

Stowaway
(1936) Fox
One of the more touching Temple vehicles has little Shirley on the run after the missionaries who were raising her are murdered in China. The runaway hides in Young's car, which is loaded onto a ship bound for America. Young and Faye decide to adopt Temple, but their marriage runs into rough seas. Temple calms the waters. **Cast:** Shirley Temple, Alice Faye, Robert Young, Eugene Pallette, Helen Westley, Arthur Treacher, Julius Tannen. **Credits:** Dir: William A. Seiter; Prod: B. G. DeSylva; Writer: William Conselman, Arthur Sheekman, Nat Perrin; Story: Samuel G. Engel; DP: Arthur C. Miller; Ed: Lloyd Nosler; Art Director: William S. Darling. B&W, 86 min. **VHS**

Straight Time
(1978) Warner Bros.
Hoffman creates a riveting portrait of a career criminal who tries unsuccessfully to make it on the outside. After being paroled for an armed robbery stretch, Hoffman takes a stream of steady abuse from his parole officer (Walsh), meets employment counselor Russell, and sees two contrasting scenarios for straight life—drug addict pal Busey's scratching for survival and the comfortable, but dull life of Stanton. After finally snapping under Walsh's needling, Hoffman recruits Stanton and then Busey for a series of robberies. Hoffman aimed for unvarnished reality in a project that he meant to direct himself, but turned over the helm to theater director Grosbard. Hoffman's intense performance and the support of fine actors such as Stanton, Walsh, and Busey make this compelling viewing. **Cast:** Dustin Hoffman, Gary Busey, Theresa Russell, M. Emmet Walsh, Harry Dean Stanton, Kathy Bates, Eddie Bunker, Fran Ryan. **Credits:** Dir: Ulu Grosbard; Prod: Stanley Beck, Tim Zinnemann; Writer: Alvin Sargent, Eddie Bunker, Jeffrey Boam; DP: Owen Roizman; Ed: Sam O'Steen, Randy Roberts; Prod Design: Stephen Grimes; Composer: David Shire; Art Director: Richard J. Lawrence. Color, 114 min. **VHS**

Strait Jacket
(1964) Columbia
Wow! The teaming of *Psycho* scripter Bloch, screamer impresario Castle, and a high-camp Crawford makes for an entertaining watch. Crawford was sent to the asylum for chopping the heads off her husband and his lover as her three-year-old watched. She returns to daughter Baker 20 years later, and heads start to roll again. Crawford's naturally the main suspect, but someone else may have taken up her ax. **Cast:** Joan Crawford, Leif Erickson, Diane Baker, George Kennedy, Edith Atwater, Mitchell Cox, Lee Yeary, Patti Lee. **Credits:** Dir: William Castle; Prod: William Castle; Writer: Robert Bloch; DP: Arthur E. Arling; Ed: Edwin Bryant; Prod Design: Boris Leven; Composer: Van Alexander. B&W, 89 min. **VHS**

The Strange Affair of Uncle Harry
(1945) Universal
Siodmak directed this thriller with Sanders as a fabric designer henpecked by the spinster twin sisters with whom he lives (Fitzgerald and MacGill). When he meets and woos Raines, his jealous sister, Fitzgerald, drives him to a murder plot. The wrong sister gets the poison, but Sanders gets the torment. Produced by Harrison, an associate of Hitchcock, who collaborated on the screenplays for *Rebecca* (1940), *Foreign Correspondent* (1941), *Suspicion* (1941), and later produced *Alfred Hitchcock Presents* on TV. The studio enforced the disappointing ending. **Cast:** George Sanders, Geraldine Fitzgerald, Ella Raines, Sara Allgood, Moyna MacGill, Samuel S. Hinds, Harry Von Zell, Judy Clark, Craig Reynolds. **Credits:** Dir: Robert Siodmak; Prod: Joan Harrison; Writer: Stephen Longstreet, Keith Winter; DP: Paul Ivano; Ed: Arthur Hilton; Prod Design: John B. Goodman, Eugene Lourie; Costumes: Travis Banton. B&W, 82 min. **VHS, LASER**

Strange Bedfellows
(1965) Universal
An American oilman (Hudson) on assignment in London meets and marries an Italian woman (Lollobrigida) on his first day in town. Discovering they don't have anything in common other than passion, he returns to the States. Seven years later, Hudson goes back to London to get a divorce, but, hoping to secure a promotion, he courts her again with the help of PR man Young—and this time they fall in love. **Cast:** Rock Hudson, Gina Lollobrigida, Gig Young, Edward Judd, Howard St. John, Nancy Kulp, Bernard Fox, Terry-Thomas. **Credits:** Dir: Melvin Frank; Prod: Melvin Frank; Writer: Melvin Frank, Michael Pertwee; Story: Norman Panama; DP: Leo Tover; Ed:

Gene Milford; Prod Design: Alexander Golitzen, Joseph C. Wright; Composer: Leigh Harline. Color, 114 min. **VHS**

Strange Cargo
(1940) MGM
An unusual Christian allegory dressed as a hard-boiled prison picture, this is not as odd as it sounds, and quite effective, with terrific performances from Gable, Hunter, and Crawford. Gable is imprisoned on Devil's Island. He meets saloon girl Crawford on one of his escapes, but is returned to the prison where he joins Dekker, Lukas, Bromberg, the filthy Lorre, and the strangely inspirational Hunter. When Hunter organizes an escape, Gable joins in and convinces Crawford to escape her life as well. As the men face various deaths, Hunter is able to comfort even the most hardened criminal and bring them peace. Gable faces off with Hunter and learns to accept his fate. **Cast:** Joan Crawford, Clark Gable, Ian Hunter, Peter Lorre, Paul Lukas, Edward Bromberg, Albert Dekker, Eduardo Ciannelli, Victor Varconi, John Arledge. **Credits:** Dir: Frank Borzage; Prod: Joseph L. Mankiewicz; Writer: Lawrence Hazard, Lesser Samuels; Story: Richard Sale; DP: Robert Planck; Ed: Robert J. Kern; Prod Design: Cedric Gibbons; Composer: Franz Waxman. B&W, 105 min. **VHS**

Strange Interlude
(1932) MGM
In this early talkie, Gable steps up in class to join Shearer, the queen of the MGM lot, in an abridged version of Eugene O'Neill's play. When Shearer loses the love of her life in WWI having never tasted the sweetness of passion, she volunteers to nurse the wounded. There she meets doctor Gable, who presses her to marry either Kirkland or Morgan. When Kirkland, her new husband, proves uninterested in consummating the marriage, Shearer turns to Gable to father her child. The child grows up to be Young and the secret of his parentage comes out when he hopes to marry. Gable grew the famous mustache for this role. **Cast:** Clark Gable, Norma Shearer, May Robson, Alexander Kirkland, Ralph Morgan, Maureen O'Sullivan, Robert Young, Henry B. Walthall, Mary Alden. **Credits:** Dir: Robert Z. Leonard; Writer: Bess Meredyth, C. Gardner Sullivan; DP: Lee Garmes; Ed: Margaret Booth; Costumes: Adrian. B&W, 110 min. **VHS**

The Strange Love of Martha Ivers

(1946) Paramount

This brutal, black-as-night noir stars Stanwyck as a woman who dominates her small town—and the men in her life—with her family fortune. She also controls her D.A. husband (Douglas), who guards a secret from her past involving the death of Stanwyck's wealthy aunt (Anderson). When Stanwyck's first love (Heflin) appears on the scene, Douglas assumes blackmail is the reason and their twisted lives come unraveled in a violent confrontation. Veteran director Milestone's only film noir features the unforgettable screen debut of Douglas and a script by future director Rossen. Dependable thriller composer Rozsa contributes a notable score. Academy Award Nomination for Best Original Story. **Cast:** Barbara Stanwyck, Kirk Douglas, Van Heflin, Lizabeth Scott, Judith Anderson, Roman Bohnen, Darryl Hickman, Janis Wilson, Ann Doran, Frank Orth. **Credits:** Dir: Lewis Milestone; Prod: Hal B. Wallis; Writer: John Patrick, Robert Riskin, Robert Rossen; DP: Victor Milner; Ed: Archie Marshek; Composer: Miklos Rozsa; Costumes: Edith Head. B&W, 117 min. **VHS, LASER**

The Strange One

(1957) Columbia

Gazzara plays an upperclassman at a southern military academy who sadistically preys on incoming plebes until challenged by Peppard's revolt of the underclassmen. An edgy film that is still unsettling, based on Calder Willingham's novel *End As a Man*, which originated with his own experiences at a military academy. The MPAA code forced cuts in scenes that intimated homosexual activity by Richman and Storch, the primary victims of Gazzara's abuse. The movie directing debut of theater director Garfein, and Peppard's screen debut. **Cast:** Ben Gazzara, Pat Hingle, George Peppard, Mark Richman, Arthur Storch, Paul Richards, Larry Gates, Clifton James, Geoffrey Horne, James Olson, Julie Wilson. **Credits:** Dir: Jack Garfein; Prod: Sam Spiegel; Writer: Calder Willingham; DP: Guffey Burnett; Ed: Sidney Katz; Prod Design: Joseph C. Wright; Composer: Kenyon Hopkins. B&W, 100 min. **VHS**

The Stranger

(1946) RKO

Welles's first thriller is the story of a ruthless Nazi war criminal (Welles) hiding as a teacher at a New England prep school. War-crimes investigator Robinson trails Welles around the world until he uncovers the monster living quietly among the white clapboard churches and village greens, and preparing to be married. Robinson gets to Welles through a former associate, released by the tribunal to unwittingly guide the search for Welles. The former Nazi strangles the man as Robinson gets closer to his quarry, eventually convincing Welles's bride (Young) of his crimes. This exhibits wonderful Wellsian touches, including an over-the-top finale on a church tower, and has great performances from Welles and Robinson. Director John Huston had an uncredited hand in the screenplay. Academy Award Nomination for Best Original Story. **Cast:** Orson Welles, Edward G. Robinson, Loretta Young, Richard Long, Konstantin Shayne, Martha Wentworth, Philip Merivale, Byron Keith, Billy House, Isabel O'Madigan. **Credits:** Dir: Orson Welles; Prod: Sam Spiegel; Writer: Anthony Veiller, Orson Welles; Story: Victor Trivas, Decla Dunning; DP: Russell Metty; Ed: Ernest Nims; Composer: Bronislau Kaper; Art Director: Perry Ferguson. B&W, 95 min. **VHS, LASER**

Stranger on the Third Floor

(1940) RKO

This film is considered by some movie historians to be the first film noir for its atmospheric, Expressionist sets and its anxious story of brutal crimes and guilt. When reporter McGuire's testimony convicts an innocent man for murder, he's haunted by regrets. His guilt seems to attract trouble in the form of a lurking stranger (Lorre) and the murder of his neighbor, a murder for which McGuire gets blamed. Ingster's directorial debut. **Cast:** Peter Lorre, John McGuire, Margaret Tallichet, Charles Waldron, Elisha Cook, Jr., Charles Halton, Ethel Griffies, Cliff Clark. **Credits:** Dir: Boris Ingster; Prod: Lee Marcus; Writer: Frank Partos; DP: Nicholas Musuraca; Ed: Harry Marker; Prod Design: Van Nest Polglase; Composer: Roy Webb. B&W, 64 min. **VHS**

Strangers on a Train

(1951) Warner Bros.

This Hitchcock masterpiece provided the iconic images of the tennis match at which the swiveling heads reveal a dangerous presence, the murder seen in the fallen glasses of the victim, and the crushing, out-of-control merry-go-round. In a brilliantly sinister performance, Walker plays a witty, urbane young madman who offhandedly suggests to tennis star Granger, a man he had just met on a train, that they solve each other's problems by exchanging murders. Though Granger shrugs off the suggestion as insane, Walker persists, stalking the tennis player until Granger nearly succumbs to Walker's plan. After Walker accomplishes his murder of Granger's wife at an amusement park, he redoubles his pursuit of Granger to ensure he fulfills his end of the deal, and threatens to drop evidence that would implicate Granger in his wife's murder. A terrified Granger rushes to retrieve the evidence and clear his name, leading to the climactic struggle on the merry-go-round. A terrific situation conceived by novelist Patricia Highsmith, and developed by famed mystery writer Raymond Chandler (with a polish by Ben Hecht). A primer in film style, gripping plotting, and technical mastery from Hitchcock. Academy Award Nomination for Best (Black-and-White) Cinematography. **Cast:** Farley Granger, Robert Walker, Ruth Roman, Leo G. Carroll, Patricia Hitchcock, Laura Elliot, Marion Lorne, Jonathan Hale. **Credits:** Dir: Alfred Hitchcock; Prod: Alfred Hitchcock; Writer: Raymond Chandler, Czenzi Ormonde; DP: Robert Burks; Ed: William Ziegler; Prod Design: Ted Haworth; Composer: Dimitri Tiomkin. B&W, 101 min. **VHS, LASER, DVD**

The Stranger's Return

(1933) MGM

Hopkins runs away from New York and her husband for the sanctuary of her grandfather Barrymore's farm. She quickly becomes his favorite, making his stepdaughter jealous. Hopkins also finds illicit romance with a local married man (Tone), and the fate of Barrymore's farm becomes the object of a bitter struggle in the family. **Cast:** Lionel Barrymore, Miriam Hopkins, Franchot Tone, Stuart Erwin, Irene Hervey, Beulah Bondi, Grant Mitchell, Tad Alexander, Aileen Carlyle. **Credits:** Dir: King Vidor; Prod: Lucien Hubbard; Writer: Brown Holmes, Richard Fantl; Story: Phil Strong; DP: William Daniels; Ed: Ben Lewis; Prod Design: Edwin B. Willis; Art Director: Frederic Hope. B&W, 89 min.

Strangers When We Meet

(1960) Columbia

Sex and guilt among the suburban lawns in a soaper starring Douglas and Novak. Douglas, a gifted architect whose wife doesn't appreciate him, falls in love with Novak, also stuck in a loveless marriage. Both resist leaving their spouses, but the issue comes to a head when Douglas gets a commission to build a city in Hawaii. A chance to see TV comedy genius Kovacs in a feature. **Cast:** Kirk Douglas, Kim Novak, Ernie Kovacs, Barbara Rush, Walter Matthau, Virginia Bruce, Kent Smith, Helen Gallagher. **Credits:** Dir: Richard Quine; Prod: Richard Quine; Writer: Evan Hunter; DP: Charles B. Lang; Ed: Charles Nelson; Prod Design: Ross Bellah; Composer: George Duning. Color, 117 min. **VHS**

Strategic Air Command
(1955) Paramount
Stewart plays a starring St. Louis Cardinals third baseman (and WWII vet) who answers the call of duty when he takes another tour piloting the giant bombers of the SAC. Wife Allyson (appearing as Stewart's spouse for the third time!) doesn't appreciate Stewart being away from their newborn, and he grumbles about missing baseball. But his mission is exciting and there's a job to be done. Stewart was himself a pilot and a patriotic, longtime officer in the air reserves. Academy Award Nomination for Best Original Screenplay. **Cast:** James Stewart, June Allyson, Barry Sullivan, Frank Lovejoy, Alex Nicol, Bruce Bennett, Jay C. Flippen, James Millican. **Credits:** Dir: Anthony Mann; Prod: Samuel J. Briskin; Writer: Valentine Davies; DP: William Daniels; Ed: Eda Warren; Prod Design: Hal Pereira; Composer: Victor Young. Color, 114 min. **VHS, LASER**

The Stratton Story
(1949) MGM
This is the popular, sentimental recounting of the life of Chicago White Sox pitcher Monty Stratton (Stewart), who lost his leg as a result of a hunting accident yet returned to play baseball in the minor leagues. One of the most popular of Hollywood baseball films, it features some noted major leaguers (Bill Dickey, Jimmy Dykese) in cameo roles. The story follows the now familiar triumph over physical adversity formula, complete with scenes of self-pity and disappointing setbacks. Allyson plays Stewart's supportive wife in the first of three features they made together; the others are *The Glenn Miller Story* (1954) and *Strategic Air Command* (1955). **Academy Awards:** Best Original Screenplay. **Cast:** James Stewart, June Allyson, Frank Morgan, Agnes Moorehead, Bill Williams, Bruce Cowling, Cliff Clark. **Credits:** Dir: Sam Wood; Prod: Jack Cummings; Writer: Douglas Morrow, Guy Trosper; DP:

Harold Rosson; Ed: Ben Lewis; Prod Design: Cedric Gibbons, Paul Groesse. B&W, 106 min. **VHS**

The Strawberry Blonde
(1941) Warner Bros.
An ex-con dentist at the turn of the century gets a chance for revenge in this spirited romantic comedy. Cagney and Carson are streetwise pals with an eye on the local beauty queen, Hayworth. Cagney's disappointed when he gets stuck with Hayworth's mousy friend de Havilland, but when Hayworth runs off and marries Carson, Cagney marries de Havilland. Years later, Hayworth insists that crooked contractor Carson hire Cagney and his father, and Cagney becomes the fall guy when one of Carson's buildings collapses. After taking a correspondence course in dentistry, Cagney and de Havilland struggle along until the fateful call about Carson's aching tooth. Revenge crosses Cagney's mind, but he decides he's been the luckier of the two. Filmed as *One Sunday Afternoon* in 1933 with Gary Cooper, and again by Walsh in 1948, this time as a musical, with Dennis Morgan. Academy Award Nomination for Best Scoring of a Musical Picture. **Cast:** James Cagney, Olivia de Havilland, Rita Hayworth, Alan Hale, George Tobias, Jack Carson, Una O'Connor, George Reeves. **Credits:** Dir: Raoul Walsh; Prod: William Cagney; Writer: Julius J. Epstein, Philip G. Epstein; Story: James Hogan; DP: James Wong Howe; Ed: William Holmes; Composer: Heinz Roemheld; Art Director: Robert M. Haas. B&W, 100 min. **VHS**

The Strawberry Statement
(1970) MGM
Producers Winkler and Chartoff make a halfhearted attempt to exploit the youth market with a drama about Vietnam-era campus upheavals. Playwright Israel Horovitz, who also appears in a small role, adapted the novel of the same title about the Columbia University protests of 1968. A '60s time capsule featuring a sound track that includes music from Crosby, Stills, Nash & Young; Buffy Saint-Marie; and John Lennon. **Cast:** Bruce Davison, Kim Darby, Bud Cort, James Coco, Bob Balaban, Israel Horovitz, Eddra Gale, John Hill. **Credits:** Dir: Stuart Hagmann; Prod: Robert Chartoff, Irwin Winkler; Writer: Israel Horovitz; Story: James Simon Kunen; DP: Ralph Woolsey; Ed: Marjorie Fowler, Fredric Steinkamp, Roger J. Roth; Composer: Ian Freebairn Smith; Art Director: George W. Davis, Preston Ames. Color, 109 min. **VHS**

A Streetcar Named Desire
(1951) Fox
Brando's performance as a sexually electrifying brute established him as the premier actor of his day, and gave us the timeless image of him holding his head in bewildered rage as he bellows, "Stella!" Director Kazan brought most of his Broadway cast to Hollywood for the screen version of Tennessee Williams's stage triumph (the only exception being Jessica Tandy, the stage Blanche). Brando had become a sensation in the stage role of Stanley, and he shows why in the film adaptation as he exposes pure,

A Streetcar Named Desire (1951)

animal energy to the audience. When unstable Blanche DuBois (Leigh) moves in with her pregnant sister Stella (Hunter) and brother-in-law, Stanley Kowalski (Brando), Stanley and Blanche circle each other like wary animals. The sexual tension and mistrust build to a violent crescendo after Brando learns Leigh has squandered their family's estate. The film was rereleased in 1993, with an additional four minutes of footage that did not make it past censors in 1951. Golden Globe for Best Supporting Actress: Kim Hunter. Academy Award Nominations: 12, including Best Picture; Best Director; Best Actor: Marlon Brando; Best Screenplay. **Academy Awards:** Best Actress: Vivien Leigh; Best Supporting Actress: Kim Hunter; Best Supporting Actor: Karl Malden; Best Art Direction. **Cast:** Vivien Leigh, Marlon Brando, Kim Hunter, Karl Malden, Rudy Bond, Nick Dennis, Wright King, Richard Garrick. **Credits:** Dir: Elia Kazan; Prod: Charles K. Feldman; Writer: Tennessee Williams, Oscar Saul; DP: Harry Stradling; Ed: David Weisbart; Prod Design: Richard Day; Composer: Alex North. B&W, 122 min. **VHS, LASER, DVD**

Street Scene
(1931) Paramount
The teeming New York tenements reach a combustible temperature in this successful early-talkie potboiler that set the stage for the social-problem dramas, such as *Dead End* (1937), that were soon to follow. Vidor depicts the street life of New York's Hell's Kitchen, with the neighbors chatting, hanging out of windows, and trying to stay cool. The main topic is the affair between Taylor and milkman Hopton, an affair that leads to a double murder when Taylor's husband (Landau) finds them together. Sidney sees her mother dead and knows that the neighbors, including her fiancé Montor, could have stopped the violence. Bondi's screen debut. **Cast:** Sylvia Sidney, William Collier, Jr., Estelle Taylor, David Landau, Beulah Bondi, Matt McHugh, Russell Hopton, Greta Granstedt, Max Montor. **Credits:** Dir: King Vidor; Prod: Samuel Goldwyn; Writer: Elmer Rice; DP: George Barnes; Ed: Hugh Bennett; Composer: Alfred Newman; Art Director: Richard Day. B&W, 80 min. **VHS**

The Street with No Name
(1948) Fox
Widmark follows his terrifying debut as a psychotic killer in *Kiss of Death* (1947) with another role as a quirky

murderer in this pseudo-documentary crime thriller. The murder of an innocent woman during a holdup leads to an F.B.I. investigation of the city's crime syndicate. Stevens goes undercover to penetrate the gang and uncover the leak in the police commissioner's office. Widmark, whose character fears fresh air and uses an inhaler, creates another remarkably creepy character. **Cast:** Mark Stevens, Richard Widmark, Lloyd Nolan, Barbara Lawrence, Ed Begley, Donald Buka, Joseph Pevney, John McIntire. **Credits:** Dir: William Keighley; Prod: Samuel G. Engel; Writer: Harry Kleiner; DP: Joseph MacDonald; Ed: William H. Reynolds; Prod Design: Lyle Wheeler; Composer: Lionel Newman. B&W, 91 min. **VHS**

Strike Me Pink
(1936) United Artists
The Mob's after Eddie Pink (Cantor) in this musical adventure. Eddie, a poor tailor, becomes an amusement park mogul after reading a self-help book, and the gangs want part of his action. Merman and Cantor sing "The Lady Dances," "Shake It Off with Rhythm," and "Calabash Pipe." **Cast:** Eddie Cantor, Ethel Merman, Sally Eilers, William Frawley, Helen Lowell, Gordon Jones, Brian Donlevy, Jack LaRue. **Credits:** Dir: Norman Taurog; Prod: Samuel Goldwyn; Writer: Frank Butler, Walter DeLeon, Francis Martin, Philip Rapp; DP: Gregg Toland; Ed: Sherman Todd; Composer: Harold Arlen; Art Director: Richard Day. B&W, 100 min. **VHS, LASER**

Strike Up the Band
(1940) MGM
Berkeley turns the usual Rooney and Garland let's-put-on-a-show routine into a witty romp. Rooney's desperate to be a big-band drummer, so he organizes his high school friends into a swinging ensemble. They set out to raise enough money to enter a contest judged by bandleader Paul Whiteman. Garland stands by to sing for the band, but when Rooney's friend needs an operation, Rooney donates the band's cash. Whiteman himself pops by, though, to save the day. Watch for an inventive sequence in which Rooney uses animated fruit (by George Pal) to explain a number ("Do the Conga"). Songs performed include Garland's rendition of "(I Ain't Got) Nobody," "Our Love Affair," and "Drummer Boy." Academy Award Nominations: 3, including Best Score. **Academy Awards:** Best Sound Recording. **Cast:** Mickey Rooney, Judy Garland, Paul Whiteman,

June Preisser, William Tracy, Ann Shoemaker, Francis Pierlot, Margaret Early. **Credits:** Dir: Busby Berkeley; Prod: Arthur Freed; Writer: Herbert Fields, Kay Van Riper, John Monks, Fred Finklehoff; DP: Ray June; Ed: Ben Lewis; Prod Design: Cedric Gibbons, John Detlie. B&W, 120 min. **VHS, LASER**

The Stripper
(1963) Fox
This is the film adaptation of William Inge's forgotten play *A Loss of Roses*, about the impact a fading dancer has on a small-town Kansas teenager (Beymer). When Woodward comes to the town she grew up in with a traveling show, her lover and the show's manager ditch her. She takes refuge in the home of an old friend whose 19-year-old son becomes enamored of her. Woodward gently thwarts his ardor though she's warmed by the innocent affection. Woodward does more than expected with the material. The directorial debut of Schaffner (*Patton*, 1970, and *Planet of the Apes*, 1968). Academy Award Nomination for Best (Black-and-White) Costume Design. **Cast:** Joanne Woodward, Richard Beymer, Claire Trevor, Carol Lynley, Robert Webber, Louis Nye, Gypsy Rose Lee, Michael J. Pollard. **Credits:** Dir: Franklin J. Schaffner; Prod: Jeff Wald; Story: Meade Roberts, William Inge; DP: Ellsworth Fredricks; Ed: Robert Simpson; Art Director: Walter M. Simonds, Jack Martin Smith; Set Designer: Stuart A. Reiss, Norman Rockett. B&W, 95 min. **VHS**

The Struggle
(1931) United Artists
In Griffith's final film, a low-budget talkie that in effect ended his career, he returns to his early preoccupation with social issues: this time the ravages of alcoholism. A once-industrious man falls prey to demon drink and drags his family and home down with him. Mostly of historic interest. **Cast:** Hal Skelly, Zita Johann, Evelyn Baldwin, Charles Richman, Helen Mack, Scott Moore, Charlotte Wynters. **Credits:** Dir: D. W. Griffith; Prod: D. W. Griffith, William N. Selig; Writer: Anita Loos, John Emerson, D. W. Griffith; DP: Joseph Ruttenberg; Ed: Barney Rogan; Composer: D. W. Griffith, Philip Scheib. B&W, 77 min. **VHS**

The Student Prince
(1954) MGM
Another go-round for Sigmund Romberg's once popular operetta about the young Prince of Heidelberg (Purdom), who is forced to abandon

the barmaid he loves (Blyth) to marry the princess selected for him by the court. Mario Lanza supplied Purdom's singing voice, and was scheduled to star until a conflict with the studio. Previously filmed in 1927 by Ernst Lubitsch with Ramon Navarro. **Cast:** Ann Blyth, Edmund Purdom, John Ericson, Louis Calhern, Edmund Gwenn, S. Z. Sakall, Betta St. John, John Williams. **Credits:** Dir: Richard Thorpe; Prod: Joe Pasternak; Writer: William Ludwig, Sonya Levien; Story: Dorothy Donnelly, Sigmund Romberg; DP: Paul C. Vogel; Ed: Gene Ruggiero; Prod Design: Cedric Gibbons; Composer: Sigmund Romberg; Art Director: Randall Duell. Color, 107 min. **VHS**

The Subject Was Roses
(1968) MGM
Frank D. Gilroy adapted his Pulitzer Prize–winning play about a WWII vet's homecoming and his attempt to break down the walls of alienation between his father and mother. Sheen and Albertson re-create their stage roles as the vet and his troubled, alcoholic father, and stage director Grosbard also helms this powerful screen drama. Neal's comeback film after her stroke three years earlier. Academy Award Nominations: 2, including Best Actress: Patricia Neal. **Academy Awards:** Best Supporting Actor: Jack Albertson. **Cast:** Patricia Neal, Jack Albertson, Martin Sheen, Elaine Williams, George Jenkins. **Credits:** Dir: Ulu Grosbard; Prod: Edgar Lansbury; Writer: Frank D. Gilroy; DP: Jack Priestley; Ed: Jerry Greenberg; Composer: Lee Pockriss. Color, 107 min. **VHS**

Submarine Patrol
(1938) Fox
Ford's WWI seagoing adventure follows the inexperienced crew of S-599, one of the submarine chasers that set sail from Brooklyn in 1917 on a mission to track down U-boats. Navy man Foster gets demoted into his command of the questionably seaworthy freighter, and the even less promising crew, including playboy Greene. He gets them in shape and all hands are on deck for depth-charging the U-boats. **Cast:** Richard Greene, Nancy Kelly, Preston Foster, George Bancroft, Slim Summerville, John Carradine, Joan Valerie, Henry Armetta, Warren Hymer, Douglas Fowley. **Credits:** Dir: John Ford; Prod: Darryl F. Zanuck; Writer: Rian James, Darrell Ware, Jack Yellen, Ray Milholland; DP: Arthur Miller; Ed: Robert Simpson; Composer: Arthur Lange; Art Director: William S. Darling, Hans Peters. B&W, 95 min.

Success at Any Price
(1934) RKO
A bitter young man (Fairbanks) works his way to the top of an advertising agency, and along the way he sells his employers short in order to put himself in the spotlight. Fairbanks marries his boss's mistress, and when he's betrayed by her, he attempts to end his life. Though he fails, Fairbanks wins the heart of steadfast Moore when he makes known the company's shady financial dealings. An anticapitalist tract scripted by Hollywood Ten member Lawson. **Cast:** Douglas Fairbanks, Jr., Genevieve Tobin, Frank Morgan, Colleen Moore, Edward Everett Horton, Nydia Westman, Allen Vincent, Henry Kolker, Spencer Charters. **Credits:** Dir: J. Walter Ruben; Prod: H. N. Swanson, Merian C. Cooper; Writer: Howard J. Green, John Howard Lawson; DP: Henry Gerrard; Ed: Jack B. Hively; Composer: Max Steiner; Art Director: Alfred Herman, Van Nest Polglase. B&W, 75 min.

Sudden Fear
(1952) RKO
A wealthy playwright (Crawford) suspects her actor husband (Palance) of having murderous designs on her fortune in this classic noir drama. Palance makes contact with former gal pal Grahame and tells her of his marriage of convenience. They do some snooping and discover a will that leaves Crawford's estate to a charity, and decide to act quickly. But Crawford, who works with a dictaphone, accidentally tapes their plotting and takes her defense into her own hands. Academy Award Nominations: 4, including Best Actress: Joan Crawford; Best Supporting Actor: Jack Palance; Best Cinematography. **Cast:** Joan Crawford, Jack Palance, Gloria Grahame, Bruce Bennett, Touch Connors, Virginia Huston. **Credits:** Dir: David Miller; Prod: Joseph Kaufman; Writer: Lenore Coffee, Robert Smith; DP: Charles Lang; Ed: Leon Barsha; Composer: Elmer Bernstein; Art Director: Boris Leven. B&W, 111 min. **VHS, LASER**

Suddenly
(1954) United Artists
Sinatra followed his comeback role in *From Here to Eternity* (1953) with this shocking portrayal of a psychopathic assassin hired to kill the president. The chilling story takes place in a small California town as the president is due to arrive by train for a fishing trip. But most of the action is confined to the house of a retired government

agent as Sinatra and his henchmen commandeer the hilltop home. The tension rises as the train's arrival nears and the captives search for a way to prevent the sniper from shooting. When told that Oswald had watched this days before the Kennedy assassination, the film was shelved and Sinatra tried to have the prints destroyed. **Cast:** Frank Sinatra, Sterling Hayden, Nancy Gates, James Gleason, Kim Charney, Paul Frees, Christopher Dark, Willis Bouchey. **Credits:** Dir: Lewis Allen; Prod: Robert Bassler; Writer: Richard Sale; DP: Charles G. Clarke; Ed: John F. Schreyer; Prod Design: F. Paul Sylos; Composer: David Raksin. B&W, 114 min. **VHS**

Suddenly, It's Spring
(1947) Paramount
MacMurray and Goddard play lawyers whose marriage is hanging by a thread but whose one-way express to divorce is derailed by WWII. Goddard returns from WAC service to find MacMurray playing footsie with Whalen, a client, and her resolve to finalize the divorce is somehow sapped. The more MacMurray pleads, the stiffer Goddard's resolve becomes. She wins. **Cast:** Paulette Goddard, Fred MacMurray, Macdonald Carey, Arleen Whelan, Lillian Fontaine, Frank Faylen, Frances Robinson, Victoria Horne, George Backus. **Credits:** Dir: Mitchell Leisen; Prod: Claude Binyon; Writer: P. J. Wolfson, Claude Binyon; DP: Daniel L. Fapp; Ed: Alma Macrorie; Composer: Victor Young; Costumes: Mary Kay Dodson; SFX: Farciot Edouart; Art Director: Hans Dreier, John Meehan. B&W, 87 min.

Suddenly Last Summer
(1959) Columbia
Some of the greatest actors of the time appear in this bleak adaptation of Tennessee Williams's play. It stretched the boundaries of permissible subject matter for a movie, and it remains, at this late date, rather shocking. Surgeon Clift practices at a Louisiana state mental hospital where he lobotomizes the patients. In pursuit of funding, he ventures to Hepburn's Garden District mansion where he learns of her sensitive poet son, and his sudden death the previous summer. The son was in the company of his cousin (Taylor), now a resident in the asylum. Hepburn wants Taylor lobotomized, but when Clift interviews her, he discovers a sickening story of Hepburn soliciting boys for her homosexual son, and the boys' murderous

revenge. A Gothic horror film of the psyche, adapted by Vidal and Williams. Golden Globe for Best Actress in a Drama: Elizabeth Taylor. Academy Award Nominations: Best Actress: Katharine Hepburn; Best Actress: Elizabeth Taylor; Best Art Direction. **Cast:** Katharine Hepburn, Elizabeth Taylor, Montgomery Clift, Albert Dekker, Mercedes McCambridge, Gary Raymond, Joan Young, Maria Britneva. **Credits:** Dir: Joseph L. Mankiewicz; Prod: Sam Spiegel; Writer: Gore Vidal, Tennessee Williams; DP: Jack Hildyard; Ed: Thomas Stanford, William Hornbeck; Composer: Buxton Orr, Malcolm Arnold; Art Director: William Kellner. B&W, 114 min. **VHS, LASER**

Suez
(1938) Fox
This is an elaborately constructed myth about Ferdinand de Lesseps (Power), the man who conceived of the Suez Canal and persevered until it was constructed. His struggle is shadowed by his relationship with Young, a courtesan who became the Empress Eugénie, and his first backer. Useless as history, but Dwan's characteristic brio with exotic action is apparent and the leads are attractive. The story is far enough off the mark that the de Lesseps family sued. Academy Award Nominations: 3, including Best Cinematography; Best Sound. **Cast:** Tyrone Power, Loretta Young, Annabella, J. Edward Bromberg, Joseph Schildkraut, Henry Stephenson, Sidney Blackmer, Maurice Moscovich, Sig Rumann,

Nigel Bruce. **Credits:** Dir: Allan Dwan; Prod: Darryl F. Zanuck; Writer: Sam Duncan, Philip Dunne, Julien Josephson; DP: Peverell Marley; Ed: Barbara McLean; Composer: Louis Silvers; Art Director: Bernard Herzbrun, Rudolph Sternad. B&W, 100 min.

The Sugarland Express
(1974) Universal
Spielberg's first theatrical film is an extended car chase with Hawn a convict's wife who springs husband Atherton from jail in an attempt to prevent the involuntary adoption of their child. They take a policeman (Johnson) hostage and the trio are soon chased by a long line of squad cars and reporters through hundreds of miles of the American west. Some wonderful performances highlight this stylish and energetic adventure before the inevitable tragic ending. **Cast:** Goldie Hawn, Ben Johnson, William Atherton, Michael Sacks, Gregory Walcott, Steve Kanaly, Jessie Lee Fulton. **Credits:** Dir: Steven Spielberg; Prod: Richard D. Zanuck, David Brown; Writer: Hal Barwood, Matthew Robbins; Story: Steven Spielberg; DP: Vilmos Zsigmond; Ed: Edward Abroms, Verna Fields; Composer: John Williams; Art Director: Joe Alves. Color, 109 min. **VHS, LASER**

The Sullivans
(1944) Fox
This is the real-life story of sacrifice that inspired one aspect of Steven Spielberg's *Saving Private Ryan*

(1998). Five brothers—Al, Frank, George, Matt, and Joe Sullivan—from Waterloo, Iowa, enlist in the navy after Japan's attack on Pearl Harbor. Al (Ryan) is married to Baxter with a family on the way, but he's encouraged to join his brothers as they've been a team throughout their lives. Leaving home, the brothers go through boot camp, request assignment together, and board the *Juneau*, a battleship doomed to go down at Guadalcanal. After all five lives are lost, the government issued an order forbidding family members to serve in the same unit. Unsparing in its depiction of the pain of loss, it's also unsentimental in demonstrating the patriotic pride that drives men to serve. Academy Award Nomination for Best Original Screenplay. **Cast:** Anne Baxter, Thomas Mitchell, Selena Royle, Edward Ryan, Trudy Marshall, John J. Campbell, James Cardwell, John Alvin, George Offerman, Roy Robert. **Credits:** Dir: Lloyd Bacon; Prod: Sam Jaffe; Writer: Mary C. McCall; Story: Edward Doherty, Jules Schermer; DP: Lucien N. Androit; Ed: Louis Loeffler; Prod Design: James Basevi, Leland Fuller; Composer: Cyril Mockridge, Alfred Newman. B&W, 111 min. **VHS**

Sullivan's Travels
(1941) Paramount
Perhaps the greatest of Sturges's many great comedies, this balances a gimlet-eyed satire of Hollywood with an unsentimental affirmation of the movies' ability to lift people from their daily lives. When director McCrea tires of the witless comedies for which he has a natural talent, he determines to illustrate on-screen the suffering of the American people in their darkest hour. The studio bosses correctly remind him that he knows nothing about suffering, so McCrea sets out on a mission to acquire firsthand experience of real people's lives. In his first attempt, the studio flacks and his gentleman's gentleman (Blore, in a typically hilarious performance) make a sham of his sincerity, though he hooks up with waitress and aspiring actress Lake. But on his next outing, McCrea loses everything: his money, his name, his memory, and his freedom when he's given the bum's rush by a railroad cop. But in the work camp, McCrea and his hardened, beaten-down companions revel in a Mickey Mouse cartoon, and the director resolves to find a way back to his calling. The script is fast, twisty, and funny, and Sturges's usual sup-

Sullivan's Travels (1941)

porting characters are magnificent. Selected for the National Film Registry. **Cast:** Joel McCrea, Veronica Lake, Robert Warwick, Eric Blore, William Demarest, Franklin Pangborn, Porter Hall, Byron Foulger, Margaret Hayes. **Credits:** Dir: Preston Sturges; Prod: Paul Jones; Writer: Preston Sturges; DP: John F. Seitz; Ed: Stuart Gilmore; Prod Design: Hans Dreier; Composer: Leo Shuken, Charles Bradshaw; Art Director: Earl Hedrick. B&W, 91 min. **VHS, LASER**

Summer and Smoke
(1962) Paramount
A marvelous portrayal by Page of longing, regret, and repressed sensuality is featured in this adaptation of Tennessee Williams's play. After a childhood together in a rural town in Mississippi, spinster Page moons over doctor Harvey, but flees when he responds with warmth to her overtures. He retreats to his medical practice, and first a dalliance with dance-hall girl Moreno, and then engagement to bland nice girl Tiffin. Page takes comfort with a traveling salesman (Holliman). Golden Globe for Best Actress in a Drama: Geraldine Page. Academy Award Nominations: 4, including Best Actress: Geraldine Page; Best Supporting Actress: Una Merkel; Best Score. **Cast:** Geraldine Page, Laurence Harvey, Rita Moreno, Una Merkel, John McIntire, Pamela Tiffin, Thomas Gomez, Earl Holliman, Casey Adams, Lee Patrick. **Credits:** Dir: Peter Glenville; Prod: Hal B. Wallis; Writer: James Poe, Meade Roberts; DP: Charles Lang; Ed: Warren Low; Composer: Elmer Bernstein; Art Director: Hal Pereira, Walter Tyler. Color, 118 min. **VHS, LASER**

Summer Holiday
(1948) MGM
Eugene O'Neill's *Ah, Wilderness!* served as the basis for stage musicals, and both musical and nonmusical movies. Rooney starred in both the 1935 version as the little brother and took the lead in this Freed-unit musical. O'Neill's story depicts with hazy nostalgia the simpler days in New England at the turn of the century as a young man stretches his boundaries while growing toward adulthood. Forbidden to woo DeHaven, Rooney goes on a bender and romances show girl Maxwell. A stern talking-to by his father (Huston) puts all to right. The Warren and Blane songs include "It's Our Home Town," "Afraid to Fall in Love," and "Independence Day." **Cast:** Mickey Rooney, Walter Huston,

Frank Morgan, Agnes Moorehead, Butch Jenkins, Selena Royle, Marilyn Maxwell, Gloria DeHaven, Anne Francis. **Credits:** Dir: Rouben Mamoulian; Prod: Arthur Freed; Writer: Frances Goodrich, Albert Hackett, Irving Brecher, Jean Holloway; DP: Charles Schoenbaum; Ed: Albert Akst; Prod Design: Cedric Gibbons; Composer: Harry Warren, Ralph Blaine; Art Director: Jack Martin Smith. Color, 92 min. **VHS**

Summer Magic
(1963) Disney
This is a Disney version of the venerable old wheeze, *Mother Carey's Chickens*. Widow McGuire, her teenage daughter Mills, and her sons are forced to move to rural Maine from Boston and make an adjustment to farm life. Ives eases the rough spots. **Cast:** Hayley Mills, Burl Ives, Dorothy McGuire, Deborah Walley, Una Merkel, Eddie Hodges, Michael J. Pollard, Peter Brown. **Credits:** Dir: James Neilson; Prod: Walt Disney, Ron Miller; Writer: Sally Benson; Story: Kate Douglas Wiggin; DP: William E. Snyder; Ed: Robert Stafford; Prod Design: Carroll Clark, Robert Clatworthy; Composer: Buddy Baker. Color, 116 min. **VHS, LASER**

Summer of '42
(1971) Warner Bros.
A gentle, nostalgic memoir of an adolescent's loss of innocence one summer to a beautiful young war bride on an island off New England. Mulligan and writer Raucher (who claimed the story is based on his experiences) supply plenty of period detail, and the performances are charming and funny. Academy Award Nominations: 4, including Best (Original) Story and Screenplay; Best Cinematography. **Academy Awards:** Best Original Dramatic Score. **Cast:** Jennifer O'Neill, Gary Grimes, Jerry Houser, Oliver Conant, Christopher Norris, Lou Frizzell, Walter Scott, Robert Mulligan. **Credits:** Dir: Robert Mulligan; Prod: Richard Roth; Writer: Herman Raucher; DP: Robert Surtees; Ed: Folmar Blangsted; Prod Design: Albert Brenner; Composer: Michel Legrand. Color, 104 min. **VHS, LASER**

A Summer Place
(1959) Warner Bros.
An innkeeper's wife (McGuire) and a vacationing businessman (Egan) rekindle a love they shared 20 years prior, before parental interference tore them apart. Their resumed affair destroys their shaky marriages, and their passion is reflected in a new generation

when her son (Donahue) and his daughter (Dee) fall in love. This sudsy melodrama won a wide audience, appealing to both teenagers as well as their parents, and made movie stars out of Dee and Donahue. **Cast:** Troy Donahue, Sandra Dee, Dorothy McGuire, Richard Egan, Arthur Kennedy, Constance Ford, Beulah Bondi, Jack Richardson. **Credits:** Dir: Delmer Daves; Prod: Delmer Daves; Writer: Delmer Daves; DP: Harry Stradling; Ed: Owen Marks; Composer: Max Steiner; Art Director: Leo K. Kuter. Color, 130 min. **VHS, LASER**

Summer Stock
(1950) MGM
This old-fashioned musical was Garland's last performance for MGM. Farmer Garland asks for help from her sister DeHaven, who has fled the canebrake for the bright lights of Broadway. She arrives with her entire summer stock company, including leading man Kelly. The whole gang decides to raise money to save the farm by putting on a show, and Garland gets the lead when Kelly and DeHaven have a tiff. Pleasant Harry Warren, Mack Gordon songs, along with the famous Harold Arlen number, "Get Happy," featuring Garland in black tights and fedora. **Cast:** Judy Garland, Gene Kelly, Gloria DeHaven, Phil Silvers, Marjorie Main, Eddie Bracken, Ray Collins, Carleton Carpenter, Nita Bieber. **Credits:** Dir: Charles Walters; Prod: Joe Pasternak; Writer: George Wells, Sy Gomberg; DP: Robert Planck; Ed: Albert Akst; Prod Design: Cedric Gibbons; Composer: Johnny Green; Art Director: Jack Martin Smith. Color, 110 min. **VHS, LASER**

Summer Storm
(1944) United Artists
Sirk directs this first Hollywood screen adaptation of an Anton Chekhov story, "The Shooting Party." Ten years after the murder of Darnell, Sanders offers himself up to the police as the killer. In flashback, he tells Darnell's story, as she used her beauty to snare a young farmer, Hass, to escape her poor home, and then flaunted her affairs. Sanders was one of the men she attracted, and he left a wife and child to pursue his passion, a guilty lust that led to murder. Hass is found guilty of the crime, and Sanders maintains his secret for 10 years. Academy Award Nomination for Best Score. **Cast:** Linda Darnell, George Sanders, Anna Lee, Hugo Hass, Edward Everett Horton, Lori Lahner, John Philliber, Sig Rumann, John Abbott, Andre Charlot.

"She had this great inner luminosity in life and in the film. Deborah just emits goodness and humanity."

Dina Merrill on Deborah Kerr in *The Sundowners* (1960)

Credits: Dir: Douglas Sirk; Prod: Islin Auster; Writer: Rowland Leigh; Story: Anton Chekhov; DP: Archie Stout; Ed: Gregg C. Tallas; Prod Design: Rudi Feld; Composer: Frank Skinner. B&W, 105 min.

Summertime
(1955) United Artists
In a touching romantic drama about a lonely, middle-aged American woman, Hepburn experiences the wonder and the pain of romance on holiday in Venice. As Hepburn marvels (along with the audience) at the sights of Venice that surround her, she meets a charming Italian boy who shows her around, including to Brazzi's antiques store. The handsome merchant finds her charming and she relishes the attention. Hepburn eventually acknowledges that, though their interlude may be the most romantic time she will ever experience, she must return to her life. Director Lean (*Brief Encounter*, 1945) captures wonderful Hepburn moments that express longing, fear, joy, and regret in one bittersweet performance. Based on Arthur Laurent's play, *The Time of the Cuckoo*. Academy Award Nominations: 2, including Best Director; Best Actress: Katharine Hepburn. **Cast:** Katharine Hepburn, Rossano Brazzi, Isa Miranda, Darren McGavin, Mari Aldon, Jane Rose, MacDonald Parke, Gaitano Audiero, Andre Morell, Jeremy Spenser. **Credits:** Dir: David Lean; Prod: Ilya Lopert; Writer: David Lean, H. E. Bates; DP: Jack Hildyard; Ed: Peter Taylor; Prod Design: Vincent Korda; Composer: Alessandro Cicognini. Color, 99 min. **VHS, LASER**

Summer Wishes, Winter Dreams
(1973) Columbia
This is a fine, quiet drama about a middle-aged woman (Woodward) who begins to dwell on childhood memories after the death of her mother (Sidney) as she slowly works herself into a deep depression. Her husband (Balsam) tries to find the meaning in his life when he also explores the past— his terrifying experiences during WWII.

Academy Award Nominations: Best Actress: Joanne Woodward; Best Supporting Actress: Sylvia Sidney. **Cast:** Joanne Woodward, Martin Balsam, Dori Brenner, Sylvia Sidney, Tresa Hughes, Minerva Pious, Gaetano Lisi, David Thomas. **Credits:** Dir: Gilbert Cates; Prod: Jack Brodsky; Writer: Stewart Stern; DP: Gerald Hirschfeld; Ed: Sidney Katz; Prod Design: Peter Dohanos; Composer: Johnny Mandel; Costumes: Anna Hill Johnstone. Color, 95 min. **VHS**

The Sun Also Rises
(1957) Fox
One of the most faithful of Ernest Hemingway adaptations follows the rootless wanderings of American expatriates in Europe following WWI. Power searches for cheap sensation to salve his impotence, the result of a war wound. He's joined in this pursuit by a beautiful aristocrat (Gardner) who had ministered to him during the war, his best friend (Albert), a Greek tycoon (Ratoff), an alcoholic writer (Ferrer), and a devil-may-care Scot (Flynn, in his penultimate role). The group ventures to Pamplona for the running of the bulls, and against that colorful backdrop, the emotional tension rises as each of the men pursues Gardner and she opts to attach herself to a handsome young matador (Evans). Beautifully rendered locations and slyly charming support from Flynn make this particularly enjoyable. Power has more trouble portraying restless youth; this was his next-to-last film and he died the following year. Gardner evidently liked the setting. After divorcing Frank Sinatra in 1957, she returned to Madrid and took up with famous matadors herself. **Cast:** Tyrone Power, Ava Gardner, Mel Ferrer, Errol Flynn, Eddie Albert, Gregory Ratoff, Juliette Greco, Marcel Dalio, Robert Evans, Henry Daniell, Bob Cunningham. **Credits:** Dir: Henry King; Prod: Darryl F. Zanuck; Writer: Peter Viertel, Ernest Hemingway; DP: Leo Tover; Ed: William Mace; Composer: Hugo Friedhofer. Color, 129 min.

Sundown
(1941) United Artists
This straightforward WWII drama depicts the Nazis stirring up trouble among the natives in Africa. Tierney, the daughter of an Arab merchant, goes undercover to help derail a German gunrunning operation. Hathaway moves the proceedings along briskly. Academy Award Nominations: 3, including Best (Black-and-White) Cinematography; Best Score. **Cast:** Gene Tierney, Bruce Cabot, Harry Carey, George Sanders, Cedric Hardwicke, Joseph Calleia, Reginald Gardiner, Carl Esmond, Marc Lawrence, Jeni Le Gon. **Credits:** Dir: Henry Hathaway; Prod: Walter Wanger; Writer: Barre Lyndon, Charles G. Booth; DP: Charles Lang; Ed: Dorothy Spencer; Prod Design: Alexander Golitzen; Composer: Miklos Rozsa; Costumes: Walter Plunkett; SFX: Ray Binger. B&W, 91 min. **VHS**

The Sundowners
(1960) Warner Bros.
By the late '50s, American studios were experimentally shooting an occasional feature in Australia. This colorful story, set in the '20s and directed by Zinnemann, features Mitchum and Kerr as a hardworking drover and his wife who wander the continent working toward their dream of buying a farm. Their family's travels bring them into contact with outsized characters (including former ship's captain Ustinov) and Mitchum engages in his share of fighting and drinking. Their dreams nearly come to pass when Mitchum wins a horse that turns out to be a swift runner. The exotic vistas of Australia provide a harshly beautiful backdrop for drama and adventures. Based on Jon Cleary's novel. Golden Globe for Special Achievements. Academy Award Nominations: 5, including Best Picture; Best Director; Best Actress: Deborah Kerr. **Cast:** Deborah Kerr, Robert Mitchum, Peter Ustinov, Michael Anderson, Glynis Johns, Dina Merrill, Chips Rafferty, Michael Anderson, Jr. **Credits:** Dir: Fred Zinnemann; Prod: Fred Zinnemann, Gerry Blattner; Writer: Isobel Lennart; Story: Jon Cleary; DP: Jack Hildyard; Ed: Jack Harris; Composer: Dimitri Tiomkin; Art Director: Michael Stringer. Color, 133 min. **VHS, LASER**

Sunrise
(1927) Fox
Subtitled *A Song of Two Humans*, this is one of the most visually beautiful and emotionally touching films in movie history. If one needs convincing that the silent cinema reached a

higher level of artistic achievement than the talkies that immediately followed, this is required viewing. Murnau constructs a morality tale with elements of Expressionist anxiety, joyous humor, and passionate love. Rustic farmer O'Brien meets city vamp Livingston, and her feminine wiles prod O'Brien to abandon his loving, child-like wife (Gaynor) and their newborn. But O'Brien suffers the torments of the damned, eventually resolving to murder his wife by faking a boating accident. When the time comes to shove her overboard, Gaynor's scream awakens O'Brien's conscience. He chases his frightened wife to the big city, where she softens and they play and marvel at the city's wonders. On their way home across the lake, the couple draw closer together than ever before, until a thunderous storm heaves Gaynor from the boat. Thinking she is lost, O'Brien dissolves in grief, and threatens Livingston—but Gaynor is found safe and the lovers are reunited as they beam at their child. A cinema treasure that rewards every viewing. Selected for the National Film Registry. **Academy Awards:** Best Actress: Janet Gaynor (also for her work in *Seventh Heaven* and *Street Angel*); Best Cinematography; Best Artistic Quality of Production. **Cast:** George O'Brien, Janet Gaynor, Margaret Livingston, Arthur Housman, J. Farrell MacDonald. **Credits:** Dir: F. W. Murnau. B&W, 110 min. **VHS, LASER**

Sunrise at Campobello
(1960) Warner Bros.
Film producer Schary turned to writing and authored this memorable portrait of FDR's early career, and the personal and political consequences of the future president's battle with polio. Garson received deserved praise for her portrayal of Eleanor Roosevelt and the eloquent determination with which she rallied her husband to the nation's service. Based on Schary's Tony-winning play. Golden Globe for Best Actress in a Drama: Greer Garson. Academy Award Nominations: 4, including Best Actress: Greer Garson; Best Art Direction. **Cast:** Ralph Bellamy, Greer Garson, Hume Cronyn, Jean Hagen, Ann Shoemaker, Alan Bunce, Tim Considine, Zina Bethune, Lyle Talbot, David White. **Credits:** Dir: Vincent J. Donehue; Prod: Dore Schary; Writer: Dore Schary; DP: Russell Harlan; Ed: George Boemler; Prod Design: Edward Carrere; Composer: Franz Waxman; Costumes: Marjorie Best. Color, 144 min. **VHS, LASER**

Sunset Boulevard
(1950) Paramount
Wilder's acid-etched portrait of Hollywood must be placed at the top of any classic-movie fan's required-viewing list. From the macabre opening scene, which establishes the film's narrator as a dead man, through Swanson's final, sweeping exit, there is not a frame or line out of place. B-movie screenwriter Holden floats facedown in a pool as he begins the story of his demise. Ditching his about-to-be-repossessed car in a Hollywood mansion's driveway, Holden wanders the premises until he's mistaken for the undertaker meant to preside at a funeral for aging silent-film queen Swanson's pet monkey. When she discovers that Holden is instead a screenwriter, Swanson envelops him in a web of gifts, flattery, money, and curiosity that makes Holden the monkey's stand-in. Holden continues to feed Swanson's delusions, aided by her faithful butler–former director–former husband von Stroheim, until he can't find a way out—even when studio script reader Olson offers her heart and help with a screenplay. Out of many resonant moments, the highlights include the weekly card game with silent-era stars Keaton, Anna O. Nilsson, and H. B. Warner; Swanson's viewings of her own performance in *Queen Kelly*, a disastrous silent picture actually directed by von Stroheim; and Swanson's slow march down the grand staircase, fully lost in her past, as her eloquent face portrays all the elation and fear that lead to the film's last line, "All right, Mr. DeMille, I'm ready for my close-up now." Golden Globes for Best Motion Picture, Drama; Best Director; Best Score; Best Actress in a Drama: Gloria Swanson. Selected for the National Film Registry. Academy Award Nominations: 11, including Best Picture; Best Director; Best Actor: William Holden; Best Actress: Gloria Swanson; Best Supporting Actor: Erich von Stroheim; Best Supporting Actress: Nancy Olson. **Academy Awards:** Best Music Score of a Drama/Comedy; Best Story and Screenplay; Best Art Direction—Set Decoration (B&W). **Cast:** Gloria Swanson, William Holden, Erich von Stroheim, Nancy Olson, Buster Keaton, Fred Clark, Lloyd Gough, Jack Webb, Cecil B. DeMille, Hedda Hopper. **Credits:** Dir: Billy Wilder; Prod: Charles Brackett; Writer: Billy Wilder, Charles Brackett, D. M. Marshman; DP: John Seitz; Ed: Doane Harrison, Arthur Schmidt; Prod Design: Hans Dreier, John Meehan; Composer: Franz Waxman, Richard Strauss; Costumes: Edith Head; SFX: Gordon Jennings, Farciot Edouart. B&W, 110 min. **VHS, LASER**

The Sunshine Boys
(1975) United Artists
This Neil Simon stage comedy makes a successful transition to the screen with Matthau and Burns playing a feuding comedy team who almost reunite for a nostalgic TV special. Irascible Matthau continues to work in commercials, and reluctantly agrees to his nephew Benjamin's invitation to

Sunset Boulevard (1950)

put together the old act again, though he hasn't spoken to Burns in years. After much negotiation, the two funny men get together and nearly come to blows. Wise, funny performances from the leads and great support from the script and cast. Academy Award Nominations: 4, including Best Actor: Walter Matthau; Best (Adapted) Screenplay. **Academy Awards:** Best Supporting Actor: George Burns. **Cast:** George Burns, Walter Matthau, Richard Benjamin, Lee Meredith, Howard Hesseman, James Cranna, Ron Rifkin, Archie Hahn. **Credits:** Dir: Herbert Ross; Prod: Ray Stark; Writer: Neil Simon; DP: David M. Walsh; Ed: John F. Burnett; Prod Design: Albert Brenner. Color, 111 min. VHS, LASER

The Sun Shines Bright

(1953) Republic
Reportedly, this turn-of-the-century story of a common-sense jurist (Winninger) in rural Kentucky was director Ford's favorite film. In fact, he was so fond of the Irvin S. Cobb stories that he filmed them twice, first as *Judge Priest* in 1934 with Will Rogers. This time, Winninger runs for reelection against a Yankee carpetbagger, while defending a black youth from a lynching, and supporting a prostitute to keep her off the streets. This often charming piece of Americana is unfortunately stained by some embarrassing interludes and a performance by black comedian Stepin Fetchit that will today prompt more winces than the intended laughs. **Cast:** Charles Winninger, Arleen Whelan, John Russell, Stepin Fetchit, Francis Ford, Paul Hurst, Mitchell Lewis, Grant Withers. **Credits:** Dir: John Ford; Prod: John Ford, Merian C. Cooper; Writer: Laurence Stallings; Story: Irvin S. Cobb; DP: Archie Stout; Ed: Jack Murray; Composer: Victor Young; Art Director: Frank Hotaling. B&W, 100 min. VHS

Sun Valley Serenade

(1941) Fox
The first of only two screen appearances by Glenn Miller, this Technicolor musical provides a spectacular setting for the big-band swing. The Glenn Miller Orchestra gets a booking at the Sun Valley resort (recently opened, the resort became a trendy vacation spot for Hollywood types), where they're met by a Norwegian immigrant (Henie) sponsored by pianist Payne. Her talents on ice come in handy when vocalist Bari exits in a jealous huff. Mostly a pleasant backdrop for terrific Miller tunes such as "Chattanooga Choo Choo" (with a dance

routine by the Nicholas Brothers and vocals by Dorothy Dandridge), "It Happened in Sun Valley," and the inevitable "In the Mood." Academy Award Nominations: 3, including Best Song ("Chattanooga Choo Choo"); Best Cinematography. **Cast:** Sonja Henie, John Payne, Glenn Miller, Milton Berle, Lynn Bari, Joan Davis, Dorothy Dandridge, Nicholas Brothers, William B. Davidson, Almira Sessions. **Credits:** Dir: H. Bruce Humberstone; Prod: Milton Sperling; Writer: Robert Ellis, Helen Logan, Edward Cronjager; Ed: James B. Clark; Prod Design: Richard Day, Lewis Creber; Choreographer: Hermes Pan. B&W, 86 min. VHS

Superfly

(1972) Warner Bros.
In an icon of the '70s with a memorable soul score from Curtis Mayfield, O'Neal plays a cocaine dealer who becomes a local hero in Harlem as he beats "the man" and amasses an illicit fortune. He's a cool head who's not in the game for the action, and he plans to retire after one more big score. Authentic street feel from the son of photographer-director Gordon Parks (*Shaft*). Followed by *Superfly T.N.T.* (1973). **Cast:** Ron O'Neal, Carl Lee, Julius W. Harris, Charles McGregor, Sheila Frazier, K.C., Sig Shore. **Credits:** Dir: Gordon Parks, Jr.; Prod: Sig Shore; Writer: Phillip Fenty; DP: James Signorelli; Ed: Bob Brady; Composer: Curtis Mayfield. Color, 93 min. VHS

Superman: The Movie

(1978) Warner Bros.
The Superman comic-book myth well told, from his birth on the doomed planet Krypton to his childhood in a small Kansas town, and to life in the big city, Metropolis. Hiding his super powers as mild-mannered reporter Clark Kent, Superman saves the world from supervillain Lex Luthor (Hackman) and his henchmen Beatty and Perrine. He also brings his beloved Lois Lane (Kidder) back to life by reversing the earth's rotation. Reeve has become forever associated with the role (despite a full career spent out of the blue tights) because of his easy, nearly bashful manner. The effects are fun, and the cast seems to enjoy themselves. This also features the notorious cameo by Brando as Superman's father, Jor-El. Note the all-star scripters, including *Godfather* author Mario Puzo and director Robert Benton. Followed by three sequels (*Superman 2,* 1980; *Superman 3,* 1983; and *Superman 4: The Quest for Peace,* 1987) and *Supergirl* (1984).

Academy Award Nominations: 3, including Best Editing; Best Score. **Academy Awards:** Best Visual Effects. **Cast:** Christopher Reeve, Margot Kidder, Marlon Brando, Glenn Ford, Terence Stamp, Gene Hackman, Ned Beatty, Jackie Cooper, Valerie Perrine, Trevor Howard. **Credits:** Dir: Richard Donner; Prod: Pierre Spengler; Writer: Mario Puzo, David Newman, Leslie Newman, Robert Benton; DP: Geoffrey Unsworth; Ed: Stuart Baird; Composer: John Williams, John Barry; Costumes: Yvonne Blake; SFX: Colin Chilvers, Roy Field, Derek Meddings, Zoran Perisic, Denys Coop, Les Bowie. Color, 143 min. VHS, LASER

Super Sleuth

(1937) RKO
This madcap murder mystery has Oakie as a movie star who starts to believe he's actually the tough private eye he portrays on the silver screen. He takes a break from acting to solve an actual murder. In the process, he hires the evil Prof. Horman (Cianelli), the real villain, as his assistant and mixes things up so badly that his lovely publicist, Sothern, has to come to the rescue. **Cast:** Jack Oakie, Ann Sothern, Edward Cianelli, Alan Bruce, Edgar Kennedy, Joan Woodbury, Bradley Page, Paul Guilfoyle, Willie Best, William Corson. **Credits:** Dir: Benjamin Stoloff; Prod: Edward Small; Writer: Ernest Pagano, Gertrude Purcell, Harry Segall; DP: Joseph H. August; Ed: William Hamilton; Prod Design: Van Nest Polglase. B&W, 75 min.

Support Your Local Gunfighter

(1971) United Artists
Another chapter in the Support Your . . . series of movie Western spoofs this time features Garner as a con man on the run from a madam he's promised to marry. When he rides through a town called Purgatory, he discovers to his crooked delight that the townspeople believe he's a deadly gunslinger. He fills his pockets and woos Pleshette. Just as much fun as the first entry. **Cast:** James Garner, Suzanne Pleshette, Jack Elam, Harry Morgan, John Dehner, Joan Blondell, Dub Taylor, Ellen Corby, Henry Jones, Marie Windsor. **Credits:** Dir: Burt Kennedy; Prod: William Finnegan; Writer: James Edward Grant; DP: Harry Stradling; Ed: William Gulick; Prod Design: Phil Barber; Composer: Jack Elliott, Allyn Ferguson; Costumes: Lambert Marks, Patricia Norris; SFX: A. D. Flowers; Set Designer: Chester L. Bayhi. Color, 93 min. VHS

Support Your Local Sheriff
(1969) United Artists
This gentle parody of Western clichés features a wry performance by Garner. Though he's just passing through, Garner becomes the sheriff of a town, hires drunkard Morgan as his deputy, and arrests Dern (and builds a jail with Dern's help). The action climaxes in a showdown with Brennan. Good fun. **Cast:** James Garner, Joan Hackett, Walter Brennan, Harry Morgan, Jack Elam, Bruce Dern, Henry Jones, Walter Burke. **Credits:** Dir: Burt Kennedy; Prod: William Bowers; Writer: William Bowers; DP: Harry Stradling; Ed: George W. Brooks; Composer: Jeff Alexander. Color, 92 min. **VHS, LASER**

Suppose They Gave a War and Nobody Came?
(1970) Cinerama
Petty despot Ewell leads a clash between a small southern town and the nearby army base when soldier Curtis is caught smooching with Pleshette. Ewell calls out the reserves for an assault on the base. Mildly amusing. **Cast:** Tony Curtis, Brian Keith, Ernest Borgnine, Suzanne Pleshette, Ivan Dixon, Tom Ewell, Bradford Dillman, Arthur O'Connell. **Credits:** Dir: Hy Averback; Prod: Fred Engel; Writer: Don McGuire, Hal Captain; DP: Burnett Guffey; Ed: John F. Burnett; Prod Design: Jack Poplin; Composer: Jerry Fielding. Color, 113 min. **VHS**

Susan and God
(1940) MGM
This is a terrific performance by Crawford as a self-absorbed society matron. After alienating her husband (March) and daughter (Quigley), Crawford returns from Europe where she has embraced a faddish new religious practice that encourages total confession as a means of wiping away sin. Crawford baffles her cynical friends, and her family nearly splits until she has a real epiphany and begins to sincerely practice her belief. Cukor directs a sparkling script by Loos. **Cast:** Joan Crawford, Rita Hayworth, Ruth Hussey, Nigel Bruce, Bruce Cabot, Fredric March, John Carroll, Rose Hobart, Rita Quigley, Marjorie Main. **Credits:** Dir: George Cukor; Prod: Hunt Stromberg; Writer: Anita Loos; Story: Rachel Crothers; DP: Robert Planck; Ed: William Terhune; Composer: Herbert Stothart; Art Director: Cedric Gibbons; Costumes: Adrian. B&W, 117 min. **VHS**

Susan Lenox (Her Fall and Rise)
(1931) MGM
The only screen pairing of Garbo and Gable comes in this adaptation of a novel that was hot stuff in the '20s. Garbo flees her impoverished father's plan to marry her off to a well-to-do farmer (Hale) into a rustic romantic idyll with Gable. But her father's on her trail, and Garbo takes refuge with a carnival, becoming the owner's mistress. Brokenhearted, Gable runs to South America, and Garbo becomes a courtesan until her past catches up with her. Now determined to find her true love, Garbo sets sail for South America. Not many sparks between the leads as they're separated for much of the story. Interesting for the familiar faces in an early talkie melodrama. **Cast:** Greta Garbo, Jean Hersholt, John Miljan, Alan Hale, Clark Gable, Hale Hamilton, Russell Simpson, Cecil Cunningham, Ian Keith, Helene Millard. **Credits:** Dir: Robert Z. Leonard; Writer: Wanda Tuchock, Zelda Sears, Leon Gordon, Edith Fitzgerald; DP: William Daniels; Ed: Margaret Booth. B&W, 77 min. **VHS**

Susannah of the Mounties
(1939) Fox
Poor little Shirley—she has the hardest time keeping parents. The perennial orphan this time loses her frontier family to an Indian attack. After her rescue by mountie Scott, he and his wife (Lockwood) adopt her, and Temple helps quell the Indian uprising while teaching the rugged mountie to dance. By 1939, it's getting late in the day for little Shirley, but this has its charms. **Cast:** Shirley Temple, Martin Good Rider, Randolph Scott, Margaret Lockwood, Farrell McDonald, Maurice Moscovich, Moroni Olsen, Victor Jory, Lester Matthews, Leyland Hodgson. **Credits:** Dir: William A. Seiter; Prod: Kenneth MacGowan; Writer: Robert Ellis, Helen Logan; DP: Arthur Miller; Ed: Robert Bischoff. B&W, 79 min. **VHS**

Susan Slept Here
(1954) RKO
Debbie Reynolds a juvenile delinquent?! Nah. But otherwise a bouncy comedy with Powell a screenwriter delving into troubled youth. He gets quite a project when a policeman pal delivers Reynolds for the holidays. Occasionally funny. Academy Award Nominations: Best Sound Recording; Best Song ("Hold My Hand"). **Cast:** Glenda Farrell, Anne Francis, Alvy Moore, Dick Powell, Debbie Reynolds,

Herb Vigran, Les Tremayne, Maidie Norman, Rita Johnson, Ellen Corby. **Credits:** Dir: Frank Tashlin; Prod: Harriet Parsons; Writer: Alex Gottlieb, Steve Fisher; DP: Nicholas Musuraca; Ed: Harry Marker; Prod Design: Carroll Clark; Composer: Leigh Harline, Jack Lawrence, Richard Myers; Costumes: Michael Woulfe; Art Director: Albert S. D'Agostino. Color, 98 min. **VHS, LASER**

The Suspect
(1944) Universal
In a gripping psychological thriller from director Siodmak, Laughton plays a mild-mannered shopkeeper in Victorian London married to a mean-spirited woman. When he meets Raines, a pretty stenographer, he falls madly in love with her and murders his wife. After beating her to death with a cane, Laughton tells the police that she fell down the stairs. All seems to go according to plan until an irksome neighbor (Daniell), suspecting foul play, decides to blackmail Laughton. After taking care of the busybody, he must now also dispose of his neighbor and the second death heightens police curiosity. **Cast:** Charles Laughton, Ella Raines, Dean Harens, Stanley Ridges, Henry Daniell, Rosalind Ivan, Molly Lamont, Raymond Severn, Eve Amber, Maude Eburne. **Credits:** Dir: Robert Siodmak; Prod: Islin Auster; Writer: Arthur T. Horman, Bertram Millhauser; Story: James Ronald; DP: Paul Ivano; Ed: Arthur Hilton; Composer: Frank Skinner. B&W, 85 min.

Suspicion
(1941) RKO
This Hitchcock thriller has a disappointing, studio-mandated ending, but also winning performances from Grant and Fontaine. In order to escape the oppression of her rigid, wealthy parents, Fontaine embraces the attention of Grant though she knows his reputation as a cad. When his friend Bruce turns up dead, Fontaine begins to think she's next and frets about the nightly glass of milk Grant brings her. Her fears reach a crescendo on a careening drive on a twisting road. Academy Award Nominations: 3, including Best Picture; Best Score. **Academy Awards:** Best Actress: Joan Fontaine. **Cast:** Cary Grant, Joan Fontaine, Cedric Hardwicke, Nigel Bruce, Dame May Whitty, Isabel Jeans, Heather Angel, Reginald Sheffield, Leo G. Carroll, Robert Curtis-Brown. **Credits:** Dir: Alfred Hitchcock; Prod: Alfred Hitchcock; Writer: Samson Raphaelson, Joan Harrison, Alma Reville; DP: Harry Stradling; Ed: William Hamilton;

Prod Design: Van Nest Polglase, Carroll Clark; Composer: Franz Waxman; Costumes: Edward Stevenson; SFX: Vernon L. Walker; Set Designer: Darrell Silvera. B&W, 99 min. **VHS, LASER**

Suzy
(1936) MGM
Chorus girl Harlow weds inventor Tone, but before they can have a honeymoon, a spy (Hume) shoots Tone. Harlow flees to Paris thinking Tone is dead, though he's only wounded. There she becomes involved with and marries dashing WWI aviator Grant, who refuses to give up his dalliances, one of which is with Hume. The spy plot and the tangled amours come unraveled when Tone solicits Grant to fly his experimental plane. The only screen pairing of Harlow and Grant. Script partially by Dorothy Parker. Academy Award Nomination for Best Song ("Did I Remember"). **Cast:** Jean Harlow, Franchot Tone, Cary Grant, Lewis Stone, Benita Hume, Inez Courtney, Elspeth Dudgeon, Tyler Brooke, Robert Livingston, Dennis Morgan. **Credits:** Dir: George Fitzmaurice; Prod: Maurice Revnes; Writer: Dorothy Parker, Alan Campbell, Horace Jackson, Lenore Coffee; DP: Ray June; Ed: George Boemler; Prod Design: Cedric Gibbons, Gabriel Scognamillo, Edwin B. Willis; Composer: William Axt; Costumes: Dolly Tree. B&W, 93 min. **VHS**

Svengali
(1931) Warner Bros.
In a bizarre early talkie, the Great Profile plays the master manipulator. When artists' model Marsh wants to marry into wealth, Barrymore uses mind control to train her singing voice and to promote her musical career. He then begins to dominate her life. Academy Award Nominations: 2, including Best Cinematography. **Cast:** John Barrymore, Marian Marsh, Donald Crisp, Carmel Myers, Lumsden Hare, Luis Alberni, Paul Porcasi. **Credits:** Dir: Archie Mayo; Writer: J. G. Alexander, George L. du Maurier; DP: Barney McGill; Ed: William Holmes; Prod Design: Anton Grot. B&W, 82 min. **VHS**

Swamp Water
(1941) Fox
Great French director Renoir's first Hollywood project takes him far from the boulevards of Paris and into the murky backwaters of the rural South. Brennan is wrongly accused of murder and sent to jail to await execution. He escapes and hides out in Georgia's swamps, where he encounters and befriends Andrews. When Andrews brings Brennan's share of their earnings from trapping to his Brennan's daughter (Baxter), Andrews's jealous girlfriend reveals the whereabouts of the fugitive. Andrews and Baxter desperately try to prove Brennan's innocence. Brennan played the same role again in *Lure of the Wilderness* (1952). **Cast:** Walter Brennan, Walter Huston, Anne Baxter, Dana Andrews, Virginia Gilmore, John Carradine, Mary Howard, Eugene Pallette, Ward Bond, Guinn "Big Boy" Williams. **Credits:** Dir: Jean Renoir; Prod: Irving Pichel; Writer: Dudley Nichols; Story: Vereen Bell; DP: J. Peverell Marley; Ed: Walter Thompson; Prod Design: Richard Day, Joseph C. Wright; Composer: David Buttolph. B&W, 94 min.

The Swan
(1956) MGM
Kelly's last screen production (*High Society* was shot earlier) finds the princess-to-be playing a princess. In this remake of a Lillian Gish film based on a creaky Ferenc Molnar Ruritanian drama, Kelly's mother (Landis) wants to see her married off to the local crown price, Guinness. Kelly, however, loves her tutor, Jourdan. Stylish and charming, with a magnificent supporting cast including Landis and Moorehead as the Queen Mother. **Cast:** Grace Kelly, Alec Guinness, Louis Jourdan, Agnes Moorehead, Jessie Royce Landis, Brian Aherne, Leo G. Carroll, Estelle Winwood, Van Dyke Parks. **Credits:** Dir: Charles Vidor; Prod: Dore Schary; Writer: John Dighton; Story: Ferenc Molnar; DP: Joseph Ruttenberg, Robert Surtees; Ed: John Dunning; Prod Design: Cedric Gibbons; Composer: Bronislau Kaper; Art Director: Randall Duell. Color, 112 min. **VHS, LASER**

Sweet and Lowdown
(1944) Fox
Take a look if you're a fan of Benny Goodman. Young trombone player Cardwell realizes a dream when he is given the chance to play with the Benny Goodman Orchestra. His ego soon swells, and ambitious girlfriend Darnell encourages him to start his own band, which fails miserably. He swallows his pride and returns to the factory job, but Benny gives him another chance. Goodman's swinging tunes include "I'm Making Believe," "Hey, Bub, Let's Have a Ball," "Jersey Bounce," "Let's Dance," and "I Yi Yi Yi Yi, I Like You." Academy Award Nomination for Best Song (" I'm Making Believe"). **Cast:** Benny Goodman, Linda Darnell, Lynn Bari, Jack Oakie, James Cardwell, Allyn Joslyn, John J. Campbell, Roy Benson, Dickie Moore. **Credits:** Dir: Archie Mayo; Prod: William LeBaron; Writer: Richard English; DP: Lucien Ballard; Ed: Dorothy Spencer; Prod Design: Maurice Ransford, Lyle Wheeler; Composer: Charles Henderson, Emil Newman. B&W, 76 min.

Sweet Bird of Youth
(1962) MGM
This is a tour de force for Page in another adaptation of a Tennessee Williams play. Page, always a strong interpreter of Williams fragile heroines, plays a fading, middle-aged movie star who clings to a handsome roughneck (Newman) who has designs on a Hollywood career. First, Newman wants to square things with his hometown girl (Knight), which leads to seamy revelations about Newman and Knight's father (Begley), and a violent climax. Newman, Page, Torn, and Sherwood were all in the Broadway production of the play, which was cleaned up considerably for the movies. Academy Award Nominations: 3, including Best Actress: Geraldine Page; Best Supporting Actress: Shirley Knight. **Academy Awards:** Best Supporting Actor: Ed Begley. **Cast:** Paul Newman, Geraldine Page, Shirley Knight, Ed Begley, Rip Torn, Mildred Dunnock, Madeleine Sherwood, Philip Abbott, Corey Allen. **Credits:** Dir: Richard Brooks; Prod: Pandro S. Berman; Writer: Richard Brooks; DP: Milton Krasner; Ed: Henry Berman; Prod Design: George W. Davis; Composer: Robert Armbruster; Costumes: Orry-Kelly. Color, 120 min. **VHS**

Sweet Charity
(1968) Universal
Tattooed love girl MacLaine gets dumped (literally, off a bridge) by her thug of a boyfriend but finds unlikely romances with an Italian movie star (Montalban) and a nebbishy insurance company clerk (McMartin). Though neither amour works out in the end, MacLaine keeps her trademark twinkle in the eye. Fosse's directing debut shows plenty of his energy, and MacLaine could not be more beautiful (especially with a tattoo). Neil Simon adapted Federico Fellini's *Nights of Cabiria* for his Broadway musical. Songs include "Big Spender," "If My

Sweet Charity (1968)

Friends Could See Me Now," and "Rhythm of Life." Academy Award Nominations: 3, including Best Score; Best Art Direction. **Cast:** Shirley MacLaine, John McMartin, Chita Rivera, Sammy Davis, Jr., Ricardo Montalban, Paula Kelly, Stubby Kaye, Barbara Bouchet. **Credits:** Dir: Bob Fosse; Prod: Robert Arthur; Writer: Peter Stone; DP: Robert Surtees; Ed: Stuart Gilmore; Prod Design: Alexander Golitzen; Composer: Cy Coleman. Color, 148 min. **VHS**

Sweethearts
(1938) MGM
This terrific musical makes wonderful use of Eddy and MacDonald's familiar, devoted screen personas—and a script from Parker and Campbell that's more than a few notches above the singing duo's usual operettas. The couple have been starring in a Broadway production of *Sweethearts*, a Victor Herbert musical, for their entire married lives. They want a break, and consider Hollywood. But the theater crowd and sponging relatives that depend on them for a livelihood won't allow it, and pull a mean trick to keep them together in New York. Academy Award Nominations: Best Sound Recording;

Best Score. **Cast:** Jeanette MacDonald, Nelson Eddy, Ray Bolger, Frank Morgan, Florence Rice, Mischa Auer, Fay Holden, Terry Kilburn. **Credits:** Dir: W. S. Van Dyke; Prod: Hunt Stromberg; Writer: Dorothy Parker, Alan Campbell; DP: Oliver T. Marsh, Allen M. Davey; Ed: Robert J. Kern; Prod Design: Cedric Gibbons; Choreographer: Albertina Rasch; Composer: Victor Herbert, Herbert Stothart. Color, 120 min. **VHS, LASER**

Sweet Rosie O'Grady
(1943) Fox
This is the prototypical Fox Technicolor musical, with the queen of the genre, Grable. After a triumphant tour on the English stage, Grable returns to her Brooklyn home with the besotted and well-pedigreed Duke of Trippingham (Gardiner) in tow. A tabloid reporter and former boyfriend, Young, reveals her rather more humble beginnings as Rosie O'Grady, burlesque princess, and featured attraction at Flugelman's Beer Gardens in the Bowery. As the pair do public battle, they rekindle romance. The songs include "My Heart Tells Me," "My Sam," "Going to the Country Fair," and the title number. **Cast:** Betty Grable, Robert Young, Adolphe Menjou, Reginald Gardiner, Virginia Grey, Phil Regan, Sig Ruman, Alan Dinehart. **Credits:** Dir: Irving Cummings; Prod: William Perlberg; Writer: Ken Englund; Story: William Lipman, Frederick Stephani, Edward Van Every; DP: James Basevi, Joseph C. Wright; Composer: Harry Warren. Color, 74 min.

Sweet Smell of Success
(1957) United Artists
New York's a tough town, and this is one tough movie. A film-noir masterpiece that's lit with the pulsing neon of Broadway, set in the world of tabloid gossip and populated with desperate characters who live on other people's misery. Lancaster rules the newspaper columns, making and breaking careers from his corner table, and Curtis (in the finest performance of his career) prostrates himself at the big man's feet, clawing for column inches for his clients. Curtis gets a shot at a PR flack's dream, an open door for his items into Lancaster's column—if he can stop a romance between Lancaster's sister (Harrison) and a jazz musician (Milner). Terrific performances and moody atmospherics from famed cameraman Howe. Selected for the National Film Registry. **Cast:** Burt Lancaster, Tony Curtis, Martin Milner, Susan Harrison,

Sam Levene, Barbara Nichols, Jeff Donnell, Edith Atwater, Emile Meyer. **Credits:** Dir: Alexander Mackendrick; Prod: James Hill; Writer: Clifford Odets; DP: James Wong Howe; Ed: Alan Crosland, Jr.; Composer: Elmer Bernstein; Art Director: Edward Carrere. B&W, 97 min. **VHS, LASER**

The Swimmer
(1968) Columbia
This is the only feature film adapted from the work of John Cheever, the master chronicler of upper-middle-class American suburbia circa the '50s and '60s. Lancaster plays an alienated middle-aged man who navigates through an affluent Connecticut community by attempting to swim home from one backyard pool to another. Each pool and each encounter reveals more about Lancaster's character: his past, dreams, and failures. An original, literate, and underrated fable from Frank and Eleanor Perry about contemporary American life and the illusions of success and happiness. **Cast:** Burt Lancaster, Janet Landgard, Janice Rule, Tony Bickley, Marge Champion, Kim Hunter, Rose Gregorio, Charles Drake. **Credits:** Dir: Frank Perry; Prod: Frank Perry, Roger Lewis; Writer: Eleanor Perry, John Cheever; DP: David Quaid, Michael Nebbia; Ed: Sidney Katz, Carl Lerner; Composer: Marvin Hamlisch; Art Director: Peter Dohanos. Color, 94 min. **VHS, LASER**

Swing High, Swing Low
(1937) Paramount
This is an overly familiar reworking of the stage production *Burlesque,* which was filmed previously as *Dance of Life* and, following this, as *When My Baby Smiles at Me* (1948). In this trot around the block, MacMurray plays a trumpeter smitten by singer Lombard (Lombard sang on-screen for the first time here) on a ship to Panama. After he becomes a hit in Central America, he takes a gig in New York backing up sultry Lamour. Lombard gets the picture and splits, and MacMurray hits the skids until true love prevails. The songs include the title number and "Spring Is in the Air." **Cast:** Carole Lombard, Fred MacMurray, Dorothy Lamour, Charles Butterworth, Jean Dixon, Franklin Pangborn, Harvey Stephens, Cecil Cunningham, Charles Arnt. **Credits:** Dir: Mitchell Leisen; Prod: Arthur Hornblow; Writer: Virginia Van Upp; DP: Ted Tetzlaff; Ed: Eda Warren; Prod Design: Hans Dreier; Composer: Boris Morros. B&W, 95 min. **VHS**

Swing Time

(1935) RKO

Here is one of the high points of the Astaire-Rogers team, and, therefore, one of the greatest of Depression-era song-and-dance spectaculars. The story involves a gambler and dancer (Astaire—and how many times do you see that combination?) who's engaged to marry Furness, but first must raise $25,000 to prove he can support her. When he meets dance teacher Rogers at Blore's dance academy, all thoughts of money fly away. The scene in which Rogers teaches Astaire to dance and the justly famous "The Way You Look Tonight" sequence are standouts. Stevens gives the familiar formula a witty lift and the Kern-Fields numbers delight. Priceless. The laserdisc edition includes audio commentary by John Mueller (author of *Astaire Dancing: The Musical Films*), a photo scrapbook of behind-the-scenes stills, and a clip for the 1935 RKO film *Hooray for Love*, with Bill "Bojangles" Robinson and Fats Waller. **Academy Awards:** Best Song ("The Way You Look Tonight"). **Cast:** Fred Astaire, Ginger Rogers, Victor Moore, Helen Broderick, Eric Blore, Betty Furness, Georges Metaxa, Landers Stevens. **Credits:** Dir: George Stevens; Prod: Pandro S. Berman; Writer: Howard Lindsay; DP: David Abel; Ed: Henry Berman; Prod Design: Van Nest Polglase; Composer: Jerome Kern, Dorothy Fields. B&W, 120 min. VHS, LASER

Swiss Family Robinson

(1940) RKO

Johann Wyss's novel gets its first big-budget movie adaptation. Mitchell pulls his family together after they're shipwrecked on their way from London to Australia. They adapt to their tropical surroundings with ingenuity and learn to love their new home. Academy Award Nomination for Best Visual Effects. **Cast:** Thomas Mitchell, Edna Best, Freddie Bartholomew, Tim Holt, John Wray, Herbert Rawlinson, Christian Rub. **Credits:** Dir: Edward Ludwig; Prod: Gene Towne, Graham Baker; Writer: Walter Ferris, Gene Towne, Graham Baker; DP: Nicholas Musuraca; Ed: George Crone; SFX: Vernon Walker. B&W, 92 min. VHS

Swiss Family Robinson

(1960) Disney

This Disney favorite is the third, and most lavish, adaptation of the family classic. Mills and McGuire lead their family from the despotic regime of Napoleon, and get chased off course by a band of pirates. They are shipwrecked on a tropical island, where they begin a new, adventuresome life. Good fun that holds adult attention, too, with lush dreams of a desert island home. **Cast:** John Mills, Dorothy McGuire, James MacArthur, Janet Munro, Sessue Hayakawa, Tommy Kirk, Kevin Corcoran, Cecil Parker. **Credits:** Dir: Ken Annakin; Prod: Bill Anderson; Writer: Lowell S. Hawley; Story: Johann Wyss; DP: Harry Waxman; Ed: Peter Boita; Prod Design: John Howell; Composer: William Alwyn, Muir Mathieson. Color, 127 min. VHS, LASER

The Sword and the Rose

(1953) Disney

This British Disney swashbuckler stars Todd as a mercenary in love with Mary Tudor (Johns), sister of Henry VIII (Justice). A jealous Duke of Buckingham (Gough) seeks to thwart the lovers, resulting in much court intrigue, imprisonment in the Tower of London, and a final duel. Adapted from Charles Major's novel *When Knighthood Was in Flower*, previously filmed in 1923. **Cast:** Richard Todd, Glynis Johns, James Robertson Justice, Michael Gough, Jane Barrett, Peter Copley, Rosalie Crutchley, Ernest Jay. **Credits:** Dir: Ken Annakin; Prod: Perce Pearce; Writer: Lawrence Edward Watkin; DP: Geoffrey Unsworth; Ed: Gerald Thomas; Prod Design: Carmen Dillon; Composer: Clifton Parker. Color, 92 min. VHS, LASER

Sylvia Scarlett

(1935) RKO

A cult curiosity that finds Hepburn in boyish drag for most of the movie. Hepburn dons boys' clothes to evade detection by the police and to help her father, Gwenn, smuggle some expensive stolen lace. They're caught when jewel thief Grant tips the cops. Hepburn gives Grant a pop in the nose, but earns a place in his racket. When she meets wealthy Aherne, their mutual attraction has Aherne scratching his head, until he figures out the gender switch. Hepburn gets to perform much derring-do, something she couldn't have done in a role that required a dress. **Cast:** Katharine Hepburn, Cary Grant, Brian Aherne, Edmund Gwenn, Dennis Moore, Lennox Pawle, Daisy Belmore, Elsa Buchanan. **Credits:** Dir: George Cukor; Prod: Pandro S. Berman; Writer: Gladys Unger; DP: Joseph H. August; Ed: Jane Loring; Composer: Roy Webb; Art Director: Van Nest Polglase. B&W, 94 min. VHS, LASER

Syncopation

(1942) RKO

Young trumpeter Cooper takes the big river up to the Windy City to start his own band. In Chicago, he falls for jazz-singing Granville, who has just lost her man in the war. As their romance and careers develop, we get to meet the greatest names in '40s jazz, including Gene Krupa and Benny Goodman. The picture ends with one of the hottest all-star jam sessions ever caught on celluloid. Numbers include "Goin' Up the River," "You Made Me Love You," "Chicago Ragtime," and "Slave Market." **Cast:** Adolphe Menjou, Jackie Cooper, Bonita Granville, George Bancroft, Ted North, Connee Boswell, Frank Jenks, Jessica Grayson, Mona Barrie, Gene Krupa. **Credits:** Dir: William Dieterle; Prod: William Dieterle; Writer: Frank Cavett, Phillip Yordan; DP: J. Roy Hunt; Ed: John Sturges; Prod Design: Albert S. D'Agostino; Composer: Leith Stevens. B&W, 88 min.

Tabu

(1931) Paramount
This visually stunning work of cinema art was created by a mismatched pair of geniuses, documentary trailblazer Flaherty and expressionist Murnau. The result tells a poetic story of man, nature, and ritual. A South Sea island beauty, Chevalier, has been deemed "taboo" to all men because she has been offered to the gods. But she and a pearl diver fall deeply in love and their doomed relationship must eventually come to a tragic end. As interesting—and tragic—as the film itself is the story of its production. Flaherty, who co-scripted the film with Murnau based on his observations of life on the island, left in the middle of production due to artistic differences. Then, just days before the film's release, Murnau was killed in an automobile accident. Selected for the National Film Registry. **Academy Awards:** Best Cinematography. **Cast:** Anna Chevalier, Matahi. **Credits:** Dir: F. W. Murnau, Robert J. Flaherty; Writer: Edgar G. Ulmer, F. W. Murnau, Robert J. Flaherty; DP: Floyd Crosby; Ed: Arthur A. Brooks; Composer: Hugo Riesenfeld, Frederic Chopin, Bedrich Smetana. B&W, 82 min. **VHS, LASER**

Take a Letter, Darling

(1942) Paramount
This gender-bending screwball comedy has Russell, an advertising executive, facing a delicate problem: Her male clients' wives jump to the wrong conclusions about the way she handles their accounts. She hires artist MacMurray as her assistant and stand-in when a phony fiancé would be handy. But her one female client, Moore, seems too much attracted to MacMurray and the usually buttoned-up Russell realizes she's gaga for her guy Friday. Watch for Benchley's wry humor in support. Academy Award Nominations: 3, including Best Cinematography. **Cast:** Rosalind Russell, Fred Mac-

Murray, Macdonald Carey, Constance Moore, Robert Benchley, Charles Arnt, Cecil Kellaway, Kathleen Howard, Margaret Seddon, Dooley Wilson. **Credits:** Dir: Mitchell Leisen; Prod: Mitchell Leisen; Writer: Claude Binyon; Story: George Beck; DP: John J. Mescall; Ed: Doane Harrison, Thomas Scott; Composer: Victor Young. B&W, 92 min.

Take Me Out to the Ballgame

(1949) MGM
Williams takes over a turn-of-the-century baseball team and comes into conflict with two of the team's best players, Sinatra and Kelly (who take their song-and-dance act on the road in the off-season). But Williams comes to the rescue when Kelly gets involved with gambler Arnold. This was Berkeley's last directorial effort; Kelly and Donen directed the musical sequences, preparing them for *On the Town* the following year. The title song, "O'Brien to Ryan to Goldberg," and "The Hat My Father Wore on St. Patrick's Day" are musical home runs. **Cast:** Gene Kelly, Frank Sinatra, Esther Williams, Betty Garrett, Edward Arnold, Jules Munshin, Richard Lane, Tom Dugan, Murray Alper, Wilton Graff. **Credits:** Dir: Busby Berkeley; Prod: Arthur Freed; Writer: Harry Tugend, Harry Crane, George Wells; DP: George J. Folsey; Ed: Blanche Sewell; Prod Design: Cedric Gibbons, Daniel B. Cathcart; Choreographer: Stanley Donen; Composer: Roger Edens; Costumes: Helen Rose; SFX: Warren Newcombe, Peter Ballbusch; Set Designer: Edwin B. Willis, Henry Grace. Color, 90 min. **VHS, LASER**

Take the High Ground

(1953) MGM
This WWII film focuses on men in boot camp as they turn from civilians into soldiers. Top sergeant Widmark drives them hard and C.O. Malden soothes their fears. Among the troops are a poet, a gymnast, and a Texan, all fac-

ing the uncertainty of war, conflicts among themselves, and the absence of their wives and girlfriends. Academy Award Nomination: Best Original Screenplay. **Cast:** Richard Widmark, Karl Malden, Elaine Stewart, Carleton Carpenter, Russ Tambly, Jerome Courtland, Steve Forrest, Robert Arthur. **Credits:** Dir: Richard Brooks; Prod: Dore Schary; Writer: Millard Kaufman; DP: John Alton; Ed: John Dunning; Composer: Dimitri Tiomkin, Ned Washington; Art Director: Cedric Gibbons. Color, 101 min.

Take the Money and Run

(1969) Cinerama
In Allen's directorial debut, he also stars as Virgil Starkwell, a bumbling small-time criminal whose career unfolds in a hilarious mockumentary. A nonstop barrage of sight gags and hysterical one-liners spoofs every aspect of crime and prison movies, and will delight anyone who loves the Warner Bros. gangster genre. **Cast:** Woody Allen, Janet Margolin, Marcel Hillaire, Jacquelyn Hyde, Lonny Chapman, Jan Merlin, James Anderson, Howard Storm, Mack Gordon. **Credits:** Dir: Woody Allen; Prod: Charles H. Joffe; Writer: Woody Allen, Mickey Rose; DP: Lester Shorr, Fouad Said; Ed: Ralph Rosenblum, James Heckert, Ron Kalish; Composer: Marvin Hamlisch. Color, 85 min. **VHS, LASER**

The Taking of Pelham One Two Three

(1974) United Artists
A gang, led by the relentless Shaw, hijacks a subway train carrying the usual cross section of New York City humanity. They threaten to shoot one each minute unless a $1 million ransom is paid in one hour. After the ransom is delivered, the men attempt an escape by sending the subway car careening down the tunnel without a driver. Matthau is the transit authority's chief of security who must try to

end the incident without casualties. A claustrophobic setting and the crackling dialogue between Matthau and Shaw raise the tension. **Cast:** Walter Matthau, Robert Shaw, Martin Balsam, Hector Elizondo, Earl Hindman, James Broderick, Dick O'Neill, Lee Wallace. **Credits:** Dir: Joseph Sargent; Prod: Gabriel Katzka, Edgar J. Scherick; Writer: Peter Stone, John Godey; DP: Owen Roizman; Ed: Jerry Greenberg, Robert Q. Lovett; Composer: David Shire; Art Director: Gene Rudolf. Color, 105 min. **VHS**

A Tale of Two Cities
(1935) MGM
In a striking adaptation of the oft-filmed Dickens tale set during the French Revolution, Colman portrays Sydney Carton, a carefree lawyer who springs into action, aiding victims of the Reign of Terror, sparking love and, eventually, an ultimate sacrifice. Haunting, dark photography adds mood to the proceedings, and the supporting performances are all standouts (in particular, screen rookie Yurka's Mme. Defarge). This was an immediate blockbuster and boosted Selznick's fortunes. Jacques Tourneur directed the second-unit crowd scenes. Academy Award Nominations: Best Picture and Best Film Editing. **Cast:** Ronald Colman, Elizabeth Allan, Basil Rathbone, Edna May Oliver, Blanche Yurka, Reginald Owen, Henry B. Walthall, Donald Woods, Walter Catlett. **Credits:** Dir: Jack Conway; Prod: David O. Selznick; Writer: W. P. Lipscomb, S. N. Behrman; Story: Charles Dickens; DP: Oliver T. Marsh; Ed: Conrad A. Nervig; Prod Design: Cedric Gibbons, Fred Hope; Composer: Herbert Stothart. B&W, 128 min. **VHS, LASER**

Tales of Manhattan
(1942) Fox
Thirteen screenwriters (including Hecht, Stewart, and even an uncredited Keaton) and a long list of stars come together for this episodic narrative about the path a tailcoat takes from swanky Manhattan soirees to scarecrow tatters and the effects it has on each owner. The stories range from comedic to touching to ironic, dealing with various issues such as love and passion, crime and punishment. Fields's contribution was edited out of the film, but it has been restored to the video release. **Cast:** Charles Boyer, Rita Hayworth, Thomas Mitchell, Ginger Rogers, Henry Fonda, Charles Laughton, Edward G. Robin-

son, W. C. Fields, Paul Robinson, Eddie Anderson. **Credits:** Dir: Julien Duvivier; Prod: Boris Morros, Sam Spiegel; Writer: Ben Hecht, Ferenc Molnar, Donald Ogden Stewart, Samuel Hoffenstein, Alan Campbell, Ladislaus Fodor, Laszlo Vadnay, Laszlo Gorog, Lamar Trotti, Henry Blankfort, Buster Keaton, Edmund Beloin, William Morrow; DP: Joseph Walker; Prod Design: Richard Day, Boris Leven; Composer: Sol Kaplan; Costumes: Irene; Set Designer: Thomas Little. B&W, 118 min. **VHS**

Talk About a Stranger
(1952) MGM
The first film of director Bradley, the auteur responsible for *They Saved Hitler's Brain*, featured future White House occupant Davis as the mistress of a citrus farmer. When their son's (soon-to-be-sitcom-star Gray) dog gets poisoned, the whole town hums with rumors about mysterious new townsman, Stone. **Cast:** George Murphy, Nancy Davis, Billy Gray, Lewis Stone, Maude Wallace, Kurt Kazsnar, Katharine Warren, Teddy Infuhr, Stanley Andrews, Anna Glomb. **Credits:** Dir: David Bradley; Prod: Richard Goldstone; Writer: Charlotte Armstrong, Margaret Fitts; DP: John Alton; Ed: Newell Kimlin; Composer: David Buttolph; Art Director: Cedric Gibbons, Eddie Imazu. B&W, 65 min.

The Talk of the Town
(1942) Columbia
The combination of a tight, witty script and the talents of the leading threesome make this a smart, must-see comedy. Grant, accused of arson and murder in a factory fire, hides out in the attic of old friend Arthur's country house. She also lets a room to law professor Colman, as he awaits word of his Supreme Court nomination. Grant's case and Arthur both intrigue Colman, and he comes to Grant's defense when he's pursued by a lynch mob. Two endings were shot, and a viewer poll determined who gets the girl. Academy Award Nominations: 7, including Best Picture, Best Original Story, Best Screenplay. **Cast:** Cary Grant, Jean Arthur, Ronald Colman, Edgar Buchanan, Glenda Farrell, Charles Dingle, Emma Dunn, Rex Ingram. **Credits:** Dir: George Stevens; Prod: George Stevens; Writer: Irwin Shaw, Sidney Buchman, Sidney Harmon; DP: Ted Tetzlaff; Ed: Otto Meyer; Prod Design: Rudolph Sternad; Composer: Frederick Hollander; Art Director: Lionel Banks. B&W, 118 min. **VHS, LASER**

Tall in the Saddle
(1944) RKO
Wayne wanted Ford to direct this, and it would have added an interesting element to an entertaining Western that combines gunplay with mystery and a look at women's roles in the West. Wayne, a cowhand who refuses to work for women, encounters two women ranch owners, including the feisty Raines, as he looks for work. When he helps Long keep control of her ranch, he runs afoul of the corrupt town leaders led by Bond. He changes his point of view toward women when Raines helps him out of a jam and he learns he is the rightful owner of a ranch. **Cast:** John Wayne, Ella Raines, George "Gabby" Hayes, Ward Bond, Audrey Long, Elisabeth Risdon, Don Douglas, Russell Wade, Frank Puglia, Paul Fix, Harry Woods. **Credits:** Dir: Edwin L. Marin; Prod: Robert Fellows; Writer: Michael Hogan, Paul Fix; DP: Robert de Grasse; Ed: Philip Martin; Prod Design: Albert S. D'Agostino, Ralph Berger; Composer: Roy Webb; SFX: Vernon L. Walker. B&W, 87 min. **VHS, LASER**

The Tall Men
(1955) Fox
This sturdy Western from Walsh features Gable and Mitchell as ex-Confederate soldiers who turn to thievery in order to survive. When they waylay Ryan, he signs them up for his cattle drive. Along the way, they battle the elements and each other after they pick up Indian attack survivor Russell. Russell has big dreams and chooses her man accordingly. **Cast:** Clark Gable, Robert Ryan, Jane Russell, Cameron Mitchell, Juan Garcia, Harry Shannon, Emile Meyer, Steve Darrell, Will Wright, Robert Adler. **Credits:** Dir: Raoul Walsh; Prod: William A. Bacher, William B. Hawks; Writer: Sydney Boehm, Frank S. Nugent; Story: Clay Fisher; DP: Leo Tover; Ed: Louis Loeffler; Prod Design: Lyle Wheeler, Mark-Lee Kirk; Composer: Victor Young. Color, 122 min. **VHS**

Tall Story
(1960) Warner Bros.
This is a mild romantic comedy mostly notable for Fonda's debut as a tall girl who enrolls in a college known for its basketball team. She becomes a cheerleader and quickly falls for star player Perkins. The romance throws off Perkins's studies and their marriage plans get him mixed up with gamblers who want him to throw an important game against the Russians. Based on Lindsay and Crouse's play.

Cast: Anthony Perkins, Jane Fonda, Ray Walston, Marc Connelly, Anne Jackson, Murray Hamilton, Elizabeth Patterson, Bob Wright, Gary Lockwood, Bart Burns. **Credits:** Dir: Joshua Logan; Prod: Joshua Logan; Writer: Julius J. Epstein; Story: Russel Crouse, Howard Lindsay, Howard Nemerov; DP: Ellsworth Fredericks; Ed: Philip Anderson; Composer: Cyril Mockridge. B&W, 92 min. VHS, LASER

The Tall Target
(1951) MGM
Abraham Lincoln's bodyguard, John Kennedy (Powell), speeds toward Baltimore on a train from Washington as he unravels an assassination plot. His suspicions were ignored by his superiors so he's faced with finding the suspect on a trainful of passengers on the Night Express alone. Trusting no one, Powell keeps track of at least 5 suspicious passengers, and will encounter not one, but multiple would-be assassins. An intriguing historical mystery directed by Mann. **Cast:** Dick Powell, Paula Raymond, Adolphe Menjou, Marshall Thompson, Ruby Dee, Will Geer, Richard Rober, Florence Bates, Voctor Killian, Katherine Warren. **Credits:** Dir: Anthony Mann; Prod: Richard Goldstone; Writer: George Worthing, Arthur Cohn, Geoffrey Homes, George Worthing Yates; DP: Paul C. Vogel; Prod Design: Cedric Gibbons, Eddie Imazu. B&W, 78 min.

The Taming of the Shrew
(1967) Columbia
Director Zeffirelli established his reputation for Shakespearean adaptations with this bawdy setting of the Bard. The audience's familiarity with the Battling Burtons gives another dimension to Burton and Taylor's portrayals of bickering and squabbling Petruchio and Katherine. He wants to win her heart (and her pocketbook) but she seems to hate every man that she meets. When Burton tames Taylor, fulfilling her father's demand that his shrewish daughter marry before sweet Pyne, York makes his move on Pyne. One of the most-filmed Shakespearean stories, going before the cameras eight times. Features an excellent score by Rota. Academy Award Nominations: Best Art Direction; Best Costume Design. **Cast:** Elizabeth Taylor, Richard Burton, Michael York, Natasha Pyne, Vernon Dobtcheff, Michael Hordern, Alfred Lynch, Alan Webb, Victor Spinetti, Roy Holder. **Credits:** Dir: Franco Zeffirelli; Prod: Richard Burton, Elizabeth Taylor, Franco Zeffirelli; Writer: Paul Dehn, Suso Cecchi D'Am-

ico, Franco Zeffirelli; Story: William Shakespeare; DP: Luciano Trasatti, Oswald Morris; Ed: Peter Taylor, Carlo Fabianelli; Prod Design: John DeCuir; Composer: Nino Rota; Art Director: Giuseppe Mariani, Elven Webb. Color, 126 min. VHS, LASER

Tammy and the Bachelor
(1957) Universal
A backwoods country girl (Reynolds) nurses a crashed pilot back to health and falls in love with him in the process. When she meets his uppity family, they don't know how to respond. Of course, she eventually charms them with her simple "down-home" attitude, and the rest is history (history, in this case, being two sequels and a television series). Reynolds's hit song "Tammy" brought even more attention to the picture. Academy Award Nomination for Best Song ("Tammy"). **Cast:** Debbie Reynolds, Leslie Nielsen, Walter Brennan, Mala Powers, Sidney Blackmer, Mildred Natwick, Fay Wray, Philip Ober, Craig Hill, Louise Beavers. **Credits:** Dir: Joseph Pevney; Prod: Ross Hunter; Writer: Oscar Brodney; DP: Arthur E. Arling; Ed: Ted J. Kent; Composer: Ray Evans, Jay Livingston, Frank Skinner; Costumes: Bill Thomas. Color, 89 min. VHS

Tammy and the Doctor
(1963) Universal
In this sequel to *Tammy and the Bachelor*, Dee takes over the duties from Debbie Reynolds. Dee plays a nurse's aide who becomes the target of a charming doctor's affections. Pretty standard fare, but notable for being Peter Fonda's film debut. **Cast:** Sandra Dee, Peter Fonda, Macdonald Carey, Beulah Bondi, Margaret Lindsay, Reginald Owen, Alice Pearce, Adam West, Stanley Clements, Doodles Weaver. **Credits:** Dir: Harry Keller; Prod: Ross Hunter; Writer: Oscar Brodney; DP: Russell Metty; Ed: Milton Carruth; Prod Design: Alexander Golitzen, George C. Webb; Composer: Frank Skinner; Costumes: Rosemary Odell; Set Designer: Howard Bristol. Color, 88 min. VHS

Tarantula
(1955) Universal
This is considered by many to be the best entry in the "horrifically enlarged bug" genre popular at the height of Cold War paranoia. A well-intentioned scientist's new growth formula keeps working and working, until his tarantula subject gets loose in the Arizona desert, grows to mammoth propor-

tions, and develops a taste for humans. It's up to the Air Force and their jet squadron leader (Eastwood) to put an end to this threat to civilization as we know it. Great special effects. **Cast:** John Agar, Mara Corday, Leo G. Carroll, Nestor Paiva, Ross Elliott, Raymond Bailey, Steve Darrell, Eddie Parker, Clint Eastwood, Billy Wayne. **Credits:** Dir: Jack Arnold; Prod: William Alland; Writer: Robert M. Fresco, Martin Berkeley; DP: George Robinson, Clifford Stine; Ed: William Morgan; Prod Design: Alexander Golitzen, Alfred Sweeney; Composer: Henry Mancini; Costumes: Jay Morley; SFX: David Horsley. B&W, 81 min. VHS

Targets
(1968) Paramount
Bogdanovich's sterling directorial debut came when producer Corman had a few more days left on Karloff's contract when he finished *The Terror* early. It still resonates creepily. By telling the parallel stories of an aging horror star (Karloff) who decides to retire, convinced that the real world is too frightening for his films to have any impact, and the boy-next-door psychopathic sniper (O'Kelly) who supports this theory far too well, Bogdanovich makes a powerful point in an inventive story. The tense climax takes place as O'Kelly snipes through a drive-in screen (showing *The Terror*) as star Karloff stalks him offscreen. **Cast:** Boris Karloff, Tim O'Kelly, Randy Quaid, Nancy Hsueh, Arthur Peterson, Mary Jackson, Tanya Morgan, Sandy Baron, Stafford Morgan, Timothy C. Burns. **Credits:** Dir: Peter Bogdanovich; Prod: Peter Bogdanovich; Writer: Peter Bogdanovich, Polly Platt; DP: Laszlo Kovacs; Ed: Peter Bogdanovich; Composer: Brian Stonestreet, Charles Greene. Color, 90 min. VHS

The Tarnished Angels
(1957) Universal
Sirk gives Faulkner a stirring adaptation. His version of the novelist's *Pylon*, a story based on Faulkner's barnstorming brother, reunites the three leads of Sirk's *Written on the Wind* (1957). In Depression-era New Orleans, journalist Hudson gets the assignment to cover a trio of stuntfliers, pilot Stack, his wing-walker wife Malone, and mechanic Carson. He becomes intrigued by the former WWI ace Stack, and feels sympathy for Malone, who offers herself to a leering businessman to get her husband access to an experimental plane. The plane brings the barnstorming family tragedy. Well-acted, well-produced

The Kings of Swing: A Tarzan Timeline

Elmo Lincoln (1918–1921). Three films. Former railroad engineer. Donned wild wig, killed actual lion in *Tarzan of the Apes* (1918).

Gene Pollar (1920). One film. Former New York City fireman. "As an actor, Gene was a great fireman."—Edgar Rice Burroughs on Pollar's performance in *The Revenge of Tarzan* (1920).

James Hubert Pierce (1927). One film, the last Tarzan silent, *Tarzan and the Golden Lion* (1927). All-American football hero. Married Edgar Rice Burroughs's daughter.

Frank Merrill (1928–1929). Two films. Champion weightlifter and gymnast. Usurped lead in *Tarzan the Mighty* (1928) when original star broke leg during vine-swinging mishap.

Johnny Weissmuller (1932–1948). Twelve films, including *Tarzan and His Mate* (1934) and *Tarzan Finds a Son!* (1939). Five-time Olympic gold-medalist swimmer. Model for BVD swimwear. Invented Tarzan yell. Buried in Acapulco, Mexico, site of his last Tarzan shoot.

Lawrence "Buster" Crabbe (1933). One film, the rarely screened *Tarzan the Fearless* (1933). Olympic gold-medalist swimmer. Went on to star in Flash Gordon and Buck Rogers serials. Wrote 1970 bestseller *Energetics*.

Herman Brix (1935, 1938). Two films. Olympic shot-putter hand-picked by Edgar Rice Burroughs for *The New Adventures of Tarzan* (1935) and *Tarzan and the Green Goddess* (1938).

Glenn Morris (1938). One film, *Tarzan's Revenge* (1938). Olympic decathlete. Only appeared in one other movie, *Hold That Coed* (1938).

Lex Barker (1949–1953). Five films, including *Tarzan's Savage Fury* (1952). Princeton University dropout. Appeared in *The Farmer's Daughter* (1947) and *Mr. Blandings Builds His Dream House* (1948). Ex-wives include Arlene Dahl and Lana Turner.

Gordon Scott (1955–1960). Five films, including *Tarzan's Hidden Jungle* (1955). Former fireman, drill sergeant, cowboy, and lifeguard; was discovered working poolside at Las Vegas's Sahara by Hollywood agent.

Denny Miller (1959). One film, 1959's *Tarzan, the Ape Man*. UCLA basketball star. Played Duke Shannon on television's *Wagon Train*.

Jock Mahoney (1962–1963). One film, *Tarzan Goes to India* (1962). Stuntman, WWII fighter pilot, horse breeder. Played the villain in *Tarzan the Magnificent* (1960).

Mike Henry (1966–1968). Three films, including *Tarzan and the Valley of Gold* (1966). Former linebacker for Pittsburgh Steelers and Los Angeles Rams.

Ron Ely (1970). Two films, including *Tarzan's Deadly Silence* (1970). Former pro football player. Host of Miss America pageant 1979 to 1981 and '80s game show *Stop the Music!*

Miles O'Keeffe (1981). One film, *Tarzan, the Ape Man*, with Bo Derek. Spoke no words in whole film, beyond jungle call. Played prehistoric warrior Ator in three films, including 1984's *The Blade Master*.

Christopher Lambert (1984). One film, *Greystoke: The Legend of Tarzan, Lord of the Apes*. U.N. diplomat's son. Starred as Scottish warrior in '90s Highlander films. Attended Paris Conservatoire.

---

melodrama. **Cast:** Rock Hudson, Robert Stack, Dorothy Malone, Jack Carson, Troy Donahue, Robert Middleton, Robert J. Wilke, Phil Harvey. **Credits:** Dir: Douglas Sirk; Prod: Albert Zugsmith; Writer: George Zuckerman; Story: William Faulkner; DP: Irving Glassberg; Ed: Russell Schoengarth; Composer: Frank Skinner; Art Director: Alexander Golitzen, Alfred Sweeney. B&W, 91 min. **VHS**

Tarnished Lady

(1931) Paramount
In Cukor's first solo outing and Bankhead's first talkie, a gold digger (Bankhead) marries a well-to-do but mild-mannered man (Brook) for his money. After growing bored with society niceties, she finds action and thrills in the hot Harlem nightclubs. But when an unexpected pregnancy is paired with a financial downfall, the once ambitious woman finds that there's "not a thing convenient about a marriage of convenience." Bankhead got the big studio build-up for her debut, but she never succeeded in translating an outsized personality into screen stardom. **Cast:** Tallulah Bankhead, Clive Brook, Phoebe Foster, Alex Kirkland, Osgood Perkins, Elizabeth Patterson, Eric Blore, Edward Gargan. **Credits:** Dir: George Cukor; Prod: Walter Wanger; Writer: Donald Ogden Stewart; DP: Larry Williams; Ed: Barney Rogan. B&W, 83 min.

Tarzan

Over the years, no less than 10 beefcake actors have stripped to their loincloths to play Tarzan, but one remains etched in our memory: Olympic swimmer Johnny Weissmuller. Indeed, MGM's most memorable Tarzan entries featured the chiseled Weissmuller and Jane as played by Maureen O'Sullivan. They teamed up for six films between 1932 and 1942, beginning with *Tarzan, the Ape Man*. *Tarzan and His Mate* (1934) marked the last Tarzan film geared for an adult audience; it even features a nude underwater ballet of sorts that still draws gasps at screenings of restored prints. With the motion-picture industry's newly established Code in place, the subsequent entries became family fare. The first Tarzan, 1918's silent *Tarzan of the Apes*, was most faithful to Edgar Rice Burroughs's Lord of the Jungle. While later installments strayed from Burroughs's original characters, the production values of the films of the 1930s and '40s were consistently high. Many of the films were shot in tropical locations, such as Africa and Guatemala, providing lush settings and lending authenticity to the films. And the movies were never short on action, with Tarzan often battling greedy poachers or hunters invading his territory. The series' later entries became contrived, though they made for unusually exotic Saturday-afternoon TV fare for baby-boomer kids.

Tarzan of the Apes *(1918)*
The Romance of Tarzan *(1918)*
Son of Tarzan *(1920)*
The Revenge of Tarzan *(1920)*
The Adventures of Tarzan *(1921)*
Tarzan and the Golden Lion *(1927)*
Tarzan the Mighty *(1928)*
Tarzan, the Ape Man *(1932)*
Tarzan the Fearless *(1933)*
Tarzan and His Mate *(1934)*
The New Adventures of Tarzan *(1935)*
Tarzan Escapes *(1936)*
Tarzan's Revenge *(1938)*
Tarzan and the Green Goddess *(1938)*
Tarzan Finds a Son! *(1939)*
Tarzan's Secret Treasure *(1941)*
Tarzan's New York Adventure *(1942)*
Tarzan Triumphs *(1943)*
Tarzan's Desert Mystery *(1941)*
Tarzan and the Amazons *(1945)*
Tarzan and the Leopard Woman *(1946)*
Tarzan and the Huntress *(1947)*
Tarzan and the Mermaids *(1948)*
Tarzan's Magic Fountain *(1949)*
Tarzan and the Slave Girl *(1950)*
Tarzan's Peril *(1951)*
Tarzan's Savage Fury *(1952)*
Tarzan and the She-Devil *(1953)*
Tarzan's Hidden Jungle *(1955)*
Tarzan and the Lost Safari *(1957)*
Tarzan's Fight for Life *(1958)*
Tarzan and the Trappers *(1958)*
Tarzan's Greatest Adventure *(1959)*
Tarzan, the Ape Man *(1959)*
Tarzan the Magnificent *(1960)*
Tarzan Goes to India *(1962)*
Tarzan's Three Challenges *(1963)*
Tarzan's Jungle Rebellion *(1965)*
Tarzan and the Valley of Gold *(1966)*
Tarzan and the Great River *(1967)*
Tarzan and the Perils of Charity Jones *(1967)*
Tarzan and the Four O'Clock Army *(1968)*
Tarzan and the Jungle Boy *(1968)*
Tarzan's Deadly Silence *(1970)*

Taxi!
(1932) Warner Bros.
Here is the famous, slam-bang Warner Bros. tough-guy movie in which Cagney mouths off in Yiddish with an Irish brogue and dances the Peabody. Inde-

Taxi Driver (1976)

pendent cabbie Cagney and Kibbee topple the viciously corrupt taxi racket that sent Cagney's friend to jail and killed his brother. Cagney brings his signature ferocity, Young is the girl he loves who would tame him, and Raft (a pal of Cagney's from New York hoofing days) does a mean Peabody. **Cast:** James Cagney, Loretta Young, Georgie Stone, George Raft, Guy Kibbee, Ray Cooke, Leila Bennett, Dorothy Burgess, Matt McHugh, David Landau. **Credits:** Dir: Roy Del Ruth, William H. Cannon; Writer: Kubec Glasmon, Kenyon Nicholson, John Bright; DP: James Van Trees; Ed: James Gibbon, Ralph Dawson; Composer: Leo F. Forbstein; Art Director: Esdras Hartley. B&W, 70 min.

Taxi Driver
(1976) Columbia
In an intense hallmark of '70s filmmaking, director Scorsese and writer Schrader created one of the most horrifying portraits of an unhinged mind and urban alienation ever committed to celluloid. De Niro gives an unforgettable, career-making performance as Travis Bickle, a Vietnam vet and New York City cab driver who becomes obsessed with ridding New York of "scum" after a misbegotten attempt to date an icy, blond political-campaign aide (Shepherd). He also tries to help a prepubescent prostitute (played perfectly by Foster) escape from her pimp, Sport (Keitel). When Shepherd rejects De Niro, he retreats even further into isolation and hatred, seeing his only chance at redemption in a one-man

assault on the world. The film climaxes in a burst of violence (made all the more powerful by Scorsese's understated direction), resolving the story, but not the disturbing portrait of neon-smeared urban life seen through De Niro's windshield. Haunting and brilliant. The effective score by Herrmann was his last. The laserdisc edition includes a second audio track with commentary by Scorsese and Schrader. Winner of the Palme d'Or at Cannes and selected as a National Film Registry Outstanding Film. Academy Award Nominations: Best Picture; Best Actor: Robert De Niro; Best Supporting Actress: Jodie Foster; Best Score. **Cast:** Robert De Niro, Cybill Shepherd, Peter Boyle, Jodie Foster, Diahnne Abbott, Victor Argo, Albert Brooks, Harvey Keitel, Peter Savage, Ralph S. Singleton. **Credits:** Dir: Martin Scorsese; Prod: Julia Phillips, Michael Phillips; Writer: Paul Schrader; DP: Michael Chapman; Ed: Tom Rolf, Melvin Shapiro; Prod Design: Charles Rosen; Composer: Bernard Herrmann; Costumes: Ruth Morley; SFX: Dick Smith. Color, 118 min. **VHS, LASER, DVD**

Tea and Sympathy
(1956) MGM
This is a solid (yet much tamer) version of the hit Broadway play about a sexually confused prep school youth (John Kerr) who is the target for bullying by his father and his schoolmates. Desperate to unravel his sexual confusion, he relies increasingly on his housemaster's wife (Deborah Kerr) for emotional support. When she learns

he's in danger of harming himself after a disastrous attempt to prove his manhood, Kerr offers more than a sympathetic ear. The three leads reprise their stage roles, giving solid, assured performances, and though Minnelli worked with what he had, the screen adaptation (by playwright Anderson) was watered down by the censors. **Cast:** Deborah Kerr, Leif Erickson, John Kerr, Edward Andrews, Darryl Hickman, Dean Jones, Norma Crane, Jacqueline De Wit, Tom Laughlin, Peter Votrian. **Credits:** Dir: Vincente Minnelli; Prod: Pandro S. Berman; Writer: Robert Anderson; DP: John Alton; Ed: Ferris Webster; Composer: Adolph Deutsch. Color, 122 min. **VHS, LASER**

Teacher's Pet
(1958) Paramount
This delightful romantic comedy stars Gable as a cynical newspaper reporter who graduated only from the school of hard knocks. When his editor insists he comply with a request to guest lecture at the local college, he first encounters journalism professor Day criticizing a letter he had written. But liking what he sees, he pretends to be a new student. When he impresses Day with his assignments, she recommends him for a job—at his own paper. After dispensing with her boyfriend, Young (in a winning role), love blossoms. Academy Award Nominations: Best (Original) Story and Screenplay and Best Supporting Actor: Gig Young. **Cast:** Clark Gable, Doris Day, Gig Young, Mamie Van Doren, Nick Adams, Charles Lane, Jack Albertson, Harry Antrim, Terry Becker, Elizabeth Harrower. **Credits:** Dir: George Seaton; Prod: William Perlberg; Writer: Fay Kanin, Michael Kanin; DP: Haskell Boggs; Ed: Alma Macrorie; Prod Design: Hal Pereira, Earl Hedrick; Composer: Roy Webb; Costumes: Edith Head; SFX: Farciot Edouart; Set Designer: Sam Comer, Robert R. Benton. B&W, 120 min. **VHS, LASER**

Tea for Two
(1950) Warner Bros.
In an entertaining musical, Day finds that she has lost all her money due to the stock-market crash. Unfortunately, she had promised to back and star in a Broadway show, so her uncle promises the money if she can answer "no" to every question for an entire day. If she manages to pull it off, the money and opportunity are hers. Difficulties arise when the charming MacRae appears, posing a threat every time he poses a question. Loosely based on the play *No, No, Nanette*, with terrific songs by the

Gershwins, Harry Warren, and others. **Cast:** Doris Day, Gordon MacRae, Gene Nelson, Eve Arden, Billy De Wolfe, S. Z. Sakall, Bill Goodwin, Virginia Gibson, Crauford Kent, Elinor Donahue. **Credits:** Dir: David Butler; Prod: William Jacobs; Writer: Harry Clork; DP: Wilfrid M. Cline; Ed: Irene Morra; Prod Design: Douglas Bacon; Choreographer: Leroy Prinz; Costumes: Leah Rhodes; Set Designer: Lyle Reifsnider. Color, 98 min. **VHS**

The Teahouse of the August Moon
(1956) MGM
Adapted by Patrick from his hit Broadway play, this sly culture-clash comedy is set during the American occupation of post–WWII Okinawa. Bumbling officer Glenn Ford gets exiled to a small village in Okinawa to bring democracy and industry to the noncomprehending villagers. He eventually, through the manipulation of interpreter Brando, sees the wisdom of establishing a much-desired teahouse staffed with geishas and setting up a network of stills to produce the local brandy. The brass (Paul Ford) doesn't consider his efforts sufficiently industrious. **Cast:** Marlon Brando, Glenn Ford, Machiko Kyo, Eddie Albert, Paul Ford, Jun Negami, Nijiko Kiyokawa, Mitsuko Sawamura. **Credits:** Dir: Daniel Mann; Prod: Jack Cummings; Writer: John Patrick; Story: John Patrick; DP: John Alton; Ed: Harold F. Kress; Composer: Saul Chaplin; Art Director: William A. Horning, Eddie Imazu. Color, 124 min. **VHS, LASER**

Telefon
(1977) United Artists
Action master Siegel directs Bronson as a KGB agent who teams up with CIA double agent Remick to intercept brainwashed Americans who are programmed to blow up American military bases. Twisty, taut script by director-cinematographer Hyams (*2010*) and TV-film writer Silliphant. **Cast:** Charles Bronson, Lee Remick, Donald Pleasence, Tyne Daly, Patrick Magee, Sheree North, Frank Marth, Roy Jenson. **Credits:** Dir: Don Siegel; Prod: James Harris; Writer: Peter Hyams, Sterling Silliphant; DP: Michael Butler; Ed: Douglas Stewart; Prod Design: Ted Haworth; Composer: Lalo Schifrin. Color, 102 min. **VHS**

Tell Me That You Love Me, Junie Moon
(1970) Paramount
In a heart-wrenching drama from late-career Preminger, a disfigured

woman (Minnelli), a homosexual paraplegic (Moore), and a quiet epileptic (Howard) once thought to be retarded decide to circle their wagons and move in together. Each has their troubles and leans on the others for emotional and physical support, and, in the case of Minnelli and Howard, a tender, tentative romance. Minnelli's raw-nerve performance was heightened when her mother, Judy Garland, died during production. **Cast:** Liza Minnelli, Ken Howard, Robert Moore, James Coco, Kay Thompson, Fred Williamson, Ben Piazza, Emily Yancy, Pete Seeger. **Credits:** Dir: Otto Preminger; Prod: Otto Preminger; Writer: Marjorie Kellogg; DP: Boris Kaufman; Ed: Henry Berman, Dean Ball; Prod Design: Lyle Wheeler; Composer: Philip Springer. Color, 112 min.

Tell Them Willie Boy Is Here
(1969) Universal
This underrated drama marked blacklisted Polonsky's return to the director's chair for the first time in 21 years (though he had written many screenplays under other names). A character-driven Western that sharply observes the friction between whites and Indians, the story follows sheriff Redford as he ambivalently pursues Blake, an Indian who murdered, in self-defense, his white lover's father. Moody and atmospheric. **Cast:** Robert Redford, Katharine Ross, Robert Blake, Susan Clark, Barry Sullivan, John Vernon, Charles Aidman, Charles McGraw. **Credits:** Dir: Abraham Polonsky; Prod: Philip A. Waxman; Writer: Abraham Polonsky; DP: Conrad Hall; Ed: Melvin Shapiro; Prod Design: Alexander Golitzen; Composer: Dave Grusin. Color, 98 min. **VHS, LASER**

The Ten Commandments
(1923) Paramount
DeMille's original silent version of DeMille's biblical epic employed thousands and left Paramount's Adolph Zukor quaking. The director's grand vision appears in a two-strip Technicolor depiction of the Book of Exodus as Moses (Roberts) leads his people out of Egypt, including an eye-popping (at the time) parting of the Red Sea. The second half of the film presents a contemporary morality tale as Chapman raises two sons, one (Dix) who follows the Commandments and another (La Rocque) who flouts them. DeMille returned to the scene of his triumph more than 30 years later with even bigger success. **Cast:** Theodore Roberts, Rod La Rocque, Richard Dix, Charles De Roche, Estelle Taylor,

Edythe Chapman. **Credits:** Dir: Cecil B. DeMille; Prod: Cecil B. DeMille; Writer: Jeanie MacPherson; DP: Bert Glennon, J. Peverell Marley, Edward S. Curtis, Fred West-erberg, Donald Keyes, Archibald Stout, Ray Renahan; Ed: Anne Bauchens; Prod Design: Paul Iribe; Costumes: Claire West. B&W, 146 min. **VHS**

The Ten Commandments

(1956) Paramount
For DeMille's last picture, Hollywood's undisputed master of the cast-of-thousands epic pulled out all the stops, topping even his 1923 silent telling of the Exodus story. Heston, in a role that became his signature, gives a highly charged performance as Moses, the Hebrew who became an Egyptian prince and then led his people out of slavery, and there isn't a false note in the production. The parting of the Red Sea, an effect that manages to remain glorious even in our age of computer graphics, was accomplished by massive amounts of water being poured into a tank and then reversed (the effects took the Oscar). The 35th anniversary video edition features an uncut 245-minute version, with Dolby stereo sound and an on-screen introduction by DeMille. The collector's edition includes a signed card from Heston. Academy Award Nominations: 7, including Best Picture. **Academy Awards:** Best Special Effects. **Cast:** Charlton Heston, Yul Brynner, John Derek, Anne Baxter, Yvonne De Carlo, H. B. Warner, Edward G. Robinson, Debra Paget, Nina Foch, Cedric Hardwicke. **Credits:** Dir: Cecil B. DeMille; Prod: Cecil B. DeMille; Writer: Aeneas MacKenzie, Jesse Lasky, Jr., Jack Gariss, Fredric M. Frank; DP: Loyal Griggs, John F. Warren, Wallace Kelley, Peverell Marley; Ed: Anne Bauchens; Composer: Elmer Bernstein; Art Director: Hal Pereira, Walter Tyler. Color, 219/245 min. **VHS, LASER**

Tender Comrade

(1943) RKO
A WWII homefront melodrama from director Dmytryk and writer Trumbo is mostly of historical interest. The depiction of war's effects on the women left behind became evidence of subliminal communist propaganda in the hands of the HUAC. War widow Rogers moves into a house shared by other military wives and mothers and they live communally, sharing their meager material possessions as well as their hopes and fears for the future. **Cast:** Ginger Rogers, Robert Ryan, Ruth Hussey, Patricia Collinge,

Kim Hunter, Jane Darwell, Mary Forbes, Richard Martin. **Credits:** Dir: Edward Dmytryk; Prod: David Hempstead; Writer: Dalton Trumbo; DP: Russell Metty; Ed: Roland Gross; Prod Design: Albert S. D'Agostino; Composer: Leigh Harline. Color, 102 min. **VHS**

Tender Is the Night

(1961) Fox
The last film supervised by David Selznick features his wife, Jones, as the mentally unbalanced wife of her former therapist, Robards. She leads him away from his practice in Zurich to a wild life of parties and drinking among the wealthy expatriates on the Riviera. The experience saps Robards of his ability to work as Jones loses interest in her former savior. Fitzgerald himself tried to sell his novel to Hollywood for years before his estate found a fan of the book in Selznick. **Cast:** Jennifer Jones, Jason Robards, Tom Ewell, Joan Fontaine, Jill St. John, Sanford Meisner. **Credits:** Dir: Henry King; Prod: Henry Weinstein; Writer: Ivan Moffat; Story: F. Scott Fitzgerald; DP: Leon Shamroy; Ed: William Reynolds; Prod Design: Jack Martin Smith, Malcolm Brown; Composer: Bernard Herrmann. Color, 146 min.

The Tender Trap

(1955) MGM
In a sophisticated romantic comedy, New York agent Sinatra shows his midwestern friend Wayne his ring-a-ding lifestyle, but realizes how lonely he is after meeting virginal Reynolds. He faces the marriage dilemma by proposing to both Reynolds and Holm, losing both, but love wins out in the end. Academy Award Nomination for Best Song ("Love Is the Tender Trap"). **Cast:** Frank Sinatra, Debbie Reynolds, Celeste Holm, David Wayne, Carolyn Jones, Lola Albright, Tom Helmore, Willard Sage. **Credits:** Dir: Charles Walters; Prod: Lawrence Weingarten; Writer: Julius J. Epstein; Story: Max Shulman, Robert Paul Smith; DP: Paul C. Vogel; Ed: John Dunning; Prod Design: Cedric Gibbons, Arthur Lonergan; Composer: Jeff Alexander. Color, 116 min. **VHS, LASER**

Ten Gentlemen from West Point

(1942) Fox
The first class at West Point also endured the first drill-sergeant, played here by Cregar in Hathaway's version of the military academy's founding. By graduation time, only the toughest are standing. Among these are the farm-

boy Montgomery and rich-kid Sutton, rivals for the hand of the lovely O'Hara. Only when the cadets successfully beat back an Indian attack will Cregar accept them as soldiers. **Cast:** George Montgomery, Maureen O'Hara, John Sutton, Laird Cregar, Shepperd Strudwick, Victor Francen, Harry Davenport, Ward Bond, Douglass Dumbrille, Ralph Byrd. **Credits:** Dir: Henry Hathaway; Prod: William Perlberg; Writer: Ben Hecht, Richard Maibaum, George Seaton; Story: Malvin Wald; DP: Leon Shamroy; Ed: James B. Clark; Prod Design: Richard Day, Nathan Juran; Composer: Alfred Newman. B&W, 102 min.

Tennessee Johnson

(1942) MGM
Here is a torn-from-the-headlines, behind-the-scenes exposé of the impeachment proceedings—of the 1860s. Heflin stars as the Tennessee lad who learns to read and write from a kindly schoolmarm (Hussey), leads a voting-rights campaign, and becomes the first president to face impeachment when Barrymore doesn't cotton to his conciliatory attitude toward the defeated South. Sturdy biopic that portrays the recently much-referenced blueprint for impeachment. **Cast:** Van Heflin, Ruth Hussey, Lionel Barrymore, Marjorie Main, Regis Toomey, Montagu Love, Porter Hall, Charles Dingle, J. Edward Bromberg, Grant Withers. **Credits:** Dir: William Dieterle; Prod: J. Walter Ruben; Writer: John L. Balderston, Wells Root; Story: Milton Gunzburg, Alvin Meyers; DP: Harold Rosson; Ed: Robert J. Kern; Prod Design: Cedric Gibbons; Composer: Herbert Stothart. B&W, 100 min.

Tennessee's Partner

(1955) RKO
This quiet, but enjoyable, Western by Dwan is the third screen version of the Bret Harte story. Reagan breaks up a fight between two men he doesn't know and ends up befriending the gambler he saves (B-star Payne, in one of his more memorable performances). Reagan then saves Payne from romantic disaster, and the gambler finds true love with the fiery Fleming, the proprietor of the local saloon and bawdy house. **Cast:** John Payne, Rhonda Fleming, Ronald Reagan, Coleen Gray, Anthony Caruso, Morris Ankrum, Chubby Johnson, Leo Gordon. **Credits:** Dir: Allan Dwan; Prod: Benedict E. Bogeaus; Writer: Milton Krims; DP: John Alton; Ed: James Leicester; Prod Design: Van Nest Polglase; Composer: Louis Forbes. Color, 86 min. **VHS**

Teresa

(1951) MGM

Finding love in Angeli's bleak Italian village does not prepare Ericson and his war bride for life in the crowded tenements of New York. When they move in with his parents after the war, the uncomfortable situation exacerbates Angeli's cultural dislocation. When she makes the difficult choice to leave the tenement after giving birth, he must decide whether or not to follow. Steiger's debut. Academy Award Nomination: Best Original Screenplay. **Cast:** Pier Angeli, John Ericson, Patricia Collinge, Pat Bishop, Peggy Ann Garner, Ralph Meeker, Bill Mauldin, Ave Ninchi, Edward Binns, Rod Steiger. **Credits:** Dir: Fred Zinnemann; Prod: Arthur M. Loew; Writer: Stewart Stern, Alfred Hayes; DP: William J. Miller; Ed: Frank Sullivan; Prod Design: Leo Kerz; Composer: Jack Schaindlin. B&W, 102 min.

Terror in a Texas Town

(1958) United Artists

The last film by director Lewis (*Gun Crazy*, 1949) is typically economical and inventive. The always terrific Hayden plays a Scandinavian seaman who returns to his father's Texas farm to discover that he has been murdered by a greedy land baron in pursuit of oil. The stunning finale features a showdown between six-gun and harpoon. **Cast:** Sterling Hayden, Sebastian Cabot, Carol Kelly, Eugene Martin, Ned Young, Sheb Wooley, Fred Kohler, Jr., Steven Mitchell. **Credits:** Dir: Joseph H. Lewis; Prod: Frank N. Seltzer; DP: Ray Rennahan; Ed: Frank Sullivan. B&W, 80 min. **VHS**

Test Pilot

(1938) MGM

This whizzy story with heart-stopping flying sequences is about the dangerous life of a test pilot and its effect on the people who love him. With the cast assembled here, this turned out to be one of MGM's biggest hits of the day. Gable is an adventurous test pilot who falls in love with Loy when he's forced to land in her family's Kansas cornfield. He settles down, thanks to the watchful eye of his loyal mechanic Tracy, and starts a family, but tensions arise when Loy objects to his testing of a new Air Force bomber. Cinematographer June provides a breathtaking experience. Academy Award Nominations: 3, including Best Picture and Best Original Screenplay. **Cast:** Clark Gable, Myrna Loy, Spencer Tracy, Lionel Barrymore, Samuel S. Hinds, Marjorie

Main, Gloria Holden, Louis Jean Heydt. **Credits:** Dir: Victor Fleming; Prod: Louis D. Lighton; Writer: Vincent Lawrence, Waldemar Young, Howard Hawks; DP: Ray June; Ed: Tom Held; Composer: Franz Waxman. B&W, 118 min. **VHS**

The Texan

(1930) Paramount

Bandit Cooper rides into town, kills a cheating gambler, hooks up with a crooked con game, and then falls in love with his mark (Wray). Standard Western based on an O. Henry story that was Paramount's follow-up to the Cooper sensation caused by *The Virginian* (1929). Future director Henry Hathaway was Cromwell's assistant. **Cast:** Gary Cooper, Fay Wray, Emma Dunn, Oscar Apfel, James Marcus, Donald Reed. **Credits:** Dir: John Cromwell; Writer: Daniel Rubin, Oliver Garret; Sytory: O. Henry; DP: Victor Milner; Ed: Verna Willis. B&W, 72 min. **VHS**

The Texans

(1938) Paramount

Scott stars as a former rebel soldier who attempts to create a new life for himself as a trail boss. His challenges include moving ten thousand cattle to Abilene while fighting the elements, rustlers, and Indians. Along the way, he encounters Bennett and her plan to re-ignite the war between the states. Strong performances all around. A remake of the 1924 silent *North of '36*. **Cast:** Randolph Scott, Joan Bennett, Walter Brennan, May Robson, Robert Cummings, Raymond Hatton, Harvey Stephens, Robert Barratt. **Credits:** Dir: James Hogan; Prod: Lucien Hubbard; Writer: Bertram Millhauser, Paul Sloane, William Wister Haines; Story: Emerson Hough; DP: Theodor Sparkuhl; Ed: LeRoy Stone. B&W, 93 min. **VHS**

Texas

(1941) Columbia

Two young drifters, Ford and Holden, wander Texas after the Civil War getting into scrapes and going their separate ways after a holdup. They meet again when Ford, now a ranch foreman, guards his herd against the rustlers led by Holden. They also compete for Trevor, the daughter of the ranch owner. **Cast:** William Holden, Glenn Ford, Claire Trevor, George Bancroft, Edgar Buchanan, Don Beddoe, Andrew Tombes, Addison Richards. **Credits:** Dir: George Marshall; Prod: Samuel Bischoff; Writer: Horace McCoy, Lewis Meltzer, Michael

Blankfort; DP: George Meehan; Ed: William A. Lyon; Art Director: Lionel Banks. B&W, 94 min. **VHS**

Texas Across the River

(1966) Universal

This is a tongue-in-cheek Western with half the Rat Pack up to frontier silliness. Dino is a gunrunner and Bishop his Indian (!) sidekick. They hook up with Spanish nobleman Delon to chase skirts across the Texas countryside. **Cast:** Dean Martin, Rosemary Forsyth, Tina Marquand, Peter Graves, Joey Bishop, Alain Delon, Michael Ansara, Linden Chiles. **Credits:** Dir: Michael Gordon; Prod: Harry Keller; Writer: Wells Root, Harold Greene, John Gay, Ben Starr; DP: Russell Metty; Ed: Gene Milford; Prod Design: Alexander Golitzen; Composer: Frank DeVol. Color, 101 min. **VHS, LASER**

The Texas Chainsaw Massacre

(1974) New Line

Hooper's horrifying nightmare follows a van full of young people driving through Texas on a scorching summer afternoon and happening upon a psychopathic family intent on turning them into butcher's meat. One by one, the characters fall prey to Leatherface's now-infamous weapon of choice, and when the last remaining survivor discovers that she has fallen into yet another trap, the murderous family brings in Grandpa to deal the last blows. Unrelentingly tense, though surprisingly ungory, this has deservedly earned its cult status as one of the most frightening experiences on celluloid. Future TV star Larroquette narrates. **Cast:** Marilyn Burns, Paul A. Partain, Gunnar Hansen, Ed Neal, Allen Danzinger, William Vail, Teri McMinn, Jim Siedow, John Larroquette. **Credits:** Dir: Tobe Hooper; Prod: Tobe Hooper; Writer: Kim Henkel, Tobe Hooper; DP: Daniel Pearl; Ed: Larry Carroll, Sallye Richardson; Composer: Wayne Bell, Tobe Hooper; Art Director: Robert A. Burns. Color, 84 min. **VHS, LASER, DVD**

Texas Terror

(1935) Monogram

Here is an early Wayne Western role as a Texas lawman who retires when he thinks he has shot his best friend. Later, he saves his friend's sister (Browne) and begins to fall in love. He also discovers that he wasn't guilty of the crime after all, and, learning who the real killers are, he begins exacting his revenge. **Cast:** John Wayne, George "Gabby" Hayes, Yakima

Canutt, Lucille Browne, Leroy Mason, Lloyd Ingraham, Bobby Nelson, Fern Emmett. **Credits:** Dir: Robert N. Bradbury; Prod: Paul Malvern; Writer: Robert N. Bradbury; DP: Archie Stout; Ed: Carl Pierson. B&W, 58 min. **VHS**

Thanks a Million
(1935) Fox
This musical satire on politics has Powell the leader of a song-and-dance troupe who, on a lark, stands for the governorship when the candidate is too soused to run. The party bosses like what they see and, before you know it, Powell's on the road to the governor's mansion. After he discovers that the bosses are corrupt, and he risks losing girlfriend Dvorak, Powell quits the race but his hat's back in the ring when he becomes the people's choice. Radio star Allen made his move to pictures here. Songs include "Happy Days Are Here Again," "Thanks a Million," "Pocketful of Sunshine," and "High on a Hilltop." **Cast:** Dick Powell, Ann Dvorak, Fred Allen, Patsy Kelly, Raymond Walburn, Benny Baker, Alan Dinehart, Andrew Tombes, Paul Harvey, Edwin Maxwell. **Credits:** Dir: Roy Del Ruth; Prod: Darryl F. Zanuck; Writer: Nunnally Johnson; DP: J. Peverell Marley; Ed: Fred Allen, Gene Fowler, Jr.; Composer: Arthur Lange, Arthur Johnston, Gus Kahn. B&W, 87 min.

Thank You, Jeeves
(1936) Fox
Fox translated Wodehouse's Jeeves stories, which are terribly British after all, into mysteries for the American audience. Treacher makes a terrific Jeeves, the archetypical gentleman's gentleman, and Niven a perfectly bird-brained Wooster. But here they tail enemy spies in a tepid comic spy tale. The first of two Jeeves mysteries that Fox hoped would blossom into a series. They didn't. **Cast:** Arthur Treacher, Virginia Field, David Niven, Lester Matthews, Colin Tapley, John Graham Spacey, Ernie Stanton, Gene Reynolds, Douglas Walton, Willie Best. **Credits:** Dir: Arthur Greville Collins; Prod: Sol M. Wurtzel; Writer: Joseph Hoffman, Ernie Stanton, P. G. Wodehouse; Ed: Nick DeMaggio; Composer: Samuel Kaylin. B&W, 57 min.

Thank Your Lucky Stars
(1943) Warner Bros.
This is the Warner Bros. entry into the cavalcade of stars wartime benefits that saw all the actors' salaries donated to the Hollywood Canteen. Virtually every Warner contract player

shows up here in a silly story of a variety show and Cantor's efforts to be involved while his double convinces everyone that he's the real Cantor. A lollapalooza of song and dance, even including a controversial routine by Flynn. The numbers include "They're Either Too Young or Too Old" (a rare glimpse of Davis singing), "That's What You Jolly Well Get," "Blues in the Night," "Ridin' for a Fall," and many more. Shore's screen debut. Academy Award Nomination for Best Song ("They're Either Too Young or Too Old"). **Cast:** Humphrey Bogart, Bette Davis, Errol Flynn, Eddie Cantor, John Garfield, Dinah Shore, Olivia de Havilland, Ann Sheridan. **Credits:** Dir: David Butler; Prod: Mark Hellinger; Writer: Norman Panama, Melvin Frank, James V. Kern; DP: Arthur Edeson; Ed: Irene Morra; Prod Design: Anton Grot; Art Director: Leo K. Kuter. B&W, 127 min. **VHS**

That Certain Age
(1938) Universal
In a winning Durbin vehicle, the young singer is infatuated with her family's houseguest, Douglas, a handsome journalist who is older, wiser, and charming. This doesn't bode well for Durbin's boyfriend, who is soon out on the curb, unable to compete. Douglas slyly uses the crush to get out of social obligations, but steers her gently back to her hometown beau. The memorable musical numbers include the Oscar-nominated "My Own." Note the Brackett-Wilder script. Academy Award Nominations: Best Song; Best Sound. **Cast:** Deanna Durbin, Melvyn Douglas, Jackie Cooper, Irene Rich, Nancy Carroll, John Halliday, Juanita Quigley, Jackie Searl, Charles Coleman. **Credits:** Dir: Edward Lugwig; Prod: Joe Pasternak; Writer: Bruce Manning, Charles Brackett, Billy Wilder; DP: Joseph A. Valentine; Ed: Bernard W. Burton; Prod Design: Jack Otterson. B&W, 101 min. **VHS**

That Certain Woman
(1937) Warner Bros.
This early role for Fonda is a weeper saved from bathos by Davis's magnetic screen presence. The widow of a gangster, Davis starts anew as a secretary in a law firm, where she meets Fonda, the rich playboy son of one of the clients. Love blossoms, but daddy Crisp demands the marriage be annulled under threat of disinheritance. A baby complicates the situation and leads to reconciliation years later. This remake of an earlier silent

picture, *The Trespasser* (starring Gloria Swanson), is powerfully acted. Apparently Fonda's appearance was a direct order from Davis, who wanted to revisit a crush she'd experienced when the two were performers in a theater group years before. The torch she carried shines in her face. **Cast:** Bette Davis, Henry Fonda, Donald Crisp, Ian Hunter, Minor Watson, Sidney Toler, Anita Louise, Katherine Alexander. **Credits:** Dir: Edmund Goulding; Prod: Robert Lord; Writer: Edmund Goulding; DP: Ernest Haller; Ed: Jack Killifer; Prod Design: Max Parker; Composer: Max Steiner. B&W, 96 min. **VHS**

That Cold Day in the Park
(1969) Commonwealth
This is director Altman's strange study of claustrophobia and obsession. Dennis, in one of her more memorable roles in a long line of lulus, plays a disturbed, frustrated spinster who meets an apparently mute drifter on a Vancouver park bench and takes him home. Once there, she throws herself at him, and even engages a prostitute for him, which pushes her over the murderous edge. A look at the formative years of a cinematic rule-breaker. **Cast:** Sandy Dennis, Michael Burns, Susanne Benton, John Garfield, Jr., Luana Anders, Michael Murphy, Ray Brown, Edward Greenhalgh, Frank Wade. **Credits:** Dir: Robert Altman; Prod: Leon Mirell, Donald Factor; Writer: Gillian Freeman; Story: Richard Miles; DP: Laszlo Kovacs; Ed: Danford B. Greene; Composer: Johnny Mandel; Art Director: Leon Ericksen. Color, 110 min. **VHS**

That Darn Cat
(1965) Disney
This Disney comedy mystery begins with a cuddly feline (D.C. for "Darn Cat") following her appetite around the neighborhood. When she returns home with a watch that belongs to the kidnapped hostage from a local bank robbery, her owners (Mills and Provine) inform the authorities. In comes F.B.I. agent Jones, and D.C. leads the investigation of the crime. Remade in 1996. **Cast:** Hayley Mills, Dean Jones, Dorothy Provine, Roddy McDowall, Neville Brand, Elsa Lanchester, William Demarest, Frank Gorshin. **Credits:** Dir: Robert Stevenson; Prod: Bill Walsh, Ron Miller; Writer: Gordon Gordon, Mildred Gordon; DP: Edward Colman; Ed: Cotton Warburton; Prod Design: Carroll Clark, William H. Tuntke; Composer: Robert F. Brunner. Color, 116 min. **VHS**

That Hamilton Woman (1941)

That Forsyte Woman
(1949) MGM
A lavish screen adaptation of the first book of John Galsworthy's trilogy is about the stifled romantic intrigues that roil a wealthy Victorian family. Leigh has been sheltered by the Forsytes from the influence of her artist father, Pidgeon. His cousin, Flynn, is married to a fiery Garson, who agrees to intercede with the family when Leigh wishes to marry architect Young. After meeting Young, however, neither is sure that they want the marriage to happen. After much ruffling of skirts and starched shirts, love finds the proper partners. Remade more completely for TV by the BBC. Academy Award Nomination: Best Costume Design. **Cast:** Errol Flynn, Greer Garson, Walter Pidgeon, Robert Young, Janet Leigh, Harry Davenport, Stanley Logan, Lumsden Hare. **Credits:** Dir: Compton Bennett; Prod: Leon Gordon; Writer: Jan Lustig, Ivan Tors, James B. Williams, Arthur Wimperis; DP: Joseph Ruttenberg; Prod Design: Cedric Gibbons; Composer: Bronislau Kaper; Art Director: Daniel B. Cathcart. B&W, 112 min. **VHS**

That Girl from Paris
(1936) RKO
This musical treat displays the vocal talents of French opera star Pons. She's an opera singer who flees a jealous lover in Paris on an ocean liner without a passport. She hides out in a swinging band and falls in love with the bandleader (Raymond). The songs are the highlight and include: "Seal It with a Kiss," "The Blue Danube," "Una Voce Poco Fa," and "The Call to Arms." Academy Award Nomination: Best Sound Recording. **Cast:** Lily Pons, Jack Oakie, Gene Raymond, Lucille Ball, Herman Bing, Mischa Auer, Frank Jenks, Vinton Haworth. **Credits:** Dir: Leigh Jason; Prod: Pandro S. Berman; Writer: P. J. Wolfson, Dorothy Yost, Joseph Fields; DP: J. Roy Hunt; Ed: William Morgan; Composer: Nathaniel Shilkret, Andre Kostelanetz; Art Director: Van Nest Polglase. B&W, 106 min. **VHS**

That Hamilton Woman
(1941) United Artists
This is the story of Emma Hamilton (Leigh), who raised herself from poverty to become the wife of a British ambassador and the mistress of one of history's most famous warriors, Lord Admiral Nelson (Olivier). Their affair begins in Naples and continues as they defy the gossips by setting up housekeeping in England before Emma sends him back to war and his death at Trafalgar. This was seen as an attempt to inspire pro-British sentiments before America's entry into WWII and was, therefore, said to be Winston Churchill's favorite movie. Academy Award Nominations: 4, including Best Cinematography; Best Visual Effects. **Academy Awards:** Best Sound Recording. **Cast:** Laurence Olivier, Vivien Leigh, Henry Wilcoxon, Gladys Cooper, Alan Mowbray, Sara Allgood, Heather Angel, Halliwell Hobbes. **Credits:** Dir: Alexander Korda; Prod: Alexander Korda; Writer: Walter Reisch, R. C. Sherriff; DP: Rudolph Mate; Ed: William Hornbeck; Prod Design: Vincent Korda; Composer: Miklos Rozsa. B&W, 125 min. **VHS, LASER**

That Lady in Ermine
(1948) Fox
This Technicolor Fox musical is set in 19th-century Europe, where the princess of tiny Graustarkia (Grable) finds her country and castle besieged by a conquering Hungarian colonel (Fairbanks). After first heeding the advice of a dream, she bewitches the gruff colonel, saves the day, and finds true love. This is listed as Lubitsch's last film, but he died eight days into production. Otto Preminger took over but insisted that the master of cinema style be credited. Songs include "This Is the Moment," "There's Something About Midnight," and "The Jester's Song." Academy Award Nomination: Best Song ("This Is the Moment"). **Cast:** Betty Grable, Douglas Fairbanks, Jr., Cesar Romero, Walter Abel, Reginald Gardiner, Harry Davenport, Virginia Campbell, Whit Bissell, Edmund MacDonald. **Credits:** Dir: Ernst Lubitsch, Otto Preminger; Prod: Ernst Lubitsch; Writer: Samson Raphaelson; DP: Leon Shamroy; Ed: Dorothy Spencer; Prod Design: J. Russell Spencer, Lyle Wheeler; Composer: Alfred Newman, Frederick Hollander, Leo Robin. Color, 89 min.

That Night in Rio
(1941) Fox
In a patented Fox south-of-the-border musical, Ameche plays a dual role as wealthy businessman Baron Manuel Duarte and nightclub entertainer Larry Martin. The Baron hires look-alike Larry to impersonate him while he secures financing overseas for his troubled airline. Larry fumbles through his new position, but manages to charm the Baroness (Faye), who is willing to suspend disbelief. Larry's girlfriend, singer Miranda, isn't so willing to go along. The sixth and last pairing of Fox's romantic duo, Ameche and Faye, and Miranda's second Hollywood role. A remake of *Folies Bergere* with Warren and Gordon songs added, and remade as *On the Riviera* (1951) with Danny Kaye. **Cast:** Alice Faye,

Don Ameche, Carmen Miranda, S. Z. Sakall, J. Carrol Naish, Curt Bois, Leonid Kinskey, Frank Puglia, Lillian Porter, Maria Montez. **Credits:** Dir: Irving Cummings; Prod: Fred Kohlmar, Darryl F. Zanuck; Writer: Hal Long, Bess Meredyth, George Seaton; Story: Hans Adler, Rudolph Lothar; DP: Ray Rennehan, Leon Shamroy; Ed: Walter Thompson; Prod Design: Richard Day, Joseph C. Wright; Composer: Mack Gordon, Alfred Newman, Harry Warren. B&W, 90 min.

That's Entertainment!
(1974) MGM
A delight for cinephiles, this picture is a nostalgic journey into the past as stars introduce scenes from a cornucopia of MGM musicals. Ranging from 1929's *Broadway* to 1958's *Gigi*, this was so well received that it was followed by two sequels and 1985's *That's Dancing!* The original is still the best, though each installment features outtakes and interviews that provide fascinating insight into the moviemaking process. **Cast:** Fred Astaire, Bing Crosby, Gene Kelly, Peter Lawford, Liza Minnelli, Donald O'Connor, Debbie Reynolds, Frank Sinatra, James Stewart, Elizabeth Taylor. **Credits:** Dir: Jack Haley, Jr.; Prod: Jack Haley, Jr.; Writer: Jack Haley, Jr.; DP: Alan Green, Ennio Guarnieri, Ernest Laszlo, Russell Metty, Gene Polito; Ed: David Blewitt, Bud Friedgen; Composer: Henry Mancini. Color, 137 min. **VHS, LASER**

That's My Boy
(1951) Paramount
This is mid-level Martin and Lewis as Jerry plays "Junior" Jackson, son of an overbearing former football great at Ridgeville College sent by his father to play for the Ridgeville squad. The coach must honor the wishes of such a prominent alum, but is fortunate to have ringer Martin looking out for Lewis. **Cast:** Dean Martin, Jerry Lewis, Ruth Hussey, Eddie Mayehoff, Marion Marshall, Polly Bergen, Hugh Sanders, John McIntire, Francis Pierlot, Lillian Randolph. **Credits:** Dir: Hal Walker; Prod: Hal B. Wallis; Writer: Cy Howard; DP: Lee Garmes; Ed: Warren Low; Prod Design: Franz Bachelin, Hal Pereira; Composer: Leigh Harline. B&W, 98 min.

That Touch of Mink
(1959) Universal
Here's another coy sex comedy starring Day (and again penned by Shapiro, the author of *Pillow Talk*, 1959), though this is elevated by the presence of Grant. Unemployed New York secretary Day gets a Cinderella brush with destiny when financier Grant's limo splashes her with mud. After making amends, Grant squires her around the country (the scene at Yankee Stadium featuring Mickey Mantle, Yogi Berra, and Roger Maris is a hoot) before offering a romantic tryst in Bermuda. Day accepts, but true to form, comes down with splotches before the deed can be done. She pursues Grant with help from Meadows and commentary from Young (who seemed to become the Technicolor era's Ralph Bellamy) until the trip to the altar—and another case of splotches on Grant. Academy Award Nominations: 3, including Best Original Screenplay. **Cast:** Cary Grant, Doris Day, Audrey Meadows, Gig Young, Alan Hewitt, John Astin, Richard Sargent, John Fiedler. **Credits:** Dir: Delbert Mann; Prod: Stanley Shapiro, Martin Melcher; Writer: Stanley Shapiro, Nate Monaster; DP: Russell Metty; Ed: Ted J. Kent; Prod Design: Alexander Golitzen, Robert Clatworthy; Composer: George Duning. Color, 99 min. **VHS**

That Uncertain Feeling
(1941) United Artists
Lubitsch remakes his 1925 silent, *Kiss Me Again*, this time with an updated script by sophisticated Stewart. Oberon wilts as her complacent husband Douglas works. When her attempts to light a fire with her husband fizzle, pianist Meredith is just the tonic she needs until divorce court looms. Academy Award Nomination: Best Score. **Cast:** Merle Oberon, Melvyn Douglas, Burgess Meredith, Alan Mowbray, Eve Arden, Harry Davenport, Sig Rumann, Richard Carle. **Credits:** Dir: Ernst Lubitsch; Prod: Ernst Lubitsch; Writer: Walter Reisch, Donald Ogden Stewart; DP: George Barnes; Ed: William Shea; Prod Design: Alexander Golitzen; Composer: Werner Richard Heymann; Costumes: Irene. B&W, 86 min. **VHS**

That Wonderful Urge
(1948) Fox
In this remake of *Love Is News* (1937), also starring Power, a cynical reporter for a tabloid newspaper is assigned to get the dirt on a beautiful heiress to a supermarket fortune (Tierney). In order to get the goods, he poses as a small-town reporter who'll set the record straight. Tierney learns of the ruse and turns the tables, telling the papers that she and Power are wed. Fired for letting other papers get the scoop, the reporter must now prove he's still a bachelor, a condition he's willing to forgo when he realizes how much he adores Tierney. **Cast:** Tyrone Power, Gene Tierney, Reginald Gardiner, Arleen Whelan, Lucile Watson, Gene Lockhart, Lloyd Gough, Porter Hall, Richard Gaines, Taylor Holmes. **Credits:** Dir: Robert B. Sinclair; Prod: Fred Kohlmar; Writer: Jay Dratler, William Lipman, Frederick Stephani; DP: Charles G. Clarke; Ed: Louis Loeffler; Prod Design: Lyle Wheeler, George W. Davis; Composer: Cyril Mockridge. B&W, 82 min.

Them!
(1954) Warner Bros.
Atomic radiation once again transforms tiny harmless creatures into gigantic holy terrors. Probably the best of the '50s Cold War paranoia phenomenon, this top-notch thriller presents giant ants spawned by nuclear testing using the sewer systems of Los Angeles like a vast ant farm. Ant expert Gwenn and his daughter Weldon direct the efforts and Whitmore makes sure they go in but they don't come out. Stellar effects and dignified performances make this better than average. Academy Award Nomination: Best Special Effects. **Cast:** James Whitmore, Edmund Gwenn, Joan Weldon, James Arness, Onslow Stevens, Sean McClory, Christian Drake, Sandy Descher. **Credits:** Dir: Gordon Douglas; Prod: David Weisbart; Writer: Ted Sherdeman; DP: Sid Hickox; Ed: Thomas Reilly; Composer: Bronislau Kaper; Prod Design: Stanley Fleischer; SFX: Ralph Ayres, William Mueller, Francis Scheid. B&W, 93 min. **VHS, LASER**

Theodora Goes Wild
(1936) Columbia
Dunne's first comedic role finds her a small-town writer who pens a saucy best-seller about a small Connecticut town not unlike her own. When she meets the bohemian New Yorker (Douglas) who illustrated her novel, they go on a whirlwind tour of the big city where she discovers that the city has a few characters of its own. Director Boleslawski was trained at the Moscow Art Theater and also directed *Clive of India* (1934) and *Les Miserables* (1935). Academy Award Nominations: Best Actress: Irene Dunne; Best Film Editing. **Cast:** Irene Dunne, Melvyn Douglas, Thomas Mitchell, Thurston Hall, Rosalind Keith, Spring Byington, Elisabeth Risdon, Margaret McWade. **Credits:** Dir: Richard Boleslawski; Prod: Everett Riskin;

Writer: Sidney Buchman; DP: Joseph Walker; Ed: Otto Meyer; Composer: Morris Stoloff; Art Director: Stephen Goosson. B&W, 94 min. **VHS**

There Goes My Heart

(1938) United Artists
This film is among the last in the Depression-era string of newsman-chasing-runaway-heiress routines. Here Bruce becomes a sales clerk in a department store owned by her grandfather through the recommendation of sympathetic clerk Kelly. Newsman March, hot on the story, tails her to the store, but, of course, falls in love with her as they hide out from her grandfather at his shack. Academy Award Nomination: Best Score. **Cast:** Fredric March, Virginia Bruce, Patsy Kelly, Alan Mowbray, Nancy Carroll, Eugene Pallette, Claude Gillingwater, Etienne Girardot, Arthur Lake, Irving Bacon. **Credits:** Dir: Norman Z. McLeod; Prod: Milton Bren; Writer: Jack Jevne, Eddie Moran, Ed Sullivan; DP: Norbert F. Brodine; Prod Design: Charles Hall; Composer: Marvin Hatley. B&W, 81 min.

There's Always a Woman

(1938) Columbia
Blondell and Douglas make a snappy team in a mystery comedy that unfolds after Astor plunks 300 dollars on investigator Douglas's desk. Douglas, however, can't take her case as he has accepted a job as an investigator for the district attorney. That leaves Douglas's wife, Blondell, a would-be detective, to take the case herself. She ends up in hot water and Douglas ends up on the case. Rita Hayworth makes a brief appearance, and Columbia followed with a sequel, *There's That Woman Again*, in which Virginia Bruce took Blondell's role. **Cast:** Joan Blondell, Melvyn Douglas, Mary Astor, Frances Drake, Jerome Cowan, Robert Paige, Thurston Hall, Pierre Watkin, Walter Kingsford, Lester Matthews. **Credits:** Dir: Alexander Hall; Prod: William Perlberg; Writer: Gladys Lehman; Story: Wilson Collison; DP: Henry Freulich; Ed: Viola Laurence; Composer: Benjamin Stoloff; Art Director: Lionel Banks, Stephen Goosson. B&W, 82 min.

There's Always Tomorrow

(1956) Universal
Sirk takes a 1934 melodrama (itself worth seeing for Frank Morgan's knockout performance) and turns it into an up-to-the-minute portrait of quiet desperation. MacMurray, a toy company executive whose latest prod-

uct is a perfectly appropriate robot, exists from day to day locked without love in a household that values only his financial contribution. When he runs into old flame Stanwyck, possibilities multiply in his mind but never come to pass despite his family's dark suspicions. Chillingly effective domestic drama. **Cast:** Barbara Stanwyck, Fred MacMurray, Joan Bennett, Pat Crowley, William Reynolds, Gigi Perreau. **Credits:** Dir: Douglas Sirk; Prod: Ross Hunter; Writer: Bernard Schoenfeld; DP: Russel Metty; Ed: William Morgan; Composer: Herman Stein, Heinz Roemheld; Art Director: Alexander Golitzen, Eric Orbom. B&W, 84 min.

There's No Business Like Show Business

(1954) Fox
This pinnacle of the Fox Technicolor backstage musical features Berlin songs and a signature role by Merman. Dailey and Merman expand their vaudeville act as they add kids. O'Connor and Gaynor join the family troupe and encounter romantic trials as they get older. O'Connor falls for aspiring singer Monroe and she joins the show; Gaynor meets a lyricist (O'Brian). When O'Connor and Dailey have a falling out, Merman carries on alone, but Gaynor brings everyone back for the rousing rendition of the title song. The tunes include the famous title song as well as "Remember," "Heat Wave," "When the Midnight Choo-Choo Leaves for Alabam'," "Let's Have Another Cup of Coffee," and "Play a Simple Melody." Academy Award Nominations: Best Motion Picture Story; Best Scoring of a Musical Picture; Best (Color) Costume Design. **Cast:** Ethel Merman, Donald O'Connor, Marilyn Monroe, Dan Dailey, Johnny Ray, Mitzi Gaynor, Richard Eastham, Hugh O'Brian. **Credits:** Dir: Walter Lang; Prod: Sol C. Siegel; Writer: Phoebe Ephron, Henry Ephron; DP: Leon Shamroy; Ed: Robert Simpson; Composer: Irving Berlin; Art Director: Alfred Newman. Color, 117 min. **VHS, LASER**

There Was a Crooked Man

(1970) Warner Bros.
This bitterly black-comic vision of the West (written by the team that penned *Bonnie and Clyde*, 1967) deserves a bigger reputation. Douglas hides a half million in booty and then ends up in the pen where he matches wits with progressive warden Fonda. After Douglas betrays Fonda and his fellow inmates (a terrific supporting cast,

including Oates and Meredith) by escaping and heading for his loot, Fonda becomes the beneficiary of Douglas's deadly bad luck. **Cast:** Kirk Douglas, Henry Fonda, Warren Oates, Burgess Meredith, John Randolph, Arthur O'Connell, Martin Gabel, Michael Blodgett. **Credits:** Dir: Joseph L. Mankiewicz; Prod: Joseph L. Mankiewicz; Writer: David Newman, Robert Benton; DP: Harry Stradling; Ed: Gene Milford; Composer: Charles Strouse; Art Director: Edward Carrere. Color, 125 min. **VHS, LASER**

These Thousand Hills

(1959) Fox
Murray, an ambitious cowboy, rejects his lowlife friends in favor of the local town's more upmarket citizens. After setting up a ranch—with money borrowed from Remick, a saloon girl—he marries the local banker's daughter and ingratiates himself with her society friends, even refusing to lend a hand when an old pal is hunted down by a posse and hanged. Yet when Remick's life is in danger, he rushes to her side, but she takes the decisive action. An unusual Western drama. **Cast:** Don Murray, Richard Egan, Lee Remick, Patricia Owens, Stuart Whitman, Albert Dekker, Harold J. Stone, Royal Dano, Jean Willes, Douglas Fowley. **Credits:** Dir: Richard Fleischer; Prod: David Weisbert; Writer: Alfred Hayes; Story: A. B. Guthrie; DP: Charles G. Clarke; Ed: Hugh Fowler; Composer: Leigh Harline; Art Director: Lyle Wheeler, Herman A. Blumenthal. Color, 96 min.

These Three

(1936) United Artists
Hellman successfully adapts her play *The Children's Hour* to the screen, and Wyler provides straightforward, sensitive direction. Hopkins and Oberon are kind, devoted schoolteachers and friends who become the target of a vicious student's lies. The student (Granville) accuses one of the teachers of sleeping with the other's fiancé (McCrea), to the horror of the other faculty and parents. Though Hellman's adaptation sidesteps the lesbian implications in the stage version, the omission somehow adds to the oppressive atmosphere. Wyler tried this again in 1961, under the play's original title. Academy Award Nomination: Best Supporting Actress: Bonita Granville. **Cast:** Merle Oberon, Miriam Hopkins, Joel McCrea, Bonita Granville, Alma Kruger, Catharine Doucet, Marcia Mae Jones, Margaret Hamilton. **Cred-

its: Dir: William Wyler; Prod: Samuel Goldwyn; Writer: Lillian Hellman; Story: Lillian Hellman; DP: Gregg Toland; Ed: Daniel Mandell; Composer: Alfred Newman; Art Director: Richard Day. B&W, 93 min. VHS

They All Kissed the Bride
(1942) MGM
Crawford once again brings out the ice-queen persona for her role as a take-no-prisoners businesswoman whose demanding demeanor softens when she unexpectedly falls in love with a journalist (Douglas) out to expose how the men in her employ feel about their boss. When her father dies, Crawford takes control of her family's trucking business and cares for her flighty mother (Burke) and sister (Parrish). Douglas shows her the lighter side of life and her knees buckle. The part was meant for Carole Lombard before her death in a plane crash while on a war-bond tour. **Cast:** Joan Crawford, Melvyn Douglas, Roland Young, Billie Burke, Allen Jenkins, Helen Parrish, Andrew Tombes, Mary Treen. **Credits:** Dir: Alexander Hall; Prod: Edward Kaufman; Writer: P. J. Wolfson; DP: Joseph Walker; Ed: Viola Lawrence; Prod Design: Lionel Banks; Composer: Werner Richard Heymann. B&W, 87 min. VHS

They Call It Sin
(1932) Warner Bros.
This is a familiar story about small-town dreams and painful big-city realizations. Young falls in love with the producer of a Broadway show and is crushed to discover, after following him to the Big Apple, that he's already married. She must stand by and wait for her opportunity to arrive. A pre-Code potboiler mostly notable for lovely Young. **Cast:** Loretta Young, David Manners, George Brent, Louis Calhern, Una Merkel, Elizabeth Patterson, Erville Alderson, Nella Walker. **Credits:** Dir: Thornton Freeland; Prod: Hal B. Wallis; Writer: Lillie Hayward; DP: James Van Trees; Ed: James Gibbon; Art Director: Jack Okey. B&W, 75 min. VHS

They Came to Cordura
(1959) Columbia
A troubled production and an ailing Cooper (in one of his last roles) still don't defeat this intriguing military drama. When Cooper gets branded a coward during the Mexican War, his C.O. sees an opportunity to grab some glory and assigns Cooper to research Medal of Honor winners. When he's not rewarded with a place

on the list, he makes Cooper shepherd the supposed heroes through the desert to Cordura, with traitor Hayworth in tow. The heroes show their dark sides and Cooper shines. Rossen tried to buy back his film when the studio recut it; he died before he could complete the deal. This bears more than a passing resemblance to *Courage Under Fire* (1996). **Cast:** Gary Cooper, Rita Hayworth, Tab Hunter, Van Heflin, Richard Conte, Michael Callan, Dick York, Robert Keith. **Credits:** Dir: Robert Rossen; Prod: William Goetz; Writer: Ivan Moffat; DP: Burnett Guffey; Ed: William A. Lyon; Composer: Elie Siegmeister; Art Director: Cary Odell. B&W, 123 min. VHS, LASER

They Died with Their Boots On
(1941) Warner Bros.
This stirring biopic of General George Custer has Flynn cutting a dashing figure in the lead. The story follows Flynn from his West Point days and the beginning of his fateful rivalry with Ned Sharp (Kennedy) to his marriage to de Havilland to his posting with the 7th Cavalry in Nebraska. Walsh treats the Sioux (led by Quinn as Crazy Horse) with understanding and Flynn finds the combination of ambition, vanity, and courage that inspired the famous last stand. **Cast:** Errol Flynn, Olivia de Havilland, Arthur Kennedy, Anthony Quinn, Charley Grapewin, Gene Lockhart, Stanley Ridges, John Litel. **Credits:** Dir: Raoul Walsh; Writer: Wally Klein; DP: Bert Glennon; Ed: William Holmes; Composer: Max Steiner; Art Director: John Hughes. B&W, 141 min. VHS

They Drive by Night
(1940) Warner Bros.
This small masterpiece features Raft's greatest role and Walsh's typically gritty direction. Bogart and Raft are truck-driving brothers who buy a truck and start driving for themselves. When Bogart gets into an accident, Raft must return to working for a trucking company as traffic manager. Along comes Lupino, the boss's seductive wife, who takes a liking to Raft. Though he has no interest (he's married to Sheridan), Lupino murders her husband in order to take over the business and pursue Raft. When he rejects her advances, she tries to pin the murder on him. **Cast:** George Raft, Ann Sheridan, Ida Lupino, Humphrey Bogart, Gale Page, Alan Hale, Roscoe Karns, John Litel. **Credits:** Dir: Raoul Walsh; Prod: Mark Hellinger; Writer:

Jerry Wald; DP: Arthur Edeson; Ed: Oliver S. Garretson; Composer: Adolph Deutsch; Art Director: John Hughes. B&W, 96 min. VHS, LASER

They Got Me Covered
(1943) RKO
This is a wartime Hope vehicle, which he carries single-handedly, about two journalists in Washington who become involved in a triangle of kidnapping, romance, and murder. Sight gags, as well as one-liners, abound, as do many fun-to-spot cameos and early roles for Doris Day and others. And who's that singing every time Hope opens his cigarette case? You got it: Bing. Butler directed the best of the Road movies, *Road to Morocco* (1942). **Cast:** Bob Hope, Dorothy Lamour, Eduardo Ciannelli, Otto Preminger, Marion Martin, Donald Meek, Phyllis Ruth, Philip Ahn. **Credits:** Dir: David Butler; Prod: Samuel Goldwyn; Writer: Harry Kurnitz; DP: Rudolph Maté; Ed: Daniel Mandell; Composer: Leigh Harline; Art Director: Perry Ferguson. B&W, 93 min. VHS, LASER

They Live by Night
(1949) RKO
In Nicholas Ray's directorial debut, his visionary style becomes clear from the opening scenes. Granger plays a naive young man drawn deeper into crime by two older, hardened outlaws (Da Silva and Flippen). O'Donnell nurses him to health after he's injured in a robbery and a touching love affair ensues, made all the more poignant because the experience is new to them. Though Granger and O'Donnell want only to go straight and be together, Granger's first step into crime sealed their fate. Based on the novel *Thieves Like Us* by Edward Anderson, which was given a lighter treatment in Robert Altman's 1974 version. Note the Woody Guthrie contribution to the sound track. **Cast:** Cathy O'Donnell, Farley Granger, Howard Da Silva, Jay C. Flippen, Helen Craig, Will Wright, Ian Wolfe, William Phipps. **Credits:** Dir: Nicholas Ray; Prod: John Houseman; Writer: Charles Schnee; DP: George E. Diskant; Ed: Sherman Todd; Composer: Woody Guthrie; Art Director: Albert S. D'Agostino. B&W, 96 min. VHS, LASER

They Made Me a Criminal
(1939) Warner Bros.
Musical fantasist Berkeley takes on the Warner Bros. crime genre and the result is a fascinating portrait of a man with a second chance. Garfield, a drunken lout of a boxing champion,

hightails it when the headlines say he killed a reporter and then died in a fiery car wreck. He lands at a camp for troubled kids and sees a chance for redemption in the faces of the Dead End Kids. Berkeley's choreographic skills pay off in terrific boxing action. Remake of *The Life of Jimmy Dolan* (1933). **Cast:** John Garfield, Claude Rains, Ann Sheridan, May Robson, Billy Halop, Bobby Jordan, Leo Gorcey, Huntz Hall. **Credits:** Dir: Busby Berkeley; Prod: Benjamin Glazer; Writer: Sig Herzig; DP: James Wong Howe; Ed: Jack Killifer; Prod Design: Anton Grot; Composer: Max Steiner. B&W, 92 min. **VHS, LASER**

They Met in Bombay
(1941) MGM
In an action-comedy with exotic locales and Gable and Russell, two jewel thieves pick up on each other's plans and make the hit together. They flee from Bombay to Hong Kong on Lorre's boat, but he tries a double cross. Finally in China, Gable dons a disguise that leads him to a heroic new life and he makes Russell an honest woman. Ladd pops up for a second. **Cast:** Clark Gable, Rosalind Russell, Peter Lorre, Jessie Ralph, Reginald Owen, Eduardo Ciannelli, Alan Ladd, Matthew Boulton. **Credits:** Dir: Clarence Brown; Prod: Hunt Stromberg; Writer: Edwin Justus Mayer; DP: William Daniels; Ed: Blanche Sewell; Prod Design: Cedric Gibbons; Composer: Herbert Stothart. B&W, 93 min. **VHS**

They Might Be Giants
(1971) Universal
In a bizarre film with engaging performances from Scott and Woodward, Scott, a retired judge, mourns the loss of his wife and slips into a delusion in which he is convinced that he's Sherlock Holmes. His conniving brother (Rawlins) wants him committed to get his hands on the family estate, and takes him to visit Woodward, a psychiatrist named Dr. Watson. When Scott intrigues her by seeing the root of another patient's problem, Scott leads the therapist on a merry chase through New York that ends with her as loopy as he is. Produced by Woodward's husband, Paul. **Cast:** George C. Scott, Joanne Woodward, Jack Gilford, Lester Rawlins, Rue McClanahan, Ron Weyand, Kitty Winn, Sudie Bond. **Credits:** Dir: Anthony Harvey; Prod: John Foreman, Paul Newman; Writer: James Goldman; DP: Victor J. Kemper; Ed: Jerry Greenberg; Prod Design: John Barry. Color, 98 min. **VHS**

They Shall Have Music
(1939) United Artists
Goldwyn's noble attempt to bring classical music to the masses and make a star of violinist Jascha Heifetz. A poor young boy who witnesses a performance by Heifetz is drawn into the world of music. He joins Brennan's music school, which is just barely solvent, and tries to convince Heifetz to play a benefit concert for the troubled institution. Musical numbers include "Rondo Capriccioso," "Hora Staccato,"

"Melody," "Estrellita," and many more. William Wyler directed some of the Heifetz segments. Academy Award Nomination: Best Score. **Cast:** Jascha Heifetz, Walter Brennan, Joel McCrea, Gene Reynolds, Marjorie Main, Andrea Leeds, Terry Kilburn, Tommy Kelly, Alfred Newman. **Credits:** Dir: Irmgard Von Cube; Prod: Samuel Goldwyn; Writer: Irmgard Von Cube; DP: Gregg Toland; Ed: Sherman Todd; Prod Design: James Basevi; Composer: Alfred Newman. B&W, 102 min. **VHS**

They Shoot Horses, Don't They?
(1969) Cinerama
A drama about marathon dancers in the Depression era becomes a poignant metaphor for spiritual defeat in a poverty-battered society. A competition for $1,500 becomes a deadly struggle for survival as master of ceremonies Young goads the contestants into increasing degradations. Fonda's first dramatic role is courageous and physically powerful as she survives to the end, but is so crushed she asks to be put out of her misery. One of the enduring works of '60s cinema. Golden Globe for Best Supporting Actor: Gig Young. Academy Award Nominations: 9, including Best Director; Best Actress: Jane Fonda; Best (Adapted) Screenplay. **Academy Awards:** Best Supporting Actor: Gig Young. **Cast:** Jane Fonda, Michael Sarrazin, Gig Young, Susannah York, Red Buttons, Bonnie Bedelia, Bruce Dern, Allyn Ann McLerie. **Credits:** Dir: Sydney Pollack; Prod: Irwin Winkler, Robert Chartoff, Sydney Pollack; Writer: James Poe, Robert Thompson; Story: Horace McCoy; DP: Philip H. Lathrop; Ed: Fredric Steinkamp; Composer: Johnny Green; Art Director: Harry Horner. Color, 123 min. **VHS, LASER**

They Were Expendable
(1945) MGM
Ford returned from making wartime documentaries when he was convinced that this wouldn't be just another war movie. It isn't. It is an inspiring, bleak tribute to the quiet dignity and courage of the American military even as they faced certain defeat in the early days of the Pacific campaign. The true story details America's PT-boat squadrons supporting the naval war in the Philippines. Montgomery (based on real-life Medal of Honor winner John Bulkeley) commands the boats and Wayne learns the importance of duty and sacrifice as a PT-boat officer. Wayne and Reed have a

They Shoot Horses, Don't They? (1969)

sweet, tender romance when he's ordered to sick bay. Ford agreed to the movie after meeting Bulkeley at Normandy. His direction was so impassioned he fell from a scaffold and broke his leg; Montgomery finished the last two weeks of shooting (and went on to direct a few interesting features and much TV). Academy Award Nominations: Best Sound Recording; Best Special Effects. **Cast:** Robert Montgomery, John Wayne, Donna Reed, Ward Bond, Marshall Thompson, Paul Langton, Leon Ames, Donald Curtis. **Credits:** Dir: John Ford; Prod: John Ford; Writer: Frank Wead; DP: Joseph H. August; Ed: Frank Hull; Prod Design: Cedric Gibbons; Composer: Herbert Stothart. B&W, 136 min. **VHS, LASER**

They Won't Believe Me
(1947) RKO
America's father figure a philandering playboy who's tried for murdering his wife? Young makes a surprisingly effective louse who uses his wife (Johnson) for her money, and romances his partner's secretary (a typically sexy Hayward) after canoodling with Greer. Along the way, two of the women meet bad ends. Young gets his, though, in an ironic twist of fate. Well acted and entertaining. **Cast:** Robert Young, Susan Hayward, Jane Greer, Rita Johnson, Tom Powers, George Tyne, Don Beddoe, Frank Ferguson. **Credits:** Dir: Irving Pichel; Prod: Joan Harrison; Writer: Jonathan Latimer; DP: Harry Wild; Ed: Elmo Williams; Prod Design: Albert S. D'Agostino; Composer: Roy Webb. B&W, 95 min. **VHS, LASER**

The Thief
(1952) United Artists
A spy-thriller noir set in New York City employs an interesting experiment: no dialogue! By leaving motivations unspoken, the creeping paranoia fills the plot's gaps. Milland gives an impressive performance as an Atomic Energy Commission scientist who commits treason. The film follows his agonizing attack of conscience as the F.B.I. moves closer to uncovering him. Gam's debut. Academy Award Nomination: Best Score. **Cast:** Ray Milland, Rita Gam, Harry Bronson, Martin Gabel, John McKutcheon, Rex O'Malley. **Credits:** Dir: Russell Rouse; Prod: Clarence Greene; Writer: Clarence Greene, Russell Rouse; DP: Sam Leavitt; Ed: Chester Schaeffer; Composer: Herschel Burke Gilbert; Costumes: Maria Donovan. B&W, 85 min. **VHS**

The Thief of Bagdad
(1924) United Artists
This is perhaps the most sumptuous spectacle of the silent era, with inventive director Walsh teaming with the production genius of two future directors, Menzies and Leisen, to create a magical setting in which Fairbanks shines. The swashbuckling hero portrays the thief who wins the heart of a princess when he sneaks into her castle. He then sets off on an adventurous journey to make himself worthy of her hand and to defeat the evil Mongol prince. Dazzling even now. Selected for the National Film Registry. **Cast:** Douglas Fairbanks, Anna May Wong, Julianne Johnston. **Credits:** Dir: Raoul Walsh; Writer: Lotta Woods; DP: Arthur Edeson; Ed: William Nolan; Prod Design: William Cameron Menzies; Costumes: Mitchell Leisen. B&W, 155 min. **VHS, LASER, DVD**

Thieves' Highway
(1949) Fox
Dark drama of disillusionment and thwarted ambition uses stylized camera work to depict the return of veteran Conte to the bitter realities of civilian life. His truck-driving father has been crippled in a confrontation with shady produce commission operative Cobb. Conte forsakes his own dreams and goes into the trucking business, where he quickly runs afoul of Cobb, but finds truth in the unlikely figure of a prostitute, and partners for his vengeance in Cobb's former gang members. Dassin's last film before facing the HUAC blacklist. **Cast:** Richard Conte, Valentina Cortesa, Lee J. Cobb, Jack Oakie, Millard Mitchell, Joseph Pevney, Morris Carnovsky, Tamara Shayne, Kasia Orzazewski, Barbara Lawrence. **Credits:** Dir: Jules Dassin; Prod: Robert Bassler; Writer: A. I. Bezzerides; DP: Norbert F. Brodine; Ed: Nick DeMaggio; Art Director: Lyle Wheeler, Chester Gore. B&W, 94 min.

Thieves Like Us
(1974) United Artists
Altman remakes Nicholas Ray's 1949 *They Live by Night* with an innocent charm that focuses the story of bank robbers in the '30s on the surprisingly sweet romance between Carradine and Duvall. Carradine, a young criminal, gets caught up with Schuck and Remsen in a prison escape. They immediately return to their chosen profession, even if it's painfully obvious that they aren't very talented at their craft. Hiding out at Skerritt's, Carradine meets and falls in love with the rather naive Duvall, and after a few notorious heists, they hope to leave crime behind. But the law pursues the thieves to the fatal end. A masterwork of the '70s from a sterling trio of screenwriters and Hollywood's most idiosyncratic voice. Fletcher's debut. **Cast:** Keith Carradine, Shelley Duvall, John Schuck, Bert Remsen, Louise Fletcher, Ann Latham, Tom Skerritt, Joan Tewkesbury. **Credits:** Dir: Robert Altman; Prod: Jerry Bick; Writer: Calder Willingham, Joan Tewkesbury, Robert Altman; DP: Jean Boffety; Ed: Lou Lombardo. Color, 123 min. **VHS, LASER**

The Thing
(1951) RKO
This masterpiece of sci-fi horror builds a Cold War metaphor of the shadowy beast that infiltrates an American installation and scatters its treacherous seeds. An Air Force squad joins a group of scientists exploring the top of the world when they report the discovery of an alien spaceship. When they unthaw its inhabitant (Arness), terror spreads when the group realizes it has unleashed a bloodsucking vegetable. They try frying and boiling, but not until they manage to electrocute the thing can they proclaim victory over the first alien invasion. Hawks only receives producer credit, but his influence can be seen throughout in the snappy dialogue, the Sheridan character's tomboy appeal, and the clash between men of principal with opposing goals. Remade by John Carpenter in 1982. **Cast:** Kenneth Tobey, James Arness, Margaret Sheridan, Robert Cornthwaite, Douglas Spencer, James Young, Dewey Martin, Robert Nichols, William Self, Eduard Franz. **Credits:** Dir: Christian Nyby; Prod: Howard Hawks; Story: Charles Lederer, Donald Stuart; DP: Russell Harlan; Ed: Roland Gross; Composer: Dimitri Tiomkin; Art Director: Albert S. D'Agostino, John Hughes. B&W, 80 min. **VHS, LASER**

Thin Ice
(1937) Fox
This charming romantic musical gives Henie plenty of room to shine. She plays an ice-skating teacher who meets, by chance, a European prince (Power) who is passing through her country. Unaware of his royalty, they fall in love. In the process, she helps him to solve his troubles (political and romantic), and the rest is musical history. Henie's second film role and her biggest success as Power adds class to her Cinderella sparkle.

The Thin Man (1934)

Cast: Sonja Henie, Tyrone Power, Sig Rumann, Raymond Walburn, Joan Davis, Alan Hale, Melville Cooper, Maurice Cass, George Givot. **Credits:** Dir: Sidney Lanfield; Prod: Raymond Griffith; Writer: Boris Ingster; DP: Robert Planck; Ed: Robert Simpson; Prod Design: Mark-Lee Kirk. Color, 86 min. **VHS**

The Thin Man

Nick and Nora Charles, played by William Powell and Myrna Loy, an urbane, fun- and martini-loving husband-and-wife detective team, were known as much for their snappy repartee as for their sleuthing. The couple's wire-haired terrier, Asta, was an important part of the team, getting lost or hiding under the bed, paws over ears, at just the wrong moment. The birth of Nick, Jr., in *Another Thin Man* (1939) didn't dampen the Charleses' enthusiasm for investigative capers, though it did somewhat curtail their debauchery (the all-night parties became kiddie birthday bashes—complete with babies stolen for the occasion by some of Nick's less savory acquaintances). Incidentally, Nick was not the lean man of the title—Edward Ellis was. He played an inventor whose death Nick and Nora investigated in *The Thin Man* (1934), which was based on Dashiell Hammett's novel. The Thin Man collection remains one of

the best of its genre, attributable to the breezy pace of the films and the chemistry between Powell and Loy. Look for James Stewart playing a suspect in *After the Thin Man* (1936).

The Thin Man *(1934)*
After the Thin Man *(1936)*
Another Thin Man *(1939)*
Shadow of the Thin Man *(1941)*
The Thin Man Goes Home *(1944)*
Song of the Thin Man *(1947)*

The Thin Red Line

(1964) Allied Artists
The first screen version of Jones's WWII novel; the second, director Terrence Malick's (*Days of Heaven*, 1978) return to the screen after 20 years, was the most anticipated movie of 1998. The bloody carnage of Guadalcanal provides the setting for a depiction of war's effect on men's souls. Sergeant Warden has the deadened eyes of a man who has seen too much death; private Dullea is at first horrified by his killing and then performs with sadistic efficiency. Grim war-is-hell drama. **Cast:** Keir Dullea, Jack Warden, Kieron Moore, James Philbrook, Steve Rowland, Stephen Levy, Mark Johnson. **Credits:** Dir: Andrew Marton; Prod: Sidney Harmon; Writer: Bernard Gordon, James Jones; DP: Manuel Berenguer; Ed: Derek Parsons; Composer: Malcolm Arnold; Art Director: Jose Alguero. Color, 99 min. **DVD**

The Third Man on the Mountain

(1959) Disney
This fine Disney adventure is about a young man (MacArthur) anxious to prove himself by climbing a yet unconquered mountain peak that claimed his father's life. Shot on location in the Swiss Alps. **Cast:** Michael Rennie, James MacArthur, Janet Munro, Herbert Lom, Laurence Naismith, Lee Patterson, Walter Fitzgerald, Nora Swinburne. **Credits:** Dir: Ken Annakin; Prod: William H. Anderson; Writer: Eleanore Griffin; Story: James Ramsey Ullman; DP: Harry Waxman; Ed: Peter Boita; Prod Design: John Howell; Composer: William Alwyn. Color, 106 min. **VHS, LASER**

Thirteen Hours by Air

(1936) Paramount
Ace commercial pilot MacMurray attempts to take passengers traveling from Newark to San Francisco through a violent snowstorm. Things are further complicated by the fact that three jewel thieves fresh from a $50,000 heist board the plane and are eager to have him make an unscheduled stop. MacMurray refuses and must contend with the thieves as well as the panic that breaks out among the passengers. **Cast:** Fred MacMurray, Joan Bennett, ZaSu Pitts, Anne Baxter, Fred Keating, Brian Donlevy, John Howard, Ruth Donnelly, Ben Barlett. **Credits:** Dir: Mitchell Leisen; Prod: E. Lloyd Sheldon; Writer: Kenyon Nicholson; DP: Theodor Sparkuhl; Prod Design: Hans Dreier, John B. Goodman. B&W, 77 min.

The Thirteenth Guest

(1932) Monogram
This classic Poverty Row thriller helped popularize the spooky dinner-party mystery and was boosted by the popularity of Rogers in her second screen appearance. A group gathers at an eerie mansion to remember the passing of the host of a dinner party thrown 13 years earlier. When the reading of an enigmatic will is interrupted by a stranger's appearance, the party-goers must solve the mystery of the "thirteenth guest," the invitee to whom the deceased host left his estate. Highly entertaining. **Cast:** Ginger Rogers, Lyle Talbot, J. Farrell MacDonald, Eddie Phillips, Erville Alderson, Robert Klein, Crauford Kent, Lynton Brent. **Credits:** Dir: Albert Ray; Prod: M. H. Hoffman; Writer: Frances Hyland, Arthur Hoerl, Armitage Trail; DP: Harry Neumann, Tom Galligan; Ed: L. R. Brown; Art Director: Gene Hornbostel. B&W, 70 min. **VHS**

Thirty Seconds over Tokyo

(1944) MGM

This dramatic, near-documentary telling of America's first bombing attack on Japan is based on the recollections of one of the surviving pilots. Tracy plays mission leader Lt. Colonel James Doolittle as he reveals their suicidal mission: rain bombs over two Japanese cities and then crash-land in enemy-occupied China. The journey begins aboard an aircraft carrier and follows a plane piloted by Johnson as it delivers its payload and crashes off the coast of China where sympathetic villagers hide the airmen and nurse the wounded. Academy Award Nominations: 2, including Best (Black-and-White) Cinematography. **Academy Awards:** Best Special Effects. **Cast:** Spencer Tracy, Van Johnson, Robert Walker, Phyllis Thaxter, Robert Mitchum, Scott McKay, Don Defore, John Reilly. **Credits:** Dir: Mervyn LeRoy; Prod: Sam Zimbalist; Writer: Dalton Trumbo; DP: Harold Rosson; Ed: Frank Sullivan; Prod Design: Cedric Gibbons; Composer: Herbert Stothart. B&W, 139 min. **VHS**

This Above All

(1942) Fox

A wartime romantic drama set in Britain tells the story of working-class Power as he overcomes his resentment of the upper classes and rejoins the war effort. Wounded in action at Dunkirk, the bitter Power returns to London where he is fixed up with Fontaine, a rich heiress who's joined up with the regular London girls of the WAAF. As love grows between them, he discovers her background and she discovers that he is about to be branded a deserter. An air raid changes both their lives when Power's courage leads to a life-threatening injury. Academy Award Nominations: 4, including Best Cinematography; Best Editing. **Cast:** Tyrone Power, Joan Fontaine, Thomas Mitchell, Henry Stephenson, Nigel Bruce, Gladys Cooper, Philip Merivale, Sara Allgood, Alexander Knox, Queenie Leonard. **Credits:** Dir: Anatole Litvak; Prod: Darryl F. Zanuck; Writer: R. C. Sherriff; Story: Eric Knight; DP: Arthur C. Miller; Ed: Walter Thompson; Prod Design: Richard Day, Joseph C. Wright, Thomas Little; Composer: Alfred Newman. B&W, 110 min.

This Could Be the Night

(1957) MGM

Musical comedy about a shy, quiet schoolteacher (Simmons) who takes an after-hours job as a secretary at a nightclub. Little does she realize that the owners (Douglas and Franciosa) also dabble as gangsters. She falls under one's spell, to the dismay of the other, who understands that if she found out about his partner's wicked ways her affections would quickly disappear. A minor, but appealing, musical directed by Wise with songs by Duke Ellington, Sammy Cahn, and Cole Porter. **Cast:** Jean Simmons, Paul Douglas, Anthony Franciosa, Joan Blondell, Neile Adams, ZaSu Pitts, J. Carrol Naish, Rafael Campos. **Credits:** Dir: Robert Wise; Prod: Joe Pasternak; Writer: Isobel Lennart; DP: Russell Harlan; Ed: George Boemler; Choreographer: Jack Baker. B&W, 105 min. **VHS, LASER**

This Day and Age

(1933) Paramount

DeMille's only gangster movie pits the young people who participate in a youth-week celebration against dangerous hoodlums. Bickford puts the protection strong-arm racket on a defenseless tailor, and then kills him as an example to other noncooperative merchants. When the mayor turns over the reins of government to the kids for the day, they use their new powers to terrify the mobster into a confession. **Cast:** Charles Bickford, Judith Allen, Richard Cromwell, Harry Green, Eddie Nugent, Ben Alexander, Oscar Rudolph, Billy Gilbert, Lester Arnold, Fuzzy Knight. **Credits:** Dir: Cecil B. DeMille; Prod: Cecil B. DeMille; Writer: Bartlett Cormack; DP: J. Peverell Marley; Ed: Anne Bauchens; Prod Design: Hans Dreier; Composer: L. W. Gilbert. B&W, 85 min.

This Gun for Hire

(1942) Paramount

Ladd emerges as a major screen presence as a paid killer who gets mixed up in a sabotage ring. The story follows the cold-blooded killer as he goes about his day's work, and then to a double cross by Cregar, a client who smuggles poison gas to the enemy. With both the police and Cregar's henchmen on his tail, nightclub singer Lake teaches Ladd that he doesn't have to kill and the murderer makes a too-late decision to do the noble thing. Ladd's performance, a frightening exercise in cold, somber detachment (watch his eyes as he decides whether or not to slay a little girl), made him an instant sensation. He and Lake made three more pictures together, including *The Blue Dahlia* (1946). Remade with Jimmy Cagney directing as *Short Cut to Hell* (1957). **Cast:** Alan Ladd, Veronica Lake, Robert Preston, Marc Lawrence, Mikhail Rasumny, Pamela Blake, Harry Shannon, Frank Ferguson, Bernadene Hayes. **Credits:** Dir: Frank Tuttle; Prod: Richard M. Blumenthal; Writer: W. R. Burnett; DP: John F. Seitz; Ed: Archie Marshek; Prod Design: Hans Dreier; Composer: David Buttolph. B&W, 81 min. **VHS, LASER**

This Happy Feeling

(1958) Universal

Innocent young Reynolds (in a seeming reprise of her *Tammy* role) falls hard for former actor Jurgens, now her employer on a horse farm. Into the mix enters Saxon, Jurgens's young neighbor, who falls even harder for Reynolds, and Jurgens's paramour, Smith. An early effort from Edwards. **Cast:** Debbie Reynolds, Curt Jurgens, John Saxon, Mary Astor, Alexis Smith, Estelle Winwood, Troy Donahue, Hayden Rorke. **Credits:** Dir: Blake Edwards; Prod: Ross Hunter; Writer: Blake Edwards; DP: Arthur E. Arling; Ed: Milton Carruth; Prod Design: Alexander Golitzen; Composer: Frank Skinner. Color, 92 min. **VHS**

This Island Earth

(1955) Universal

This is top-of-the-line '50s sci-fi with the best effects of the day. Two scientists from Earth (Reason and Domergue) are tricked into helping aliens save their doomed planet, Metaluna. The apocalyptic wasteland is about to be swallowed by an artificially-bred race of disgusting mutants that are ravaging the planet. A notable distinction (good or bad, depending upon how you look at it): this was the target of *Mystery Science Theater 3000*'s first trip to the big screen. **Cast:** Jeff Morrow, Faith Domergue, Rex Reason, Russell Johnson, Lance Fuller, Robert Nichols, Douglas Spencer, Karl L. Lindt. **Credits:** Dir: Jack Arnold, Joseph M. Newman; Prod: William Alland; Writer: Franklin Coen, Edward O'Callaghan; DP: Clifford Stine; Ed: Virgil Vogel; Prod Design: Alexander Golitzen; Composer: Herman Stein. Color, 86 min. **VHS, LASER, DVD**

This Is My Affair

(1937) Fox

This crime drama with an intriguing historical twist is based on a story by producer Zanuck. Turn-of-the-century naval officer Taylor gets decommissioned so he can go undercover and expose a ring of bank robbers whose methods are so successful they endanger the monetary system. He infiltrates the gang by sweet-talking saloon singer Stanwyck and they complicate the mission by falling in love. The only person to know of Taylor's assignment is President McKinley (Conroy). Just as the police move in on the gang and round up Taylor with them, McKinley is assassinated. Desperate Stanwyck must bring Taylor's case straight to Teddy Roosevelt (Blackmer) before it's too late. **Cast:** Robert Taylor, Barbara Stanwyck, Victor McLaglen, Brian Donlevy, Frank Conroy, John Carradine, Douglas Fowley, Alan Dinehart, Sig Ruman, Robert McWade, Sidney Blackmer. **Credits:** Dir: William A. Seiter; Prod: Darryl F. Zanuck, Kenneth MacGowan; Writer: Allen Rivkin, Lamar Trotti; DP: Robert Planck; Ed: Allen McNeil; Prod Design: Rudolph Sternad; Composer: Mack Gordon, Harry Revel. B&W, 100 min.

This Is the Army
(1943) Warner Bros.
This Irving Berlin flag-waving musical has a finale that features Berlin along with 300 soldiers in the all-time greatest USO show. Murphy was a song-and-dance man who enlisted in WWI and put on a big benefit show. His son, Reagan, gets drafted for WWII and follows in his father's soft-shoe footsteps. The many songs include "Your Country and My Country," "My Sweetie," "We're On Our Way to France," "I'm on K.P.," and "Poor Little Me." Academy Award Nominations: 3, including Best Sound; Best Art Direction. **Academy Awards:** Best Scoring of a Musical. **Cast:** George Murphy, Joan Leslie, Ronald Reagan, Dolores Costello, Kate Smith, Joe Lewis, Alan Hale, Charles Butterworth. **Credits:** Dir: Michael Curtiz; Prod: Jack L. Warner; Writer: Casey Robinson, Claude Binyon; DP: Bert Glennon; Ed: George Amy; Composer: Irving Berlin; Art Director: John Hughes. Color, 121 min. **VHS**

This Land Is Mine
(1943) RKO
Renoir's second American film is a well-presented story of heroism called forth by brutality. Laughton delivers an inspired performance as a passive, shy schoolteacher during the Nazi occupation who rises to the occasion when his mentor and the woman he loves (O'Hara) become involved in the Resistance. He uses his show trial for a rousing speech rallying the town, knowing he will pay with his life. **Academy Awards:** Best Sound Recording. **Cast:** Charles Laughton, Maureen O'Hara, George Sanders, Walter Slezak, Kent Smith, Una O'Connor, Philip Merivale, Thurston Hall. **Credits:** Dir: Jean Renoir; Prod: Jean Renoir, Dudley Nichols; Writer: Dudley Nichols; DP: Frank Redman; Ed: Frederic Knudtson; Prod Design: Eugene Lourie; Composer: Lothar Perl. B&W, 103 min. **VHS, LASER**

This Love of Ours
(1945) Universal
This lush soaper (based on a Pirandello play) stars Oberon as she runs into her ex-husband (Korvin), who left her 15 years prior when he incorrectly suspected her of having an affair. She later attempts suicide over the encounter, but her ex-husband, a doctor, saves her. He tells her that she has a daughter who needs her, and wins her love once again. Now Oberon must win over her own daughter, who thinks her mother died years earlier. An expensively mounted remake of the 1932 Garbo vehicle *As You Desire Me*. Academy Award Nomination: Best Score. **Cast:** Merle Oberon, Charles Korvin, Claude Rains, Carl Esmond, Sue England, Jess Barker, Harry Davenport, Ralph Morgan, Fritz Leiber. **Credits:** Dir: William Dieterle; Prod: Howard Benedict; Writer: John Klorer, Leonard Lee, Bruce Manning; Story: Luigi Pirandello; DP: Lucien Ballard; Ed: Frank Gross; Prod Design: Robert Clatworthy, John B. Goodman; Composer: Hans J. Salter. B&W, 90 min.

This Man's Navy
(1945) MGM .
Another Wellman war picture set in the air, this time among blimp pilots. Beery annoys his fellow pilots with stories of his family and his son's heroic exploits in the Navy, though he doesn't have a son or a wife. When Beery meets a widow with a sick son and strikes up a friendship with the pair, he encourages the boy to recover and join the Navy, where he becomes a hero. The pilot and the widow marry, fulfilling Beery's fantasies. **Cast:** Wallace Beery, Tom Drake, James Gleason, Jan Clayton, Selena Royle, Noah Beery, Henry O'Neill, Steve Brodie, George Chandler. **Credits:** Dir: William Wellman; Prod: Samuel Marx; Writer: Hugh Allen, Borden Chase, Allen Rivkin, John Twist; DP: Sidney Wagner; Ed: Irvine Warburton; Prod Design: Howard Campbell, Cedric Gibbons; Composer: Nathaniel Shilkret. B&W, 100 min.

This Property Is Condemned
(1966) Paramount
This steamy film version of Tennessee Williams's play about a young man's eventful visit to a small-town boarding-house survives meddling by the producer, a script worked over by director Coppola and legendary producer Coe, and the town used as a location rising up in outrage. Wood plays a flirty southern belle who dreams of the day when a handsome traveler will come to take her away. When Redford arrives at her mother's boarding-house, she's convinced that she's found her man. Her mother's interference drives Redford away, and Wood makes a disastrous match with her mother's violent lover, Bronson. Notable for the chemistry between Wood and Redford and photography by Howe. **Cast:** Robert Redford, Natalie Wood, Charles Bronson, Kate Reid, Mary Badham, Dabney Coleman, Robert Blake, Alan Baxter, Jon Provost. **Credits:** Dir: Sydney Pollack; Prod: John Houseman; Writer: Francis Coppola, Fred Coe, Ediith Sommer; Story: Tennessee Williams; DP: James Wong Howe; Ed: Adrienne Fazan; Prod Design: Hal Pereira; Composer: Kenyon Hopkins. Color, 110 min. **VHS, LASER**

This Thing Called Love
(1940) Columbia
This sophisticated sex comedy was risqué in its day. Russell is an independent business executive who marries Douglas but refuses to consummate their nuptials until they have survived a three-month trial period. Douglas unwillingly agrees, but finds it more difficult than he first imagined, and he attempts to seduce his wife in an increasingly desperate series of humiliating defeats. When Russell finally gives in, her husband's triumph is deflated by a case of poison oak. **Cast:** Rosalind Russell, Melvyn Douglas, Binnie Barnes, Lee J. Cobb, Gloria Holden, Paul McGrath, Leona Maricle, Don Beddoe, Allyn Joslyn. **Credits:** Dir: Alexander Hall; Prod: William Perlberg; Writer: Ken Englund, George Seaton, P. J. Wolfson; Story: Edwin Burke; DP: Joseph Walker; Ed: Viola Lawrence; Prod Design: Lionel Banks; Composer: Werner R. Heymann. B&W, 98 min.

This Woman Is Dangerous
(1952) Warner Bros.
Crawford's last at Warner is a pot-boiler combo of gangster movie and soap opera (gangster opera?). She's the brains behind a vicious circle of thieves, with the brawn supplied by her jealous lover, Brian. Concealing her criminal past, Crawford checks herself into a hospital for corrective eye surgery by Morgan. Naturally, she

and the doctor fall in love and she even charms his daughter. Now repentant and reformed, Crawford worries that her past will resurface in the form of an attack by Brian, who indeed turns up in Morgan's operating room. Routine, but Crawford's always entertaining. **Cast:** Joan Crawford, Dennis Morgan, David Brian, Richard Webb, Mari Aldon, Philip Carey, Katherine Warren, George Chandler, William Challee, Sherry Jackson. **Credits:** Dir: Felix E. Feist; Prod: Robert Sisk; Writer: Geoffery Homes, George Yeats; DP: Ted McCord; Ed: James Moore; Prod Design: Leo Kuter. B&W, 100 min.

The Thomas Crown Affair
(1968) United Artists
Director Jewison combines the heist film with romance and stirs it with the very latest in '60s film style. McQueen stars as a millionaire who hatches a plan for the perfect bank robbery. Dunaway is the insurance investigator out to expose him. As she closes in, they do a warily sexy tango as each tries to deduce the other's motives as they fall in love. The chess scene is famously seductive. Academy Award Nominations: 2, including Best Original Score. **Academy Awards:** Best Song ("The Windmills of Your Mind"). **Cast:** Steve McQueen, Faye Dunaway, Paul Burke, Yaphet Kotto, Todd Martin, Sam Melville, Addison Powell, Judy Pace. **Credits:** Dir: Norman Jewison; Prod: Norman Jewison; Writer: Alan R. Trustman; DP: Haskell Wexler; Ed: Hal Ashby, Ralph E. Winters, Byron Brandt; Composer: Michel Legrand; Art Director: Robert Boyle. Color, 102 min. **VHS, LASER**

Thoroughbreds Don't Cry
(1937) MGM
Rooney and Garland appear together for the first time in this trip to the racetrack. Rooney is a jockey who takes a dive in order for his shiftless father to earn a large enough payoff to cover his "medical troubles." When the horse's owner (Smith) dies, Rooney asks his father to borrow the money back so that the owner's grandson can run the horse in another race. His father rejects him, but Rooney takes the money anyway. When his father finds out, he tells the authorities about his son's earlier incident. Garland, in her first starring role, takes a few opportunities to introduce us to how well she can sing. **Cast:** Judy Garland, Mickey Rooney, Sophie Tucker, C. Aubrey Smith, Frankie Darro, Henry Kolker, Helen Troy,

Charles D. Brown. **Credits:** Dir: Alfred E. Green; Prod: Harry Rapf; Writer: Lawrence Hazard; DP: Leonard Smith; Ed: Elmo Veron. B&W, 80 min. **VHS**

Thoroughly Modern Millie
(1967) Universal
Small-town girl Andrews is on a mission when she moves from Kansas to the Big Apple in the Roaring '20s: become a fashionable stenographer and fall in love with the president of the company. She hooks up with Moore and together they face the romantic trials and tribulations of being modern women. Overly long (it was designed for wide-screen road shows), but stuffed with nostalgic music and huge set pieces, including the title song, "The Tapioca," "The Jewish Wedding Song," and "Jimmy." Golden Globe for Best Supporting Actress: Carol Channing. Academy Award Nominations: 7, including Best Supporting Actress: Carol Channing; Best Song ("Thoroughly Modern Millie"). **Academy Awards:** Best Original Musical or Comedy Score. **Cast:** Julie Andrews, Mary Tyler Moore, Carol Channing, John Gavin, Beatrice Lillie, Jack Soo, Noriyuki Morita, Philip Ahn. **Credits:** Dir: George Roy Hill; Prod: Ross Hunter; Writer: Richard Morris; DP: Russell Metty; Ed: Stuart Gilmore; Prod Design: Alexander Golitzen; Composer: Elmer Bernstein. Color, 138 min. **VHS, LASER**

Those Calloways
(1965) Disney
Enjoyable family entertainment from Disney has Keith as the Indian-reared head of a small-town New England family who spends all his money to maintain a nearby lake as a sanctuary for migrating geese. Abbott sees the possibilities for a game-hunting area and the two end up in a dramatic clash. **Cast:** Brian Keith, Vera Miles, Ed Wynn, Walter Brennan, Brandon De Wilde, Linda Evans, Philip Abbott, John Larkin. **Credits:** Dir: Norman Tokar; Prod: Winston Hibler; Writer: Louis Pelletier; DP: Edward Colman; Ed: Grant K. Smith; Prod Design: Carroll Clark; Composer: Max Steiner. Color, 130 min. **VHS**

Those Daring Young Men in Their Jaunty Jalopies
(1969) Paramount
The follow-up to *Those Magnificent Men in Their Flying Machines* boasts an equally expansive international cast and expensive production. The story follows a '20s automobile race that travels 1,500 miles to Monte

Carlo. The British team is the comedy duo of Cook and Moore, members of England's fabled Goon Show. **Cast:** Tony Curtis, Terry-Thomas, Dudley Moore, Peter Cook, Susan Hampshire, Walter Chiari, Lando Buzzanca, Jack Hawkins. **Credits:** Dir: Ken Annakin; Prod: Ken Annakin; Writer: Ken Annakin, Jack Davies; DP: Gabor Pogany, Walter Wottitz, Bert Palmgren; Ed: Peter Taylor; Art Director: Elven Webb, Boris Jurga, Marc Frederix; Composer: Ron Goodwin. Color, 125 min. **VHS, LASER**

Those Magnificent Men in Their Flying Machines
(1965) Fox
An international comedy spectacular with Morley a rich English publisher who sponsors a London to Paris "air race." The stars and their fabulous flying machines come from all over the world to participate. The film winningly combines romance and slapstick, double crosses and midair hijinks for harmless fun. Academy Award Nomination: Best (Original) Story and Screenplay. **Cast:** Terry-Thomas, James Fox, Stuart Whitman, Sarah Miles, Alberto Sordi, Robert Morley, Gert Frobe, Jean-Pierre Cassel. **Credits:** Dir: Ken Annakin; Prod: Stan Margulies; Writer: Ken Annakin, Jack Davies; DP: Christopher Challis; Ed: Gordon Stone, Ann Coates; Prod Design: Tom Morahan; Composer: Ron Goodwin. Color, 138 min. **VHS, LASER**

A Thousand and One Nights
(1945) Columbia
An entertaining satire on Arabian Nights tales finds Aladdin, played by a charming Wilde, pining for Princess Armina (Jergens). He thinks he's found the answer in a magic lamp, but when the genie emerges, it's another beautiful woman (Keyes). Keyes, immediately recognizing her attraction to Wilde, does her best to extinguish his passion for the princess. Silvers plays Wilde's comic sidekick, and don't blink or you'll miss Shelley Winters, who flashes by as a handmaiden. Academy Award Nominations: Best Art Direction; Best Visual Effects. **Cast:** Cornel Wilde, Evelyn Keyes, Phil Silvers, Adele Jergens, Dusty Anderson, Dennis Hoey, Rex Ingram, Richard Hale. **Credits:** Dir: Alfred E. Green; Prod: Samuel Bischoff; Writer: Richard English, Jack Henley, Wilfrid H. Pettitt; DP: Ray Rennahan; Ed: Gene Havlick; Prod Design: Stephen Goosson, Rudolph Sternad; Composer: Marlin Skiles. B&W, 92 min. **VHS**

A Thousand Clowns

(1965) United Artists
Gardner successfully adapts his Broadway play about the whimsically misanthropic former writer for a Soupy Sales–like children's program and his wise-before-his-time young nephew. Robards and Gordon have to forsake their nonconformist routine when the social service agency (in the persons of a sympathetic Harris and her bureaucratic fiancé Daniels) threatens to remove Gordon from their home. The possibility of losing each other forces Robards to reenter the 9-to-5. Wonderfully translated by legendary TV-drama producer Coe with standout performances all around, including a bitingly funny role for theater director Saks as Chuckles the Chipmunk. Academy Award Nominations: 4, including Best Picture; Best (Adapted) Screenplay. **Academy Awards:** Best Supporting Actor: Martin Balsam. **Cast:** Jason Robards, Barbara Harris, Martin Balsam, Barry Gordon, Gene Saks, William Daniels. **Credits:** Dir: Fred Coe; Prod: Fred Coe; Writer: Herb Gardner; DP: Arthur J. Ornitz; Ed: Ralph Rosenblum; Composer: Don Walker; Set Designer: Herbert F. Mulligan. B&W, 118 min. **VHS**

Thousands Cheer

(1943) MGM
MGM's version of the benefit flag-waver put the entire back lot on dress parade (see *Hollywood Canteen* and *This Is the Army*) and features Kelly in one of his earliest starring roles as a reluctant army private who falls for the colonel's daughter (Grayson). Soon enough, plans are being made for a USO show that will bring out all the stars and entertain the servicemen. Let the dancing begin. Featured songs include "Honeysuckle Rose" and Garland's "The Joint Is Really Jumping Down at Carnegie Hall." Academy Award Nominations: 3, including Best (Color) Cinematography. **Cast:** Kathryn Grayson, Gene Kelly, Mary Astor, Judy Garland, John Boles, Jose Iturbi, Richard Simmons, Ben Blue, Frank Jenks, Mickey Rooney, Judy Garland, Lena Horne, Lucille Ball. **Credits:** Dir: George Sidney; Prod: Joe Pasternak; Writer: Paul Jarrico, Richard Collins; DP: George Folsey, Jr.; Ed: George Boemler; Prod Design: Cedric Gibbons, Daniel Cathcart; Composer: Herbert Stothart. Color, 126 min. **VHS, LASER**

Three Blind Mice

(1938) Fox
Familiar plot of three Kansas sisters (Young, Weaver, and Moore) seeking wealthy husbands in sunny California gets the royal treatment from the wonderful actors in the leads. Young poses as a wealthy visitor with her sisters as household staff. She falls for McCrea, who pretends to be wealthy to impress Young but is as poor as she. **Cast:** Loretta Young, David Niven, Joel McCrea, Stuart Erwin, Marjorie Weaver, Pauline Moore, Binnie Barnes, Jane Darwell. **Credits:** Dir: William Seiter; Prod: Rymond Griffith; Writer: Brown Holmes, Lynn Starling; DP: Ernest Palmer; Ed: James Morley. B&W, 75 min.

The Three Caballeros

(1945) RKO
This wonderful Disney feature leaps from Donald Duck's birthday presents to an animated, fun-filled journey through Latin America. One of those timeless pictures that holds up just as well today as it did upon its initial release. Academy Award Nominations: Best Sound Recording; Best Score. **Cast:** Joaquin Garay, Sterling Holloway, Frank Graham, Aurora Miranda, Carmen Molina, Dora Luz. **Credits:** Dir: Norman Ferguson, Clyde Geronimi, Jack Kinney, Bill Roberts, Harold Young; Prod: Norman Ferguson; Writer: Homer Brightman, Ernest Terrazzas, Ted Sears, Bill Peet, Ralph Wright, Elmer Plummer, Roy Williams, William Cottrell, Del Connell, James Bodrero; DP: Ray Rennahan; Ed: John Haliday; Art Director: Rich Irvine; Composer: Edward Plumb, Paul J. Smith, Charles Wolcott. Color, 72 min. **VHS, LASER**

Three Came Home

(1950) Fox
In a gripping wartime drama with powerhouse performances, Colbert portrays the wife of a British administrator living on Borneo at the outbreak of WWII. The Japanese invasion brings internment in a prison camp, where Colbert struggles to keep her spirit in the face of brutal conditions. Hayakawa gives a nuanced characterization of the camp commander who overcomes his essential humanity to perform his duty and exact revenge. Based on the actual experiences of Agnes Newton Keith; the same situation appears in Bruce Beresford's *Paradise Road* (1997) with Glenn Close. **Cast:** Claudette Colbert, Patric Knowles, Sessue Hayakawa, Helen Westcott, Leslie Thomas, John Burton, George Leigh, Melinda Plowman. **Credits:** Dir: Jean Negulesco; Prod: Nunnally Johnson; Writer: Nunnally Johnson; DP: Milton Krasner; Ed: Dorothy Spencer; Prod Design: Lyle Wheeler; Composer: Hugo Friedhofer. B&W, 106 min. **VHS**

Three Coins in the Fountain

(1954) Fox
In this handsomely photographed romance, three American women (Peters, McGuire, McNamara) pin their hopes for love on wishes they make by tossing coins into the Trevi Fountain in Rome. Each finds romance; who wouldn't in a Rome this beautiful? Ol' Blue Eyes lends his vocal talents to the title song. Negulesco tried this one again in 1964 as *The Pleasure Seekers*. Academy Award Nominations: 3, including Best Picture. **Academy Awards:** Best Song ("Three Coins in the Fountain"); Best Color Cinematography. **Cast:** Clifton Webb, Dorothy McGuire, Jean Peters, Louis Jourdan, Maggie McNamara, Rossano Brazzi, Howard St. John, Kathryn Givney, Cathleen Nesbitt, Vicente Padula. **Credits:** Dir: Jean Negulesco; Prod: Sol C. Siegel; Writer: John Patrick; Story: John H. Secondari; DP: Milton Krasner; Ed: William Reynolds; Prod Design: Lyle Wheeler; Composer: Jule Styne, Sammy Cahn, Victor Young. Color, 102 min. **VHS**

Three Comrades

(1938) MGM
Three German veterans of WWI (Tone, Taylor, and Young) set up an auto business in a postwar Berlin suffocating in poverty and defeat. Determined to give their lives meaning, they build their business and Taylor weds high-spirited Sullavan, though they both know she will soon die of tuberculosis. When Young dies in a street skirmish, the dark cloud of Nazism looms larger on the horizon. Based on the novel by Erich Maria Remarque, this was Fitzgerald's only official screen credit. Powerful, ominous drama with Sullavan's best performance. Academy Award Nomination: Best Actress: Margaret Sullavan. **Cast:** Robert Taylor, Margaret Sullavan, Franchot Tone, Robert Young, Guy Kibbee, Lionel Atwill, Henry Hull, George Zucco. **Credits:** Dir: Frank Borzage; Prod: Joseph L. Mankiewicz; Writer: F. Scott Fitzgerald, Edward Paramore; DP: Joseph Ruttenberg; Ed: Frank Sullivan; Prod Design: Cedric Gibbons; Composer: Franz Waxman. B&W, 99 min. **VHS**

Three-Cornered Moon

(1933) Paramount
In an early screwball comedy, Boland tries to hold together her eccentric family (including saucy daughter Col-

bert, law student Ford, and Bakewell, a would-be actor) after they lose their fortune in the stock-market crash. While Colbert works in a shoe factory and tries to help her brothers find jobs, she falls in love with a melancholy writer, but marries a wealthy doctor. **Cast:** Claudette Colbert, Richard Arlen, Mary Boland, Wallace Ford, Lyda Roberti, Tom Brown, Joan Marsh, Hardie Albright, William Bakewell, Sam Hardy. **Credits:** Dir: Elliott Nugent; Prod: B. P. Schulberg; Writer: S. K. Lauren, Ray Harris; Story: Gertrude Tonkonogy; DP: Leon Shamroy. B&W, 77 min.

Three Daring Daughters
(1948) MGM
A charming comedy that is also an above-average musical. MacDonald, a divorced fashion editor with three daughters (Donahue, Powell, and Todd), meets famed pianist Iturbi on a cruise ship. They fall in love and get married, a decision that her daughters greet with a plot to get rid of Iturbi and get back their father. True love brings the girls around. Packed with Iturbi's playing and standards such as "Route 66," "Alma Mater," "Fleurette," and "The Dickey Bird Song." **Cast:** Jeanette MacDonald, Jose Iturbi, Elinor Donahue, Jane Powell, Edward Arnold, Harry Davenport, Ann Todd, Tom Helmore. **Credits:** Dir: Fred M. Wilcox; Prod: Joe Pasternak; Writer: Albert Mannheimer, Frederick Kohner, Sonya Levien, John Meehan; DP: Ray June; Ed: Adrienne Fazan; Prod Design: Cedric Gibbons, Preston Ames; Composer: George Stoll. Color, 115 min. **VHS**

Three Days of the Condor
(1975) Paramount
Jaw-clenching suspense with Redford as a bookworm CIA employee in New York who comes back from lunch one day to discover that the entire staff at his office has been massacred. Paranoid and convinced that he's still being targeted, he kidnaps Dunaway for a place to hide. He tracks the killer as the killer tracks him, getting closer with each deadly near-miss. Eventually, with Dunaway's help, Redford encounters the coolly efficient assassin (Von Sydow) and receives a warning: Never trust a smiling face offering a ride. Based on the novel *Six Days of the Condor* by James Grady. Academy Award Nominations: Best Film Editing. **Cast:** Robert Redford, Faye Dunaway, Cliff Robertson, Max Von Sydow, John Houseman, Addison Powell, Walter McGinn, Tina Chen, Michael Kane.

Credits: Dir: Sydney Pollack; Prod: Stanley Schneider; Writer: Lorenzo Semple, Jr., David Rayfiel; DP: Owen Roizman; Ed: Fredric Steinkamp, Don Guidice; Prod Design: Stephen Grimes; Composer: Dave Grusin. Color, 118 min. **VHS, LASER**

The Three Faces of Eve
(1957) Fox
Woodward gives a tour-de-force portrayal of a schizophrenic young woman who seeks psychiatric help in dealing with her three distinct personalities: a housewife, a seductress, and an even-keeled, highly intelligent woman. The scene in which Woodward introduces all three of these distinct characters to the audience remains emotionally powerful. Based on an actual case study. Golden Globe for Best Actress in a Drama: Joanne Woodward. **Academy Awards:** Best Actress: Joanne Woodward. **Cast:** Joanne Woodward, Lee J. Cobb, David Wayne, Nancy Kulp, Douglas Spencer, Terry Rossio, Ken Scott, Mimi Gibson. **Credits:** Dir: Nunnally Johnson; Prod: Nunnally Johnson; Writer: Nunnally Johnson; DP: Stanley Cortez; Ed: Marjorie Fowler; Prod Design: Lyle Wheeler, Herman Blumenthal; Composer: Robert Emmett Dolan. B&W, 95 min. **VHS, LASER**

Three Faces West
(1940) Republic
In an original blend of Western melodrama and anti-Nazi moralizing, an Austrian refugee doctor (Coburn) helps Wayne aid a group of Dust Bowl farmers who are struggling to survive in the Pacific Northwest. Wayne romances the doctor's daughter, Gurie, who pines for her lost Austrian love. **Cast:** John Wayne, Charles Coburn, Sigrid Gurie, Spencer Charters, Roland Varno, Trevor Bardette, Sonny Bupp, Wade Boteler. **Credits:** Dir: Bernard Vorhaus; Prod: Sol C. Siegel; Writer: F. Hugh Herbert, Joseph Moncure March, Samuel Ornitz, Doris Anderson; DP: John Alton; Ed: William Morgan; Composer: Victor Young; Art Director: John MacKay. B&W, 80 min. **VHS**

Three Girls About Town
(1941) Columbia
Faith, Charity, and Hope (Blondell, Barnes, and Blair) are three sisters who join forces to investigate the mysterious murder of a guest at a fancy hotel where two of the sisters work as waitresses. The hotel is full of suspects, as the victim was found dead during a busy convention. Blondell

enlists the aid of Howard, an eager reporter in search of a story. Benchley adds a humorous lift. **Cast:** Robert Benchley, John Howard, Binnie Barnes, Janet Blair, Hugh O'Connell, Paul Harvey, Frank McGlynn, Eric Blore, Una O'Connor, Joan Blondell. **Credits:** Dir: Leigh Jason; Prod: Samuel Bishoff; Writer: Richard Carroll; DP: Franz Planer; Ed: Charles Nelson; Prod Design: Lionel Banks; Composer: Morris Stoloff. B&W, 73 min.

Three Godfathers
(1936) MGM
Three badmen traveling across the desert after robbing the New Jerusalem bank come across a wagon in the sand. Inside, they find a dying mother (Hervey) and, by her side, a newborn baby. The mother pleads with the men to look after the child and see that it is returned safely to civilization. Reluctant at first, they eventually agree and take the baby with them. As time passes, the life of the young foundling becomes more important than the money they've stolen or even their own lives. This Western version of the Three Wise Men story was made for the screen five times. **Cast:** Willard Robertson, John Sheehan, Chester Morris, Lewis Stone, Walter Brennan, Irene Hervey, Sidney Toler, Dorothy Tree, Roger Imhof. **Credits:** Dir: Richard Boleslawski; Prod: Joseph L. Mankiewicz; Writer: Robert Livingston, Manuel Seff; Story: Peter B. Kyne; DP: Joseph Ruttenberg; Ed: Frank Sullivan; Prod Design: Cedric Gibbons; Composer: William Axt. B&W, 82 min.

Three Godfathers
(1948) MGM
Ford's first color feature is the last, and best, version of this story that had been filmed four times previously (once in the silent days by Ford). Three outlaws risk their lives and freedom by rescuing and taking care of a small child that they discover in the desert. Wayne survives the brutal heat of Death Valley to fulfill his pledge to the child's dying mother (Natwick). This film was dedicated to Harry Carey, Sr., who participated in Ford's first attempt at this story, 1919's *Marked Men.* Touching and sweet. **Cast:** John Wayne, Ward Bond, Harry Carey, Jr., Pedro Armendariz, Mildred Natwick, Mae Marsh, Ben Johnson, Jane Darwell, Charles Halton. **Credits:** Dir: John Ford; Prod: John Ford; Writer: Laurence Stallings; DP: Winton C. Hoch; Ed: Jack Murray; Prod Design: James Basevi; Composer: Richard Hageman. Color, 105 min. **VHS**

Three Hours to Kill

(1954) Columbia
This tough-guy Western follows Andrews, who is nearly lynched for allegedly killing the brother of his fiancée, as he tracks the real killer. No-nonsense direction from Werker. **Cast:** Dana Andrews, Donna Reed, Dianne Foster, Stephen Elliot, Richard Coogan, Lawrence Hugo, James Westerfield, Richard Webb, Carolyn Jones, Charlotte Fletcher. **Credits:** Dir: Alfred L. Werker; Prod: Harry J. Brown; Writer: Roy Huggins, Richard Alan Simmons, Maxwell Shane; Story: Alex Gottlieb; DP: Charles Lawton; Ed: Gene Havlick; Composer: Paul Sawtell; Art Director: George Brooks. Color, 77 min.

Three Husbands

(1950) United Artists
When a playboy, who has recently passed away, leaves behind letters for three husbands to read, they are not pleased to discover that each of their wives (Arden, Warrick, Brown) had an affair. The rest of the film is spent, somewhat comically, trying to decide who's guilty. Writer Caspary previously used the same gag for her *A Letter to Three Wives* (1949). **Cast:** Eve Arden, Ruth Warrick, Vanessa Brown, Emlyn Williams, Shepperd Strudwick, Howard Da Silva, Robert Karnes, Billie Burke. **Credits:** Dir: Irving Reis; Prod: Isadore Goldsmith; Writer: Vera Caspary, Edward Eliscu; DP: Franz Planer; Ed: Louis Sackin; Prod Design: Rudolph Sternad; Composer: Herschel Burke Gilbert. Color, 78 min. **VHS**

Three Little Girls in Blue

(1946) Fox
This second-string Fox musical has three friends (Vera-Ellen, Haver, Blaine) traveling to Atlantic City to pass themselves off as rich women in order to attract beaux. The heart can't be tamed, though, and two fall in love with impoverished suitors, while the third finds a wealthy beau. **Cast:** June Haver, George Montgomery, Vivian Blaine, Thurston Hall, Ruby Dandridge, Charles Halton, Celeste Holm, Vera-Ellen, Frank Latimore, Clinton Rosemond. **Credits:** Dir: H. Bruce Humberstone; Prod: Mack Gordon; Writer: Valentine Davis, Brown Holmes, Lynn Starling, Robert Ellis, Helen Logan; Story: Stephen Powys; DP: Ernest Palmer; Ed: Barbara McLean; Choreographer: Seymour Felix, Babe Pearce; Composer: Josef Myrow, Harry Warren, Mack Gordon, Alfred Newman; Costumes: Bonnie Cashin; Art Director: Lyle Wheeler, Joseph C. Wright. Color, 90 min.

Three Little Words

(1950) MGM
This musical biopic of the vaudeville songwriting team of Kalmar and Ruby features exuberant performances from Astaire and Skelton as the songsmiths. Injured hoofer Astaire meets pianist Skelton on Coney Island and they become the Broadway and movie team that wrote everything from "I Wanna Be Loved By You" (performed here by a young Reynolds, though her voice is dubbed by the original performer, Helen Kane) to Groucho's famous "Hooray for Captain Spaulding." Golden Globe for Best Actor in a Musical or Comedy: Fred Astaire. Academy Award Nomination: Best Scoring of a Musical Picture. **Cast:** Red Skelton, Vera-Ellen, Debbie Reynolds, Fred Astaire, Keenan Wynn, Gale Robbins, Gloria De Haven, Phil Regan. **Credits:** Dir: Richard Thorpe; Prod: Jack Cummings; Writer: George Wells; DP: Harry Jackson; Ed: Ben Lewis; Prod Design: Cedric Gibbons; Composer: Andre Previn. Color, 104 min. **VHS, LASER**

The Three Lives of Thomasina

(1963) Disney
When a turn-of-the-century Scottish girl's veterinarian father (McGoohan) puts her beloved, but tetanus-infected, cat to sleep, she (Dotrice) is despondent. The cat, meanwhile, journeys through cat heaven until a strange woman from the woods (Hampshire) appears who has the power to bring the animal back to life and return her to the little girl. She also manages to soften the father in the process. Another Disney gem, based on a story by Gallico. **Cast:** Patrick McGoohan, Susan Hampshire, Karen Dotrice, Matthew Gerber, Laurence Naismith, Jean Anderson, Wilfred Brambell, Finlay Currie. **Credits:** Dir: Don Chaffey; Prod: Hugh Attwooll; Writer: Robert Westerby; Story: Paul Gallico; DP: Paul Beeson; Ed: Gordon Stone; Composer: Paul Smith, Eric Rodgers; Art Director: Michael Stringer. Color, 97 min. **VHS, LASER**

Three Men on a Horse

(1936) Warner Bros.
McHugh plays a greeting-card poet who also happens to have a knack for picking winning horses. When three gamblers discover his talent, they abduct McHugh and force him to come up with a big payout. Meanwhile, boss Kibbee is facing the Mother's Day crunch without his best writer, and his wife thinks his "little black book" contains code names for his girlfriends. Blondell stands out in support. **Cast:** Frank McHugh, Sam Levene, Joan Blondell, Teddy Hart, Guy Kibbee, Carol Hughes, Allen Jenkins, Edgar Kennedy, Eddie Anderson. **Credits:** Dir: Mervyn LeRoy; Prod: Samuel Bischoff; Writer: Laird Doyle; DP: Sol Polito; Ed: Ralph Dawson; Prod Design: Robert M. Haas; Composer: Leo F. Forbstein. B&W, 96 min. **VHS**

The Three Musketeers

(1921) United Artists
Fairbanks's first no-expenses-spared costume swashbuckler defined his screen image as an adventure hero. This extravagant production remains fairly faithful to the novel, and is cast with the most intriguing faces of the period, including a slimmer Pallette as Aramis. A silent-era landmark. **Cast:** Douglas Fairbanks, Leon Barry, George Siegmann, Eugene Pallette, Boyd Irwin, Thomas Holding, Sidney Franklin, Charles Stevens, Nigel De Brulier, Willis Robards. **Credits:** Dir: Fred Niblo; Writer: Douglas Fairbanks, Lotta Woods, Edward Knoblock; Story: Alexandre Dumas; DP: Arthur Edeson; Ed: Nellie Mason; Prod Design: Edward M. Langley; Composer: Louis Gottschalk. B&W, 120 min. **VHS**

The Three Musketeers

(1933)
This 12-episode serial starring Wayne updates the characters from the Alexandre Dumas story to members of the French Foreign Legion battling the nefarious leader of the Circle of Death. **Cast:** John Wayne, Ruth Hall, Noah Beery, Lon Chaney, Jr., Jack Mulhall, Raymond Hatton, Ralph Bushman, Al Ferguson, Hooper Atchley. **Credits:** Dir: Armand Schaefer, Colbert Clark; Prod: Nat Levine; Writer: Colbert Clark, Bennett Cohen, Wyndham Gittens, Norman S. Hall, Ella Arnold; DP: Tom Galligan, Edgar Lyons, Ernest Miller; Ed: Ray Snyder; Composer: Lee Zahler. B&W, 230 min. **VHS, LASER**

The Three Musketeers

(1939) Fox
The charming, hilarious musical version of the Dumas tale stars Ameche as spirited swashbuckler D'Artagnan. Ameche sings his way through the festivities, as the three bumbling Ritz brothers impersonate the Musketeers. Songs include "Chicken Soup," "Song of the Musketeers," and "My Lady." Lighthearted fun from Dwan, a director who knew a little something about swashbucklers. **Cast:** Don Ameche,

Ritz Brothers, Lionel Atwill, Binnie Barnes, Miles Mander, Gloria Stuart, Pauline Moore, John Carradine, Joseph Schildkraut. **Credits:** Dir: Allan Dwan; Prod: Raymond Griffith; Writer: M. M. Musselman, William A. Drake, Sam Hellman, Sid Kuller, Ray Golden; Story: Alexandre Dumas; DP: Peverell Marley; Ed: Jack Dennis. B&W, 73 min. **VHS**

The Three Musketeers
(1948) MGM
This zesty, all-star, Technicolor version of Dumas's swashbuckler stars Kelly as a marvelously athletic D'Artagnan. Kelly links up with the famed swordsmen (Heflin, Young, and Coote) and fights for their king (Morgan) against the machinations of Richelieu (a wonderful role for Price) and his mistress, Countess de Winter (Turner, electrifying in her first color screen appearance). Allyson pins her heart on Kelly and passes on information about the Queen's (Lansbury) affair. The story has been made for the screen several times, including the landmark 1921 silent version starring Douglas Fairbanks and the first talking version in 1935 with Paul Lukas, but this stands out for energy and sheer star power. Academy Award Nomination: Best (Color) Cinematography. **Cast:** Gene Kelly, Lana Turner, June Allyson, Angela Lansbury, Vincent Price, Frank Morgan, Keenan Wynn, Van Heflin, John Sutton, Gig Young, Robert Coote. **Credits:** Dir: George Sidney; Prod: Pandro S. Berman; Writer: Robert Ardrey; Story: Alexandre Dumas; DP: Robert Planck; Ed: George Boemler; Prod Design: Cedric Gibbons; Composer: Herbert Stothart; Art Director: Malcolm F. Brown. Color, 127 min. **VHS, LASER**

The Three Musketeers
(1974) Fox
In this extravagant version of Dumas's classic, director Lester brings energy and a light touch with comedy to create a swashbuckling romp. York plays D'Artagnan with an innocent good nature, and Reed, Chamberlain, and Finlay engage in convincing swordplay (each of the stars told *AMC Magazine* about injuries received in the fight sequences). York falls for a bountiful Welch and Dunaway makes a delightfully scheming Milady. The producers created a sequel, *The Four Musketeers* (1975), from the footage, much to the displeasure of the cast who had been paid for just one picture. **Cast:** Oliver Reed, Raquel Welch, Richard Chamberlain, Michael York, Faye Dun-

away, Charlton Heston, Christopher Lee, Joss Ackland, Roy Kinnear, Frank Finlay. **Credits:** Dir: Richard Lester; Prod: Alexander Salkind, Ilya Salkind; Story: Alexandre Dumas; DP: David Watkin; Ed: John Victor Smith; Prod Design: Brian Eatwell; Composer: Michel Legrand; Costumes: Yvonne Blake, Ron Talsky. Color, 108 min. **VHS, DVD**

Three on a Match
(1932) Warner Bros.
Three school friends—Davis, a stenographer; Blondell, a showgirl; and Dvorak, a bored society dame—rekindle their acquaintance after 10 years. Later, at a going-away party for Dvorak, she ditches her husband to run off with Blondell's gangster boyfriend (Talbot). Her impulsive act leads to blackmail and suicide, the deadly fate reserved for the third to light a cigarette from one match. A snappy production that features Bogart's first role as a gangster and a pre-Code glimpse at the Roaring '20s. Remade in 1938 as *Broadway Musketeers*. **Cast:** Bette Davis, Joan Blondell, Ann Dvorak, Warren William, Humphrey Bogart, Lyle Talbot, Glenda Farrell, Anne Shirley, Edward Arnold. **Credits:** Dir: Mervyn LeRoy; Prod: Samuel Bischoff; Writer: Lucien Hubbard; DP: Sol Polito; Ed: Ray Curtiss; Prod Design: Robert M. Haas. B&W, 65 min. **VHS**

Three Secrets
(1950) Warner Bros.
In a heavy drama that calls for plenty of tissues, a five-year-old child is the only remaining survivor of a plane crash that claims his foster parents. Three women (Parker, Neal, Roman) must wait to find out if the boy is the one they gave up for adoption just after birth. Flashbacks reveal the secrets that must come out if each woman is to make her case to reclaim her son. **Cast:** Eleanor Parker, Patricia Neal, Frank Lovejoy, Leif Erickson, Ruth Roman, Arthur Franz, Katharine Warren, Edmond Ryan. **Credits:** Dir: Robert Wise; Prod: Milton Sperling; Writer: Martin Rackin, Gina Kaus; DP: Sid Hickox; Ed: Thomas Reilly; Prod Design: Charles H. Clarke; Composer: David Buttolph. B&W, 98 min. **VHS**

Three Smart Girls
(1936) Universal
Here is Durbin's electric big-screen debut at age 14. In this music-filled comedy, Durbin and her two sisters (Grey and Read) are on a mission to reunite their parents. The only prob-

lem is that their father has already met someone else (a conniving gold digger) and is about to take her to the altar. It's up to the daughters to sing enough charming numbers that will make their parents fall in love again. Even the sisters find beaux. Songs include "Someone to Care for Me" and "My Heart Is Singing." Academy Award Nominations: 3, including Best Picture; Best Story. **Cast:** Deanna Durbin, Binnie Barnes, Alice Brady, Ray Milland, Charles Winninger, Mischa Auer, Nan Grey, Barbara Read. **Credits:** Dir: Henry Koster; Prod: Joe Pasternak; Writer: Adele Comandini, Austin Parker; DP: Joseph A. Valentine; Ed: Ted J. Kent; Prod Design: John Harkrider. B&W, 84 min. **VHS**

Three Smart Girls Grow Up
(1939) Universal
The sequel to *Three Smart Girls* again stars Durbin as the charming little sister. This time her mission is to play matchmaker for her two sisters (Parrish replaces Barbara Read) when they both long for the same fella. Of course Deanna sings, including her big hit, "Because." This sequel was as popular as the original, and ended up being one of the year's biggest money earners. **Cast:** Deanna Durbin, Charles Winninger, Nan Grey, Helen Parrish, Nella Walker, Robert Cummings, William Lundigan, Ernest Cossart. **Credits:** Dir: Henry Koster; Prod: Joe Pasternak; Writer: Bruce Manning, Felix Jackson; DP: Joseph A. Valentine; Ed: Ted J. Kent; Costumes: Vera West. B&W, 88 min. **VHS**

Three Strangers
(1946) Warner Bros.
A terrifically entertaining crime thriller about three lost souls who meet on the eve of the Chinese New Year. The group includes a woman deserted by her husband (Fitzgerald), a scheming lawyer (Greenstreet), and an alcoholic petty criminal (Lorre). Fitzgerald shows the other two a strange statue and relays the fable of it granting a wish to three strangers on Chinese New Year's. They test the story by cosigning a lottery ticket, but each is then plagued with murderously bad luck. Lorre keeps the lottery ticket, which turns out to be a big winner, but burns it rather than risk more bad luck. Another wonderful pairing of Greenstreet and Lorre in a story written by Huston after he bought an odd statue in London. Hitchcock showed early interest in directing, but Negulesco adds all the necessary atmosphere. **Cast:** Peter Lorre, Sydney Green-

street, Geraldine Fitzgerald, Robert Shayne, Joan Lorring, Margorie Riordan, Arthur Shields, Rosalind Ivan, John Alvin, Peter Whitney. **Credits:** Dir: Jean Negulesco; Prod: Wolfgang Reinhardt; Writer: John Huston, Howard Koch, Jr.; DP: Arthur Edelson; Ed: George Amy; Composer: Adolph Deutsch, Leo F. Forbstein; Art Director: Ted Smith. B&W, 92 min.

Three Violent People
(1957) Paramount
Confederate soldier Heston returns to post–Civil War Texas and marries former prostitute Baxter. Once there, he must struggle to maintain the family's land. His brother (Tryon) wants him to sell the place for his share of the proceeds, and then Heston learns about Baxter's shady past. After surviving a murder attempt, Heston and Baxter reconcile. A Western melodrama. **Cast:** Anne Baxter, Tom Tryon, Charlton Heston, Gilbert Roland, Forrest Tucker, Bruce Bennett, Elaine Stritch, Barton MacLane. **Credits:** Dir: Rudolph Maté; Prod: Hugh Brown; Writer: James Grant; DP: Loyal Griggs; Ed: Alma Macrorie; Prod Design: Hal Pereira; Composer: Walter Scharf. Color, 100 min. **VHS**

Three Wise Girls
(1932) Columbia
In the standard small-town girls take on Manhattan routine, Harlow plays a sweet, shy gal who journeys to the bright lights after hearing her pal Clarke's having a blast. After fending off cads, Harlow takes a job modeling (a chance for pre-Code peeks at ladies in lingerie) and kept-woman Clarke commits suicide after her married boyfriend goes back to his wife. That sends Harlow back to her small town, but her married beau does the right thing and trails after her. Mostly interesting for pre-MGM Harlow and the Depression-era trappings. **Cast:** Jean Harlow, Mae Clarke, Walter Byron, Marie Prevost, Andy Devine, Natalie Moorhead, Lucy Beaumont, Jameson Thomas, Walter Miller. **Credits:** Dir: William Beaudine; Writer: Agnes Christine Johnston, Robert Riskin, Wilson Collison; DP: Ted Tetzlaff; Ed: Jack Dennis. B&W, 66 min.

Three Women
(1977) Fox
This enigmatic narrative plays like Ingmar Bergman's *Persona* set in a flea-bitten Southern California desert town, supposedly inspired by a dream Altman had while his wife was in the hospital. Spacek arrives from small-

town Texas and begins working at a rehabilitation center. She latches on to Duvall, who gladly assumes the role of social tutor, unaware that the other residents mock her. Spacek moves in with Duvall, and, after a halfhearted suicide attempt following a disastrous party, a transformation of roles takes place. When the pregnant wife (Rule) of their brutal, drunken landlord (Fortier) delivers a stillborn son, the cycle of change reverses itself again and the three women set up uneasy housekeeping. Reverberant imagery and astonishing performances hold attention through a challenging work. **Cast:** Sierra Pecheur, Craig Richard Nelson, Maisie Hoy, Belita Moreno, Shelley Duvall, Sissy Spacek, Janice Rule, Robert Fortier, Ruth Nelson, John Cromwell. **Credits:** Dir: Robert Altman; Prod: Robert Altman; Writer: Robert Altman; DP: Charles Rosher; Ed: Dennis M. Hill, William A. Sawyer; Prod Design: James Vance; Composer: Gerald Busby. Color, 122 min.

The Thrill of It All
(1963) Universal
Day and Garner give winning performances in this Reiner-penned satire of television and advertising. Housewife Day contentedly takes care of home and family for gynecologist Garner until she unwittingly becomes the perfect pitchwoman for Happy Soap washing powder. When she begins neglecting household chores for her more glamorous advertising duties, Garner's chauvinistic side rears its head and he schemes to keep her close to home. Watch for Reiner's several cameos. Pitts's last role. **Cast:** Doris Day, James Garner, Arlene Francis, Edward Andrews, Elliott Reid, Carl Reiner, ZaSu Pitts, Hayden Rorke. **Credits:** Dir: Norman Jewison; Prod: Ross Hunter, Martin Melcher; Writer: Carl Reiner; Story: Larry Gelbart; DP: Russell Metty; Ed: Milton Carruth; Prod Design: Alexander Golitzen, Robert Boyle; Composer: Frank DeVol. Color, 108 min. **VHS**

Thunderball
(1965) United Artists
The fourth chapter of the James Bond series features Connery preventing SPECTRE from dropping an atomic bomb on Miami (for a measly one-hundred-million-pound ransom) after hijacking a NATO bomber. Still exciting, with striking effects and a great underwater battle. Based on Ian Fleming's 1961 novel, it was remade in 1983 as *Never Say Never Again*, with Connery returning to the role after an

extended absence. Bad girl Auger won the role over Raquel Welch and Julie Christie. **Academy Awards:** Best Special Visual Effects. **Cast:** Sean Connery, Claudine Auger, Adolfo Celi, Luciana Paluzzi, Bernard Lee, Guy Doleman, Molly Peters, Desmond Llewelyn. **Credits:** Dir: Terence Young; Prod: Kevin McClory; Story: Richard Maibaum, John Hopkins; DP: Ted Moore; Ed: Peter Hunt; Prod Design: Ken Adam; Composer: John Barry. Color, 132 min. **VHS, LASER**

Thunder Bay
(1953) Universal
The Stewart-Mann team leaves the Wild West for the rolling swells of the Louisiana offshore oil rigs. Stewart and Duryea deliver solid performances as two Louisiana wildcatters who are convinced that oil can be found at the bottom of the Gulf of Mexico. When they find a backer for their oil platform, the town's local shrimp fishermen take violent exception to their plans and their romances with two local girls (Dru and Henderson) take a back seat. A hurricane—and a big oil strike—save the day. **Cast:** James Stewart, Joanne Dru, Gilbert Roland, Marcia Henderson, Dan Duryea, Jay C. Flippen, Harry Morgan, Antonio Moreno, Fortunio Bonanova. **Credits:** Dir: Anthony Mann; Prod: Aaron Rosenberg; Writer: Gil Doud, John Michael Hayes; DP: William Daniels; Ed: Russell Schoengarth; Prod Design: Alexander Golitzen, Richard Reidl; Composer: Frank Skinner. Color, 102 min. **VHS**

Thunder Birds
(1942) Fox
Another wartime aeronautical adventure is directed by former pilot Wellman. This outing focuses on the pilots' training and features Foster as a veteran of WWI who must content himself with training young pilots for action overseas in WWII. Much of the story centers on a romantic triangle between Foster, local girl Tierney, and his most difficult student, Sutton. Watch for a photo of Wellman as a young flier to come out of Foster's wallet at a crucial point in the story. **Cast:** Gene Tierney, Preston Foster, John Sutton, Jack Holt, May Whitty, George Barbier, Richard Haydn, Reginald Denny, Ted North, Janis Carter. **Credits:** Dir: William Wellman; Prod: Lamar Trotti; Writer: Lamar Trotti; Story: Darryl F. Zanuck; DP: Ernest Palmer; Ed: Walter Thompson; Prod Design: James Basevi, Richard Day; Composer: David Buttolph. Color, 78 min.

Thunderbirds

(1952) Republic

As the United States is suddenly thrust into WWII, Oklahoma National Guard airmen Barrymore and Derek find their squadron bound for Europe. Once there, with engines screaming and machine guns blazing, these all-American aviators wing their way to air dominance in the skies over Italy, France, and ultimately Germany. War-hardened vet Bond, who is revealed as Barrymore's long-lost and presumed-dead father, shepherds them through danger. **Cast:** John Drew Barrymore, John Derek, Gene Evans, Mona Freeman, Wally Cassell, Ward Bond, Eileen Christy, Mae Clarke, Ben Cooper, Benny Baker. **Credits:** Dir: John H. Auer; Prod: John H. Auer; Writer: Mary C. McCall; DP: Reggie Lanning; Ed: Richard Van Enger; Prod Design: Frank Hotaling; Composer: Victor Young. B&W, 98 min.

Thunderbolt and Lightfoot

(1974) United Artists

Cimino's film debut is a funny, well-paced story of an ex-con (Eastwood) who teams up with a young drifter (Bridges). Eastwood's old partners (Kennedy and Lewis) believe that he's hiding money from their last heist, and once he convinces them not to kill them both, Bridges decides that the only way to get the money back is to pull off the same robbery, using the same means. The heist blows up (literally) and Eastwood is left alone, but rich. Bridges's happy-go-lucky, would-be thief leaps off the screen. Academy Award Nomination: Best Supporting Actor: Jeff Bridges. **Cast:** Clint Eastwood, Jeff Bridges, George Kennedy, Geoffrey Lewis, Catherine Bach, Gary Busey, Jack Dodson. **Credits:** Dir: Michael Cimino; Prod: Robert Daley; Writer: Michael Cimino; DP: Frank Stanley; Ed: Ferris Webster; Prod Design: Tambi Larsen; Composer: Dee Barton. Color, 117 min. **VHS, LASER**

Thunder on the Hill

(1951) Universal

A monstrous storm traps this mystery thriller's participants inside a convent situated high above a badly flooded British town. Villagers seeking shelter within the convent's walls are joined by a nun (Colbert), the convent doctor (Douglas), the doctor's wife (Crawford), and a woman set to hang (Blyth) for the murder of her brother. The nun senses that the woman is innocent, and as rain and thunder smash against the sanctuary, she sets out to solve the crime. A less-melodramatic but still stylish Sirk effort. **Cast:** Claudette Colbert, Ann Blyth, Anne Crawford, Philip Friend, Robert Douglas, Gladys Cooper, Michael Pate, John Abbott, Connie Gilchrist, Gavin Muir, Phyllis Stanley, Norma Varden. **Credits:** Dir: Douglas Sirk; Prod: Michel Kraike; Writer: Oscar Saul, Andrew Solt; DP: William Daniels; Ed: Ted J. Kent; Prod Design: Bernard Herzbrun, Nathan Juran, Russell A. Gausman, John Austin; Composer: Hans J. Salter, Alfred Newman. B&W, 84 min.

Thunder Road

(1958) United Artists

Mitchum shines (as in "moonshines") in this southern melodrama as he performs quadruple duties as writer, producer, star, and composer of the theme song (which he made a hit). Mitchum comes home from Korea to pick up where he left off with the family's moonshine business, and battles with both the federal authorities and the local mob. Mitchum's son makes his debut playing his dad's younger brother. A film close to Mitchum's heart, and it shows. **Cast:** Robert Mitchum, Gene Barry, Keely Smith, Jim Mitchum, Sandra Knight, Mitchell Ryan, Peter Breck, Jerry Hardin, James Phillips, Jacques Aubuchon. **Credits:** Dir: Arthur Ripley; Prod: Robert Mitchum; Writer: Walter Wise; Story: Robert Mitchum; DP: Alan Stensvold, David Ettinson; Ed: Harry Marker; Composer: Jack Marshall. B&W, 94 min. **VHS**

THX 1138

(1971) Warner Bros.

This Orwellian vision of the 25th century comes from the future creator of the more optimistic *Star Wars* universe. In an underground world, robotic work and drugs suffocate emotion and feeling. When two workers (Duvall and McOmie) avoid their "medication," they begin to fill with repressed sexuality and then fall in love. As they battle the authorities, McOmie discovers that she's pregnant. Lucas expanded his thesis film at USC (with Francis Ford Coppola as executive producer) for this feature release. Mandatory viewing for *Star Wars* fanatics. **Cast:** Robert Duvall, Donald Pleasence, Maggie McOmie, Ian Wolfe, Sid Haig, Marshall Efron, Johnny Weissmuller, Irene Forrest. **Credits:** Dir: George Lucas; Prod: Lawrence Sturhahn; Writer: George Lucas; DP: David Myers; Ed: George Lucas; Composer: Lalo Schifrin; Art Director: Michael Haller. Color, 90 min. **VHS, LASER**

Tickle Me

(1965) Allied Artists

Elvis stars as a singing rodeo cowboy who gets a job at an all-female dude ranch. Once there, he romances the owner (Adams) but falls in love with one of the staff (Lane), who has a treasure map that makes her the target of kidnappers. The King's job? Ward off the evil men and sing as many songs as humanly possible in an hour and a half, including "Night Rider," "It Feels So Right," and "(It's a) Long, Lonely Highway." **Cast:** Elvis Presley, Jocelyn Lane, Julie Adams, Jack Mullaney, Merry Anders, Bill Williams, Edward Faulkner, Connie Gilchrist. **Credits:** Dir: Norman Taurog; Prod: Ben Schwalb; Writer: Edward Bernds, Ellwood Ullman; DP: Loyal Griggs; Ed: Archie Marshek; Composer: Walter Scharf; Art Director: Hal Pereira, Arthur Lonergan. Color, 90 min. **VHS**

Tiger Shark

(1932) Warner Bros.

Robinson portrays a tuna fisherman who loses a hand to a shark and then his wife's affections to his friend (Arlen). This early Hawks outing portrays the dangers of the fisherman's life, and Robinson finds the tenderness that turns to murderous revenge in his character. In a vague allusion to *Moby Dick*, Robinson meets his shark nemesis again and is dragged to his death by a rope attached to a harpoon. **Cast:** Edward G. Robinson, Richard Arlen, Zita Johann, Leila Bennett, J. Carrol Naish, Vince Barnett, William Ricciardi. **Credits:** Dir: Howard Hawks, Richard Rosson; Prod: Raymond Griffiths; Writer: Houston Branch, Wells Root, John Lee Mahin; DP: Tony Gaudio; Ed: Thomas Pratt; Composer: Leo F. Forbstein; Costumes: Orry-Kelly; Art Director: Jack Okey. B&W, 80 min.

Tight Spot

(1955) Columbia

This hard-hitting film noir has leggy model Rogers falsely imprisoned as a gangster's moll released into the custody of DA Robinson. When she's asked to testify against bigshot gangster Greene, she refuses as none of the other witnesses have lived long enough to take the stand. When one of her bodyguards is killed, Robinson figures out that the other guard (Keith) works for Greene. Karlson also directed the highly regarded noirs *Scandal Sheet* (1952) and *The Phenix City Story* (1955). **Cast:** Ginger Rogers, Edward G. Robinson, Brian

Keith, Lucy Marlow, Lorne Greene, Katherine Anderson, Allen Nourse, Peter Leeds, Doye O'Dell, Eve McVeagh. **Credits:** Dir: Phil Karlson; Prod: Lewis J. Rachmil; Writer: William Bower, Leonard Kantor; DP: Burnett Guffey; Ed: Viola Lawrence; Prod Design: Carl Anderson; Composer: George Duning. B&W, 97 min.

Tillie and Gus
(1933) Paramount
In a classic Fields comedy, two old con artists (Fields and Skipworth) return home seeking part of an inheritance to find a young couple being swindled by an evil attorney. To win back their niece and nephew's inheritance, the wily cardsharks must fix and win a paddleboat race, a race that becomes unintentionally explosive. **Cast:** W. C. Fields, Alison Skipworth, Baby LeRoy, Julie Bishop, Philip Trent, Clarence Wilson, George Barbier, Barton MacLane, Edgar Kennedy, Bob McKenzie. **Credits:** Dir: Francis Martin; Prod: Douglas Maclean; Writer: Walter DeLeon, Francis Martin; Story: Rupert Hughes; DP: Ben F. Reynolds; Prod Design: Hans Dreier, Harry Oliver. B&W, 58 min.

Till the Clouds Roll By
(1946) MGM
Musical biopic of songwriter Jerome Kern, starring MGM's brightest talent. Garland, Grayson, Horne, Sinatra (singing "Ol' Man River"), and many others appear for brief sequences, lighting up the screen. The story portrays Kern (Walker) as he moves to England, finds a wife and a songwriting partner (Heflin), tries his hand on Broadway and eventually creates *Show Boat*. The fabled Freed unit works its magic with an endless list of Kern tunes and magnificent performances (Garland's scenes were directed by her husband, Vincente Minnelli). Of particular note: Horne singing "Can't Help Lovin' Dat Man," "Till the Clouds Roll By" sung by June Allyson, "Smoke Gets in Your Eyes" with Cyd Charisse, and "Sunny" sung by Garland. **Cast:** Van Johnson, Lena Horne, Robert Walker, Frank Sinatra, Judy Garland, Tony Martin, Lucille Bremer, Van Heflin, Joan Wells, Kathryn Grayson. **Credits:** Dir: Richard Whorf; Prod: Arthur Freed; Writer: Myles Connolly, Jean Holloway; Story: Guy Bolton; DP: Harry Stradling, George J. Folsey; Ed: Albert Akst; Composer: Conrad Salinger, Lennie Hayton, Roger Edens; Art Director: Cedric Gibbons, Daniel B. Cathcart. Color, 138 min. VHS, LASER

Till the End of Time
(1946) RKO
This sobering portrait of postwar life was overshadowed by the superior production of *The Best Years of Our Lives*. Three G.I.'s (Mitchum, Madison, and Williams) return from combat and try to settle back into their lives. Madison gets heat from his parents to marry and finds solace with war widow McGuire, Mitchum loses his mustering-out pay, and crippled Williams has to adjust to his disability. A battle with the Klan refreshes their memory of why they fought, and gives the trio a push back to the world. This is a solid adaptation of Busch's novel *They Dream of Home* that deserves more recognition. **Cast:** Dorothy McGuire, Guy Madison, Robert Mitchum, Bill Williams, Tom Tully, William Gargan, Jean Porter, Johnny Sands. **Credits:** Dir: Edward Dmytryk; Prod: Dore Schary; Writer: Allen Rivkin; Story: Niven Busch; DP: Harry Wild; Ed: Harry Gerstad; Composer: Leigh Harline; Art Director: Albert S. D'Agostino, Jack Okey. B&W, 105 min. VHS, LASER

'Til We Meet Again
(1940) Warner Bros.
This weepy remake of *One Way Passage* (1932) is elevated by the performances of Oberon and Brent. Two ill-starred lovers meet on an ocean liner: Suave criminal Brent is on his way to San Quentin's electric chair; Oberon is suffering from a fatal heart condition. Perennial cop O'Brien allows the romance to blossom, and he pitches a little woo with tourist Fitzgerald on the side. Brent gets a chance to escape, but when he learns of Oberon's fate, he returns to the ship and they face their certain fate together. **Cast:** Merle Oberon, George Brent, Pat O'Brien, Geraldine Fitzgerald, Binnie Barnes, Frank McHugh, Eric Blore, George Reeves, Victor Kilian, Cy Kendall. **Credits:** Dir: Edmund Goulding; Prod: Hal B. Wallis; Writer: Warren Duff; Story: Robert Lord; DP: Tony Gaudio; Ed: Ralph Dawson; Prod Design: Robert M. Haas; Composer: Leo F. Forbstein. B&W, 99 min.

Time After Time
(1979) Warner Bros.
H. G. Wells (McDowell), while comfortably living in Victorian England, discovers that his time machine has been borrowed by an acquaintance, Jack the Ripper. Jack has transported himself to 1979 San Francisco, where he hopes to do even more damage. Wells follows the killer into the machine to stop the Ripper before he can slay

again. Once in San Francisco, the famous prognosticator marvels at a world he never could have foreseen and falls in love with a daffy bank employee (Steenburgen, in her first big role; she and McDowell would marry soon after). Clever entertainment from the writer of *The Seven Percent Solution* (1976), another historical-fictional speculation. **Cast:** David Warner, Mary Steenburgen, Malcolm McDowell, Charles Cioffi, Corey Feldman, Laurie Main, Andonia Katsaros, Patti D'Arbanville. **Credits:** Dir: Nicholas Meyer; Prod: Herb Jaffe; Writer: Nicholas Meyer, Steven Hayes, Karl Alexander; DP: Paul Lohmann; Ed: Donn Cambern; Prod Design: Edward C. Carfagno; Composer: Miklos Rozsa. Color, 112 min. VHS, LASER

Time Limit
(1957) United Artists
Basehart, a former Korean War POW charged with treason, admits his guilt and offers no defense for his action. Unwilling to settle for the apparent open-and-shut case, the investigating colonel (Widmark) digs deeper and discovers that he acted to save the lives of those imprisoned with him. An intriguing drama, directed by actor Malden and produced by Widmark, that offers no easy answers to the moral dilemma it poses. **Cast:** Richard Widmark, Richard Basehart, Dolores Michaels, June Lockhart, Carl Benton Reid, Martin Balsam, Rip Torn, Khigh Dhiegh, Yale Wexler, Alan Dexter. **Credits:** Dir: Karl Malden; Prod: Richard Widmark, William Reynolds; Writer: Henry Denker, Ralph Berkey; DP: Sam Leavitt; Ed: Aaron Stell; Composer: Fred Steiner. B&W, 96 min.

The Time Machine
(1960) MGM
An exciting, faithful production of H. G. Wells's 1895 classic in which a scientist (Taylor) journeys into the distant future to explore man's fate. After peeking at war and nuclear devastation, he arrives in the year 802,701 where he inspires the peaceful Elois to revolt against the subterranean Morlocks and falls in love with an Eloi woman, Mimieux. Pal's interpretation of Wells's vision of the future is a sight to behold. **Academy Awards:** Best Special Effects. **Cast:** Rod Taylor, Alan Young, Yvette Mimieux, Sebastian Cabot, Tom Helmore, Whit Bissell, Paul Frees. **Credits:** Dir: George Pal; Prod: George Pal; Writer: David Duncan; Story: H. G. Wells; DP: Paul C. Vogel; Ed: George Tomasini; Composer: Rus-

sell Garcia; Art Director: George W. Davis; SFX: Gene Warren, Tim Baar. Color, 103 min. VHS, LASER

The Time of Your Life

(1948) United Artists

In a winning adaptation of Saroyan's Pulitzer Prize–winning ensemble comedy about the various characters who populate Nick's Saloon, Restaurant and Entertainment Palace, a waterfront dive, Cagney stars as a philosophical barfly who comments on the world from his comfortable stool. This was a Cagney brothers project (it even featured a small role for sister Jeanne) that was dear to Jimmy Cagney's heart. It met with great critical acclaim (and Saroyan's approval), but little box office. **Cast:** James Cagney, William Bendix, Broderick Crawford, Ward Bond, James Barton, Paul Draper, Gale Page, James Lydon. **Credits:** Dir: H. C. Potter; Prod: William Cagney; Writer: Nathaniel Curtis; Story: William Saroyan; DP: James Wong Howe; Ed: Walter Hannemann, Truman Wood; Composer: Carmen Dragon; Art Director: Wiard Ihnen. B&W, 109 min. VHS

A Time to Love and a Time to Die

(1958) Universal

Sirk's brooding romance set among the ruins of war reflects the troubling experience of his early career in Nazi Germany. Gavin portrays a German soldier on furlough who discovers that his town has been destroyed and that his parents are missing. As he searches for traces of his former life, he falls in love with the daughter of his family's doctor (Pulver). They marry, a hopeful, forlornly romantic gesture as they know he must return to the Russian front and she's unlikely to survive the collapse of their homeland. Based on a novel by Remarque, who has a small cameo role. Academy Award Nomination: Best Sound. **Cast:** John Gavin, Lilo Pulver, Jock Mahoney, Keenan Wynn, Erich Maria Remarque, Dieter Borsche, Barbara Rutting, Thayer David. **Credits:** Dir: Douglas Sirk; Prod: Robert Arthur; Writer: Orin Jannings; Story: Erich Maria Remarque; DP: Russell Metty; Ed: Ted J. Kent; Composer: Miklos Rozsa; Art Director: Alexander Golitzen, Alfred Sweeney. Color, 133 min. VHS

The Tingler

(1959) Columbia

This introduced audiences to "Percepto," Castle's device of placing joy buzzers under selected theater seats to get the joint really jumping. Price plays a coroner who discovers that fear comes from a creature that settles on the base of a person's spine. The only way to get rid of it? Screaming. He decides to test his theory on a deaf mute. Black-and-white water becomes colorful blood, followed by a scene of mind alteration that many consider to be cinema's first acid trip. After a theater owner dies, the critters get loose in the theater and the buzzers start buzzing. **Cast:** Vincent Price, Judith Evelyn, Darryl Hickman, Patricia Cutts, Pamela Lincoln, Philip Coolidge. **Credits:** Dir: William Castle; Prod: William Castle; Writer: Robb White; DP: Wilfrid M. Cline; Ed: Chester Schaeffer; Composer: Von Dexter; Art Director: Phillip Bennett. B&W, 81 min. VHS

Tin Pan Alley

(1940) Fox

Top-of-the-line Fox musical stars Oakie and Payne as two struggling songwriters in New York's fabled Tin Pan Alley who meet singing sisters Faye and Grable. Faye joins their music-publishing biz for a while, but when Grable hits it big in London, she's back in the act and the boys can't get a break. When the two songsmiths enlist in WWI, they head to London and a rendezvous with their old flames. The first pairing of Faye with Grable, the up-and-comer who would replace the veteran star as queen of the Fox musical. The nostalgic numbers include "Sheik of Araby," "K-K-K-Katy," and "Honeysuckle Rose." **Academy Awards:** Best Score. **Cast:** Alice Faye, Betty Grable, Jack Oakie, John Payne, Esther Ralston, Allen Jenkins, Harold Nicholas, Fayard Nicholas. **Credits:** Dir: Walter Lang; Prod: Kenneth MacGowan; Writer: Robert Ellis, Helen Logan; Story: Pamela Harris; DP: Leon Shamroy; Ed: Walter Thompson; Composer: Alfred Newman; Art Director: Richard Day, Joseph C. Wright. B&W, 94 min. VHS

The Tin Star

(1957) Paramount

In this Mann Western, Fonda is an ex-lawman turned bounty hunter who drops his guard long enough to get involved with a small town's inexperienced sheriff (Perkins) and to fall in love with a young boy's mother (Palmer). This well-written Western (compliments of Nichols) looks behind the façade of the stereotypical Western loner. Academy Award Nomination: Best (Original) Story and Screenplay. **Cast:** Henry Fonda, Anthony Perkins,

Betsy Palmer, Neville Brand, Lee Van Cleef, John McIntire, Michel Ray, Howard Petrie. **Credits:** Dir: Anthony Mann; Prod: William Perlberg, George Seaton; Writer: Dudley Nichols; Story: Barney Slater, Joel Kane; DP: Loyal Griggs; Ed: Alma Macrorie; Prod Design: Hal Pereira, Joseph MacMillan Johnson; Composer: Elmer Bernstein. B&W, 93 min. VHS, LASER

The Tip Off

(1931) RKO

In this sweet, unassuming early talkie, naive Quillan is unaware of the danger he's in by having an affair with a vicious gangster's girlfriend. He gets bailed out by two friends, boxer Armstrong and his girl, Rogers. An early role for Rogers and her first for RKO. **Cast:** Eddie Quillan, Robert Armstrong, Ginger Rogers, Joan Peers, Ralf Harolde, Charles Sellon, Ernie Adams, Jack Herrick, Frank Darien, Luis Alberni. **Credits:** Dir: Albert Rogell; Prod: Harry Joe Brown; Writer: Earl Baldwin; Story: George Kibbe Turner; DP: Edward Snyder; Ed: Charles Craft; Prod Design: Carroll Clark. B&W, 75 min. VHS

Titanic

(1953) Fox

Here's the melodramatic depiction of history's most memorable shipwreck (carried by Brackett, Reisch, and Breen's Oscar-winning script). Though not on a technical level with James Cameron's visual spectacle, this remains a solid portrayal of the tragic voyage. Stanwyck's marital problems with Webb make up the rather soapy narrative, but the re-creation of the tragedy and its human cost is moving. Academy Award Nominations: 2, including Best Art Direction. **Academy Awards:** Best Story and Screenplay. **Cast:** Clifton Webb, Barbara Stanwyck, Robert Wagner, Richard Basehart, Thelma Ritter, Audrey Dalton, Brian Aherne, Bobby Breen. **Credits:** Dir: Jean Negulesco; Prod: Charles Brackett; Writer: Charles Brackett, Walter Reisch, Richard Breen; DP: Joseph MacDonald; Ed: Louis Loeffler; Composer: Sol Kaplan, Lionel Newman; Art Director: Lyle Wheeler, Maurice Ransford. Color, 98 min. VHS, LASER

T-Men

(1947) Eagle-Lion Films

Director Mann's first of his dark films noir is one of the highlights of the genre. Its pseudo-documentary camera work and violent action raise disturbing questions of how far society is willing to go to preserve order.

To Be or Not to Be (1942)

Two Treasury Department agents (O'Keefe and Ryder) go undercover to infiltrate a Detroit counterfeiting ring and then follow a lead to L.A. where they become tangled in the web so completely that O'Keefe must stand by and watch as his partner dies, unable to step in for fear of blowing his own cover. He must then move quickly to stay one step ahead of the murderous McGraw. The scene of McGraw killing an associate in a steam bath is horrifying, and one of the most famous in film noir. Academy Award Nomination for Best Sound Recording. **Cast:** Dennis O'Keefe, June Lockhart, Alfred Ryder, Charles McGraw, Wallace Ford, Jane Randolph, Art Smith, Herbert Heyes, Jack Overman, John Wengraf. **Credits:** Dir: Anthony Mann; Prod: Aubrey Schenck; Writer: John C. Higgins; DP: John Alton; Ed: Fred Allen; Composer: Paul Sawtell; SFX: Edward C. Jewell, George J. Teague. B&W, 93 min. **VHS, LASER**

The Toast of New Orleans
(1950) MGM
Here's an excuse to get Lanza singing on-screen again with Grayson after their success in *That Midnight Kiss* (1949). Lanza plays a turn-of-the-century New Orleans fisherman smitten with opera star Grayson. When her manager (Niven) hears him sing, he offers the tenor a less briny career. Songs include "Be My Love," and arias from *Carmen, Madame Butterfly,* and *La Traviata.* Academy Award Nomination: Best Song ("Be My Love"). **Cast:** Mario Lanza, Kathryn Grayson, David Niven, Rita Moreno, J. Carrol Naish, James Mitchell, Richard Hageman, Clinton Sundberg, Sig Arno, Romo Vincent. **Credits:** Dir: Norman Taurog; Prod: Joe Pasternak; Writer: Sy Gomberg, George Wells; DP: William E. Snyder; Ed: Gene Ruggiero; Prod Design: Cedric Gibbons; Art Director: Daniel B. Cathcart. Color, 98 min. **VHS, LASER**

The Toast of New York
(1937) RKO
Arnold gives a fine performance as the infamous Wall Street financier Jubilee Jim Fisk, who went from medicine shows to cotton smuggling in the Civil War to duping railroad magnate Vanderbilt to cornering the market in gold and bringing down the economy. Grant plays his sidekick who warms to the big guy's gal, Farmer. Those curious about the real actress portrayed so movingly by Jessica Lange in *Frances* (1982) will want to see Farmer in this, one of her too-few featured roles. **Cast:** Edward Arnold, Cary Grant, Frances Farmer, Jack Oakie, Donald Meek, Clarence Kolb, Marianne Marks, Winter Hall. **Credits:** Dir: Rowland V. Lee; Prod: Edward Small; Writer: Dudley Nichols, John Twist, Joel Sayre, Matthew Josephson; DP: Peverell Marley; Ed: George Hively, Samuel E. Beetley; Art Director: Van Nest Polglase. B&W, 109 min. **VHS, LASER**

Tobacco Road
(1941) Fox
An oddball, flip side of the coin to Ford's *Grapes of Wrath* takes a humorous look at a family of layabouts in the Georgia backwoods during the Great Depression. Facing monthly bills of $100, Grapewin and his wife Rambeau worry about their inability to come up with the cash. Grapewin faces the hard times that surround him with a gleeful sense of humor that seems as much a tribute to his spirit as it is to his unwillingness to work. His children are no different: Tracy is more interested in cars than work, and Tierney in snaring boy-next-door Bond. They all remain cheerful, hopeful that someday all will be well. **Cast:** Charley Grapewin, Marjorie Rambeau, Gene Tierney, William Tracy, Elizabeth Patterson, Dana Andrews, Slim Summerville, Ward Bond, Grant Mitchell, Zeffie Tilbury. **Credits:** Dir: John Ford; Prod: Darryl F. Zanuck; Writer: Nunnally Johnson; Story: Erskine Caldwell, Jack Kirkland; DP: Arthur C. Miller; Ed: Barbara McLean; Prod Design: James Basevi, Richard Day; Composer: David Buttolph. B&W, 84 min.

To Be or Not to Be
(1942) United Artists
Lubitsch, Benny, and Lombard (in her final screen appearance) are all at their best in this classic black comedy. The two leads portray a husband-and-wife acting team in Nazi-occupied Warsaw. When flier Stack, who is mad for Lombard, discovers an impostor being sent from England to destroy the underground resistance, he passes word to the actress and the theater troupe goes into action. Benny is masterful as he dons disguise after disguise while baffling the inquisitive Nazis. Controversial upon its release for using humor as a weapon against tyranny, this is now considered one of Lubitsch's and Hollywood's finest moments. Selected for the National Film Registry. Academy Award Nomination for Best Score. **Cast:** Jack Benny, Carole Lombard, Robert Stack, Lionel Atwill, Sig Rumann, Felix Bressart, Stanley Ridges, Tom Dugan. **Credits:** Dir: Ernst Lubitsch; Prod: Ernst Lubitsch; Writer: Edwin Justus Mayer; DP: Rudolph Mate; Ed: Dorothy Spencer; Prod Design: Vincent Korda; Composer: Miklos Rozsa. B&W, 102 min. **VHS, LASER**

Tobruk

(1966) Universal
In a WWII tale, three soldiers (Hudson, Green, and Peppard) lead an unusual commando squadron of British soldiers posing as POWs and German Jews posing as their Nazi captors on a mission to destroy Rommel's fuel supply in the North African desert. Effective action and an inventive situation. Academy Award Nomination: Best Special Visual Effects. **Cast:** Rock Hudson, George Peppard, Guy Stockwell, Nigel Green, Jack Watson, Norman Rossington, Percy Herbert, Liam Redmond. **Credits:** Dir: Arthur Hiller; Prod: Gene Corman; Writer: Leo Gordon; DP: Russell Harlan, Nelson Tyler; Ed: Robert Jones; Prod Design: Alexander Golitzen; Composer: Bronislau Kaper; SFX: Howard Anderson, Albert Whitlock. Color, 110 min. **VHS**

Toby Tyler

(1959) Disney
Angry at his stern uncle, a young orphan boy (Corcoran) fulfills every kid's dream (circa 1960 anyway) when he runs away and joins the circus. There he befriends a chimpanzee, and saves the day when he takes over a horseback act. He even gets the attention of his aunt and uncle—like we said, every kid's dream, a Disney specialty. **Cast:** Kevin Corcoran, Henry Calvin, Gene Sheldon, Bob Sweeney, Richard Eastham, James Drury, Edith Evanson, Tom Fadden. **Credits:** Dir: Charles Barton; Prod: Bill Walsh; Writer: Bill Walsh; DP: William E. Snyder; Ed: Stanley Johnson; Prod Design: Carroll Clark; Composer: Buddy Baker. Color, 96 min. **VHS, LASER**

To Catch a Thief

(1955) Paramount
Hitchcock Lite describes this detour into comedy-suspense. Grant plays a (supposedly) retired jewel thief who finds himself once again under suspicion when a rash of jewel heists hits the aristocrats of Monaco. He woos elegant American heiress Kelly, and, as she tempts him with her jewelry and her charms, they pursue the thief to clear Grant's name. Famously sexy, with swirling kisses, fireworks, and come-hither dialogue. Academy Award Nominations: 3, including Best Costume Design. **Academy Awards:** Best Color Cinematography. **Cast:** Cary Grant, Grace Kelly, Brigitte Auber, Jessie Royce Landis, John Williams, Charles Vanel, Wee Willie Davis, Georgette Anys. **Credits:** Dir: Alfred Hitchcock; Prod: Alfred Hitchcock; Writer: John Michael Hayes; DP: Robert

Burks; Ed: George Tomasini; Prod Design: Joseph MacMillan Johnson; Composer: Lyn Murray; Art Director: Hal Pereira. Color, 103 min. **VHS, LASER**

Today We Live

(1933) MGM
Faulkner coauthored (loosely adapted from his short story "Turn About") and Hawks directed the aerial sequences with elan, but the rather soapy melodrama on the ground makes for tough going. British party girl Crawford first grabs the attention of her brother's (Tone) navy buddy (Young)—until flyboy Cooper shows up. The posturing between the rivals begins over whose duty is more hazardous until all concerned opt to die rather than get in the way of Crawford and Cooper's true romance. Early days for one and all, and interesting mostly for that. **Cast:** Joan Crawford, Gary Cooper, Robert Young, Franchot Tone, Roscoe Karns, Louise Closser Hale. **Credits:** Dir: Howard Hawks; Prod: Howard Hawks; Writer: Edith Fitzgerald, Dwight Taylor, William Faulkner; Story: William Faulkner; DP: Oliver T. Marsh; Ed: Edward Curtiss; Prod Design: Cedric Gibbons; Costumes: Adrian. B&W, 113 min. **VHS**

To Each His Own

(1946) Paramount
Leisen's superior drama features de Havilland as an unwed woman who encounters the son she gave up for adoption as a young man (Lund). Her story unfolds in flashback as she walks her air-raid warden beat: a passionate, brief affair in a small town, the father (also Lund) killed in action in WWI, the painful adoption, years of devotion to a successful business while her son knows her only through presents as a friend of his "mother." When he visits and lets his attachment to Welles be known, de Havilland's confidant (Culver) helps the romance as he opens the son's eyes to the identity of his real mother. This was de Havilland's first role after winning the landmark court ruling that limited studio control of actors to seven years. Lund's debut after work on Broadway. Academy Award Nominations: 2, including Best Original Story. **Academy Awards:** Best Actress: Olivia de Havilland. **Cast:** Olivia de Havilland, Mary Anderson, Roland Culver, Virginia Welles, Bill Goodwin, John Lund, Philip Terry, Victoria Horne. **Credits:** Dir: Mitchell Leisen; Prod: Charles Brackett; Writer: Charles Brackett, Jacques Thery; DP: Daniel Fapp; Ed: Alma Macrorie; Prod Design:

Hans Dreier; Composer: Victor Young; Art Director: Roland Anderson. B&W, 122 min. **VHS**

Together Again

(1944) Columbia
In a lighthearted romantic comedy, Dunne is the mayor of a small Vermont town, a position she inherited when her husband died five years previous. When her husband's statue is struck by lightning and the head knocked off, Dunne's father-in-law (Coburn) sees it as a sign that she must move on and marry again. He sends her to New York to interview a sculptor (Boyer) to fix the statue. He takes the job and becomes a potential prospect, but first Dunne's teenaged daughter gets in the way. **Cast:** Irene Dunne, Charles Boyer, Charles Coburn, Mona Freeman, Jerome Courtland, Elizabeth Patterson, Charles Dingle, Walter Baldwin, Fern Emmett, Frank Puglia. **Credits:** Dir: Charles Vidor; Prod: Virginia Van Upp; Writer: Hugh Herbert, Virginia Van Upp; Story: Herbert J. Biberman, Stanley Russell; DP: Joseph Walker; Ed: Otto Meyer; Prod Design: Stephen Goosson, Van Nest Polglase; Composer: Werner R. Heymann. B&W, 93 min.

To Have and Have Not

(1945) Warner Bros.
One of the best–loved classic movies of all time is famous for the offscreen romance that sparked on-screen electricity between Bogart and Bacall. This prototypical Hawks story (with help from William Faulkner) began with a bet between the director and Ernest Hemingway that he could film Hemingway's worst book, which was, in the author's own estimation, *To Have and Have Not*. Hemingway shouldn't have paid because Hawks threw out the story. He placed Bogart in WWII Martinique as a charter-boat captain squiring rich folks around to fish. The apolitical sailor turns down requests for help from the French Resistance until Bacall appears at his doorway looking for a match. After smoldering glances (and some of the funniest banter ever in movies), he discovers she also needs a way back to the U.S. To secure the price of her ticket, Bogart takes an assignment to smuggle Dalio and Moran into Martinique and winds up on the lam from the Vichy police and nursing a wounded Dalio. Bacall turns in her ticket and throws in with the reluctant hero. Bacall was a 19-year-old model when Hawks's wife spotted her on a magazine cover, and she is perhaps the most luminous,

enticing character ever to grace the screen. Bogart must have thought so, too, for theirs is a famous Hollywood love story that everyone who sees this can watch blossoming. Magic. **Cast:** Humphrey Bogart, Lauren Bacall, Walter Brennan, Hoagy Carmichael, Dolores Moran, Sheldon Leonard, Marcel Dalio, Walter Sande. **Credits:** Dir: Howard Hawks; Prod: Howard Hawks; Writer: Jules Furthman, William Faulkner; DP: Sid Hickox; Ed: Christian Nyby; Composer: Franz Waxman; Art Director: Charles Novi. B&W, 101 min. VHS, LASER

To Hell and Back
(1955) Universal
Murphy, WWII's most decorated soldier, stars in his own autobiography. The picture follows the soldier from his upbringing as the son of Texas sharecroppers to his enlistment at an early age to his heroic actions in battle. Murphy's extraordinary efforts earned him 24 medals, one of which was the Congressional Medal of Honor. Murphy already had a somewhat lackluster movie career when this was made; his own story is his highest screen accomplishment. **Cast:** Audie Murphy, Marshall Thompson, Charles Drake, Gregg Palmer, Jack Kelly, Paul Picerni, David Janssen, Paul Langton. **Credits:** Dir: Jesse Hibbs; Prod: Aaron Rosenberg; Writer: Gil Doud; DP: Maury Gertsman; Ed: Edward Curtiss; Prod Design: Alexander Golitzen, Robert Clatworthy; Composer: Joseph Gershenson. Color, 106 min. VHS

To Kill a Mockingbird
(1962) Universal
One of the most beloved of classic movies speaks at once with the wisdom of years and with childlike innocence, capturing both voices flawlessly. Foote's adaptation of the Lee novel gives us a story of quiet courage and unexpected deliverance from the point of view of Scout (Badham), a six-year-old girl in the Depression-era South. She and her brother live with their widowed father Atticus (Peck), a lawyer and well-respected pillar of the community. Their world of play also contains the mystery of Boo Radley (Duvall), the reclusive boy next door rumored to be chained to his bed by his vicious father. The children's world parallels the serious business of Atticus's defense of a black man accused of attacking a white woman. The dignity of the accused and Peck's impassioned defense aren't enough to overcome the jury's racism. But the real

attacker wants revenge, and the adult business and the children's world collide on a dark wooded path. All the performances seem to emerge from the dusty southern ground and the atmosphere clings like August heat. A beautifully realized drama cherished with each new generation. Selected for the National Film Registry. Golden Globes for Best Score; Best Actor in a Drama: Gregory Peck,; Best Film Promoting International Understanding. Academy Award Nominations: 8, including Best Picture; Best Supporting Actress: Mary Badham; Best Director. **Academy Awards:** Best Actor: Gregory Peck; Best Screenplay Based on Material from Another Medium; Best Art Direction—Set Decoration (B&W). **Cast:** Gregory Peck, Mary Badham, Philip Alford, Brock Peters, Robert Duvall, John Megna, Frank Overton, Rosemary Murphy, Ruth White, Estelle Evans. **Credits:** Dir: Robert Mulligan; Prod: Alan J. Pakula; Writer: Horton Foote; Story: Harper Lee; DP: Russell Harlan; Ed: Aaron Stell; Prod Design: Alexander Golitzen, Henry Bumstead; Composer: Elmer Bernstein. B&W, 149 min. VHS, LASER, DVD

Tomahawk
(1952) Universal
When gold is found in the Dakotas, the U.S. Army is quick to build an outpost at the site, but their actions enrage the land's rightful owners, the Sioux. The conflict escalates to the point of violence, despite the efforts of a peace-loving Army scout (Heflin). A thoughtful reflection on real events, revealed through the shifting perspectives of characters on either side of the standoff. **Cast:** Van Heflin, Yvonne De Carlo, Preston Foster, Jack Oakie, Alex Nicol, Tom Tully, Ann Doran, Rock Hudson, Susan Cabot, Arthur Space. **Credits:** Dir: George Sherman; Prod: Leonard Goldstein; Writer: Silvia Richards, Maurice Geraghty; DP: Charles Boyle; Ed: Danny B. Landres; Prod Design: Richard H. Riedel; Composer: H. J. Salter; Art Director: Bernard Herzbrun. Color, 82 min. VHS

Tom Brown of Culver
(1932) Universal
In this coming-of-age film, a young ruffian (Brown) becomes a fine cadet believing he's walking in the footsteps of his dead military-hero father. When he discovers that his father is alive, shell-shocked, and a deserter, he pieces together his own life and his father's story. Watch for Power's debut playing an upperclassman. **Cast:** Tom Brown, Slim Summerville,

Richard Cromwell, H. B. Warner, Sidney Toler, Russell Hopton, Andy Devine, Willard Robertson, Ben Alexander, Tyrone Power. **Credits:** Dir: William Wyler; Prod: Carl Laemmle; Writer: George Green, Dale Van Every, Tom Buckingham, Clarence Marks; DP: Charles Stumar; Ed: Frank Gross. B&W, 82 min.

Tom Brown's School Days
(1940) RKO
This is one of child actor Bartholomew's finest performances. Tom Brown arrives at Rugby School and encounters the hazing of the school bullies in an institution where discipline has been nearly replaced by anarchy. While a stern new headmaster (Hardwicke) attempts to bring order, Tom and his friends stage their own revolution against the bullies, employing tricks, fisticuffs, and ingenious practical jokes such as nailing the ringleader's furniture to the ceiling. The Hughes novel has received several less than satisfying screen renditions; this is the best of the lot. **Cast:** Freddie Bartholomew, Cedric Hardwicke, Jimmy Lydon, Gale Storm, Billy Halop, Polly Moran, Hughie Green, Ernest Cossart. **Credits:** Dir: Robert Stevenson; Prod: Gene Towne; Writer: Walter Ferris; Writer: Thomas Hughes; DP: Nicholas Musuraca; Ed: William Hamilton; Composer: Anthony Collins; Art Director: Van Nest Polglase. B&W, 86 min. VHS

Tom, Dick and Harry
(1941) RKO
In a sparkling comedy directed by Kanin, Rogers is a telephone operator who must choose from three attractive suitors. Will it be wealthy Marshal, the charming nonconformist Meredith, or the earnest salesman Murphy? She always dreamed of a millionaire but it's the heart (and the kiss) of Meredith that wins. Remade in 1957 as *The Girl Most Likely*. Academy Award Nominations: Best Original Screenplay. **Cast:** Ginger Rogers, George Murphy, Burgess Meredith, Alan Marshal, Joe Cunningham, Jane Seymour, Phil Silvers, Sidney Skolsky. **Credits:** Dir: Garson Kanin; Prod: Robert Sisk; Writer: Paul Jarrico; DP: Merritt Gerstad; Ed: John Sturges; Prod Design: Mark-Lee Kirk; Composer: Roy Webb; Art Director: Van Nest Polglase. B&W, 87 min. VHS

Tomorrow
(1971) Filmgroup
Duvall's first major film role reveals the talent that would blossom in one

of the screen's most affecting actors. Based on the William Faulkner story, and scripted with understated elegance by Foote, the quiet, somber story follows a solitary backcountry farmer who encounters a pregnant young girl, cares for her, and then loses her soon after her child is delivered and their marriage. After years of caring for the boy, he again faces a wrenching loss when the woman's kin come for the child. Duvall finds the tiny nuances that reveal emotion in a stoic man unaccustomed to expression. Foote had written the story once before for a *Playhouse 90* adaptation. Worth searching for. **Cast:** Robert Duvall, Richard McConnell, Sudie Bond, Olga Bellin, Peter Masterson, William Hawley, James Franks, Johnny Mask. **Credits:** Dir: Joseph Anthony; Prod: Paul Roebling, Gilbert Pearlman; Writer: Horton Foote; Story: William Faulkner; DP: Alan Green; Ed: Reva Schlesinger; Composer: Irwin Stahl. B&W, 102 min. **VHS**

Tomorrow Is Forever
(1946) RKO
Welles and Colbert (how's that for an odd couple?) star in this wartime melodrama. Shortly after Welles and Colbert marry, he's wounded and scarred in WWI. Rather than burden his new wife and child, he vanishes into a new life in Austria. Colbert marries again and carries on happily until fate brings Welles to her husband Brent's factory. Six-year-old Wood's debut. **Cast:** Claudette Colbert, Orson Welles, George Brent, Lucile Watson, Richard Long, Natalie Wood, John Wengraf, Ian Wolfe. **Credits:** Dir: Irving Pichel; Prod: David Lewis; Writer: Lenore Coffee; DP: Joseph A. Valentine; Ed: Ernest Nims; Composer: Max Steiner; Art Director: Wiard Ihnen. B&W, 105 min. **VHS, LASER**

Tom Sawyer
(1973) United Artists
This is a well-made musical version of Twain's tale of life on the Mississippi. Tom (Whitaker) and his friend Becky Thatcher (a 10-year-old Foster) embark on a series of adventures, singing their way through Hannibal, Missouri. Songs include "River Song," "Gratification," "Freebootin'," "Aunt Polly's Soliloquy," and the title tune. Academy Award Nominations: 3, including Best Score; Best Art Direction. **Cast:** Johnnie Whitaker, Jodie Foster, Warren Oates, Celeste Holm, Jeff East, Lucille Benson, Henry Jones, Dub Taylor. **Credits:** Dir: Don Taylor; Prod: Arthur P. Jacobs; Writer: Robert B. Sherman,

Richard M. Sherman; Story: Mark Twain; DP: Frank Stanley; Ed: Marion Rothman; Prod Design: Philip M. Jefferies; Composer: John Williams, Richard M. Sherman, Robert B. Sherman. Color, 104 min. **VHS**

Tom Thumb
(1958) MGM
Pal's effects bring to life the Brothers Grimm story of five-inch-tall Tom Thumb (Tamblyn). Sellers and Terry-Thomas try to steal the little boy from the peasant family that took him in. A timeless family classic. **Academy Awards:** Best Special Effects. **Cast:** Russ Tamblyn, Peter Sellers, Terry-Thomas, Alan Young, Jessie Matthews, June Thorburn, Bernard Miles, Peter Butterworth. **Credits:** Dir: George Pal; Prod: George Pal; Writer: Ladislaus Fodor; DP: Georges Perinal; Ed: Frank Clarke; Composer: Douglas Gamley, Kermit Goell, Peggy Lee, Fred Spielman, Janice Torre, Ken E. Jones; Costumes: Olga Lehmann; Art Director: Elliot Scott; SFX: Tom Howard. Color, 98 min. **VHS, LASER**

Tonight and Every Night
(1945) Columbia
Based on the real heroism of London's Music Box Theater, this unique musical depicts a theater that believes the show must go on despite the bombs raining down during the Blitz. Hayworth charms RAF pilot Bowman, and song-and-dance team Blair and Platt fall in love but meet a tragic end. The Styne and Sammy Cahn songs include "Cry and You Cry Alone," "Anywhere," and "The Boy I Left Behind." Academy Award Nominations: Best Song ("Anywhere"); Best Score. **Cast:** Rita Hayworth, Lee Bowman, Marc Platt, Leslie Brooks, Shelley Winters, Janet Blair, Dusty Anderson, Stephen Crane. **Credits:** Dir: Victor Saville; Prod: Victor Saville; Writer: Lesser Samuels, Abem Finkel; DP: Rudolph Maté; Ed: Viola Lawrence; Prod Design: Rudolph Sternad; Composer: Jule Styne; Art Director: Stephen Goosson, Lionel Banks. Color, 92 min. **VHS**

Tonka
(1958) Disney
A young Sioux Indian (Mineo, fresh from his role in *Rebel Without a Cause*) captures a magnificent stallion but has to give it to his insolent older cousin in accordance with custom. Rather than see his cousin beat the horse, he releases it into the wild, only to discover it has been captured for use by the hated U.S. cavalry.

Mineo risks capture to be near his beloved horse, and becomes a young cavalry mascot after the horse is the only survivor of Little Big Horn. **Cast:** Sal Mineo, Philip Carey, Jerome Courtland, Rafael Campos, Joy Page, Herbert Rudley, Slim Pickens, Buzz Henry. **Credits:** Dir: Lewis R. Foster; Prod: James Pratt; Writer: Lewis R. Foster, Lillie Hayward; DP: Loyal Griggs; Ed: Ellsworth Hoagland; Composer: Oliver Wallace; Art Director: Robert Smith. Color, 97 min. **VHS**

Tony Rome
(1967) Fox
Sinatra takes on a private-eye role. The easy life on his Miami houseboat gets rocky when he agrees to escort home an erratic heiress (Lyon). When the girl's diamond pin goes missing, the trail leads to Sinatra. St. John helps him unravel the girl's underworld connections while dodging fists and bullets. Followed by *Lady in Cement* (1968). **Cast:** Frank Sinatra, Jill St. John, Gena Rowlands, Richard Conte, Sue Lyon, Simon Oakland, Jeffrey Lynn, Lloyd Bochner. **Credits:** Dir: Gordon Douglas; Prod: Aaron Rosenberg; Writer: Richard Breen; DP: Joseph Biroc; Ed: Robert Simpson; Composer: Billy May; Art Director: Jack Martin Smith, James Roth. Color, 110 min. **VHS**

Too Hot to Handle
(1938) MGM
Gable and Loy star in a fast-paced insider's look at the rough-and-tumble world of newsreel producers (the story was written by a newsreel producer). Gable and assistant Carillo come to the aid of lady flier Loy when her brother is captured by an Amazonian tribe. After impressing the natives with movie voodoo, Gable and Carillo snatch the captive and make for the States with a scoop. An entertaining look at manufactured news with more than a little contemporary relevance. **Cast:** Clark Gable, Myrna Loy, Walter Pidgeon, Leo Carrillo, Walter Connolly, Virginia Weidler, Henry Kolker, Marjorie Main. **Credits:** Dir: Jack Conway; Prod: Lawrence Weingarten; Writer: Laurence Stallings, John Lee Mahin; DP: Harold Rosson; Ed: Frank Sullivan; Composer: Franz Waxman. B&W, 108 min. **VHS**

Too Late the Hero
(1969) Cinerama
As in *The Dirty Dozen*, Aldrich once again assembles a motley squad of reluctant heroes. Because he can speak Japanese, Robertson is

recruited for a mission led by Elliott to knock out a Japanese observation post on a Pacific island. Skeptical enlisted man Caine and Robertson survive to match wits with the Japanese commandant. **Cast:** Michael Caine, Cliff Robertson, Ian Bannen, Henry Fonda, Harry Andrews, Denholm Elliott, Ronald Fraser, Lance Percival. **Credits:** Dir: Robert Aldrich; Prod: Robert Aldrich; Writer: Robert Aldrich, Lukas Heller; DP: Joseph Biroc; Ed: Michael Luciano; Composer: Gerald Fried; Art Director: James Vance. Color, 133 min. VHS

Too Many Girls
(1940) RKO
This engaging Rodgers and Hart musical is directed by Mr. Broadway himself, Abbott. Heiress Ball escapes her many suitors by enrolling in a small New Mexico college where the coeds outnumber the men ten to one. Her bodyguards come in handy on the gridiron. Film debuts for Johnson, Arnaz, and Bracken. Lucy and Desi married soon after production. Songs include "Love Never Went to College," "The Conga," "I Didn't Know What Time It Was," and "You're Nearer." **Cast:** Lucille Ball, Richard Carlson, Eddie Bracken, Ann Miller, Hal LeRoy, Frances Langford, Desi Arnaz, Van Johnson. **Credits:** Dir: George Abbott; Prod: George Abbott, Harry E. Edington; Writer: John Twist; DP: Frank Redman; Ed: William Hamilton; Composer: Richard Rodgers, Lorenz Hart; Art Director: Van Nest Polglase. B&W, 85 min. VHS, LASER

Too Many Husbands
(1940) Columbia
Unintentional bigamy must have tickled the funnybone in classic Hollywood because the mistakenly-deceased-spouse routine shows up again and again. This is one of the best trots around the block for the old wheeze as Arthur believes her husband MacMurray to have perished in a shipwreck. She finds solace with Douglas, but when MacMurray turns up alive, healthy and quite handsome, Arthur's in a delightful pickle as the center of attention. The men become friends and sort things out themselves. The leads make this worthwhile. Remade as *Three for the Show* in 1955 with Betty Grable. Academy Award Nomination: Best Sound. **Cast:** Jean Arthur, Fred MacMurray, Melvyn Douglas, Harry Davenport, Dorothy Peterson, Melville Cooper, Edgar Buchanan, Tom Dugan. **Credits:** Dir:

Wesley Ruggles; Prod: Wesley Ruggles; Writer: Claude Binyon; Story: W. Somerset Maugham; DP: Joseph Walker; Ed: William A. Lyon, Otto Meyer; Prod Design: Lionel Banks; Composer: Frederick Hollander. B&W, 84 min.

Topaz
(1969) Universal
Hitchcock delves into the murky waters of international espionage as French spy Stafford uncovers the Russian missile sites on Cuba. When CIA man Forsythe learns of the missile movements from a defector, he requests help from Stafford to infiltrate a Cuban spy ring and bring back documentation of the plot. His Cuban girlfriend, Dor, puts her staff at his disposal and, after close calls and assassinations, film of the missiles makes its way to the CIA. Stafford then solves the close-to-home leaks of NATO secrets. Based on Leon Uris's best-selling novel. **Cast:** John Forsythe, Philippe Noiret, Michel Piccoli, Frederick Stafford, John Vernon, Dany Robin, Karin Dor, Claude Jade. **Credits:** Dir: Alfred Hitchcock; Prod: Alfred Hitchcock; Writer: Samuel Taylor; DP: Jack Hildyard; Ed: William Ziegler; Prod Design: Henry Bumstead; Composer: Maurice Jarre. Color, 126 min. VHS, LASER

Topaze
(1933) RKO
The great Barrymore becomes a mousy teacher in this winning comedy. After being discharged from his position due to meddling from chemical magnate Mason's wife, he applies for a job at Mason's bottled-water company. Barrymore throws himself into his work and develops a sparkling, healthy water that becomes a hit with the public. When he discovers that Mason is selling tap water instead of his concoction, Barrymore finds the man's man within and challenges the tycoon. He winds up with a share of the business and Mason's mistress, Loy. Hecht adapted Pagnol's play for its first English-language screen version (it was filmed 4 times). **Cast:** John Barrymore, Myrna Loy, Albert Conti, Luis Alberni, Jobyna Howland, Jackie Searl, Frank Reicher, Reginald Mason. **Credits:** Dir: Harry D'Arrast; Prod: David O. Selznick; Writer: Ben Hecht, Benn W. Levy; Story: Marcel Pagnol; DP: Lucien Andriot; Ed: William Hamilton; Composer: Max Steiner; Art Director: Van Nest Polglase. B&W, 78 min. VHS, LASER

Top Hat
(1935) RKO
Astaire, Rogers, Irving Berlin, choreography by Hermes Pan and Astaire: all the elements that define the classic Astaire-Rogers picture and, therefore, the height of the '30s musical. When dancer Astaire hits London for the debut of his new show, his tap practice in his agent's (Horton) hotel room wakes his downstairs neighbor, Rogers. With one look at her face, a smitten Astaire chases her all over London and even to Venice after she believes he's really married to Horton's wife, Broderick. Despite her marriage in a fury to an Italian designer, the lovers are reunited in a gondola at the end. The plot's made meaningless, of course, by the elegance and bravura of the Deco sets, the perfectly integrated musical set pieces, and the justly famous pairing of Astaire and Rogers, including their renowned interpretation of "Cheek to Cheek." All 5 Berlin tunes, including "Cheek to Cheek" and "Top Hat," made it to the top of the charts. Selected for the National Film Registry. Academy Award Nominations: 3, including Best Picture; Best Song ("Take My Breath Away"). **Cast:** Fred Astaire, Ginger Rogers, Edward Everett Horton, Helen Broderick, Eric Blore, Erik Rhodes, Lucille Ball, Leonard Mudie. **Credits:** Dir: Mark Sandrich; Prod: Pandro S. Berman; Writer: Dwight Taylor, Allan Scott; DP: David Abel; Ed: William Hamilton; Prod Design: Carroll Clark; Composer: Max Steiner; Art Director: Van Nest Polglase. B&W, 103 min. VHS

Topkapi
(1964) United Artists
A team of daring (and quite amusing) thieves contrive a diabolically clever plot to steal a priceless dagger decorated with four dazzling emeralds from the Topkapi Palace Museum in Turkey. Mercouri and Schell enlist electronics expert Morley, acrobat Segal, muscleman Hahn, and bumbling driver Ustinov for their scheme. Though Ustinov turns informer, all goes well (including a dangling stunt to avoid the floor-wired alarm that must have been borrowed by the writers of 1996's *Mission: Impossible*) until a bird blows their cover. A tongue-in-cheek caper from Dassin based on Eric Ambler's *The Light of Day*. **Academy Awards:** Best Supporting Actor: Peter Ustinov. **Cast:** Melina Mercouri, Peter Ustinov, Maximilian Schell, Robert Morley, Gilles Segal, Akim Tamiroff, Jess Hahn, Titos Vandis, Joseph Dassin.

Credits: Dir: Jules Dassin; Prod: Jules Dassin; Writer: Monja Danischewsky, Gilles Segal; DP: Henri Alekan; Ed: Roger Dwyre; Composer: Manos Hadjidakis; Art Director: Max Douy. Color, 122 min. **VHS, LASER**

Topper
(1937) MGM
One of the greatest delights of '30s cinema. Happy-go-lucky married couple Grant and Bennett fritter away their time and considerable wealth with parties, driving fast cars, and annoying stuffy banker Young with their inattention to important matters such as boring board meetings. When they run their roadster into a tree, their consternation at being only halfway to heaven turns to a conviction that they must liven up Young's life. So the specters instigate parties, purchases of roadsters, and holidays at the shore. Young's wife is outraged at his newfound zest until she starts to have fun too. Young could not be better as he reacts to his invisible visitors (the scene in which the ghosts help the drunken Young down hotel steps and through the lobby is priceless physical comedy). A treasure. Followed by two sequels and a TV series. Academy Award Nominations: Best Supporting Actor: Roland Young; Best Sound Recording. **Cast:** Cary Grant, Roland Young, Constance Bennett, Billie Burke, Alan Mowbray, Eugene Pallette, Arthur Lake, Hedda Hopper. **Credits:** Dir: Norman Z. McLeod; Prod: Hal Roach; Writer: Jack Jevne, Eric Hatch, E. Edwin Moran; DP: Norbert F. Brodine; Ed: William Terhune; Composer: Edward B. Powell, Hugo Friedhofer; Art Director: Arthur Rouce. B&W, 97 min. **VHS, LASER**

Topper Returns
(1940) MGM
The third of the *Topper* movies finds Young a detective after ghostly murder victim Blondell asks him to intercede and save potential victim Landis's life. Young next took the *Topper* act to TV. Academy Award Nominations: Best Sound Recording; Best Special Effects. **Cast:** Roland Young, Joan Blondell, Carole Landis, Eddie Anderson, George Zucco, Billie Burke, Patsy Kelly, Dennis O'Keefe. **Credits:** Dir: Roy Del Ruth; Prod: Hal Roach; Writer: Gordon Douglas, Jonathan Latimer; DP: Norbert F. Brodine; Ed: James E. Newcom; Composer: Werner Richard Heymann; Costumes: Royer; Art Director: Nicolai Remisoff. B&W, 87 min. **VHS, LASER**

Topper Takes a Trip
(1939) MGM
Bennett tackles Young's marital problems without the benefit of hubby Grant in this follow-up to *Topper*. When Burke spots her husband (Young) with Bennett, she assumes he's having an affair and flies off to Paris. Bennett and her equally invisible dog (who provides many of the laughs here) put things to right, and she joins Grant in the great beyond. Academy Award Nomination for Best Visual Effects. **Cast:** Roland Young, Constance Bennett, Billie Burke, Carole Landis, Alan Mowbray, Veree Teasdale, Franklin Pangborn. **Credits:** Dir: Norman Z. McLeod; Prod: Hal Roach; Writer: Eddie Moran, Jack Jevne, Corey Ford; DP: Norbert F. Brodine; Ed: William Terhune; Art Director: Charles Hall; Effects: Roy Seawright; SFX: Roy Seawright. B&W, 85 min. **VHS, LASER**

Tora! Tora! Tora!
(1970) Fox
A hands-across-the-waters production has Japanese directors depicting the preparation to attack Pearl Harbor and an American director showing the U.S.'s cluelessness. The actual invasion makes the first hour worth enduring. Japanese master Akira Kurosawa shot the first few days of this before fleeing the studio strictures. Academy Award Nominations: 5, including Best Cinematography; Best Art Direction. **Academy Awards:** Best Special Visual Effects. **Cast:** Martin Balsam, E. G. Marshall, James Whitmore, Jason Robards, Ned Wertimer, Joseph Cotten, So Yamamura, Tatsuya Mihashi, Takahiro Tamura, Eijiro Tono. **Credits:** Dir: Richard Fleischer, Toshio Masuda, Kinji Fukasaku; Prod: Elmo Williams; Writer: Larry Forrester, Hideo Oguni, Ryuzo Kikushima; DP: Charles F. Wheeler, Sinsaku Himeda, Osami Furuya, Masamichi Satoh; Ed: James E. Newcom, Pembroke Herring, Inoue Chikaya; Prod Design: Yoshiro Muraki; Composer: Jerry Goldsmith; Art Director: Jack Martin Smith, Richard Day, Taizoh Kawashima; SFX: A.D. Flowers, L.B. Abbot. Color, 144 min. **VHS, LASER**

Torch Song
(1953) MGM
In a backstage potboiler, a typically hard-as-nails Crawford portrays a Broadway musical star who chews up people when she's not chewing scenery. After all around her flee, she engages a blind pianist (Wilding) as her arranger. He won't stand for her abuse, which intrigues the imperious star. When Crawford discovers an

early clipping written by Wilding, she understands that he loved her then and loves her still. Academy Award Nominations: Best Supporting Actress: Marjorie Rambeau. **Cast:** Joan Crawford, Michael Wilding, Marjorie Rambeau, Gig Young, Harry Morgan, Dorothy Patrick, James Todd, Eugene Loring. **Credits:** Dir: Charles Walters; Prod: Henry Berman, Sidney Franklin; Writer: John Michael Hayes, Jan Lustig; DP: Robert Planck; Ed: Albert Akst; Prod Design: Cedric Gibbons; Composer: Adolph Deutsch; Art Director: Preston Ames. Color, 90 min. **VHS, LASER**

Torchy Blane
Glenda Farrell charmed as the acerbic, wisecracking reporter Torchy Blane, whose pluck came in handy in solving crimes that confounded police. In each entry of this snappy Warner Bros. series, Torchy Blane teamed up—or butted heads with—police lieutenant Steve McBride, played by Barton MacLane, who was also her fiancé. Fast-talking Torchy clearly was the brains of the couple and inevitably solved the mystery, leaving McBride in the dust. Torchy Blane was based on Frederick Nebel's pulp magazine stories, though Nebel's character was a male reporter named Kennedy. The gender change worked well, mostly because Farrell is so darned appealing. Farrell and MacLane starred in all but two of the films. Lola Lane and Paul Kelly took over in *Torchy Blane in Panama* (1938) and Jane Wyman and Allen Jenkins paired in *Torchy Plays with Dynamite* (1939).

Smart Blonde *(1936)*
Fly-Away Baby *(1937)*
Adventurous Blonde *(1937)*
Blondes at Work *(1938)*
Torchy Blane in Panama *(1938)*
Torchy Gets Her Man *(1938)*
Torchy Blane in Chinatown *(1939)*
Torchy Runs for Mayor *(1939)*
Torchy Plays with Dynamite *(1939)*

Torn Curtain
(1966) Universal
Middling Cold War Hitchcock features one of his starriest casts. Newman plays a nuclear physicist who goes undercover in East Germany to recover a secret formula. Once behind the Iron Curtain, he and fiancée Andrews have to get out alive. Just okay Hitchcock, but that's better than most. **Cast:** Paul Newman, Julie Andrews, David Opatoshu, Lila Kedrova, Peter Lorre, Ludwig Donath,

Hansjoerg Felmy, Tamara Toumanova. **Credits:** Dir: Alfred Hitchcock; Prod: Alfred Hitchcock; Writer: Brian Moore; DP: John F. Warren; Ed: Bud Hoffman; Composer: John Addison; Art Director: Frank Arrigo. Color, 125 min. **VHS, LASER**

Tortilla Flat

(1942) MGM
Tracy and Garfield play two friends just trying to get by in Steinbeck's world of Monterey, California's canneries and fishermen. Tracy and Tamiroff move in when Garfield inherits two houses, seeming to bring him bad luck as Garfield fights with the beautiful cannery worker he adores (Lamarr) and one of his houses burns down. Tracy gets ideas when Morgan shows up with his dog and a small fortune. Whimsical humor and realistically portrayed, colorful characters make this an overlooked gem. Academy Award Nomination for Best Supporting Actor: Frank Morgan. **Cast:** Spencer Tracy, Hedy Lamarr, John Garfield, Frank Morgan, Akim Tamiroff, Sheldon Leonard, John Qualen, Donald Meek. **Credits:** Dir: Victor Fleming; Prod: Sam Zimbalist; Writer: John Lee Mahin, Benjamin Glazer; Story: John Steinbeck; DP: Karl Freund; Ed: James E. Newcom; Prod Design: Cedric Gibbons, Paul Groesse; Composer: Franz Waxman. B&W, 105 min. **VHS, LASER**

To the Ends of the Earth

(1948) Columbia
A pseudo-documentary whodunit has narcotics agent Powell following the drug-trade trail around the world from San Francisco to Shanghai, Egypt, Havana, and the New Jersey coast. Powell tracks a Japanese steamer suspected of drug smuggling, but, before he can board the boat, its Chinese plantation slaves are mercilessly jettisoned, and so the narc must travel to Shanghai to infiltrate the drug ring. After following them to Egypt where their opium is grown and then to Havana (a shipping point), he ends up in New York during a United Nations commission on drug control. **Cast:** Dick Powell, Signe Hasso, Ludwig Donath, Vladimir Sokoloff, Edgar Barrier, John Hoyt, Marcel Journet, Luis Van Rooten, Fritz Leiber. **Credits:** Dir: Robert Stevenson; Prod: Sidney Buchman; Writer: Jay Richard Kennedy; DP: Burnett Guffey; Ed: William A. Lyon; Prod Design: Stephen Goosson; Composer: George Duning, Morris Stoloff. B&W, 104 min.

To the Last Man

(1933) Paramount
This, one of Paramount's Hathaway-Scott Westerns, is based on the novels of Zane Grey, and follows a feud between clans in 1880s Arizona and a romance between Scott and Ralston. You might spot five-year-old Temple in her second role. **Cast:** Randolph Scott, Esther Ralston, Noah Beery, Shirley Temple, Buster Crabbe, Jack LaRue, Barton MacLane, Muriel Kirkland. **Credits:** Dir: Henry Hathaway; Prod: Harold Hurley; Writer: Jack Cunningham; DP: Ben Reynolds; Art Director: Earl Hedrick. B&W, 70 min. **VHS**

To the Victor

(1948) Warner Bros.
Set in Paris shortly after WWII, an American veteran (Morgan) who has stayed behind to make money in the black market meets a French woman (Lindfors) on the run from a bunch of thugs associated with her husband, a traitor and collaborator who's been brought back to France for trial. Despite the danger, the woman testifies against her husband, and in the process attempts to reform the American vet who's fallen in love with her. Lindfors's first Hollywood role. **Cast:** Dennis Morgan, Viveca Lindfors, Victor Francen, Bruce Bennett, Dorothy Malone, Tom D'Andrea, Eduardo Cianelli, Douglas Kennedy, Joseph Buloff, William Conrad. **Credits:** Dir: Delmer Daves; Prod: Jerry Wald; Writer: Richard Brooks; DP: Robert Burks; Ed: Folmar Blangsted; Prod Design: Leo K. Kater; Composer: David Buttolph. B&W, 100 min.

A Touch of Class

(1973) Avco Embassy
This wistful romantic comedy is elevated by Jackson's perfectly straight-faced comic performance. Businessman Segal lives with his wife and kids in London, where he meets fashion illustrator Jackson. She agrees to a tryst in Spain, a romantic excursion foiled by the intrusions of Sorvino and his wife, back spasms, and miscommunications. After the tension's off, though, real romance begins and continues in London until the emotions become too real and the consequences too high. Academy Award Nominations: 5, including Best Picture; Best Original Screenplay; Best Song ("All That Love Went to Waste"). **Academy Awards:** Best Actress: Glenda Jackson. **Cast:** George Segal, Glenda Jackson, Paul Sorvino, Cec Linder, K. Callan, Mary Barclay, Michael Elwyn, Nadim Sawalha. **Credits:** Dir: Melvin

Frank; Prod: Melvin Frank; Writer: Melvin Frank, Jack Rose; DP: Austin Dempster; Ed: Bill Butler; Prod Design: Terence Marsh, Alan Tomkins; Composer: John Cameron. Color, 103 min. **VHS**

Touch of Evil

(1958) Universal
A story of studio meddling became one of the most talked about movies of 1998 upon release of a restored version based on notes that Welles had sent to Universal in response to their reediting. Right from the first shot, which many consider the finest opening sequence in movie history (and which the studio decided to run credits over), Welles takes a tawdry crime melodrama and turns it into dark poetry. Heston, a Mexican cop, is heading for a honeymoon with Leigh, but they are distracted by a car bombing as they cross the border. When Heston offers to help in the investigation, he begins a twisted journey into a seedy night time world of drug smugglers, prostitutes, and, most magnificently, "a great detective, but a bad cop" played by Welles. Leigh falls into a snare set by drug kingpin Tamiroff as her husband goes *mano a mano* with a murderous Welles. An absorbing noir, and a triumphant story of film preservation. Selected for the National Film Registry. **Cast:** Charlton Heston, Janet Leigh, Orson Welles, Joseph Calleia, Akim Tamiroff, Marlene Dietrich, Zsa Zsa Gabor, Ray Collins. **Credits:** Dir: Orson Welles, Harry Keller; Prod: Albert Zugsmith; Writer: Orson Welles; DP: Russell Metty; Ed: Virgil Vogel, Aaron Stell; Prod Design: Alexander Golitzen, Robert Clatworthy; Composer: Henry Mancini. B&W, 108 min. **VHS, LASER**

The Towering Inferno

(1974) Fox
Producer-director Allen here perfects the big-budget disaster epic that he introduced with *The Poseidon Adventure* (1972). This time, the setting is San Francisco and the grand opening of the world's tallest skyscraper. When a fire begins to engulf the building, it's up to firefighters McQueen and Newman to save the day. Golden Globe for Best Supporting Actor: Fred Astaire. Academy Award Nominations: 8, including Best Picture; Best Supporting Actor: Fred Astaire. **Academy Awards:** Best Film Editing; Best Cinematography; Best Song ("We May Never Love Like This Again"). **Cast:** Steve McQueen, Paul Newman, William Holden, Faye Dunaway, Fred

Astaire, O. J. Simpson, Robert Vaughn. **Credits:** Dir: Irwin Allen, John Guillermin; Prod: Irwin Allen; Writer: Stirling Silliphant; DP: Fred Koenekamp, Joseph Biroc; Ed: Harold F. Kress, Carl Kress; Prod Design: William J. Creber; Composer: John Williams; Costumes: Paul Zastupnevich; Art Director: Ward Preston. Color, 165 min. **VHS, LASER**

The Tower of London
(1939) Universal
This chilling melodrama set in the 15th century recounts the deeds that earned Richard III (Rathbone) his place as the most despised monarch in English history and established The Tower as the most dreaded building in the world. The gruesome tale of Richard of Gloucester's rise to the throne through the executions of powerful noblemen and the haunting murder of his two crown-prince nephews. Karloff plays Mord, his coldhearted executioner, and Price portrays the Duke of Clarence, who meets his end in a vat of wine. Due to the brutality of some scenes (which had to be trimmed before the film's theatrical release), many mistake this for a horror film. It is instead a graphic and disturbing historical drama. **Cast:** Basil Rathbone, Boris Karloff, Barbara O'Neil, Ian Hunter, Vincent Price, Nan Grey, Leo G. Carroll, John Sutton, Miles Mander. **Credits:** Dir: Rowland V. Lee; Prod: Rowland V. Lee; Writer: Robert N. Lee; DP: George Robinson; Ed: Edward Curtiss; Composer: Frank Skinner; Art Director: Jack Otterson. B&W, 93 min. **VHS**

Toys in the Attic
(1963) United Artists
This screen adaptation of Lillian Hellman's play depicts the dark family doings when wayward Martin returns to New Orleans with his child bride (Mimieux) in tow. His overprotective, aging spinster sisters (Page and Hiller) are first delighted with his gifts, then wonder where his money comes from. When Page and Mimieux eavesdrop, they uncover Martin's phony real-estate dealings and Mimieux's mother's affair with a black chauffeur. Page convinces a stung Mimieux to rat on her husband in the hope that he will drive her away, but she ends up alone with her scheming. Great performances by Hiller, Page, and Martin. Academy Award Nominations: Best (Black-and-White) Costume Design. **Cast:** Dean Martin, Geraldine Page, Yvette Mimieux, Wendy Hiller, Gene Tierney, Nan Martin, Larry Gates,

Frank Silvera. **Credits:** Dir: George Roy Hill; Prod: Walter Mirisch; Writer: James Poe; DP: Joseph Biroc; Ed: Stuart Gilmore, Marshall M. Borden; Composer: George Duning; Art Director: Cary Odell. B&W, 90 min. **VHS**

Trader Horn
(1931) MGM
Hollywood takes its first excursion to Africa and the experience nearly killed cast and crew. Carey plays a trader who goes on a search for a missionary's daughter (Booth) in the deepest jungles near a waterfall where her father had died. He makes a shocking discovery when taken captive by fierce natives: the missionary's daughter now rules the tribe as a goddess. Shot on location in 1929 by Van Dyke, but pieced together by Irving Thalberg with reshoots over the course of the next year. The result was a surprise hit. Academy Award Nomination for Best Picture. **Cast:** Harry Carey, Edwina Booth, Duncan Renaldo, Olive Golden, Mutia Omoolu, Olive Carey, C. Aubrey Smith. **Credits:** Dir: W. S. Van Dyke II; Writer: Richard Schayer, Cyril Hume, Dale Van Every, John T. Neville; DP: Clyde De Vinna; Ed: Ben Lewis. B&W, 120 min. **VHS**

Trade Winds
(1938) United Artists
Bennett, accused of shooting and killing a man who drove her sister to suicide, leads investigators March and Bellamy on a merry jaunt around the world. Before March can cash the reward being offered, he falls in love with his beautiful quarry. Garnett created this in order to use the footage he shot while sailing his boat around the world, but it also features snappy dialogue from Parker and her husband, Campbell. **Cast:** Fredric March, Joan Bennett, Ralph Bellamy, Ann Sothern, Sidney Blackmer, Thomas Mitchell, Robert Elliott, Patricia Farr, Wilma Francis, Phyllis Barry. **Credits:** Dir: Tay Garnett; Prod: Walter Wagner; Writer: Frank R. Adams, Alan Campbell, Dorothy Parker; Story: Tay Garnett; DP: Rudolph Maté; Ed: Walt Reynolds, Dorothy Spencer; Composer: Alfred Newman. B&W, 98 min.

The Trail of the Lonesome Pine
(1936) Paramount
Three-strip Technicolor makes its first trip outdoors with this story of a long-running backwoods feud and its collision with the modern world. The Tollivers and the Falins are Kentucky families who have been at each

other's throats forever. Enter MacMurray, an engineer who wants to build a railroad through their land, who saves Fonda from a rival clan. Fonda's not that grateful, though, as he fears that his sister Sidney will run off with the city man. MacMurray does arrange for her to go to school, but when her brother, MacFarland, gets killed in an assault on the railroad's workers, Sidney reverts to her upbringing and calls for retaliation. This was filmed twice before in silent days and was old hat by the time of this first sound treatment, but Hathaway gives it some energy. Fonda's first color role. Academy Award Nomination for Best Original Song ("A Melody from the Sky"). **Cast:** Fred MacMurray, Sylvia Sidney, Henry Fonda, Fred Stone, Nigel Bruce, Beulah Bondi, Spanky McFarland, Fuzzy Knight, Robert Barratt. **Credits:** Dir: Henry Hathaway; Prod: Walter Wanger; Writer: Grover Jones, Harvey Thew, Horace McCoy; Story: John Fox, Jr.; DP: W. Howard Greene, Robert C. Bruce; Ed: Robert Bischoff; Prod Design: Hans Dreier. Color, 100 min. **VHS**

Trail of the Vigilantes
(1940) Universal
Dwan took a standard Western yawner and turned it into a sprightly parody with Tone a tenderfoot newspaperman joining up with Crawford, Auer, and Devine to bust William's rackets. Tone has some hilarious moments as he adjusts to the rigors of the West, falls off horses, and avoids the violent attentions of randy cowgirl Moran. **Cast:** Franchot Tone, Warren William, Broderick Crawford, Andy Devine, Mischa Auer, Porter Hall, Peggy Moran, Samuel S. Hinds, Charles Trowbridge, Max Wagner. **Credits:** Dir: Allan Dwan; Prod: Allan Dwan; Writer: Harold Shumate; DP: Joseph A. Valentine; Ed: Edward Curtiss; Prod Design: Jack Otterson; Composer: Hans J. Salter. B&W, 75 min.

Trail Street
(1947) RKO
Scott plays legendary lawman Bat Masterson as he joins with land agent Ryan to take sides with peaceful farmers against treacherous ranchers. Standard mythmaking but with a better-than-average cast. **Cast:** Randolph Scott, Robert Ryan, Anne Jeffreys, George "Gabby" Hayes, Madge Meredith, Steve Brodie, Billy House, Virginia Sale. **Credits:** Dir: Ray Enright; Prod: Nat Holt; Writer: Norman Houston, Gena Lewis; DP:

J. Roy Hunt; Ed: Lyle Boyer; Prod Design: Ralph Berger; Composer: Paul Sawtell; Art Director: Albert S. D'Agostino. B&W, 84 min. **VHS**

The Train
(1965) United Artists
Frankenheimer crafts (after taking over from Arthur Penn and rewriting the script) a memorable WWII suspenser. During the last days of the German occupation of Paris, a German colonel (the magnificent Scofield) is ordered to steal all of the city's most revered works of art and send them on a train to Germany. When the French Resistance discovers the plan, Lancaster, the train inspector, reluctantly agrees to sabotage the train, not wanting to risk lives for paintings. He concocts an elaborate scheme to keep the train in France, but Scofield becomes obsessed with his mission and persists through derailments and murder, an obsession matched by Lancaster's determination to foil the shipment. Academy Award Nomination for Best (Original) Story and Screenplay. **Cast:** Burt Lancaster, Paul Scofield, Michel Simon, Jeanne Moreau, Albert Remy, Wolfgang Preiss, Richard Munch, Jacques Marin. **Credits:** Dir: John Frankenheimer; Prod: Jules Bricken; Writer: Franklin Coen, Frank Davis, Walter Bernstein, Albert Husson; DP: Jean Tournier, Walter Wottitz; Ed: David Bretherton; Prod Design: Willy Holt; Composer: Maurice Jarre. B&W, 133 min. **VHS, LASER**

The Train Robbers
(1973) Warner Bros.
The Duke gets involved in an elaborate ruse involving a hidden cache of money and a beautiful widow (Ann-Margret). Civil War vet Wayne rides to Mexico to retrieve the loot, only to discover that he's being followed by Montalban and 20 men. Wayne and his men fight off the mystery riders (with help from a shotgun-wielding Ann-Margret) and offers his share to the widow's little boy. He then gets a nasty surprise that sets him riding in pursuit of the "widow." Standard late-period Wayne. **Cast:** John Wayne, Ann-Margret, Rod Taylor, Ben Johnson, Christopher George, Bobby Vinton, Jerry Gatlin, Ricardo Montalban. **Credits:** Dir: Burt Kennedy; Prod: Michael Wayne; Writer: Burt Kennedy; DP: William Clothier; Ed: Frank Santillo; Composer: Dominic Frontiere; Art Director: Alfred Sweeney. Color, 92 min. **VHS, LASER**

Tramp, Tramp, Tramp
(1926) First National
Unduly overlooked silent comic genius Langdon stars in his first feature as a participant in a cross-country walking race. Along the way, Crawford, the daughter of the race sponsor, appears on advertising billboards and Harry falls in love. After hilarious mishaps, Crawford appears and the two end up married. Written in part by future director Capra. **Cast:** Harry Langdon, Joan Crawford. **Credits:** Dir: Harry Edwards, Mack Sennett; Writer: Frank Capra, Tim Whelan, Hal Conklin, J. Frank Holliday, Gerald Duffy, Murray Roth; DP: Elgin Lessley; Composer: Philip Carli. Tinted 84 min. **VHS**

Trapeze
(1956) United Artists
Lancaster revisits the circus acrobatics of his youth as the impaired aerialist who once risked his life and achieved the "triple," three midair somersaults. Curtis is the son of a former Lancaster colleague who wants to know the secret, and Lollobrigida the tumbler who romances both aerialists to move up on the circus ladder. **Cast:** Burt Lancaster, Tony Curtis, Gina Lollobrigida, Katy Jurado, Thomas Gomez, Johnny Puleo, Minor Watson, Gerard Landry. **Credits:** Dir: Carol Reed; Prod: James Hill; Writer: James R. Webb, Liam O'Brien; DP: Robert Krasker; Ed: Bert Bates; Composer: Malcolm Arnold; Art Director: Rino Mondellini. Color, 105 min. **VHS**

Travels with My Aunt
(1972) MGM
Banker McCowen gets drawn into the wild life of his aunt (Smith) when she informs him at his mother's cremation that the ashes are not his mother. From London to Paris to an excursion on the Orient Express to Turkey and back to Paris, McCowen and Smith go on a wild goose chase attempting to ransom Smith's errant lover, Stephens. A whirlwind of a performance from Smith (replacing Katharine Hepburn!) in a late-period, less energetic Cukor outing. From Graham Greene's best-selling novel. Academy Award Nominations: 4, including Best Actress: Maggie Smith; Best Cinematography. **Academy Awards:** Best Costume Design. **Cast:** Maggie Smith, Alec McCowen, Robert Stephens, Cindy Williams, Louis Gossett, Jr., Robert Flemyng, Jose Luis Lopez Vazquez, Daniel Emilfork. **Credits:** Dir: George Cukor; Prod: Robert Fryer, James Cresson; Writer: Jay Presson Allen, Hugh Wheeler; DP:

Douglas Slocombe; Ed: John Bloom; Composer: Tony Hatch; Art Director: Gil Parrondo, Bob Laing. Color, 109 min. **VHS, LASER**

Treasure Island
(1934) MGM
Fleming's sure hand with sprawling costume epics comes in handy in the first sound version (and the best ever) of Robert Louis Stevenson's adventure tale. Cooper is perfectly cast as young Jim Hawkins, who receives a map to pirate treasure from old salt Barrymore. He boards a ship to take him to the island, but discovers the vessel's crawling with the pirates who want their treasure back, led by Beery as Long John Silver. Great family entertainment produced in grand style. **Cast:** Wallace Beery, Jackie Cooper, Lionel Barrymore, Otto Kruger, Lewis Stone, Nigel Bruce, Charles Sale, William V. Mong. **Credits:** Dir: Victor Fleming; Prod: Hunt Stromberg; Writer: John Lee Mahin, Leonard Praskins, John Howard Lawson; DP: Ray June, Harold Rosson, Clyde De Vinna; Ed: Blanche Sewell; Prod Design: Cedric Gibbons; Composer: Herbert Stothart; Art Director: Merrill Pye, Edwin B. Willis. B&W, 105 min. **VHS, LASER**

Treasure Island
(1950) Disney
Disney's first all-live-action film is a beautiful, expensively mounted production of the Robert Louis Stevenson pirate tale. Driscoll makes an engaging Jim Hawkins and Newton pulls out all the stops as Long John Silver. Well done and worth watching as many times as the kids demand to see it. **Cast:** Bobby Driscoll, Robert Newton, Basil Sydney, Walter Fitzgerald, Denis O'Dea, Ralph Truman, Finlay Currie, John Laurie. **Credits:** Dir: Byron Haskin; Prod: Perce Pearce; Writer: Lawrence Edward Watkin; DP: Freddie Young; Ed: Alan Jaggs; Prod Design: Tom Morahan; Composer: Clifton Parker. Color, 96 min. **VHS, LASER**

Treasure of Lost Canyon
(1952) Universal
A frontier doctor (Powell) takes an orphaned boy raised in a traveling medicine show under his wing, but changes his altruistic tune when the boy discovers a treasure chest. Transformed by the thought of how the cash could bankroll his return to the bright lights of San Francisco, the doctor wants the chest for himself. But the boy's former guardian, an unscrupulous lawyer (Hull), has competing designs on the

money, which the boy has wisely concealed under a raging waterfall. Powell reforms in time to keep the lawyer at bay. **Cast:** William Powell, Julie Adams, Charles Drake, Rosemary DeCamp, Tommy Ivo, Chubby Johnson, John Doucette, Marvin Press, Henry Hull. **Credits:** Dir: Ted Tetzlaff; Prod: Leonard Goldstein, William Alland; Writer: Brainerd Duffield, Emerson Crocker; Story: Robert Louis Stevenson; DP: Russell Metty; Ed: Milton Carruth; Composer: Joseph Gershenson; Art Director: Bernard Herzbrun, Alexander Golitzen. Color, 82 min.

The Treasure of the Sierra Madre
(1948) Warner Bros.
Many consider this to be John Huston's finest moment, though he supplied many to choose from. It is in any case a classic tale of greed and its corrosive effect on the human soul. Two drifters on the bum in Mexico (Bogart and Holt) see their fortunes rise after working for some pocket money and Bogart wins a lottery. They take their new means and team up with an old prospector they meet in a flophouse (Walter Huston) to venture into the mountains to dig for gold. Bogart declares that he won't fall prey to Huston's warning about riches turning men's heads, wanting only his fair share. Their luck seems to hold after surviving a bandit attack and hitting a strike, but as the gold dust piles up, the wariness sets in. Bogart is magnificent as he slowly lets the greed and suspicion eat him alive, pulling a gun on his onetime partner and succumbing at last to the bandit's gun. Essential viewing for any classic-movie fan. Golden Globes for Best Director: John Huston; Best Supporting Actor: Walter Huston; Best Motion Picture, Drama. Selected for the National Film Registry. Academy Award Nominations: 4, including Best Picture. **Academy Awards:** Best Director; Best Supporting Actor: Walter Huston; Best Screenplay. **Cast:** Humphrey Bogart, Walter Huston, Tim Holt, Bruce Bennett, Robert Blake, John Huston, Jack Holt, Jose Torvay. **Credits:** Dir: John Huston; Prod: Henry Blanke; Writer: John Huston; Story: B. Traven; DP: Ted McCord; Ed: Owen Marks; Composer: Max Steiner; Art Director: John Hughes. B&W, 126 min. **VHS, LASER**

A Tree Grows in Brooklyn
(1945) Fox
In Kazan's directorial debut, standout performances make a touching adaptation of Smith's beloved novel.

Set in turn-of-the-century Brooklyn, the story follows a family of Irish who struggle to simply survive in their teeming neighborhood. Dunn makes a sometime-living as a waiter, mother McGuire stretches every penny to the exasperation of the local merchants, and Garner dreams of a better life as she reads her way alphabetically through the library hoping to become a writer. The scenes of Garner and her brother (Donaldson) in the streets of Brooklyn are detailed and evocative; the emotional connections in the family seem palpably real. Sincere, moving family drama. Academy Award Nominations: 2, including Best Screenplay. **Academy Awards:** Best Supporting Actor: James Dunn; Special Oscar for Best Child Actress: Peggy Ann Garner. **Cast:** Dorothy McGuire, Joan Blondell, James Dunn, Lloyd Nolan, Peggy Ann Garner, Ted Donaldson, James Gleason, Mae Marsh. **Credits:** Dir: Elia Kazan; Prod: Louis D. Lighton; Writer: Tess Slesinger, Frank Davis; Story: Betty Smith; DP: Leon Shamroy; Ed: Dorothy Spencer; Prod Design: Lyle Wheeler; Composer: Alfred Newman. B&W, 128 min. **VHS, LASER**

Trial
(1955) MGM
This taut, political courtroom drama manages to attack racism and social injustice while denouncing communism. Ford is an idealistic young attorney certain the young Mexican-American boy he's defending, Campos, didn't commit the murder for which he's standing trial, and the angry, white lynch mob outside the courtroom won't convince him otherwise. The judge is willing to let Ford have his say, but communist agitator Kennedy tries to make the case into something it's not. Academy Award Nomination for Best Supporting Actor: Arthur Kennedy. **Cast:** Juano Hernandez, Rodney Bell, Glenn Ford, Dorothy McGuire, John Hodiak, Arthur Kennedy, Katy Jurado, Rafael Campos, John Hoyt, Paul Guilfoyle. **Credits:** Dir: Mark Robson; Prod: Charles Schnee; Writer: Don Mankiewicz; DP: Robert Surtees; Ed: Albert Akst; Prod Design: Cedric Gibbons, Randal Duell; Composer: Daniele Amfitheatrof. B&W, 105 min.

Tribute to a Bad Man
(1956) MGM
Cagney, in one of his few Westerns, plays a ruthless horse breeder whose brutality toward his hands and the rustlers he summarily hangs costs him the love of his companion, Papas (in her Hollywood debut). She sees an

opportunity to escape her life when younger man Dubbins comes to work on the ranch and they begin an affair. When Cagney reluctantly lets the two leave without taking revenge, Papas recognizes the man she first fell in love with. Originally slated to star Spencer Tracy and Grace Kelly. **Cast:** James Cagney, Don Dubbins, Stephen McNally, Irene Papas, Vic Morrow, Royal Dano, Lee Van Cleef, James Griffith. **Credits:** Dir: Robert Wise; Prod: Sam Zimbalist; Writer: Michael Blankfort; DP: Robert Surtees; Ed: Ralph E. Winters; Prod Design: Cedric Gibbons, Paul Groesse; Composer: Miklos Rozsa. Color, 95 min. **VHS**

The Trip
(1967) AIP
Take a trip yourself back to the halcyon days of drug experimentation when all was groovy. TV producer Fonda can't get it together, so his friend Dern suggests a little mind expansion courtesy of pusher Hopper. Buckle your seat belts for a hallucinogenic ride along with Fonda as he experiences death, sex, and rebirth, all in one night. Nicholson wrote the script for this cult favorite Corman quickie. **Cast:** Peter Fonda, Susan Strasberg, Dennis Hopper, Bruce Dern, Salli Sachse, Luana Anders, Katherine Walsh. **Credits:** Dir: Roger Corman; Prod: Roger Corman; Writer: Jack Nicholson; DP: Arch Dalzell; Ed: Ronald Sinclair; Composer: American Music Band. Color, 85 min. **VHS**

Trouble Along the Way
(1953) Warner Bros.
Former pro coach Wayne lends his sideline skills to tiny St. Anthony's College when his former wife mounts a custody battle for their daughter. His team starts to win, but Wayne's hardball tactics offend the college president (Coburn). When he's fired, caseworker Reed comes to his defense and loses her heart. Pleasant enough. **Cast:** John Wayne, Donna Reed, Charles Coburn, Sherry Jackson, Marie Windsor, Tom Tully, Tom Helmore, Dabbs Greer. **Credits:** Dir: Michael Curtiz; Prod: Melville Shavelson; Writer: Melville Shavelson, Jack Rose; DP: Archie Stout; Ed: Owen Marks; Composer: Max Steiner; Art Director: Leo K. Kuter. B&W, 110 min. **VHS, LASER**

Trouble for Two
(1936) MGM
Prince Florizal (Montgomery), the son of a European monarch, travels to London for an arranged marriage to

the beautiful Princess Brenda (Russell). While in London, however, he gets involved with a mysterious organization called the Suicide Club. Before Montgomery can marry, he must outwit the murderers. Based on Robert Louis Stevenson's Suicide Club stories. **Cast:** Robert Montgomery, Rosalind Russell, Frank Morgan, Reginald Owen, Louis Hayward, E. E. Clive, David Holt, Walter Kingsford, Ivan Simpson, Tom Moore. **Credits:** Dir: J. Walter Ruben; Prod: Louis D. Lighton; Writer: Manuel Seff, Edward E. Paramore, Jr.; DP: Charles G. Clarke; Ed: Robert J. Kern; Prod Design: Cedric Gibbons; Composer: Franz Waxman. B&W, 75 min.

Trouble in Paradise

(1932) Paramount
This continental confection from Lubitsch features a sharp script full of tangy double entendres and a strong cast. Marshall and Hopkins, a pair of sophisticated thieves (and former lovers), travel from Venice to Paris, where they compete with each other as they insinuate themselves into the life of a wealthy owner of a perfume boutique (Francis) as secretary and maid. The urbane Marshall finds himself romantically inclined, putting the big heist in jeopardy, but Francis's beau Horton thinks he smells a rat. A sumptuously Deco-designed, pre-Code bedroom farce without equal since. **Cast:** Miriam Hopkins, Kay Francis, Herbert Marshall, Charlie Ruggles, Edward Everett Horton, C. Aubrey Smith, Robert Greig, George Humbert, Rolfe Sedan, Luis Alberni. **Credits:** Dir: Ernst Lubitsch; Prod: Ernst Lubitsch; Writer: Laszlo Aladar, Grover Jones, Samson Raphaelson; DP: Victor Milner; Composer: Franke Harling, Leo Robin; Costumes: Travis Banton; Art Director: Hans Dreier. B&W, 83 min.

The Trouble with Angels

(1966) Columbia
Two boisterous young girls (Mills and Harding) wreak havoc on mother superior Russell's convent school, though she sees good souls under the mischief. After Russell discovers Harding's hidden talents and lets Mills see the simple beauty of devotion, the girls completely reform. Lupino's first outing in 13 years, and it's a little creaky, though Russell and the two girls are endearing. Followed by *Where Angels Go, Trouble Follows* in 1968. **Cast:** Hayley Mills, June Harding, Rosalind Russell, Binnie Barnes, Gypsy Rose Lee, Camilla Sparv, Mary

Wickes. **Credits:** Dir: Ida Lupino; Prod: William Frye; Writer: Blanche Hanalis; Story: Jane Trahey; Ed: Robert C. Jones; Composer: Jerry Goldsmith; Art Director: John Beckman. Color, 112 min. **VHS, LASER**

The Trouble with Harry

(1955) Paramount
Hitchcock winks at his predilection for the macabre with this black comedy romp around a troublesome dead body. MacLaine's son (a pre-*Beaver* Mathers) finds a corpse who turns out to be MacLaine's ex. Gripped with guilt and panic, she buries the body, but it keeps moving thanks to other guilty parties such as batty old lady Natwick and sea captain Gwenn. Romance follows for the guilty parties and accessory-after-the-fact Forsythe. Herrmann's first of many brilliant scores for the famed director, and MacLaine's first screen appearance. **Cast:** John Forsythe, Shirley MacLaine, Edmund Gwenn, Mildred Natwick, Mildred Dunnock, Jerry Mathers, Royal Dano. **Credits:** Dir: Alfred Hitchcock; Prod: Alfred Hitchcock; Writer: John Hayes; Story: Jack Trevor; DP: Robert Burks; Ed: Alma Macrorie; Composer: Bernard Herrmann; Art Director: Hal Pereira, John B. Goodman. Color, 100 min. **VHS, LASER**

True Grit

(1969) Paramount
Wayne enters his lion-in-winter phase, subverting his screen image as Western hero to provide a darker, richer portrayal of the real true grit called for on the frontier. Overweight, drunken, and one-eyed, Wayne, as marshal Rooster Cogburn, would seem an unpromising candidate to track a murderous cowboy into Indian Territory. But he's Darby's choice to find the man who killed her father. They're joined by bounty hunter Campbell (in his first screen role) as they follow Corey and Duvall's gang to their hideout. After much gunplay and a quiet confessional scene between Darby and Wayne that Wayne considered his best on film, Wayne proves an old cowboy with true grit can still get the job done. Followed by the somewhat lighter *Rooster Cogburn* in 1975 with Katharine Hepburn. Academy Award Nominations: 2, including Best Song ("True Grit"). **Academy Awards:** Best Actor: John Wayne. **Cast:** John Wayne, Glen Campbell, Kim Darby, Robert Duvall, Jeff Corey, Jeremy Slate, Dennis Hopper, Alfred Ryder, Strother Martin. **Credits:** Dir: Henry Hathaway; Prod: Hal B. Wallis; Writer: Marguerite

Roberts; Story: Charles Portis; DP: Lucien Ballard; Ed: Warren Low; Prod Design: Walter Tyler; Composer: Elmer Bernstein. Color, 128 min. **VHS**

The True Story of Jesse James

(1957) Fox
A remake of the 1939 Tyrone Power-Henry Fonda version of the much-filmed Western myth with director Ray's trademark visual style. Die-hard rebels Wagner and his brother Hunter turn to crime after the Civil War. After pulling a few robberies just to survive, they find their rebellious life outside society exciting until they can't find a way back. Interesting, seldom-seen Western with Ray's deep understanding of the outsider (made two years after his better-known *Rebel Without a Cause*). **Cast:** Robert Wagner, Jeffrey Hunter, Hope Lange, Agnes Moorehead, Alan Hale, John Carradine, Rachel Stephens. **Credits:** Dir: Nicholas Ray; Prod: Herbert Swope; Writer: Walter Newman; Story: Nunnally Johnson; DP: Joseph MacDonald; Ed: Robert Simpson; Prod Design: Lyle Wheeler, Addison Hehr; Composer: Leigh Harline. Color, 92 min.

True to Life

(1943) Paramount
Powell and Tone, bachelor writing partners on a family drama serial for radio, are quickly running out of situations to write about since neither has any experience with families. When they pick waitress Martin's family to observe, they open the door to a hilariously screwball bunch, including her inventor father (Moore) and his layabout brother (Demarest). As they broadcast the family's eccentricities to a growing listening audience, Tone takes a shine to Martin and Powell tries to prevent her family from hearing their monkeyshines on the radio. Sly satire and great fun. **Cast:** Mary Martin, Franchot Tone, Dick Powell, Victor Moore, Mabel Paige, William Demarest, Yvonne De Carlo. **Credits:** Dir: George Marshall; Prod: Paul Jones; Writer: Harry Tugend, Don Hartman; Story: Ben Barzman, Bess Taffel, Sol Barzman; DP: Charles Lang; Composer: Victor Young. B&W, 94 min.

Tugboat Annie

(1933) MGM
A star turn for character actors Dressler and Beery as a tugboat captain and her drunken husband. Their son, Young, has become captain of an ocean liner, and he encourages

Dressler to give up her little boat. She refuses to leave the life she knows and the man she loves, even after he wrecks the tug and they must work together hauling garbage to make ends meet. Beery gets a chance at redemption when Young's liner sends out an SOS. A sentimental favorite that became a huge hit. **Cast:** Marie Dressler, Wallace Beery, Robert Young, Maureen O'Sullivan, Willard Robertson, Tammany Young, Frankie Darro, Jack Pennick, Paul Hurst, Oscar Apfel. **Credits:** Dir: Mervyn LeRoy; Prod: Harry Rapf; Writer: Zelda Sears, Norman Reilly Raine; Story: Eve Greene; DP: Gregg Toland; Ed: Blanche Sewell; Prod Design: Merill Pye. B&W, 87 min.

Tulsa

(1949) Eagle-Lion
A rancher's daughter (Hayward) first fights the oil prospector (Gough) she blames for killing her father, then becomes a wildcatter herself after fortuitously ending up with a fistful of land leases. With the help of geologist Preston and Indian rancher Armendariz, Hayward builds an oil empire, but endangers her relationships by working with her one-time nemesis. Academy Award Nomination for Best Special Effects. **Cast:** Susan Hayward, Robert Preston, Chill Wills, Ed Begley, Lloyd Gough, Pedro Armendariz, Harry Shannon, Jimmy Conlin, Paul E. Burns. **Credits:** Dir: Stuart Heisler; Prod: Walter Wanger; Writer: Frank S. Nugent, Curtis Kenyon; DP: Winton C. Hoch; Ed: Terry Morse; Composer: Frank Skinner; Art Director: Nathan Juran. Color, 90 min. **VHS**

The Tunnel of Love

(1958) MGM
Kelly shows a light touch with comedy as he directs a sophisticated sex comedy with Day and Widmark. They're a happily married couple that has everything . . . except a baby. When they decide to adopt a child, the beautiful adoption agency investigator (Scala) turns her nose up at Widmark. He makes a comeback—a big comeback—after too much wine, and, months later, Scala informs him she has a child for him to adopt. Day threatens divorce, but, in the end, the babies and couples are evenly distributed. **Cast:** Doris Day, Richard Widmark, Gig Young, Gia Scala, Elisabeth Fraser, Elizabeth Wilson, Doodles Weaver, Charles Wagenheim, Robert B. Williams. **Credits:** Dir: Gene Kelly; Prod: Joseph Fields, Martin Melcher; Writer: Joseph Fields, Peter De Vries,

The Turning Point (1979)

Jerome Chodorov; DP: Robert Bronner; Ed: John MacSweeney; Costumes: Helen Rose. B&W, 98 min. **VHS, LASER**

Turn Back the Clock

(1933) MGM
After a fight with his wife (Clarke), a drunken Tracy runs into the street and gets walloped by an automobile. While unconscious, the poor man imagines trading places with his rich friend, marrying a wealthy woman and leaving behind the doldrums of the Depression. A collective fantasy shared by millions, cowritten by Hecht. **Cast:** Lee Tracy, Mae Clarke, Otto Kruger, George Barbier, Peggy Shannon, C. Henry Gordon, Gil Lamb, Clara Blandwick. **Credits:** Dir: Edgar Selwyn; Prod: Harry Rapf; Writer: Edgar Selwyn, Ben Hecht; DP: Harold Rosson; Ed: Frank Sullivan; Prod Design: Edwin B. Willis; Composer: Douglas Shearer. B&W, 77 min.

The Turning Point

(1952) Paramount
This is a tough noir featuring state prosecutor O'Brien enlisting his pal, investigative reporter Holden, in his commission's battle with an organized crime syndicate at the root of their city's political corruption. Holden discovers O'Brien's cop father (Tully) is in Mob boss Begley's back pocket. He's torn between his friendship with O'Brien and exposing the bribery, but Begley orders Tully killed first. As the commission closes in, Begley employs murder and arson, killing dozens when

he burns down a tenement he owns to prevent the investigators from finding papers hidden there. Holden romances O'Brien's girl Smith, but his involvement earns him a bullet in a tense showdown at a boxing match. **Cast:** William Holden, Edmond O'Brien, Alexis Smith, Tom Tully, Ed Begley, Danny Dayton, Ray Teal, Ted De Corsia, Don Porter, Howard Freeman. **Credits:** Dir: William Dieterle, Friedrich Ermler; Prod: Irving Asher; Writer: Warren Duff; Story: Horace McCoy; DP: Lionel Lindon; Ed: George Tomasini; Composer: Irvin Talbot; Art Director: Hal Pereira, Joseph MacMillan Johnson. B&W, 85 min.

The Turning Point

(1979) Fox
This is an involving drama about the choices women make when balancing career and family, and the rewards of each path. The story reunites old friends Bancroft, an internationally renowned ballerina at the end of her career, and MacLaine, who gave up her career in order to raise a family with fellow dancer Skerritt. They reconnect when MacLaine's daughter (Browne), a promising ballerina, pursues her talent to New York where she comes under Bancroft's wing. The daughter's choice brings up old rivalries and regrets in the older women as the younger one tests her blossoming talent. Baryshnikov's film debut. Academy Award Nominations: 11, including Best Picture; Best Director; Best Actress: Anne Bancroft; Best Actress: Shirley MacLaine; Best (Origi-

Twelve O'Clock High (1949)

nal) Screenplay. **Cast:** Shirley Mac-Laine, Anne Bancroft, Leslie Browne, Mikhail Baryshnikov, Tom Skerritt, Martha Scott, Antoinette Sibley, Starr Danias. **Credits:** Dir: Herbert Ross; Prod: Herbert Ross, Arthur Laurents; Writer: Arthur Laurents; DP: Robert Surtees; Ed: William Reynolds; Prod Design: Albert Brenner; Composer: John Lanchbery. Color, 119 min. **VHS**

The Tuttles of Tahiti
(1942) RKO
In a comedic Romeo and Juliet story set on a Pacific paradise, the Tuttles, led by patriarch Laughton, glory in their life on Tahiti, lounging away the days, avoiding work and the industrious family headed by matriarch Bates. Their mutual animosity gets tested when Hall falls for Drake. Negligible, but fun. **Cast:** Charles Laughton, Jon Hall, Peggy Drake, Victor Francen, Gene Reynolds, Florence Bates, Curt Bois, Adeline de Walt Reynolds, Ray Mala. **Credits:** Dir: Charles Vidor; Prod: Sol Lesser; Writer: Lewis Meltzer, James Hilton, Robert Carson; DP: Nicholas Musuraca; Ed: Frederic Knudtson. B&W, 91 min. **VHS, LASER**

Twelve Angry Men
(1957) United Artists
This is perhaps the most famous classic-movie courtroom drama. The jurors get their instructions in a murder case and enter a hot, close jury room to begin deliberating. The first count shows only Fonda holding out for acquittal. After going through the evidence, four vote acquittal. Then the

fireworks begin, fueled by fatigue, heat, and the different personalities and experiences of the jurors. In Lumet's debut, he breaks every rule of cinema action, setting his story in one claustrophobic room and using multiple takes from different angles to provide movement. Originally a teleplay, this was Fonda's only experiment with producing. Remade for cable TV with Jack Lemmon. **Cast:** Henry Fonda, Lee J. Cobb, Ed Begley, E. G. Marshall, Jack Warden, Martin Balsam, Jack Klugman, John Fiedler. **Credits:** Dir: Sidney Lumet; Prod: Henry Fonda, Reginald Rose; Writer: Reginald Rose; DP: Boris Kaufman; Ed: Carl Lerner; Prod Design: Robert Markell; Composer: Kenyon Hopkins. B&W, 95 min. **VHS, LASER**

The Twelve Chairs
(1970)
The most sophisticated Brooks comedy involves a wild goose chase across Russia by Moody for a dining chair, his rich mother confided on her deathbed, that is filled with jewels. The chair was one of a set of 12 that are scattered across the country, some used as props in a theater, some in a high-wire act, and one in a railway waiting room. Moody and DeLuise battle for the loot and then become a team. **Cast:** Mel Brooks, Frank Langella, Ron Moody, Bridget Brice, Dom DeLuise, Robert Bernal, David Lander, Andreas Voutsinas, Vlada Petric, Diana Coupland. **Credits:** Dir: Mel Brooks; Prod: Michael Hertzberg; Writer: Mel Brooks; DP:

Dorde Nikolic; Ed: Alan Heim; Composer: John Morris, Jonathan Tunick. Color, 94 min. **VHS, LASER**

Twelve O'Clock High
(1949) Fox
This compelling WWII drama focuses on the emotional effects the fear and anxiety of war have on fighting men. When a compassionate bomber-squadron leader (Merrill) resists taking his scarred, jumpy men on one more near-suicidal daytime mission, he's replaced by by-the-book general Peck. After exposure to the dangers his men face, Peck becomes more uncertain than his predecessor, even suffering a nervous collapse from the stress. One of the few war films to depict the real human costs of war (based on the true story of Gen. Frank Armstrong), it also includes terrifying aerial sequences that make real the dangers the fliers faced. Academy Award Nominations: 4, including Best Picture, Best Actor: Gregory Peck. **Academy Awards:** Best Supporting Actor: Dean Jagger; Best Sound Recording. **Cast:** Gregory Peck, Hugh Marlowe, Gary Merrill, Millard Mitchell, Dean Jagger, Robert Arthur, Paul Stewart. **Credits:** Dir: Henry King; Prod: Darryl F. Zanuck; Writer: Sy Bartlett, Beirne Lay, Jr.; DP: Leon Shamroy; Ed: Barbara McLean; Prod Design: Lyle Wheeler, Maurice Ransford; Composer: Alfred Newman. B&W, 132 min. **VHS, LASER**

Twentieth Century
(1934) Columbia
Here's another whip-smart comedy from Hawks-Hecht-MacArthur, the *His Girl Friday* (1940) team. Theater producer Barrymore molds Lombard into a Broadway smash, but their hectic life leads her to the saner climes of Hollywood where she becomes an even bigger star. Without his former wife, Barrymore can't get a show together and he's on the run from Chicago to New York aboard the famous Twentieth Century Limited. As luck and romantic farce demand, Lombard's on the same train with her new beau, slow-witted football star Karns. After much hilarious wheedling, wooing, door-slamming, and conniving, Lombard's ready once again for the Great White Way. Barrymore at his best, and a terrific warm-up for even bigger things for the creators. **Cast:** John Barrymore, Carole Lombard, Walter Connolly, Roscoe Karns, Etienne Girardot, Ralph Forbes, Edgar Kennedy, Dale Fuller. **Credits:** Dir: Howard Hawks; Prod: Howard Hawks; Writer: Charles MacArthur, Ben Hecht; DP: Joseph H. August; Ed: Gene Havlick. B&W, 91 min. **VHS**

Twice-Told Tales

(1963) United Artists

Vincent Price stars in a trio of Nathaniel Hawthorne thrillers. "Dr. Heidegger's Experiment" presents the discovery of an eternal youth serum that also raises the dead. Unfortunately for the inventor, it creates a witness to a murder: the victim. The serum in "Rappaccini's Daughter" causes everyone who touches the inventor's daughter to die, inconvenient now that she's in love with the student next door. And, in the famous "The House of the Seven Gables," Price's visit to his ancestral home raises spectral issues that should have been left alone. **Cast:** Vincent Price, Sebastian Cabot, Brett Halsey, Joyce Taylor, Beverly Garland, Mari Blanchard, Abraham Sofaer, Edith Evanson. **Credits:** Dir: Sidney Salkow; Prod: Robert E. Kent; Writer: Robert E. Kent; DP: Ellis W. Carter; Ed: Grant Whytock; Prod Design: Franz Bachelin; Composer: Richard LaSalle. Color, 120 min. **VHS**

Two-Faced Woman

(1941) MGM

In Garbo's last film appearance, she strains to duplicate her success as a comedienne in *Ninotchka* (1939), but this light romance has its winning moments. Garbo meets Douglas when she gives him skiing lessons, and they quickly marry. When she hears about his beautiful, brainy playwright girlfriend (Bennett) back in New York, she tests his affection by posing as her own, vampier, twin sister. Douglas immediately gets the idea and plays along, and Garbo exits in a huff, but her amused husband retrieves her from the slopes. Additional scenes were added to Cukor's film when the Catholic Legion of Decency objected to the original premise that Douglas fell for Garbo's trick and pursued her, believing Garbo was really her sister. **Cast:** Melvyn Douglas, Constance Bennett, Roland Young, Greta Garbo, Robert Sterling, Ruth Gordon, George Cleveland, G. P. Huntley. **Credits:** Dir: George Cukor, Charles Dorian, Andrew Marton; Prod: Gottfried Reinhardt; Writer: S. N. Behrman, Salka Viertel, George Oppenheimer; DP: Joseph Ruttenberg; Ed: George Boemler; Prod Design: Cedric Gibbons; Composer: Bronislau Kaper; Art Director: Daniel B. Cathcart. B&W, 94 min. **VHS**

Two for the Seesaw

(1962) United Artists

Wise directs Mitchum and MacLaine in a sweetly comic romance. Lawyer Mitchum flees a bad marriage in Nebraska and, at the urging of old friend Firestone, starts again in New York. There the straitlaced lawyer meets free-spirited dancer MacLaine and they begin an on-again, off-again romance. Arthur Penn directed Henry Fonda and Anne Bancroft in the Broadway production. Academy Award Nominations: 2 Best Cinematography; Best Song ("Second Chance"). **Cast:** Robert Mitchum, Shirley MacLaine, Edmond Ryan, Elisabeth Fraser, Eddie Firestone, Billy Gray, Vic Lundin, Colin Campbell. **Credits:** Dir: Robert Wise; Prod: Walter Mirisch; Writer: Isobel Lennart; DP: Ted McCord; Ed: Stuart Gilmore. Color, 109 min. **VHS, LASER**

Two Girls and a Sailor

(1944) MGM

A singing-dancing sister act (Allyson and DeHaven) who entertain the soldiers in their cramped apartment open a USO showplace in an old warehouse bought for them by sailor Johnson. The whole gang puts on a show, and that's the point here. There are terrific numbers and rare chances to see great performers doing signature routines, such as Durante and his "Inka Dinka Doo," Xavier Cugat swinging "The Thrill of a New Romance," Harry James backing "The Young Man with a Horn," and even Allen doing "Concerto for Index Finger." Academy Award Nomination for Best Original Screenplay. **Cast:** Van Johnson, June Allyson, Gloria DeHaven, Lena Horne, Donald Meek, Jimmy Durante, Gracie Allen, Tom Drake. **Credits:** Dir: Richard Thorpe; Prod: Joe Pasternak; Writer: Richard Connell, Gladys Lehman; DP: Robert Surtees; Ed: George Boemler; Prod Design: Cedric Gibbons. Color, 125 min. **VHS, LASER**

Two-Lane Blacktop

(1971) Universal

Director Hellman has one of America's most individual film voices, bringing a brooding, existential wonder to low-budget genre pictures such as his Westerns, *The Shooting* and *Ride the Whirlwind* (both 1967), and this refreshing take on the commonplace road movie. Rock stars Taylor and Wilson wander from race to race in a souped-up '55 Chevy, taking their winnings and moving on, picking up hitchhikers (Bird and Stanton), and getting involved in a cross-country race with Oates. The race fails to hold their attention, and their shared lover Bird takes off with Oates, so they hit the pedal and roar off to the horizon. **Cast:** James Taylor, Dennis Wilson, Warren Oates, Rudy Wurlitzer, Harry Dean Stanton, Laurie Bird, David Drake, Richard Ruth. **Credits:** Dir: Monte Hellman; Prod: Michael Laughlin; Writer: Rudy Wurlitzer, Will Corry; DP: Jack Deerson; Ed: Monte Hellman; Composer: Billy James. Color, 101 min.

The Two Mrs. Carrolls

(1947) Warner Bros.

In this less well known Bogart thriller, he portrays a twisted painter who dispatches with his wives after finding a new lover and painting the current Mrs. Carroll as the Angel of Death. When Bogart takes up with Smith, Stanwyck discovers his plot when her stepdaughter resists going away to school; she returned to find her mother dead the last time she was sent away. Stanwyck turns to old flame O'Moore for help just in the nick of time. **Cast:** Humphrey Bogart, Barbara Stanwyck, Alexis Smith, Nigel Bruce, Isobel Elsom, Patrick O'Moore, Ann Carter, Anita Bolster, Barry Bernard. **Credits:** Dir: Peter Godfrey; Prod: Mark Hellinger; Writer: Thomas Job; DP: Peverell Marley, Robert Burks; Ed: Frederick Richards; Prod Design: Anton Grot; Composer: Franz Waxman. B&W, 99 min. **VHS**

Two Mules for Sister Sara

(1969) Universal

In this Siegel-Eastwood Western, Eastwood delivers a prostitute posing as a nun (MacLaine) to the Mexican revolutionaries she's helping. They take up arms with the Mexicans and lead an invasion of the French garrison. An okay action flick that depends on the chemistry between Eastwood and MacLaine. **Cast:** Shirley MacLaine, Clint Eastwood, Manolo Fabregas, Alberto Morin, John Kelly, Enrique Lucero, Ada Carrasco, Pancho Cordova. **Credits:** Dir: Don Siegel; Prod: Martin Rackin, Carol Case; Writer: Albert Maltz; DP: Gabriel Figueroa; Ed: Robert F. Shugrue, Juan Jose Marino; Composer: Ennio Morricone; Art Director: Jose Rodriguez Granada. Color, 105 min. **VHS**

Two Rode Together

(1961) Columbia

In a lesser, later Ford Western, Stewart is a corrupt small-town sheriff who goes on a bounty hunt with army officer Widmark to return white settlers from their Indian captors.

When Kent, who has thoroughly assumed an Indian identity, is turned loose back at the fort, he kills the woman who claims him and is hung before Jones recognizes him as her brother. Cristal, who had become chief Strode's squaw, is shunned by the white women and bitterly longs for her life with the Indians. When Stewart learns he has lost his position, the two outcasts ride away together. **Cast:** James Stewart, Richard Widmark, Shirley Jones, Andy Devine, Linda Cristal, John McIntire, Paul Birch, Willis Bouchey, David Kent, Woody Strode. **Credits:** Dir: John Ford; Prod: Stan Shpetner; Writer: Frank S. Nugent; DP: Charles Lawton, Jr.; Ed: Jack Murray; Composer: George Duning; Art Director: Robert Peterson. Color, 109 min. VHS, LASER

Two Seconds
(1932) Warner Bros.
Two seconds is the time it takes for the juice to flow after the switch is flipped on the electric chair, and in that interval we see the circumstances that brought Robinson to his reckoning. Robinson, a high-steel worker, kills his best friend (Foster) after he reveals Robinson's wife's (Osborne) faithlessness, but Robinson fries for killing his tarty wife. **Cast:** Edward G. Robinson, Preston Foster, Vivienne Osborne, J. Carrol Naish, Guy Kibbee, Fredrick Burton, Adrienne Dare, Dorothea Wolbert, Edward McWade, Berton Churchill. **Credits:** Dir: Mervyn LeRoy; Prod: Hal B. Wallis; Writer: Harvey F. Thew; Story: Elliot Lester; DP: Sol Polito; Ed: Terrill Morse; Composer: Leo F. Forbstein; Art Director: Anton Grot. B&W, 68 min.

Two Weeks in Another Town
(1962) MGM
A reteaming of the writer, director, producer, and star of *The Bad and the Beautiful* (1952) in another tale of Hollywood's dark side. Douglas gets out of a sanitarium to a washed-up career, and latches on to a minor role in past-collaborator Robinson's cheapie being filmed in Rome (they even reminisce about their glory days by watching scenes from *The Bad and the Beautiful*). After soapy goings-on with Douglas's ex-wife Charisse, Robinson's wife Trevor, and misbehaving star Hamilton, Douglas takes the reins of the production and finds a new career. Based on an Irwin Shaw novel. **Cast:** Kirk Douglas, Cyd Charisse, Edward G. Robinson, George Hamilton, Claire Trevor, Daliah Lavi, Constance Ford, Rosanna Schiaffino. **Credits:** Dir: Vincente Minnelli; Prod: John Houseman; Writer: Charles Schnee; DP: Milton Krasner; Ed: Adrienne Fazan, Robert J. Kern; Prod Design: Urie McCleary; Composer: David Raksin; Art Director: George W. Davis. Color, 107 min. LASER

Two Years Before the Mast
(1946) Paramount
Ladd, a wealthy shipowner's son, gets snagged out of a Boston waterfront dive and shipped out on a freighter heading for California. Skipper Da Silva is renowned for his cruelty (backed up by plug-ugly Bendix) and the ship's conditions are shocking. When Da Silva refuses to supply fruit and water when they reach California, even Bendix objects. The captain's brutal slaying of his enforcer causes a mutiny, which leads to a courtroom appeal for better conditions for sailors. Harrowing maritime adventure, with Ladd giving a fine performance as the callow young man who grows up under the captain's oppression. **Cast:** Alan Ladd, Brian Donlevy, William Bendix, Barry Fitzgerald, Howard Da Silva, Albert Dekker, Darryl Hickman. **Credits:** Dir: John Farrow; Prod: Seton Miller; Writer: Seton Miller, George Bruce; DP: Ernest Laszlo; Ed: Eda Miller; Prod Design: Hans Dreier, Franz Bachelin; Composer: Victor Young. B&W, 98 min. VHS

Typhoon
(1940) Paramount
Lamour struts her sarong in eye-popping Technicolor, and Preston gets every man's dream come true when he's rescued by Lamour from an attack by natives as he leads a pearl-diving expedition. She drags him back to her treetop lair on a deserted island, and there they await the gathering storm. All in all, a fair trade-off for enduring a little rain. Academy Award Nomination for Best Visual Effects. **Cast:** Dorothy Lamour, Robert Preston, Lynne Overman, J. Carrol Naish, Chief Thundercloud, Frank Reicher, John Rogers, Paul Harvey, Norma Nelson, Jack Carson. **Credits:** Dir: Louis King; Prod: Anthony Veiller; Writer: Steve Fisher, Allen Rivkin; DP: William Mellor; Ed: Alma Macrorie; Prod Design: Hans Dreier, John B. Goodman; Composer: Frederick Hollander; SFX: Farciot Eduoart, Gordon Jennings, Loren Ryder. Color, 70 min.

The Ugly American
(1963) Universal
Brando turns in a fascinating performance in a thinly-veiled critique of American foreign policy in Southeast Asia. A powerful newspaper publisher back in the States, Brando is the new ambassador to an Asian nation wracked by civil war and communist insurgency. He learns that an old comrade (Okada) is leading the guerrillas and comes to question America's policy in the region. Okada is best remembered for his leading role in Alain Resnais's *Hiroshima, Mon Amour* (1959). **Cast:** Marlon Brando, Sandra Church, Eiji Okada, Pat Hingle, Arthur Hill, Jocelyn Brando, Judson Pratt, Judson Laire, Philip Ober. **Credits:** Dir: George Englund; Prod: George Englund; Writer: Stewart Stern; Story: William J. Lederer, Eugene Burdick; DP: Clifford Stine; Ed: Ted J. Kent; Composer: Frank Skinner; Art Director: Alexander Golitzen, Alfred Sweeney. Color, 120 min. **VHS**

Ulzana's Raid
(1972) Universal
Slam-bang director Aldrich's work has been reappreciated in recent years for its rawhide tough, grimly realistic action and fast pace. This is a fine example, with Lancaster (an Aldrich favorite) playing a scout working for young cavalry leader Davison as they pursue a band of Apaches led by Martinez. Each has a different view of their opponent and their mission, leading to tension as they prepare to face their quarry. **Cast:** Burt Lancaster, Bruce Davison, Richard Jaeckel, Jorge Luke, Joaquin Martinez, Lloyd Bochner, Karl Swenson, Douglas Watson. **Credits:** Dir: Robert Aldrich; Prod: Carter DeHaven; Writer: Alan Sharp; DP: Joseph Biroc; Ed: Michael Luciano; Composer: Frank DeVol; Art Director: James Vance. Color, 103 min. **VHS, LASER**

Uncertain Glory
(1944) Warner Bros.
Here is a Walsh "quickie" (according to the director), but it's an interesting situation for what amounts to a detective story. Flynn is a murderer in occupied Paris about to be guillotined when Allied bombs come to his rescue. He escapes to Spain with detective Lukas on his trail. When Nazis round up innocent hostages to flush out a pair of saboteurs, Flynn volunteers to make a surprising sacrifice. **Cast:** Errol Flynn, Paul Lukas, Jean Sullivan, Lucile Watson, Faye Emerson, James Flavin, Douglas Dumbrille, Dennis Hoey. **Credits:** Dir: Raoul Walsh; Prod: Robert Buckner; Writer: Laszlo Vadnay, Max Brand; DP: Sid Hickox; Ed: George Amy; Prod Design: Robert M. Haas; Composer: Adolph Deutsch. B&W, 102 min. **VHS**

Unconquered
(1947) Paramount
DeMille's typically grandiose version of early colonial days was an extremely expensive ($5 million) bust, but with Cooper and Goddard in the leads it makes an enjoyable watch. Militia officer Cooper vies with evil da Silva for indentured servant Goddard's contract as da Silva stirs up a war with the Seneca Indians (his in-laws). Worth seeing just to witness Karloff speaking Seneca. Academy Award Nomination: Best Visual Effects. **Cast:** Gary Cooper, Paulette Goddard, Howard da Silva, Boris Karloff, Cecil Kellaway, Ward Bond, Katherine DeMille, Henry Wilcoxon. **Credits:** Dir: Cecil B. DeMille; Prod: Cecil B. DeMille; Writer: Charles Bennett, Fredric M. Frank, Jesse Lasky, Jr.; DP: Ray Rennahan; Ed: Anne Bauchens; Prod Design: Hans Dreier; Composer: Victor Young; Art Director: Walter Tyler. Color, 147 min. **VHS**

The Undefeated
(1969) Fox
A late Wayne role, but not up to the standard of *True Grit* (1969) or the lion-in-winter eloquence of *The Shootist* (1976). Former Union officer Wayne and his adopted son ride with a herd of cattle toward Mexico where they link up with former Confederate officer Hudson and his band of proud rebels against Mexican bandits and the French army. **Cast:** John Wayne, Rock Hudson, Antonio Aguilar, Lee Meriwether, Tony Aguilar, Ben Johnson, Bruce Cabot. **Credits:** Dir: Andrew V. McLaglen; Prod: Robert L. Jacks; Writer: James Lee Barrett; Story: Stanley L. Hough; DP: William Clothier; Ed: Robert Simpson; Composer: Hugo Montenegro; Art Director: Carl Anderson. Color, 119 min. **VHS, LASER**

Under Capricorn
(1949) Warner Bros.
This is a rare costume melodrama from Hitchcock. Cotten has been transported to Australia for killing wife Bergman's brother. She follows him, and he becomes a wealthy landowner but socially isolated because of his violent history. Bergman begins to drink and Leighton takes the opportunity to inveigle her way into Cotten's household. When Bergman's cousin Wilding arrives from Ireland and discovers her degraded condition, he does his best to cheer her—and falls in love with her. Leighton seizes the chance to solidify her position, which leads to a deadly showdown and shocking revelations. A less-successful curiosity in Hitchcock's career. **Cast:** Ingrid Bergman, Joseph Cotten, Michael Wilding, Cecil Parker, Margaret Leighton, Denis O'Dea, Jack Watling, Harcourt Williams. **Credits:** Dir: Alfred Hitchcock; Prod: Lord Sidney Lewis Bernstein, Alfred Hitchcock; Writer: James Bridie, Hume Cronyn; DP: Jack Cardiff, Paul Beeson, Ian Craig, David McNeilly, Jack Haste; Ed: Bert Bates; Prod Design: Tom Morahan; Composer: Richard Addinsell. Color, 117 min. **VHS, LASER**

The Undercover Man

(1949) Columbia
Derived from the Treasury Department's pursuit of Al Capone, this follows T-men Ford and Whitmore in their quest for the facts and figures of a mobster's tax evasion. The underworld gang permanently silences witnesses, and even Ford's wife is placed in danger, but the angry daughter of a Mob victim rouses Ford to action. **Cast:** Glenn Ford, James Whitmore, Nina Foch, Barry Kelley, David Wolfe, Frank Tweddell, Howard St. John, J. Frank Hamilton, Leo Penn, Joan Lazer. **Credits:** Dir: Joseph H. Lewis; Prod: Robert Rossen; Writer: Frank Wilson, Sidney Boehm, Marvin Wald, Jerry Rubin; DP: Burnett Guffey; Ed: Al Clark; Composer: Morris Stoloff; Costumes: Jean Louis; Art Director: Walter Holscher. B&W, 85 min.

Under Two Flags

(1936) Fox
Ouida's novel was already wheezy by the time of this first talking version, but Colman gives a dashing performance as a British gentleman who vanishes (with his valet) into the French Foreign Legion after taking the rap for a murder he didn't commit. At the desert outpost, he attracts the attention of Colbert, who throws herself at the handsome soldier. Colman also attracts the unwelcome attention of McLaglen, his commander and Colbert's former flame. Though Colman jilts her for an English lady (Russell), Colbert comes to his rescue in the desert. Theda Bara played the Colbert role in a silent-screen version. **Cast:** Ronald Colman, Claudette Colbert, Victor McLaglen, Rosalind Russell, Gregory Ratoff, Nigel Bruce, C. Henry Gordon, Herbert Mundin, John Carradine, Lumsden Hare. **Credits:** Dir: Otto Brower, Frank Lloyd; Prod: Raymond Griffith, Darryl F. Zanuck; Writer: Walter Ferris, W. P. Lipscomb; Story: Ouida; DP: Ernest Palmer; Ed: Raph Dietrich; Prod Design: William S. Darling; Composer: Louis Silvers. B&W, 96 min.

Under Western Stars

(1938) Republic
Singing cowboy Roy stars in his first big role as a congressman from the drought-stricken dustbowl who goes to battle in Washington (with Dale and sidekick Smiley at his side) for the folks back home. This is the first of director Kane's 41 pictures with Rogers. Academy Award Nomination for Best Song ("Dust"). **Cast:** Roy Rogers, Dale Evans, Trigger, Smiley Burnette, Carol Hughes, Guy Usher, Kenneth Harlan, Stephen Chase. **Credits:** Dir: Joseph Kane; Prod: Sol C. Siegel; Writer: Dorrell McGowan, Stuart McGowan, Betty Burbridge; DP: Jack Marta; Ed: Lester Orlebeck. B&W, 54 min. VHS

Underworld, U.S.A.

(1960) Columbia
This is another of Fuller's dark, brutal tales of a man taking on all sides alone. Robertson vows to avenge the brutal murder of his father, and enters the violent criminal world where, while in prison, he discovers the identity of the killers and then sets out to destroy them. In the meantime, the murderers have become Mob bosses, which means they interest government investigator Emhardt, who uses Robertson's vendetta to further his own agenda of toppling the Mob. **Cast:** Cliff Robertson, Dolores Dorn, Beatrice Kay, Robert Emhardt, Larry Gates, Richard Rust, Gerald Milton, Tina Rome. **Credits:** Dir: Samuel Fuller; Prod: Samuel Fuller; Writer: Samuel Fuller; DP: Hal Mohr; Ed: Jerome Thoms; Composer: Harry Sukman; Art Director: Robert Peterson. B&W, 99 min. VHS

Unfaithfully Yours

(1948) Fox
A stylish, cerebral concoction from Sturges, this film builds fantasy and laughter from the themes of the classical music heard on the sound track. Harrison plays an orchestra conductor happily married to Darnell until his brother-in-law (Vallee) hires a private detective to follow her. Though he goes to great lengths to avoid looking at the report, Harrison sees three different visions of infidelity and murder as he conducts three pieces on a symphonic program. His attempt to carry out one of the revenge fantasies leads to a cheerful reconciliation. The unsuccessful release may be partially attributed to the scandal surrounding the suicide of Harrison's lover, troubled actress Carole Landis. Remade in 1984 with Dudley Moore. **Cast:** Rex Harrison, Linda Darnell, Kurt Kreuger, Barbara Lawrence, Rudy Vallee, Lionel Stander, Edgar Kennedy, Alan Bridge. **Credits:** Dir: Preston Sturges; Prod: Preston Sturges; Writer: Preston Sturges; DP: Victor Milner; Ed: Robert Fritch; Prod Design: Lyle Wheeler, Joseph C. Wright; Composer: Gioacchino Rossini, Richard Wagner, Pyotr Ilich Tchaikovsky. B&W, 105 min. VHS, LASER

The Unforgiven

(1960) MGM
This spectacularly ill-starred Huston production has a great story (from the author who wrote the novel that was the basis for *The Searchers*) and a great cast, including Lancaster, Hepburn, and Gish. A Western set in 1850s Texas finds Gish's family struggling with raising cattle and battling Indians. When suspicions surface that adopted daughter Hepburn may be of Indian birth, Gish kills the messenger but can't prevent the Kiowas from trying to reclaim their kin. One son, Murphy, refuses to defend her, the other, Lancaster, falls in love with her. During the course of shooting, Hepburn broke her back and had a miscarriage, Murphy nearly drowned, and three crew members died in a plane crash. Lackluster box office torpedoed Lancaster's production company, too. **Cast:** Burt Lancaster, Audrey Hepburn, Lillian Gish, Audie Murphy, John Saxon, Charles Bickford, Albert Salmi, Joseph Wiseman. **Credits:** Dir: John Huston; Prod: James Hill; Writer: Ben Maddow, Alan LeMay; DP: Franz Planer; Ed: Russell Lloyd; Composer: Dimitri Tiomkin; Art Director: Stephen Grimes. Color, 125 min. VHS, LASER

Unholy Partners

(1941) MGM
In this solid, hard-hitting LeRoy newspaper saga, war correspondent Robinson returns home to his newspaper job but needs more action after being on the front lines. He starts a tabloid with gangster Arnold, a partnership that ends with guns blazing. **Cast:** Edgar G. Robinson, Lorraine Day, Edward Arnold, Marsha Hunt, William Orr, Don Beddoe, Charles Dingle, Charles Crane, Walter Kingsford, Charles Halton. **Credits:** Dir: Mervyn LeRoy; Prod: Samuel Marx; Writer: Earl Baldwin, Bartlett Cormack, Lesser Samuels; DP: George Barnes; Ed: Harold F. Kress; Prod Design: Cedric Gibbons; Composer: David Snell. B&W, 94 min.

The Uninvited

(1944) Paramount
An engaging ghost story with a suspenseful story. Soon after moving into a creepy house on Cornwall's cliffs, a house purchased at a suspiciously low price, music critic Milland and his sister Hussey experience unusual occurrences. Flowers wilt, the smell of mimosas wafts through the rooms, and Russell seems drawn to the house despite her grandfather Crisp's warnings. The mystery of Russell's

mother's death unravels when not one but two spirits reappear. Academy Award Nomination for Best (Black-and-White) Cinematography. **Cast:** Ray Milland, Ruth Hussey, Cornelia Otis Skinner, Gail Russell, Donald Crisp, Dorothy Stickney, Alan Napier, George Kirby. **Credits:** Dir: Lewis Allen; Prod: Charles Brackett; Writer: Dodie Smith, Frank Partos; DP: Charles Lang; Ed: Doane Harrison; Composer: Victor Young; Art Director: Hans Dreier, Ernst Fegte. B&W, 99 min. VHS, LASER

Union Depot
(1932) Warner Bros.
Released only three months prior to *Grand Hotel*, this snappy film uses a similarly episodic structure, but the action here is packed into a railroad station where hobo Fairbanks and his buddy (Kibbee) find a wallet in the washroom and a claim ticket for a violin. When the instrument case turns out to be filled with cash, they're unwittingly mixed up with counterfeiters on the lam from federal agents, but help out struggling chorine Blondell with a loan. **Cast:** Douglas Fairbanks, Jr., Joan Blondell, Guy Kibbee, Alan Hale, George Rosener, Dickie Moore, Ruth Hall, Mae Madison, Polly Walters, David Landau. **Credits:** Dir: Alfred E. Green; Writer: Gene Fowler, Douglas Durkin, Joe Laurie; Story: Kenyon Nicholson, Walter DeLeon, John Bright, Kubec Glasmon; DP: Sol Polito; Ed: Jack Killifer; Composer: Leo F. Forbstein; Art Director: Jack Okey. B&W, 75 min.

Union Pacific
(1939) Paramount
American history according to DeMille; here he adds rich detail to the story of the first transcontinental railroad. McCrea plays the construction foreman who wards off rival Preston's attempts to slow progress through theft and vice. Preston's also his rival for Union Pacific postmistress Stanwyck who, in one Indian attack, proves she can sling lead as well as the boys. Based on the book by Ernest Haycox. Academy Award Nomination: Best Visual Effects. **Cast:** Barbara Stanwyck, Joel McCrea, Akim Tamiroff, Robert Preston, Lynne Overman, Brian Donlevy, Robert Barrat, Anthony Quinn. **Credits:** Dir: Cecil B. DeMille; Prod: Cecil B. DeMille; Writer: Walter DeLeon, C. Gardner Sullivan, Jesse Lasky, Jr., Jack Cunningham; DP: Victor Milner, Dewey Wrigley; Ed: Anne Bauchens; Prod Design: Hans Dreier; Composer:

An Unmarried Woman (1978)

George Antheil, Sigmund Krumgold, John Leipold; Art Director: Roland Anderson. B&W, 136 min. VHS

An Unmarried Woman
(1978) Fox
This is the best of Mazursky's efforts to plot the emotional and sexual landscape of the '70s as men and women sorted out new definitions for their relationships. Clayburgh gets blindsided by the news that her husband of 15 years (Murphy) is leaving her for a woman he met at Bloomingdale's. She puts her new life as an independent woman back together again with the help of friends, therapy, sexual experiments (with Gorman in a painful, funny scene), and, finally, love on her terms with soulful artist Bates. Academy Award Nominations: Best Picture; Best Actress: Jill Clayburgh; Best Original Screenplay. **Cast:** Jill Clayburgh, Alan Bates, Michael Murphy, Cliff Gorman, Pat Quinn, Kelly Bishop. **Credits:** Dir: Paul Mazursky; Prod: Paul Mazursky, Tony Ray; Writer: Paul Mazursky; DP: Arthur Ornitz; Ed: Stuart Pappe; Composer: Bill Conti; Prod Design: Pato Guzman. Color, 124 min. VHS

The Unsinkable Molly Brown
(1964) MGM
The trademark vivacious performance by Reynolds in this charming musical adaptation of a Broadway hit is based on a true story. Reynolds plays the title role of a country girl born under a lucky star as she marries Presnell, who soon becomes wealthy, and then conquers Denver society by bringing royalty back for a visit after her first grand tour of the continent. She earns her nickname with her heroic efforts during the sinking of the *Titanic*. Songs include "Belly Up to the Bar, Boys," "Colorado Is My Home," "I Ain't Down Yet," and "Up Where the People Are." Academy Award Nominations: 6, including Best Actress: Debbie Reynolds; Best Cinematography; Best (Adapted) Score. **Cast:** Debbie Reynolds, Ed Begley, Harve Presnell, Jack Kruschen, Hermione Baddeley, Vassili Lambrinos, Harvey Lembeck, George Mitchell. **Credits:** Dir: Charles Walters; Prod: Lawrence Weingarten; Writer: Helen Deutsch; Story: Meredith Willson, Richard Morris; DP: Daniel Fapp; Ed: Fredric Steinkamp; Composer: Meredith Willson; Art Director: George Davis, Preston Ames. Color, 128 min. VHS, LASER

Untamed
(1955) Fox
Hayward and Power clash and clinch in an adventurous romance. Hayward plays a high-spirited Irish country lass who meets Power, a dashing Boer who's in Ireland to buy horses. Years later, she immigrates to South Africa with her husband. When he is killed in a Zulu raid, Power rides to the rescue, though he must battle Egan for Hay-

ward's attention. The romance endures absences, economic hardships, and battles with natives and the elements. **Cast:** Tyrone Power, Susan Hayward, Richard Egan, John Justin, Agnes Moorehead, Rita Moreno, Hope Emerson, Brad Dexter, Henry O'Neill. **Credits:** Dir: Henry King; Prod: William A. Bacher, Bert Friedlob; Writer: William A. Bacher, Michael Blankfort, Frank Fenton, Talbot Jennings, Helga Moray; DP: Leo Tover; Ed: Barbara McLean; Prod Design: Addison Hehr; Composer: Franz Waxman. Color, 111 min.

Until They Sail
(1957) MGM
An early role for Newman and one that made him a favorite of the female half of the audience. During WWII, a troop of American soldiers descends on the New Zealand city of Christchurch turning the emotional lives of the citizens upside down. The story follows four sisters and their fraternization with the soldiers. Fontaine falls deeply and tragically in love, Dee waits for her hometown boyfriend, Laurie takes on most of the troop after a hasty marriage, and widowed Simmons falls reluctantly for officer Newman. Based on a James Michener story. **Cast:** Jean Simmons, Joan Fontaine, Piper Laurie, Sandra Dee, Paul Newman, Charles Drake, Dean Jones, Patrick MacNee. **Credits:** Dir: Robert Wise; Prod: Charles Schnee; Writer: Robert Anderson; DP: Joseph Ruttenberg; Ed: Harold F. Kress; Prod Design: William A. Horning, Paul Groesse; Composer: David Raksin. Color, 95 min. VHS

Up in Arms
(1944) RKO
Nightclub performer Kaye became a star with this, his first feature film. Based on the Eddie Cantor vehicle *Whoopee!* (1930), the story follows hypochondriac elevator operator Kaye as he's drafted into the Army during WWII. When Kaye tells girlfriend Dowling that he and pal Andrews are shipping out, she and pal Shore, who really loves Kaye, tag along all the way to an Army base in the Pacific. Kaye lets loose with his multiple skills of mimicry, double-talk, and light song and dance—especially in a Max

Sennett–esque finale with invading Japanese soldiers. Songs by both Harold Arlen and Kaye's future wife, Sylvia Fine. Academy Award Nominations: Best Song ("Now I Know"); Best Score. **Cast:** Danny Kaye, Dinah Shore, Constance Dowling, Dana Andrews, Virginia Mayo, Louis Calhern, George Mathews, Benny Baker. **Credits:** Dir: Elliott Nugent; Prod: Don Hartman; Writer: Don Hartman, Allan Boretz, Robert Pirosh; DP: Ray Rennahan; Ed: Daniel Mandell; Prod Design: McClure Capps; Composer: Ray Heindorf; Art Director: Perry Ferguson, Stewart Chaney. Color, 105 min. VHS, LASER

Upperworld
(1934) Warner Bros.
Hecht penned the story of a lonely millionaire businessman (William) who strays from his socially ambitious wife (Astor) only to find himself mixed up in a double murder. William gets involved with a showgirl (Rogers), whose employer (Naish), despite her objections, tries to blackmail him. A fight ensues, and two corpses later the millionaire finds himself being pursued by cop Toler. **Cast:** Warren William, Mary Astor, Ginger Rogers, Andy Devine, Dickie Moore, Henry O'Neill, Sidney Toler, J. Carrol Naish, Theodore Newton, Ferdinand Gottschalk, Robert Barrat. **Credits:** Dir: Roy Del Ruth; Writer: Ben Markson; Story: Ben Hecht; DP: Tony Gaudio; Ed: Owen Marks; Prod Design: Robert Lord; Art Director: Anton Grot. B&W, 72 min.

Up the River
(1930) Fox
Tracy's first screen appearance (and Bogart's second) in a prison comedy by Ford. Ex-con Tracy gets himself and former cell-mate Hymer thrown back into a pen, only this time it's a comfy medium-security prison with lots of athletics, amateur theatricals, and romance with the women just over the wall. They're joined by cell-mate Bogart, who gets mixed up in a romance with Luce and a blackmail plot by Wallace. **Cast:** Spencer Tracy, Humphrey Bogart, William Collier, Warren Hymer, Joan Marie Lawes, Claire Luce, Sharon Lynn, George MacFarlane, Robert Emmett O'Connor, Gaylord

Pendleton. **Credits:** Dir: John Ford; Prod: William Fox; Writer: William Collier, Sr., John Ford; Story: Maurine Watkins; DP: Joseph H. August; Ed: Frank E. Hull; Prod Design: Duncan Cramer; Composer: Joseph McCarthy, James F. Hanley. B&W, 92 min.

Up the Sandbox
(1972) National General
This is an interesting experiment from the height of the women's liberation movement, and an early indication that Streisand would use her celebrity to further social and political issues. Streisand portrays the wife of a college professor and mother of two whose third pregnancy sends her into various reveries of revenge, adventure, and romance. Her daydreams blend with the day-to-day realities of being a wife and mother and what that means in a world that offers women more opportunities. **Cast:** Barbra Streisand, David Selby, Jane Hoffman, John C. Becher, Ariane Heller, Gary Smith, Terry Smith, Jacobo Morales. **Credits:** Dir: Irvin Kershner; Prod: Robert Chartoff, Irwin Winkler; Writer: Paul Zindel; Story: Anne Roiphe; DP: Gordon Willis; Ed: Robert Lawrence; Prod Design: Harry Horner; Composer: Billy Goldenberg. Color, 98 min. VHS, LASER

Uptown Saturday Night
(1974) Warner Bros.
This is the first of the "Uptown" movies directed by and starring Poitier (the others are *Let's Do It Again*, 1975, and *A Piece of the Action*, 1977), which feature the biggest black stars of the day. When factory worker Poitier and taxi driver Cosby relax at an illegal gambling joint, gangsters rob the players. When Poitier loses his wallet in the robbery, he also loses a lottery ticket worth $50,000. The pals pursue the wallet into the underworld, meeting up with Mob boss Belafonte. **Cast:** Bill Cosby, Sidney Poitier, Flip Wilson, Harry Belafonte, Richard Pryor, Rosalind Cash, Roscoe Lee Browne, Paul Kelly. **Credits:** Dir: Sidney Poitier; Prod: Melville Tucker; Writer: Richard Wesley; DP: Fred Koenekamp; Ed: Pembroke Herring; Prod Design: Alfred Sweeney; Composer: Tom Scott. Color, 104 min. VHS

Valdez Is Coming
(1971) United Artists
This odd oater features an interesting performance by Lancaster as a Mexican-American lawman who intercedes in a lynching and finds himself the target of the rich man who wanted the black victim dead. Sherin's first shot as a film director, coming after a long, successful stint on Broadway. Based on a novel by Elmore Leonard. **Cast:** Burt Lancaster, Susan Clark, Frank Silvera, Richard Jordan, Jon Cypher, Barton Heyman, Hector Elizondo, Phil Brown. **Credits:** Dir: Edwin Sherin; Prod: Ira Steiner; Writer: Roland Kibbee, David Rayfiel; DP: Gabor Pogany; Ed: James Heckert; Composer: Charles Gross; Art Director: Jose Marie Tapiador, Jose Maria Alarcon. Color, 90 min. **VHS**

The Valley of Decision
(1945) MGM
Period soaper set in 1870s Pittsburgh has poor Irish girl Garson becoming part of steel-mill owner Crisp's family when she takes a job as their maid. She steals the hearts of the entire family, particularly Peck, but because of the differences in their social status they can never be together. A strike supported by Garson's father (Barrymore) drives another wedge between them. Based on Davenport's 1942 novel. Academy Award Nominations: 2, Best Actress: Greer Garson; Best Score. **Cast:** Gregory Peck, Greer Garson, Donald Crisp, Lionel Barrymore, Preston Foster, Marsha Hunt, Gladys Cooper, Reginald Owen, Dan Duryea, Jessica Tandy. **Credits:** Dir: Tay Garnett; Prod: Edwin H. Knopf; Writer: John Meehan, Sonya Levien; Story: Marcia Davenport; DP: Joseph Ruttenberg; Ed: Blanche Sewell; Prod Design: Cedric Gibbons; Composer: Herbert Stothart; Art Director: Paul Groesse. B&W, 111 min. **VHS**

Valley of the Dolls
(1967) Fox
This is the high-water mark of modish Hollywood camp, adapted from the deliciously pulpy novel by Jacqueline Susann. Three ambitious young women from different walks of life (Parkins, Tate, and Duke) each suffer in the show business meat grinder. The scene in which a hysterical Duke cries to her pills, "My dolls! My beautiful dolls!" and Hayward's entire performance as an aging chanteuse have launched a thousand drag shows. Academy Award Nomination for Best Score. **Cast:** Sharon Tate, Patty Duke, Barbara Parkins, Susan Hayward, Richard Dreyfuss, Martin Milner, Charles Drake, Alexander Davion, Lee Grant, Naomi Stevens. **Credits:** Dir: Walter Grauman; Prod: David Weisbart; Writer: Helen Deutsch, Dorothy Kingsley; DP: William Daniels; Ed: Dorothy Spencer; Composer: John Williams; Art Director: Jack Martin Smith, Richard Day. Color, 124 min. **VHS, LASER**

The Vampire Bat
(1933) Majestic
Here is an intriguing sideshow to the horror boom of the early '30s from an ambitious Poverty Row studio. Townspeople in a village plagued by murders get suspicious when mad scientist Atwill sends his helper Frye (in a reprise of his *Dracula* role) to gather liquid nourishment for his latest experiment. Wray stars as one of the victims of his blood lust. The story takes place on familiar creepy territory, with the village from *Frankenstein*, the house from *The Old Dark House*, and the sets from *The Cat and the Canary* being borrowed from Universal for the production. **Cast:** Lionel Atwill, Fay Wray, Melvyn Douglas, Dwight Frye, Robert Frazer, Lionel Belmore, William V. Mong, Fern

Valley of the Dolls (1967)

Emmett. **Credits:** Dir: Frank Strayer; Prod: Phil Goldstone; Writer: Edward T. Lowe; DP: Ira Morgan; Ed: Otis Garrett; Prod Design: Charles D. Hall, Daniel Hall. B&W, 71 min. VHS

Vanishing Point
(1971) Fox
A road movie loaded with all the existential angst of its day. Professional driver Newman bets he can run a pumped-up Dodge Challenger from San Francisco to Denver in just 15 hours, and the cops along the way try to stop him. He gets spiritual guidance from a blind deejay played by Little. This has long enjoyed a cult following for its Benzedrine-fueled vibe and great songs spun by Little. A scene with Charlotte Rampling was cut from the American release. **Cast:** Barry Newman, Dean Jagger, Cleavon Little, Paul Koslo, Robert Donner, Timothy Scott, Gilda Texter, Anthony James. **Credits:** Dir: Richard C. Sarafian; Prod: Norman

Spencer; Writer: Guillermo Cain; DP: John A. Alonzo; Ed: Stefan Arnsten; Composer: Jim Bowen, Peter Carpenter, Tom Thacker. Color, 98 min. VHS, LASER

Variety Girl
(1947) Paramount
This slim backstage story has two ingenues (Hatcher and San Juan) wandering Paramount's back lot and getting involved in a benefit show for the Variety Clubs. If anyone called in sick that day, it's not apparent, as everyone from Cecil B. DeMille to the immortal Sonny Tufts punches the clock and helps to put on that big charity show. Movie fans will enjoy the time-capsule tour of Paramount Studios and postwar Hollywood hot spots. Better than it might have been. **Cast:** Mary Hatcher, Olga San Juan, DeForest Kelley, Bing Crosby, Gary Cooper, Ray Milland, Alan Ladd, Barbara Stanwyck, Paulette Goddard. **Credits:** Dir: Gregory

Marshall; Prod: Daniel Dare; Writer: Edmund Hartman, Frank Tashlin, Robert Welch, Monte Brice; DP: Lionel Lindon, Stuart Thompson; Ed: LeRoy Stone; Composer: Joseph J. Lilley; Art Director: Hans Dreier, Robert Clatworthy. B&W and Color, 83 min.

The Velvet Touch
(1948) RKO
In this drama of conscience, Russell portrays an actress whose ambition to play the lead role in *Hedda Gabler* gets her into real trouble. When Ames, a theatrical producer, tries to undermine her efforts, Russell kills him, but rival actress Trevor, Ames's former lover, gets convicted for Russell's crime. A fine performance from Russell and solid support from Greenstreet as a theater-buff detective. The first production from Russell's own company. **Cast:** Rosalind Russell, Leo Genn, Claire Trevor, Sydney Greenstreet, Leon Ames, Frank McHugh, Walter Kingsford,

Vertigo (1958)

Dan Tobin. **Credits:** Dir: John Gage; Prod: Frederick Brisson; Writer: Leo Rosten, Walter Reilly; Story: Anabel Ross; DP: Joseph Walker; Ed: Chandler House; Prod Design: William Flannery; Composer: Leigh Harline. B&W, 97 min. **VHS**

Vera Cruz

(1954) United Artists
Action director Aldrich guides a Western adventure of two mercenaries (Cooper and Lancaster) choosing between the lure of vast riches from siding with Mexico's Emperor Maximilian and the appeal of Montiel's revolutionary fervor. The two sign up to guard heiress Darcel and a shipment of gold but end up on opposite sides after general Romero seizes the gold. **Cast:** Gary Cooper, Burt Lancaster, Denise Darcel, Cesar Romero, Sarita Montiel, George Macready, Ernest Borgnine, Morris Ankrum. **Credits:** Dir: Robert Aldrich; Prod: James Hill; Writer: Roland Kibbee, James R. Webb; DP: Ernest Laszlo; Ed: Alan Crosland, Jr.; Composer: Hugo Friedhofer. Color, 94 min. **VHS, LASER**

The Verdict

(1946) Warner Bros.
Director Siegel's first feature is a clever mystery featuring the last screen pairing of Greenstreet and Lorre. Greenstreet retires from Scotland Yard after sending the wrong man to the gallows. His replacement as chief, Coulouris, boasts of his modern techniques, methods he gets to try when a baffling murder occurs. Greenstreet and his friend Lorre, a ghoulish illustrator, take a keen interest in the case. A neat twist at the end reveals the construction of the perfect crime. **Cast:** Sydney Greenstreet, Peter Lorre, Joan Lorring, George Coulouris, Rosalind Ivan, Paul Cavanagh, Arthur Shields, Morton Lowry, Holmes Herbert. **Credits:** Dir: Don Siegel; Prod: Williams Jacobs, Jack Warner; Writer: Peter Milne; Story: Israel Zangwill; DP: Ernest Haller; Ed: Thomas Reilly; Prod Design: Ted Smith; Composer: Frederick Hollander. B&W, 86 min.

Vertigo

(1958) Paramount
When the restored version of *Vertigo* debuted in theaters, it reignited interest in and appreciation for what is generally considered to be Hitchcock's most personal work. It also underlined Hitchcock's technical mastery in the use of color and camera effects (the famous zoom-in-dolly-out shot used to simulate vertigo) and the importance of Herrmann's jittery score. Stewart plays another character (as in *Rear Window*) who, because he is psychically or physically separated from his real life, creates an imaginary, anxiety-provoking substitution. Stewart leaves the San Francisco police force after his vertigo leads to a partner's death. He takes a job tailing the wife (Novak) of a school friend who has been behaving strangely. When he saves her from a suicidal plunge, his fascination turns to longing, a longing that comes to a bitter end when she seemingly succeeds in dying, again due to Stewart's vertigo, in a leap from a bell tower. After gathering his shattered mind in an institution, Stewart spots a woman with an uncanny likeness to his lost love. His obsession drives him to re-create her in the exact image of his suicidal lover, forcing a confrontation with the truth of her identity. Critics have long discussed the relevance of the Stewart character's manipulating of the Novak character and the director's own obsession with creating the ideal cool-blonde heroine. Among the most fascinating and suspenseful of classic movies. The special edition video release has been restored and remastered from the original negative. Based on the novel *D'Entre Les Morts* by Boileau and Narcejac, the authors of the story for French director Henri-Georges Clouzot's *Diabolique*. Selected as a National Film Registry Outstanding Film. Academy Award Nominations: Best Art Direction; Best Sound. **Cast:** James Stewart, Kim Novak, Barbara Bel Geddes, Tom Helmore, Henry Jones, Raymond Bailey, Ellen Corby, Konstantin Shayne, Lee Patrick, Paul Bryar. **Credits:** Dir: Alfred Hitchcock; Prod: Alfred Hitchcock; Writer: Alec Coppel, Samuel W. Taylor; Story: Pierre Boileau, Thomas Narcejac; DP: Robert Burks; Ed: George Tomasini; Prod Design: Henry Bumstead; Composer: Bernard Herrmann; Costumes: Edith Head; Art Director: Hal Pereira. Color, 126 min. **VHS, LASER, DVD**

Victory

(1940) Paramount
This is the third screen interpretation of Conrad's novel *Victory*. March forsakes the evils of the world and casts himself away on a remote island. When he visits a neighboring island, he meets Field, a musician struggling to keep out of the clutches of the hotel owner. March takes her with him to his island, where their idyll is interrupted by three islanders goaded by the hotel owner to steal March's nonexistent cache of gold. **Cast:** Fredric March, Betty Field, Cedric Hardwicke, Jerome Cowan, Sig Rumann, Margaret Wycherly, Fritz Feld, Lionel Royce, Rafaela Ottiano. **Credits:** Dir: John Cromwell; Prod: John Cromwell; Writer: John L. Balderston; Story: Joseph Conrad; DP: Leo Tover; Ed: William Shea; Prod Design: Hans Dreier, Robert Usher; Composer: Frederick Hollander. B&W, 79 min.

Vigil in the Night

(1940) RKO
A medical potboiler with stirring performances by Lombard and Shirley as sister nurses working in English working-class hospitals. Lombard takes the rap for a fatal mistake of Shirley's and is banished to a poor hospital where she works alongside and longs for Aherne, and rebuffs the advances of Mitchell. Shirley repays her spiritual debt by sacrificing her life to save Mitchell's child. **Cast:** Carole Lombard, Anne Shirley, Brian Aherne, Julien Mitchell, Robert Coote, Peter Cushing, Ethel Griffies, Brenda Forbes, Rita Page, Doris Lloyd. **Credits:** Dir: George Stevens; Prod: George Stevens; Writer: Fred Guinol, Rowland Leigh, P. J. Wolfson; Story: A. J. Cronin; DP: Robert De Grasse; Ed: Henry Berman; Prod Design: Van Nest Polglase; Composer: Alfred Newman. B&W, 96 min.

The Vikings

(1958) United Artists
Pseudo-historical claptrap but with rousing action, this tale set during the Viking assault on England revolves around two half-brothers (Douglas and Curtis), sons of the Viking king, vying for the throne of Northumbria. But the real star is the bleak natural beauty of the Norwegian tundra where much of the movie was shot. **Cast:** Kirk Douglas, Ernest Borgnine, Janet Leigh, Tony Curtis, James Donald, Alexander Knox, Frank Thring, Maxine Audley. **Credits:** Dir: Richard Fleischer; Prod: Jerry Bresler; Writer: Dale Wasserman, Calder Willingham; Story: Edison Marshall; DP: Jack Cardiff; Ed: Elmo Williams; Composer: Mario Nascimbene. Color, 124 min. **VHS, LASER**

The Village Tale

(1935) RKO
In this grim drama, gossip, claustrophobia, and the petty viciousness of small-town society destroy the lives of two men and one lovely lady. Beautiful, bored housewife Johnson falls hopelessly in love with Scott. Their passion remains unconsummated, but the ill-will of the townspeople causes her husband (Hohl) to attempt Scott's murder. In the mean-

time, gossip drives another innocent man to suicide. **Cast:** Kay Johnson, Randolph Scott, Arthur Hohl, Robert Barrat, T. Roy Barnes, Janet Beecher, Dorothy Burgess, Andy Clyde, Edward Ellis, De Witt Jennings. **Credits:** Dir: John Cromwell; Prod: David Hempstead; Writer: Allan Scott; DP: Nicholas Musuraca; Ed: William Morgan; Prod Design: Van Nest Polglase; Composer: Alberto Colombo. B&W, 80 min.

The Violent Men
(1955) Columbia
This uneven but action-packed Western has Ford as a farmer pushed to violence by bitter, disabled rancher Robinson. Robinson's wife (Stanwyck) and his brother (Keith) goad him to expand his empire while carrying on an affair. Ford loses his wife because of his pacifist beliefs, which were forged in the horror of the Civil War. When one of his farmhands gets killed by one of Robinson's men, he turns his knowledge of war to his advantage in a violent all-out assault. **Cast:** Barbara Stanwyck, Glenn Ford, Edward G. Robinson, Dianne Foster, Brian Keith, Richard Jaeckel, James Westerfield, Jack Kelly. **Credits:** Dir: Rudolph Maté; Prod: Lewis J. Rachmil; Writer: Harry Kleiner; DP: W. Howard Greene, Burnett Guffey; Ed: Jerome Thoms; Composer: Max Steiner; Art Director: Carl Anderson. Color, 96 min. **VHS**

Violent Saturday
(1955) Fox
This harrowing crime drama focuses on the pent-up energies that are on the verge of destroying a small town's deceptive tranquillity. When a hard-boiled gang of crooks shows up planning to knock over the bank, they find themselves in a town ripe to explode. The robbery sets off a violent catharsis and the film ends as bullets fly, bodies fall, and an Amish farmer (Borgnine) violates his sect's most sacred commandment by sticking a pitchfork into a sadist's back. Marvin is particularly effective as a gas-huffing gunman. **Cast:** Victor Mature, Richard Egan, Stephen McNally, Virginia Leith, Tom Noonan, Lee Marvin, Margaret Hayes, J. Carrol Naish, Sylvia Sidney, Ernest Borgnine. **Credits:** Dir: Richard Fleischer; Prod: Buddy Adler; Writer: Sidney Boehm, William L. Heath; DP: Charles G. Clarke; Ed: Louis Loeffler; Prod Design: George Davis, Lyle Wheeler; Composer: Hugo Friedhofer. Color, 90 min.

Virginia City
(1940) Warner Bros.
Curtiz's Civil War–era follow-up to 1939's *Dodge City* finds Flynn, a Union officer escapee from a Confederate prison, chasing gold being sent from the north by Scott to finance the rebel cause. Along the way, he fights off outlaw Bogart and rebel spy Hopkins, who sets him a tender trap. **Cast:** Humphrey Bogart, Errol Flynn, Randolph Scott, Miriam Hopkins, Frank McHugh, Alan Hale, John Litel, Guinn "Big Boy" Williams. **Credits:** Dir: Michael Curtiz; Prod: Robert Fellows; Writer: Robert Buckner, Norman Reilly Raine, Howard Koch; DP: Sol Polito; Ed: George Amy; Composer: Max Steiner; Art Director: Ted Smith. B&W, 121 min. **VHS**

The Virginian
(1929) Paramount
Owen Wister's novel was one of the best-known and best-loved Western tales of its day: it was produced twice for the silent screen before this first talking version; it made a star of future silent Western hero William S. Hart in its stage incarnation; and it received a color treatment in the '40s and a long-running TV series adaptation in the '60s. Cooper's first talking role set his heroic image in the public mind as the ranch hand who reluctantly helps lynch his one-time rival in love. On his wedding day, he redeems himself in the eyes of his fiancée when he guns down the man who led his friend to crime. **Cast:** Gary Cooper, Walter Huston, Mary Brian, Richard Arlen, Eugene Pallette, Chester Conklin. **Credits:** Dir: Victor Fleming; Prod: Louis Lighton; Writer: Edward Paramore, Howard Estabrook, Grover Jones, Keene Thompson; DP: J. Roy Hunt, Edward Cronjager; Ed: William Shea. B&W, 92 min. **VHS**

The Virginian
(1946) Paramount
In the Technicolor remake of the 1929 Cooper-Huston Western classic, McCrea is the hero rancher and Donlevy the rustling heavy. McCrea is fine and so is the color production, but the Cooper version remains more memorable. **Cast:** Joel McCrea, Barbara Britton, Sonny Tufts, Brian Donlevy, Fay Bainter, Tom Tully, Henry O'Neill, James Burke. **Credits:** Dir: Stuart Gilmore; Prod: Paul Jones; Writer: Frances Goodrich, Albert Hackett, Edward Paramore, Howard Estabrook; Story: Owen Wister; DP: Harry Hallenberger; Ed: Everett Douglas; Composer: Daniele Amfitheatrof; Art Director: Hans Dreier, John Meehan. Color, 87 min. **VHS**

The Virgin Queen
(1955) Fox
Davis takes the role of Elizabeth I for the second time (the first was *The Private Lives of Elizabeth and Essex*, 1939) in this outing depicting the queen's later years. When Todd, as dashing Walter Raleigh, makes a gallant impression at court, Davis seems to become a blushing young girl again, doting on him and making him captain of the guards. Just as she is to send him off to the New World with ships and a knighthood, she learns that he and lady-in-waiting Collins have been secretly wed. The nuptials earn Todd a stay in the Tower of London before he sails. Academy Award Nomination for Best (Color) Costume Design. **Cast:** Bette Davis, Richard Todd, Joan Collins, Herbert Marshall, Dan O'Herlihy, Robert Douglas, Romney Brent, Leslie Parrish. **Credits:** Dir: Henry Koster; Prod: Charles Brackett; Writer: Harry Brown, Mindret Lord; DP: Charles G. Clarke; Ed: Robert Simpson; Prod Design: Lyle Wheeler; Composer: Franz Waxman; Costumes: Mary Wills; Art Director: Leland Fuller. Color, 92 min. **VHS**

Vivacious Lady
(1938) RKO
Stewart, a small-town botany teacher, and Rogers, a flashy New York nightclub singer, marry on a whim and return to his home to set up housekeeping. They try to keep the wedding a secret from Stewart's father (Coburn), a stuffy college president, and mother (Bondi), who is subject to phony heart palpitations. Culture-clash comedy follows. Stevens provides Rogers's natural comedic talent good support and her platinum beauty glows in every scene. Academy Award Nominations: Best Cinematography; Best Sound. **Cast:** Ginger Rogers, James Stewart, Beulah Bondi, James Ellison, Charles Coburn, Phyllis Kennedy, Alec Craig, Franklin Pangborn. **Credits:** Dir: George Stevens; Prod: George Stevens; Writer: P. J. Wolfson, Ernest Pagano; DP: Robert de Grasse; Ed: Henry Berman; Prod Design: Carroll Clark; Composer: Roy Webb; Art Director: Van Nest Polglase. B&W, 90 min. **VHS, LASER**

Viva Las Vegas
(1963) MGM
Elvis is at his best with the only woman who could equal his on-screen energy, Ann-Margret. They were reportedly an item during production, and the sparks fly on the screen, too. Presley plays a race driver who needs money to keep

his Grand Prix car humming. He works as a waiter on the Las Vegas strip when he isn't busy romancing Ann-Margret and singing songs that include the lounge-favorite title number, "I Need Somebody to Lean On," "Come On Everybody," and "The Lady Loves Me." **Cast:** Elvis Presley, Ann-Margret, Cesare Danova, William Demarest, Jack Carter, Nicky Blair, Robert B. Williams, Eddie Quillan. **Credits:** Dir: George Sidney; Prod: Jack Cummings, George Sidney; Writer: Sally Benson; DP: Joseph Biroc; Ed: John McSweeney; Composer: George Stoll; Art Director: George W. Davis, Edward C. Carfagno. Color, 86 min. **VHS, LASER, DVD**

Viva Villa
(1934) MGM
The action-filled life of Mexican rebel Pancho Villa offered Beery one of his best roles. From the time a young Villa watched his father being whipped by soldiers, he seethed with hatred for the wealthy who controlled Mexico. He and his band earned the loyalty of the peasants by robbing landowners and distributing some of the proceeds to the poor. Beery throws his support to the rebel army led by Walthall and the rebels sweep to victory, but internal rivalries lead to dissension and murder. Hawks had an uncredited hand in the direction. Academy Award Nominations: 3, including Best Picture; Best Adapted Screenplay. **Cast:** Wallace Beery, Leo Carrillo, Fay Wray, Donald Cook, Stuart Erwin, George E. Stone, Henry B. Walthall, Joseph Schildkraut, Katherine De Mille. **Credits:** Dir: Jack Conway,

Howard Hawks; Prod: David O. Selznick; Writer: Ben Hecht; DP: James Wong Howe; Ed: Robert J. Kern; Composer: Herbert Stothart; Art Director: Harry Oliver. B&W, 115 min. **VHS, LASER**

Viva Zapata!
(1952) Fox
Brando brings dignity and strength to his portrayal of Mexican revolutionary Emiliano Zapata. A reluctant hero, Zapata leads the peasants in a quest to seize their land back from the wealthy after first trying to ignore his calling. He promises Peters a quiet life and finds work on a horse farm. But the indignities and cruelty of the government are finally too much, and Brando takes command, with his brother, Quinn, of a peasant army. He joins the revolution being waged in the north by Villa and, after they come to power, is faced with the complexities of governing. A breakthrough for both Kazan and Brando, it continued their collaboration, begun with the stage production of *A Streetcar Named Desire* and three powerful films in four years, *Streetcar, Zapata,* and *On the Waterfront.* Steinbeck wrote the Oscar-nominated screenplay. Academy Award Nominations: 5, including Best Actor: Marlon Brando; Best Story and Screenplay. **Academy Awards:** Best Supporting Actor: Anthony Quinn. **Cast:** Marlon Brando, Anthony Quinn, Jean Peters, Joseph Wiseman, Arnold Moss, Alan Reed, Harold B. Gordon, Lou Gilbert. **Credits:** Dir: Elia Kazan; Prod: Darryl F. Zanuck; Writer: John

Steinbeck; DP: Joseph MacDonald; Ed: Barbara McLean; Prod Design: Lyle Wheeler; Composer: Alex North; Art Director: Leland Fuller. B&W, 114 min. **VHS, LASER**

Vogues of 1938
(1937) United Artists
In this gorgeous musical fashion show, Bennett is a rebellious rich girl who decides to become a model and Baxter is the owner of a chic boutique battling his rival and his wife (Vinson). Mostly an excuse to see the fashions of the day in glorious early Technicolor. Academy Award Nominations: Best Interior Decoration; Best Song ("That Old Feeling"). **Cast:** Warner Baxter, Joan Bennett, Helen Vinson, Mischa Auer, Alan Mowbray, Jerome Cowan, Alma Kruger, Marjorie Gateson. **Credits:** Dir: Irving Cummings; Prod: Walter Wanger; Writer: Bella Spewack, Samuel Spewack; DP: Ray Rennahan; Ed: Otho S. Lovering, Dorothy Spencer; Composer: Boris Morros; Art Director: Alexander Toluboff. Color, 110 min. **VHS**

The Voice of the Turtle
(1947) Warner Bros.
One of Reagan's best performances is in this solid translation to film of a hit Broadway play. Sergeant Reagan comes to New York for a date with actress Arden, but she dumps him for a higher-ranking officer. Fellow actress Parker gives him a place to stay, and, of course, one thing leads to another. Arden decides she made a bad deal, though, and does her best to intervene. Considered the height of sophisticated comedy in its day. **Cast:** Ronald Reagan, Eleanor Parker, Eve Arden, Wayne Morris, Kent Smith, John Emery, Erskine Sanford, John Holland, Nino Pepitone, Helen Wallace. **Credits:** Dir: Irving Rapper; Prod: Charles Hoffman; Writer: John Van Druten, Charles Hoffman; DP: Sol Polito; Ed: Rudi Fehr; Composer: Max Steiner, Leo F. Forbstein; Art Director: Robert M. Haas. B&W, 103 min.

Von Ryan's Express
(1965) Fox
Sinatra stars in a WWII thriller as an American flier who leads the inmates of an Italian POW camp on a daring run for freedom in Switzerland. With the help of newly liberated Italians, the POWs commandeer a freight train heading north, and the Germans do their best to stop it. Great action sequences as Nazi planes make a last-ditch effort to halt the escape. Academy Award Nomination for Best Sound Effects Editing. **Cast:** Frank

Von Ryan's Express (1965)

Sinatra, Trevor Howard, Luther Adler, James Brolin, Brad Dexter, Edward Mulhare, Raffaella Carra, Sergio Fantoni. **Credits:** Dir: Mark Robson; Prod: Saul David; Writer: Wendell Mayes, Joseph Landon; DP: William Daniels; Ed: Dorothy Spencer; Composer: Jerry Goldsmith; Art Director: Jack Martin Smith. Color, 117 min. **VHS, LASER**

Voyage to the Bottom of the Sea

(1961) Fox

Written, produced, and directed by Allen, the father of the '70s disaster specta-cle, this is a colorful, entertaining under-water science-fiction tale. Pidgeon plays an admiral who has invented a nuclear submarine that allows him to evade the naval forces of the world's superpowers while he pursues his mission to counter-act the effects of the Van Allen radiation belt with nuclear missles. Other chal-lenges include a giant squid and the devious plotting of psychologist Fontaine. The basis for the long-running TV series. **Cast:** Walter Pidgeon, Joan Fontaine, Peter Lorre, Robert Sterling, Barbara Eden, Michael Ansara, Frankie Avalon, Regis Toomey. **Credits:** Dir: Irwin Allen; Prod: Irwin Allen; Writer: Irwin Allen, Charles Bennett; DP: Winton C. Hoch; Ed: George Boemler; Composer: Paul Sawtell, Bert Shefter; Art Director: Jack Martin Smith, Herman A. Blumenthal. Color, 109 min. **VHS**

The WAC from Walla Walla

(1952) Republic
This musical WWII caper finds country comedienne Canova accidentally enlisted in the WACs. Determined to do her long line of Army ancestors proud, however, the bungling recruit makes the best of things, ultimately foiling two foreign agents when she stumbles upon their plot to spirit the top-secret schematics for America's newest guided missile out of the country. **Cast:** Judy Canova, Stephen Dunne, George Cleveland, June Vincent, Irene Ryan, Roy Barcroft, Allen Jenkins, George Chandler, Elizabeth Slifer, Thurston Hall. **Credits:** Dir: Michael Witney; Prod: Sydney Picker; Writer: Arthur T. Horman; DP: Jack Marta; Ed: Tony Martinelli; Composer: R. Dale Butts, Jack Elliot, Harold Spina; Art Director: Fred A. Ritter. B&W, 83 min.

The Wackiest Ship in the Army

(1961) Columbia
Lemmon commands a broken-down WWII navy vessel with an inexperienced crew through waters patrolled by the Japanese. Nelson costars as a particularly green recruit who does some fine singing, but Lemmon's comedic exasperation carries the day. **Cast:** Jack Lemmon, Ricky Nelson, Chips Rafferty, John Lund, Tom Tully, Joby Baker, Warren Berlinger, Patricia Driscoll. **Credits:** Dir: Richard Murphy; Prod: Fred Kohlmar; Writer: Richard Murphy, Herbert Margolis, William Raynor; Story: Herbert Carlson; DP: Charles Lawton, Jr.; Ed: Charles Nelson; Composer: George Dunning; Art Director: Carl Anderson. Color, 99 min. **VHS, LASER**

Wagon Master

(1950) RKO
Fine Ford Western about two rugged cowhands (Ford stalwarts Johnson and Bond) who join a wagon train of faith-ful, hardy Mormons heading for Utah. One of Ford's exemplary tales of human survival that contrast ideals (the expression of the Mormons' beliefs in their quest for the "promised land") with reality (the harsh Western terrain, the threat of Indian attack and outlaws). The inspiration for the television show *Wagon Train* (which also starred Bond). **Cast:** Ben Johnson, Joanne Dru, Ward Bond, Harry Carey, Jr., Charles Kemper, Alan Mowbray, Jane Darwell, Ruth Clifford. **Credits:** Dir: John Ford; Prod: Merian C. Cooper, John Ford; Writer: Patrick Ford, Frank S. Nugent; DP: Bert Glennon; Ed: Jack Murray; Composer: Richard Hageman. B&W, 86 min. **VHS, LASER**

Waikiki Wedding

(1937) Paramount
Bing plays a laid-back PR man for a Hawaiian pineapple company, enjoying his life in tropical paradise, until beautiful Ross arrives on the island as winner of a public relations contest for the company. He's charged with escorting her and concocts some elaborate schemes to keep her entertained, with the help of Burns and Ross's friend Raye. Naturally, there's plenty of romance and crooning, including "Blue Hawaii" and "Sweet Leilani." Academy Award Nominations: 2. **Academy Awards:** Best Song ("Sweet Leilani"). **Cast:** Bing Crosby, Shirley Ross, Martha Raye, Bob Burns, Leif Erikson, Anthony Quinn, Grady Sutton, George Barbier. **Credits:** Dir: Frank Tuttle; Prod: Arthur Hornblow, Jr.; Writer: Frank Butler, Don Hartman, Walter DeLeon, Francis Martin; DP: Karl Struss; Ed: Paul Weatherwax; Composer: Boris Morros; SFX: Farciot Edouart. B&W, 89 min. **VHS**

Wait 'Till the Sun Shines, Nellie

(1952) Fox
David Wayne plays a barber desperately clinging to the simple ways of rural, small-town life who finds his marriage on the rocks when his wife, Peters, who longs for the bright lights of the big city, takes a lover and abandons him. Nothing that happens to him, including the death of his estranged wife, raising their kids on his own, his son's eventual violent demise as a mobster, or the loss of his barbershop to fire, ever shakes his belief in his way of life. Wayne turns in a fine performance, aging half a century during the film. **Cast:** David Wayne, Jean Peters, Hugh Marlowe, Warren Stevens, Albert Dekker, Helene Stanley, Tom Morton, Joyce MacKenzie, Alan Hale, Richard Karlan. **Credits:** Dir: Henry King; Prod: George Jessel; Writer: Allan Scott, Maxwell Shane; Story: Ferdinand Reyher; DP: Leon Shamroy; Ed: Barbara McLean; Composer: Alfred Newman; Art Director: Lyle Wheeler, Maurice Ransford. Color, 108 min.

Wait Until Dark

(1967) Warner Bros.
A gripping tale of a blind woman (Hepburn) confronted in her apartment by three criminals conspiring to retrieve a heroin-filled doll that's unwittingly come into her household. Hepburn turns in an utterly convincing performance as the blind woman who outwits the crazed gang leader, Arkin, when she plunges him into darkness, too. One of the great, edge-of-your-seat suspense movies as the audience watches the sinister machinations that the heroine can't. Based on a Broadway play (directed by Arthur Penn); it returned to Broadway in 1998 with Quentin Tarantino in the Arkin role. Academy Award Nomination for Best Actress: Audrey Hepburn. **Cast:** Audrey Hepburn, Alan Arkin, Efrem Zimbalist, Jr., Jack Weston, Richard Crenna, Samantha Jones, Gary Morgan, Jean Del Val. **Credits:** Dir: Terence Young; Prod: Mel Ferrer; Writer: Jane-Howard Carrington,

Wait Until Dark (1967)

Robert Carrington; DP: Charles Lang; Ed: Gene Milford; Composer: Henry Mancini; Art Director: George Jenkins. Color, 108 min. **VHS, LASER**

Wake Island
(1942) Paramount
This immensely popular wartime hit stirred the nation in the darkest days of WWII. A hearty handful of Marines bravely attempt the impossible: with no chance for reinforcements, they struggle to hold the remote outpost of Wake Island in the days following the Japanese attack on Pearl Harbor. Donlevy and Bendix are superb in a picture that set the standard for wartime flag-wavers (and was used by the Marines at boot camps!). Academy Award Nominations: Best Picture; Best Director; Best Supporting Actor; William Bendix; Best Original Screenplay. **Cast:** Robert Preston, Brian Donlevy, William Bendix, Macdonald Carey, Albert Dekker, Walter Abel, Mikhail Rasumny, Don Castle. **Credits:** Dir: John Farrow; Prod: Joseph Sistrom; Writer: W. R. Burnett, Frank Butler; DP: Theodor Sparkuhl; Ed: LeRoy Stone; Prod Design: Hans Dreier; Composer: David Buttolph; Art Director: Earl Hedrick. B&W, 88 min. **VHS**

Wake Me When It's Over
(1960) Fox
Shawn, a successful restaurant owner, is mistakenly drafted and sent to a military outpost on a flyspeck island in the Pacific Ocean. Red tape delays his return home but, in the meantime, he's inspired to build a resort hotel

and enlists the help of his bored fellow servicemen. A fine service comedy with Shawn's first big role and a too-rare opportunity to see TV legend Kovacs in a major part. **Cast:** Margo Moore, Jack Warden, Dick Shawn, Don Knotts, Ernie Kovacs, Robert Strauss, Noreen Nash, Parley Baer, Robert Emhardt, Nobu McCarthy. **Credits:** Dir: Mervyn LeRoy; Prod: Mervyn LeRoy; Writer: Richard Breen; Story: Howard Singer; DP: Leon Shamroy; Ed: Aaron Stell; Prod Design: Lyle Wheeler, John Beckman; Composer: Cyril Mockridge. Color, 126 min.

Wake of the Red Witch
(1948) Republic
A roaring, salty adventure tale with Wayne battling ship owner Adler over pearls, $5 million in gold, and the love of lovely Russell. Wayne wins her love but loses her hand in marriage and wages a long battle to get her back, a battle that ends with the couple together in eternity. **Cast:** John Wayne, Gail Russell, Gig Young, Luther Adler, Eduard Franz, Jeff Corey, Adele Mara, Grant Withers. **Credits:** Dir: Edward Ludwig; Prod: Edmund Grainger; Writer: Harry Brown, Kenneth Gamet; Story: Garland Roark; DP: Reggie Lanning; Ed: Richard L. Van Enger; Composer: Nathan Scott; Art Director: James Sullivan. B&W, 106 min. **VHS**

Wake Up and Live
(1937) Fox
This delightful musical depicts the radio personality wars of the '30s and features big-time radio stars Winchell

and Bernie giving a big-screen rendition of their broadcast battle. Unknown crooner Haley is biding his time as station tour guide while trying to make it big over the airwaves; he gets a lucky break thanks to a mistaken live mike and also wins the chance to woo Faye. Songs include "There's a Lull in My Life," "I Love You Too Much Muchacha," "Wake Up and Live," and "De Camptown Races." Fascinating glimpse at radio history. **Cast:** Walter Winchell, Ben Bernie, Alice Faye, Pat Kelly, Ned Sparks, Jack Haley, Walter Catlett, Grace Bradley, Leah Ray, Joan Davis. **Credits:** Dir: Sidney Lanfield; Prod: Darryl F. Zanuck, Kenneth MacGowan; Writer: Harry Tugend, Jack Yellen, Curtis Kenyon; Story: Dorothea Brande; DP: Edward Cronjager; Ed: Robert Simpson; Prod Design: Mark-Lee Kirk; Composer: Louis Silvers. B&W, 91 min.

Walk, Don't Run
(1966) Columbia
Grant's last film performance finds him an English businessman who arrives in Tokyo and discovers it impossible to find lodging with the influx of tourists for the upcoming Olympic Games. He is able to talk his way into sharing an apartment with a beautiful British woman (Eggar) despite the objections of her fiancé, and finds himself matchmaking between her and an American Olympic athlete (Hutton). In this remake of *The More the Merrier* (1943), Grant gallantly refused to play the romantic lead, and deferred to the younger Hutton. Music by Quincy Jones. **Cast:** Cary Grant, Samantha Eggar, Jim Hutton, John Standing, Miiko Taka, Ted Hartley, A. Ben Astar, George Takei. **Credits:** Dir: Charles Walters; Prod: Sol C. Siegel; Writer: Sol Saks; DP: Harry Stradling; Ed: Walter Thompson, James D. Wells; Prod Design: Joseph Wright; Composer: Quincy Jones. Color, 114 min. **VHS**

Walk East on Beacon
(1952) Columbia
F.B.I. chief Hoover wrote the *Reader's Digest* article on which this docudrama-like spy yarn is based. When a U.S.-born Soviet spy disappears, his wife calls in the F.B.I. Murphy tracks the spy ring through Boston, nabbing the ringleader (Stepanek) just as he is about to slip onto a waiting sub. Notable for the realistic depiction of espionage operations. **Cast:** George Murphy, Finlay Currie, Virginia Gilmore, Karel Stepanek, Louisa Horton, Peter

Capell, Wick Bruno, Jack Manning, Karl Weber. **Credits:** Dir: Alfred Werker; Prod: Louis de Rochemont; Writer: Emmett Murphy, Leo Rosten, Virginia Shaler; Story: J. Edgar Hoover; DP: Joseph Brun; Ed: Angelo Ross; Composer: Louise Applebaum; Art Director: Herbert Andrews. B&W, 98 min.

The Walking Dead
(1936) Warner Bros.
Karloff, in another of his patented back-from-the-grave roles, plays a reformed criminal framed for the murder of the judge who sentenced him, and executed in the electric chair. His innocence is discovered too late, but he is revived by the Lindbergh heart (a mechanical pump actually invented by the famous flier) and sets out to wreak revenge on his framers. Curtiz's moody atmosphere makes this a standout. **Cast:** Boris Karloff, Ricardo Cortez, Edmund Gwenn, Marguerite Churchill, Henry Hull, Barton MacLane, Henry O'Neill, Joe King, Addison Richards, Paul Harvey. **Credits:** Dir: Michael Curtiz; Prod: Louis F. Edelman; Writer: Robert Adams, Ewart Adamson, Joseph Fields, Lillian Hayward, Peter Milne; DP: Hal Mohr; Ed: Thomas Pratt; Prod Design: Hugh Reticker. B&W, 66 min.

The Walking Hills
(1949) Columbia
Director John Sturges's first film is an excellent Western about a group of eight men who stumble into information that might lead to a 100-year-old wagon train loaded with gold. The men, led by Scott, are joined by Raines, who brings a romantic competition to the already tense group. A sandstorm uncovers the gold but doesn't resolve who gets to keep it. **Cast:** Randolph Scott, Ella Raines, John Ireland, Arthur Kennedy, Reed Howes, Houseley Stevenson, Russell Collins, William Bishop, Edgar Buchanan, Jerome Courtland. **Credits:** Dir: John Sturges; Prod: Harry J. Brown, Randolph Scott; Writer: Alan LeMay, Virginia Roddick; DP: Charles Lawton, Jr.; Ed: William A. Lyon; Composer: Arthur Morton; Art Director: Robert Peterson. B&W, 78 min.

Walking Tall
(1973) Cinerama
Real-life Tennessee sheriff Buford Pusser (Baker) becomes a larger-than-life folk hero in the first of the movies celebrating his righteous anger. When he sets out to rid his community of organized crime, prostitution, and gambling, a vicious war ensues that claims the life of his wife. He gets out his big stick and fights back with a vengeance. A surprise, people's-choice hit that earned $17 million on its release. **Cast:** Joe Don Baker, Elizabeth Hartman, Noah Beery, Gene Evans, Pepper Martin, John F. Brascia, Bruce Glover, Arch Johnson. **Credits:** Dir: Phil Karlson; Prod: Mort Briskin; Writer: Mort Briskin; DP: Jack A. Marta; Ed: Harry Gerstad; Prod Design: Stan Jolley; Composer: Walter Scharf, Johnny Mathis. Color, 126 min. **VHS, DVD**

Walking Tall, Pt. II
(1975) AIP
Sheriff Buford Pusser (Svenson) comes back to town with the intention of avenging the murder of his wife. The plot's pretty much a repeat of the prequel, though not quite as violent. The real Pusser was supposed to star but was killed in a mysterious car crash right before filming began. **Cast:** Bo Svenson, Richard Jaeckel, Noah Beery, Luke Askew, John Davis Chandler, Robert Doqui, Bruce Glover, Brooke Mills. **Credits:** Dir: Earl Bellamy; Prod: Charles A. Pratt; Writer: Howard B. Kreitsek; DP: Keith Smith; Ed: Art Seid; Composer: Walter Scharf. Color, 113 min. **VHS, LASER**

Walk in the Spring Rain
(1970) Columbia
In a romantic melodrama with the less-common angle of mid-life love, Bergman, the wife of a dry-as-dust college professor (Weaver), accompanies her husband on sabbatical to the mountains of Tennessee. There she meets a simple, compassionate handyman (Quinn) whose lust for life ignites a passionate affair that leads to tragedy. Notable for a script by the usually reliable Silliphant. **Cast:** Ingrid Bergman, Fritz Weaver, Anthony Quinn, Katherine Crawford, Tom Fielding, Virginia Gregg, Mitchell Silverman. **Credits:** Dir: Guy Green; Prod: Stirling Silliphant; Writer: Stirling Silliphant; DP: Charles Lang; Ed: Ferris Anderson; Composer: Elmer Bernstein. Color, 98 min. **VHS**

A Walk in the Sun
(1945) Fox
The second, WWII chapter of Milestone's great war trilogy (following *All Quiet on the Western Front*, 1930, and preceding *Pork Chop Hill*, 1959), this is one of the most revealing films of the interior life of a foot soldier ever made. Just six miles on the Italian coast measures the distance traveled in the film, and in those six miles the troops encounter death, madness, and weary triumph. The audience listens in to the soldiers' thoughts as they face danger, making this an intimate, gripping experience. **Cast:** Dana Andrews, Richard Conte, Lloyd Bridges, John Ireland, George Tyne, Sterling Holloway, Herbert Rudley, Norman Lloyd, Steve Brodie. **Credits:** Dir: Lewis Milestone; Prod: Lewis Milestone; Writer: Robert Rossen; Story: Harry Brown; DP: Russell Harlan; Ed: Duncan Mansfield; Composer: Freddie Rich; Art Director: Max Bertisch. B&W, 117 min. **VHS**

Walk on the Wild Side
(1962) Columbia
In the '30s, a good-natured man (Harvey) train-hops from Texas to Louisiana in search of his lost love (Capucine). After linking up with loose lady Fonda, he learns that she is working in a brothel run by Stanwyck and must fight for his life, as well as hers, to free her. Loosely based on a Nelson Algren novel, the script had help from Clifford Odets and Ben Hecht and was credited to novelist Fante. The Stanwyck character's lesbian interest in Capucine raised eyebrows at the time. Academy Award Nomination for Best (Original) Score. **Cast:** Jane Fonda, Laurence Harvey, Barbara Stanwyck, Capucine, Anne Baxter, Joanna Moore, Richard Rust, Karl Swenson. **Credits:** Dir: Edward Dmytryk; Prod: Charles K. Feldman; Writer: John Fante, Edmund Morris; DP: Joseph MacDonald; Ed: Charles J. Rice; Prod Design: Richard Sylbert; Composer: Elmer Bernstein. B&W, 114 min. **VHS**

Walk Softly, Stranger
(1950) RKO
Cotten plays a petty grifter who flees his past to a small-town factory job and reluctantly falls in love with his boss's daughter, Valli, a wheelchair-bound young woman he intended to scam with romance. Love transforms him but some shady characters from his past catch up with him and derail his new life. Release was held up to build on Cotten and Valli's success in *The Third Man* (1949). **Cast:** Joseph Cotten, Jack Parr, Alida Valli, Spring Byington, Paul Stewart, Jeff Donnell, John McIntire, Howard Petrie. **Credits:** Dir: Robert Stevenson; Prod: Robert Sparks; Writer: Frank Fenton; DP: Harry Wild; Ed: Frederic Knudtson; Composer: Frederick Hollander. B&W, 81 min. **VHS**

Walk the Proud Land

(1956) Universal

An affecting Western with the always-honorable Murphy as the famous honest Indian agent John P. Clum. Trapped between Geronimo's Apaches, the Army, and the land-grabbing pioneers and with a dash of matrimonial discord thrown in when squaw Bancroft takes a liking to him, this biopic culminates in the surrender of Geronimo. Silverheels, better known as Tonto on the TV series *The Lone Ranger*, played Geronimo for the third time in his career. **Cast:** Audie Murphy, Anne Bancroft, Pat Crowley, Charles Drake, Jay Silverheels, Thomas Rall, Robert Warwick, Eugene Mazzola. **Credits:** Dir: Jesse Hibbs; Prod: Aaron Rosenberg; Writer: Gil Doud, Jack Sher; DP: Harold Lipstein; Ed: Sherman Todd. Color, 89 min. **VHS**

Wanda Nevada

(1979) United Artists

Peter Fonda directs for the first time and dad Henry makes an appearance in this updated Western variant on *Little Miss Marker*. A cowboy (Peter Fonda) wins a plucky orphaned girl (Shields) in a poker game, and together they set out to prospect for gold in the Grand Canyon while pursued by a gang looking for the same loot. **Cast:** Peter Fonda, Brooke Shields, Fiona Lewis, Luke Askew, Ted Markland, Henry Fonda, Severn Darden, Paul Fix. **Credits:** Dir: Peter Fonda; Prod: Neal Dobrofsky, Dennis Hackin; Writer: Dennis Hackin; DP: Michael Butler; Ed: Scott Conrad; Composer: Ken Lauber; Art Director: Lynda Paradise. Color, 109 min. **VHS**

The Wanderers

(1979) Orion

A moody, wistful movie about an Italian-American teen gang from the Bronx in the early '60s. Wahl leads the Fordham Baldies with little Manz (again a scene-stealing tough-little-girl role as in *Days of Heaven*, 1978) tagging along as they face the near-mythic Duckie Boys. Novelist Price, whose story this was based on, later became even better known as a screenwriter, and intriguing director Kaufman also helmed *Invasion of the Body Snatchers* (1978) and *The Unbearable Lightness of Being* (1988). The evocative sound track includes tunes by Dion, The Shirelles, The Four Seasons, and others. **Cast:** Ken Wahl, John Friedrich, Karen Allen, Olympia Dukakis, Alan Rosenburg, Jim Youngs, Tony Ganios, Linda Manz. **Credits:** Dir: Philip Kaufman; Prod: Martin Ransohoff; Writer: Rose Kauf-man, Philip Kaufman; Story: Richard Price; DP: Michael Chapman; Ed: Ronald Roose, Stuart Pappe; Art Director: John Moore. Color, 117 min. **VHS**

War and Peace

(1956) Paramount

This Technicolor epic version of Tolstoy's historical romance set in Czarist Russia was in preproduction for 10 years and took almost 2 years to shoot, with producers De Laurentiis and Ponti spending $6 million on 18,000 actors and 3,000 horses. Even though much of the novel is omitted in this three-hour version, this is a stirring and mostly successful attempt to bring a famously difficult narrative to life. The story follows illegitimate aristocrat Fonda and his star-crossed romance with Hepburn that survives ill-advised marriages and the war-torn backdrop of Napoleon's assault on Russia. The superlative 1968 Russian version directed by Sergei Bondarchuk runs nearly seven hours. Academy Award Nominations: 3, including Best Director; Best Cinematography. **Cast:** Audrey Hepburn, Henry Fonda, Mel Ferrer, Vittorio Gassman, John Mills, Herbert Lom, Oscar Homolka, Anita Ekberg. **Credits:** Dir: King Vidor; Prod: Dino De Laurentiis; Writer: Bridget Boland, Robert Westerby, King Vidor, Mario Camerini, Ennio De Concini, Ivo Perilli, Irwin Shaw; Story: Leo Tolstoy; DP: Jack Cardiff, Aldo Tonti; Ed: Stuart Gilmore, Leo Catozzo; Prod Design: Franz Bachelin; Composer: Nino Rota; Art Director: Mario Chiari, Giani Polidori. Color, 208 min. **VHS, LASER**

Warlock

(1959) Fox

This is a terrific end-of-the-West Western, with Fonda in the role of the aging gunfighter brought to a small mining town to clean up the community. He brings adoring sidekick Quinn with him, and former hoodlum Widmark signs on as deputy. Once the bad guys are run off, jealousies surface and the town questions having a gunslinger, even a fading one, around. Fonda establishes his dominance and rides off into history. An emotionally complex Western balanced with believable action, and an unusual outing for director Dmytryk. **Cast:** Henry Fonda, Anthony Quinn, Richard Widmark, Dorothy Malone, Dolores Michaels, Wallace Ford, Tom Drake, Richard Arlen. **Credits:** Dir: Edward Dmytryk; Prod: Edward Dmytryk; Writer: Robert Alan Aurthur; DP: Joseph MacDonald; Ed: Jack W. Holmes; Prod Design: Lyle Wheeler; Composer: Leigh Harline; Art Director: Herman A. Blumenthal. Color, 122 min. **VHS**

The War Lord

(1965) Universal

Heston stars as Chrysagon (in one of his personal favorite roles), an 11th-century Norman knight and war lord, who falls in love with a peasant girl (Forsyth) who is already engaged to the son of the tribe's chieftain. This sets the stage for betrayal, bloody battles, murder, and forbidden love as Heston and Forsyth vow never to part. Carefully crafted historical drama. **Cast:** Charlton Heston, Richard Boone, Rosemary Forsyth, Guy Stockwell, Niall MacGinnis, Henry Wilcoxon, James Farentino, Maurice Evans. **Credits:** Dir: Franklin J. Schaffner; Prod: Walter Seltzer; Writer: John Collier, Millard Kaufman; Story: Leslie Stevens; DP: Russell Metty; Ed: Folmar Blangsted; Composer: Jerome Moross; Art Director: Alexander Golitzen, Henry Bumstead. Color, 121 min. **VHS, LASER**

War of the Wildcats

(1943) Republic

Wayne plays a cowboy who battles with Dekker, an oil tycoon, for drilling rights on Indian lands in Oklahoma during the oil boom days. They also feud over the heart of Scott. The terrific wagon chase through flaming oil fields was directed by legendary stunt man Yakima Canutt. Evans's first Western: she went on to greater fame as Roy Rogers's sweetheart. **Cast:** John Wayne, Albert Dekker, Martha Scott, George "Gabby" Hayes, Marjorie Rambeau, Dale Evans, Grant Withers, Sidney Blackmer. **Credits:** Dir: Albert Rogell; Prod: Robert North; Writer: Ethel Hill, Eleanore Griffin, Thomson Burtis; DP: Jack Marta; Ed: Ernest Nims; Composer: Walter Scharf; Art Director: Russell Kimball. B&W, 102 min. **VHS**

The War of the Worlds

(1953) Paramount

H. G. Wells's 1898 novella of Martian invasion terrified radio audiences with Orson Welles's Mercury Theater production (1938) and this film adaptation continues to be a science-fiction favorite. Special-effects maestro Pal set the screen version in the U.S. (just as Welles did) as Martians looking for a new home land in the desert in what appear to be meteors and make a worldwide assault, easily defeating the human weapons, until they encounter a microscopic line of defense. Russian director Sergey Eisenstein was briefly considered for the project! Academy Award Nominations: 3, including Best Sound Recording; Best Editing. **Academy Awards:** Best Visual Effects. **Cast:** Gene Barry, Ann Robinson, Les Tremayne, Jack Kruschen, Houseley Stevenson, Paul Frees, Henry Brandon, Pierre Cressoy. **Credits:** Dir: Byron Haskin; Prod: George Pal; Writer: Barre Lyndon; Story: H. G. Wells; DP: George Barnes; Ed: Everett Douglas; Composer: Leith Stevens; Art Director: Hal Pereira, Albert Nozaki; SFX: Gordon Jennings, Paul Lerpae, Wallace Kelly, Ivyl Burks, Jan Domela, Irmin Roberts, Walter Hoffman, Chesley Bonestell. Color, 88 min. VHS, LASER

The Warriors
(1979) Paramount
Action-master Hill's opera of urban lawlessness follows New York City street gangs as they try to form one massive army of the night. When a double-cross killing gets pinned on the Warriors, the gang fights its way back to their Coney Island home turf. Atmospheric, stylized look at the street brutality that dehumanizes teenagers. **Cast:** Michael Beck, James Remar, Deborah Van Valkenburgh, Thomas Waites, David Harris, David Kelly, Lynne Thigpen, Robert Wightman. **Credits:** Dir: Walter Hill; Prod: Lawrence Gordon; Writer: David Shaber, Walter Hill; Story: Sol Yurick; DP: Andrew Laszlo; Ed: David Holden; Composer: Barry Devorzon. Color, 94 min. VHS, LASER

The War Wagon
(1967) Universal
Old hands Wayne and Douglas give this action-packed Western a wry humor. A daring rancher and an egocentric gunslinger put aside their differences in order to rob a ruthless cattle baron of his payroll and overcome an Indian attack and the defense by a "war wagon" bristling with gunmen. **Cast:** John Wayne, Kirk Douglas, Howard Keel, Robert Walker, Keenan Wynn, Bruce Cabot, Joanna Barnes, Valora Noland. **Credits:** Dir: Burt Kennedy; Prod: Marvin Schwartz; Writer: Clair Huffaker; DP: William Clothier; Ed: Harry Gerstad; Composer: Dimitri Tiomkin; Art Director: Alfred Sweeney. Color, 111 min. VHS, LASER, DVD

Washington Merry-Go-Round
(1932) Columbia
Tracy plays Button Gwinnett Brown, a descendant of three Georgia signers

War of the Worlds (1953)

of the Declaration of Independence, and an honest politician whose temporary defeats at the hands of the evil bosses will not deter him from his duty. Helped by an elderly, honest senator and the senator's cute granddaughter, Tracy cleans up the capitol. Interesting mostly as a later effort by renowned director Cruze from the pen of Swerling. **Cast:** Lee Tracy, Constance Cummings, Walter Connolly, Alan Dinehart, Arthur Vinton, Arthur Hoyt, Berton Churchill, Frank Sheridan, Clay Clement, Clarence Muse. **Credits:** Dir: James Cruze; Prod: James Cruze; Writer: Jo Swerling; Story: Maxwell Anderson; Ed: Richard Cahoon. B&W, 78 min.

Washington Story
(1952) MGM
A cub reporter (Neal) gets an assignment to write a puffy, flattering magazine feature about politicians, but is really looking for skeletons in the closet of earnest congressman Johnson. When she realizes that he really is as honest and hardworking as he appears, she falls in love with him. Eventually she's forced to choose between her heart and her desire to get the "big story" when the political heat gets turned up. Filmed on location in the capital and at the Pentagon. **Cast:** Van Johnson, Patricia Neal, Philip Ober, Louis Calhern, Sidney Blackmer, Elizabeth Patterson, Jimmy Fox, Raymond Greenleaf, Gregory Marshall. **Credits:** Dir: Robert Pirosh; Prod: Dore Schary; Writer: Robert Pirosh; DP: John Alton; Ed:

John Dunning, John Durant; Composer: Conrad Salinger; Art Director: Daniel B. Cathcart, Cedric Gibbons. B&W, 81 min.

Watch on the Rhine
(1943) Warner Bros.
In this well-made adaptation of Hellman's play, Davis and Lukas are German anti-Nazi underground leaders who flee the country, only to be hurled back into danger when suspected by Nazi agents operating in the U.S. One of the first American films to present the dangers of fascist thought, this benefits from performances by the leads. Hellman teamed with her companion Hammett for the screen adaptation. Golden Globe for Best Actor: Paul Lukas. Academy Award Nominations: 4, including Best Picture; Best Screenplay. **Academy Awards:** Best Actor: Paul Lukas. Irving G. Thalberg Memorial Award. **Cast:** Bette Davis, Paul Lukas, Geraldine Fitzgerald, Beulah Bondi, George Coulouris, Donald Woods, Henry Daniell, Donald Buka. **Credits:** Dir: Herman Shumlin; Prod: Hal B. Wallis; Writer: Lillian Hellman, Dashiell Hammett; DP: Merritt Gerstad; Ed: Rudi Fehr; Composer: Max Steiner; Art Director: Carl Jules Weyl. B&W, 113 min. VHS

Waterloo Bridge
(1940) MGM
A heart-tugging wartime romance begins with officer Taylor's memories of the woman he loved and lost. Just before he departs for the trenches of WWI, Taylor meets and falls for balle-

rina Leigh. She loses her position to bid him adieu, and later, in desperate straits, sinks to prostitution, walking the Waterloo Bridge. There, after the war, she encounters Taylor, who she believed had been killed. She hides her new profession and picks up their life anew though she comes to believe all will resurface. Leigh gives a heartfelt performance (perhaps fueled by her new romance with Laurence Olivier, which followed on the heels of her success in *Gone With the Wind* (1939). Academy Award Nominations: Best (Black-and-White) Cinematography; Best Original Score. **Cast:** Vivien Leigh, Robert Taylor, Lucile Watson, Virginia Field, Leo G. Carroll, Steffi Duna, Leonard Mudie, C. Aubrey Smith. **Credits:** Dir: Mervyn LeRoy; Prod: Sidney Franklin; Writer: S. N. Behrman; DP: Joseph Ruttenberg; Ed: George Boemler; Prod Design: Cedric Gibbons; Composer: Herbert Stothart. B&W, 109 min. **VHS, LASER**

The Watermelon Man
(1970) Columbia
Biting (and funny) social satire and the first studio effort from black filmmaker Van Peebles concerns a white bigot who wakes one morning to find himself transformed into a black man (both played to great effect by Cambridge). **Cast:** Godfrey Cambridge, Estelle Parsons, Howard Caine, D'Urville Martin, Paul Williams, Mantan Moreland, Kay Kimberly, Kay E. Kuter. **Credits:** Dir: Melvin Van Peebles; Prod: John B. Bennett; Writer: Herman Raucher; DP: Wallace Kelley; Ed: Carl Kress; Composer: Melvin Van Peebles; Art Director: Malcolm Bert, Sydney Litwack. Color, 97 min. **VHS, LASER**

Wattstax
(1973) Columbia
This is a documentary capturing the all-black music festival "Wattstax," which took place in the Los Angeles Coliseum on August 20, 1972. Richard Pryor provides a comic introduction, and the music ranges from Gospel and rhythm and blues to soul and the blues. Dialogues and discussions are intercut with performances, providing candid insights into the black experience of the early '70s. **Cast:** Richard Pryor, Ted Lange, Rufus Thomas, Isaac Hayes. **Credits:** Dir: Mel Stuart; Prod: Larry Shaw, Mel Stuart; DP: Robert Marks, Jose Mignone, Roderick Young, Larry Clark, John A. Alonzo; Ed: Robert Lambert; Composer: Jerry Manning. Color, 102 min.

Way Back Home
(1932) RKO
Based on Lord's radio serial, this RKO drama deals with the problems of a Maine preacher as he attempts to shelter a boy from the effects of living with his alcoholic father. Notable mostly for an early appearance by an unknown Davis. **Cast:** Bette Davis, Phillips Lord, Frank Albertson, Oscar Apfel, Stanley Fields, Dorothy Peterson, Frankie Darro. **Credits:** Dir: William A. Seiter; Prod: Pandro S. Berman; Writer: Jane Murfin; DP: J. Roy Hunt; Composer: Max Steiner; Art Director: Max Ree. B&W, 81 min. **VHS**

Way Down East
(1920) United Artists
This Griffith silent melodrama (and the first time he had worked from a scenario developed by another) ranks second only to his *Birth of a Nation* (1915) in importance. The story follows a poor woman (Gish) trapped by a vicious scoundrel (Sherman) into a sham marriage so he can have his way with her. He leaves her alone and pregnant. Scorned as a now-unwed mother and grieving for her dead infant, she finally attracts the interest of proper Squire Bartlett (Barthlemess) and his family, but she can't let herself love due to her troubled past. Barthlemess's father learns the truth and throws her out into the snow, where she drifts away on passing ice floes when she tries to cross a river. Barthlemess realizes he loves her and saves her with thrilling leaps from floe to floe. Poetic and heartbreaking. Remade in 1935 with Henry Fonda. **Cast:** Lillian Gish, Lowell Sherman, Richard Barthelmess, Mary Hay, Creighton Hale. **Credits:** Dir: D. W. Griffith; Prod: D. W. Griffith; Writer: Anthony Paul Kelly, D. W. Griffith, Joseph R. Grismer; DP: Billy Bitzer, Henrik Sortov; Ed: James Smith, Rose Smith; Composer: Louis Silvers, William F. Peters. B&W, 119 min. **VHS, DVD**

Way of a Gaucho
(1952) Fox
An unusual, and unusually beautiful, Western filmed by Tourneur in the high Andes. Calhoun agrees to serve a tour of duty in the Argentine military to avoid doing hard time behind bars but flees into the rugged mountains, where he raids trains making their way across the pampas. When he is eventually apprehended by his former commanding officer, the outlaw gaucho decides he has tempted fate too long and swears to go straight. **Cast:** Rory Calhoun, Gene Tierney, Richard

Boone, Hugh Marlowe, Everett Sloane, Enrique Chaico, Jorge Villoldo, Roland Dumas. **Credits:** Dir: Jacques Tourneur; Prod: Philip Dunne; Writer: Philip Dunne; Story: Herbert Childs; DP: Harry Jackson; Ed: Robert Fritch; Composer: Sol Kaplan, Alfred Newman; Art Director: Lyle Wheeler, Mark-Lee Kirk. Color, 91 min.

The Way to Love
(1933) Paramount
Chevalier plays a Paris vagabond who advertises the services of a love doctor but who would give anything to become a tour guide and pursue his relationship with Dvorak, a circus performer who acts as a target for a knife-thrower. For Chevalier fans only. Songs include "Lover of Paree," "Way to Love," and "Lucky Guy." **Cast:** Maurice Chevalier, Ann Dvorak, Edward Everett Horton, Arthur Pierson, Minna Gombell, Blanche Frederici, Douglass Dumbrille, John Miljan, Sidney Toler, George Hagen. **Credits:** Dir: Norman Taurog; Prod: Benjamin Glazer; Writer: Gene Fowler, Jr., Benjamin Glazer, Claude Binvon, Frank Butler; DP: Charley Lang; Ed: William Shea; Prod Design: Hans Dreier; Composer: Nathaniel Finston. B&W, 80 min.

The Way West
(1967) United Artists
There has been no more heartfelt chronicler of America's western migration than author Guthrie, and here one of his best-known works gets a less-than-majestic treatment. But old hands Mitchum, Douglas, and Widmark make the proceedings interesting as a wagon train rolls slowly on the Oregon Trail through Indian attacks and tragic romances. **Cast:** Kirk Douglas, Robert Mitchum, Richard Widmark, Lola Albright, Michael Witney, Stubby Kaye, Sally Field, Jack Elam. **Credits:** Dir: Andrew V. McLaglen; Prod: Harold Hecht; Writer: Ben Maddow, Mitchell Lindemann; Story: A. B. Guthrie; DP: William Clothier; Ed: Otto Lovering; Prod Design: Ted Haworth; Composer: Bronislau Kaper. Color, 122 min. **VHS**

The Way We Were
(1973) Columbia
A star-crossed love between opposites captured the hearts of romantics. Campus radical Streisand meets preppy Redford in college and sparks fly, an attachment that would be enflamed and then quenched through war, marriage, children, Hollywood, and divorce. Redford at his eye-twinkling best and Streisand convincing as the

strident, but lovable, activist. This began a fruitful collaboration between Redford and director Pollack that included *Out of Africa* (1985). Academy Award Nominations: 6, including Best Actress: Barbra Streisand. **Academy Awards:** Best Song; Best Original Dramatic Score. **Cast:** Barbra Streisand, Robert Redford, Bradford Dillman, Murray Hamilton, Lois Chiles, Patrick O'Neal, Herb Edelman, Roy Jenson. **Credits:** Dir: Sydney Pollack; Prod: Ray Stark; Writer: Arthur Laurents; DP: Harry Stradling; Ed: Margaret Booth; Prod Design: Stephen Grimes; Composer: Marvin Hamlisch. Color, 118 min. **VHS, LASER**

We Are Not Alone
(1939) Warner Bros.
In this tragic romance, Muni (in one of his favorite roles) portrays a doctor in an English country town at the outbreak of WWI who treats a despairing Austrian dancer (Bryan), and hires her as a nanny for his son. This sparks conflict with his already difficult wife, Robson, who retaliates by shipping the boy off to his uncle. The mother accidentally dies when the son unknowingly mixes up two medicines, and the Great War breaks out, placing the dancer in danger because of her origins. Muni helps her, and they are falsely accused of the murder of Muni's wife, an accusation that can only be disputed by his son, who Muni swears to silence. From the Hilton novel. **Cast:** Paul Muni, Jane Bryan, Flora Robson, Raymond Severn, Una O'Connor, Alan Napier, James Stephenson, Montagu Love, Henry Daniell, Stanley Logan. **Credits:** Dir: Edmund Goulding; Prod: Henry Blanke; Writer: Milton Krims; Story: James Hilton; DP: Tony Gaudio; Ed: Warren Low; Composer: Max Steiner; SFX: Byron Haskins, H. F. Koenekamp. B&W, 112 min.

A Wedding
(1978) Fox
A massive cast in a trademark Altman narrative depends on fleeting moments gathered from overlapping stories. A wedding between southern gentry and a wealthy family with Mob ties offers more than enough opportunity for slamming doors, bungled affairs, and flamboyant performances. Gish's 100th screen appearance. **Cast:** Desi Arnaz, Jr., Carol Burnett, Geraldine Chaplin, Howard Duff, Mia Farrow, Vittorio Gassman, Lillian Gish, Paul Dooley. **Credits:** Dir: Robert Altman; Prod: Robert Altman; Writer: John Considine, Patricia Resnick, Allan Nicholls,

Robert Altman; DP: Charles Rosher; Ed: Tony Lombardo; Composer: John Hotchkis. Color, 125 min. **VHS**

The Wedding Night
(1935) United Artists
A troubled writer (Cooper) and his wife (Vinson) find seclusion at a Connecticut farmhouse after his latest manuscript receives a lackluster reaction. Cooper, looking for a new theme, becomes intrigued with Polish farmgirl Sten and the simplicity of her life. His wife soon returns to the city while the attraction grows between the writer and the farmgirl, and his new novel is based on her life. Forced into an arranged marriage with Bellamy by her father, she vows to fight it, though the writer's wife returns. Sten gets married, but fends off Bellamy on their wedding night by implying she has been with the writer, forcing a violent and revealing confrontation. Another of Goldwyn's efforts to elevate Sten to stardom. **Cast:** Milla Davenport, Gary Cooper, Anna Sten, Helen Vinson, Ralph Bellamy, Sig Rumann, Leonid Snegoff, Elinor Wesselhoeft. **Credits:** Dir: King Vidor; Prod: Samuel Goldwyn; Writer: Edith Fitzgerald, Edwin H. Knopf; DP: Gregg Toland; Ed: Stuart Heisler; Prod Design: Richard Day; Composer: Alfred Newman. B&W, 82 min.

Weekend at the Waldorf
(1945) MGM
An updating of *Grand Hotel* (predating Neil Simon's *Plaza Suite*) follows romantic mix-ups between Rogers and Pidgeon and Turner and Johnson with music by Xavier Cugat and humor courtesy of Benchley. No better than expected, but good fun. **Cast:** Ginger Rogers, Lana Turner, Walter Pidgeon, Van Johnson, Edward Arnold, Phyllis Thaxter, Keenan Wynn, Robert Benchley, Leon Ames, Porter Hall. **Credits:** Dir: Robert Z. Leonard; Prod: Arthur Hornblow, Jr.; Writer: Samuel Spewack, Bella Spewack, Guy Bolton; DP: Robert Planck; Ed: Robert J. Kern; Prod Design: Cedric Gibbons; Composer: Johnny Green. B&W, 130 min. **VHS**

Weekend in Havana
(1941) Fox
Classic-period Fox musical has shopgirl Faye getting the grand tour of Havana after her cruise ship runs aground. Payne guides her through the lively nightlife of the pre-Castro Carribean paradise, where she meets gambler Romero and his nightclubsinger girlfriend Miranda. Romance and singing ensue, including

"Romance and Rhumba," "Weekend in Havana," and "Tropical Magic." **Cast:** Alice Faye, John Payne, Carmen Miranda, Cesar Romero, Sheldon Leonard, George Barbier, Billy Gilbert, Leonid Kinskey, Chris-Pin Martin. **Credits:** Dir: Walter Lang; Prod: William LeBaron; Writer: Karl Tunberg, Darrell Ware; DP: Ernest Palmer; Ed: Allen McNeil; Composer: Mack Gordon, Harry Warren; Art Director: Richard Day. Color, 80 min. **VHS**

Wee Willie Winkie
(1937) Fox
Little Miss Sunshine directed by Ford! Temple and her widowed mother (Lang) travel to India to visit her grandfather (Smith), an officer in the British Army, and she becomes their little mascot. She soon befriends an Indian prisoner (Romero) who was the leader of the rebelling natives and eventually negotiates for peace between the warring factions. Based on an 1889 story by Rudyard Kipling. Academy Award Nomination for Best Interior Decoration. **Cast:** Shirley Temple, Cesar Romero, Victor McLaglen, C. Aubrey Smith, June Lang, Michael Whalen, Constance Collier, Douglas Scott. **Credits:** Dir: John Ford; Prod: Gene Markey; Writer: Ernest Pascal; DP: Arthur Miller; Ed: Walter Thompson; Composer: Louis Silvers; Art Director: William S. Darling. B&W, 103 min. **VHS**

Welcome Stranger
(1947) Paramount
Bing plays an affable young doctor (who loves to sing) who comes to a small town and meets with suspicion until he saves the old doctor (Fitzgerald) who runs a local clinic and four boys laid low with a mysterious illness. Crosby and Fitzgerald (the *Going My Way* team) together again for one more heartwarming outing. **Cast:** Bing Crosby, Barry Fitzgerald, Joan Caulfield, Wanda Hendrix, Frank Faylen, Elizabeth Patterson, Robert Shayne, Larry Young, Don Beddoe, Percy Kilbride. **Credits:** Dir: Elliott Nugent; Prod: Sol C. Siegel; Writer: Arthur Sheekman; DP: Lionel Lindon; Ed: Everett Douglas; Prod Design: Hans Dreier; Composer: Robert Emmett Dolan. B&W, 107 min. **VHS**

Welcome to Hard Times
(1967) MGM
In a bleak revisionist Western, Fonda, the mayor of Hard Times, is unwilling to stand up to local menace Ray, who murders indiscriminately and sets the entire town on fire. The town rebuilds, and when Ray comes around again,

Fonda finds the courage to gun him down. Great supporting cast; based on a novel by Doctorow. **Cast:** Henry Fonda, Janice Paige, John Anderson, Warren Oates, Fay Spain, Edgar Buchanan, Aldo Ray, Elisha Cook, Jr., Lon Chaney, Jr., Denver Pyle, Keenan Wynn. **Credits:** Dir: Burt Kennedy; Prod: Max E. Youngstein, David Karr; Writer: Burt Kennedy; Story: E. L. Doctorow; DP: Harry Stradling; Ed: Aaron Stell; Prod Design: George W. Davis, Carl Anderson; Composer: Harry Sukman. Color, 103 min.

We Live Again
(1934) United Artists
Set in 1875 and based on Tolstoy's *Resurrection*, this stirring melodrama depicts the redemption of a callow Russian nobleman (March) and the servant girl (Sten) he grew up with, then seduced and betrayed in his youth. When he encounters her later in a courtroom, after their child dies and she has sunk to prostitution, accused of a crime she did not commit, he makes a noble sacrifice. Note the contributions by Sturges, playwright Anderson, and author Wilder, and the cinematography by Toland. A first-class literary drama handled with typical elegance by Mamoulian. **Cast:** Anna Sten, Fredric March, Jane Baxter, C. Aubrey Smith, Ethel Griffies, Gwendolyn Logan, Jessie Ralph, Sam Jaffe, Cecil Cunningham, Jessie Arnold. **Credits:** Dir: Rouben Mamoulian; Prod: Samuel Goldwyn; Writer: Leonard Praskins, Preston Sturges, Maxwell Anderson, Thornton Wilder; Story: Leo Tolstoy; DP: Gregg Toland; Ed: Otho Lovering; Composer: Alfred Newman; Art Director: Richard Day, Sergei Soudeikin. B&W, 85 min.

The Well
(1951) United Artists
An incisive study of racial bitterness and crowd psychology as a black child disappears and then is discovered in a dry well. Construction foreman Morgan is pinned with kidnapping her, but then faces a test of conscience when he's proved innocent and his expertise is needed for the child's rescue. Academy Award Nominations: Best Story and Screenplay; Best Film Editing. **Cast:** Richard Rober, Harry Morgan, Barry Kelley, Christine Larson, Maidie Norman, Ernest Anderson, Richard Simmons. **Credits:** Dir: Russell Rouse, Leo Popkin; Prod: Clarence Greene; Writer: Russell Rouse, Clarence Greene; DP: Ernest Laszlo; Ed: Chester Schaeffer; Composer: Dimitri Tiomkin. B&W, 85 min. **VHS**

Wells Fargo
(1937) Paramount
The vast, episodic history of America's western expansion is told in the story of its expanding communications and transportation industries. Nineteenth-century America comes to life through the episodes depicting the Overland Mail, the Pony Express, Indian Wars, the Civil War, and, finally, the uniting of the country by the railroads. While Wells Fargo founder O'Neill dispatches trusty aid Ramsay Mackay (McCrea) through action-packed adventures, McCrea and his wife Dee (also man and wife offscreen) must heal the wound to their marriage the Civil War brings. Academy Award Nomination: Best Sound. **Cast:** Joel McCrea, Bob Burns, Frances Dee, Lloyd Nolan, Henry O'Neill, Mary Nash, Ralph Morgan, John Brown, Porter Hall, Jack Clark. **Credits:** Dir: Frank Lloyd; Prod: Frank Lloyd, Howard Estabrook; Writer: Gerald Geraghty, Frederick J. Jackson, Paul Schofield Jackson; Story: Stuart N. Lake; DP: Theodor Sparkuhl; Ed: Hugh Bennett; Prod Design: Hans Dreier; Composer: Victor Young. B&W, 115 min.

We're No Angels
(1955) Paramount
Master of suspenseful atmosphere Curtiz creates a comic crime caper that features Bogart in a rare light-hearted role. Bogart, Ray, and Ustinov escape from Devil's Island during the holiday season, and prepare to rob and kill a family that runs a clothing store. Mistaken for repairmen, Carroll welcomes the dastardly trio and charms them into sticking around and helping out with his business. All goes well until greedy uncle Rathbone shows up for an audit, but the new storekeepers know how to dispatch with his sort. A cheery wink at Bogart's tough-guy persona. **Cast:** Humphrey Bogart, Aldo Ray, Joan Bennett, Peter Ustinov, Basil Rathbone, Leo G. Carroll, John Baer, Gloria Talbott. **Credits:** Dir: Michael Curtiz; Prod: Pat Duggan; Writer: Ranald MacDougall; DP: Loyal Griggs; Ed: Arthur Schmidt; Composer: Frederick Hollander; Art Director: Hal Pereira. Color, 106 min. **VHS, LASER**

We're Not Dressing
(1934) Paramount
Deckhand Crosby gets the upper hand on the upper classes when Lombard's yacht runs aground. Previously responsible only for walking the heiress's pet bear, Crosby takes charge of the survival tactics, while pitching woo with

Lombard, and singing a little, too. Burns and Allen happen by as botanists exploring the island. A satirical, musical adaptation of J. M. Barrie's *The Admirable Crichton* that features "Let's Play House" and "Once in a Blue Moon." **Cast:** Bing Crosby, Carole Lombard, Ethel Merman, Ray Milland, George Burns, Gracie Allen, Leon Errol. **Credits:** Dir: Norman Taurog; Prod: Benjamin Glazer; Writer: Horace Jackson, Francis Martin; DP: Charles Lang; Ed: Stuart Heisler; Prod Design: Hans Dreier. B&W, 74 min. **VHS, LASER**

Werewolf of London
(1935) Universal
This is the original Universal werewolf movie (coming a full six years before Chaney howled in *The Wolf Man*) and a classic in its own right. Renowned botanist Hull discovers a rare Tibetan flower that blooms only under the full moon and has to fight off a werewolf, who bites him in the attack, for possession of the bloom. Once back in London, he receives a visit from Oland, who tells him the flower can cure the curse of the werewolf. Oland also reveals that he was the werewolf who bit him in Tibet and that Hull must prepare for a transformation at the next full moon. Hull struggles with his murderous side as he tries to get the flower to blossom before he kills again. A great, overlooked horror chiller. **Cast:** Henry Hull, Warner Oland, Valerie Hobson, Lester Matthews, Spring Byington, Clark Williams, J. M. Kerrigan, Charlotte Granville. **Credits:** Dir: Stuart Walker; Prod: Robert Harris; Writer: John Colton; DP: Charles Stumar; Ed: Russell Schoengarth; Art Director: Albert S. D'Agostino. B&W, 75 min. **VHS, LASER**

The Westerner
(1940) United Artists
An enduring Western with a memorable central performance by Brennan. Judge Roy Bean (known as the hanging judge) ruled his western domain with a despotic hand. When Cooper comes into his courtroom, he knows the deadly outcome, and uses his wits to escape by promising a lock of hair from the judge's dream, Lily Langtry. He also takes sides with the homesteaders (including Davenport) against the judge, which leads to a rousing final showdown in a gaslit theater. Note the cinematography by Toland. Debuts for Andrews and Tucker. Academy Award Nominations: 3, including Best Original Story. **Academy Awards:** Best Supporting Actor: Walter Bren-

nan. **Cast:** Gary Cooper, Walter Brennan, Doris Davenport, Dana Andrews, Paul Hurst, Chill Wills, Charles Halton, Forrest Tucker. **Credits:** Dir: William Wyler; Prod: Samuel Goldwyn; Writer: Jo Swerling, Niven Busch; Story: Stuart N. Lake; DP: Gregg Toland; Ed: Daniel Mandell; Prod Design: James Basevi; Composer: Alfred Newman, Dimitri Tiomkin. B&W, 100 min. **VHS, LASER**

Western Union
(1941) Fox
Lang's loving depiction of the old West follows the "singing wire" of the telegraph as Western Union men rush to complete their job so the Union can stay in touch with the western territories. Scott, a former outlaw looking for a way back to the right side of the law, signs on as a scout and finds himself caught between his new role and his outlaw brother (MacLane), a Confederate sympathizer. Stirring action, and one of Lang's favorites of his own films. **Cast:** Randolph Scott, Vance Shaw, Robert Young, Barton MacLane, Virginia Gilmore, Chill Wills, Russell Hicks, Victor Kilian. **Credits:** Dir: Fritz Lang; Prod: Harry Joe Brown; Story: Robert Carson; DP: Edward Cronjager; Ed: Robert Bischoff; Composer: David Buttolph; Art Director: Richard Day. Color, 95 min. **VHS**

The West Point Story
(1950) Warner Bros.
In a song-and-dance role, Cagney is a Broadway producer who stages a show written by a plebe (MacRae) at West Point and gets a taste of the harsh Academy life. Jimmy's in fine form, and Day has a turn as a star who entices MacRae to go AWOL in Hollywood. Academy Award Nomination for Best Scoring of a Musical Picture. **Cast:** James Cagney, Virginia Mayo, Doris Day, Gordon MacRae, Gene Nelson, Alan Hale, Roland Winters, Wilton Graff. **Credits:** Dir: Roy Del Ruth; Prod: Louis F. Edelman; Writer: John Monks, Charles Hoffman, Irving Wallace; DP: Sid Hickox; Ed: Owen Marks; Prod Design: Charles H. Clarke. Color, 113 min. **VHS**

West Side Story
(1961) United Artists
This is a jumping, heart-throbbing leap forward for film musicals, full of melodies you know by heart, frenetic dancing, and a time-tested romance. Based loosely on *Romeo and Juliet*, Laurents's stage production follows two New York street gangs and the ill-starred romance between Wood and

Beymer that crosses the line between them. Moreno sparkles and Wood's luminous beauty would have any young gangster singing her name. Robbins clashed with Wise (who also brought stage smash *The Sound of Music* to the screen) and choreographed only four numbers (including "I Feel Pretty" and "America") but they're athletic, balletic stunners. The immortal songs (by Bernstein and Sondheim) also include "Maria," "The Jet Song," "Officer Krupke," and "Tonight." Selected for the National Film Registry and winner of Golden Globes for Best Supporting Actor: George Chakiris; Best Supporting Actress: Rita Moreno; Best Motion Picture, Musical. Academy Award Nominations: 11, including Best (Adapted) Screenplay. **Academy Awards:** Best Picture; Best Director; Best Supporting Actor: George Chakiris; Best Supporting Actress: Rita Moreno; Best Film Editing; Best Sound; Best Color Cinematography; Best Scoring of a Musical; Best Costume Design (Color); Best Art Direction—Set Decoration (Color). **Cast:** Natalie Wood, Richard Beymer, Rita Moreno, Russ Tamblyn, George Chakiris, Simon Oakland, Tony Mordente, Eliot Feld. **Credits:** Dir: Robert Wise, Jerome Robbins; Prod: Robert Wise; Writer: Ernest Lehman; Story: Arthur Laurents; DP: Daniel Fapp; Ed: Thomas Stanford; Prod Design: Boris Leven; Composer: Leonard Bernstein, Stephen Sondheim. Color, 155 min. **VHS, LASER, DVD**

Westward Ho
(1935) Republic
The Duke sings! In this early appearance, Wayne forms a warbling vigilante group to catch a band of vicious outlaws. While on the trail, he comes face-to-face with his brother, the leader of the gang that kidnapped him many years before. **Cast:** John Wayne, Sheila Bromley, Frank McGlynn, Jack Curtis, Yakima Canutt, Hank Bell, Dick Jones, Glenn Strange. **Credits:** Dir: Robert Bradbury; Prod: Paul Malvern; Writer: Lindsley Parsons; DP: Archie Stout; Ed: Carl Pierson. B&W, 61 min. **VHS**

Westward the Women
(1951) MGM
An unusual Western from old hand Wellman depicts the arduous wagon-train passage of 150 women from Chicago to California. Most of the hazards along the way are posed by the men hired to protect them, and wagon master Taylor has his hands full dispatching the love-struck cowhands while fighting Indians and battling the

elements. The women emerge as real Western heroes. **Cast:** Robert Taylor, Denise Darcel, John McIntire, Hope Emerson, Julie Bishop, Beverly Dennis, Marilyn Erskine, Frankie Darro. **Credits:** Dir: William Wellman; Prod: Dore Schary; Writer: Charles Schnee; DP: William Mellor; Ed: James E. Newcom; Prod Design: Cedric Gibbons; Composer: Jeff Alexander. B&W, 118 min. **VHS**

Westworld
(1973) MGM
Tenderfoot businessmen Brolin and Benjamin look down the business end of the wrong gun when the Western-themed amusement park they visit goes murderously out of control. Brynner is a steely-eyed automaton gunned down by Benjamin who returns for unprogrammed vengeance. Writer-director Crichton would later create another amusement park out of control with *Jurassic Park* (1993). **Cast:** Yul Brynner, James Brolin, Richard Benjamin, Norman Bartold, Alan Oppenheimer, Victoria Shaw, Jared Martin, Dick Van Patten. **Credits:** Dir: Michael Crichton; Prod: Paul Lazarus; Writer: Michael Crichton; DP: Gene Polito; Ed: David Bretherton; Composer: Fred Karlin; Art Director: Herman A. Blumenthal. Color, 90 min. **VHS, LASER, DVD**

We Were Strangers
(1949) Columbia
Huston's suspenseful thriller follows Garfield, a Cuban-born American citizen, who is returning to his native country to join his people's revolution that resulted in the 1933 overthrow of Cuban president Machado. He and three fellow conspirators (including Jones) band together to build a tunnel under a Havana cemetery where they will detonate a bomb as members of the government attend a state funeral. But the family of the assassinated man decides against burying the victim in that particular cemetery and the plot is discovered by police. Despised by both left- and right-wingers, but interesting for Huston's treatment of politics mixed with adventure. Based on the novel *Rough Sketch* by Sylvester. **Cast:** Jose Perez, John Garfield, Jennifer Jones, David Bond, Wally Cassell, Robert Tafur, Paul Monte, Ramon Novarro, Gilbert Roland, Tito Renaldo. **Credits:** Dir: John Huston; Prod: Sam Spiegel; Writer: John Huston, Peter Viertel; DP: Russell Metty; Ed: Al Clark; Composer: George Antheil; Art Director: Cary Odell. B&W, 106 min.

What a Life

(1939) Paramount

The first of the Henry Aldrich movies was written by Wilder and Brackett, and starred Cooper as the adolescent Henry who has a talent for trouble. Jackie's dad is a Phi Beta Kappa Princetonian, and poor Cooper struggles to live up to that standard, though his grades are a mess and he's always in hot water. **Cast:** Dorothy Stickney, Kathleen Lockhart, Jackie Cooper, Betty Field, John Howard, Janice Logan, Vaughan Glaser, Lionel Stander, Hedda Hopper, James Corner. **Credits:** Dir: Jay Theodore Reed; Prod: Jay Theodore Reed; Writer: Charles Brackett, Billy Wilder; Story: Clifford Goldsmith; DP: Victor Milner; Ed: William Shea; Art Director: Hans Dreier, A. Earl Hedrick. B&W, 75 min.

What a Way to Go!

(1964) Fox

MacLaine plays a widow who is the victim of the strangest of curses: whenever she marries, her husband suddenly gets fabulously rich and then kicks the bucket. The marvelously overblown production—half a million dollars were spent on MacLaine's costumes alone—unfolds in a series of flashbacks on the psychiatrist's couch, where each one of her affairs (with a devastatingly debonair lineup of movie hunks) is presented as a spoof on a different movie genre. In the end, she convinces the IRS to take all her money, and she weds Martin, a poor janitor. Academy Award Nominations: Best Art Direction; Best Costume Design. **Cast:** Shirley MacLaine, Paul Newman, Robert Mitchum, Dean Martin, Gene Kelly, Bob Cummings, Dick Van Dyke, Reginald Gardiner, Margaret Dumont, Lou Nova. **Credits:** Dir: J. Lee Thompson; Prod: Arthur P. Jacobs; Writer: Betty Comden, Adolph Green, Gwen Davis; DP: Leon Shamroy; Ed: Marjorie Fowler; Prod Design: Jack Marton Smith, Ted Haworth; Composer: Nelson Riddle; Costumes: Edith Head. Color, 111 min.

What Ever Happened to Aunt Alice?

(1969) Cinerama

Gordon goes sleuthing when her friend and maid goes missing after starting work for Page. Page is an elderly widow having trouble making ends meet . . . and keeping maids. Gordon goes in disguise to investigate. Produced by Aldrich, the creator of *What Ever Happened to Baby Jane?* (1962)

and *Hush, Hush Sweet Charlotte* (1965). **Cast:** Geraldine Page, Ruth Gordon, Rosemary Forsyth, Robert Fuller, Mildred Dunnock, Peter Bonerz, Richard Angarola, Claire Kelly. **Credits:** Dir: Lee H. Katzin; Prod: Robert Aldrich; Writer: Theodore Apstein; DP: Joseph Biroc; Ed: Frank J. Urioste; Composer: Gerald Fried; Costumes: Renie; Art Director: William Glasgow. Color, 101 min. **VHS**

What Ever Happened to Baby Jane?

(1962) Warner Bros.

The collision of classic movie stars Davis and Crawford is like matter and antimatter, resulting in a dark star of a movie thriller. Wicked satire of their own diva personas underlines the performances of the two stars as sisters who were once stars, Davis a cutesy child act named Baby Jane and Crawford a drama queen. Trapped for years in their house (Davis demented by the bottle, Crawford in a wheelchair from an accident seemingly caused by Davis) with only their maid (Norman) to separate them, their mutual antagonism explodes when Davis hears of Crawford's plan to sell the house and institutionalize her. By turns astonishing and grotesque, this is great fun for classic movie fans seeing the stars wink at their early careers and for glimpses of the stars in authentic early film roles. Academy Award Nominations: 5, including Best Actress: Bette Davis; Best Supporting Actor: Victor Buono; Best Cinematography (B&W). **Academy Awards:** Best Costume Design (B&W). **Cast:** Bette Davis, Joan Crawford, Victor Buono, Anna Lee, Maidie Norman, Marjorie Bennett, Dave Willock, Bert Freed. **Credits:** Dir: Robert Aldrich; Prod: Robert Aldrich; Writer: Lukas Heller; DP: Ernest Haller; Ed: Michael Luciano; Composer: Frank DeVol; Art Director: William Glasgow. B&W, 134 min. **VHS, LASER, DVD**

What Every Woman Knows

(1934) MGM

Hayes stars in an early sound version of a favorite story from the silent period. Hayes is neither beautiful nor glamorous, but as wife of the rising Scottish politician Aherne, she knows what every woman knows: that behind every good man is a better woman. Their marriage begins lovelessly and is tested when a sparkling aristocrat arrives on the scene, but Hayes's hand advances her husband's career, and he is left to decide which woman to admire. **Cast:** Helen Hayes,

Brian Aherne, Davison Clark, Leonid Kinsky, Edgar Norton, Fritzie Ridgeway, Madge Evans, Lucile Watson, Dudley Digges, Donald Crisp, David Torrence. **Credits:** Dir: Gregory La Cava; Writer: Nydia Westman, James Kevin McGuinness, John Meehan; DP: Charles Rosher; Ed: Blanche Sewell; Composer: Herbert Stothart; Art Director: Cedric Gibbons, Lansing C. Holden, Edwin B. Willis. B&W, 90 min.

What Price Glory?

(1952) Fox

Ford remakes a Raoul Walsh silent set in WWI France. An unusual war comedy (particularly from Ford!) finds Cagney and Dailey escorting a ragtag group up to the trenches and battling for the attention of a cafe owner's daughter, Calvet. Originally intended to be a musical, the final cut features two songs. **Cast:** James Cagney, Dan Dailey, Craig Hill, Corinne Calvet, William Demarest, Robert Wagner, Marisa Pavan, Max Showalter, James Gleason. **Credits:** Dir: John Ford; Prod: Sol C. Siegel; Writer: Henry Ephron, Phoebe Ephron; DP: Joseph MacDonald; Ed: Dorothy Spencer; Prod Design: Lyle Wheeler; Composer: Alfred Newman. Color, 111 min. **VHS**

What Price Hollywood?

(1932) RKO

Cukor's movie breakthrough was a film that producer Selznick considered to be fairly straight reportage of backstage Hollywood. Bennett, a waitress at the Brown Derby, convinces sozzled director Sherman to squire her around Hollywood and get her a screen test, a toe in the movie waters that leads to Oscars, romance, suicide, marriage, separation, and reconciliation. Cukor revisited the scene of this early success with the more melodramatic *A Star Is Born* (1954). Academy Award Nomination for Best Original Screenplay. **Cast:** Constance Bennett, Lowell Sherman, Neil Hamilton, Gregory Ratoff, Brooks Benedict, Louise Beavers, Eddie Anderson, Bryant Washburn. **Credits:** Dir: George Cukor; Prod: David O. Selznick; Writer: Jane Murfin; DP: Charles Rosher; Ed: Jack Kitchin; Prod Design: Carroll Clark; Composer: Max Steiner. B&W, 88 min. **VHS, LASER**

What's New, Pussycat?

(1965) United Artists

A swinging dose of '60s silliness with the first screen appearance (and screenplay) by Allen, as the nebbishy friend of Schneider, a lovely teacher who is just one of a long line of women hot on the trail of O'Toole, a French fashion-magazine editor. While O'Toole can't number his paramours, Allen, an "undresser" for chorus girls at the Crazy Horse saloon, is driven mad by his fruitless proximity to scantily clad dancers. Lounge lizards will want to check out the Bacharach-David songs and bachelor-pad decor throughout. Academy Award Nomination for Best Song ("What's New, Pussycat?"). **Cast:** Peter Sellers, Peter O'Toole, Romy Schneider, Paula Prentiss, Woody Allen, Capucine, Ursula Andress, Eddra Gale. **Credits:** Dir: Clive Donner; Prod: Charles K. Feldman; Writer: Woody Allen; DP: Jean Badal; Ed: Fergus McDonell; Composer: Burt Bacharach, Hal David; Art Director: Jacques Saulnier. Color, 110 min. VHS, LASER

What's the Matter with Helen?

(1971) United Artists
The mothers (Reynolds and Winters) of two murderers are hounded all the way to Hollywood where they open a school to train little Shirley Temples for the movies. When a mysterious visitor seems to bring back the past, Winters quickly dispatches him, a murderous act that, it turns out, she had practiced previously. A creepy thriller with aging actresses in the mode of *What Ever Happened to Baby Jane?* (1962). Academy Award Nomination for Best Costumes. **Cast:** Debbie Reynolds, Shelley Winters, Dennis Weaver, Agnes Moorehead, Michael MacLiammoir, Lee Jones, Robbie Morgan, Helen Winston. **Credits:** Dir: Curtis Harrington; Prod: George Edwards; Writer: Henry Farrell; DP: Lucien Ballard; Ed: William Reynolds; Composer: David Raksin; Art Director: Eugene Lourie. Color, 101 min. VHS

What's Up, Doc?

(1972) Warner Bros.
Director (and film historian) Bogdanovich's homage to the great screwball comedies of the '30s lifts the absentminded-professor-meets-madcap-girl routine from *Bringing Up Baby* (1938) and makes it his own. On his way to a musicologists' convention, mild-mannered O'Neal's suitcase full of rocks gets mixed up with flamboyant Streisand's valise. Chases and confusion ensue. Kahn's debut. **Cast:** Barbra Streisand, Ryan O'Neal, Madeline Kahn, Kenneth Mars, Austin Pendleton, Sorrell Booke, Stefan Gierasch, Mabel Albertson, Michael Murphy. **Credits:** Dir: Peter Bogdanovich; Prod: Peter Bogdanovich; Writer: Buck Henry,

David Newman, Robert Benton; Story: Peter Bogdanovich; DP: Laszlo Kovacs; Ed: Verna Fields; Prod Design: Polly Platt; Composer: Artie Butler. Color, 90 min. VHS, LASER

What's Up, Tiger Lily?

(1966) AIP
Allen makes egg salad of an actual Japanese spy film (*Kagi No Kagi*, or "Key of Keys") by dubbing one-liners in English, supposedly much of it improvised with then-wife Lasser and writing partner Rose. Allen, the self-described master of danger, spins a new story of the world being saved by one man's recipe for egg salad. A surreal, hilarious treat. Music (and appearance) by the Lovin' Spoonful. **Cast:** Woody Allen, Tatsuya Mihashi, Hana Miya, Tadao Nakamura, Louise Lasser, Mickey Rose, Frank Buxton, Len Maxwell. **Credits:** Dir: Woody Allen; Prod: Woody Allen; Writer: Kazuo Yamada, Woody Allen, Frank Buxton, Len Maxwell, Louise Lasser, Mickey Rose, Bryna Wilson, Julie Bennett; DP: Kazuo Yamada; Ed: Richard Krown; Composer: Jack Lewis. Color, 90 min. VHS, LASER

Wheeler and Woolsey

RKO produced 21 pictures starring the comedy team of Bert Wheeler and Robert Woolsey, and, fortunately for the studio, some of these— *Diplomaniacs* (1933); *Hips, Hips, Hooray* (1934); and *Cockeyed Cavaliers* (1934)—were among the most successful films of the 1930s. Wheeler, who had become a star in his own right, thanks to his role in Broadway's *The Ziegfeld Follies,* was introduced to his future partner in comedy by Flo Ziegfeld in 1927. The pair starred in the Broadway musical *Rio Rita,* which featured Wheeler as a man desperate to arrange a quickie divorce and Woolsey as his shady lawyer. The musical was so successful that RKO signed the comedians for the film version. Thus began a collaboration that would span nine years. The partnership came to a premature end with Robert Woolsey's untimely death in 1939.

Rio Rita *(1929)*
Dixiana *(1930)*
Half-Shot at Sunrise *(1930)*
Hook, Line, and Sinker *(1930)*
The Cuckoos *(1930)*
Caught Plastered *(1931)*
Cracked Nuts *(1931)*
Peach O'Reno *(1931)*
Hold 'em Jail *(1932)*
Girl Crazy *(1932)*

Diplomaniacs *(1933)*
So This Is Africa *(1933)*
Cockeyed Cavaliers *(1934)*
Hips, Hips, Hooray *(1934)*
Kentucky Kernels *(1934)*
The Nitwits *(1935)*
The Rainmakers *(1935)*
Mummy's Boys *(1936)*
Silly Billies *(1936)*
High Flyers *(1937)*
On Again—Off Again *(1937)*

The Wheeler Dealers

(1963) MGM
Wall Street gets a ribbing when a Texas oilman (Garner) pretends to be penniless and seeks investment advice from Remick. The "worthless" stock her boss (Backus) pushes on him repays millions when oil is discovered on the company's property. Garner gets the millions and the girl. **Cast:** Lee Remick, James Garner, Jim Backus, Phil Harris, Shelley Berman, Chill Wills, John Astin, Louis Nye. **Credits:** Dir: Arthur Hiller; Prod: Martin Ransohoff; Writer: George J. W. Goodman, Ira Wallach; DP: Charles Lang; Ed: Tom McAdoo; Composer: Frank DeVol; Art Director: George W. Davis, Addison Hehr. Color, 110 min. VHS

When in Rome

(1952) MGM
On the lam after a prison break, con man Douglas tries to give the authorities the slip by ducking aboard a ship bound for Italy. To avoid detection, he steals the robe and ID of a priest making a pilgrimage to the Vatican City (Johnson). The priest follows him on his tour of sacred sites, and while eluding his pursuers on Rome's scenic streets and plazas, the clergyman steers Douglas from his thieving ways, inspiring a pious conversion. **Cast:** Van Johnson, Paul Douglas, Joseph Calleia, Carlo Rizzo, Tudor Owen, Dino Nardi, Aldo Sivani, Mario Siletti, Argentina Brunetti. **Credits:** Dir: Clarence Brown; Prod: Clarence Brown; Writer: Charles Schnee, Dorothy Kingsley; DP: William Daniels; Ed: Robert J. Kern; Composer: Carmen Dragon; Art Director: Cedric Gibbons, Edward C. Carfagno. B&W, 78 min.

When Ladies Meet

(1933) MGM
When two women (mistress Loy and wife Harding) are brought together by Montgomery to discuss the characters of a new book, they are unaware that they both love the same man, publisher Morgan. Academy Award Nomination for Best Interior Decoration. **Cast:** Ann Harding, Robert Mont-

gomery, Myrna Loy, Alice Brady, Frank Morgan, Luis Alberni. **Credits:** Dir: Harry Beaumont; Prod: Lawrence Weingarten; Writer: John Meehan, Leon Gordon; DP: Ray June; Ed: Basil Wrangell. B&W, 73 min. **VHS**

When Ladies Meet
(1941) MGM
Crawford is a novelist with advanced ideas about women's liberation, including free love with her married publisher Marshall. Taylor has his cap set for Crawford, so when Crawford decides to steal Marshall away from wife Garson, Taylor arranges for the two women to spend time together. They become friends and it becomes clear what kind of man Marshall is. The two female leads give sharp portrayals in an interesting look at the period's picture of the modern woman. Academy Award Nomination: Best Art Direction. **Cast:** Joan Crawford, Greer Garson, Robert Taylor, Herbert Marshall, Spring Byington. **Credits:** Dir: Robert Z. Leonard; Prod: Robert Z. Leonard; Orville Dull; Writer: S. K. Lauren, Anita Loos; DP: Robert Planck; Ed: Robert Kern; Prod Design: Cedric Gibbons; Composer: Bronislau Kaper. B&W, 105 min. **VHS**

When My Baby Smiles at Me
(1948) Fox
The quintessential Fox Technicolor musical: Grable and a hoary backstage plot set in the nostalgic days of vaudeville. Skid and Bonny (Dailey and Grable) partner onstage and off. When success comes to comedian Skid, he develops an oversized ego and a taste for booze. With help from Oakie and Havoc, he gets back on the stage and reclaims his place in Grable's act—and heart. Songs include "When My Baby Smiles at Me," "Don't Bring Lulu," "What Did I Do?" and "By the Way." Academy Award Nominations: Best Actor: Dan Dailey; Best Score. **Cast:** Betty Grable, Dan Dailey, Jack Oakie, June Havoc, Richard Arlen, James Gleason, Vanita Wade, Kenny Williams, Jean Wallace, Pat Behrs. **Credits:** Dir: Walter Lang; Prod: George Jessel; Writer: Lamar Trotti, Elizabeth Reinhardt; Story: George Manker Watters, Arthur Hopkins; DP: Harry Jackson; Ed: Barbara McLean; Prod Design: Lyle Wheeler, Leland Fuller; Composer: Alfred Newman, Mack Gordon, Josef Myrow. Color, 98 min.

When Strangers Marry
(1944) Monogram
This tight little thriller directed by a young Castle (from a script by an

equally young Yordan) didn't sound promising upon release by Poverty Row studio Monogram after a 10-day shooting schedule. But with plenty of twists and one of the first roles for Mitchum, it's worth searching out. Hunter heads to New York to meet Jagger, the man she recently married after a brief courtship. When Jagger fails to meet her, Hunter turns to Mitchum, an old flame, for help. Meanwhile, the police, who are searching for the murderer of a conventioneer, begin to suspect Mitchum. When Jagger does turn up he pleads his innocence, and Hunter comes to suspect Mitchum. Features a score by the already celebrated Tiomkin. **Cast:** Robert Mitchum, Kim Hunter, Dean Jagger, Neil Hamilton, Dick Elliot, Milton Kibbee, Lou Lubin, Rhonda Fleming, Marta Mitrovich, George Lloyd. **Credits:** Dir: William Castle; Prod: Frank King, Maurice King; Writer: Dennis J. Cooper, Phillip Yordan; Story: George Moskov; DP: Ira H. Morgan; Ed: Martin G. Cohn; Prod Design: Frank Paul Sylos; Composer: Dimitri Tiomkin. B&W, 67 min.

When the Daltons Rode
(1940) Universal
This sophisticated Western from director Marshall stars Scott, but in a courtroom rather than the range. The Dalton boys are upstanding western Americans, self-reliant and honorable, but when the railroad company resorts to stealing the Dalton land, and one company man gets himself killed, the boys are forced into the outlaw life. When the brothers are nabbed by the law, Scott mounts a defense. **Cast:** Randolph Scott, Kay Francis, Brian Donlevy, George Bancroft, Broderick Crawford, Stuart Erwin, Andy Devine, Frank Albertson, Mary Golden, Harvey Stephens. **Credits:** Dir: George Marshall; Writer: Harold Shumate, Lester Cole, Stuart Anthony; Story: Emmett Dalton, Jack Jungmeyer; DP: Hal Mohr; Ed: Edward Curtiss; Prod Design: Jack Otterson; Composer: Frank Skinner. B&W, 81 min.

When the Legends Die
(1972) Fox
Forrest, a rebellious Ute Indian, finds his way to the rodeo circuit where aging rider Widmark spots his natural talent and makes the young man a bronc-busting contender. But Widmark's gambling and drinking break up the relationship, and Forrest goes on to compete for the national championship. After Forrest recovers from an injury, the two are reunited as the

older man fades toward the final roundup. **Cast:** Frederic Forrest, Richard Widmark, Luana Anders, Vito Scotti, Herbert Nelson, John War Eagle, John Gruber, Jack Mullaney. **Credits:** Dir: Stuart Millar; Prod: Stuart Millar; Writer: Robert Dozier; DP: Richard H. Kline; Ed: Luis San Andres; Prod Design: Angelo Graham; Composer: Glenn Paxton. Color, 105 min. **VHS**

When Tomorrow Comes
(1939) Universal
Here is a melodramatic étude of brilliant artist, unbalanced wife, acts of God, labor agitation, and doomed love. Boyer portrays a concert pianist in a troubled marriage who meets waitress and aspiring labor organizer Dunne, and whisks her off to scenic Long Island, where a storm maroons them. First the love tempest, then the morning after and revelations about Boyer's marriage, are succeeded by Dunne's surrendering Boyer to his wife. Remade as *Interlude* in 1957 and 1968. **Academy Award:** Best Sound. **Cast:** Irene Dunne, Charles Boyer, Nydia Westman, Onslow Stevens, Fritz Feld, Barbara O'Neil, Nella Walker, Constance Moore, Jerry Marlowe. **Credits:** Dir: John M. Stahl; Prod: John M. Stahl; Writer: Dwight Taylor; Story: James M. Cain; DP: John J. Mescall; Ed: Milton Carruth; Composer: Charles Previn; Costumes: Orry-Kelly. B&W, 90 min.

When Worlds Collide
(1951) Paramount
A Pal-produced, special-effects and science-fiction feast has a rogue planet hurtling through space toward Earth. Only a rich industrialist takes action, commissioning a spaceship to carry him to a new world. But who will be among the 40 allowed onboard? The craft rises just as tidal waves wipe out New York and the planet begins to break up. Academy Award Nominations: 2, including Best (Color) Cinematography. **Academy Awards:** Best Special Effects. **Cast:** Richard Derr, Barbara Rush, Larry Keating, Peter Hanson, John Hoyt, Judith Ames, Stephen Chase, Frank Cady. **Credits:** Dir: Rudolph Maté; Prod: George Pal; Writer: Sydney Boehm; DP: John Seitz; Ed: Arthur Schmidt; Prod Design: Hal Pereira; Composer: Leith Stevens. Color, 82 min. **VHS, LASER**

Where Do We Go from Here?
(1945) Fox
This unusually engaging WWII musical fantasy features songs by Weill and Ira Gershwin. MacMurray longs to

serve but minor ails make him 4F. He throws himself into war drives where one day he discovers a lantern that houses a genie and the solution to his deferral. The genie is a bit out of practice, however, and MacMurray winds up serving at Valley Forge, but with George Washington. When the genie tries to repair his handiwork, the time-traveler sails with Christopher Columbus and then buys Manhattan from an Indian for $24. Genial, escapist fun. **Cast:** Fred MacMurray, Joan Leslie, June Haver, Herman Bing, Gene Sheldon, Anthony Quinn, Carlos Ramirez, Fortunio Bonanova. **Credits:** Dir: Gregory Ratoff; Prod: William Perlberg; Writer: Morrie Ryskind, Sig Herzig; DP: Leon Shamroy; Ed: J. Watson Webb; Composer: Ira Gershwin, Kurt Weill, David Raksin; Art Director: Leland Fuller, Lyle Wheeler. Color, 77 min.

Where Eagles Dare
(1968) MGM
This is one of the great '60s WWII films, from an era that was distant enough from the real events to turn that global conflagration into nothing more serious than the backdrop for fantasy derring-do. This is better than most, with a story by MacLean that has action, suspense, and a surprise ending. A group of commandos led by Burton and Eastwood don Nazi uniforms and parachute into Bavaria to rescue a captured American general. Except the mission isn't what it seems, nor are the commandos all on the same side. **Cast:** Richard Burton, Clint Eastwood, Mary Ure, Michael Hordern, Donald Houston, Peter Barkworth, Robert Beatty, William Squire. **Credits:** Dir: Brian G. Hutton; Prod: Elliott Kastner; Writer: Alistair MacLean; Story: Alistair MacLean; DP: Arthur Ibbetson; Ed: John Jympson; Composer: Ron Goodwin; Art Director: Peter Mullins. Color, 158 min. **VHS, LASER**

Where Love Has Gone
(1964) Paramount
This soapy melodrama from the pen of novelist Harold Robbins is built on the schematic of the Johnny Stompanato killing by Lana Turner's teenage daughter. Davis dominates a San Francisco family that includes daughter Hayward, a sculptor. When Hayward meets war hero Connors, Davis tries to buy a marriage, but Connors rejects the offer. But he and Hayward begin a relationship, marry, and have a daughter, though Connors eventually comes under Davis's rule

and begins drinking, and Hayward's eye begins wandering. They divorce and Hayward's restlessness leads to ruin and tragedy. Academy Award Nomination for Best Song ("Where Love Has Gone"). **Cast:** Bette Davis, Susan Hayward, Michael Connors, Jane Greer, Joey Heatherton, George Macready, DeForest Kelley, Anne Seymour. **Credits:** Dir: Edward Dmytryk; Prod: Joseph E. Levine; Writer: John Michael Hayes; DP: Joseph MacDonald; Ed: Frank Bracht; Prod Design: Hal Pereira; Composer: Walter Scharf. Color, 114 min. **VHS**

Where's Charley?
(1952) Warner Bros.
Love-struck Oxford college students Bolger and Shackleton (Bolger was in his forties!) desperately want to date McLerie and Germaine, but are stymied by a school policy that prohibits unchaperoned dating. Necessity being the mother of invention, the pair hatches a plot to create a chaperone, and thus Charley adopts the feminine guise of his aunt. Trouble ensues when McLerie's uncle falls in love with Charlie's "aunt," and to make matters worse, the real aunt shows up for a visit as well. A sprightly musical remake of the too oft filmed *Charley's Aunt* story, which had graced movie screens since silent days. **Cast:** Ray Bolger, Horace Cooper, Mary Germaine, Allyn Ann McLerie, Margaretta Scott, Robert Shackleton, Howard Marion-Crawford, Henry Hewitt, H. G. Stoker. **Credits:** Dir: David Butler; Prod: Cy Feuer, Ernest Martin; Writer: John Monks; DP: Erwin Hiller; Ed: Reginald Mills; Composer: Louis Levy; Art Director: David Folkes. Color, 97 min.

Where's Poppa?
(1970) United Artists
This surreal, often hilariously tasteless comedy has lawyer Segal (now starring on TV's *Just Shoot Me*) saddled with the worst mother ever put on-screen (Gordon). He can't bring himself to put her in a home though she has fouled up every romance he has begun, eats like a pig, swears like a sailor, and has a habit of pulling his pants down and biting his tush. Inspiration to find a solution comes in the form of nurse Van Devere. **Cast:** George Segal, Ruth Gordon, Trish Van Devere, Ron Leibman, Rae Allen, Vincent Gardenia, Alice Drummond, Tom Atkins. **Credits:** Dir: Carl Reiner; Prod: Jerry Tokofsky; Writer: Robert Klane; DP: Jack Priestley; Ed: Bud Molin; Prod Design: Warren Clymer; Composer: Jack Elliott. Color, 84 min. **VHS, LASER**

Where the Boys Are
(1960) MGM
Four young women (Hart, Mimieux, Prentiss, Francis) sharing a hotel room in Fort Lauderdale during spring break also share a common desire—to meet boys. Their experiences vary from finding Ivy League soul mates to being used and abandoned by the frat boys. Camp fun with '50s moralizing. Remade in 1984. **Cast:** George Hamilton, Paula Prentiss, Jim Hutton, Yvette Mimieux, Dolores Hart, Barbara Nichols, Connie Francis, Chill Wills, Frank Gorshin. **Credits:** Dir: Henry Levin; Prod: Joe Pasternak; Writer: George Wells; DP: Robert Bronner; Ed: Fredric Steinkamp; Composer: George Stoll; Art Director: George W. Davis. Color, 100 min. **VHS, LASER**

Where the Lillies Bloom
(1974) United Artists
Four Appalachian children carry on by themselves when their father dies, and keep the news of his death a secret so they won't be taken away by the state. Together they overcome obstacles such as mean landlord Stanton. Written by the creator of *The Waltons*; music by bluegrass legend Scruggs. **Cast:** Julie Gholson, Jan Smithers, Matthew Burril, Helen Harmon, Harry Dean Stanton, Rance Howard, Sudie Bond. **Credits:** Dir: William A. Graham; Prod: Robert B. Radnitz; Writer: Earl Hamner, Jr.; DP: Urs Furrer; Ed: Nick Brown; Composer: Earl Scruggs. Color, 97 min. **VHS**

Where There's Life
(1947) Paramount
Hope antics as a disk jockey about to be married who learns he is heir to the throne of a kingdom in the throes of a revolution. Hope throws off the one-liners while avoiding revolutionaries, and Bendix is his intended's brother. **Cast:** Bob Hope, Signe Hasso, George Coulouris, Vera Marsh, William Bendix, George Zucco. **Credits:** Dir: Sidney Lanfield; Prod: Paul Jones; Writer: Allan Boretz, Melville Shavelson; DP: Charles Lang; Ed: Archie Marshek; Prod Design: Hans Dreier; Costumes: Edith Head. B&W, 75 min. **VHS**

While the City Sleeps
(1956) RKO
An exploitative newspaper publisher (Price) pits three of his staff against each other in a crime-solving contest for the paper's top job in this dark thriller by Lang. The Lipstick Killer (Barrymore) stalks the night, preying on women. The three newspapermen

(Mitchell, Sanders, and Craig) pursue the murderer, each enlisting help from streetwise reporter Andrews and the women in their lives. A must-see for film noir and Lang fans. **Cast:** Dana Andrews, Rhonda Fleming, George Sanders, Howard Duff, Sally Forrest, Thomas Mitchell, Vincent Price, Ida Lupino, John Drew Barrymore, James Craig. **Credits:** Dir: Fritz Lang; Prod: Bert Friedlob; Writer: Casey Robinson; DP: Ernest Laszlo; Ed: Gene Fowler, Jr.; Prod Design: Carroll Clark; Composer: Herschel Burke Gilbert. B&W, 100 min. **VHS**

Whirlpool
(1949) Fox
In an interesting crime tale with a psychological premise, Tierney plays the wife of a prominent Los Angeles psychiatrist who has been plagued, since her youth, by kleptomania. Caught attempting to steal a brooch, she's aided by an enigmatic hypnotist (Ferrer). He hypnotizes Tierney, inducing her to visit a former mistress's house, where she is discovered by police with the body of the dead mistress. Though unsure whether or not she committed the crime, her husband (Conte) stands up for her, disproving the hypnotist's alibi and setting up a final confrontation. **Cast:** Gene Tierney, Jose Ferrer, Richard Conte, Charles Bickford, Barbara O'Neil, Eduard Franz, Constance Collier, Fortunio Bonanova, Larry Keating, Ruth Lee. **Credits:** Dir: Otto Preminger; Prod: Otto Preminger; Writer: Ben Hecht, Andrew Solt; Story: Guy Endore; DP: Arthur C. Miller; Ed: Louis Loeffler; Prod Design: Leland Fuller, Lyle Wheeler; Composer: David Raksin. B&W, 97 min.

Whispering Smith
(1948) Paramount
This is the Technicolor remake of a silent horse opera in which pistol-savvy railroad detective Ladd is offered the job of foreman on a ranch owned by an old friend (Preston). He turns down the offer because he doesn't like his pal's new shady friends and wonders how his buddy, a lowly freight-car overseer, can afford to own a ranch. Preston loses his railroad job and joins his shady ranch hands in a post office stickup, forcing Ladd to hunt down his old friend. **Cast:** Alan Ladd, Donald Crisp, Brenda Marshall, William Demarest, Murvyn Vye, Frank Faylen, John Eldredge, Robert Preston, Fay Holden, Robert Wood. **Credits:** Dir: Leslie Fenton;

Prod: Mel Epstein; Writer: Frank Butler, Karl Kamb; Story: Frank H. Spearman; DP: Ray Rennahan; Ed: Archie Marshek; Prod Design: Hans Dreier, Walter Tyler; Composer: Adolph Deutsch. Color, 88 min.

Whistling in Brooklyn
(1943) MGM
This is the third of Skelton's "Whistling" mysteries that follow the crime-solving adventures of radio wise man Wally Benton. This time, Skelton tracks the "Constant Reader," a cop killer, to Brooklyn's Ebbets Field. **Cast:** Red Skelton, Ann Rutherford, Jean Rogers, Rags Ragland, Ray Collins, Henry O'Neill, William Frawley, Sam Levene. **Credits:** Dir: S. Sylvan Simon; Prod: George Haight; Writer: Nat Perrin; DP: Lester White; Ed: Ben Lewis; Prod Design: Cedric Gibbons; Composer: George Basserman. Color, 87 min. **VHS**

Whistling in Dixie
(1942) MGM
This is the second of Skelton's appearances as goofy radio-show sleuth Wally "The Fox" Benton. Fiancée Rutherford convinces Skelton to help out a relative who's hiding a cache of Confederate gold. **Cast:** Red Skelton, Ann Rutherford, George Bancroft, Guy Kibbee, Diana Lewis, Peter Whitney, Rags Ragland, Celia Travers. **Credits:** Dir: S. Sylvan Simon; Prod: George Haight; Writer: Nat Perrin; DP: Clyde De Vinna; Ed: Frank Sullivan; Prod Design: Cedric Gibbons. B&W, 73 min. **VHS**

Whistling in the Dark
(1941) MGM
Skelton became a star with the short series of crime capers that began with this. As radio crime-show host Wally "The Fox" Benton, Skelton, his girlfriend Rutherford, and his sponsor's daughter (Grey) get kidnapped by the sinister leader of a phony moon-worshiping cult (Veidt), who stands to inherit a huge bequest once he gets rid of an inconvenient heir. Skelton is forced to use his knowledge of mysteries to create the perfect crime with which the heir can be dispatched. Originally seen in 1933 with Ernest Truex. **Cast:** Red Skelton, Ann Rutherford, Virginia Grey, Conrad Veidt, Rags Ragland, Eve Arden, Don Douglas, Don Costello. **Credits:** Dir: S. Sylvan Simon; Prod: George Haight; Writer: Robert MacGunigle; DP: Sidney Wagner; Ed: Frank Hull; Prod Design: Cedric Gibbons. B&W, 78 min. **VHS**

White Cargo
(1942) MGM
In the role that made Lamarr an international sex symbol she is an irresistible native beauty who preys on the hormones of the men who struggle to survive life on a remote rubber plantation. Pidgeon has already lost one man to Lamarr's wiles and he's determined not to lose Carlson, but to no avail. He marries the jungle queen, but she soon tires of him and plots his demise. Lamarr did her part for WWII morale with her clingy sarong. **Cast:** Hedy Lamarr, Walter Pidgeon, Frank Morgan, Richard Carlson, Reginald Owen, Henry O'Neill, Bramwell Fletcher, Clyde Cook. **Credits:** Dir: Richard Thorpe; Prod: Victor Saville; Writer: Leon Gordon; DP: Harry Stradling; Ed: Fredrick Y. Smith; Prod Design: Cedric Gibbons; Composer: Bronislau Kaper. B&W, 90 min. **VHS**

White Christmas
(1954) Paramount
Curtiz directs what amounts to a Technicolor spin-off of the Crosby-Astaire holiday salute, *Holiday Inn* (1942). Crosby appears again (this time with Kaye) as half of a song-and-dance duo who come to the rescue of a ski resort run by their former commanding officer (Jagger) by putting on a show. A veritable treasury of Irving Berlin classics includes "Sisters," "Blue Skies," and, of course, "White Christmas." The 40th anniversary video release included a fully remastered letterboxed edition, an audio CD, a collector's brochure, a copy of Clooney's personal script, and a glossy photo from the film. Academy Award Nomination for Best Song ("Count Your Blessings Instead of Sheep"). **Cast:** Bing Crosby, Danny Kaye, Dean Jagger, Vera Ellen, Rosemary Clooney, Mary Wickes, John F. Brascia. **Credits:** Dir: Michael Curtiz; Prod: Robert Emmett Dolan; Writer: Norman Krasna, Norman Panama, Melvin Frank; DP: Loyal Griggs; Ed: Frank Bracht; Prod Design: Hal Pereira. Color, 120 min. **VHS, LASER**

The White Cliffs of Dover
(1944) MGM
This stirring, sentimental elegy for Britain's losses in world wars was meant (like *Mrs. Miniver*, 1942) to rally support for our closest allies. Dunne stars as an American-born Red Cross worker in Britain who lost her beloved husband (Marshal) in the WWI trenches, and then sees her son pass through her hospital (played first by

McDowall, then Lawford) as he comes home to die from his wounds in WWII. Academy Award Nomination for Best (Black-and-White) Cinematography. **Cast:** Irene Dunne, Alan Marshal, Van Johnson, Frank Morgan, C. Aubrey Smith, Roddy McDowall, Gladys Cooper, Peter Lawford, Dame May Whitty. **Credits:** Dir: Clarence Brown; Prod: Sidney Franklin; Writer: Claudine West, Jan Lustig, George Froeschel; Story: Alice Duer Miller; DP: George J. Folsey; Ed: Robert J. Kern, Al Jennings; Prod Design: Cedric Gibbons; Composer: Herbert Stothart; Art Director: Randall Duell. B&W, 127 min. **VHS**

White Heat
(1949) Warner Bros.
"Made it, Ma. Top of the world!" The last explosion of the Warner Bros. gangster movies, a decade after their '30s heyday, was one of the best, with Cagney unleashing a merciless portrayal of the warped personality that becomes a ruthless killer. Based on the mother-son gang led by "Ma" Barker, the story opens with Cagney's gang holding up a train and then hiding out in a freezing cabin with an injured member and his wife (Mayo) and mother (Wycherly). Dissension in the gang and an attraction between Mayo and a rebellious gangster (Cochran) lead to a police tail in Southern California, a stint in prison for Cagney, and a blazing final showdown. The climactic shoot-out in the oil refinery has become a movie icon and it remains one of Cagney's and director Walsh's greatest moments. Academy Award Nomination for Best Motion Picture Story. **Cast:** James Cagney, Virginia Mayo, Margaret Wycherly, Edmond O'Brien, Steve Cochran, John Archer, Wally Cassell, Fred Clark, Ford Rainey. **Credits:** Dir: Raoul Walsh; Prod: Louis F. Edelman; Writer: Ivan Goff; DP: Sid Hickox; Ed: Owen Marks; Composer: Max Steiner; Art Director: Edward Carrere. B&W, 114 min. **VHS, LASER**

White Line Fever
(1975) Columbia
This is the first studio feature for intriguing director Kaplan (*Over the Edge*, 1979, *Heart Like a Wheel*, 1983) after working on Roger Corman quickies. A young trucker (Vincent) and his childhood sweetheart (Lenz) battle the corruption that plagues the nation's long-haul trucking industry, organizing support from other independent truckers to fight Pickens and his leg-breakers. **Cast:** Jan-Michael Vincent, Kay Lenz, Slim Pickens, L. Q.

Jones, Don Porter, Johnny Ray Mc-Ghee, Leigh French, R. G. Armstrong. **Credits:** Dir: Jonathan Kaplan; Prod: John Kemeny; Writer: Jonathan Kaplan; DP: Fred Koenekamp; Ed: O. Nicholas Brown; Prod Design: Sydney Litwack; Composer: David Nichtern. Color, 92 min. **VHS**

The White Tower
(1950) RKO
Just after WWII, recreational climbers make a dangerous assault on a forbidding Alpine peak. Restless vet Ford lets Valli, who has a fixation on the mountain that claimed her father's life, goad him into joining the climb with aging naturalist Hardwicke, former Nazi Bridges, bitter writer Rains, and guide Homolka. The well-rendered, arduous climb reveals truths and takes lives. **Cast:** Glenn Ford, Alida Valli, Claude Rains, Cedric Hardwicke, Oscar Homolka, Lotte Stein, Lloyd Bridges. **Credits:** Dir: Ted Tetz- laff; Prod: Sid Rogell; Writer: Paul Jarrico; Story: James Ramsey Ullman; DP: Ray Rennahan; Ed: Samuel E. Beetley; Prod Design: Albert S. D'Agostino, Ralph Berger; Composer: Roy Webb. Color, 98 min. **VHS**

White Zombie
(1932) United Artists
This early horror film with Lugosi remains a rarely screened treat. Inspired by a contemporary book on Haiti, the story follows a couple arriving in Haiti for their wedding who are introduced to the island with a zombie parade near a burial. The blushing-bride-to-be is quickly transformed into a pallid, soulless zombie by voodoo master Lugosi (who had just given his *Dracula* performance) and becomes the object of desire for a creepy landowner and Lugosi. **Cast:** Bela Lugosi, Madge Bellamy, Robert Frazer, John Harron, Clarence Muse, Brandon Hurst, John Peters, Dan Crimmins. **Credits:** Dir: Victor Halperin; Prod: Edward Halperin; Writer: Garnett Weston; Story: William Seabrook; DP: Arthur Martinelli; Ed: Harold McLernon; Composer: Abe Meyer. B&W, 79 min. **VHS**

Who Is Killing the Great Chefs of Europe?
(1978) Warner Bros.
A humorous mystery with an international cast finds Morley under doctor's orders to lose weight. He finds it difficult to lay off the delicacies until his favorite European chefs begin dying, murdered as if they were being prepared for their most famous entrées.

Cast: George Segal, Jacqueline Bisset, Robert Morley, Jean-Pierre Cassel, Philippe Noiret, Jean Rochefort, Stefano Satta Flores, Peter Sallis, Tim Barlow, John Le Mesurier. **Credits:** Dir: Ted Kotcheff; Prod: William Aldrich, Merv Adelson; Writer: Peter Stone; DP: John Alcott; Ed: Thom Noble; Composer: Henry Mancini; Costumes: Judy Moorcroft. Color, 112 min. **VHS**

The Whole Town's Talking
(1935) Columbia
Robinson balances comedy and action in a classic-era gangster movie by Ford. Robinson portrays both a timid hardware-store clerk and a ruthless gangster with subtlety and finesse. When the gang boss learns that he has an identical double, he uses the clerk's identity card to move about more openly, and insures his cooperation by kidnapping the clerk's would-be girlfriend (Arthur) and his aunt. The clerk rouses himself to action when he learns the gangster plans to eliminate him in a mistaken-identity killing at a holdup. **Cast:** Edward G. Robinson, Jean Arthur, Arthur Hohl, Arthur Byron, Wallace Ford, Donald Meek, Etienne Girardot, Edward Brophy, Paul Harvey, Lucille Ball. **Credits:** Dir: John Ford; Prod: Lester Cowan; Writer: Jo Swerling, Robert Riskin; Story: W. R. Burnett; DP: Joseph H. August; Ed: Viola Lawrence. B&W, 95 min. **VHS**

Who'll Stop the Rain?
(1978) United Artists
A violent, somber trip through the early-'70s struggles with drugs and disillusionment. Nolte is a Merchant Marine enlisted by war-weary journalist Moriarty to make a big score by smuggling heroin from Southeast Asia to California. The deal goes south and Nolte hits the road with Weld and federal agents in tow. Their wanderings expose the soulless life of upscale L.A. and the last days of the hippie communes. Great performances and sound track, including the Creedence Clearwater Revival title song. Based on Stone's award-winning novel *Dog Soldiers*. **Cast:** Nick Nolte, Tuesday Weld, Michael Moriarty, Charles Haid, David Opatoshu, Gail Strickland, Ray Sharkey, Richard Masur, Anthony Zerbe. **Credits:** Dir: Karel Reisz; Prod: Herb Jaffe, Gabriel Katzka; Writer: Judith Rascoe, Robert Stone; DP: Richard H. Kline; Ed: John Bloom; Prod Design: Dale Hennesy; Composer: Laurence Rosenthal; Costumes: William Ware Theiss. Color, 126 min. **VHS, LASER**

Whoopee!

(1930) United Artists

This early Technicolor musical transposes a Broadway hit to the screen complete with Goldwyn Girls (including a young Grable), choreography by Berkeley, and a star-making turn by Cantor. The slim story follows hypochondriac Cantor west with his nurse as he mixes with cowboys and Indians and complicates the romantic life of Hunt until he gets her together with the right guy, Gregory. Cantor's version of "Makin' Whoopee" became a hit and his signature tune. Remade with Danny Kaye as *Up in Arms* (1944). Academy Award Nomination for Best Interior Decoration. **Cast:** Eddie Cantor, Eleanor Hunt, Paul Gregory, John Rutherford, Albert Hackett, Dean Jagger, Betty Grable, Virginia Bruce, Claire Dodd. **Credits:** Dir: Thornton Freeland; Prod: Samuel Goldwyn, Florenz Ziegfeld; Writer: William Conselman; DP: Lee Garmes, Ray Rennahan, Gregg Toland; Ed: Stuart Heisler; Prod Design: Richard Day; Choreographer: Busby Berkeley; Costumes: John Harkrider. Color, 93 min. **VHS, LASER**

Who's Afraid of Virginia Woolf?

(1966) Warner Bros.

Here is a blistering dissection of the compromises, hidden and not-so-hidden animosities, and ultimate acceptance that make marriage merely a détente in the war between men and women. Nichols's debut as director couldn't have been more auspicious as he applied theatrical experience to Albee's scandalous Broadway success and managed the notoriously combative Burtons to their finest work on-screen. The bitter recriminations begin shortly after 2 A.M. and end at dawn as a tweedy, ineffectual professor and his braying wife (Burton and Taylor) welcome the preppy new prof and his wispy wife (Segal and Dennis) to their home for a nightcap. The following hours are a foul-mouthed, drunken brawl of lust and disappointments that ends with the knowledge that the characters need the emotional roughhousing simply to feel anything at all. An astonishing feat for the actors, the director, and for cinematographer Wexler, who makes his camera waltz and duck punches. Academy Award Nominations: 13, including Best Picture; Best Director; Best Actor: Richard Burton; Best (Adapted) Screenplay. **Academy Awards:** Best Actress: Elizabeth Taylor; Best Supporting Actress: Sandy Dennis; Best Black-and-White Cinematography; Best Costume Design (B&W); Best Art Direction—Set Decoration (B&W or Color). **Cast:** Richard Burton, Elizabeth Taylor, George Segal, Sandy Dennis, Nichelle Nichols. **Credits:** Dir: Mike Nichols; Prod: Ernest Lehman; Writer: Ernest Lehman; Story: Edward Albee; DP: Haskell Wexler; Ed: Sam O'Steen; Prod Design: Richard Sylbert; Composer: Alex North; Costumes: Irene Sharaff; Set Designer: George James Hopkins. B&W, 133 min. **VHS, LASER, DVD**

Who's Minding the Mint?

(1967) Columbia

Hilarious farce as Hutton, an employee of the U.S. mint, accidentally disposes of $50,000 then constructs a Rube Goldberg machine of a plot to reprint the cash to cover his losses. As he recruits a gang of oddballs, including Brennan, Gilford, and Berle, for his plot, he needs to print more and more cash. The plan goes delightfully awry. **Cast:** Jim Hutton, Walter Brennan, Jack Gilford, Milton Berle, Joey Bishop, Victor Buono, Dorothy Provine, Jamie Farr, David J. Stewart, Jackie Joseph. **Credits:** Dir: Howard Morris; Prod: Norman Maurer; Writer: R. S. Allen, Harvey Bullock; DP: Joseph Biroc; Ed: Adrienne Fazan; Prod Design: John Beckman; Composer: Lalo Schifrin; SFX: Richard Albain. Color, 97 min. **VHS**

Who's That Knocking at My Door?

(1968) Warner Bros.

Scorsese's debut feature (and Keitel's big-screen debut) depicts streetwise Keitel and his friends from New York's Little Italy as they discover the world and ways of thinking that lie beyond their neighborhood. Keitel's horizons expand when he meets Bethune, a free spirit with an intellectual bent who he can't pigeonhole as a candidate for sex or marriage. This was developed from Scorsese's NYU film school project, and was meant to be the second part of a trilogy that included *Mean Streets*, his breakthrough feature. A fascinating glimpse into the creative development of an American master. **Cast:** Zina Bethune, Harvey Keitel, Anne Collette, Lennard Kuras, Michael Scala, Bill Minkin, Harry Northrup, Catherine Scorsese. **Credits:** Dir: Martin Scorsese; Prod: Haig Manoogian, Joseph Weill; Writer: Martin Scorsese, Betzi Manoogian; DP: Michael Wadleigh, Richard A. Coll; Ed: Thelma Schoonmaker; Prod Design: Vic Magnotta. B&W, 90 min. **VHS**

Who Was That Lady?

(1960) Columbia

Leigh catches her husband, Curtis, a Columbia University professor, kissing one of his students and prepares for divorce. Turning to his friend Martin for advice, the men concoct a tale that he's an F.B.I. agent on undercover duty and that the kiss was part of his cover. Leigh believes the story—but she's not the only one. The farce continues with Russian spies, TV news crews, U.S. agents all chasing each other until a truth serum reveals the romantic escapades that led to espionage. **Cast:** Tony Curtis, Dean Martin, Janet Leigh, James Whitmore, John McIntire, Barbara Nichols, Joi Lansing, Simon Oakland, Marion Javits, Larry Keating. **Credits:** Dir: George Sidney; Prod: Norman Krasna; DP: Harry Stradling; Ed: Viola Lawrence; Composer: Andre Previn. B&W, 115 min.

Wife, Husband and Friend

(1939) Fox

Young and Baxter have separately been convinced that they have more vocal talent than they really do, and it requires several operatic and very public humiliations to convince them of the wisdom of surrendering their dreams of stardom. Probably one of the very few films with a musical credit for Rudyard Kipling (for "The Road to Mandalay"). Based on a lighter novel by pulp writer Cain. Remade in 1949 as *Everybody Does It* with Paul Douglas and Linda Darnell. **Cast:** Loretta Young, Warner Baxter, Binnie Barnes, Cesar Romero, George Barbier, J. Edward Bromberg, Eugene Pallette, Ruth Terry, Helen Westley, Alice Armand. **Credits:** Dir: Gregory Ratoff; Prod: Darryl F. Zanuck; Writer: Nunnally Johnson; Story: James M. Cain; DP: Ernest Palmer; Ed: Walter Thompson; Composer: David Buttolph, Samuel Pokrass, Walter Bullock, Armando Hjauser; Art Director: Richard Day, Mark-Lee Kirk. B&W, 80 min.

Wife vs. Secretary

(1936) MGM

What a cast—Gable, Harlow, Loy, Stewart—in a better-than-average romantic melodrama. Gable's a devoted husband whose relationship with his voluptuous secretary (Harlow) is all business. His wife (Loy) listens to her mother's (Robson) suspicions, though, and flies off the handle when Gable and Harlow celebrate a business deal in Havana. An early role for Stewart as Harlow's marriage-minded boyfriend. **Cast:** Clark Gable, Jean

Harlow, Myrna Loy, May Robson, George Barbier, James Stewart, Hobart Cavanaugh, Gilbert Emery, Margaret Irving, William Newell. **Credits:** Dir: Clarence Brown; Prod: Hunt Stromberg; Writer: Norman Krasna, Alice Duer Miller, John Lee Mahin; DP: Ray June; Ed: Frank Hull; Prod Design: Cedric Gibbons; Composer: Herbert Stothart; Costumes: Adrian; Set Designer: Edwin B. Willis. B&W, 89 min. **VHS**

The Wild Angels
(1966) AIP
A pre-*Easy Rider* Fonda leads a decadent motorcycle gang through violent, drug-fueled mayhem in this early biker flick from the Corman factory. When Fonda and Co. bust injured Dern out of his hospital bed, the gang succeeds in killing him, which leads to a sacrilegious funeral orgy (Dern spends much of the time out of his coffin and propped up in a chair with a cigarette shoved in his lifeless mouth). Director and film historian Peter Bogdanovich rewrote the script, and future director Hellman edited. A surprise hit, the low-budget shocker was even invited to the Venice Film Festival. **Cast:** Peter Fonda, Nancy Sinatra, Bruce Dern, Diane Ladd, Norman Alden, Michael J. Pollard, Joan Shawlee, Gayle Hunnicutt, Art Baker, Frank Maxwell. **Credits:** Dir: Roger Corman; Prod: Roger Corman; Writer: Charles B. Griffith; DP: Richard Moore; Ed: Monte Hellman; Composer: Mike Curb; Art Director: Leon Ericksen. Color, 87 min. **VHS**

Wild Boys of the Road
(1933) Warner Bros.
Here is Wellman's fascinating pre-Code look at the economic and spiritual chaos caused by the Depression. Darro and Phillips hit the rails, leaving behind a comfortable life in California when their families are thrown out of work. As they make their way east, they hook up with two tough girls (Hudson and Coonan), drift into petty thievery, suffer from want and violence, and join the mass of kids just like them out on the road. In one of the most interesting sequences, they create a community from discarded sewer construction materials and establish a kind of commune of the dispossessed. By the time Darro and Phillips reach New York, they've become hardened and weary, and no longer are they boys. **Cast:** Frankie Darro, Rochelle Hudson, Dorothy Coonan, Edwin Phillips, Ann Hovey, Arthur Hohl, Sterling Holloway. **Credits:** Dir:

William Wellman; Prod: Robert Presnell; Writer: Earl Baldwin; DP: Arthur Todd; Ed: Thomas Pratt; Prod Design: Esdras Hartley. B&W, 68 min.

The Wild Bunch
(1969) Warner Bros.
Peckinpah's landmark of operatic violence sounded the death knell of the traditional Western as it depicted the last days of the Old West code of honor even among outlaws. The brutal men in Peckinpah's world kill without regret, but find themselves in a world where the rules seemed to have changed. Bounty hunter Ryan stalks his former friend, aging outlaw legend Holden, from a robbery that turns into an ambush to Mexico where his gang is double-crossed in an arms deal with a Mexican warlord. The savagery of the Mexican general leads to the famous slow-motion gun battle that seems to bathe the screen in blood as each bullet makes its impact. Peckinpah's difficult relationship with the producers led to a famously butchered release (after it was shown to enthusiastic critics). The wide-screen, original director's cut has recently been digitally restored, and the laserdisc version features interviews, the original trailer, and more. Academy Award Nominations: Best (Original) Screenplay; Best Original Score. **Cast:** William Holden, Robert Ryan, Ernest Borgnine, Edmond O'Brien, Warren Oates, Bo Hopkins, Ben Johnson, Strother Martin, Albert Dekker. **Credits:** Dir: Sam Peckinpah; Prod: Phil

Feldman; Writer: Walon Green, Sam Peckinpah; Story: Roy N. Sickner; DP: Lucien Ballard; Ed: Lou Lombardo; Composer: Jerry Fielding; Art Director: Edward Carrere. Color, 145 min. **VHS, LASER, DVD**

Wild in the Country
(1961) Fox
Acclaimed dramatist Odets tackled this Elvis vehicle and then wrote off Hollywood. But Presley acquits himself well as a backwoods troublemaker who turns literary lion under the guidance of psychiatrist Lange. She has eyes for the troubled young man, but competes for his attention with Weld, Perkins, and his books. Songs include "I Slipped, I Stumbled, I Fell" and "In My Way." **Cast:** Elvis Presley, Hope Lange, John Ireland, Tuesday Weld, Millie Perkins, Gary Lockwood, William Mims, Raymond Greenleaf, Christina Crawford, Robin Raymond. **Credits:** Dir: Philip Dunne; Prod: Jerry Wald; Writer: Clifford Odets; DP: William Mellor; Prod Design: Jack Martin Smith, Preston Ames; Composer: Kenyon Hopkins; Costumes: Don Feld; Set Designer: Walter Scott, Stuart A. Reiss. Color, 114 min. **VHS**

Wild in the Streets
(1968) AIP
Cool '60s political satire has acid dealer and rock star Jones influencing a candidate for senator (Holbrook, of course), getting the voting age lowered to 14. From that point, it's open season on anyone over 30 . . . until

The Wild Angels (1966)

> ## "When he came for his screen test, he didn't say a word. He just sat there tearing up an envelope into little pieces. So I figured he must be a genius and signed him."
>
> Director Nicholas Ray on Marlon Brando

the even younger crowd gets restless. Great B-level rock sound track and appearances by Dick Clark and Walter Winchell. Academy Award Nomination for Best Film Editing. **Cast:** Christopher Jones, Shelley Winters, Diane Varsi, Hal Holbrook, Richard Pryor, Ed Begley, Bert Freed, Kevin Coughlin, Larry Bishop. **Credits:** Dir: Barry Shear; Prod: James H. Nicholson, Samuel Z. Arkoff; Writer: Robert Thom; DP: Richard Moore; Ed: Fred Feitshans, Eve Newman; Costumes: Richard Bruno; Art Director: Paul Sylos; Set Designer: Harry Reif. Color, 97 min. **VHS**

The Wild North
(1952) MGM
After killing a man in self-defense, Granger flees into the Canadian wilderness, where he is pursued by Royal Canadian Mounted Police officer Corey. A lifelong trapper and savvy survivalist, Granger turns the tables on Corey, leading him straight into backwoods dangers. When Corey's injured, Granger risks his own life to return the hobbled Mountie safely back to civilization. **Cast:** Stewart Granger, Wendell Corey, Cyd Charisse, J. M. Kerrigan, Ray Teal, Houseley Stevenson. **Credits:** Dir: Andrew Marton; Prod: Stephen Ames; Writer: Robert Surtees; Ed: John Dunning; Composer: Bronislau Kaper; Art Director: Preston Ames, Cedric Gibbons. Color, 97 min.

The Wild One
(1954) Columbia
This Beat-like portrait of rebellion against the safe choices of the Eisenhower years created a movie icon of Brando's brooding biker-gang leader. Brando and his fellow bikers descend on a small California town after being run off from a motorcycle race. They occupy themselves with drinking and making a nuisance of themselves until a rival gang, led by Marvin, rolls into town. Meanwhile, Brando has been ingratiating himself with the sheriff's

daughter, who's fascinated by the troubled biker's sensitivity and the possibility of splitting from Dullsville. A rumble gets out of control, leading to accidental death and a lynch mob. Still cool. **Cast:** Marlon Brando, Mary Murphy, Robert Keith, Lee Marvin, Jay C. Flippen, Petty Maley, Hugh Sanders, Ray Teal. **Credits:** Dir: Laslo Benedek; Prod: Stanley Kramer; Writer: John Paxton; Story: Frank Rooney; DP: Hal Mohr; Ed: Al Clark; Prod Design: Rudolph Sternad, Walter Holscher; Composer: Leith Stevens. B&W, 79 min. **VHS, LASER, DVD**

Wild River
(1960) Fox
Clift portrays an agent for the Tennessee Valley Authority assigned to move people out of the valley to make way for a dam. He encounters resistance from an 80-year old woman (Van Fleet, who was only 40 at the time!) and racism from those who don't appreciate his evenhanded treatment of local blacks. Remick, Van Fleet's granddaughter, finds him admirable, however, and they eventually marry. Perhaps only Kazan could have cajoled a performance of this caliber out of Clift at this point in his career. **Cast:** Montgomery Clift, Lee Remick, Jo Van Fleet, Albert Salmi, Jay C. Flippen, James Westerfield, Barbara Loden, Frank Overton, Malcolm Atterbury, Bruce Dern. **Credits:** Dir: Elia Kazan; Prod: Elia Kazan; Writer: Paul Osborn; Story: William Bradford Huie, Borden Deal; DP: Ellsworth Fredericks; Ed: William Reynolds; Prod Design: Lyle Wheeler; Composer: Kenyon Hopkins. Color, 110 min.

Will Penny
(1968) Paramount
An aging cowboy (Heston) looking for work falls in love with a beautiful woman (Hackett) heading west to join her husband. When he rides into an ambush set by Pleasence and his sons, it ignites a blood feud. Though

offered a chance to stay and try farming with Hackett and her sons, Heston knows that the open range is his only home. An uncompromising depiction of the hardships of the west on the cusp of the modern world. **Cast:** Charlton Heston, Joan Hackett, Donald Pleasence, Lee Majors, Bruce Dern, Ben Johnson, Slim Pickens, Clifton James, Anthony Zerbe, Roy Jenson. **Credits:** Dir: Tom Gries; Prod: Fred Engel, Walter Seltzer; Writer: Tom Gries; DP: Lucien Ballard; Ed: Warren Low; Prod Design: Hal Pereira, Roland Anderson; Composer: David Raksin; Costumes: John Anderson, Ruth Stella; SFX: Paul K. Lerpae; Set Designer: Robert R. Benton, Ray Moyer. Color, 109 min. **VHS, LASER**

Will Success Spoil Rock Hunter?
(1957) Fox
In a hilarious satire of TV and advertising, Randall, a buttoned-up ad agency junior exec, gets a taste of Hollywood tabloid excess when he convinces bosomy starlet Mansfield to endorse his client's Stay-Put lipstick. In exchange for her endorsement, the sly pinup enlists Randall as her new flame to incite her jealous, jungle-movie-star boyfriend (Hargitay, Mansfield's offscreen husband). Director Tashlin was a former animation director with an eye for color and frenetic comedy; he became a favorite of French New Wave director and film theorist Jean-Luc Godard. **Cast:** Tony Randall, Jayne Mansfield, Betsy Drake, Joan Blondell, John Williams, Henry Jones, Mickey Hargitay, Groucho Marx, Robert Adler, Larry Kerr. **Credits:** Dir: Frank Tashlin; Prod: Frank Tashlin; Writer: Frank Tashlin; DP: Joseph MacDonald; Ed: Hugh S. Fowler; Prod Design: Lyle Wheeler, Leland Fuller; Composer: Cyril J. Mockridge; Costumes: Charles LeMaire; SFX: L. B. Abbott. Color, 94 min. **VHS**

Willy Wonka and the Chocolate Factory
(1971) Paramount
In an amusing musical adapted by Dahl from his famous kids' book, a candymaker (Wilder) hides five golden tickets in candy bars for lucky children to win a lifetime supply of candy and a tour of his wonderful confectionery factory. Young Ostrum resists the temptation to steal and gets a bigger reward than he could have imagined. Fine family fun. Academy Award Nomination for Best Song Score. **Cast:** Gene Wilder, Jack Albertson, Peter Ostrum, Michael Bollner, Ursula Reit,

Denise Nickerson, Leonard Stone, Julie Dawn Cole. **Credits:** Dir: Mel Stuart; Prod: David L. Wolper, Stan Margulies; Writer: Roald Dahl; DP: Arthur Ibbetson; Ed: David Saxon; Composer: Walter Scharf; Art Director: Harper Goff. Color, 100 min. VHS, LASER, DVD

Wilson
(1944) Fox
Richly detailed screen biography of President Woodrow Wilson depicts his life from Princeton University president and political historian to surprise success as governor and road to the White House. Producer Zanuck remained fiercely proud of this prestige picture and remained equally baffled by its chilly public reception. Golden Globe for Best Actor: Alexander Knox. Academy Award Nominations: 10, including Best Picture; Best Director; Best Actor: Alexander Knox. **Academy Awards:** Best Film Editing; Best Sound Recording; Best Color Cinematography; Best Original Screenplay; Best Color Interior Decoration; Irving G. Thalberg Memorial Award. **Cast:** Alexander Knox, Charles Coburn, Geraldine Fitzgerald, Thomas Mitchell, Ruth Nelson, Cedric Hardwicke, Vincent Price, William Eythe, Mary Anderson, Ruth Ford. **Credits:** Dir: Henry King; Prod: Darryl F. Zanuck; Writer: Lamar Trotti; DP: Leon Shamroy; Ed: Barbara McLean; Prod Design: James Basevi; Composer: Alfred Newman; Art Director: Wiard Ihnen. Color, 154 min. VHS

Winchester '73
(1950) Universal
This is the first of the Mann-Stewart Westerns that brought a new, adult sophistication to the genre, and perhaps the best. Stewart, on the trail of his father's killer, wins a Winchester rifle in a shooting contest against McNally. McNally steals the weapon and Stewart relentlessly pursues the rifle as it changes hands from outlaws to homesteaders and back again. The story comes full circle when Stewart discovers the identity of his father's killer. An interesting characterization of a decent man consumed by a dark passion for revenge. The laserdisc includes a personal narration by Stewart. **Cast:** James Stewart, Shelley Winters, Dan Duryea, Tony Curtis, Rock Hudson, Stephen McNally, Millard Mitchell, Charles Drake. **Credits:** Dir: Anthony Mann; Prod: Aaron Rosenberg; Writer: Robert L. Richards, Borden Chase; DP: William Daniels; Ed: Edward Curtiss; Composer: Joseph Gershenson; Costumes: Yvonne Wood; Art Director: Bernard

Herzbrun, Nathan Juran, Russell A. Gausman, A. Roland Fields. B&W, 82 min. VHS, LASER

The Wind
(1928) MGM
One of the great stylistic accomplishments of the silent screen, this film features a bravura performance by Gish as a simple woman who finds life harsh on the Texas prairies. When she comes to live with her cousin, she clashes with the cousin's wife and she's put out of the house. Taking her chances, she marries a cowhand (Hanson) who rides off for a roundup. She endures a violent windstorm and an equally violent attack by Love, a married man she had spurned. Gish kills him and watches in mounting horror as the windstorm uncovers the shallow grave she dug. She is nearly mad by the time Hanson returns to comfort her. Now available with a sound track by silent-movie music specialists, The Alloy Orchestra. Selected for the National Film Registry. **Cast:** Lillian Gish, Lars Hanson, Montagu Love, Dorothy Cumming. **Credits:** Dir: Victor Seastrom; Writer: Frances Marion. B&W, 82 min. VHS, LASER

The Wind and the Lion
(1975) United Artists
Stirring historical balderdash as Arab chieftain Connery kidnaps lovely Bergen and Teddy Roosevelt (Keith) sends in the Marines. After spending time with Connery's gallantry, Bergen may not want saving. **Academy Awards:** Best Sound; Best Original Score. **Cast:** Sean Connery, Candice Bergen, Brian Keith, John Huston, Geoffrey Lewis, Steve Kanaly, Vladek Sheybal, Nadim Sawalha. **Credits:** Dir: John Milius; Prod: Herb Jaffe; Writer: John Milius; DP: Billy Williams; Ed: Robert L. Wolfe; Prod Design: Gil Parando; Composer: Jerry Goldsmith; Art Director: Antonio Paton. Color, 120 min. VHS, LASER

The Window
(1949) RKO
Former Disney child star Driscoll stars in a murderous variation on the boy who cries wolf tale. While sleeping on the fire escape of his Lower East Side tenament, Driscoll witnesses a murder. His parents discount his story and make him apologize to the murderers after they discover he has already notified the police, marking him as a witness. Driscoll tries to evade murderer Stewart while also trying to convince skeptical adults. Gripping story with an on-location

authenticity. Director Tetzlaff was formerly a cinematographer and had clearly learned from the master while shooting *Notorious* for Hitchcock. Based on the novel *The Boy Who Cried Murder* by Woolrich. Academy Award Nomination for Best Film Editing. **Academy Awards:** Special Achievement Award: Bobby Driscoll. **Cast:** Bobby Driscoll, Barbara Hale, Arthur Kennedy, Paul Stewart, Ruth Roman, Anthony Ross, Richard Benedict, Jim Nolan. **Credits:** Dir: Ted Tetzlaff; Prod: Frederic Ullman; Writer: Mel Dinelli; Story: Cornell Woolrich; DP: William Steiner; Ed: Frederic Knudtson; Composer: Roy Webb; Art Director: Walter E. Keller. B&W, 73 min. VHS

Wing and a Prayer
(1944) Fox
A Hathaway men-under-fire tale follows the crew of a Pacific-based aircraft carrier as they battle the Japanese in the early days of WWII. Ameche plays the flight commander and Andrews the squadron leader. Academy Award Nomination for Best Original Screenplay. **Cast:** Don Ameche, Dana Andrews, William Eythe, Richard Jaeckel, Charles Bickford, Richard Crane, Glenn Langan, Robert Bailey. **Credits:** Dir: Henry Hathaway; Prod: Walter Morosco, William A. Bacher; Writer: Jerry Cady; DP: Glen MacWilliams; Ed: J. Watson Webb; Prod Design: Lyle Wheeler, Lewis Creber; Composer: Hugo Friedhofer. B&W, 100 min. VHS

Winged Victory
(1944) Fox
This flag-waver dedicated to the men of the Army Air Force is directed by Cukor, a director better known for deft handling of drama than wartime action. But that may explain the main interest being the lives of the wives left behind as the men go first to training and then to war. Holliday shines in the first of several films she would appear in for Cukor. **Cast:** Jane Ball, Richard Benedict, Lee J. Cobb, Jeanne Crain, Mark Daniels, Jo-Carroll Dennison, Peter Lind Hayes, Judy Holliday, Lon McCallister, Jim Nolan. **Credits:** Dir: George Cukor; Prod: Darryl F. Zanuck; Writer: Moss Hart; DP: Glen MacWilliams; Ed: Barbara McLean; Prod Design: Lyle Wheeler, Lewis H. Creber; Composer: David Rose. B&W, 130 min.

Wings
(1927) Paramount
This is the winner of the first Best Picture Oscar and the story of its produc-

tion is by now well-known Hollywood lore, but as pure cinematic excitement, it still leaps off the screen. Directed by 28-year-old "Wild Bill" Wellman (a former flier with the Lafayette Escadrille) who marshaled the resources of the War Department to create what remains among the most thrilling aerial sequences on film. The story follows two friends as they prepare to become fliers in WWI. Rogers and Arlen leave for camp where they meet a young veteran (Cooper, in his breakthrough role), whose death doesn't quench their thirst for action. Their pal Bow follows the two to France as a Red Cross nurse so she can keep her eye on Rogers. After engaging in aerial combat, Arlen's plane is shot down over German lines. Thinking his friend dead, Rogers rushes to his plane to wreak revenge. Meanwhile, Arlen has commandeered a German triplane and heads toward base, leading to a fateful confrontation. Wellman planted cameras in real planes so none of the action is faked; some of the fliers went on to illustrious Air Force careers. A stirring, emotional film and one of the silent greats. **Academy Awards:** Best Picture; Best Engineering Effects. **Cast:** Clara Bow, Charles "Buddy" Rogers, Richard Arlen, Gary Cooper, Jobyna Ralston, Henry Walthall. **Credits:** Dir: William Wellman; Prod: Lucien Hubbard; Writer: Hope Loring, Louis Lighton; Story: John Monk Saunders; Ed: Lucien Hubbard; Prod Design: Laurence Hitt; Costumes: Edith Head. B&W, 139 min. **VHS, LASER**

The Wings of Eagles

(1957) MGM
This rarely screened Ford drama is among his most deeply felt, personal pictures. Frank "Spig" Wead (Wayne) was a screenwriter (*Dirigible, Ceiling Zero, They Were Expendable*) and one of the fathers of naval aviation. A man of action obsessed with his naval career, he was less successful sustaining a family life, eventually alienating wife O'Hara and unable to reach her even as their child dies. Features a dead-on impersonation of Ford himself by stock company player Bond. **Cast:** John Wayne, Dan Dailey, Maureen O'Hara, Ward Bond, Sig Rumann, Kenneth Tobey, Edmund Lowe. **Credits:** Dir: John Ford; Prod: Charles Schnee; Writer: Frank Fenton, William Wister Haines; Story: James Todd, Frank Wead; DP: Paul C. Vogel; Ed: Gene Ruggiero; Composer: Jeff Alexander; Art Director: William A. Horning, Malcolm F. Brown. Color, 118 min. **VHS**

Winning

(1969) Universal
Winning Indy circuit driver Newman hits a rough patch when he marries Woodward, losing a string of races to his rival Wagner. The duel culminates at the Indy 500 with real footage from the disastrous 1968 race. **Cast:** Paul Newman, Joanne Woodward, Robert Wagner, Richard Thomas, David Sheiner, Clu Gulager, Toni Clayton, Maxine Stuart. **Credits:** Dir: James Goldstone; Prod: John Foreman; Writer: Howard A. Rodman; DP: Richard Moore; Ed: Edward A. Biery, Richard C. Meyer; Prod Design: Alexander Golitzen; Composer: Dave Grusin; Costumes: Edith Head; Art Director: John Lloyd, Joe Alves. Color, 123 min. **VHS, LASER**

The Winning Team

(1953) Warner Bros.
Reagan's favorite role was his portrayal of Hall of Fame baseball pitcher Grover Cleveland Alexander. His astonishing natural talent lifted Alexander quickly from the bush leagues to a stellar rise with the Philadelphia Athletics. His career took a turn after being hit in the head and then serving in WWI, when he began seeing double and suffering headaches, a condition not helped by his drinking. Wife Day sticks by his side as he slides back to the minors. The movie skirts Alexander's real battle with epilepsy, but is an entertaining watch for any baseball fan. **Cast:** Doris Day, Ronald Reagan, Frank Lovejoy, Eve Miller, James Millican, Russ Tamblyn, Walter Baldwin, Dorothy Adams. **Credits:** Dir: Lewis Seiler; Prod: Bryan Foy; Writer: Ted Sherdeman, Seeleg Lester, Merwin Gerard; DP: Sid Hickox; Ed: Alan Crosland, Jr.; Composer: David Buttolph; Art Director: Douglas Bacon. B&W, 98 min. **VHS, LASER**

Winter Kills

(1979) Avco Embassy
Here is a hidden gem worth searching for. The younger brother of an assassinated U.S. president (Bridges) launches a private investigation into the murder, and finds the plot leading back to his father (Huston), a wealthy industrialist. A clever satire on the political system that was barely noticed upon its theatrical release, but has wickedly funny performances from Huston, Bridges, and Perkins. **Cast:** Jeff Bridges, John Huston, Anthony Perkins, Belinda Bauer, Sterling Hayden, Eli Wallach, Dorothy Malone, Tomas Milian. **Credits:** Dir: William Richert; Prod: Fred Caruso; Writer: William Richert; DP: Vilmos

Zsigmond; Ed: David Bretherton; Composer: Maurice Jarre; Art Director: Norman Newberry. Color, 97 min. **VHS, LASER**

Winterset

(1936) RKO
Based on Maxwell Anderson's Broadway play, this drama follows Meredith's struggle to clear the name of his father who was wrongly executed for killing a cop during a robbery. During his investigation, he becomes involved with the daughter (Margo) of the man who drove the getaway car. Meredith's screen debut in a role he first played on the stage. Academy Award Nominations: Best Score; Best Art Direction. **Cast:** Burgess Meredith, John Carradine, Margo, Eduardo Ciannelli, Mischa Auer, Myron McCormick, Paul Guilfoyle, Edward Ellis. **Credits:** Dir: Alfred Santell; Prod: Pandro S. Berman; Writer: Anthony Veiller; DP: Peverell Marley; Ed: William Hamilton; Composer: Roy Webb; SFX: Vernon L. Walker. B&W, 85 min. **VHS**

Wintertime

(1943) Fox
In this last major musical entry in Henie's frosty crowd pleasers the novelty is starting to wear as thin as spring ice. Here she visits the great white north and brings hope to a struggling old Canadian hotel that houses some retired, old vaudevillians. Wilde and Romero are appropriately dashing as they compete for Henie's attention. **Cast:** Sonja Henie, Jack Oakie, Cesar Romero, Carole Landis, Cornel Wilde, S. Z. Sakall, Woody Herman, Don Douglas. **Credits:** Dir: John Brahm; Prod: William LeBaron; Writer: E. Edwin Moran, Jack Jevne, Lynn Starling; DP: Joseph MacDonald, Glen MacWilliams; Ed: Louis Loeffler; Prod Design: James Basevi, Maurice Ransford; Composer: Alfred Newman. B&W, 82 min. **VHS**

Wise Blood

(1979) New Line
Huston's scathing satire of evil men duping the spiritually needy in the garb of evangelical preachers captures the sultry atmosphere found in Flannery O'Connor's novel. Dourif sheds his army uniform for a preacher's robes and wanders the back roads with a supposedly blind preacher picking up what wisdom he can find. **Cast:** Brad Dourif, Ned Beatty, Harry Dean Stanton, Dan Shor, Amy Wright, Mary Nell Santacroce, John Huston. **Credits:** Dir: John Huston; Prod: Michael Fitzgerald, Kathy Fitzgerald; Writer: Benedict

Fitzgerald; DP: Gerry Fisher; Ed: Roberto Silvi; Composer: Alex North. Color, 106 min. VHS

Wise Girl

(1937) RKO

In this charming screwball comedy, society girl Hopkins masquerades as a starving Greenwich Village artist in order to find her lost sister's two children and their penniless artist father, Milland. Mostly fun for the look at the bohemian life of the mid-'30s. **Cast:** Miriam Hopkins, Ray Milland, Alec Craig, Guinn Williams, Margaret Dumont, Jean De Briac, Ivan Lebedev, Rafael Storm, Richard Lane, Gregory Gaye. **Credits:** Dir: Leigh Jason; Prod: Edward Kaufman; Writer: Charles Norman, Allan Scott; DP: Peverell Marley; Ed: Jack Hively; Prod Design: Van Nest Polglase. B&W, 70 min.

With a Song in My Heart

(1952) Fox

In another of Hayward's portrayals of plucky heroines overcoming long odds (and another great performance in support by Ritter), this biopic of '30's chanteuse Jane Froman traces her career from her first big break at a Cincinnati radio station to Radio City Music Hall and stardom. Froman marries her pianist, Don Ross (Wayne), who helps launch her career but who grows increasingly jealous of her success. As WWII rages, Froman tours with the USO, entertaining the troops. But when her plane crashes in Lisbon, she is partially paralyzed and must return home, where she endures painful surgeries (and falls for fellow patient Calhoun) before mounting a successful comeback. Froman dubbed her own voice in a long list of the era's most popular songs. Academy Award Nominations: 5, including Best Actress: Susan Hayward; Best Supporting Actress: Thelma Ritter. **Academy Awards:** Best Score. **Cast:** Susan Hayward, Rory Calhoun, David Wayne, Thelma Ritter, Robert Wagner, Una Merkel, Helen Westcott, Jane Froman, Casey Adams. **Credits:** Dir: Walter Lang, Phillipe Labro; Prod: Lamar Trotti; Writer: Lamar Trotti; DP: Leon Shamroy; Ed: J. Watson Webb; Composer: Alfred Newman; Art Director: Lyle Wheeler, John De Cuir. Color, 117 min.

Without Love

(1945) MGM

Tracy and Hepburn star in a pleasant wartime comedy written by the *Philadelphia Story* team of playwright Philip Barry and screenwriter Stewart. A widow (Hepburn) in overpopulated WWII Washington, D.C., allows a scientist (Tracy) working on a new pilot's helmet to set up a laboratory in her basement to conduct secret experiments—if they agree to a platonic marriage for appearance's sake. His eccentricity clashes with her well-bred manner, but love blossoms. Not as well known, but the leads and writers guarantee a movie worth watching. **Cast:** Spencer Tracy, Katharine Hepburn, Lucille Ball, Keenan Wynn, Carl Esmond, Patricia Morison, Felix Bressart, Gloria Grahame. **Credits:** Dir: Harold S. Bucquet; Prod: Lawrence Weingarten; Writer: Donald Ogden Stewart; DP: Karl Freund; Ed: Frank Sullivan; Prod Design: Cedric Gibbons; Composer: Bronislau Kaper; Art Director: Harry McAfee. B&W, 113 min. VHS, LASER

Without Reservations

(1946) RKO

Wayne steps into Gable's shoes and walks the unfamiliar terrain of light romantic comedy as novelist Colbert becomes convinced that he's the right man for the lead in the movie of her latest book. Marine Wayne and his buddy Defore are heading to San Diego to report for duty; Colbert's on her way to Hollywood. She hides her identity and pals around with the fliers through mishaps, jailings, and the stirrings of romance. **Cast:** John Wayne, Claudette Colbert, Don Defore, Anne Triola, Phil Brown, Frank Puglia, Thurston Hall, Dona Drake. **Credits:** Dir: Mervyn LeRoy; Prod: Jesse L. Lasky; Writer: Andrew Solt; DP: Milton Krasner; Ed: Jack Ruggiero; Prod Design: Ralph Berger; Composer: Roy Webb; Art Director: Albert S. D'Agostino. B&W, 101 min. VHS, LASER

With Six You Get Eggroll

(1968) National General

Doris Day's last big-screen role finds her a widow with three sons who gets fixed up with a widower, Keith, who has a daughter. After initial reluctance they elope and return to find their families (even the dogs) at war. An attempt at détente through a camping excursion ends in comic mayhem. Mildly amusing family fare. **Cast:** Doris Day, Brian Keith, Alice Ghostley, Barbara Hershey, Jamie Farr, George Carlin, Pat Carroll, John Findlater. **Credits:** Dir: Howard Morris; Prod: Martin Melcher; Writer: Gwen Bagni, Paul Dubov, Harvey Bullock, R. S. Allen; DP: Ellsworth Fredricks, Harry Stradling; Ed: Adrienne Fazan; Art Director: Cary Odell. Color, 95 min. VHS

Witness for the Prosecution

(1957) United Artists

Wilder pumps up the pace of Agatha Christie's play and adds even more suspense in a twisty, impossible-to-predict mystery. Laughton is ready to retire his barrister's wig at his wife Lanchester's insistence when a colleague presents him with an intriguing murder case involving drifter Power and the murder of a wealthy widow. Power's only alibi is his wife, Dietrich, and she's not the witness either Power or Laughton expects. A terrific, engaging whodunit. Golden Globe for Best Supporting Actress: Elsa Lanchester. Academy Award Nominations: 6, including Best Picture; Best Director; Best Actor: Charles Laughton. **Cast:** Marlene Dietrich, Tyrone Power, Charles Laughton, Elsa Lanchester, John Williams, Henry Daniell, Ian Wolfe, Torin Thatcher. **Credits:** Dir: Billy Wilder; Prod: Arthur Hornblow, Jr.; Writer: Billy Wilder, Harry Kurnitz, Larry Marcus; DP: Russell Harlan; Ed: Daniel Mandell; Prod Design: Alexander Trauner; Composer: Matty Malneck. B&W, 116 min. VHS, LASER

Witness to Murder

(1954) United Artists

Stanwyck witnesses her neighbor, Sanders, commit a murder. She calls the police but since they can't find a body, they think she is mistaken, but Sanders learns she saw his deed, enters her apartment, forges letters on her typewriter that make her appear insane, and takes them to the police. Stanwyck endures a trip to the mental hospital, after which she confronts the murderer. A clever crime melodrama. **Cast:** Barbara Stanwyck, George Sanders, Gary Merrill, Jesse White, Harry Shannon, Claire Carleton, Lewis Martin, Dick Elliott, Harry Tyler, Juanita Moore. **Credits:** Dir: Roy Rowland; Prod: Chester Erskine; Writer: Chester Erskine; DP: John Alton; Ed: Robert Swink; Composer: Herschel Burke Gilbert; Art Director: William Ferrari. B&W, 81 min.

The Wizard of Oz

(1939) MGM

Treasured by millions with each new screening, this colorful musical fantasy defines for many the greatest achievements of Hollywood's classic period. MGM put every resource into the production, from dazzling Technicolor (an early use of the three-strip process; the colors astonished audiences of the day), marvelous songs from Arlen and Harburg that would become standards, a star-making performance from Garland (actually the studio's third choice for the role), and the thousands of studio artisans who created hundreds of costumes and 70 sets for an ambitious, months-long production led by three of the studio's most-trusted directors (and early sequences, not in the final cut, by Richard Thorpe). The result follows a Kansas farmgirl (Garland) who escapes her black-and-white life and Hamilton's threat to do away with her beloved dog, Toto, to a Technicolor world that lies over the rainbow. After becoming the hero of Munchkin Land, Garland and Toto link arms with Bolger, Haley, and Lahr (the Scarecrow, Tin Man, and Cowardly Lion) to place each of their desires in front of the fabled Wizard, desires that they learn are really always within their reach. One of the classics that rewards each viewing. The special 50th anniversary video edition includes 17 minutes of extra footage, including Ray Bolger's scarecrow dance and the rehearsal and sound track from the jitterbug dance, both of which were edited out of the film; Buddy Ebsen (the initial Tin Man) performing "If I Only Had a Heart"; Judy Garland receiving her Oscar; the original theatrical promotional trailer; and a 32-page souvenir booklet. Selected as a National Film Registry Outstanding Film. The collector's edition also includes a documentary hosted by Angela Lansbury and behind-the-scenes footage. Academy Award Nominations: 5, including Best Picture. **Academy Awards:** Best Song ("Somewhere over the Rainbow"); Best Original Score; Best Juvenile Actress: Judy Garland. **Cast:** Judy Garland, Jack Haley, Ray Bolger, Bert Lahr, Billie Burke, Margaret Hamilton, Frank Morgan, Charley Grapewin, Clara Blandick, Pat Walshe. **Credits:** Dir: Victor Fleming, King Vidor, George Cukor; Prod: Arthur Freed, Mervyn LeRoy; Writer: Noel Langley, Florence Ryerson, Edgar Allan Woolf; Story: L. Frank Baum; DP: Harold Rosson; Ed: Blanche Sewell; Prod Design: Cedric Gibbons; Choreographer: Bobby Connolly; Composer: Harold Arlen, E. Y. Harburg; George Bassman, Robert W. Stringer, Herbert Stothart, George E. Stoll; Costumes: Adrian; SFX: A. Arnold Gillespie. B&W and color, 103 min. **VHS, LASER, DVD**

The Wolf Man
(1941) Universal
The last of Universal's classic horror quintet deserves its place in the monster pantheon. British heir Chaney returns home after college and notices shopkeeper Ankers. He visits her curiosity shop and picks up a sil-

ver-headed cane with a pentagram motif—the sign of the werewolf. At a Gypsy festival, Ankers has her palm read by Lugosi and his mother (famous Moscow Art Theater actress Ouspenskaya) and the news isn't good. After hearing a wolf's cries on the moors, Chaney rushes toward the cries and fights off a snarling creature, though he's bitten in the process. He wakes to discover Lugosi dead. Returning to Ouspenskaya, she tells him he is now a werewolf as was her son. Chaney struggles in vain to suppress the wild beast within him until he dies by the cane that he picked up at the curiosity shop. Chaney resisted following in his silent-star father's horror-film steps, but this was the role with which he became most closely associated, wearing the yak-hair makeup six times. One of the most sophisticated of the Universal monster movies. **Cast:** Claude Rains, Lon Chaney, Jr., Bela Lugosi, Ralph Bellamy, Warren William, Patric Knowles, Maria Ouspenskaya, Evelyn Ankers. **Credits:** Dir: George Waggner; Prod: George Waggner; Writer: Curt Siodmak; DP: Joe Valentine; Ed: Ted J. Kent; Art Director: Jack Otterson. B&W, 71 min. **VHS, LASER**

Woman Chases Man
(1937) United Artists
In this madcap comedy architect Hopkins will do anything it takes to overcome the difficulties she faces as a professional woman in a man's business by securing a job designing a development project for real estate mogul Winninger. She tricks Winninger's millionaire son McCrea into financing the project by getting him hopelessly drunk. Love follows the commerce. Famous mostly for the number of name directors who rejected the project, the script doctoring by Dorothy Parker and her husband, Alan Campbell, and Goldwyn's determination to see the picture made. Crawford's debut. **Cast:** Miriam Hopkins, Joel McCrea, Erik Rhodes, Charles Winninger, Ella Logan, Leona Maricle, Broderick Crawford, Charles Halton, Manuel Seff. **Credits:** Dir: John G. Blystone; Prod: Samuel Goldwyn, George Haight; Writer: Joseph Anthony, David Hertz, Frank Fenton; DP: Gregg Toland; Ed: Daniel Mandell; Composer: Alfred Newman; Art Director: Richard Day. B&W, 71 min.

The Woman in the Window
(1944) RKO
A tense, engrossing film noir from Lang follows staid college professor

Robinson into the dangerous world that awaits just a momentary lapse in judgment. When he admires a beautiful portrait in a gallery, he's pleased to notice the model (Bennett) standing next to him. When he accepts her invitation to visit, her boyfriend bursts in and a deadly struggle ensues. Fearing scandal, Bennett and Robinson dispose of the body. Meanwhile, Robinson's friend Massey becomes the D.A. on the case and the noose grows tighter. The ending, forced by the Production Code's insistence that no crime go unpunished, spoils the whole only a little. Academy Award Nomination: Best Score. **Cast:** Edward G. Robinson, Joan Bennett, Dan Duryea, Raymond Massey, Robert Blake, Dorothy Peterson, Frank Melton, Don Brodie. **Credits:** Dir: Fritz Lang; Prod: Nunnally Johnson; Writer: Nunnally Johnson; DP: Milton Krasner; Ed: Marjorie Johnson, Gene Fowler, Jr.; Composer: Arthur Lange; Art Director: Duncan Cramer. B&W, 99 min. **VHS**

The Woman in White
(1948) Warner Bros.
Based on a 19th-century British novel, this is a mystery about a rich young woman (Parker) and an evil plot by Greenstreet and Emery to swindle her through marriage. Parker gets a warning from a mysterious woman in a white dress, her twin sister, who the men have had committed to a private insane asylum. The plotters get theirs when Greenstreet's wife Moorehead comes unhinged. **Cast:** Alexis Smith, Eleanor Parker, Sydney Greenstreet, Gig Young, Agnes Moorehead, John Emery, Curt Bois, Emma Dunn, Matthew Boulton, John Abbott. **Credits:** Dir: Peter Godfrey; Prod: Henry Blanke; Writer: Stephen Morehouse Avery; Story: Wilkie Collins; DP: Carl E. Guthrie; Ed: Clarence Kolster; Prod Design: Stanley Fleischer; Composer: Max Steiner, Leo F. Forbstein. B&W, 108 min.

A Woman of Distinction
(1950) Columbia
Russell has an easy charm in this romantic comedy. As dean of Benton College, Russell has no time for romance. So she is shocked to discover her name linked romantically with a handsome British astronomer (Milland) on a lecture tour. That's okay with her father, Gwenn. **Cast:** Rosalind Russell, Ray Milland, Edmund Gwenn, Francis Lederer, Jerome Courtland, Alex Gerry, Charlotte Wynters, Charles Evans. **Credits:** Dir: Edward Buzzell; Prod: Buddy Adler; Writer: Charles

Hoffman, Frank Tashlin; Story: Hugo Butler, Ian McLellan Hunter; DP: Joseph Walker; Ed: Charles Nelson; Composer: Werner Richard Heymann; Art Director: Robert Peterson. B&W, 85 min. VHS, LASER

The Woman of the Town
(1943) United Artists
In a sturdy depiction of colorful Western character Bat Masterson (Dekker), this depicts the time he spent as marshal of Dodge City, his battle with cattle baron Sullivan, and his tragic romance with dance-hall girl Trevor. Academy Award Nomination for Best Scoring of a Dramatic or Comedy Picture. **Cast:** Claire Trevor, Albert Dekker, Barry Sullivan, Henry Hull, Marion Martin, Porter Hall, Percy Kilbride, Beryl Wallace. **Credits:** Dir: George Archainbaud; Prod: Lewis J. Rachmil; Writer: Aeneas MacKenzie; Story: Norman Houston; DP: Russell Harlan; Ed: Carroll Lewis; Art Director: Ralph Berger. B&W, 90 min. VHS

Woman of the Year
(1942) MGM
This is the first of the Hepburn-Tracy on-screen sparring matches, and perhaps the best. Hepburn and Tracy work for the same newspaper, he a sports writer and she a political commentator. They meet after his angry response to her opinion that baseball should be called off during the war. To the surprise of all, they marry. The odd-couple pairing results in sharply observed scenes from a marriage: her fumbling at housework and devotion to her work, his drinking and resentment of her career. The inevitable bumps lead Hepburn to consider divorce just as she's chosen Woman of the Year. Originally developed by Garson Kanin, he turned it over to Lardner and his brother Michael, who earned Oscars. Academy Award Nominations: 2, including Best Actress: Katharine Hepburn. **Academy Awards:** Best Original Screenplay. **Cast:** Katharine Hepburn, Spencer Tracy, Fay Bainter, Reginald Owen, William Bendix, Minor Watson, Gladys Blake, Dan Tobin. **Credits:** Dir: George Stevens; Prod: Joseph L. Mankiewicz; Writer: Michael Kanin, Ring Lardner; DP: Joseph Ruttenberg; Ed: Frank Sullivan; Composer: Franz Waxman; Art Director: Cedric Gibbons, Randall Duell. B&W, 118 min. VHS, LASER, DVD

The Woman on Pier 13
(1950) RKO
This sharp little Cold War quickie has Ryan as a happily married man with a high-ranking position at a shipping firm in San Francisco—and a murderous, communist past. The Party tries to blackmail him into participation in a strike plot. When they resort to threatening his wife (Day) and murdering her brother (Agar), Ryan picks up a gun and goes hunting for Reds. **Cast:** Laraine Day, Robert Ryan, John Agar, Thomas Gomez, Janis Carter, Richard Rober, William Talman, Paul E. Burns, Paul Guilfoyle, Patrick Collins. **Credits:** Dir: Robert Stevenson; Prod: Jack J. Gross; Writer: Charles Grayson, Robert Hardy Andrews, George F. Slavin; DP: Nicholas Musuraca; Ed: Roland Gross; Prod Design: Darrel Silvera, James Altwies; Composer: Leigh Harline; Art Director: Albert S. D'Agostino, Walter E. Keller. B&W, 73 min.

The Woman on the Beach
(1947) RKO
The last of French master Renoir's Hollywood films is a brooding, richly-textured depiction of human relationships haunted by remorse and longing for the final release of death. Ryan, a married veteran plagued by memories of combat, encounters Bennett on the beach. Bennett's husband is a brilliant painter (Bickford) now blind after Bennett lashed out at him. Ryan falls in love with Bennett but becomes convinced the painter knows about them. After tests of their willingness to sacrifice the security of their unsatisfying but stable lives, Bennett proves her devotion to her husband and Ryan retreats to his wife. **Cast:** Joan Bennett, Robert Ryan, Charles Bickford, Nan Leslie, Walter Sand, Irene Ryan, Frank Darien, Jay Norris, Glenn Vernon. **Credits:** Dir: Jean Renoir; Prod: Jack J. Gross; Writer: Mitchell Wilson, Jean Renoir, Michael Hogan, Frank Davis; DP: Leo Tover, Harry Wild; Composer: Hanns Eisler, C. Bakaleinikoff; Art Director: Albert S. D'Agostino. B&W, 71 min.

Woman on the Run
(1950) Universal
A struggling artist (Elliott) witnesses a murder that forces him into hiding. The police desperately want to find the missing man and so does his wife (Sheridan), when she learns Elliott has a heart condition of which he is unaware. A newspaper reporter (O'Keefe) offers suspect advice. **Cast:** Ann Sheridan, Dennis O'Keefe, Robert Keith, Frank Jenks, Ross Elliott, John Qualen, J. Farrell MacDonald, Tom Dillon. **Credits:** Dir: Norman Foster; Prod: Howard Welsch; Writer: Alan Campbell, Norman Foster; DP: Hal Mohr; Ed: Otto Ludwig; Composer: Emil Newman, Arthur Lange; Art Director: Boris Leven. B&W, 77 min. VHS

A Woman's Face
(1941) MGM
Cukor strays near film noir territory with this intriguing melodrama of a woman disfigured from childhood who carries her scars inside as well. Bitter, lonely Crawford runs a blackmailing operation, and gets mixed up in a more serious crime, a murder plot, in order to win the heart of callous heir Veidt. When she tries to blackmail the wife of a surgeon, the unwitting doctor takes an interest in her case and

The Woman in the Window (1944)

repairs her face. Now that she can turn a new face to the world, she begins to see the evil of the murder plot. A remake of a Swedish film starring a young Ingrid Bergman. **Cast:** Joan Crawford, Conrad Veidt, Melvyn Douglas, Osa Massen, Donald Meek, Connie Gilchrist, Richard Nichols, Charles Quigley. **Credits:** Dir: George Cukor; Prod: Victor Saville; Writer: Donald Ogden Stewart, Elliot Paul; DP: Robert Planck; Ed: Frank Sullivan; Prod Design: Wade B. Rubottom; Composer: Bronislau Kaper. B&W, 107 min. **VHS**

A Woman's Secret
(1949) RKO
Ray directs a complex plot that answers the mystery of why fading thrush O'Hara shot her protégée Grahame (then Ray's wife). The story of their Svengali-puppet relationship leads to a surprise twist. **Cast:** Maureen O'Hara, Melvyn Douglas, Gloria Grahame, Bill Williams, Victory Jory, Mary Philips, Jay C. Flippen, Robert Warwick. **Credits:** Dir: Nicholas Ray; Prod: Herman J. Mankiewicz; Writer: Herman J. Mankiewicz; Story: Vicki Baum; DP: George E. Diskant; Ed: Sherman Todd; Prod Design: Albert S. D'Agostino, Carroll Clark; Composer: Frederick Hollander. B&W, 85 min. **VHS**

A Woman's Vengeance
(1947) Universal
The woman of the title is Tandy and her vengeance is that of a woman scorned. Boyer is the unfortunate object of her devotion. Working with accomplice Natwick, she murders his invalid wife and stands back to let the clouds of suspicion gather around his subsequent remarriage to Blyth, with whom he was having an affair before his wife's murder. It doesn't take long before he is arrested, tried, and sentenced to die, but Hardwicke, in a masterful role, begins to suspect Tandy. She breaks as the clock moves closer to the hour of his execution. One of the few screenplays by Huxley, adapted from his own story, "The Giaconda Smile." **Cast:** Charles Boyer, Ann Blyth, Jessica Tandy, Cedric Hardwicke, Mildred Natwick, Cecil Humphreys, Rachel Kempson, Hugh French, Valerie Cardew, Carl Harbord. **Credits:** Dir: Zoltan Korda; Prod: Zoltan Korda; Writer: Aldous Huxley; DP: Russell Metty; Ed: Jack Wheeler; Composer: Miklos Rozsa; Art Director: Bernard Herzbrun, Eugene Lourie. B&W, 96 min.

Woman's World
(1954) Fox
Each of three women (Bacall, Allyson, and Dahl) uses a different facet of feminine wiles and graces to help their husbands when an auto executive searching for a general manager makes his decision based on his impression of their wives. The right man gets the job despite being with the wrong woman. Interesting glimpse at social roles of the mid-'50s, with smart direction by Negulesco. **Cast:** Clifton Webb, June Allyson, Van Heflin, Lauren Bacall, Fred MacMurray, Arlene Dahl, Cornel Wilde, Elliott Reid. **Credits:** Dir: Jean Negulesco; Prod: Charles Brackett; Writer: Claude Binyon, Mary Loos, Richard Sale, Howard Lindsay, Russel Crouse; Story: Mona Williams; DP: Joseph MacDonald; Ed: Louis Loeffler; Composer: Cyril J. Mockridge; Art Director: Lyle Wheeler. Color, 94 min. **VHS**

A Woman Under the Influence
(1974) Faces
Perhaps Cassavetes's most successful work, this features a gripping, fascinating performance from his wife, Rowlands. A middle-class, Italian-American housewife with three children loves her family deeply though she has no definition of herself other than through her family. When her flights of fancy and frustrated lashing-out become too much to handle, she is committed to an institution by her husband, Falk. She comes out six months later, shaky and unmoored from the only anchor she had, her family. An emotionally draining, powerful film. Selected as a National Film Registry Outstanding Film. Academy Award Nominations: Best Actress: Gena Rowlands; Best Director. **Cast:** Peter Falk, Gena Rowlands, Matthew Cassel, Matthew Laborteaux, Christina Grisanti, Katherine Cassavetes, Lady Rowlands, Fred Draper, Mario Gallo, John Finnegan. **Credits:** Dir: John Cassavetes; Prod: Sam Shaw; Writer: John Cassavetes; DP: Mitch Breif; Ed: David Armstrong, Elizabeth Bergeron, Sheila Viseltear, Tom Cornwell; Composer: Bo Harwood; Art Director: Phedon Papamichael. Color, 155 min. **VHS, LASER, DVD**

The Women
(1939) MGM
In a social satire as sharp as a cat's claw, Cukor pulls back the curtains of drawing rooms and ladies' lounges to expose the machinations that go into the war between women over men.

Shearer has what she thinks is a happy marriage until meddlesome Russell connives to have her learn the truth about her husband's affair with store clerk Crawford. After a trip to Reno for a quickie divorce, she learns that her husband isn't pleased with Crawford. So Shearer paints her nails jungle red and enlists her friends to snare her husband from Crawford's clutches. Snappy, spiteful dialogue from Loos, based on the play by Luce, delivered by MGM's best actresses. **Cast:** Norma Shearer, Joan Crawford, Rosalind Russell, Joan Fontaine, Paulette Goddard, Lucile Watson, Phyllis Povah, Virginia Weidler. **Credits:** Dir: George Cukor; Prod: Hunt Stromberg; Writer: Anita Loos, Jane Murfin; Story: Clare Boothe Luce; DP: Oliver T. Marsh, Joseph Ruttenberg; Ed: Robert J. Kern; Prod Design: Cedric Gibbons, Wade B. Rubottom; Composer: Edward Ward, David Snell. B&W, 133 min. **VHS, LASER**

The Wonderful World of the Brothers Grimm
(1962) Cinerama
Pal produced this fantasy-bio that combines a look at how the brothers came to write their tales with stagings of the tales themselves. The stories include "The Dancing Princess," about a young royal who runs through the shoes, "The Cobbler and the Elves," about a kindly shoemaker who tends to local orphans instead of his customers, and "The Singing Bone," about a dragonslayer whose bad end comes back to haunt his killer. Academy Award Nominations: 4. **Academy Awards:** Best Costume Design (Color). **Cast:** Laurence Harvey, Claire Bloom, Jim Backus, Yvette Mimieux, Buddy Hackett, Barbara Eden, Oscar Homolka, Arnold Stang. **Credits:** Dir: Henry Levin, George Pal; Prod: George Pal; Writer: David P. Harmon, Charles Beaumont, William Roberts; Story: Hermann Gerstner; DP: Paul C. Vogel; Ed: Walter Thompson; Composer: Leigh Harline; Art Director: George Davis, Edward C. Carfagno. Color, 134 min. **VHS, LASER**

Wonder Man
(1945) RKO
In another patented dual role, Kaye plays both a song-and-dance man killed by gangsters and his librarian twin brother. When the milquetoast bookworm refuses his brother's spirited request to help catch the criminals, the ghost takes over, impressing the librarian's fiancée, Mayo. Academy Award Nominations: 4, including

Best Song ("So in Love"). **Academy Awards:** Best Special Effects. **Cast:** Danny Kaye, Virginia Mayo, Vera Ellen, Donald Woods, S. Z. Sakall, Allen Jenkins, Edward Brophy, Steve Cochran. **Credits:** Dir: H. Bruce Humberstone; Prod: Samuel Goldwyn; Writer: Don Hartman; DP: Victor Milner; Ed: Daniel Mandell; Composer: Ray Heindorf; Art Director: Ernst Fegte. Color, 98 min. VHS, LASER

Ed Wood

The King of Cheese, the Prince of Sleaze, call him what you like, but Ed Wood, the lovable transvestite, was one persistent director-producer-writer-actor. Wood's unique vision infused many of his films, which dealt with such diverse subjects as crime, aliens, atomic radiation, vampires, and cross-dressing. Production value was never Wood's main concern; indeed, the paper-plate flying saucers featured in *Plan 9 from Outer Space* (1956) became a symbol of his joyful use of any means at hand to get a movie made. Though bizarre and often featuring horrendous performances, his films earned Wood a cult following that endures to the present day, exemplified by director Tim Burton's loving semibiographical portrait, *Ed Wood* (1994).

The Streets of Laredo *(1948)*
Glen or Glenda *(1953)*
Jail Bait *(1954)*
Bride of the Monster *(1956)*
The Violent Years *(1956)*
Plan 9 from Outer Space *(1956)*
Final Curtain *(1957)*
The Bride and the Beast *(1958)*
Night of the Ghouls *(1959)*
The Sinister Urge *(1960)*
The Shotgun Wedding *(1963)*
Orgy of the Dead *(1965; screenplay)*

Woodstock

(1970) Warner Bros.
The festival of peace and love that named a generation is documented with a gritty, knowing style that portrays as much of the community that grew up at the festival as the music on the stage. This was a musical and cultural watershed, with performances by Richie Havens, Joan Baez, The Who, Crosby, Stills & Nash, Arlo Guthrie, Jimi Hendrix, Canned Heat, Joe Cocker, Creedence Clearwater Revival, Janis Joplin, Santana, Jefferson Airplane, and many more. Note Scorsese among the editors. The digitally remastered, wide-screen edition released in celebration of the festival's 25th anniversary includes 40 minutes of footage not included in the original. Academy Award Nominations: 2. **Academy Awards:** Best Documentary Feature. **Credits:** Dir: Michael Wadleigh; Prod: Bob Maurice; DP: Don Lenzer, David Myers, Richard Pearce, Michael Wadleigh, Al Wertheimer; Ed: Jere Huggins, Thelma Schoonmaker, Martin Scorsese, Stanley Warnow, Yeu-Bun Yee, Michael Wadleigh. Color, 225 min. VHS, LASER, DVD

The Working Man

(1933) Warner Bros.
In this entertaining, early-talkie comedy, two rival families run shoe-factory empires. When Arliss, one of the footwear magnates, goes on vacation, he leaves his nephew in charge and unwittingly spends time with the heirs (Davis and Newton) to the rival firm. Because he's pretending to be a bum, the fun-loving duo offer him a job. Before long he's running their factory, and brewing a romance between Davis and his nephew. **Cast:** George Arliss, Bette Davis, Hardie Albright, Theodore Newton, Gordon Westcott, John Farrell MacDonald, Charles Evans, Fredrick Burton, Pat Wing, Edward Van Sloan. **Credits:** Dir: John G. Adolfi; Prod: Lucien Hubbard; Writer: Charles Kenyon, Maude Howell; Story: Edward Franklin; DP: Sol Polito; Ed: Owen Marks; Prod Design: Jack Okey. B&W, 74 min.

The World Changes

(1933) Warner Bros.
Muni plays a pioneer turned businessman in this epic drama that depicts three generations of a midwestern family from 1852 to 1929. Muni builds a fortune raising cattle and devising a way to ship beef in refrigerated rail cars. As time goes by, though, his wife (Astor) begins to look down on his business as she has aspirations for a society marriage for their son. Muni supports his son's stock brokerage only to see it crash along with the economy in 1929. **Cast:** Paul Muni, Aline MacMahon, Mary Astor, Donald Cook, Patricia Ellis, Jean Muir, Margaret Lindsay, Guy Kibbee, Theodore Newton, Alan Dinehart. **Credits:** Dir: Mervyn LeRoy; Prod: Robert Lord; Writer: Edward

---

Michael Azerrad Picks Rock Movies

1. *Woodstock* (1970). Not only does this film capture the late '60s rock zeitgeist, it documents the beginning of rock's decline into festival spectacle. Some great performances, too.

2. *Gimme Shelter* (1970). The depressing and horrific end of the '60s, happening right in front of your eyes.

3. *A Hard Day's Night* (1964). Perfectly captures the Beatles' wit, energy, and sterling music. A funny movie by any standard.

4. *The Decline of Western Civilization* (1981). PUNK ROCK!

5. *Don't Look Back* (1967). Dylan in wisecracking, speedfreak mode, dismantling *Time* reporters and blowing minds.

6. *Saturday Night Fever* (1977). The definitive disco document, complete with 18-carat sound track.

7. *The Rocky Horror Picture Show* (1975). The seminal glam-rock fest.

8. *Cocksucker Blues* (1972). Look up "decadence" in the dictionary: It says "See *Cocksucker Blues*."

9. *Yellow Submarine* (1968). Psychedelia even a kid could love, with absolutely beautiful animation and fantastic music.

10. *Let It Be* (1970). Eyewitness report of the dissolution of the greatest band ever; dense, moving, unforgettable.

Michael Azerrad is a veteran rock journalist and author of the forthcoming *Just Gimme Indie Rock!: The American Indie Scene 1981–1991*, to be published in the fall of 1999.

Chodorov, Sheridan Gibney; DP: Tony Gaudio; Ed: William Holmes; Prod Design: Jack Okey; Composer: Leo F. Forbstein. B&W, 90 min.

The World in His Arms
(1952) Universal

In a rollicking romantic adventure set in 1850s San Francisco, Peck and Quinn are seal poachers and rivals. Peck becomes enamored of a Russian princess (Blyth) on the lam from an arranged marriage, and the two prepare to marry—until her Russian fiancé (Esmond) sails into the harbor and snatches her away before sailing for Alaska. Peck goes on a bender and loses all, but then makes a wager with Quinn based on a seal-catching race to Alaska. Peck wins, but the two are nabbed by the Russians and jailed, until Blyth comes to the rescue. The sailors return the favor by kidnapping her as she prepares to walk down the aisle with Esmond. **Cast:** Gregory Peck, Ann Blyth, Anthony Quinn, John McIntire, Carl Esmond, Andrea King, Hans Conried, Bryan Forbes. **Credits:** Dir: Raoul Walsh; Prod: Aaron Rosenberg; Writer: Borden Chase, Horace McCoy; DP: Russell Metty; Ed: Frank Gross; Composer: Frank Skinner; Art Director: Bernard Herzbrun, Alexander Golitzen. Color, 104 min. **VHS**

The World Moves On
(1934) Fox

Ford directs this historical drama, which begins in 19th-century New Orleans. The story follows the fortunes of the Warburton and Girard families, who expand the cotton business overseas to Germany, England, and France. Carroll weds Tone and their sons run the families' operations overseas, operations that come to ruin through war and economic disasters. Powerful war sequences punctuate the story. **Cast:** Madeleine Carroll, Franchot Tone, Mort Shuman, Louise Dresser, Reginald Denny, Franklin Melton, Seigfried Rumann, Walter McGrall, Marcelle Corday, Barry Norton. **Credits:** Dir: John Ford; Prod: Winfield R. Sheehan; Writer: Reginald Berkeley; DP: George Schneiderman; Prod Design: William S. Darling; Composer: Max Steiner. B&W, 104 min.

The World of Henry Orient
(1964) United Artists

In this light romantic comedy, two teenage girls who idolize eccentric pianist Sellers follow him around New York City to the consternation of his mistress, Prentiss. Sweet and engaging. **Cast:** Peter Sellers, Paula Prentiss, Tom Bosley, Angela Lansbury, Phyllis Thaxter, Bibi Osterwald, Peter Duchin, Al Lewis. **Credits:** Dir: George Roy Hill; Prod: Jerome Hellman; Writer: Nora Johnson, Nunnally Johnson; DP: Boris Kaufman, Arthur J. Ornitz; Ed: Stuart Gilmore; Prod Design: James Sullivan; Composer: Elmer Bernstein, Ken Lauber; Costumes: Ann Roth. Color, 106 min. **VHS, LASER**

The World of Suzie Wong
(1961) Paramount

In this exotic soaper, a struggling artist in Hong Kong (Holden) meets and becomes enamored with a prostitute, Kwan. At first rejecting her and pursuing Syms, he begins to see the loveliness under the hard life Kwan leads. A hidden baby's tragic death brings the two together for the last time. **Cast:** William Holden, Nancy Kwan, Sylvia Syms, Michael Wilding, Laurence Naismith, Jacqui Chan, Bernard Cribbins, Lionel Blair. **Credits:** Dir: Richard Quine; Prod: Ray Stark; Writer: John Patrick; Story: Richard Mason, Paul Osborn; DP: Geoffrey Unsworth; Ed: Bert Bates; Composer: George Dunning; Art Director: John Box. Color, 129 min. **VHS**

Written on the Wind
(1956) Universal

The most exaggerated (and absorbing) of Sirk's melodramas depicts the corrupt souls of a Texas oil dynasty. Hudson plays the calm, moral center of a familial storm as the nearly adopted favorite son of clan leader Keith. The domineering father trusts geologist Hudson more than his weak son Stack and his sex-obsessed daughter Malone (in a slinky, wildly erotic performance). When Hudson and Stack meet ad exec Bacall on a trip to New York, she falls for Stack's easy charm and is reluctantly dazzled by his wealth, though she recognizes Hudson's strength and character. The family settles into an uneasy peace until Malone's flagrant catting around brings a tragic final showdown. Sirk painted '50s American materialistic dreams in vibrant colors, but also deep shadow, finding the underlying emptiness within the gaudy display. Academy Award Nominations: 3, including Best Supporting Actor: Robert Stack; Best Song ("Written on the Wind"). **Academy Awards:** Best Supporting Actress: Dorothy Malone. **Cast:** Rock Hudson, Lauren Bacall, Robert Stack, Dorothy Malone, Grant Williams, Robert Keith, Bob Wilke, Edward Platt. **Credits:** Dir: Douglas Sirk; Prod: Albert Zugsmith; Writer: George Zuckerman; DP: Russell Metty; Ed: Russell Schoengarth; Prod Design: Alexander Golitzen; Composer: Frank Skinner. Color, 99 min. **VHS**

The Wrong Man
(1956) Warner Bros.

This is a Hitchcock thriller based on actual events and filmed in authentic locations. Stork Club bass player Fonda goes to an insurance office to get money for his wife's (Miles) dentist visit, and finds himself accused of a theft. He slips up while giving a handwriting sample and his spelling inadvertently matches a ransom note, whereupon he is jailed. Miles cracks under the strain of his imprisonment and trial, and has to be institutional-

Romance Classics Picks the Greatest Romantic Movies of All Time

1. *An Affair to Remember* (1957)

2. *Casablanca* (1942)

3. *Breakfast at Tiffany's* (1961)

4. *Wuthering Heights* (1939)

5. *Love in the Afternoon* (1957)

Romance Classics is a 24-hour entertainment service devoted entirely to romance. The programming features a mix of great romantic films, popular miniseries and teleplays, adaptations of romantic literature, and original lifestyle programs.

Wuthering Heights (1939)

ized. Bleak, unforgiving, and wholly unlike his more entertaining thrillers, Hitchcock walks the audience through the tedium and minutiae of police procedure, building a mountain of authentic incident that weighs heavily on the film. Splendid music score by Herrmann. **Cast:** Henry Fonda, Vera Miles, Anthony Quayle, Harold J. Stone, Esther Minciotti, Charles Cooper, Nehemiah Persoff, Laurinda Barrett. **Credits:** Dir: Alfred Hitchcock; Prod: Alfred Hitchcock; Writer: Maxwell Anderson, Angus MacPhail; DP: Robert Burks; Ed: George Tomasini; Composer: Bernard Herrmann; Art Director: Paul Sylbert, William L. Kuehl. B&W, 126 min. **VHS, LASER**

Wuthering Heights
(1939) United Artists
Classic Hollywood's most enduring romance is a sumptuously rendered adaptation of Brontë's 1847 novel. The story of eternal lovers Cathy and Heathcliff (Oberon and Olivier) begins in their childhood. Gypsy boy Olivier and manor-born Oberon become playmates and soul mates as they spend the years frolicking in their imaginary castle among the heather. As they grow to adulthood, jealousy drives Olivier away and ambition drives Oberon into the arms of Niven. Olivier returns a wealthy man, but possessed of a desire for revenge. Knowing Oberon loves him, he lovelessly marries Niven's sister (Fitzgerald), dooming them both to lives of bitterness. But the lovers are reconciled and make a pact to be together for eternity as Oberon slips into death. Beautifully photographed by Toland, with Wyler's characteristic care in composition and performances. Academy Award Nominations: 8, including Best Picture; Best Director; Best Actor: Laurence Olivier; Best Screenplay. **Academy Awards:** Best Black-and-White Cinematography. **Cast:** Laurence Olivier, Merle Oberon, David Niven, Flora Robson, Geraldine Fitzgerald, Donald Crisp, Hugh Williams, Leo G. Carroll. **Credits:** Dir: William Wyler; Prod: Samuel Goldwyn; Writer: Ben Hecht, Charles MacArthur; Story: Emily Brontë; DP: Gregg Toland; Ed: Daniel Mandell; Prod Design: James Basevi; Composer: Alfred Newman. B&W, 104 min. **VHS, DVD**

The Yakuza

(1975) Warner Bros.
In an exotic action picture that opens a window onto Japanese culture and its *yakuza* crime gangs, Mitchum reluctantly agrees to go to Japan to help rescue wealthy businessman Keith's daughter, who is being held hostage for money Keith owes the *yakuza.* Mitchum begins his search by visiting his lost love, a Japanese woman (Keiko) he met during the war. Her brother (Ken) is now a *yakuza,* and a traditionalist clinging to the old rituals of warfare. The two band together to free the hostage and settle old scores, Mitchum armed with a gun and Ken with his sword. Slashing action realistically treated and balanced with tender feelings of loss in a script by thinking-man's action director Schrader. **Cast:** Robert Mitchum, Takakura Ken, Brian Keith, Herb Edelman, Richard Jordan, Kishi Keiko, Okada Eiji, James Shigeta. **Credits:** Dir: Sydney Pollack; Prod: Sydney Pollack; Writer: Paul Schrader, Robert Towne; Story: Leonard Schrader; DP: Okazaki Kozo, Duke Callaghan; Ed: Fredric Steinkamp, Thomas Stanford, Don Guidice; Prod Design: Stephen Grimes; Composer: Dave Grusin; Art Director: Ishida Yoshiyuki. Color, 112 min. VHS

A Yank at Oxford

(1938) MGM
A spirited fish-out-of-water comedy, and MGM's first British-made film, follows brash, young American Taylor as he learns to fit in at Oxford. Taylor gets some of his rough edges sanded down, and wins the heart of O'Sullivan, his rival's sister. The screenplay received a polish from F. Scott Fitzgerald. **Cast:** Robert Taylor, Lionel Barrymore, Maureen O'Sullivan, Vivien Leigh, Edmund Gwenn, Griffiths Jones, C. V. France, Edward Rigby, Morton Selten, Claude Gillingwater. **Credits:** Dir: Jack Conway; Prod: Michael Balcon; Writer: Malcolm Stu-

art Boylan, Walter Ferris, George Oppenheimer; Story: Sidney Gilliatt, Leon Gordon, Michael Hogan; DP: Harold Rosson; Ed: Charles Frend; Composer: Hubert Bath, Edward Ward. B&W, 100 min.

Yankee Buccaneer

(1952) Universal
Disguising his U.S. navy ship as a pirate vessel, Chandler and his second in command, Brady, sail into the dangerous waters of the Caribbean to battle the scores of privateers plundering America's merchant fleet. The two sailors fight amongst themselves while battling the pirates, and a lovely Portuguese countess (Ball) they welcome aboard wants to warn her government of a pirate-backed coup being plotted by a Spanish governor. **Cast:** Jeff Chandler, Scott Brady, Suzan Ball, Joseph Calleia, Rodolfo Acosta, George Mathews, James Parnell, David Janssen, Michael Ansara, Joseph Vitale. **Credits:** Dir: Frederick De Cordova; Prod: Howard Christie; Writer: Charles K. Peck, Jr.; DP: Russell Metty; Ed: Frank Gross; Composer: Joseph Gershenson; Art Director: Bernard Herzbrun, Robert Boyle. Color, 86 min.

Yankee Doodle Dandy

(1942) Warner Bros.
This grand musical features Cagney's personal favorite performance. The life of George M. Cohan, one of the great entertainers of the first half of the century, is a textbook on the development of American pop culture. As played by Cagney, it's great fun, too. Cohan, who produced 40 Broadway shows and wrote more than 1,000 songs, sprang from his family's vaudeville act, and eventually makes his way to Tin Pan Alley's song factory. Once he's a hit, he performs in and writes his own spectacular productions. An endless list of songs, and endless energy from Cagney.

Selected as a National Film Registry Outstanding Film. Academy Award Nominations: 8, including Best Picture; Best Director; Best Original Story. **Academy Awards:** Best Actor: James Cagney; Best Sound Recording; Best Scoring of a Musical. **Cast:** James Cagney, Joan Leslie, Walter Huston, Richard Whorf, George Tobias, Irene Manning, Rosemary DeCamp, Jeanne Cagney. **Credits:** Dir: Michael Curtiz; Prod: William Cagney; Writer: Robert Buckner; DP: James Wong Howe; Ed: George Amy; Art Director: Carl Jules Weyl. B&W, 128 min. VHS, LASER

A Yank in the RAF

(1941) Fox
Hollywood pitched in with Britain's war effort in this WWII romance. Power flies planes bound for Britain up to Canada, then takes an assignment to cross the Atlantic. When in London, he meets old flame Grable, a nightclub singer doing war work, and he's convinced to sign up for the RAF. The aerial sequences include actual air-combat footage. Grable sings "Another Dream Won't Do Us Any Harm" and "Hi-Ya Love." Academy Award Nomination for Best Special Effects. **Cast:** Tyrone Power, Betty Grable, John Sutton, Reginald Gardiner, Donald Stuart, Richard Fraser, Claud Allister. **Credits:** Dir: Henry King; Prod: Darryl F. Zanuck; Writer: Darrell Ware, Karl Tunberg; Story: Melville Crossman; DP: Leon Shamroy, Ronald Neame; Ed: Barbara McLean; Prod Design: Richard Day, James Basevi; Composer: Leo Robin, Ralph Rainger, Alfred Newman; SFX: Fred Sersen, E. H. Hansen. B&W, 98 min. VHS

Yanks

(1979) Universal
From early 1942 until D-day, waves of Americans landed in Britain on their way to fight at the European front. This follows three couples formed from the troop movements: brash

Gere, who can't woo proper Eichhorn from her boyfriend; married lovers Redgrave and Devane; and young, passionate Vennera and Morgan. Unexceptional story, but an interesting historical setting for romance. **Cast:** Richard Gere, Vanessa Redgrave, William Devane, Lisa Eichhorn, Rachel Roberts, Chick Vennera, Arlen Dean Snyder, Annie Ross, Tom Nolan, John Ratzenberger, Wendy Morgan. **Credits:** Dir: John Schlesinger; Prod: Joseph Janni, Lester Persky; Writer: Colin Welland, Walter Bernstein; DP: Dick Bush; Ed: Jim Clark; Prod Design: Milly Burns; Choreographer: Eleanor Fazan; Costumes: Shirley Russell. Color, 139 min. **VHS, LASER**

The Yearling
(1946) MGM
Based on the novel by Marjorie Kinnan Rawlings, this is the enduring family story of a boy (Jarman) who grows up as he says good-bye to his animal friend. Peck and Wyman barely scratch out a living from their small Florida farm. Their only surviving child, Jarman, has a lonely life and wishes he had a pet. Given their circumstances, that's out of the question, until Peck orphans a fawn. The boy and deer grow closer until the deer starts eating the family's hard-won crops and a painful decision is made. Originally a project for Spencer Tracy to be directed by Victor Fleming, MGM revived the production and made it a great success. Remade for TV in 1994. Golden Globe for Best Actor: Gregory Peck. Academy Award Nominations: 7, including Best Picture; Best Director; Best Actor: Gregory Peck; Best Actress: Jane Wyman. **Academy Awards:** Best Color Cinematography; Best Interior Decoration (Color); Special Achievement Awards. **Cast:** Gregory Peck, Jane Wyman, Claude Jarman, Jr., Chill Wills, Clem Bevans, Margaret Wycherly, Henry Travers, Forrest Tucker. **Credits:** Dir: Clarence Brown; Prod: Sidney Franklin; Writer: Paul Osborn; Story: Marjorie Kinnan Rawlings; DP: Charles Rosher, Leonard Smith, Arthur E. Arling; Ed: Harold F. Kress; Prod Design: Cedric Gibbons, Paul Groesse; Composer: Herbert Stothart. Color, 129 min. **VHS, LASER**

The Yellow Cab Man
(1950) MGM
Cabbie Skelton doesn't spend his idling time idle: he dreams up inventions, including unbreakable, elastic glass. Some mobsters see the potential and give him a run for his money. One of Skelton's big-screen best.

Cast: Red Skelton, Gloria De Haven, Walter Slezak, Edward Arnold, James Gleason, Jay C. Flippen, Polly Moran, Paul Harvey. **Credits:** Dir: Jack Donohue; Prod: Richard Goldstone; Writer: Devery Freeman; DP: Harry Stradling; Ed: Albert Akst; Prod Design: Cedric Gibbons; Composer: Scott Bradley. B&W, 85 min. **VHS**

Yellow Jack
(1938) MGM
This gripping drama tells the true story of five soldiers who volunteer to be subjects in research to find a cure for the then-fatal disease of yellow fever. In Cuba, just after the Spanish-American War, Major Walter Reed conducted experiments meant to determine the source of the disease the soldiers nicknamed "yellow jack." Montgomery draws the assignment of being bitten by infected mosquitoes. This effectively captures the soldiers' sacrifice for their fellow man. James Stewart played the Montgomery role on Broadway. **Cast:** Robert Montgomery, Virginia Bruce, Lewis Stone, Andy Devine, Henry Hull, Charles Coburn, Buddy Ebsen, Henry O'Neill, Janet Beecher, William Henry. **Credits:** Dir: George B. Seitz; Prod: Jack Cummings; Writer: Edward Chodorov, Sidney Howard, Paul DeKruif; DP: Lester White; Ed: Blanche Sewell; Composer: Dr. William Axt. B&W, 83 min.

Yellow Sky
(1948) Fox
Peck leads a gang of saddle tramps robbing banks across the post–Civil War frontier. After robbing a bank, the posse in pursuit drives them to a salt flat, the only escape route. The gang trudges slowly across the parched, blistered earth until they come to a ghost town with a population of two, prospector Barton and his granddaughter Baxter. The thieves see possibilities in both the old man's claim and Baxter, but Peck develops a liking for both, too, and defends them to the death. **Cast:** Gregory Peck, Anne Baxter, Richard Widmark, Harry Morgan, Robert Arthur, John Russell, James Barton, Charles Kemper, Robert Adler, Victor Kilian. **Credits:** Dir: William Wellman; Prod: Lamar Trotti; Writer: Lamar Trotti; DP: Joseph MacDonald; Ed: Harmon Jones; Prod Design: Lyle Wheeler, Albert Hogsett. B&W, 98 min. **VHS**

The Yellow Ticket
(1931) Fox
This early talkie from Walsh is set in pre-revolutionary Russia. A peasant

Jewish girl (Landi) tries to visit her dying father imprisoned in St. Petersburg. The young girl can travel only under the guise of a "yellow ticket," which brands her a prostitute. When she arrives, Landi learns that her father has died. She finds comfort in the arms of a British reporter (Olivier) who publishes her horrifying tale, shedding light on the miseries of Czarist Russia. Soon the couple is on the run from the government secret service and its boss, Barrymore. **Cast:** Elissa Landi, Mischa Auer, Lionel Barrymore, Boris Karloff, Laurence Olivier, Sarah Padden, Walter Byron, Rita La Roy, Edwin Maxwell. **Credits:** Dir: Raoul Walsh; Writer: Guy Bolton, James Furthman; DP: James Wong Howe; Ed: Jack Murray; Prod Design: William S. Darling; Composer: Carli D. Elinor, R. H. Bassett. B&W, 78 min.

Yolanda and the Thief
(1945) MGM
In this less well known MGM musical fantasy, Astaire plays a slippery con man out to swindle devout heiress Yolanda (Bremer) by posing as her guardian angel. As he becomes closer to her, he falls further in love, but has to square himself with her real guardian angel before he can marry her. Songs include "Yolanda," "Coffee Time," and "Will You Marry Me?" **Cast:** Fred Astaire, Lucille Bremer, Frank Morgan, Leon Ames, Mildred Natwick, Mary Nash, Ludwig Stossel, Jane Green, Remo Bufano. **Credits:** Dir: Vincente Minnelli; Prod: Arthur Freed; DP: Charles Rosher; Ed: George White; Composer: Arthur Freed, Harry Warren; Costumes: Irene Sharaff. Color, 109 min. **VHS, LASER**

You and Me
(1938) Paramount
Lang brews an odd gumbo of gangsters, romance, comedy, and music in his third Hollywood picture. Ex-con Raft works in a store staffed largely with parolees, including Sidney, with whom he begins a romance only to discover that she's also a con. The news sends him back to the underworld unaware that she's carrying his baby. Sidney uses humorous good sense, though, to foil his backsliding and leads him to the altar. **Cast:** George Raft, Sylvia Sidney, Robert Cummings, Harry Carey, Julia Faye, Joyce Compton, Arthur Hoyt, Warren Hymer, Juanita Quigley. **Credits:** Dir: Fritz Lang; Prod: Fritz Lang; Writer: Virginia Van Upp; Story: Norman Krasna; DP: Charles Lang; Ed: Paul Weather-

wax; Prod Design: Hans Dreier; Composer: Kurt Weill; Art Director: Ernst Fegte. B&W, 90 min. **VHS**

You Belong to Me
(1941) Columbia
In this rematch of *The Lady Eve*'s romantic pairing, idle millionaire Fonda gets distracted by the sight of Stanwyck while skiing. The resulting accident brings Stanwyck, the local doctor, rushing to treat his injuries. The pair fall in love and marry, but because he has time on his hands, Fonda constantly badgers Stanwyck with jealous fantasies. In order to save her marriage, Stanwyck pushes her husband into a job. When denounced for taking a low-level job from someone more deserving, Fonda finds a use for his money that's beneficial for his marriage and the community. **Cast:** Barbara Stanwyck, Henry Fonda, Edgar Buchanan, Roger Clark, Ruth Donnelly, Melville Cooper, Ralph Peter, Maude Eburne, Renie Riano, Ellen Lowe. **Credits:** Dir: Wesley Ruggles; Prod: Wesley Ruggles; Writer: Claude Binyon; Story: Dalton Trumbo; DP: Joseph Walker; Ed: Viola Lawrence; Prod Design: Lionel Banks; Composer: Frederick Hollander. B&W, 94 min.

You Came Along
(1945) Paramount
This is a romantic melodrama (penned by Ayn Rand!) in which three fliers go on a war-bond drive with a pretty Treasury Department employee (Scott). She falls for Cummings, but he doesn't reveal his battle with leukemia. They marry and Scott is soon a widow, but she receives comfort from his friends. **Cast:** Robert Cummings, Lizabeth Scott, Don Defore, Charles Drake, Julie Bishop, Kim Hunter, Rhys Williams, Franklin Pangborn, Minor Watson. **Credits:** Dir: John Farrow; Prod: Hal B. Wallis; Writer: Ayn Rand, Robert Smith; DP: Daniel L. Fapp; Ed: Eda Warren; Composer: Victor Young; Art Director: Hans Dreier, Hal Pereira. B&W, 103 min.

You Can't Cheat an Honest Man
(1939) Universal
Fields's first feature for Universal survived on-set battles with director Marshall to become one of his best. Fleabag circus operator Fields sees an opportunity to improve his station in life when his daughter (Moore) gets a proposal from a rich suitor. This breaks circus performer Bergen's heart and sets up big-screen skirmishes between radio combatants

Fields and Charlie McCarthy, Bergen's dummy sidekick. **Cast:** W. C. Fields, Edgar Bergen, Constance Moore, James Bush, Mary Forbes, Thurston Hall. **Credits:** Dir: George Marshall; Prod: Lester Cowan; Writer: George Marion, Richard Mack, Everett Freeman; DP: Milton Krasner; Ed: Otto Ludwig; Prod Design: Jack Otterson. B&W, 79 min. **VHS**

You Can't Have Everything
(1937) Fox
In this musical romantic comedy, Faye plays a struggling playwright and direct descendant of Edgar Allan Poe. When Ameche, a show-biz insider, gets her play made, as a musical, he falls head over heels for her. His girlfriend, Lee, in her film debut, isn't amused. The picture features gems by the Ritz Brothers, Louis Prima, and some nifty tap dancing by Samuel Green and Ted Fraser. Songs include "Danger, Love at Work," "Please Pardon Us We're in Love," "The Loveliness of You," and "Long Underwear." **Cast:** Alice Faye, The Ritz Brothers, Don Ameche, Charles Winninger, Gypsy Rose Lee, Arthur Treacher, Tony Martin, Phyllis Brooks, Louis Prima, Samuel Green. **Credits:** Dir: Norman Taurog; Prod: Darryl F. Zanuck, Lawrence Schwab; Writer: Harry Tugend, Karl Tunberg, Jack Yellen; DP: Lucien N. Andriot; Ed: Hanson T. Fritch; Prod Design: Duncan Cramer; Composer: Mark Gordon, Harry Revel. B&W, 100 min.

You Can't Take It with You
(1938) Columbia
The Pulitzer Prize–winning play by George S. Kaufman and Moss Hart gets an endearing Capra treatment. Arthur fears she may never lead a normal life as she's surrounded by her family's lovable lunacy. Grandfather Barrymore amassed a pile of cash and decided that he and his family were going to spend it doing only what they really want, which includes xylophone playing, ballet dancing, mystery writing, and experimenting with fireworks. Into this eccentric household comes Arthur's dubious beau, Stewart, the son of Arthur's boss, Arnold. After hilarious mishaps, love wins out. Academy Award Nominations: 7, including Best Supporting Actress: Spring Byington; Best Screenplay. **Academy Awards:** Best Picture; Best Director. **Cast:** Jean Arthur, James Stewart, Lionel Barrymore, Edward Arnold, Mischa Auer, Ann Miller, Spring Byington, Samuel S. Hinds. **Credits:** Dir: Frank Capra; Prod: Frank Capra; Writer:

Robert Riskin; DP: Joseph Walker; Ed: Gene Havlick; Composer: Dimitri Tiomkin; Art Director: Stephen Goosson. B&W, 128 min. **VHS, LASER**

You for Me
(1952) MGM
Film noir queen Greer takes a shot at romantic comedy. When philanthropist playboy Lawford takes a double-barrel load of buckshot in the rump while on a hunting trip, he ends up in a hospital his financial contributions have helped to keep in the black. Hospital administrator Young encourages Greer to be nice to her VIP patient, but she treats Lawford just like every other stubbed-toe that comes through her ward, a strategy that makes her only more attractive to the playboy. **Cast:** Jane Greer, Peter Lawford, Gig Young, Rita Corday, Julia Dean, Howard Wendell, Otto Hulett, Barbara Brown, Barbara Ruick, Kathryn Card. **Credits:** Dir: Don Weis; Prod: Henry Berman; Writer: William Roberts; DP: Paul C. Vogel; Ed: Newell P. Kimlin; Composer: Alberto Colombo; Art Director: Cedric Gibbons, Eddie Imazu. B&W, 71 min.

You Gotta Stay Happy
(1948) Universal
In this screwball confection with the unlikely pairing of Stewart and Fontaine, she takes wedding-night refuge from her ill-advised marriage in Stewart's hotel room. When she can't be revived the next day, bankrupt air-cargo executive Stewart takes her on a cross-country trip with a plane full of eccentrics including a chain-smoking chimp. By the time the plane crashlands, Stewart and Fontaine are in love. **Cast:** James Stewart, Joan Fontaine, Eddie Albert, Percy Kilbride, Roland Young, Stanley Prager, Edith Evanson, Porter Hall, William Bakewell, Emory Parnell. **Credits:** Dir: H. C. Potter; Prod: Karl Tunberg; Writer: Karl Tunberg; Story: Robert Carson; DP: Russell Metty; Ed: Paul Weatherwax; Prod Design: Alexander Golitzen; Composer: Danielle Amfitheatrof; Costumes: Jean Louis; SFX: David Horsley. B&W, 101 min. **VHS**

You'll Find Out
(1940) RKO
Radio star Kyser and his crew head to a creepy house for Parrish's 21st birthday party, where it seems the other guests (including Karloff, Lugosi, and Lorre) are determined that the birthday girl (and beneficiary of a large bequest) won't see 22. Academy Award Nomination: Best Song ("I'd

Know You Anywhere"). **Cast:** Kay Kyser, Boris Karloff, Peter Lorre, Bela Lugosi, Helen Parrish, Dennis O'Keefe, Alma Kruger, Leonard Mudie. **Credits:** Dir: David Butler; Prod: David Butler; Writer: James V. Kern; DP: Frank Redman; Ed: Irene Morra; Composer: Roy Webb; Art Director: Van Nest Polglase. B&W, 97 min. **VHS**

You'll Never Get Rich
(1941) Columbia
Astaire and Hayworth make a smart, sexy pair, perhaps even more electric than the better-known screen coupling of Astaire and Rogers. Choreographer Astaire leads Hayworth through a few steps and she leads him on a merry romantic chase. Producer Benchley uses Astaire as a cover for his own aspirations toward Hayworth, though at first she's cool toward the choreographer. Her army captain boyfriend lets the show go on when Astaire is drafted in the middle of their show. The Cole Porter songs include "Since I Kissed My Baby Goodbye," "Wedding Cake Walk," and "Dream Dancing." Academy Award Nominations: Best Song ("Since I Kissed My Baby Goodbye"); Best Scoring of a Musical Picture. **Cast:** Fred Astaire, Rita Hayworth, John Hubbard, Robert Benchley, Osa Massen, Frieda Inescort, Guinn "Big Boy" Williams, Donald MacBride. **Credits:** Dir: Sidney Lanfield; Prod: Samuel Bischoff; Writer: Michael Fessier; DP: Phillip Tannura; Ed: Otto Meyer; Choreographer: Robert Alton; Art Director: Lionel Banks. B&W, 88 min. **VHS, LASER**

You Never Can Tell
(1951) Universal
Surely here is one of the highest concepts (or perhaps the writers were the highest) in the history of Hollywood. A murdered dog who was heir to a fortune asks for and receives the chance to reincarnate as private investigator Powell (along with sidekick Holden, a former racehorse) to track the killer. He and the filly must return to Beastatory before the next moon or forever remain humanimals, but, after falling in love with Dow, the prime suspect, Powell may not return. **Cast:** Dick Powell, Peggy Dow, Joyce Holden, Charles Drake, Albert Sharpe, Sara Taft, William Vedder, Watson Downs, Mort Shuman, Lou Polan. **Credits:** Dir: Lou Breslow; Prod: Leonard Goldstein; Writer: Lou Breslow, George Chandler; DP: Maury Gertsman; Ed: Frank Gross; Prod Design: Bernard Herzbrun, Alexander Golitzen; Composer: Hans J. Salter. B&W, 78 min.

Young and Innocent
(1937) Gaumont
In one of Hitchcock's early British mysteries, a police chief's plucky teenage daughter (Pilbeam) flees with a charming, wrongfully accused fugitive (Marmont) as they try to clear his name and catch the real murderer. Much of the film is a chase, but there are well-known sequences (the dolly shot in the final sequence up to the real killer's twitching face) that show the touch of the future master. **Cast:** Derrick Demarney, Nova Pilbeam, Percy Marmont, Mary Clare, John Longden, George Curzon, Basil Radford, George Merritt. **Credits:** Dir: Alfred Hitchcock; Prod: Edward Black; Writer: Charles Bennett; DP: Bernard Knowles; Ed: Charles Frend; Prod Design: Alfred Junge; Composer: Louis Levy. B&W, 84 min. **VHS, LASER**

Young and Willing
(1942) United Artists
A young Holden and Hayward shine in a story of struggling young actors and actresses trying to get a break in New York. The three actors and three actresses share one apartment, leading to romantic entanglements, a marriage, and a crack at the big time when their landlady finds an unproduced play by their downstairs neighbor, Benchley. **Cast:** Susan Hayward, William Holden, Robert Benchley, Eddie Bracken, Martha O'Driscoll, Barbara Britton, Mabel Paige, James Brown. **Credits:** Dir: Edward H. Griffith; Prod: Edward H. Griffith; Writer: Virginia Van Upp; DP: Leo Tover; Ed: Eda Warren; Prod Design: Hans Dreier. B&W, 84 min. **VHS**

Young at Heart
(1954) Warner Bros.
In this musical romantic melodrama sisters Day and Malone compete for the attention of composer Young. He and Day prepare to marry until Day discovers Malone's feelings for Young and defers to her sister. Day marries Young's moody friend Sinatra, and they learn to love each other as the years go by. Great songs by George and Ira Gershwin, Cole Porter, Harold Arlen, and more. A musical remake of 1938's *Four Daughters*. **Cast:** Doris Day, Frank Sinatra, Gig Young, Ethel Barrymore, Dorothy Malone, Robert Keith, Elisabeth Fraser, Alan Hale, Jr., Lonny Chapman, Frank Ferguson. **Credits:** Dir: Gordon Douglas; Prod: Henry Blanke; Writer: Liam O'Brien; DP: Ted McCord; Ed: William Ziegler;

Composer: Ray Heindorf; Art Director: John Beckman. Color, 117 min. **VHS**

Young Bess
(1953) MGM
In a lavishly mounted and engagingly performed historical romance, Simmons plays the young princess who would become Elizabeth I. She deals with the heartbreak of first love with an admiral (Granger, Simmons's off-screen husband) and the machinations of jealous courtiers. Laughton again in one of his most acclaimed roles, Bess's father, Henry VIII. Academy Award Nominations: Best (Color) Art Direction—Set Decoration; Best (Color) Costume Design. **Cast:** Jean Simmons, Stewart Granger, Charles Laughton, Deborah Kerr, Cecil Kellaway, Leo G. Carroll, Guy Walsh, Guy Rolfe. **Credits:** Dir: George Sidney; Prod: Sidney Franklin; Writer: Jan Lustig; DP: Charles Rosher; Ed: Ralph E. Winters; Prod Design: Cedric Gibbons; Composer: Miklos Rozsa. Color, 112 min. **VHS**

Young Frankenstein
(1974) Fox
The high point of Brooks's genre parodies depends for many of its laughs on closely observed and lovingly re-created situations (the blind man scene, the little girl and the lake) taken from the original *Frankenstein* (1931) and *Bride of Frankenstein* (1935)—even the mad doctor's laboratory set is the original. Wilder plays a scientist and descendant of the good doctor (though he insists the name is pronounced "Fronk-en-steen") who inherits the creepy old house and his predecessor's experiments. Brooks's stock company are all in top form, particularly Wilder and Kahn. A treat for any classic-movie fan. Academy Award Nominations: 2, including Best Adapted Screenplay. **Cast:** Gene Wilder, Peter Boyle, Marty Feldman, Madeline Kahn, Cloris Leachman, Teri Garr, Kenneth Mars, Gene Hackman. **Credits:** Dir: Mel Brooks; Prod: Michael Gruskoff; Writer: Gene Wilder, Mel Brooks; DP: Gerald Hirschfeld; Ed: John C. Howard; Prod Design: Dale Hennesy; Composer: John Morris. B&W, 108 min. **VHS, LASER, DVD**

The Young in Heart
(1938) United Artists
This is great fun as a family of con artists (Young, Burke, Fairbanks, and Gaynor) set their sights on elderly Dupree's fortune. She turns the tables and gives all four a lesson in life and

the value of hard work. Academy Award Nominations: Best Cinematography; Best Original Score. **Cast:** Minnie Dupree, Janet Gaynor, Douglas Fairbanks, Jr., Roland Young, Billie Burke, Richard Carlson, Paulette Goddard, Henry Stephenson, Eily Malyon, Tom Ricketts. **Credits:** Dir: Richard Wallace; Prod: David O. Selznick; Writer: Paul Osborn, Charles Bennett; DP: Leon Shamroy; Ed: Hal C. Kern; Prod Design: Lyle Wheeler; Composer: Franz Waxman. B&W, 91 min. **VHS**

The Young Lions
(1958) Fox
This dramatic portrayal of men at war is based on the novel by Irwin Shaw. The story follows two Nazis (Brando, a young, idealistic officer, and Schell, a ruthless career soldier) and two Americans (Clift, a Jew facing prejudice in the army, and carefree Martin) from training to the disillusionment of war and the shock of the concentration

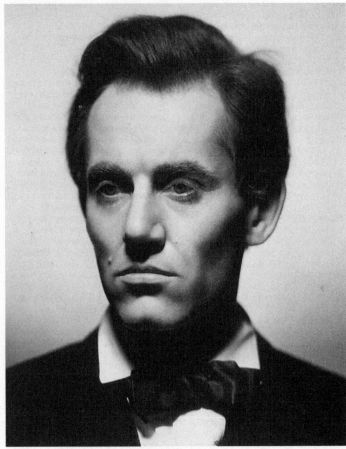

Young Mr. Lincoln (1940)

camps. The combination of Brando and Clift promises fireworks, and, though both were pleased with their performances, there were more fireworks on the set than on the screen. Academy Award Nominations: 3, including Best (Black-and-White) Cinematography; Best Sound. **Cast:** Marlon Brando, Montgomery Clift, Dean Martin, Hope Lange, Barbara Rush, Maximilian Schell, May Britt, Lee Van Cleef. **Credits:** Dir: Edward Dmytryk; Prod: Al Lichtman; Writer: Edward Anhalt; Story: Irwin Shaw; DP: Joseph MacDonald; Ed: Dorothy Spencer; Prod Design: Lyle Wheeler; Composer: Hugo Friedhofer. B&W, 167 min. **VHS, LASER**

Young Man with a Horn
(1950) Warner Bros.
Curtiz directs a dark portrait of a musician obsessed with giving voice to the music he hears in his head. Based loosely on the life of Bix Beiderbecke, Douglas plays a trumpeter (his parts

were dubbed by Harry James) who pursues a sound that he first hears as a boy on the shadowy streets of the wrong side of town, through firings for playing the wrong kind of jazz, through success, and through a long tumble down to the gutter. Bacall plays a slinky, soulless viper who temporarily lures him away from his calling. Day cheers him on and lifts him up when he needs it. A gutsy, emotional portrayal for Douglas, with great feeling for the music. **Cast:** Kirk Douglas, Lauren Bacall, Doris Day, Hoagy Carmichael, Juano Hernandez, Jerome Cowan, Mary Beth Hughes, Nestor Paiva. **Credits:** Dir: Michael Curtiz; Prod: Jerry Wald; Writer: Carl Foreman, Edmund H. North; DP: Ted McCord; Ed: Alan Crosland, Jr.; Composer: Ray Heindorf; Art Director: Edward Carrere. B&W, 112 min. **VHS, LASER**

Young Man with Ideas
(1952) MGM
In a light romantic comedy from Leisen, Ford plays a legal clerk studying to pass the California bar exam who faces romantic challenges to his happy marriage from a fellow student (Foch) and singer Darcel. Then his wife (Roman) lands them in hot water with some mobsters when she jokingly accepts a bet from an unknown caller who thinks he's reached the bookie that had previously owned their telephone number. In the climactic courtroom scene, the new young lawyer successfully defends himself against criminal charges. **Cast:** Glenn Ford, Donna Corcoran, Ray Collins, Denise Darcel, Nina Foch, Sheldon Leonard, Ruth Roman. **Credits:** Dir: Mitchell Leisen; Prod: Gottfried Reinhardt, William H. Wright; Writer: Arthur Sheekman, Ben Barzman; Ed: Frederick Smith; Composer: David Rose; Art Director: Cedric Gibbons, Arthur Longeran. B&W, 85 min.

Young Mr. Lincoln
(1940) Fox
Ford's depiction of Lincoln's early career finds the statesman in the shy, shambling young lawyer. Fonda plays the future president in the period from the Whig convention of 1832 to his decision to pursue his law career to his first major trial. Particularly telling and poetic is the loss of his first love (Moore), with the scene dissolving from their meeting by a river to her grave site on the same spot next to the now-frozen river. Fine historical drama with a great performance from Fonda. Academy Award Nomination for Best Original Screenplay. **Cast:** Henry

Fonda, Alice Brady, Marjorie Weaver, Donald Meek, Pauline Moore, Arleen Whelan, Richard Cromwell, Ward Bond. **Credits:** Dir: John Ford; Prod: Kenneth MacGowan; Writer: Lamar Trotti; DP: Bert Glennon, Arthur Miller; Ed: Walter Thompson; Prod Design: Richard Day; Composer: Alfred Newman. B&W, 100 min. VHS, LASER

The Young Philadelphians
(1959) Warner Bros.
In this melodrama, Newman is an ambitious lawyer sacrificing his true love for social advancement and his principles for career advancement. Raised believing he was fathered by a prominent Philadelphia lawyer, Newman scratches his way back into Main Line society with his own law career and his assignations with powerful women. He reclaims his values defending his war buddy, Vaughn. Academy Award Nominations: 3, including Best Supporting Actor: Robert Vaughn. **Cast:** Paul Newman, Barbara Rush, Brian Keith, Alexis Smith, Diane Brewster, Billie Burke, John Williams, Robert Vaughn. **Credits:** Dir: Vincent Sherman; Prod: James Gunn; DP: Harry Stradling; Ed: William Ziegler; Composer: Ernest Gold; Art Director: Malcolm Bert. B&W, 148 min. VHS

The Young Savages
(1961) United Artists
An assistant D.A. (Lancaster) from the mean streets of an Italian–Puerto Rican neighborhood gets the assignment when his politically ambitious boss prosecutes a gang murder. Lancaster's knowledge of the streets and his sympathy for the young gang members lead to surprising revelations about the turf war that led to murder. A fast-paced urban drama that was Frankenheimer's second feature, with a script from Miller and Anhalt, his frequent collaborators from TV drama. Based on *A Matter of Conviction* by Evan Hunter. **Cast:** Burt Lancaster, John Davis Chandler, Telly Savalas, Chris Robinson, Milton Selzer, Dina Merrill, Shelley Winters, Edward Andrews, Pilar Seurat. **Credits:** Dir: John Frankenheimer; Prod: Pat Duggan; Writer: Edward Anhalt, J. P. Miller; Story: Evan Hunter; DP: Lionel Lindon; Ed: Eda Warren; Prod Design: Burr Smidt; Composer: David Amram. B&W, 103 min. VHS

Young Tom Edison
(1940) MGM
Rooney brings his trademark vitality to the role of the young inventor. The

story depicts two years in Edison's life as his experiments cause an uproar in the lives of his family and friends. **Cast:** Mickey Rooney, Fay Bainter, George Bancroft, Virginia Weidler, Eugene Palette, Victor Kilian, Bobby Jordan, Lloyd Corrigan. **Credits:** Dir: Norman Taurog; Prod: John Considine; Writer: Bradbury Foote, Dore Schary; DP: Sidney Wagner; Ed: Elmo Veron; Prod Design: Cedric Gibbons; Composer: Edward Ward. B&W, 82 min. VHS

You Only Live Once
(1937) United Artists
Lang's finest Hollywood film depicts the haunting story of a man plagued by his past and driven to desperation. Ex-con Fonda swears to go straight and marries long-suffering Sidney. But because of his criminal record, he loses his job and their apartment, and, on circumstantial evidence, is sentenced to death for a murder he didn't commit. After a last-ditch prison break, Fonda and Sidney make their way through the cold, gray Depression-era land toward Canada. Lang reportedly worked the cast relentlessly, keeping them awake nearly around the clock to achieve a worn, hopeless tone in their performances. **Cast:** Sylvia Sidney, Henry Fonda, Barton MacLane, William Gargan, Jean Dixon, Warren Hymer, Charles "Chic" Sale, Margaret Hamilton. **Credits:** Dir: Fritz Lang; Prod: Walter Wanger; Writer: Gene Towne, Graham Baker; DP: Leon Shamroy; Ed: Daniel Mandell; Composer: Alfred Newman; Art Director: Alexander Toluboff. B&W, 90 min. VHS

You Only Live Twice
(1967) United Artists
This is a middling Bond thriller in which SPECTRE agent Pleasence snares Russian and U.S. satellites knowing it will precipitate WWIII. Screenplay by Roald Dahl. **Cast:** Sean Connery, Akiko Wakabayashi, Tetsuro Tamba, Donald Pleasence, Teru Shimada,

Karin Dor, Lois Maxwell, Desmond Llewelyn. **Credits:** Dir: Lewis Gilbert; Prod: Albert R. Broccoli, Harry Saltzman; Writer: Roald Dahl, Harold Jack Bloom; DP: Freddie Young; Ed: Peter Hunt; Composer: John Barry; Art Director: Harry Pottle. Color, 118 min. VHS, LASER

You're a Big Boy Now
(1966) Warner Bros.
This whimsical early effort from Coppola follows a young man (Kastner) as he escapes his smothering mother (Page) and ventures to New York in the swinging '60s for an education in the ways of the world. Thanks to more experienced Bill, Kastner pursues a go-go girl and finds true love with pal Black. Sound track songs by The Lovin' Spoonful. Academy Award Nomination: Best Supporting Actress: Geraldine Page. **Cast:** Elizabeth Hartman, Peter Kastner, Geraldine Page, Julie Harris, Michael Dunn, Tony Bill, Karen Black, Dolph Sweet. **Credits:** Dir: Francis Ford Coppola; Prod: Phil Feldman; Writer: Francis Ford Coppola; DP: Andrew Laszlo; Ed: Aram Avakian; Composer: Robert Prince; Art Director: Vassilis Fotopoulos. Color, 98 min. VHS, LASER

You're in the Navy Now
(1951) Fox
In a comedy about an inexperienced naval officer, Cooper is assigned to an experimental, steam-powered patrol vessel that gets dubbed the U.S.S. *Teakettle*. Everything that can go wrong does, despite efforts by Mitchell, the only sea-tested crewman aboard, but they are nevertheless awarded for their perseverance. The debut for Bronson. **Cast:** Gary Cooper, Millard Mitchell, Eddie Albert, John McIntire, Ray Collins, Harry Von Zell, Jack Webb, Lee Marvin, Charles Bronson. **Credits:** Dir: Henry Hathaway; Prod: Fred Kohlmar; Writer: John W. Hazard, Richard Murphy; DP: Joe MacDonald; Ed: James B. Clark; Prod

"Between us we arrived at the idea that Christian was someone who had gone into the war openly, then he learned that the war, like all wars, was useless."

Edward Dmytryk on directing Marlon Brando in *The Young Lions* (1958)

Design: J. Russell Spencer, Lyle Wheeler; Composer: Cyril Mockridge. B&W, 93 min.

You're Never Too Young
(1955) Paramount
Jerry disguises himself as a schoolboy and ends up in Dino's classroom. He wants to become a barber, but when a bunch of stolen diamonds winds up in his hands, he's too scared to let them go. Thief Burr will stop at nothing to get the loot and, donning a pint-sized sailor suit, Jerry hides out at a girls' school and proceeds to make suave teacher Martin's life miserable. Left-field remake of *The Major and the Minor* (1942). **Cast:** Dean Martin, Jerry Lewis, Diana Lynn, Nina Foch, Raymond Burr, Mitzi McCall, Veda Ann Borg, Margery Maude, Ron Vincent, Nancy Kulp. **Credits:** Dir: Norman Taurog; Prod: Paul Jones; Writer: Sidney Sheldon, Fanny Kilbourne; DP: Daniel Fapp; Ed: Archie Marshek; Prod Design: A. Earl Hedrick, Hal Pereira; Composer: Sammy Cahn, Arthur Schwartz. Color, 102 min.

You're Telling Me
(1934) Paramount
This hilarious Fields vehicle features some of his most famous routines. Fields, an unsuccessful inventor of hilariously useless items, sinks to despair and the bottle. When his daughter (Marsh) announces her engagement to rich boy Crabbe, Fields pulls out all the stops to redeem himself and comes up with puncture-proof tires. When a mix-up foils the demon-stration, he turns to suicide but even that goes awry. A helpful princess puts all to right. A remake of his 1926 silent, *So's Your Old Man.* **Cast:** W. C. Fields, Joan Marsh, Larry Buster Crabbe, Adrienne Ames, Louise Carter, Kathleen Howard, James B. Kenton, Robert McKenzie, Dell Henderson, Nora Cecil. **Credits:** Dir: Erle C. Kenton; Prod: William Le Baron. Writer: Paul Jones, Walter DeLeon, Russell Streiner, J. P. McEvoy; DP: Alfred Gilks; Ed: Otto Lovering; Composer: Howard I. Young; Art Director: Robert Odell. B&W, 67 min.

Yours, Mine and Ours
(1968) United Artists
Widower Fonda (who has 10 kids) meets and marries Ball (who has eight kids). This features the expected humorous complications of having 18 kids under one roof, but also warm, good-natured performances from the leads. **Cast:** Lucille Ball, Henry Fonda, Van Johnson, Tom Bosley, Ben Murphy, Kimberly Beck, Mitch Vogel, Eric Shea. **Credits:** Dir: Melville Shavelson; Prod: Robert F. Blumofe; Writer: Melville Shavelson; DP: Charles F. Wheeler; Ed: Stuart Gilmore; Composer: Fred Karlin; Art Director: Arthur Lonergan. Color, 114 min. **VHS, LASER**

You Said a Mouthful
(1932) Warner Bros.
This is an early Rogers appearance (mostly in a bathing suit) in a vehicle for satchel-mouthed comedian Brown, who, despite being afraid of the water, invents a bathing suit that will not sink. He gets a chance to test it when he's mistaken for a swimming champion by heiress Rogers. **Cast:** Joe E. Brown, Ginger Rogers, Sheila Terry, Guinn "Big Boy" Williams, Harry Gribon, Oscar Apfel, Edwin Maxwell, Frank Hagney, Selmer Jackson, Mia Marvin. **Credits:** Dir: Lloyd Bacon; Prod: Raymond Griffith; Writer: Robert Lord, Bolton Mallory; Story: William B. Dover; DP: Richard Towers; Ed: Owen Marks; Art Director: Jack Okey. B&W, 75 min.

You Were Never Lovelier
(1942) Columbia
This is the stylish second outing for Astaire and Hayworth (following their equally enjoyable *You'll Never Get Rich,* 1941). Astaire blows his money on the horses and finds himself at loose ends in Argentina. He pursues Menjou for a booking in his nightclub, and finds himself pursuing his daughter, Hayworth, for her hand. Besides the title song, the film score features "I'm Old-Fashioned" and "Dearly Beloved." Academy Award Nominations: 3, Best Sound Recording; Best Song ("Dearly Beloved"); Best Scoring of a Musical Picture. **Cast:** Fred Astaire, Rita Hayworth, Adolphe Menjou, Leslie Brooks, Adele Mara, Isobel Elsom, Gus Schilling, Barbara Brown. **Credits:** Dir: William A. Seiter; Prod: Louis F. Edelman; Writer: Michael Fessier; DP: Ted Tetzlaff; Ed: William A. Lyon; Prod Design: Lionel Banks; Composer: Jerome Kern. B&W, 98 min. **VHS, LASER**

Zabriskie Point
(1970) MGM
In Italian master Michelangelo Antonioni's first American film, he tracks the rebelliousness of the early '70s from a meeting of campus radicals to Frechette's search for experience in the expanses of Death Valley. All the hallmarks of the time are here with its abundantly trippy music and dialogue. A curious interpretation of American culture from an outside observer who happens to be one of the cinema's great visual artists. **Cast:** Mark Frechette, Daria Halperin, Rod Taylor, Paul Fix, G. D. Spradlin, Bill Garaway. **Credits:** Dir: Michelangelo Antonioni; Prod: Carlo Ponti; Writer: Michelangelo Antonioni, Fred Gardner, Sam Shepard, Tonino Guerra, Claire Peploe; DP: Alfio Contini; Ed: Franco Arcalli; Prod Designer: Dean Tavoularis. Color, 112 min.

Zaza
(1939) Paramount
The almost incredible durability of this plot would seem to point to an enduring public appetite for the mildly prurient. It saw service as a successful play, an opera, and no less than three silent films, the last in 1923 with Gloria Swanson. Cukor directs the fourth outing for this story of an affair between Marshall's married man and Colbert's steamy French chanteuse, who leaves him to become the toast of Gay Paree. Comic Lahr's performance is the high point. **Cast:** Claudette Colbert, Herbert Marshall, Bert Lahr, Helen Westley, Constance Collier, Genevieve Tobin, Walter Catlett, Ann Todd, Rex O'Malley, Ernest Cossart. **Credits:** Dir: George Cukor; Prod: Albert Lewin; Writer: Zoe Akins; Story: Pierre Breton, Charles Simon; DP: Charles Lang, Jr.; Ed: Edward Dmytryk; Composer: Frank Loesser, Frederick Hollander; Art Director: Hans Dreier, Robert Usher. B&W, 83 min.

Zenobia
(1939) United Artists
Hardy gamely tests his comic wings without perennial sidekick Laurel; instead, we get a taste of silent veteran Langdon as Hardy's foil. The plot is essentially a pachyderm romance: Langdon is a carnie who loves Zenobia the elephant, but her affections stray when Dr. Hardy delicately undoes a knot in her tail. The miffed Langdon takes Hardy to court to win back Zenobia's love, but she comes back on her own. **Cast:** Oliver Hardy, Harry Langdon, Billie Burke, Alice Brady, James Ellison, Jean Parker, June Lang, Olin Howland, J. Farrell MacDonald, Stepin Fetchit. **Credits:** Dir: Gordon Douglas; Prod: Hal Roach, A. Edward Sutherland; Writer: Corey Ford; Story: Walter DeLeon, Arnold Belgard; DP: Karl Struss; Ed: Bert Jordan; Composer: Marvin Hatley; Costumes: Omar Kiam; SFX: Roy Seawright; Art Director: Charles D. Hall. B&W, 74 min.

Ziegfeld Follies
(1946) MGM
A lavish salute from MGM's Freed musical unit to Broadway's most opulent producer—the third MGM tribute and the second time around for Powell playing the great showman, now in heaven and dreaming of the shows he could put on. Mostly an excuse for glorious musical set-pieces directed by the studio's best musical helmsman, Minnelli, the highlights include a duet for Astaire and Kelly (a first!) in a rare song by the Gershwins, "The Babbit and the Bromide," Esther Williams in the water, and Garland teasing Greer Garson. **Cast:** Fred Astaire, Lucille Ball, William Powell, Judy Garland, Gene Kelly, Red Skelton, Fanny Brice, Edward Arnold, Lucille Bremer. **Credits:** Dir: Vincente Minnelli; Prod: Arthur Freed; Writer: Jack McGowan,

Guy Bolton; DP: George J. Folsey; Ed: Albert Akst; Prod Design: Cedric Gibbons. Color, 115 min. **VHS, LASER**

Ziegfeld Girl
(1941) MGM
The rise and (in some cases) fall of three Ziegfeld Girls, Garland, Lamarr, and Turner, rendered in high MGM style. Young stage vet Garland leaves her father's act for a crack at the bright lights, Turner chases rainbows with the Park Avenue crowd and breaks truck driver Stewart's heart, and Lamarr has to choose between the stage and her struggling violinist husband. Mainly, though, lots of singing and dancing. Among the highlights: Garland singing "I'm Always Chasing Rainbows." **Cast:** James Stewart, Lana Turner, Judy Garland, Hedy Lamarr, Tony Martin, Jackie Cooper, Ian Hunter, Edward Everett Horton, Al Shean, Eve Arden. **Credits:** Dir: Robert Z. Leonard; Prod: Pandro S. Berman; Writer: Marguerite Roberts; DP: Ray June; Ed: Blanche Sewell; Prod Design: Cedric Gibbons; Composer: Herbert Stothart. B&W, 133 min. **VHS**

Zoo in Budapest
(1933) Fox
This whimsical drama follows Young as a young orphan, who hides at the zoo in Budapest, where she meets an animal keeper devoted to his charges. When he steals a woman's fur coat, he also has to hide out in the zoo, where he saves both Young from assault and a child stuck in a tiger's cage. A lost gem. **Cast:** Loretta Young, Gene Raymond, O. P. Heggie, Wally Albright, Paul Fix, Murray Kinnell, Ruth Warren, Roy Stewart, Frances Rich, Niles Welch. **Credits:** Dir: Rowland V. Lee; Prod: Jesse L. Lasky; Writer: Dan Totheroh, Louise Long, Melville Baker, John Kirkland, Rowland V. Lee; DP: Lee Garmes; Ed: Harold Schuster. B&W, 85 min.

Zorba the Greek

(1964) Fox

This is the career-defining role for Quinn as Kazantzakis's colorful, free-spirited Greek hero. When restless young Englishman Bates comes to a small Greek island to explore his roots and his future, he meets Quinn and joins him at the hotel run by aging prostitute Kedrova. He also catches the eye of local beauty Papas, which leads to shame and anguish when a heartbroken local commits suicide. The islanders turn on Papas, stoning her to death, and, soon after, Kedrova dies in Quinn's arms. The two men console themselves with Quinn's soulful dance to the beauty of life that shines through the pain. Originally meant for the art houses, its international success earned Oscars and spawned a musical stage adaptation, which also starred Quinn. Academy Award Nominations: 7, including Best Picture; Best Director; Best Actor: Anthony Quinn; Best (Adapted) Screenplay. **Academy Awards:** Best Supporting Actress: Lila Kedrova; Best Black-and-White Cinematography; Best Art Direction—Set Decoration (B&W). **Cast:** Anthony Quinn, Alan Bates, Irene Papas, Lila Kedrova, George Foundas, Takis Emmanuel, Yorgo Voyagis. **Credits:** Dir: Michael Cacoyannis; Prod: Michael Cacoyannis; Writer: Michael Cacoyannis; Story: Nikos Kazantzakis; DP: Walter Lassally; Ed: Michael Cacoyannis; Composer: Mikis Theodorakis; Art Director: Vassilis Fotopoulos. B&W, 142 min. **VHS, LASER**

Zorba the Greek (1964)

Filmographies

Actors

June Allyson
(Oct. 17, 1917)
1978 Blackout
1972 They Only Kill Their Masters
1959 A Stranger in My Arms
1957 My Man Godfrey; Interlude
1956 The Opposite Sex; You Can't Run Away from It
1955 The McConnell Story a.k.a. Tiger in the Sky; Strategic Air Command; The Shrike
1954 A Woman's World; The Glenn Miller Story; Executive Suite
1953 Remains to Be Seen; Battle Circus
1952 The Girl in White
1951 Too Young to Kiss
1950 The Reformer and the Redhead; Right Cross
1949 Little Women; The Stratton Story
1948 The Bride Goes Wild; The Three Musketeers; Words and Music
1947 The High Barbaree; Good News
1946 The Sailor Takes a Wife; The Secret Heart; Two Sisters from Boston; Till the Clouds Roll By
1945 Her Highness and the Bellboy
1944 Music for Millions; Two Girls and a Sailor; Meet the People
1943 Best Foot Forward; Thousands Cheer; Girl Crazy

Don Ameche
(May 31, 1908–1993)
1994 Corrina, Corrina
1993 Homeward Bound: The Incredible Journey
1992 Folks!
1991 Oddball Hall; Oscar
1988 Cocoon: the Return a.k.a. Cocoon 2; Coming to America; Things Change
1987 Harry and the Hendersons
1985 Cocoon
1983 Trading Places
1970 Suppose They Gave a War and Nobody Came? a.k.a. War Games; The Boatniks
1966 Picture Mommy Dead a.k.a. Color Mommy Dead; Rings Around the World
1961 A Fever in the Blood
1955 Fire One
1954 Phantom Caravan
1949 Slightly French
1948 Sleep, My Love
1947 That's My Man
1946 So Goes My Love; A Genius in the Family
1945 Guest Wife; It's in the Bag a.k.a. The Fifth Chair
1944 Greenwich Village; A Wing and a Prayer

1943 The Happy Land; Something to Shout About; Heaven Can Wait
1942 Girl Trouble; The Magnificent Dope
1941 Kiss the Boys Goodbye; That Night in Rio; Confirm or Deny; Moon over Miami; The Feminine Touch a.k.a. The Gentle Touch
1940 Lillian Russell; Four Sons; Down Argentine Way
1939 Midnight; The Story of Alexander Graham Bell a.k.a. The Modern Miracle; Swanee River; The Three Musketeers; Hollywood Cavalcade
1938 Gateway; In Old Chicago; Josette; Happy Landing; Alexander's Ragtime Band
1937 You Can't Have Everything; Love Is News; Love Under Fire; Fifty Roads to Town a.k.a. Fifty Races to Town
1936 One in a Million; Ladies in Love; Ramona; Sins of Man
1935 Clive of India; Dante's Inferno

Julie Andrews
(Oct. 1, 1935)
1992 A Fine Romance
1991 Tchin-Tchin
1986 Duet for One; That's Life!
1983 The Man Who Loved Women
1982 Victor/Victoria
1981 S.O.B.
1980 Little Miss Marker
1979 10
1974 The Tamarind Seed
1970 Darling Lili
1968 Star!
1967 Thoroughly Modern Millie; The Singing Princess
1966 Torn Curtain; Hawaii
1965 The Sound of Music
1964 The Americanization of Emily; Mary Poppins

Alan Arkin
(Mar. 26, 1934)
1998 Slums of Beverly Hills
1997 Four Days in September; Grosse Pointe Blank; Gattaca
1996 Mother Night
1995 The Jerky Boys; Steal Big, Steal Little; Heck's Way Home
1994 North; Bullets over Broadway
1993 Indian Summer; So I Married an Axe Murderer
1992 Glengarry Glen Ross
1991 The Rocketeer
1990 Havana; Edward Scissorhands; Coupe De Ville
1986 Big Trouble
1985 The Fourth Wise Man; Joshua Then and Now; Bad Medicine

1983 The Return of Captain Invincible
1982 Full Moon High; The Last Unicorn
1981 Chu Chu and the Philly Flash; Improper Channels
1980 Simon
1979 The In-Laws; The Magician of Lublin
1977 Fire Sale
1976 The Seven-Per-Cent Solution
1975 Hearts of the West; Rafferty and the Gold Dust Twins
1974 Freebie and the Bean
1972 Last of the Red Hot Lovers; Deadhead Miles
1971 Little Murders
1970 Catch-22
1969 The Monitors; People Soup; Popi
1968 Inspector Clouseau; The Heart Is a Lonely Hunter
1967 Sette Volte Donna a.k.a. Woman Times Seven; Wait Until Dark
1966 The Russians Are Coming, the Russians Are Coming!
1957 Calypso Heat Wave

Jean Arthur
(Oct. 17, 1905–1991)
1953 Shane
1948 A Foreign Affair
1944 The Impatient Years
1943 A Lady Takes a Chance a.k.a. The Cowboy and the Girl; The More the Merrier
1942 The Talk of the Town
1941 The Devil and Miss Jones
1940 Arizona; Too Many Husbands
1939 Only Angels Have Wings; Mr. Smith Goes to Washington
1938 You Can't Take It with You
1937 Easy Living; History Is Made at Night
1936 The Plainsman; Adventure in Manhattan; The Ex-Mrs. Bradford; More Than a Secretary; Mr. Deeds Goes to Town
1935 If You Could Only Cook; Diamond Jim; Party Wire; Public Hero No. 1; Public Menace; The Whole Town's Talking
1934 Whirlpool; The Defense Rests
1933 The Past of Mary Holmes; Get That Venus
1931 The Lawyer's Secret; Ex-Bad Boy; The Virtuous Husband a.k.a. What Wives Don't Want; The Gang Buster
1930 The Return of Dr. Fu Manchu; The Silver Horde; Street of Chance; Paramount on Parade; Danger Lights; Young Eagles
1929 The Mysterious Doctor Fu Manchu; Half Way to

Heaven; The Canary Murder Case; The Saturday Night Kid; Stairs of Sand; The Greene Murder Case
1928 Sins of the Fathers; Easy Come, Easy Go; Warming Up; Brotherly Love
1927 Horse Shoes; Flying Luck; Broken Gate; Husband Hunters
1926 Under Fire; The Fighting Cheat; Double Daring
1925 Drug Store Cowboy; The Fighting Smile; A Man of Nerve; Seven Chances; Tearin' Loose; Hurricane Horseman
1924 Fast and Fearless; Biff Bang Buddy; Travelin' Fast; Thundering Romance; Bringin' Home the Bacon
1923 Cameo Kirby; The Temple of Venus

Fred Astaire
(May 10, 1899–1987)
1984 Gotta Dance, Gotta Sing; George Stevens: A Filmmaker's Journey
1981 Ghost Story
1977 Un Taxi Mauve a.k.a. The Purple Taxi
1976 The Amazing Dobermans; That's Entertainment, Part II
1974 The Towering Inferno; That's Entertainment
1969 Midas Run
1968 Finian's Rainbow
1962 The Notorious Landlady
1961 The Pleasure of His Company
1959 On the Beach
1957 Silk Stockings; Funny Face
1955 Daddy Long Legs
1953 The Band Wagon
1952 The Belle of New York
1951 Royal Wedding a.k.a. Wedding Bells
1950 Three Little Words; Let's Dance
1949 The Barkleys of Broadway
1948 Easter Parade
1946 Ziegfeld Follies; Blue Skies
1945 Yolanda and the Thief
1943 The Sky's the Limit
1942 Holiday Inn; You Were Never Lovelier
1941 You'll Never Get Rich
1940 Broadway Melody of 1940; Second Chorus
1939 The Story of Vernon and Irene Castle
1938 Carefree
1937 Shall We Dance?; A Damsel in Distress
1936 Follow the Fleet; Swing Time
1935 Top Hat; Roberta
1934 The Gay Divorcee a.k.a. Gay Divorce
1933 Dancing Lady; Flying Down to Rio
1915 Fanchon the Cricket

Mary Astor
(May 3, 1906–1987)
1965 Hush . . . Hush, Sweet Charlotte
1964 Youngblood Hawke
1961 Return to Peyton Place
1959 A Stranger in My Arms
1958 This Happy Feeling
1957 The Devil's Hairpin
1956 The Power and the Prize; A Kiss Before Dying
1949 Little Women; Act of Violence; Any Number Can Play
1947 Cass Timberlane; Cynthia; Desert Fury; Fiesta
1946 Claudia and David
1944 Meet Me in St. Louis; Blonde Fever
1943 Thousands Cheer; Young Ideas
1942 The Palm Beach Story; Across the Pacific
1941 The Great Lie; The Maltese Falcon
1940 Brigham Young— Frontiersman *a.k.a.* Brigham Young; Turnabout
1939 Midnight
1938 No Time to Marry; Paradise for Three; There's Always a Woman; Woman Against Woman; Listen, Darling
1937 The Prisoner of Zenda; The Hurricane
1936 Dodsworth; The Murder of Dr. Harrigan; And So They Were Married; Trapped by Television; The Lady from Nowhere
1935 Dinky; I Am a Thief; Man of Iron; Page Miss Glory; Red Hot Tires; Straight from the Heart
1934 The Man with Two Faces; Easy to Love; Return of the Terror; Upper World; The Case of the Howling Dog
1933 Jennie Gerhardt; The Little Giant; Convention City; The World Changes; The Kennel Murder Case
1932 Men of Chance; A Successful Calamity; Those We Love; Red Dust; The Lost Squadron
1931 Other Men's Women *a.k.a.* The Steel Highway; The Sin Ship; Smart Woman; The Royal Bed *a.k.a.* Queen's Husband; Behind Office Doors; White Shoulders
1930 The Runaway Bride; Holiday; Ladies Love Brutes; The Lash *a.k.a.* Adios
1929 New Year's Eve; The Woman from Hell; Show of Shows
1928 Romance of the Underworld *a.k.a.* Romance and Bright Lights; Dressed to Kill; Three-Ring Marriage; Dry Martini; Heart to Heart
1927 The Sea Tiger; The Sunset Derby; Rose of the Golden West; No Place to Go; Two Arabian Knights; The Rough Riders
1926 High Steppers; Forever After; Don Juan; The Wise Guy
1925 Scarlet Saint; Don Q, Son of Zorro; Enticement;

Playing with Souls; The Pace That Thrills; Oh! Doctor
1924 The Fighting Coward; Unguarded Women; Inez from Hollywood *a.k.a.* The Good Bad Girl; The Fighting American; The Price of a Party; Beau Brummell
1923 Marriage Maker; Woman-Proof; Bright Shawl; Hollywood *a.k.a.* Joligud; Success; Puritan Passions; Second Fiddle; To the Ladies; The Rapids
1922 The Man Who Played God; The Scarecrow; The Young Painter; John Smith
1921 The Bashful Suitor; The Beggar Maid

Lew Ayres
(Dec. 28, 1908–1998)
1978 Damien: Omen II
1977 The End of the World
1973 Battle for the Planet of the Apes
1972 The Biscuit Eater; The Man; Tomorrow's Champion
1971 The Last Generation
1966 Kill No More
1964 The Carpetbaggers
1962 Advise and Consent
1953 City on a Hunt; No Escape; Donovan's Brain
1951 New Mexico
1950 The Capture
1948 Johnny Belinda
1947 The Unfaithful
1946 The Dark Mirror
1942 Fingers at the Window; Dr. Kildare's Victory *a.k.a.* The Doctor and the Debutante
1941 Maisie Was a Lady; The People vs. Dr. Kildare *a.k.a.* My Life Is Yours; Dr. Kildare's Wedding Day *a.k.a.* Mary Names the Day
1940 The Golden Fleecing; Dr. Kildare's Crisis; Dr. Kildare's Strange Case; Dr. Kildare Goes Home
1939 Remember?; The Secret of Dr. Kildare; Calling Dr. Kildare; These Glamour Girls; Ice Follies; Broadway Serenade *a.k.a.* Serenade
1938 King of the Newsboys; Rich Man, Poor Girl; Scandal Street; Spring Madness; The Young Dr. Kildare; Holiday
1937 Hold 'em Navy!; The Crime Nobody Saw; The Last Train from Madrid
1936 Panic on the Air; Murder With Pictures; The Leathernecks Have Landed; Shakedown; Lady Be Careful
1935 Spring Tonic; Silk Hat Kid; Lottery Lover
1934 She Learned About Sailors; Servants' Entrance; Cross Country Cruise; Let's Be Ritzy
1933 State Fair; Don't Bet on Love; My Weakness
1932 Okay, America!; The Impatient Maiden; Night World
1931 Heaven on Earth *a.k.a.* Mississippi; The Spirit of Notre Dame; Many a Slip;

Up for Murder; The Iron Man
1930 All Quiet on the Western Front; East Is West; Common Clay; The Doorway to Hell *a.k.a.* A Handful of Clouds
1929 The Kiss; The Sophomore; Big News

Lauren Bacall
(Sept. 16, 1924)
1997 Le Jour et la Nuit *a.k.a.* Day and Night
1996 My Fellow Americans; The Mirror Has Two Faces
1994 Pret-A-Porter *a.k.a.* Ready to Wear
1993 A Foreign Field
1991 All I Want for Christmas
1990 Innocent Victim *a.k.a.* Tree of Hands; Misery
1989 A Little Piece of Sunshine
1988 Mr. North; Appointment with Death
1981 The Fan
1979 H.E.A.L.T.H.
1976 The Shootist
1974 Murder on the Orient Express
1972 Monuments
1966 Harper
1964 Sex and the Single Girl; Shock Treatment
1959 Flame over India
1958 The Gift of Love
1957 Designing Woman
1956 Written on the Wind
1955 Blood Alley; The Cobweb
1954 A Woman's World
1953 How to Marry a Millionaire
1950 Bright Leaf; Young Man with a Horn
1948 Key Largo
1947 Dark Passage
1946 The Big Sleep; Two Guys from Milwaukee
1945 Confidential Agent
1944 To Have and Have Not

Lucille Ball
(Aug. 6, 1911–1989)
1974 Mame
1973 Lucky Luciano
1968 Yours, Mine and Ours
1967 A Guide for the Married Man
1963 Critic's Choice
1960 The Facts of Life
1956 Forever Darling
1954 The Long, Long Trailer
1951 The Magic Carpet
1950 Fancy Pants; The Fuller Brush Girl; A Woman of Distinction
1949 Miss Grant Takes Richmond *a.k.a.* Innocence Is Bliss; Sorrowful Jones; Easy Living
1947 Her Husband's Affairs; Lured
1946 Ziegfeld Follies; Easy to Wed; Lover Come Back; The Dark Corner; Two Smart People
1945 Abbott and Costello in Hollywood; Without Love
1944 Meet the People; Thousands Cheer; Du Barry Was a Lady; Best Foot Forward
1942 Valley of the Sun; Seven Days' Leave; The Big Street
1941 A Girl, a Guy and a Gob; Look Who's Laughing
1940 Too Many Girls; You Can't

Fool Your Wife; Dance, Girl, Dance; The Marines Fly High
1939 Beauty for the Asking; Five Came Back; Panama Lady; That's Right—You're Wrong; Twelve Crowded Hours
1938 Annabel Takes a Tour; Next Time I Marry; Having Wonderful Time; The Affairs of Annabel; Go Chase Yourself; Joy of Living; Room Service
1937 Stage Door; Don't Tell the Wife; Hitting a New High
1936 Bunker Bean; Winterset; The Farmer in the Dell; Follow the Fleet; That Girl from Paris; Chatterbox
1935 Roberta; I Dream Too Much; Top Hat; Old Man Rhythm; The Whole Town's Talking; Carnival
1934 Jealousy; The Affairs of Cellini; Kid Millions; Men of the Night; Nana; Fugitive Lady; Broadway Bill; Bottoms Up; Three Little Pigskins; Bulldog Drummond Strikes Back
1933 Blood Money; Broadway Through a Keyhole; The Bowery; Roman Scandals; The Kid from Spain
1929 Bulldog Drummond

Tallulah Bankhead
(Jan. 31, 1903–1968)
1965 Die! Die! My Darling! *a.k.a.* Fanatic
1953 Main Street to Broadway
1945 A Royal Scandal
1944 Lifeboat
1943 Stage Door Canteen
1932 The Devil and the Deep; Faithless; Make Me a Star; Thunder Below
1931 My Sin; The Cheat; Tarnished Lady
1928 His House in Order; A Woman's Law
1919 Trap
1918 When Men Betray; 30 a Week

John Barrymore
(Feb. 15, 1882–1942)
1941 Playmates; World Premiere; The Invisible Woman
1940 The Great Profile
1939 Midnight
1938 The Great Man Votes; Marie Antoinette; Bulldog Drummond's Peril; Hold That Co-Ed; Romance in the Dark; Spawn of the North
1937 Maytime; Bulldog Drummond Comes Back; Bulldog Drummond's Revenge; Night Club Scandal; True Confession
1936 Romeo and Juliet
1934 Twentieth Century; Long Lost Father
1933 Topaze; Counselor-at-Law; Dinner at Eight; Night Flight; Reunion in Vienna
1932 Arsene Lupin; Grand Hotel; A Bill of Divorcement; Rasputin and the Empress; State's Attorney
1931 The Mad Genius; Svengali
1930 The Man from Blankley's; Moby Dick

1929 Eternal Love; General Crack; The Show of Shows
1928 Tempest
1927 When a Man Loves; The Beloved Rogue
1926 Don Juan; The Sea Beast
1924 Beau Brummell
1922 Sherlock Holmes
1921 The Lotus Eater
1920 Dr. Jekyll and Mr. Hyde
1919 Here Comes the Bride; The Test of Honor
1918 On the Quiet
1917 Raffles the Amateur Cracksman
1916 The Lost Bridegroom; The Red Widow; Nearly a King
1915 Are You a Mason?; The Incorrigible Dukane; The Dictator
1914 The Man from Mexico; An American Citizen

Lionel Barrymore
(Apr. 28, 1878–1954)
1953 Main Street to Broadway
1952 Lone Star
1951 Bannerline
1950 Malaya; Right Cross
1949 Down to the Sea in Ships
1948 Key Largo
1947 Dark Delusion
1946 Duel in the Sun; It's a Wonderful Life; The Secret Heart; Three Wise Fools
1945 The Valley of Decision
1944 Dragon Seed; Since You Went Away; Between Two Women; Three Men in White
1943 A Guy Named Joe; Thousands Cheer; Dr. Gillespie's Criminal Case
1942 Calling Dr. Gillespie; Dr. Gillespie's New Assistant; Tennessee Johnson
1941 Lady Be Good; The Bad Man; Dr. Kildare's Victory; The Penalty; The People vs. Dr. Kildare
1940 Dr. Kildare's Strange Case; Dr. Kildare Goes Home; Dr. Kildare's Crisis
1939 On Borrowed Time; Calling Dr. Kildare; Let Freedom Ring; The Secret of Dr. Kildare
1938 Test Pilot; You Can't Take It with You; A Yank at Oxford; Young Dr. Kildare
1937 Navy Blue and Gold; Saratoga; Captains Courageous; A Family Affair; Camille
1936 The Road to Glory; The Devil Doll; The Gorgeous Hussy; The Voice of Bugle Ann
1935 David Copperfield; The Little Colonel; Mark of the Vampire; The Return of Peter Grimm; Ah, Wilderness!; Public Hero No. 1
1934 Treasure Island; Carolina; This Side of Heaven; The Girl from Missouri
1933 Christopher Bean; Looking Forward; Night Flight; One Man's Journey; Dinner at Eight; Should Ladies Behave?; The Stranger's Return; Sweepings; Berkeley Square
1932 Rasputin and the Empress; Grand Hotel; Mata Hari; Broken Lullaby;

Washington Masquerade; Arsene Lupin
1931 A Free Soul; Ten Cents a Dance (dir.); The Yellow Ticket; Guilty Hands
1930 Free and Easy; Love Comes Along
1929 The Mysterious Island; Stark Mad; The Hollywood Revue of 1929
1928 Sadie Thompson; Drums of Love; The River Woman; Road House; Alias Jimmy Valentine; The Lion and the Mouse
1927 Body and Soul; The Show; Women Love Diamonds; The Thirteenth Hour
1926 Lucky Lady; The Temptress; Brooding Eyes; The Barrier; Bells
1925 The Girl Who Wouldn't Work; The Iron Man; Wildfire; The Splendid Road
1924 Decameron Nights; America; I Am the Man; Meddling Women
1923 The Enemies of Women; Eternal City; Unseeing Eyes
1921 Jim the Penman; The Great Adventure
1920 The Master Mind; The Copperhead; The Penalty; The Devil's Garden
1917 His Father's Son; The Millionaire's Double; Life's Whirlpool
1916 The Brand of Cowardice; The Quitter; The Upheaval
1915 A Yellow Streak; Flaming Sword; A Modern Magdalen; The Romance of Elaine; The Exploits of Elaine
1914 Classmates; Judith of Bethulia; The Seats of the Mighty; The Battle at Elderbush Gulch; Strongheart; Men and Women
1913 An Adventure in the Autumn Woods; Brute Force; Death's Marathon; The Enemy's Baby; A Girl's Stratagem; The House of Darkness; The House of Discord; Just Gold; The Lady and the Mouse; A Misunderstood Boy; Near to Earth; Oil and Water; The Perfidy of Mary; The Ranchero's Revenge; The Sheriff's Baby; So Runs the Way; The Telephone Girl and the Lady; Three Friends; A Timely Interception; The Yaqui Cur; Fate; The Wanderer
1912 Musketeers of Pig Alley; The Chief's Blanket; A Cry for Help; The God Within; Gold and Glitter; Home Folks; The Informer; The Massacre; My Baby; My Hero; The New York Hat; The One She Loved; So Near, Yet So Far; Friends; Brutality
1911 Fighting Blood; The Miser's Heart; Battle

Warren Beatty
(Mar. 30, 1937)
1998 Bulworth
1994 Love Affair

1991 Bugsy
1990 Dick Tracy
1987 Ishtar
1984 George Stevens: A Filmmaker's Journey
1981 Reds
1978 Heaven Can Wait
1975 Shampoo; The Fortune
1974 The Parallax View
1971 $ (Dollars); McCabe and Mrs. Miller
1970 The Only Game in Town
1967 Bonnie and Clyde
1966 Kaleidoscope; Promise Her Anything
1965 Mickey One
1964 Lilith
1962 All Fall Down
1961 Splendor in the Grass; The Roman Spring of Mrs. Stone

Wallace Beery
(Apr. 1, 1885–1949)
1949 Big Jack
1948 A Date with Judy; Alias a Gentleman
1946 Bad Bascomb; The Mighty McGurk
1945 This Man's Navy
1944 Barbary Coast Gent; Rationing
1943 Salute to the Marines
1942 Jackass Mail
1941 The Bad Man; Barnacle Bill; The Bugle Sounds
1940 The Man from Dakota; 20-Mule Team; Wyoming
1939 Sergeant Madden; Stand up and Fight; Thunder Afloat
1938 The Bad Man of Brimstone; Port of Seven Seas; Stablemates
1937 The Good Old Soak; Slave Ship
1936 A Message to Garcia; Old Hutch
1935 O'Shaughnessey's Boy; Ah, Wilderness!; China Seas; West Point of the Air
1934 The Mighty Barnum; Treasure Island; Viva Villa!
1933 The Bowery; Dinner at Eight; Tugboat Annie
1932 Flesh; Grand Hotel
1931 The Secret Six; Hell Divers; The Champ
1930 Derelict; Billy the Kid; A Lady's Morals; The Big House; Min and Bill; Way for a Sailor
1929 Chinatown Nights; River of Romance; Stairs of Sand
1928 Partners in Crime; The Big Killing; Beggars of Life; Wife Savers
1927 Fireman, Save My Child; Now We're in the Air; We're in the Navy Now; Casey at the Bat; Two Flaming Youths
1926 Old Ironsides; Behind the Front; The Wanderer; The Volcano
1925 The Night Club; The Devil's Cargo; Adventure; The Lost World; Coming Through; Rugged Water; In the Name of Love; The Pony Express
1924 Red Lily; The Sea Hawk; The Signal Tower; Dynamite Smith; So Big; Another Man's Wife; Madonna of the Streets; The Great Divide

1923 Ashes of Vengeance; The Three Ages; Spanish Dancer; Bavu; Stormswept; The Eternal Struggle; White Tiger
1922 I Am the Law; Trouble; Robin Hood; Man from Hell's River; Only a Shop Girl; Wild Honey; Rosary; The Sagebrush Trail
1921 The Four Horsemen of the Apocalypse; Last Trail; Patsy; Golden Snare; The Rookie's Return; A Tale of Two Worlds
1920 Virgin of Stamboul; The Last of the Mohicans; Behind the Door; The Mollycoddle; The Round Up
1919 Life Line; Love Burglar; Unpardonable Sin; Victory
1918 Johanna Enlists
1917 Little American; Teddy at the Throttle
1915 The Slim Princess
1914 Sweedie series

Constance Bennett
(Oct. 22, 1904–1965)
1966 Madame X
1954 It Should Happen to You
1951 As Young As You Feel
1948 Angel on the Amazon; Smart Woman
1947 The Unsuspected
1946 Centennial Summer
1945 Paris Underground
1942 Madame Spy; Sin Town
1941 Law of the Tropics; Two-Faced Woman; Wild Bill Hickok Rides; Topper Returns
1940 Escape to Glory
1939 Tail Spin; Topper Takes a Trip
1938 Merrily We Live; Service De Luxe
1937 Topper
1936 Everything Is Thunder; Ladies in Love
1935 After Office Hours
1934 The Affairs of Cellini; Moulin Rouge; Outcast Lady
1933 Our Betters; Bed of Roses; After Tonight
1932 Lady with a Past; Rockabye; What Price Hollywood?; Two Against the World
1931 The Easiest Way; Born to Love; Bought; The Common Law
1930 Son of the Gods; Three Faces East; Sin Takes a Holiday; Common Clay
1929 This Thing Called Love; Rich People
1926 Married?
1925 The Goose Woman; My Son; Pinch Hitter; Code of the West; Goose Hangs High; Wandering Fires; Sally, Irene and Mary
1924 Cytherea; Into the Net
1922 Reckless Youth; What's Wrong with the Women?; Evidence
1916 Valley of Decision

Joan Bennett
(Feb. 27, 1910–1990)
1977 Suspiria
1970 House of Dark Shadows
1967 Those Fantastic Flying Fools
1965 San Ferry Ann

1960 Desire in the Dust
1956 Navy Wife; There's Always Tomorrow
1955 We're No Angels
1954 Highway Dragnet
1951 Father's Little Dividend; The Guy Who Came Back
1950 For Heaven's Sake; Father of the Bride
1949 The Reckless Moment
1948 The Scar; The Secret Beyond the Door
1947 The Macomber Affair; The Woman on the Beach
1945 Scarlet Street; Nob Hill; Colonel Effingham's Raid
1944 The Woman in the Window
1943 Margin for Error
1942 Girl Trouble; Twin Beds; The Wife Takes a Flyer
1941 Man Hunt; She Knew All the Answers; Wild Geese Calling; Confirm or Deny
1940 The Son of Monte Cristo; Green Hell; The Man I Married; The House Across the Bay
1939 The Man in the Iron Mask; The Housekeeper's Daughter
1938 I Met My Love Again; Artists and Models Abroad; The Texans; Trade Winds
1937 Vogues of 1938
1936 Big Brown Eyes; Thirteen Hours by Air; Two in a Crowd; Wedding Present
1935 The Man Who Broke the Bank at Monte Carlo; Private Worlds; She Couldn't Take It; The Man Who Reclaimed His Head; Two for Tonight; Mississippi
1934 The Pursuit of Happiness
1933 Arizona to Broadway; Little Women
1932 She Wanted a Millionaire; The Trial of Vivienne Ware; Week-Ends Only; Careless Lady; Wild Girl; Me and My Gal
1931 Hush Money; Doctors' Wives; Many a Slip
1930 Maybe It's Love; Crazy That Way; Puttin' on the Ritz; Moby Dick; Scotland Yard
1929 The Divine Lady; The Mississippi Gambler; Three Live Ghosts; Disraeli; Bulldog Drummond
1928 Power
1923 Eternal City
1916 Valley of Decision

Candice Bergen
(May 8, 1946)
1985 Stick
1984 2010
1982 Gandhi
1981 Rich and Famous
1979 Starting Over
1978 A Night Full of Rain *a.k.a.* The End of the World (In Our Usual Bed in a Night Full of Rain); Oliver's Story
1977 The Domino Principle
1975 The Wind and the Lion; Bite the Bullet
1974 11 Harrowhouse
1971 T. R. Baskin; The Hunting Party; Carnal Knowledge
1970 The Adventurers; Soldier Blue; Getting Straight

1968 The Magus
1967 Vivre Pour Vivre; The Day the Fish Came Out
1966 The Sand Pebbles; The Group

Ingrid Bergman
(Aug. 29, 1915–1982)
1978 Autumn Sonata
1976 A Matter of Time
1974 Murder on the Orient Express
1973 From the Mixed-Up Files of Mrs. Basil E. Frankweiler
1970 A Walk in the Spring Rain
1969 Cactus Flower
1964 The Yellow Rolls-Royce; The Visit
1961 Goodbye Again
1958 The Inn of the Sixth Happiness; Indiscreet; Paris Does Strange Things; Anastasia
1955 Angst
1954 Joan at the Stake
1953 The Voyage to Italy; We the Women
1952 The Greatest Love
1950 Stromboli
1949 Under Capricorn
1948 Arch of Triumph; Joan of Arc
1946 Notorious
1945 Saratoga Trunk; The Bells of St. Mary's; Spellbound
1944 Gaslight
1943 For Whom the Bell Tolls
1942 Casablanca
1941 Rage in Heaven; Dr. Jekyll and Mr. Hyde; Adam Had Four Sons
1940 June Night
1939 Intermezzo
1938 A Woman's Face; Only One Night; Dollar; The Four Companions
1936 On the Sunnyside; Intermezzo
1935 Swedenhielms; Walpurgis Night; Ocean Breakers
1934 The Count of the Monk's Bridge

Humphrey Bogart
(Dec. 25, 1899–1957)
1956 The Harder They Fall
1955 The Desperate Hours; The Left Hand of God; We're No Angels
1954 The Caine Mutiny; The Barefoot Contessa; Sabrina; The Love Lottery
1953 Beat the Devil; Battle Circus
1952 Deadline U.S.A.; Road to Bali
1951 The Enforcer; The African Queen; Sirocco
1950 Chain Lightning; In a Lonely Place
1949 Knock on Any Door; Tokyo Joe
1948 Key Largo; The Treasure of the Sierra Madre
1947 Dead Reckoning; Dark Passage; The Two Mrs. Carrolls; Always Together
1946 The Big Sleep; Two Guys from Milwaukee
1945 Conflict
1944 Passage to Marseilles; To Have and Have Not
1943 Action in the North Atlantic; Sahara; Thank Your Lucky Stars
1942 In This Our Life; All Through the Night; Across

the Pacific; The Big Shot; Casablanca
1941 The Maltese Falcon; High Sierra; The Wagons Roll at Night
1940 Brother Orchid; They Drive By Night; Virginia City; It All Came True
1939 The Oklahoma Kid; Invisible Stripes; Dark Victory; King of the Underworld; The Roaring Twenties; The Return of Doctor X; You Can't Get Away with Murder
1938 The Amazing Dr. Clitterhouse; Crime School; Angels with Dirty Faces; Men Are Such Fools; Swing Your Lady; Racket Busters
1937 Kid Galahad; The Great O'Malley; Stand-In; Marked Woman; Black Legion; San Quentin; Dead End
1936 The Petrified Forest; Isle of Fury; Bullets or Ballots; China Clipper; Two Against the World
1934 Midnight
1932 Love Affair; Big City Blues; Three on a Match
1931 Body and Soul; A Holy Terror; Women of All Nations; Bad Sister
1930 A Devil with Women; Up the River

Ernest Borgnine
(Jan. 24, 1917)
1998 Small Soldiers; BASEketball
1997 McHale's Navy; Gattaca
1996 All Dogs Go to Heaven 2; Merlin's Shop of Mystical Wonders
1991 Mistress
1990 Laser Mission; Tides of War; Any Man's Death
1989 Moving Target
1988 Uppercut Man; Spike of Bensonhurst
1987 Skeleton Coast
1984 Vengeance Is Mine; Codename: Wildgeese
1983 The Young Warriors; Carpool
1981 Escape from New York; Deadly Blessing; Super Fuzz
1980 When Time Ran Out
1979 The Black Hole; The Double McGuffin; The Ravagers
1978 Convoy; Crossed Swords
1977 The Greatest
1976 Shoot
1975 Hustle; Sunday in the Country; The Devil's Rain
1974 Law and Disorder
1973 The Neptune Factor; Emperor of the North
1972 The Poseidon Adventure; The Revengers; Guns of the Revolution
1971 Willard; Ripped-Off; Bunny O'Hare; Rain for a Dusty Summer; Hannie Caulder
1970 A Bullet for Sandoval; Suppose They Gave a War and Nobody Came?; The Adventurers
1969 Vengeance Is Mine; The Wild Bunch
1968 The Legend of Lylah Clare; The Split; Ice Station Zebra

1967 The Dirty Dozen; Chuka
1966 The Oscar
1965 The Flight of the Phoenix
1964 McHale's Navy
1962 Barabbas
1961 The Italian Brigands; Go Naked in the World
1960 Man on a String; Pay or Die
1959 The Rabbit Trap; Season of Passion
1958 The Vikings; Torpedo Run; The Badlanders
1957 Three Brave Men
1956 Jubal; The Catered Affair; The Best Things in Life Are Free; The Square Jungle
1955 The Last Command; Run for Cover; Violent Saturday; Marty; Bad Day at Black Rock
1954 The Bounty Hunter; Demetrius and the Gladiators; Vera Cruz
1953 The Stranger Wore a Gun; Johnny Guitar; From Here to Eternity
1951 The Whistle at Eaton Falls; China Corsair; The Mob

Charles Boyer
(Aug. 28, 1897–1978)
1976 A Matter of Time
1974 Stavisky
1973 Lost Horizon
1969 The Madwoman of Chaillot; The April Fools
1968 The Day the Hotline Got Hot
1967 Casino Royale; Barefoot in the Park
1966 Is Paris Burning?; How to Steal a Million
1965 A Very Special Favor
1963 Love Is a Ball
1962 The Four Horsemen of the Apocalypse; Adorable Julia; Midnight Folly
1961 Fanny
1959 Paris Hotel
1958 La Parisienne; Maxime; The Buccaneer; Lucky to Be a Woman
1956 Around the World in 80 Days
1955 Nana; The Cobweb
1953 The Earrings of Madame De . . .
1952 The Happy Time
1951 Thunder in the East; The Thirteenth Letter; The First Legion
1948 Arch of Triumph
1947 A Woman's Vengeance
1946 Cluny Brown
1945 Confidential Agent
1944 Gaslight; Together Again
1943 The Constant Nymph; Flesh and Fantasy; The Heart of a Nation
1942 Tales of Manhattan
1941 Hold Back the Dawn; Back Street; Appointment for Love
1940 All This and Heaven Too
1939 Love Affair; When Tomorrow Comes
1938 Algiers
1937 Tovarich; Conquest; History Is Made at Night
1936 The Garden of Allah; Mayerling
1935 Break of Hearts; Liliom; Private Worlds; Shanghai
1934 Caravan; The Battle

1933 Heart Song; The Empress and I
1932 The Man from Yesterday; Red-Headed Woman
1931 The Magnificent Lie
1929 Le Capitaine Fracasse
1920 L' Homme Du Large

Marlon Brando
(Apr. 3, 1924)
1997 The Brave
1996 The Island of Dr. Moreau
1995 Don Juan DeMarco
1992 Christopher Columbus: The Discovery
1990 The Freshman
1989 A Dry White Season
1985 Marlon Brando (documentary)
1980 The Formula
1979 Apocalypse Now
1978 Superman
1976 The Missouri Breaks
1973 Last Tango in Paris
1972 The Godfather
1971 The Nightcomers
1969 The Night of the Following Day; Burn!
1968 Candy
1967 Reflections in a Golden Eye; A Countess from Hong Kong
1966 The Chase; The Appaloosa
1965 The Saboteur, Code Name Morituri
1964 Bedtime Story
1963 The Ugly American
1962 Mutiny on the Bounty
1961 One-Eyed Jacks
1960 The Fugitive Kind
1958 The Young Lions
1957 Sayonara
1956 The Teahouse of the August Moon
1955 Guys and Dolls
1954 The Wild One; On the Waterfront; Desiree
1953 Julius Caesar
1952 Viva Zapata!
1951 A Streetcar Named Desire
1950 The Men

George Brent
(Mar. 15, 1904–1979)
1978 Born Again
1973 Lucky Luciano
1956 Death of a Scoundrel
1953 Mexican Manhunt; Tangier Incident
1952 Man Bait; Montana Belle
1951 F.B.I. Girl
1949 Bride for Sale; Illegal Entry; The Kid from Cleveland; Red Canyon
1948 Angel on the Amazon; Luxury Liner
1947 Out of the Blue; Christmas Eve; The Corpse Came C.O.D.; Slave Girl
1946 The Spiral Staircase; Tomorrow Is Forever; Lover Come Back; Temptation; My Reputation
1945 The Affairs of Susan
1944 Experiment Perilous
1942 In This Our Life; The Gay Sisters; Silver Queen; Twin Beds; You Can't Escape Forever
1941 Honeymoon for Three; International Lady; The Great Lie; They Dare Not Love
1940 The Fighting 69th; The Man Who Talked Too

Much; South of Suez; Till We Meet Again; Adventure in Diamonds
1939 The Rains Came; Dark Victory; The Old Maid; Wings of the Navy
1938 Jezebel; Gold Is Where You Find It; Secrets of an Actress; Racket Busters
1937 Mountain Justice; Submarine D-1; The Go-Getter; God's Country and the Woman
1936 The Case Against Mrs. Ames; More Than a Secretary; Snowed Under; Give Me Your Heart; The Golden Arrow
1935 The Right to Live; Special Agent; The Goose and the Gander; Front Page Woman; Living on Velvet; In Person; Stranded
1934 Stamboul Quest; The Painted Veil; Desirable; Housewife
1933 From Headquarters; Man Killer; Baby Face; 42nd Street; Lilly Turner; Luxury Liner; The Keyhole; Female
1932 They Call It Sin; Miss Pinkerton; So Big; Week-End Marriage; The Rich Are Always with Us; The Purchase Price; The Crash
1931 Fair Warning; Lightning Warrior series; Once a Sinner; Ex-Bad Boy; Charlie Chan Carries On; The Homicide Squad
1930 Under Suspicion

Richard Burton
(Nov. 10, 1925–1984)
1984 Nineteen Eighty-Four
1983 Wagner
1980 Circle of Two
1979 Tristan and Isolde; Absolution; Lovespell
1978 Breakthrough; The Medusa Touch; The Wild Geese
1977 Equus; Exorcist II: The Heretic
1974 The Klansman; The Voyage
1973 Massacre in Rome Sutjeska a.k.a. The Fifth Offensive
1972 Bluebeard; Hammersmith Is Out; The Assassination of Trotsky
1971 Raid on Rommel; Under Milk Wood; Villain
1969 Anne of the Thousand Days; Staircase
1968 Where Eagles Dare; Boom!; Candy
1967 Doctor Faustus; The Taming of the Shrew; The Comedians; Casino Royale
1966 Who's Afraid of Virginia Woolf?
1965 What's New Pussycat?; The Sandpiper; The Spy Who Came in from the Cold
1964 The Night of the Iguana; Zulu; Hamlet; Becket
1963 The V.I.P.s; Cleopatra
1962 The Longest Day
1960 The Bramble Bush; Ice Palace
1959 Look Back in Anger
1957 Bitter Victory; Sea Wife
1956 Alexander the Great

1955 Prince of Players; The Rains of Ranchipur
1954 Demetrius and the Gladiators
1953 The Robe; The Desert Rats
1952 Waterfront Women; My Cousin Rachel
1951 Green Grow the Rushes
1950 Her Panelled Door; Waterfront
1949 Woman of Dolwyn; Now Barabbas Was a Robber

James Cagney
(July 17, 1899–1986)
1981 Ragtime
1968 Arizona Bushwackers
1961 One, Two, Three
1960 The Gallant Hours
1959 Never Steal Anything Small; Shake Hands with the Devil
1957 Man of a Thousand Faces; Short Cut to Hell
1956 These Wilder Years; Tribute to a Badman
1955 Love Me or Leave Me; The Seven Little Foys; Mr. Roberts; Run for Cover
1953 A Lion Is in the Streets
1952 What Price Glory?
1951 Come Fill the Cup; Starlift
1950 The West Point Story; Kiss Tomorrow Goodbye
1949 White Heat
1948 The Time of Your Life
1946 13 Rue Madeleine
1945 Blood on the Sun
1943 Johnny Come Lately; Show Business at War
1942 Yankee Doodle Dandy; Captains of the Clouds
1941 The Strawberry Blonde; The Bride Came C.O.D.
1940 City for Conquest; The Fighting 69th; Torrid Zone
1939 The Oklahoma Kid; Each Dawn I Die; The Roaring Twenties
1938 Angels with Dirty Faces; Boy Meets Girl
1937 Something to Sing About
1936 Great Guy
1935 Frisco Kid; The Irish in Us; Ceiling Zero; G-Men; Devil Dogs of the Air; A Midsummer Night's Dream
1934 Jimmy the Gent; The St. Louis Kid; He Was Her Man; Here Comes the Navy
1933 Lady Killer; Hard to Handle; The Mayor of Hell; Picture Snatcher; Footlight Parade
1932 Taxi!; The Crowd Roars; Winner Take All
1931 Other Men's Women; Smart Money; The Millionaire; Blonde Crazy; The Public Enemy
1930 Sinner's Holiday; The Doorway to Hell

Michael Caine
(Mar. 14, 1933)
1996 Blood and Wine
1995 Bullet to Beijing
1994 On Deadly Ground; Then There Were Giants, Part 2
1992 Death Becomes Her; The Muppet Christmas Carol; Blue Ice; Noises Off
1991 King Midas and the Golden Touch

1990 Bullseye!; Mr. Destiny; A Shock to the System
1988 Dirty Rotten Scoundrels; Without a Clue
1987 The Fourth Protocol; Jaws: the Revenge; Surrender; The Whistle Blower
1986 Half Moon Street; Hannah and Her Sisters; Mona Lisa; Sweet Liberty
1985 The Holcroft Covenant; Water
1984 The Jigsaw Man; Blame It On Rio
1983 Educating Rita; Beyond the Limit
1982 Deathtrap
1981 Victory; The Hand
1980 Dressed to Kill; The Island
1979 Beyond the Poseidon Adventure; Ashanti
1978 The Swarm; California Suite
1977 A Bridge Too Far; Silver Bears
1976 Harry and Walter Go to New York; The Eagle Has Landed
1975 The Romantic Englishwoman; The Wilby Conspiracy; Peeper; The Man Who Would Be King
1974 The Black Windmill; The Destructors
1972 Pulp; X, Y and Zee; Sleuth
1971 Get Carter; Kidnapped
1970 The Last Valley; Too Late the Hero
1969 The Italian Job; Play Dirty; Battle of Britain
1968 Deadfall; The Magus
1967 Billion Dollar Brain; Sette Volte Donna; Hurry Sundown
1966 Funeral in Berlin; Gambit; The Wrong Box; Alfie
1965 The Ipcress File
1964 Zulu
1963 The Wrong Arm of the Law
1962 The Day the Earth Caught Fire
1960 The Bulldog Breed; Foxhole in Cairo
1959 Breakout
1958 The Two-Headed Spy; The Key
1957 How to Murder a Rich Uncle
1956 A Hill in Korea

Harry Carey, Jr.
(May 16, 1921–1998)
1996 The Sunchaser
1993 Tombstone
1990 Back to the Future 3
1989 Breaking in; Bad Jim
1988 Cherry 2000
1987 Illegally Yours; The Whales of August
1986 Crossroads
1985 Mask
1984 Gremlins
1982 Endangered Species
1981 Uforia
1980 The Long Riders
1976 Nickelodeon
1975 Take a Hard Ride
1974 Challenge to White Fang
1973 Cahill: United States Marshal
1972 A Man from the East; White Fang
1971 One More Train to Rob; Trinity Is Still My Name; Something Big; Big Jake
1970 Dirty Dingus Magee; The Moonshine War
1969 One More Time; The

Undefeated; Death of a Gunfighter
1968 The Devil's Brigade; Bandolero!
1967 The Ballad of Josie; The Way West
1966 Alvarez Kelly; Man from Tomorrow; The Rare Breed
1965 Billy the Kid vs. Dracula; Shenandoah
1964 Taggart; Cheyenne Autumn; The Raiders
1962 A Public Affair; Texas John Slaughter; Wild Times
1961 The Comancheros; The Great Impostor; Two Rode Together
1960 Noose for a Gunman
1959 Escort West; Rio Bravo; Gundown at Sandoval
1958 From Hell to Texas
1957 Gun the Man Down; Kiss Them for Me; The River's Edge
1956 The Great Locomotive Chase; The Searchers; Seventh Cavalry
1955 House of Bamboo; Mr. Roberts; The Long Gray Line
1954 Silver Lode; The Outcast
1953 San Antone; Sweethearts on Parade; Gentlemen Prefer Blondes; Beneath the 12-Mile Reef; Island in the Sky
1952 Monkey Business; Niagara; The Raiders; The Wild Blue Yonder
1951 Warpath
1950 Copper Canyon; Rio Grande; Wagonmaster
1949 She Wore a Yellow Ribbon; So Dear to My Heart
1948 The Three Godfathers; Red River; Moonrise
1947 Pursued

John Cassavetes
(Dec. 9, 1929–1989)
1986 Big Trouble
1984 I'm Almost Not Crazy . . . : John Cassavetes: The Man and His Work; Love Streams
1983 Marvin and Tige
1982 Incubus; Tempest
1981 Whose Life Is It Anyway?
1980 Gloria
1978 The Fury; Brass Target
1977 Opening Night
1976 Mikey and Nicky; Two-Minute Warning
1975 Capone
1971 Minnie and Moskowitz
1970 Husbands
1969 Machine Gun McCain
1968 Rosemary's Baby
1967 Devil's Angels; Rome Like Chicago; The Dirty Dozen
1964 The Killers
1962 The Webster Boy
1959 Virgin Island
1958 Saddle the Wind
1957 Edge of the City; Affair in Havana
1956 Crime in the Streets
1955 I'll Cry Tomorrow; The Night Holds Terror
1953 Taxi
1951 Fourteen Hours

Lon Chaney, Jr.
(Feb. 10, 1906–1973)
1971 Dracula vs. Frankenstein
1969 A Time to Run; Dracula's Castle
1968 The Frontiersman; Buckskin; Fireball Jungle
1967 Dr. Terror's Gallery of Horrors; Hillbillies in a Haunted House; Alien Massacre; Welcome to Hard Times
1966 Johnny Reno; Apache Uprising
1965 House of the Black Death; Black Spurs; Town Tamer; Young Fury
1964 Spider Baby; Law of the Lawless; Stage to Thunder Rock; Witchcraft
1963 The Haunted Palace
1961 The Phantom; Chivato
1959 Night of the Ghouls a.k.a. Revenge of the Dead (U.S. title); The Alligator People; Face of the Screaming Werewolf
1958 The Defiant Ones; Money, Women and Guns
1957 The Cyclops
1956 Manfish; The Black Sleep; The Indestructible Man; Pardners; Daniel Boone, Trail Blazer; Along the Mohawk Trail
1955 Not As a Stranger; The Silver Star; I Died a Thousand Times; Big House, USA; The Indian Fighter
1954 Passion; Casanova's Big Night; The Black Pirates; The Boy from Oklahoma; Lost Treasure of the Amazon; The Big Chase
1953 A Lion Is in the Streets; Raiders of the Seven Seas
1952 Battles of Chief Pontiac; The Black Castle; The Bushwhackers; Springfield Rifle; Thief of Damascus; High Noon; The Bushwackers
1951 Behave Yourself!; Bride of the Gorilla; Flame of Araby; Inside Straight
1950 Only the Valiant; Once a Thief
1949 Captain China; There's a Girl in My Heart
1948 The Counterfeiters; 16 Fathoms Deep; Abbott and Costello Meet Frankenstein
1947 My Favorite Brunette; Albuquerque
1945 The Mummy's Curse; House of Dracula; The Daltons Ride Again; The Frozen Ghost; Pillow of Death; Strange Confession; Here Come the Co-Eds
1944 Dead Man's Eyes; Follow the Boys; Ghost Catchers; Weird Woman; Cobra Woman; The Mummy's Ghost; House of Frankenstein
1943 Frankenstein Meets the Wolfman; Son of Dracula; Crazy House; Calling Dr. Death; Eyes of the Underworld; Scream in the Night; Frontier Badmen
1942 North to the Klondike; The Ghost of Frankenstein; Sherlock Holmes and the Voice of Terror; The Mummy's Tomb
1941 The Wolf Man; Billy the Kid; Man Made Monster; Badlands of Dakota; San Antonio Rose; Too Many Blondes; Riders of Death Valley; Overland Mail
1940 Northwest Mounted Police; One Million B.C.; Of Mice and Men
1939 Charlie Chan in the City of Darkness; Jesse James; Union Pacific; Frontier Marshal
1938 Alexander's Ragtime Band; City Girl; Road Demon; Happy Landing; Passport Husband; Cheyenne Rides Again; Josette; Mr. Moto's Gamble
1937 Slave Ship; Life Begins in College; Midnight Taxi; Thin Ice; Angel's Holiday; Wife, Doctor and Nurse; Wild and Woolly; Love and Hisses; Charlie Chan on Broadway; Second Honeymoon; Secret Agent X-9 series
1936 Rose Bowl; Ace Drummond series; Killer at Large; The Old Corral; Sharad of Atlantis; The Singing Cowboy
1935 Captain Hurricane; Shadow of Silk Lennox; Accent on Youth; Girl of My Dreams
1934 Sixteen Fathoms Deep; The Life of Vergie Winters
1933 Lucky Devils; The Three Musketeers; Scarlet River; Son of the Border
1932 Bird of Paradise; Girl Crazy; The Last Frontier

Charles Chaplin
(Apr. 16, 1889–1977)
1967 The Countess from Hong Kong
1957 A King in New York
1952 Limelight
1947 Monsieur Verdoux
1940 The Great Dictator
1936 Modern Times
1931 City Lights
1928 Show People; The Circus
1925 The Gold Rush
1923 A Woman of Paris; The Pilgrim; Souls for Sale
1922 Pay Day; The Kid; The Idle Class; The Nut
1919 A Day's Pleasure; Sunnyside
1918 Easy Street; A Dog's Life; The Bond; Shoulder Arms; Triple Trouble; How to Make Movies
1917 The Immigrant; The Adventurer
1916 The Vagabond; The Floorwalker; The Fireman; The Rink; Police; Easy Street; The Burlesque of Carmen; Behind the Screen; The Count; One A.M.; The Pawnshop; Triple Trouble
1915 The Bank; The Champion; His New Job; By the Sea; Shanghaied; In the Park; A Jitney Elopement; A Night in the Show; The Tramp; Work; A Woman
1914 His Prehistoric Past; The Property Man; The Knockout; The Dough and Dynamite; Recreation; The Rounders; The Star Boarder; Tango Tangles; Those Love Pangs; Twenty Minutes of Love; Tillie's Punctured Romance; Between Showers; A Busy Day; Caught in a Cabaret; Caught in the Rain; Cruel, Cruel Love; The Face on the Bar Room Floor; The Fatal Mallet; A Film Johnnie; Gentlemen of Nerve; Getting Acquainted; Her Friend the Bandit; His Favorite Pastime; His Musical Career; His Trysting Place; Kid Auto Races at Venice; Laughing Gas; Mabel at the Wheel; Mabel's Busy Day; Mabel's Married Life; Mabel's Strange Predicament; Making a Living; The Masquerader; The New Janitor; His New Profession

Maurice Chevalier
(Sept. 12, 1888–1972)
1970 The Aristocats (song)
1966 Monkeys, Go Home!
1964 I'd Rather Be Rich
1963 A New Kind of Love; Panic Button
1962 In Search of the Castaways; Jessica
1961 Fanny
1960 A Breath of Scandal; Black Tights; Can-Can; Pepe
1959 Count Your Blessings
1958 Gigi
1957 Love in the Afternoon
1956 My Seven Little Sins; Cento Anni D'Amore
1953 Schlager-Parade
1950 Just Me; A Royal Affair
1947 Man About Town
1939 Personal Column; Break the News; With a Smile
1936 The Beloved Vagabond; The Man of the Hour
1935 Folies Bergère
1934 The Merry Widow
1933 A Bedtime Story; The Way to Love
1932 Make Me a Star; Love Me Tonight; One Hour with You
1931 The Smiling Lieutenant
1930 The Big Pond; Playboy of Paris; Paramount on Parade
1929 The Love Parade; Innocents of Paris

Julie Christie
(Apr. 14, 1941)
1997 Afterglow
1996 Dragonheart; Hamlet
1990 Fools of Fortune
1988 Secret Obsession; Dadah Is Death
1986 Miss Mary; Power; Sins of the Fathers
1982 The Return of the Soldier; Heat and Dust
1981 Memoirs of a Survivor; The Animals Film
1978 Heaven Can Wait
1977 Demon Seed
1975 Nashville; Shampoo
1973 Don't Look Now
1971 McCabe and Mrs. Miller; The Go-Between
1970 In Search of Gregory
1968 Petulia
1967 Far from the Madding Crowd

1966 Fahrenheit 451
1965 Young Cassidy; Darling; Doctor Zhivago
1963 The Fast Lady; Billy Liar
1962 Crooks Anonymous

Jill Clayburgh
(Apr. 30, 1944)
1997 Going All the Way; Fools Rush In
1994 Naked in New York
1993 Rich in Love
1992 Whispers in the Dark; Day of Atonement
1987 Shy People
1985 Where Are the Children?
1983 Hanna K.
1982 I'm Dancing As Fast As I Can
1981 First Monday in October
1980 It's My Turn
1979 Starting Over; Luna
1978 An Unmarried Woman
1977 Semi-Tough
1976 Silver Streak; Gable and Lombard
1974 The Terminal Man
1973 The Thief Who Came to Dinner
1972 Portnoy's Complaint
1971 The Telephone Book
1969 The Wedding Party

Montgomery Clift
(Oct. 17, 1920–1966)
1966 The Defector
1962 Freud
1961 The Misfits; Judgment at Nuremberg
1960 Wild River
1959 Suddenly, Last Summer
1958 The Young Lions; Lonelyhearts
1957 Raintree County
1953 I Confess; From Here to Eternity; Indiscretion of an American Wife
1951 A Place in the Sun
1950 The Big Lift
1949 The Heiress
1948 Red River; The Search

Claudette Colbert
(Sept. 13, 1905–1996)
1961 Parrish
1957 Funny Face
1956 Texas Lady
1955 Royal Affairs in Versailles
1954 Daughters of Destiny
1952 Outpost in Malaya
1951 Let's Make It Legal; Thunder on the Hill
1950 Three Came Home; The Secret Fury
1949 Bride for Sale
1948 Family Honeymoon; Sleep, My Love
1947 The Egg and I
1946 Without Reservations; The Secret Heart; Tomorrow Is Forever
1945 Guest Wife
1944 Since You Went Away; Practically Yours
1943 No Time for Love; So Proudly We Hail!
1942 The Palm Beach Story
1941 Remember the Day; Skylark
1940 Arise, My Love; Boom Town
1939 It's a Wonderful World; Midnight; Drums Along the Mohawk; Zaza
1938 Bluebeard's Eighth Wife
1937 Maid of Salem; I Met Him in Paris; Tovarich
1936 Under Two Flags
1935 Private Worlds; The Bride

Comes Home; She Married Her Boss; The Gilded Lily
1934 Cleopatra; Four Frightened People; It Happened One Night; Imitation of Life
1933 I Cover the Waterfront; Three-Cornered Moon; Torch Singer
1932 Tonight Is Ours; The Phantom President; The Misleading Lady; Make Me a Star; The Man from Yesterday; The Wiser Sex; The Sign of the Cross
1931 Honor Among Lovers; The Smiling Lieutenant; Secrets of a Secretary; His Woman
1930 L'Enigmatique Monsieur Parkes; Young Man of Manhattan; Manslaughter; The Big Pond
1929 The Hole in the Wall; The Lady Lies
1927 For the Love of Mike

Ronald Colman
(Feb. 9, 1891–1958)
1957 The Story of Mankind
1956 Around the World in 80 Days
1950 Champagne for Caesar
1947 A Double Life; The Late George Apley
1944 Kismet
1942 Random Harvest; The Talk of the Town
1941 My Life with Caroline
1940 Lucky Partners
1939 The Light That Failed
1938 If I Were King
1937 Lost Horizon; The Prisoner of Zenda
1936 Under Two Flags
1935 Clive of India; A Tale of Two Cities; The Man Who Broke the Bank at Monte Carlo
1934 Bulldog Drummond Strikes Back
1933 The Masquerader
1932 Cynara
1931 Arrowsmith; The Unholy Garden
1930 Raffles; The Devil to Pay
1929 Bulldog Drummond; Condemned; The Rescue
1928 Two Lovers
1927 Magic Flame; The Night of Love
1926 Kiki; Beau Geste; The Winning of Barbara Worth
1925 Romola; Her Sister from Paris; Lady Windermere's Fan; Sporting Venus; Stella Dallas; Thief in Paradise; The Dark Angel; His Supreme Moment
1924 Tarnish; Her Night of Romance; 20 Dollars a Week
1923 The White Sister; The Eternal City
1921 Handcuffs or Kisses?
1920 Anna the Adventuress; Black Spider; A Son of David
1919 Snow in the Desert; Sheba; A Daughter of Eve; The Toilers
1917 The Live Wire

Gary Cooper
(May 7, 1901–1961)
1961 The Naked Edge
1959 The Hanging Tree; They Came to Cordura; The

Wreck of the Mary Deare; Alias Jesse James
1958 Man of the West; Ten North Frederick
1957 Love in the Afternoon
1956 Friendly Persuasion
1955 The Court Martial of Billy Mitchell
1954 Garden of Evil
1953 Return to Paradise; Blowing Wild; Vera Cruz
1952 High Noon; Springfield Rifle
1951 Distant Drums; It's a Big Country; Starlift; You're in the Navy Now
1950 Bright Leaf; Dallas
1949 The Fountainhead; Task Force; It's a Great Feeling
1948 Good Sam; Unconquered; Variety Girl
1946 Cloak and Dagger
1945 Along Came Jones; Saratoga Trunk
1944 Casanova Brown; The Story of Dr. Wassell
1943 For Whom the Bell Tolls
1942 The Pride of the Yankees
1941 Ball of Fire; Sergeant York; Meet John Doe
1940 The Westerner; Northwest Mounted Police
1939 The Real Glory; Beau Geste
1938 The Adventures of Marco Polo; Bluebeard's Eighth Wife; The Cowboy and the Lady
1937 Souls at Sea
1936 The Plainsman; Hollywood Boulevard; The General Died at Dawn; Mr. Deeds Goes to Town; Desire
1935 The Lives of a Bengal Lancer; Peter Ibbetson; The Wedding Night
1934 Now and Forever; Operator 13; Alice in Wonderland; One Sunday Afternoon; Today We Live; Design for Living
1932 If I Had a Million; A Farewell to Arms; Make Me a Star; The Devil and the Deep
1931 His Woman; I Take This Woman; City Streets; Fighting Caravans
1930 A Man from Wyoming; Only the Brave; Seven Days Leave; The Spoilers; Morocco; The Texan; Paramount on Parade
1929 Wolf Song; Betrayal; The Virginian
1928 The Shopworn Angel; Legion of the Condemned; Half a Bride; Beau Sabreur; Lilac Time; Doomsday; First Kiss
1927 Arizona Bound; Wings; Nevada; Children of Divorce; It; Last Outlaw
1926 The Enchanted Hill; Watch Your Wife; Three Pals; The Winning of Barbara Worth; Old Ironsides
1925 The Lucky Horseshoe; Wild Horse Mesa; Thundering Herd; The Eagle

Joseph Cotten
(May 15, 1905–1995)
1983 The House Where Death Lives; Syndicate Sadists
1982 The House Where Evil Dwells

1981 Churchill and the Generals; Delusion
1980 The Hearse; Heaven's Gate
1979 Concorde Affaire '79
1978 The Perfect Crime; The Fish Men; The Wild Geese; Caravans
1977 Airport '77; Twilight's Last Gleaming
1975 Timber Tramps; A Delicate Balance
1973 Soylent Green
1972 Doomsday Voyage; The Scientific Cardplayer; The Blood Baron; Lady Frankenstein
1971 The Abominable Dr. Phibes
1970 Tora! Tora! Tora!
1969 The Grasshopper; Latitude Zero; Hour of Vengeance
1968 Petulia; Days of Fire; White Comanche
1967 The Hellbenders; Jack of Diamonds; Some May Live; Brighty of the Grand Canyon
1966 The Money Trap; The Oscar; The Tramplers
1965 The Great Sioux Massacre; Hush . . . Hush, Sweet Charlotte
1964 The Search
1961 The Last Sunset
1960 The Angel Wore Red
1958 From the Earth to the Moon; Touch of Evil
1957 The Halliday Brand
1956 The Killer Is Loose; The Bottom of the Bottle
1955 Special Delivery
1953 Egypt by Three; A Blueprint for Murder
1952 The Steel Trap; Untamed Frontier; Niagara
1951 Peking Express; Othello; Half Angel; The Man with a Cloak
1950 Two Flags West; September Affair; Walk Softly, Stranger; Gone to Earth
1949 The Third Man; Under Capricorn; Beyond the Forest
1948 Portrait of Jennie
1947 The Farmer's Daughter
1946 Duel in the Sun
1945 Love Letters
1944 Since You Went Away; I'll Be Seeing You; Gaslight
1943 Hers to Hold; Shadow of a Doubt
1942 The Magnificent Ambersons; Journey into Fear;
1941 Lydia; Citizen Kane
1938 Too Much Johnson

Broderick Crawford
(Dec. 9, 1911–1986)
1988 Ransom Money; Upper Crust
1982 Liar's Moon
1980 Harlequin; There Goes the Bride
1979 A Little Romance
1977 The Private Files of J. Edgar Hoover; Proof of the Man
1976 Won Ton Ton, the Dog Who Saved Hollywood
1973 Terror in the Wax Museum
1972 Embassy; The Candidate
1971 The Yin and Yang of Mr. Go
1970 Hell's Bloody Devils; How Did a Nice Girl Like You Get Into This Business?

1968 Gregorio and the Angel
1967 The Vulture; Red Tomahawk; Manutara
1966 Kid Rodelo; The Texican; The Oscar
1965 Up from the Beach; Mutiny at Fort Sharp
1964 A House Is Not a Home; Brilliant Benjamin Boggs
1963 Square of Violence; The Castilian
1962 Convicts Four
1960 Goliath and the Dragon; The Last of the Vikings
1958 The Decks Ran Red
1956 The Fastest Gun Alive; Between Heaven and Hell
1955 Big House, USA; New York Confidential; Il Bidone; Not As a Stranger
1954 Night People; Down Three Dark Streets; Human Desire
1953 The Last Posse
1952 Lone Star; Scandal Sheet; Stop, You're Killing Me; Last of the Comanches
1951 The Mob
1950 Cargo to Capetown; Convicted; Born Yesterday
1949 Night unto Night; Anna Lucasta; Bad Men of Tombstone; All the King's Men; A Kiss in the Dark
1948 Sealed Verdict; The Time of Your Life
1947 Slave Girl; The Flame
1946 The Runaround; The Black Angel
1942 Men of Texas; Butch Minds the Baby; North to the Klondike; Sin Town; I Married a Witch; Larceny, Inc.; Broadway
1941 The Black Cat; Tight Shoes; South of Tahiti; Badlands of Dakota
1940 Texas Rangers Ride Again; When the Daltons Rode; Trail of the Vigilantes; I Can't Give You Anything but Love, Baby; Seven Sinners; Slightly Honorable
1939 The Real Glory; Undercover Doctor; Eternally Yours; Beau Geste; Ambush; Island of Lost Men; Sudden Money
1938 Start Cheering
1937 Submarine D-1; Woman Chases Man

Joan Crawford
(Mar. 23, 1904–1977)
1970 Trog
1967 Berserk!; The Karate Killers
1965 I Saw What You Did
1964 Strait-Jacket; Fatal Confinement; Della
1963 The Caretakers
1962 What Ever Happened to Baby Jane?
1959 The Best of Everything
1957 The Story of Esther Costello
1956 Autumn Leaves
1955 Female on the Beach; Queen Bee
1953 Johnny Guitar; Torch Song
1952 Sudden Fear; This Woman Is Dangerous
1951 Goodbye, My Fancy
1950 The Damned Don't Cry; Harriet Craig
1949 Flamingo Road; It's a Great Feeling

1947 Possessed; Daisy Kenyon
1946 Humoresque
1945 Mildred Pierce
1944 Hollywood Canteen
1943 Above Suspicion
1942 Reunion in France; They All Kissed the Bride
1941 When Ladies Meet; A Woman's Face
1940 Susan and God; Strange Cargo
1939 The Women; The Ice Follies of 1939
1938 The Shining Hour
1937 Mannequin; The Last of Mrs. Cheyney; The Bride Wore Red
1936 Love on the Run; The Gorgeous Hussy
1935 I Live My Life; No More Ladies
1934 Chained; Forsaking All Others; Sadie McKee
1933 Today We Live; Dancing Lady
1932 Letty Lynton; Rain; Grand Hotel
1931 Dance Fools Dance; Laughing Sinners; Possessed; This Modern Age
1930 Montana Moon; Our Blushing Brides; Paid
1929 The Duke Steps Out; The Hollywood Revue; Untamed; Our Modern Maidens
1928 Rose-Marie; Our Dancing Daughters; Dream of Love; The Law of the Range; West Point; Four Walls; Across to Singapore
1927 Spring Fever; Twelve Miles Out; Understanding Heart; The Taxi Dancer; The Unknown
1926 Tramp, Tramp, Tramp; Boob; Paris
1925 Old Clothes; Proud Flesh; Pretty Ladies; Only Thing; Sally, Irene and Mary

Bing Crosby
(May 2, 1904–1977)
1974 That's Entertainment
1972 Cancel My Reservation
1966 Stagecoach
1964 Robin and the Seven Hoods
1962 The Road to Hong Kong
1960 Let's Make Love; High Time; Pepe
1959 Alias Jesse James; Say One for Me
1957 Man on Fire
1956 Anything Goes; High Society
1954 Hollywood Goes to War; White Christmas; The Country Girl
1953 Scared Stiff; Off Limits; Little Boy Lost
1952 Son of Paleface; Road to Bali; Just for You; The Greatest Show on Earth
1951 Here Comes the Groom; Angels in the Outfield
1950 Mr. Music; Riding High
1949 The Adventures of Ichabod and Mr. Toad; Top o' the Morning; A Connecticut Yankee in King Arthur's Court
1948 The Emperor Waltz
1947 My Favorite Brunette; Road to Rio; Variety Girl; Welcome Stranger

1946 Blue Skies; Monsieur Beaucaire
1945 Road to Utopia; The Bells of St. Mary's; Duffy's Tavern; Out of This World
1944 Here Come the Waves; The Princess and the Pirate; Going My Way
1943 Dixie
1942 The Road to Morocco; Holiday Inn; My Favorite Blonde; Star Spangled Rhythm
1941 Road to Zanzibar; Birth of the Blues
1940 Road to Singapore; Rhythm on the River; If I Had My Way
1939 Paris Honeymoon; The Starmaker; East Side of Heaven
1938 Sing You Sinners; Dr. Rhythm
1937 Waikiki Wedding; Double or Nothing
1936 Rhythm on the Range; Anything Goes; Pennies from Heaven
1935 Two for Tonight; The Big Broadcast of 1936; Mississippi
1934 She Loves Me Not; We're Not Dressing; Here Is My Heart
1933 Blue of the Night; College Humor; Going Hollywood; Too Much Harmony; Sing, Bing, Sing
1932 The Big Broadcast; Confessions of a Co-Ed
1931 I Surrender Dear; Reaching for the Moon
1930 The King of Jazz

Dan Dailey
(Dec. 14, 1914–1978)
1978 The Private Files of J. Edgar Hoover
1962 Hemingway's Adventures of a Young Man
1960 Pepe
1958 Underwater Warrior; The Wings of Eagles
1957 Oh, Men! Oh, Women!; The Wayward Bus
1956 The Best Things in Life Are Free; Meet Me in Las Vegas
1955 It's Always Fair Weather
1954 There's No Business Like Show Business
1953 The Girl Next Door; The Kid from Left Field; Taxi
1952 Meet Me at the Fair; What Price Glory?; The Pride of St. Louis
1951 I Can Get It for You Wholesale; Call Me Mister
1950 I'll Get By; My Blue Heaven; A Ticket to Tomahawk; When Willie Comes Marching Home
1949 You're My Everything; Chicken Every Sunday
1948 Give My Regards to Broadway; When My Baby Smiles at Me; You Were Meant for Me
1947 Mother Wore Tights
1942 Sunday Punch; Mokey; Panama Hattie; Give Out, Sisters
1941 Washington Melodrama; Ziegfeld Girl; Down in San Diego; The Wild Man of Borneo; Moon over Her Shoulder; The Get-Away;

Lady Be Good; Keeping Company
1940 The Captain Is a Lady; Dulcy; The Mortal Storm

Dorothy Dandridge
(Nov. 9, 1923–1965)
1960 Moment of Danger
1959 Tamango; Porgy and Bess
1958 The Decks Ran Red
1957 Island in the Sun
1954 Carmen Jones
1953 Bright Road; Remains to Be Seen
1951 The Harlem Globetrotters; Tarzan's Peril
1947 Flamingo
1946 Jungle Queen
1945 Pillow to Post
1944 Since You Went Away; Atlantic City
1943 Hit Parade of 1943
1942 Lucky Jordan; Drums of the Congo
1941 Lady from Louisiana; Bahama Passage; Sun Valley Serenade; Sundown
1940 Condemned Men
1937 A Day at the Races

Linda Darnell
(Oct. 16, 1921–1965)
1965 Black Spurs
1963 The Castilian
1957 Zero Hour
1956 Dakota Incident
1955 Gli Ultimi Cinque Minuti
1954 This Is My Love
1953 Second Chance; Angels of Darkness
1952 Blackbeard the Pirate; Island of Desire; Night Without Sleep
1951 Saturday Island; The Guy Who Came Back; The Lady Pays Off; The Thirteenth Letter
1950 No Way Out; Two Flags West
1949 Everybody Does It; Slattery's Hurricane; A Letter to Three Wives
1948 Unfaithfully Yours; The Walls of Jericho
1947 Forever Amber
1946 Anna and the King of Siam; My Darling Clementine; Centennial Summer
1945 Hangover Square; The Great John L.; Fallen Angel
1944 Summer Storm; Sweet and Lowdown; It Happened Tomorrow; Buffalo Bill
1943 The Song of Bernadette; City Without Men
1942 The Loves of Edgar Allan Poe
1941 Rise and Shine; Blood and Sand
1940 Star Dust; Brigham Young; The Mark of Zorro; Chad Hanna
1939 Daytime Wife; Hotel for Women

Marion Davies
(Jan. 3, 1897–1961)
1937 Ever Since Eve
1936 Cain and Mabel; Hearts Divided
1935 Page Miss Glory
1934 Operator 13
1933 Going Hollywood; Peg O' My Heart

1932 Blondie of the Follies; Polly of the Circus
1931 The Bachelor Father; Five and Ten; It's a Wise Child
1930 Not So Dumb; The Floradora Girl
1929 Marianne; The Hollywood Revue of 1929
1928 Cardboard Lover; Show People; Patsy
1927 Quality Street; The Red Mill; The Fair Co-Ed; Tillie the Toiler
1926 Beverly of Graustark
1925 Zander the Great; Lights of Old Broadway
1924 Yolanda; Janice Meredith
1923 Little Old New York; The Pilgrim; Adam and Eva
1922 Beauty's Worth; When Knighthood Was in Flower; Young Diana; Bride's Play
1921 Buried Treasure
1920 Restless Sex; April Folly; Enchantment; Cinema Murder
1919 Getting Mary Married; The Dark Star; The Belle of New York
1918 The Burden of Proof; Cecelia of the Pink Roses
1917 Runaway Romany

Bette Davis
(Apr. 5, 1908–1989)
1989 The Wicked Stepmother
1987 The Whales of August
1981 The Watcher in the Woods
1978 Return from Witch Mountain; Death on the Nile
1976 Burnt Offerings
1971 Bunny O'Hare
1969 Connecting Rooms
1968 The Anniversary
1965 The Nanny; Hush . . . Hush, Sweet Charlotte
1964 The Empty Canvas; Where Love Has Gone; Dead Ringer
1962 What Ever Happened to Baby Jane?
1961 Pocketful of Miracles
1959 John Paul Jones; The Scapegoat
1956 Storm Center; The Catered Affair
1955 The Virgin Queen
1952 The Star; Phone Call from a Stranger
1951 Another Man's Poison; Payment on Demand
1950 All About Eve
1949 Beyond the Forest
1948 Winter Meeting; June Bride
1946 Deception; A Stolen Life
1945 The Corn Is Green
1944 Mr. Skeffington; Hollywood Canteen
1943 Watch on the Rhine; Thank Your Lucky Stars; Old Acquaintance
1942 Now, Voyager; In This Our Life
1941 The Man Who Came to Dinner; The Bride Came C.O.D.; Shining Victory; The Little Foxes; The Great Lie
1940 The Letter; All This and Heaven Too
1939 Juarez; The Private Lives of Elizabeth and Essex; The Old Maid; Dark Victory
1938 Jezebel; The Sisters
1937 It's Love I'm After; Marked Woman; Kid Galahad; That Certain Woman
1936 The Petrified Forest; Satan Met a Lady; The Golden Arrow
1935 Special Agent; Front Page Woman; The Girl from Tenth Avenue; Dangerous; Bordertown
1934 Fashions of 1934; Of Human Bondage; Fog over Frisco; Jimmy the Gent; The Big Shakedown; Housewife
1933 20,000 Years in Sing-Sing; The Working Man; Ex-Lady; Bureau of Missing Persons; Parachute Jumper
1932 The Man Who Played God; Way Back Home; The Menace; Hell's House; The Cabin in the Cotton; The Rich Are Always with Us; So Big; Three on a Match; The Dark Horse
1931 Seed; Bad Sister; Waterloo Bridge

Doris Day
(Apr. 3, 1924)
1968 Where Were You When the Lights Went Out?; With Six You Get Eggroll
1967 The Ballad of Josie; Caprice
1966 The Glass Bottom Boat
1965 Do Not Disturb
1964 Send Me No Flowers
1963 The Thrill of It All!; Move Over, Darling
1962 That Touch of Mink; Billy Rose's Jumbo
1961 Lover Come Back
1960 Midnight Lace; Please Don't Eat the Daisies
1959 Pillow Talk; It Happened to Jane
1958 Teacher's Pet; The Tunnel of Love
1957 The Pajama Game
1956 Julie; The Man Who Knew Too Much
1955 Love Me or Leave Me
1954 Lucky Me; Young at Heart
1953 By the Light of the Silvery Moon; Calamity Jane
1952 April in Paris; The Winning Team
1951 The Lullaby of Broadway; On Moonlight Bay; I'll See You in My Dreams; Starlift
1950 The West Point Story; Young Man with a Horn; Tea for Two; Storm Warning
1949 My Dream Is Yours; It's a Great Feeling
1948 Romance on the High Seas

James Dean
(Feb. 8, 1931–1955)
1956 Giant
1955 East of Eden; Rebel Without a Cause
1953 Trouble Along the Way
1952 Has Anybody Seen My Gal?
1951 Fixed Bayonets; Sailor Beware

Olivia de Havilland
(July 1, 1916)
1978 The Swarm; The Fifth Musketeer
1977 Airport '77
1972 Pope Joan
1970 The Adventurers
1965 Hush . . . Hush, Sweet Charlotte

1964 Lady in a Cage
1962 Light in the Piazza
1959 Libel
1958 The Proud Rebel
1956 The Ambassador's Daughter
1955 That Lady; Not As a Stranger
1952 My Cousin Rachel
1949 The Heiress
1948 The Snake Pit
1946 The Dark Mirror; Devotion; To Each His Own; The Well-Groomed Bride
1944 Hollywood Canteen
1943 Government Girl; Princess O'Rourke; Thank Your Lucky Stars
1942 In This Our Life; The Male Animal
1941 The Strawberry Blonde; Hold Back the Dawn; They Died with Their Boots On
1940 My Love Came Back; Santa Fe Trail
1939 Gone with the Wind; Raffles; The Private Lives of Elizabeth and Essex; Wings of the Navy; Dodge City
1938 The Adventures of Robin Hood; Four's a Crowd; Hard to Get; Gold Is Where You Find It
1937 Call It a Day; It's Love I'm After; The Great Garrick
1936 Anthony Adverse; The Charge of the Light Brigade
1935 Captain Blood; A Midsummer Night's Dream; The Irish in Us; Alibi Ike

Robert De Niro
(Aug. 17, 1943)
1998 Great Expectations; Ronin
1997 Cop Land; Jackie Brown; Wag the Dog
1996 Faithful; The Fan; Marvin's Room; Sleepers
1995 A Hundred and One Nights of Simon Cinema; Casino; Heat
1994 Mary Shelley's Frankenstein
1993 Mad Dog and Glory; This Boy's Life; A Bronx Tale
1992 Night and the City
1991 Mistress; Guilty by Suspicion; Cape Fear; Backdraft
1990 Stanley and Iris; Goodfellas; Awakenings
1989 We're No Angels; Jacknife
1988 Midnight Run
1987 Angel Heart; The Untouchables
1986 The Mission
1985 Brazil
1984 Once Upon a Time in America; Falling in Love
1983 The King of Comedy
1981 True Confessions
1980 Raging Bull
1978 The Deer Hunter
1977 New York, New York
1976 Taxi Driver; 1900; The Last Tycoon
1974 The Godfather, Part II
1973 Mean Streets; Bang the Drum Slowly
1971 The Gang That Couldn't Shoot Straight; Born to Win; Jennifer on My Mind
1970 Bloody Mama; Hi, Mom!; The Wedding Party; Sam's Song
1968 Greetings

Marlene Dietrich
(Dec. 27, 1901–1992)
1978 Just a Gigolo
1964 Paris When It Sizzles
1961 Judgment at Nuremberg
1958 Touch of Evil
1957 Witness for the Prosecution; The Monte Carlo Story
1956 Around the World in 80 Days
1952 Rancho Notorious
1951 No Highway in the Sky
1950 Stage Fright
1949 Jigsaw
1948 A Foreign Affair; The Room Upstairs
1947 Golden Earrings
1944 Follow the Boys; Kismet
1942 The Spoilers; The Lady Is Willing; Pittsburgh
1941 The Flame of New Orleans; Manpower
1940 Seven Sinners
1939 Destry Rides Again
1937 Angel; Knight Without Armour
1936 Desire; The Garden of Allah
1935 The Devil Is a Woman
1934 The Scarlet Empress
1933 Song of Songs
1932 Blonde Venus; Shanghai Express
1931 Dishonored
1930 The Blue Angel; Morocco

Kirk Douglas
(Dec. 9, 1916)
1994 Greedy
1991 Oscar
1986 Tough Guys
1983 Eddie Macon's Run
1982 The Man from Snowy River
1980 The Final Countdown; Saturn 3
1979 Home Movies; The Villain
1978 The Fury; The Chosen
1975 Posse; Once Is Not Enough
1973 Scalawag; The Master Touch
1971 Catch Me a Spy; Gunfight; The Light at the Edge of the World
1970 There Was a Crooked Man
1969 The Arrangement
1968 The Brotherhood; A Lovely Way to Die
1967 The War Wagon; The Way the West Was Won
1966 Is Paris Burning?; Cast a Giant Shadow; The Heroes of Telemark
1965 In Harm's Way
1964 Seven Days in May
1963 For Love or Money; The List of Adrian Messenger; The Hook
1962 Two Weeks in Another Town; Lonely Are the Brave
1961 Town Without Pity; The Last Sunset
1960 Spartacus; Strangers When We Meet
1959 The Devil's Disciple; The Last Train from Gun Hill
1958 The Vikings
1957 Paths of Glory; Gunfight at the O.K. Corral; Top Secret Affair
1956 Lust for Life
1955 The Indian Fighter; Man

Without a Star; Ulysses;
The Racers
1954 20,000 Leagues Under
the Sea
1953 Act of Love; The Juggler;
The Story of Three Loves
1952 The Bad and the
Beautiful; The Big Trees;
The Big Sky
1951 Detective Story; The
Big Carnival; Along the
Great Divide
1950 The Glass Menagerie;
Young Man with a Horn
1949 Champion; A Letter to
Three Wives
1948 The Walls of Jericho; My
Dear Secretary
1947 Mourning Becomes
Electra; Out of the Past; I
Walk Alone
1946 The Strange Loves of
Martha Ivers

Melvyn Douglas
(Apr. 5, 1901–1981)
1981 Ghost Story
1980 Tell Me a Riddle
1979 The Seduction of Joe
Tynan; Being There; The
Changeling
1977 Portrait of Grandpa Doc;
Twilight's Last Gleaming
1976 The Tenant
1972 The Candidate; One Is a
Lonely Number
1970 I Never Sang for My
Father
1967 Hotel; Companions in
Nightmare
1965 Rapture
1964 Advance to the Rear; The
Americanization of Emily
1963 Hud
1962 Billy Budd
1951 On the Loose; My
Forbidden Past
1949 A Woman's Secret; The
Great Sinner
1948 Mr. Blandings Builds His
Dream House; My Own
True Love
1947 The Sea of Grass; The
Guilt of Janet Ames
1943 Three Hearts for Julia
1942 They All Kissed the Bride;
We Were Dancing
1941 Our Wife; Two-Faced
Woman; That Uncertain
Feeling; A Woman's Face;
This Thing Called Love
1940 He Stayed for Breakfast;
Third Finger, Left Hand;
Too Many Husbands
1939 Ninotchka; Tell No Tales;
The Amazing Mr.
Williams; Good Girls Go
to Paris
1938 The Shining Hour; That
Certain Age; Arsene Lupin
Returns; There's Always
a Woman; There's That
Woman Again; Fast
Company; The Toy Wife
1937 I'll Take Romance; Angel;
Women of Glamour;
Captains Courageous; I
Met Him in Paris
1936 The Lone Wolf Returns;
And So They Were
Married; The Gorgeous
Hussy; Theodora Goes
Wild
1935 She Married Her Boss;
The People's Enemy;
Annie Oakley; Mary
Burns, Fugitive
1934 Woman in the Dark;

Dangerous Corner;
Nagana
1933 Counsellor-at-Law; The
Vampire Bat
1932 The Wiser Sex; As You
Desire Me; Prestige; The
Old Dark House; The
Broken Wing
1931 Tonight or Never

Faye Dunaway
(Jan. 14, 1941)
1998 Gia
1997 The Twilight of the Golds;
In Praise of Older Women
1996 Dunston Checks In; Albino
Alligator; The Chamber
1995 Don Juan DeMarco;
Drunks
1994 Even Cowgirls Get the
Blues
1993 The Temp; Arizona Dream
1992 Double Edge; Scorchers
1990 The Handmaid's Tale;
The Two Jakes; Wait Until
Spring, Bandini
1989 On a Moonlit Night
1988 The Gamble;
Burning Secret
1987 Midnight Crossing; Barfly
1984 Supergirl; Ordeal by
Innocence
1983 The Wicked Lady
1981 Mommie Dearest
1980 The First Deadly Sin
1979 The Champ
1978 The Eyes of Laura Mars
1976 Voyage of the Damned;
Network
1975 The Four Musketeers;
Three Days of the Condor
1974 The Towering Inferno;
Chinatown
1973 Oklahoma Crude; The
Three Musketeers
1971 The Deadly Trap; Doc
1970 Puzzle of a Downfall Child;
Little Big Man
1969 The Extraordinary
Seaman; A Place for
Lovers; The Arrangement
1968 The Thomas Crown Affair
1967 The Happening; Bonnie
and Clyde; Hurry Sundown

Irene Dunne
(Dec. 20, 1898–1990)
1952 It Grows on Trees
1950 Never a Dull Moment; The
Mudlark
1948 I Remember Mama
1947 Life with Father
1946 Anna and the King of
Siam
1945 Over 21
1944 The White Cliffs of Dover;
A Guy Named Joe;
Together Again
1942 Lady in a Jam
1941 Penny Serenade;
Unfinished Business
1940 My Favorite Wife
1939 Invitation to Happiness;
Love Affair; When
Tomorrow Comes
1938 Joy of Living
1937 High, Wide and
Handsome; The Awful
Truth
1936 Theodora Goes Wild;
Show Boat
1935 Sweet Adeline;
Magnificent Obsession;
Roberta
1934 Stingaree; This Man Is
Mine; The Age of
Innocence
1933 No Other Woman; The

Secret of Madame
Blanche; The Silver Cord;
Ann Vickers; If I Were Free
1932 Back Street; Thirteen
Women; Symphony of Six
Million
1931 Consolation Marriage; The
Great Lover; Bachelor
Apartment; Cimarron
1930 Leathernecking

Deanna Durbin
(Dec. 4, 1921)
1950 Summer Stock
1948 For the Love of Mary; Up
in Central Park
1947 I'll Be Yours; Something in
the Wind
1946 Because of Him
1945 Lady on a Train
1944 Christmas Holiday; Can't
Help Singing
1943 His Butler's Sister; Hers
to Hold; The Amazing Mrs.
Holliday
1941 Nice Girl?; It Started with
Eve
1940 It's a Date; Spring Parade
1939 Three Smart Girls Grow
Up; First Love
1938 That Certain Age; Mad
About Music
1937 One Hundred Men and a
Girl
1936 Three Smart Girls

Robert Duvall
(Jan. 5, 1931)
1998 The Gingerbread Man;
Deep Impact
1997 The Apostle
1996 A Family Thing; Sling
Blade; Phenomenon
1995 The Stars Fell on
Henrietta; Something to
Talk About; Scarlet Letter
1994 The Paper
1993 Falling Down; Geronimo:
An American Legend;
Wrestling Ernest
Hemingway
1992 Newsies; The Plague
1991 Rambling Rose; Convicts
1990 The Handmaid's Tale;
Days of Thunder; A Show
of Force
1988 Colors
1987 Let's Get Harry; The
Roarer
1986 The Lightship; Belizaire
the Cajun
1984 The Natural; The Stone
Boy
1983 Angelo My Love; Hotel
Colonial
1982 Tender Mercies; The
Pursuit of D. B. Cooper
1981 True Confessions
1979 Apocalypse Now; The
Great Santini
1978 Invasion of the Body
Snatchers; The Betsy
1977 The Greatest
1976 Network; The Eagle Has
Landed; The Seven
Percent Solution
1975 Breakout; The Killer Elite
1974 The Conversation; The
Godfather, Part II; The
Outfit
1973 Lady Ice; Badge 373;
Tomorrow; The Godfather;
The Great Northfield,
Minnesota Raid
1972 Joe Kidd
1971 THX 1138; Lawman
1970 The Revolutionary;
M*A*S*H

1969 The Rain People; True Grit
1968 The Detective;
Countdown; Bullitt
1966 The Chase
1964 Nightmare in the Sun
1963 Captain Newman, M.D.
1962 To Kill a Mockingbird

Clint Eastwood
(May 31, 1930)
1997 Absolute Power
1995 The Bridges of Madison
County; Casper
1993 In the Line of Fire; A
Perfect World
1992 Unforgiven
1990 The Rookie; White Hunter,
Black Heart
1989 Pink Cadillac
1988 The Dead Pool; Bird
1986 Heartbreak Ridge
1985 Pale Rider
1984 Tightrope; City Heat
1983 Sudden Impact
1982 Firefox; Honkytonk Man
1980 Bronco Billy; Any Which
Way You Can
1979 Escape from Alcatraz
1978 Every Which Way But
Loose
1977 The Gauntlet
1976 The Outlaw Josey Wales;
The Enforcer
1975 The Eiger Sanction
1974 Thunderbolt and Lightfoot
1973 High Plains Drifter;
Magnum Force; Breezy
1972 Joe Kidd
1971 Play Misty for Me; Dirty
Harry; The Beguiled
1970 Two Mules for Sister Sara;
Kelly's Heroes
1969 Paint Your Wagon
1968 Where Eagles Dare; Hang
'em High; Coogan's Bluff
1966 The Witches; The Good,
the Bad and the Ugly; For
a Few Dollars More
1964 A Fistful of Dollars
1958 Ambush at Cimarron
Pass; Lafayette Escadrille
1957 Escapade in Japan
1956 The First Traveling
Saleslady; Never Say
Goodbye; Star in the Dust;
Away All Boats
1955 Lady Godiva; Revenge of
the Creature; Francis in
the Navy; Tarantula

Douglas Fairbanks
(May 23, 1883–1939)
1934 The Private Life of Don
Juan
1932 Mr. Robinson Crusoe
1931 Reaching for the Moon
1929 The Iron Mask; The
Taming of the Shrew
1928 Show People; The Gaucho
1927 Kiss for Mary Pickford
1926 The Black Pirate
1925 Don Q, Son of Zorro
1924 The Thief of Baghdad
1922 Robin Hood
1921 The Three Musketeers;
The Nut
1920 The Mark of Zorro; The
Mollycoddle
1919 His Majesty the American;
The Knickerbocker
Buckaroo; Till the Clouds
Roll By
1918 Arizona; Bound in
Morocco; He Comes Up
Smiling; Headin' South;
Mr. Fix-It; Say! Young
Fellow
1917 Down to Earth; The Man

from Painted Post; In
Again–Out Again;
Reaching for the Moon;
A Modern Musketeer;
The Americano; Wild and
Woolly
1916 The Matrimaniac;
Intolerance; The Good Bad
Man; Manhattan
Madness; The Habit of
Happiness; An American
Aristocracy; Flirting with
Fate; Half Breed; His
Picture in the Papers;
Reggie Mixes In
1915 The Lamb; The Martyrs of
the Alamo; Double Trouble

Douglas Fairbanks, Jr.
(Dec. 9, 1909)
1981 Ghost Story
1957 The Silken Affair
1954 Thoroughbred; Destination
Milan; Forever My Heart;
The Last Moment; The
Red Dress
1953 The Genie; Three's
Company
1951 Mr. Drake's Duck
1950 State Secret
1949 The Fighting O'Flynn; The
Great Manhunt
1948 That Lady in Ermine
1947 The Exile; Sinbad the
Sailor
1941 The Corsican Brothers
1940 Green Hell; Safari; Angels
over Broadway
1939 Rulers of the Sea;
The Sun Never Sets;
Gunga Din
1938 Carnival Boat; Joy of
Living; Having Wonderful
Time; The Rage of Paris;
The Young in Heart
1937 When Thief Meets Thief;
The Prisoner of Zenda
1936 The Amateur Gentleman;
Accused; Crime over
London
1935 Man of the Moment;
Mimi
1934 Success at Any Price;
Catherine the Great
1933 The Life of Jimmy Dolan;
Captured; The Narrow
Corner; Parachute
Jumper; Morning Glory
1932 Love Is a Racket; Scarlet
Dawn; It's Tough to Be
Famous; Union Depot
1931 I Like Your Nerve;
Chances; Little Caesar
1930 Party Girl; Loose Ankles;
One Night at Susie's;
Outward Bound; The Little
Accident; The Way of All
Men; The Dawn Patrol
1929 Party Incorporated; The
Careless Age; The
Forward Pass; The Jazz
Age; Our Modern
Maidens; The Show of
Shows; Fast Life
1928 Dead Man's Curve; The
Barker; The Toilers;
Modern Mothers; A
Woman of Affairs; The
Power of the Press
1927 Women Love Diamonds; A
Texas Steer; Is Zat So?
1926 Man Bait; Padlocked;
Broken Hearts of
Hollywood; The American
Venus
1925 Wild Horse Mesa; The Air
Mail; Stella Dallas
1923 Stephen Steps Out

Alice Faye
(May 5, 1912–1998)
1978 Every Girl Should Have
One; The Magic of Lassie
1976 Won Ton Ton, the Dog
Who Saved Hollywood
1962 State Fair
1945 Fallen Angel
1944 Four Jills in a Jeep
1943 The Gang's All Here;
Hello, Frisco, Hello
1941 That Night in Rio;
Weekend in Havana; The
Great American Broadcast
1940 Lillian Russell; Little Old
New York; Tin Pan Alley
1939 Hollywood Cavalcade;
Rose of Washington
Square; Tail Spin;
Barricade
1938 Sally, Irene and Mary;
Alexander's Ragtime
Band; In Old Chicago
1937 On the Avenue; Wake Up
and Live; You Can't Have
Everything; You're a
Sweetheart
1936 King of Burlesque; Sing,
Baby, Sing; Poor Little
Rich Girl; Stowaway
1935 George White's Scandals;
Every Night at Eight;
Music is Magic
1934 Now I'll Tell; George
White's Scandals; 365
Nights in Hollywood; She
Learned About Sailors

W. C. Fields
(Feb. 10, 1879–1946)
1944 Sensations of 1945;
Follow the Boys; Song of
the Open Road
1942 Tales of Manhattan *(scene
deleted)*
1941 Never Give a Sucker an
Even Break
1940 My Little Chickadee; The
Bank Dick
1939 You Can't Cheat an
Honest Man
1937 The Big Broadcast of
1938
1936 Poppy
1935 David Copperfield; The
Man on the Flying
Trapeze; Mississippi
1934 It's a Gift; The Old-
Fashioned Way; Six of a
Kind; You're Telling Me;
Mrs. Wiggs of the
Cabbage Patch
1933 The Fatal Glass of Beer;
The Barber Shop; Alice in
Wonderland; International
House; Tillie and Gus
1932 If I Had a Million; Million
Dollar Legs; The
Pharmacist; The Dentist
1931 Her Majesty Love; The
Golf Specialist
1928 Tillie's Punctured
Romance; Fools for
Luck
1927 The Potters; Two Flaming
Youths; Running Wild
1926 It's the Old Army Game;
So's Your Old Man
1925 That Royle Girl; Sally of
the Sawdust
1924 Janice Meredith
1915 Pool Sharks

Errol Flynn
(June 20, 1909–1959)
1959 Cuban Rebel Girls
1958 The Roots of Heaven; Too
Much, Too Soon

1957 The Big Boodle; Istanbul;
The Sun Also Rises
1955 King's Rhapsody; Let's
Make Up; The Warriors
1954 Crossed Swords
1953 The Master of Ballantrae
1952 Mara Maru; Against All
Flags
1951 Adventures of Captain
Fabian; Hello God; Kim
1950 Montana; Rocky Mountain
1949 It's a Great Feeling; That
Forsyte Woman; The
Adventures of Don Juan
1948 Silver River
1947 Escape Me Never; Always
Together; Cry Wolf
1946 Never Say Goodbye
1945 San Antonio; Objective,
Burma!
1944 Hollywood Canteen;
Uncertain Glory
1943 Northern Pursuit; Edge of
Darkness; Thank Your
Lucky Stars
1942 Desperate Journey;
Gentleman Jim
1941 Dive Bomber; Footsteps in
the Dark; They Died with
Their Boots on
1940 The Sea Hawk; Santa Fe
Trail; Virginia City
1939 The Private Lives of
Elizabeth and Essex;
Dodge City
1938 The Adventures of Robin
Hood; The Sisters; The
Dawn Patrol; Four's a
Crowd
1937 The Perfect Specimen;
The Prince and the
Pauper; The Green Light;
Another Dawn
1936 The Charge of the Light
Brigade
1935 Captain Blood; Don't Bet
on Blondes; Murder at
Monte Carlo; The Case of
the Curious Bride
1933 In the Wake of the Bounty

Henry Fonda
(May 16, 1905–1982)
1981 On Golden Pond
1980 The Jilting of Granny
Weatherall
1979 Meteor; Wanda Nevada;
City on Fire
1978 The Swarm; Fedora
1977 The Great Battle; The Blue
Hotel; Tentacles; Roller
Coaster; The Last of the
Cowboys
1976 Midway
1974 My Name Is Nobody;
Mussolini's Last Stand
1973 Ash Wednesday; Night
Flight from Moscow
1971 Sometimes a Great
Notion; The American
West of John Ford
1970 The Cheyenne Social
Club; There Was a
Crooked Man; Too Late
the Hero
1968 Once Upon a Time in the
West; The Boston
Strangler; Yours, Mine and
Ours; Firecreek; Madigan
1967 Welcome to Hard Times
1966 A Big Hand for the Little
Lady; The Dirty Game
1965 Battle of the Bulge; The
Rounders; In Harm's Way
1964 Sex and the Single Girl;
Fail-Safe; The Best Man
1963 Spencer's Mountain
1962 How the West Was Won;

Advise and Consent; The
Longest Day
1959 Warlock; The Man Who
Understood Women
1957 The Tin Star; 12 Angry
Men; Stage Struck; The
Wrong Man
1956 War and Peace
1955 Mr. Roberts
1953 Main Street to Broadway
1949 Jigsaw
1948 Fort Apache; On Our
Merry Way
1947 The Fugitive; Daisy
Kenyon; The Long Night
1946 My Darling Clementine
1943 The Immortal Sergeant;
The Ox-Bow Incident
1942 The Male Animal; Rings
on Her Fingers; Tales of
Manhattan; The Big
Street; The Magnificent
Dope
1941 The Lady Eve; Wild Geese
Calling; You Belong to Me
1940 The Grapes of Wrath; The
Return of Frank James;
Lillian Russell; Chad
Hanna
1939 The Story of Alexander
Graham Bell; Let Us Live;
Drums Along the Mohawk;
Young Mr. Lincoln; Jesse
James
1938 The Mad Miss Manton;
Spawn of the North; I Met
My Love Again; Blockade;
Jezebel
1937 Slim; You Only Live Once;
That Certain Woman;
Wings of the Morning
1936 Spendthrift; The Moon's
Our Home; The Trail of the
Lonesome Pine
1935 The Farmer Takes a Wife;
Way Down East; I Dream
Too Much

Joan Fontaine
(Oct. 22, 1917)
1966 The Devil's Own
1961 Voyage to the Bottom of
the Sea; Tender Is the
Night
1958 South Pacific; A Certain
Smile; Until They Sail;
Island in the Sun
1956 Serenade; Beyond a
Reasonable Doubt;
Casanova's Big Night
1953 The Bigamist; Decameron
Nights; Flight to Tangier
1952 Ivanhoe; Something to
Live For; Othello
1951 Darling, How Could You!
1950 Born to Be Bad;
September Affair
1948 The Emperor Waltz; Kiss
the Blood off My Hands; A
Letter from an Unknown
Woman; You Gotta Stay
Happy
1947 Ivy
1946 From This Day Forward
1945 The Affairs of Susan
1944 Frenchman's Creek; Jane
Eyre
1943 The Constant Nymph
1942 This Above All
1941 Suspicion
1940 Rebecca
1939 Man of Conquest; The
Women; Gunga Din
1938 Sky Giant; Maid's Night
Out; The Duke of West
Point; Blonde Cheat
1937 You Can't Beat Love;
Quality Street; A Damsel

in Distress; Music for
Madame; A Million to One;
The Man Who Found
Himself
1935 No More Ladies

Glenn Ford
(May 1, 1916)
1990 Border Shootout
1982 Virus
1981 Happy Birthday to Me
1980 The Visitor
1978 Superman
1976 Midway
1973 Santee
1969 Heaven with a Gun; Smith!
1968 Day of the Assassin
1967 The Last Challenge; A
Time for Killing
1966 The Money Trap; Rage; Is
Paris Burning?
1965 The Rounders
1964 Advance to the Rear; Dear
Heart; Fate Is the Hunter
1963 Love Is a Ball
1962 The Courtship of Eddie's
Father; The Four
Horsemen of the
Apocalypse; Experiment in
Terror
1961 Cry for Happy; Pocketful
of Miracles
1960 Cimarron
1959 The Gazebo; It Started
with a Kiss
1958 Cowboy; Imitation
General; The Sheepman;
Torpedo Run
1957 3:10 to Yuma; Don't Go
Near the Water
1956 The Fastest Gun Alive;
The Teahouse of the
August Moon; Jubal
1955 Interrupted Melody;
Ransom; The Violent Men;
The Blackboard Jungle;
The Americano; Trial
1954 Human Desire
1953 Plunder of the Sun; Terror
on a Train; The Man from
the Alamo; Appointment in
Honduras; The Big Heat
1952 Young Man with Ideas;
Affair in Trinidad; The
Green Glove
1951 The Secret of Convict
Lake; Follow the Sun
1950 The Redhead and the
Cowboy; The Flying
Missile; The White Tower;
Convicted
1949 The Undercover Man; Mr.
Soft Touch; Lust for Gold;
The Doctor and the Girl
1948 The Return of October;
The Man from Colorado;
The Mating of Millie; The
Loves of Carmen
1947 Framed; Gilda; A Stolen
Life; Gallant Journey
1943 The Desperadoes;
Destroyer
1942 Flight Lieutenant; The
Adventures of Martin
Eden
1941 Go West, Young Lady;
Texas; So Ends Our Night
1940 The Lady in Question;
Babies for Sale; Men
Without Souls; Blondie
Plays Cupid; Convicted
Woman
1939 Heaven with a Barbed
Wire Fence

Jodie Foster
(Nov. 19, 1963)
1997 Contact

1994 Maverick; Nell
1993 Sommersby
1992 Shadows and Fog
1991 Little Man Tate; The
Silence of the Lambs
1989 Backtrack
1988 Stealing Home; Five
Corners; The Accused
1987 Siesta
1986 Mesmerized
1984 The Hotel New
Hampshire; The Blood of
Others
1982 O'Hara's Wife
1980 Foxes; Carny
1977 Candleshoe; Moi, Fleur
Bleue; Il Casotto
1976 Taxi Driver; Freaky Friday;
Echoes of a Summer; The
Little Girl Who Lives Down
the Lane; Bugsy Malone
1974 Alice Doesn't Live Here
Anymore
1973 Tom Sawyer; One Little
Indian
1972 Kansas City Bomber;
Napoleon and Samantha

Clark Gable
(Feb. 1, 1901–1960)
1961 The Misfits
1960 It Started in Naples
1959 But Not for Me
1958 Run Silent, Run Deep;
Teacher's Pet
1957 Band of Angels
1956 The King and Four Queens
1955 Soldier of Fortune; The
Tall Men
1954 Betrayed
1953 Mogambo; Never Let Me
Go
1952 Lone Star
1951 Across the Wide Missouri;
Callaway Went Thataway
1950 Key to the City; To Please
a Lady
1949 Any Number Can Play
1948 Command Decision;
Homecoming
1947 The Hucksters
1945 Adventure
1942 Somewhere I'll Find You
1941 Honky Tonk; They Met in
Bombay
1940 Strange Cargo; Comrade
X; Boom Town
1939 Gone with the Wind;
Idiot's Delight
1938 Test Pilot; Too Hot to
Handle
1937 Saratoga; Parnell
1936 San Francisco; Wife vs.
Secretary; Love on the
Run; Cain and Mabel
1935 Mutiny on the Bounty; The
Call of the Wild; China
Seas; After Office Hours
1934 It Happened One Night;
Forsaking All Others; Men
in White; Manhattan
Melodrama; Chained
1933 Night Flight; Hold Your
Man; The White Sister;
Dancing Lady
1932 Polly of the Circus; No
Man of Her Own; Red
Dust; Strange Interlude
1931 Hell Divers; Night Nurse;
The Painted Desert; A
Free Soul; Susan Lenox:
Her Fall and Rise;
Laughing Sinners; The
Secret Six; Sporting
Blood; Dance Fools
Dance; The Possessed;
The Easiest Way; The
Finger Points

1925 North Star; The
Johnstown Flood; The
Plastic Age; The Merry
Widow
1924 Forbidden Paradise; White
Man; The Iron Horse

Greta Garbo
(Sept. 18, 1905–1990)
1941 Two-Faced Woman
1939 Ninotchka
1937 Conquest; Camille
1935 Anna Karenina
1934 The Painted Veil
1933 Queen Christina
1932 As You Desire Me; Grand
Hotel
1931 Mata Hari; Inspiration;
Susan Lenox: Her Fall and
Rise
1930 Romance; Anna Christie
1929 The Single Standard; The
Kiss; Wild Orchids; A
Man's Man
1928 The Mysterious Lady; A
Woman of Affairs; The
Divine Woman
1927 Love
1926 Flesh and the Devil; The
Temptress; The Torrent
1925 The Joyless Street
1924 The Atonement of Gosta
Berling
1922 Peter the Tramp

Ava Gardner
(Dec. 24, 1922–1990)
1982 Regina
1981 Priest of Love
1980 The Kidnapping of the
President; City on Fire
1977 The Cassandra Crossing;
The Sentinel
1976 The Blue Bird
1975 Permission to Kill
1974 Earthquake
1972 The Life and Times of
Judge Roy Bean
1971 The Devil's Widow
1968 Mayerling
1966 The Bible—In the
Beginning
1964 The Night of the Iguana;
Seven Days in May
1963 55 Days at Peking
1960 The Angel Wore Red
1959 On the Beach; The Naked
Maja
1957 The Little Hut; The Sun
Also Rises
1956 Bhowani Junction
1954 The Barefoot Contessa;
Knights of the Round
Table
1953 The Band Wagon;
Mogambo; Ride, Vaquero!
1952 The Snows of Kilimanjaro;
Lone Star
1951 My Forbidden Past;
Pandora and the Flying
Dutchman; Show Boat
1950 The Killer That Stalked
New York
1949 The Bribe; The Great
Sinner; East Side, West
Side
1948 One Touch of Venus
1947 The Hucksters;
Singapore
1946 Whistle Stop; The Killers
1945 She Went to the Races
1944 Two Girls and a Sailor;
Maisie Goes to Reno;
Music for Millions; Blonde
Fever; Three Men in White
1943 Pilot No. 5; Lost Angel;
Hitler's Madman; Ghosts
on the Loose; Swing

Fever; Young Ideas; Du
Barry Was a Lady
1942 This Time for Keeps; Joe
Smith, American; We Were
Dancing; Calling Dr.
Gillespie; Kid Glove Killer;
Sunday Punch; Reunion in
France
1941 H. M. Pulham, Esq.

John Garfield
(Mar. 4, 1913–1952)
1951 He Ran All the Way
1950 The Breaking Point; Under
My Skin
1949 Jigsaw; We Were
Strangers
1948 Force of Evil
1947 Gentleman's Agreement;
Body and Soul; Daisy
Kenyon
1946 The Postman Always
Rings Twice; Humoresque;
Nobody Lives Forever
1945 Pride of the Marines
1944 Between Two Worlds;
Hollywood Canteen
1943 Thank Your Lucky Stars;
The Fallen Sparrow; Air
Force; Destination Tokyo
1942 Tortilla Flat; Dangerously
They Live
1941 Out of the Fog; The Sea
Wolf
1940 East of the River; Flowing
Gold; Castle on the
Hudson; Saturday's
Children
1939 Four Wives; Juarez; Dust
Be My Destiny; Daughters
Courageous; They Made
Me a Criminal; Blackwell's
Island
1938 Four Daughters
1933 Footlight Parade

Judy Garland
(June 10, 1922–1969)
1963 A Child Is Waiting; I Could
Go on Singing
1962 Gay Purr-Ee
1961 Judgment at Nuremberg
1960 Pepe
1954 A Star Is Born
1950 Summer Stock
1949 In the Good Old
Summertime
1948 The Pirate; Easter Parade;
Words and Music
1946 The Harvey Girls; Till the
Clouds Roll By; Ziegfeld
Follies
1945 The Clock
1944 Meet Me in St. Louis
1943 Thousands Cheer; Girl
Crazy; Presenting Lily
Mars
1942 For Me and My Gal; We
Must Have Music
1941 Life Begins for Andy
Hardy; Ziegfeld Girl;
Babes on Broadway
1940 Andy Hardy Meets
Debutante; Strike Up the
Band; Little Nellie Kelly
1939 The Wizard of Oz; Babes
in Arms
1938 Listen, Darling; Everybody
Sing; Love Finds Andy
Hardy
1937 Thoroughbreds Don't Cry;
Broadway Melody of 1938
1936 Pigskin Parade

James Garner
(Apr. 7, 1928)
1998 Twilight
1996 My Fellow Americans

1994 Maverick
1993 Fire in the Sky
1992 The Distinguished Gentleman
1988 Sunset
1985 Murphy's Romance
1984 Tank
1982 Victor/Victoria
1981 The Fan
1979 H.E.A.L.T.H.
1974 The Castaway Cowboy
1973 One Little Indian
1972 They Only Kill Their Masters
1971 Support Your Local Gunfighter; Skin Game
1970 A Man Called Sledge
1969 Support Your Local Sheriff!; Marlowe
1968 The Pink Jungle; How Sweet It Is
1967 Hour of the Gun
1966 Duel at Diablo; A Man Could Get Killed; Mister Buddwing; Grand Prix
1965 The Art of Love; 36 Hours
1964 The Americanization of Emily
1963 The Wheeler Dealers; Move Over, Darling; The Great Escape; The Thrill of It All!
1962 Boys' Night Out
1961 The Children's Hour
1960 Cash McCall
1959 Up Periscope
1958 Darby's Rangers
1957 Shoot-Out at Medicine Bend; Sayonara
1956 Toward the Unknown; The Girl He Left Behind

Greer Garson
(Sept. 28, 1908–1996)
1967 The Happiest Millionaire
1966 The Singing Nun
1960 Sunrise at Campobello; Pepe
1955 Strange Lady in Town
1954 Her Twelve Men
1953 Julius Caesar; Scandal at Scourie
1951 The Law and the Lady
1950 The Miniver Story
1949 That Forsyte Woman
1948 Julia Misbehaves
1947 Desire Me
1945 Adventure; The Valley of Decision
1944 Mrs. Parkington
1943 Madame Curie; The Youngest Profession
1942 Random Harvest; Mrs. Miniver
1941 Blossoms in the Dust; When Ladies Meet
1940 Pride and Prejudice
1939 Goodbye, Mr. Chips; Remember?

Paulette Goddard
(June 3, 1905–1990)
1964 Time of Indifference
1954 The Unholy Four; The Charge of the Lancers
1953 Vice Squad; Paris Model; Sins of Jezebel
1952 Babes in Bagdad
1950 The Torch
1949 Bride of Vengeance; Anna Lucasta
1948 An Ideal Husband; A Miracle Can Happen; Hazard
1947 Suddenly It's Spring; Variety Girl; Unconquered
1946 Kitty; Diary of a Chambermaid

1945 Duffy's Tavern
1944 Standing Room Only; I Love a Soldier
1943 The Crystal Ball; So Proudly We Hail
1942 The Lady Has Plans; Reap the Wild Wind; The Forest Rangers; Star Spangled Rhythm
1941 Second Chorus; Pot o' Gold; Hold Back the Dawn; Nothing But the Truth
1940 Northwest Mounted Police; The Great Dictator; Ghost Breakers
1939 The Cat and the Canary; The Women
1938 The Young in Heart; Dramatic School
1936 Modern Times
1934 Kid Millions
1933 Roman Scandals
1932 The Kid from Spain; Girl Grief; The Mouthpiece; Pack Up Your Troubles; Young Ironsides; Show Business
1931 The Girl Habit; City Streets
1929 The Locked Door

Betty Grable
(Dec. 18, 1916–1973)
1955 How to Be Very, Very, Popular; Three for the Show
1953 How to Marry a Millionaire; The Farmer Takes a Wife
1951 Call Me Mister; Meet Me After the Show
1950 My Blue Heaven; Wabash Avenue
1949 The Beautiful Blonde from Bashful Bend
1948 That Lady in Ermine; When My Baby Smiles at Me
1947 Mother Wore Tights; The Shocking Miss Pilgrim
1946 Do You Love Me?
1945 Diamond Horseshoe; The Dolly Sisters
1944 Four Jills in a Jeep; Pin-Up Girl
1943 Coney Island; Sweet Rosie O'Grady
1942 Song of the Islands; Footlight Serenade; Springtime in the Rockies
1941 A Yank in the R.A.F.; Moon over Miami; I Wake Up Screaming
1940 Down Argentine Way; Tin Pan Alley
1939 Man About Town; Million Dollar Legs; The Day the Bookies Wept
1938 Give Me a Sailor; College Swing; Campus Confessions
1937 This Way Please; Thrill of a Lifetime
1936 Don't Turn 'em Loose; Follow the Fleet; Pigskin Parade
1935 The Nitwits; Collegiate; Old Man Rhythm
1934 By Your Leave; Student Tour; The Gay Divorcee
1933 Child of Manhattan; The Sweetheart of Sigma Chi; Cavalcade; Melody Cruise; What Price Innocence?
1932 Hold 'em Jail; The Greeks Had a Word for Them;

Probation; The Kid from Spain
1931 Kiki; Palmy Days
1930 Movietone Follies of 1930; Whoopee!; Let's Go Places; Happy Days

Gloria Grahame
(Nov. 28, 1925–1981)
1980 Melvin and Howard; Phobia
1979 A Nightingale Sang in Berkeley Square; Chilly Scenes of Winter
1976 Mansion of the Doomed
1974 Mama's Dirty Girls
1973 Tarot
1972 The Loners
1971 The Todd Killings; Blood and Lace; Chandler
1970 The Merry Wives of Windsor
1966 Ride Beyond Vengeance
1959 Odds Against Tomorrow
1957 Ride Out for Revenge
1956 The Man Who Never Was
1955 Not As a Stranger; Oklahoma!; The Cobweb
1954 The Good Die Young; Naked Alibi; Human Desire
1953 The Glass Wall; Man on a Tightrope; Prisoners of the Casbah; The Big Heat
1952 The Greatest Show on Earth; The Bad and the Beautiful; Sudden Fear; Macao
1950 In a Lonely Place
1949 Roughshod; A Woman's Secret
1947 Merton of the Movies; It Happened in Brooklyn; Song of the Thin Man; Crossfire
1946 It's a Wonderful Life
1945 Without Love
1944 Blonde Fever

Cary Grant
(Jan. 18, 1904–1986)
1966 Walk, Don't Run
1964 Father Goose
1963 Charade
1962 That Touch of Mink
1961 The Grass Is Greener
1959 North by Northwest; Operation Petticoat
1958 Houseboat; Indiscreet
1957 An Affair to Remember; The Pride and the Passion; Kiss Them for Me
1955 To Catch a Thief
1953 Dream Wife
1952 Monkey Business; Room for One More
1951 People Will Talk
1950 Crisis
1949 I Was a Male War Bride
1948 Mr. Blandings Builds His Dream House; Every Girl Should Be Married
1947 The Bachelor and the Bobby-Soxer; The Bishop's Wife
1946 Night and Day; Notorious; Without Reservations
1944 None But the Lonely Heart; Arsenic and Old Lace; Once Upon a Time
1943 Destination Tokyo; Mr. Lucky
1942 The Talk of the Town; Once Upon a Honeymoon
1941 Suspicion; Penny Serenade

1940 The Philadelphia Story; The Howards of Virginia; My Favorite Wife; His Girl Friday
1939 Only Angels Have Wings; In Name Only; Gunga Din
1938 Holiday; Bringing Up Baby
1937 The Toast of New York; The Awful Truth; The Amazing Adventure; When You're in Love; Topper
1936 The Amazing Quest; Suzy; Wedding Present; Big Brown Eyes
1935 Enter Madame; The Last Outpost; Wings in the Dark; Sylvia Scarlett
1934 Kiss and Make Up; Born to Be Bad; Ladies Should Listen; Thirty-Day Princess
1933 The Eagle and the Hawk; I'm No Angel; She Done Him Wrong; Alice in Wonderland; Gambling Ship; The Woman Accused
1932 Sinners in the Sun; Merrily We Go to Hell; This Is the Night; The Devil and the Deep; Madame Butterfly; Hot Saturday; Blonde Venus

Sydney Greenstreet
(Dec. 27, 1879–1954)
1950 Malaya
1949 Flamingo Road; It's a Great Feeling
1948 The Velvet Touch; Ruthless; The Woman in White
1947 The Hucksters; That Way with Women
1946 Devotion; Three Strangers; The Verdict
1945 Pillow to Post; Christmas in Connecticut; Conflict
1944 Between Two Worlds; The Conspirators; The Mask of Dimitrios; Passage to Marseilles; Hollywood Canteen
1943 Background to Danger
1942 Across the Pacific; Casablanca; In This Our Life
1941 The Maltese Falcon; They Died with Their Boots On

Jane Greer
(Sept. 9, 1924)
1989 Immediate Family
1986 Just Between Friends
1984 Against All Odds
1973 The Outfit
1965 Billie
1964 Where Love Has Gone
1957 Man of a Thousand Faces
1956 Run for the Sun
1953 Down Among the Sheltering Palms; The Prisoner of Zenda; The Clown; Desperate Search; You for Me
1951 You're in the Navy Now
1950 The Company She Keeps
1949 The Big Steal
1948 Station West
1947 Out of the Past; Sinbad the Sailor; They Won't Believe Me
1946 The Bamboo Blonde; Sunset Pass; The Falcon's Alibi
1945 Pan-Americana; Two O'Clock Courage; George White's Scandals; Dick Tracy, Detective

Gene Hackman
(Jan. 30, 1931)
1998 Twilight
1997 Absolute Power
1996 The Birdcage; The
 Chamber; Extreme
 Measures
1995 The Quick and the Dead;
 Crimson Tide; Get
 Shorty
1994 Wyatt Earp
1993 The Firm; Geronimo: An
 American Legend
1992 Unforgiven
1991 Class Action
1990 Loose Cannons; Narrow
 Margin; Postcards from
 the Edge
1989 The Package
1988 Mississippi Burning; Full
 Moon in Blue Water; Split
 Decisions; Bat 21;
 Another Woman
1987 No Way Out; Superman IV
1986 Hoosiers; Power
1985 Target; Twice in a
 Lifetime
1984 Misunderstood
1983 Uncommon Valor; Under
 Fire
1981 Reds; Eureka; All Night
 Long
1980 Superman II
1978 Superman
1977 The Domino Principle; A
 Bridge Too Far; March or
 Die
1975 Lucky Lady; The French
 Connection II; Bite the
 Bullet; Night Moves
1974 The Conversation; Young
 Frankenstein; Zandy's
 Bride
1973 Scarecrow
1972 Prime Cut; The Poseidon
 Adventure
1971 The Hunting Party; The
 French Connection; Cisco
 Pike
1970 I Never Sang for My
 Father; Doctors' Wives
1969 Marooned; The Gypsy
 Moths; Downhill Racer
1968 Riot; The Split
1967 First to Fight; Bonnie and
 Clyde; Banning
1966 Hawaii; A Covenant with
 Death
1964 Lilith
1961 Mad Dog Coll

Jean Harlow
(Mar. 3, 1911–1937)
1937 Saratoga; Personal
 Property
1936 Libeled Lady; Suzy; Wife
 vs. Secretary
1935 China Seas; Reckless;
 Riff Raff
1934 The Girl from Missouri
1933 Hold Your Man;
 Bombshell; Dinner at
 Eight
1932 Red Dust; Red-Headed
 Woman; The Beast of the
 City; Three Wise Girls
1931 Platinum Blonde; Goldie;
 The Iron Man; The Secret
 Six; The Public Enemy;
 City Lights
1930 Hell's Angels
1929 New York Nights; The
 Saturday Night Kid;
 Fugitives; This Thing
 Called Love; The Love
 Parade; Close Harmony;
 Bacon Grabbers; Double
 Whoopee; Liberty; The

Unkissed Man; Weak but
 Willing
1928 Moran of the Marines

Rex Harrison
(Mar. 5, 1908–1990)
1983 A Time to Die
1979 Ashanti
1978 Shalimar—The Deadly
 Thief
1977 The Prince and the
 Pauper; The Fifth
 Musketeer
1969 Staircase
1968 A Flea in Her Ear
1967 Doctor Dolittle; The Honey
 Pot
1965 The Agony and the
 Ecstasy; The Yellow Rolls-
 Royce; My Fair Lady
1963 Cleopatra
1962 The Happy Thieves
1960 Midnight Lace
1958 The Reluctant Debutante
1955 The Constant Husband
1954 King Richard and the
 Crusaders
1953 Main Street to Broadway
1952 The Four Poster
1951 The Long Dark Hall
1948 Escape; Unfaithfully Yours
1947 The Foxes of Harrow; The
 Ghost and Mrs. Muir
1946 Anna and the King of
 Siam; Journey Together
1945 A Yank in London; Blithe
 Spirit; Notorious
 Gentleman
1941 Major Barbara
1940 Night Train to Munich
1939 Ten Days in Paris;
 Continental Express
1938 Over the Moon; The
 Citadel; St. Martin's
 Lane
1937 School for Husbands;
 Storm in a Teacup
1936 Men Are Not Gods
1935 All at Sea
1934 Leave It to Blanche; Get
 Your Man
1930 The Great Game; The
 School for Scandal

Helen Hayes
(Oct. 10, 1900–1993)
1977 Candleshoe
1975 One of Our Dinosaurs Is
 Missing
1974 Herbie Rides Again
·1970 Airport
1959 The Third Man on the
 Mountain
1956 Anastasia
1955 Richard III
1953 Main Street to Broadway
1952 My Son, John
1948 Anna Karenina
1943 Stage Door Canteen
1939 The Spy in Black
1938 St. Martin's Lane
1937 Wings of the Morning
1935 Vanessa, Her Love
 Story
1934 Crime Without Passion;
 What Every Woman Knows
1933 The White Sister; Another
 Language; Night Flight
1932 A Farewell to Arms; The
 Son-Daughter; The Skin
 Game
1931 Arrowsmith; The Sin of
 Madelon Claudet
1924 Riders of the Range
1920 Babs
1917 The Weavers of Life
1910 Jean and the Calico
 Doll

Susan Hayward
(June 30, 1918–1975)
1972 The Revengers
1967 The Honey Pot; Valley of
 the Dolls
1964 Where Love Has Gone
1963 The Stolen Hours
1962 I Thank a Fool
1961 Ada; Back Street; The
 Marriage-Go-Round
1959 Thunder in the Sun;
 Woman Obsessed
1958 I Want to Live!
1957 Top Secret Affair
1956 The Conqueror
1955 Soldier of Fortune; I'll Cry
 Tomorrow; Untamed
1954 Garden of Evil; Demetrius
 and the Gladiators
1953 The President's Lady;
 White Witch Doctor
1952 The Snows of Kilimanjaro;
 with a Song in My Heart;
 The Lusty Men
1951 David and Bathsheba; I
 Can Get It for You
 Wholesale; I'd Climb the
 Highest Mountain;
 Rawhide
1950 My Foolish Heart
1949 Tulsa; House of Strangers
1948 The Saxon Charm; Tap
 Roots
1947 Smash-Up: The Story of a
 Woman; The Lost
 Moment; They Won't
 Believe Me
1946 Canyon Passage;
 Deadline at Dawn
1944 The Fighting Seabees; The
 Hairy Ape; And Now
 Tomorrow
1943 Jack London; Change of
 Heart; Young and Willing
1942 Star Spangled Rhythm; I
 Married a Witch; The
 Forest Rangers; Reap the
 Wild Wind
1941 Adam Had Four Sons;
 Among the Living; Sis
 Hopkins
1939 Beau Geste; $1,000 a
 Touchdown; Our Leading
 Citizen
1938 The Amazing Dr.
 Clitterhouse; Girls on
 Probation; The Sisters;
 Comet over Broadway
1937 Hollywood Hotel

Rita Hayworth
(Oct. 17, 1918–1987)
1972 The Wrath of God
1970 The Naked Zoo
1969 Road to Salina
1968 Sons of Satan
1967 The Rover
1966 The Money Trap; The
 Poppy Is Also a Flower
1964 Circus World
1962 The Happy Thieves
1959 They Came to Cordura;
 The Story on Page One
1958 Separate Tables
1957 Pal Joey; Fire Down
 Below
1953 Miss Sadie Thompson;
 Salome
1952 Affair in Trinidad
1948 The Loves of Carmen; The
 Lady from Shanghai
1947 Down to Earth
1946 Gilda
1945 Tonight and Every Night
1944 Cover Girl
1942 You Were Never Lovelier;
 My Gal Sal; Tales of
 Manhattan

1941 You'll Never Get Rich;
 Affectionately Yours; The
 Strawberry Blonde; Blood
 and Sand
1940 The Lady in Question;
 Susan and God; Music in
 My Heart; Blondie on a
 Budget; Angels over
 Broadway
1939 Homicide Bureau; The
 Lone Wolf Spy Hunt; The
 Renegade Ranger; Only
 Angels Have Wings;
 Special Inspector
1938 Rebellion; Juvenile Court;
 Convicted; There's Always
 a Woman; Who Killed Gail
 Preston?
1937 Old Louisiana; Paid to
 Dance; Hit the Saddle;
 Trouble in Texas;
 Criminals of the Air; The
 Game That Kills; Hard to
 Hold; Girls Can Play
1936 Meet Nero Wolfe; Human
 Cargo; Dancing Pirate
1935 Under the Pampas Moon;
 Paddy O'Day; Dante's
 Inferno; Charlie Chan in
 Egypt

Audrey Hepburn
(May 4, 1929–1993)
1989 Always
1981 They All Laughed
1979 Bloodline
1976 Robin and Marian
1967 Two for the Road; Wait
 Until Dark
1966 How to Steal a Million
1964 Paris When It Sizzles; My
 Fair Lady
1963 Charade
1962 The Children's Hour
1961 Breakfast at Tiffany's
1960 The Unforgiven
1959 Green Mansions; The
 Nun's Story
1957 Love in the Afternoon;
 Funny Face
1956 War and Peace
1954 Sabrina
1953 Roman Holiday
1952 The Secret People
1951 Young Wives' Tale;
 One Wild Oat; Monte
 Carlo Baby; Laughter
 in Paradise; The
 Lavender Hill Mob

Katharine Hepburn
(Nov. 9, 1907)
1994 Love Affair
1984 Grace Quigley
1981 On Golden Pond
1978 Olly Olly Oxen Free
1975 Rooster Cogburn
1973 A Delicate Balance
1971 The Trojan Women
1969 The Madwoman of Chaillot
1968 The Lion in Winter
1967 Guess Who's Coming
 to Dinner
1962 Long Day's Journey
 into Night
1959 Suddenly, Last Summer
1957 Desk Set
1956 The Rainmaker; The
 Iron Petticoat
1955 Summertime
1952 Pat and Mike
1951 The African Queen
1949 Adam's Rib
1948 State of the Union
1947 Song of Love; The Sea
 of Grass
1946 Undercurrent
1945 Without Love

1944 Dragon Seed
1943 Stage Door Canteen
1942 Woman of the Year;
     Keeper of the Flame
1940 The Philadelphia Story
1938 Holiday; Bringing Up Baby
1937 Stage Door; Quality Street
1936 A Woman Rebels; Mary of
     Scotland
1935 Sylvia Scarlett; Break of
     Hearts; Alice Adams
1934 The Little Minister; Spitfire
1933 Christopher Strong; Little
     Women; Morning Glory
1932 A Bill of Divorcement

Charlton Heston
(Oct. 4, 1923)
1998 Armageddon
1997 Hercules
1996 Alaska; Hamlet; The
     Adventures of Mowgli
1995 In the Mouth of Madness
1994 True Lies
1993 Wayne's World 2;
     Tombstone
1990 Solar Crisis; Almost an
     Angel
1982 Mother Lode
1980 The Mountain Men; The
     Awakening
1978 Gray Lady Down
1977 The Prince and the Pauper
1976 Two-Minute Warning;
     Midway; The Last Hard
     Men
1975 The Four Musketeers
1974 Earthquake; Airport 1975;
     The Three Musketeers
1973 Soylent Green
1972 Call of the Wild;
     Skyjacked; Anthony and
     Cleopatra
1971 The Omega Man
1970 Beneath the Planet of the
     Apes; The Hawaiians;
     Julius Caesar
1969 Number One
1968 Planet of the Apes; Will
     Penny; Counterpoint
1966 Khartoum
1965 The Agony and the
     Ecstasy; Major Dundee;
     The Greatest Story Ever
     Told; The War Lord
1963 55 Days at Peking;
     Diamond Head
1962 The Pigeon That Took
     Rome
1961 El Cid
1959 Ben-Hur; The Wreck of the
     Mary Deare
1958 The Big Country; The
     Buccaneer; Touch of Evil
1957 Three Violent People
1956 The Ten Commandments
1955 The Private War of Major
     Benson; Lucy Gallant; The
     Far Horizons
1954 Secret of the Incas; The
     Naked Jungle
1953 Bad for Each Other;
     Arrowhead; The
     President's Lady; The
     Pony Express
1952 The Greatest Show on
     Earth; The Savage; Ruby
     Gentry
1950 Dark City; Julius Caesar
1942 Peer Gynt

Dustin Hoffman
(Aug. 8, 1937)
1998 Sphere
1997 Mad City; Wag the Dog
1996 American Buffalo;
     Sleepers
1995 Outbreak

1992 Hero
1991 Hook; Billy Bathgate
1990 Dick Tracy
1989 Family Business
1988 Rain Man
1987 Ishtar
1985 Death of a Salesman
1982 Tootsie
1979 Kramer vs. Kramer;
     Agatha
1978 Straight Time
1976 Marathon Man; All the
     President's Men
1974 Lenny
1973 Papillon
1972 Alfredo, Alfredo
1971 Who Is Harry Kellerman
     and Why Is He Saying
     Those Terrible Things
     About Me?; Straw Dogs
1970 Little Big Man
1969 Midnight Cowboy; John
     and Mary
1968 Madigan's Millions
1967 The Tiger Makes Out; The
     Graduate

William Holden
(Apr. 17, 1918–1981)
1981 S.O.B.
1980 The Earthling; When Time
     Ran Out
1979 Escape to Athena; Ashanti
1978 Damien: Omen II; Fedora
1976 Network
1974 The Towering Inferno;
     Open Season
1973 Breezy
1972 The Revengers
1971 Wild Rovers
1969 The Christmas Tree; The
     Wild Bunch
1968 The Devil's Brigade
1967 Casino Royale
1966 Alvarez Kelly
1964 Paris When It Sizzles; The
     Seventh Dawn
1962 Satan Never Sleeps; The
     Counterfeit Traitor; The
     Lion
1960 The World of Suzie Wong
1959 The Horse Soldiers
1958 The Key
1957 The Bridge on the River
     Kwai
1956 Toward the Unknown; The
     Proud and Profane
1955 The Bridges at Toko-Ri;
     Love Is a Many
     Splendored Thing; Picnic
1954 Executive Suite; Sabrina;
     The Country Girl
1953 The Moon Is Blue; Escape
     from Fort Bravo; Forever
     Female; Stalag 1
1952 The Turning Point; Boots
     Malone
1951 Force of Arms; Submarine
     Command
1950 Union Station; Father Is a
     Bachelor; Born Yesterday;
     Sunset Boulevard
1949 Dear Wife; Miss Grant
     Takes Richmond; Streets
     of Laredo; The Dark Past
1948 Apartment for Peggy; The
     Man from Colorado;
     Rachel and the Stranger
1947 Blaze of Noon; Dear Ruth;
     Variety Girl
1943 Young and Willing
1942 Meet the Stewarts; The
     Remarkable Andrew; The
     Fleet's In
1941 Texas; I Wanted Wings
1940 Those Were the Days;
     Arizona; Invisible Stripes;
     Our Town

1939 Golden Boy; Million Dollar
     Legs
1938 Prison Farm

Judy Holliday
(June 21, 1922–1965)
1960 Bells Are Ringing
1956 Full of Life; The Solid Gold
     Cadillac
1954 Phffft!; It Should Happen
     to You
1952 The Marrying Kind
1950 Born Yesterday
1949 Adam's Rib
1944 Greenwich Village;
     Something for the Boys;
     Winged Victory

Bob Hope
(May 29, 1903)
1985 Spies Like Us
1979 The Muppet Movie
1972 Cancel My Reservation
1969 How to Commit a
     Marriage
1968 The Private Navy of Sgt.
     O'Farrell
1967 Eight on the Lam
1966 Boy, Did I Get a Wrong
     Number!; The Oscar; Not
     with My Wife, You Don't!
1965 I'll Take Sweden
1963 A Global Affair; Call Me
     Bwana; Critic's Choice
1962 The Road to Hong Kong
1961 Bachelor in Paradise
1960 The Facts of Life
1959 The Five Pennies; Alias
     Jesse James
1957 Paris Holiday; Beau James
1956 The Iron Petticoat; That
     Certain Feeling
1955 The Seven Little Foys
1954 Casanova's Big Night
1953 Scared Stiff; Here Come
     the Girls; Off Limits
1952 Road to Bali; The Greatest
     Show on Earth; Son of
     Paleface
1951 The Lemon Drop Kid; My
     Favorite Spy
1950 Fancy Pants
1949 Sorrowful Jones; The
     Great Lover
1948 The Paleface
1947 My Favorite Brunette;
     Variety Girl; Where There's
     Life; Road to Rio
1946 Road to Utopia; Monsieur
     Beaucaire
1944 The Princess and the
     Pirate
1943 Let's Face It; They Got Me
     Covered
1942 The Road to Morocco;
     Star Spangled Rhythm; My
     Favorite Blonde
1941 Road to Zanzibar; Nothing
     But the Truth; Louisiana
     Purchase; Caught in the
     Draft
1940 Road to Singapore; The
     Ghost Breakers
1939 Some Like It Hot; Never
     Say Die; The Cat and the
     Canary
1938 Thanks for the Memory;
     College Swing; Give Me a
     Sailor
1937 The Big Broadcast of
     1938

Lena Horne
(June 30, 1917)
1978 The Wiz
1969 Death of a Gunfighter
1956 Meet Me in Las Vegas
1950 The Duchess of Idaho

1948 Words and Music
1946 Till the Clouds Roll By;
     Ziegfeld Follies
1944 Two Girls and a Sailor;
     Broadway Rhythm; Boogie-
     Woogie Dream
1943 Thousands Cheer; I Dood
     It; Cabin in the Sky;
     Stormy Weather; Swing
     Fever
1942 Panama Hattie
1938 The Duke Is Tops

Rock Hudson
(Nov. 17, 1925–1985)
1984 The Ambassador
1980 The Mirror Crack'd
1978 Avalanche
1976 Embryo
1973 Showdown
1971 Pretty Maids All in a Row
1970 Darling Lili; The Hornet's
     Nest
1969 A Fine Pair; The
     Undefeated
1968 Ice Station Zebra
1967 Tobruk
1966 Blindfold; Seconds
1965 Strange Bedfellows; A
     Very Special Favor
1964 Send Me No Flowers;
     Man's Favorite Sport?
1963 A Gathering of Eagles
1962 The Spiral Road
1961 The Last Sunset; Come
     September; Lover Come
     Back
1959 This Earth Is Mine; Pillow
     Talk
1958 Twilight for the Gods; The
     Tarnished Angels
1957 Something of Value; Battle
     Hymn; A Farewell to Arms
1956 Never Say Goodbye;
     Written on the Wind; Four
     Girls in Town; Giant; All
     That Heaven Allows
1955 Captain Lightfoot; One
     Desire
1954 Taza, Son of Cochise;
     Magnificent Obsession;
     Bengal Brigade
1953 Seminole; The Golden
     Blade; Back to God's
     Country; Sea Devils; Gun
     Fury
1952 Here Come the Nelsons;
     Scarlet Angel; Has
     Anybody Seen My Gal?;
     Bend of the River;
     Horizons West; The
     Lawless Breed
1951 The Iron Man; The Fat
     Man; Bright Victory; Air
     Cadet; Tomahawk
1950 I Was a Shoplifter; The
     Desert Hawk; Shakedown;
     Winchester '73; One Way
     Street; Peggy
1949 Undertow
1948 Fighter Squadron

Ben Johnson
(June 13, 1920–1998)
1996 The Evening Star
1994 Angels in the Outfield
1992 Radio Flyer
1991 My Heroes Have Always
     Been Cowboys
1990 Back to Back
1989 Dark Before Dawn
1988 Cherry 2000
1986 Let's Get Harry
1987 Trespasses
1984 Red Dawn
1983 Champions
1982 Tex; Ruckus
1980 Terror Train

1978 The Swarm; Grayeagle
1977 The Greatest
1976 The Town That Dreaded Sundown; Breakheart Pass
1975 Hustle; Bite the Bullet
1973 The Train Robbers; Kid Blue; Dillinger
1972 The Getaway; Corky; Junior Bonner
1971 Something Big; The Last Picture Show
1970 Chisum
1969 The Undefeated; The Wild Bunch
1968 Hang 'em High; Will Penny
1966 The Rare Breed
1965 Major Dundee
1964 Cheyenne Autumn
1961 One-Eyed Jacks; Tomboy and the Champ
1960 Ten Who Dared
1957 Slim Carter; War Drums
1956 Rebel in Town
1955 Oklahoma!; Simba
1953 Shane
1952 Wild Stallion
1951 Fort Defiance
1950 Rio Grande
1949 Mighty Joe Young; She Wore a Yellow Ribbon
1948 Fort Apache; Three Godfathers
1945 The Naughty Nineties
1943 The Outlaw

Van Johnson
(Aug. 25, 1916)
1985 The Purple Rose of Cairo
1980 The Kidnapping of the President
1970 Company of Killers
1968 Where Angels Go, Trouble Follows; Yours, Mine and Ours
1967 Divorce American Style
1963 Wives and Lovers
1960 The Enemy General
1959 Web of Evidence
1958 The Last Blitzkrieg
1957 Action of the Tiger; Kelly and Me
1956 The Bottom of the Bottle; Miracle in the Rain; Slander; 23 Paces to Baker Street
1955 The End of the Affair
1954 Men of the Fighting Lady; The Siege at Red River; The Caine Mutiny; Brigadoon; The Last Time I Saw Paris
1953 Remains to Be Seen; Confidentially Connie; Easy to Love
1952 Invitation; The Plymouth Adventure; Washington Story; When in Rome
1951 It's a Big Country; Three Guys Named Mike; Too Young to Kiss; Go for Broke!
1950 The Duchess of Idaho; Grounds for Marriage; The Big Hangover
1949 Scene of the Crime; Mother Is a Freshman; Battleground; In the Good Old Summertime
1948 The Bride Goes Wild; State of the Union; Command Decision
1947 The High Barbaree; The Romance of Rosy Ridge
1946 Ziegfeld Follies; Till the Clouds Roll By; No Leave, No Love; Easy to Wed

1945 Weekend at the Waldorf; Thrill of a Romance
1944 The White Cliffs of Dover; Three Men in White; Thirty Seconds over Tokyo; A Guy Named Joe; Between Two Women; Two Girls and a Sailor
1943 The Human Comedy; Pilot No. 5; Madame Curie; Dr. Gillespie's Criminal Case
1942 Somewhere I'll Find You; The War Against Mrs. Hadley; Murder in the Big House; Dr. Gillespie's New Assistant
1940 Too Many Girls

James Earl Jones
(Jan. 17, 1931)
1997 Gang Related; What the Deaf Man Heard
1996 A Family Thing; Good Luck
1995 Jefferson in Paris; Cry, the Beloved Country
1994 Clean Slate; The Lion King; Clear and Present Danger
1993 The Meteor Man; The Sandlot; Sommersby; Excessive Force; Dreamrider
1992 Patriot Games; Scorchers; Sneakers
1991 True Identity; Convicts
1990 The Hunt for Red October; The Ambulance; Terrorgram
1989 Three Fugitives; Grim Prairie Tales; Field of Dreams; Best of the Best
1988 Coming to America
1987 Gardens of Stone; Allan Quatermain and the Lost City of Gold; Pinocchio and the Emperor of the Night; Matewan
1986 My Little Girl; Soul Man
1985 City Limits
1983 Return of the Jedi *(voice of Vader)*
1982 Conan the Barbarian; Blood Tide
1981 Demon Island
1980 The Empire Strikes Back *(voice of Vader)*
1977 A Piece of the Action; The Last Remake of Beau Geste; Exorcist II: The Heretic; The Greatest; King Lear; Star Wars *(voice of Vader)*
1976 Swashbuckler; The River Niger; The Bingo Long Traveling All-Stars and Motor Kings
1975 Deadly Hero
1974 Claudine
1972 The Man
1970 End of the Road; The Great White Hope
1967 The Comedians
1964 Dr. Strangelove or: How I Learned to Stop Worrying and Love the Bomb

Jennifer Jones
(Mar. 2, 1919)
1974 The Towering Inferno
1969 Angel, Angel, Down We Go
1966 The Idol
1962 Tender Is the Night
1957 The Barretts of Wimpole Street; A Farewell to Arms
1956 The Man in the Gray Flannel Suit
1955 Love Is a Many Splendored Thing; Good Morning, Miss Dove
1954 Beat the Devil
1953 Indiscretion of an American Wife
1952 Carrie; Ruby Gentry
1950 Gone to Earth
1949 Madame Bovary; We Were Strangers
1948 Portrait of Jennie
1946 Cluny Brown; Duel in the Sun
1945 Love Letters
1944 Since You Went Away
1943 The Song of Bernadette
1939 Dick Tracy's G-Men; New Frontier

Boris Karloff
(Nov. 23, 1887–1969)
1968 Curse of the Crimson Altar; House of Evil; The Sinister Invasion; The Snake People; Targets
1967 Mad Monster Party; The Sorcerers; The Venetian Affair; Cauldron of Blood
1966 The Daydreamer; The Ghost in the Invisible Bikini
1965 Die, Monster, Die!
1964 Bikini Beach
1963 The Comedy of Terrors; The Raven; The Terror; Black Sabbath
1962 Corridors of Blood
1958 The Haunted Strangler; Frankenstein 1970
1957 Voodoo Island
1953 Island Monster; Sabaka; Abbott and Costello Meet Dr. Jekyll and Mr. Hyde
1952 The Black Castle
1951 The Strange Door
1949 Abbott and Costello Meet the Killer, Boris Karloff
1948 Tap Roots
1947 The Secret Life of Walter Mitty; Dick Tracy Meets Gruesome; Lured; Unconquered
1946 Bedlam
1945 Isle of the Dead; The Body Snatcher
1944 The Climax; House of Frankenstein
1942 The Boogie Man Will Get You
1941 The Devil Commands
1940 Doomed to Die; The Ape; You'll Find Out; Black Friday; Devil's Island; The Man with Nine Lives; British Intelligence; Before I Hang; The Fatal Hour
1939 Son of Frankenstein; The Mystery of Mr. Wong; The Man They Could Not Hang; Mr. Wong in Chinatown; The Tower of London
1938 Mr. Wong, Detective; The Invisible Menace
1937 Juggernaut; Night Key; West of Shanghai
1936 The Invisible Ray; Charlie Chan at the Opera; The Walking Dead; The Man Who Lived Again
1935 The Raven; The Black Cat; The Black Room; The Bride of Frankenstein
1934 Gift of Gab; The House of Rothschild; The Lost Patrol
1933 The Ghoul
1932 The Cohens and Kellys in Hollywood; The Mask of Fu Manchu; Business and Pleasure; Behind the Mask; The Miracle Man; The Mummy; Night World; The Old Dark House; Alias the Doctor; Scarface
1931 Graft; The Guilty Generation; Cracked Nuts; I Like Your Nerve; The Last Parade; The Mad Genius; Frankenstein; The Public Defender; The Criminal Code; Tonight or Never; The Yellow Ticket; Donovan's Kid; Smart Money; Pardon Us; Five Star Final; King of the Wild; Mothers Cry
1930 The Sea Bat; The Utah Kid; The Bad One
1929 Devil's Chaplain; King of the Kongo; Burning the Wind; Phantom of the North; The Unholy Night; Anne Against the World; Behind That Curtain; The Fatal Warning; Two Sisters
1928 The Little Wild Girl; Vultures of the Sea
1927 Phantom Buster; The Princess from Hoboken; Let It Rain; Soft Cushions; Tarzan and the Golden Lion; Two Arabian Knights; Meddlin' Stranger
1926 The Bells; Eagle of the Sea; Greater Glory; Flaming Fury; Valencia; Old Ironsides; Her Honor the Governor; Golden Web; The Man in the Saddle; The Nickel Hopper
1925 The Prairie Wife; Never the Twain Shall Meet; Lady Robin Hood; Forbidden Cargo; Parisian Nights
1924 Dynamite Dan; Riders of the Plains; The Hellion
1923 The Prisoner
1922 The Altar Stairs; Man from Downing Street
1921 Cheated Hearts; The Cave Girl
1920 The Last of the Mohicans; Deadlier Sex
1919 His Majesty the American; The Prince and Betty; The Lightning Raider
1916 The Dumb Girl of Portici

Danny Kaye
(Jan. 18, 1913–1987)
1969 The Madwoman of Chaillot
1963 The Man from the Diners' Club
1961 On the Double
1959 The Five Pennies
1958 Me and the Colonel; Merry Andrew
1956 The Court Jester
1954 White Christmas; Knock on Wood
1952 Hans Christian Andersen
1951 On the Riviera
1949 The Inspector General; It's a Great Feeling
1948 A Song Is Born
1947 The Secret Life of Walter Mitty
1946 The Kid from Brooklyn
1945 Wonder Man
1944 Up in Arms

Buster Keaton
(Oct. 4, 1895–1966)
1970 Four Clowns
1966 War, Italian Style; A Funny

Thing Happened on the Way to the Forum

1965 Beach Blanket Bingo; How to Stuff a Wild Bikini; Sergeant Deadhead
1964 Pajama Party
1963 It's a Mad, Mad, Mad, Mad World
1960 The Adventures of Huckleberry Finn
1956 Around the World in 80 Days
1952 Limelight
1950 Sunset Boulevard
1949 In the Good Old Summertime; The Lovable Cheat; You're My Everything
1946 God's Country; Boom in the Moon
1945 She Went to the Races; That Night with You; That's the Spirit
1944 San Diego, I Love You
1943 Forever and a Day
1940 The Villain Still Pursued Her; New Moon; Li'l Abner; The Taming of the Snood; Nothing But Pleasure
1939 Hollywood Cavalcade; Pest from the West
1937 Ditto; Jail Bait; Love Nest on Wheels
1936 Blue Blazes; The Chemist; Grand Slam Opera; Mixed Magic; An Old Spanish Custom
1934 Allez Oop; The Gold Ghost
1933 What! No Beer?
1932 The Passionate Plumber; Speak Easily
1931 Parlor, Bedroom and Bath; The Sidewalks of New York
1930 Doughboys; Free and Easy
1929 The Spite Marriage; The Hollywood Revue
1928 The Cameraman; Steamboat Bill, Jr.
1927 The General; College
1926 Battling Butler
1925 Go West; Seven Chances
1924 The Navigator; Sherlock, Jr.
1923 The Three Ages; The Balloonatic; Our Hospitality
1922 Day Dreams; Love Nest; The Blacksmith; Cops; The Electric House; The Frozen North
1921 Two Houses of Keaton; The Boat; The Saphead; The Goat; Hard Luck; The High Sign; The Paleface; The Playhouse; Haunted House; Skirts
1920 One Week; The Scarecrow; Convict 13 Neighbors
1919 A Desert Hero; The Garage; The Hayseed; Back Stage
1918 The Cook; Moonshine; Out West; Good Night, Nurse!; The Bell Boy
1917 A Reckless Romeo; The Rough House; The Butcher Boy

Diane Keaton
(Jan. 5, 1946)
1997 The Only Thrill
1996 Marvin's Room; The First Wives Club
1995 Unstrung Heroes; Father of the Bride 2
1993 Manhattan Murder Mystery; Look Who's Talking Now
1991 Father of the Bride
1990 The Lemon Sisters; The Godfather, Part III
1988 The Good Mother
1987 Radio Days; Baby Boom; Heaven
1986 Crimes of the Heart
1984 Mrs. Soffel; The Little Drummer Girl
1982 Shoot the Moon
1981 Reds
1979 Manhattan
1978 Interiors
1977 Looking for Mr. Goodbar; Annie Hall
1976 Harry and Walter Go to New York; I Will, I Will...for Now
1975 Love and Death
1974 The Godfather, Part II
1973 Sleeper
1972 The Godfather; Play It Again, Sam
1970 Lovers and Other Strangers

Gene Kelly
(Aug.23, 1912–1996)
1994 That's Entertainment!, III
1985 That's Dancing!
1980 Xanadu
1977 Viva Knievel!
1976 That's Entertainment! II
1974 That's Entertainment!
1973 40 Carats
1970 The Cheyenne Social Club
1969 Hello, Dolly!
1967 A Guide for the Married Man; The Young Girls of Rochefort
1964 What a Way to Go!
1962 Gigot
1960 Let's Make Love; Inherit the Wind
1958 The Tunnel of Love; Marjorie Morningstar
1957 Les Girls; The Happy Road
1955 It's Always Fair Weather
1954 Deep in My Heart; Crest of the Wave; Brigadoon
1952 Love Is Better Than Ever; The Devil Makes Three; Singin' in the Rain
1951 It's a Big Country; An American in Paris
1950 Summer Stock; The Black Hand
1949 On the Town; Take Me Out to the Ball Game
1948 The Pirate; The Three Musketeers; Words and Music
1947 Living in a Big Way
1946 Ziegfeld Follies
1945 Anchors Aweigh
1944 Christmas Holiday; Cover Girl
1943 The Cross of Lorraine; Pilot No. 5; Du Barry Was a Lady; Thousands Cheer
1942 For Me and My Gal

Grace Kelly
(Nov. 12, 1928–1982)
1956 High Society; The Swan
1955 The Bridges at Toko-Ri; To Catch a Thief
1954 Green Fire; Dial M for Murder; Rear Window; The Country Girl
1953 Mogambo
1952 High Noon
1951 Fourteen Hours

Deborah Kerr
(Sept. 30, 1921)
1985 The Assam Garden; Reunion at Fairborough

1969 The Gypsy Moths; The Arrangement
1968 Prudence and the Pill
1967 Casino Royale; Eye of the Devil
1965 Marriage on the Rocks
1964 The Night of the Iguana; The Chalk Garden
1961 The Naked Edge; The Innocents; The Grass Is Greener
1960 The Sundowners
1959 Beloved Infidel; Count Your Blessings; The Journey
1958 Separate Tables
1957 Bonjour Tristesse; Heaven Knows, Mr. Allison; Kiss Them for Me; An Affair to Remember
1956 The King and I; The Proud and Profane; Tea and Sympathy
1955 The End of the Affair
1953 Dream Wife; From Here to Eternity; Julius Caesar; Thunder in the East; Young Bess
1952 The Prisoner of Zenda
1951 Quo Vadis?
1950 Please Believe Me; King Solomon's Mines
1949 Edward, My Son
1948 Hatter's Castle
1947 The Hucksters; If Winter Comes; Black Narcissus
1946 I See a Dark Stranger
1945 Vacation from Marriage
1943 The Life and Death of Colonel Blimp
1942 The Day Will Dawn
1941 Hatter's Castle; The Courageous Mr. Penn; Love on the Dole; Major Barbara

Alan Ladd
(Sept. 3, 1913–1964)
1964 The Carpetbaggers
1962 13 West Street
1960 All the Young Men; Guns of the Timberlands; One Foot in Hell
1959 The Man in the Net
1958 The Proud Rebel; The Badlanders; The Deep Six
1957 The Big Land; The Boy on a Dolphin
1956 Santiago
1955 Hell on Frisco Bay; The McConnell Story
1954 Drum Beat; The Black Knight; Hell Below Zero; Paratrooper; Saskatchewan
1953 Shane; Desert Legion; Thunder in the East; Botany Bay
1952 The Iron Mistress
1951 Appointment with Danger; Red Mountain
1950 Captain Carey, U.S.A; Branded
1949 Chicago Deadline; The Great Gatsby
1948 Beyond Glory; Saigon; Whispering Smith
1947 Calcutta; My Favorite Brunette; Variety Girl; Wild Harvest
1946 The Blue Dahlia; O.S.S.; Two Years Before the Mast; Santa Fe Uprising
1945 Duffy's Tavern; Salty O'Rourke
1944 And Now Tomorrow
1943 China
1942 This Gun for Hire; Lucky Jordan; Joan of Paris; Star

Spangled Rhythm; The Glass Key
1941 The Reluctant Dragon; Citizen Kane; Petticoat Politics; They Met in Bombay; Cadet Girl; Gangs, Inc.; The Black Cat; Great Guns
1940 Meet the Missus; Light of the Western Stars; Captain Caution; The Light of Western Stars; Cross Country Romance; The Howards of Virginia; Those Were the Days; Her First Romance; Brother Rat and a Baby; In Old Missouri; Wildcat Bus; Gangs of Chicago
1939 Rulers of the Sea; Hitler—Beast of Berlin
1938 Come On, Leathernecks!; Freshman Year; Helltown; The Goldwyn Follies
1937 Hold 'em Navy!; The Last Train from Madrid; Souls at Sea
1936 Pigskin Parade
1932 Tom Brown of Culver; Once in a Lifetime

Veronica Lake
(Nov. 14, 1919–1973)
1970 Flesh Feast
1952 Stronghold
1949 Slattery's Hurricane
1948 Isn't It Romantic?; Saigon; The Sainted Sisters
1947 Ramrod; Variety Girl
1946 The Blue Dahlia
1945 Duffy's Tavern; Hold That Blonde; Out of This World; Bring on the Girls; Miss Susie Slagle's
1944 The Hour Before the Dawn
1943 So Proudly We Hail!
1942 This Gun for Hire; I Married a Witch; Star Spangled Rhythm; The Glass Key
1941 I Wanted Wings; Sullivan's Travels; Hold Back the Dawn
1940 Forty Little Mothers; Young As You Feel
1939 Sorority House; All Women Have Secrets; Dancing Co-Ed

Dorothy Lamour
(Dec. 10, 1940–1996)
1987 Creepshow 2
1976 Won Ton Ton, the Dog Who Saved Hollywood
1970 The Phynx
1964 Pajama Party
1963 Donovan's Reef
1962 The Road to Hong Kong
1953 Road to Bali
1952 The Greatest Show on Earth
1951 Here Comes the Groom
1949 The Lucky Stiff; Manhandled; Slightly French
1948 The Girl from Manhattan; Lulu Belle; On Our Merry Way
1947 Road to Rio; Variety Girl; Wild Harvest; My Favorite Brunette
1946 Road to Utopia
1945 Duffy's Tavern; Masquerade in Mexico; A Medal for Benny
1944 And the Angels Sing; Rainbow Island

1943 Dixie; Riding High; They Got Me Covered
1942 The Road to Morocco; Beyond the Blue Horizon; Star Spangled Rhythm; The Fleet's In
1941 Road to Zanzibar; Caught in the Draft; Aloma of the South Seas
1940 Johnny Apollo; Moon over Burma; Road to Singapore; Chad Hanna; Typhoon
1939 Disputed Passage; St. Louis Blues; Man About Town
1938 Spawn of the North; Tropic Holiday; Her Jungle Love; The Big Broadcast of 1938
1937 High, Wide and Handsome; Thrill of a Lifetime; The Hurricane; The Last Train from Madrid; Swing High, Swing Low
1936 College Holiday; The Jungle Princess
1933 Footlight Parade
1930 Dixiana

Burt Lancaster
(Nov. 2, 1930–1994)
1990 The Jeweller's Shop
1989 Field of Dreams
1988 Rocket Gibraltar
1986 Tough Guys
1985 Little Treasure
1983 Local Hero; The Osterman Weekend
1981 Cattle Annie and Little Britches
1980 Atlantic City
1979 Zulu Dawn
1978 Go Tell the Spartans
1977 The Island of Dr. Moreau; Twilight's Last Gleaming
1976 Buffalo Bill and the Indians, or Sitting Bull's History Lesson; The Cassandra Crossing; 1900
1974 The Midnight Man
1973 Scorpio; Executive Action
1972 Ulzana's Raid
1971 Valdez Is Coming; Lawman
1970 Airport
1969 Castle Keep; The Gypsy Moths
1968 The Swimmer; The Scalphunters
1966 The Professionals
1965 The Hallelujah Trail
1964 The Train; Seven Days in May
1963 The Leopard; The List of Adrian Messenger; A Child Is Waiting
1962 Birdman of Alcatraz
1961 Judgment at Nuremberg; The Young Savages
1960 The Unforgiven; Elmer Gantry
1959 The Devil's Disciple
1958 Run Silent, Run Deep; Separate Tables
1957 Gunfight at the O.K. Corral; Sweet Smell of Success
1956 The Rainmaker; Trapeze; The Kentuckian; The Rose Tattoo
1954 Apache; Vera Cruz
1953 South Sea Woman; Three Sailors and a Girl; His Majesty O'keefe; From Here to Eternity

1952 Come Back, Little Sheba; The Crimson Pirate
1951 Jim Thorpe–All American; Vengeance Valley; Ten Tall Men
1950 Mister 880; The Killer That Stalked New York; The Flame and the Arrow
1949 Criss Cross; Rope of Sand
1948 I Walk Alone; Kiss the Blood off My Hands; All My Sons; Sorry, Wrong Number
1947 Brute Force; Variety Girl; Desert Fury
1946 The Killers

Harry Langdon
(June 15, 1884–1944)
1945 Swingin'on a Rainbow
1944 Block Busters; Hot Rhythm
1943 House of Errors
1941 Road Show; All American Co-Ed; Double Trouble; Misbehaving Husbands
1940 Saps at Sea; A Chump at Oxford
1939 The Flying Deuces; Zenobia
1938 Block-Heads; There Goes My Heart
1937 Wise Guys
1935 Atlantic Adventure
1933 Hallelujah, I'm a Bum; My Weakness
1931 Mad About Money; A Soldier's Plaything
1930 See America Thirst; The Big Kick; The Fighting Parson; The Head Guy; King
1929 Hotter Than Hot; Sky Boy; Skirt Shy
1928 The Chaser; Heart Trouble
1927 Three's a Crowd; Long Pants
1926 Baby Face Harry Langdon; The Strong Man; Ella Cinders; Tramp, Tramp, Tramp; His First Flame
1925 Lucky Stars
1924 All Night Long; Smile Please; The Cat's Meow; The Luck of the Foolish

Angela Lansbury
(Oct. 16, 1925)
1984 The Company of Wolves
1983 The Pirates of Penzance
1982 The Last Unicorn
1980 The Mirror Crack'd
1979 The Lady Vanishes
1978 Death on the Nile
1975 The First Christmas
1971 Bedknobs and Broomsticks
1970 Something for Everyone
1966 Mister Buddwing
1965 The Greatest Story Ever Told; Harlow; The Amorous Adventures of Moll Flanders
1964 The World of Henry Orient; Dear Heart
1963 In the Cool of the Day
1962 The Manchurian Candidate; All Fall Down
1961 Blue Hawaii
1960 The Dark at the Top of the Stairs; A Breath of Scandal
1959 Season of Passion
1958 The Reluctant Debutante; The Long, Hot Summer
1956 Please Murder Me; The Court Jester

1955 The Purple Mask; A Lawless Street
1954 Remains to Be Seen
1952 Mutiny
1951 Kind Lady
1949 Samson and Delilah; The Red Danube
1948 If Winter Comes; Tenth Avenue Angel; State of the Union; The Three Musketeers
1947 The Private Affairs of Bel Ami
1946 Till the Clouds Roll By; The Harvey Girls; The Hoodlum Saint
1945 The Picture of Dorian Gray
1944 National Velvet; Gaslight

Charles Laughton
(July 1, 1899–1962)
1962 Advise and Consent
1960 Spartacus; Under Ten Flags
1957 Witness for the Prosecution
1955 The Night of the Hunter
1954 Hobson's Choice
1953 Young Bess; Salome
1952 O. Henry's Full House; Abbott and Costello Meet Captain Kidd
1951 The Blue Veil; The Strange Door
1949 The Bribe
1948 The Big Clock; The Girl from Manhattan; The Man on the Eiffel Tower; Arch of Triumph
1947 The Paradine Case
1946 Because of Him
1945 Captain Kidd
1944 The Canterville Ghost; The Suspect
1943 The Man from Down Under; This Land Is Mine; Forever and a Day
1942 The Tuttles of Tahiti; Stand by for Action; Tales of Manhattan
1941 It Started with Eve
1940 They Knew What They Wanted
1939 The Hunchback of Notre Dame; Jamaica Inn
1938 Sidewalks of London; The Beachcomber
1936 Rembrandt
1935 Les Miserables; Mutiny on the Bounty; Ruggles of Red Gap
1934 The Barretts of Wimpole Street
1933 White Woman; The Private Life of Henry VIII
1932 Payment Deferred; The Devil and the Deep; The Old Dark House; The Sign of the Cross; Island of Lost Souls; If I Had a Million
1931 Down River
1930 Wolves
1929 Piccadilly

Janet Leigh
(July 6, 1927)
1998 Halloween: H20
1980 The Fog
1979 Boardwalk
1972 Night of the Lepus; One Is a Lonely Number
1969 Hello Down There
1968 Grand Slam
1966 Harper; Kid Rodelo; The Spy in the Green Hat; Three on a Couch; An American Dream

1963 Wives and Lovers; Bye Bye Birdie
1962 The Manchurian Candidate
1960 Pepe; Who Was That Lady?; Psycho
1959 The Perfect Furlough
1958 The Vikings; Touch of Evil
1957 Jet Pilot
1956 Safari; My Sister Eileen
1955 Pete Kelly's Blues
1954 Rogue Cop; Prince Valiant; Living It Up; The Black Shield of Falworth
1953 Walking My Baby Back Home; Confidentially Connie; The Naked Spur; Houdini; Here Come the Girls
1952 Fearless Fagan; Scaramouche; It's A Big Country; Just This Once
1951 Strictly Dishonorable; Two Tickets to Broadway; Angels in the Outfield
1950 That Forsyte Woman
1949 The Doctor and the Girl; Little Women; The Red Danube; Act of Violence; Holiday Affair
1948 Words and Music; If Winter Comes; Hills of Home
1947 The Romance of Rosy Ridge

Vivien Leigh
(Nov. 5, 1913–1967)
1965 Ship of Fools
1961 The Roman Spring of Mrs. Stone
1955 The Deep Blue Sea
1951 A Streetcar Named Desire
1948 Anna Karenina
1946 Caesar and Cleopatra
1941 That Hamilton Woman
1940 Waterloo Bridge
1939 Gone With the Wind; Twenty-one Days Together
1938 Sidewalks of London; A Yank at Oxford
1937 Fire Over England; Dark Journey; Storm in a Teacup
1935 Look Up and Laugh

Jack Lemmon
(Feb. 8, 1925)
1998 Neil Simon's The Odd Couple II
1997 Out to Sea
1996 Hamlet; My Fellow Americans; The Grass Harp; Getting Away with Murder
1995 Grumpier Old Men
1993 Grumpy Old Men; Short Cuts
1992 Glengarry Glen Ross; The Player
1991 JFK
1989 Dad
1986 That's Life!
1985 Macaroni
1984 Mass Appeal
1982 Missing
1981 Buddy Buddy
1980 Tribute
1979 The China Syndrome
1977 Airport '77
1976 Alex and the Gypsy
1975 The Prisoner of Second Avenue
1974 The Front Page
1973 Save the Tiger
1972 Avanti!; The War Between Men and Women
1971 Kotch

1970 The Out-of-Towners
1969 The April Fools
1968 The Odd Couple
1967 Luv
1966 The Fortune Cookie
1965 The Great Race; How to Murder Your Wife
1964 Good Neighbor Sam
1963 Under the Yum-Yum Tree; Irma La Douce
1962 The Notorious Landlady
1960 The Wackiest Ship in the Army; Pepe; The Apartment
1959 It Happened to Jane; Some Like It Hot
1958 Bell, Book and Candle; Cowboy
1957 Operation Mad Ball; Fire Down Below
1956 You Can't Run Away from It
1955 My Sister Eileen; Mr. Roberts; Three for the Show
1954 Phffft!; It Should Happen to You

Jerry Lewis
(Mar. 16, 1926)
1995 Funny Bones
1993 Arizona Dream
1992 Mr. Saturday Night
1989 Cookie
1984 Slapstick of Another Kind
1983 Cracking Up; The King of Comedy
1981 Hardly Working
1970 Which Way to the Front?; One More Time
1969 Hook, Line and Sinker
1968 Don't Raise the Bridge, Lower the River
1967 The Big Mouth
1966 Three on a Couch; Way . . . Way Out
1965 Boeing Boeing; The Family Jewels
1964 The Patsy; The Disorderly Orderly
1963 It's a Mad, Mad, Mad, Mad World; Who's Minding the Store?; The Nutty Professor
1962 It's Only Money; The Ladies' Man
1961 The Errand Boy
1960 Visit to a Small Planet; The Bellboy; Cinderfella
1959 Don't Give up the Ship
1958 Rock-a-Bye Baby; The Geisha Boy
1957 The Sad Sack
1956 Pardners; The Delicate Delinquent; Hollywood or Bust
1955 You're Never Too Young; Artists and Models
1954 Three Ring Circus; Living It Up
1953 Scared Stiff; The Stooge; Here Come the Girls; The Caddy; Money from Home
1952 Jumping Jacks; The Road to Bali; Sailor Beware
1951 That's My Boy
1950 At War with the Army; The Milkman; My Friend Irma Goes West
1949 My Friend Irma

Harold Lloyd
(Apr. 20, 1888–1960)
1962 Harold Lloyd's World of Comedy
1947 The Sin of Harold Diddlebock
1942 My Favorite Spy

1941 A Girl, a Guy and a Gob
1938 Professor Beware
1936 The Milky Way
1934 The Cat's Paw
1932 Movie Crazy
1930 Feet First
1929 Welcome Danger
1928 Speedy
1927 The Kid Brother
1926 For Heaven's Sake
1925 The Freshman
1924 Girl Shy; Hot Water
1923 Safety Last; Why Worry?
1922 Doctor Jack; Grandma's Boy
1921 A Sailor-Made Man; Among Those Present; I Do; Never Weaken; Now or Never
1920 Get Out and Get Under; Haunted Spooks; High and Dizzy; An Eastern Westerner; Number, Please
1919 His Royal Slyness; Don't Shove; I'm on My Way; At the Old Stage Door; Ask Father; Bumping into Broadway; Captain Kidd's Kids; From Hand to Mouth
1918 Are Crooks Dishonest?; On the Jump
1917 Luke's Lost Liberty; Luke's Trolley Troubles; Lonesome Luke on Tin Can Alley; Over the Fence; Stop! Luke! Listen!; Lonesome Luke's Honeymoon; Luke Wins Ye Ladye Faire; Luke's Busy Day; Lonesome Luke's Lively Life; Lonesome Luke's Wild Women; Lonesome Luke, Lawyer; Lonesome Luke, Mechanic; Lonesome Luke, Messenger; Lonesome Luke, Plumber; All Aboard; Bliss
1916 Lonesome Luke Leans to the Literary; Lonesome Luke Lolls in Luxury; Lonesome Luke, Circus King; Luke and the Bang-Tails; Luke and the Bomb Throwers; Luke and the Mermaids; Luke and the Rural Roughnecks; Luke Does the Midway; Luke Foils the Villain; Luke Joins the Navy; Luke Laughs Last; Luke Locates the Loot; Luke Lugs Luggage; Luke Pipes the Pippins; Luke Rides Roughshod; Luke's Double; Luke's Fatal Flivver; Luke's Fireworks Fizzle; Luke's Late Lunchers; Luke's Lost Lamb; Luke's Movie Muddle; Luke's Newsie Knockout; Luke's Shattered Sleep; Luke's Society Mixup; Luke's Speedy Club Life; Luke's Washful Waiting; Luke, Crystal Gazer; Luke, Patient Provider; Luke, Rank Impersonator; Luke, the Candy Cut-Up; Luke, the Chauffeur; Marriage a la Carte; Them Was the Happy Days!
1915 Giving Them Fits; Keystone Comedies, Vol. 5; Great While It Lasted; Fresh from the Farm; Just

Nuts; Bughouse Bellhops; Lonesome Luke; Peculiar Patients' Pranks; Lonesome Luke, Social Gangster; Ragtime Snap Shots; Some Baby; Miss Fatty's Seaside Lovers; Once Every Ten Minutes
1913 Fatty and His Funny Friends

Carole Lombard
(Oct. 6, 1908–1942)
1942 To Be or Not to Be
1941 Mr. and Mrs. Smith
1940 They Knew What They Wanted; Vigil in the Night
1939 Made for Each Other; In Name Only
1938 Fools for Scandal
1937 Nothing Sacred; Swing High, Swing Low; True Confession
1936 Love Before Breakfast; My Man Godfrey; The Princess Comes Across
1935 Hands Across the Table; Rumba
1934 Bolero; The Gay Blade; Lady By Choice; Now and Forever; Twentieth Century; We're Not Dressing
1933 Brief Moment; The Eagle and the Hawk; From Hell to Heaven; White Woman
1932 No One Man; No More Orchids; No Man of Her Own; Virtue; Sinners in the Sun
1931 I Take This Woman; It Pays to Advertise; Ladies' Man; Man of the World; Up Pops the Devil
1930 The Arizona Kid; Fast and Loose; Safety in Numbers
1929 Big News; High Voltage; The Racketeer
1928 The Divine Sinner; Me Gangster; Ned McCobb's Daughter; Show Folks
1925 Hearts and Spurs; Durand of the Badlands; Marriage in Transit
1921 A Perfect Crime

Peter Lorre
(June 26, 1904–1964)
1964 The Comedy of Terrors; Muscle Beach Party; The Patsy
1963 The Raven
1962 Five Weeks in a Balloon; Tales of Terror
1961 Voyage to the Bottom of the Sea
1960 Scent of Mystery
1959 The Big Circus
1957 Hell Ship Mutiny; The Sad Sack; Silk Stockings; The Buster Keaton Story; The Story of Mankind
1956 Meet Me in Las Vegas; Congo Crossing; Around the World in 80 Days
1954 20,000 Leagues Under the Sea
1953 Beat the Devil
1951 The Lost One
1950 Quicksand; Double Confession
1949 Rope of Sand
1948 Casbah
1947 My Favorite Brunette
1946 The Chase; The Black Angel; The Beast with Five Fingers; Three Strangers; The Verdict

1945 Confidential Agent; Hotel Berlin
1944 Arsenic and Old Lace; Passage to Marseilles; The Conspirators; Hollywood Canteen; The Mask of Dimitrios
1943 Background to Danger; The Constant Nymph; The Cross of Lorraine
1942 Invisible Agent; Casablanca; All Through the Night; In This Our Life; The Boogie Man Will Get You
1941 The Face Behind the Mask; Mr. District Attorney; They Met in Bombay; The Maltese Falcon
1940 You'll Find Out; I Was an Adventuress; Island of Doomed Men; Stranger Cargo; The Stranger on the Third Floor
1939 Mr. Moto in Danger Island; Mr. Moto's Last Warning; Mr. Moto Takes a Vacation
1938 Mr. Moto Takes a Chance; Mr. Moto's Gamble; Mysterious Mr. Moto; I'll Give a Million
1937 Nancy Steele Is Missing!; The Crack-Up; Thank You, Mr. Moto; Think Fast, Mr. Moto; Lancer Spy
1936 The Secret Agent
1935 Mad Love; Crime and Punishment
1934 The Man Who Knew Too Much
1931 M

Myrna Loy
(Aug. 2, 1905–1993)
1980 Just Tell Me What You Want
1978 The End
1974 Airport 1975
1969 The April Fools
1960 From the Terrace; Midnight Lace
1958 Lonelyhearts
1956 The Ambassador's Daughter
1952 Belles on Their Toes
1950 Cheaper by the Dozen
1949 The Red Pony; That Dangerous Age
1948 Mr. Blandings Builds His Dream House
1947 The Senator Was Indiscreet; Song of the Thin Man; The Bachelor and the Bobby-Soxer
1946 So Goes My Love; The Best Years of Our Lives
1944 The Thin Man Goes Home
1941 Shadow of the Thin Man; Love Crazy
1940 I Love You Again; Third Finger, Left Hand
1939 Lucky Night; The Rains Came; Another Thin Man
1938 Too Hot to Handle; Man-Proof; Test Pilot
1937 Parnell; Double Wedding
1936 Wife vs. Secretary; The Great Ziegfeld; After the Thin Man; Libeled Lady; Petticoat Fever; To Mary—with Love
1935 Whipsaw; Wings in the Dark
1934 Evelyn Prentice; Men in White; Manhattan Melodrama; Stamboul

Quest; Broadway Bill; The Thin Man
1933 Topaze; When Ladies Meet; Night Flight; The Barbarian; Penthouse; The Prizefighter and the Lady
1932 Love Me Tonight; New Morals for Old; Vanity Fair; The Mask of Fu Manchu; Thirteen Women; Emma; The Wet Parade; The Woman in Room 13; The Animal Kingdom
1931 The Naughty Flirt; Rebound; Skyline; Body and Soul; Transatlantic; A Connecticut Yankee; Consolation Marriage; Arrowsmith; Hush Money
1930 Renegades; The Devil to Pay; Isle of Escape; The Jazz Cinderella; Bride of the Regiment; Last of the Duanes; The Truth About Youth; Under a Texas Moon; Cameo Kirby; Cock o' the Walk; Rogue of the Rio Grande
1929 The Great Divide; Fancy Baggage; The Squall; Hardboiled Rose; The Show of Shows; The Desert Song; The Black Watch; Evidence
1928 State Street Sadie; A Girl in Every Port; Pay As You Enter; Turn Back the Hours; Beware of Married Men; The Crimson City; Noah's Ark; The Midnight Taxi
1927 Ham and Eggs at the Front; The Girl from Chicago; Simple Sis; A Sailor's Sweetheart; The Jazz Singer; Bitter Apples; If I Were Single; The Heart of Maryland; Finger Prints
1926 So This Is Paris; Across the Pacific; The Caveman; Don Juan; The Exquisite Sinner; The Gilded Highway; Ben-Hur: A Tale of the Christ; Why Girls Go Back Home
1925 Pretty Ladies

Bela Lugosi
(Oct. 20, 1882–1956)
1956 Plan 9 from Outer Space; Bride of the Monster; The Black Sleep
1953 Glen or Glenda
1952 Bela Lugosi Meets a Brooklyn Gorilla; My Son, the Vampire
1948 Abbott and Costello Meet Frankenstein
1947 Dick Tracy Meets Karloff; Scared to Death
1946 Genius at Work
1945 The Body Snatcher; Zombies on Broadway
1944 One Body Too Many; Return of the Ape Man; Voodoo Man
1943 The Ape Man; Ghosts on the Loose; The Return of the Vampire; Frankenstein Meets the Wolfman
1942 The Ghost of Frankenstein; Black Dragons; The Corpse Vanishes; Night Monster; Bowery at Midnight
1941 Spooks Run Wild; The Wolf Man; The Black Cat; The Invisible Ghost; The Devil Bat
1940 The Saint's Double Trouble; You'll Find Out; Black Friday
1939 The Human Monster; The Phantom Creeps (serial); Son of Frankenstein; The Gorilla; Ninotchka
1937 S.O.S. Coast Guard (serial)
1936 Shadow of Chinatown (serial); Postal Inspector; The Invisible Ray
1935 Phantom Ship; Murder by Television; The Raven; The Best Man Wins; Mark of the Vampire; The Mysterious Mr. Wong
1934 The Return of Chandu; The Black Cat; Gift of Gab
1933 The Devil's in Love; The Whispering Shadow (serial); International House; Night of Terror; The Death Kiss
1932 Chandu the Magician; Murders in the Rue Morgue; Island of Lost Souls; White Zombie
1931 The Black Camel; Women of All Nations; Dracula; Broadminded
1930 Renegades; Such Men Are Dangerous; Wild Company
1929 The Thirteenth Chair; Prisoners
1928 How to Handle Women; The Veiled Woman
1925 Midnight Girl; Daughters Who Pay
1924 The Rejected Woman
1923 The Silent Command;

Ida Lupino
(Feb. 4, 1918–1995)
1978 My Boys Are Good Boys
1976 The Food of the Gods
1975 The Devil's Rain
1972 Junior Bonner; Deadhead Miles
1969 Backtrack
1966 The Trouble with Angels
1956 While the City Sleeps; Strange Intruder
1955 The Big Knife; Women's Prison
1954 Private Hell 36
1953 Jennifer; The Bigamist; The Hitch-Hiker
1952 Beware, My Lovely; On Dangerous Ground
1951 Hard, Fast and Beautiful
1949 Woman in Hiding; Lust for Gold
1948 Road House
1947 Deep Valley; Escape Me Never
1946 The Man I Love; Devotion
1945 Pillow to Post
1944 In Our Time; Hollywood Canteen
1943 Forever and a Day; Thank Your Lucky Stars
1942 Life Begins at 8:30; Moontide; The Hard Way
1941 Out of the Fog; Ladies in Retirement; High Sierra; The Sea Wolf
1940 They Drive By Night
1939 The Lone Wolf Spy Hunt; The Lady and the Mob; The Adventures of Sherlock Holmes; The Light That Failed
1937 Let's Get Married; Artists and Models; Sea Devils; Fight for Your Lady

1936 Yours for the Asking; Anything Goes; The Gay Desperado; One Rainy Afternoon
1935 Paris in Spring; Peter Ibbetson; Smart Girl
1934 Ready for Love; Search for Beauty; Come On, Marines
1933 Money for Speed; I Lived with You; High Finance; Prince of Arcadia; The Ghost Camera; Her First Affair

Shirley MacLaine
(Apr. 24, 1934)
1997 A Smile Like Yours
1996 Mrs. Winterbourne; The Evening Star
1994 Guarding Tess
1993 Wrestling Ernest Hemingway
1992 Used People
1991 Defending Your Life
1990 Postcards from the Edge; Waiting for the Light
1989 Steel Magnolias
1988 Madame Sousatzka
1984 Cannonball Run II
1983 Terms of Endearment
1980 A Change of Seasons; Loving Couples
1979 Being There
1977 The Turning Point
1972 The Possession of Joel Delaney
1971 Desperate Characters
1970 Two Mules for Sister Sara
1969 Sweet Charity
1968 The Bliss of Mrs. Blossom
1967 Woman Times Seven
1966 Gambit
1965 John Goldfarb, Please Come Home
1964 The Yellow Rolls-Royce; What a Way to Go!
1963 Irma La Douce
1962 Two for the Seesaw; My Geisha; The Children's Hour
1961 Two Loves; All in a Night's Work
1960 Ocean's Eleven; Can-Can; The Apartment
1959 Career; Ask Any Girl
1958 Hot Spell; The Sheepman; Some Came Running; The Matchmaker
1956 Around the World in 80 Days
1955 Artists and Models; The Trouble with Harry

Fred MacMurray
(Aug. 30, 1908–1991)
1978 The Swarm
1973 Charley and the Angel
1967 The Happiest Millionaire
1966 Follow Me, Boys!
1964 Kisses for My President
1963 Son of Flubber
1962 Bon Voyage!
1961 The Absent-Minded Professor
1960 The Apartment
1959 The Shaggy Dog; Face of a Fugitive; The Oregon Trail
1958 Day of the Bad Man; Good Day for a Hanging
1957 Gun for a Coward; Quantez
1956 There's Always Tomorrow
1955 At Gunpoint; The Far Horizons; The Rains of Ranchipur
1954 The Caine Mutiny; The Pushover; A Woman's World
1953 Fair Wind to Java; The Moonlighter
1951 Callaway Went Thataway; A Millionaire for Christy
1950 Borderline; Never a Dull Moment
1949 Father Was a Fullback; Family Honeymoon
1948 An Innocent Affair; On Our Merry Way; The Miracle of the Bells
1947 Singapore; Suddenly It's Spring; The Egg and I
1946 Smoky
1945 Captain Eddie; Murder, He Says; Pardon My Past; Where Do We Go from Here?
1944 Practically Yours; Standing Room Only; Double Indemnity; And the Angels Sing
1943 Flight for Freedom; Above Suspicion; No Time for Love
1942 The Forest Rangers; Star Spangled Rhythm; Take a Letter, Darling; The Lady Is Willing
1941 New York Town; One Night in Lisbon; Virginia; Dive Bomber
1940 Rangers of Fortune; Remember the Night; Too Many Husbands; Little Old New York
1939 Cafe Society; Honeymoon in Bali; Invitation to Happiness
1938 Sing You Sinners; Men with Wings; Cocoanut Grove
1937 Exclusive; Champagne Waltz; Swing High, Swing Low; Maid of Salem; True Confession
1936 The Texas Rangers; Thirteen Hours by Air; The Trail of the Lonesome Pine; The Princess Comes Across
1935 The Bride Comes Home; The Gilded Lily; Alice Adams; Hands Across the Table; Men Without Names; Car 99; Grand Old Girl
1934 Friends of Mr. Sweeney; Tiger Rose; Girls Gone Wild; Glad Rag Doll

Karl Malden
(Mar. 22, 1913)
1987 Nuts
1986 Billy Galvin
1983 The Sting II; Twilight Time
1979 Beyond the Poseidon Adventure; Meteor
1974 Ricco
1972 The Summertime Killer
1971 The Wild Rovers; The Cat O' Nine Tails
1970 Patton
1968 Blue; Hot Millions
1967 Billion Dollar Brain; Hotel
1966 Murderers' Row; The Adventures of Bullwhip Griffin; Nevada Smith
1965 The Cincinnati Kid
1964 Dead Ringer; Cheyenne Autumn
1963 Come Fly with Me
1962 How the West Was Won; Birdman of Alcatraz; All Fall Down; Gypsy

1961 Parrish; The Great Impostor; One-Eyed Jacks
1960 Pollyanna
1959 The Hanging Tree
1957 Fear Strikes Out; Bombers B-52
1956 Baby Doll
1954 Phantom of the Rue Morgue; On the Waterfront
1953 Take the High Ground; I Confess
1952 Diplomatic Courier; Operation Secret; Ruby Gentry
1951 A Streetcar Named Desire; The Sellout; Decision Before Dawn
1950 Where the Sidewalk Ends; The Gunfighter; Halls of Montezuma
1947 Boomerang!; Kiss of Death; 13 Rue Madeleine
1944 Winged Victory
1940 They Knew What They Wanted

Fredric March
(Aug. 31, 1897–1975)
1973 The Iceman Cometh
1970 Tick, Tick, Tick
1967 Hombre
1964 Seven Days in May
1962 The Condemned of Altona
1961 The Young Doctors
1960 Inherit the Wind
1959 Middle of the Night
1956 The Man in the Gray Flannel Suit; Alexander the Great
1955 The Bridges at Toko-Ri; The Desperate Hours
1954 Executive Suite
1953 Man on a Tightrope
1951 Death of a Salesman; It's a Big Country
1949 Christopher Columbus
1948 An Act of Murder; Another Part of the Forest
1946 The Best Years of Our Lives
1944 The Adventures of Mark Twain; Tomorrow the World
1942 Bedtime Story; I Married a Witch
1941 One Foot in Heaven; So Ends Our Night
1940 Susan and God; Victory
1938 The Buccaneer; There Goes My Heart; Trade Winds
1937 Nothing Sacred; A Star Is Born
1936 Mary of Scotland; The Road to Glory; Anthony Adverse
1935 Anna Karenina; Les Miserables; The Dark Angel
1934 Good Dame; All of Me; The Barretts of Wimpole Street; We Live Again; Death Takes a Holiday; The Affairs of Cellini
1933 Design for Living; Tonight Is Ours; The Eagle and the Hawk
1932 Merrily We Go to Hell; Strangers in Love; The Sign of the Cross; Smilin' Through; Make Me a Star; Dr. Jekyll and Mr. Hyde
1931 Honor Among Lovers; My Sin; The Night Angel
1930 The Royal Family of Broadway; Manslaughter; True to the Navy; Ladies

Love Brutes; Paramount on Parade; Laughter; Sarah and Son
1929 The Wild Party; The Studio Murder Mystery; The Marriage Playground; Jealousy; The Dummy; Footlights and Fools; Paris Bound

Lee Marvin
(Feb. 19, 1924–1987)
1986 The Delta Force
1984 Dog Day
1983 Gorky Park
1981 Death Hunt
1980 The Big Red One
1979 Avalanche Express
1976 The Great Scout and Cathouse Thursday; Shout at the Devil
1974 The Klansman; The Spikes Gang
1973 Emperor of the North; The Iceman Cometh
1972 Pocket Money; Prime Cut
1970 Monte Walsh
1969 Paint Your Wagon
1968 Hell in the Pacific; Sergeant Ryker
1967 The Dirty Dozen; Point Blank
1966 The Professionals
1965 Ship of Fools; Cat Ballou
1964 The Killers
1963 Donovan's Reef
1962 The Man Who Shot Liberty Valance
1961 The Comancheros
1958 The Missouri Traveler
1957 Raintree County
1956 Attack; Pillars of the Sky; The Rack; Seven Men from Now
1955 A Life in the Balance; I Died a Thousand Times; Pete Kelly's Blues; Violent Saturday; Shack Out on 101; Not As a Stranger; Bad Day at Black Rock
1954 Gorilla at Large; The Wild One; The Raid; The Caine Mutiny
1953 The Big Heat; The Stranger Wore a Gun; Seminole; The Glory Brigade; Gun Fury; Down Among the Sheltering Palms
1952 Eight Iron Men; We're Not Married; The Duel at Silver Creek; Diplomatic Courier; Hangman's Knot
1951 You're in the Navy Now; Hong Kong

Marx Brothers
Groucho: (Oct. 2, 1890–1977)
Harpo: (Nov. 21, 1888–1964)
Chico: (Mar. 26, 1886–1961)
Zeppo: (Feb. 25, 1901–1979)
1968 Skidoo *(Groucho)*
1957 Will Success Spoil Rock Hunter? *(Groucho)*; The Story of Mankind *(Groucho, Harpo, Chico)*
1952 A Girl in Every Port *(Groucho)*
1951 Double Dynamite *(Groucho)*
1950 Mr. Music *(Groucho)*
1949 Love Happy *(Groucho, Harpo, Chico)*
1947 Copacabana *(Groucho)*
1946 A Night in Casablanca *(Groucho, Harpo, Chico)*
1941 The Big Store *(Groucho, Harpo, Chico)*

1940 Go West *(Groucho, Harpo, Chico)*
1939 At the Circus *(Groucho, Harpo, Chico)*
1938 Room Service *(Groucho, Harpo, Chico)*
1937 A Day at the Races *(Groucho, Harpo, Chico)*
1935 A Night at the Opera *(Groucho, Harpo, Chico)*
1933 Duck Soup *(all four)*
1932 Horse Feathers *(all four)*
1931 Monkey Business *(all four)*
1930 Animal Crackers *(all four)*
1929 The Cocoanuts *(all four)*

James Mason
(May 15, 1909–1984)
1984 The Assisi Underground; The Shooting Party
1983 Yellowbeard; Alexandre
1982 Evil Under the Sun; The Verdict
1981 A Dangerous Summer
1980 Ffolkes
1979 Murder by Decree; The Water Babies; Bloodline; The Passage
1978 The Boys from Brazil; Heaven Can Wait
1977 Cross of Iron; Hot Stuff
1976 Voyage of the Damned
1975 Inside Out; The Kidnap Syndicate; Mandingo; The Flower in His Mouth; The Left Hand of the Law
1974 The Destructors; 11 Harrowhouse; Trikimia; Nostro Nero in Casa Nichols
1973 The Last of Sheila; The Mackintosh Man
1972 Bad Man's River; Child's Play; Kill! Kill! Kill!
1971 Cold Sweat
1970 The Third Eye; Spring and Port Wine
1969 Age of Consent
1968 Duffy; Mayerling; The Sea Gull
1967 Stranger in the House; The Deadly Affair
1966 The Blue Max; Georgy Girl
1965 Lord Jim; Genghis Khan; The Uninhibited
1964 The Pumpkin Eater; The Fall of the Roman Empire
1963 Torpedo Bay
1962 Escape from Zahrain; Hero's Island; Lolita; Tiara Tahiti
1960 The Marriage-Go-Round; A Touch of Larceny; The Trials of Oscar Wilde
1959 North by Northwest; Journey to the Center of the Earth
1958 Cry Terror!; The Decks Ran Red
1957 Island in the Sun
1956 Bigger Than Life; Forever Darling
1954 Prince Valiant; 20,000 Leagues Under the Sea; A Star Is Born
1953 The Man Between; Julius Caesar; Botany Bay; The Story of Three Loves; The Desert Rats; Charade
1952 A Lady Possessed; The Prisoner of Zenda; Five Fingers; Face to Face
1951 Pandora and the Flying Dutchman; The Desert Fox
1950 One Way Street
1949 The Reckless Moment;

Caught; Madame Bovary; East Side, West Side
1947 Odd Man Out; The Patient Vanishes; The Upturned Glass
1946 The Seventh Veil
1945 They Met in the Dark; They Were Sisters; The Wicked Lady; A Place of One's Own; The Man in Grey
1944 Fanny By Gaslight; Secret Mission; Candlelight in Algeria; Hotel Reserve
1943 The Bells Go Down; The Alibi
1942 Thunder Rock; The Night Has Eyes; Hatter's Castle
1941 This Man Is Dangerous
1939 I Met a Murderer
1938 The Return of the Scarlet Pimpernel
1937 The Mill on the Floss; Catch As Catch Can; Fire Over England; The High Command
1936 Troubled Waters; Prison Breaker; Cauldron of Blood; The Secret of Stamboul
1935 Late Extra

Walter Matthau
(Oct. 1, 1920)
1998 Neil Simon's The Odd Couple II
1997 Out to Sea
1996 I'm Not Rappaport; The Grass Harp
1995 Grumpier Old Men
1994 I.Q.
1993 Grumpy Old Men; Dennis the Menace
1991 JFK
1988 The Little Devil; The Couch Trip
1986 Pirates
1985 Movers and Shakers
1983 The Survivors
1982 I Ought to Be in Pictures
1981 First Monday in October; Buddy Buddy
1980 Hopscotch; Little Miss Marker
1978 House Calls; Casey's Shadow; California Suite
1976 The Bad News Bears
1975 The Sunshine Boys
1974 Earthquake; The Taking of Pelham One, Two, Three; The Front Page
1973 Charley Varrick; The Laughing Policeman
1972 Pete 'n' Tillie
1971 Plaza Suite; A New Leaf; Kotch
1969 Cactus Flower; Hello, Dolly!
1968 The Secret Life of an American Wife; The Odd Couple; Candy
1967 A Guide for the Married Man
1966 The Fortune Cookie
1965 Mirage
1964 Goodbye Charlie; Fail-Safe; Ensign Pulver
1963 Island of Love; Charade
1962 Lonely Are the Brave; Who's Got the Action?
1960 Strangers When We Meet; Gangster Story
1958 Ride a Crooked Trail; Onionhead; King Creole; The Voice in the Mirror
1957 A Face in the Crowd; Slaughter on Tenth Avenue

1956 Bigger Than Life
1955 The Indian Fighter; The Kentuckian

Victor Mature
(Jan. 29, 1915–1994)
1979 Firepower
1976 Won Ton Ton, the Dog Who Saved Hollywood
1972 Every Little Crook and Nanny
1968 Head
1966 After the Fox
1962 The Tartars
1960 Hannibal
1959 The Bandit of Zhobe; The Big Circus; Escort West; Timbuktu
1958 China Doll; No Time to Die
1957 The Long Haul; Pickup Alley
1956 Safari; The Sharkfighters; Zarak
1955 Chief Crazy Horse; The Last Frontier; Violent Saturday
1954 Dangerous Mission; The Egyptian; Demetrius and the Gladiators; Betrayed
1953 The Glory Brigade; The Veils of Bagdad; Affair with a Stranger; The Robe
1952 Androcles and the Lion; Million Dollar Mermaid; Something for the Birds; The Las Vegas Story
1950 I'll Get By; Stella; Gambling House; Wabash Avenue
1949 Red, Hot and Blue; Easy Living; Samson and Delilah
1948 Fury at Furnace Creek; Cry of the City
1947 Kiss of Death; Moss Rose
1946 My Darling Clementine
1942 My Gal Sal; Footlight Serenade; Seven Days Leave; Song of the Islands
1941 I Wake Up Screaming; The Shanghai Gesture
1940 Captain Caution; One Million B.C.; No, No Nanette
1939 The Housekeeper's Daughter

Joel McCrea
(Nov. 5, 1905–1990)
1976 Mustang Country
1970 Cry Blood, Apache
1962 Ride the High Country
1959 The Gunfight at Dodge City
1958 Cattle Empire; Fort Massacre
1957 Gunsight Ridge; The Tall Stranger; Trooper Hook; The Oklahoman
1956 The First Texan
1955 Stranger on Horseback; Wichita
1954 Black Horse Canyon; Border River
1953 The Lone Hand; Shoot First
1952 The San Francisco Story
1951 Cattle Drive; The Hollywood Story
1950 Frenchie; The Outriders; Stars in My Crown; Saddle Tramp
1949 Colorado Territory; South of St. Louis
1948 Four Faces West
1947 Ramrod
1946 The Virginian

1945 The Unseen
1944 The Great Moment; Buffalo Bill
1943 The More the Merrier
1942 The Great Man's Lady; The Palm Beach Story
1941 Sullivan's Travels; Reaching for the Sun
1940 Foreign Correspondent; He Married His Wife; The Primrose Path
1939 They Shall Have Music; Espionage Agent; Union Pacific
1938 Three Blind Mice; Youth Takes a Fling
1937 Internes Can't Take Money; Dead End; Wells Fargo; Woman Chases Man
1936 These Three; Come and Get It; Two in a Crowd; Banjo on My Knee; Adventure in Manhattan
1935 Private Worlds; Splendor; Our Little Girl; Woman Wanted; The Barbary Coast
1934 The Richest Girl in the World; Gambling Lady; Half a Sinner
1933 Bed of Roses; Scarlet River; The Silver Cord; Chance at Heaven; One Man's Journey
1932 Bird of Paradise; The Sport Parade; Rockabye; The Lost Squadron; Business and Pleasure; The Most Dangerous Game
1931 Girls About Town; Born to Love; Once a Sinner; Kept Husbands; The Common Law
1930 The Silver Horde; Lightnin'
1929 So This Is College; Dynamite; The Jazz Age; The Thirteenth Chair
1928 Dead Man's Curve
1927 The Enemy; The Fair Co-Ed

Roddy McDowall
(Sept. 17, 1928–1998)
1998 Something To Believe In
1997 Kipling's Second Jungle Book: Mowgli and Baloo
1996 It's My Party
1995 The Grass Harp; Last Summer in the Hamptons; Unknown Origin
1994 Mirror, Mirror 2: Raven Dance
1991 Double Trouble; Going Under
1989 Cutting Class; Heroes Stand Alone; Shakma; The Big Picture
1988 Doin' Time on Planet Earth; Fright Night Part 2
1987 Dead of Winter; Overboard
1985 Fright Night
1982 Evil Under the Sun; Class of 1984
1981 Charlie Chan and the Curse of the Dragon Queen
1979 Scavenger Hunt; Circle of Iron
1978 Rabbit Test; Laserblast; The Cat from Outer Space
1977 Sixth and Main
1976 Embryo; Mean Johnny Barrows
1975 Funny Lady
1974 Dirty Mary, Crazy Larry
1973 Arnold; The Legend of Hell

House; Battle for the Planet of the Apes
1972 The Poseidon Adventure; The Life and Times of Judge Roy Bean; Conquest of the Planet of the Apes
1971 Pretty Maids All in a Row; Escape from the Planet of the Apes; Bedknobs and Broomsticks
1969 Hello Down There; Midas Run; Cult of the Damned
1968 Five Card Stud; Planet of the Apes
1967 The Cool Ones; It!; The Adventures of Bullwhip Griffin
1966 The Defector; Lord Love a Duck
1965 The Third Day; That Darn Cat; The Greatest Story Ever Told; Inside Daisy Clover; The Loved One
1964 Shock Treatment
1963 Cleopatra
1962 The Longest Day
1960 The Subterraneans; Midnight Lace
1952 The Steel Fist
1950 Killer Shark; Big Timber; Everybody's Dancin'
1949 Tuna Clipper; Black Midnight
1948 Rocky; Macbeth; Kidnapped
1946 Holiday in Mexico
1945 Molly and Me; Thunderhead, Son of Flicka
1944 The Keys of the Kingdom; The White Cliffs of Dover
1943 My Friend Flicka; Lassie Come Home
1942 The Pied Piper; Son of Fury; On the Sunny Side
1941 Poison Pen; Confirm or Deny; How Green Was My Valley; Man Hunt; This England; You Will Remember
1940 Saloon Bar
1939 The Outsider; Murder Will Out; Dead Man's Shoes; Just William
1938 I See Ice; The Yellow Sands; Hey! Hey! USA; Kidnapped; Scruffy; John Halifax, Gentleman; Murder in the Family

Steve McQueen
(Mar. 24, 1930–1980)
1980 The Hunter; Tom Horn
1979 An Enemy of the People
1974 The Towering Inferno
1973 Papillon
1972 Junior Bonner; The Getaway
1971 Le Mans
1969 The Reivers
1968 Bullitt; The Thomas Crown Affair
1966 Nevada Smith; The Sand Pebbles
1965 The Cincinnati Kid; Baby the Rain Must Fall
1963 Love with the Proper Stranger; Soldier in the Rain; The Great Escape
1962 The War Lover; Hell Is for Heroes
1961 The Honeymoon Machine
1960 The Magnificent Seven
1959 Never So Few; The Great St. Louis Bank Robbery
1958 Never Love a Stranger; The Blob

1956 Somebody Up There Likes Me

Carmen Miranda
(Feb. 9, 1909–1955)
1953 Scared Stiff
1950 Nancy Goes to Rio
1948 A Date with Judy
1947 Copacabana
1946 Doll Face; If I'm Lucky
1944 Four Jills in a Jeep; Greenwich Village; Something for the Boys
1943 The Gang's All Here
1942 Springtime in the Rockies
1941 That Night in Rio; Weekend in Havana
1940 Down Argentine Way

Robert Mitchum
(Aug. 6, 1917–1997)
1996 Dead Man
1995 Backfire
1993 Woman of Desire; Tombstone
1991 Cape Fear
1988 Mr. North; Scrooged
1984 Maria's Lovers; The Ambassador
1982 That Championship Season
1981 Agency
1980 Nightkill
1979 Breakthrough
1978 Matilda; The Big Sleep
1977 The Amsterdam Kill
1976 Midway; The Last Tycoon
1975 The Yakuza; Farewell, My Lovely
1973 The Friends of Eddie Coyle
1972 The Wrath of God
1971 Going Home
1970 Ryan's Daughter
1969 The Good Guys and the Bad Guys; Young Billy Young
1968 Villa Rides; Secret Ceremony; Five Card Stud; Anzio
1967 The Way West; El Dorado
1965 Mister Moses
1964 Man in the Middle; What a Way to Go!
1963 Rampage; The List of Adrian Messenger
1962 The Longest Day; Two for the Seesaw; Cape Fear
1961 The Last Time I Saw Archie
1960 The Night Fighters; The Grass Is Greener; Home from the Hill; The Sundowners
1959 The Angry Hills; The Wonderful Country
1958 Thunder Road; The Hunters
1957 Heaven Knows, Mr. Allison; The Enemy Below; Fire Down Below
1956 Bandido; Foreign Intrigue
1955 The Night of the Hunter; Man with the Gun; Not As a Stranger
1954 Track of the Cat; River of No Return; She Couldn't Say No
1953 Angel Face; Second Chance; White Witch Doctor
1952 Macao; One Minute to Zero; The Lusty Men
1951 My Forbidden Past; The Racket; His Kind of Woman
1950 Where Danger Lives
1949 The Red Pony; Holiday Affair; The Big Steal

1948 Rachel and the Stranger;
     Blood on the Moon
1947 Crossfire; Hoppy's
     Holiday; Pursued; Out of
     the Past; Desire Me
1946 Till the End of Time;
     Undercurrent; The Locket
1945 The Story of G.I. Joe;
     West of the Pecos
1944 Thirty Seconds over
     Tokyo; Nevada; Johnny
     Doesn't Live Here Any
     More; When Strangers
     Marry; Mr. Winkle Goes to
     War; The Girl Rush
1943 We've Never Been Licked;
     Doughboys in Ireland;
     Bar-20; Aerial Gunner; The
     Leather Burners; Hoppy
     Serves a Writ; Cry Havoc;
     The Human Comedy;
     Minesweeper; Beyond the
     Last Frontier; Riders of
     the Deadline; The Dancing
     Masters; Border Patrol;
     Colt Comrades; Gung Ho!;
     The Lone Star Trail; False
     Colors; Follow the Band;
     Corvette K-225

Marilyn Monroe
(June 1, 1926–1962)
1961 The Misfits
1960 Let's Make Love
1959 Some Like It Hot
1957 The Prince and the
     Showgirl
1956 Bus Stop
1955 The Seven Year Itch
1954 River of No Return;
     There's No Business Like
     Show Business
1953 How to Marry a
     Millionaire; Gentlemen
     Prefer Blondes
1952 Don't Bother to Knock;
     Niagara; Monkey
     Business; We're Not
     Married; Clash by Night;
     O. Henry's Full House
1951 Let's Make It Legal; Home
     Town Story; Love Nest; As
     Young As You Feel
1950 All About Eve; A Ticket to
     Tomahawk; The Asphalt
     Jungle; Love Happy; Right
     Cross; The Fireball
1949 Ladies of the Chorus
1948 Scudda Hoo! Scudda Hay!
1947 Dangerous Years

Robert Montgomery
(May 21, 1904–1981)
1960 The Gallant Hours;
     College Confidential
1959 A Private's Affair; Say One
     for Me
1950 Your Witness
1949 Once More, My Darling
1948 June Bride; The Saxon
     Charm
1947 Ride the Pink Horse
1946 Lady in the Lake
1945 They Were Expendable
1941 Here Comes Mr. Jordan;
     Rage in Heaven; Mr. and
     Mrs. Smith; Unfinished
     Business
1940 The Earl of Chicago;
     Haunted Honeymoon
1939 Fast and Loose
1938 The First Hundred Years;
     Three Loves Has Nancy;
     Yellow Jack
1937 Ever Since Eve; Live, Love
     and Learn; Night Must
     Fall; The Last of Mrs.
     Cheyney

1936 Petticoat Fever; Piccadilly
     Jim; Trouble for Two
1935 No More Ladies; Vanessa,
     Her Love Story; Biography
     of a Bachelor Girl
1934 Forsaking All Others; The
     Mystery of Mr. X; Rip Tide;
     Hide-Out; Fugitive Lovers
1933 Night Flight; Hell Below;
     Made on Broadway; When
     Ladies Meet; Another
     Language
1932 Blondie of the Follies; But
     the Flesh Is Weak; Letty
     Lynton; Faithless; Lovers
     Courageous
1931 Shipmates; Strangers May
     Kiss; Private Lives; The
     Easiest Way; The Man in
     Possession; Inspiration
1930 Free and Easy; Our
     Blushing Brides; Sins of
     the Children; The Big
     House; War Nurse; The
     Divorcee; Love in the
     Rough
1929 So This Is College; Their
     Own Desire; Three Live
     Ghosts; Untamed

Agnes Moorehead
(Dec. 6, 1906–1974)
1973 Charlotte's Web; The
     Death of a Lumberjack
1972 Dear Dead Delilah
1971 What's the Matter with
     Helen?
1966 The Singing Nun
1965 Hush . . . Hush, Sweet
     Charlotte
1963 Who's Minding the Store?
1962 How the West Was Won;
     Jessica
1961 Bachelor in Paradise;
     Twenty Plus Two
1960 Pollyanna
1959 Night of the Quarter
     Moon; The Bat; The
     Tempest
1957 Jeanne Eagels; The Story
     of Mankind; The True
     Story of Jesse James;
     Raintree County
1956 The Swan; The Conqueror;
     Meet Me in Las Vegas;
     The Opposite Sex;
     Pardners; The Revolt of
     Mamie Stover
1955 All That Heaven Allows;
     The Left Hand of God;
     Untamed
1954 Magnificent Obsession
1953 Scandal at Scourie; The
     Story of Three Loves;
     Those Redheads from
     Seattle; Main Street to
     Broadway
1952 The Blazing Forest;
     Captain Blackjack
1951 Fourteen Hours; Show
     Boat; Adventures of
     Captain Fabian; The Blue
     Veil
1950 Caged
1949 The Stratton Story;
     Without Honor; The Great
     Sinner
1948 The Woman in White;
     Summer Holiday; Station
     West; Johnny Belinda
1947 The Lost Moment; Dark
     Passage
1945 Keep Your Powder Dry;
     Her Highness and the
     Bellboy; Our Vines Have
     Tender Grapes
1944 Since You Went Away;
     Tomorrow the World; Jane

     Eyre; Dragon Seed; The
     Seventh Cross; Mrs.
     Parkington
1943 Government Girl; The
     Youngest Profession
1942 The Big Street; Journey
     into Fear; The Magnificent
     Ambersons
1941 Citizen Kane

Paul Muni
(Sept. 22, 1895–1967)
1959 The Last Angry Man
1953 Stranger on the Prowl
1946 Angel on My Shoulder
1945 A Song to Remember;
     Counter Attack
1943 The Commandos Strike at
     Dawn; Stage Door
     Canteen
1940 Hudson's Bay
1939 Juarez; We Are Not Alone
1937 The Life of Emile Zola;
     The Good Earth; The
     Woman I Love
1936 The Story of Louis Pasteur
1935 Dr. Socrates; Black Fury;
     Bordertown
1934 Hi, Nellie!
1933 The World Changes
1932 I Am a Fugitive from a
     Chain Gang; Scarface
1929 The Valiant; Seven Faces

Paul Newman
(Jan. 26, 1925)
1998 Twilight
1994 The Hudsucker Proxy;
     Nobody's Fool
1990 Mr. and Mrs. Bridge
1989 Fat Man and Little Boy;
     Blaze
1986 The Color of Money
1984 Harry and Son
1982 The Verdict
1981 Absence of Malice; Fort
     Apache, the Bronx
1980 When Time Ran Out
1979 Quintet
1977 Slap Shot
1976 Buffalo Bill and the
     Indians, or Sitting Bull's
     History Lesson; Silent
     Movie
1975 The Drowning Pool
1974 The Towering Inferno
1973 The Mackintosh Man; The
     Sting
1972 The Life and Times of
     Judge Roy Bean; Pocket
     Money
1971 Sometimes a Great
     Notion; They Might Be
     Giants
1970 WUSA
1969 Butch Cassidy and the
     Sundance Kid; Winning
1968 The Secret War of Harry
     Frigg
1967 Cool Hand Luke; Hombre
1966 Torn Curtain; Harper
1965 Lady L
1964 The Outrage; What a Way
     to Go!
1963 A New Kind of Love; Hud;
     The Prize
1962 Sweet Bird of Youth;
     Hemingway's Adventures
     of a Young Man
1961 Paris Blues; The Hustler
1960 From the Terrace;
     Exodus
1959 The Young Philadelphians
1958 Rally 'Round the Flag,
     Boys!; The Long, Hot
     Summer; Cat on a Hot Tin
     Roof; The Left-Handed
     Gun

1957 The Helen Morgan Story;
     Until They Sail
1956 The Rack; Somebody Up
     There Likes Me
1954 The Silver Chalice

Jack Nicholson
(Apr. 22, 1937)
1997 As Good As It Gets; Blood
     and Wine
1996 The Evening Star; Mars
     Attacks!
1995 The Crossing Guard
1994 Wolf
1992 A Few Good Men; Hoffa;
     Man Trouble
1990 The Two Jakes
1989 Batman
1987 Ironweed; The Witches of
     Eastwick; Broadcast News
1986 Heartburn
1985 Prizzi's Honor
1983 Terms of Endearment
1982 The Border
1981 The Postman Always
     Rings Twice; Reds
1980 The Shining
1978 Goin' South
1976 The Missouri Breaks; The
     Last Tycoon
1975 One Flew Over the
     Cuckoo's Nest; Tommy;
     The Passenger; The
     Fortune
1974 Chinatown
1973 The Last Detail
1972 The King of Marvin
     Gardens
1971 Drive, He Said; A Safe
     Place; Carnal Knowledge
1970 Five Easy Pieces; On a
     Clear Day You Can See
     Forever
1969 Rebel Rousers; Easy Rider
1968 Psych-Out
1967 Ride in the Whirlwind; The
     St. Valentine's Day
     Massacre; The Trip; The
     Shooting; Hell's Angels on
     Wheels
1966 Flight to Fury
1964 Back Door to Hell; Ensign
     Pulver
1963 Thunder Island; The
     Terror; The Raven
1962 The Broken Land
1960 The Wild Ride; Studs
     Lonigan; The Little Shop
     of Horrors; Too Soon to
     Love
1958 The Cry Baby Killer

Kim Novak
(Feb. 13, 1933)
1991 Liebestraum
1990 The Children
1980 The Mirror Crack'd
1979 Just a Gigolo
1977 The White Buffalo
1973 Tales That Witness
     Madness
1969 The Great Bank Robbery
1968 The Legend of Lylah Clare
1965 The Amorous Adventures
     of Moll Flanders
1964 Of Human Bondage; Kiss
     Me, Stupid
1962 Boys' Night Out; The
     Notorious Landlady
1960 Strangers When We Meet;
     Pepe
1959 Middle of the Night
1958 Vertigo; Bell, Book and
     Candle
1957 Jeanne Eagels; Pal Joey
1956 Picnic; The Eddy Duchin
     Story
1955 Five Against the House;

Son of Sinbad; The Man with the Golden Arm
1954 Phffft!; The Pushover; The French Line

Merle Oberon
(Feb. 19, 1911–1979)
1973 Interval
1967 Hotel
1966 Oscar
1963 Of Love and Desire
1956 The Price of Fear
1954 Deep in My Heart; Desiree
1952 Affair in Monte Carlo
1951 Pardon My French
1948 Berlin Express
1947 Night Song
1946 Night in Paradise; Temptation
1945 A Song to Remember; This Love of Ours
1944 The Lodger; Dark Waters
1943 Forever and a Day; Stage Door Canteen; First Comes Courage
1941 Affectionately Yours; Lydia; That Uncertain Feeling
1940 Till We Meet Again
1939 The Lion Has Wings; Wuthering Heights
1938 The Cowboy and the Lady; The Divorce of Lady X
1937 Over the Moon
1936 Beloved Enemy; These Three
1935 Dark Angel; Folies Bergere; The Scarlet Pimpernel
1934 The Private Life of Don Juan; The Broken Melody; Thunder in the East
1933 The Private Life of Henry VIII
1932 Men of Tomorrow; Wedding Rehearsal

Maureen O'Hara
(Aug. 17, 1920)
1991 Only the Lonely
1971 Big Jake
1970 How Do I Love Thee?
1966 The Rare Breed
1965 The Battle of the Villa Fiorita
1963 McLintock!; Spencer's Mountain
1962 Mr. Hobbs Takes a Vacation
1961 The Parent Trap; The Deadly Companions
1959 Our Man in Havana
1957 The Wings of Eagles
1956 Everything But the Truth; Lisbon
1955 The Magnificent Matador; Lady Godiva; The Long Gray Line
1954 Fire Over Africa
1953 The Redhead from Wyoming; War Arrow
1952 Against All Flags; At Sword's Point; The Quiet Man; Kangaroo
1951 Flame of Araby
1950 Comanche Territory; Rio Grande; Tripoli
1949 Bagdad; Father Was a Fullback; The Forbidden Street; A Woman's Secret
1948 Sitting Pretty
1947 The Foxes of Harrow; The Homestretch; Miracle on 34th Street; Sinbad the Sailor
1946 Do You Love Me?; Sentimental Journey

1945 The Spanish Main
1944 Buffalo Bill
1943 The Fallen Sparrow; The Immortal Sergeant; This Land Is Mine
1942 The Black Swan; To the Shores of Tripoli; Ten Gentlemen from West Point
1941 How Green Was My Valley; They Met in Argentina
1940 Dance, Girl, Dance; A Bill of Divorcement
1939 Little Miss Molly; Jamaica Inn; The Hunchback of Notre Dame
1938 The Playboy

Laurence Olivier
(May 22, 1907–1989)
1988 War Requiem
1985 The Wild Geese 2
1984 The Jigsaw Man; The Bounty
1981 Clash of the Titans; Inchon
1980 The Jazz Singer
1979 A Little Romance; Dracula
1978 The Betsy; The Boys from Brazil
1977 A Bridge Too Far
1976 Marathon Man; The Seven Percent Solution
1972 Sleuth; Lady Caroline Lamb
1971 Nicholas and Alexandra
1970 The Three Sisters
1969 Battle of Britain; Oh! What a Lovely War
1968 Romeo and Juliet; The Shoes of the Fisherman; The Dance of Death
1966 Khartoum
1965 Bunny Lake Is Missing; Othello
1963 Uncle Vanya
1962 Term of Trial
1960 The Entertainer; Spartacus
1959 The Devil's Disciple
1957 The Prince and the Showgirl
1955 Richard III
1953 The Beggar's Opera
1952 The Magic Box; Carrie
1948 Hamlet
1944 Henry V
1943 The Demi-Paradise
1941 That Hamilton Woman; The 49th Parallel
1940 Pride and Prejudice; Rebecca
1939 Wuthering Heights; Q Planes
1938 The Divorce of Lady X; 21 Days Together
1937 Fire Over England
1936 As You Like It
1935 I Stand Condemned
1934 No Funny Business
1933 Perfect Understanding
1932 Westward Passage
1931 The Yellow Ticket; Friends and Lovers; Her Strange Desire
1930 The Temporary Widow; Too Many Crooks

Peter O'Toole
(Aug. 2, 1932)
1998 Phantoms
1997 Fairy Tale: A True Story
1992 The Seventh Coin; Rebecca's Daughters; Worlds Apart
1991 King Ralph
1990 Wings of Fame; Isabelle

Eberhardt; The Rainbow Thief; Buried Alive
1989 On a Moonlit Night
1988 High Spirits
1987 The Last Emperor
1986 Club Paradise
1985 Creator
1984 Supergirl
1982 My Favorite Year
1980 The Stunt Man
1979 Zulu Dawn; Caligula
1978 Power Play
1976 Foxtrot
1975 Rosebud; Man Friday
1972 The Ruling Class; Man of La Mancha
1971 Under Milk Wood; Murphy's War
1970 Country Dance
1969 Goodbye, Mr. Chips
1968 Great Catherine; The Lion in Winter
1967 Casino Royale; The Night of the Generals
1966 How to Steal a Million; The Bible
1965 Lord Jim; What's New Pussycat?; The Sandpiper
1964 Becket
1962 Lawrence of Arabia
1960 The Day They Robbed the Bank of England; Kidnapped
1959 The Savage Innocents

Gregory Peck
(Apr. 5, 1916)
1991 Cape Fear; Other People's Money
1989 The Old Gringo
1987 Amazing Grace and Chuck
1980 The Sea Wolves
1978 The Boys from Brazil
1977 MacArthur
1976 The Omen
1974 Billy Two Hats
1971 Shoot Out
1970 I Walk the Line
1969 The Chairman; MacKenna's Gold; Marooned; The Stalking Moon
1966 Arabesque
1965 Mirage
1964 Behold a Pale Horse
1963 Captain Newman, M.D.
1962 Cape Fear; How the West Was Won; To Kill a Mockingbird
1961 The Guns of Navarone
1959 Pork Chop Hill; On the Beach; Beloved Infidel
1958 The Big Country; The Bravados
1957 Designing Woman
1956 The Man in the Gray Flannel Suit; Moby Dick
1954 The Million Pound Note; Night People; The Purple Plain
1953 Roman Holiday
1952 The Snows of Kilimanjaro; The World in His Arms
1951 Captain Horatio Hornblower; David and Bathsheba; Only the Valiant
1950 The Gunfighter
1949 The Great Sinner; Twelve O'Clock High
1948 Yellow Sky; The Paradine Case
1947 Gentleman's Agreement; The Macomber Affair
1946 The Yearling; Duel in the Sun
1945 Spellbound; The Valley of Decision

1944 The Keys of the Kingdom; Days of Glory

Sidney Poitier
(Feb. 20, 1924)
1997 The Jackal
1992 Sneakers
1988 Little Nikita; Shoot to Kill
1977 A Piece of the Action
1975 Let's Do It Again; The Wilby Conspiracy
1974 Uptown Saturday Night
1973 A Warm December
1972 Buck and the Preacher
1971 The Organization
1970 Brother John; They Call Me Mister Tibbs!
1969 The Lost Man
1968 For Love of Ivy
1967 Guess Who's Coming to Dinner; To Sir, with Love; In the Heat of the Night
1966 Duel at Diablo
1965 The Bedford Incident; The Greatest Story Ever Told; A Patch of Blue; The Slender Thread
1964 The Long Ships
1963 Lilies of the Field
1962 Pressure Point
1961 Paris Blues; A Raisin in the Sun
1960 All the Young Men
1959 Porgy and Bess
1958 The Defiant Ones; Virgin Island
1957 The Mark of the Hawk; Something of Value; Edge of the City; Band of Angels
1956 Goodbye, My Lady
1955 The Blackboard Jungle
1954 Go, Man, Go!
1952 Red Ball Express
1951 Cry, the Beloved Country
1950 No Way Out

Dick Powell
(Nov. 14, 1904–1963)
1954 Susan Slept Here
1952 The Bad and the Beautiful
1951 Cry Danger; Callaway Went Thataway; The Tall Target; You Never Can Tell
1950 The Reformer and the Redhead; Right Cross
1949 Mrs. Mike
1948 The Pitfall; Station West; Rogues' Regiment; To the Ends of the Earth
1947 Johnny O'Clock
1945 Cornered
1944 It Happened Tomorrow; Meet the People; Murder, My Sweet
1943 Happy Go Lucky; Riding High; True to Life
1942 Star Spangled Rhythm
1941 In the Navy; Model Wife
1940 I Want a Divorce; Christmas in July
1939 Naughty But Nice
1938 Going Places; Hard to Get; The Cowboy from Brooklyn
1937 Hollywood Hotel; On the Avenue; The Singing Marine; Varsity Show
1936 Gold Diggers of 1937; Hearts Divided; Colleen; Stage Struck
1935 Page Miss Glory; Shipmates Forever; A Midsummer Night's Dream; Thanks a Million; Broadway Gondolier; Gold Diggers of 1935
1934 Dames; Happiness Ahead; Twenty Million

Sweethearts; Wonder Bar;
Flirtation Walk
1933 Gold Diggers of 1933;
Convention City; 42nd
Street; The King's
Vacation; Footlight
Parade; College Coach
1932 Blessed Event; Big City
Blues; Too Busy to Work

William Powell
(July 29, 1892–1984)
1955 Mr. Roberts
1953 The Girl Who Had
Everything; How to Marry
a Millionaire
1952 The Treasure of Lost
Canyon
1951 It's a Big Country
1949 Dancing in the Dark; Take
One False Step
1948 Mr. Peabody and the
Mermaid
1947 Life with Father; The
Senator Was Indiscreet;
Song of the Thin Man
1946 The Hoodlum Saint;
Ziegfeld Follies
1944 The Thin Man Goes Home
1943 The Heavenly Body; The
Youngest Profession
1942 Crossroads
1941 Shadow of the Thin Man;
Love Crazy
1940 I Love You Again
1939 Another Thin Man
1938 The Baroness and
the Butler
1937 The Last of Mrs. Cheyney;
The Emperor's
Candlesticks; Double
Wedding
1936 After the Thin Man;
Libeled Lady; The Ex-Mrs.
Bradford; My Man
Godfrey; The Great
Ziegfeld
1935 Reckless; Escapade;
Rendezvous; Star of
Midnight
1934 Fashions of 1934;
Manhattan Melodrama;
Evelyn Prentice; The Thin
Man; The Key
1933 Double Harness; Lawyer
Man; Man Killer; The
Kennel Murder Case
1932 High Pressure; Jewel
Robbery; One Way
Passage
1931 Ladies' Man; Man of the
World; The Road to
Singapore
1930 For the Defense; The
Benson Murder Case;
Behind the Makeup;
Pointed Heels; Shadow of
the Law; Street of
Chance; Paramount on
Parade
1929 Charming Sinners; The
Greene Murder Case; The
Canary Murder Case
1928 Beau Sabreur; The
Dragnet; Partners in
Crime; The Four Feathers;
Feel My Pulse; Vanishing
Pioneer; The Last
Command; Interference;
Forgotten Faces
1927 Paid to Love; Senorita;
Love's Greatest Mistake;
She's a Sheik; Special
Delivery; Time to Love;
Nevada; New York
1926 Aloma of the South Seas;
Desert Gold; Tin Gods;
The Great Gatsby; White

Mice; Beau Geste; The
Runaway; Sea Horses
1925 Too Many Kisses;
Beautiful City; My Lady's
Lips; Faint Perfume;
Romola
1924 Dangerous Money
1923 Bright Shawl; Under the
Red Robe
1922 When Knighthood Was in
Flower; Outcast; Sherlock
Holmes

Tyrone Power
(May 5, 1913–1958)
1957 Witness for the
Prosecution; Seven Waves
Away; The Rising of the
Moon; The Sun Also Rises
1956 The Eddy Duchin Story
1955 The Long Gray Line;
Untamed
1953 King of the Khyber Rifles;
The Mississippi Gambler
1952 Diplomatic Courier; Pony
Soldier
1951 Rawhide; I'll Never
Forget You
1950 An American Guerrilla in
the Philippines; The Black
Rose
1949 Prince of Foxes
1948 The Luck of the Irish; That
Wonderful Urge
1947 Captain from Castile;
Nightmare Alley
1946 The Razor's Edge
1943 Crash Dive
1942 Son of Fury; The Black
Swan; This Above All
1941 Blood and Sand; A Yank in
the R.A.F.
1940 The Mark of Zorro;
Brigham Young; Johnny
Apollo
1939 The Rains Came; Jesse
James; Rose of
Washington Square;
Second Fiddle; Day-Time
Wife
1938 Suez; In Old Chicago;
Alexander's Ragtime
Band; Marie Antoinette
1937 Second Honeymoon; Thin
Ice; Cafe Metropole; Love
Is News
1936 Ladies in Love; Girls'
Dormitory; Lloyds of
London
1934 Flirtation Walk
1932 Tom Brown of Culver

Elvis Presley
(Jan. 8, 1935–1977)
1969 Charro!; The Trouble with
Girls; Change of Habit
1968 Live a Little, Love a Little;
Speedway; Stay Away,
Joe
1967 Double Trouble; Easy
Come, Easy Go; Clambake
1966 Paradise, Hawaiian Style;
Spinout; Frankie and
Johnny
1965 Girl Happy; Harum
Scarum; Tickle Me
1964 Roustabout; Kissin'
Cousins; Viva Las Vegas
1963 Fun in Acapulco; It
Happened at the World's
Fair
1962 Girls! Girls! Girls!; Kid
Galahad; Follow That
Dream
1961 Blue Hawaii; Wild in the
Country
1960 G.I. Blues; Flaming Star
1958 King Creole

1957 Loving You; Jailhouse
Rock
1956 Love Me Tender

Robert Preston
(June 8, 1918–1987)
1984 The Last Starfighter
1982 Victor/Victoria
1981 S.O.B.
1977 Semi-Tough
1975 My Father's House
1974 Mame
1972 Junior Bonner; Child's
Play
1963 Island of Love; All the Way
Home
1962 How the West Was Won;
The Music Man
1960 The Dark at the Top of the
Stairs
1956 The Last Frontier
1952 Face to Face
1951 Best of the Badmen; My
Outlaw Brother;
Cloudburst; When I Grow
Up
1950 The Sundowners
1949 The Lady Gambles; Tulsa
1948 Whispering Smith; Blood
on the Moon; The Big City
1947 The Macomber Affair;
Variety Girl; Wild Harvest
1943 Night Plane from
Chungking
1942 Star Spangled Rhythm;
Wake Island; Reap the
Wild Wind; This Gun
for Hire
1941 Parachute Battalion; New
York Town; The Night of
January 16th; Pacific
Blackout; The Lady from
Cheyenne
1940 Moon Over Burma;
Northwest Mounted
Police; Typhoon
1939 Beau Geste; Disbarred;
Union Pacific
1938 Illegal Traffic; King of
Alcatraz

Vincent Price
(May 27, 1911–1993)
1990 Edward Scissorhands
1988 Dead Heat
1987 The Offspring; The Whales
of August
1986 Escapes; The Great
Mouse Detective
1984 Bloodbath at the House
of Death
1982 House of the Long
Shadows
1981 The Monster Club
1979 Scavenger Hunt
1975 Journey into Fear
1974 Percy's Progress;
Madhouse
1973 Theatre of Blood
1972 Dr. Phibes Rises Again
1971 The Abominable Dr. Phibes
1970 Scream and Scream
Again; Cry of the Banshee
1969 The Oblong Box; The
Trouble with Girls
1968 Spirits of the Dead; More
Dead Than Alive; The
Conqueror Worm
1967 The Jackals; House of
1000 Dolls
1966 Dr. Goldfoot and the "S"
Bombs
1965 The Black Pirate; Dr.
Goldfoot and the Bikini
Machine; War Gods of
the Deep
1964 The Comedy of Terrors;
The Masque of the Red

Death; The Tomb of
Ligeia; The Last Man
on Earth
1963 The Graveside Story;
Twice-Told Tales; The
Haunted Palace; Beach
Party; The Raven; The
Black Buccaneer; Diary of
a Madman
1962 Tower of London;
Confessions of an Opium
Eater; Convicts Four
1961 Tales of Terror; Pit and the
Pendulum; Queen of the
Nile; Master of the World
1960 The House of Usher
1959 The Big Circus; The
Return of the Fly; The
Tingler; The Bat
1958 The Fly; House on
Haunted Hill
1957 The Story of Mankind
1956 While the City Sleeps; The
Ten Commandments;
Serenade; The Vagabond
King
1955 Son of Sinbad
1954 The Mad Magician;
Dangerous Mission;
Casanova's Big Night
1953 House of Wax
1952 The Las Vegas Story
1951 Adventures of Captain
Fabian; His Kind of
Woman
1950 The Baron of Arizona;
Curtain Call at Cactus
Creek; Champagne for
Caesar
1949 The Bribe; Bagdad
1948 The Three Musketeers;
Rogues' Regiment; Up in
Central Park; Abbott and
Costello Meet
Frankenstein
1947 Moss Rose; The Web; The
Long Night
1946 Shock!; Dragonwyck
1945 Leave Her to Heaven;
Guest in the House; A
Royal Scandal
1944 Wilson; The Keys of the
Kingdom; Laura; The Eve
of St. Mark
1943 The Song of Bernadette
1940 The House of the Seven
Gables; Green Hell;
Hudson's Bay; The
Invisible Man Returns;
Brigham Young
1939 The Private Lives of
Elizabeth and Essex; The
Tower of London
1938 Service De Luxe

Anthony Quinn
(Apr. 21, 1915)
1996 Seven Servants; The
Mayor; Gotti
1995 A Walk in the Clouds;
Somebody to Love
1993 Last Action Hero
1991 Jungle Fever; Mobsters;
Only the Lonely
1990 Ghosts Can't Do It;
Revenge
1981 The Salamander
1979 The Passage; Caravans
1978 The Greek Tycoon; The
Children of Sanchez
1976 The Message; The Switch;
The Inheritance
1974 Marseille Contract
1973 The Don Is Dead; Deaf
Smith and Johnny Ears;
The Deadly Kiss
1972 Across 110th Street
1970 A Walk in the Spring Rain;

R.P.M. *a.k.a.* Revolutions Per Minute; Flap
1969 The Secret of Santa Vittoria; A Dream of Kings
1968 The Shoes of the Fisherman; Guns for San Sebastian; The Magus
1967 The Happening; The Rover; The 25th Hour
1966 The Lost Command
1965 A High Wind in Jamaica; Marco the Magnificent
1964 Zorba the Greek; The Visit; Behold a Pale Horse
1962 Lawrence of Arabia; Requiem for a Heavyweight
1961 Barabbas; The Guns of Navarone
1960 Portrait in Black; Heller in Pink Tights
1959 Last Train from Gun Hill; Warlock; The Savage Innocents; The Black Orchid
1958 Attila; Hot Spell
1957 The Ride Back; The River's Edge; Wild Is the Wind
1956 The Hunchback of Notre Dame; Lust for Life; Man from Del Rio; The Wild Party
1955 Seven Cities of Gold; The Naked Street; The Magnificent Matador
1954 The Long Wait; Blowing Wild; Ulysses; La Strada
1953 City Beneath the Sea; Fatal Desire; Ride, Vaquero; Angels of Darkness; Seminole; East of Sumatra
1952 The World in His Arms; The Brigand; Viva Zapata!; Against All Flags
1951 High Treason; Mask of the Avenger; The Brave Bulls
1947 The Imperfect Lady; Black Gold; Sinbad the Sailor; Tycoon
1946 California
1945 China Sky; Where Do We Go from Here?; Back to Bataan
1944 Buffalo Bill; Roger Touhy, Gangster!; Irish Eyes Are Smiling; Ladies of Washington
1943 The Saint Meets the Tiger; Guadalcanal Diary; The Ox-Bow Incident
1942 The Road to Morocco; Larceny, Inc.; The Black Swan
1941 Thieves Fall Out; Bullets for O'Hara; The Perfect Snob; Blood and Sand; They Died with Their Boots On; Knockout
1940 The Ghost Breakers; Road to Singapore; Parole Fixer; Emergency Squad; Texas Rangers Ride Again; City for Conquest
1939 Island of Lost Men; Television Spy; Union Pacific; King of Chinatown
1938 The Buccaneer; King of Alcatraz; Tip-Off Girls; Hunted Men; Dangerous to Know; Bulldog Drummond in Africa
1937 Swing High, Swing Low; Partners in Crime; Daughter of Shanghai; The Last Train from Madrid; Waikiki Wedding

1936 The Milky Way; The Plainsman; Night Waitress; Sworn Enemy; Parole

George Raft
(Sept. 26, 1895–1980)
1980 The Man with Bogart's Face
1978 Sextette
1972 Hammersmith Is Out
1971 Deadhead Miles
1968 Madigan's Millions; Skidoo
1967 Five Golden Dragons; Casino Royale
1966 The Upper Hand
1964 The Patsy; For Those Who Think Young
1962 The Ladies' Man
1960 Ocean's Eleven
1959 Jet over the Atlantic; Some Like It Hot
1956 Around the World in 80 Days
1955 A Bullet for Joey
1954 The Man from Cairo; Rogue Cop; Black Widow
1953 I'll Get You; Loan Shark
1952 Man Bait
1951 Lucky Nick Cain
1949 A Dangerous Profession; Johnny Allegro; Red Light; Outpost in Morocco
1948 Race Street
1947 Christmas Eve; Intrigue
1946 Whistle Stop; Nocturne; Mr. Ace
1945 Johnny Angel; Nob Hill
1944 Follow the Boys
1943 Background to Danger; Stage Door Canteen
1942 Broadway
1941 Manpower
1940 They Drive By Night; Invisible Stripes
1939 The House Across the Bay; The Lady's from Kentucky; Each Dawn I Die; I Stole a Million
1938 Spawn of the North; You and Me
1937 Souls at Sea
1936 Yours for the Asking; It Had to Happen
1935 Every Night at Eight; Rumba; She Couldn't Take It; Stolen Harmony; The Glass Key
1934 Bolero; All of Me; Limehouse Blues; The Trumpet Blows
1933 The Bowery; Pick-Up; Midnight Club
1932 Madame Racketeer; Taxi!; Love Is a Racket; Under Cover Man; Dancers in the Dark; Winner Take All; Night World; If I Had a Million; Scarface; Night After Night
1931 Quick Millions; Palmy Days; Hush Money; Goldie
1929 Queen of the Nightclubs

Basil Rathbone
(June 13, 1892–1967)
1967 Hillbillies in a Haunted House
1966 Planet of Blood; The Ghost in the Invisible Bikini; Voyage to a Prehistoric Planet
1963 The Comedy of Terrors
1962 The Magic Sword; A Christmas Carol; Two Before Zero; Tales of Terror

1958 The Last Hurrah
1956 The Court Jester; The Black Sleep
1955 We're No Angels
1954 Casanova's Big Night
1949 The Adventures of Ichabod and Mr. Toad
1946 Terror by Night; Dressed to Kill; Heartbeat
1945 Pursuit to Algiers; The Woman in Green; The House of Fear
1944 Bathing Beauty; The Spider Woman; The Pearl of Death; Frenchman's Creek; The Scarlet Claw; Sherlock Holmes Faces Death; Above Suspicion; Sherlock Holmes in Washington; Sherlock Holmes and the Secret Weapon; Crazy House
1942 Sherlock Holmes and the Voice of Terror; Crossroads; Fingers at the Window; Paris Calling
1941 The Black Cat; International Lady; The Mad Doctor
1940 The Mark of Zorro; Rhythm on the River
1939 The Adventures of Sherlock Holmes; The Hound of the Baskervilles; The Tower of London; Son of Frankenstein; Sherlock Holmes Double Feature; Rio; The Sun Never Sets
1938 The Adventures of Marco Polo; The Dawn Patrol; If I Were King; The Adventures of Robin Hood
1937 Love from a Stranger; Make a Wish; Tovarich; Confession
1936 Romeo and Juliet; Private Number; The Garden of Allah
1935 Kind Lady; The Last Days of Pompeii; Captain Blood; A Feather in Her Hat; Anna Karenina; A Tale of Two Cities; House of Menace; David Copperfield
1933 Loyalties; One Precious Year
1932 A Woman Commands
1930 The Bishop Murder Case; A Lady Surrenders; The Lady of Scandal; This Mad World; The Flirting Widow; Sin Takes a Holiday; A Notorious Affair
1929 The Last of Mrs. Cheyney
1926 Great Deception
1925 Masked Bride
1924 Trouping with Ellen
1921 Innocent

Robert Redford
(Aug. 18, 1937)
1998 The Horse Whisperer
1996 Up Close and Personal
1993 Indecent Proposal
1992 Sneakers
1990 Havana
1986 Legal Eagles
1985 Out of Africa
1984 The Natural
1980 Brubaker
1979 The Electric Horseman
1977 A Bridge Too Far
1976 All the President's Men
1975 Three Days of the Condor; The Great Waldo Pepper
1974 The Great Gatsby

1973 The Sting; The Way We Were
1972 The Hot Rock; The Candidate; Jeremiah Johnson
1970 Little Fauss and Big Halsy
1969 Downhill Racer; Butch Cassidy and the Sundance Kid; Tell Them Willie Boy Is Here
1967 Barefoot in the Park
1966 The Chase; This Property Is Condemned
1965 Situation Hopeless But Not Serious; Inside Daisy Clover
1962 War Hunt

Burt Reynolds
(Feb. 11, 1936)
1997 Meet Wally Sparks; Bean; Boogie Nights
1996 Striptease; Mad Dog Time; Citizen Ruth; The Maddening
1993 Cop and a Half
1992 The Player
1990 Modern Love
1989 Physical Evidence; Breaking in; All Dogs Go to Heaven
1988 Switching Channels; Rent-a-Cop
1987 Heat; Malone
1985 Stick
1984 Cannonball Run II; City Heat
1983 Smokey and the Bandit 3; Stroker Ace; The Man Who Loved Women
1982 Best Friends; The Best Little Whorehouse in Texas
1981 Sharky's Machine; Paternity; The Cannonball Run
1980 Rough Cut; Smokey and the Bandit II
1979 Starting Over
1978 Hooper; The End
1977 Semi-Tough; Smokey and the Bandit
1976 Nickelodeon; Silent Movie; Gator
1975 Hustle; Lucky Lady; W. W. and the Dixie Dancekings; At Long Last Love
1974 The Longest Yard
1973 The Man Who Loved Cat Dancing; White Lightning; Shamus
1972 Deliverance; Everything You Always Wanted to Know About Sex, but Were Afraid to Ask; Fuzz
1970 Skullduggery
1969 Impasse; Sam Whiskey; Shark!; 100 Rifles
1968 Fade-In
1967 Navajo Joe
1965 Operation C.I.A.
1961 Angel Baby; Armored Command

Debbie Reynolds
(Apr. 1, 1932)
1997 In & Out
1996 Wedding Bell Blues; Mother
1994 That's Entertainment! Part 3
1993 Heaven and Earth
1992 The Bodyguard
1984 That's Singing: The Best of Broadway
1974 That's Entertainment!
1973 Charlotte's Web

1971 What's the Matter with Helen?
1967 Divorce American Style
1966 The Singing Nun
1964 The Unsinkable Molly Brown; Goodbye Charlie
1963 Mary Mary; My Six Loves
1962 How the West Was Won
1961 The Pleasure of His Company; The Second Time Around
1960 Pepe; The Rat Race
1959 It Started with a Kiss; The Gazebo; The Mating Game; Say One for Me
1958 This Happy Feeling
1957 Tammy and the Bachelor
1956 Meet Me in Las Vegas; Bundle of Joy; The Catered Affair
1955 The Tender Trap; Hit the Deck
1954 Susan Slept Here; Athena
1953 I Love Melvin; Give a Girl a Break; The Affairs of Dobie Gillis
1952 Skirts Ahoy!; Singin' in the Rain
1951 Mr. Imperium
1950 Two Weeks with Love; Three Little Words; The Daughter of Rosie O'Grady
1948 June Bride

Jason Robards, Jr.
(July 22, 1922)
1998 Heartwood
1997 A Thousand Acres
1994 The Paper; Little Big League
1993 The Adventures of Huck Finn; The Trial; Philadelphia
1992 Jonah and the Whale; Lincoln; Storyville
1991 Pure Luck
1990 Quick Change
1989 Parenthood; Dream a Little Dream
1988 The Good Mother; Bright Lights, Big City
1987 Square Dance
1983 Something Wicked This Way Comes; Max Dugan Returns
1982 Burden of Dreams
1981 The Legend of the Lone Ranger; Cabolblanco
1980 Melvin and Howard; Raise the Titanic
1979 Hurricane
1978 Comes a Horseman
1977 Julia
1976 All the President's Men
1975 A Boy and His Dog
1974 Mr. Sycamore
1973 Pat Garrett and Billy the Kid
1972 The War Between Men and Women
1971 Murders in the Rue Morgue; Johnny Got His Gun
1970 Tora! Tora! Tora!; Operation Snafu; Fools; Julius Caesar; The Ballad of Cable Hogue
1968 Isadora; Once Upon a Time in the West; The Night They Raided Minsky's
1967 Hour of the Gun; The St. Valentine's Day Massacre; Divorce American Style
1966 A Big Hand for the Little Lady; Any Wednesday
1965 A Thousand Clowns
1964 Act One

1962 Long Day's Journey into Night
1961 By Love Possessed; Tender Is the Night
1959 The Journey

Paul Robeson
(April 9, 1898–1976)
1942 Native Land; Tales of Manhattan
1941 The Proud Valley
1937 King Solomon's Mines; Big Fella; Jericho
1936 Song of Freedom; Show Boat
1935 Sanders of the River
1933 The Emperor Jones
1925 Body and Soul

Edward G. Robinson
(Dec. 12, 1893–1973)
1973 Soylent Green
1970 Song of Norway
1969 MacKenna's Gold
1968 Never a Dull Moment; The Biggest Bundle of Them All
1965 The Cincinnati Kid
1964 Robin and the Seven Hoods; Good Neighbor Sam; The Outrage; Cheyenne Autumn
1963 The Prize; A Boy Ten Feet Tall
1962 My Geisha; Two Weeks in Another Town
1960 Seven Thieves; Pepe
1959 The Hole in the Head
1956 The Ten Commandments; Nightmare
1955 The Violent Men; Tight Spot; Black Tuesday; Illegal; A Bullet for Joey; Hell on Frisco Bay
1953 The Big Leaguer; The Glass Web; Vice Squad
1952 Actors and Sin
1950 Operation X
1949 It's a Great Feeling; House of Strangers
1948 Key Largo; All My Sons; Night Has a Thousand Eyes
1947 The Red House
1946 The Stranger; Journey Together
1945 Our Vines Have Tender Grapes; Scarlet Street; The Woman in the Window
1944 Mister Winkle Goes to War; Double Indemnity; Tampico
1943 Flesh and Fantasy; Destroyer
1942 Larceny, Inc.; Tales of Manhattan
1941 Manpower; The Sea Wolf; Unholy Partners
1940 A Dispatch from Reuters; Dr. Ehrlich's Magic Bullet; Brother Orchid
1939 Blackmail; Confessions of a Nazi Spy
1938 I Am the Law; A Slight Case of Murder; The Amazing Dr. Clitterhouse
1937 The Last Gangster; Kid Galahad; Thunder in the City
1936 Bullets or Ballets
1935 The Whole Town's Talking; The Barbary Coast
1934 The Man with Two Faces; Dark Hazard
1933 I Loved a Woman; The Little Giant
1932 Tiger Shark; Two Seconds; Silver Dollar; The Hatchet Man
1931 Smart Money; Five Star Final
1930 Outside the Law; The Widow from Chicago; East Is West; Little Caesar; A Lady to Love; Night Ride
1929 The Hole in the Wall
1923 Bright Shawl

Ginger Rogers
(July 16, 1911–1995)
1965 Harlow
1964 Quick, Let's Get Married
1957 Oh, Men! Oh, Women!
1956 The First Traveling Saleslady; Teenage Rebel
1955 Tight Spot
1954 Black Widow; Twist of Fate
1953 Forever Female
1952 Monkey Business; We're Not Married; Dreamboat
1951 The Groom Wore Spurs
1950 Storm Warning; Perfect Strangers
1949 The Barkleys of Broadway
1947 It Had to Be You
1946 Heartbeat; Magnificent Doll
1945 Weekend at the Waldorf
1944 I'll Be Seeing You; The Lady in the Dark
1943 Tender Comrade
1942 Once Upon a Honeymoon; The Major and the Minor; Roxie Hart; Tales of Manhattan
1941 Tom, Dick and Harry
1940 The Primrose Path; Lucky Partners; Kitty Foyle
1939 Fifth Avenue Girl; The Story of Vernon and Irene Castle; Bachelor Mother
1938 Vivacious Lady; Having Wonderful Time; Carefree
1937 Stage Door; Shall We Dance?
1936 Follow the Fleet; Swing Time
1935 Roberta; Star of Midnight; Top Hat; In Person
1934 Romance in Manhattan; Rafter Romance; Change of Heart; Twenty Million Sweethearts; Upper World; The Gay Divorcee; Finishing School
1933 42nd Street; Flying Down to Rio; Professional Sweetheart; Chance at Heaven; Sitting Pretty; Don't Bet on Love; Broadway Bad; Gold Diggers of 1933; A Shriek in the Night; Carnival Boat
1932 The Thirteenth Guest; Hat Check Girl; The Tenderfoot; You Said a Mouthful
1931 Honor Among Lovers; The Tip-Off; Suicide Fleet
1930 Young Man of Manhattan; The Sap from Syracuse; Queen High; Follow the Leader

Mickey Rooney
(Sept. 23, 1920)
1998 Animals (and the Tollkeeper); Babe II: Pig in the City
1994 Revenge of the Red Baron
1992 The Legend of Wolf Mountain; Little Nemo: Adventures in Slumberland; Sweet Justice
1991 My Heroes Have Always Been Cowboys; Silent Night, Deadly Night 5: The Toymaker
1989 Erik the Viking
1986 Lightning: The White Stallion
1985 The Care Bears Movie
1981 The Fox and the Hound
1980 Honeysuckle Rose
1979 The Black Stallion; Arabian Adventure
1977 The Magic of Lassie; Pete's Dragon; The Domino Principle
1975 Find the Lady
1974 Ace of Hearts
1972 Pulp; Richard
1971 B.J. Presents; Journey Back to Oz
1970 Santa Claus Is Coming to Town; Hollywood Blue
1969 The Comic; 80 Steps to Jonah; The Extraordinary Seaman; A Woman for Charlie
1968 Skidoo
1966 Ambush Bay; 24 Hours to Kill
1965 How to Stuff a Wild Bikini
1964 The Secret Invasion
1963 It's a Mad, Mad, Mad, Mad World
1962 Requiem for a Heavyweight
1961 King of the Roaring Twenties: The Story of Arnold Rothstein; Breakfast at Tiffany's; Everything's Ducky
1960 The Private Lives of Adam and Eve; Platinum High School
1959 The Big Operator; The Last Mile
1958 A Nice Little Bank That Should Be Robbed; Andy Hardy Comes Home
1957 Baby Face Nelson; Operation Mad Ball
1956 The Bold and the Brave; Francis in the Haunted House; The Magnificent Roughnecks; Jaguar
1955 The Twinkle in God's Eye; The Bridges at Toko-Ri
1954 Drive a Crooked Road; The Atomic Kid
1953 All Ashore; Off Limits; A Slight Case of Larceny
1952 Sound Off
1951 The Strip; My Outlaw Brother; Guilty of Treason
1950 He's a Cockeyed Wonder; Quicksand; The Fireball
1949 The Big Wheel; The Sun Comes Up
1948 Summer Holiday; Rusty Leads the Way; Words and Music
1947 Killer McCoy
1946 Love Laughs at Andy Hardy
1944 Andy Hardy's Blonde Trouble; National Velvet
1943 Girl Crazy; Thousands Cheer; The Human Comedy; Show Business at War
1942 The Courtship of Andy Hardy; Andy Hardy's Double Life; A Yank at Eton
1941 Babes on Broadway; Men of Boys Town; Life Begins

for Andy Hardy; Andy Hardy's Private Secretary
1940 Strike Up the Band; Young Tom Edison; Andy Hardy Meets Debutante
1939 The Hardys Ride High; Andy Hardy Gets Spring Fever; Babes in Arms; Judge Hardy and Son; Mickey the Great; The Adventures of Huckleberry Finn
1938 Judge Hardy's Children; Out West with the Hardys; Stablemates; You're Only Young Once; Lord Jeff; Boys Town; Hold That Kiss; Love Finds Andy Hardy; Love Is a Headache
1937 Slave Ship; Thoroughbreds Don't Cry; A Family Affair; Live, Love and Learn; Captains Courageous; Hoosier Schoolboy
1936 The Devil Is a Sissy; Little Lord Fauntleroy; The Healer; Down the Stretch
1935 Reckless; The County Chairman; Ah, Wilderness!; A Midsummer Night's Dream; Riff Raff
1934 Death on the Diamond; Love Birds; Beloved; Blind Date; Half a Sinner; Chained; Hide-Out; Upper World; The Lost Jungle; I Like It That Way
1933 The Big Chance; The World Changes; The Life of Jimmy Dolan; The Chief; Broadway to Hollywood; The Big Cage
1932 Fast Companions; Emma; The Beast of the City; High Speed; Sin's Payday; My Pal, the King
1930 Those Darn Kids
1927 Orchids and Ermine

Jane Russell
(June 21, 1921)
1970 Darker Than Amber
1967 The Born Losers
1966 Johnny Reno; Waco
1964 Fate Is the Hunter
1957 The Fuzzy Pink Nightgown
1956 Hot Blood; The Revolt of Mamie Stover
1955 The Tall Men; Underwater!; Foxfire; Gentlemen Marry Brunettes
1954 The French Line
1953 Gentlemen Prefer Blondes; Road to Bali
1952 Montana Belle; Son of Paleface; Macao; The Las Vegas Story
1951 Double Dynamite; His Kind of Woman
1948 The Paleface
1946 Young Widow
1943 The Outlaw

Rosalind Russell
(June 4, 1908–1976)
1971 Mrs. Pollifax—Spy
1968 Where Angels Go, Trouble Follows
1967 Oh Dad, Poor Dad, Mama's Hung You in the Closet and I'm Feelin' So Sad; Rosie!
1966 The Trouble with Angels

1962 Gypsy; Five Finger Exercise
1961 A Majority of One
1958 Auntie Mame
1956 The Feminine Touch
1955 The Girl Rush; Picnic
1952 Never Wave at a Wac
1950 A Woman of Distinction
1949 Tell It to the Judge
1948 The Velvet Touch
1947 The Guilt of Janet Ames; Mourning Becomes Electra
1946 Sister Kenny
1945 Roughly Speaking; She Wouldn't Say Yes
1943 Flight for Freedom; What a Woman!
1942 My Sister Eileen; Take a Letter, Darling
1941 The Feminine Touch; Design for Scandal; This Thing Called Love; They Met in Bombay
1940 Hired Wife; His Girl Friday; No Time for Comedy
1939 The Women; Fast and Loose
1938 Man-Proof; Four's a Crowd; The Citadel
1937 Night Must Fall; Live, Love and Learn
1936 Craig's Wife; It Had to Happen; Trouble for Two; Under Two Flags
1935 The Casino Murder Case; Rendezvous; China Seas; West Point of the Air; Reckless; The Night Is Young
1934 Forsaking All Others; The President Vanishes; Evelyn Prentice

Susan Sarandon
(Oct. 4, 1946)
1998 Twilight; Illuminata; Stepmom
1996 James and the Giant Peach
1995 Dead Man Walking; The Celluloid Closet
1994 The Client; Little Women; Safe Passage
1992 Lorenzo's Oil; Light Sleeper; The Player; Bob Roberts
1991 Thelma & Louise
1990 White Palace
1989 A Dry White Season; The January Man
1988 Sweet Hearts Dance; Bull Durham
1987 The Witches of Eastwick
1985 Compromising Positions
1984 The Buddy System
1983 The Hunger
1982 Tempest
1980 Loving Couples; Atlantic City
1979 Something Short of Paradise
1978 Pretty Baby; King of the Gypsies
1977 The Other Side of Midnight
1976 Checkered Flag or Crash; Dragonfly; The Great Smokey Roadblock
1975 The Great Waldo Pepper; The Rocky Horror Picture Show
1974 The Front Page; Lovin' Molly
1972 Lady Liberty
1970 Joe

George C. Scott
(Oct. 18, 1926)
1995 Angus

1993 Malice
1990 The Rescuers Down Under; The Exorcist 3
1984 Firestarter
1983 The Indomitable Teddy Roosevelt
1981 Taps
1980 The Formula; The Changeling
1979 Hardcore
1978 Movie, Movie
1977 The Prince and the Pauper; Islands in the Stream
1975 The Hindenburg
1974 The Savage Is Loose; Bank Shot
1973 Oklahoma Crude; The Day of the Dolphin
1972 Rage; The New Centurions
1971 The Hospital; The Last Run; They Might Be Giants
1970 Patton
1968 Petulia
1967 The Flim-Flam Man
1966 The Bible. . . In the Beginning; Not with My Wife, You Don't!
1965 The Yellow Rolls-Royce
1964 Dr. Strangelove or How I Learned to Stop Worrying and Love the Bomb
1963 The List of Adrian Messenger
1961 The Hustler
1959 The Hanging Tree; Anatomy of a Murder

George Segal
(Feb. 13, 1934)
1996 It's My Party; Flirting with Disaster; The Cable Guy; The Mirror Has Two Faces
1995 To Die For; The Babysitter Now
1993 Look Who's Talking Now
1994 Army of One
1992 Me, Myself and I
1991 For the Boys
1989 Look Who's Talking; All's Fair
1985 Stick
1981 Carbon Copy
1980 The Last Married Couple in America
1979 Lost and Found
1978 Who Is Killing the Great Chefs of Europe?
1977 Fun with Dick and Jane; Rollercoaster
1976 The Duchess and the Dirtwater Fox
1975 Russian Roulette; The Black Bird
1974 California Split; The Terminal Man
1973 A Touch of Class; Blume in Love
1972 The Hot Rock
1971 Born to Win
1970 Where's Poppa?; Loving; The Owl and the Pussycat
1969 The Girl Who Couldn't Say No; The Southern Star; The Bridge at Remagen
1968 Bye-Bye Braverman; No Way to Treat a Lady
1967 The St. Valentine's Day Massacre
1966 The Quiller Memorandum; The Lost Command; Who's Afraid of Virginia Woolf?
1965 Ship of Fools; King Rat
1964 The New Interns; Invitation to a Gunfighter
1963 Act One
1961 The Young Doctors

Peter Sellers
(Sept. 8, 1925–1980)
1982 The Trail of the Pink Panther
1980 The Fiendish Plot of Dr. Fu Manchu
1979 The Prisoner of Zenda; Being There
1978 The Revenge of the Pink Panther
1976 Murder by Death; The Pink Panther Strikes Again
1975 The Great McGonagall; Undercovers Hero
1974 The Return of the Pink Panther
1973 The Blockhouse; The Optimists
1972 Alice's Adventures in Wonderland; Where Does It Hurt?
1970 There's a Girl in My Soup; A Day at the Beach; Hoffman
1969 The Magic Christian
1968 The Party; I Love You, Alice B. Toklas
1967 The Bobo; Casino Royale; Woman Times Seven
1966 The Wrong Box; After the Fox
1965 What's New Pussycat?
1964 A Shot in the Dark; The World of Henry Orient; The Pink Panther; Dr. Strangelove or How I Learned to Stop Worrying and Love the Bomb
1963 The Wrong Arm of the Law; Heavens Above!
1962 Lolita; Waltz of the Toreadors; The Road to Hong Kong; Only Two Can Play; The Dock Brief
1961 I Like Money
1960 The Millionairess; The Battle of the Sexes; Two-Way Stretch; Never Let Go
1959 The Mouse That Roared; Carlton Browne of the F.O.; I'm All Right Jack
1958 Up the Creek; Your Past Is Showing; Tom Thumb
1957 John and Julie; The Smallest Show on Earth; The Man Who Never Was
1955 The Ladykillers
1954 Orders Are Orders
1952 Down Among the Z Men
1951 Penny Points to Paradise

Norma Shearer
(Aug. 10, 1900–1983)
1942 Her Cardboard Lover; We Were Dancing
1940 Escape
1939 Idiot's Delight; The Women
1938 Marie Antoinette
1936 Romeo and Juliet
1934 The Barretts of Wimpole Street; Riptide
1932 Smilin' Through
1931 A Free Soul; Private Lives; Strangers May Kiss
1930 Let Us Be Gay; The Divorcee
1929 The Last of Mrs. Cheyney; Their Own Desire; The Trial of Mary Dugan; The Hollywood Revue of 1929
1928 The Actress; A Lady of Chance; The Latest from Paris
1927 After Midnight; Demi Bride; The Student Prince

1926 Devil's Circus; The Waning Sex
1925 Pretty Ladies; His Secretary; Slave of Fashion; Excuse Me; The Tower of Lies; Lady of the Night; Waking Up the Town
1924 He Who Gets Slapped; Broken Barriers; The Snob; Broadway After Dark; Trail of the Law; Married Flirts; The Wolf Man; Empty Hands
1923 The Devil's Partner; The Wanters; Lucretia Lombard; Pleasure Mad
1922 Channing of the Northwest; The Man Who Paid
1921 The Sign on the Door
1920 Restless Sex; The Flapper; The Stealers; Way Down East

Jean Simmons
(Jan. 31, 1929)
1995 How to Make an American Quilt
1988 The Dawning
1985 Going Undercover
1984 A Moment in Time
1979 Dominique Is Dead
1974 Mr. Sycamore
1971 Say Hello to Yesterday
1969 The Happy Ending
1967 Rough Night in Jericho; Divorce American Style
1966 Mister Buddwing
1965 Life at the Top
1963 All the Way Home
1960 The Grass Is Greener; Spartacus; Elmer Gantry
1959 This Earth Is Mine
1958 Home Before Dark; The Big Country
1957 This Could Be the Night; Until They Sail
1956 Hilda Crane
1955 Footsteps in the Fog; Guys and Dolls
1954 Desiree; A Bullet Is Waiting; The Egyptian
1953 The Actress; Affair with a Stranger; Young Bess; The Robe; Angel Face
1952 She Couldn't Say No; Androcles and the Lion
1951 So Long at the Fair
1950 The Clouded Yellow; Cage of Gold; Trio
1949 Adam and Evelyn; The Blue Lagoon
1948 Hamlet
1947 The Woman in the Hall; The Inheritance; Black Narcissus
1946 Great Expectations; Hungry Hill; Caesar and Cleopatra
1945 The Way to the Stars
1944 Kiss the Bride Goodbye; Mr. Emmanuel; Meet Sexton Blake; Give Us the Moon

Frank Sinatra
(Dec. 12, 1915–1998)
1990 Listen Up
1989 Entertaining the Troops
1984 Cannonball Run II
1980 The First Deadly Sin
1974 That's Entertainment
1970 Dirty Dingus Magee
1968 Lady in Cement; The Detective
1967 Tony Rome; The Naked Runner
1966 Assault on a Queen; The

Oscar; Cast a Giant Shadow
1965 None But the Brave; Von Ryan's Express; Marriage on the Rocks
1964 Robin and the Seven Hoods
1963 The List of Adrian Messenger; Come Blow Your Horn; 4 for Texas
1962 The Manchurian Candidate; The Road to Hong Kong; Sergeants 3
1961 The Devil at 4 O'Clock
1960 Ocean's Eleven; Pepe; Can-Can
1959 Never So Few; A Hole in the Head
1958 Some Came Running; Kings Go Forth
1957 Pal Joey; The Joker Is Wild; The Pride and the Passion
1956 High Society; Johnny Concho; Around the World in 80 Days; Meet Me in Las Vegas
1955 Guys and Dolls; The Tender Trap; The Man with the Golden Arm; Not As a Stranger
1954 Young at Heart; Suddenly; Hollywood Goes to War
1953 From Here to Eternity
1952 Meet Danny Wilson
1951 Double Dynamite
1949 Take Me Out to the Ball Game; On the Town
1948 The Kissing Bandit; The Miracle of the Bells
1947 It Happened in Brooklyn
1946 Till the Clouds Roll By
1945 The House I Live In; Anchors Aweigh
1944 Step Lively; Higher and Higher
1943 Show Business at War; Reveille with Beverly
1942 Ship Ahoy
1941 Las Vegas Nights

Barbara Stanwyck
(July 16, 1907–1990)
1964 The Night Walker; Roustabout
1962 A Walk on the Wild Side
1957 Crime of Passion; Forty Guns; Trooper Hook
1956 There's Always Tomorrow; These Wilder Years
1955 The Maverick Queen; The Violent Men; Escape to Burma
1954 Cattle Queen of Montana; Executive Suite; Witness to Murder
1953 Blowing Wild; All I Desire; Jeopardy; The Moonlighter; Titanic
1952 Clash by Night
1951 The Man with a Cloak
1950 The Furies; No Man of Her Own; To Please a Lady
1949 The File on Thelma Jordon; The Lady Gambles; East Side, West Side
1948 Sorry, Wrong Number; B.F.'s Daughter; Cry Wolf; The Two Mrs. Carrolls; The Other Love
1947 Variety Girl
1946 The Bride Wore Boots; California; The Strange Love of Martha Ivers; My Reputation
1945 Christmas in Connecticut

1944 Double Indemnity; Hollywood Canteen
1943 Flesh and Fantasy; Lady of Burlesque
1942 The Gay Sisters; The Great Man's Lady
1941 Meet John Doe; The Lady Eve; You Belong to Me; Ball of Fire
1940 Remember the Night
1939 Golden Boy; Union Pacific
1938 The Mad Miss Manton; Always Goodbye
1937 Stella Dallas; This Is My Affair; Breakfast for Two; Interns Can't Take Money
1936 A Message to Garcia; The Plough and the Stars; His Brother's Wife; The Bride Walks Out; Banjo on My Knee
1935 Red Salute; The Secret Bride; Annie Oakley; The Woman in Red
1934 A Lost Lady; Gambling Lady
1933 Ladies They Talk About; The Bitter Tea of General Yen; Ever in My Heart; Baby Face
1932 Shopworn; The Purchase Price; Forbidden; Always Goodbye; So Big
1931 Illicit; Night Nurse; Ten Cents a Dance
1930 Ladies of Leisure
1929 The Locked Door; Mexicali Rose
1927 Broadway Nights

Rod Steiger
(Apr. 14, 1925)
1998 Animals (and the Tollkeeper)
1997 Truth or Consequences, N.M.; Incognito; Shiloh
1996 Carpool; Mars Attacks!
1995 Out There; Little Surprises; Demolition Day; Op Center
1994 The Specialist; Seven Sundays; The Last Tattoo
1993 The Neighbor
1992 The Player; Guilty As Charged
1991 The Ballad of the Sad Cafe
1990 Men of Respect; That Summer of White Roses; The Twilight Murders
1989 The January Man
1988 American Gothic
1987 The Kindred; Catch the Heat
1986 The Last Contract
1984 The Naked Face
1982 The Magic Mountain
1981 Cattle Annie and Little Britches; The Chosen; Lion of the Desert
1980 The Lucky Star; Klondike Fever
1979 Wolf Lake; Love and Bullets; The Amityville Horror; Breakthrough
1978 F.I.S.T.
1977 Portrait of a Hitman
1976 W. C. Fields and Me
1975 Hennessy; Dirty Hands
1974 Mussolini: The Last Four Days
1973 Lolly Madonna XXX; Lucky Luciano; The Heroes
1972 Duck, You Sucker!
1971 Happy Birthday, Wanda June
1970 Waterloo

1969 Three Into Two Won't Go; The Illustrated Man
1968 The Sergeant; No Way to Treat a Lady
1967 In the Heat of the Night; The Girl and the General
1965 And There Came a Man; The Loved One; Doctor Zhivago; The Pawnbroker
1964 Time of Indifference
1963 Hands Over the City
1962 The World in My Pocket; The Longest Day; Convicts Four; 13 West Street
1961 On Friday at Eleven; The Mark
1960 Seven Thieves
1959 Al Capone
1958 Cry Terror
1957 The Unholy Wife; Across the Bridge; Run of the Arrow
1956 Back from Eternity; Jubal; The Harder They Fall
1955 The Big Knife; The Court Martial of Billy Mitchell; Oklahoma!
1954 On the Waterfront
1951 Teresa

James Stewart
(May 20, 1908–1997)
1991 An American Tail II
1981 Tale of Africa
1978 The Big Sleep; The Magic of Lassie
1977 Airport '77
1976 The Shootist
1974 That's Entertainment
1971 The Fool's Parade
1970 The Cheyenne Social Club
1968 Bandolero!; Firecreek
1966 The Flight of the Phoenix; The Rare Breed
1965 Dear Brigitte; Shenandoah
1964 Cheyenne Autumn
1963 Take Her She's Mine
1962 Mr. Hobbs Takes a Vacation; How the West Was Won; The Man Who Shot Liberty Valance
1961 Two Rode Together; X-15
1960 The Mountain Road
1959 Anatomy of a Murder; The FBI Story
1958 Bell, Book and Candle; Vertigo
1957 Night Passage; The Spirit of St. Louis
1956 The Man Who Knew Too Much
1955 The Far Country; The Man From Laramie; Strategic Air Command
1954 The Glenn Miller Story; Rear Window
1953 The Naked Spur; Thunder Bay
1952 Bend of the River; Carbine Williams; The Greatest Show on Earth
1951 No Highway in the Sky
1950 Broken Arrow; The Jackpot; Harvey; Malaya
1949 The Stratton Story; You Gotta Stay Happy
1948 Call Northside 777; On Our Merry Way; Rope
1947 Magic Town
1946 It's a Wonderful Life
1941 Come Live with Me; Pot o' Gold; Ziegfeld Girl
1940 The Mortal Storm; No Time for Comedy; The Philadelphia Story; The Shop Around the Corner
1939 Destry Rides Again; Ice Follies of 1939; It's a

Wonderful World; Made
for Each Other; Mr. Smith
Goes to Washington
1938 Of Human Hearts;
Vivacious Lady; The
Shopworn Angel; You
Can't Take It with You
1937 The Last Gangster; Navy
Blue and Gold; Seventh
Heaven
1936 After the Thin Man; Born
to Dance; The Gorgeous
Hussy; Next Time We
Love; Small Town Girl;
Speed; Wife vs. Secretary
1935 The Murder Man;

Meryl Streep
(Apr. 22, 1949)
1998 One True Thing
1996 Before and After;
Marvin's Room
1995 The Bridges of Madison
County
1994 The River Wild
1993 The House of the Spirits
1992 The Night Before Christmas; Death Becomes Her
1991 Defending Your Life
1990 Postcards from the Edge
1989 She-Devil
1988 A Cry in the Dark
1987 Ironweed
1986 Heartburn
1985 Plenty; Out of Africa
1984 Falling in Love
1983 Silkwood
1982 Still of the Night; Sophie's
Choice
1981 The French Lieutenant's
Woman
1979 The Seduction of Joe
Tynan; Manhattan; Kramer
vs. Kramer
1978 The Deer Hunter
1977 Julia

Barbra Streisand
(Apr. 24, 1942)
1996 The Mirror Has Two Faces
1991 The Prince of Tides
1990 Betsy's Wedding
1987 Nuts
1983 Yentl
1981 All Night Long
1979 The Main Event
1976 A Star Is Born
1975 Funny Lady
1974 For Pete's Sake
1973 The Way We Were
1972 Up the Sandbox; What's
Up, Doc?
1970 On a Clear Day You Can
See Forever; The Owl and
the Pussycat
1969 Hello, Dolly!
1968 Funny Girl

Donald Sutherland
(July 17, 1934)
1998 Fallen; Without Limits
1997 Shadow Conspiracy; The
Assignment; Natural Enemy
1996 Hollow Point; A Time to
Kill
1995 Outbreak
1994 Disclosure; Oldest Living
Confederate Widow Tells
All; The Puppet Masters
1993 Six Degrees of
Separation; Younger and
Younger; Benefit of the
Doubt
1992 Shadow of the Wolf; Buffy
the Vampire Slayer
1991 Eminent Domain; JFK;
Scream of Stone;
Backdraft

1989 Lock Up; Lost Angels;
Bethune: The Making of a
Hero; A Dry White Season
1988 Apprentice to Murder
1987 The Rosary Murders; The
Trouble with Spies; The
Wolf at the Door
1985 Revolution; Heaven Help
Us
1984 Ordeal by Innocence;
Crackers
1983 Max Dugan Returns
1981 Eye of the Needle;
Threshold;
Disappearance; Gas
1980 Nothing Personal;
Ordinary People; Bear
Island
1979 Murder by Decree; The
Great Train Robbery; A
Man, a Woman, and a
Bank
1978 Invasion of the Body
Snatchers; Animal House
1977 Disappearance; Blood
Relatives; The Kentucky
Fried Movie
1976 The Eagle Has Landed;
1900; Fellini's Casanova
1975 End of the Game; The Day
of the Locust
1974 S*P*Y*S
1973 Lady Ice; Steelyard Blues;
Alien Thunder; Don't Look
Now
1971 Johnny Got His Gun; Little
Murders; Klute
1970 The Act of the Heart;
Kelly's Heroes;
M*A*S*H; Start the
Revolution Without Me;
Alex in Wonderland
1968 Sebastian; Interlude;
Joanna; Oedipus the King;
The Split
1967 Billion Dollar Brain; The
Dirty Dozen
1966 Promise Her Anything
1965 Die! Die! My Darling!; Dr.
Terror's House of Horrors;
The Bedford Incident
1964 Castle of the Living Dead

Jessica Tandy
(June 7, 1907–1994)
1994 Nobody's Fool; Camilla
1992 Used People
1991 Fried Green Tomatoes
1989 Driving Miss Daisy
1988 The House on Carroll
Street; Cocoon: The
Return
1987 *batteries not included
1985 Cocoon
1984 The Bostonians
1982 Still of the Night; The
World According to Garp;
Best Friends
1981 Honky Tonk Freeway
1974 Butley
1963 The Birds
1962 Hemingway's Adventures
of a Young Man
1958 The Light in the Forest
1951 The Desert Fox
1950 September Affair
1947 A Woman's Vengeance;
Forever Amber
1946 Dragonwyck; The Green
Years
1945 The Valley of Decision
1944 The Seventh Cross
1938 Murder in the Family
1932 Indiscretions of Eve

Elizabeth Taylor
(Feb. 27, 1932)
1994 The Flintstones

1988 Young Toscanini
1980 The Mirror Crack'd
1979 Winter Kills
1977 A Little Night Music
1976 The Blue Bird
1974 The Driver's Seat
1973 Ash Wednesday
1972 Night Watch; X, Y and
Zee; Hammersmith Is Out
1971 Under Milk Wood
1970 The Only Game in Town
1969 Anne of the Thousand
Days
1968 Secret Ceremony; Boom!;
Doctor Faustus
1967 Reflections in a Golden
Eye; The Taming of the
Shrew; The Comedians
1966 Who's Afraid of Virginia
Woolf?
1965 The Sandpiper; The Love
Goddesses
1963 The V.I.P.s; Cleopatra
1960 Scent of Mystery;
Butterfield 8
1959 Suddenly Last Summer
1958 Cat on a Hot Tin Roof
1957 Raintree County
1956 Giant
1954 The Last Time I Saw Paris;
Rhapsody; Elephant Walk;
Beau Brummell
1953 The Girl Who Had
Everything
1952 Love Is Better Than Ever;
Ivanhoe
1951 Callaway Went Thataway;
A Place in the Sun; Quo
Vadis?; Father's Little
Dividend
1950 Father of the Bride; The
Big Hangover
1949 Conspirator; Little Women
1948 Julia Misbehaves; A Date
with Judy
1947 Cynthia; Life with Father
1946 Courage of Lassie
1944 The White Cliffs of Dover;
National Velvet; Jane Eyre
1943 Lassie Come Home
1942 There's One Born Every
Minute

Robert Taylor
(Aug. 5, 1911–1969)
1968 Where Angels Go, Trouble
Follows; The Day the
Hotline Got Hot
1967 The Glass Sphinx
1966 Savage Pampas; Johnny
Tiger
1964 The Night Walker; A House
Is Not a Home
1963 Miracle of the White
Stallions; Cattle King
1960 Killers of Kilimanjaro
1959 The Hangman; The House
of the Seven Hawks
1958 The Law and Jake Wade;
Party Girl; Saddle the
Wind
1957 Tip on a Dead Jockey
1956 The Last Hunt; The Power
and the Prize; D-Day, the
Sixth of June
1955 Many Rivers to Cross;
Quentin Durward
1954 Rogue Cop; Valley of the
Kings
1953 Knights of the Round
Table; I Love Melvin; All
the Brothers Were Valiant;
Ride, Vaquero; Above and
Beyond
1952 Ivanhoe
1951 Quo Vadis?; Westward the
Women
1950 Devil's Doorway

1949 The Bribe; Ambush;
Conspirator
1947 The High Wall
1946 Undercurrent
1943 Song of Russia; The
Youngest Profession;
Bataan
1942 Stand By for Action; Her
Cardboard Lover;
1941 Johnny Eager; Billy the
Kid; When Ladies Meet
1940 Escape; Flight Command;
Waterloo Bridge
1939 Stand Up and Fight;
Remember?; Lucky Night;
Lady of the Tropics
1938 The Crowd Roars; A Yank
at Oxford; Three Comrades
1937 This Is My Affair;
Broadway Melody of 1938;
Personal Property
1936 Small Town Girl; Private
Number; His Brother's
Wife; The Gorgeous
Hussy; Camille
1935 Buried Loot; Society
Doctor; Broadway Melody
of 1936; Magnificent
Obsession; West Point of
the Air; Times Square
Lady; Murder in the Fleet
1934 A Wicked Woman; There's
Always Tomorrow; Handy
Andy

Shirley Temple
(Apr. 23, 1928)
1949 The Story of Seabiscuit;
Adventure in Baltimore;
Mr. Belvedere Goes to
College; A Kiss for Corliss
1948 Fort Apache
1947 The Bachelor and the
Bobby-Soxer; Honeymoon;
That Hagen Girl
1945 Kiss and Tell
1944 Since You Went Away; I'll
Be Seeing You
1942 Miss Annie Rooney
1941 Kathleen
1940 The Blue Bird; Young
People
1939 Susannah of the
Mounties; The Little
Princess
1938 Rebecca of Sunnybrook
Farm; Just Around the
Corner; Little Miss
Broadway
1937 Wee Willie Winkle; Heidi
1936 Stowaway; Dimples;
Captain January; Poor
Little Rich Girl
1935 The Little Colonel; Our
Little Girl; Curly Top; The
Littlest Rebel
1934 Carolina; Change of
Heart; Baby, Take a Bow;
Stand Up and Cheer;
Mandalay; Bright Eyes;
Now and Forever; Now I'll
Tell; Little Miss Marker
1933 To the Last Man; Out All
Night
1932 The Red-Haired Alibi; Glad
Rags to Riches

Gene Tierney
(Nov. 20, 1920–1991)
1964 The Pleasure Seekers
1963 Toys in the Attic
1962 Advise and Consent
1955 The Left Hand of God
1954 Personal Affair; Black
Widow; The Egyptian
1953 Never Let Me Go
1952 The Plymouth Adventure;
Way of a Gaucho

1951 The Mating Season; Close to My Heart; The Secret of Convict Lake; On the Riviera
1950 Night and the City; Where the Sidewalk Ends
1949 Whirlpool
1948 The Iron Curtain; That Wonderful Urge
1947 The Ghost and Mrs. Muir
1946 Dragonwyck; The Razor's Edge
1945 A Bell for Adano; Leave Her to Heaven
1944 Laura
1943 Heaven Can Wait
1942 Thunder Birds; The Shanghai Gesture; Son of Fury; Rings on Her Fingers; China Girl
1941 Belle Starr; Tobacco Road; Sundown
1940 The Return of Frank James; Hudson's Bay

Spencer Tracy
(Apr. 5, 1900–1967)
1967 Guess Who's Coming to Dinner
1963 It's a Mad, Mad, Mad, Mad World
1962 How the West Was Won
1961 Judgment at Nuremberg; The Devil at 4 O'clock
1960 Inherit the Wind
1958 The Last Hurrah; The Old Man and the Sea
1957 Desk Set
1956 The Mountain
1955 Bad Day at Black Rock
1954 Broken Lance
1953 The Actress
1952 Pat and Mike; The Plymouth Adventure
1951 Father's Little Dividend; The People Against O'Hara
1950 Father of the Bride; Malaya
1949 Adam's Rib; Edward, My Son
1948 State of the Union
1947 Cass Timberlane; The Sea of Grass
1945 Without Love
1944 The Seventh Cross; Thirty Seconds over Tokyo
1943 A Guy Named Joe
1942 Tortilla Flat; Woman of the Year; Keeper of the Flame
1941 Dr. Jekyll and Mr. Hyde; Men of Boys Town
1940 Northwest Passage; Boom Town; I Take This Woman; Edison the Man
1939 Stanley and Livingstone
1938 Boys Town; Test Pilot
1937 The Big City; Captains Courageous; Mannequin; They Gave Him a Gun
1936 Libeled Lady; Fury; San Francisco
1935 Vᵢⱼⱼpsaw; The Murder Man; Dante's Inferno; Riff Raff; It's a Small World
1934 Looking for Trouble; Now I'll Tell; Bottoms Up; The Show-Off; Marie Galante
1933 The Mad Game; Shanghai Madness; The Face in the Sky; 20,000 Years in Sing Sing; A Man's Castle; The Power and the Glory
1932 Sky Devils; Society Girl; She Wanted a Millionaire; Young America; Painted Woman; Me and My Gal; Disorderly Conduct

1931 Quick Millions; Six Cylinder Love; Goldie
1930 Up the River

John Travolta
(Feb. 18, 1954)
1998 Primary Colors
1997 Face/Off; She's So Lovely; Mad City; Get Shorty
1996 Broken Arrow; Phenomenon; Michael
1995 White Man's Burden
1994 Pulp Fiction
1993 Look Who's Talking Now
1991 Shout; Boris and Natasha
1990 Look Who's Talking Too
1989 Look Who's Talking; The Experts
1985 Perfect
1983 Staying Alive; Two of a Kind
1981 Blow Out
1980 Urban Cowboy
1978 Moment by Moment; Grease
1977 Saturday Night Fever
1976 Carrie
1975 The Devil's Rain

Lana Turner
(Feb. 8, 1920)
1979 Witches' Brew
1976 Bittersweet Love
1974 Persecution
1969 The Big Cube
1966 Madame X
1965 Love Has Many Faces
1963 Who's Got the Action?
1961 Bachelor in Paradise; By Love Possessed
1960 Portrait in Black
1959 Imitation of Life
1958 Another Time, Another Place; The Lady Takes a Flyer
1957 Peyton Place
1956 Diane
1955 The Prodigal; The Sea Chase; The Rains of Ranchipur
1954 Betrayed; The Flame and the Flesh
1953 Latin Lovers
1952 The Bad and the Beautiful; The Merry Widow
1951 Mr. Imperium
1950 A Life of Her Own
1948 The Three Musketeers; Homecoming
1947 Cass Timberlane; Green Dolphin Street
1946 The Postman Always Rings Twice
1945 Weekend at the Waldorf; Keep Your Powder Dry
1944 Marriage Is a Private Affair
1943 Du Barry Was a Lady; Slightly Dangerous; The Youngest Profession
1942 Johnny Eager; Somewhere I'll Find You
1941 Honky Tonk; Ziegfeld Girl; Dr. Jekyll and Mr. Hyde
1940 Two Girls on Broadway; We Who Are Young
1939 Dancing Co-Ed; Calling Dr. Kildare; These Glamour Girls
1938 Love Finds Andy Hardy; Rich Man, Poor Girl; The Chaser; Dramatic School; Four's a Crowd; The Adventures of Marco Polo
1937 The Great Garrick; A Star Is Born; They Won't Forget

John Wayne
(May 26, 1907–1979)
1976 The Shootist
1975 Rooster Cogburn; Brannigan
1974 McQ
1973 The Train Robbers; Cahill: United States Marshal
1972 The Cowboys; Cancel My Reservation
1971 Big Jake
1970 Rio Lobo; Chisum
1969 True Grit; The Undefeated; Hellfighters
1968 The Green Berets
1967 The War Wagon; El Dorado
1966 Cast a Giant Shadow
1965 The Greatest Story Ever Told; In Harm's Way; The Sons of Katie Elder
1964 Circus World
1963 Donovan's Reef; McLintock!
1962 Hatari!; How the West Was Won; The Longest Day; The Man Who Shot Liberty Valance
1961 The Comancheros
1960 North to Alaska; The Alamo
1959 The Horse Soldiers; Rio Bravo
1958 The Barbarian and the Geisha; I Married a Woman
1957 Jet Pilot; Legend of the Lost; The Wings of Eagles
1956 The Searchers; The Conqueror
1955 Blood Alley; The Sea Chase
1954 The High and the Mighty
1953 Trouble Along the Way; Hondo; Island in the Sky
1952 The Quiet Man; Big Jim McLain
1951 Operation Pacific; Flying Leathernecks; The Bullfighter and the Lady
1950 Rio Grande
1949 Sands of Iwo Jima; She Wore a Yellow Ribbon; The Fighting Kentuckian; The Three Godfathers
1948 Red River; Fort Apache; Wake of the Red Witch
1947 Angel and the Badman; Tycoon
1946 Without Reservations
1945 Dakota; Back to Bataan; They Were Expendable; Flame of the Barbary Coast
1944 The Fighting Seabees; Tall in the Saddle
1943 A Lady Takes a Chance; In Old Oklahoma
1942 Reap the Wild Wind; Lady for a Night; The Flying Tigers; The Spoilers; In Old California; Reunion in France; Pittsburgh
1941 Lady from New Orleans; The Shepherd of the Hills; Wheel of Fortune
1940 The Three Faces West; The Dark Command; The Long Voyage Home; Seven Sinners
1939 Three Texas Steers; Allegheny Uprising; Wyoming Outlaw; The Night Riders; Stagecoach; New Frontier
1938 Santa Fe Stampede; Pals of the Saddle; Red River Range; Overland Stage Raiders

1937 Conflict; Hell Town; Adventure's End; California Straight Ahead; I Cover the War; Idol of the Crowds
1936 Winds of the Wasteland; King of the Pecos; The Lonely Trail; The Lawless Nineties; The Sea Spoilers; The Oregon Trail
1935 Paradise Canyon; Westward Ho; Rainbow Valley; The Dawn Rider; Lawless Range; The Desert Trail; Texas Terror
1934 The New Frontier; The Lawless Frontier; The Trail Beyond; Randy Rides Alone; The Man from Utah; The Star Packer; The Lucky Texan; West of the Divide; 'Neath the Arizona Skies; Blue Steel
1933 Central Airport; College Coach; The Life of Jimmy Dolan; The Man from Monterey; Sagebrush Trail; Somewhere in Sonora; The Telegraph Trail; His Private Secretary; Riders of Destiny; Baby Face; The Three Musketeers *(serial)*
1932 Lady and Gent; Texas Cyclone; Ride Him, Cowboy; The Big Stampede; That's My Boy; Haunted Gold; The Hollywood Handicap; The Hurricane Express; Two-Fisted Law; The Shadow of the Eagle
1931 The Range Feud; Girls Demand Excitement; The Deceiver; Three Girls Lost; Arizona; Maker of Men
1930 Rough Romance; Born Reckless; Cheer Up and Smile; The Big Trail; Men Without Women
1929 The Black Watch; Words and Music; Salute; Speakeasy; The Forward Pass
1928 Noah's Ark; Hangman's House; Four Sons; Mother Machree
1927 Annie Laurie; The Dropkick

Orson Welles
(May 6, 1915—1985)
1987 Someone to Love
1985 The Greenstone
1984 Slapstick of Another Kind; Where Is Parsifal?
1981 The History of the World— Part I; Butterfly
1979 The Muppet Movie; Tesla; The Double McGuffin
1976 Voyage of the Damned
1975 Ten Little Indians
1972 Treasure Island; Necromancy; Get to Know Your Rabbit; Malpertius; The Canterbury Tales
1971 Ten Days' Wonder; A Safe Place
1970 Catch-22; Waterloo; The Kremlin Letter; Start the Revolution Without Me; 12 Plus 1
1969 The Southern Star; Battle of Neretva
1968 House of Cards; The Last Roman; Oedipus the King; Tepepa
1967 I'll Never Forget What's 'is

Name; The Sailor from Gibraltar; Casino Royale
1966 A Man for All Seasons; Is Paris Burning?
1965 Marco the Magnificent
1963 The V.I.P.s
1962 Lafayette
1961 The Tartars; King of Kings
1960 The Battle of Austerlitz; Crack in the Mirror; David and Goliath
1959 Compulsion; Ferry to Hong Kong
1958 Touch of Evil; The Long Hot Summer; The Roots of Heaven; The Vikings
1957 Man in the Shadow; Pay the Devil
1956 Moby Dick
1955 Mr. Arkadin; Three Cases of Murder; Napoléon
1954 Trouble in the Glen; Royal Affairs in Versailles
1952 Trent's Last Case; Othello
1951 The Little World of Don Camillo
1950 The Black Rose
1949 Prince of Foxes; Black Magic; The Third Man
1948 The Lady from Shanghai; Macbeth
1947 Monsieur Verdoux
1946 Duel in the Sun; Tomorrow Is Forever; The Stranger
1944 Follow the Boys; Jane Eyre
1943 Show Business at War
1942 Journey into Fear; The Magnificent Ambersons
1941 Citizen Kane
1940 Swiss Family Robinson
1938 Too Much Johnson
1929 Trent's Last Case

Mae West
(Aug. 17, 1892–1980)
1978 Sextette
1970 Myra Breckenridge
1943 The Heat's On
1940 My Little Chickadee
1937 Every Day's a Holiday
1936 Go West, Young Man; Klondike Annie
1935 Goin' to Town
1934 Belle of the Nineties
1933 I'm No Angel; She Done Him Wrong
1932 Night After Night

Richard Widmark
(Dec. 26, 1914)
1995 Wild Bill: Hollywood Maverick
1991 True Colors
1984 Against All Odds
1982 Final Option; Hanky Panky
1981 National Lampoon's Movie Madness
1980 Bear Island
1978 Coma; The Swarm
1977 The Perfect Killer; Twilight's Last Gleaming; The Domino Principle
1976 The Sell Out; To the Devil, a Daughter
1974 Murder on the Orient Express
1972 When the Legends Die
1970 The Moonshine War
1969 Death of a Gunfighter
1968 Madigan
1967 The Way West
1966 Alvarez Kelly
1965 The Bedford Incident
1964 Flight from Ashiya; The Long Ships; Cheyenne Autumn
1963 How the West Was Won
1961 Judgment at Nuremberg;

The Secret Ways; Two Rode Together
1960 The Alamo
1959 Warlock; The Trap
1958 The Tunnel of Love; The Law and Jake Wade
1957 Saint Joan; Time Limit
1956 The Last Wagon; Run for the Sun; Backlash
1955 A Prize of Gold; The Cobweb
1954 Hell and High Water; Garden of Evil; Broken Lance
1953 Pickup on South Street; Take the High Ground; Destination Gobi
1952 Red Skies of Montana; Don't Bother to Knock; O. Henry's Full House; My Pal Gus
1951 The Frogmen
1950 Panic in the Streets; Halls of Montezuma; No Way Out; Night and the City
1949 Down to the Sea in Ships; Slattery's Hurricane
1948 The Street with No Name; Road House; Yellow Sky
1947 Kiss of Death

Gene Wilder
(June 11, 1935)
1991 Another You
1990 Funny About Love
1989 See No Evil, Hear No Evil
1986 Haunted Honeymoon
1984 The Woman in Red
1982 Hanky Panky
1980 Stir Crazy; Sunday Lovers
1979 The Frisco Kid
1977 The World's Greatest Lover
1976 Silver Streak
1975 The Adventures of Sherlock Holmes' Smarter Brother
1974 Blazing Saddles; Young Frankenstein; Rhinoceros; The Little Prince
1972 Everything You Always Wanted to Know About Sex (But Were Afraid to Ask)
1971 Willy Wonka and the Chocolate Factory
1970 Start the Revolution Without Me; Quackser Fortune Has a Cousin in the Bronx
1968 The Producers
1967 Bonnie and Clyde

Natalie Wood
(July 20, 1938–1981)
1983 Brainstorm
1980 The Last Married Couple in America; Willie and Phil
1978 Meteor
1975 Peeper
1972 The Candidate
1969 Bob & Carol & Ted & Alice
1966 This Property Is Condemned; Penelope
1965 The Great Race; Inside Daisy Clover
1964 Sex and the Single Girl
1963 Love with the Proper Stranger
1962 Gypsy
1961 Splendor in the Grass; West Side Story
1960 All the Fine Young Cannibals
1959 Cash McCall
1958 Kings Go Forth; Marjorie Morningstar
1957 Bombers B-52
1956 A Cry in the Night; The Girl

He Left Behind; The Burning Hills; The Searchers
1955 One Desire; Rebel Without a Cause
1954 The Silver Chalice
1952 The Star; Just for You; The Rose Bowl Story
1951 Dear Brat; The Blue Veil
1950 No Sad Songs for Me; Our Very Own; Never a Dull Moment; The Jackpot
1949 Father Was a Fullback; The Green Promise
1948 Scudda-Hoo? Scudda-Hay?; Chicken Every Sunday
1947 Miracle on 34th Street; Driftwood; The Ghost and Mrs. Muir
1946 Tomorrow Is Forever; The Bride Wore Boots
1943 Happy Land

Joanne Woodward
(Feb. 27, 1930)
1993 Philadelphia
1990 Mr. and Mrs. Bridge
1987 The Glass Menagerie
1984 Harry and Son
1978 The End
1975 The Drowning Pool
1973 Summer Wishes Winter Dreams
1972 The Effect of Gamma Rays on Man-in-the-Moon Marigolds
1971 They Might Be Giants
1970 WUSA
1969 King; Winning
1968 Rachel Rachel
1966 A Big Hand for the Little Lady; A Fine Madness
1965 Signpost to Murder
1963 The Stripper; A New Kind of Love
1961 Paris Blues
1960 The Fugitive Kind; From the Terrace
1959 The Sound and the Fury
1958 Rally 'Round the Flag, Boys!; The Long Hot Summer
1957 The Three Faces of Eve; No Down Payment
1956 A Kiss Before Dying
1955 Count Three and Pray

Jane Wyman
(Jan. 4, 1914)
1995 Wild Bill: Hollywood Maverick
1969 How to Commit a Marriage
1962 Bon Voyage!
1960 Pollyanna
1959 Holiday for Lovers
1956 Miracle in the Rain
1955 All That Heaven Allows; Lucy Gallant
1954 Magnificent Obsession
1953 Let's Do It Again; So Big
1952 Just for You; The Story of Will Rogers
1951 Here Comes the Groom; The Blue Veil; Starlift; Three Guys Named Mike
1950 The Glass Menagerie; Stage Fright
1949 A Kiss in the Dark; The Lady Takes a Sailor; It's a Great Feeling
1948 Johnny Belinda
1947 Cheyenne; Magic Town
1946 Night and Day; One More Tomorrow; The Yearling
1945 The Lost Weekend
1944 The Doughgirls; Make

Your Own Bed; Crime by Night; Hollywood Canteen
1943 Princess O'Rourke
1942 Larceny, Inc.; My Favorite Spy; Footlight Serenade
1941 Honeymoon for Three; Bad Men of Missouri; The Body Disappears; You're in the Army Now
1940 Brother Rat and a Baby; My Love Came Back; Gambling on the High Seas; An Angel from Texas; Flight Angels; Tugboat Annie Sails Again
1939 Kid Nightingale; Private Detective; Tail Spin; Torchy Plays with Dynamite; The Kid from Kokomo
1938 The Spy Ring; Brother Rat; Wide Open Faces; The Crowd Roars; He Couldn't Say No; Fools for Scandal
1937 Public Wedding; Ready, Willing and Able; The Singing Marine; Slim; Smart Blonde; The King and the Chorus Girl; Mr. Dodd Takes the Air
1936 Gold Diggers of 1937; Stage Struck; Anything Goes; Cain and Mabel; My Man Godfrey; Polo Joe; King of Burlesque
1935 Stolen Harmony; All the King's Horses; Rumba
1934 College Rhythm
1933 Elmer the Great
1932 The Kid from Spain

Loretta Young
(Jan. 6, 1913)
1953 It Happens Every Thursday
1952 Because of You; Paula
1951 Half Angel; Cause for Alarm
1950 Key to the City
1949 Come to the Stable; Mother Is a Freshman
1948 Rachel and the Stranger; The Accused
1947 The Farmer's Daughter; The Bishop's Wife
1946 The Perfect Marriage; The Stranger
1945 Along Came Jones
1944 And Now Tomorrow; Ladies Courageous
1943 China; Show Business at War
1942 A Night to Remember; Bedtime Story
1941 The Lady from Cheyenne; The Men in Her Life
1940 He Stayed for Breakfast; The Doctor Takes a Wife
1939 Eternally Yours; The Story of Alexander Graham Bell; Wife, Husband and Friend
1938 Four Men and a Prayer; Kentucky; Suez; Three Blind Mice
1937 Cafe Metropole; Love Is News; Love Under Fire; Second Honeymoon; Wife, Doctor and Nurse
1936 Ladies in Love; Private Number; Ramona; Secret Interlude; The Unguarded Hour
1935 Shanghai; The Crusades; Clive of India; The Call of the Wild
1934 Caravan; Bulldog Drummond Strikes Back; The House of Rothschild;

Born to Be Bad; The White Parade
1933 Grand Slam; Employees' Entrance; A Man's Castle; Midnight Mary; She Had to Say Yes; The Devil's in Love; The Life of Jimmy Dolan; Zoo in Budapest; Heroes for Sale
1932 The Hatchet Man; Life Begins; They Call It Sin; Week-End Marriage; Play Girl
1931 The Ruling Voice; I Like Your Nerve; Three Girls Lost; Too Young to Marry; The Right of Way; Big Business Girl; Platinum Blonde; Beau Ideal
1930 Loose Ankles; The Second Floor Mystery; The Truth About Youth; Kismet; The Devil to Pay; Road to Paradise; The Man from Blankley's; Broken Dishes
1929 Scarlet Seas; The Careless Age; Fast Life; The Girl in the Glass Cage; The Forward Pass; Show of Shows; The Squall
1928 Laugh, Clown, Laugh; The Whip Woman; The Head Man; The Magnificent Flirt
1927 Naughty But Nice
1921 The Sheik

Directors

Woody Allen
(Dec. 1, 1935)
1998 Celebrity
1997 Deconstructing Harry
1996 Everyone Says I Love You
1995 Mighty Aphrodite
1994 Bullets Over Broadway
1993 Manhattan Murder Mystery
1992 Husbands and Wives; Shadows and Fog
1990 Alice
1989 Crimes and Misdemeanors; New York Stories
1988 Another Woman
1987 September; Radio Days
1986 Hannah and Her Sisters
1985 The Purple Rose of Cairo
1984 Broadway Danny Rose
1983 Zelig
1982 A Midsummer's Night Sex Comedy
1980 Stardust Memories
1979 Manhattan
1978 Interiors
1977 Annie Hall
1975 Love and Death
1973 Sleeper
1972 Everything You Always Wanted to Know About Sex (but Were Afraid to Ask)
1971 Bananas
1969 Take the Money and Run

Robert Altman
(Feb. 20, 1925)
1997 The Wild Card; The Gingerbread Man
1996 Kansas City
1994 Ready to Wear
1993 Short Cuts
1992 The Player
1990 Vincent & Theo
1988 Aria
1987 Beyond Therapy
1985 OC and Stiggs; Fool for Love
1984 Secret Honor
1983 Streamers
1982 Come Back to the Five and Dime, Jimmy Dean, Jimmy Dean
1980 Popeye
1979 A Perfect Couple; Quintet; Health
1978 A Wedding
1977 Three Women
1976 Buffalo Bill and the Indians, or Sitting Bull's History Lesson
1975 Nashville
1974 Thieves Like Us; California Split
1973 The Long Goodbye
1972 Images
1971 McCabe and Mrs. Miller
1970 M*A*S*H; Brewster McCloud
1969 That Cold Day in the Park
1968 Countdown
1957 The Delinquents; The James Dean Story

Dorothy Arzner
(Jan. 3, 1900–1975)
1943 First Comes Courage
1940 Dance, Girl, Dance
1937 The Bride Wore Red
1936 Craig's Wife
1934 Nana
1933 Christopher Strong
1932 Merrily We Go to Hell
1931 Working Girls; Honor Among Lovers
1930 Paramount on Parade; Sarah and Son; Anybody's Woman
1929 The Wild Party
1928 Manhattan Cocktail
1927 Get Your Man; Ten Modern Commandments; Fashions for Women

Busby Berkeley
(Nov. 29, 1895–1976)
1949 Take Me Out to the Ball Game
1946 Cinderella Jones
1943 The Gang's All Here
1942 For Me and My Gal
1941 Blonde Inspiration; Babes on Broadway
1940 Forty Little Mothers; Strike Up the Band
1939 Fast and Furious; Babes in Arms; They Made Me a Criminal
1938 Men Are Such Fools; Garden of the Moon; Comet Over Broadway
1937 Hollywood Hotel; The Go-Getter
1936 Stage Struck
1935 Gold Diggers of 1935; Bright Lights; I Live for Love
1933 She Had To Say Yes

Budd Boetticher
(July 29, 1916)
1971 A Time for Dying
1960 Comanche Station; The Rise and Fall of Legs Diamond
1959 Westbound; Ride Lonesome
1958 Buchanan Rides Alone
1957 Decision at Sundown; The Tall T
1956 Seven Men from Now; The Killer Is Loose
1955 The Magnificent Matador
1953 Wings of the Hawk; The Man from the Alamo; Seminole; East of Sumatra; City Beneath the Sea
1952 Horizons West; Bronco Buster; Red Ball Express
1951 The Bullfighter and the Lady; The Sword of d'Artagnan; The Cimarron Kid
1950 Killer Shark
1949 The Wolf Hunters; Black Midnight
1948 Behind Locked Doors; Assigned to Danger
1945 Youth on Trial; A Guy, a Gal and a Pal; Escape in the Fog
1944 The Missing Juror; One Mysterious Night

Peter Bogdanovich
(July 30, 1939)
1993 The Thing Called Love
1992 Noises Off
1990 Texasville
1988 Illegally Yours
1985 Mask
1982 They All Laughed
1979 Saint Jack
1976 Nickelodeon
1975 At Long Last Love
1974 Daisy Miller
1973 Paper Moon
1972 What's Up, Doc?
1971 The Last Picture Show
1968 Voyage to the Planet of Prehistoric Women; Targets

Frank Borzage
(Apr. 23, 1893–1962)
1959 The Big Fisherman
1958 China Doll
1949 Moonrise
1947 That's My Man
1946 Magnificent Doll; I've Always Loved You
1945 The Spanish Main
1944 Till We Meet Again
1943 Stage Door Canteen; His Butler's Sister
1942 The Vanishing Virginian; Seven Sweethearts
1941 Flight Command; Smilin' Through
1940 Strange Cargo; The Mortal Storm
1939 Disputed Passage
1938 Mannequin; Three Comrades; The Shining Hour
1937 The Green Light; History Is Made at Night; The Big City
1936 Desire; Hearts Divided
1935 Stranded; Shipmates Forever; Living on Velvet
1934 No Greater Glory; Little Man, What Now?; Flirtation Walk
1933 Secrets; A Man's Castle
1932 Young America; A Farewell to Arms; After Tomorrow
1931 Young as You Feel; Bad Girl; Doctor's Wives
1930 Liliom; Song o' My Heart
1929 The River; They Had to See Paris; Lucky Star
1928 Street Angel
1927 Seventh Heaven
1926 Dixie Merchant; Marriage License?; Early to Wed; The First Year
1925 Daddy's Gone-a-Hunting; Wages for Wives; Lazybones; The Lady; The Circle
1924 Secrets
1923 The Nth Commandment; Age of Desire; Children of the Dust
1922 Back Pay; Billy Jim; The Good Provider; The Valley of Silent Men; The Pride of Palomar
1921 The Duke of Chimney Butte; Get-Rich-Quick Wallingford
1920 Humoresque
1919 Toton; Prudence of Broadway; Whom the Gods Would Destroy; Ashes of Desire
1918 The Curse of Iku; Society for Sale; The Ghost Flower; Who Is to Blame?; Shoes That Danced; Innocent's Progress; An Honest Man; Gun Woman; The Atom
1917 Wee Lady Betty; Flying Colors; Until They Get Me
1916 That Gal of Burke's; The Silken Spider; Nell Dale's Men Folks; Mammy's Rose; Life's Harmony; Code of Honor; The Forgotten Prayer; The Courtin' of Calliope Clew; Immediate Lee; Enchantment; Pride and the Man; Dollars of Dross

Frank Capra
(May 18, 1897–1991)
1961 Pocketful of Miracles
1959 A Hole in the Head
1951 Here Comes the Groom
1950 Riding High
1948 State of the Union
1946 It's a Wonderful Life
1944 Arsenic and Old Lace
1941 Meet John Doe
1939 Mr. Smith Goes to Washington
1938 You Can't Take It with You
1937 Lost Horizon
1936 Mr. Deeds Goes to Town
1934 It Happened One Night; Broadway Bill
1933 Lady for a Day; The Bitter Tea of General Yen
1932 Forbidden; American Madness
1931 The Miracle Woman; Dirigible; Platinum Blonde
1930 Ladies of Leisure; Rain or Shine
1929 The Younger Generation; Flight; The Donovan Affair
1928 The Matinee Idol; The Way of the Strong; Submarine; So This Is Love?; Say It with Sables; The Power of the Press; That Certain Thing
1927 For the Love of Mike; Long Pants
1926 Tramp, Tramp, Tramp; The Strong Man

John Cassavetes
(Dec. 9, 1929–1989)
1986 Big Trouble
1984 Love Streams
1980 Gloria
1977 Opening Night
1976 The Killing of a Chinese Bookie
1974 A Woman Under the Influence
1971 Minnie and Moskowitz
1970 Husbands
1968 Faces
1963 A Child Is Waiting

1962 Too Late Blues
1961 Shadows

Charles Chaplin
(Apr. 16, 1889–1977)
1957 A King in New York
1952 Limelight
1947 Monsieur Verdoux
1940 The Great Dictator
1936 Modern Times
1931 City Lights
1928 The Circus
1925 The Gold Rush
1923 The Pilgrim; A Woman of Paris
1922 Pay Day
1921 The Idle Class; The Kid; The Nut
1919 Sunnyside; A Day's Pleasure
1918 Triple Trouble; Shoulder Arms; A Dog's Life; The Bond
1917 The Adventurer; Easy Street; The Cure; The Immigrant
1916 The Count; The Vagabond; One A.M.; The Pawnshop; Behind the Screen; The Fireman; The Floorwalker; A Woman; The Burlesque of Carmen; The Rink
1915 His New Job; The Champion; Behind the Screen; A Jitney Elopement; In the Park; Work; The Tramp; A Night in the Show; By the Sea; Bank; Shanghaied; Police
1914 Caught in a Cabaret; Caught in the Rain; The Fatal Mallet; Her Friend the Bandit; Mabel's Married Life; Mabel's Busy Day; Dough and Dynamite; His Prehistoric Past; Knockout; His New Profession; The New Janitor; The Masquerader; Gentlemen of Nerve; Getting Acquainted; Laughing Gas; His Trysting Place; His Musical Career; The Face on the Bar Room Floor; Her Friend the Bandit; A Busy Day; The Rounders; The Property Man; Recreation; Those Love Pangs

Merian C. Cooper
(Oct. 24, 1893–1973)
1933 The Four Feathers; King Kong
1927 Chang: A Drama of the Wilderness
1924 Grass

Francis Ford Coppola
(Apr. 7, 1939)
1997 The Rainmaker
1996 Jack
1992 Bram Stoker's Dracula
1990 The Godfather, Part III
1989 New York Stories
1988 Tucker: The Man and His Dream
1987 Gardens of Stone
1986 Peggy Sue Got Married
1984 The Cotton Club
1983 Rumble Fish; The Outsiders
1982 One From the Heart
1979 Apocalypse Now
1974 The Conversation; The Godfather, Part II
1972 The Godfather

1969 The Rain People
1968 Finian's Rainbow
1967 You're a Big Boy Now
1963 Battle Beyond the Sun; Dementia 13
1962 The Bellboy and the Playgirls
1961 Tonight For Sure

George Cukor
(July 7, 1899–1983)
1981 Rich and Famous
1976 The Blue Bird
1972 Travels with My Aunt
1969 Justine
1964 My Fair Lady
1962 The Chapman Report
1960 Song Without End; Let's Make Love; Heller in Pink Tights
1957 Wild Is the Wind; Les Girls
1956 Bhowani Junction
1954 It Should Happen to You; A Star Is Born
1953 The Actress
1952 The Marrying Kind; Pat and Mike
1951 The Model and the Marriage Broker
1950 A Life of Her Own; Born Yesterday
1949 Adam's Rib; Edward, My Son
1947 Desire Me; A Double Life
1944 Winged Victory; Gaslight
1943 Keeper of the Flame
1942 Her Cardboard Lover
1941 Two-Faced Woman; A Woman's Face
1940 Susan and God; The Philadelphia Story
1939 The Women
1938 Holiday; Zaza
1937 Camille
1936 Romeo and Juliet
1935 Sylvia Scarlett; David Copperfield; No More Ladies
1933 Little Women; Our Betters; Dinner at Eight
1932 A Bill of Divorcement; What Price Hollywood?; Rockabye; One Hour with You
1931 Tarnished Lady; Girls About Town
1930 The Virtuous Sin; The Royal Family of Broadway; Grumpy

Michael Curtiz
(Dec. 24, 1888–1962)
1961 Francis of Assisi; The Comancheros
1960 The Adventures of Huckleberry Finn; The Breath of Scandal
1959 The Man in the Net; The Hangman
1958 The Proud Rebel; King Creole
1957 The Helen Morgan Story
1956 The Vagabond King; The Scarlet Hour; The Best Things in Life Are Free
1955 We're No Angels
1954 The Boy from Oklahoma; White Christmas; The Egyptian
1953 The Jazz Singer; Trouble Along the Way
1952 I'll See You in My Dreams; The Story of Will Rogers
1951 Force of Arms; Jim Thorpe—All American
1950 Bright Leaf; The Breaking Point; Young Man with a Horn

1949 The Lady Takes a Sailor; Flamingo Road; My Dream Is Yours
1948 Romance on the High Seas
1947 The Unsuspected; Life with Father
1946 Night and Day
1945 Roughly Speaking; Mildred Pierce
1944 Passage to Marseilles; Janie
1943 Mission to Moscow; This Is the Army
1942 Casablanca; Captains of the Clouds; Yankee Doodle Dandy
1941 Dive Bomber; The Sea Wolf
1940 The Sea Hawk; Virginia City; Santa Fe Trail
1939 Elizabeth the Queen; Dodge City; Four Wives; Daughters Courageous; The Private Lives of Elizabeth and Essex
1938 Four Daughters; Angels with Dirty Faces; Gold Is Where You Find It; The Adventures of Robin Hood; Four's a Crowd
1937 Kid Galahad; Stolen Holiday; The Perfect Specimen; Mountain Justice
1936 The Walking Dead; The Charge of the Light Brigade
1935 Front Page Woman; Black Fury; The Case of the Curious Bride; Captain Blood; Little Big Shot
1934 British Agent; Mandalay; The Key; Jimmy the Gent
1933 The Mystery of the Wax Museum; Goodbye Again; 20,000 Years in Sing Sing; The Kennel Murder Case; Female; The Keyhole; Private Detective 62; Man Killer
1932 Doctor X; The Woman from Monte Carlo; The Strange Love of Molly Louvain; Alias the Doctor; The Cabin in the Cotton
1931 Mad Genius; God's Gift to Women
1930 The Matrimonial Bed; Under a Texas Moon; Mammy; Bright Lights; A Soldier's Plaything; River's End
1929 Noah's Ark; The Gamblers; The Glad Rag Doll; Hearts in Exile; The Madonna of Avenue A
1928 Tenderloin
1927 The Third Degree; Million Bid; Good Time Charlie; Desired Woman
1924 Moon of Israel
1922 Sodom and Gomorrah
1917 The Colonel

Cecil B. DeMille
(Aug. 12, 1881–1959)
1956 The Ten Commandments
1952 The Greatest Show on Earth
1949 Samson and Delilah
1947 Unconquered
1944 The Story of Dr. Wassell
1942 Reap the Wild Wind
1940 Northwest Mounted Police
1939 Union Pacific
1938 The Buccaneer
1937 The Plainsman
1935 The Crusades

1934 Four Frightened People; Cleopatra
1933 This Day and Age
1932 The Sign of the Cross
1931 The Squaw Man
1930 Madame Satan
1929 The Godless Girl; Dynamite
1927 The King of Kings
1926 The Volga Boatman
1925 The Road to Yesterday; The Golden Bed
1924 Feet of Clay; Triumph
1923 Adam's Rib; The Ten Commandments
1922 Saturday Night; Manslaughter
1921 Forbidden Fruit; The Affairs of Anatol; Fool's Paradise
1920 Why Change Your Wife?; Something to Think About
1919 For Better, for Worse; Male and Female; Don't Change Your Husband
1918 Till I Come Back to You; The Whispering Chorus; You Can't Have Everything; The Squaw Man; Old Wives for New
1917 Joan the Woman; The Woman God Forgot; The Little American; The Devil Stone; Romance of the Redwoods
1916 The Golden Chance; The Girl of the Golden West; Temptation; Sweet Kitty Bellairs; The Dream Girl; Heart of Nora Flynn; Maria Rosa; Trail of the Lonesome Pine
1915 The Captive; Kindling; The Arab; Unafraid; Out West; Carmen; The Wild Goose Chase; Lost and Won; The Warrens of Virginia; The Cheat; Chimmie Fadden
1914 The Squaw Man; The Man from Home; The Man on the Box; The Ghost Breaker; What's His Name?; The Call of the North; Brewster's Millions; Rose of the Rancho; The Virginian; The Only Son

Edward Dmytryk
(Sept. 4, 1908)
1976 The Human Factor; He Is My Brother
1972 Bluebeard
1968 Anzio; Shalako
1966 Alvarez Kelly
1965 Mirage
1964 Where Love Has Gone; The Carpetbaggers
1962 The Reluctant Saint; A Walk on the Wild Side
1959 The Blue Angel; Warlock
1958 The Young Lions
1957 Raintree County
1956 The Mountain
1955 The Left Hand of God; Soldier of Fortune
1954 The Caine Mutiny; Broken Lance; The End of the Affair
1953 The Juggler
1952 The Sniper; Mutiny; Eight Iron Men
1949 Salt to the Devil; Give Us This Day; The Hidden Room
1947 So Well Remembered; Crossfire
1946 In Old New Mexico; Till the End of Time

1945 Cornered; Back to Bataan
1944 Tender Comrade; Murder, My Sweet
1943 Captive Wild Woman; Hitler's Children; The Falcon Strikes Back; Behind the Rising Sun
1942 Counter-Espionage; Seven Miles from Alcatraz
1941 Confessions of Boston Blackie; Secrets of the Lone Wolf; The Devil Commands; The Blonde from Singapore; Underage; Sweetheart of the Camp; The Devil Commands
1940 Emergency Squad; Her First Romance; Golden Gloves; Mystery Sea Raider
1939 Television Spy
1935 The Hawk

Stanley Donen
(Apr. 13, 1924)
1984 Blame It on Rio
1980 Saturn 3
1978 Movie, Movie
1975 Lucky Lady
1974 The Little Prince
1969 Staircase
1967 Two for the Road; Bedazzled
1966 Arabesque
1963 Charade
1960 Surprise Package; Once More, with Feeling; The Grass Is Greener
1958 Indiscreet; Damn Yankees
1957 Kiss Them for Me; The Pajama Game; Funny Face
1955 It's Always Fair Weather
1954 Deep in My Heart; Seven Brides for Seven Brothers
1953 Give a Girl a Break
1952 Love Is Better Than Ever; Fearless Fagan; Singin' in the Rain
1951 Royal Wedding
1949 On the Town

Allan Dwan
(Selected list)
(Apr. 3, 1885–1981)
1961 The Most Dangerous Man Alive; Calendar Girl
1958 Enchanted Island
1957 The River's Edge; The Restless Breed
1956 Hold Back the Night; Slightly Scarlet
1955 Escape to Burma; The Pearl of the South Pacific; Tennessee's Partner
1954 Flight Nurse; Cattle Queen of Montana; Silver Lode; Passion
1953 The Woman They Almost Lynched; Sweethearts on Parade
1952 Montana Belle; I Dream of Jeannie
1951 Surrender; Belle Le Grande; The Wild Blue Yonder
1949 Sands of Iwo Jima
1948 The Inside Story; Angel in Exile
1947 Calendar Girl; Northwest Outpost; Driftwood
1946 Rendezvous with Annie
1945 Brewster's Millions; Getting Gertie's Garter
1944 Abroad with Two Yanks; Up in Mabel's Room
1943 Around the World
1942 Here We Go Again!; Friendly Enemies

1941 Rise and Shine; Look Who's Laughing
1940 Young People; Trail of the Vigilantes; Sailor's Lady
1939 The Three Musketeers; The Gorilla; Frontier Marshal
1938 Rebecca of Sunnybrook Farm; Suez; Josette
1937 Woman-Wise; That I May Live; One Mile from Heaven; Heidi
1936 The Song and Dance Man; High Tension; Human Cargo; 15 Maiden Lane
1935 Black Sheep; Navy Wife
1934 I Spy; Hollywood Party
1933 Her First Affair; Counsel's Opinion
1932 While Paris Sleeps
1931 Chances; Wicked
1930 What a Widow!; Man to Man
1929 The Iron Mask
1927 West Point; East Side, West Side
1923 Zaza
1922 Robin Hood
1911 The Yiddisher Cowboy

Blake Edwards
(July 26, 1922)
1993 Son of the Pink Panther
1991 Switch
1989 Skin Deep
1988 Sunset
1987 Blind Date
1986 That's Life!; A Fine Mess
1984 Micki + Maude
1983 The Curse of the Pink Panther; The Man Who Loved Women
1982 Victor/Victoria; The Trail of the Pink Panther
1981 S.O.B.
1979 10
1978 The Revenge of the Pink Panther
1976 The Pink Panther Strikes Again
1975 The Return of the Pink Panther
1974 The Tamarind Seed
1972 The Carey Treatment
1971 The Wild Rovers
1970 Darling Lili
1968 The Party
1967 Gunn
1966 What Did You Do in the War, Daddy?
1965 The Great Race
1964 The Pink Panther; A Shot in the Dark
1963 Soldier in the Rain
1962 Experiment in Terror
1961 Breakfast at Tiffany's
1960 High Time
1959 Operation Petticoat; The Perfect Furlough
1958 This Happy Feeling
1957 Mister Cory
1956 He Laughed Last
1955 Bring Your Smile Along

John Ford
(Selected list)
(Feb. 1, 1895–1973)
1976 Chesty
1966 Seven Women
1965 Young Cassidy
1964 Cheyenne Autumn
1963 Donovan's Reef
1962 Two Rode Together; The Man Who Shot Liberty Valance; How the West Was Won
1960 The Trial of Sergeant Rutledge

1959 The Horse Soldiers; Gideon of Scotland Yard
1958 The Last Hurrah
1957 The Rising of the Moon; The Wings of Eagles
1956 The Searchers
1955 Mr. Roberts; The Long Gray Line
1953 The Sun Shines Bright; Mogambo
1952 What Price Glory?; The Quiet Man
1950 When Willie Comes Marching Home; Rio Grande
1949 The Three Godfathers; She Wore a Yellow Ribbon
1948 Fort Apache
1947 The Fugitive
1946 My Darling Clementine
1945 They Were Expendable
1941 Tobacco Road; How Green Was My Valley
1940 The Grapes of Wrath; The Long Voyage Home
1939 Drums Along the Mohawk; Stagecoach; Young Mr. Lincoln
1938 Wee Willie Winkie; The Hurricane; Submarine Patrol; Four Men and a Prayer
1936 Mary of Scotland; The Prisoner of Shark Island; The Plough and the Stars
1935 The Whole Town's Talking; The Informer; Steamboat Round the Bend
1934 The Lost Patrol; The World Moves On; Judge Priest
1933 Doctor Bull; Pilgrimage
1932 Air Mail; Flesh
1931 The Brat; Seas Beneath; Arrowsmith
1930 Up the River; Men Without Women; Born Reckless
1929 The Black Watch; Strong Boy; Salute
1928 Mother Machree; Hangman's House; Four Sons; Riley the Cop
1926 Three Bad Men
1925 Thank You; Lightnin'
1924 Hearts of Oak; The Iron Horse
1923 Little Miss Smiles; North of Hudson Bay
1922 Silver Wings
1921 The Big Punch; The Wallop
1920 Riders of Vengeance; The Outcasts of Poker Flat; The Price of Avenue A
1917 Straight Shootin'

Bob Fosse
(June 23, 1927–1987)
1983 Star 80
1979 All That Jazz
1974 Lenny
1972 Cabaret
1969 Sweet Charity

John Frankenheimer
(Feb. 19, 1930)
1996 The Island of Dr. Moreau
1991 Year of the Gun
1990 The Fourth War
1989 Dead Bang
1986 The Holcroft Covenant; 52 Pick-Up
1982 The Challenge
1979 The Prophecy
1977 Black Sunday
1975 The French Connection II
1974 99 and 44/100 Percent Dead
1973 The Iceman Cometh; Impossible Object

1971 The Horsemen
1970 I Walk the Line
1969 The Gypsy Moths; The Extraordinary Seaman
1968 The Fixer
1966 Seconds; Grand Prix
1964 Seven Days in May; The Train
1962 All Fall Down; The Manchurian Candidate; The Birdman of Alcatraz
1961 The Young Savages
1957 The Young Stranger

William Friedkin
(Aug. 29, 1939)
1995 Jade
1994 Blue Chips
1992 Rampage
1990 The Guardian
1985 To Live and Die in L.A.
1983 Deal of the Century
1980 Cruising
1979 The Brink's Job
1977 Sorcerer
1973 The Exorcist
1971 The French Connection
1970 The Boys in the Band
1968 The Birthday Party; The Night They Raided Minsky's
1967 Good Times

Sam Fuller
(Aug. 12, 1911)
1989 Street of No Return
1984 Thieves After Dark
1982 White Dog
1980 The Big Red One
1972 Dead Pigeon on Beethoven Street
1969 Shark!
1965 The Naked Kiss
1963 Shock Corridor
1962 Merrill's Marauders
1961 Underworld U.S.A.
1959 The Crimson Kimono; Verboten!
1957 Run of the Arrow; China Gate; Forty Guns
1955 House of Bamboo
1954 Hell and High Water
1953 Pickup on South Street
1952 Park Row
1951 Fixed Bayonets
1950 The Steel Helmet; The Baron of Arizona
1949 I Shot Jesse James

D. W. Griffith
(Selected list)
(Jan. 22, 1875–1948)
1930 Abraham Lincoln
1929 Lady of the Pavements
1928 The Battle of the Sexes
1924 America
1923 The White Rose
1922 Orphans of the Storm
1920 Way Down East
1919 Broken Blossoms
1918 Hearts of the World
1916 Intolerance
1915 The Birth of a Nation
1914 Judith of Bethulia; Home Sweet Home

Henry Hathaway
(Mar. 13, 1898–1985)
1974 Hangup
1971 Shoot Out; Raid on Rommel
1969 True Grit
1968 Five Card Stud
1967 The Last Safari
1966 Nevada Smith
1965 The Sons of Katie Elder
1964 Circus World; Spartacus and the Ten Gladiators; Of Human Bondage

1962 How the West Was Won
1960 Seven Thieves; North to Alaska
1959 Woman Obsessed
1958 From Hell to Texas
1957 Legend of the Lost
1956 23 Paces to Baker Street; The Bottom of the Bottle
1955 The Racers
1954 Garden of Evil; Prince Valiant
1953 Niagara; White Witch Doctor
1952 Diplomatic Courier; O. Henry's Full House
1951 You're in the Navy Now; U.S.S. Teakettle; The Desert Fox; 14 Hours
1950 The Black Rose
1949 Down to the Sea in Ships
1948 Call Northside 777
1947 13 Rue Madeleine; Kiss of Death
1946 The Dark Corner
1945 Nob Hill; The House on 92nd Street
1944 Home in Indiana; A Wing and a Prayer
1943 China Girl
1942 Ten Gentlemen from West Point
1941 Sundown; The Shepherd of the Hills
1940 Johnny Apollo; Brigham Young
1939 The Real Glory
1938 Spawn of the North
1937 Souls at Sea
1936 The Trail of the Lonesome Pine; Go West, Young Man
1935 The Lives of a Bengal Lancer; I Loved a Soldier; Peter Ibbetson
1934 The Witching Hour; The Last Round-Up; Now and Forever; Come On, Marines
1933 Man of the Forest; The Thundering Herd; Under the Tonto Rim; To the Last Man; Heritage of the Desert; Sunset Pass
1932 When the West Was Young; Wild Horse Mesa; Buffalo Stampede

Howard Hawks
(May 30, 1896–1977)
1970 Rio Lobo
1967 El Dorado
1965 Red Line 7000
1964 Man's Favorite Sport?
1962 Hatari!
1959 Rio Bravo
1955 Land of the Pharaohs
1953 Gentlemen Prefer Blondes
1952 The Big Sky; Monkey Business; Henry's Full House
1949 I Was a Male War Bride
1948 Red River; A Song Is Born
1946 The Big Sleep
1944 To Have and Have Not
1943 Air Force
1942 Ball of Fire
1941 Sergeant York
1940 His Girl Friday
1939 Only Angels Have Wings
1938 Bringing Up Baby
1936 Ceiling Zero; The Road to Glory; Come and Get It
1935 The Barbary Coast
1934 Viva Villa!; Twentieth Century
1933 Today We Live
1932 Scarface; Tiger Shark; The Crowd Roars; The Shame of a Nation

1931 The Criminal Code
1930 The Dawn Patrol
1929 Trent's Last Case; Masked Emotions
1928 A Girl in Every Port; The Air Circus; Fazil
1927 Cradle Snatchers; Paid to Love
1926 Road to Glory; Fig Leaves

Alfred Hitchcock
(Aug. 13, 1899–1980)
1976 Family Plot
1972 Frenzy
1969 Topaz
1966 Torn Curtain
1964 Marnie
1963 The Birds
1960 Psycho
1959 North by Northwest
1958 Vertigo
1957 The Wrong Man
1956 The Man Who Knew Too Much
1955 The Trouble with Harry; To Catch a Thief
1954 Dial M for Murder; Rear Window
1953 I Confess
1951 Strangers on a Train
1950 Stage Fright
1949 Under Capricorn
1948 The Paradine Case; Rope
1946 Notorious
1945 Spellbound
1944 Lifeboat; Bon Voyage; Madagascar Landing
1943 Shadow of a Doubt
1942 Saboteur
1941 Mr. and Mrs. Smith; Suspicion
1940 Foreign Correspondent; Rebecca
1939 Jamaica Inn
1938 The Lady Vanishes
1937 Sabotage; Young and Innocent
1936 The Secret Agent
1935 The 39 Steps
1934 The Man Who Knew Too Much
1933 Waltzes from Vienna; Strauss's Great Waltz
1932 Number 17; Rich and Strange
1931 The Skin Game
1930 Elstree Calling; Mary; Murder; Juno and the Paycock
1929 Blackmail; The Manxman; Harmony Heaven
1928 Champagne; The Farmer's Wife
1927 Easy Virtue; Downhill; The Ring
1926 Mountain Eagle; The Lodger; Fear o' God; The Case of Jonathan Drew
1925 The Pleasure Garden

John Huston
(Aug. 5, 1906–1987)
1987 The Dead
1985 Prizzi's Honor
1984 Under the Volcano
1982 Annie
1981 Victory
1980 Phobia
1976 Independence
1975 The Man Who Would Be King
1973 The Mackintosh Man
1972 The Life and Times of Judge Roy Bean; Fat City
1970 The Kremlin Letter
1969 A Walk with Love and Death; Sinful Davey; De Sade

1967 Casino Royale; Reflections in a Golden Eye
1966 The Bible—The Beginning
1964 The Night of the Iguana
1963 Freud; The List of Adrian Messenger
1961 The Misfits
1960 The Unforgiven
1958 The Barbarian and the Geisha; The Roots of Heaven
1957 Heaven Knows, Mr. Allison
1956 Moby Dick
1954 Beat the Devil
1952 Moulin Rouge
1951 The African Queen; The Red Badge of Courage
1950 The Asphalt Jungle
1949 We Were Strangers
1948 Key Largo; The Treasure of the Sierra Madre
1942 In This Our Life; Across the Pacific
1941 The Maltese Falcon

Elia Kazan
(Sept. 7, 1909)
1976 The Last Tycoon
1972 The Visitors
1969 The Arrangement
1963 America, America
1961 Splendor in the Grass
1960 Wild River
1957 A Face in the Crowd
1956 Baby Doll
1955 East of Eden
1954 On the Waterfront
1953 Man on a Tightrope
1952 Viva Zapata!
1951 A Streetcar Named Desire
1950 Panic in the Streets
1949 Pinky
1947 Gentleman's Agreement; Boomerang!; The Sea of Grass
1945 A Tree Grows in Brooklyn

Buster Keaton
(Oct. 4, 1895–1966)
1938 The Hollywood Handicap; Life in Sometown USA
1928 The General
1926 Battling Butler
1925 Seven Chances; Go West
1924 Sherlock Jr.; The Navigator
1923 Love Nest; Day Dreams; Our Hospitality; Balloonatic/One Week; The Three Ages
1922 Two Houses of Keaton; The Frozen North; The Electric House; Cops; The Blacksmith
1921 Haunted House; The Playhouse; The Paleface; The High Sign; Hard Luck; The Boat
1920 Neighbors; Convict 13; The Scarecrow; One Week

Gene Kelly
(Aug. 23, 1912–1996)
1970 The Cheyenne Social Club
1969 Hello, Dolly!
1967 A Guide for the Married Man
1962 Gigot
1958 The Tunnel of Love
1957 The Happy Road
1956 Invitation to the Dance
1955 It's Always Fair Weather
1952 Singin' in the Rain
1949 On the Town

Stanley Kramer
(Sept. 23, 1913)
1979 The Runner Stumbles

1977 The Domino Principle
1973 Oklahoma Crude
1971 Bless the Beasts and Children
1970 R.P.M.
1969 The Secret of Santa Vittoria
1967 Guess Who's Coming to Dinner
1965 Ship of Fools
1963 It's a Mad, Mad, Mad, Mad World
1961 Judgment at Nuremberg
1960 Inherit the Wind
1959 On the Beach
1958 The Defiant Ones
1957 The Pride and the Passion
1955 Not as a Stranger

Stanley Kubrick
(July 26, 1928–1999)
1987 Full Metal Jacket
1980 The Shining
1975 Barry Lyndon
1971 A Clockwork Orange
1968 2001: A Space Odyssey
1964 Dr. Strangelove or: How I Learned to Stop Worrying and Love the Bomb
1962 Lolita
1960 Spartacus
1957 Paths of Glory
1956 The Killing
1955 Killer's Kiss
1953 Fear and Desire
1951 Flying Padre
1950 Day of the Fight

Fritz Lang
(Dec. 5, 1890–1976)
1960 The Thousand Eyes of Dr. Mabuse
1959 The Tiger of Bengal; The Indian Tomb
1956 Beyond a Reasonable Doubt; While the City Sleeps
1955 Moonfleet
1954 Human Desire
1953 The Big Heat; The Blue Gardenia
1952 Clash by Night; Rancho Victorious
1950 The House by the River; An American Guerilla in the Philippines
1948 The Secret Beyond the Door
1946 Cloak and Dagger
1945 Scarlet Street
1944 The Woman in the Window; Ministry of Fear
1943 Hangmen Also Die!
1941 Manhunt; Western Union
1940 The Return of Frank James
1938 You and Me
1937 You Only Live Once
1936 Fury
1934 Liliom
1933 The Crimes of Dr. Mabuse
1931 M
1929 Girl in the Moon
1928 Spies
1927 Metropolis
1924 Siegfried's Death
1920 The Wandering Image; Destiny; Dr. Mabuse: The Gambler; Siegfried; Kriemhilde's Revenge
1919 The Spiders; Madame Butterfly; The Half Caste

David Lean
(Mar. 25, 1908–1991)
1984 A Passage to India
1970 Ryan's Daughter
1965 Doctor Zhivago

1962 Lawrence of Arabia
1957 The Bridge on the River Kwai
1955 Summertime
1954 Hobson's Choice
1952 Breaking the Sound Barrier
1950 Madeleine
1949 The Passionate Friends
1948 Oliver Twist
1946 Great Expectations
1945 Brief Encounter
1944 This Happy Breed
1942 In Which We Serve

Mitchell Leisen
(Oct. 6, 1898–1972)
1957 The Girl Most Likely
1955 Bedeviled
1953 Tonight We Sing
1951 Darling, How Could You!; The Mating Season; Young Man with Ideas
1950 No Man of Her Own; Captain Carey, U.S.A.
1949 Song of Surrender; Bride of Vengeance
1948 Dream Girl
1947 Suddenly It's Spring; Golden Earrings
1946 To Each His Own
1945 Masquerade in Mexico; Kitty
1944 Practically Yours; The Lady in the Dark; Frenchman's Creek
1943 No Time for Love
1942 The Lady Is Willing; Take a Letter Darling
1941 I Wanted Wings; Hold Back the Dawn
1940 Remember the Night; Arise, My Love
1939 Midnight
1938 The Big Broadcast of 1938; Artists and Models Abroad
1937 Swing High, Swing Low; Easy Living
1936 Thirteen Hours By Air; The Big Broadcast of 1937
1935 Behold My Wife; Hands Across the Table; Four Hours to Kill
1934 Murder at the Vanities; Death Takes a Holiday
1933 Cradle Song

Richard Lester
(Jan. 19, 1932)
1991 Get Back
1990 The Return of the Musketeers
1984 Finders Keepers
1983 Superman III
1980 Superman II
1979 Butch and Sundance: The Early Days; Cuba
1976 Robin and Marian; The Ritz
1975 Royal Flash; The Four Musketeers
1974 The Three Musketeers; Juggernaut
1969 The Bed Sitting Room
1968 Petulia
1967 How I Won the War
1966 A Funny Thing Happened On the Way to the Forum
1965 The Knack
1964 A Hard Day's Night
1963 The Mouse on the Moon
1962 Ring-a-Ding Rhythm
1960 The Running Jumping & Standing Still Film

Jerry Lewis
(Mar. 16, 1926)
1983 Cracking Up

1981 Hardly Working
1970 One More Time; Which Way to the Front?
1967 The Big Mouth
1966 Three on a Couch
1965 The Family Jewels
1964 The Patsy
1963 The Nutty Professor
1961 The Errand Boy; The Ladies' Man
1960 Cinderfella; The Bellboy

Ernst Lubitsch
(Jan. 28, 1892–1947)
1948 That Lady in Ermine
1946 Cluny Brown
1945 A Royal Scandal
1943 Heaven Can Wait
1942 To Be or Not to Be
1941 That Uncertain Feeling
1940 The Shop Around the Corner
1939 Ninotchka
1938 Bluebeard's Eighth Wife
1937 Angel
1934 The Merry Widow
1933 Design for Living
1932 Un Heure Pres De Toi; Trouble in Paradise; If I Had a Million; Broken Lullaby
1931 The Smiling Lieutenant
1930 Paramount on Parade; Monte Carlo
1929 Eternal Love; The Love Parade
1928 The Patriot
1927 The Student Prince; Old Heidelberg
1926 So This Is Paris
1925 Montmartre; Lady Widermere's Fan; Kiss Me Again
1924 Forbidden Paradise; Three Women
1923 Rosita
1922 Loves of Pharaoh
1921 Sumurun; Vendetta
1920 Anna Boleyn; Romeo and Juliet in the Snow; One Arabian Night
1919 Passion; Rausch; Meyer from Berlin; Oyster Princess
1918 Gypsy Blood; Carmen
1917 Wenn Vier Dasselbe Tun
1916 Schuhpalast; Pinkus; Wo Ist Mein Schatz?
1915 Blindekuh

George Lucas
(May 14, 1944)
1977 Star Wars
1973 American Graffiti
1971 THX 1138

Sidney Lumet
(June 25, 1924)
1997 Night Falls on Manhattan
1993 Guilty as Sin
1992 A Stranger Among Us
1990 Q and A
1989 Family Business
1988 Running on Empty
1986 Power; The Morning After
1984 Garbo Talks
1983 Daniel
1982 The Verdict; Deathtrap
1981 Prince of the City
1980 Just Tell Me What You Want
1978 The Wiz
1977 Equus
1976 Network
1975 Dog Day Afternoon
1974 Lovin' Molly; Murder on the Orient Express
1973 Serpico; The Offence

1972 Child's Play
1971 The Anderson Tapes
1970 The Last of the Mobile Hotshots
1969 The Appointment
1968 The Seagull; Bye-Bye Braverman
1967 The Deadly Affair
1966 The Group
1965 The Pawnbroker; The Hill
1964 Fail-Safe
1962 Long Day's Journey Into Night; A View from the Bridge
1960 The Fugitive Kind
1959 That Kind of Woman
1958 Stage Struck
1957 12 Angry Men

Ida Lupino
(Feb. 4, 1918–1995)
1966 The Trouble with Angels
1953 The Hitch-Hiker; The Bigamist
1951 Hard, Fast and Beautiful
1950 Outrage; Never Fear

Rouben Mamoulian
(Oct. 8, 1898–1987)
1957 Silk Stockings
1948 Summer Holiday
1942 Rings on Her Fingers
1941 Blood and Sand
1940 The Mark of Zorro
1939 Golden Boy
1937 High, Wide and Handsome
1936 The Gay Desperado
1935 Becky Sharp
1934 We Live Again
1933 Queen Christina; Song of Songs
1932 Dr. Jekyll and Mr. Hyde; Love Me Tonight
1931 City Streets
1929 Applause

Joseph Mankiewicz
(Feb. 11, 1909–1993)
1972 Sleuth
1970 There Was a Crooked Man
1967 The Honey Pot
1963 Cleopatra
1959 Suddenly, Last Summer
1958 The Quiet American
1955 Guys and Dolls
1954 The Barefoot Contessa
1953 Julius Caesar
1952 Five Fingers
1951 People Will Talk
1950 No Way Out; All About Eve
1949 House of Strangers; A Letter to Three Wives
1948 Escape
1947 The Late George Apley; The Ghost and Mrs. Muir
1946 Somewhere in the Night; Dragonwyck

Anthony Mann
(June 30, 1906–1967)
1968 A Dandy in Aspic
1965 The Heroes of Telemark
1964 The Fall of the Roman Empire
1961 El Cid
1960 Cimarron
1958 Man of the West; God's Little Acre
1957 The Tin Star; Men in War
1956 Serenade
1955 The Last Frontier; Strategic Air Command; The Far Country; The Man from Laramie
1954 The Glenn Miller Story
1953 The Naked Spur; Thunder Bay
1952 Bend of the River

1951 The Tall Target
1950 Side Street; The Furies; Devil's Doorway; Winchester '73
1949 Reign of Terror; Border Incident
1948 T-Men; Raw Deal
1947 Desperate; Railroaded
1946 Strange Impersonation; The Bamboo Blonde
1945 Sing Your Way Home; Two O'Clock Courage; The Great Flamarion
1944 My Best Gal; Strangers in the Night
1943 Nobody's Darling
1942 Moonlight in Havana; Dr. Broadway

Delbert Mann
(Jan. 30, 1920–1991)
1983 Bronte
1982 Night Crossing
1976 The Birch Interval
1971 Kidnapped
1968 The Pink Jungle
1967 Fitzwilly
1966 Mr. Buddwing
1965 Quick, Before It Melts
1964 Dear Heart
1963 A Gathering of Eagles
1962 That Touch of Mink
1961 Lover Come Back; The Outsider
1960 The Dark at the Top of the Stairs
1959 Middle of the Night
1958 Separate Tables; Desire Under the Elms
1957 The Bachelor Party
1955 Marty

Paul Mazursky
(Apr. 25, 1930)
1996 Faithful
1993 The Pickle
1991 Scenes from a Mall
1989 Enemies, A Love Story
1988 Moon Over Parador
1986 Down and Out in Beverly Hills
1984 Moscow on the Hudson
1982 Tempest
1980 Willie and Phil
1978 An Unmarried Woman
1976 Next Stop, Greenwich Village
1974 Harry and Tonto
1970 Alex in Wonderland; Blume in Love
1969 Bob and Carol and Ted and Alice

Leo McCarey
(Oct. 3, 1898–1969)
1962 Satan Never Sleeps
1958 Rally 'Round the Flag, Boys!
1957 An Affair to Remember
1952 My Son, John
1948 Good Sam
1945 The Bells of Saint Mary's
1944 Going My Way
1942 Once Upon a Honeymoon
1939 Love Affair
1937 Make Way for Tomorrow; The Awful Truth
1936 The Milky Way
1935 Ruggles of Red Gap
1934 Six of a Kind; Belle of the Nineties
1933 Duck Soup
1932 The Kid from Spain
1931 Indiscreet
1930 Part Time Wife; Let's Go Native; Wild Company
1929 Wrong Again; The Unkissed Man; Sky Boy;

Liberty; Big Business; The
Sophomore; Red Hot
Rhythm
1928 The Finishing Touch
1927 We Slip Up; Should
Married Men Go Home?;
Pass the Gravy; Habeas
Corpus
1926 Dog Shy; Crazy Like a
Fox; Be Your Age; Eve's
Love Letters
1925 Bad Boy; Innocent
Husbands
1924 All Wet

Vincente Minnelli
(Feb. 28, 1903–1986)
1976 A Matter of Time
1970 On a Clear Day You Can
See Forever
1965 The Sandpiper
1964 Goodbye Charlie
1963 The Courtship of Eddie's
Father
1962 Two Weeks in Another
Town; The Four Horsemen
of the Apocalypse
1960 Bells Are Ringing; Home
from the Hill
1959 Some Came Running
1958 The Reluctant Debutante;
Gigi
1957 Designing Women
1956 Tea and Sympathy; Lust
for Life
1955 The Cobweb; Kismet
1954 Brigadoon; The Long,
Long Trailer
1953 The Story of Three Loves;
The Band Wagon
1952 The Bad and the Beautiful
1951 Father's Little Dividend;
An American in Paris
1950 Father of the Bride
1949 Madame Bovary
1948 The Pirate
1946 Undercurrent; Ziegfeld
Follies
1945 The Clock; Yolanda and
the Thief
1944 Meet Me in St. Louis
1943 Cabin in the Sky; I Dood It

Mike Nichols
(Nov. 6, 1931)
1998 Primary Colors
1996 The Birdcage
1994 Wolf
1991 Regarding Henry
1990 Postcards from the Edge
1988 Biloxi Blues; Working
Girl
1986 Heartburn
1983 Silkwood
1975 The Fortune
1973 The Day of the Dolphin
1971 Carnal Knowledge
1970 Catch-22
1967 The Graduate
1966 Who's Afraid of Virginia
Woolf?

Sam Peckinpah
(Feb. 21, 1925–1984)
1983 The Osterman Weekend
1978 Convoy
1977 Cross of Iron
1975 The Killer Elite
1974 Bring Me the Head of
Alfredo Garcia
1973 Pat Garrett and Billy
the Kid
1972 The Getaway; Junior
Bonner
1971 Straw Dogs
1970 The Ballad of Cable Hogue
1969 The Wild Bunch
1965 Major Dundee

1962 Ride the High Country
1961 The Deadly Companions

Arthur Penn
(Sept. 27, 1922)
1997 Inside
1989 Penn and Teller Get Killed
1987 Dead of Winter
1985 Target
1981 Four Friends
1976 The Missouri Breaks
1975 Night Moves
1970 Little Big Man
1969 Alice's Restaurant
1967 Bonnie and Clyde
1966 The Chase
1965 Mickey One
1962 The Miracle Worker

Sydney Pollack
(July 1, 1934)
1995 Sabrina
1993 The Firm
1990 Havana
1985 Out of Africa
1982 Tootsie
1981 Absence of Malice
1979 The Electric Horseman
1977 Bobby Deerfield
1975 The Yakuza; Three Days of
the Condor
1973 The Way We Were
1972 Jeremiah Johnson
1969 Castle Keep; They Shoot
Horses, Don't They?
1968 The Scalphunters
1966 This Property Is
Condemned
1965 The Slender Thread

Otto Preminger
(Dec. 5, 1905–1986)
1980 The Human Factor
1975 Rosebud
1971 Such Good Friends
1970 Tell Me That You Love Me,
Junie Moon
1968 Skidoo
1967 Hurry Sundown
1965 Bunny Lake Is Missing; In
Harm's Way
1963 The Cardinal
1962 Advise and Consent
1960 Exodus
1959 Porgy and Bess; Anatomy
of a Murder
1958 Bonjour Tristesse
1957 Saint Joan
1955 The Court Martial of Billy
Mitchell; The Man with the
Golden Arm
1954 Carmen Jones; River of
No Return
1953 The Moon Is Blue; Angel
Face
1951 The Thirteenth Letter
1950 Whirlpool; Where the
Sidewalk Ends
1949 The Fan
1948 That Lady in Ermine
1947 Forever Amber; Daisy
Kenyon
1946 Centennial Summer
1945 A Royal Scandal; Fallen
Angel
1944 In the Meantime, Darling;
Laura
1943 Margin for Error
1937 Danger: Love at Work
1936 Under Your Spell

Nicholas Ray
(Aug. 7, 1911–1979)
1963 55 Days at Peking
1961 King of Kings
1960 The Savage Innocents
1958 Wind Across the
Everglades; Party Girl

1957 The True Story of Jesse
James
1956 Hot Blood; Bigger
Than Life
1955 Run for Cover; Rebel
Without a Cause
1954 Johnny Guitar
1952 On Dangerous Ground;
The Lusty Men
1951 Flying Leathernecks
1950 Born to Be Bad; In a
Lonely Place
1949 A Woman's Secret; Knock
on Any Door; They Live
By Night

John Schlesinger
(Feb. 16, 1926)
1996 Cold Comfort Farm
1995 Eye for an Eye
1993 The Innocent
1990 Pacific Heights
1988 Madame Sousatzka
1987 The Believers
1985 The Falcon and the
Snowman
1981 Honky Tonk Freeway
1979 Yanks
1976 Marathon Man
1975 The Day of the Locust
1971 Sunday, Bloody Sunday
1969 Midnight Cowboy
1967 Far from the Madding
Crowd
1965 Darling
1963 Billy Liar
1962 A Kind of Loving

Martin Scorsese
(Nov. 17, 1942)
1998 Kundun
1995 Casino
1993 The Age of Innocence
1991 Cape Fear
1990 Goodfellas
1989 New York Stories
1988 The Last Temptation of
Christ
1986 The Color of Money
1985 After Hours
1983 The King of Comedy
1980 Raging Bull
1978 New York, New York;
American Boy
1976 Taxi Driver
1975 Alice Doesn't Live Here
Anymore
1974 Italianamerican
1973 Mean Streets
1972 Boxcar Bertha
1968 Who's That Knocking at
My Door
1967 The Big Shave
1964 It's Not Just You, Murray!
1963 What's a Nice Girl Like
You Doing in a Place
Like This?

Don Siegel
(Oct. 26, 1912–1991)
1982 Jinxed!
1980 Rough Cut
1979 Escape from Alcatraz
1977 Telefon
1976 The Shootist
1974 The Black Windmill
1973 Charley Varrick
1971 The Beguiled; Dirty Harry
1970 Two Mules for Sister Sara
1969 Death of a Gunfighter
1968 Madigan; Coogan's Bluff
1964 The Killers
1962 Hell Is for Heroes
1960 Flaming Star
1959 Hound-Dog Man; Edge of
Eternity
1958 Spanish Affair; The
Lineup; The Gun Runners

1957 Baby Face Nelson
1956 Invasion of the Body
Snatchers; Crime in
the Streets
1955 An Annapolis Story
1954 Private Hell 36; Riot in
Cell Block 11
1953 No Time for Flowers;
China Venture; Count the
Hours
1952 The Duel at Silver Creek
1946 The Verdict; The Big Steal;
Night Unto Night

Douglas Sirk
(Apr. 26, 1900–1987)
1959 Imitation of Life; Harvey
Middleman, Fireman
1958 The Tarnished Angels; A
Time to Love and a Time
to Die
1957 Never Say Goodbye;
Written on the Wind;
Battle Hymn; Interlude
1956 All That Heaven Allows;
There's Always Tomorrow
1955 Captain Lightfoot
1954 Taza, Son of Cochise;
Sign of the Pagan;
Magnificent Obsession
1953 All I Desire; Take Me
to Town
1952 Has Anybody Seen My
Gal?; No Room for the
Groom; Meet Me at the
Fair
1951 The First Legion; Weekend
with Father; Thunder on
the Hill; The Lady Pays Off
1950 Mystery Submarine
1949 Slightly French;
Shockproof
1948 Sleep, My Love
1947 Lured
1946 Thieves' Holiday; A
Scandal in Paris
1944 Summer Storm
1943 Hitler's Madman

Steven Spielberg
(Dec. 18, 1947)
1998 Saving Private Ryan
1997 Amistad; The Lost World:
Jurassic Park II
1993 Schindler's List;
Jurassic Park
1991 Hook
1989 Always; Indiana Jones and
the Last Crusade
1987 Empire of the Sun
1985 The Color Purple
1984 Indiana Jones and the
Temple of Doom
1983 Twilight Zone: The Movie
1982 E.T.
1981 Raiders of the Lost Ark
1979 1941
1977 Close Encounters of the
Third Kind
1975 Jaws
1971 Duel

George Stevens
(Dec. 18, 1904–1975)
1970 The Only Game in Town
1965 The Greatest Story Ever
Told
1959 The Diary of Anne Frank
1956 Giant
1953 Shane
1952 Something to Live For
1951 A Place in the Sun
1948 I Remember Mama
1943 The More the Merrier
1942 Woman of the Year; The
Talk of the Town
1941 Penny Serenade
1940 Vigil in the Night

1939 Gunga Din
1938 Vivacious Lady
1937 Quality Street
1936 Swing Time
1935 Alice Adams; The Nitwits;
 Laddie; Annie Oakley
1934 Kentucky Kernels;
 Bachelor Bait
1933 The Cohens and Kellys in
 Trouble

Preston Sturges
(Aug. 29, 1898–1959)
1956 The French, They Are a
 Funny Race
1949 The Beautiful Blonde from
 Bashful Bend
1948 Unfaithfully Yours
1947 The Sin of Harold
 Diddlebock
1944 Hail the Conquering Hero;
 The Miracle of Morgan's
 Creek; The Great Moment
1942 The Palm Beach Story
1941 The Lady Eve; Sullivan's
 Travels
1940 Christmas in July; The
 Great McGinty

Orson Welles
(May 6, 1915–1985)
1993 It's All True
1968 The Immortal Story
1966 Chimes at Midnight
1962 The Trial
1958 Touch of Evil
1955 Mr. Arkadin
1948 Macbeth; The Lady from
 Shanghai; Othello
1946 The Stranger
1942 The Magnificent
 Ambersons
1941 Citizen Kane
1938 Too Much Johnson

William Wellman
(Feb. 29, 1896–1975)
1958 Lafayette Escadrille;
 Darby's Rangers
1956 Goodbye My Lady
1955 Blood Alley
1954 Track of the Cat; The High
 and the Mighty

1953 Island in the Sky
1952 My Man and I; Westward
 the Women
1951 Accross the Wide Missouri
1950 The Next Voice You Hear;
 The Happy Years
1949 Battleground
1948 Yellow Sky; The Iron
 Curtain
1947 Magic Town
1946 Gallant Journey
1945 The Story of G.I. Joe; This
 Man's Navy
1944 Buffalo Bill
1943 Lady of Burlesque; The
 Ox-Bow Incident
1942 Thunderbirds; The Great
 Man's Lady; Roxy Heart
1941 Reaching for the Sun
1939 The Light That Failed;
 Beau Geste
1938 Men with Wings
1937 Nothing Sacred; A Star Is
 Born
1936 Small Town Girl; The
 Robin Hood of El Dorado
1935 Call of the Wild
1934 The President Vanishes;
 Stingaree; Looking for
 Trouble
1933 College Coach; Wild Boys
 of the Road; Heroes for
 Sale; Midnight Mary; Lilly
 Turner; Central Airport;
 Frisco Jenny
1932 The Conquerers; The
 Purchase Price; Love Is a
 Racket; So Big; The
 Hatchet Man
1931 Safe in Hell; The Star
 Witness; Night Nurse;
 The Public Enemy; Other
 Men's Women
1930 Maybe It's Love; Young
 Eagles; Dangerous
 Paradise
1929 Woman Trap; The Man I
 Love; Chinatown Nights;
 Wings
1928 Beggars of Life; Ladies
 of the Mob; The Legion
 of the Condemned
1927 Wings

1926 You Never Know Women;
 The Cat's Pajamas; The
 Boob
1925 When Husbands Flirt
1924 The Circus Cowboy; Not a
 Drum Was Heard; The
 Vagabond Trail
1923 Cupid's Fireman; Big Dan;
 Secondhand Love; The
 Man Who Won

James Whale
(July 22, 1896–1957)
1941 They Dare Not Love
1940 Green Hell
1939 The Man in the Iron Mask
1938 Port of Seven Seas;
 Wives Under Suspicion;
 Sinners in Paradise
1937 The Road Back; The Great
 Garrick
1936 Showboat
1935 The Bride of Frankenstein;
 Remember Last Night?
1934 One More River
1933 The Invisible Man; The
 Kiss Before the Mirror; By
 Candlelight
1932 The Impatient Maiden;
 The Old Dark House
1931 Waterloo Bridge;
 Frankenstein
1930 Journey's End; Hell's
 Angels

Billy Wilder
(June 22, 1906)
1981 Buddy Buddy
1978 Fedora
1974 The Front Page
1972 Avanti!
1970 The Private Life of
 Sherlock Holmes
1966 The Fortune Cookie
1964 Kiss Me, Stupid!
1963 Irma La Duce
1961 One, Two, Three
1960 The Apartment
1959 Some Like It Hot
1958 Witness for the Prosecution
1957 Love in the Afternoon; The
 Spirit of St. Louis
1955 The Seven Year Itch

1954 Sabrina
1953 Stalag 17
1951 Ace in the Hole
1950 Sunset Boulevard
1948 A Foreign Affair; The
 Emperor Waltz
1945 The Lost Weekend
1944 Double Indemnity
1943 Five Graves to Cairo
1942 The Major and the Minor

Robert Wise
(Sept. 10, 1914)
1989 Rooftops
1979 Star Trek—The Motion
 Picture
1977 Audrey Rose
1975 The Hindenburg
1973 Two People
1971 The Andromeda Strain
1968 Star
1966 The Sand Pebbles
1965 The Sound of Music
1963 The Haunting
1962 Two for the Seesaw
1961 West Side Story
1959 Odds Against Tomorrow
1958 I Want to Live; Run Silent,
 Run Deep
1957 Until They Sail; This Could
 Be the Night
1956 Somebody Up There Likes
 Me; Tribute to a Bad Man
1955 Helen of Troy
1954 Executive Suite
1953 So Big; Destination Gobi;
 The Desert Rats
1952 Something for the Birds;
 The Captive City
1951 The Day the Earth Stood
 Still; The House on
 Telegraph Hill
1950 Three Secrets; Two
 Flags West
1949 The Set-Up
1948 Blood on the Moon;
 Mystery in Mexico
1947 Born to Kill
1946 Criminal Court
1945 A Game of Death; The
 Body Snatcher
1944 Mademoiselle Fifi; The
 Curse of the Cat People

Academy Awards® 1927–1980

The Academy Awards enshrine the movie industry's high opinion of its own achievements, and, therefore, make a fascinating capsule history of Hollywood. In just the short list of most familiar categories, one can see the rise and fall of careers, new technologies blossom, and the influence of social trends and historic events on the filmmakers. The Oscar night ceremony has also become the most anticipated night on the movie fan's calendar, growing from the first, rather intimate, industry gathering at the Hollywood Roosevelt Hotel on May 16, 1929, to today's glamorous event that's broadcast to billions.

1927/1928
Best Picture: *Wings*
Best Actor: Emil Jannings, *The Last Command*; *The Way of All Flesh*
Best Actress: Janet Gaynor, *Seventh Heaven*; *Street Angel*; *Sunrise*
Best Director: Frank Borzage, *Seventh Heaven*; Lewis Milestone, *Two Arabian Knights*

1928/1929
Best Picture: *Broadway Melody*
Best Actor: Warner Baxter, *In Old Arizona*
Best Actress: Mary Pickford, *Coquette*
Best Director: Frank Lloyd, *The Divine Lady*; *Weary River*; *Drag*

1929/1930
Best Picture: *All Quiet on the Western Front*
Best Actor: George Arliss, *Disraeli*
Best Actress: Norma Shearer, *The Divorcée*
Best Director: Lewis Milestone, *All Quiet on the Western Front*

1930/1931
Best Picture: *Cimarron*
Best Actor: Lionel Barrymore, *A Free Soul*
Best Actress: Marie Dressler, *Min and Bill*

Best Director: Norman Taurog, *Skippy*

1931/1932
Best Picture: *Grand Hotel*
Best Actor: Wallace Beery, *The Champ*; Fredric March, *Dr. Jekyll and Mr. Hyde*
Best Actress: Helen Hayes, *The Sin of Madelon Claudet*
Best Director: Frank Borzage, *Bad Girl*

1932/1933
Best Picture: *Cavalcade*
Best Actor: Charles Laughton, *The Private Life of Henry VIII*
Best Actress: Katharine Hepburn, *Morning Glory*
Best Director: Frank Lloyd, *Cavalcade*

1934
Best Picture: *It Happened One Night*
Best Actor: Clark Gable, *It Happened One Night*
Best Actress: Claudette Colbert, *It Happened One Night*
Best Director: Frank Capra, *It Happened One Night*

1935
Best Picture: *Mutiny on the Bounty*
Best Actor: Victor McLaglen, *The Informer*
Best Actress: Bette Davis, *Dangerous*

Best Director: John Ford, *The Informer*

1936
Best Picture: *The Great Ziegfeld*
Best Actor: Paul Muni, *The Story of Louis Pasteur*
Best Actress: Luise Rainer, *The Great Ziegfeld*
Best Supporting Actor: Walter Brennan, *Come and Get It*
Best Supporting Actress: Gale Sondergaard, *Anthony Adverse*
Best Director: Frank Capra, *Mr. Deeds Goes to Town*

1937
Best Picture: *The Life of Emile Zola*
Best Actor: Spencer Tracy, *Captains Courageous*
Best Actress: Luise Rainer, *The Good Earth*
Best Supporting Actor: Joseph Schildkraut, *The Life of Emile Zola*
Best Supporting Actress: Alice Brady, *In Old Chicago*
Best Director: Leo McCarey, *The Awful Truth*

1938
Best Picture: *You Can't Take It with You*
Best Actor: Spencer Tracy, *Boys Town*
Best Actress: Bette Davis, *Jezebel*
Best Supporting Actor: Walter Brennan, *Kentucky*
Best Supporting Actress: Fay Bainter, *Jezebel*
Best Director: Frank Capra, *You Can't Take It with You*

1939
Best Picture: *Gone With the Wind*
Best Actor: Robert Donat, *Goodbye, Mr. Chips*
Best Actress: Vivien Leigh, *Gone With the Wind*
Best Supporting Actor: Thomas Mitchell, *Stagecoach*
Best Supporting Actress: Hattie McDaniel, *Gone With the Wind*
Best Director: Victor Fleming, *Gone With the Wind*

1940

Best Picture: *Rebecca*
Best Actor: James Stewart, *The Philadelphia Story*
Best Actress: Ginger Rogers, *Kitty Foyle*
Best Supporting Actor: Walter Brennan, *The Westerner*
Best Supporting Actress: Jane Darwell, *The Grapes of Wrath*
Best Director: John Ford, *The Grapes of Wrath*

1941

Best Picture: *How Green Was My Valley*
Best Actor: Gary Cooper, *Sergeant York*
Best Actress: Joan Fontaine, *Suspicion*
Best Supporting Actor: Donald Crisp, *How Green Was My Valley*
Best Supporting Actress: Mary Astor, *The Great Lie*
Best Director: John Ford, *How Green Was My Valley*

1942

Best Picture: *Mrs. Miniver*
Best Actor: James Cagney, *Yankee Doodle Dandy*
Best Actress: Greer Garson, *Mrs. Miniver*
Best Supporting Actor: Van Heflin, *Johnny Eager*
Best Supporting Actress: Teresa Wright, *Mrs. Miniver*
Best Director: William Wyler, *Mrs. Miniver*

1943

Best Picture: *Casablanca*
Best Actor: Paul Lukas, *Watch on the Rhine*
Best Actress: Jennifer Jones, *The Song of Bernadette*
Best Supporting Actor: Charles Coburn, *The More the Merrier*
Best Supporting Actress: Katina Paxinou, *For Whom the Bell Tolls*
Best Director: Michael Curtiz, *Casablanca*

1944

Best Picture: *Going My Way*
Best Actor: Bing Crosby, *Going My Way*
Best Actress: Ingrid Bergman, *Gaslight*
Best Supporting Actor: Barry Fitzgerald, *Going My Way*
Best Supporting Actress: Ethel Barrymore, *None but the Lonely Heart*
Best Director: Leo McCarey, *Going My Way*

1945

Best Picture: *The Lost Weekend*
Best Actor: Ray Milland, *The Lost Weekend*
Best Actress: Joan Crawford, *Mildred Pierce*
Best Supporting Actor: James Dunn, *A Tree Grows in Brooklyn*
Best Supporting Actress: Anne Revere, *National Velvet*
Best Director: Billy Wilder, *The Lost Weekend*

1946

Best Picture: *The Best Years of Our Lives*
Best Actor: Fredric March, *The Best Years of Our Lives*
Best Actress: Olivia de Havilland, *To Each His Own*
Best Supporting Actor: Harold Russell, *The Best Years of Our Lives*
Best Supporting Actress: Anne Baxter, *The Razor's Edge*
Best Director: William Wyler, *The Best Years of Our Lives*

1947

Best Picture: *Gentleman's Agreement*
Best Actor: Ronald Colman, *A Double Life*
Best Actress: Loretta Young, *The Farmer's Daughter*
Best Supporting Actor: Edmund Gwenn, *Miracle on 34th Street*
Best Supporting Actress: Celeste Holm, *Gentleman's Agreement*
Best Director: Elia Kazan, *Gentleman's Agreement*

1948

Best Picture: *Hamlet*
Best Actor: Laurence Olivier, *Hamlet*
Best Actress: Jane Wyman, *Johnny Belinda*
Best Supporting Actor: Walter Huston, *The Treasure of the Sierra Madre*
Best Supporting Actress: Claire Trevor, *Key Largo*
Best Director: John Huston, *The Treasure of the Sierra Madre*

1949

Best Picture: *All the King's Men*
Best Actor: Broderick Crawford, *All the King's Men*
Best Actress: Olivia de Havilland, *The Heiress*
Best Supporting Actor: Dean Jagger, *Twelve O'Clock High*
Best Supporting Actress: Mercedes McCambridge, *All the King's Men*
Best Director: Joseph L. Mankiewicz, *A Letter to Three Wives*

1950

Best Picture: *All About Eve*
Best Actor: José Ferrer, *Cyrano de Bergerac*
Best Actress: Judy Holliday, *Born Yesterday*

Best Supporting Actor: George Sanders, *All About Eve*
Best Supporting Actress: Josephine Hull, *Harvey*
Best Director: Joseph L. Mankiewicz, *All About Eve*

Going My Way (1944)

1951
Best Picture: *An American in Paris*
Best Actor: Humphrey Bogart, *The African Queen*
Best Actress: Vivien Leigh, *A Streetcar Named Desire*
Best Supporting Actor: Karl Malden, *A Streetcar Named Desire*
Best Supporting Actress: Kim Hunter, *A Streetcar Named Desire*
Best Director: George Stevens, *A Place in the Sun*

1952
Best Picture: *The Greatest Show on Earth*
Best Actor: Gary Cooper, *High Noon*
Best Actress: Shirley Booth, *Come Back, Little Sheba*
Best Supporting Actor: Anthony Quinn, *Viva Zapata!*
Best Supporting Actress: Gloria Grahame, *The Bad and the Beautiful*
Best Director: John Ford, *The Quiet Man*

1953
Best Picture: *From Here to Eternity*
Best Actor: William Holden, *Stalag 17*
Best Actress: Audrey Hepburn, *Roman Holiday*
Best Supporting Actor: Frank Sinatra, *From Here to Eternity*
Best Supporting Actress: Donna Reed, *From Here to Eternity*
Best Director: Fred Zinnemann, *From Here to Eternity*

1954
Best Picture: *On the Waterfront*
Best Actor: Marlon Brando, *On the Waterfront*
Best Actress: Grace Kelly, *The Country Girl*
Best Supporting Actor: Edmond O'Brien, *The Barefoot Contessa*
Best Supporting Actress: Eva Marie Saint, *On the Waterfront*
Best Director: Elia Kazan, *On the Waterfront*

1955
Best Picture: *Marty*
Best Actor: Ernest Borgnine, *Marty*
Best Actress: Anna Magnani, *The Rose Tattoo*
Best Supporting Actor: Jack Lemmon, *Mister Roberts*
Best Supporting Actress: Jo Van Fleet, *East of Eden*
Best Director: Delbert Mann, *Marty*

1956
Best Picture: *Around the World in 80 Days*
Best Actor: Yul Brynner, *The King and I*

Best Actress: Ingrid Bergman, *Anastasia*
Best Supporting Actor: Anthony Quinn,*Lust for Life*
Best Supporting Actress: Dorothy Malone, *Written on the Wind*
Best Director: George Stevens, *Giant*

1957
Best Picture: *The Bridge on the River Kwai*
Best Actor: Alec Guinoess, *The Bridge on the River Kwai*
Best Actress: Joanne Woodward, *The Three Faces of Eve*
Best Supporting Actor: Red Buttons, *Sayonara*
Best Supporting Actress: Miyoshi Umeki, *Sayonara*
Best Director: David Lean, *The Bridge on the River Kwai*

1958
Best Picture: *Gigi*
Best Actor: David Niven, *Separate Tables*
Best Actress: Susan Hayward, *I Want to Live!*
Best Supporting Actor: Burl Ives, *The Big Country*
Best Supporting Actress: Wendy Hiller, *Separate Tables*
Best Director: Vincente Minnelli, *Gigi*

1959
Best Picture: *Ben-Hur*
Best Actor: Charlton Heston, *Ben-Hur*
Best Actress: Simone Signoret, *Room at the Top*
Best Supporting Actor: Hugh Griffith, *Ben-Hur*
Best Supporting Actress: Shelley Winters, *The Diary of Anne Frank*
Best Director: William Wyler, *Ben-Hur*

1960
Best Picture: *The Apartment*
Best Actor: Burt Lancaster, *Elmer Gantry*
Best Actress: Elizabeth Taylor, *Butterfield 8*
Best Supporting Actor: Peter Ustinov, *Spartacus*
Best Supporting Actress: Shirley Jones, *Elmer Gantry*
Best Director: Billy Wilder, *The Apartment*

1961
Best Picture: *West Side Story*
Best Actor: Maximilian Schell, *Judgment at Nuremburg*
Best Actress: Sophia Loren, *Two Women*
Best Supporting Actor: George Chakiris, *West Side Story*

Best Supporting Actress: Rita Moreno, *West Side Story*
Best Director: Robert Wise and Jerome Robbins, *West Side Story*

1962
Best Picture: *Lawrence of Arabia*
Best Actor: Gregory Peck, *To Kill a Mockingbird*
Best Actress: Anne Bancroft, *The Miracle Worker*
Best Supporting Actor: Ed Begley, *Sweet Bird of Youth*
Best Supporting Actress: Patty Duke, *The Miracle Worker*
Best Director: David Lean, *Lawrence of Arabia*

1963
Best Picture: *Tom Jones*
Best Actor: Sidney Poitier, *Lilies of the Field*
Best Actress: Patricia Neal, *Hud*
Best Supporting Actor: Melvyn Douglas, *Hud*
Best Supporting Actress: Margaret Rutherford, *The V.I.P.s*
Best Director: Tony Richardson, *Tom Jones*

1964
Best Picture: *My Fair Lady*
Best Actor: Rex Harrison, *My Fair Lady*
Best Actress: Julie Andrews, *Mary Poppins*
Best Supporting Actor: Peter Ustinov, *Topkapi*
Best Supporting Actress: Lila Kedrova, *Zorba the Greek*
Best Director: George Cukor, *My Fair Lady*

1965
Best Picture: *The Sound of Music*
Best Actor: Lee Marvin, *Cat Ballou*
Best Actress: Julie Christie, *Darling*
Best Supporting Actor: Martin Balsam, *A Thousand Clowns*
Best Supporting Actress: Shelley Winters, *A Patch of Blue*
Best Director: Robert Wise, *The Sound of Music*

1966
Best Picture: *A Man for All Seasons*
Best Actor: Paul Scofield, *A Man for All Seasons*
Best Actress: Elizabeth Taylor, *Who's Afraid of Virginia Woolf?*
Best Supporting Actor: Walter Matthau, *The Fortune Cookie*
Best Supporting Actress: Sandy Dennis, *Who's Afraid of Virginia Woolf?*
Best Director: Fred Zinnemann, *A Man for All Seasons*

1967
Best Picture: *In the Heat of the Night*
Best Actor: Rod Steiger, *In the Heat of the Night*
Best Actress: Katharine Hepburn, *Guess Who's Coming to Dinner*
Best Supporting Actor: George Kennedy, *Cool Hand Luke*
Best Supporting Actress: Estelle Parsons, *Bonnie and Clyde*
Best Director: Mike Nichols, *The Graduate*

1968
Best Picture: *Oliver!*
Best Actor: Cliff Robertson, *Charly*
Best Actress: Katharine Hepburn, *The Lion in Winter*, Barbra Streisand, *Funny Girl*
Best Supporting Actor: Jack Albertson, *The Subject Was Roses*
Best Supporting Actress: Ruth Gordon, *Rosemary's Baby*
Best Director: Carol Reed, *Oliver!*

1969
Best Picture: *Midnight Cowboy*
Best Actor: John Wayne, *True Grit*
Best Actress: Maggie Smith, *The Prime of Miss Jean Brodie*
Best Supporting Actor: Gig Young, *They Shoot Horses, Don't They?*
Best Supporting Actress: Goldie Hawn, *Cactus Flower*
Best Director: John Schlesinger, *Midnight Cowboy*

1970
Best Picture: *Patton*
Best Actor: George C. Scott, *Patton*
Best Actress: Glenda Jackson, *Women in Love*
Best Supporting Actor: John Mills, *Ryan's Daughter*
Best Supporting Actress: Helen Hayes, *Airport*
Best Director: Franklin J. Schaffner, *Patton*

1971
Best Picture: *The French Connection*
Best Actor: Gene Hackman, *The French Connection*
Best Actress: Jane Fonda, *Klute*
Best Supporting Actor: Ben Johnson, *The Last Picture Show*
Best Supporting Actress: Cloris Leachman, *The Last Picture Show*
Best Director: William Friedkin, *The French Connection*

1972
Best Picture: *The Godfather*
Best Actor: Marlon Brando, *The Godfather*
Best Actress: Liza Minelli, *Cabaret*
Best Supporting Actor: Joel Grey, *Cabaret*

Best Supporting Actress: Eileen Heckart, *Butterflies Are Free*
Best Director: Bob Fosse, *Cabaret*

1973
Best Picture: *The Sting*
Best Actor: Jack Lemmon, *Save the Tiger*
Best Actress: Glenda Jackson, *A Touch of Class*
Best Supporting Actor: John Houseman, *The Paper Chase*
Best Supporting Actress: Tatum O'Neal, *Paper Moon*
Best Director: George Roy Hill, *The Sting*

1974
Best Picture: *The Godfather Part II*
Best Actor: Art Carney, *Harry and Tonto*
Best Actress: Ellen Burstyn, *Alice Doesn't Live Here Anymore*

Best Supporting Actor: Robert De Niro, *The Godfather Part II*
Best Supporting Actress: Ingrid Bergman, *Murder on the Orient Express*
Best Director: Francis Ford Coppola, *The Godfather Part II*

1975
Best Picture: *One Flew over the Cuckoo's Nest*
Best Actor: Jack Nicholson, *One Flew over the Cuckoo's Nest*
Best Actress: Louise Fletcher, *One Flew over the Cuckoo's Nest*
Best Supporting Actor: George Burns, *The Sunshine Boys*
Best Supporting Actress: Lee Grant, *Shampoo*
Best Director: Milos Forman, *One Flew over the Cuckoo's Nest*

The Sound of Music (1965)

1976
Best Picture: *Rocky*
Best Actor: Peter Finch, *Network*
Best Actress: Faye Dunaway, *Network*
Best Supporting Actor: Jason Robards, *All the President's Men*
Best Supporting Actress: Beatrice Straight, *Network*
Best Director: John G. Avildsen, *Rocky*

1977
Best Picture: *Annie Hall*
Best Actor: Richard Dreyfuss, *The Goodbye Girl*
Best Actress: Diane Keaton, *Annie Hall*
Best Supporting Actor: Jason Robards, *Julia*
Best Supporting Actress: Vanessa Redgrave, *Julia*
Best Director: Woody Allen, *Annie Hall*

1978
Best Picture: *The Deer Hunter*
Best Actor: Jon Voight, *Coming Home*
Best Actress: Jane Fonda, *Coming Home*
Best Supporting Actor: Christopher Walken, *The Deer Hunter*
Best Supporting Actress: Maggie Smith, *California Suite*
Best Director: Michael Cimino, *The Deer Hunter*

1979
Best Picture: *Kramer vs. Kramer*
Best Actor: Dustin Hoffman, *Kramer vs. Kramer*
Best Actress: Sally Field, *Norma Rae*
Best Supporting Actor: Melvyn Douglas, *Being There*

Best Supporting Actress: Meryl Streep, *Kramer vs. Kramer*
Best Director: Robert Benton, *Kramer vs. Kramer*

1980
Best Picture: *Ordinary People*
Best Actor: Robert De Niro, *Raging Bull*
Best Actress: Sissy Spacek, *Coal Miner's Daughter*
Best Supporting Actor: Timothy Hutton, *Ordinary People*
Best Supporting Actress: Mary Steenburgen, *Melvin and Howard*
Best Director: Robert Redford, *Ordinary People*

Kramer vs. Kramer (1979)

The Most Popular Movies 1939–1980

The list below, based on film rentals—the money the movie studio receives from exhibitors—provides a snapshot of the top-earning movies through the decades, and an interesting comparison with the industry favorites as voted by the Academy. Think of the list below as the popular vote. The film rental figures were derived from *Variety* and other industry publications.

1939
1. Gone With the Wind $77,641,106
2. The Wizard of Oz 4,544,851
3. The Hunchback of Notre Dame *(tie)* 1,500,000
3. Jesse James *(tie)* 1,500,000
3. Mr. Smith Goes to Washington *(tie)* 1,500,000

1940
1. Fantasia $41,660,000
2. Pinocchio 40,442,000
3. Boom Town 4,586,415
4. Rebecca *(tie)* 1,500,000
4. Santa Fe Trail *(tie)* 1,500,000

1941
1. Sergeant York $6,135,707
2. Dive Bomber *(tie)* 1,500,000
2. Honky Tonk *(tie)* 1,500,000
2. The Philadelphia Story *(tie)* 1,500,000
2. A Yank in the R.A.F. *(tie)* 1,500,000

1942
1. Bambi $47,265,000
2. Mrs. Miniver 5,390,009
3. Yankee Doodle Dandy 4,719,681
4. Random Harvest 4,665,501
5. Casablanca 4,145,178

1943
1. This Is the Army $8,301,000
2. For Whom the Bell Tolls 7,100,000
3. The Outlaw 5,075,000
4. The Song of Bernadette 5,000,000
5. Stage Door Canteen 4,339,532

1944
1. Going My Way $6,500.000
2. Meet Me in St. Louis 5,132,202
3. Since You Went Away 4,924,756
4. 30 Seconds over Tokyo 4,471,080
5. White Cliffs of Dover 4,045,250

1945
1. The Bells of St. Mary's $8,000,000
2. Leave Her to Heaven 5,500,000
3. Spellbound 4,970,583
4. Anchors Aweigh 4,778,679
5. The Valley of Decision 4,566,374

1946
1. Song of the South $29,228,717
2. The Best Years of Our Lives *(tie)* 11,300,000
2. Duel in the Sun *(tie)* 11,300,000
4. The Jolson Story 7,600,000
5. Blue Skies 5,700,000

1947
1. Welcome Stranger $6,100,000
2. The Egg and I 5,500,000
3. Unconquered 5,250,000
4. Life with Father 5,057,000
5. Forever Amber 5,000,000

1948
1. The Red Shoes $5,000,000
2. Red River 4,506,825
3. The Paleface 4,500,000
4. The Three Musketeers 4,306,876
5. Johnny Belinda 4,266,000

1949
1. Samson and Delilah $11,500,000
2. Battleground 5,051,143
3. Jolson Sings Again *(tie)* 5,000,000
3. The Sands of Iwo Jima *(tie)* 5,000,000
5. I Was a Male War Bride 4,100,000

1950
1. Cinderella $41,087,000
2. King Solomon's Mines 5,586,000
3. Annie Get Your Gun 4,919,394
4. Cheaper by the Dozen 4,425,000
5. Father of the Bride 4,054,405

1951
1. Quo Vadis? $11,901,662
2. Alice in Wonderland 7,196,000
3. Show Boat 5,533,000
4. David and Bathsheba 4,720,000
5. The Great Caruso 4,531,000

1952
1. This Is Cinerama $15,400,000
2. The Greatest Show on Earth 14,000,000
3. The Snows of Kilimanjaro 6,500,000
4. Ivanhoe 6,258,000
5. Hans Christian Andersen 6,000,000

1953
1. Peter Pan $37,584,000
2. The Robe 17,500,000
3. From Here to Eternity 12,200,000
4. Shane 9,000,000
5. How to Marry a Millionaire 7,300,000

1954
1. White Christmas $12,000,000
2. 20,000 Leagues Under the Sea 11,267,000
3. Rear Window 9,812,271
4. The Caine Mutiny 8,700,000
5. The Glenn Miller Story 7,590,994

1955
1. Lady and the Tramp $40,249,000
2. Cinerama Holiday 12,000,000
3. Mister Roberts 8,500,000
4. Battle Cry 8,100,000
5. Oklahoma! 7,100,000

1956
1. The Ten
   Commandments $43,000,000
2. Around the World in
   80 Days 23,120,000
3. Giant 14,000,000
4. Seven Wonders of
   the World 12,500,000
5. The King and I 8,500,000

1957
1. The Bridge on the
   River Kwai $17,195,000
2. Peyton Place 11,500,000
3. Sayonara 10,500,000
4. Old Yeller 10,050,000
5. Raintree County 5,962,839

1958
1. South Pacific $17,500,000
2. Auntie Mame 9,300,000
3. Cat on a Hot Tin Roof 8,785,162

The Ten Commandments (1956)

4. No Time for Sergeants 7,500,000
5. Gigi 7,321.423

1959
1. Ben-Hur $36,992,088
2. Sleeping Beauty 21,998,000
3. The Shaggy Dog 12,317,000
4. Operation Petticoat 9,321,555
5. Darby O'Gill and the
   Little People 8,336,000

1960
1. Swiss Family
   Robinson $20,178,000
2. Psycho 11,200,000
3. Spartacus 10,300,454
4. Exodus 8,331,582
5. The Alamo 7,918,776

1961
1. 101 Dalmatians $68,648,000
2. West Side Story 19,645,570

3. The Guns of
   Navarone 13,000,000
4. El Cid 12,000,000
5. The Absent-Minded
   Professor 11,426,000

1962
1. How the West
   Was Won $20,932,883
2. Lawrence of Arabia 20,310,000
3. The Longest Day 17,600,000
4. In Search of the
   Castaways 9,975,000
5. The Music Man 8,100,000

1963
1. Cleopatra $26,000,000
2. It's a Mad, Mad,
   Mad,Mad World 20,849,786
3. Tom Jones 16,925,988
4. Irma La Douce 11,921,784
5. The Sword in
   the Stone 10,475,000

1964
1. Mary Poppins $45,000,000
2. Goldfinger 22,997,706
3. The Carpetbaggers 15,500,000
4. My Fair Lady 12,000,000
5. From Russia with Love 9,924,279

1965
1. The Sound of Music $79,975,000
2. Doctor Zhivago 47,116,811
3. Thunderball 28,621,434
4. Those Magnificent
   Men in Their
   Flying Machines 14,000,000
5. That Darn Cat 12,628,000

1966
1. Hawaii $15,553,018
2. The Bible 15,000,000
3. Who's Afraid of
   Virginia Woolf? 14,500,000
4. A Man for All Seasons 12,750,000
5. Lt. Robin Crusoe, USN 10,164,000

1967
1. The Jungle Book $60,964,000
2. The Graduate 44,090,729
3. Guess Who's Coming
   to Dinner 25,500,000
4. Bonnie and Clyde 22,800,000
5. The Dirty Dozen 20,403,826

1968
1. Funny Girl $26,325,000
2. 2001: A Space
   Odyssey 25,521,917
3. The Odd Couple 20,000,000
4. Bullitt 19,000,000
5. Romeo and Juliet 17,473,000

1969
1. Butch Cassidy and
   the Sundance Kid $46,039,000

2. The Love Bug 23,150,000
3. Midnight Cowboy 20,499,282
4. Easy Rider 19,100,000
5. Hello, Dolly! 15,200,000

1970
1. Love Story $50,000,000
2. Airport 45,220,118
3. M*A*S*H 36,720,000
4. Patton 28,100,000
5. The Aristocats 26,462,000

1971
1. Fiddler on the Roof $38,251,196
2. Billy Jack 32,500,000
3. The French Connection 26,315,000
4. Summer of '42 20,500,000
5. Diamonds Are Forever 19,726,829

1972
1. The Godfather $86,691,000
2. The Poseidon
   Adventure 42,000,000
3. What's Up Doc? 28,000,000
4. Deliverance 22,600,000
5. Jeremiah Johnson 21,900,000

1973
1. The Exorcist $89,000,000
2. The Sting 78,212,000

3. American Graffiti 55,128,175
4. Papillon 22,500,000
5. The Way We Were 22,457,000

1974
1. The Towering Inferno $52,000,000
2. Blazing Saddles 47,800,000
3. Young Frankenstein 38,823,000
4. Earthquake 35,849,994
5. The Trial of Billy Jack 31,100,000

1975
1. Jaws $129,549,325
2. One Flew over the
   Cuckoo's Nest 59,939,701
3. The Rocky Horror
   Picture Show 49,782,690
4. Shampoo 23,822,000
5. Dog Day Afternoon 22,500,000

1976
1. Rocky $56,524,972
2. A Star Is Born 37,100,000
3. King Kong 36,915,000
4. Silver Streak 30,018,000
5. All the President's Men 30,000,000

1977
1. Star Wars $270,918,000
2. Close Encounters

of the Third Kind 82,750,000
3. Saturday Night Fever 74,100,000
4. Smokey and the Bandit 58,949,939
5. The Goodbye Girl 41,839,170

1978
1. Grease $96,300,000
2. Superman 82,800,000
3. National Lampoon's
   Animal House 70,826,000
4. Every Which Way
   but Loose 51,900,000
5. Jaws 2 50,431,964

1979
1. Kramer vs. Kramer $59,986,335
2. Star Trek: The
   Motion Picture 56,000,000
3. The Jerk 42,989,656
4. Rocky II 42,169,387
5. Alien 40,300,000

1980
1. The Empire
   Strikes Back $173,814,000
2. 9 to 5 59,100,000
3. Stir Crazy 58,364,420
4. Airplane! 40,610,000
5. Any Which Way
   You Can 40,500,000

Wish List

Pondering the American Film Institute 100

by Alicia Potter

So notorious is its stature that, among certain cinephiles, you could simply say "The List" and a furor of Vesuvian proportions would erupt. Yes, we're talking about the American Film Institute's roster of what it deems America's 100 greatest movies. Few have embraced it; some have excoriated it. However, one thing's for sure: The List has trumped *Titanic* director James Cameron's Oscar acceptance speech/ego-leak as 1998's greatest cinematic controversy.

It's inspired column inches of analyses and pontifications and, of course, yards of alternative lists. In all, the hoopla distills American film to three rudimentary questions: What's good? What's bad? and Where's Buster Keaton?

First, some background. The American Film Institute (AFI) started the selection process in November 1996, when its archivists and historians whittled down a century of cinema (1896–1996) to 400 feature films of varying noteworthiness.

Ballots listing all 400 were then sent to a wide range of movie folk—actors, directors, producers, cinematographers, studio executives, exhibitors, critics—and a few outside the biz, most notably President and Mrs. Clinton and Vice President and Mrs. Gore. The process of selecting the final 100 was truly "secret ballot": AFI won't reveal who received the ballots, or how many of the 1,500 voters actually participated.

The voting may have been hushed, but the aftermath has crescendo'd into a cacophony of rants. And, we agree, some of the list's exclusions are deeply distressing. With the exception of *Double Indemnity* (1944; No. 38), film noir gets blacked out; and, save for *The Birth of a Nation* (1915; No. 44), so do silent dramas, easily some of the most beautiful—and seminal—films of all time. Like other critics of the list, we gasped over who got snubbed at the door: no Fred and Ginger, no Buster, no Greta, no Preston, no Ernst.

Seth Oster, spokesman for AFI, responds, "If you criticize the list because of one film or one actor that either made it or didn't, you're losing sight of the others that are there."

Still, the list inspires considerable head-scratching. Consider the AFI's definition of American film: *Lawrence of Arabia* (1962; No. 5), *The Bridge on the River Kwai* (1957; No. 13)—both by British director David Lean and financed overseas. Also, while it's not in the top 100, 1996's *The English Patient,* the work of a Canadian author, a British director and screenwriter, and a predominantly European cast, appeared on the top-400 list. In this case, as long as American dollars are behind a film, that's American enough.

Across The Pond, the British Film Institute (BFI) issued its own list earlier this year with nary a breath of controversy. It generously opened its slate to 360 films (yes, Buster Keaton's there) of international origins. Interestingly, BFI wrapped the list at 1981, because, as it argues, a film needs

Alicia Potter is a staff writer for American Movie Classics Magazine. *She also writes for the* Boston Phoenix *and the* Boston Herald.

time to "settle in one's mind and mature." The British archivists also opted not to rank the films, and instead filed them by year.

That's where AFI derailed. To say Steven Spielberg's *E.T.: The Extra-Terrestrial* (1982; No. 25) is better, or more influential, than D. W. Griffith's *The Birth of a Nation* is not to compare apples and oranges but apples and guavas. By nature, film eludes such narrow comparison—the lines between entertainment and art, style and substance, have always been delightfully wavy.

Meanwhile, the notion of compressing a century of cinema into a neat, wholly marketable list digs at what's most troubling about the film industry today. It smacks of the commercial juggernaut, that publicity machine that turns actors into action figures, and holds its breath to see what direction a critic's thumb will take.

Yet despite the list's drawbacks it's impossible not to admit that many of the films in the top 100 are in exceptionally good company: *Citizen Kane* (1941); *Casablanca* (1942); *On the Waterfront* (1954); *The Searchers* (1956); *All Quiet on the Western Front* (1930); and two John Ford films, the starkly powerful *The Grapes of Wrath* (1940) and the peerless *Stagecoach* (1939), to name but a few. Oster himself pshaws the backlash. "We wanted to shift cocktail conversation away from box-office grosses to how movies have changed our culture," he says. "The talk means we've been successful. I'm not surprised by it. I'm encouraged by it."

Touché. Indeed, no matter on which side of the water-cooler debate you fall, it's hard to fault AFI for getting a nation riled about film, especially classic film. If the list inspires an 18-year-old to rent *Citizen Kane*—or, for that matter, an 80-year-old to rent *Pulp Fiction*—so be it.

And who can predict the power of the films that didn't make the list but still received a waterfall of publicity? Perhaps, somewhere, someone is watching *The Navigator* (1924) for the first time and figuring out what the big deal is about that Keaton chap.

The Birth of a Nation (1915)

The American Film Institute List of 100 Greatest Movies

1. Citizen Kane (1941)
2. Casablanca (1942)
3. The Godfather (1972)
4. Gone With the Wind (1939)
5. Lawrence of Arabia (1962)
6. The Wizard of Oz (1939)
7. The Graduate (1967)
8. On the Waterfront (1954)
9. Schindler's List (1993)
10. Singin' in the Rain (1952)
11. It's a Wonderful Life (1946)
12. Sunset Boulevard (1950)
13. The Bridge on the River Kwai (1957)
14. Some Like It Hot (1959)
15. Star Wars (1977)
16. All About Eve (1950)
17. The African Queen (1951)
18. Psycho (1960)
19. Chinatown (1974)
20. One Flew over the Cuckoo's Nest (1975)
21. The Grapes of Wrath (1940)
22. 2001: A Space Odyssey (1968)
23. The Maltese Falcon (1941)
24. Raging Bull (1980)
25. E.T.: The Extra-Terrestrial (1982)
26. Dr. Strangelove or: How I Learned to Stop Worrying and Love the Bomb (1964)
27. Bonnie and Clyde (1967)
28. Apocalypse Now (1979)
29. Mr.Smith Goes to Washington (1939)
30. The Treasure of the Sierra Madre (1948)
31. Annie Hall (1977)
32. The Godfather Part II (1974)
33. High Noon (1952)
34. To Kill a Mockingbird (1962)
35. It Happened One Night (1934)
36. Midnight Cowboy (1969)
37. The Best Years of Our Lives (1946)
38. Double Indemnity (1944)
39. Doctor Zhivago (1965)
40. North by Northwest (1959)
41. West Side Story (1961)
42. Rear Window (1954)
43. King Kong (1933)
44. The Birth of a Nation (1915)
45. A Streetcar Named Desire (1951)
46. A Clockwork Orange (1971)
47. Taxi Driver (1976)
48. Jaws (1975)
49. Snow White and the Seven Dwarfs (1937)
50. Butch Cassidy and the Sundance Kid (1969)
51. The Philadelphia Story (1940)
52. From Here to Eternity (1953)
53. Amadeus (1984)
54. All Quiet on the Western Front (1930)
55. The Sound of Music (1965)
56. M*A*S*H (1970)
57. The Third Man (1949)
58. Fantasia (1940)
59. Rebel Without a Cause (1955)
60. Raiders of the Lost Ark (1981)
61. Vertigo (1958)
62. Tootsie (1982)
63. Stagecoach (1939)
64. Close Encounters of the Third Kind (1977)
65. The Silence of the Lambs (1991)
66. Network (1976)
67. The Manchurian Candidate (1962)

The Details

Many critics have brooded that the American Film Institute's list was a "popularity contest," that, from the start, it was top-heavy with recent movies. Indeed, the original list of 400 films contains some, well, curious choices—*Pretty Woman* (1990), *Ferris Bueller's Day Off* (1986), and *Beverly Hills Cop* (1984)—that nudge out timeless movies like a game of musical chairs. However, here's how classic film fared overall:

• The 1950s is the most represented decade on the list, with 20 films.

• The year 1939 has 5 films in the top 100: *Gone With the Wind, The Wizard of Oz, Stagecoach, Wuthering Heights,* and *Mr. Smith Goes to Washington.*

• Charlie Chaplin is the most celebrated actor-director, with 3 films. Among the unhyphenated, Alfred Hitchcock made the list with 4 titles, John Huston with 3, and Steven Spielberg leads all with 5.

• Marlon Brando is the only actor to star in 2 of the top 10 films.

• Katharine Hepburn is the most represented leading actress, with 4 films.

• Four silent films made the list.

Chinatown (1974)

68. An American in Paris *(1951)*
69. Shane *(1953)*
70. The French Connection *(1971)*
71. Forrest Gump *(1994)*
72. Ben-Hur *(1959)*
73. Wuthering Heights *(1939)*
74. The Gold Rush *(1925)*
75. Dances With Wolves *(1990)*
76. City Lights *(1931)*
77. American Graffiti *(1973)*
78. Rocky *(1976)*
79. The Deer Hunter *(1978)*

80. The Wild Bunch *(1969)*
81. Modern Times *(1936)*
82. Giant *(1956)*
83. Platoon *(1986)*
84. Fargo *(1996)*
85. Duck Soup *(1933)*
86. Mutiny on the Bounty *(1935)*
87. Frankenstein *(1931)*
88. Easy Rider *(1969)*
89. Patton *(1970)*
90. The Jazz Singer *(1927)*
91. My Fair Lady *(1964)*

92. A Place in the Sun *(1951)*
93. The Apartment *(1960)*
94. Goodfellas *(1990)*
95. Pulp Fiction *(1994)*
96. The Searchers *(1956)*
97. Bringing Up Baby *(1938)*
98. Unforgiven *(1992)*
99. Guess Who's Coming to Dinner *(1967)*
100. Yankee Doodle Dandy *(1942)*

The British Film Institute List

The British Film Institute developed a list of 360 classics of world cinema in the course of its ongoing effort to ensure the availability of prints for theatrical screening. As demand from the repertory cinemas declined, distributors vanished, television outlets turned to video editions of the classics, and the number of classic-movie prints dwindled. BFI archivist David Meeker began the project in 1982 as the first step in his effort to build a library of perfect show-prints to be screened at the Museum of the Moving Image in London. He insists that his isn't a "greatest hits" list, and that the choices reflect his own (unusually well-informed) opinions. However, the BFI list makes a wonderful primer on the history of world cinema and a "must see" checklist that will last a lifetime.

1914
Cabiria *(Giovanni Pastrone)*

1915
The Birth of a Nation *(D. W. Griffith)*
The Cheat *(Cecil B. DeMille)*

1916
Les Vampires *(Louis Feuillade)*
Intolerance, Love's Struggle Throughout the Ages *(D. W. Griffith)*
Judex *(Louis Feuillade)*

1918
J'accuse *(Abel Gance)*
Tih Nimh *(Louis Feuillade)*

1919
Karin Ingmarsdotter *(Victor Sjostrom)*
True Heart Susie *(D. W. Griffith)*
Die Austernprinzessin ("The Oyster Princess") *(Ernst Lubitsch)*

1920
Das Cabinet des Dr. Caligari *(Robert Wiene)*

1921
La Roue *(Abel Gance)*

1922
Foolish Wives *(Erich Von Stroheim)*

1923
Gunnar Hedes saga *(Mauritz Stiller)*

Die Nibelungen, Ein deutsches Heldenlied I: Siegfrieds Tod *(Fritz Lang)*

1924
Die Nibelungen, Ein deutsches Heldenlied II: Kriemhilds Rache *(Fritz Lang)*
Der letzte Mann (The Last Laugh) *(Friedrich W. Murnau)*
The Navigator *(Buster Keaton, Donald Crisp)*
Inhumaine *(Marcel L'Herbier)*
Neobychainiye Priklucheniya Mistera Vesta v Stranye Bolshevikov ("The Extraordinary Adventures of Mr. West in the Land of the Bolsheviks") *(Lev Kuleshov)*
Greed *(Erich Von Stroheim)*

1925
Stachka ("Strike") *(Sergei M. Eisenstein)*
The Gold Rush *(Charles Chaplin)*
The Freshman *(Fred Newmeyer, Sam Taylor)*
Visages d'enfants ("Faces of Children") *(Jacques Feyder)*
The Unholy Three *(Tod Browning)*
Variete ("Vaudeville") *(E. A. Dupont)*
Tumbleweeds *(King Baggot)*
Bronenosets Potyomkin ("Battleship Potemkin") *(Sergei M. Eisenstein)*
Metropolis *(Fritz Lang)*

1926
Mat' ("Mother") *(V. I. Pudovkin)*
Dura Lex ("By the Law") *(Lev Kuleshov)*
Hands Up! *(Clarence Badger)*
Flesh and the Devil *(Clarence Brown)*
The Lodger: A Story of the London Fog *(Alfred Hitchcock)*
The Strong Man *(Frank Capra)*
Geheimnisse einer Seele ("Secrets of a Soul") *(G. W. Pabst)*
Faust-eine deutsche Volkssage *(Friedrich W. Murnau)*
Kurutta Ippeiji ("A Page of Madness") *(Teinosukel Cinugasa)*
Napoleon *(Abel Gance)*

1927
Sunrise, a Song of Two Humans *(F. W. Murnau)*
Un chapeau de paille d'Italie ("An Italian Straw Hat") *(Rene Clair)*
Berlin, die Sinfonie der Grosstadt ("Berlin, Symphony of a City") *(Walther Ruttmann)*
The Crowd *(King Vidor)*
Love *(Edmund Goulding)*
La Passion de Jeanne d'Arc *(Carl Theodor Dreyer)*
The Man Who Laughs *(Paul Leni)*

1928
The Docks of New York *(Josef von Sternberg)*
Steamboat Bill, Jr. *(Charles F. Reisner)*
Dom na Trubnoi ("The House on Trubnaya Square") *(Boris Barnet)*
Oktyabr ("October") *(Sergei M. Eisenstein, Grigori Alexandrov)*
The Wind *(Victor Sjostrom)*
Queen Kelly *(Erich Von Stroheim)*
Heimkehr *(Joe May)*
Chelovyek S Kinoaparatom ("The Man with a Movie Camera") *(Dziga Vertov)*
L'Argent *(Marcel L'Herbier)*
Asphalt *(Joe May)*
Spione ("The Spy") *(Fritz Lang)*

1929

Blackmail *(silent version; Alfred Hitchcock)*
Die Wunderbare Luge Der Nina Petrowna *(Hans Schwarz)*
Piccadilly *(silent version; E. A. Dupont)*
Die Buchse der Pandora (Variationen Auf Das Thema Frank Wedekind's Lulu) *(G. W. Pabst)*
Menschen am Sonntag ("People on Sunday") *(Robert Siodmak, Edgar G. Ulmer)*
Applause *(Rouben Mamoulian)*

1930

The Big Trail *(Raoul Walsh)*
Zemlja ("Earth") *(Alexander P. Dovzhenko)*
Der Blaue Engel ("The Blue Angel") *(Josef von Sternberg)*
L'Age d'or *(Luis Buñuel)*
Little Caesar *(Mervyn LeRoy)*
All Quiet on the Western Front *(Lewis Milestone)*
Ariane *(Paul Czinner)*

1931

Frankenstein *(James Whale)*
The Public Enemy *(William A. Wellman)*
M *(Fritz Lang)*
La Chienne *(Jean Renoir)*
City Lights *(Charles Chaplin)*
Le Million *(Rene Clair)*
Marius *(Alexander Korda)*
Die 3-Groschen-Oper ("The Threepenny Opera") *(German version; G. W. Pabst)*

1932

Love Me Tonight *(Rouben Mamoulian)*
Vampyr Der Traum des Allan Gray *(Carl Theodor Dreyer)*
Boudu sauve des eaux ("Boudu Saved from Drowning") *(Jean Renoir)*
Tavaszi Zapor/Marie, Legende hongroise *(Paul Fejos)*
Scarface *(Howard Hawks)*
The Most Dangerous Game *(Ernest B. Schoedsack, Irving Pichel)*
Liebelei *(Max Ophuls)*

1933

42nd Street *(Lloyd Bacon)*
King Kong *(Ernest B. Schoedsack, Merian C. Cooper)*
Chuncan ("Spring Silkworms") *(Cheng Bugao)*
Tanming ("Daybreak") *(Sun Yu)*
Queen Christina *(Rouben Mamoulian)*
Hallelujah I'm a Bum *(Lewis Milestone)*
Duck Soup *(Leo McCarey)*

1934

L'Atalante *(Jean Vigo)*
La signora di tutti *(Max Ophuls)*
It Happened One Night *(Frank Capra)*
It's a Gift *(Norman Z. McLeod)*
The Scarlet Empress *(Josef von Sternberg)*

Shennu ("The Goddess") *(Wu Yonggang)*

1935

Toni *(Jean Renoir)*
Novyi Gulliver *(Aleksander Ptushko)*
La Kermesse heroique ("Carnival in Flanders") *(French version; Jacques Feyder)*
First a Girl *(Victor Saville)*
A Night at the Opera *(Sam Wood)*
Tsuma Yo Bara No Yoni ("Wife, Be Like a Rose") *(Mikio Naruse)*
Bride of Frankenstein *(James Whale)*

1936

La Belle Equipe *(Julien Duvivier)*
Triumph des Willens ("Triumph of the Will") *(Leni Riefenstahl)*
Modern Times *(Charles Chaplin)*
Le Roman d'un tricheur ("Diary of a Cheat") *(Sacha Guitry)*
Rembrandt *(Alexander Korda)*
Things to Come *(William Cameron Menzies)*
Swing Time *(George Stevens)*
Show Boat *(James Whale)*
Cesar *(Marcel Pagnol)*
Way Out West *(James W. Horne)*

1937

Pepe Le Moko *(Julien Duvivier)*
Nothing Sacred *(William A. Wellman)*
La Grande Illusion *(Jean Renoir)*
Malu Tanshi ("Street Angel") *(Yuan Muzhi)*
Les Perles de la Couronne ("The Pearls of the Crown") *(Sacha Guitry, Christian-Jaque)*
Snow White and the Seven Dwarfs *(David Hand)*
Un carnet de bal *(Julien Duvivier)*
Oh, Mr Porter! *(Marcel Varnel)*

1938

Bringing Up Baby *(Howard Hawks)*
Jezebel *(William Wyler)*
Olympia *(Leni Riefenstahl)*
La Bête humaine *(Jean Renoir)*
Quai des brumes *(Marcel Carne)*
Aleksandr Nevskii ("Alexander Nevsky") *(Sergei M. Eisenstein, Dmitri Vasiliev)*
Varastettu kuolema ("Stolen Death") *(Nyrki Tapiovaara)*

1939

The Wizard of Oz *(Victor Fleming)*
Only Angels Have Wings *(Howard Hawks)*
La Regle du jeu *(Jean Renoir)*
Stagecoach *(John Ford)*
Le Jour se leve *(Marcel Carne)*
Zangiku monogatari ("The Story of Late Chrysanthemums") *(Kenji Mizoguchi)*

1940

The Grapes of Wrath *(John Ford)*
The Thief of Bagdad *(Ludwig Berger, Michael Powell, Tim Whelan)*
Fantasia *(Walt Disney Productions)*

1941

Remorques *(Jean Gremillon)*
Citizen Kane *(Orson Welles)*
Sullivan's Travels *(Preston Sturges)*
The Maltese Falcon *(John Huston)*

1942

La Nuit fantastique *(Marcel L'Herbier)*
The Magnificent Ambersons *(Orson Welles)*
Aniki Bobo *(Manoel De Oliveira)*
Ossessione *(Luchino Visconti)*
Went the Day Well? *(Alberto Cavalcanti)*

Greed (1924)

The Palm Beach Story
  (Preston Sturges)
To Be or Not to Be (Ernst Lubitsch)
Casablanca (Michael Curtiz)
Le Corbeau (Henri-Georges Clouzot)

1943
Douce (Claude Autant-Lara)
Cat People (Jacques Tourneur)
The Life and Death of Colonel Blimp
  (Michael Powell,
  Emeric Pressburger)
Fires Were Started
  (Humphrey Jennings)
I Walked with a Zombie
  (Jacques Tourneur)
Millions Like Us (Frank Launder,
  Sidney Gilliat)

1944
The Chronicle History of King
  Henry the Fifth with His
  Battell Fought at Agincourt in
  France (Laurence Olivier)
Meet Me in St. Louis
  (Vincente Minnelli)
Laura (Otto Preminger)
Double Indemnity (Billy Wilder)
To Have and Have Not
  (Howard Hawks)
Ivan Groznyi ("Ivan the Terrible," Parts
  One and Two; Part Two, 1946)
  (Sergei M. Eisenstein)

1945
Les Enfants du Paradis (Marcel Carne)
Brief Encounter (David Lean)
Roma citta aperta ("Rome, Open
  City") (Roberto Rossellini)
A Walk in the Sun (Lewis Milestone)
I Know Where I'm Going!
  (Michael Powell,
  Emeric Pressburger)
Les Dames du Bois de Boulogne
  (Robert Bresson)
G.I. Joe (William A. Wellman)

1946
La Belle et la bête (Jean Cocteau)
The Big Sleep (Howard Hawks)
My Darling Clementine (John Ford)
The Best Years of Our Lives
  (William Wyler)
A Matter of Life and Death
  (Michael Powell,
  Emeric Pressburger)
Leave Her to Heaven (John M. Stahl)
Great Expectations (David Lean)

1947
Odd Man Out (Carol Reed)
The Ghost and Mrs. Muir
  (Joseph Mankiewicz)
Quai des Orfevres
  (Henri-Georges Clouzot)
Black Narcissus (Michael Powell,
  Emeric Pressburger)
Red River (Howard Hawks)
Yijiang Chunshui Xiang Dong Liu

("The Spring River Flows East")
  (Cai Chusheng, Zheng Junli)
Jour de fête (Jacques Tati)

1948
Ladri di biciclette ("The Bicycle Thief")
  (Vittorio De Sica)
Letter from an Unknown Woman
  (Max Ophuls)
Fort Apache (John Ford)
The Red Shoes (Michael Powell,
  Emeric Pressburger)
Moonrise (Frank Borzage)
Une si jolie petite plage (Yves Allegret)

1949
White Heat (Raoul Walsh)
Gun Crazy (Joseph H. Lewis)
Wuya Yu Maque ("Crows and
  Sparrows") (Zheng Junli)
Kind Hearts and Coronets
  (Robert Hamer)
She Wore a Yellow Ribbon (John Ford)
Les Enfants terribles
  (Jean-Pierre Melville)
The Third Man (Carol Reed)
La Beauté du diable (René Clair)

1950
Cyrano de Bergerac (Michael Gordon)
In a Lonely Place (Nicholas Ray)
The Asphalt Jungle (John Huston)
Los Olvidados (Luis Buñuel)
Orphée (Jean Cocteau)
Rio Grande (John Ford)
Wagon Master (John Ford)
Sunset Boulevard (Billy Wilder)
Rashomon (Akira Kurosawa)
La Ronde (Max Ophuls)

1951
The Medium (Gian-Carlo Menotti)
Fröken Julie ("Miss Julie")
  (Alf Sjoberg)
Strangers on a Train (Alfred Hitchcock)
The Thing from Another World
  (Christian Nyby)
Singin' in the Rain (Stanley Donen,
  Gene Kelly)

1952
Les Vacances de M. Hulot
  (Jacques Tati)
High Noon (Fred Zinnemann)
Ikiru ("Living") (Akira Kurosawa)
The Quiet Man (John Ford)
Jeux interdits ("Forbidden Games")
  (Rene Clement)
Casque d'or (Jacques Becker)
El (Luis Buñuel)
Shane (George Stevens)

1953
The Band Wagon (Vincente Minnelli)
From Here to Eternity
  (Fred Zinnemann)
Tokyo Monogatari ("Tokyo Story")
  (Yasujiro Ozu)
The Big Heat (Fritz Lang)
The Sun Shines Bright (John Ford)

I vitelloni (Federico Fellini)

1954
Sansho Dayu (Kenji Mizoguchi)
Shichinin No Samurai ("The Seven
  Samurai") (Akira Kurosawa)
Pokolenie ("A Generation")
  (Andrzej Wajda)
On the Waterfront (Elia Kazan)
A Star Is Born (George Cukor)

1955
Lola Montès/Lola Montez
  (Max Ophuls)
Richard III (Laurence Olivier)
French Cancan (Jean Renoir)
Kiss Me Deadly (Robert Aldrich)
The Man from Laramie (Anthony Mann)
The Night of the Hunter (Charles
  Laughton)
Shin Heike monogatari ("New Tales of
  Taira Clan") (Kenji Mizoguchi)
Pather Panchali (Satyajit Ray)

1956
The Searchers (John Ford)
Aparajito ("The Unvanquished")
  (Satyajit Ray)
Bob le flambeur (Jean-Pierre Melville)
Un condamne a mort s'est
  echappe ("A Man Escaped")
  (Robert Bresson)
Written on the Wind (Douglas Sirk)
Det sjunde inseglet ("The Seventh
  Seal") (Ingmar Bergman)
Invasion of the Body Snatchers
  (Don Siegel)

1957
The Tall T (Budd Boetticher)
Smultronstället ("Wild Strawberries")
  (Ingmar Bergman)
Kanal (Andrzej Wajda)
Buye Cheng ("City Without Night")
  (Tang Ziaodan)
Sweet Smell of Success
  (Alexander Mackendrick)
Paths of Glory (Stanley Kubrick)
Kumonosu-Jo ("Throne of Blood")
  (Akira Kurosawa)
La casa del angel ("The House of the
  Angel") (Leopoldo Torre Nilsson)
Forty Guns (Sam Fuller)

1958
Apur Sansar ("The World of Apu")
  (Satyajit Ray)
Popiol i diament ("Ashes and
  Diamonds") (Andrzej Wajda)
Eroica (Andrzej Munk)
Vertigo (Alfred Hitchcock)
Enjo ("Conflagration") (Kon Ichikawa)
Touch of Evil (Orson Welles)
Rio Bravo (Howard Hawks)
Jalsaghar ("The Music Room")
  (Satyajit Ray)

1959
Ningen no joken I ("The Human
  Condition: No Greater Love")

(*Masaki Kobayashi*)
Ningen no joken II ("The Human
    Condition: Road to Eternity")
    (*Masaki Kobayashi*)
Hiroshima mon amour (*Alain Resnais*)
Les Cousins (*Claude Chabrol*)
Some Like It Hot (*Billy Wilder*)
Pickpocket (*Robert Bresson*)
L'Avventura/L'Aventure
    (*Michelangelo Antonioni*)
À bout de souffle ("Breathless")
    (*Jean-Luc Godard*)

1960

Shadows (*John Cassavetes*)
Peeping Tom (*Michael Powell*)
Ningen No Joken III ("The Human
    Condition: A Soldier's Prayer")
    (*Masaki Kobayashi*)
Paris nous appartient
    (*Jacques Rivette*)
Rocco e i suoi fratelli/Rocco et ses
    freres (*Luchino Visconti*)
Psycho (*Alfred Hitchcock*)
Lola/Donna di vita (*Jacques Demy*)
One-Eyed Jacks (*Marlon Brando*)
Damas Sobachkoi ("The Lady with the
    Little Dog") (*Josef Heifitz*)

1961

Viridiana (*Luis Buñuel*)
Accattone (*Pier Paolo Pasolini*)
L'Année dernière à Marienbad/Lanno
    scorso a Marienbad (*Alain Resnais*)
Il posto (*Ermanno Olmi*)
Jules et Jim (*François Truffaut*)
Lolita (*Stanley Kubrick*)

1962

Cleo de 5 à 7 (*Agnès Varda*)
Nóz w wodzie ("Knife in the Water")
    (*Roman Polanski*)
The Manchurian Candidate
    (*John Frankenheimer*)
The Man Who Shot Liberty Valance
    (*John Ford*)
Lawrence of Arabia (*David Lean*)

1963

The Nutty Professor (*Jerry Lewis*)
The Servant (*Joseph Losey*)
Le Feu follet/Fuocofatuo (*Louis Malle*)
Yukinójo henge ("An Actor's Revenge")
    (*Kon Ichikawa*)
Le Mépris/Il disprezzo (*Jean-Luc
    Godard*)
The Birds (*Alfred Hitchcock*)
Judex (*Georges Franju*)
8½ (*Federico Fellini*)

1964

Vidas Secas Nelson
    (*Pereira Dos Santos*)
Marnie (*Alfred Hitchcock*)
Charulata (*Satyajit Ray*)
Les Parapluies de Cherbourg
    (*Jacques Demy*)
Wutai Jiemei ("Two Stage Sisters")
    (*Xie Jin*)

1965

Szegenylegenyek ("The Roundup")
    (*Mikos Jancso*)
Repulsion (*Roman Polanski*)
Pierrot le fou (*Jean-Luc Godard*)
I pugni in tasca ("Fists in the Pocket")
    (*Marco Bellocchio*)

1966

Abschied von Gestern
    (*Alexander Kluge*)
Le Deuxième Souffle
    (*Jean-Pierre Melville*)
Mouchette (*Robert Bresson*)
Andrei Rublev (*Andrei Tarkovsky*)

1967

Le Samourai/Frank Costello faccia
    d'angelo (*Jean-Pierre Melville*)
Horri, ma panenko ("The Firemen's
    Ball") (*Milos Forman*)
The St. Valentine's Day Massacre
    (*Roger Corman*)
Bonnie and Clyde (*Arthur Penn*)
Belle de Jour (*Luis Buñuel*)

1968

if. . . . (*Lindsay Anderson*)
Night of the Living Dead
    (*George A. Romero*)
2001: A Space Odyssey
    (*Stanley Kubrick*)
La hora de los hornos ("Hour of the
    Furnaces") (*Octavio Getino,
    Fernando Solanos*)
C'era una volta il west ("Once
    Upon a Time in the West")
    (*Sergio Leone*)
Memorias del subdesarrollo
    ("Memories of Underdevelopment")
    (*Tomas Gutierrez Alea*)

1969

The Wild Bunch (*Sam Peckinpah*)
Xia Nu ("A Touch of Zen") (*Hu Jinquan*)
M*A*S*H (*Robert Altman*)

1970

Le Boucher (*Claude Chabrol*)
Hsi, Nu, Ai, Le ("Four Moods")
    (*Li Han-Hsiang, Li Hsing,
    Cai Ching-Jui, Hu Jinquan*)
Strategia del ragno ("The Spider's
    Stratagem") (*Bernardo
    Bertolucci*)
Il conformista ("The Conformist")
    (*Bernardo Bertolucci*)
Performance (*Nicolas Roeg,
    Donald Cammell*)

1971

Blanche (*Walerian Borowczyk*)

1972

Viskningar och rop ("Cries and
    Whispers") (*Ingmar Bergman*)
Tout va bien (*Jean-Luc Godard,
    Jean-Pierre Gorin*)
The Godfather
    (*Francis Ford Coppola*)

1973

Mean Streets (*Martin Scorsese*)
Angst essen Seele auf ("Fear Eats the
    Soul") (*Rainer Werner Fassbinder*)
El espiritu de la colmena ("Spirit of
    the Beehive") (*Victor Erice*)
La Nuit americaine (*François Truffaut*)

1974

Chinatown (*Roman Polanski*)
Alice in den Stadten ("Alice in the
    Cities") (*Wim Wenders*)
The Godfather Part II
    (*Francis Ford Coppola*)

1975

Maynila: Sa Mga Kuko Ng Liwanag
    ("Manila: In the Claws of Neon")
    (*Lino Brocka*)
O thiassos ("The Traveling Players")
    (*Theo Angelopoulos*)

1976

Ai No Corrida ("In the Realm of the
    Senses") (*Nagisa Oshima*)
The Shootist (*Don Siegel*)
Assault on Precinct 13
    (*John Carpenter*)
Taxi Driver (*Martin Scorsese*)
Cadaveri eccellenti ("Illustrious
    Corpses") (*Francesco Rosi*)
Voskhozhdenie ("The Ascent")
    (*Larissa Shepitko*)

1977

Close Encounters of the Third Kind
    (*Steven Spielberg*)
Annie Hall (*Woody Allen*)

1978

Prae Kow ("The Scar") (*Cherd Songsri*)
L'albero degli zoccoli ("The Tree of
    Wooden Clogs") (*Ermanno Olmi*)

1979

Apocalypse Now
    (*Francis Ford Coppola*)
Stiru ("The Herd") (*Zeki Okten*)

1980

Raging Bull (*Martin Scorsese*)

1981

Mad Max 2 (*George Miller*)

The Modern Library List

The Modern Library has selected and ranked what it considers to be the best novels published in the English language since 1900. Its board of nominators included Daniel J. Boorstin; A. S. Byatt; Christopher Cerf; Shelby Foote; Vartan Gregorian; Edmund Morris; John Richardson; Arthur Schlesinger, Jr.; William Styron; and Gore Vidal. This list annotates with asterisks those titles that have been adapted into films and includes U.S. release date and director.

1. Ulysses
    *by James Joyce ***
    (1967; Joseph Strick)

2. The Great Gatsby
    *by F. Scott Fitzgerald ****
    (1949; Elliott Nugent)
    (1974; Jack Clayton)

3. A Portrait of the Artist as a Young Man
    by James Joyce
    (1979; Joseph Strick)

4. Lolita
    *by Vladimir Nabokov ****
    (1962; Stanley Kubrick)
    (1998; Adrian Lyne)

5. Brave New World
    by Aldous Huxley
    (made for television)

6. The Sound and the Fury
    *by William Faulkner ***
    (1959; Martin Ritt)

7. Catch-22
    *by Joseph Heller ***
    (1970; Mike Nichols)

8. Darkness at Noon
    by Arthur Koestler

9. Sons and Lovers
    *by D. H. Lawrence ***
    (1960; Jack Cardiff)

10. The Grapes of Wrath
    *by John Steinbeck ***
    (1940; John Ford)

11. Under the Volcano
    by Malcolm Lowry
    (1984; John Huston)

12. The Way of All Flesh
    *by Samuel Butler ****
    (1927; silent)
    (1940; Louis King)

13. 1984
    *by George Orwell ****
    (1956; Michael Anderson)
    (1984; Michael Radford)

14. I, Claudius
    by Robert Graves
    (made for television)

15. To the Lighthouse
    by Virginia Woolf

16. An American Tragedy
    *by Theodore Dreiser ****
    (1931; Josef von Sternberg)
    (1951; George Stevens, A Place in the Sun)

17. The Heart Is a Lonely Hunter
    *by Carson McCullers ***
    (1968; Robert Ellis Miller)

18. Slaughterhouse-Five
    *by Kurt Vonnegut ***
    (1972; George Roy Hill)

19. Invisible Man
    by Ralph Ellison

20. Native Son
    *by Richard Wright ****
    (1950; Pierre Chanal)
    (1986; Jerold Freedman)

21. Henderson the Rain King
    by Saul Bellow

22. Appointment in Samarra
    by John O'Hara

23. U.S.A.
    Trilogy,
    by John Dos Passos

24. Winesburg, Ohio
    by Sherwood Anderson

25. A Passage to India
    *by E. M. Forster ***
    (1984; David Lean)

26. The Wings of the Dove
    *by Henry James ***
    (1997; Iain Softley)

27. The Ambassadors
    by Henry James

28. Tender Is the Night
    *by F. Scott Fitzgerald ***
    (1962; Henry King)

29. The Studs Lonigan Trilogy
    *by James T. Farrell ***
    (1960; Irving Lerner)
    (also made for television)

30. The Good Soldier
    by Ford Madox Ford

31. Animal Farm
    *by George Orwell ***
    (1955; John Halas)

32. The Golden Bowl
    by Henry James

33. Sister Carrie
    *by Theodore Dreiser ***
    (1952; William Wyler)

34. A Handful of Dust
    *by Evelyn Waugh ***
    (1988; Charles Sturridge)

35. As I Lay Dying
    by William Faulkner

36. All the King's Men
    *by Robert Penn Warren ***
    (1949; Robert Rossen)

37. The Bridge of San Luis Rey
    *by Thornton Wilder ***
    (1944; Rowland Lee)

38. Howards End
    *by E. M. Forster ***
    (1992; James Ivory)

39. Go Tell It on the Mountain
    *by James Baldwin ***
    (1984; made for television)

40. The Heart of the Matter
    by Graham Greene *
    (1954; George More O'Farrall)

41. Lord of the Flies
    by William Golding **
    (1963; Peter Brook)
    (1990; Harry Hook)

42. Deliverance
    by James Dickey *
    (1972; John Boorman)

43. A Dance to the Music of Time
    Series,
    by Anthony Powell

44. Point Counter Point
    by Aldous Huxley

45. The Sun Also Rises
    by Ernest Hemingway *
    (1957; Henry King)

46. The Secret Agent
    by Joseph Conrad **
    (1936; Alfred Hitchcock)
    (1996; Christopher Hampton)

47. Nostromo
    by Joseph Conrad *
    (made for television)

48. The Rainbow
    by D. H. Lawrence *
    (1989; Ken Russell)

49. Women in Love
    by D. H. Lawrence *
    (1969; Ken Russell)

50. Tropic of Cancer
    by Henry Miller *
    (1970; Joseph Strick)

51. The Naked and the Dead
    by Norman Mailer *
    (1958; Raoul Walsh)

52. Portnoy's Complaint
    by Philip Roth *
    (1972; Ernest Lehman)

53. Pale Fire
    by Vladimir Nabokov

54. Light in August
    by William Faulkner

55. On the Road
    by Jack Kerouac

56. The Maltese Falcon
    by Dashiell Hammett ***
    (1931; Roy del Ruth)
    (1936; William Dieterle, Satan
    Met a Lady)
    (1941; John Huston)

57. Parade's End
    by Ford Madox Ford

58. The Age of Innocence
    by Edith Wharton **
    (1934; Phillip Moeller)
    (1993; Martin Scorsese)

59. Zuleika Dobson
    by Max Beerbohm

60. The Moviegoer
    by Walker Percy

61. Death Comes for the Archbishop
    by Willa Cather

62. From Here to Eternity
    by James Jones *
    (1953; Fred Zinnemann)

63. The Wapshot Chronicles
    by John Cheever

64. The Catcher in the Rye
    by J. D. Salinger

65. A Clockwork Orange
    by Anthony Burgess *
    (1971; Stanley Kubrick)

66. Of Human Bondage
    by W. Somerset Maugham ***
    (1934; John Cromwell)
    (1946; Edmund Goulding)
    (1964; Ken Hughes)

67. Heart of Darkness
    by Joseph Conrad **
    (1979; Francis Ford Coppola,
    basis for Apocalypse Now)
    (1994; made for television)

68. Main Street
    by Sinclair Lewis

69. The House of Mirth
    by Edith Wharton *
    (in production at press time)

70. The Alexandria Quartet
    by Lawrence Durrell *
    (1964; George Cukor, Justine)

71. A High Wind in Jamaica
    by Richard Hughes *
    (1965; Alexander Mackendrick)

72. A House for Mr. Biswas
    by V. S. Naipaul

73. The Day of the Locust
    by Nathanael West *
    (1975; John Schlesinger)

74. A Farewell to Arms
    by Ernest Hemingway **
    (1932; Frank Borzage)
    (1957; Charles Vidor)

75. Scoop
    by Evelyn Waugh

76. The Prime of Miss Jean Brodie
    by Muriel Spark *
    (1969; Ronald Neame)

77. Finnegans Wake
    by James Joyce *
    (1965; Mary Ellen Bute)

78. Kim
    by Rudyard Kipling **
    (1950; Victor Saville)
    (1984; made for television)

79. A Room with a View
    by E. M. Forster *
    (1986; James Ivory)

80. Brideshead Revisited
    by Evelyn Waugh *
    (1982; made for television)

81. The Adventures of Augie March
    by Saul Bellow

82. Angle of Repose
    by Wallace Stegner

83. A Bend in the River
    by V. S. Naipaul

84. The Death of the Heart
    by Elizabeth Bowen

85. Lord Jim
    by Joseph Conrad *
    (1965; Richard Brooks)

86. Ragtime
    by E. L. Doctorow *
    (1981; Milos Forman)

87. The Old Wives' Tale
    by Arnold Bennett

88. The Call of the Wild
    by Jack London ****
    (1935; William Wellman)
    (1972; Ken Annakin)
    (made twice for television)

89. Loving
    by Henry Green

90. Midnight's Children
    by Salman Rushdie

91. Tobacco Road
    by Erskine Caldwell *
    (1941; John Ford)

92. Ironweed
    by William Kennedy *
    (1987; Hector Babenco)

93. The Magus
    by John Fowles *
    (1968; Guy Green)

94. Wide Sargasso Sea
    by Jean Rhys *
    (1993; John Duigan)

95. Under the Net
    by Iris Murdoch

96. Sophie's Choice
    by William Styron *
    (1982; Alan J. Pakula)

97. The Sheltering Sky
    by Paul Bowles *
    (1990; Bernardo Bertolucci)

98. The Postman Always Rings Twice
    by James M. Cain ****
    (1946; Tay Garnett)
    (1981; Bob Rafelson)
    (also made in France and Italy)

99. The Ginger Man
    by J. P. Donleavy *
    (in production at press time)

100. The Magnificent Ambersons
     by Booth Tarkington *
     (1942; Orson Welles)

Movies Selected for the National Film Registry

Adam's Rib *(1949)*

The Adventures of Robin Hood *(1938)*

The African Queen *(1951)*

All About Eve *(1950)*

All Quiet on the Western Front *(1930)*

All That Heaven Allows *(1955)*

American Graffiti *(1973)*

An American in Paris *(1951)*

Annie Hall *(1977)*

The Apartment *(1960)*

The Awful Truth *(1937)*

Badlands *(1973)*

The Band Wagon *(1953)*

The Bank Dick *(1940)*

The Battle of San Pietro *(1945)*

Ben-Hur *(1926)*

The Best Years of Our Lives *(1946)*

Big Business *(1929)*

The Big Parade *(1925)*

The Big Sleep *(1946)*

The Birth of a Nation *(1915)*

The Black Pirate *(1926)*

Blacksmith Scene *(1893)*

Blade Runner *(1982)*

The Blood of Jesus *(1941)*

Bonnie and Clyde *(1967)*

The Bridge on the River Kwai *(1957)*

Bringing Up Baby *(1938)*

Broken Blossoms *(1919)*

Cabaret *(1972)*

Carmen Jones *(1954)*

Casablanca *(1942)*

Castro Street *(1966)*

Cat People *(1942)*

Chan Is Missing *(1982)*

The Cheat *(1915)*

Chinatown *(1974)*

Chulas Fronteras *(1976)*

Citizen Kane *(1941)*

City Lights *(1931)*

The Conversation *(1974)*

The Cool World *(1963)*

Cops *(1922)*

A Corner in Wheat *(1909)*

The Crowd *(1928)*

Czechoslovakia 1968 *(1968)*

David Holzman's Diary *(1968)*

The Day the Earth Stood Still *(1951)*

The Deer Hunter *(1978)*

Destry Rides Again *(1939)*

Detour *(1946)*

Dodsworth *(1936)*

Dog Star Man *(1964)*

Double Indemnity *(1944)*

Dr. Strangelove or: How I Learned to Stop Worrying and Love the Bomb *(1964)*

Duck Soup *(1933)*

Eaux D'artifice *(1953)*

El Norte *(1983)*

E.T.: The Extra-Terrestrial *(1982)*

The Exploits of Elaine *(1914)*

Fantasia *(1940)*

Fatty's Tintype Tangle *(1915)*

Flash Gordon *(serial, 1936)*

Footlight Parade *(1933)*

Force of Evil *(1948)*

The Forgotten Frontier *(1931)*

The Four Horsemen of the Apocalypse *(1921)*

Frankenstein *(1931)*

Frank Film *(1973)*

Freaks *(1932)*

The Freshman *(1925)*

Fury *(1936)*

The General *(1927)*

Gerald McBoing Boing *(1951)*

Gertie the Dinosaur *(1914)*

Gigi *(1958)*

The Godfather *(1972)*

The Godfather Part II *(1974)*

The Gold Rush *(1925)*

Gone With the Wind *(1939)*

The Graduate *(1967)*

The Grapes of Wrath *(1940)*

Grass *(1925)*

The Great Dictator *(1940)*

The Great Train Robbery *(1903)*

Greed *(1924)*

Harlan County, U.S.A. *(1976)*

Harold and Maude *(1972)*

The Heiress *(1949)*

Hell's Hinges *(1916)*

High Noon *(1952)*

High School *(1968)*

Hindenburg *disaster newsreel footage (1937)*

His Girl Friday *(1940)*

Hospital *(1970)*

The Hospital *(1971)*

How Green Was My Valley *(1941)*

How the West Was Won *(1962)*

The Hustler *(1961)*

I Am a Fugitive from a Chain Gang *(1932)*

Intolerance *(1916)*

Invasion of the Body Snatchers *(1956)*

The Italian *(1915)*

It Happened One Night *(1934)*

It's a Wonderful Life *(1946)*

Jammin' the Blues *(1944)*

The Jazz Singer *(1927)*

Killer of Sheep *(1977)*

King Kong *(1933)*

Knute Rockne, All American *(1940)*

The Lady Eve *(1941)*

Lassie Come Home *(1943)*

The Last of the Mohicans *(1920)*

Lawrence of Arabia *(1962)*

The Learning Tree *(1969)*

Letter from an Unknown Woman *(1948)*

The Life and Death of 9413— A Hollywood Extra *(1927)*

The Life and Times of Rosie the Riveter *(1980)*

The Little Fugitive *(1953)*

Louisiana Story *(1948)*

Love Me Tonight *(1932)*

Magical Maestro *(1952)*

The Magnificent Ambersons *(1942)*

The Maltese Falcon *(1941)*

The Manchurian Candidate *(1962)*

Manhatta *(1921)*

March of Time: Inside Nazi Germany— 1938 *(1938)*

Marty *(1955)*

M*A*S*H *(1970)*

Mean Streets *(1973)*

Meet Me in St. Louis *(1944)*

Meshes of the Afternoon *(1943)*

Midnight Cowboy *(1969)*

Mildred Pierce *(1945)*

Modern Times *(1936)*

Morocco *(1930)*

Motion Painting No. 1 *(1947)*

A Movie *(1958)*

Mr. Smith Goes to Washington *(1939)*

The Music Box *(1932)*

My Darling Clementine *(1946)*

The Naked Spur *(1953)*

Nanook of the North *(1922)*

Nashville *(1975)*

A Night at the Opera *(1935)*

The Night of the Hunter *(1955)*

Ninotchka *(1939)*

North by Northwest *(1959)*

Nothing But a Man *(1964)*

One Flew over the Cuckoo's Nest *(1975)*

On the Waterfront *(1954)*

The Outlaw—Josey Wales *(1976)*

Out of the Past *(1947)*

Paths of Glory *(1957)*

The Philadelphia Story *(1940)*

Pinocchio *(1940)*

A Place in the Sun *(1951)*

Point of Order *(1964)*

The Poor Little Rich Girl *(1917)*

Primary *(1960)*

The Prisoner of Zenda *(1937)*

The Producers *(1968)*

Psycho *(1960)*

Pull My Daisy *(1959)*

Raging Bull *(1980)*

Rear Window *(1954)*

Rebel Without a Cause *(1955)*

Red River *(1948)*

Republic Steel strike riot newsreel footage (1937)

Return of the Secaucus 7 *(1980)*

Ride the High Country *(1962)*

Rip Van Winkle *(1896)*

The River *(1937)*

Road to Morocco *(1942)*

Safety Last *(1923)*

Salesman *(1969)*

Salt of the Earth *(1954)*

Scarface *(1932)*

The Searchers *(1956)*

Seventh Heaven *(1927)*

Shadow of a Doubt *(1943)*

Shadows *(1960)*

Shane *(1953)*

She Done Him Wrong *(1933)*

Sherlock, Jr. *(1924)*

Shock Corridor *(1963)*

Show Boat *(1936)*

Singin' in the Rain *(1952)*

Snow White *(1933)*

Snow White and the Seven Dwarfs *(1937)*

Some Like It Hot *(1959)*

Stagecoach *(1939)*

Star Wars *(1977)*

Sullivan's Travels *(1941)*

Sunrise *(1927)*

Sunset Boulevard *(1950)*

Sweet Smell of Success *(1957)*

Tabu *(1931)*

Taxi Driver *(1976)*

Tevye *(1939)*

The Thief of Bagdad *(1924)*

The Thin Man *(1934)*

To Be or Not to Be *(1942)*

To Fly *(1976)*

To Kill a Mockingbird *(1962)*

Topaz *(1943–45; home-movie footage taken at Japanese-American Internment Camp, the Topaz War Relocation Authority Center)*

Top Hat *(1935)*

Touch of Evil *(1958)*

The Treasure of the Sierra Madre *(1948)*

Trouble in Paradise *(1932)*

Tulips Shall Grow *(1942)*

2001: A Space Odyssey *(1968)*

Verbena Tragica *(1939)*

Vertigo *(1958)*

West Side Story *(1961)*

What's Opera, Doc? *(1957)*

Where Are My Children? *(1916)*

The Wind *(1928)*

Wings *(1927)*

Within Our Gates *(1920)*

The Wizard of Oz *(1939)*

A Woman Under the Influence *(1974)*

Woodstock *(1970)*

Yankee Doodle Dandy *(1942)*

Zapruder film (1963; footage of the assassination of President John F. Kennedy)

TV Guide's 50 Greatest Movies on TV and Video

1. The Godfather Part II *(1974)*
2. Casablanca *(1942)*
3. Citizen Kane *(1941)*
4. The Wizard of Oz *(1939)*
5. To Kill a Mockingbird *(1962)*
6. Singin' in the Rain *(1952)*
7. The Godfather *(1972)*
8. Psycho *(1960)*
9. Chinatown *(1974)*
10. Bonnie and Clyde *(1967)*
11. Vertigo *(1958)*
12. It's a Wonderful Life *(1946)*
13. Pinocchio *(1940)*
14. Bringing Up Baby *(1938)*
15. The Philadelphia Story *(1940)*
16. Sunset Boulevard *(1950)*
17. Some Like It Hot *(1959)*
18. The Searchers *(1956)*
19. Duck Soup *(1933)*
20. Raging Bull *(1980)*
21. Annie Hall *(1977)*
22. Ninotchka (1939)
23. All About Eve *(1950)*
24. Double Indemnity *(1944)*
25. A Streetcar Named Desire *(1951)*
26. The Exorcist *(1973)*
27. The Empire Strikes Back *(1980)*
28. Gone With the Wind *(1939)*
29. The Lion King *(1994)*
30. The Palm Beach Story *(1942)*
31. Rebel Without a Cause *(1955)*
32. Dr. Strangelove or: How I Learned to Stop Worrying and Love the Bomb *(1964)*
33. Schindler's List *(1993)*
34. Apollo 13 *(1995)*
35. The African Queen *(1951)*
36. The Graduate *(1967)*
37. American Graffiti *(1973)*
38. Jaws *(1975)*
39. Laura *(1944)*
40. On the Waterfront *(1954)*
41. Saturday Night Fever *(1977)*
42. Modern Times *(1936)*
43. Raiders of the Lost Ark *(1981)*
44. Babe *(1995)*
45. Top Hat *(1935)*
46. Butch Cassidy and the Sundance Kid *(1969)*
47. Cabaret *(1972)*
48. The Quiet Man *(1952)*
49. Dirty Harry *(1971)*
50. Bride of Frankenstein *(1935)*

Citizen Kane (1941)

Classic-Movie Web Sites

The number of movie-related Web sites is staggering, from insider tip sheets to fan chats to the most obscure technological or historical preoccupations. The links below will get you launched on an Internet exploration of classic movies in the digital information age.

AFI Online
afionline.org
In addition to film news and resources for directors and writers, the site offers information on film preservation, the AFI's top 100 movies of all time, and features on classic Hollywood. Also:

afi.100movies.com
"The AFI's 100 Years, 100 Films" site. The American Film Institute's List of America's 100 Greatest Movies, with film news, photos, and a classic-movie game.

American Movie Classics
amctv.com
Feature articles; behind-the-scenes looks at the classics; programming information; filmographies and biographies of the stars, from Bergman to Keaton to Weismuller; classic-movie references, and resources for purchasing videos, books, and sound tracks.

Big Star
bigstar.com
One-stop shopping for classics and contemporary hits. Nicely organized and easy to use, with thorough descriptions and links to stars and directors.

Class Act
zianet.com/jjohnson/classact.htm
A history of the golden age of movie musicals, with synopses, cast and crew information, awards, features, and more.

The Classic Movie Cafe
geocities.com/Hollywood/
Boulevard/2442

Created by classic-movie fans, the site includes their picks of the best films of all time, an in-depth look at a featured movie and star of the month, trivia, chat, links, and posters.

Elizabeth Anthony's Classic Homepage
reelclassics.com
Not as comprehensive as the reference sites, but an intelligent site that includes pictures and posters of Elizabeth's favorite movies and stars, biographies and filmographies, sound bites, movie clips, memorabilia resources, and links.

Film 100
film100.com/
An opinionated site that lists the most influential people in Hollywood history, ranked in order of their contribution to film, from directors and cinematographers to costume designers and actors. Also features an interesting two-screen format.

The Greatest Films
filmsite.org
In addition to its own list of the top 100 films of all time, the site includes comparative lists from *Movieline* magazine, *TV Guide,* the American Film Institute, Mr. Showbiz, and more, as well as posters, a timeline, and list of Oscar winners. The descriptions emphasize story and dialogue.

Hollywood Online
hollywoodonline.com
News, chat, clips, bios, synopses of classics as well as current films, and links to buying videos.

Homevideos.com
homevideos.com
Classics as well as recent films on video, listed by genre, with links to star bios; helpful for hard-to-find videos.

The Mining Company
classicfilm.miningco.com
Feature articles, thousands of links, a newsletter, and a chat area—a must bookmark for classic-movie fans.

Mr. Showbiz
mrshowbiz.com
In addition to current news and releases, search for the classics, star bios, and links to other biographical databases.

The Palace
moderntimes.com/palace
A popular classic-movie site with feature articles, biographies, audio clips, and links for poster resources, awards, features, biographies, and video sales.

Reel.com
reel.com
Buy (new or used) or rent movies and DVDs; includes summaries, links to titles with common cast members and director, and a guide to components of the films, such as suspense, sex, action, drama.

TV Gen
tvgen.com/movies
TV Guide's Web site features TV news and personalities but also a terrific reference for movies: includes the cast, credits, and reviews, as well as thousands of filmographies and biographies.

UCLA Film and TV Archive
cinema.ucla.edu
UCLA's archive site outlines the history of film, from the silents to talkies to film noir, and gives background on the major studios and directors.

Movie Magazines and Journals

American Cinematographer
A.S.C. Holding Corp.
1782 N. Orange Dr.
Los Angeles, CA 90028
(213) 876-5080

American Movie Classics Magazine
P.O. Box 469082
Escondido, CA 92046
(888) 262-4700

Camera Obscura: A Journal of Feminism and Film Theory
Indiana University
601 N. Morton St.
Bloomington, IN 47404
(812) 855-9449

Cinefantastique
P.O. Box 270
Oak Park, IL 60603
(708) 366-5566

Fangoria
Starlog Group
475 Park Avenue South
New York, NY 10016-6989
(212) 689-2830

Film Comment
Film Society of Lincoln Center
165 W. 66th St.
New York, NY 10023-6910
(800) 783-4903

Filmfax
Box 1900
Evanston, IL 60204-1900
(708) 866-7155

Filmmaker Magazine
Independent Feature Project
104 W. 29th St., 12th Floor
New York, NY 10001
(800) FILMMAG

Film Quarterly
University of California Press
2120 Berkeley Way
Berkeley, CA 94702
(510) 642-4247

Film Threat Video Guide
Film Threat Video, Inc.
2805 Magnolia Blvd.
Burbank, CA 91505
(818) 848-8971

The Independent
Association for Independent
Video and Film
625 Broadway, 9th Floor
New York, NY 10012-2611
(212) 807-1400

Millennium Film Journal
66 E. Fourth St.
New York, NY 10003
(212) 673-0090

Movieline
P.O. Box 469004
Escondido, CA 92046
(310) 282-0711

Moviemaker
2265 Westwood Blvd. #47
Los Angeles, CA 90064
(888) MAKEMOVIES

Outré
Box 1900
Evanston, IL 60204-1900
(708) 866-7155

Premiere
1633 Broadway
New York, NY 10019
(800) 289-2489

Spectator—USC Journal of Film and Television Criticism
USC School of Cinema and TV
Division of Critical Studies
University of Southern California
Los Angeles, CA 90089-2211
(213) 740-3334

Velvet Light Trap
University of Texas Press
Box 7819
Austin, TX 78713-7819
(512) 471-4531

Movie Palace Memories

While many people are content to see the latest blockbuster at the local, boxy multiplex, there's a growing appreciation for the opulent grandeur of movie palaces. These theaters were usually built in the '20s and provided their audiences with as much excitement as the feature film. The list of restored theaters below is far from comprehensive, so check your area for a movie palace. They're dazzling historical and architectural wonders and they may also introduce you to a classic-film series or some of the other community arts ventures that now put these restored gems to good use.

Augusta Theatre
523 State Street
Augusta, KS 67010
(316) 775-3661

The Augusta was the first theater completely lit by neon when it was opened in 1935. In addition, architect L. P. Larson embellished the walls with painted murals of classical scenes. These two features make it a showcase example of Art Deco style. The theater is now home to the Augusta Arts Council.

Castro Theatre
429 Castro Street
San Francisco, CA 94114
(415) 621-6120

Architect Timothy Pflueger launched his career in theater design with the opening of the Castro in 1922. This theater is reminiscent of a Spanish Colonial cathedral—replete with gilt mirrors, frescoed murals, elaborate mullioned windows, and grand staircases. The Castro is an active movie house and each show includes musical intermissions with performances on the theater's Wurlitzer Opus organ.

The 5th Avenue Theater
1308 5th Avenue
Seattle, WA 98101
(206) 625-1900

Here's a movie palace with a Chinese flair. Architects Robert Reimer and Gustav Liljestrom veered away from the popular Spanish and French looks of the '20s and opted instead for a theater styled after the Temple of Imperial Peace. They included such rarities as Ho-Ho birds and Foo dogs in the plasterwork and copied the dome from Peking's Imperial Palace.

The Fox Theatre
660 Peachtree Street NE
Atlanta, GA 30365
(404) 881-2100

This Moorish fantasy, opened just months after the beginning of the Depression, features a romantic night sky of sparkling stars and wispy clouds, minarets, bronze onion domes, and a striped canopy above the balcony seating. The large Moller organ, nicknamed Mighty Mo, still rolls on as thunderously as ever when it's not imitating exotic birdcalls and animal sounds.

The Gusman Center for the Performing Arts
174 East Flagler Street
Miami, FL 33131
(305) 374-2444

Originally known as the Olympia, this John Eberson–designed theater is famous for its nearly perfect acoustics and its restored Wurlitzer pipe organ. This '20s gem was created to simulate an outdoor Roman coliseum and now has a restored hand-painted fire curtain, ticket booth, and orchestra pit. It's a centerpiece of Miami's cultural life and home to the Miami Philharmonic Orchestra and the Miami Film Festival.

The Ohio Theatre
55 East State Street
Columbus, OH 43215
(614) 469-0939

Famous movie-palace designer Thomas Lamb inaugurated his Spanish Baroque style here in 1928. There are also Moroccan flourishes throughout, including authentic African decorations brought back from a safari. The Columbus Association for the Performing Arts now operates the Ohio.

The Paramount Theatre
352 Cypress Street
Abilene, TX 79601
(915) 676-9620

The Paramount reflects a Spanish style in keeping with its Texas roots. Conquistador helmets decorate the facade, mission bell towers frame the stage, and the ceiling is lit by thousands of electric stars. This 1987 award-winning restoration now hosts opera, ballet, theater, and a classic-film series.

The Polk Theatre

121 South Florida Avenue
Lakeland, FL 33801
(941) 682-7553

After opening in 1928, the Polk became the venue for first runs of *Snow White and the Seven Dwarfs, Gone With the Wind,* and *The Wizard of Oz.* The Polk also hosted such major entertainers as Tommy Dorsey, Harry James, and Gene Autry. These top acts were housed in an elegant Art Deco theater, designed in the Italian Renaissance style, artfully painted and bedecked to replicate a Venetian palazzo at sunset. A 100-ton Air Wash Carrier, which required a full-time employee to regulate the temperature, made this the coolest theater in Florida. Still under restoration, the Polk is now a focal point of local civic activity.

The Rialto Square Theatre

102 North Chicago Street
Joliet, IL 60431
(815) 726-7171

The Rialto Square is widely considered to be one of the ten best theaters in the country and features seven different styles of architecture, including Roman, Greek, Renaissance, and Baroque. There's a grand hall modeled after Versailles' Hall of Mirrors and the Arc de Triomphe. In the lobby hangs the largest cut-glass chandelier in the country, nicknamed the Duchess. The 1981 renovation restored the many beautiful details that make this a movie palace not to be missed.

The Senator Theater

5904 York Road
Baltimore, MD 21212
(410) 435-8338

In 1991 *USA Today* voted this friendly neighborhood theater one of the four best in the country. It's a great example of Art Deco style and continues to be run as a movie theater by the grandson of the man who first brought movies to Baltimore, back in 1909.

The State Theatre

805 Hennepin Avenue
Minneapolis, MN 55402
(612) 339-0075

The Gusman Center

The Orpheum Theatre

910 Hennepin Avenue
Minneapolis, MN 55402
(612) 339-0075

The recent restoration of these two neighboring theaters, which both date from 1921, has reinvigorated a previously down-and-out area. The State is resplendent in gilded Italian Renaissance style, while the Orpheum's majesty lies in the grand stairways, columns, and friezes of the Beaux Arts school. These two gems were once a big stopping place on the vaudeville circuit, and they continue to thrive as home to musical theater and classic-film festivals.

Syracuse Area Landmark Theater

362 South Salina Street
Syracuse, NY 13201
(315) 475-7979

The 1977 restoration of this Baroque theater led the revitalization of downtown Syracuse. The showplace features a Louis Comfort Tiffany chandelier, a Musicians' Gallery, and a Japanese pagoda fish pond. Thomas Lamb designed this 1928 landmark with an Indo-Persian atmosphere that actually incorporates European, Byzantine, and Romanesque flourishes. Now the home of the Syracuse Symphony, SALT also brings touring Broadway shows and a wide range of live music to area residents.

The Tampa Theatre

711 North Franklin Street
Tampa, FL 33602
(813) 274-8286

Architect John Eberson, who designed more than 50 movie theaters, created this Florida-Mediterranean theater to give moviegoers the impression of being outdoors. The electric-lit stars embedded in the ceiling were wired to dim and brighten, and a machine known as the Brenography Junior added special effects like wispy clouds to the illusion. Potted plants, stuffed birds, and hanging vines increased the tropical nature feeling. The Tampa has been almost completely restored to its former grandeur, thanks to local fund-raising efforts, and now hosts an acclaimed film series, concerts, and other special events. It has also become a favorite field trip for local schoolchildren.

The Wang Center for the Performing Arts

268 Tremont Street
Boston, MA 02116
(617) 482-9393

The Metropolitan, as this movie palace was known in 1925, extended over a full city block and was five stories tall. Architect Clarence Blackall designed this theater to be Boston's cultural hub—it housed ornamental statuary, a theater that featured vaudeville performances and movies, and was a host to the best jazz music of its time. In its current incarnation as the Wang Center for the Performing Arts, it presents touring Broadway shows, concerts, ballet, and film series.

The Warner Theatre

1299 Pennsylvania Avenue
Washington, D.C. 20004
(202) 783-4000

This neoclassical auditorium, which was opened in 1924, was immaculately restored using original materials and with great attention to authentic details as small as carpet and fabric swatches. A 15-by-6-feet chandelier illuminates a gold-leaf ceiling, and a restaurant and ballroom are located in the basement. The Warner is still an active participant in Washington's cultural life, and offers music, theater, and film.